WILLIAM A. SODEMAN, M.D., Sc.D., F.A.C.P.

PROFESSOR EMERITUS OF MEDICINE, FORMERLY DEAN AND VICE PRESIDENT
FOR MEDICAL AFFAIRS, JEFFERSON MEDICAL COLLEGE

WILLIAM A. SODEMAN, Jr., M.D.

CHIEF, GASTROENTEROLOGY SECTION,
ANN ARBOR VETERANS ADMINISTRATION HOSPITAL;
INSTRUCTOR, DEPARTMENT OF
INTERNAL MEDICINE, UNIVERSITY OF MICHIGAN
MEDICAL SCHOOL

W. B. SAUNDERS COMPANY

PHILADELPHIA AND LONDON

Fourth Edition

PATHOLOGIC
PHYSIOLOGY

Mechanisms of disease

W. B. Saunders Company: West Washington Square,
Philadelphia, Pa. 19105

12 Dyott Street
London, W.C.1

Reprinted April, 1968

Pathologic Physiology

Contributors

BERNARD J. ALPERS, M.D., Sc.D.
Professor Emeritus, Jefferson Medical College; Neurologist, Jefferson Hospital; Consultant, Pennsylvania Hospital; Neurologist and Consultant, Institute of the Pennsylvania Hospital, Philadelphia.

WILLIAM B. BEAN, M.D., F.A.C.P.
Professor and Head of the Department of Internal Medicine, College of Medicine, State University of Iowa; Physician-in-Chief, University Hospitals, Iowa City, Iowa; formerly Commanding Officer, Armored Medical Research Laboratory, Fort Knox, Kentucky.

NORMAN BRACHFELD, M.D., F.A.C.P., F.A.C.C.
Assistant Professor of Medicine, Cornell University Medical College; Assistant Attending Physician, The New York Hospital; Assistant Visiting Physician, Second Division, Bellevue Hospital; Associate Member and Head, Division of Myocardial Metabolism, Institute for Muscle Disease; Career Scientist, Health Research Council, City of New York.

SIR F. MACFARLANE BURNET, M.D., Ph.D.
Emeritus Professor of Experimental Medicine, Melbourne University; formerly Director, Walter and Eliza Hall Institute, Royal Melbourne Hospital, Melbourne, Australia.

WILLIAM B. CASTLE, M.D., S.M. (Hon.), M.D. (Hon.), S.D. (Hon.), LL.D., L.H.D., M.A.C.P.
Francis Weld Peabody Faculty Professor of Medicine, Harvard University; Honorary Director, Thorndike Memorial Laboratory, Boston City Hospital; Consulting Physician, Second and Fourth (Harvard) Medical Services, Boston City Hospital, Boston.

ARTHUR C. CORCORAN, M.D., C.M.
Late Professor of Internal Medicine, University of Michigan Medical School, Ann Arbor, Michigan.

BERTRAM D. DINMAN, M.D., Sc.D.
Professor of Industrial Health, School of Public Health, Research Associate, Institute of Industrial Health, and Associate Professor, University of Michigan Medical School, Ann Arbor, Michigan.

RICHARD H. FREYBERG, M.D., M.S.
Clinical Professor of Medicine, Cornell University Medical College; Director, Department of Rheumatic Diseases, Hospital for Special Surgery, New York Hospital–Cornell University Medical College, New York.

BENJAMIN R. GENDEL, M.D.
Professor of Internal Medicine, Emory University School of Medicine; Attending Physician, Grady Memorial Hospital, Atlanta; Consultant, Veterans Administration Hospital, Atlanta, and Martin Army Hospital, Fort Benning, Georgia.

v

FRANZ GOLDSTEIN, M.D.
Associate Professor of Medicine, Jefferson Medical College; Assistant Attending Physician, Jefferson Medical College Hospital and Philadelphia General Hospital, Philadelphia.

EDGAR HULL, M.D.
Professor of Medicine and Head, Department of Medicine, Louisiana State University School of Medicine; Senior Visiting Physician in Medicine, Louisiana State University Division, Charity Hospital of Louisiana at New Orleans, New Orleans, Louisiana.

FRANZ J. INGELFINGER, M.D.
Conrad Wesselhoeft Professor of Medicine, Boston University School of Medicine; Director, Fifth and Sixth (Boston University) Medical Services, Boston City Hospital; Chief, Gastrointestinal Section, University Hospital, Boston.

JAMES H. JANDL, M.D.
Associate Professor of Medicine, Harvard Medical School; Associate Physician, Thorndike Memorial Laboratory; Assisting Physician, Boston City Hospital, Boston.

FRANKLIN D. JOHNSTON, M.D.
Professor of Internal Medicine, University of Michigan Medical School; Director of Heart Station, University Hospital, Ann Arbor, Michigan.

JOHN H. KILLOUGH, Ph.D., M.D.
Associate Professor of Medicine, Jefferson Medical College; Attending Physician and Director of Cardiopulmonary Laboratory, Jefferson Medical College and Hospital, Philadelphia.

JOSEPH B. KIRSNER, M.D., Ph.D.
Professor of Medicine and Head of Gastroenterology, Department of Medicine, University of Chicago; Attending Physician, A. M. Billings Hospital, Chicago.

MAURICE E. KRAHL, Ph.D.
Professor of Physiology, University of Chicago, Chicago.

JOHN S. LA DUE, M.D., Ph.D., F.A.C.P.
Associate Professor of Clinical Medicine, Cornell University Medical College; Associate Attending Physician, Memorial Cancer Center; Assistant Attending Physician, The New York Hospital, New York.

ELLIOTT L. MANCALL, M.D.
Professor of Medicine (Neurology), Hahnemann Medical College; Senior Attending Neu-

rologist, Hahnemann Medical College Hospital, Philadelphia.

C. THORPE RAY, M.D.
Professor and Chairman, Department of Medicine, University of Missouri School of Medicine; Chief, Department of Medicine, University of Missouri Medical Center, Columbia, Missouri.

EDWARD C. REIFENSTEIN, Jr., M.D., F.A.C.P.
Consultant in Endocrinology and Metabolism, Senior Associate Clinical Research Director, The Squibb Institute for Medical Research, Squibb Pharmaceutical Company, E. R. Squibb and Sons, Inc., Olin Mathieson Chemical Corporation; Assistant Clinical Professor of Medicine, New York Medical College; Assistant Attending Physician, Flower and Fifth Avenue Hospitals, New York.

HENRY T. RICKETTS, M.D.
Professor of Medicine, University of Chicago; Attending Physician, University of Chicago Hospitals and Clinics, Chicago.

JOSEPH T. ROBERTS, M.D., Ph.D., F.A.C.P.
Assistant Professor of Clinical Medicine, State University of New York at Buffalo; formerly Dean, Professor of Medicine and Head of Department of Medicine, University of Arkansas School of Medicine; Chief, Medical Service, Veterans Administration Hospital, Fort Howard, Maryland; formerly Chief, Cardiology Section, Veterans Administration Hospital, Buffalo, New York.

LEON SCHIFF, M.D., Ph.D.
Professor of Medicine, University of Cincinnati College of Medicine; Director, Gastric Laboratory and Division of Gastroenterology, Department of Internal Medicine, University of Cincinnati College of Medicine and Cincinnati General Hospital, Cincinnati.

JOHN H. SEABURY, M.S., M.D.
Professor of Medicine, Louisiana State University School of Medicine; Senior Visiting Physician and Director of the Lung Station, Charity Hospital of Louisiana at New Orleans, New Orleans, Louisiana.

WILLIAM B. SHERMAN, M.D.
Associate Clinical Professor of Medicine, College of Physicians and Surgeons, Columbia University; Director, Institute of Allergy, Roosevelt Hospital; Associate Attending Physician, Presbyterian Hospital, New York.

WILLIAM A. SODEMAN, M.D., Sc.D., F.A.C.P.
Professor Emeritus of Medicine, Formerly Dean and Vice President for Medical Affairs, Jefferson Medical College, Philadelphia.

WILLIAM A. SODEMAN, Jr., M.D.
Instructor, Department of Internal Medicine, University of Michigan Medical School; Chief, Gastroenterology Section, Ann Arbor Veterans Administration Hospital, Ann Arbor, Michigan.

JOHN P. UTZ, M.D.
Professor of Medicine, Medical College of Virginia; Chief, Division of Infectious Diseases, Medical College of Virginia Hospitals, Richmond, Virginia.

JOHN M. WELLER, M.D.
Professor of Internal Medicine, University of Michigan Medical School, Ann Arbor, Michigan.

Preface to the Fourth Edition

Knowledge in medical science is advancing at an ever increasing pace. With the Fourth Edition of this text the editors and contributors have been confronted with the task of sorting and interrelating this mass of newer knowledge in a meaningful way. Further extension of the molecular and chemical nature of disease, for example, can be seen throughout the book and an introductory chapter on the subject has been included. Newer concepts in autoimmune diseases and in genetics have been added. Thorough revision of the chapters on infectious diseases has been attempted with a reduction of data to basic concepts in mechanisms of disease. The chapter on the spleen and reticulo-endothelial system has been entirely redone. In every chapter an attempt has been made to reach deeper into subcellular mechanisms to promote a greater understanding of how and why symptoms appear.

Again the esprit de corps of the contributors in completing the fourth edition has been high. The W. B. Saunders Company and its staff have been most patient and cooperative. The editors wish to thank their wives, Mary Agnes Sodeman and Marjorie Christian Sodeman, for their support through the long hours of preparation of this work and for their help in reading manuscripts.

Philadelphia, Pennsylvania　　　　　　　　　　　　WILLIAM A. SODEMAN, M.D.
Ann Arbor, Michigan　　　　　　　　　　　WILLIAM A. SODEMAN, JR., M.D.

Preface to the First Edition

This volume, a collaborative effort by 25 authors, approaches problems of disease in the field of internal medicine from the standpoint of disturbed physiology. Unlike the usual text, which is devoted to discussions of etiology, pathology, symptoms and treatment, this work analyzes symptoms and signs and the mechanisms of their development. The monograph is not intended to take the place of standard texts on physiology or textbooks of medicine. It does not aim at the completeness of either, but does try to bridge the gap between them by presenting a clinical picture of disease seen as physiologic dysfunction. An attempt is made to promote understanding of how and why symptoms appear, so that the student or physician may have a reasonable explanation for the findings he elicits. Neurologic problems are considered only as they are related to the various disease groups. The same is true of metabolic disturbances and disorders of acid-base balance.

The Editor thanks the contributors for their ready cooperation in covering certain aspects of disease in which presentation of material is at times most difficult. He thanks the Saunders Company for their help and guidance, and also Miss Brent S. Robertson for her long hours of hard work and patience in reading and checking manuscripts.

New Orleans, Louisiana   WILLIAM A. SODEMAN, M.D.

Contents

xiii

PART II   GENETICS AND DISEASE

Chapter Four

PART III   METABOLISM AND THE ENDOCRINE GLANDS

Chapter Five

Chapter Six

Chapter Seven

Chapter Thirteen

PART V   PHYSICAL, TOXIC AND CHEMICAL AGENTS

Chapter Fourteen

Chapter Fifteen

PART VI   CIRCULATORY SYSTEM

Chapter Twenty

CONGESTIVE HEART FAILURE, CORONARY INSUFFICIENCY AND MYOCARDIAL
INFARCTION 448

Norman Brachfeld and John S. La Due

PART VII   RESPIRATORY SYSTEM

Chapter Twenty-One

PULMONARY VENTILATION AND RESPIRATION; TESTS OF RESPIRATORY FUNCTION 505

John H. Seabury

Chapter Twenty-Two

PROTECTIVE MECHANISMS OF THE LUNGS; PULMONARY DISEASE; PLEURAL
DISEASE 539

John H. Killough

PART XI   MUSCULOSKELETAL SYSTEM

Chapter Thirty-Two

THE JOINTS 935

Richard H. Freyberg

PART XII   NERVOUS SYSTEM

Chapter Thirty-Three

THE NERVOUS SYSTEM 963

Bernard J. Alpers and Elliott L. Mancall

Part I

Pathologic Physiology

Chapter One

Pathologic Physiology

WILLIAM A. SODEMAN

Pathologic physiology, as the term implies, is concerned with disturbances in normal physiology, the mechanisms producing these disturbances and the ways in which they express themselves as symptoms and signs. Such abnormalities may accompany or result from anatomic defects, but they frequently occur in the absence of any pathologic anatomic change, for "biochemical lesions" may be expressions of cellular dysfunction before the process is severe enough, or has been present long enough, to cause damage detectable grossly or microscopically. Indeed much study is now being carried out in subcellular biologic phenomena to establish the mechanisms whereby external agents or developmental defects produce changes leading to disturbed physiologic functions. Examples of these mechanisms are developed in later chapters.

Pathologic physiologic disturbances include the many phases of pathogenesis of disease. They represent the mechanisms whereby etiologic agents effect their damage—the reaction pattern between causative factors and the body itself. Discussions in this text, therefore, center, not around agents producing disease, but around the mechanisms whereby these agents bring about bodily changes resulting in symptoms and signs.

Etiology of Disease

The understanding of disease has tradition-

ally been based upon knowledge of causative agents. Before the medical world had any understanding of causation of disease, medicine consisted largely of symptomatic care. As the result of the use of thousands of concoctions and procedures, tried upon the basis of superstition, magic and other grounds, certain medicines and procedures were found to be helpful. These were used to suppress symptoms until the natural course of events effected cure. Some curative agents were empirically stumbled upon by such methods. Putting iron into solution by the rusting process and its use in certain anemias are examples in many of the systems of primitive medicine throughout the world, and there are dozens of such examples.

PRIMARY FACTORS

The real era of modern medicine started with the upsurge in interest in cause of disease brought about by the demonstration of microorganisms as etiologic agents. It then became possible, in the laboratory, to take the inciting agent of disease and manipulate it at will, expose a susceptible animal to it and study the developing changes from the beginning. Varying mechanisms responsible for action of these agents were uncovered. Some produced poisons (toxins) which selected peripheral nerves or the spinal cord; some acted directly on involved structures. Others invaded the blood stream and over-

3

whelmed the body by general growth, or chose certain sites to locate and destroy tissue, such as the meninges. Against some of these the body reacted by producing protective agents. In short, a vast and complex group of reactions, mechanisms of disease and means of recovery were found.

Understanding went beyond the inciting agent alone, beyond the concept merely of an organism as the cause of the disease, into the very ways and means of its action in producing the disease and its manifestations. Thus we could understand how the diphtheria bacillus could remain and grow in the throat and still kill by absorbed toxins affecting the heart. Important as is the causative agent of diphtheria, the elucidation of the mechanisms of its action and the ways in which it affects and disturbs normal physiology gives us the basis for the development of means of prevention and cure. In carbon monoxide (CO) poisoning the affinity of hemoglobin for CO can be reversed, at least in part, by exposure to high pressures of oxygen. This mechanism, therefore, is helpful in the application of hyperbaric oxygenation to facilitate this process in the patient and increase elimination of CO through the lungs. In short, the unraveling of the pathologic physiology and the understanding of the process profoundly affected and directed the approach to control and treatment. Much of the discussions which follow, therefore, concerns etiologic factors and agents. But it is the way in which they act that is our field of interest, not the inciting agents themselves.

SECONDARY FACTORS

As progress led to the discovery of additional factors important in the cause of disease, certain events or states at times were found necessary to precipitate disease, and in the absence of these events the inciting factor, or primary etiologic agent, was not effective. For example, experimental pneumococcal infection in dogs has been shown to occur only sporadically if the pneumococcus is sprayed into the upper respiratory passages. If a starch paste is instilled first, the spraying of the pneumococcus into the upper respiratory passages regularly produces pneumonia. The stasis produced by the paste is important in permitting the pneumococcus to become established, just as is stasis postoperatively, or as is the Saturday night alcoholic bout in breaking down the protective respiratory barriers. In such patients these precipitating events are just as important in the production of that bout of pneumonia, just as important as etiologic factors, as is the pneumococcus. Thus, in addition to the inciting agent, certain other etiologic factors may be necessary to produce the disease, and the action and interaction of these constitute a part of the mechanisms of the disease. They may represent disturbances produced by processes unrelated to the inciting agent, yet important in the final disease picture. The etiology of disease is always multiple, and our interest rests in the mechanisms of all these multiple agents. Causation is a composite of many pathogenic factors.

In many diseases the primary causative agents or factors are unknown and may or often may not rest in the environment. We may know a host of precipitating and perpetuating factors. This is true in peptic ulcer. The study of the precipitating and perpetuating factors, the mechanism of their action and the pathologic physiologic responses they bring about give us an understanding of the development of symptoms and signs, and lead to procedures in therapy effective in blocking these mechanisms and bringing about control of the disease despite the fact that basic causation is not understood. Similar situations occur in peripheral vascular disease, certain arthritic states, hypertensive disease and many other processes in which the primary etiologic factors are not established. A study of the multiple factors known to be active leads to the demonstration of mechanisms which help clarify our understanding of the afflicted patients.

Body Responses to Etiologic Agents

Our concern with pathologic physiology and mechanisms of disease relates to the effects and changes brought about by these agents within the body. A multiplicity of etiologic factors concerns the external inciting agent, if there is one, in the environment and the reaction in the body. The interaction of this varying group of factors makes up the expression of disease we encounter. It is the process going on in the patient, both as a total organism and as the possessor of many individually conditioned cell types and masses, which alters the normal reaction pattern of cells and groups of cells to disturb normal mechanisms. The study of these processes within the cell, and how they are modified, is the real basis for the understanding of pathologic physiology.

Important as these processes are, some of those not directly affecting the host do not concern us in the mechanisms of the disease in the individual patient. They bear on occurrence of disease in groups and distribution of disease in the environment, so that epidemiologically they are important. This is true of rainfall and vegetation in maintenance of the vector of malaria, factors so important etiologically that their control will eradicate not only the vector in an area, but the disease also. These aspects, however, do not bear upon the mechanisms in the afflicted patient and do not concern us directly in our discussions of pathologic physiology. However, as such climatic factors directly affect the host, they do concern us.

Whether or not the primary factors are known, the host reaction may be studied, and the mechanisms of these changes we may understand. Reaction patterns and the mechanism of bodily expression may many times be similar with dissimilar inciting agents. Outstanding examples of this are the greatly dissimilar causes of the stress and adaptation syndrome. All agents acting upon the body exert a nonspecific as well as a specific effect. Man's adaptive and protective capabilities are limited, and his response to many sorts of noxious agents and threats may be similar. The form of the reaction to any one agent may depend more on the person's nature and past experience and on similar effects of the noxious agent on cellular mechanisms, enzyme patterns and so forth than upon the particular noxious agent evoking it. Later in the text the concept of diseases of adaptation is developed. This adaptive protective reaction may be far more damaging to the individual than the effects of the noxious agent per se, be it direct effects of microorganisms, climate, physical forces, disruption of customs and habits, or others. Here one can see why chronic psychic trauma and chronic infection might give similar reactions and symptoms.

How important the host may be is shown in a study of a group of adult men, homogeneous in economic, social and cultural background, physical and social environment, occupation and general exposure to infection who were observed for as long as 35 years. Every illness was recorded. It was found that 28 per cent of the men had 77 per cent of the episodes of illness and 80 per cent of the days of disability during the first year of observation. The distribution was similar in each subsequent year, and the group with the highest frequency of illness during the first year continued to have the highest frequency during the whole period. These studies held for illnesses of all body systems, psychologic disturbances, surgical operations and accidents. These data were reported as indicating that disease syndromes are transient aspects of the reaction of the whole individual to his total environment, and that their occurrence is governed as much by the relation of the individual to his social environment as by his random contact with specific etiologic factors. The effect of the stimulus depends in great degree not only on the type of stimulus but on the state of the individual and his response. Some adapt more readily than others. These data tell us how little we really know of the underlying factors producing host reactions. Still, the nature of the response may depend upon the state of the individual when stimulated, so that similar situations may have entirely different effects on two individuals or the same individual at different times. Thus the tubercle bacillus may produce pulmonary disease in one person and renal disease in another, or it may take one form on first exposure and a different form on later contacts in the same individual.

Subsequent chapters describe some functions of cells and the phenomena within them. In development the means by which single cells give rise to many different types of cells —that is, to their development and differentiation—has not been established. Studies in depth on DNA and RNA are in progress to determine what in the cell regulates these definite structural formations. An eventual understanding of these processes and the mechanisms of inherent defects, for example, may lead in the future to their alteration or neutralization in such diseases as galactosemia, phenylketonuria and sickle-cell anemia. Such understanding, too, may lead to ways in which external agents affecting cellular function may be blocked.

It must be kept in mind that the various mechanisms of disease described in this monograph are incomplete and fragmentary. For some diseases they are much better known than for others. In some instances fragmentary knowledge must be combined with much anatomic description to show satisfactorily the present incomplete state of our knowledge. This is true, for example, in disease of the joints. In other fields, such as in the infections, in which extensive investigation has been done, greater knowledge demands less interpolation and permits of a more clear-cut picture. Still in hypertensive disease, in which tremendous amounts of work have also been done, many important points are not settled. Concepts enjoyed today may be out of fashion tomorrow without concrete proof pro or con.

It is only through an understanding of the impact of the multiple etiologic factors in disease on the host, both on individual cellular and total bodily function, that the mechanisms whereby they disturb normal physiology can be elucidated. Only then can one grasp a truly basic understanding of disease processes and lay a groundwork for satisfactory symptomatic interpretation and establishment of sound curative procedures.

REFERENCES

Hinkle, L. E., Jr., and Plummer, N.: The "host factor" in human illness: The occurrence of differences in general susceptibility to illness among a group of adult men. Clin. Res. Proc., 2:102, 1954.

Wiener, N.: Dynamical systems in physics and biology. New Scientist, 21:211, 1964.

Wolf, S.: Stress and heart disease. Mod. Concepts Cardiovas. Dis., 29:599, 1960.

Chapter Two

Subcellular Biology and Pathologic Physiology

WILLIAM A. SODEMAN, Jr.

Introduction

The cell membrane is a mechanical barrier to the study of disturbances of intracellular physiology. Histologic staining has been for years the standard tool for the demonstration of pathologic intracellular structures. However, it is apparent that even under the best of circumstances the differentiation of cytoplasmic and nuclear structures by their affinity for one of a mixture of dyes can yield only minimal information about normal and disordered intracellular structures. The study of intracellular physiology is only slightly less unsatisfactory.

Cell-free systems have been used to approach problems of intracellular physiology and have had particular utility in shaping our understanding of metabolic steps and pathways. Major qualitative and quantitative differences have become apparent between the physiology of the extracellular and intracellular environments. The intracellular environment may be characterized as functioning at a molecular level. Accordingly, subcellular biology has been more commonly called molecular biology. The technological pillars upon which the newer investigations of subcellular physiology have been based are *electron microscopy* and the tools of *macromolecular biochemistry,* particularly protein biochemistry and enzymology.

The electron microscope has enriched our understanding of the intracellular environ-ment in both health and disease by its display of structurally distinct organelles. Extensive correlation of alteration of organelles with disease states has been possible, but this static demonstration of a pathologic process is not easily interpreted in terms of physiologic mechanisms.

Physiologic measurements made outside the limiting membrane of the cell wall represent a summation of individual but interdependent subcellular processes. This extracellular image of an intracellular environment, regardless of whether it is formed at the level of the single cell, an organ, or the body as a whole, can be distorted like a reflection in an imperfect mirror by the discontinuity of the cell wall separating the two compartments. Measurement of the product of a cell or cellular activity does not imply an understanding of the molecular mechanisms producing it.

Our understanding of the pathologic physiology of many disease processes is arrested far above the level of intracellular mechanisms. It does not always serve clinical utility to pursue the mechanism further. In this case the molecular mechanism represents a secondary factor in the understanding of the pathologic physiology of the disease. The patient will demarcate and the surgeon amputate the gangrenous tissue following arterial embolization to a limb without knowledge of the molecular mechanisms leading to cell death. Conversely, when a disease is understood only in terms of secondary factors, a

7

search for primary molecular mechanisms may be rewarding.

The remainder of this chapter illustrates some successful applications of molecular biology to the problems of interpretation of pathophysiology.

Molecular Biology

Molecular biology includes the study of all subcellular processes: replication, growth, metabolism, secretion, and absorption. Proteins, particularly nucleoproteins and those proteins differentiated as enzymes and antibodies, have been accorded special attention by the molecular biologist. Without a clear understanding of the molecular mechanisms related to protein synthesis and function, significant progress in the study of other aspects of cellular biology will be impeded. Nonprotein compounds have been studied extensively, particularly those that have a demonstrated function such as the vitamins and some hormones. Proteins that function in a metabolic role rather than primarily as structural agents have been of particular interest. A selection of the basic principles fundamental to the current approach to molecular biology are outlined here.

MOLECULAR DISEASES

The credit for recognition of inborn errors of metabolism is given to Garrod, who described alkaptonuria in 1902. Pauling added the term *molecular diseases* and equated this with diseases of the protein molecules. These represent diseases caused by lack of production, excess production, or production of altered molecules. Interest has centered about molecular diseases involving enzymes, hemoglobins, and immunoglobulins. Originally attention was drawn to these diseases because of a functional defect. Protein synthesis is under genetic control. The investigations of molecular diseases and of molecular genetics have become closely related disciplines. It cannot be assumed that a 1:1 relationship exists between molecular disease and abnormality of genetic control—for instance, it remains to be shown that the myeloma protein is an abnormal molecule, and it *may* be that the underlying factor is a nongenetic stimulus to produce a normal molecule rather than the production of an abnormal molecule—but most instances studied have at least an implied genetic abnormality as an etiologic mechanism. Pauling has raised the interest-

ing speculation that many molecular diseases have been acquired during the evolutionary process, but have been masked by environmental adaptation. Specifically, the loss of the enzymatic mechanisms to synthesize vitamins, essential amino acids, and polyunsaturated fats would illustrate these masked molecular diseases. This ability has been retained by many simpler organisms and plants on which we depend for our supply.

PROTEIN STRUCTURE

As will be discussed, the function of a protein molecule is related to the structure. The structural characteristics of proteins have been grouped under five headings by Linderstrøm-Lang and by Haber and associates. Their outline is followed here.

Random Coil. Most biologically active proteins have a specific spatial structure. Molecules that in solution are without a fixed three-dimensional structure are termed random coils.

Primary Structure. The chemical structure, meaning the number and sequence of amino acids linked in a chain or chains by peptide bonds, a covalent bond, is called the primary structure.

Secondary Structure. Parts of the amino acid chains are folded in a regular manner to form a coil or helix. Most commonly this is a right-handed coil or alpha helix, though left-handed coils are known. The helical structure is stabilized by hydrogen bonds linking carbonyl and imide groups in the spiral. This coiling of chains is termed secondary structure.

Tertiary Structure. Helical segments of the chain may be folded into a specific spatial configuration that yields a compact structure. This folding is stabilized by covalent bonds, the most important of which is the disulfide (-S-S-) bond, and by other noncovalent interactions. This folding is termed tertiary structure.

Quaternary Structure. If a protein is formed by specific aggregation of subunits such as peptide chains, the aggregation is termed quaternary structure.

GENETIC FACTORS

The basic concepts of molecular genetics have been summarized by Tatum. This outline follows his interpretation. Inheritance in a biochemical sense is based on several special characteristics of nucleic acids. Deoxyribonucleic acid (DNA) forms the fundamental genetic material except in some viruses, in which ribonucleic acid (RNA) performs this function. These special characteristics include the ability of the DNA molecule to replicate itself under the stimulus of the dividing cell and in the presence of a full complement of cellular enzymes and organelles. Also there is the capacity to store all the information necessary to direct synthesis of functional molecules. Genetic information directing the synthesis of protein molecules resides in the base sequences of the DNA molecule. The intact cell has the ability to interpret the DNA sequence called the genetic code in terms of its meaning for protein synthesis, and it also has the appropriate stored energy, enzymes, messenger and transfer RNA, and ribosomes to implement the synthesis. This mechanism of decoding is discussed in Chapter 4.

It is pertinent to this discussion to mention that on the DNA strand sequences of three bases (triplets) specify complementary triplets of RNA bases. Each of the 20 amino acids has one or more specific trinucleotides which specify the inclusion of the amino acid in the protein chain. The primary structure of the protein is determined by a succession of triplets in the polynucleotide. The framework for activation and control of specific genes on the DNA strand, the regulatory function, apparently may arise in part from within other areas of the DNA strand. For a more detailed evaluation of the genetic code and the source of this discussion the report by Ochoa should be consulted.

The presence of nonchromosomal mechanisms of inheritance seems to be clearly established, though their role, if any, in molecular disease is not clear. It has been suggested that nonchromosomal genes are nucleic acids and that patterns of replication and activity resemble those of their chromosomal counterparts. There is ample evidence for the presence of nonchromosomal DNA that could fulfill this function.

ACTIVE SITE

Many molecular diseases represent the deficiency of a functional molecule. Active transport or metabolism of a substrate presumably occurs by reversible specific interaction with an enzyme or carrier, usually a protein, though activators and cofactors may also be necessary. The function or activity is a product of the dynamics of the making, holding, and breaking of this interaction, the substrate thus being altered or transported. Specificity is conferred on the reaction by a structurally differentiated area of the molecule termed the active site. The spatial orientation of reactive and inert groups in the active site is complementary to a specific structure in the substrate. This represents in effect the old lock and key hypothesis for specific reactions. A specific steric configuration on the molecule can interact with a specific configuration on the substrate. As examples, immunoglobulins have an active site permitting combination with specific antigens, hemoglobins have an active site for combination with oxygen and carbon monoxide, and enzymes have an active site for combination with the substrate. Haber and co-workers have stressed that in all proteins except random coils the steric configuration giving rise to the active site is a product of molecular folding, i.e., the secondary and tertiary structures. Protein molecules are of such a size that the active site may occupy only a limited part of the molecular surface. Because of molecular folding, widely separated areas of the primary sequence may participate in the active site.

Of significant importance is the demonstration that for many proteins the steric configuration giving rise to the active site is determined by the primary amino acid sequence. Specific antibodies, ribonuclease, amylase A, trypsin, egg white lysozyme, and bacteriophage lysozyme all have been subjected to nondegrading denaturation by reduction with unfolding of secondary and tertiary structure until the protein is essentially a random coil in solution. Primary sequence was not altered. Loss of specific activity was noted. With oxidation under appropriate conditions refolding of the molecule occurred and specific immunologic or enzymatic activity has been recovered. Further discussion of reversible denaturation may be found in Haber and co-workers, Epstein and Anfinsen, Isemura and co-workers, Merigan and Dreyer, Whitney and Tanford, and White. Studies demonstrating reversible denaturation by uncoiling and recoiling suggest that with at least some proteins the genetic mechanisms determining the primary sequence also fix the structure of the completed molecule. If alterations of the primary sequence occur that can give rise to steric changes in the configuration of the active site, the molecule may not function in a physiologic manner. Thus the substitution of a single amino acid in the beta chain of the hemoglobin molecule gives rise to sickle hemoglobin.

There may be more than a single active site per molecule. Bivalent antibody is a well characterized demonstration of two active sites. Enzyme activation may depend on the binding of a coenzyme or other cofactor to the molecule. This binding may require an active site. Efron has suggested that in cystathioninuria, an amino-aciduria associated with multiple congenital anomalies, mental retardation, and psychoses, such an enzyme defect may be at fault. Cystathioninase, which is thought to be the deficient enzyme, is dependent on vitamin B_6. Defective binding of this coenzyme by the apoenzyme could explain this defect and the response to high concentrations of vitamin B_6.

Mechanisms of Primary Molecular Disease

A disease the etiology of which may be traced to a molecular abnormality may be termed a primary molecular disease. If the apparent molecular abnormality does not play an etiologic role in a disease process, it may be termed a secondary molecular disease. It should be noted that the term secondary molecular disease is a semantic orphan, as it is clinically more useful to consider diseases in terms of their primary causative factors. Secondary molecular changes are considered in a later section of this chapter.

Molecular abnormalities affecting fundamental aspects of cellular development and metabolism result in deletion of the cell and the trait. These are lethals. Less severe defects may permit cell survival, and the alteration may be recognized as a primary molecular disease. The molecular alteration may be qualitative, that is, an altered or changed molecule is produced; quantitative, that is, a molecule is produced in excess or in subnormal quantity; or both. The mechanism of these abnormalities usually seems to be genetic, yet this does not exclude the possibility of a defect in molecular synthesis or release at an acquired level. Genetic abnormalities may involve regulator, operator, or structural genes. If the regulator or operator locus is involved, production will be impaired, whereas alterations at a structural locus may either affect production or result in the appearance of an abnormal molecule.

Because of the complexity of the etiologic mechanisms, there is difficulty in preparing a meaningful classification of molecular diseases with our present level of understanding. No attempt at such a classification is intended in this discussion. A detailed listing of all known molecular derangements is also beyond the scope of this chapter. The rapid addition of new molecular diseases would make such a list quickly out of date.

Mechanisms of molecular disease are considered here under three headings: molecular deletion, or the absence of a functioning molecule; molecular alteration, or the production of a functioning but altered molecule; and molecular addition, or the production of a molecule not ordinarily present or production in excess. Diseases have been assigned to categories for illustrative purposes only. In many cases the discussion concerns the phenotypic expression of an imperfectly understood genetic defect, and the assumed mechanism may yet prove invalid.

MOLECULAR DELETION

No group of diseases exemplifies the effects of molecular deletion better than the primary amino-acidurias. With this group of diseases abnormal quantities of one or more amino acids appear in the urine. The accumulation results from a defect in the metabolism or transport of the amino acid. In many cases a specific enzyme defect has been demonstrated, and in any case the enzyme deficit is assumed. It is not clear whether the enzyme is not made or whether an altered, i.e., inactive molecule is produced. Table 2–1 includes a partial listing of known syndromes, the amino acid involved, and the enzyme defect when known. This discussion and table have been drawn from the review by Efron.

The amino-acidurias in general tend to produce cerebral manifestations, including mental retardation, convulsions, and psychosis. In addition to central nervous system symptoms, each individual disease usually has a constellation of other abnormalities that are polysystemic and represent not only the results of amino acid metabolism but a more fundamental genetic defect. Examples are the association of white hair with Oasthouse urine disease or congenital anomalies with cystathioninuria. If the accumulated unmetabolized amino acid is excreted in the urine without reabsorption, blood amino acid levels are low. Those amino acids that can be reabsorbed by the kidney accumulate to abnormally elevated levels in the blood and spill into the urine when the reabsorptive mechanism is saturated. Amino-aciduria also can result from a defect in active reabsorption be-

TABLE 2–1. PRIMARY AMINO-ACIDURIA.*

Disease	Amino Acid in Blood or Urine	Faulty Enzyme
Phenylketonuria	Phenylalanine	Phenylalanine hydroxylase
Tyrosinosis	Tyrosine	? P-hydroxyphenylpyruvic acid
Histidinemia	Histidine	Histidase
Maple-syrup-urine disease	Valine, leucine, isoleucine	Branched chain keto acid decarboxylase
Hypervalinemia	Valine	? Valine transaminase
Hyperglycinemia	Glycine (leucine on high-protein diet)	Unknown
Hyperprolinemia I	Proline	Proline oxidase
Hyperprolinemia II	Proline	Δ^1-pyrroline-5-carboxylate dehydrogenase
Hydroxyprolinemia	Hydroxyproline	Hydroxyproline oxidase
Homocystinuria	Methionine, homocystine	Cystathionine synthetase
Hyperlysinemia	Lysine	Unknown
Citrullinemia	Citrulline	Argininosuccinic acid synthetase
Congenital lysine intolerance	Lysine, arginine	Unknown
Oasthouse urine disease	? Phenylalanine, methionine, valine, leucine, isoleucine, tyrosine	Unknown
Argininosuccinic aciduria	Argininosuccinic acid, citrulline	Argininosuccinase
Cystathioninuria	Cystathionine	Cystathioninase
Hypophosphatasia	Phosphoethanolamine	Serum alkaline phosphatase
Beta-aminoisobutyric-aciduria	Beta-aminoisobutyric acid	Unknown
Familial amaurotic idiocy (juvenile form)	Histidine, methyl histidines, carnosine, anserine	Unknown
Cystinuria	Cystine, lysine, arginine, ornithine	Transport abnormality
Hartnup disease	Monoaminomonocarboxylic amino acids	Transport abnormality
Joseph's syndrome	Proline, hydroxyproline, glycine	Transport abnormality
Glycinuria	Glycine	Unknown

* Modified from Efron, M. L.: New England J. Med., *272*:1058, 1965.

cause of a defective transport protein. Blood levels are not elevated. Diagnosis of the disorder depends on demonstration of elevated levels of the appropriate amino acid(s) in blood or urine. Chromatographic and electrophoretic methods have been used as well as bacterial inhibition assays to demonstrate amino acids.

Treatment of primary amino-aciduria when available is based upon the understanding of the above mechanisms and is usually by dietary adjustment. It should be noted that at least one amino-aciduria, beta-aminoisobutyric-aciduria, is apparently harmless and has been used as a genetic marker. Secondary amino-acidurias are as a rule best treated by attention to the primary disease. Dietary treatment of primary amino-aciduria implies the use of purified diets to eliminate the substances that cannot be metabolized, thus preventing their accumulation to toxic levels. Dietary control is limited to those diseases characterized by an accumulation of essential amino acids. In disorders of the urea cycle, low protein diets are of assistance in preventing ammonia intoxication. An exception in terms of treatment is cystathioninuria, mentioned above, which appears to respond to high doses of vitamin B_6.

MOLECULAR ALTERATION

Alteration of the primary sequence may affect the secondary and tertiary structure of a protein. If the change leaves the active site functionally intact, an altered molecule results. If the change can alter the functional capacity of the active site, a molecular disease results. Hemoglobin is a molecule in which many primary sequence alterations have been identified. Hemoglobin is a heme-containing protein with the ability to combine reversibly with oxygen. The active site is related to this iron-containing heme moiety. Ingram has characterized vertebrate hemoglobin as a symmetrical molecule made up of four polypeptide chains. Molecules contain two each of two different chains termed alpha and beta chains in normal adult human hemoglobin A. The iron heme moiety is oriented in the folded globin structure to form the active site. Many single amino acid substitutions in the globin sequence have been identified. There do appear to be forbidden areas

in which alterations do not appear. Braunitzer and associates have identified several of
these areas, which they term "basic centers."
These lie between amino acids 56 and 61 in
the alpha chain (total length, 141 residues)
and 61 and 66 in the beta chain (total length,
146 residues). Known substitutions in the primary sequence can be explained by single
alterations in the nucleic acid triplet sequence, that is, the genetic code.

Ingram's review of the pertinent literature
concerning normal and abnormal hemoglobins serves as the primary source for this
discussion. Most of these alterations do not
seem to be related to disease, though several
are associated with well described syndromes.
Sickle cell disease represents one of these
syndromes. Sickle hemoglobin, also called
hemoglobin S, is electrophoretically distinct
from normal adult (A) hemoglobin. This
charge difference, which can be demonstrated
by electrophoresis, is due to the substitution
of a valine residue for a glutamic acid residue at the sixth position on the beta polypeptide chain resulting in the loss of two negative
charges per molecule. This change also evidently alters some of the solubility characteristics of the molecule. Intracellular hemoglobin is soluble. Sickle hemoglobin, unlike
hemoglobin A, when deoxygenated precipitates to form paracrystalline aggregates also
called tactoids. This change from a soluble
substance to a relatively rigid crystal-like
mass distorts the cell membrane and gives rise
to the characteristic sickle-shaped cell.
Clumping of distorted cells in the vascular
tree and prompt removal of sickled cells by
the spleen give rise to the classic features of
this syndrome—infarcts, splenomegaly, and
anemia. The mechanism of the solubility
change is not well understood. It is known
that deoxygenation results in a small conformational change in the normal molecule.
Ingram has summarized the information on
this point. He indicates that deoxygenation
results in a change in the beta chains such
that the beta chains move out a few angstroms from the center of the molecule. The
valine substitution in sickle hemoglobin must
then result in a conformational change so
that deoxygenation permits aggregation into
tactoids.

A second example of a change resulting in
an altered molecule and disease is illustrated
by the M group of hemoglobins. This group of
hemoglobins has been described in association
with hereditary methemoglobinemia. Hemoglobin M$_{Boston}$, hemoglobin M$_{Saskatoon}$, and

hemoglobin M$_{Milwaukee}$ have been investigated
carefully. Hemoglobin M$_{Boston}$ contains an
aspartic acid substitution for histidine at residue 58 on the alpha polypeptide chain. Hemoglobin M$_{Saskatoon}$ and hemoglobin M$_{Milwaukee}$
contain beta chain substitutions of tyrosine for
histidine at residue 63 and a glutamic acid for
valine substitution at residue 67, respectively.
In each case the substitution places an amino
acid with a reactive side chain in an area that
is thought to be spatially related near the
heme group in the folded molecule. The iron
atom is usually in the ferrous state, but occasionally it will be oxidized spontaneously to
the ferric state. When this happens it can
form a stable complex with the reactive side
chains of the substituted amino acids of the
hemoglobin M group. This complex prevents
the combination with oxygen and is stable
enough to resist reduction by red cell enzymes. Thus, half the molecule is in the
methemoglobin form. In this case knowledge
of a molecular arrangement has permitted
the understanding of an unusual syndrome.

MOLECULAR ADDITION

This mechanism produces a molecular disease by addition of a molecule with a new
functional capacity or by production of a
molecule in an excess over that normally
present. The demonstration of a new molecule or new enzyme is understandably difficult, and this remains a mechanism in search
of a disease. There is evidence suggesting
that enzyme overproduction is an etiologic
mechanism in at least one disease. Acute intermittent porphyria has been thought to have
a part of its etiology in such a mechanism.
Tschudy, in a recent review of the biochemical lesions in porphyria, has summarized the
evidence in this regard. Hepatic porphyrin
synthesis has as its rate-limiting reaction the
decarboxylation of alpha-amino-beta-ketoa-
dipic acid to form delta-aminolevulinic acid.
This is catalyzed by delta-aminolevulinic acid
synthetase (ALA synthetase). This enzyme
has been demonstrated in excess in the liver
of a patient with acute intermittent porphyria.
This enzyme is an inducible enzyme and is
known to be subject to dietary manipulation
and to estrogen therapy. This may be in fact
a secondary disorder, with the primary abnormality a genetic defect leading to induction of ALA synthetase rather than direct genetic control of the enzyme. Tschudy points
out that there are other presumably secondary biochemical changes in acute intermittent

porphyria and that the induction of the enzyme alone does not explain the cause of the clinical manifestations of porphyria. The final word is clearly not yet written, but it is instructive from the standpoint of mechanisms to recognize that production of an otherwise normal enzyme in excess can be part of a clinical molecular disease.

Mechanisms of Secondary Molecular Disease

We have suggested that alterations in the molecular pattern in a tissue may be induced by other than genetic events. Such alterations as have been demonstrated at this time have been related both to molecular deficit and to localized changes in cellular metabolism.

Dawson and his co-workers have provided an excellent illustration of such a change in molecular pattern by the demonstrations of alterations in lactic dehydrogenase (LDH) isozymes in denervated muscle. The enzyme molecule is a tetramere of two kinds of molecular subunits or parent forms. The two parent forms are called muscle and heart. A heart type has four heart subunits and a muscle type four muscle subunits. Three hybrid types have been isolated. Heart forms can be distinguished from muscle forms by functional criteria in addition to electrophoretic and immunologic differences. The heart form catalyzes reactions in an aerobic environment, and the muscle form in an anaerobic environment. Dawson and associates point out that denervation of the rabbit gastrochemius muscle, normally high in muscle subunits, results after a month in a reduction of demonstrable muscle subunits without a reduction in number of heart subunits. The alteration in muscle metabolism from an actively contracting anaerobic metabolic environment to a paralyzed aerobic environment is reflected in the enzyme pattern. A similar alteration has been noted in muscular dystrophy of chickens. Molecular patterns then appear responsive to both genetic and environmental determinants.

This text is replete with explanations of mechanisms of disease extending to the molecular and chemical levels of disease. Vitamin absence has been alluded to already. The effects of hormones and cell secretions on metabolism form another broad area to be discussed. Other examples include fluid and electrolyte balance, fat absorption, and cellular destructive diseases with their release of cellular components into the circulation. It appears that major advances have been made in the understanding of subcellular biology in both health and disease. A large constellation of diseases clearly have their primary etiology in derangements of the molecular mechanisms discussed here. At this time the observed diseases for the most part represent gross alterations in metabolic or functional activity. The technical advances that have brought our understanding to its present state will continue, and we can look forward to identification of more subtle influences of molecular biology on pathologic physiology. This chapter serves chiefly to establish concepts and varying mechanisms of action. To a greater extent these concepts are found throughout the text integrated into interpretations relative to disease groups and categories under discussion.

REFERENCES

Braunitzer, G., Hilschmann, N., Rudloff, V., Hilsey, K., Liebohl, B., and Müller, R.: The hemoglobin particles: Chemical and genetic aspects of their structure. Nature, *190*:480, 1961.

Dawson, D. M., Goodfriend, T. L., and Kaplan, N. O.: Lactic dehydrogenases: Functions of the two types. Science, *143*:929, 1964.

Efron, M. L.: Aminoaciduria. New England J. Med., *272*:1058, 1107, 1965.

Epstein, C. J., and Anfinsen, C. B.: The reversible reduction of disulfide bonds in trypsin and ribonuclease coupled to carboxymethyl cellulose. J. Biol. Chem., *237*:2175, 1962.

Epstein, C. J., and Anfinsen, C. B.: Reversible reduction and reoxidation of poly-DL-alanyl trypsin. J. Biol. Chem., *237*:3464, 1962.

Garrod, A. E.: Inborn Errors of Metabolism, 2nd ed. London, Henry Frowde and Hodder & Stoughton, 1923.

Haber, E.: Recovery of antigenic specificity after denaturation and complete reduction of disulfides in a papain fragment of antibody. Proc. Nat. Acad. Sc., *52*:1099, 1964.

Haber, E., Bennett, J. C., and Mills, J. A.: The relationship of the three-dimensional conformation of proteins to their antigenic specificity. Medicine, *43*:305, 1964.

Ingram, V. M.: The Hemoglobins in Genetics and Evolution. New York, Columbia University Press, 1963.

Isemura, T., Takagi, T., Maeda, Y., and Imai, K.: Recovery of enzymatic activity of reduced Taka-Amylase A and reduced lysozyme by air oxidation. Biochem. & Biophys. Res. Comm., *5*:373, 1961.

Isemura, T., Takagi, T., Maeda, Y., and Yutani, K.: Recovery of the intact structure of Taka-Amylase A after reduction of all disulfide linkages in 8 M urea. J. Biochem., *53*:155, 1963.

Linderstrøm-Lang, K. U., and Schellman, J. A.: Protein structure and enzyme activity. In Boyer, P. D.,

Lardy, H., and Myrbäck, K. (eds.): The Enzymes, Volume I, p. 443. New York, Academic Press, 1959.

Merigan, T. C., and Dreyer, W. J.: Studies on the antigenic combining sites in bacteriophage lysozyme. Ann. New York Acad. Sc., *103*:765, 1963.

Ochoa, S.: The chemical basis of heredity—the genetic code. Bull. New York Acad. Med., *40*:387, 1964.

Pauling, L.: Molecular disease and evolution. Bull. New York Acad. Med., *40*:334, 1964.

Sager, R.: Nonchromosomal heredity. New England J. Med., *271*:352, 1964.

Tatum, E. L.: Medicine and molecular genetics. Bull. New York Acad. Med., *40*:361, 1964.

Tschudy, D. P.: Biochemical lesions in porphyria. J.A.M.A., *191*:718, 1965.

White, F. H., Jr.: Regeneration of native secondary and tertiary structures by air oxidation of reduced ribonuclease. J. Biol. Chem., *236*:1353, 1961.

White, F. H., Jr.: Reduction of lysozyme and regeneration of enzymatic activity by air-oxidation of the reduced form. Fed. Proc., *21*:233, 1962.

Whitney, P. L., and Tanford, C.: Recovery of specific activity after complete unfolding and reduction of an antibody fragment. Proc. Nat. Acad. Sc., *53*:524, 1965.

Chapter Three

Autoimmune Disease

F. M. BURNET

Immunopathology is concerned with those phenomena resulting from the action of immunologic processes which give rise to signs and symptoms of disease, and with the experimental and theoretical bases of their understanding. Broadly speaking, we can divide the conditions involved into *allergic disease,* which we define as a reaction to *foreign* material which provokes bodily harm, and *autoimmune disease,* in which the reaction is against substances *natural to the body.* As is the way of biologic definitions there are difficult intermediate situations in which, apparently as part of the reaction to a foreign substance, an immunologic attack on body components is also manifested.

In this discussion no further mention will be made of typical allergic disease, as exemplified in hay fever, asthma, and eczema, in which the sensitizing antigen can usually be identified. In a rather different category are the conditions exemplified by rheumatic fever, in which a bacterial antigen with a stereochemical relationship to an antigenic determinant in certain body tissues appears to provoke an immunologic response directly harmful to the target tissues concerned. Such conditions conform to our definition of autoimmune disease and will call for some comment. There has, in fact, been a strong tendency among immunologists who still hold instructionist views of antibody production to look to processes of this type as the pre-

dominant cause of autoimmune disease (Stevens).

Also to be considered are several types of abnormal reactions to drugs, notably those which mimic autoimmune disease. These include Sedormid or quinidine purpura and stibophen hemolytic anemia, in which platelets or red cells are destroyed by a well-defined immunologic process. Here again, it has been suggested that autoimmune disease in general differs from these only in that the (extrinsic) antigen is unknown (Shulman).

In discussing the pathologic physiology of autoimmune disease it will be necessary to avoid the temptation to draw a clear line of demarcation between autoimmune diseases in which the whole pathogenesis is related to intrinsic processes, and other conditions in which extrinsic agents play a significant part in leading to broadly similar disease. The main objective of this contribution will be, in fact, to bring out the factors responsible for this gradient-like disposition of the diseases with which we must be concerned. It is equally important, however, to concentrate most attention on those conditions which represent the autoimmune diseases par excellence in, for the present at least, showing no evidence that individual environmental factors are directly concerned. Our approach is therefore first to consider the common factors present in two accepted autoimmune diseases of man, acquired hemolytic anemia (AHA)

15

and systemic lupus erythematosus (SLE), and in the genetically based disease seen in mice of strain NZB and its hybrids, which has many of the qualities of both AHA and SLE and, to a certain extent at least, can serve as a laboratory model of autoimmune disease in general.

Salient Features of Human and Murine Autoimmune Disease

If we take as our first model acquired hemolytic anemia of Dacie's "warm type," its essential features can be summarized as follows.

The disease depends on the accelerated removal and hemolysis of the patient's red cells due to the attachment to the cell surface of antibody of varying degrees of avidity and completeness. This is recognized by the Coombs antiglobulin test in which washed patient's red cells are agglutinated by an antiserum active only against human Ig G (γ_2, 7S) globulin. The specificity of the antibodies present varies from case to case, but in general antibody reacts with all types of human erythrocytes and, apart from a weak reaction with cells from some other primates, not with other mammalian red cells.

In similar brief outline, systemic lupus erythematosus is a rare disease predominantly affecting young women. It has a protean symptomatology that may involve many organs. Renal lesions are present in 70 to 75 per cent of cases, and the most common cause of death is renal failure. The disease is characterized immunologically by the presence of a constellation of antibodies directed against components of mammalian nuclei. These include the LE cell factor, as well as antibodies against DNA, nucleoprotein, and histones. Other antibodies of some clinical importance are also found, including those giving biologic false positive results in serologic tests for syphilis and, when hemolytic phenomena are present, incomplete antibodies against one or more of the human red cell antigens.

The mouse strain NZB was described by Bielschowsky et al. and has been extensively studied in Dunedin and in Melbourne. All individuals become Coombs positive at some time between 15 and 40 weeks of age and (particularly in the males) show most of the signs of a more or less adequately compensated hemolytic anemia. As in AHA there are antibodies present in the serum of many established cases which react with any type of

mouse red cell, weakly with rat cells, but not with those of other species.

In older mice, especially females, renal failure with gross histologic lesions is common. This is even more characteristic of the F1 hybrid NZB/NZW (Helyer and Howie), in which all females are dead from renal disease by 1 year of age. In both NZB and the hybrid, a proportion of sera are positive by LE cell tests and for antinuclear factor.

We can summarize the features common to all these conditions as follows:

1. Genetic factors are certainly crucial in the murine disease, are generally accepted as significant for SLE, but have not been established for AHA.

2. In all, the individual appears healthy up to a certain age. A process is then initiated which persists throughout life in most cases, although in AHA there is a relatively small proportion of complete recoveries.

3. In both AHA and SLE and in the murine disease, antibodies are present in serum which react with normal constituents of other individuals as well as autologous material.

4. Secondary autoimmune hemolytic disease is relatively common in human SLE, and as has been mentioned the NZB mice show, in addition to hemolytic anemia, a relatively distinct set of pathologic changes highly reminiscent of SLE.

5. Dacie points out that detailed clinical and hematologic study will show such a wide range of differences that no two cases of AHA are alike. The polymorphism of signs and symptoms in SLE is one of the characteristics of the disease. Even NZB disease in a genetically uniform population shows significant variation from one individual to the next.

6. The thymus shows significant changes in NZB disease (Burnet, 1962, 1964b) and in SLE. In one instance of AHA in an infant successfully treated by thymectomy, the thymus showed gross proliferation of plasmocytic cells.

In addition to these features common to all three conditions some others may be added which, though not seen in AHA, are common to a number of other autoimmune conditions as well as SLE and have been spoken of by Mackay and Burnet as useful "markers" of autoimmune disease.

7. An increase of serum gamma globulin is common.

8. In local lesions, whether in kidney, skin, or elsewhere, mononuclear infiltrates, including particularly lymphocytes and plasma cells, are usual.

9. Appropriate tests with fluorescent anti-globulin serum will show deposition of gamma globulin in affected tissues, notably in kidney and skin in SLE.

10. Enlargement of lymph nodes and spleen is common.

A General Approach to Autoimmune Disease

This survey of some of the general features of three typical autoimmune situations allows us to particularize the problems which need to be clarified before the phenomena of autoimmune disease can be brought into line with the general concepts of immunology and pathology.

1. By its nature, autoimmune disease represents a breakdown in the process usually referred to as natural immunologic tolerance, by which the normal constituents of the body do not provoke the appearance of antibodies (or immunologically reactive cells) against them. Tolerance has become a complex topic in recent years, but some attempt to understand its mechanism and meaning is clearly needed in the present context.

Modern discussion of immunologic theory has centered very largely on the nature of tolerance. All "elective" theories, including clonal selection theory, which at present provides the most suitable basis for the consideration of all pathologic aspects of immunity, are mainly justified by their relevance to tolerance phenomena.

2. Study of tissue extracts and components as antigens has uncovered many phenomena of special interest for autoimmune disease. The thyroid gland is especially prone to immunologic attack, with current opinion ascribing not only Hashimoto's thyroiditis and myxedema but also thyrotoxicosis to autoimmune processes. Experimental studies in both human and animal material point strongly to the antigens concerned being "segregated" or "inaccessible" antigens which are not subject to the same rules for tolerance as apply to material commonly found in both blood and lymph circulations.

There must be a very wide range of potential antigenic determinants, i.e., distinctive stereochemical patterns of appropriate configurations, present in such inaccessible situations in the body. This raises the important possibility, first exemplified by Kaplan's work on the streptococcus and cardiac antigens, that some of these inaccessible body antigens may have a significant cross reactivity with a microorganismal antigen. Stevens has emphasized the possibility that in this way an antibody provoked by an infecting or saprophytic microorganism might quite accidentally become pathogenic for the host.

3. Three features of autoimmune disease strongly suggest the importance of somatic mutation. The first is the regularity of specific age incidence curves in a given autoimmune disease, and their characteristic differences from one disease to another (Burch). The second is the random-appearing character of the range of antibodies produced and tissues affected in such a disease as SLE. The third and most cogent is the *homogeneity* of the specific antibodies in many cases of human AHA, for which the only reasonable interpretation is that a single mutant clone is responsible for producing the pathogenic antibody.

4. Following a suggestion by Thomas in 1959, there has been much recent interest in what may be called the function of immunologic surveillance. The basic assumption is that when, as a result of somatic mutation, new antigenic determinants arise and the mutant cell proliferates sufficiently for a significant concentration of the new antigen to be present, an immunologic response equivalent to homograft rejection takes place eliminating the mutant clone. The evidence for this is indirect and is derived mainly from the demonstration of the antigenicity of some autochthonous tumors, but it could be of sufficient significance in autoimmune disease to justify brief discussion.

5. Interest in thymic disease in relation to autoimmune disease has been generated mainly in the author's laboratory, and the hypotheses on the matter have not been widely accepted. Nevertheless, the germinal centers of myasthenia gravis, the characteristic thymic picture in SLE, the regular thymic lesions in NZB mice and most of their hybrids, and the plasmablasts in the thymus described by Kariaklis et al. are all observational facts which in one way or another must be fitted into the picture of autoimmune disease.

Each of these themes will therefore be considered in its relation to autoimmune disease.

Immunologic Tolerance

It is axiomatic that any mammalian individual normally shows no evidence of immune reaction against components of his own body. It is well known, however, that tissue grafts from any individual other than an identical twin will be rejected by an immunologic mechanism and that in most cases injection of foreign blood cells will provoke antibody production. As a first approach which will need qualification later, we may say that the body is tolerant of its own components and reacts immunologically only against material carrying chemical patterns not found in the body. This tolerance might at first sight be regarded simply as a genetic character; but a simple observation, due originally to Owen, makes this interpretation impossible.

If we take two consecutive calves from the same cow, sired by the same bull, they will usually show some difference in their blood groups. If one has combination X the other will have Y, and if the first is injected with blood of the second it will almost certainly produce antibody anti-Y. If, however, the cow has dizygotic twins similarly with X and Y blood genotypes, fusion of the placental circulations will result in the two calves, each having a mixture of X and Y blood cells. They will retain these mixtures for life and no anti-X or anti-Y responses will be recognizable. Here tolerance is clearly not genetic in origin but is developed by a process taking place during embryonic life.

There is no uniformity among immunologists as to how tolerance is to be interpreted, but there are two broad approaches, both of which are based on "elective" theories of antibody formation. In any elective theory it is assumed that the specific pattern of reactivity of an antibody is determined by genetic mechanisms within the cell, and that the function of antigen is not to instruct the cell to produce a corresponding antibody, but to select and stimulate cells with inbuilt capacity to produce such an antibody (Burnet, 1959, 1964a; Jerne; Talmage; Lederberg).

The first type of explanation is based on what Lederberg called subcellular theories by which any reactive cells can potentially produce a wide range of antibody patterns. When an immature cell capable potentially of producing antibodies A B -----Z makes effective contact with antigen A, it is assumed that union of antigen and receptor blocks channel A but leaves B C -----Z capable, subsequently, of reacting with any corresponding antigen. As long as antigen A persists in the body, the blocked cell and its descendants are unresponsive, i.e., tolerant to A, but respond normally by antibody production to any of the other antigens within its repertoire.

The second approach to tolerance (the clonal selection approach) assumes that any given lymphoid cell has only a very limited range of reactivity. With the vast majority of antigens it cannot react at all. With an antigen with which it can react, the alternatives are essentially the same as in the first approach. If the cell is physiologically immature and in an appropriate internal environment—the thymic cortex may be especially important in this respect—it will be vulnerable to antigen. Exposure to an adequate intensity or sequence of antigenic contact will either destroy the cell or permanently inactivate any immunologic capacity. In any other circumstances, antigenic stimulation will lead to positive immunologic manifestations, including the production of antibody and the eventual emergence in one form or another of descendant cells with the same range of immunologic reactivity.

The central role played by clones of cells with immune reactivity in an approach such as this calls for an appropriate name for such cells. The term "immunologically competent cell" has been much used, but for compactness I shall use Dameshek's suggestion, "immunocyte," with exactly the same connotation for any cell, lymphocyte, plasma cell, or macrophage which can react recognizably and specifically with antigen.

On the first approach, cells are tolerant because one of their potential activities is blocked by persisting antigen. On the second, tolerance represents a simple absence of cells which can react with the antigenic determinant in question. Either interpretation allows an understanding of why the body's own accessible constituents are tolerated. Every immunocyte capable of reaction will have been eliminated or inactivated during the course of development and differentiation. This process of eliminating self-reactive clones is conveniently referred to as immunologic homeostasis.

So far only the cellular aspect of immunity and tolerance has been considered, and no thought has been given as to how an antigen stimulates an immunocyte to produce antibody. In all probability there is more than one process involved. Many of the difficulties that arise, for instance, in the interpretation of the results of experiments on the "breaking" of tolerance by related or chemically altered antigens, require some elaboration of the role of macrophages. Of particular interest are the dendritic macrophages found in primary lymph follicles and studied by Nossal et al. In rats and perhaps in other species, it seems that production of Ig G (7S) antibody results from the stimulation of cells by antigen which has been processed in some way by these follicular macrophages. In order to be taken up by such cells the antigen requires to be opsonized by combination with antibody which in unimmunized animals will be "natural antibody" Ig M or Ig A in character. Acquired or natural tolerance will then depend on one or more of the following factors: (1) absence of natural antibody which can react with native antigen and by implication of cells which can produce it; (2) absence of cells which can react directly with the antigen to produce antibody of Ig M or Ig A character; (3) absence of cells subject to stimulation with antigenic determinants as processed by follicular macrophages.

There is a growing certainty that the influence of a given antigenic macromolecule or particle on a potentially reactive immunocyte depends both on the physiologic state of the cell and the physiochemical disposition of the relevant antigenic determinants.

When theoretical matters need to be introduced in this consideration of autoimmune disease they will be discussed in terms of clonal selection, but it must be recognized that all such statements can be modified so as to conform to a subcellular theory of tolerance. In addition, the parts played by the reticuloendothelial system, especially the follicular macrophages, and the various physical types of antibody must always be borne in mind in considering any clinical or experimental situation.

From the point of view of understanding autoimmune disease the essential feature is the process of immunologic homeostasis, which may be defined as the process by which the immunocytes of the body become nonreactive to any antigenic determinants that are present in significant concentration in the blood or lymph circulations or in the lymphoid tissues including the thymus. Autoimmune disease represents a breakdown of this process. There are two ways in which this can be pictured. The internal environment may be abnormal, or clones of cells may arise which as a result of somatic mutation are resistant to what should be a tolerance-producing contact with antigen.

Inaccessible Antigens

Many years ago it was recognized that protein from the lens of the rabbit's eye could provoke an antibody response when it was injected into another rabbit. This gave rise to the concept that there were certain tissues in the body which were segregated from the general metabolic traffic and could therefore contain antigens or antigenic determinants which essentially were as foreign to the body as a bacterial antigen. More recently the term inaccessible antigen has come into use, and it has become steadily clearer that such antigens may be involved in a wide range of autoimmune conditions.

The classic example of local autoimmune disease is Hashimoto's disease of the thyroid. The ease and regularity with which antibodies against thyroid constituents can be detected in the patient's serum, plus the existence of accurate methods for the study of thyroid function and the accessibility of the gland to biopsy, have combined to make this one of the most intensively cultivated fields of academic medicine in the last decade. Additional interest also arose from the simultaneous experimental work which showed that immunization of rabbits with homologous thyroid tissue could produce histologic and serologic findings analogous to those in the human disease. For these reasons it is convenient to discuss immunologic disease of the thyroid in some detail to exemplify principles which will probably be found applicable to a range of other conditions as well.

It is well known that Hashimoto's disease and its sequel myxedema involve females almost exclusively and usually affect women over 50. There are reports of Hashimoto's disease in uniovular twins (Irvine et al.), and several studies (Hall et al.) have shown that siblings and other close relatives of patients with autoimmune thyroid disease have a much higher incidence of positive serologic tests with thyroid antigens than is found in any appropriate control group. Many of these are asymptomatic. As would be expected from such a finding a small but significant proportion of individuals, particularly older women in all "normal control" series, show antibody against thyroglobulin or microsomal thyroid antigen. Moreover, in a random series of thyroids from routine autopsies examined by Goudie et al., about 23 per cent of women over 55 showed significant lymphoid infiltration of the organ.

Hashimoto's disease thus appears to be the extreme manifestation of a rather common process basically genetic in origin by which autoantibody production and lymphocytic infiltration of the thyroid develop.

A clue to the nature of the anomaly that leads to the development of autoimmune reactions may be found in the range of conditions in which there is an unusually high proportion of serologic reactors with one or other of the antithyroid tests. These include first, other thyroid conditions, particularly thyrotoxicosis and in addition, SLE, pernicious anemia, Paget's disease of bone, active chronic hepatitis, and idiopathic Addison's disease. With the exception, for the time being at least, of Paget's disease, all these are known or suspected to be of autoimmune origin. The fault that leads to Hashimoto's disease also predisposes apparently to autoimmune processes directed against other tissues and vice versa.

In recent years there has been an increasing interest in the possibility that thyrotoxicosis may be part of an autoimmune process. Apart from Hashimoto's disease and its sequel myxedema, patients with thyrotoxicosis show the highest incidence ($\pm$ 70 per cent) of positive serologic reactions. A proportion of patients show the clinical sequence thyrotoxicosis, Hashimoto's disease, myxedema. Most early cases of Hashimoto's disease show increased functional activity of the thyroid with a high radioiodine uptake and a high level of protein-bound iodine in the circulation. Other reasons may be given for this, but there is much to suggest that there is a reality about the sequence and that we are dealing with a unitary syndrome whose manifestations are to a large extent determined by the age of the patient at the time of onset of the disease. Other features pointing toward an autoimmune component in thyrotoxicosis are (1) its predominant occurrence in females, (2) the presence of lymphoid cell infiltration in many surgically removed glands, (3) the presence of lymphocytic infiltration in the ocular muscles in exophthalmos and ophthalmoplegia, and (4) the demonstration that the long-acting thyroid stimulator (LATS), present particularly in cases with ocular changes and pretibial myxedema, has the characteristics of an immunoglobulin.

There may be cases of thyrotoxicosis in which autoimmune processes play no part and others in which the presence of antibody is no more than the result of stimulation by an "inaccessible" antigen functioning simply as a foreign substance. On the other hand, a self-consistent picture can be given if we regard the whole complex of thyrotoxicosis, Hashimoto's disease, and myxedema as representing varying phases and manifestations of autoimmunity, i.e., as resulting from the emergence of immunocytes with aberrant reactivity to one or more of the antigenic determinants specific to thyroid cells. The anomalies may be either (1) a heightened reactivity to what is normally a poor antigen or (2) an abnormal resistance to inhibition by a high concentration of antigen, with the further possibility of (3) an increased invasiveness, in the sense of ability to pass from the circulation to a site containing the corresponding antigen.

The first possibility will be discussed at more length in the next section owing to its relevance to drug sensitivity; but it seems likely that if a combining site has undue avidity for a body antigen, the clone carrying it is more likely to become pathogenic than one with a less avid receptor. This would be likely to hold irrespective of whether the antibody or cells carrying the equivalent receptor (fixed antibody) were the pathogenic agents.

The essence of the forbidden clone hypothesis of autoimmune disease is that cells of such clones are resistant to inhibition or destruction by antigen excess. This holds primarily for cells in the sensitive physiologically young phase but will be expected to hold relatively at other physiologic stages. The presence of lymphoid cells, particularly germinal centers and plasma cells, in the substance of a target organ is interpreted as an index of immunocytes reacting positively in the presence of a large concentration of antigen and therefore possessing the second quality of a pathogenic forbidden clone mentioned above.

The third quality of increased invasiveness is not yet properly understood, but it is a characteristic feature of experimental models of autoimmune disease that the target organs are invaded by mononuclear cells. Perhaps the two findings that may be most relevant to the human thyroid situation are (1) Paterson's demonstration that the appearance of circulating antibody provides *protection* against cellular invasion of the central nervous system in experimental allergic encephalomyelitis in rats and (2) Roitt's finding that rats given singly either Freund adjuvant or a substantial dose of rabbit antithyroid serum show no more than trivial evidence of thyroiditis, but when both are given a severe inflammation with cellular invasion results. It is evident that quite minor individual factors may determine whether or not circulating antibody is damaging—by being able to penetrate the target organ—or protective, presumably by preventing access of antigen to potentially pathogenic immunocytes.

Without being able to define the parameters in detail we may assume that immune attack on the thyroid may be mediated either by antibody or by cells. Antibody in the form of the circulating "long-action thyroid stimulator" (LATS), which has the physical qualities of a 7S immunoglobulin (Meek et al.), may provoke abnormal functional activity. Entry of cells into the thyroid will lead to diffuse infiltration and perhaps proliferation of lymphocytes with slow progressive damage to structure and function. In a proportion local antigenic stimulation will lead to the appearance of germinal centers and accumulation of plasma cells presumably with local production of antibody.

Perhaps the most persuasive indication that thyrotoxicosis is usually an autoimmune disease is its age and sex incidence. If we accept Burch's general approach, any disease arising in the absence of recognizable environmental cause in women from young adult life onward is likely to have an autoimmune origin.

It will be for the future to show to what extent this general approach holds for other tissues. Subject to the qualifications discussed in the next section there is substantial though sometimes minority opinion that pernicious anemia, idiopathic Addison's disease of the suprarenals, pemphigus vulgaris, and some forms of male sterility have a basically similar pathogenesis.

Extrinsic Antigens in Relation to Autoimmune Disease

Immunologic processes are involved in a very wide range of physiologic and pathologic conditions, and it is often difficult to be sure what antigen is involved in a given example of what appears to be autoimmune disease. In this chapter the aim has been to confine the subject matter to conditions in which antibodies or immunologically active cells directly damage target cells of the host. This does not, however, automatically eliminate extrinsic antigens from playing a part in the pathogenesis of what are by this definition autoimmune diseases. There are probably thousands of chemical configurations in the specialized tissues of the body which are both potentially capable of serving as antigenic determinants and normally inaccessible. It would be surprising if some of these were not equivalent in pattern to a bacterial or other

extrinsic antigenic determinant capable of reaching parenteral tissues in quantity. Under such circumstances, immune reaction against the foreign antigen might build up a population of cells and antibody with pathogenic potentiality against the organ carrying the corresponding antigenic determinant.

The only example for which this situation has been virtually established is the induction of rheumatic fever by preceding streptococcal throat infection. Kaplan's work has established that certain hemolytic streptococci carry antigenic determinants which cross-react serologically with antigens in cardiac muscle. It is almost certain that antigens similarly related to this or some other streptococcal antigenic determinant are also present in synovial tissue.

The current picture of rheumatic fever is of a persisting streptococcal infection in the tonsillar region which both liberates toxic products such as streptolysin S and stimulates the production of a variety of antibodies against bacterial antigens. In addition we have a situation in the infected tonsils which may be similar to what obtains in the granuloma produced by the use of Freund adjuvant in the experimental animal, and the suggestion from Hirschhorn's recent work that streptolysin S may be a nonspecific stimulant of lymphocytes to activity. A special opportunity may well be provided for the emergence of "aggressive" clones of immunocytes, including those potentially reactive with the antigenic determinants of the target organs. Once access to a damaged cell is achieved, further damage to adjacent cells will result in a spreading involvement of the organ.

With immunologic damage there will necessarily be liberation eventually into the circulation of normally inaccessible antigen now capable of itself serving as a stimulus to immune response. In this way it becomes possible for an immune response to an extrinsic agent (the streptococcus) to initiate a process which can proceed after the elimination of the infection and so become in the strictest sense an autoimmune condition. Perhaps the postcommissurotomy syndrome is of this nature.

A rather different effect of microorganismal infection on autoimmune disease may arise as a result of antibody production and the coating of specific globulin molecules on antigenic particles such as living or dead bacteria. This results in some degree of denaturation of the gamma globulin by which new antigenic determinants are exposed. In at least a proportion of people, such denatured gamma globulin (DGG) can serve as an antigen.

Human antibodies against various aspects of DGG are highly heterogeneous and, in Kunkel and Tan's opinion, can be divided into three major groups: (1) those associated with entry of gamma globulin from another individual by maternal transfer or by transfusion, (2) those generated by the existence of a continuing bacterial infection, notably subacute bacterial endocarditis, and (3) those associated with rheumatoid arthritis. The characteristic serologic abnormalities in rheumatoid arthritis are all directed against and tested with one or another form of DGG. There is also growing evidence that in the affected joint tissues there is excess antigamma globulin and diminished complement as well as lymphocytes and plasma cells. All this provides a reasonable basis for assuming that abnormal immunologic activity directed against DGG is an essential part of the pathogenesis of rheumatoid arthritis.

The existence of rheumatic fever plus the involvement of joints in serum sickness and as a late manifestation in a rather wide range of mild viral infections, such as rubella, all point toward a vulnerability of the synovial tissue to immunologic damage. Rheumatoid arthritis in comparison with the arthritis of rheumatic fever is a continuing process at a subacute level as against a rapidly evolving self-limited local process. The simplest, but not necessarily the correct, way to bring the various immunologic features of rheumatoid arthritis into relationship is to assume an initiation of the lesion as a result of some microorganism-antibody relationship. This may be either a Kaplan-type situation with a streptococcal antigen cross-reacting with an inaccessible synovial antigenic determinant, or a simple deposition of antigen-antibody complex in the synovia. Under either circumstance, denatured gamma globulin (DGG) will lodge in synovial tissue. In the normal individual this will be harmlessly disposed of, but in those with inadequate capacity for immunologic homeostasis, in whom clones of immunocytes reactive with DGG can emerge, the potentiality of an autocatalytic process arises. Especially if facilitated by cold and minor trauma, entry of cells reactive with DGG will lead to local plasma cell formation and the eventual deposition of some of their antibody as DGG, thus increasing the concentration of the antigen. Mellors' findings suggest that concomitantly germinal centers

(? of the same clones) arise in draining lymph nodes. From these, either directly or indirectly, antibody (anti-DGG) passes into the circulation.

Extrinsic antigenic determinants may also enter the body in the form of drugs or industrial poisons and give rise to immunologically based disease that may closely simulate autoimmune disease. In some instances of drug hypersensitivity a drug-antibody complex has a damaging effect on one or another of the circulating cells, particularly red cells or platelets, more rarely leukocytes. The best known examples are Sedormid purpura, studied in detail by Ackroyd, quinine and quinidine purpura, stibophen anemia, and, according to Shulman, post-transfusion purpura. The essence of the serologic reactions used in diagnosing these conditions is that they occur only when antiserum from the patient, drug, and target cell suspension are brought together. Since the drugs concerned are of small molecular weight the test tube situation can readily be analyzed by dialysis techniques. Work by Shulman and associates has led to the interpretation that hemolysis or platelet lysis results from the adsorption to the target cell of a firmly bound drug-antibody complex with or without the subsequent attachment of complement. In the examples cited by Shulman, when the antibody concerned is 7S the haptene antibody complex attaches to platelets and when 19S to red cells, but this may not invariably be the case.

The crucial feature of this type of disease is its rarity; single cases occur among thousands who receive the drug without ill effect. In most animal experiments with haptenes, the drug must be appropriately bound to a protein carrier if it is to be either antigenic or reactive in the ordinary sense in vitro. No precipitation between haptene and antibody occurs, and in vitro effects are limited to a displacement of dialysis equilibrium and a capacity of relatively high concentrations of haptene to inhibit reaction between antibody and carrier-bound haptene. In quinidine purpura, however, the haptene is bound firmly to antibody and the complex then attaches to platelets causing their lysis. The observable quality then is the existence of antibody of very high avidity capable of binding the drug firmly, and we must assume that this is based on some genetic anomaly in the cells producing this antibody. By far the simplest hypothesis is that in susceptible individuals there are present as a result of genetic and somatic genetic processes some lymphoid cells carrying immunologic receptors (bound antibody) which, for steric reasons, bind the drug in question with the same firmness usually reserved for haptene-carrier combinations. This results in the initiation of the antibody producing process, clonal proliferation, and the production of antibody of abnormally high avidity.

Somatic Mutation

It is impossible to discuss immunity and especially autoimmune disease without introducing the concept of somatic mutation. This has been largely neglected in discussions of health and disease, but it is easy to see its potential importance. There are now many examples of (genetic) mutation whose frequency per generation is known. For most it lies between 1 in 10^5 to 1 in 10^7. Mutation is equivalent to error or accident in DNA replication which still leaves the segment in question functionally active. There is no reason to believe that errors in replication are less frequent in somatic than in germinal cells, and there is a real possibility that in the regions of the somatic cell genome that are active in guiding the specific function of the cell they may be more frequent. In any large long-lived animal such as man, if somatic mutation occurs at the rate suggested by Orgel of 10^{-8} per nucleotide per replication, there will inevitably be a relatively rapid accumulation of mutant somatic cells unless there is some specific process by which they are eliminated.

A mutation is something which occurs at random and very rarely. It involves only a particular segment of DNA in a single cell and in general will result in a modification of chemical structure in some functional protein. This may or may not have a significant effect on the functioning of the cell involved. When one mutant cell is associated with 10^6 or 10^8 unmutated cells of the same tissue, the effect of the mutation, no matter how extreme, will usually be quite undetectable. The effect of a mutation will only become recognizable chemically, microscopically, or clinically, if in some way the change in the original mutant can be *magnified*. If we neglect some very far-fetched speculations, this can only occur when the cell in which the mutation occurs can undergo extensive proliferation. If, for instance, a somatic mutation should occur in a cell at an early stage in the division of the fertilized ovum, the resulting effect might involve a substantial proportion of the cells of the body. Perhaps the classic example in mammals is the fleece mosaicism in sheep described by Fraser and Short, in which the proportion of the skin area carrying the "mutant" type of fleece appears to be determined by how early in the course of primary segmentation of the ovum the mutation occurred.

When a somatic mutation occurs in a fully developed organism, if its effect is to be detectable, proliferation of the mutant must be capable of outstripping that of its unmutated congener cells. Whatever part the accelerating environmental factors (carcinogen, radiation, or virus) may play in carcinogenesis, the operational result is the emergence of a mutant clone of cells which produces a persisting mass of descendant cells far beyond that arising from any normal clone. In pathology, neoplasia is the most common indication of the occurrence of somatic mutation or of a sequence of mutations.

Some years ago the concept of the forbidden clone was introduced as a theoretical basis of autoimmune disease (Burnet, 1959). Before discussing this it is desirable first that one define a clone as the progeny derived by asexual multiplication from a single cell. Whenever mutation or other inheritable modification occurs, the cell involved is taken as initiating a new clone. When two clones differ this may be as a result of genetic differences in the ordinary sense that they arise from two dissimilar fertilized ova. On the other hand, two clones within the same organism may differ because one or both have undergone somatic mutation or some equivalent inheritable change in the course of their differentiation and subsequent proliferation. There is no reason why mutations of similar type and with the same phenotypic result should not occur at either level.

The lymphoid cell system more than any other population of cells in the body is in a particularly favorable situation to show the effects of somatic mutation and selective proliferation. There are a rapid normal turnover of cells and a perpetual liability to massive proliferation (during infection or immunization) and massive destruction (under any corticosteroid mediated stress situation). Quite minor mutational differences will therefore be liable to give rise to conspicuous changes in the character of the lymphoid cell population.

The most important mutational change that could be relevant to autoimmune disease would be the development of a resistance to that destructive action of antigenic contact which normally eliminates cells capable of reacting with accessible antigens before they enter the general lymphoid cell population of the body. Cells of such "forbidden clones" would then react to the corresponding body antigen as normal immune clones do to the corresponding foreign antigen, by proliferation and antibody production. If, in view of its abnormal mutant character, the clone had pathogenic capacities, these could be manifested either by the production of antibody damaging to the target cells or by the accumulation of descendant cells capable of damaging the target cells by contact and surface interaction.

In addition to the development of resistance to the destructive effect of appropriate antigenic contact, there are several other possibilities of mutational change that are relevant to the general theme. A mutation might, without changing the general pattern of the combining site of antibody, increase its avidity for the specific antigen, it might produce a pattern with a wider range of activity, it might produce a clone of cells with abnormally high capacity to infiltrate into areas containing the corresponding antigen, and separately or as part of any of these mutational changes, a changed *antigenicity* of some component of the cell might arise.

Recently experimental evidence directly supporting this point of view for our type autoimmune disease AHA has been provided by Leddy and Bakemeier. They found that, while virtually all typical antibodies in human beings can be shown to be made up of Ig G globulins with both L and K antigens on the light chains, AHA antibodies eluted from Coombs positive cells were much more homogeneous. Their 20 cases of AHA included nine that had L type chains only and four with K type light chains. Several others had such an abnormal preponderance of one or the other that one could easily postulate a selective advantage or a prior appearance of the clone responsible for the dominant antibody type. The obvious and only simple interpretation is that the cells involved in producing the homogeneous antibody globulin are monoclonal in character and arise from a single mutational event.

In a subsequent section (p. 28) it will be necessary to consider the need for some control over the potential dangers of somatic mutation and the bearing of this on the char-

acteristic variability in intensity of autoimmune disease during its course and on the "burning out" that sometimes terminates it.

Function of the Thymus and Its Relation to Autoimmune Disease

The thymus occupies a key situation in all modern considerations of immunologic function, but there is no unanimity in the formulation of its role. The following statements are each substantiated by experimental or clinical work and are probably wrong only when other controlling mechanisms not yet recognized or understood play a part in functions at present ascribed to the thymus.

1. The thymus is a derivative of branchial epithelium, and at a relatively early stage in mammalian embryonic life lymphocytes develop from thymic epithelium. They are the first lymphocytes to be found in the body, and the primary colonization of the lymphoid organs with the cells forming lymph follicles is from these thymic lymphocytes.

2. In pre- and postnatal life the thymus reaches its maximal activity as a producer of lymphocytes, the relative activity at different stages varying considerably from species to species. The thymus remains an active site of lymphocytic mitosis as long as cortical tissue persists.

3. The thymus throughout its existence is a lymphoepithelial organ in which the epithelial component provides essentially an appropriate environment for multiplication and differentiation of lymphocytes. There is evidence of varying degrees of cogency that the epithelial cells produce products with the following activities: (a) to stimulate proliferation of lymphocytes in the thymic cortex; (b) to direct "stem cells" to differentiation as lymphocytes; (c) to maintain the viability of lymphocytic clones liberated from the thymus at the prenatal or perinatal period; and (d) to provide an internal environment in which immunocytes making contact with the corresponding antigenic determinant are inactivated or destroyed.

4. The lymphocytes of the thymus are subject to a rapid turnover. An acceptable thymic graft is completely repopulated with host cells within 2 to 3 weeks. Subject to considerable uncertainties, one current interpretation is as follows:

There are stem cells circulating in the blood which probably develop in the bone marrow. The cytologic origin of these stem cells is unknown, but there is an increasing opinion that they have the morphologic character of small lymphocytes. It is in fact becoming expedient to regard the small lymphocytes simply as a common mobile carrier of a wide variety of "information" and to give up any attempt to trace their cytologic origin. They may in the last analysis all be of thymic origin. In the living animal, however, what is important is that the stem cells lodge in the thymic cortex and under the influence of "epithelial hormone" proliferate and differentiate to immunocytes. A constant stream (in the young animal) or trickle (in older individuals) of such newly differentiated immunocytes passes to the various lymphoid organs.

5. Since removal of the thymus from half-grown or adult individuals has only minimal effects on immune function, any vital activities of the thymus are either confined to the pre- and perinatal period or, more likely, are progressively taken over by the other lymphoid tissues of the body. There are experimental studies, however, which suggest that even in adult life absence of a thymus can be a relatively severe immunologic handicap. It is possible that throughout life the thymus may be necessary if *new* immune patterns are to be produced.

6. The pattern of lymphoid cell multiplication in the cortex of the thymus is unique in mammals, and normally there are no germinal centers in either cortex or medulla, while plasma cells are inconspicuous and are seen only in relation to blood vessels. If antigenic material is injected directly into the substance of the thymus, both germinal centers and plasma cells may develop, so that their absence in the normal organ is presumably dependent on the maintenance of structural integrity. We are strongly disposed to Clark's interpretation that the tenuous epithelial framework of the cortex is the controlling factor in inhibiting germinal center and plasma cell formation.

7. Again following Clark, we believe that there is no clear distinction between cortex and medulla. The thymus is a spongy epithelial structure, the portion packed with proliferating lymphoid cells being cortex, the less heavily infiltrated area being medulla. Depletion of cortex and expansion of medulla are seen in many conditions.

If this outline of the function of the thymus is correct, it may obviously play a significant part in autoimmune disease. Earlier it has been mentioned that lesions may be seen in the thymus in some cases of SLE and of AHA,

and in the NZB mouse disease (p. 16). There are some other relevant pathologic conditions of the thymus that should be mentioned.

1. Failure of the lymphocyte-producing function of the thymus to develop has now been observed in a small number of infants (Hitzig et al.). In general, these infants show no circulating lymphocytes, they will accept skin homografts, they are extremely susceptible to infection, and all reported cases have died.

2. In a majority of cases of myasthenia gravis in young women the thymus removed at operation shows large numbers of germinal centers (Sloan). It should be noted that myasthenia gravis is the *only* autoimmune disease in which the thymus is often removed surgically and therefore available for satisfactory histologic examination. There are isolated observations to suggest that in active chronic hepatitis and rheumatoid arthritis as well as SLE such lesions would be more frequently found in material obtained at biopsy if this were practical than in the material normally examined at autopsy. Gunn et al. have found that 32 per cent of thymus biopsy samples taken in the course of surgery for thyrotoxicosis show germinal centers.

3. Nonmalignant tumors of the thymus, lymphoepitheliomatous in character, may be associated with systemic disease, particularly myasthenia gravis. Much more rarely erythroid aplasia and acquired agammaglobulinemia may be associated with thymoma. In none of these conditions is removal of the thymoma curative, and in all three there is insufficient evidence to allow a full interpretation of the syndrome on an autoimmune basis. Myasthenia gravis associated with thymoma, however, usually shows even more marked serologic tests than the nontumorous variety, and it is hard to believe that both are not basically autoimmune in character. Perhaps the most likely interpretation is that the thymoma formation is secondary to chronic stimulation of the thymic epithelium when it contains antigenic determinants in common with the other target organ of an immune process.

If the forbidden clone hypothesis is used as a basis, there are four ways in which the thymus may theoretically be involved in autoimmune disease.

1. During infancy and childhood the thymus is the most active center of lymphoid cell multiplication and is therefore the most likely *site of origin* of somatic mutations pathogenic or otherwise in such cells.

2. By hypothesis a clone of autoimmune cells can behave in the thymus as normal immunocytes do in the general lymphoid tissue, i.e., in producing germinal centers and plasma cells. These findings in the thymus may therefore serve as an *index* of the presence of autoimmune clones in the body.

3. Extensive proliferation of autoimmune cells in the thymus may make the organ a *major source* of pathogenic antibodies and cells. In myasthenia gravis removal of the thymus at an early stage is often curative and is associated with a disappearance of specific antibody in a high proportion.

4. The thymus may be a *target organ* against which part of the autoimmune process is directed. In myasthenia gravis the thymic epithelium reacts apparently with the same antibody that combines with the A band of voluntary muscle (van der Geld et al.). In SLE there are many plasma cells in the region of the lost cortical tissue, and the characteristic whorled proliferation of epithelial cells has much in common with the histologic appearance of nonmalignant thymomas. For a variety of reasons it seems likely that epithelial proliferation is a secondary result of autoimmune disease rather than a primary aspect of the process, and both appearances are therefore best regarded as a response of target tissue to chronic stimulation and damage.

The Pathogenesis of Autoimmune Disease

The presence of demonstrable antibody that reacts with a normal body component may be an important piece of the evidence that leads to a diagnosis of autoimmune disease, but it is important not to equate the presence of antibody with disease. Antibody is probably the most important factor when the autoimmune process involves the highly accessible antigens on the surface of any circulating cells of the blood, but in other conditions a direct attack by cells is probably more important. Other factors which must not be neglected are the potentially damaging action of soluble antigen-antibody complexes, particularly on the kidney, and the possible participation of complement.

Evidence for these types of immunopathogenic action has been derived in the first instance from the study of a range of experimental models.

Experimental Models of Autoimmune Disease

It has been known for many years that by immunizing an animal of species A with cells derived from species B, the antiserum so obtained when given intravenously to a B animal would be likely to cause serious damage to the cells used for immunization. Hemolytic anemia, thrombocytopenic purpura, and the so-called Masugi nephritis can be produced in this fashion. In general, simple injection of cells into an animal of the species providing the cells will produce at most isoantibodies defining antigenic differences between strains within the species; an animal's own cells are not antigenic. The main value of these experiments in which disease is produced by the passive administration of serum produced in a foreign species has been (a) to underline the significance of tolerance to "self" tissues, and (b) to show that antibody can in fact serve as a pathogenic agent. Antibodies produced in autoimmune processes are in general far less avid and effective than these experimentally produced antibodies, and in recent years relatively little interest has been shown in this type of experiment. On the other hand there has been a considerable concentration of effort in showing that the statement that constituents naturally present in an animal are nonantigenic is incorrect.

With the use of adjuvants, particularly Freund complete adjuvant (FCA) of paraffin, emulsifier, and killed acid-fast bacilli, and large amounts of semipurified and concentrated antigen, it is possible to produce a wide range of autoantibodies and to induce severe and lethal disease. If hemithyroidectomy is performed on a rabbit and the thyroid tissue used for its own immunization with FCA, antibodies against thyroglobulin will be produced, and an infiltration of the remaining portion of the thyroid with lymphocytes becomes demonstrable (Witebsky et al.). With still more strenuous treatment, rabbits immunized with large amounts of ribonucleoprotein from rabbit tissues in FCA gave rise to almost as extensive a range of antibodies as are found in sera from patients with SLE.

The effect of heavy immunization with FCA in overriding the normal ban on production of antibody against accessible components and accentuating the immune response against many inaccessible antigens is probably to be related to the cellular constitution of the granuloma which develops and within which most of the antibody is produced. Here apparently normal controls break down, and in addition to the development of autoantibody we also observe or deduce the appearance of aggressive cells capable of specific attack on a target tissue. The conditions in experimental allergic encephalomyelitis are especially interesting because of the evidence that the *antibody* produced antagonizes the lesion-producing power of the aggressive cells, both being produced by the same immunization with isologous brain material in FCA. The extent to which these "aggressive" cells are equivalent to the cells of "forbidden clones" in human autoimmune disease is unknown.

The next experimental model to be mentioned is the so-called "graft vs. host" reaction. In broad terms this results when viable lymphoid cells are introduced parenterally into an animal which is not genetically similar to the donor of the cells but which, for one reason or another, will allow the cells to colonize its tissues. These requirements can be fulfilled (1) when parental type cells are injected into an F1 hybrid, (2) when lymphoid cells from an adult donor are injected into an embryonic or newborn recipient, or (3) when lymphoid cells from a different strain are injected into a heavily irradiated recipient.

Extensive experiments with each of these situations have shown that proper choice of strains and of conditions of experiment is essential if clear and reproducible results are to be obtained. Features common to all types of successful experiment are (1) multiplication of the donor cell type with, when this is technically demonstrable, the production of donor type gamma globulin; (2) damage to a variety of host tissues often with a phase of host cell proliferation (the splenic enlargement and the chorioallantoic foci in the Simonsen reaction are predominantly due to accumulation of host cells); (3) in the late stages usually severe "runting" with great atrophy of lymphoid tissues.

Particularly in the "parent into F1" system when the injection is made into young recipients, a wide variety of damaging effects resembling those of autoimmune disease can be observed. In this situation we have a variety of adult cells not susceptible to any controls present in the juvenile host and therefore in virtually the same position as is postulated for forbidden clones in human disease.

The pathogenic action of antigen-antibody complexes is perhaps best seen in the study by Dixon et al. of the result of injecting relatively large amounts of soluble antigens daily

in rabbits. Animals show wide individual differences in their capacity to produce antibody, and in these experiments three groups could be recognized: (A) rabbits actively producing antibody so that the standard dose of antigen given intravenously was rapidly removed; (B) poor producers in which the cir-

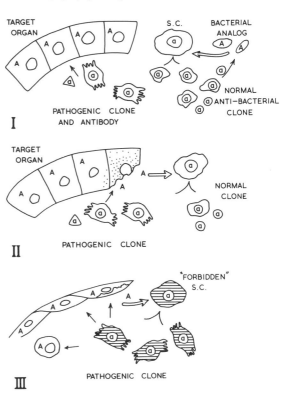

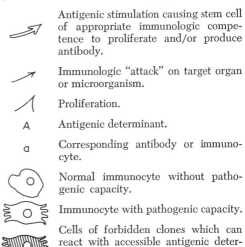

Figure 3–1. Schematic diagram to illustrate theoretical concepts used in discussing autoimmune disease. I—Rheumatic fever. II—Hashimoto's disease. III—Systemic lupus erythematosus.

Symbols used have the following significance:

Antigenic stimulation causing stem cell of appropriate immunologic competence to proliferate and/or produce antibody.

Immunologic "attack" on target organ or microorganism.

Proliferation.

A   Antigenic determinant.

a   Corresponding antibody or immunocyte.

Normal immunocyte without pathogenic capacity.

Immunocyte with pathogenic capacity.

Cells of forbidden clones which can react with accessible antigenic determinants.

culating antibody united with a portion of the injected antigen and the resulting complex was kept soluble by the persisting presence of excess of antigen; and (C) rabbits producing no antibody so that no antigen-antibody complex resulted. With only minor exceptions, group A rabbits showed some acute glomerulitis with proteinuria and recovery; of group B rabbits, 43 of 49 showed chronic glomerulonephritis with proteinuria, hematuria, and azotemia, while those in group C had no kidney lesions. Electron microscopic study of the lesions in group B kidneys showed thickening of the glomerular basement membrane and deposition of foreign material on the epithelial side of the membrane.

McCluskey et al. produced rather similar lesions in mice by direct injection of soluble antigen-antibody complexes. Whenever we have antigen-antibody complexes in the body, complement is likely to be involved, and absorption of Ag-Ab-C[1] to the surface of cells may produce a variety of effects including hemolysis, the formation of platelet thrombi and fibrin, and the discharge of lysosomes in polymorphonuclear leukocytes and other cells.

The Direct Activity of Cells Against Target Tissues

The origin and character of immunocytes are matters of current controversy, but no one can doubt the existence of cells capable of reacting with appropriate foreign antigens, and opinion is virtually unanimous that the significant cell types concerned are lymphocytes—large, medium, or small—plasma cells, and monocytes. It is simplest and common usage to regard these as essentially different functional forms of the same clones of immunocytes. This, however, has not been established, and there is a growing impression that activities common to different morphologic cell types may result from "informational transfer" of some less far-reaching type than direct somatic inheritance.

For the present discussion, however, all that is needed is the recognition of the existence of reactive mononuclear cells and the potentiality for their relatively rapid increase in numbers.

The destructive action of specifically immune lymphoid cells, usually on neoplastic target cells both in vitro and in vivo, has now been clearly demonstrated in a number of situations. Rosenau and Moon used lymphocytes from mice immunized with L cells (of C3H origin) and showed that in tissue culture the lymphocytes attached to the target cells and destroyed them. No added complement was needed for the action. In their experiments the motility of the lymphocytes was lost in the process; there are other indications that the interaction of competent cell and target cell may be lethal or damaging to both (e.g., Baker et al., McKhann). Others have found, however, that in similar situations no damage to the lymphocytes could be recognized (Wilson). The cytotoxic action of immune lymphocytes is presumably a result of mutual or one-sided liberation of pharmacologically active agents with a damaging increase in cell surface permeability. This is probably always associated with more or less damage to lysosomes and liberation of their enzymes. It is the type of process which histologic sections suggest is occurring in the villi of the synovium of a rheumatoid joint or around the liver lobules in lupoid hepatitis.

Recent studies of the development of the delayed hypersensitivity reaction to tuberculin indicate that only a proportion of the mononuclear cells that accumulate are immunologically specific. Spector's interpretation is that a relatively small number of specifically reactive cells can produce a local increase in capillary permeability that allows all types of circulating leukocytes to enter the tissues. The nature of the cellular accumulation will then depend mainly on the relative speed with which different sorts of leukocytes are removed from the region. When we are dealing with an autoimmune situation involving a relatively inaccessible intracellular antigen a somewhat similar situation may arise. In an intact organ none of the antigen may be accessible to circulating cells, but following infection or trauma blood cells will enter the tissue nonspecifically. If these include cells reactive against the antigen in question, the reaction will be damaging to adjacent tissue cells, thus allowing more antigen to become accessible and opening up the possibility of an expanding and self-perpetuating pathologic process.

Controlling Processes in Autoimmune Disease

Perhaps the most outstanding impression one receives from a detailed study of any type of autoimmune disease is the lack of uniformity between cases. This holds for the duration and intensity of clinical manifestations and equally for the range and concentration of antibodies in the circulation. A wide diversity of character would be expected on the twofold assumption of the forbidden clone hypothesis that modification of antibody pattern is dependent on somatic mutation and that resistance to the primary homeostatic process by which tolerance is safeguarded is also due to somatic mutation. For both we can adopt a strictly darwinian approach that any mutant which under the existing circumstances has a short-term advantage for proliferation and survival will prosper.

Taken alone, this is probably too simple a formulation. Having regard to the frequency of opportunity for somatic mutation in any large long-lived animal such as man, it is necessary to postulate and if possible to imagine the form of controls which can prevent an early and lethal onset of a wide variety of malignant and autoimmune processes.

Many autoimmune diseases undergo partial or complete regression, sometimes after splenectomy or thymectomy, sometimes after tapered-off courses of corticosteroids, or quite spontaneously. If one examines a large series of "normal" individuals for low titer autoantibodies of almost any type, a significant proportion of positive tests will be obtained; there are apparently normal people who have a hypergammaglobulinemia, of either the diffuse type (polyclonal) or the monoclonal myeloma type, and sections of "normal" thymuses often show an occasional germinal center. It seems that minor autoimmune processes are often initiated but do not progress to overt disease. The process by which this control is exerted is unknown, but there are indications that it may be of the same nature as the "immunologic surveillance" of mutant cells that Thomas, Prehn, and others consider an important protective mechanism against neoplastic disease. This is most simply pictured as resulting from the association with the mutant of a new and therefore foreign antigenic determinant against which what is equivalent to homograft immunity can develop, with eventual elimination of the mutant clone.

There is indirect evidence of a quite distinct controlling mechanism in relation to antibody quality. In acquired hemolytic anemia the antibodies produced, or at least those demonstrable in the circulation, differ considerably from those obtained if, for example, a rabbit is immunized with human red cells. The antibodies are of such a quality that they do not cause agglutination or lysis in vivo; they are incomplete in that their effect on red cells is not to cause direct agglutination but merely to render them agglutinable by an antiglobulin (the direct Coombs test). Or they are "cold agglutinins" only effective at temperatures well below 37° C. No adequate explanation of this "temperate" quality of autoimmune antibodies has yet been provided. One feels intuitively that we are in the presence of a homeostatic process that has not been completely overcome.

Principles and Potentialities of Treatment

Experience indicates that the only currently helpful modes of treatment of serious autoimmune disease are by the anti-inflammatory corticosteroids on the one hand and immunosuppressive drugs, 6-mercaptopurine and its derivative Imuran, on the other.

A variety of derivatives of the natural hormone cortisol are used in the treatment of rheumatoid arthritis and other conditions, but there is no indication that their action differs from that of cortisol (hydrocortisone), which is also the effective form into which cortisone is converted in the body. The term cortisol will therefore be considered synonymous for most purposes with anti-inflammatory corticosteroids in general, including prednisone, prednisolone, and cortisone.

The pharmacologic effects of cortisol which may be relevant to its use in autoimmune disease are as follows:

1. With large doses there is a striking lymphocytolytic effect, particularly in the thymic cortex, and a diminution in the total number of medium and small lymphocytes.

2. Circulating eosinophils are reduced or absent perhaps as a secondary result.

3. There is a diminution in surface permeability of most cells, and a simple and possibly correct way of generalizing a wide range of cortisol activities is that it weakens or depresses all immunologically relevant reactions in which cell surfaces are concerned. These may include phagocytosis, stimulation of cells to proliferation or antibody production by contact with antigen, the release of pharmacologically active substances by stimulated cells, and the exposure of intracellular antigens.

Corticosteroids may have different effects in different species, and clinical experience indicates that there are important individual differences in human beings. Antibody production is much less influenced in man, monkey, and guinea pig than in rabbit, rat, and mouse.

A number of cytotoxic drugs have been shown to be capable of inhibiting an antibody response when given in doses close to a toxic level. These include 6-mercaptopurine, cyclophosphamide, and methotrexate. Of these, 6-MP and its derivative azathioprine (Imuran) have been those most commonly used in therapy and discussion will be limited to them.

In the rabbit it has now been established that an adequate dose of 6-MP over several days, during which a relatively large dose of an antigen such as bovine serum albumin (BSA) is given, will not only prevent antibody production against BSA but will leave the animal tolerant after the drug is stopped. It has been shown that such tolerant animals will react normally to an unrelated antigen.

In terms of clonal selection ideas, it seems that a certain concentration of drug is lethal to any cell activated to a potential antibody-producing status by contact with antigen. In order to produce effective tolerance *all* cells capable of reacting with the antigen must be stimulated and simultaneously exposed to the drug. This requires a relatively high dose of antigen and a near toxic dosage of 6-MP. In the guinea pig, which is much less susceptible to the general toxic action of 6-MP, the immunosuppressive effect is not shown.

When these experimental findings are transferred to the clinical situation it becomes evident that neither group of drugs is likely to have curative powers. An adequate short course of prednisolone or its equivalent will almost regularly greatly ameliorate any acute phase of autoimmune disease. Failure to do so can, in fact, be used as a significant criterion against a diagnosis of an autoimmune process. There is, however, no elimination of any pathogenic clones of cells, and with continuing treatment there are serious dangers of hormonal side effects as well as a tendency for the autoimmune manifestations sooner or later to escape from control. The handling of corticosteroid therapy in autoimmune disease is a matter of empirical skill not yet logically describable.

Imuran therapy is in the early stages and might be expected to be effective (a) when only a limited number of forbidden clones are involved, (b) when the autoantigen concerned is present in relatively high concentration, and (c) when the drug can be maintained for a few weeks at least. It is interesting therefore that probably the most optimistic report has come from Mackay et al. for the treatment of lupoid hepatitis. Of all the autoimmune diseases this is the one which fits nearest to the three conditions required.

General Conclusions

Throughout this discussion of generalized autoimmune disease and of the various less well defined localized forms and mixed allergic and autoimmune conditions, there is an inescapable contrast between the normal and the disease-prone individual. In the normal person most or all organs containing inaccessible antigens must suffer occasional minor trauma or infection, allowing liberation of the antigen. Nothing more than an occasional minimal production of antibody results. In a small minority local autoimmune disease arises as in the thyroid, liver, or adrenal glands. The vast majority of individuals given such drugs as quinidine and Sedormid experience only the normal pharmacologic effects; the exceptional individual develops thrombocytopenic purpura. Similarly, there must be small amounts of denatured globulin produced in the body every day, but both detectable antibody of RF type and rheumatoid arthritis are rare. So are all the other diseases ascribed to autoimmune processes and a wide range of idiosyncratic drug reactions.

Within each apparent nosological entity too, there is a degree of individuality that hardly allows two cases to be alike. When refined serologic tests are possible, as in the acquired hemolytic anemias, in SLE when there is a sophisticated approach to nucleic acid antigens, or in rheumatoid arthritis when a battery of allotypes is available, the individuality of each serum is equally evident.

This heterogeneity of allergic and autoimmune disease is the key to its understanding —just as the intense heterogeneity of antibody points to what has been called the darwinian approach to immunological theory. To understand immunity and the diseases or accidents that arise by immunologic malfunction, it is necessary to regard the lymphoid cell populations of the body from which the immunologically competent cells arise as a semi-autonomous population subject to storms of proliferation and episodes in which vast numbers are destroyed. Lymphoid cells have the same chromosomal inheritance as all other somatic cells of the body; but being subject, like every type of replicating cell or organism, to mutation (in this case, somatic mutation), the detailed structure of the population is necessarily determined by what can only be described as an evolutionary process involving mutation, selection and survival.

Mutation is blind error within the limitations of a continuing capacity for replication and transcription of the nucleic acid segment involved. Its results are insignificant unless the phenotypic expression of the mutation is such as to give the clone concerned an advantage over its unchanged congeners. In the mammalian body the lymphoid cell system is the only free population of cells with an active traffic throughout the body. If the clonal selection approach to immunity has any relevance at all, the whole function of the system is dependent on a balance between selective proliferation on the one hand and both specific and nonspecific destruction on the other. It is in this system above all others that we can expect the effects of somatic mutation to be magnified until they are expressed as disease.

Mutation is a random process, but it takes place against a background of macromolecular structure determined by the genetic history of the organism or cell. Modification of the background may greatly influence both the frequency with which a given somatic mutation can occur and the probability that its occurrence will allow the emergence of a phenotypically mutant cell line. This provides a reasonable basis for the fact that different strains or individuals of the same species may differ greatly in the frequency with which a certain type of somatic mutant can be detected.

What may become one of the most important intellectual approaches to autoimmune disease has been opened up by Burch's use of the epidemiologic data, especially age and sex specific incidence in standard populations, to deduce the general character of the random process concerned. This is derived basically from early studies of the specific age and sex incidence of cancer, but has been elaborated by Burch in an attempt to assess the relative effects of genetic (germinal) abnormality and of the somatic mutations which are presumed to be the rare random events occurring over the whole life period. His conclusion about rheumatoid arthritis is that about half the population is genetically "at risk" and that the disease arises by a sequence of somatic mutations, four or five in females and two or three in males being needed

to cause rheumatoid arthritis of classic intensity. One's impression is that detailed interpretations of this sort will require progressive modification as more accurate data and better understanding of pathogenesis are obtained. The essential features, however, seem likely to hold despite any changes of immunologic opinion. They are (1) that noninfectious diseases now generally regarded as of autoimmune type each have their own characteristic age specific incidence curves and that these have significant resemblances, both among themselves and to the age incidence curves of malignant diseases; (2) the mathematical study and interpretation of such regularities in terms of the probable biologic processes concerned is a legitimate scientific activity; (3) somatic mutation is the only concept which provides the necessary qualities and flexibility to provide a basis for these regularities.

However important somatic mutation may be in providing cells with antibody patterns and individual capacities or anomalies from which new significant clones of lymphoid cells may arise, the selective internal environment must always play an equally significant part. At various points in this discussion we have mentioned the possibility of trauma, infection, or autoimmune attack in making accessible otherwise hidden antigens, of pathogens with an accidental antigenic similarity to body constituents provoking a potentially pathogenic immune response, and of drugs which are effectively antigenic only in a small minority of people. There are probably still many other relevant aspects of the internal environment yet to be discovered. There are insistent suggestions that emotional factors may be concerned in immunopathology presumably through hormonal changes, that chronic granulomatous conditions may produce effects analogous to the experimental use of Freund complete adjuvant and that there is still much to be learned about the immunologic functions of spleen and thymus.

A full understanding of autoimmune disease is still far away, but one can feel confident that such an understanding will be in the framework used here—somatic mutation as a source of both immune patterns and potentially pathogenic anomalies of behavior, and the internal environment with all its physiologic and traumatic changes plus the chance of microbial infection or drug ingestion, to serve as the selective agent that will decide whether pathogenic clones flourish or disappear.

As in every biologic situation, heredity and environment, nature and nurture, must be given equal significance or our interpretation and our actions will be unbalanced and ineffective.

REFERENCES

Ackroyd, J. F.: Platelet agglutinins and lysins in the pathogenesis of thrombocytopenic purpura with a note on platelet groups. Brit. Med. Bull., *11:*28, 1954.

Baker, P., Weiser, R. S., Jutila, J., Evans, C. A., and Blandau, R. J.: Mechanism of tumor homograft rejection: The behavior of Sarcoma I Ascites tumor in the A/Jax and C57B1/6K mouse. Ann. New York Acad. Sc., *100:*46, 1962.

Bielschowsky, M., Helyer, B. J., and Howie, J. B.: Spontaneous haemolytic anaemia in mice of the NZB/BL strain. Proc. Univ. Otago Med. Sch., *37:*9, 1959.

Burch, P. R. J.: Autoimmunity: Some etiological aspects. Lancet, *1:*1253, 1963.

Burnet, F. M.: The Clonal Selection Theory of Acquired Immunity. (The Abraham Flexner Lectures of Vanderbilt University 1958.) Nashville, Cambridge University Press and Vanderbilt University Press, 1959.

Burnet, F. M.: The immunological significance of the thymus: An extension of the clonal selection theory of immunity. Austral. Ann. Med., *11:*79, 1962.

Burnet, F. M.: A darwinian approach to immunity. Nature, *203:*451, 1964(a).

Burnet, F. M.: The pathology of the thymus (with special reference to autoimmune disease). Sommer Memorial Lecture delivered at Portland, Oregon, April 22, 1964. Northwest. Med., *63:* 519–601, 1964(b).

Burnet, F. M.: Somatic mutation and chronic disease. Brit. Med. J., *1:*338, 1965.

Clark, S. L., Jr.: The thymus in mice of strain 129/J studied with the electron microscope. Am. J. Anat., *112:*1, 1963.

Dameshek, W.: Discussion. In Good, R. A., and Gabrielsen, A. E. (eds.): The Thymus in Immunobiology, p. 738. New York, Hoeber Medical Division, Harper & Row, 1964.

Dixon, F. J., Feldman, J. D., and Vaquez, J. J.: Experimental glomerulonephritis. The pathogenesis of a laboratory model resembling the spectrum of human glomerulonephritis. J. Exper. Med., *113:* 899, 1961.

Feldman, M., Globerson, R., and Nachtigal, D.: Discussion. In Conceptual Advances in Immunology and Oncology, p. 442. New York, Hoeber Medical Division, Harper & Row, 1963.

Fraser, A. S., and Short, B. F.: Studies of sheep mosaic for fleece type. I. Patterns and origin of mosaicism. Austral. J. Biol. Sc., *11:*200, 1958.

Goudie, R. B., Anderson, J. R., and Gray, K. C.: Complement fixing anti-thyroid antibodies in hospital patients with asymptomatic thyroid lesions. J. Path. Bact., 77:389, 1959.

Gunn, A., Michie, W., and Irvine, W. J.: The thymus in thyroid disease. Lancet, *2:*776, 1964.

Hall, R., Owen, S. G., and Smart, G. A.: Evidence for genetic pre-disposition to formation of thyroid antibodies. Lancet, *2:*187, 1960.

Helyer, B. J., and Howie, J. B.: Renal disease associated with positive LE tests in a cross-bred strain of mice. Nature, *197:*197, 1963.

Hirschhorn, K., Schreibman, R. R., Verbo, S., and Gruskin, R. H.: The action of Streptolysin S on peripheral lymphocytes of normal subjects and patients with rheumatic fever. Proc. Nat. Acad. Sc., *52:*1151, 1964.

Hitzig, W. H., Biro, Z., Bosch, H., and Huser, H. J.: Agammaglobulinemie und Alymphocytose mit Schwund des lymphatisches Gewebes. Helve. Paediat. Acta, *6:*551, 1958.

Irvine, W. J., Macgregor, A. C., Stuart, A. E., and Hall, G. H.: Hashimoto's disease in uniovular twins. Lancet, *2:*850, 1961.

Jerne, N. K.: Immunological speculations. Ann. Rev. Microbiol., *14:*341, 1960.

Kaplan, M. H.: Immunological relation of streptococcal and tissue antigens: I. Properties of an antigen in certain strains of group A streptococci exhibiting an immunologic cross reaction with human heart tissue. J. Immunol., *90:*595, 1963.

Kariaklis, A., Valaes, T., Pantelakis, S. N., and Doxiadis, S. R.: Thymectomy in an infant with autoimmune haemolytic anaemia. Lancet, *2:*778, 1964.

Kunkel, H. C., and Tan, E. M.: Autoantibodies and disease. Adv. Immunol., *4:*351, 1964.

Leddy, J. P., and Bakemeier, R. F.: Structural aspects of human erythrocyte autoantibodies. I. L chain types and electrophoretic dispersion. J. Exper. Med., *121:*1, 1965.

Lederberg, J.: Genes and antibodies. Science, *129:*1649, 1959.

Mackay, I. R., and Burnet, F. M.: Autoimmune Diseases. Springfield, Charles C Thomas, 1963.

Mackay, I. R., Ungar, B., and Weiden, S.: The treatment of active chronic hepatitis and lupoid hepatitis with 6-mercaptopurine and azothioprine. Lancet, *1:*899, 1964.

Marshall, A. H. E., and White, R. G.: The immunological reactivity of the thymus. Brit. J. Exper. Path., *42:*379, 1961.

McCluskey, R. T., Benacerraf, B., and Miller, F.: Passive acute glomerulonephritis induced by antigen-antibody complexes. Proc. Soc. Exper. Biol. Med., *111:*764, 1962.

McKhann, C. F.: Destruction of immune lymphoid cells in transplantation immunity. J. Immunol., *91:* 693, 1963.

Meek, J. C., Jones, A. E., Lewis, W. J., and Vanderlaan, W. P.: Characterization of the long acting thyroid stimulator of Graves disease. Proc. Nat. Acad. Sc., *52:*342, 1964.

Mellors, R. C., Nowoslawski, A., and Korngold, L.: Rheumatoid arthritis and the cellular origin of rheumatoid factors. Am. J. Path., *39:*533, 1961.

Nossal, G. J. V., Ada, G. L., and Austin, C. M.: Antigens in immunity. IV. Cellular localization of ^{125}I and ^{131}I-labelled flagella in lymph nodes. Austral. J. Exper. Biol., *42:*311, 1964.

Orgel, L. E.: The maintenance of the accuracy of protein synthesis and its relevance to ageing. Proc. Nat. Acad. Sc., *49:*517, 1963.

Owen, R. D.: Immunogenetic consequences of vascular

anastamoses between bovine twins. Science, 102:400, 1945.

Paterson, P. Y., and Martin, H. S.: Suppression of allergic encephalomyelitis in rats by means of antibrain serum. J. Exper. Med., 117:755, 1963.

Prehn, R. T.: Tumor specific immunity to transplanted dibenz[a,h]-anthracene induced sarcomas. Cancer Res., 20:1614, 1960.

Roitt, I. M., Jones, H. E. H., and Doniach, D.: Mechanisms of tissue damage in human experimental autoimmune thyroiditis. Second Int. Symp. Immunopath., Basel, p. 174, 1962.

Rose, N. R., and Witebsky, E.: Studies on organ specificity. V. Changes in the thyroid glands of rabbits following active immunization with rabbit thyroid extracts. J. Immunol., 76:417, 1956.

Rosenau, W., and Moon, H. D.: Lysis of homologous cells by sensitized lymphocytes in tissue culture. J. Nat. Cancer Inst., 27:471, 1961.

Schwartz, R., and Dameshek, W.: Drug induced immunological tolerance. Nature, 183:1682, 1959.

Shulman, N. R.: A mechanism of cell destruction in individuals sensitized to foreign antigens and its implications in autoimmunity. Ann. Int. Med., 60:506, 1964.

Sloan, H. E.: The thymus in myasthenia gravis. Surgery, 13:154, 1943.

Stevens, K. M.: The aetiology of systemic lupus erythematosus. Lancet, 2:506, 1964.

Strauss, A. J. L., van der Geld, H. W. R., Kemp, P. G., Dexum, E., and Goodman, H. C.: Immunological concomitants of myasthenia gravis. Ann. New York Acad. Sc., 124:744, 1965.

Talmage, D. W.: Immunological specificity. Science, 129:1643, 1959.

Thomas, L.: Discussion. In Lawrence, H. C. (ed.): Cellular and Humoral Aspects of the Hypersensitive States, p. 529. New York, Hoeber Medical Division, Harper & Row, 1959.

ven der Geld, H., Feltkampf, T. E. W., and Osterhuis, H. J. G. H.: Reactivity of myasthenia gravis serum γ-globulin with skeletal muscle and thymus demonstrated by immuno-fluorescence. Proc. Soc. Exper. Biol. Med., 115:782, 1964.

Wilson, D. B.: The reaction of immunologically activated lymphoid cells against homologous target tissue cells in vitro. J. Cell & Comp. Physiol., 62:273, 1963.

Witebsky, E., and Rose, N. R.: Studies on organ specificity. IV. Production of rabbit thyroid antibodies in the rabbit. J. Immunol., 76:408, 1956.

Witebsky, E., Rose, N. R., Terplan, K., Paine, J. R., and Egan, R. W.: Chronic thyroiditis and autoimmunization. J.A.M.A., 164:1439, 1957.

Part II

Genetics and Disease

Chapter Four

Genetics and Disease

BENJAMIN R. GENDEL

Introduction

During the past two decades an extraordinary amount of progress has been made in genetics, particularly in the human and clinical aspects. Advances in biochemistry, especially in the techniques of chromatography, enzymology, and microchemical analysis, have resulted in the clarification of the pathophysiology of a number of metabolic disorders known to the clinician for many years, and also have uncovered an increasing number of new diseases. The analysis of urine, blood, and other body fluids for abnormal metabolites has become feasible and should lead to still further advances. New cytologic techniques have improved the study of human chromosomes. To the physician all of this has resulted in a new importance of genetics which will undoubtedly increase in the future. This chapter reviews briefly the essentials of genetics as they apply to clinical medicine, and points out the pathophysiologic mechanisms in the development of some disease states. It will not be possible to point out all the diseases in which genetic factors play a role. Disease states selected will be those which illustrate a mechanism, and the selection therefore is arbitrary.

The Physical Basis of Inheritance

Genes

Hereditary information is carried by the genes, which are arranged in a linear order along the length of the chromosomes. Since half the chromosomes are derived from the ovum and the other half from the sperm, the fertilized ovum, or *zygote*, contains hereditary information from each parent. As the zygote develops and grows by mitosis, the genes are reduplicated and appear in each nucleated cell of the body. The chromosomes of man contain many thousands of pairs of genes so minute that they are not visible under the microscope. However, genes have been localized on the giant chromosomes found in the salivary gland cells of larvae of the fruit fly, *Drosophila melanogaster*.

The information carried by the genes is coded in the *deoxyribonucleic acid* of the chromosomes (DNA). This is reproduced by replication of the DNA in the nuclei of the somatic cells by mitosis. The information is transcribed from the DNA to messenger RNA (mRNA) which is synthesized in the nucleus and serves to transmit information from the gene to the ribosomes of the cytoplasm where proteins are formed. Messenger RNA has a purine and pyrimidine base composition which is complementary to the DNA and in this manner can transmit genetic information from the genes in the nucleus to the ribosomes in the cytoplasm. In the ribosomes another variety of RNA, transfer or soluble RNA (sRNA) specific for each amino acid, carries the amino acids to the ribosomes. There the amino acids are arranged in the proper sequence to form a specific protein, according

37

to the code of the mRNA. The 20 amino acids which occur in proteins are coded by the appropriate order of nucleotide bases in the messenger RNA. The sequence of 3 bases or triplets acts as a code and spells out a particular amino acid. For example, the sequence of three consecutive uridylic acids (UUU) in RNA is known to designate phenylalanine; CCC designates proline, and the code letters for the 18 other amino acids have been worked out. A tentative dictionary of the amino acids and the corresponding triplets which are their code words has been developed.

The concept of the gene and its action has become more complex as a result of fundamental work on gene action in microbiological systems. As a result of work by Jacob and Monod, it is now believed that some genes are responsible for the synthesis of a particular enzyme or protein. These are called *structural genes*. Other genes are concerned with the regulation and control of the protein production. These genes are *operator genes* and are located adjacent to the corresponding structural gene on the chromosome. The operator gene controls the action of its adjacent structural gene, either allowing it or not allowing it to produce or release its mRNA. The operator gene itself is under the control of another gene which may be at a distance away or even on another chromosome. This gene is called a *regulator gene* and is responsible for switching the operator gene to the "off or on" position. The interaction of all three genes and their products is necessary for the production of the specific protein or enzyme. This controlling mechanism for the operation of the genes is consistent with the well-known fact that although every somatic cell in the body has all the genes contained in the zygote, only some of these are operative in any particular cell. For example, pancreatic acinar cells produce pancreatic secretions but do not produce many other substances. The genes, other than those controlling pancreatic secretion, are kept in abeyance through control of the operator genes so that these do not permit the structural genes to form or release their mRNA.

Chromosomes

The study of human chromosomes has been facilitated by improved cytologic techniques. These have included (1) the use of short-term tissue culture, including blood and bone marrow aspirates; (2) the use of colchicine to arrest mitosis before the formation of the

spindle in the metaphase; (3) the use of hypotonic solutions to cause the cells to swell and disperse the chromosomes; and (4) the use of phytohemagglutinin which acts as a mitogenic agent, stimulating mitoses of the lymphocytes in cultures of peripheral blood. With these newer techniques the chromosomes appear, in metaphase, as double rod-shaped structures, the *chromatids*, which lie adjacent to each other and are connected at a point called the *centromere* (Fig. 4–1). An analysis of the types of chromosomes has permitted a preliminary classification based on the size and shape of the chromosome. The position of the centromere determines the shape. The centromere may be approximately in the center of the chromosome, in which case the arms are equal in length. This chromosome is called a metacentric chromosome (Fig. 4–1, group A). The centromere may be toward one end, in which case the arms are unequal, two being longer than the other two. This is called a submetacentric chromosome (group C). The attachment of the centromere may be at one end, making the chromosomes V-shaped; these are called acrocentric chromosomes (group G). For many years it was thought that the number of human chromosomes was 48; but in 1956, with the use of more modern techniques, Tjio and Levan reported that the correct number was really 46—22 pairs of autosomes, chromosomes which look alike, and one pair of sex chromosomes, alike in the female (XX), but dissimilar in the male (XY).

The chromosomes are numbered in descending order based on their lengths and may be divided into groups depending upon the position of the centromere. The X chromosome is of the size of the larger chromosome of group C, and the Y chromosome is a small acrocentric chromosome similar to group G.

Mitosis and Meiosis

The many cells of the body are derived from the division of preceding cells; hence it is essential that we review briefly mitosis and meiosis. The resting cell is referred to as being in the *interphase*. As the cell divides in mitosis, it goes through successive stages. In the *prophase* physical changes occur in the chromosomes, which become thicker and more discrete. In the following stage, the *metaphase,* the chromosomes may be seen as two halves, the two chromatids, held together at the centromere. The chromosomes then migrate to the equatorial plate, and some of

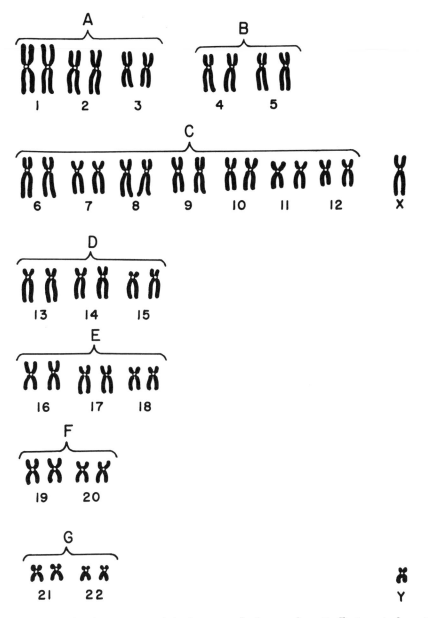

Figure 4–1. The chromosomes of the human male shown schematically in metaphase. The chromosomes are shown in pairs, and in metaphase each chromosome is composed of two chromatids attached at the centromere, which is the lighter staining constriction. The chromosomes are separated into groups as indicated. The 22 pairs of autosomes are numbered. The X chromosome is very much like chromosomes of group C and is nearest chromosome 6 in size and appearance. The Y chromosome approximates the two acrocentric chromosome pairs in group G.

the mitotic spindle fibers attach to the centromere. During the next phase, the *anaphase*, the chromatids move apart, apparently pulled by the spindle fibers to each pole of the dividing cell. The *telophase* is the stage during which the nuclear membrane forms about each group of daughter chromosomes, and the cell divides in two. Thus, each newly formed cell nucleus has the same number and

kind of chromosomes as the original cell from which it was derived. This paired number of chromosomes in each cell is called the *diploid number*.

During the formation of the reproductive cells, a modification of the above process occurs, called meiosis or meiotic division. Here, during the course of two successive cell divisions, the duplication of the chromosomes occurs only once so that the germinal cells have only one of each pair of chromosomes. This number is called the *haploid number* of chromosomes. The chromosomes, instead of remaining independent as in mitosis, line up in pairs during the division of the primary spermatocyte or primary oocyte. The chromosome pairs intertwine, permitting the opportunity for transfer of parts of the chromosomes to each other. When the cell divides in the first meiotic division the chromosomes are not duplicated; instead, one of each pair of chromosomes goes to each newly formed cell, giving rise to the haploid number. In the second meiotic division, the haploid number of chromosomes is duplicated in each daughter cell. This is essential in sexual reproduction because fertilization re-establishes the diploid number of chromosomes. If this were not the case, fertilization would result in a doubling of the chromosome number with each event.

Determination of Sex

The sex chromosomes in the human female, a pair equal in size, are called the X chromosomes. In the male there is one X chromosome which is paired with a smaller acrocentric chromosome, the Y chromosome. Thus, the sex chromosome makeup of females is XX and of males, XY. As a result of experimental work in the Drosophila, Bridges formulated the *genic balance* theory of sex determination. This theory held that the determination of sex was based on a balance between genes for maleness, distributed among the autosomes, and genes of femaleness, distributed along the X chromosomes. The implication was that the Y chromosome was inert, at least in the Drosophila. For example, a fly with a normal number of autosomes but only one X chromosome and no Y chromosome (XO genotype) was a male fly, despite the absence of the Y chromosome. In the human, however, it would appear that the Y chromosome is important in promoting the development of the male. The human who is XO is a female in appearance, and the XXY human is male in appearance. How these peculiar genotypes occur was clarified in a series of remarkable biologic experiments on the fruit fly which led to the discovery of a process called *nondisjunction*. Until recently this seemed of little importance to medicine, but newer developments make it necessary to review this phenomenon.

Nondisjunction

During meiosis the chromosomes initially form in pairs and then separate or disjoin from each other during the first meiotic division. This is known as disjunction. Ordinarily this separates the two X chromosomes, and we would expect each ovum formed after the reduction division to contain only one X chromosome. By the same token, sperm would be either X chromosome-containing or Y chromosome-containing. Nondisjunction is the failure of two members of a pair of chromosomes to separate at the first meiotic division. Under these circumstances it would be possible for ova to contain either both X chromosomes or no X chromosome. In spermatogenesis nondisjunction results in sperm containing no sex chromosomes or having both the X and Y chromosomes. Such chromosomal accidents are now known to occur in humans as a result of finding individuals with XO and XXY patterns.

Nondisjunction may also involve any pair of chromosomes and is not confined to the sex chromosomes. Nondisjunction involving the autosomes is the basis for the development of Down's syndrome (mongolism) and the other forms of autosomal trisomy.

The factors which lead to the production of nondisjunction are not understood. In Down's syndrome, the incidence of such births increases with increasing age of the mother. Similar but less marked maternal age effects are also noted in other forms of trisomy. A possible explanation may be that the potential ova proceed to the first maturation division and then remain quiescent for many years in the ovary. Meiosis is not completed until after the sperm enters the ovum. Thus ova have remained dormant for many more years in the older mother than in the younger mother. This may give more opportunity for something to go wrong.

Hereditary Variations

Variations among individuals may be nonhereditary or hereditary. The nonhereditary variations are those imposed upon the individual by his environment. These influences are considerable and although there are conditions in which the genetic constitution is the major factor in determining the nature of the individual, in general there is an interaction between hereditary factors and the individual's environment. Roberts points out that it is useful to think of this interaction as follows:

1. A particular disease or characteristic always occurs in those individuals who inherit the appropriate gene. In these individuals

there is complete hereditary determination. This is seen in the *blood groups, hemophilia, albinism,* and *achondroplastic dwarfism.*

2. A characteristic occurs in individuals of a particular genetic constitution but does not express itself in others because of environmental influences which are necessary for the development of the trait. Drug-induced *hemolytic anemia,* occurring in individuals whose erythrocytes have the inherited deficiency of glucose-6-phosphate dehydrogenase, is an example of this situation. These individuals show no evidence of disease unless they are exposed to certain drugs or other compounds.

3. A disease may occur in individuals of any genetic constitution with the same frequency and with no relation to the genetic constitution. Under these circumstances the condition is entirely determined by environment.

Hereditary variations may be due to a number of disturbances which involve the genes. These may be classified in two major categories, either as *gene mutations* or as *chromosomal accidents* (Fig. 4-2). In the former, the number and appearance of the chromosomes is normal. The gene mutation which may also be called a point mutation is a change so small that it is not visible but is nonetheless potentially capable of being transmitted. A mutation may occur in germinal cells and thus may be transmitted to offspring, or it may occur in somatic cells. If it occurs in the somatic cell, only the descendants of that cell are affected; therefore there is no transmission of the abnormality to subsequent generations. Roberts points out

that a blue segment in a brown iris is an example of the effects of a somatic mutation.

Differences in individuals may also result from chromosomal aberrations. The chromosomes may be normal in number but abnormal in structure, or the chromosomal abnormality may be a numerical variation from the normal number of 46 chromosomes. Chromosomal aberrations have been known in plants and animals for a long time, but only in recent years have human cytogenetic techniques been advanced sufficiently to prove that they occur in humans as well. Nondisjunction, mentioned previously, may result in a fertilized ovum containing more or less chromosomes than the diploid number. The chromosomes which are involved may be either autosomes or sex chromosomes. The term *polyploidy* refers to the duplication, one or more times, of a whole set of chromosomes; the term *triploid* refers to a cell having three of each kind of chromosome, and *tetraploid* to a cell having four of each kind. *Aneuploidy* is the term applied to an increase or decrease in the normal (euploid) number of chromosomes but not involving a full set. *Trisomy* is a form of aneuploidy in which three chromosomes of a specific pair are present instead of two. Such individuals are referred to as *trisomic.*

Structural abnormalities in individual chromosomes also occur even though the total number is normal. These include *translocations,* which occur when a piece of one chromosome is broken off and is attached to another chromosome. *Deletions* are the losses of parts of chromosomes. Other structural ab-

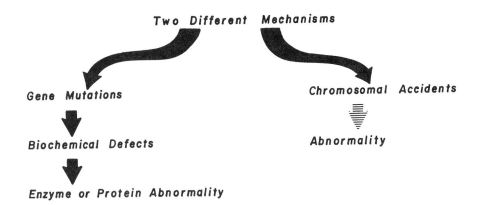

Pathophysiology of Genetic Diseases

Two Different Mechanisms

Gene Mutations   Chromosomal Accidents

Biochemical Defects   Abnormality

Enzyme or Protein Abnormality

Figure 4-2. See text. The interrupted arrow pointing from chromosomal accidents indicates that the mechanisms for production of the effects are uncertain.

normalities occur, and these will be discussed later in this chapter.

Mosaics are individuals with two distinct genetic cell types. These may be cells with two or more distinct chromosomal constitutions. Mosaics may arise during early embryogenesis, as a result of either anaphase lag or nondisjunction in the course of cell division. The resultant daughter cells, therefore, do not obtain the same number of chromosomes from the parent cell. Nondisjunction has already been discussed. Anaphase lag is the phenomenon which occurs when a chromosome lags behind in mitosis and may be lost. The daughter cells, therefore, have nuclei which differ in their chromosomal number. Each daughter cell with a different chromosomal number then perpetuates that number by continued mitosis. The individual under such circumstances will have some somatic cells with a normal number of chromosomes and other somatic cells with the deficient number of chromosomes. Mosaics having two cell types are derived in this way. Some cells, for example, would have 45 chromosomes and others 46 chromosomes.

Mechanisms of Inheritance

The patterns of inheritance in man are fundamentally the same as those in lower animals and plants. Genes affecting a particular trait are carried on each of the pair of homologous chromosomes, and are located on the corresponding point, or *locus,* of each of the chromosomes. The locus may contain a gene for the normal state, or it may be occupied by a mutant gene which controls an alternative trait. Although several different kinds of mutations are possible for a given locus, no more than one may be present at a locus at a single time. The hemoglobins illustrate diverse mutations for one locus. The locus may have the gene for normal β-chains which lead to normal hemoglobin, or it may be replaced by the mutant genes for either sickle β-chains or β-chains for hemoglobin C. Genes for alternative characters occupying the same locus on homologous chromosomes are called *alleles.* If both chromosomes of a given pair have the same gene at each locus, the individual is referred to as *homozygous* for that gene pair. If different alleles are present at corresponding loci, the individual is called *heterozygous.* Under these circumstances the trait controlled by one gene may be demonstrated in the individual, whereas the characteristic transmitted by the other

gene may not be demonstrated. The trait which is evident is referred to as dominant and the inheritance as *dominant inheritance.* The trait which is not expressed is referred to as *recessive.* If both chromosomes have an allele for the same recessive trait, this condition will appear in that individual. This is referred to as *recessive inheritance.* Another possibility is that neither trait may be dominant or recessive. Under these circumstances the heterozygous condition produces some effect but the homozygous condition produces a more marked effect. This is illustrated also by the hemoglobinopathies, in which one gene for normal hemoglobin and another for sickle hemoglobin result in sickle cell trait but two genes for sickle hemoglobin result in a greater degree of abnormality, sickle cell anemia. This type of inheritance is referred to as intermediate inheritance or *incomplete dominance.* It must be pointed out that it is not the gene which is dominant, recessive, or intermediate but the characteristic controlled by the gene.

Dominant Inheritance

The mechanism of inheritance for a disease transmitted as a dominant characteristic may be demonstrated by Huntington's chorea. The gene for Huntington's chorea can be designated as H, and the gene for the normal state as h. The normal individual will have the genotype hh and the individual with Huntington's chorea will be Hh. The mode of transmission is shown in Figure 4–3. It can be seen that there is a 50 per cent chance of any offspring's having Huntington's chorea and a 50 per cent chance of the child's being normal. This is the classical 1:1 ratio of the marriage of affected individuals to normals in dominant inheritance. Another possibility, the marriage of two affected but heterozygous individuals with a dominant trait, is demonstrated in Figure 4–3B. It will be noted that there is now a new ratio of only one normal child to each three affected children. One-fourth of the offspring may be homozygous for the dominant trait. It is possible that this homozygous individual may be affected equally as the heterozygotes for the trait, or the homozygote may be more severely affected. For many rare conditions, the clinical appearance (phenotype) of such a homozygous individual is unknown.

Under some circumstances the homozygous state for a dominant condition may be lethal and the individual may die in utero or shortly after birth. It is quite likely that some otherwise unexplained instances of abortion may result from lethal genes present in the fetus. The occurrence of a homozygous lethal condition has been reported in a case of hereditary hemorrhagic telangiectasia in which two affected parents were reported to have produced an infant with rapidly progressing hemangiomata and early death.

The criteria for recognizing dominant inheritance are: (1) Each affected individual has an affected parent unless the condition is the result of a new mutation. (2) Affected individuals married to normals have affected and normal offspring in the ratio of 1:1. (3) The normal children of affected individuals when they marry normals have only normal offspring. (4) Direct transmission of a *rare* trait through three generations (in the absence of consanguinity) is practically diagnostic of dominant inheritance.

Factors Modifying Dominant Ratios. There are a number of factors which may modify the ratios expected in dominant inheritance. The possibility that the homozygous state will be lethal, resulting in death in utero and a high incidence of abortions, has been mentioned. This situation would result, in the case of two affected parents, in an apparent ratio of only two affected offspring to each normal child. The expected 3:1 ratio would not be noted because the homozygote would die in utero.

Penetrance is another factor which may modify the expected 1:1 ratio. Penetrance may be defined as the frequency with which a gene produces its effect. Genes producing their effect in each individual possessing them may be said to have 100 per cent penetrance. Other genes produce their effect in only one of each 10 individuals who possess the gene. Such genes are said to have 10 per cent penetrance. Various other percentages of penetrance are possible. Those factors responsible for reduced penetrance are not clear, but there is a possibility that other genes elsewhere on the chromosomes may influence the action of the gene in question. In plants and animals the influence of modifying genes at different loci or even on different chromosomes is known to occur, and is referred to as *epistasis.* The occurrence of albinism in the Negro demonstrates the influence of genes resulting in failure of pigmentation of the skin, despite the presence of other genes which would result in pigmentation of the skin. Environmental factors may influence the expression of the genotype, and play some role in reducing penetrance of a gene. Unless penetrance is complete, or nearly so, the interpetation of mechanisms of human inheritance is very difficult.

Expressivity refers to the variability in the manifestation of the same gene in different individuals. This also may be the result of modifying genes or environmental factors and may produce milder o atypical forms of the

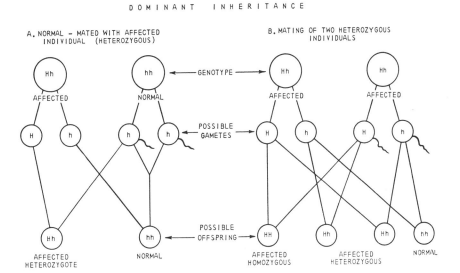

Figure 4–3. Dominant inheritance. *A* shows a normal individual mated with an affected heterozygous individual. The reduction division in the affected female permits ova of two types, *H* and *h*. The normal male has only one type of sperm, *h*. The combinations show the classical 1:1 ratio of affected to normal individuals. *B* shows the mating of two affected heterozygous individuals and the different ratio of offspring.

inherited condition, which consequently may not be recognized.

Lastly, the age at onset of the hereditary disorder may modify the dominant ratio. Such a situation is demonstrated in the inheritance of Huntington's chorea, in which the average age of onset is about 35 years. Affected individuals may appear perfectly normal during childhood and young adult life. If death occurs prior to the age at which the disease usually manifests itself, these individuals are not recognized as abnormal.

Pernicious anemia and diabetes mellitus constitute two other examples of inherited disorders which do not necessarily appear until later in life.

Recessive Inheritance

In the recessive mode of inheritance, a gene for the recessive condition must be carried on both members of a chromosome pair for the condition to be manifested in the individual. There are a number of criteria which permit the recognition of recessive inheritance. (1) The majority of affected individuals have normal appearing parents. (2) The condition has a definite familial incidence, but a statistically significant number of sibships will show a ratio of three normals to one affected individual. (3) If the abnormality is rare, evidence of consanguinity may be noted among parents of affected individuals; first cousins have one-eighth of their genes in common. (4) Affected individuals who marry normals have normal-appearing offspring in the majority of cases. If an affected child occurs, this implies that the normal-appearing mate is heterozygous and the proportion of normal children to affected children will be 1:1. (5) Affected individuals who marry other affected individuals will have only affected offspring, provided the abnormality is due to the same gene. In this connection it should be noted that some conditions which appear to be similar clinically are different genetically. They may be due to entirely different genes at other loci. For example, deaf mutism may be caused by one of several pairs of recessive genes at different loci; thus it is possible for two deaf mute parents, who are each homozygous for deaf mutism, to have normal children—if the gene responsible for the deaf mutism in each parent is different. Another possibility to account for normal offspring from two deaf mute parents is that one or both of the parents may be deaf mutes due to environmental influences, such as infection, rather than to hereditary

factors. This type of superficial simulation of a hereditary clinical syndrome through acquired causes is called a *phenocopy*.

Intermediate Inheritance or Incomplete Dominance

In this type of inheritance, the heterozygous individual has characteristics intermediate between the normal person and the individual who has both genes for the particular condition. In other words, the presence of one gene for a condition produces some effect, but the presence of both genes for the condition produces a greater abnormality. This is exemplified by the inheritance of *sickle cell anemia*. The presence of one gene for sickle hemoglobin results in sickle cell trait. This condition is compatible with good health and the carriers of the trait characteristically do not have hemolytic anemia, crises, leg ulcers, or the other manifestations of sickle cell anemia. The presence of both genes for sickle hemoglobin results in the clinical picture of sickle cell anemia. It is noteworthy that the heterozygote with sickle cell trait does show evidence that the gene is present. Sickle hemoglobin may be demonstrated by reducing agents such as sodium metabisulfite or by electrophoresis of hemoglobin. Although carriers of sickle cell trait are asymptomatic, under exceptional circumstances of hypoxia, as in flights in unpressurized airplanes, they have been reported to develop splenic infarctions presumably as a result of intravascular sickling. In addition, carriers of the trait may show in later years an inability to concentrate their urine or recurrent hematuria.

Thalassemia is another condition in which the individual homozygous for the thalassemia gene shows the severe manifestations of the disease and the heterozygote shows a mild, sometimes asymptomatic, condition.

It is very likely that many other conditions which are believed to be inherited by either dominant or recessive types of inheritance more properly should be considered as examples of intermedate inheritance. The phenotype (clinical appearance) of the homozygote is unknown for many rare traits inherited as mendelian dominants. The homozygous individual may be more severely affected than the heterozygote, and this situation could be designated as a provisional dominant until the phenotype of the homozygote becomes known. In addition, the development of new biochemical methods has permitted the identification of partial biochemical defects in the recessive carrier of a number of diseases. It is thus obvious that the terms "dominant" and "recessive"—so entrenched in our vocabulary—are relative and refer more to the clinical characteristic than to the action of the gene.

Sex-Linked Inheritance

Although sex chromosomes are concerned with determination of the sex of the individual, they also carry genes for unrelated conditions. Since such genes are located on the sex chromosomes, the characteristics they control are linked with sex. There are several possible mechanisms for sex-linked transmission of hereditary diseases, but only one type has been definitely known to occur in man. This type is the classic sex-linked inheritance and occurs by way of the X chromosomes (Fig. 4–4). *Hemophilia* (AHG or factor VIII and PTC or factor IX deficiencies but not PTA, factor XI deficiency), *red-green color blindness*, and *pseudohypertrophic muscular dystrophy* are some examples of sex-linked recessive inheritance. In the female this is similar to autosomal recessive inheritance in that both chromosomes must have the mutant gene for the disease to be expressed. If only one chromosome has the sex-linked recessive gene, the normal gene on the other chromosome is dominant and will prevent its expression. In the male, however, since there is only one X chromosome, the presence of the

mutant gene for the recessive condition on that chromosome will result in the development of the trait. In the male with only one X chromosome, the terms homozygous and heterozygous do not apply. The male is said to be *hemizygous* for genes carried on the X chromosome. If the gene is rare, as in the case of hemophilia, the disease is transmitted through unaffected females to half of their sons (i.e., those who receive the X chromosome containing the mutation from the mother). If the gene is not too uncommon, as in the case of red-green color blindness, homozygous color-blind females will occur but they will be much less frequent than color-blind men. The following may be considered criteria for sex-linked recessive inheritance: (1) Most of the affected individuals are males. (2) The daughters of an affected male may appear normal but will transmit the condition to half their sons, since one of the two X chromosomes of the daughter must have come from the affected father, whose only X chromosome carried the mutation. (3) An affected female may occur through the marriage of an affected male and a carrier (normal-appearing) female. (4) The normal male children of a carrier female do not transmit the disease.

Although affected homozygous females do occur (Fig. 4–4 III), some affected females

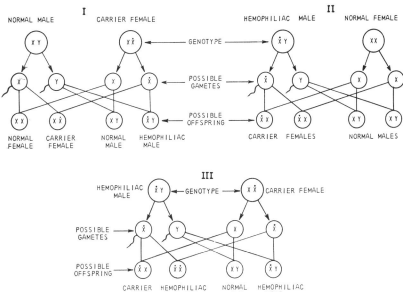

Figure 4–4. Inheritance of hemophilia (AHG deficiency). *X* represents a normal X chromosome; *Ẋ* represents an X chromosome with the mutant gene for AHG deficiency. Several different types of mating and the possible offspring are shown.

who did not come from the mating of a carrier female and an affected male have been observed. From the family history, some of these affected females should have been heterozygous carriers. As noted above, the heterozygous female with a sex-linked recessive condition should be asymptomatic, but these individuals showed variable degrees of the basic condition, as for example, classic hemophilia (factor VIII deficiency). Such heterozygous individuals have been called "manifesting heterozygotes."

This phenomenon can be explained by the Lyon hypothesis, which holds that there is inactivation (lyonization) of an X chromosome. This hypothesis is supported by the present view concerning the nature of the Barr chromatin body. The current view is that the Barr body represents an inactive heterochromatic or dark-staining X chromosome. Normal females have one Barr body, representing one inactive X chromosome (the other X chromosome is the active one). Females with three X chromosomes (XXX) have two Barr bodies. Indeed, females with even more X chromosomes have one Barr body for each X chromosome present over one. To put it another way, the number of X chromosomes is equal to the number of Barr bodies plus one.

The *Lyon hypothesis* suggests that (1) in the female all or part of one X chromosome is genetically inactive and goes to form the Barr body; (2) the decision whether the maternal or the paternally derived X chromosome is the inactive one is made early in embryonic life and is random; (3) all cells derived from each cell at the time of lyonization of the X chromosome have the same inactive X chromosome, either maternal or paternal, and therefore have the same active X chromosome. This hypothesis offers an explanation for the "manifesting heterozygote." Although we do not know the site of formation of factor VIII (antihemophilic globulin), if the tissues responsible are controlled by an X chromosome which is normal, the level of AHG will be normal and the female will be asymptomatic. If, however, the tissues responsible for factor VIII formation have as their active X chromosome the one with the mutant gene for hemophilia, then a severe deficiency will be present in such a heterozygous female. It is also possible that the tissues responsible may have some cells with the normal X chromosome and other cells with the mutant X chromosome. Under these circumstances an intermediate amount of

factor VIII will be produced, and if the deficiency is severe enough the patient may have bleeding episodes, spontaneously or especially during operative procedures.

The lyonization of an X chromosome in the normal female provides an explanation as to why the female with two X chromosomes shows no more effect of the genes on the X chromosome than the normal male with only one X chromosome. One would logically expect females to have twice as much factor VIII or G6PD (see p. 45) as the male. This is not the case and is consistent with the Lyon hypothesis. This hypothesis has also led to the view that females are mosaics with respect to the X chromosome, some tissues containing the maternal X and other tissues the paternal X in a random fashion.

Another, but even more rare, explanation for the occurrence of a female hemophiliac has been proposed by the report of a 16-month-old girl with severe hemophilia (factor VIII deficiency). Her mother belonged to a hemophiliac family, suggesting she could be a heterozygous carrier, but her father was normal. Several explanations were considered, but an investigation of the child's "nuclear sex" showed the chromatin-negative pattern characteristic of the male. Study of the chromosomes of the child showed an XY pattern! There is no satisfactory explanation for this discrepancy between the male sex-chromosome pattern and the female phenotype. A possible explanation is that this male child had a feminizing testicular tumor, but that the sexual status could not be determined at this early age. A similar discrepancy has been reported in a family with sex-linked muscular dystrophy of the Duchenne type, in which an affected girl was reported. Study of her nuclear sex showed a male type; chromosomal studies were not done. It is possible that other similar cases will be found.

An additional mechanism for a sex-linked recessive disease to be manifest in the female is its development in a patient with Turner's syndrome. If the X in the XO female has the gene for the disease it will be expressed freely, just as in the hemizygous male. This indicates the need to study females who have sex-linked recessive diseases without a compatible family history. Examination of their cells for Barr bodies and cytogenetic studies are indicated.

Sex-linked dominant inheritance by way of the X chromosomes may occur, but is rare. Vitamin D-resistant rickets (familial hypophosphatemia), a disease in which there is decreased renal tubular reabsorption of in-

organic phosphate leading to hypophosphatemia, is an example of a disease inherited as
a sex-linked dominant. In this form of inheritance both males and females are affected,
but the affected male cannot transmit the disease to his sons, who receive his Y chromosome but not his X chromosome. All his
daughters receive the affected X chromosome
and thus would show the condition.

Two other types of sex-linked transmission
are possible. One type depends upon genes
carried on the Y chromosome. Conditions inherited in this manner can occur only in the
male and obviously would be transmitted to
all the sons. This mechanism of inheritance
has been suggested for a condition characterized by hairy ears seen in men in India.
Nonetheless, this type of inheritance has not
been unequivocally proved. The other type is
based on the assumption that homologous
parts of the X and Y chromosomes exist. Thus
there would be genes at paired loci on these
homologous parts of the sex chromosomes.
This type of inheritance has been called *partial sex-linkage*. In a recent review the evidence for partial sex-linkage was considered
not to be statistically significant.

Sex-Influenced Inheritance

Genes for conditions inherited through this
mechanism are carried on the autosomes but
are influenced by the sex of the individual,
probably through endocrine secretions. The
mechanism of inheritance appears as a dominant in the male and as a recessive in the
female. The common type of inherited baldness (pattern baldness) is transmitted in this
manner. If the gene for baldness is designated
as B and the gene for lack of baldness is designated as b, the homozygous (BB) and the
heterozygous (Bb) male have the condition
but only the homozygous female (BB) has
it. The heterozygous (Bb) and normal female
(bb) do not have the condition. It is possible
for the heterozygous female who develops an
androgen-secreting tumor to develop baldness.
The criteria for the recognition of the sex-
influenced type of inheritance are: (1) the
condition is more common in men than in
women, and (2) an affected male transmits
the trait to one-half of his sons. The latter
is important in distinguishing sex-influenced
from sex-linked inheritance.

Polygenic or Multifactorial Inheritance

The traits considered previously have been
striking conditions such as sickle cells compared to normal cells and Huntington's chorea
compared to the normal individual. These
traits are considered *discontinuous,* that is,
the trait is either present or it is absent. There
are other fundamental characteristics which
cannot be separated as easily. These form a
continuous series from one extreme to the
other, as for example height, intelligence, and
others. Measurements of these traits form the
well-known bell-shaped curve of a normal
distribution. They differ quantitatively with
a continuous variation from one extreme to
the other. These conditions are believed to
result from many sets of alleles which are
cumulative in their effect. This type of inheritance is called *polygenic* or *multifactorial*.
It is more difficult to study than single-factor
inheritance, particularly in man. Skin color
is believed to be inherited in this fashion, and
there is also an opinion that essential hypertension is inherited in the same manner.

Types of Genetic Diseases

A completely satisfactory classification of
the various types of genetic defects is not yet
possible. At the present time it appears useful to divide the genetic disturbances into
two major types. One type includes the disorders which are inherited from the parents
through gene mutations. The other type is
the result of a chromosomal accident which
may occur either in the parents or in the
individual.

THE MUTANT GENE AND MECHANISMS OF GENE ACTION

Inherited changes are brought about by
mutations which occur in genes. The mutation
occurs in a single gene and produces an abnormal template which results in a defect in
a single enzyme or the formation of an abnormal polypeptide chain. This is the basis
of the "one gene—one enzyme" theory. The
enzyme defect produces a single and fundamental biochemical disorder—the primary
gene effect. This leads to a number of consequences culminating in the characteristic
clinical picture. Although a biochemical defect is believed to underlie all hereditary conditions produced by a gene mutation, the
biochemical abnormality cannot always be
demonstrated in our present state of knowledge. A pathophysiologic classification of the
various types of abnormalities resulting from
a gene mutation is shown in Table 4–1. The

TABLE 4–1. PATHOPHYSIOLOGIC CLASSIFICA-
TION OF GENETIC DISORDERS RESULTING FROM
GENE MUTATIONS.

1. Lethals
2. Morphologic-embryologic defects
3. Inborn errors of metabolism
4. Abiotrophic disturbances
5. Immunologic disturbances
6. Susceptibility to infectious diseases
7. Abnormal drug metabolism

subdivisions are arbitrary, but it is believed that they aid in understanding the different courses from the gene mutation to the clinical picture.

Lethals

The gene mutation may result in such a degree of biochemical abnormality that the condition is not compatible with life. Little is known about such conditions, but they probably exist and may result in death in utero. Homozygous states which are not compatible with life have already been mentioned. These conditions have been called lethals and the genes responsible for them, lethal genes.

Morphologic-Embryologic Defects

There are a number of hereditary disease states which result in a morphologic defect for which a genetically induced biochemical abnormality has not been demonstrated at the present time. Nonetheless it would appear likely that such an abnormality results from a mutant gene during the early stages of embryonic development. It is thus possible for an individual to have a supernumerary digit, as in *polydactylism*, or to have a deformity of bone, eye, or skin. At present the chemical abnormality can no longer be detected after birth. It is also possible that improved techniques may ultimately result in the detection of the biochemical defect, particularly when these techniques are applied to experimental embryology. A number of congenital defects are believed to be controlled (in part at least) by heredity. *Polycystic kidney disease* occurs in families. There seem to be two different genetic varieties, the adult form inherited as a dominant and the infantile type which is probably inherited in a recessive manner. The disease is thought to occur as a result of embryologic failure of the union of the convoluted tubules and collecting ducts. Other congenital defects, such as cleft palate, harelip, club foot, and congeni-

tal hypertrophic pyloric stenosis, tend to occur in families more frequently than would be expected by chance. The type of transmission is not clear, but the view that genetic factors are important is supported by studies of identical twins, who have the same genes, correlated with fraternal twins, who do not. Studies showing the degree of concordance or discordance between sets of twins are of some value in assessing the role of genetic vs. environmental factors. In a study of 65 pairs of twins, one or both having harelip, it was found that in 33 per cent of identical twins, both had harelip, whereas this occurred in only 5 per cent of fraternal twins. These figures tend to support a genetic basis for harelip. Conversely, the importance of environmental factors is demonstrated by the finding of only one of a pair of identical twins who had harelip in 67 per cent of these identical twins. It should be apparent from this that both genetic and environmental factors contribute to the pathogenesis of harelip.

Although with most morphologic defects the biochemical disturbance is unknown, *hereditary spherocytosis* is an example of a morphologic defect in which biochemical disturbances within the erythrocyte have been demonstrated. The primary defect in this disorder would appear to reside in the cell membrane. An early suggestion was that there was a possible enzymatic defect somewhere in the Embden-Meyerhof oxidative pathway of carbohydrate metabolism in the erythrocyte. A defect in intracellular glycolysis which can be largely restored to normal upon incubation of the red cells with adenosine has been demonstrated. Recently a defect in the sodium pump mechanism of the erythrocyte has been proposed as the basic defect leading to the spherocyte.

Inborn Errors of Metabolism

Dent has defined an inborn metabolic error as "a permanent inherited condition due to a primary enzyme abnormality. As a result one or more chemical compounds may follow an altered metabolic pathway and may be found in some body fluids in greatly increased or decreased quantities." In the synthesis of compounds this can be schematically represented as shown in Figure 4–5. In the figure it can be assumed that substance A is serially converted in the course of normal metabolism to substances B, C, and D by specific enzymes designated as E_1, E_2, E_3. The normal end-product D is likely to be found in various body fluids in measurable quantities, while the preceding compounds may be assumed to be present in insignificant amounts because of a rapid rate of turnover. If we assume a genetic defect for the enzyme E_3, which converts substance C into substance D, a block would occur which would lead to either of two different types of disturbances: (1) an increase of the intermediate metabolic product C, as for example the accumulation of phenylalanine in *phenylketonuria,* or (2) there may be a deficiency in the final end-product, D, but no apparent increase in the precursor, C. This latter mechanism is exemplified by *albinism.*

In *phenylketonuria* there is a deficiency of the enzyme phenylalanine hydroxylase, which converts phenylalanine to tyrosine (Fig. 4–6). The sequential failure in metabolism results in the accumulation of phenylalanine in the blood and spinal fluid. The excess of phenylalanine is converted by a transaminase to phenylpyruvic acid and is excreted in the urine, where it may be detected by various tests. In addition a failure to convert phenylalanine to tyrosine results in a decreased production of melanin, which is believed to be responsible for the relative absence of pigment in the skin and hair. Patients with phenylketonuria tend to have blond hair and a fair skin. The excessive accumulation of phenylalanine or perhaps of one of its products damages the central nervous system, resulting in mental deficiency. Because the damage results from a failure to metabolize phenylalanine normally, it is rational to treat these patients with a low phenylalanine diet, which, if started soon after birth, may be effective in preventing the mental retardation. Although this condition is uncommon, it is believed to account for about 1 per cent of all mental defectives in institutions. Previously the incidence was considered to be 1 in every 20,000 to 40,000 births, but routine testing of the newborn has shown an incidence of 1:10,000. It is transmitted as a recessive trait; therefore, a family with an affected child and normal parents has one in four chances of having another affected child with each succeeding pregnancy. Although the parents appear normal, each must be a heterozygous carrier of the gene for phenylketonuria. Until recently there was no way of being certain whether a normal-appearing individual was a carrier of the gene for phenylketonuria. It is possible now to detect most of the heterozygous carriers by means of a phenylalanine tolerance test, similar to a glucose tolerance test. The heterozygous carrier demonstrates a curve between the normal response and that of the patient with phenylketonuria. This indicates that the presence of one gene for the disease gives rise to a partial defect but not enough to produce the disease. The heterozygous carriers for a number of recessively inherited conditions can now be detected.

Albinism represents a deficiency of the final end-product, melanin (substance D in Fig. 4–5), but no detectable increase in the precursor. In this condition the mutant gene results in a deficiency of the enzyme tyrosinase in the melanocytes of the skin. The melanocytes, however, are present in normal numbers. The deficiency of tyrosinase inter-

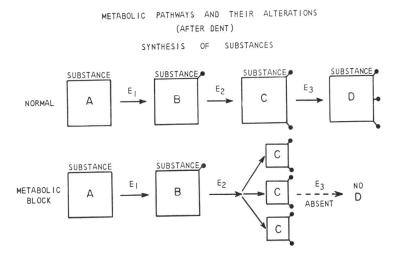

Figure 4–5. Alterations in the metabolic pathways involved in the synthesis of substances. See text for explanation.

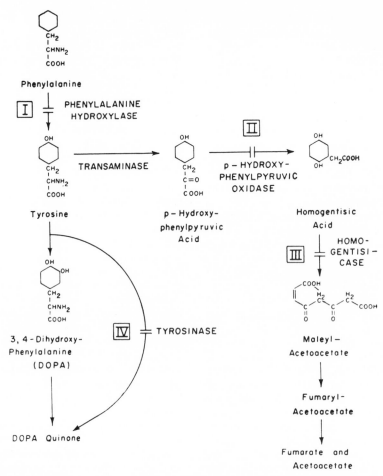

Figure 4–6. The normal metabolic pathway for phenylalanine. *I,* The deficiency of phenylalanine hydroxylase results in phenylketonuria. *IV.* The deficiency of the enzyme, tyrosinase, results in albinism. *II* and *III* represent deficiencies of enzymes which lead to tyrosinosis and alkaptonuria, which are not discussed in the text. (From Hsia, D. Y.: Inborn Errors of Metabolism. Chicago, Year Book Publishers, 1959.)

feres with the conversion of tyrosine to dopa, which is ultimately converted to melanin (Fig. 4–6). Since melanin cannot be produced in adequate amounts, albinos have a non-pigmented white skin, white hair, and a non-pigmented iris.

Conditions such as albinism are readily recognized at birth. There are other diseases in which an enzyme defect is present at birth but in which there would be no disturbance in the individual if it were not for the effect of extrinsic factors which occur after birth. *Galactosemia* is a condition in which there is a deficiency or absence of the enzyme galactose-1-phosphate uridyltransferase, which is required to convert galactose to glucose. Newborn infants with this condition appear to be normal, but after several days of milk feeding the metabolic block is manifested in the accumulation of galactose. The infants vomit, fail to thrive, become lethargic, and develop marked hepatomegaly. The accumulation of galactose in the blood and tissues results in galactosemia, cirrhosis, and cataracts. As a result of the metabolic block, there is a decrease in the blood glucose level which may lead to convulsions and mental deficiency. The syndrome may be reversed by omission of milk and milk products from the diet. If the child can be tided over, milk can later be reintroduced into the diet in small quantities without adverse effect because of the development of other pathways of galactose metabolism.

Another example of the normal-appearing individual who has an inherited enzyme defect, but in whom the defect does not become manifest until even later in life, or perhaps not at all, is the inherited deficiency of glucose-6-phosphate dehydrogenase in the erythrocytes. These individuals appear to be perfectly normal until they receive certain drugs, at which time *hemolytic anemia* will occur. This condition was discovered as a by-product of research on antimalarial drugs. It was noted that when primaquine was administered, a hemolytic anemia occurred in 10 per cent of Negro males but only rarely in Caucasians. In asymptomatic periods between attacks, the erythrocytes of affected individuals showed no spherocytosis or other morphologic abnormality and no underlying hemolytic mechanism could be demonstrated. Studies to clarify the basic defect underlying this type of anemia have shown that there is a deficiency of the enzyme glucose-6-phosphate dehydrogenase (G6PD). This enzyme plays a key role in the pentose phosphate pathway of carbohydrate metabolism in the erythrocyte and is concerned in the important step of converting glucose-6-phosphate to 6-phosphogluconate. This step permits the conversion of TPN to TPNH. The latter is essential in the protection of the erythrocyte from oxidation and subsequent destruction such as might occur with many oxidant drugs used in clinical medicine. The ingestion of primaquine causes hemolysis and its effects —anemia, jaundice, and reticulocytosis. Heinz-Ehrlich bodies appear in the erythrocytes. Other drugs, including sulfonamides and nitrofurantoin, have also been found to produce the hemolytic anemia, and it has been shown that *favism* and *naphthalene*-induced anemia occur in individuals with a deficiency of this enzyme.

Further study of G6PD deficiency showed that this condition was not a single genetic disorder. Two types of sex-linked recessively inherited G6PD deficiency are now known, one type occurring in Negroes as noted above. The other type occurs in Mediterranean Caucasians who suffer from a more severe degree of enzyme deficiency. In Caucasians, hemolytic anemia may be induced by a wider spectrum of drugs, some of which do not produce hemolytic anemia in the Negro. In addition to these sex-linked types, at least one other type of G6PD deficiency is known to occur in white children. These have an even more severe deficiency of the enzyme than the other types, and for this reason have a chronic hemolytic anemia which appears in childhood.

In addition to the enzyme deficiencies or abnormalities, gene mutation may result also in the formation of an abnormal protein which may produce a disease. This is exemplified by the mutations producing the abnormal hemoglobins, some of which result in serious disease. Work in this area has been very intensive and rewarding and has led to a better understanding of the chemistry of hemoglobin and to many important contributions to basic genetics.

The hemoglobin molecule is composed of four polypeptide chains, each one attached to a heme group. The four polypeptide chains make up the globin portion of the molecule and consist of two pairs of identical chains designated arbitrarily as α- and β-chains. The formula for normal hemoglobin (Hb-A) can be written as $\alpha_2^A \beta_2^A$. The superscript A indicates that the polypeptide chain is normal. The amino acid sequences for both these chains have been worked out, and the α-chain consists of a sequence of 141 amino acids, whereas the β-chain has 146 amino acids. In addition to Hb-A, which comprises about 96 per cent of all the adult hemoglobin, there are two other minor normal hemoglobins which are important. Hb-A$_2$ comprises 1.5 to 3.0 per cent of the total hemoglobin. It can be distinguished from Hb-A by its slower electrophoretic mobility and can also be separated from it by various types of chromatography. It also is made up of four polypeptide chains, two of which are the same as the α-chains of Hb-A; the other two chains differ by a number of amino acids from the β-chains, and these have been designated as δ-chains. The formula for Hb-A$_2$ can be written as $\alpha_2^A \delta_2^{A_2}$. The other important hemoglobin is fetal hemoglobin (Hb-F), which is the major form in fetal life. It gradually decreases after birth until about 6 months of age, after which it constitutes 0.5 to 2.0 per cent of the total hemoglobin as determined by the alkali denaturation technique. This hemoglobin can be separated from Hb-A by special electrophoretic techniques or by its greater resistance to alkali denaturation. The α-chains are common to all three types of hemoglobin, and hemoglobin F has the same α-chains as Hb-A and Hb-A$_2$. The other pair of chains differs from both β-chains and δ-chains; these are called γ-chains. The formula for Hb-F can be written $\alpha_2^A \gamma_2^F$. Several other minor adult, fetal, and even embryonic hemoglobins are known, but these will not be considered here.

Thus, four different polypeptide chains, α, β, γ, and δ, make up Hb-A, A$_2$ and F. Each chain is controlled by a different genetic locus. The α-chain locus determines the production of α-chains; the β-chain locus, β-chains; the γ-chain locus, γ-chains; and the δ-chain locus, δ-chains. These genes are structural genes and are responsible for the amino acid content and sequence of each chain. As mentioned earlier, the structural genes are set in motion by adjacent operator genes, and these are controlled by still other genes, the regulatory genes.

A mutation at the locus for α-chains will result in the production of abnormal α-chains and therefore an abnormal hemoglobin. Similarly mutations at the loci for β-, γ-, or δ-chains will result in the production of abnormal polypeptide chains. Sickle cell hemoglobin is the result of a mutation in the β-chain locus. Ordinarily the sixth amino acid in the β-chain is a glutamic acid. If a valine is substituted, sickle hemoglobin will be produced. The β-chain of sickle hemoglobin can be written as $\beta^{6\ val}$ to indicate that there is a valine in the sixth amino acid position instead of the normal amino acid for this position. Since there are two loci for β-chains, a single mutation will result in production of some $\beta^{6\ val}$-chains, but the normal locus will produce normal β^A-chains. Thus patients with sickle cell trait have both normal and sickle hemoglobins. If the same mutation is present at both loci, only abnormal β-chains will be produced and therefore only sickle hemoglobin will be present as in sickle cell anemia. A more detailed description will be presented in Chapter 30.

The abnormal hemoglobin of sickle cell anemia differs from normal hemoglobin in being less soluble, especially in the reduced form. When exposed to decreased oxygen tension, it forms tactoids. These are molecular rearrangements which lead to erythrocytic sickling. The consequence of this is increased viscosity of blood, stasis leading to further hypoxia, and a vicious cycle. Thrombosis, infarction, and hemorrhage may follow. Simultaneously the red cell abnormality results in increased mechanical fragility and hemolytic anemia with all its characteristics. Thus we can see the sequence of a genetic abnormality which produces an altered protein molecule leading to a disease state. This is the basis for the term "molecular disease."

During intrauterine life Hb-F is the major hemoglobin, but after birth this decreases and is replaced by Hb-A. This changeover can be explained by the regulatory or controller genes which control the rates of synthesis of the various polypeptide chains. The structural genes control the structure or amino acid sequences, and mutation at the structural loci produces abnormal hemoglobins. On the other hand a mutation at the regulatory locus would change the *rate* of synthesis, the structure remaining normal. Some individuals continue to have a very high proportion of fetal hemoglobin, and this is believed to be due to a failure of the regulatory genes to shut off γ-chains and produce more β-chains instead. This is a hereditary condition and is called the "hereditary persistence of fetal hemoglobin."

Another pathophysiologic mechanism is demonstrated in the disorders resulting from disturbances in transport mechanisms. These may involve either renal tubular transport alone or intestinal absorption associated with renal transport disturbances. The basic nature of both these defects is not clear but may relate to the absence or abnormality of an enzyme essential to the transport mechanism or a defect in a protein which mediates transport. Unfortunately the precise mechanisms are unknown. *Nephrogenic diabetes insipidus* is an example of a hereditary failure of the renal tubules to reabsorb water. Its exact mode of inheritance is controversial. Early studies suggested a sex-linked recessive inheritance, but more recent studies suggest an autosomal inheritance, probably a dominant with decreased penetrance in the female. A characteristic feature of the disease is the failure of the renal tubules to respond to antidiuretic hormone. *Renal glycosuria* results from an abnormality of the renal transport of glucose. It is characterized by glucosuria in the face of normal blood sugar levels and is inherited as an autosomal dominant. In the *Fanconi syndrome* the failure of reabsorption involves not only one substance but several, including glucose, water, amino acids, phosphate, and uric acid. The resultant clinical picture includes a form of vitamin D-resistant rickets and low levels of serum phosphate and uric acid as well as albuminuria, aminoaciduria, and glucosuria. This results in severe and progressive inanition and dwarfism.

Hartnup disease, described in 1956, is an example of a more widespread defect in transport mechanisms. The disease is characterized by a pellagra-like skin eruption, episodic cerebellar ataxia, and aminoaciduria. The biochemical defect results from a disturbance in tryptophan metabolism. This amino acid is poorly absorbed from the jejunum and also poorly reabsorbed from the renal tubules. There is also a deficiency in the conversion of tryptophan to nicotinic acid which leads to the pellagra-like skin lesions.

Abiotrophic Disturbances

Some hereditary disorders are not present at birth but develop over a period of years, despite the fact that the inherited mutant gene for the condition must have been present at the time of fertilization. Gowers coined the term *abiotrophy* to describe the concept of an inherited weakness of a tissue which appears normal for a time but in the course of time results in premature degeneration of the tissue. The mechanism for this is not clear, but it points up the important clinical observation that all inherited diseases do not become manifest at birth, but rather may appear many years later. Gowers called attention to the occurrence of *pattern baldness* in young men, but he particularly emphasized the gradual failure of the neurons in degenerative diseases of the nervous system, using *Friedreich's ataxia* as one example. The child with this disease may appear perfectly healthy for some years after birth. The disease begins, however, between 6 and 15 years of age, when degenerative changes appear in the spinal cord involving the posterior columns, the spinocerebellar tracts, and the pyramidal tracts; the peripheral nerves are also involved. The child develops ataxia, absence of deep reflexes, and a positive Babinski sign. Huntington's chorea has an even later age of onset than Friedreich's ataxia. Unfortunately, there is no information available concerning the basic mechanisms of these disorders.

McKusick has suggested that various connective tissue diseases are also in the nature of abiotrophies. In *pseudoxanthoma elasticum,* skin changes are not usually noted until the second decade of life or later. The areas of predilection are those subject to more than the usual wear and tear, such as flexural areas and areas exposed to the weather and to irritation by clothing. In the *Marfan syndrome* the innate weakness in the media of the aorta and pulmonary artery might not be detected in those patients who die in infancy and childhood, but by the time adult life is reached, the dilatation of these vessels may be noted, or actual disruption of the media with dissecting aneurysm may be found. Although the biochemical disturbances in these hereditary connective tissue disorders have not been completely worked out, available information suggests the following: (1) *Marfan's syndrome* probably results from a defect in elastic tissue. (2) In *Ehlers-Danlos syndrome,* the fundamental defect is probably in the formation of the collagen wickerwork, the term applied to the crossing and tightly interlacing collagen fibers. (3) In *pseudoxanthoma elasticum,* there is believed to be a dystrophy of collagen. (4) In *Hurler's syndrome,* an abnormality in the formation of a mucopolysaccharide is believed to be the fundamental defect. (5) In *osteogenesis imperfecta,* the collagen fibers are abnormal and the basic abnormality is believed to be in the maturation of collagen.

Immunologic Disturbances

These disturbances involve the blood groups and their antibodies, both natural and acquired. Mismatched transfusion reactions present the simplest type of this disorder. The discovery of the *Rh blood groups* clarified the cause of erythroblastosis fetalis. The mechanism for the development of erythroblastosis fetalis is basically under the control of genes, inasmuch as all blood groups are controlled by genes. In fact the genetic control of the blood groups is such that environmental influences play virtually no role. If Rh incompatibility exists between mother and fetus, it is possible for antibodies to be formed by the mother against the erythrocytes of the fetus. The antibodies in turn destroy the fetal erythrocytes and produce a hemolytic anemia of variable severity. In approximately 10 per cent of erythroblastosis fetalis cases, the incompatibility is in the ABO system rather than the Rh system.

Recently, clarification of the *P blood group system* has shown the extremely rare occurrence of a new gene, p. Individuals who were formerly P+ are now designated as P_1 and the formerly P— individuals are called P_2. The rare individuals who are homozygous for the new gene (pp) have anti-P_1 and anti-P_2 in their serum. These are extremely potent antibodies, and the women who possess these antibodies and who happen to have P_1 or P_2 children have a high percentage of miscarriages early in pregnancy. Only eight such families have been described thus far.

Susceptibility to Infectious Diseases

The severity of an infectious disease depends upon three factors: (1) the number of invading organisms, (2) the virulence of the infectious agents, and (3) the resistance of the host. Host resistance is a complex phenomenon governed by genes which control the body chemistry so that there may be more resistance or less resistance to a particular infectious agent. The mechanisms which operate to make one individual more susceptible than another to infection are for the most part unknown. In one particular instance we do have an explanation for poor resistance on the part of the host. In *hereditary agammaglobulinemia,* a sex-linked recessive disease, the patient is subject to frequent and recurrent bacterial infections. These infections result from the inability of the host to produce antibodies.

Genetic factors are of some importance in the development of tuberculosis. It has been known for many years that the Negro is more susceptible to tuberculosis than the Caucasian. Studies of the occurrence of tuberculosis show that both identical twins developed tuberculosis in 52 of 78 pairs of identical twins. On the other hand, in fraternal twins both developed the disease in only 53 of 230 pairs. This lends support to the hypothesis of a genetic influence on the susceptibility to tuberculosis because identical twins are genetically the same whereas fraternal twins have a different genotype. The increased susceptibility of patients with sickle cell anemia to Salmonella infection, especially to Salmonella osteomyelitis, is well known. The susceptibility to rheumatic fever is also believed to be under some genetic control.

The genetics of susceptibility to disease is not simple, and its dependence upon a single pair of genes similar to most conditions already discussed is extremely unlikely. It is more likely that susceptibility to disease depends upon a number of genes at different loci all acting together. This type of inheritance is called *polygenic.* Each set of alleles produces a small but cumulative effect.

Detoxification of Drugs

Some people inherit a defect in regard to the inactivation of certain drugs. For example, some patients receiving the muscle relaxant suxamethonium for electroshock therapy or in anesthesia for operative procedures were found to have an unduly prolonged response to the drug. Ordinarily the drug is destroyed rapidly by the enzyme pseudocholinesterase present in the blood, but in affected individuals an inherited deficiency of pseudocholinesterase was found. In addition, in a study of plasma isoniazid concentrations following administration of this drug for the treatment of tuberculosis, it was found that the population could be divided into rapid inactivators, who have a low INH level, and slow inac-

tivators, who maintain a high INH level. Both suxamethonium and INH inactivation appear to be inherited as autosomal recessive characteristics. It is interesting that neither of these conditions would have been detected if drugs had not been used in otherwise normal-appearing individuals. These conditions point up the importance of environmental factors. Since the genetic disorder was disclosed by a pharmacologic agent, the term *pharmacogenetics* has come into use.

Other pathophysiologic mechanisms certainly must exist, and remain to be worked out in the future. The clarification of these is beset with the difficulties inherent in the separation of genetic effects in man from environmental factors. For many common conditions the basic problem of the existence of genetic factors still needs to be answered unequivocally. In *coronary artery disease,* there is no general agreement as to the influence of heredity. This complex problem has been reviewed by McKusick, who believes that genetic factors are of significance. In this condition, multiple pathophysiologic mechanisms exist. Disturbances of lipid metabolism, such as idiopathic hypercholesteremia and hyperlipemia, are known to predispose to coronary artery disease. Idiopathic hyperlipemia appears to be inherited as an autosomal recessive, but there are several different ideas of the genetic mechanism for the inheritance of idiopathic hypercholesteremia. It may be inherited as a dominant or as an incomplete dominant with the homozygous state accounting for the more severe form of the condition. An alternative view is that it may be the upper end of the bell-shaped curve of distribution of levels of serum cholesterol in the population. In this case polygenic inheritance would be a more likely explanation. In addition to a biochemical defect in lipid metabolism, it is also possible that morphologic differences in the anatomy of the coronary arteries might be genetically determined. Thus, the predominance of the left coronary artery in the development of the vascular tree could predispose to coronary occlusion. Information on the inheritance of the vascular pattern of the coronary tree is difficult to obtain, but there is an analogy in the inheritance of other vascular patterns in man, such as the antecubital fossa, aortic arch, and anterior chest wall. Other factors under the control of genes, such as diabetes mellitus, also influence the occurrence of coronary artery disease. Personality and temperament may be still other factors which play a role in its incidence. These characteristics may also be under genetic control. It is thus apparent that several different pathophysiologic mechanisms, such as a biochemical disturbance, a morphologic abnormality, and other factors, may be important in the development of a single clinical condition.

Another complex problem is presented by the relationship of heredity and the development of *cancer* in man. Ideas concerning inherited cancer in mice need to be revised in light of recent studies of viruses. There is no agreement about heredity and cancer in man. The familial aggregation of cancer, or even a specific type of cancer, has been offered as support of the role of genetics. The difficulty with this type of evidence is that one cannot be sure that the occurrence was not a matter of chance alone. Nevertheless, in one form of cancer of the eye, retinoblastoma, there is strong evidence that the condition is inherited. For most other forms of cancer, the information at the present time is not definite, and obviously genetic mechanisms or pathophysiologic mechanisms cannot be discussed.

Chromosomal Abnormalities

The normal diploid number of chromosomes of man is 46. This number is present in all the somatic cells. In the gametes, however, the number of chromosomes is reduced by half during meiosis. This haploid number, or single set of chromosomes, is 23. In view of the fact that the genes are located on the chromosomes, it is apparent that any variation in *number* of the chromosomes or abnormalities in *structure* resulting from loss of or addition of a piece of a chromosome could lead to an abnormality in the individual. Such chromosomal abnormalities have been de-

TABLE 4–2. CLASSIFICATION OF CHROMOSOMAL ABNORMALITIES.

1. Numerical
   A. Polyploidy
   B. Aneuploidy
      (1) Autosomal
      (2) Sex chromosomal
   C. Trisomy
2. Structural
   A. Translocations
   B. Deletions
   C. Duplications
   D. Inversions
   E. Isochromosomes
   F. Ring chromosomes

scribed in clinical disorders (in contrast to gene mutations, in which the chromosomal number and structure are normal). The relationship of the chromosomal abnormality to the disease state in terms of the mechanism for the production of the effect is not certain. The chromosomal abnormalities may be divided into two major groups, numerical abnormalities and structural abnormalities (Table 4–2).

NUMERICAL ABNORMALITIES OF THE CHROMOSOMES

Aneuploid States

The aneuploid state may result from abnormal numbers of the autosomes or the sex chromosomes or sometimes of both. Trisomy is clearly established as an important cause of clinical disease, and several well-documented autosomal trisomic conditions are known. Although the extra chromosome can usually be assigned to a particular group, it is difficult sometimes to specify which chromosome in the group is the trisomic one. Under these circumstances the condition is referred to as trisomy for a particular group rather than for a specific chromosome. The three conditions which have been clearly established are (1) trisomy for chromosome 21, which results in Down's syndrome or mongolism; (2) trisomy for a chromosome of group D, which produces a rare form of congenital malformation; and (3) trisomy for a chromosome of group E, which produces another type of congenital malformation.

Monosomy is the state in which only one of a particular chromosome pair is present instead of two. Autosomal monosomic conditions have not been clearly established, although monosomy for the X chromosome is known and is the basis for Turner's syndrome. Other aneuploid states may occur which are more complex, involving trisomy of several chromosomal pairs. This would produce karyotypes with 48, 49, 50 or more chromosomes. No important or consistent clinical condition has been produced in this manner, with the exception of the combination of Down's syndrome and Klinefelter's syndrome in the same individual.

AUTOSOMAL ANEUPLOIDY

Trisomy 21

Lejeune in 1959 was the first to find that patients with Down's syndrome had 47 chro-

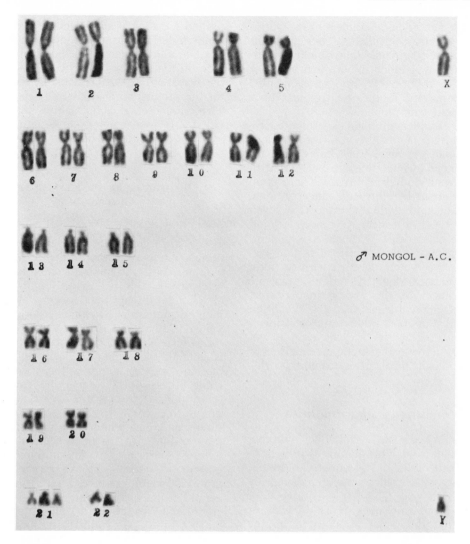

Figure 4–7. The karyotype of a male child with Down's syndrome. Note that chromosome 21 is present three times, whereas all the other autosomes are present in duplicate. (Photograph supplied through the courtesy of Dr. Mary E. Walker, Department of Pediatrics, Emory University School of Medicine.)

mosomes instead of 46. The extra one was an acrocentric chromosome belonging to the smallest group (G) and now accepted as chromosome 21. Subsequently many other workers have confirmed that the common type of mongolism is characterized by the presence of trisomy 21 and that this is the basic defect in this condition (Fig. 4–7). The mechanism which is responsible for the trisomic state is believed to be meiotic nondisjunction. Mongolism is more frequent with advancing age in the mother, and this has its analogy in the fruit fly in which nondisjunction occurs more frequently with increasing age of the flies.

While most children with Down's syndrome

are born of older mothers, some exceptions to this were soon discovered. These had the following characteristics which permitted their differentiation from the more common classic cases: (1) there was a familial occurrence; (2) the mothers were younger; (3) the children had 46 instead of 47 chromosomes, but one chromosome was a peculiar large one; (4) the mother had 45 chromosomes but one of these was the same peculiar large chromosome which the child also had. It became apparent from a study of the chromosomes of the normal mother that she had only one chromosome 15 and only one chromosome 21. The abnormal chromosome consisted of chromosomes 21 and 15 stuck together. In effect, therefore, the mother really had a full diploid complement of chromosomes including two 15's and 21's, one of each chromosome separately and the other two stuck to each other. The explanation of this is that chromosome 21 has become translocated to the 15. If her oocyte splits to form 2 possible ova (Fig. 4–8), it is possible for the children with Down's syndrome to receive a separate 21 from the mother and also a 15 (the one with the translocated 21), and therefore in effect the ovum would have two 21's and one 15. When this ovum is fertilized by a sperm containing a 21 and a 15, the zygote would be trisomic for 21 and have a pair of chromosome 15. This type of mongolism has been called translocation mongolism. There is another type of translocation mongolism which is due to translocation of one chromosome 21 to another chromosome 21. This has been called 21/21 or G/G translocation. Both these types of translocations involve the acrocentric chromosomes, and these may have a predilection for adhering to each other.

In addition to the classic and translocation types of mongolism, there are some patients with mongolism who have some but not all of the features of the disease. These appear to be mosaics who have two or more different cell lines and on occasion have been called *partial mongolism.* In one variety of mosaic mongolism, the patient has cells with 46 chromosomes and other body cells with 47, the latter being trisomic for 21. The mechanism for the development of this variant is believed to be *mitotic* rather than meiotic nondisjunction. It probably has its origin in early embryogenesis when a cell in mitosis has its chromosomes split unevenly so that some daughter cells have 47 instead of 46 chromosomes. This would result in some, but not all, of the cells of the body having the trisomic state; therefore the full picture of mongolism would not be present. These mosaics have a chromosomal number of 46/47 or normal/trisomy 21.

Another unusual variety of mongolism is associated with 48 chromosomes. This occurs in patients with Down's syndrome due to trisomy 21 combined with Klinefelter's syndrome with XXY chromosomal constitution.

Trisomy D Syndrome

Patau and his coworkers described a patient with retarded development, failure to thrive, and a very striking constellation of congenital malformations including harelip, cleft palate, microphthalmia, polydactyly, con-

Figure 4–8. The mechanism for the production of a 15/21 translocation mongol. See text for detailed explanation. It should be noted that only the split of the zygote which could produce the translocation mongol is shown. Other splits are possible but for the sake of simplicity are not depicted.

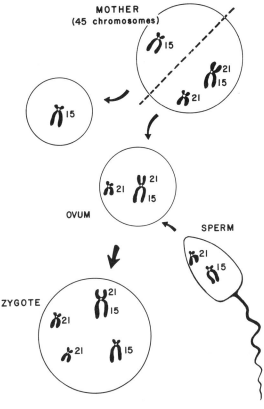

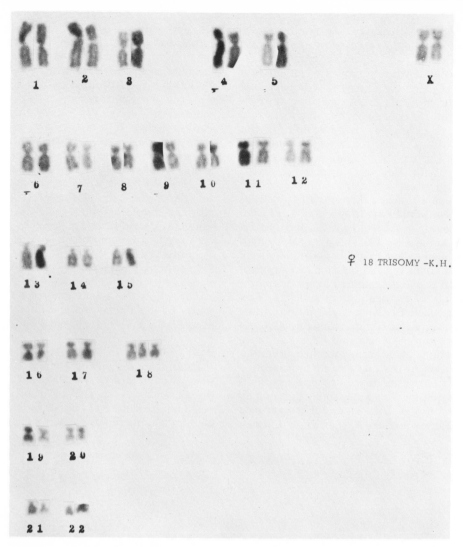

Figure 4–9. The karyotype of a female with the syndrome of trisomy 18. Note that this chromosome is represented three times, whereas all the other autosomes are present in duplicate. (Photograph supplied through the courtesy of Dr. Mary E. Walker, Department of Pediatrics, Emory University School of Medicine.)

genital heart defects, and mental retardation. The child had an extra chromosome which had the appearance of a group D chromosome (13-15). This observation has been confirmed by many subsequent case reports. In addition to the manifestations noted, deafness, seizures, hypotonicity, horizontal palmar creases, and capillary hemiangiomata also may occur. Meiotic nondisjunction is probably the basis for this trisomic condition, but the mechanism for the production of the various defects is not understood.

Trisomy E Syndrome

A more common type of congenital malformation was described by Edwards. In this

there is trisomy of one of the group E chromosomes, most likely chromosome 18. These patients have developmental and mental retardation, failure to thrive associated with hypertonicity, low-set pixie-like ears, a peculiar flexion deformity of the fingers with the index finger overlapping the third finger, and various congenital cardiac abnormalities. These patients usually survive only a few months, although one patient is reported in whom the diagnosis was made at 10 years of age. The karyotype of a patient with trisomy E syndrome is shown in Figure 4–9. When the full clinical picture is present both group E and group D trisomy can be suspected or diagnosed clinically.

Sex Chromosomal Aneuploidy

During production of the gametes, meiosis brings about a reduction from the diploid number of 46 chromosomes to a haploid number of 23. If nondisjunction occurs with respect to the sex chromosomes, some ova or sperm will have either none or both of the sex chromosomes. Fertilization leads to several possible sex chromosomal constitutions, and this appears to be the basis for the development of Turner's syndrome and Klinefelter's syndrome (Fig. 4–10).

Turner's Syndrome (Ovarian Dysgenesis)

This syndrome is a form of primary hypogonadism in phenotypic females who have gonadal aplasia with infantile genitalia, lack of secondary sex characteristics, amenorrhea, short stature, and sometimes a variety of congenital defects, including webbing of the neck and coarctation of the aorta. They have a high gonadotropin excretion in the urine and low urinary estrogens, as would be expected in primary gonadal failure. About 60 to 80 per cent of these individuals are chromatin-negative, and cytogenetic studies have

shown that they have only 45 chromosomes and an XO constitution. The possible mechanisms for production are schematically represented in Figure 4–10.

In contrast to the majority of patients with Turner's syndrome, some patients with ovarian dysgenesis are chromatin positive or have Barr bodies. The karyotypes of these patients had 46 chromosomes and therefore did not show aneuploidy. The 44 autosomes were all normal, as would be expected, and a single normal-appearing X chromosome was present. The other (46th) chromosome was a large metacentric chromosome that looked more like chromosome 3 than any other. This structurally abnormal chromosome is generally believed to be an *isochromosome* X. This term is applied to an abnormal chromosome which arises as a result of transverse division rather than the normal longitudinal division of the metaphase chromosome (Fig. 4–11). Each chromatid is therefore composed of the same two long arms of the X. Therefore, individuals who have a normal X and an isochromosome X have the short arms of the X represented only once on the normal X chromosome, whereas the long arms are represented

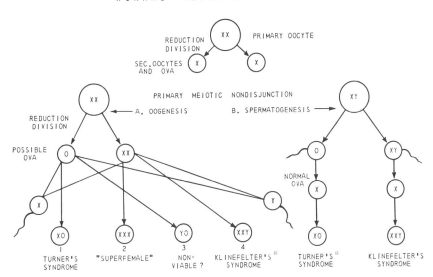

Figure 4–10. Meiotic division and nondisjunction. In normal meiotic division of a primary oocyte, each of the secondary oocytes and ova contains one X chromosome. For simplification, the polar bodies are ignored. The same process in spermatogenesis leads to X or Y chromosome–containing sperm. *A*, In primary meiotic nondisjunction involving oogenesis, an ovum with no X chromosomes and another with both X chromosomes are shown. In each instance the result of fertilization by an X-containing sperm and the result of fertilization by a Y-containing sperm are depicted. The possible combinations could lead to Turner's syndrome, a "superfemale" or Klinefelter's syndrome. The YO offspring has not yet been shown for humans and is nonviable in the Drosophila. *B*, Primary meiotic nondisjunction is shown occurring in spermatogenesis. Each possible sperm is shown fertilizing a normal ovum. The asterisk indicates that the current evidence favors that particular mechanism for Klinefelter's syndrome and Turner's syndrome.

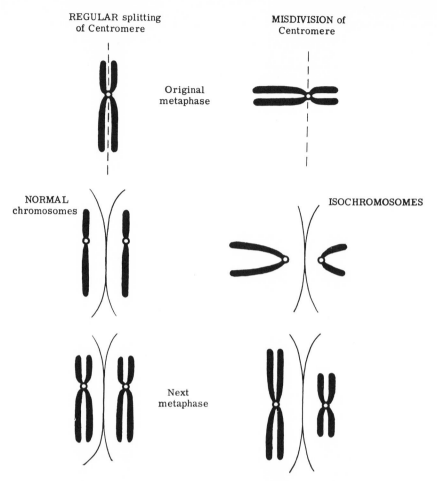

Figure 4–11. The mechanism for production of an isochromosome. (From Hamerton, J. L. (ed.): Chromosomes in Medicine. London, William Heinemann Medical Books, Ltd., 1962.)

three times, once on the normal X and twice on the isochromosome. This and other observations suggest that the genes involved in the production of Turner's syndrome are located on the short arm of the X chromosome. It is interesting that isotopic studies show that the isochromosome X is the late-labeling one (i.e., the normal X chromosome synthesizes its DNA first). In the decision as to which X chromosome becomes the Barr body, the isochromosome X always appears to become the Barr body and hence becomes the inactive or partially inactive one. This would appear to be logical, as there must be many important genes on the short arms of the X.

Turner's syndrome with one normal X and another chromosome which appears to be a smaller X has been described. These patients are said to have a partial Turner's syndrome in that some clinical features are lacking. Others with an abnormal X chromosome in the shape of a ring have also been described.

In addition to these two rarer varieties, a form of the syndrome due to mosaicism has been described also. These have been mosaics with 45/46 chromosomes, XO/XX, or XO/XY; 45/47 chromosomes, XO/XXX, or XO/XYY, and even more complex mosaics with three different cell types of 45/46/47 chromosomes, XO/XX/XXX. The mosaics may be chromatin positive or negative depending upon the number of X chromosomes present.

Klinefelter's Syndrome

This is a fairly common type of hypogonadism in phenotypic males who have small testes, azoospermia, gynecomastia in many cases, and high titers of gonadotropin in the urine. As a result of studies of nuclear chromatin, it was found that the cells of most of these individuals were chromatin positive. Not all clinical cases of Klinefelter's syndrome are chromatin positive; hence it is likely that this syndrome is not homogeneous but rather is composed of several separate conditions. Some of the chromatin negative cases may be acquired following mumps orchitis or other conditions and thus may be phenocopies. The group of patients with chromatin-positive Klinefelter's syndrome were first assumed to have an XX makeup, because one Barr body implies the presence of two X chromosomes. Later, cytogenetic studies on these individuals showed that 47 chromosomes were present. Indeed there were two X chromosomes, but there also was a Y chromosome and the sex chromosome constitution was XXY. This, like other types of aneuploidy discussed earlier, is believed to result from meiotic nondisjunction (Fig. 4–10). Since maternal aging appears to be a factor in nondisjunction, it is noteworthy that some effect of maternal age has been shown for XXY Klinefelter's syndrome, but this is not as striking as for mongolism.

Klinefelter's syndrome with one Barr body and 48 chromosomes has been described. This occurs in association of XXY with trisomy 21, that is, the combination of mongolism and Klinefelter's syndrome in the same individual. Another type in which the sex chromosomes were XXYY has also been described and produced the characteristic clinical picture.

Several additional varieties of Klinefelter's syndrome, other than the chromatin positive type with one Barr body, have been described. One type has 48 chromosomes, two Barr bodies, and the sex chromosomes are XXXY; another has three Barr bodies, XXXXY, and a total of 49 chromosomes. The clinical picture of hypogonadism is present, but there seems to be a greater degree of mental retardation with each additional X chromosome. In addition, based on a limited number of cases, the XXXXY variety seems to have several additional phenotypic features including skeletal anomalies. Radioulnar synostoses have occurred in some of these cases. It is also characterized by a more severe hypogonadism with hypoplasia of the penis and scrotum. The explanation for the more marked mental retardation with increasing numbers of X chromosomes is unknown, as is the explanation for the associated skeletal anomalies.

Multi-X Females

The normal female has two X chromosomes, but females with more than two X chromosomes are known. The "superfemale" or triple-X syndrome is a female who has two Barr bodies and 47 chromosomes. This term, the "superfemale," is used frequently because this was the original designation applied to female fruit flies with three X chromosomes. Although the first patient with this disorder had secondary amenorrhea, no characteristic clinical picture has been defined except for a tendency to a subnormal mental state. Tetra-X females with XXXX, three Barr bodies, and 48 chromosomes, and the penta-X state with XXXXX, four Barr bodies, and 49 chromosomes have also been described.

STRUCTURAL ABNORMALITIES OF THE CHROMOSOMES

Under some circumstances the total number of chromosomes is normal, but individual chromosomes may be abnormal in appearance. This may be the result of the loss of some chromosomal material, exchange of material with another chromosome, or other abnormalities. The result is an alteration in the specific structure of a particular chromosome or chromosomes. This may occur during meiosis or mitosis when chromosomes may break. In most instances the pieces join together again and there is no basic change. It would appear that if the separated piece of chromosome does not attach itself to other chromosomal material which has a centromere, it degenerates and is lost. This results in deletions, or losses of a part of a chromosome.

Translocations

If the separated chromosomal fragment becomes attached to another chromosome, it is said to be translocated. Sometimes parts of two different chromosomes exchange places with each other; this is called a reciprocal translocation. If the translocated piece of chromosome is large enough, the other chromosome to which it has become attached will be morphologically altered in such a way as to be recognized as different. If, however, the translocated piece is very small, this is impossible to recognize under the microscope at present and would be overlooked. It is quite likely that many small translocations are undetected for this reason.

Translocations which have been recognized thus far in human cytogenetics involve either a whole chromosome or the major portion of a chromosome. This has been discussed already in connection with Down's syndrome and the 21/15 and 21/21 translocations. Another possible example of translocation in man is represented by the Sturge-Weber syndrome. This is characterized by mental retardation, epileptic seizures, a port wine type nevus over the face usually in the distribution of the trigeminal nerve or its branches, and a characteristic intracranial calcification found on x-ray. In one reported patient trisomy for a chromosome of the G group was found, but this was not confirmed by others. Studies by Patau suggested that a translocation of part of a chromosome of group G to a chromosome of group D might be responsible. He proposed the name of "partial trisomy" for this condition. Studies in Sturge-Weber syndrome are still needed to confirm whether a translocation of a small fragment of a G group chromosome is the basis for this disorder.

Deletions

In 1960 Nowell and Hungerford in Philadelphia reported the association of a chromosomal abnormality with chronic granulocytic leukemia. They found that chromosome 21 had lost about one-half of the material of its longer arm. This is believed to be a deletion of part of the long arm of chromosome 21, although a translocation to another larger chromosome can not be ruled out entirely. This abnormality is called the Ph[1] chromosome or Philadelphia chromosome. This finding represented a milestone in that, although chromosomal abnormalities in malignant disease were known for many years, this was the first time that a *specific* chromosomal abnormality was associated with a specific neoplasm. The Ph[1] chromosome is believed to be a somatic mutation which occurred in a relatively undifferentiated hemopoietic cell; cultures of other tissues such as skin or even lymphocytes have not shown the Ph[1] chromosome. It is present in most if not all cases of chronic granulocytic leukemia. The Ph[1] negative cases which have been reported present atypical features and may represent a separate group from the classic cases of chronic granulocytic leukemia. It is also noteworthy that the abnormality can be found in cells in the marrow even in complete remission of the disease characterized by normalization of blood counts, regression of splenomegaly, and the return of a normal leukocytic alkaline phosphatase in the blood. The Ph[1] chromosome has been found also in the terminal phase of chronic granulocytic leukemia when the acute blast crisis has supervened.

The causative factors leading to the production of the Ph[1] chromosome are not clear. Radiation is known to induce damage to the chromosomes, leading to deletions, and this may be a factor in some cases. In addition other mutagenic agents such as chemicals or viruses may be ultimately implicated as factors leading to the original somatic mutation.

An interesting point concerning chronic granulocytic leukemia is that it is associated with a low or absent leukocytic alkaline phosphatase (LAP) level. Therefore this has prompted the suggestion that the genes for LAP production are located on the 21 chromosome. With this in mind, it was anticipated that children with Down's syndrome due to trisomy 21 would have higher levels of LAP than normal diploid individuals because of the presence of three chromosomes. Indeed this was found by several investigators. There are, however, several serious objections to concluding that the LAP gene is located on chromosome 21. (1) Studies of patients with myeloid metaplasia, in which one-third of the patients have a low LAP, have not shown the Ph[1] chromosome. The same is true for paroxysmal nocturnal hemoglobinuria which also may be associated with a low LAP. (2) If the alleged locus for LAP production on chromosome 21 is deleted by the somatic mutation responsible for chronic granulocytic leukemia, then it would be logical to assume that the LAP level would be reduced in half, because the gene on the normal 21 chromosome would be operative. This is not the case; the reduction in LAP level is more than half and often the level is close to zero. (3) Another objection to the location of the gene for LAP production is that when complete remissions in chronic granulocytic leukemia are achieved, normalization of LAP levels may occur, yet the Ph[1] chromosome can still be found in the marrow.

Chromosomal studies in other types of leukemia have not been as fruitful as those in chronic granulocytic leukemia. No specific chromosomal abnormality has been found as the basis for the other leukemias. In chronic lymphocytic leukemia, the karyotype has been found to be normal or the abnormalities found have not been consistent. On the other hand, Gunz and Fitzgerald from Christchurch, New Zealand, have reported finding an abnormal chromosome of group G in two siblings with chronic lymphocytic leukemia and several normal members of their family. This chromosome was designated Ch[1]. Unfortunately the investigators were unable to find this abnormality in subsequent studies. At the moment the status of the Ch[1] chromosome and its relationship to chronic lymphocytic leukemia are not clear.

In acute leukemia, many cytogenetic abnormalities have been found, but these have not been consistent. Both numerical and structural abnormalities of the chromosomes have been noted. The chromosomal abnormalities have been found to disappear when complete remission of the disease has been induced by treatment. Subsequent relapse of the disease has resulted in the reappearance of the identical chromosomal abnormalities which existed originally. This would indicate a significant relationship of the chromosomal abnormalities to the disease state, although it does not necessarily indicate a causal relationship as with the Ph[1] chromosome.

An interesting speculative area is the relationship of Down's syndrome (trisomy 21) to leukemia. It is well known that Down's syndrome carries with it a twentyfold increase in the incidence of leukemia. Chronic granulocytic leukemia is also associated with an abnormality of chromosome 21, but the type of leukemia seen in Down's syndrome is not chronic but acute leukemia. These associations are intriguing, but unfortunately there is no satisfactory explanation for these associations with chromosome 21.

Another chromosomal deletion has been suggested as the basis for a particular form of mental retardation associated with a moon-face, round head, wide-set eyes, low ears, presence of an epicanthic fold, and a simian crease. The major feature of this disorder, however, is the characteristic *cri du chat*, the cry of the suffering kitten. Lejeune in reporting several cases of this disorder noted a partial deletion of the short arm of chromosome 5. This finding has been confirmed by others.

Duplications

During the exchanges of chromosomal material which occur in chromosomal divisions, it is possible that some inequalities may occur. As a consequence it is possible for one chromosome to emerge with a particular gene locus represented two times on the chromosome instead of once. In the diploid state it would then be represented three times instead of twice. This abnormality is called a duplication. Little is known concerning this abnormality and its present relationship to clinical medicine.

Other Structural Abnormalities

Inversions have been mentioned previously but at present have not been detected in the human, and their relationship to disease in man is unknown. It is almost impossible to detect an inversion in a chromosome in man with our present cytogenetic techniques. Isochromosomes and ring chromosomes have also been discussed in relationship to Turner's syndrome.

The acrocentric chromosomes of groups D and G have small satellites extending from the short arms of the chromosomes. These are small, poorly defined, and weakly staining portions of the chromosome separated from the remainder by a constriction, called the secondary constriction. (The primary constriction is at the location of the centromere.) Although it has been suggested that some cases of Marfan's syndrome have enlarged satellites, this could not be confirmed in subsequent studies.

The mechanisms for the production of the disease states produced by the chromosomal abnormalities discussed above are not clear. Deletions obviously result in the loss of genes located on the deleted part of the chromosome. Additional genes made available by trisomy or duplications also have some effect. Even inversions by altering the linear order of genes could have an effect on the individual. All of this must result in a biochemical disturbance which at present is obscure. These disturbances may be elucidated in the course of time, and a clearer understanding of the pathophysiology will be available at that time.

REFERENCES

Allison, A. C., and Blumberg, B. S.: Dominance and recessivity in medical genetics. Am. J. Med., 25:933, 1958.

Baglioni, C.: Correlations between genetics and chemistry of hemoglobins. In Taylor, J. H.: Molecular Biology. New York, Academic Press, 1963.

Blank, C. E.: Some aspects of chromosome mosaicism in clinical medicine. Lancet, 2:903, 1964.

Childs, B., and Sidbury, J. B.: A survey of genetics as it applies to problems in medicine. Pediatrics, 20:177, 1957.

Childs, B., and Young, W. J.: Genetic variation in man. Am. J. Med., 34:663, 1963.

Clarke, C. A.: Genetics for the Clinician, 2nd ed. Philadelphia, F. A. Davis Co., 1964.

Dent, C. A.: Foreword to symposium on inborn errors of metabolism. Am. J. Med., 22:671, 1957.

Efron, M. L.: Aminoaciduria. New England J. Med., 272:1058, 1107, 1965.

Ferguson-Smith, M. A.: Karyotype-phenotype correlations in gonadal dysgenesis and their bearing on the pathogenesis of malformations. J. Med. Genet., 2:142, 1965.

Ferrier, P., Barnatter, F., and Klein, D.: Muscular dystrophy (Duchenne) in a girl with Turner's syndrome. J. Med. Genet., 2:38, 1965.

Fraser, F. C.: Recent advances in genetics in relation to pediatrics. J. Ped., 52:734, 1958.

Gunz, F. W., and Fitzgerald, P. H.: Chromosomes and leukemia. Blood, 23:394, 1964.

Hamerton, J. L. (ed.): Chromosomes in Medicine. London, William Heinemann Medical Books, Ltd., 1962.

Huehns, E. R., and Shooter, E. M.: Human hemoglobins. J. Med. Genet., 2:48, 1965.

Hungerford, D. A.: The Philadelphia chromosome and some others. Ann. Int. Med., 61:789, 1964.

Hsia, D. Y.: Inborn Errors of Metabolism. Chicago, Year Book Publishers, 1959.

Jacob, H. S., and Jandl, J. H.: Increased cell membrane permeability in the pathogenesis of hereditary spherocytosis. J. Clin. Invest., 43:1704, 1964.

Jandl, J. H.: The Heinz body hemolytic anemias. Ann. Int. Med., 58:702, 1963.

Knox, W. E., and Hsia, D. Y.: Pathogenetic problems in phenylketonuria. Am. J. Med., 22:687, 1957.

Landing, B. H.: Hereditary metabolic diseases—general considerations. Metabolism, 9:198, 1960.

Lejeune, J.: Quoted by MacIntyre et al. (see below).

Lyman, F. L.: Phenylketonuria. Springfield, Charles C Thomas, 1963.

Lyon, M. F.: Sex chromatin and gene action in the mammalian X-chromosome. Am. J. Human Genet., 14:135, 1962.

MacIntyre, M. N., Staples, W. I., LaPolla, J., and Hempel, J. M.: The "cat cry" syndrome. Am. J. Dis. Child., 108:538, 1964.

McKusick, V. A.: Mechanisms in genetic diseases of man. Am. J. Med., 22:676, 1957.

McKusick, V. A.: Genetic factors in cardiovascular diseases: I. The four major types of cardiovascular disease. Mod. Concepts Cardiovas. Dis., 28:535, 1959.

McKusick, V. A.: Heritable Disorders of Connective Tissues, 2nd ed. St. Louis, C. V. Mosby Co., 1960.

McKusick, V. A.: Human Genetics. Englewood Cliffs, N. J., Prentice-Hall, Inc., 1964.

Nilsson, I. M., Bergman, S., Reitalu, J., and Waldenström, J.: Hemophilia in a "girl" with male sex-chromatin pattern. Lancet, 2:264, 1959.

Ochoa, S.: The chemical basis of heredity—the genetic code. Bull. New York Acad. Med., 40:387, 1964.

Ozonoff, M. B., Steinbach, H. L., and Mamunes, P.: The trisomy 18 syndrome. Am. J. Roentgenol., 91:618, 1964.

Parker, W. C., and Bearn, A. G.: Application of genetic regulatory mechanism to human genetics. Am. J. Med., 34:680, 1963.

Price Evans, D. A.: Pharmacogenetics. Am. J. Med., 34:639, 1963.

Reed, S. C.: Counseling in Medical Genetics, 2nd ed. Philadelphia, W. B. Saunders Co., 1963.

Roberts, J. A. F.: An Introduction to Medical Genetics, 2nd ed. New York, Oxford University Press, 1963.

Rosenfield, R. L., Breibart, S., Isaacs, H. J., Klevit, H. D., and Mellman, W. J.: Trisomy of chromosomes 13–15 and 17–18: Its association with infantile arteriosclerosis. Am. J. Med. Sc., 244: 763, 1962.

Snyder, L. J., and Doan, C. A.: Studies in human inheritance: XXV. Is the homozygous form of multiple telangiectasia lethal? J. Lab. & Clin. Med., 29:1211, 1944.

Sohval, A. R.: Recent progress in human chromosome analysis and its relation to the sex chromatin. Am. J. Med., 31:397, 1961.

Stern, C.: Principles of Human Genetics, 2nd ed. San Francisco and London, W. H. Freeman and Co., 1960.

Sutton, H. E.: An Introduction to Human Genetics. New York, Holt, Rinehart and Winston, 1965.

Tarlov, A. R., Brewer, G. J., Carson, P. E., and Alving, A. S.: Primaquine sensitivity, glucose-6-phosphate dehydrogenase deficiency: An inborn error of metabolism of medical and biological significance. Arch. Int. Med., 109:209, 1962.

Wittinghill, M.: Human Genetics and its Foundations. New York, Reinhold Publishing Corp., 1965.

Zellweger, H.: Familial mongolism: History and present status. Clin. Ped., 3:291, 1964.

Part III

Metabolism
and the
Endocrine Glands

Chapter Five

Nutritional Factors; Protein and Fat Metabolism

WILLIAM A. SODEMAN

Introduction

Nutrition is the process which results in a state of nourishment, and the nourishment of the body represents that of the various cells. Included in nutrition are the metabolic processes in the cells along with the factors related to them, such as provision of energy, the building of protoplasm and the synthesis of factors related to growth and metabolism of cells. Some have divided the factors necessary for such nourishment into aliments, nonspecific substances used for energy production and for growth and repair (carbohydrate, fat, protein) and nutrients, or specific substances not synthesized by the body in adequate amounts which must be supplied (either per se or as closely related compounds) because of their essentialness for metabolism, growth and repair. These compounds include some of the elements such as iron and iodine, certain fatty and amino acids, vitamins and provitamins. Water and oxygen are also necessary.

The term vitamin is used to indicate an organic compound, aside from carbohydrate, protein and fat, present in food in very small quantities, needed for growth and health maintenance, and not synthesized by the host. In some animals certain vitamins, for example vitamin C, can be synthesized and for them vitamin C is a hormone. For man and other primates it is a vitamin.

Certain vitamins are synthesized in the gastrointestinal tract, some in amounts which make them usually no problem in bodily economy (vitamin K). However, at times when production is disturbed, symptoms arise. Niacin, riboflavin and thiamine are among others produced in some amount in the intestine. Vitamin D is also produced in the body by irradiation of the provitamin in the skin.

A diet which contains a sufficient quantity of the factors necessary for proper growth, maturation, reproduction and maintenance of good health may be considered adequate. The requirements of such a diet are not entirely known, but the work of a host of investigators in the past 50 years has led to the recognition of certain basic substances known to be essential to proper nutrition. These are adequate (1) caloric intake, (2) protein intake, (3) water, (4) minerals and (5) vitamins. No doubt other factors are important. Certain unsaturated fatty acids appear to be essential. Digestibility, palatability, satiety and an adequate residue are important factors.

The inability of the patient to satisfy his bodily needs may arise in at least three ways: (1) There may be an inadequate supply in the environment. The patient may lack food or the proper types of food because it is not available or because of his inability to choose the proper food. (2) The patient may

67

be unable to utilize the supply of foodstuffs available in the environment. (3) The patient's state may so change that his usual intake is no longer adequate because of increased needs (p. 82). He does not feel the necessity for increased intake. Inadequate supply usually depends upon economic factors, war, famine, a lack of productiveness in the community, faddism in diet and psychic states. Failure to utilize foodstuffs, when adequate amounts are ingested, depends on a variety of factors, such as chronic diarrhea, short-circuiting operations on the intestine which interfere with absorption in the face of apparently adequate intake, absence from the gastrointestinal tract of bile—an essential for proper absorption of vitamins A and K—and liver disease (for a normal liver is also essential for the utilization of these same vitamins). Increased need for vitamins or minerals may occur—for example, in pregnancy and hyperthyroidism—when the patient's dietary habits may not change and intake is not increased to meet the new metabolic levels. It is apparent, then, that nutritional "deficiency" disease does not merely imply lack of essential factors in the diet. Such substances must be present in adequate quantities, and then must be ingested, assimilated and properly utilized by the body. It is understandable why malnutrition is frequent in patients with hepatic cirrhosis, chronic ulcerative colitis, peptic ulcer, or advanced heart failure.

In the patient, deficiencies of a single factor alone are rare. The very nature of foods and the distribution of minerals and vitamins are such that a diet seriously lacking in one of these factors is likely to be lacking in others. At times there are striking exceptions to these statements, but this is not the rule. Diet faddists, for example, may greatly reduce protein intake while maintaining vitamin, mineral and caloric intake. The obese person, subsisting largely on carbohydrates, may be lacking in various vitamins. Nutritional disturbances may occur in spite of gain in weight, or leanness may occur without obvious avitaminosis. Most frequently, however, the patient deficient in one essential nutritive factor is deficient in some others. He usually ingests an inadequate supply of the various factors for variable periods and may have symptoms produced by each, but not sufficiently specific for diagnosis of one or the other deficiency. Care must be taken, when such a patient becomes sufficiently deficient in one factor to show characteristic or pathog-

nomonic evidence of a specific deficiency, that labeling it scurvy or beriberi, for example, will not cause neglect of his other, less evident deficiencies.

Some deficiency states are not well classified at all. This is true of *kwashiorkor*, a nutritional disturbance first found in Africa, but known to occur in many areas now. It causes growth retardation in children, disturbed pigmentation of the hair and skin, edema associated with disturbed serum proteins, and hepatic damage. The liver damage is sometimes thought to result in cirrhosis later on in life. This disease seems to occur in persons existing on diets poor in protein, but the exact nutritional relations are not clear. Continuous undernutrition in infancy and childhood affects skeletal growth. There is a reduction in height and weight levels.

The effects produced by the vitamin deficiencies are best classified, from the clinical standpoint, into three categories: (1) absence of symptoms and physical signs, when diagnosis may be made only by special procedures and tests; (2) symptoms and signs which may or may not be characteristic of vitamin deficiency, but are not pathognomonic or diagnostic of a specific deficiency; and (3) the typical clinical picture of frank specific deficiency. In group 2 the evidences of group 1 are also present, and in 3 those of 1 and 2. The reverse, however, is not true. In general, these categories represent increasingly greater deficiency, and the frequency of occurrence is, therefore, greater in 1 than in 2, and in 2 than in 3. In the following pages the tests and procedures which permit diagnosis in group 1 will be given in conjunction with remarks concerning groups 2 and 3, and these three will be referred to, for the sake of convenience, as the minimal, moderate and advanced pictures, respectively.

General principles underlying the treatment of all deficiency diseases include:

1. The immediate administration of emergency and lifesaving measures to a patient in a serious or critical state. This often entails the use of symptomatic and supportive measures, together with specific heroic measures directed at the etiology of the disease. In vitamin C deficiency, for example, hemorrhage and shock may demand immediate transfusion, warmth and fluids before vitamin C is given, and this, in turn, may be required intravenously for immediate effects rather than by the conventional oral route.

2. The outstanding deficiency, or deficiencies, accounting for the main diagnosis must

be treated in adequate dosage, at times as stated before, as an emergency measure, in the form of the purified vitamin supplemented by various concentrates.

3. The diet should be adequate in all known factors, especially those mentioned previously, to ensure correction of the other deficiencies present, less evident, but necessarily important in prevention of attainment of good health. Administration of vitamins and minerals in the natural state is most important, for it also includes the possible administration of other factors essential to health, but still unknown to medical science.

4. Symptomatic care and correction of related and unrelated defects are important.

Clinically, the abnormalities of structure and function and the signs and symptoms of disease caused by a deficiency of the various essential nutrients are likely to be obscured or distorted. This is because such deficiencies are frequently complicated by other disease which has led to such a deficiency and because these deficiencies are usually multiple. Thus the clinical picture is complex and often reflects more than one disease. Furthermore, many of the pathologic changes and the related symptoms and signs are clinically nonspecific. Even in those instances in which nutrients, such as the vitamins, are concerned with highly specific biochemical reactions which can be identified with great accuracy in vitro or in the experimental animal, it may be difficult or impossible to determine why and in what manner those biochemical lesions cause the clinical signs and manifestations associated with them.

An attempt will be made to describe the clinical manifestations of an excess or a deficiency of the various aliments and nutrients and to indicate in what manner that excess or deficiency has produced such a result. Because there is confusion at times about the meaning of the terms, clinical signs and symptoms are taken here to mean any abnormality detectable in any test or procedure of examination applicable to human subjects.

The aliments and nutrients which will be considered are protein, calories (carbohydrates and fats), thiamine, riboflavin, niacin, pteroylglutamic acid (folic acid) group, vitamins A, B_{12}, C, D, K and E, and the minerals calcium, iron, fluorine and iodine. Because of their doubtful significance in human nutrition, a variety of other vitamins and vitamin-like substances will not be discussed. Carbohydrate metabolism is discussed in Chapter 6.

Proteins

Proteins enter into the structure of all tissues, and of some—muscle, for example—to a much greater extent than others. Unlike carbohydrates and fats, they contain—in addition to carbon, hydrogen and oxygen—nitrogen, sulfur and usually phosphorus.

The bodily functions that depend on protein metabolism include practically all the physiologic processes of the body. Tissue growth and repair are both dependent upon protein. Hemoglobin is an important protein, and the enzymes, genes, antibodies and hormones are protein products. Protein affects water balance through its oncotic pressure as well as its participation in acid-base balance. The cellular proteins are not fixed after cell formation. Continued regeneration requires new amino acids. Both plasma and cellular proteins represent parts of a pool of circulating products for cell maintenance.

The protein molecule consists of a great number of primary units called *amino acids,* which are linked together. Twenty-one such amino acids are known to enter into protein structure, and the various proteins contain these units in varying amounts, numbers and combinations, so that the molecular weights of proteins may be small—35,000 for egg albumen—or very large—5,000,000 for hemocyanin. Such proteins, in large part, assume an elliptical or *globular* shape by coiling of the peptide chains and are soluble in salt solution or water. Albumins and globulins fall in this category. *Fibrous* proteins are elongated and held together in parallel bundles. Collagens and elastins of connective tissue fall in this category. Many proteins combine with nonprotein substances to make *conjugated* proteins. Nucleoproteins, lipoproteins and mucoproteins are in this category.

When proteins are ingested, digestive processes break them down into their primary constituents. This breakdown for absorption by the gastrointestinal tract is described in Chapters 24 to 26. Only negligible amounts are absorbed unchanged. The effects of such unchanged protein and those of parenterally introduced protein are described in Chapter 13, and the internal metabolic processes concerned with protein are discussed in the appropriate chapters (Chaps. 8, 27 and 30). After digestion and absorption the amino acids needed for the building of body protein, hormones and enzymes are utilized for this purpose. From the blood the amino acids are absorbed by cells through transport mechanisms, which also prevent active loss through the kidneys unless plasma levels get remarkably high. Amino acids are conjugated into proteins, some of which are stored, especially in some organs such as the liver, for breakdown and resynthesis elsewhere when necessary. Proteins are synthesized in all cells, the cellular genes controlling the proteins' types and consequently the functions and character of the particular cell. The rate of synthesis is influenced by many factors. Growth hormone acts in this way as does insulin. These effects and those of other hormones are indicated in Chapter 8. Excess amino acids are broken up, and the amino group (NH_2) is split off and converted, probably through an ammonia stage and combination with carbon dioxide, to urea, which is excreted in the urine. The remainder, now a fatty acid, is either oxidized for energy or converted into glucose. The progressive changes in the liver are discussed extensively in Chapter 27.

Although some nitrogen is lost to the body in saliva, hair and sweat, the amount is negligible. Hence the difference between the nitrogen intake and the fecal and urinary excretion represents the nitrogen or protein balance of the body. If these values are equal, nitrogen equilibrium is said to exist; if intake exceeds output, positive balance occurs; and if the reverse, negative balance. Normally, protein intake is required to replace loss of tissue protein. If an excess is ingested, the excess nitrogen is excreted. On inadequate intake, destruction of tissues continues and a negative balance results. In growing animals, in pregnancy and after wasting diseases the balance is positive when the intake is adequate.

Of the amino acids which make up proteins, at least ten are considered essential in the diet, i.e., are not synthesized at all or are inadequately synthesized in the body; hence outside sources are necessary. Others may be produced in the body. Thus, not only is an adequate protein intake necessary, but this adequacy implies a sufficient supply of the essential amino acids. For proper nitrogen balance the essential acids must be present —methionine, for example, as well as valine, leucine, isoleucine, threonine, phenylalanine, tryptophane, histidine and lysine. Not only must all the essential amino acids be present, but they must be present at the same time and in the proper proportions. The constant breakdown and reconstitution of proteins brings about a constant interchange between amino acids in tissues and free amino acids, requiring a continued supply in the diet. Arginine can be synthesized, but not at rates necessary for normal growth. Specific RNA molecules act as "templates," "line up" the activated amino acids, and cause them to combine in the proper order for the protein concerned. All necessary amino acids must be available for synthesis or the protein is not formed. Although the chief sign of protein deficiency has always been considered to be edema, profound effects of protein deficiency develop long before edema appears. The lack of a dramatic singular expression of such deficiencies has been a factor in retarding recognition of the importance and frequency of protein deficiency.

Certain amino acids are recognized as having specific functions. For example, phenylalanine is basic for the synthesis of thyroxine. Methionine is a source of methyl groups for synthesis of choline and creatine. Evidence points to the need for an adequate supply of all necessary amino acids for the building of a particular tissue. When protein depletion occurs, losses from various tissues are not uniform. Some proteins are depleted more rapidly than others, and some tissues more severely than others.

In the presence of a negative nitrogen balance from deficiency of essential amino acids, symptoms that include loss of appetite, fatigue and nervous irritability develop. The clinical syndromes of the various qualitative protein deficiencies are not yet well enough elucidated to warrant inclusion here. The minimal requirements of these various acids are not well established. In animals, deficiency results in loss of weight even though the caloric intake is adequate. Some proteins contain inadequate numbers or amounts of essential amino acids, whereas others are rich in them. Hence animal protein, rich in essential amino acids and containing them in proportions more closely resembling those of the body protein, is required in smaller amounts than is vegetable protein. If inferior protein exclusively is fed, even in large amounts, a negative nitrogen balance may result. Therefore the qualitative as well as quantitative aspects of protein requirements must be considered. In growth periods the requirement obviously is higher, and has been set in children from 4 gm. per kilogram at one year to about 2 gm. at six. These are estimates which exceed the common estimate of 0.66 to 1 gm. per kilogram per day for an adult. Obviously in pregnancy, hyperthyroidism and other conditions in which total metabolism is increased, such as in fever and infectious processes, the requirement is increased. In the infections, protein is also necessary for the synthesis of specific immune globulins. With protein depletion or restriction the capacity to produce agglutinins has been shown to be reduced in experimental animals. Noninfectious toxic agents, such as liver poisons, are more effective in protein depletion.

Aminoaciduria is at times important in some disease states. In phenylketonuria phenylalanine blood levels are elevated because of defective conversion of phenylalanine to tyrosine. Severe liver damage and some renal diseases also produce abnormal aminoaciduria. The Fanconi syndrome, with renal tubular injury, shows increased values in the urine, as well as elevated values for phosphate and glucose.

Fibrinogen and albumin are formed chiefly in the liver, some of the globulins elsewhere (see Chap. 27). Amino acids disappear rapidly from the blood after absorption and are integrated into tissue and plasma proteins, as studies of tagged acids show. The complexity of the factors bringing about the process is great and not clear. Emotional stress may affect protein metabolism and produce negative nitrogen balance. There is definite evidence that the pituitary growth hormone is involved. Endocrine relationships in these processes are discussed in Chapter 8.

Studies on labeled amino acids show the entrance of the dietary fraction into tissues rather promptly, indicating a constant and dynamic interchange of dietary and tissue nitrogenous products.

The dietary carbohydrate and fat supply is important in the nitrogen balance. If a man is placed on an exclusively protein diet, negative nitrogen balance will develop, for there is an inadequate supply of protein for energy requirements, and, after the carbohydrate and fat stores of the body have been depleted, tissue protein is utilized for energy. If carbohydrate and fat supply sufficient calories, protein intake may be reduced to a minimum, that is, to the requirement for tissue "wear and tear." Thus carbohydrate and fat "spare" protein; they relieve tissue protein of the necessity for supplying energy. Carbohydrate exceeds fat in this property.

Protein storage, whose existence was denied for many years, actually occurs, and the protein so stored is called *deposit protein*. In man it is said to amount to 2 kg. and, if held with 10 kg. of water, would make up about 17 per cent of the body weight. On a nonprotein or starvation diet, this store is utilized and, when protein is ingested, reaccumulates. The site of storage is not clear, but experiments in rats show that various organs become enriched with protein on a high protein diet. Protein is continually being built up and broken down in all cells. When there is acute need, catabolic processes are set up and protein is released from many cells. In this way, tissue structural protein also acts as storage protein. The relation of protein metabolism to endocrine function is discussed in Chapter 8.

Plasma proteins also act as a store, and fractionation has shown well over 30 components. The usual clinical estimates of plasma proteins are based on a salting out process which divides serum albumin from serum globulin. Actually, a fraction of the globulin remains with the albumin. A more adequate clinical division is based upon electrophoresis. By this process the proteins may be grouped into three large fractions, with subgroups. Specific physiologic function can be related to some of these components. The greater part consists of two albumin groups with molecular weight around 70,000, three globulin groups (alpha, beta, gamma) with molecular weights around 175,000, and fibrinogen. These fractions may be further subdivided, for example, the gamma globulins, representing a number of different immune bodies, probably representing a number of different protein complexes. In some diseases abnormal fractions appear (Chap. 2). For example, in myeloma a variable fraction appears between the beta and gamma globulin. Not included in these divisions are the prothrombin, hormones, enzymes and other protein fractions too low in concentration for the technique to determine. Lipoproteins are largely a part of the alpha and beta globulins. Advances in fractionation of the serum proteins have developed some important divisions. For example, the gamma globulins are useful in the establishment of passive immunity, and purified albumin is of importance in the treatment of certain protein deficiency states.

Protein Deficiency

Hypoproteinemia may be a sign of protein deficiency before edema develops. This may result from inability to take food, as in surgical patients; from inability to utilize ingested protein, as in ulcerative colitis; from excessive utilization of protein when calories from other sources are lacking; or, finally, from excessive loss of protein through proteinuria, drainage from wounds and repeated paracenteses in cirrhosis. Amino acid therapy with hydrolyzed proteins has become a popular supplement to the diet when there is insufficient intake or inability to absorb proteins properly, for example, in the presence of gastrointestinal barriers or severe diarrhea. Such products have been used extensively in peptic ulcer, not only for the added protein intake, but for the buffering action against gastric acid as well.

Primary protein deficiency is an uncommon phenomenon in the United States when characterized by the development of edema in the absence of cardiovascular, renal or hepatic causes. Loss of weight, weakness, muscle wasting, pigmentary changes in the skin, poor wound healing, and normocytic or macrocytic anemia may appear. If long continued, the edema, at first dependent, may become generalized and associated with weakness and muscle atrophy. Finally circulatory, renal, hepatic and central nervous system dystrophies ensue. Kwashiorkor has been discussed already. More commonly, protein deficiency is associated with caloric deficiency, either primary or secondary, and the picture is confused by associated phenomena, but edema remains a prominent finding except in slow and severe starvation, in which, with serum protein levels under 4 gm., or even 2.5 gm., per 100 ml., there may be no demonstrable edema.

Protein deficiency is an extremely important complication of chronic abscesses draining large amounts of pus. Fifty to 200 gm. of protein may be lost per day from a lung abscess or a decubitus ulcer, and healing may become impossible unless this loss is recognized and corrected. There is some evidence that such ulcers may be in part a function of the total circulating protein. Below a fairly critical level decubitus ulcers form and will not heal, and above that level they either do not form or heal fairly well. In such bedridden patients edema may be difficult to demonstrate. Protein losses from large burns and from draining osteomyelitis are also tremendous. Protein losses through the genitourinary tract may be large in nephrotic states and in certain blood dyscrasias, such as multiple myeloma, and some leukemias. Such losses, regardless of the cause, if not restored in utilizable form in the diet, will lead to the signs and symptoms of protein deficiency.

Apparently all persons, sick or well, except those who are severely undernourished and already in a state in which the excretion of metabolites of protein metabolism exceeds intake, who are put to bed go into a phase of negative nitrogen balance regardless of the protein intake. It is a matter of dispute whether this phenomenon is an asset or a liability, just as some years ago fever, in association with disease, was subject to the same argument. Apparently a preliminary and tentative conclusion is justified to the effect that if this state can be altered in the first four days of bedfastness, it is probably of relatively long standing and not just a phenomenon associated with acute illness, is a liability and should be corrected. There is little evidence that, in acute illness of short duration, it needs to be given serious consideration. Bedridden patients with simple fractures go into negative nitrogen balance. The same is true with simple elective herniorrhaphies and appendectomies. Even the simple experiment of putting a well and healthy young medical student to bed for several days will produce this phenomenon. It appears to be associated with acute infections and with vascular accidents such as coronary occlusion and cerebrovascular thrombosis. Normally this state is short-lived and intractable to therapy. However, if it continues beyond three or four days to a week, it constitutes protein deficiency, which will delay all healing processes and must be corrected by adequate protein intake. The value of adequate protein intake cannot be overestimated in the proper management of fractures, burns, all chronic abscesses and chronic systemic diseases, and proper protein intake may possibly shorten the course of acute severe but self-limited infections of many kinds.

The mechanism of production of edema in protein deficiency has been thought to be a simple osmotic pressure phenomenon. The lowered circulating blood proteins do not have a water-holding capacity equal to the capacity of the fixed tissue proteins; hence water accumulates in the tissues at the expense of the blood volume. That this explanation is not the whole story is manifested by the edema of starvation, but there is little evidence that this explanation does not hold in true primary protein deficiency from either extrinsic or intrinsic causes. In famine edema there appears to be no great fall in plasma colloid osmotic pressure and no rise in tissue osmotic pressure. In spite of protein-deficient diets the plasma protein concentration may be normal in the presence of edema, low in the absence of edema or very low in the presence of moderate edema without demonstrable pressure differences between tissue and circulating blood. Both arterial and venous pressures are usually low, and the presence of edema might be thought to be explainable on a circulatory basis, except that in equally deranged circulatory states and in the presence of lowered plasma protein, edema may be conspicuous by its absence. Changes in renal blood flow with disturbed salt excretion have recently been postulated. Keys has shown in experimental subjects placed on low calorie diets, but with blood protein levels maintained, that edema appears without increase in the measured extracellular space. When there is sufficient loss of cellular tissue so that the unchanged extracellular space finally exceeds the reduced tissue (cellular) structure by a volume of approximately 10 per cent over normal, edema appears. In most famine areas pure calorie deficiency is not usually seen, and accompanying vitamin and protein deficiency adds to the complexity of the picture. Sodeman has demonstrated in famine victims shifts in water between the nutritionally depleted tissue cells and the extracellular space. Changes in osmolarity related to salt balance across the tissue cell membrane probably enter into the mechanism. The anemia of protein deficiency is probably due to a lack of stroma-forming substance in the reticuloendothelial system and reflects a phenomenon common to all new cell formation in the body.

It is evident that protein deficiency must play an important role in the vitamin B complex deficiency states, because the enzymes involved are probably always carried by protein molecules. Tryptophane deficiency results in reduced niacin activity. Tryptophane appears to be necessary for the synthesis of niacin in the body. Also it is known that amino acids and vitamin B_6 have a metabolic relationship. The vitamin B complex and proteins are both associated with liver function. Prolonged impaired liver function is likely to give rise to protein deficiency. In advanced cirrhosis and, prophylactically, early in liver damage, adequate vitamin B complex, proteins and calories are important in treatment (see Chap. 27). Increasing knowledge of the action of the endocrine substances suggests that here too metabolic disturbances may present variable chemical pictures depending upon the state of protein nutrition quantitatively and perhaps also qualitatively. The Selye alarm reaction, the curious response of animals to multiple noxious stimuli, may be materially affected quantitatively by protein metabolism. The first phase, acclimatization to activity in a noxious environment and the final phase, dissolution, may be intimately connected with qualitative or quantitative intracellular protein deficiencies.

In the evaluation of the state of protein metabolism, determinations of the plasma proteins are valuable. However, blood levels may be normal in the face of important protein loss, and patients with rapid loss of nitrogen may have low plasma levels which do not reflect the same degree of depletion seen with similar levels in gradually developing prolonged imbalance. A general evaluation of the patient is important. Rapid losses in weight, as well as remarkable underweight, are strongly indicative of protein deficiency. Clinical states in which there is disturbed intake or disturbed absorption in the intestinal tract, such as in ulcerative colitis, are likely to indicate protein deficiency.

Therapeutically, protein deficiency must be corrected by replacement. When losses exceed 150 gm. per day, this usually cannot be accomplished by the oral route alone. In cases in which the loss is renal the situation may not be altered by any form of therapy. The fundamental nature of this problem is still unknown. The significance of moderate or marked protein deficiency, either primary from lack of intake, or secondary from a myriad of causes, in relation to antibody formation and the normal cellular response to disease, is also poorly understood. It is known that antibody formation is disturbed by protein deficiency. However, this should be given serious consideration in the management of the critically, and particularly the chronically, ill. Undoubtedly the importance of protein, in proper amount and of correct quality, in the management of disease is rapidly increasing as our knowledge of the subject grows.

Fats

Fats, combinations of fatty acids and glycerol, provide an important source of energy. These are the neutral fats or triglycerides. *Fatty acids,* combined with cholesterol, carbohydrate and phosphoric acid, participate in other stages of fatty acid metabolism considered under other headings. The term *lipids* includes these compounds which contain, along with fatty acids, nitrogen with or without phosphorus. Phospholipids are an important group. *Cholesterol esters* are cholesterol compounds of fatty acids. Free cholesterol represents another group of compounds.

The body fats are usually a mixed variety, having a molecule containing two or more fatty acids. They function chiefly as a source of easily stored energy. Fat-free diets in animals have indicated that some unsaturated fatty acids, particularly linoleic, linolenic, and arachidonic, are "essential" and that their absence from the diet produces disturbed growth and skin lesions. Elsewhere it is pointed out that unsaturated fatty acids are not atherogenic, as are the saturated group. They may be related to cholesterol transport, and possibly there is a requirement relative to the saturated fat in the diet.

The digestion of fats is discussed in Chapters 25 to 27.

On passage through the intestinal mucosa the split glycerol and fatty acids are resynthesized to new triglyceride molecules which enter the lymph as droplets about 0.5 micron in size called *chylomicrons.* The cholesterol and phospholipids absorbed enter these chylomicrons in small amounts. It is the increase in chylomicrons after a fatty meal which produces a turbid plasma, for the lymphatics transmit them to the venous blood via the thoracic duct. *Lipoprotein lipase,* the so-called clearing factor, breaks down the triglyceride of the chylomicrons, glycerol being metabolized as a carbohydrate, and fatty acids being carried with albumen to body cells for oxidation or storage. Some chylomicrons enter the liver directly to be metabolized. The fatty acids combined with serum albumen, unesterified fatty acid, represent an important fraction, for they are transmitted rapidly to body cells for energy use. In the American diet almost half the calories are derived from fats. In addition carbohydrate is converted to fat for storage. Thiamine is thought to be involved in this conversion, and other members of the B complex (riboflavin, pyridoxine and nicotinic acid) may also participate in the reaction. Protein is converted to carbohydrate and may then be converted to fat. These fat stores are active metabolically and are available for carbohydrate and protein synthesis. Fat is no longer regarded only as a final storage form of excess food. It is a part of the active metabolic pool of the body. Besides acting as caloric stores, carriers of fat-soluble vitamins

and adding palatability and satiety to the diet, fats relate to the development of important disease processes.

Normally oxidation of fatty acids in the body is complete. The degradation takes place by progressive release of two carbon segments in the form of acetyl coenzyme A (acetyl Co-A), the beta oxidation process, with entrance of acetyl Co-A into the tricarboxylic acid cycle, as in the metabolic handling of carbohydrate. Over half the initial degradation takes place in the liver, where a portion of acetyl Co-A is transformed to acetoacetic acid and carried to peripheral tissues to be reconverted for energy oxidation.

Accumulation of acetoacetic acid, a keto acid, in the blood results in ketosis. Betahydroxybutyric acid and acetone are formed from acetoacetic acid. These substances are called ketone bodies. This abnormality occurs with interference in carbohydrate metabolism, such as in diabetes mellitus, in starvation when energy must come from stored fats, or in the use of high fat diets. Cellular limits on ability to oxidize acetoacetic acid, together with the excess produced, lead to high blood levels and severe acidosis. The acidosis results from the increase in acids present tending to lower the blood pH and from the combination of these acids with cations of the blood, chiefly sodium, which is lost through urinary excretion of these products. Ketone bodies are oxidized to carbon dioxide and water to supply energy in both normal and diabetic animals. Their function and use continue during satisfactory metabolism of carbohydrate. Both protein and carbohydrate are antiketogenic, the former less so than the latter, for some amino acids are ketogenic. This process of ketone depression takes place in the liver. Elevation of liver fat is accompanied by the replacement of carbohydrate (glycogen) by fat in metabolism and by increased ketogenesis.

In diabetic animals, insulin favors deposition of glycogen in the liver and inhibits fat deposition, so that insulin has an antiketogenic action. In normal persons insulin may reduce liver glycogen and is then ketogenic. Aside from insulin, other hormones affect fat metabolism and are important in development of pathologic states. Corticotropin and growth hormone have a fat-mobilizing effect. Glucocorticoids increase the rate of fat mobilization, and in their absence mobilization of fat is depressed. Their need for fat mobilization is important in the development of ketosis. Hence they are said to be keto-genic. Thyroid hormone causes mobilization of fats as does epinephrine.

The long-recognized high caloric value of fat is now being used in the makeup of emulsions with carbohydrate for liquid high caloric, low volume diets. In addition to the high caloric value, fats have an important function in the absorption of fat-soluble vitamins, especially A, D, K and other factors. Need for essential fatty acids has already been mentioned.

Cholesterol is of both dietary and endogenous origin. All cells may produce cholesterol, but the endogenous source is overwhelmingly the liver. If dietary sources are high, less is produced in the liver and blood levels change but little. However, diets high in saturated fats increase cholesterol levels, and those high in unsaturated fats usually have a depressing effect. Cholesterol is used in the body to form cholic acid for bile salt production, to form certain hormones, such as adrenocortical hormone, progesterone and testosterone, and in the corneum of skin to give it water-protective properties. Along with phospholipids it enters into cell membranes to control permeability and into cell structures themselves for cell stability.

Of great interest today is the place of cholesterol and lipids in atherogenesis, especially since atheromatous plaques contain large amounts of cholesterol and experimental atherosclerosis is easily produced in rabbits by high cholesterol feeding. In addition dietary fats affect the occurrence of atherosclerosis.

The amount of fat necessary in the diet is not established. In the United States fat calories represent up to 40 per cent of the intake, a figure which some believe excessive and predisposing to atherosclerosis. In some countries, Japan, for example, fat calories represent only 10 per cent of the diet. With diets of comparable fat content serum cholesterol levels are lower when the dietary fat is largely made up of unsaturated fatty acids. Thus types of fat as well as amounts are important.

The relationships of fat intake to the development of atherosclerosis are not clear. Men are more markedly affected than women. Either male sex hormone accelerates the process or female sex hormone protects against it. Blood lipids have been increased in males on carbohydrate enriched diets. Levels of cholesterol, total fatty acids, and distribution of saturated and unsaturated fatty acids in the serum may relate to age, sex, family history of heart disease, presence of diabetes, hypothyroidism, hypertension and other diseases and are discussed in appropriate sections of this text.

Calories

General Metabolism

All the various chemical reactions responsible for growth, maintenance of vital functions and energy production constitute the metabolic activity of the body. Metabolic processes causing breakdown of tissue are termed catabolic; those concerned with construction, anabolic. Ingested food provides the energy for these various processes, including physical activity. Since energy is transformed and not created or destroyed, there is a definite relation between energy of intake and that of output and storage. The dietary sources of energy are carbohydrates, proteins and fats, substances which, on oxidation, produce approximately 4.1, 4.1 and 9.3 calories per gram, respectively, usually given in tables as 4.0, 4.0 and 9.0.

Carbohydrates, fats and proteins are utilized by cells to synthesize adenosine triphosphate (ATP) which is used as an energy source in these chemical reactions and if in excess is lost as heat. Such reactions take place in protein and glucose synthesis, in synthesis of fatty acids, and in other processes, including muscle contraction, transport of substances across membranes, nerve conduction and glandular secretions. ATP relates as well to creatine phosphate in energy storage.

In the transfer of energy from foodstuff to ATP 60 per cent is lost as heat. If added to heat loss in ATP conversions, the total lost becomes about 75 per cent and only 25 per cent is used in functional systems—and even this is further reduced in tissue turnover. Increased bodily activity (muscular) also expends energy by its transfer to the environment.

In the combustion of each of the foodstuffs, oxygen is utilized and carbon dioxide is given off. The ratio of carbon dioxide given off to oxygen utilized (the *respiratory quotient*) is constant for each, being 1.0 for carbohydrate, 0.80 for protein, and 0.70 for fats. Thus, for fats and proteins, the oxygen required exceeds the carbon dioxide given off. When the food oxidized is chiefly carbohydrate, the respiratory quotient approaches unity. If it drops to 0.70, the mixture oxidized is chiefly fat. On usual diets the respiratory quotient is about 0.85, but may exceed 1.0 when fat is being formed from carbohydrate, for oxygen is given up in this process.

Since the production of heat is related to the amount of carbon dioxide given off and oxygen utilized, the determination of the quantity of either the oxygen consumed or the carbon dioxide given off in a definite period of time permits the calculation of the amount of heat produced in the body during that period. The amount of heat produced for specific quantities of these two gases varies with the type of food oxidized, but the variations in oxygen are less than those for carbon dioxide. Oxygen is, therefore, usually used to calculate heat production, and even then correction for the food mixture must be made. This is done by correction for the non-protein respiratory quotient with an additional calculation for protein based on the urinary nitrogen excretion. Usually, in clinical measurements of the basal metabolic rate, the respiratory quotient is assumed to be 0.82, and such fine calculations are not made.

Heat production at rest is related to the surface area of the body, so that small animals with a greater surface area in relation to body weight produce more heat per unit of body weight than do larger animals. Heat is produced by metabolic processes in the tissues, including the organs and muscles, and is obviously increased by work, ingestion of food, reduced environmental temperature and elevation in body temperature.

Oxygen consumption by the body is determined clinically in the subject who is awake, but whose digestive processes are at a minimum—that is, 12 hours after a light meal—who is at rest physically and mentally, having refrained from strenuous exercise for 24 hours and having had a satisfactory night's rest. The temperature of the room should be comfortable. The subject rests, lying down for 30 minutes before the determination is made. Oxygen consumption is usually measured by a recorder attached to a closed circuit which indicates the variations in volume of oxygen in a tank as respiration proceeds. Carbon dioxide is chemically removed from the system, the change in base line of the respiratory curve representing the change in oxygen; that is, presumably the amount utilized over a recorded period of time. Corrections for body temperature and variations in oxygen volume due to environmental temperature and barometric pressure are based on charts.

A respiratory quotient of 0.82 is assumed. From the patient's height and weight an estimation of the surface area is made. The heat production per square meter of body surface per hour is then calculated, and the determination is compared with normal standards. Results are expressed in percentage above (+) or below (−) the assumed normal. Likewise, from the calories produced per hour, the total *basal* heat production per day may be estimated. In general, for adults this ranges from 1400 to 1800 calories per day.

It is obvious that such determinations are far from exact. When leaks occur in the appliance fitted into the mouth to insure breathing into the machine, through a punctured ear drum, or in the nose clip used to stop nasal breathing, or when real basal conditions do not prevail as a result of physical exercise, ingestion of food or lack of mental rest, oxygen values too high may be obtained. Mistakes in calculation or changes in the resting position of the chest after the determination has been started may give values too low or too high. The assumed respiratory quotient, the technique of estimation of body surface and variations in atmospheric conditions also add some errors.

The values vary with age and sex. Heat production diminishes with age. Premature infants and the newborn have lower rates than infants several weeks old. In females the rates are slightly lower than in males. There are racial differences, and warm climates reduce the basal metabolic rate. Pregnancy increases the rate in the later months, when the metabolism represents that of the mother and the fetus. Dietary factors, barometric pressure and drugs also influence the rate. Disturbances in basal metabolism and their mechanisms are discussed in the appropriate sections, such as undernutrition, endocrine disturbances, leukemia and polycythemia.

Ingestion of food increases heat production, as stated before. This effect, called the specific dynamic action, or SDA, starts within an hour after ingestion of food and is at its height in three hours. It is generally thought, but not proved, that this effect is greatest as a result of protein ingestion, an effect not ascribed to digestion, for digestive activity without food does not produce it and intravenous administration of amino acids does. Specific amino acids (glycine, alanine, leucine, glutamic acid, tyrosine and phenylalanine) are thought to be responsible. It is possible that the effect is the result of direct stimulation of the metabolism of tissue cells, and some investigators have ascribed part of the protein effect to work performed by the kidney in the excretion of urea. Others believe that the work of deaminization and urea formation is responsible for the specific dynamic action of protein. This action occurs in the liver. The specific dynamic action of carbohydrate and fat probably arises on a different basis. Proof of exact mechanisms is not forthcoming, but that of carbohydrate is thought due to conversion of glucose to glycogen and that of fat to the speeding up of the oxidation of fat following ingestion.

The energy requirement for an individual is generally calculated upon the basis of the basal metabolism with additions for the specific dynamic action of food, needs for work, requirements for temperature regulation and for growth. The last three components are variable and difficult to estimate. Since clinically determined basal metabolism is usually above the true figure, and since in sleep the level is below the basal estimate, the effects of specific dynamic action are usually considered to be included in the figures for basal metabolism. Requirements for work vary so greatly that the reader should refer to various tables indicating the general requirements for various activities.

Obesity

When caloric intake exceeds the output, calories must be stored, for energy cannot be created or destroyed. Excessive protein and carbohydrate, as already stated, are converted to fat. Continuous excess of caloric intake thus leads to overweight due to fat storage. This is termed obesity.

Though the causes for obesity may not always be clear in any particular person, it is obvious that the remarks given previously on energy balance must hold. That some persons, who are otherwise normal, indulge in foods to such an extent that intake exceeds use is obvious. The average person without much thought keeps intake and output of energy in balance with normal unchanging weight, often for many years. Apparently his desire for food and his activity are balanced by a satisfactory regulatory mechanism. If this mechanism, presumably an unknown one controlling appetite, is disturbed and intake is stepped up, weight increases because of fat deposition. If, after years of regulation, the appetite is "set" for the usual activity and, with aging and more sedentary activity, it is not changed, obesity may develop. This may occur from extraneous factors affecting the person at any age, and is likely to be responsible for increases in weight as age progresses.

Many factors apparently affect food intake and increase intake above calories necessary for activity. Family habits and customs in eating, emotional factors causing frustration and dissatisfaction, and hereditary factors appear to be some of these. Heredity in obesity is a much disputed factor. Often family or racial groups tend to be obese. Habits and customs in eating may be responsible. Some have tried to demonstrate metabolic anomalies to account for the changes, but in general such anomalies cannot be demonstrated. Digestion is no more efficient than usual; the basal metabolic rate is not changed; fat metabolism cannot be shown to deviate from normal; and other metabolic processes show no real error. In some strains of rats with a hereditary tendency to obesity ineffective mobilization of fat from adipose tissue has been demonstrated while storage was normal. Obesity does "run in families" and may relate through hereditary psychic factors, genetically set feeding centers, or otherwise. At times, and in the minority of patients, some metabolic errors are found. In hypothyroidism, metabolism is low. In some obese subjects Hetenyi found blood lipids lower than in normal persons. Such a change could be responsible for reduction in the feeling of satiety and cause desire for carbohydrate foods. Experimentally, lesions in the diencephalon have led to development of obesity in animals. This area is considered to be the one in which hunger and satiety sensations originate. The lateral nuclei of the hypothalamus have been labeled the hunger center and the ventromedial nuclei, stimulation of which in animals produces satiety, the satiety center. In some endocrine disturbances, distribution of fat varies, and such terms as "pituitary" or "gonadal" obesity have been used. Still, dietary restriction of calories will cause loss of weight in such patients, and any action of such glands in the production of obesity must relate to the intake or output of energy.

Obesity predisposes to certain diseases and makes some diseases worse. The increased work of carrying the load of fatty tissue adds to the strain of the patient with heart disease. Relationships to diabetes are discussed in Chapter 6.

The only satisfactory plan for treatment of the obese patient is to reduce intake of calories below output. This is logically accomplished by reduction of dietary intake. Increase in output through exercise or drugs to increase metabolism is not generally successful without dietary control and, in circumstances in which related disease is present, may be harmful.

Caloric Deficiency

Perhaps the best understood and most generally recognized nutritional deficiency encountered in medical practice is simple primary caloric deficiency. In the United States its most common cause is economic want or illness which increases the need for, or interferes with the intake or absorption of, foods. Elsewhere in the world, periodically, inadequate availability of food plays a significant role, but even in famine regions the economic factor usually dominates. Early, the only finding is asymptomatic weight loss followed shortly by weakness and easy fatigability. Progressively there is diminished ability to work, apathy, mental depression, intense hunger, abdominal and muscular pains, amenorrhea, diminished to absent libido, loss of fertility, emotional imbalance, dizzy spells and fainting spells. These symptoms are accompanied by emaciation, dryness and pigmentation of the skin, bradycardia, hypotension, dyspnea on slight exertion, lowered basal metabolic rate, anemia, dependent edema, diminished organ and blood volume, albuminuria and acidosis. Specific nutrient deficiency signs may be absent or occur irregularly. As death from starvation approaches, especially if the starvation has been gradual in development, all body requirements are tremendously lowered, and the patient may remain motionless for days to weeks in a semistuporous state, subsisting on almost nothing.

The mechanism of production of the dominant findings, loss of weight and strength, are relatively well understood. The body has specific caloric requirements for the maintenance of normal body functions plus a caloric requirement for work. If these are not provided daily by calorically equivalent food, weight loss promptly ensues. For a short time work output is not diminished, but soon the body spares itself by diminishing and finally eliminating the caloric requirement for external work by doing no external work. Progressively, if metabolic requirements are not met, body tissue is metabolized. At this point caloric deficiency becomes protein deficiency as well. However, as this begins, metabolic requirements progressively diminish. Cell respiration slows and, whereas metabolic needs for a normal 150 pound man may be 2000 calories per day, when his weight has fallen to 100 pounds, his needs may fall to 1200 calories, and to 900 to 1000 calories when his weight reaches approximately 60 per cent of normal. There is some evidence that under some circumstances minimal life-saving requirements for bedridden patients may get as low as 500 calories per day for short periods. As with all other deficiency states, acute severe privation will result in rapid decline and early death without the adjustments which take place in slow, moderate and gradual privation. Basically, however, in either state it is a matter of simple arithmetic. Caloric expenditure must be met by caloric intake, or deterioration will ensue. As soon as fat and glycogen stores are exhausted, protein catabolism begins. Not until then do the more serious stigmata of caloric deficiency appear.

The mechanism of some of the phenomena of caloric deficiency is not understood. Conspicuous among these is the brownish pigmentation of the skin about the mouth, eyes and in skin folds. Another is edema when serum proteins are not low or the occasional absence of edema when serum proteins are very low.

As caloric requirement falls in slow starvation, vitamin and mineral requirements must also fall, because evidences of the specific deficiencies such as pellagra, scurvy and the like, are not striking in many starving people, even though the intake of the specific nutrients is far below known requirements for health.

Leanness, body weight below the average without obvious disease to account for it and without the factors leading to starvation, occurs, and again must present a discrepancy between caloric intake and output. Some persons, presumably in perfect health otherwise, seem to maintain a state of underweight in the face of apparently adequate intake of food. Programs to increase their intake often fail to cause an increase in weight because of inadequacies in the program. No metabolic defect is found in them. Still, the relationship between energy intake and output must hold, and factors to disturb this relationship must be present. Often such persons are of asthenic habitus and display other symptoms: lack of stamina, presence of nervous symptoms, poorly developed musculature.

Vitamins

Vitamins, or derivatives of them, function with proteins in promotion of catalysis in certain body processes. Commonly, the vitamin derivatives are coenzymes which activate enzymes in metabolic processes, for example in hydrogenation, dehydrogenation, ester hydrolysis and carbon bond cleavage. Much fundamental knowledge in these areas remains to be discovered.

Vitamins, like other organic compounds, may have pharmacologic effects not explained by their nutritional actions. This is especially true when they may be used in large amounts. Niacin is such an example.

Vitamin A

Aside from the limitation of growth and development in children, the generally accepted subjective symptoms and discernible objective signs of vitamin A deficiency are hemeralopia, or night blindness, xerosis and xerophthalmia, a dermatosis and perhaps a vaginitis. Other manifestations are either impossible to detect clinically or are so nonspecific as to defy designation as signs of the deficiency. These latter include changes in the bronchial mucosa, sometimes with accompanying atelectasis and terminal pneumonia in children, and changes in the epithelium of the urinary tract with excessive epithelial cells in the urine. Congenital abnormalities, particularly those resulting from disturbances in skeletal growth with mechanical injury to the nervous system, have not been reported in man.

Vitamin A is a higher alcohol which is ingested preformed as such, or is formed in the body, probably in the liver or in the intestinal wall, from the provitamin A carotenoids. There are numbers of compounds with this action, for example retinol, retinal and retinoic acid. Storage is largely (95 per cent) in the liver. Its mode of action, that is, the actual chemical mechanism, process or system involved, is not clear. It exerts an influence on glycogen neogenesis and its action also affects adrenal cortical function. It affects the production of mucous types of mucopolysaccharides. It is essential to proper vision, to the maintenance of normal epithelial cells and to proper growth. This includes bone growth. If one reasons from the effects of its deficiency, the vitamin functions primarily by stimulating the development of new cells. Growing tissue deficient in vitamin A increases in purine content when furnished vitamin A, suggesting the growth of new cell nuclei. Vitamin A also joins with a protein to form visual purple. These two actions, indefinite as the first is at present, explain the production of the clinical manifestations of its deficiency.

Clinically, its effect on cell growth is most noticeable in the epithelium. In general the effect may be described as a metaplasia, the replacement of specialized types of epithelium by a stratified, cornified, hyperkeratotic type. Objection has been raised to the use of the term "metaplasia" in describing the pathologic changes in the skin, the epithelium of which is normally squamous and keratinizing. This may be correct, but the process in other sites is essentially a metaplasia, and even in the skin the involvement of sebaceous and sweat glands warrants the use of this term, which can be used to advantage to describe the changes elsewhere.

In the skin this change characteristically leads to a perifollicular papular hyperkeratosis. The sebaceous glands become atrophic, and the ducts are plugged with keratinized epithelium which often projects as a horny plug from the mouth of the gland. With this there is loss of hair, broken shafts remaining in the follicles, and dryness because of lack of sebaceous secretion and sweat, the sweat glands likewise becoming atrophic. There is some general thickening of the epidermis with increased desquamation and pigmentation, particularly about the follicles. This pigmentation may persist when the papule has disappeared. Infection is not common when the skin is kept clean.

In the eye there is a similar process, affecting first the cornea, then the sclera, with increased desquamation or cornification of the epithelium producing superficial, grayish, foamlike lesions called *Bitot's spots,* edema and vascularization of the cornea, and a decrease or loss of lacrimation because of atrophy of the lacrimal glands. Later stages result in opacities of the cornea and are complicated by infection, perforation and loss of the eye (keratomalacia).

In the bronchi and upper air passages, ureters and kidney pelves, uterus, vagina, esophagus and perhaps other parts of the gastrointestinal tract, pancreas and elsewhere, similar changes occur. The developing tooth structure is seriously affected. In infants the desquamated cells may plug the bronchi, leading possibly to bronchiectasis and to infection and terminal pneumonia in advanced cases.

The effect of vitamin A deficiency on vision varies from delayed dark adaptation to frank night blindness (nyctalopia). The mechanism of this functional abnormality is better understood than that of the morphologic effects of the deficiency. Except for a slight increase in sensitivity of the cones possibly affected by vitamin A lack, dark adaptation is accomplished by use, and greater sensitivity, of the rods. The rods are stimulated by changes in the visual purple, a complex substance containing vitamin A. Visual purple, or rhodopsin, is rapidly broken down by light to visual yellow, a mixture of retinene and a protein. In this reversible reaction rhodopsin is reformed, but in the recurring process a certain amount of vitamin A disappears and must be replaced if function of the rods is to be maintained. Thus deficiency of vitamin A may impair function of the rods and hence dark adaptation and vision in dim light.

Additional factors affecting the formation of visual purple are the supply of oxygen to the retina (anoxia) and the length of time the retina has previously been exposed to bright light. There is the possibility that structural changes in rods or retinal nerves occur as the result of alterations in the visual purple, and such injury may interfere with their adjustments to dark. The structural changes would be slower to respond to treatment with vitamin A than would the chemical changes associated with the visual purple.

The daily requirement of vitamin A is not known but is proportional to body weight. Recommendations exceed minimal requirements and approach optimal needs. In children this varies from 1500 I.U. under one year to 4500 I.U. at ten to twelve years. In adults it approximates 2500 I.U., including a margin of safety, and up to 5000 to 6000 I.U. have been recommended.

The Vitamin B Complex

The vitamin B complex now consists of more than 20 factors. They are, as a group, water-soluble, but differ greatly in their functions in the body. However, coenzymes containing thiamine, riboflavin, niacin, pyridoxine and pantothenic acid have important roles in carbohydrate metabolism. Only five of the group, *thiamine* (B_1), *riboflavin, nicotinic acid, folic acid* and *vitamin* B_{12}, will be discussed here.

Of the others, *vitamin* B_6, or *pyridoxine,* deficiency in animals has shown acrodynia, anemia and convulsions. In man induced deficiency has produced skin lesions about the eyes, nose and mouth. Lymphocytopenia develops also. There are active structurally related compounds. Pellagrins have improved when vitamin B_6 was added to their diets with other factors. The typical lesions of cheilitis have been reported to heal with its use. Infants placed on a pyridoxine-free diet show disturbances in tryptophane metabolism, and suffer a hypochromic anemia and convulsions. Infants placed upon artificial formulas low in pyridoxine have shown hyperirritability and convulsions which were relieved by pyridoxine injections. Adult volunteers placed on pyridoxine-deficient diets which were poor in all B complex, have had seborrheic dermatitis starting in the nasolabial folds and later spreading. Intertrigo developed under the breasts. Cheilosis, glossitis and stomatitis of the type seen in niacin and riboflavin deficiency have also occurred. Lymphopenia was also present. Deficiency of *pantothenic acid* has been known to produce graying of hair as well as other symptoms in animals. It plays an important role in human nutrition but deficiency appears to be rare. Its place in human nutrition is not settled. It is active in an enzyme system in adrenal function, and induced deficiency in volunteers is accompanied by findings suggesting adrenal cortical insufficiency.

Choline appears to be related to mobilization of fatty acids in the body, for in experimental animals its deficiency leads to development of fatty liver and hemorrhagic and renal lesions. It is thought to be a donor of labile methyl groups. It also stimulates the formation of phospholipids and enters into the production of acetylcholine. In human beings it is widely used in the treatment of hepatic disorders with fatty degeneration. Its exact place in human nutrition has not yet been evaluated.

Biotin deficiency produces skin changes in rats. Diets high in egg white produce such damage, presumably through a biotin-inactivating factor (avidin) in egg white. It appears to function in the carboxylation of pyruvate to oxalacetate. Human requirements are not established, but skin changes presumably due to biotin deficiency have been produced in man from feeding large amounts of egg white. Naturally occurring biotin deficiency syndrome has been described in infants, characterized by seborrheic dermatitis (Leiner's disease).

Inositol has no known importance in clinical disease. It appears to be necessary for formation of some cephalins.

Para-aminobenzoic acid was once thought to have a possible role in graying of hair, but at present its need in the diet of human beings has not been established. Chemotherapeutically, it has been used in the treatment of certain rickettsial diseases.

Thiamine (*Vitamin* B_1). The primary

clinical manifestations of this deficiency are a peripheral neuritis and congestive heart failure. The two may be combined and in the more advanced stages form the classical pictures of dry and wet beriberi, respectively. Additional features are disturbances in gastrointestinal function and mental symptoms resembling those of psychoneurosis and neurasthenia. Involvement of the second and the eighth cranial nerves, possibly leading to permanent optic atrophy and deafness, may apparently occur in severe prolonged deficiency. Whether certain other effects, such as testicular atrophy, gynecomastia and other changes in secondary sex characteristics, recently described, are the result of thiamine deficiency alone cannot at present be stated.

The signs and symptoms of the peripheral neuritis are those which would be expected from such a lesion and are similar to those seen in peripheral neuritis due to other causes. They include fatigue, muscular weakness, heaviness and stiffness of the extremities, with paresthesias and tenderness of the nerve trunks and muscles. The symptoms begin distally and first in the lower extremities. Later there are pain and cramps, severe paresthesias, and partial to complete paralysis with atrophy of the muscles which show the reaction of degeneration. Hyperesthesia and paresthesia are followed by anesthesia. Deep sensation is present and painful. Vibratory sense is lost early. Reflexes are at first increased and then diminished to absent. Loss of sphincter control may occur late. Accompanying these signs there may be headache, insomnia, nervousness, defects of memory and personality changes. Edema may be present.

With these signs and symptoms there are clearly demonstrable histologic changes in the peripheral nerves, though they are late in appearing. The distal part of the nerve is affected first. There is degeneration of the myelin sheath, with pigmentation and later degeneration of the Schwann cells. There may also be degeneration of the nerve cells of the sympathetic system. In the central nervous system medullary degeneration has been observed in spinal tracts, posterior columns and posterior nerve roots. In Wernicke's syndrome, in which some clinicians have felt that thiamine deficiency plays a part, there is involvement of the oculomotor nerves and focal degeneration and hemorrhage in the brain. Chastek paralysis in foxes, which is definitely related to thiamine deficiency, causes pathologic changes in the brain similar to those seen in Wernicke's syndrome. A factor destructive to vitamin B_1 has been found in fish, and foxes with paralysis have been on diets high in fish content.

The congestive heart failure of thiamine deficiency differs somewhat from that seen in other forms of heart disease. The cardiac enlargement is mainly to the right, there is a peripheral dilatation of arterioles, and the circulation time is shortened (faster) with lessened arteriovenous oxygen difference. The cardiac output is increased. Pulsations of the peripheral arteries are prominent, and the pulse pressure is likely to be increased, the pulse collapsing and labile. Dyspnea may be severe. Functional systolic murmurs are common. The electrocardiogram shows distinct but not specific changes. QRS voltage is low, with depressed or inverted T waves. Arrhythmias are uncommon. Edema may be extensive and include effusions into serous cavities. Edema may appear as the result of, or independently of, the cardiac state. In multiple deficiency it may be similar to that seen in caloric deficiency or in famine edema. The mechanism is not always clear.

The gastrointestinal symptoms consist in the main of anorexia, sometimes nausea and vomiting and constipation. These are early findings and precede neuritis and cardiac effects. On roentgenographic examination so-called puddling of barium in the small intestine is observed, but whether this can be related solely to thiamine deficiency and to the decreased tone and motility of the gastrointestinal tract that has been described experimentally is not clear.

In infantile beriberi the disease is liable to be more acute, with anorexia, abdominal distention and tenderness, colic and constipation. There is edema, tachycardia, dyspnea and aphonia, the last-named causing the "beriberi grunt" or cry. Cyanosis, congestive cardiac failure, and later rigidity, muscular twitching, coma and death, may occur with great rapidity.

It is clear that some of the signs and symptoms are the result of involvement of the peripheral (and possibly the central) nervous system, while others, particularly those referable to the cardiovascular system and the edema, are not. It has been suggested that the cardiovascular abnormalities are the result of changes in the cardiac nerves, particularly the vagus. Direct evidence for such a mechanism is, however, not convincing. There is likewise no evidence of a direct nervous effect on capillaries leading to an increased permeability and the production of edema. Such data as are available suggest that the edema fluid in beriberi is low in protein and hence not the result of any gross lesions in the capillaries.

Structural changes are not, however, a necessary accompaniment of altered function. Symptoms and signs of neuritis may be present even though the myelin sheath is normal on microscopic examination. Nervous tissue utilizes only glucose for energy. Thiamine in its phosphorlyated form, as cocarboxylase, is enzymatically active in the oxidation of glucose, specifically required for the oxidation and decarboxylation of pyruvic acid. Pyruvic acid is formed in one of the steps of the oxidation of glucose. In the absence of an adequate supply of thiamine, pyruvic acid (and lactic acid) accumulates in the blood and tissues in amounts easily measured chemically, and oxygen uptake is decreased. It is not implied that this accumulation is of itself the cause of the changes occurring in thiamine deficiency. Structural and functional changes cannot be reproduced by injection of this and related substances. Nevertheless, this is definite evidence of disturbance in the metabolism of nerve tissues which might cause functional changes and, if sufficiently severe and long continued, result in structural damage, temporary or permanent.

Such an explanation may account in part for the cardiovascular changes. Alteration in nerve function could conceivably produce the vasodilatation with resulting increases in blood flow and the related cardiocirculatory phenomena, including increased transudation of fluid from the blood vessels. In addition to such a postulated nervous influence, there is the possibility of a direct effect on other tissues. Thiamine is present in relatively high concentration in the heart. In experimental animals thiamine deficiency causing cardiac abnormalities is accompanied by areas of focal necrosis of the myocardium, a finding not observed in other deficiencies. "Hydropic" degeneration and edema of the heart muscle have been found in man. Therefore the cardiovascular manifestations of thiamine deficiency may represent a combined neurogenic and direct myocardial lesion, the congestive failure resulting from an increased work load and a damaged myocardium.

The mechanism of the gastrointestinal symptoms is less clear. A loss of gastrointestinal tone and motility might result from nervous or direct muscle injury. Significant lesions in the intestinal plexuses or in the muscularis have not been satisfactorily demonstrated. The cause of the anorexia is unknown.

Daily requirements approximate 1 mg. and are increased during active growth, pregnancy, lactation and in fevers, hyperthyroidism and other conditions which cause a general increase in metabolism.

Riboflavin. In 1938 and 1939 Sebrell and Butler experimentally produced in women on a diet low in riboflavin content lesions characterized by cheilosis and seborrheic dermatitis about the nose. These were cured by synthetic crystalline riboflavin and their appearance prevented by the same substance. This syndrome had been described previously by Goldberger, Wheeler and Sydenstricker as "pellagra sine pellagra," but to Sebrell should go the credit for his conviction that these lesions were a separate entity not due to nicotinic acid deficiency.

Within a year after Sebrell's publication, vascularization of the cornea as seen by the slit lamp (the ophthalmoscope and the hand slit lamp are not reliable in the demonstration of this lesion) was described as part of the riboflavin deficiency syndrome, and shortly thereafter the magenta-colored tongue with large flat-topped papillae was included as a probable additional sign of the disease. Subsequently, from all over the world have come descriptions of additional signs such as dermatitis of the hands (but not the feet), anal fissure, angular conjunctivitis, vernal conjunctivitis and grossly visible circumcorneal injection. The etiology of this latter group of signs has not been well substantiated in any instance, and, since the difficulties of proving the etiology, much less the mechanism of production of the lesions, are great even in Sebrell's experimental subjects, it seems unwise to accept them as bona fide evidences of riboflavin deficiency at this time.

The clinical syndrome generally attributed to riboflavin deficiency at present is characterized by weakness, angular stomatitis with shallow fissures filled with a nonpurulent yellow exudate, cheilosis with a bright vermilion color at the mucocutaneous junction, a tongue with burning sensation, magenta color and large flat-topped papillae, and circumciliary corneal vascularization by a network of minute anastomosing capillaries demonstrable with certainty only by the use of the slit lamp and ocular microscope.

The nature of this syndrome is not entirely clear. There is some question concerning the etiology of these lesions, and riboflavin deficiency is not necessarily the whole story. A lesion of the mouth indistinguishable from this cheilosis has been seen occasionally in an excellently nourished gourmet when he became constipated. Not all Sebrell's subjects had these lesions. Only a relatively few of the seriously B-deficient patients in Spies' clinic showed them in 1939. Two patients who did show these lesions also had diarrhea. When treated with parenteral crystalline riboflavin plus oral Epsom salts (to continue their diarrheic state), they did not respond in twenty-one days. In another the lesions disappeared in five days after a single large dose of paregoric. A fourth with this syndrome plus constipation was cured by magnesium sulfate. The eye lesions may have many environmental causes. People with poor-fitting artificial dentures may have angular stomatitis indistinguishable from that ascribed to riboflavin deficiency.

Riboflavin, or other substances of similar and related chemical structure, appears in almost all living cells. It has become increasingly clear that by no means all people whose diets appear to be deficient in riboflavin will exhibit this syndrome. People whose diets are not deficient may occasionally show some of its stigmata.

Experimentally in animals, even fatal riboflavin deficiency is not associated with an absence of this substance in the tissues. There are grounds to suspect that riboflavin may be essential for life. Serious deficiency in dogs over a protracted period results in sudden death unless they are treated by intravenous riboflavin within a few minutes after the beginning of coma and convulsions. Similar phenomena are seen in other animals experimentally. In still others, ruminants particularly, deficiency cannot be produced under anything simulating normal conditions, because riboflavin material is synthesized by bacteria in the gut. There is clear-cut evidence that riboflavin can be synthesized in the cecum of rats on some diets and not on others. It is synthesized in man under certain conditions.

Riboflavin, together with adenine and nicotinic amide, phosphorylated and attached to a protein carrier, forms an important enzyme in the oxidation-reduction mechanism essential to carbohydrate metabolism. In addition it is an essential part of the oxidase enzyme necessary for the deaminization of d-amino acids in protein metabolism. Its relation to deaminization of l-amino acids is not yet clear. Finally, it probably plays a similar role in xanthine metabolism.

There is no information which will relate these intricate intracellular metabolic chemical functions of riboflavin to the formation of cheilosis, nasal seborrheic dermatosis or corneal vascularization. In animals riboflavin is essential for growth and tissue repair.

It is relatively easy to hypothesize the mechanism of sudden death in dogs (cessation of intracellular respiration), but even here it is only hypothesis. Experimental evidence has shown that in borderline deficient rats the riboflavin content of the cornea at the time of beginning vascularization is not altered by either visible or ultraviolet light, even though corneal vascularization is increased by such treatment. Furthermore, the corneal riboflavin content of deficient rats at the time of beginning corneal vascularization is not significantly different from its content some weeks later when they suddenly die in convulsions and coma (with far more marked corneal vascularization). The oxygen uptake of the cornea early in the disease is increased and decreases to less than normal late in the disease. However, experimentally in rats, the beginning of corneal vascularization does appear to be associated with a critical level of concentration of riboflavin in local tissue.

It must be concluded that the clinical syndrome described as riboflavin deficiency (Sebrell's term "ariboflavinosis" must be rejected, because even fatal deficiency in animals is not a state characterized by *absence* of riboflavin in the tissues) and characterized by cheliosis, dermatosis, magenta tongue, corneal vascularization and perhaps other phenomena may be a manifestation of riboflavin deficiency. All the aspects of the syndrome may be produced by other seemingly unrelated agents. Patients whose diets are seriously deficient in riboflavin will not certainly show the syndrome.

The daily requirement for man relates to body weight and is somewhat under 2 mg.

Alteration of bacterial flora in the intestinal tract may be as effective therapeutically as riboflavin in some cases. Finally, the relation between the known chemical functions of riboflavin and the production of this syndrome in patients whose diets are deficient in riboflavin, and whose urinary and fecal excretion of riboflavin is less than normal, is unknown. There is no evidence that quantities of riboflavin in excess of daily requirements normally obtained in most American diets can or do serve any useful purpose.

Nicotinic Acid. The symptom complex generally attributed to niacin (nicotinic acid) deficiency is that of pellagra. Dermatitis, particularly on exposed surfaces and areas previously injured by trauma or diminished blood supply; enteritis from buccal mucosa to the anal orifice, and most easily demonstrated in the mouth by glossitis and stomatitis, in the gut by diarrhea, and around the anus by proctitis; central nervous system damage characterized clinically by varying degrees of dementia—make up the classical picture of fully developed pellagra. More commonly only parts of the syndrome are seen. Atrophy of the papillae along the lateral margins of the tongue and redness and soreness of the tip and edges plus local edema are perhaps the earliest clearly recognizable diagnostic findings. Pure pellagra, without any evidence of thiamine deficiency or folic acid or protein deficiency, is an extreme rarity, if it occurs naturally at all. As a result, the usual clinical picture is confused by additional findings characteristic of the signs of the other B-complex deficiencies plus caloric and protein deficiency in most instances.

The lesions of pellagra promptly respond to niacin therapy. However, if the etiologic deficient diet is maintained and the curative daily dose of niacin is maintained for several weeks, the lesions will frequently reappear, to respond again only to a larger dose of niacin. This phenomenon is demonstrable in patients when the disease is epidemic and is rarely, if ever, a pure entity. I am not aware of any experimental work in man in which the only deficiency was niacin and in which this curious phenomenon could be demonstrated. In practice, only an adequate diet will permanently cure the disease.

Niacin occurs in the body as an amide, loosely linked to a number of other substances to form two coenzymes, di- and tri-phosphopyridine nucleotide. These coenzymes are an essential part of one of the oxidation-reduction systems of intracellular metabolism. The coenzyme is not formed when nicotinic acid is deficient in the diet, because the body cannot synthesize adequate amounts of nicotinic acid.

The mechanism by which diminution in the body's supply of nicotinic acid or coenzymes produces acute inflammatory lesions of the skin and enteric tract and the changes in the brain is not known. It seems probable that the deficiency is manifested in most body cells, but that some variety of local trauma to the skin or enteric tract or both is the added burden which causes objective cellular change to take place. This trauma may be as mild as sunshine (without burn), or may be wind, locally applied moderate heat, a bruise or even the scar of an old injury. However, the reasons why the reaction should be an acute inflammation rather than primarily a degenerative process are in no way explained by this hypothesis, which also does not explain the cerebral lesions. (They occur late, when parenchymatous change is also demonstrable in other protected organs.)

Evidence indicates that tryptophan may reduce the amount of niacin necessary. It serves as a precursor of niacin (an inadequate supply may contribute to niacin deficiency) and can be used in the treatment of pellagra. Low tryptophan and niacin content of corn diets accounts for their pellagra producing effects.

The daily requirement of nicotinic acid is not definitely known. Recommendations, far exceeding needs, approximate 12 to 18 mg.

Folic Acid. The compounds variously designated as vitamin B_c, liver *L. casei* factor, the fermentation *L. casei* factor, and rhizopterin have a similar nucleus, 4-[(2-amino-4-hydroxy-6-pteridyl) methyl] aminobenzoic acid. Folinic acid, the citrovorum factor, is a metabolite of folic acid. Pteroylglutamic acid is the simplest of these compounds to show activity. First found to be antianemic for the chick, some variation in the different compounds has been established, especially their microbiologic activity and activity in the chick.

The manifestations in man of a deficiency of "folic" acid are not fully known and for the present must be deduced from the effect of its administration on various abnormalities, signs, symptoms and evidence of disease which can be detected clinically. They apparently include, so far as is known at present, (1) gastrointestinal disturbances, (2) a macrocytic anemia of the kind known as nutritional and as tropical anemia, (3) leukopenia, (4) granulocytopenia and (5) possibly dermatosis. Although the substance is effective in relieving at least the hematologic aspects of pernicious anemia, it is settled that this disease is not a natural result of such a deficiency. The exact biochemical relationship between pteroylglutamic acid and vitamin B_{12} is not clear. Both appear to be necessary for erythropoiesis.

In the American tropics the manifestations of sprue—glossitis, diarrhea, increased fat content of stools, loss of weight, characteristic macrocytic, hyperchromic anemia, as well as decreased intestinal absorption (glucose, vitamin A and carotene)—are partially relieved by its use. A number of factors relate to the development of tropical sprue. Changes in intestinal flora are thought to be of importance. Folic acid is thought to be secondary. The problem is discussed further in Chapters 25 and 30.

The mechanism of the action of the vitamin is unknown. Pteroylglutamic acid exists in several forms, including a conjugated form occurring in the various food sources. It is associated metabolically with ascorbic acid, is involved in amino acid metabolism, and is essential to the formation of labile methyl groups. Its principal function may be related to intestinal absorption. It is not the red cell-maturating factor. Neither it nor the conjugated form is the extrinsic factor of Castle. Though it causes a hematopoietic response in pernicious anemia, nerve lesions progress or develop with its use.

Antagonists to pteroylglutamic acid and related compounds are known. Pteroylaspartic acid is such a compound; some sulfonamide compounds and pteridines are as well. The sulfonamides are said to be antagonistic through interference with biologic synthesis, and aminopterin by interference with use.

Vitamin B₁₂. This vitamin (cobalamin) has been isolated from liver as a crystalline compound. A group of compounds show its action. It contains cobalt. It is active in the growth of *Lactobacillus lactis.* It is the most highly active substance, by weight, in pernicious anemia, and is effective as well in the pernicious-like anemias. It is necessary for the function of all cells in the body and is the only pure chemical known which will relieve the cord lesions in pernicious anemia. Vitamin B₁₂ is synthesized by many microorganisms, including those in the gastrointestinal tract. Its relationship to pernicious anemia is discussed in Chapter 30. It also enters into the metabolism of labile methyl groups and has a lipotropic effect.

Ascorbic Acid (Vitamin C)

The classical expression of vitamin C lack is scurvy, the slight or earlier stages of the deficiency being manifested by the signs and symptoms in lesser degree. For the most part these consist in hemorrhage of varying severity in various locations—in the skin, subcutaneous tissue and muscle, the mucous membranes and, less often, elsewhere. Epistaxis is common.

In infants and children there is a disturbance of growing bone which is pathognomonic and readily apparent on roentgenologic examination. It may be confused with rickets. The earliest change is in the osteoblasts, which lose their shape, leave the trabeculae, and tend to resemble fibroblasts. The normal "lattice" of calcified cartilage is replaced by *irregular* masses of calcified cartilage in fibrous tissue. Until growth stops these are pushed forward in an area of the shaft normally occupied by marrow tissue. The lattice

is widened and irregular, and microscopic fractures lead to its disorganization. The osteoblasts fail to form new bone and new trabeculae. Between old trabeculae and the calcified matrix there is a zone of rarefaction free of trabeculae, a fibrous area, resulting in epiphysial fractures and separations. Bone resorption continues while formation occurs, and there is atrophy throughout, including the cortex. Normal hematopoietic marrow at the epiphysis is replaced by "framework" marrow, loose connective tissue with few cells, much intercellular ground substance, and resembles embryonic connective tissue. With the zone of rarefaction, it constitutes the *Trümmerfeld* and *Gerüstmark* seen on roentgen examination. Gross changes include fractures and separation of the periosteum.

There is defective formation of the teeth and, in adults, resorption of normal dentin and cementum, with hyperemia and edema of the pulp, followed by atrophy and degeneration of the odontoblast layer. Hemorrhage into the pulp may result in the formation of cysts and calcification or the formation of osteoid tissue. Rarefaction of the alveolar processes leads to loosening and loss of teeth. The characteristic gingivitis is the result of hyperemia, edema and hemorrhage, often followed by infection and ulceration.

Less specific changes include lassitude, weakness, apathy and depression, with loss of appetite. The skin may become pigmented, with a hemorrhagic perifollicular papillary eruption similar to that seen in vitamin A deficiency. There is pain and swelling of the legs, and in infants the pain may be so severe as to cause immobility and lead to a mistaken diagnosis of paralysis. There is an anemia, especially in infants, and in this group too fever occurs. Interference with the healing of wounds and fractures and an increased susceptibility to superimposed infections also develop. The tensile strength of healing wounds is lessened, the healing process delayed, and scar tissue defective.

The basic defect responsible for all or nearly all these phenomena appears to be a failure of the formation of the normal intercellular ground substance of mesothelial tissue and hence of structure derived from this tissue, notably connective tissue. Vitamin C has a respiratory function as an oxidation-reduction catalyst. Although no morphologic changes have been demonstrated in the capillaries nor in a cement substance binding their endothelial cells, it is assumed that the hemorrhages are the result of increased capillary fragility. The latter is one of the most characteristic findings in vitamin C deficiency, but is not constant (as tested) or specific.

Although lesions of the capillaries cannot be demonstrated, there is no doubt of the defective formation of intercellular ground substance. Normally, the intercellular ground substance contains a reticulum-forming wavy band of collagen. In vitamin C deficiency, formation of reticulum and collagen is deficient. Collagen bundles disappear and are not re-formed. With a partially deficient supply of vitamin C, a defective or imperfect ground substance may be formed. In the absence of the vitamin none is formed, and that previously present disappears. After the administration of vitamin C the return to normal is rapid. Within 24 hours there are signs of regeneration of normal connective tissue, fibroblasts put out collagen fibers, and capillary buds invade blood clots.

It is clear that the failure of formation of normal connective tissue is responsible for the defects in bone, tooth structures and wound healing. Whether it is also responsible for the bleeding is uncertain because the actual defect in the capillaries has not been demonstrated. Inconsistencies between the level of vitamin C nutrition and capillary fragility are reported, but many factors are concerned, and data often have not been properly interpreted.

It has been suggested that the so-called vitamin P is the factor concerned with capillary resistance, but this has not been confirmed, and for the present a capillary defect resulting from vitamin C deficiency may be assumed. The same explanation will account for the edema. Whether or not the group of substances related to vitamin P, such as hesperidin or rutin, influence capillary resistance, there is no evidence of relationship to an essential food factor.

The mechanism of the anemia is not clear. Anemia is not constant, though frequent in severe deficiency (scurvy). A reticulocytosis following the administration of ascorbic acid suggests that the vitamin is necessary for the maturation or manufacture of red cells. Among other factors are the changes in the bone marrow already described. Loss of blood directly due to hemorrhage from the disease may produce microcytic anemia. Finally, severe deficiencies are likely to be accompanied by severe deficiencies of other nutrients which may be the cause of an anemia. However, the available evidence indicates that vitamin C lack, of itself, may induce an anemia, possibly brought about through the effect of vitamin C on the absorption or utilization of other nutrients.

In addition to the imperfect formation of the intercellular ground substance and changes in form and formation of the osteoblasts in growing bone, vitamin C apparently has an effect on the deposition of lime salts in osteoid tissue. A deficiency of vitamin C is accompanied by a decrease in the alkaline phosphatase in the blood and in bone.

Although the principal pathologic changes, and hence most of the clinical signs and symptoms, are easily explained on the basis of the defect in the intercellular ground substance, the biochemical function of ascorbic acid in relation to this process remains unknown. The chemical nature and action of the acid in vitro are clearly understood. It is a highly soluble substance whose most striking property is a strong, reversible oxidation-reduction reaction in acid solution. The reaction, which is unique in most animal and plant tissues, is strongly suggestive of a specific function, but so far no place for such function among the various enzyme systems has been found. The activation of certain enzymes seems to be nonspecific. Detoxification processes, though suggested by some animal experimentation, remain unestablished. Perhaps the most promising lead is the fact that in vitamin C-deficient guinea pigs and premature infants, who are incapable of metabolizing phenylalanine and tyrosine properly, this defect is corrected when additional amounts of vitamin C are supplied. Apparently vitamin C enters into the conversion of pteroylglutamic acid into citrovorum factor, and also enters into adrenal function.

Besides the specific effect of vitamin C on the lesions caused by its deficiency, the vitamin has been shown experimentally to affect basal metabolism, glucose tolerance, the production of complement and various antibodies, susceptibility to various poisons such as diphtheria toxin, and resistance to certain infective agents, particularly viruses. A virucidal effect in vitro is also described. None of these appears to be specific or related to the mechanism responsible for the production of, or freedom from, scurvy.

Vitamin C requirements are unknown. Estimates average about 50 mg. daily, with increases in pregnancy, lactation, infection and in some gastrointestinal diseases.

Vitamin D and Calcium

Rickets in the child is the outstanding clinical manifestation of vitamin D deficiency.

Osteomalacia, the counterpart in the adult, is rare in the United States and limited in large part to conditions in which vitamin D is not absorbed from the intestine, as in the sprue syndrome when absorption from the small intestine is impaired, in pancreatic disease in which fat hydrolysis, necessary for fat absorption, is reduced, and in some types of chronic biliary obstruction, when bile acids, important in fat absorption, do not reach the intestine. Such patients often do not get adequate exposure to sunshine, either. Inadequate intake, together with lack of exposure to sunlight, is a likely cause of deficiency both in adults and children. Antirachitic properties given substances by irradiation are due to certain activated 9, 10-secosterols. The term vitamin D_1 is no longer used. D_2 is ergocalciferol and D_3 cholecalciferol. Inadequate intake, together with lack of exposure to sunlight, is a likely cause of deficiency both in children and in adults.

In bone formation, osteoid bone, first laid down, is impregnated with calcium salts, chiefly hydroxy-calcium phosphate. The exact mechanism of the precipitation of calcium and phosphorus is not clear. It is evident that the solubility product of the two ions must be exceeded, for such precipitation and depletion of the body of either may interfere with the action and prevent calcification of osteoid. In children rickets develops. Lack of vitamin D produces this disturbance by interference with absorption of calcium from the intestine. Calcium is taken in, but lost in the feces. Serum calcium and phosphorus are low. A fall in serum calcium stimulates parathormone production, which increases phosphorus excretion through the kidneys and tends to raise serum calcium. With sufficient stimulation serum calcium may return to normal and serum phosphorus remains depressed. Thus calcium levels may be normal or low in rickets. If parathormone stimulation fails, serum calcium may be very low and serum phosphorus normal. The concentration of alkaline phosphatase is increased.

The symptoms and signs of rickets vary from those detected only on roentgenographic examination or biochemical tests (blood alkaline phosphatase) to death from asphyxia caused by collapse of a softened bony thorax. There is softening of the bones; enlargement of the epiphysial junctions; thinning and thickening of flat bones, as in the skull (craniotabes and "bosses"); fractures, often multiple and "greenstick" in type. Microscopically, the pattern of bone structure and development becomes disorderly, with failure of cartilage cells to develop normally in the zone of proliferation, and irregular destruction of cartilage cells by advancing capillaries in the intermediate zone. These abnormalities, gross and microscopic, result in deformities which later may persist as scars of the deficiency. Besides these skeletal lesions there may be such findings as "head sweating," irritability, restlessness, nystagmus and "pot belly." The infants, though often fat, are flabby and the muscles hypotonic.

When vitamin D is supplied, there is an immediate decrease in phosphorus and calcium excretion, a retention of both calcium and phosphorus, an increase in all forms of phosphorus in the plasma with a rise in the calcium-phosphorus complex, and a resumption of orderly development of osteoblasts and deposition of salts in osteoid tissue. The absorption of calcium and phosphorus is improved, and this presumably is one of the preliminary actions. The retention of both calcium and phosphorus is then greater than normal. However, the exact mechanism by which vitamin D induces these changes is unknown. It has been suggested that it may act in some way with an enzyme system in the formation of the calcium-phosphorus complex, or cause a flooding of the special local area of osteoid tissue with phosphate ions, thus raising the concentration of the calcium-phosphorus complex and leading to a precipitation of that salt in the osteoid tissue. Vitamin D, available calcium and parathyroid hormone relate in a system which regulates metabolism of calcium and phosphorus. The action of vitamin D in the absorption of calcium (and indirectly phosphorus) from the intestine and that of parathyroid hormone as a regulating mechanism sets up an interplay among intake, absorption, excretion and balance which is influenced significantly if one or several factors are disturbed. Calcium deficiency may be added to vitamin D deficiency (rickets) in children. When present, it exaggerates the deficiency of vitamin D and introduces additional changes, those of tetany. It is likely to occur during treatment of rickets with vitamin D, the demand for, and deposition of, calcium under the conditions of improved and restored bone growth exceeding the available supply of calcium and precipitating calcium deficiency. In some patients blood calcium levels are normal and blood phosphorus levels low.

The *tetany* of calcium deficiency reflects a state of hyperirritability caused by hypocalcemia. It is manifested by carpopedal spasm, Chvostek's sign, laryngeal spasm and convulsions. It may be precipitated or induced by hypoxia (tourniquet test), fever and other secondary factors. It is the result of increased nerve excitability caused by a decrease in the concentration of ionizable calcium in blood and tissue fluids and can be promptly relieved by an ionizable form of calcium. Vitamin D, by increasing the absorption of calcium and improving its utilization, may relieve a mild calcium deficiency or make a borderline supply more adequate, but cannot compensate for an actual, in contrast to a relative, deficiency. In some other forms of tetany, such as parathyroid tetany, the administration of calcium and vitamin D, though sometimes helpful, does not remove or relieve the basic cause of the tetany.

The osteomalacia of adults has already been discussed. In some parts of the world, as in north China, lack of exposure to sunshine and poor vitamin D intake combine to make osteomalacia common in women. Frequent pregnancies and prolonged breast feeding contribute. Under these circumstances increased calcium intake without added vitamin D is not remarkably beneficial. However, actual dietary deficiency of calcium may contribute, and its occurrence is nearly always conditioned by factors which increase calcium requirements or deplete calcium reserves, such as pregnancy and lactation. In sprue, and disturbances interfering with fat absorption, vitamin D and calcium are both lost. However, vitamin D lack is of major importance in the negative calcium balance. Lack of absorption of calcium and phosphorus leads to osteomalacia through failure of calcification of newly laid down osteoid, which is continually replacing the small amount of bone resorbed day by day. Bones weaken, pains are present and demineralization and even pathologic fractures develop. Pseudofractures also appear. Low serum calcium and phosphorus appears, as in rickets.

Certain types of demineralization of bone, such as that seen at or following the menopause and in senility, are believed to be related to disturbances in endocrine function rather than to calcium deficiency. In such cases the administration of calcium, which is effective in true calcium deficiency, gives no relief. Calcium ions in blood and tissue fluids exchange rapidly with those of bone as shown in radioisotopic studies. This turnover is reduced in older women and those with osteoporosis. Rest and inactivity tend to increase calcium excretion.

The daily requirement of vitamin D is not

known. It is synthesized in the body through irradiation of the skin, and in the adult in normal circumstances an unknown and probably chief source is endogenous. In infants 135 to 400 I.U. are the minimum.

Vitamin E

There are no symptoms or pathologic states generally considered to be the result of a deficiency of vitamin E in man. Various forms of "sterility" in women, as well as actual abortion, ascribed to vitamin E deficiency have not been clearly shown to be due to such a cause, and the evidence that vitamin E is an essential factor for normal parturition in the human being has not been confirmed. Similarly, the testicular degeneration which occurs in the rat deficient in vitamin E has not been shown to have a counterpart in man, and the atrophy of muscle produced in animals by this deficiency has not been shown to occur in human beings. Attempts to affect favorably the various "muscular dystrophies" by administration of vitamin E have been generally unsuccessful. A syndrome of macrocytic anemia and elevated creatine excretion in the urine has been relieved by vitamin E therapy. A relationship between vitamin E and vitamin B_{12} has been postulated. Vitamin E may play a role in the transport or metabolism of vitamin B_{12}.

Vitamin E is a tocopherol occurring in three natural forms, alpha (α), beta (β) and gamma (γ) tocopherol. Some related compounds show vitamin E "activity."

Two ways in which vitamin E might affect human structure or function are suggested. It is related chemically to certain sex hormones, and it has been suggested that it may affect hormone production and balance. The vitamin has strong antioxidant activity and has been thought of as a protector of vitamin A and carotene against destruction by oxidation, particularly oxidation by unsaturated fatty acids. Vitamin E *might* thus determine the adequacy or inadequacy of a minimal dietary supply of vitamin A and carotene. As an antioxidant it has a function in muscle metabolism.

Vitamin K

The clinical expressions of vitamin K deficiency are hemorrhage and the defective clotting of blood which causes it. The hemorrhage occurs principally in the newborn, accompanying the trauma of birth and clinically known as "hemorrhagic disease of the newborn," and in association with jaundice and gastrointestinal disease which interfere with the production or absorption of vitamin K in and from the intestinal tract.

In hemorrhagic disease of the newborn, hemorrhage of varying severity occurs in one or more sites—skin, mucous membranes, brain, lungs and other viscera. This bleeding, which rarely begins before the second or third day of life, is usually ended by the seventh or eighth day, but occasionally is prolonged until the tenth or twelfth day. If not fatal, usually in the first or second day, the disease is self-limited. The bleeding may be concealed, as in cerebral hemorrhage, and it is the belief of some clinicians that many cases of so-called cerebral injuries are the result of such bleeding. Fever may be present, prostration is common, and there may be diarrhea, sometimes bloody.

In jaundice and gastrointestinal disease similar spontaneous bleeding into the skin, mucous membranes or viscera may occur, but the persistent bleeding following surgical incisions and procedures is more characteristic and a dangerous complication. A similar bleeding with liver disease is primarily the result of failure to utilize vitamin K rather than of a deficiency of vitamin K. The clinical results, as far as vitamin K function is concerned, are much the same.

Vitamin K is a naphthoquinone. There are many natural compounds, $K_{1(20)}$ (phylloquinone) from alfalfa meal and $K_{2(35)}$ from putrefied fish meal being examples. Many related compounds have vitamin K activity, and some are more active than the natural vitamins. Vitamin K is fat soluble, and adequate absorption of it depends on the presence of fat in the intestinal contents and factors favorable to fat absorption; hence the deficiency in jaundice. In man it is ordinarily supplied for the most part as the result of bacterial action in the intestine, relatively little coming from the food.

Vitamin K is used in, and is necessary for, the formation of prothrombin. Prothrombin is the precursor of thrombin, which in turn converts fibrinogen to usable fibrin. Fibrin is essential to the clotting of blood. When vitamin K is deficient, prothrombin is deficient, and blood clotting is delayed, incomplete and, with a severe deficiency, indefinitely prolonged. The manner in which vitamin K participates in the formation of prothrombin is unknown. Supposedly these vitamins function in the respiratory enzyme system in coupled electron transport and phosphorylation.

In the newborn the deficiency of vitamin K is thought to be due to a failure of the fetus to receive from the mother a supply adequate to tide the infant over the first prenatal days during which the bacterial flora is being established in the intestine. When this has occurred, the infant supplies its own vitamin K. This explains the natural limitation of the disease to eight or nine days, and the correctness of the assumption is supported by the uniformly satisfactory result of treatment of the mother with vitamin K a few days before birth, or of the infant shortly after delivery.

In jaundice or gastrointestinal disease the deficiency of vitamin K is the result of failure to absorb the fat-soluble vitamin even though there is production of vitamin K by bacteria in the gastrointestinal tract. Certain strains of *Escherichia coli* have been shown to synthesize vitamin K to a greater degree than many other species of bacteria. Naturally, factors affecting the growth and activity of intestinal bacteria may affect greatly the production of vitamin K in the intestine. Treatment with sulfonamides may have such an effect. Synthetic, water-soluble forms of vitamin K are absorbed without the presence of bile salts or fat. They are also effective parenterally.

Since vitamin K loses its ability to maintain prothrombin production with severe liver damage, the presumption is that the reaction of prothrombin formation takes place in the liver. In the presence of adequate vitamin K in the body (by parenteral injection), persistence of low prothrombin values is interpreted as resulting from liver disease.

It may be seen that four factors are necessary to prevent and control hypoprothrombinemia in man: (1) bile of normal composition in the gastrointestinal tract, (2) a diet adequate in vitamin K or materials from which it can be made and a bacterial flora capable of synthesis, (3) a normal absorptive surface in the small intestine, and (4) a liver capable of functioning in the synthesis of prothrombin. In treatment, parenteral administration will circumvent the necessity of the first three.

The normal daily requirement is not known, chiefly because of synthesis in the intestine. In the newborn, 1 mg. daily is adequate.

Hypervitaminoses

The isolation of pure vitamins and the development of highly potent sources have made possible the administration of doses exceeding by many hundred times the small quantities needed as nutritional factors. This brings up the possibility that these agents may produce toxic symptoms. Such action could occur either through an excess of the vitamin as a nutritional agent or through its action as a drug or allergen independent of its nutritional function. Much has been written on these aspects of the vitamins, but little is definitely proved.

Hypervitaminosis A. This has been described in children one to three years of age fed large quantities of carotenoids or vitamin A, 75,000 I.U. up, for six to fifteen months. Hyperirritability, dry skin, sparse hair and swellings over the long bones develop. Plasma vitamin A levels reach 300 I.U. per 100 ml., and serum alkaline phosphatase is elevated. The long bones show hyperostoses by roentgenogram. Symptoms ascribed to other substances in the fish oils have been reported. Experimentally in the human hypervitaminosis A is associated not only with high blood levels of vitamin A but with severe headaches, polyarthralgia and skin changes. Still other clinicians have used over a million units of vitamin A daily with no ill effects. Carotenemia appears to be the only result of high carotene intake, and its effects are only temporary cosmetic ones.

Hypervitaminoses B, C and E. Vitamin B_1 in large doses produces no ill effects. In animals 25,000 times the estimated requirement has been given without ill effect. Spasm of smooth muscle and herpes zoster have been reported following large doses, yet the vitamin has been used to treat herpes zoster. When impure preparations have been used parenterally, dyspnea, precordial distress, nausea and a fall in blood pressure have occurred. These effects appear to be those of the impurities. *Niacin* has the remarkable effect, already described, of dilating blood vessels and causing flushing of the face, headache, vomiting and epigastric distress.

Vitamin C in doses of 10,000 mg. has been given without the development of toxic effects.

Information on *vitamin* E is lacking.

Hypervitaminosis D. This develops from prolonged excessive intake. In rats doses 100 times the protective dose cause injury. Loss of weight, anorexia, nausea, vomiting, muscular weakness, apathy, hypercalcemia and phosphatemia, and the calcification of cartilage, blood vessels and organs, including the kidneys, develop. Calcium and phosphorus levels of serum and urine are increased, partially as the result of demineralization of bone. Bone changes simulate those of osteitis fi-

brosa cystica, and symptoms related to changes in the blood calcium appear. These findings have developed in arthritic patients under treatment with huge doses of 200,000 to 1,000,000 units, but usual clinical doses for vitamin D deficiency have not caused symptoms.

Minerals

Many physiologic processes depend upon an adequate supply of minerals. These include, among others: (1) maintenance of pH at proper levels, (2) a poorly known role in cellular function, (3) maintenance of osmotic pressure values and (4) the formation of the body framework. Many of the minerals are required in small amounts and abound in nature, so that the deficiency is unusual (zinc, aluminum, magnesium, cobalt, nickel, copper). *Zinc* enters into the structure of the enzyme carbonic anhydrase. It is present in the pancreas and combines readily with insulin. It is also present in lactic dehydrogenase and peptidases. Zinc deficiency has been suggested as an explanation for the arrested growth of a group of dwarfs studied in Iran and Egypt. Other minerals, however, may be inadequate in the food (iodine, sodium, calcium, phosphorus, iron, fluorine). Of the latter group, sodium, potassium, calcium and phosphorus are discussed elsewhere. Only magnesium, cobalt, copper, iodine, fluorine and iron will be discussed here.

Magnesium

Quantitative needs in man are not clear. Required for growth and maintenance, the element is found in bone and in soft tissues, where it functions as a catalyst in intracellular enzymatic reactions. Low levels are associated with muscle twitching and convulsions, and may occur in diabetic acidosis, in chronic alcoholism and in chronic debilitating disease. A cellular deficit appears to be responsible. There is little relationship between serum levels and symptoms.

Cobalt

A deficiency state is not recognized. However, the element enters into the activity of certain enzymes and is a part of the vitamin B_{12} molecule. Excess cobalt in the diet may produce polycythemia.

Copper

Hypocupremia has been found in the newborn and in hepato-lenticular degeneration.

Tissue stores are elevated in these states. Increased losses occur in nephrotic syndrome. In infants copper lack is related to anemia.

Iodine

The result of iodine deficiency is a simple goiter. Carried through several generations, it results in cretinism, with or without goiter. Simple goiter may be accompanied by hypothyroidism, but usually is not. Therefore the clinical manifestation of iodine lack is usually the unsightly goiter, with or without purely mechanical pressure symptoms such as those resulting from compression of the trachea.

Iodine is required for the formation of thyroxine, the secretory product of the thyroid gland. Thyroxine in turn is a catalyst involved in the metabolism of the tissue cells, presumably of all the cells. Its action maintains metabolism, particularly oxygen consumption, at a higher level than would otherwise occur.

With an insufficiency of iodine there result hyperplasia and hypertrophy of the thyroid gland in response to the increased work of extracting iodine and manufacturing thyroxine: thus, the goiter. If the deficiency of iodine continues and the supply is inadequate, then and only then does a deficiency of the thyroid hormone occur. With this deficiency of thyroxine, the metabolism of the cells and the body drops to a lower level, affecting the following functions: calorigenic action; growth, maturation and differentiation of tissue; distribution of body water, salts and colloids; carbohydrate metabolism; nerve functions; muscular function; circulation; and other endocrine functions. Clinically, this is manifested in the various symptoms and signs of hypothyroidism and cretinism. The calorigenic effect is manifested by the lowered oxygen consumption (basal metabolic rate). In the cretin there is lack of growth, delayed union of the epiphyses, delayed and imperfect ossification, faulty and delayed dentition and incomplete development of the brain. In the milder hypothyroid states, which are the only ones commonly seen in simple goiter, other clinical changes appear besides the goiter. There may be mild disturbances in salt and water metabolism (water retention), increased glucose tolerance, some muscular weakness, menstrual disturbances, susceptibility to infection and fatigability.

The shortage of iodine required to cause pathologic changes (goiter) has been accurately determined. When the concentration of iodine in the thyroid falls below 0.1 per cent (dry weight), hyperplasia occurs. Iodine arrests hyperplasia and hypertrophy and, in favorable (early) cases, causes resolution of the goiter. Iodine also restores the secretion of thyroxine and relieves the symptoms of hypothyroidism, except as follows: (1) Immediately after the administration of iodine to a patient with simple goiter there may be a sudden cessation of secretory activity, a filling of the gland with colloid and an intensification of the hypothyroidism (lowered basal metabolic rate). Later, secretion is resumed and the hypothyroidism relieved. (2) Iodine has little effect on the hypofunction or lack of function (athyreosis) of cretinism or the result of such lack of function. In either hypothyroidism or cretinism the goiter itself, if present, may be little affected, except perhaps to become firmer, nodular and fibrous. In iodine deficiency, prevention is much more important than cure.

Fluorine

There is evidence that fluorine plays a part in dental health. Ingestion of excessive amounts during the period of enamel formation produces mottled enamel. When the water supply has an excess of one to two parts per million of fluoride, this condition begins to appear in the population. Prolonged exposure also produces osteosclerosis. Positive calcium retention results. This is common in certain geographic areas. Higher levels of fluoridation of water or industrial intoxication produce anemia, gastrointestinal symptoms and calcification of ligaments and muscle attachments. When one part per million occurs in the water of a population, dental caries decreases in that group and mottling is not seen. This has been done experimentally with water supplies. Topical application of fluorides to teeth retards caries formation.

Iron

The only known clinical effect of a deficiency of iron is an anemia. The anemia is characteristically a hypochromic, microcytic anemia, primarily a lack of hemoglobin, though the red blood cells are often reduced in number. Accompanying the anemia there may be a glossitis, cheilosis (angular fissures or perlèche), the Plummer-Vinson syndrome and such symptoms as pallor, weakness, shortness of breath and edema. An actual (dietary) deficiency of iron is uncommon, and relative deficiencies occur almost exclusively in growing children, women in the childbearing period and those who have suffered losses of blood. Except for such persons, the requirement of iron is almost negligible.

The principal function of hemoglobin is to transport oxygen to the tissues and to act as a buffering agent. With insufficient hemoglobin there may be pallor and tissue anoxia. The anoxia is responsible for such symptoms as shortness of breath and weakness. Increased work of the heart resulting from the decreased hemoglobin and oxygen-carrying capacity of the blood, combined with injury to the heart itself from the anoxia, may cause heart failure with such signs and symptoms as cardiac enlargement and edema.

The mechanism of the production of glossitis, cheilosis and related symptoms is unknown. Iron is used in the oxidation of metabolites by means of iron-containing enzymes such as the cytochrome, but the amounts of iron needed for this purpose are small, and deficiencies of this kind, if they exist, are as yet unrecognized clinically (see Chap. 30).

The administration of iron readily relieves the anemia in true uncomplicated iron deficiency anemia and causes a disappearance of the related glossitis and cheilosis. For infants, fortification of milk with iron has been used as a preventive. Ferrous iron is more readily absorbed than ferric iron, the latter being reduced to the ferrous state in the intestine before absorption. When radioactive iron is used, the ready uptake of iron constitutes a test of iron deficiency anemia. Normally, very little is absorbed. It is believed that the intestinal absorption is brought about in the intestinal wall by the protein *apoferritin,* which takes up iron to become *ferritin.* Experimentally, this material is capable of producing shock when released into the blood stream. Possibly in iron intoxication in children there may be excessive absorption of iron, excess formation of ferritin and subsequent shock. Excessive iron may be toxic. Frequent transfusions and intravenous injections of iron produce excessive stores. In hemochromatosis, excessive absorption produces deposits in the liver, pancreas, adrenals and other tissues. In iron deficiency anemia the serum iron is low. Low levels are also found in anemias associated with infections. Determination of the iron-binding capacity of plasma will differentiate hypoferremia due to iron deficiency from that due to infection. Serum iron is high in many other nutritional anemias. The administration of iron in iron deficiency anemia characteristically produces a significant reticulocytosis. Phytic acid interferes with the absorption of dietary iron, but in true iron deficiency anemia, dietary iron is inadequate, and cure of the anemia requires the administration of therapeutic doses of inorganic iron, which in true iron deficiency anemia are well absorbed.

REFERENCES

Aaes-Jorgensen, E.: Essential fatty acids. Physiol. Rev., *41:*1, 1961.

Avioli, L. V., McDonald, J. E., and Williams, F. T.: Abnormal metabolism of vitamin D_3 in vitamin D-resistant rickets and familial hypophosphatemia. Presented before American Society for Clinical Investigation, May 2, 1966.

Bean, W. B., Hodges, R. E., and Daum, K.: Pantothenic acid deficiency induced in human subjects. J. Clin. Invest., *34:*1073, 1955.

Berneske, G. M., Butson, A. R. C., Gauld, E. N., and Levy, D.: Clinical trial of high dosage vitamin E in human muscular dystrophy. Canad. M. A. J., *82:*418, 1960.

Birkhead, N. C., Blizzard, J. J., Daly, J. W., Haupt, G. J., Issekutz, B., Myers, R. N., and Rodahl, K.: AMRL-TD4-64-61. Wright-Patterson Air Force Base, Ohio, 1964.

Flink, E. B., McCollister, R., Prasad, A. S., Melby, J. C., and Doe, R. P.: Evidences for clinical magnesium deficiency. Ann. Int. Med., *47:*956, 1957.

Gribetz, D., Silverman, S. H., and Sobel, A. E.: Vitamin A poisoning. Pediatrics, *7:*372, 1951.

Keys, A.: Caloric undernutrition and starvation, with notes on protein deficiency. J.A.M.A., *138:*500, 1948.

MacDonald, I.: The lipid response of young women to dietary carbohydrates. Am. J. Clin. Nutrit., *16:*458, 1965.

Majaj, A. S.: Vitamin E responsive macrocytic anemia in protein-calorie malnutrition. Am. J. Clin. Nutrit., *18:*362, 1966.

Majaj, A. S., Dinning, J. S., Azzam, S. A., and Darby, W. J.: Vitamin E responsive megaloblastic anemia in infants with protein-calorie malnutrition. Am. J. Clin. Nutrit., *12:*374, 1963.

Marsh, A., Long, H., and Stierwalt, E.: Comparative hematologic response to iron fortification of a milk formula. Pediatrics, *24:*404, 1959.

Pandit, C. G., Raghavachari, T. N. S., Rao, D. S., and Krishnamati, V.: Endemic fluorosis in South India. Indian J. M. Res., *28:*533, 1940.

Sandler, M., and Bourne, G. H. (eds.): Atherosclerosis and its Origin. New York, Academic Press, 1963.

Scrimshaw, N. S., Habicht, J., Piché, M., Cholakos, B., and Arroyave, G.: Protein metabolism of young men during university examinations. Am. J. Clin. Nutrit., *18:*321, 1966.

Smith, J. P.: The pathology of ferrous sulfate poisoning. J. Path. Bact., *64:*467, 1952.

Smith, W. O., and Hammarsten, J. F.: Intracellular magnesium in delerium tremens and uremia. Am. J. Med. Sc., *237:*413, 1959.

Sodeman, W. A., and Mukherji, K. L.: Some observations on malnourished patients with edema. J. Lab. & Clin. Med., *42:*954, 1953.

Stein, W. H., and Moore, S.: The structure of proteins. Sci. Am., *204*:81, 1961.

Steinbaum, E. A., and Miller, N. E.: Obesity from eating elicited by daily stimulation of hypothalamus. Am. J. Physiol., *208*:1, 1965.

Underwood, E. J.: Trace Elements in Human and Animal Nutrition, 2nd ed. New York, Academic Press, 1962.

Vilter, R. W., and others: The effect of vitamin B_6 deficiency induced by desoxypyridoxine in human beings. J. Lab. & Clin. Med., *42*:335, 1953.

Wiese, H. F., Bennett, M. J., Braun, I. H., Yamanaka, W., and Coon, E.: Blood serum lipid patterns during infancy and childhood. Am. J. Clin. Nutrit., *18*:155, 1966.

Chapter Six

Carbohydrate Metabolism

HENRY T. RICKETTS
and
MAURICE E. KRAHL

The Chemistry of Carbohydrate Utilization

According to current concepts, glucose and glycogen are normally utilized as outlined in Figure 6–1. Each tissue varies in the degree to which a given pathway is operative, but in general one mole of glucose is split to form two moles of pyruvic acid, then each of these is oxidized to carbon dioxide and water or converted to other substances such as fat or protein. These reactions serve the double purpose of yielding energy for cellular function and intermediates for synthesis of necessary cellular components. The great flexibility provided by these interconversions helps to insure that tissues which have special nutritional requirements, such as the nervous system has for glucose, are supplied with what is needed even during extended periods of starvation.

Energy derived from these processes by the generation of so-called "high energy" phosphate groups is accumulated via ATP:

Each ATP has readily available about 7500 calories (7.5 kilocalories in the units used in nutritional calculations) for synthetic processes or for muscular contraction and other work. "High energy" phosphate groups are generated at several points, one each during formation of 3-phosphoglyceric acid, pyruvic acid, and succinic acid; three during the reoxidation of each DPNH to DPN and H_2O; and two during reoxidation of $FADH_2$ to FAD and H_2O. It may be calculated from Figure 6–1 that a maximum of 20 ATP can be generated during oxidation of each 3-phosphoglyceraldehyde to CO_2 and H_2O; this amounts to 38 for each glucose (2×20 minus the two ATP required for formation of glucose-6-phosphate and fructose diphosphate) and 39 for each glucosyl residue of glycogen.

The carbons of glucose are convertible to a large number of products, which will be discussed below in relation to various pathologic states.

$$\underset{\text{Adenosine diphosphate}}{\text{ADP}} \quad + \quad \underset{\substack{\text{High energy}\\\text{phosphate}}}{\sim \text{P}} \rightleftarrows \quad \underset{\text{Adenosine triphosphate}}{\text{ATP}}$$

Regulatory Mechanisms of Carbohydrate Metabolism

Despite wide variation in intake, storage, and oxidation of carbohydrate, the blood sugar is maintained within fairly narrow limits by a complex series of homeostatic mechanisms. These regulatory factors may be classified roughly into two groups: those which control the supply of glucose and those which control its utilization.

The Pancreas

The pancreas produces two substances which have opposite effects on blood sugar: *insulin,* which lowers it, and *glucagon,* which raises it.

Insulin facilitates anabolic processes. In mammals it has been shown to stimulate directly the use of glucose by muscle and adipose tissue, the synthesis of glycogen in muscle, the synthesis of fatty acids in adipose tissue and mammary gland, and the incorporation of amino acids into protein of muscle or adipose tissue. The stimulatory effect of insulin on glucose uptake is correlated with its promotion of the entry of glucose into muscle cells, thereby making more glucose available for possible conversion to glucose-6-phosphate by hexokinase (translocation theory). It has also been proposed that insulin may relieve an inhibition of hexokinase (transformation theory).

The enhancement of glycogen synthesis by insulin may stem in part from the increase in glucose-6-phosphate, discussed above, and the consequent increased concentration of intermediates of the UDP-G or phosphorylase pathways. But insulin stimulates glycogen formation under conditions in which increase in glucose supply does not; this has been explained by Larner's finding that insulin increases the concentration of glucose-6-phosphate-independent glycogen synthetase.

Similarly, the enhancement of fat synthesis by insulin is dependent on an extracellular supply of glucose and is therefore considered to be, in part at least, the consequence of the following events: increased formation of glucose-6-phosphate; increased formation of TPNH via the phosphogluconate pathway, and an increased rate of hydrogenation of precursors to fatty acids. Other effects of insulin upon fatty acid synthesis are under investigation.

The stimulation by insulin of amino acid incorporation into muscle protein (usually referred to as protein synthesis) may in certain circumstances, especially in fasting animals, be correlated with increased glucose use. But insulin has another action on protein synthesis, as shown by the fact that it can enhance amino acid incorporation into protein of isolated muscle in the absence of extracellular glucose; the nature of this direct effect on protein synthesis has yet to be elucidated.

The liver is a special case in its response to insulin. Normally this organ forms blood glucose from glycogen, protein, or possibly in small amounts from fatty acids, via the synthetic pathways of Figure 6–1; the final step for all precursors is hydrolysis of glucose-6-phosphate by its specific phosphatase. The liver also synthesizes glycogen, fats, and proteins. The question whether insulin has a direct action on glucose uptake and output or on glycogen, fat, or protein synthesis of *normal* liver is a matter of debate. However, there are a number of well-documented defects in the metabolism of the liver in severe diabetes: Studies of isolated liver preparations show that the conversion of glucose to its phosphorylated products and the synthesis of fatty acids and of protein are decreased while the output of glucose and levels of liver glucose-6-phosphatase are increased relative to normal values. These defects are corrected by injection of insulin into the diabetic animal, the return to normal requiring some hours. It has been proposed that, in diabetes, there is a decrease in one or more enzymes of anabolic pathways and an increase in enzymes for gluconeogenesis, and that the delayed effect of insulin on the diabetic liver is concerned with restoration of these enzyme systems to normal levels.

Adipose tissue is another special case. Normally, in the fed animal, about one-fourth or one-fifth of the glucose available to the animal is converted to fat which may be deposited in adipose tissue. The deposition of such storage fat is increased by insulin and decreased in diabetes, in which fat leaves the depots to be converted to ketone bodies in the liver. The mechanism of transport from adipose tissue to liver is not wholly clear. It has been found, however, that a lipase contained in adipose tissue can liberate fatty acids, facilitating their combination with serum albumin to form a transport system. The liberation of these nonesterified, or free, fatty acids (NEFA, FFA) into the plasma is suppressed by insulin and by glucose if insulin is present, and is increased in starvation and diabetes. Diabetic acidosis is not caused

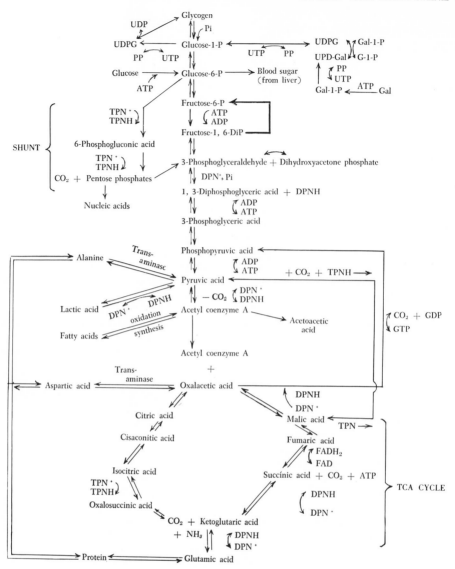

Figure 6–1. Pathways of carbohydrate metabolism.

ABBREVIATIONS: *ADP, ATP:* adenosine di- and triphosphate, respectively. *DPN+* and *DPNH:* diphosphopyridine nucleotide, oxidized and reduced forms. *G-1-P:* glucose-1-phosphate. *Gal-1-P:* galactose-1-phosphate. *GDP* and *GTP:* guanosine di- and triphosphates. *Pi* and *PP:* inorganic ortho- and pyrophosphate. *TPN+* and *TPNH:* triphosphopyridine nucleotide, oxidized and reduced forms. *UDP* and *UTP:* uridine di- and triphosphates. *UDPG:* uridine diphosphoglucose. *UDP-Gal:* uridine diphosphogalactose. *FAD* and *FADH₂:* flavin-adenine dinucleotide, oxidized and reduced forms.

by FFA, as these comprise only about 5 per cent of the total blood lipids.

Each of the anabolic processes that occur normally in the cell as a result of the action of insulin is impaired in the diabetic organism, and this impairment is reflected in clinical manifestations. The effects of insulin deficiency must be regarded not only as loss of carbohydrate and the compensatory overconsumption of body protein and fat, all con-

tributing to malnutrition, but also as a failure of synthesis of these essential components, so that their destruction cannot be repaired. Thus, when lack of insulin causes glycogenolysis it also prevents resynthesis of glycogen, which indirectly favors ketosis. When tissue protein is broken down for fuel because glucose cannot be used, failure of new protein synthesis exaggerates the depletion of muscle mass and body weight. The metabolism of fat is similarly, perhaps more importantly, affected.

Several methods for estimating circulating insulin or insulin-like activity (ILA) have been developed. In each, a specific insulin-like effect or property of the test serum or plasma is compared with the effect or property of known amounts of crystalline insulin added to an otherwise identical system under similar conditions. These assays are of two sorts. In one, the fluid to be tested is incubated with rat tissue in a medium containing glucose; when rat diaphragm is the tissue used, its glucose uptake or glycogen synthesis is the index of ILA; when rat epididymal fat pad is used, the index is glucose uptake, fat synthesis, or production of $C^{14}O_2$ from C^{14} glucose. Other methods utilize various immunologic techniques. The sample to be tested, with or without prior extraction with acid ethanol, is incubated with tracer amounts of I^{131}-labeled insulin and insulin antiserum derived from immunized guinea pigs; the endogenous insulin of the sample competitively inhibits the binding of labeled insulin to antibody, and the ratio of bound to unbound (free) insulin in the mixture, determined by counting the radioactivity of these fractions after their separation by electrophoresis or precipitation, gives an estimate of the insulin concentration of the unknown when compared with the bound-to-free ratio obtained with known concentrations of unlabeled insulin.

There is some doubt as to what, precisely, is being measured by any of these methods. Although the *rat diaphragm* would seem to be measuring true, active insulin because the insulin-like effect (ILA) can be completely blocked by anti-insulin serum, confidence in the method is shaken by the fact that diluted plasma yields disproportionately higher results (up to 4600 μU./ml. in fasting human subjects) than does undiluted plasma (generally less than 100 μU./ml. and averaging about 40 μU./ml.). By the *fat pad* procedure, ILA values of from 33 to 940 μU./ml. have been observed in fasting subjects. A possible explanation for the apparently greater sensitivity of the fat than the diaphragm method is that adipose tissue may contain an enzyme which frees insulin from a protein-bound, "complexed," or partially inactive form (see Antoniades et al.). This would suggest that in the intact organism, bound insulin is able to act on fat for lipogenesis while only "free" insulin can act on muscle for glycogenesis. Astonishingly, normal fasting levels of ILA are found by the fat pad method in the to-

tally depancreatized dog, and these are increased by administration of glucose. Clearly something besides insulin as we know it is operating on adipose tissue under these conditions. The high degree of specificity and sensitivity provided by *immunologic methods* would appear to favor the immunoassay over the bioassays described. Immunoassay yields values of the same order of magnitude as the diaphragm. It is possible, as Berson points out, that immunologically reactive insulin in plasma may not be biologically active, but this is unlikely.

Despite the imperfections and uncertainties of available insulin assays, they have greatly advanced our knowledge of normal and pathologic physiology. They have shown, by all methods, a sharp rise in insulin or ILA following administration of glucose and of tolbutamide in normal subjects; mean normal fasting levels with a delayed but finally normal or supernormal rise after glucose in diabetes of adult onset; generally high values in obesity; and mean high levels in acromegaly (rat diaphragm and immunoassay), in leucine-induced hypoglycemia, and in most cases (why not all?) of insuloma. Plasma insulin is low or undetectable in patients with growth-onset diabetes.

Glucagon, the second pancreatic substance affecting carbohydrate metabolism, raises blood sugar by stimulating the activity of the phosphorylase system which converts glycogen to glucose-1-phosphate. This is accomplished by favoring formation of an activator of phosphorylase (3′, 5′-cyclic adenosinemonophosphate). There is increasing evidence that glycogen is synthesized via one pathway (UDPG), which may be stimulated by insulin, and broken down by a second pathway (phosphorylase), which is stimulated by glucagon in liver and by epinephrine in both liver and muscle.

Radioimmunochemical methods for measuring the small amounts of glucagon present in blood have permitted observations indicating that this hormone may play a significant role in regulation of the blood sugar. Unger and his colleagues have shown in dogs that the induction of hypoglycemia by insulin or phloridzin is followed by increased concentrations of glucagon in the pancreaticoduodenal vein blood, and that the administration of glucose to the hypoglycemic animals results in a prompt fall in glucagon secretion. In man, peripheral venous glucagon levels are increased three- to fourfold after 3 days of total starvation. In normal human subjects given a glucose load, glucagon levels decline sharply with the rising blood sugar and increase again 2 or 3 hours after normoglycemia has been restored.

The existence of true glucagon-secreting islet cell tumors has recently been established. There is no evidence that diabetes is caused by overproduction of this hormone.

Other Endocrine Glands

Since the influence of other endocrine glands on carbohydrate metabolism is discussed in Chapter 8, only the salient features of the subject will be summarized here.

The anterior lobe of the hypophysis produces a number of hormones that directly or indirectly affect the metabolism of carbohydrate. Growth hormone, or a closely associated impurity (for which the term "growth hormone" will henceforth be employed), elevates the blood sugar of normal, depancreatized, hypophysectomized-depancreatized, and adrenalectomized-depancreatized animals. There is good evidence that this effect is brought about both by a decreased utilization of glucose in the peripheral tissues and by increased hepatic gluconeogenesis. The decreased utilization in the periphery is due in part to interference with the action of insulin. Hypophysectomy, on the other hand, tends to lower blood sugar if insulin supplies are normal.

These effects of growth hormone on blood glucose are reciprocated by an influence of blood glucose on growth hormone secretion. Immunoassay methods recently have shown that circulating growth hormone levels are sharply increased by hypoglycemia and suppressed by hyperglycemia. Thus, the growth hormone-insulin system resembles the glucagon-insulin system, but appears to be more readily triggered, in facilitating homeostatic control of the blood sugar. That the glucagon response to hypoglycemia may be initiated by a primary rise in growth hormone levels is suggested by the work of Unger (referred to above), who found that release of growth hormone preceded that of glucagon in the normoglycemic phase of the glucose tolerance curve.

Under certain conditions growth hormone not only produces hyperglycemia but is truly diabetogenic: its administration causes in normal animals (dog and cat), first, stimulation and, later, exhaustion and degeneration of the beta cells of the islands of Langerhans so that, with suitable dosage, permanent diabetes results. Since this outcome can be prevented by the simultaneous administration of insulin, it is suggested that the destruction of the beta cells is attributable at least in part to the peripheral hyperglycemic, as opposed to a direct pancreatotropic, action of growth hormone. These observations offer a ready explanation for the high prevalence of diabetes (up to 25 per cent) in acromegaly.

Two other pituitary hormones, the adrenotropic and the thyrotropic, likewise have significant although indirect influences on sugar metabolism by way of their target organs. The effects of the adrenal glucocorticoids are in part similar to those of growth hormone, and account for the frequency of diabetes in Cushing's syndrome. These glucocorticoids also enhance gluconeogenesis by increasing the activity of four enzymes of liver: glucose-6-phosphatase, fructose-1,6-diphosphatase, phosphoenolpyruvate carboxykinase, and pyruvate kinase. The adrenal medulla, when stimulated by stress, also increases blood sugar by releasing epinephrine which favors breakdown of hepatic glycogen to glucose through activation of phosphorylase. This effect, however, is transitory, and the occurrence of chronic hyperglycemia (diabetes) in some patients with epinephrine-secreting tumors (pheochromocytoma) remains unexplained. Thyroid hormone increases both gluconeogenesis and glycogenolysis, thus tending to elevate the blood sugar. Such elevation would doubtless be greater were it not for the accompanying hypermetabolism, which increases the rate of glucose oxidation.

As might be expected from the preceding discussion, the *absence* of the pituitary, adrenal, and thyroid hormones that tend to increase blood sugar is accompanied by a tendency toward hypoglycemia, particularly during fasting, and by a remarkable sensitivity to injected insulin.

Effect of Nonhormonal Drugs on Blood Sugar

The blood sugar is influenced to some degree by many drugs. Only those which have a significant effect and which have been subjected to recent investigation will be discussed here.

DRUGS WITH HYPERGLYCEMIC ACTION

Benzothiadiazine Derivatives. In 1959, chlorothiazide was reported to increase blood sugar in some diabetic patients. It has now been shown that similar compounds, some diuretic, others not, have a hyperglycemic effect even in normal human subjects and large and small animals. Wolff et al. have reported two hypertensive, nonobese patients in whom apparently permanent diabetes developed after treatment with chlorothiazide for 7 months and 3 years respectively. One had a family history of diabetes but normal fasting blood sugars in the midcourse of therapy, rising later to more than 400 mg. per 100 ml. Diazoxide,* either alone or in combination with chlorothiazide or trichlormethiazide, is especially "diabetogenic." In rats, the increase in blood sugar caused by diazoxide is prevented by tolbutamide and by potassium and diminished by adrenalectomy; results following hypophysectomy are conflicting. The drug increases plasma cortisol. It is reported to have no effect on ILA (fat pad) in rats, but chronic administration of chlorothiazide has been followed by decreased ILA (fat pad) in some patients who developed diabetes.

DRUGS WITH HYPOGLYCEMIC ACTION

Sulfonylureas. The therapeutically useful and available drugs of this group include tolbutamide, acetohexamide, and chlorpropamide. They are most effective in "maturity-onset" diabetes of mild degree, in which the beta cells have retained some of their functional capacity. They are of little or no avail in juvenile or unstable diabetes, in which that capacity has been lost, for it is certain that the presence of insulin is required. In lowering the blood sugar of both normal and diabetic organisms, these agents inhibit hepatic glucose output and increase hepatic glycogen. It is uncertain whether these effects are produced in part by a direct action on the liver, but there is convincing evidence that the principal action of the drugs is to release pancreatic insulin. The mechanism by which this occurs is not fully known. Antoniades et al. have reported experiments suggesting that tolbutamide frees insulin from its bound form in the beta cells. There is also evidence that the drug liberates insulin from its postulated binding to protein in the circulation.

Biguanides. Members of this group, represented by phenformin, differ considerably

from the sulfonylureas. They do not lower the blood sugar of normal individuals, do not produce true hypoglycemia in diabetic patients, and do not stimulate the release of pancreatic insulin. Indeed, many of the effects of phenformin are opposite to those of insulin: it decreases liver glycogen, fat synthesis, the rate of disappearance of lactate, pyruvate, and citrate, and the oxidation of glucose. It increases blood lactate to high levels. Although it resembles insulin in diminishing gluconeogenesis and increasing peripheral glucose uptake, it does so in a different manner, perhaps related to its demonstrated production of tissue anoxia with resulting decrease of oxidative phosphorylation and stimulation of anaerobic glycolysis.

Aspirin. Aspirin has long been known to have a hypoglycemic action, but large doses are required and better agents are available.

Clinical Abnormalities of Carbohydrate Metabolism

INBORN METABOLIC ERRORS

Galactosemia. Certain individuals have an impaired utilization of ingested galactose, with accumulation of galactose-1-phosphate in the tissues. The disease occurs in infancy and is manifested by vomiting, weight loss, jaundice, mental retardation, cataracts, hepatomegaly, amino-aciduria and hypoglycemia. The symptoms are due to the hereditary absence of both the enzyme that forms UDP-Gal from UDPG and galactose-1-phosphate and the enzyme that forms UDP-Gal from UTP and galactose-1-phosphate (Fig. 6–1). The latter enzyme appears to increase with age and thus to improve galactose metabolism in these patients.

Glycogen Storage (Including von Gierke's) Disease. This is another, probably familial, disease of infants and children caused by enzymatic defects and characterized by excessive deposition of glycogen in liver, kidney, muscle (including cardiac), and other tissues. Patients exhibit enlargement of the liver, kidneys, and heart, retarded development, hypoglycemia, ketosis, acidosis, and hyperlipemia. Deficiencies of at least three enzymes have been found in individual cases of glycogen storage disease: glucose-6-phosphatase of liver, the glucosidase which splits the 1,6-glucosidic branching linkages of glycogen, and phosphorylase.

---

* Released and then withdrawn for clinical trial in 1962.

DIABETES MELLITUS

Definition, Pathogenesis and Pathologic Physiology

Advances of the last few years have made it difficult to offer a satisfactory definition of diabetes mellitus. In its classic form it is a genetically determined disease transmitted probably in a recessive manner. Its full expression is manifested by persistent hyperglycemia, glycosuria, and ketosis; impairment of the synthesis of glycogen, protein, and fat; and markedly decreased amounts of extractable insulin in the pancreas and of insulin or insulin-like activity (ILA) in the blood.

There can be no quarrel with defining the severe form of diabetes in these terms. But as one moves backward, so to speak, through milder and milder degrees of the disorder and toward the "prediabetic" state, one finds elements of the definition dropping out and some even reversing themselves. Ketosis disappears, glycosuria may be minimal or absent, and hyperglycemia does not occur during fasting and can be induced only after a meal or after ingestion of glucose. Pancreatic insulin, though usually subnormal, is substantial; levels of circulating insulin and ILA after an overnight fast are within normal limits, and their increase in response to a load of glucose, while delayed, tends in the end to be excessive. Whether an individual at this stage can be called truly diabetic is determined, for want of a better criterion, by the degree of abnormality of the glucose tolerance test (GTT), and the decision is bound to be somewhat arbitrary. Many, if not most, authorities accept the carefully worked out standards of Fajans and Conn by which the GTT is interpreted: After ingestion of 1.75 gm. of glucose per kilogram of standard body weight by a properly prepared subject, a 1-hour blood sugar value (true glucose in venous blood) of 160 mg. or more per 100 ml. *and* a 2-hour value of 120 or more denote diabetes; a 2-hour value between 120 and 110 indicates probable diabetes; and a 1-hour value below 160 with a 2-hour value below 110 is interpreted as normal. It is common knowledge, of course, that the genetically predisposed individual may display a normal tolerance for glucose one year and become diabetic the next. He may then be said to have been prediabetic the previous year.

At this point it is essential to be clear about the term "prediabetes." It carries prognostic implications which are not always valid. It is like the so-called precancerous lesion, leu-koplakia, which sometimes develops into cancer but often does not. Prediabetes cannot be used as a diagnosis except in retrospect: Every diabetic *has been* a prediabetic. These strictures are necessary because even among persons with a maximal genetic push toward diabetes, i.e., the offspring of two diabetic parents, the disease develops in far less than 100 per cent of cases. It is permissible to call persons with such an inheritance "predisposed" but not "prediabetic." Many of them, it is true, show some deviations from normal. These include, among other things, an abnormally elevated blood sugar curve during the cortisone glucose tolerance test but a normal curve with the standard GTT, a tendency to hypoglycemia several hours after ingestion of carbohydrate, and high fasting levels of plasma ILA as determined by bioassay with the rat epididymal fat pad, although normal levels are found by other methods.

The occurrence of hypoglycemia and the presence of normal or increased, rather than low, ILA in predisposed individuals have opened up new possibilities concerning the pathogenesis of diabetes. The genetic defect may lie not in the pancreas, as has been generally assumed, but in circulating or tissue antagonists to insulin, or substances that bind insulin, thus rendering it more or less ineffectual; the resulting deficiency of active insulin stimulates the pancreas to make more, and the vicious cycle continues until the beta cells become exhausted. Further evidence for partial interference with insulin action is the fact that in the frank but mild diabetes of adult onset, the response to glucose of both true (immunologically determined) insulin and ILA, though actually greater than normal, is nevertheless inadequate to yield a normal glucose tolerance curve.

The nature and source of these interfering substances are not known with certainty. Naturally occurring growth hormone, glucocorticoids, thyroxin, and glucagon antagonize insulin action, but there is no evidence that these are present to excess in ordinary diabetes or in persons predisposed to it. Antoniades has presented experiments which seem to show that insulin (really ILA) circulates in two forms, one free, or active in the rat diaphragm preparation, and the other bound to "basic protein," from which the active form is liberated by administration of glucose and by incubation of serum with adipose tissue or extracts thereof; release of the active form after glucose occurs more slowly in diabetic than in normal subjects. Vallance-Owen has reported finding in the blood of normal persons, but in greater concentrations in diabetics and their relatives, a polypeptide attached to albumin which he calls "synalbumin" and which interferes with the action of insulin on the rat diaphragm.

The hypothesis that insulin antagonists may play a leading role in the pathogenesis of diabetes has not been proved. It should be borne in mind that it is based on determinations of circulating insulin and ILA by methods that differ widely in principle and yield results of different orders of magnitude, probably because they measure different things.

Regardless of the mechanisms involved, there is much to be said for the concept, well expressed by Conn, that the development of diabetes is a continuum that begins with fertilization of the ovum and ends when the beta cells are finally overpowered by whatever diabetogenic influences have been at work. For reasons completely unknown, frank diabetes may appear during the first year of life or not until senility, though both the infant and the old man may be congenitally predisposed to the disease.

The origin of the excess glucose in diabetes was in dispute for many years. One school of thought maintained that hyperglycemia was due to inability to utilize carbohydrate, while the opposing school held that overproduction of glucose from noncarbohydrate sources was responsible, with little or no impairment of its oxidation or storage.

It was finally shown that glucose utilization in diabetes is not an all-or-none affair. Even in the completely diabetic organism some glycogen deposition can be forced and ketosis diminished by the administration of sufficient glucose. On the other hand, utilization is far from normal. It has been shown by the use of isotopic techniques that glucose oxidation in totally depancreatized dogs is reduced about 60 per cent below that found in normal dogs or in diabetic dogs maintained with insulin, and Stetten, Ingle and co-workers have demonstrated both decreased glucose utilization and increased glucose production in diabetic rats.

The large nitrogen excretion and the relatively constant dextrose-nitrogen ratio in the urine of the phlorizined or depancreatized dog fed exclusively on meat leave little doubt that extra sugar is formed from protein. Whether the blood sugar in severe diabetes also receives a significant contribution from fat was debated vigorously for years. It has long been known that the catabolism of fat yields acetate. It has now been shown that the carbon of C^{14}-labeled acetate administered to both normal and diabetic animals can be recovered from the glycogen of the liver. It can no longer be doubted, therefore, that the products of fat breakdown are capable of forming carbohydrate. It is still questionable, however, whether this occurs in large enough measure to constitute an appreciable addition to the sources of blood glucose.

If hyperglycemia is the chief biochemical manifestation of diabetes, ketosis is next in importance. It is essential to be clear on the point that one does not cause the other. Both are due to a common underlying mechanism. Fundamentally, ketosis is the result of lack of available glucose. In starvation, glucose is unavailable because it and its immediate precursors are not ingested. In diabetes it is unavailable because, despite increased levels in the blood, lack of insulin prevents its full acceptance and utilization by the cells. In either event the exclusion, or near exclusion, of glucose from the metabolism forces the body to call upon protein and fat for its energy. Calculations based on urinary nitrogen excretion in these circumstances make it certain that the amount of protein catabolized cannot possibly supply all the requisite calories and that the principal source of heat must be the oxidation of fat.

The free fatty acids liberated for this purpose from adipose tissue by action of its lipase are normally broken down (Fig. 6–1) to acetyl coenzyme A (CoA). The acetyl CoA can then be reformed into fatty acid by another pathway requiring TPNH (which is obtainable in effective quantities from carbohydrate only) and ATP. It can be oxidized to CO_2 or it can be transformed via acetoacetyl CoA into acetoacetic acid, beta-hydroxybutyric acid and acetone (ketones). Acetoacetic acid, in turn, can be oxidized by peripheral tissues, but only up to a certain maximum rate, estimated by Stadie to be about 34 millimoles of ketones per kg. per day. In diabetes the net formation of ketone bodies is increased, owing to increased conversion of fat to acetyl CoA and nonavailability of carbohydrate to facilitate recombination of acetyl CoA into fatty acid. Thus, the magnitude of fat catabolism is governed by, and is essentially the reciprocal of, the amount of carbohydrate being metabolized. Ketosis occurs when the rate of fat catabolism becomes rapid enough to provide ketone bodies in excess of the tissues' ability to consume them. When, but not before, ketosis becomes severe enough to lower the CO_2-combining power of the blood, the condition is referred to as ketoacidosis.

CLINICAL DIABETES

Let us now follow the course of events in a clinical case of diabetes from its inception to its termination in coma. Some time before the onset of symptoms, and this may be days or years, hyperglycemia has developed as a result of deficiency of insulin in available or effective form. As the blood sugar rises to levels between 160 and 200 mg. per 100 ml., the amount of glucose filtered through the renal glomeruli exceeds the capacity of the tubules to reabsorb it, and glycosuria results. This so-called "renal threshold" may be elevated in older individuals and those with some forms of nephritis.

The concentration of sugar in the urine may vary from a trace to 10 per cent or higher. Small amounts do not cause symptoms, but large quantities of urinary glucose lead to profound changes in the fluid and electrolyte economy of the body. The excretion of sugar requires considerable water, and the urine volume is consequently increased (polyuria). This naturally causes thirst (polydipsia). For a time, fluid loss is compensated by an equivalent intake. Eventually, however, owing in part to a washing out of electrolytes in the process of diuresis, this compensation fails and dehydration occurs.

A 24-hour output of 4 L. of urine containing 5 per cent glucose means the loss of 200 gm. of carbohydrate, or 800 calories, per day. This is a substantial part of the total calories required for maintenance. Thus deprived of part of his normal nutriment, the patient feels hungry and eats more (polyphagia). For a while he is able to maintain equilibrium, but since most of the extra carbohydrate he eats is promptly excreted in the urine, the caloric balance soon becomes negative again, and loss of weight inevitably supervenes. In addition, the increased glycosuria occasioned by overeating causes further diuresis, dehydration, and salt depletion, a truly vicious cycle. Aggravating the loss of weight incident to glycosuria is the breakdown of depot fat and muscle protein, which are called upon as fuel in the absence of usable glucose.

At this stage ketosis appears. Whether the ketone bodies are toxic in themselves, i.e., in addition to their acid properties, has not been finally settled. However, except for acetone,

they are certainly acids, and they behave as such in the blood and tissues. Up to a point their noxious effects are prevented by the natural defenses of the body. Chief among these are the phosphate and bicarbonate buffer systems of the blood. The relatively strong acid, acetoacetic, for example, combines with sodium bicarbonate to yield a weak acid, H_2CO_3, and sodium acetoacetate; H_2CO_3 readily dissociates to carbon dioxide and water, and the former is blown off through the lungs, while the sodium acetoacetate is excreted in the urine. Similarly, acetoacetic acid combines with disodium acid phosphate to form another weak acid, H_2NaPO_4, and sodium acetoacetate, which is eliminated by the kidneys. These processes, while for a time preventing a serious fall in serum pH, do result in a depletion of the alkali reserve and a loss of fixed base in the urine. Such loss would be greater were it not for the fact that the kidneys exchange some H^+ directly for the Na^+ of tubular urine and furthermore increase their manufacture of ammonia which combines with the acid radical and thus minimizes urinary sodium excretion.

As ketosis becomes more severe, these defenses break down. In particular, sodium, potassium, and magnesium leave the body in large amounts. The pH of the blood falls, sometimes as low as 7.0, with resulting stimulation of the respiratory center and hyperpnea (Kussmaul breathing). With the onset of vomiting, which is caused by a mechanism not well understood, the loss of base, chloride, and water becomes extreme. Abdominal pain, probably the result of salt depletion (as in heat stroke), is common at this stage and may be mistaken for the pain of an acute surgical condition. The patient's progression from drowsiness to stupor and finally to coma is probably caused by a combination of factors, among which are a lowered serum pH, dehydration, and deficiency of electrolytes. No doubt these factors also are responsible for the terminal circulatory collapse and renal failure.

The treatment of acidosis has as its prime objectives the resumption of glucose utilization and the restoration of fluids and electrolytes. These aims must be achieved at the earliest possible moment—delay may be fatal. Large doses of insulin, usually several hundred units, are necessary. Ordinarily this puts a sufficient brake on ketone production to cause regression of the acidosis, but in severe cases the additional administration of sodium bicarbonate intravenously may be advisable.

For replacement of water and salt, isotonic sodium chloride solution is most widely used. This does not correct the shortage of potassium, magnesium, and phosphate, and moreover it supplies an excess of chloride in relation to needs so that hyperchloremia sometimes results. For these reasons, hypotonic solutions of sodium chloride, to which are added sodium bicarbonate, potassium, and phosphate, have been proposed, but, because of the more ready availability of physiologic saline itself, have not found general acceptance.

Serious hypokalemia may occur during the treatment of diabetic acidosis by ordinary means. At the height of acidosis the depletion of total body potassium that has taken place through proteolysis and excretion in the urine is not reflected in serum potassium levels because of hemoconcentration. During treatment, however, these levels tend to fall for several reasons. Chief of these is hemodilution by administered fluids not containing potassium. Additionally, under the influence of insulin, potassium is carried from the extracellular fluid space back into the cells along with glucose and amino acids for the reconstitution of glycogen and protein. The resulting decline in serum potassium concentration is manifested clinically by muscular weakness which may profoundly, or even fatally, affect respiratory efforts, and by depression of the T waves and the S-T segments of the electrocardiogram. The electrocardiographic changes are often used to detect hypokalemia when chemical methods are not available. Treatment of course consists in giving potassium chloride, by mouth if possible, but intravenously if necessary. The latter route should not be used in the presence of renal failure. There is little point in giving glucose when the blood sugar is already too high. As this subsides under the action of insulin, however, the severely negative carbohydrate balance should be corrected by the administration of sugar.

LACTIC (NONKETOTIC) ACIDOSIS

Recently a number of cases of lactic acidosis have been reported in diabetic patients. Many of them have been associated with nonketotic diabetes, though in an occasional case diabetic ketoacidosis and lactic acidosis have coexisted.

The physician's attention is directed to the possibility of lactic acidemia when, in a patient with symptoms of acidosis (hyperpnea, confusion, and stupor) and a low serum CO_2 level, the sum of the measured serum anions (principally HCO_3^-, Cl^-, and protein, and in diabetics the ketone acids) is significantly less than the sum of the measured serum cations (principally Na^+, Ca^{++}, and K^+) expressed as mEq./L. Lactate may be found to make up the anion deficit, although acidosis due to conditions such as salicylate or methanol poisoning should be kept in mind.

The origin of lactic acid must be traced briefly. When the breakdown of glycogen or glucose reaches the stage of pyruvic acid (Fig. 6–1), the latter normally (in the presence of oxygen) enters the tricarboxylic cycle for oxidative dissimilation to CO_2 and H_2O. In the absence of oxygen, however, aerobic oxidation in the cycle is blocked and part of the accumulated pyruvate is converted to lactate by the DPN-DPNH system. This is what happens during the temporary hypoxia and "oxygen debt" occasioned by muscular activity. The lactate so produced is carried to the liver where it is reoxidized to pyruvate for synthesis of glycogen. In conditions leading to more severe degrees of anoxia, production of lactic acid may exceed the ability of the liver to dispose of it. Such conditions include strenuous muscular exercise, pulmonary disease, massive hemorrhage, and other events resulting in shock, such as myocardial infarction, mesenteric thrombosis, and overwhelming infection. In these circumstances blood lactate levels, which in health and with subjects at rest do not exceed 1.25 mM./L., may reach 20 to 30 mM./L.

Huckabee has defined the relation between lactate and pyruvate in which an excess of lactate (XL) occurs:

$$XL = (Ln-Lo) - (Pn-Po)\frac{Lo}{Po}, \text{ where}$$

Ln = lactate found
Lo = normal basal lactate (0.618 mEq./L.)
Pn = pyruvate found
Po = normal basal pyruvate
   (0.142 mEq./L.)
$$\frac{Lo}{Po} = \frac{0.618}{0.142} = 4.35$$

The normal values shown are for arterial blood in the basal state.

In studying patients with hyperlactatemia Huckabee identified two major groups. In Group 1, with a wide variety of unrelated diseases, lactate and pyruvate were elevated proportionately, maintaining a ratio of 10:1 or less. In Group 2, lactate was increased out of proportion to pyruvate (> 10:1) and therefore was interpreted as "excess lactate."

This group was composed of two subgroups: A, patients with hypoxia or gastrointestinal hemorrhage, in whom the hyperlactatemia was apparently not serious, for none died; and B, patients without hypoxia or circulatory or respiratory disturbance but with true acidosis, all of whom died. Group 2B was considered to represent "idiopathic" lactic acidosis. Since Huckabee's publication, several cases belonging in his Group 2A and ending fatally despite vigorous alkali therapy have been reported. Some of these were diabetic patients taking phenformin, a drug which is known to increase blood lactate by its promotion of anaerobic glycolysis. Most of these patients, however, had conditions which in themselves could have been lethal, and the studies of Bernier et al. make it unlikely that phenformin has contributed importantly to the lactic acidosis in such cases.

HYPEROSMOLAR (NONACIDOTIC) COMA IN DIABETES

Instances of hyperosmolar coma in diabetes are being reported with increasing frequency. Danowski has compiled from the literature a useful tabulation of the available data in such cases. Most patients exhibit little or no ketonuria or ketonemia and little or no depression of serum CO_2. Coma is the result of extremely high levels of blood glucose, usually in the neighborhood of 1000 mg./100 ml. or higher, with or without elevated concentrations of serum sodium, which may reach 170 mEq./L. Serum osmolality, measured in some cases but in others estimated from glucose concentrations (18 mg. glucose/100 ml. = 1 mOsm./kg. H_2O), has ranged from 321 to 462 mOsm./kg. (normal, c. 290). Such extremes of hyperglycemia are encountered in patients with uncontrolled diabetes of recent onset or during an acute illness, and are accompanied by severe dehydration. Hemoconcentration may explain some of the hypernatremia, but potassium levels are normal, so that failure of the kidneys to excrete sodium must be considered as a possibility.

Treatment of hyperosmolar coma in diabetes must include hypotonic or isotonic fluids and insulin. The mortality, however, is high, frequently because of complicating disease.

HYPOGLYCEMIA

Conn has given an etiologic classification of spontaneous hypoglycemia, which is outlined in abridged and amended form here:

I. Organic—recognizable anatomic lesion
  A. Hyperinsulinism
    1. Pancreatic island cell adenoma
    2. Pancreatic island cell carcinoma
    3. Generalized hypertrophy and hyperplasia of the islands of Langerhans
  B. Hepatic disease, including glycogenosis (von Gierke's disease)
  C. Pituitary hypofunction (anterior lobe)
  D. Adrenal hypofunction (cortex)
  E. Central nervous system lesion (hypothalamus or brain stem; interference with nervous control of blood sugar)
  F. Some hepatomas
  G. Some fibrosarcomas
II. Functional—no recognized anatomic lesion, but explainable on basis of unusual somatic function
  A. Hyperinsulinism (imbalance of the autonomic nervous system); hypoglycemic fatigue; nervous hypoglycemia; functional hypoglycemia; reactive hypoglycemia
  B. Alimentary hyperinsulinism (rapid intestinal absorption)
    1. After gastroenterostomy
    2. After gastric resection (partial or total)
  C. Renal glycosuria (severe degrees of low renal threshold for dextrose)
  D. Lactation
  E. Severe continuous muscular work
III. Miscellaneous
  A. L-leucine
  B. Ethanol
  C. Factitious (surreptitious insulin administration)
  D. Postoperative hypoglycemia
  E. Severe inanition
  F. Unknown

Organic Hypoglycemia

In benign or malignant tumor or diffuse hyperplasia of the islands of Langerhans, there is a relatively constant excessive output of insulin, which is further increased by the ingestion of carbohydrate. The blood sugar sinks to subnormal levels when food is withheld for more than a few hours. The glucose tolerance curve begins with a low fasting value and is again low between 2 and 5 hours after administration of the test dose. This test, however, is of less diagnostic value than the 24-hour starvation test, followed, if no symptoms appear, by exercise. Muscular exertion hastens and intensifies the fall in blood sugar occasioned by abstention from food.

Intravenous injection of sodium tolbutamide causes a distinctly greater fall in blood sugar in cases of islet cell tumor than in other forms of hypoglycemia. Symptoms may be bizarre, and cases of organic hyperinsulinism have often been mistaken for psychoneurosis, psychosis, epilepsy, and brain tumor. Dietary treatment in these cases is of little or no avail. Surgical removal of the islet cell tumor, which incidentally may be very small and difficult to find, or subtotal pancreatectomy in cases of diffuse hyperplasia, is indicated.

Certain diseases of the liver, when they are severe, occasionally result in hypoglycemia owing to interference with the enzyme systems responsible for either the storage or breakdown of glycogen. Such conditions include the glycogenoses, cholangiolitic hepatitis, toxic hepatitis (acute yellow atrophy), diffuse carcinomatosis, and fatty degeneration. Portal cirrhosis, on the other hand, is more commonly associated with a decreased tolerance for glucose. Severe hypoglycemia, resembling clinically that caused by insuloma, occurs in some cases of hepatoma and retroperitoneal fibrosarcoma. The explanation is elusive. In only one case have significant amounts of insulin or an insulin-like substance been extracted from the tumor.

Hypoglycemia caused by deficiencies of the anterior pituitary lobe and the adrenal cortex requires little comment here, since its physiologic basis is discussed elsewhere. Suffice it to say that failure of production of somatotropin and corticotropin by the hypophysis and of the 11-oxysteroids by the adrenal cortex is usually accompanied by an increased tolerance for glucose and frequently by low levels of blood sugar during fasting. The clinical conditions in which these effects may be manifest are, for the pituitary, destructive lesions such as chromophobe tumors and cysts, and atrophy or degeneration (Simmonds' disease); and, for the adrenal, Addison's disease. Primary myxedema, in which tolerance for glucose is commonly increased, rarely if ever presents serious hypoglycemia. Myxedema secondary to panhypopituitarism may exhibit hypoglycemic tendencies, but more because of adrenal than thyroid deficiency.

Functional Hypoglycemia

In the functional type of hyperinsulinism, insulin secretion proceeds at a normal rate during fasting, but is excessively responsive to ordinary stimuli such as changes in autonomic activity or the ingestion of carbohy-

drate. The glucose tolerance test reveals a normal fasting blood sugar and a normal rise after the test dose, but a sharp fall to hypoglycemic levels between 2 and 4 hours. The blood sugar is well maintained during starvation.

One type of functional hyperinsulinism is seen in patients who have had gastroenterostomy or gastric resection. In such cases the rapid emptying of the remaining stomach floods the small intestine with food, which, if it contains large amounts of carbohydrate, leads to a transitory but marked hyperglycemia. This stimulates the pancreas to secrete more insulin than normal, thus "overshooting the mark" and producing hypoglycemia. Patients with these kinds of gastric operation frequently experience the "dumping syndrome," a symptom complex composed of weakness, dizziness, flushing, warmth, perspiration, epigastric fullness, palpitation and nausea which appear soon after eating and are precipitated reflexly by the sudden mechanical dilatation of the small bowel. The symptoms are easily confused with those of hypoglycemia, which, although sometimes a part of this picture, generally occurs an hour or two later.

The most frequent type of functional hyperinsulinism is that observed in high-strung, nervous persons with what is called, for want of a better term, autonomic imbalance. In such cases starvation is well tolerated, but the blood sugar falls to abnormally low levels 2 to 4 hours after the ingestion of carbohydrates, particularly under conditions of physical or emotional stress. Complete proof that this is due to hypersecretion of insulin is lacking, but indirect evidence suggests that this is the most plausible explanation.

Functional hyperinsulinism is treated with a low carbohydrate, high protein and relatively high fat diet which, by minimizing postprandial hyperglycemia, also minimizes insulin secretion.

Leucine Hypoglycemia

In 1956 Cochran et al. reported that, in some cases of "idiopathic" hypoglycemia of infants (McQuarrie's syndrome), oral administration of L-leucine caused a marked fall in blood sugar with convulsions. Later it was found that this amino acid has a similar effect in some patients with insuloma. Hypoglycemia is also produced in leucine-sensitive subjects by isoleucine and alpha-ketoisocaproic acid, the keto analogue of L-leucine, but not by D-leucine or other amino acids. L-leucine given orally induces slight but insignificant lowering of blood sugar in normal human beings; the effect is exaggerated, though not to the point of symptoms, with intravenous administration. However, when such tests are preceded by chlorpropamide therapy, leucine causes marked hypoglycemia and this is accompanied by a sharp increase in plasma insulin levels (immunoassay). A similar rise in plasma insulin concentrations has been reported in leucine-sensitive subjects following ingestion of leucine without pretreatment with chlorpropamide. Release of pancreatic insulin, then, would seem to be a major action of leucine in predisposed individuals. There is some evidence that it potentiates circulating insulin, and it may have a direct but minor effect on the liver in reducing glucose output (animal experiments). The failure of leucine to produce hypoglycemia in all cases of McQuarrie's syndrome and of islet cell tumor remains unexplained.

Recent evidence indicates that intravenous injection of mixtures of amino acids not containing leucine or isoleucine causes a significant increase in plasma insulin levels in healthy subjects.

Alcohol Hypoglycemia

The occasional occurrence of hypoglycemia in acute alcoholism has been known for many years. In persons who drank denatured alcohol solvents (Solox), this reaction was originally attributed to methanol or other constituents of such products rather than to their content of ethanol, but later studies have exonerated these substances insofar as hypoglycemia is concerned, and it has been abundantly established that ethyl alcohol is generally the responsible agent. In the typical case, hypoglycemia, often with coma, develops following excessive intake of ordinary spirituous beverages and prolonged (2 or 3 days) abstinence from food. Freinkel and associates showed, in chronic alcoholics studied in the hospital, that ingestion of moderate doses of alcohol after only an overnight fast produced some fall in blood sugar, while longer fasting accentuated the effect. The hypoglycemia so induced did not respond to glucagon, suggesting that liver glycogen had been depleted. Hypoglycemia-unresponsiveness after intravenously injected insulin, decreased glucose tolerance, and delayed but prolonged depression of blood sugar after intravenous tolbutamide was demonstrated in these subjects. Plasma insulin levels (immunoassay) were not increased during alcohol-induced hypoglycemia but rose normally after administration of glucose. The fall in blood sugar could be partially prevented by pretreatment with cortisone. Severe liver disease was not found in any subject. For the present, alcohol hypoglycemia can best be explained by diminished hepatic glucose output following exhaustion of liver glycogen (increased glycogenolysis or failure of synthesis) and coupled with defective gluconeogenesis. The latter is probably brought about by decreased concentrations of hepatic DPN, a coenzyme which is involved in the conversion of glucose precursors to glucose and which suffers depletion during both starvation and the oxidation of alcohol.

Whatever the cause, a *rapid* drop in blood sugar to levels below normal evokes a sympathomimetic response, presumably through stimulation of epinephrine secretion, consisting of nervousness, trembling, palpitation, and sweating (the last via a cholinergic mechanism). A *slow* fall of the blood sugar may also produce these symptoms, but in addition affects the brain, resulting in drowsiness, diplopia, peculiar behavior, paresthesias, and headache. Severe hypoglycemia, whether of sudden or gradual onset, may involve all the foregoing symptoms and may terminate in unconsciousness, convulsions and death. All these effects depend upon the fact that the nervous system requires adequate amounts of glucose for proper functioning.

REFERENCES

Antoniades, H. N., Bougas, J. A., Camerini-Davalos, R., and Pyle, H. M.: Insulin regulatory mechanisms and diabetes mellitus. Diabetes, *13:*230, 1964.

Antoniades, H. N., Bougas, J. A., Camerini-Davalos, R., Pyle, H. M., Mazurkie, S. J., Lozano-Castaneda, O., and Marble, A.: Insulin-regulatory mechanisms and diabetes mellitus: Effect of tolbutamide on the insulin regulatory mechanisms. New England J. Med., *269:*386, 1963.

Bernier, G. M., Miller, M., and Springate, C. S.: Lactic acidosis and phenformin hydrochloride. J.A.M.A., *184:*43, 1963.

Berson, S. A., and Yalow, R. S.: The present status of insulin antagonists in plasma. Diabetes, *13:*247, 1964.

Bornstein, J., and Lawrence, R. D.: Two types of diabetes, with and without available plasma insulin. Brit. M. J., *1:*732, 1951.

Cochran, W. A., Payne, W. W., Simpkiss, M. J., and Woolf, L. I.: Familial hypoglycemia precipitated by amino acids. J. Clin. Invest., *35:*411, 1956.

Colwell, A. R., Jr., and Colwell, J. A.: Pancreatic action of the sulfonylureas. J. Lab. & Clin. Med., *53:*376, 1959.

Conn, J. W.: The diagnosis and management of spontaneous hypoglycemia. J.A.M.A., *134:*130, 1947.

Conn, J. W., and Fajans, S. S.: The prediabetic state: A concept of dynamic resistance to a genetic diabetogenic influence. Am. J. Med., *31:*839, 1961.

Danowski, T. S., and Nabarro, J. D. N.: Hyperosmolar and other types of nonketoacidotic coma in diabetes. Diabetes, *14:*162, 1965.

Daughaday, W. H., Lipicky, R. J., and Rasinski, D. C.: Lactic acidosis as a cause of nonketotic acidosis in diabetic patients. New England J. Med., *267:*1010, 1962.

Dole, V. P.: A relation between non-esterified fatty acids in plasma and the metabolism of glucose. J. Clin. Invest., *35:*150, 1956.

Duncan, G. G. (ed.): Diseases of Metabolism, 5th ed. Philadelphia, W. B. Saunders Company, 1964.

Fajans, S. S.: Leucine-induced hypoglycemia. New England J. Med., *272:*1224, 1965.

Fajans, S. S., and Conn, J. W.: An approach to the prediction of diabetes mellitus by modification of the glucose tolerance test with cortisone. Diabetes, *3:*296, 1954.

Field, J. B., Williams, H. E., and Mortimore, G. E.: Studies on the mechanism of ethanol-induced hypoglycemia. J. Clin. Invest., *42:*497, 1963.

Freinkel, N., Singer, D. L., Arky, R. A., Bleicher, S. J., Anderson, J. B., and Silbert, C. K.: Alcohol hypoglycemia. I. Carbohydrate metabolism of patients with clinical alcohol hypoglycemia and the experimental reproduction of the syndrome with pure ethanol. J. Clin. Invest., *42:*1112, 1963.

Froesch, E. R., Bürgi, H., Ramseier, E. B., Bally, P., and Labhart, A.: Antibody-suppressible and nonsuppressible insulin-like activities in human serum and their physiologic significance. An insulin assay with adipose tissue of increased precision and specificity. J. Clin. Invest., *42:*1816, 1963.

Grodsky, G. M., and Forsham, P. H.: An immuno-chemical assay of total extractable insulin in man. J. Clin. Invest., *39:*1070, 1960.

Hasselblatt, A.: Liberation of insulin bound to serum protein by tolbutamide. Metabolism, *12:*302, 1963.

Houssay, B. A.: Diabetes as a disturbance of endocrine regulation. Am. J. M. Sc., *193:*581, 1937.

Huckabee, W. E.: Abnormal resting blood lactate. I. The significance of hyperlactatemia in hospitalized patients. Am. J. Med., *30:*833, 1961.

Huckabee, W. E.: Abnormal resting blood lactate. II. Lactic acidosis. Am. J. Med., *30:*840, 1961.

Isselbacher, K. J.: A mammalian uridine diphosphate galactose pyrophosphorylase. J. Biol. Chem., *232:*429, 1958.

Kalckar, H. M., and Maxwell, E. S.: Biosynthesis and metabolic function of uridine diphosphoglucose in mammalian organisms and its relevance to certain inborn errors. Physiol. Rev., *38:*77, 1958.

Krahl, M. E.: The Action of Insulin on Cells. New York, Academic Press, 1961.

Krall, L. P., and Bradley, R. F.: Clinical evaluation of formamidinyliminourea, a new biguanide oral blood sugar lowering compound: Comparison with other hypoglycemic agents. Ann. Int. Med., *50:*586, 1959.

Krebs, H. A.: Considerations concerning the pathways of synthesis in living matter: Synthesis of glycogen from non-carbohydrate precursors. Bull. Johns Hopkins Hospital, *95:*19, 1954.

Kvam, D. C., and Stanton, H. C.: Studies on diazoxide hyperglycemia. Diabetes, *13:*639, 1964.

Larner, J., and Villar-Palasi, C.: Enzymes in a glycogen storage myopathy. Proc. Nat. Acad. Sc., *45:*1234, 1959.

Leloir, L. F., and Cardini, C. E.: Biosynthesis of glycogen from uridine diphosphate glucose. J. Am. Chem. Soc., *79:*6340, 1957.

Levine, R., and Goldstein, M. S.: On the mechanism of action of insulin. Recent Progress in Hormone Research, *11:*343, 1955.

Lipmann, F.: Biosynthetic mechanisms. Harvey Lect., *44:*99, 1948–1949.

Lochner, A., and Madison, L. L.: The mechanism of ethanol-induced hypoglycemia (abstr.). Program, Twenty-third Annual Meeting, American Diabetes Association, 1963.

Loubatières, A.: General pharmacodynamics of the hypoglycemic arylsulfonamides. Ann. New York Acad. Sc., *74:*413, 1959.

Lukens, F. D. W.: Insulin and protein metabolism. Diabetes, *13:*451, 1964.

Lukens, F. D. W., and Dohan, F. C.: Pituitary-diabetes in the cat: Recovery following insulin or dietary treatment. Endocrinology, *30:*175, 1942.

Manchester, K. L., and Young, F. G.: Insulin and protein metabolism. Vitamins and Hormones, *19:*95, 1961.

Morgan, C. R., and Lazarow, A.: Immunoassay of insulin using a two-antibody system. Proc. Soc. Exper. Biol. Med., *110:*29, 1962.

Ochoa, S.: Enzyme mechanisms in the citric acid cycle. Adv. Enzymol., *15:*183, 1954.

Raben, M. S., and Hollenberg, C. H.: Effect of glucose and insulin on the esterification of fatty acids by isolated adipose tissue. J. Clin. Invest., *39:*435, 1960.

Racker, E.: Alternate pathways of glucose and fructose metabolism. Adv. Enzymol., *15:*141, 1954.

Randle, P. J.: Plasma-insulin activity in acromegaly assayed by the rat diaphragm method. Lancet, *1:*441, 1954.

Renold, A. E., Hastings, A. B., Nesbitt, F. B., and Ashmore, J.: Studies on carbohydrate metabolism in rat liver slices. J. Biol. Chem., *213:*135, 1955.

Roth, J., Glick, S. M., Yalow, R. S., and Berson, S. A.: The influence of blood glucose on the plasma concentration of growth hormone. Diabetes, *13:*355, 1964.

Samaan, N., Dollery, C. T., and Fraser, R.: Diabetogenic action of benzothiadiazines. Lancet, *2:*1244, 1963.

Siperstein, M. D., and Fagan, V. M.: Studies on the relationship between glucose oxidation and intermediary metabolism. II. The role of glucose oxidation in lipogenesis in diabetic rat liver. J. Clin. Invest., *37:*1185, 1958.

Smith, R. W., Jr., Gaebler, O. H., and Long, C. N. H.: The Hypophyseal Growth Hormone: Nature and Actions. New York, McGraw-Hill Book Co., 1955.

Sprague, R. G., and Power, M. H.: Electrolyte metabolism in diabetic acidosis. J.A.M.A., *151:*970, 1953.

Stadie, W. C.: Fat metabolism in diabetes mellitus. J. Clin. Invest., *19*:843, 1940.

Stanbury, J. B., Fredrickson, D. S., and Wyngaarden, J. B.: The Metabolic Basis of Inherited Disease. New York, Blakiston Division, McGraw-Hill Book Co., 1960.

Steinke, J., Sirek, A., Lauris, V., Lukens, F. D. W., and Renold, A. E.: Measurement of small quantities of insulin-like activity with rat adipose tissue. III. Persistence of serum insulin-like activity after pancreatectomy. J. Clin. Invest., *41*:1699, 1962.

Steinke, J., Soeldner, J. S., Camerini-Davalos, R. A., and Renold, A. E.: Studies on serum insulin-like activity (ILA) in prediabetes and early overt diabetes. Diabetes, *12*:502, 1963.

Sterne, J.: The present state of knowledge on the mode of action of the anti-diabetic diguanides. Metabolism, *13*:791, 1964.

Stetten, D., Jr., Welt, I. D., Ingle, D. J., and Morley, E. H.: Rates of glucose production and oxidation in normal and diabetic rats. J. Biol. Chem., *192*:817, 1952.

Sutherland, E. W., and Rall, T. W.: The relation of adenosine-3′,5′-phosphate and phosphorylase to the actions of catecholamines and other hormones. Pharmacol. Rev., *12*:265, 1960.

Unger, R. H., and Eisentraut, A. M.: Studies of the physiologic role of glucagon. Diabetes, *13*:563, 1964.

Unger, R. H., Eisentraut, A. M., and Lochner, J. d'V.: Glucagon-producing tumors of the islets of Langerhans (abstr.). J. Clin. Invest., *42*:987, 1963.

Vagelos, P. R.: Lipid metabolism. Ann. Rev. Biochem., *33*:139, 1964.

Vallance-Owen, J.: Synalbumin insulin antagonism. Diabetes, *13*:241, 1964.

Villar-Palasi, C., and Larner, J.: Insulin-mediated effect on the activity of UDPG-glycogen transphosphorylase of muscle. Biochim. Biophys. Acta, *39*:171, 1960.

Waters, W. C., III, Hall, J. D., and Schwartz, W. B.: Spontaneous lactic acidosis. Am. J. Med., *35*: 781, 1963.

Weber, G., Singhal, R. L., and Srivastava, S. K.: Insulin: Suppressor of biosynthesis of hepatic gluconeogenic enzymes. Proc. Nat. Acad. Sc., *53*:96, 1965.

Williams, R. H. (ed.): Diabetes. New York, Paul B. Hoeber, Inc., 1960.

Wolff, F. W., and Parmley, W. W.: Further observations concerning the hyperglycemic activity of benzothiadiazines. Diabetes, *13*:115, 1964.

Wool, I. G., and Krahl, M. E.: Incorporation of C^{14} amino acids into protein of isolated diaphragms: An effect of insulin independent of glucose entry. Am. J. Physiol., *196*:961, 1959.

Wrenshall, G. A., Bogoch, A., and Ritchie, R. C.: Extractable insulin of pancreas: Correlation with pathological and clinical findings in diabetic and nondiabetic cases. Diabetes, *1*:87, 1952.

Yalow, R. S., and Berson, S. A.: Immunoassay of endogenous plasma insulin in man. J. Clin. Invest., *39*:1157, 1960.

Young, F. G.: Permanent experimental diabetes produced by pituitary (anterior lobe) injections. Lancet, *2*:372, 1937.

Chapter Seven

Water and Electrolyte Balance

C. THORPE RAY

When all fields of clinical medicine are considered, the most frequently encountered problems are prevention and correction of disorders in fluid and electrolyte balance. Establishing values of concentration of the various ions in the serum is necessary, but the use of these values alone leads to empirical maneuvers unless the mechanisms producing these end results are carefully considered. Many factors influencing water and electrolyte balance remain to be identified and quantitated, but much is known, and all existing knowledge should be fully utilized.

The substances in solution in the fluids of the body serve several physiologic functions which are best understood when the solutes are quantitated in terms of their individual chemical activities. Chemical activity in this instance refers to the chemical combining power (milliequivalent) and osmotic pressure (milliosmol). An explanation of the various units of measurement is essential to an understanding of the body fluids.

1. *Mol.* A mol of a substance is the molecular weight in grams. For example, one mol of NaCl = 23 + 35.5 = 58.5 grams. These same units may be applied to ions. A mol of an ion is the sum of its atomic weights expressed in grams; for example, a mol of K^+ is 39 grams, Cl^-, 35.5 grams, Ca^{++}, 40 grams, SO_4^{--}, 96 grams and HCO_3^-, 61 grams.

2. *Millimol.* A millimol is 1/1000 of a mol,

or, using the previous example of NaCl, 58.5 mg.

These units quantitate substances by weights but do not express the chemical activities of these substances nor ions in the body fluids. For this reason, the term "equivalent" was introduced to portray the chemical combining power of substances of different weights. The weights of ions are unimportant, but the electrochemical reaction between ions is of paramount importance.

3. *Equivalent.* An equivalent of an ion is the sum of its atomic weights divided by the valence. In the case of univalent ions the equivalent is equal to a mol. Thus 1 gram of hydrogen has equivalent combining power to 23 grams Na^+, 39 grams K^+, 61 grams HCO_3^- and 35.5 grams Cl^-.

In the case of divalent ions each mol has double the combining power, and thus an equivalent is 0.5 mol. For example, a mol of Ca^{++} would be 40 grams, but this has the combining power equivalent to 2×35 grams Cl^-. Accordingly one equivalent of Ca^{++} is 0.5 mol, or 20 grams; and a mol of SO_4^{--} is 96 grams, and an equivalent is 48 grams.

4. *Milliequivalent.* A milliequivalent is 1/1000 of an equivalent. The term milliequivalent is used to describe the contents of body fluids, since concentrations of ions normally are in the range of thousandths of mols or equivalents.

By using the terms equivalents and milli-

109

equivalents, a means is available to quantitate the chemical combining power of solutes in the body fluids. The next major function to be quantitated is that of maintenance of proper osmotic forces in the body. The substances present in a solution tend to "hold" water, i.e., to reduce the chemical potential of water. The osmotic pressure of a solution is the pressure which would have to be exerted to counteract this "water holding" tendency of the substances in solution and thereby restore the chemical potential of the solvent, water, to that of pure water. The osmotic pressure of any solution is proportional to the number of particles in solution, whether ionized or un-ionized. Furthermore, it is the total number of particles and not their individual sizes which contributes to the osmotic pressure. For example, one sodium ion and one proteinate ion each contribute the same amount to the osmotic pressure of body fluids despite great differences in their individual sizes.

Illustrated in Figure 7–1 are two compartments, X and Y, separated by a semipermeable membrane, M, which is entirely permeable to water. In example a, both compartments contain pure water, and, since the concentration, temperature and pressure are equal on both sides of the membrane, water molecules would move at equal rates in both

directions. In example b, a solute is added in equal concentration to the water in both X and Y. The total osmotic pressure of the solution is increased, but the particles present in solution tend to "hold" water equally well in compartments X and Y. Water has freedom of movement across the membrane, but, since the tendency to "hold" water is equal on the two sides, there will be no net movement in either direction. The solutions X and Y are *isosmolar*.

In example c, additional solute has been added to compartment X, and this solution is now hyperosmolar to that in compartment Y, and Y is now hyposmolar to X. The immediate effect is to increase the tendency to hold water in compartment X. There are two possible effects from this increase in the number of particles in solution. If the new substance traverses the membrane, it will become equally distributed in both compartment X and Y, and they again become isosmolar. There will be no net gain or loss of fluid on either side, yet the total osmotic pressure in both compartments is increased as shown in example d. If, however, the substance added to compartment X in example c cannot cross the membrane, a different osmotic pressure will exist between compartments X and Y. In consequence of the increased tendency to hold water in compartment X, water moves from Y to X until the level of fluid in X rises to a sufficient height that the resulting hydrostatic column exactly counteracts the increased tendency to hold water in compartment X. The difference in height of the column of fluid in X and Y is a measure of osmotic pressure difference.

The osmotic pressure of a solution is proportional to the molal concentration of the solutes contained therein. The millimol is used to denote concentration of a solute, and the effect of substances in solution on osmotic pressure is defined by another unit, the *milliosmol*. The millimol and milliosmol are equal when substances do not dissociate. For example, glucose does not dissociate, and 180 mg. is both a millimol and a milliosmol. If substances completely dissociate into two ions, a millimol will equal two milliosmols.

It is obvious from the explanation of units of measurement that the content of water and salt in the body is related, as are their metabolic balances. Each is meaningful principally in relation to the other. However, many factors influence either water or salt primarily and the other secondarily. To ap-

OSMOTIC PRESSURE

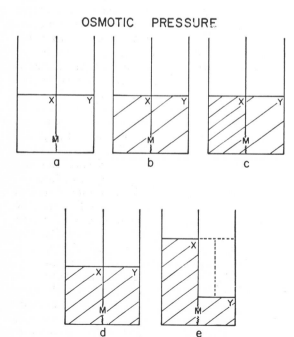

Figure 7–1. See text for explanation.

proach an understanding of the genesis of abnormal patterns of concentration and balance of electrolytes and water, the two will be considered separately as much as possible.

Volumes and Composition of Body Fluids

Measurements of the Volumes of Body Fluids

Measurements of total body water have been achieved by the dilution principle, utilizing tracer substances which are evenly distributed throughout the fluids of the body. The substances most commonly used for this purpose are antipyrine and the isotopes of hydrogen, deuterium and tritium. The various organs and tissues of the body vary widely in their content of water. Adipose tissue is lowest in content of water and skeletal muscle is highest. Consequently, the total body water of "normal" people varies from 50 to 75 per cent of total body weight, depending on the ratio of lean body mass to the amount of adipose tissue present.

It is convenient and useful to divide the water in the body into extracellular and intracellular phases. While estimates of total body water are reasonably accurate, studies of the volume of extracellular fluid entail three serious assumptions: (1) The tracer substance to be measured is distributed equally in all the extracellular fluid. (2) The test substance does not enter the cellular pool. (3) The tracer substance is not metabolized in the body. Many tracer substances have been used for estimations of extracellular fluid volume, and all suffer serious limitations. Furthermore, the extent of the errors is unknown. The high concentration of sulfate in cellular water should discourage serious attempts to estimate extracellular fluid with this substance. The use of the chloride space as a measure of extracellular water has little to recommend

it, since isotope dilution studies utilizing Cl^{36} demonstrated approximately one-third of the chloride in the body to be in the cellular pool. Inulin and sucrose are likewise not entirely limited to extracellular water. In summary, there is no really satisfactory method for measuring extracellular water, and, since intracellular water is the difference between the total and the extracellular volumes, calculations of intracellular water are likewise suspect.

With the limitations of accuracy indicated previously, the approximate values for partitioning of water are presented in Table 7–1. The subject in this example is the mythical "standard" 70-kilogram adult male commonly encountered in writings on this subject.

Characteristics of Intracellular and Extracellular Fluids

In addition to the differences in volumes of the extracellular and intracellular fluid compartments, there are more striking differences in the substances held in solution within them. The cell membrane is a relatively permeable structure, yet chemical gradients of crystalloids exist between the cellular and extracellular fluid compartments. Maintenance of gradients of this magnitude across a membrane with fluids of identical physical state and osmolality on either side would require an enormous expenditure of energy. To account for the obvious differences in the concentration of sodium across the cell membranes an energy-dependent sodium pump has been postulated to keep the concentration of sodium low in the intracellular fluid. Since there are gradients of other ions across cell membranes one would need either to postulate additional pump-systems or to reduce the specificity of the sodium pump to a nonspecific cation pump. The mechanism of action of such cation pumps has been the subject of an enormous volume of literature, much of which is inconclusive and conflicting. A number of important factors have been demonstrated to influence the cation pump. Such factors include a source of energy, the presence of calcium, the presence and configuration of lipid-protein complexes at the cell membrane and metabolic inhibitors and stimulants. The difference in the sizes of the hydrated ions of potassium and sodium may in part be responsible for the cellular-extracellular gradients of these ions without requiring expenditure of energy to drive the pump.

TABLE 7–1. PARTITIONING OF BODY WATER IN A 70-KILOGRAM ADULT.

	Liters	Per Cent of Body Weight
Total body water	49	70
1. Extracellular	14	20
a. Intravascular	3	4
b. Extravascular	11	15
2. Intracellular	35	50

TABLE 7–2.

	Serum, mEq./L.	Intracellular Fluid, mEq./L.
Na$^+$	138	10
K$^+$	4	150
Ca^{++} & Mg^{++}	7	
Mg^{++}		40
Cl$^-$	102	15–20
HCO$_3^-$	26	10
PO$_4^{---}$ & SO$_4^{--}$	3	150
Organic acids	3	
Protein	15	40

TABLE 7–3.

	Serum, mEq./L.	Serum* Water, mEq./L.	Interstitial† Fluid mEq./L.
Na$^+$	138	147.7	140.5
K$^+$	4	4.3	4.1
Ca^{++} & Mg^{++}	7	7.5	7.1
Cl$^-$	102	109.1	114.5
HCO$_3^-$	26	27.8	29.2
PO$_4^{---}$ & SO$_4^{--}$	3	3.2	3.4
Organic acids	3	3.2	3.4
Protein	15	16.1	

* Correction to concentration per liter of serum water is based on the value of 93 per cent of serum.

† Values derived by use of Donnan factors of 0.95 for cations in serum water and 1.05 for anions in serum water. These factors do not consider special binding of cations or anions, nor the effect of polyvalence of ions.

The magnitude of some of the differences in chemical content of intracellular and extracellular fluids is shown in Table 7–2.

Samples of intracellular water are not available for analysis in the normal state. These values presented in Table 7–2 must be regarded as estimates involving some rather important assumptions. There are very few data bearing on the forms and physicochemical states in which materials exist within the cells. Regardless of the chemical gradients and the extent to which ions are bound or dissociated, the fluids within the cells are in osmotic equilibrium with the extracellular fluids. As long as the cell membrane is freely permeable to water, osmotic equilibrium must exist.

A variety of extracellular fluids, serum, lymph and serosal fluid, for example, have been available for extensive analysis of chemical content. While these examples may not be chemically identical to all types of extracellular fluid, the knowledge of their chemical content allows the prediction that extracellular fluid is an ultrafiltrate of plasma. Non-inflammatory edema fluid has the chemical characteristics of a predictable ultrafiltrate of plasma. Differences in the concentration of certain ions in the vascular and extravascular spaces would be expected. The non-

diffusible proteins are negatively charged, and thus, in order to maintain electroneutrality, a higher concentration of sodium and other cations must remain in the vascular compartment (Gibbs-Donnan equilibrium). The effects of this phenomenon are shown in Table 7–3.

Exchanges of Fluids between Cellular and Extracellular Spaces

As in the case of exchanges of fluids between vascular and extravascular spaces, the *total* exchange of fluids between extracellular and cellular spaces is enormous. Water crosses cellular membranes almost too rapidly to estimate the rate of transfer. The *net* exchanges of fluids between extracellular and intracellular spaces are governed by the osmotic pressures which exist in these two compartments. Water moves across cellular membranes to maintain an isosmolar state. The relationship of changes in osmotic pressure to net exchanges of fluids is shown in

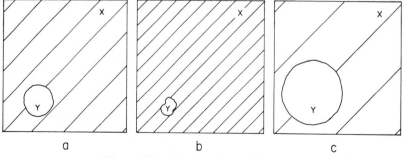

Figure 7–2. See text for explanation.

Figure 7–2. In example *a*, an isosmolar state exists between compartment *X* and compartment *Y*. If compartment *X* represents extracellular fluids with 300 mOs./L. of NaCl, and compartment *Y* represents cellular space containing cellular substances in solution at a concentration of 300 mOs./L., an isosmotic state is present. Water is passing freely between compartments, but no net gains or losses are observed. If an additional 300 mOs./L. of NaCl is added to compartment *X*, and differential osmotic pressure results since NaCl cannot gain access to the cells (example *b*) we then have 600 mOs./L. in *X* and 300 mOs./L. in *Y*. Consequently fluid moves from the cellular compartment until osmotic equilibrium is again re-established. In this instance osmotic equilibrium would be reached at slightly less than 600 mOs./L., due to the movement of water from *Y* to *X*. The mechanism of cellular dehydration involves net loss of water from cells to re-establish osmotic equilibrium with hyperosmolar extracellular compartment.

The mechanism of cellular hydration is depicted in example *c*. If the osmolality of the fluid in *X* is reduced from 300 mOs./L. to 150 mOs./L., the cellular fluid becomes hyperosmolar to that in *X*. Consequently, water moves from the extracellular to the intracellular space until osmotic equilibrium is re-established. In this instance the two compartments would become isosmolar at a value greater than 150 mOs./L., due to movement of water from *X* to *Y*. Cellular hydration, which occurs with electrolyte depletion from the extracellular fluids, occurs by the same mechanism as illustrated in example *c*.

Exchanges of Fluids between Vascular and Extravascular Spaces

The vascular and extravascular spaces are separated by capillary membranes which are freely permeable to water and salts. In consequence of the free ingress and egress of these substances from the vascular space, the *total exchange* of water and salts between these compartments is enormous. Previous studies of rates of exchange of sodium indicated that about 50 pounds of sodium chloride was exchanged daily between these two compartments. This figure is very close to the amount of sodium chloride which is contained in the normal daily cardiac output. When the tracer substance was administered intravascularly, the limiting factor on the rate of diffu-

sion was the rate of the circulation of blood. When radioisotopes of potassium, chloride, mercury, rubidium and cesium were used, the limiting factor on diffusion was still the rate of circulation of blood. The surface area of the capillary bed of man is about 5000 square meters, or roughly one-half a city block. Since this area is permeable to salt, it is analogous to a large sieve of similar dimensions. If one had a beaker of sand to spread over this area, the limiting factor on the rate of passage of sand through the sieve would be the rate at which the sand was spread (the rate of circulation in the instance of human capillaries). When the rates of *total* exchange were studied without the limiting factor of the rate of circulation, the amount of sodium chloride crossing the capillary walls of man was estimated to be about 50,000 pounds each day. If water crossed the capillary wall in the same proportion as exists between sodium and water in serum, the amount of water involved would be about 250,000 gallons daily. In the case of water and crystalloids, the capillary wall hardly exists as a barrier. Increasing the permeability of the capillary to these substances would be hard to imagine.

It must be emphasized that these *total exchanges* do not of themselves govern the net exchanges of fluids between the vascular and extravascular compartments. Since the greatest possible *net* exchange is such a small per cent of the *total* exchange, other factors must be sought. The net exchanges of fluid between vascular and extravascular compartments are very small, since both of these fluid volumes must normally remain within relatively fixed limits.

Maintenance of a relatively fixed vascular volume is due to the presence of protein on one side of a semipermeable membrane. The protein molecules are too large to pass freely through the membrane. The restraint of proteins to the vascular space results in an oncotic force which tends to hold water. At normal concentrations of protein in plasma, this oncotic force is about 24 mm. Hg. The presence of the oncotic force to counteract the hydrostatic force in the capillary forms the basis of Starling's hypothesis of factors governing the net exchange of fluid between vascular and extravascular compartments. Somewhat oversimplified, the hypothesis states that hydrostatic forces in the arterial side of the capillary tend to exceed the oncotic force of the plasma protein which results in fluid loss. In the venous limb of the capillary, hydrostatic forces are less than on-cotic force, and fluid returns to the vascular space. When hydrostatic forces in the arterial limb are increased, more fluid leaves, and, in consequence of the greater loss of fluid, the protein becomes more concentrated and exerts a greater oncotic force. Pressure within the interstitial spaces favors return of water to the vascular system. An abnormally low concentration of plasma protein would favor loss of fluid to the extravascular space. These and other factors involved in capillary fluid exchange may be combined in an idealized model of the circulation, and their individual effects on fluid exchange may be postulated and measured.

Certainly, all these factors contribute to the control of net exchange of fluids, but, when these factors are studied individually in clinical disease states, their effect is not always clear. For example, there is a very poor correlation between venous pressure and edema in circumstances wherein only the venous pressure is altered. The relationship of low plasma protein to edema in the nephrotic syndrome is well known. However, the edema may disappear without measurable change in the concentration of plasma protein. Such observations indicate that many factors are involved in the control of net exchanges of fluids.

The altered permeability of the capillary membrane has been invoked as a mechanism of unbalancing net exchanges of fluids between compartments. Capillaries normally are not completely impermeable to protein. The capillary wall may be injured by inflammation and physical and chemical trauma so that a greater amount of protein escapes from the vascular space. However, there are no data to establish an increased loss of protein into the interstitial fluid in many of the diseases in which edema has been attributed to increased capillary permeability. A notable example is acute glomerulonephritis. In any disorder characterized by generalized increase in extravascular fluids, sodium imbalance, rather than abnormal capillary permeability, should be suspected.

External Exchanges of Fluids—Water Balance

The rejection or conservation of water by the body is meaningful only when considered in light of the normal relationships of water and electrolytes in the body fluids.

An adequate intake of both water and electrolytes is necessary to maintain the volume and contents of the body fluids within normal limits. The average intake of water, foods and salts by healthy individuals usually provides an excess. In a system such as the body of man, a steady state (zero balance) may be achieved by regulation of either intake or output. While thirst and hunger exert a regulatory influence over intake of water and salts, their importance is minimized by renal adjustments. Derangements of body fluids in consequence of excessive or inadequate intakes occur only after the deficits or excesses are beyond the normal corrective capacity of strong renal responses. The efficiency of the kidney in regulation of fluid volume is apparent in the normal stability of body weight, despite the quantitatively indiscriminate nature of intestinal absorption. Furthermore, in clinical conditions characterized by fluid volume distortion, such as generalized edema, there is usually no change in intake but rather a diminution in output. However, with progressive degrees of impairment of renal function, the intake becomes more important.

The intake of water must equal output in order to maintain zero balance. The intake of water must meet minimal needs of the body for obligatory water loss if progressive dehydration is to be prevented. The "average" daily water losses are shown in Table 7–4.

The evaporative water loss from the skin and lungs is considered an obligatory loss, although the amount may be influenced by temperature and humidity. For example, an additional 50 to 75 cc. of water is lost by this route for every degree F. rise in the body temperature above normal.

The amount of water lost in normal stools is negligible—100 cc. to 200 cc. daily. However, in the presence of diarrhea this route of loss of both water and electrolytes becomes very important. There are about eight liters of secretions daily throughout the length of

TABLE 7–4.

"AVERAGE" DAILY WATER LOSS Comfortable Environment	
Skin and lungs* (insensible)	800 to 1200 cc.
Stool	100 to 200 cc.
Urine†	1500 cc.

* This value is only the obligatory evaporative loss and does not include loss by sensible perspiration.
† Average urinary volume is not synonymous with obligatory urine volume.

the intestinal tract. If not reabsorbed, these fluids must be replaced by an increased intake.

The great variable in water loss is sensible perspiration, which may vary from zero to several liters daily. There is no way to predict the amount which will be lost by this route. Consequently, the defenses of water balance against such variables are the satisfaction of the sense of thirst and the ability of the kidney to vary the concentration of urine from four times the concentration of plasma to about one-sixth that of plasma (1400 mOs./L. to 50 mOs./L.).

The rate of water loss by the kidneys is governed by two principles, defense of osmolality of the body fluids and defense of volume of the body fluids. The defense of osmolality involves the response of the kidney to the antidiuretic hormone and to the rate of excretion of solutes in the urine. The mechanism of the defense of volume is unknown.

The Effect of Solute Load on Water Excretion

The average daily solute load to be excreted is about 1200 mOs. However, this solute load is quite variable, being increased by fever, destruction of tissue and increased protein catabolism. The kidney does not concentrate the urine maximally when the load of solutes is large, and the larger the solute load the nearer the urinary osmolarity approaches that of plasma. Thus many substances, such as $NaCl$, Na_2SO_4, mannitol, urea, sucrose, etc., are osmotic diuretics. The administration of concentrated salt solutions (sea water included) actually results in more dehydration because of this phenomenon.

The obligatory water loss by normal kidneys is difficult to establish without information about the solute load. The solute load may vary from 1200 mOs. for an average diet to as low as 300 mOs. in a diet principally of glucose. In circumstances in which an increase in the solute load is expected, the symptom of thirst becomes extremely important. In unconscious or confused patients who cannot experience nor express their desire for water, the additional obligatory needs for large urinary solute excretion must be anticipated and provided.

The preceding remarks regarding obligatory urinary volumes apply to normal kidneys. With progressive degrees of impairment of renal function, the ability to excrete a urine hyperosmolar to plasma decreases. A stage is reached at which the average solute load keeps the kidneys in a state of constant osmotic diuresis. In such circumstances the obligatory water loss by this route is increased considerably.

The Effect of the Antidiuretic Hormone on Water Excretion

In addition to the effect of the solute load on urinary volume, the presence or absence of antidiuretic hormone (ADH) is extremely important in determining the amount of water conserved or rejected by the kidney. The influence of the solute load may become more important either by increasing the solute load, such as occurs in infections, or by decreasing the renal mass with a normal solute excretory load, as occurs in chronic renal disease. Under normal circumstances the ADH mechanism is the more important determinant of urinary volume. The precise mechanism by which ADH decreases water excretion is unknown, but the speed and the precision with which the kidneys respond are largely responsible for the maintenance of the remarkable constancy of the effective osmotic pressure of the extracellular fluids.

Verney clearly demonstrated that small changes in the effective osmotic pressure of the extracellular fluids result in reactions appropriate to defend the steady state. Injection of small amounts of sodium chloride result in abrupt cessation of a water diuresis. The exquisitely sensitive receptors are located in the hypothalamus. The antidiuretic hormone is elaborated in the hypothalamus and stored in the posterior pituitary gland, awaiting release in response to proper stimuli.

Many stimuli are known to result in ADH release. Any circumstances which result in an increase in the *effective* osmotic pressure of the extracellular fluids result in water conservation by the kidney. Loss of water out of proportion to loss of salt results in ADH secretion, just as does the injection of salt, glucose or sucrose, all of which increase the effective osmolality of the extracellular fluids, since they do not have free access to the intracellular fluid. Urea enters many cellular compartments without restraint, and, while administration of urea increases the total osmolality of both extracellular and intracellular fluids, there is no increase in the effective osmotic pressure in the extracellular fluid and therefore no resultant ADH release. If the osmotic pressure of the extracellular fluid is increased, a shift of water from intracellular to extracellular compartments must result.

The final stimulus to ADH secretion may be the reduction in intracellular water, but the primary change is in the osmotic pressure in the extracellular fluid. By maintaining a steady state in the extracellular pool, ADH defends the volumes of intracellular water.

There are other stimuli which are effective in stimulating secretion and release of ADH without having any known effect on osmolality of the extracellular fluid. Pain and severe emotional stimuli cause an antidiuresis. Various drugs, such as morphine, anesthetic agents, histamine, acetylcholine and nicotine, result in secretion of ADH. A decrease in blood volume produced by bleeding and a redistribution of blood produced, for example when the subject is standing quietly, or when he is reclining on a tilting table, also result in secretion of ADH. The mechanism by which acute changes in blood volume cause this effect is unknown.

Ingestion of water without salt results in a decrease in effective osmotic pressure of the extracellular fluids and a suppression of ADH secretion. In consequence of the absence of antidiuretic hormone effect, water is rejected by the kidney and a "water diuresis" results. The excretion of a dilute urine thus defends the rather narrow limits of osmolality of the body fluids.

The effect of insufficient amounts of ADH in the genesis of distortions of volume of body fluids and electrolytes is clearly established. The relative or complete absence of ADH results in varying degrees of diabetes insipidus. The polyuria so characteristic of this disease is due to an inability of the renal tubules to absorb water appropriately. Excretion of large volumes of hyposmolar urine results in a deficit of water in the body. Loss of water in excess of salt results in hyperosmolality of the extracellular fluids and thus of all body fluids. Thirst is the natural result of this distortion of osmolality and volume.

While the role of ADH in dehydration is clear-cut, there is no clearly established role of ADH in the genesis of the positive water balance which occurs during periods of excessive fluid accumulations, such as in congestive heart failure and nephrotic syndrome. The period of active gain in weight and fluid volume is characterized by a diminished output of urine, but this is not attributable to the ADH mechanism. The end-organ, the kidney, is unable to respond to ADH in the presence of an osmotic diuresis originating from a large solute load or from the presence of renal dis-

ease. In these circumstances, the "apparent" inappropriate response is attributable to failure of the end-organ to respond rather than to inappropriate secretion or release of ADH.

From the previous discussions it is apparent that water loss by way of the kidney is regulated by physiologic mechanisms which respond to changes in osmolality of the body fluids. There is a second, and entirely separate, regulatory mechanism mediated by way of the kidneys—the regulation of volume of the body fluids. The volume regulatory mechanism is independent of osmoreceptors and of changes in osmolarity of the body fluids. For example, if water is administered as isotonic glucose, a water diuresis ensues. If the water is administered as isotonic saline, there is no immediate effect on the rate of water excretion. The body fluids are expanded, weight increases, and there are all the evidences of a positive water balance. This added fluid is lost slowly over the next few days until the former weight and fluid volumes are achieved. The mechanisms of correction of isosmolar volume distortions have been debated at length, particularly the role of "volume" receptors somewhere within the cranium and in the vascular structures within the thorax. The means by which such receptors could influence the kidneys is not known. Despite these defects in knowledge of the mechanisms involved, volume regulation must be accepted as an important part of water balance.

Up to this point, water balance has been considered almost entirely from the standpoint of water loss. A steady state or zero balance can occur only when intake of water is sufficient to meet losses by all routes, obligatory or otherwise. The acquisition of enough water to maintain balance ultimately depends on the sensation of thirst. Thirst, the desire to drink water, is a complex reaction in man, and it may be the result of psychologic as well as physiologic stimuli. Physiologically, thirst is stimulated by factors which increase the osmolality of the extracellular fluids. Administration of substances which are limited to the extracellular fluids increases the effective osmotic pressure therein and results in a stimulus to drink water. However, substances, which have free access to the cellular pool, such as urea, do not stimulate thirst. Either water deficit or salt excess may result in the stimulus to drink water. Dryness of the mucous membranes of the mouth and pharynx results in the sensation of thirst, even in the absence of changes in the body fluids.

Changes in the circulating vascular volume effect the thirst mechanism. Thirst has long been recognized as a concomitant of bleeding. In such a circumstance, no changes in effective osmolality of the extracellular fluids exist. The finding of thirst with the syndrome of hyponatremia is contrary to expectations on the basis of changes in osmolality. The stimulus to drink water, arising from the reduced vascular volume, produces a response which is entirely inappropriate to defend the osmolality of the body fluids. The same response may be observed immediately following abdominal paracenteses in cirrhotics.

Despite the demonstration of inappropriate thirst in certain diseases, this sensation still remains the only natural determinant of water intake. For thirst to provide for enough water to meet obligatory daily losses, there must be consciousness, access to water, and the strength to obtain it. There are numerous clinical states in which these three circumstances do not exist and in which progressive dehydration occurs if water is not "arbitrarily" provided.

Turnover of Body Water

The turnover of body water reflects a phenomenon which is not necessarily related to net balance. Turnover reflects the rate of exchange of body water with the intake and output. Since water is freely diffusible into all areas of the body, ingested water equilibrates with the water existing in the body and with the evaporative and urinary losses. Turnover is a description of the average length of residence of a specifically identified volume of water in the body. Since turnover is exponential in nature, the value is usually expressed as half-life; for example, one-half the water in the body is completely exchanged in from four to nine days. This exchange rate can be increased by ingesting greater quantities of water. If the volume of total body water and the water intake are known, calculations of half-life are reasonably accurate without the need for administration of tracer substances.

Electrolyte Balance

Electrolyte balance will be considered from the standpoint of the basic functions of electrolytes in the body, which are (1) the maintenance of proper osmolality and volume of the body fluids, (2) specific physiologic effects of certain ions in the body, such as the effect of Ca^{++} on neuromuscular excitability, and (3) the maintenance of proper acid-base equilibrium. An effort will be made to treat electrolyte metabolism separately from that of water.

SODIUM

Sodium constitutes over 90 per cent of the cations in the extracellular fluids, and thus, with its accompanying anions, sodium determines the osmotic pressure of the extracellular fluids. Through its effect on osmolality, the sodium content of the body helps to determine the volume of the extracellular fluid compartment. Since osmotic equilibrium must exist between cellular and extracellular compartments, net transfers of water result from variations in concentration of sodium in the extracellular fluid. In this manner the content of fluids in the various compartments is conditioned by the concentration of sodium in one compartment.

In maintenance of acid-base equilibrium, the role of sodium, as the major fixed cation, is equal in importance to the predominant role played by this ion in the control of osmolality and fluid volume. A study of chemical contents of the blood indicates that the concentration of sodium determines the amount of "available base." The metabolism and balance of sodium are closely related to its role in maintenance of proper pH of body fluids.

The presence of sodium ion is necessary for maintenance of normal membrane potentials. The many phenomena in the body which depend on electrical events require Na^+ in proper balance with other ions, notably K^+. Ringer clearly demonstrated the need for Na^+ in the maintenance of the heart beat. Proper neuromuscular function also requires Na^+, as evidenced by weakness and hyporeflexia in hyponatremia.

Sodium Content of the Body

Measurements of the total sodium content of the body have been attempted by both standard chemical methods and the isotope dilution technique. Considerable variation exists in the results. Isotope dilution techniques give a value for total sodium of about 40 mEq./kg. of body weight, or 2800 mEq. for a 70-kg. man.

The partitioning of sodium in the body gives rise to two phases, exchangeable and non-exchangeable fractions. The exchangeable fraction includes the sodium in the extracellular fluids, that in the intracellular fluids, and about 15 per cent of the sodium content of bone. The extracellular fluid compartment would normally contain about 2000 mEq. of sodium. Approximately 10 per cent of body sodium is in intracellular fluid.

The cell may be visualized as a structure with many canals communicating through it. The presence of sodium in cellular water may represent the solutes in transit through the canals.

There is a large quantity of sodium in bone, and only a small part (10 to 15 per cent) of the sodium content of bone enters into immediate exchange with that in the remainder of the extracellular compartment. For this reason the isotope dilution techniques do not equilibrate with all the sodium, and therefore do not give an accurate estimate of the total content of sodium in the body. The term "exchangeable sodium" is often used incorrectly. One may measure all the exchangeable sodium, but the isotope dilution techniques measure only the "exchanging sodium." Some sodium may be exchangeable but not exchanging at the time of measurement. The non-exchangeable sodium fraction which is fixed in bone does not participate in the usual functions of sodium in the body.

Shifts of Sodium between Compartments

Under normal conditions the amounts of sodium in the various compartments are remarkably constant. The sodium in extracellular fluids and that within the cellular compartment are probably in free exchange. The gradient in concentration is maintained by mechanisms discussed previously. Under certain circumstances, some of the extracellular sodium may enter the cells. For example, in alkalemia associated with potassium loss, the Na^+ enters the cell and replaces K^+. In diseases accompanied by severe cellular injury, there may be an increased Na^+ content in the cellular fluids.

Sodium may be mobilized from bone to replace sodium loss from the extracellular fluids. Continued acid loads from metabolic defects or administration of acid salts may shift sodium from bone to the extracellular fluids. Sodium may be taken from the extracellular fluids and stored in bone during periods of positive sodium balance.

Evidences for deposition of sodium in bone are frequently encountered in isotope and balance studies. Sodium is retained (positive balance) without change in body weight,

osmolality of the extracellular fluids or in the concentration of sodium in the serum. This set of circumstances is best explained by deposition of sodium on the surface of bone crystals.

Sodium Balance

The content of sodium in the body remains relatively constant in health. Intake of sodium must equal total losses for zero balance to be maintained. Since very little control is exercised over the intake of sodium, attention must be directed toward control of excretion of this ion. In a comfortable environment the losses of sodium via the skin are unimportant. Sensible perspiration may result in significant losses of sodium and even greater losses of water since sweat is a hypotonic solution. The loss of sodium by way of normal stools is only 1 or 2 per cent of the total excretion. Except in the event of sensible perspiration, the nonurinary losses of sodium are unimportant in healthy subjects. Of great importance are the factors which allow the kidney to achieve zero balance of sodium with an extremely variable intake.

Factors Which Influence Sodium Excretion by the Kidneys

The kidneys have the ability to excrete a urine of very low or very high sodium content. There are many factors acting simultaneously to influence the tubular function of the kidney. The functional behavior at any one instant may represent a compromise between various stimuli acting to produce opposite results.

The Effect of Volume of Body Fluid Compartments. The effect of expanded fluid volumes on water and salt excretion has been previously discussed. The mechanisms involved in regulation of body fluids through the control of sodium excretion are not clear. Isosmotic expansion of the extracellular fluids evokes a slow response but the additional fluid and salt are lost in time. Increased sodium excretion in response to expanded fluid volumes may occur even with decreased glomerular filtration rates. The mechanism which influences the kidney to retain or excrete sodium in response to volume changes obviously has to alter renal tubular function. This function of renal tubules may be independent from that which defends concentration of ions in the fluids of the body.

Contraction of body fluid volume results

in sodium retention by the kidney. This has led to the postulation of a sensitive volume receptor in the cephalic end of the body. The exact nature and mode of stimulation of such receptors remain unknown. A tempting explanation of these saluretic or antisaluretic responses exists on the basis of aldosterone secretion. Increased aldosterone secretion has been shown to follow contraction of the circulating blood volume. However, there are many aspects of the antisaluresis of volume regulation which are not attributable to aldosterone.

The Effect of Anion Excretion. The average dietary intake of foods and salts requires the kidney to excrete an acid urine. This is accomplished normally without depletion of fixed base by virture of H^+ exchange and ammonia secretion. When the acid load to be excreted by the kidney increases beyond a certain capacity of ammonia formation and H^+ exchange, the excretion of anions removes Na^+, K^+, Mg^{++} and Ca^{++} from the body.

The Effect of Adrenal Cortical Hormones. The influence of adrenal cortical hormones on sodium excretion is best exemplified by the effects of their absence. In classic Addison's disease there is an inability to excrete sodium immediately in response to a salt load. Likewise, there is an inability to retain sodium in response to salt deprivation. Addisonian patients can respond to salt loading but they do so slowly. Administration of hydrocortisone restores the normal renal tubular response. The precise site or sites of action in the tubules and the mode of action of adrenal cortical hormones are unknown.

Sodium excretion and balance can be influenced by many steroid compounds. The most potent is aldosterone, which has been the subject of extensive reports. The role of aldosterone in normal sodium metabolism has been established; however, the role of aldosterone in abnormal sodium retention in disease is not clear. In common clinical syndromes, the attributing of all aspects of increased sodium retention and expanded fluid volumes to excessive aldosterone is attractive but probably inaccurate.

Clinical Examples of Disorders in Sodium Balance

Despite the precision of regulatory mechanisms governing sodium balance in normal man, clinical disorders of this function are commonly encountered. The abnormalities of sodium metabolism and the genesis of abnormal concentrations of electrolytes in body fluids are well understood in some diseases. In others, the mechanisms are still debatable, for example, the pathogenesis of expanded fluid volumes in congestive heart failure. It is possible to present only a few examples of disease states to illustrate the principles involved.

Loss of sodium by way of large amounts of sensible perspiration may lead to *hyponatremia*. Since sweat contains less sodium than plasma, the first deficit is water, with consequent hyperosmolality of extracellular fluids. Movement of water from cells to extracellular fluid (Fig. 7–2) minimizes this change in osmolality. Some sodium is lost in sweat and some is excreted in the urine. If the water deficit is replaced without salt the extracellular fluids become hyposmolar to the cells, and water moves from the extracellular into the cellular compartments.

An inability both to conserve salt and to excrete water is seen in Addison's disease. As long as the intake of salt is adequate to meet the needs created by salt wastage, there are no obvious defects in sodium metabolism. However, when salt intake is restricted, the kidney continues to lose sodium into the urine in excess of the intake. This negative balance results in contraction of fluid volume, hyponatremia and hyperkalemia. Administration of sodium-retaining steroids stops the salt wasting by the kidney and corrects the balance.

Primary renal disease of many varieties may result in an inability to conserve salt. The homeostatic functions are usually fulfilled quite satisfactorily, despite obvious failure to serve other excretory functions for as long as the individual continues to ingest moderate amounts of salt (five to seven grams). But, if salt is restricted, the renal tubules of diseased kidneys may no longer be able to respond to the stimuli which cause sodium retention. An example of sodium wasting is shown in Figure 7–3. The disease illustrated is chronic glomerulonephritis with azotemia. The initial blood urea nitrogen was 90 mg. per cent, K^+:5 mEq./L., HCO_3^-:13 mEq./L., Cl^-:112 mEq./L. and Na:138 mEq./L. Severe sodium restriction (0.5 grams of sodium) was initiated because of the presence of edema. The effect of restriction of intake and failure of renal conservation of salt was to continue negative sodium balance. Progressive hyponatremia and hypochloremia ensued until the concentration of sodium fell from an initial 138 mEq./L. to 105 mEq./L., and the chloride from 112

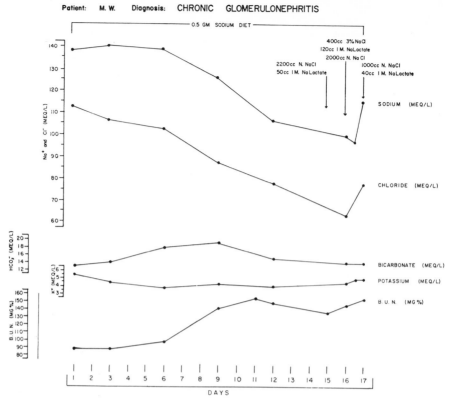

Figure 7–3. See text for explanation.

mEq./L. to 65 mEq./L. There was progressive deterioration in renal function evidenced by a rising blood urea nitrogen. The extent of the sodium deficit incurred by renal salt wasting in this instance is reflected by the small corrective effect of administration of over 1000 mEq. of sodium (over one-half the sodium normally present in the extracellular fluids) in the last three days. Depletion of solutes in the extracellular fluids results in a differential osmotic pressure which favors shifts of fluids into the cellular compartment (Fig. 7–2). The loss of fluid into the cellular compartment tends to maintain the concentration of sodium in extracellular fluids so that the deficit of sodium is actually greater than the hyponatremia alone would indicate. The failure of the serum sodium to rise very much after administration of 1000 mEq. of sodium was due to the large proportion given as isotonic saline. Some of the sodium was, however, administered in hypertonic solutions (3 per cent NaCl, 500 mEq./L.). The increase in osmolality of the extracellular fluids in consequence of administration of hyperosmolal solutions causes water to move from cells to the extracellular fluid to maintain osmotic equilibrium. It is apparent that

sodium depletion influences the osmolality of total body water and, further, that administration of salt solutions modifies the osmolality of all fluids in the body. Isosmolar expansion of extracellular fluids does not correct the existing individual electrolyte or water deficits.

The normal kidney may be converted into a salt-wasting organ by administration of diuretic agents. The purpose of diuretics is to create a negative sodium balance. If the saluretic effect of diuretics is exhibited intermittently, the defenses of the body are able to compensate; but administration of potent diuretics each day for prolonged periods is a frequent cause of electrolyte depletion. There is a greater likelihood of solute depletion when the dietary intake of salt is small. Figure 7–4 illustrates the effect of continued negative balance of sodium due to drugs. The patient had an appendectomy on the third day of observation. There had been considerable edema present prior to admission to the hospital. Because of large volumes of fluids and salt in the postoperative period, the edema increased. The dietary intake of sodium was restricted first to one gram per day, then increased to two and later to three grams daily. Both sodium loss and chloride loss were apparent, but chloride was lost in excess of sodium. The result was hyposmolality of extracellular fluids and alkalemia. In this instance the depletion of solutes occurred yet considerable edema still coexisted. Water had shifted from extracellular to intracellular compartments because of osmotic pressure. Signs and symptoms of cellular overhydration (water intoxication) occurred at the time of the lowest concentrations of sodium and chloride. Thirst is often experienced inappropriately under such circumstances and was seen in this case. Increased intake of water should have aggravated the defect in this state. In such ways impressive deficits of sodium may result from daily administration of diuretics. The rapidity of development of solute depletion in this instance indicates the need for frequent observations.

The concentration of sodium in the intestinal secretions makes this route of extrarenal loss of sodium a very important one. The pancreatic juice, bile and the secretions of the small intestines contain about the same concentration of sodium as does plasma. Yet, very little sodium is lost by way of the gastrointestinal tract normally. In the event of diarrhea, the loss of sodium into the stools reaches significant amounts. The losses of

sodium are accompanied by losses of water, chloride and potassium. Depending on the relative deficits of these substances, various chemical patterns in the plasma may result. The loss of water usually results in hyperosmolality. Hyponatremia may not exist until the water deficit is corrected. The deficit of sodium may be quite large, particularly with diarrhea of long duration.

The effect of fistulas and of intestinal drainage is the same as from diarrhea. These abnormalities may be regarded as interruptions in the normal sequence of events as the bowel handles the fluid and salt of the diet. The average daily intake is three liters of water and ten grams of sodium chloride; if this were a solution it would be hyposmolal to plasma, especially with regard to sodium. In transit through the lumen of the gastrointestinal tract, the osmolality of the contents is increased to that of plasma. This requires the temporary addition of solutes from the body. When the content of the intestine is lost via fistulas before reabsorption of solutes has occurred, a serious deficit of sodium, chloride and potassium ensues.

The clinical examples of disorders in sodium metabolism which have been presented have involved principally disorders of exces-

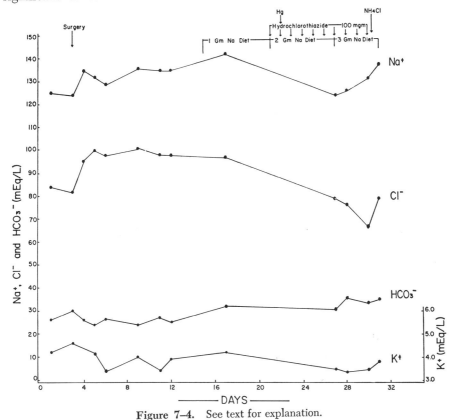

Figure 7–4.   See text for explanation.

sive loss. In some of these examples the organs which normally conserve sodium are presumed to be unable to respond to normal regulatory mechanisms. There are other clinical disorders of sodium metabolism which are due to failure or change in the regulatory mechanism itself. Asymptomatic hyponatremia is not infrequently encountered in chronic diseases. The manifest disorders of sodium metabolism in these circumstances have been described by Welt. There appears to be a new steady state of sodium balance which is achieved at a lower concentration of sodium in the plasma. These individuals are in zero balance and, if an additional amount of sodium is administered, it is excreted promptly in the urine. The new steady state with hyponatremia is defended in the same manner as normal man defends the normal concentrations of sodium in the extracellular fluids.

There are quite obviously many other clinical disorders of sodium metabolism which were not considered here. The positive sodium balance in congestive heart failure, in the nephrotic syndrome, and in cirrhosis with ascites, have only been alluded to. These and other disorders are considered in other chapters.

Chloride

The Chloride Content of the Body

The total content of chloride in the body has been estimated to be 60 to 85 grams. Conventional techniques for tissue analysis result in loss of chloride by volatilization and hence permit rather large errors. Calculations of the total exchanging chloride in the body by isotope dilution indicate that there are approximately 2000 mEq. (70 gm.) in an average adult (70 kg.). The chloride space is approximately 30 per cent of body weight in normal adults, and if extracellular fluid is 20 per cent of body weight then one-third of the exchanging chloride in the body must exist intracellularly or in bone. Large net shifts of chloride between extracellular and intracellular compartments may be identified in disease states such as congestive heart failure and in disturbances in acid-base equilibrium.

Chloride Balance

In normal man, the concentration of chloride in the plasma is defended with a precision equaling that observed in defense of the concentration of sodium. Changes in dietary intake result in prompt changes of renal excretion of chloride. An average diet results in a close relationship between the urinary content of sodium and chloride. The kidney is able to maintain zero balance of chloride for long periods of time with an extremely small dietary intake (200 mg. NaCl). However, in disorders of acid-base equilibrium, the concentration of chloride in plasma is more variable than is that of sodium. The defenses of acid-base equilibrium involve an adjustment of total anions to total cations. Electroneutrality between total anions and total cations must be maintained at all times. There are only two readily variable constituents among the anions, namely HCO_3^- and Cl^-.

Changes in acid-base equilibrium involving a primary alteration in the content of bicarbonate are reflected by a reciprocal change in chloride. Primary changes in the concentration of bicarbonate occur in disorders of respirations, in both hypo- and hyperventilation. Under these circumstances, the concentration of chloride in the plasma may vary independently from that of sodium. Likewise, the urinary content of chloride and of sodium varies independently under these circumstances.

A large amount of chloride is excreted into the gastric contents in the form of hydrochloric acid. Intestinal absorption of chloride is virtually complete since loss by this route is normally only 1 to 2 per cent of total excretion. However, in the event of vomiting and diarrhea, losses of chloride may be quite large. Chloride lost with the insensible water from the skin is negligible, but in large volumes of sensible perspiration there may be significant quantities of chloride.

Factors Influencing Renal Excretion of Chloride

In general the factors which influence renal excretion of sodium affect the excretion of chloride also. The mechanism involved in regulation of fluid volume affects both sodium and chloride proportionately. In renal disease the tubules may be unable to reabsorb either sodium or chloride adequately to defend either concentration or fluid volume. With this tubular defect, sodium and chloride are usually lost proportionately (Fig. 7–3).

The disparate excretion of sodium and chloride in renal defense of acid-base equilibrium is to be anticipated. The variations in the concentration of chloride in the extracellular fluids which are necessary in defense of acid-base equilibrium can occur only by renal excretion or by shifts between compartments. The contribution of the latter to the control of the chloride content of plasma is limited. Therefore renal excretion of chloride must vary in a manner designed to serve the defense of acid-base equilibrium.

The action of mercurial and thiazide diuretics on the renal tubules results in increased excretion of chloride. The response to these drugs results in a greater loss of chloride than of sodium.

Clinical Examples of Disorders in Chloride Balance

The disorders of chloride balance which are associated with disorders in sodium balance have been considered (Figs. 7-3 and 7-4). Likewise, those associated with disorders in potassium balance and disorders of acid-base equilibrium will be considered with those subjects.

One of the more common disorders of chloride balance is that encountered as a result of loss of gastric juice, usually resulting from continuous gastric suction or excessive vomiting. While there is some loss of sodium and potassium by this route, there is even greater loss of chloride. The primary effect is that of reducing the concentration of chloride in the plasma with a concomitant increase in bicarbonate. The latter is achieved through retention of CO_2 by reducing ventilation. In consequence of the *hypochloremia* and alkalemia both hydrogen and sodium enter the cellular compartment to displace potassium. Correction of the deficit usually requires chloride, potassium, water and sodium.

POTASSIUM

The potassium ion serves a number of functions in the body. It is the major cation in the intracellular fluids. All cellular activities involving electrical phenomena, such as cardiac and skeletal muscle contractions, as well as nerve impulse conduction, are dependent upon the gradients of potassium and sodium across the cell membrane. These and many other functions make the proper concentration of potassium of paramount importance.

Potassium Content of the Body

The total potassium content of the body has been estimated to be 3,000 to 4,000 mEq., or 40 to 60 mEq./kg., of body weight. The large variations are due to differences in techniques and the variability of the ratio of lean body mass to adipose tissue in normal man. The conventional techniques of chemical analysis of tissues are likely to give higher values than with K^{42} isotope dilution techniques, which suffer serious limitations in estimating the potassium content of the body. This radioisotope dilution technique involves an error of unknown magnitude due to failure of the isotope to achieve an equilibrium with all the potassium in the body. Potassium is compartmented into many functionally separate units which are exchanging with the plasma at different rates. For this reason, the injected tracers do not enter into equilibrium with the potassium to be measured. With the use of whole body counters, however, it is now possible to determine the potassium content of the body. This approach determines the content of the naturally occurring radioisotope of potassium, K^{40}. Man has spent his entire life equilibrating with this isotope. Thus, more reliable data about potassium metabolism in health and in disease states have resulted.

Shifts of Potassium between Compartments

There are several unique characteristics of the compartmentation of potassium. The un-

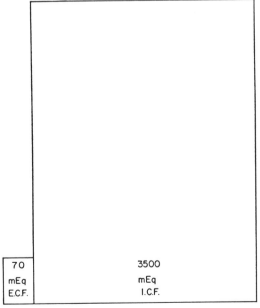

| 70 mEq E.C.F. | 3500 mEq I.C.F. |

RELATIVE CONTENTS OF POTASSIUM IN THE E.C.F. AND CELLULAR SPACE

Figure 7-5. See text for explanation.

usual distribution of potassium exerts profound effects on potassium metabolism and therefore deserves special notice. The distribution of potassium in the body is illustrated in Figure 7–5. The extracellular fluids comprise roughly 20 per cent of body weight, yet contain only two per cent of the potassium in the body. This disproportion in distribution must serve many functions, but at the same time it creates an ideal situation for the development of life-threatening changes in the concentration of potassium in the extracellular fluids. For example, a net gain of only one per cent of the potassium content of cells would reduce the concentration in the extracellular fluids to one-half the original concentration. For similar reasons, a sudden release of only a small percentage of the potassium in cells can overload the extracellular fluids. Again, the potassium content of tissues is further divided into separate units which take up and release potassium at different rates. The exchange of potassium between different tissues must occur by way of the extracellular fluids and the plasma.

There are many metabolic processes which result in a shift of potassium between compartments. The transfer of glucose from extracellular to intracellular fluids requires potassium. The amount of potassium required for transfer of glucose and for glycogenesis may vary among species. Studies of rat and human erythrocytes revealed that erythrocytes utilized one-half to one millimol of glucose for each millimol of potassium entering the cells. The amount of potassium required for the transfer of one millimol of glucose into hepatic and muscle cells is not established, but there is a shift of potassium into cells during glycogenesis. The development of hypokalemia in the correction of diabetic acidosis is evidence that this intercompartmental shift of potassium may be quite significant. Glycogenolysis releases potassium from the cellular compartment.

Tissue repair and growth require potassium. The formation of new protein within cells creates a demand for added potassium to enter the cellular compartments, and protein breakdown releases potassium from cells. Cellular injury and hypoxia also result in release of potassium from the cells.

Potassium may be shifted between compartments in response to disorders in acid-base equilibrium. In alkalemia potassium may be replaced in cells by sodium and hydrogen. In severe acidemia potassium may enter the extracellular fluids to be excreted with the urine in combination with strong anions.

In addition to "net" shifts of potassium, there is a rather specialized reciprocal shift of sodium and potassium at the cell border in association with nerve impulse transmission and cardiac and skeletal muscle contraction. Potassium shifts from the cellular to the extracellular compartment with stimulation, and the reverse shift occurs during restitution of the resting membrane potential. The shift of sodium is exactly opposite to that of potassium under these circumstances.

Potassium Balance

The relative constancy of the concentration of potassium in the serum points to the presence of effective regulatory mechanisms. The existence of regulatory mechanisms is further suggested by the zero balance of potassium which exists normally. Loss in normal stools constitutes about 10 per cent of the total daily excretion of potassium. Losses may become very large in diarrheal stools, whether they are caused by disease or laxatives.

As in the case of sodium, the kidneys occupy the key position in the regulation of balance of potassium. However, the renal conservation of potassium is not so efficient as it is for sodium or chloride. Serious deficits of potassium in the body may exist with continued loss of significant amounts of this ion in the urine, even in the normal individual. In many disease states the renal conservation of potassium is impaired even further. Under these conditions, the result of deprivation of potassium intake can be a serious deficit in the body. The development of potassium deficits in patients maintained on potassium-free intravenous fluids is a common example of the operation of the above mechanisms.

Factors Which Influence Renal Excretion of Potassium

The adrenal cortical hormones promote the excretion of potassium in the urine. The mechanisms of action of such hormones on the renal tubular cells are unknown. The increased excretion of potassium in these circumstances may be related to the increased conservation of sodium in a tubular exchange mechanism. Sodium is conserved by H^+ or K^+ ion exchanging with Na^+ in the tubular urine.

The excretion of potassium is also influenced by disturbances in acid-base equilibrium. The ion exchange mechanism involves an exchange of either hydrogen or potassium for sodium. In disorders of acid-base equilibrium, either hydrogen or potassium may dominate the exchange. In instances of systemic alkalemia from hyperventilation, it is the potassium ion which is dominant in this exchange process; in alkalemia associated with hypochloremia, it is the hydrogen ion.

Excretion of potassium is also influenced by the state of the kidney itself. Potassium loss may be excessive in many types of chronic renal disease with polyuria. A serious deficit may also occur from excessive urinary loss of potassium in the diuretic phases of recovery from acute lower nephron disease. In still another renal disease, renal tubular acidosis, abnormal amounts of bicarbonate are excreted in the urine along with accompanying fixed cations, including potassium. During periods of oliguria, whether from acute renal shutdown or chronic renal disease, there is inadequate excretion of potassium to defend the concentration in the plasma. Fatalities from hyperkalemia are not uncommon under these circumstances.

Clinical Examples of Disorders in Potassium Balance

Numerous clinical disorders are accompanied by abnormalities in the concentration of potassium in the plasma. The small amount of potassium in the extracellular fluids with a very large amount located intracellularly makes defense of concentration difficult.

The common clinical manifestations of *hypokalemia* are weakness and paralysis of skeletal muscle, intestinal ileus, bladder atony, apathy, and hyporeflexia. *Hyperkalemia* may result in muscle paralysis and disturbances in reflexes. There are serious cardiac manifestations in both hypokalemia and hyperkalemia. The occurrence and severity of the clinical manifestations of these disturbances are not predictable on the basis of the concentration of potassium alone. An abnormally low level of potassium is more likely to cause difficulty if the amount of sodium is normal or high, and this same concentration of potassium may result in no clinical manifestations of hypokalemia if the sodium concentration is low. Similarly, an abnormally high level of potassium is po-

Lead I Continuous

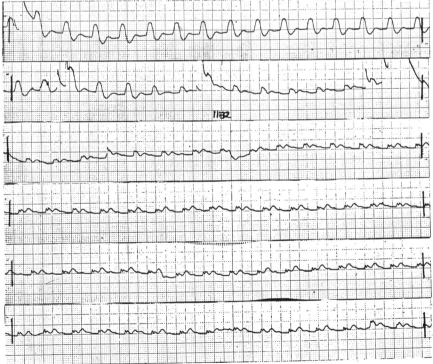

Figure 7–6. See text for explanation.

RELATIVE   HYPERKALEMIA

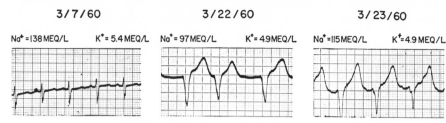

Figure 7–7.   See text for explanation.

tentiated by a low concentration of sodium but counteracted if it is high. Calcium also is antagonistic to some of the physiologic effects of potassium, particularly those involving neuromuscular and cardiac manifestations.

The effect of the proportion of sodium to potassium is shown in Figure 7–6. In this illustration the electrocardiogram is continuous. The initial strip illustrates an extreme hyperkalemic effect. The concentration of potassium in the plasma was 9.4 mEq./L. and the concentration of sodium was 128 mEq./L. An infusion of sodium lactate was begun twenty seconds before the beginning of the first strip in this illustration. Within a very short time the electrocardiographic effects of hyperkalemia began to decrease as shown in these continuous strips. Within one minute after the last strip all effects of hyperkalemia had disappeared from the electrocardiogram. Simultaneously with these electrocardiographic changes were (1) return of consciousness, (2) resumption of normal respiratory efforts, (3) restoration of normal blood pressure, and (4) disappearance of gallop rhythm. In the two minutes involved, no changes in the concentration of potassium in the plasma could have occurred. The improvement can therefore be attributed to the physiologic antagonism of the sodium ion for potassium. The antagonism between sodium and potassium continues at both ends of the spectrum. Figure 7–7 illustrates the electrocardiogram in an instance of "relative" hyperkalemia. The patient suffered from chronic glomerulonephritis with azotemia. In consequence of a markedly restricted intake of sodium the extremely low value of 97 mEq./L. of sodium was achieved. The "normal" concentration of potassium (4.9 mEq./L.) would have been relatively hyperkalemic to this extremely low value for sodium. The effects of this ionic imbalance on the electrocardiogram were essentially the same as in hyperkalemia. The partial correction of the concentration of sodium in the plasma, without change in the concentration

of potassium, resulted in some improvement of the electrocardiographic abnormalities. The continual interaction of sodium, calcium and potassium makes for inaccuracy in the definition of clinical syndromes based on concentration of a single ion in the plasma.

A high concentration of potassium in the plasma is seen in a number of clinical disorders. The principles involved can be illustrated by a few examples.

The release of potassium from the intracellular compartment with consequent increase in concentration of potassium in the plasma is exemplified clinically by acute hemolytic reactions and crushing injury to tissue. Under these circumstances the only defense against hyperkalemia is by renal excretion or shifting into some other cellular compartment.

The intravenous administration of potassium may result in transiently excessive arterial plasma concentrations. In this instance the problem is largely one of rate of injection. The effects of hyperkalemia resulting from too rapid administration are best detected by the electrocardiogram. Potassium is rapidly extracted in one circulation through capillary beds, and consequently venous plasma potassium concentrations may not reflect that in coronary arterial blood during intravenous administration of potassium. It is not unusual to encounter electrocardiographic effects of hyperkalemia during treatment for hypokalemia, and when the rate of injection is reduced the electrocardiogram reverts quite promptly to the pattern of hypokalemia.

Another clinical example of disordered potassium balance with hyperkalemia occurs in renal diseases. In chronic renal disease with polyuria, excretion of potassium is usually adequate to protect its concentration in the plasma. With terminal renal failure and oliguria, the excretion of potassium is usually inadequate. At this stage of the disease poor appetite, nausea and vomiting are frequently encountered. Inadequate nutrition results in increased breakdown of glycogen and protein with release of additional amounts of potassium into the extracellular fluids. With failing renal function, a reduction in the concentration of potassium in the extracellular compartment depends on shifting potassium back into the cells with glucose.

The hyperkalemia in uncontrolled diabetes with acidemia is another commonly encountered clinical example of hyperkalemia due to shifting of potassium from the cellular to the extracellular compartment. In these circumstances potassium is lost from the cells as a consequence of glycogen and protein breakdown and a loss of fixed base from the extracellular fluid. The dehydration which accompanies the severe acidemia in uncontrolled diabetes increases the degree of hyperkalemia (Fig. 7–8).

The pathogenesis of hypokalemia is always either intercompartmental shifting of potassium, faulty intake, excessive loss or a combination of these factors.

An example of hypokalemia resulting from an intercompartmental shift of potassium is frequently encountered during treatment of uncontrolled diabetes with acidemia. There

may be hyperkalemia before insulin therapy is started. Figure 7–8 illustrates a case involving both hyperkalemia and hypokalemia. The patient presented evidences of acidemia (HCO_3^-: 10 mEq./L.), hyperkalemia (K^+: 5.8 mEq./L.), hyponatremia (Na^+: 125 mEq./L.) and a blood sugar of 360 mg. per cent. The concentration of potassium fell from the initial hyperkalemic value of 5.8 mEq./L. to 2.8 mEq./L. within three hours. There had been no change in the bicarbonate content of the plasma and only a slight decrease in blood sugar in three hours. The shift of potassium from the small compartment (70 mEq.) in an effort to repair a sizable deficit in a very large compartment resulted in depletion of potassium in the extracellular fluids. Administration of potassium-free fluids further aggravates the defect. An indication of the size of the deficit of cellular potassium is obtained from the fact that hypokalemia continued despite vigorous attempts at correction. The potassium deficit incurred during development of acidemia in uncontrolled diabetes may be quite large, often amounting to 20 per cent of the total

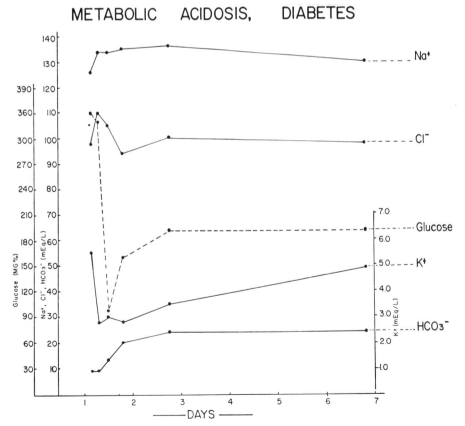

Figure 7–8.   See text for explanation.

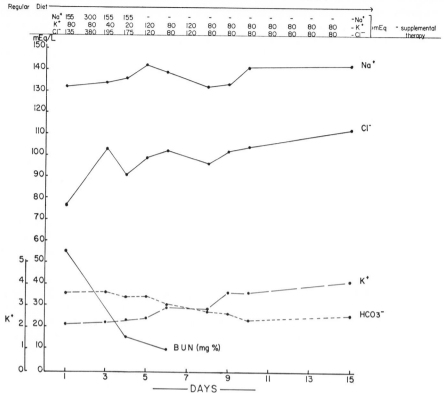

Figure 7–9.   See text for explanation.

potassium in the body. Again, attention is directed to the injudicious planning of the compartmentation of potassium which requires correction of a deficit of 700 mEq. (20 per cent of total) from a compartment containing not over 70 mEq. of potassium.

Serious deficits of potassium and hypokalemia may result from a faulty intake. The average diet contains adequate amounts of potassium to maintain balance, but, in diseases requiring intravenous feedings for a long period of time, an adequate amount of potassium may not be supplied. In a normal man who is not taking in potassium, there is continued loss in the urine. The renal conservation of potassium is even less in disease states. A deficit develops because urinary losses continue to exceed the intake of potassium.

An example of hypokalemia and potassium depletion from excessive extrarenal loss is encountered in diarrhea. Normally, only a small amount of potassium is lost in the stools, but in diarrhea the losses may be quite large. The electrolyte abnormalities often include

deficits of sodium, chloride and water in addition to potassium. The effects of severe diarrhea are shown in Figure 7–9. Diarrhea had been present for three weeks prior to admission. Initial observations indicated dehydration, hypokalemia (K+: 2.0 mEq./L.), hypochloremia and alkalemia, which frequently accompany hypokalemia. There had been no vomiting to explain the hypochloremia, and the concentration of sodium was nearly normal. The stools became normal by the third day. A severe deficit was indicated by the slow correction of the electrolyte abnormalities in this patient despite a regular diet plus supplemental therapy consisting of 1100 mEq. of potassium and 1760 mEq. of chloride in 15 days.

Another mechanism for development of potassium deficiency and hypokalemia is excessive renal excretion of potassium, which may be caused by a variety of clinical disorders. This effect is exemplified by the potassium deficiency and hypokalemia in primary aldosteronism, in Cushing's disease, and with exogenous adrenal steroid therapy. Although the precise mechanism of action of adrenal steroids on the renal tubular cells is not known, it is clear that negative balance occurs in these circumstances with an average daily intake of potassium. With the excessive loss in the urine, supplemental potassium must be administered if serious deficits are to be avoided.

Calcium and Magnesium

These two substances constitute no more than three to five per cent of the total cations in the extracellular fluid. Their role in acid-base equilibrium is therefore quite small. Likewise, they are relatively unimportant in the control of the volume and osmolality of the body fluids. However, both calcium and magnesium are essential to the body for their specific ion effects.

CALCIUM

Functions of the calcium ion include its influence on cell membrane permeability, neuromuscular excitability, transmission of nerve impulses, blood coagulation and its role in activation of certain enzyme systems. These activities of calcium are determined by the extent of ionization, which is influenced by changes in acid-base equilibrium. Alkalemia decreases the amount of calcium existing in the ionized state without necessarily changing the total amount of calcium in the plasma. This effect of alkalemia is exemplified by the occurrence of tetany with the hyperventilation syndrome, in which the total serum calcium is normal, yet the ionized fraction is quite low. The ionization of calcium is increased in the presence of acidemia. In uremia with an abnormally low serum calcium present, the ionized form constitutes a greater percentage of the total calcium present, and thus maintains a concentration of calcium ions sufficient to avoid tetany. If the pH of the blood is shifted back toward the normal values, ionization of calcium is decreased, and tetany may ensue.

The daily metabolic requirements of calcium, the routes of excretion, and its functions in bone metabolism are considered in other chapters (see pp. 144 and 150).

MAGNESIUM

The difficulties encountered in the chemical techniques for quantitation of magnesium have delayed an understanding of magnesium balance. Like calcium, magnesium is transported in the plasma in two phases, the ionized and the protein bound. Their relative proportions vary with techniques, but the ratio of ionized to bound magnesium in plasma is estimated at approximately 2:1.

Daily balance requirements of magnesium are not established. The average diet provides a daily intake of 20 to 40 mEq. of magnesium, which is enough to maintain balance in normal man. About one-third of the ingested magnesium is absorbed from the intestinal tract, and, once absorbed, excretion from the body is principally by the kidney.

The roles of magnesium in the body are under extensive investigation. It is known to activate a number of enzyme systems, but the details of the genesis of the clinical manifestations of disorders in magnesium metabolism are not known. Neuromuscular manifestations of magnesium deficiency include delirium, confusion, muscle twitchings, cramps, tetany and convulsions. Data on magnesium metabolism are insufficient to attribute the clinical effects specifically to the concentration of magnesium in the plasma, to its concentration at certain crucial areas, or to its concentration within cells. The signs and symptoms of excess or deficiency of magnesium, which are recognized today, involve the neuromuscular and cardiovascular systems. Magnesium excess results in depression of the nervous system with loss of deep tendon reflexes, drowsiness and sometimes coma.

The cardiovascular manifestations of magnesium deficiency are not clearly defined, but tachycardia and mechanismal disorders may result. An excess of magnesium may cause bradycardia and depression of conduction through the junctional tissues and within the ventricles.

Changes in the concentration and content of magnesium in the body may be influenced by alterations in intake, absorption or excretion. In addition there may be significant shifts of magnesium between compartments in the body. The clinical circumstances in which *magnesium deficiency* may be encountered include disorders of intake, such as vomiting, prolonged gastric suction, and maintenance of caloric intake on magnesium-free foods (e.g., alcohol) or intravenous fluids (as in the postoperative state). Magnesium excess occurs with loss of the normal renal excretory route in acute and chronic renal failure; some of the clinical manifestations of uremia may be due to hypermagnesemia. Intravenous administration of magnesium may also result in *hypermagnesemia.*

Acid-Base Equilibrium

It is difficult to imagine a more commonly encountered or more thoroughly studied problem than disorders in acid-base equilibrium in the body, and yet it is equally difficult to imagine a topic about which so much terminological confusion exists. Terms of definition in use for many years have different meanings for physiologists, biochemists and clinicians. These language barriers have interfered seriously with understanding of disorders in acid-base equilibrium and the application of long-established facts to current clinical problems. There is now a certain amount of agreement on definitions of terms and subsequent literature should be easier to interpret.

The availability of measurements of non-buffer ions such as sodium, potassium and chloride and the difficulty in obtaining accurate measurements of arterial pCO_2 and pH tended to focus attention away from the central role of the hydrogen ion in neutrality regulation of the body fluids. Such measurements of pCO_2 and pH are now available to the clinician and should result in a more careful consideration of the effect of disease on hydrogen ion metabolism. (See Chapter 21 for further discussion of this entire concept.)

The concentration of the hydrogen ion, commonly expressed as the negative logarithm (pH), is the parameter of greatest importance in acid-base equilibrium. Thus, pH 7 indicates that the concentration of hydrogen ions is 1/10,000,000 (i.e., 10^{-7}) of an equivalent per liter. In the instance of hydrogen, one gram is equal to one equivalent, so there is 0.0000001 gram per liter at pH 7. At pH 7.4 there is 0.000000039 gram H^+ per liter, and at pH 7.1 there is about twice this amount. The efficiency of the mechanisms of defense of pH is apparent when one considers that body metabolism produces from 50 to 70 mEq. of hydrogen per day and that the daily turnover is about 30,000 times as great as the amount of H^+ dissociated at any time in the body.

In describing substances as acids or bases the Bronsted-Lowry system has certain advantages from the standpoint of conceptual clarity. It emphasizes the central role played by water in acid-base reactions in aqueous systems such as the body fluids. In the Bronsted-Lowry system an acid is a compound or ion which gives up a *proton (H+)* and a base is a compound or ion which accepts a proton. It should be emphasized that the proton (H+) does not exist as such in solution; in water it is hydrated to form the hydronium ion. This may be exemplified as follows:

$$CH_3COOH + H_2O \leftrightharpoons CH_3COO^- + H_3O^+$$
$$\text{acid} \qquad \text{base} \qquad \text{base} \qquad \text{acid}$$

In this instance acetic acid and acetate ion form one conjugate acid-base pair and hydronium ion and water form the other. In the Bronsted-Lowry theory "acidity" is regarded as the level of proton availability or the "proton activity." The acidity is an expression of the ease with which protons can be removed from existing combinations to react with a new base that may be introduced into the solution. A high proton activity would mean that the protons are bound loosely.

The ability to defend the pH of body fluids within the narrow limits compatible with life involves *buffer systems,* buffer being defined as substances which minimize the change in pH in the solution when acids or bases are added. Weak acids with their conjugate bases act as buffers in biologic fluids. Carbonic, phosphoric and organic acids along with the acid groups of proteins act as buffers. Anions and cations such as chloride, sodium and potassium do not function as buffers; they are neither acids nor bases. They are, however, important in maintenance of electroneutrality of the body fluids within which the concentration of the hydrogen ion may vary.

One needs to consider separately the buffers that minimize changes in pH during transport of CO_2 and those that minimize the change produced when acids or bases other than H_2CO_3 and bicarbonate are introduced. The bicarbonate system (HCO_3/H_2CO_3) is the principal buffer utilized when acids other than H_2CO_3 enter the body. This system is not the buffer employed in buffering H_2CO_3 itself.

The metabolic processes in the body produce CO_2 which is hydrated to H_2CO_3. There is very little change in pH associated with the transport of H_2CO_3. This buffering capacity of whole blood for H_2CO_3 is due largely to hemoglobin. When whole blood is exposed to increased CO_2 tension in vitro the pCO_2 in the blood rises and so does the bicarbonate. This is a reflection of the buffering capacity of hemoglobin for H_2CO_3, but in this instance the rise in bicarbonate is insufficient to prevent a decrease in pH. The relation of pH, H_2CO_3 and HCO_3 is expressed in the Henderson-Hasselbalch equation:

$$pH = pK' + \log\frac{(HCO_3^-)}{(H_2CO_3)}$$

$$pH = pK' + \log\frac{(HCO_3^-)}{\alpha\,pCO_2}$$

$$= 6.10 + \log\frac{24}{.03 \times 40} \text{ at } 38°$$

$$= 6.10 + \log 20$$

$$= 7.4$$

The compensatory mechanisms of the body are designed to restore the proper proportion of bicarbonate to H_2CO_3 and thus change abnormalities of pH to or toward normal.

When acids other than H_2CO_3 enter the body the principal buffer is the bicarbonate system itself. This system is unusually well suited for this purpose since the large amount of CO_2 produced each day provides an abundant supply of bicarbonate and the concentration of its paired acid is rapidly altered by respiratory action. The reaction to the addition of an acid into the system can be illustrated as follows:

$$HCl + NaHCO_3 \rightarrow NaCl + H_2CO_3$$

The carbonic acid dissociates into water and carbon dioxide, the latter being removed by the lungs. The effect is that of removing more bicarbonate than there is reduction in pCO_2. The pH would decrease as indicated in the Henderson-Hasselbalch equation. Compensatory responses become operative in an attempt to restore the bicarbonate $-pCO_2$ ratio to normal and thus correct the deviation of pH from normal. The compensatory mechanisms involve appropriate changes in pulmonary ventilation and renal excretion. In addition to the buffers in the blood there are buffers in the other extracellular fluid and in the intracellular compartment. Evidence for such buffers is derived from infusion of acid substances and observations on acute hypercapnia. The studies on buffering in muscle indicate that this intracellular compartment is not as well buffered as is the blood for changes in pCO_2.

The renal responses in defense of pH are quite slow in contrast to the immediate effects of blood buffers and the rapid respiratory response. The kidneys bear the ultimate responsibility for maintaining pH within narrow limits. The kidney can excrete a urine containing a hydrogen ion concentration several hundred times that in plasma at pH 7.4. When coupled with urinary buffers this H^+ concentration in the urine defends against metabolic acid production. The acidification of the urine is accomplished by bicarbonate reabsorption, acidification of *diphasic* phosphate buffer and ammonia formation and its subsequent excretion as ammonium ion. The regulation of these renal responses is predominantly through the pH and pCO_2 of the perfusing blood.

MECHANISMS OF PRODUCTION OF DISORDERS IN ACID-BASE EQUILIBRIUM

Clinical disorders in acid-base equilibrium are derived from either a respiratory or metabolic origin or a combination of the two. Attempts to assess the metabolic component have given rise to much disagreement in approach and confusion in terminology. The terms "acidosis" and "alkalosis" have had many uses and meanings. These terms should be restricted to indicate the process or condition which would result in a deviation of pH if there were no secondary changes in response to the primary etiologic factor. In this usage the terms "alkalosis" and "acidosis" may be modified by general terms such as "respiratory" or "metabolic" or more specific terms such as "diabetic," "renal," and so forth, to denote the process or condition without dependence on deviation of pH per se. The deviation of pH can best be described numerically, but the terms "acidemia" and "alkalemia" are acceptable substitutes for numerical values. Thus, it would be possible to have "acidosis" without "acidemia" if compensatory mechanisms are adequate.

The characterization of the acid-base status of the blood has given rise to considerable controversy. There is general agreement that measurement of pCO_2 is the only adequate measure of the respiratory component of acid-base equilibrium. The best measure of the metabolic component is still debated. The use of the "whole blood base excess" by one group and "bicarbonate" by others has been the central point of lengthy discussions. The "whole blood base excess" may be independent of pCO_2 in a physicochemical sense as studied in vitro but it is not totally independent of pCO_2 in vivo. There is limited clinical importance of the differences revealed by the in vitro and in vivo measurements. The need for assessing the pertinent clinical information is the same regardless of which approach is used. The immediate availability of accurate determinations of pCO_2 and pH are probably more important clinically than is the difference in the third parameter, "whole blood base excess" versus "bicarbonate."

The following types of acidosis and alkalosis are presented as simple (versus mixed) varieties of disturbance in acid-base equilibrium. The presence of more than one primary process, such as a mixed disorder of respiratory alkalosis and metabolic acidosis, frequently occurs.

Respiratory Acidosis

The primary event in respiratory acidosis is the retention of CO_2 in consequence of alveolar hypoventilation (Fig. 7–10). As a result of a retention of CO_2 there is a fall in pH predictable from the Henderson-Hasselbalch equation (see Chap. 21). The bicarbonate rises as a consequence of tissue buffers and renal reabsorption of bicarbonate. The level of bicarbonate achieved is usually 5 to 10 mM./L. below that which would be required for complete compensation. The plasma chloride usually follows a time course

reciprocal to that of bicarbonate. The chloride is excreted by the kidney, and during periods of rapidly increasing hypercapnia the chloride is not excreted as rapidly as the rise in pCO_2. The data presented in Figure 7–10 were derived from a patient with emphysema. The initial values were almost normal, and during the next 18 days the concentration of bicarbonate and chloride decreased. One usually expects chloride and bicarbonate to vary reciprocally, but in this instance the progressive decline in sodium would limit the values of the anions. This is an illustration of the role of sodium in maintenance of electroneutrality. Subsequently, the respiratory status of the patient deteriorated and there was a rise in bicarbonate to 50 mEq./L. and a fall in chloride to a value of 75 mEq./L. It is important to recognize that repair of these chemical defects may be delayed if the intake of chloride is low, but the intake of chloride should not be increased until the primary respiratory defect has been improved. The values for serum electrolytes in this patient are commonly encountered in patients with chronic lung disease with worsening of pulmonary function due to pulmonary infections. The serum potassium is not shown but was found to be normal initially and rose during the period of exacerbation. Occasionally one encounters

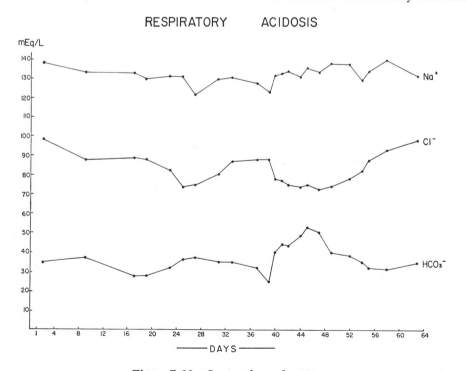

Figure 7–10. See text for explanation.

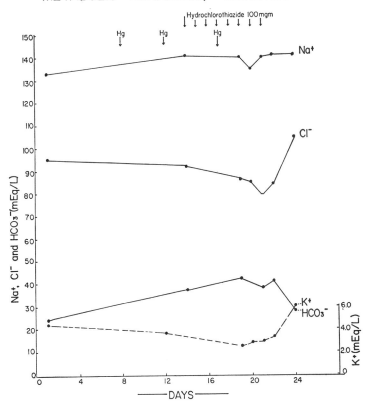

Figure 7–11. See text for explanation.

hypokalemia with hypercapnia and extracellular alkalemia in chronic lung disease.

Respiratory Alkalosis

Excessive loss of CO_2 through hyperventilation constitutes the primary defect in this disorder of acid-base equilibrium (see Chap. 21). The excessive loss of CO_2 from the lung results in an increase in the ratio of bicarbonate to carbonic acid. In addition to buffering, the compensatory mechanisms include a shift of sodium from the extracellular fluids into cells and an increase in the rate of urinary excretion of potassium and bicarbonate with simultaneous renal retention of chloride and hydrogen. The primary defect of excessive CO_2 loss may be corrected by decreasing alveolar ventilation or increasing the CO_2 content of inspired air. A normal value for pH with a reduced pCO_2 defines the state of complete compensation.

Metabolic Acidosis

The primary process in metabolic acidosis is the accumulation of H^+, the source of which is acids other than carbonic. In uncontrolled diabetes the source of the excess H^+ is the ketoacids. The source of the excess hydrogen may be endogenously produced acids or substances administered. Loss of bicarbonate from the body may result in an excess of hydrogen ion in the body. The first buffering occurs with the bicarbonate system. The loss of bicarbonate results in a lowered bicarbonate to carbonic acid ratio. With increased respiratory loss of CO_2 partial compensation occurs. The renal adjustments consist of excretion of a more acid urine, increased ammonia formation, and reabsorption of bicarbonate. Incomplete compensation is reflected by a decrease in pH and decrease in bicarbonate in excess of the decrease in pCO_2. The serum electrolyte values vary widely, depending on the degree of dehydration, accumulation of unmeasured anions and a number of other factors. In instances of renal failure, diabetic acidosis and lactic acidosis there are unmeasured anions which may be estimated by $Na^+ - (Cl^- + HCO_3^- + 14)$.

Metabolic Alkalosis

Metabolic alkalosis is the process which causes or tends to cause a nonrespiratory deficit in extracellular hydrogen ion concentration. An increased bicarbonate and an elevated pH reflect the hydrogen ion deficit. The respiratory compensation for metabolic alkalosis is relatively ineffective; the pCO_2 may be slightly elevated, normal or decreased. Values for serum electrolytes usually reveal an elevated bicarbonate, low chloride, low potassium and a variable concentration of sodium. There is usually a low serum potassium in chronic metabolic alkalosis. Potassium is lost in the urine so that serious potassium deficiency occurs. There is a peculiar relationship between metabolic alkalosis and potassium loss in that each can result in the other.

Figure 7–11 presents commonly encountered values for serum electrolytes in an instance of metabolic alkalosis from the use of diuretics. Over the first 20 days there was a progressive fall in chloride to 80 mEq./L. There was a simultaneous rise in the bicarbonate to 40 mEq./L. During this same interval of time the serum potassium fell to 2.5 mEq./L. The administration of potassium chloride resulted in a prompt return of all values to normal.

The preceding illustrations have purposely dealt with single etiologic processes in the genesis of abnormalities in acid-base equilibrium. Mixed disturbances occur rather frequently, and treatment sometimes converts one type of acid-base disturbance into another. With careful appraisal of repeated laboratory data and changes in the clinical state of the individual these mixed disturbances can be identified and properly managed.

REFERENCES

Anderson, E. C.: Three-component body composition analysis based on potassium and water determinations. Ann. New York Acad. Sc., *110*:189, 1963.

Astrup, P.: VIII. Ultra-micro method for determining pH, pCO_2 and standard bicarbonate in capillary blood. In Woolner, R. F. (ed.): A Symposium on pH and Blood Gas Measurements. Boston, Little, Brown & Co., 1959.

August, J. T., Nelson, D. H., and Thorn, G. W.: Aldosterone. New England J. Med., *259*:917, 967, 1958.

Barger, A. C.: The pathogenesis of sodium retention on congestive heart failure. Metabolism, *5*:480, 1956.

Barker, E. S.: Physiologic and clinical aspects of magnesium metabolism. J. Chron. Dis., *11*:278, 1960.

Bartter, F. C.: The role of aldosterone in normal homeostasis and in certain disease states. Metabolism, *5*:369, 1956.

Bates, R. G.: Acids, bases and buffers. Ann. New York Acad. Sc., *133*:25, 1966.

Brackett, N. C., Jr., Cohen, J. J., and Schwartz, W. B.: Carbon dioxide titration curve in normal man. New England J. Med., *272*:6, 1965.

Bresler, E. H.: The problem of the volume component of body fluid homeostasis. Am. J. Med. Sc., *232*:93, 1956.

Brown, E. B.: Blood and tissue buffers. Arch. Int. Med., *116*:665, 1965.

Elkington, J. R.: Hydrogen ion turnover in health and in renal disease. Ann. Int. Med., *57*:660, 1962.

Elkington, J. R.: Editorial. Acid-base disorders and the clinician. Ann. Int. Med., *63*:893, 1965.

Elkington, J. R.: Acid-base disturbances in renal disease. Ann. New York Acad. Sc., *133*:195, 1966.

Holmes, J. H., and Gregersen, M. I.: Observations on the drinking induced by hypertonic solutions. Am. J. Physiol., *162*:326, 1950.

Huckabee, W. E.: Abnormal resting blood lactate, II. Am. J. Med., *30*:840, 1961.

Lenzi, F., and Canniggia, A.: Nature of myocardial contraction and action potentials. Acta Med. Scand., *146*:300, 1953.

Love, W. D., Romney, R. B., and Burch, G. E.: A comparison of the distribution of potassium and exchangeable rubidium in the organs of the dog, using rubidium[86]. Circ. Res., *2*:112, 1954.

Moore, F. D., McMurrey, J. D., Parker, H. V., and Magnus, I. C.: Body composition; total body water and electrolytes: Intravascular and extravascular phase volumes. Metabolism, *5*:447, 1956.

Muller, A. F., and O'Connor, C. M. (eds.): Aldosterone: An International Symposium. Boston, Little, Brown & Co., 1957.

Nichols, G., Jr., and Nichols, H.: The role of bone in sodium metabolism. Metabolism, *5*:438, 1956.

Nuttall, F. Q.: Serum electrolytes and their relation to acid-base balance. Arch. Int. Med., *116*:670, 1965.

Pinson, E. A.: Water exchange and barriers as studied by the use of hydrogen isotopes. Physiol. Rev., *32*:123, 1952.

Randall, R. E., Jr., Rossmeisl, E. C., and Bleifer, K. H.: Magnesium depletion in man. Ann. Int. Med., *50*:257, 1959.

Ray, C. T., and Burch, G. E.: Vascular response in man to ligation of the inferior vena cava. Arch. Int. Med., *80*:587, 1947.

Ray, C. T., and Burch, G. E.: Rates of transfer of Rb[86], K[42], K[39], Cl[36], Cl[35], Na[22], and Na[23] across a blister surface on the forearm of normal man and patients with chronic congestive heart failure. Internat. J. Appl. Rad. & Isotopes, *4*:129, 1959.

Ray, C. T., and Burch, G. E.: Relationship of equilibrium of distribution, biologic decay rates, and space and mass of H^3, Cl^{36}, and Rb^{86} observed simultaneously in a comfortable and in a hot and humid environment in control subjects and in patients with congestive heart failure. J. Lab. & Clin. Med., *53*:69, 1959.

Relman, A. S.: The participation of cells in disturbances of acid-base balance. Ann. New York Acad. Sc., *133*:160, 1966.

Robin, E. D.: Abnormalities of acid-base regulation in chronic pulmonary disease, with special reference to hypercapnia and extracellular alkalosis. New England J. Med., *268*:917, 1963.

Seal, U. S.: The chemistry of buffers. Arch. Int. Med., *116*:658, 1965.

Schwartz, W. B.: Defense of extracellular pH during acute and chronic hypercapnia. Ann. New York Acad. Sc., *133*:125, 1966.

Schwartz, W. B., Hayes, R. M., Polak, A., and Haymie, G. D.: Effects of chronic hypercapnia on electrolyte and acid-base equilibrium. II. Recovery, with special reference to the influence of chloride intake. J. Clin. Invest., *40*:1238, 1961.

Schwartz, W. B., and Relman, A. S.: A critique of the parameters used in the evaluation of acid-base disorders. New England J. Med., *268*:1382, 1963.

Siggaard-Andersen, O.: The pH-log CO_2 blood acid-base nomogram revised. Scand. J. Clin. & Lab. Invest., *14*:598, 1962.

Siggaard-Andersen, O.: Titratable acid or base of body fluids. Ann. New York Acad. Sc., *133*:41, 1966.

Skou, J. C.: Enzymatic basis for active transport of Na^+ and K^+ across cell membrane. Physiol. Rev., *45*:596, 1965.

Threefoot, S. A., Burch, G. E., and Ray, C. T.: Chloride "space" and total exchanging chloride in man measured with long-life radiochloride, Cl^{36}. J. Lab. & Clin. Med., *42*:16, 1953.

Threefoot, S. A., Ray, C. T., and Burch, G. E.: Study of the use of Rb^{86} as a tracer for the measurement of Rb^{86} and K^{39} space and mass in intact man with and without congenital heart failure. J. Lab. & Clin. Med., *45*:395, 1955.

Weller, J. M., and Taylor, I. M.: Rate of potassium exchange in the rat erythrocyte. Proc. Soc. Exper. Biol. & Med., *78*:780, 1951.

Welt, L. G.: The renal regulation of water balance. Metabolism, *5*:395, 1956.

Welt, L. G.: Clinical Disorders of Hydration and Acid-Base Equilibrium, 2nd ed. Boston, Little, Brown & Co., 1959.

Wilde, W. S.: Transport through biological membranes. Ann. Rev. Physiol., *17*:17, 1955.

Winters, R. W.: Terminology of acid-base disorders. Ann. Int. Med., *63*:873, 1965.

Chapter Eight

Endocrine Glands

EDWARD C. REIFENSTEIN, Jr.

In order to trace the sequence of events in the disordered function of the human tissues in states of disease, a knowledge of the sequence of events in the normal physiology of these tissues in states of health is a prerequisite. For the glands of internal secretion, such information is still confusing and incomplete. Because of the gaps in our knowledge we must utilize theories and guesses if we wish to present a logical arrangement and a smooth transition of events to explain the manifestations of glandular activity in health and in disease. From the viewpoint of the reader there is considerable advantage in such an orderly, organized system of interpretation. The author, while mindful of controversial issues in the subjects to be discussed, will be dogmatic in many instances to render these gaps in the factual knowledge less conspicuous and hence less confusing to the reader.

General Considerations

Definitions

Endocrinology is defined as the study of the ductless or endocrine glands and their internal secretions. These secretions regulate the rates of various physiologic processes. Since these processes are involved in all phases of health and disease, the study of the endocrine glands merges indistinguishably with the studies of general physiology, pathology, and medicine. We have come to recognize that there is an endocrine component to all dis-

orders. The endocrinologist of today is the internist, the general practitioner, or the specialist in any field who evaluates the role that the glands of internal secretion play in the pathologic physiology of each of his patients and utilizes hormone preparations in his diagnostic and therapeutic armamentarium.

General Outline of Hormone Relations

The requirements of the body tissues for alterations in the rates of various physiologic processes are basically responsible for initiating the physiologic adjustments in hormonal activity. The components of the endocrine system are influenced by these requirements, in some instances via a direct effect upon the central nervous system with secondary effects upon the endocrine glands, in other instances via a direct effect upon the anterior pituitary gland, with secondary effects upon the "tissue-affecting" glands, and in still other instances via a direct effect upon the "tissue-affecting" glands. The anterior part of the pituitary gland is the hormone-regulating center of most of the other endocrine glands. The anterior pituitary is connected by neurohumoral pathways via the hypothalamus with the central nervous system; thus the hormonal system of the body is to a major extent subject to nervous control. The anterior pituitary exerts its influence on other glands by means of "tropic" hormones, in response to which these "target" glands in turn produce "tissue-affecting" hormones. In certain instances to be mentioned later this basic pattern of interrelationship has been modified to the extent that the tropic hormones of the anterior pituitary affect the body tissues directly. Furthermore, in some instances no tropic hormones to certain of the tissue-affecting glands have been detected, although these glands seem to be under the control of the central nervous system. Finally, in some instances both the nervous and the anterior pituitary tropic hormone control seem to be lacking, so that the "tissue-affecting" gland responds directly to the body tissues.

Classification of Hormone Actions

The known actions of the hormones may be classified as illustrated in Figure 8–1. The first action of a hormone is to affect all body tissues to a greater or less degree, depending upon their sensitivity to this hormone (arrow 1). The second action of a hormone is to inhibit the gland that produces it (arrow 2). For example, the tissue-affecting hormones inhibit or decrease the production of the anterior pituitary tropic hormones that originally cause their production, and, in the instances in which no pituitary tropic hormone is

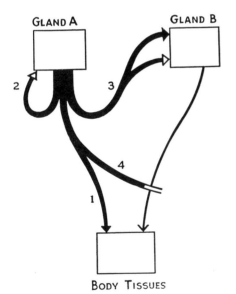

Figure 8–1. Diagram to illustrate the known actions of hormones. Solid-headed arrows indicate stimulation; open-headed arrows indicate inhibition; open bar (arrow 4) indicates neutralization or augmentation. Arrow 1, action on all body tissues; arrow 2, inhibiting action on parent endocrine gland (*Gland A*); arrow 3, stimulating or inhibiting action on another endocrine gland (*Gland B*); arrow 4, neutralizing or augmenting action on effect of some other hormone on body tissues. For further discussion, see text.

known, the tissue-affecting hormones inhibit directly the tissue-affecting gland. The third action of a hormone from one gland (*Gland A*) is to affect another gland (*Gland B*) by either stimulation or inhibition (arrow 3). It will be seen that the actions indicated by arrows 2 and 3 are simply special instances of the first action; in other words, other glands and the gland originating the hormone are included in the body tissues affected by the hormone. Finally a hormone can inhibit (neutralize) or accelerate (augment) the action of some other hormone in the end-organ tissues (arrow 4).

It follows from what has been said that continuous administration of an excess of any hormone (tropic or tissue-affecting) may result in the atrophy of the gland that is the endogenous source of this hormone. Likewise a hormone-producing tumor frequently will be associated with an atrophy of the remaining normal glandular tissue that produces the same hormone; for example, a tumor of one adrenal gland often will be accompanied by atrophy of the remaining adrenal gland. This is termed "compensatory atrophy." Such atrophy may or may not be permanent when the hormone excess is eliminated. Furthermore, prolonged stimulation via an excess of a pituitary tropic hormone or via the nervous system may result in "exhaustion atrophy" of the gland being stimulated. If a gland has been deprived of part of its functioning tissue by disease or surgery, the remaining tissue tends to become hyperplastic to make up the hormone deficit; thus a mild degree of hypothyroidism rarely persists for long. The existence in the body of a condition which can be restored toward normal only by an excess of a hormone serves to produce hyperplasia of the gland that produces this hormone; e.g., a low serum calcium level in chronic nephritis induces hyperplasia of the parathyroid glands. A glandular change of this type is termed "compensatory hyperplasia or hypertrophy." The state of responsiveness of body tissues to a hormone may vary from time to time for reasons which are not always clear; for example, insulin resistance may appear unexpectedly in some patients with diabetes mellitus. Some syndromes are known in which body tissues are congenitally resistant to a hormone; e.g., lack of growth in "end-organ" dwarfs.

Figure 8–2 has been constructed to illustrate some special relationships that are present when Figure 8–1 is applied to the situation in which there is an anterior pituitary tropic hormone stimulating a target gland. As shown in Figure 8–2, *Hormone A* stimulates (arrow *1*) the target gland, which produces a tissue-affecting hormone (arrow *2*) with the property (arrow *3*) of inhibiting *Hormone A* and also the property (arrow *4*) of stimulating *Hormone B*.

Objectives of Hormone Therapy

As a corollary to the classification of the general pattern of hormone actions, we may list the following objectives that should be kept in mind in the exogenous administration of hormones for therapeutic reasons: (1) the simple replacement of hormone deficiency, (2) the stimulation of an underfunctioning gland so that it produces more of its own hormone, (3) the inhibition of an overfunctioning gland so that it produces less of its own hormone, (4) the neutralization or augmentation in the end-organ tissues of the effect of a "tissue-affecting" hormone, and (5) the utilization of some specific pharmacologic property of a hormone.

Natural vs. Artificial "Hormones"

The discussion which follows will be confined as far as possible to the naturally occurring hormones. However, some of our knowledge of the physiology of the hormones has been derived from the study of artificial substances (those producing effects similar to those of natural hormones, but not found in nature), and we must recognize that there may be some quantitative or even qualitative differences between the actions of these artificial substances and those of natural hormones. Furthermore, inasmuch as some natural hormones have been synthesized (and indeed are available chiefly as synthetic preparations), the term "synthetic hormone" cannot be used as a synonym for "artificial hormone."

The Hormone Content of the Glands

Some glands, such as the thyroid, store within themselves considerable quantities of the hormone they produce. In many other glands, however, the content of hormone found on extraction of the gland is exceedingly small; hence the hormone is made and released when needed rather than accumulated in any quantity in the parent gland. This fact has greatly hampered investigators in their efforts to isolate some of the hormones from the glands.

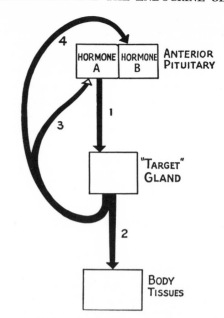

Figure 8–2. Diagram to illustrate the hormone relationships between the anterior pituitary glands, the "target" glands, and the body tissues. Solid-headed arrows indicate stimulation; open-headed arrows indicate inhibition. *Hormone A* produced by the anterior pituitary gland stimulates (arrow *1*) the "target" gland to produce its hormone, which stimulates (arrow *2*) all body tissues, inhibits (arrow *3*) the production of more *Hormone A* by the anterior pituitary, and stimulates (arrow *4*) the production of more *Hormone B* by the anterior pituitary. For further discussion, see text.

The action of a tropic hormone on a tissue-affecting gland also depends to some extent upon the content of tissue-affecting hormone stored in the gland. In some instances the tropic hormone may release stored tissue-affecting hormone and empty the tissue-affecting gland; in others the tropic hormone may stimulate the tissue-affecting gland to begin producing its hormone, which is released as fast as it is produced. Since the exact actions of the tropic hormones have not been fully established, the expression "production and/or release" will be used to indicate this unsettled state of affairs.

Intermediary Metabolism in Disease

One generalization needs to be emphasized in relation to the disorders of metabolism that occur in disease. This is the concept of "normal" vs. "abnormal" hormones. In some conditions there may be an excessive production of "normal" hormones, which then induce in the body tissues manifestations of excessive amounts of these hormones. On the other hand, some disease processes may give rise to "abnormal" hormones which have unusual actions. In these conditions it is not known whether the glands produce "normal" hormones which are then distorted in the process of metabolism or whether the glands produce "abnormal" hormones directly. This latter situation applies particularly to the disorders involving the steroid hormones, that is, the estrogens, androgens, progestogens, and adrenocortical compounds. Only minor alterations in the chemical structure of a steroid hormone are required to produce a considerable change in its biologic activity. We wonder about the origin of some of the steroid metabolites isolated from the urine of diseased patients which have never been found in the urine of normal persons. Do they arise from abnormal precursors elaborated by the glands, or do they originate from the abnormal metabolism of normal precursors?

Résumé of Glandular Physiology

In addition to the basic concepts peculiar to the endocrine system that already have been outlined, the gross physiology of the various glands must be considered before the pathologic physiology and mechanisms of disease can be discussed in relation to these glands.

Hypothalamus

The hypothalamus is connected by neurohumoral pathways to the pituitary gland. These pathways to the anterior pituitary are particularly concerned with the production and/or release from the basophile cells of the gonadotropic hormone, which is termed the luteinizing hormone (LH) in the female, and the interstitial cell-stimulating hormone (ICSH) in the male. However, pathways also exist to the adrenocorticotropic hormone (ACTH), the thyrotropic or thyroid-stimulating hormone (TSH), and the follicle-stimulating hormone (FSH). Other nerve pathways to the posterior pituitary regulate the release of the antidiuretic and oxytocic principles.

Anterior Pituitary

The anterior pituitary gland is composed of at least three types of cells: the acidophile (A), the basophile (B), and the chromophobe (C). Only the first two of these are known to produce hormones, which are chiefly "tropic."

The hormones produced by the acidophile cells include (1) *somatotropic or growth hormone* (STH), (2) *thyrotropic or thyroid-stimulating hormone* (TSH), (3) *adrenocortico-*

tropic hormone (ACTH), (4) *"glycotropic or glycostatic" hormone,* and (5) *luteotropic (lactogenic) hormone* (LTH). One of the gonadotropic hormones (LH) may be produced by the acidophile cells, but the evidence is not complete, so that for the present it is included in the group produced by the basophile cells. The evidence that there may be tropic hormones to the pancreas, the parathyroids, and the adrenal medulla is not convincing. The hormones produced by the basophile cells are both gonadotropic: (1) *follicle-stimulating hormone* (FSH) and (2) *luteinizing hormone* (LH) in the female, or *interstitial cell-stimulating hormone* (ICSH) in the male. As pointed out earlier, neurohumoral pathways from the hypothalamus have a role in the production and/or release of these tropic hormones. This relationship is well demonstrated for LH (ICSH); some lesions in the hypothalamus cause an increase and others a decrease in this hormone.

The functions of the tropic hormones of the A group may be summarized briefly as follows: (1) The somatotropic (growth) hormone (STH) produces growth of tissues by stimulating the growth of cartilage and by inducing protein-tissue anabolism. (2) The thyrotropic hormone (TSH) is the thyroid-stimulating hormone. (3) The adrenocorticotropic hormone (ACTH) stimulates the adrenal cortex to produce and/or release one or more of the hormones (cortisol or cortisone) which have to do particularly with gluconeogenesis (the conversion of protein or fat into carbohydrate), and hence are termed "sugar" or "S" hormones. The adrenal cortex also produces and/or releases a hormone of the desoxycorticosterone type (aldosterone), a hormone of the androgenic type (which has an anabolic effect on protein tissue and hence is termed the "nitrogen" or "N" hormone), and a hormone of the estrogenic type. The production and/or release of aldosterone appears to be independent of anterior pituitary "tropic" hormone control. Investigators are not agreed as to whether the production and/or release of the "N" hormone is the result of stimulation with this same ACTH or is the result of stimulation with another "adrenocorticotropic" hormone such as LH (ICSH) or LTH. A partial synthesis of the polypeptide chain of ACTH has been achieved. (4) The "glycotropic or glycostatic" hormone reduces the effectiveness and temporarily increases the production of insulin, and prevents the fall of muscle glycogen in pituitarectomized animals. It is not clear whether this hormone is the same substance which is spoken of sometimes as the diabetogenic hormone; some investigators believe that the diabetogenic action of anterior pituitary extracts can be explained by the combination of STH with ACTH and the glycotropic hormone. Recent evidence suggests that the "glycotropic" or "glycostatic" properties may be inherent in the somatotropic (growth) hormone. Finally, (5) the lactogenic (LTH) hormone induces lactation in the suitably primed breast.

The functions of the tropic hormones of the basophile group must be considered in greater detail. It should be pointed out that the tropic hormones of the B group are qualitatively identical in both sexes, although in animals there is a suggestion that there may be a quantitative difference.

The interrelationship of the gonadotropic hormones in the female gonad can be dogmatically summarized as follows: The follicle-stimulating hormone (FSH) causes the follicles of the ovary to develop and to produce estrogen if there is present a small amount of luteinizing hormone (LH). There is some evidence that if no LH is released, the stimulated follicle still produces some substance which, while not estrogenic, has the property of inhibiting FSH. The estrogen inhibits the FSH and in small amounts stimulates the production of more LH. The increased LH (in the presence of a small amount of FSH) induces ovulation and the formation of a nonfunctioning corpus luteum. Luteotropic hormone (LTH) maintains the corpus luteum for about two weeks and causes the release from it of the corpus luteum hormones, progestogen and estrogen. It is to be noted that a trace of LH seems to be needed with FSH hormone to cause estrogen to be produced by the ovary, and likewise that a trace of FSH seems to be needed with LH to induce ovulation. Furthermore, the production of and/or release of LH and probably of luteotropic hormone (LTH) by the anterior pituitary gland is inhibited by progestogen and by estrogen (in large amounts).

In the male the relationships are not as well understood. The sequence of events seems to be: The male androgenic hormone brings about the development of the testicular tubules; then FSH stimulates the *mature* tubules to produce spermatozoa and probably another hormone (inhibin?) which inhibits FSH and possibly stimulates the production of interstitial cell-stimulating hormone (ICSH). ICSH stimulates the Leydig cells to develop and

with LTH to produce the male androgenic hormone. The production and/or release of ICSH and probably of LTH by the anterior pituitary is inhibited by the androgen.

Some mention must be made of the effect of gonadotropic hormones on the adrenal cortex. There is fairly convincing evidence that LH and/or LTH stimulates the adrenal cortex, probably the so-called X-zone, to produce in both sexes an androgenic hormone (the "nitrogen" or "N" hormone) similar to the androgen produced by the testis, which has, like this latter hormone, protein anabolic properties and which leads to the excretion of 17-ketosteroids in the urine. The effect of FSH on the adrenal cortex has not been established. ACTH also may stimulate the adrenal cortex to produce the "nitrogen" hormone.

Posterior Pituitary

The posterior pituitary gland produces at least two hormones, oxytocin (*Pitocin*) and vasopressin (*Pitressin*). Du Vigneaud has established the polypeptide structure of these hormones and synthesized both. Pitocin has an oxytocic action, causing contraction of the uterus during the interval when it is under the influence of estrogen alone, but not during the period when it is under the influence of progestogen with estrogen. The production of Pitressin is regulated by nerve fibers from the vagus and the supraopticohypophyseal tract. Pitressin exerts an antidiuretic action by inducing tubular reabsorption in the kidney; the diuretic effect is apparently maintained by the anterior pituitary. Pitressin also induces peripheral vasoconstriction and stimulates smooth muscle. The hormone arising from the intermediate lobe of the pituitary gland causes a dispersion of black pigment granules in the epidermal melanophores.

Ovary

The relation of the anterior pituitary gonadotropic hormones to the ovary already has been mentioned. Under the influence of these hormones the follicle produces and/or releases estrogen (estradiol), and the corpus luteum produces and/or releases progestogen (progesterone) and estrogen. Chorionic gonadotropin also causes the corpus luteum to produce and/or release progestogen and estrogen.

Estradiol has the following effects: (1) It inhibits FSH. (2) It stimulates in small doses and inhibits in large doses the production of LH. (3) It neutralizes some of the effects of androgen on the tissues. (4) It causes growth, thickening and cornification of the vaginal mucosa with deposition of glycogen and formation of a more acid secretion. (5) It causes growth of the myometrium and proliferation of the endometrium of the uterus with a growth of the glands. (If continued long enough, it produces marked hyperplasia.) (6) It increases uterine motility by augmenting the action of Pitocin. (7) It induces development of the nipples in the mammary glands (growth of the ducts and possibly of the alveoli). (8) In large doses it inhibits the luteotropic (lactogenic) hormone (LTH). (9) It stimulates the osteoblasts and hence bone formation with retention of calcium. (10) It produces a moderate transitory increase of protein tissue formation. (11) It maintains the skin and mucous membranes. (12) It tends to lower the serum phosphorus level. (13) It tends to decrease the gland cells and increase the stroma of the prostate, perhaps through effect (3). (14) It causes atrophy of the testicular tubules. (15) It decreases libido. (16) It stimulates the production and/or release of ACTH. (17) It tends to raise the serum phospholipids and to lower the serum cholesterol and the cholesterol/phospholipid ratio. (18) It affects the renal tubules so that water, sodium and chloride are conserved and potassium is excreted. If continued long enough in the female, it will prevent ovulation through effect (1). Lack of estrogen will cause the opposite of effects (1) through (9). Withdrawal of or rapid reduction in the amount of estrogen, therefore, tends to be followed by uterine bleeding. Bone formation [effect (9)] is augmented when androgen is administered in combination with estrogen. Attention is called to the fact that alpha estradiol is not only an estrogen as far as genital structures are concerned, but also an anabolic agent as far as certain other tissues are concerned. There is no convincing evidence that estrogen induces malignant growth in human tissues.

Progesterone has the following effects: (1) It inhibits LH and probably LTH. (2) It seems to stimulate the production of FSH. (3) It converts the endometrial glands into a secretory state and prepares the endometrium for the implantation of the ovum. (4) It decreases uterine motility by inhibiting the action of Pitocin. (5) It maintains the functional activity of the placenta. (6) It promotes the development of the acinar (secretory) tissue of the breast. (7) It neutralizes the effect of aldosterone on the renal tubules so that water, sodium and chloride are excreted and potassium is conserved. (8) It is thought to facilitate the metabolism of estradiol so that the less active metabolites, estrone and estriol, are more readily formed. (9) In large doses it has an "anesthetic" or sedative effect upon the central nervous system. Progestogen also is formed by the placenta during the second and third trimesters. Progesterone has no significant effect on the endometrium not primed with estrogen; but in the presence of estrogen the withdrawal of progesterone is usually followed by uterine bleeding and desquamation of a secretory endometrium. Similarly, the withdrawal of the influence of a progestogen in the presence of continued estrogenic activity results in secretory bleeding and endometrial desquamation.

Testis

The relation of the pituitary gonadotropins to this gland also has been mentioned. As a result of these tropic hormones, the testis produces and/or releases androgen (testosterone) and another hormone (? inhibin).

Testosterone has the following effects: (1) It inhibits ICSH (LH). (2) In small doses it may stimulate, but in large doses it will inhibit FSH. (3) It neutralizes some of the effects of estrogen on the tissues. (4) It causes growth of the penis, scrotum, seminal vesicles and prostate. (5) It causes growth of the facial and body hair. (6) In small doses it inhibits, in large doses it develops, the immature tubules; it depresses the Leydig cells through effect (1). (7) It induces marked formation of protein tissue and hence causes growth in general, particularly of the muscles, skin, bones, larynx and kidneys. (8) It increases the libido. (9) It increases the vascularity and the blood flow in the tissues. (10) It inhibits the luteotropic (lactogenic) hormone. (11) It affects the renal tubules so that water, sodium and chloride are conserved and potassium is excreted. (12) It causes involution of the thymus. (13) It tends to elevate moderately the basal metabolic rate. (14) It inhibits the production and/or release of ACTH. (15) In large doses it markedly stimulates erythropoiesis. (16) It tends to lower the serum phospholipids and to raise the serum cholesterol and the cholesterol/phospholipid ratio. Bone formation [effect (7)] is augmented when estrogen is administered in combination with androgen. There is no convincing evidence that androgen induces malignant growth in human tissues.

The testis also produces *another hormone* the functions of which are relatively unknown. This hormone resembles estrogen and may be a substance which was called by the McCullaghs "inhibin." It apparently (1) inhibits FSH; (2) stimulates the production of ICSH (LH) and LTH; (3) neutralizes some of the effects of androgen on the tissues, particularly on the breast and prostate. The cellular origin of the second testicular hormone is not established; for purposes of discussion it is assumed that the second hormone is produced and/or released by the tubules of the testis, although the evidence is not complete. In some respects this hormone resembles estrogen.

Adrenal Cortex

The adrenal cortex produces a number of hormones, the best understood of which are: (1) *aldosterone,* which is similar in its action to desoxycorticosterone, but more potent. This hormone affects the renal tubules so that water, sodium and chloride are conserved and potassium is excreted; it apparently is necessary for life. Although the production and/or release of aldosterone appears to be independent of anterior pituitary "tropic" hormone control, the amount of aldosterone produced seems to be increased by ACTH until this effect is offset by increased cortisol produced in response to the ACTH. The production of aldosterone appears to be increased by several different mechanisms: (a) a fall in the serum sodium level, (b) a rise in serum potassium level, (c) constriction of the inferior vena cava, and (d) constriction of the common carotid artery. Gordon Farrell has presented evidence suggesting that aldosterone secretion by the zona glomerulosa of the adrenal cortex is regulated by a neurohumoral substance, *glomerulotropin,* arising in the posterior commissure-pineal area of the brain stem. It is of interest that the sodium-retaining effect of aldosterone can be inhibited by progestogens. (2) *Cortisol* and its derivative, *cortisone.* These corticosteroid or glucocorticoid hormones have as one of their prime actions the stimulation of the rate of glucose formation from noncarbohydrate precursors, either by diverting amino acids from protein synthesis to gluconeogenesis, or by diverting fatty acids from fat synthesis to gluconeogenesis. It appears that when a sufficient excess of either of these two groups of noncarbohydrate precursors is present, the other is spared as source material for cortisol-induced gluconeogenesis. Usually, however, there are not enough fatty acids available to prevent the utilization of amino acids for glucose formation; this leads to an insufficiency of amino

acids for protein synthesis. Under these circumstances, therefore, cortisol and cortisone have an *anti-anabolic effect.* The inhibition of protein anabolism involves all protein tissue, including the matrix of cartilage and of bone. When the available amino acids and fatty acids simultaneously are markedly reduced, there is a breakdown of protein tissues and of fatty tissues as well as an inhibition of new tissue formation in order to correct the deficit and to maintain the hormone-induced gluconeogenesis from these noncarbohydrate precursors. Under these extreme conditions, cortisol and cortisone have a *catabolic effect* as well as an anti-anabolic effect. In addition, these hormones appear to affect carbohydrate metabolism by increasing the deposition of glycogen in the liver, by decreasing the utilization of carbohydrate in the tissues, and by lowering the renal carbohydrate threshold. Cortisol and cortisone also cause a temporary increase in muscular efficiency, a reduction in fibrous tissue proliferation, a decrease in membrane permeability, an atrophy of lymphoid tissue, and sometimes a retention of sodium and water with a diuresis of potassium. These hormones are the precursors of the urinary corticosteroid metabolites and of some of the urinary 17-ketosteroid metabolites which have an adrenal origin. Because of their action on carbohydrate metabolism these compounds are sometimes referred to as *"sugar"* or *"S"* hormones. (3) An androgenic hormone. This substance (like the androgenic hormone of the testis) has a stimulating effect on protein tissue anabolism; this hormone stimulates the growth of axillary hair, has some other androgenic properties, and probably is the precursor of some of the 17-ketosteroid metabolites in the urine which have an adrenal origin. Because of the effect of this hormone on nitrogen metabolism, it is spoken of as the *"nitrogen"* or *"N"* hormone.

In addition, in the adrenal cortex there are substances necessary to maintain a normal renal function and to insure growth at a normal rate; these substances are found in the amorphous fraction of whole adrenal cortical extract. Sodium salts will decrease and potassium salts will increase the need for aldosterone. Substances are also present in the whole adrenal cortical extract which cause atrophy of the adrenal and the thymus glands. The "sugar" hormones of the adrenal cortex are produced by the stimulus of ACTH. Recent studies suggest that the "nitrogen" hormone of the adrenal cortex may be produced by the stimulus of this same ACTH; it also may be produced by the stimulation of another type of "adrenocorticotropic" hormone: LH (ICSH) and/or LTH and chorionic gonadotropin. The evidence favors the interpretation that the production and/or release of aldosterone is independent of anterior pituitary "tropic" hormone control. Estrogen and progestogen also are produced by the adrenal cortex; their role is unknown.

Although children almost from birth excrete in the urine cortisol metabolites in amounts that are normal for adults, children excrete practically no urinary 17-ketosteroid metabolites until they reach approximately 8 years of age. About the eighth year there is an important alteration in adrenal cortical function which has been termed the "adrenarche." This is to be differentiated from the onset at about the twelfth year of adult gonadal function, which is called "menarche" in the female and "Leydigarche" in the male. Recent studies have shown that the adrenal cortex can as readily be stimulated by ACTH to produce urinary 17-ketosteroid metabolites before the "adrenarche" as it can be after this event; furthermore, the administration of androgens leads to the same kinds and amounts of urinary 17-ketosteroid metabolites before the "adrenarche" as it does after this alteration. Thus it is probable that before the eighth year the adrenal cortex is not being stimulated by the pituitary "tropic" hormone that leads to the production of the "nitrogen" hormone. Since the adrenal cortex is being stimulated to produce adult amounts of cortisol almost from birth, these findings provide strong support for the concept that the anterior pituitary gland produces at least two different types of adrenocorticotropic hormones, one concerned with cortisol production, the other with "nitrogen" hormone production.

It has been demonstrated that the administration of ACTH leads to the release of cortisol, as indicated by a fall in the blood eosinophile level and a rise in the urinary uric acid to creatinine ratio; this provides a test of the responsiveness of the adrenal cortex for cortisol production. It has been shown also that the administration of epinephrine leads to stimulation of the central nervous system, which produces a release of ACTH from the anterior pituitary gland and then a release of cortisol from the adrenal cortex as indicated by alterations in the same indices (the blood eosinophile level and the urinary uric acid to creatinine ratio); this provides a test of the responsiveness of the anterior pituitary gland for ACTH production. Obviously, the test of pituitary gland responsiveness is not valid if the adrenal cortex is not responsive. These procedures are of value in determining the integrity of the pituitary-adrenal cortical system.

Adrenal Medulla

The adrenal medulla produces *epinephrine*, which causes in general the effect of stimulation of the sympathetic nervous system (sympathomimetic effects). Epinephrine constricts the peripheral blood vessels, thus raising the blood pressure, dilates the coronary arteries, increases the blood sugar and blood lactic acid by accelerating the rate of enzymatic breakdown of glycogen in the liver and the muscles, and increases the basal metabolic rate. It also stimulates the release of ACTH and TSH from the anterior pituitary gland. The evidence for an anterior pituitary "tropic" hormone affecting the adrenal medulla is meager. The release of epinephrine, however, does seem to be under the influence of stimulation from the central nervous system.

Thyroid

The thyrotropic, or thyroid-stimulating, hormone (TSH) of the anterior pituitary stimulates the thyroid gland to produce its hormone, *thyroxine*. The thyroid hormone has the following effects: (1) It raises the basal metabolism. (2) It is necessary for normal growth. (3) It maintains the normal excretion of water, salt and colloids. (4) It tends to reduce the level of the blood lipids, particularly cholesterol. (5) It decreases liver glycogen. (6) It increases protein catabolism. (7) It is necessary for normal emotional responsiveness, cerebral activity, sensory acuity, alertness, vasomotor and peristaltic activity. (8) It increases creatinuria. (9) It increases the irritability of the cardiac muscle. (10) It increases the tolerance to some types of drugs, particularly morphine and digitalis. (11) It increases the rate of absorption from the gastrointestinal tract. (12) It inhibits the production of TSH. (13) It causes enlargement of the adrenal cortex. (14) It increases the sensitivity of the organism to epinephrine. (15) It increases the production of gonadal hormones. (16) It increases bone resorption. Lack of the thyroid hormones causes the reverse of most of these effects. In the absence of adequate iodine, normal thyroid hormone is not produced.

The thyroid hormone, thyroxine (tetraiodothyronine), is formed in the follicles of the thyroid gland by the combination of iodide (trapped from the blood) and amino acids (tyrosine) to form diiodotyrosine and then thyroglobulin. The thyroglobulin is hydrolyzed in the gland to release thyroid hormones (chiefly thyroxine) under the influence of enzymes (protease and peptidase) which are activated by TSH. The released thyroxine in the blood is transported bound to a thyroxine-binding protein. In the peripheral tissues, the thyroxine is released from its protein carrier and converted to compounds with less iodine, chiefly triiodothyronine. The mechanisms by which thyroxine or other thyroid hormones exert their actions in the peripheral tissues are not clear. One suggestion advanced is that thyroxine increases the rate of metabolic processes by decreasing the efficiency of the enzyme activities by which cellular oxidations are coupled with phosphorylation. Thus, by "uncoupling" oxidative phosphorylations, the hormone makes available an increased amount of utilizable "high phosphate" energy so that oxidation is accelerated as phosphorylation is depressed. Other investigators believe that the action of thyroxine on the peripheral tissues is concerned with the control of some structural property rather than with the enzymes of oxidative phosphorylation.

A number of compounds have been utilized in the therapy of thyroid disorders because they exhibit antithyroid properties. These compounds have been shown to act: (1) by inhibiting the trapping of iodide by the thyroid gland, (2) by inhibiting the iodination steps in the synthesis of thyroxine, or (3) by a combination of (1) and (2). The net effect of these agents is to decrease the production of thyroid hormone. The antithyroid compounds include such substances as: (1) monovalent anions (perchlorate, chlorate, hypochlorite, periodate, iodate, biiodite, and nitrate), (2) thiocyanate and thiosulfate, (3) thiocarbamides (thiourea, thiouracil, and so forth), (4) aminobenzenes (sulfonamides, p-aminosalicylic acid), and (5) polyhydric phenols (resorcinol).

A substance called *thyrocalcitonin* in the physiologic state prevents an excessive hypercalcemic response to the parathyroid hormone by reducing a greater than physiologic amount of calcium in the plasma to a normal level. Whether this is a second hormone made by the thyroid gland or is really the hormone *calcitonin* made by the parathyroid glands but stored in the thyroid gland remains to be determined. The role of thyrocalcitonin in pathologic disorders of the thyroid and/or the parathyroid glands is not known.

Parathyroids

The *parathyroid hormone* regulates the calcium and phosphorus metabolism, through its actions on the excretion of these minerals by the kidney, on the release of these minerals from the skeleton (bone resorption), and on the absorption of calcium from the gastrointestinal tract. The hormone exerts its mineral effects by increasing the absorption of calcium from the gastrointestinal tract, by increasing the renal tubular reabsorption of calcium, and by increasing the excretion of phosphorus in the urine; this in turn leads to a decrease in the serum phosphorus level. The action of the parathyroid hormone in inducing phosphorus diuresis has been attributed to a decreased tubular reabsorption of phosphorus; recent evidence suggests that this effect of the hormone may result from an increased tubular secretion of phosphorus. The physical-chemical properties of the blood serum and the other body fluids tend to keep the product of the ions of calcium and phosphorus a constant. To maintain this constancy, more calcium is held in the serum when the serum inorganic phosphorus level is low. This added calcium comes from one of two sources: (1) the calcium which normally is circulating from the gastrointestinal tract by absorption to the serum and back again to the gastrointestinal tract by secretion with the enteric juices, or (2), failing this, the calcium which is stored in the skeleton. The net result of the added calcium is to raise the serum calcium level. When the serum calcium level becomes sufficiently elevated, hypercalciuria occurs which masks the increased renal tubular reabsorption of calcium. The parathyroid hormone exerts its protein effect by activating the osteoclasts to produce proteolytic enzymes which cause resorption of bone. A permissive level of vitamin D appears to be necessary for the parathyroid hormone to exert its actions. A low serum calcium level stimulates the parathyroid glands to increase their hormone production, and vice versa; when the serum calcium level is normal, a high serum phosphorus level may act as a stimulus to increased hormone production. There is little evidence that the anterior pituitary produces a "tropic" hormone which stimulates the parathyroid glands.

The parathyroid gland appears to produce a second hormone, *calcitonin*, which in the physiologic state prevents an excessive hypercalcemic response to the parathyroid hormone by reducing a greater than physiologic amount of calcium in the plasma to a normal level. The role of this hormone in pathologic disorders of the parathyroid gland is unknown. A substance with a similar action, *thyrocalcitonin,* has been isolated from the thyroid gland. Whether this is a second hormone made by the thyroid gland or is really calcitonin made by the parathyroid gland but stored in the thyroid gland remains to be determined.

Pancreas

The islands of Langerhans consist of two types of cells: the alpha cells, which appear to produce a hormone called *glucagon* (hyperglycemia-glycogenolytic factor, HGF); and the beta cells, which produce *insulin.* Glucagon appears to induce hyperglycemia by mobilizing liver glycogen through activation of phosphorylase; it may be under the control of an anterior pituitary tropic hormone which is either identical or closely associated with the growth hormone (somatotropic hormone, STH). At present the use of this hormone is still in the experimental stage. When the concentration of dextrose in the blood passing through the pancreas rises to a certain level, insulin production is increased. Insulin lowers the blood sugar level by increasing the oxidation of carbohydrate and the deposition of glycogen in the muscles and the liver. When there is a low blood sugar level, the low carbohydrate "fire" in the brain in turn stimulates the nervous system, and a stimulus is sent through the sympathetic nervous system (via the adrenal medulla) to the liver, resulting in increased glycogenolysis. This increases the blood dextrose level and, as a result, the carbohydrate oxidation. In insulin lack, when less carbohydrate is oxidized, more fat is burned, resulting in ketosis. Increased glycogenolysis causes the liver glycogen to fall; this stimulates the adrenal cortex to produce more of the "sugar" hormone, which increases the conversion of proteins into sugar (gluconeogenesis) with a resultant increase in the nitrogen excretion in the urine. Exogenous insulin therefore: (1) decreases fat combustion (hence decreases ketosis); (2) decreases gluconeogenesis from protein; (3) accelerates the formation of glycogen; (4) increases the combustion of carbohydrate; (5) decreases the insulin content of the pancreas; (6) protects the islet cells; and (7) counteracts the effect of the adrenocortical "sugar" hormone. The combination of (2), (3) and (4) lowers the blood sugar level. Insulin also induces an increase in the appetite. The synthesis of insulin is discussed in Chapter 6.

It has been proposed that there is only one basic mechanism for the action of insulin: to increase the permeability of the cell membrane to glucose. It is suggested that insulin could induce this change in cell permeability at the membrane surface either by facilitating the conversion of glucose through phosphorylation or oxidation into more lipid-soluble and hence more permeable compounds, or by altering the physical structure of the cell wall through the combining of the insulin protein with the membrane protein so that glucose can pass more easily into the cell. The other effects of insulin are believed to be the consequences of the increase in intracellular glucose. The same mechanism is used to explain the action of insulin on the liver, since it is assumed that the increased transfer of glucose into the cells of the anterior pituitary gland leads to an increase in the production and/or release of ACTH with its effects on adrenal cortical hormone production and/or release and thus on the metabolic processes in the liver. According to this theory, under certain circumstances cells may elaborate their own insulin-like lipoproteins which, by interfering with permeability, may be responsible for the development of insulin resistance.

Placenta

The placenta produces several types of hormones: (1) *anterior pituitary-like hormone,* (2) *progestogen (progesterone),* (3) *estrogen,* (4) *glucocorticoid,* and (5) *placental growth hormone—lactogen.* Anterior pituitary-like hormone is a *chorionic gonadotropin,* but has many similarities to LH (ICSH) or LTH of the anterior pituitary and induces most of the same effects. During the first few weeks of pregnancy, anterior pituitary-like hormone maintains the corpus luteum of pregnancy; this is spoken of as the period of "pituitary adoption." Hypophysectomy after this time does not interrupt pregnancy in animals. About the second or third month the placenta produces enough progestogen and estrogen so that the ovary may be removed in the human being without interruption of pregnancy. This is called the period of "ovarian adoption." The progestogen and estrogen seem to be identical with those produced by the ovary and produce the effects that have been described for these organs. Some of the steroid metabolites of adrenal glucocorticoid origin which are present in the

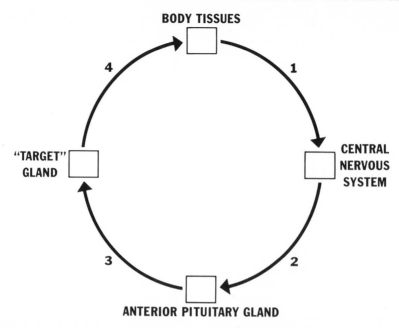

Figure 8–3. Diagram to illustrate the relations in an endocrine system of four components: the body tissues, the central nervous system, the anterior pituitary gland, and the "target" gland. The body tissue requirements stimulate (arrow *1*) the central nervous system to initiate or to stop the cycle; the central nervous system stimulates (arrow *2*) the anterior pituitary gland; this gland produces a hormone which stimulates (arrow *3*) the "target" gland; and the "target gland" produces a hormone which stimulates (arrow *4*) the body tissues. For further discussion, see text.

urine of the normal nonpregnant woman are markedly decreased in amount or absent in the urine of the normal pregnant woman, particularly during the eighth and ninth months; furthermore, after delivery the nonpregnant pattern of metabolite excretion quickly reappears. Since the normal pregnant woman has no manifestations of adrenal cortical insufficiency, these urinary metabolite changes suggest that the placenta also may produce hormones with glucocorticoid activity, which supply all the requirements for hormones of this type and hence temporarily suppress the production of the hormones of adrenal cortical origin, and which do not give rise to the same urinary metabolites as do the hormones of adrenal cortical origin. This phase of placental activity may be called the period of "adrenal cortical adoption." There is no evidence that either the central nervous system or the anterior pituitary gland has much influence on the placenta, at least after the first few days of pregnancy. A growth hormone has been isolated from the placenta; it may play an important role in the remarkable growth of the fetus that occurs during gestation. A lactogenic principle also has been identified; some evidence suggests that it may be identical with the placental growth hormone. Further discussion of the placental

growth hormone lactogen is given in Chapter 6.

Dynamic Physiology of the Hormones

From an anatomic viewpoint it is possible, with the knowledge available at present, to divide the various endocrine gland systems into groups depending upon the number of different tissues which are thought to participate in the function of each system. This classification, although arbitrary, is useful in the formulation of a concept of the integrated action of the hormones with each other and with the body as a whole.

The most complicated of these systems contains four components: the central nervous system, the anterior pituitary gland, the "target" gland, and the body tissues. The relations of this system are illustrated schematically in Figure 8–3. *It is probable that body tissue requirements always are basically responsible for the initiation of the physiologic adjustments in hormone activity.* Changes in the body tissues influence (arrow *1*) the central nervous system, and thus set in motion the cycle of hormone activity. The central nervous system, by way of neurohumoral pathways (arrow *2*) from the hypothalamus, influences the anterior pituitary gland to alter its production and/or release of a "tropic" hormone (arrow 3), which affects the "target" gland so that it changes its production and/or release of a "tissue-affecting" hormone (arrow 4), which brings about an adjustment in the body tissues.

A number of examples of the system shown in Figure 8–3 can be cited. The best, perhaps, is the mechanism involved in the onset of adolescence. In this, for reasons unknown, stimulating impulses arise in the central nervous system which travel by way of the neurohumoral pathways from the hypothalamus to the anterior pituitary gland, and lead to the production and/or release of the gonadotropic hormones (FSH, LH, and LTH). These gonadotropic hormones in the female stimulate the ovary to produce estrogen and progestogen, and in the male stimulate the testis to produce androgen and (?) inhibin; these "tissue-affecting" hormones produce the feminizing or masculinizing alterations, respectively, in the body tissues which constitute the clinical picture of developing puberty. Another example is the mechanism which induces ovulation in some women. Intercourse sets up nerve impulses from the hypothalamus which cause the anterior pituitary to release LH; this in turn stimulates the ovarian follicle to ovulate and to form a corpus luteum, which then produces progestogen and estrogen; progestogen with estrogen produces secretory changes in the endometrium and thus prepares the way for implantation of the ovum if fertilization occurs.

A striking example of the influence of the body tissues on hormone activity is found in the syndrome of adaptation (Selye) which the body exhibits to any type of noxious stimulus, such as a fracture, a burn, an infection, an operation, exposure to heat or cold, or a drug reaction. The stimulus arising from the local tissue damage in some obscure way acts upon the central nervous system, which in turn causes release from the anterior pituitary gland of ACTH; ACTH stimulates the adrenal cortex so that there is an increase in the production of "sugar" hormone (cortisol), which then inhibits the anabolism of protoplasm in the nondamaged parts of the body tissues, and thus floods the damage site with materials for tissue repair. The local stimulus for repair overrides the systemic adjustment against anabolism of protoplasm. The TSH-thyroid hormone system also appears to follow the scheme shown in Figure 8–3.

A somewhat less complicated system is illustrated in Figure 8–4. In this the requirements of the body tissues stimulate (arrow 1) the central nervous system; in turn the central nervous system stimulates (arrow 2) the pituitary gland, which puts out a hormone (arrow 3) which directly affects the body tissues. The anterior pituitary growth hormone and the posterior pituitary hormones (Pitocin and Pitressin) probably are endocrine secretions whose mechanism of regulation follows this scheme. Another example of this type of control is found in lactation, in which suckling stimulates the central nervous system, which then influences the anterior pituitary so that the lactogenic hormone is released, thereby causing the breast to secrete milk.

A different system of three components is shown in Figure 8–5. Here the requirements of the body tissues influence (arrow 1) the central nervous system, which in turn stimulates a gland other than the pituitary directly (arrow 2) and causes it to secrete a hormone (arrow 3) which affects the tissues of the body. The mechanism of regulation of epinephrine secretion probably follows this scheme. For example, emotion stimulates the

Figure 8–4. Diagram to illustrate the relations in an endocrine system of three components: the body tissues, the central nervous system, and the pituitary gland. The body tissue requirements stimulate (arrow 1) the central nervous system to initiate or to stop the cycle; the central nervous system stimulates (arrow 2) the pituitary gland; and this gland produces a hormone which stimulates (arrow 3) the body tissues. For further discussion, see text.

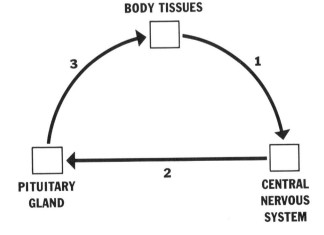

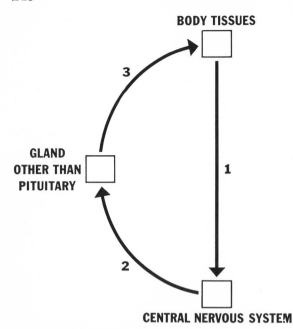

BODY TISSUES

GLAND OTHER THAN PITUITARY

CENTRAL NERVOUS SYSTEM

Figure 8–5. Diagram to illustrate the relations in an endocrine system of three components: the body tissues, the central nervous system, and a gland other than the pituitary. The body tissue requirements stimulate (arrow *1*) the central nervous system to initiate or to stop the cycle; the central nervous system stimulates (arrow *2*) a gland other than the pituitary; and this gland produces a hormone which stimulates (arrow *3*) the body tissues. For further discussion, see text.

central nervous system, which sends impulses to the adrenal medulla; this gland in turn releases epinephrine, which then affects body tissues.

Certain of the hormone-regulating systems seem to follow the simple pattern illustrated in Figure 8–6. In this, the body tissue deficit stimulates the endocrine gland, which then produces more hormone and corrects the body deficit. The activities of the parathyroid glands and of that part of the adrenal cortex which produces aldosterone apparently are regulated by such a mechanism. The hormone activity of the placenta also seems to be under this type of control.

When the central nervous system and the body tissues are not considered, we can see certain general interrelations between pituitary tropic hormones and the tissue-affecting hormones which are stimulated by them. The best known example of these is shown in Figure 8–7. In this, FSH stimulates (arrow *1*) the production of estrogen, which in turn stimulates (arrow *2*) the production of LH and LTH from the anterior pituitary. These two gonadotropic hormones in turn stimulate (arrow *3*) the production of progestogen, which then stimulates (arrow *4*) the production of FSH, thus completing a cycle. On the other hand, the estrogen that is produced inhibits (arrow *5*) the production and/or release of FSH, and similarly the progestogen that is produced inhibits (arrow *6*) the production and/or release of LH and LTH. Because of a lack of pure pituitary preparations, it has not been possible to demonstrate

whether LH and LTH have an inhibitory effect upon estrogen production, or whether FSH has an inhibitory effect upon progestogen production.

Similarly, the effect of various hormones on the sugar level of the blood may be presented diagrammatically (Fig. 8–8). In the normal person the influences which tend to raise it above normal must be balanced by the in-

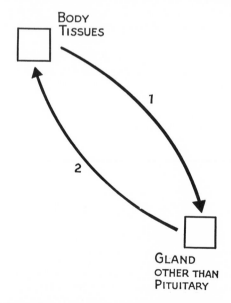

BODY TISSUES

GLAND OTHER THAN PITUITARY

Figure 8–6. Diagram to illustrate the relations in an endocrine system of two components: a gland other than the pituitary, and the body tissues. The body tissue requirements stimulate (arrow *1*) the gland to produce a hormone which stimulates (arrow *2*) the body tissues. For further discussion, see text.

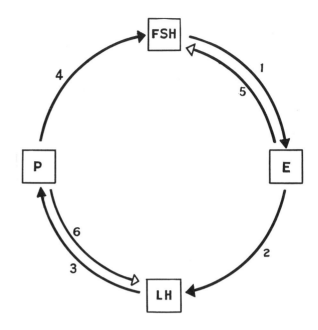

Figure 8–7. Diagram to illustrate certain relations between the anterior pituitary gonadotropic hormones and the gonadal hormones. Solid-headed arrows indicate stimulation; open-headed arrows indicate inhibition; FSH = follicle-stimulating hormone; E = estrogen; LH = luteinizing hormone; P = progestogen. The anterior pituitary gonadotropic hormone *FSH* stimulates (arrow *1*) the production of estrogen (*E*); *E* stimulates (arrow *2*) the production of the anterior pituitary gonadotropic hormone *LH*; *LH* stimulates (arrow *3*) the production of progestogen (*P*); and *P* stimulates (arrow *4*) the production of *FSH*. In contrast, *E* inhibits (arrow *5*) the production of *FSH*; and *P* inhibits (arrow *6*) the production of *LH*. It is not known whether *LH* inhibits the production of *E* or whether *FSH* inhibits the production of *P*. For further discussion, see text.

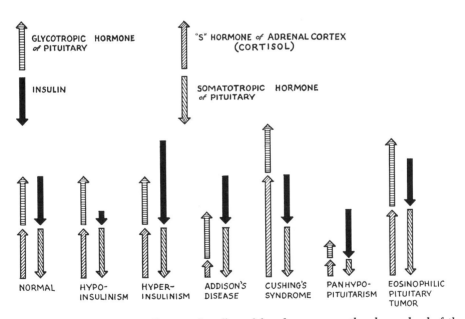

Figure 8–8. Diagrams to illustrate the effect of four hormones on the glucose level of the blood serum in various endocrine conditions. For discussion, see text.

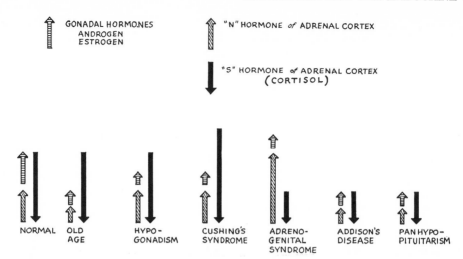

Figure 8–9. Diagrams to illustrate the effect of three hormones on endosteal bone formation. For discussion, see text.

fluences which tend to lower it below normal. In Figure 8–8 an influence which tends to raise the glucose level is represented by an arrow which points upward, and one which tends to lower the level by an arrow which points downward. Only four influences are represented: insulin, somatotropic hormone, glycotropic hormone, and "sugar" hormone. It is assumed that other influences, such as liver, muscle, and epinephrine, are constant and in the normal range. Insulin, of course, is depicted as a glucose level-lowering influence. Since the somatotropic hormone of the anterior pituitary causes anabolism of protoplasm, it reduces the gluconeogenesis from protein; hence it is depicted as a glucose level-lowering influence. The glycotropic hormone is represented as a glucose level-raising influence because it antagonizes insulin. The "sugar" hormone of the adrenal cortex (cortisol) promotes gluconeogenesis from protein and hence is shown as a glucose level-raising influence. The various disease entities involving these four hormones also are represented in Figure 8–8. In this diagram only the arrows depicting the hormones directly affected are shortened or lengthened. In most conditions *an abnormality of one hormone is partially offset by a compensatory change in another.*

The same type of analysis may be made diagrammatically (Fig. 8–9) of the effect of various hormones on endosteal bone formation. The influences which cause decreased bone formation are balanced against those which cause increased bone formation in the normal person. In Figure 8–9 an influence which tends to increase bone formation is

depicted as an arrow which points upward, and one which tends to decrease bone formation by an arrow which points downward. Only three influences are represented: the gonadal hormones, the "nitrogen" hormone of the adrenal cortex, and the "sugar" hormone of the adrenal cortex (cortisol). It is assumed that other influences, such as the parathyroid hormone, the thyroid hormone, and the somatotropic hormone of the pituitary gland, are constant and in the normal range. The gonadal hormones are depicted as bone formation-increasing influences, since their lack leads to osteoporosis; and adrenal cortical "nitrogen" hormone is depicted as a bone formation-increasing influence, since children with an excess of this hormone (adrenogenital syndrome) grow much more rapidly than do normal children. The "sugar" hormone of the adrenal cortex (cortisol) is represented as a bone formation-decreasing influence, since excess of this hormone (Cushing's syndrome) leads to osteoporosis. Various disease entities resulting from these three influences also are represented in Figure 8–9.

In a similar way graphic representations can be made of the effect of opposing hormonal influences on various body tissues, e.g., prostate, breast, muscles, and others.

Pathologic Physiology of the Main Endocrine Abnormalities

It is beyond the scope of this chapter to discuss in detail the pathology of the various disturbances recognized as endocrine dysfunction. These disturbances may be divided roughly into (1) hyperfunction, (2) hypofunction, and (3) dysfunction. There is probably some degree of dysfunction in almost all states of hyperfunction. In general, it is clear from Figure 8–3 that hyperfunction may result because any one of the four arrows is too great. The body tissue requirements may be increased as a result of fever or damage, or the body tissues may be resistant to the effects of the hormones, and hence larger amounts must be produced. Arrow 2 may be too great because of lesions in the central nervous system which stimulate excessively the neurohumoral pathways to the anterior pituitary and thus increase the width of the arrows all around the diagram. The anterior pituitary may be hyperfunctioning because of a tumor or a hyperplasia of the gland. Finally, the target gland may be hyperfunctioning because of a tumor or a hyperplasia.

In a similar way, hypofunction can be induced by a break in the cycle at almost any point. With destructive lesions in the hypothalamus, the central nervous system may fail to stimulate the anterior pituitary; in turn, with destructive lesions in the anterior pituitary, the target gland may not receive the hormone stimulation; with destruction of the target gland, the body tissues no longer receive hormones. As indicated earlier, there is a compensatory increase in the production of some hormones when those that follow are eliminated by disease. For example, if arrow 4 is removed because of the destruction of the target gland, arrows 3 and 2 usually show a compensatory increase in an effort to get the system back into adjustment. Similarly, if there is destruction of the anterior pituitary, it might be expected that the impulses from the hypothalamus would be greater than normal.

In addition, we can conceive of conditions in which the metabolism of the hormone produced by the target gland is abnormal, and hence upon body tissues the secretion has some of the effects of a normal hormone, but not all; this is a form of hormonal imbalance that cannot be adjusted by an increase or decrease in the size of the arrows in Figure 8–3. Some recent experiments have illustrated this type of mechanism in animals. In these the ovaries were transplanted into the spleen. The hormones produced by the ovaries were carried by the portal circulation directly to the liver and inactivated. As a result the ovarian hormones were not able to exert their usual inhibitory effect upon the pituitary gon-adotropins. Pituitary gonadotropins were released in excessive amounts and produced excessive stimulation of the ovary, so that finally granulosa cell tumors were produced. It is conceivable that hormone imbalance may thus eventually lead to tumor formation in man.

Recently attention has been focused on the "autoimmune" diseases (see Chap. 3). In these conditions because of damage to the hormone-producing cells, prehormonal moieties and fragments normally retained within the cells escape into the circulating blood and serve as antigens for inducing antibodies or cytotoxic substances which cause inflammation, gland cell destruction, and interference with or inhibition of normal hormonal actions. Chronic thyroiditis and exophthalmic goiter may represent disorders of this type.

An attempt will now be made to analyze the pathologic physiology and mechanism of disease for some of the better known endocrine disorders.

Hypothalamic Precocity

Lesions in the hypothalamus may lead to an early release of impulses to the anterior pituitary gland. If these impulses activate the release of gonadotropins, the gonads will be stimulated to precocious activity. There is a suggestion that lesions in the region of the mammillary bodies may lead to release of FSH, and lesions in the region of the pineal body may lead to release of LH (ICSH) and/or LTH. In the female the release of FSH will start the cycle of ovarian activity and, if a little LH also is present, will lead to estrogen production, feminization, corpus luteum formation, progestogen and estrogen production and menstruation; in the male the release of FSH will have little effect on the testes unless they first have been matured by androgen. The release of LH (ICSH) and/or LTH alone will have little effect in the female, but in the male will lead to stimulation of the Leydig cells, androgen production, and masculinization. It is pertinent to this discussion that lesions in the pineal body lead to precocity in males, but not in females, while lesions in the mammillary bodies have been found in polyostotic fibrous dysplasia, a condition characterized by precocity in females, but not in males.

It should be pointed out that true precocity which arises from lesions in the hypothalamus must be distinguished from pseudoprecocity which results from hormone-producing neoplasms of the gonads or the adrenal cortex.

Fröhlich's Syndrome

A great many fat children who are slow in developing are thought by some physicians to have Fröhlich's syndrome, or adiposa dystrophia genitalis. It is preferable, however, to limit the diagnosis of Fröhlich's syndrome to cases in which there is a definite pathologic lesion: a tumor or a craniopharyngioma in the region of the hypothalamus which destroys the neurohumoral pathways to the anterior pituitary. As a result of this destruction, these children do not show any evidences of adolescence, because the release of gonadotropic hormones cannot occur, although they are normal from an endocrinologic viewpoint up to the time of puberty. In addition, the lesion in the hypothalamus often results in stimulation of the hypothalamic appetite center, and, because of excessive appetite, the children become obese. These children, although lacking the neurohumoral stimulation for the release of gonadotropins, seem to be able to produce adequate amounts of TSH and ACTH. Children with Fröhlich's syndrome are differentiated from those with panhypopituitarism by the fact that they lack the evidences of thyroid underfunction and adrenal cortical insufficiency. These patients should be ideal candidates for stimulation therapy with the pituitary gonadotropic hormones when adequate preparations of these substances become available. For example, males can be successfully stimulated to increased testicular function by the administration of chorionic gonadotropin.

The majority of obese children who are slow in passing through puberty do not have Fröhlich's syndrome or dystrophia adiposa genitalis; in fact, they do not have any endocrine abnormality. Such children constitute one of the commonest problems of pediatric endocrinology. Boys with this condition usually do not have genitalia that actually are underdeveloped for their chronologic age; the genital structures merely appear small in relation to the excessive mass of body fat in which they are hidden. Occasionally, however, true underdevelopment may occur. As soon as these obese boys and girls begin to lose weight, they develop sexually at an unusually rapid rate. The explanation probably is found in the fact that the gonadal hormones are very soluble in fat. Although the gonads of these obese children are producing normal amounts of hormones for children of their age, the hormones, as fast as they are produced, are being taken up and stored in the excessive body fat that is being deposited. Thus the hormones do not have the opportunity to exert their normal effects on the development of the genital and secondary sexual structures as long as these children are increasing their body content of fatty tissue. However, as soon as weight reduction begins with destruction of fatty tissue, the stored gonadal hormones are released from the fat, and by augmenting the hormones that currently are being produced by the gonads bring about an accelerated rate of development. The basic therapeutic approach to most children with obesity, therefore, is weight reduction rather than hormone administration.

Adolescent Mammoplasia

In females, as indicated earlier, ovarian function cannot be initiated until FSH is released, since LH and/or LTH alone seems to have no effect on the ovary in the absence of FSH. Menarche cannot appear, therefore, until FSH release occurs; ovulation cannot take place before LH release occurs.

In the male, however, ICSH (LH) and LTH must be released for testicular androgen production to begin. The tubules of the testis are not responsive to FSH until they have been considerably developed by the androgen; only then do they begin to produce their hormone, which, for purposes of discussion, is called inhibin. Thus, for a time, the adolescent boy is under the influence of androgen without inhibin. The androgen in the absence of inhibin causes enlargement of the breasts and the prostate; then, as tubular function increases and inhibin production occurs, the stimulating effect of the androgen on the breasts and prostate is neutralized, and these tissues regress. This enlargement and then regression of the breasts is a physiologic process referred to as adolescent mammoplasia.

Hypothalamic or Psychogenic Amenorrhea

In this condition, it is thought that, as a result of some emotional trauma, there is a block to the normal continuous release of impulses from the hypothalamus to the anterior pituitary for the production and/or release of LH. With the cessation of production of LH, the ovarian follicle can no longer make estrogen, and amenorrhea develops. However, since there is no block to the release of FSH, the excretion level of FSH in the urine is not reduced. It is postulated that in the absence of LH the stimulated follicle still produces some substance which, while not estrogenic, has the property of inhibiting FSH. In hypothalamic amenorrhea this substance prevents the FSH production from becoming increased as it is in those types of amenorrhea in which the primary defect is in the ovary.

Patients with hypothalamic amenorrhea are the women who stop having periods after a violent emotional episode, such as fear in a hurricane, a bombing, or a fire, or the women who have emotional maladjustments, marital troubles or similar difficulties. This condition occurs commonly in students and nurses away from home for the first time, in women whose husbands have gone away to war, in women who have had one pregnancy and fear another, and so on. In some women it is not possible to find the underlying psychologic difficulty without considerable probing by a competent psychiatrist. The incidence of this type of amenorrhea has dropped considerably since the cessation of World War II. Women with hypothalamic amenorrhea always give a history of normal, regular periods with abrupt cessation of menstruation after an emotional event. Examination of the pelvic organs reveals a lack of estrogen as indicated by an atrophic vaginal mucosa on smear and an atrophic endometrium on biopsy. The atrophic endometrium can be demonstrated also by giving these patients a course of progestogen and finding that they fail to bleed after the progestogen has been discontinued. It should be pointed out that manipulation of the pelvic organs during examination or biopsy may produce sufficient stimulation of the central nervous system to overcome the block temporarily so that LH is released; after such procedures these patients frequently ovulate within 24 hours and have normal menstruation from a secretory endometrium in about 14 days. One wonders whether the interruption of regular coitus is partially responsible for the development of this type of amenorrhea in the married woman; in this respect she develops a pattern that resembles that of the rabbit, which does not ovulate unless it copulates. Although these women lack estrogen, the urinary gonadotropin titer is normal rather than high, as it is in postmenopausal women who lack estrogen because of ovarian failure.

The steps in establishing the diagnosis of "hypothalamic amenorrhea" are as follows: (1) the history of psychic trauma just preceding the onset of amenorrhea is obtained if possible; (2) the excretion of the FSH in the urine is tested and found to be normal, thus eliminating amenorrhea that results from a disturbance primary in the anterior pituitary gland (where the FSH excretion is low) and amenorrhea that results from a disturbance primary in the ovaries (where the FSH excretion is high); (3) the absence of estrogenic effects in the pelvic tissues is established by endometrial biopsy, vaginal smear, or failure to bleed after an adequate course of progestogen; and (4) the ability of the endometrium to respond to estrogen withdrawal with bleeding is demonstrated by administering and then terminating an adequate course of estrogen. If bleeding does not occur, a history of exposure of the endometrium to infection, to radium or other radioactive materials, or to x-radiation should be sought, and, if obtained, usually will eliminate the diagnosis of "hypothalamic amenorrhea." A moderate decrease in the urinary excretion of 17-ketosteroids is consistent with the diagnosis of hypothalamic amenorrhea.

The administration of LH in the form of chorionic gonadotropin replaces the missing hormone and causes these patients to produce estrogen, so that they will then bleed after a course of progestogen. Furthermore, small amounts of estrogen will stimulate the anterior pituitary to release LH, and, in some patients at least, the continuous administration of small doses of estrogen has been followed by the return of regular ovarian cycles with ovulation. It will be recalled that, once some release of LH has been induced by the estrogenic therapy, the follicle will then make more estrogen. This in turn will stimulate the pituitary to release further amounts of LH, which will then be sufficient to induce ovulation and corpus luteum formation. Thus the small amount of estrogen may restore the entire situation to normal. In some patients the return of regular bleeding (from the mechanism just given or from cyclic hormone therapy with estrogen followed by progestogen and estrogen) is sufficient reassurance to remove the psychologic block. Psychotherapy, of course, plays a considerable role in the treatment of these patients. An effective regimen for inducing cyclic hormone therapy with long-acting parenteral preparations is the following: *Injection A*—20 mg. of estradiol valerate (Delestrogen) intramuscularly on Day 1, *Injection B*—250 mg. of 17-alpha-hydroxyprogesterone caproate (Delalutin) combined with 5 mg. of estradiol valerate intramuscularly on Day 14, and then *Injection A* alternating with *Injection B* once every 14 days starting on Day 28. Uterine bleeding with endometrial desquamation usually takes place on about Day 28 and recurs every 28 days as long as the regular schedule of alternating injections every 14 days is followed. A preparation (Deluteval) is now available in which the estrogenic ester and the progestational ester are combined in the ratio of *Injection B.*

It is probable that the amenorrhea in anorexia nervosa and in the women incarcerated in concentration camps during the war is also in part of the "hypothalamic" type, since in many cases the cessation of menses occurred before any significant loss in weight. Chronic starvation, of course, is a well-recognized cause of cessation of pituitary, ovarian, and uterine activity.

Acromegaly

Acromegaly is the clinical syndrome which arises when the eosinophile (acidophile) cells of the anterior pituitary produce excessive amounts of hormones because of adenoma formation. It will be recalled that the anterior pituitary can be divided into three types of cells: the acidophile, or "A," cells, the basophile, or "B," cells, and the chromophobe, or "C," cells. Only the "A" and "B" cells are thought to produce hormones. Adenoma of the "A" cells may lead to three groups of clinical manifestations: (1) symptoms due to the pressure of the expanding lesion within the sella turcica; (2) symptoms due to the excessive amounts of the hormones produced by the "A" cells; and (3) symptoms due to the inadequate amounts of the hormones produced by the "B" cells because of interference of the expanding "A" cell tumor with the hormone production of these "B" cells. The progressive stages, therefore, in the gradual development of acromegaly and in the gradual expansion in the size of the adenoma of the eosinophile cells would be (1) the development of evidences of excessive production of hormones of the "A" cells without other evidences of intracranial pressure or of interference with "B" cell function; (2) the appearance of interference with "B" cell function, which would include chiefly a loss of gonadal function in the males and amenorrhea in the females; and finally (3) the development of pressure symptoms, which indicate that the lesion within the sella turcica has expanded to the point where it is impinging upon the bony structures and thus giving headache, lassitude, insomnia, and irritability, or upon the optic nerves and thus producing visual difficulties and, ultimately, blindness.

The manifestations of excessive "A" cell activity are chiefly those produced by the growth (somatotropic) hormone (STH). There is an increase in the size of all the organs of the body: the heart, the lungs, the kidneys, the spleen, and other structures. At the same time there is a marked increase in the size of the acral parts: the nose, the chin, the hands, the feet, and the ears. It is this enlargement of the acral parts that gives the name to the syndrome. Of course, if the eosinophile adenoma arises before closure of the epiphyses at the end of adolescence, gigantism may result. In addition to the evidences of increased growth hormone, there also is evidence of increased production of lactogenic hormone. Almost all these patients will be found to have persistent lactation; in other words, if one examines the breast carefully, he can usually express some secretion from it. In some patients there is spontaneous lactorrhea.

Another hormone produced by the anterior pituitary "A" cells is the "diabetogenic" or glycotropic hormone. This hormone may be responsible for the carbohydrate abnormalities found in acromegaly. However, some investigators think that a combination of STH and ACTH is responsible for the carbohydrate abnormalities in this condition. A diabetic type of glucose tolerance curve is found, and at the same time these patients are frequently insulin-resistant.

There is little to indicate that ACTH is produced in excess in this condition. In a few instances excessive production of adrenal cortical "sugar" hormone (cortisol) has been demonstrated by biologic tests, and in a few cases the 17-ketosteroid excretion has been elevated; but, by and large, these biologic and chemical tests of adrenal cortical hormone production have given results within normal limits in acromegaly.

TSH also may be produced in excess in these patients, and this may account for the fact that many of them have an elevated basal metabolic rate. At the same time their thyroid glands are large, and it is not possible to determine whether this is the result of excessive stimulation from TSH or part of the general "megaly" of all organs. Other manifestations of hyperthyroidism usually are not apparent. The growth hormone itself causes an increase in the rate of cellular metabolism.

Attention is called to the fact that in most of these patients there is a moderate to marked elevation in the serum inorganic phosphorus level of the blood without a concomitant fall in the serum calcium level. There is considerable evidence to indicate that under such circumstances the elevation of the serum inorganic phosphorus level is an index of the pituitary growth hormone activity. Furthermore, it can be shown that therapeutic measures, such as removal of the tumor, x-radiation to the pituitary, or gonadal hormone administration (*vide infra*), which are inducing a beneficial response, will at the same time cause a fall in the elevated serum inorganic phosphorus level.

Recent investigations have shown that many patients with acromegaly are markedly benefited during the administration of moderate to large doses of estrogens and/or androgens, which alleviate the symptoms of headache, insomnia, irritability, lassitude, numbness, and tingling in the hands, and decrease the size of the hands and feet. At the same time these hormones also cause a fall in the serum inorganic phosphorus level which appears to be an index of the improvement of these patients with therapy. It is thought that the hormones produce these beneficial effects directly by inhibiting the action or production of the anterior pituitary growth hormone rather than indirectly by replacing gonadal hormone deficiency. It is of interest that the serum inorganic phosphorus level usually is not elevated in those acromegalic women who still are having normal cyclical ovarian function; this finding is interpreted as indicating some degree of inhibition of the growth hormone by the endogenous estrogen.

When a suitable ratio of androgen to estrogen is used, the unwanted actions of the individual hormones on the genital organs and the accessory sexual structures are neutralized and thus practically eliminated without interfering with the beneficial pituitary growth hormone-inhibiting and anabolic effects of these substances in acromegaly. The therapy with the proper combination is applicable, therefore, to women and children as well as to men. The administration of both types of gonadal hormone in combination has been facilitated by the development of esters of these steroids, such as testosterone enanthate (Delatestryl) and estradiol valerate (Delestrogen), which in appropriate doses (200 mg. of the testosterone ester and 20 mg. of the estradiol ester) are effective for about one month after a single intramuscular injection. Larger and more frequent doses probably are indicated in treating acromegaly. Also, a preparation (Deladumone) is available in which both the androgenic ester and the estrogenic ester are combined into one formulation (in the ratio of 90 mg. of testosterone enanthate to 4 mg. of estradiol valerate).

A suitably balanced preparation of androgen with estrogen should be useful in reducing the pituitary growth hormone hyperactivity of preadolescent children of either sex with gigantism while still preserving the existing potential of these children for normal sexual development and function. Large doses of androgen alone, estrogen alone, or androgen and estrogen in combination, cause a marked acceleration in the rate of skeletal maturation with fusion of the growing ends (epiphyses) of the long bones to the shafts (i.e., closure of the epiphyses). This will terminate linear growth and prevent further gigantism. It should be noted that such therapy will not convert these excessively tall children into acromegalic individuals, because the excess pituitary growth hormone production also is suppressed by the hormone combination.

In certain fulminating cases of acromegaly or gigantism with a rapidly growing tumor accompanied by progressing visual field defects and increasing local pressure symptoms, hormone therapy may be ineffective. If such patients do not respond promptly to large doses of hormones, they should be hypophysectomized without delay.

Attention also is called to the fact that acromegalic patients frequently show a generalized osteoporosis, which involves the bones of the spine in particular. The osteoporosis is present in the bodies of the vertebrae even though there is evidence of marked increase in the size of the vertebrae. This overgrowth of the vertebrae is particularly pronounced in the thoracic and lumbar spine, and occurs in the antero-posterior diameter in such a way that the enlarged bodies of the vertebrae interfere with each other as the patient attempts to bend over, so that he can no longer touch the floor. At the same time there is no loss of lateral motion. This test is of some value in the diagnosis of acromegaly. Patients with acromegaly also have an overgrowth of the mandible, but not of the teeth, and hence the teeth become separated; this manifestation may be useful in diagnosis. When these patients are studied on a metabolic regimen, they are found to be in a negative calcium balance, and some investigators think that there is a correlation between the negative calcium balance and the negative nitrogen balance. In other words, in these patients there is not enough protein to go around, and the bones, because of a low "priority rating," do not get enough to keep on forming matrix. This situation also is corrected by the administration of estrogens and/or androgens, in that these patients are then put into a positive calcium balance.

Panhypopituitarism (Simmonds' Cachexia, Sheehan's Syndrome, Pituitary Dwarfism)

Under this heading we shall discuss the syndromes in which there is hypofunction of all the hormones produced by the anterior pituitary gland. There can be, of course, all degrees of panhypopituitarism.

The etiology of the condition varies considerably. In the pituitary dwarf the pituitary gland is probably congenitally abnormal and thus fails to function. In the Sheehan syndrome there is thrombosis in the blood vessels of the anterior pituitary gland in a woman during a difficult labor, and thereafter there develops, slowly but unmistakably over a period of years, the full-blown picture of hypofunction of all activities of the anterior pituitary. Other cases of panhypopituitarism arise as a result of the destruction of the pituitary gland with the growth of a chromophobe adenoma (which is not in itself producing hormones); however, this lesion usually does not lead to the characteristic picture of Simmonds' cachexia. The lesion responsible for this latter condition is not entirely clear; in this disorder not only is there hypofunction of all the elements of the anterior pituitary, but also superimposed on this a marked degree of malnutrition. The difference may be simply a matter of degree.

The loss of the tropic hormones from the "A" and "B" cells of the anterior pituitary results in the loss of stimulation to all the target glands. Thus there is no stimulation to the adrenal cortex, the thyroid, and the gonads, and these glands in turn produce inadequate amounts of their hormones. These patients are hypoglycemia-unresponsive; that is, they do not produce from their adrenal cortices steroids of the "sugar" hormone type (cortisol) when the blood sugar has been reduced with insulin. The 17-ketosteroid excretion is practically zero, indicating that the precursors of these substances are not produced by the adrenal or the male gonad. The basal metabolic rate is low, and the patients have other evidences of myxedema (so-called pituitary myxedema). Finally, they have hypofunction of the gonads with loss of libido, aspermatogenesis, amenorrhea, loss of body hair, and weakness.

Attention is called to the fact that there is no good evidence for a pituitary tropic hormone that regulates the activity of the parathyroid glands. Thus in panhypopituitarism there is no abnormality in the levels of serum calcium and serum phosphorus. Similarly, the glomerulosa of the adrenal cortex, which produces aldosterone, is not under the influence of the anterior pituitary. For this reason, an abnormality in serum sodium or serum potassium concentration is rare in panhypopituitarism. In this respect these patients differ sharply from patients with Addison's disease, in whom there is evidence of a defect in the production of aldosterone as well as in the production of the "sugar" and "nitrogen" types of hormones. These patients also can be differentiated from those with adrenal insufficiency of the Addison's type by the fact that the latter have pigmentation, while the patients with adrenal insufficiency due to panhypopituitarism do not. The reason for this discrepancy is not clear.

Since these patients lack the hormones produced by the target glands, the most obvious therapy is to replace these hormones. However, it should be pointed out that the administration of any one of these compounds greatly upsets the endocrine balance, since none of the other hormones is present in appreciable amounts. For this reason thyroid, insulin, androgen, estrogen and adrenal cortical steroids must be administered to these patients with considerable caution, and the dosage gradually increased. This mechanism accounts for the unusual sensitivity of patients with panhypopituitarism to any kind of medication. Complete replacement therapy consists in the administration of (1) adrenal cortical "sugar" hormone (cortisol); (2) androgenic compounds to replace the "nitrogen" hormone of the adrenal cortex (which is similar to androgen); (3) thyroid; and (4) gonadal hormones, such as estrogen and progestogen in the female, or androgen in the male. These hormones then will bring about developmental changes in the panhypopituitary dwarfs, or restore the tissues toward normal to a considerable degree in those patients in whom the panhypopituitarism developed after they had become adults.

Ideal replacement therapy, of course, would be the administration of the pure pituitary tropic hormones to induce physiologic stimulation of the target glands. Human anterior pituitary growth hormones are effective, but not available in sufficient quantity for practical therapy. Pure adrenocorticotropic hormone has been prepared. This substance is potent, and can be used in such patients. Thyrotropic hormone and the gonadotropic hormones have been prepared by various methods, but none of the preparations is pure, although some are potent. These latter pituitary hormone preparations are open to the objection that they are made from animal glands and hence are foreign protein derivatives; because of their lack of purity they tend to induce antibody and foreign protein reactions in the patients to whom they are administered. Perhaps the most purified of the pituitary tropic hormones is Prolactin, the lactogenic hormone [identical with the luteotropic hormone (LTH)]. This has been available, but its use has not been of much benefit to patients with panhypopituitarism. It seems best, therefore, since these patients are extremely sensitive to reactions of all sorts, to avoid the expensive and reaction-producing impure protein preparations of the pituitary for the time being, and to give these patients replacement therapy in the form of the steroids and of the thyroid hormone.

Pituitary Amenorrhea and Pituitary-Ovarian Hypofunction

A considerable number of women have a decreased production of the gonadotropins from the basophile cells without evidences of any decreased production of the hormones from the "A" cells. When this condition occurs before puberty, it is analogous to Fröhlich's syndrome. However, the condition also occurs in some women who previously have had normal menstrual periods and who for unknown reasons have stopped producing gonadotropic hormones. Since it is known that the pituitary tropic hormones, particularly the gonadotropins, are sensitive to the loss of certain of the vitamin B fractions and to protein starvation, these patients may have early manifestations of anorexia nervosa. On the other hand, the loss of gonadotropins and the cessation of menses occur in many of these patients before there has been any appreciable weight loss, so that it is hard to believe that anorexia is the sole cause. The gonadotropin titer is very low, and as a result the gonad is not stimulated; consequently there is no production of estrogen, no ovulation, and no corpus luteum to produce progestogen and estrogen. The breasts are flat; the uterine endometrium and the vaginal mucosa show atrophy.

In some women, the decreased production of the pituitary gonadotropins results in menstrual irregularities with lack of ovulation rather than in amenorrhea. These patients usually present themselves as infertility problems.

Rational therapy is the administration of pituitary gonadotropic substances. Recently, two preparations of human origin containing a high level of FSH activity have been used clinically: (1) a human pituitary gland preparation, and (2) a post-menopausal urine preparation. When one of these preparations in a suitable dosage is injected in the proper sequence with chorionic gonadotropin, a hormone also of human origin which has many of the effects found in LH (and perhaps LTH), follicle maturation and ovulation occurs. This results in the elimination of the amenorrhea and/or the resumption of normal ovulatory menstrual cycles. About half of these previously infertile women have become pregnant after this therapy. Unfortunately, superfetation with multiple births occurs with considerable frequency. Whether this can be eliminated by adjustment of the amount or the timing of the dosage, by greater purification of the preparations, or by the addition of other hormonal agents, or whether the development of multiple follicles simultaneously is inherent in this form of therapy remains to be determined. Human gonadotropin therapy for infertility is most effective in women with low endogenous gonadotropin titers, is infrequently effective in women with normal endogenous gonadotropin levels, and is never effective in women with elevated gonadotropin levels.

Very similar results are being obtained also in the same type of women with pituitary-ovarian hypofunction and infertility from the administration of clomiphene citrate, an analogue of the nonsteroidal estrogen, chlorotrianisene. This compound may act either directly on the hypothalamicopituitary axis causing an increase in FSH output, or on the ovary sensitizing it to respond more readily to endogenous gonadotropins. However, most of the evidence suggests that clomiphene citrate has marked antiestrogenic activity and thus by removing the inhibitory effect of the estrogen causes an increase in the endogenous FSH production. It is not clear whether the compound primarily also causes an increase in the LH or the LTH production by the pituitary. The women who respond with ovulation to clomiphene citrate may be only those in whom the pituitary gland is capable of producing LH and LTH once follicle maturation and estrogen production have been initiated. Cystic enlargement of the ovaries, probably related to the use of larger doses of clomiphene citrate than are required for follicle maturation and ovulation, has been troublesome during the early studies on this compound, and should be watched for in all patients in whom the agent is used. Approximately three-quarters of the anovulatory women have become ovulatory, and about half of the treated women have become pregnant. The incidence of multiple births has been somewhat higher than normal with clomiphene citrate as well as with human gonadotropin therapy. Clomiphene citrate is not effective in women with elevated gonadotropin levels. The current data suggest that in women with inherent damage to the gonadotropin-producing mechanism of the anterior pituitary gland, ovulation and even pregnancy might be induced by administering human pituitary and chorionic gonadotropic substances but not by giving clomiphene citrate.

An occasionally effective therapeutic regimen for patients with pituitary amenorrhea is (1) the use of cyclic courses of estrogen alone or of estrogen and progestogen in sequence as "corrective" or "rebound stimulation" therapy (see p. 153), and (2) when the possibilities of restoring normal ovarian function have been exhausted, the use of cyclic courses of estrogen and progestogen in sequence, or preferably of continuous medication with a suitably balanced androgen-estrogen combination as "replacement" therapy (see p. 155).

Cushing's Syndrome

It is difficult to discuss the pathologic physiology of Cushing's syndrome because of the lack of agreement as to the pathologic lesions in the patients comprising the group of cases with manifestations recognized as Cushing's syndrome. There appears to be good evidence that the final target gland involved in this syndrome is the adrenal cortex. It is clear in some cases that a malignant tumor of the adrenal cortex produces the clinical manifestations of Cushing's syndrome. Other cases are found in which there is a definite hyperplasia of the adrenal cortex. At the same time, ever since the observations of Cushing in 1932, attention has been focused on the anterior pituitary basophile cells, and particularly on the basophilic adenoma, as possibly a causative lesion in the condition we call Cushing's syndrome. (In those patients in whom this pituitary tumor is present and is thought to be responsible for the characteristic manifestations of the syndrome, it is more accurate to call the condition "Cushing's disease.") The occurrence of many cases of adenoma of the basophile cells without the picture of Cushing's syndrome or indeed without any clinical manifestations, and the occurrence of cases of Cushing's syndrome without any evidence of a basophile adenoma, make it difficult to consider the basophile adenoma as an important feature in the etiology of most cases. It is just as reasonable to assume that the basophilic adenomas are due to the effects on the pituitary gland of excessive amounts of adrenal cortical steroids as to assume that the adrenal cortical overactivity is due to the effects of excessive amounts of pituitary tropic substances from basophilic adenomas. A more common finding in the anterior pituitary is the so-called Crooke cell changes, which again may just as well be a result of the action of excessive adrenal cortical steroids on the pituitary as a manifestation of some primary disturbance in the anterior pituitary. Finally, to complete the confusion, cases of Cushing's syndrome have been described which at postmortem examination had definite lesions in the paraventricular nuclei of the hypothalamus, and no recognizable anatomic abnormalities in either the anterior pituitary or the adrenal cortical tissues.

We can make some sense out of this pathologic confusion if we consider that the final common body-tissue manifestations of Cushing's syndrome are brought about by an excess of adrenal cortical hormones. The excess of adrenal cortical hormones may be induced by cancer or hyperplasia of the adrenal cortex. If it is produced by hyperplasia, the adrenal cortices may receive excessive stimulation from the anterior pituitary, so that some cases arise primarily from the anterior pituitary. Finally, there are a few cases in which the primary lesions appear to be in the hypothalamus with a resulting increase in stimulation of the anterior pituitary, which in turn produces excessive amounts of the hormones that stimulate the adrenal cortex, which finally secretes excessive amounts of the steroids that induce the manifestations of Cushing's syndrome.

In this syndrome the primary type of adrenal cortical steroids produced in excess is that which has to do with the carbohydrate metabolism, in other words, cortisol and its derivative, cortisone (the "sugar" or "S" hormones). As a result of the excessive production of this hormone the patient exhibits manifestations of too much sugar and usually of too little protein. One of the prime actions of cortisol is the stimulation of the rate of glucose formation from noncarbohydrate precursors, either by diverting amino acids from protein synthesis to gluconeogenesis, or by diverting fatty acids from fat synthesis to gluconeogenesis. When a sufficient excess of either of these two groups of noncarbohydrate precursors is present, it appears that the other is spared as source material for the cortisol-induced gluconeogenesis. Usually, however, there are not enough fatty acids available to prevent the utilization of amino acids for glucose formation; this leads to an insufficiency of amino acids for protein synthesis. Under these circumstances, therefore, cortisol has an antianabolic effect. When the available amino acids and the available fatty acids both are markedly reduced, there is a breakdown of protein tissues and of fatty tissues in addition to an inhibition of new tissue formation in order to correct the deficit and to maintain the cortisol-induced gluconeogenesis. Under these more severe conditions cortisol has a catabolic effect as well as an antianabolic effect.

The manifestations of too little protein are muscular weakness, cessation of growth, osteoporosis, thin skin, and perhaps amenorrhea; the manifestations of too much sugar are those of insulin-resistant diabetes. Cortisol inhibits insulin, increases gluconeogenesis, induces increased glycogen deposition in the liver, lowers the renal sugar threshold, and decreases the sugar utilization by the tissues. In addition, an excess of "sugar" hormone (cortisol) causes an increased breakdown of lymphoid tissues, and, as a result, lymphocytopenia; also at times it causes a disturbance in electrolyte metabolism with a tendency toward high serum sodium and carbon dioxide levels coupled with low serum potassium and chloride levels. A large amount of 11-oxysteroids is found in the urine by chemical test, and of compounds with corticoid activity by biologic test. The normal diurnal rhythm of adrenocortical metabolite excretion usually is absent in Cushing's syndrome. The adrenal cortex also may produce steroids which cause a decreased utilization of fat in these cases to account for the moon face, the buffalo hump and the other evidences of abnormal fat distribution; on the other hand, these abnormalities of fat metabolism may be the result of the efforts of the body to handle the excess of carbohydrate by reconverting some of it to fat, but this interpretation provides no explanation for the characteristic location of the abnormal fat deposits. It is difficult to attribute to excessive cortisol production some of the other manifestations—for example, the hirsutism without other evidences of virilism, the hypertension, the polycythemia, and the acne. There does seem to be some compensatory increase in "nitrogen" hormone production, which might account for the hirsutism, the polycythemia, and the acne in some cases.

Thorn and Albright showed that the administration of purified ACTH to patients with panhypopituitarism results in an increased urinary excretion not only of 11-oxysteroids, but also of 17-ketosteroids. This mechanism may be responsible for increased adrenal androgen production in those cases of Cushing's syndrome resulting from an increased production and/or release of ACTH. Furthermore, ACTH increases the production of aldosterone until this effect is offset by increased cortisol production. Excessive aldosterone production may account for the findings of hypertension, sodium retention, and potassium diuresis. It is of interest that the chloride ion shifts with the potassium rather than with the sodium in this syndrome; in other words, since there is a loss of potassium, there is also a loss of chloride, even though there is a retention of sodium. Some of the weakness complained of by these patients may be due to the loss of intracellular potassium, and increased amounts of potassium are of benefit in the treatment of this condition.

In the therapy of Cushing's syndrome it is also difficult to generalize. If there is a malignant tumor of the adrenal cortex, the only treatment is surgical. On the other hand, in the presence of hyperplasia of the adrenal cortex there are several possible routes of approach. Partial resection of the hyperplastic adrenal cortical tissue is of benefit, and now that cortisol and its various new derivatives are available as replacement therapy, complete resection of both adrenal cortices has been carried out successfully in some cases. In certain patients the syndrome develops as the result of excessive activity of the anterior pituitary, and in them x-radiation to the pituitary is followed by marked improvement. However, x-radiation to the adrenal cortices has not been followed by any appreciable improvement in the patients reported. Considerable benefit has been observed in patients with Cushing's syndrome who are treated with gonadal hormones.

In approximately 10 per cent of the cases of Cushing's syndrome, pituitary tumors become apparent following adrenalectomy. These individuals have x-ray findings in the skull or changes in visual fields; all have an increase in pigmentation greater than in Addison's disease. At this time it is not established whether small tumors were present preoperatively and continued to grow postoperatively or whether adrenalectomy has acted as a stimulus to such growth.

In this disease the effect of estrogenic substances is transitory as far as nitrogen retention and the induction of a positive calcium balance are concerned. Androgenic compounds, on the other hand, have a much more pronounced effect upon the retention of nitrogen and also of phosphorus, potassium, and sulfur in the proportions in which these substances exist in protoplasm. In these patients a demonstrable increase can be induced in the thickness of the skin, and presumably in the muscles and bone matrix as well. Furthermore, after the matrix has been formed, these patients begin to retain calcium and also additional phosphorus in the proportion to calcium that exists in bone, so that there is objective evidence that they are forming bone as well as storing protoplasm. Further indication of the beneficial effects of androgen is obtained from the changes that occur in the excretion of 11-oxysteroids, which is sharply reduced in most of the patients after the administration of testosterone compounds. Since these patients already are hirsute, there is no great objection to giving them a virilizing hormone if they are women. Furthermore, the administration of androgen practically will eliminate the lymphocytopenia and eosinopenia, which are useful indices of the status of patients with this condition.

Since the anabolic effects of androgen and estrogen augment each other, the most effective therapy to induce repletion of protein and osseous tissues in Cushing's syndrome is the simultaneous administration of androgen and estrogen. The administration of both types of hormone in combination has been facilitated by the development of esters of gonadal hormones, such as testosterone enanthate (Delatestryl) and estradiol valerate (Delestrogen) (see p. 155). The administration of additional potassium also is of benefit in reducing the complications of adrenal cortical hormone excess.

In many patients with Cushing's syndrome the degree of abnormal function of the adrenal cortex fluctuates considerably from day to day, so that, whereas for a few days the patient may be producing excessive amounts of 11-oxysteroids, a few days later he may be excreting practically normal quantities. Spontaneous remissions may occur.

Primary Hyperaldosteronism (Conn's Syndrome)

In 1954, Jerome W. Conn described the syndrome of primary aldosteronism characterized by high titers of aldosterone-like materials in the urine, hypokalemia, hypernatremia, alkalosis, Pitressin-resistant polyuria with a renal tubular defect in the reabsorption of water, polydipsia, intermittent tetany, muscular weakness, hypomagnesemia, hypertension, absence of edema, severe headache, paresthesias of the hands and feet, and resistance to potassium therapy. Several hundred cases now have been described. Adrenal cortical tumors were found in the original cases, but a recent tabulation indicates that single or multiple adenomas occur in 85 per cent, bilaterally enlarged glands with hyperplasia in 9 per cent, and normal-sized glands with either focal nodular hyperplasia or no recognizable pathologic lesion in 6 per cent of the cases. The cases should be diagnosed early and treated before irreversible renal damage has occurred. Surgical excision of the hyperfunctioning tissue usually results in a dramatic disappearance of the entire syndrome.

Primary Hypoaldosteronism

Skanse and Hokfelt recently have described the syndrome of primary hypoaldosteronism, characterized by dizziness, fainting spells, weakness, fatigability, hypotension, hyponatremia, and complete absence of aldosterone in the urine. The patient responded satisfactorily to desoxycorticosterone acetate. Hypoaldosteronism also occurs in some patients as part of the clinical picture of Addison's disease (adrenal cortical insufficiency).

Adaptation Syndrome

In relation to Cushing's syndrome a word should be said about the "adaptation syndrome" of Selye. He has demonstrated that, in response to all kinds of damaging events —such as exposure to cold, heat, reactions to drugs, fracture, infection, operation, burns, or other trauma—the individual responds, as part of his adaptative mechanism, with a hormone pattern that during the initial phase is similar to that of Cushing's syndrome. The sequence of events seems to be (1) damaging event; (2) by some means the hypothalamus is stimulated; (3) the impulses travel to the anterior pituitary and result in the release of adrenocorticotropic hormone, which (4) releases a large amount of adrenal cortical "sugar" hormone (cortisol); (5) this initiates changes in the body in the direction of preventing the systemic anabolism of tissues. At the same time the "sugar" hormone causes a breakdown of lymphoid tissue with a release of immune globulins which help to combat the damaging event if it is an infection. The interference with anabolism of protoplasm floods the system with all manner of building materials for the anabolism of protoplasm, and these materials are thus made available in large amounts to the site of injury. It is postulated that at the site of injury there is a local stimulating factor which is able to override the general systemic effect of the "sugar" hormone and induce a maximal amount of tissue regeneration. After this "catabolic" phase the patient passes into an "anabolic" phase, during which there is a marked anabolism of tissues in all parts of the system as well as in the local site of injury; this continues until convalescence is completed. In the "anabolic" phase there is no longer an excess of "sugar" hormone, but instead there is an excess of "nitrogen" hormone. According to Selye, the individual passes through a succession of steps or stages. First he goes through the shock stage, and then the countershock stage, both of which together are known as the "alarm reaction." After this he goes through a stage in which his resistance to the same type of damaging event is much greater than it was before, but during which his resistance to other types of damaging events is much lowered; finally, if the damaging event is continued, he enters a stage of exhaustion and ultimately dies, or, if the damaging event is terminated, he enters a stage of convalescence and eventually recovers.

The sequence of events in the "adaptation syndrome" can be continued as follows: (6) The large amount of the "sugar" hormone which is released inhibits the "nitrogen" hormone and aldosterone; this prevents the systemic accumulation of protoplasm and of extracellular fluid; and (7) when the excess production of the "sugar" hormone ceases and the inhibitory activity disappears, the "nitrogen" hormone and aldosterone are produced in increased amounts which stimulate the systemic anabolism of protoplasm and the reestablishment of electrolyte and water equilibrium during the period of convalescence. The concept of the "adaptation syndrome" provides another addition to the homeostatic mechanisms which are set in motion in an effort to maintain the optimal conditions in the individual. Cushing's syndrome, as a more prolonged counterpart of the transitory initial phase in the adaptation syndrome, becomes of great importance to the clinical investigator.

Disorders of Adaptation; Effects of Pituitary Adrenocorticotropic Hormone and of Adrenal Cortical Steroid Hormones in Nonendocrine Disorders

When the concept of the "adaptation syndrome" is applied to clinical medicine, it follows that there is an endocrine component in the manifestations of all disease conditions, and that the term "nonendocrine" disorder is correct only in reference to the locus of the primary or initial pathologic state. Important contributions to our knowledge of the pathologic physiology, the diagnosis, and the treatment of all systemic illness may be anticipated from further study of the role of this endocrine component.

It has become apparent that there are conditions in which the homeostatic mechanism of the "adaptation syndrome" does not function properly. Thus there has developed the concept of "diseases of adaptation." These diseases may involve defective or abnormal function of the body tissues, the central nervous system, the anterior pituitary gland, or the adrenal cortex. In other words, in terms of Figure 8–3 (p. 146), arrows 1, 2, 3 or 4 may be decreased or increased in size in relation to the normal. Furthermore, the disturbance in adaptation may be manifested during the stage of the "alarm reaction," during the "catabolic" phase or during the "anabolic" phase.

Disorders of Adaptation During the "Alarm Reaction." Disordered adaptation during the "alarm reaction" has been commonly observed. It is obvious that a noxious stimulus will lead to the clinical manifestations of "shock" in any person if it is of sufficiently intense degree. It is not yet clear, however, why the identical insult to the organism which produces a relatively mild reaction in one person will cause an extremely severe response in another. Certain acute fulminating infections are usually associated with a profound "alarm reaction." An example of this is infection with meningococci, in which such severe demands are made on the adrenal cortex for cortisol production that the gland breaks down with hemorrhage and destruction; this is the Waterhouse-Friderichsen syndrome. The administration of massive amounts of cortisol is indicated.

Disorders of Adaptation During the "Catabolic Phase." Many disorders of adaptation occur during the "catabolic" phase of the "adaptation syndrome." In a group of human disease conditions, lesions are present which are similar (if not identical) to the pathologic changes that can be induced in animals by the administration of large doses of aldosterone, and as a result the suggestion has been advanced that in man these disease states arise because of the excessive production of aldosterone by the adrenal cortex. These disease conditions include particularly disturbances in the cardiovascular system, such as periarteritis nodosa, rheumatic diseases such as rheumatoid arthritis and rheumatic fever, hypertension, and renal arteriolar diseases with nephrosclerosis. One of the most exciting recent developments in medicine has been the dramatic beneficial response of many of the patients with these conditions to the administration of large doses of anterior pituitary adrenocorticotropic hormone (ACTH) or of large doses of "sugar" hormone preparations (such as cortisol). Equally spectacular responses to these agents have been obtained in a considerable number of other human disease conditions in which the evidence suggesting an increase in the production of aldosterone by the adrenal cortex is less clear. These include disseminated lupus erythematosus, diffuse collagen diseases, dermatomyositis, scleroderma, psoriasis and psoriatic arthritis, pemphigus, gout, acute nephritis, chronic nephritis, nephrosis, status asthmaticus, bronchial asthma, allergic rhinitis, atopic dermatitis, drug hypersensitivity and other allergic states, ulcerative colitis, myasthenia gravis, acute alcoholic intoxication, certain psychiatric states, and certain acute infections. As far as present knowledge goes, these beneficial alterations must be considered only temporary remissions and not permanent changes or "cures." In some disease conditions, however, the administration of adrenocorticotropic hormone or cortisol has either produced no effect or possibly made the patients worse; these include viral hepatitis, tuberculosis, poliomyelitis, certain chronic neurologic disorders, and certain psychiatric states.

The following sequence of events is proposed as an explanation for the disorder in adaptation in these conditions: (1) The disease process initiates a reaction at the site of local injury in the tissues. (2) By some unknown mechanism this affects (arrow *1* of Figure 8–3) the central nervous system, which in turn "fires" (arrow *2* of Figure 8–3) the anterior pituitary gland to bring about increased release of ACTH; this hormone stimulates (arrow *3* of Figure 8–3) the adrenal cortex to produce the "sugar" hormone (cortisol), which then acts (arrow *4* of Figure 8–3) on the body tissues. (3) The increased release of ACTH results in an increased production of aldosterone, which also acts on the body tissues. (4) In the patient with a physiologic course of adaptation events, the rise in aldosterone production is prevented from becoming abnormally high by the inhibiting action of the increased amount of cortisol, which restores the aldosterone production to the physiologic range in a relatively short time as the "catabolic" phase progresses. (5) In the patient with a pathologic course of adaptation events, the rise in aldosterone production becomes abnormally high or persists unduly long because of an inadequate or insufficiently sustained increase in cortisol production. (6) In the patient with a pathologic course of adaptation events, the inadequate or insufficiently sustained increase in cortisol production develops because a "block" or "resistance" is established between the site of local injury and the central nervous system, thus shutting off further increased release of ACTH and hence of cortisol in response to this particular local stimulus. (7) The pituitary-adrenal cortical system is still capable of responding to other stimuli, and hence there is no evidence of adrenal cortical insufficiency. (8) The abnormal excess of aldosterone leads to the "disorder of adaptation" in some patients, and the lack of sufficient cortisol leads to a failure to complete the "catabolic" phase in other patients, and thus to a "disorder of adaptation" in them.

This sequence of events for the pathologic physiology of "disorders of adaptation," if correct, would provide an explanation for the beneficial effects of the administration of ACTH or cortisol, since these agents would bring about an inhibition of the production of aldosterone and would induce a progression of the disease process through the "catabolic" phase into the convalescent or "anabolic" stage with ultimate recovery. The demonstration in some of the "disorders of adaptation" that the adrenal cortex is normally responsive for cortisol production to ACTH, and that the anterior pituitary gland is normally responsive for ACTH production to epinephrine, favors the interpretation that the locus of the "block" or "resistance" in these "disorders of adaptation" is between the site of local injury and the central nervous system.

Disorders of Adaptation During the "Anabolic Phase." Still other types of "disorders of adaptation" are encountered during the "anabolic" phase of the "adaptation syndrome." Many patients respond normally to the "catabolic" phase, but fail to progress into the "anabolic" phase. This is a common occurrence in chronic debilitating diseases. The signs of the chronic disease process subside, but the recovery from the wasting and the protein and osseous tissue depletion is unduly protracted. Such patients respond dramatically, with marked anabolism of protoplasm and bone, and increase in weight, appetite, strength and well-being, to the administration of a combination of androgen and estrogen. When a suitable ratio of these gonadal hormones is used, the unwanted actions of the individual hormones on the genital organs and the accessory sexual structures are neutralized and thus practically eliminated without interfering with their beneficial anabolic effects. The therapy is applicable, therefore, to women and children as well as to men. The administration of both types of gonadal hormone in combination has been facilitated by the recent development of esters of these steroids, such as testosterone enanthate (Delatestryl) and estradiol valerate (Delestrogen), which in appropriate doses are effective for about one month after a single intramuscular injection. Also, a preparation (Deladumone) is available in which both the androgenic ester and the estrogenic ester are combined into one formulation in the desired ratio.

Some of the conditions in which the combination of androgen and estrogen may be given advantageously for its anabolic action to combat tissue depletion and chronic debility include malnutrition, starvation, cachexia, vitamin deficiencies, fractures, surgical trauma, burns, chronic wounds, spinal cord injuries, chronic neurologic disorders, chronic arthritis, chronic orthopedic conditions, convalescence from acute diseases (such as rheumatic fever, Still's disease, and so forth), chronic psychiatric states, anorexia nervosa, hyperthyroidism, Cushing's syndrome, adrenal cortical insufficiency, Addison's disease, diabetes mellitus, ulcerative colitis, steatorrhea, chronic pancreatitis, cirrhosis of the liver, chronic gastrointestinal tract disease, nephrotic syndrome and nephrosis, and other wasting conditions. The restoration of patients with these disorders to good health involves not only the treatment of the underlying condition and the administration of anabolic steroids, but also the use of other measures which will stimulate or accelerate tissue repletion and recovery from debility. These measures include proper diet, vitamin and mineral supplements, appropriate physical activity and therapy, and the administration of other adjuvant therapeutic agents.

Furthermore, the administration of an anabolic steroid combination may be of value even in conditions without protein depletion or chronic debility. Such therapy may accelerate convalescence from major surgery; may have a renotropic effect and cause hypertrophy of the surviving kidney before and after unilateral nephrectomy; may induce a moderate gain in weight in persons of constitutionally lean habitus; may protect the protein tissues of obese persons from catabolism while they are on a low-calorie reducing diet; and may improve the muscle tone of the urinary tract with the elimination of nocturnal enuresis, incontinence, poor sphincter control, or similar disturbances. The fact that most patients in whom such therapy is desirable are not suffering from general protein depletion or chronic debility diminishes the degree of protein anabolism that can be achieved, but does not eliminate the potential for a considerable amount of beneficial response. However, in well-nourished, physically-trained adolescent individuals and mature young adults, the administration of anabolic steroids does not improve physical performance as in athletic events. Therapy with an anabolic steroid combination is of value, also, in conditions in which accelerated bone tissue anabolism is desired. These include osteoporosis of various types; fractures, particularly in elderly patients; Paget's disease of bone (osteitis deformans); osteogenesis imperfecta (brittle-bones-and-blue-sclerae syndrome; fragilitas ossium); and delayed skeletal growth in children.

Addison's Disease and Adrenal Cortical Insufficiency

Addison's disease is adrenal cortical insufficiency due primarily to disease in the adrenal cortex. This disease may be either tuberculosis or a condition of unknown etiology which produces bilateral atrophy of the adrenal cortices. As a result of the disease in the adrenal cortex, there is decreased production of all types of hormones produced by the adrenal cortex. There is, therefore, a decrease in the production of the steroids that have to do with regulation of the carbohydrate metabolism—in other words, the "sugar" hormones (cortisol and its derivatives); in those that have to do with masculinization and nitrogen metabolism—namely, the "nitrogen" hormones; and finally in the hormone that regulates the electrolyte balance, particularly of sodium and potassium—namely, aldosterone. Clinical manifestations can be traced directly to the absence of these hormones. With the loss of some of these adrenal cortical hormones there will be a compensatory increase in the pituitary tropic hormones, particularly ACTH. The gonadotropic hormones, LH (ICSH) and LTH, which are thought to affect the adrenal cortex, also may be considerably increased.

In contrast to adrenal cortical insufficiency due primarily to disease in the adrenals, adrenal cortical insufficiency may occur as part of the picture of panhypopituitarism. In these cases the anterior pituitary tropic hormones are not produced in adequate amounts and the adrenal cortex is not stimulated to produce some of its hormones. This applies to the "sugar" and the "nitrogen" hormones. However, the evidence indicates that aldosterone, which regulates the sodium and potassium metabolism, is not controlled by tropic substances from the pituitary; hence the electrolyte balance is not greatly disturbed in panhypopituitarism.

Another differential point of considerable interest between these two types of adrenal cortical insufficiency is the difference in pigmentation in the two conditions. In Addison's disease there is marked pigmentation, whereas in panhypopituitarism increased pigmentation is rare. It may be that the sequence of events in Addison's disease is (1) loss of a hormone from the adrenal cortex which inhibits a hormone from the intermediate lobe of the pituitary, (2) loss of the regulatory function of this intermediate lobe hormone on the dispersion of black pigment granules in the melanophores, and (3) pigmentation. In panhypopituitarism the intermediate lobe hormone would be lacking. These two different types of adrenal cortical insufficiency also can be told apart by their response to adrenocorticotropic hormone. In Addison's disease the adrenal gland is unresponsive; hence, after the administration of adrenocorticotropic hormone there is no sharp fall in the eosinophils and lymphocytes and no rise in the uric acid

excretion such as is found in patients who have hypofunctioning adrenal cortices because of the lack of pituitary stimulation.

In treatment, patients with Addison's disease require replacement of all the adrenal cortical hormones. Adrenal cortical insufficiency in association with panhypopituitarism will respond to stimulation therapy with ACTH or to replacement therapy with preparations of corticosteroid and androgenic hormones; in addition, the underfunction of the thyroid and the gonads must be treated.

A recently developed compound, 9-alpha-fluorohydrocortisone (Florinef), is a potent agent for controlling the electrolyte balance in patients with Addison's disease. A daily dose of 0.1 to 0.3 mg. orally produces satisfactory salt retention in such patients; when enhanced glucocorticoid effect is desired, 6.25 to 25 mg. of cortisone, 5 to 20 mg. of cortisol, or 4 to 12 mg. of triamcinolone (Kenacort) daily by mouth may be administered concomitantly.

Adrenogenital Syndrome

This condition, which may be congenital or acquired, results from hyperfunction of the adrenal cortex. It is usually due to bilateral hyperplasia, but can be due to tumor. When this condition occurs in the female, there is an increased production of masculinizing ("nitrogen") hormones which also have to do with the maintenance of normal nitrogen anabolism. As a result these women become masculinized and develop a large clitoris, a deep voice, hirsutism, amenorrhea and strong muscles. Hyperfunction of the adrenal cortex due to bilateral hyperplasia or tumor with the production of androgenic (or estrogenic) hormones is not common in males, in whom it produces the clinical manifestations of macrogenitosomia precox or, rarely, feminization. In these cases arising primarily in the adrenal cortex it would be expected that the production of tropic hormone(s) from the anterior pituitary would be reduced. On the other hand, most cases arise as a result of excessive production of tropic hormone(s) (adrenocorticotropic and/or luteinizing and luteotropic) by the pituitary gland with secondary overstimulation of the adrenal cortex to hyperfunction. As a further manifestation of the excessive masculinizing hormones produced by these patients, one usually finds an elevated 17-ketosteroid excretion. There is evidence that this elevation can be reduced somewhat by inhibition of pituitary tropic hormone production with androgenic compounds. The administration of estrogens, x-radiation of the pituitary, and partial resection of the adrenal cortices have not been very satisfactory for this condition.

Wilkins and his associates and Bartter and his colleagues have shown that the elevated 17-ketosteroid excretion in the adrenogenital syndrome can be reduced practically to zero by the administration of a potent "sugar" hormone (cortisol or cortisone). The demonstration that cortisol can suppress the "nitrogen" hormone production by the hyperplastic adrenal cortices of patients with the adrenogenital syndrome represents an important advance in the therapy of this condition. The clinical status of these patients is improved by such therapy.

The recently developed compound, 9-alpha-fluorohydrocortisone (Florinef), is very potent in inhibiting the excessive "nitrogen" hormone production by the hyperplastic adrenal cortices in such patients. Daily doses of 1 or 2 mg. orally will maintain the urinary 17-ketosteroid excretion at or near the normal levels. Since 9-alpha-fluorohydrocortisone causes a retention of sodium and water, and a marked diuresis of potassium, these patients should be placed on a low sodium diet supplemented with potassium chloride.

Three recent observations contribute to an understanding of the pathologic physiology of the adrenogenital syndrome: there are (1) a reduced production of cortisol; (2) an increased production of ACTH; and (3) an increased excretion of pregnanetriol by these patients. The pregnanetriol arises as a metabolite of 17-alpha-hydroxyprogesterone, an intermediate compound in the biosynthesis of hydrocortisone (cortisol) by the adrenal cortex. The present concept of the pathologic physiology of the adrenogenital syndrome is as follows: (1) there is a block (probably at an enzyme level) in the conversion of 17-alpha-hydroxyprogesterone to hydrocortisone; (2) the excess of 17-alpha-hydroxyprogesterone is metabolized and excreted in the urine as an excess of pregnanetriol; (3) the insufficiency of hydrocortisone causes the anterior pituitary gland to produce an excess of ACTH; (4) the excess of ACTH stimulates the adrenal cortices to produce an excess of the "nitrogen" hormones; (5) the excess of the "nitrogen" hormones causes the masculinization and other clinical features of the syndrome; and (6) the excess of the "nitrogen" hormones is metabolized and excreted in the urine as an excess of 17-ketosteroid compounds. This concept provides an explanation for the effectiveness of cortisol and its potent derivatives in correcting the pathologic physiology. Some children with a congenital adrenogenital syndrome also have a persistent loss of sodium in the urine. This may be a manifestation of hypoaldosteronism resulting from pressure atrophy of the zona glomerulosa from compression by the hyperfunctioning androgen-producing adrenal cortical tissue.

Adrenal Androgen Hyperfunction Syndromes (Stein-Leventhal Syndrome; Large, Pale Ovary Syndrome)

During the past two decades there has been increasing recognition of the fact that many women have certain manifestations resembling disturbances of ovarian and adrenal cortical function without having the clinical features characteristic of a typical adrenogenital syndrome. These women exhibit one or more of the following manifestations: (1) disturbances of ovarian function with irregular and infrequent menses, infrequent or absent ovulation, or amenorrhea, (2) infertility, (3) mild hirsutism, (4) acne, (5) chronic cystic mastitis, and (6) a urinary 17-ketosteroid excretion at the upper limit of the range which has been called "normal." The available evidence suggests that these women are producing more than a physiologic amount of androgen from the adrenal cortex, and that the excessive amount of this hormone interferes with physiologic cyclic ovarian function.

Many of these patients have a syndrome described in 1935 by Stein and Leventhal of large, pale ovaries containing many follicle cysts and covered with a thick fibrous capsule. It was postulated that the follicles could not rupture through this thick capsule. This led to the use of a deep wedge resection, of stripping off the capsule, and of splitting the ovary and turning the organ "inside out." In many instances these surgical procedures have been followed by restoration of cyclic ovarian function, conception, and some recession in the androgenic manifestations.

Recently, it has been demonstrated that in many of the patients with the adrenal androgen hyperfunction syndrome (including women with the Stein-Leventhal syndrome) the administration of small doses of corticosteroids (2.5 mg. of cortisone three times a day to 5 mg. four times a day) results in the restoration of cyclic ovarian function and frequently in conception, provided the dosage of the corticosteroid medication is adjusted so that the urinary 17-ketosteroid excretion is between 8 and 10 mg. per 24 hours. Larger doses with suppression of the 17-ketosteroid excretion below 8 mg. per 24 hours do not appear to be effective. It seems to be desirable to continue the maintenance dosage of the corticosteroid medication throughout gestation in this regimen. It has been suggested that these beneficial responses to corticosteroids are brought about by a reduction in the adrenal androgen production following an inhibition of ACTH by the corticosteroid medication.

Similar beneficial effects have been observed in some women with adrenal androgen hyperfunction following the repeated administration of a potent long-acting progestational compound, 17-alpha-hydroxyprogesterone caproate (Delalutin). It has been demonstrated that LH and LTH increase the androgen production by the human adrenal cortex, and that this progestational compound (Delalutin) reduces the production and/or release of LH in man. It is suggested that the beneficial responses of women with the adrenal androgen hyperfunction syndrome to the progestational compound are brought about by a reduction in adrenal androgen production following an inhibition of the LH and LTH production by the progestational compound.

The available evidence suggests, therefore, that there are two pathologic mechanisms which may result in an increased production of androgen by the adrenal cortex and which result in the same group of clinical manifestations. The following sequence of events is proposed as an explanation for these two pathologic mechanisms: (1) for reasons unknown regular ovulation does not occur; (2) under the influence of continued FSH and LH a number of follicles partially develop and produce a continuous supply of estrogen; (3) the continuous supply of estrogen exerts a stimulating effect upon the anterior pituitary tropic hormones, and one of two responses occurs, depending on the reactivity of the anterior pituitary gland: either ACTH production is increased by the estrogen, or LH and LTH production is increased by the estrogen; (4) if ACTH production is increased, then (a) the adrenal cortex is stimulated by the ACTH to an increased production of adrenal androgen; (b) the adrenal androgen inhibits LH and thus prevents further ovulation; (c) the adrenal androgen causes mild hirsutism, acne, chronic cystic mastitis; and urinary 17-ketosteroid values that are at the upper limit of the physiologic range; (5) if LH and LTH production is increased, then

(a) further ovulation is prevented by the continuous release of excessive amounts of these gonadotropins, (b) the adrenal cortex is stimulated by the LH and LTH to an increased production of adrenal androgen; (c) the adrenal androgen causes mild hirsutism, acne, chronic cystic mastitis, and urinary 17-ketosteroid excretion values that are at the upper limit of the physiologic range. This proposal does not provide a satisfactory explanation for the thickening of the capsule of the ovary. It does supply a partial rationale for the beneficial response of patients with the Stein-Leventhal syndrome to surgical procedures involving the ovary, since it is now recognized that these measures have a much greater chance of being effective if all the follicle cysts are aspirated. In effect this greatly reduces the excess of estrogen which has been inducing an abnormal increase in either the ACTH or the LH and LTH production. It also suggests that patients with the adrenal androgen hyperfunction syndrome who fail to respond to corticosteroid medication should be given a trial on 17-alpha-hydroxyprogesterone caproate (Delalutin) medication, and vice versa. Tests for measuring the urinary excretion of ACTH and of LH (LTH) are now being evaluated experimentally; it should be possible with these tests to determine in a given patient which of the two mechanisms of pathologic physiology is present and which of the two types of hormonal agents should be used as therapy.

Pheochromocytoma

Pheochromocytomas are tumors of the chromaffin tissue of the body, particularly the adrenal medulla. These tumors produce excessive amounts of epinephrine or norepinephrine, either continuously or paroxysmally. When predominantly epinephrine or a large amount of norepinephrine is released, the symptoms are those of excessive sympathetic nervous system stimulation, particularly hypertension and vasomotor disturbances, hyperhidrosis, hypermetabolism, and frequently hyperglycemia. The attacks can be brought on by palpating the tumor and squeezing out the epinephrine from it; this is not without danger. The attacks also can be induced at times by the administration of histamine, which leads to the release of epinephrine and thus induces a typical attack. When a small amount of norepinephrine with little or no epinephrine is released, the syndrome of essential hypertension is closely simulated. The hypertension of pheochromocytoma persists after the administration of tetraethylammonium chloride, which paralyzes the sympathetic nervous system, and also after sedation and cold tests. These procedures normally evoke a hypotensive response in other forms of hypertension. The benzodioxane and Regitine tests are positive. Patients with pheochromocytoma excrete 12 to 50 times the normal amount of pressor substances (epinephrine plus norepinephrine) in the urine, a determination that is of value in establishing the diagnosis. The demonstration and location of the tumor by gas insufflation x-ray studies also may be helpful.

Diabetes Insipidus

In this condition a lesion in the brain stem interrupts the nerve fibers from the vagus and from the supraoptic nuclei which pass down to the hypophysis. As a consequence the posterior pituitary no longer produces its hormones, vasopressin (Pitressin) and oxytocin (Pitocin). The loss of Pitressin is followed by disappearance of the normal antidiuretic action of this hormone, which causes tubular reabsorption of water in the kidney. As a result, there is a diuresis of water which is maintained by an undefined factor in the anterior pituitary gland. It has been shown that when a patient who has diabetes insipidus develops panhypopituitarism—that is, destruction of the anterior pituitary—the diabetes insipidus disappears. As a result of the excessive diuresis of water, patients with diabetes insipidus have a marked thirst.

Menopause and the Menopausal Syndrome

One of the most puzzling problems in endocrinology for which no adequate explanation has been found is the reason for the failure of ovarian function that occurs in women between the ages of 45 and 50. A reasonable teleologic argument can be advanced that menopause is good for the race because it prevents women from bearing children at an age when they would not produce good offspring. However, this is certainly not an advantageous situation for any given woman, even though it may be an evolutionary development. The cessation of ovarian function, or perhaps it would be better said, the decrease in ovarian function to the point below adequate amounts for adult activity, results in a hormone imbalance which in some patients produces no manifestations and in others produces marked symptoms. The loss of estrogenic hormones results in a marked increase in the production and/or release of pituitary gonadotropins of the FSH type. It is not so clearly established that the loss of ovulation and progestogen is followed by an increase in the production of the pituitary gonadotropins, LH and LTH, although this is probably true. Along with this shift in hormone balance, in many patients there appears to be a marked disturbance in the stability of the autonomic nervous system; as a result, there are frequent discharges of sympathetic activity which result in the symptom called "hot flushes" and in nervousness, and so forth. Though these symptoms usually run parallel to the increase in gonadotropins, they are not necessarily so, and are perhaps better thought of as manifestations of estrogen deficiency than of gonadotropin excess. For example, I have seen two postmenopausal women with acromegaly, high gonadotropin excretion, and frequent hot flushes, in whom all the basophile cells of the pituitary were destroyed by the enlarging tumor. Although there was a fall in the gonadotropin excretion to such a low level that it could not be measured, there was no change in the frequent occurrence of the hot flushes.

As a woman approaches and passes through the menopause, she undergoes also an alteration in the function of the adrenal cortex. The production of gonadal-like hormones (particularly androgen and estrogen) by the adrenal cortex diminishes steadily with aging; in contrast, the production of glucocorticoid hormones by the adrenal cortex persists at the mature young adult level almost unchanged into the ninth decade. The gonadal hormones, androgen and estrogen, have an anabolic action upon protein and osseous tissues; the glucocorticoid hormones have an antianabolic (and under severe conditions, a catabolic) action upon these tissues. In the mature young adult woman and man, the production of these two types of hormones with opposing influences upon protein and osseous tissues is balanced. However, with aging, women and men develop a relative excess of antianabolic steroids over anabolic steroids in part as a result of the decreased production of the gonadal hormones, and in part as a result of the sustained production of the glucocorticoid hormones.

The other symptoms which appear during and after the onset of the menopause—in other words, in women from age 45 onward—are due to the gradually increasing lack of estrogen (and androgen) combined with the gradually increasing relative excess of cortisol. This hormonal imbalance makes itself manifest in a gradual decrease in the thickness of the skin and in the size and tone of the muscles; in the appearance of atrophy of the vagina, the endometrium and the breasts; and particularly in a decrease in the formation of bone matrix by the osteoblasts. This latter condition results in osteoporosis from the failure to provide an organic matrix for the deposition of calcium. Osteoporosis is the most common systemic bone disorder.

The Menopausal Syndrome. The majority of patients with the menopausal syndrome respond well to estrogen alone. However, there is a small group which must have progestogen also in order to eliminate all unpleasant symptoms. If estrogen is used alone as therapy in these women, I favor its administration in cyclical courses of 4 or 5 weeks, followed by a period of a week to 10 days without therapy so that the proliferative endometrium can be shed and the excessive stimulation of the breast and uterus eliminated. Or, preferably, the estrogen can be given continuously, and a course of progestogen administered at regular intervals to assure the shedding of the proliferated endometrium every 4 weeks. There are no convincing statistics that estrogen administered to such patients increases the incidence of neoplastic disease; in fact, there is some evidence that some forms of neoplastic disease in older women may be less prone to occur during estrogenic therapy.

After the menopause most women and their physicians prefer to avoid cyclic uterine bleeding as a result of therapy. The menopausal symptoms can be controlled satisfactorily in such patients with a combination of androgen and estrogen; in addition, both hormones inhibit the production and/or release of the gonadotropic hormones from the anterior pituitary gland and thus correct the hormone imbalance that follows ovarian failure. Therapy with an androgen-estrogen combination is indicated, furthermore, to offset the relative excess of antianabolic glucocorticoid hormones and thus to maintain protein and osseous tissue anabolism regardless of whether or not the woman has or has had menopausal symptoms. When androgen and estrogen are combined in a suitable ratio, the potentials for stimulating or maintaining tissue anabolism and for achieving hormone homeostasis are retained, but the unwanted actions of the individual gonadal hormones on the genital organs and accessory sexual structures are neutralized and thus practically eliminated as a consequence of therapy with such a combination. Hence control of menopausal symptoms, correction of pituitary gonadotropic hormone imbalance and maintenance of tissue anabolism can be achieved with a suitable androgen-estrogen combination without inducing the unwanted complication of uterine bleeding. Such therapy can be administered conveniently by a single intramuscular injection once a month of appropriate amounts of a preparation (Deladumone), which combines into one formulation testosterone enanthate and estradiol valerate in the desired ratio (90 mg. of the testosterone ester to 4 mg. of the estradiol ester).

Postmenopausal and Senile Osteoporosis

In a large group of women, for some additional reason (which may be related to an inadequate calcium intake), the osteoporosis becomes much more marked, and in a matter of 5 to 6 years after the menopause a clinical degree of disability develops. This is manifested in collapse of the vertebrae and sometimes in a sufficient excretion of calcium through the urine to form kidney stones. The usual story is that a patient, typically about 5 years after the menopause, while riding in an automobile, goes over a bump, feels a pain in her back, and fractures a vertebra. This is an alarming situation to her, and sometimes to her physician, but, as a matter of fact, I have never seen a serious nerve injury result from such a collapse of vertebrae. Similar clinical manifestations of decreased bone formation appear also in a smaller group of aging men (and in some postmenopausal women during the seventh decade of life). Although the osseous disorder in these elderly patients is called senile osteoporosis, it is distinguishable from postmenopausal osteoporosis only by the age at which the clinical syndrome becomes manifest.

The bone mass in osteoporosis becomes less dense in the roentgenograms, but the bones actually do not become smaller. Osteoporosis of the postmenopausal and senile types is a chronic condition which has been developing for some years before the clinical diagnosis is made. In such patients the serum calcium, inorganic phosphorus, alkaline phosphatase and total protein levels are in the normal range, which aids in differentiating osteoporosis from the other systemic or local bone disorders with too little calcified mass, in which one or more of these serum constituents usually show abnormal values. These other disorders include, particularly, osteomalacia (rickets in the child), osteitis fibrosa generalisata (the bone complication of hyperparathyroidism), and multiple myeloma. The diminished rate of bone matrix formation that leads to postmenopausal and senile osteoporosis retards the rate of fracture healing in elderly patients. This complication is favorably influenced by the same treatment (see below) that improves the osteoporosis.

The sequence of the events in the development of postmenopausal and senile osteoporosis is as follows: (1) endogenous gonadal hormones are reduced below the effective levels by the cessation of ovarian function while endogenous glucocorticoid hormones are maintained at effective levels by the continuation of this type of adrenal cortical function; (2) the activity of the osteoblasts in forming the protein matrix (osteoid) of bone is greatly diminished by the deficiency of the gonadal hormones combined with the relative excess of the glucocorticoid hormones; (3) the formation of mineralized bone decreases because there is no matrix laid down into which the minerals can be deposited; (4) the physiologic process of bone resorption continues unabated, and hence bone no longer is in a state of dynamic equilibrium; (5) as a result, the total mass of calcified bone gradually becomes reduced, although the units of calcified bone that remain still have a normal chemical composition; (6) eventually the weakened bones become tender, painful, and more susceptible to fractures; (7) at the same time the thin bones are more responsive to the stresses and strains of weight-bearing, and this excessive physiologic stimulus causes the osteoblasts to resume approximately normal activity (hence the normal level in the serum of the osteoblastic enzyme, alkaline phosphatase); and (8) the end result is a reduced total calcified bone mass that is almost restored to a state of dynamic equilibrium.

The patients with postmenopausal and senile osteoporosis are improved clinically by the administration of estrogen alone, and markedly benefited by the administration of androgen and estrogen in combination. When androgen and estrogen are combined in a suitable ratio (see below), the potential for maintaining osseous tissue anabolism is retained, but the unwanted actions of the individual gonadal hormones in the sexual sphere are practically eliminated. The administration of both types of gonadal hormones in combination has been facilitated by the development of esters of these hormones (see p. 155).

Anabolic steroid therapy does not eliminate the existing osteoporosis, but merely prevents further progression of the osseous disorder. In addition to anabolic hormone therapy, patients with post-menopausal, senile, and other types of osteoporosis should be given a high protein diet, large doses of ascorbic acid, an adequate amount of water and during the initial weeks of hormone therapy a limited intake of calcium (milk, milk products, and calcium-containing medications) and of calciferol (Vitamin D) to avoid any tendency to hypercalciuria, as much physical activity as can be tolerated with deliberate avoidance of immobilization in any form (except for splinting of acutely fractured areas), and instructions on the proper use of their muscles to avoid undue strain on the weakened bones. When normal osteoblastic activity has been restored by several months of anabolic steroid therapy, the amount of calcium in the diet should be gradually increased until it reaches approximately twice the normal adult intake; thereafter, this level should be maintained as long as the patient continues on hormonal therapy. The patients respond with clinical improvement in weeks, but the therapeutic regimen must be continued for years to prevent further reduction in the calcified bone mass and thus to arrest the osseous disorder. The use of calcium alone without hormone therapy apparently does not arrest the progress of the osseous condition.

Gonadal Dysgenesis (Ovarian Agenesis, Turner's Syndrome, Ovarian Short-Stature Syndrome, Functional Prepuberal Castration)

Gonadal dysgenesis is found in children who are born with rudimentary gonadal tissue. These individuals commonly have a female phenotype, although about 80 per cent have a male sex chromosome constitution. These "females" have sexual infantilism, never go through the menarche, and have evidences of lack of estrogenic hormones, as shown by inadequate development of the breast and atropic vaginal mucosa and endometrium. Furthermore, because of the lack of ovarian hormones, there is a high titer of gonadotropin in the urine.

In addition, these "female" patients show some decreased stature, which causes them to be called "ovarian dwarfs." "Ovarian dwarfs" differ from pituitary dwarfs in the following respects: (1) The FSH test is strongly positive rather than negative. (2)

The patients are of short stature, about 4 feet 8 inches tall, rather than actually dwarfs. (3) The epiphysial union is slightly, rather than markedly, delayed. (4) The 17-ketosteroid excretion in the urine is low, but not almost absent. (5) The axillary and pubic hair is decreased, but not absent. (6) The strength and nutrition are only slightly impaired, rather than markedly so. (7) The insulin tolerance tests give normal results rather than hypoglycemia unresponsiveness. (8) These patients have a marked propensity to have congenital abnormalities, notably coarctation of the aorta and Turner's syndrome (webbing of the neck, sexual and somatic infantilism, and increased carrying angle of the arms). These patients resemble pituitary dwarfs in having complete lack of uterine and breast development, but in addition they have a marked tendency to osteoporosis and precocious senility. The evidence favors the theory that the shortness of the stature is just another manifestation of the congenital abnormalities in these patients. It has been suggested that the corresponding syndrome in males is functional prepuberal castration.

In phenotypic females with gonadal dysgenesis the administration of estrogen has resulted in considerable increase in general well-being, development of the breasts, increase in axillary and pubic hair, and increase in the rate of growth in those subjects whose epiphyses are still ununited. Cyclic therapy with estrogen and progestogen in sequence may be given to satisfy the desire of many of these patients to have regular uterine bleeding simulating the monthly menstruation of their normal sisters. The administration of such cyclic therapy has been facilitated by the development of certain long-acting hormone preparations, such as estradiol valerate (Delestrogen) and 17-alpha-hydroxyprogesterone caproate (Delalutin). In appropriate doses, the estradiol valerate (20 mg.) is effective for about 3 weeks and the 17-alpha-hydroxyprogesterone caproate (250 mg.) for about 2 weeks after a single intramuscular injection. An effective regimen for inducing cyclic hormone therapy with these long-acting parenteral preparations is described on page 153.

Amenorrhea

Disorders involving the ovary may arise from functional or organic disturbances in the ovary, the anterior pituitary gland, the central nervous system (especially the hypothalamus), and the general body tissues. The manifestations of these disorders (amenorrhea, derangement of the menstrual cycle, sterility, and the other clinical features of insufficiency of ovarian hormones) give no clue as to the underlying pathologic physiology. Amenorrhea is classed as *primary* when menarche has failed to occur by 17 or 18 years of age, and *secondary* when menstruation ceases after previously normal ovarian function. However, both primary and secondary amenorrhea can arise from organic as well as from functional disturbances in the various anatomic components. The classification, therefore, gives no clear indication of the underlying pathologic condition.

For example, amenorrhea may be a manifestation of a variety of conditions: physiologic states (pregnancy, primary amenorrhea of the premenarchal girl, and secondary amenorrhea of the postmenopausal woman), primary amenorrhea, secondary amenorrhea, hypogonadotropic hypogonadism, hypergonadotropic hypogonadism, pituitary amenorrhea, prepuberal ovarian failure (gonadal dysgenesis, ovarian agenesis, Turner's syndrome, "ovarian-short-stature syndrome," primary hypo-ovarianism, congenital hypoestrinism, premenarchal menopause), postpuberal ovarian failure (castration, menopause praecox, physiologic menopause, artificial menopause), panhypopituitarism, pituitary dwarfism, Simmonds' cachexia, Sheehan's syndrome, hypothalamic or psychogenic amenorrhea, early anorexia nervosa, Fröhlich's syndrome, malnutrition, chronic debilitating disease, anemia, thyroid disease, adrenal disease, amenorrheic phase of metropathia haemorrhagia, and so forth. In many instances it is possible to establish the basic pathologic physiology of the ovarian disorder by careful diagnostic procedures and to determine from this whether or not normal ovarian function can be restored by suitable therapy. In the absence of such information, however, it must be assumed that the disturbance in ovarian function is amenable to correction. Therapy should be administered with this objective in mind until the futility of such a course of action is established. The use of estrogen and progestogen in this manner can be termed "corrective therapy" or "rebound stimulation therapy." In all cases of amenorrhea other ancillary therapy should be given as indicated, and underlying defects (such as malnutrition and anemia) should be corrected. When the possibilities of restoring normal ovarian function have been exhausted, cyclic courses of estrogen and progestogen or continuous medication with a suitably balanced androgen-estrogen combination may be considered for "replacement therapy."

In most instances, the ovarian disturbance that leads to amenorrhea is a failure to ovulate. In many women, the inadequately functioning ovary continues to produce some estrogen. This estrogen causes some proliferation of the endometrium, which must be eliminated before "rebound stimulation therapy" is initiated. This can be accomplished by administering a large dose of progestogen, which converts the proliferated endometrium to the secretory type and then as its action terminates results in uterine bleeding with endometrial desquamation. This is spoken of as a "medical D. and C." It has an advantage over surgical curettage in that all areas of the endometrium are converted to the secretory phase and shed, whereas with the surgical procedure some areas may be missed unless the curettage is performed very carefully. A "medical D. and C." can be carried out very conveniently by administering 375 to 500 mg. of the long-acting progestational agent, 17-alpha-hydroxyprogesterone caproate (Delalutin), as a single intramuscular injection; uterine bleeding with endometrial desquamation usually occurs in 8 to 12 days. As soon as the endometrial desquamation is completed, the patient is ready for a trial of "rebound stimulation therapy."

The use of estrogen and progestogen for "rebound stimulation therapy" is based on the following facts. In the human ovarian cycle under physiologic conditions, estrogen is produced by the follicle during the first two weeks (the proliferative phase), and progestogen and estrogen are produced by the corpus luteum during the second two weeks (the secretory phase). With these cyclic variations in the gonadal hormone production during the proliferative and the secretory stages, there are sequential compensatory alterations in the production and/or release of the gonadotropic hormones by the anterior pituitary gland and likewise cyclic alterations in the structure and activity of the endometrium. When the gonadal hormones are used for "rebound stimulation therapy" in patients with amenorrhea, they are administered in the amounts and at the times required to induce sequential changes in the gonadotropic hormones and the endometrium which simulate the physiologic responses of the endogenously induced menstrual cycle. To assure a complete restoration of the physiologic responses by the anterior pituitary gland and the endometrial tissues, the regimen of cyclic hormone therapy is continued without deviation or interruption for 4 consecutive months. Such therapy creates a favorable situation for the pituitary and the ovary to resume normal cyclic function. At this point, the administration of the gonadal hormones is discontinued for 4 months in order to permit the "rebound" to take place; the patient is kept under close observation during these 4 months to detect the onset of physiologic cyclic ovarian function if this is going to occur. Many patients resume normal ovarian activity after one single course (4 months) of cyclic therapy; others, after repeated courses of hormone treatment alternated with intervals (each 4 months in duration) with no hormonal medication. An effective regimen for inducing cyclic hormone therapy with long-acting parenteral preparations has been described above.

In patients with amenorrhea who fail to resume cyclic ovarian function following the use of repeated courses of gonadal hormones as "rebound stimulation therapy," it is rational to attempt a restoration of gonadal activity with gonadotropic substances of pituitary and chorionic origin. The use of these gonadotropic agents for this purpose is described in the section on pituitary amenorrhea (see above).

When it is decided that there is no further possibility or desire to attempt to restore ovarian function in a patient with amenorrhea, she is treated as an individual with the menopause. Younger women who wish to have regular monthly menses are continued on cyclic hormone therapy (as described above) without interruption until it is decided to terminate monthly menstruation. At that point these women, and their older sisters who prefer to avoid cyclic uterine bleeding as the result of treatment, are given "replacement therapy" with a suitably balanced androgen-estrogen combination. Such therapy can be administered conveniently by giving a single intramuscular injection once a month of appropriate amounts of a preparation (Deladumone) which combines into one formulation testosterone enanthate and estradiol valerate in the desired ratio (90 mg. of the testosterone ester to 4 mg. of the estradiol ester). The rationale for the use of such hormonal medication is described in the section on menopause and the menopausal syndrome (see p. 167).

Dysfunctional Uterine Bleeding
(Metropathia Hemorrhagica)

Dysfunctional uterine bleeding is primarily a manifestation of lack of ovulation. For reasons which are not clear, the ovary stops ovulating, although the follicles are stimulated to produce estrogen. There is a suggestion that in some cases the amount of estrogen produced is too much, and that in other cases the amount is normal or too little. The end result, however, is that estrogen affects the uterus for too long a time and the proliferative changes in the endometrium increase until finally there results marked hyperplasia and a "Swiss-cheese" type of endometrium. This ultimately breaks down and bleeds, probably because there is insufficient estrogen to maintain it. During the interval when the proliferation of the endometrium is going on, the patient has amenorrhea, and then, when the endometrium begins to break down, there is bleeding, so that the clinical manifestations usually include amenorrhea alternating with irregular bleeding. These patients have no evidence of secretory endometrium and hence are not ovulating. Whether this failure to ovulate results from some primary difficulty in the ovary or from some disturbance in the pituitary is not known.

Patients with dysfunctional uterine bleeding during the amenorrheic phase are treated in the same manner as patients with other forms of amenorrhea. The steps are: (1) to get rid of the proliferated endometrium of the uterus by doing a "medical D. and C."; this is accomplished by administering progestogen (see p. 171); (2) to attempt to restore cyclic ovarian function by the use of cyclic hormone therapy with estrogen and progestogen for "rebound stimulation therapy" (see p. 153), or if this fails, by the use of gonadotropic substances (see p. 153); and (3) if the possibilities of restoring ovarian function have been exhausted, to provide "replacement therapy" with continuous cyclic hormone therapy in younger women who desire regular menses (see p. 153), or with a suitably balanced androgen-estrogen combination.

Patients with dysfunctional uterine bleeding during a bleeding episode respond to hormone therapy so dramatically that surgery rarely is indicated. These women can be divided into two groups on the basis of the severity of the clinical manifestations. (1) The majority of such patients have had only a moderate amount of uterine bleeding and do not require correction of the blood loss and the anemia before the pathologic condition in the uterus is eliminated. These patients respond very satisfactorily to a "medical D. and C." (see p. 171). A large dose of progestogen is administered which converts the bleeding proliferative endometrium into the secretory stage, temporarily stops the hemorrhaging, and then induces endometrial desquamation with its accompanying bleeding. As soon as the pathologic condition in the uterus is thus corrected, the patient is ready for therapy aimed at restoring or replacing ovarian function. (2) The small remaining group of women with dysfunctional uterine bleeding who present themselves during a bleeding episode and have had severe uterine hemorrhaging require correction of the blood loss and the anemia before they are subjected to a "medical D. and C." with its attendant additional blood loss. The first step is to control the bleeding. This can be achieved by administering a sufficient amount of estrogen to induce hemostasis and to maintain the proliferative endometrium for an additional 3 to 4 weeks. During this interval in which there is no further uterine bleeding, the exsanguinated patient is given blood transfusions, hematinics, and other measures to combat the blood loss and the anemia. When these women are in condition to withstand further uterine bleeding, they are given a very large dose of progestogen to induce a "medical D. and C." with endometrial desquamation and correction of the pathology in the uterus. As soon as this is achieved, the patient is ready for therapy aimed at restoring or replacing ovarian function.

Once the uterine changes have been corrected in the women with dysfunctional uterine bleeding who have presented themselves for medical care during a bleeding episode, the disturbance in ovarian function is treated in exactly the same manner as in the women with dysfunctional uterine bleeding who have consulted the physician during the amenorrheic phase (see above). In the past, androgenic compounds have been used to control bleeding episodes in some of the women with dysfunctional uterine bleeding; these hormone preparations induce atrophy of the endometrium. However, the possibility of inducing masculinization limits the usefulness of androgenic hormones in women with this functional disturbance.

Presumptive Test for Pregnancy

The possibility of pregnancy must be considered in all women of child-bearing age with secondary amenorrhea of short duration (one to three months). The levels of chorionic gonadotropin in the blood or the urine of pregnant women do not become sufficiently elevated to give reliable positive biologic responses in animal assays until about the sixth week of gestation. However, from the onset of conception, the corpus luteum of pregnancy and later the placenta produce increased amounts of progestogen and estrogen. In such patients, the withdrawal of the progestational and estrogenic influences of hormone medication after a short course of administration is not followed by uterine bleeding with endometrial desquamation because the decidual state of the endometrium is maintained by the continuous presence of increased amounts of endogenously produced progestogen and estrogen. The lack of uterine bleeding, therefore, following a short course of progestogen and estrogen (i.e., 2.5 mg. of norethindrone acetate combined with 50 mcg. of ethinyl estradiol in one tablet [Gestest] taken two times a day for two days) in a woman of child-bearing age with secondary amenorrhea of short duration is a positive response for pregnancy; the use of hormonal agents in this manner constitutes a presumptive test for pregnancy. In women of child-bearing age with a secondary amenorrhea of short duration which is not caused by pregnancy, the withdrawal of the hormonal medication is followed by a "medical D. and C." with uterine bleeding and endometrial desquamation. The occurrence of uterine bleeding, therefore, following a short course of progestogen and estrogen in such a woman is a negative response for pregnancy. The employment of these hormones as a presumptive test for pregnancy is useful particularly in the early weeks of amenorrhea to provide indirect evidence of the presence or the absence of pregnancy before the biologic tests for the presence or the absence of increased gonadotropin production are reliable.

Dysmenorrhea and Endometriosis

Very severe cramps occur at the time of menstruation in some women who have no other manifestations of an ovarian disorder. This condition sometimes is termed "essential dysmenorrhea." The dysmenorrhea appears to be associated with abnormal uterine contractions resulting from increased uterine irritability. The cause of the increased irritability is obscure; it may be secondary to psychic and emotional stress. Psychotherapy appears to be important in the management of dysmenorrhea in many patients. It frequently is desirable to provide relief from the dysmenorrhea, particularly in younger women in whom the severe prostration and pains cause sufficient disability to interfere for several days with school attendance or work. Patients with true "essential" dysmenorrhea have cramps only when they desquamate a secretory endometrium. Therefore, inhibition of ovulation and thus of corpus luteum formation with the production of progestogen (and estrogen) affords temporary relief.

Ovulation can be inhibited by the administration of several types of hormonal medications. When progestational preparations are given shortly after the start of an ovarian cycle and before ovulation has taken place, and continued until shortly before the expected time of menstruation, the production of LH and LTH is inhibited and ovulation is prevented. In the patient with true "essential" dysmenorrhea, however, the progestational medications induce secretory changes in the endometrium, and the desquamation of secretory endometrium by such patients is associated with cramps. Thus, progestational agents usually do not relieve the dysmenorrhea. Androgenic medications administered in a similar manner will inhibit the production of LH and LTH and thus prevent ovulation. If bleeding occurs in such patients with true "essential" dysmenorrhea following androgen therapy, it is painless. However, the estrogen-induced proliferation of the endometrium usually is inhibited by the androgenic compounds so that uterine bleeding does not occur. Furthermore, when androgens are administered in sufficient amounts to inhibit ovulation, there is a hazard of inducing masculinization in the women. Therefore, the most satisfactory hormonal medication for preventing ovulation in women with "essential" dysmenorrhea is estrogen.

If estrogen is administered in sufficient dosage soon enough after the onset of any regular period (it usually is sufficient to start the hormone therapy on the second day), and if the estrogenic effect is maintained for 3 or more weeks, LH and LTH are inhibited, ovulation is prevented, and the proliferated endometrium is shed by estrogen-withdrawal bleeding when the action of the estrogen is terminated. This is painless in "essential" dysmenorrhea. If the dysmenorrhea is the result of other conditions such as endometriosis, however, the pain will not be relieved, and even may be made worse following the estrogen therapy. This point is utilized as a therapeutic test with estrogen to differentiate "essential" dysmenorrhea from other conditions with painful uterine bleeding.

Endometriosis is a common condition in which pathologic tissue which resembles the uterine endometrium histologically and which responds to hormonal stimulation with estrogen in a similar manner occurs aberrantly (chiefly in the pelvic cavity). The usual manifestations of endometriosis include menstrual disturbances, infertility, dysmenorrhea, and symptoms from pressure on structures adjacent to the endometriosis implants. The masses of aberrant tissue grow under the influence of estrogen and they atrophy when the estrogenic action is eliminated.

The administration of androgenic hormone preparations has been effective in many patients with endometriosis in inducing relief of pain and in reducing the size of the aberrant pelvic masses. However, androgenic therapy must be used with caution and has not been utilized widely because of the potential hazard of inducing masculinization.

It has been known for years that, when a patient who has endometriosis becomes pregnant, there is a considerable improvement in the symptoms and the signs of the endometriosis during the gestation and for about 2 years after the pregnancy has been terminated. This observation has led to the use of a hormone-induced pseudopregnancy state as a treatment for endometriosis with gratifying results in many patients. The pseudopregnancy is brought about by administering progestogenic and estrogenic hormones in a suitable ratio to maintain a decidual state in the endometrium starting a few days after ovulation. The decidual reaction cannot be maintained on progestogen alone, and cannot be maintained with progestogen and estrogen in a constant dosage for more than about 2 months. Thereafter, there is some degeneration of the decidual endometrium with "breakthrough" bleeding. This can be avoided by increasing the maintenance dosage of progestogen and estrogen every 6 weeks. With such a regimen it is possible to carry a decidual endometrium without "breakthrough" bleeding for as long as 9 months. As the endometrium is being maintained by the continuous presence of gradually increasing amounts of progestogen and estrogen, the endometriosis tissue degenerates and practically disappears. When the hormonal therapy is discontinued after 6 to 9 months of uninterrupted treatment, there usually is desquamated a decidual cast of the entire internal lining of the uterus.

Clinically in true endometriosis there is a marked relief of pain with the hormonally induced pseudopregnancy; this occurs so consistently that if this symptom is not alleviated by the third month of treatment the diagnosis of endometriosis is questioned. In addition, there is a marked reduction in the size of the aberrant endometriosis masses with a restoration of the normal mobility of the pelvic organs. Some patients respond very satisfactorily to hormone-induced pseudopregnancy and do not require surgical procedures; in other women, the hormone regimen is employed prior to conservative or radical surgical measures in the belief that the hormone therapy facilitates the operative procedure by reducing the vascularity and the size of the lesions; and, in some women, the hormone program is instituted following the surgical procedure in an attempt to control the lesions that are not amenable to excision. In women with endometriosis in whom infertility has been a problem, conception frequently occurs shortly after the hormone-induced pseudopregnancy is terminated. The patients resume normal cyclic ovarian function promptly when the administration of the hormones is discontinued. This form of hormonal management of endometriosis has not been used for a sufficient time to determine whether or not the benefits of the treatment will be permanent, or, if they are not, how soon the manifestations of the pathologic condition will reappear. Hormone-induced pseudopregnancy appears to be a physiologic method of controlling endometriosis which preserves the ovarian function and the child-bearing capacity of the woman afflicted with this disorder.

Both progestogen and estrogen are required to induce a pseudopregnancy state with hormones. These substances should be given in a ratio which brings about and maintains a mature secretory endometrium in the decidual stage. This can be accomplished very effectively with the long-acting injectable hormone preparations if 250 mg. of 17-alpha-hydroxy-progesterone caproate (Delalutin) and 5 mg. of estradiol valerate (Delestrogen) are administered simultaneously. A new preparation (Deluteval), in which these two esters are combined in the desired ratio, facilitates such therapy. In inducing a pseudopregnancy state, the progestogen-estrogen preparation is injected once a week, starting a few days after ovulation with 125 mg. of the caproate ester and 2.5 mg. of the valerate ester per injection and increasingly the weekly injections by 125 mg. of the caproate ester and 2.5 mg. of the valerate ester every 6 weeks for a total of 36 weeks of treatment.

Hormones and Conception Control

Ovulation can be inhibited by the administration of several types of hormonal preparations. When progestational preparations are given in sufficient dosage shortly after the start of an ovarian cycle and before ovulation has taken place, and continued until shortly before the expected time of menstruation, the production of LH and LTH is inhibited and ovulation is prevented. However, progestogens have an antiestrogenic action and tend to neutralize or inhibit the endogenous production of estrogen. Since the uterine endometrium cannot be maintained in a pseudo-decidual state by progestogenic activity alone in the absence of estrogenic activity, the administration of progestogens alone usually results in premature desquamation of immature secretory endometrium and "breakthrough" bleeding. Estrogen alone, instead of the progestogen, when administered in the same regimen also will inhibit the production of the pituitary gonadotropins and prevent ovulation. If the estrogen therapy is interrupted after 3 weeks, the proliferated uterine endometrium is shed by estrogen-withdrawal bleeding. However, all of the proliferated endometrium usually is not shed each time the estrogen therapy is withdrawn, and thus after some months of treatment the patient may have irregular and unpredictable bleeding from an induced metropathia hemorrhagica (see above). The most satisfactory method of inducing inhibition of ovulation with hormones is to give progestogen combined with estrogen so that the pituitary gonadotropin production is inhibited by both agents and following cessation of therapy the lining of the uterus is completely desquamated as secretory endometrium. The combined hormone preparations are administered orally each day from the fifth to the twenty-fifth days of the cycle or parenterally as a single injection on the eighth day of the cycle (Deladroxate).

Hormones are effective in conception control not only by inhibiting ovulation, but also by other mechanisms such as premature aging of the endometrium so that it no longer will accept implantation, alteration of the cervical mucus so that it interferes with sperm penetration, and acceleration of ovum passage through the tubes so that it arrives prematurely. A few patients taking progestogen-estrogen combinations for conception control experience the occasional menstrual cycle manifestations (bloating, edema, premenstrual tension) observed in normally ovulating women; a few have breakthrough bleeding or amenorrhea. Following the withdrawal of continuous exogenously induced hormone levels maintained for several years for conception control, the pituitary-ovarian activities resume a normal pattern of cyclic function in almost all patients in 8 to 12 weeks, just as these activities resume a normal pattern in almost all patients in 8 to 12 weeks following the cessation of continuous endogenously induced hormone levels maintained for 9 months for gestation.

Premenstrual Tension

Premenstrual tension is a syndrome characterized by the cyclical recurrence for about 5 to 10 days preceding each menstruation of a variety of symptoms (in various combinations and in varying intensity), such as nervousness, sensations of intolerable tension, irritability, emotional instability, depression, insomnia, vertigo, headache, nausea, premenstrual "bloating," and edema. The manifestations disappear shortly after the onset of menstruation. The mechanism by which the psychic and emotional changes are related to the hormones involved in the ovarian cycle is not entirely clear, and many theories have been advanced. Psychosomatic factors appear to be important, and psychotherapy is valuable in these patients. Other factors that have been suggested include (1) autonomic nervous system imbalance, (2) increase in antidiuretic hormone, (3) menstrual toxins, (4) hypoglycemia, (5) allergic reactions to ovarian hormones, (6) increased estrogenic activity, (7) decreased progestational activity, (8) vitamin deficiency, and (9) gonadotropin-ovarian hormone imbalance.

The most plausible mechanism at present is an imbalance in the production of progestogen and estrogen from the corpus luteum after ovulation so that too little progestogen is produced for the amount of estrogen. Estrogen (and androgen) stimulates the production and/or release of aldosterone; progestogen antagonizes the action of aldosterone on the renal tubules. In the presence of too little progestogen, aldosterone production and/or release is greater than normal, leading to sodium retention and clinical manifestations suggesting a mild hyperaldosteronism. The administration of progestational compounds with no inherent estrogenic (or androgenic) activity, by restoring the balance with estrogen and by neutralizing the peripheral effect of the excess of aldosterone, causes a marked clinical improvement with the elimination of the symptoms. A very effective regimen is the administration of a single injection of 125 mg. of the long-acting progestational preparation, 17-alpha-hydroxyprogesterone caproate (Delalutin), one or two days after ovulation each month. This usually completely relieves the condition. Some of the symptoms can be eliminated also by the use of diuretics.

Anorexia Nervosa

In this condition the patient is suffering from a disorder similar to that described earlier as "hypothalamic" amenorrhea. In fact, anorexia nervosa could be classified as a subform of "hypothalamic" amenorrhea. Patients with anorexia nervosa have a psychoneurotic state which results in anorexia. The psychologic state also results in a block to the release of neurohumoral impulses from the hypothalamus so that LH is not released and amenorrhea develops. In the differentiation of these patients from those with amenorrhea as a result of pituitary hypofunction following malnutrition, it is significant that in anorexia nervosa the amenorrhea begins before the patients have lost any considerable degree of weight. It should be pointed out that in time, as these patients fail to eat and become extremely malnourished, there is hypofunction of all the tissues of the body, including the pituitary gland, the thyroid, the adrenals, and the gonads; in other words, a state of panhypopituitarism becomes superimposed upon the anorexia nervosa if it has persisted for a sufficient length of time. The main therapy is psychotherapy, but hormone medication may be given as a supplement in order to stimulate the target glands or replace their hormones if the condition has persisted for a long time.

Arrhenoblastoma

An arrhenoblastoma is an ovarian tumor which produces hormones similar to those produced by the male testis. Some patients show evidences of masculinization with hir-

sutism, atrophy of the breasts, hypertrophy of the clitoris, and changes in the voice. Other patients are remarkably free from these manifestations. It is suggested that these latter patients have tumors which are producing the type of hormone thought to be produced by the tubules of the male testis; and it is expected that these patients will have a decreased secretion of pituitary gonadotropin of the FSH type. At least one case is on record in which the tumor produced excessive amounts of steroids with an effect on carbohydrate metabolism. These tumors are sometimes malignant and metastasize. The gonadotropic hormone levels in this condition need further study.

Granulosa Tumors, Theca Cell Tumors, and Luteomas

The granulosa and theca cell tumors arise in the ovary and produce excessive amounts of estrogen. The luteomas also arise in the ovary and produce increased amounts of estrogen and progestogen. As a result of the excessive production of estrogen, these patients have large breasts and excessive amounts of axillary hair, and there may be accelerated body growth in the preadolescent. Amenorrhea alternating with irregular bleeding may occur from metropathia hemorrhagica as a result of the continuous presence of large amounts of estrogen. The FSH production by the pituitary is considerably decreased.

Investigations by Li and Gardner and by Furth and Sobel suggest that these tumors may arise in an interesting way. These investigators transplanted an ovary to the spleen of rats and then removed the other ovary. They showed that in animals thus prepared atrophic changes developed in the uterus, indicating that the hormones produced by the transplanted ovary were being inactivated by the liver. At the same time the pituitaries produced an excessive amount of gonadotropin such as in found in the castrate. When the animals were kept sufficiently long periods of time, the excessive gonadotropin stimulated the ovary to the point at which granulosa cell tumors and luteomas developed. Some of the animal tumors were malignant and metastasized. Whether these tumors in the human being are due to excessive effect of gonadotropin upon the ovary because of a lack of ovarian hormones or because of some derangement in their metabolism so that they are no longer available to neutralize or inhibit the gonadotropin is not known.

Hypoleydigism

This term is used to describe a condition in which the Leydig cells of the testis produce a decreased amount of androgen. This may result from intrinsic disease in the testis, in which case the situation is analogous to castration, or from a lack of stimulation from the pituitary. The latter situation may result from a failure of the neurohumoral impulses to reach the pituitary from the hypothalamus (as in Fröhlich's syndrome), or from a deficiency in the pituitary itself (as in panhypopituitarism, or in a selective deficiency in the production of gonadotropins, such as is found in the usual type of eunuchoid patient). When the disease is intrinsic in the testis, there is an increased production of ICSH (LH) and/or LTH by the pituitary; in the other forms of hypoleydigism ICSH (LH) and LTH production is decreased. In many cases there is also an increased production of FSH when the disease causing hypoleydigism is intrinsic in the testis, and a decreased production of FSH in the other forms of hypoleydigism.

The symptoms and clinical manifestations vary, depending upon whether the condition occurs before puberty or after. There are surprisingly few clinical manifestations of hypoleydigism when the disorder arises after puberty. There is atrophy of the testes, some decrease in the rate of growth of the body and facial hair, and slight decrease in the size of the testes along with inability to secure erection of the phallus; there may be manifestations of emotional instability analogous to those found in the castrate female. A patient in whom hypoleydigism occurs before puberty retains the physical characteristics of a child, with soft skin, high-pitched voice, lack of beard, and preadolescent muscular and genital development. Spermatogenesis is always decreased or absent in the presence of hypoleydigism.

Treatment is based upon whether the cause is primary in the testis or results from inadequate stimulation from the pituitary. When the primary changes are in the testis, the only treatment that can be given is replacement therapy with androgenic hormones. When the primary defect is inadequate stimulation from the pituitary, it is rational to give stimulation therapy in the form of ICSH or, since no adequate preparations of this hormone are available, chorionic gonadotropin.

Another possible method of increasing the endogenous production of ICSH by the anterior pituitary gland is to utilize the principle of "rebound stimulation therapy." Androgen in appropriate doses when administered for a suitable period of time will suppress the ICSH production by the pituitary gland; after the withdrawal of the androgen, however, there may be a "rebound" increase in the production of ICSH which in certain cases is sufficient to provide the Leydig cells with enough stimulation to maintain function. For this reason the administration of androgen therapy to patients with hypoleydigism from inadequate pituitary stimulation should be interrupted temporarily for 3 or 4 months after 4 or 5 months of medication in order to permit the "rebound" to take place and to detect the onset of spontaneous testicular function if it is going to occur. The gradual decrease of androgenic activity following the administration of certain long-acting testosterone esters, such as testosterone enanthate (Delatestryl), also may provide a physiologic stimulus for a "rebound" in the endogenous ICSH production. In appropriate doses (200 to 400 mg.), testosterone enanthate is effective for about one month after a single intramuscular injection.

Hypospermatogenesis

Hypospermatogenesis can occur in the presence of normal Leydig cell function, but normal spermatogenesis does not occur in the presence of decreased Leydig cell function. When normal amounts of androgenic hormones are not present, the functional state of the tubules is not maintained and spermatogenesis cannot proceed at a normal rate; in other words, hypoleydigism is a primary cause of hypospermatogenesis. In those patients who have normal Leydig cell function, hypospermatogenesis may occur either because there is disease in the testis which destroys the tubules and results in an increase in FSH such as is found in seminiferous tubule dysgenesis (see below), or because there is lack of stimulation from the pituitary due to a decrease in the FSH production.

The tubules of the testis are thought to produce, in addition to sperm, a hormone which has been called "inhibin." This hormone is postulated to inhibit the production of FSH from the pituitary and to inhibit the effect of androgen on the breast and the prostate. In patients who have been castrated and lack the tubules and their hormone, or in those who have primary disease of the testis with damage to the tubules, the lack of "inhibin" is thought to account for the occasional development of gynecomastia after treatment with androgenic preparations. In those patients with hypospermatogenesis in whom there are evidences of hypoleydigism, treatment for the inadequate Leydig cell function should be instituted first, and then the administration of preparations containing FSH may be of value.

Seminiferous Tubule Dysgenesis (Gynecomastia-and-Small-Testes Syndrome, Klinefelter's Syndrome)

In 1942 Klinefelter, Reifenstein and Albright called attention to a syndrome in males, characterized by gynecomastia, aspermatogenesis without aleydigism, and increased excretion of FSH. Further cases of this syndrome subsequently were described by Heller and Nelson, and it now is recognized to be a very common disorder. The endocrine manifestations (such as gynecomastia and a variable degree of eunuchoidism) are not prominent in many cases, and the only essential features are the typical pathologic lesions in the testes and azoospermia. The testes are less than normal size and the FSH excretion is elevated in most adult patients. The increased incidence of mental deficiency in this syndrome has been stressed in recent reports. A most interesting finding has been the demonstration that the majority of these patients have a female (positive) sex chromatin pattern with an increased number (greater than 46) and/or an abnormal constitution (XXY, XXXY, XXXXY, mosaic patterns, and so forth) of the sex chromosomes. This has made it possible to discover many cases in adults with minimal physical manifestations and to detect this disorder in preadolescent individuals. The lesions in the tubules of the testis show thickening of the basement membranes with a loss of all of the spermatogenic elements and frequently complete hyalinization; large clumps of Leydig cells are visible and may be present in greater numbers than can be accounted for by the atrophy of the tubular elements. There is some histologic evidence that these Leydig cells are not normal. I believe that, as a consequence of the lesions in these tubules, there is a loss of the hormone which has been called "inhibin." As a result of this loss, the pituitary produces excessive amounts of gonadotropic hormone of the FSH type. The hyalinization of the tubules does not begin until the onset of puberty, and probably is a response to the increase in anterior pituitary gonadotropins at

that time. Similarly, the FSH excretion in patients with this syndrome does not become elevated until the onset of puberty.

How these patients acquire gynecomastia is not clear. I favor the theory that the loss of "inhibin" leads to the unopposed action on the breast of androgen from the Leydig cells. Another school of thought favors the thesis that abnormal steroids produced either from the Leydig cells or from the adrenal cortex cause the development of the breast. There is little evidence that these patients are producing excessive amounts of estrogen or that they have abnormal liver function which alters the metabolism of the steroids. No therapy has been found which will reduce the gynecomastia or affect the hypospermatogenesis of these patients.

Hereditary Male Pseudohermaphroditism with Hypogonadism, Hypospadias, and Gynecomastia (Reifenstein's Syndrome)

In 1947, Reifenstein described a hereditary disorder affecting sexual differentiation in the male which resembles the Klinefelter syndrome clinically (with post-pubertal testicular atrophy, weak or absent virilization, aspermatogenesis and infertility, and to a variable extent, gynecomastia) but has in addition hypospadias in all the affected members. Increased excretion of FSH may be present in both syndromes. In contrast to patients with the Klinefelter syndrome, those with the Reifenstein syndrome have a male (negative) sex chromatin pattern with a normal 46 (XY) karyotype chromosome count. Data reported recently on 21 affected members of three separate families indicate that the disorder is inherited through phenotypically normal female carriers and affects only genetic males as either an X-linked recessive or an autosomal dominant, male-limited trait. In these three families, linkage data, using the X_g^a blood type or color vision as marker traits, were either uninformative or inconclusive, and provided no evidence for or against the view that the gene for the Reifenstein syndrome is carried on the X chromosome. The Y chromosome was of average length and normal morphology in the Reifenstein syndrome. Since many of the clinical manifestations in the Reifenstein syndrome are the same as those in the Klinefelter syndrome, it is clear that these clinical defects cannot be related per se to the abnormal number (over 46) and/or constitution (XXY, XXXY, XXXXY, mosaic patterns, and so forth) of the sex chromosomes which are found in the Klinefelter syndrome because these abnormalities are not found in the Reifenstein syndrome.

Cryptorchidism

The testes, which normally migrate into the scrotum by the end of the eighth month of fetal life, fail to descend in some individuals. About 30 per cent of premature male infants, 10 per cent of full term male infants, 2 per cent of boys at puberty, and 0.2 per cent of adult men have undescended testes. Thus, the majority of preadolescent boys with bilateral cryptorchidism will achieve spontaneous descent of the testes by the time of puberty. The undescended testis apparently is not harmed by leaving it in the ectopic position until puberty; however, after puberty the retained testis generally shows involution of the germinal elements and rarely is able to achieve spermatogenesis in adult life. Some workers contend that most testes which have failed to descend during normal development are inherently defective and hence are usually sterile even though they are brought into the scrotum by surgical or hormonal therapy.

All the factors which contribute to the lack of testicular descent are not known. Those which have been recognized include (1) congenital abnormalities in development; (2) mechanical obstructions in the retroperitoneal areas or inguinal canals; and (3) endocrine disturbance during fetal life, particularly inadequate chorionic gonadotropin production by the placenta during the latter part of pregnancy. Unilateral cryptorchidism usually is caused by a mechanical obstruction rather than by congenital or endocrine factors. Many boys have migratory testes which are retracted into the inguinal canals by excitement or cold; the migratory organs usually can be found in the scrotum if the patient is placed in a hot bath. The diagnosis of undescended testes should be established beyond question before any therapy is instituted.

It has been recommended that the abnormal position of the testes be corrected before adult life for the following reasons: (1) to avoid irreversible tubular damage from the higher temperature of the internal body cavities with consequent sterility; (2) to eliminate the increased hazard of trauma to the testis because of its malposition (particularly if it lies over the symphysis or in the inguinal canal); (3) to reduce the psychologic trauma of being different from other males; and (4) to avoid any tendency to carcinomatous degeneration in the aberrantly placed genital organs. Opinion varies as to the optimal age at which treatment for undescended testes should be instituted: (1) The majority of physicians consider 7 to 11 years of age (just prior to puberty) as the ideal time for treatment. (2) Some advocate waiting until puberty has started. (3) Others advise correction of the malposition before the patient has reached the age of 3 years. The psychologic trauma of having undescended testes and of being different from other boys is stressed by those who advocate early correction of cryptorchidism.

Procedures designed to bring the malplaced testes into their normal scrotal position involve surgical and hormonal considerations. Several therapeutic regimens have been proposed: (1) Surgery alone without any hormone medication. A few surgeons still believe that hormone therapy is of no value, and operate in all cases of cryptorchidism. (2) Surgery after priming with androgenic hormone therapy for anatomic development. Prior to surgically transplanting the testes into the scrotum, some surgeons administer androgens for 6 to 8 weeks to induce growth and development of the testes and the scrotum and elongation of the spermatic cord; they believe that such treatment improves the chance of success in the operation. Androgenic preparations not infrequently induce testicular descent. (3) Chorionic gonadotropin therapy followed immediately by surgery if the testes fail to descend after an adequate trial of the hormonal medication. The majority of physicians favor an initial trial of chorionic gonadotropin in an effort to induce descent, and reserve surgical intervention for the cases which fail to respond to hormone therapy. It is claimed that the percentage of preadolescent cryptorchid boys who have testicular descent following the administration of chorionic gonadotropin is approximately the same as the percentage of these same boys who would have spontaneous descent when they undergo puberty. This has led some workers to suggest that the testes which can be brought down by chorionic gonadotropin before puberty would have come down spontaneously during adolescence.

In approximately 25 per cent of preadolescent cryptorchid boys, the testes descend with chorionic gonadotropin therapy. If descent is going to occur, the signs usually appear within the first 6 to 8 weeks of treatment, and then the hormone administration is continued until the testes have descended well into the scrotal sac. If no signs of descent have appeared within this time, further administration of chorionic gonadotropin usually is of no avail, and should be discontinued. A satisfactory dosage regimen of chorionic gonadotropin (Follutein) is 1000 to 2000 I.U. by intramuscular injection three times a week or 2500 to 5000 I.U. once a week. This amount of the hormone preparation usually induces evidence of a slight to moderate increase in endogenous androgen production by the Leydig cells of the testes within 6 to 8 weeks in boys whose gonads are responsive to this gonadotropic hormone. Preadolescent boys who are being treated with chorionic gonadotropin should be watched carefully to avoid the premature development which will occur if the endogenous androgen production is stimulated sufficiently to achieve adult levels at too early an age. However, there is no danger of excessive androgen production because the ability of the Leydig cells to respond to the chorionic gonadotropin limits the amount of androgen produced to the maximum adult level (a quantity which is optimal for tissue growth). Thus, the interstitial cells of the testis may be "prematurely stimulated" but not "overstimulated" by this gonadotropic hormone. Since the chorionic material is of human origin (homologous) it does not induce antihormone production.

In prepuberal boys who have achieved evidence of androgen production but not testicular descent following chorionic gonadotropin therapy, surgical transplantation should be instituted without delay. It is claimed that testes which have been stimulated by the hormone therapy (1) are more susceptible to damage from the higher internal body temperature with resulting sterility, and (2) are more prone to develop malignant lesions if they are not removed to the normal scrotal position. If evidence is obtained of androgen production and testicular descent does not occur, a mechanical barrier can be assumed. In the rare cases in which androgenic manifestations do not follow the administration of chorionic gonadotropin, unresponsive, damaged, or rudimentary testicular tissue probably is present. Endocrine therapy with an androgenic preparation then is indicated for such patients in an effort to induce testicular descent. Even if descent is not achieved, the anatomic changes induced by the androgen in the genital organs and accessory sexual structures facilitate the subsequent operative procedure, providing that this is undertaken before there is a regression of these androgenic responses.

The final success of the therapeutic procedures must be judged by the subsequent function of the cryptorchid testes which have been brought into the scrotum by treatment with chorionic gonadotropin and/or surgery. In general, these gonads (1) usually are capable of spontaneously producing androgenic hormones and thus inducing normal sexual maturation and libido, and (2) frequently have some impairment of spermatogenesis which makes many of these individuals relatively infertile. Prolonged observation of adequately studied cases is needed.

In postadolescent cryptorchid patients with adequate endogenous androgen production and no evidence of hypogonadism, treatment with chorionic gonadotropin or androgen usually does not induce testicular descent. Unilateral cryptorchidism in a postadolescent patient with manifestations of adequate androgen production commonly indicates a mechanical barrier on the side which has failed to descend.

Male "Climacteric"

A great many older men complain of vasomotor symptoms, fatigue, and decreased genital function which some physicians believe to represent a male "climacteric or menopause." When the production of excessive amounts of gonadotropin by the pituitary is used to establish the decrease in activity of the testis, there are few cases that satisfy the requirements of hormone imbalance. There is no doubt, however, that this hormone deficiency syndrome occasionally does occur in aging men. The sequence of events seems to be (1) failure of testicular function, (2) loss of the testicular hormones, androgen and "inhibin," (3) increase in the pituitary gonadotropins, FSH, ICSH(LH), and LTH, and (4) the appearance of symptoms of autonomic nervous system instability. In general, increase in the gonadotropins goes along with the symptoms of vasomotor instability. Since much larger amounts of androgen than of estrogen are required to inhibit FSH, it has been my practice first to give estrogen to inhibit FSH, and then in addition to administer sufficient androgen for the patient to have erections. On this therapy these patients are considerably improved.

Teratoma, Chorioepithelioma, and Choriocarcinoma

These tumors of the male and female gonads secrete large amounts of anterior pituitary-like hormones, which are similar in action to the anterior pituitary-like hormone secreted by the placenta, that is, chorionic gonado-tropin. There is some indication that these tumors also may secrete large amounts of estrogen. In the male the tumors are frequently associated with the development of gynecomastia. This may be due to several mechanisms: (1) the increased production of estrogen, with its effect on the male breast; (2) atrophy of the testicular tubules as a consequence of the excess estrogen so that the hormone "inhibin" is lost, and as a result there is unopposed action of the androgen on the breast; (3) an increased production of androgen as a result of the stimulation of the Leydig cells by the chorionic gonadotropin, resulting in inhibition of the tubules by the androgen, loss of "inhibin," and unopposed action of the androgen on the breast; or (4) a direct action of the chorionic gonadotropin on the breast. In some patients with these trophoblastic tumors, temporary remissions have been achieved recently with the administration of repeated courses of the folic acid antagonist 4-amino-N^{10} methylpteroylglutamic acid (Methotrexate) in toxic quantities. In the cases that responded favorably, the amounts of chorionic gonadotropin excreted in the urine were reduced from extremely high levels to the physiologic range.

Leydig Cell Tumor

Tumors of the Leydig cells of the testis are rare. They produce large quantities of androgenic hormones, and patients with this condition exhibit manifestations of the excessive amounts of these hormones. These individuals are very hirsute, remain strong in spite of the malignant disease, and have an excessive excretion of 17-ketosteroids in the urine. It is assumed that the ICSH(LH) and LTH production by the anterior pituitary is inhibited by the large amounts of androgens.

Cretinism and Myxedema (Hypothyroidism)

When an infant has hypothyroidism at birth, he is said to be a cretin; when he acquires hypothyroidism after birth, he is said to develop myxedema (juvenile myxedema). The primary disturbance is a loss of adequate thyroid hormone production. Although the evidence is not complete, patients with hypothyroidism may be classified in two groups: (1) those in whom the disease arises primarily in the thyroid gland with a loss of the thyroid hormone and then an increase in TSH production, and (2) those in whom the disease arises primarily in the pituitary gland with a loss of TSH and then decreased production of thyroid hormone. Included in this latter group are the so-called pituitary myxedema patients, who are really suffering from panhypopituitarism. This latter group might be expected to respond to potent preparations of TSH; the former group would not respond at all. In general, both groups are treated with thyroid extract, thyroxine, or triiodothyronine, which appear to be equally effective when given in appropriate doses. Myxedema coma, a state of hypothermic cachexia in untreated and uncomplicated myxedema, is reported to respond successfully to triiodothyronine intravenously.

Thyrotoxicosis (Hyperthyroidism)

The manifestations of this disorder are the result of excessive production and/or release of the thyroid hormone (thyroxine) from either (1) a toxic diffuse or hyperplastic goiter (Graves' disease, exophthalmic goiter) or (2) a toxic nodular goiter (or a toxic adenoma). There is no evidence that an abnormal secretion is released by the diseased thyroid gland in either condition. The excessive production and/or release of thyroxine results from one or two basic mechanisms: (1) increased stimulation of the thyroid gland because of increased amounts and/or activity of TSH from the anterior pituitary gland or (2) disease which is primary in the thyroid gland. The first mechanism is present in Graves' disease (exophthalmic goiter).

The increased amount and/or activity of TSH is brought about in several ways: (1) iodine deficiency leading to decreased inactivation of TSH combined with decreased thyroxine production and hence decreased inhibition of TSH production and/or release from the anterior pituitary gland; (2) increased neurogenic stimulation via the hypothalamus with increased production and/or release of neurohumoral materials which stimulate the production and/or release of TSH from the anterior pituitary gland; (3) increased production and/or release of TSH from the anterior pituitary gland because of hyperfunctioning disorders originating in the pituitary gland; (4) increased production and/or release of TSH because the pituitary gland becomes resistant to the inhibitory action of thyroxine on TSH production and/or release; and (5) increased production and/or release of TSH because the thyroid gland produces insufficient thyroxine to inhibit TSH production and/or release. Thyroxine production may be inadequate as a result of (1) iodine deficiency; (2) thyroidectomy; (3) destruction of thyroid gland tissue by x-ray irradiation; (4) destruction of thyroid gland tissue by radioiodine; (5) inhibition of the thyroid iodide-serum iodide gradient by antithyroid chemical agents such as thiocyanate; (6) inhibition of the synthesis of thyroxine by antithyroid chemical agents such as thiourea; and (7) inhibition of thyroxine activity outside the thyroid gland by chemical thyroxine antagonists.

The effects of an increased amount and/or activity of TSH on the thyroid gland are (1) increased proteolysis of thyroglobulin with more rapid transfer of thyroxine into the blood stream; (2) decreased storage of thyroid hormone; (3) increased thyroid iodide-serum iodide gradient with increased trapping of iodide by the thyroid; (4) increased oxidation of iodide to iodine in the thyroid; (5) increased rate of synthesis of diiodotyrosine and thyroxine; and (6) hypertrophy and hyperplasia of the acinar cells. Disorders which are primary in the thyroid gland, such as adenoma or carcinoma, also can cause increased production of thyroid hormone and hyperthyroidism. Following the administration of a tracer dose of radioiodine, there is an increased concentration of the radioactive element in the thyroid gland and a decreased excretion of it in the urine in patients with hyperthyroidism; these alterations are useful indices in establishing the diagnosis.

In treating hyperthyroidism, a number of therapeutic procedures are used either alone or in combination, depending upon the factors which appear to participate in the mechanism underlying the hyperfunction of the thyroid gland. These measures include: (1) The administration of iodine. This provides satisfactory control only in mild cases. (2) The use of psychotherapy. This is indicated and is effective only occasionally. (3) Irradiation of the pituitary gland with roentgen rays. This is not sufficiently effective to warrant its use as therapy. (4) Thyroidectomy. Subtotal surgical removal of the thyroid gland cures the disease in most patients, brings the hyperfunctional state and the pressure manifestations from the goiter under control very rapidly, and eliminates thyroid lesions which are suspected of being cancerous. It has the following disadvantages: persistence or recurrence of thyrotoxicosis, myxedema, hypoparathyroidism, paralysis of the vocal cords, mortality, physical discomfort, acute emotional upset, and time lost from work. Thyroid storm (flooding of the system with excess thyroxine) is avoided by a preliminary course of antithyroid compounds. (5) Roentgenotherapy

to the thyroid gland. This shrinks the goiter in patients treated with antithyroid agents. By itself, it induces a cure of the hyperthyroidism in only about one-third of the cases. It involves the hazards of toxic effects of x-rays on the skin (burns) and on the other adjacent structures (tracheitis and esophagitis). (6) Irradiation of the thyroid gland with radioiodine. Radioiodine therapy is definitive, causes a pronounced regression or disappearance of the goiter, can always be effective, rarely is followed by relapse or subsequent attacks, and avoids the unfavorable features of surgery. The disadvantages include: (a) it induces permanent myxedema in a sizable proportion of cases, (b) it is difficult to administer because of uncertainty in determining the appropriate dosage for complete treatment in one administration, (c) it requires a protracted period of management to achieve a maximal beneficial response, and (d) it has the theoretical hazards of inducing carcinogenic effects and mutation of genes. Radioiodine therapy is the treatment of choice in older patients. (7) The use of antithyroid compounds. Antithyroid drugs control the hyperthyroidism in all cases in a reasonably short time; do not induce damage in the thyroid gland, irreversible changes, or permanent myxedema; are easily regulated from the point of view of dosage; and avoid the unfavorable features of surgery. The disadvantages include: (a) these agents fail to induce a lasting remission in a proportion of patients; (b) they require a protracted period of administration to control the thyrotoxicosis; and (c) they may induce toxic reactions. In general, toxic reactions are seldom seen, are usually mild, and either subside spontaneously or else respond promptly to a change to another compound. Therapy with antithyroid agents is the treatment of choice in children, in pregnant women, and in cases in which the diagnosis of hyperthyroidism is in question. (8) The use of chemical thyroxine antagonists. At present, no compounds with sufficient activity are available for general use.

Exophthalmic Goiter (Graves' Disease)

In this disease there is present, in addition to thyrotoxicosis, exophthalmos, which may become severe and malignant so that blindness finally results. The primary mechanism is thought to be an increased production by the anterior pituitary gland of TSH and of another distinct component, called the exophthalmos-producing substance (E.P.S.); the increased amounts of these two materials affect not only the thyroid, resulting in thyrotoxicosis, but also the eyes, resulting in exophthalmos. Evidence suggests that in some instances the thyroid becomes exhausted and cannot produce enough hormone to inactivate these two factors, and, as a result, the increased amounts of these factors stimulate the eyes and lead to progressive exophthalmos. Some cases are improved by the administration of thyroid extract and are made worse by thyroidectomy. However, thyroid hormone cannot be given to many of these patients, because it aggravates the thyrotoxicosis already present. Roentgen irradiation of the orbits or pituitary region; hypophysectomy or section of the pituitary stalk; retro-ocular injection of hyaluronidase, of triiodothyronine, or of an adrenal glucocorticoid compound; and administration of estrogen or iodide have been tried in such patients with indifferent results. Large doses of corticosteroids not infrequently cause temporary improvement by relieving the "inflammatory" components of the disorder and sometimes induce regression of the exophthalmos. Recently a gamma globulin, called long-acting thyroid stimulator (LATS), has been isolated from the serum of patients with significant exophthalmos and/or pretibial myxedema. This may represent altered TSH which has escaped from the thyroid gland in some manner associated with a specific antigen-antibody response; thus exophthalmic goiter may be one of the "autoimmune" disorders. The serum level of LATS may be depressed by large doses of corticosteroids.

Simple Goiter

In this condition, it is believed that, at the onset, an insufficient amount of thyroid hormone is produced (usually because of an inadequate intake of iodine), and as a consequence initially there is an increased production of TSH by the anterior pituitary gland. This stimulates the thyroid gland to increased growth and to increased thyroxine production. The increased growth leads to the formation of the goiter, and, in most patients, the increase in thyroid hormone production compensates for the increase in TSH production. As a result, a dynamic equilibrium is re-established between TSH and thyroid hormone, and the measurable levels of hormone production are in the physiologic range.

Thyroiditis

Subacute thyroiditis, apparently the result of a viral infection, is the most frequently encountered inflammatory condition. When damage to the gland is extensive, thyroid hormone production may be inadequate. Moderately severe thyroiditis often responds to thyroid hormone medication. Corticosteroid hormones effectively suppress the symptoms in cases of short duration, and may be used with thyroid hormone in protracted cases. Antibodies to thyroglobulin have been demonstrated in some patients. Chronic thyroiditis, including Hashimoto's disease and the rare Riedl's struma, seldom is diagnosed. These disorders apparently respond to the same hormonal management. Antibodies to thyroglobulin have been found also in these chronic conditions. The sequence of events in "autoimmune" thyroiditis, particularly Hashimoto's disease, may be (1) damage to the thyroid (by infection, hemorrhage, surgery, irradiation, genetic mutation, excessive TSH, malignant invasion, or other factors); (2) destruction of acinar cells with liberation of two types of antigens: microsomal particles and colloid; (3) interaction of the thyroid cells with the antigens to produce cytotoxic substances; (4) induction of interstitial inflammation and antibody formation by the cytotoxic substances; and (5) sufficient destruction of the thyroid by the antibodies in some cases to lead to post-thyroiditis myxedema.

Hypoparathyroidism

This disorder, which is due to insufficient parathyroid hormone, arises either as an idiopathic state or as a result of the loss of the function of the parathyroid glands after damage or removal at thyroidectomy. There is no indication of hypoparathyroidism in patients with panhypopituitarism. This is strong evidence that there is no parathyrotropic hormone secreted by the anterior pituitary gland.

After the loss of the parathyroid hormone, the excretion of phosphorus in the urine is decreased, and phosphorus piles up in the blood serum. As a result, the ion product of phosphorus *times* calcium activities rises, and the blood becomes relatively more saturated with these minerals in relation to bone. As a consequence, less than normal amounts of calcium and phosphorus are resorbed from bone, and the calcium level in the blood tends to fall. With the fall in the blood calcium level, less calcium is excreted in the urine. At the same time, since less bone is resorbed, the bones of the body tend to become more dense; since the blood is more saturated in terms of the ion product, there is a tendency to metastatic calcification, which may occur in the choroid plexus of the brain, in the lens and conjunctiva of the eye, in the lung, and in the gastric mucosa. The fall in the level of calcium in the blood results in alterations in the excitability of nervous tissue which lead to tetany, and abnormalities of the electrocardiogram and electroencephalogram.

These patients respond to the administration of parathyroid hormone; however, a sufficiently purified preparation is not yet available for general use. The chief therapy used is dihydrotachysterol (A.T.–10) by mouth, either alone or supplemented with calciferol (vitamin D_2). In addition, these patients are given a high calcium, low phosphorus diet.

With the demonstration that the parathyroid glands also produce the serum calcium-lowering hormone, calcitonin, the possibility exists that some cases of hypoparathyroidism may be the result of an excessive production of calcitonin. Also some cases of hypoparathyroidism could occur as a consequence of an excessive production of the similarly acting thyrocalcitonin by the thyroid gland.

Pseudohypoparathyroidism

This interesting disease is an excellent example of the lack of end-organ response to a normal hormone production. Albright and his associates described four patients with this condition, and other investigators have reported a number of additional patients. The hormone production may be increased because biopsy of a parathyroid gland in several cases has revealed hyperplastic tissue; increased bone resorption also has been reported in some patients. The blood findings, however, are those of hypoparathyroidism, with a high serum inorganic phosphorus level and a low serum calcium level. The patients have tetany and the other symptoms of true hypoparathyroidism. These patients are extremely resistant to parathyroid extract and show little phosphorus diuresis after the intravenous administration of large amounts of this hormone. The patients are controlled, however, when large amounts of dihydrotachysterol (A.T.–10) are administered. All the patients have a peculiar physiognomy characterized by a round face and a rather thickset figure; they also tend to have brachydactyly due to shortness of the metacarpal or occasionally the metatarsal bones. An approximate estimate of the length of time that the patient has had pseudohypoparathyroidism can be obtained from the number of short metacarpals. Because of the short metacarpals, no knuckles are apparent for the involved fingers when the hand is clenched into a fist.

These patients also tend to have areas of calcification in soft tissues, a tendency that is more marked than in ordinary hypoparathyroidism. Congenital defects commonly are present in other members of the family. The concomitant occurrence of diabetes insipidus and decreased glucose tolerance has been described in one patient with pseudohypoparathyroidism. Abortive cases (called pseudo-pseudohypoparathyroidism) with the developmental anomalies but without the abnormal chemical findings have been described.

Hyperparathyroidism

In this condition there is primarily disease in the parathyroid glands which may be an adenoma, a hypertrophy, a hyperplasia, or a carcinoma. The pathologic physiology is brought about by excessive amounts of parathyroid hormone. A pituitary tropic hormone affecting the parathyroid glands has not been demonstrated. Hyperplasia of the parathyroids usually is thought to be secondary to some alteration in the requirements of the body tissues; for example, with the loss of calcium as a fixed base in the urine, the serum calcium level falls, and there is a stimulus to the parathyroids to increase the hormone production in order to restore the serum calcium level. A small number of unusual cases have been reported in which a functioning parathyroid adenoma has been associated with a functioning adenoma of the pancreatic islets and/or a chromophobe (nonfunctioning) adenoma of the anterior pituitary gland. Not even a reasonable speculation has been advanced as to the pathologic physiology of this curious combination of endocrine disturbances.

The usual sequence of events when excessive production of parathyroid hormone occurs is (1) an increase in the excretion of inorganic phosphorus in the urine; (2) a loss of phosphorus from the serum; (3) an undersaturation of the serum in relation to calcium *times* phosphorus; (4) an increase in the concentration of calcium that is maintained in the serum to make up the phosphorus deficit; (5) to meet the increased calcium requirement in the serum, either the hormone-induced increase in the absorption of calcium from the gastrointestinal tract (if the calcium intake has been adequate) or the hormone-induced increase in the resorption of calcium (and phosphorus) from bone (if the calcium intake has been insufficient); (6) a rise above normal in the serum calcium level; and (7) an excretion of excessive amounts of calcium in the urine. It is obvious that an imbalance between the increased resorption of bone and the compensatory increased formation of bone does not occur if sufficient amounts of calcium and phosphorus are taken in through the gastrointestinal tract to restore the normal saturation of calcium *times* phosphorus in the blood. This mechanism accounts for the increasing incidence of cases of hyperparathyroidism without overt bone disease, in which there is no evidence of any decalcification. Furthermore, these patients have no cysts or brown tumors, such as are found in the "classical cases" in association with decalcification; therefore we believe that in the "classical cases" the excess amount of bone resorption must in some way be responsible for these bone lesions as well as for the decalcification. Radioisotope studies reveal that all patients with hyperparathyroidism have an increased rate of bone turnover with an excessive amount of bone resorption. In those cases without overt (histologic or radiologic) evidence of bone involvement, the increase in the rate of bone resorption is nearly balanced by a compensatory increase in the rate of bone formation; in those cases with obvious bone involvement, it is not.

I favor the interpretation also that the parathyroid hormone has a lytic action on bone, probably by stimulating the osteoclasts to produce proteolytic enzymes; it is postulated that these enzymes destroy the bone to support the mineral homeostasis of the body fluids. This proteolytic action of the parathyroid hormone may account for the marked muscular weakness, for the occurrence of duodenal ulceration, and for a number of other symptoms (such as fatigue, apathy, and weight loss) which frequently are associated with hyperfunction of the parathyroid glands.

As a result of the excessive excretion of calcium through the kidney, there very commonly is kidney damage and the formation of renal calculi. About 5 per cent of all renal calculi are caused by hyperparathyroidism. Many cases of "hidden" hyperparathyroidism with predominantly renal complications currently are being missed because physicians do not think of the possibility of parathyroid hyperfunction unless obvious bone involvement is present. The true incidence of hyperparathyroidism cannot be determined until there is more alertness and skill in diagnosing the condition. Renal disease without overt bone changes represents the commonest finding in hyperparathyroidism, but in a sufficiently large series of patients four different types of clinical expression are found: (1) chemical hyperparathyroidism without overt bone or kidney disease, (2) hyperparathyroidism with overt bone but without kidney disease, (3) hyperparathyroidism with kidney but without overt bone disease, and (4) hyperparathyroidism with both kidney and overt bone disease. From what has been said, it is clear that both bone involvement and kidney involvement must be considered to be important features of hyperparathyroidism. The treatment of the condition is surgical removal of the parathyroid adenoma, or subtotal resection of the hypertrophied parathyroid glands.

Since it now appears that the parathyroid glands also produce the serum calcium-lowering hormone, calcitonin, the possibility exists that some cases of hyperparathyroidism may be the result of an inadequate production of calcitonin. Also some cases of hyperparathyroidism could occur as a consequence of an inadequate production of the similarly acting thyrocalcitonin by the thyroid gland. It is possible that very severe, intractable, or fulminating cases of hyperparathyroidism may result from deficient production of both calcitonin and thyrocalcitonin, or from an excessive production of parathyroid hormone combined with an inadequate production of calcitonin.

Diabetes Mellitus

The chief disturbance in this condition is inadequate production of insulin from the pancreas. There is evidence in man that excessive production of pituitary growth hormone occurs in certain patients with diabetes mellitus and may be responsible for some cases of diabetes mellitus, in addition to those associated with acromegaly. However, there is no evidence that other patients with diabetes mellitus lack a tropic substance and hence do not produce insulin. The concept of "prediabetes" and other aspects of the pathogenesis of diabetes mellitus are discussed in Chapter 6. Diabetes mellitus due to insulin lack must be differentiated from the diabetes that results from the excessive production of the "sugar" hormones (cortisol and cortisone) by the adrenal cortex as in Cushing's syndrome. In this syndrome a "diabetic" type of glucose tolerance curve is seen, but the patient is insulin-resistant in contrast to the usual ordinary diabetic. The "diabetic" type of glucose tolerance curve found at times in acromegaly may be a manifestation of increased production of pituitary tropic substance which interferes with the action of insulin. The opposing influences which affect the level of the blood sugar have been discussed previously (p. 149). Some aspects concerning the assay, the protein binding, and the synthesis of insulin are presented in Chapter 6.

In the last 5 years, there has been much interest in the development of oral hypoglycemic agents (chiefly sulfonylurea compounds). Although the mechanism of action of these substances still is controversial, most investigators believe that these compounds act by stimulating the diseased pancreas to increase its output of insulin. Consequently, the sulfonylurea compounds are ineffective in the complete absence of insulin, and cannot replace insulin in severe or well-established juvenile diabetes or in diabetic acidosis and other emergencies. However, in 50 to 60 per cent of the milder diabetics who have required small to moderate doses of insulin and who presumably still can produce some hormone of their own, injected insulin can be replaced by the oral compounds. For the most part, patients have been selected for maintenance on the oral agents on the basis of a trial of routine management with them over a period of days or weeks. Sustained administration of the new oral hypoglycemic compounds for many years in a life-long disease must be undertaken with caution until the prolonged effects of these substances are established. Other comments on insulin antagonism and antibodies are found in Chapter 6.

Hyperinsulinism

Excessive production of insulin results from an adenoma of the islet cells of Langerhans or from an overresponsiveness of these islet cells to a normal physiologic stimulation. Islet cell adenomas produce excessive amounts of insulin continuously and cause marked hypoglycemia. The overresponsive islet cells produce excessive amounts of insulin only in response to a physiologic stimulus and hence intermittently. Patients with this latter condition show a marked hypoglycemic reaction a few hours after the ingestion of carbohydrate (see Chap. 6), but do not exhibit a hypoglycemic reaction when fasted, in contrast to patients with hyperinsulinism from an adenoma of the islet cells.

The action of insulin in carbohydrate metabolism is discussed in detail in another chapter (Chap. 6). It has been proposed that there is only one basic mechanism for the action of insulin: to increase the permeability of the cell membrane to glucose. It is suggested that insulin could induce this change in cell permeability at the membrane surface either by facilitating the conversion of glucose through phosphorylation or oxidation into more lipid-soluble and hence more permeable compounds, or by altering the physical structure of the cell wall through the combining of the insulin protein with the membrane protein so that glucose can pass more easily into the cell. The other effects of insulin are believed to be the consequences of the increase in intracellular glucose. The action of insulin on the liver is explained by the same mechanism, since it is assumed that the increased transfer of glucose into the cells of the anterior pituitary gland leads to an increase in the production and/or release of ACTH with its effects on adrenal cortical hormone production and/or release and thus on the metabolic processes in the liver.

In brief, the sequence of events following the excessive production of insulin is (1) an increase in carbohydrate oxidation; (2) a decrease in the stimulation to the central nervous system tissue which occurs when carbohydrate oxidation is inadequate; (3) hence a decrease in the stimulus to the adrenal medulla; (4) a decrease in the amount of epinephrine produced; (5) a decrease in glycogenolysis in the liver; (6) a reduction in the amount of glucose that enters the blood; and (7) the onset of hypoglycemia. In the overresponsive type of hyperinsulinism there is a stimulus to insulin production with the ingestion of carbohydrate. This initiates the sequence just described.

Hyperinsulinism when due to an adenoma is treated by surgical removal of the tumor. The overresponsiveness of the islet cells can be controlled by a reduction in the carbohydrate intake and maintenance of the patient on a high protein and high fat diet, so that the amount of carbohydrate in the blood as the result of digestion is kept relatively constant and does not serve as a marked stimulus to the production of insulin.

Pregnancy Toxemia Complicating Diabetes Mellitus

The hormonal abnormalities that occur in pregnancy are not well understood. There is some evidence, however, that in the toxemias of pregnancy, particularly in those that develop in patients with diabetes mellitus, there is a defective hormone production by the placenta. A most plausible mechanism at present is an imbalance in the production of progestogen and estrogen by the placenta so that too little progestogen is produced for the amount of estrogen. As a result of the decrease in the progestogen, the amount of gonadotropin in the blood may rise. Large doses of progestogen and/or estrogen will inhibit the production and/or release of the pituitary gonadotropins, LH and LTH; presumably these gonadal hormones also will reduce the production of chorionic gonadotropin. Priscilla White and her associates administered large amounts of progestogen and/or estrogen to pregnant diabetic patients, and claimed that by this therapy they decreased the incidence of fetal and maternal complications in these patients. Recent evidence indicates that estrogen stimulates the production and/or release of aldosterone, and that progestogen antagonizes the action of aldosterone on the renal tubules. In the presence of too little progestogen, aldosterone production and/or release is greater than normal, leading to sodium retention and clinical manifestations of hyperaldosteronism. These contribute to the symptoms of toxemia. On this basis, the most rational and effective therapy for toxemias of pregnancy in patients without or with diabetes mellitus should be the administration of large amounts of a progestational compound with no inherent estrogenic (or androgenic) activity, for example, 17-alpha-hydroxyprogesterone caproate (Delalutin). Treatment with such an agent should restore the balance with estrogen, should neutralize the peripheral effects of the excess of aldosterone, and thus should cause marked clinical improvement with elimination of the symptoms.

Recurrent and Threatened Abortion

Loss of the products of conception before viability is called abortion. The chief causative factors include (1) congenital abnormalities, (2) mechanical difficulties, and (3) failure in the hormonal support of the pregnancy. In about 60 per cent of women with repeated abortion, the loss of the fetus in successive gestations is attributed to a recurrence of the same pathologic factor. In the majority of women with recurrent abortion, failure of the hormonal support is responsible for the unfavorable outcome of the pregnancy. The inadequate hormonal support may arise from (1) a defective trophoblast, which produces insufficient chorionic gonadotropin to maintain an adequate production of progestogen and estrogen by the corpus luteum of pregnancy and by the placenta; (2) a defective corpus luteum of pregnancy which fails to respond adequately to physiologic amounts of chorionic gonadotropin and hence does not produce sufficient quantities of progestogen and estrogen; and (3) a defective placenta which fails to respond adequately to physiologic amounts of chorionic gonadotropin and hence does not produce sufficient quantities of progestogen and estrogen when the corpus luteum of pregnancy reaches the end of its period of activity.

In most women with recurrent abortion, the failure of hormonal support is the result of a functional disturbance; in a few patients, it is the result of an organic condition in the trophoblast, the corpus luteum of pregnancy, or the placenta. Failure of hormonal support with insufficient progestational activity must be assumed to be present in all pregnant women who have a history of recurrent abortion or who are threatening to abort. Since the amount of progestational activity must be adequate for pregnancy to run an uncomplicated course, this hormonal activity must be made available in such women regardless of whether the insufficiency results from an organic or a functional disturbance. I prefer to rely on the administration of progestational agents rather than to attempt to stimulate the endogenous production of progestogen either by formal psychotherapy or by unrecognized psychotherapy (in the guise of non-hormonal medications and reassurance); it is obvious that non-hormonal agents cannot supply the essential progestational activity in those cases which are not amenable to psychotherapy because the hormone insufficiency arises from organic defects.

Adequate progestational hormone therapy in women with recurrent abortion induces several beneficial effects: (1) It causes approximately three times as many successful pregnancies with live babies in women with secondary habitual abortion (a fetal salvage rate of about 70 per cent), and it brings about the first successful pregnancy with a live baby in over 60 per cent of women with primary habitual abortion. (2) It induces a useful acceleration of fetal maturation to term, which may result in a mature infant in a shortened period of gestation. (3) It prolongs the survival and improves the state and function of the placenta during the early weeks of gestation. Adequate hormonal support will not prevent abortions which result from congenital abnormalities or mechanical difficulties. Progestational compounds which are derivatives of androgens or which have inherent androgenic effects are contraindicated in pregnant women because of the hazards of masculinization of the mother and of virilization of the female fetus with the development of pseudo-hermaphroditism.

A very satisfactory progestational agent for treating women with obstetrical complications, particularly recurrent and threatened abortion, is 17-alpha-hydroxyprogesterone caproate (Delalutin), a compound which is not, and never becomes, an androgen. Optimal therapy for recurrent abortion consists of a single injection of 375 to 500 mg. intramuscularly once a week, starting as soon as possible and continuing to within 2 weeks of the expected date of delivery. In threatened abortion, 500 mg. or more is injected every 8 hours until the manifestations subside, and then 500 mg. twice a week for 2 additional weeks; thereafter, the patient is treated with 375 to 500 mg. once a week to within 2 weeks of the expected date of delivery. For these indications, this steroid ester is more advantageous than other progestational substances because its longer duration of action and greater solubility in oil permit the repeated injection of large amounts of progestational activity, in a smaller volume of vehicle, at less frequent intervals, with minimal local irritation, and without any hazard to the mother or to the developing infant.

Postpartum Breast Manifestations

In the United States, approximately 70 per cent of postpartum women do not nurse their newborn infants. The emptying of the gravid uterus and the loss of the large amounts of hormones produced by the placenta result in an increased production and/or release of the lactogenic hormone (LTH). If the mother does not nurse her infant, the breasts usually become engorged and painful, and there is leakage of milk; these unpleasant manifestations persist for 10 days to 2 weeks when they are not treated. Prior to the introduction of hormone therapy, the postpartum breast responses were controlled ineffectively with tight binders, ice packs, and occasionally analgesics.

The production and/or release of the lactogenic hormone (LTH) can be inhibited by appropriate doses of estrogens, of androgens, or of progestogens. In the past, the inhibition of LTH has been difficult to achieve, because oral therapy could not be started for some hours after delivery, which often was too late to prevent the release of the pituitary tropic hormone and to control the breast manifestations. Furthermore, the use of inhibiting (large) doses of preparations with single hormone activity not infrequently was followed by undesirable effects, such as uterine bleeding with estrogen or masculinization with androgen. Finally, secondary (delayed) breast manifestations (pain, leakage, and/or engorgement) appeared unless the inhibition of LTH was maintained for over 2 weeks; this required the repeated administration of short-acting injectable or oral preparations. A solution for some of these difficulties was found to be the use of androgen combined with estrogen in an appropriate ratio to reduce the unwanted single hormone effects to the minimum.

The most satisfactory hormonal therapy for the control of postpartum breast manifestations that has been evolved to date is the use of a single intramuscular injection of a long-acting preparation (Deladumone) in which testosterone enanthate and estradiol valerate are combined in the desired ratio (90 mg. of the testosterone ester to 4 mg. of the estradiol ester per cc.). A single injection of 4 cc. of this preparation at the end of the first stage of labor eliminates the initial and the secondary postpartum breast manifestations in over 90 per cent of women. This therapy (1) does not interfere with the subsequent course of the labor or the postpartum recovery period; (2) does not cause uterine bleeding, persistent lochia, or delayed involution of the uterus; (3) does not delay the resumption of normal cyclic ovarian function; (4) does not interfere with the physiologic stimulus of suckling so that the patient can nurse the infant if she changes her mind; (5) can be given sufficiently early to prevent the production and/or release of LTH because it is a parenteral preparation which does not depend for its administration upon the patient's recovering from the delivery procedure sufficiently to take it (as is the case with oral preparations which must be swallowed); (6) is convenient for the nursing staff of a busy obstetrical service; (7) is convenient for the patient during the hospitalization because she is not subjected to repeated medication; (8) is convenient for the patient and the physician when the mother leaves the hospital because arrangements to continue the administration of medication are not necessary; and (9) produces a minimum of undesirable single hormone actions on the genital organs and accessory sexual structures.

Endocrine Therapy for Neoplastic Disease

The mechanisms by which alterations in the endocrine system induce temporary beneficial responses in neoplastic lesions of the accessory sexual structures (breast, prostate, endometrium) are not understood. Objective remissions have been induced by (1) gonadectomy, (2) hypophysectomy, (3) adrenalectomy, (4) administration of androgen, (5) administration of estrogen, (6) administration of progestogen, (7) administration of corticosteroids, and (8) administration of steroid compounds in combination. Furthermore, steroid substances modified structurally so that they appear to have none of the usual gonadal or adrenal hormone-like activities in human beings have been reported to induce objective remissions in women with advanced mammary cancer. The effect of these modified steroids on the neurohumeral substances of the central nervous system and on some of the anterior pituitary tropic hormones remains to be established. Therefore, at present there is no rationale for the beneficial effects upon neoplastic lesions of the secondary sexual structures which are induced at times by alterations in the endocrine environment. Hormone therapy is administered empirically, usually in pharmacologic doses. Surgical treatment and irradiation, singly or in combination, still are considered to be the primary forms of treatment.

Summary

An attempt has been made to outline in a general way the dynamic interrelations between the various glands of internal secretion, and to describe some of the adjustments that occur when disease processes alter the status of these endocrine glands. It is recognized that many of the steps in the sequence of events of the various disorders, as outlined, will have to be modified, and that the entire presentation is, at best, only a first approximation. The necessity is stressed of considering the function of all the glands of the endocrine system when one is faced with a disorder that appears to involve only one of these glands.

REFERENCES

Albright, F.: Cushing's syndrome: Its pathological physiology, its relationship to the adrenogenital syndrome, and its connection with the problem of the reaction of the body to injurious agents ("alarm reaction" of Selye). Harvey Lect., 38: 123, 1942–1943.

Albright, F.: The gonads. In Musser, J. H.: Internal Medicine: Its Theory and Practice, 4th ed. Philadelphia, Lea & Febiger, 1945, Chap. XVI, pp. 951–979.

Albright, F., Forbes, A. P., and Bartter, F. C.: The effect of adrenocorticotrophic hormone in patients with panhypopituitarism. Tr. Conference Metabol. Aspects of Convalescence, 15th meet-ing, Mar. 31–April 1, 1947. New York, Josiah Macy, Jr., Foundation, pp. 118–127.

Albright, F., Forbes, A. P., Fraser, R., Miller, R. B., and Reifenstein, E. C., Jr.: A classification of the causes of hypoleydigism. Tr. A. Am. Physicians, 50:43, 1941.

Albright, F., and Reifenstein, E. C., Jr.: The Parathyroid Glands and Metabolic Bone Disease: Selected Studies. Baltimore, Williams & Wilkins Co. 1948, pp. 1–393.

Albright, F., Smith, P. H., and Fraser, R.: A syndrome characterized by primary ovarian insufficiency and decreased stature; report of 11 cases with a digression on hormonal control of axillary and pubic hair. Am. J. Med. Sc., 204:625, 1942.

Astwood, E. B.: Management of thyroid disorders. In The Centennial Lectures Commemorating the One Hundredth Anniversary of E. R. Squibb & Sons. New York, G. P. Putnam's Sons, 1959, pp. 203–214.

Bartter, F. C., and others: The effects of adrenocorticotropic hormone and cortisone in the adrenogenital syndrome associated with congenital adrenal hyperplasia: An attempt to explain and correct its disordered hormonal pattern. J. Clin. Invest., 30:237, 1951.

Bowen, P., Lee, C. S. N., Migeon, C. J., Kaplan, N. M., Whalley, P. J., McKusick, V. A., and Reifenstein, E. C., Jr.: Hereditary male pseudohermaphroditism with hypogonadism, hypospadias, and gynecomastia. Ann. Int. Med., 62: 252, 1965.

Bowman, W. E., and Reifenstein, E. C., Jr.: Influence of the central nervous system on the menstrual cycle. In Soskin, S. (ed.): Progress in Clinical Endocrinology. New York, Grune & Stratton, Inc., 1950, pp. 327–334.

Cahill, G. F.: Pheochromocytoma. In Craig, R. L. (ed.): Hormones in Health and Disease. New York, Macmillan Company, 1954, Chap. 10, pp. 131–147.

Conn, J. W.: Evolution of primary aldosteronism as a highly specific clinical entity. J.A.M.A., 172: 1650, 1960.

Ferguson-Smith, M. A.: Cytogenetics in man. A.M.A. Arch. Int. Med., 105:627, 1960.

Fraser, R., Albright, F., and Smith, P. H.: Carbohydrate metabolism; the value of the glucose tolerance test, the insulin tolerance test, and the glucose-insulin tolerance test in the diagnosis of endocrinologic disorders of glucose metabolism. J. Clin. Endocrinol., 1:297, 1941.

Furth, J., and Sobel, H.: Neoplastic transplantation of granulosa cells in grafts of normal ovaries into spleens of gonadectomized mice. J. Nat. Cancer Inst., 8:7, 1947.

Gemzell, C.: Induction of ovulation with human gonadotropins. Recent Progress in Hormone Research, 21:179, 1965.

Gillespie, L., Sexton, L. T., and White, P.: Treatment of human diabetic pregnancies with estradiol valerate and 17 α-hydroxyprogesterone 17-n-caproate. Ann. New York Acad. Sc., 71:794, 1958.

Greenblatt, R. B., and Maheesh, V. B.: Induction of ovulation with clomiphene citrate. Year Book of Endocrinology, pp. 248–268, 1964–1965.

Greep, R. O., and Deane, H. W.: Cytochemical evidence for the cessation of hormone production in the zona glomerulosa of the rat's adrenal cortex after prolonged treatment with desoxycorticosterone acetate. Endocrinology, *40*:417, 1947.

Heller, C. G., and Nelson, W. O.: Hyalinization of the seminiferous tubules associated with normal or failing Leydig-cell function. Discussion of relationship to eunuchoidism, gynecomastia, elevated gonadotrophins, depressed 17-ketosteroids, and estrogens. J. Clin. Endocrinol., *5*:1, 1945.

Klinefelter, H. F., Jr., Albright, F., and Griswold, G. C.: Experiences with a quantitative test for normal or decreased amounts of follicle-stimulating hormone in the urine in endocrinological diagnosis. J. Clin. Endocrinol., *3*:529, 1943.

Klinefelter, H. F., Jr., Reifenstein, E. C., Jr., and Albright, F.: Syndrome characterized by gynecomastia, aspermatogenesis without a-leydigism, and increased excretion of follicle-stimulating hormone. J. Clin. Endocrinol., *2*:615, 1942.

Levine, R., and Goldstein, M. S.: On the mechanism of action of insulin. Recent Progress in Hormone Research, *11*:343, 1955.

Li, C. H., Evans, H. M., and Simpson, M. E.: Isolation and properties of the anterior hypophyseal growth hormone. Science, *99*:183, 1944; J. Biol. Chem., *159*:353, 1945.

Li, M. H., and Gardner, W. U.: Tumors in intrasplenic ovarian transplants in castrated mice. Science, *105*:13, 1947.

Means, J. H.: Diseases of the endocrine glands. In Musser, J. H.: Internal Medicine: Its Theory and Practice, 4th ed. Philadelphia, Lea & Febiger, 1945, Chap. XVI, pp. 901–951.

Nelson, D. H., and Sprunt, J. G.: Pituitary tumors postadrenalectomy for Cushing's syndrome. Proc. Second International Congress Endocrinol., Excerpta Medica Foundation, International Congress Series No. 83, Part II, pp. 1053–1057, 1965.

Rasmussen, H., and Reifenstein, E. C., Jr.: The parathyroid glands. In Williams, R. H. (ed.): Textbook of Endocrinology, 3rd ed., Philadelphia, W. B. Saunders Co., 1962, Chap. 11, pp. 731–879.

Rawson, R. W.: Today's thyroidologists and their beckoning frontiers. J. Clin. Endocrinol. and Metab., *16*:1405, 1956.

Reifenstein, E. C., Jr.: Endocrinology: A synopsis of normal and pathologic physiology, diagnostic procedures, and therapy. M. Clin. North America, *28*:1232, 1944.

Reifenstein, E. C., Jr.: Psychogenic or "hypothalamic" amenorrhea. M. Clin. North America, *30*:1103, 1946.

Reifenstein, E. C., Jr.: Hereditary familial hypogonadism (abstract). Proc. Am. Fed. Clin. Res., *3*:86, 1947.

Reifenstein, E. C., Jr.: The metabolism of convalescence. In Gordon, E. S. (ed.): A Symposium on Steroid Hormones. Madison, University of Wisconsin Press, 1950, pp. 374–380.

Reifenstein, E. C., Jr.: The relation of the adrenal cortex to gynecology. In Meigs, J. V., and Sturgis, S. H.: Progress in Gynecology. New York, Grune & Stratton, Inc., 1950, Vol. 2, pp. 270–283.

Reifenstein, E. C., Jr.: Diseases of the parathyroid glands. In Williams, R. H. (ed.): Textbook of Endocrinology, 2nd ed. Philadelphia, W. B. Saunders Co., 1955, Chap. 8, pp. 483–581.

Reifenstein, E. C., Jr.: The rationale for the use of anabolic steroids in controlling the adverse effects of corticoid hormones upon protein and osseous tissues. South. Med. J., *49*:933, 1956.

Reifenstein, E. C., Jr.: The relationships of steroid hormones to the development and the management of osteoporosis in aging people. Clin. Orth., *10*: 206, 1957.

Reifenstein, E. C., Jr.: Introduction of marked as well as prolonged biologic activity by esterification: 17-Alpha-hydroxyprogesterone caproate, a unique progestational compound. Fertil. & Steril., *8*:50, 1957.

Reifenstein, E. C., Jr.: Clinical use of 17 α-hydroxyprogesterone 17-*n*-caproate in habitual abortion. Ann. New York Acad. Sc., *71*:762, 1958.

Reifenstein, E. C., Jr.: The endocrine aspects of senile osteoporosis. Read as part of the Panel on Diseases Among the Aged in the Session on New Concepts in Aging, conducted by the Committee on Aging of the Council on Medical Services, before the American Medical Association, Atlantic City, 1959.

Reifenstein, E. C., Jr.: Metabolic disorders of bone. In Harrison, T. R. (ed.): Principles of Internal Medicine, 4th ed. New York, Blakiston Division, McGraw-Hill Book Co., 1962, Section 3, Chaps. 77–82, pp. 690–721.

Reifenstein, E. C., Jr., and Albright, F.: The metabolic effects of steroid hormones in osteoporosis. J. Clin. Invest., *26*:24, 1947.

Reifenstein, E. C., Jr., and Howard, R. P.: The parathyroid glands. In Glandular Physiology and Therapy, 5th ed., prepared under the auspices of the Council on Pharmacy and Chemistry, American Medical Association. Philadelphia, J. B. Lippincott Co., 1954, Chap. 11, pp. 351–385.

Reifenstein, E. C., Jr., Kinsell, L. W., and Albright, F.: Observations on the use of the serum phosphorus level as an index of pituitary growth hormone activity; the effect of estrogen therapy on acromegaly. Endocrinology, *39*:71, 1946.

Selye, H.: The general adaptation syndrome and the diseases of adaptation. J. Clin. Endocrinol., *6*: 117, 1946.

Selye, H.: The general-adaptation-syndrome and the diseases of adaptation. In Textbook of Endocrinology. Montreal, Acta Endocrinologica, 1947, Chap. XII, pp. 837–867.

Sohval, A. R.: Sex chromatin, chromosomes and male infertility. Fertil. & Steril., *14*:180, 1963.

Stein, I. F., and Leventhal, M. L.: Amenorrhea associated with bilateral polycystic ovaries. Am. J. Obst. & Gynec., *29*:181, 1935.

Thorn, G. W., Prunty, F. T. G., and Forsham, P. H.: Clinical studies on the effects of pituitary adrenocorticotrophic hormone. Tr. A. Am. Physicians, *60*:143, 1947.

White, P., and Hunt, H.: Pregnancy complicating diabetes. A report of clinical results. J. Clin. Endocrinol., *3*:500, 1943.

Wilkins, L. and others: Treatment of congenital adrenal hyperplasia with cortisone. J. Clin. Endocrinol., *11*:1, 1951.

Part IV

Infection and Allergy

Chapter Nine

Role of the Invading Organism

JOHN P. UTZ

Introduction

For the purposes of these chapters infection is defined as the invasion and multiplication of a microorganism in the tissues of man. Disease is defined as an abnormal state or function in man. These terms are frequently and incorrectly used interchangeably to mean an infectious disease. It is obvious that a disease need not be of infectious origin, but it is less well recognized that infection can occur in the absence of clinical disease. The latter is described by such a term as subclinical infection. There is similarly a confusion of the terms contagious and infectious and an erroneous tendency to use them interchangeably. Some infectious diseases are noncontagious, in which man-to-man or animal-to-man spread is not known to occur.

With such distinctions in mind, one can appreciate that infectious disease and the symptoms and findings that result are functions of the microorganisms involved, the inflammatory response elicited and such predisposing or defensive factors that may exist at the time of infection. The organization of this section is based on these three considerations.

Biologic Characteristics of Microbial Agents of Disease

Man may be infected and disease may be produced by a great variety of microorganisms, grouped commonly as viruses, rickettsia, bacteria, fungi (of the plant kingdom), and parasites (of the animal kingdom). Those characteristics of these organisms that lead directly to disease in man concern us here.

Physical Size

The microorganisms grouped as above have an almost unlimited variation both in form and size. The smallest of them, measuring approximately 20 mμ, are members of the arbovirus group which cause such illnesses in the United States as St. Louis and western and eastern equine encephalitis. Somewhat midway in size is the staphylococcus, which measures approximately 1000 mμ. At the other terminal of the range are those animal parasites of the Platyhelminthes phylum (e.g., beef or pork tapeworm) that may measure 10 meters in length. Thus there exists an approximately 10^{10}-fold range in size among microorganisms that infect man.

Obstructive and Pressure Phenomena

The mere physical presence of microorganisms within man may be enough to induce symptoms. By virtue of their great size, the fish, beef, or pork tapeworms may produce intestinal obstruction. Though much smaller in size, ascarids tend to form tangled balls in the intestine with the same effect. The Dracunculus worm (1 meter in

193

length) produces a visible and palpable subcutaneous swelling, and another smaller (2 to 5 cm.) filaria, *Loa loa,* may be present momentarily beneath the conjunctiva of the eye. Other filariae, such as *Wuchereria bancrofti,* obstruct the lymphatic vessels and produce elephantiasis. Various flukes, including *Fasciola hepatica,* occlude the bile ducts to induce jaundice and other symptoms of posthepatic obstruction. The larval form of *Taenia solium* may encyst in the brain, with subsequent focal symptoms, calcification and occasionally jacksonian epilepsy.

However, organisms need not be of such large size to produce pressure effects, if the site of their multiplication is sufficiently sensitive to change. For example, partial or even total blindness may result from the multiplication of the fungus *Cryptococcus neoformans* in the confines of the optic nerve. One of the explanations for death in the patient with anthrax is vascular occlusion, necrosis and gangrene from blockage of capillaries by large numbers of *Bacillus anthracis.*

Chemical Characteristics

Other than instances just mentioned and even in severely infected patients, the total bulk of all infecting bacteria is minute relative to the size of the host. Manifold greater numbers of carbon particles can be injected into the body without producing a mechanical effect similar to disease in the infected patient. It is obvious that most infecting microorganisms produce disease by a means other than physical.

A major mechanism by which microorganisms cause disease is the production of a *toxin,* a harmful chemical substance elaborated and excreted (exotoxin) or liberated chiefly after disintegration (endotoxin) by the microorganism. These two general types are distinguished by additional criteria of importance to the present subject. Exotoxins, which are usually proteins, may be potent in amounts one thousandfold less than those required for endotoxic effect. Exotoxins are relatively tissue specific in their site of action, e.g., central nervous system, myocardium and adrenals, whereas endotoxins, which are lipopolysaccharides, have more generalized and diverse effects. Exotoxins are more highly antigenic and result in rapid development of neutralizing antibodies (see Chap. 10). A variety of bacteria; at least one fungus, *Aspergillus fumigatus;* members of the psittacosis (Bedsonia) group of microorganisms; and mumps, influenza and poliomyelitis

viruses are known to liberate an endotoxin. In human disease, only the endotoxins of gram-negative bacteria, identical to the species specific antigens, are thought to be important.

The infusion of endotoxin in man results in a variety of effects including chills, nausea, vomiting, myalgias, fever, headaches, tachycardia and, in large enough doses, hypotension. These will be discussed in the next chapter.

Perhaps the most dramatic example of *exotoxin* activity is seen with *Clostridium botulinum,* whose toxin, produced in food kept under anaerobic conditions, can induce disease in the complete absence of bacterial multiplication. Five types of toxin are known, and two of these, A and B, have been highly purified. These toxins resist intestinal enzymes and are absorbed and act by paralyzing cholinergic nerve endings within 12 to 100 hours after ingestion. At the terminal branches of these nerve fibers acetylcholine release and neuromuscular transmission are blocked. Adrenergic nerve endings are not affected. Patients lose their ability to accommodate their vision to near objects, lose pupillary light reflex and sometimes develop diplopia. Speaking and swallowing become difficult. Salivation is decreased with resulting dry mouth. Intestinal muscle activity is diminished to the point of paralytic ileus. Postural hypotension and faintness develop, and difficulty in urinary voiding may occur. The most dangerous effect is respiratory muscle weakness with resultant anoxia and death.

In diphtheria the exotoxin of *Corynebacterium diphtheriae* directly affects cardiac muscle with the development of gallop rhythm, shock, and cardiac failure due to myocarditis. The electrocardiogram shows delayed conduction time, bundle branch block and, terminally, ventricular fibrillation. Neurotoxic effects result in paralysis of the soft palate (cranial 9), and the ocular muscles with convergent squint and loss of accommodation (cranial 3, 4, 6) and less commonly the muscles of the face (cranial 7) and larynx (cranial 10). It has been suggested that this toxin is the protein moiety of the respiratory pigment cytochrome B, and that the toxin blocks production of this enzyme intracellularly.

Tetanus exotoxin acts on the motor cells of the spinal cord producing increased muscle tone and spasm. When such spasm affects the respiratory muscles, anoxia, cyanosis and death may result. In addition the toxin is hemolytic and probably inactivates phagocytic cells. Other exotoxins, lecithinases and hemolysins produced by other Clostridium species are important contributing causes in the anemia and renal tubular necrosis that occasionally develop.

The *erythrogenic toxin* produced by group A Streptococcus is responsible for the erythematous and hemorrhagic skin eruption seen in scarlet fever. *Streptolysin S* (for extractibility from cultures by use of serum) may play a role in producing generalized symptoms in human disease. The enterotoxin produced by many strains of *Staphylococcus aureus* is associated with the severe enteritis frequently seen with infection by this microorganism. Another exotoxin, *streptolysin O* (for oxygen lability), kills rabbits and acts on human cells in culture, but is probably not an important factor in inducing disease in man.

In cell culture systems the action of some toxins has been more specifically localized. The addition of large doses of diphtheria toxin to human epithelial and monkey kidney cells produces an almost immediate decrease in adenosine triphosphate synthesis. This effect is compatible with an inhibition of a cytochrome-linked oxidative phosphorylation. The action is reversible when antitoxin is added. In other studies protein synthesis in cells is inhibited.

Capsules

A number of bacteria and one fungus, *Cryptococcus neoformans*, have a polysaccharide capsule, which in some instances increases the ability of the microorganism to produce disease. So far as is known, the "concept of capsule action" is that the capsule (1) prevents phagocytosis in cell systems, (2) increases virulence when capsule material is added to noncapsulated bacteria in animals and (3) may produce "immunologic paralysis" (of Felton) by presenting an overwhelming amount of antigen to animals. The capsule of the *Diplococcus pneumoniae* markedly impedes phagocytosis by protective cells (leukocytes). Capsular material is sufficiently soluble so that it can dissolve in body fluids and combine with and neutralize circulating antibody. *Pasteurella pestis* has a protein capsule that similarly impedes phagocytosis. The capsule of *Bacillus anthracis* is a polypeptide that facilitates infection by neutralizing an antibacterial substance which is rich in lysine and present in a variety of tissues. A theoretical explanation for capsule action is the production of "immunologic paralysis" seen in animals following injection of pneumococcal antigen in amounts that render the animal incapable of producing detectable antibody.

Enzymes

There are a number of enzymes that are not toxins but that when produced by microorganisms may facilitate their ability to induce disease. *Hyaluronidase*, produced by some strains of Streptococcus, Staphylococcus, *Clostridium welchii* and *Corynebacterium diphtheriae*, hydrolyzes hyaluronic acid, an essential constituent of the intracellular ground substance of tissues. By such enzymatic activity bacteria may spread more readily. The enzyme is known, after its discoverer, as the Duran-Reynals spreading factor.

One of the characteristics of those strains of Staphylococcus that seem to be more important in human disease is the production of an enzyme *coagulase*, which coagulates citrated or oxalated human blood. It has been suggested that this enzyme is important in laying down fibrin in the periphery of a Staphylococcus lesion (so that it becomes a walled abscess) in the center of which phagocytosis may be impaired.

Somewhat contrariwise, most virulent strains of *Streptococcus pyogenes* and other bacteria as well produce an enzyme, *streptokinase*, which liquefies clots. This enzyme acts on a normal blood constituent, plasminogen, which then forms plasmin, an active proteolytic agent. Plasmin also inactivates complement, a circulating protein important in defense against infection. The action of streptokinase is thus twofold: it inactivates a circulating defense mechanism and, by preventing clot formation and localization, promotes spread of infection.

Deoxyribonuclease, produced by most virulent strains of Streptococcus, splits deoxyribonucleotides into simpler nucleotides. This enzyme has been reported capable of liquefying exudates, e.g., pleural fluid after intrapleural injection into man, and of producing lesions after intravenous injection into rabbits. Its role in inducing human disease is probably similar to that of streptokinase. Virulent strains of *Francisella tularensis* possess the enzyme citrulline uridase, whereas most nonvirulent strains lack the enzyme.

Members of the myxovirus group, notably influenza and mumps, produce an enzyme that results in the release of neuraminic acid, and the enzyme is thus sometimes termed *neuraminidase.* The enzymatic activity was discovered as a result of the observation that various members of this group of viruses can agglutinate erythrocytes of various species of animals or birds. Hemagglutination occurred by means of adsorption of virus to cells, but later there was spontaneous elution of virus from red cells. Virus could again agglutinate other red cells, but cells to which virus had once adsorbed and eluted could not be agglutinated again. This action seemed characteristically enzymatic, and this property of these viruses was first known as the receptor-destroying enzyme. It has been clearly shown that neuraminidase is important in the adsorption of viruses to cells in vivo as well, but the analogue of elution has not been so clearly demonstrated in vivo. Nevertheless, neuraminidase appears to be an important and specific enzymatic mechanism by which one form of infection is achieved.

"Invasiveness"

This term refers to the property of many microorganisms of being able to enter tissue. Except for the few enzymes previously mentioned, virtually nothing is known of the mechanism by which such invasion occurs. Quantitatively, microorganisms vary from being almost unable to invade tissue to having the power of early, extensive and fulminant spread. An example of the former would be *Corynebacterium diphtheriae,* which is capable of invading only the superficial epithelial cells of the upper respiratory tract, from which site it exerts its deleterious effect by elaboration of an absorbed toxin. *Clostridium tetani* after implantation beneath the skin similarly shows no tendency to spread but from that site produces a toxin. This toxin passes to motor nerve endings in the anterior horn cells and interferes with impulses that inhibit motor activity. Such interference results in increased muscle contraction and spasm. (The modes of absorption, of carriage to nerve endings, of passage from blood to brain when it occurs or of the action on nerve endings are not known.) The rhinovirus likewise does not invade deep tissue but induces a common cold by acting on superficial cells alone. Influenza virus is more puzzling, as it produces marked systemic symptoms, but only rarely and under unusual circumstances is it recoverable from deep tissues. *Candida albicans,* a fungus, occasionally produces severe and painful oral mucosal disease (thrush) but under normal host conditions usually does not invade tissue.

On the other hand a variety of microorganisms are able under special circumstances to invade contiguous tissue from superficial cells. Examples of this among the fungi include Actinomyces which produces an indolent, slowly spreading "wooden" type of subcutaneous cellulitis. This organism, as well as *Entamoeba histolytica,* is capable of destroying and passing through such tough fibrous tissues as the diaphragm, pleura, thoracic wall and even skin. The herpes simplex virus invades tissues near the mucocutaneous border of the lip and produces the typical vesicular "cold sore." The virus remains at the site and may induce a second crop of lesions years later. In experimental studies with cell cultures it seems probable that infection of a few cells may generate enough interferon to prevent infection of other cells. It has also been suggested that virus is "stored" at cell sites from which cell penetration is not possible. Under experimental conditions of cell cultures, the herpes zoster virus spreads from one cell to another via cell bridges without entering the extracellular fluid. Adenoviruses are similarly long-term residents in tonsillar or adenoidal tissue. In latent infections with adenoviruses, reactivation or delayed illness in the adenoidal tissues is not recognizable clinically. It is doubtful whether the recurrent attacks of tonsillitis (for which surgery is done, presumably) represent a clinical aspect of the latent infection. The factors that reactivate herpes virus are usually described as local trauma or "decreased generalized resistance."

A third degree of invasive ability is that manifest by microorganisms which produce a lesion at the portal of entry and then invade the lymphatic system. The fungus, *Sporotrichum schenckii,* entering through a small barberry or rose thorn scratch, produces lesions at the site and along the draining lymphatic vessels central to the site. Local pain and systemic symptoms such as fever are characteristically absent. The Staphylococcus, however, entering through such an abrasion, produces an acute lymphangitis with much local pain, heat, swelling and systemic symptoms of fever and malaise.

In primary infection *M. tuberculosis* multiplies in lymph nodes and spreads centrally to produce gross lesions in chains of nodes. In the lung the involved draining lymph node and the parenchymal pulmonary lesion constitute the classic Ghon complex. *Treponema pallidum* also enters the lymphatics and from there passes to the sentinel regional lymph node in early syphilis infection. Although less commonly thought of as invading in this fashion, vaccinia virus spreads to the lymphatics draining from the primary lesion at the time of vaccination. Under natural conditions of infection poliovirus spreads from its intestinal epithelial site of multiplication by way of the lymphatics to the regional lymph nodes.

A fourth degree of invasiveness is microbial penetration of blood vessel walls and hematogenous dissemination. Among the bacteria the gram-negative rod forms characteristically spread in this way. The most virulent of these is *Salmonella typhosa,* but under proper conditions a less virulent genus, such as *Escherichia coli,* or even a relatively avirulent organism, such as *Pseudomonas aeruginosa,* does so. Among fungi those species of Absidia and Rhizopus that induce sinusitis or orbital cellulitis rather promptly invade vessel walls and spread by the blood to remote organs. Mumps virus, although detectable in the blood on only rare occasions, spreads hematogenously from the parotids to the testis and the kidney. After infectious and serum hepatitis, the virus may persist in the blood for more than a year and be a threat to anyone else who receives such blood or plasma by transfusion. In dengue, yellow fever and Colorado tick fever, viremia is sufficiently constant and prolonged so that blood culture for virus is the best means of confirming the diagnosis. Similarly in malaria and filariasis the microorganisms in the blood may be sufficiently numerous as to be visible in a single drop of blood when examined by thick smear technique.

Virulence

After a discussion of all the foregoing properties there still remain other mechanisms, grouped under the term virulence, by which a microorganism induces disease. Basically virulence is the degree of disease produced by a *strain* of a microorganism. One speaks of a "pathogenic" species of Clostridia, but of a virulent strain of *D. pneumonia.* It is basic to the definition that there is not some specific enzymatic or biochemical difference to account for the virulence. Indeed, an organism so assigned to a species could hardly have such differences without becoming a new species.

Virulence is most strikingly observed by comparing two strains of the same species which may differ solely in their ability to produce disease. Among types of *Diplococcus pneumoniae,* I, II and especially III are highly virulent, and infection with them is accompanied by the highest case fatality rates. In a less direct way types 12 and Red Lake of the Group A *Streptococcus pyogenes* are associated with an increased frequency of subsequent acute glomerulonephritis. Among polioviruses the Mahoney strain is known for its virulence. The Louisiana and Illinois strains of the psittacosis group of microorganisms were associated with high fatality rates in man. One must still consider with awe and dread the virulence of the strain of influenza virus which in the years 1917 to 1919 killed 20,000,000 people. Considered from a completely contrary point of view, some strains of microorganisms are noteworthy and useful for their lack of virulence. The bacillus of Calmette-Guerin (BCG) is used in active immunization programs against tuberculosis, on the basis that this bovine strain of *M. tuberculosis* has a consistently low virulence. The development of active, attenuated poliovirus vaccine was based on the selection of poliovirus strains that are of low virulence.

The mechanisms responsible for virulence are of natural interest and of crucial importance. In experimental infections in laboratory animals it is well recognized that serial passage of an agent in a susceptible animal host results in increasing virulence, whereas serial passage on artificial media diminishes virulence. Similarly, growing a virulent strain of microorganism in a medium lacking optimal growth factors can reduce virulence, as can exposure of the microorganism to ultraviolet light.

Organ Affinity

Among the properties that microorganisms possess enabling them to induce disease, there is probably none so clinically important as organ affinity. Mumps, as just one example, is universally known for its parotitis and for the feared and painful orchitis. *Diplococcus pneumoniae, Neisseria meningitidis, Bedsonia lymphogranulomatis,* and poliovirus derive their names from the organ each affects most dramatically.

The experimental studies of the phenomenon of organ affinity are basically negative. Some organs are not affected by some microorganisms, perhaps because the former contain antimicrobial substances. The thymus, pancreas, thyroid and other organs have been shown to produce polypeptides active against *E. coli* and the Streptococcus. Tuberculostatic activity has been found in the lymph nodes, spleen, and liver of infected animals. Some of these substances are rich in arginine, others in lysine, amino acids not otherwise known to have antimicrobial properties.

It is possible, however, to magnify out of all proper proportion this organ affinity. For example mumps virus affects many organs: the meninges, pancreas, ovaries, thyroid, spleen and, as most recently demonstrated, the kidneys. The symptoms produced by pneumococcus infections are due in considerable part to a generalized bacteremia. In North American blastomycosis the skin lesion is so striking that it was not appreciated for almost 50 years that the primary site of infection is probably the lung.

Sources in Nature

One may understand more readily the pathologic physiology of disease in man if one knows the source in nature from which a microorganism infects tissue.

Microorganisms Already Present in Tissue

The possibility exists that a microorganism that begins to multiply and cause disease in man has already been present in a dormant state in tissues. An example of this is herpes simplex virus, which after primary infection persists for long periods only occasionally to multiply and produce a "cold sore." It has been postulated that latent viruses may be present in genetic material and that such viruses may be unmasked to produce disease much later in life. Proof of this is lacking, and the diseases in which this mechanism has been suggested, e.g., leukemia, are not those considered to be infections in the classic sense of the word.

Commensal Flora

The mouth, the upper respiratory tract, the lower gastrointestinal tract and the skin have a bacterial and fungal flora which is "normal" and yet a source of potential disease. On normal skin *Staphylococcus epidermis, Pseudomonas aeruginosa, Escherichia coli* and other gram-negative rod-form bacteria can similarly be considered commensal microorganisms. Among potential pathogens of the gastrointestinal tract are various species of the Enterobacteriaceae and Bacteroides. Although one, two or sometimes even three

viruses can be recovered from a simple stool specimen, especially in children, there does not seem to be a consistent viral microflora. The conjunctiva of the eye, the terminal portion of the urethra and the vagina have a lesser variety and fewer total numbers of microorganisms. The paranasal sinuses, terminal bronchi, upper urinary tract, stomach and upper intestine, though contiguous with areas mentioned before, are virtually free of flora or are sterile on culture.

Thus man is in intimate contact with a great number and variety of microorganisms that are known to be potential pathogens. Furthermore, absence of disease as a result of this contact cannot be ascribed to the skin or mucous membrane acting as an impenetrable barrier. In one study bacteremia was demonstrated following a 30-minute period of chewing a bolus of paraffin in over 50 per cent of persons with varying degrees of caries. Furthermore, minute abrasions, cracks, cuts and other breaches of the wall between the tissues of man and his microflora appear daily. In many of these instances there is visible bleeding and ample opportunity for blood invasion. Despite this resistance to disease, there is nevertheless a substantial relationship of this microflora to disease in man. Urinary tract infection early in its course is virtually always due to a bacterial species common in the lower gastrointestinal tract or on the perineum. Respiratory diseases such as pharyngitis, sinusitis, and pneumonia are due to organisms commonly in the mouth. Wound or skin infections are usually due to organisms such as *Staphylococcus aureus* and *Pseudomonas aeruginosa* that are occasionally a part of the microflora of the skin (see Chap. 11).

Soil

Soil is the natural habitat of the greatest variety and numbers of microorganisms in our environment, but fortunately only a few are commonly pathogenic. Dust from soil contaminated by chicken or bird droppings is probably the means by which great numbers of people (85 per cent of the population in some areas) are infected with the fungus *Histoplasma capsulatum*. In the southwestern part of the United States the fungus infection acquired virtually as frequently from the soil is *Coccidioides immitis*. Various species of Clostridium survive in and infect man from soil. In a different way dust in barracks or in hospitals may provide the source from which man may acquire Group A hemolytic *Strep-*

tococcus pyogenes pharyngitis. Man also acquires hookworm infection by walking barefoot in soil. Though various picornaviruses (poliovirus and Coxsackie) are quite resistant and capable of surviving transiently in soil, this occasional habitat is of less importance in man than stool-hand-mouth spread.

Other Humans

There are large numbers of diseases of man that have as their only source another human being. *Mycobacterium tuberculosis*, human strain, is an outstanding example of a microorganism that a patient acquires from prolonged or intimate contact with another infected person. The venereal diseases as a group are characteristically but not exclusively acquired by sexual contact with another person. The dermatophytoses due to *Microsporum audouini* and *Trichophyton mentagrophytes* spread from person to person. Many of the common viral infections do not have a host other than man. These include measles, mumps, varicella, rubella, rubeola, infectious and serum hepatitis, and poliovirus.

The human source of infection may be a patient clinically ill with disease or a convalescent or healthy carrier. In the case of smallpox healthy carriers are unknown, whereas virulent strains of *Diplococcus pneumoniae* may be carried by otherwise healthy persons. In some instances the carrier state is directly related to an abnormal process or disease. The site of *Salmonella typhosa* localization in man is commonly the gallbladder, the bile and, most specifically, a gallstone. Such an infected stone may be most resistant to antibiotic therapy, and cholecystectomy may be necessary to cure the carrier state. The site of the infection may further influence the degree of contagion, as in nasal carriers of *Staphylococcus aureus*, who pose a greater threat than do pharyngeal carriers. A single Salmonella carrier, such as the notorious Typhoid Mary, may account for 50 cases of typhoid over a 15-year period, whereas there may be 50 asymptomatic Group A *Streptococcus pyogenes* carriers for one case of severe pharyngitis.

Water

With the improvements in sanitation during the past 50 years, water is a source of infection only when such methods break down. In rural areas contamination occurs through the use of shallow springs, and in urban areas there may be contamination of fresh water pipes by broken sewer pipes, failure in chlorination process, or back siphonage. Disease resulting from water sources is almost always gastrointestinal in origin and character. *Entamoeba histolytica* infections occurred in over 1000 persons in Chicago in 1933 because of faulty plumbing in a large hotel. *Shigella sonnei* infection resulted in gastroenteritis in 188 persons as a consequence of contamination of city drinking water by river water in Leicester, England. In Asia, *Vibrio cholerae* infections have their source in drinking water contaminated by sewage. Among the viruses only the agents that cause infectious hepatitis are spread with any frequency from water.

The exceptions to the gastrointestinal type of disease from microorganisms in water occur with *Leptospira icterohaemorrhagiae* which infects man percutaneously, and certain Schistosomes that produce a local dermatitis in those who swim in infested lakes.

Milk

Disease produced by drinking milk containing microorganisms is more diverse than that seen in the case of water. At one time *Mycobacterium tuberculosis* from infected cows was the cause of frequently encountered gastrointestinal and osseous tuberculosis in man. Brucellosis may result from drinking milk contaminated by *Brucella abortus* from infected cows. Similarly, in the past *Streptococcus pyogenes* mastitis in cows resulted in epidemic pharyngitis in populations that drank the contaminated milk. More common than any of these infections today, however, is Q fever, resulting from the ingestion of milk containing the rickettsia, *Coxiella burnetii*. It is not necessary for the animals to be infected themselves for milk to serve as a source of infection. By virtue of its nutrient content, e.g., protein, and the warm temperature at time of collection, milk serves as an excellent medium for growth, or simply as a vehicle for spread of responsible microorganisms, e.g., Salmonella, infectious hepatitis, or poliovirus present in the milk handlers.

Food

There are four ways in which disease results from microorganisms in food. The first is by direct infection of the gastrointestinal tract occurring with a gastroenteritis due usually to infection with a Staphylococcus or Salmonella species or rarely some other enteric bacteria. Salmonella are found commonly in eggs and dried egg powder used in fillings or frostings. Food allowed to stand after exposure to Staphylococcus may permit growth of large numbers of organisms and the production of a potent enterotoxin.

A second mechanism of disease is that exemplified by infectious hepatitis occasionally acquired from raw oysters and clams. Although virus has been demonstrated in duodenal content and in stool, multiplication is not known to occur in the gastrointestinal tract. By an unknown route, presumably either lymph or blood, the virus reaches the liver where it produces its major manifestations of illness.

Third, food improperly canned or bottled and kept under anaerobic conditions may be contaminated by *Clostridium botulinum* and may result in the disease previously described (p. 194). In this instance disease results from a toxin acting at multiple sites distant from the gastrointestinal tract.

Fourth, hepatic abscess may result from infection by *Entamoeba histolytica* acquired from uncooked vegetables. In this infection ulcerative lesions are produced in the cecum by a microorganism that releases a lytic enzyme and enters tissues by its ameboid motion. When mesenteric vessels are eroded, the parasite is carried by the portal circulation to the liver, where the classic liver abscess may develop.

Animals

Animals are reservoirs of a number of microorganisms that produce severe disease in man. We have previously described tuberculosis, brucellosis, epidemic pharyngitis, and Q fever acquired from cows. A severe dermatitis and cellulitis result from infection with *Bacillus anthracis* acquired from sheep and cows. Rabbits and rodents are the source of infection in man with *Pasteurella tularensis*. Psittacotic pneumonia results from exposure to birds infected with *Bedsonia ornithosis*. Rabies results from the bite of dogs, foxes or bats infected with the virus. Among parasites, *Taenia solium* has its source in swine and *Taenia saginata* in cattle. Muscle pain, periorbital edema, fever and occasionally paralysis may result from infection with *Trichinella spiralis* from infected swine. It has recently been shown that the malarial parasites, *Plasmodium cynomolgi* and *Plasmodium knowlesi*, which infect monkeys, are capable of infecting man and inducing a clinical illness indistinguishable from that caused by human strains of malaria parasites.

The disease produced depends to a great extent on the animal activity or contact—from a bite of the animal (rabies), from ingestion of animal meat containing a parasite (tapeworm infection), from handling the animal (tularemia), from handling only the skin or fur (anthrax), from inhaling dust from birds (psittacosis), or only indirectly by way of a vector (malaria).

Insect and Arthropod Sources

Mention of malaria immediately draws attention to the mosquito which is the source for naturally acquired disease in man. In the Anopheles mosquito, as in the Culex mosquito which transmits filariasis, the plasmodia and filaria pass through important developmental stages necessary for subsequent infection in man.

In a second type of infection the microorganisms merely multiply in the insect. In the plague of the fourteenth century, during which 25,000,000 persons or one-quarter of the world's population perished, the common rat flea, *Xenopsylla cheopis*, was the source of infection for man. The tick, *Dermacentor andersoni*, is an important source of both *Pasteurella tularensis* and *Rickettsia rickettsii*, agents that cause respectively tularemia and Rocky Mountain spotted fever. Mosquitoes, ticks and mites are the source of infection in man of the large number of arbovirus infections, including St. Louis encephalitis, dengue, Rift Valley fever and Russian spring-summer disease. The diseases Colorado tick fever and phlebotomous fever derive their names from their insect hosts.

In a third type of infection disease is acquired not by the insect bite but rather by the patient's accidental abrasion of the skin at the site of fecal deposition. Flies may also be an indirect source of infection for man in contaminating food with microorganisms they have ingested or carried on their legs or bodies. Poliovirus has been recovered from flies, but this is not an important source of this disease in man. In contrast, flies are important in infecting man with Shigella species.

Disease in man thus depends on the vector activity or contact—from a bite and direct percutaneous injection of the parasite (malaria), from defecation onto the skin of contaminated excreta of the vector (plague), or from transfer by the vector of a microorganism to food subsequently eaten (shigellosis).

Placental

Even before birth humans are subject to infection when the usually germ-free environment of the embryo is invaded by the transplacental route. One of the earliest recognized examples of such infection was congenital lues. In many instances the infection is fatal and the pregnancy is aborted or a stillborn child is delivered. In utero infection with *Toxoplasma gondii* is similarly severe and markedly in contrast to the much milder disease or inapparent infection in adults. Of considerable contemporary interest is transplacental infection with rubella virus. The isolation and characterization of the virus has resulted in proof that infection of the fetus is a definitive event in the teratogenetic effects (cataracts, deafness, cardiac lesions) of infection of the mother during the first trimester of pregnancy.

Intravenous Fluids

A number of diseases are spread by the intravenous or intramuscular route, and for one disease, serum hepatitis, this is the only route, so far as is known, by which disease is acquired. By definition all diseases acquired by this route are induced by man either legitimately and as an accepted risk in a hospital, or unlawfully, as for example in a narcotic addict who accidentally induces disease in himself. Malaria and lues are other diseases acquired by this route under these conditions. In these instances needles, syringes, whole blood, plasma, fibrinogen, or albumin may be contaminated with the microorganism. In these three diseases, with immediate hematogenous spread there is evidence of disease in widespread areas of the body.

REFERENCES

Bullock, W.: History of Bacteriology. New York, Oxford University Press, 1938.

Dubos, R. J., and Hirsch, J. G.: Bacterial and Mycotic Infections in Man, 4th ed. Philadelphia, J. B. Lippincott Co., 1965.

McDermott, W.: Conference on air borne infections. Bact. Rev., 25:173, 1961.

Smith, D. T., Conant, N. F., and Overman, J. R.: Zinsser Microbiology, 13th ed. New York, Appleton-Century-Crofts, 1964.

Wilson, G. S., and Miles, A. A.: Topley and Wilson's Principles of Bacteriology and Immunity, 4th ed. Baltimore, Williams & Wilkins Co., 1964.

Chapter Ten

Role of the Host Response

JOHN P. UTZ

Introduction

As mentioned in Chapter 9, it should be remembered that there are numbers of commonly encountered true infections in which there is no clinical host response to invasion of the microorganism. In the western part of the United States it is presumed on the basis of skin hypersensitivity studies that there has been infection by *Coccidioides immitis* in as high as 80 per cent of the population, very few of whom have had an identifiable illness. Similarly, mumps virus may produce illness in only one or a few members of the family, though the remaining members, on the basis of a persisting immunity or a rise in antibody titer, are infected. Of course, an antibody titer rise or the production of an immune state is a host response to infection, but since the attention of this chapter is directed to disease with its symptoms and signs, host response limited only to such immune reactions will not be considered further.

General Responses

Just as some infections do not produce clinical disease, many inflammatory responses are not due to infection. However, infectious agents are so common that in the presence of inflammation an infectious origin is the first consideration. Inflammation is defined as a reaction to injury in which there are multiple microscopic, functional, chemical and clinically apparent characteristics. We shall be concerned here with those reactions that are not localized.

Fever

Fever may be defined as an elevation of the body temperature above normal. The normal body temperature is generally considered to be 37° C. (98.6° F.). In studies of "normal" people, however, there seems to be a rather striking distribution of morning temperatures with standard deviations of from 0.47 to 0.50° F. from a mean of 98.6° F. It has even been suggested on the basis of a statistical study that the theoretical distribution of oral temperatures in normal persons during a 24-hour period should be from 97.0 to 100.4° F.

It has been widely thought that a rectal temperature recording is a more accurate measure of body temperature and less subject to deliberate or inadvertent modification by previous oral fluids or other agents. However, the rectal temperature has been shown in some studies to be less responsive than the oral temperature to changes in body heat balance, and thus perhaps less reflective of temperature changes in infection.

There are a number of physiologic factors and normal activities of man which affect body temperature. There is first of all a diurnal variation such that there may be 2 to 3° F. difference in temperature between a maximal value after 6:00 in the evening and

202

a minimal value in the early morning before awakening. Heavy physical exercise may markedly increase body temperatures (as much as 4 to 5° F.), and localized muscular activity, such as vigorous gum chewing, may elevate oral temperature 1° F. Increased body temperature has been noted after ingestion of a heavy meal. Just after onset of menstruation there is in most women a fall of from 0.5 to 0.75° F. in early morning body temperature, which value continues daily until the time of ovulation. On this day there is a clinically important and abrupt rise of 0.5 to 0.75° F. in the morning temperature that continues to the onset of menstruation.

Fever is said to be intermittent when some recordings are normal or below normal in a 24-hour period. When there is marked (at least 1° C.) variation, but not a completely normal value during a 24-hour period, fever is said to be remittent. It is continuous when there is little (0.5° C. or less) variation within a 24-hour period. Fever may also be described as quotidian (daily), factitial (fraudulent or self-induced), autumnal (occurring in the fall season) or tertian (every other day). Other qualifications of the term may not refer to the fever per se, but instead may connote an extensive symptomatologic complex, e.g., scarlet fever, Rocky Mountain spotted fever and Rift Valley fever, in which temperature elevation is not even the most distinctive feature. Lastly there remains the somewhat ludicrous and inappropriate use of the term for disease in which elevated temperature virtually never occurs, e.g., hay fever.

Temperature elevation results from two factors, either increased heat production without adequate dissipation or decreased heat dissipation with normal heat production. Heat is lost from the body by radiation (transferred to cooler objects), by vaporization (from skin or lungs) or by convection (transferred to air). Under a few circumstances fever results from a failure of the heat loss mechanism. Under rather unusual conditions of a high external temperature combined with high humidity, heat loss by way of sweating or evaporation may be impaired. Under usual circumstances, however, fever is a function principally of increased production that exceeds the rate of dissipation.

When fever is intermittent it is usually possible to distinguish clinically three phases: first, rising temperature, the chill; second, a steady state, the flush; and third, falling temperature, the sweating.

During the steady state of fever, the patient is conscious of the warmth of his body and may recognize the characteristic flush of his face. In addition most patients have a general malaise and not unusually aching in joints or muscles, nausea and headache. Sustained high fever, occurring usually in the young or elderly, is frequently accompanied by disorientation, irrationality, hallucinations, inappropriate responses and combativeness, which together form the picture of delirium or the acute brain syndrome. In children fever is often accompanied as well by a convulsion which, like delirium, represents deranged cortical function.

The pathogenesis of fever is intimately related to mechanisms that control and regulate normal body temperature. It has been known for over 50 years that the hypothalamus plays a crucial role in temperature regulation. It has been suggested that in the hypothalamus there are at least two thermoregulatory centers, one that initiates responses to a lowered body temperature and one that operates to decrease body temperature. These two centers have multiple neural connections, and activity of one inhibits activity of the other. In animals experimental electrical stimulation of either leads to appropriate response. The center for heat production is relatively insensitive, and prolonged electrical stimulation increases temperature only 0.5° C. In contrast, stimulation of another area results in a decrease in temperature of as much as 9° C.

The factors, chemical or electrical, that affect the hypothalamic centers are not well known under natural conditions of disease. Most of our knowledge of the mechanism of fever is based on the response to endotoxin. As little as 0.0005 μg./kg. of purified endotoxin administered intravenously is capable of inducing fever. The febrile response to endotoxin has been well studied in animals and in man. Following administration of endotoxin there is a latent period before the appearance of fever, variable according to species, but of from 15 to 90 minutes in duration. During this period in animals, but not in man, there is a marked fall in circulating polymorphonuclear leukocytes. This disappearance is attributed to their adherence to the endothelial lining of blood vessels. This latent period has suggested that there may be an intermediary product that more directly induces fever.

Following administration of endotoxin there appears in the blood a protein, different from endotoxin, that can induce fever without a latent period. This factor, endogenous pyrogen (EP), may be extracted from polymorphonuclear leukocytes and from other tissues as well. There seems to be a direct correlation between the amount of this material present and the degree of fever. When polymorphonuclear leukocytes are completely eliminated by the effect of nitrogen mustard, rabbits do not develop fever after usual doses of endotoxin. These same animals can react to the administration of endogenous pyrogen from an extraneous source.

In animals production of endogenous pyrogen can be induced by a number of substances besides bacterial endotoxin that are important in infection: myxoviruses, gram-positive bacteria, fungi, and under appropriate circumstances, inflammatory exudate.

At the moment the degree to which these studies in animals applies to man is controversial and under active productive investigation.

The release of endogenous pyrogen from cells appears to be an active metabolic process. Appropriate concentrations of such ions as potassium and calcium can prevent release presumably by maintaining a more intact cell membrane.

In summary, fever with infection seems most directly related to hypothalamic nervous activity. The hypothalamus can probably be activated by a number of stimuli. Important among these is an endogenous pyrogen released from various body cells but notably from polymorphonuclear leukocytes. Release of endogenous pyrogen is induced in turn by cell injury resulting from a number of extraneous sources, among which are bacterial endotoxin, gram-positive bacteria, some viruses and fungi.

Chills

It is common for many patients to have chilliness or, less frequently, shaking chills (or rigor) with infection. As mentioned before, a chill commonly precedes fever and may be considered the first phase of rising temperature. Depending on the study, however, temperature rise may occur immediately before or after the chill. It is essential to the definition of a chill that the patient feel cold. Without this sensation such shaking is better called tremor. Shaking, clinically indistinguishable from a chill, may accompany an acute emotional reaction either of fear or of great tension and excitement. In a true chill the patient is usually sufficiently distressed that he puts on additional clothes or blankets. In many instances these are not helpful, and he begins to shake. The rigor is visibly apparent so that the whole bed may shake. He sits huddled in a chair or drawn up in the fetal position in bed. Speaking becomes difficult because of chattering of the teeth and twitching of the facial muscles. The skin is pale or occasionally slightly cyanotic, and there is cutis anserina ("goose flesh"). A chill may last from approximately 10 to 60 minutes.

Two processes are involved in the pathogenesis of the chill. The first is a rise in the internal body temperature, as reflected by a rectal thermometer (see Fever). The second is a fall in, or at least an inappropriately low, skin temperature. The low skin temperature is a result of marked vasoconstriction. The resulting markedly decreased blood flow in the capillaries accounts for the pallor and cyanosis. The shaking of a chill results in a marked increase in metabolism and an increase in heat production.

The anatomic center for initiating a chill and the impulses which affect it are not known. Some experimental evidence suggests that there is a shivering center in the hypothalamus, but other evidence contradicts this. This center is presumably sensitive, not to an increased internal temperature, but to the decreased external temperature produced experimentally by cold exposure. The efferent impulses from this center are severed by anterior root or spinal cord section. Shivering in hemiplegic and in sympathectomized extremities suggests that the effect is not mediated through the pyramidal tract or the sympathetic nervous system. Some evidence indicates that the efferent fibers from the hypothalamus are in the lateral white columns, the tectospinal or rubrospinal tracts. The fact that shivering may occur within a few seconds of a blast of cold air to a cold subject has been used to support the hypothesis that there are receptors in the skin independently capable of initiating shivering.

Sweating

The inordinate sweating accompanying fever is a common response to infection. In this instance, sweating is considered the hallmark of the falling or defervescent phase of fever. Sweating is generalized, though perhaps more profuse in the axillary and genital areas, where sudoriferous glands are more numerous. Palms and soles, which sweat under emotional stimuli, do not sweat as a result of thermal stimulation. The skin and sometimes the hair are wet. In this stage the patient feels warm and throws off the bedclothes. With severe sweating the patient may be intensely thirsty and with increasing salt loss may have fatigue, nausea, headache, muscle cramps and weakness.

A more unusual type of sweating, which may not be accompanied by fever and yet is characteristic of infection, is that occurring during sleep, the so called "night sweats." These are rather poorly understood and though dramatic in nature have not been well studied. Characteristically the patient is not aware of any great feeling of warmth, but awakes instead because of drenched clothes and covers. Sweating may be so severe that clothing must be changed. It is not unusual for multiple sweats of this sort to occur in one night. Occasionally the perspiration is malodorous. When night sweats persist, lassitude, weight loss and malaise are frequently encountered.

Sweating is probably initiated by thermoreceptive hypothalamic centers. Moderate warming of the hypothalamus results in a prompt increase in sweating, whereas warming of the skin to 34.5° C. results in sweating only after a distinct latent period. From multiple laboratory studies skin thermoreceptors appear unable to initiate sweating independently.

Sweating results in heat loss from the body by means of markedly increased evaporation. This degree of evaporation may thus accompany and to some degree account for the fall in temperature ending a febrile episode. Much less is known, however, of the effects of night sweats. In these instances sweating is independent of fever and may be a direct effect of infection per se. There is virtually no experimental evidence bearing on the mechanism of night sweats.

Anorexia

One of the most common manifestations of infection is anorexia, a loss of appetite for food or a loss of interest in eating. Even foods formerly attractive to the patient fail to excite his interest. Anorexia may occur before any fever is evident, and experimental hyperthermia does not necessarily depress the appetite.

The cause for anorexia in infections is undoubtedly complex. Environmental factors, such as unpleasant sights, odors or sounds, may psychologically inhibit appetite. To a great extent appetite is a psychological perception, and a number of "purely" emotional states, such as worry, anxiety or depression, decrease appetite. Such fear, conscious or unconscious, of the implications of other symptoms may directly lead to anorexia.

To a considerable degree the anorexia of infection has been ascribed to "toxicity" of illness. This explanation is inexact, deceptive and unfortunate. In most infections no circulating toxin can be detected, and to use the term "toxic" 'in this instance debases the concept.

Decreased corticosteroid production, as in Addison's disease, may be accompanied by profound anorexia. Although often suggested, there is no proof that a slight degree of corticosteroid deficiency may occur in infections and induce mild anorexia.

In infections localized to the abdominal viscera, reflexes that decrease gastrointestinal activity and otherwise affect the bowel may result in loss of appetite.

When such visceral reflexes are not involved, anorexia is explained on the basis of action by an unknown factor on the brain stem or hypothalamus. This center of Borison and Wang has chemoreceptors capable of detecting and directly responding to such circulating agents as amphetamine to produce anorexia.

Generalized Cutaneous Reactions

The skin is an extraordinarily sensitive indicator of the presence of generalized infection. Furthermore, skin changes are frequently pathognomonic of the infection present and establish the diagnosis before the etiologic agent can be identified in cultures or microscopically in tissue sections. There is an almost unlimited variety to the lesions produced in the skin in infection, and mechanisms differ in most of them.

One example of a diffuse cutaneous and mucosal skin lesion is jaundice. Elevated bilirubin is characteristic of infectious hepatitis, but this finding may occur in other illnesses as well, such as Weil's disease, malaria, yellow fever, and even pneumococcal pneumonia and typhoid fever. In these instances there is diffuse hepatic inflammation or increased hemolysis. In contrast, abscesses in the liver due to *Entamoeba histolytica* or with pylephlebitis rarely produce jaundice unless there is incidental compression of the biliary system.

In other diseases the diffuse cutaneous lesion is due to a direct effect on the vascular endothelium of the skin with hyperemia and dilation. Such a lesion is seen in scarlet fever and measles.

In still other instances there are lesions that result from active bacterial proliferation in the small vessels so that thrombosis, occlusion and petechiae formation are present. Such lesions occur in typhoid fever, meningococcemia, ecthyma gangrenosum (due to *Pseudomonas aeruginosa* infection) and bacterial or fungal endocarditis.

Multiple skin lesions that are vesicular in nature are seen in varicella (chickenpox), smallpox, rickettsialpox, and sometimes in *Pseudomonas aeruginosa* infections. From these lesions as well the microorganisms can be cultured.

North American blastomycosis and sporotrichosis are two of the systemic mycoses which may produce multiple skin lesions from which the fungi can be readily recovered.

Malaise

It is an almost universal experience that malaise is both one of the most frequent and most distressing symptoms encountered. Repeatedly patients, after speaking of one complaint or another, attest that they could bear with one or many of them if they did not feel "so bad" or "so terrible" or so "generally ill." More colloquial equivalents of these expressions are even more numerous and vivid without, unfortunately, describing the symptom more accurately. The antonym or contrary expression can be described only vapidly as "feeling good." The absence of malaise is a striking event to both patient and physician, so that the statement is often heard, "Despite his illness he felt surprisingly well." It must be admitted that the symptom malaise, no matter how common, cannot be measured or expressed quantitatively. Without such measurements elucidation of cause has seemed virtually impossible, and description of "possible mechanisms" would inappropriately perpetuate a delusion of some knowledge.

Generalized Weakness

In many patients there are various manifestations of generalized weakness. This weakness usually can be distinguished by patient and physician from the true paralysis or paresis that results so directly from actual anterior horn cell damage in poliomyelitis. Generalized weakness is almost never localized or complete and consists of an impairment in sustained activity and of an early and inappropriate fatigue.

In some instances these complaints may represent direct invasion of muscle by the infecting organisms. Among the viruses, Coxsackie B strains clearly infect the heart muscle to produce myocarditis, characteristically in children. Various fungi, including *Actinomyces israelii* and *Sporotrichum schenckii*, can produce muscle lesions. Pyogenic bacteria can induce multiple abscesses in muscle tissue. The persistence of infection and inactivity may result in visible atrophy of muscle groups and lead to further weakness. Such muscle groups may show vacuoles and edema microscopically.

None of these mechanisms, however, seem to explain the generalized type of weakness. It seems more likely that this symptom represents a nonspecific manifestation in muscle tissue. In this regard eosinophilic, hyaline changes in muscle have been described in a number of chronic infections including tuberculosis, typhoid fever and yellow fever. The degree of severity of lesions has seemed to relate directly to the degree of illness present.

As mentioned before, some muscle weakness is due to sodium loss that follows sweating.

Loss of Interest and Enthusiasm

These terms merely hint at a wide variety of emotional or psychophysiologic manifestations of infection. Patients ill from infections of many causes almost always show a loss of interest in their families, usual work and previously enjoyable pleasures. Their thought and speech content shrink to become exclusively limited to their complaints and their emotional reactions. In addition, their motor activity lessens, they take to their beds, and complain of weariness and loss of energy and interest. In part these symptoms reflect the direct effects of a high fever, drenching sweat, hyponatremia, or dehydration. It is tempting to attribute some reactions to a teleologic protective action of the body to limit inflammation and further tissue damage and destruction.

In some patients, however, particularly those with such infections as infectious mononucleosis and brucellosis, there seems to be a disproportionate severity and prolongation of such reactions. Some such illnesses are truly multiphased, i.e., relapsing or undulant. However, in some patients there is no evidence of continuing infection. Recent studies of this phenomenon suggest that such patients may be depression prone before infection, and develop this reaction after such trauma as an acute illness.

REFERENCES

Bennett, I. L., Jr., and Nicastri, A.: Fever as a mechanism of resistance. Bact. Rev., *24:*16, 1960.

Beslin, R. D., and Wood, W. B.: Studies on the pathogenesis of fever. J. Exper. Med., *119:*697, 1964.

Best, C. H., and Taylor, N. B.: The Physiological Basis of Medical Practice, 7th ed. Baltimore, Williams & Wilkins Co., 1961.

Imboden, J. B., Canter, A., and Cluff, L. E.: Symptomatic recovery from medical disorders. Influence of psychological factors. J.A.M.A., *178:* 1182, 1961.

Thomas, L.: The physiological disturbances produced by endotoxins. Ann. Rev. Physiol., *16:*467, 1956.

Chapter Eleven

Factors Predisposing to Infectious Disease

JOHN P. UTZ

Introduction

In Chapters 9 and 10 were described the role of the invading microorganism and the body response to this invasion in the production of symptoms. There is a third element that strongly affects the degree of illness in the host, an element that in turn is twofold and at cross purposes. In every person infected there are factors at work that predispose to disease and others that limit or protect against it. Each of these is in part natural and in part artificial—that is to say, produced in our modern world by the effects of civilization and, in particular, by the mechanical and chemical interventions of the physician.

Predisposing Factors

Natural

Age. The two extremes of life, infancy and old age, are periods when various infections are more common and more severe than at other ages. These infections include notably bacterial pneumonia and tuberculosis. The common infections of mumps, measles, poliomyelitis, varicella, and infectious hepatitis are more severe in adults than in children. However, it is noteworthy that respiratory disease of viral origin is less common in the elderly than in the young. Among the systemic mycoses, disseminated histoplasmosis is more frequent in infants, cryptococcosis is a di-

sease of the middle period and blastomycosis is more common in older age groups.

The mechanism responsible for frequent infections in the child would appear related to antibody formation. The antibody, passively transferred in utero from the mother, is gradually lost over the first six months of life. Following the disappearance of maternal antibody, the child begins to manufacture antibody with repeated exposures to antigen in the form of invading microbes. In the elderly there is a decrease in responsiveness to antigenic stimulation. The greater prevalence of some infections in the middle years is less readily explained. Increased exposure as a result of occupational activities, e.g., brucellosis in stockyard workers, explains only a part of these differences in prevalence.

Sex. Occupation similarly accounts for differences in prevalence rates between the sexes. However, such an explanation does not account for the high risk of severe poliomyelitis in women of child-bearing age. Urinary tract infection occurs ten times more frequently in the female than in the male, and the explanation in this instance seems to be obstruction of the ureters from a gravid uterus or other anatomic factors such as urethral trauma during sexual intercourse and the shorter female urethra. In children, severe infections (meningitis and septicemia) are almost twice as frequent in males as in females. Osteomyelitis is more common in boys, and tuberculosis and cryptococcosis in

208

men, without an adequate available explanation.

Race. It is a frequent observation and an important clue to the diagnosis that some infections, e.g., tuberculosis, are more frequent in Negro populations than in white. When tuberculosis does occur it appears, furthermore, to be more severe as well. Coccidioidomycosis in disseminated form occurs three times more often in the Mexican, 15 times more often in the Negro and five times more often in the Filipino than in the white.

It is difficult to ascribe these observed differences to race per se, as it is evident that in these populations there are important social differences in such factors as housing, prolonged occupational exposure to dust, likelihood of crowded living quarters, customs in consulting physicians, ease of obtaining medical care, ability to purchase drugs and faithfulness to treatment programs. These differences are probably more important than differences in race.

Nutrition. It is a curious fact that both malnutrition and good nutrition are predisposing factors to disease. Memories are still vivid of the decimating effect of infection in concentration camp prisoners. These clinical observations are corroborated by controlled experimental studies with fewer variables in which deprivation of particular dietary factors of protein and vitamins A, D, C and B has increased susceptibility to infection with Salmonella, Pneumococcus, and Rickettsia microorganisms. On the other hand, a vitamin B deficiency in experimental studies in mice may decrease susceptibility to poliovirus. Hypoproteinemic rats and rabbits have a lowered resistance to *D. pneumoniae* infections.

The mechanism for increased susceptibility with dietary deficiency has been ascribed to "inanition with decreased resistance," or to impairment in antibody production.

Fatigue. There is a general impression that fatigue predisposes to infection and illness, particularly in poliomyelitis in man. In animals, exercise before and following inoculation with poliovirus or the Pneumococcus results in increased rates of infection and death. In other studies fatigue appears to activate a latent Salmonella infection and lead to wide dissemination of microorganisms.

The mechanism of enhancement of infection by fatigue appears from some studies not to be due to depressed antibody production. One can only speculate on the role of lactic acid or other metabolites in the increased susceptibility.

Occupation. In the vast majority of occupations the role of the work in increased infection is merely the opportunity for increased exposure to the infecting microorganism. Thus one expects brucellosis in stockyard workers, sporotrichosis in gardeners, tuberculosis in nurses, tularemia in hunters, and anthrax in wool workers. Tuberculosis is also more common than the usual in miners and stonecutters. In these workers susceptibility is due to increased exposure, not to *M. tuberculosis,* but to silica which is known both clinically and experimentally to predispose to this infectious disease. In experimental studies pulmonary damage by calcium chloride, comparable to that by silica, is not accompanied by increased susceptibility. Silica appears to have a direct stimulating effect on the growth of *M. tuberculosis.* How this stimulation is effected is not known.

Temperature Extremes. There is a widespread belief that exposure to cold and, to a lesser degree, heat predisposes to infection. The great English mathematician George Boole—as well as many less noteworthy persons—after a long walk in the cold and rain, "took cold" and died of pneumonia. On the other hand, enteroviral infections including poliomyelitis and herpangina are more common in the summer.

It is likely that a number of mechanisms are at work in temperature effects on infection. Experimentally, cold temperature results in lower bacterial multiplication but also in suppression of antibody formation. At temperatures slightly higher than normal bacterial multiplication may be more rapid, but antibody response to an antigen is also more rapid. At temperatures only a little higher still, multiplication of *Cryptococcus neoformans,* for example, may be completely suppressed. Experimental studies in man have shown that changes in environmental temperature are followed by detectable changes in the nasal mucosa. Cold decreases ciliary movement in the tracheal mucosa, and impairment of this defensive measure may also be important.

Physiologic and Metabolic Defects. There are small numbers of conditions which might be termed diseases but which are fundamentally physiologic or metabolic defects predisposing to disease. Patients with hypogammaglobulinemia and others with dysproteinemias or macroglobulinemia who produce abnormal globulins are especially prone to repeated bacterial infection. It is of interest that patients with these defects do not seem to have recurrent viral infections.

Diabetes mellitus is properly considered a disorder of carbohydrate metabolism, and patients with this disorder are especially prone to infection. Tuberculosis is four times more common in diabetic than in nondiabetic patients; phycomycosis (mucormycosis) among the fungal illnesses occurs almost always in a patient with diabetes mellitus. Pyelonephritis due to gram-negative bacteria, skin infections due to Staphylococcus and Candida, are additional important clinical illnesses.

Since gamma globulin is virtually all antibody, failure to produce or production of abnormal gamma or gamma-related globulins seems an adequate explanation for predisposing to infection. In diabetes mellitus the mechanism is less clear. It is reasonable to explain some infections (pyelonephritis, candidosis) on the basis of the increased urine and blood levels of glucose, a substrate important for the growth in culture media of Candida and some bacteria. In other experimental fungal infections, acidosis rather than hypoglycemia appears crucial to increased susceptibility. In these studies acidosis was accompanied by a markedly delayed and decreased migration of phagocytic cells into the site of infection.

Other Diseases. So-called "intercurrent infection" is a frequent cause of death in the typically prolonged course of a number of common diseases such as rheumatoid arthritis. In this instance there is little to suggest a predisposing effect. However, in emphysema and bronchiectasis mechanical factors such as bronchial obstruction and inadequate drainage of sputum are probably directly responsible for the increased frequency of a terminal infectious disease. In other diseases, notably chronic lymphatic leukemia and Hodgkin's disease, the increased frequency of infection has been associated with diminished antibody production. Lastly it should be remembered that one infection can predispose to another, e.g., influenza viral disease is often followed by a severe Staphylococcus or *H. influenzae* pneumonia. The mechanisms at work in these latter instances are undoubtedly multiple and include mechanical damage to tissue and impaired response.

Induced Factors

There is a wide variety of artificially induced factors predisposing to disease in man.

The point of separating the artificial from the natural is to remind us that many of the former result from actions by the physician. In most instances, but regrettably not all, the predisposing factors are induced deliberately for the good of the patient, with a careful consideration beforehand of the risks and an intelligent attempt to prevent illness when possible.

Corticosteroids. The immeasurable beneficial effects of corticosteroid therapy have been accompanied by a striking increase in frequency of complicating infectious diseases. Therapy has resulted, for example, in reactivation of tuberculosis, dissemination of a well localized or tolerated commensal organism (Candida), fatal outcome of an otherwise mild illness (chickenpox) and increased frequency of such illnesses as pneumococcal pneumonia and gram-negative bacterial pyelonephritis and septicemia. These dire complications seem to occur more frequently in artificially induced hyperadrenocorticism than in the naturally occurring Cushing syndrome.

The increased susceptibility to infection in man has been so striking that it has resulted in a large number of studies of the phenomenon in animals. At present the administration of corticosteroids is one of the earliest considered steps in making a resistant animal susceptible to an infection. Notable examples of increased severity of laboratory animal disease include infections with Brucella in guinea pigs, Staphylococcus in rabbits, poliovirus in mice, and mumps in the embryonated hens' eggs.

Studies of the mechanisms of susceptibility have been equally voluminous. Virtually every step in host defense has been shown in one study or another to be affected by steroids. The most important of these effects seem to be, in summary, the general lessening of inflammatory response and the impairment in antibody formation.

Ionizing Radiation. Although small amounts have the opposite effect, larger doses of x-irradiation result in increased susceptibility to disease. After large, whole body exposure, most dramatically at Hiroshima and Nagasaki but also in industrial accidents, disease due to infection appeared approximately two to three days after exposure. In patients irradiated deliberately and carefully, frequency of infection is increased but the onset is delayed.

In experimental studies in animals larger doses of radiation lead to septicemia due to commensal gram-negative bacteria or the

Streptococcus approximately two weeks after exposure. Smaller amounts of radiation result in increased lethality when the animal is challenged subsequently with live or heat-killed bacteria or fungi.

In increased susceptibility to infection following radiation two mechanisms seem to be at work. The first of these is early marked cellular damage and destruction. Lymphocytes, important in host defense, are among the most radiosensitive cells. Death of other cells with edema, hemorrhage and mucosal sloughing seems to remove the barriers to microbial invasion and dissemination. The second mechanism, resulting from destruction of plasma cells, is impaired antibody synthesis. This immunosuppression is a more delayed effect and with proper dosage of irradiation has been deliberately utilized recently to enhance host acceptance after organ transplantation.

Immunosuppressive Drugs. For the purpose of suppressing host rejection of organ transplants, a number of different drugs— 6-mercaptopurine, dactinomycin, and azothiopurine—have been carefully employed. By use of such agents before and after transplantation, antibody production and host rejection have been suppressed for prolonged periods of time. In as many as a third of such patients death from infection has occurred. Although antibiotic therapy effective against more commonly encountered bacteria may be partly responsible, increased susceptibility in general seems to explain the preponderance of such unusual infectious agents as cytomegalovirus, *Pneumocystis carinii,* Aspergillus species or, among commensals, Candida species.

Antimicrobial Drugs. The first effective antibiotic agent, penicillin, had been employed less than a year before it was recognized that its use was accompanied by superinfection, the growth of a new bacterium with resulting disease. One of the earliest examples was otitis media and meningitis due to *H.*

influenzae, in patients treated for pneumococcal pneumonia. Tetracycline or combinations of other antibiotics to achieve a "broad coverage" predisposes to *Pseudomonas aeruginosa* infection, which in septicemic form is fatal in a high percentage of patients. Candida endocarditis similarly is known clinically and experimentally to follow antibacterial therapy.

The mechanisms of this reaction are manifold. Probably most important is the opportunity for a commensal bacterium resistant to the antimicrobic agent to multiply by virtue of the increased nutrient material available to it. This increased nutrient is a function in turn of the suppression of growth of other microorganisms and a derangement of the normal ecology of the body's bacterial flora. A second mechanism is a direct stimulatory effect on one microorganism by an "antibiotic" for another. As an extreme example of this, it is possible under laboratory conditions to make a bacterium antibiotic dependent. Third, chloramphenicol directly inhibits antibody production. Finally, it seems reasonable that the antianabolic effect of an antibiotic such as tetracycline may depress generally the body's immune responses.

REFERENCES

Elberg, S. S.: Factors affecting resistance to infection. Ann. Rev. Microbiol., *10:*1, 1956.

Florey, H.: General Pathology, 3rd Ed. Philadelphia, W. B. Saunders Co., 1962.

Nungester, W. J.: Nonspecific factors in immunity. Ann. Rev. Microbiol., 8:363, 1954.

Perez-Tamayo, R.: Mechanisms of Disease. Philadelphia, W. B. Saunders Co., 1961.

Raffel, S. (guest ed.): Basic and clinical immunology. M. Clin. North America, Nov., 1965.

Spector, W. B.: The acute inflammatory response. Ann. New York Acad. Sci., *116:*747, 1964.

Thomas, L., Uhr, J. W., and Grant, L.: Injury, Inflammation and Immunity. Baltimore, Williams & Wilkins Co., 1964.

Chapter Twelve

Factors Tending to Prevent Infectious Disease

JOHN P. UTZ

Introduction

There is danger in use of the term "defense mechanisms" of ascribing teleologic roles to body cells or fluids. The response of the body is not directly "defensive," and the microorganism is not really "invasive." We are really speaking of those host responses, biochemically or otherwise induced, which in the evolutionary development of man have resulted in survival, selectively, of the fittest.

In any event, there are a number of factors, natural and artificially induced, which serve to protect man from disease in the presence of infection.

Local Defenses

In one sense the body may be considered a hollow tube open on the external surface (skin) and the internal surface (mucosa of the respiratory, oral-gastrointestinal and genitourinary tracts). These surfaces are hardly ever completely intact but are marred or penetrated by sweat and sebaceous glands, gross or microscopic cuts and abrasions, cavities in teeth, minute ulceration of bowel and so forth. Despite such defects, however, these surfaces contain many thousand times more microorganisms than they permit to enter.

Skin

Commensal microorganisms of the skin include various species of Staphylococcus and Corynebacterium, lipophilic fungi, *Pseudomonas aeruginosa* and, at times, other microorganisms as well. This population quantitatively and qualitatively represents a selective persistence (or viewed conversely, a rejection) of many microorganisms present in the environmental air. In the skin such factors as desiccation, desquamation, acid pH and the presence of fatty acids appear to be important mechanisms in the control of bacterial, fungal and viral colonization. Oleic acid, for example, as well as other fatty acids on the skin, is active in suppressing Candida growth on body surfaces. Indeed, recent work suggests that these natural mechanisms are more effective than prolonged washing, as in a surgical scrub, in decreasing bacterial counts.

Respiratory Tract

The second surface of the body exposed to microorganisms is the respiratory tract. If the air exchanged in a single respiration is 500 ml., if the respiratory rate is 15 times per minute, and if the bacterial population of air is approximately 25 colonies per liter, then the cells of the respiratory tract are exposed each hour to about 1000 colonial units of bacteria alone. Because of the two right angle turns in the direction of air and because of the additional obstacles to flow in the turbinates, most of the particulate matter in air has been in contact with the mucosal surfaces between the external nares and the glottal opening to the trachea. Mucin, secreted at a rate of 1 liter a day by the glands of the upper respiratory tract, retains most of the microorganisms that strike the mucosal surface. Mucin is known to have a degree of antiviral action mediated by the mucoproteins which adsorb some myxoviruses. Mucin usually has antibacterial activity as well, particularly in the form of lysozyme, secreted in tears and passed into the pharynx by way of the lacrymal nasal duct. The mucin in turn is directed by the action of cilia toward the hypopharynx from which it is swallowed. By an undulant vigorous movement the cilia move mucin at a rate of 2.5 to 7.5 mm. per minute. Mucin that is not swallowed and that may strike the glottis induces coughing, which still more forcefully expels material from the lower respiratory tract. Particles of greater than 10 microns virtually never reach the alveoli, and over 95 per cent of particles less than that size are similarly trapped. Those rare bacteria that do reach the terminal bronchioles, alveolar ducts and alveoli are removed by phagocytes. In addition, antibody to a number of viruses has been demonstrated in nasal secretions.

Digestive Tract

The mechanisms at work in the upper respiratory tract also operate in the upper digestive tract. In addition to the action of mucin and cilia it is important to remember that saliva has bactericidal activity, notably against *Corynebacterium diphtheriae*. Gastric juice has an even greater bactericidal activity, especially against such pathogens as *Brucella abortus* and Salmonella and Shigella species. The acid contents of the stomach serve to depress bacterial growth in the duodenum and upper half of the jejunum as well. Although bile has the property of lysing *Diplococcus pneumoniae*, its alkalinity serves to neutralize the antibacterial activity of the acid contents from the stomach and hence to increase bacterial growth. By the time ingested food and intestinal secretions reach the lower small intestine and the colon, the bacterial population has increased at least a millionfold. The huge commensal bacterial populations of the bowel may exert an antibiotic effect against potential pathogens or competitively deprive them of nutrients. Other than these activities and an intact mucosa, little is known of factors in the distal gastrointestinal tract that prevent tissue invasion and disease.

Genitourinary Tract

The mechanical flushing effect and the acidity of the urine are the major mechanisms by which infection and disease are prevented in the urethral or external end of the urinary tract. However, there are additional factors at work including lysozyme, a mucoprotein capable of inhibiting some functions of various myxoviruses, minute amounts of antibody and gamma globulin, and other antibacterial and antimycobacterial (tuberculosis) substances.

Vagina

The vagina, another surface exposed to microorganisms, has a remarkable resistance to invasion that is a function of the commensal organisms normally present. These in turn result from endocrine effects on the epithelial lining. Estrogens naturally secreted by the ovaries favor the deposition of glycogen in the epithelial cells. Desquamated, glycogen-laden cells support the growth of *Lactobacillus acidophilus*. The large amount of lactic acid produced by this microorganism is capable of depressing growth of such serious pathogens as *Pseudomonas aeruginosa* and *Staphylococcus aureus*.

Systemic Defenses

It would be repetitious to cite previously discussed factors such as age, sex, race and nutrition (Chap. 11), which, when considered contrariwise from previously, result in increased resistance.

Antibodies

Even at the first moment of extrauterine life, the infant has substances circulating in his blood that prevent disease on exposure to infectious agents. One of these substances is called antibody, usually a gamma immunoglobulin, present in blood or other body fluid, which is the result of and reacts specifically with a stimulant termed antigen. Such an antigen-antibody reaction, with notable exceptions, is usually considered protective for the host. The infant acquires his antibody passively across the placenta in utero. Such maternally acquired antibody seems undoubtedly a factor in the relative rarity of such illnesses as measles, streptococcal pharyngitis and pneumococcal infections in the newborn. This maternal antibody disappears during the first 6 months of life, and from that time on antibody present represents the production by the child after stimulation by an antigen. In most instances such antibody effectively protects against later disease so that only the first exposure to the microorganism results in illness. In some instances, the common cold for example, the protection from further illness is less apparent, but this lack of immunity is the result of a large number of causative agents, in the rhinovirus family for example, that so differ in antigenic makeup that antibodies to one do not protect against disease from another.

The mechanism by which antibody protects against disease is generally clearly evident from the measures used to detect antibody presence. Pneumococcal antibody results in marked swelling of the pneumococcal capsule. Antibodies to *Vibrio cholera* clearly distort and kill this organism. Antibody to various toxins (antitoxin) is capable of inactivating the specific toxin in vitro.

Another serum factor, opsonin, renders bacteria more susceptible to phagocytosis by directly uniting with the bacteria to change their external electrical charge. In viral infections an additional protective protein material, interferon, is released from infected cells so that they or other cells become insusceptible to another viral infection. The protective effect of interference has been demonstrated experimentally by the relatively mild degree of illness developing when virulent dengue virus is given simultaneously with an attenuated yellow fever virus.

Other Humoral Substances

These materials differ from antibody in being nonspecific in their general antimicrobic activity. Such a substance is complement, a heat-labile component of normal serum. Lipid fractions, e.g., lecithin-like, of normal animal serum are capable of neutralizing in vitro the ineffectiveness of a number of viruses including influenza. Leukocytes release a heat-stable substance, leukin, which is bactericidal for a few species of bacteria.

Properdin, a euglobulin which does not require antigen for induction, has antibacterial activity in the presence of magnesium ions and complement. In contrast, antibody requires antigen but does not need complement.

More recently there has been described a serum factor in the euglobulin and β globulin group that is active against Candida species and that seems to be absent from the serum of infected or susceptible patients.

Cellular Factors

One need reflect only on the patients with chronic lymphatic leukemia, who are so prone to both bacterial and fungal infection, to appreciate the importance of cells, in this case the polymorphonuclear leukocytes, in the prevention of disease. Physiologically active phagocytic circulating cells are clear determinants of death or survival in many instances of infection.

In addition there are other cells, fixed in tissue, especially in such reticuloendothelial organs as the spleen and liver, that are important in preventing disease. In experimental infections passage through such organs results in a marked reduction in circulating microorganisms. Larger macrophages, foreign body giant cells, for example, are important in addition in the engulfment and killing of such fungal pathogens as *Histoplasma capsulatum* and *Blastomyces dermatitidis*.

Induced Factors

Every therapeutic effort by the physician is intended to lessen the severity of or even prevent disease. These measures include general supportive care, such as rest, proper diet, replacement of fluids and electrolytes, sedation, and symptomatic therapy to control diarrhea, vomiting and cough.

In addition there are three specific antimicrobic measures which should be emphasized.

Vaccines. A variety of vaccines have been developed, which, in an occasionally spectacular degree, limit or prevent disease. The principle of deliberate exposure to limited amounts of a noxious material to prevent serious disease probably antedates written history. The term vaccination originates, however, with the work of Jenner who established on experimental grounds that exposure to cowpox (vaccinia) protected the recipient from smallpox (variola). Since the time of this demonstration in 1796, a variety of products have been developed to the point that today many are standard preventive medical measures for virtually everyone. Disease rarely occurs subsequently in persons properly vaccinated with such products as tetanus toxoid and attenuated poliomyelitis virus. Only slightly less protection is afforded by use of pertussis, diphtheria and more recently measles vaccine.

The mechanism by which vaccines protect was established as early as 1890, with the demonstration that after exposure to diphtheria toxin a protective factor, antitoxin, appears in serum. The artificially induced antibodies are similar in action to those developing after natural infection.

Antiserums. Beginning with the work of Ehrlich, antiserums produced in animals with the use of vaccines have been important means of modifying or occasionally preventing disease. Antitoxins such as those against diphtheria and botulinism relieve symptoms of disease and prevent fatal outcome. Administered after exposure, hyperimmune gamma globulin, according to the dosage employed, can completely prevent infection and disease or so modify the infection that an immune state is produced with relatively few and minor symptoms.

This means of protection from disease is considered to be "passive" since the recipient of the serum plays no role himself in modifying the illness. It is important to remember, however, that the state of immunity resulting from such passive transfer is short lived, i.e., protection from disease is afforded for no more than a month usually.

Chemotherapy. No method of preventing or modifying disease is more important or more widely employed today than that of antimicrobic drugs. The use of these agents began in the mid-1930s, and new agents still become available for clinical evaluation and general use each year. This large number of drugs allows for varying routes and frequency of administration, duration of chemotherapeutic activity and localization of action. The use of these agents has profoundly affected the severity of symptoms, the duration of illness, the frequency of sequelae and the case fatality rates of almost all infectious diseases.

In preventing disease by an infecting organism chemotherapy has its effect on the microorganism itself. This action may result in killing of the bacteria, which action is thus "bactericidal," or in merely suppressing the growth or multiplication of the microorganism, a "bacteriostatic" effect. Chemotherapeutic agents effect this suppression of growth by various means. Penicillin acts on the bacterial cell wall, polymyxin acts on the cell membrane, tetracycline interferes with protein synthesis, griseofulvin interferes with nucleic acid synthesis, and the sulfonamides affect intermediary metabolism.

As already mentioned, but worthy of reemphasis, chemotherapy has not been and probably never will be "broad" enough to prevent disease from all possible microbial agents. As some pathogenic microorganisms are suppressed, different illnesses appear, the result of infection with agents previously considered minimally pathogenic for man. Also, success of chemotherapy is still dependent on intact host defenses, and serious disease still results under circumstances previously mentioned of lowered or absent resistance to disease. Lastly, the use of these agents has been attended by increasing frequency of side-effects, either as idiosyncratic reactions in the unusual patient or as predictable and to some extent only partially preventable effects of the basic action of the drugs.

REFERENCES

Austrian, R., and others: Symposium on antibiotics. Am. J. Med., *39:*689, 1965.

Aycock, W. L., Hopper, S., and Long, D. A.: Seasonal prevalence as a principle in epidemiology. Am. J. Med. Sc., *209:*395, 1965.

Kass, E. H.: Hormones and host resistance to infections. Bact. Rev., *24:*177, 1960.

Miles, A. A., Miles, E. M., and Burke, G.: The value and duration of defense reactions of the skin to primary lodgement of bacteria. Brit. J. Exper. Path., *38:*79, 1956.

Scrimshaw, N. S., Taylor, C. E., and Gordon, J. E.: Interactions of nutrition and infection. Am. J. Med. Sc., *273:*367, 1959.

Spector, W. G., and Willoughby, D. A.: The inflammatory response. Bact. Rev., *27:*117, 1963.

Chapter Thirteen

Allergy

WILLIAM B. SHERMAN

Introduction

The term *allergy* was suggested by von Pirquet in 1906 to describe the altered reaction of organisms and tissues to repeated contacts with infective and antigenic agents such as vaccine virus, tuberculin, and foreign serums.* Acquired hypersensitivity of this type, manifest as anaphylaxis, contact dermatitis, and tuberculin sensitivity, has been studied extensively in experimental animals. These experimental studies have contributed greatly to the understanding of several common human diseases such as hay fever, bronchial asthma, infantile eczema, contact dermatitis, and acute urticaria.

The phenomena of allergy can be divided into two general classes:* *immediate reactions* occurring within a few minutes after exposure to the antigen, and *delayed reactions* which are manifested after a period of 12 to 24 hours or more. Both types show the high degree of specificity characteristic of immunologic reactions. In those cases in which the time of onset of sensitization can be clearly established, the incubation period is of the order of 5 to 10 days. In the immediate type of sensitization the circulating plasma usually contains antibodies capable of transferring the sensitization to nonallergic individuals of the same, and occasionally other, species. In the delayed type of allergy, the plasma or serum shows no evidence of antibody activity. This type of sensitization apparently resides in lymphoid cells.† In certain typical examples, such as experimental contact dermatitis and tuberculin sensitization, sensitivity can be transferred from one animal to another by the injection of lymphoid cells.

The present use of the term allergy is intended to include those reactions which have a proved or probable immunologic mechanism, but not other individual idiosyncrasies in which a completely different mechanism is involved, such as galactosemia in which the intolerance of galactose depends upon the absence of a specific enzyme mechanism.

Experimental Anaphylaxis

Many basic features of the allergic reaction are illustrated by experimental anaphylaxis. This phenomenon may be induced in most common species of mammals, but the guinea pig, which is highly susceptible and easily handled, is most commonly used for the study of the phenomenon. If 0.1 to 1 ml. of a nontoxic heterologous protein solution, such as horse serum or egg white, is injected parenterally into a normal guinea pig, there is no visible effect. However, this injection induces a state of sensitization in the animal, and if a second similar injection is given 7 to 10

---

* For concepts related to altered reactions of the host's own tissues see Chapter 3, Autoimmune Disease.

† For participation of the spleen and thymus in antigen-antibody reactions see Chapter 31.

days later there is an immediate violent re-action characterized by restlessness, labored respiration, and convulsions, usually causing death within a few minutes. The state of sensitization may be shown to persist through most of the life of the guinea pig.

When an active antigen is used, sensitization may be produced by any parenteral route, intravenous, intraperitoneal, intramuscular, intracerebral, or subcutaneous, and in some cases, by ingestion or inhalation of the foreign protein. The shocking dose may also be given by any of these routes, but the symptoms are usually more severe and rapid if the antigen is injected intravenously or intraperitoneally.

Concomitant with the development of sensitivity, antibodies may appear in the serum of the sensitizing animal and have the properties of precipitins, which also induce passive sensitization in other animals of the same and, in many instances, of other species. This antibody has been shown to pass through the placenta of the guinea pig, so that if the mother has been actively sensitized before or during pregnancy, the young are born in a state of passive sensitization which persists for several weeks but is not passed on to the third generation.

The symptoms of anaphylactic shock in each species are typical regardless of the antigen used, but vary greatly in different species. In the guinea pig the outstanding manifestation is bronchospasm and death results from asphyxia. Anaphylactic shock in a rabbit is characterized by circulatory failure resulting from obstruction of the pulmonary circulation. In the dog there is marked splanchnic congestion, apparently due to spasm of the hepatic veins.

The anaphylactic reaction can also be readily demonstrated with such excised smooth muscle of the sensitized guinea pig as a strip of intestinal or uterine muscle suspended in a water bath. The excised muscle reacts with spasm when the specific antigen is added to the bath. This phenomenon is called the *Schultz-Dale reaction.*

Most of the physiologic manifestations of anaphylaxis are due to pharmacologically active substances which are released as a result of the antigen-antibody reaction. The most important such substance is histamine, but slow reacting substance SRS-A, serotonin, heparin, acetylcholine, and bradykinin have also been shown to be released during the anaphylactic reaction in the various species.

When an actively sensitized animal has received a sublethal dose of antigen, a temporary state of desensitization is produced. During this period the antibodies of the plasma are partially depleted and the animal can tolerate injections of antigen considerably larger than those which would previously have produced fatal shock.

When the antigen to which the animal has been sensitized is injected intracutaneously or subcutaneously, it produces a local inflammatory reaction which becomes grossly apparent after 24 to 48 hours and often progresses to necrosis. Although this *Arthus phenomenon* has the gross appearance of a delayed reaction, microscopic study shows that changes occur in small blood vessels within a few minutes after the injection of antigen. It is properly considered a manifestation of the immediate type of allergy.

Anaphylactic Sensitization in Man

When man is injected with a heterologous protein such as antitoxin derived from another species of animal, the immunologic and physiologic changes produced are essentially similar to those observed in experimental anaphylaxis in animals. Heterologous protein such as bovine serum globulin introduced intravenously is, during the first few days, metabolized in much the same manner as the individual's own serum proteins. After 5 to 7 days there is an abrupt change as the individual reacts immunologically to the foreign protein. The heterologous protein remaining in the circulation disappears abruptly, and antibody reacting specifically with the antigen becomes demonstrable.

It is at the time of this change that symptoms of *serum sickness* occur. The most common manifestations are enlargement of the superficial lymph nodes, fever, skin rashes, and arthralgia. If a single pure antigen has been introduced, the symptoms of serum sickness are usually of brief duration. Prolonged and recurrent attacks result from the injection of crude heterologous serum which contains a number of different protein antigens that induce sensitization with slightly different incubation periods.

The clinical symptoms of serum sickness are most effectively controlled by the use of corticosteroid drugs or corticotropin which inhibit the physiologic reaction without appreciably affecting the immunologic changes.

The individual who has recovered from serum sickness is anaphylactically sensitized to the causative antigen. His plasma and serum contain a typical gamma globulin antibody which forms a precipitate with the antigen in the test tube and will induce passive general and local anaphylaxis when injected into guinea pigs. Injection of minute quantities of the specific heterologous serum into the skin of the sensitized individual produces an immediate urticarial reaction. A somewhat similar local reaction with edema and erythema may be produced by instilling the specific antigen into the conjunctival sac.

During this state of active sensitization, which may last for months or even years, further injections of the same heterologous antigen are apt to produce anaphylactic shock manifested by urticaria, asthma, and failure of the peripheral circulation. Such reactions are fatal within a few minutes in some cases.

The risk of such severe reactions makes it essential to consider the possibility of sensitization before any heterologous serum is injected for a prophylactic or therapeutic purpose. Such sensitivity may be suspected on the basis of the history of previous injections of heterologous serum, especially if serum sickness has resulted therefrom, and may be proved by careful skin and eye tests with the serum to be injected.

Most persons who have been actively sensitized by a previous injection of heterologous serum can be temporarily *desensitized* by the careful administration of a series of graduated doses of serum injected at first subcutaneously, then intramuscularly or intravenously. The first dose is only slightly larger than that used in the skin test for sensitization; the final injection makes up the full therapeutic dose. Detailed schedules for such desensitization have been published by MacKenzie and others, and should be followed carefully as severe reactions have resulted from attempts at more rapid desensitization.

It should be remembered that a considerable proportion of the serious reactions to heterologous serum occur in individuals who have *not* been sensitized by previous injections, but are atopically sensitive to the animal from which the serum is derived. Most of these patients have asthma or rhinitis upon contact with animals, and also show positive skin and eye tests to the heterologous serum. In such atopic sensitization to heterologous serum, desensitization is far more difficult than in individuals who have acquired sensitivity from a previous injection. A cautious series of injections may permit the injection of relatively small amounts of antiserum, such as the prophylactic dose of tetanus antitoxin,

but full therapeutic doses can rarely be accomplished. The immunologic mechanisms involved in such atopic sensitization are discussed in the next section.

Individuals who have been sensitized by a previous injection of heterologous serum but who have lost their circulating antibody with the passage of time, often show anamnestic response to a subsequent injection of the same heterologous serum, manifested by the appearance of *accelerated serum sickness* occurring after a shorter interval than the typical incubation period, with clinical features intermediate between typical primary serum sickness and the anaphylactic reaction.

These reactions to heterologous serum protein appear to be normal responses to the conditions artificially imposed. Heredity has not been shown to be an important predisposing factor, and the incidence of reactions varies with the amount of serum injected. When large injections of antipneumococcus serum were used in the treatment of lobar pneumonia, more than 90 per cent of the individuals treated developed some manifestations of serum sensitivity.

Anaphylactic Reactions to other Antigens

Reactions with the clinical features of anaphylactic shock, occasionally fatal, may also occur after injections of penicillin and occasionally other drugs, and after the stings of insects of the order Hymenoptera. Such reactions occur in a sporadic fashion. Statistically they are more frequent in individuals who have a family or personal history of atopic sensitization, but they are not limited to this group. Individuals showing such relations usually have immediate urticarial reactions to the insect venom or to penicillin. Their serum or plasma often contains antibodies capable of inducing passive sensitization in normal human skin, but the precipitating antibodies characteristic of serum allergy are rarely demonstrable. Effects of particulate antigens and effects of splenic function are described in Chapter 31.

In allergy to insect venoms a degree of desensitization can be attained by repeated injections of small doses of the venom subcutaneously. The chemical nature of the antigens involved and the details of the immunologic reactions are only partially understood. The reactions to penicillin are further discussed in the section on drug allergies.

Atopy

Many of the most common allergic diseases of man, including hay fever, bronchial asthma, infantile eczema, and atopic dermatitis, are not attributable to any unusual exposure to antigen but develop sporadically in certain individuals, after the casual contacts of ordinary life which do not induce sensitization in most individuals. Numerous studies have shown that individuals who have suffered from one disease of this group are significantly more susceptible to other diseases of the group than is the general population. A significant proportion of the patients so afflicted also give a family history of disease of the same group. In the development of these diseases, hereditary predisposition appears to play a role comparable in importance to that of exposure to antigens. Coca and Cooke classified these allergic diseases as manifestations of *atopy* and emphasized the apparent importance of heredity in their development.

In the case of antigens of fixed and known geographic distribution, such as pollens, it is readily shown that such individuals develop sensitization only to antigens with which they have had contact. Additional evidence of the importance · of exposure to the antigen is furnished by studies of atopic sensitization to potent but rarely encountered antigens such as castor bean. In the case of common food antigens which may be transmitted from the mother to the child through the placenta or in the breast milk, previous exposure is difficult to exclude, and the occurrence of atopic symptoms after the first known contact with the antigen is not unusual.

The atopic form of sensitization was believed by Coca and Cooke to be peculiar to man, but similar sensitivities, with almost identical immunologic manifestations, have since been shown to occur in dogs, cattle, and other species.

The basic facts of the inheritance of this group of allergies were established by Cooke and Vander Veer in 1916. They showed that the infant was not born sensitive, but inherited equally from the mother and father a tendency to develop such sensitizations. They noted that neither the particular disease manifestation nor sensitivity to a specific allergen was inherited. Subsequent studies have shown that the sensitizing antibody of an atopic mother is not transmitted through the placenta to the infant, confirming the impression that the acquisition of sensitization depends upon genetic rather than placental factors. The infant develops active sensitization after birth, rather than being born passively sensitized as in the case of the young of an anaphylactically sensitive female guinea pig.

Many other studies have confirmed the influence of heredity in the development of atopic sensitization, but various authors have differed in their interpretations of the mendelian mechanism involved. Cooke and Vander Veer believe that the atopic tendency is determined by a single pair of genetic factors and that the allergic factor is dominant. On the basis of another early study, Adkinson suggested that the allergic factor was recessive. Neither of these views was entirely consistent with the statistics offered to support them. Wiener, Zieve, and Fries suggested that if a single pair of factors was involved the allergic factor was a partial dominant. Most subsequent writers have accepted this hypothesis but have differed as to the degree of penetrance of the allergic factor. On the other hand Pearson has pointed out that the observed facts are equally consistent with the view that a number of pairs of hereditary factors are involved.

Although the exact genetic mechanism remains in doubt, recognition of the hereditary factor is an important aid in diagnosis. The past history of diseases of this group in a given individual greatly increases the probability that other symptoms of unknown cause may have an atopic basis. A family history of similar diseases is also of definite significance. On the other hand, the history of serum sickness, contact dermatitis, or other allergic manifestations not in this hereditary group, is of no significance.

The substances giving rise to atopic sensitization are in general organic materials such as pollens, mold spores, animal danders, vegetable dust, and foods. Those that have been studied by immunodiffusion or by chemical methods have been shown to be complex mixtures of many different antigens. The antigens which have been separated from them by chemical means have proved to be typical proteins or chemically similar substances of lower molecular weight.

In a few instances, clinically and immunologically typical atopic sensitization has been shown to be due to substances of known and relatively simple chemical structure, such as phthalic anhydride, halazone, tannic acid, and chlorogenic acid. Such compounds are believed to act as haptenes combining with body protein to produce compound antigens which are active in producing sensitization.

Antibodies in Atopic Sensitization

The individual with atopic sensitization characteristically shows an immediate urticarial reaction when minute quantities of the specific antigen are injected intracutaneously as a skin test. This reaction is essentially similar to that observed in individuals who have been sensitized to heterologous serum by previous injections.

On the other hand, the plasma or serum of the atopically sensitized individual does not contain the precipitating antibodies found in acquired serum allergy, and does not induce local or general anaphylaxis when injected into the guinea pig. By suitably sensitive techniques the serum will in most cases produce agglutination of erythrocytes or other particles coated with the specific antigen.

Characteristically the serum contains an antibody, the *skin-sensitizing antibody or reagin,* which produces passive sensitization when injected intravenously into normal humans and local passive sensitization when injected intracutaneously into normal skin. Sites in normal human skin which have been passively sensitized by this *Prausnitz-Kuestner phenomenon* react to tests with a specific antigen essentially as do those of the actively sensitized individual.

This type of passive sensitization cannot be transferred to most common laboratory animals, but the skin of many species of monkeys has been shown to accept sensitization. The reactions observed in monkeys are less definite than those in normal human skin, but may be readily demonstrated by the intravenous injection of a dye such as Evans blue which is extravasated at the site of the allergic reaction. While the monkey is proving increasingly useful in the detection and study of skin-sensitizing antibodies, the basic method of their detection remains the local passive sensitization of normal human skin. No in vitro method has proved an adequate substitute.

There is no quantitative method for determining the amount of skin-sensitizing antibody or reagent in serum. The relative activity of different sera can be estimated only by the titer to which the sera can be diluted and still elicit a positive reaction.

Sera containing skin-sensitizing antibody have been studied extensively by various chemical and physical means of fractionation such as protein precipitation, electrophoresis, ultracentrifugation, and chromatography. None of these methods has permitted isolation of the skin-sensitizing antibody in quantities and purity which permit precise chemical characterization. However, they have provided considerable indirect and negative evidence as to the nature of the serum component which carries passive atopic sensitization. Neither the typical Ig G-globulin nor the macromolecular Ig M-globulin seems to be significantly involved. It appears probable that the activity may be carried either by Ig A-globulin or by a variety of complexes of protein molecules which differ in their physical and chemical properties.

Injections of Antigen

A common method of specific treatment of atopic sensitization is an attempt to desensitize (or immunize) the patient by a series of injections of the specific antigen. Carefully controlled statistical studies have shown that such treatment renders the patient less sensitive, but the immunologic mechanism by which it produces its effect remains obscure. Such treatment has been shown to produce a two- to fourfold increase in the titer of skin-sensitizing antibody during the first few months, but if the treatment is continued, this slight initial rise is followed by a progressive drop in the titer leading in 5 or 10 years to almost complete desensitization.

The repeated injections of antigen also produce other manifestations of antibody activity in the serum. Cooke and coworkers in 1935 reported the development in the serum of treated hay fever patients of a blocking antibody, which reacted with the same antigen as the skin-sensitizing antibody but did not sensitize human skin. Loveless showed that this blocking antibody could be readily demonstrated in the sera of treated patients after the skin-sensitizing activity had been destroyed by heat. Titers of hemagglutinating antibody in hay fever sera are greatly increased after treatment with injections of antigen. More recently, such sera have been shown to bind specifically pollen antigen labeled with I^{131}.

These blocking, hemagglutinating, and binding antibodies have been shown to be developed by nonatopic volunteers who are given injections of pollen antigens. They do not passively sensitize normal skin, but may inhibit allergic reactions in it, by inactivating antigen.

Fractionation of sera showing such activity indicates that it is in general associated with the Ig G-globulins and essentially unrelated to the skin-sensitizing antibody.

All these forms of antibody are adsorbed from serum by specific immunoadsorbents. Reports that blocking antibody may specifically displace skin-sensitizing antibody from immunoadsorbents suggest that the antibodies induced by injections of antigen have a greater affinity for the specific antigen than the pre-existing skin-sensitizing antibodies.

The tolerance for increasing doses of antigen produced by injection treatment is apparently related to the development of such blocking antibodies. Their role in protecting the patient against natural exposure to pollens is less clearly established. The most recent studies suggest that the reactivity of the patient after treatment is primarily related to the titer of skin-sensitizing antibody and that blocking antibody plays a secondary role in protection.

Physiology of Atopic Reactions

The reaction of the atopic individual when exposed to the specific antigen consists in general of dilatation of the smaller blood vessels, transudation of fluid to the tissues, spasm of smooth muscles, and increased secretion of mucous glands. These physiologic reactions apparently result from the liberation of chemical mediators by the antigen-antibody reaction. The most important of such mediators is believed to be histamine. Katz and Cohen have shown that when the specific antigen is added in the test tube to the blood of a hay fever patient, measurable quantities of histamine are liberated from the cells into the plasma. The effects of temperature and various chemical agents on this reaction suggest that it is an enzymatic reaction.

Schild and associates showed that the bronchial smooth muscle of a patient with atopic asthma, when suspended in a water bath, contracted on exposure to the specific antigen. A similar contraction was produced when histamine was added to the water bath. The reaction of the bronchial muscle to histamine was readily inhibited by antihistamine drugs, but the reaction to antigen was only partially inhibited by high concentrations of these drugs. These workers also showed that lung tissue from the asthmatic patient released histamine when perfused with the specific antigen.

In subsequent studies, Brocklehurst showed that when the asthmatic lung was perfused with antigen it released not only histamine but also the slow reacting substance, SRS-A. The two active substances are quite different chemically and can be separated by adsorption and elution with suitable solvents.

These studies clearly show that the atopic reaction takes place when all connections to the central or autonomic nervous system have been removed. They suggest that histamine and SRS-A are important chemical mediators released by the antigen-antibody reaction and produce the physiologic reaction. They do not exclude the possibility that other pharmacologically active substances such as serotonin, bradykinin, and acetylcholine may also be involved.

While these studies indicate that atopic reactions may occur in isolated cells and tissues without connections to the nervous system, it should be remembered that allergic reactions in the intact individual occur primarily in blood vessels, smooth muscles, and mucous glands which are innervated by the autonomic nervous system. It appears probable that atopic reactions in the living body may be considerably augmented or inhibited by the synergistic or antagonistic impulses of the autonomic nervous system. Holmes and associates have studied the effect of autonomic nervous control on the reactions of the nasal mucosa of a patient with pollen hay fever. They showed that if the sympathetic innervation of one side of the nose was removed by paralyzing the stellate ganglion, the reaction of the mucosa to the specific pollen antigen was greatly augmented on the treated as compared to the untreated side.

There is considerable clinical evidence that the atopic reaction, whic his basically an immunologic phenomenon, may be influenced not only by nervous influences but also by nonspecific irritants and by the state of physiologic activity of the organ involved.

Atopic Eczema

One of the common diseases generally believed to be due to atopic sensitization is the itching, eczematoid lesion diagnosed in infants as infantile eczema and in older children and adults as atopic dermatitis. Although many children affected in infancy show spontaneous remissions by the age of 5 years, there is little doubt that atopic dermatitis seen in older children and adults usually represents a persistence or recurrence of the same disease. Hellström reported that 86 per cent of adults treated for atopic dermatitis reported that the onset had occurred during the first five years of life.

The relationship of this disease to atopic sensitization is indicated not only by the positive family history, which is elicited in more than 50 per cent of the cases, but also by the striking tendency of infants with infantile eczema to develop manifestations of respiratory atopic disease later in life. Pasternack* reported that 30 per cent of infants with eczema develop asthma by the age of 6. Stiffler* reported that of 40 children with infantile eczema followed after 21 years, only 11 showed no manifestations of atopic disease. In 50 to 75 per cent of cases of infantile eczema, the atopic tendency is also manifested by definite, immediate, urticarial reactions to skin tests with extrinsic allergens.

The relationship of the disease to the specific extrinsic allergens which react in skin tests is less simple than in the respiratory allergies. In many clinical trials eating foods which have given marked reactions in skin tests has failed to produce an exacerbation of the eczema, and the disease has persisted when presumed causative factors have been eliminated. There is considerable evidence that other factors are involved. The skin which is not directly involved in the eruption is not entirely normal, typically showing a white dermatographia and blanching after intracutaneous injection of acetylcholine. The eczematous individual appears to be abnormally susceptible to itching produced by any stimulus, and there is little doubt that many of the visible manifestations result from or are aggravated by scratching. Details of the pathogenesis remain obscure, but the allergic approach to diagnosis and treatment has proved less successful than in the respiratory allergies.

Atopic Reactions to Infective Agents

In bronchial asthma, evidence of typical atopic sensitization to extrinsic antigens can be demonstrated in 50 to 75 per cent of cases. The remaining cases, in which no evidence of sensitization to an extrinsic factor can be demonstrated, have similar hereditary backgrounds, often have simultaneously, or have had in the past, hay fever or other obvious atopic diseases, and show the same clinical

* See Conference on Infantile Eczema, pp. 164, 166.

manifestations and laboratory findings such as eosinophilia of the sputum and blood. On the basis of history and response to therapeutic measures, the asthma in most of these cases appears to be related to respiratory infection. Cooke and others have suggested that such cases represent an atopic reaction to bacterial infection. The classic manifestations of atopic sensitization, immediate urticarial skin reactions to intracutaneous injections of antigen, and the presence of the skin sensitizing antibody in the serum, are not demonstrable with the bacterial antigens presently available. However, strong suggestive evidence is offered by the frequent occurrence of exacerbations of asthma after intracutaneous or subcutaneous injections of minute doses of bacterial vaccine. Clinically, this type of asthma has been found to be frequently associated with hyperplastic changes in the sinus membranes, nasal polyps, and allergy to aspirin. Patients showing these features may also give positive skin reactions to extrinsic antigens, but satisfactory relief is rarely obtained by treatment directed entirely at these extrinsic factors. The occurrence of an atopic sensitization to infective agents has not been satisfactorily proved, but treatment based on the assumption of its occurrence has given many satisfactory results.

This presumed atopic reaction to bacterial antigens is distinct from the delayed type of bacterial allergy typified by the tuberculin reaction, from the anaphylactic skin reaction to pneumococcus polysaccharide reported by Tillet and Francis, and from acute rheumatic fever which is believed to result from sensitization to the hemolytic streptococcus.

Delayed Allergies

The delayed type of hypersensitivity is manifested in clinical medicine by allergic contact dermatitis, and by delayed reactions to infective agents such as the tuberculin reaction. Both types of reactions are readily reproduced and studied in experimental animals such as guinea pigs. In neither instance does the serum of the sensitized individual contain demonstrable antibodies. Sensitization appears to depend upon lymphoid cells. This has been demonstrated both by the transfer of sensitivity from actively sensitized to normal animals by injecting suspensions of lymphoid cells, and also by the occurrence of specific reactions to antigen in cultures of lymphoid cells from actively sensitized animals.

Allergic Contact Dermatitis

Contact dermatitis both in experimental animals and in man is caused by a wide variety of agents, including both inorganic and organic compounds, of simpler chemical structure and lower molecular weight than typical proteins. These include salts of metals such as nickel and mercury, simple organic compounds such as formaldehyde, numerous drugs applied topically, and the lipoid-soluble compounds of poison ivy and other plants. Most of these substances are not antigenic but are thought to act as haptenes combining with body proteins to produce sensitization.

When an active sensitizing agent such as an extract of poison ivy is applied to the unbroken skin of a previously unexposed man, there is no visible reaction. However, if the same material is applied to another site 10 to 14 days later, a vesicular dermatitis appears within 24 to 48 hours. Although the skin is generally the site of both sensitization and the reaction, Haxthausen has shown that skin grafts from a person with contact dermatitis transferred to a nonsensitive identical twin did not remain sensitive, while those transferred from the nonsensitive to the sensitive twin acquired the sensitization of the recipient. This is consistent with the view that sensitization actually depends upon wandering cells of the lymphoid series rather than the cells of the skin itself.

In contact dermatitis due to poison ivy and other plants, partial desensitization may be produced by injections of suitable extracts of the allergen. The results of such treatment are not entirely satisfactory, and the mechanism of relief has not been established.

Delayed Sensitization to Infective Agents

Sensitization of the tuberculin type in general results from infection with viable organisms including vaccination with attenuated strains such as BCG. In experimental animals, similar sensitization may be accomplished by injecting a considerable volume of killed organisms or by injecting killed organisms in conjunction with adjuvants which produce a local tissue reaction.

Sensitization of this type occurs in a wide variety of infectious diseases such as brucellosis, glanders, syphilis, coccidioidomycosis and lymphopathia venereum, caused by bacteria, spirochetes, fungi, or viruses. In many of these diseases the specific skin reaction is a helpful diagnostic procedure.

The course of many chronic infections such as tuberculosis and syphilis is greatly influenced by the development in the host of hypersensitivity to the infectious agent. This changes the infection from one in which the organisms spread rapidly through the body with relatively little inflammatory reaction, to one in which they become localized in foci marked by severe inflammatory reaction with tissue necrosis and scarring.

Drug Allergies

Allergic reactions to drugs present special problems. Most of the naturally encountered antigens, which are causes of allergic disease in susceptible individuals, are relatively inert in other individuals. Drugs, on the other hand, have definite pharmacologic and toxic effects in their susceptibility to which individuals vary slightly. With a few exceptions, such as insulin and papain, drugs are not proteins and not typical antigens. In the case of allergy to simple nonprotein drugs, immunologic mechanisms are rarely demonstrable. Skin tests may be unreliable or hazardous or both.

While typically allergic manifestations, such as asthma, rhinitis, urticaria, and contact dermatitis may be produced by nonprotein drugs, these substances may also produce fever, unusual types of rashes, blood dyscrasias, and hepatic reactions which are unusual or unknown as manifestations of allergy to naturally encountered antigens. Some of these unusual manifestations are presumed to be allergic reactions, in the absence of any demonstrable antibody mechanism, because of their clinical course. Characteristically, there are no symptoms after the first dose. Fever or skin rash or both develop after an incubation period of 7 to 14 days, and subside when the drug is discontinued and eliminated from the body, but recur within a few hours when a subsequent dose is given.

Contact dermatitis due to topically applied medications does not differ significantly from contact dermatitis due to other causes. In general, the causative agents are not antigens but are presumed to act as haptenes combining with body proteins to induce sensitization. The causative relationship can usually be established by the patch test in which the lesion is reproduced in previously uninvolved skin by an application of the suspected allergen.

The complexity of allergic reactions to

other nonprotein drugs is suggested by the extensive investigations of penicillin allergy. This drug, although relatively nontoxic in normal individuals, is a frequent cause of allergic reactions. These take many forms, including a delayed urticarial reaction similar to serum sickness, an "id" reaction simulating a dermatophytid associated with fungus infections of the skin, and various other forms of dermatitis. However, the most interesting and most important clinical manifestation is the immediate, severe anaphylactic shock reaction following injection of the drug, which has been the cause of many fatalities. Careful studies have shown that penicillin, as marketed, is neither antigenic nor able to form the stable chemical compounds with protein, which would permit it to act as the haptene. In the body it undergoes rapid chemical changes into a variety of degradation products, including penicillenic acid and penicilloic acid, which can combine with protein and act as a haptene.

In many cases of acute anaphylactic sensitization to penicillin, skin tests with penicillin G itself elicit immediate urticarial reactions but they cannot be relied upon to detect all sensitive individuals. Penicilloyl polylysine has been suggested as an artificial conjugate which will detect sensitivity to the penicilloyl group without inducing sensitization in normal persons. It appears to offer promise as a diagnostic agent in penicillin allergy.

These careful studies of penicillin allergy are a model for the investigation of sensitivities to other nonprotein drugs, but the results of such work are not yet available.

REFERENCES

Adkinson, J.: The behavior of bronchial asthma as an inherited character. Genetics, 5:363, 1920.

Ciba Foundation Symposium: Histamine. Boston, Little, Brown & Co., 1956.

Conference on Infantile Eczema. Sponsored by The John A. Hartford Foundation. J. Ped., 66:153, 1965.

Cooke, R. A.: Allergy in Theory and Practice. Philadelphia, W. B. Saunders Co., 1947.

Cooke, R. A., and Vander Veer, A.: Human sensitization. J. Immunol., 1:201, 1916.

Feldberg, W.: Histamine and anaphylaxis. Ann. Rev. Physiol., 3:671, 1941.

Haxthausen, H.: Allergic dermatitis: Studies in identical twins. Acta Dermatovener., 23:438, 1943.

Henry Ford Hospital: Mechanisms of Hypersensitivity. International Symposium. Boston, Little, Brown & Co., 1959.

Katz, G., and Cohen, S.: Experimental evidence of histamine release in allergy. J.A.M.A., 117:1782, 1941.

Lawrence, H. S.: Cellular and Humoral Aspects of the Hypersensitive States. New York, Hoeber Medical Division, Harper & Row, 1959.

Loveless, M. H.: Immunological studies of pollinosis. I. The presence of two antibodies related to the same antigen in the serum of treated hay fever patients. J. Immunol., 38:25, 1940.

Nomenclature for immunoglobulins. Bull. World Health Org., 30:447, 1964.

Parker, C. W.: Penicillin allergy. Am. J. Med., 34:747, 1963.

Rich, A. R.: The role of hypersensitivity in the pathogenesis of rheumatic fever and periarteritis nodosa. Proc. Inst. Med. Chicago, 15:270, 1945.

Schild, H. O., Hawkins, D. F., Mongar, J. L., and Herheimer, H.: Reactions of isolated human asthmatic lung and bronchial tissue to a specific antigen. Lancet, 2:376, 1951.

Sherman, W. B., and Kessler, W. R.: Allergy in Pediatric Practice. St. Louis, C. V. Mosby Co., 1957.

Part V

Physical, Toxic and Chemical Agents

Chapter Fourteen

Physical and Toxic Agents

WILLIAM B. BEAN

Introduction

Man's body is so ordered that each tolerable challenge or stimulus calls forth activities to compensate for, nullify, or repair the resulting disturbances. With advance in the scale of structural and operational complexities these balancing adaptations increase in power, scope, and intricacy. They constitute the adaptive talents which have permitted man to endure in a hostile world. Their compass is nothing less than life itself. But man, one of the few creatures on the face of the earth whose chance for survival is even partly within the grasp of his own wit and strength, has shown scant interest in a rational solution of his problems. Indeed, the adaptive capacities of man, his potential for living the full life, only recently have had any systematic study at all. Application of a well-developed knowledge of adaptation may eventually extend the field of public health as that, in turn, has extended the field of general medicine. This chapter will consider some of man's responses to physical and toxic agents, conditions, and forces.

The reactions evoked in human beings by such agents are profoundly affected by the rate as well as by the degree of change. The end result is influenced by the presence or absence of an acquired adjustment to new environmental conditions. Protection by external modifications may alter or eliminate the effect, as in air conditioning or the use of oxygen at high altitudes; or internal adjustments may permit new conditions to be met successfully, as in acclimatization to high or low temperatures. The intricacies of man's inner mechanisms are not yet reducible to simple equations. Clinical judgment, the wisdom of experience, must be ready to point out the paradox that some men with a pulse rate of 150 are in better condition than others with a rate of 130 under the same stress. The physician, whose interest is an individual person or patient, must supply a corrective for the mathematician, who may too readily ascribe final significance to a chart, logarithm, or equation. With our present knowledge we cannot evaluate the whole man from formulas, though some aspects can be quantitated with precision.

In this chapter I survey the common ancient physical forces which affect man, emphasizing environmental temperature and aviation and space medicine. As far as possible the discussion will include a definition of the physical agent or force, the terms of its measurement, the disorders it produces, internal adaptations and external protective measures which prevent disabling or lethal effects, and therapeutic means to alleviate or correct any damage which may be done. Since understanding of the disorders produced by physical and toxic agents depends directly on a knowledge of the physiologic changes, these will be stressed.

227

Environmental Temperature

HEAT

Source of Heat

Environmental heat comes from the sun, which warms earth, air, and man. The effects of heat in the air are dependent on its capacity of convection, and are greatly influenced by moisture content because of its influence on evaporation. According to Blum, perplexing difficulties assail the physicist who attempts to measure exactly such an obvious factor as the heat load contributed by sunlight. One must evaluate separately, and then try to unify, effects relating to wavelength; spectral distribution; absorption by ozone, water vapor, and dust; reflection and absorption by skin or clothing; profiles exposed to direct "sky" and terrain radiation; and other factors. The laboratory cannot duplicate field conditions where physiologic measurements are limited. Quantitation of solar radiation in terms of reaction of human subjects is but a rough approximation.

Heat Load

Heat load consists of internal and external heat and varies in degree, type, and duration. Results range from mild discomfort to incineration. Environmental and metabolic heat are measured in calories,* a large *calorie* representing the quantity of heat needed to raise a kilogram of water from 0° to 1° C. *Temperature scales* are arbitrary measures of heat content based on (1) the freezing and boiling points of water at sea level (*Centigrade*), (2) whimsy (*Fahrenheit*), and (3) the cessation of molecular activity producing heat (*absolute*). *Dry bulb temperature* (D.B.T.) is the true air temperature not influenced directly by radiation or conduction. *Wet bulb temperature* (W.B.T.) is that obtained when the bulb of a mercury thermometer covered by a moistened jacket is subjected to an air current, the cooling effect decreasing as evaporation declines with increasing moisture. From the dry and wet bulb temperature we derive the *relative humidity,* the percentage of saturation of air with moisture in terms of

---

* A *British thermal unit* is the amount of heat required to raise the temperature of 1 pound of water from 39° to 40° F. Ventilation engineers use this quantum as well as grains of water per cubic foot—perverse survivals of fossilized units of measure, others being the still prevalent medical use of Fahrenheit instead of Centigrade thermometry and still other departures from the logic of the metric system.

a maximal quantity it could contain without precipitation at a given temperature. *Effective temperature* is a measure of subjective equivalence for various combinations of dry and wet bulb temperatures. *Radiation* is the transfer of energy between bodies by electromagnetic waves; the net flow is from warmer to cooler, the amount varying as the fourth power of the temperature of the emitting body. The wavelength varies inversely with the absolute temperature. Radiation may be reflected at the same wavelength, transmitted, or absorbed and give rise to heat. *Conduction* is the flow of heat through a substance from one molecule to another. It varies with the conductivity of the material. Its transfer from one object to another is influenced by gradient (the difference between the temperatures of two objects), surface, and contact. *Convection* is the flow in moving gas or liquid of heat added by conduction at one point and removed at another. *Evaporation* of sweat, the transformation of a liquid to a gas, removes heat from the skin surface, each liter accounting for 580 kilogram-calories of heat. Vaporization from the respiratory passages and insensible perspiration act similarly.

The Basic Heat Equation

The laws governing heat regulation in man are simple. Their application is difficult. The human body has a normal temperature of about 98.6° F. or 37° C. Body heat is generated by oxidative processes and may be increased through convection, conduction, and radiation. Heat is lost by evaporation, radiation, convection, conduction, and the trifling loss through excreta and unevaporated sweat. Ingesting hot or cold substances affects the balance slightly. The equilibrium equation is:

$$M - W - E \pm R \pm V \pm D \pm X = O,$$

where M = metabolism, W = mechanical work done, E = evaporative heat loss, R = radiation (gain or loss), V = convection (gain or loss), D = conduction (gain or loss), and X = ingesta, excreta, or unevaporated sweat (gain or loss).

Departures from equilibrium imply heat loss or storage, S, which is conventionally given a positive sign when the body is cooling. The general equation thus becomes:

$$M \pm S - W - E \pm R \pm V \pm D \pm X = O.$$

Production of heat cannot cease, but its rate may be reduced. Channels for heat dissipation vary with ambient air temperature, moisture, and movement; the direction and gradient of transfer of radiant energy to or from the surroundings; and contact with hot or cold surfaces for conduction. When air temperature is higher than skin temperature, heat can be lost by evaporation of moisture; in saturated air, heat must be lost by other means. When saturated air has a temperature higher than that of the skin, heat cannot be lost; fever results, and the situation rapidly becomes intolerable.

Internal heat must be brought to the surface of the body to be lost. It moves by molecular conduction in quantities dependent upon specific conductivity of tissues, gradient from center to surface, and linear depth. The quantity carried by circulating blood depends on the specific heat of blood, the volume flow to the skin, and the gradient. In general, raising body temperature and skin temperature, increasing the volume flow of blood to the skin per unit of time, or decreasing the depth of the thermal gradient facilitates heat loss, while opposite changes conserve heat. Conduction in the body can be measured by thermocouples inserted in needles or by intubation. Both techniques introduce uncontrollable factors. Rectal and oral thermometry are the conventional methods of measuring body heat and have limitations, but are useful because of their unique simplicity. Skin temperature is best measured by radiometry. The circulation, however, can be measured in a variety of ways ranging from heart rate to cardiac output and blood volume determinations. Since the heat exchange by radiation is frequently beyond the adjusting mechanisms in man, homeostasis is largely dependent on control of blood flow and sweating.

A study of the avenues of heat exchange must deal with body mass, surface and heat production, and the four ways it can be lost. Evaporation can be measured by accurate determination of the weight of a subject before and after standard work in a controlled environment, but all other factors present difficulties. Radiation to or from the body depends on the silhouette of surfaces. The constant motion inherent in work presents a kaleidoscopic multitude of surfaces for emission or absorption of radiant energy which so far has defied exact measurement. In such standard procedures as walking on a treadmill or standing still in a regulated air current, the intimate eddies and larger turbulences can only be guessed. Conduction between feet and floor is another troublesome factor. Though a great deal has been learned from partitional calorimetry in the resting subject, study of man at work is scant.

Acclimatization

When first exposed to very hot environments, even fit men cannot work long or strenuously. By a process of acclimatization they adapt themselves to work in the heat. When this adaptation is advanced, performance may be nearly as effective in extreme heat as in temperate surroundings. The mechanisms whereby work in the heat becomes tolerable are concerned with fitness for work and the changes which constitute acclimatization. Men at rest can endure hotter environments than they can work in. The physical effects of heat are accentuated by work. The harmful consequences of heat depend on many factors, among which are heat load, work load, state of acclimatization, hydration, salt and electrolyte balance, physical fitness, training, age, rest, and fatigue.

The upper limits of tolerable heat load have been defined in terms of work, of capacity to approach or reach a steady state. The effects of clothing in adding to heat load have been measured. Study of salt and water metabolism focused attention on the adrenal. Studies in the field dispelled the bugbear of peculiar dietary requirements for desert or tropical sojourns of up to at least 2 to 3 years. They cast grave doubt on the reality of deterioration from any climatic hazard peculiar to the tropics.

Ability to do a given task depends on physical fitness for that task and implies adequate physical structure, satisfactory physiologic and physiochemical state, and proper motivation. Superior fitness in a temperate environment carries no assurance that work can be done when a man is suddenly thrust into desert or tropical heat. When fit young men, adequately trained in such work as marching, are exposed to a dry bulb temperature of 120° F. (48.9° C.) and 20 per cent relative humidity, or dry bulb temperature of 91° F. (32.8° C.) at 95 per cent relative humidity, they are incapable of work for long periods. Compared with their performance in a temperate environment, the pulse is higher, internal and skin temperatures are higher, and the blood pressure is unstable, especially in the erect position. The face and upper body are flushed. The eyes and nasal mucosa may be injected. Lacrimation and sniffles occur. The hands and sometimes the feet swell. The rate of sweating increases. There is a sense of overwhelming oppression which rapidly takes

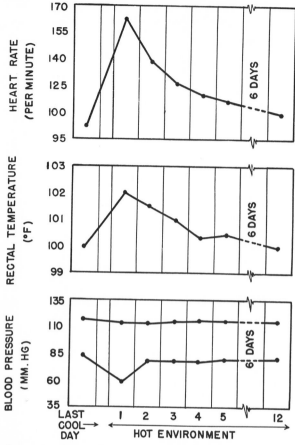

Figure 14–1. The process of acclimatization as represented by changes from day to day in heart rate, rectal temperature, and blood pressure. Average data from 14 men at the end of the fifth 1-hour work period, except for the first day in the heat, when the fourth period data were used. Although the hot environment here was moist with 95 per cent relative humidity and D.B.T. of 91° F., similar changes are seen in dry heat at D.B.T. of 120° F.

the spirit out of men. In desert, jungle, or laboratory hot room, caloriphobia may be intense. Trifling work is fatiguing, and more burdensome work rapidly leads to exhaustion. Throbbing headache may reach cruel intensity. Dizziness occurs, accentuated in the standing position. Dyspnea may be a problem. Thirst, which rapidly becomes intense if water is withheld, proves a lagging guide to water replacement. The loss is never voluntarily replaced during work. Nausea, vomiting, and loss of appetite are commonplace. Lack of coordination reduces efficiency. The eyes become glazed and stare vacantly. Apathy may be interrupted by outbursts of irritability. Judgment and morale decline. Occasionally hysteria or hyperventilation with tetany may add their bizarre signs and symptoms. The walking man may collapse. The standing man may faint. Unwillingness to continue work or the onset of physical disability may rapidly disorganize well-motivated persons. A severe and alarming albeit usually innocuous illness has produced almost complete ineffectiveness.

Contrast with this picture that of a man

after 4 or 5 days of work in the heat. He now performs his work with only slightly higher pulse and temperature than in a cool environment. He is cheerful, alert, and vigorous. No longer does he exhibit the flushed, sometimes edematous skin and engorged mucous membranes of earlier exposures. He can stand without peril of syncope, even after 4 hours of continuous work. Water is drunk eagerly, though thirst still is not an adequate incentive for complete fluid replacement. Sweating continues at a rapid rate, somewhat faster than on first exposure. Thus the essential gains of cardiovascular-thermal acclimatization have been made, though improvement may continue at a slow rate for days or weeks. The changes may be portrayed graphically if the pulse, rectal temperature, and blood pressure are used as indices of overall improvement (see Fig. 14–1).

The more fit man becomes acclimatized faster than the less fit man, but even the best may be totally disabled on first exposure to heat. When acclimatization is complete, fit and unfit men retain their relative positions. Activity is essential to full adjustment, but enough dry heat taxes the heat-dissipating mechanism of the resting man and so induces partial acclimatization, whereas resting in moist heat does not. Working to exhaustion and the occurrence of postexercise syncope do not retard acclimatization if rest, water, and salt are given. Performance in the heat after loss of sleep, ingestion of alcohol, and restriction of water causes reversion to the unacclimatized state.

Adaptation to heat, characterized by lower body and skin temperatures, must depend on either enhanced elimination or reduced production of heat, or both. In terms of actual calories responsible for an elevation of rectal temperature by 2 or 3° F., the quantity of heat is small. Thus extra heat might be eliminated by a more rapid onset of sweating, more rapid achievement of maximal rate of sweat output, or sweating which began rapidly at a high level. Reduced production of heat might result from increased skill and facility of performance or increased fitness in a given task.

A phenomenon which deserves further study is the variable relationship between elevations of pulse rate and of temperature which may be observed during and after acclimatization. Though most subjects respond with roughly parallel declines in pulse and temperature from the high levels of initial exposure, some may have a slow pulse and high temperature, while others have a fast pulse but low temperature. By other criteria there is little to choose between these types, although there is an impression that those with slow pulse may be more fit. Presumably the thermostat is set lower in some than in others. The circulation makes the needed adjustments.

The prevention of accumulation of body heat is accomplished by an increase in evaporative cooling from an increased sweating rate, which accounts for three-fourths of the reduction, and by a decrease in metabolic heat production, which accounts for the remainder. The increase in sweating rate parallels the fall in rectal temperature, while the decrease in metabolism is gradual.

Conn and his co-workers demonstrated a second type of adaptation to heat consisting of changes related to activity of the adrenocortical hormones, the main characteristic of which is a reduction in the salt content of sweat. This change takes place gradually and reaches its peak many days after cardiovascular thermoregulatory acclimatization has been achieved.

Syncope

Men suddenly exposed to hot environments have a fast pulse and widespread peripheral vasodilatation. There is little change in blood volume in acute experiments if hydration is encouraged. Orthostatic syncope is common when the subject stands or is tilted erect after work, or even after resting in very hot surroundings. Fainting is known on every drill field, and its relation to heat is recognized. Syncope can be prevented by (1) moderate contraction of leg muscles, (2) inflation of pressure cuffs applied with the subject supine to prevent hypostatic pooling of blood, (3) maintenance of the erect position, but with the legs at hip level, and (4) repeated work in the heat. Syncope is heralded by dizziness, yawning, sighing respiration, blurred vision, sometimes gunbarrel in type, pallor, low arterial and pulse pressures, and sudden bradycardia. All these symptoms disappear when fainting or voluntary movement effects recumbency. This reaction has no relation to fitness nor is it particularly prevalent in those whose pulse rate or rectal temperature indicates heat intolerance.

Upper Environmental Limits

A definition of a number of upper environmental limits for work in heat is influenced by variables such as subjects (age, sex, race, physique, training, diet, hydration, salt and water balance, acclimatization, fitness, motivation, and others), work pattern, energy output, environmental factors, and the criterion of limit. The resultant definition is necessarily arbitrary. The wet bulb temperature is the best measure of top limits. As intolerable zones are approached, a narrow temperature range, 4 to 5° F., separates easy from "impossible" ranges. In general, work at wet bulb temperature below 91° F. (32.8° C.) is easy, from 91 to 94° F. (32.8 to 34.4° C.) is difficult, and above 94° F. (34.4° C.) is intolerable (see Fig. 14–2). At the upper limits sweating is profuse, averaging about 2.5 liters per hour and in some cases reaching 3.5 liters per hour. Men acclimatized to work at one level of heat must be reacclimatized at each higher level. If they are initially acclimatized in the range of an upper limit, the same work may be done at a lower heat load for longer periods and at less physiologic cost.

Disease Due to Effect of Heat

It has been customary to divide the diseases which result from excessive heat into

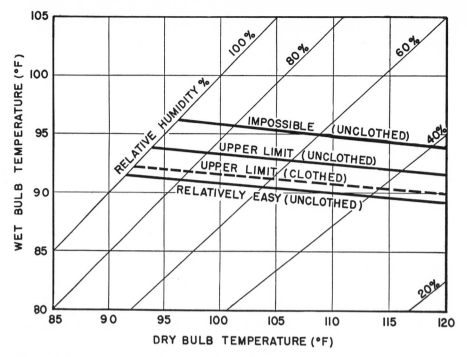

Figure 14–2. Diagram indicating equivalent zones of "impossible," difficult (upper limit), and relatively easy combinations of dry and wet bulb temperatures; the effect of relative humidity and of clothing on acclimatized men working for 4 hours at an energy expenditure of about 300 calories per hour.

exhaustion, stroke, and cramps. To these has been added another, thermogenic anhidrosis. At least part of the syndrome of heat exhaustion results from dehydration. Much doubt has been cast upon salt depletion as the cause of heat cramps. The symptoms of any one type tend to reduce activity enough to prevent others from occurring. In the final analysis all result from the disparity between the internal (metabolic) plus environmental (climatic) heat load and the capacity for eliminating heat.

Heatstroke is accompanied by irritability, visual disturbances, delirium, collapse, and coma eventuating in death if not treated. Nausea and vomiting may foreshadow an attack, which may start suddenly. There are dry, hot, flushed skin, flaccid muscles, a high rectal temperature, 105 to 110° F. (40.6 to 43.3° C.), tachycardia, deep breathing, bounding pulse, high pulse pressure, and elevated systolic pressure. Cardiac failure, peripheral circulatory failure, and sodium chloride depletion do not appear to be causally related to heatstroke; but protracted exposure to unusual degrees of heat, especially when nights do not cool, old age, degenerative diseases, and the acute effects of alcohol are important predisposing conditions. High body heat causes signs and symptoms. The acute attack begins with cessation of sweating. It is universal, not sparing the face and neck, and is presumably of central origin. Effective treatment consists of rapid cooling of the body by immersion in tubs of ice water, together with massage. The vasoconstriction produced in the skin by the use of extreme surface cooling, as in ice tubs or alcohol, water, and a fan, reduces the interchange of blood between the interior and surface of the body, so that the actual temperature deep within the tissues may be rising at a time when the surface is extremely cool. Thus it is important that massage be used to increase the circulation between surface and interior. Strong vasodilating agents might help.

Heat exhaustion is characterized by weakness, hypotension, and only moderately elevated rectal temperature. Pallor may appear, especially when fainting occurs. The skin is not dry. Physical findings are not of special note. The condition does not differ significantly from the state produced in a person well acclimatized to heat who works after dehydration, acute alcoholism, or loss of sleep. Similar changes occur after protracted moderate salt depletion. Fainting and peripheral vascular collapse may occur with or without a prodrome of thirst, nausea, vomiting, headache, dizziness, subjective exhaustion, mental fogginess, irritability, and complete incapacity for work. Lack of fitness from any cause favors its occurrence. It is probable that the exhaustion following protracted physical exercise in comfortable surroundings is of the same nature. The vascular instability, orthostatic syncope, and other changes produced by brief exhausting exercise may have the same mechanism. Similar results follow work after severe calorie deprivation.

Painful spasms of voluntary muscles during or after work in hot environments have been attributed to salt depletion; the predisposing roles of acute alcoholism and ill health have been noted. I am not aware that heat cramp has been produced by salt depletion in normal men under controlled conditions. In industry, prevention of heat cramps has followed the prophylactic use of salt tablets and water, but much of the published work was hardly controlled. More careful studies are needed. Physiologic saline solution intravenously has given dramatic relief, and is also effective in dehydration and heat exhaustion.

Thermogenic anhidrosis was observed in previously healthy acclimatized soldiers toward the end of a summer spent in a desert. Profuse sweating for several days ended suddenly except on the face and neck. Illness began abruptly with weakness, warmth, discomfort, dizziness, an "all-in" feeling, headache, and shakiness during exposure to severe heat. The warm and dry skin had a fine papular eruption or branny desquamation. Body temperature was generally below 99° F. (37.2° C.). Severe prickly heat was an invariable antecedent. There was hyperkeratotic plugging of sweat ducts. The mechanism appears to be a physiologic exhaustion or physical obstruction of sweat glands which produces a state similar to the congenital ectodermal disorder of absent sweat glands. The role of prickly heat in its genesis is important. There is usually prompt recovery with rest and return to a cool environment.

Ultraviolet Radiation. At least two types of harm may result from exposure to sunlight, one a true photochemical reaction from photosensitivity, and the other an accentuation of sunburn. The minimal erythema dose is not a sensitive measure. Effects can not be explained as photochemical reactions in a homogeneous system. Skin layers react differently. Erythema seems to depend on the release of vasodilator substances from injured epidermal cells. Erythema threshold varies in

a given subject from time to time and is influenced by sweating or wetting of the skin. The degree of protection against sunlight given by sunburn preventives varies with the subject, the spectrum of the light, and the spectrum of the material. These explain differences in estimated protection. Experimental conditions cannot be defined in terms of the laws of physics which govern the results.

Danger to the eyes is real. Since injury is not painful early the eyes may be damaged by less than a skin erythema dose. Therapeutic lamps, laboratory instruments, and devices for control of air-borne infection are important hazards.

Burns will not be considered here, except to point out that the time and temperature combination required to produce erythema is a simple logarithmic function. At any temperature, vesiculation is produced by exposures 2½ times as long as that required for erythema.

COLD

Source of Cold

Environmental cold indicates lack of heat; its geographic variation is common knowledge. The same physical laws regulate temperature exchange in heat and cold. Convective cooling by winds may be considerable, and its reduction by wind-impervious material is of basic importance in the design of arctic clothing. Wearing wet clothing and footwear in temperatures around freezing causes much cold injury. The moisture content of air below freezing temperatures is very low.

Man's ability to survive in arctic regions depends more on protective clothing and experience than upon physiologic adaptations. Cold water removes heat from the body much more readily than does air at the same temperature, unless the air is moving rapidly. Thus immersion in water at temperatures near the freezing point is likely to be fatal to a normal person after 30 to 60 minutes, whereas he survives in still air at this temperature for many hours.

Acclimatization

Kane, a physician with wide experience in both hot and cold regions, noted over 100 years ago that "the mysterious compensations by which we adapt ourselves to climate are more striking here [Arctic] than in the Tropics"; and he was impressed with the need for outdoor work to achieve acclimatization.

Skill in combating cold weather must have developed with the survival of ancient man in the glacial epochs. In relatively modern times the problem has recurred for people living in arctic and subarctic regions and to a lesser degree in cool temperature zones. Polar explorations have been a fertile field for experiment in finding the best methods and materials for protection and survival, in part by utilization of the wisdom of the Eskimo.

Effects of Cold

The effects of cold vary from the unpleasantness of goose pimples and shivering to gangrene or death from extreme or protracted exposure. Cold evokes the physiologic converse of heat. There is increasing evidence that there is no essential difference in the reactions of tissues to different types of cold or in the various sequelae of severe chilling and ischemia. Data from Baron Larrey's writings on the retreat from Moscow, observations in the Crimean War, and the attacks on Everest indicate a fundamental similarity. Trench foot, shelter foot, and immersion foot are all variants of a single disorder, modified by duration of exposure, wetness, and chilling. They are akin to frostbite, in which damage is more severe because of cell disruption from freezing. Because of the relation of surface to mass and the gradients existing from center to periphery, the extremities are most liable to damaging effects of cold.

Cold produces constriction of blood vessels in response to hypothalamic impulses and by direct contraction of smooth muscle. When skin temperature closely approaches freezing, an intermittent increase in blood flow mediated by axon reflexes to arteriovenous anastomoses sustains the sluggish metabolic needs for a time. Immersion of the normal hand or foot in water at 41° F. (5° C.) for 2 hours produces swelling which may increase the volume by 15 per cent. If such exposure is general, serious losses of circulating fluid may result. On removal from ice water the chilled extremity exhibits the triple response of vasodilatation, reddening, and fluid extravasation. Whealing may occur. The picture is one of simple acute inflammation.

Trench foot has borne testimony to ignorance, unpreparedness, or disaster as its cause. The main predisposing causes are stasis, constriction of limbs, and failure to change the footgear, especially the socks, sufficiently often. Coldness and wetness at temperatures around freezing precipitate trench foot. In the cold, pain may occur, but numbness slowly supervenes, followed by edema and blistering of which the victim may be unaware. This may be followed by infection or gangrene, or the tissues may survive when circulation becomes re-established. Vasoneurosis with severe pain may be a stubborn residual. Pain has been attributed to selective involvement of sensory nerves, to anoxia, and to scar tissue. It may be reduced by keeping the limb cold (below 80° F., 26.7° C.). In experimental animals circulation cannot be demonstrated by the fluorescein method within 30 to 120 minutes after application of cold. The dye spreads into the affected area in greater degree than normal some hours after exposure. Thrombosis and gangrene follow. Treatment with heparin greatly reduces the damage.

The physical effects of cold are intimately associated with *protective clothing*. Fabrics and their insulating capacity and practical usefulness have been studied. For human subjects the heat loss through a clothing assembly is equivalent to the sum of metabolic heat production and heat lost through the lungs by vaporization of moisture and warming of the inspired air, and of the heat lost through evaporation of perspiration. A practical unit, the *clo*,* has been advanced as a measure of insulation, but is not an absolute index because (1) with uneven distribution of insulation, local cooling at poorly insulated points diminishes the adequacy of the outfit; (2) accumulation of sweat markedly reduces insulation; and (3) movement increases loss of heat by convection so much that a given clo value may decrease by two-thirds when a subject works. Just as in problems of heat, when the physicist leaves models and deals with man, the complexity and multiplicity of ever-changing situations defy complete formulation.

With hard work in an arctic clothing assembly, the private environment approaches that of the humid tropics; heat loss must be facilitated by removal of clothes lest the accumulation of sweat impair insulating capacity further and lead to serious local cooling. Especially when the great convective cooling effect of cold wind comes to bear this is important.

Subjects clad in arctic uniform, sitting qui-

---

* The clo, a unit for thermal insulation of clothing, is "the amount of insulation necessary to maintain comfort in a sitting-resting subject in a normally ventilated room (air movement 20 ft./min. or 10 cm./sec.) at a temperature of 70° F. (21° C.) and a humidity of the air which is less than 50 per cent."

etly in an environment of 32 to −40° F. (0 to −40° C.) and remaining 3 hours, experience an increase of metabolism which may amount to 60 to 80 per cent during the third hour at −40° C. There is a rough correlation between metabolic rate and severity and duration of exposure to cold. Shivering does not usually occur when the metabolism first rises, although often it is severe by the end of the second or third hour. Skin temperatures decline rapidly at first, but usually stabilize during the third hour. Individual toe temperatures below 0° C. may be recorded at the end of very cold exposures. Rectal temperatures fall rapidly at first, but tend to level off 1 to 1.5° C. below the control value. There is no uniform relation between metabolism and skin and rectal temperatures. Considerable variation in a subject from time to time, variability among subjects, and other irregularities in responses reduce the significance of the trends.

Diet is of great importance in the cold because of the requirements for increased heat production. Pemmican—dehydrated meat and fat in equal parts—has been used by polar explorers, but because of its high satiety level it is unacceptable. Unsupplemented by carbohydrate, pemmican has never been used successfully for long periods. High fat, high carbohydrate, and high protein diets are effective, in declining order, in maintaining psychomotor efficiency, body temperature, and metabolism in cool environment. Frequent small meals are better than eating the same total quantity in large ones. The diet for sustained activity in extreme cold has not been defined. Acceptability of food is a major consideration.

Allen stressed the use of cold in the production of anesthesia for amputation of limbs. He defined the indications for and limitations of such procedures. The production of deep narcosis and a kind of human hibernation by refrigeration which induces marked hypothermia has been used to treat neoplastic disease in man. The results have not yet established in cryotherapy in practice, though useful information concerning disturbed physiologic processes has been obtained. As a method for anesthesia in surgical operations on the heart it is in the experimental stage, but offers some promise.

Treatment

Treatment of injury from cold should be preventive. When prophylactic measures cannot be applied, general and local treatment is helpful. In extreme degrees of exposure of the whole body to cold it has been found that rapid application of external warmth is lifesaving, just as the opposite procedure is essential in heatstroke.

Ultrasonic Energy

Man's ear cannot hear frequencies much above 16,000 cycles per second, so waves of higher frequency are called *ultrasonic*. For practical purposes very high frequencies do not propagate well through the air and are hard to transfer from air to liquid or solid and back again. As the terms are generally used in medicine, ultrasonic frequencies deal with millions of cycles, rather than thousands. They are transmitted through solid or liquid media and not across a vacuum and not well through air. As with almost every form of energy in its biologic effects, ultrasound usually terminates by being turned into heat. Indeed the earliest medical use of ultrasound was as a heat generator acting as diathermy does in heating deep tissues. The physics concerned is very complex. The elasticity rather than the density of the object impinged on is a major factor in converting ultrasonic energy to heat. In addition, cells can be disrupted, or necrosis can be produced without disruption of cell walls, and perhaps suspension of function may be produced without necrosis. By converging several beams of energy, none of which injures cells or tissue along its path, and focusing by using stereotaxic localization a tiny area can be affected. Nerve tracts can be disrupted without leaving the necessary track which a needle, a knife, or a laser beam must make along its path of entry and exit. The tolerance of different cells and tissues varies. The method, still experimental, has promise of producing lesions or destroying tissue deep inside the body without leaving a trail of destruction. As a medical magic wand its beams converge deep inside to produce the pinpointed effect desired, its degree determined by time and intensity of exposure.

The technical production of ultrasonic energy depends on a reversed piezo electric effect. The piezo phenomenon consists of generation of an electrical charge between the two sides of a crystal when it is compressed or exposed to pressure. The reverse process produces a tiny physical alteration in the dimensions of a crystal by changing the potential.

Using echo techniques one can obtain what

amounts to tomography by ultrasonic scans which enable one to get accurate measures of normal internal structures as well as their deformity in disease. Ultrasonics has been used experimentally in producing small isolated lesions in inaccessible portions of the central nervous system. Ultrasonosurgery has been used in Parkinson's disease. But the long-term results have yet to be evaluated. The physics of such problems is very complex. It is not yet known whether tumor destruction, disruption of calculi, psychosurgery, or other uses will prove of benefit beyond enlarging our ideas. The techniques are complicated. They have not yet had sufficient trial. The use of ultrasonics for diagnostic techniques for long periods may introduce dangers, but they are not worked out in detail.

Lasers

The invention and rapid development of the laser (Light Amplification by Stimulated Emission of Radiation) are producing a speedy revolution in some scientific and technical realms of biology. In the ordinary physics of light, waves are rather topsy-turvy. The light source produces a beam with light waves of many different lengths, side by side and in close juxtaposition. They follow one another in temporal sequence. Increasing the intensity of light by concentrating it in space is limited by chromatic aberration. Laser light is not coherent in space and time, and since all its electromagnetic waves are nearly the same length the crest of adjacent waves falls on the same plane. Monochromatic light with huge wattage can be focused to produce intense power density measured in billions of watts per square centimeter. Prodigious magnetic and electrostatic fields can be created and focused.

Laser radiation can be delivered continuously or blasted out in fractions of a millisecond. Ophthalmologists had already used other forms of light for coagulation of retinal lesions and immediately saw possible application of laser beams. There is some danger that workers might harm their own eyes or skin. The effect depends on the ordinary physical and biochemical constituents of tissues and whether dyes or chemicals are on the skin.

The capacity to focus intense energy in a small compass means that one can aim a controlled bundle of energy with great precision but, as with a bullet shot from a gun, it may destroy whatever gets in the way. It leaves a hole and tract, differing thus from focused ultrasonic energy. Whether or not it will be an effective device to attack cancer is now obscure.

One surprising use that has already been exploited is to employ the laser in ultramicrodissection of living cells in tissue cultures. Furious energy in needle-like microprobes can be focused on vacuoles, nuclei, or other microstructures which can be blasted out of existence without bursting the cell. Perhaps at very much lower levels of energy and using the affinity of special dyes for certain tissue one may be able to get localized concentration for large destructive effects. Such a procedure has some analogy to the thyroid's binding of radioactive iodine. Perhaps by the use of such highly concentrated energy a single cell or an organelle of a cell can be volatilized, and the gas analyzed by a spectrograph. A new dimension in biologic analysis may allow us to explore even tinier specks of matter. Much has to be worked out concerning the transmission of laser beams through tissues. We must remember the slow development of knowledge of x-ray and the scandalous lack of understanding of the damage that was being done by casual overexposure. We need to go slowly with all due caution.

Aeromedicine

When man ascends to high altitudes, he encounters *reduced atmospheric pressure, reduced temperature,* and, in a plane, the problems of *acceleration, gravity,* and *motion.* Except for apparatus the main effects of reduced atmospheric pressure are found in alterations in concentrations of gases, oxygen and nitrogen being of chief concern. Since man is an obligatory aerobe, high altitudes cannot be endured unless additional oxygen is available. Failure of oxygen apparatus may cause an emergency which, unless immediately corrected, leads to death. Very high altitudes cannot be reached without pressurized cabins or pressure breathing. When pure oxygen is delivered at a pressure of 8 to 12 inches of water throughout the respiratory cycle, some persons can reach altitudes of 50,000 feet. Above pressure of 8 inches circulatory failure may develop.

The symptoms and signs which occur when subjects breathing 100 per cent oxygen in a decompression chamber make a simulated ascent to 35,000 feet at a rate of 5000 feet a minute include (1) those occurring during ascent or just after reaching altitude—anxiety, ear clicks, and abdominal distention and its relief by belching and expulsion of flatus; (2) those taking place after an interval at altitude —"bends," i.e., pain in extremities, "chokes," or burning pains and coughing accentuated by deep breathing, "faints" from disturbed systemic circulation, and skin lesions; and (3) those occurring after descent (focal neurologic manifestations, syncope, shock, otitis media, fatigue, and disorders of the respiratory passages, locomotor system, and skin).

Since 100 per cent oxygen obviates systemic hypoxia at 35,000 feet, these troubles are not the result of inadequacy of inspired oxygen. Since carbon dioxide tension of atmospheric air is zero, reduced barometric pressure does not alter the partial pressure of carbon dioxide in the blood. Therefore, physical effects of high altitude must arise from changes in internal pressure-volume relationships and pressure changes in atmosphere and body tissues which affect the solubility of gases in body fluids. The effect on body tissues, fluids, and pulmonary gas in free contact with the surrounding atmosphere is negligible. Gas in cavities such as the middle ear, sinuses, and intestinal tract, without free exit, expands and produces symptoms when the ambient pressure decreases. The hydrostatic pressure head (absolute tissue pressure minus atmospheric pressure) in cerebrospinal fluid, veins, arteries, subcutaneous tissue, and normal joint spaces is not immediately influenced by changes in environmental pressure. Changes in cerebrospinal fluid pressure may result from the distention produced by increased intra-abdominal pressure.

The absolute pressures of nitrogen, oxygen, carbon dioxide, and water vapor within the liquid components of the body are governed by the surrounding atmospheric pressure. At ground levels of 760 mm. of mercury pressure, nitrogen tension in tissues is far higher than that of oxygen, carbon dioxide, or water vapor because of its relatively high partial pressure. Supersaturation and bubble formation will occur in tissues when absolute pressure (the surrounding ambient pressure plus tissue hydrostatic pressure) decreases faster than the partial pressure of dissolved nitrogen. Since nitrogen is eliminated much more slowly than in the brief time of rapid ascents, nitrogen forms gas bubbles which expand, distort tissues, impinge upon sensitive nerve endings, and cause symptoms. The localization of bubbles is influenced by the greater potential volume of nitrogen available in fatty than in nonfatty tissue. Nitrogen clearance of various tissues is regulated by effective blood flow and the level of alveolar nitrogen tension.

Syndromes Produced by Free Gas

During ascent, all subjects hear hissing or clicking noises associated with relief of middle ear tension facilitated by yawning, swallowing, or chewing. Release of expanded air from the middle ear is through the eustachian tube. When equilibrium is reached at altitude, symptoms cease. The pharyngeal opening of the tube is collapsed. With increasing external pressure during descent, air must enter it to prevent painful compression of the drum, with tinnitus and impaired hearing. Swelling caused by infection, allergy, or emotion contributes to tubal blockade. There is great individual variation in symptoms. Pharyngeal maneuvers open the tube and reduce this source of trouble. Positive pressure breathing or a moderate Valsalva procedure may help. If equilibration is not achieved during descent, pain, fullness, and deafness persist. Outpouring of sterile fluid may occur. Rarely, a drum ruptures. Aero-otitis media heals spontaneously. With frequently repeated ascents it tends to persist, and infection may occur.

Air trapped in the nasal sinuses produces symptoms in the same way. Involvement of the maxillary sinus may produce pain referred to the teeth and may be confused with true dental pain. It is generally agreed that only diseased teeth become painful and that expansion of gas in minute apical pockets probably is responsible. Stirring up dormant infection may account for delayed episodes of pain.

Gas normally present in the alimentary canal expands upon ascent and produces cramping pains until belching or passage of flatus. Gas pains rarely begin after altitude has been maintained for 10 minutes. Diet has not been demonstrated to have a primary role in abdominal cramps. Innate capacity to expel gas accounts for great individual variation in susceptibility, and training accounts for the sharp decrease with repeated ascents.

Pre-existing pneumothorax, by expanding, may shift the mediastinum and embarrass respiration and circulation. Spontaneous pneumothorax is no more likely to occur at altitude than on the ground.

Syndromes from protracted exposure to altitude with adequate oxygen supply are bends, chokes, circulatory collapse, skin changes, and neurologic disorders. *Bends,* the

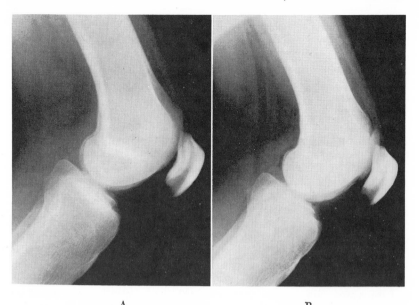

A   B

Figure 14–3. *A*, X-ray photograph of the knee before exposure to reduced atmospheric pressure. *B*, The collection of bubbles and bands of gas along vessels and fascial planes within the joint space, and as discrete collections in the tissues. (Courtesy of Dr. E. B. Ferris.)

commonest manifestation of decompression sickness, denotes pain and disability—usually in a joint, sometimes radiating up or down a limb—which result from exposure to high altitude. The pain is deep, aching, constant, and not throbbing. When it is severe, local numbness, weakness, and faintness resemble the sickening pain of a blow on the testicle. It is likely to occur in joints subjected to weight-bearing stress. Distribution rarely follows peripheral vessels or nerves. Signs of local inflammation are wanting. Gas in joint spaces, though usual, is not responsible for bends. Pain is relieved by recompression, partial descent, immersion of the limb in mercury, compression with a blood pressure cuff, arterial occlusion, or meticulous relaxation of the part. Reascent, even after several hours at ground level, may cause recurrence at the same site. Selective straining exercise is of the utmost importance in the precipitation and localization of bends. The time of onset, rate of progression, and severity of pain in bends vary widely. It generally commences 20 to 30 minutes after an altitude of 35,000 feet is reached, and rarely begins after 90 minutes at altitude. Though it may reach peak intensity explosively, about 15 minutes usually elapse before it becomes unbearable.

Above the critical altitude, bends increases in frequency, severity, and speed of onset with increasing altitude. Preflight inhalation of 100 per cent oxygen for half an hour gives measurable protection which becomes complete when inhalation lasts 8 hours. Roentgen rays may reveal air bubbles in implicated joints, and crepitus may be felt. In the knee they appear as discrete round bubbles in periarticular tissues, usually behind or beside the femur in the popliteal fat, or as longitudinal ribbons in fascial planes along tendon or muscle bundles in the popliteal fossa (see Fig. 14–3). The presence of gas in a joint space does not correlate well with bends, but that in fascial planes does. Repeated attacks may be followed for a few months by minor joint pains, but these ultimately vanish without sequel. The fact that denitrogenation prevents bends demonstrates the primary role of nitrogen in its genesis.

The site of bubble formation and the mechanism of pain have evoked much controversy. The term aero-embolism epitomizes one school of thought. Extravascular bubble formation is a more tenable theory, however, because there is no local cyanosis, pallor, or cooling to implicate defective blood supply. Roentgenograms have no consistent vascular distribution of bubbles. Local compression and vascular obstruction, which should increase aero-embolic signs, relieve bends, presumably by compressing bubbles. Recurrence of bends at the original site upon reascent 4 to 6 hours after onset suggests that incompletely absorbed bubbles trapped in extravascular spaces re-expand. The pain of bends is unlike ischemic pain. Since arterial, alveolar, and atmospheric nitrogen are in equilibrium, arterial blood cannot become supersaturated. The role of exercise in localizing bends, the importance of pressure mechanics and muscle insertion tension with focal negative pressure all indicate that local rather than systemic effects of exercise are responsible.

In addition to a sense of coolness and prickling, relatively mild and late *changes in the skin* may develop. Subcutaneous blebs of uncertain nature sometimes appear. Subcutaneous emphysema occurs rarely, usually over fat. A mottled, creeping, burning eruption is more common. It commences as a small pallid area over the torso, shoulders, forearms, or thighs, spreading peripherally as the center becomes erythematous and 1 to 2° C. warmer than uninvolved skin. No crepitus is present, but there is moderate pain and tenderness. It is related to underlying fat rather than nerves or vessels and is prone to occur in older persons, especially in those susceptible to chokes. There is presumably initial obstruction of small arteries and veins, producing pallor. When this is overcome, reactive hyperemia supervenes. A spreading factor of H-substance may account for the circular spread. Since denitrogenation prevents it, it probably results from nitrogen bubbles, most likely extravascular. No bubbles can be felt in the skin. Thus the indirect evidence implicates intermittent transient small vessel spasm and reactive hyperemia secondary to extravascular bubbles and trauma of fatty tissue under the skin.

Chokes is a term indicating burning in the retrosternal region during deep inspiration. As it waxes in intensity, an uncontrollable urge to cough occurs unless respiration is shallow and quiet. It soon encompasses the whole respiratory cycle, and paroxysms of cough with increased ventilation tend to perpetuate a chain reaction. Cyanosis, faintness, apprehension, and a moderate increase in blood pressure presage the advent of vasodepressor syncope, which will occur unless recompression speedily comes to the rescue. If the pharynx is involved, it displays a fiery red color; this, with the symptoms, indicates acute inflammation of part or all of the pharyngotracheobronchial system such as follows inhalation of irritant gases or a brisk run in extreme cold.

Chokes generally begins gradually and can be moderated by quiet breathing. It occurs later than bends, the mean onset time being 44 minutes as compared with 30 minutes for bends in a group of subjects experiencing both at 35,000 feet. Chokes rarely develops after 2 hours at altitude. With exercise, bends may force descent before chokes appears, whereas in bends-resistant subjects exercise may shorten the time when chokes occurs. There is more individual variation in susceptibility to chokes than to bends. Older and fatter subjects are affected more frequently. Return to ground level relieves chokes, but not so dramatically as it relieves bends. Soreness, coughing spells, and retrosternal burning may persist for hours or, if they were very severe or protracted, for a couple of days. In severe cases a roentgenogram may reveal pulmonary congestion. Available evidence points to a basic similarity between the mottled skin lesion and chokes, suggesting that submucosal nitrogen bubbles produce the disorder. No recent support has been found for air embolism of coronary or pulmonary arteries as the cause. Symptoms are not reproduced by accidental intravenous infusion of air.

The *neurologic manifestations* of decompression sickness follow a stereotyped pattern. Their relation to syncope is that both occur in severe reactions. Homonymous scintillating scotomas are common, with subjective blindness in the affected part of the visual field, but with intact central vision. Transitory palsies, convulsions, aphasia, and other phenomena are rare. When focal signs clear, a throbbing headache usually occurs, very like migraine in its concomitants. Subjects with a history of migraine are specially prone to neurologic changes. Severe reactions, often leaving residual disorders for days, are usually associated with vascular collapse, but are rare. Electroencephalograms reveal irregular slow waves in foci corresponding to the neurologic abnormalities. Decompression sickness, especially with chokes and skin changes, is usually well established before focal neurologic signs appear. They often occur during or after descent. Vasodilator drugs induce a prompt diminution of symptoms. Though the implication of major branches of arteries supplying large cortical areas is manifest, aeroembolization is considered highly unlikely. Random emboli would hardly pick the branches of the posterior cerebral artery so regularly. The onset after recompression and the failure of relief with descent militate against the theory of mechanical obstruction by intra-arterial bubbles. It would appear that the same mechanism operates as in clinical migraine with focal signs from cerebral arterial spasm and headache from dilatation of extracranial arteries.

Syncope and *collapse* may be vasodepressor or nondepressor, or may follow hyperventilation. *Vasodepressor* syncope is similar to that provoked by other stimuli. Weakness, dizziness, pallor, nausea, sweating, falling blood pressure, and fainting characterize it. Recumbency usually prevents or corrects unconsciousness promptly. During unconsciousness high voltage slow waves appear in the electroencephalogram. Psychic, reflex, or traumatic factors or anoxia may precipitate the syncopal reaction. The sharp reduction of attacks with repeated exposure to altitude emphasizes the psychic element, though there may be a physical adaptation. Later, faints are generally found only in severe decompression sickness, which suggests that reflexes and tissue damage may be partly responsible. A *nondepressor* type, usually associated with the coughing spells of chokes and manifest by lightheadedness, rarely eventuates in syncope. Anoxia may be the cause. *Hyperventilation* presents the usual train of symptoms. Postflight syncope may happen immediately on descent as a continuation of in-flight vasodepression, and is usually brief. A delayed reaction may take place 1 to 5 hours after descent, or, less often, may persist as a continuation of the immediate type. Shock characterizes the delayed type with hypotension, cold mottled cyanotic skin, restlessness, sighing respiration, reduced consciousness, and focal neurologic signs, progressing to coma. It usually but not invariably occurs in subjects suffering from advance decompression sickness, suggesting widespread tissue damage such as might occur from release of proteolytic enzymes, H-substances, or inhibition of respiratory enzyme systems.

Psychologic reactions in subjects undergoing decompression vary tremendously with circumstances. In highly motivated subjects they are minor; in air cadets, in whom anticipation of the hazards of combat looms large, they may be severe. Anxiety might be anticipatory or the result of any of the more or less alarming reactions induced by decompression. Muscular and mental fatigue (boredom) fail to account for the appearance of a cumulative type of fatigue after repeated exposures. It closely resembles the fatigue which follows anxiety situations, but its nature is unclear. When confidence, experience, and absence of danger in decompression chambers are established, psychologic reactions are insignificant.

Each of the components of the syndrome of decompression disease at altitude appears to arise from the formation of bubbles, the main constituent of which is nitrogen. Its elimination from a tissue depends on effective blood flow and gradient from tissue to blood. Thus, when absolute tissue pressure is decreased at altitude, nitrogen bubbles should form in a tissue before its intimate blood supply develops bubbles. If extravascular bubbles and vascular spasm produce stasis, equilibrium is established between tissue and blood, in both of which bubbles now form with equal readiness. Intravascular bubbles may accentuate focal changes. Intravascular bubbles found in divers dying with bends, or in the vena cava of decompressed animals, may also be secondary and arise after symptoms occur. In altitude decompression the return to ground level at once halts the mechanisms producing decompression sickness. Descent into caissons and the current passion for underwater activity of all sorts have emphasized all the problems of increased oxygen, nitrogen, and carbon dioxide pressures. Since they may not act as inert gases at increased pressures, concentrations innocuous at one atmosphere may produce toxic effects at high pressures. In the diver whose decompression occurs when he comes up to the surface, the conditions favorable to bubble formation continue as long as he is not recompressed. Bubbles may go on forming after death. Even in experimental animals, bubbles have not been found in arterial blood. Thus, although some competent investigators disagree, the weight of evidence supports the secondary formation of intravenous bubbles in animals after stasis or stagnation following vasospasm.

The pathogenesis of altitude decompression disease is pictured as follows: Decompression permits the formation and enlargement of nitrogen bubbles in tissues, but mostly outside vessels. Distortion causes pain. Each bubble is a minute traumatic agent which may call forth a variety of vascular responses locally and at a distance. These reactions, varying with the tissue implicated and the amount of bubble formation, account for the symptoms at altitude and their progression and sequels after descent. Stasis from local spasms or systemic shock favors intravascular development of bubbles with all its disastrous complications. Intravenous bubbles, though they may terminate decompression sickness fatally, are not its cause and need not figure in its ordinary symptoms.

Hyperbaric Medicine

Man never stops seeking superlatives, though in therapy the idea that if some is good, more is better is true only within narrow limits. The do-it-yourself person can get into serious trouble if in his enthusiasm in autodosing he moves from therapeutic to toxic levels. The notion of a physiologic supercharger has occurred to physiologists for a long time. In recent years the development of hyperbaric oxygenation has made one of the dreams a reality. The equipment is costly. Scrupulous attention to details of management and safety are essential, with the special hazards of fire with high oxygen concentration in a small space. Sudden technical failure may cause explosive decompression.

The bends and related disorders result from accumulation of nitrogen bubbles in tissues. Nitrogen narcosis may be a problem.

In the normal state the pulmonary access route of oxygen is very efficient. In pulmonary or circulatory disease, hyperbaric therapy might help, but unhappily, though pulmonary venous blood can be given a high oxygen content, mixing with large extrapulmonary venoarterial shunts may leave general systemic oxygen concentrations lower than desired. So far, getting oxygen into solution in the plasma has not been as effective practically as might be expected theoretically. Circulatory arrest can be prolonged with hyperbaric oxygenation, especially under hypothermia.

When man undergoes hyperbaric oxygenation, the retinal arteries become narrow, the heart rate slows, the cardiac output decreases, and the peripheral resistance increases. This might take a load off the heart. Efforts to treat patients having severe myocardial infarction by such means have not been particularly successful. The most consistently favorable therapeutic results have been in the treatment of gas gangrene. There is some indication that malignant tumors respond to irradiation more completely in the presence of hyperbaric oxygenation.

Lurking in the background is the ever-present problem of oxygen toxicity. Acute disorders of central nervous system function with convulsions and neurologic abnormalities put a sharp brake on prolonged exposure at several atmospheres. Irreversible pulmonary changes may occur if exposure to more than 2 atmospheres of oxygen lasts more than 3 hours. In the presence of venoarterial shunts outside the pulmonary system profound systemic acidosis may follow hyperbaric oxygenation.

I am aware of no studies on the hyperbaric effects of exposure in deep mines. Perhaps some gain in work tolerance or extra acclimatization was obtained from increased oxygen pressure. Captain Workman of the U.S. Navy Medical Corps, using Daniel L. Gilbert's data on "Cosmic and geophysical aspects of the respiratory gases," extrapolates to give figures for 5 miles below ground which gives $P_B = 1667$ mm. Hg. There the PO_2 is equal to 348 mm. Hg in the air inspired and would be 339 mm. Hg in alveolar air, equivalent to that of 47 per cent oxygen at 760 mm. Hg total pressure. The problem in mines and in hyperbaric chambers needs intense further study.*

Space Medicine

When the last edition of this book was written, there were no records of man having been sustained weightless for any extended period. The discussion was based largely on observations obtained in parabolic flight of very short duration. We now have records of hundreds of man-hours of weightlessness in various space craft with one or more crewmen. The problems encountered and their solutions have been surprisingly close to what was postulated from meager experience.

Man has evolved in a physical world with narrow limits of variation of temperature, gravity, gases, diurnal change of light and dark, and ordinary altitudes. He did not discover their essential qualities, reactions, and relations until recent times. The commonplace does not excite much curiosity or interest. A bird would never discover air or a fish, water. Nonetheless, man is altogether dependent upon contact with his surroundings for orientations essential for normal behavior and indeed for sanity. The continual bombardment of innumerable stimuli sorted out by his nervous system evokes those fantastic adjustments by which individual man makes his way in a world which is neutral at best and usually hostile. Deprive man of sensory stimuli and he goes to sleep. If the deprivation continues, an erratic stage of disorganization

---

* Mining is unusual at levels more than two miles below the surface, and at levels less than that below sea level.

and disorientation supervenes. The real world cannot be told from a world of dreams in which hallucinations and delusions deprive the person of his usual control of himself.

When man ventures into space, he is separated from the customary orienting stimuli of his surroundings. Physical and physiologic supports are gone. Intellectual, social, and domestic adjustments melt away. Although every man lives in a world of his own, no man is an island. When he ventures into space bundled up in a small vehicle, he does became a distant and deserted if not desert island. In this Alice in Wonderland world his immediate environment has no up or down, nor any top or bottom for his eyes to see and his touch to perceive. Noise will be what he makes or what is sent to him over instruments punctuating the vast silence of the spheres. Often only such light as he brings along relieves his sensorium of the blackness of an uneasy solstice. Smell, taste, and to some extent touch constitute the main normal sensations. Plunged into loneliness of a new order of profundity he is assailed by forces of radiation and magnetic fields and perhaps bits of interstellar stardust or debris that already is littering up the nearby space. He is linked to earth by gravitational forces, propelled by the mighty thrust of a new spirit *vis a tergo;* he and his fate are sealed in a capsule which he can control only in part, as he is shepherded by men and calculating machines of prodigious smallness. Man now gropes in a new order of complexity and perplexity, paradoxical because most of the ordinary complexities and perplexities of life have been removed *en bloc.*

Though the space vehicle of the future may have a large crew, our present concern is for the small crew or solitary rider. Except for the loneliness of the solo performer, the problems of a crew consist of the mighty magnifications of gravity at take-off, temperature changes, radiation, water and excretion, food, weightlessness, claustrophobia, and a sense of unreality and concern for the outcome of the venture, which may run all the way from a safe return to incineration or vanishing in limbo.

Aside from the increasing apprehension of the countdown period and occasional postponements or cancellations, the problems of the take-off include the sudden liberation of great pressures and strains from the almost instantaneously multiplying effects of gravity at blast-off together with noise, heat, vibration, and the risk of damage from leaking

gases. Since the possibility of failure shortly after the blast-off are real, an escape or separation of an entire chamber has to be built into the design with emergency release effected by the astronaut, a ground monitor, or an automatic release mechanism.

The problems of acceleration and deceleration in an escape capsule do not differ in kind, though they differ sharply in magnitude, from those of escape from supersonic planes. The problem of an acceleration environment has been described in terms of duration and complexity of pattern, with its flux of various linear and angular components, its rate of onset and decline, as well as magnitude. Physical and physiologic effects must be described in terms of the three major axes of the body, the top-bottom, the right-left, and the front-back.

In physiologic terms acceleration (a) measured as a multiple of (g) and any force (F) is a multiple of the standard weight (W) of the body on which it is acting. For practical considerations G is equal to $\frac{a}{g}$ or G is equal to $\frac{F}{W}$. Angular and linear accelerations have the same definition as in classic mechanics. Zero gravity, sub-gravity, weightlessness, and impact acceleration are the major recurring dimensions to be considered. Vibration has its own specific characteristics which act on vectors of the three axes of the body. Vibration or oscillation is the rapid alternate variation in acceleration, as a displacement swings a body or craft back and forth across the reference path. Amplitude, frequency, intensity, and cycles in the pattern of larger acceleration are important.

It is not known to what extent sub-gravity during orbiting will lower man's tolerance for the great impacts of deceleration on re-entry. Tolerance to gravity may be measured by visibility of lights and the stage of consciousness. Blurred vision, pain in the eyeballs, headache, excessive lacrimation, redout and retinal hemorrhage are untoward effects. Tolerance to gravity is a function of several primary acceleration variables, such as the direction of G force with regard to the axes of the body, the rate of onset and decline of G, the magnitude of peak G, and the duration and the total time of acceleration. Effects are influenced by physical fitness, physiologic state, and possibly adaptations, training, and the negative effect of removal of stimuli associated with prolonged weightlessness.

Various factors are used as end points to

measure tolerance, type and degree of protective devices and restraints, body position including the axes and exact location of the angles of the back, head and legs, environment temperature, pressure, and light. Some importance is given to age, emotional stability, motivation, stoicism, confidence, drive for recognition or reward, techniques of breathing, training in muscular performance, and the nature of the tasks required during peak gravitational stress. These elements make the problem one of kaleidoscopic complexity.

Part of the effect on vision of rapid acceleration is the mechanical pressure on the eyes and the accumulation of tears. Blood flow to the retina and brain is decreased. Positive pressure breathing of 100 per cent oxygen before exposure to gravity may be of some value in improving vision, but the advantage probably is not great. The input of sensory stimuli for orientation includes the eyes, the labyrinthine system, and peripheral nerves conveying impulses of pressure and postural and muscle sense. Illusions confuse or falsify interpretations. Wrong ideas of direction and a sense of tumbling or moving may occur with changes of velocity and acceleration. When pilots are trained in the performance of a complex cycle of jobs and subjected to steady state acceleration on a centrifuge, efficiency in skills decreases before physiologic performance.

Motion sickness may occur with the blast-off, with vibration soon after the blast-off and the tumbling, revolving, spiraling, or canting of the craft in its course, as well as with corrective measures to stabilize erratic progression. How these might be managed by a gyro-stabilizer is not yet known.

Weightlessness has been studied intensely for brief periods by neutralizing the effect of gravity against the centrifugal counter thrust in a plane traversing part of an outside parabolic loop. In weightlessness lasting approximately a minute, orientation remains good. The subject has a feeling that his eyes rotate upward and laterally. The sensation of a full bladder disappears, while blood pressure and other cardiovascular phenomena apparently remain normal. Swallowing presents some problems to the airway. Individual reactions may vary from stolid *savoir faire* to giggles, frustration, temper outburst, embarrassment, or mild hysteria with hyperventilation. Small experimental animals seem to be able to withstand much longer periods of weightlessness quite comfortably; what will happen to man during very long periods can be determined only by actual experience since we cannot extrapolate from the experience of a single minute at zero gravity.

Claustrophobia and solitude have been tested for many days in mockup capsules. Some of the present plans have the spaceman literally bolted into place. The symbolic entry into a coffin, a preview of death, may be a powerful factor in inducing an awe-inspiring emotional strain. One can speculate that under such circumstances anxiety might give rise to panic, panic to hopelessness, and hopelessness to complete operational inertia. Death without any physical injury might occur, as in Curt Richter's dewhiskered wild rats which died under the supreme frustration of despair and hopelessness. In these creatures an overwhelming bradycardia leads to asystole.

Cosmic ray and other forms of radiation present hazards which are slowly being met by those who interpret messages sent back by man-made satellites. The Van Allen belt has already posed an unexpected new problem for man in space. No doubt there are many more hazards. The unreality induced by the loss of divisions between day and night and many other matters which tend to swing the feeling of improbability into one of unreality constitute hazards which vary with the individual but inevitably present special difficulties.

The extent to which special filters in the skin of the capsule will be needed to protect the man but still preserve some outside vision is an added problem.

Putting aside weightlessness at zero G in space, the inner and outer man confronts new problems of internal and external environments. There are complex issues of food, water, excretion, and temperature control. Heat generated in the almost explosive burning at launching must be blocked by insulation. There is no room for refrigeration. Within the atmosphere aerodynamic heating presents problems during re-entry or escape. They are similar to those in high speed jets, though of a much greater magnitude. If the imagination boggles at such new hazards for man in space, at least we can form a clear view of the fetid environment which would exist if anything went wrong with the air-purifying or excreta-removing systems. Fortunately, olfactory senses fatigue rapidly and human effluvia are less noisome to their producer than to others.

Adequate drinking water must be provided. With the water of combustion of foods it must maintain equilibrium, balancing losses by sweat, insensible perspiration, and urine. Many ingenious ideas for recycling of water require very cumbersome apparatus. The condensation of moisture on clothes, gear, and walls of the chamber and the control of humidity without the discard of water present special problems.

Since there is no effectual counterpressure in atmosphereless space, the capsule must maintain pressures well within the tolerable range. Presumably they will not be fixed at sea level but at some immediate altitude where the relationship between the partial pressure of essential gases could be controlled most readily. Emergency measures for counterpressure in the event of a small air leak or to exhaust noxious gases must be considered. For an extended voyage in a space vehicle, chemical or biosynthetic gas exchanges of oxygen and carbon dioxide must be used. Photosynthesis by some form of green algae could utilize carbon dioxide, but a method of capturing just enough radiation from the sun presents extravagantly complex problems. Perhaps new, efficient strains of algae could be found. The toxic effects of ozone and other materials must be prevented. While a system employing interstellar hydroponics to clear the air of carbon dioxide and synthesize edible protein fires the imagination of the amateur astronaut, it presents problems of weight, water, energy and gas exchange, and solar radiation of unearthly complexity. Experience with acceptability of packaged emergency rations during World War II and some of the near disasters when pemmican was tried make me skeptical about any long-term program using dehydrated foods or the nourishing but repulsive protein produced by algae. Presumably the constraint of the very confined quarters would keep the metabolism at a low ebb.

Food and excreta, water and gases, pose an excessively complex maze of puzzles for which many solutions are ruled out by the considerations of space. With present apparatus it takes about 200 times the weight of the payload to get an instrument or vehicle into orbit. Considerations of weight exclude many otherwise satisfactory solutions. Unpleasant food leading to satiety, and anorexia almost impervious to starvation, can demoralize a man and render him totally ineffective just as easily as can anoxia, slow poisoning by noxious gases, radiation, or destruction by a flake of stardust.

The personal gear and harness of space suits have fascinated the fabricators of television programs. What is needed is supportive and protective clothing for attaining rigidity and immobility at times of sudden increases in gravity on leaving or entering the atmosphere, protection against radiation, and temperature and moisture control in an outfit which leaves very little mobility beyond wrist action. The problems of the complexity and the size of an apparatus for landing safely even on the moon, getting off and returning to the earth's atmosphere, and finally landing are of great complexity.

The requirements for space add new stresses and strains and thus new dimensions to the effects of physical forces and man's adjustments to them. No form of adaptation to space can be predicted. How it could be achieved best and to what extent learning and training might help are unknown. It may not be possible or feasible. This underscores the problem of general fitness. We begin with a person with many superlative qualities and without serious flaw. His physique must be good, his intelligence splendid. He must have many inherent skills and by learning and training must acquire others. But the overriding and limiting factors are those which deal with mental and temperamental attributes and capacities. Claustrophobia, physical constraint, detachment, a confusion of reality in hallucinations, boredom, unaccustomed silence, loneliness, unused touch, vision, hearing, perhaps smelling—these must all be brought under control lest the very unreality of the environment, leading to fatal mental aberrations or mounting and uncontrolled anxiety, cause the astronaut to destroy himself through inadvertence or panic.

EXPERIENCES FROM SPACE FLIGHTS

Reactions following more prolonged flights, such as the 34-hour flight of astronaut Cooper in 1963, revealed that orthostatic intolerance might occur during or just after re-entry. Unfortunately, medical data from Russian flights have not been obtained with ease. There are suggestions of biomedical difficulties, but their nature or extent is not clear. It has been found that cardiac arrhythmias may follow the hypodynamic state, and in some experiences there may be periods of arrhythmias requiring drug treatment. There are some suggestions, however, though the evidence is not completely evaluated, that dynamic alterations in control of the peripheral circulation as well as venous return and cardiac output occur. There is little evidence that active exercise during weightlessness counteracts such events, but detailed studies have not been practicable.

The problems of oculogyral and oculogravic illusory afterimage of targets and similar problems must be studied. Up to now the confined astronaut seeing what is about him with occasional visual clues from sightings of the earth has not become disoriented. Without visual clues during weightlessness, positional sense might be impaired or lost. Is this true disorientation? New terminology may be needed. Perhaps with improved instrumentation, monitoring, and better clinical tests, the purely or mainly physiologic indices ultimately may provide information of the necessary kind. At present a good psychomotor task gives the best functional measure of the state of the astronaut and his fitness. At the physiologic level, the three major concerns are lability of blood pressure, deterioration of musculoskeletal capacity, and disorientation. To combat these problems, efforts have been made along several lines. First are the multiextremity tourniquets. Second, there are drugs such as metaraminol (Aramine) and phenylephrine (Neo-Synephrine), but we have no information about their value. The third is the use of exercise. It has not yet been discovered how effective exercise may be in preventing the difficulties people face when exposed to prolonged weightlessness.

The physiologic atrophy of disuse is what happens to a physiologic system when for a season it is not needed. The living surviving organism can have no knowledge of sustained physiologic blackout. No true equivalent of hibernation or aestivation has been achieved by man, although many adaptations can be developed and extended by gradually increasing extremes. When the cardiovascular, postural, and baroreceptive reflexes are deprived of hitherto invariable gravitational stimuli, they undergo a kind of deconditioning, atrophy, or failure. The almost infinite number of variables which one can test and measure, the ever-increasing variety of drugs which can be used, and the impressive responsibility for gaining knowledge rapidly for the strange state of weightlessness are not the kinds of information which have been accumulated patiently during the life of the race. In the last hundred years cardiovascular and circulatory processes, stimuli, responses, and limitations were discovered under the ordinary circumstances of the usual environment of one G. Now suddenly they are taxed to the limit. Might dwarfs, somatic or achondroplastic,

turn out to be especially suited to the problem of space and weightlessness? The cardiovascular system of a man who spends his time reclining or sitting becomes that of a dwarf. Diuretic responses to recumbency exemplify the prices our adaptive mechanism has to pay when the erect posture is suddenly changed in a kind of guilty inertia superimposed on weightlessness.

Mundane problems of overheating, hydration, and excessive sweating, as well as the vividly described breakdown in a simple system for collecting urine, suddenly claim attention. The basic question of adaptation concerns the fixation of baroreceptors. Will man with his now long heritage of the acquired upright posture adjust? One astronaut we had in orbit suffered from a recurring tendency to postural hypotension for 24 hours after landing. Venous engorgement of the dependent extremities, slight speeding of the heart rate, and decreased systolic blood pressure were observed during quiet standing.

Only the surface of these problems has been scratched. Difficulties in comprehension are bound to occur because of the multifactorial nature of the physiologic, physical, and psychological problems with their infinite number and variety of stresses of different strength, length, and direction. Who can find the integrating elements? We need the unique extrapolation into space of problems of human experimentation carried far beyond and above the call of duty. The result of prolonged incarceration in what amounts to a physiologic vacuum with its shifting net effects upon unitary and combined physiologic systems must be observed in relation to concurrent and concomitant as well as sequential environmental factors. We can measure only some of these, but only after we consider the transient excesses of acceleration and the blighting confinement which has been used as supreme punishment. Biomedical devices, delicate sensing machinery, and electronic calculators must help us with the insistent and largely unanswered questions of the space age.

The time between the invention of the wheel and the use of electricity was but a tiny flick of time's eyelash. The few generations since our partial mastery of electricity and our bold venturing into space have compressed eons of time. Man must try to become a partner if not a master of the great forces he has peered at and unleashed.

On relatively short flights the problems of increased urinary calcium and the formation of urinary calculi are not of concern. For the longer missions, however, one cannot safely extrapolate from experience on shorter ones. Prolonged immobilization without weight bearing and exercise with the general sulggishness of metabolism resulting from relative inactivity may present altogether new problems. Recent reports, not always clearly or certainly documented, suggest that Soviet scientists have not found increased calcium loss attributable to a few days of weightlessness. Studies of American astronauts following the Gemini IV flight indicate no substantial or significant loss of calcium. In such reports as are available from Russia, albuminuria, hematuria, increased excretion of casts, and changes in hydroxycorticosteroid excretion, a cholesterol level recorded in their cosmonauts, returned to normal within less than a month of the termination of flight. Thus, it would appear that the physical effect of such things might be the equivalent of a hard week's work, a grueling crew race, a football game, or similar activity. But whether such alterations are related to vibration, to gravitational forces, to radiation, or to the physiologic attributes of weightlessness cannot be answered at present. Observations on electrophysiologic processes relating to the eye, the skin, and the brain suggest that the changes are transitory. Occasional orthostatic hypotension and difficulties with eighth nerve function are not yet explained.

The medical and biologic applications of space telemetry present fantastic challenges but equally great opportunities. New developments will come rapidly.

Mechanical and Hydraulic Factors

Physical forces produce effects which vary with their nature and scope and with the points of impact on the victim, his position, physical state, and protective paraphernalia. Physical trauma, coeval with man's existence on earth, has assumed ever larger proportions as industry has used more complex machines and as warfare has advanced from slings and arrows to cordite and nuclear energy. The question of whether mankind will be hoist with its own petard has passed from philosophic to urgently practical stages. Only a few aspects of mechanical and hydraulic injury are mentioned here. Selection is random, for a survey can be contained only in encyclopedias.

Missile Injury

Missile injury has been investigated inten-

sively by the use of high speed photography. The transfer of energy from bullet into disruption of tissues has been quantitated. Little of utility has been added to the knowledge gained from previous experience of man's inhumanity to man. Though shock waves produce bizarre effects, physical laws are followed.

Blast

Blast transmitted through air or water injuries by wave propagation, bomb fragments, dislodgment of objects or victims, burns, asphyxiation, or drowning. Since a positive pressure wave from blast is followed by a negative wave, it is idle to speculate on, and academic to test, the precise role of each in the production of trauma. Air blast causes hemorrhage from ruptured small vessels, especially in the ear, thorax, and abdomen, and rupture of viscera and large vessels. Because of compressible gas in pulmonary alveoli, middle ear, and gut, overlying tissues are liable to injury. Pain, dyspnea, hemoptysis, and, later, infection may result from damage to the respiratory system. Pain, abdominal rigidity, hematemesis, melena, ruptured viscera or large vessels, and peritonitis may follow injury to abdominal structures. They are much more frequent after underwater blast from depth charges than as a result of air blast. There is a degree of protection if the back rather than the front of the subject receives the wave directly. Ear injuries range from congestion and hemorrhage to rupture of the drum with temporary or permanent deafness. An indirect effect of blast may occur when the victim, trapped in debris, suffers extensive muscle injury, with autolysis liberating myohemoglobin and other substances, which induce a lower nephron nephrosis and renal failure. Physical motion of the body through space may produce mild reactions from effects upon the vestibular apparatus; the sudden accelerating, decelerating and centrifugal forces of linear flight and deviations from it may cause death.

Motion Sickness and Seasickness*

Motion sickness results from the effects of certain movements upon the semicircular canals and is characterized by nausea, vomiting, pallor, cold sweating, apathy, drowsiness, malaise, and depression. It appears to be an

---

* Car, train, and plane sickness are of a similar nature.

altogether useless reaction, a relic perhaps of some ancient, purposeful response.

Gravity and Acceleration

Before the use of high speed airplanes man's dealings with gravity and acceleration were ordinarily in terms of small forces and moderate changes. Postural adjustments to gravity had been evaluated chiefly in static position. Abrupt deceleration in automobile or railroad accidents caused injury by physical trauma. Planes are subject to forces which far exceed the adaptive capacity of their human operators. Man's body, unprotected, is not able to deal effectively with the suddenly built-up power of gravity impinging upon him when sharp turns, banks, or loops produce abrupt deviation from linear flight at high velocity. A large part of the resulting difficulty comes from circulatory incapacity resulting in pooling of blood. Blackout and redout are the terms for symptoms of cerebral anemia and plethora produced by centrifugal and centripetal forces.

In small animals subjected to large gravitational forces in a centrifuge the lethal limits are a function of gravity (G) times time (T). Guinea pigs and rats are resistant to G effects, monkeys moderately resistant, and rabbits little resistant. Young animals are more susceptible than adult animals, and males more than females. Exposure to sublethal G for days or months increases tolerance. Abdominal belts or inflated rubber bags give protection. Hypoxia sufficient to induce prostration once every 2 or 3 days for a month increases resistance to high acceleratory forces. A similar effect follows a 5-minute exposure to water at 5° C. just before the test. Exhausting exercise just before exposure reduces tolerance substantially.

Centrifugation causes great displacement of blood. Moderate G forces of brief duration retard respiration, while longer ones produce slow, deep breathing. Short runs increase the pulse rate. Blood pressure is reduced immediately after moderate exposure. Permanent disorientation and rigidity may occur after severe exposure. Delta brain waves often occur during centrifugation and disappear soon afterward; an inhibition of all waves for 5 to 7 minutes sometimes occurs.

Human subjects exposed for 60 seconds to 4.2 G suffer loss of peripheral vision or blackout, retinal in origin, which improves after the first 10 seconds. Blood pressure may fall 20 to 30 mm. per G increase in acceleration. Physiologic reactions during acceleration have been divided into the period of progressive failure and the period of compensation. During the first period, pulse rate increases, pulse in the ear may disappear, blood pressure at brain level decreases, vision is reduced, and consciousness is lost. Six to 11 seconds after onset of acceleration the second phase begins. Blood pressure rises, ear pulse returns, the pulse may slow, and vision and consciousness may return. Immersion in water or the use of positive pressure gravity suits provides a considerable degree of protection. The most important region for pressure is over the abdomen, and some additional effect can be obtained from pressure on the legs. Hydrostatic effects are reduced in the prone or supine position.

Elaborate equipment has been constructed to measure the force and determine the effects of crash, impact deceleration, ejection from speeding planes, or pick-up by flying planes, and of other situations in which nearly instantaneous stress of many times the force of gravity may affect the subject. The data obtained are of great importance, but no new concept has evolved, the effects produced being merely an exaggeration of those to which the careless acrobat is liable.

Aside from the effects of blast, noise may be merely annoying or may lead to permanent impairment of hearing. Machle studied the effects of exposure to repeated gun blasts in gunnery instructors and artillerists. Since recovery from a single period of gun blast may require about a week, much of the permanent injury appeared to arise from the daily repetition of exposure. Individual variations and uncontrollable variables in the behavior of blast waves prevented a systematic prediction of loss hearing.

Radium, Roentgen Rays, Radioactive Substances, and Atomic Factors

There is nothing magical about the workings of radioactive energy upon human tissues. Much has been learned about it in the relatively short period since the discovery of radioactivity at the end of the last century. Radiation includes invisible electromagnetic waves, similar to light, heat, ultraviolet, and radio waves, which travel in straight lines at a speed of 186,300 miles per second. Electromagnetic rays of a wavelength of 10 to 0.05 angstrom units are commonly used in medicine. Similar effects may be produced by isotopes of elements rendered radioactive by corpuscular radiation in the form of alpha and beta radiation and by neutrons. The biologic effect of these forms of radiation occurs when, impinging upon living tissue, the energy initiates a temporary separation of atoms and molecules into electrically charged particles, i.e., ionization, and the release of energy as chemical change or heat. The effects are proportional to the amount of ionization produced and depend on the tissues affected. They differ in quantity, but not in kind. Radiation may be blocked by lead or concrete screens and shields, or lead-impregnated gloves or aprons. Once tissues have been exposed, a sequence of changes is set in motion which cannot be stopped.

Roentgen rays are produced in vacuum tubes with two electrodes at opposite ends separated by a gap across which a current of electricity under high voltage is passed between the cathode and the anode, or target. On striking the anode, some of the energy is converted into roentgen rays which escape through the walls of the vacuum tube much as light escapes from an electric bulb. Roentgen rays are true electromagnetic waves quite different from an electric current. Usually, to screen out all but a small beam which can be directed to a particular part of the body, the tube is covered with lead except for a small exit aperture in which are placed thin layers of copper or aluminum, or both, to absorb rays of longer wavelength, but to allow rays of shorter wavelength and greater penetrating power to pass. Very high voltages are used to generate rays for the treatment of deep-seated disease. Lower voltages are suitable for roentgenograms and the treatment of superficial disease.

The *roentgen or "r,"* a measure of ionization produced in a known quantity of air through which a beam of roentgen rays passes, is the yardstick for the measurement of doses. A dose administered at low intensity over a long period or with intervening rest periods or to a large area will produce less change than the same dose at high intensity, at short intervals, or over a small area. The wavelength, the filtration, and the skin-target distance complicate the problem. No unit will accurately foretell the degree of tissue damage. An *erythema dose* is the amount of radiation which will produce a slight reddening of the skin of the average human subject. This dose does not bear a predictable relation to roentgens. The erythema dose for single exposures may vary from about 300 r with very long wavelength, or "soft" radiation, up to as much as 1000 r in "hard" radiation gen-

erated at 1,000,000 volts. An erythema dose of soft radiation produces less damage to deep structures than one caused by hard rays.

The character of the pathologic changes depends on the tissue involved and the degree and extent of exposure. Cellular changes include functional derangements, swelling, vacuolization, necrosis, or death. Intracellular changes may affect collagen, osteoid, or elastica. Vascular injury may produce an early endothelial swelling and thrombosis and late telangiectasis with partial or complete occlusion, and all combinations of subsequent trophic changes. Chromosomal changes may affect later generations of cells, leading to perverted function, blighted structure, or death.

Any living cell can be destroyed by sufficient radiation. Cells differ in susceptibility and resistance. Germ cells, bone marrow cells, and lymphocytes are highly radiosensitive. Cells of bone, cartilage, muscle, brain, kidney, liver, thyroid, pancreas, pituitary, adrenal, and parathyroid are radioresistant. There is no exact correlation between the microscopic appearance of cellular tumors and their response to radiation. Undifferentiated cells in general are more readily damaged than mature cells. All cells are particularly vulnerable to radiation damage during mitosis. Irradiation less than that which kills a cell may interfere with one or many functions. A stimulating effect, once suspected, is now denied. The effects of radiation are frequently delayed. Since man has no sensory Geiger counter, severe damage may occur without knowledge of exposure. A mild erythema may appear rapidly and disappear before evidence of a burn appears a week or two later. Even though apparently complete recovery may follow exposure of the skin to radiation, a latent change can be demonstrated by re-exposing to a moderate dose the same area, which is now much more vulnerable to injury than adjacent normal skin. Divided doses are cumulative, but show incomplete summation. The *tolerance dose* is the most radiation which can be received without a tissue losing its main function. A syndrome of *radiation sickness* characterized by nausea, vomiting, loss of appetite, headache, and malaise may occur shortly after exposure. There is some evidence that it results from a depression of respiratory enzyme systems. Various vitamins, liver extract, and insulin have been hailed as preventive or curative agents, but have not been proved so. Depression of bone marrow function of mild or severe degree may occur and progress for months.

Despite emphasis on the immediate physical and chemical changes in irradiated tissues, attention has been concentrated on the disordered physiology of the entire organism as indicated by the influence on growth and development, by pancytopenia, bleeding, inanition, altered immune reactions, carcinogenesis, and infection. The manifestations of injury and recovery are influenced greatly by the physiologic interactions of the whole organism. The biologic effects of ionizing radiation are similar, but their efficiency varies considerably, depending on the absorption of energy in relation to tissue mass, time, and distribution. The biologic effectiveness of radiation increases with increase in linear energy transfer. Complexities of the problem of dose distribution so far have defied exact quantitation. Thus, in experimental lymphosarcoma the dose required for regression of a subcutaneous implant is less than that required for intramuscular implant. Furthermore, general body irradiation which does not directly reach a tumor may induce regression.

The metabolic upheaval induced by high energy radiation may come from inhibition or destruction of enzyme systems. Other biochemical aberrations have been recognized; the exact role each plays in the mechanism of injury is not known. Most emphasis has been given to sulfhydryl-obligate enzymes, which are very radiosensitive.

Respiration of tissues irradiated in vitro or obtained from irradiated animals is either unchanged or decreased. The oxygen consumption of the whole animal is not altered to any significant degree. One primary effect of irradiation is alteration of nucleoprotein metabolism. Even here the significance of the derangements is not clearly understood. Nucleic acid turnover and the concentration of nucleic acid as measured by isotope uptake are decreased in many tissues. Synthesis of desoxyribonucleic acid and ribonucleic acid may be corrupted, disrupted, or stopped. Experiments to date have not revealed impairment of protein synthesis. Glucose metabolism may be decreased immediately after exposure to irradiation, and liver glycogen is greatly depleted after massive irradiation. Lipids, phospholipids, cholesterol, and vitamin A are not affected acutely.

In terms of the cellular changes, most emphasis is focused on the antimitotic effect of irradiation. The depression of cellular elements of blood is a result of both antimitotic action and necrotizing effect. Irradiating pelvic carcinoma produces hemolysis. Anemia occurs in spite of increased activity of bone marrow. In addition to hemolysis, a hemorrhagic tendency is prominent in some forms of irradiation toxicity. It is the result of thrombocytopenia. Alteration in vascular integrity may play a part in some hemorrhagic syndromes. Necrosis and infection, as well as vascular permeability and fragility, may influence the results.

The severe effects of x-rays on mice are associated with septicemia caused by microorganisms of enteric origin. The effect is delayed. Bacterial invasion reaches a peak near the middle of the second week, well after the morphologic changes in the gut have occurred. This suggests that general body resistance or some other mechanism must be responsible rather than anything which facilitates the invasion of the blood by microorganisms from the alimentary canal. To some extent antibiotics have been effective in reducing mortality. There is good evidence that irradiation may impair or inhibit antibody formation. Irradiated animals are much less able to stand various nonspecific forms of trauma, stimuli, and stress. Injury has been modified in certain animals by inducing either hypothermia or hypoxia, and it is generally agreed that the main effect of hypothermia is the associated hypoxia.

A good summary of the problem is given by Patt:

> Since high energy radiations are dissipated at random in the heterogeneous and highly integrated system many different effects may ensue, some of which are not a direct consequence of energy absorption. This situation differs only in degree from cell to tissue to total organism. It is necessary, therefore, to contend with the physiological interplay in the system as a whole. It is well known that injury and recovery are dependent to some extent upon the interactions between irradiated and nonirradiated areas. The damage of specific regions, e.g. a lymph-node or a tumor, is also generally more severe at the total body exposure than after local irradiation. These effects may be attributed to the liberation of non-specific toxic materials from irradiated tissues to hormonal influences, to the sparing action of non-irradiated tissues.

In man acute radiation injury usually occurs from accidental exposure to high energy accelerators, radioactive materials, or nuclear fission reactors. The injury and occasionally the death which follow result from disturbances at the cell level. The acute radiation syndrome is the sickness produced by exposure of most or all of the body to penetrating radiation. It differs radically from the chronic effects of repeated exposure exemplified by the early radiologic victims with their destructive and sometimes neoplastic lesions from repeated unguarded exposure.

Radiation injuries uncomplicated by blasts, wounds, or burns fall into four phases. One is prostration, nausea, vomiting, and diarrhea beginning within an hour after exposure and lasting up to 2 days. Phase two is a period of relative well-being which lasts until phase three, which is characterized by fever, diarrhea, hemorrhages into the skin and internal organs, loss of hair, and ulceration of mouth and throat. Those who survive this febrile illness enter phase four, a long period of convalescence leading usually to apparently complete recovery. Even under experimental circumstances it is not easy to get an exact measure of the quantity of radiation impinging upon a person, so that data from those exposed in Japan are necessarily somewhat vague.

In reactor accidents moderately fast neutrons are chiefly responsible for the severe damage, mostly in the superficial layers of flesh near the reactors. The body is not uniformly exposed. Fairly accurate measurements of the quantity affecting the entire body have been made on the basis of the induced radioactivity in serum sodium. This correlated surprisingly well with the clinical severity in the few persons studied. The illness consisted of overwhelming prostration and toxicity with high fever, weight loss, severe gastrointestinal symptoms, shock, and, in the worst exposures, death, with little or no response to appropriate therapeutic agents. Some of the effects were attributed to necrosis of the most exposed tissues. Persons with less exposure had relatively few symptoms.

In contrast to the illness produced by exposure of the entire body to a single dose of ionizing radiation, the overexposure of a small portion of the body produces less severe effects. In persons receiving beta ray burns from overexposure of the hands to fission fragments, severe itching and burning of the skin occurred. Later the fingers swelled and blistered. Pain occurred. There was slight fever and slight leukocytosis. Treatment was disappointing. Blood transfusions have not been particularly helpful and are indicated only as replacement therapy. Broad-spectrum antibiotics have not been notably valuable.

Electrical Injuries

The forces of electric current are measured in terms of *voltage* and *amperage.* Its flow through the body is determined by the points of entrance and exit, and the amount of current is determined by the resistance at the points of contact. The unit of electromotive force is the *volt;* that of resistance is the *ohm.* The unit of intensity is the *ampere,* which is the current produced by 1 volt acting through the resistance of 1 ohm. Until modern times injury from electric forces was limited to that resulting from lightning, but with widespread use of electricity accidental injury has become an important problem. The physical changes which occur when the human body becomes a conductor of electric current have been investigated carefully.

There is a close analogy between the injuries produced by electricity and those produced by simple mechanical trauma. The quantity of current received depends on the resistance at the point of contact and the duration of exposure. The enormous voltage of lightning may produce extraordinary effects, but precise quantitation of the current is impossible. In legal electrocution so much heat is produced that the tissue changes are in a class by themselves and do not throw much light on the effects of accidental nonfatal injury. The resistance of the human skin may vary from about 1,000,000 ohms on a callused hand to about 1000 ohms on moist skin. In a given period of time the effective voltage of alternating current is about 0.71 that of direct current of the same voltage, although at certain phases the effective current may be 1.4 times that of direct current per volt and thus be more dangerous. Currents of a given voltage with frequencies of 2000 are less dangerous; hence high voltage alternating current is used in radiologic treatment and in surgery. The manner and mechanism of death differ with high and low voltage current. High voltages are especially prone to cause ventricular fibrillation and physiologic asystole; low voltages "freeze" the muscles of respiration. The apparent cessation of function should not deter one from efforts at resuscitation, since recovery has followed apparent death.

The effect produced by electric current depends on the pathway it takes. In the living body, current passes through tissues by the most direct route between points of entry and exit, regardless of the structures traversed. Physiologic effects may result from the stimulation of tissues which react to current, as in the case of nerves, or from the heat generated. Functional damage may occur in vital organs and tissues. Persons shocked by electric current may be thrown or fall and be injured.

Gross and microscopic examination of tissues traversed by the electric current may reveal damage which, in some respects and in certain tissues, may be characteristic of injury from electricity, although other agents may produce similar changes. Sufficient current will produce primary inflammatory and, later, degenerative reactions in nerve cells and fibers. These changes may be due in part to heat generation and in part to a local reaction after the current has passed through. If the pathway directly involves the brain, death from paralysis of the respiratory center may occur. If the current traverses the heart immediate death from ventricular fibrillation or standstill may result. Injury to the nervous system may be direct and local from the current or indirect, the result of circulatory changes secondary to the action of the current on heart or nerve centers. In the brain, changes in the caliber of blood vessels and in the flow of blood through them, as well as abrupt shifts in blood pressure, may be the result of pathologic impulses from the sympathetic nerves and ganglia. Consequently there may be temporary or permanent damage to an area of the brain with disturbed blood supply. Severe convulsions or prolonged coma produced by electric current may be followed by lesions of the brain.

Injury from *diathermy* may result from short circuits or local overheating, which is guarded against by the patient's subjective feelings. Exposure to ordinary *radar* apparatus and equipment does not cause injury in man.

Concluding Remarks

With the exception of the delayed effects of radioactive substances, it may be stated as a general rule that physical agents do not give rise to injury which appears as a delayed reaction or is progressive in nature once the deleterious factor is removed. If the immediate effects are survived without evidence of hurt, subsequent disorders may not be attributed to the exposure to physical agents. As an illustration, although the syndrome of trench foot may not be full blown directly after removal from exposure, trench foot will not suddenly appear later in someone formerly exposed to cold who did not manifest early signs of cold injury. Similarly, heatstroke may leave permanent neurologic sequelae, but these arise at the time of the disorder rather than at a late date.

I have found no evidence that a person who suffers from the effects of a physical stimulus is particularly susceptible to injury on second exposure, if recovery from the initial trouble has been complete. Certainly in young healthy men, heat, cold, and high altitude produce fewer ill effects with repeated exposure. Not only is man's inherent resistance to injury great, but he has many latent capacities which enable him to acquire more resistance to repeated physical stimuli.

Now that man has been put in orbit and brought back safely many factors which concern man in space are unknown. The future will decide whether all the effort is a majestic farce as man tries to outdo himself, or whether some new insights will help the vast majority of earthbound persons face and endure those mundane problems from which they cannot fly away.

A study of the adaptations and adjustments within the latent capacity of man is in its infancy. It is a field which must attract its workers and philosophers if man is to survive and keep growing in an environment neutral at best and often hostile. Here more than elsewhere chimeras and pontifications call down the relentless hand of nature, for nature excuses neither false dreams nor flimsy data. We must continue the study of total man and total environment. It must be built upon a firm base of contemporary knowledge backed by historical wisdom. In the hard writings of the petrified past we see many mistakes, creatures whose adaptations led to their dying out. Nature neither forgives weakness nor forgets illusion; and in evolution the price of failure is extinction.

I wish to acknowledge great indebtedness to my former associates at the Armored Medical Research Laboratory at Fort Knox, and to my present colleagues at the University of Iowa and elsewhere.

REFERENCES

Aerospace Medical Center, School of Aviation Medicine, U.S.A.F., Brooks Air Force Base, Texas. Numerous brochures, papers, lectures and pamphlets.

Ashe, W. F., and Roberts, L. B.: Experimental human burns. Partial report. War Med., 7:82, 1945.

Bean, W. B.: Nutrition survey of American troops in the Pacific. Nutrition Rev., 4:257, 1946.

Bean, W. B., and Eichna, L. W.: Performance in relation to environmental temperature; reactions of normal young men to simulated desert environment. Fed. Proc., 2:144, 1943.

Bean, W. B., Spies, T. D., and Vilter, R. W.: A note on irradiation sickness. Am. J. Med. Sc., 208:46, 1944.

Blum, H.: The solar heat load: Its relationship to total heat load and its relative importance in the design of clothing. J. Clin. Invest., 24:712, 1945.

Britton, S. W., Corey, E. L., and Stewart, G. A.: Effects of high acceleratory forces and their alleviation. Am. J. Physiol., 146:33, 1946.

Cohen, H., and Biskind, G. R.: Pathologic aspects of atmospheric blast injuries in man. Arch. Path., 42:12, 1946.

Conn, J. W.: Electrolyte composition of sweat. Arch. Int. Med., 83:416, 1949.

Di Giovanni, C., Jr., and Chambers, R. M.: Physiologic and psychologic aspects of the gravity spectrum. New England J. Med., 270:35, 88, 134, 1964.

Dunlap, C. E.: Medicolegal aspects of injuries from exposure to roentgen rays and radioactive substances. Occup. Med., 1:237, 1946.

Eichna, L. W., Ashe, W. F., Bean, W. B., and Shelley, W. B.: The upper limits of environmental heat and humidity tolerated by acclimatized men working in hot environments. J. Indust. Hyg. & Toxicol., 27:59, 1945.

Eichna, L. W., Bean, W. B., Ashe, W. F., and Nelson, N.: Performance in relation to environmental temperature; reactions of normal young men to hot, humid (simulated jungle) environment. Bull. Johns Hopkins Hospital, 76:25, 1945.

Evans, T. C.: Biological and Medical Effects of Radiation at Low Levels. Manual of Lectures presented at the Institute In-service Training Course in Radiological Health, University of Michigan, School of Public Health, February 5-8, 1951.

Ferris, E. B., Blankenhorn, M. A., Robinson, H. W., and Cullen, G. E.: Heat stroke; clinical and chemical observations on 44 cases. J. Clin. Invest., 17:249, 1938.

Gordon, D.: Ultrasound as a Diagnostic Surgical Tool. Baltimore, Williams and Wilkins Co., 1964.

Hamilton, W.: Personal comments.

Hammond, C. W., Tompkins, M., and Miller, C. P.: Studies on susceptibility to infection following ionizing radiation. J. Exper. Med., 99:405, 1954.

Hyslop, G. H.: Effects of electrical injuries, with particular reference to the nervous system. Occup. Med., 1:199, 1946.

Ionides, M., Plummer, J., and Siple, P. A.: Report: Climatology and environmental protection section. Office Quartermaster General, 17 September 1945.

Kane, E. K.: Arctic Explorations, Vol. I. Philadelphia, J. B. Lippincott Co., 1856, p. 245.

Ladell, W. S. S., Waterlow, J. C., and Hudson, M. F.: Desert climate: Physiological and clinical observations. Lancet, 2:491, 1944.

Lamport, H., Ward, A. A., and Schorr, M. G.: Appraisal of rapid killing power of high velocity bullets. Mil. Surgeon, 99:215, 1946.

Lewis, T.: Observations on some normal and injurious effects of cold upon the skin and underlying tissues. Brit. Med. J., 2:795, 837, 869, 1941.

Machle, W.: Effects of gun blast on hearing. Arch. Otolaryng., 42:164, 1945.

Machle, W., and Hatch, T. F.: Heat: Man's exchanges and physiological responses. Physiol. Rev., 27:200, 1947.

McCally, M., and Graveline, D. E.: Physiologic aspects of prolonged weightlessness. New England J. Med., 269:508, 1963.

National Aeronautics and Space Administration, SP-5023: Medical and biological applications of space telemetry.

Pockett, W. O., McElroy, W. D., and Harvey, E. N.: Studies of wounds of the abdomen and thorax produced by high velocity missiles. Mil. Surgeon, 98:427, 1946.

Selye, H.: The general adaptation syndrome and the diseases of adaptation. J. Clin. Endocr., 6:117, 1946.

Selye, H.: On the acquisition of tissue resistant to digestion by gastric juice. Gastroenterology, 26:221, 1954.

Taylor, H. L., Henschel, A., Mickelson, O., and Keys, A.: The effect of the sodium chloride intake on the work performance of man during exposure to dry heat and experimental heat exhaustion. Am. J. Physiol., 140:439, 1943.

Tunbridge, R. E.: Cause, effect and treatment of air blast injuries. War Med., 7:3, 1945.

Warren, S.: The histopathology of radiation lesions. Physiol. Rev., 24:225, 1944.

White, J. C.: Vascular and neurologic lesions in survivors of shipwreck. New England J. Med., 228:211, 1943.

Wolkin, J., Goodman, J. I., and Kelley, W.: Failure of the sweat mechanism in the desert. J.A.M.A., 124:478, 1944.

Workman, R. D.: Personal letter, November 26, 1965.

Chapter Fifteen

Chemical Agents and Disease

B. D. DINMAN

Introduction

In his attempt to gain mastery over the environment, man and his technology have brought into being new molecules which the world has never before known. In the latter half of the twentieth century, new chemical agents have been synthesized which have the capability of regulating the growth rates of plants and animals, or which can differentially cause weeds to wither while sparing crop growth. A host of such agents ubiquitously find their way into channels of commerce leading directly to the household, whether intended for domestic use, e.g., detergents, or as a residue associated with foodstuffs. Hence there is a need among all physicians for some understanding of the interaction of such exogenous chemical agents with biological systems.

Before this era, relatively few chemicals were readily available to the public at large, while food additives were of a simple nature and frequently of biological origin. Formerly the study of the effect of chemicals was directed toward post-mortem examination of end results of tissue response. This yielded a static visualization of both agent-specific and nonspecific tissue alteration. But with advent of the doctrine of "prevention of occurrence" or "prevention of progression" of disease, only a conceptualization of the dynamic functional changes induced by a chemical at *all* stages of tissue response will permit the development of effective clinical preventatives. It should be apparent that study of chemically induced lesions seen from the viewpoint of morphology alone can give little insight into the early clinical events associated with chemical intoxication. Thus if we are to intervene effectively to prevent these pathologic processes, an understanding of the earliest functional events is required.

Basic to this chapter is the concept that dose as a function of time is the determinant of tissue response. While this is almost a priori recognized by the practitioner dealing with therapeutic chemicals, for some unknown reason dose as a determinant of response is ignored when he considers chemical "poisons." It will become apparent in this chapter that enzymatically controlled metabolic systems capable of handling exogenous chemicals have rate limits. These systems are to varying degrees self replicative, and may be supplemented by alternate metabolic pathways which also operate under similar limitations. If in general these limitations in the rate of metabolic transformation or regeneration of metabolic pathways are not exceeded by the dose or the time over which the dose is given, there are few if any chemical agents with which a biological system cannot cope.

In addition to these determinants of the dose-response relationship, still another factor controls the course and outcome of an individual's reaction to chemical agents. This response is based upon the genetically de-

253

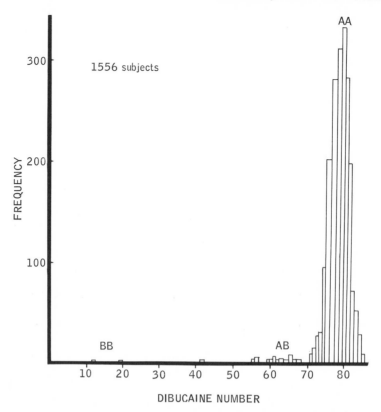

Figure 15–1. The distribution of the genotypes controlling cholinesterase within a population, as demonstrated by techniques expressing degree of inhibition of serum cholinesterase obtained with dibucaine. (After Kalow and Staron, 1957.)

termined availability of an enzyme(s) required for metabolic degradation or detoxification. Such a genetically determined phenomenon is exemplified by the case of those enzymes responsible for the splitting of the bond between choline and its ester, i.e., the cholinesterases. Whereas most individuals have the usual form of this enzyme that attacks the choline-ester bond readily, some small group (1:5100) within the population is endowed with a relatively large proportion of an atypical form of this enzyme exhibiting a *lower* affinity for cleavage of this bond. It must be pointed out that the normal process producing hydrolytic cleavage of the ester-choline bond is to some extent available to such persons, so that physiologic concentrations of acetylcholine normally present can be degraded and inactivated. Only upon administration of the muscle relaxant succinylcholine is there clinical manifestation of the presence of this atypical catalyst among these persons. As a result of the failure of enzymatic breakdown of this compound, such patients given the agent at surgery respond with a severe, persistent apnea.

Utilizing special techniques, Kalow has shown that acetylcholine esterase distributes itself within a population in three groupings, i.e., a rare number of individuals with little of the "normal" enzyme activity (1:5100), a second (and major) group with the usual enzyme activity, and a third, infrequent group whose enzyme activity is intermediate in "quantity" (1:30). Most observations on the inheritance of these characteristics indicate the presence of two autosomal allelic genes without dominance, with each gene causing the formation of one of the two types of enzyme. The typical genotype leading to "usual" enzyme elaboration can be expressed as AA; the atypical, low enzyme activity is expressed by the genotype BB, while intermediate enzyme activity would possess one of each allele, i.e., AB (Fig. 15–1). Except under conditions of drug administration discussed above there probably would not be clinical expression of this defect in the heterozygous group AB. Nevertheless, by appropriate techniques an intermediate amount of enzyme activity can be demonstrated. Other inborn errors of metabolism, e.g., phenylketonuria, galactosemia, in general appear to distribute and express themselves similarly in large populations.

The foregoing bears directly upon the concept of the genetically determined variation of response to chemicals. The statistical origin of the concept of "normal" is clinically all too often forgotten. Thus, while the "normal" individual represents the population within the large middle portion of the bell-shaped curve or "gaussian" distribution, there still remain those persons at the upper and lower portions (or "tails") of this distribution of occurrences. Accordingly if the physician gives a similar dose of therapeutic agent to enough patients over the years, eventually he will be faced with a patient who responds as if he were given gross overdosage. This person probably represents one of the few such individuals at the lower tail of the distribution of responses normally found in the population. Such a clinically susceptible individual may not possess the necessary enzymatic integrity of a chemical degradation pathway to the required extent, and thus the chemical agent may persist over a longer period of time in relatively high concentrations. It appears that the efficacy with which a metabolic pathway carries out its function is related in part to genetic endowment. Just as this atypical individual expresses a homozygosity (BB) of allelic endowment, the vast majority of individuals in the population on the rising slope of the normal curve are either heterozygous or more frequently homozygous in their genetic endowment. While the heterozygous may have somewhat less of the usual form of the enzyme, nevertheless such patients in the main have sufficient catalyst to escape clinical detection.

The Interaction of Biological Systems and Chemical Agents

INTRODUCTION

For rational understanding of the clinical response resulting from the encounter of a biological system with a toxic chemical agent, insight into the characteristics of the two interacting components is necessary. The delicately balanced, energy-dependent biological host with its range of compensatory mechanisms can only return to a position of homeostasis within certain limits; the chemical agent can effect a change upon such systems only as a function of certain physicochemical char-

acteristics. Study of the effect of each of these variables can lead to discernment of the essentials producing the symptom complex or the diffuse clinical picture resulting from such an encounter.

CHARACTERISTICS OF CHEMICAL INTOXICANTS GOVERNING THEIR BIOLOGICAL ACTIVITY

The effect that a chemical agent may exert upon the body economy is dependent not only upon the host's biological characteristics, but also upon the physicochemical nature of that exogenous agent. A three-dimensional matrix might be constructed consisting of the physicochemical, quantitative and temporal parameters responsible for the specific effects of these agents.

As for the first of these, the physicochemical, given a compound whose energy state is close to or at ground level, such material is less capable of transferring energy to another compound. The energy state of a chemical compound, in terms of everyday language, is usually referred to as its "reactivity." If a chemical is relatively insoluble or inert in reference to other adjacent molecules, it may act simply as a foreign body by virtue of its low reactivity. However, it must be understood that the inertness or minimal reactivity of any specific chemical compound in a relatively simple in vitro system frequently bears no relevance to the complex and relatively reactive biological milieu. Thus silica dioxide outside the body is extremely insoluble; its capability of inciting a severe pulmonary proliferative reaction is well established.

The potential for chemical reaction occurs if an exogenous chemical is less stable energetically or is more highly soluble and is made available to the normal constituents of a cell. However, both conditions of "availability" and solubility must be met before any interaction can occur. It is not surprising therefore, in view of the predominantly aqueous internal environment, that chemical agents which have relatively higher levels of biological activity usually ionize and are water soluble. By contrast, truly nonpolar compounds should less readily interact with cellular constituents unless these cellular components are themselves nonpolar. However, such lipid-soluble compounds react with aqueous cellular components because of the presence of naturally occurring emulsifying components such as phospholipids, or because of the presence of lipid components in subcellular structures.

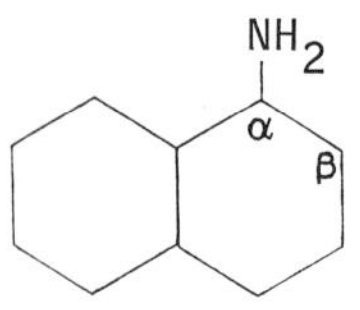

α - Naphthylamine

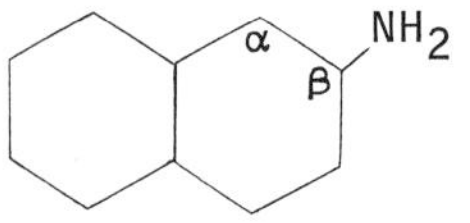

β - Naphthylamine

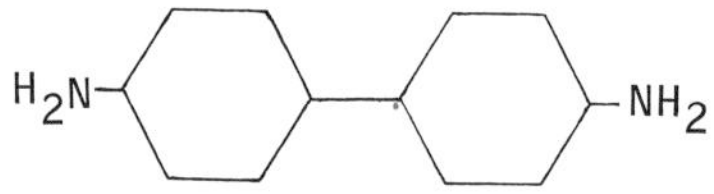

Figure 15–2. While the α-naphthylamine is not carcinogenic, the β isomer is clearly oncogenic, as is benzidine. Note that the *para* positions of both carcinogenic materials are inaccessible to metabolic alteration, in contrast to the noncarcinogenic α isomer.

Benzidine

The molecular configuration of an exogenous chemical agent can markedly alter tissue response. This is exemplified by the naphthylamines, wherein the position of the amine substituent on the naphthylic nucleus determines whether this chemical is carcinogenic. With the amine substituted at the alpha position this agent does not produce bladder tumors; amine substitution at the beta position produces a potent carcinogen (Fig. 15–2). Since the same applies with benzidine, the accessibility of the *para* position for further metabolic alteration (hydroxylation?) may aid in determining carcinogenic behavior.

The principle that pharmacodynamic response is dose dependent is clearly applicable to the area of toxicology. The observation of Hutchinson, that a biological system will interact only when 10^4 atoms of an element are present within a cell, might well set a lower limit of dosage. From this level and upward, the net result of the presence of a foreign compound to the host organism becomes dependent upon quantitative considerations, such as degree of energy change in a cell system, the numbers of cells involved and the primacy of the organ at risk. Thus, given the most toxic chemical known, there appears to be a dose level below which no detectable signs or symptoms appear. Though there may be functional biochemical or anatomic change at the cellular level, unless relatively large numbers of cells are altered clinical response will not be manifest. With the passage of time, the extraneous detritus resulting from such an interaction may be excreted or deactivated and the damaged cell ultimately replaced (except in the central nervous system). With these adjustments the total body economy returns to normal without any residual evidence of chemical damage. Accordingly it can be stated that for *any*

chemical there is a lower limit below which toxicity cannot be demonstrated in the intact animal except by the most subtle and sophisticated methodologies. And even with these techniques, with small doses no meaningful functional alteration can be defined.

In addition to the chemical reactivity of the material in question, the wide variation in toxic potential among any large numbers of chemicals (e.g., hydrogen sulfide in contrast to sulfur dioxide) is also a reflection of the relative rates of operation of available detoxification pathways. Considered from a different viewpoint, chemical intoxication will result only when the rate at which the agent or its metabolite is presented to the body is in excess of rate limits placed on the pertinent degradative or excretory processes that inactivate the chemical.

This principle can be clearly demonstrated in the case of exposure to soluble lead acetate. If an individual ingests this compound at levels which exceed 2.0 mg. daily, he can be shown to be slowly and progressively increasing his body burden of lead. His blood lead level will slowly rise over a 4-week period from a level within the normal range of 0.02 to 0.05 mg./100 gm. of blood to a new level of the order of 0.07 to 0.09 mg./100 gm. of blood. While this laboratory indicator demonstrates absorption of lead, in many cases there will be no distinctive clinical alteration, even though there may be an elevation of coproporphyrin and a disturbance in delta-amino levulinic acid metabolism. Under these conditions of dosage, it can be seen that the metabolic reaction rates controlling bone sequestration of lead have not been exceeded. Accordingly the amount of lead presented over the time period under consideration can be stored at this site where it is relatively inert. Rapid removal of this individual from exposure will be followed over several weeks by a gradual decrease in blood and bone lead levels, without his being aware that exposure to a toxic chemical has occurred. If the dose is doubled, over a shorter period of time lead absorption sufficient to elevate blood lead levels to 0.1 to 0.12 mg./100 gm. of blood will occur and the individual so exposed might well have symptoms. In this case the rate of absorption exceeds the gross rate of bony uptake. Consequently, the lead which remains outside the bony matrix has a greater opportunity to wreak clinical mischief.

Given a still larger dose in the same short time period, the rate at which lead can be stored in the bony matrix is rapidly exceeded. Whereas clinical lead intoxication makes its appearance after several weeks of low level exposure, under these conditions of acute dosing clinical alterations rapidly become manifest. Thus the third component of our chemical agent matrix, i.e., the time parameter, is interdependent in the main on the quantitative consideration of dose. That is, the occurrence of an acute biological response is dependent upon the algebraic sum* of (a) the *amount* of chemical presented to the body economy per unit time minus (b) the *rate* of metabolic deactivation or sequestration and excretion. Ultimately these rates are dependent upon the rate characteristics of each individual enzyme-mediated metabolic reaction occurring as one step in a multiple sequence of biochemical events.

Inherent, of course, in the concept of rate is the basic premise that time is its prime component, this variable being an integral member of the physicochemical and quantitative factors of our triad.

The Energetics of Cellular Activity and the Control of Its Equilibrium

The multiple, complex processes whereby a cell reproduces itself, constructs new or replacement components or communicates, are ultimately dependent upon the availability of usable energy. Further, in addition to the driving forces necessary to run these processes, their effectiveness depends upon the integration of intracellular control mechanisms which initiate, moderate the rate of and terminate these activities in ordered sequences.

It should be apparent that if an exogenous chemical is introduced into this delicately balanced interdependent cellular system, potentials for interruption and disorder exist. The mechanisms that produce energy to sustain these processes are a particularly crucial point whereat potential chemical interference may occur. The energy utilized to drive the engines of our civilization is derived from the chemical bonds of fossil fuels. The degradation of these bonds unlocks these bonds with the attendant release of heat. Living systems similarly obtain free energy by opening the chemical bonds of fuel stuffs, and utilize this energy or store it as its needs dictate. However, since the cell can only operate within a relatively narrow temperature range, it is unable to use heat energy to function, since thermal energy is usable only when it can be passed from one locus to a second when the latter is at lower temperature. The cell cannot burn its fuel at the 1400° F. combustion temperature of fossil fuels. Thus within a relatively low, constant temperature range, within a narrow range of hydrogen ion concentration and in a dilute aqueous medium, a more sophisticated means of energy extraction has evolved.

Free energy extracted from foodstuffs by oxidation is stored in the physiologically usable form as the bond of the terminal phosphate group of the adenosine triphosphate (ATP) molecule, rather than liberated as heat. The process of glycolysis, whereby glucose is broken down and energy potentials extracted, is not simply brought about by a drastic hydrolysis of this energy source, but rather occurs in a stepwise, ordered manner proceeding through at least 11 stages, each catalyzed by a specific enzyme, the process finally ending in pyruvate.

Following glycolysis pyruvate is broken down, and the two carbon products are recombined with a four-carbon moiety, oxalacetate, in the Krebs or citric acid cycle. Energized electrons are extracted from the intermediates of this cycle by specific enzymes and are fed into a series of electron carrier molecules of the respiratory chain. These are once more available for storage as available energy in the form of the high energy phosphate bond of ATP. The Krebs cycle and this latter process, referred to as oxidative phosphorylation, both occur within specific structural components of the mitochondria.

---

* In other than short-term, acute conditions of exposure, such algebraic summation of these two factors, i.e., dose vs. deactivation rate, requires that the dose response curve be linear. With chronic dosing this straight-line relationship between dose and response is usually not linear; accordingly under such chronic conditions these relationships cannot be expressed by simple algebraic summation.

It should be apparent that this orderly process is dependent upon the integrity of enzymes that initiate and control the rate of each intervening step. Clearly, each succeeding step in this multiphase process is dependent upon the successful completion of the immediately prior process. These crucial enzymes may be readily altered, since functioning of these proteins depends upon the integrity of a specific amino acid sequence, active site relationships, three-dimensional spatial configuration of their molecular arrangements, and so forth.

When a heavy metal ion is brought into contact with such an enzyme molecule, a binding site is usually available to the metal. This binding site may take the form of a ligand, e.g., $-SH$, $-NH_2$, $-OH$, and so on. The resulting complexing or ionic binding of such a heavy metal to the enzyme molecule may change this catalyst's functional characteristics. In the case of any one step of the energy-producing processes described above, if a single enzyme necessary for any one step is blocked, this imperatively requisite source of power will cease to operate and the dependent process will run down and cease.

These enzymatically controlled processes depend not only upon the stereochemical intactness of the protein molecule; in many cases enzymes require specific spatial relationships to subcellular structural entities. Thus, while the molecular integrity of the enzyme glucose-6-phosphatase may not be compromised, this enzyme also appears to require an intact endoplasmic reticulum or ergastoplasmic membrane system. If these membranes, or the plasma membrane, are considered a bimolecular layer of a lipoprotein nature, such exogenous chemicals as nonpolar lipid solvents (e.g., CCl_4) may readily be seen to possess considerable potentials for damaging effects. By changing this membrane's physical-chemical state, morphologic integrity is compromised; but in addition there is impairment of the activity of those enzyme systems dependent upon the intactness of this structure.

The electron-transport chain, the final step in this energy-producing mechanism, has been shown to be located within an elementary particle on another lipoprotein membrane within the mitochondria. These particles too are apparently dependent upon an organized and ordered three-dimensional pattern. The specific spatial separation of these particles bearing the electron transport process allows enzymes of the citric acid cycle (contained in the nonparticulate matrix of the mitochondria) "access" to the elementary particles. If a lipid solvent disrupts these mitochondrial membranes, the structural relationships of the electron transfer particles to the membrane are destroyed. In the absence of the electron transport system, any precedent energy-yielding reactions (e.g., glycolysis or Krebs citrate cycle) that yield energized electrons are less effective, since transfer of this energy—as in the formation of ATP from ADP—is no longer as effectively accomplished. Under such conditions less usable energy is stored or accumulated. Thus, as previously accumulated high energy phosphate bonds are utilized, in the absence of their replacement the energy level of the cell runs down. Accordingly, such vital energy-dependent functions, such as control of permeability, synthesis, and so forth, are impaired and finally blocked, with cell breakdown following apace.

In the test tube, as the products of a chemical reaction accumulate, a gradual slowing of interaction occurs in keeping with physicochemical laws. Within the cell the products of one reaction sequentially enter into successive reactions, so that ultimately the products of this activity are either synthesized into a cell component, serve as a source of energy or are transferred from the cell. If a reaction product accumulates within a cell, one can conclude that the reaction yielding this material is operating at a rate in excess of the capability of the succeeding process. In vitro, physicochemical considerations would eventually halt the reaction producing this product, but not until considerable product accumulates. Within the cell, however, while it appears that metabolic processes are responsive to such reaction dynamics, more subtle means of cellular function control are also available. The key to these control devices lies in the fact that enzymes influence both the quantitative and qualitative functions of metabolic pathways. Thus any mechanism that can influence activity of enzymes in turn controls cellular metabolic processes.

The concept of "end-product inhibition" provides one such mechanism for influencing enzyme action (Fig. 15–3). This device is brought into play by the accumulation of a product which may be elaborated as a result of a sequence of enzymatically mediated chemical transformations. This accumulation of product appears to inhibit the synthesis of new enzyme and/or its activity per se. It should be noted that the enzyme so influenced

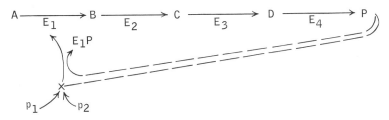

A – D = Substrate and/or products

P   = End-product

$E_1 - E_4$ = Individual enzymatic mediators

p_1, p_2 = Precursor components of E_1

$E_1 P$ = Complex of E_1 and P, inactive

Figure 15–3. End-product inhibition mechanisms. The product (P) of a series of enzymatically mediated reactions may inhibit or moderate the reaction A → B by means of two possible mechanisms. It can inhibit synthesis of E, from its precursors p_2 and p_1 or it can join with the enzyme E, to form the inactive complex E_1P.

is usually not directly involved with the elaboration of the triggering product, but rather is several reactions precedent to the "product." Thus the process of "end-product inhibition," by acting upon the enzyme mediating one step in a chain of metabolic activity, can bring to a halt or control the rate of this cellular sequence of chemical events.

Another mechanism whereby an enzyme's activity may be regulated has been demonstrated in the case of glutamic dehydrogenase. It appears that this enzyme under the proper conditions may have its catalytic activity abolished upon depolymerization into four smaller molecular fragments. Quite remarkably these four monomeric forms still are active enzymes, but now act in quite another reaction involving the oxidation of alanine. But given the proper conditions within the cell, these four fragments can again polymerize to express their presence as the enzyme glutamic dehydrogenase once more. This unique chain of events provides still another autoregulatory method whereby metabolic activity controlled by enzymes may be controlled within the cell. It should be pointed out that the quantitative aspects of many factors controlling this remarkable depolymerization and repolymerization are critically controlling parameters.

In summary, these brief discussions suggest various sites at which the cell's dynamic equilibrium may be disturbed by structural as well as biochemical alteration. Agents which affect the molecular arrangement of the structural components of the cell may ultimately alter specific enzymatically controlled function. The physicochemical arrangement of the protein molecules that constitute the enzymes may be altered directly by chemical agents, leading to loss of catalytic activity. We have seen but a few examples of how metabolic activity is controlled by exquisitely balanced autoregulatory systems which utilize enzymes as their operants.

These quantitative and time-dependent variables all may apparently affect the delicate interactions required to maintain a state of dynamic equilibrium in conformation with general laws of physics and chemistry. This equilibrium is not static as is a stone lying on a flat level surface; rather it is similar to the equilibrium of a tightrope walker who sways to one side and then another, but necessarily about a single balance point. These cellular systems are similarly in a dynamic equilibrium, with the degree of stability of this system similarly limited by an allowable degree of "sway" which will or will not permit restoration toward an equilibrium point when such displacements occur.

Portals of Entry of Chemicals

Dependent upon physiochemical considerations previously discussed, chemicals can enter the body through (1) the lungs, (2) the skin and mucous membranes and (3) the gastrointestinal tract. Aside from medicaments, the entry of a chemical agent through this last route was formerly either the result of criminal or suicidal intent. However, with modern advances in the development of chemical agents for multiple applications in agriculture (e.g., selective plant poisons, defoliants, pesticides, growth accelerators) or in the household (detergents, polishes, chemical bleaches and whiteners), there exist numerous opportunities for chemical compounds to enter the body through the gastrointestinal tract. By contrast, occupational exposure to chemicals usually leads to absorption in the order of frequency indicated by the three portals of entry mentioned above.

INHALATION OF CHEMICALS

While entry of chemicals into the body is commonly thought of as pursuing the oral pathway, entry through the respiratory tract affords a remarkably effective route of ingress. The surface area of the pulmonary capillary-gas exchange surface has been estimated to cover approximately 140 square meters. This compares favorably with the gastrointestinal absorptive surface, and is at least 50 times greater than the adult skin surface area. Thus, given the proper physicochemical circumstances, the pulmonary portal represents a considerable potential exchange surface for gas, vapors, fumes and even particulates.

Furthermore, following lung absorption, carriage of chemicals directly to the brain and other vital organs occurs without prior passage through the liver, in which organ detoxification mechanisms might inactivate the agent. Accordingly possibilities are enhanced for exposure to the undegraded chemical in these organs.

The degree of absorption through the pulmonary portal of entry is primarily dependent upon the physical state of the chemical under consideration. Fumes, vapors, mists and gases, being molecular or in the submicron size range, are absorbed into the capillary bed of the lungs in accordance with definite physicochemical laws. While in the main the locus of action of materials in these physical states is determined by their solubility, the dose of such materials presented to the respiratory tract may also play a role in determining the site of damage.

Given a highly soluble vapor, e.g., hydrochloric acid or ammonia, unless the respiratory tract is presented with large doses, there is "scrubbing out" of this irritant gas in the aqueous mucus cover of the turbinates and pharynx, with the consequence that little if any of the vapor reaches the lower respiratory tract. Under these conditions, the effects of small doses of such highly soluble irritant gases are mainly manifest by erythema and discomfort in the nose and throat and of the conjunctiva. If presented in large doses, however, the "scrubbing" capacity of the upper respiratory tract may be overwhelmed, with the result that sufficient of the irritant gases reach the lower respiratory tract to produce a chemical burn of the lungs. Under these conditions patchy or—in very large doses—massive pulmonary edema occurs. By contrast, gases of relatively low solubility in aqueous media will produce little upper respiratory tract irritation, though they quite readily reach the lower branches of the pulmonary tree—even in small doses—producing lung pathology here. This is exemplified by relatively insoluble phosgene gas, which even in small doses will largely reach the alveoli, gradually go into solution, slowly hydrolyze to HCl and some hours later produce pulmonary edema. Thus, mol for mol, such gases or vapors of lower water solubility are frequently more capable than the more water-soluble gases of producing serious pathologic alterations in the lower reaches of the respiratory tree, since the former readily by-pass the protective aqueous mucus layer serving as an absorptive medium in the upper respiratory tract.

Rates of diffusion of vapors or gases are dependent upon the partial pressure differentials between the alveolar air and vascular compartment. The instantaneous partial pressure of such gases or vapors in the blood is in the main a function of their solubilities in what is essentially an aqueous medium. Accordingly, though fresh blood rapidly replaces aerated blood in the pulmonary capillaries, if the vapor is nonpolar—and thus only slightly soluble in this aqueous system—saturation of the blood occurs at a rate directly proportional to pulmonary blood flow. Because of this marked limitation placed on uptake by low solubility in blood, nonpolar vapors or gases in the alveoli rapidly come into equilibrium with the vascular compartment, in contrast to the more water-soluble (polar) vapors or gases. As this equilibrium approaches, the pressure differential between blood and alveolar air decreases, and there is less of the driving force from ambient air to the body interior. In the case of the soluble gases or vapors, the rate of blood saturation is directly proportional to alveolar partial pressure, since the rate of uptake is not limited by solubility considerations.

This rate of pulmonary uptake may be

altered by extrapulmonary considerations. The rate of movement of these dissolved vapors or gases from the vascular compartment to the internal milieu directly affects the blood partial pressure of these materials. Such movement from the liquid phase of the circulation may be due to renal excretion, specific tissue pick-up (e.g., CO by the erythrocyte) or a partition coefficient more favorable to extravascular localization. This last case is seen when DDT appears to move selectively from the blood to organs of relatively higher lipid concentration than the blood, e.g., the mesenteric fat depots.

While the rate of absorption is to a large degree a function of the specific physicochemical nature of the material under consideration, this rate can be altered by physiologic activity or pathologic alteration. If blood flow and ventilation rates are altered by physical activity, the rate of absorption is increased as larger volumes of relatively unsaturated blood are presented to more alveoli containing the gas in question. The rate of absorption accordingly is greatly increased with increased physical exertion. Among individuals with impairment in excretory (i.e., kidney) or detoxification (i.e., liver) function, a more rapid buildup of toxicants occurs on respiratory exposure than is the case among normals. Though equilibrium is reached more rapidly, nevertheless smaller doses produce toxicity in such persons more rapidly, as the net gain in retention of the chemical toxicant occurs more promptly.

The lungs should also be considered as a potential organ of passive excretion following exposure to gases or vapors. If a person so exposed is removed to a contaminant-free atmosphere, this effectively diminishes the alveolar partial pressure of the gas in question, assuming continued ventilation and lung perfusion. With a gradient now established in the direction *from* the capillary to the alveolus, the absorbed gas or vapor leaves the blood. While maintenance of ventilation and circulation permits body desaturation of such gaseous contaminants, measures intended to stimulate either respiration or circulation should be considered with reservation, as the toxic properties of the inhaled gas may have imposed an undue circulatory load. Under these circumstances, any attempt to drive these functions more vigorously may precipitate decompensation.

The ability of particulate matter entering the pulmonary tree to produce a local and systemic effect depends largely upon its physical nature. The chemical nature of such materials may be of secondary importance, since particles too large to reach the lower segments of the lungs have relatively less pathologic potential, regardless of chemical properties. Thus size, density and surface area of particulates determine biological activity to a large extent. Particles larger than 5 microns in size are usually not particularly active as far as inciting pulmonary disease or permitting absorption. As mass usually is related to size, large particles, once set in motion, have a higher inertia than smaller particles. In view of the numerous changes of direction of air flow in the pulmonary tree, it follows that particles having a high kinetic energy and inertia (i.e., having less physical ability to change direction of motion) also have a greater probability of impingement, and lesser probabilities of deeper penetration of the lungs. It should also be apparent that variations in particle density may determine impingement probabilities. Thus, given a particle of uranium oxide with a density of 11 and a diameter of 1 micron, it will behave in the respiratory tract as a particle of lower density several microns larger in diameter. From this stems the observation that, given a similarity in particle size, deep pulmonary penetration and deposition of uranium oxide (which particle is of high density) are less than those of a low density particle. Another factor making large particles more likely to impinge on a portion of the tracheobronchial tree is the fact that larger and/or denser particles tend to remain suspended in air for only a short period in contrast to smaller or lighter ones. Both these factors, size and density, combine to determine probability of deposition. Impaction in the air conduction passages leads ultimately to pulmonary cleansing effected by the upward-moving escalator of the cilia-propelled tracheobronchial mucus. This "moving stairway" acts from the alveolar duct level upward, continuously carrying out of the lung those particulates entrapped in this tenacious moving carpet.

Other physical properties of particulates appear to be determinants of biological activity. The crystalline lattice structure peculiar to silica, which exists chemically as free silicon dioxide, elicits a potent fibrogenic response in the lung. By contrast, noncrystalline amorphous silicates are essentially inert. It has been pointed out that the intra-atomic distance of the two oxygen atoms of this crystal is similar to the relationship of similar atoms on the surface of the endotoxin molecule of the pneumococcus bacillus. What relationship this may have to the immune nature of the response, which in some aspects is common to these dissimilar agents, is as yet obscure.

In addition, the elastic properties of the particulate may play a role in determining biological response, since particulate fibers of similar sizes, e.g., fiberglass and asbestos, produce quite different results in the lung. While fiberglass responds to elastic deformation quite readily and does not produce pulmonary damage, asbestos fibers are relatively inelastic and do produce pathologic alteration when they lodge in the constantly changing diameters of bronchioles. Undoubtedly, the specific chemical nature of the asbestos fiber plays a role in inciting pathologic alteration. Indeed, the chemical nature of the asbestos fiber in contrast to the glass fiber may be the major determinant of the pulmonary reaction. However, such response may well be also dependent upon its peculiar mechanical properties.

Finally, the chemical nature of the particle which impinges in the lungs may determine the nature of the biological response. Particulates of lead oxide impinging on alveolar surfaces allow for leaching and systemic absorption, while similar particles of lead sulfide are associated with little if any absorption.

The ultimate fate of particles that impinge on the pulmonary surfaces is variable, though such final disposal loci also determine the site of response. Particulates which are deposited in the alveoli may be phagocytized by macrophages. In the case of crystalline silica, these particles most frequently are conveyed by dust cells along the peribronchial and perivascular lymphatics, though some few of these cells may migrate upward through the air conduction pathways.

Phagocytes that have ingested such crystals eventually reach the hilar lymph nodes where they are filtered out. This accumulation leads to a fibrous response, which in turn produces enlargement of these nodes early in the disease. Subsequent distortion of the tracheobronchial tree may lead to inadequate drainage with accumulation of small amounts of mucus and a scanty cough. Many of the phagocytes—for reasons yet unclear—break down in the course of this passage through these lymphatic channels, with the development of a localized inflammatory response in association with this necrotic debris. With the inflammatory response there is an impairment of lymphatic movement and phagocytic ac-

tivity, resulting in stasis, retention of silica locally and the formation of fibrotic nodules at these sites. Later, after years of exposure to free silica, increased lung markings and typical fibrotic nodules of silicosis are found along the course of the lymphatics. The typical silica nodule of the lung parenchyma, characterized by a circumferentially oriented, onion-skin-like hyalin deposition, is also seen in the hilar lymph node. In addition such individuals appear to be highly susceptible to tuberculous infection. When this complication supervenes, a more diffuse fibrosis and associated pulmonary obstructive disorder result. As these dense nodules begin to calcify, the roentgenogram will clearly demonstrate these radiopaque nodular structures, each of which might be considered the tombstone of a silica crystal.

ABSORPTION VIA THE CUTANEOUS ROUTE

The skin is usually considered as constituting an effective barrier to entry into the internal milieu. Inorganic electrolytes, high molecular weight substances, molecular aggregates and particulates quite clearly cannot penetrate the uninjured epidermal layer. To a very slight extent some gases may pass directly through the cutaneous barricade.

The barriers to transcutaneous movement are found at several points in and on the skin. Immediately on the epidermal surface is a water and oil emulsion, liberated by keratinizing cells and secretions of the sebaceous and sweat glands. While the pH (4.5 to 6.0) of this "acid mantle" is said to have antifungal and antibacterial properties, it poses little resistance to passage of most compounds. Since the keratin layer is fairly porous, it is at the area directly above the granular layer (between the stratum granulosum and stratum corneum) that one finds the first major mechanism appearing to block further passage of many compounds across the skin barrier.

The causes of the relatively high degree of impermeability found here are not fully understood. These cells have been shown by electron microscopy to be extremely dense, consisting of a uniform keratin material, and to contain less than 10 per cent water. Furthermore, at this location there has been demonstrated an electronegatively charged, horizontally oriented field which is believed to repel anions and prevent cations from penetrating more deeply. Furthermore, passage around these cells becomes more difficult since at this level the cells are most densely packed.

However, for certain groups of chemicals the skin poses no significant hindrance to percutaneous passage. Nonpolar materials of an ether:water partition coefficient greater than 1 most readily traverse this percutaneous route. It is assumed that, since most such lipid-like materials pass directly through cells, the lipid content of these cutaneous cell membranes permits such passage. In the case of aniline or carbon tetrachloride, this apparently appears to be true, since these nonpolar compounds pass through the intact skin almost as readily as any other portal. Though this theory applies in many cases, there are, however, some exceptions to this concept. Indeed, phenol, which is soluble in both aqueous and lipid media, passes extremely readily through the skin barrier.

While the skin surface per se is the major entry route as a result of its larger surface area, the dermal appendages also permit entrance to the internal environment of the body. The termination of the granulosum barrier described above occurs at the level where the sebaceous gland enters the follicle. This barrier layer may thus be by-passed, for chemicals can diffuse through the continuum of the liquid phase or mantle on the skin surface and thence eventually to these glands. The cells of the pilosebaceous apparatus with their extensive blood supply appear to be quite permeable. By contrast, it is believed that the sweat glands do not provide a significant portal of entry.

In addition, the foregoing premises are based upon an intact skin surface. Therefore, breaks in the epidermal continuity may afford a significant portal of entry for highly toxic chemicals. Systemic distribution may occur following penetration of the skin by flying objects contaminated by such agents, or through lacerations or abrasions. However, here again systemic absorption usually is dependent upon solubility and particle size, since these determine the potential for leaching of the chemical constituents of such bodies.

GASTROINTESTINAL TRACT AND MUCOUS MEMBRANE ABSORPTION

As previously noted, absorption via this route is a result of specific and peculiar situations rather than occurrences that usually arise from occupational or the more common environmental exposures. The potential for gastrointestinal tract absorption must be considered, however, under such circumstances when toxic materials are inadvertently carried to the mouth by contamination of cigarettes, food or the hands themselves. Such contamination is commonly noted in work places characterized by inadequate environmental hygiene.

While the rate of absorption for numerous materials is variable, the small intestine is apparently the major site of gastrointestinal absorption. Except for ethyl alcohol, few if any chemical agents are absorbed directly through the gastric mucosa. Those agents absorbed at the remainder of the small intestine do so as a function of various physicochemical factors.

The rate of absorption is frequently decreased in the presence of food, since liquids dilute and solid particulates may react to form insoluble complexes or allow adsorption of toxic materials onto their surfaces. Thus the presence of the casein of milk on contacting caustics forms a curd-like mass due to protein coagulation, thus leading to adsorption and decreased gastrointestinal tract absorption.

Solubility also plays a role in the rate of gastrointestinal absorption. More carbon tetrachloride is absorbed in the presence of a fatty meal or alcohol, as the concentration of this solvent per unit volume of gastrointestinal contents is decreased. In the presence of a relatively high concentration at an absorbing surface, transmembrane movement is impeded by rate limits of absorption in contrast to low concentrations. Such rate limits appear to be operative in the gastrointestinal tract. The "selectivity" of absorption that prevents the uptake of "unnatural" substances appears to be an expression of such concentration-dependent rate limits.

Systemic effects are also modified by the fact that materials absorbed through the gastrointestinal tract must first pass through the liver via the portal system. This transit introduces the potential for metabolic transformations such as detoxification or degradation and/or excretion via the biliary duct. Thus, in the case of lead and arsenic, entry into the general circulation is prevented to a degree by excretion into the biliary system.

Absorption of various chemicals at the surfaces of the gastrointestinal tract, as with any body interface, may lead to local damage. With ingestion of corrosive agents, irreversible alteration of protein components may readily occur, leading to the potentials for discontinuity of such epithelial surfaces. The clinical expression of this change is seen in the denaturation of the protein of the mucosa by caustics, resulting in a typical white, friable appearance. Since coagulated protein is relatively less elastic, normal gastrointestinal movement may lead to disruption of the mucosa. If these destructive corrosive effects extend deeper than the superficial mucosa, rupture of the superficial blood vessels with associated hemorrhage may develop.

What is frequently considered a local effect in the gastrointestinal tract may actually be an expression of a systemic alteration in which the intestinal tract may also participate. Such is the case with the ulcerations of the upper bowel seen in arsenic ingestion. Apparently one of the basic lesions of arsenic intoxication is a marked alteration in capillary permeability. This primary lesion is expressed by leakage at the glomerular tuft with the resultant hematuria and proteinuria. However, because of the dramatic changes within the gastrointestinal tract, the renal lesion usually present is not sought and thus not detected. In the gut, leakage of the fluid phase from the superficial capillary bed leads to extravasation and collection of serum in the submucosa. With further accumulation, stretching of the mucosa continues until rupture occurs, which in turn leads to frank bleeding from what appears to be an ulcerated mucosa. Fluid and protein continue to be lost via this discontinuity, while hypermotility, cramping and severe abdominal pain appear due to the irritation produced by such luminal contents and rupture of the mucosa. In acute arsenic intoxication a fatal termination may supervene due to fluid losses from the vascular bed, shock and circulatory collapse. Yet that which is seen as a local effect is in fact a manifestation of a systemic alteration in capillary permeability at the molecular level. Since permeability maintenance is energy dependent, it has been suggested that the known interference by arsenic with pyruvate dehydrogenase activity in the Embden-Meyerhof pathway may reduce energy availability to endothelial cells. With ensuing entropy, loss of permeability control in such structures may be one of the earliest functional alterations.

The mucous membranes offer a varying degree of protection of the internal environment from hostile agents. Women with no known contact to mercury other than certain mercury-containing contraceptive preparations can be demonstrated to absorb considerable amounts of inorganic mercury salts; a degree of absorption via this route is possible even to the point of producing a fatal outcome. The absorption of nitroglycerin or even larger molecules, e.g., progesterone, via the buccal mucous membrane is well known. In former years the absorption of silver salts following nasal instillation was sufficient to cause the generalized body discoloration of argyria. While these portals of entry are well demonstrated, the elucidation of the mechanism of absorption and factors affecting this process are not clear at this time.

Cellular Biology and Enzymatic Alteration as the Determinant of Clinical Response to Toxic Chemical Absorption

For the rational understanding of the clinical symptom complex which may result from absorption of a toxic chemical, the study of the interrelations between organ systems, i.e., physiologic response, is of itself inadequate. That this is true arises from knowledge that chemical-induced alteration of organ function may stem from causes other than direct modification of its constituent cells. Changes in any one of several organs demonstrating a pathologic alteration may result from changes far removed from that organ, e.g., changes in blood flow, or hormone-mediated and/or direct neurogenic activity. Such changes are seen following absorption of hexavalent uranium producing renal tubular damage and resultant accumulation of waste products of metabolism. Their buildup in the circulation appears to play a role in liver injury with resultant fatty metamorphosis. Yet study of hepatic physiology would provide an inadequate basis for building a rational, mechanistic understanding of the clinical complex stemming from uranium intoxication.

Similarly, pathologic alteration described in terms of structural change contributes only in part to comprehension of the mechanisms underlying clinical response. The structural entities contained within the cell are not the static, fixed entities suggested by morphologic study. The delimiting boundary of the cell, i.e., the plasma membrane, cytoplasm and associated organelles, the nucleus and its contents—all these cell components in health and disease are constantly in a state of flux or turnover. The replacement and renewal inherent in this state are clearly dependent upon energy sources. This driving force is necessary for the activity involved in synthesis of replacement components and the dynamic functions carried out by and among these structures. The integration of this system and its synthetic or energy-producing activity are ultimately dependent upon catalysts which determine the rate of these reactions. Accordingly, in the final analyses, these crucial activities are dependent upon enzymatic control. While it must be understood that enzymes do not contribute to the net energy required for such chemical reactions, it should be pointed out that such catalysis accelerates such reactions, permitting them to proceed within restricted temperature and concentration ranges.

Thus we have arrived at our premise, i.e., that much of the clinical picture of chemically induced morbidity will be more clearly explicable when we can describe the interactions of toxic agents on enzymes and the metabolic systems they control. Though the details of such interactions constitute an as yet ill-perceived horizon, undoubtedly the biochemical approach will in turn be succeeded by the viewpoint that considers such dynamics purely in a biophysical frame of reference. Since these intimate biophysical insights are not yet within our grasp, our discussion here centers mainly about the mechanisms whereby chemicals alter intracellular enzymatic processes.

Mode of Action of Chemicals Upon Enzyme Systems

Enzymatic Inactivation or Denaturation

As is the case with other proteins, the functional status of an enzyme is dependent upon its three-dimensional structural integrity. Exposure of any protein system to drastic chemical or thermal conditions may produce irreversible alteration of these requisite spatial relationships. On contact with strong acids or alkaline agents skin surfaces and mucous membranes demonstrate the formation of an irreversible protein coagulum. The changes induced by thermal coagulation of egg white are clearly analogous to alterations seen following tissue contact by chemical coagulants. Thus there are similar alterations of the structural characteristics (e.g., elasticity, flexibility) and the functional nature (e.g., permeability) of the target tissues. These become whitened, biologically inert and readily friable. Given undue mechanical stress, such surfaces can be ruptured readily. This clearly serves to explain

the clinical basis for the contraindication of gastric tube passage through an alkali-burned esophagus; such a devitalized organ is structurally weakened and presents a high risk of perforation. With the passage of time, phagocytic removal of detritus occurs, and this protein coagulum is replaced by fibrous tissue, scarring and subsequent contracture. All these changes can occur at any body surface so contacted.

However, enzymatic activity can be irreversibly inactivated by means less drastic than protein denaturation. Such interactions are at the root of chemical toxicity, and their specific mechanisms are here considered individually.

Direct Enzyme-Chemical Combination

This type of interaction is one of the most obvious manners in which toxicity may be produced. A chemical agent may combine with an enzyme so as to alter the catalyst's structural relationships, and especially its active-site or active-group spatial associations. The significance of such alterations is readily apparent, since it is at such sites that the substrate (i.e., the material acted upon and changed by the enzyme) combines with the enzyme. The very brief association of these two components (enzyme and substrate) leads to the formation of a complex. This combination is succeeded by a change in the substrate, which becomes "activated," i.e., the substrate becomes particularly susceptible to chemical reaction or change.

The combination of the cyanide ion with an atom of iron produces a metal-cyanide complex; this combination inhibits the activity of cytochrome A_3 in the terminal segment of the electron transfer chain. With inhibition of this reaction, there is a cessation of the oxidative mechanism. This process plays a vital role in the metabolic reaction providing a major source of energy for cellular activity. Clinically, the first symptom of mild poisoning is manifest by that system with the highest level of oxidative metabolic needs and whose aberration is most rapidly reflected by clinical alteration. Given these requirements, one expects the central nervous system to be the first to demonstrate clearly symptomatic alterations analogous to a lack of oxygen, since the net effect of impairment of cellular oxidation (or the ability to utilize oxygen) is essentially the same as that produced by hypoxia. Thus headache, lassitude and nausea appear as manifestations of nerve cell hypoxia, but in more severe poisonings—as anoxia, in this peculiar sense, supervenes—these manifestations are replaced by signs of oxygen lack at motor centers. The convulsions resulting from this type of cellular "anoxia" at these sites are succeeded by collapse and respiratory paralysis. Death may occur quite rapidly as a consequence of anoxia of the vital brain stem nuclei controlling cardiovascular and respiratory functions.

The lethal propensities of cyanide are somewhat unusual, since the block of a critical step in the electron transfer chain cannot be readily by-passed by a shunt or alternate pathway. Arsenic by contrast is lethal only in relatively larger doses than cyanide, since enzymatic blocks produced by its salts or oxides may be by-passed. Arsenic, by combining with the sulfhydryl groups associated with numerous enzymes, e.g., pyruvate oxidase, forms an inactive complex. However, in those organs which can utilize fatty acids as a source of energy substrate, these lipid moieties may be utilized in energy production by their entry into the citric acid cycle independent of carbohydrate sources. Accordingly an arsenic-induced block in carbohydrate oxidative energy metabolism at the point of pyruvate oxidation can be by-passed and energy needs met. Thus in chronic arsenic poisoning the myocardium demonstrates only minor clinical manifestations of functional change because of the existence of such shunts in these cells. This alternate energy source may not be as readily available to peripheral nervous tissue. Such possibility of "by-pass" potential may account for the observation that in subacute and chronic arsenic intoxication, peripheral nerve degeneration produces clinical symptoms of motor and sensory dysfunction in contrast to relatively few changes in cardiac function.

An exceptionally clear picture of direct enzyme inhibition is afforded by examination of the effects of the organophosphate insecticides upon the enzyme acetylcholine esterase (AChE). It should be recalled that acetylcholine acts as the chemical mediator transmitting nervous impulses across the synapse. This enzyme AChE causes hydrolysis or breakdown of acetylcholine secreted at such neural synapses. By virtue of this usual action of AChE at these sites there is termination of the nerve impulse at the synaptic junction or motor end-plate.

The organophosphate pesticides are of such a molecular size and configuration that they attach at the two active sites of the AChE molecule whereat acetylcholine ordinarily would be bound, activated and then cleaved by this esterase. This phosphorylated enzyme complex (i.e., the AChE-organophosphate combination) is quite abnormally stable. Furthermore, access to the active site on AChE where acetylcholine normally is cleaved, is blocked, leading to failure of acetylcholine breakdown. Therefore this mediator acetylcholine persists and continues to stimulate at postganglionic parasympathetic synapses and striated muscle motor end-plates. Protracted stimulation of the motor nerves of the gastrointestinal tract produces vomiting, diarrhea and abdominal cramps, while continued ciliary body stimulation causes contraction and resultant blurring of vision and miosis. Persistent parasympathetic stimulation leads to increased secretions by glandular cells, as manifested by salivation, lacrimation and diaphoresis. In addition parasympathetically induced bronchoconstriction causes airway obstruction and increased secretions in the tracheobronchial tree, so that expiratory wheezing and moist rales are heard. Persons thus affected complain of a tightness in the chest (bronchoconstriction?) and dyspnea. With progression of this intoxication resulting from enzyme inhibition, the fine muscle tremors or fasciculation caused by continuous motor end-plate stimulation are succeeded by gross convulsions, stemming from both central motor stimulation and continued peripheral nerve activity. Ultimately, malcoordinated respiratory muscle activity and central nervous system hyperactivity lead to impaired respiratory exchange with cyanosis, exhaustion, coma and death. That all of these result mainly from continued acetylcholine-mediated activity at these various receptor sites of the involved synapses is clearly demonstrated by administration of large doses of atropine. This compound produces a striking reversal of the signs of toxicity described above by blocking responsiveness to acetylcholine at receptor portions of the synaptic junction.

Competitive Inhibition

This mechanism applies to that situation wherein a toxic material competes with other metabolites or cofactors for the active site of an enzyme. Such competitive inhibition reaches a maximum when the competing material structurally is highly similar to the chemical configuration of the constituent (i.e., metabolite or cofactor) normally acted upon by the enzyme (see above).

An unusual but probably not unique example of pharmacologic competitive inhibition is seen in the behavior of two organophosphate pesticides which compete for a single specific enzymatic detoxification system. One of these, malathion, is approximately 30 times less toxic than another such pesticide, EPN. Yet when given in combination, the toxicity of malathion is remarkably enhanced. It appears that EPN more successfully competes for the same enzyme that ordinarily would rapidly hydrolize malathion. It is believed that malathion cannot be acted upon by this enzyme that would ordinarily render it metabolically inactive, i.e., reduce its toxicity. Accordingly, this unsuccessful competition of malathion for the degrading enzyme leads to its persistence and accumulation as a toxicologically active agent. Though other similar combinations of organic thiophosphates are known to produce similar enhancements of toxicity, similar situations not involving organic thiophosphates undoubtedly exist.

INDUCTION OF TOXICITY BY METABOLIC ALTERATION OF CHEMICALS

Though the word "detoxification" implies a mechanism that reduces toxic potentials inherent in a compound, it should be understood that these processes whereby the animal economy produces such metabolic transformations phylogenetically stem mainly from an ability to utilize food substances. Thus "detoxification" pathways that exist do so largely insofar as nonfood substances exhibiting structural similarities to food components may be acted upon. Indeed, these relatively nondiscriminating biological enzyme systems may produce the apparent paradox of enhanced toxicity following this peculiar metabolic transformation, i.e., "detoxification."

Oxidation

This is one of the most common mechanisms whereby metabolic transformations may be achieved. For example, toluene is oxidized to benzoic acid, biologically a relatively innocuous compound. However, such metabolic oxidations may form products of greatly enhanced toxicity, a conspicuous example being the product of methanol oxidation, formaldehyde. This oxidative product is of relatively high cytotoxic potential, causing irreversible alteration of protein. The specific effect of wood alcohol on the retina is explained in part on the basis that retinal cells—as well as hepatocytes—are believed to be specific loci whereat the enzyme alcohol dehydrogenase catalyzes the biological oxidation of alcohols.

Accordingly it has been suggested that intracellular oxidation by this enzyme produces within the retinal cells minute quantities of formaldehyde. However, despite the small quantities elaborated, such intracellular formation of formaldehyde is sufficient to produce cellular damage. The blindness that may follow methanol intoxication is an expression of the minimal capacity for regeneration of injured central nervous system tissue. Concurrently, hepatocytic death is readily succeeded by regenerative replacement of necrotized liver cells so that permanent liver damage does not ensue following such an insult. Other examples of enhanced toxicity following oxidative change are found following successive oxidation of the benzene molecule to di- and trihydroxybenzene. This successive transformation appears to lead to successively increasing acute toxicity. In yet another instance, the replacement of sulfur by oxygen leads to the oxidation of inert parathion to the highly toxic paraoxon with resultant severe physiologic embarrassment (see discussion of acetylcholine esterase inhibition).

Reduction

Though reduction represents a somewhat less frequent body metabolic activity than oxidation, several groups of foreign compounds are altered by this mechanism. Nitrobenzenes or certain organic compounds composed of an aromatic ring with an attached nitrogen (e.g., primaquine, sulfanilimide) ordinarily can be metabolized by reduction without serious consequences. The additional hydrogen atom to carry out this reduction is ordinarily supplied by reduced triphosphopyridine nucleotide (TPNH) which normally is in adequate supply in most tissues. The formation of TPNH is in certain cells, e.g., erythrocytes, probably dependent in the main upon the action of the enzyme glucose-6-phosphate dehydrogenase (G-6-PD).

An unusual example of failure of the reductive process stems from a genetically determined metabolic defect. This abnormality occurs in certain racial groups which genetically develop erythrocytes deficient in G-6-PD. As a consequence of deficiency there is a diminution of red cell TPNH. Because of the deficiency of TPNH, there is a concurrent diminution in the rate of glutathione reduction, the hydrogen ion donated by TPNH being required to carry out this reduction. Both of these compounds, TPNH and reduced glutathione, are in turn required to maintain hemoglobin and ferro-catalase in the reduced state.

This defect and the attendant deficiencies are not expressed under normal conditions in individuals carrying this genetic abnormality.

However, with the absorption of oxidizing chemicals there is a conversion of hemoglobin to the oxidized form, i.e., methemoglobin. To reduce this oxidized hemoglobin to the physiologically functional (i.e., reduced) form requires an increased supply of hydrogen atoms. Among persons having decreased G-6-PD and resultant diminished TPNH to act as a hydrogen ion donor, this peculiar enzyme deficiency leads to serious consequences. With impairment of erythrocytic ability to re-establish a reducing environment, the rate of reduction of this oxidized hemoglobin (i.e., methemoglobin) formed by nitrogen-containing aromatic chemicals is markedly decreased. This ultimately leads to a temporal persistence of methemoglobin in persons with this genetic defect in contrast to individuals possessing normal G-6-PD activity in the erythrocyte. Furthermore, reduced glutathione appears to be required for cellular integrity. Among such susceptibles, with both of these loads upon cellular homeostasis, absorption of these oxidizing compounds frequently results in massive hemolysis and/or prolonged methemoglobinemia. Thus what had previously been empirically described as "hypersensitivity" can be explained by hereditary factors determining the integrity of this metabolic pathway.

As previously noted in the discussion of oxidation reactions, a reductive type alteration resulting in a more toxic product is seen in the reduction of nitrobenzene to aminobenzene and coincident oxidation to para-aminophenol. This metabolic product is approximately 50 to 80 times more toxic than the parent material, nitrobenzene.

Conjugation

Conjugative metabolic alterations resulting in synthesis of new compounds occur commonly in the course of normal body activity. Such additions of normal tissue constituents, e.g., glucuronate or sulfate, to the molecule of a foreign material usually result in solubilization of the original exogenous molecule. While in most cases this results in a compound of lesser toxicity, continued utilization of the endogenous constituent involved in conjugative processes may lead to depletion of these vital substances. A depletion of cysteine, utilized in the conjugation of p-bromobenzene, is seen when this chemical is fed to growing animals in excess of certain quantities. These feedings lead to a cessation of growth, since the animal is unable to provide sufficient cysteine for both growth and conjugation of the excessive amounts of p-bromobenzene.

The fact that cysteine is utilized for detoxification of p-bromobenzene has been utilized in the treatment of selenium intoxication. In areas where selenium is present in soils, body burdens of this element become relatively high. The selenium ingested in vegetation and water in such locations displaces the sulfur of cysteine and methionine of body tissues with a resultant deficiency of these amino acids. Selenized individuals have been given p-bromobenzene in the hope of removing from their bodies some of the selenium-containing cysteine. In these cases conjugation of the selenium-containing cysteine with the p-bromobenzene occurred. This was confirmed by the observation that selenium blood levels dropped considerably and that urinary excretion of selenium as a mercapturic acid rose with this therapy.

Lethal Synthesis

In contrast to detoxification effected by conjugative synthesis, the metabolic transformation by the body of one chemical into a new compound can have untoward results. In addition to the oxidative, reductive and conjugative processes previously considered, a somewhat different type of synthesis by the body has been demonstrated following absorption of sodium fluoroacetate (1080). The metabolic transfer to citric acid of the fluorine atoms in this toxic compound leads to the biological synthesis of fluorocitrate. This citrate is an inhibitor of the enzyme aconitase, with the result that the normal product of this enzyme's activity, cis-aconitate, is not formed. This deficiency of cis-aconitate blocks the completion of the Krebs or citric acid cycle necessary for oxidative energy metabolism and cell respiration. Those cells requiring the highest rates of oxidation, i.e., myocardial and central nervous system cells, are the first to demonstrate this energy source depletion. Absorption of 1080 leads to severe cardiac irregularities of rhythm, failure and collapse, accompanied by a rapid onset of convulsions and finally coma. The result of this block of the Krebs cycle apparently cannot be effectively reversed, since the fluorocitrate aconitase complex formed cannot be degraded by any known enzyme system.

The possibility exists for entry into the Krebs cycle of other normally available metabolites, e.g., α-ketoglutarate, oxaloacetate, beyond the point of the fluorocitrate-induced block. However, the potential for such by-passes appears limited in view of the extreme toxicity of this compound 1080.

SOME BIOPHYSICAL DETERMINANTS OF CHEMICAL INTOXICATION

A mechanism of toxicity due to direct combination by an exogenous chemical with a body component is clearly illustrated by the remarkable affinity of carbon monoxide for hemoglobin. Carbon monoxide forms a moderately stable complex with the ferrous tetrapyrrole respiratory pigment hemoglobin. As a result of this association CO blocks the accessibility of reactive sites on the hemoglobin molecule ordinarily available for oxygen carriage. In such a competition between CO and O_2, the attraction of carbon monoxide for hemoglobin is approximately 210 times greater than that of oxygen.

From these considerations it follows that while this affinity of CO for hemoglobin is so much greater than that of oxygen, nevertheless this is a *relative* affinity for the hemoglobin molecule. Accordingly the partial pressures of these two gases act as determinants of the quantities of each gas taken up. Thus, given a fixed concentration of carbon monoxide in the ambient air (and concurrently in the alveolus), ultimately a point of equilibrium between CO in blood and alveolar air is reached. As this event approaches, the rate of hemoglobin conversion gradually decreases, since the "back pressure" of CO in the blood approaches the alveolar CO partial pressure. This increasing "back pressure" gradually decreases the pressure differential or gradient across the alveolar membrane, with the result that the rate of CO absorption slows, and the proportion of CO absorbed from the inspired mixture decreases steadily from its initial value of about 50 per cent. When equilibrium is reached, the net transfer of CO between blood and air and the rate of increase in carboxyhemoglobin become zero.

Achievement of this steady state can readily serve to illustrate the concept of dose dependency in a responsive biological system at the molecular and physiologic levels. If the concentrations of CO in air occur in the range of 50 parts per million (0.005 per cent), an equilibrium between blood and ambient air is eventually reached. This event occurs with conversion of approximately 8 per cent of the available hemoglobin. At such time, if the exposure concentration remains at 50 ppm, there is no longer an increase or decrease in the net amount of hemoglobin existing as the carboxyhemoglobin form.

Furthermore, this example of the conversion of hemoglobin by carbon monoxide can serve also to illustrate clearly the time parameter which is a major determinant of chemical intoxication. As previously stated, this conversion occurs at a rate dependent upon the alveolar partial pressure. At a concentration of approximately 50 ppm, approximately 9 hours must elapse for this concentration to come into equilibrium, i.e., the 8 per cent carboxyhemoglobin conversion level. By contrast, because of the CO arising from tobacco combustion, moderately heavy cigarette smokers are commonly found to have this concentration of carboxyhemoglobin. Yet Goldsmith and coworkers have shown that levels of 400 to 450 ppm (0.04 to 0.045 per cent) CO are attained in the inhaled cigarette smoke stream. In the face of such relatively higher CO exposure levels of cigarette smokers, one is led to inquire why smokers have a level of carboxyhemoglobin formation comparable to that of individuals exposed to 50 ppm. Plainly, what is occurring with cigarette-induced CO exposure is repeated *short-term* peak concentration exposures. The result is a high gradient of short duration across the alveolar membrane during the act of smoke inhalation. As smoking ceases this gradient is subsequently reversed because of a relatively high "back pressure" from the blood to the alveoli. Over several hours of intermittent smoking the net effect results in an equilibration at approximately 8 per cent hemoglobin conversion, despite the peak exposure levels. Thus the high peaks over a period of time average out to levels which only very indirectly reflect these high levels of CO found in the cigarette smoke stream.

However, these hemoglobin conversion rates are also dependent upon physiologic factors, a prime consideration being the pulmonary ventilation parameter. Thus, by increasing the volume of air moved per unit time, one readily sees that a greater quantity of CO can be presented to the gas exchange membrane per unit time. Consequently, rates of hemoglobin conversion can reflect a change in physical activity, since in going from the resting state to one of heavy work it has been found that the rate of conversion is increased by a factor of 366 per cent.

The fact that this alteration of an intrinsic property of hemoglobin, i.e., its ability to carry oxygen, does not produce a permanent structural change in the hemoglobin molecule points up another possible manner by which chemicals may interact with many biological molecules. This CO-hemoglobin molecular complex is an example of an interaction that produces only a functional modification of the hemoglobin molecule. Concurrently the underlying structural nature of the hemoglobin molecule remains relatively intact and can express its preintoxication functional characteristics given once more the proper conditions of oxygen tension.

There is yet another functional change in hemoglobin as a result of its combination with CO. Douglas and Haldane quite clearly stated that "oxygen is given off from oxyhemoglobin in a totally abnormal manner when the blood is highly saturated with carbon monoxide . . . the dissociation of oxygen being altered in such a way that the oxygen comes off less readily, or only at a lower pressure than in normal bloods." As a consequence of the reluctance to give up oxygen peculiar to this mixture of oxygenated and carbon monoxide-heme complexes on a single hemoglobin molecule, the release of oxygen from such erythrocytes to the tissue goes on much less *readily*. The rate of release of oxygen normally required by the tissues occurs in the presence of carboxyhemoglobin only when tissue oxygen pressure falls to very low tensions. That this shift in the oxyhemoglobin dissociation curve becomes significant only with relatively high carboxyhemoglobin levels (i.e., greater than 30 to 40 per cent conversion) is not clearly appreciated. Nevertheless, this shift in the oxygen dissociation curve can pose problems if a sudden increased tissue demand—as with exercise—is imposed upon this already fragilely balanced system of oxygen supply and demand at the tissues. A clinical example of this impediment to oxygen release is seen in those individuals who have suffered CO intoxication. On attempting to rise and walk about from the semiconscious state, they may take only a few steps before they once more collapse. Thus, while their tissue needs are met at rest, the increased tissue demand associated with work of motion cannot be met due to this

oxygen dissociation shift and lowered O_2 carrying capacity.

Depending on several circumstances, such combinations of chemicals and body constituents may have either a beneficial or deleterious effect. Most drugs form reversible complexes with plasma proteins and intracellular components. These nonspecific, loose chemical attachments may provide a reservoir from which the compound can be released in response to a decrease in the circulating, unbound form of the chemical in question. This dynamic equilibrium may ultimately serve to permit prolongation of drug action as a consequence of slow release from such binding stores. In the case of lead, the storage of this ion in the bony matrix may permit buildup in concentration of this potentially toxic agent in this depot without the manifestation of intoxication despite prolonged low level absorption. However, with stress situations, e.g., heat (?), mobilization of such stores leads to symptoms of acute intoxication, though the patient may no longer be in lead exposure. Such a dynamic equilibrium between the lead bound in the bony compartment and that in the vascular compartment has implications in regard to chelation therapy.

Chelation has been defined as the incorporation of a metal ion into a heterocyclic ring structure. The metal is bound by two or more ions of the complexing molecule, the latter being referred to as a ligand. Certain atoms in the ligand "donate" electrons to the metal atoms and thus "share" electron pairs with the metal ions. By reason of this electron "sharing," the metal ion is sequestered within the "ionic cage" of the donor molecule, inhibiting expression of the toxic nature of many metal ions.

At present, available chelating agents, e.g., Versene, or calcium disodium ethylenediaminetetracetic acid (EDTA), are capable of chelating only circulating lead and other ions. While the acute symptoms due to unsequestered lead are rapidly abated by chelation, therapy directed toward removal of body burdens of lead outside the vascular compartment is ineffectual. Thus, if the patient is given a rest period of about 1 week, an equilibrium between lead bound in bone and circulating lead will be re-established. At this time another 3 to 5 days of EDTA therapy leads to chelation of the circulating lead with diminution of this compartment's loading. By such an alternating, stepwise program the clinician may achieve diminution of the total body burden of lead.

The Structural and Functional Consequences of Chemical Toxicity

THE RELATIONSHIP OF ULTRASTRUCTURE TO CELL FUNCTION

The cell membrane may be considered as constituting the interface of the cell with the external environment. This applies even to innermost cells of the body, since the extracellular fluid medium serving as a transport medium produces relatively little change in chemicals of extracorporeal origin. Most frequently exogenous materials carried in the extracellular compartment are only moderately and/or reversibly altered, e.g., the loosely bound complexes of drugs and plasma protein.

The cell membrane takes the form of a double-layered structure. Each of the two layers is 35 to 40 angstroms thick and consists of a lipoprotein complex. Various modifications of these layers occur in specific cell types, e.g., microvilli in secretive and absorptive cells, or invaginations of various other plasma membranes. Transport across physically unaltered membranes is achieved as the result of active, energy-dependent and probably enzymatically controlled activity. The process of phagocytosis or pinocytosis, whereby materials are transported across the membrane, produces a physical modification of these membranes. Phagocytosis causes incorporation of particulate material, while the pinocytosis incorporates extracellular fluid. These processes are probably a common method whereby most cells take up water and solutes.

Though the enzymatic processes controlling and mediating these activities are as yet not clear, it appears that this complex activity can be readily disturbed by chemical agents. Additionally it is obvious that alteration of structural integrity may also produce changes in cell wall function. In the case of mercuric or cupric chloride, changes in potassium and phosphate concentrations within the cell probably stem from the alteration of the membrane's normal cross-linking of sulfhydryl groups. The effects of lipid solvent, e.g., CCl_4, may also stem from a disturbance of the physical stability of the cell membrane's lipid components.

The endoplasmic reticula or ergastoplasm, membranous channels which dip down into and course through the cell matrix, are considered by some to be an invagination of the cell membrane. Both morphologically and functionally these are differentiated into two specific types. One of these is associated with electron-dense particles that lie on what might be considered the intracellular side of these membranous channels. These particles, the polyribosomes, are one of the sites of intracellular protein synthesis. Here messenger RNA from the nucleus meets the activated amino acids carried by transfer RNA. Linkage of these amino acid moieties into the proper sequence, as directed by the sequence code carried by messenger RNA, leads to the synthesis of a specific protein. If this concept is real, that the interior of the endoplasmic reticular channel does represent an intruding continuum of the cell membrane, and this communicates with the external cell environment, synthesis of protein occurring at this locus on the endoplasmic reticulum would provide for ready egress of such newly formed protein from the interior milieu of the cell.

Another portion of these membranes has no associated granules. These smooth membranes appear to be the site of numerous processes. The enzyme glucose-6-phosphatase (G-6-Pase) is located on these smooth membranes. The spatial association of the enzyme with this membrane appears to be prerequisite for its catalytic function. For the transport of glucose out of liver cells for use in other organs of the body, dephosphorylation of glucose-6-phosphate by this enzyme is required before secretion from the cell can occur. Once more, the location of G-6 Pase at the endoplasmic reticulum may afford a convenient site for communication with the external environment. In addition several enzymatically controlled detoxification processes such as oxidation of hexobarbital, dealkylation of codeine and aminopyrine and hydroxylation of acetanilid are localized in these smooth membranes. Undoubtedly many more chemical agents will be found to be structurally altered or transformed in this portion of the cell. Also inherent in such structural association is the implication that any chemical agent affecting this locus may cause unexpected drug responses. Exposure to chlordane or DDT appears to stimulate the detoxifying enzyme activities associated with these structures. Accordingly, drugs given to animals pretreated with these pesticides have been shown to be metabolized at an accelerated rate for some months after this pretreatment.

Equally as important might be the inhibition of metabolic transformation activity in this structure. The result of such enzyme inhibition on the detoxification process has been previously considered.

Other functions have been ascribed to this reticulum. It has been suggested by Siekevitz that control of cell permeability also resides in part in this structure. If indeed the reticulum is an extension of the plasma membrane into the cell, control of movement to and from the cell at this interface would not be unreasonable.

The mitochondria are another of the cytoplasmic organelles affording a structural matrix upon which are placed vital biochemical functions. These structures within the cytoplasm are variegated in shape and size in life. They consist of a dual membrane, the inner membrane being involuted into "shelves" or cristae. On these shelves are seen "elementary particles," approximately 80 to 100 angstroms in diameter. These particles apparently are the site of the respiratory (or electron-transport chain) and phosphorylating enzymes. The semifluid matrix within the mitochondria carries the Krebs (citric acid) cycle enzymes. Thus within this organelle is found an important part of the process mediating oxidation of foodstuffs and yielding electrons, which are in turn transferred to the respiratory enzyme chain. It is at this elementary particle in the mitochondria that the cyanide ion complexes with the iron-containing cytochrome enzymes of the electron-transfer chain, leading in turn to cessation of cellular respiration.

There also occurs within the mitochondria the transfer of electrons that provide the energy to be stored in ATP. The process whereby energy is stored as high energy chemical bonds for later release is referred to as oxidative phosphorylation. This process is susceptible to an interference that may be exerted by several chemicals, such as dinitrophenol and dinitro-ortho-cresol. Absorption of these chemicals results in failure of ATP formation. Under these conditions oxidative processes continue to operate in the absence of ATP formation. As a result heat, rather than energy-rich phosphate bonds, is produced. The clinical picture of acute hyperthermia and a rapid increase of 20 to 30 per cent in metabolic rate reflects an ill-fated attempt to replace ATP stores. There is a marked tachycardia, perspiration and eventual collapse. Though this picture simulates hyperthyroid crisis, there is no elevation in cardiac output and no alleviation of the symptoms of myxedema, and in contrast to such crises there is depression of levels of circulating protein-bound iodine and decreased I^{131} uptake.

CELL TOXICITY—A CHEMICOPHYSIOLOGIC SYNTHESIS

The effects at the cell level of a typical hepatotoxin, carbon tetrachloride, and the physiologic consequences of its cellular effect serve as a possible prototype of integrated response to toxic agents occurring at multiple levels. It appears that a major change in permeability occurs, possibly due to this compound's lipid solvent effect at the cell membrane and at the endoplasmic reticulum. While the intimate mechanisms of this alteration in permeability are not clear, the consequences are rather well defined. One of the earliest changes consists of increases in intracellular calcium, water and sodium and a loss of potassium. Each of these shifts represents an impairment of the processes responsible for normal permeability maintenance. The increase in calcium and decrease in potassium potentially lead to diminution of oxidative phosphorylation. (However, this is not actually seen till later in the course of this process.) The increase in intracellular sodium and water in turn produces the microscopic picture of a swollen hydropic cell.

As another consequence of damage to the endoplasmic reticulum, there is a decrease in glucose-6-phosphatase (G-6-Pase) activity concurrent to or following apace with a rapid diminution in hepatic glycogen. It should be recalled that before glucose can be secreted from a hepatocyte, the enzyme G-6-Pase must dephosphorylate (remove phosphate) from glucose-6-phosphate. Accordingly, damage to the endoplasmic reticulum and its associated enzyme G-6-Pase probably leads to failure of glucose secretion by the liver, with a concurrent drop in blood glucose noted. At the same time there is evidence of a stress response characterized by increased adrenal cortical and medullary activity. The adrenal medullary release of such catecholamines as norepinephrine and epinephrine may represent a response of failure of hepatic glucose secretion and the resultant hypoglycemia. At the same time, the adrenal cortical response may represent another attempt to correct the diminished oxidizable circulating substrate, i.e., glucose. The glucosteroids, by activating and/or leading to synthesis of the transaminases (pyruvic, oxaloacetic) bring about conversion of the amino acids alanine and aspartic acid (aspartate) to pyruvate and oxaloacetate respectively. Thus products resulting from these transformations can be utilized in the Krebs cycle. The end result is conversion of protein (i.e., gluconeogenesis). Thus a noncarbohydrate source can provide an oxidizable substrate.

Unfortunately the secretion of epinephrine and related neurohumors secreted in response to CCl_4 absorption may cause other untoward effects. Brody has suggested that stimulation of the nerves to the hepatic blood vessels produces restriction of blood supply to the liver, hypoxia and central lobular necrosis. In addition the catecholamines appear to mobilize nonesterified fatty acids from depots. These lipid precursors presented in large quantities to a damaged liver play an important role in the etiology of "fatty" liver associated with this type of intoxication.

Hypoxia in turn leads to a shift toward utilization of anaerobic pathways. This in turn produces a decrease in pH, due to an accumulation of lactate and because the process of glycolysis produces phosphate by-products. The change in cell pH plays a role in the breakdown of lysosomes which release their proteolytic enzymes; in addition, lowering of pH activates these catalysts. These proteolytic enzymes cause a breakdown of cell structure protein, which leads in turn to accumulation of osmotically active molecules. Despite a leaky membrane this damaged cell continues the swelling which previously had been precipitated by calcium and sodium uptake noted above.

Concurrently, other energy-dependent processes begin to fail. Protein synthesis slows and then is practically halted. While many enzyme systems continue to operate—especially those in the mitochondria until relatively late in the course of cell damage—there begins a fragmentation of the coordinated multilinked activity characteristic of the normal organized, metabolic system. With a failure of this coordination, structure begins to fragment and nuclear breakdown is seen. This results in the spill of nucleoprotein into the extracellular spaces among other cellular debris. Before this stage, examination of the cell demonstrates persistence of nuclear outlines. Nevertheless this unit has become an inert, foreign object which then becomes the subject of phagocytosis or "heterolysis."

Though this sequence of morphologic breakdown may take 8 to 12 hours, in the course of the alterations herein described the cell actually has reached a point of no return at about the second or third hour. It is noteworthy that while structurally the hepatocyte might have appeared intact or at worst reversibly altered (e.g., hydropic and/or granular alteration), functionally this unit of life has advanced far down the road toward cell death.

The net result of these changes is an area of necrosis within the liver. If this area is small, detection of this damage may be demonstrable only by an increased serum enzyme activity, a change in alpha globulin synthesis or a qualitative change in albumin. These latter two changes, which reflect a defect in protein synthesis, are expressed by a positive cephalin-cholesterol flocculation test. This abnormality probably results from damage to the rough-surfaced endoplasmic reticulum where protein synthesis occurred (see above). Such structural alteration as seen by electron microscopy correlates quite clearly with early failure in protein synthesis by the liver resulting from CCl_4 poisoning.

If, however, the quantitative volume of cell damage is larger, breakdown of the parenchymal cells leads to decreased synthesis of osmotically active molecules with a resultant edema. In addition, defects in coagulation due to the failure of synthesis of prothrombin and other clotting factors may lead to intravascular thrombosis. With cell breakdown, physical obstruction to biliary egress via the bile radicles produces clinical jaundice.

It should be pointed out that the effect of CCl_4 in acute intoxication is not limited to hepatic alteration. Indeed, in acute cases in the absence of lethal central nervous system depression, the cause of death is usually renal failure. While the sequence of changes described here has been more clearly elaborated for the hepatocyte, future investigations will undoubtedly cast more light upon renal alteration that frequently leads to demise in acute CCl_4 poisoning.

REFERENCES

Belknap, E. L., and Belknap, E. L., Jr.: Clinical control of health in the storage battery industry. Indust. Med. & Surg., 28:94, 1959.

Beutler, E.: The hemolytic effect of primaquine and related compounds: A review. Blood, 24:103, 1959.

Boyer, P. D.: Mechanisms of enzyme action. Ann. Rev. Biochem., 29:15, 1960.

Brodie, B. B., Cosmides, G. J., and Rael, D. P.: Toxicology and the biomedical sciences. Science, 148:1547, 1965.

Brody, T. M., Calvert, D. N., and Schneider, A. F.: Alterations of carbon tetrachloride-induced pathologic changes in the rat by spinal transection, adrenalectomy and adrenergic blocking agents. J. Pharmacol. & Exper. Therap., 131:341, 1961.

Cell Regulatory Mechanisms. Cold Spring Harbor Symposia on Quantitative Biology, Volume XXVI. Cold Spring Harbor, N.Y., Long Island Biologic Association, 1961.

Chenoweth, M. B.: Monofluoroacetic acid and related compounds. Pharmacol. Rev., 1:383, 1949.

Dinman, B. D.: Arsenic: Chronic human intoxication. J. Occup. Med., 2:137, 1960.

Dinman, B. D., and Ashe, W. F.: Arsenic intoxication. In Harvey, J. C. (ed.): Tice's Practice of Medicine. Hagerstown, Md., W. F. Prior Co., 1962.

Douglas, C. G., and Haldane, J. B. S.: The laws of combination of hemaglobin with carbon monoxide and oxygen. J. Physiol., 44:275, 1912.

Durham, W. F., and Hayes, W. J., Jr.: Organic phosphorus poisoning and its therapy; with special reference to modes of action and compounds that reactivate inhibited cholinesterase. Arch. Environ. Health, 5:21, 1962.

Fernández-Morán, H.: Cell-membrane ultrastructure. Low-temperature microscopy and x-ray diffraction studies of lipoprotein components in lamellar systems. Circulation, 26:1039 (supplement, part II), 1962.

Fouts, J. R.: Interaction of drugs and hepatic microsomes. Fed. Proc., 21:1107, 1962.

Fox, C. F.; Dinman, B. D., and Frajola, W. J.: CCl₄ poisoning: II. Serum enzymes, free fatty acids and liver pathology; effects of phenoxybenzamine and Phenergan. Proc. Soc. Exper. Biol. Med., 111:721, 1962.

Goldsmith, J. R., Terzaghi, J., and Hackney, J. D.: Evaluation of fluctuating carbon monoxide exposure. Arch. Environ. Health, 7:647, 1963.

Henderson, Y., and Haggard, H. W.: Noxious Gases and the Principles of Respiration Influencing Their Action, 2nd ed. New York, Reinhold Publishing Corp., 1943.

Hutchinson, G. E.: The influence of the environment. Proc. Nat. Acad. Sc., 51:930, 1964.

Kalow, W.: Pharmacogenetics: Heredity and the Response to Drugs. Philadelphia, W. B. Saunders Co., 1962.

Kehoe, R. A.: The metabolism of lead in man in health and disease. The Harben Lectures, 1960. J. Roy. Inst. Pub. Health & Hyg., 24:81, 1961.

Lanza, A. J. (ed.): The Pneumoconioses. New York, Grune and Stratton, 1963.

Lilienthal, J. L., Jr.: Carbon monoxide. J. Pharmacol. & Exper. Therap., 99:324, 1950.

Majno, G.: Death of liver tissue. Chapter XX in Rouiller, C. (ed.): The Liver, Vol. II. New York, Academic Press, 1964.

Malkinson, F. D.: Permeability of the stratum corneum. In Montagna, W., and Lobitz, W. C. (eds.): The Epidermis. New York, Academic Press, 1964, p. 435.

Murphy, S. D., and Dubois, K. P.: Quantitative measurement of inhibition of the enzymatic detoxification of malathione by EPN. Proc. Soc. Exper. Biol. Med., 96:813, 1957.

Passow, H., and Rothstein, A.: The binding of mercury by the yeast cell in relation to changes in permeability. J. Gen. Physiol., 43:621, 1960.

Patty, F. A. (ed.): Industrial Hygiene and Toxicology, 2nd ed. Vol. II. New York, Interscience Publishers, 1963.

Peters, R. A.: The study of enzymes in relation to selective toxicity in animal tissues. Sympos. Soc. Exper. Biol., 3:36, 1949.

Ponder, E.: The cell membrane and its properties. In Brachet, J., and Mirsky, A. E. (eds.): The Cell, Vol. II, pp. 1–84. New York, Academic Press, 1961.

Reynolds, E. S.: Liver parenchymal injury. J. Cell. Biol., 19:139, 1963.

Rouiller, C.: Experimental toxic injury of the liver. Chapter 22 in Rouiller, C. (ed.): The Liver, Vol. II. New York, Academic Press, 1964.

Rosen, F., Roberts, N. R., and Nichol, C. A.: Glucocorticosteroids and transaminase activity. J. Biol. Chem., 234:476, 1959.

Schotz, M. C., and Recknagel, R. O.: Rapid increase of rat liver triglycerides following CCl₄ poisoning. Biochim. Biophys. Acta, 41:151, 1960.

Siekevitz, P.: On the meaning of intracellular structure for metabolic regulation. In Wolstenholme, G. E. W., and O'Connor, C. M. (eds.): Ciba Foundation Symposium on The Regulation of Cell Metabolism. Boston, Little, Brown and Co., 1959.

Stokinger, H. E.: Means of contact and entry of toxic agents. In Occupational Diseases, A Guide To Their Recognition. U. S. Public Health Service Publication 1097. Washington, D. C., U. S. Government Printing Office, 1964.

Thiers, R. E., Reynolds, E. S., and Vallee, B. L.: The effect of carbon tetrachloride poisoning on subcellular metal distribution in rat liver. J. Biol. Chem., 253:2130, 1960.

Umbarger, H. E.: Endproduct inhibition of the initial enzyme in a biosynthetic sequence as a mechanism of feedback control. In Bonner, D. M. (ed.): Control Mechanisms in Cellular Processes. New York, Ronald Press, 1961, pp. 67–85.

Williams, R. J. P.: Nature and properties of metal ions of biological interest and their coordination compounds. Fed. Proc., 20:5 (supplement 10, part II), 1961.

Williams, T. R.: Detoxification Mechanisms. The Metabolism and Detoxification of Drugs, Toxic Substances and Other Organic Compounds, 2nd ed. London, Chapman and Hall, 1959.

Yielding, K. L., and Tomkins, G. M.: Structural alteration in crystalline glutamic dehydrogenase induced by steroid hormones. Proc. Nat. Acad. Sc., 46:1483, 1960.

Circulatory System

Chapter Sixteen

Hemodynamics: The Blood Vessels

WILLIAM A. SODEMAN

General Hemodynamics

The blood vessels together with the heart form a closed system, the vascular system, in which the blood circulates, propelled by the heart. This system varies in anatomic structure to fit its function and location in the circulation, the differences being important in normal physiology as well as in pathologic physiology. The vessels conducting blood away from the heart, the arteries, have thick walls which, in the largest vessels—the aorta in the greater circuit and the pulmonary artery in the lesser circuit—consist largely of elastic fibers with little muscular tissue. In the medium-sized arteries the elastic tissue becomes less prominent and the muscular tissue increases, and this change continues into the smaller arteries, in which the muscular structures greatly predominate. As these vessels continue to divide, the walls of the smallest vessels still having a medial coat, the arterioles, with an outside diameter of approximately 0.2 mm., consist almost entirely of smooth muscle. These vessels in turn divide into smaller vessels, the capillaries, which are about 5 to 20 microns in diameter and 0.4 to 0.7 mm. long and entirely devoid of a coating, the bare endothelial lining remaining with only isolated cells, the Rouget cells, covering them. The capillaries gradually come together forming small veins or venules which eventually form larger venous channels and carry the blood back to the heart. These vessels, with a much smaller internal pressure, have much thinner walls.

The ejection of blood into the great vessels creates variations in pressure and velocity of blood flow which are complex and difficult to analyze. Knowledge in the science of flow of fluids in tubes—that is, rheology—has increased greatly in recent years, so that there is now some understanding of these changes in the circulation. Exactly what happens when blood is ejected from the heart into the great vessels will depend upon the nature of these vessels and the amount of blood in the system, as well as upon the resistance to outflow. If the great vessels were perfectly rigid tubes, such as water pipes, the introduction of a new volume of noncompressible fluid would produce a pressure wave front, traveling through the fluid at the rate of almost 1 mile per second. As the inertia of the fluid in the vessel was overcome, there would be an increased flow of blood until an amount of blood was ejected from the vessels equal to the amount forced in. The pressure would then return rapidly to its original level, presumably zero, until a new injection of fluid into the vessel occurred.

The Effects of Elasticity

In elastic vessels different circumstances prevail. If the amount of blood in the vessel is sufficient to distend it, as is usual in the circulation, the distended walls of the elastic vessel exert a pressure on the contained fluid.

277

If additional fluid is forced into the vessel, as happens in cardiac systole, the blood could either be forced out of the vessel, or, if the resistance to its forward passage were greater than the pressure required to distend the vessel, the latter would be further distended. This happens in the normal circulation. The elasticity of the walls permits the aorta to store nearly half the blood of each systole, to be moved onward during diastole by the elastic recoil. This gives a smoother outflow through the arterioles. The vessel, because of its elasticity, tends to resist this distention, and energy is stored in the elastic vessel wall. At the end of the ejection of blood into the vessel, the pressure is highest, and the distended vessel acts through its elasticity to force blood forward, an action which continues until the volume of blood is reduced to an amount which distends the vessel to a pressure equalling the energy needed for outflow. In the circulation a new ejection of blood appears before this level is reached, and a pulsatile flow with a maximum (systolic) and minimum (diastolic) pressure is maintained. Thus, with each heart beat, potential energy is stored in the vessel walls and is released again as kinetic energy during diastole.

Arteriosclerosis

The ejected blood enters the large, elastic arteries, which act as a compression chamber to buffer the more peripheral arteries from too sudden an increase in pressure and flow. In systole only a portion of the blood is moved along and a portion is stored by expansion of the vessels to allow a "run off" into the capillaries during diastole. The more peripheral muscular arteries function otherwise to contract and reduce their lumen to adapt to varying volumes of circulating blood (carotids, brachial, radial, femoral). Changes in the vessel walls affect not only the diameter of the vessels, but also hemodynamic factors based upon the characteristics of the blood vessel wall. Thus, with reduction in the elasticity of the vessels, other things being constant, a higher pressure is found at the height of injection and a lower pressure in the interval. In man increased size of the aorta may partially compensate for such changes. Comparable change may occur in pressure relations if the vessel is distended beyond its usual limits, as in thyrotoxicosis, for the vessel is then more rigid. Aortic arteriosclerosis is one of the most common of all conditions affecting arterial elasticity. Thus in overdis-

tention of the aorta or in disease reducing the elasticity of the aortic wall, systolic pressures may be elevated with normal or low diastolic pressures, resulting in so-called "systolic hypertension."

The term "arteriosclerosis" is applied to a group of diseases characterized by loss of elasticity of arteries as a result of structural changes in the medial and intimal layers. Medial change is common in the peripheral arteries with the aging process and produces tortuosity and stiffening of the vessel wall. This process goes on to some degree in other arteries as well. This is the well known *Mönckeberg type* of arteriosclerosis. *Atherosclerosis,* an entirely different process, also takes place in the intima of certain arteries. Thickening of the intima, with localized deposits of lipid, may occur at points of trauma, such as the orifices of the intercostal arteries, in the lower aorta where pressure relations are higher, and in the epicardial portions of the coronary arteries, for example. The lipid deposits, on coalescing, and with cholesterol deposits, make up atheromatous plaques associated with reactive fibroblastic changes. This process impinges upon the lumen and impairs blood flow. Slowing of the circulation in the areas predisposes to thrombosis. The vascularity of the lesions in the involved areas subjects them to hemorrhagic change, and rupture of vasa vasorum may lead to sudden closure. Although this process occurs with aging, diastolic hypertension, diabetes, gout and conditions associated with disturbed fat metabolism are all factors which play a part in its production. Dietary factors, especially increased dietary fat, appear important.

Theories on the cause of atherosclerosis vary greatly. Virchow believed that the mechanical trauma of pulsations was responsible. Localization in the lower extremities and in the lower portion of the aorta favors this concept at least as a contributing factor. Atherosclerotic change in the pulmonary vessels in the hypertension of mitral stenosis also shows the importance of trauma. The acceleration of atherosclerosis by diastolic hypertension is well known and also indicates the importance of mechanical strain. However, in some parts of the world, for example, West Africa, hypertension is common and clinical atherosclerosis is not, suggesting that some other factor, currently thought by many to be an atherogenic diet, may be important in conditioning the vessels for the action of mechanical trauma. However, the general place of this factor or its primary importance is in doubt. If such a strain is a prime factor in the process, lipid changes would be secondary. Some believe, with little experimental support, that changes in intercellular ground substance are primary. In either instance, disturbed fat metabolism would not be the initiating factor. In groups of patients with atherosclerotic changes at clinical level, cholesterol determinations tend to be high on the average, and abnormal fractions of lipoprotein appear in the blood of a large number but not all of those afflicted. The frequency of diseases due to atherosclerosis (coronary occlusion, for example) seems to correlate with high fat intake in the diet in studies carried out throughout the world. Saturated fatty acids appear to be atherogenic, the unsaturated group generally not. Further evidence connects atheromas with diseases characterized by hypercholesterolemia and hyperlipemia, e.g., hypothyroidism, diabetes mellitus and nephrosis. These data, together with animal studies on the feeding of fat and cholesterol with the production of atheromatous changes, establish the importance of lipid metabolism in the process. Whether, in patients with no obvious lipid disturbances, local changes in the vessels predisposed to the laying down of lipid and the production of atheromas or whether unknown disturbances in lipid metabolism predispose to such a process is not known. Likewise, the exact mechanisms at work in the process are not clear. However, at present, measures are applied to correct such disturbances through dietary control, such as early adequate control of diabetes, and by other means. Some believe carbohydrate-fat relationships in the diet are important. Blood lipids have been increased in males on carbohydrate enriched diets (Chap. 5).

Familial studies suggest that genetic factors are at work. Differences in occurrence of overt disease in male and female are not adequately explained on mechanistic grounds. That an interrelationship of genetic factors, sexual influences, mechanical trauma, and disturbed fat metabolism occurs in the process seems evident. However, the real place of each of these factors, either in cause or in a mechanism of development, is not clear.

Atheromatosis may result in two changes responsible for inadequacy of the arteries: rupture of the vessel and obstruction. Both these changes produce serious results and, if they occur in a vital organ (heart, brain), may lead to death. General narrowing of vessels from arteriosclerosis must be greatly advanced to reduce blood supplies to a point at which symptoms appear, unless an accident of the type mentioned occurs. The gradually developing symptoms along with manifestations of peripheral vessel occlusion are discussed later in this chapter.

Changes in Velocity and Pressure

If the amount of blood ejected into a normal vessel were increased and the vessel more distended than usual, or if the diastolic pressure were elevated and distended the vessel further, the wall would tend to reach its elastic limits and become a rigid tube. Under this circumstance, too, the pulse pressure would be greater, as happens in diastolic hypertension and in increased cardiac output with exercise or hyperthyroidism.

When fluid flows through a tube of constant diameter with a constant pressure head, the velocity remains constant, but there is a drop in lateral pressure as flow progresses along the tube. This is due to loss of energy by friction, the energy being dissipated as heat. If flow is increased by the use of a constant pressure head and diminished resistance to outflow (open valve or stopcock, for example), the velocity becomes greater. Since the energy in the stream is a combination of potential and kinetic energy and since an increase in one effects a diminution in the other, increases in flow would diminish the lateral pressure. In short, the greater the velocity of flow, the lower the lateral pressure (and vice versa). The energy of pressure is converted to the energy of flow. With increased velocity, also, friction on the walls is greater. (Frictional resistance is proportional to the velocity squared.) Both these factors reduce the lateral pressure and diminish it more rapidly as flow progresses along the tube. The pressure gradient then becomes more marked.

This is true in the circulation. In the larger arteries, where the pressure is generally high, frictional loss is not great. It increases greatly in the arterioles, however. In general, the fall in pressure from the aorta to the small arteries is in the range of approximately 20 mm. of mercury, whereas in the arterioles the drop is as much as 50 to 60 mm. of mercury. This is not due directly to a larger capacity of these vessels. It is true that the arterioles consist of a great number of small vessels resulting from the division of the larger arteries into smaller channels, but calculations have shown that the actual cross-sectional area of the arterioles increases above that of the arteries only moderately. This factor, therefore, should not affect velocity and volume flow in these vessels greatly, for, in artificial systems with a constant pressure, the velocity of flow is proportional to the cross-sectional area, and the volume flow, the actual amount of fluid passing through the tube, is proportional to the fourth power of the diameter (Poiseuille's law). However, frictional resistance is greatly increased, for, although it is proportional to the velocity squared, it is also proportional to the surface area, and the surface area, of course, is remarkably increased. The great drop in pressure occurs, therefore, where the frictional resistance is greatly increased, that is, in the arterioles. These vessels also change their caliber, varying the cross-sectional area, and resistance is greater if cross-sectional area is reduced, thus permitting the passage of more or less blood from the arteriole into the capillary. The variation in the outflow of blood from the arteriole has a great influence upon the pressure in the artery and a reverse tendency in the capillaries and veins. Arteriolar control of arterial pressure is, therefore, of major importance. This will be discussed further under *Hypertension*.

It is difficult to explain on physical grounds the energy relationships in the arteries, because of their branching, their variation in size, their elasticity and the pulsatile flow. The total energy imparted to the blood by the heart and present at a given place in the arterial system may be broken down into several components. There will have been a certain energy loss from that originally present due to friction in the tubes, as already stated. The remaining energy will consist of two components: an energy of flow, or kinetic energy, and a potential energy, which will be represented by the lateral pressure, or the pressure upon the walls of the vessel. The greater the velocity of the blood, the less will be the lateral pressure, for the energy of flow and the lateral pressure will equal a constant, and an increase in one is represented by a reduction in the other. Changes in one area or organ may produce a shift of blood to other areas. For example, dilatation of skin vessels to dissipate heat in hot weather may be accompanied by reduced circulation to the kidney and other internal structures. Such changes affect flow, volume of flow, and pressure relations in both regions. Likewise, if there is a localized dilatation in the tube and the energy supplied to that area remains

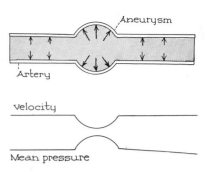

Figure 16–1. Diagram showing change in lateral pressure (indicated by arrows), velocity and mean pressure in an artery with aneurysmal dilatation.

constant, then in the locally dilated area the velocity will be diminished and the pressure upon the walls will be increased (Fig. 16–1). Thus it can be seen that when a portion of a vessel becomes abnormally dilated, as in aneurysm or in varicosities of the vein, the pressure upon the walls in this area is increased, tending to dilate the walls further. Such aneurysms or varicosities, therefore, tend to become greater and greater because of the increased lateral pressure. If the localized dilatation in the blood vessel is primarily the result of disease which has reduced the elasticity of, and weakened, the walls of the aorta, such as the change in the media in syphilis, the process of increased dilatation may then advance more rapidly because of this added factor.

In a similar fashion, if there is constriction of the vessel so that its cross-sectional area is reduced, the velocity in that area is increased and, along with it, the kinetic energy, while the potential energy is reduced. With constriction of the vessel, therefore, the pressure upon the walls is diminished, and, depending upon the characteristics of the tube, the rate of flow, the pressure and the characteristics of the fluid, eddy currents may develop. Also if the velocity is increased for other reasons and exceeds a critical value, the differences between the axial and peripheral streams produce new components resultant in eddy currents causing vibrations which may be heard or felt. Compression of an artery against a firm structure, such as a bone, with the chest piece of the stethoscope may constrict the vessel and increase the velocity so that audible vibrations occur, and the turbulence will be heard as a murmur. In coarctation of the aorta the constriction may be such that this type of murmur may be heard when the stethoscope is placed between the scapulas posteriorly on the chest. With dilatation of the vessel and development of eddy currents in aneurysms, such murmurs may be heard and, if they are sufficiently great, may be felt as thrills.

If, for any reason, the viscosity of the blood is diminished and the circulation is speeded up, even though the blood vessels remain intact, turbulence may reach the point at which sounds develop. This happens in anemias. Likewise in conditions in which the blood flow is unusually increased the same set of circumstances may develop. Murmurs may be heard over the heart or over some of the great vessels when exercise increases blood velocity or when hyperthyroidism or emotional excitement has the same effect. When there is no organic disease in the heart to account for the murmur and it arises from changes in blood viscosity or velocity, such murmurs are usually termed functional. A better term is physiologic. However, when some local anatomic disturbance accounts for the change, with constriction or dilatation of the area to produce eddy currents, the murmurs are commonly called organic.

The technique commonly used clinically to determine blood pressure is based upon the hearing of the eddy currents of the turbulent flow produced by the constriction of the vessel with the blood pressure cuff. (See discussion of blood pressure.)

ARTERIAL PULSE

Whereas the pulse wave front in a perfectly rigid tube moves rapidly—at the rate of almost 1 mile per second, as stated previously—in elastic tubes, such as the blood vessel, the transmission of the pulsatile phenomenon is slow, and, since the tubes are not perfectly elastic, the pulse wave is gradually dampened as it progresses along the vessel. With the great reduction in pressure in the arteriole the dampening effect upon the pulse is great and little pulsation may be seen in the capillaries. If the arterioles dilate, as they do in hot weather and after exercise, the pulsations reaching the capillaries are greater and may even visibly extend into the venules. Likewise, in diseases in which the pulse pressure is greatly increased—for example, in aortic regurgitation, hyperthyroidism or arteriosclerotic disease—pulsations reaching the capillaries are increased and may be detected when pressure is properly made upon the fingernail or upon the skin or mucous membrane. At the edge of the blanched area produced by the pressure of a glass slide, careful inspection will show the slight movement of the blanched margin with each pulsation in the blood-filled capillaries at this margin. If the part is brought slightly below heart level, the phenomenon will show up better. Pulsations may also be seen in the reddened area produced by brisk rubbing of the skin over the forehead. In general, however, in the capillaries the blood flow tends to lose its pulsatile character and become a steady flow.

The pulsation following the ejection of blood from the left ventricle is transmitted throughout the arteries and is felt as the pulse wave. The more rigid the artery becomes, the more rapidly the pulse wave progresses. Normally, this velocity is between 5 and 9 meters per second. It is slower in the aorta and increases as the peripheral arteries are reached. The time interval required for the pulsation to reach a peripheral artery, such as the radial, may be great enough to equal the time intervals of some of the events in the cardiac cycle, so that if, on auscultation of the heart, attempts are made to time cardiac events by utilizing the radial pulse as the onset of systole, confusion and mistiming may result. Either the apical beat or the carotid pulse should be used for timing such events in the heart. The blood flow is not synchronous with the pulse wave, the latter traveling more rapidly. Still, flow is affected by the waves, not unlike the phenomenon that occurs when a stone is dropped in a moving stream.

Means of Recording and Studying the Pulse

A graphic representation of the pulsation may be made (Fig. 16–2) by use of a small glass funnel placed over the artery and connected through an air system to a rubber diaphragm to which is attached a mirror. The compression of the air within the system by

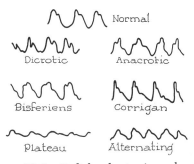

Figure 16–2. Radial pulse tracings, showing the various types of arterial pulse.

the pulsations of the artery moves the rubber diaphragm and the mirror, which reflects a light beam to a recording instrument. Such an instrument, termed a sphygmograph, may also record pulsatile phenomena in veins when used, for example, over the jugular vein. These instruments were used in the pre-electrocardiographic era to record simultaneous jugular and arterial pulsations in the study of disturbances in cardiac activity. Similar instruments have been devised to record the pulsations in the distal part of the finger tip. These methods give recordings of *volume pulses*. By strain gauge and similar electronic techniques *pressure pulses* may be recorded from varying areas of the circulatory system and are very useful in studies of congenital and other types of heart disease. Examples are given in that section. The recording of such pulsations over a considerable period of time may show fluctuations in the height and form of the pulse curve and changes in base line which reflect not only general changes in the circulation, but also local changes in the caliber and properties of the vessel under the influences of hormonal and nervous control. Increases or reductions in vasomotor tone may be detected in this way, and the effect of psychic influences and traumatic and operative procedures on the nerves, such as sympathetic block, may be evaluated.

The form, frequency and regularity of the pulse may be studied in this way as well. Such waves have a steep upstroke (anacrotic) and more leisurely downstroke (catacrotic). In the descending limb a negative wave (dicrotic notch) is seen. The dicrotic notch represents the elastic rebound of the arterial wall as ventricular systole ends and the pressure in the ventricle falls below the aortic pressure. The blood column sweeps toward the heart, and a negative wave is set up. The aortic valves then become taut and move away from the ventricular cavity, and the blood column rebounds, producing an incisure. The pressure pulse is transmitted through the aorta to the periphery, the vessels expanding and elongating to accommodate it. The character of the vessel walls, the stroke output of the heart, the duration of systole and the diastolic pressure all influence the shape of the wave. As the waves proceed toward the periphery, friction, damping and vessel elasticity produce a change in the shape of the wave. The ascent is more gradual, and a smoothing out of its general

form occurs. Secondary waves develop owing to new vibrations set up and to reflected waves. By the time the wave reaches the radial artery it shows a primary and a dicrotic wave with an intervening dicrotic notch. This notch results from a variable summation effect of a damped incisure and the trough of the reflected dicrotic wave. Underfilling of the arterial system from dilatation of vessels, from loss of blood volume (hemorrhage) or from many causes of low diastolic pressure makes the dicrotic wave prominent. In hypertensive states the damped incisure accounts for the prominence of the notch.

Clinically, the pulse is generally studied by palpation. Because the frequency and regularity of the pulse reflect the frequency and regularity of the heart beat, these aspects of the pulse are considered in the section on the heart. The form of the pulse wave may be detected in some degree by palpation; for example, a wave that rises and falls rapidly, as does the water-hammer pulse of aortic insufficiency, or one that rises slowly and has a prolonged plateau-like peak, as sometimes occurs in aortic stenosis (Fig. 16–2). In clinical medicine, pulsations are usually not graphically recorded, except for special studies, and the skill of the physician in palpation is utilized for their recognition. The compressibility of the pulse, as an index of the pulse pressure and arterial pressure, is not depended upon, although it may be estimated by palpation of the pulse. Before precise diagnostic methods were devised, clinicians often depended to a great extent upon palpation of the pulse in such diseases as typhoid fever, in which the pulse may be soft and a notch may occur after its peak sufficiently deep to give a double peaklike sensation to the palpating finger, called the dicrotic pulse. However, graphic records of the subclavian pulse sometimes give important information not obtained otherwise. In aortic stenosis the pressure first goes up, sharply followed by a notch and then a gradual rise until the end of systole. An early systolic rise and diastolic collapse characterizes the pulse of aortic regurgitation. In the radial pulse (Fig. 16–2) similar helpful findings occur.

Pressure upon arteries, by tumors of various types, or intra-arterial obstruction to flow may slow the pulse wave. Either graphic registration or palpation of the pulse on both sides—in the radials, for example, with aneurysm—will disclose a difference in time of arrival of the pulses or in volume or character. Obstruction of an artery may completely obliterate the pulse, and palpation of the pulse in various locations in the extremities (carotid, femoral, posterior tibial, dorsalis pedis, brachial, radial) should be routine. Constriction of an artery (as in coarctation of the aorta) may obliterate the pulsations below the area when complete obstruction is not present. Spasm may reduce the size of the pulsations so greatly that there may be difficulty in detection of the pulse even by graphic means. The techniques described later for release of spasm will cause return of the pulse when this factor is important. Organic obstruction may be due to embolism, thrombosis or compression.

Impaired pulsations and symptoms may be manifested in areas remote from the obstruction itself. A unique example is the *pulseless disease* or thrombotic obliteration of the great vessels arising from the aortic arch. Reduced pulsations may occur in the arms and neck. Systolic murmurs often occur in the neck. Carotid obstruction may give rise to ocular or cerebral symptoms and may be mistaken for obstruction in the cerebral vessels. Such cerebral arterial insufficiency frequently occurs in attacks. Claudication of the masseter muscles may occur. Increased collateral circulation may result in hypertension of the lower extremities which, along with reduced pulsations in the upper body, has been termed "reversed coarctation." Rarely are the lower extremities involved.

At the other end of the aorta, at or near the bifurcation, partial or complete obstruction may develop due to intravascular clotting on atherosclerotic damage. This produces the *Leriche syndrome*. Pulsations may disappear in the lower extremities, even though the process is segmental and localized at the aortic bifurcation. "Trophic" changes in the legs are infrequent. Murmurs may appear over the obstructed area. Claudication of the thighs, rather than of the calves or foot, occurs. Impotence may be present. Recognition of the process and localization by aortography is important, because replacement or by-pass arterial grafts may be curative since the lesion is often localized and segmental (Fig. 16–3).

Another unique situation occurs in dissecting aneurysm. It is generally thought that rupture begins in the intima at, or close to, an atheromatous ulcer, but some investigators

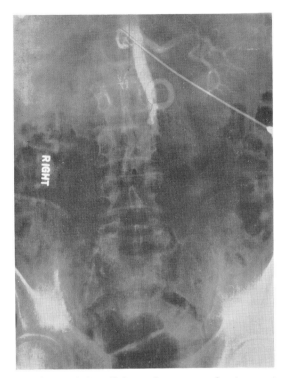

Figure 16–3. Abdominal aortogram showing complete occlusion of distal aorta.

believe that cystic medial necrosis is important. Dissection progresses and, if branches of the aorta are reached, may occlude pulsations in them (the subclavian and, with it, the arteries in the arm, for example) when pulsations are easily felt in the leg. Other arch vessels, if occluded, will produce cerebral symptoms. If the aortic ring is reached, it may be destroyed and aortic regurgitation develop. If the gastrointestinal and renal vessels are involved, abdominal and renal symptoms appear, and, with dissection into the femorals, gangrene may occur in the legs.

The most accurate measurements of pressure within the vessels can be recorded with manometers, connected to a needle inserted into the artery, if the sensitivity and quickness of the manometer are adequate. The strain gauge manometer is such a device. This instrument is more accurate than the indirect methods used clinically and is useful in experimental procedures when high degrees of accuracy are desirable. Direct measurements of pressure pulses are made by catheterization of the veins with insertion of the catheter to various areas to be studied— the right atrium, right ventricle, pulmonary artery, left ventricle, for example. (See section on congenital heart disease.)

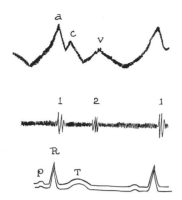

Figure 16–4. Simultaneous tracings of venous pulse (above), heart sounds (center) and electrocardiogram (below), showing the time relations of the various events.

Venous Pulse

Venous pulse does not describe the pulsations which are at times transmitted from the arteriole through the capillaries to the veins, but refers to pulsations observed in the jugular and other veins near the heart. These pulsations arise from impulses transmitted to the veins, not through the capillaries, but from the heart and underlying arteries in proximity to the great veins. Hence the term *cardiac venous pulse*. They are best seen with the subject in recumbency to distend the vein. Quite different is the *respiratory venous pulse*, the collapse and distention seen alternately with inspiration and expiration. Cardiac venous pulse curves have the forms shown in Figure 16–4, typically with the three waves marked, *A, C* and *V*. The *A* wave is due to atrial contraction, the *C* wave to the increase in pressure in the atrium produced by the bulging of the atrioventricular valve into the atrium during ventricular contractions. It is thought also that the pulsation of the carotid artery contributes to the C wave. Finally the *V* wave represents the increase in atrial pressure attending the filling of the atrium with venous blood. Thus it can be seen that cardiac events may be timed from the venous pulsation, and, if tracings of the carotid artery are taken simultaneously, not only cardiac events, but left- and right-sided cardiac events may be correlated with each other.

Detailed analyses of such records in the past contributed greatly to our knowledge of cardiac activity and, before the days of the electrocardiogram, were used clinically to study cardiac events. Mackenzie devised an instrument, the ink polygraph, for recording these events in ink upon a moving paper. It was in great vogue at the turn of the century. Many variations in the tracings were useful in the study of cardiac irregularity. The disappearance of the *A* wave, for example, produced a tracing which was called the ventricular pulse and, with absolutely irregularly occurring *C* and *V* waves, was indicative of what we now know to be atrial fibrillation. Atrioventricular dissociation and prolongation of the atrioventricular conduction time could be diagnosed by the relation of the *A* and *C* waves to each other. Extrasystoles and their origin, whether atrial or ventricular, could also be detected in this way. An *A* wave precedes the atrial type. In nodal rhythm, with simultaneous atrial and ventricular contraction, *A* and *C* summate.

Evidences of Peripheral Vascular Disease

Peripheral vascular disease implies disturbances in blood flow through the periphery, especially the extremities, whether due to structural disturbances, either remote or in the area, or not. The terms "functional" and "organic" are in common use. Functional disturbances imply the absence of structural changes in the vessels *as a cause* of the disorder, for example, Raynaud's disease. Organic changes may result from such functional disorders. Organic disturbance implies disturbed circulation *as the result* of structural damage to vessels, for example, atherosclerotic obstruction involving the vessels of the area, or cervical rib involving the vessels beyond the structural defect. If such disturbances prevent an adequate circulation through the arteries, arterial insufficiency develops and may result in a train of symptoms, including reduced or absent pulsations, pain, color change with change in position, coldness, pallor, ulceration and gangrene. The extremities and especially the digits are commonly involved, for they are more greatly exposed to trauma and temperature changes.

The complex regulation of the vascular system through inherent tone, hormonal and chemical influences, as well as by vasomotor nerves, makes it susceptible to a multitude of disturbances in disease. The peripheral arteries themselves are subject to disturbances resulting from vasomotor imbalance and its results, as well as structural changes from inflammation, aneurysm, arteriovenous fistula and occlusive disease. Many of the manifestations of disease are the same whether or not actual organic damage is present. The changes may be local or general in extent.

The importance of examination of the patient for evidences of disturbed peripheral vascular structure cannot be too strongly stressed. The symptoms and signs important in the establishment of a diagnosis are listed as follows: (1) pain, (2) changes in color, (3) ulceration or gangrene, scleroderma and impaired nail growth, (4) enlargement or shrinkage of extremities, (5) excessively cold or warm extremities, and (6) abnormal pulsations of, or enlarged, veins. With any of these findings, disease of the peripheral circulation should be suspected and more detailed examination carried out. Swelling, atrophy, elongation or shortening of the limbs; ulceration, gangrene, scleroderma, eczema, varices or thrombophlebitis; abnormal temperature of the skin; altered color of the skin and unusual change with elevation and dependency; impaired arterial pulsations; auscultatory evidence of arteriovenous fistula or aneurysm may be found.

In the absence of all these findings, important peripheral vascular disease, with the exception of Raynaud's disease or erythromelalgia, is not likely to be present. Certainly the presence of any one of the findings indicates the need for further investigation.

In the study of a patient for disturbances in the circulation, it may be desirable to test the effects of factors and agents known to disturb the circulation. For such tests it is essential that influences of extraneous factors on the circulation be removed and the circulation brought to a steady state. Since food, smoking, exercise and emotional factors influence the circulation, patients should be studied in a postabsorptive state (eight hours or longer), with freedom from the effects of smoking tobacco (two hours or longer) in a comfortable environment not tending to produce arteriolar constriction or dilatation. A constant temperature of about 68 to 70° F. is most desirable.

Much of the symptomatology results from vasodilatation, vasoconstriction and vasospasm. Investigation for local factors and remote factors acting reflexly is essential. Organic damage to vessels may interfere with normal local and reflex mechanisms for dilatation or constriction and produce symptoms.

PAIN

Pain is an outstanding symptom in many peripheral vascular disorders. It may be of several types, and varies in mechanism. Pain at rest in sudden arterial occlusion may be sudden and severe. At times it may come on gradually over several hours. Usually pain due to embolism or thrombosis is associated with coldness, loss of, or diminished, pulsations and sensation, and some paresis, all resulting from ischemia and all being manifestations of *acute arterial insufficiency*. The cause for such pain is not entirely clear. Slowly developing complete occlusions often occur without any pain at all. However, in acute occlusion there is spasm of associated collateral vessels, a factor which some believe important in the causation of the pain, for sympathetic block relieves it. Spasm is partially responsible, also, for pallor and the other ischemic symptoms mentioned.

With complete acute obstruction, as in embolism, immediate diagnosis is necessary, for delay in treatment may necessitate amputation. The part should be kept down, by elevation of the head of the bed if the lower extremity is involved, cold applied to reduce metabolism in the already undersupplied area, and procedures used to relieve spasm. Surgical removal of the obstruction is considered in early cases. Arteries may be temporarily obstructed with production of some of the symptoms mentioned. Hyperabduction of the arms in sleep may occlude the subclavian artery, even to the point at which gangrene develops.

In ulceration and gangrene, as seen, for example, in Buerger's disease (and before ulceration in so-called pretrophic pain of ischemia), pain is common. It is, however, different in type and may be constant and severe, interfering with sleep so that the patient sits up, with the feet dependent, for relief. Heat may give partial relief, as may the dependent position. Elevation and cold accentuate the pain. The fact that cold and elevation do this suggests that the cause is related to ischemia of the part. Necrosis from impaired circulation is responsible for gangrene, and, when severe, ulceration is a common part of the picture. Less marked changes result in a number of disturbances, such as thickened nails, large corns and callus formation on the parts exposed to friction or weight bearing. This type of pain is related to the degree and type of impaired circulation and not to the nature of the process itself. *Arteriosclerotic endarteritis obliterans* may produce the same pain as that in Buerger's disease.

Other types of pain associated with vascular disease may be burning, sharp, shooting, tearing or throbbing. Pain may be severe and extensive, involving a part of the extremity, or may have paroxysmal exacerbations, especially at night. This type of pain is thought to be due to ischemic neuritis and is common in arteriosclerosis obliterans. In general, arteriosclerosis causes no pain until diminished circulation impairs the transport of blood or until thrombosis or rupture takes place. The acute inflammation of arteries (and of veins and lymphatics as well) may be painful, but the pain is mild, often only a dull ache associated with tenderness on pressure, findings of the type seen in acute inflammation in general.

It has been stated that pain of ischemia may be accentuated by cold and elevation of the extremity and relieved by heat and dependency. Contrariwise, in some patients pain may be accentuated by heat and dependency. Such types of pain are usually burning, often with an aching or pricking component. The pain is usually produced when the temperature of the skin is elevated to between 32 and 36° C., and redness appears as well. Lewis thought that a local injury to the skin produced this susceptibility. The term *erythromelalgia* is applied to this reaction, which occurs without known cause as well as in a number of well known diseases, including hypertension, gout and polycythemia. The pain may be reproduced by increasing the skin temperature either reflexly or by direct heat, and the correlation of distress and skin temperature establishes the nature of the pain.

Most important of the types of intermittent pain, because of its frequency, is *intermittent claudication,* which results from an inadequate supply of blood to contracting muscles, though various types of occlusive arterial disease reducing arterial (and oxygen) supply to active muscular tissues may also produce it. Occasionally, severe anemia with intact arteries will produce it. Lewis and his associates studied intermittent claudication in normal subjects, producing it by exercise after interrupting the blood supply to the limb. They demonstrated its presence when the arteries were dilated, indicating that spasm is not the cause, and concluded that a chemical stimulus in the muscle from metabolic changes in the muscle fibers acting in the tissue spaces, a "factor P," was responsible. This substance, they found, was acid and nonvolatile.

Intermittent claudication is not to be con-fused with *nocturnal cramps,* which do not signify arterial disease and seldom occur in patients with arterial disease. Nocturnal cramps occur at rest, particularly when the patient is in bed, and are relieved by exercise. The mechanism of such pain is not clear, but it has been suggested that sudden muscular contractions, not met by expected resistance and without the check of antagonistic groups, occur and that the excess energy is converted into muscle spasm.

Skin Color

Skin color is an important sign of changes in the peripheral circulation, for a portion of the color of the skin is attributable to the vessels down to and including those of the subpapillary plexus. Changes in color may result from changes in the color of the blood itself or in the amount of blood contained in the vessels. Pallor, for example, results from acute arterial obstruction, be it due to thrombus or embolus in a large vessel or to constriction as in a digital artery in Raynaud's disease. Arteriolar spasm, or constriction, also produces pallor and coldness. Arteriolar dilatation, on the other hand, produces redness, and, if capillary dilatation occurs with it and the circulation is sufficiently slowed so that the tissues take up excessive oxygen, cyanosis may appear. These changes may be modified by other factors affecting the skin, as in redness from subcutaneous hemorrhage, for example.

Raynaud's disease exemplifies the changes described. Most physicians agree with Lewis that it results from abnormal sensitivity of the involved arteries (the digitals, for example) to low temperatures. Some believe that a neurogenic element enters into the picture, but Lewis' theory is most widely held. In the early stages of an attack, exposure to cold causes arteriolar spasm leading to pallor. Later, with dilatation of the arterioles and capillaries, redness, dusky cyanosis, or cyanosis may develop. Thus pallor, redness, and cyanosis are produced by Raynaud's disease, the color varying with the state of the small vessels. Venous obstruction may lead to stasis and cyanosis also.

In Raynaud's disease color changes are produced by cold, or at times by emotion. Attacks may be artificially produced by immersion of the hand in iced water. In general, in Raynaud's disease no cause can be assigned, such as cervical rib, arterial obstruction, or the like, and spontaneous attacks are bilateral. Obstruction to arteries may be secondary and, if present, involves only minute peripheral arteries, so that gangrene, if produced, is superficial and usually only on the fingertips or acral parts. Similar color changes (and changes in state of small vessels) are caused by occlusive vascular disease and are then termed secondary Raynaud's phenomena. These may happen in Buerger's disease (thromboangiitis obliterans), in pneumatic hammer disease, intoxication with ergot or heavy metals, cervical rib and neurogenic lesions.

Buerger's disease, unlike Raynaud's disease, is accompanied by actual large vessel occlusion. Indeed there is controversy as to Buerger's disease as an entity separate from arteriosclerosis obliterans. Relationship with smoking and differences in distribution between upper and lower extremities and unique occlusive changes by arteriography suggest separate entities, as does the occurrence in the Orient in an epidemiological setting in which atherosclerosis is uncommon. For this reason, differentiation of Raynaud's phenomena accompanying Buerger's disease (and other occlusive disease) from Raynaud's disease must be made. In Buerger's disease some unknown cause produces intimal and endothelial proliferation and thrombosis. Obstructive signs appear. This occurs in the arteries and, in about 40 per cent of patients, in the veins as well. Hemoconcentration has been suggested as important in this picture, and smoking has been incriminated. Increased tendency to clot formation has been postulated. No matter what the fundamental cause of Buerger's disease, obstruction and spasm both play a role in the arterial insufficiency accompanying it, and these factors must be evaluated for proper therapy. Sympathectomy, for example, does increase blood supply and minimize gangrene. It is of more value when the spastic factor is important. It does not affect the manifestations due to occlusion, such as claudication, and does not prevent recurrent phlebitis and progress of the arterial lesions.

In *arteriosclerosis* local obstructive symptoms appear, precipitated by atheromas and thrombus formation. This condition, termed arteriosclerotic endarteritis obliterans, or arteriosclerosis obliterans, is one of the most common of arterial occlusive diseases. The symptoms depend upon location, degree of involvement of branches and the rapidity of development. Localized obstruction in vessels of sufficient size may be treated with surgical grafting if diagnosis is accurate. With a greater reactivity of tissues to reduced circulation, as in diabetes mellitus, more damage results from the occlusion. All the peripheral changes seen in Buerger's disease may develop, usually without phlebitis, however. In older patients the differentiation of these diseases may not be possible, and there is some evidence that Buerger's disease may be a form of localized atherosclerotic damage. Symptoms vary from those of acute occlusion to chronic insufficiency with claudication, muscle weakness, atrophy of skin and deeper structures, and stiffness of joints. Infection may be a serious problem by aggravation, through pressure, of impaired circulation, and by increased metabolic need which the vessels cannot supply.

Position of the extremity, through changes in the degree and rate of filling of small vessels, may modify color greatly. If spasm of arterioles or obstruction to arteries produces pallor, or reduced blood flow develops without pallor, elevation of the part may accentuate it or bring it out, if not present previously. Dependency may, contrariwise, produce redness, and, if blood flow is impaired, excessive removal of O_2 by the tissues with the stasis may produce cyanosis. Abnormalities in circulation may, therefore, produce deviations from normal which are accentuated by postural change. Changes in the speed with which color returns to normal at heart level may be an important finding, especially in disease obstructing arteries. Usually, if the hand and arm are elevated and blanching appears normally, the return of the color to the normal hue will occur within five seconds after return of the part to, or slightly below, heart level. In the lower extremity the time for similar change is about ten seconds. The appearance of redness on dependency and its disappearance are also to be compared with the normal.

Tests for changes in skin color, other than postural changes, have been devised. Obstruction of an artery, with a blood pressure cuff, followed by release produces a hyperemia with a rush of redness. The timing of the speed of the flushing is one such procedure. Application of cold has already been mentioned, and application of heat is also done.

Permanent color changes in the skin may occur from vascular disease. Acrocyanosis, with constant blueness of the fingers, results from obstruction to small peripheral arteries. With venous stasis, especially on the anterior lateral aspects of the legs, various shades of brownish pigmentation may occur along with dusky redness to blueness, finally ending in ulceration.

In reactions to cold, color changes are common. In acute pernio with dermatitis, edema and a bluish redness develop. This persists for several days and, if repeated, may become chronic. In trench foot the moisture increases the dissipation of heat from the part. Continued exposure for some days (two to six) may produce the color changes. Immersion foot appears to develop similarly, though the mechanisms underlying it are not clear. A peripheral vasoneuropathy and intravascular agglutinative thrombi are possibilities. Immersion foot, caused by exposure to cold in a wet environment, and frostbite, caused by exposure to cold in an atmosphere of air, are probably on different bases. The intravascular agglutinative phenomena of frostbite have been found lacking in experimental immersion foot. Tissue and nerve anoxia is thought to be important. In frostbite local vasoconstriction is prolonged until nutritional disturbances appear locally. There is pallor from vasoconstriction, and ischemia may lead to local death of tissues and gangrene. The tissues themselves may be actually frozen. Hyperemia and color changes accompany thawing.

Skin Temperature

The temperature of the part may be helpful in diagnosis. The temperature of the skin represents a balance between the heat brought to the part by the blood and that lost through the surface. When conditions governing dissipation of heat do not change, increased heat indicates an increase in, and diminished heat a decrease in, blood flow to the part. If the part is the skin, it may or may not reflect the total circulation to the extremity. The skin may be cold when adequate circulation is maintained through deeper vessels.

Skin temperature varies widely, especially with the environmental temperature, smoking, the basal metabolism, fever, exercise and other factors. Generally the skin temperature is lower in the lower extremities than in the upper. Vessel tone tends to keep the feet at a temperature just above that of the room, so that their temperature varies usually from 24 to 36° C. In the upper extremities the range is generally higher, for the hands act as

a part of the mechanism for heat dissipation. When the room temperature rises, skin temperature rises. At 25° C. (77° F.) the fingers are about 33° and the toes about 26 or 27°. At 28° C. (82.4° F.) the toe temperature rises to 28 or 29°. Thus coldness of the extremities may be normal, and, to show abnormality, controlled conditions for measurement may be necessary (see below). Comparison of both sides under similar conditions is helpful.

Since variability in skin temperatures makes for difficulty in interpretation of these measurements in diagnosis, measurements are best made at physical and mental rest, without food, without smoking, and with the room temperature constant. Under such conditions the two sides may be compared; in general, they vary less than 1 degree C. Variations of 2 degrees or more indicate a disturbance in circulation. Instead of skin temperatures, calorimetry may be used to test the heat eliminated by a part.

Unilateral differences in blood volume, and effects of dilating and constricting agents on the part may be shown by use of *radioactive isotopes*.

Many techniques have been utilized to show the presence of spasm and to help differentiate the spastic factor from organic occlusion, a fact of great importance, for sympathectomy is of greatest value when vasospasm is marked. This may be done by study of pulsations, registered graphically by the plethysmograph, and by determinations of skin temperature in a part after procedures which are known to relieve spasm. Sympathetic block is one such procedure. Reflex vasodilatation, in which an extremity not under study—for example, one arm—is placed in warm water, usually at 110° F. or in that range, is another. The warmed blood from the part causes a reflex stimulation of the sympathetic nerves to the opposite arm, that is, the one under study, and, normally, vasodilatation occurs in it. The vessels of the legs may be stimulated by immersion of the arms, or vice versa. Spinal anesthesia and artificial fever accomplish the same purpose. Autonomic blocking agents, especially those reducing adrenergic vasoconstriction, are also useful. When typhoid vaccine is given intravenously, the relation between the rise in oral temperature (used in lieu of blood temperature) and the rise in cutaneous temperature may be stated as the so-called vasomotor index.

The limits of organic occlusion may be estimated by the reactive hyperemia test, the histamine test, the oscillometer, distribution of isotopes in the blood, and by visualization of vessels. The *histamine test* is done in a warm atmosphere by puncturing histamine (1:1000) into the skin of the horizontally held extremity. Failure of a wheal and flare to appear in five minutes is indicative of impaired flow in the area tested. The *reactive hyperemia test* consists in occlusion of the circulation for five minutes after the warm extremity has been emptied of blood. Sudden release of occlusion is normally followed by hyperemia indicated by a flush which reaches the tips of the digits in less than five seconds.

OSCILLOMETRIC INDEX

Examination of the pulse is discussed elsewhere. In addition, the oscillometer, used to indicate changes in volume of pulse, gives the oscillometric index, or the maximal pulsations. There is considerable variation in this index. It may demonstrate pulsations in deep-lying arteries which could not be examined otherwise. Some clinicians believe that it is not a reliable guide. It does not register the development of collateral circulation, and certain pulsations may not register. It is also possible to change the cuff in the same area and vary the pulsations. Furthermore, it does not differentiate organic from vasomotor disturbances. But it will at times show the site of arterial occlusion, though at other times it is not reliable. It is not a good index of collateral blood supply and does not correlate well with skin temperature.

VISUALIZATION OF VESSELS

Direct inspection of arteries, veins and capillaries is possible only to a limited extent. Visualization of the retinal vessels with the ophthalmoscope should be a routine practice. In hypertensive states and in arteriosclerosis various changes in these vessels are readily discernible. The actual blood column is seen, and its width, variations in its contour and its tortuosity represent changes in the vessel walls. Secondary changes, such as papilledema, hemorrhage and exudation, may be detected. With obstruction to the central retinal artery, a pale ischemic retina is seen. These changes will not be described in detail here.

The blood vessels may be seen directly in other areas of the body—in the rectum and sigmoid colon through the sigmoidoscope, for example. However, this procedure is cumbersome for this purpose and is little used.

The capillary loops may be seen in the nail fold, with the aid of a microscope, an oblique light and a transparent oil applied to the area. A normal pattern consists of loops of uniform size arranged in parallel rows. The loops are hairpin in type, the venous side being slightly wider than the arterial loop. The blood stream, and not the wall, is seen as a smooth column of blood.

With increased age the loops increase in length and become tortuous. Capillary flow diminishes. In the fifth decade these changes are accompanied by a tendency towards stasis, and by segmentation of the stream, which is interrupted by some spaces filled with clear plasma.

Congestive failure slows the stream, which appears granular and shows some stasis. In hypertension, flow increases. In arteriosclerosis, loops at times appear moth-eaten and blood flow sluggish. In polycythemia the loops are filled and bulging with blood. In Raynaud's disease the stages described in the discussion of skin color are visible. In Buerger's disease less dilatation is seen and the blood flow is not so greatly disturbed.

Disturbances in small arteries, not amenable to examination otherwise, as well as in large ones, may be detected in *arteriograms,* roentgenograms following intra-arterial injections either directly into the vessels or through catheters placed strategically for the parts to be studied (see Fig. 16–3). Such injected arteries are normally smooth, and the contour of the lumen is not interrupted. Tortuosity of marked degree is absent and collateral circulation normal. Spasm is manifested by a smooth diminution in caliber; obstruction due to Buerger's disease or arteriosclerosis appears as incomplete filling (filling defect); patchy obstruction, which may be segmental, gives irregularity in the size of the lumen and variations in collateral circulation. Arteriovenous fistulas may be demonstrated. *Venography* may be performed as well. More recently demonstration of the large veins, the right and left sides of the heart and the aorta by such techniques has been perfected, and congenital defects, fistulas and other abnormalities may be visualized. For this, the radiopaque solution must be rapidly injected into the peripheral veins.

Blood Pressure

Long before scientific proof was available it was known that the pressure was high in the arteries and low in the veins. This was demonstrated in traumatic incidents in which the arteries and veins were cut. Blood was seen to spurt from the arteries, and considerable pressure was necessary to stop it, whereas from the veins the flow was not pulsating, it was slower, and little force was necessary to compress the veins and stop bleeding. The pressures in the arteries and the veins were first measured in 1733 by Stephen Hales, who inserted a cannula into an artery and into a vein of a mare and noted the rise of the blood column in a tube. The arterial column rose approximately 8 feet, whereas the venous column rose only 12 inches.

An explanation has already been given of the main transition from the high pressure in the arteries to the low pressure in the capillaries and veins. The frictional resistance to blood flow in the arteries in general is low and is represented by a drop of only approximately 20 mm. of mercury in pressure from the aorta to the arteriole. The friction is in large part in the blood stream itself and not against the vessel wall. There is a fine film of blood against the arteriolar wall which moves but little. Another thin layer inside this external one moves along the external layer, another inside it against the second, and so on until the central area of blood in the vessel is reached. Thus in the center of the blood vessel the friction is least and the velocity greatest. In a large vessel, such as the aorta, in which the cross section is great, there is a large central core of blood having little frictional resistance, and the loss of energy by friction in such vessels, and consequently the drop in pressure, is small. However, in small vessels, such as the arterioles, in which the central core of frictionless blood is small and a large part of the blood stream is in the area closer to the walls, the friction is greatly increased and the drop in blood pressure great. Since in the arterioles the blood velocity is not remarkably reduced, or is reduced only moderately, there is no reduction in friction as a result of reduction in velocity, and this factor cannot compensate for the resistance due to the increased surface area.

In the capillaries it might be thought that, because the vessels increase greatly in number and the surface area is, therefore, much greater than in the arterioles, a much greater drop in pressure would occur. However, unlike the arteriolar cross section, that of the capillaries is greatly increased and has been estimated to be from 600 to 800 times greater than the cross section of the aorta. This great increase in cross-sectional area reduces greatly the velocity of flow of blood, a factor which, in itself, would tend to increase the pressure. At the same time this reduction in velocity of flow reduces the frictional resistance at the wall and helps to compensate for any further drop in pressure resulting from increases in capillary surface area. Ordinarily, therefore, the drop in pressure across the capillary, as a result of summation of these opposing factors, amounts to essentially the same drop in pressure as in the greater arteries. The greatest decrease in pressure on the arterial side can, therefore, be seen to occur in the arterioles.

The blood leaves the capillaries and enters the small venules and is carried through these vessels as they coalesce into larger and larger veins until the venae cavae are reached. In these venous channels, as the heart is approached, the cross-sectional area of the vascular bed is again reduced, until, at the entrance of the veins into the heart, the cross-sectional area is about twice that of the aorta. The velocity of blood is increased as it passes along the veins, propelled in part by muscular contractions, and the frictional loss is small so that by the time the blood stream again reaches the heart the pressure is about 5 mm. of water.

ARTERIAL BLOOD PRESSURE

Measurement

The cumbersomeness of Hales' technique for measuring the blood pressure in the mare gave way in 1828 to the use of the U-tube mercury manometer, with much smaller apparatus and tubing. Pressures measured with this instrument were read in millimeters of mercury, and these units for the expression of arterial blood pressure are still used almost exclusively.

The intra-arterial insertion of a needle connected to a manometer containing mercury through the medium of a sodium citrate solution has been commonly used to record blood pressure upon a kymograph. In this way the height of the blood pressure, and the varying synchronous changes resulting from the periodic ejection of blood into the arteries, may be recorded and the effects of respiration and other influences noted in the record. Such an apparatus does not record accurately, however, the variations in the pulsatile change in pressure because of the inertia of the column of mercury. The Hamilton manometer removes this factor. Such an instrument will record the maximum pressure at the height of the pulse wave, which represents the height of systole and is called the systolic pressure, and the minimum pressure between the pulse waves, the so-called diastolic pressure. Catheterization of the heart or pulmonary or peripheral arteries permits direct pressure recordings by use of the strain gauge manometer and accurate and continuous records of blood pressure may be made with these instruments (see section on congenital heart disease, Chapter 19), giving accurate systolic and diastolic levels. The difference between these two represents a calculation called the pulse pressure. The integrated mean of the systolic and diastolic pressures, the so-called mean pressure, is used extensively experimentally, but has found little use in clinical medicine. The average variation in normal pressure seen in man is given in Figure 16–5.

It can be seen that the diastolic pressure represents a constant minimal load which the artery must bear at all times and also represents a load against which the left ventricle must exert pressure before any blood may be ejected from the heart. The diagram in Figure 16–6 shows clearly that, as the small arteries are reached and the arterioles are entered, the pulse pressure is gradually reduced and the systolic and diastolic levels

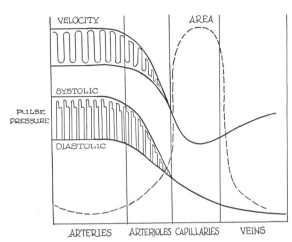

Figure 16–6. Diagram (modified from Best and Taylor) indicating the pressure and velocity of the blood in the vascular system. The relation between velocity and vascular area is shown. Note also the absence of pulsatile phenomena in the pressure and velocity curves in the capillaries and veins.

approach each other. In the capillaries the flow becomes essentially a steady one.

The arterial blood pressure in man is usually measured in the arm at the brachial artery. The patient should be seated or lying down with the arm slightly flexed and at heart level. Time should be allowed for recovery from recent exercise or excitement. Clothing should not constrict the arm. At times the standing position may be used for special purposes. This is true in a check of postural hypotension. The position of the arm is then important, and the arm should be at heart level to avoid erroneous readings.

Since cannulization of the artery is not practical for usual studies, methods have been devised for determining the blood pressure indirectly. The instrument universally used for measurement of arterial pressure in man is the sphygmomanometer, the principle of which is the balancing of air pressure against the blood pressure and the estimation of the former, either by a mercury column or by an aneroid manometer calibrated against a mercury column. This is accomplished by inflation of a cloth-covered rubber bag, 12 to 13 cm. wide and 23 cm. long, placed firmly and snugly around the upper arm with the lower edge about 1 inch above the antecubital space, until the pressure in the bag exceeds that in the artery. The pressure in the bag is read upon the manometer. There should be no bulging or displacement of the bag. The pressure is then gradually

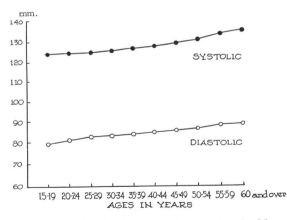

Figure 16–5. Blood pressure (average) in healthy men. (From data by Symonds: J.A.M.A., Vol. 80.)

reduced until the blood pressure is determined.

Blood pressure determination can be accomplished in three ways. The first, the *palpatory,* involves palpation of the radial pulse and noting the pressure at which it returns, after it has been obliterated by elevation of the pressure in the cuff above the pressure in the brachial artery. This is accomplished by a slow reduction of the pressure in the cuff by manipulation of a controllable leak valve. This method is not used extensively for several reasons. In the first place, only the systolic pressure can be determined, and, in general, it is inaccurate, being too low by approximately 5 to 10 mm. of mercury. The method is useful, however, in part at least, in assuring that, by the absence of the radial pulse, the brachial pulse is exceeded, a point that cannot always be settled by the auscultatory method.

In the *auscultatory* method, pressure is raised above that of the brachial artery, as controlled by palpation of the radial pulse, and then is gradually lowered while a stethoscope is applied over the artery at the bend of the elbow. As the pressure is lowered, a series of sounds, called the Korotkoff sounds, are heard. The first is a clear, sharp snapping sound, the appearance of which is taken as the systolic pressure, that is, the break-through of the pulse wave. This sound, which signals the beginning of phase 1, becomes louder during approximately 10 mm. of drop in pressure. Then phase 2 develops, signaled by a softening of the sound, which becomes swishing, or murmur-like, and lasts for a drop of approximately 15 mm. in pressure. Phase 3 appears when the sound again increases in intensity for approximately another 15 mm. of mercury. Phase 4 is ushered in as the sound is suddenly reduced in intensity and becomes muffled. The beginning of phase 4 is commonly taken as the diastolic pressure and should be recorded as such. As the pressure is further lowered, the sound disappears altogether. This signals the fifth phase and again is commonly recorded in the blood pressure, so that a blood pressure is recorded as, for example, 120/82/76. The first two figures are those usually recorded as the systolic and diastolic pressures; the last is commonly not recorded.

At times there may be a silent period, as the transition is made from phase 1 to phase 4, and this period may last through a pressure drop of 10 or more mm. of mercury, as low as 40 to 50 mm. below true systolic level

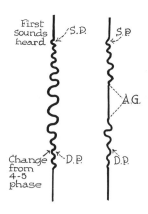

Figure 16–7. Graphic representation of the auscultatory events during the taking of blood pressure by the auscultatory method. *S.P.* = systolic pressure; *D.P.* = diastolic pressure; *A.G.* represents the silent period, known as the auscultatory gap, noted frequently in hypertensive patients.

(Fig. 16–7). This is the so-called auscultatory gap. If the pressure in the cuff is initially raised to this level, the observer may believe that he has exceeded the systolic pressure in the patient when he actually has not, and record the blood pressure erroneously. This can always be controlled by raising the pressure above the level at which the radial pulse may be palpated.

A third method of recording the blood pressure is the *oscillometric.* In the Pachon type oscillometer two rubber bags are contained in the cuff, and the pressure in these is transmitted to a recording manometer. The mechanism is so arranged that when the column of blood reaches the lower cuff, the pulsation is reversed on the record. The entrance of the column of blood into the artery under the second cuff and the reversal of the record signal the systolic pressure. As the pressure is further reduced, the oscillations become greater and greater until they suddenly diminish markedly in size. This point is commonly taken as the diastolic pressure, but the precise point on the record at which the change occurs is not always evident.

The blood pressure may be taken in other parts of the body, particularly in the leg. When this is done, the patient rests in the horizontal position and the cuff is placed around the thigh, the sound being elicited over the artery in the popliteal space by application of the chest piece of the stethoscope there. The usual sphygmomanometer is made for use on the arm, and the cuff does not fit well around the thigh, particularly in large and obese subjects. This difficulty may be overcome by applying the cuff around the thigh close to the popliteal space and wrapping firmly, but not too tightly, a number of turns of roller bandage over it. A special cuff with a rubber bag 15 cm. wide should be used. The systolic pressure in the leg is commonly 20 to 30 points higher than in the arm, and the diastolic pressure 10 or more points higher.

In the brachial artery the pressure is commonly considered to be the lateral pressure in the aorta, so that the subclavian and brachial arteries represent extensions, or side-arms, from the wall of the aorta, the pressure recorded representing essentially this component of the energy of the blood in the aorta. Much of the energy in the aorta is kinetic energy, or energy of flow. In the leg, however, the femoral arteries represent, in essence, an extension of the aorta, and, when the pressure is taken there, the blood flow is stopped in that vessel. The energy of flow is, during the blockage of the vessel, converted into potential energy, or energy of pressure, and this then is represented in the determination made in the leg. The pressure as taken in the leg, therefore, is normally always higher than that in the arm, and is lowered only when there is some interference with blood flow to the lower extremity. This may be the result of embolic phenomena, of encroachment of tumors upon the aorta or its branches, and, outstanding clinically, of coarctation of the aorta.

The blood pressure should be taken in both arms; in general, the readings in both arms agree within a few millimeters. If there is any great difference, the pressure should again be taken in the first arm, for there may have been a general change in blood pressure between the two readings. Compression of vessels by aneurysm or tumors in the mediastinum may cause remarkable differences in the arms. At times in certain patients the pressure may vary in the two arms as much as 10 or 15 mm. of mercury or even to a greater extent without representing significant disease. Distortion of the vessels coming off from the aorta may at times account for such differences. At other times local occlusive disease or scalenus anticus syndrome may be accountable for the differences.

Factors Maintaining Pulse Pressure

The pulse pressure is maintained, not by a single factor, but by a group of factors which interplay with each other. These factors are (1) the pumping action of the heart, (2) the peripheral resistance, (3) the amount of blood in the arteries, (4) the viscosity of the blood, and (5) the elasticity of the arterial walls. The first of these factors has to do with the cardiac output. It has already been noted that the blood ejected by the left ventricle into the aorta cannot immediately displace blood already in that structure and that the pressure rises and the arterial walls become stretched. If the amount of blood put into the aorta per minute remains constant and the heart rate increases, diastole is shortened and the next systole comes along before the previous diastolic level is reached. The diastolic level, therefore, is elevated and the systolic pressure also, for the vessel is further distended. Conversely, a decrease in the heart rate will produce opposite effects. If, however, the amount of blood per minute is increased, the aorta is further distended and the systolic pressure elevated.

Of the other four factors, that of change in blood viscosity is of least importance clinically in blood pressure changes. If the viscosity of a liquid increases, greater pressures are necessary to move it through tubes, for its internal friction is elevated. Reductions in cells (anemia) and in protein reduce blood viscosity; the reverse elevates it. Many other factors—hyperglycemia, carbon dioxide content, elevated blood calcium and others—elevate it. In chronic hypertensive and hypotensive states these factors are of little importance. The increase in blood volume is at times important, for, if the arterial system becomes overfilled and the arterial walls are distended, systolic and diastolic pressures will be elevated. Loss of blood drops the blood pressure. The capacity of the blood vessels is very large and, if sufficiently dilated in certain parts of the body (abdominal area, for example), may cause pooling of blood and marked reduction in pressure due to the discrepancy between the vascular volume and the blood volume. (See the discussion of Shock.) In vascular disease the changes in peripheral resistance and the change in elasticity of the arterial walls are most important. Increased peripheral resistance in the arterioles increases primarily the diastolic pressure, and decreased peripheral resistance reduces it. (See the discussion below.) Peripheral resistance varies directly with the pressure and inversely with the flow.

In conditions in which these relationships are disturbed, changes in blood pressure may be marked. In arteriovenous aneurysm, for example, a large leakage of blood from the arterial to the venous system would act as a reduction in peripheral resistance. There is an increased output of blood by the heart to compensate for that lost through the leak, so that momentarily the systolic pressure is higher because of this added blood. Its sudden leakage to the veins, however, drops the pressure rapidly, and high systolic and low diastolic pressures result. This may be manifested by increased visible pulsations in the large vessels (carotid), a large pulse and increased capillary pulse. Where pulsations reach the veins in areas that can be felt, murmurs and palpable thrills may be found. In aortic regurgitation the circumstances in the arteries are similar except that blood leaks back into the heart. The wide pulse pressure, low diastolic pressure, Corrigan's pulse, capillary pulse are thus explained.

It has already been explained that arteriosclerosis raises the systolic pressure by a reduction in the elasticity of the arterial walls. According to the explanation given, the diastolic pressure in arteriosclerosis would, in general, be lowered, and indeed that is at times seen. However, it is elevated if the peripheral vessels are also involved. The interplay of these various factors in the control of the blood pressure is important. A change in one may lead to a compensatory effect from the other. In hemorrhage, for example, when a quantity of blood is lost from the arterial system and the blood pressure drops markedly, there is a tendency toward constriction of the arterial system to make up for the lost blood volume. The blood volume may also be increased to great degrees—for example, in polycythemias—without remarkable changes in blood pressure because of the compensation for this increase by dilatation of vessels.

A number of factors normally affect the arterial blood pressure. Although in most normal young adults the systolic pressure averages around 120 mm. and the diastolic around 80 mm. of mercury, the usual variation in systolic pressure is from 100 to 140 mm. and of diastolic from 60 to 85 mm. Under usual activities the blood pressure (casual) is somewhat higher than after ten to twelve hours postprandially and after rest for a half hour in a warm room (basal pressure). A slight variation occurs from moment to moment and during the day, the pressure being 5 to 10 mm. of mercury higher in the afternoon than in the morning. Bodily movement, pain, position and emotional stress vary

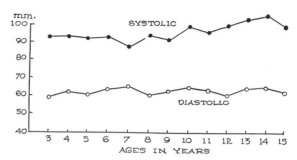

Figure 16–8. Average blood pressure values in 2300 healthy children. (From data by Judson and Nicholson: Am. J. Dis. Child., Vol. 27.)

it. Until adult life is reached, age may make a remarkable difference (Fig. 16–8), and in the older age groups the figures are somewhat higher than average, but still within the range just stated. The figures given are average with a scatter of about 10 per cent. It is difficult to assess normal values and impossible to define a truly normal level. The farther from average, the more likely is the reading to be pathologic. In general, those of ptotic build have a lower pressure level than the pyknic type. Exercise has a profound effect upon the blood pressure; when exercise becomes strenuous, the systolic pressure may even reach levels of 200 mm. of mercury, with diastolic levels reaching as high as 100 mm. or more.

If the pressure is taken with the patient lying down and then standing, it will be found that, in general, on standing the diastolic pressure rises to a slight degree, a few millimeters of mercury, and the systolic pressure drops slightly. At times the systolic pressure may rise to a slight degree.

Arteriolar Innervation. The arterioles are supplied by at least two sets of nerves, the vasomotor nerves: one, the vasoconstrictors, which cause contraction (and constriction) of the arteriole by stimulating the circularly arranged smooth muscle, and the other, the vasodilators, which relax the smooth muscle and produce dilatation. The activities of these two sets of nerves keep the arterioles in their normal state through a balance between them. The term "vasodilatation" (or "vasodilation") is used in general discussions to signify arteriolar widening with increased blood flow; "vasoconstriction," to mean arteriolar constriction. Both terms are applied to similar changes in other vessels.

Sympathetic nerve fibers exert the vasoconstrictor influence, and arise in the thoracolumbar chain. These vascular nerves, to both the upper and lower extremities, come directly from the sympathetic chain and pass to the vessel walls. Another supply reaches the smaller vessels through the somatic nerve trunks, such as the ulnar, so that the arterioles and capillaries are innervated solely in this latter fashion. This distribution is important in surgery, for stripping the greater vessels of their nerve supply will not affect the smaller vessels.

The vasodilator group arises, as do the vasoconstrictor nerves, over the parasympathetic branches and posterior spinal routes. Facts concerning the vasodilator group are not well established. Application of heat, as to the hand, may produce reflex vasodilatation in other parts—the legs, for example. This occurs presumably through return of the warmed blood to the brain, where the sympathetic nerves are stimulated.

These vasomotor nerves are under the influence of a vasomotor center situated in the medulla. The constrictor center has tone, and, if a part is separated from this control, the blood vessels in it dilate with a fall in blood pressure which lasts until the spinal and lower areas take over a tonic effect, produced locally. Removal of lumbar sympathetic nerves has increased the flow for a matter of several months.

Tonic impulses result from afferent impulses from the various regions of the body, including the blood vessels themselves (carotid sinus, aortic nerve), from the nervous centers in the brain, from general somatic and visceral afferents and from blood chemical changes. For example, vagal afferent fibers terminating in the aortic arch, or heart, control heart rate, blood pressure and caliber of blood vessels. Lowering of the venous pressure produces vasoconstriction, thereby minimizing the effects of reduced venous pressure, as in shock. Elevations in venous pressure, if sufficiently high, give a vagotonic response and vasoconstriction, just as an elevation in pressure in the right atrium causes an increase in heart rate (Bainbridge reflex). In the carotid sinus (enlargement of the common carotid artery at its bifurcation) rest afferent fibers of a reflex arc which is completed through the vagus nerve, stimulation resulting in slowing of the heart rate. Peripheral vasodilatation may occur from stimulation of the carotid sinus also, with a drop in blood pressure. The arc may be completed through cerebral vessels also producing, on stimulation, cerebral ischemia and syncope, even though peripheral dilatation or vagal

slowing of the heart does not occur. Pressure on the carotid sinus will set off this reflex and, if it is hyperactive, produce dramatic symptoms or through vagal influences correct certain cardiac irregularities. It is more sensitive in arteriosclerosis and after digitalization. Pressure below the carotid sinus may have the opposite effect of pressure upon it. Hypersensitivity of the carotid sinus produces symptoms on slight pressure, such as shaving or wearing a tight collar.

The carotid sinus and aortic nerves are important in maintenance of cerebral circulation and of arterial blood pressure—for example, in postural changes. In shock or hemorrhage, with a fall in blood pressure, these mechanisms produce vasoconstriction and reduce the size of the vascular bed. If blood pressure is excessive, the depressor reflex is activated.

Afferent impulses from the skin, muscles and other structures also are important in the adjustment of vasomotor tone and control of the peripheral vessels. Muscular exercise constricts splanchnic vessels. Emotional factors may markedly affect the arterial tone through their effect upon the vasomotor centers as well as upon the activity of the heart and even through the liberation of epinephrine. Although a number of factors such as carbon dioxide tension influence the arterial tone, those of greatest interest clinically are the factors causing persistent deviations of the pressure from normal, be it an elevation or a depression. The carotid and aortic bodies have afferent fibers which are stimulated by changes in the composition of the blood in them. Carbon dioxide is one of the important chemicals which influence vasomotor state in this way as well as through direct action on the vasomotor centers of the spine and medulla.

Metabolic Influences. Metabolites (CO_2, O_2, H^+ and OH^-) also influence the arterioles directly, as do hormones (renin-angiotensin, sympathin, epinephrine) and certain other agents such as alcohol and tobacco. Carbon dioxide, lactic acid and reduced oxygen content of an area which is active produce dilatation of the arterioles and increased blood flow, effects differing from those in the carotid body, so that general rise of blood pressure is added to the local dilation to increase blood flow through the area concerned. Increased activity of an organ causes an increase in oxygen requirement, and elevated local metabolic requirements lead to increased blood flow. Local nervous and hormonal mechanisms control these. If insufficient to maintain blood pressure, the sympathetic system is further excited and constricts arterioles to organs which are not active. Blood flow to these is diminished and blood is shunted where needed. If deprivation is severe, ischemic damage to organs and irreversible changes with circulatory insult (heat stroke, shock) result.

Epinephrine causes constriction of the arterioles, especially in the skin, splanchnic area and mucous membranes. Its effects on the coronary arteries are dilating. Histamine produces arteriolar dilatation. Angiotensin is discussed later. Nervous influences affect peripheral resistance in response to definite stimuli and situations which resemble an emergency.

Arterial Hypertension

The factors already discussed which are known to influence the blood pressure may all at some time or other account for elevated readings. Such hypertension by itself is not a diagnosis. It is the result of a number of diseases and disturbances, some serious and progressive, others transient. As Grollman points out, the patient with elevated blood pressure readings must be evaluated to determine whether he has hypertensive disease or a transient, unimportant rise in blood pressure due to some of these factors. Intermittent diastolic hypertension may therefore be en-

TABLE 16–1.   AN ETIOLOGICAL CLASSIFICATION OF HYPERTENSION.

I. ARTERIAL HYPERTENSION (elevation of systolic and diastolic blood pressures)
  A. *Essential Hypertension*
    1. Labile (intermittent)
    2. Established ("fixed")
  B. *Renal Hypertension*
    1. Bilateral kidney disease
      a. Glomerulonephritis
      b. Chronic pyelonephritis
      c. Diabetic glomerulosclerosis
      d. Congenital polycystic kidneys
      e. Periarteritis nodosa
      f. Scleroderma
      g. Lupus erythematosus
      h. Gouty nephritis
      i. Nephrocalcinosis
      j. Necrotizing nephrosis
      k. Renal amyloidosis
      l. Radiation nephritis
      m. Obstructive uropathy
    2. Unilateral kidney disease
      a. Inflammatory, thrombotic, embolic or atherosclerotic obstruction of renal artery or of branches
      b. Chronic pyelonephritis
      c. Obstructive uropathy
      d. Renal tumor
      e. Perinephritis
      f. Renal hematoma
  C. *Endocrine Hypertension*
    1. Pheochromocytoma
    2. Primary aldosteronism
    3. Cushing's syndrome
    4. Adrenogenital syndrome
    5. Pituitary eosinophilic adenoma
    6. Ovarian arrhenoblastoma
  D. *Neurogenic Hypertension*
    1. Brain tumors
    2. Concussion of brain
    3. Epilepsy
    4. Increased intracranial pressure
    5. Encephalitis
    6. Diencephalic syndrome
    7. Lead encephalopathy
    8. Bulbar poliomyelitis
    9. Tabes dorsalis
    10. Transverse myelitis
    11. Transection of the cord
    12. Polyneuritis
    13. Postdiphtheritic neuritis
    14. Porphyria
    15. Anxiety states
    16. Asphyxia
  E. *Hypertension of Coarctation of the Aorta*
  F. *Hypertension of Toxemia of Pregnancy*
    1. Preeclampsia
    2. Eclampsia
II. SYSTOLIC HYPERTENSION
  A. Caused mainly by an increased stroke output of the left ventricle
    1. Complete heart block
    2. Aortic regurgitation
    3. Patent ductus arteriosus
    4. Thyrotoxicosis
    5. Arteriovenous fistula
    6. Severe anemia
    7. Beriberi
    8. Paget's disease of bone
  B. Caused mainly by a decreased distensibility of the aorta
    1. Arteriosclerosis of aorta
    2. Coarctation of aorta

(Modified from Hollander, W.: Med. Clin. North America, p. 1408, Sept. 1957.)

countered in emotional stress and anxiety when there is no evidence of disease. Still, intermittent hypertension may be part of hypertensive disease, the forerunner of persistent changes, and the earliest manifestation of developing hypertensive disease. Actuarial reports show that even those patients with "high normal" levels are more prone to vascular disease than those with "low normal" levels. In a large group of hypertensives decreased survival is a function of increasing levels. Obviously, whatever mechanisms are active, they may be intermittent. In general, in persistent pictures, the increased peripheral resistance accounts for the continually present hypertensive state seen in the patient. There are many classifications of such persistent hypertensive states. The one given in Table 16-1 is suitable.

Secondary Hypertension. Of those with known cause, most patients fall into a group associated with chronic renal disease. The association with renal disease has been known since the time of Richard Bright. Clinically, at least 90 per cent of the hypertensive patients seen are not in a known secondary group and fall into an unknown or essential group. There is thought, based upon experimental evidences given below, to believe that the essential group may be mediated through the kidney in the absence of obviously disturbed renal function. Final proof is lacking (see also Chap. 29).

In both essential hypertension and hypertension secondary to renal disease the cause of the elevation in blood pressure is an increase in the peripheral resistance, that is, an increased resistance in the arteriole. How this change is mediated is a matter of great dispute, but its study, particularly with reference to action through the kidneys, has received great impetus since the observations of Goldblatt. This observer experimentally constricted in part the renal artery in animals with a silver clamp and produced renal ischemia with a subsequent elevation in blood pressure which simulated the essential variety seen in human beings both in the benign and malignant phases. This procedure, although it produces ischemia of the kidney, may lead to persistent elevations in blood pressure when there are no remarkable changes in kidney function detectable by the usual clinical means. Hypertension produced by such renal ischemia, be it through the use of a Goldblatt clamp, by obstruction of the ureters, as a result of renal damage by roentgen ray, or by

impairment of renal circulation by surrounding the kidneys with cellophane or silk, is thought to result from a vasoconstrictor substance produced in the ischemic kidney. It is not nervous in origin, for denervation operations do not prevent or modify the experimental hypertension produced by the ischemia.

Elaborate experiments have been performed to demonstrate the presence of a pressor substance in the circulation of hypertensive animals. Transfusion and cross transfusion experiments have not been successful or have given equivocal results. Still, an animal with normal tension may acquire hypertension if the ischemic kidney of a hypertensive animal is transplanted into its tissues. In fact a pressor substance has been collected from the venous blood of the ischemic kidney, a substance called *renin,* apparently produced in the cortex of the kidney and apparently present in or near the cells of the juxta-glomerular body. Perfusion experiments show little activity of renin unless a normal constituent of blood, a component of the alpha globulin fraction, is added. Renin hydrolyzes this agent to produce angiotensin I, which is then converted to angiotensin II. How angiotensin II acts is not clear. It may stimulate secretion of aldosterone by the adrenal cortex. The relationship of renin to essential hypertension, if any, is not established. Renin inhibitors have been used in therapy. In renal hypertension itself angiotensin is probably only one of many components in this complex problem (see Chap. 29). Satisfactory results have not been obtained with renin inhibitor, and the place of these substances in the mechanism of essential hypertension is not clear.

Whether the events that occur in the Goldblatt experiment are comparable to those of naturally occurring hypertensive disease in man has been a matter of great dispute. The cardiac output, heart rates, blood volume and peripheral blood flow are normal in the experimental animals as in the human disease. Blood flow through extremities, muscles and brain is essentially normal, unlike the findings in increased activity of epinephrine. The splanchnic bed and renal arterioles participate in vasoconstriction, but blood flow is normal due to the elevated pressure. The blood pressure appears to be "set" at a higher level than normal. Sympathectomy neither prevents nor cures the experimental disease. However, how important this renal mechanism may be in essential hypertensive disease in man is not established, although many investigators believe that this, or a comparable mechanism, produces the hypertension through some type of renal action.

In acute hemorrhagic nephritis, in which the hypertensive picture is often sudden in onset and may not be persistent, and in eclampsia as well, renin has been found in the circulating blood in amounts which could account for the hypertensive picture.

The Goldblatt mechanism appears to be active in certain types of renal disease other than in the diffuse nephritic pictures mentioned. In pyelonephritis with atrophic renal damage, unilateral or bilateral, the mechanism appears to be active. Removal of the unilaterally involved atrophic kidney frequently results in relief of the hypertension. Congenital anomalies of the renal artery or atherosclerotic disease impinging on renal arterial blood flow may cause hypertension. Renin release has been shown to be influenced by pressure changes within the kidney in the absence of changes in flow and oxygen uptake, possibly in the gradient between the intraluminal pressure at the glomerular capillary and the pressure in renal tissue. Since correction of these defects may produce cure, their recognition is important. The frequency of these groups in the usual run of hypertensions is low, perhaps one to five per cent. Since results of the usual renal function studies are normal, demonstration of a mechanism different from that of essential hypertension is not possible. However, sudden onset, occurrence in a young patient, rapid development of a malignant phase in an older patient and presence of flank or abdominal pain preceding the hypertension may suggest the possibility. Demonstration of disparity of size of the kidneys by roentgenogram contributes to the diagnosis. Differential renal function studies by ureteral catheterization with reduced volume, sodium excretion, or dye appearance on one side (Howard test) are helpful; the radioisotopic renogram may also be an aid. However, angiography is finally necessary to show the defect and the cause for a unilateral Goldblatt mechanism and to rule out essential hypertension.

Attempts to relate certain instances of hypertension to *endocrine disease* have not been successful. Hypertension does occur in such diseases as pituitary basophilism, aldosteronism and pheochromocytoma, but none of these conditions occurs in essential hypertension. Recently much interest in saluretic diuretics and low sodium diets in hypertension has led to consideration of possible relationships between hypertension and the adrenal cortex. The mechanisms in primary aldosteronism are discussed elsewhere. Primary aldosteronism may exist with normal serum electrolyte values and be mistaken for essential hypertension. Plasma renin activity is suppressed and aldosterone production increased in such patients. At times also diminished carbohydrate tolerance occurs.

Experimentally, hypertension may be produced by the administration of ACTH, especially when sodium intake is not restricted. Circumstances are similar to those in Cushing's disease. This is apparently mediated by the adrenal cortex, and is due to increased peripheral resistance. In hypertensive disease which appears to be based upon other factors, such as that seen in acute hemorrhagic nephritis and in toxemia of pregnancy, there is a more direct relation between sodium intake and blood pressure level. In essential hypertension some relation is evident, but it is not clear how important it is. While hypertension is associated with some disturbance in salt and water metabolism, serum sodium and chloride determinations are normal in hypertensive subjects generally. Some hypertensives, in early phases, are huge salt excretors. Low sodium diets, when rigid, reduce blood pressure. Effective agents producing negative sodium and water balance reduce plasma and extracellular fluid volume and increase responsiveness to ganglion-blocking drugs.

Most interesting and unusual is the hypertensive state associated with pheochromocytoma, a tumor of the medullary portion of the adrenal gland. These tumors contain large amounts of epinephrine and norepinephrine in varying proportions. Hypertension may be persistent, but is often paroxysmal. Symptoms result from release of the hormones from the tumor, causing sudden rapid rises in blood pressure, tachycardia, anxiety, headache, nausea and epigastric and precordial pain. All symptoms do not always appear. Norepinephrine produces no tachycardia and does not affect the cardiac output. Epinephrine does, and produces hypermetabolism and hyperglycemia as well. Variations in the clinical picture depend in large part on these variables, but there are exceptions. Since blood epinephrine is difficult to determine, certain tests may be helpful in diagnosis. Intravenous histamine (0.025 mg.) may bring on an attack and more recently tyramine has been used as a provocative agent. Benodioxane intravenously, 10 mg. per square meter of body surface, through adrenolytic action, drops the blood pressure elevation, if due to epinephrine or norepinephrine, as do certain other adrenergic blocking agents (Regitine, Dibenamine). Thus, in persistent hypertension of this type, these agents, especially Regitine, are useful. Dibenamine and Regitine have a similar action. There is considerable variability in results with the various testing agents. The finding of abnormal levels of catecholamines and their metabolites in the blood and in the urine has become available through precise chemical tests and may indicate excessive production of pressor agents by the adrenal gland, thus becoming helpful in diagnosis.

Toxic disturbances are at times the cause of hypertension. Lead produces hypertensive crises, it is true, but no association of lead or any other toxic substance with essential hypertension has been established.

Big vessel *arteriosclerosis* produces an entirely different change in the blood pressure, with elevation of the systolic level and no elevation, or a drop, in the diastolic level (see p. 278), and can be dismissed as a cause of essential hypertension. At times arteriosclerotic disease extends into small vessels and into the arterioles. It is possible that peripheral resistance is increased under these circumstances and that diastolic elevations could occur. However, such changes do not appear early in essential hypertension, and their late occurrence can be explained only as a result of the hypertension, or with the hypertension accelerating the arteriosclerotic process, rather than vice versa. Thus an arteriosclerotic mechanism for essential hypertension is not established.

In Table 16–1, neurogenic causes for hypertension are listed. Known neurogenic mechanisms affecting the blood pressure have been reviewed on p. 294

Essential Hypertension. Much of the discussion under secondary hypertension has concerned the possible relationships of known mechanisms to essential hypertension and should be reviewed, particularly as related to possible renal factors. In over 80 per cent of patients with diastolic hypertension the cause, for the individual and to medical science, is unknown. Possible mechanisms have been reviewed above. Those instances with cause unestablished by medical science are termed *essential hypertension,* a term indicating hypertension of unknown origin.

There are data to suggest the presence of hereditary factor, at least as a predisposing cause. Ayman's studies show a high incidence of hypertension in the offspring (46 per cent) if both parents were hypertensive and a low incidence (3 per cent) in the children of those who are normotensive. There are also racial differences in incidence. The frequency of the characteristic constitutional build, of a stocky, thick-set, muddy-complexioned person with hypertension, is well known. Some inherited error of metabolism is possible.

The relationship between hypertension and the underlying disease is not clear. The problem of hypertension causing basic organ damage or that damage and the hypertension stem from the same cause is unsettled. Therapy to reduce blood pressure is based on the assumption that control of hypertension is paramount to the control of the hypertensive disease. There is evidence to incriminate *nervous impulses.* The assumption has long been made that increased peripheral resistance results from a hypersensitivity of the vasoconstrictor nerves supplying the arterioles. The type of hypertension produced in animals by section of carotid sinuses and aortic nerves does not bear any real resemblance to essential hypertension. It is accompanied by wide swings of blood pressure, tachycardia, and changes in cardiac output and blood volume. There is also increased peripheral blood flow. Such hypertension is practically eradicated by complete sympathectomy. However, many hypertensive, as well as nonhypertensive, subjects show prolonged increase in blood pressure with emotional disturbances. Change in the reaction to the cold pressor test from hyperreactive to hyporeactive has occurred, depending upon the psychologic problem presented to the patient at the time. Emotional factors affect neural control of blood vessels, and, despite block of sympathetic impulses with tetraethylammonium and similar agents, blood pressure may be varied by emotional stimuli.

Our chief concern is to find out what activates these neurogenic reactions. Sympathetic nervous hyperactivity may not be necessary to produce changes in nervous activity. If arterioles were sensitized or hyperactive to epinephrine or norepinephrine, or if there were limited ability to inactivate norepinephrine, normal sympathetic outflow might produce increased vasoconstrictor activity. However, there is little evidence to support this view.

Some implications of the effects of neurogenic impulses may be gained from current drug therapy, which is based upon ganglion-blocking agents and upon agents otherwise affecting nervous impulses. Reserpine is known to produce in animals a depletion of catecholamines and serotonin in the brain and of norepinephrine in sympathetic nerves. Other drugs, such as guanethidine, also deplete catecholamines from neuroeffector junctions as well as from other storage sites. Ganglion-blocking agents function through reduction of transmission of impulses through the ganglia by inhibition of acetylcholine action. Although many agents exert their major effects at the sympathetic neuroeffector site, the precise actions are not identical. Both sympathetic and parasympathetic blockade occurs; side effects result from the parasympathetic block. Parasympathetic blockade is commonly incomplete, and the fact that the impulses affecting pressure during standing are involved accounts for postural hypotension. Since antipressor therapy may reverse malignant hypertension, participation of the nervous system in the mechanisms seems likely.

Effects of deranged *sodium* metabolism have already been discussed. Low sodium diets combined with saluretic diuretics produce hypotensive responses. High salt intake in certain areas of the world correlates with increased incidence of hypertension. The mechanisms involved are not clear, nor is the importance of the factor in the hypertensive reaction established.

Symptomatology. Usually hypertension itself causes few symptoms. Most symptoms are those of atherosclerotic complications as expressed in specific organs—the heart, kidneys or brain, for example. In the heart both the strain of increased diastolic pressure from arteriolar constriction and the acceleration of coronary atherosclerosis are active in production of congestive heart failure. Some general symptoms are at times elicited. Fatigue, insomnia, headache, vertigo are such, although some investigators believe that many of these have been produced after discussions with physicians. Patients who are told of possible heart changes, stroke, or the like, may experience anxiety, and minor symptoms may be exaggerated. Those with rapidly progressing hypertension entering the malignant phase with arteriolar necrosis have symptoms of severe arteriolar disease referred to the organs involved—the eye with hemorrhage and exudates and papilledema, the kidney with renal insufficiency, the heart with severe cardiac damage, and the brain with severe

ischemia producing hypertensive encephalopathy.

The convulsive disorders accompanying certain hypertensive states—for example, the convulsions of acute nephritis or eclampsia of pregnancy—are thought to be the result of cerebral ischemia produced by hypertensive crises and constriction of the arterioles. In some patients edema of the brain may be present and may act as a contributing factor. Convulsions often occur in the absence of edema. Control of these convulsions, therefore, is based upon therapy to relax arteriolar spasm or therapy to render the brain less responsive.

"Malignant" and "benign" hypertension appear to be phases of a similar process. In the malignant type, a more severe acute phase develops accompanied by arteriolar constriction severe enough to be associated with necrosis. In experimental hypertension, with the Goldblatt clamp, the process may be made "benign" or "malignant" by the degree of constriction of the renal artery. One can visualize any cause of arteriolar constriction, if severe enough, producing the malignant phase. Some varieties of hypertension, therefore, may be more commonly malignant than others, and some causes, if acute and severe enough from onset, may produce an acute, fulminating, rapidly progressing picture of malignant hypertension without any intermediate developments. Benign phases are likely to be prolonged, and the mechanism of the clinical findings is through the development of complications secondary to atherosclerosis. Malignant types are more likely to present findings resulting directly from arteriolar damage.

Place of Surgery. Obviously, patients with hypertension of known cause, such as chronic hemorrhagic nephritis, unilateral pyelonephritis, pheochromocytoma and coarctation of the aorta, must be evaluated by proper investigation to establish if possible a known correctable cause. Anomalies of the renal artery when corrected result in return of blood pressure to normal. The removal of a unilateral atrophic kidney, when function of the opposite kidney is adequate, often results in a drop in blood pressure. Generally, those most favorable are candidates under fifty years of age. Experience has shown that patients with prolonged hypertension, especially those over fifty years of age and those with severe functional damage to the brain, eyegrounds, heart and kidneys, are not favorable subjects; but, when a removable cause of hypertension is present, it should be eliminated.

In essential hypertension the attack by sympathectomy has, in large part, given way to the use of antihypertensive drugs. Sympathectomy is confined chiefly to instances in which the drugs cannot be given successfully.

Hypotension

Hypotension may accompany many disease states. Systolic pressures below 100 are usually considered low. When occurring without demonstrable cause, hypotension is called essential, or primary, and such patients show no ill effects except, at times, increased fatigue, loss of vitality and vigor, and headaches. Such symptoms occur in hypertensive and normotensive subjects as well, so that relationship to hypotension is doubtful. In shock hypotension is dramatic. It may occur in wasting and debilitating diseases, such as tuberculosis. In marked nutritional deficiency states hypotension is common, and in such conditions as Addison's disease it is an outstanding finding.

The mechanism of hypotension, aside from that related to shock when there is a loss of blood volume or a sudden increase in the intravascular space, is little understood. Addison's disease and the hypotension of acute infection probably fall into this group. Hypotension related to syncope is discussed below.

Postural hypotension, a condition occasionally met clinically, is characterized by a marked drop in blood pressure on assumption of the standing position. The reflex mechanisms which maintain the blood pressure and counterbalance the effects of gravity are reduced, and the systolic pressure drops to low levels along with the diastolic pressure. Vertigo and even faintness develop.

There are two general sets of conditions which produce it: (1) Exaggerated venous pooling of blood in the presence of a normally functioning sympathetic nervous system. This is seen in older people, in those standing at attention, in Addison's disease, in marked varicosities, after partial sympathectomy and after the use of ganglion-blocking agents. Some believe that the hypotension resulting from meprobamate ingestion in some individuals, acting at times in very small doses, may be the result of direct action on the vasomotor center of the medulla. (2) In failure of the sympathetic nervous impulses to respond to the normal pooling of blood on assuming the upright position, that is, in loss of reflex vasoconstrictor response to the fall in blood

pressure, a similar picture may be seen. If only the postural vasoconstrictor reflexes are affected, it may be an isolated finding. However, if the lesions are extensive enough to involve other portions of the autonomic nervous system, other disturbances in function may be present. These include inhibition of sweating, paleness of the skin, and failure of the heart rate to increase with drop in pressure. These changes may be secondary to disease involving the central nervous system, such as multiple sclerosis, or may occur in the absence of any obvious associated disease.

SYNCOPE

Transient sudden loss of consciousness of short duration is termed syncope. Confusion with shock is discussed under Shock. If gradual in onset and prolonged and not spontaneously reversible, the loss of consciousness is called coma. Both conditions differ from sleep in that noninjurious stimuli do not affect the state of unconsciousness. Events leading to syncope may stop short of a stimulus sufficient to cause unconsciousness, so that lightheadedness, a sinking sensation, numbness of the hands and feet, epigastric or precordial uneasiness, weakness, yawning and nausea may constitute the episode without actual loss of consciousness. The patient, usually standing or sitting, collapses, and the body lies limp and motionless. Facial pallor is marked, the pupils are dilated, and respiration is slowed. The attack usually terminates when the horizontal position is assumed. Two such episodes described as the same by patients or onlookers may be different in origin and require different therapy.

Syncope may be divided into three types. The first includes those patients in whom the mechanism underlying disturbed blood flow to the brain effects a pooling or deviation of blood which interferes with return of flow to the heart. In this group, blood does not return to the heart in sufficient amounts to maintain adequate cerebral circulation. Since the disturbance in circulation occurs before blood gets to the heart, it is termed *precardiac*.

The second category includes those in whom return of blood to the heart is adequate, but in whom the heart fails to function adequately as a pump, as in extreme tachycardia, or asystole. This is called *cardiac* syncope, although it does not necessarily imply organic heart disease. Nathanson defined cardiac syncope as sudden loss of consciousness due to cerebral anemia of cardiac origin, and sudden cardiac death as fatal cardiac syncope.

The third group includes those in whom both factors are normal, but in whom there is an interference in blood flow to the brain somewhere between the heart and the brain itself. This is the *postcardiac* type.

The precardiac type includes common fainting attacks, a condition to which Lewis applied the term *vasovagal syncope*. The syncope of postural hypotension falls into the precardiac group with changes in pulse pressure and pulse quite similar to those in common fainting attacks. The peripheral type of carotid sinus syndrome, that resulting in dilatation of peripheral vessels with drop in blood pressure when the carotid sinus is stimulated, is also in the same group, as are certain types of pleural and peritoneal "shock." All the reactions that occur when the pleural space is invaded by a needle are not explained as precardiac syncope, but precardiac syncope is one of the reactions which result from such procedures. So-called peritoneal shock, in which there is sudden loss of pressure in the peritoneal cavity, falls into the same category.

The condition described by Weiss as central vasomotor syncope, and exemplified by syncopal reactions to local anesthetics and brain tumors, also falls into this group. Here also go pulmonary vascular changes that result, for example, from the Valsalva experiment, after which venous return is temporarily stopped, as well as pulmonary vascular disturbances resulting from sudden release of pressure following compression of the thorax, which produces some pooling of blood in the chest.

All the pictures of precardiac syncope are characterized by some disturbance in return of blood to the heart, resulting in inadequate output and disturbed cerebral circulation.

Cardiac syncope may be broken down into at least three categories, all characterized by extreme changes in heart rate with accompanying blood pressure changes. This finding differentiates the syncope from the other two groups, narrows the problem of differential diagnosis and immediately points out the direction which therapy must take.

The first of the three categories in this group is that of vagal stimulation resulting in asystole or a markedly slowed ventricular rate. Such vagal stimulation, if sufficient to produce an inadequate minute output of blood, despite the fact that the output produced by each beat is greater than normal, will result in asystole with the blood pressure approaching zero, or slow heart rate in which the change in blood pressure is less marked. Such pictures of vagal stimulation may be the result of hyperactive carotid sinus or other reflexes, such as the oculovagal or vagovagal reflex. The last is characterized by afferent stimuli arising from a vagal source and being sent as efferent stimuli again down the vagus. These reactions have been described in patients with syncope on swallowing when a diverticulum of the esophagus has instigated the reflex. Pleural shock falls into this group if the reflex produced by the pleural stimulation is manifested in vagal stimulation.

Obviously this train of events may occur in the absence of organic heart disease. It is not usual for more than one of these reflexes to be hyperactive at a time. For example, the oculovagal reflex may be hyperactive when the carotid sinus reflex is normal.

Second, cardiac syncope may be produced when organic disease of the heart interferes with conduction from the atrium to the ventricle. This is the so-called Stokes-Adams syndrome of organic heart disease. The change from normal conduction or partial heart block to complete heart block may occur with a latent period before the ventricle takes up its own rhythm. If this period is sufficiently long, syncope may develop along with convulsions and the other symptoms characteristic of Stokes-Adams attacks. The same picture may develop if the ventricle does not stop beating, but the ventricular pacemaker, although becoming active quickly, is sufficiently slow, let us say 8 beats per minute, to produce long intervals between each beat. The Stokes-Adams syndrome may also develop in complete heart block, as is infrequently appreciated by many physicians, when the ventricular pacemaker shifts to another center which discharges at a slow rate or with transient seizures of ventricular fibrillation.

In the third category, under the cardiac grouping, the heart rate is extremely rapid, as in paroxysmal tachycardia or 1:1 atrial flutter, the efficiency of the heart as a pump is markedly reduced, and the cardiac output is so diminished that cerebral circulation is impaired. When this abnormality becomes sufficiently advanced, syncope develops.

Cardiac syncope, therefore, may result from extremely slow hearts or extremely rapid hearts, both producing an inadequate output of blood. It may occur in the absence or presence of organic heart disease. Under either circumstance the picture is a dramatic one which requires effective treatment.

Under the term "cardiac syncope" there should also be considered certain episodes of fainting associated with aortic stenosis and congestive and anginal heart failure. Proper classification of this group is not possible, but it is mentioned here because some investigators believe that with congestive or anginal heart failure, particularly with exertion, the heart may not be able to increase its output sufficiently to meet the demands in the periphery. Here, despite the fact that blood pressure and heart rate may not be remarkably out of the range of normal, syncope might develop because of the inadequate response of the heart to exercise. That this mechanism is active in some patients and does enter into the development of syncope is not definitely established. For the present, however, since heart rate and pulse pressure are not remarkably altered and cardiac output is probably not reduced, these types are included in the postcardiac grouping.

The postcardiac group is characterized by syncope in the absence of lowered pulse pressure and extreme changes in heart rate. In their absence the entities already discussed, except syncope on exertion with angina pectoris and aortic stenosis, need not be considered in the differential diagnosis. Postcardiac syncope is most clearly exemplified by the third type of carotid sinus syndrome, that is, the cerebral type. Since this can be produced experimentally in patients by digital pressure on the carotid sinus, it has been studied thoroughly, particularly by Weiss and his group. It is well known that carotid sinus stimulation may result in syncope despite the fact that the blood pressure is not lowered and the heart rate is not disturbed. In patients in whom mixed types of carotid sinus reflex occur, thorough atropinization to eliminate vagal effects does not stop the occurrence of syncope. In attacks these patients become extremely pale and faint, apparently from vascular effects in the brain. Weiss was able to show that there was no evidence of sufficient disturbance in the total cerebral circulation to account for the syncope. He suggested that there may be localized disturbances in circulation affecting the portion of the midbrain which controls consciousness. Such attacks are frequently accompanied by convulsions, which leads to their being regarded as epileptic seizures, particularly

when they occur spontaneously. This part of the problem will not be discussed here except to state that there is adequate evidence to indicate that such episodes are not of the nature of epilepsy.

Syncope may also develop under other circumstances when the precardiac and cardiac mechanisms are not active, with disturbances in the circulation to the brain in the absence of diminished output by the heart. Syncope of hypertensive crises falls into this category, as does that accompanying cerebral engorgement. Syncope associated with dissecting aneurysm likewise may fall into this group, but it is not clear in some of these patients that stimulation of the aortic nerves and vagal effects may not be responsible for the syncope. The transient, sudden loss of consciousness which occurs in hypoglycemic reactions is considered in the same category and possibly is explained by biochemical changes in the brain rather than by circulatory disturbances. These transient losses of consciousness do fit the definition of syncope and are certainly postcardiac in type.

Angina pectoris and aortic stenosis are two conditions in which syncope has been noted and in which, in certain patients, changes in the blood pressure and pulse have not occurred. This would indicate, then, a disturbance in cerebral circulation not accounted for by reduction in cardiac output. It is possible, since these episodes of syncope occur on exertion, that the explanation of syncope in some of these patients lies in inadequate increase in cardiac output, as stated in the discussion of cardiac syncope, but there is little evidence to make this differentiation, and, in the absence of remarkable changes in blood pressure and heart rate, they seem to belong in this group. In both angina pectoris and aortic stenosis in some instances it is known that other types of syncope, both precardiac and cardiac, are active in the production of fainting attacks. In those in whom this is not true, the postcardiac mechanism is most likely active.

Heart disease may produce syncope which falls into any of these three groups.

SHOCK

The term "shock" in medicine is used in many ways. Such conditions as shock therapy, nervous shock, and so forth, fall into other fields. Peripheral circulatory insufficiency or failure and its findings are the presenting picture in the condition "true shock," discussed here. The picture is usually described as one characterized by a reduced venous return and lowered blood pressure accompanied by a circulatory impairment which tends to progress and eventuate in an irreversible circulatory failure and death. The set of symptoms and signs varies with severity of causative factors, the individual involved, and the time sequence of the development of the picture. An adjective such as medical, traumatic, hemorrhagic, septic, surgical, is used often to connote the condition producing it. Since syncope or coma sometimes accompanies shock, it is necessary to consider in the differential diagnosis the various types of syncope and at times of coma. The early changes which develop in the circulation—pallor, venous collapse, falling blood pressure—are quite comparable in common fainting attacks and in the picture of shock. Since syncope is a transient loss of consciousness, it may be associated with shock and therefore cannot be differentiated from that under the definitions we are using. Shock can be differentiated from common fainting attacks, for here there is implied not only transient unconsciousness, but also a reversible vascular mechanism. In essence, common fainting attacks and shock pictures differ in that, with common fainting attacks, changes in the circulation are temporary and reversible, whereas in the usual shock picture the circulatory changes are prolonged. The differentiation goes back to the cause. Syncopal states seen in emotional conditions and with severe colicky pain have often been termed primary shock. These immediately follow such events or injuries, and do not represent true shock.

True shock, as the term is used here, represents a syndrome in which there is a loss of adequate effective perfusion of vital organs. Complex interrelated hemodynamic, metabolic and hematologic changes develop in which there is a critical impairment of effective circulating blood volume. There is a great diversity of etiologic factors. The cause may rest in the heart or arteries when forward flow of blood is impaired (certain instances of acute myocardial infarction, acute cardiac tamponade, pulmonary embolism). To compensate for the inadequate cardiac output arteriolar constriction may take place, through aortic carotid sinus or other mechanisms. Failure of such compensations leaves a pale patient with tachycardia, lowered blood pressure, and output of blood inadequate for cellular metabolism. In tamponade

venous pressure is also elevated. When the cause is an infection, such as a gram-negative rod septicemia, the endotoxin may react with certain components of blood and trigger off a histamine release. This has been shown experimentally in animals. A direct action on heart muscle is thought to occur. The response appears to be anaphylactoid. Venous pooling with portal venous hypertension develops. Metabolic acidosis appears. In humans these mechanisms are not entirely worked out. In surgical trauma blood may be pooled or sequestered in venocapillary segments and plasma lost to the tissues. Isotopic studies indicate the importance of the former rather than the latter. Indeed a number of factors may be so interwoven that many of them may be responsible for the final clinical picture. Seepage from wounds or burned areas, effects of vomiting or diarrhea, electrolyte disturbances, with fluid shifts, plasma loss to the tissues, and, most obviously, hemorrhage, at times are responsible. When the changes result from hemorrhage, the onset is a sudden drop in blood pressure, resulting from the reduced circulating blood volume. The loss of blood usually must be greater than 10 per cent for any appreciable effect to develop. The resulting tachycardia occurs from carotid sinus and aortic reflexes. The spleen contracts to put out its contained blood. Air hunger appears. The skin becomes pale, for its small vessels, as well as those of the intestine and less essential organs, constrict to diminish the vascular bed to approach the reduced blood volume and increase venous return, cardiac output and blood pressure. Faintness and giddiness may appear from cerebral ischemia. Later fluids are poured into the circulation from the tissues to help compensate for the reduced volume. Cyanosis occurs, especially in the fingertips, the metabolic rate and the body temperature drop, and the pulse is rapid and thready. Venous pressure is low as is the cardiac output. Tissue perfusion becomes more impaired, oxygenation of tissues is further embarrassed, aerobic metabolism is reduced and anaerobic pathways come into play.

At first compensatory factors may be partially effective. However, as circulatory volume and venous return continue to diminish, the cardiac output drops greatly and the blood pressure may continue to fall. Alpha adrenergic stimuli result in venular constriction and increased venous return.

Late in shock the peripheral vessels become

unresponsive to continued vasoconstrictor discharges and they dilate. Fluid passes to the tissues as the result of the increased capillary pressure. Blood is shunted from these tissues. Later, with depletion of epinephrine and norepinephrine stores, there is terminal vasodilatation and impaired cardiac function. Metabolic acidosis may contribute further to vasomotor and cardiac collapse. However, such possibilities, evident in animal research, are not clearly established for humans. The lethal effects of prolonged shock probably result from an accumulation of toxic products secondary to poor tissue perfusion and anoxia resulting from the anaerobic metabolic processes.

The multiplicity of factors initiating shock and the variable mechanisms stimulated as it progresses emphasize the division of therapeutic measures into two groups: one, emergency measures applied to correct underlying circulatory failure and the disturbed vascular volume, the other directed at etiologic factors.

There is evidence that some "vasopressor" agents selectively act on arterial vessels and others primarily on venules and veins, a matter of practical importance. Angiotensin II causes arterial constriction experimentally in dogs with increased portal venous pressure and venous pooling. Isoproterenol causes a fall in arterial and portal venous pressures and increased venous return. Epinephrine participates in both reactions. Direct observation of the microcirculation in experimental animals shows that norepinephrine intensifies arteriolar constriction and capillary ischemia, reduces microcirculatory vasomotion and predisposes to venular stasis. Octapressin tends to sustain venous tone and increase venous return. Vasopressor agents have a limited place in the treatment of shock, particularly in cardiogenic and septic shock, and occasionally in hemorrhage.

The treatment of nonhemorrhagic shock by transfusion, is not constantly effective, and in animals death occurs when the amount of fluid loss is insufficient to explain it. Hemodilution follows hemorrhage; hemoconcentration, other types of shock. Blood chemical changes vary, nonhemorrhagic shock producing prolonged coagulation time and elevated nitrogen and potassium levels, while hemorrhage either does not affect or has opposite effects upon these factors. There is no doubt that all these factors play some part in the production of shock, but no one has been able to show that they are primarily responsible.

In shock many organs may be profoundly affected. The kidneys, for example, filter little blood through the glomeruli, and the tubular function may be impaired. Shock depletes the heart of substances necessary for its function. In general, sodium ion exchange is disturbed.

VENOUS PRESSURE

A glance at Figure 16–6 shows that the pressure in the veins drops from that in the capillaries. This reduction is aided to some degree by an increase in the velocity of the flow of blood as the venous cross section becomes smaller when the larger veins are entered, for the increase in velocity is accompanied by a reduction in lateral pressure. However, loss of pressure due to friction, although small, appears to be the important cause of the slight drop, and the pressure gradient is not great.

The energy imparted to the blood by its ejection from the left ventricle into the aorta is largely responsible for the continued flow of blood back to the heart through the veins. The pressure, therefore, represents in a large part this energy. If the arterioles are widened, the pressure increases. But this is modified to a considerable extent by the fact that the small venules and the capillaries may dilate to adjust themselves to the amount of blood coming into them from the arteries, and thus little variation in pressure may appear. The reverse may also be true. If the arterioles constrict and send less blood into the capillaries, these vessels may constrict through nervous control and reduce their capacity and thereby maintain the pressure.

The flow of blood to the heart through the veins may also be influenced by the thoracic pressure, for, in inspiration, the pressure inside the thorax is actually less than atmospheric pressure by approximately 6 mm. of mercury and, during expiration, may amount to as much as —2.5 mm. of mercury. The average is —4 mm. of mercury in the right atrium. If the positive pressure in the vein, resulting from the remaining force of the left ventricle in transmitting the blood through the vein, is added to the negative pressure in the thorax, the total pressure effective in driving the blood forward toward the heart will be obtained. This is called the effective venous pressure.

Respiration may also help venous return in other ways. For example, the descent of the diaphragm in inspiration may cause compression of abdominal structures and increase the pressure in the inferior vena cava. Because of the presence of valves in the veins, the flow of blood to the heart is increased. Respiratory effects are exaggerated in the Valsalva experiment as well as in the Müller experiment.

Other influences, collectively termed the *venopressor mechanism,* may help the flow of blood through the venous channels to the heart. The valves in the veins are so arranged that, if pressure is produced upon the veins, the valves will close and the blood flow be directed toward the heart. In veins between, or influenced by, muscular structures surrounding them, the movement of the muscles massages the veins, particularly during exercise, which helps considerably in increasing the venous return. This is effective in abdominal muscles as well as others. During exercise especially, this action of the muscles prevents the pooling of blood in the veins as the cardiac output is increased and more blood is sent through the arterial system to the venous circulation. A loss of this effect upon the veins with relaxation of muscular tone may impede venous return.

When the person is in the erect position, the gravitational effects of the column of blood between the point of the vessel studied and the heart act as a hydrostatic influence on the venous pressure. Since the pressures are relatively low in the venous system, the effects of gravity upon the venous system represent a large component of the total pressure and exert more influence on the venous pressure than on the arterial pressure. Above heart level gravity aids veins and hinders arteries. Below heart level the reverse is true. The arterial pressure is high enough to overcome the drag of gravity above the heart level.

Nervous control is important in the regulation of the circulation with postural change. The nervous control maintains the venous and capillary tone by adjusting the caliber of these small vessels in the splanchnic area. The small venules and veins receive sympathetic vasoconstrictor impulses, and a tonic state normally exists. Venipuncture causes constriction, and carbon dioxide is thought to produce local dilatation. The factors which influence arterial tone in general also affect venous tone.

A number of clinical syndromes develop as a result of inadequacies in some of the stimulating mechanisms. Some of the weakness, the giddiness and at times the syncope which occur when a patient first assumes the erect position after prolonged rest in bed are the result of the loss of tone in the muscles as well as lowered tone in the nervous control of the vessels. Blood pools in the abdominal veins and capillaries, venous return to the heart diminishes, and output of blood is reduced. The brain receives less blood, and symptoms leading to syncope appear. The drop in blood pressure in these episodes amounts to 25 mm. or more. Fainting in soldiers kept at attention for a long time results apparently from the same mechanism, that is, the loss of the massaging effect of the muscles. These changes are counteracted by the assumption of the horizontal position, which naturally ensues when the individual faints.

Measurement

Techniques for the measurement of venous pressure differ greatly from those for the measurement of arterial pressure. The low pressures obtaining in the veins, particularly when the part is brought to heart level, require a more delicate instrument than the sphygmomanometer to record such minor changes in pressure as occur. The simplest and crudest method is to raise the arm, when the vessels are unrestricted by clothing, until the vein, distended in the lowered position, collapses. If this level is sighted off against the heart level, the elevation of venous pressure may be estimated. Other techniques have been utilized to cause collapse of a vein, particularly the placing of a transparent chamber over a part of a vein. An increase in pressure in the chamber can be seen to cause collapse of the vein, and, when this is read at heart level on a suitable manometer connected to the chamber, an indirect determination of pressure may be obtained. Heart level should represent the level of the left atrium. Various points are used; the mid-axillary line in the supine position is satisfactory, since there is difficulty in obtaining the true physiologic zero point, which itself is variable. Pressures in the right atrium itself are obtained by catheterization.

Direct determination of venous pressure by insertion of a needle into the vein is the most reliable technique. A column of citrated solution is placed in a vertical tube connected with the needle, the vein is brought to heart level, and, as the citrate flows into the vein, it will seek its level at the height of the venous pressure, which may then be read in millimeters or centimeters of citrate solution (Fig. 16-9).

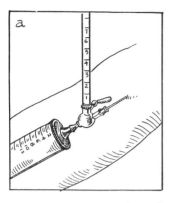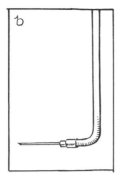

Figure 16–9. *a,* The technique for direct determination of venous pressure, using syringe and 3-way stopcock. *b,* L-tube also used in direct venous pressure determinations. (From Sodeman in Pullen: Medical Diagnosis.)

When the vein is brought to heart level and the pressure taken in a normal person, the figure is usually between 50 and 100 mm. of water. If the pressure is taken below heart level, the effects of gravity must be considered in the determination.

Elevation of Venous Pressure

Venous pressure is elevated when there is some obstruction to flow toward the heart. This may be the result of constricting clothing, tumors or other factors exerting pressure upon the vein locally. If the heart cannot take all the blood returning to it through the veins, there will be a damming back of blood, and the pressure increases. This is one of the theories of congestive heart failure, and, in the absence of mediastinal pressure or pressure peripherally to account for the elevation, such rises in venous pressure may be interpreted as the inability of the heart to take care of the blood reaching it. This may be due to myocardial weakness, to tamponade of the heart from pericardial effusion or to constriction of the heart by a thickened abnormal pericardium. A general rise in venous pressure distends the liver and causes engorgement of other structures—the kidneys, with reduced secretion; cerebral veins, with slowing of the circulation there. The effects on capillary filtration are given in the section on water balance. This effect and the effect upon other structures are described in Chapter 20.

Blood flow through small vessels is reduced, and cyanosis may appear. It must be pointed out here that, in arterial hypertension, capillary and venous pressures are not increased. The reduction in pressure across the arterioles is sufficient to reduce the pressure in the capillaries and veins to their usual normal level, and venous pressure is not increased in hypertensive states unless there is cardiac failure or elevation of venous pressure for other reasons.

Locally, venous pressure may be elevated from gravitational effects and at times from connections directly to an artery, that is, through arteriovenous aneurysm. In growing structures, as in children before the epiphyses close, this arterialization of the venous blood may result in an increased growth of the involved extremity, and an asymmetry may appear upon this basis. Elevations in pulmonary venous pressure are described in Chapter 20.

Reduction in Venous Pressure

Abnormal reductions in venous pressure also occur. These are seen chiefly in shocklike states, whether medical shock, such as that occurring with coronary thrombosis, or surgical shock following operative procedures, hemorrhage, and so on. Under these circumstances the veins may be so collapsed that it may be difficult to enter them with a needle. When an airplane is pulled out of a power dive, the force of gravity may be so great that inertia keeps the blood of the occupant temporarily in the lower part of the body, venous return to the heart is diminished, and cerebral blood pressure falls with loss of vision and consciousness ("blackout"). This occurs when the force equals 5 to 6 G, that is, five to six times the force of gravity. The opposite effects force blood to the head and cause engorgement, headache, feeling of fullness, increased venous return to the heart, and even mental confusion and cerebral hemorrhage. Spasm of veins, or venospasm, caused by many physical and chemical stimuli as cold or venipuncture, for example, produces constriction of these structures. Spasm of veins is not important in disturbances of the peripheral vascular system, but does occur in some such disorders—for example, thrombophlebitis.

Disturbances in Venous Circulation

With inadequate venous circulation, venous insufficiency exists. This may result from acute processes (thrombophlebitis) and cause swelling of the extremity and distended veins, or chronic disorders (varicose veins) which result in pigmentation, stasis dermatitis and ulceration. Pain is not an important symptom, but aching and heaviness develop on standing. Varicose veins may be palpated if thrombosis develops in them. With inflammation of thrombophlebitis, tenderness occurs. Varicosities and some of the factors related to their progress have already been discussed. Distention is the most constant sign. The emptying of veins in the elevated position and the speed of filling when dependency is assumed give an index of arteriolar circulation. If valves are defective, similar maneuvers cause a reflux of blood.

Many tests for incompetency of veins have been devised, all involving elevation of the part to empty the vein and noting the speed and character of filling, at rest or with exercise. Exercise may be necessary to demonstrate the adequacy or inadequacy of the deep veins. Inadequacy of the deep veins of the lower extremity is also indicated by the precipitation of pain by exercise when the superficial veins are occluded by a pressure bandage.

The color of veins is such that infra-red photography will bring out the superficial venous pattern of the leg, chest, abdomen or other part. Frequently such demonstrations in selected cases will indicate the presence of obstruction or of collateral circulation developed for other reasons.

Varicosities may be primary (caused by unknown, possibly hereditary factors or endocrine changes) or secondary, when obstruction is evident. If the valves are incompetent and the patient is erect much of the time, blood flow may actually be reversed. In the presence of obstruction and disturbed blood flow, a state of chronic venous insufficiency may develop, manifested by edema, eczematous eruptions and ulceration, especially with minor trauma and poor nutrition to the part.

Changes in venous walls may be extensive without the development of symptoms. In phlebosclerosis, for example, the veins may not be dilated and may not show the calcium deposits seen in the degenerative sclerosis of old age. Hyalinization with loss of the endothelium may develop. Fibrosis appears, but causes few clinical symptoms. Obstruction does not occur and there is no pain. Palpation of the veins discloses hard cords which are small, mobile, smooth and diminished in caliber.

Thrombophlebitis results from inflammation of the venous wall. It may occur without obvious cause, although it is ascribed to perivenous lymphangitis resulting from organisms transmitted from the lymphatics, or to a known inflammatory process. It is often asso-

ciated with inflammatory or neoplastic disease. As a result of the inflammation there are changes in the endothelium which predispose to clot formation, and partial or complete occlusion may result. Such changes are common postoperatively, when white or mixed clots tend to form and are firmly attached to the wall. Complete block of venous return may lead to massive engorgement and edema in fascial compartments of a limb with pressure adequate to impair arterial blood supply. Except in instances in which a coagulation thrombus forms proximal to an area of thrombophlebitis and is not well attached, and except in suppurative thrombophlebitis with proteolytic ferments which liquefy the clot and permit fragments to break off, embolism is uncommon.

In *phlebothrombosis,* in which the thrombus results from slowing of the blood stream and increased coagulability of the blood rather than from inflammation, the clot is a red thrombus and is loosely attached to the venous wall. It may become detached easily and frequently causes embolism. The reason for increased coagulability of the blood in phlebothrombosis is not clear, but there is an acceleration of blood coagulability which favors clotting. It may be related to the trauma of operation. The frequency of involvement of the veins of the lower extremities is no doubt due to the slowing of the circulation there. Age, cardiovascular disease and possibly digitalis are predisposing factors.

Not all agree that phlebothrombosis and thrombophlebitis are sharply defined entities as just described. In phlebothrombosis, inflammation is said to develop within a few hours, and thrombophlebitis may have associated phlebothrombosis, so that from the standpoint of the type of clot the pictures may be mixed.

The symptoms in thrombophlebitis are well defined—fever, pain and swelling—the first two as the result of inflammation and infection, the last from other factors. The venous flow is reduced, and this may be a factor in increasing capillary anoxia, which in turn may be partially responsible for the eczema, cellulitis, and even necrosis and skin ulcers seen at times. Vasoconstrictor impulses may be active in the segment involved, and spasm of the arterioles and venules may develop distally, contributing to the edema and obstruction. This is the basis for therapy by sympathetic block. The extremity may show some loss of color, and the skin may be cool. If the involved veins are superficial, redness and warmth are felt in them.

In phlebothrombosis there may be no symptoms until embolism develops. Slight rises in pulse rate occur, the sedimentation rate is elevated, and there may be tenderness on pressure of the affected part or on putting it on stretch (pain in the calf on dorsiflexion of the foot, Homans' sign, for example). Such findings are diagnostic and justify ligation above the involved area to prevent embolism.

Outstanding example of obstructive phenomena in veins are the *superior* and *inferior vena caval syndromes*. In superior vena caval obstruction from neoplasm, aneurysm or mediastinitis, the head and upper extremities are involved. There is cerebral congestion with headache, vertigo, throbbing and even mental confusion. Dilated veins and cyanosis of the face appear. Stooping and bending forward or exercise accentuates these symptoms. If the venous plexus is enlarged over the sternum, obstruction is above the azygos vein. If the azygos vein is also obstructed, blood must go through the inferior vena cava and large collaterals to cross the costal margin. Blood flow is in a downward direction over the anterior abdominal wall. Venous pressure is higher if the obstruction is below the azygos vein. In inferior vena caval syndrome due to neoplasm or aneurysm, adhesions, or the like, both lower extremities are enlarged with edema. There is prominence of the superficial veins of the legs, and dilated, often tortuous, superficial abdominal veins will extend up to the thorax. Ascites is not the result, but a possible cause, of the picture. Venous pressure is normal in the upper extremities.

Capillaries

Blood flow through the capillaries varies with location and need. In the human skin, for example, regardless of need, variations in blood flow are not accompanied by great changes in the number of open capillaries. In the muscles, however, the number open and transmitting blood depends upon need. With exercise and increased blood flow and oxygen supply, twenty to fifty times as many capillaries are open as when the tissues are at rest. The capillaries communicating directly from arteriole to venule remain open, but other branching channels are not.

The thin endothelial cells making up the capillary walls are usually regarded as semipermeable membranes (the permeability of which is influenced by stretching), but at times red blood cells, white blood cells, injected particles and even larger structures (microfilariae) go through apparently uninjured capillaries. These probably pass at the junction of the endothelial cells, and there is the possibility that much of the so-called capillary permeability may depend on the cement substance at these junctions rather than on the cells themselves. This is a relatively unexplored field. (See the section on water balance.)

The pressure in the capillaries has been measured by direct cannulization and the micropipet, and it has been shown to be, at rest at heart level, above the osmotic pressure of the plasma proteins on the arterial side and below that pressure on the venular side. Constriction of arterioles causes some drop in the capillary pressure, and dilatation an increase. But this is not the only factor which affects the pressure. The ability of the capillaries to contract and relax influences the pressure, as do the tissue pressure and the effects of varying venous pressure, either on a hypostatic basis or on the basis of disease. These relations and their bearing upon transmission of fluid into and out of the capillaries are described in the section on water balance. The variations in capillary permeability are also discussed in that section.

The fragility of the capillaries may be tested with negative pressure (suction) or with positive pressure (raising of pressure to or above diastolic pressure by application of a blood pressure cuff). Capillaries vary in fragility, owing to many factors: physiologic states, such as menstruation, menopause, thinness of skin, blondness; drugs, such as sulfadiazine, gold salts, aspirin, Dicumarol overdosage; toxins, as those of scarlet fever and diphtheria; metabolic disorders, such as uremia; vitamin deficiencies, as lack of vitamin C; endocrine disorders, as hyperthyroidism; blood dyscrasias, such as the purpuras; degenerative diseases, particularly arteriosclerosis; many dermatologic states, allergic disorders and some diseases of the nervous system. Hypertension may produce increased capillary fragility. In various organs, including the skin, direct arteriovenous shunts which by-pass the capillaries have been demonstrated. They function as aids to produce sudden necessary shifts in blood—for example, in the skin for heat elimination and in the lungs to adjust the volume of blood contacting alveolar air.

Blood Velocity and Circulation Time

The various types of flowmeters and stromuhrs used in experimental physiology are not applicable to the clinic. Velocity of blood flow varies in different parts of the circulation (Fig. 16–6). In the large arteries, in which it is greatest, it fluctuates with ventricular systole, being greatest at the height of systole and least in diastole. As the capillaries are approached and the pulsatile flow disappears, these variations in blood velocity also disappear. The velocity diminishes slightly in the arteries as the periphery is reached and drops slightly in response to the pressure in the arterioles. In the capillaries, where the cross section is 600 to 800 times that of the aorta, velocity diminishes to a greater extent than pressure and again increases in the bigger veins as the pressure drops again. The blood velocity increases to some degree in the venous side as the venous channels coalesce and the total cross section becomes smaller (Fig. 16–6).

Circulation Time

In clinical medicine the velocity of blood flow is expressed as the circulation time. If this time is longer than normal, the circulation time is prolonged or slowed; if shorter than normal, the time is fast. Since the routes over which the blood may travel in its journey from and back to the heart are greatly varied in their length, there is no such thing as a single definite circulation time. Clinical techniques measure the circulation time from one point in the circulation to another. For example, a material which may be tasted is injected into the arm vein, and the length of time required for the blood to reach the heart, go through the lungs, back to the heart, and out to the tongue in sufficient concentration for the test material to be tasted is measured. The technique just described is commonly used, either with Decholin, a bitter-tasting preparation of bile salts, or with saccharin, which may be detected by its sweetish taste. If a material which may be detected on the breath (ether) or may cause a cough when it reaches the lungs (paraldehyde) is used, the arm-to-lung circulation time may be measured. Thus techniques are available to measure the circulation time through the right side of the heart and through the combined right and left sides of the heart. Circulation time through the left side of the heart may be calculated by difference.

The great difficulty with measurements of circulation time of the first type described is that the end point is purely subjective and the patient's senses must be depended upon. If a dye, such as fluorescein, and apparatus to determine fluorescence in the eyes are used, it is possible to determine the arm-to-eye circulation time and have an objective end point. Similarly, radioactive substances may be injected and a Geiger counter used to determine the end point. Normally, the arm-to-lung circulation time is about six seconds, the arm-to-tongue circulation time approximately eighteen seconds. When calcium salts which give a warm sensation are used, the arm-to-tongue circulation time may be measured and the arrival of the substance in various parts of the body—in the arms, the perineum, the legs, for example—may be detected by the patient as a warm sensation and the time of arrival noted, so that the circulation time to various parts of the body may be determined. This may be of help at times when local disease of the cardiovascular system interferes with flow of blood to one part of the body or another—for example, in Buerger's disease or arteriosclerosis obliterans.

Prolongation of the circulation time is at times a valuable observation when the problem of heart failure is not well established. In left ventricular failure, for example, without right ventricular failure, there is a prolongation of the circulation time which is absent in allergic asthma.

A reduction in the circulation time, that is, a shortening of the circuit, occurs in anemia and hyperthyroidism. In overriding of the aorta, in which blood enters the aorta directly from the right ventricle and bypasses the lungs, the time is greatly shortened if sufficient blood traverses the abnormal route to carry enough test material for recognition.

Circulation Rate

Experimentally, the circulation rate, or output of the heart, is often measured in order to study the effects of disease upon the circulation. This has little application in the clinic. The same is true of the volume of blood flowing through an organ or extremity. This, too, can be measured with a plethysmograph applied to the part or by a calorimeter, which measures the heat dissipated from the part in a definite period of time. With knowledge of the specific heat of blood and the temperatures of the arterial and venous blood, the circulation through the area—that is, the blood flow—may be calculated by formula. Further discussion appears in Chapter 19.

The Lesser Circulation

The discussions of circulation through the lungs, the coronary system and the liver are found in the sections dealing with those systems. However, some factors concerned in the lesser circulation may be mentioned here. The volume of blood passing through the lesser circulation per minute must equal that passing through the greater circuit, or an accumulation of blood would occur in one or the other of these circuits. The blood pressure in the lesser circuit is about one-sixth that of the aorta, a figure usually given as a mean pressure of 20 mm. of mercury when the pressure is near zero in the pulmonary veins. Variations occur with respiration. Tone in the pulmonary arterioles is low, for the vascular bed is distensible, and, in the presence of resistance to flow due to left-sided heart failure or mitral stenosis, the pressure in the pulmonary circuit readily increases and engorgement of vessels results.

Respiration has a distinct influence of pulmonary arterial pressure, which falls in inspiration and rises in expiration. These changes are caused by changes in the capacity of pulmonary vessels as a result of respiration despite increased intake of blood into the right ventricle in inspiration. Forced expiration, particularly the Valsalva experiment (with glottis closed), compresses the arteries and raises the pressure.

Further discussion of the pulmonary circulation is found in Chapters 21 and 22.

The Lymphatics

The tissue spaces are drained by a network of vessels called the lymphatics. There is considerable discussion as to whether this series of vessels begins as blind closed tubes or whether these vessels are open into the tissue spaces. The endothelium is not selective and passes material forced from the outer surface. These vessels coalesce into plexuses which reach the larger lymphatic trunks entering the venous channels through the thoracic duct. The larger lymphatic trunks contain valves comparable to those in the veins which permit the movement of lymph in only one direction. These channels are interrupted from time to time by lymph nodes through which the lymph must pass on its way to the thoracic duct. The function of the nodes is defense against invasion by bacteria traveling through the lymphatic passages. Bacteria reaching the nodes meet with a reaction of phagocytes which attack and tend to destroy them. In this way the pathway of bacterial invasion into the blood is interrupted.

The tissue fluid of the extracellular spaces,

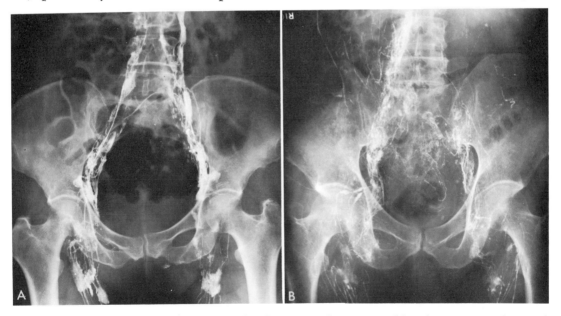

Figure 16–10. Lymphangiograms taken with radiopaque media. *A,* Normal lymphangiogram made immediately following injection. It reveals numerous lymph nodes and their connecting lymphatic channels. *B,* Abnormal lymphangiogram. This exposure, made immediately following injection, reveals innumerable collateral lymphatic channels. There was extensive invasion by a malignancy of the retroperitoneal lymphatics blocking normal lymphatic flow. Note that collaterals cross the midline. (Courtesy of Dr. Philip J. Hodes.)

together with its solutes and with the small amount of protein which is extravasated from the capillaries, drains into the lymphatics. Hence the composition of the lymph is similar to that of the fluid in the tissue spaces and has a low protein content. It clots. An increased production of tissue fluid causes an increase in the lymphatic drainage, this mechanism keeping the tissue pressure low. The lymphatic volume, therefore, is dependent on the amount of fluid filtered from the capillaries and not reabsorbed at their venous ends. Obstruction to the lymph vessels interferes with this drainage mechanism and may be responsible for the development of edema (Fig. 16–10).

The movement of lymph depends to a great extent upon the contraction of muscles surrounding lymphatic channels and on the pressure of the fluid filtered from the capillaries. Active motion of the part will, therefore, increase the lymph production. Lymph production is also increased by anything that results in venous obstruction, for venous obstruction increases capillary pressure and the filtration of fluid from the capillaries to the tissue spaces. Edema is thus produced. Lymphedema is, therefore, essentially a stasis edema, and, if the vessels dilate and the valves become incompetent, the process is furthered by added stasis. In such areas, especially when the protein content of the fluid is high, infection develops more easily and attacks of acute lymphangitis with fever often occur. These may gradually further the obstructive process, finally resulting in elephantiasis. There may be aching and a feeling of heaviness on standing. The high protein content also favors fibroblastic proliferation, giving a hard, woody feel to these areas. Often the mechanism of obstruction is unknown. Congenital hypoplasia, inflammatory disease, pressure from neoplasms, scars and fibrosis may occur.

The Effect of Pregnancy on the Circulation

The metabolic increases that occur after the third month of pregnancy affect the circulation. Cardiac output is increased. With enlargement of the fetus there is compression upon the diaphragm and displacement of the heart. The effects of such displacement may be elicited by physical examination of the heart. Development of the placenta results in a circulatory pattern in which arteriovenous shunts appear. These are comparable to arteriovenous leaks of other sorts and have the same effect on the circulation—diastolic pressure diminishes; the heart rate is increased; cardiac output is increased. The effects of mechanical displacement, of the increased burden of the tissue on circulation, and of the arteriovenous shunt mechanism, all contribute to the total picture seen in the pregnant woman.

REFERENCES

Ayman, D.: Arterial Hypertension. New York, Oxford University Press, 1948.

Babb, R. R., Alarcon-Segovia, D., and Fairbairn, J. F., II: Erythermalgia. Circulation, 29:136, 1964.

Bechgaard, P., Kopp, H., and Nielsen, J.: One thousand hypertensive patients followed 16–22 years. Acta Med. Scand. Suppl., 312:175, 1956.

Burton, A. C.: Physiology and Biophysics of the Circulation. Chicago, Year Book Publishers, 1965.

Conn, J. W., Rovner, D. R., Cohen, E. L., and Nesbit, R. M.: Normokalemic primary aldosteronism. J. A. M. A., 195:21, 1966.

Crawford, E. S., DeBakey, M. E., Morris, G. C., Jr., and Cooley, D. A.: Thrombo-obliterative disease of the great vessels arising from the aortic arch. J. Thoracic & Cardiovasc. Surg., 43:38, 1962.

Currens, J. H.: A comparison of the blood pressure in the lying and standing positions; a study of 500 women. Am. Heart J., 35:646, 1948.

Cywes, S., and Louw, J. H.: Phlegmasia cerulea dolens: Successful treatment by relieving fasciotomy. Surgery, 51:169, 1962.

Dahl, L. K.: Salt, fat, and hypertension: The Japanese experience. Nutrit. Rev., 18:97, 1960.

Danaraj, T. J., and Ong, W. H.: Obliterative brachiocephalic arteritis (pulseless disease). Am. J. Cardiol., 5:277, 1960.

Engelman, K., and Sjoerdsma, A.: New test for pheochromocytoma based on pressor responsiveness to tyramine. Clin. Res., 12:181, 1964.

Hershey, S. G., Mazzia, V. D. B., Altura, B. M., and Gyure, L.: Effects of vasopressors on the microcirculation and on survival in hemorrhagic shock. Anesthesiology, 26:179, 1965.

Hollander, W.: Current diagnosis of systemic arterial hypertension. M. Clin. North America, 38:1407, 1957.

Lange, K., Werner, D., and Boyd, L. J.: The functional pathology of experimental immersion foot. Am. Heart J., 35:238, 1948.

Lewis, C., Whigham, H., Pasette, A., and Weil, M. H.: Circulatory effects of various vasopressor agents with implications for their selective use in treatment of hypotension and shock. Am. J. Cardiol., 13:116, 1964.

Lewis, T.: Vascular Disorders of the Limbs. New York, Macmillan, 1936.

Lewis, T.: Pain. New York, Macmillan, 1942.

McKusick, V. A., Harris, W. S., Ottesen, O. E., Goodman, R. M., Shelley, W. M., and Bloodwell, R. P.: Buerger's Disease. J. A. M. A., 181:5, 1962.

Myers, K. A.: Hemodynamic changes determining the treatment of shock. Med. Bull. Presbyterian-St. Luke's Hosp., 5:68, 1966.

Ochsner, A.: Venous thrombosis. J.A.M.A., 132:827, 1946.

Pickering, G.: The concept of essential hypertension as a quantitative disease (and discussion). Proceedings of the Prague Symposium, Section One, 23, 1962.

Ruch, T. C., and Fulton, J. F.: Medical Physiology and Biophysics, 18th ed. Philadelphia, W. B. Saunders Co., 1960.

Sodeman, W. A.: Direct venous pressure determinations by use of a new instrument. Am. Heart J., 43:687, 1952.

Sodeman, W. A., and Engelhardt, H. T.: The causes of syncope, with special reference to the heart. New Orleans M. & S. J., 97:307, 1945.

Stahl, W. M.: The pressure control of renin release by the kidney. Am. J. Cardiol., 17:139, 1966.

Chapter Seventeen

Dynamics and Circulation of Heart Muscle; Cardiac Reserve; Heart Pain; The Cardiac Cycle*

JOSEPH T. ROBERTS

A patient with heart failure suffers from the effects of abnormalities in the dynamics of his cardiac muscle. There are important relations among the cardiac circulation, the cardiac cycle and the cardiac dynamics. Each of these mechanisms affects the other and, if altered, may lead to the loss of cardiac reserve. Many chemical and cytologic changes at intercellular and intracellular levels have damaging effects on these cardiac mechanisms and probably can be affected reciprocally by them also. Application of knowledge concerning these matters helps the physician to understand the manifestations of diseases affecting the heart and contributes to more helpful treatment of heart disease.

Cardiac Dynamics

The dynamics of the heart are functional attributes depending upon the arrangement

* Reviewed in the Veterans Administration and published with the approval of the Chief Medical Director. The statements and conclusions published by the author are the result of his own study and do not necessarily reflect the opinion or policy of the Veterans Administration.

of the organ's structural units and upon the biochemical phenomena of these units. Although the integration of these two determinants is not clearly understood, it seems certain that they are dependent upon each other.

STRUCTURE OF THE HEART

The heart is a rhythmically pulsating part of the vascular system. It consists of (1) the endocardium, (2) the myocardium, (3) the pericardium, (4) a blood and lymphatic supply, (5) a nerve supply and (6) a supportive system.

The *endocardium* is a smooth lining membrane, composed of a layer of simple squamous endothelium and an under layer of connective tissue. Normal endothelium provides a smooth surface for contact with the blood to reduce friction and clotting. When damaged, as by infection, infarction, aging, stasis or trauma, this surface may provide a site for formation of an intracardiac thrombus. From this an embolus may be detached to float to some branch of the pulmonary or aortic arterial system. Infarction of a segment of the lung, brain, spleen, leg or some other organ

314

may follow. Four ringlike shelves of reflected endocardium form the cardiac valves, which normally make the heart a unidirectional pump. These valves are the atrioventricular or receiving (tricuspid, mitral) and semilunar or discharging (pulmonary, aortic) valves. Their shape and attachments are excellently adapted so they fold out of the path of forward moving blood but snap shut to prevent backward flow. The edges of the atrioventricular valves float against each other, with several millimeters of surface in contact. The semilunar valves touch along their edges only. Strings of endothelially covered collagen fibers (chordae tendineae) serve, like lines on a sail, to anchor the atrioventricular valve leaflets to the muscle of the ventricle. These structures are often injured by acute, subacute, or chronic endocarditis, trauma, one of the collagen diseases or dilation of the chambers. Other incompetent valves "guard" the orifices of the coronary sinus (valve of Thebesius), the inferior vena cava (valve of Eustachius) and the accessory coronary veins in the right atrium, as well as the minute openings of the luminal or Thebesian veins in all four chambers. Occasionally, at the left end of the coronary sinus is a small incomplete valve. Rarely, a large "network of Chiari" is formed by larger perforated residuals of the embryonic right sinus venosus valve, instead of the smaller valves of Eustachius and Thebesius, and these may be enmeshed in thrombi or emboli.

Often reported recently is thickening and fibrosis of the mural subendocardium, at times bad enough to interfere with either the blood supply of the heart or its dilation during diastole. Atrial endocardial fibrosis is common in rheumatic heart disease and most severe in the left atrium; ventricular fibrosis of the endocardium usually follows coronary artery disease, hypertension, aortic valvular defect or cor pulmonale. The constricting form of endocardial fibrosis may be acquired, but is more commonly seen with congenital cardiac anomalies.

The *pericardium* is an inelastic covering which helps anchor the heart, reduces friction between the pulsating heart and its environment, and limits the distention of the heart during diastole. Of its four layers two are smooth, simple, squamous mesothelial layers which glide smoothly against each other with the movement of the heart. Between them is the pericardial cavity, a closed sac containing normally only a few drops of lubricating serous fluid. If roughened by infarction, infection, inflammation, as well as by cancer or hemorrhage from trauma, these surfaces may produce a friction rub. The inner or visceral layer of the pericardium is attached firmly to the myocardium by a fibrous layer in which run the coronary vessels and nerves. The epicardium is made up of these two layers. The outer mesothelial layer is loosely attached to the other mediastinal structures by an outer fibrous layer. These thin, flexible layers may be changed into rigid, even calcified, scars which seriously constrict or angulate parts of the heart or its vessels. The parietal and visceral layers of the pericardium are continuous with each other around the great vessels entering and leaving the heart. Fluid (serum, pus or blood) may appear between the two layers. If this pericardial effusion appears slowly, the parietal pericardium may be stretched very greatly with no clinical effect until very late. If the effusion is formed quickly, the outer pericardium will not stretch any and the softer parts of the heart (atria, pulmonary veins, right ventricle and venae cavae) will be collapsed. This "tamponade" effect prevents filling of the heart, with obstruction to venous return, loss of cardiac output, fall in coronary flow, arrhythmias and death. Fibrosis, sometimes calcified, may form bands or sheets around the heart with chronic cardiac constriction and slow cardiac failure. Removal of such constrictions of bands or fluid often prevents death or at least improves cardiac reserve. After chronic cardiac constriction, "atrophy of disuse" often shrinks the myocardial fibers (Roberts and Beck) so that decortication may be followed by abrupt fatal overdilation of the atrophic fibers. Beck has stressed the probable minor importance of adhesions between the heart and adjacent structures as the cause of cardiac failure in such cases. Hypertrophy when present is due to other causes such as valvular disease or hypertension.

Pericarditis (infectious, hemorrhagic, chemical, traumatic or neoplastic) often injures the underlying muscles, nerves and coronary vessels, with electrocardiographic and clinical changes. The *myocardium*, a muscular layer between the epicardium and endocardium, is designed to provide the power for pushing blood throughout the body. When it ceases to do this, life ends. The cardiac muscle fibers branch and anastomose to form a syncytial mass arranged in large sheets or bundles. The smaller bundles are sheathed in rather dense fibrous tissue. They are grouped into four

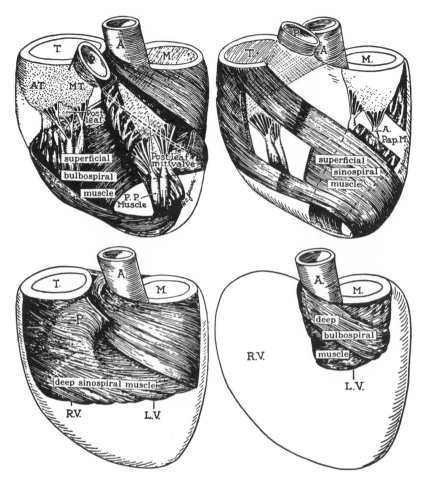

Figure 17–1. The muscle bundles of the heart. (From Robb and Robb: Am. Heart J., 1942.)

main bundles in the ventricles (according to McCallum, Mall and Robb) arranged as follows: (1) the deep bulbospiral bundle, (2) the superficial bulbospiral bundle, (3) the deep sinospiral bundle, (4) the superficial sinospiral bundle. These bundles encircle the ventricular chambers in characteristic patterns (Fig. 17–1). The bundles of muscle fibers are attached to the apical surface of the fibrous skeleton of the heart, in the region of the atrioventricular groove, directly at one end and at the other end through insertions of the papillary muscles into the chordae tendineae and atrioventricular (mitral and tricuspid) valve cusps. The ventricular blood is expelled by the contraction of these spirally arranged bundles, fixed at each end, in a manner similar to the wringing out of a wet rag. Injury of the deep bulbospiral bundle, according to Robb, causes a sharp fall in blood pressure and death. Injury of the other bundles produces less clearly related effects. Changes in the mass of these bundles have

not been correlated with cardiac hypertrophy or specific diseases. Rupture of a papillary muscle or its attached chordae tendineae and related valvular leaflets is usually due to myocardial infarction, endocarditis or trauma by contusion or penetrating wounds, and may cause loud, bizarre murmurs, intense thrills and severe abrupt heart failure. The same results follow rupture of an interventricular septum after myocardial infarction. Fortunately, with earlier diagnosis and better treatment, both these complications are rare.

In a rare entity recently emphasized, subaortic muscular hypertrophic stenosis, a localized band of hypertrophied muscle subdivides the left ventricle. This may cause great inefficiency in left ventricular output, especially after exercise or some other mechanism has increased the contractions of this band. This strange entity may be accompanied by severe atypical angina *after* exercise has reduced cardiac output and coronary flow. Histochemically, increased norepinephrine concentration has been found in the hypertrophic muscle; use of antagonists of norepinephrine for treatment has been tried with uncertain benefit.

The atrial chambers have thinner muscular walls which consist of more delicate bundles. As in the ventricles, these bundles encircle the cavities spirally in two layers and are attached at each end to the basal side of the *fibrous skeleton* of the heart. This anchoring, supportive site for all the chambers, valves and outflow tracts is made of dense fibrous connective tissue in four rings and two trigones. These may become calcified, unrelated to calcification of the valves or vessels. Abnormal dilation of these rings gives weakened support of the cusps with regurgitation of blood.

The myocardial fibers of the atria and ventricles are separated by the fibrous skeleton of the heart, with certain significant exceptions. In 1893 Kent, and later His, described an atrioventricular bundle of specialized cardiac muscle tissue (commonly called the bundle of His) connecting the atria and ventricles. In 1895 Kent reported another similar bundle, since referred to as the atrioventricular column of Kent. Most authorities have denied the existence in mammalian hearts of any other muscular connections. Some authors, on evidence not entirely convincing, have described many other muscular connections, but no significant function has been established

for these probably vestigial fibers. The majority opinion favors the belief that no contraction is transmitted between the ventricles and the atria, and that no electrical activity passes between the two regions except over the specialized conduction tissue of the bundle of His or, rarely, the column of Kent.

Sino-atrioventricular System

The specialized sino-atrioventricular conduction system, sometimes called the "Purkinje system," is especially adapted for the initiation and propagation of the rhythmically formed electrical activity which stimulates the heart beat. In the anterior sulcus (Fig. 17–2) between the right atrium and the superior vena cava there is a small spindle-shaped mass of specialized tissue, the sino-atrial node of Keith and Flack, about 7 mm. long and 3 mm. wide, where the normal heart beat originates. This node is called the "pacemaker." Delicate strands of specialized conduction tissue extend from this node up on the wall of the superior vena cava and downward to the left over the walls of the two atria to merge with the ordinary cardiac muscle fibers of these two chambers. At the upper right posterior end of the atrioventricular bundle of Kent and His, there is an expanded, club-shaped mass called the atrioventricular node of Tawara (Fig. 17–3). To this node a few delicate, specialized branches come from the atrial muscle fibers. The node

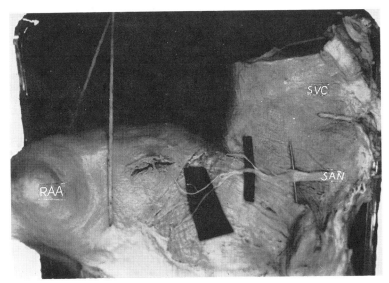

Figure 17–2.   The sino-atrial node (SAN) with its branches in the sulcus terminale, between the right auricular appendage (RAA) and the orifice of the superior vena cava (SVC) on the anterior surface of the atrium (dissection of a horse's heart). Note wire under node and black paper under branches. A prominent artery (usually from the right coronary artery) leads into the SA node.

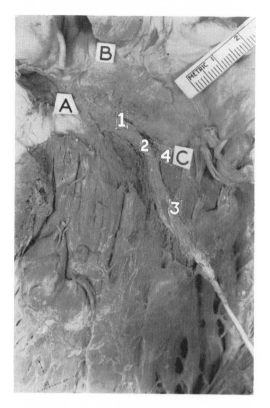

Figure 17–3. The atrioventricular node (1), bundle of His (2), and right branch (3), with the subendocardial plexus of the right ventricle. Barium sulfate injection of the conduction system in a beef heart. The left branch (4) can be seen entering the septum near point *C*. (*A*, Orifice of coronary sinus; *B*, cusp of inferior vena cava; *C*, septal cusp of tricuspid valve.)

lies in a triangle formed by the mouth of the coronary sinus, the cusp of the inferior vena cava and the septal cusp of the tricuspid valve. The atrioventricular bundle extends from this node forward, to the left and toward the apex, penetrating the fibrous skeleton to reach the interventricular fibrous septum at a thin portion called the undefended space of Peacock. Here the bundle divides into right and left branches. The right branch of the bundle goes along the right side of the interventricular septum, between the endocardium and myocardium for a variable distance before it bends to the right. It crosses the cavity of the right ventricle as the so-called moderator band. In many human hearts there is no distinct "moderator band" or bridge of muscle across the cavity. On reaching the anterior wall of the right ventricle, the right branch divides into delicate strands which form a subendocardial plexus of light-colored Purkinje fibers. The right branch is a

long, narrow, round bundle which is more prone to injury by stretching or touching than is the wide, flattened multi-stranded left bundle branch. The latter also follows the lining of the ventricle more closely. This anatomic arrangement may be the reason that the electrocardiogram reveals depolarization of the right side of the interventricular septum after the left side. The left branch (Fig. 17–4) of the bundle pierces the membranous septum at its thinnest or "undefended" area (space of Peacock), just below the aortic valve at the commissure between the right coronary and noncoronary cusps. It then divides into anterior and posterior bands which go along the septum toward the apical part of the left ventricle to form a plexus in the subendocardium. From the subendocardial plexus in each ventricle fibers go out into the myocardium to merge with the ordinary cardiac fibers, and in places there is communication through the septum. According to Robb, the branches of the conduction tissue are distributed in a rather specific manner to each of the four ventricular contracting muscle bundles. Occasional aberrant atrioventricular conduction tissue has been assumed to be present outside the myocardium and inside the epicardium of the back of the left ventricle to explain rare cases of accelerated atrioventricular conduction (Wolff-Parkinson-White syndrome, Type A), according to Barker. Several other locations of conduction tissue have been described but are not generally recognized (listed by Roberts and Luisada, 1959). The embryological history of the conduction system as two shrinking cones of specialized tissue around the sino-atrial and atrio-ventricular funnels may explain the variability of its less constant parts.

The amount of glycogen in the conduction apparatus (more than in ordinary heart muscle) makes possible differential staining and also rapid (though transient) visualization by application of Lugol's or other iodine solutions. In fresh hearts this facilitates the finding of the conduction apparatus during an autopsy or possibly even during open-heart surgery. The difficulty of unaided dissection has often led to doubt as to the existence of the system. Simple experiments on animals and accidental or unknowing injury in human patients (e.g., by application of ligatures, cuts or cold) can clearly demonstrate the presence and role of the system. The AV bundle is often vulnerable during efforts to close an interventricular septal defect. Its branches are very often "blocked" in patients, most

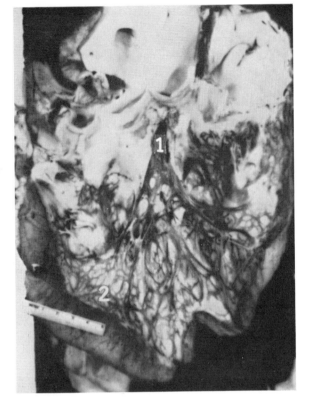

Figure 17–4. Left branch (1) of the bundle of His, penetrating the septum below the aortic commissure and forming the subendocardial plexus (2) of the left ventricle. Beef heart with India ink injected into the conduction system.

often by coronary artery disease with or without infarction. "Parietal block," in which the electrocardiogram resembles the pattern of left ventricular hypertrophy without prolongation of the QRS interval, has been blamed on infarction or ischemia of the anterior strands of the left bundle branch (called "superior" by Grant).

The small arteries in the SA or AV node or other parts of the conduction system may be narrowed by any vascular disease, e.g., atherosclerosis, collagen disease, bacteremia and others, with resulting effects on the rhythm. The large or smaller anterior (superior) or posterior (inferior) branches of the left bundle branch may be injured alone and in various combinations by vascular and other disease with resulting patterns of the electrocardiogram and vectorcardiogram. For example the "parietal block" pattern is very common with left ventricular enlargement. According to Grant, this is due to injury of the superior left bundle branch.

Muscle Fibers

Cardiac muscle fibers (Fig. 17–5) are branching and anastomosing cylinders which on cross section appear as circles or ovals. Each fiber is composed of many smaller strands, the myofibrils, which are made of

alternating segments of differentially staining material. The segmented structure of the myofibrils accounts for the transversely striated appearance of stained longitudinal sections. It is believed that the contractile molecules, probably myosin or actomyosin, are arranged in such a way that in each

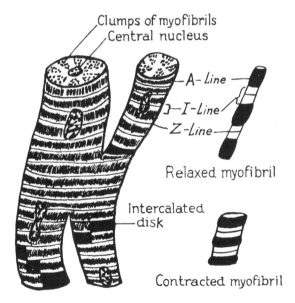

Figure 17–5. Diagram of cardiac muscle fibers.

myofibril there are alternate groups of molecules with their long axes directed across or parallel to the long axis of the fiber. Shifting the proportions of molecules in these groups accounts for the shortening of the fiber that occurs with cardiac contraction during its isotonic phase. As seen in a transversely cut fiber, the ends of the myofibrils are clumped in wedge-shaped groups near the periphery of the muscle fiber, just inside the condensation of sarcoplasm which surrounds the fiber. In cardiac muscle fibers the sarcolemma is thin and delicate, contrasting with the sturdy sarcolemma of striated skeletal muscle fibers. The nucleus in a cardiac muscle fiber is found in the center of the fiber, with a clear zone of sarcoplasm around it, differing again from skeletal muscle structure. The nucleus itself is ovoid, large and vesicular except in cardiac hypertrophy, in which it may be much larger, more vesicular and brick-shaped, and in cardiac atrophy, in which it is smaller, pyknotic and not squared at the ends. Besides the cross striations, there are other markings in stained sections, called intercalated disks, which are due to unexplained differences in chemical composition at irregular points on the myofibrils. Fragmentation of the myofibrils may occur at these intercalated disks or other points and may be an important feature of cardiac strain and failure.

A newer biophysical theory of muscle contractions, as described by Guyton, visualizes billions of small protein fibrils of two types, myosin and actin, which interdigitate with each other to only a slight extent in a resting state. (See p. 324 for discussion of an earlier theory.) With flow of an impulse over the surface of a fiber, permeability of the membrane lets sodium diffuse into the fiber; this generates energy to send the impulse farther down the fiber. Calcium ion permeability is also increased slightly. The calcium reacts with myosin to form an enzyme called adenosine triphosphatase (ATP-ase) which catalyzes the release of energy from the ATP surrounding the muscle fibrils. This energy creates a momentary electrostatic charge between the myosin and actin fibrils. The actin fibrils are pulled into the spaces between the myosin fibrils by this charge and so shortening of the muscle occurs.

In turn the calcium ions are bound by the relaxing substance within a fraction of a second after they enter the fiber. With the un-ionized calcium only being then present, no more energy is released from the ATP. Relaxation occurs as the electrostatic charges

between the actin and myosin fibrils are lost.

This mechanism has been used to explain why the greatly overdistended muscle of heart failure does not contract as well as normal. It is believed that the actin fibrils are pulled so far apart from the myosin fibrils that they do not interdigitate at all. Thus the charges between the two groups of fibrils are too weak to pull them together.

Digitalis, by increasing calcium permeability of cardiac muscle membranes, causes its well-known increase in the strength of muscle contraction. Conversely, the old fear of using calcium with digitalis is substantiated by this theory.

Imbalance of other ions, e.g., potassium, magnesium and manganese, may be suspected of altering these mechanisms when either increased or decreased. Potassium excess may stop the heart in diastole by blocking the entry of sodium ions and preventing the start of contraction. Hypokalemia is well known to predispose dangerously to digitalis toxicity also.

In the interstitial spaces between the syncytial myocardial fibers there are similar plexuses of hemic and lymphatic capillaries, fibrous connective tissue in small amounts, the end plates and terminal fibers of the cardiac nerves, tissue fluid and small numbers of wandering cells. Derangements of each of these units can be related with the mechanisms of cardiac dysfunction. Quantitative study of these structural units in various disorders is gradually contributing valuable information to the problems of cardiac function. Within the last few years it has been seen that changes in the composition and abundance of collagen or white fibrous connective tissue may be found in all organs and tissues of the body. These changes are most apparent in the group of somewhat related "collagen diseases," such as rheumatic fever, rheumatoid arthritis, periarteritis nodosum, disseminated lupus erythematosus, scleroderma, and others. Clumps of reactive cells, perivascular changes or intravascular changes add to the damage caused by the changes in the collagen fibers in each unit of the heart. These elements have been given much greater importance in medicine recently, with better understanding of some disturbed mechanisms and hope for better treatment in the future.

The specialized muscle fibers resemble the ordinary cardiac fibers. However, in the two nodes the fibers are thinner, more closely striated transversely and longitudinally, and there is less interstitial space. In other parts of the conduction system the fibers are thicker, have more abundant sarcoplasm and have the appearance of being more "water-soaked." They are lighter in color, both in the stained and unstained condition, and contain more abundant stores of glycogen. Their capillary blood supply is poorer than in ordinary cardiac muscle, and this may cause their greater susceptibility to coronary insufficiency or electrolyte change. Cardiac muscle fibers can often be found extending on the pulmonary veins near the atrial walls but probably have only a vestigial role.

The sequence of dilatation (with stretched fibers) and hypertrophy is usually steplike. Heart disease of various forms causes hypertrophy or atrophy of cardiac muscle fibers, with change in fiber diameter and heart weight. Fibrosis may develop from hyperplasia of the interstitial tissue or replacement of ischemic or injured muscle. These changes are variable, progressive, local or generalized. The histochemical changes in all such areas are poorly known but probably of great importance in disordered function.

Smooth muscle in a hypertrophic layer may be found outside the endocardium and its hyperplastic elastic lamellae in endocardial elastomyofibrosis (EEMF) of unknown etiology in congenital and acquired forms (Fisher and Davis). This condition, often associated with eosinophilic or other myocarditis, can cause clinical signs resembling those of constrictive pericarditis because of lost distensibility of the heart during diastole. Less likely to do so is the endocardial and other scarring of the heart after myocardial infarction. The latter is free of elastic fibers and often results in an aneurysm of the heart (Rokitansky aneurysm), with reciprocal bulging of the area during systole. This causes cardiac failure by loss of contracting muscle, mitral insufficiency from weakness of infarcted papillary muscle, or increased ventricular volume with poor emptying of the enlarged cavity. Both types of endocardial fibrosis create bizarre electrocardiographic abnormalities of long duration and confuse or obscure diagnosis of changing processes.

DYNAMIC PROPERTIES OF CARDIAC MUSCLE

When the structure of the sino-atrioventricular conduction system became understood about 1910, a great advance occurred in the explanation of the way in which the heart beat occurs. The cardinal feature of cardiac muscle is its dynamic property of *rhythmicity* in both the *origination* and *transmission* of *electrical impulses*. Each fiber, ordinary as well as specialized, has these properties. However, there is a normal gradient for these properties in different parts of the heart. The sino-atrial node has the most highly specialized ability rhythmically to form and discharge differences in electrical potential at an optimal rate (65 to 90 times per minute in the normal adult human heart). Therefore this node serves as the normal pacemaker of the heart; that is, it starts each heart beat.

The mechanism by which this impulse formation occurs is unknown. A tentative explanation is that the ionic charges on the inside and outside of the cell membranes differ, so that rhythmically negative charges are thrown off the outside of the membrane because of cyclic chemical changes on the inside. Once formed, this electrical impulse normally leaves the sino-atrial node over its specialized branches to reach the atrial and ventricular muscle fibers. During this time, when the person is connected to an electrocardiographic recording machine, a deflection from the isoelectric line is inscribed, and this wave has been named the "P wave." Normally an interval of about 0.10 second elapses during the writing of the P wave. The P wave occurs as a result of "depolarization" of the atria.

The current of electricity is then passed from the atrial ordinary cardiac muscle fibers to the specialized fibers making up the small arms of the atrioventricular node of Tawara and then to the node itself. Here the impulse is thought to be temporarily halted before it passes along the atrioventricular bundle of Kent and His. During this halt there is no difference in potential between the electrodes, and so there is an isoelectric phase which is called the P-QR interval. This segment of the electrocardiogram is normally flat and horizontal, and lasts for 0.04 to 0.10 second.

Near its end there is a very short wave representing the "repolarization" of the atria. Because this stands for the same event called the T wave when occurring in the ventricle instead of the atria it is called the "atrial T or T_A wave." The T_A wave is usually obscured, except in AV block, by coinciding with the QRS complex. During the next interval of 0.06 to 0.10 second, the impulse passes from the atrioventricular bundle and its two branches to the subendocardial plexus, and goes into the ordinary ventricular muscle, where it inscribes the QRS complex on the electrocardiogram. An isoelectric segment then follows, called the RS-T segment, after which an upright T wave is found. During the isoelectric T-P interval the sino-atrial node prepares and emits the charge which initiates the next cycle. The normal characteristics of each part of the electrocardiogram are discussed in Chapter 18. The rate of transmission varies in different areas and is subject to great effects by changes in oxygen supply, heart rate and electrolyte concentrations.

The property of rhythmicity of impulse formation is also present in other cardiac muscle fibers. If for some reason the sino-atrial node fails to function properly, an impulse may be formed somewhere else. Thus the pacemaker may be shifted to the atrial muscle, to the atrioventricular node or bundle, to the branches or to the ordinary ventricular muscle fibers. When this happens, the normal sino-atrial rhythm is replaced by one of the dysrhythmias, all of which are less efficient. Clinical improvement in the efficiency of the heart is obtained by conversion of one of the severe arrhythmias to regular sinus rhythm or, if this is not possible, to one of the less disturbing arrhythmias. Pacemaking functions may be aberrant in origin, also because of increased irritability in areas outside the sino-atrial node. Such changes are common with coronary artery insufficiency, inflammation or general weakness of any cause, with toxic doses of many drugs (such as digitalis) or with excessive smoking, fatigue, hypoxia, or changes in electrolyte and hormone balance.

Blood supply damage in the SA node may cause atrial arrhythmias such as atrial fibrillation. Transplantation of the SA node to the ventricular myocardium might improve complete atrioventricular block if the node's blood supply could be kept intact.

The loss of the ability of the SA node to serve as the pacemaker for the ventricle with complete AV block shifts this role to the AV node or an idioventricular pacemaker. Usually the heart rate then falls to as low as 28 to 40 cycles per minute and this causes fall in cerebral blood flow, convulsions, coronary insufficiency, heart failure and death. Great benefit in this condition often results from implanting an artificial pacemaker in the ventricle, as introduced by Chardack, Greatbatch and Gage.

A fourth cardinal feature or property of cardiac muscle is *refractoriness*. This property prevents a cardiac muscle fiber, ordinary or specialized, from responding to a stimulus until an interval of time has elapsed after the previous stimulus. The period after receipt of a stimulus, during which the fiber is refractory and fails to transmit or respond to this or other stimuli, no matter how strong in intensity, is referred to as the absolute refractory period. The duration of this period can vary within normal limits and also in response to disease or drugs. Refractoriness is an important property which prevents the heart from responding to needless stimulation, but, when excessive, it may block the normal transmission of impulses and lead to the various types of heart block. In the normal heart beat the fibers are "absolutely or totally refractory" during the earlier part of the cycle, but become less refractory later. During the phase of "partial refractoriness' (the relatively refractory period) a response may follow stimulation of greater intensity than is needed to cause response in the nonrefractory or irritable period. The relative lengths of the nonrefractory and the refractory periods will determine the cardiac rate in response to stimulation at any give rate.

Irritability is a fifth property of cardiac muscle and in a reverse way is closely related to refractoriness. By irritability is meant the property of the heart muscle which allows it to respond to a stimulus. During the phase of the cardiac cycle when the muscle is irritable it will respond to every stimulus of sufficient intensity, and will respond with most forceful contraction of which it is capable at that particular time. This accounts for the "all or none" law, by which is meant that the heart muscle fiber will respond with its maximal contraction to any adequate stimulus or it will not respond in any way under the conditions present at the time. The intensity and duration of the stimulus, the degree of stretch to which the fiber is subjected at the moment, the influence of neural, hormonal and nutritional balance, of oxygen supply, salts, drugs and the products of infection are some of the factors which can modify the degree of irritability of cardiac muscle. During the phase when refractoriness is greatest, irritability is lowest, and vice versa. Thus there are the cyclic phases of non-irritability, grading through increasing degrees of relative irritability to the phase of irritability. The relative lengths of these phases are subject to variation, just as is the threshold of irritability in the irritable phase. Most cells of protoplasm have this property of irritability, through which they are caused to move by an irritating stimulus, but in the animal body the cardiac muscle fibers have this property most highly developed.

The response which these fibers make to an adequate stimulus is contraction, due to a sixth physical property of *contractility*. The fibers shorten and, being attached at each end and spirally arranged, reduce the lumen to push blood out of the cardiac chambers. The force of contraction varies as a result of such factors as initial length at the time of the stimulation beginning the contraction, oxygen supply of the fibers, viscosity of the blood upon which the chamber contracts, and nutritional equilibrium of the muscle cells. Of these, most attention has been given to the relation between fiber lengths and force of contraction. Within certain limits, increasing the diastolic length of a fiber increases the force of its contraction proportionately. This accounts for the so-called Starling's law of the heart, which states that when these fibers are stretched, the heart contracts with greater force. Up to a certain point this law holds true, but when a fiber is stretched beyond that, or probably when the recurrent overstretching has happened too many times, the force of contraction fails to increase proportionately and may even fall below its former level with resultant heart failure.

The rate of contraction is another important variable, influenced by many factors. Contraction is divided into two phases: (1) the isometric period, when the fiber's length is unshortened, but when its "tension" is increasing to a point at which shortening must occur; and (2) the isotonic period, when the fiber is shortening, but the tension remains unchanged.

Contractility is the first dynamic property of heart muscle to appear in the early weeks of embryonic life, beginning in the fetal cardiac tube in a segment later to form the sinus venosus. Normally the rate of contraction is 65 to 80 times per minute in the adult heart and 120 to 140 in the infant heart, and the rhythm is quite regular.

Relaxation of the heart muscle is an invaluable seventh property which is the reverse of contraction. Relaxation occurs between periods of contraction, and enables the heart to become filled again with blood for expulsion in the following cycle. Its two phases are (1) the isometric period, with unchanged fiber length, but with declining fiber tension, which begins at the end of isotonic contraction and ends with the onset of (2) the isotonic period of relaxation, during which the fiber tension remains constant, but the fiber length increases until the commencement of isometric contraction. The power of relaxation might better be called expansion, or *expansibility*, and is just as significant as contractility, for without expansibility the cardiac chambers cannot become filled with blood in adequate amounts. Expansibility may be limited physically by the normally inelastic pericardium and decreased below normal by such conditions as (1) cardiac tamponade, in which the pericardial cavity becomes filled with blood or other fluid; (2) pericardial constrictive disease, in which bands or sheets of thickened, stiffened or even calcified pericardium occur; (3) compression by tumors, pleural fluids, deformed vertebrae and ribs or depressed sternum (*trichterbrust, or funnel chest*); (4) endocardial fibroelastosis; or (5) severe myocardial fibrosis such as that produced by scleroderma, dermatomyositis and chronic myocarditis. (6) The progressive diastolic dilation of the heart with incomplete emptying in systole and with progressive hypertrophy gives such an enlarged heart that expansibility may be limited by the chest wall and its other contents. Irreversible enlargement with poorly coordinated expansibility and contraction is common with chronic heart failure as with the cardiomyopathy of hypertension, alcoholism, infection, coronary disease, trauma and other injuries.

Relaxation of the heart muscle is ordinarily considered to be a passive phenomenon caused by cessation of contraction and the rush of venous blood into the chambers during diastole. While it is evident that these factors are operative, a little thought indicates that they alone cannot explain the property of expansibility. Expansion of the heart chambers occurs in the isolated beating heart, including that of a human being, where no venous return to the chambers can occur through the severed caval and pulmonary veins. This cyclic dilation, alternating with contraction, also is seen in patients with shock or peripheral vascular collapse; in these states the venous return and circulating blood volume are less than normal. The thud of the heart wall against the thorax may be just as forceful over an enlarged chamber during diastole as during the systolic impulse. Therefore it seems plain that diastolic expansion or relaxation of heart muscle is an active, forceful phenomenon resembling its reverse, contraction. This dynamic property of forceful relaxation was repeatedly noted in the isolated, beating human hearts revived by Roberts and Wearn by perfusion through the coronary arteries. It has also been plainly seen during operations as well as in the successful restoration of heart beats by cardiac massage after certain types of cardiac stand-still.

The loss of expansibility is evident conspicuously in the atria. With severe mitral stenosis or insufficiency the left atrium gets very big, with "left atrial overload"; with pulmonary disease or chronic left heart failure, "right or biatrial overload" appears on the ECG.

Molecular phenomena must be understood to explain these two properties, but biochemical and biophysical data in this field are just beginning to be accumulated. From evidence obtained by roentgenologic and double refraction methods, it is believed that there is a definite molecular orientation on the myofibril, especially of stretched-out protein molecules in parallel chains. These molecules are now thought to be myosin and actin or actomyosin, a contractile protein molecule which has the property of contracting and elongating in different conditions of acidity, heat or water content. This material is coagulated and shrunken by increase in acidity or heating, and this coagulability is reversible. In the resting state most of the molecules of myosin are arranged so that their long axes are parallel to that of the fiber, probably in the anisotrophic, dark A-disk. Between adjacent A-disks (Fig. 17–5) there are isotrophic, light, or I-disks, in the middle of which is the Z-line or disk. The Z-line is continuous with the sarcolemma, and the mass between two adjacent Z-lines is one sarcomere. In the light band or I-disk the molecules of the contractile protein are arranged with their long axes crossing that of the fiber. After arrival of an adequate stimulus to contraction, the proportion between molecules lying longitudinally and transversely changes, so that most of them lie transversely. This results in shortening of the sarcomeres and so of the fibers. With another theory, moving of actin fibrils into clefts between myosin fibrils under changing ionic conditions occurs. (See Chap. 20 for further discussion of the mechanism of contraction.)

What sets off this slipping together of actin and myosin fibers or the reorientation of the myosin molecules? It may be that with the breakdown of phosphocreatine into adenylic acid, adenosine triphosphate and lactic acid, the pH of the sarcomere is so changed that greater coagulability of the myosin molecules must occur. The adenosine triphosphate (ATP) may act as a catalyst to bring together actin and myosin as the contractile molecule of actomyosin. With adequate oxygen in the sarcoplasm, attracted there from the capillary blood by myoglobin (or muscle hemoglobin) and concentrated there, phosphocreatine is cyclically resynthesized, returning the pH to its former state and so causing the reorientation of the long axis of myosin molecules to the former proportion or expelling the actin fibrils further out of the myosin clefts. During this phase the sarcomere becomes elongated, and so does the fiber. Heat is formed during this cycle, chiefly during the breakdown of phosphocreatine, and is utilized only partially in the resynthesis. Thus energy in the form of heat is provided during both systole and diastole, but mostly during diastole. Expansibility is one of the most widespread observable results of heat formation. The reorientation of the myosin molecules and the formation of heat during this time account for the elongation of the fiber during diastole. If these explanations are correct, it is apparent that relaxation of the heart must be looked upon as an active process, not just a passive dilation due to the inrush of venous blood. When the heart has used up all its reserve ability to stretch, heart failure usually may be found, just as after loss of the power of contraction. In fact exceeding expansibility limits may be the dominant cause of lost cardiac reserve.

If cardiac relaxation or expansion is partially an active process, it might be expected that the cardiac chambers would exert some aspirating effect upon the returning venous blood. This possibility has been established experimentally by (1) observing that a beating excised heart of an animal will aspirate fluid in which it is submerged and will expel it so as to resemble jet propulsion or the movements of a squid and by (2) noting the suction at the entrance to the ventricles by palpation and watching the sucking in of water when isolated but beating and revived human hearts were submerged (Roberts, in Wearn's laboratory, 1936–1940) and by (3) recently more precise hemodynamic studies by Brecker (1958). The relative roles of diastolic suction and systolic pushing of blood are not clear, but suction by the heart may also be lost with failing cardiac reserve.

Catheterization of the coronary sinus, human as well as animal, has given much help in studying overall changes in the extraction and utilization of substrates of the heart beating in its normal environment and in furnishing leads on the mechanism of enzyme release by the necrotic heart muscle. It aids in differentiating between changes in energy production and utilization of the heart and in studying coronary flow and myocardial oxygen consumption (cf. Bing and others, and Zimmerman). The cannulated coronary sinus has been of use for perfusion to maintain life during cardiac operations.

The biochemical cycle of the heart beat is receiving great study still, because many experimental results are difficult to confirm or harmonize. For example, recent studies by Mommaerts have failed to confirm the expectation that phosphocreatine derivatives fluctuated in concentration during the heart beat. At present we still await clear proof of the chemical or physical nature of cardiac contraction and expansion.

Circulation in the Heart

The capillaries of the heart are its most essential vessels. They are tiny tubes with a simple endothelial wall and vary in diameter between about 3 and 12 microns. This variation in size may be the effect of constriction by cardiac muscle fibers, degrees of stasis of blood at the spot, and occasional distention into "sinusoids." The capillaries branch and anastomose with each other, between the meshes of the muscle fiber, so that each fiber is closely surrounded by a capillary net. In general the capillaries parallel the fibers. Transverse sections of fibers, after injections of dye into the capillary bed, show the capillaries to be spaced rather uniformly in the interstitial spaces. Normally, an optimal capillary concentration is maintained throughout life. Roberts and Wearn found this to be about 3342 capillaries per square millimeter in normal adult human hearts which had an average muscle fiber diameter of 13.9 microns and a ratio of one capillary for each fiber. In the hearts of newly born infants with average fiber diameters of 6.4 microns the capillary concentration was the same (3365 capillaries per square millimeter), but there was only one capillary for each six of the small muscle fibers. This indicates that, during the interval from birth to maturity, the capillaries increase in number so as to maintain the same concentration in the growing heart as at birth, despite the increase in size of each muscle fiber. As a result the capillary:fiber ratio of 1:6 at birth changes to a ratio of 1:1 by adolescence and remains so throughout life in all hearts (Fig. 17–6). On the other hand, when hypertrophy occurs as a result of heart disease and failure, the capillary:fiber ratio remains constant, but the capillary concentration falls in proportion to the increase in fiber diameter and heart weight (Figs. 17–7 and 17–8). Thus the hypertrophied heart is ischemic in proportion to its degree of hypertrophy because of this relative decrease in the capillary blood supply. This condition is easily recognized clinically, for it is rare to find a patient with a clinically enlarged heart

Figure 17–6. Changes in the fiber:capillary ratio during growth and hypertrophy of human hearts. (From Roberts and Wearn: Am. Heart J., 1941.)

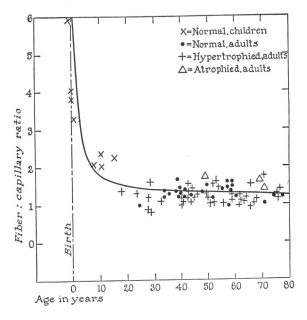

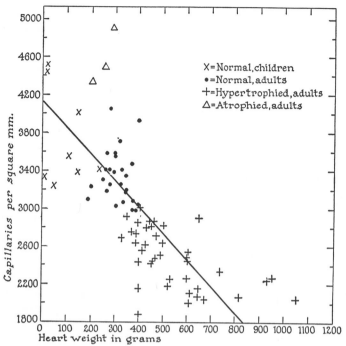

Figure 17–7. Concentration of capillaries in normal, hypertrophied and atrophied human hearts. (From Roberts and Wearn: Am. Heart J., 1941.)

who does not have some indication of cardiac inefficiency or even clear-cut cardiac failure. With recent experiences in the surgical relief of advanced heart disease, such as mitral stenosis, the tolerance of the heart is good in small hearts, but proportionally bad with hypertrophy. As a large heart improves in function, its size is often found to get smaller; this may be due to decrease in both hypertrophy and dilatation. Only myocardial biopsy with critical measuring of muscle fibers or careful measuring of size of cardiac chambers related to ventricular mural thickness, before and after correction of cardiac enlargement, will tell whether hypertrophy is reversible. The mechanisms causing hypertrophy of fibers are not known but are probably related to capillary permeability and intramuscular diffusion indexes. In these studies on the cardiac capillary bed, the diameter of the capillaries remained essentially unchanged with hypertrophy. It must be assumed that the length of the capillaries increased with the increased diameter and length (or volume) of the heart's chambers. With the muscle stretching of dilation as well as compression by the swollen fibers of hypertrophy many capillaries are expected to be compressed. Each of these mechanisms is assumed to make the hypertrophied heart even more ischemic, although hypothetically increased blood flow or diffusion may help with "compensation."

The interstitial fluid spaces, fibers and cells enter into the changes in the environment of heart muscle fibers by ebb and flow tides between them and the blood vascular and lymphatic capillaries.

Enlargement of the heart (as seen on physical or radiological examination) usually involves both dilatation and hypertrophy. In some conditions, such as myxedema, beriberi or atrioventricular fistula, correction of the condition causes such quick shrinkage in cardiac size that dilatation seems to be the predominant defect. Clinically efforts to separate cardiac dilatation from hypertrophy (e.g., by cineangiocardiography) are needed much more than usually attempted.

The capillary concentration is increased with cardiac atrophy (as in Addison's disease, starvation or pericardial constriction) and, strangely, also in the scar areas of cardiac infarction. This increase in capillaries per unit area is of no functional benefit as it is due to capillaries' coming closer together, with atrophy or loss of muscle fibers. Many inflammatory conditions (especially myocarditis of rheumatic fever, other collagen diseases or infections) cause obstruction, rupture or thrombosis of myocardial capillaries. Shock, lymphomas, purpura and many other diseases may damage these capillaries also. Such changes are probably of great significance in myocarditis or so-called myocardiopathies of any cause.

An adequate blood supply to the capillary

bed is most important if cardiac function is to be maintained. This capillary blood supply to the heart is safeguarded (Fig. 17–9) by several extraordinary mechanisms:

1. Two large coronary arteries, arising from the right and left anterior aortic sinuses of Valsalva, divide into branches which form a coronary ring in the atrioventricular sulcus and also in the interventricular sulcus. The pattern is fairly constant, the left coronary artery dividing into its anterior descending and left circumflex branches. However, the pattern varies in different hearts, especially in the supply to the posterior surface of the heart. According to Barnes, in 74 per cent of hearts most of the posterior surface is supplied by the right coronary artery. The secondary and smaller branches of each coronary artery anastomose with each other and also with branches from the other main artery.

The extent to which this anastomosis occurs may be great, so that complete occlusion of a main artery may be endured without infarction of the muscular territory which it supplies if the main arteries which supply the anastomosing small branches are open. Later, however, when the collateral circulation is occluded by the progress of disease, infarc-

tion of the heart is seen to affect chiefly the area supplied by the vessel occluded earlier. These "intercoronary anastomoses" appear to be the mcst valuable source of collateral cardiac circulation. They develop slowly as a rule, but at times may expand from minute capillaries to vessels of important size within a few hours or days. The intercoronary arteries may be narrowed by proliferative, thrombotic or embolic disease, and probably by spasm with loss of their protective role.

2. Extracardiac anastomoses connect branches of the coronary arteries and other branches of the aorta. These are usually minute channels lying in the pericardial reflections about the aorta, pulmonary artery and veins and venae cavae. Although their existence is recognized, they seldom seem to be dilated enough to serve as important sources of collateral circulation after stenosis of the coronary artery. Efforts to increase the extracardiac anastomoses have been made by Beck, O'Shaughnessy, Thomson and others by placing irritants in the pericardial cavity or by attaching the pectoral muscle, lung or omentum to the myocardium. Roberts has connected the coronary arteries and veins of animals to the internal mammary artery or other

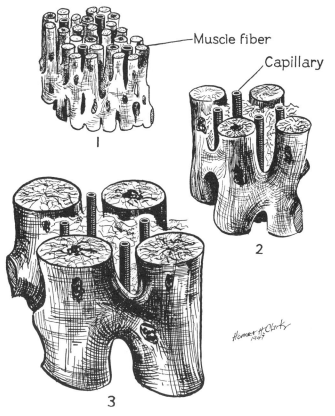

Muscle fiber

Capillary

Figure 17–8. Sketch showing the vascular changes in heart muscle attending growth and hypertrophy. *1,* From a newly born heart with normal concentration of capillaries, each supplying about six small fibers. *2,* From a normal adult heart with the same concentration of capillaries in the ratio of one fiber for each capillary. *3,* From a hypertrophied heart with a low concentration of capillaries which have not multiplied with increased size of fibers. (Based on data of Roberts and Wearn, 1938, 1941.)

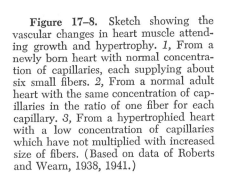

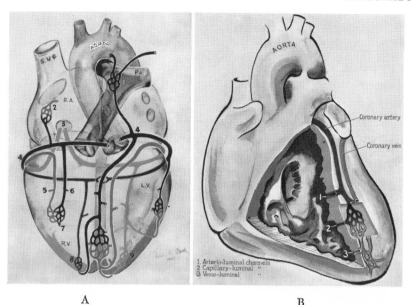

A   B

Figure 17–9. *A,* Diagram of the collateral circulation supplying blood to the heart. *1,* Extracardiac anastomoses between the coronary arteries and other branches of the aorta. *2,* Accessory coronary veins opening directly into the right atrium. *3,* Coronary veins ending in the coronary sinus above the tricuspid valve. *4,* The left and right main coronary arteries with inter-coronary arterial anastomoses. *5,* Veno-luminal channel (Thebesian vein). *6,* Arterio-luminal anastomoses. *7,* Sinusoido-capillary-luminal anastomosis. *8,* Interarterial anastomosis through capillaries. *9,* Intervenous anastomoses. *B,* Diagram of the collateral luminal anastomosis of the right ventricle. *1,* Arterio-luminal vessels; *2,* Capillary-luminal anastomosis. *3,* Veno-luminal anastomosis.

aortic branches. Vineberg tunneled the internal mammary artery through the myocardium as a source of anastomoses with small local coronary vessels, and this has become one of the most popular current methods for "revascularizing" the hearts of coronary artery disease. Roberts has similarly carried pectoral or intercostal muscles, nerves, edges of the lung, and larger arteries and veins through myocardial tunnels for anastomosis with coronary vessels. The use of these procedures in the treatment of cardiac ischemia is still in the experimental stage. An exaggerated concept of the size and role of the extracardiac anastomosis followed Glover's claim to relieve angina pectoris by cutting the upper internal mammary arteries. This procedure, discarded earlier, did not shunt blood through pericardial connections to the ischemic coronary arteries in carefully evaluated experiments on animals and patients. The relief found with some patients is explained as due to (1) a placebo effect, (2) raising the threshold for pain psychologically, or (3) correction of a reflex vasoneuropathy similar to that in temporal arteralgia, as diagramed in Figure 17–13).

3. Retrograde flow into the capillary bed

may occur through the coronary sinus and veins. This may be an ebb and flow mechanism. Valves in the coronary veins are absent or incompetent. However, in ordinary conditions the blood reaching the capillary bed by this route would be low in oxygen content and probably of little value. Experimentally, it is possible to bring a new arterial blood supply to dogs' ischemic hearts by an anastomosis between the subclavian artery and coronary sinus (Fig. 17–10) or between the internal mammary artery and the coronary vein or artery. Nourishment of the ischemic heart by way of the coronary sinus and veins was first proposed for coronary disease when J. T. Roberts in 1938 devised an operation for arterializing the coronary vessels by a connection to the aorta. This was confirmed in 1948 by C. S. Beck and has been used by him on patients with apparent protection against the effects of coronary disease. Bailey, Bakst, Blalock, Sengstrom and De-Bakey with their co-workers and others gave clinical and experimental evidence supporting the belief that arteriolization of coronary veins should protect against coronary artery disease (cf. Roberts, Browne and Roberts, 1943). Although not being used at present because of late thromboses in some of the fistulas, possible excessive arteriovenous fistula effect in some operations, with too much atrial run-off, and the very great technical difficulties, *this method still seems the most promising from a physiological standpoint* and may become feasible with improvements in such techniques as "cardiac arrest surgery" and easier techniques of anastomoses.

4. The luminal system of vessels is composed of minute channels connecting the cardiac cavities with (1) the coronary arteries and arterioles, (2) the cardiac capillaries and sinusoids, and (3) the coronary veins. Usually these channels are microscopic, only a few being grossly visible. However, in occasional hearts with sclerotic vessels the ostia of the luminal vessels are easily seen and may approach 1 mm. in diameter. The direction of flow through luminal vessels depends upon the gradient of pressure between the cardiac chamber and vessel concerned and in acute experiments was shown to occur in either direction, with changes in the gradient between coronary artery and ventricular cavity on either the right or left side of the heart. If the pressure in the coronary arteries exceeds that in the left ventricle, for example, the luminal channels serve as accessory drainage routes. On the other hand, if the pressure in the left ventricle exceeds that in the coronary arteries, as it may in patients with coronary stenosis, aortic stenosis or aortic insufficiency,

the blood from the left ventricle may reach the cardiac capillary bed by way of the luminal anastomoses. If the pressure in the right ventricle is lower than that in the left ventricle, the luminal channels of the right ventricle do not nourish the myocardium, but may drain it. When this normal situation is altered so that the right ventricular pressure exceeds that in the left ventricle and coronary arteries, the myocardium may be nourished from the right ventricle through the luminal vessels. This situation may exist, for example, in patients with pulmonary stenosis, left ventricular failure, mitral stenosis or coronary artery stenosis. The magnitude of flow through the luminal channels is not known. However, it is suspected from Wearn's experiments that as much as 60 per cent of the coronary blood may be drained through the luminal vessels into the cavities under some conditions. In rare hearts in which both main coronary arteries are completely occluded the luminal vessels may acquire a major role in nourishing the heart, as O'Leary and Wearn inferred from two hearts with syphilitic occlusion of both coronary ostia. In many other hearts with partial stenosis of the coronary arteries the luminal vessels may help maintain life by supplementing the coronary arteries. This surmise has not been proved experimentally on a chronic basis although several studies support such a mechanism in acute experiments (cf. Roberts, 1945). Artificially, acces-

Figure 17–10. Diagram of experimental anastomosis between the coronary sinus (C.S.) and a branch of the aorta for bringing arterial blood supply to the ischemic myocardium after coronary artery occlusion. (According to Roberts, Browne and Roberts: Fed. Proc., 1943, and M. Ann., District of Columbia, Vol. 14, 1945.)

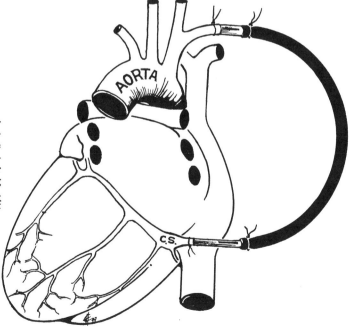

sory luminal vessels have been created by puncturing holes in the endocardium or by carrying vessel segments across the ventricular cavity by tunneling through the ventricular wall.

The coronary veins accompany the branches of the coronary arteries and end in the coronary sinus except for a few which open directly into the right atrium. The latter, known as accessory coronary veins, drain the anterior surface of the right ventricle.

The lymphatic supply of the heart consists of three plexuses: (1) endocardial, (2) myocardial, (3) epicardial. All cardiac lymphatic channels drain to the epicardial plexus, which in turn drains into a single large lymphatic channel lying in the arch of the pulmonary artery. This system has an active flow of lymph and is probably of great importance in the metabolism of heart muscle. Red blood cells enter the lymphatics on massage, contusion, or other injury of the heart. It has been suspected that there is some relation between damage of the cardiac lymphatics and various forms of heart disease, but mechanisms of the relation remain unsolved.

Coronary Arteriosclerosis

By far the most serious and frequent disease affecting the coronary blood vessels is atherosclerosis with thrombosis. Often this condition completely or partially closes the major or secondary coronary arteries and is nearly always present in patients having myocardial infarction. Either the right or left ventricle may be infarcted by this process, but the left ventricle is nearly always affected to a much greater extent because it is much thicker and less well supplied with protecting anastomoses. Partial or patchy ischemia of the myocardium may occur without complete occlusion of the arteries when the metabolic needs are not met by the volume of blood carried through the narrowed channels. Embolism occurs infrequently; usually it is caused by bacterial endocarditis, granulation and cracking of a stenotic aortic valve, mural thrombosis of a left ventricular infarction, or the left atrial thrombosis associated with rheumatic mitral stenosis. Air or gas embolism of coronary arteries, as shown experimentally by Moore, may be produced in patients by faulty pneumothorax, by rupture of overdistended alveoli or blebs into pulmonary venules in emphysematous patients or overventilating divers, in victims of nitrogen bubbles and in the "bends" or caisson disease. Embolism from such bubbles, even if small, on the left side of the heart is a much greater hazard than on the right side. Narrowing of the coronary vessels, especially the capillaries, lymphatics, arterioles and venules, may result from generalized processes, such as rickettsial or other infectious diseases, sensitization reactions or any of the so-called collagen diseases, vasospasm, thrombosis, and compression by hemorrhage, petechiae or abscesses.

When arteriosclerosis affects the coronary arteries, the lumina of many coronary arteries are stenosed by eccentric plaques of lipoid, fibrinous, edematous, hemorrhagic or calcified material. These plaques elevate the endothelium and sometimes invade the media. The severity of the process varies in different branches. Usually thrombosis occurs on or near the stenosing plaque. Subintimal hemorrhage or edema, as well as "fibrinoid" changes so often found in the collagen diseases, may obliterate the lumen. The main trunks or primary branches of the coronary arteries are affected with about equal frequency. However, infarction of the right ventricle is much less common than of the left. Whitten attributed this to a difference in the angle at which the penetrating branches leave the main trunks and enter the myocardium. In the right ventricle this angle of penetration is obtuse and gradual, whereas in the left ventricle the angle is acute and abrupt. He suggested that the bending of the penetrating branches with each heart beat increased the trauma and rate of degeneration of the left coronary arteries. This does not explain why the disease most often affects the main trunks or primary branches, which may be injured most by the bending near the coronary groove.

Coronary arteriosclerosis affects men more frequently, earlier and more severely than women. Dock attributed this to a congenital difference in the thickness of the intima when he found that the coronary arteries of male infants had thicker intimas than those of female children. This observation has not been confirmed. It seems more probable that incidence of this disease is related to differences in ancestry, dietary habits, physical and psychic trauma, and the demand placed upon the coronary arteries by greater exertion. At present, faulty metabolism of cholesterol, or other derivatives of fat, is thought to be an important factor causing arteriosclerosis. These fatty substances may pass through the intima or plug the tiny vasa vasorum in the wall of the arteries. Fat globules may be seen in the capillaries of fasting animals, more abundantly so after fatty meals. The molecules containing cholesterol vary greatly in size and probably in significance. According to some authors, elevated serum and tissue levels of cholesterol or related fractions are statistically related to the incidence of coronary or other atherosclerosis; but many believe these associations to be inconstant and not causal relations. Dietary reduction in fat precursors may lower serum cholesterol and decrease coronary insufficiency, although these effects are closely related to other benefits of weight control. The long-term effects of preventing the change of cholesterol precursors to cholesterol are still unknown and raise many doubts about the advisability of routine use of this method until further information accumulates.

Coronary Blood Flow

Coronary blood flow has not been measured reliably even in animals because of the many variables acting upon the rate and volume of flow in this complicated vascular system. Some of the determinants of coronary flow are (1) the aortic blood pressure at the mouths of the coronary arteries, (2) resistance offered by the coronary arteries, capillaries and veins, (3) viscosity of the blood, (4) caliber of the vessels, as increased by anoxia, vasodilatation or stasis and decreased by (a) spasm, (b) narrowing by their elongation in diastole or dilatation and hypertrophy, (c) compression of vessels by hypertrophied fibers or myocarditic nodules, or (d) proliferative and thrombotic lesions, (5) extravascular support offered to intramural vessels by the cardiac muscle during systole and diastole, (6) heart rate, (7) the temperature and (8) chemical composition of the blood, (9) cardiac rhythm, the action of (10) neurohumors and (11) drugs, (12) degrees of cardiac failure and (13) the pressure within the cardiac chambers, especially the right atrium and left ventricle.

Flow in coronary vessels is a doubly biphasic phenomenon depending largely upon the resultant of two factors: the aortic blood pressure and the state of the coronary vessels. The greatest flow usually occurs during diastole. Three main phases are recognized. During isometric contraction of the ventricles the coronary flow falls sharply because the aortic pressure is lowest then. During the isotonic or ejection phase the coronary flow rises with the rise of aortic pressure and then falls, but the volume of flow is less than expected from the rise in coronary artery pressure be-

cause there is still great intramural tension with constriction of the coronary vessels. During the isometric relaxation period the coronary flow again rises to its greatest peak and stays near the high level throughout the rest of diastole with a slow, gradual fall during isotonic diastole until the abrupt fall at isometric systole begins. It may be that there is even some backward flow through the major coronary arteries and ostia at this time due to squeezing of the vessels.

With tachycardia the coronary flow is proportionately decreased, largely because of the shortened diastolic period and relatively prolonged systole. With severe bradycardia the coronary flow is also diminished, for reasons poorly understood. Within normal ranges of heart rate, the experimentally perfused mean aortic pressure being kept the same, the coronary artery flow varies in proportion to the heart rate. These observations explain to some extent the frequency with which signs of cardiac ischemia, such as cardiac pain, dyspnea, or alterations of the RS-T segments or T waves are found in patients with abnormal heart rates. With partial AV block, the filling of the ventricles may be increased by the prolonged atrial systole, giving an accentuated atrial (fourth) and first heart sound, but with poor efficiency. This handicap is sometimes even greater with complete AV block or AV dissociation or even with accelerated conduction (W.P.W. syndrome) because of the lack of correlated action of the atria and ventricles. However, the tolerance for these defects is often very good for long periods.

Cardiac ischemia is expected in hypertension because (1) the increased aortic pressure is opposed by increased intramyocardial pressure; (2) the cardiac metabolism is increased and more blood is needed but not available; and (3) arteriosclerosis of the larger coronary arteries, arteriolar sclerosis and arteriospasm narrow the coronary vessels. Similarly, in cor pulmonale the flow, especially through the right coronary artery, is lowered because of increased intramural pressure in the right ventricle. Also, stretching of pulmonary artery walls, compression of the coronary arteries by the dilated pulmonary artery, angulation of pulmonary and caval veins by cardiac rotation, and poor oxygenation of blood through the damaged lung may be causes of the common anginal and electrocardiographic abnormalities with either chronic or acute cor pulmonale. In mitral stenosis or insufficiency and in aortic stenosis the flow falls because the aortic pressure 'is low. The low diastolic aortic pressure of aortic insufficiency, together with the increased intramural pressure and left ventricular hypertrophy, decreases the coronary flow, especially during the diastolic phase, when, normally, flow is greatest. In syphilitic heart disease there often is added the harmful factor of stenosis or occlusion of the coronary ostia; the same factor may obstruct the coronary ostial inflow in patients with dissecting aneurysms. In any of these and other diseases, if the cardiac chambers are enlarged or if the pulmonary veins and venae cavae are bent, coronary insufficiency is to be expected from compression of the coronary arteries or veins with a fall in coronary inflow or drainage.

Viscosity of the blood is a modifier of coronary flow which is seldom considered clinically. With increased viscosity, such as may occur during dehydration, shock, polycythemia, azotemia, hyperglycemia, hyperprothrombinemia, hypercholesterolemia, hyperglobulinemia and other states, the coronary flow is decreased. On the other hand, in anemia with hypervolemia or after excessive administration of intravenous fluid, the viscosity of the blood is decreased and coronary blood flow increased; however, because the capacity of the blood to carry oxygen is low, the myocardium often becomes ischemic. Anoxemia causes dilatation of the coronary arteries, and, if other conditions were the same, this would raise the coronary flow. However, the myocardium may suffer from oxygen lack despite this attempted compensatory mechanism. Asphyxia or hypercapnia plays a minor role also by raising the coronary artery flow. The mechanism of these increases is not clear, but possibly involves the effect of metabolites accumulating as a result of failure of aerobic oxidation in the muscle cells. For example, adenosine, adenine and adenylic acid, breakdown products of nucleic acids, are related to the xanthines and presumably cause vasodilatation and increase in the strength of ventricular contraction, in heart rate and in blood pressure.

Cardiac rhythm may influence coronary flow significantly. During experimental ventricular fibrillation the intramural pressure is low, so that the coronary flow during perfusion is increased. However, this is of no practical aid because the aortic and coronary artery pressures are also too low unless raised artificially by retrograde aortic perfusion promptly. Atrial fibrillation and flutter have little apparent effect on coronary flow except as they may alter the rate and strength of ventricular contraction; when the latter are abnormal, correction by digitalis, quinidine, oxygen or even by specific therapy such as antithyroxin substances may improve the coronary flow. Premature contractions from any cause, if frequent, may cause coronary flow to be inadequate by lowering the cardiac output and aortic pressure as well as by increasing the intervals of ventricular systole; correction by quinidine, digitalis, sedation or removal of the cause is likely to be needed.

The coronary vessels are richly supplied with nerve fibers, but these fibers have not been satisfactorily traced to their sources because of the close anatomic association between the sympathetic and parasympathetic nerve trunks. Acetylcholine, the parasympathetic neurohumor, decreases the coronary flow in dogs, but its effect in man is unknown. Sympatheticomimetic epinephrine increases perfused coronary flow in dogs, cats and man, apparently by dilatation of the coronary arteries, but it increases the heart rate, irritability and energy utilization and is likely to precipitate ventricular fibrillation, particularly in ischemic hearts, so that its clinical use in such states is dangerous.

Sympathetic nervous stimulation increases coronary blood flow in the isolated beating heart, the heart-lung preparation and in the intact animal. Vagal stimulation constricts the coronary vessels in the isolated or intact beating heart of dogs, but in the fibrillating heart the vagus dilates the coronary vessels as it does elsewhere in the body. In the dog continual tonic activity of the vagi regulates coronary flow, but apparently sympathetic tone is negligible. Parasympathetic nerve fibers reach the smallest vessels, whereas few sympathetic fibers extend beyond the larger coronary vessels. Such experiments on animals cannot explain the role of tonic nervous control of the coronary arteries in human beings. Coronary sinus outflow is increased by weak stimulation of afferent cardiac nerves and decreased by stronger stimulation. Distention of the stomach, gallbladder, colon, urinary bladder or peritoneal cavity usually decreases coronary arterial flow, as indicated by the frequency of associated anginal pain, probably by (1) shifting of significant volumes of blood, (2) viscerocardiac reflexes, (3) angulation of the heart, (4) interference with venous return to the heart, and (5) lowering of the psychological threshold for angina by summation of these other discomforts. The flow may be increased by exercise, cooling of the skin or cutaneous pain, but not enough to compensate for the increased cardiac work or to prevent anginal attacks. Coronary flow activated through the carotid sinus varies inversely with cerebral blood pressure.

Nitrates, papaverine, ephedrine, atropine and perhaps morphine increase coronary flow in concentrations comparable to those used clinically. In such concentrations the xanthines, Coramine and Metrazol, do not affect coronary flow, although in far greater concentrations they may increase it. Prolonged and severe coronary arterial constriction is caused by Pituitrin and Pitressin. Digitalis-like substances, although decreasing coronary flow in toxic concentrations, are without effect in nontoxic doses. Therefore their use should not be withheld in patients with suspected coronary artery disease when heart failure, atrial fibrillation or atrial tachycardia indicate that they would be of benefit. Frequently digitalis seems to improve coronary flow clinically by correcting arrhythmias or the insufficient circulation of heart failure. However, it is unsafe to give toxic doses to such patients. Quinidine affects coronary flow only by its effect upon the cardiac rate, rhythm and muscular tone. Histamine increases coronary flow in human, dog and cat hearts, but is not used clinically. Many substances (e.g., pentaerythritol tetranitrate) introduced in recent years may increase effective coronary artery blood flow, according to many reports based upon indirectly related criteria such as clinically counting the number and severity of anginal episodes, use of nitroglycerine, tolerance for daily activity and protection of the electrocardiogram against the effects of exercise, hypoxia, stress, vasoconstrictors (e.g., epinephrine) or stimulants of cardiac activity and demands such as ergotamine. Evaluation of these by direct inspection, injections of dye, and flowmeters has been confined usually to normal animals; those with coronary lesions might have very different responses.

In acutely hypertensive animals the coronary flow increases with the aortic pressure, but the problem has not been studied in chronically hypertensive animals. The effect of renin and angiotensin is unknown. The great frequency of insufficient coronary flow in hypertensive patients is well known and is probably the result of the commonly associated atherosclerosis, emotional and physical stress, general vasospasm, obesity with associated rise of the chylomicrons or large lipid molecules in the blood, hypertrophy of the ventricle with capillary insufficiency, and other mechanisms. In experimental hyperthyroidism blood flow through all vessels, including the coronary arteries, is increased, and this is probably true in clinical hyperthyroidism as well. However, tachycardia, atrial fibrillation and increased metabolism frequently counteract this and produce evidence of coronary insufficiency. In myxedema, thyroid substance often causes angina, even in small doses, by increasing the work of the heart. Smaller doses often control the common coronary insufficiency of myxedema.

The effect of congestive heart failure upon coronary flow to the heart is not clearly described. It is useful to visualize the coronary vessels as a third system (Fig. 17–11) of arteries, capillaries and veins beginning on one side of the heart and emptying into the other side as do the aortic and pulmonary vascular beds. Each of these three vascular systems may be affected by either forward or backward failure of one or both sides of the heart. For example, any factor interfering with the normal or required inflow of blood to the coronary arteries will cause cardiac ischemia by "forward failure" of the coronary circulation (e.g., coronary artery stenosis or vasoconstriction, valvular disease, pulmonary obstruction, angulation of the cardiac vessels, especially the pulmonary veins and venae cavae, shock, hypoxia or anemia). When the need for coronary blood supply under conditions acting at any given time cannot be met by the available coronary blood flow, congestive heart failure of one or both ventricles may be expected. Backward failure of the left ventricle may temporarily increase coronary flow, chiefly through the right coronary artery, when pulmonary arterial pressure rises, but soon coronary flow through the right ventricle is impaired as its intramural pressure increases, and right ventricular failure follows quickly. Backward failure with its increase of pressure in the cardiac chambers may briefly raise the volume of blood entering the myocardium through veno-luminal and arterio-luminal channels, but this blood is likely to be hypoxic and of little prolonged value. Stasis of myocardial blood is also expected from elevated pressure in cardiac chambers, especially the right atrium and ventricle, because of decreased coronary venous outflow. Experimentally, obstruction of the coronary sinus or of single coronary veins seems to improve nutrition to areas supplied by a ligated coronary artery, possibly because of increased utilization of venous

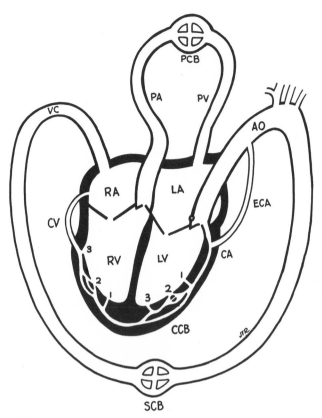

Figure 17–11. Diagram of the circulation, showing (1) the three capillary beds: systemic (*SCB*), pulmonary (*PCB*), and coronary (*CCB*); and (2) the anastomoses of the coronary vessels: extracardiac anastomoses (*ECA*), and luminal (Thebesian) vessels (*1, 2, 3*). *1,* Arterio-luminal vessels; *2,* sinusoidal-luminal or capillary-luminal anastomoses; *3,* veno-luminal anastomoses. *CA,* Coronary arteries; *CV,* coronary veins; *VC,* venae cavae; *RA,* right atrium; *RV,* right ventricle; *PA,* pulmonary artery; *PV,* pulmonary veins; *LA,* left atrium; *LV,* left ventricle; *AO,* aorta. (From Roberts: Texas State J. Med., 1942.)

oxygen with slowed flow. The work of L. Gross, of Beck and Mako, and of Fouteaux on ligation of coronary veins to combat coronary artery stenosis is not yet an indication for such procedures in clinical practice. Congestive heart failure probably impairs coronary blood flow by many mechanisms at a time when need for better cardiac nutrition is urgent. Drugs are of questionable value in increasing the volume of collateral circulation during cardiac ischemia except by indirectly aiding the toleration of ischemia during the interval required for development of collateral circulation. With the use of cineangiography, as developed especially by Sones, dilation of anastomoses between coronary arteries after gradual occlusion was found increased in pigs after prolonged use of pentaerythritol nitrate, and similar dilation has been seen on an acute basis in patients receiving this and similar agents. Despite this and widespread clinical use, prevention of progressive coronary artery disease by known vasodilators seems improbable thus far.

Cardiac Reserve

Normally the heart has a remarkable reserve amount of the energy needed for its ability to perform its function of propelling enough blood to meet the demands of the body even under unusual conditions of exertion. The heart meets the demand for greater volumes of circulating blood, required by exercise, digestion, excitement, fever, cold, acceleration or deceleration and various abnormal states, by increasing its output by the following mechanisms: (1) increase in rate, or decrease, as needed, (2) increased diastolic filling and systolic emptying of the ventricles, (3) dilatation of the ventricles, and (4) possibly hypertrophy. Other mechanisms may include: (5) improvement of the venous oxygen reserve (normally negligible in heart muscle, according to Carlson and Rushmer and others), (6) augmented oxygen extraction from coronary blood, (7) improved biochemical efficiency of the heart beat, as with fever, (8) improved ratio between (a) "useful work" (with its two fractions of potential and kinetic energy) and (b) energy waste, a widely variable ratio averaging about 2 per cent, (9) improved diffusion rates of oxygen and other materials between capillary and muscle fiber in the heart wall. These variants upon which effective circulation to tissues depends are usefully grouped into four components of cardiac reserve: venous oxygen reserve, the maximum cardiac output which can be maintained, the efficiency of myocardial energy release and the oxygen release to the heart muscle. Training, avoidance of excessive demands and many other adjustments in some degree often gradually improve cardiac reserve, although the basic lesion may not be removed. This is usually the object of treatment, even in the occasional situations where surgery, healing of infection or chemical regulation can improve a specific abnormality. The ability of the heart to make these adjustments with biochemical efficiency varies in different persons and in the same person from time to time.

Cardiac reserve is the capacity of the heart to meet the extra demands placed upon it. Clinically, the following grades of cardiac reserve can be recognized: (1) normal cardiac reserve, the power of the normal heart to respond to even excessive demands without the production of symptoms and signs of cardiac inefficiency; (2) slightly decreased reserve, the ability to meet ordinary demands with efficiency despite inability to fulfill excessive demands for increased circulation without breathlessness, tachycardia, palpitation, discomfort and other complaints which do not disappear promptly on rest; (3) moderately decreased cardiac reserve, the inability to meet even slightly unusual demands without such evidences of cardiac inefficiency; (4) severely diminished reserve, the inability to meet any unusual demands, and occasional evidence of cardiac inefficiency even when resting; (5) completely lost cardiac reserve, the inability to maintain an efficient circulation even at rest without signs or symptoms of heart failure. Each of these grades of cardiac reserve may merge into the others and may seem to reflect weakness of either ventricle. Most physicians forget that cardiac reserve may get better or worse suddenly, paroxysmally or gradually. Often these variations in cardiac reserve occur in many cycles, but sometimes loss of reserve results in sudden death or chronic, resistant heart failure.

In any patient change from one grade of cardiac reserve to another may be expected. As the heart disease of a patient advances in severity and duration, cardiac reserve is progressively lost. With proper treatment some degree of cardiac reserve may be regained, temporarily in most cases. Unless the etiologic form of heart disease is a reversible type of heart disease (e.g., the heart disease of hyperthyroidism, myxedema, beriberi, patent ductus arteriosus, coarctation, mitral stenosis, atrial septal defect, tetralogy of Fallot, anemia, hypertension or subacute bacterial endocarditis), the loss of cardiac reserve continues, despite temporary improvements with or without treatment, to the state of completely lost cardiac reserve and the stopping of the heart when its own circulation cannot be maintained. An important goal is the recognition of the loss of cardiac reserve in its earliest stages. In the earlier stages much better results are expected from proper treatment. Too frequently patients with known heart disease are not treated until the last stage of lost cardiac reserve is reached, manifested by edema of legs or lungs, enlarged liver, ascites or pleural effusion, and at that time the ability of the heart to regain reserve is limited.

The mechanisms governing cardiac reserve are poorly understood and are seldom measured well, even experimentally. Probably each of the many known and unknown factors in cardiac structure, mechanics, muscular chemistry and circulation influences cardiac reserve. If the cardiac rate is much above 100 or below 50, cardiac reserve is usually limited, probably because of (1) decreased coronary blood flow and (2) either too little or too great filling of the ventricular cavities during diastole. When the venous return is limited (for example, by cardiac tamponade, pericardial constrictions, vena caval thrombosis, mediastinal tumors or backward failure), cardiac reserve is lost in proportion. Obstruction to the outflow of blood from either chamber, by valvular stenosis or regurgitation or by recirculation through abnormal shunts (congenital or acquired), increases the demand upon the heart muscle and in time leads to excessive strain upon one or both ventricles, followed soon by loss of cardiac reserve. The same result follows a prolonged strain on the cardiac reserve when the circulating blood volume is increased, as in congestive cardiac failure and excessive sodium retention or hypo-albuminemia.

If the normal, regular cardiac cycle is altered, cardiac reserve is decreased, often very soon. Complete loss of cardiac reserve always accompanies ventricular fibrillation and tachycardia, and usually is, at best, moderately severe with frequent premature beats from any source, atrial fibrillation or flutter. The various degrees of heart block seldom limit cardiac reserve seriously, but, if of high grade, they usually indicate the presence of

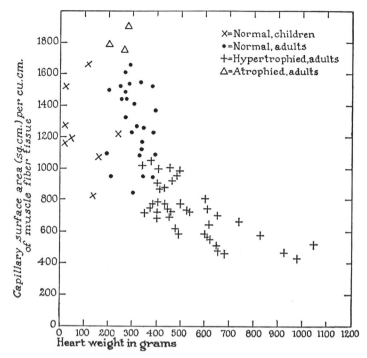

Figure 17-12. Capillary surface area (sq. cm.) per cu. cm. of muscle fiber tissue in relation to heart weight, of normal, hypertrophied and atrophied human hearts. (From Roberts and Wearn: Am. J. Heart., 1941.)

types of heart disease which by other mechanisms destroy cardiac reserve. It is desirable to correct any cardiac arrhythmia as soon as possible so that loss of cardiac reserve may be arrested. Toxic, inflammatory, chemical, endocrine or vascular injury of the myocardium may cause severe loss of cardiac reserve which frequently is temporary and may improve after the condition has been corrected. However, during the activity of such processes the limitation of cardiac reserve should be recognized clearly and the patient spared as much exertion as possible. Otherwise, the demands upon the heart may exceed its reserve and acute or irremediable heart failure will be precipitated.

The role of cardiac hypertrophy in cardiac reserve is poorly understood by many physicians. Cardiac hypertrophy, like excessive dilatation or prolonged tachycardia, is a harmful mechanism in itself and never occurs unless the heart has already lost some of its reserve and will probably lose more. Often patients with hypertension or valvular disease maintain good cardiac reserve until hypertrophy begins to be recognizable by roentgenologic or physical examination. Thereafter, loss of cardiac reserve is usually prompt and progressive unless the cardiac enlargement can be corrected. Practically without exception, patients with recognizable cardiac enlargement have poor cardiac reserve. Roberts and Wearn showed that the capillary bed of

the hypertrophied human myocardium is decreased in proportion to the increase in heart weight. As the muscle fibers enlarge, the capillaries are pushed so far apart that there is a great increase in the distance through which oxygen and other metabolized substances must diffuse in going between the capillary endothelium and the muscle nucleus. The capillary surface area per cubic centimeter of contracting muscle fibers is 1184 sq. cm. normally, but was found to average only 625 sq. cm. in a group of hypertrophied hearts. The actual diffusion in normal and hypertrophied hearts has not been measured, but it is evidently impaired by hypertrophy through this great relative loss of capillary diffusing surface (Fig. 17-12).

Fundamentally, cardiac reserve probably depends upon the maintenance in the cardiac muscle cells of the following abilities: (1) to fragment rhythmically and resynthesize phosphocreatine for the liberation of energy in the muscle fibers and stimulate the next phase; (2) to rotate rhythmically the myosin molecules on the myofibrils from the long to the short status so as to shorten the muscle fiber length with contraction and (vice versa) lengthen them with relaxation; or according to another theory, to increase the cyclic sliding of the actin fibrils in and out of the spaces between the myosin fibrils with cyclic building up and discharge of electrostatic charges; and (3) to attract rhythmically, by the action of myoglobin, oxygen from the adjacent capillaries into the cardiac muscle fibers for the resynthesis of phosphocreatine, and for the liberation of carbon dioxide with the breakdown of the latter. Any factor (such as change in fiber diameter, decrease in diffusion rate, lack of oxygen supply, irregular rhythm, abnormal rate or excessive demands) which interferes with these adjustments is likely to cause loss of reserve power and, if prolonged, obvious congestive heart failure. The sarcosomes of the heart muscle are believed by Kisch to be important enzyme-bearing organelles of microscopic and partly ultramicroscopic size. The ability of the normal heart to work steadily without prolonged rest periods is safeguarded by their great number. He believed that their osmiophilic degeneration in patients dying of severe heart failure was a factor causing malfunction of the enzyme system of the heart in heart failure.

Measurement

Clinically, the measurement of cardiac reserve must be indirect. Two mistakes are commonly made, namely, (1) failure to recognize and correct loss of cardiac reserve before it is too far advanced and (2) erroneous ascribing of certain symptoms to cardiac failure when they are really noncardiac. Evidence of cardiac inefficiency should be carefully evaluated when any of the following exist: breathlessness; palpitation; fast heart action or rate of breathing; undue fatigue; sensations of pressure or constriction, even pain, over the sternum, precordium, shoulders or arm; unexplained drowsiness or sleeplessness; increased number of premature beats; paroxysmal arrhythmia of any type, pulsus alternans, gallop rhythm, diffuse apex beats; faint or abnormal heart sounds; exaggerated diastolic impact; edema; enlarged heart or liver; pulmonary rales or basal dullness. Elevation of the venous pressure (above a maximum of 15 cm.), prolongation of the circulation time (beyond 10 seconds, arm-to-lung, and 20 seconds, arm-to-tongue), a rise in venous pressure of more than 1.5 cm. on pressure over the liver, decrease in the vital capacity (below 3000 cc. for women or 4500 cc. for men or according to the tables of DuBois) and loss of ability to hold the breath for more than 30 seconds are useful signs of impaired cardiac reserve, but usually when they are significantly abnormal the reserve is so far lost that cardiac failure is obvious by simple inspection. Electrocardiographically, evidence of "strain" of one or more chambers may be found, occasionally alone, but usually with other evidence of lowered cardiac reserve. The electrocardiogram of "strain" usually has similarity to or mixture with the characteristics of hypertrophy, coronary insufficiency, drug effects or of electrolytic disturbance; these basic disturbances are often combined in a ventricle which has lost some of its reserve or is being "strained."

Several efforts have been made to test cardiac reserve clinically by observation of the time required for heart rate, blood pressure or respiration to return to normal after a standard exercise, but to date none of these has been found to have value greater than simple observation of a change in a person's tolerance of his own usual exertion. The stair test and the ability to blow at a definite rate against slight resistance have the same status.

Unusually small hearts are likely to have diminished cardiac reserve also, a fact often overlooked. For example, the atrophic heart of any emaciating illness (such as tuberculosis, carcinoma, Simmonds' disease or starvation) or of Addison's disease is always prone to heart failure. This is often acute and severe, even fatal. Usually the failure is precipitated by some mild strain which normally would cause no difficulty. Acute dilatation and congestive failure may occur in such states, but more frequent is simple arrest of cardiac action due to failure in the properties of rhythmicity of impulse formation, irritability or contractility. Basic disturbances include (1) lack of salts, minerals, vitamins and other substances in the atrophied fibers due to nutritional deficiency; (2) shrinkage of muscle fibers to such a small size that they lose the power to contract with the needed force; (3) loss of many muscle fibers and replacement by fibrous tissue, especially in extensive coronary artery disease or after "healing" of myocarditis; and (4) "atrophy of disuse" in constrictive pericardial disease. In case of the last type, acute heart failure may follow relief of the constriction by surgical intervention because of excessive stretching of the weakened atrophic muscle fibers.

In "functional cardiovascular disease" (neurocirculatory asthenia), lowered cardiac reserve is often suspected, but cannot be explained except on the supposition of psychologic or neurogenic imbalance of the autonomic nervous system. In the situation known as "stress," changes are expected in the collagenous fibers of small blood vessels, the surfaces of endothelial cells, the tendency of blood to sludge or clot, or the electrolyte : water ratios in cells and tissues. If stress is severe, prolonged or repeated, functional or organic heart disease may result to some degree. Some of these effects may be reversed by rest or hormonal treatment as with cortisone or ACTH or with salicylates.

Cardiac Pain and Cardiac Nerves

The neural mechanisms for the control of the heart and coronary circulation and for the production and perception of cardiac pain are not established at present because of difficulty in tracing anatomic connections of the cardiac nerves. These nerves, both afferent and efferent, are vagal and sympathetic. Efferent cardiac nerves, from the vagal ganglion nodosum and ansa hypoglossi and from the superior, middle and inferior cervical sympathetic ganglions, form complex superficial and deep plexuses behind the base of the heart. From the deep plexus, branches enter the heart. Those fibers from the right cardiac nerves supply chiefly the sino-atrial node and atrial muscle, while the ventricles and atrioventricular conduction tissue are supplied almost entirely by the left cardiac nerves. Ganglions with cell bodies lie in the coronary sulcus, but few if any nerve cell bodies are found below there. In animals it is rather well established that the vagus nerves slow impulse formation and conduction, increase refractoriness, lower irritability and inhibit contractility in their respective territories, while the sympathetic cardiac nerves oppose these actions in a sort of balanced dual innervation. Their motor effects on the coronary arteries have been mentioned before.

The afferent cardiac nerves are much less well understood. Sensory nerve endings, both of the branching bare and the whorled encapsulated types, are present in the heart muscle, endocardium, epicardium and adventitia of the coronary arteries, according to Stohr. Axons of the more specialized end organs acquire a myelin sheath, while many of the less specialized pain fibers remain unmyelinated. In the plexus around the coronary arteries both types mingle with the nonmyelinated autonomic motor neurons and traverse the deep and superficial cardiac plexuses (where their definitive course is easily lost in any presently known method of study). Apparently, regulatory or subconscious stimuli reach the medulla over the vagus nerves, and possibly over the sympathetic cardiac nerves. The afferent fibers conducting impulses resulting in the sensation of pain enter the upper thoracic segments of the spinal cord over the superior, middle and inferior sympathetic cardiac nerves, which end in the corresponding ganglions of the sympathetic chain; these fibers with few exceptions descend from these ganglions to the upper thoracic ganglions of the chain and then pass via the white rami communicantes to cell bodies in the dorsal root ganglions of the upper five dorsal nerves. Along these same paths, plus the other thoracic nerves, stimuli arising in the thoracic aorta reach the spinal cord, so that anesthetic or surgical block of these sympathetic neurons may stop either cardiac or aortic painful stimuli. Such relief of pain is occasionally sought clinically when it is not feared that removal of the warning signal of pain may allow a careless patient to overexert himself.

Beyond the dorsal root ganglion cells the course by which sensations of cardiac and all other types of "referred" visceral pain reach consciousness is quite unknown. Making use of studies showing the important role of vasa nervorum in the function of all nerves, Roberts proposed a circuit or reflex arc (Fig. 17–13) to explain referred cardiac pain and consisting of the following components: (1) myocardial nerve anoxia stimulates (2) impulses along afferent cardiac nerves to (3) dorsal root ganglion cell bodies and their central axons in the cervical and upper thoracic spinal cord segments, terminating in (4) association neurons on (5) cell bodies in the dorsolateral or intermediolateral cell body groups of the gray substance; these send (6) efferent sympathetic effector axons via the white rami communicantes, synapses in the sympathetic ganglions, and gray rami communicantes and somatic nerves, to (7) the smooth muscle in the vasa nervorum of peripheral somatic nerves distributed to the areas of "cardiac pain"; (8) spasm of these vasa nervorum results in ischemia of the somatic nerves, causing impulses to go over the lateral spinothalamic tracts from these peripheral nerves with resulting consciousness of pain in the area supplied by the ischemic somatic nerves. This is a "trigger" mechanism which may persist, unless interrupted, after the initial stimulus has stopped. At times, relief of such pain may be obtained by anesthesia of the painful area in the chest wall (skin or muscle) or arm, or by surgical or chemical blocking of the pathway at any point. Spasm and dilatation of living vasa nervorum, as well as stasis and sludging of blood in them, has been seen by Roberts and co-workers, using quartz rod visualization. They found that the vasa nervorum of living animals constrict under the systemic or local influence of drugs like epinephrine and dilate with nitrites.

This proposed reflex has been given strong support by their recent work, which showed that ligation of a coronary artery is quickly followed by reversible spasm of the vasa nervorum of the left arm with no changes in the right arm's nerves. This parallels the ordinary clinical "referral" of coronary pain to the left arm more than to the right. Such reflex spasm of the blood vessels of the hand and upper limb after coronary occlusion may explain the common sequel of "shoulder-hand syndrome," "Raynaud's phenomenon" and "Dupuytren's contracture" in patients surviving coronary disease. The latter can be explained, on this basis, by spasticity of the

unopposed palmaris longus muscle due to irritability of its ischemic nerve supply.

The sensation called "cardiac pain" may be one of heat, cold, tingling, cutting, stabbing, tearing, pressure or compression, according to the degree of involvement of the different types of somatic axons conducting thermal, painful or proprioceptive impulses. The small nerve fibers and endings which lie between the cardiac muscle fibers and in the coats of the coronary vessels receive and transmit stimuli created by ischemia. Such stimuli may be due to lack of oxygen, to failure of impaired local circulation to remove the products of metabolism (e.g., lactic acid), to some hypothetical pain-producing substance of unknown nature, to spasm of the coronary artery or distention of its wall above an occlusion causing compression of the local nerve fibers. Also, according to Roberts' work on peripheral nerves, partial ischemia of these intrinsic cardiac nerves (by thrombosis or other changes in their vasa nervorum) may cause painful sensations to arise from

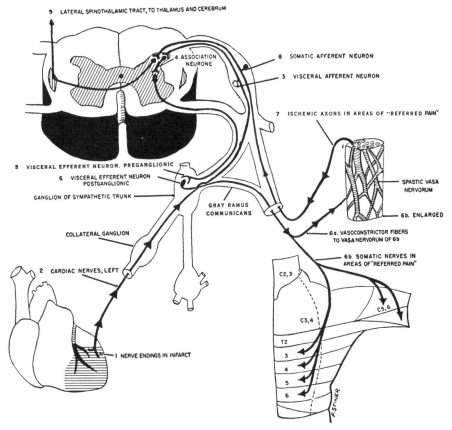

Figure 17–13. Scheme showing circuit for referred cardiac pain on basis of spastic vaso-neuropathy. Spasm of the vasa nervorum causes ischemia of somatic nerves. The impulse follows the sequence of the numerals 1 to 9. (From Roberts: Am. Heart J., 1948.)

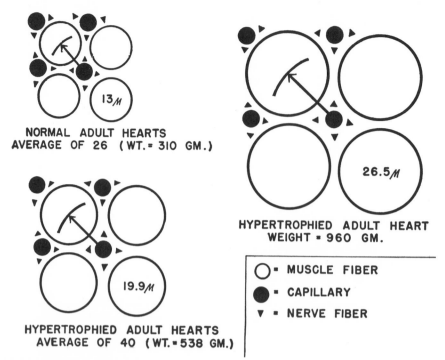

Figure 17–14. Diagrams of the relationship of myocardial fibers, capillaries and nerves in normal and hypertrophied human hearts. With hypertrophy the muscle fibers become ischemic with increase in the distance for diffusion between the capillary wall and the center of the muscle fibers, but the terminal nerve fibers remain close to the capillaries. (From Roberts: M. Ann., District of Columbia, 1945.)

them. However, if the blood supply to such nerves is completely lost, they soon lose the power of transmitting any stimuli. Such mechanisms help explain such clinical observations as the frequent disappearance of angina pectoris after myocardial infarction or the occasional occurrence of painless infarction; these may have caused infarction of the myocardial nerves with loss of receptivity of sensations. (See also Chap. 20.)

This mechanism is also involved in explanation of the rarity with which cardiac pain is felt by patients with great cardiac hypertrophy who have no other cause for chest pain. In the hearts of such patients the minute cardiac nerves remain close to their blood supply (the myocardial capillaries) and so are not ischemic, even when the capillaries have been pushed so far apart that the hypertrophied muscle fibers are seriously ischemic (Fig. 17–14). It is believed that uncomplicated cardiac hypertrophy is seldom the cause of cardiac pain. As cardiac hypertrophy and failure progress, however, other mechanisms will commonly produce the pain of myocardial infarction, pericarditis, fear or pulmonary infarction.

The common site of most severe heart pain

—near the sternum—is well known but seldom explained. The intercostal nerves from the two sides overlap across the midline in this area so that there are more nerve endings here than elsewhere. When these nerves are ischemic, as a result of the reflex neural vasospasm described above, such an excess innervation creates an area of greater acuity for pain and other sensory disturbance near the sternum. The referral of angina pectoris, coronary insufficiency or myocardial infarction is more often to the left arm, chest, or jaw than to the right. This can be explained as due to (1) the embryological formation of the left ventricle and septum from the left part of the cardiac tube, (2) the distribution of the left cardiac nerves to the derivations of the left cardiac tube as it was left behind with the cephalad growth of the embryo, (3) the fact that the usual infarction of the heart is in the left ventricle and septum, which is related to the left arm, chest, and jaw. Referral of heart pain or other sensations to unusual or even distant areas is explained by referral over variable association pathways in the cord to the abdomen or feet. There are many variants in the clinical forms of coronary deficiency. For example, reflex vasospastic ischemia of motor, autonomic, or proprioceptive axons causes muscular spasm or cramps, shoulder-hand syndromes, swelling, sweating, color and temperature changes, and even sclerodermal or Raynaud's phenomena. The common sensations of squeezing, vise- or ropelike compression or of tearing apart in the chest (complaints often met) are explained as due to reflex vasoneuropathy involving the axons of proprioception, which, when stimulated, give sensations of a change of position in space.

After infarction it is not unusual for patients to regain a large share of their cardiac reserve and tolerance for activity without pain. This is due to good flow in the coronary vessels of the remaining cardiac muscle, hinted at by the frequent observation of post-infarction patients with no signs of "coronary insufficiency" after an exercise tolerance test.

The Cardiac Cycle

The numerous cyclic events, except for biochemical events, occurring with each normal heart beat can be correlated, as in Figure 17–15. The chemicals undergo cyclic changes of the greatest importance, but the proportions of such vital substances as phosphocreatine, myosin, salts, and so on, have not been adequately determined during each phase of the heart beat except as discussed above. There is serious doubt of the acceptability of even these previously believed chemical cycles.

All the cyclic events should be correlated with each other, by projecting vertical lines on Figure 17–15. Since the primary function of the heart is to pump, with blood flowing into its left ventricle and being pushed out into the aorta, the cyclic events of the cardiac volume may be taken as the basis for correlation of the other cycles. The consecutive phases (and their basal durations) of the cardiac cycle are listed below, and the known events occurring during each phase are discussed.

I. Dynamic Interval of Atrial Systole (0.05 second)

At the end of the period of diastasis of the preceding cardiac cycle, the atria are filled to their greatest capacity with blood which has returned via the superior and inferior venae cavae and the pulmonary veins. The atrial muscle fibers are stretched to their greatest length during this momentary pause in the heart's activity. At this time phosphocreatine has been resynthesized in the atrial muscle, and in the ventricular muscle this process is nearing completion. Electrical energy is liberated from the sino-atrial node and passes over the atrial muscle to stimulate the reorientation of molecules, e.g., of actomyosin, from their long phase to the short phase and thus produces, first, increased tension and then beginning shortening of the atrial muscle fibers or atrial systole. During this time the P wave can be recorded electrocardiographically, and frequently small vibrations called the "atrial sound" can be recorded phonocardiographically, although seldom heard. The recorded curves of atrial pressure, as well as ventricular, aortic and coronary artery pressures, are at their base lines.

II. Inflow Phase of Atrial Systole (0.06 second)

The isometric phase of atrial systole ends, and its isotonic phase occurs, with peristaltic contraction of the atria. The end of atrial ejection of blood into the ventricles occurs, most of the atrial blood having flowed into the ventricles previously during the isotonic phase of ventricular diastole. The isoelectric P-R interval is recorded. (Occasionally an "atrial" T wave is recorded as a result of atrial repolarization, but usually this is buried in the QRS complex.) The atrial pressure curve rises to its peak and falls. Small rises in ventricular pressure, aortic pressure and cardiac volume and also the "a" wave of the jugular pulse occur. At the end of this phase ventricular diastole ends and ventricular systole begins.

III. Isometric Ventricular Contraction (0.05 second)

During this brief phase the atrioventricular valves, previously open, begin to float shut because of the eddies of ventricular blood beneath the valve cusps and because of the cessation of excessive pressure on their atrial sides. These eddies probably account for the small initial vibrations of the first heart sound, which rises in intensity through this phase. The semilunar valves are shut. Pressures in the atria and ventricles are about the same at the beginning of this phase, but near its end the ventricular pressures rise rapidly until they exceed the aortic and pulmonic pressures and force the semilunar valves to open. During this phase the muscle fibers are not shortening because they are contracting

DIAGRAM OF TWO CYCLES OF THE HEART BEAT, SHOWING IMPORTANT CORRELATIONS.

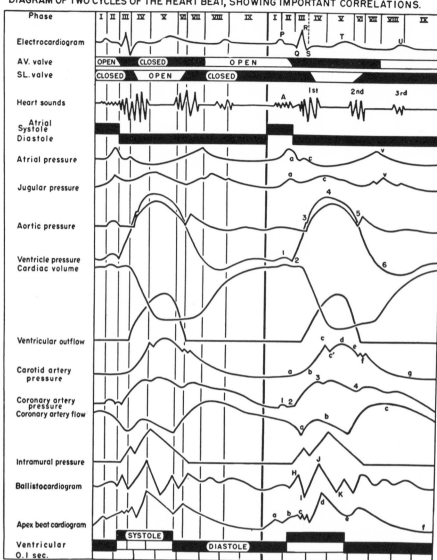

Figure 17–15. Correlations of cyclic events during the heart beat. On the left, in the first cycle, vertical lines show projection on each phenomenon of the nine phases of the heart beat. On the right, in the second cycle, the waves or events on each record are labeled. (Modified from Lewis, Wiggers, Orías and Braun-Menéndez and others.)

on incompressible liquid which has no outlet. A small short rise in coronary artery pressure occurs, due to compression of these vessels by rising intramural tension at a time when the peak of ventricular inflow coincides with the rising tension of the ventricular muscle fibers just before they begin to shorten. Cardiac output has not yet begun to occur. Ventricular myosin molecules are starting to rotate from the long to the short axis, and in the atrial muscle the reverse is beginning. The atrial pressure rises sharply to a short low

peak as a result of the slight herniation of the atrioventricular valves into the atria which accompanies the rapid rise in ventricular pressure.

IV. Isotonic Ventricular Contraction with Maximum Ejection Phase (0.09 second)

The contractile molecules of the ventricular muscle fibers have been rotated, producing their abrupt and forceful shortening which marks this phase of cardiac systole. Because of the spiralled arrangement of these fibers, the lumen of the heart shrinks and the cardiac volume plunges abruptly to its lowest point. The pressures in the two ventricles continue to rise precipitously, reaching a much higher level in the left side, because of (1) the greater mass of contracting muscle and (2) the greater peripheral resistance to be overcome in the aortic branches as compared with the resistance in the pulmonary branches. The first heart sound, reaching its maximum intensity and duration, is produced by the friction of the contracting muscle fibers against each other and against the blood in the ventricle, and by the abrupt closure of the atrioventricular valve cusps. The chordae tendineae also are abruptly and forcibly tensed to keep the valve cusps from stretching out into the atria, adding to the vibrations of this sound. These cusps are triangular shelves (composed of reflections of endocardium with some dense connective tissue and a few muscle fibers and blood vessels) with notched edges. At the points of these edges the fibrous chordae tendineae are attached so as to anchor these valves to the papillary muscles, like guy lines on a sail. As the ventricular pressures near their peaks, the semilunar aortic and pulmonic valves abruptly open and the maximum ejection of blood occurs into the aorta and pulmonary artery from the respective ventricles.

After the opening of these outlet valves, the ventricular pressure continues its rapid rise for a short time, but then gradually the rapidity of this rise diminishes as the peak is reached. Thus the summit of the curve is rounded. The aortic pressure curve during this and the next phase follows the left ventricular pressure curve closely (at a slightly lower level and slightly later time), and the pulmonic arterial and right ventricular curves bear similar relations. The atrial pressure, which had risen at the end of the preceding phase, falls abruptly when the semilunar valves open, but then begins a slow, low rise along with the ventricular pressure. After the fall in cardiac volume (with maximum ejection) has begun to be less abrupt, the intensity of the first heart sound wanes. The isoelectric S-T segment is recorded during this time. A low short rise in coronary artery pressure occurs and accompanies a sharp fall in the volume of coronary artery blood flow to its lowest level during this time. These last changes may be related to the rise of intramural pressure to its highest level before aortic pressure begins to rise.

V. Ventricular Contraction with Reduced Ejection Phase
(0.13 second)

As the contraction of the ventricles continues it becomes less forceful when the fibers have shortened greatly and most of the blood has been ejected. The curve of cardiac volume falls more gradually instead of precipitously as during the preceding phase and reaches its lowest point at the end of this phase. The curves of the ventricular and aortic pressures decline gradually with a pattern which is the reverse of the latter part of that in the preceding phase. The atrial pressure rises gradually as venous blood flows into the heart. The heart is silent during this phase, and the T wave is found on the electrocardiogram. The coronary artery pressure parallels the aortic pressure, while volume of flow through the coronary arteries rises to the lower of its two peaks as the aortic pressure forces blood on through the coronary arteries against the declining intramural resistance.

VI. Protodiastolic Phase of Diastole (0.04 second)

During this brief phase the contraction of the ventricles has ceased, but relaxation has not yet started. Cardiac volume remains practically unchanged. Ventricular, aortic, pulmonary artery and coronary artery pressures, which had started a slow fall, now begin to fall rapidly. When the ventricular pressures fall below those in their outflow tracts, the semilunar valves begin to float away from the aortic or pulmonary walls. This creates eddies in the current of blood as well as vibrations of the valves and vessel walls, which account for the second heart sound. This sound is heard throughout this short phase, which ends when the semilunar valves are completely closed. During this time, also, the incisura of the central arterial pulse (e.g., the subclavian) is recorded. Atrial blood pressure continues its slow rise as before, for venous blood enters the atria at all times except during its systole. This short phase is considered a part of diastole by Wiggers, as seems most logical because contraction has stopped, but some other authors include it as part of systole.

VII. Isometric Relaxation Phase of Diastole (0.08 second)

This phase begins with the closing of the semilunar valves and ends when the atrioventricular valves open. Each of these events is caused by the sharply falling ventricular pressure being exceeded by the more slowly falling aortic pressure and by the rising atrial pressure. After the aortic semilunar valves have closed, the sharp postincisural rise occurs on the aortic, coronary and other arterial pressure curves. Accompanying this are the last few vibrations of the second sound and the end of the T wave. The cardiac volume curve shows a small, steplike rise.

VIII. Rapid Inflow or Rapid Filling Phase of Ventricular Diastole (0.11 second)

After the atrioventricular valves have opened and floated back against the walls of the ventricles, the blood accumulated in the atria rushes into the ventricles. The ventricular myosin molecules are changing from the short to the long state so that the muscle fibers can elongate as this blood pours into the cavity. During this isotonic phase, i.e., with unchanging fiber tension, the cardiac volume rises rapidly, nearly to reach its highest point. Ventricular and atrial pressures fall in a parallel manner to attain a plateau maintained throughout the next phase. Near the end of this phase, or about 0.08 second after the second sound, the third heart sound is occasionally heard. The mechanism of its production is obscure, although it may be attributed to (1) vibrations of the ventricular muscle from the impact of the inrushing blood, (2) prolonged after-vibrations of the aortic valves, (3) an opening snap of the atrioventricular valves, (4) asynchronous closure of the aortic and pulmonary valves (improbable) or (5) stretching of the pericardium by the expanding heart. The coronary artery pressure curve resembles the aortic curve with a slight delay. The rate and volume of blood flow through the coronary arteries rise to the highest point during this phase, because of the steadily falling intramural resistance coinciding with the maintenance of aortic pressure at the diastolic level by the closed aortic valves. The electrocardiogram usually remains at an isoelectric level during this and the following phases, although occasionally a U wave, of unknown significance and cause, may be found. In the chemical cycle the ventricular phosphocreatine is probably being resynthesized as more oxygen is attracted into the muscle cells from the large volume of coronary arterial blood flowing through the capillaries.

IX. Diastasis Phase (0.19 second)

During this phase the heart is at its most complete rest. Little or no change occurs in any of the plateaus reached by the several curves at the end of the preceding phase, except that the ventricular pressure curve may continue a much slower rise as the venous blood goes through the resting atria into the ventricles. The chemical events preparing for the next cycle are being brought into readiness. Diffusion of oxygen and metabolites probably occurs at the greatest rate during this time. This phase is the first part of the cycle to be shortened or lost when the heart rate increases; with bradycardia it is prolonged. Near the end of this phase, electrocardiographic, chemical and atrial pressure changes are prepared for the initiation of the first phase of the next cycle in the heart beat.

ABNORMALITIES OF CARDIAC RATE AND RHYTHM

Because of physiologic or pathologic changes in the regulators of the heart beat, in the conduction apparatus or in the ability of some part of the heart to respond to stimulation, variations in cardiac rate and rhythm are frequently encountered clinically. At times useful information may be obtained from records of the venous or central arterial pulses, from phonocardiograms, ballistocardiograms, apex cardiograms (tracings of the precordial motions), fluoroscopy, cinefluoroscopy or from roentgen kymocardiograms (records of the moving cardiac borders over a slit placed on a fluoroscopic screen), but the electrocardiogram is much more commonly relied upon for the definition of abnormal rates and rhythms. By its use combined with skillful physical examination, a physician can create useful concepts of the changes which an abnormal rate or rhythm may cause in any of the cyclic events shown in Figure 17-15, many of which cannot be determined by physical examination. These abnormalities will be considered briefly at this point.

Cardiac rate may be normal, rapid (tachycardia) or slow (bradycardia). The normal range varies somewhat with age, physical state, training for exertion, and with different normal persons according to their vagal tone. However, a rate above 100 or below 60 per minute is significantly rapid or slow. The pacemaker for either of these kinds of rates may be in the sino-atrial node (sinus rhythm), in the atrial muscle (atrial rhythm), in the atrioventricular node or bundle (A-V nodal rhythm) or at any point in the ventricles (ventricular rhythm). The cardiac rate is usually given according to the ventricular rate, which normally is equal to the atrial rate. In abnormal mechanisms, however, either the atrial or ventricular rate may exceed the other.

Disturbances of rhythm and rate, of any type, may be paroxysmal (i.e., beginning and/or stopping under observation or according to symptoms) or persistent. The paroxysms may be occasional or frequent, severe or mild, symptomatic or asymptomatic, and may have a duration of only several beats or as long as many days. Tachycardia should be treated in accordance with its probable etiology, cardiac or noncardiac. If noncardiac, e.g., due to infection, hemorrhage, shock or emotion, correction must be made by relief of these states. If tachycardia is of cardiac origin, its precise type must always be determined, electrocardiographically if possible. Treatment of ventricular tachycardia with digitalis may be fatal because of conversion to ventricular fibrillation, but the disorder may be relieved by quinidine; other tachycardias of cardiac origin may be benefited by digitalis, vagus stimulation (by pressure on the carotid sinus, eyeballs or epiglottis), by sedation, Pronestyl or Mecholyl. For these arrhythmias with rapid rates conversion by electric shock (either alternating or now preferably direct current) has become very useful as developed by Wiggers, Beck, Zoll, Lown and others.

Any type of *tachycardia* may be thought of as an attempt at compensation for inadequate cardiac output, brought about by such mechanisms as (1) the Marey reflex (wherein a rise in aortic or carotid sinus pressure causes a fall in heart rate, and vice versa), (2) the Bainbridge reflex (wherein a rise in venous or right atrial blood pressure initiates a rise in heart rate, and vice versa) or (3) the Alam-Smirk reflex (whereby impulses from contracting ischemic muscle raise the rate). However, like dilatation and hypertrophy, this so-called attempt at compensation has deleterious effects upon a damaged heart and in time causes more serious injury than it attempts to relieve (see p. 336). Therefore tachycardia should be brought under control

as soon as possible. With tachycardia of any type, the diastolic phases of the cycle are shortened more than the systolic periods, with the result that work is being performed without sufficient time for relaxation, cardiac filling or restoration of the biochemical state to that needed for most efficient contraction. For example, there is less time for the coronary blood flow, which occurs to its greatest extent and with most efficiency during diastole. Therefore the myocardial fibers are less well nourished, with poorer supply of oxygen to the fibers for resynthesis of phosphocreatine. Energy is produced by relatively anoxic fibers; lowered mechanical efficiency and loss of cardiac reserve follows to such a degree that cardiac ischemic pain or heart failure and death may ensue. This is especially prone to occur if other abnormalities are present, as is often the case. After a paroxysm of tachycardia, inverted T waves or deviated S-T segments may indicate damage to the myocardium by the ischemia, angina pectoris may be initiated, or even myocardial infarction may become evident. Ventricular contraction may occur on a partially filled chamber while the atria are still distended with inflowing venous blood, resulting in inefficient cardiac output. Often a "gallop rhythm" may be heard, caused by (1) intensification of the atrial sound (presystolic gallop), (2) intensification of the third heart sound (protodiastolic gallop) or (3) merging of the atrial and third heart sounds (summation gallops). Systole of the ventricles may be inefficient or wasteful of energy also when it occurs before the semilunar valves can open, and this event cannot take place until the run-off of blood ejected previously has occurred. Tachycardia is more inefficient if it is ventricular or A-V nodal in origin because the contracting ventricles may oppose the inflow of atrial blood. Strangely, A-V nodal rhythm of normal rate does not produce clinical signs of such inefficiency as might be expected. The Valsalva maneuver may sharply reduce the rate and blood pressure briefly.

Bradycardia is usually of sinus origin and is due to preponderance of vagal effect over the sympathetic innervation of the heart. It is found in many otherwise normal people, in well-trained athletes or after exercise. This mechanism may be responsible for a person's great endurance. In certain diseases—for example, typhoid fever—relative bradycardia may be found due probably to excessive vagotonia in proportion to the degree of fever or other abnormalities ordinarily increasing the heart rate. Digitalis or other drugs in toxic doses often cause bradycardia, usually moderate, by excessive vagal inhibition of the sinus node's pacemaking function or by raising the refractoriness of the atrioventricular bundle. *Sinus bradycardia* must be distinguished by the electrocardiogram from slow idioventricular rhythms. These conditions frequently indicate the presence of serious organic heart disease with structural damage to the nodes or bundle. Infectious or chemical toxicity, ischemia or fatigue may reduce the ability of the normal pacemaker to form and discharge rhythmically the energy needed for the heart beat, and other parts of the heart may likewise have this property depressed to such a degree that extra-sinus rhythms do not occur. In the dying heart sinus bradycardia is often seen, sometimes without transmission of impulses beyond the atrial muscle. Bradycardia which develops during cardiac or other surgery, or with myocardial infarction, pneumonia, or other serious disease is a critical sign of impending disaster, and emergency measures should be taken to correct the trend.

Sinus arrest is due probably to the same mechanisms as sinus bradycardia. The cessation of sinus impulses may be only momentary with omission of one cycle (followed by a return to sinus, or some other, rhythm) or prolonged for several seconds. When the latter occurs, cerebral ischemia produces syncope, convulsion or death unless the heart beat is restored promptly. Frequently this is produced by an idioventricular rhythm, but it may be corrected occasionally by a blow over the heart, by pricking the myocardium with a needle or by injecting a sympatheticomimetic drug (e.g., epinephrine) into the left ventricle. Cardiac massage through the opened chest or diaphragm, combined with artificial respiration, may be lifesaving occasionally by maintaining the coronary and cerebral circulation until spontaneous cardiac rhythm is restored. This opportunity usually exists only in the operating room, where, however, patients are particularly prone to sinus arrest because of hypoxic anesthesia. Useful cerebral function seldom returns after cerebral ischemia lasting as long as three minutes. The degree of mental recovery varies with (1) the interval between cardiac arrest and effective cardiac output being started by either massage or intrinsic rhythms, (2) the level of cerebral reserve before the moment of cardiac arrest, (3) the efficiency with which oxygenation and cardiac output are maintained by the

new rhythm, and (4) removal of the agent causing the cardiac arrest. Isolated cerebral functions may strangely come and go for a long time after such a catastrophe. This makes special care worth while in even badly deteriorated patients. Recently external cardiac massage has become generally used. Combined promptly and skillfully with aided respiration, electrical control of the heart beat, improvement in levels of electrolytes, acid-base imbalance, vasopressors and other factors, cardiac massage has saved many lives. In the great majority of cardiac arrests revival fails because of underlying disease or delay in use of all needed efforts.

Sinus arrhythmia is an irregular rhythm of sinus (i.e., SA nodal) origin caused by fluctuating ratios between vagal and sympathetic tone. Usually this is related to respiration with transitory slowing of the heart rate during expiration and a quickening with inspiration. Within moderate ranges this arrhythmia may be considered normal and, in fact, is sometimes used as a rough test of cardiac reserve, for normally it is exaggerated by forced held inspiration and expiration. A heart with poor cardiac reserve usually is unable to respond with sinus arrhythmia during such a test. On superficial physical examination sinus arrhythmia may be confused with other irregularities. Sometimes this rhythm must be distinguished from *wandering pacemaker* with serially changing P-wave contours or P-R intervals indicating a shift in location of the pacemaker.

Sinus premature systole results when the sinus node prematurely discharges an impulse which is followed by systole. It indicates a state of increased irritability and probably diminished refractoriness in the node and other parts of the heart. This may be only a transitory state of no significance or an indication of more serious underlying disease. The interval between the premature impulse and the subsequent one is usually normal rather than prolonged. *Atrial premature systole* is quite similar except that altered contour of the P waves indicates its origin in the atrial muscle outside the sinus node, and the pause following it is prolonged. When they recur frequently, these two disorders may cause erroneous suspicion of more serious irregularities, such as atrial fibrillation, and so may lead to unnecessary or even harmful treatment unless checked by the electrocardiogram. When a short P-R interval accompanies a leftward P-wave axis, the pacemaker is believed to be near the lower posterior wall of the right atrium, causing *coronary sinus* rhythm; this seems more often associated with pulmonary disease than not.

Atrial tachycardia resembles sinus tachycardia except that the P wave may be abnormal in contour. If the tachycardia is very rapid, however, the P waves may be merged in the preceding T waves so that it is impossible to locate the pacemaker precisely. It indicates increased irritability in the atrial muscle or lowered irritability in the sinoatrial node.

Atrial flutter and fibrillation are serious disorders of mechanism and nearly always indicate serious myocardial disease, such as caused by rheumatic fever, coronary artery disease, thyrotoxicosis or poisoning. These irregularities are attributed to the so-called circus mechanism, wherein an atrial impulse follows a ringlike pathway throughout the atria at a rapid rate. This circus pathway in the case of flutter usually follows a fixed course around the ends of the venae cavae at a rate of 200 to 400 times a minute, producing rapid "f" or abnormal P waves. There is some recent evidence to indicate that a single regularly discharging ectopic focus rather than circus movement may be responsible for flutter. These "f" waves in flutter are usually regular and of similar contour. The ventricles usually respond to only a fraction of the circuits of atrial depolarization because the relatively long refractory period of the atrioventricular node produces an incomplete atrioventricular block. The ventricular rate therefore usually varies between 75 and 150 per minute. The ratio between the atrial and ventricular complexes defines such a rhythm as a flutter with 2:1, 3:1, 4:1, or other, rhythm which may vary from moment to moment. Occasionally, when the atrial rate is not too fast, and possibly as a result of treatment with quinidine, a 1:1 rhythm may exist. The object of treatment is to increase the refractory period of the atrioventricular node to such a degree that ventricular response will be at a normal rate or to convert the mechanism to a normal sinus rhythm. In occasional cases surgical interruption (by cutting or ligature) of the AV bundle might be useful with control of the ventricular rhythm by an artificial pacemaker of the Chardack or other type.

Atrial fibrillation resembles flutter except that the circuits of depolarization are small, numerous, variable in size and constantly changing in pattern. This is attributed to the greatly increased irritability and lowered refractoriness of the atrial muscle. On the electrocardiogram the atrial complexes ("f" waves) are usually small, of short duration and so variable that no fixed pattern can be detected, and the rate varies between 400 and 550 per minute. At times the small, rapid circuits counterbalance each other so that practically no deflections of the isoelectric line are evident. The ventricular response is much slower than the atrial rate and usually irregular, but still so rapid that ventricular efficiency is so seriously impaired that loss of cardiac reserve and heart failure will follow unless the ventricular rate is slowed. Obviously, the peristaltic contraction of the atria is lost in either flutter or fibrillation, but this may not prevent moderately good ventricular filling if ventricular diastasis is long enough. With either of these disturbances of rhythm, small rapid abnormal waves may replace the atrial ("a") waves on tracings of the jugular or atrial pressure. (These can be made by polygraphs, optical or mechanical recorders or direct catheterization.) The phonocardiograph may also detect the loss of atrial systole. Records of ventricular pressure, cardiac volume, coronary flow or of the QRS-T complex on the electrocardiogram vary from one cycle to the next because of variations in ventricular filling and in the force of ventricular systole.

The atrial complexes may vary slightly in contour and rhythm. If this variation is only slightly different from flutter, the rhythm is referred to as *impure flutter,* or as *flutter-fibrillation* if the rhythm resembles flutter for a moment and then approaches fibrillation at another moment.

Prinzmetal, Scherf and their associates have thrown doubt on the validity of the circus movement theory for explaining the atrial arrhythmias. Their experiments indicate that atrial extrasystole, paroxysmal atrial tachycardia, atrial flutter and atrial fibrillation are of a unitary nature and are due to impulses emitting from a single ectopic focus. The particular arrhythmia observed depends on the rate and regularity of discharge of impulses from this focus.

Atrioventricular (AV) nodal mechanisms occur when the pacemaker is in this node. They include AV *nodal premature systole, regular rhythm, tachycardia and escape* (also theoretically, *bradycardia*). The impulse arises in the atrioventricular node and may stimulate both the ventricles and atria if these two regions are not refractory at the time. The P wave is usually inverted, diphasic or bizarre in contour. It may follow or be super-imposed upon the QRS complex; if the P wave precedes the QRS, the P-R interval is less than 0.12 second. Similar changes in the relation of atrial and ventricular complexes may be expected in tracings of the jugular or atrial pressure or of the heart sounds. Atrioventricular nodal mechanisms indicate a relative decrease in the irritability and rhythmicity of the sino-atrial node or atria. There is little or no pathogenic significance in these disorders, however. Cardiac efficiency may not be impaired by such dislocation of the pacemaker unless the tachycardia or frequency of premature systole is excessive.

Supraventricular tachycardia must be diagnosed when the P waves cannot be detected or defined as either atrioventricular nodal, atrial or sinus nodal in origin. At the same time ventricular complexes indicate that the pacemaker lies above the branching of the bundle of His. The significance and other characteristics of this disturbance are the same as for atrial tachycardia. Supraventricular tachycardia can often be proved to be a more specific arrhythmia by use of esophageal or chest leads or by using vagal stimulation.

Ventricular rhythms usually indicate serious myocardial disease with excessive ventricular irritability, except when there are only occasional premature ventricular systoles. *Idioventricular rhythm* is characterized by heart beats for which the pacemaker lies in the ventricle. The rate is usually slow (20 to 50 per minute) or occasionally may be more rapid. This disorder is usually found in cases of complete atrioventricular block in which none of the supraventricular impulses can get through to the ventricles, or in sinus arrest. Then, because of the irritability of the ventricular myocardium, the patient is kept alive by idioventricular contraction. The rate of ventricular contraction is usually about half as rapid as the rate of atrial depolarization. Atrial waves may be of normal configuration, but the QRS-T complexes are abnormal in shape because of the aberrant pathway followed by the electrical impulse. The contour of the QRS complex depends upon the site of the ventricular pacemaker and probably also to some degree upon variation in the pathway from the focus of impulse formation during different cardiac cycles. Ventricular impulses may arise in any point of the ventricles—for example, in the septum or in either ventricle, in either the apical or basal part, and on the anterior or posterior surface. The contour of the individual QRS-T complexes

resembles that of ventricular premature systoles arising at the same focus. Frequently, idioventricular rhythm may arise from a single focus, but at times there is a *shifting ventricular pacemaker* with ventricular complexes of variable contour due to impulses from more than one place. At times the pacemaker may shift regularly so that there is a regular pattern of variation in contour of these complexes. For example, every second or third complex may be similar. The latter situation is usually more precarious, since it indicates that many parts of the ventricular myocardium are unusually irritable and ventricular tachycardia or fibrillation is more likely to ensue. When the idioventricular rhythm is slow and regular, cardiac function may be moderately efficient at rest or with minimal exertion, because adequate time is allowed for ventricular filling and outlet and for coronary blood flow. Cardiac reserve, however, is never so efficient as with a normal mechanism, possibly because the coronary flow is lowered, the ventricles are overfilled and the normal cycle of chemical changes is altered. However, even more important is the probability that serious myocardial damage has been caused by the underlying disease. These patients are prone to Stokes-Adams attacks from ventricular arrest, with cerebral ischemia, syncope and often sudden death. This is most likely to occur at a time when idioventricular rhythm changes to supraventricular rhythm, or vice versa, or when the ventricular rhythm abruptly changes to a fraction of its former rate—for example, from 60 to 20 beats per minute. On tracings of other types, such as the venous or atrial pressure, or of heart sounds, the normal relation of atrial and ventricular waves is altered as on the electrocardiogram, where it may be shown that the atria and ventricles are beating independently of each other. With fatal cardiac arrest life may be restored occasionally by use of (1) Zoll's or other "pacemaker" (a rhythmic stimulator) or (2) cardiac massage. At times a "defibrillator" may be needed because ventricular fibrillation must be stopped before normal rhythm can be restored.

Interference dissociation is a disturbance in mechanism involving a moderately rapid ventricular rate arising in the ventricle or atrioventricular node, but with the atria contracting at a slower rate. This is usually produced by toxic doses of digitalis. Occasionally an apparently premature ventricular complex of normal contour may be superimposed upon the basic ventricular rhythm when an atrial impulse reaches the atrioventricular node and ventricles when they are not in a refractory condition. With complete atrioventricular heart block, normal atrioventricular conduction is not likely to occur. When the excessive digitalis is eliminated from the body, interference dissociation may disappear.

When the atrioventricular node or bundle is only partially blocked by increased refractoriness, a state of *partial or incomplete atrioventricular block* exists. The atrioventricular conduction time is prolonged, resulting in prolongation of the P-R interval above the accepted limits of normal for the patient's age and heart rate. This is most frequent in active rheumatic fever or coronary artery disease or after excessive use of digitalis. In some patients, especially those with digitalis intoxication, there may be *dropped ventricular beats* due to periodic or occasional increase in the atrioventricular block from partial to complete block. This complete block may occur at regular intervals. If a ventricular beat is dropped every second, third or fourth atrial complex, for example, there may be 2:1 block or various other degrees, such as 3:2, 4:3 and so on. When the P-R interval (or atrioventricular conduction time) varies in a cyclic manner, progressively lengthening during each succeeding beat until the atrial impulse is completely blocked at the atrioventricular node, the abnormal mechanism is referred to as the *Wenckebach phenomenon*. Venous or atrial pulse tracings will reflect these abnormal mechanisms by similarly changed ratios between the atrial and ventricular waves.

Ventricular paroxysmal tachycardia has the characteristics of the tachycardias already described except that the QRS complexes are wide and slurred and resemble those of ventricular premature contractions or idioventricular rhythm. As in these disorders, the ventricular pacemaker may be located in any part of the ventricles and may shift from time to time with resultant variation in the contour of the ventricular waves. The atrial rhythm is not disturbed except when there is retrograde conduction from the ventricles to the atria. Occasionally the location of P waves can be identified at regular intervals on the bizarre ventricular complexes. This disorder is always paroxysmal, for it so seriously interferes with cardiac reserve that heart failure and death occur if it is prolonged. It always indicates a high degree of irritability in the ventricles and practically always provides reliable indication of serious heart disease. The disorder may be produced by digitalis, quinidine, anesthesia, epinephrine and other drugs, by cardiac trauma, coronary occlusion or any other form of heart disease. It is not affected by carotid sinus pressure or vagal stimulation. It may be improved by oxygen, sedation, local anesthesia of the heart, intravenous procaine (experimentally) or quinidine. Its recognition electrocardiographically is urgent because of the frequency with which it is converted quickly to ventricular fibrillation, especially by digitalis. Cardiac reserve is always lower after an attack of ventricular tachycardia than it was before the paroxysm began.

Ventricular fibrillation is the most serious of all disturbances of cardiac mechanism and almost without exception leads to cardiac standstill and death. It is seldom seen electrocardiographically except when records are being made on a dying patient. Rarely, however, it may be detected in patients undergoing anesthesia or after coronary thrombosis. Presumably, circus mechanisms begin simultaneously at a great many spots in the ventricular myocardium. At the onset of the disorder these circuits are rather large in diameter and the QRS complexes are of large size and long duration, although absolutely irregular and markedly deformed. Within a minute or so, however, experimentally and in the human being, the circuits become smaller and smaller, reflected in smaller QRS complexes. Soon the entire ventricle is a shivering mass of contractions arising at innumerable points and extending for small distances before being blocked by refractory areas or by circuits arising from adjacent foci. By this time the QRS complexes have become very small and of short duration, although still irregular in contour and timing. Within a few minutes ventricular standstill occurs and is followed before long by atrial standstill and death. No effective ventricular contractions occur in this disorder, so that syncope or a Stokes-Adams attack results. Cardiac sounds have no characteristic pattern, but are irregular, weak and variable. Coronary flow is decreased and then stopped, because there is no effective cardiac output or ventricular systole. As a result, the myocardium becomes anoxic and resynthesis of phosphocreatine ceases. The disorder may be initiated by weak electrical stimulation at the point in the cycle when the ventricle is least refractory. Experimentally, and occasionally in patients, the disorder may be interrupted by appropriate stimulation with electrodes placed upon the heart or chest wall before the chemical reserve is completely lost, so that after an interval of inactivity an idioventricular or even normal sinus mechanism may begin.

Ventricular premature systole occurs when some spot in the ventricle is so irritable that it initiates an impulse without reference to the basic cardiac rhythm. This focus may be at any point in the ventricle. Occasional heart beats of this type occur even in the most normal people, but they are more likely to be symptomatic or frequent in patients with ventricular damage. Following the ventricular premature systole there usually is a compensatory pause. This is an interval sufficient to counterbalance the shortening of the preceding intersystolic intervals so that the subsequent QRS complex occurs at the time expected. When premature ventricular systoles occur regularly with every alternate heart beat, the alternation of compensatory pauses and short intervals between heart beats produces an apparent coupling of the pulse or heart beat referred to as *bigeminy;* similarly, *trigeminy, quadrigeminy* or other rhythms may be found occasionally, most commonly due to digitalis intoxication. With premature ventricular systole the ventricular output is low, the pulse is low in volume, the heart sounds are weak, and the pulse may not reach the peripheral arteries. Conversely, with the succeeding heart beat, each of these characteristics may be augmented by the greater ventricular filling. Such "extrasystoles" may be multifocal. Within the cardiac cycle premature ventricular systoles are most prone to occur at the point where large "U waves" exist, and possibly are due to a deficiency of potassium in many cases. Such a potassium deficiency is often correlated with coronary artery insufficiency or sensitivity to digitalis or other drugs.

In *pulsus alternans* the pulse volume, cardiac output and blood pressure vary with alternate beats of the heart. Occasionally this is reflected in the electrocardiogram by alternation in the amplitude of the QRS complexes ("electrical alternans"). Its origin is uncertain, but it is probably due to incomplete restoration of phosphocreatine or other factors of partial contraction in some ventricular muscle fibers, so that with alternate beats only a fraction of the ventricular fibers are contracted. Almost always it is a serious prognostic sign of extensive myocardial fatigue or weakening. The heart sounds may alternate in intensity also in this disorder.

Disturbed *intraventricular conduction* occurs frequently in patients with heart disease and occasionally in normal people, owing to abnormal rates or routes in the spread of depolarization and repolarization throughout the two ventricles. These changes may be due to generalized alterations in the conductivity of these chambers or to sharply localized lesions in one of the branches of the bundle of His. In *partial intraventricular block* there is only slight prolongation in the spread of the impulse through the ventricles and the QRS interval is between 0.10 and 0.12 second in duration. There is some slurring and notching of the QRS complexes due to disturbances in the ventricular musculature. This partial block may affect either bundle branch to a greater degree than the other. If conduction is defective in the smaller branches of the Purkinje system, and QRS complexes are of low amplitude, *arborization block* exists. Partial right bundle branch block, especially as seen with a pattern of rSr′ in lead V1, is very common with emphysema or chronic pulmonary disease of any cause, or transiently with pulmonary embolism. Large or distorted P waves in leads 2, 3, and aVF and inverted P waves in lead aVL with rightward, vertical or clockwise cardiac rotation are often associated with this conduction defect.

Complete bundle branch block (right or left) may be caused by any condition (such as coronary artery disease, gumma, rheumatic fever, tumor, myocarditis) which blocks the transmission of the impulse coming normally from the atria and keeps it from going through one of the bundle branches. When the impulse is blocked in one branch, the myocardium supplied by it is stimulated by impulses coming by abnormal routes from the ventricle supplied by the opposite bundle. The QRS interval is always prolonged to at least 0.12 second by bundle branch block when the heart rate is normal, and varies slightly with more rapid heart rates. In *complete left bundle branch block* the main deflection (i.e., the one of greatest duration) is upward in lead I with no significant S wave. In *complete right bundle branch block* a significant S wave occurs in lead I. Usually these complexes are deformed by slurring or notching, but not always so. The T wave and frequently the RS-T segment are deviated to the direction opposite the main deflection. Bundle branch block may be paroxysmal or may occur at regular intervals in a sequence of normal complexes. The intrisicoid deflection is delayed in Lead V5 or V6, (i.e., R is prolonged) with left bundle branch block, in contrast to this conspicuous finding in Lead

V1 with right bundle branch block. With the latter (RBBB) the conduction delay may be transient as with stretching of the right ventricle by failure or by touching the exposed right bundle branch during right cardiac catheterization. The left branch in contrast is flat and branches soon after it goes through the septum. For this reason and because LBBB is more often a sequel of coronary artery disease, it is often considered to have a more ominous prognosis.

False bundle branch block (column of Kent, or Wolff-Parkinson-White syndrome) is an electrocardiographic picture showing P-R interval (usually less than 0.11 second), a wide QRS complex (usually 0.11 to 0.14 second) and a normal or short P-T interval. A "delta wave" or notch on the upstroke of R is often seen. It is believed to be due to rapid transmission of atrial impulses through the bundle of Kent (originally called the atrioventricular column of Kent) without the delay of passage through the atrioventricular node and bundle of His. Since the column of Kent is on the extreme right margin of the heart rather than in the septum, the right ventricle is depolarized first and the impulse then spreads over the rest of the ventricle in an abnormal way through the ventricular muscle or Purkinje system. Another possible explanation for the disorder may be the coincidence of atrioventricular nodal rhythm and a bundle branch block. The disorder usually occurs in those without demonstrable heart disease, but predisposes to attacks of paroxysmal tachycardia, usually of the supraventricular type. *Accelerated conduction* is another term for this so-called W-P-W syndrome. Although usually believed to be of little clinical significance, W-P-W syndrome may be followed by sudden unexpected death in some cases.

Combined disorders of rhythm and rate are frequently encountered, especially in patients who have serious forms of heart disease or who have had excessive doses of digitalis, quinidine, stimulants or depressants.

Cardiac Sounds, Murmurs and Thrills

Vibrations of the heart and chest wall produce audible and palpable phenomena, the normal and abnormal cardiac sounds or murmurs and thrills. No known device approaches the efficiency of the trained human ear and hand in interpretation of these cyclic phenomena of the heart beat. However, study of records made by either optical or electrical recording devices is of value in acquiring skill at auscultation, in correlating these vibrations with other cyclic events and for making permanent records for subsequent study. Occasionally, inspection of a phonocardiogram or its correlation with pulse records may establish a diagnosis when other measures fail.

Heart sounds have the following characteristics: (1) time of occurrence in the cardiac cycle, (2) duration, (3) quality, (4) intensity, (5) variability, (6) mode of formation, (7) pitch, (8) resemblance to common noncardiac sounds. Of these characteristics, *quality* is the most difficult to define or record. To accomplish this graphically in an interesting way, McKusick has added a third dimension to the usual recording in two planes. This is called spectrophonocardiography.

The first heart sound, a few small, coarse vibrations rapidly increasing to large, more rapid vibrations which then rapidly diminish to a silent period, marks the beginning of ventricular systole. Usually it is the loudest sound heard over the heart, is of moderate pitch and, when the heart is beating quietly, is uniform from beat to beat except as it is modified by respiration or position. With exercise, emotion, breathing, change in position, pulmonary or pericardial abnormality or poor cardiac reserve the character of the sound varies greatly from beat to beat. It is probably formed by several mechanisms rather than by one alone, as claimed by many writers. Friction of the contracting muscle fibers against themselves and against the blood in the cavities causes a large part of the sound, as indicated by the fact that the sound may be heard over the isolated perfused heart. Vibrations of the atrioventricular valves as they begin to float shut and after they have completely closed cause the so-called valvular or snapping quality of the sound. Vibrations of the chordae tendineae (as they are stretched by the contracting papillary muscles) and of the semilunar valves (as they are being opened) may contribute some vibrations to the sound. Atrial contraction adds a component also. Many of the variations in quality and intensity of this sound are due to unknown factors. The *ejection sound* is that loud short snap produced as the blood is abruptly discharged.

The second heart sound is usually short, occurs during the protodiastolic phase, and consists of rather uniform vibrations of higher pitch and intensity than the first heart sound. Its vibrations are caused by the semilunar valves floating away from the aortic and pulmonic artery walls during the brief period between the end of isotonic contraction and isometric relaxation of the ventricles. In other words, when the ventricles stop expelling blood, the elasticity of the great arteries causes a rebound of the blood column which snaps shut the semilunar valves. Normally this occurs simultaneously on the two sides of the heart, so that the sound is rather uniform throughout. However, the sound may be abnormal when for any reason the two ventricles do not contract at the same time and with equal force, when the two valves do not close with equal ease and effectiveness or when peripheral resistance in the aortic and pulmonary beds is altered. The first part of the second heart sound will be exaggerated when the right ventricle contracts earlier (as in left bundle branch block) or more forcibly, and when the peripheral resistance is increased in the pulmonary bed. If the aortic or pulmonary valve is ruptured or damaged by syphilitic, rheumatic or other infection, so that it is incompetent, the second heart sound is diminished or lost except for the part formed by closing of the undamaged valve. On the other hand, when the semilunar valves themselves are competent, but permit regurgitation of blood because of dilatation of the weakened fibrous supporting ring, the second sound is not altered or increased, although the murmur of aortic regurgitation is present. Lesions causing stenosis of the semilunar valves often interfere with their closure and decrease the sound.

The third heart sound occurs normally in two-thirds of all children and young adults who have good cardiac health. It is a short sound with few vibrations of low amplitude, and occurs near the end of isotonic relaxation of the ventricles. Its mechanism is not understood, but has been attributed to vibrations (1) of the semilunar valves, (2) of the atrioventricular valves when blood rushes from the atria into the ventricles and, with better evidence, to vibrations (3) of the muscular or tendinous ventricular walls. It may be due in part also to stretching of the pericardium or slapping of the apex against the chest wall during diastole. Frequently, when confused with abnormal heart sounds or murmurs, a normal third sound leads to an erroneous diagnosis of gallop rhythm or valvular disease.

The *atrial heart sound* is a *fourth* normal sound which occurs earlier in the cycle than the first heart sound. It is seldom heard, but is frequently recorded by sensitive phonocardiographs. It is of low pitch and intensity, rather uniform in quality and lasting during most of both phases of atrial systole. Often it is continuous with the early part of the first heart sound. The atrial sound is produced by contraction of the atrial muscle, by vibrations in the ventricular walls from the impact of blood forced into them by atrial contraction and probably by vibrations of other structures during atrial systole. This sound varies considerably in intensity during respiration, is greatest over the middle of the sternum and is exaggerated with atrial distention, hypertrophy or irritability. The atrial sound may be recorded most clearly when a "wandering atrial pacemaker" causes a shifting relation between the P and QRS waves.

At times the atrial sound may be confused with a *splitting* or *reduplication* of the first heart sound. The latter may be due to mechanisms similar to those causing duplication of the second heart sound by the unequal and asynchronous contraction of the two ventricles or closing of the two atrioventricular valves. The first heart sound may be really split with a silent phase between its two parts. In other cases either the early or late part of the sound, or both, may be exaggerated.

Gallop rhythm occurs when an extra heart sound is heard, usually in tachycardia, in such a way that a triple rhythm of the sounds is present. It has a cadence like the sound of a galloping horse. It is an important and usually ominous clinical sign indicating serious loss of cardiac reserve of either one or both ventricles. As mentioned before, gallop rhythm may be of the presystolic, protodiastolic or summation type. It may be of either ventricular or atrial origin; the former is malignant and the latter benign in prognosis. For diagnosis and prognosis it is important to distinguish a gallop rhythm from accentuation of normal heart sounds (especially the third and atrial sounds), from reduplicated sounds and from short murmurs. The mechanisms producing each of these are so different that their proper definition gives much information about the organic and functional changes in the heart.

A systolic *shock* and diastolic *impact* due to pounding of the heart against the thorax may be felt, especially when certain chambers are enlarged. These forces may be felt, seen or recorded by tambours during the first and second sounds. Rarely the other sounds may be marked by movements of the chest wall. These evidences of the cyclic writhing, contraction and relaxation of the heart are the best known manifestations of the heart beat, but they have not been adequately studied by mechanical means because of confusion due to many modifying factors, such as the chest wall, lungs and heart sounds. At present more frequent use of apex cardiograms helps evaluate mechanisms of muscular contraction and is used in coordination with PCG, ECG and pressure recordings.

Cardiac murmurs are abnormal sounds produced by vibrations of either normal or damaged parts of the heart. *Thrills* are the palpable phenomena due to the same vibrations. At times both can be detected when a murmur is present, but often carelessness or lack of skill in palpation prevents recognition of a thrill. Some physicians, especially those with impaired hearing, can develop their skill so highly as to recognize by palpation the existence of abnormalities overlooked by others in listening for murmurs or abnormal sounds.

Murmurs may be classified according to (1) time and duration in the cardiac cycle, (2) quality, (3) pitch, (4) intensity, (5) crescendo or decrescendo nature of the murmur, (6) alterability by position, respiration or other factors, (7) mechanism, and (8) etiology. In order to evaluate the significance of any murmur, the patient's history and all other information must be correlated.

The production of murmurs depends upon eddies or whirlpools in the current of blood going through the heart or other vessels. If one listens or feels over a rubber hose while it is compressed or has a diaphragm in its lumen, a murmur and thrill can be detected. As the stream of fluid goes through the tubing to an area of altered diameter, the velocity of the stream is changed. As the stream divides or goes around a bend, or through a constriction, the velocity of each particle must be increased. When the constriction is passed or the lumen abruptly becomes dilated, the velocity of the moving current is decreased. The eddies at the point where the lumen changes size set up vibrations in the wall of the tubing or in the diaphragm. The murmur is usually transmitted with greater intensity toward the direction in which the stream is moving. Other modifying factors in production of a murmur are (1) the viscosity of the fluid, (2) the rigidity or flexibility of the diaphragm and vessel walls, (3) the ease with which the vibrations of a specific character are transmitted through the surrounding structures, (4) absence of confusing or dampening factors, and (5) the duration and intensity of propelling forces.

Cardiac murmurs due to similar mechanisms occur most often when one or more of the cardiac valves are damaged by disease so as to produce (1) stenosis, (2) insufficiency or (3) dilatation of the supporting fibrous ring. Stenosis, usually due to rheumatic endocarditis, sclerosis or calcification, causes stiffening or fusion of the valve cusps so that the cusps cannot open properly. Thus, during the time when there should be unhindered flow through the valvular orifice, an abnormal diaphragm is present in the stream. If the stenosis affects the tricuspid or mitral valve, the murmur is produced during diastole, i.e., the phase when blood is running from the atrium into the ventricle. This murmur will vary in time and quality with each of the events of atrial systole and ventricular diastole. When stenosis affects the aortic or pulmonary valve, the murmur will occur during systole, i.e., the phases when blood is running from the ventricles into the great arteries.

Currently, murmurs are often called *"ejection"* or *"regurgitant"* types. *Ejection* murmurs are those due to "ejection" of the blood forward from the contracting ventricle, with alteration of the sound by stenosis of aortic or pulmonary valves. *Regurgitant* murmurs are due to blood running backward through incompetent mitral, tricuspid or other valves.

In addition to stenosis, which prevents the valves from opening properly, insufficiency of either valve may be caused by infection, trauma and aging, or by weakening of the myocardium and fibrous skeleton of the heart to such an extent that the supporting fibrous ring of a valve is dilated. When the valves are incapable of closing completely at the proper time, the blood will flow in the direction from which it has been expelled. Besides vibrations thus caused by blood running back through an unclosed valvular diaphragm, additional vibrations will result from eddies set up when the regurgitant column of blood meets the forward-moving blood behind the insufficient valve. For example, regurgitation through the aortic or pulmonary valve produces a murmur during diastole, a time when normal closure of these valves should prevent regurgitation of the cardiac output into the ventricles. When the mitral or tricuspid valve is incapable of closing completely, the blood runs from the ventricle into the atrium during ventricular contraction. Thus a fraction of the cardiac energy is wasted in pushing blood backward against the forward-moving stream. The amount of energy wasted varies according to the degree of valvular insufficiency. Similarly, cardiac energy is wasted in proportion to the degree of stenosis which increases the resistance to the forward-moving column of blood. If stenosis and insufficiency are mild, the wasted energy will be small and will not require much extra work to maintain the amount of cardiac output needed under resting conditions or even in response to extra demands. However, each of these conditions is usually progressive and in time becomes severe (see also Chapter 19).

Stenosis and insufficiency often exist at the same time, especially after injury by rheumatic fever or sclerosing processes. When the increased resistance caused by a narrow valvular stenosis or the amount of regurgitant blood through an insufficient valve becomes great, most of the available cardiac energy will be wasted in producing the cardiac work needed to counteract these valvular defects. This leads inevitably to loss of cardiac reserve after an interval which may vary from a few hours to many years in different cases.

Murmurs and thrills are produced in similar ways when the blood stream goes through an abnormal communication between the chambers of the heart or of the blood vessels, or when the stream of blood whirls around and around in a localized dilatation such as a cardiac or aortic aneurysm. Murmurs often help a great deal in the diagnosis of congenital cardiovascular anomalies. The intensity of the murmur often varies inversely with the size of the aperture and directly with the propelling force causing it. Murmurs due to narrowing of blood vessels by angulation or compression may be produced when the heart is displaced toward one side of the chest by tumors or thoracic deformities. Murmurs may also be produced when the blood is of low viscosity, as it may be with severe anemia.

Details of specific murmurs are described in detail elsewhere. With mitral stenosis a presystolic apical murmur of crescendo rumbling tone is sharply localized; it usually disappears with atrial fibrillation or flutter because it is caused by atrial systole not occurring with these arrhythmias. With mitral insufficiency a harsh, widespread systolic murmur radiates from the apex, often to the back as blood is pushed back into the left atrium. With severe mitral disease, in which usually both stenosis and regurgitation exist, high pulmonary vascular pressure builds up and causes so much dilatation of the pulmonary valve as right ventricular failure develops that a pulmonic diastolic murmur is heard. This is the Graham Steell murmur, a functional one. Contrasted with these combinations is the aortic diastolic murmur of aortic insufficiency (an organic lesion), with an associated functional presystolic mitral rumbling murmur resembling that of rheumatic mitral stenosis. This is the Austin Flint murmur, explained as due to (1) pushing back into the mitral diastolic stream of the anterior mitral leaflet by the regurgitant stream against the posterior dilated aortic ring; (2) deflection from the dropped right anterior aortic cusp (Gouley); (3) flow of atrial blood into a left ventricle dilated by aortic regurgitation or (4) eddies formed by the mixing of the atrial and aortic jets of blood running into the left ventricle at the same time, and by (5) the usual thickening of the mitral valve even in syphilitic heart disease after prolonged failure.

The diastolic murmur of aortic regurgitation is usually short, high pitched and of low intensity, occurring early in diastole and decrescendo as the pressure of the aortic regurgitant stream is falling soon after isotonic diastole. It may last into mid-diastole or later. As with the other murmurs of mitral stenosis, it occurs often throughout diastole, with decrescendo and crescendo or hour-glass shape on a phonocardiogram. These contours contrast with the diamond-shaped murmur recorded over aortic or pulmonary stenosis as the vibrations build up to a maximum and then fade. Murmurs of tricuspid insufficiency or stenosis resemble those of similar mitral lesions, except for distribution and intensity. A "continuous or machinery-shop" murmur occurs over an arteriovenous fistula, or the similar patent ductus arteriosus, where blood flows continuously from a high pressure area to a low pressure one with systolic accentuation. Systolic murmurs are heard as blood is compressed and released in going through an interventricular septal defect or coarctation. Many variations of murmurs and sounds occur with other lesions and with changes in dilatation or shape of valve rings, leaflets or chambers with changing heart failure. Endocarditis often causes changing murmurs by altering the shape of valve leaflets.

Friction rubs are audible or palpable vibratory phenomena which may resemble murmurs. Their mechanism is quite different, however. Such rubs are caused by vibrations in the pericardium when its two surfaces roughened by disease scrape over each other during the heart beat.

Several other infrequent sounds related to

the heart beat need brief mention here. A *protodiastolic* sound (loud, sharp, high-pitched) may be associated with *localized* calcification of the pericardium. Faintness or absence of heart sounds may be due to thickening of the pericardium, with or without effusion. A *pericardial splash* (a waterwheel murmur) may be heard when both gas and fluid are in the sac, as after aspiration with introduction of air, or in traumatic lesions of the sac. The *pericardial knock* (often loud and tapping in quality) may be due to (1) free diastolic fling of the heart against the left diaphragm over a distended, hollow abdominal viscus or (2) uncushioned systolic impact of the heart against the chest wall in left pneumothorax. A *ventricular knock* is a short, loud sound early in diastole, occasionally heard when a very large left ventricle expands against the ribs; this may be similar to a *ventricular gallop,* except that the latter is faint or lower in intensity. The two may have similar underlying mechanisms.

A *gastrocardiac splashing sound* may be produced by (1) a large overactive heart with (2) a suitable mixture of gas and fluid in the stomach. We have heard similar transient *"cardioesophageal" sounds,* at times quite alarming, in patients who had air and fluid in the esophagus as demonstrated by fluoroscopy. Apparently a combination of transient cardiospasm, drinking of liquid and air-swallowing had trapped the air in the esophagus so that it bubbled with each heart beat. The sound (bubbling, loud and at times audible to the patient) was heard best over the midsternum, but shifted its level of greatest intensity from moment to moment. Similar phenomena may occur over an esophageal or gastric hiatal hernia.

Mediastinal emphysematous noises (Hamman's sign) are crackling, popping or crepitant noises, sometimes very loud, over a mediastinum in which air has accumulated. This may occur with interstitial pulmonary emphysema, perirenal injection of air, paravertebral injection of Novocain, or trauma. The sounds are loudest during systole, but may occur in diastole and are caused by movements of the heart against the air trapped in the loose fibrous tissue of the mediastinum.

A *semilunar opening click* or ejection click may be heard over either of these valves at the instant they open and allow ventricular ejection to begin. The sound is loud, high-pitched, short and clicking. The vibrations are probably made by sharp shaking of the semilunar cusps when the ventricular blood begins to meet the aortic column of blood, or vibrations of the dilated pulmonary artery or aortic wall.

REFERENCES

Bakst, A. A., Costas-Durieux, J., Goldberg, H., and Bailey, C. P.: Protection of the heart by arteriolization of the coronary sinus. J. Thoracic Surg., 27:433, 1954.

Beck, C. S., and Leightninger, D. S.: Operations for coronary artery disease. J.A.M.A., 156:1226, 1954.

Beck, C. S., Stanton, E., Batiuchok, W., and Leiter, E.: Revascularization of the heart by grafting a systemic artery or a new branch from the aorta into the coronary sinus. J.A.M.A., 137:436, 1948.

Bellet, S.: Recent advances in the treatment of cardiac arrhythmias. Am. Heart J., 56:479, 1958.

Bing, R. J., Hammond, M. N., Handelsman, J. C., Powers, S. R., Spencer, F. W., Eckenhoff, J. B., Goodale, W. T., Hafkenschiel, J. H., and Kety, S. S.: The measurement of coronary blood flow, oxygen consumption and efficiency of the left ventricle in man. Am. Heart J., 38:1, 1949.

Chardack, W. M.: Heart block treated with implantable pacemaker. Prog. Cardiovasc. Dis., 6:507, 1964.

Chardack, W. M., Gage, A. A., and Dean, D. C.: Slowing of the heart by paired pulse pacemaking. Am. J. Cardiol., 14:374, 1964.

Chardack, W. M., Gage, A. A., and Greatbatch, W.: A transistorized, self-contained, implantable pacemaker for the long-term correction of complete heart block. Surgery, 48:643, 1960.

Eckstein, R. W., Roberts, J. T., Gregg, D. E., and Wearn, J. T.: Observations on the role of the Thebesian veins and luminal vessels of the right ventricle. Am. J. Physiol., 132:648, 1941.

Fisher, E. R., and Davis, E. R.: Myocarditis with endocardial elastomyofibrosis (EEMF). Am. Heart J., 56:537, 1958.

Fisher, E. R., and Davis, E. R.: Observations concerning the pathogenesis of endocardial thickening in the adult heart. Am. Heart J., 56:553, 1958.

Gouley, B. A.: The aortic valvular lesion associated with the Austin Flint murmur. Am. Heart J., 22:208, 1941.

Hollander, W., and Chobanian, A.: The effects of an inhibitor of cholesterol biosynthesis, triparanol (MER-29), in subjects with and without coronary artery disease. Boston Med. Quart., 10:2, 1959.

James, T. J.: Anatomy of the Coronary Arteries. New York, Paul B. Hoeber, Inc., 1961.

Kisch, B.: A new concept of cardiac failure. Am. J. Cardiol., 5:383, 1960.

Klemperer, P.: Pathology of systemic lupus erythematosus. In McManus, J. E. A.: Progress in Fundamental Medicine. Philadelphia, Lea & Febiger, 1952.

Levine, S. A., and Harvey, W. P.: Clinical Auscultation of the Heart. Philadelphia, W. B. Saunders Co., 1959.

Luisada, A. A.: From Auscultation to Phonocardiography. St. Louis, C. V. Mosby Co., 1965.

McKusick, V. A.: Cardiovascular Sounds in Health and Disease. Baltimore, Williams & Wilkins Co., 1958.

Mommaerts, W. F. H. M.: The fundamental aspects of the chemistry and behavior of contractile proteins. Paper presented at the Second World Congress of Cardiology, Washington, D.C., Sept. 12–17, 1954.

Mommaerts, W. F. H. M.: Physiology of muscular contraction; metabolism of the heart. In Luisada, A. A. (ed.): Cardiovascular Functions, pp. 2–3 to 2–23. New York, McGraw-Hill Book Co., 1962.

Patterson, J. C.: Coronary artery disease. In McManus, J. E. A.: Progress in Fundamental Medicine. Philadelphia, Lea & Febiger, 1952.

Roberts, J. T.: The role of the small vessels and nerves of the heart in heart failure, coronary artery thrombosis and cardiac pain. Med. Ann. D.C., *14*:483, 1945.

Roberts, J. T.: A case of congenital aortic atresia with hypoplasia of ascending aorta, normal origin of coronary arteries, left ventricular hypoplasia and mitral stenosis. Am. Heart J., *12*:448, 1936.

Roberts, J. T.: Newer conceptions of the mechanism of heart failure. Texas State J. Med., *38*:221, 1942.

Roberts, J. T.: The role of the vasa nervorum, especially in regard to referred pain. Fed. Proc., 7:1948.

Roberts, J. T.: A new blood supply for ischemic hearts. Fed. Proc., 8:1949.

Roberts, J. T.: Anatomy of the conduction system. Chapter 5 in Luisada, A. A. (ed.): Encyclopedia of Cardiology. New York, McGraw Hill-Blakiston, Vol. 1 (of 4): 61–84, 1959.

Roberts, J. T.: Anatomy of the arteries, veins and lymphatic vessels of the heart. Chapter 6 in Luisada, A. A. (ed.): Encyclopedia of Cardiology. New York, McGraw Hill-Blakiston, Vol. 1 (of 4): 85–118, 1959.

Roberts, J. T.: Specific pathology of the coronary arteries. Chapter VIII in Abramson, D. I. (ed.): Blood Vessels and Lymphatics. New York, Academic Press, 1961.

Roberts, J. T.: Supplementing coronary blood supply directly by: endocardial puncturing; left ventricular implant of coronary sinus, vein or artery segments; arterial connections to coronary vessels; arteriolization of coronary sinus and veins. Am. J. Physiol., *187*:627, 1956.

Roberts, J. T., and Beck, C. S.: The effect of chronic cardiac compression on the size of the heart muscle fibers. Am. Heart J., *22*:314, 1941.

Roberts, J. T., Browne, R. S., and Roberts, G.: Nourishment of the heart muscle by way of the coronary sinus. Fed. Proc., *2*:90, 1943.

Roberts, J. T., Murdock, H. R., Jr., Campo, J. L., Tanner, C. J., and Paparella, J. A.: Blood vessels of nerves as seen in living animals with quartz rod illumination. Fed. Proc., *9*:169, 1950.

Roberts, J. T., and Spencer, F. D., Jr.: The accessory mechanism for drainage and nourishment of the myocardium by the Thebesian or arterio-luminal vessels, especially in the left ventricle. Proc. Am. Fed. Clin. Res., 3:1947, and Anat. Rec., *94*:547, 1946.

Roberts, J. T., and Wearn, J. T.: Quantitative studies of the capillary:muscle relationship in human hearts during normal growth and hypertrophy. Am. Heart J., *21*:617, 1941.

Roberts, J. T., Wearn, J. T., and Badal, J. J.: The capillary:muscle ratio in normal and hypertrophied human hearts. Proc. Soc. Exper. Biol. Med., *38*:322, 1938.

Rushmer, R. F.: Cardiovascular Dynamics, 2nd ed. Philadelphia, W. B. Saunders Co., 1961.

Rytand, D. A.: The circus movement (entrapped circuit wave) hypothesis and atrial flutter. Ann. Int. Med., *65*:125, 1966.

Sears, G. A., and Manning, G. W.: Routine electrocardiography: postprandial T-wave changes. Am. Heart J., *56*:591, 1958.

Sevelius, G., and Johnson, P. C.: Myocardial blood flow determined by surface counting and ratio formula. J. Lab. & Clin. Med., *54*:669, 1959.

Szent-Gyorgy, A.: Chemical Physiology of Contraction in Body and Heart Muscle. New York, Academic Press, 1953.

Torp, K. H.: Congenital aortic stenosis with hyperplasia of the endocardium of the left ventricle. Acta Path. Microbiol. Scand., *29*:109, 1951.

Wearn, J. T.: Morphological and functional alterations of the coronary circulation. Harvey Lect., *35*:243, 1939–1940.

Chapter Eighteen

The Electrocardiogram

FRANKLIN D. JOHNSTON

Introduction

Electrocardiograms are records obtained by suitable instruments, called electrocardiographs, from electrodes or electrode systems usually located on the surface of the body. This is possible because with each heart beat relatively large voltages are generated in the heart muscle, and these in turn cause potential differences to appear on the body surface. These potential differences are actually due to currents that flow through the heart and much of the torso but that do not pass for any significant distance into the extremities. The importance of the latter fact will be pointed out later in discussion of electrocardiograms obtained from electrodes placed on the extremities, that is, the limb or extremity leads.

It is clear that if ordinary electrocardiograms, obtained with electrodes on the surface of the body, are to be of much value to the physician in deciding whether heart disease of any kind is or is not present he must be able to relate findings in these tracings to electrical events occurring in the heart. To do this he must understand normal pathways of excitation and recovery in the heart, how various pathologic lesions may alter these electrical events, and especially how various types of leads (electrode arrangements) depict normal or abnormal excitation and recovery. Some physicians are content with a purely descriptive approach to electrocardiographic diagnosis. These individuals learn

from books or lectures that with certain cardiac lesions alterations of a particular kind are likely to be seen in certain electrocardiographic leads, but they do not understand what has "gone wrong" inside the heart or why evidences of this will appear in certain leads and not in others. Perhaps this kind of electrocardiographic interpretation is better than none, but physicians who use it are "in trouble" when unusual or atypical records appear. Most of this section will be devoted to discussion of normal and abnormal passage of electrical phenomena in the heart and how leads or lead systems work. Hopefully this may help some budding electrocardiographers.

A few words should be said about the term "lead." Unfortunately it is used with two distinct but closely related meanings. It is used first to describe an arrangement of electrodes; thus, lead I means that electrodes are placed on the right and left arms. Lead I is also used to refer to the electrocardiogram that is obtained when the electrodes on the two arms are connected to the recording instrument.

It is important for physicians using electrocardiograms to remember that although electrocardiograms are purely electrical records two types of help may be got from them. Some tracings give specific diagnostic information. For example, a record showing definite QRS and T wave changes in leads II, III, and AVF is diagnostic of inferior myocardial infarction, and the physician will need no further clinical or laboratory evidence to make the diagnosis. Similar specific diagnostic help may be given by tracings showing arrhythmias, such as atrial paroxysmal tachycardia; other tracings may show T wave and perhaps other changes, making it certain that hyperkalemia is present.

Many electrocardiograms give nonspecific information and do not point to any single cardiac lesion, but when combined with other clinical data they may be of diagnostic help. Examples of this are found in records which indicate that right or left ventricular hypertrophy is present; similar nonspecific help may be got from tracings showing bundle branch block, and T wave abnormalities. It should be emphasized that the T waves are more easily altered by many things, related or unrelated to heart disease, than are any of the other deflections in the electrocardiogram. Consequently, physicians should be cautious in making a diagnosis of coronary artery or other heart disease on the basis of T wave "abnormalities" alone.

Basic Electrophysiology of the Heart

This is not the place for a detailed discussion of the current concepts of how voltages are produced in the muscle cells in the heart and how in turn these voltages combine and become available for registration by suitable electrodes on the heart or more commonly by electrodes on the surface of the body. As a matter of fact, some of the factors involved in these complicated phenomena are not well understood. Nevertheless, so much work has been done in this area in recent years and some of it has such direct bearing on changes occurring in ordinary electrocardiograms that a brief review of the important aspects of this field will be given.

After the development of suitable microelectrodes by Ling and Gerard in 1949, many investigators including Draper and Weidmann, Woodbury, Hecht, and Christopherson, Hoffman and Suckling, and others began to record transmembrane potentials with the tip of the electrode inside single heart muscle cells. Extensive studies of this kind on animals of many different species have been done in the past 15 years, and presumably the findings on mammals, especially dogs, are much like those that would be found in human subjects. Interesting differences have been found in the form of these records, depending on the type of heart muscle under study. Thus, records obtained from ordinary atrial and ventricular muscle cells are quite similar in form but differ in several respects from those recorded from Purkinje fibers and especially from cells in the sino-atrial or atrioventricular nodes. Figure 18–1 shows the types of transmembrane action potentials obtained from the atrial, ventricular, and S-A nodal muscle cells. It should be emphasized that in the resting state the inside of the cell is negative by the surprising amount of about 90 millivolts (M.V.) with respect to tissues outside the

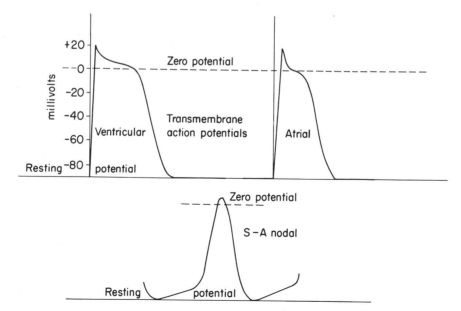

Figure 18–1. Transmembrane action potentials of the kind that are recorded with a microelectrode inside a single mammalian heart muscle cell. See text.

cell, and when excitation (depolarization) of the cell occurs there is abrupt loss of intracellular negativity with overshooting above the zero potential line and relative positivity of the inside of the cell for a short time. As repolarization of the cell (recovery) begins there is a rapid loss of the intracellular positivity followed by more gradual building up of negativity within the cell until the resting state is reached.

It is known that the transmembrane action potentials are caused by movements of ions, primarily potassium (K) and sodium (Na), across the cell membrane during excitation and recovery, and it is certain that the resting membrane potential is largely due to the potassium and chloride concentration gradients between the inside and outside of the cell. The rapid upstroke of the action potential is now believed to be due primarily to passage of sodium ions across the cell membrane into the cell, and this is probably associated with loss of potassium ions from the inside of the cell. The ionic movements occurring during the much longer period of repolarization are not clearly understood but must in essence represent a reversal of the events occurring during excitation. Thus sodium ions must be removed from inside to the outside of the cell and potassium ions must migrate in the opposite direction during this period.

Although the transmembrane action potentials recorded from single heart muscle cells (Fig. 18–1) show little resemblance to ordinary electrocardiograms, it is clear that a close relationship between them must exist. The rapid upstrokes seen in action potentials from cells in the atrial or ventricular muscle correspond to waves in the electrocardiogram (P waves and QRS complexes) caused by excitation of the atria and ventricles respectively, while the rest of the action potentials relate to the R-ST segments and T waves. Atrial T waves are rarely seen in ordinary electrocardiograms because the voltages involved are small and they are usually hidden by the larger ventricular complexes.

Two questions may be properly asked at this point. Why are the durations of the P waves and QRS complexes so much greater than those of the rapid upstrokes observed when single muscle cells are excited, and why are the voltages recorded in all kinds of ordinary electrocardiograms so much smaller than those known to exist across the membranes in single heart muscle cells? The answer to the first question is easy if one remembers that the durations of P waves and QRS complexes, in ordinary electrocardiograms, reflect the time required for excitation of all the muscle cells in the atria and ventricles and really represent the mean direction and magnitude of voltages produced as the waves of excitation pass from cell to cell over these chambers.

The reasons why voltages found in tracings taken with an electrode on the surface of the heart (direct leads), with electrodes on the precordium (semidirect leads), or with electrodes on the extremities (indirect or remote leads), are so much smaller than transmembrane action potentials are not as easy to explain.

Figure 18–2 illustrates the relative size of these different kinds of records. It will be observed that the largest voltage found in direct leads is about 20 per cent of the voltage represented by the rapid upstroke of the action potential, while the voltage recorded in limb leads is only 1 to 2 per cent of the transmembrane voltage. The explanation for these voltage differences may be found in part from the laws which govern the distribution of electrical potentials when a source of voltage exists in a volume conductor. Thus, if a muscle fiber undergoing excitation may at any instant be considered as an equivalent dipole of voltage E, with l the distance between the positive and negative poles, the potential caused at any point P in the volume conductor will be given by the expression

$$V_p = \frac{El \cos \phi}{r^2} \text{ , where } \phi \text{ is the angle between}$$

Figure 18–2. Comparative sizes of voltages existing across the membrane of a single heart muscle cell and QRS complexes recorded by direct, semidirect, and indirect (limb) leads. See text.

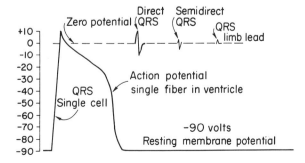

point P and the straight line joining the positive and negative poles of the dipole and r is the distance between the midpoint of this straight line and point P. Although E, as we have seen, may be large, l will be very small, so the dipole moment (El) due to excitation and recovery of a single cell will also be small. Furthermore, since the effects of the dipole on the potential at P vary inversely as the square of the distance (r) one would expect only small potential changes, if P is any significant distance from the dipole. It is believed that voltages recorded in any type of electrocardiogram do not reflect transmembrane action potentials directly but are due to electrical effects produced as excitation followed by recovery occurs in more or less orderly sequence, in the millions of muscle cells that make up the atrial and ventricular muscle. These matters will be discussed in more detail later.

Referring again to Figure 18–1, it will be seen that the action potentials of ordinary atrial and ventricular muscle cells are similar with only minor differences during the repolarization period. In both, when the resting transmembrane potential is reached, this potential remains constant until the cell is again excited. The action potential from a cell in the S-A node shows a more gradual upstroke and quite rapid repolarization; almost immediately after this phase is complete, gradual depolarization with an upward slope of the base line occurs. When this gradually decreasing negativity within the cell reaches a certain critical level, spontaneous excitation of the cell takes place. These latter characteristics have been found only in muscle cells in the S-A and A-V nodes and in Purkinje tissue, making it clear that under ordinary circumstances active or potential pacemakers in the heart occur only in these specialized fibers and not in ordinary atrial and ventricular muscle. These facts have important implications in connection with cardiac arrhythmias and in normal excitation of atrial and ventricular muscle.

The size, duration, and form of transmembrane action potentials may be changed by altering the environment of the heart muscle cells under study. Increase or decrease in the extracellular concentration of ions normally present (K, Na, Ca, etc.) or the presence of drugs like digitalis or quinidine changes the action potentials in specific ways; studies of this kind are the basis of much current knowledge regarding ionic shifts across cell membranes and the resulting electrical potentials.

These studies have also helped to explain changes observed in ordinary electrocardiograms. For example, digitalis decreases the duration of the action potentials in ventricular muscle cells, and this is reflected in the shortening of the Q-T interval in electrocardiograms. Further correlations between changes known to occur in action potentials under certain circumstances and electrocardiograms may help to explain many findings in the latter which are poorly understood at the present time. Readers interested in more information on these matters are referred to Hoffman and Cranefield's *Electrophysiology of the Heart.*

Spread of Excitation and Recovery in the Heart

It is logical to discuss the important features of excitation and recovery of the atria and ventricles at this point and to consider the behavior of electrocardiographic leads later. It must be pointed out, however, that these matters are very closely related, and most of our knowledge about the former is based on the findings in and proper interpretation of electrical records (leads) obtained by electrode arrangements (leads) of many different kinds. For the proper understanding of one a clear understanding of the other is necessary, and the reader should keep this in mind.

Figure 18–3 illustrates the relations between the electrocardiogram and mechanical events in the heart and also indicates the three basic complexes (P, QRS, and T) seen in most electrocardiograms. The important intervals (P-R, QRS, and QT) are also shown. The electrocardiogram shown in Figure 18–3 is normal and could be either standard leads I or II or one of the chest leads taken over the left side of the precordium (V_4, V_5, or V_6). Many matters involved in electrocardiographic interpretation, such as measurement of the heart rate or important intervals and the whole field of the cardiac arrhythmias, are covered in books on electrocardiography and will not be discussed here. Referring again to Figure 18–3, we note that the P waves are caused by excitation of the atria and immediately precede contraction of these chambers; the QRS complexes are due to excitation of the ventricles and are followed shortly by ventricular contraction. The period from the end of the QRS complex to the end of the T wave reflects electrical recovery or repolarization of ventricular muscle, and this

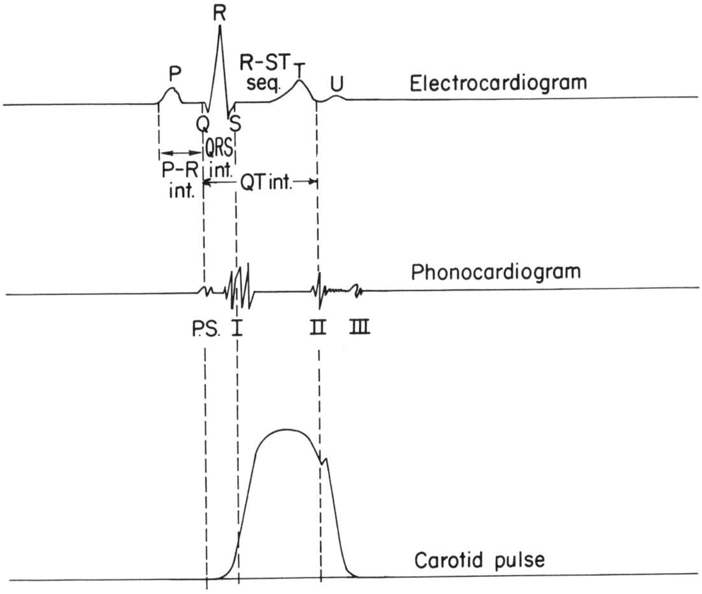

Figure 18–3. The temporal relationship between the electrocardiogram and mechanical events in the heart. I, II, and III are the first, second, and third heart sounds respectively; P.S. is a presystolic extra sound.

process (just as is true in single muscle fibers) lasts much longer than excitation. The first part of this recovery period is usually isoelectric and is referred to as the R-ST segment. As mentioned earlier, atrial recovery (Ta) waves also occur but are usually not seen. U waves are occasionally seen in tracings taken from entirely normal human subjects but are also seen (often with some depression of the R-ST segments or flat T waves) in patients with hypokalemia. The U waves are probably due to delay in recovery in part of the ventricular muscle and, when they occur in patients with hypokalemia, are caused by slow migration of potassium ions back into the cardiac muscle cells.

When the usual normal sinus rhythm is present, the pacemaker for the heart is in the sino-atrial (S-A) node, located in the right atrium close to the junction of the superior vena cava with this chamber. Since under ordinary circumstances there are probably no functioning special conducting tissues in the atria, excitation passes from the S-A node over the rest of the atrial muscle in a general downward, leftward, and somewhat anterior direction. The passage of this wave of excitation over the atria is responsible for the P waves, and its average direction is such as to result in upright P waves in leads I, II, aV_F, and most of the chest leads. Inverted P waves are seen in lead aV_R, and these waves may be upright, diphasic, or inverted in leads III, aV_L, and the right chest leads.

At this point, the excitation wave and what it means must be defined more precisely. In the previous section we have seen that heart

muscle cells, only in the S-A and A-V nodes and in special conducting (Purkinje) tissue in the ventricles, have the ability to depolarize spontaneously or to serve as pacemakers. When normal sinus rhythm is present, cells in the S-A node, regulated by mediators from the vagus nerve and sympathetic nervous system, depolarize at a faster rate than is present in other potential pacemaking tissue and for this reason serve as the pacemaker for the entire heart. With excitation of a cell (or cells) in the S-A node adjacent cells in the node or in surrounding atrial tissue in turn undergo excitation, and this process spreads uniformly (like ignition of a fuse on a firecracker) in all directions at a rate of about 1000 mm./sec. over all the atrial muscle. This is what we mean by the terms excitation wave or wave of activation. From the electrical point of view this may be represented by a double layer or surface studded with positive and negative charges which passes over the muscle as it becomes excited. The positive charges always face resting muscle or the direction toward which the excitation wave is passing. Excitation of the atria as we have seen above is a relatively simple process and may be represented by an arrow (vector) originating in the S-A node and oriented downward and to the left (Fig. 18–4).

Suppose that for some reason the rate of impulse formation in the S-A node decreases below that in the A-V node and that the latter takes over as the pacemaker for the heart. Since the A-V node is located near the orifice of the coronary sinus below most of the atrial muscle, spread of excitation over

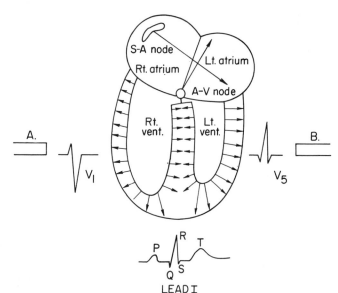

A.

B.

V_I

V_5

R
T
P
Q S

LEAD I

Figure 18–4. Diagrammatic illustration of the course of atrial excitation when normal sinus rhythm and A-V nodal rhythm are present. Arrows in the septum and free walls of the ventricles indicate the general pathways of ventricular excitation. The time sequence of ventricular excitation is roughly as follows:

0.00-0.02 sec.—Left side of septum—midportion.

0.015-0.025 sec.—Right lower septum and endocardial surface of both ventricles.

0.020-0.070 sec.—Apex and free walls of both ventricles and septum except basal portions.

0.065-0.080 sec.—Basal portions of septum and both ventricles.

the atria will be from below, upward and usually slightly to the left (Fig. 18–4), so that P waves will be inverted in leads II, III, and aV_F when A-V nodal rhythm is present.

As excitation of the atria nears completion the excitation wave reaches the A-V node and passes through this structure. It is known that transmission in or near this node is slow and that much of the P-R interval, as measured in ordinary electrocardiograms, is due to slow conduction in this area. After the excitation wave passes through the A-V node it enters the main stem of the His bundle and passes very rapidly through this structure, the right and left bundle branches into the Purkinje network which spreads over much of the endocardial surfaces of both ventricles and may penetrate into the ventricular muscle in some areas. The rate of transmission of excitation through these special conducting pathways is approximately 4000 mm./sec. It should be pointed out that no evidence of excitation of these special conducting pathways is seen in ordinary electrocardiograms, even in direct leads with an electrode on the surface of the heart. This is true because the amount of muscle undergoing excitation during this brief period of time is very small. Experimental studies, however, employing suitable small electrodes placed directly on these special fibers have not only proved that excitation passes rapidly over these structures but that this occurs immediately before excitation of ordinary muscle fibers in the ventricles.

The excitation of ordinary ventricular muscle is triggered by impulses arriving over Purkinje fibers, and this excitation (which is the cause for QRS complexes) is a much more complicated affair than is atrial excitation. The general pathways of normal intraventricular excitation are indicated by the arrows in Figure 18–4, and the time sequence of excitation is also indicated in this figure. Thus, part of the left side of the septum is excited first, and excitation from left to right and anteriorly in this region causes normal septal Q waves to appear in lead I and in the left chest leads. The initial part of the small R waves, seen in right chest leads, is also caused by this early left-sided septal excitation. Very shortly, excitation of the right septal surface and adjacent portions of the right ventricular wall begin with nearly simultaneous excitation of the endocardial muscle of the left ventricle. The apical regions of the two ventricles and the septum are excited relatively early followed by excitation of the rest of the ventricular muscle, with the basal parts of the right ventricle and septum and the posterobasal wall of the left ventricle the last to be excited.

The summary of ventricular excitation given above is based largely on experimental studies on dogs by Scher and Young, and excitation in the human heart is probably similar. Although there are differences in opinion among investigators about the details of ventricular excitation, it is likely that the septum is excited from both sides and excitation of the free walls of both ventricles passes from within outward as indicated by the arrows in Figure 18–4. It is clear that, during much of the period of excitation, waves of depolarization pass simultaneously in many different directions over ventricular muscle, and cancellation effects, for waves traveling in opposite directions, must greatly modify potentials recorded at points outside of the heart. Nevertheless, if it is remembered that when the mean direction of excitation at any instant is approaching an electrode this electrode will be positive, giving an upward deflection, and when excitation is on the average passing away from an electrode, making it negative and causing a downward deflection, it is possible to explain deflections in the QRS complex in terms of excitation occurring in various parts of the ventricles. To do this, one must know the location of an electrode or electrodes, employed for certain leads, with respect to the heart and how these leads function. The best evidence we have that the ideas regarding ventricular excitation and behavior of leads are correct is found in the fact that when excitation is abnormal or abolished in certain parts of the ventricles (as occurs with bundle branch block or myocardial infarction) anticipated changes in the form of QRS complexes are actually found. These matters will be discussed again later.

Before electrocardiographic leads and their behavior are considered, the electrical recovery process in atrial and ventricular muscle and how these events are depicted in electrocardiograms must be discussed. It is clear that in any single muscle cell in the heart repolarization or recovery must represent electrical events that are equal but opposite in sign to those which occur with depolarization or excitation of the cell, even though the former lasts much longer than the latter. One would therefore expect the T waves always to be opposite in direction to the chief deflections of the QRS complexes and the P waves. This is probably true of atrial recovery (Ta) waves because, when they are visible, they are usually opposite in direction to the P waves. Not a great deal of work has been done relative to atrial recovery, but it seems likely that repolarization here occurs in the same general order as excitation.

If one refers again to the normal electrocardiogram shown in Figure 18–3, he sees that the QRS complex and the T wave are both primarily upward deflections. The question arises as to how this peculiar situation, which is seen in many normal electrocardiograms, may be explained. Although many aspects of recovery in normal ventricular muscle are poorly understood, it is almost certain that recovery occurs more slowly (or the excited state lasts longer) in subendocardial muscle than in muscle at or near the epicardial surface, so that the spread of repolarization is opposite in direction (from the epicardial toward the endocardial surface) to the paths of excitation. Thus normal recovery may be thought of as a wave of repolarization which passes relatively slowly across the ventricular walls from outside inward, but here the electrical representation would require a surface studded with negative and positive charges with the negative charges oriented toward the cavities of the ventricles. The cause or causes for this situation are not entirely clear. It has been suggested that a temperature gradient across the walls of the ventricles, with the epicardial muscle slightly warmer than subendocardial muscle, may play a role. Recent studies by Reynolds and Yu on dogs and humans indicate that while such a temperature gradient does exist, other factors such as variation of the blood supply to ventricular muscle, must also be present.

Wilson and associates, many years ago, were concerned with the above matters, and the concept of the ventricular gradient was introduced to explain the unexpected direction of T waves in many tracings. Although Ashman, Gardberg, and others have done extensive work in more recent years on the ventricular gradient, it is a rather difficult and theoretical concept and has never proved to be of much value in clinical electrocardiography. For these reasons, the ventricular gradient will not be discussed further here.

As was pointed out in the introduction to this section, the T waves are very easily altered by many factors, some related to heart disease and some not. This is not surprising since repolarization of muscle involves not only ionic movements which are essential for re-excitation of the cells but storage of energy, subsequently released by muscular contraction, must also occur during this period. The rate at which biochemical processes responsible for repolarization occur is dependent on temperature, the blood supply, and environmental factors such as concentration of essential ions (Na, K, Cl, Ca, etc.). Some of these variables also modify excitation to some extent but to a much lesser degree than is true of recovery.

It is clear that in normal hearts (and probably in many abnormal hearts as well) recovery does not follow excitation in regular time sequence in ventricular muscle, thus causing QRS complexes and T waves oriented in the same direction. Many experimental and clinical observations indicate, however, that this usual unexpected order or direction of recovery is very easily disturbed, often resulting in oppositely directed QRS complexes and T waves. Thus when excitation is abnormal, as in bundle branch block, recovery appears to follow its time sequence more closely than usual and the T waves and QRS complexes are commonly opposite in direction. Such T wave changes are called secondary because they are dependent on abnormal excitation. If the epicardial muscle is cooled in any way, or if the arterial circulation to part of the left ventricle is reduced by partial ligation of a coronary artery in an experimental animal, electrocardiograms taken with an exploring electrode close to the affected region will show marked T wave alterations due to delayed recovery in the involved muscle. Changes of this kind are referred to as primary T wave changes and are due to many different things that alter repolarization locally in ventricular muscle. Most T wave "abnormalities" seen in clinical electrocardiography are of this type. If physicians remember that T wave "abnormalities" of the same kind may occur in a patient with narrowing of a coronary artery and in a normal subject who has just eaten a large meal finished off with ice cream (with cooling of the posterior and inferior aspects of the heart), it should make them careful about attributing the "abnormal" T waves to any specific cause.

This is the appropriate place to discuss changes in the R-ST segments and T waves caused by injury or ischemia of ventricular muscle. A great deal of confusion and uncertainty has existed in connection with these matters over the years, but in recent years work by Alzamora-Castro and associates, Katcher and associates, Samson and Scher, and Sodi-Pallares and associates has clarified many aspects of this rather complicated field. Perhaps the easiest way to approach this matter is to consider a simple experiment of the kind done by Bayley and associates over 20 years ago. A loose ligature is placed around a branch of the anterior descending coronary artery in a dog, and a suitable electrode is applied to the surface of the left ventricle directly over the region nourished by this artery. An electrocardiogram taken before the ligature is tightened would appear like the one shown in Figure 18–5A, provided precautions are taken to avoid cooling of the epicardial surface of the heart. It will be observed that the chief deflection of the QRS complex, as well as the T wave, is upright.

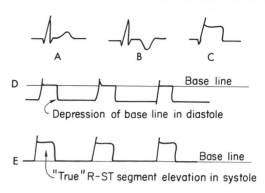

Figure 18–5. *A, B, C,* Normal direct lead, inverted T wave due to local ischemia, and elevation of the R-ST segment due to acute injury respectively. *D,* Depression of the base line in diastole due to injury current and elevation of the R-ST segment due to disappearance of the injury current in systole. *E,* "True" elevation of the R-ST segment. See text.

As the ligature is gradually tightened, thus decreasing arterial flow to the area under study, no change is observed initially, but soon the upright T wave becomes inverted (Fig. 18–5B). If the ligature is now loosened the T wave will soon again become upright. It is clear that decrease in the blood supply has delayed repolarization in the epicardial muscle beneath the electrode sufficiently to reverse the order of recovery and invert the T wave. Suppose that the ligature is now tightened sufficiently to obstruct the artery almost completely. Within a few seconds elevation of the R-ST segment begins to appear, and shortly a tracing like that seen in Figure 18–5C is recorded. This type of change always occurs when heart muscle is injured by cutting off its blood supply, by trauma, or other insults such as application of a concentrated solution of KCl. Injured muscle is unable to repolarize at all or its repolarization is subnormal, so that *during the resting state* such muscle is negative with respect to surrounding normally repolarized muscle and a so-called injury current exists. Since the polarity of direct (or indirect) leads is always arranged so that positivity of the exploring electrode will cause an upward deflection and negativity a downward deflection in the tracing obtained, it may seem strange that elevation and not depression of the R-ST segment is seen when the exploring electrode is located on or is facing injured muscle. The explanation for this situation is obvious if one remembers that injured muscle is negative only during the resting (polarized) state of uninjured ventricular muscle and that this negativity disappears when the uninjured muscle is excited (depolarized). This would cause depression of the base line between heartbeats and an *upward* movement of this base line which *seems to indicate positivity of injured muscle* during excitation and much of the recovery period. The negativity of injured muscle, with base line depression between beats, can only be appreciated when special equipment with great stability and a D.C. response is used to record the electrocardiograms. Figure 18–5D illustrates what is actually occurring with injury to ventricular muscle.

Another cause has been described for elevation of the R-ST segment. It is attributed by some workers not to injury but to factors which prevent the wave of excitation from entering an area of heart muscle, so that *this area, although it is able to polarize, is not excited.* An electrode located on or facing such an area would therefore remain positive during excitation and recovery of the balance of the ventricular muscle, thus causing what might be called *true elevation* of the R-ST segment. In tracings taken with ordinary electrocardiographs this type of R-ST segment elevation cannot be distinguished from the kind due to injury, but with special equipment of the type mentioned above the differentiation is possible. Figure 18–5E illustrates the mechanism involved when excitation is blocked and an area of depolarized muscle is not excited. Alzamora-Castro and associates have produced this type of R-ST segment elevation in dogs by injecting cocaine into a coronary artery; they believe that blocking of excitation, as well as injury, may be responsible for R-ST segment elevation seen with acute myocardial infarction. Although there is general agreement that R-ST segment elevation occurs as a result of factors other than the disappearance of negativity of injured muscle during electrical systole, Samson and Scher have presented some evidence that blocking of excitation may not be an important factor in this "true" R-ST segment elevation.

In the above, nothing has been said about depression of the R-ST segments that are seen most often in tracings taken on patients with coronary artery disease. If an electrocardiogram is taken during a spontaneous attack of angina pectoris or if a patient with coronary disease is exercised and tracings are taken during or shortly after the exertion, significant depression of the R-ST segments (as compared with a control tracing) is likely to appear in the standard leads and in the left chest leads (V_4-V_6). These changes are usu-

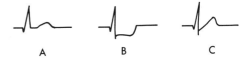

Figure 18–6. *A*, Normal chest lead (V_5) from a patient with angina pectoris, free of chest discomfort. *B*, Depression of the R-ST segment in this lead during an anginal attack or after exertion. *C*, Depression of the junction between QRS and T often seen in normal subjects with tachycardia due to exertion. See text.

ally transient and often disappear entirely within 5 to 10 minutes after the end of the anginal attack or the termination of exercise. Figure 18–6A illustrates a normal record (chest lead V_5 taken in a patient with angina pectoris when free of chest discomfort), and Figure 18–6B shows the type of change found in this lead during an anginal attack or immediately after exertion. How can this alteration be explained? Although a certain answer to this question cannot be given at this time, it is likely that during effort or at the time of an anginal attack the blood supply is reduced more in subendocardial than in epicardial muscle and transient injury appears in the subendocardium of the left ventricle. This would cause *elevation* of the R-ST segment in a tracing taken with an exploring electrode in the cavity of the left ventricle (as is often reflected in lead aV_R) but causes depression of the R-ST segments in most leads from the surface of the body. This is known as a reciprocal change and occurs here in V_5 because the exploring electrode for this lead does not face the injured area but is directed toward the relatively normal part of the left ventricular wall. A similar type of reciprocal deviation of the R-ST segment is seen occasionally in the usual anterior chest leads when an acute strictly posterior myocardial infarction occurs. Here depression of the R-ST segments will appear in several of these leads, and elevation of the R-ST segment will be found only in leads taken with an exploring electrode on the left posterior chest or in the esophagus behind the left ventricle.

Stress tests of different kinds, usually exercise tests, are being increasingly used to help in the diagnosis of coronary artery disease and to decide whether chest discomfort is or is not angina pectoris. The writer may be old fashioned but still believes that a complete and accurate history is the best way to reach a decision on this matter. Exercise tests have a place, especially relating to insurance matters (when an applicant for a large policy might not report chest symptoms fully to the examining physician), but they should not be done in lieu of a good history, and when they are done they must be properly supervised and interpreted. As a result of sinus tachycardia induced by exercise many normal individuals develop depression of the junction between the QRS complex and the T wave, as shown in Figure 18–6C. This is not true depression of the R-ST segment and should be considered a normal response to exercise.

Leads and Lead Systems and Their Behavior

Leads used ordinarily in clinical electrocardiography are of two types, bipolar and "unipolar." Standard leads I, II, and III, suggested by Einthoven many years ago, are bipolar leads, and aV_R, aV_L, aV_F, and the six chest leads usually taken are "unipolar" leads.

The standard leads are recorded from suitable electrodes placed on the right arm, left arm, and left leg and are represented by the following equations:

$$\text{Lead I} = V_L - V_R$$
$$\text{Lead II} = V_F - V_R$$
$$\text{Lead III} = V_F - V_L$$

where V_R, V_L, and V_F are the electrical potentials present in the right arm, left arm, and left leg respectively. Although the potentials of these three extremities vary in magnitude, they are in general of about the same size; this is the reason why the standard leads are called bipolar leads. Lead I thus represents the difference in potential between the left arm and right arm, lead II the difference in potential between the left leg and right arm, and lead III the difference in potential between the left leg and the left arm.

There is, strictly speaking, no such thing as a unipolar lead, because no electrocardiogram can be recorded with a single electrode located anywhere on the surface of or within the body. There must always be a closed circuit in the input to an electrocardiograph, and this means there must be two electrodes attached directly or indirectly to the body. There is no single point on the surface of the body where the potential variations due to cardiac activity are zero or negligibly small, but Wilson and associates suggested many years ago that if electrodes on the right arm, left arm, and left leg are connected through large, equal resistances to a common point, this central terminal has quite small potential variations and may be used as an indifferent electrode. If an exploring electrode is placed anywhere on the body and this is used, with the central terminal, to record an electrocardiogram, the tracing obtained represents fairly accurately the potential variations at the site of the exploring electrode alone and is, in this sense, a unipolar lead. Connections from the electrocardiograph to the exploring electrode and the central terminal are always made so that *positivity of the former* will give an upward deflection in the tracing recorded. Figure 18–7A illustrates the central terminal arrangement. Here the exploring electrode is located on the anterior chest wall at the fourth I.C.S. left sternal edge. This is the position employed for the second routine chest lead and the record obtained is referred to as chest lead V_2.

If the wire, used with the exploring electrode, is connected to electrodes on the right arm, left arm, and left leg in turn, the "unipolar" extremity leads V_R, V_L, and V_F will be recorded. Figure 18–7B shows the connections for lead V_L. Goldberger pointed out many years ago that if the connection between the electrode on any of the above extremities and the central terminal is broken while the unipolar extremity lead is being recorded, the resulting tracings will be identical in form but 50 per cent larger in size than V_R, V_L, and V_F. These are the augmented unipolar extremity leads aV_R, aV_L, and aV_F. Figure 18–7C shows the minor change in the circuit to obtain aV_L. Augmented unipolar extremity leads are commonly recorded in routine electrocardiography so that with the three standard (bipolar) leads, six limb leads are obtained. Six chest leads are also usually recorded, making up the conventional 12 lead electrocardiogram.

In the introduction it was pointed out that currents due to electrical activity in the heart flow through much of the torso but do not pass for any significant distance into the extremities. One might therefore ask if the arms and legs receive any electrical potential from the heart. The answer to this is that they do but that *all* areas in the arms and legs have the *same electrical potential*, which is the potential existing at the regions where each of the extremities joins the torso. This explains why it makes no difference where electrodes are placed on the arms and legs, and this is a unique advantage of the limb leads. The reverse is true relative to the location of an exploring electrode on the thorax, especially if it is close to the heart, and is the reason why the positions of the electrode for chest leads must be carefully located with respect

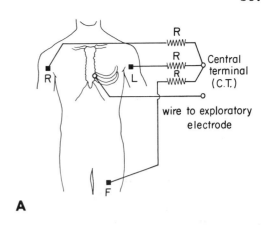

A

Figure 18–7. Central terminal arrangement for recording "unipolar" leads. *A*, The circuit for registration of chest lead V₂. *B, C*, The connections for leads V$_L$ and aV$_L$ respectively. R and r are large (at least 25,000 ohms) equal resistances. (*B, C*, From Luisada, A. A. [ed.]: Cardiology: An Encyclopedia of the Cardiovascular System, Volume II. New York, Blakiston Division, McGraw-Hill Book Co.)

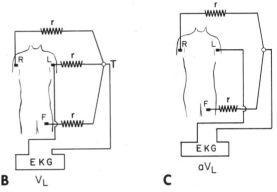

B   V$_L$ **C**   aV$_L$

to bony landmarks on the surface of the chest.

Although during the early years when chest leads were being taken there was no general agreement as to the number of such leads, where on the chest wall the exploring electrode should be placed, and what should be used as the indifferent electrode (the left leg, the right arm, a point on the left posterior chest behind the heart, or the central terminal), almost all physicians now record six chest leads at specified points on the chest and use the central terminal for the indifferent electrode.

The positions on the chest surface used routinely for the chest leads are as follows:

1. Fourth I.C.S—right sternal edge.
2. Fourth I.C.S.—left sternal edge.
3. Halfway between 2 and 4.
4. Fifth I.C.S.—left midclavicular line.
5. Left anterior axillary line—same level as 4.
6. Left midaxillary line—same level as 4.

If additional chest leads are taken further to the left than usual they are designated as follows:

7. Left posterior axillary line—same level as 4.

8. Left midscapular line—same level as 4.
9. Midline over spine—same level as 4.

Extra leads on the anterior portion of the right chest in positions corresponding to the usual locations over the left side are labeled V$_{3R}$, V$_{4R}$, etc., and if chest leads are taken at a higher or lower level than usual they are designated as 3V₂ or 5V₂. Thus lead 5V₂ would be taken at the left sternal edge in the fifth I.C.S. rather than in the fourth I.C.S.

When the central terminal is used for the indifferent electrode (as is usually true) all the chest leads are referred to as V̇ leads and are designated as V₁, V₂, etc. If, however, the right arm or left leg should be employed for the indifferent electrode, the chest leads are labeled CR-1, CR-2, etc., or CF1, CF2, etc.

Before other kinds of leads used primarily for vectorcardiography are described, matters relating to the behavior of leads of any kind must be presented. Since the same series of electrical events is going on in the heart with every heart cycle and the resulting electrical effects on the surface of the body may be recorded with two electrodes (provided they are not close together) located in an infinite number of different places on the skin surface, what is the point of taking more than a single electrocardiogram? The simplest answer to this question is that different leads give different views of the continually repeating electrical activity in the heart and thereby help the physician to build up a more complete picture of this cardiac activity. The situation is analogous to what an art critic would do when deciding whether he should or should not purchase an expensive statue. He would almost certainly walk around this object and view it from different directions. The statue would not change but it would appear different to the critic, depending on his position. Electrocardiographic leads differ because with various orientations of electrodes with respect to the heart the leads pick up or emphasize voltages caused by excitation or recovery passing in certain directions and not in others.

Although the equilateral triangle reference system, proposed by Einthoven many years ago, has been used for over 50 years to relate deflections seen in the standard limb leads to electrical events occurring in the heart, the behavior of the limb and especially leads of other kinds has not been well understood until relatively recent years. Burger and van Milaan made a great contribution nearly 20 years ago when they introduced the concept of the lead vector, and Schmitt and Frank have done extensive work elaborating on this powerful technique. Unfortunately the lead vector is not easily appreciated and understood by the average physician, and the waters were muddied even more when the terms "transfer impedance" and "image vector" rather than lead vector were used by Schmitt and Frank respectively.

The lead field described by McFee and Johnston is closely related to the lead vector but is easier to understand and use. It is essentially the same idea proposed earlier by Lepeschkin under the name of "tubes of influence" of a lead, and the lead field for any lead may be drawn fairly accurately if a battery is connected to the lead terminals and the paths of current flow that must pass through the torso, including the heart, are visualized. Figure 18–8A illustrates the lead field of standard lead I. Here the battery is connected to electrodes on the two arms and the lines joining the two shoulder areas indicate the general direction and current density of these flow lines. This is the lead field *and the part of it that passes through the heart determines the behavior of lead I.* This may

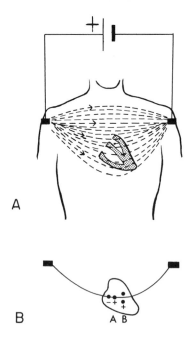

Figure 18–8. *A,* The lead field for lead I. *B,* A single element of the lead field passing through the heart. A voltage in the heart oriented parallel to this element (A) will contribute maximally to lead I, while a voltage (B) oriented at right angles to the element will contribute nothing to the lead. (*A,* Modified from Luisada.)

still seem to be a queer idea, but using the reciprocity theorem of Helmholz it has been shown not only to be correct but to be a generalization of the lead vector concept. How is it used to clarify the behavior of a lead? This is very simple indeed. If the course of excitation (or recovery) in the heart is parallel to the lead field, these cardiac voltages will contribute maximally to the electrocardiogram recorded, and if the paths of excitation (or recovery) are oriented at right angles to the lead field these voltages will contribute nothing to the electrocardiogram recorded by the lead (Fig. 18–8B). Furthermore, if the current density of the lead field is high (indicated by lines of current flow drawn close together as shown in Figure 18–8A at the base of the heart), a certain voltage in the heart oriented parallel to the lead field would produce a larger deflection in lead I than would the same voltage parallel to the lead field near the apex of the heart where the current density of the lead field is lower.

With the above ideas in mind, what can one say about the behavior of lead I? Since its lead field through the heart (Fig. 18–8A) is oriented chiefly in a transverse direction, it is clear that this lead records the effects of

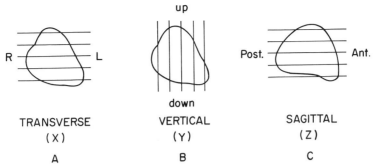

Figure 18–9. *A, B, C,* Lead fields through the heart for ideal transverse (X), vertical (Y), and sagittal (Z) leads. See text.

excitation and recovery that pass primarily from right to left or left to right. In other words, lead I is a fairly good one for recording transverse components of cardiac voltages. It is not ideal for this purpose because the lead field has considerable curvature in the apical regions of the heart, and this means that voltages with vertical components in this location are also recorded in lead I. It should be quite obvious that leads providing transverse, vertical, and sagittal components of heart voltages in purest form must have uniform lead fields passing through the heart in strictly transverse, vertical, and sagittal directions, as shown in Figure 18–9A, B, and C. Such leads are called orthogonal leads and are important in vectorcardiography and for other reasons. It should be pointed out here that it is easy to devise lead arrangements which will give lead fields of the kind illustrated in Figure 18–9; these lead systems will be discussed later.

What about the behavior of the other commonly used electrocardiographic leads as defined by their lead fields? If the lead fields for leads II, III, aV$_R$, aV$_L$ and aV$_F$ are visualized, it will be clear that II, III, aV$_R$, and aV$_L$ record voltages having vertical and to a somewhat lesser degree transverse components in the heart, and that aV$_F$ records primarily vertical components since its lead field is nearly vertical in direction through the heart. These conclusions are not new, of course, and have been fairly well understood from the equilateral triangle arrangement and the equivalent triaxial reference system that have been used for many years. Figure 18–10 shows the equilateral triangle construction and how a series of voltages during excitation of the ventricles (represented by the arrows O$_1$, O$_2$, O$_3$, etc.) are related to deflections of the QRS complexes in leads I, II, and III. Figure 18–10 shows the scheme for angular measurement of voltages in the frontal plane

and also indicates in the simplest possible manner the relationship between ordinary scalar electrocardiograms and vectorcardiograms. If the heads of the arrows (*vectors*) (O$_1$, O$_2$, O$_3$, O$_4$, etc.) that represent the *average* direction and magnitude of voltages

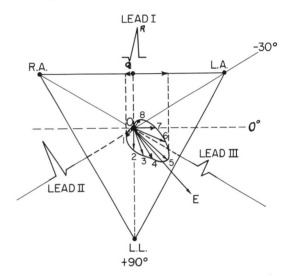

Figure 18–10. The Einthoven triangle construction for relating voltages existing at any instant in the heart (O$_1$, O$_2$, etc.) to deflections occurring in the standard leads I, II, and III. Thus, perpendiculars dropped from the two ends of the small voltage O$_1$ on the line of lead I give a small voltage with the right arm (R.A.) positive and the left arm (L.A.) negative, causing the initial downward deflection (Q wave) in this lead. The larger R wave in lead I corresponds approximately to the projection of O$_5$ on the line of lead I. The deflections in leads II and III are found by a similar projection of voltages O$_1$, O$_2$, O$_3$ . . . O$_8$ on the lines of leads II and III. An upward deflection in these leads occurs when the vectors O$_1$, O$_2$, O$_3$, . . . etc. or the arrows representing their projections on the lines of leads II and III point toward the left leg (L.L.). The smooth curve connecting the heads of all the vectors O$_1$, O$_2$, O$_3$, . . . O$_8$ is the vectorcardiogram or vector loop representing the QRS complex in the frontal plane. The vectors and loops for the P and T waves are not shown in this figure.

caused by excitation *of the ventricles* at successive instants of time are joined by a smooth curve, the vectorcardiogram is obtained. Thus the loop seen in Figure 18–10 is the vectorcardiogram in the frontal plane. It is clear that vectorcardiograms are more closely related to electrical events in the heart than are scalar tracings, but it is also obvious that the vector loops are only a different way of displaying information that is also present in the scalar records.

Referring again to Figure 18–10, the arrows O_1, O_2, O_3, etc. represent the magnitude and direction of the mean voltage of excitation at successive instants and are referred to as the instantaneous electrical axes of QRS. If all of these are added vectorally the mean axis of QRS, OE, will be obtained. If this mean axis lies in the quadrant between 0 and $+90°$ this is the usual normal range and no axis deviation is present. If the mean electrical axis rotates in a counterclockwise direction so that it lies at $-10°$, $-30°$, $-60°$, etc., left axis deviation is present, and if it is located beyond $+90°$ right axis deviation is said to exist.

It will be observed that the sides of the equilateral triangle (Fig. 18–10) or the lines of leads I, II, and III are roughly parallel to the direction of the part of the lead fields of these leads that passes through the heart. This is the reason why the triangle arrangement has been so useful as an approximate method for relating the limb leads to voltages in the heart. It should be pointed out that the assumptions underlying the Einthoven equilateral triangle are not fully met and that an oblique triangle, often called a Burger triangle (Fig. 18–11), would be a more accurate construction.

Little has been said about the polarity employed in the limb leads. This must be specified, of course, if we are to know whether excitation passing in a certain direction in the heart will give an upward or a downward deflection in these leads. From the earlier discussion of unipolar leads, upward deflections will occur in aV_R, aV_L, and aV_F when the average direction of excitation in the heart is passing toward the right shoulder, left shoulder, and left leg respectively. Although standard leads I, II, and III are bipolar leads, connections are made so that excitation passing from right to left (toward the left shoulder) gives an upward deflection in I and excitation passing from above downward (toward the left leg) gives an upward deflection in leads II and III.

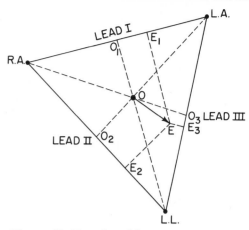

Figure 18–11. The oblique (Burger) triangle shown gives a more accurate relationship between a voltage (OE) in the heart and the deflection occurring in the standard leads than does the equilateral triangle construction. This is true because in the oblique triangle the lines of leads I, II, and III are more nearly parallel to the directions of the lead fields of these leads through the heart.

It should be clear that the limb leads record voltages in the heart that are passing in transverse and vertical directions but would not depict voltages having primarily anterior-posterior or posterior-anterior (sagittal) directions. The first four (or five) chest leads are recorded from exploring electrodes located on the anterior chest wall, and since their lead fields have a primarily anterior-posterior direction through the heart, these leads record chiefly the sagittal components of cardiac voltages. Since the sixth chest lead, V_6, is located in the left midaxillary line its lead field is oriented more transversely than sagittally, and it responds mostly to transverse components, particularly those arising in the left side of the heart. This is the reason why lead V_6 often resembles lead I. The distribution of the lead field that must exist when a unipolar chest lead with the central terminal as the indifferent electrode is taken, is shown in Figure 18–12. Here an electric current entering at the exploring electrode on the chest wall will divide as it passes through the heart and leave the torso in equal amounts to enter the right arm, left arm, and left leg and then through the large equal resistances to the central terminal. Since the lead field is more concentrated in parts of the heart close to the exploring electrode than in more remote regions of the heart, voltages existing in the former areas contribute more to the record obtained than do voltages more distant from the exploring electrode.

Chest leads yield records similar to those

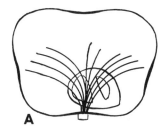 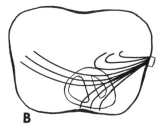

Figure 18–12. *A, B,* The lead fields of chest leads V_1 or V_2 and V_6 respectively. See text. (From Luisada, A. A. [ed.]: Cardiology: An Encyclopedia of the Cardiovascular System, Volume II. New York, Blakiston Division, McGraw-Hill Book Co.)

that would be obtained in direct leads with an electrode on the surface of the heart beneath the location of the precordial electrode, although the record obtained with the direct lead is approximately ten times larger (greater in voltage) than is the corresponding chest (semidirect) lead. Chest leads may therefore be considered as a method of sampling the voltages that exist on the accessible surfaces of the heart. If chest leads are taken over the posterior left chest, the tracings obtained do not reflect very well the type of record that would be obtained by direct leads from the posterior surface of the heart. This is true because, since the heart is a considerable distance from the posterior chest electrode, the lead field through the heart will be weak and different in form from the field of a direct posterior lead. Tracings taken with a suitable exploring electrode in the esophagus may be used to sample voltages existing on the posterior aspect of the heart and may be very useful in clarifying the type of atrial mechanism that is present if the electrode is located at the atrial level. Esophageal leads have been taken occasionally for many years but have not been employed as often as they would be if their advantages were generally known. Brody and associates have recently

described a new and better technique for taking esophageal leads, using both unipolar and bipolar electrodes.

We should now be able to understand or even predict changes in the QRS complexes occurring with bundle branch block and myocardial infarction. Figure 18–13A and B indicates the major changes in excitation and the types of QRS complexes seen in lead I and chest leads V_1 and V_5 (or V_6) in right and left bundle branch block respectively. Since there is delay in or complete blocking of conduction in the main right or left bundle branch when incomplete or complete bundle branch block exists, the time required for excitation of the ventricles will be increased, and QRS intervals will be from 0.10 to 0.12 second in incomplete and 0.12 second or more in complete branch block.

In complete right branch block (Fig. 18–13A), the septum is excited primarily from left to right, the left ventricle is excited at its normal time, and the right ventricle only when events in the septum and left ventricle are nearly complete. In V_1 the initial R wave is due to septal excitation (passing toward the electrode), the downstroke is due to excitation in the left ventricle (passing away from the electrode), and the secondary R wave,

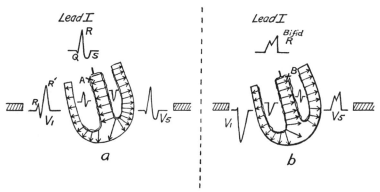

Figure 18–13. The spread of the electrical impulse over the ventricles in *a*, complete right bundle branch block, and *b*, complete left branch block.

R¹, is caused by late excitation of the free wall of the right ventricle with the excitation wave again passing toward the electrode. In V₅, the Q wave is due to excitation of the septum from left to right, the R wave to normal excitation of the left ventricle toward the electrode, and the broad S wave to the delayed excitation of the right ventricle. The form of the QRS complex in lead I is similarly explained.

When complete left branch block is present (Fig. 18–13B), the septum is excited from right to left during the time the right ventricle is also being activated, while the left ventricle is excited later. In V₁ initial R waves are small or may be absent, and the QRS complex consists entirely of a broad downward deflection (QS wave). Any R wave present is due entirely to excitation of the free wall of the right ventricle, but this may be canceled by excitation passing in the opposite (right to left) direction in the septum. In V₅ the QRS complex consists of a broad notched R wave. The first part of the R wave is of course septal in origin, and the balance is due to late excitation of the free wall of the left ventricle. Excitation of the ventricles is thus mostly from right to left throughout the period of activation, and this is the reason why Q waves are not seen in lead I or in the left chest leads when left branch block is present.

Myocardial infarction causes abnormalities of the QRS complexes because living muscle capable of excitation becomes electrically inert and voltages due to activation disappear. How characteristic the QRS changes are depends on how large the infarct is, whether it is transmural or not, where it is located, and how close it is to the exploring electrode of a lead. Infarcts involving the septum primarily are often not associated with QRS changes suggesting infarction but may cause intraventricular block and A-V block. Subendocardial infarction in the free wall of the left ventricle usually does not cause alterations in the QRS complexes typical of infarction, although some decrease in size of R waves in leads with electrodes over the area involved may occur. Inverted T waves may appear in several chest leads when an anterior subendocardial infarct is fairly recent, presumably owing to the fact that recovery is abnormal in living muscle on the epicardial surface overlying the infarct.

Figure 18–14A illustrates a transmural infarct with more extensive involvement of the subendocardial muscle and the type of QRS complexes that would be obtained with direct and semidirect leads over the area of infarc-

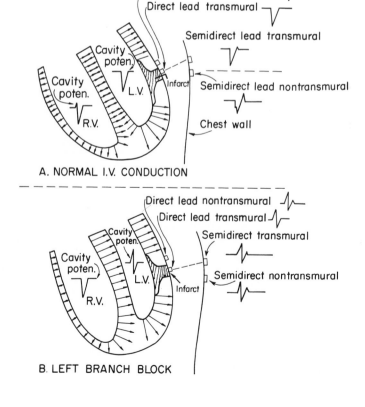

Figure 18–14. *A,* Illustrates the cause for QRS changes occurring with transmural or extensive nontransmural infarction in direct and semidirect leads when normal intraventricular conduction is present. *B,* Indicates why these changes are not seen when left branch block is also present. See text.

tion. Tracings from the center of the infarct show QS waves because there is no living muscle in the wall of the left ventricle between the electrode and the cavity of the left ventricle and therefore no excitation wave passing toward the electrode to make it positive and to give an upward deflection. This may also be expressed in terms of the potential of the cavity of the left ventricle. Except when left bundle branch block is present, the potential within this cavity is negative throughout the period of ventricular excitation, and with transmural infarction external leads with an electrode on or facing the infarct assume the potential within the cavity.

A direct or indirect lead, taken from a more peripheral area *of the infarct* where living responsive muscle is present on the epicardial surface of the ventricle (Fig. 18–14A), will show an abnormally large, broad Q wave and a final (often late) R wave of varying size. The large Q wave is due to transmission of negativity from the cavity of the left ventricle to the external electrode until the epicardial muscle is excited. If the area of subendocardial infarction is large, excitation of living epicardial muscle may be delayed, and this is peri-infarction block. Here the QRS interval is usually increased primarily in the leads with electrodes located close to the infarct.

If the above matters are clearly understood and it is remembered that electrodes, direct, semidirect, or remote, facing an infarct will show either abnormally large Q waves or QS waves, the QRS changes to be expected with infarction in both limb and chest leads will be obvious. Thus, with strictly anterior infarction QRS changes are seen in one or more of the routine chest leads, and if the infarct is anterolateral in location, changes are found in the left chest leads (V_5 and V_6) and also in leads I and aV_L because the infarct faces the left shoulder and modifies the potential of the left arm. With inferior or diaphragmatic infarcts the infarct faces downward and causes QRS changes to appear in aV_F and in leads II and III. Strictly posterior infarcts are not very common but may not be recognized in ordinary electrocardiograms largely because chest leads are not taken over the left posterior chest very often. For reasons mentioned earlier, such posterior leads are not as valuable for sampling potentials on the posterior surface of the heart as are the usual anterior chest leads for studying potentials present on its anterior surface.

Figure 18–14B illustrates why QRS changes due to infarction are usually absent when left bundle branch block is also present. Since the septum is excited from right to left, the potential in the cavity of the left ventricle is initially positive, and therefore Q waves and QS waves will not be seen in leads taken with an electrode facing an infarct. This means, of course, that when left branch block is present, electrocardiograms have less value in the diagnosis of myocardial infarction than when normal intraventricular conduction is present. This difficulty does not arise when right branch block exists, because here the cavity of the left ventricle has a negative potential throughout the period of ventricular excitation and the usual QRS changes due to infarction are preserved.

Vectorcardiography

Enough has already been said about ordinary scalar electrocardiograms and vectorcardiograms to make it clear that the latter are closely related to the former. The vector figures contain no information not present in the two scalar records that are combined, usually by means of the cathode ray tube, to produce them.

Einthoven, many years ago, was aware of the vectorcardiogram in the frontal plane. Mann, about 45 years ago, constructed vector figures from two of the standard leads and called them monocardiograms. The idea of vectorcardiography is therefore not new, but little attention was paid to it until necessary electronic equipment and the cathode ray tube became available, making it possible to record the vector loops in a simple and accurate fashion. Wilson and Johnston assembled the necessary equipment and began to take vectorcardiograms in the frontal plane in 1937, and at about the same time Schellong and Hollmann and Hollmann in Germany described similar work. Figure 18–15 shows the arrangements and circuits employed to obtain the vectorcardiogram in the frontal plane by Wilson and Johnston. Here lead I is amplified and connected to the horizontal deflecting plates of the cathode ray tube and V_F is amplified and connected to the vertical plates of the tube. The voltages of lead I cause the electron beam within the tube to move back and forth transversely, and those of V_F cause the beam to move simultaneously up and down in a vertical direction. The beam of electrons causes a bright blue fluorescent spot when it strikes a suitable coating on the inner surface of the base of the tube, and with each heartbeat the spot traces out a series of three loops which correspond to

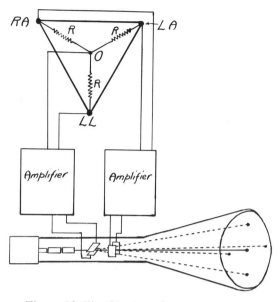

Figure 18–15. Circuit and equipment used by Wilson and Johnston to record vectorcardiograms in the frontal plane. See text. (From Wilson, F. N., and Johnston, F. D.: Am. Heart J., *16*:14, 1938.)

the P waves, QRS complexes, and T waves. The polarity is arranged so that an upward deflection in lead I causes the spot to move toward the right of an observer facing the base of the tube and an upward deflection in V_F (or aV_F) causes a downward movement of the spot. Figure 18–16*A* shows a vectorcardiogram taken with this technique on a subject with a normal heart, and Figure 18–16*B* is a vectorcardiogram taken on a patient with left axis deviation due to left ventricular hypertrophy. The loops corresponding to the relatively small P and T waves are not well seen in these vectorcardiograms, but with greater amplification and other special electronic techniques available today these loops may be clearly visualized and recorded.

From the earlier discussion concerning the behavior of the limb leads it should be clear that the vectorcardiograms shown in Figure 18–16 are not entirely accurate figures in the frontal plane. This is true largely because lead I does not provide transverse (X) components of cardiac voltages in pure form, and

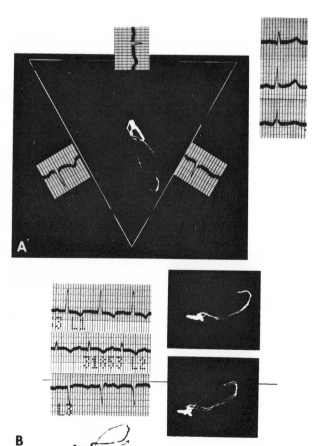

Figure 18–16. Vectorcardiograms in the frontal plane taken with arrangements shown in Figure 18–15. *A* was taken from a normal subject and *B* from a patient with left axis deviation and left ventricular hypertrophy.

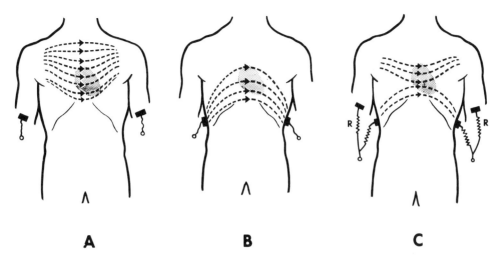

Figure 18–17. Corrected lead I to obtain a better X lead. *A,* Lead field of lead I alone. *B,* Lead field of a lead with electrodes in each midaxilla below the level of the heart. *C,* When lead I and the lead shown in *B* are combined, the resulting lead field has a more transverse direction through the heart. (From McFee, R., and Johnston, F. D.: Circulation, 9:868, 1954.)

a lead arrangement that would have a uniform transversely oriented lead field through the heart (Fig. 18–9A) combined with V_F or a lead with one electrode on the neck and the other on the left leg would give more accurate frontal plane vector figures. Corrected lead I suggested by McFee and Johnston (Fig. 18–17) would be superior to ordinary lead I for the X lead; a lead arrangement with several electrodes, each connected through large equal resistances to a common terminal, placed in the two axillae at the cardiac level would be even better.

If vectorcardiograms in the horizontal plane are desired, a lead providing transverse (X) components of cardiac voltages is connected to the horizontal plates and a lead giving

sagittal (Z) components to the vertical plates of the cathode ray tube. Polarity is arranged so that an upward deflection in the X lead causes the fluorescent spot to move to the right of an observer facing the tube and an upward deflection in the Z lead causes the spot to move downward. To record a vectorcardiogram in the sagittal plane, the Z lead is connected to the horizontal plates and the vertical (Y) lead to the vertical plates of the tube. If right sagittal vector figures (the sagittal plane being viewed from the patient's right side) are to be recorded, the polarity to obtain this requires that an upward deflection in the Z lead will move the spot toward the observer's right and an upward deflection in the Y lead will cause the spot to

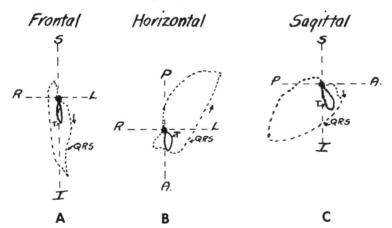

Figure 18–18. Vectorcardiograms taken in the frontal, horizontal, and right sagittal planes on a normal subject. R—right, L—left, S—superior, I—inferior, A—anterior, and P—posterior. (From Johnston, F. D.: Circulation, 23:297, 1961.)

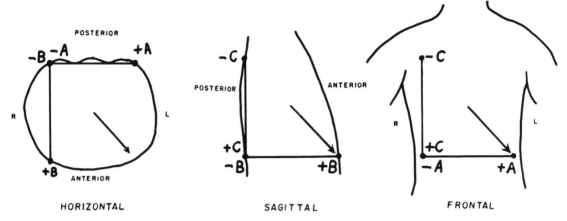

Figure 18–19. Scheme for placement of electrodes used in the cube system for vectorcardiography. See text. (From Grishman, A., and Scherlis, L.: Spatial Vectorcardiography. Philadelphia, W. B. Saunders Co., 1952.)

move downward. Figure 18–18 shows vectorcardiograms in the frontal, horizontal, and sagittal planes taken on a subject with a normal heart.

Duchosal and Sulzer carried out extensive early vectorcardiographic studies recording many records of this kind in the horizontal and sagittal planes as well as in the frontal plane. From the vector figures in any two of these three planes they constructed wire loop models which represented the spatial vectorcardiogram. These workers used a lead system with four electrodes on the thorax as far away from and as nearly equidistant from the heart as possible. Grishman and Sherlis have introduced a similar arrangement known as the cube system which has been extensively used in this country (Fig. 18–19). Burch and associates have used the equilateral tetrahedron system for vectorcardiography. Here, lead I is used for the transverse (X) component of heart voltages, V_F (or aV_F) for the vertical (Y) component, and a unipolar lead with an electrode on the left posterior chest, directly behind the heart, is used to provide the sagittal (Z) component.

We have seen earlier that lead I is not a very good X lead and the lead field of the sagittal (Z) component, used with the tetrahedron system, shows so much curvature especially in anterior parts of the heart (Fig. 18–20C) that of the three leads used in this system the vertical (Y) lead is the only one that is satisfactory. If one visualizes the lead fields that exist with the cube system, it is obvious that this arrangement cannot provide even approximately accurate representations of the transverse, vertical, and sagittal components of heart voltages. For example, the

electrodes for the "sagittal" component are located on the right lower anterior and posterior aspects of the chest, and the only place where the lead field would have a primarily anterior-posterior direction would be between these electrodes. The lead field through the heart is weak and has marked transverse and vertical curvature (Fig. 18–20A). What do these things mean? Unless leads that yield reasonably accurate X, Y, and Z components of cardiac voltages are employed for vectorcardiography, the figures obtained will not be in the frontal, horizontal, and sagittal planes at all but in warped uncertain planes. Nevertheless, they are referred to as vectorcardiograms in the frontal, horizontal, and sagittal planes, and some of the most enthusiastic vectorcardiographers use and defend the cube system as providing information not available in ordinary scalar records. It is possible, of course, that by chance some electrocardiographic alterations helpful in diagnosis may appear in exaggerated form in almost any kind of lead and hence in vector figures obtained by combining this lead with another.

One of the greatest problems in vectorcardiography today is the lack of general agreement concerning the kinds of leads that should be employed, but in the last few years there has been increasing use of arrangements that provide reasonably good orthogonal components of cardiac voltages, and hopefully this trend will continue.

There has been enough work done recently to indicate that vectorcardiograms, taken with systems devised by Frank, Schmitt and Simonson, McFee and Parungao, and with other multiple electrode arrangements, are similar and are quite accurate representations of the

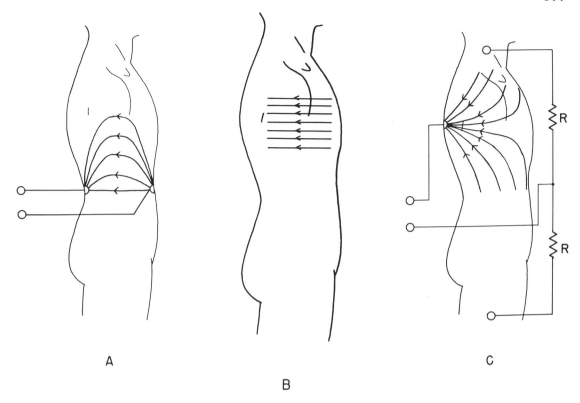

A

B

C

Figure 18–20. *A,* Marked curvature of the lead field through the heart when the cube system is used for the sagittal (Z) lead. *B,* The lead field of an ideal sagittal lead. *C,* The lead field for the sagittal lead used with the tetrahedron system. (From McFee, R., and Johnston, F. D.: Circulation, 9:255, 1954.)

spatial loops in the frontal, horizontal, and sagittal planes.

The writer believes that a good orthogonal lead system should be equally good to record ordinary scalar electrocardiograms and vectorcardiograms and hopes to see the day arrive when for many purposes three scalar tracings, X, Y, and Z, will take the place of the 12 lead electrocardiogram now routinely recorded. Physicians having the equipment and interest in vector presentation may take vectorcardiograms as well. Johnston has discussed these and related matters in more detail elsewhere.

A great deal of space could be devoted to illustrative figures and discussion of the changes occurring in vectorcardiograms in various cardiac abnormalities such as myocardial infarction and bundle branch block. If one remembers, however, that the vector figures represent the termini of the instantaneous electrical axes that exist during excitation (and recovery) projected on frontal, horizontal, and sagittal planes (see Fig. 18–10), and also knows how various cardiac lesions will alter excitation in the ventricles, the nature of changes that appear in QRS

loops when certain lesions are present should be obvious. Thus with inferior or diaphragmatic myocardial infarction the instantaneous electrical axes occurring during the early part of and sometimes throughout excitation of the ventricles point from below upward. These vectors cause the broad Q waves or QS waves seen in leads aV_F, II, and III and must also alter the form of the vector figures in the frontal and sagittal planes where the *abnormal* vertical (Y) component is combined with the transverse (X) and sagittal (Z) components respectively. Figure 18–21 shows the limb and chest leads and the vectorcardiograms that are found with inferior myocardial infarction. Figure 18–22 shows the conventional scalar electrocardiograms and vectorcardiograms when complete right branch block is present. If the reader understands the relations between scalar tracings and vector figures, how right branch block alters intraventricular conduction, and how leads work, he should have no trouble understanding Figure 18–22, and this section on electrocardiography will have been worthwhile.

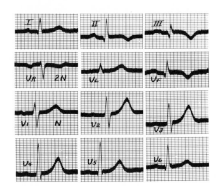

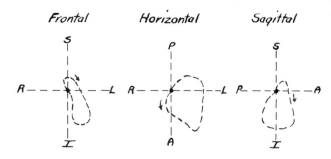

Figure 18–21. The scalar electrocardiogram and vectorcardiograms from a patient with fairly recent inferior infarction. QRS loops only are shown in the vector figures. See text.

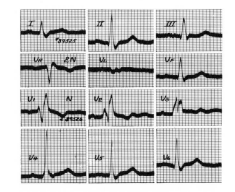

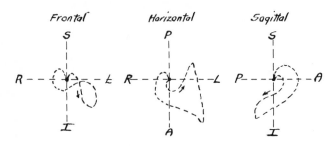

Figure 18–22. Scalar electrocardiograms and vectorcardiograms from a patient with complete right branch block.

REFERENCES

Alzamora-Castro, V., Battilana, G., and Abugattas, R.: The electrical manifestations observed in damaged or injured cardiac muscle. An experimental study. Am. Heart J., 54:254, 1957.

Ashman, R.: The normal human ventricular gradient. Am. Heart J., 26:495, 1943.

Bayley, R. H., LaDue, J. S., and York, D. J.: Electrocardiographic changes (local ventricular ischemia and injury) produced in the dog by temporary occlusion of a coronary artery, showing a new stage in the evolution of myocardial infarction. Am. Heart J., 27:164, 1944.

Brody, D. A., Harris, T. R., and Romans, W. E.: A simple method of obtaining esophageal electrocardiograms of good diagnostic quality. Am. Heart J., 50:923, 1955.

Burch, G. E., Abildskov, J. A., and Cronvich, J. A.: The Spatial Vectocardiogram. Philadelphia, Lea and Febiger, 1954.

Burger, H. C., and van Milaan, J. B.: Heart vector and leads I, II, III. Brit. Heart J., 8:157, 1946; 9:154, 1947; 10:229, 1948.

Draper, M. H., and Weidmann, S.: Cardiac resting and action potentials recorded with an intracellular electrode. J. Physiol. (London), 115:74, 1951.

Duchosal, P. W., and Sulzer, R.: La Vectorcardiographie. Basle, S. Karger, 1949.

Frank, E.: Spread of current in volume conductors of finite extent. The electrophysiology of the heart. Ann. New York Acad. Sc., 65:980, 1957.

Frank, E.: An accurate, clinically practical system for spatial vectocardiography. Circulation, 13:737, 1956.

Gardberg, M., and Rosen, I. L.: The ventricular gradient of Wilson. The electrophysiology of the heart. Ann. New York Acad. Sc., 65:873, 1957.

Goldberger, E.: A simple indifferent electrocardiographic electrode of zero potential and a technique of obtaining augmented unipolar extremity leads. Am. Heart J., 23:483, 1942.

Grishman, A., and Scherlis, L.: Spatial Vectocardiography. Philadelphia, W. B. Saunders Co., 1952.

Hoffman, B. F., and Cranefield, P. F.: Electrophysiology of the Heart. New York, Blakiston Division, McGraw-Hill Book Co., 1960.

Hoffman, B. F., and Suckling, E. E.: Cellular potentials of intact mammalian hearts. Am. J. Physiol., 170:357, 1952.

Hollmann, W., and Hollmann, H. E.: Neue elektrokardiographische Untersuchungsmethode. Ztschr. f. Kreislaufforsch., 29:546, 1937.

Johnston, F. D.: Electrocardiography. In Glasser, O. (ed.): Medical Physics. Chicago, Year Book Publishers, 1960, Vol. 3, p. 237.

Johnston, F. D.: The clinical value of vectorcardiography. Circulation, 23:297, 1961.

Katcher, A. H., Pierce, G., and Sayen, J. J.: Effects of experimental regional ischemia and levarterenol on the RS-T segment and baseline of ventricular surface electrocardiograms obtained by direct-coupled amplification. Circ. Res., 8:29, 1960.

Lepeschkin, E.: Modern Electrocardiography. Baltimore, Williams & Wilkins Co., 1951.

Ling, G., and Gerard, R. W.: The normal membrane potential of frog sartorius fibers. J. Cell. & Comp. Physiol., 34:383, 1949.

Mann, H.: A method of analyzing the electrocardiogram. Arch. Int. Med., 25:283, 1920.

McFee, R., and Johnston, F. D.: Electrocardiographic leads I, II, and III. Circulation, 8:554, 1953; 9:255, 1954; 9:868, 1954.

McFee, R., and Parungao, A.: An orthogonal lead system for clinical electrocardiography. Am. Heart J., 62:93, 1961.

Reynolds, E. W., Jr., and Yu, P. N.: Transmyocardial temperature gradient in dog and man. Relation to the polarity of the T wave of the electrocardiogram. Circ. Res., 15:11, 1964.

Samson, W. E., and Scher, A. M.: Mechanism of S-T segment alteration during acute myocardial injury. Circ. Res., 8:780, 1960.

Schellong, F.: Vektordiagraphie des Herzens als klinische Methode. Klin. Wchnschr., 17:453, 1938.

Scher, A. M., and Young, A. C.: The pathway of ventricular depolarization in the dog. Circ. Res., 4:461, 1956.

Schmitt, O. H.: Lead vectors and transfer impedance. The electrophysiology of the heart. Ann. New York Acad. Sc., 65:1092, 1957.

Sodi-Pallares, D., and Calder, R. M.: New Bases of Electrocardiography. St. Louis, C. V. Mosby Co., 1956.

Wilson, F. N., and Johnston, F. D.: The vectorcardiogram. Am. Heart J., 16:14, 1938.

Wilson, F. N., Johnston, F. D., MacLeod, A. G., and Barker, P. S.: Electrocardiograms that represent the potential variations of a single electrode. Am. Heart J., 9:447, 1934.

Wilson, F. N., MacLeod, A. G., and Barker, P. S.: The T deflection of the electrocardiogram. Tr. A. Am. Physicians, 46:29, 1931.

Woodbury, L. A., Hecht, H. H., and Christopherson, A. R.: Membrane resting and action potentials of single cardiac muscle fibers of the frog ventricle. Am. J. Physiol., 164:307, 1951.

Chapter Nineteen

Cardiac Output;
Hypertrophy and Dilatation;
Valvular Diseases; Congenital
Defects; Pericardial Diseases;
Extracardiac Factors

EDGAR HULL

The Output of the Heart

METHODS OF ESTIMATION

The only methods in common use which permit reasonably accurate estimation of the cardiac output in man are those which apply the Fick principle or the dye dilution principle.

The Fick Principle

In 1870 Fick pointed out that the difference between the concentrations of oxygen in arterial and mixed venous blood represents the amount of oxygen taken up by each unit of blood as it flows through the lungs. If, in addition, the total amount of oxygen absorbed in a given period of time is known, the amount of blood flowing through the lungs during that period may be calculated by means of the following formula:

$$\frac{O_2 \text{ absorption}}{\text{Arterial } O_2 \text{ content} - \text{venous } O_2 \text{ content}} = \text{blood flow}$$

Obviously, the blood flow through the lungs represents the output of the right ventricle. In the absence of shunting, the output of the left ventricle is the same.

For application of the formula, assume oxygen consumption to be 240 ml. per minute, arterial oxygen content 19 volumes per 100 ml., venous oxygen content 13 volumes per 100 ml.

$$\frac{240}{19 - 13} \times 100 = 4000 \text{ ml./min. (4 liters)}$$

Direct Fick Method. Oxygen intake is determined in the usual way. A sample of arterial blood is obtained by puncture of an accessible artery. Mixed venous blood is obtained from the pulmonary artery by venous catheterization (Fig. 19–1), the assumption being made that blood from the two venae cavae and the coronary sinus is thoroughly mixed at this site. Both samples are analyzed for oxygen content, and the Fick equation is applied. Indirect methods employing the Fick principle were very valuable before the advent of cardiac catheterization, but are no longer used.

The Dye Dilution Principle

In 1897 Stewart pointed out that, if a known amount of a detectable substance is rapidly injected into a vein, its subsequent concentration during the time of its passage through an artery must be inversely related to the amount of blood which flows from the vein to the artery during this time—i.e., to the circulation rate or cardiac output—and devised a method for estimation of the cardiac output in dogs, using sodium chloride as the detectable substance.

Many years later Hamilton and associates devised a dye injection method based upon this principle, indicating the relations by the formula

$$f = \frac{I}{ct}$$

where f is the flow rate, I is the amount of dye injected into the vein, c the average concentration of the dye in multiple samples drawn from an artery during the first circulation of the dye, and t the time required for this first circulation.

The validity of the formula is obvious. I is of course a known factor, but there are difficulties in determining c and t, since recirculation begins before all the dye has passed the point of sampling on the first circulation.

The authors found, however, in working with models which did not permit recirculation that the concentration curve of the dye in samples taken, if plotted on semilogarithmic paper, descended in a straight line (Fig. 19–2, *A*). In models which permit recirculation, the onset of recirculation is marked by a break in the straight line of the descending limb, usually followed by a secondary rise (Fig. 19–2, *B*); they found, further, that when the dye is injected into an animal the concentration curve of arterial samples is much like that of the recirculating models. They then assumed that by extrapolation downward of the straight portion of the descending limb a curve may be constructed which would have been obtained if the dye had not recirculated (Fig. 19–3). From this curve the values of c and t are obtainable.

Dye Injection (Indicator-Dilution) Method

In the currently used modification of Hamilton's technique, Evans blue dye is injected rapidly intravenously, and the curve of its subsequent arterial concentration recorded directly by the use of a cuvette oximeter. The

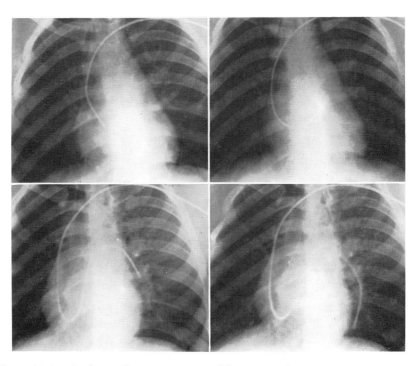

Figure 19–1. Cardiac catheterization, normal heart. Tip of catheter shown successively in right atrium, right ventricle, left pulmonary artery, pulmonary "capillary."

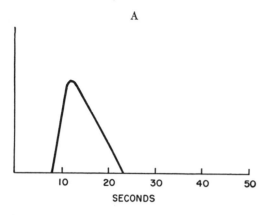

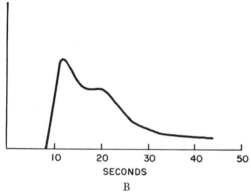

Figure 19–2. *A,* Dye concentration curve (schematic) in a nonrecirculating model (see text). *B,* Dye concentration curve (schematic) in a model which permits recirculation (see text).

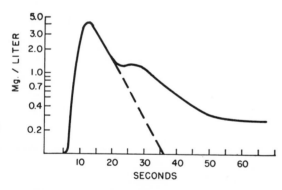

Figure 19–3. Extrapolated curve of dye concentration as described in text.

curve is replotted on semilogarithmic paper, then extrapolated as described above, its duration (t) measured, and the average concentration of the dye (c) calculated.

Example: Suppose that the amount of dye injected (I) is 5 mg., its average arterial concentration as calculated from the curve is 3.33 mg. per liter (c), the duration of the curve is thirty seconds (t). Then:

$$f = \frac{5}{3.33 \times 30} = 0.05 \text{ liter per second, or 3 liters per}$$
minute.

Estimations of output by indicator-dilution methods are unreliable in the presence of shunts between the sites of injection and sampling (although useful in the detection of shunts) or if there is significant valvular insufficiency (though useful in studying the hemodynamics of such cases), because "abnormal" curves are recorded due to early recirculation in one instance and "back and forth" movement of blood in the other.

Expression of the Cardiac Output

Figures for cardiac output may be expressed in three ways:

(1) *Minute volume,* or *circulation rate*—the output per minute
(2) *Stroke volume*—the output per beat
(3) *Cardiac index*—the minute volume per square meter of body surface

Methods using the Fick or dye principle yield the minute volume, from which the stroke volume may be determined by dividing by the heart rate. The cardiac index is determined by dividing the minute volume by the body surface in square meters.

Normal Cardiac Output

In normal persons the output is most closely related to body size and rate of metabolism; hence the most constant and most accurately predictable value is the cardiac index in the basal state. In this state the *cardiac index* averages about 3 liters in normal adults, with a range of 2 to 4. The basal *minute volume,* which varies with body size, ranges from 2 to 6 or 7 liters. The *stroke volume,* which in addition varies with heart rate, ranges from about 50 to 100 ml. In a 70 kg. man the normal minute output is about 5 liters per minute, the stroke volume (at a heart rate of 70) about 70 ml. There are no strictly normal factors which will reduce the circulation rate below the basal level; hence practically all the normal variations relate to increase of output above that in the basal state.

In essence, stroke volume depends upon three factors: the amount of blood in the ventricle(s) when systole begins, the contractile power of the ventricle(s) at any given end-diastolic volume, and the resistance which opposes ejection. Augmentation of stroke volume may therefore be effected by increase in return flow during any given diastolic period, by primary increase in contractile power, or by decrease in arteriolar "tone." Further, within limits minute volume may be augmented by increase in rate (more beats per unit of time with little or no decline in filling per beat).

Increase in return flow may be afforded on a short-term basis by exercise or by mobilization of blood stores from the splanchnic region, on a long-term basis by increase of blood volume; primary strengthening of contractile power through mediation of the adrenergic nerves and epinephrine and norepinephrine; decrease of peripheral resistance by autonomic interplay and by the effect of epinephrine.

Interplay of the three factors (Fig. 19–4) enables the heart to vary its output in accordance with the demands of the body. Normal factors which increase the need or demand for blood flow therefore bring about an increase in the circulation rate; these include exercise, excitement, eating, high environmental temperature, and pregnancy.

ABNORMALITIES OF CARDIAC OUTPUT NOT RELATED TO CARDIOVASCULAR DISEASE

Abnormal conditions which increase or decrease the need or demand for blood flow (principally, probably the demand for oxygen) affect in corresponding manner the output of the heart, whether it is healthy or diseased. Thus the output is increased in anxiety states, in hyperthyroidism, fever and other hypermetabolic conditions, in severe anemia, obesity,* emphysema and other hypoxic states, and in beriberi (defective tissue oxidation). It is reduced in myxedema, Sheehan's disease, starvation and other hypometabolic states.

Abnormal increase or decrease of output may occur, however, without respect to oxygen demand; such abnormalities are due to primary increase or decrease of venous return

---

*In fat persons without heart disease the increase in cardiac output is entirely attributable to flow through the adipose tissue; renal, cerebral, splanchnic and muscle flow are normal, not increased.

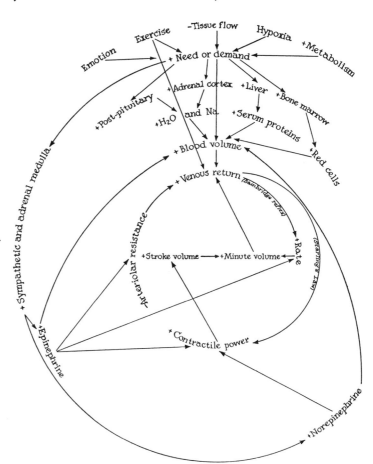

Figure 19–4. Mechanisms for increasing cardiac output.

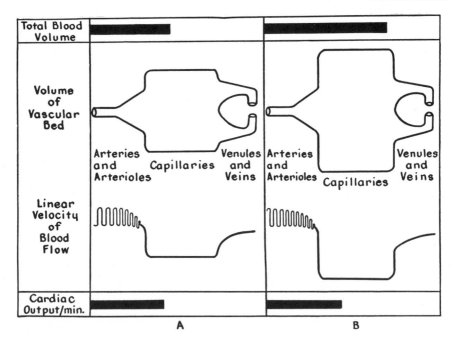

Figure 19–5. Explanation of normal cardiac output despite increase of blood volume in polycythemia vera.

to the heart. The outstanding example of decrease is severe diminution of effective blood volume such as occurs in hemorrhage, trauma, burns, splanchnic pooling in bacteremia, etc.; in these cases the deficit in venous return cannot be overcome without outside help, regardless of the need for restoration of tissue flow. Examples of primary increase in venous return (and of output) are arteriovenous shunting in the bones in cases of Paget's disease, and venous shunting between the portal and caval systems in some cases of portal cirrhosis of the liver. Interestingly, in polycythemia vera, the one disease characterized by primary increase of blood volume, cardiac output is not increased; it appears that in this instance effective blood volume is maintained at a normal level by accommodation of the excess volume in the capillary bed (Fig. 19–5).

THE CARDIAC OUTPUT IN CARDIOVASCULAR ABNORMALITIES

Except in the case of shunting (discussed below), heart disease per se is never responsible for an increase in the circulation rate above the normal. Disease of the heart muscle, deformity of the valves, or increase in peripheral resistance—each of these factors would tend to reduce output, and, if any of these factors exist in severe form, or appear

suddenly, or persist for long periods, reduction of output, or heart failure, does in fact occur. In order to prevent or to overcome reduction of output, the same mechanisms are brought into play which enable the normal heart to increase its output on demand. That these devices are often successful is attested by the fact that for many years cardiac output may be maintained at normal or near normal levels in spite of extensive destruction of heart muscle by infarction, or in the presence of marked hypertension; and, further, by the fact that within a few days or weeks following a catastrophic occurrence such as acute massive myocardial infarction, the circulation rate, at first critically reduced, may be reasonably adequate.

This background should enable the reader to understand the status of the cardiac output in the conditions mentioned below; details are to be found in sections which deal with the different conditions individually.

Cardiac Arrhythmias

The period of most rapid ventricular filling occurs early in diastole, while intraventricular pressure is yet low. Moderate *increases* in heart rate therefore do not affect the minute volume, although they cause diminution of the stroke volume. The minute volume of a normal heart, other factors being equal, is not altered by rates up to 150 per minute. The anticipated increase of output does not occur; there is no need for it. Extremely rapid rates, such as those which occur in the *paroxysmal tachycardias,* encroach upon the period of rapid filling and result in significant reduction of output in some cases, but probably not in all. In *sinus bradycardia* with rates as slow as 50 or even lower, minute volume is not altered if the heart is normal, stroke volume being considerably increased.

In *atrial fibrillation* the minute output is usually reduced, because (1) ventricular rhythm being grossly irregular, many of the ventricular beats occur so early as to shorten the period of rapid filling; and (2) the absence of atrial contraction diminishes late diastolic ventricular filling and brings about less efficient closure of the atrioventricular valves.

In the presence of normal coordinated contractions of atria and ventricles, the increased rate of atrioventricular flow produced by atrial contraction causes the a-v valves to move upward to a position of near-closure just before the onset of ventricular systole. If the atria are not beating (or if their contraction is not coordinated with the onset of ventricular systole) this upward movement fails to occur and the a-v valves are more widely open when ventricular contraction begins. Since the papillary muscles contract simultaneously with the ventricles, closure of the a-v valves may be delayed resulting in some early regurgitation, particularly through the mitral orifice. (The mitral valve is less efficient than the tricuspid.)

Regurgitation due to this factor must be of slight degree, significant only if other more serious factors are operating which tend to reduce cardiac output. There is no doubt, however, that in patients with heart disease and atrial fibrillation in whom the rate is well controlled with digitalis, conversion to sinus rhythm is often followed by prompt increase in cardiac output and dramatic clinical improvement. Conversely, recurrence of atrial fibrillation in such patients may again precipitate heart failure.

In other arrhythmias in which the rate is rapid, the rhythm irregular, or the sequence of atrial and ventricular beats uncoordinated, cardiac output may be reduced, particularly if the heart is diseased. Examples are *ventricular tachycardia, a-v nodal rhythms,* various types of atrioventricular dissociation, and frequent *ventricular* or *a-v nodal premature beats.* In ventricular tachycardia abnormal sequence of ventricular contraction itself (asynergy) may contribute to reduced output.

In most persons with *complete atrioventricular block* basal cardiac output is subnormal even though the ventricular rate is not extremely slow, but in some cases with rates as slow as 30 the minute volume at rest is within the lower limits of normal; undoubt-

edly the condition of the myocardium is critical in this regard. Exercise in all cases induces much less than normal increase of output (or no increase at all) because of inability of the ventricles to accelerate.

If (as in most cases of complete a-v block) ventricular rate is slow and output subnormal, and the rate is stepped up by medication (isoproterenol) or by the use of an electrical pacemaker, output almost invariably improves and signs of heart failure (if previously present) usually ameliorate. The ideal rate in such cases appears to be in the range of 65 to 75. Such a rate can be maintained with safety by use of a pacemaker, but not with isoproterenol.

The heart which is normal (except as regards its rate and rhythm) can withstand rather marked increase or decrease in its rate and considerable chaos in its rhythm with little or no decrease in output, but in the diseased heart arrhythmias often seriously compromise its ability to maintain an output which is minimally adequate for tissue perfusion. Particularly pernicious are the arrhythmias which complicate acute myocardial infarction, and digitalis therapy in congestive heart failure.

Valvular Disease

In *insufficiency* it is perhaps reasonably accurate to say that the *net* output is not altered if the myocardium remains fully competent, although the *gross* stroke volume of the ventricle affected by the leak is increased by the extra amount of blood which flows into it during diastole. Nevertheless, output is often distinctly subnormal in cases of high grade mitral insufficiency in the absence of overt signs of heart failure. Full compensation for severe regurgitation through either of the a-v orifices is practically impossible (p. 401).

In high grade *stenosis* of either the mitral or the tricuspid valve, cardiac output is reduced; the obstruction causes diminished filling of the affected ventricle; its output, and therefore the output of the other ventricle as well, is reduced. In stenosis of slight or moderate degree the cardiac output is usually found to be normal. Stenosis of either semilunar valve does not alter the basal cardiac output so long as hypertrophy compensates for the obstruction, but inability of the heart quickly to increase its output in cases of high grade stenosis may lead to characteristic symptoms (p. 396).

Heart Failure

In congestive heart failure the cardiac out-

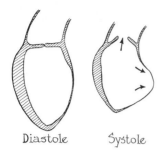

Figure 19–6. Paradoxical bulge during systole of large myocardial "scar."

put at rest is diminished in most but not in all cases. Decrease of cardiac output is therefore not a constant or essential feature of the physiologic picture of congestive failure. It appears, however, that a subnormal output, not necessarily in relation to the basal metabolic requirements, but to the need of the tissues for oxygen during activity, sets into play mechanisms for augmenting the circulation rate, and that one of these, increase of blood volume, is in large part responsible for the congestion of congestive failure.

Stewart and associates found, in a series of patients with organic heart disease, but without evidences of congestion, that average values for cardiac index and stroke volume were below normal. With the onset of congestive failure these average values were further reduced. It may be supposed that the following states obtain in persons with heart disease: If compensation is perfect, output is normal under all circumstances; if myocardial reserve is impaired, less than normal increase in output occurs with increasing metabolic needs; with more impairment, but still without congestive phenomena, output may be subnormal even at rest. Finally, it should be noted that in conditions which per se cause increased cardiac output—such as chronic hypoxic states (emphysema), hyperthyroidism, anemia and beriberi—the picture of congestive failure may occur in the presence of a high cardiac index; in this instance the stimulus to increased blood volume (and the consequent congestion) is inadequate output in proportion to demand (see Chap. 20).

With recovery from congestive failure (in chronic heart disease), cardiac output, if previously subnormal, usually but not always increases, but in most cases remains below normal even though freedom from congestion is maintained by therapy. There is no obligate relation between low output and congestive phenomena.

Myocardial Infarction

Cardiac output is reduced temporarily in the vast majority of cases of acute infarction (even the "mild" ones), because of cessation of contraction in the infarcted region and diminished power of adjacent ischemic muscle. Cardiac shock is the expression of sudden critical decline in cardiac output.

Even after clinically severe infarctions output may return to normal within a few weeks; in "mild" infarctions it usually does if the heart was previously normal.

After the infarct has healed, the victim of acute myocardial infarction is essentially a person with chronic organic heart disease, which may be of minor, intermediate or severe degree, and his status as regards cardiac output depends upon the size of the myocardial scar and the compensatory ability of the muscle which has escaped infarction. Large healed infarctions not only fail to contract, but actually bulge paradoxically as the healthy regions contract; considerable increments of contractile energy are expended thus rather than in moving blood onward (Fig. 19–6). This energy waste is particularly great in the case of ventricular aneurysms.

Other Cardiovascular Abnormalities

In *constrictive pericarditis*, large *pericardial effusions*, and *restrictive cardiomyopathies*, output is reduced because of interference with ventricular filling. Congenital and acquired *communications* between the chambers of the heart, between the aorta and the pulmonary artery, and between arteries and veins act to increase the output of one or both ventricles, and/or to alter the relative and absolute circulation rates in the greater and lesser circulations. The pathologic physiology of some of these conditions is considered later in this chapter.

Hypertrophy and Dilatation of the Heart

Hypertrophy refers to increase in the *diameter* of the muscle fibers of the heart; it is characterized by thickening of the walls of the chambers and by increase in heart weight. *Dilatation* refers to increase in the *length* of the fibers; it is characterized by increase in the volume of the cavities of the heart.

VENTRICULAR DILATATION AND HYPERTROPHY

Dilatation

Dilatation is one of the three mechanisms whereby the normal heart increases its output (see p. 382). *Physiologic dilatation* results from increased ventricular filling which stretches the muscle fibers and increases their diastolic length. This in accordance with Starling's law brings about increase of contractile force and augmentation of stroke volume. Although physiologic dilatation is a very important mechanism, its role in augmentation of rate in response to exercise is minor except in athletes and other persons adapted to strenuous exertion; in most of us increase in rate and to a lesser extent "primary" increase in contractile power (due to autonomic nerve interplay) are responsible for most of the increase in minute volume.

Starling stated the law of the heart as follows: "The energy of contraction is a function of the length of the muscle fiber." Again: "The larger the diastolic volume of the heart (within physiologic limits) the greater is the energy of its contraction. . . ." "The oxygen consumption . . . is determined by its diastolic volume, and therefore by the initial length of its muscular fibers. This rule applies whatever the physiologic condition of the heart."

Sonnenblick et al. have recently furnished an ultrastructural basis for Starling's law: "The force of contraction of cardiac muscle is a function of sarcomere length prior to the onset of contraction." Their work showed that increase in sarcomere length (and in muscle length) occurs by increase in the length of the I bands only without change in the A band or H zone (Fig. 19–7). The force of contraction appears to depend in part upon the disposition of the thinner actin filaments (which "slide" as the sarcomere lengthens and shortens) relative to the thicker fixed myosin filaments. (See also p. 458.)

If the fibers (sarcomeres) are stretched beyond physiologic limits, contractile force (as would be expected) falls off (Fig. 19–8). In the cat papillary muscle contractile power declines when sarcomere length exceeds 2.2μ.

In valvular insufficiency, septal defects, patent ductus arteriosus and arteriovenous fistulae, diastolic inflow to one or both ventricles is "permanently" augmented. In such conditions *physiologic dilatation* due to a *pathologic state* occurs. By this mechanism (and the hypertrophy which follows) the heart is often able to maintain a normal or near-normal circulation rate even if the leak or shunt is quite large.

If the contractile power of the heart muscle is weakened because of disease or ischemia or other factors affecting its metabolism, the ventricles may dilate because of increase in residual volume (at the end of systole) above the normal 60 ml. or so. This is *pathologic dilatation*. Pathologic dilatation also results in greater energy production so that for a time or in part the heart itself may compensate for its weakness.

There are, of course, limits to compensation by dilatation, attested to by the fact that the circulation rate in persons with very large hearts is nearly always subnormal. In the first place when fiber length exceeds a certain maximum (perhaps corresponding to sarcomere lengths of 0.2μ) contractile power falls off as the "hump" of Starling's curve is passed (Fig. 19–9). Excessive dilatation is self-defeating.

In the second place dilatation itself imposes a mechanical disadvantage upon the ventricle. As ventricular volume expands, a progressively larger portion of the mechanical energy of contraction is expended in imparting tension to the fibers and a correspondingly smaller portion in producing shortening of them. Burton estimates that if one heart

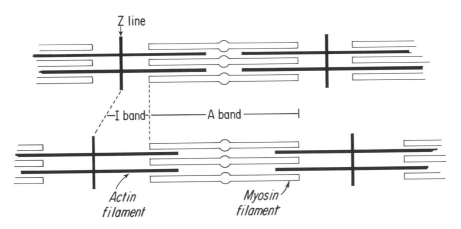

Figure 19–7. Diagram of sarcomere structure at shorter (above) and longer lengths. Lengthening is due only to increase in the I band. Myosin filaments (only in A band) do not participate. (From Sonnenblick, Spiro, and Spotnitz: American Heart Journal, *68*:336, 1964. The C. V. Mosby Co., St. Louis.)

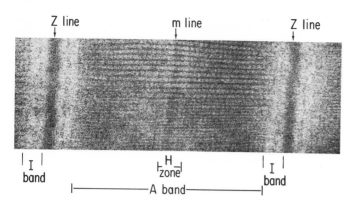

Figure 19-8. Electron microphotograph of a sarcomere. In this specimen the I band is quite narrow (short). If the sarcomere is stretched excessively (I band quite wide), contractile power falls off. Compare with Figure 19-7. (Courtesy of Dr. James A. Freeman.)

were twice as big in its linear dimensions as another, four times as much contractile power would be required to produce the same systolic pressure (or the same force directed toward the center of the ventricular cavity) in the larger heart. This disadvantage, however, is mitigated by the fact that the larger the heart the less shortening of its fibers is needed to produce a given stroke volume.

1. The law of Laplace states (in essence) that the pressure within a curved body of any shape is proportional to the tension in its walls and its principal radii of curvature according to the following equation:

$$P = T\left(\frac{1}{R_1} + \frac{1}{R_2}\right),$$

where P is pressure, T is tension, and R_1 and R_2 the principal radii of curvature. If both radii are doubled and P remains the same, T is quadrupled.

2. For simplicity's sake consider only a cross section of the left ventricle and assume it to be circular in shape. If the diastolic area is 15 cm.², the circumference is about 13.8 cm. If the systolic area were reduced by

7.5 cm.², the circumference would be reduced to 9.7 cm., representing shortening of the fibers by some 4 cm. If on the other hand the diastolic area is 30 cm.², and the circumference is about 19.4 cm., reduction of the area by 7.5 cm.² would be accomplished by diminution of the systolic circumference to 16.8 cm., and shortening of the fibers by only 2.2 cm.

The greatly dilated heart also works at a metabolic disadvantage, since regardless of its contractile power its metabolic rate (O_2 consumption) depends upon its diastolic volume.

Hypertrophy

Hypertrophy develops if dilatation persists for any considerable period of time. It also occurs in the absence of detectable enlargement of the heart (either clinically or at autopsy), in the latter instance usually in association with conditions which cause increased resistance to the outflow of blood during systole, as for example stenosis of one of the semilunar valves or increased peripheral resistance (hypertension). In some cases the factors which lead to hypertrophy are more subtle and sometimes not apparent. Hypertrophied fibers contract with greater power than their normal counterparts and (other things being equal) consume more oxygen and other substances which furnish energy for their contraction.

There is experimental evidence that both the ultrastructure and the metabolism of hypertrophied heart muscle are altered, as, for example, elongated mitochondria with disordered arrangement of the cristae, and decline in the oxidative and phosphorylative power of the mitochondria. As expected, protein synthesis in heart muscle has been found to be increased as hypertrophy develops.

Interestingly, Linzbach has reported that sarcomere length is not increased in the dilated, hypertrophied hearts of persons who have died in chronic congestive failure. His findings cast doubt upon the concept that overstretching of individual fibers plays a major role in chronic myocardial "weakness." Linzbach contends that the total number of fibers in hypertrophied hearts

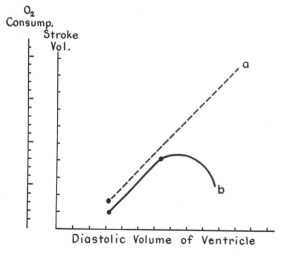

Figure 19-9. Effect of increasing diastolic volume on oxygen consumption (*a*) and output per beat (*b*).

is increased; that is, that there is also hyperplasia, that these hearts have "grown" bigger.

The Genesis of Hypertrophy.

Teleologically, the basis of cardiac hypertrophy is the need for more powerful contraction. *Pathogenetically,* the stimulus which induces hypertrophy appears to be the production, with each beat over a period of time, of total energy in excess of the normal or usual amount. It is likely that tension rather than diastolic length is crucial in the genesis of hypertrophy; were initial fiber length solely responsible, hypertrophy in the absence of dilatation could not occur.

1. Although resting tension rises with increasing diastolic fiber length, hypertrophy in the absence of dilatation obviously cannot be explained on the basis of an increase in resting tension. The common stimulus to hypertrophy (if indeed it *is* tension) must be the tension developed during systole, most likely related also to the duration of contraction. (In skeletal muscle total energy production is proportional to the force developed and the time it is maintained.)

2. This is not to say that diastolic tension may not be increased in hypertrophied but undilated hearts. Without doubt hypertrophied fibers resist stretching more than normal fibers do, and at a given diastolic volume the resting tension of hypertrophied fibers is probably increased. A hypertrophied chamber may therefore accept less blood at a given filling pressure; this mechanism may explain the occasional finding at necropsy of *concentric hypertrophy,* in which the cavity of a hypertrophied left ventricle is actually smaller than normal.

3. Although longstanding dilatation is always accompanied by hypertrophy, the latter is not infrequently absent or minimal in cases of longstanding hypertension and in congenital aortic stenosis. This apparent paradox may be explained as follows: for the undilated ventricle (as compared to one considerably dilated) the systolic tension required to produce a given intraventricular pressure is much less (see p. 388). Burch's calculations led him to conclude that "in the presence of hypertension, the 'load' or total force exerted upon the left ventricle of a heart of normal size is not considerably different . . . from that of the subject without hypertension and a normal sized heart."

Like dilatation, hypertrophy is *specific,* developing only in fibers subjected to stretching or increased tension (or to as yet unknown pathogenetic factors). Hypertrophy of the walls of a single chamber is therefore of common occurrence, and in many cases some portions of a ventricular wall are more hypertrophied than others. Less commonly hypertrophy is confined largely to one or another region of a ventricle.

In fact, hypertrophy seldom involves all regions of a given chamber to the same degree, nor indeed does dilatation. Undoubtedly a major factor in this lack of uniformity is the difference in principal radii of curvature in different portions of one or the other ventricle, which in accordance with the law of Laplace (see p. 388) affects differentially the tension of the fibers, tension being greater where the curvature of the walls is less (radii larger) (Fig. 19–10). This factor also (at least in some cases) is responsible for localized encroachment of hypertrophied regions upon the lumen during systole. Further, with dilatation comes change in shape, and with this come differences in tension and therefore differences in degree of hypertrophy. Even the sequence of contraction, whether or not it is altered by conduction defects, may play a role. Purely regional hypertrophy is probably best explained by localized disease or metabolic disorder.

The Causes of Dilatation and Hypertrophy.

From the physiologic viewpoint there are two causes of *ventricular dilatation:* increased diastolic filling and myocardial "weakness."

Increased ventricular filling may be due to normal factors, such as muscular exercise, or to abnormal conditions, such as valvular insufficiency, arteriovenous fistula and defects in the cardiac septa. Normal factors usually exist temporarily, lead only to transient dilatation, and affect both ventricles. Abnormal factors often exist permanently, cause permanent dilatation, and may affect either or both ventricles.

Myocardial "weakness" (by which is meant diminution of the contractile power of the ventricles at a given diastolic filling) is caused by destruction or degeneration of myocardial fibers or by factors which affect unfavorably the chemical changes that occur during contraction or during "recovery" between contractions. Such factors include, among others, the following: infarction; myocarditis or myocardial degeneration due to rheumatic fever, diphtheria or filtrable viruses or to protozoal, metazoal or mycotic organisms; amyloidosis, progressive systemic sclerosis, sarcoidosis or cancer involving the heart muscle; hypoxia due to ischemia or anemia; and thiamine or amino acid deficiency.

Ventricular hypertrophy is caused indirectly by the factors which cause dilatation, provided dilatation persists, and directly by con-

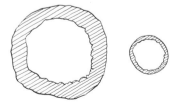

Figure 19–10. Schematic showing relative thickness of left ventricular muscle near apex (at right) and at a higher level where cavity is larger and curvature is less (at left).

ditions which cause increased resistance to the outflow of blood or interfere mechanically with ventricular contraction. Thus left ventricular hypertrophy occurs in systemic hypertension, aortic stenosis, coarctation of the aorta; the right ventricle hypertrophies in pulmonary stenosis and in conditions which cause increased resistance in the pulmonary circuit, such as mitral stenosis, emphysema and prolonged failure of the left ventricle.

In the majority of cases, hypertrophy which is detected by clinical methods or encountered at necropsy can be ascribed to one or more of the causes which we have mentioned. The hypertrophy in infantile *subendocardial fibroelastosis* may perhaps be ascribed to increased resistance to shortening of the fibers by the thickened, stiffened subendocardium. The same mechanism may operate in the restrictive type of so-called *primary cardiomyopathy*. In the congestive type of cardiomyopathy, dilatation probably precedes hypertrophy; in the more rare obstructive type, disease or metabolic disorder affecting principally the subaortic or submitral myocardium may be responsible for the hypertrophy which obstructs outflow or filling. The myocardiopathies themselves may be secondary to myocarditis due to some of the causes listed above, or due to alcoholism, or to genetically determined disorders of myocardial metabolism.

Normal Hypertrophy. Hypertrophy of the heart has been induced in dogs and rats by vigorous exercise over a period of time. The process is reversible, gradually receding after termination of the exercise period. Whether analogous hypertrophy develops in the hearts of athletes or other normal persons who engage in strenuous muscular exercise is not definitely known. It has been shown, however, that during exercise the hearts of trained athletes, as compared to those of untrained persons, compensate for increased venous return with relatively slight increases in rate; this must mean that the heart of the trained athlete undergoes relatively great physiologic dilatation during exercise. It is reasonable to assume that great physiologic dilatation, frequently repeated, may lead to the development of hypertrophy, which should be called "normal hypertrophy." There is no good evidence that normal hypertrophy, if it occurs, has any harmful effects.

The Reversibility of Hypertrophy. There is no way of telling whether or not hypertrophy of the human heart is reversible, since there are at present no methods whereby the progress of hypertrophy can be studied independently of dilatation and other myocardial changes. However, upon teleologic grounds and by analogy with experimental hypertrophy, it would be supposed that hypertrophy, being a compensatory process, is potentially reversible. It is highly probable that hypertrophy can at least be partially reversed by surgical or medical measures designed to remove or ameliorate its causes.

The Limitations of Dilatation and Hypertrophy. There are, of course, limits beyond which dilatation and hypertrophy fail to compensate for the abnormal conditions which caused them to develop. In the first place, compensation by dilatation is limited, fundamentally, by the degree of optimal dilatation beyond which the power of contractions diminishes, although oxygen consumption continues to increase as dilatation progresses.

An excellent example of the consequences of excessive dilatation is to be found in the effect of venesection on the cardiac output of patients with severe congestive heart failure. In such cases, rapid blood-letting may cause the output promptly to *increase*, the reverse of what would happen in normal subjects. The mechanism is as follows: The rapid removal of blood causes diminution of return flow to the heart. Diastolic intraventricular pressure falls, and dilatation diminishes. The ventricular muscle, previously overstretched, now more closely approaches the optimal degree of dilatation; it contracts more powerfully, and the output of the heart is increased.

Secondly, even though the degree of optimal dilatation has not been exceeded, the energy requirements of the dilated heart, and hence the need for coronary flow, are increased. A greatly dilated heart may therefore be hypoxic and its contractile power lessened even if coronary flow is unimpaired, much more so if irrigation of the heart muscle is diminished because of coronary artery disease.

Finally, dilatation cannot compensate adequately for sudden great increase in the load upon the heart occasioned, for example, by rupture of chordae tendineae or a sizable perforation of the ventricular septum; or for the weakness which immediately follows thrombosis of a major coronary artery. In such instances it seems likely that inadequate compensation is due in part to the fact that because of resistance to sudden stretching the fibers cannot elongate sufficiently; the degree of dilatation which can occur quickly is limited.

The limits of compensation by hypertrophy are also without doubt related at least in part to blood supply, since the need for energy-producing substances increases along with the progressive development of hypertrophy. Further, Roberts, Wearn and Boten have demonstrated that during hypertrophy the capillaries of the myocardium do not increase in number, but are pushed farther apart as the muscle fibers enlarge; the concentration of capillaries is thus decreased, and each capillary has to supply an increasing mass of muscle as the heart hypertrophies.

HYPERTROPHY AND DILATATION OF THE ATRIA

Qualitatively atrial hypertrophy and dilatation are identical with the same processes that affect the ventricles; they are due to the same factors, serve the same purpose, and are subject to the same limitations. They occur in conditions characterized by increased filling of the atria or by increased resistance to the outflow of blood from them. Within limits, dilated and hypertrophied atria contract with more power and thus compensate for the factors which caused them to dilate and which led to their hypertrophy.

Quantitatively atrial compensation compares quite favorably with that of the ventricles, especially when one considers that the atria are not equipped with valves to prevent backflow into their tributary veins during atrial systole. Witness, for example, the considerable hypertrophy with only slight dilatation of the left atrium often observed in severe longstanding mitral stenosis; without doubt atrial hypertrophy plays an important role in filling the ventricle in such cases.

Since no valves guard the inlets of the atria pathologic dilatation of these chambers is accompanied by dilatation of the thin-walled veins which empty into them, and increased resistance to atrial outflow necessarily results in increased resistance to flow in the tributary veins.

Augmented filling of *both* atria occurs in the presence of increased cardiac output; of the *left atrium* in mitral insufficiency and patent ductus arteriosus; of the *right atrium* in tricuspid insufficiency and atrial septal defect.

Increased filling seems to lead to atrial failure—i.e., pathologic dilatation—only if the augmented load is retrograde; that is, if it is due to backflow through either or both of the atrioventricular orifices. If augmented atrial flow comes via the veins or even through an atrial septal defect, only physiologic dilatation occurs in the absence of increased resistance to outflow.

The most important causes of *increased re-sistance to atrial outflow* are obstruction of the appertaining atrioventricular orifice, and impairment of the contractile power of the corresponding ventricle; in the latter instance the resistance to ventricular filling is increased because of the abnormally large amount of residual blood in the ventricle. Increased resistance alone seldom leads to great atrial dilatation; in "pure" mitral stenosis, for example, the left atrium is usually only slightly or moderately enlarged. Giant atria are observed frequently only when inflow and resistance to outflow are both increased; the left atrium in mitral insufficiency *and* left ventricular failure, the right atrium in tricuspid insufficiency or atrial septal defect with right ventricular failure.

Valvular Disease of the Heart

GENERAL CONSIDERATIONS

Distinction should be made between the effects of valve lesions per se and disturbances due to superimposed myocardial failure. Each type of lesion has effects which are specific so long as compensation is maintained, whereas with the supervention of myocardial failure nonspecific effects are added.

Three further distinctions are also necessary.

1. Dynamically significant lesions and those so minor as to be manifested only by murmurs.

2. Acute and chronic lesions, the latter being much more common. Suddenly developing insufficiency, due to ruptured (or perforated) cusps, chordae tendineae or papillary muscles is not very rare; sudden obstruction, due to large emboli or pedunculated thrombi, is decidedly so. Only the atrioventricular orifices are subject to sudden obstruction. Chronic insufficiency is due (except as noted below) to acquired or congenital deformity of the cusps; stenosis is due to fusion of the cusps resulting from inflammation, or to congenital deformity.

3. Insufficiency and incompetence, the former term referring to leakage due to deformity of the cusps, the latter to leakage which occurs when normal cusps fail to close completely the orifice which they guard. This distinction, however, is clinical and anatomic rather than dynamic or physiologic, and will ordinarily not be made in the discussions of this section.

Incompetence of the *a-v valves* may be due to dilatation of the ring of the valve (Fig. 19–11), ven-

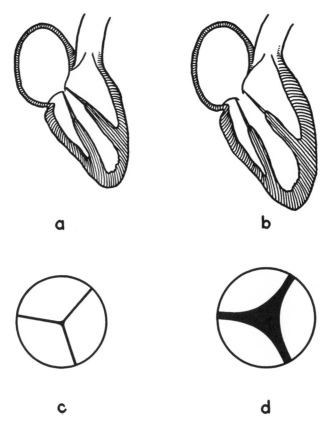

Figure 19–11. Genesis of valvular incompetence. *a,* Left chambers of normal heart, ventricular systole. *b,* Mitral incompetence due to dilatation of left ventricle with consequent relative shortening of chordae tendineae. *c,* Normal pulmonary valve seen from above, ventricular diastole. *d,* Pulmonary incompetence due to dilatation of pulmonary orifice with "trigonization" of the valve.

tricular dilatation with resultant downward displacement of the sites or origin of the papillary muscles (Fig. 19–11), weakened contraction of the papillary muscles ("papillary muscle dysfunction"), or combinations of these factors. Severe incompetence is due most commonly to ventricular failure, in which all three factors may operate. Not rarely insufficiency and incompetence coexist, as would be expected.

Incompetence of the *pulmonary valve,* usually not significant dynamically, is due most commonly to dilatation of the valve ring resulting from prolonged pulmonary hypertension or greatly increased pulmonary flow over a period of time (Fig. 19–11). *Aortic incompetence* due to these factors is rather rare, presumably because of the greater strength of the aortic annulus. Severe aortic incompetence may occur in syphilitic aortitis involving the root of the aorta, distortion of the aortic root by dissecting aneurysm, or genetic disorders of connective tissue.

THE CAUSES OF VALVULAR DISEASE

Rheumatic fever: Mitral, aortic, tricuspid insufficiency, stenosis; involvement of pulmonary valve is very rare.

Syphilis: Aortic insufficiency, aortic incompetence.

Congenital: Pulmonary stenosis, insufficiency; aortic stenosis, insufficiency; mitral and tricuspid stenosis, insufficiency; pulmonary incompetence in atrial and ventricular septal defects, patent ductus, etc.

Bacterial and mycotic endocarditis: Acute, subacute, chronic insufficiency of aortic, mitral, tricuspid, rarely pulmonary valve (vegetations, destruction or perforation of cusps, ruptured chordae tendineae, etc.).

Heritable disorders (Marfan, Hurler, l-cystinuria, etc.): aortic, mitral incompetence.

Trauma: Ruptured aortic cusp (external force), penetrating wound involving cusps or chordae.

Miscellaneous and "idiopathic": Cardiomyopathies (mitral, tricuspid incompetence; subaortic, inframitral stenosis); practically all causes of myocardial disease and heart failure including systemic and pulmonary hypertension, collagen diseases, myocardial infarction; chirurgenic (damage of valves incident to cardiac surgery); etc.

Insufficiency and Incompetence. Rather different conditions obtain in the case of incompetent a-v valves on the one hand and semilunar valves on the other, and in the case of valves of the right and the left sides of the heart.

1. In all cases, of course, leakage occurs when the valve ought to be closed. In insufficiency of an a-v valve leaking occurs during systole, part of the gross stroke volume of the ventricle being propelled backward, the other part forward. In semilunar valve insufficiency the entire stroke output is propelled forward during systole but a portion regurgitates back into the ventricle during diastole. In either case the net stroke volume equals the gross output (per beat) minus backward or regurgitant flow.

2. The ratio *regurgitant flow to onward flow* obviously is dependent upon the ratio *resistance regurgitant flow to resistance onward flow*. The latter, in turn, is determined by (a) the size (area) of the aperture in the closed valve, (b) the peripheral resistance which opposes forward flow and (c) the resistance proximal to the valve which opposes backward flow. Therefore, at a given gross stroke volume and at a hole in the valve of a given size, the volume of blood which leaks backward is proportional to the differences in pressures proximal and distal to the valve during the time it is closed.

3. In insufficiency of the *aortic valve,* the peripheral resistance is that of the systemic circulation during diastole; the proximal, the resistance of the muscle fibers of the left ventricle to stretching. In *pulmonary insufficiency* the peripheral and proximal resistances are respectively the diastolic resistance of the pulmonary circulation and the resistance to stretching offered by the right ventricular muscle. The thicker walls of the left ventricle offer somewhat greater resistance to stretching, but the resistance (pressure) distal to the aortic valve is many times that in the pulmonary circuit; it is likely, therefore, that with a given degree of deformity the aortic valve leaks worse than its counterpart of the right side.

4. In *mitral insufficiency* the resistance distal to the valve is that of the greater circulation during systole; the proximal resistance is that which opposes distention of the left atrium and the pulmonary veins. In *tricuspid insufficiency* the distal and proximal resistances are respectively that of the pulmonary circuit during systole and that which opposes distention of the right atrium and venae cavae. Resistance to backward flow is undoubtedly less on the right side because of the much larger capacity of the veins of the greater circulation, but the pressure in the aorta during systole is six to eight times that in the pulmonary artery; hence with a given degree of deformity the mitral valve leaks worse than the tricuspid.

5. The ventricles resist stretching more than do the atria and their tributary veins; hence with a given aperture of insufficiency the atrioventricular valves leak worse than the semilunar valves. *The mitral valve leaks worst of all.*

6. Backflow usually follows the onset of systole immediately if an a-v valve is incompetent, and begins immediately following the onset of diastole if one of the semilunar valves leaks. In most cases, therefore, the period of isometric contraction or isometric relaxation (as the case may be) is absent. Backflow usually continues throughout systole when an a-v valve leaks, and throughout diastole in the case of a semilunar valve, but is ordinarily greatest shortly after the incompetent valve closes, when the difference in the pressures on the two sides of the valve is maximal.

In some cases of mitral and tricuspid insufficiency the valve does not leak when it first closes, but only after pressure on its ventricular side has reached a certain critical level. In such cases regurgitation is probably of slight degree as a rule, due either to weakened contraction of papillary muscles or to minor deformity of the cusps.

In other cases (or in the same cases) backflow may cease while systole is yet in progress. Regurgitation of minor moment confined to early systole may occur if atrial and ventricular systole are incoordinated (a-v dissociation) or if the atria are not contracting at all (atrial fibrillation).

If one were to equate the velocity of regurgitant flow with the intensity of murmurs (which one should not do), it would seem that in some cases of aortic and pulmonary insufficiency little or no regurgitation occurs during the last part of diastole; perhaps in such cases when aortic pressure falls below a critical level apposition of the cusps is sufficient to close the orifice almost or quite completely.

7. When regurgitation is free or severe, perfect or near-perfect compensation (i.e., normal or near-normal net output and absence of symptoms) is much more readily attained if the lesion affects a semilunar valve rather than one which guards an atrioventricular orifice, for the following reasons: (1) In semilunar insufficiency the entire stroke volume of the ventricle (increased above normal by approximately the volume of regurgitation) is propelled forward, and all or nearly all of the onward flow occurs before regurgitation begins; while in a-v insufficiency backward and

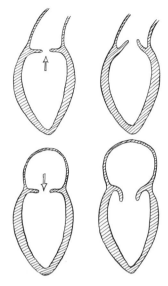

Figure 19–12. Semilunar stenosis (above) and atrioventricular stenosis (below). In each instance the resistance to flow is greater in the sketches on the right because the *length* of the narrowed regions is greater.

forward flow occur simultaneously, in effect competing one against the other, backward flow being favored because of lesser resistance to flow in this direction. (2) In semilunar insufficiency no "back pressure" into the atrium and great veins occurs so long as the appertaining ventricle remains competent; while back pressure is a sine qua non of severe insufficiency of either a-v valve.

It should now be clear that with an aperture of given size (when the valve ought to be closed) pulmonary insufficiency is borne best, mitral insufficiency worst. One could get along quite well without a pulmonary valve. Severe aortic insufficiency may be borne well for many years. Severe tricuspid insufficiency results in elevation of right atrial and systemic venous pressure, but the elevated pressure of itself increases resistance to backflow and tends to reduce the volume of regurgitation. In severe mitral insufficiency elevation of left atrial pressure, even though it be considerable, can cause but little reduction of regurgitant flow because of the much greater pressure in the left ventricle. A normal circulation rate cannot be attained in the presence of severe mitral insufficiency.

Whenever the circulation rate is considerably reduced, mechanisms are brought into play whereby blood volume is increased (see p. 383). Increase of blood volume, really in the absence of myocardial failure, plays a considerable role in the physiologic and clinical pictures of mitral and tricuspid insufficiency.

Stenosis. Rather considerable stenosis must exist before the orifice of an open valve offers appreciable resistance to the onward flow of blood, the critical reduction in the orifice area having been determined to be about

three-fourths, or to about 1 cm.^{2}. Below the critical area, however, increasing degrees of stenosis lead to progressively severe physiologic disturbances.

Resistance to flow through a normal valve orifice and one which is moderately narrowed is almost negligible because of the very small *length* of the orifice. Since resistance in a segment of a tube is directly proportional to its length and inversely proportional to its caliber (R $\propto \dfrac{1}{r^4}$, Poiseuille's law), so long as length is negligible resistance cannot be appreciable. If the length (thickness) of a stenotic aperture is only a millimeter or two, rather marked narrowing must therefore occur before resistance to flow becomes significant, even though (if the orifice is round) resistance is increased four times if the area is reduced by one-half and 16 times if it is reduced by three-fourths. However, once resistance become significant it increases much more steeply in absolute terms as the orifice becomes more and more narrowed.

It is now clear that the significance of stenosis depends not only upon the minimal cross-section area of the orifice but also upon its length and its shape (Fig. 19–12). Mention should also be made of stenosis due to hypertrophy of heart muscle in localized regions, which increases in degree when the muscle contracts. Valvular, infravalvular and supravalvular stenosis have effects upon resistance to flow which differ considerably.

If no gradient of pressure exists across a valve, whatever stenosis may be present is obviously insignificant. If a gradient exists, the physiologic significance of the stenosis may be evaluated by reference to Poiseuille's equation $R = \dfrac{mG}{F}$, where R is resistance, mG *is* the mean difference of pressures across the valve while blood is flowing through it, and F is the volume of blood which flows. Since R obviously is inversely proportional to the "functional size" of the orifice, the following ratio obtains: FA $\propto \dfrac{F}{mG}$, where FA is the "functional area" (size) of the stenotic orifice. The Gorlin equation for estimating FA in cm.^{2} is derived from this ratio, the ratio being converted to equations by the use of empirical constants.

The Gorlin formula for estimating the mitral valve area (MVA), for example, is as follows:

$$MVA = \frac{MVF}{0.7 \times 44.5 \sqrt{LAP - LVDP}},$$

where *MVF* is flow through the mitral valve in ml. per second of diastole, *LAP* is mean left atrial pressure, and *LVDP* is mean left ventricular diastolic pressure.

As regards maintenance of a normal or near-normal circulation rate the heart compensates best for *aortic stenosis,* perhaps because of the inherently great power of a hypertrophied left ventricle; even in high grade stenosis of this valve cardiac output at rest may remain normal for many years. In *pulmonary stenosis,* on the other hand, cardiac output is usually subnormal if the orifice is significantly narrowed, but the circulation rate may change but little as years pass. The circulation rate is reduced in most cases of high grade *mitral* and *tricuspid stenosis,* but often to a surprisingly small degree.

Stenosis vs. Insufficiency. In *stenosis* the muscle of the affected chamber(s) of the heart must overcome increased resistance to emptying, and therefore work against an *overload of pressure; in insufficiency,* on the other hand, the heart works under a *volume overload.* It is really impossible to say which of these challenges is more difficult for the heart to cope with, particularly in a given patient; there are too many variable factors to consider, often unpredictable as to whether or when, such as related or unrelated disease or disturbance in the lungs or the coronary circulation, arrhythmias, etc. It is said that the right ventricle is better able to cope with volume overload than the left, and that the reverse obtains for pressure overloading, but this statement is at best only partly true. Certainly pulmonary insufficiency is borne well (although it is rare in severe form), but of all common lesions free aortic insufficiency is perhaps borne best of all, while sudden death is an ever-present danger in severe aortic stenosis; again, congestive failure eventually ensues in most cases of aortic stenosis, but is rare in isolated pulmonary stenosis. The truth is that (1) the heart performs remarkably well even though its valves are seriously deformed, and (2) marked stenosis or very free insufficiency cannot be borne indefinitely (nor indeed can the "normal" heart go on indefinitely).

Insufficiency and Stenosis. It is inevitable that a valve so deformed as to leak may not be capable of opening fully, and vice versa; stenosis and insufficiency therefore commonly coexist. It is obvious, however, that if the orifice of a valve is markedly stenotic it cannot leak very badly; nor can the orifice of a valve which leaks severely be markedly narrowed. For this reason in most cases of severe valvular disease either insufficiency or stenosis predominates, the physiologic effects of the lesser lesion being negligible or minimal.

Probably in all cases of severe aortic stenosis regurgitation can be no more than minimal; and certainly free regurgitation precludes the existence of significant stenosis. However, for reasons which are now clear, significant mitral stenosis can coexist with fairly free insufficiency, since other factors being equal the mitral valve leaks worse than the aortic (p. 393).

MITRAL VALVE DISEASE

Mitral Insufficiency

When mitral insufficiency develops gradually, complete compensation for an indefinite period of time can probably be maintained if less than half of the left ventricular stroke volume regurgitates into the atrium; in such cases dilatation of the left atrium and left ventricle does not exceed physiologic limits. If regurgitant exceeds forward flow (and in severe insufficiency backward flow may be three to five times onward flow), it is impossible for the left ventricle to maintain a normal circulation rate even though it is fully competent in the physiologic sense (Fig. 19–13).

During ventricular systole the regurgitated blood is added to that which flows into the left atrium from the lungs; the atrium dilates and in time becomes hypertrophied. So long as the left ventricle remains competent, however, and its end diastolic pressure is not elevated, the walls of the atrium are stretched only intermittently (during ventricular systole), and only a normal amount of blood remains in this chamber at the end of ventricular diastole. The atrium, therefore, does not tend to dilate progressively (except insofar as the degree of insufficiency increases); mean left atrial pressure is only slightly to moderately elevated, and there is no great increase of resistance in the pulmonary circuit (Fig. 19–13).

During ventricular diastole ventricular filling is increased in proportion to the degree of insufficiency; the left ventricle therefore dilates and hypertrophies. As explained above, in severe mitral insufficiency it is impossible for the left ventricle to maintain a normal circulation rate because of the dynamics of this lesion. In severe but well compensated mitral insufficiency the only symptoms (principally easy fatigability and muscular weakness) are related to the low net cardiac output.

Dynamically significant mitral insufficiency tends of itself to get worse as time passes due to the superimposition of incompetence (p. 393). In time, as the left ventricle "weakens,"

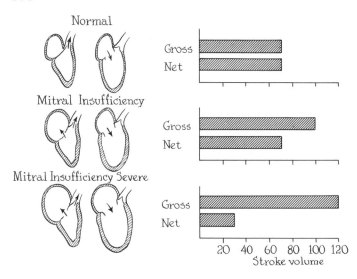

Figure 19–13. Comparison of gross and net stroke volumes in the normal, slight or moderate mitral insufficiency, and severe mitral insufficiency.

residual blood in this chamber is increased and end diastolic pressure is elevated. There follows more pronounced elevation of left atrial pressure and greater dilatation of the left atrium, which may attain great size. Resistance in the pulmonary circuit is now definitely (but usually not markedly) increased, and pressure elevated. Right ventricular hypertrophy, usually not of great degree, occurs (Fig. 19–14). Atrial fibrillation often supervenes, and finally congestive heart failure. Dyspnea is probably not a symptom of mitral insufficiency per se, but occurs only after the left ventricle has begun to fail.

Should severe mitral insufficiency occur suddenly, the initial picture is that of cardiac shock, often rapidly fatal, as is the case in most other circumstances under which the previously normal (or nearly normal) heart is suddenly confronted with an insufferable burden (see heart failure). Although the left atrium dilates and a degree of pulmonary congestion occurs, most of the symptoms are due to marked decrease of the circulation rate. If the patient survives the initial critical stage, pulmonary edema and other congestive phenomena are apt to appear during recovery from cardiac shock.

In some cases of bacterial endocarditis involving the mitral valve, insufficiency of slight or moderate degree may worsen suddenly due to rupture of a chorda tendinea. Because of preexisting adaptation to the valvular lesion, in this event the sudden decrease of output may be less pronounced, the shock state less severe and transitory, and the subsequent physiologic and clinical picture that of rapidly but not suddenly worsening mitral insufficiency, with increase of left pressure, pulmonary congestion, dyspnea, etc. In such cases left atrial enlargement is not so great as in severe mitral insufficiency which has developed gradually, but left atrial and pulmonary artery pressures are considerably higher.

Mitral Stenosis

Significant narrowing interferes with the free passage of blood from the left atrium into the left ventricle, with resultant increase of pressure in the left atrium and the pulmonary vascular system in proportion to the severity of the stenosis. The left atrium and right ventricle undergo hypertrophy, and in time the former dilates, usually only to a slight or moderate degree. Compensation is maintained through the efforts of the left atrium and right ventricle, at the expense of congestion of the lungs and typically with a slight or moderate decrease in the circulation rate. At this stage, which may last for some years, the patient may be asymptomatic during rest or usual activity, but short of breath on unusual exertion.

The degree of pulmonary engorgement at which a balance is established between the volume of blood which enters the lungs and the amount which flows through the constricted mitral orifice depends upon the output of the right ventricle and the severity of the stenosis. If the right ventricle is fully competent, the degree of engorgement in a given case thus varies with the venous return to the right side of the heart. Rest will diminish the engorgement; activity will increase it. Sudden exertion, such as running, may so increase the output of the right ventricle as to upset the balance, with the production of sudden, extreme, even fatal, congestion of the lungs.

When congestion is severe or prolonged, reflex constriction of arterioles occurs, more pronounced in dependent portions of the lungs. Such constriction tends to limit the degree of congestion by limiting flow into the capillaries, but also causes increase of pulmonary vascular resistance and further elevation of pulmonary arterial pressure.

With the passage of time (and increase in the degree of stenosis), the arterioles and small arteries undergo sclerotic changes not unlike those which occur in the systemic arterioles in cases of greater-circulation hypertension, with pronounced narrowing of their lumina (Fig. 19–15); in this instance resistance to flow through the lungs is further increased, and pressure in the pulmonary arteries further elevated.

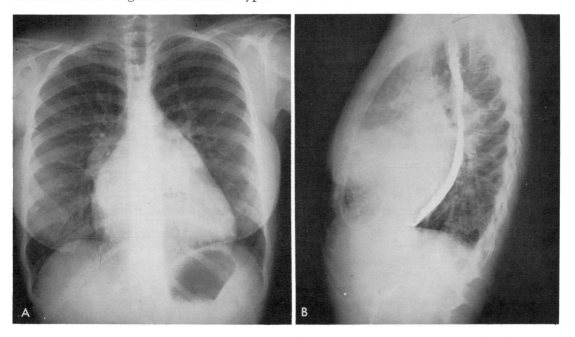

Figure 19–14. *A* and *B,* Severe mitral insufficiency. Enlargement of both ventricles, left atrium.

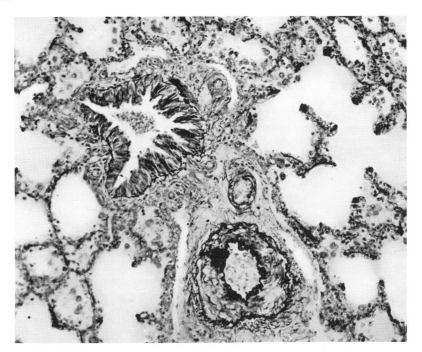

Figure 19–15. Pulmonary arteriosclerosis. The media of the small pulmonary artery near the bottom of the figure is markedly thickened, the lumen narrowed. Similar changes are seen in two smaller vessels above, nearer the bronchiole. (Courtesy of Dr. W. E. Jaques.)

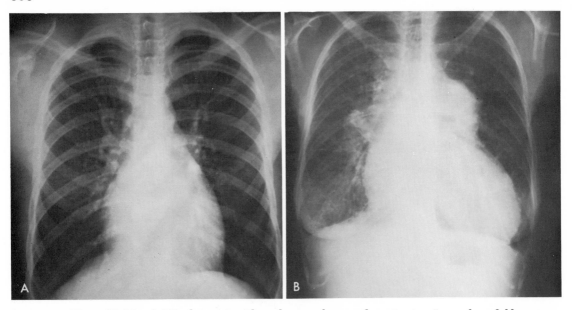

Figure 19–16. *A,* Mitral stenosis with moderate pulmonary hypertension. Lower lung fields relatively hypovascular. *B,* Mitral stenosis with marked longstanding pulmonary hypertension. Mitral commissurotomy 5 years before, benefit only temporary. Great dilatation of main pulmonary arteries.

Marked pulmonary hypertension (systolic pressure above 80) in mitral stenosis is always significant of advanced pulmonary vascular changes, the clinical counterparts being signs of dilatation of the pulmonary artery, great or considerable right ventricular hypertrophy and enlargement, and, by x-ray, evidence of greater perfusion of the upper portions of the lungs as compared to the dependent portions (Fig. 19–16). Although dyspnea on exertion is present, frank pulmonary edema is uncommon; symptoms are mostly due to low cardiac output and right ventricular backward failure.

Continued high pressure in the smaller pulmonary veins causes reversal of flow through the anastomotic venules which connect the pulmonary and bronchial systems of veins, so that the submucosal veins of the bronchi may be engorged with blood which is by-passing the left side of the heart (Fig. 19–17).

The changes just mentioned set the stage for thrombosis of small vessels in the lungs and for hemorrhage into the bronchi. During periods of great engorgement, edema of the lungs occurs; continued engorgement and recurrent edema may lead to fibrosis.

It will be remembered, also, that the veins of the visceral pleura drain into the bronchial veins. Pressure may therefore be increased in veins and capillaries of the pleura with the production of recurrent hydrothorax more frequent on the right side.

Atrial fibrillation may set in at any time; it

may be transient and recurrent, or permanent. With the onset of fibrillation the left atrium loses whatever contractile power it had and the efficiency of the compensating right ventricle is compromised. Further, the combination of mitral obstruction and atrial fibrillation predisposes to the formation of thrombi in the left auricle, which may become sources of embolism.

A greatly dilated left pulmonary artery may compress the left recurrent nerve and give rise to hoarseness (Fig. 19–18). Persistent cough, most commonly due to pulmonary congestion, is in some instances due to compression of the left bronchus by a dilated pulmonary artery.

Thus it is evident that dyspnea on exertion, cough, hemoptysis, fatigability, hydrothorax and embolic phenomena are signs of mitral stenosis per se, and may occur even though the compensating right ventricle is functioning adequately. The collateral physical signs of mitral stenosis—accentuation of the pulmonary second sound, pulmonary systolic murmur and the Graham Steell murmur of pulmonary incompetence—can be correlated with pulmonary hypertension and dilatation of the pulmonary artery.

Sudden obstruction of a normal mitral orifice (as by a pedunculated tumor) is manifested predominantly by signs of pronounced

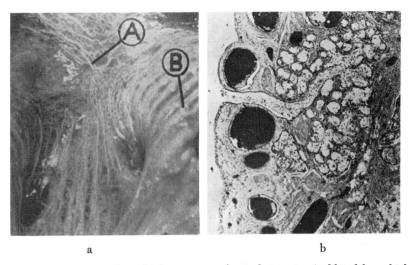

a   b

Figure 19–17. a, Large bronchi from a case of mitral stenosis: *A*, dilated bronchial veins; *B*, mucosal gold. b. Section of large bronchus, same case. Dilated bronchial veins close to mucosa are seen. (From F. C. Ferguson et al., Am. Heart J., Vol. 28.)

diminution of output rather than by those of pulmonary congestion. Most commonly, however, sudden obstruction is superposed upon chronic narrowing (left atrial tumor, atrial thrombi in cases of mitral stenosis); and severe forward failure and intense pulmonary congestion occur together. In cases of myxoma of the left atrium the usual physiologic picture is that of rapidly (but not suddenly) developing mitral stenosis.

Mitral Insufficiency and Stenosis

In very "tight" mitral stenosis significant insufficiency cannot occur because of the small size of the orifice and the elevation of left atrial pressure. If stenosis is slight or moderate, however, significant or even free regurgitation may occur. Even so, the physiologic (and clinical) picture is apt to be that of either one of the entities with only a few features of the other. If stenosis predominates, for example, concomitant moderate insufficiency results in greater enlargement of the left atrium than is usual in mitral stenosis and in enlargement of the left ventricle. If insufficiency is predominant (and free), great dilatation of the left atrium may occur as an effect of concomitant stenosis. Whichever lesion predominates, the circulation rate is reduced more greatly than would be the case were a "pure" lesion of the same severity present. Other things being equal, combined stenosis and insufficiency are worse than either lesion alone.

Cardiac Catheterization in Mitral Disease

By right heart catheterization cardiac output may be estimated (p. 380), right ventricular, pulmonary, arterial, and pulmonary "wedge" pressures measured (Fig. 19–1), and pulmonary vascular resistance calculated,

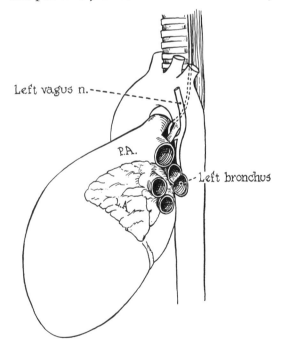

Figure 19–18. Relation of pulmonary artery and left atrium to left recurrent nerve and left bronchus.

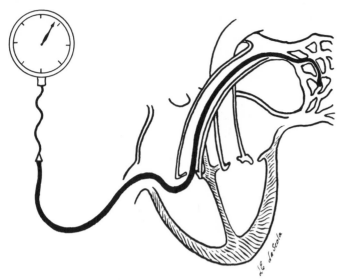

Figure 19–19. How "wedge" pressure may approximate pressure in the left atrium.

as well as the resistance to flow through the mitral valve.

Pulmonary "wedge" pressure is that measured at the site where the advancing catheter becomes wedged into one of the small branches of a pulmonary artery and can be moved onward no farther (Fig. 19–1), flow around the catheter being prevented by the snug fit. The blood column between its open tip and the left atrium serves in effect as a manometer connected with the cavity of the left atrium (Fig. 19–19).

Usual values for these pressures in normal subjects are shown in Table 19–1.

Resistances are estimated by application of Poiseuille's law, which states that rate of flow (Q) is directly proportional to the pressure gradient (PG) and inversely proportional to resistance (R). That is, $Q = \dfrac{PG \times K}{R}$, and $R = \dfrac{PG \times K}{Q}$. The constant K becomes 1332 if PG is expressed in mm./Hg and Q in ml./sec., R then being expressed in dynes/sec./cm.$^{-5}$. The equation then becomes $R = \dfrac{1332 PG}{Q}$.

Ordinarily (since the estimation is only semiquantitative at best), it is assumed that mean diastolic pressure in the left ventricle is zero (which it isn't), in which case PG = pressure (P), and the following formulas are used, in the knowledge that they are reasonably valid only in the absence of left ventricular failure and other factors which cause elevation of

diastolic pressure in this chamber. (In the formulas, Q is cardiac output, P_A is mean pressure in the pulmonary artery, and P_W mean wedge pressure.)

Total pulmonary resistance (TPR) $= \dfrac{1332 P_A}{Q}$

Mitral orifice resistance (MR) $= \dfrac{1332 P_W}{Q}$

Pulmonary arteriolar resistance (PAR) = TPR-MR,

or PAR $= \dfrac{1332 (P_A - P_W)}{Q}$

Normal figures for TPR, MR, and PAR with the subject at rest are in the neighborhood of 200, 120 and 80, respectively; these figures would be obtained, for example, if Q is 100 ml./sec. (6 liters/min.) P_A is 15, P_W, 9. With exercise, P_A usually declines because of a decrease in PAR.

In *mitral stenosis* the most characteristic features are elevation of P_W and increase of MR. Wedge pressure may be as high as 35 in severe cases, but more commonly is about 25 to 30. Unless cardiac output (Q) is substantially reduced, P_W is nearly always above 20 in cases of significant stenosis, but if Q is very small P_W may be only slightly elevated.

The calculated resistance of the mitral valve (MR) is always increased, usually to more than twice normal in cases of significant stenosis. Pulmonary artery pressure is also elevated, the systolic seldom above 60 unless the pulmonary arteriolar resistance is considerably increased.

Let us consider three cases: In case 1, P_A is 30(45/ 20), P_W 25, Q 80 (approximately 5 liters/min.). TPR is about 500, MR 415, PAR 85.

In case 2, P_A is 20(28/15), P_W 16, Q 40 (2.5 liters/ min.). TPR is about 650, MR 525, PAR 125.

In case 3, P_A is 50(75/38), P_W 22, Q 60 (3.5 liters/ min.). TPR is about 1300, MR 500, PAR 800.

In all three cases the severity of the stenosis is

TABLE 19–1. NORMAL PRESSURES IN LESSER CIRCULATION (MM. OF MERCURY).

	Range	Average
Right ventricle, systolic	20–30	25
Right ventricle, diastolic	0	0
Pulmonary artery, systolic	20–30	25
Pulmonary artery, diastolic	6–12	9
Pulmonary artery, mean	13–17	15
Pulmonary "wedge," mean	6–12	9

roughly the same. In case 1, with the highest cardiac output, wedge pressure is highest but, since pulmonary arteriolar resistance is normal, pulmonary artery pressure is only moderately elevated.

In case 2, because of the low cardiac output, wedge pressure is but slightly elevated and pulmonary artery pressure is hardly elevated at all. The gradient $P_A - P_W$ is only 4 mm./Hg.

In case 3 pressure in the pulmonary artery is greatly elevated because of marked increase in pulmonary arteriolar resistance.

In most cases of mitral stenosis cardiac output at rest has been found to be subnormal; exercise often does not induce the normal increase of output, which may remain unchanged, increase slightly or actually decrease. Even if output decreases with exercise, pulmonary artery and wedge pressures rise considerably or markedly. In some cases the graphic record of wedge pressure reveals prominent *a* waves synchronous with atrial systole (Fig. 19–20), transmitted backward (with considerable dampening) from the left atrium.

In *chronic mitral insufficiency*, for reasons which are now clear, P_W is elevated only slightly or moderately in the absence of left ventricular failure; in some cases of free regurgitation, with great enlargement of the left atrium, mean wedge pressure has been found to be normal. In subacute cases, such as a few weeks after rupture of a chorda in bacterial endocarditis, P_W has been found to be considerably elevated, the left atrium only moderately enlarged. Typically the wedge pressure curve in mitral insufficiency displays large waves synchronous with ventricular systole, the "regurgitant" or *cv* wave transmitted backward from the left atrium (Fig. 19–20). As a rule PAR is normal or only slightly increased in cases of mitral insufficiency. As expected, cardiac output is subnormal, often markedly so, in free mitral regurgitation, even in the absence of heart failure.

By *left heart* catheterization pressures may be measured, and the forms of the pressure curves recorded, in the left atrium and left ventricle (Fig. 19–21). By this method, in *mitral stenosis* mean left atrial pressure is elevated, corresponding almost exactly to P_W in nearly all cases. During ventricular diastole a definite pressure gradient can be demonstrated across the mitral valve which varies with the degree of stenosis from about 10 to 25 mm. Hg in most cases. With a given degree of

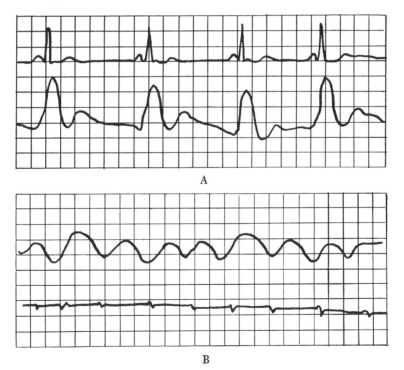

A

B

Figure 19–20. *A*, "Wedge" pressure curve in mitral stenosis. Marked exaggeration of presystolic *a* waves. *B*, "Wedge" pressure curve in mitral insufficiency. Large broad "regurgitant" waves are seen which reach their peaks late in ventricular systole. Atrial fibrillation. ECG is above pressure curve in *A*, below in *B*. (Traced from actual pressure curves.)

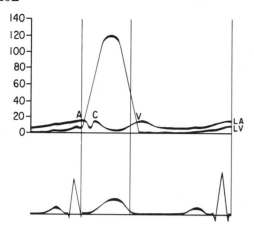

Figure 19–21. Normal pressure relationships in left atrium (LA) and left ventricle (LV). *a, c. v* waves as labeled. EKG below. Compare with Figures 19–22 and 19–23.

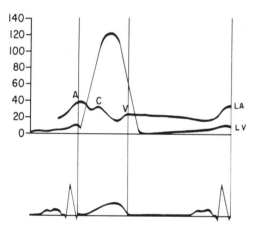

Figure 19–22. Mitral stenosis. Pressure relationships in left atrium and left ventricle. Note prominent A wave of LA pulse, diastolic gradient between LA and LV pressures. Compare with Figures 19–21 and 19–23. Semischematic.

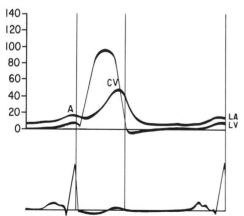

Figure 19–23. Mitral insufficiency. Pressure relationships in left atrium and left ventricle. Note large *cv* wave in left atrial pressure pulse. Compare with Figures 19–21 and 19–22. Semischematic.

stenosis left atrial pressure and the gradient across the open valve vary, obviously, with the cardiac output. In the left atrial pressure curve the *a* wave is characteristically prominent, occasionally quite large (Fig. 19–22), an effect of contraction of the hypertrophied atrial muscle against the resistance of the stenosis.

In *free mitral insufficiency* the descent between the *c* and *v* waves is absent, the two waves combined to form a large or giant *cv* or regurgitant wave, which often resembles the pressure curve of the left ventricle ("ventricularization of the atrium") (Fig. 19–23). If only slight stenosis is additionally present (as is often the case), a considerable gradient may exist across the valve during ventricular diastole because of the great increase in atrioventricular flow.

According to Poiseuille's law (p. 394), $Q \propto \frac{G}{R}$, where G is the pressure gradient. Hence, $G \propto \frac{Q}{R}$; with a given resistance, the gradient varies directly with the rate of flow.

Surgery of the Mitral Valve

The clinical improvement following successful surgery for mitral stenosis is attributable to diminution of the resistance to atrioventricular flow in the left side of the heart, and in the physiologic sphere is attended by lessening of the pulmonary hypertension, decrease in right ventricular work and increase of cardiac output. Shortly after commissurotomy there may be only a modest decrease of pulmonary arterial pressure, but after some months the decrease may be much more pronounced; this delayed, presumably gradual decline of the pressure toward normal suggests regression of the pulmonary arteriolar lesions and decrease in pulmonary arteriolar resistance. Seldom, however, do dynamics and pressures return to normal; rather, the physiologic and clinical pictures are changed to those of less severe stenosis.

In mitral insufficiency treated successfully by valve replacement or valvuloplasty, hemodynamic as well as clinical improvement occurs, but only rarely are normal parameters restored. The size of the left ventricle and left atrium often diminishes, dyspnea may disappear and weakness lessen, but seldom is a normal cardiac output regained, probably for the following reasons: (1) the left ventricle, overburdened for a long time, dilated, hypertrophied, and probably in a state of chronic failure, is incapable of full recovery; (2) neither a prosthetic nor a patched valve can function perfectly.

DISEASE OF THE AORTIC VALVE

The left ventricle alone bears the brunt of compensation for defects of the aortic valve. If aortic stenosis is present, the ventricle must overcome the increased resistance to the egress of blood by more powerful contraction; this it accomplishes by the development of hypertrophy, often with relatively slight dilatation. If the aortic valve leaks, the ventricle must increase its gross output by the amount of the regurgitated blood in order to maintain normal flow to the periphery; this it achieves by dilatation and hypertrophy. The ventricle performs these tasks well, so that good compensation for high grade lesions may be maintained for many years.

Aortic Stenosis

Obstruction of the aortic orifice becomes significant only if the aperture is reduced to about one-fourth its normal area, or to 0.075 sq. cm. Obstruction of this degree or greater leads to hypertrophy of the left ventricle and results in disturbances of the circulation even though compensation is reasonably well maintained. The most important of these disturbances are related to slow discharge of the left ventricle, to inability of the ventricle to increase its output quickly and to inadequacy of coronary flow. The clinical counterparts of these three physiologic disturbances are, respectively (1) plateau pulse, (2) syncopal attacks and (3) cardiac pain.

Plateau Pulse. The left ventricle cannot force blood through a markedly narrowed aortic orifice at normal speed. Blood is ejected into the aorta at a slower rate, but the ejection phase is prolonged, so that the cardiac output is maintained at normal levels under ordinary circumstances. With slow ejection, intra-aortic pressure rises more gradually than is normally the case, and reaches its peak late. The slope of the ascending limb of the central arterial pulse is therefore gentle and prolonged. Transmitted to the periphery, these changes become manifest in a radial pulse which rises slowly and seems to be long sustained—the *plateau pulse*. Because of its slow rise, the pulse is apparently reduced in amplitude, although actually, unless the stroke volume of the left ventricle is reduced, pulse pressure is affected but little. The pulsus parvus et tardus is characteristic of aortic stenosis with considerable reduction of stroke volume (Fig. 19–24).

In some cases the gradual upstroke of the recorded radial pulse is interrupted by a notch. Rarely the notch is so deep as to be palpable, giving the examiner the impression of an additional wave as the pulse rises—the *anacrotic* pulse, which beats on the way up.

Anacrotism is related to a similar but more marked change in the shape of the aortic pressure pulse. During the isometric phase of systole, pressure within the left ventricle reaches a great height before the stiffened valve is opened. As the resistance is suddenly overcome, ejection at first is rapid, and the aortic pressure curve rises steeply. The sharp rise in pressure increases the resistance to outflow, so that, again rather suddenly, the speed of ejection decreases, to continue slowly through the remainder of systole. The anacrotic notch occurs as the velocity of ejection drops off suddenly, after which the pressure pulse again rises slowly until the end of systole.

The plateau pulse is often not sufficiently pronounced to be detected by palpation, but is clearly

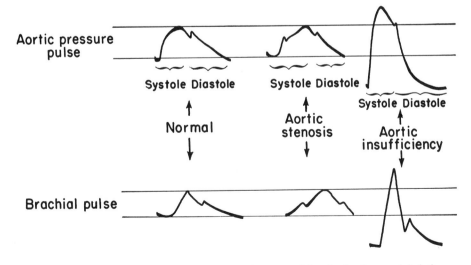

Figure 19–24.   Schematic representation of aortic and brachial pulses, as labeled.

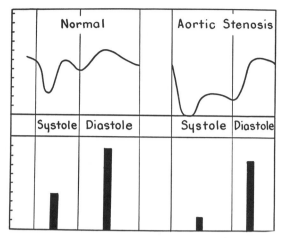

Figure 19–25. Coronary flow in high grade aortic stenosis, contrasted with the normal. Black columns below intended to indicate total volume of flow during systole and diastole, curves above to indicate variation in rates of flow throughout cardiac cycle. (Schematic, after Wiggers.)

evident if the pressure waves are recorded directly from the radial, brachial or carotid artery or from the aorta, or indirectly from the carotid.

Syncope. During exercise the arterioles of skeletal muscle dilate, so that a large part of the cardiac output is diverted to the active muscles. If the heart is normal, adequate flow to the brain is maintained because of the great increase in cardiac output. In normal subjects and in most persons with heart disease strenuous exertion is limited by dyspnea (due principally to engorgement of the lungs), which usually appears only after several seconds or minutes of exercise. As return flow to the right side of the heart is rapidly and progressively augmented, blood is ejected into the pulmonary artery somewhat more rapidly than it enters the left ventricle, mainly because of the lag between each increase of right ventricular output and the consequent increase of left ventricular output. As exercise continues, the total quantity of blood in the lungs therefore continues to increase; the elasticity of the lungs is thereby diminished with resultant progressive diminution of breathing reserve to the point of conscious respiratory effort.

The net decrease of arteriolar tone which accompanies exercise tends per se to diminish the resistance of the arterial system and thus enables the left ventricle to increase its output with a proportionally slight increase of mechanical work. Hence the left ventricle, in the absence of aortic obstruction, is able to increase its output quickly and, within limits, progressively in response to the demands of exercise.

If, however, the aortic orifice is markedly narrowed, the unyielding obstruction largely prevents the alleviating effect of decreased arteriolar tone upon resistance, so that the ventricle must perform a relatively great amount of work in order to increase its systolic discharge. For this reason the ventricle may fail to increase its output quickly and adequately, so that in some cases of high grade aortic stenosis sudden exertion is abruptly halted by inadequacy of the left ventricular output before significant engorgement of the lungs has developed. A large part of the inadequate output is diverted to the active muscles, cerebral ischemia ensues, and syncope occurs; the subject may faint promptly or quickly become weak and dizzy whenever he attempts suddenly to increase his activity—to run, to climb stairs rapidly or even to walk fast.

Cardiac Pain. The flow of blood through the coronary vessels is phasic; during the cardiac cycle its velocity varies with changes in the head of pressure in the aorta, and with changes in the resistance of the coronary system related to the mechanical effects of ventricular systole. Of themselves, contraction of the muscle and the consequent elevation of intraventricular pressure tend to diminish coronary flow by their squeezing effect upon intramural vessels, but this tendency is in part counterbalanced by the rising intra-aortic pressure during systole. During the isometric phase of ventricular systole, when intra-aortic pressure is at its lowest, the velocity of coronary flow decreases markedly; during the stage of early, rapid ejection it increases, and then declines progressively until the end of systole. With the onset of diastole the velocity increases sharply and then gradually decreases. Flow is greater during diastole than during systole, but the systolic component is an important fraction of the total flow.

In severe aortic obstruction the isometric phase of ventricular systole is prolonged, and intraventricular pressure is markedly elevated throughout systole, while intra-aortic pressure is relatively or absolutely low. Systolic coronary flow is thus markedly decreased, and since systole is prolonged and diastole shortened, total coronary flow is significantly reduced (Fig. 19–25).

This reduction of coronary flow is a factor in the ultimate development of heart failure, but is also responsible for the attacks of cardiac pain which are characteristic of severe, longstanding aortic stenosis. The pain may have all the characteristics of classic angina pectoris, but individual attacks of pain often persist for hours, and are especially liable to occur at night, waking the patient from sleep.

The cause of the episodes of nocturnal pain has not been clearly established; they have been attributed to reduction of the cardiac output during sleep with consequent decline of intra-aortic pressure and further decrease of coronary flow out of proportion to the decreased metabolic needs of the cardiac muscle. It should be mentioned that nocturnal attacks are not unusual in patients with angina pectoris due to coronary artery disease; nocturnal angina is not specifically related to aortic stenosis.

Some patients with aortic stenosis are subject to episodes of syncope, others to anginal attacks, some to both, some to neither. In some cases the earliest symptoms are those of heart failure, and in most the terminal picture is that of congestive failure. Some die suddenly, often during exercise, of ventricular fibrillation or other arrhythmia probably related to sudden decrease of coronary flow; syncope may in some instances be due to transient arrhythmias.

Congenital Aortic Stenosis. The pathologic physiology of congenital obstruction of the aortic orifice differs only slightly from that of its acquired counterpart. Perhaps because the obstruction has existed since fetal life, congenital stenosis is on the whole borne well, and in many cases the condition during childhood is manifested only by objective signs in the complete absence of subjective symptoms. Syncope, angina, heart failure may not appear until middle-age, although sudden death in childhood is not very rare. Poststenotic dilatation of the aorta (see p. 410), is encountered in most cases of congenital valvular stenosis, less commonly in the slowly developing acquired form. Such dilatation does not occur in congenital subvalvular (subaortic) stenosis. In supravalvular stenosis, characterized by narrowing of the ascending aorta often accompanied by segmental stenosis of branches of the

aortic arch and pulmonary artery, angina is common because the free edges of the aortic cusps may be adherent to the constricted segment and thereby obstruct flow into the coronary ostia.

In *hypertrophic subaortic stenosis,* considered to be a variant of the cardiomyopathies (p. 434), there seems to be disproportionately great hypertrophy of the upper portion of the ventricular septum so that, when the ventricles contract, the left ventricular outflow tract is obstructed, producing a pressure gradient below the valve. Some investigators contend that the gradient is artifactual, maintaining that the apparently very high pressure in the region of the apex is due to early obliteration of the ventricular cavity in this region so that the force of ventricular contraction is exerted directly against the catheter at and near its tip. It is certain that this situation obtains in some cases, but almost just as certainly not in all. Characteristically in these cases there is a hump early on the downstroke of the carotid pulse, before the dicrotic notch and wave (Fig. 19–26), probably produced as follows: early in ventricular systole, when contraction is confined mostly to the apical regions, there is but little obstruction to outflow; the ascent of the pulse wave is normal or quickened. Later, as the basal portion contracts, outflow obstruction supervenes, and the pulse wave descends more rapidly than is normal, but the descent is halted as blood is forced past the obstruction, producing the hump. The dicrotic notch, it will be remembered, marks the end of ventricular systole.

Aortic Insufficiency

Backflow of less than a fourth of the gross output of the left ventricle is considered to be physiologically insignificant unless aortic stenosis coexists (see p. 408), and is manifested only by the characteristic diastolic murmur. More free regurgitation leads to characteristic changes in the arterial pulse and in the chronology of arterial blood flow, to dilatation and hypertrophy of the left ventricle, and eventually in some cases to heart failure. Leaks which are not severe enough to cause detectable enlargement of the heart may suffice to produce prominent effects upon the peripheral circulation.

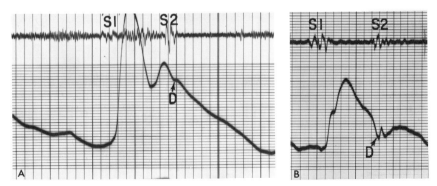

Figure 19–26. *A,* Carotid pulse in idiopathic hypertrophic subaortic stenosis. Note sharp dip during systole followed by later rise, well before the dicrotic notch and wave (D). *B,* Normal carotid pulse for comparison.

Even very free aortic regurgitation is borne well provided it develops gradually and eventually reaches a stationary stage. Patients with extreme degrees of insufficiency due to rheumatic valvulitis are often relatively asymptomatic for two decades or more. Persons with syphilitic insufficiency usually do not fare so well, for two reasons: (1) the leak progresses in severity more rapidly, and tends never to reach a stationary stage; (2) myocardial circulation is often compromised by narrowing or occlusion of the coronary ostia.

With a given degree of valvular deformity, aortic insufficiency is borne better than mitral insufficiency. In the first place, the volume of backflow is less: in mitral insufficiency regurgitation takes preference over forward flow because of the great difference between pressures in the aorta and left atrium; in aortic insufficiency, on the other hand, a major part of flow into the periphery has already occurred before the end of ventricular systole, at which time intra-aortic pressure is falling off very rapidly (see below). In the second place, in aortic insufficiency the patient is spared the baneful effects of prolonged pulmonary hypertension; only with the development of congestive failure do pressures in the lesser circulation become elevated.

Reflux through the defective valve is most pronounced early in diastole, when intra-aortic pressure is relatively high. The backflow causes a sudden drop in aortic pressure early in diastole, followed by a more gradual decline as the reflux continues and blood flows to the periphery. At the end of diastole, pressure in the aorta is below normal. This low pressure decreases the resistance to ejection during the early part of systole; also, because its walls are stretched by the addition of regurgitated blood, the left ventricle contracts with greater power and increases its output. During the first part of systole, therefore, the ventricle empties rapidly, and aortic pressure rises more abruptly than is normally the case to a height greater than normal. The sudden rise in aortic pressure increases the resistance to ejection, so that during the latter part of systole little blood is expelled; as a result, aortic pressure falls rather sharply near the end of systole. This fall is halted momentarily by elastic recoil of the overdistended aorta, the recoil being of greater power than normally and exerting its effect earlier; it results in the propagation of a prominent positive wave into the arteries which is superimposed upon the descending limb of the pulse wave (Fig. 19–24).

The aortic pressure pulse, then, shows an abrupt rise early in systole, a sharp decline late in systole and a precipitous drop early in diastole. Systolic pressure is elevated, diastolic pressure diminished; pulse pressure is increased. Also, the major part of the flow into the aorta, and from it to the periphery, occurs during the early part of systole; at this time the arteries are overfilled and the velocity of flow is abnormally great. During the latter part of systole and during diastole, flow to the periphery decreases markedly; at the end of diastole the arteries are relatively empty and the velocity of flow is abnormally slow.

These abnormalities of pressure and flow, altered somewhat in their transmission to smaller vessels, are responsible for the peripheral signs of aortic insufficiency—the wide pulse pressure, the throbbing arteries, the Corrigan pulse, Quincke's capillary pulse, the arterial sounds and murmurs.

Blood Pressure. The systolic pressure is elevated and the diastolic pressure decreased in proportion to the size of the reflux; such pressures as 200/30 may be encountered if regurgitation is free. In some cases the diastolic pressure falls so low that, as estimated indirectly by the auscultatory method, its value is zero. The visible *throbbing* of the carotid and brachial arteries, and even of smaller ones such as the superficial temporal and dorsalis pedis, is due not only to the wide pulse pressure, but also to the abrupt rise and fall of the pulse wave.

Corrigan Pulse. The Corrigan or water-hammer pulse is the peripheral representation of the aortic pressure pulse, modified during its transmission to the radial artery in such a manner as to change its rounded peak into a sharp apex. The pulse therefore rises quickly and immediately collapses; the beat strikes the palpating finger suddenly and with great force, and just as suddenly is gone.

The water-hammer phenomenon is accentuated by elevation of the arm. According to Wiggers, this accentuation is due to the summation of reflected waves with the rise of the pulse beat, the reflected waves being better transmitted when the artery is relatively empty. It may, however, be due to reversal or near reversal of flow in the arteries of the arm during ventricular diastole as an effect of gravity, with resultant precipitous decline of pressure; in this case the brachial system would participate in the retrograde flow which occurs in the aorta in all cases of significant aortic insufficiency.

Quincke's Capillary Pulse. Normally the pulse wave is small when it reaches the arterioles, and is lost as the blood passes through them. In free aortic insufficiency, however, a relatively large pulse with a steep ascending limb is propagated into the arterioles; the pulse wave may therefore be transmitted into the capillaries. To put it another way, the rapid and great fall of arterial pressure during late systole and during diastole results in greatly diminished flow into the capillaries, so that at the end of diastole they are relatively empty, and the tissues are blanched. Early in systole arterial pressure rises sharply, and flow into the capillaries increases suddenly; the capillaries fill up quickly, and the tissues are hyperemic. Hence the alternate blushing and blanching, elicited most readily in the nail beds and lips, especially if gentle pressure is applied so as to exaggerate the blanching.

Arterial Sounds and Murmurs. Under normal circumstances, if the right amount of pressure is exerted with the bell of a stethoscope upon the femoral or brachial artery, a swishing murmur is heard with each pulse beat. The murmur is related to the flow of blood past the site of compression, and is analogous to phase II or III of the Korotkoff sounds. It occurs synchronously with the ascending limb of the pulse wave, at a time when the velocity of flow is great, and disappears as the pulse wave begins to fall. If the pressure of the stethoscope is carefully increased, the murmur may be replaced by a faint tapping sound, analogous to phase I of the Korotkoff sounds; this sound, short and single, is due to sudden expansion of the compressed segment as blood enters it, the velocity of flow now being insufficient to produce a murmur.

In aortic insufficiency, and in other conditions characterized by large pulse pressure and increased velocity of systolic flow, the murmur, for obvious reasons, becomes louder. In some cases, if just the right amount of pressure is applied, the murmur is doubled—two separate murmurs are heard with each beat; this double murmur is *Duroziez's sign.* It may be explained thus: As the large, steep pulse wave strikes the obstruction, blood flows through with considerable velocity, giving rise to the first phase of the murmur; this is loud, but of short duration. Because of reduced flow through the obstructed site, pressure is built up in the segment just proximal to it, and the artery becomes distended, while pressure in the segment below does not reach its usual height. When the pulse collapses, its steep descent is quickly halted by recoil of the distended proximal segment, and a strong dicrotic wave is propagated forward, at a time when pressure below the obstruction is falling rapidly. Flow through the narrowed region is therefore increased, and the second phase of the murmur is produced (Fig. 19–27).

More constantly present in aortic insufficiency is the *pistol shot sound of Traube,* elicited by the application of increasing pressure to the artery until maximal sound is produced. Traube's sound, analogous to greatly exaggerated phase I Korotkoff sounds, is loud and short, and popping or cracking in quality. In some cases a tapping sound, synchronous with the pulse beat, is heard when the stethoscope is applied without pressure over the vessel; rarely, a double tone is heard. The tone is related to sudden expansion of the artery; when doubled, its genesis is similar to that of the double murmur.

Blood Flow to the Tissues. Total flow to the tissues is normal as long as the left ventricle remains competent. The chronology of *coronary flow* is necessarily affected profoundly, velocity decreasing markedly as aortic pressure falls off, and increasing considerably during systole as pressure rises to high levels. Whether or not the balance permits adequate total flow must depend upon a number of factors, such as the severity of the leak, the degree of dilatation and hypertrophy of the left ventricle, and the presence

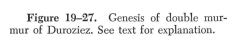

Figure 19–27. Genesis of double murmur of Duroziez. See text for explanation.

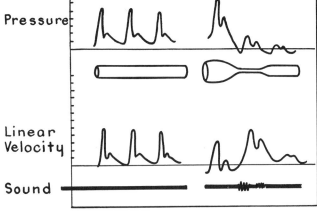

or absence of narrowing of the coronary arteries or of their ostia. In experimental lesions total coronary flow has been found to be normal or increased in some cases, diminished in others.

The majority of persons with pure aortic insufficiency due to syphilis do not complain of cardiac pain unless the coronary ostia are involved in the syphilitic process. On the other hand, angina pectoris is common in persons with rheumatic aortic regurgitation. Perhaps in these cases the concomitance of even slight aortic stenosis causes sufficient diminution of systolic coronary flow to result in significant reduction of total flow, and thus to produce myocardial ischemia. As in the case of mitral insufficiency, the sudden development of aortic insufficiency is manifest initially by forward rather than by backward failure, by shock rather than dyspnea (see p. 396).

Aortic Stenosis and Insufficiency

The combination of aortic stenosis and insufficiency is common in rheumatic heart disease. For obvious reasons free regurgitation is not possible in the presence of high grade stenosis; nevertheless, even slight regurgitation in the presence of significant stenosis, or slight stenosis in the presence of significant regurgitation, produces a baneful effect, since in each case the left ventricle is required to eject an increased volume of blood against an abnormally great resistance. Perhaps of equal or greater importance is the effect of the combination on coronary flow.

Cardiac Catheterization in Aortic Valve Disease

By *left heart* catheterization, pressures are measured and the forms of the pressure curves recorded in the left ventricle and aorta (or brachial artery). If cardiac output is also estimated, the resistance of the aortic valve can be calculated. In *aortic stenosis* the most characteristic feature is a pressure gradient across the valve, the magnitude of which varies with the degree of stenosis (and with the cardiac output). The gradient of systolic pressure between ventricle and aorta may be as great as 200 mm. Hg, systolic ventricular pressure as high as 300. In most typical cases the systolic gradient has been found to be from 50 to 150.

Surgery of the Aortic Valve

Successful replacement of the deformed aortic valve by a prosthetic device results, in the case of *aortic insufficiency,* in complete disappearance of the peripheral phenomena. In most of these cases some degree of heart failure was present prior to surgery; heart size and cardiac output seldom return to normal,

although clinical improvement may be gratifying. In *aortic stenosis* a small gradient persists across the artificial valve, which offers some obstruction to blood flow. Cardiac output, often reduced before surgery, increases, but usually not to a normal value.

TRICUSPID VALVE DISEASE

Slight deformity of the tricuspid valve, not sufficiently pronounced to produce significant effects upon the heart or circulation, is common in rheumatic heart disease, associated in nearly all instances with more marked defects of the mitral or aortic valves, or of both. Significant tricuspid lesions are usually associated with more severe mitral or aortic defects, which therefore dominate in the production of physiologic disturbances and clinical signs. Occasionally, however, pictures related predominantly to tricuspid defects are seen. The pathologic physiology of tricuspid disease is quite analogous to that of mitral disease, with the important exception that in the former hypertension in the greater circulation is limited to the veins and capillaries; because of the relatively great resistance which normally resides in the systemic arterioles, tricuspid disease results in no appreciable increase in the total resistance of the greater circulation and in no arterial hypertension. It should also be noted that tricuspid disease never leads to congestion of the lungs, even in the presence of heart failure; rather, it tends to reduce the volume of blood in the pulmonary vascular bed.

Tricuspid Insufficiency

In proportion to the size of the leak, dilatation and hypertrophy of the right ventricle occur, and, intermittently with each contraction of the ventricle, distention of the right atrium. Reflux of blood during ventricular systole causes the propagation of a large positive pressure wave into the great veins, the peak of which occurs late in systole at about the time of the normal v wave (Fig. 19–28). This may be manifested by exaggerated *systolic pulsation* of the neck veins and by pulsation of the liver. If the right ventricle remains competent and regurgitation is not very great, there are no other signs, and no symptoms. With the onset of right ventricular failure, progressive dilatation of the right atrium may occur, together with considerable or marked increase in venous pressure, the effects of which are described below under the heading Tricuspid Stenosis.

Tricuspid Stenosis

Constriction of the tricuspid aperture results in increase of the normally slight resistance which opposes the movement of blood through the systemic veins into the right atrium and thence into the ventricle. The atrium undergoes hypertrophy, venous pressure is elevated, and the veins are distended; contraction of the hypertrophied right atrium causes increase in the amplitude of the *a* wave of the venous pulse (Fig. 19–28), which may be expressed as prominent *presystolic pulsation* of the veins of the neck. For reasons which are not clear (perhaps due to chance), giant *a* waves in atrial pressure curves have been recorded more consistently in tricuspid than in mitral stenosis.

If the orifice is markedly narrowed, the great resistance opposing flow through the veins and capillaries results in marked elevation of venous pressure, passive congestion and *enlargement of the liver, ascites* and, in some cases, *edema* of the lower extremities. However, as in constrictive pericarditis, it is characteristic for subcutaneous edema to be slight or absent even in the presence of a large amount of fluid in the peritoneal cavity.* Cardiac output may be normal or subnormal at rest; exercise results in further elevation of atrial and venous pressure without concomitant increase of output. Tolerance to activity and exercise is limited by fatigue and weakness, but the fairly good state of general health which may be maintained for several years, despite the recurrence of ascites after numerous paracenteses, speaks against the existence of continuous tissue hypoxia of severe degree.

The only chamber of the heart which compensates at all for tricuspid stenosis is the right atrium. Obviously, hypertrophy of the right atrium alone cannot compensate for severe obstruction. If no other means were available for overcoming the great resistance opposing flow through a markedly narrowed tricuspid orifice, filling of the right ventricle, and consequently the output of both ventricles, inevitably would be reduced to an extreme degree, with corresponding reduction in the rate of flow into the venous system, which would automatically limit the degree of venous hypertension that could develop. One would then expect a circulation rate so low as to cause severe, permanent hypoxia

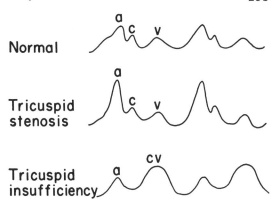

Figure 19–28. Venous pulse in tricuspid stenosis and in tricuspid insufficiency, contrasted to the normal. (Schematic.)

of the tissues, and no more than moderate elevation of venous pressure; it would be unlikely that intracapillary pressures (which in general depend upon the rate of tissue flow on the one hand, and the venous pressure on the other) would be sufficiently elevated to produce edema and ascites.

Clearly, then, some other compensating factor operates in high grade tricuspid stenosis to maintain cardiac output. This factor is increase in the volume of circulating blood, the mechanisms by which blood volume is increased probably being the same as those which operate in congestive heart failure and concretio cordis. Per se, increase of blood volume results in augmentation of ventricular filling and output and of peripheral blood flow; in the presence of tricuspid obstruction a further effect is disproportionate elevation of venous pressure.

Tricuspid Insufficiency and Stenosis

The clinical and physiologic picture of this combination of lesions is identical in most respects with that of tricuspid stenosis or of free insufficiency. Great dilatation of the right atrium is a characteristic finding.

PULMONARY VALVE DISEASE

In nearly all cases of pulmonary stenosis the obstruction is congenital and is frequently accompanied by other defects. Chronic pulmonary insufficiency is a rarity, although the valve may become incompetent because of great dilatation of the pulmonary artery, which may occur in mitral stenosis and in other conditions in which pressure and/or flow in the pulmonary artery is greatly in-

---

* The unique distribution of edema in tricuspid stenosis and concretio cordis is considered on page 432.

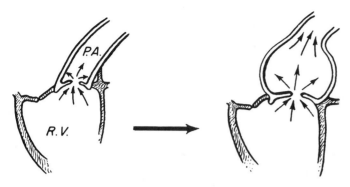

Figure 19–29. How jet effect may lead to dilatation of the pulmonary artery in cases of valvular stenosis.

creased. In congenital valvular stenosis slight incompetency is not uncommon because of poststenotic dilatation of the artery (see below). In rare cases of infundibular stenosis the pulmonary valve is absent, giving a combination of stenosis and insufficiency. Acute insufficiency is uncommon and due in most instances to bacterial endocarditis, which leads to serious difficulty more from emboli thrown into the lung than from leakage of the valve.

Pulmonary Stenosis

In most respects this lesion is analogous to aortic stenosis, its effects being exerted on the right ventricle instead of the left. In a good many cases the stenosis is dynamically insignificant, manifested only by a murmur. If the orifice is reduced by three-fourths, or to about 1 cm.^{2} or less, hypertrophy of the right ventricle occurs, which may become very marked without the occurrence of detectable dilatation. If the lesion is not complicated by the presence of other congenital defects, circulatory dynamics are not detectably changed as long as the right ventricle remains competent. In the average case compensation is well maintained during childhood; only during adolescence or adult life do definite symptoms appear. It is interesting, however, that, following surgical amelioration of the obstruction, some of these "asymptomatic" patients have become more alert and energetic and have developed considerably improved exercise tolerance; not until after surgery does it become evident that cardiac output was not completely adequate before. As the right ventricle "weakens," it dilates, and its output falls off; particularly, its output fails to meet the needs of normal activities. Fatigue and pronounced weakness or even fainting on exertion are characteristic symptoms. Unlike cases of aortic stenosis, cardiac pain is rare, for obvious reasons (see p. 404). Dyspnea on exertion may occur, but is neither severe nor prolonged, since there is no pulmonary engorgement and arterial oxygen saturation is normal; rather, the dyspnea is related to low-output hypoxia. Great dilatation of the right ventricle may occur before the final appearance of frank congestive failure.

The site of congenital pulmonary stenosis may be in the infundibulum of the right ventricle (infundibular stenosis) or at the valve orifice (valvular stenosis); the latter is more common in cases of isolated pulmonary stenosis, the former in cases accompanied by other congenital anomalies. In most cases of valvular stenosis the main pulmonary artery just beyond the valve is considerably or greatly dilated, the branches smaller than normal. The dilatation is believed to be due to a "jet" effect.

Analogous to the situation in aortic stenosis, right ventricular systolic pressure is elevated and systole prolonged. Over a longer than normal period, therefore, blood is ejected forcibly through the narrowed aperture. As it passes through the orifice into the pulmonary artery the column of blood suddenly widens, so that a considerable part of its total force is directed laterally and obliquely against the walls of the artery rather than onward along its lumen (Fig. 19–29). To put it another way: as the column of blood widens, its linear velocity suddenly decreases; lateral pressure, therefore, suddenly increases.

Pulmonary Insufficiency

This lesion, although occasionally dynamically significant, is borne well and rarely of itself leads to heart failure. It is characterized by dilatation and hypertrophy of the right ventricle and increase of pulse pressure in the pulmonary arteries, analogous to the Corrigan pulse of aortic insufficiency. Under the fluoroscope vigorous pulsation of the pulmonary artery and its larger branches may be observed.

Cardiac Catheterization in Pulmonary Stenosis

As expected, systolic and mean pressures in

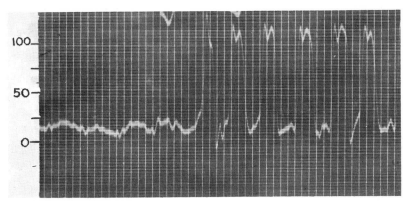

Figure 19–30. Pulmonary stenosis; record of pressures in the pulmonary artery and right ventricle. Note the great increase of pressure as tip of catheter was withdrawn from pulmonary artery into right ventricle.

the right ventricle are elevated, while systolic and mean pressures in the pulmonary artery are much lower, often but not always below normal. The pulse wave in the pulmonary artery is of the plateau type (see p. 403), its amplitude often diminished. Diastolic pressure is normal in most cases, but may be somewhat elevated if pulse pressure is small and mean pressure only slightly reduced (see p. 403). In severe stenosis the systolic pressure gradient between right ventricle and pulmonary artery may exceed 100 mm. Hg.

In valvular stenosis the pressure transition occurs as the catheter is pulled back from the pulmonary artery through the valve orifice; in infundibular stenosis, when it is withdrawn from the infundibulum into the ventricular cavity proper (Fig. 19–30). If, as occasionally happens, there is stenosis at both sites, a double transition may be recorded.

Surgery for Pulmonary Stenosis

Surgical amelioration of pulmonary stenosis, both valvular and infundibular, has now become commonplace, its value definitely established. It is interesting that in some cases of valvular stenosis right ventricular systolic pressure does not return to near normal levels until several months after successful valvulotomy; this phenomenon is attributable to narrowing of the right ventricular outflow tract due to hypertrophy, which gradually regresses after the stimulus to hypertrophy has been removed. A murmur of pulmonary insufficiency is commonly present after the surgeon has corrected the stenosis; occasionally the regurgitation is sufficiently marked to cause dilatation of the right ventricle, but this chirurgenic lesion is borne well.

COMBINED VALVULAR DISEASE

Lesions of more than one valve are in nearly all instances due to scarring which follows rheumatic valvulitis. The most frequent combination is mitral and aortic disease; the less frequent combination of tricuspid disease with mitral or aortic lesions, or both, has been mentioned previously. Not uncommonly, two or more valves are only slightly deformed. If one valve is seriously involved, the deformity of the others is commonly slight and insignificant. If two or more valves are significantly deformed, one is usually affected much more seriously than the others. Most frequently mitral involvement is preponderant; less commonly, aortic; rarely, tricuspid. Perhaps the most common combination is mitral stenosis and aortic insufficiency.

The physiologic effects of combined lesions are due principally to the summated effects of the individual lesions. In perhaps the majority of cases, for reasons just given, there is but little summation; the principal effects are those related to the most seriously deformed valve. Not uncommonly, however, definite physiologic and anatomic changes due to both mitral and aortic defects are seen and, rather rarely, changes related to both mitral and tricuspid lesions.

Much has been written about a lesion of one valve compensating for that of another. It is obvious, however, that the more valves affected, and the more seriously each is involved, the greater the alteration of the circulation as a whole. No lesion can "compensate" for another except at the expense of venous engorgement and decrease of blood flow to the tissues of the body. For example, tight mitral stenosis, if it causes decreased filling of the left ventricle, may "compensate" for aortic insufficiency by diminishing the work of the left ventricle, but the price paid is engorgement of the lungs, decreased cardiac output and diminished coronary flow. Tricuspid stenosis may "compensate" for mitral stenosis, diminishing the burden of the right ventricle and decreasing the congestion of the lungs, but at the expense of increased venous congestion of the greater circulation and decrease of the cardiac output and blood flow to the tissues. In the latter instance, however, definite value is received for the price paid, since the diminution of pulmonary engorgement pays dividends in relief or decrease of dyspnea, and in lessened chances of pulmonary complications; at the same time, the increase in congestion of the systemic veins is proportionately slight. Whether or not this "compensation" often prolongs life is not known; undoubtedly it does in some cases. On the whole, persons with disease of both the mitral and tricuspid valves do not live so long as those with mitral disease alone, but this may be due to the fact that when the tricuspid valve is significantly deformed, very tight mitral stenosis, which of itself would cause death at an early age, is usually present as well. As would be expected, the prognosis of combined lesions is, in general, worse than that of lesions involving a single valve.

Surgery has been successfully performed in a considerable number of cases of combined mitral and aortic lesions and in a smaller number of combined mitral and tricuspid lesions. In a few cases all three valves have been successfully replaced with prosthetic devices. Usually, if significant lesions of two valves are present, both valves are repaired or replaced at the same operation in order to avoid intolerable overburdening of the heart.

For example, if mitral stenosis and aortic insufficiency coexist, mitral commissurotomy alone would suddenly confront the left ventricle with an increased diastolic overload which it could not cope with.

Obviously, restoration of normal dynamics cannot be expected in multiple valve surgery; all that can be accomplished is physiologic and clinical improvement.

Congenital Defects

The common congenital anomalies of the heart and great vessels are atrial septal defect, ventricular septal defect, patent ductus arteriosus, pulmonary stenosis (p. 409), aortic stenosis (p. 403) and coarctation of the aorta.

All of these are encountered frequently as isolated anomalies, but each is often accompanied by other congenital defects. The pathologic physiology of the rarer anomalies can be predicted provided one understands the effects of abnormal communications and obstructions involving the heart and great vessels as exemplified by the more common congenital lesions.

Defects of the cardiac septa and patent ductus, if uncomplicated, are characterized by left-to-right shunts, so that oxygenated blood destined for the periphery is recirculated through the lungs, with resultant increase of pulmonary blood flow and often decrease of peripheral flow. The deleterious effects of these lesions are due to increased work of the heart incident to the recirculation of blood through the lungs, to the increased pulmonary flow per se, and, to a lesser extent, to reduction of peripheral flow. Right-to-left shunting does not occur in any uncomplicated, isolated, single anomaly; such shunting is due either to pulmonary stenosis (or tricuspid obstruction) plus a septal defect, or to the effects of large left-to-right shunts upon the heart or the blood vessels of the lungs.

Atrial Septal Defect

Shunting does not occur through the slit-like valvular opening in simple patency of the foramen ovale, which by its architecture permits flow only from right to left (Fig. 19–31), but the circulation may be affected profoundly by the flow of blood through large defects of the atrial septum (Figs. 19–33 and 19–40). In such defects the direction of flow is from the left atrium into the right. This flow is due to a slightly higher pressure in the left than in the right atrium, or, to put it another way, to the fact that the normal resistance to atrioventricular flow is greater in the left than in the right side of the heart. This difference in pressure is most likely related to the anatomic features of the atrioventricular orifices and ventricular cavities on the two sides of the heart. The mitral orifice is smaller than the tricuspid opening (Fig. 19–38), and the cavity of the left ventricle is narrower and longer than the right, which is shorter and of larger caliber* (Fig. 19–

* Possible additional factors are the thinner walls of the right ventricle, which may offer less resistance to distention near the end of diastole, and the more efficient construction of the tricuspid valve, whose three cusps probably lie in closer apposition to the walls of the ventricle late in diastole than the two cusps of the mitral valve.

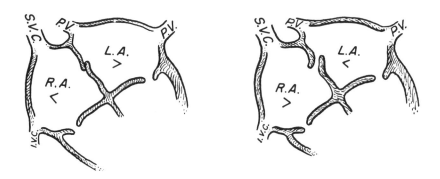

Figure 19–31. How the foramen ovale permits interatrial flow only if pressure in the right atrium is greater.

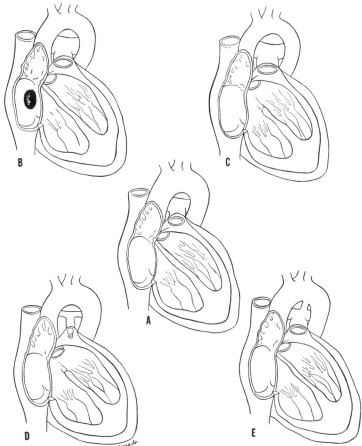

Figure 19–32. Congenital lesions. A, normal; B, atrial septum defect; C, Eisenmenger complex; D, tetralogy of Fallot; E, patent ductus arteriosus.

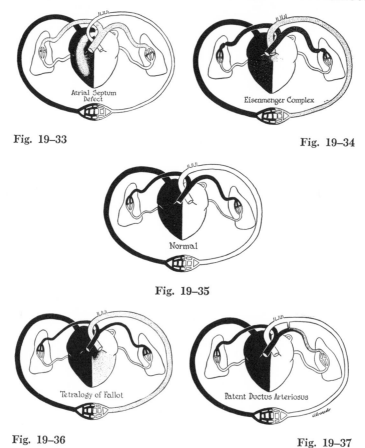

Fig. 19–33   Fig. 19–34

Fig. 19–35

Fig. 19–36   Fig. 19–37

Figures 19–33 to 19–37. Schema of circulation in congenital anomalies. (Modified from Abbott.)

39); the effect of these differences is greater resistance to atrioventricular flow on the left side of the heart than on the right. Nearly all the shunting necessarily occurs during ventricular diastole, but it is probable that because of the greater capacity of the right atrium a minor degree of left-to-right flow continues after the atrioventricular valves have closed.

The flow of extra blood into the right atrium and thence into the right ventricle causes the ventricle to dilate and hypertrophy, but has little or no effect upon the right atrium, since nearly all the shunted blood merely traverses this chamber. The minute and stroke volumes of the right ventricle are increased in proportion to the magnitude of the shunt. Systolic pressure in the pulmonary artery is elevated and pulse pressure increased. Because of the low resistance in the pulmonary circuit, pressure falls off quickly at the end of systole, and the diastolic pressure is only slightly elevated, or not increased

at all. Pulsation of the pulmonary arteries is abnormally vigorous. If compensation is perfect, filling and output of the left ventricle are normal; the net effect is recirculation through the lungs of the blood which leaks through the hole in the septum. If the shunt is very great, however, filling of the left ventricle may be subnormal, so that peripheral flow is reduced even though the right ventricle remains fully competent. Disparity between the rates of pulmonary and peripheral flow results in considerable or great dilatation of the pulmonary arterial system, and in some cases to decrease in the caliber (hypoplasia) of the aorta. Incompetence of the pulmonary valve may result if the main pulmonary artery is greatly dilated.

In time the overburdened ventricle may "weaken," so that residual blood and resistance to filling of this chamber increases; there then occurs an increase of right atrial pressure and necessarily a decrease in the volume of flow through the septal defect and de-

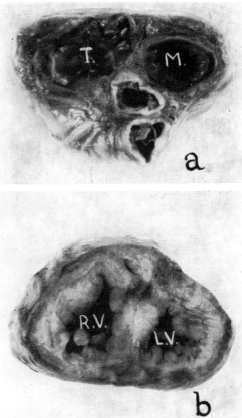

Figure 19–38. *a,* Cross section of the normal heart of a stillborn infant at term, at the level of the atrioventricular orifices: *T,* tricuspid orifice; *M,* mitral orifice. *b,* Section of same heart at a level 1 cm. below the atrioventricular orifices: *RV,* right ventricle; *LV,* left ventricle. (Courtesy of the American Heart Journal.) (E. Hull: Am. Heart J., Vol. 38.)

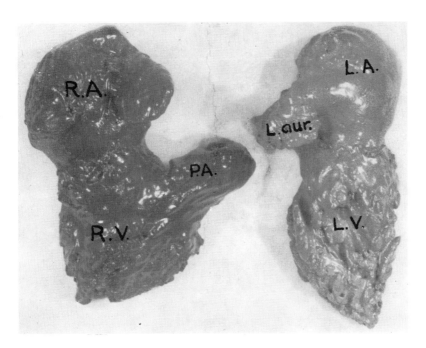

Figure 19–39. Casts of the cavities of a normal heart, viewed from their antiseptal surfaces: *RA,* right atrium; *RV,* right ventricle; *PA,* pulmonary artery; *LA,* left atrium; *LV,* left ventricle; *L. aur.,* left auricle. (Courtesy of the American Heart Journal.) (E. Hull: Am. Heart J., Vol. 38.)

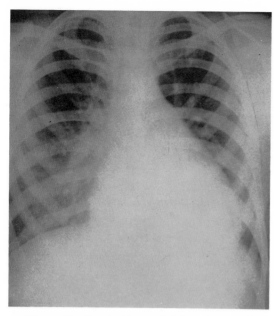

Figure 19–40. Atrial septal defect. Boy aged 10 years, asymptomatic. Catheterization studies indicated that systemic blood flow was approximately 5 liters per minute, pulmonary flow 18 liters. Pulmonary arterial pressure normal (25/15). Successfully corrected by surgery. Defect was of the secundum type, 3.5 × 1 cm.

creased filling of the weakened ventricle, whose burden is thereby diminished. This remarkable adaptation, which is probably effected with little or no further reduction in peripheral flow, is in large measure responsible for the long life and relative freedom from subjective complaints of many persons with large atrial septal defects.

The *physical signs* of atrial septal defect are due to dilatation and increased pulsation of the pulmonary artery: dullness and pulsation to the left of the upper sternum; systolic murmur in the second left interspace; accentuation and fixed splitting of the pulmonary second sound;* in some cases the diastolic murmur of pulmonary incompetence. *Roentgenologic study* (Fig. 19–40) discloses the anatomic effects of the lesion: enlargement of the right ventricle, dilatation of the pulmonary artery and its branches, and decrease in the size of the aorta. Enlargement of the right atrium occurs only after the right ventricle has "weakened." Fluoroscopic examination reveals the throbbing of the pulmonary arteries, which may be so marked as to produce the "hilar dance." The characteristic *electro-*

---

* The dilated pulmonary artery being closer to the chest wall, the sound suffers less than normal loss of intensity in transmission. Fixed splitting may occur because systole of the right ventricle is somewhat prolonged due to the larger volume of blood it discharges; the pulmonary valve then closes after the aortic during both phases of respiration, rather than only during inspiration, as is normally the case.

cardiographic pattern of "right bundle branch delay" is probably due to hypertrophy of the right ventricular outflow tract. If *subjective symptoms* are present, they are due to reduced peripheral flow, causing fatigability, decreased exercise tolerance and weakness. Hoarseness due to compression of the left recurrent nerve by the dilated pulmonary artery or cough due to compression of the left bronchus is an occasional complaint (Fig. 19–18).

Anomalous Pulmonary Veins

The picture of atrial septal defect may be closely reproduced if one (or two) of the main pulmonary veins enters the right atrium instead of the left. The effect is that of a left-to-right shunt of considerable magnitude at the atrial level. Not rarely, anomalous veins and atrial septal defect are coexistent lesions. In some such cases all the pulmonary veins drain into the right atrium ("total anomalous venous return"); in this event all the blood destined for the systemic circulation passes through the atrial septal defect from right to left.

Pulmonary Hypertension in Atrial Septal Defects

Increase of pulmonary flow would tend per se to produce pulmonary hypertension; in fact, if the vascular system of the lungs were a series of rigid tubes, resistance would be quadrupled if right ventricular output were doubled, since resistance is directly proportional to the square of velocity. It has been shown, however, that during exercise in normal subjects mean pressure in the pulmonary artery does not rise until pulmonary flow greatly exceeds the resting level, presumably because of passive (and perhaps active) dilatation of the arterioles of the lungs. This explains why, in most patients with ASD, particularly those who are asymptomatic, mean pulmonary arterial pressure is elevated only slightly or moderately in spite of an obvious considerable increase in pulmonary flow.

With the passage of time, however, severe pulmonary hypertension develops in some cases, which must be indicative of increased resistance to flow through the pulmonary arterioles. Widespread thickening of the walls of the small arteries and arterioles with encroachment upon their lumina has been found at autopsy in such cases; even if the lumina are not narrowed, the distensibility of these vessels and their ability to dilate must be markedly decreased: herein lies the cause of the severe hypertension. The lesions are presumably related pathogenetically to the increase of flow and to the moderate hypertension which it causes. Whether active constriction of the arterioles is a factor in the genesis of the hypertension and of the arteriolar lesions is not known. As would be expected, pulmonary hypertension occurs only in cases of large defects, but why it develops only in a minority of such cases is a mystery. Nor is it known why in the majority of cases it develops at an early age (see p. 418). Pulmonary hypertension has a baneful influence since it imposes an increased pressure load on the right ventricle. It is present in most cases in which serious difficulties arise during childhood.

Right-to-Left Shunting in Atrial Septal Defect

In well compensated cases of large ASD there may be slight, clinically insignificant oxygen unsaturation of arterial blood, undoubtedly due to passive mixing of right and left atrial blood at the site of the defect during ventricular systole. It should be obvious that in the presence of a large defect there can be no gradient of pressure between the atria and no active flow through the defect when the atrioventricular valves are closed. Since there can be no flow out of the freely communicating atria, there can be little or no flow from one to the other; whatever difference in pressure existed during diastole must disappear after the atrioventricular valves close. During systole, however, the atria are filling from the great veins, and some passive mixing may take place at the site of a large defect. In this sense a right-to-left shunt sufficient to cause slight oxygen unsaturation of arterial blood, is a common occurrence in well compensated cases.

Right-to-left flow sufficient to cause clinical cyanosis, however, is indicative of right ventricular failure with increase of right atrial pressure. For some time cyanosis may be noticeable only on exertion; with advancing failure it may be present constantly. It is improbable that there is ever complete reversal of flow except perhaps terminally; more likely the shunt is bidirectional—left to right early during ventricular diastole, right to left toward its end and during ventricular systole.

Even in severe heart failure, resistance to atrioventricular flow is slight during the period which follows immediately upon opening of the atrioventricular valves; during this period the pressure relations between the two atria are probably nearly normal, and blood flows from left to right. As ventricular filling proceeds resistance to flow increases more on the right side than on the left, and the direction of the shunt is reversed. Shunt reversal may again enable the failing right heart to maintain a precarious balance, since flow into the left atrium results in diminution of the volume load of the right ventricle; also, edema may fail to appear because the shunt prevents inordinate elevation of right atrial pressure. Right ventricular output is relatively small, left ventricular output relatively great but absolutely reduced considerably because the ultimate energy for its filling must derive from the failing right ventricle; tissue hypoxia is due both to anoxemia and to reduced flow. Weakness and fatigability are marked, and dyspnea may be considerable.

At this stage (or earlier) strenuous exertion (such as that of labor) may induce intense cyanosis soon followed by a severe shock-like state, the latter being due to critical overloading of the right ventricle with resultant marked decrease in its output. Interestingly, this syndrome may respond dramatically to l-norepinephrine (or metaraminol), probably not because of vasoconstriction but because it increases the contractile power of the right ventricle.

Pulmonary Stenosis with Patent Atrial Septum

In about 20 per cent of normal hearts the margins of the foramen ovale fail to fuse. In many cases of congenital pulmonary stenosis, therefore, right-to-left flow between the atria is possible. So long as the right ventricle remains fully competent, no such flow occurs, but with the onset of incipient failure right atrial pressure rises and a right-to-left shunt through the foramen ovale is initiated. Since the shunt serves to reduce the burden of the right ventricle, failure tends not to be progressive, and a fairly stable shunt of moderate to considerable magnitude is established. Persistent cyanosis is present, and the physiologic picture becomes almost identical with that of the tetralogy of Fallot (p. 420). In these cases cyanosis is apt to make its appearance during early childhood.

Less commonly pulmonary stenosis and true atrial septal defect coexist. In this event right-to-left shunting begins shortly after birth (or may continue after birth), since a left-to-right interatrial shunt in the presence of tight pulmonary stenosis confronts the right ventricle with an intolerable burden. The right-to-left shunt is of great magnitude, the physiologic picture that of a severe tetralogy.

Ostium Primum Defect

In defect of the septum primum (the partial form of endocardial cushion defect) there is a large ASD just above the a-v valves often associated with a cleft mitral valve, less commonly with deformity of the tricuspid valve also. Most commonly the physiologic picture is that of ASD plus mitral insufficiency (see p. 395). In the presence of MI, shunting through the ASD occurs during ventricular systole as well as diastole, and shunted blood is derived not only from the pulmonary veins but also from the left ventricle. The net effect is pronounced reduction in peripheral blood flow. Growth and development are retarded, easy fatigability characteristic.

If tricuspid insufficiency exists, the physiologic effects of this lesion may be manifest—increased venous pressure, systolic pulsation of neck veins, enlarged liver, etc. (see p. 408). Higher pressure in the right atrium would per se tend to reverse the shunt, but this tendency is opposed by the presence of mitral insufficiency which usually coexists.

Lutembacher's Complex

Rather rarely mitral stenosis coexists with defects of the atrial septum, the combination being known as Lutembacher's complex. It appears that in most cases the mitral stenosis is an acquired lesion of rheumatic etiology.

If the mitral obstruction is significant in degree, a larger part of the blood which enters the left atrium passes through the septal defect, and a smaller part enters the left ventricle. Thus the left atrium and the pulmonary system of veins are spared the effects of high pressure, to a degree proportional to the amount by which filling of the left ventricle is reduced. The output of the left ventricle is decreased in like amount. Return flow to the right atrium via the great veins is correspondingly diminished, while an increased amount of blood enters this chamber through the septal defect. Total filling of the right atrium and right ventricle is therefore not affected by the mitral obstruction; more blood enters by the septal defect, less by way of the venae cavae.

Hence the status of the circulation in ASD is altered in only one respect by the presence of mitral stenosis: the output of the left ventricle is decreased in proportion to the degree of obstruction. Since this change has no definite clinical expression, the clinical picture is altered only by the addition of the characteristic diastolic murmur of mitral stenosis. The left atrium does not enlarge; no signs of passive pulmonary congestion appear.

Ventricular Septal Defect

Defects of the ventricular septum usually involve the membranous portion, in close proximity to the anteromedial cusp of the aortic valve; large defects may involve the muscular septum as well. Flow through the defect occurs during ventricular systole, its left-to-right direction being determined by the high resistance offered flow into the aorta on the one hand and the low resistance of the pulmonary vascular system on the other. It is obvious that if other factors are equal the shunt through a ventricular septal defect must greatly exceed the flow through an atrial defect of the same size.

If the defect is quite small (match-sized), its own resistance sharply limits the magnitude of the shunt, and the circulation is affected but little; right ventricular systolic pressure and pulmonary arterial pressures remain nor-

mal, and there is only a slight or moderate increase in pulmonary blood flow. Such small defects, compatible with normal or near-normal longevity, comprise the classical *Maladie de Roger,* and are manifested principally by the characteristic long, loud systolic murmur.

If, on the other hand, the defect is so large as to offer but little resistance to shunting, its effect during ventricular systole is to produce a common ventricle, and the magnitude of the shunt is determined only by the difference between the resistances of the systemic and pulmonary vascular beds. Between these two extremes is the defect of moderate size which permits considerable left-to-right flow but limits its magnitude in greater or lesser degree.

The blood which is shunted through the defect recirculates through the lungs and returns to the left ventricle, the output and work of both ventricles being increased in proportion to the magnitude of the shunt. The pulmonary and systemic circuits are affected in the same way as they are in cases of atrial septum defect (p. 412), the only differences being that the right atrium does not participate in the recirculation process, whereas the left ventricle does. Heart failure may occur during infancy or even during the first few days of life in the case of large defects; persons with defects of moderate size are often free of symptoms until later childhood, adolescence, or adult life. Interestingly, severe heart failure occurring during infancy is not necessarily fatal; in some cases compensation is restored and maintained for months or years.

Not rarely VSD's close spontaneously during the first few months or years of life, and large ones may diminish considerably in size. In one of our cases the shunt amounted to 7 times systemic flow at age 8 months, to 0.7 times systemic flow at age 5 years, at which time RV and PA pressures were normal.

Pulmonary Hypertension in Ventricular Septal Defect

As expected, pulmonary hypertension is present at an early age in many cases of large defects, and eventually develops in the case of many defects of moderate size. Further, it appears that in some cases pulmonary hypertension is present from birth or persists after birth. Within limits increase of pulmonary vascular resistance is geneficial, since it results in decrease in the magnitude of the shunt and the volume load of the right ventricle.

During fetal life the pulmonary circuit is a high-resistance system, the lumina of the minor branches of the pulmonary arteries and of the arterioles being relatively small, their medial coats thick (Fig. 19–41). Most of the blood which enters the main pulmonary artery is therefore shunted through the ductus arteriosus into the aorta. After birth this "fetal hypertrophy" of the media regresses; the media of the small pulmonary vessels become thinner, their lumina larger, and pulmonary vascular resistance much lower.

In instances of very large VSD or wide patency of the ductus, the fetal state of the small pulmonary vessels may persist and thereby prevent inordinate increase in pulmonary flow. Persistence of the "fetal hypertrophy" and maintenance of "arteriolar tone" in the pulmonary system may therefore explain, as a protective or compensatory mechanism, the finding of pronounced pulmonary hypertension in infants with defects which per se would lead to left-to-right shunts of such magnitude as to preclude even reasonably adequate systemic flow and which would present the heart with an intolerable burden. In some cases of large defects the left-to-right shunt is of minor magnitude and the right ventricle, although greatly hypertrophied, is but little enlarged (Fig. 19–42).

In some cases another factor operates to reduce the magnitude of the shunt: hypertrophy of the outflow tract of the right ventricle may lead to narrowing of the infundibulum—a secondary infundibular stenosis, which increases the resistance to flow into the pulmonary artery.

Right-to-Left Shunting in Ventricular Septal Defect

Obviously, reversal of the shunt will occur whenever resistance to pulmonary flow exceeds resistance to systemic flow. In the absence of pulmonary stenosis pulmonary resistance seldom exceeds systemic resistance until after the age of 4 or 5, but after this age, and quite commonly after the age of 10 or 12, right-to-left shunting occurs through large defects. At the onset, reversal of the shunt may occur only with exercise; later, bidirectional shunting may be more or less constantly present, and finally the shunt may become predominantly right-to-left and of considerable magnitude. The picture of right-to-left shunting in ventricular septal defect constitutes the *Eisenmenger syndrome* or complex (Figs. 19–32 and 19–34).

The tetralogy originally described by Eisenmenger consists of ventricular septal defect, dextroposition of the aorta, dilatation of the pulmonary artery, and hypertrophy of the right ventricle. It is characterized by a left-to-right shunt during early childhood, with the development of cyanosis (right-to-left shunt) during later childhood, adolescence, or early adult life. Although in this anomaly the origin of the aorta is displaced to the right and overrides the defect in the top of the ventricular septum (Fig. 19–32, *C*), it should be clear from the foregoing that even with dextroposition of the aorta significant right-to-left shunting cannot occur unless or until marked pulmonary hypertension has developed. There is therefore no physiologic difference between Eisenmenger's tetralogy and the Eisenmenger syndrome.

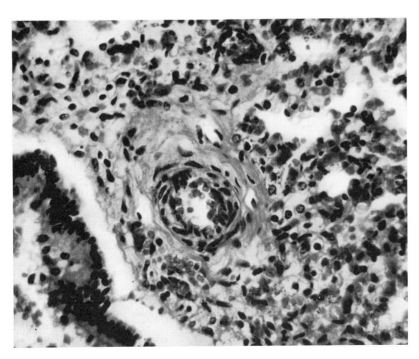

Figure 19–41. Small artery ("arteriole") in lung of a 6-7 months' fetus; normal medial "hypertrophy," small lumen. Bronchiole below and to the left. (Courtesy of Dr. W. E. Jaques.)

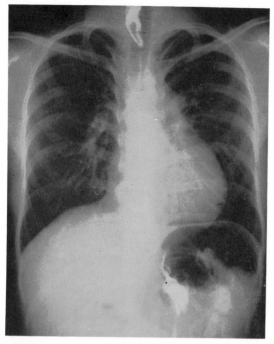

Figure 19–42. Ventricular septal defect with pulmonary hypertension. Girl age 15. Marked retardation of growth, dyspnea on slightest exertion. Catheterization studies indicated that systemic flow was approximately 2.7 liters per minute, pulmonary flow 5.5 liters. Right ventricular pressure was 110/10, pulmonary artery pressure 110/70, femoral artery pressure 110/80. Very slight right-to-left shunt (arterial O_2 saturation breathing air 83 per cent, oxygen 99 per cent). Death three weeks after surgical closure of defect, which was 3 cm. in diameter.

Ventricular Septal Defect with Aortic Insufficiency

Significant or severe aortic regurgitation develops in some cases of VSD, due as a rule to prolapse of the right aortic cusp, which is situated immediately above the defect in the membranous septum. Apparently the prolapse occurs gradually during the first decade of life, the attachment of the cusp lacking normal support or strength. In such cases the VSD is usually of only moderate size, and once the aortic insufficiency has become severe it dominates the physiologic and clinical pictures.

Ventricular Septal Defect with Pulmonary Stenosis (Tetralogy of Fallot)

The tetrad described by Fallot consists of pulmonary stenosis, ventricular septal defect, dextroposed aorta, and right ventricular hypertrophy (Fig. 19–32, *D*). The essential lesions for production of the characteristic clinical

and physiologic picture are, however, just the first two parts of the tetralogy. Right ventricular hypertrophy is secondary, dextroposition neither necessary nor constantly present.

In classic cases the septal defect is large and the pulmonary stenosis moderately severe. Because of the latter, resistance to flow into the pulmonary artery is increased so greatly that, when the ventricles contract, blood from both ventricles enters the aorta; only a part of the output of the right ventricle flows into the pulmonary circuit. The result is that venous blood, in an amount related to the degree of the pulmonary stenosis, is shunted into the aorta without passing through the lungs (Fig. 19–36); oxygen saturation of arterial blood is correspondingly reduced. Blood flow through the lungs is decreased in proportion to the degree of pulmonary stenosis, and flow into the aorta and to the periphery is increased in the same proportion.

The right ventricle undergoes hypertrophy, but little or no dilatation, since its filling is not greatly increased. The pulmonary vascular system becomes hypoplastic; the lungs are relatively bloodless.

The *clinical picture* of Fallot's tetralogy is related to increased oxygen unsaturation of blood in the capillaries, to tissue hypoxia, to hypertrophy of the right ventricle, and to hypoplasia of the pulmonary vessels and the relatively bloodless state of the lungs. Thus are explained the *cyanosis*, increasing on exertion,[*] polycythemia, which is compensatory since it enables the blood which passes through the lungs to take up more oxygen; *retardation of growth and development; dyspnea* or *fainting* or *squatting*[†] on exertion; the *coeur en sabot* configuration of the roentgenologic silhouette of the heart and the

---

[*] During exercise there is increase of venous return together with decrease in the peripheral resistance of the greater circulation, but the resistance offered by the pulmonary stenosis remains unchanged; hence the right-to-left shunt increases both relatively and absolutely.

[†] It has been shown that squatting causes more rapid return of arterial O_2 saturation to its resting value after exercise. Squatting causes an increase of resistance in the systemic circulation (exercise causes the reverse), possibly due to bending of the femoral and popliteal arteries and increase of intra-abdominal pressure; right to left shunting is therefore lessened. Further, venous return to the heart is increased, and since relatively less blood is shunted, more flows through the lungs. Undoubtedly improved pulmonary ventilation (higher expiratory position of the diaphragm) is a major reason why these patients are relieved of dyspnea by squatting.

preternaturally clear lung fields; the *electro-cardiographic signs* of right ventricular hypertrophy.

The genesis of *clubbing* of the fingers and toes, so characteristic of the cyanotic forms of congenital heart disease, is unknown. Clubbing is not peculiar to congenital heart disease, nor indeed to conditions characterized by subnormal arterial oxygen saturation; it occurs in a wide variety of conditions among which a common pathogenetic factor is difficult to find.

Mendlowitz's careful studies led him to the opinion that the common factor among the conditions in which clubbing of the digits and hypertrophic osteoarthropathy occur is increased peripreral blood flow. Mauer suggested that there must be two factors for clubbing to be produced: rapid blood flow, and tissue hypoxia. The tissue hypoxia may be due to subnormal arterial oxygen saturation, as in cardiac and pulmonary disorders, or to interference with diffusion of oxygen from the red cells because of intravascular rouleaux formation, such as occurs in conditions characterized by rapid sedimentation rates. This attractive theory accounts for the occurrence of clubbing in infections, neoplasms and metabolic disorders in which arterial hypoxia does not occur, and explains the rapid development of clubbing and osteoarthropathy in certain mediastinal and lung tumors and lung abscesses in which sedimentation rates are rapid and arterial hypoxia also exists.

If the pulmonary stenosis is very severe or there is pulmonary atresia (pseudotruncus), the major part (or all) of pulmonary blood flow reaches the lungs through anastomoses between the systemic and pulmonary arterial systems, mostly via the bronchial and intercostal arteries. In such cases cyanosis is very marked, polycythemia pronounced, hypoxic symptoms severe; in some cases continuous murmurs may be heard over dilated intercostal arteries.

If, on the other hand, the pulmonary stenosis is slight or moderate, the physiologic (and clinical) picture is that of VSD, blood shunting from left to right. In such cases, if the VSD is large, a moderate degree of pulmonary stenosis may be beneficial (see p. 417).

If there is pulmonary stenosis with a small ventricular septal defect and no overriding of the aorta, shunting is minimized by the resistance of the small septal aperture. Depending upon the degree of pulmonary stenosis there may be a small left-to-right shunt, no shunt at all, or a small or moderate right-to-left shunt; in the last case (very severe pulmonary stenosis), right ventricular failure is apt to occur at an early age.

Often in tetralogy of Fallot cyanosis is not apparent until 6 or 7 months of age. In such cases it is likely that at birth there is only slight infundibular stenosis, and that the shunt is initially left to right and of considerable magnitude. As hypertrophy of the right ventricular outflow tract progresses (see p. 417), the stenosis becomes increasingly severe so that eventually shunt reversal occurs. In many cases of tetralogy, for reasons which are now clear, bidirectional shunting is present.

PATENT DUCTUS ARTERIOSUS

In many respects patent ductus arteriosus is analogous to ventricular septal defect, since in each there is communication between the high resistance greater circulation and the low resistance pulmonary system. In both instances left-to-right shunting is considerable unless the communication is quite small; in both, large communications may lead to heart failure in early infancy, to pulmonary hypertension, and to eventual shunt reversal. The principal physiologic differences, all related to the site at which shunting occurs, are as follows:

1. In patent ductus arteriosus the right ventricle does not participate in the recirculation process, so that there is no stimulus to right sided hypertrophy unless or until pulmonary hypertension develops.

2. In patent ductus arteriosus shunting occurs throughout the cardiac cycle, the velocity of flow through the ductus being greatest late in systole when the difference in pressure between the two systems is greatest (Fig. 19–43).

3. Unless the ductus is of small caliber, the aortic pressure pulse and the peripheral arterial pulses are affected in characteristic fashion by the shunt. Typically, pulse pressure is increased, diastolic pressure diminished; the ascent and, more particularly, the descent of the pressure pulse are steepened. The aorta as well as the pulmonary artery can be seen to throb vigorously under the fluoroscope; the peripheral pulses are corriganoid, like those of aortic insufficiency.

In fact, the dynamics of patent ductus arteriosus and aortic insufficiency are quite similar. In both instances blood destined for the periphery leaks from the aorta into the left ventricle—in aortic insufficiency directly, in patent ductus arteriosus indirectly via the lungs and the left atrium. In the latter, however, the leakage is most pronounced during systole, while in the former it occurs only during diastole. Hence in patent ductus arteriosus systolic pressure tends not to be elevated, the increased pulse pressure being due principally to decline of the diastolic pressure. It is said that the diminution of diastolic pressure in patent ductus arteriosus is accentuated by exercise, but I have not been impressed with this phenomenon.

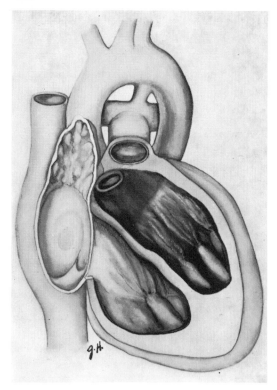

Figure 19–43. Patent ductus arteriosus. Compare with Figure 19–32.

It is further to be noted that sometimes pulse pressure is not increased in patent ductus arteriosus even though the caliber of the ductus is considerable. Presumably in these cases pulmonary vascular resistance has increased sufficiently to reduce diastolic flow through the ductus.

4. If right-to-left shunting develops, cyanosis is apt to be deeper (and arterial oxygen unsaturation more pronounced) in the lower than in the upper extremities. The difference is due to the fact that the ductus communicates with the aorta distal to the left subclavian artery, so that the greater part of the flow from pulmonary artery into aorta is directed downward.

COARCTATION OF THE AORTA

In the "adult type" of this anomaly, which is the type to be considered, there is constriction or atresia of the descending arch a short distance beyond the root of the left subclavian artery, in the region of the attachment of the ligamentum arteriosum. In occasional cases the ductus remains patent, its aortic orifice being just proximal to the stenosis (postductal coarctation). In most cases the condition is borne without symptoms

during infancy and childhood and is manifested only by objective signs related to the resistance of the coarctation and to the development of collateral vessels which permit the narrowed site to be bypassed; in some cases, however, heart failure occurs during early infancy (*vide infra*).

The channels of the bypass consist of connections between branches of the subclavian arteries (scapular branches, superior intercostals, internal mammaries) and branches of the descending aorta and the iliac arteries (intercostals, deep epigastrics) (Fig. 19–44).

The clinical picture is in part due to the dilated channels themselves, to their pulsation and to the flow of blood through them: the erosion of the posterior arcs of the ribs, the pulsations over the back, the systolic or continuous murmurs audible in some patients between the scapulas.

The physiologic disturbances are expressed principally by alteration of the relations between pressures in the arteries of the upper and lower extremities. Obviously, this alteration reflects changes of pressure in the aorta above and below the stenosis, which are due directly or indirectly to the coarctation itself.

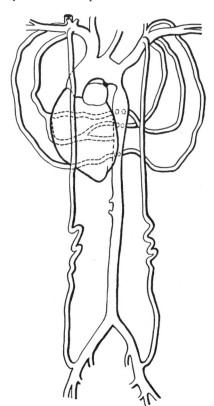

Figure 19–44. Collateral circulation in coarctation of the aorta. (Schematic.)

Pulse Pressures, Systolic Pressures, Pulse Forms

In effect, coarctation of high grade divides the aorta into two vessels, which may be called the proximal and distal aortas; these reservoirs communicate through a small aperture at the stenotic site and through a series of tortuous indirect channels.

The systolic discharge of the left ventricle (which is of normal amount in most cases) is ejected into the proximal aorta, the capacity of which is only about one-third of the normal aorta. The elastic reservoir being greatly reduced in volume, pressure in the proximal aorta rises excessively during early systole, producing a large, steep, ascending limb in the aortic pressure pulse. Late in systole and early in diastole the pressure declines rapidly, for the principal reason that, because of the small reservoir, blood is quickly propelled toward the periphery; blood flows rapidly, not only into the arteries of the upper part of the body, but also through the channels which lead into the distal aorta. Thus a pulse wave of great amplitude with quick rise and fall is propagated into the carotid and subclavian arteries (Fig. 19–45). Systolic pressure in the arms is elevated considerably.

Now propagation of the pulse is not specifically affected by factors which affect blood flow, but rather by those which affect the transmission of compressional waves; especially are the waves affected by reflection, which occurs with each change of direction or of vessel caliber. Great reflection occurs as the pressure pulse strikes the site of constriction, and as the waves are propagated over the tortuous branching and converging collateral channels; the pulse wave is therefore greatly reduced in amplitude when it reaches the distal aorta, or it may be entirely dissipated in its transmission. Also, if the wave is propagated principally through the collaterals, its arrival in the distal aorta is delayed. Since pressure waves reach the distal aorta via different channels of varying lengths and therefore at different times, the ascent and descent of its pressure pulse are gradual.

Hence a small, often delayed, plateau-like pulse (or no pulse at all) is propagated into the arteries of the abdomen and lower extremities (Fig. 19–45). Systolic pressure is considerably less than that in the arteries of the upper part of the body, but not necessarily below a normal level.

The disturbances just described constitute the most constant and most characteristic

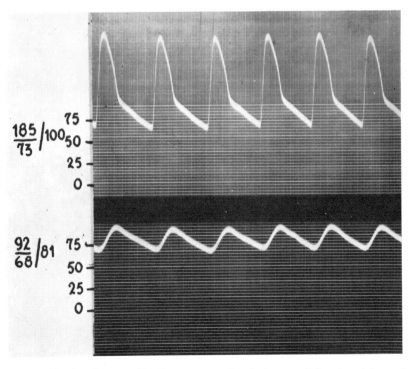

Figure 19–45. Simultaneous blood pressures in brachial artery (*above*) and femoral artery (*below*) in a case of coarctation of the aorta. Numerals at left refer to systolic, diastolic and mean pressures.

physical signs of coarctation: increase of pulse pressure in the brachial arteries, decrease in the femorals; high systolic pressure in the brachials, lower systolic pressure in the femorals; a pulse of great amplitude in the brachial and radial arteries; impalpable pulse or a small, delayed, plateau-like pulse in the femoral and dorsalis pedis arteries. They also account for the throbbing of the arteries of the neck and the frequently observed capillary pulse in the lips and fingernails (see p. 406).

Mean Pressures

Mean pressure in the aorta is determined by the cardiac output and the resistance which opposes the onward flow of blood. If the cardiac output is normal and the resistance which resides in the peripheral arterioles is unchanged, it follows that mean pressure in the proximal aorta (in cases of coarctation) must be increased above the normal in proportion to the resistance which opposes the flow of blood into the distal aorta. This obviously represents an appreciable though not necessarily a great increase in total resistance. The stenosis itself offers great resistance, which, however, is mitigated by the presence of the collateral channels; these oppose blood flow principally because of their small individual calibers. Mean pressure in the proximal aorta is therefore inevitably elevated, but not necessarily to a great height.

Just as inevitably, mean pressure in the distal aorta is decreased below that in the segment above the stenosis. There are two reasons for this: First, elevation of mean pressure in the proximal aorta in the presence of normal arteriolar resistance in the arms and head results in increased flow through the upper part of the body, so that the distal aorta receives less than its normal share of the stroke volume of the heart. Second, resistance to outflow from the distal aorta is normal, while the resistance which opposes flow out of the proximal aorta increased; this factor would operate to depress mean pressure in the distal segment below that in the proximal aorta even if selective vasoconstriction in the upper part of the body prevented increased flow through these regions and insured a normal input to the distal aorta.

Therefore, since mean pressure in the arteries is related to mean intra-aortic pressure, mean pressure in the arteries of the arms is elevated, and higher than that in the legs; the difference between the mean pressures is, however, not necessarily great.

True mean pressure has no exact clinical expression, for it is not the arithmetic mean of the systolic and diastolic pressures (the systolic pressure being the highest instantaneous pressure attained as the pulse wave passes, and the diastolic the lowest level to which pressure falls after passage of the pulse wave), but rather the average of an infinite number of instantaneous pressures which exist during the pulse cycle. If the pulse wave is of normal form, mean arterial pressure is somewhat nearer to the diastolic than to the systolic pressure. If the pulse wave rises and falls precipitously, mean pressure more nearly approaches the diastolic, while if the pulse is of plateau form, mean pressure may be at or near the arithmetic mean of the systolic and diastolic pressures. Obviously, also, if pulse pressure is large, mean pressure (in absolute terms) is farther removed from both the systolic and diastolic pressures, while if pulse pressure is small, mean pressure is nearer to both the systolic and diastolic pressures.

Diastolic Pressures

It should be noted that mean pressure, not diastolic pressure, measures the peripheral resistance. The mean pressure does not depend on the levels of systolic and diastolic pressures; rather, both systolic and diastolic pressures depend upon the level of mean pressure and upon the pulse pressure and the shape of the pulse wave.

Now we have seen that in coarctation of the aorta mean pressure and pulse pressure are both elevated in the arteries of the upper extremity, the former less than the latter. Because of the shape of the pulse wave, mean pressure is nearer to the diastolic than the systolic pressure, but because the pulse wave is large, diastolic pressure is still considerably below mean pressure. Therefore diastolic pressure may be elevated, normal or even subnormal.

In the arteries of the lower extremities mean pressure is below, but not necessarily much below, that in the upper part of the body, while pulse pressure is greatly reduced. Because the pulse wave is of small amplitude, systolic, mean and diastolic pressures are all close together. Therefore diastolic pressure is not much below mean pressure. If the reduction of mean pressure is only moderate, then diastolic pressure may not be reduced at all, or may even be elevated; in fact, it may be as high as the diastolic pressure in the upper extremities. Thus is explained the fact that in some cases of coarctation diastolic pressure in the femoral arteries is elevated, and may be as high as or occasionally even higher than diastolic pressure in the brachials; there is no need to postulate the existence of generalized constriction of arterioles throughout the body. Indeed, the fact that cerebral blood flow is considerably increased in cases of coarctation (but not in essential hypertension), as well as a body of clinical evidence which indicates that flow in the tissues supplied by branches originating from the proximal segment is increased, speaks against the opinion expressed by several authors that the hypertension of coarctation is due, not to the mechanical effects of the coarctation, but rather to widespread increase of arteriolar tone.

Suppose that in a case of coarctation mean pressure in the brachial artery is 110, pulse pressure 100; systolic pressure might then be 190, diastolic 90. Suppose that mean pressure in the femoral artery is 95,* pulse pressure 10; systolic pressure might then be 100, diastolic 90.

In some but not in most cases of coarctation mean arterial pressure in the lower extremities is considerably above normal, and pressure in the arms very high; in these cases the hypertension cannot be due solely to the effects of the coarctation per se. It is believed that the hypertension in some of these cases is of renal origin, related pathogenetically to diminution of pulse pressure in the arteries of the kidneys—to the "quality" of renal blood flow.

The hypertension of coarctation leads to hypertrophy of the left ventricle, to dilatation of the proximal aorta and to cerebral atherosclerosis; heart failure may occur eventually, but death is more commonly due to dissecting aneurysm, rupture of the aorta, cerebral hemorrhage or bacterial endocarditis. Deficient circulation in the legs may be manifested by claudication. The distal aorta is often hypoplastic (an effect of diminished pulse pressure as much as reduced flow), but the portion immediately beyond the constricted isthmus is frequently dilated. The pathogenesis of the dilatation is undoubtedly the same as that of poststenotic dilatation of the pulmonary artery—a "jet" effect (p. 410).

Not very rarely severe congestive heart failure occurs in early infancy in cases of coarctation. In some but not nearly all of these the coarctation is proximal to the ductus, which is usually widely patent (infantile or preductal type). In the majority of cases the failure responds to medical management, and cardiac compensation may be well maintained thereafter during infancy and early childhood at least through the efforts of the left ventricle and perhaps also because of enlargement of the collateral channels.

Interestingly, there are usually right axis deviation and other signs of right ventricular hypertrophy in the ECG's of infants in heart failure due to coarctation, presumably because left ventricular failure with resulting pulmonary hypertension supervenes before the normal fetal hypertrophy of the right ventricle has had time to regress.

CARDIAC CATHETERIZATION IN THE STUDY OF CONGENITAL HEART DISEASE

By the technique of right-sided cardiac catheterization, samples of blood for gas analysis may be obtained from the superior and inferior venae cavae, right atrium, right ventricle and the pulmonary artery and its branches (Fig. 19–1), and the pressures measured at these various sites. Data thus obtained are of value in establishing or confirming the diagnosis of certain congenital anomalies of the heart and great vessels, and have contributed importantly to knowledge of the quantitative aspects of the abnormalities of pressure and flow in these conditions. In some cases the catheter can be passed through a septal defect or a patent ductus or into an anomalous pulmonary vein and thereby establish a diagnosis with absolute certainty (Fig. 19–46).

Data Obtainable by Comparative Oxygen Content of Blood Samples

A left-to-right shunt between the greater and lesser circulations may be detected, its location determined and its relative magnitude estimated by comparison of the oxygen contents of samples taken at the several sites mentioned. Normally the oxygen contents of blood in the right atrium, right ventricle and pulmonary artery are nearly the same, and about equal to the average oxygen content of samples taken from the superior and inferior venae cavae. If there is shunting due to *atrial septal defect,* the oxygen content of right atrial blood exceeds that of blood from the venae cavae; the finding of a higher oxygen content in right ventricular blood than in samples from the right atrium is indicative of *ventricular septal defect;* and *patency of the ductus arteriosus* is suggested if blood from the pulmonary artery has a higher oxygen content than right ventricular blood.

In left-to-right shunts the oxygen saturation of blood drawn from a systemic artery is normal (about 95 per cent or 19 volumes per 100 ml. at a hemoglobin content of 15 gm. per 100 ml.†). If this is the case, then the

---

* Mean pressure is normally slightly greater in the femoral than in the brachial arteries.

† 100 per cent oxygen saturation in volumes per cent = hemoglobin in grams per 100 ml. $\times$ 1.34.

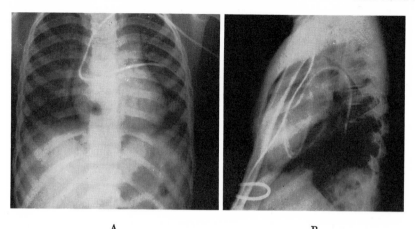

A   B

Figure 19–46. Cardiac catheterization. *A*, Atrial septal defect; tip of catheter in pulmonary vein. *B*, Eisenmenger complex; tip of catheter in descending aorta.

relative rates of systemic and pulmonary flow and hence the relative magnitude of the shunt can be estimated. If, in addition, the oxygen absorption per unit of time is determined, the absolute volume of blood shunted per unit of time may be estimated by application of the Fick principle. The accuracy of these estimations is limited, however, by incomplete mixing of shunted and nonshunted blood. In atrial septal defect, for example, the oxygen content of samples taken from different regions of the right atrial cavity or even from different regions of the right ventricle may vary considerably; the same obtains in samples from the main pulmonary artery and its right and left branches in cases of patent ductus.

Suppose that in *patent ductus arteriosus* the oxygen contents of samples obtained from the right ventricle, *mv* (mixed venous blood), pulmonary artery, *pa*, and from a systemic artery, *sa*, are respectively 13, 16 and 19 volumes per cent, and that the oxygen absorption is 240 ml. per minute.

Applying the Fick equation to determine pulmonary flow, *PF*, and systemic flow, *SF*, separately, we have

$$PF = \frac{O_2 \text{ absorption/min.}}{(O_2 \text{ sa} - O_2 \text{ pa})}$$

and

$$SF = \frac{O_2 \text{ absorption/min.}}{(O_2 \text{ sa} - O_2 \text{ mv})}$$

Then, $PF = \dfrac{240 \text{ ml.}}{0.03} = 8$ liters/min.,

$SF = \dfrac{240 \text{ ml.}}{0.06} = 4$ liters/min.

and the rate of flow through the ductus is 4 liters per minute, amounting to one-half of the output of the left ventricle.

Since the numerators of the two Fick equations are the same, it is obvious that the ratio of *PF* to *SF* varies inversely with the denominators. That is,

$$\frac{PF}{SF} = \frac{6}{3}, \text{ or PF} = 2 \text{ SF}.$$

Thus the ratio of systemic to pulmonary flow and the relative magnitude of the shunt may be estimated without determining oxygen absorption.

"Right-to-left" shunts and bidirectional shunts may be detected and studied quantitatively if the assumption is made that the oxygen saturation of blood leaving the lungs is normal (95 per cent, the same as that of normal arterial blood); or, preferably, if the sample of blood from a systemic artery is drawn while the subject is inhaling 100 per cent oxygen, for during this time the O_2 saturation of blood leaving the lungs (pv) is 100 per cent.

If there is a right-to-left shunt, O_2 saturation of systemic arterial blood will be subnormal (less than 92 per cent if the subject is breathing air, less than 99 per cent if breathing oxygen). If shunting is bidirectional, signs of a left-to-right shunt are encountered as well, in that the O_2 content of samples from the right atrium or right ventricle or pulmonary artery is higher than that of blood from the venae cavae. In both instances the rate of systemic flow is inversely proportional to the O_2 difference between mixed venous blood and systemic arterial blood, and the rate of pulmonary flow bears the same relation to the O_2 contents of pulmonary arterial blood on the one hand and the blood leaving the lungs on the other.

Suppose that in a case of *tetralogy of Fallot* the oxygen consumption is 215 ml. per minute, the hemoglobin content of the blood is 20 gm. per 100 ml. and that analyses of blood samples yield the following O_2 contents:

Superior vena cava	15.7
Inferior vena cava	16.4
Right atrium	15.8
Right ventricle	16.1
Pulmonary artery	16.0
Pulmonary veins	26.8*
Systemic artery	21.0

There is no evidence of a left-to-right shunt. The O_2 content of mixed venous blood is taken as 16.

Arterial O_2 saturation is 80 per cent, indicating a right-to-left shunt of considerable magnitude.

Applying the Fick equation, we have

$$PF = \frac{O_2 \text{ absorption/min.}}{O_2 \text{ pv} - O_2 \text{ pa}} = \frac{215}{0.268 - 0.16}$$
$$= 2 \text{ liters/min.}$$

$$SF = \frac{O_2 \text{ absorption/min.}}{O_2 \text{ sa} - O_2 \text{ mv}} = \frac{215}{0.21 - 0.16}$$
$$= 4.3 \text{ liters/min.}$$

The magnitude of the shunt is 2.3 liters per minute amounting to 55 per cent of the output of the right ventricle; $PF = 0.45 \ SF$.

The relative magnitude of right-to-left shunts may be estimated if one assumes that the O_2 saturation of mixed venous blood is normal or usual (about 65 per cent) and an arterial sample drawn while the subject is breathing oxygen. In the present case, assuming mv to be 16.4, we have

$$\frac{PF}{SF} = \frac{O_2 \text{ sa} - O_2 \text{ mv}}{O_2 \text{ pv} - O_2 \text{ pa}} = \frac{21 - 16.4}{26.8 - 16.4} = 0.43$$

Subnormal arterial O_2 saturation alone is, of course, not diagnostic of a right-to-left shunt, for in pulmonary disease the blood flowing through the lungs may escape normal saturation. Even in advanced pulmonary disease, however, arterial oxygen saturation approaches 100 per cent during the inhalation of 100 per cent oxygen. Should saturation not reach 98 or 99 per cent during oxygen inhalation, a right-to-left shunt may be assumed to be present. Such a shunt does not necessarily reside in the heart or great vessels; it may be in the lungs—pulmonary arteriovenous fistula or, more commonly, disease in which blood is flowing through unaerated regions of the lungs.

In bidirectional shunts there is a "jump up" of O_2 content in one or more of the sites explored by right heart catheterization plus subnormal oxygen saturation. By use of the Fick principle the magnitude of the shunt in each direction can be estimated.

Suppose that in a case of VSD hemoglobin is 16, and the O_2 content of brachial artery blood is 20.4 while the subject is breathing oxygen. Since O_2 saturation of sa is 95 per cent, there is a small shunt from right to left.

Suppose that on right heart catheterization the following figures are obtained:

Superior vena cava	14.3
Inferior vena cava	14.7
Right atrium	14.5
Right ventricle	16.4
Pulmonary artery	16.5

The "jump up" of O_2 content between RA and RV signifies a small shunt from left to right at the ventricular level. Hence, if no pulmonary stenosis is present, this is a case of the *Eisenmenger syndrome*.

If O_2 consumption is 200 ml. per minute, we have

$$PF = \frac{200}{O_2 \text{ pv} - O_2 \text{ pa}} = \frac{200}{21.44\dagger - 16.4}$$
$$= 4 \text{ liters/min.}$$

$$SF = \frac{200}{O_2 \text{ sa} - O_2 \text{ mv}} = \frac{200}{20.4 - 14.5}$$
$$= 3.3 \text{ liters/min.,}$$

indicating that the predominant direction of the shunt is left to right, its net amount being 0.7 liters per minute.

Although total PF is 4, this represents the mixed venous blood flowing through the lungs (effective pulmonary flow, EPF) plus the left-to-right shunt. EPF obviously is $\frac{O_2 \text{ consumption}}{O_2 \text{ pv} - O_2 \text{ mv}}$, or about 2.8 liters per minute. Then the left-to-right shunt equals 4 minus 2.80, or about 1.2 liters per minute.

Similarly, total SF represents EPF plus the shunt from right to left. Then the right-to-left shunt in this case equals 3.3 minus 2.8, or about 0.5 liters per minute. In comparative terms, about 18 per cent of mixed venous blood is shunted from right to left, and about 40 per cent of the arterialized blood is shunted from left to right.

Intracardiac and Pulmonary Arterial Pressures in Congenital Defects

Direct measurement of the pressures in the right ventricle and pulmonary artery may disclose characteristic or diagnostic abnormalities. In all the conditions which have been discussed venous and right atrial pressures are normal in the absence of complicating heart failure. In *atrial septal defect* systolic pressures in the right ventricle and pulmonary artery are considerably elevated and approximately equal; diastolic intraventricular pressure is normal (zero), and diastolic pressure in the pulmonary artery is normal or slightly to moderately elevated, the recorded pressure pulse rising and falling sharply. Similar changes are found in *ventricular septal defect* and in wide *patency of the ductus arteriosus*. In all these conditions, as discussed previously, definite or pronounced pulmonary hypertension may develop. In pulmonary stenosis, as

---

* Subject breathing O_2, saturation 100 per cent.

* 21.44 represents 100 per cent O_2 saturation.

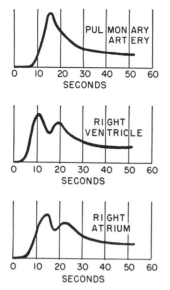

Figure 19–47. Dye concentration curves (schematic) in a right-to-left shunt at the ventricular level. The curve following injection into the pulmonary artery is normal. In the curves following injection into the right ventricle and right atrium the appearance time is shortened, and a prominent secondary rise occurs.

previously mentioned, diagnostic pressure changes are recorded if the catheter can be passed into the pulmonary artery (see p. 410).

Comparative pressures in the right side of the heart and in systemic arteries may serve to distinguish between two common types of *morbus ceruleus*—tetralogy of Fallot, and pulmonary stenosis with patent foramen ovale. In the former (p. 420) systolic pressures in the right ventricle and brachial artery are nearly equal in most cases, whereas in pulmonary stenosis with intact ventricular septum right ventricular systolic pressure may be considerably higher of the two. In an occasional case of tetralogy, however, in which there is high grade pulmonary stenosis, a small septal defect, and no overriding of the aorta, systolic pressure in the right ventricle may exceed that in the brachial artery.

Dye Injection Techniques in the Study of Congenital Anomalies

The dye dilution principle (p. 381) may be used to detect the presence of shunts, determine their direction and, perhaps with considerable error, estimate their magnitude. In left-to-right shunts, for example, the appearance and build-up times of the dye are normal, but the disappearance time is prolonged and the slope of the descending limb of the dye curve flattened because of the later appearance of dye which has recirculated through the lungs. In right-to-left shunts the curve is more characteristic: the appearance

time is short because some of the dye enters the aorta without traversing the lungs, and there is a secondary hump on the ascending limb due to the later appearance of dye which has circulated through the lungs in normal fashion (Fig. 19–47). Swan and associates have derived a formula for calculating the approximate magnitude of the shunt from the characteristics of the curve.

More important clinically is the determination of the site of a right-to-left shunt by the injection of dye into the different chambers (or vessels) into which a cardiac catheter can be passed. Injection of the dye into a chamber beyond the defect yields a curve of essentially normal form, but injection at or proximal to the site of the defect results in a curve characteristic of a right-to-left shunt (Fig. 19–47).

The dye dilution technique has also been used to study hemodynamics in coarctation of the aorta. Such studies have shown that the circulation time to the brachial artery and ear is slightly less than in normal subjects, and that the circulation time to the femoral artery is significantly prolonged.*

Gas Inhalation

Left-to-right shunts of such small magnitude as to escape recognition by analysis of blood samples for O_2 content may be detected and their site determined if the subject inhales an innocuous foreign gas during right heart catheterization. Obviously, the gas appears much more promptly in the chamber (or vessel) at which shunting occurs than is normally the case, since some of it enters the right side of the heart (or pulmonary artery) without traversing the systemic circulation (Fig. 19–48). Hydrogen is the gas usually used for this purpose, its presence being detected by a platinum-tipped electrode.

Angiocardiography

This method is a sine qua non for the definitive diagnosis of complicated defects and for studying the details of less complicated ones. The radiopaque material may be injected into the right side of the heart, into the left side, or into the aorta (Fig. 19–49). By cineangiography the movement of the "dye"

---

* Normally the dye will appear in the femoral artery about 2.5 seconds before its appearance in the brachial artery. In cases of coarctation this difference is reduced by a second or more (Beard, Wood and Clagett).

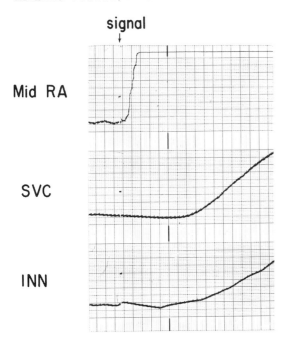

Figure 19–48. Triple platinum-tipped hydrogen electrodes in mid right atrium, superior vena cava and innominate vein. Paper speed of 2.5 mm. per second. Signal marks inhalation of hydrogen gas. The rapid rise in the curve from the mid right atrium denotes a left to right shunt at that point.

may be followed from heartbeat to heartbeat as it moves through abnormal channels or defects, past stenotic regions, etc.

SURGERY FOR CONGENITAL CARDIOVASCULAR DEFECTS

Corrective Surgery

The best results following closure of *septal defects* and excision of *patent ductus* have occurred in cases with normal or only slightly elevated pulmonary arteriolar resistances; good results have been obtained even in patients with intractable heart failure in whom pulmonary arterial pressures were only slightly or moderately elevated and in whom large left-to-right shunts were still present. Mortality has been higher and improvement less frequent if considerable or marked pulmonary hypertension existed preoperatively. Results in most instances were disastrous if right ventricular systolic pressure before operation approached or equaled systemic arterial pressure and there was little or no left-to-right shunt, but favorable results have been obtained in cases of bidirectional shunting, provided a large left-to-right shunt was still

present and pulmonary flow considerably greater than systemic. The reasons for these results appear to be as follows:

1. In the absence of pulmonary hypertension, the heart has been subjected only to volume overload, from which it is immediately relieved when the defect is closed.

2. In the presence of pulmonary hypertension, pressure overload is a major factor in the burden of the right ventricle, which is not directly relieved by closure of the defect.

3. Pulmonary hypertension may persist postoperatively because of irreversible lesions in the vessels of the lungs.

4. If there is little or no left-to-right shunt because of great increase of pulmonary vascular resistance (or, in the case of atrial septal defect, because of right ventricular failure and consequent increase of right atrial pressure), closure of the defect decreases the volume load of the heart little or not at all. Further, in such cases the defect has come to serve as a safety outlet for the right ventricle in such a way that severe failure is prevented or mitigated by right-to-left shunting in the event of increased venous return, hypoxia or arrhythmia or any other factor which would tend to overload or weaken the right ventricle acutely; closure of the defect suddenly deprives the right ventricle of its emergency outlet.

In some but not in nearly all cases of *tetralogy*, substantially complete correction of

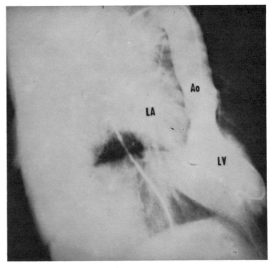

Figure 19–49. Angiocardiogram in a case of mitral insufficiency. "Dye" injected into left ventricle (LV). Note opacification of left atrium (LA) as well as aorta (Ao). (Courtesy of Drs. Ike Muslow and Rozelle Hahn.)

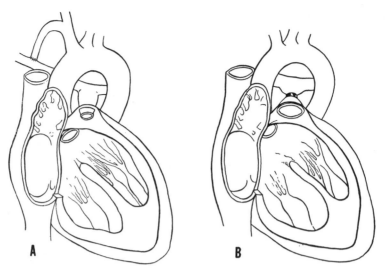

Figure 19–50. *A,* Taussig-Blalock operation for tetralogy of Fallot. *B,* Muller-Dammann operation for ventricular septal defect.

the defects has proved to be feasible, with resultant restoration of the heart to a nearly normal physiologic status; very severe infundibular stenosis and marked overriding of the aorta are the major technical obstacles to complete correction.

As expected, successful excision of the narrowed segment in *coarctation* has usually led to substantially complete restoration of normal pressure and flow relationships. Interestingly, in some cases, most of them in adults, although pressure *relationships* between the upper and lower extremities have immediately been restored to normal, hypertension has persisted for weeks or months, pressures declining to normal gradually. Perhaps these are the cases in which a renal factor has been in operation (p. 730), or in which arteriolar constriction or reversible arteriolosclerosis in the upper portion of the body has participated in the genesis of the hypertension.

Palliative Surgery

The Taussig-Blalock operation for the tetralogy of Fallot (Fig. 19–50, *A*) (and the Potts procedure) is essentially the production of an artificial ductus arteriosus (or aortic septal defect), imposing a left-to-right shunt between the systemic and pulmonary circuits with resultant increase of pulmonary flow and reduction of arterial hypoxia. After the operation there is bidirectional shunting, right-to-left at the ventricular level, left-to-right through the artificially created defect. Production of the artificial shunt results in sudden increase of return flow to the left side of the

heart, as a consequence of which left ventricular failure may occur postoperatively; usually, however, the left ventricle soon compensates for its increased volume load, and considerable long-term benefit is obtained. The Potts operation has had its greatest usefulness in infants with critical reduction of pulmonary flow, the Taussig-Blalock procedure in older children in whom corrective surgery is not feasible.

Banding of the pulmonary artery producing an artificial pulmonary stenosis (Muller-Dammann operation) (Fig. 19–50, *B*) has often brought about striking improvement in infants with heart failure due to large left-to-right shunts through *ventricular septal defects;* the aim of the procedure is to increase the resistance to right ventricular outflow sufficiently to reduce the magnitude of the shunt; its effects are identical with those of the acquired infundibular stenosis, which, in some cases, develops spontaneously, and analogous to cases of tetralogy of Fallot with large ventricular septal defect but only moderate pulmonary stenosis.

Pericardial Disease

The effects of pericardial effusion and of constrictive pericarditis upon the circulation are due to compression of the heart with resultant restriction of its diastolic volume. If this restriction is considerable, adequate ventricular filling is not possible; the output of the heart is therefore diminished, and blood is dammed back into the veins of the greater and lesser circulations.

Hemopericardium

In wounds of the heart, ruptured myocardial infarcts or intrapericardial rupture of saccular or dissecting aneurysms of the aorta, the rapid accumulation of relatively small amounts of blood in the pericardial sac (as, for example, only 200 or 300 ml.) may cause serious or fatal tamponade of the heart, because the pericardial sac is an inelastic fibrous envelope, not capable of sudden distention. In such cases the clinical picture is dominated by the effects of a rapidly falling cardiac output: blood pressure falls, pulse pressure diminishes markedly, *pulsus paradoxus* appears, and a shocklike picture rapidly supervenes. The neck veins, however, are distended, and venous pressure is elevated.

Pericardial Effusion

Fluid accumulates more slowly in instances of "idiopathic," rheumatic or tuberculous pericarditis and in the pericarditis due to pyogenic organisms or to malignant disease.

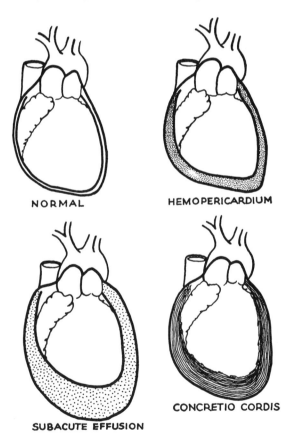

NORMAL   HEMOPERICARDIUM

SUBACUTE EFFUSION   CONCRETIO CORDIS

Figure 19–51. Types of cardiac compression. (Schematic, after Burwell and Blalock: J.A.M.A., Vol. 110.)

In such cases the fluid causes gradual distention of the pericardial sac, so that large amounts may accumulate before the heart is seriously compressed (Fig. 19–51). As the cardiac output declines pulse pressure diminishes and pulsus paradoxus may appear (p. 433). The veins of the neck become engorged, their pulsations diminished; venous pressure creased; the liver is enlarged and tender; dyspnea is present. As a consequence of venous and capillary engorgement, edema of the lungs and transudation of fluid into the pleural and peritoneal cavities may occur. However, if, as occasionally happens, the fluid accumulates very slowly over a period of weeks or months, very large effusions may exist without any signs of cardiac compression.

Constrictive Pericarditis

In cases of *concretio cordis* the consequences of venous engorgement and of diminished cardiac output gradually become manifest as the compression progresses. Venous pressure may reach great heights, much above the pressures ordinarily encountered in congestive heart failure—up to 400 mm. of water. The neck veins are distended, the liver is enlarged; ascites, hydrothorax and edema of the lower extremities may occur. The pulse is of small volume and usually fast. Fatigability, due to the diminished cardiac output, is a characteristic subjective symptom.

In most clinical cases of constrictive pericarditis the total blood volume is increased. This increase is in large part responsible for the marked elevation of venous pressure, but is beneficial in that it insures better ventricular filling and a more nearly adequate cardiac output than would otherwise be the case. However, the hypervolemia, in the presence of high venous pressure, tends to increase the formation of transudates and edema.

It is notable that most patients with concretio cordis are not dyspneic at rest, although they become short of breath on slight exertion. This phenomenon simply must mean that the total blood volume is so distributed between the greater and lesser circulations that there is not sufficient congestion of the lungs to cause dyspnea at rest. This is not surprising in the light of the fact that patients with high grade mitral stenosis of such severity as to cause diminution of cardiac output, but in whom venous pressure in the greater circulation is normal, may not be dyspneic at rest. The situation in constrictive pericarditis is much like that in combined mitral and tricuspid stenosis, in which the tricuspid obstruction tends actually to diminish pulmonary congestion. There is no justification for assuming, if the patient with concretio cordis has enlargement of the liver, but no overt evidence of pulmonary congestion at rest, that the constricting envelope is compressing the right ventricle or the venae cavae selectively.

Mention should also be made of the differences between the distribution of edema in constrictive pericarditis and in congestive heart failure. In the former, ascites tends to predominate, often with little or no edema of the feet and legs, while in congestive failure the reverse usually obtains. It is not necessary to assume the existence in concretio cordis of specific factors which produce obstruction of the hepatic veins, for the distribution of edema in this condition is the same as that in tricuspid stenosis. Rather, it is likely that edema in congestive failure, tricuspid obstruction and chronic cardiac constriction is of essentially the same cause—that in all three conditions the edema is related pathogenetically to generalized venous hypertension of the greater circulation, and results from excessive transudation through the walls of capillaries consequent to elevation of capillary blood pressure.

The predominance of ascites in concretio cordis and tricuspid obstruction is probably due for the most part to the gradual development of sustained but moderate capillary hypertension in these conditions, in contrast to the relatively rapid development of intermittent, fluctuating but more marked capillary hypertension in most cases of congestive heart failure. Efficient mechanisms operate to prevent the formation or persistence of subcutaneous edema in the event of sustained venous hypertension, but these compensating factors fail to halt the formation of edema if elevation of venous pressure develops rapidly and fluctuates in degree. No such efficient mechanisms are available to inhibit accumulation of fluid in the peritoneal cavity. Hence in constrictive pericarditis the formation of subcutaneous edema is largely or completely prevented, while ascites accumulates slowly and steadily. With the onset of congestive heart failure, on the other hand, edema of the legs, its formation augmented by the effect of gravity upon venous and capillary pressures in dependent regions, may attain considerable proportions before detectable ascites appears.

The average hydrodynamic pressure in the capil-

laries of a given region depends principally upon the rate of blood flow in that region and the height of the venous pressure, the former factor being an index of the velocity of capillary flow and the latter a measure of the resistance opposing capillary flow. Since pressure varies with the square of the velocity, but only with the first power of the "peripheral resistance," change in the rate of flow exerts relatively greater influence upon capillary pressure than does change in the venous pressure. For this reason capillary pressures in most cases of congestive failure (in which decrease of the circulatory rate is only slight or moderate) must on the average be considerably above the capillary pressures in typical clinical cases of constrictive pericarditis (in which the cardiac output is more markedly subnormal), despite the more pronounced elevation of venous pressures in the latter condition.

In both conditions under discussion venous pressure rises and cardiac output increases in response to exercise, and opposite changes occur during rest. However, the fluctuations are sharper and of relatively greater magnitude in congestive failure, and, unless failure is far advanced, the absolute increase and decrease in cardiac output are considerably greater. Hence capillary pressure (and the consequent tendency toward increased capillary filtration) fluctuates more widely from minute to minute, from hour to hour, and diurnally in heart failure than in constrictive pericarditis.

Significant reduction of cardiac output results in proportionate selective arteriolar constriction with consequent relatively great reduction of blood flow in certain regions and diversion of relatively large amounts to others. One region thus sequestered is the integument, and it is therefore probable that the relative as well as the absolute rates of blood flow in the skin and subcutaneous tissues are more markedly reduced in concretio cordis than in congestive failure. Compensatory arteriolar constriction involves the splanchnic bed as well if the cardiac output suddenly becomes inadequate, but it seems unlikely that sequestration of the splanchnic region (with consequent impairment of liver function, digestion and absorption) should persist or even occur if the cardiac output is gradually and permanently reduced to a definitely or markedly subnormal rate. Probably, therefore, slowly progressive compression of the heart affects splanchnic flow much less profoundly than flow in the integument; perhaps, on the other hand, splanchnic flow is curtailed almost as much as integumentary flow at the onset of congestive heart failure.

These considerations suggest that the unique distribution of edema in constrictive pericarditis is correlated especially with the gradual development of venous hypertension and the slowly progressive but eventually considerable decrease in the circulation rate, with the result that, on the average, capillary pressures throughout the body are moderately rather than markedly elevated and subject to relatively slight fluctuation, and that, consequent to selective arteriolar constriction, elevation of capillary pressure is relatively slight in the subcutaneous tissues and skin.

It is interesting that in some longstanding cases of congestive heart failure, in which initially dependent edema predominated over ascites, the reverse obtains as the years pass. The predominance of ascites has been attributed to "cardiac cirrhosis," but at autopsy it is rare to find anatomic evidence of severe portal obstruction. More likely the altered distribution of edema is due to longstanding considerable reduction of cardiac output and increase of hepatic venous pressure.

Resection of the constricting scar results in decrease of venous pressure, increase of cardiac output and amelioration or disappearance of the signs related to these physiologic disturbances. In certain cases, however, fatal heart failure has followed rapidly upon cardiolysis in longstanding severe cases of concretio cordis. In such cases the myocardium of the left ventricle has been found to be thin and atrophic, undoubtedly because of the diminution of its load incident to decreased filling over the years.

Pulsus Paradoxus and Inspiratory Distention of the Neck Veins

These two physical signs are quite characteristic of cardiac compression. They often coexist, so that if the pulse weakens during inspiration (*pulsus paradoxus*), the neck veins distend at the same time; this suggests that the two phenomena are related. Since they occur in cases of pericardial effusion as well as in constrictive pericarditis (indeed more often in the former), it appears that they actually are due to the effects of compression of the heart, and not to mediastinopericardial bands about the great vessels which are pulled taut as the size of the thorax increases during inspiration, nor to interference with ventricular systole by adhesions which anchor the heart to the chest wall and diaphragm.

It should be noted that the neck veins are abnormally distended and that the pulse is of reduced volume throughout the respiratory cycle in cardiac compression. Since these signs are due to reduced filling of the heart, the cause in *increased* distention of the veins and of *further* reduction in the pulse volume should be sought in factors that come into play during inspiration which might cause *greater interference* with filling of the chambers of both sides of the heart.

Under normal circumstances venous pressure declines slightly during quiet inspiration, but the output of the left ventricle and the arterial blood pressure do not change appreciably. During a deep inspiration, and especially upon an inspiratory effort against a closed glottis (Müller experiment), venous pressure declines sharply, the neck veins collapse, left ventricular output diminishes, and pulse volume decreases; pulsus paradoxus appears. This combination of pulsus paradoxus and inspiratory *collapse* of the neck veins occurs prominently in conditions characterized by great increase of the negative intrathoracic pressure during inspiration, as, for example, laryngeal stenosis and bronchial asthma. It thus appears that, although an increase of the negative pressure within the thorax causes an increased amount of blood to be sucked into the great veins of the thorax from the neck and abdomen, it causes instead *reduced* filling of the left ventricle.

Now the negative pressure within the thorax is exerted both upon the intrathoracic veins and the atria, but to a lesser extent upon the latter, which have thicker walls and are protected by the relatively indistensible pericardium. Therefore, when the negative intrathoracic pressure increases during inspiration, the fall of intra-atrial pressure is not so great as that in the veins of the caval and pulmonary systems, and the differences between venous and atrial pressures are reduced. Thus, although larger amounts are sucked into the caval and pulmonary veins, filling of the atria is not necessarily increased correspondingly during inspiration. Filling of the right side of the heart is increased, but it appears that filling of the left side is actually decreased; blood is pooled in the dilated pulmonary veins and enters the left atrium in smaller amounts. Most of this pooling must occur in veins within the lungs rather than in the four main pulmonary veins, the volume of whose extrapericardial portions is rather small.

In cardiac compression the atria are more or less completely protected from changes in intrathoracic pressure by the enveloping fluid or the rigid pericardial scar. Therefore, although the veins dilate during inspiration, the atria do not. More blood is pooled in the veins, and less enters the heart, whose output is thus reduced: hence the pulsus paradoxus.

The inspiratory distention of the neck veins may be explained as follows: During inspiration the velocity of flow into the great veins and right atrium initially increases sharply, but flow is abruptly halted or markedly slowed because the capacity of the right ventricle cannot be increased. As a result a positive pressure wave is set up which is propagated into the already distended veins of the neck. It is likely that this wave of increased pressure is superimposed upon a pressure which is slightly less than the pressure during expiration.

Cardiac Catheterization in Constrictive Pericarditis

The right ventricular pressure curve may be altered in characteristic fashion in cases of concretio cordis. At or near zero when diastole begins, the pressure rises gradually in normal subjects during the remainder of diastole as the ventricle fills. In constrictive pericarditis the ventricle (as is normal) fills rapidly at first, but rather suddenly attains maximal size as its rigid envelope halts further distention; consequently, a steep positive pressure wave is set up producing a hump in the pressure curve (Fig. 19–52). Quick and sudden cessation of ventricular filling is probably also responsible for the third heart sound ("pericardial knock"), which is frequently heard in cases of constrictive pericarditis; its genesis is not greatly different from that of the protodiastolic gallop of heart failure. Indeed, the hump in the pressure recorded in constrictive pericarditis has also been observed in heart failure.

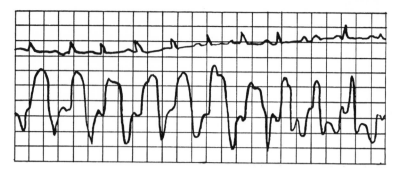

Figure 19–52. Right ventricular pressure in concretio cordis. Sharp drop followed by rebound in early diastole.

The Cardiomyopathies

In most cases of cardiomyopathy due to myocarditis or alcohol, and in the "primary" and familial cases as well, the physiologic and clinical picture is that of hypertrophy, dilatation and congestive heart failure, the so-called "congestive" type. In some, however, marked subendocardial fibrosis occurs, producing an intracardiac concretio which simulates the physiologic and clinical picture of constrictive pericarditis; this is the "restrictive" type. In still others eccentric hypertrophy, particularly of the ventricular septum, may lead to obstruction of the outflow tract of the left ventricle (hypertrophic subaortic stenosis, p. 405), or of the inflow tract of either ventricle; this is the "obstructive" type.

Extracardiac Conditions Affecting Function of the Heart

Extracardiac conditions may exert effects upon the heart by several mechanisms, one or more of which may operate in a single condition. They may cause the work of the heart to be increased; by their very nature they may cause changes in myocardial metabolism; they may bring about impairment of the nutrition of the heart, especially by decreasing its supply of oxygen; they may be accompanied by or result in anatomic lesions of the heart. In all these conditions the development of severe impairment of cardiac function is greatly favored by advancing age and by the pre-existence of organic disease of the heart or of the coronary arteries.

In this brief section we propose only to mention the mechanisms whereby certain extracardiac conditions may affect the heart. More complete discussions may be found in other parts of this book and in the references listed at the end of this section.

Hypertension

Chronic hypertension of whatever etiology causes cardiac hypertrophy and favors the development of coronary atherosclerosis. It is among the most frequent causes of congestive heart failure and is an important indirect factor in the causation of angina pectoris and myocardial infarction. Acute forms of hypertension, such as occur in acute glomerulonephritis and toxemia of pregnancy, may lead to rapid dilatation and failure of the heart in the absence of hypertrophy. In these states, however, hypertension is not the sole factor causing the heart to fail; an important additional factor is the rather sudden increase of blood volume, related to water and salt retention in in which cardiac failure plays no part. The left ventricle has not only to work against an increased peripheral resistance, but also to cope with a considerably augmented venous return. Water and salt retention alone may cause dilatation of the heart, increased venous pressure, enlargement of the liver and pulmonary edema, as exemplified by their occurrence in anuric and oliguric states which are not accompanied by hypertension, as for example cases of acute tubular necrosis of the kidneys in which fluid and salt intake have not been sufficiently curtailed.

Hypotension

Chronic hypotension, which may occur in "normal" persons and in a variety of conditions such as Addison's disease, hypopituitarism, cachectic states, etc., does not appear directly to harm the heart. It is likely, however, that in acute hypotensive states, such as hemorrhagic and bacteremic shock, reduction of coronary flow seriously compromises myocardial metabolism and is an important factor in the production of the irreversible stage of shock. There is good evidence that the failure to recover from prolonged shock is due at least in part to weakness of the myocardium.

Anemia

In persons with severe anemia cardiac output is increased in an attempt to compensate for the diminished oxygen-carrying capacity of the blood. This increase is accomplished by augmentation of the stroke volume as well as increase in heart rate. Cardiac hypertrophy, usually moderate, may therefore occur in long-standing cases of anemia. If augmentation of output does not compensate for the reduction of hemoglobin the heart muscle, like other tissues, may suffer from hypoxia. For these reasons cardiac enlargement, angina pectoris and even congestive heart failure may occur in persons with anemia, especially in elderly patients.

Hyperthyroidism

In hyperthyroidism the metabolic demands of the tissues are increased—demands which are met by an increase in the circulatory rate. Although this increase is accomplished largely by an increase in heart rate, the output per beat is also increased; augmentation of the cardiac output is aided by increase of blood volume. The metabolic needs of the heart itself are also increased. Cardiac efficiency is reduced by the onset of atrial fibrillation in many cases. The cardiac hypertrophy observed in longstanding cases of severe hyperthyroidism is therefore not unexpected, and it is not surprising to learn that heart failure is a common complication of hyperthyroidism. The coincidence of valvular disease or hypertension is important in the causation of heart failure in most of these cases; heart failure is but rarely due to hyperthyroidism alone in young people.

In other conditions characterized by prolonged increase of metabolism, notably in the chronic leukemias, cardiac hypertrophy may develop and heart failure eventually supervene. In the leukemias the concurrent anemia is probably as important as the elevated metabolism in causing the cardiopathy.

Hypothyroidism

In myxedema the cardiac output, velocity of blood flow, and blood volume are all decreased. Although the work of the heart is diminished, the silhouette of the heart is nevertheless enlarged in most cases. Hydropericardium contributes to the enlargement in some cases, but in the majority it appears that the heart is actually dilated. The cause of the dilatation is not known; presumably it is due to myocardial weakness resulting directly from the thyroid deficiency. The size of the heart decreases after therapy with thyroid substance.

Longstanding hypothyroidism, with its disturbance of lipid metabolism, favors the development of atherosclerosis, which often involves the coronary arteries; angina pectoris is therefore a common symptom. The angina may be aggravated if treatment is begun with more than minimal dosage of thyroid substance, probably because of rapid increase in the metabolic needs of the myocardium in the presence of coronary sclerosis; on the other hand, careful thyroid medication may result in diminution of the frequency and severity of anginal attacks. Congestive heart failure occurs in a rather small minority of cases of longstanding myxedema and responds to thyroid therapy. Presumably in these cases the heart is so specifically weakened by the thyroid deficiency that it fails even though its burden is reduced by the general metabolic effects of hypothyroidism.

Pulmonary Disease

In obstructive emphysema, pulmonary fibrosis and other chronic or subacute diseases of the lungs (cystic disease, sarcoidosis, sickle cell disease, Hamman-Rich syndrome, etc.) arterial hypoxia may lead to increase of cardiac output, and in many cases to pulmonary hypertension presumably due in part to constriction of pulmonary arterioles, in part to increased flow through an indistensible vascular bed. Hypertrophy, dilatation and eventually failure of the right ventricle may occur; the left ventricle, too, may undergo hypertrophy and enlargement (increased volume load, myocardial hypoxia). Coronary disease or hypertension is a contributory or principal factor in the causation of heart failure in some cases. Hypoventilation due to pronounced *kyphoscoliosis* or to extreme *obesity* may lead to the development of cor pulmonale and to heart failure by the same mechanisms which operate in emphysema and other diffuse processes in the lungs. In kyphoscoliosis the lungs are "too little"; in obesity respiratory movements are restricted by fat deposits in the abdomen and in the chest wall.

Pulmonary Embolism and Thrombosis; Primary Pulmonary Hypertension

Complete or almost complete obstruction of the pulmonary artery at its bifurcation by the lodgment of a large embolus causes sudden, almost immediate, death. High grade but incomplete obstruction causes sudden diminution of flow into the lungs and through them into the left side of the heart. The dramatic clinical picture is related to sudden diminution of the output of the left ventricle, which causes the shocklike state, and to decreased blood flow through the lungs, which may cause agonizing dyspnea. The pulmonary artery, right ventricle and great veins are quickly distended by blood which cannot be forced past the obstructed site; this distention may be manifested by physical, radiologic and electrocardiographic signs which led McGinn and White to apply the appropriate and now generally used name of *acute cor pulmonale*. Repeated smaller embolizations or a single large shower of small emboli (as for example amniotic fluid embolism during labor) may so reduce the capacity of the pulmonary vascular bed as to produce pulmonary hypertension and a subacute or chronic form of cor pulmonale. Thrombosis in the pulmonary arterial system due to propagation from emboli or appearing de novo in persons with pulmonary vascular disease, heart failure or erythremia may exert the same effect. Primary pulmonary hypertension, a disease of unknown cause affecting adolescent females for the most part and which may be a familial disorder, is a rather rare cause of cor pulmonale.

Fever

When body temperature is elevated, the rate of metabolism is stepped up; oxygen consumption increases about 13 per cent for each degree rise above 37° C. Cardiac output is increased proportionally, by increase of heart rate and stroke volume, as in exercise. The work of the heart is therefore increased, but high fevers do not last sufficiently long to embarrass the healthy heart of themselves. If, however, the victim of a febrile illness has preexisting heart disease, or if the "toxins" of the infection exert a harmful effect upon the myocardium, the additional load occasioned by the fever may cause the heart to fail. In elderly persons fever (or the effects of the toxins which cause it) may cause atrial fibrillation to appear, which may precipitate cardiac failure. Failure of the contractile power of the myocardium contributes significantly to the circulatory failure which heralds the approach of death in acute infections.

Infectious, Metabolic and Toxic States

Certain infectious diseases, notably *rheumatic fever* and *diphtheria*, may be accompanied or followed by acute degenerative processes in the heart muscle. Rarely acute or subacute degeneration may follow *pregnancy*. Occasionally acute myocardial degeneration occurs during convalescence from such conditions as *scarlet fever, bacterial pneumonia* and various *virus diseases. Polyarteritis nodosa* may involve the coronary arteries; myocardial lesions may occur in *disseminated lupus, scleroderma,* primary *amyloidosis, sarcoidosis, hemochromatosis* and *uremia*. In any of these conditions the lesions may find physiologic expression in cardiac enlargement, congestive failure, cardiac pain or cardiac arrhythmias.

Heart failure is characteristic of *thiamine deficiency. Electrolyte disturbances* may affect the heart profoundly. Of these the most important in its effects on the myocardium is potassium. *Hypokalemia* leads primarily to weakness of contractile power, *hyperkalemia* to conduction disturbances, abnormalities of impulse production, cardiac standstill. Thus the heart may be seriously or fatally affected by any condition in which there is significant loss or retention of potassium, or in which there is shift of potassium ions from extracellular fluid into cells or vice versa.

Potassium loss may occur in diarrhea, intestinal obstruction, ileus, excessive diuresis, adrenal corticoid therapy, aldosteronism, etc.; *potassium retention* may occur in renal failure, especially in acute suppression of urine. Acute hyperkalemia may be due to the transfusion of large amounts of stored blood or to the intravenous infusion of potassium salts. *Hypokalemia* due to shift of potassium ions occurs principally in association with rapid utilization of glucose, as in the therapy of diabetic acidosis and in hypoglycemia due to insulin overdosage. *Hyperkalemia* due to ionic shift occurs in severe trauma, widespread damage of body cells, and in association with mobilization of glucose from the liver (hemorrhagic, traumatic, bacteremic, and cardiac shock, severe uncontrolled diabetes mellitus).

Acidosis and *alkalosis*, particularly the former, affect the metabolism of heart muscle as well as that of other cells and tissues, and it is likely that acute failure of the heart plays an important role in death due to acidosis of whatever cause. The severe acidosis of profound shock is undoubtedly a major factor in the failure of response to usual methods of therapy.

REFERENCES

Edwards, J. E.: Congenital malformations of the heart and great vessels. In Gould, S. E., Pathology of the Heart, 2d ed. Springfield, Charles C Thomas, 1959.

Friedberg, C. K.: Diseases of the Heart, 3rd ed. Philadelphia, W. B. Saunders Co., 1966.

Gasul, B. M., Arcilla, R. A., and Lev, M.: Heart Disease in Children. Philadelphia, J. B. Lippincott Co., 1966.

Hurst, J. W., and Logue, R. B.: The Heart. New York, McGraw-Hill—Blakiston Division, 1966.

Levine, S. A.: Clinical Heart Disease. 5th ed. Philadelphia, W. B. Saunders Co., 1958.

Luisada, A. A. (ed.): Cardiology; An Encyclopedia of the Cardiovascular System. New York, McGraw-Hill—Blakiston Division, 1959.

Nadas, A. S.: Pediatric Cardiology, 2d ed. Philadelphia, W. B. Saunders Co., 1963.

Taussig, H. B.: Congenital Malformations of the Heart, 2d ed. New York, The Commonwealth Fund, 1960.

White, P. D.: Heart Disease, 3rd ed. New York, The Macmillan Company, 1944.

Wood, P.: Diseases of the Heart and Circulation, 2d ed. Philadelphia, J. B. Lippincott Co., 1956.

The Output of the Heart

Alexander, J. K.: Obesity and cardiac performance. Am. J. Cardiol., 14:860, 1964.

Benchimol, A., Akre, P. R., and Dimond, E. G.: Clinical experience with the use of computers for calculation of cardiac output. Am. J. Cardiol., 15:213, 1965.

Benchimol, A., Li, Y. B., Legler, J. F., and Dimond, E. G.: Rapidly repeated determinations of the cardiac output with the indicator-dilution technic. Am. J. Cardiol., 13:790, 1964.

Braunwald, E., and Frahm, C. J.: Studies on Starling's Law of the Heart. IV. Observations on the hemodynamic functions of the left atrium in man. Circulation, 24:633, 1961.

Broch, O. J., Humerfelt, S., Haarstad, J., and Myrhe, U. R.: Hemodynamic studies in acute myocardial infarction. Am. Heart J., 57:522, 1959.

Broch, O. J., and Muller, O.: Haemodynamic studies during auricular fibrillation and after restoration of sinus rhythm. Brit. Heart J., 19:222, 1957.

Bruce, T. A., and Shillingford, J. P.: The normal resting cardiac output: Serial determinations by a dye dilution method. Brit. Heart J., 24:69, 1962.

Burch, G. E., and DePasquale, N. P.: Cardiac performance in relation to blood volume. Am. J. Cardiol., 14:784, 1964.

Chapman, C. B., and Fraser, R. S.: Studies on the effect of exercise on cardiovascular function. I. Cardiac output and mean circulation time. Circulation, 9:57, 1954.

Cobb, L. A., Kramer, R. J., and Finch, C. A.: Circulatory effects of chronic hypervolemia in polycythemia vera. J. Clin. Invest., 39:1722, 1960.

Cournand, A., and Ranges, H. A.: Determination of cardiac output in man by the direct Fick method and the ballistocardiograph. Am. J. Physiol., 133:251, 1941.

Cournand, A., and Ranges, H. A.: Catheterization of right auricle in man. Proc. Soc. Exper. Biol. Med., 46:462, 1941.

Dow, P.: Estimations of cardiac output and central blood volume by dye dilution. Physiol. Rev., 36:77, 1956.

Ferrer, M. I., and Harvey, R. M.: Some hemodynamic aspects of cardiac arrhythmias in man. A clinicophysiologic correlation. Am. Heart J., 68:153, 1964.

Gellhorn, E.: Cardiovascular reactions in asphyxia and the postasphyxial state. Am. Heart J., 67:73, 1964.

Gilbert, R. P., Goldberg, M., and Griffin, J.: Circulatory changes in acute myocardial infarction. Circulation, 9:847, 1954.

Grollman, A.: The Cardiac Output of Man in Health and Disease. Springfield, Ill., Charles C Thomas, 1932.

Hamilton, W. F., and others: Comparison of the Fick and dye injection methods of measuring the cardiac output in man. Am. J. Physiol., 153:309, 1948.

Hamilton, W. F., and others: Measurement of the cardiac output. Section II, volume 1, chapter 17, p. 551, in Handbook of Physiology. Washington, D. C., American Physiological Society, 1962.

Hecht, H. H., Osher, W. J., and Samuels, A. J.: Cardiovascular adjustments in subjects with organic heart disease before and after conversion of atrial fibrillation to normal sinus rhythm. J. Clin. Invest., 30:647, 1951.

Katz, L. N.: The performance of the heart. Circulation, 21:483, 1960.

Kerkhof, A. C., and Baumann, H.: Minute volume determinations in mitral stenosis during auricular fibrillation and when restored to normal rhythm. Proc. Soc. Exper. Biol. Med., 31:168, 1933.

Kirklin, J. W., and others: Symposium on diagnostic applications of indicator-dilution technics. Proc. Staff Meet. Mayo Clin., 32:463, 1957.

Kory, R. C., and Meneely, G. R.: Cardiac output in auricular fibrillation with observations on the effects of conversion to normal sinus rhythm. J. Clin. Invest., 30:653, 1951.

Lind, J., Wegelius, C., and Lichtenstein, H.: The dynamics of the heart in complete A-V block. An angiocardiographic study. Circulation, 10:195, 1954.

McMichael, J., and Sharpey-Schafer, E. P.: Cardiac output in man by a direct Fick method: Effects of posture, venous pressure change, atropine, and adrenaline. Brit. Heart J., 6:33, 1944.

Merriman, J. E., Wyant, G. M., Bray, G., and McGeachy, W.: Serial cardiac output determination in man. Canad. Anaesth. Soc. J., 5:375, 1958.

Miller, D. E., and others: Effect of ventricular rate on the cardiac output in the dog with chronic heart block. Circ. Res., 10:658, 1962.

Miller, O. F., and Bellet, S.: Treatment of intractable heart failure in the presence of complete atrioventricular heart block by the use of the internal cardiac pacemaker: Report of two cases. New England J. Med., 265:768, 1961.

Mommaerts, W. F. H. M., Abbott, B. C., and Whalen, W. J.: Selected topics on the physiology of the heart. In Bourne, G. H.: The Structure and Function of Muscle, volume II, Biochemistry and Physiology, chapter XII, p. 517. New York, Academic Press, 1960.

Morris, J. J., Jr., Entman, M., North, W. C., Kong, Y., and McIntosh, H.: The changes in cardiac output with reversion of atrial fibrillation to sinus rhythm. Circulation, 31:670, 1965.

Morris, J. J., Jr., and others: Cardiac output in atrial fibrillation and sinus rhythm. Circulation, 28: 772, 1963.

Reeves, J. T., Groves, R. F., Filley, G. F., and Blount, S. G., Jr.: Cardiac output of normal resting man. J. Appl. Physiol., 16:276, 1961.

Richardson, D. W., Wyso, E. M., Hecht, A. M., and Fitzpatrick, D. P.: Value of continuous photoelectric recording of dye curves in the estimation of cardiac output. Circulation, 20:1111, 1959.

Samet, P., Bernstein, W., and Levine, S.: Significance of the atrial contribution to ventricular filling. Am. J. Cardiol., 15:195, 1965.

Samet, P., Bernstein, W. H., Medow, A., and Nathan, D. A.: Effect of alterations in ventricular rate on cardiac output in complete heart block. Am. J. Cardiol., 14:477, 1964.

Smith, W. W., Wikler, N. S., and Fox, A. C.: Hemodynamic studies of patients with myocardial infarction. Circulation, 9:352, 1954.

Stack, M. F., and others: Cardiovascular hemodynamic functions in complete heart block and the effect of isopropylnorepinephrine. Circulation, 17: 526, 1958.

Stead, E. A., and Warren, J. V.: Cardiac output in man: Analysis of mechanisms varying the cardiac output based on recent clinical studies. Arch. Int. Med., 80:237, 1947.

Stewart, H. J., and others: The cardiac output in congestive heart failure and in organic heart disease. Ann. Int. Med., 13:2323, 1940.

Visscher, M. B., and Johnson, J. A.: The Fick principle: Analysis of potential errors in its conventional application. J. Appl. Physiol., 5:635, 1953.

Hypertrophy and Dilatation of the Heart

Bing, R. J.: Metabolism of the heart. In Harvey Lectures, series L, p. 27. New York, Academic Press, 1956.

Bing, R. J., Wu, C., and Gudbjarnason, S.: Mechanism of heart failure. Circ. Res., 15: suppl. 2, 64, 1964.

Braunwald, E., and Ross, J., Jr.: Applicability of Starling's law of the heart to man. Circ. Res., 15: suppl. 2, 169, 1964.

Burch, G. E., DePasquale, N. P., and Cronvich, J. A.: Influence of ventricular size on the relationship between contractile and manifest tension. Am. Heart J., 69:624, 1965.

Burch, G. E., Ray, C. T., and Cronvich, J. A.: Certain mechanical peculiarities of the human cardiac pump in normal and diseased states. Circulation, 5:504, 1952.

Burton, A. C.: The importance of the shape and size of the heart (editorial). Am. Heart J., 54:801, 1957.

Grande, F., and Taylor, H. L.: Adaptive changes in the heart, vessels, and patterns of control under chronically high loads. In Handbook of Physiology, Section II, volume 3, chapter 74, p. 2615. Washington, D. C., American Physiological Society, 1965.

Grant, R. P.: Architectonics of the heart. Am. Heart J., 46:405, 1953.

Grant, R. P.: Aspects of cardiac hypertrophy. Am. Heart J., 46:154, 1953.

Greiner, T.: Relationship of force of contraction to high energy phosphate in heart muscle. J. Pharmacol. & Exper. Ther., 105:178, 1952.

Gudbjarnason, S., Telerman, M., and Bing, R. J.: Protein metabolism in cardiac hypertrophy and heart failure. Am. J. Physiol., 206:294, 1964.

Harrison, T. R.: Some unanswered questions concerning enlargement and failure of the heart. Am. Heart J., 69:100, 1965.

Keys, A., and Friedell, H. L.: Size and stroke of the heart in young men in relation to athletic activity. Science, 87:456, 1938.

Linzbach, A. J.: Heart failure from the point of view of quantitative anatomy. Am. J. Cardiol., 5:370, 1960.

Master, A. M.: The etiology of cardiac enlargement in coronary occlusion, hypertension, and coronary artery disease. Am. Heart J., 47:321, 1954.

Meerson, F. Z.: Compensatory hyperfunction of the heart and cardiac insufficiency. Circ. Res., 10: 250, 1962.

Olson, R. E., and Piatnek, D. A.: Conservation of energy in cardiac muscle. Ann. New York Acad. Sc., 72:466, 1959.

Roberts, J. T., Wearn, J. T., and Boten, I.: Quantitative changes in the capillary-muscle relationship in human hearts during normal growth and hypertrophy. Am. Heart J., 21:617, 1941.

Schneider, E. C., and Crampton, C. F.: Comparison of some respiratory and circulatory reactions in athletes and nonathletes. Am. J. Physiol., 129: 165, 1940.

Sonnenblick, E. H., Spiro, D., and Spotnitz, H. M.: The ultrastructural basis of Starling's law of the heart. The role of the sarcomere in determining ventricular size and stroke volume. Am. Heart J., 68:336, 1964.

Sonnenblick, E. H., Spotnitz, H. M., and Spiro, D.: Role of the sarcomere in ventricular function and the mechanism of heart failure. Circ. Res., 15: suppl. 2, 70, 1964.

Starling, E. H.: Linacre Lecture on the Law of the Heart. Cambridge, 1915. London, Longmans, Green & Co., 1918.

Stenger, R. J., and Spiro, D.: The ultrastructure of mammalian cardiac muscle. J. Biophys. & Biochem. Cytol., 9:325, 1961.

Szekeres, L., and Schein, M.: Cell metabolism of the overloaded mammalian heart in situ. Cardiologia (Basel), 34:18, 1959.

Wollenberger, A., Kleitke, B., and Raabe, G.: Some metabolic characteristics of mitochondria from chronically overloaded, hypertrophied hearts. Exper. & Molec. Path., 2:251, 1963.

Wollenberger, A., and Schulze, W.: Mitochondrial

alterations in the myocardium of dogs with aortic stenosis. J. Biophys. & Biochem. Cytol., 10:285, 1961.

Valvular Disease of the Heart

Altschule, M. D., and Blumgart, H. L.: The circulatory dynamics in tricuspid stenosis. Am. Heart J., 13:589, 1937.

Anderson, A. M., Cobb, L. A., Bruce, R. A., and Merendino, K. A.: Evaluation of mitral annuloplasty for mitral regurgitation: Clinical and hemodynamic status four to forty-one months after surgery. Circulation, 26:26, 1962.

Ankeney, J. S., Fishman, A. P., and Fritts, H. W., Jr.: An analysis of normal and abnormal left atrial pressure pulse in man. Circ. Res., 4:95, 1956.

Arnott, W. M., and Withering, W.: Physiologic problems in mitral stenosis. Am. Heart J., 68:145, 1964.

Austen, W. G., Bender, H. W., Wilcox, B. R., and Morrow, A. G.: Experimental aortic regurgitation: The magnitude and acute hemodynamic effects of regurgitant flows associated with valvular defects of various sizes. J. Surg. Res., 3:466, 1963.

Ayres, S. M., and Lukas, D. S.: Mild pulmonic stenosis: A clinical and hemodynamic study of eleven cases. Ann. Int. Med., 52:1076, 1960.

Ball, J. D., Kopelman, H., and Witham, A. C.: Circulatory changes in mitral stenosis at rest and on exercise. Brit. Heart J., 14:363, 1952.

Basu, A. K., and Sen Gupta, D.: Haemodynamics in mitral stenosis before, during, and after valvotomy. Brit. Heart J., 24:445, 1962.

Becker, D. L., Burchell, H. B., and Edwards, J. E.: Pathology of the pulmonary vascular tree. II. The occurrence in mitral insufficiency of occlusive pulmonary vascular lesions. Circulation, 3:230, 1951.

Benchimol, A., Dimond, E. G., and Shen, Y.: Ejection time in aortic stenosis and mitral stenosis. Comparison between the direct and indirect arterial tracings, with special reference to pre- and postoperative findings. Am. J. Cardiol., 5:728, 1960.

Bentivoglio, L., Uricchio, J. F., and Likoff, W.: The paradox of right ventricular enlargement in mitral insufficiency. Am. J. Med., 24:193, 1958.

Bevegard, S., Jonsson, B., and Karlöf, I.: Low subvalvular aortic and pulmonic stenosis caused by asymmetrical hypertrophy and derangement of muscle bundles of the ventricular wall. Acta Med. Scand., 172:269, 1962.

Björk, V. O.: Direct pressure measurement in the left atrium, the left ventricle, and the aorta. Acta Chir. Scand., 107:466, 1954.

Björk, V. O., Lodin, H., and Malers, E.: The evaluation of the degree of mitral insufficiency by selective left ventricular angiocardiography. Am. Heart J., 60:691, 1960.

Björk, V. O., and Malmström, G.: The diastolic pressure gradient between the left atrium and the left ventricle in cases of mitral stenosis. Am. Heart J., 58:486, 1959.

Boas, E. P.: Clinical "capillary pulsation." Heart, 11:57, 1924.

Boiteau, G. M., and Allenstein, B. J.: Hypertrophic subaortic stenosis: Clinical and hemodynamic studies with special reference to pulse contour measurement. Am. J. Cardiol., 8:614, 1961.

Borst, H. G., McGregor, M., Whittenberger, J. L., and Berglund, E.: Influence of pulmonary arterial and left atrial pressures on pulmonary vascular resistance. Circ. Res., 4:393, 1956.

Bowden, D. H., Favara, B. E., and Donahoe, J. L.: Marfan's syndrome. Accelerated course in childhood associated with lesions of mitral valve and pulmonary artery. Am. Heart J., 69:96, 1965.

Brandenburg, R. O., and Burchell, H. B.: Mitral insufficiency: Clinical consideration. Proc. Staff Meet. Mayo Clin., 33:510, 1958.

Braunwald, E., and Awe, W. C.: The syndrome of severe mitral regurgitation with normal left atrial pressure. Circulation, 27:29, 1963.

Braunwald, E., Brockenbrough, E. C., and Morrow, A. G.: Hypertrophic subaortic stenosis—A broadened concept. Circulation, 26:161, 1962.

Braunwald, E., Goldblatt, A., Aygen, M. M., Rockoff, S. D., and Morrow, A. G.: Congenital aortic stenosis. I. Clinical and hemodynamic findings in 100 patients. Circulation, 27:426, 1963.

Braunwald, E., Lambrew, C. T., Rockoff, S. D., Ross, J., Jr., and Morrow, A. G.: Idiopathic hypertrophic subaortic stenosis: I. A description of the disease based upon an analysis of 64 patients. Circulation, 30:3, 1964.

Braunwald, E., and Sarnoff, S. J.: The hemodynamics of valvular regurgitation. In Luisada, A. A. (ed.): An Encyclopedia of the Cardiovascular System, Volume 3, p. 7. New York, McGraw-Hill—Blakiston Division, 1959.

Brofman, B. L., and Feil, H.: The diagnosis of congenital subaortic stenosis. Application of hemodynamic principles. Circulation, 6:817, 1952.

Bruns, D. L., Connolly, J. E., and Stofer, R. C.: Experimental observations on poststenotic dilatation. J. Thoracic Surg., 38:662, 1959.

Burchell, H. B., and others: Symposium on the diagnostic value of simultaneous catheterization of the aorta and the right and left sides of the heart. Proc. Staff Meet. Mayo Clin., 31:105, 1956.

Buteler, B. S.: The relation of systolic upstroke time and pulse in aortic stenosis. Brit. Heart J., 24:657, 1962.

Calvin, J. L., Perloff, J. K., Conrad, P. W., and Hufnagel, C. A.: Idiopathic hypertrophic subaortic stenosis. Am. Heart J., 63:477, 1962.

Camp, F. A., McDonald, K. E., and Schenk, W. G., Jr.: Hemodynamics of experimental pulmonic insufficiency. J. Thoracic Surg., 47:372, 1964.

Carroll, D., Cohn, J. E., and Riley, R. L.: Pulmonary function in mitral valvular disease: Distribution and diffusion characteristics in resting patients. J. Clin. Invest., 32:510, 1953.

Coelho, E.: Physiopathologic study (clinical and experimental) of the tricuspid valve. Am. J. Cardiol., 3:517, 1959.

Contratto, A. W., and Levine, S. A.: Aortic stenosis, with special reference to angina pectoris and syncope. Ann. Int. Med., 10:1636, 1937.

Cooke, W. T., and White, P. D.: Tricuspid stenosis, with particular reference to diagnosis and prognosis. Brit. Heart J., 3:147, 1941.

Crawford, J. H., and Rosenberger, H.: Studies on human capillaries: Observations on the nature of capillary pulse in aortic insufficiency. J. Clin. Invest., 4:307, 1937.

Curti, P. C., and others: Respiratory and circulatory studies of patients with mitral stenosis. Circulation, 8:893, 1953.

D'Cruz, I. A., Arcilla, R. A., and Agustsson, M. H.: Dilatation of the pulmonary trunk in stenosis of the pulmonary valve and of the pulmonary arteries in children. Am. Heart J., 68:612, 1964.

Delaney, T. B., and Nadas, A. S.: Peripheral pulmonic stenosis. Am. J. Cardiol., 13:451, 1964.

DeSanctis, R. W., Dean, D. C., and Bland, E. F.: Extreme left atrial enlargement. Some characteristic features. Circulation, 29:14, 1964.

Dexter, L., and others: Aortic stenosis. Arch. Int. Med., 101:254, 1958.

Dexter, L., and others: Studies of the pulmonary circulation in man at rest. Normal variations and the interrelations between increased pulmonary blood flow, elevated pulmonary arterial pressure, and high pulmonary "capillary" pressures. J. Clin. Investigation, 29:602, 1950.

Dotter, C. T., and Gensini, G. G.: Percutaneous retrograde catheterization of the left ventricle and systemic arteries of man. Radiology, 75:171, 1960.

Dow, P.: Development of anacrotic and tardus pulse of aortic stenosis. Am. J. Physiol., 131:432, 1940.

Draper, A., and others: Physiologic studies in mitral valvular disease. Circulation, 3:531, 1951.

Edwards, J. E., and Burchell, H. B.: Pathologic anatomy of mitral insufficiency. Proc. Staff Meet. Mayo Clin., 33:497, 1958.

Ellis, F. H., Jr., and Bulbulian, A. H.: Prosthetic replacement of the mitral valve. I. Preliminary experimental observations. Proc. Staff Meet. Mayo Clin., 33:532, 1958.

Ellis, F. H., Jr., McGoon, D. C., Brandenburg, R. O., and Kirklin, J. W.: Clinical experience with total mitral valve replacement with prosthetic valves. J. Thoracic Surg., 46:482, 1963.

Ellis, L. B., Abelmann, W. H., and Harken, D. E.: Selection of patients for mitral and aortic valvuloplasty. Circulation, 15:924, 1957.

Ellis, L. B., and others: Studies in mitral stenosis. I. A correlation of physiologic and clinical findings. Arch. Int. Med., 88:515, 1951.

Epstein, E. J., and Coulshed, N.: Assessment of aortic stenosis from the external carotid pulse wave. Brit. Heart J., 26:84, 1964.

Ferguson, F. C., Kobilak, R. E., and Deitrick, J. E.: Varices of the bronchial veins as a source of hemoptysis in mitral stenosis. Am. Heart J., 28:445, 1944.

Ferrer, M. I., Harvey, R. M., Kuschner, M., Richards, D. W., Jr., and Cournand, A.: Hemodynamic studies in tricuspid stenosis of rheumatic origin. Circ. Res., 1:49, 1953.

Fisher, D. L.: The use of pressure recordings obtained at transthoracic left heart catheterization in the diagnosis of valvular heart disease. J. Thoracic Surg., 30:379, 1955.

Fowler, N. O., Cubberly, R., and Dorney, E.: Pulmonary blood distribution and oxygen diffusion in mitral stenosis. Am. Heart J., 48:1, 1954.

Fowler, N. O., Westcott, R. N., and Scott, R. C.: Normal pressure in the right heart and pulmonary artery. Am. Heart J., 46:264, 1953.

Gladstone, S. A.: A few observations on the hemodynamics of the normal circulation and the changes which occur in aortic insufficiency. Bull. Johns Hopkins Hosp., 44:83, 1929.

Goldberg, H., Bakst, A. A., and Bailey, C. P.: The dynamics of aortic valvular disease. Am. Heart J., 47:527, 1954.

Gorlin, R., and Goodale, W. T.: Changing blood pressure in aortic insufficiency; its clinical significance. New England J. Med., 255:77, 1956.

Gorlin, R., and Gorlin, S. G.: Hydraulic formula for calculation of the area of the stenotic mitral valve, other cardiac valves, and central circulatory shunts. I. Am. Heart J., 41:1, 1951.

Gorlin, R., Lewis, B. M., Haynes, F. W., and Dexter, L.: Studies of the circulatory dynamics at rest in mitral valvular regurgitation with and without stenosis. Am. Heart J., 43:357, 1952.

Gorlin, R., and others: Dynamics of the circulation in aortic valvular disease. Am. J. Med., 18:855, 1955.

Gorlin, R., and others: Studies of the circulatory dynamics in mitral stenosis. II. Altered dynamics at rest. Am. Heart J., 41:30, 1951.

Goyette, E. M., Farinacci, C. J., Forsee, J. H., and Blake, H. A.: The clinicopathologic correlation of lung biopsies in mitral stenosis. Am. Heart J., 47:645, 1954.

Gray, I. R., and Joshipura, C. S.: Retrograde left ventricular catheterization and cardioangiography in aortic stenosis. Brit. Heart J., 26:199, 1964.

Gray, I. R., Joshipura, C. S., and Mackinnon, J.: Retrograde left ventricular cardioangiography in the diagnosis of mitral regurgitation. Brit. Heart J., 25:145, 1963.

Guidry, L. D., Callahan, J. A., Marshall, H. W., and Ellis, F. H., Jr.: The surgical treatment of mitral insufficiency by mitral annuloplasty. Proc. Staff Meet. Mayo Clin., 33:523, 1958.

Hamer, N. A. J., Roy, S. B., and Dow, J. W.: Determinants of the left atrial pressure pulse in mitral valve disease. Circulation, 19:257, 1959.

Haynes, F., Novack, P., Schlant, R., Phinney, A., and Dexter, L.: Hemodynamics of mitral stenosis and regurgitation. Fed. Proc., 16:56, 1957.

Hernandez, R. R., Greenfield, J. C., and McCall, B. W.: Pressure-flow studies in hypertrophic subaortic stenosis. J. Clin. Invest., 43:401, 1964.

Honey, M.: Clinical and hemodynamic observations on combined mitral and aortic stenosis. Brit. Heart J., 23:545, 1961.

Katz, L. N., and Feil, H. S.: Clinical observations on the dynamics of ventricular systole. III. Aortic stenosis and aortic insufficiency. Heart, 12:171, 1925.

Killip, T., III, and Lukas, D. S.: Tricuspid stenosis. Physiologic criteria for diagnosis and hemodynamic abnormalities. Circulation, 16:3, 1957.

Kjellberg, S. R., Nordenström, B., Rudhe, U., Björk, V. O., and Malmström, G.: Cardioangiographic studies of the mitral and aortic valves. Acta Radiol., suppl. 204, p. 1, 1961.

Larrabee, W. F., Parker, R. L., and Edwards, J. E.: Pathology of intrapulmonary arteries and arterioles in mitral stenosis. Proc. Staff Meet. Mayo Clin., 24:316, 1949.

Lewis, B. M., and others: Clinical and physiologic correlations in patients with mitral stenosis. Am. Heart J., 43:2, 1952.

Likoff, W.: Surgical treatment of acquired valvular disease as viewed by the internist. Circulation, 21:559, 1960.

Luchsinger, P. C., Seipp, H. W., Jr., and Patel, D. J.: Relationship of pulmonary artery wedge pressure to left atrial pressure in man. Circ. Res., 11:315, 1962.

Luisada, A. A.: On the pathogenesis of the signs of Traube and Duroziez in aortic insufficiency. A graphic study. Am. Heart J., 26:721, 1943.

Luisada, A. A., and Wolff, L.: The significance of the pulmonary diastolic murmur in cases of mitral stenosis. Am. J. Med. Sc., 209:204, 1945.

Marshall, H. W., and Wood, E. H.: Hemodynamic considerations in mitral regurgitation. Proc. Staff Meet. Mayo Clin., 33:517, 1958.

Marvin, H. M., and Sullivan, A. G.: Clinical observations upon syncope and sudden death in . . . aortic stenosis. Am. Heart J., 10:705, 1935.

McDonald, L., Dealy, J. B., Jr., Rabinowitz, M., and Dexter, L.: Clinical, physiological and pathological findings in mitral stenosis and regurgitation. Medicine, 36:237, 1957.

McGinn, S., and White, P. D.: Acute pulmonary congestion and cardiac asthma in patients with mitral stenosis. Am. Heart J., 9:697, 1934.

McGuire, J., and McNamara, R. J.: Organic and relative insufficiency of the pulmonary valve. Am. Heart J., 14:562, 1937.

McMichael, J., and Shillingford, J. P.: The role of valvular incompetence in heart failure. Brit. Med. J., 1:537, 1957.

Menges, H., Jr., Brandenburg, R. O., and Brown, A. L., Jr.: The clinical, hemodynamic, and pathologic diagnosis of muscular subvalvular aortic stenosis. Circulation, 24:1126, 1961.

Messer, A. L., Hurst, J. W., Rappaport, M. B., and Sprague, H. B.: A study of the venous pulse in tricuspid valve disease. Circulation, 1:388, 1950.

Miller, G. A. H., Kirklin, J. W., and Swan, H. J. C.: Myocardial function and left ventricular volumes in acquired valvular insufficiency. Circulation, 31:374, 1965.

Morrow, A. G., Awe, W. C., and Braunwald, E.: Combined mitral and aortic stenosis. Brit. Heart J., 24:606, 1962.

Morrow, A. G., Braunwald, E., Haller, J. A., and Sharp, E. H.: Left atrial pressure pulse in mitral valve disease; a correlation of pressures obtained by transbronchial puncture with the valvular lesion. Circulation, 16:399, 1957.

Morrow, A. G., Braunwald, E., and Ross, J., Jr.: Left heart catheterization: An appraisal of techniques and their applications in cardiovascular diagnosis. Arch. Int. Med., 105:645, 1960.

Musser, B. G., and Goldberg, H.: Left heart catheterization: Evaluation of its clinical application in 450 cases. J. Thoracic Surg., 34:414, 1957.

Neustadt, J. E., and Shaffer, A. B.: Diagnostic value of the left atrial pressure pulse in mitral valvular disease. Am. Heart J., 58:675, 1959.

Nixon, P. G. F., and Wooler, G. H.: Rapid left ventricular filling and stasis in mitral regurgitation. Brit. Heart J., 23:161, 1961.

Raber, G., and Goldberg, H.: Left ventricular, central aortic, and peripheral pressure pulses in aortic stenosis. Am. J. Cardiol., 1:572, 1958.

Rapaport, E., and Dexter, L.: Pulmonary "capillary" pressure. Methods Med. Res., 7:58, 1958.

Rees, J. R., Epstein, E. J., Criley, J. M., and Ross, R. S.: Haemodynamic effects of severe aortic regurgitation. Brit. Heart J., 26:412, 1964.

Rodbard, S., Ikeda, K., and Montes, M.: Mechanisms of post-stenotic dilatation. Circulation, 28:791, 1963.

Rodbard, S., and Williams, F.: The dynamics of mitral insufficiency. Am. Heart J., 48:521, 1954.

Rodrigo, F. A.: Estimation of valve area and valvular resistance: A critical study of the physical basis of the methods employed. Am. Heart J., 45:1, 1953.

Ross, J., Jr., Braunwald, E., and Morrow, A. G.: Clinical and hemodynamic observations in pure mitral insufficiency. Am. J. Cardiol., 2:11, 1958.

Rowe, G. C.: Relative stenosis of cardiac valves. Am. Heart J., 67:334, 1964.

Selzer, A.: Effects of atrial fibrillation upon the circulation in patients with mitral stenosis. Am. Heart J., 59:518, 1960.

Selzer, A., Poppes, R. W., Lau, F. Y. K., Morgan, J. J., and Anderson, W. L.: Present status of diagnostic cardiac catheterization. New England J. Med., 268:589, 654, 1963.

Selzer, A., Willet, F. M., McCaughey, D. J., and Feichtmeir, T. V.: Uses of cardiac catheterization in acquired heart disease. New England J. Med., 257:66, 121, 1957.

Shaw, D. B.: The pressure wave form in the pulmonary artery. Brit. Heart J., 25:347, 1963.

Smith, J. E., Hsu, I., Evans, J. M., and Lederer, L. G.: Aortic stenosis: A study with particular reference to an indirect carotid pulse recording in diagnosis. Am. Heart J., 58:527, 1959.

Snellen, H. A.: Estimation of valve area and valvular resistance. Am. Heart J., 45:1, 1963.

Starr, A., and Edwards, M. L.: Mitral replacement: Clinical experience with a ball-valve prosthesis. Ann. Surg., 154:726, 1961.

Talbert, J. L., Morrow, A. G., Collins, N. P., and Gilbert, J. W.: The incidence and significance of pulmonic regurgitation after pulmonary valvulotomy. Am. Heart J., 65:590, 1963.

Taquini, A. C., Lozada, B. B., Donaldson, R. J., D'Aiutolo, R. E. H., and Ballina, E. S.: Mitral stenosis and cor pulmonale. Am. Heart J., 46:639, 1953.

Watson, H., and Lowe, K. G.: Ventricular pressure flow relationships in isolated valvular stenosis. Brit. Heart J., 24:431, 1962.

Werkä, L.: The dynamics and consequences of stenosis or insufficiency of the cardiac valves. In Handbook of Physiology, Section II, volume 1, chapter 20, p. 645. Washington, D. C., American Physiological Society, 1962.

West, J. B., and Dollery, C. T.: Distribution of blood flow and the pressure-flow relations of the whole lung. J. Appl. Physiol., 20:175, 1965.

Wiggers, C. J.: The magnitude of regurgitation with aortic leaks of different sizes. J.A.M.A., 97:1359, 1931.

Wiggers, C. J., and Feil, H.: The cardiodynamics of mitral insufficiency. Heart, 9:149, 1921–22.

Wigle, E. D.: The arterial pressure pulse in muscular

subaortic stenosis. Brit. Heart J., 25:97, 1963.

Wong, P. C. Y., and Sanders, C. A.: A nomogram for estimation of the cardiac valve areas. Circulation, 32:425, 1965.

Wood, P.: Aortic stenosis. Am. J. Cardiol., 1:553, 1958.

Yu, P. N., and others: Clinical and hemodynamic studies of tricuspid stenosis. Circulation, 13:680, 1956.

Yu, P. N., and others: Studies of pulmonary hypertension. IV. Pulmonary circulatory dynamics in patients with mitral stenosis at rest. Am. Heart J., 47:330, 1954.

Congenital Cardiovascular Defects

Abbott, M. E.: Atlas of Congenital Cardiac Disease. New York, American Heart Association, 1954.

Adams, W. R., and Veith, I.: Pulmonary Circulation. New York, Grune and Stratton, Inc., 1959.

Ainger, L. E., and Pate, J. W.: Ostium secundum atrial septal defects and congestive heart failure in infancy. Am. J. Cardiol., 15:380, 1965.

Albert, H. M., Fowler, R. L., Craighead, C. C., Glass, B. A., and Atik, M.: Pulmonary artery banding: A treatment for infants with intractable heart failure due to interventricular septal defect. Circulation, 23:16, 1961.

Arcilla, R. A., Agustsson, M. H., Bicoff, J. P., Lynfield, J., Weinberg, M., Jr., Fell, E. H., and Gasul, B. M.: Further observations on the natural history of isolated ventricular septal defects in infancy and childhood: Serial cardiac catheterization studies in 75 patients. Circulation, 28:560, 1963.

Ash, R.: Natural history of ventricular septal defects in childhood lesions with predominant arteriovenous shunts. J. Pediat., 64:45, 1964.

Auld, P. A. M., Johnson, A. L., Gibbons, J. E., and McGregor, M.: Changes in pulmonary vascular resistance in infants and children with left-to-right intracardiac shunt. Circulation, 27:257, 1963.

Beard, E. F., Wood, E. H., and Clagett, O. T.: Study of hemodynamics in coarctation of the aorta using dye dilution and direct intra-arterial pressure recording methods. J. Lab. & Clin. Med., 38:858, 1951.

Beck, W., Swan, H. J. C., Burchell, H. B., and Kirklin, J. W.: Pulmonary vascular resistance after repair of atrial septal defects in patients with pulmonary hypertension. Circulation, 22:938, 1960.

Becu, L. M., and others: Anatomic and pathologic studies in ventricular septal defect. Circulation, 14:349, 1956.

Beuren, A. J., and others: Syndrome of supravalvular aortic stenosis, peripheral pulmonary stenosis, mental retardation and similar facial appearance. Am. J. Cardiol., 13:471, 1964.

Blake, H. A., Hall, R. J., and Manion, W. C.: Anomalous pulmonary venous return. Circulation, 32:406, 1965.

Blalock, A., and Taussig, H. B.: Surgical treatment of malformations of the heart in which there is pulmonary stenosis or pulmonary atresia. J.A.M.A., 128:189, 1945.

Blount, S. G., Jr., Swan, H., Gensini, G., and McCord, M. C.: Atrial septal defect. Clinical and physiologic response to complete closure in five patients. Circulation, 9:801, 1954.

Blumgart, H. L., Lawrence, J. S., and Ernstene, A. C.: Dynamics of circulation in coarctation (stenosis of isthmus) of aorta of adult type; Relation to essential hypertension. Arch. Int. Med., 47:806, 1931.

Brannon, E. S., Weens, H. S., and Warren, J. V.: Atrial septal defect; Study of hemodynamics by the technique of right heart catheterization. Am. J. Med. Sc., 210:480, 1945.

Braunwald, N. S., Braunwald, E., and Morrow, A. G.: The effects of surgical abolition of left-to-right shunts on the pulmonary vascular dynamics of patients with pulmonary hypertension. Circulation, 26:1270, 1962.

Broadbent, J. C., Clagett, O. T., Burchell, H. B., and Wood, E. H.: Dye-dilution curves in acyanotic congenital heart disease. Am. J. Physiol., 167:770, 1951.

Broadbent, J. C., and Wood, E. H.: Indicator-dilution curves in acyanotic congenital heart disease. Circulation, 9:890, 1954.

Broadbent, J. C., Wood, E. H., and Burchell, H. B.: Left-to-right intracardiac shunts in the presence of pulmonary stenosis. Proc. Staff Meet. Mayo Clin., 28:101, 1953.

Brotchner, R. J.: Etiology of hypertension resulting from coarctation of the aorta. Arch. Path., 28:676, 1939.

Brotmacher, L.: Haemodynamic effects of squatting during recovery from exertion. Brit. Heart J., 19:567, 1957.

Burroughs, J. T., and Edwards, J. E.: Total anomalous pulmonary venous connection. Am. Heart J., 59:913, 1960.

Callahan, J. A., Brandenburg, R. O., and Swan, H. J. C.: Pulmonary stenosis and interatrial communication with cyanosis: Hemodynamic and clinical study of 10 patients. Am. J. Med., 19:189, 1955.

Campbell, M. (chairman): Symposium on congenital heart disease. Brit. Heart J., 20:261, 1958.

Cournand, A.: Some aspects of the pulmonary circulation in normal man and in chronic cardiopulmonary diseases. Circulation, 2:641, 1950.

Dailey, F. H., Genovese, P. D., and Behnke, R. H.: Patent ductus arteriosus with reversal of flow in adults. Ann. Int. Med., 56:865, 1962.

D'Cruz, I. A., Lendrum, B. L., and Novak, G.: Congenital absence of the pulmonary valve. Am. Heart J., 68:728, 1964.

Dexter, L.: Atrial septal defect. Brit. Heart J., 18:209, 1956.

Dexter, L., and others: Studies of the pulmonary circulation in man at rest. Normal variations and the interrelations between increased pulmonary blood flow, elevated pulmonary arterial pressure, and high pulmonary "capillary" pressures. J. Clin. Invest., 29:602, 1950.

Dow, J. W., and Dexter, L.: Circulatory dynamics in atrial septal defect. J. Clin. Investigation, 29:809, 1950.

Dow, J. W., and others: Studies of congenital heart disease. IV. Uncomplicated pulmonic stenosis. Circulation, 1:267, 1950.

Downing, S. E., Vidone, R. A., Brandt, H. M., and Liebow, A. A.: The pathogenesis of vascular lesions of experimental hyperkinetic pulmonary hypertension. Am. J. Path., 43:739, 1963.

Draper, A. J., and others: Physiological studies in pre- and postoperative mitral stenosis. J. Clin. Invest., 29:809, 1950.

Dresdale, D. T., Michtom, R. J., and Schultz, M.: Recent studies in primary pulmonary hypertension including pharmacodynamic observations on pulmonary vascular resistance. Bull. New York Acad. Med., 30:195, 1954.

Edwards, J. E.: Functional pathology of the pulmonary vascular tree in congenital cardiac disease. Circulation, 15:164, 1957.

Edwards, J. E., and others: An Atlas of Congenital Anomalies of the Heart and Great Vessels. Springfield, Charles C Thomas, 1954.

Edwards, J. E., and others: Symposium on total anomalous pulmonary venous connection. Proc. Staff Meet. Mayo Clin., 31:151, 1956.

Ellis, F. H., Jr., Kirklin, J. W., Callahan, J. A., and Wood, E. H.: Patent ductus arteriosus with pulmonary hypertension. J. Thoracic Surg., 31:268, 1956.

Engle, M. A., and Taussig, H. B.: Valvular pulmonic stenosis with intact ventricular septum and patent foramen ovale; report of illustrative cases and analysis of clinical syndrome. Circulation, 2:481, 1950.

Espino-Vela, J.: Rheumatic heart disease associated with atrial septal defect: Clinical and pathologic study of 12 cases of Lutembacher's syndrome. Am. Heart J., 57:185, 1959.

Evans, J. R., Rowe, R. D., and Keith, J. D.: Spontaneous closure of ventricular septal defects. Circulation, 22:1044, 1960.

Falkenbach, K. H., Zheutlin, N., Dowdy, A. H., and O'Loughlin, B. J.: Pulmonary hypertension due to pulmonary arterial coarctation. Radiology, 73:575, 1959.

Fallot, A.: Contribution à l'anatomie pathologique de la maladie bleue (cyanose cardiaque). Marseille-med., 25:77, 138, 207, 270, 341, 403, 1888.

Ginsburg, J.: Clubbing of the fingers. In Handbook of Physiology, Section II, volume 3, chapter 65, p. 2377. Washington, D. C., American Physiological Society, 1965.

Goldberg, H., Silber, E. N., Gordon, A., and Katz, L. N.: The dynamics of Eisenmenger's complex: An integration of the pathologic, physiologic and clinical features. Circulation, 4:343, 1951.

Goldblatt, A., Bernhard, W. F., Nadas, A. S., and Gross, R. E.: Pulmonary artery banding. Indications and results in infants and children. Circulation, 32:172, 1965.

Gordon, A. J., and others: Patent ductus arteriosus with reversal of flow. New England J. Med., 251:923, 1954.

Gott, V. L., Lester, R. G., Lillehei, C. W., and Varco, R. L.: Total anomalous pulmonary return: An analysis of thirty cases. Circulation, 13:543, 1956.

Green, E. W., Ziegler, R. F., and Kavanagh-Gray, D.: Clinical use of retrograde left ventricular catheterization in congenital heart disease. Circulation, 20:704, 1959.

Gross, R. E.: Coarctation of the aorta. Circulation, 7: 757, 1953.

Gross, R. E.: Complete division for the patent ductus arteriosus. J. Thoracic Surg., 16:314, 1947.

Gross, R. E.: Hypertension from coarctation of the aorta. Am. J. Surg., 107:14, 1964.

Gross, R. E.: Surgical correction for coarctation of the aorta. Surgery, 18:673, 1945.

Gross, R. E.: Surgical management of the patent ductus arteriosus. Ann. Surg., 110:321, 1939.

Gross, R. E., and Hubbard, J. P.: Surgical ligation of a patent ductus arteriosus; Report of first successful case. J.A.M.A., 112:729, 1939.

Gross, R. E., and Longino, L. A.: The patent ductus arteriosus: Observations from 412 surgically treated cases. Circulation, 3:125, 1951.

Halloran, K. H., Talner, N. S., and Browne, M. J.: A study of ventricular septal defect associated with aortic insufficiency. Am. Heart J., 69:320, 1965.

Heath, D., and Whitaker, W.: Hypertensive pulmonary vascular disease. Circulation, 14:323, 1956.

Hetzel, P. S., Swan, H. J. C., and Wood, E. H.: The applications of indicator-dilution curves in cardiac catheterization. In Zimmerman, H. A.: Intravascular Catheterization. Springfield, Charles C Thomas, 1959.

Hoffman, J. I. E., and Rudolph, A. M.: The natural history of ventricular septal defects in infancy. Am. J. Cardiol., 16:634, 1965.

Hoffman, J. I. E., Rudolph, A. M., Nadas, A. S., and Paul, M. H.: Physiologic differentiation of pulmonic stenosis with and without an intact ventricular septum. Circulation, 22:385, 1960.

Hultgren, H., Selzer, A., Purdy, A., Holman, E., and Gerbode, F.: The syndrome of patent ductus arteriosus with pulmonary hypertension. Circulation, 8:15, 1953.

Hyman, A. L., Hyman, E. S., Quiroz, A. C., and Gantt, J. R.: Hydrogen platinum electrode system in detection of intravascular shunts. Am. Heart J., 61:53, 1961.

Johnson, A. M.: Functional infundibular stenosis: Its differentiation from structural stenosis and its importance in atrial septal defect. Guy's Hosp. Rep., 108:373, 1959.

Keck, E. W. O., Ongley, P. A., Kincaid, O. W., and Swan, H. J. C.: Ventricular septal defect with aortic insufficiency: A clinical and hemodynamic study of 18 proved cases. Circulation, 27:203, 1963.

Kidd, L., Rose, V., Collins, G., and Keith, J.: Ventricular septal defect in infancy: A hemodynamic study. Am. Heart J., 69:4, 1965.

Kiely, B., Adams, P., Jr., Anderson, R. C., and Lester, R. G.: The ostium primum syndrome. J. Dis. Child., 96:381, 1958.

King, J. T.: Blood pressure in stenosis at isthmus of aorta. Ann. Int. Med., 10:1802, 1937.

Levy, L., II, Fowler, R. L., Kirkley, D., Albert, H., and Martinez-Lopez, J. I.: Multiple hydrogen-electrode catheter for determination of cardiac shunts. New England J. Med., 264:1356, 1961.

Lewis, T.: Material relating to coarctation of aorta of the adult type. Heart, 16:205, 1933.

Long, R. T. L., Braunwald, E., and Morrow, A. G.: Intracardiac injection of radioactive krypton. Clinical applications of new methods for characterization of circulatory shunts. Circulation, *21:* 1126, 1960.

Lucas, R. V., Jr., and others: The natural history of isolated ventricular septal defect: A serial physiologic study. Circulation, *24:*1372, 1961.

Lukas, D. S., Araujo, J., and Steinberg, I.: The syndrome of patent ductus arteriosus with reversal of flow. Am. J. Med., *17:*298, 1954.

Lutembacher, R.: De le stenose mitrale avec communication interauriculaire. Arch. Mal. Coeur, *9:* 237, 1916.

Lynfield, J., Gasul, B. M., Arcilla, R., and Luan, L. L.: The natural history of ventricular septal defects in infancy and childhood: Based on serial cardiac catheterization studies. Am. J. Med., *30:* 357, 1961.

Malm, J. R., Blumenthal, S., Jameson, A. G., and Humphreys, G. H., II: Observations on coarctation of the aorta in infants. Arch. Surg., *86:*96, 1963.

Marshall, H. W., Helmholz, H. F., Jr., and Wood, E. H.: Physiologic consequences of congenital heart disease. In Handbook of Physiology, Section II, volume 1, chapter 14, p. 417. Washington, D. C., American Physiological Society, 1962.

Marshall, R. J., and Warden, H. E.: Mitral valve disease complicated by left-to-right shunt at atrial level. Circulation, *29:*432, 1964.

Mauer, E. F.: On the etiology of clubbing of the fingers. Am. Heart J., *34:*852, 1947.

McDonald, L., Emanuel, R., and Towers, M.: Aspects of pulmonary blood flow in atrial septal defect. Brit. Heart J., *21:*279, 1959.

Mendlowitz, M.: Clubbing and hypertrophic osteoarthropathy. Medicine, *21:*269, 1942.

Morgan, B. C., Griffiths, S. P., and Blumenthal, S.: Ventricular septal defect. I. Congestive heart failure in infancy. Pediatrics, *25:*54, 1960.

Muller, W. H., Jr., and Dammann, J. F., Jr.: The treatment of certain congenital malformations of the heart by the creation of pulmonic stenosis to reduce pulmonary hypertension and excessive pulmonary blood flow; a preliminary report. Surg. Gynec. & Obst., *95:*213, 1952.

Mustard, W. T., Rowe, R. D., Keith, J. D., and Sirek, A.: Coarctation of the aorta with special reference to the first year of life. Ann. Surg., *141:*429, 1955.

Nadas, A. S., Scott, L. P., Hauck, A. J., and Rudolph, A. M.: Spontaneous functional closing of ventricular septal defects. New England J. Med., *264:*309, 1961.

Nadas, A. S., Thilenius, O. G., LaFarge, C. G., and Hauck, A. J.: Ventricular septal defect with aortic regurgitation: Medical and pathologic aspects. Circulation, *29:*862, 1964.

Nemickas, R., Roberts, J., Gunnar, R. M., and Tobin, J. R., Jr.: Isolated congenital pulmonic insufficiency. Differentiation of mild from severe regurgitation. Am. J. Cardiol., *14:*456, 1964.

Nieveen, J., Van der Sikke, L. B., Sien, Q. G., and DeVries, H.: Coarctation of the pulmonary artery. Cardiologia, *38:*239, 1961.

O'Donnell, T. V., and McIlroy, M. B.: The circulatory effects of squatting. Am. Heart J., *64:*347, 1962.

Omeri, M. A., Bishop, M., Oakley, C., Bentall, H. H., and Cleland, W. P.: The mitral valve in endocardial cushion defects. Brit. Heart J., *27:*161, 1965.

Rathi, L., and Keith, J. D.: Post-operative blood pressures in coarctation of the aorta. Brit. Heart J., *26:*671, 1964.

Rodbard, S., and Schaffer, A. B.: Muscular contraction in the infundibular region as a mechanism of pulmonic stenosis in man. Am. Heart J., *51:*885, 1956.

Rowe, G. G., Castillo, C. A., Maxwell, G. M., Clifford, J. E., and Crumpton, C. W.: Atrial septal defect and the mechanism of shunt. Am. Heart J., *61:* 369, 1961.

Rowe, R. D., Vlad, P., and Keith, J. D.: Experiences with 180 cases of tetralogy of Fallot in infants and children. Canad. Med. Assoc. J., *73:*23, 1955.

Rudolph, A. M., and Nadas, A. S.: The pulmonary circulation and congenital heart disease: Considerations of the role of the pulmonary circulation in certain systemic-pulmonary communications. New England J. Med., *267:*968, 1022, 1962.

Rudolph, A. M., Scarpelli, E. M., Golinko, R. J., and Gootman, N. L.: Hemodynamic basis for clinical manifestations of patent ductus arteriosus. Am. Heart J., *68:*477, 1964.

Rytand, D. A.: The renal factor in arterial hypertension with coarctation of the aorta. J. Clin. Invest., *17:*391, 1938.

Sambhi, M. P., and Zimmerman, H. A.: Pathologic physiology of Lutembacher syndrome. Am. J. Cardiol., *2:*681, 1958.

Sanders, R. J.: Use of a radioactive gas (Kr^{85}) in diagnosis of cardiac shunts. Proc. Soc. Exper. Biol. Med., *97:*5, 1958.

Saphir, O., and Lev, M.: The tetralogy of Eisenmenger. Am. Heart J., *21:*31, 1941.

Selzer, A., and Carnes, W. H.: The role of pulmonary stenosis in the production of chronic cyanosis. Am. Heart J., *45:*382, 1953.

Selzer, A., Carnes, W. H., Noble, C. A., Higgins, W. H., and Holmes, R. O.: The syndrome of pulmonary stenosis with patent foramen ovale. Am. J. Med., *6:*3, 1949.

Selzer, A., and Laqueur, G. L.: The Eisenmenger complex and its relation to the uncomplicated defect of the ventricular septum. Review of thirty-five autopsied cases of Eisenmenger's complex, including two new cases. Arch. Int. Med., *87:*218, 1951.

Sharpey-Shafer, E. P.: Effects of squatting on the normal and falling circulation. Brit. Med. J., *1:* 1072, 1956.

Siegel, J. H.: A study of the mechanisms of cardiovascular adaptation to an acute ventricular septal defect. J. Thoracic Surg., *41:*523, 1961.

Silber, E. N., Prec, O., Grossman, N., and Katz, L. N.: Dynamics of isolated pulmonary stenosis. Am. J. Med., *10:*21, 1951.

Steele, J. M.: Evidence for general distribution of peripheral resistance in coarctation of the aorta: Report of three cases. J. Clin. Invest., *20:*473, 1941.

Storstein, O., and Helle, I.: Pulmonary hypertension in patent ductus arteriosus. Acta Med. Scand., *156:*131, 1956–1957.

Swan, H. J. C., Toscano-Barboza, E., and Wood, E. H.: Hemodynamic findings in total anomalous pulmonary venous drainage. Proc. Staff Meet. Mayo Clin., 31:177, 1956.

Swan, H. J. C., and Wood, E. H.: Localization of cardiac defects by dye-dilution curves recorded after injection of T-1824 at multiple sites in the heart and great vessels during cardiac catheterization. Proc. Staff Meet. Mayo Clin., 28:95, 1953.

Swan, H. J. C., Zapata-Diaz, J., and Wood, E. H.: Dye dilution curves in cyanotic congenital heart disease. Circulation, 8:70, 1953.

Symposium on persistent atrioventricular canal. Am. J. Cardiol., 6:565, 618, 1960.

Taussig, H. B.: Congenital Malformations of the Heart, 2d ed. New York, Commonwealth Fund, 1960.

Wiederhelm, C. A., Bruce, R. A., Hamilton, C., and Parker, R.: Diagnosis of central shunts from abnormalities of peripheral dye dilution curves. Am. Heart J., 54:205, 1957.

Winchell, P., and Bashour, F.: Some physiologic features of atrial septal defect: Observations in 38 adult patients. Am. J. Cardiol., 2:687, 1958.

Wood, E. H.: Diagnostic applications of indicator-dilution techniques in congenital heart disease. Circ. Res., 10:531, 1962.

Wood, P.: The Eisenmenger syndrome, or pulmonary hypertension with reversed central shunt. Brit. Med. J., 2:701, 755, 1958.

Wood, P., Magidson, O., and Wilson, P. A. O.: Ventricular septal defect with a note on acyanotic Fallot's tetralogy. Brit. Heart J., 16:387, 1954.

Pericardial Disease

Adcock, J. D., Lyons, R. H., and Barnwell, J. B.: The circulatory effects produced in a patient with pneumopericardium by artificially varying the intrapericardial pressure. Am. Heart J., 19:283, 1940.

Beck, C. S.: Acute and chronic compression of the heart. Am. Heart J., 14:515, 1937.

Berglund, E., Sarnoff, S. J., and Isaacs, J. P.: Ventricular Function: Role of the pericardium in regulation of cardiovascular dynamics. Circ. Res., 3:133, 1955.

Blalock, A., and Burwell, C. S.: Chronic pericardial disease: Report of 28 cases of constrictive pericarditis. Surg. Gynec. & Obst., 73:433, 1941.

Burdine, J. A., and Wallace, J. M.: Pulsus paradoxus and Kussmaul's sign in massive pulmonary embolism. Am. J. Cardiol., 14:413, 1965.

Burwell, C. S.: Constrictive pericarditis. Circulation, 15:161, 1957.

Burwell, C. S., and Blalock, A.: Chronic constrictive pericarditis. Physiologic and pathologic considerations. J.A.M.A., 110:265, 1938.

Connolly, D. C., Dry, T. J., Good, C. A., Clagett, O. T., and Burchell, H. B.: Chronic idiopathic effusion without tamponade. Circulation, 20:1095, 1959.

Golinko, R. J., Kaplan, N., and Rudolph, A. M.: The mechanism of pulsus paradoxus during acute pericardial tamponade. J. Clin. Invest., 42:249, 1963.

Hansen, A. T., Eskildsen, P., and Götzsche, H.: Pressure curves from the right auricle and the right ventricle in chronic constrictive pericarditis. Circulation, 3:881, 1951.

Harvey, R. M., Ferrer, M. I., Cathcart, R. T., Richards, D. W., and Cournand, A.: Mechanical and myocardial factors in chronic constrictive pericarditis. Circulation, 8:695, 1953.

Heuer, G. J., and Stewart, H. J.: The surgical treatment of chronic constrictive pericarditis. Surg. Gynec. & Obst., 68:967, 1939.

Katz, L. N., and Gauchat, H. W.: Observations on pulsus paradoxus (with special reference to pericardial effusions). Arch. Int. Med., 33:350, 371, 1924.

Kloster, F. E., Crislip, R. L., Bristow, J. D., Herr, R. H., Ritzmann, L. W., and Griswold, H. E.: Hemodynamic studies following pericardiectomy for constrictive pericarditis. Circulation, 32:145, 1965.

Lange, R. L., Botticelli, J. T., Tsagaris, T. J., Walker, J. A., Gani, M., and Bustamante, R. A.: Diagnostic signs in compressive cardiac disorders: Constrictive pericarditis, pericardial effusion, and tamponade. Circulation, 23:763, 1966.

Lange, R. L., and Tsagaris, T. J.: Time course of factors causing exaggerated respiratory variation of arterial blood pressure. J. Lab. & Clin. Med., 63:431, 1964.

Lyons, R. H., and Burwell, C. S.: Induced changes in the circulation in constrictive pericarditis. Brit. Heart J., 8:33, 1946.

Morgan, B. C., Guneroth, W. G., and Dillard, D. H.: Relationship of pericardial to pleural pressure during quiet respiration and cardiac tamponade. Circ. Res., 26:493, 1965.

Mounsey, P.: The early diastolic sound of constrictive pericarditis. Brit. Heart J., 17:143, 1955.

Sharp, J. T., Burnell, I. L., Holland, J. F., Griffith, G. T., and Greene, D. G.: Hemodynamics during induced cardiac tamponade in man. Am. J. Med., 29:640, 1960.

Sodeman, W. A.: Chronic constrictive pericarditis. Am. J. Med. Sc., 202:127, 1941.

Wood, P.: Chronic constrictive pericarditis. Am. J. Cardiol., 7:48, 1961.

Miscellaneous

Aber, C. P., and Thompson, G. S.: Factors associated with cardiac enlargement in myxedema. Brit. Heart J., 25:421, 1963.

Abrahamsen, A. M., Haarstad, J., and Oulie, C.: Haemodynamic studies in thyrotoxicosis before and after treatment. Acta Med. Scand., 174:463, 1963.

Aguirre, C. V., and others: Corazon pulmonar agudo hidatico. Arch. Inst. Cardiol. Mex., 26:211, 1956.

Alexander, J. K.: Obesity and cardiac performance. Am. J. Cardiol., 14:860, 1964.

Andrus, E. C.: The thyroid and the circulation. Circulation, 7:437, 1953.

Balchum, O. J., McCord, M. C., and Blount, S. G., Jr.: The clinical and hemodynamic pattern in non-specific myocarditis: A comparison with other entities also impairing myocardial efficiency. Am. Heart J., 52:430, 1956.

Barker, P. S., and Johnston, F. D.: Chronic pericarditis with effusion. Circulation, 2:134, 1950.

Barry, M., and Hall, M.: Familial cardiomyopathy. Brit. Heart J., 24:613, 1962.

Blankenhorn, M. A., and Gall, E. A.: Myocarditis and myocardosis. A clinicopathologic appraisal. Circulation, *13*:217, 1956.

Brannon, E. S., Merrill, A. J., Warren, J. V., and Stead, E. A., Jr.: The cardiac output in patients with chronic anemia as measured by the technique of right atrial catheterization. J. Clin. Invest., *24*: 332, 1945.

Brogden, W. W.: Cardiomyopathies. Lancet, *2*:1179, 1243, 1957.

Burwell, C. S., and Dexter, L.: Beri-beri heart disease. Tr. A. Am. Physicians, *60*:59, 1947.

Chapman, E. M., Dill, D. B., and Graybiel, A.: The decrease in functional capacity of the lungs and heart resulting from deformities of the chest: Pulmonocardiac failure. Medicine, *27*:111, 1939.

Cohen, J., Effat, H., Goodwin, J. F., Oakley, C. M., and Steiner, R. E.: Hypertrophic obstructive cardiomyopathy. Brit. Heart J., *26*:16, 1964.

Dalton, J. C., Pearson, R. J., Jr., and White, P. D.: Constrictive pericarditis: A review and longterm follow-up of 78 cases. Ann. Int. Med., *45*: 445, 1956.

Derow, H. A.: The heart in renal disease. Circulation, *10*:114, 1954.

East, T., and Oram, S.: The heart in scleroderma. Brit. Heart J., *9*:167, 1947.

Egeli, E. S., and Berkmen, R.: Action of hypoglycemia on coronary insufficiency and mechanism of ECG alterations. Am. Heart J., *59*:527, 1960.

Ellis, L. B., and Faulkner, J. M.: The heart in anemia. New England J. Med., *220*:943, 1939.

Ellis, L. B., Mebane, J. G., Maresh, G., Hultgren, H. N., and Bloomfield, R. A.: The effect of myxedema on the cardiovascular system. Am. Heart J., *43*: 341, 1952.

Ernestene, A. C.: The cardiovascular complications of hyperthyroidism. Am. J. Med. Sc., *191*:248, 1938.

Evans, W.: Alcoholic cardiomyopathy. Am. Heart J., *61*:556, 1961.

Evans, W.: Familial cardiomegaly. Brit. Heart J., *11*: 68, 1949.

Fahr, G.: Myxedema heart: A report based upon a study of 17 cases of myxedema. Am. Heart J., *8*:91, 1932–33.

Farber, S. J.: Physiologic aspects of glomerulonephritis. J. Chron. Dis., *5*:87, 1957.

Faulkner, J. M., Place, E. H., and Ohler, W. R.: The effect of scarlet fever on the heart. Am. J. Med. Sc., *189*:352, 1935.

Ferrans, V. J., and others: Alcoholic cardiomyopathy. A histochemical study. Am. Heart J., *69*:748, 1965.

Fowler, N. O., Gueron, M., and Rowlands, D. T., Jr.: Primary myocardial disease. Circulation, *23*: 498, 1961.

Fowler, N. O., Westcott, R. N., Scott, R. C., and Hess, E.: The cardiac output in chronic cor pulmonale. Circulation, *6*:888, 1952.

Gordon, A. H.: Pericardial effusion in myxedema. Tr. A. Am. Physicians, *50*:272, 1935.

Gorlin, R.: The hyperkinetic heart syndrome. J.A.M.A., *182*:823, 1962.

Gottsegen, G., and Török, E.: A clinico-pathologic study of cor pulmonale with heart failure. Am. J. Cardiol., *2*:441, 1958.

Gouley, B. A., McMillan, T. M., and Bellet, S.: Idio-

pathic myocardial degeneration associated with pregnancy and especially the puerperium. Am. J. Med. Sc., *194*:185, 1937.

Graettinger, J. S., Muenster, J. J., Selverstone, L. A., and Campbell, J. A.: A correlation of clinical and hemodynamic studies in patients with hyperthyroidism with and without congestive heart failure. J. Clin. Invest., *38*:1316, 1959.

Gunnar, R. M., Dillon, R. F., Wallyn, R. J., and Elisberg, E. J.: The physiologic and clinical similarity between primary amyloid of the heart and constrictive pericarditis. Circulation, *12*:827, 1955.

Hamilton, J. D., and Greenwood, W. F.: Myxedema heart disease. Circulation, *15*:442, 1957.

Hickam, J. B., and Cargill, W. H.: Effect of exercise on cardiac output and pulmonary arterial pressure in normal persons and in patients with cardiovascular disease and pulmonary emphysema. J. Clin. Invest., *27*:10, 1948.

Hyman, A. L., Myers, W. D., and Meyer, A.: The effect of acute pulmonary embolus upon cardiopulmonary hemodynamics. Am. Heart J., *67*: 313, 1964.

Jones, T. D., and White, P. D.: The heart after severe diphtheria. Am. Heart J., *3*:190, 1927.

Kline, I. K., and Saphir, O.: Chronic pernicious myocarditis. Am. Heart J., *59*:681, 1960.

Kountz, W. B., Alexander, H. L., and Prinzmetal, M.: The heart in emphysema. Am. Heart J., *11*:163, 1936.

Krasnow, N.: Hypertrophic obstructive cardiomyopathy. Am. Heart J., *69*:820, 1965.

La Due, J. S.: Myxedema heart: A pathological and therapeutic study. Ann. Int. Med., *18*:332, 1943.

Lahey, F. H., Hurxthal, L. M., and Driscoll, R. E.: Thyrocardiac disease: Review of 614 cases. Ann. Surg., *118*:681, 1943.

Langendorf, R., and Pirani, C. L.: The heart in uremia: An electrocardiographic and pathologic study. Am. Heart J., *33*:282, 1947.

Leiter, L.: Metabolic heart disease. Mod. Concepts Cardiovas. Dis., *26*:403, 1957.

Lisan, P., Imbriglia, J., and Likoff, W.: Myocardial disease associated with progressive muscular dystrophy (a report of 2 cases). Am. Heart J., *58*: 913, 1959.

Marks, P. A., and Roof, B. S.: Pericardial effusion associated with myxedema. Ann. Int. Med., *39*: 230, 1953.

McBrien, D. J., and Hindle, W.: Myxoedema and heart failure. Lancet, *1*:1066, 1963.

McGinn, S., and White, P. D.: Acute cor pulmonale resulting from pulmonary embolism. J.A.M.A., *104*:1473, 1935.

Moschowitz, E.: Hypertension of the pulmonary circulation. Am. J. Med. Sc., *174*:388, 1927.

Nelson, J. R., and Smith, J. R.: The pathologic physiology of pulmonary embolism. A physiologic discussion of the vascular reactions following pulmonary arterial obstruction by emboli of varying size. Am. Heart J., *58*:916, 1959.

Neubauer, C.: Diphtheritic heart disorders of children. Brit. Med. J., *2*:91, 1942.

Pierce, J. A., Price, B. O., and Joyce, J. W.: Familial occurrence of postpartal heart failure. Arch. Int. Med., *111*:651, 1963.

Porter, W. B., and James, G. W.: The heart in anemia. Circulation, *8*:111, 1953.

Rivera-Estrada, C., Saltzman, P. W., Singer, D., and Katz, L. N.: Action of hypoxia on the pulmonary vasculature. Circ. Res., 6:10, 1958.

Rowlands, D. T., and Vilter, C. F.: A study of cardiac stigmata in prolonged human thiamine deficiency. Circulation, 21:4, 1960.

Rushmer, R. F.: Regulation of the heart's functions. Circulation, 21:744, 1960.

Sackner, M. A., Lewis, D. H., Robinson, M. J., and Beller, S.: Idiopathic myocardial hypertrophy: A review. Am. J. Cardiol., 7:714, 1961.

Sanders, V.: Idiopathic disease of the myocardium. Arch. Int. Med., 112:661, 1963.

Sanghvi, L. M., Shrama, R., and Misra, S. N.: Cardiovascular disturbances in chronic severe anemia. Circulation, 15:373, 1957.

Schlesinger, P., and Benchimol, A. B.: The pure form of thyrotoxic heart disease. Am. J. Cardiol., 2:430, 1958.

Scott, J. C., Balourdas, T. A., and Croll, M. N.: The effect of experimental hypothyroidism on coronary blood flow and hemodynamic factors. Am. J. Cardiol., 7:690, 1961.

Shearn, M. A.: The heart in systemic lupus erythematosus. Am. Heart J., 58:452, 1959.

Stewart, H. J., Crane, N. F., and Deitrick, J. E.: Studies of the circulation in pernicious anemia. J. Clin. Invest., 16:431, 1937.

Stewart, H. J., Deitrick, J. E., and Crane, N. F.: Studies of the circulation in . . . spontaneous myxedema. J. Clin. Invest., 17:237, 1938.

Summers, V. K., and Surtess, S. J.: Thyrotoxicosis and heart disease. Acta Med. Scand., 169:661, 1961.

Thomas, H. M., Jr.: Effect of thyroid hormone on circulation. J.A.M.A., 163:337, 1957.

Thomson, W. A. R.: The effect of potassium on the heart in man. Brit. Heart J., 1:269, 1939.

Treger, A., and Blount, S. G., Jr.: Familial cardiomyopathy. Am. Heart J., 70:40, 1965.

Weaver, W. F., and Burchell, H. B.: Serum potassium and the electrocardiogram in hypokalemia. Circulation, 21:505, 1960.

Weinstein, L.: Cardiovascular manifestations in some of the common infectious diseases. Mod. Concepts Cardiovas. Dis., 23:229, 1954.

Weiss, S., and Wilkins, R. W.: The nature of the cardiovascular disturbance in nutritional deficiency states. Ann. Int. Med., 11:104, 1937.

Werkö, L., and Eliasch, H.: Circulatory studies in a case of primary pulmonary hypertension. Cardiologia, 21:403, 1953.

White, P. D.: Pulmonary embolism and heart disease. Am. J. Med. Sc., 200:577, 1940.

White, P. D.: The acute cor pulmonale. Ann. Int. Med., 9:115, 1935.

Whitehill, M. R., Longcope, W. T., and Williams, R.: The occurrence and significance of myocardial failure in acute hemorrhagic nephritis. Bull. Johns Hopkins Hosp., 64:83, 1939.

Wood, P.: Pulmonary hypertension. Brit. Med. Bull., 8:348, 1952.

Wood, P.: Pulmonary hypertension. Mod. Concepts Cardiovas. Dis., 28:513, 1959.

Zondek, H.: Association of myxedema heart and arteriosclerotic heart disease. J.A.M.A., 170:1920, 1959.

Chapter Twenty

Congestive Heart Failure, Coronary Insufficiency and Myocardial Infarction

NORMAN BRACHFELD
and
JOHN S. LA DUE

Cardiac Decompensation

Cardiac decompensation can be defined as the inability of the ventricles to empty themselves adequately. This results in elevation of the end diastolic or filling pressure which, transmitted backwards, can account for many of the symptoms and signs exhibited by the patient in heart failure. Broadly speaking, one can say that this state is the result of an inability of the heart to pump sufficient blood to meet the metabolic needs of the body. The cardiac output, though usually diminished, may be normal or even elevated. Decreasing mechanical efficiency or the inability of the heart adequately to transfer oxidative energy into useful work might be considered a more fundamental definition.

In functional terms we are actually speaking of *myocardial failure,* i.e., failure of the heart muscle to perform as a competent pump. The two ventricular chambers may be likened to pumping stations in a recirculating pipeline. The efficiency of these pumps may be expressed, therefore, by their ability to maintain the forward flow of a filling load. In congestive heart failure the ratio of car-

diac output to filling load (diastolic filling pressure) is abnormally decreased. It is not possible to set arbitrary levels of output below which congestive heart failure may be said to be present. Although usually diminished in chronic, untreated congestive heart failure, total cardiac output may be high in failure occurring as a result of anemia, thyrotoxicosis, beriberi, and arteriovenous shunts. Conversely, when tissue needs are markedly reduced in myxedema or during hypothermia, cardiac output may be severely decreased without heart failure.

The term *"cardiac reserve"* defines the difference between the actual work being performed by the heart and the maximal effort of which it is capable, i.e., the increment in filling load that can be assumed without a decrease in effective pumping. Most forms of intrinsic heart disease reduce this reserve capacity. At times the heart may be the target or symptomatic organ of a remote vascular or metabolic process. Intrinsic cardiovascular homeostatic mechanisms or optimal therapy may compensate for encroachments upon this reserve and maintain cardiac output. Under these circumstances the patient

448

may be asymptomatic at rest or during ordinary activity and lead a fairly normal, if somewhat restricted life. Anything increasing the work demanded of the heart may exhaust these compensatory mechanisms; the resulting increment in cardiac output will fall short of that which would be pumped by a normal heart faced by the same degree of stress. Eventually signs and symptoms will appear. These are caused by a decrease in cardiac output and by venous congestion behind an overfilled dilated ventricle. The patient is now said to be in a state of clinical *congestive heart failure*. Objectively, diminished exercise tolerance is usually the first symptom of diminished cardiac reserve. Stress of any kind, most often infectious in origin, particularly pulmonary infection (with cough), myocarditis, severe hypertensive crisis, coronary thrombosis or pulmonary infarction, easily exhausts cardiac reserve and precipitates the signs and symptoms of congestive failure.

An inadequate cardiac output eventually leads to engorgement of the pulmonary or systemic venous systems, or both. The resulting symptoms may include weakness, fatigability, dyspnea, orthopnea, cough, hemoptysis, fever, oliguria and albuminuria. Cardiac enlargement, venous engorgement, edema, pulmonary rales, cyanosis, pleural effusion, ascites, hepatomegaly, splenomegaly and cachexia are found on physical examination. Physiologic measurements may reveal an increase in ventricular end diastolic pressure. The ratio of cardiac output to filling load falls. There follows a secondary rise in atrial, central, capillary and peripheral venous pressures and prolongation of the circulation time. Vital capacity and maximal breathing capacity fall as the increase in pulmonary blood volume decreases distensibility and increases the rigidity of the lungs. Acidosis and hypoglycemia may occur. Total body oxygen consumption is increased and is manifested by an elevation of the basal metabolic rate.

Some investigators wish to subdivide causes of circulatory congestion into cardiac and noncardiac types. According to this concept mitral stenosis and tricuspid stenosis cause congestion by a purely mechanical obstruction to flow. They claim that myocardial contractility remains normal. However, if contractility were adequate to meet the pressure demands of valvular stenosis, so as to permit sufficient emptying, congestion would not occur. One must conclude, therefore, that under these circumstances as well the myo-cardium has failed as a pump. Prolonged tachycardia may result in circulatory congestion but is again due to *failure* of the ventricles to empty adequately under this stress.

With constrictive pericarditis the venous inflow to the right and, occasionally, to the left side of the heart as well is restricted, and pulmonary and systemic venous congestion may result without failure of the myocardium.

Cases of congestive heart failure seen with severe anemia, beriberi, thyrotoxicosis and left to right shunts are examples of myocardial failure associated with increased output, so-called "high output failure." These abnormalities may exist for variable periods of time without evidence of failure until the myocardium cannot meet its pumping load.

Increased blood volume, a secondary increase in interstitial fluid, and water and salt retention may follow excessive doses of mineralocorticoids with or without congestive heart failure. The same may be seen with normal or increased fluid ingestion in the presence of anuria.

In polycythemia vera both blood volume and blood viscosity are increased. The load on the heart may be greatly enhanced, and, especially when cardiac reserve has already been reduced owing to other causes, its ability to remain in compensation may be seriously compromised.

Such causes of heart failure are especially important to recognize since the appropriate treatment of anemia, polycythemia, beriberi and anuria and surgical correction of mitral stenosis and tricuspid stenosis effectively relieve circulatory congestion. The response to digitalis and other cardiotonic agents is much less predictable in these disorders and is often ineffective unless the primary etiologic factors are attacked.

THE FRANK-STARLING MECHANISM AND THE "LAW OF THE HEART"

The normal heart is adaptable and can maintain output and pressure, after a very brief period of adaptation, despite a variety of hemodynamic stresses. At rest, an as yet unknown regulatory system fixes cardiac output within narrow bounds and matches blood flow to the metabolic needs of the body. Investigators postulate a feedback mechanism in which afferent signals, possibly the biochemical end products of metabolism, trigger efferent operative stimuli which maintain normal output. In congestive heart fail-

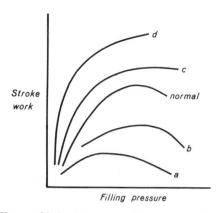

Stroke work

d

c

normal

b

a

Filling pressure

Figure 20–1. Diagrammatic representation of ventricular function (Starling) curves under varying physiologic states. Any point on the normal operative curve may shift to a differing performance level under conditions of (*a*) low output failure, (*b*) high output failure, (*c*) physiologic hypertrophy or (*d*) influence of catecholamine injection or sympathetic stimulation.

ure this mechanism no longer operates fully. The signal itself may be interfered with, but this state more probably implies failure of the target organ. The heart is no longer capable of a fully adequate response, and its efficiency as a volume pump is drastically reduced. Pressure head may be maintained, but volume output per minute falls. The heart dilates, and ventricular volume, ventricular diastolic pressure and central venous pressure rise. The circulatory system becomes congested by an increasing volume of sluggishly moving blood unless an increase in myocardial contractility can compensate for the increase in load.

The late nineteenth century physiologists described the intrinsic myogenic mechanisms whereby the heart, in the absence of its normal regulatory controls, could still alter its output in response to stress.

As early as 1898, E. H. Starling was puzzled by the fact that he was able to "increase the resistance to be overcome by the heart to three or four times the normal amount without altering in any way the quantity of blood expelled at each beat." His experiments showed that, within wide limits, the output of the heart was independent of resistance to output and that this property of the myocardium remained even if the heart was completely denervated, a circumstance determined by the heart-lung preparation with which he worked. Within certain limits, cardiac output seemed to be proportional to venous inflow. He concluded that this response must be due to an intrinsic characteristic of the myocardium. In 1895, Otto

Frank had shown that the stretched muscle of the amphibian heart contracts more forcefully than does the unstretched. In a remarkable series of papers, published in 1914, and in his famous Linacre lecture of 1918, Starling applied this concept to the mammal and described his "law of the heart" which stated: ". . . the mechanical energy set free on passage from the resting to the contracted state depends on the area of chemically active surfaces, i.e., on the length of the muscle fibers." In other words, neither the force against which the heart must pump nor its diastolic pressure but rather the diastolic fiber length determines the vigor of the subsequent systolic contraction. The greater the diastolic fiber length, the greater the contractile force it will exert.

Thus, when the normal heart is stressed by an increased venous inflow, an intrinsic myogenic autoregulatory mechanism permits the ventricular residual volume to expand which increases diastolic fiber length and permits the heart to eject whatever volume flows into it. Similarly, in the face of an increased arterial resistance, a temporary reduction in stroke volume increases residual volume and, by the same mechanism, enhances the force of contraction. Under both circumstances, a delicate adjustment of diastolic volume enables the ventricle to pump an increased output at a fixed pressure or maintain the same output against increased outflow resistance.

This concept may be expressed graphically in several ways. Since measurements of ventricular volume have only recently become possible, most curves plot filling pressure (reflecting diastolic volume) against stroke work (more reliable than cardiac output as an index of ventricular function) (Fig. 20–1, normal curve). The ascending limb of this "ventricular function curve" shows an initial steep rise. An increase of as little as 1.0 cm. H_2O in diastolic pressure may increase stroke work as much as 300 per cent. As filling pressure rises further a maximum response is evoked and the curve reaches a plateau. It then enters its so-called "descending limb" of marked decompensation during which further fiber stretch leads not to an improvement of performance characteristics, but to a depression of function. Ventricular output falls as diastolic volume rises. In Starling's words: ". . . the dilatation, which is the mechanical result of unchanging inflow and failing outflow and is the automatic means of regulating outflow to inflow, proceeds to such an extent that the tension of the muscle fibers becomes increasingly inadequate in producing a rise of intracardiac pressure. The mechanical disadvantage at which the dilated heart must act finally smashes up the system and the circulation comes to an end."

This same type of myogenic autoregulatory mechanism applies to both atrium and ventricle, although slopes vary somewhat between the different chambers. Using more modern techniques, Braunwald et al. have been able to confirm the applicability of Starling's concepts to the control of ventricular function in man. In the compensated heart, the relationship between ventricular volume and cardiac output (or stroke work) acts automatically to maintain hemodynamic balance between the right and left sides of the heart. When one side of the heart is acutely stressed, compensatory changes in diastolic fiber length occur, and the outputs of the two ventricles are brought back into balance. These changes are reflected by measurable changes in the relationship between the two atrial pressures. As examples, the increase in right ventricular filling, which accompanies inspiration, is balanced by an immediate increase in right ventricular stroke volume. The reverse occurs during exhalation. On tilting from a recumbent to a passive standing position, both atrial pressures fall as does stroke volume. In the absence of this intrinsic autoregulated responsiveness, "the lungs would become either dry or inundated in a short period of time" (Sarnoff and Mitchell). During exercise, end diastolic volume and cardiac output increase.

This concept of primary myogenic responsiveness, describing a single curve of ventricular function, holds true for the denervated Starling heart preparation. When applied to intact man, however, several inconsistencies immediately became apparent. In the intact animal or human subject cardiac output increased under certain physiologic conditions often despite significant decrease in diastolic volume. Inotropic drugs could also increase cardiac output despite a simultaneous decrease in diastolic volume. In addition, denervation removed the rate response of the heart entirely. It was evident that the original "law of the heart" could not be applied to intact man without modification. Sarnoff demonstrated that reproducible Frank-Starling curves could be obtained in man if the external factors governing myocardial response remained constant. He held that the relationship between filling pressure and stroke work was a consistent one. The theory was modified by demonstrating that the same heart would shift to a new level of performance and record a whole "family" of differing curves when its circulatory state was altered by injection of catecholamines, sympathetic nerve stimulation, restriction of coronary flow or severe anemia (Fig. 20-1).

Neither the hypertrophied heart nor the heart in failure conformed to the concepts of a single curve of function; therefore such a representation was clearly inadequate to express the true pattern of response. As the physiologic state of the organism changed, the heart responded not only by moving to a new point on its curve but by describing an entirely different Starling curve. Sarnoff emphasized that the ventricle does not "blithely skip from curve to curve" unless an important physiologic influence intervenes. Determined by differing extracardiac circulatory factors, the initial base line "set" of the ventricle adjusts itself and thus determines the level of the function curve on which it will be operating. It is worth noting that a ventricular function curve describes the total ventricular reflection of the Frank-Starling hypothesis which in actuality is applicable to the individual myocardial fiber. Under certain conditions (localized ischemia, hypertrophy) distinct areas of the same chamber may operate on different function curves and produce serious alterations in ventricular mechanics.

The Frank-Starling "law of the heart" is not the only basic mechanism enabling the ventricle to adjust to major circulatory changes. Other myogenic factors modify and interact with this mechanism and are elicited by a change in hemodynamic state. These include changes in aortic pressure (Anrep effect) and changes in heart rate (Bowditch's "staircase phenomenon" and the related concept of post-extrasystolic potentiation). Sarnoff classifies these factors as examples of "homeometric autoregulation." They call forth an increase in the contractile force of the heart and permit the ventricle to eject the same stroke volume against varying resistances without the increase in fiber length required by the Frank-Starling principle. Protection against encroachment upon Frank-Starling reserve is thus provided, and the ventricle may more adequately respond to changes in stroke volume.

Neurogenic or humoral factors, which act through the mechanism of adrenergic potentiation, may also be classified as examples of homeometric adaptation. Braunwald and Ross have recently investigated the effect of alterations in humoral environment on ventricular function and emphasize the importance of this influence over inotropic responsiveness. The increase in stroke work following an increase in venous inflow, seen in the Starling preparation, could be reproduced in man only after ganglionic blocking drugs were used to inhibit the activity of the autonomic nervous system. This suggests that the adrenergic system serves to buffer alterations in circulatory dynamics. Catecholamines have a positive inotropic effect on the myocardium and increase ventricular contractility so that the chamber now responds to any given filling pressure (diastolic fiber length) with an augmented force of contraction and functions on a Starling curve whose initial slope is steeper and shifted to the left. In man both myogenic and adrenergic mechanisms appear to be normally operative and provide sufficient reserve so that if one is interfered with, the organism may fall back on the other.

The initial response of the normal heart to an increase in load is mediated principally by neurohumoral controls. After onset of exercise, external ventricular dimensions fall significantly while the force of ventricular contraction is markedly increased. The augmentation of cardiac output appears to depend primarily on an increase in heart rate and a catecholamine-induced increase in the vigor of contraction, enhancing systolic emptying and stroke volume. Slight increases in filling pressure are also seen and suggest that the Frank-Starling mechanism does play a role, if a minor one, in this augmentation.

THE FAILING HEART

In contrast to the denervated heart preparation, it has not proved possible to alter hemodynamics to such a degree that the normal ventricle with an intact pericardium can be made to function on the descending limb of its function curve. In man, myocardial failure should not be thought of as a mechanical stretching of the muscle fiber to a point beyond which further filling produces a decrease in stroke work (descending limb). Our present knowledge would indicate that heart failure is a manifestation of an alteration in myocardial contractility. From this changed base line the failing ventricle does not ascend a normal Starling curve, but shifts to the right and now operates on a new curve of

depressed function in which the increase in filling pressure required to produce a given increase in stroke work becomes excessive. In advanced failure, there may be little or no increase in stroke output despite great increase in filling pressure. Thus, there are limits to the usual range of adaptive dilatation beyond which the Frank-Starling mechanism can no longer operate effectively. When this border is crossed the ventricle becomes hypodynamic, and the symptoms and signs of advanced cardiac decompensation ensue. Stroke output is now fixed, and an increase in cardiac output (in response to stress) can occur only through augmentation of heart rate.

Ventricular dilatation is not the *cause* of failure but a *result* of the decreased efficiency of myocardial contraction. In advanced failure the ventricle operates on the plateau of its depressed function curve. It cannot contract for any extended period of time on the descending limb of its curve, although it can be temporarily driven to this position when forced to meet an increment in work load. If the stress is prolonged, the excessive degree of dilatation may result in cardiac arrest. Cardiac function on the descending limb is probably prevented by the relatively rigid fibrous pericardium, the stiffness of the ventricular wall and the short sarcomere lengths at which the myofibrils of the myocardium normally contract.

The increase in circulating blood volume caused by renal retention of salt and water adds an additional burden to a circulatory system which may be already functioning on a depressed Starling curve and therefore may be unable to increase output in response to an increase in venous inflow.

It is clear that the adrenergic nervous system is an important factor in the control of ventricular function. It assumes even greater significance when the functional reserve of the Frank-Starling mechanism has been exhausted. An increase in physical activity in congestive heart failure is accompanied by an increase in arterial norepinephrine concentration far greater than that usually seen. The resultant augmentation of myocardial contractility may enable the failing heart to meet modest increases in demand. Administration of adrenergic blocking drugs intensifies clinical manifestations of heart failure and may completely abolish the already depressed increase in stroke volume that follows exercise. Braunwald has reported a marked reduction in concentration of norepinephrine measured in hearts that had been in prolonged failure. This reduction may be secondary to a prolonged intensive barrage of sympathetic nerve impulses. Such tissue depletion may further intensify failure.

CARDIAC DILATATION AND THE PRINCIPLE OF LAPLACE

Application of the principle of Laplace to the mechanics of the heart has helped us to understand the factors determining whether ventricular dilatation will have a harmful or beneficial effect on cardiac function. It also helps to describe the effects of such dilatation on the energy requirements of the normal and failing ventricle and may explain the apparently paradoxical observation that the heart in failure cannot maintain an adequate output although it usually is able to pump at an adequate head of pressure. Starling's original hypothesis included the concept that the oxygen cost of myocardial pressure development (an index of its mechanical efficiency) is determined by diastolic fiber length. Recent workers have shown that the principal determinant of myocardial oxygen consumption is actually the *tension* generated by the myocardial fiber (wall tension). Laplace described the physical laws relating to the contraction of hollow spheres. The human heart is certainly not a perfect sphere, but, if one assumes that the ventricle does in general conform to such dimensions, these laws may provide valuable insight into myocardial energetics. They are in accord with the observation that the normal ventricle functions at an ideal geometric shape for maximal efficiency. Burch et al. and, more recently, Levine and Wagman have utilized these laws to present theoretical analyses of ventricular contraction with particular reference to the effects of dilatation.

The internal surface area of a sphere is a function of the square of its radius ($A = 4\pi r^2$). Since the contained volume is related to the third power of the radius ($V = 4/3\pi r^3$), it is obvious that any alterations in the size of the sphere will be reflected by changes in volume that are several times greater than changes in area. Clinical application of these interrelationships depends directly on the oxygen cost of such changes in shape and requires a means of determining the contractile tension or load on the

ventricular wall as they occur. The law of Laplace states that:

$$T = P \times \pi r^2$$

where:
T = total wall tension
P = intracavitary pressure
r = radius of the sphere

During systole, despite an elevation in intracavitary pressure from end diastolic to systolic peak, there is a proportionately greater and more rapid *decrease* in internal surface area as stroke volume is ejected. Wall tension shows a progressive fall, and the load on the normal heart actually declines throughout the period of systolic ejection (Fig. 20–2). This state changes appreciably when the ventricle dilates and end diastolic volume increases to several times that of normal. Let us assume that the same increment in pressure from diastolic to systolic peak is required. Stroke volume now forms a significantly smaller percentage of total diastolic volume. Relatively little shortening is required for stroke ejection, the change in radius is minimized as is the internal surface area, and contractile wall tension (load), initially excessive, will increase progressively during the course of systole. Starling's law permits an increase in diastolic fiber length to increase stroke work, but when the energetics of contraction are considered it becomes clear that the implied increment in tension must be paid for by an increase in total energy expenditure (and a reduction in reserve capacity). Under stress, usually an exercise demand, pressure and volume, work may be increased with *greater* efficiency in the normal heart due to the exponential decrease in internal surface area. As illustrated (Fig. 20–2, A), final systolic tension (T_2) falls to below resting levels as stroke volume increases. In the dilated ventricle such increments require additional expenditures of energy and calculated efficiency falls (Fig. 20–2, B).

Thus the compensated heart performs its work with relatively small force but considerable shortening. In contrast, the decompensated dilated heart shortens little and must utilize considerable force to do so (Linzbach). The heart in failure may liberate a normal amount of energy, but as it is working at a severe mechanical disadvantage with a limited ability to shorten, this energy is no longer adequate to expel a normal stroke volume. Eventually the cost in energy of this type of adaptive dilatation becomes prohibi-

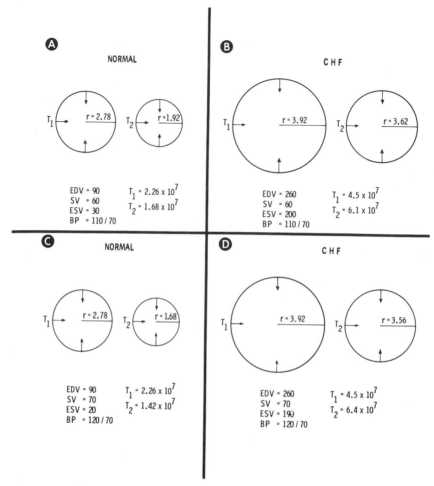

Figure 20–2. A simplified version of the energetics of cardiac systole in normal and failing hearts. *A* represents a simplified "normal" left ventricle contracting at a constant rate from a volume of 90 ml. EDV = end diastolic volume in ml.; SV = stroke volume; ESV = end systolic volume; B.P. = blood pressure in mm. Hg; T_1 = total wall tension (in dynes) at opening of aortic valve (blood pressure = 70 mm. Hg); T_2 = total wall tension at end of systolic contraction (blood pressure = 110 mm. Hg). *Note that end systolic tension (T_2) is less than initial systolic tension (T_1). B represents the same events occurring in a dilated, failing ventricle, ejecting the same stroke volume at the same pressure and duration of systole. Note that end systolic tension now exceeds initial systolic tension. C and D, The energetics of the normal* and failing ventricle are compared when each is called upon to produce a specific increment in pressure and volume work (an increase in systolic pressure [10 mm. Hg] and of stroke volume [10 ml.]). (After Levine and Wagman.)

tive, the loss of leverage cannot be compensated, mechanical difficulties inherent in fiber shortening at excessive wall tensions (decreased rate of fiber shortening) ensue, and further increase in diastolic volume no longer produces an increment in stroke work. The necessity of maintaining high intraventricular pressures diverts energy from muscle shortening and utilizes it primarily to support high initial and peak systolic tensions; blood pressure is therefore supported, but at the expense of a fall in stroke output. This hypo-

dynamic, decompensated heart is markedly dilated; its borders barely move as each systole ejects but a small fraction of total diastolic volume.

Myocardial hypertrophy may alter these relationships. As cardiac reserve is exhausted by a continuous, excessive work load, persistence of dilatation leads to an increase in muscle mass and eventually to a state of pathologic hypertrophy differing both physiologically and anatomically from the physiologic hypertrophy of the athlete or heavy laborer subjected to *intermittent* extreme work loads. Hypertrophy causes the Starling curve to shift to the left (Fig. 20–1), and in many cases compensation is sustained. Differences in the type of hypertrophy depend upon whether the load is due to a primary increase in volume flow (aortic insufficiency, mitral incompetence) or pressure (aortic stenosis, essential hypertension). In the former, dilatation and hypertrophy proceed together and lead to an increase in chamber size as well as wall thickness. The heart may weigh as much as 1000 gm. Under a pressure load the size of the heart may not initially appear to increase since the wall thickens at the expense of endocardial volume. With persistence and progression of this overload, dilatation recurs, and the law of Laplace reasserts itself. In both types the coronary arteries or coronary ostia eventually prove insufficient to maintain myocardial perfusion and hypoxia may result.

DETERMINANTS OF MYOCARDIAL OXYGEN CONSUMPTION

Bing's report in 1951 that the oxygen consumption per 100 gm. of left ventricle, approximately 9 ml. per minute, was essentially normal in patients with congestive heart failure led to a re-evaluation of the determinants of myocardial oxygen consumption (MVO_2). Starling first demonstrated that the oxygen consumption of his isolated heart preparation was related to its ventricular volume. In 1914, Evans and Matsuoka appeared to challenge this observation by showing that MVO_2 was determined primarily by the aortic blood pressure rather than by stroke volume. The development of the cardiac catheter enabled contemporary workers to substantiate and document the finding that cardiac pressure work was much more expensive in terms of oxygen cost than was flow work, and an effort was made to reconcile these apparently incompatible observations. Sarnoff approached the problem by analyzing the dynamic events of the cardiac cycle and suggested that the product of the mean systolic blood pressure and the duration of systole, a parameter termed the tension-time index (TTI), was the principal, if not the sole determinant of MVO_2. That became apparent during exercise, after administration of catecholamines or any agent augmenting the contractile state of the myocardium. Levine and Wagman emphasized that the most important single factor in MVO_2 is myocardial *tension* and that tension

depends not only on the area under the systolic pressure curve but, as may be inferred from Starling, on volume changes in the cardiac chamber during systole. Thus Starling's observations accounted for the radius variable of the Laplace principle, the pressure variable being taken into account by TTI. In general, one may say that total tension and therefore MVO_2 per beat are governed by the dynamic changes occurring in intracavitary pressure and in the mean radius of the cardiac chamber during systole. Sonnenblick refined these concepts further by his demonstration that, in addition to the tension developed by the myocardium, the *velocity* of myocardial contraction is an important determinant of MVO_2. This is a particularly important factor when myocardial contraction is augmented and may explain the marked increase in MVO_2 after administration of norepinephrine and some other catecholamines.

MYOCARDIAL OXYGEN CONSUMPTION IN CONGESTIVE HEART FAILURE

Levine and Wagman found that the oxygen cost of maintaining pressure in chronically dilated and hypertrophied hearts is the same per unit weight as in normal hearts. The increase in efficiency shown by the normal heart during effort is not seen in the diseased heart. On the contrary, initial mean efficiency is lower and does not rise on effort. They point out that when the normal heart is acutely dilated the principle of Laplace is operative and tension increases; since weight is unchanged, MVO_2 per unit weight is increased. With the onset of failure and hypertrophy, heart weight increases and MVO_2 per unit weight once again becomes normal. Note, however, that since weight is increased total MVO_2 may be *greatly* increased.

The increase in basal metabolic rate (BMR) and in total body oxygen consumption, $TBqO_2$, a hypermetabolic state thought to be due to the increased work of respiration of the severely dyspneic patient in failure, may in reality be related to MVO_2. The contribution of the oxygen consumed by the hypertrophied myocardium to the total BMR in congestive heart failure may be extremely high. In 12 patients studied by Levine and Wagman, $TBqO_2$ was elevated 19 per cent. Total MVO_2, however, was three times that of normal and accounted for 16 per cent of the $TBqO_2$. When total MVO_2 was subtracted from $TBqO_2$ in normal subjects and likewise in those with congestive heart failure, differences in calculated metabolic rate disappeared, and TBqO₂ was virtually identical in both groups.

Univentricular Heart Failure

Because the heart is composed of a spiral syncytium, the ventricles function to a great extent interdependently. Venous return to each side of the heart varies both in respect to volume and time and requires a reciprocating relationship. Indeed, Starr has shown that dogs may survive despite destruction of 85 per cent of the free wall of the right ventricle without an appreciable increase in right atrial or peripheral venous pressure; this may be due to the ability of the left ventricle or interventricular septum to facilitate right ventricular ejection. It is therefore relatively rare to find one ventricle in severe failure without some degree of decompensation in the other. Structurally, there is a significant difference between the two chambers, each being tailored to the kind of work it must perform. Thus, although the thick-walled left ventricle is not an efficient volume pump, it is ideally suited to create the mechanical force necessary to eject blood against a high outflow resistance. It often remains compensated despite chronic pathologic elevations in outflow resistance by a relatively slight degree of hypertrophy (aortic stenosis, vascular hypertension). Its reserve is quite limited, however, under an increase in volume load (aortic insufficiency), and it may dilate to a massive size to accommodate an increase in stroke volume without excessive fiber shortening.

The right ventricle is primarily a volume pump and faces a relatively low pulmonary outflow resistance. It has a thin wall, and the ratio of wall thickness to internal surface area is low. As such, it requires a much greater wall force than does the left ventricle to develop a given interventricular pressure, but can readily eject large volumes of blood with relatively little fiber shortening. It can sustain increases in volume load quite easily, by a relatively slight degree of dilatation, but is unable to maintain compensation against a chronic increase in the outflow resistance of the pulmonary circuit (pulmonic stenosis, cor pulmonale, pulmonary hypertension). In keeping with these mechanical differences, the ventricles describe quite different Starling curves. Filling pressures on the left and right side of the heart bear no direct relationship to the function of the other.

In the early stages of a disease which primarily affects the left ventricle (aortic valve disease, hypertension, ischemia of the left ventricle), this chamber may show signs of decompensation, particularly in response to exercise, at a time when right ventricular function is entirely normal. As the disease progresses, left-sided failure may dominate less severe right-sided decompensation. In most cases, impairment of the left side eventually increases pulmonary resistance, and the signs and symptoms of biventricular failure (systemic and pulmonary venous congestion) soon follow.

It is obvious that, over any period of time, the output of the right and left ventricles must be equal since one is dependent upon the other for its filling load. In the early stages of left ventricular failure, however, a temporary imbalance may occur. The venous return to the right side of the heart is easily handled by the right ventricle at normal filling pressures. The decompensated left ventricle, however, is not equal to this load and the volume of blood in the pulmonary circuit increases and causes pulmonary congestion. Eventually, if the decrease in cardiac output persists, chronic fluid retention increases pulmonary volume to an even greater degree, and pulmonary edema may ensue. The symptoms and signs refer primarily to the lungs, and there may be little systemic evidence of decompensation.

Less commonly, often in children with congenital heart disease (pulmonic stenosis) and in certain types of cardiac and noncardiac adult disease (pulmonary hypertension, cor pulmonale, tricuspid insufficiency), right ventricular failure may predominate over left ventricular failure. When acute, right heart failure may cause a precipitous drop in cardiac output. The relatively small volume of blood redistributed from the small pulmonary circuit to the large systemic venous circuit is insufficient to raise venous pressure enough to maintain an adequate gradient and to prime the right ventricle. If the patient survives, renal fluid retention occurs, blood volume and cardiac output increase, and the symptoms and signs of systemic venous congestion become manifest. In isolated right-sided failure, there may be little or no evidence of pulmonary vascular congestion since the left ventricle is capable of ejecting whatever volume is delivered to it.

The term "backward failure" of the heart was originally derived from the symptoms of pulmonary congestion following left ventricular failure. Subsequently, as a measurable decrease in cardiac output became a part of the concept of congestive heart failure, several authors suggested the term "forward failure." Unfortunately, the proponents of both sides sometimes lost sight of the obvious physiologic fact that if the heart fails to pump blood forward, this volume must dam up and produce signs of backward congestion. A good deal of tortured reasoning as well as numerous exceptions were required to make all the facts conform to each theory. As noted earlier, the venous return is obviously dependent upon the cardiac output.

The concepts of "backward" and "forward" failure proved of value in the past by stimulating investigation that has clarified our understanding of the contributions of a changing cardiac output and diastolic ventricular volume to the mechanism of congestive heart failure. They are little more than historical landmarks to contemporary cardiovascular physiologists.

Pathologic Changes in Congestive Heart Failure

By light microscopy the cell of the cardiac muscle appears as a branching fiber containing an oval, centrally placed nucleus. The sarcoplasm (muscle cytoplasm) seems filled with contractile protein arranged in parallel, longitudinally oriented linear units termed myofibrils which are frequently separated one from the other by numerous giant mitochondria strung like beads along the myofibrillar axis. Changes in the birefringence of the myofibrils produce an alternating density pattern and lend a striated appearance to the cell. A double, thin membrane, the sarcolemma, contains the cell laterally, and invaginates and fuses at its poles, often at a point of bifurcation, in a unique terminal structure identified as the intercalated disc. Although myocardium is therefore cellular in organization and not a true structural syncytium, low resistance to electrical conduction across these discs permits the fibers to function as components of an interlocking syncytial-like structure.

Pathologic changes seen under the light microscope are inconstant. Some authors have reported hydropic degeneration of the myofibrils followed by necrosis and fibrosis in degenerative, infectious and metabolic heart disease. If failure is associated with hypertrophy, there may be no evident histologic abnormality. When viewed under the electron microscope, the fine structure of the cell becomes evident; the myofibril is seen to be composed of sarcomeres, repeating subunits arranged in series along a longitudinal axis, which are the primary units of contraction (Fig. 20–3). The Z line or membrane appears as a continuous structure crossing the myofibril and forming the polar boundary of these repeating contractile units. In some cases the Z line seems to form a connecting bridge between adjacent myofibrils. The distance between each pair of Z lines as measured by Sonnenblick is from 1.5 to 2.5 microns long. The striated bandlike appearance of the fiber is due to changes in density resulting from the interdigitating of the contractile protein elements of the sarcomere, viz., *actin*, a thin filament and *myosin*, a thicker filament. Actin, the secondary filament is anchored at the Z line and extends inward toward the median H zone of the sarcomere. The heavier, primary filament myosin is confined to the central zone and partially overlaps the thin filament. The central A band is thus composed of a double array of filaments. In sequence one notes a dark terminal Z line, a light I band composed solely of thin actin filaments, and finally a very narrow lighter central H zone forming at the point where the actin filament terminates and which is composed of myosin molecules (see p. 387).

Huxley has proposed that the contraction and shortening of the muscle following excitation results from a sliding movement of actin filaments inward between myosin filaments through a finite distance. The overall sarcomere length may thus vary without a change in specific filament length. Although some objections to this theory have been raised, it remains most attractive and is supported by electron micrographs of muscle in various stages of contraction and stretch. In such sections the central A band remains fixed in its longitudinal dimension, whereas changes in sarcomere length appear to correlate well with the width of the I band.

The Frank-Starling mechanism relates an increase in the force of contraction to an increase in diastolic volume (fiber length). In an ingenious series of studies Sonnenblick has defined an ultrastructural basis for the Frank-Starling law of the heart and has suggested that the sarcomere, as the fundamental unit of contraction, provides a limit to the compensation afforded by dilatation. Electron micrographs have supported this concept by showing that a percentage change in the cir-

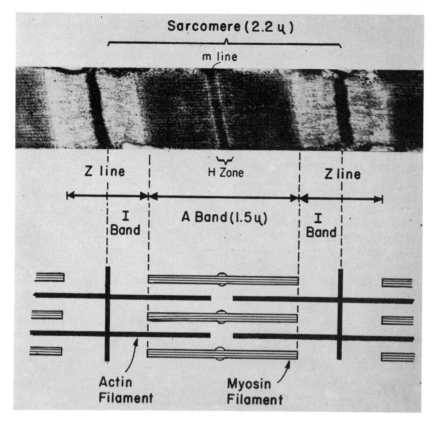

Figure 20–3. Diagrammatic representation of the structure of the sarcomere in relation to its appearance in an electron micrograph. (Reproduced with permission from Sonnenblick, E. N., Spiro, D., and Spotnitz, H. M.: Am. Heart J., *68:*336, 1964.)

cumference of the wall of the ventricle is matched by a similar percentage change in sarcomere length. By plotting a series of sarcomere length-tension curves, this investigator has demonstrated that shortening of the sarcomere by 15 to 20 per cent would provide the total contractile force necessary to maintain the normal ratio of stroke volume to end diastolic volume. Huxley and Peachey have emphasized the importance of the measurable finite length of the normal sarcomere. When this contractile unit was stretched to its maximal dimensions, that is, to a distance equal to the sum of the individual lengths of the myosin and actin elements, a state of "overstretch" was reached and contraction could no longer take place. Applying this theory to studies with cat papillary muscle, Sonnenblick found that actively developed tension was maximal at sarcomere lengths of 2.2 microns. Lengths greater than this were not reached at normal ventricular filling pressures. When pressure was elevated above normal, additional stretch was achieved, sarcomere length was in-

creased owing to a disengagement of thin actin filaments from thick myosin filaments, and the H zone was widened. At an elevated filling pressure of 12 to 15 mm. Hg, the sarcomere was stretched to a point on the descending limb of the sarcomere length-tension curve. Such overstretch may permanently impair the ability of muscle to contract. One may speculate that the relative number of contractile myocardial units overstretched in this manner may well determine the degree of ventricular decompensation. Thus the appearance of a widened H zone would seem to correspond to the plateau or descending limb of the ventricular function curve and may prove to be the major structural defect in ventricular decompensation with dilatation.

In the markedly overdistended ventricle, increased sarcomere length may not entirely account for increased ventricular volume. Linzbach has proposed that disorganization at the muscle bundle level may occur during decompensation and that sliding of fibers and their rearrangement, as well as relative slippage of myocardial cells, may contribute to ventricular dilatation. Both concepts support the physiologic observation that there is a limit to adaptive dilatation and that, when this limit is exceeded, normal shortening in response to excitation is prevented and the ventricle becomes hypodynamic.

The mitochondria from failing hearts prepared in the immediate postmortem period have been reported to show osmiophilic degeneration when examined by electron microscopy. These findings, however, have not been confirmed by examination of sections made from tissue obtained during open heart surgery.

VASCULAR RESPONSE TO CARDIAC DECOMPENSATION

The reserve capacity of the normal heart is about sixfold, permitting it to increase its output four to six times as long as venous return is maintained. Decompensation at rest occurs only when myocardial disease is so severe as to diminish this reserve. A fall in cardiac output is a challenge to circulatory homeostasis and may be brought about by congestive heart failure, shock, hemorrhage, and severe dehydration or fluid loss attributable to other causes.

Each stimulates a similar, nonspecific response: the first is an attempt to maintain perfusion of vital tissues. Mobilization of autoregulatory neurohumoral mechanisms may occur within 7 seconds and reach a maximum within 45 seconds (Guyton). The fall in cardiac output and, initially, in blood pressure stimulates the baro (stretch) receptors and an immediate increase in sympathetic activity. The concentration of circulating norepinephrine rises to abnormally high levels as does its renal excretion. Norepinephrine has been shown to cause as much as a tenfold increase in the elastic stiffness (tone) of the arterial tree. Total resistance is increased and perfusion pressure is supported. Sympathetic blocking drugs, such as hexamethonium, can prevent this response. The venous system, which is much more distensible, contains over three times the volume of blood present in the arterial system at onetenth the pressure. It responds to sympathetic stimulation by a marked increase in venomotor tone which tends to reduce the capacitance of the vascular tree. Since blood is incompressible, an augmentation in vasomotor tone must result in the transfer of blood to an area which will dilate despite this generalized increase in tone. The result is a redistribution of blood. Flow to skin, kidney, gastrointestinal tract and skeletal muscle decreases, and blood is driven centripetally toward the heart and pulmonary vascular bed.

Guyton has emphasized the contribution of the venous regulation of cardiac output. Flow into the atria is of course dependent upon the slight pressure gradient existing between the great veins and the right atrium. Sudden failure of the ventricles causes an elevation of atrial pressure. The resulting tendency toward reversal of the gradient necessary for adequate venous return is combated by the increased tone in the normally low pressure venous bed. Since elevation of venous pressure contributes to the elevation of the mean circulatory pressure (the average force pushing blood toward the heart), such elevation may not be a detriment to cardiac function but a crucial compensatory mechanism in the early stages of heart failure. The increase in venous tone causes a rise in input pressure at the point where the veins empty into the heart. To a limited degree, the failing heart may respond to this type of pump priming by an increase in cardiac output. It is important to emphasize that this is an emergency mechanism and may well prove detrimental in established congestive heart failure.

In this early stage venous pressures are only slightly elevated (4 to 8 mm. Hg). Since central blood volume is increased at the expense of the peripheral vascular system, there may be no evidence of the peripheral venous engorgement so commonly associated with chronic cardiac decompensation. With the onset of the chronic stage, some days after the acute episode, retention of salt and water by the kidney superimposes an expanded extracellular fluid volume (interstitial and total blood volume) on a venous system whose pressure is already elevated because of increased inflow resistance (elevated atrial pressure) and increased vasomotor tone. As a result, mean venous or central venous pressure rises to still higher levels causing more engorgement of the venous system and, unless compensation is recovered, may lead to further cardiac overloading and deterioration. Eventually the plasticity characteristics of the veins permit their gradual relaxation and enable them to accommodate an increase in total blood volume. Distention of the veins and of the other major venous reservoirs, the liver and spleen, soon becomes apparent. The initial acute fall in capillary pressure is reversed in chronic decompensation and rises with the increase in total blood volume and continued elevation of venous pressure.

RENAL ROLE IN CARDIAC DECOMPENSATION

The second response to a fall in cardiac output is an attempt to utilize renal compensatory mechanisms and is characterized by retention of salt and water. Almost any circulatory stress which reduces arterial filling (sequestration of blood in the extremities by venous occlusive cuffs, static standing, chronic anemia, arteriovenous anastomosis, etc.) will lead to retention of sodium and water (Barger).

In 1785, Withering suggested the role of the kidney in retaining fluid during cardiac decompensation; noting the copious diuresis after treatment with digitalis, he believed that "dropsy" was of renal rather than cardiac origin. An afferent sensor, most probably a stretch receptor within the walls of the renal afferent arterioles, alerts the kidney to the threatened collapse of the general circulatory system. The stimulus is a decrease in "true" or "effective" plasma volume. The renal response is retention of salt and water and a progressive increase in volume of interstitial fluid and blood. The increase in venous pressure originally brought about by an increase in vasomotor tone is thus augmented; in a few patients the heart retains some responsiveness to this type of inflow priming; in such patients one may see improvement in cardiac output and a reversal of these compensatory changes. This second response is usually quite ineffective, however, and fluid retention leads not to improvement, but to further functional deterioration.

In the otherwise normal patient fluid retention and expansion of extracellular volume are efficient means of correcting a fluid deficit. When volume is restored to normal this efficient homeostatic mechanism is terminated by negative feedback signals. The response is nondiscriminating and is that of a volume regulating system calculated to restore what appears to be a fall in plasma volume. As such, it is incapable of differentiating between the fall in cardiac output and perfusion pressure attributable to blood loss or fluid depletion and that caused by a depression of cardiac function. In the decompensated heart, the stimulus for retention is a fall in effective cardiac output and not in blood volume. It will persist until adequate flow is restored. Eventually the tissues and vascular system become flooded with excess fluid, advanced symptoms and signs of heart failure become evident, and, unless treated, the patient succumbs.

Many investigators have shown that the patient in severe congestive heart failure will demonstrate an increase in extracellular fluid volume, in total body water, and in total exchangeable sodium and chloride (when expressed as a percentage of body weight). Total exchangeable potassium, cell mass and body fat are reduced. Renal studies usually show a decrease in plasma flow, glomerular filtration, renal venous pressure and tubular reabsorption of sodium. Aldosterone secretion by the adrenal cortex increases concomitantly (eight- to forty-fold) and the concentration of antidiuretic hormone also increases in both blood and urine. There is clearly a drastic alteration in normal renal function.

RENAL REGULATION OF SODIUM BALANCE

Over 98 per cent of the 24,000 mEq. of sodium filtered by the glomerulus each day is reabsorbed by the tubular system. It is clear that the homeostatic controls necessary for the preservation of extracellular fluid volume are extremely active. A very slight decrease in either total fluid volume or sodium concentration causes almost complete tubular reabsorption of sodium. The *rate* of excretion is determined by the balance between glomerular filtration and tubular reabsorption. Since active secretion of sodium does not occur and the glomerular filtration rate appears to be relatively constant in the normal subject, variations in tubular reabsorption appear to play the major role. About 85 per cent of the filtered sodium is reabsorbed in the proximal tubules by a transport system that moves sodium against an electrochemical gradient (chloride moves passively in the same direction).

Sodium chloride is also reabsorbed in the collecting duct and in the ascending limb of Henle's loop, but to a much less significant degree. The remainder of the filtered sodium, not excreted in the urine, is reabsorbed in the distal tubule by ion exchange with hydrogen or potassium, a transfer which helps to maintain a physiologic pH and serves as the principal means for excretion of potassium ion. The absence of sodium ion in the tubular fluid of the distal segment may halt potassium excretion completely and may, under the proper circumstances, lead to potassium intoxication.

Little is known about normal regulation of sodium transport, particularly those mechanisms which function in the proximal tubular segment. Adrenal insufficiency is accompanied by failure of the tubules to reabsorb sodium maximally. This defect has been traced to the absence of aldosterone, a potent adrenal mineralocorticoid that enhances or perhaps plays a permissive role in the distal tubular reabsorption of sodium and in tubular secretion of potassium, hydrogen ion and ammonia. At normal concentrations the effect is a limited one, however, and even in the complete absence of aldosterone, loss of sodium rarely exceeds 150 to 200 mEq. per day.

RENAL SODIUM RETENTION IN CONGESTIVE HEART FAILURE

Sodium retention may be one of the earliest manifestations of cardiac decompensation and may possibly precede a measurable rise in venous pressure or change in glomerular filtration rate. The concepts of glomerular filtration rate (GFR), renal plasma flow (RPF) and filtration fraction (FF = GFR/RPF) are essential to an understanding of the physiologic mechanisms offered to explain this derangement. A normal balance between glomerular filtration and tubular reabsorption will lead to normal sodium excretion. Reduction in filtration with good tubular function or, conversely, the presence of normal filtration paired with an increase in tubular reabsorption will lead to reduced excretion of sodium. An increase in tubular reabsorption may also be brought about (by mechanisms to be described presently) by a reduction in renal plasma flow despite a normal GFR (increase in filtration fraction). Common to all three mechanisms is a relative or absolute increase in tubular reabsorption of sodium.

Decrease in Glomerular Filtration

The observation that glomerular filtration rate is commonly reduced to one-third or one-half the normal rate in patients with severe congestive failure leads to the postulate that the decreased filtrate was more completely absorbed by a normally functioning proximal and distal tubular transport system and was the cause of the decrease in urine flow and sodium concentration. This mechanism undoubtedly plays a role in the later stages of chronic congestive heart failure, but there is substantial evidence that it is not of primary importance. Salt retention may occur before a measurable fall in GFR. Hypophysectomy and renal arterial constriction both reduce GFR, but are usually not associated with edema or positive sodium balance. In some cardiac patients (in whom GFR was depressed) GFR remained depressed despite diuresis and clinical improvement; in others it was elevated and remained so despite accumulation of fluid. In addition, the rate of tubular reabsorption of sodium may decrease in response to a fall in GFR, thus restoring the previous glomerulotubular balance.

Increase in Tubular Reabsorption of Sodium

Barger showed that unilateral infusion of sodium into the renal artery of the normal dog is followed by a marked unilateral increase in sodium excretion. When the same infusion was given to an animal in congestive heart failure, no rise in sodium excretion occurred, although the GFR was normal. If a mercurial diuretic was then infused, sodium excretion by the injected kidney increased forty-fold. Since mercurials act to depress tubular function, it appears likely that the defect is due to an increased tubular reabsorption of sodium.

These and other experiments convinced most investigators that, whereas the fall in GFR may be a contributory factor, the increase in tubular reabsorption is most likely the earliest and most significant cause of sodium accumulation.

Increase in Filtration Fraction

Normally, 20 per cent of renal plasma flow (RPF) is filtered at the glomerulus (FF = 0.2). Merrill has shown, however, that RPF fell proportionately more than did GFR in patients with congestive heart failure; in some cases GFR was 40 per cent of RPF (FF = 0.4). RPF was similarly lowered when other causes reduced effective circulating blood volume. Furthermore, an increase in RPF will increase urine flow and sodium excretion.

Filtration at the glomerulus causes the composition of the plasma to change so that the colloid osmotic pressure of the peritubular capillaries is markedly increased (little protein is filtered at the glomerulus). Since the hydrostatic pressure within the capillaries is the same as that within the tubules, water and sodium are reabsorbed passively and are mediated by the gradient in colloid osmotic pressures between the peritubular capillaries

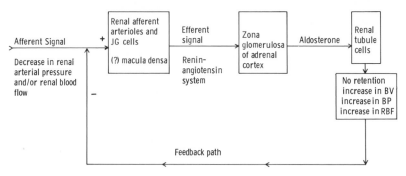

Figure 20–4. (After Urquhart and Davis.)

and the fluid in the tubular lumen (Vander). According to this theory water and sodium are transferred to restore isotonicity to the postglomerular plasma. An increase in filtration fraction raises the protein concentration of postglomerular plasma, markedly accentuates the osmotic gradient and enhances renal salt retention. Barger suggests that an increase in sympathetic tone is responsible for the renal vasoconstriction and decrease in RPF. Infusion of Dibenzyline (an adrenergic blocking agent) into the renal artery of a dog in congestive heart failure leads to an increase in RPF and sodium excretion on the infused side, but has no effect in the normal animal. Thus the increase in sympathetic tone, which accompanies congestive heart failure, may be indirectly responsible for the increase in sodium retention.

Urquhart and Davis claim that the filtration fraction is not invariably increased during pathologic sodium retention and that such an increase may occur in the absence of sodium retention. They also demonstrated almost complete sodium retention after thoracic caval constriction with protein depletion, so that postglomerular plasma colloid osmotic pressure was 40 to 50 per cent less than when sodium balance was normal.

Role of Aldosterone

Several investigators support the theory that increased tubular reabsorption of sodium is induced by the potent mineralocorticoid aldosterone. According to their reports, the tubule of the patient in failure shows an increased sensitivity to the salt-retaining actions of this hormone. They note that increased titers of aldosterone are seen in the blood and urine of patients and experimental animals in congestive failure and in other pathologic conditions of sodium retention and reduced effective circulating blood volume. Although administration of aldosterone will

not induce the signs and symptoms of failure in the normal subject, its administration to patients in failure will greatly accentuate their degree of decompensation. In the experimental animal adrenalectomy is followed by prompt natriuresis and evidence of potassium retention, both of which can be reversed by injection of aldosterone into the renal artery.

A schema for negative feedback control of aldosterone secretion, one that would be responsive to the hemodynamic changes attendant upon myocardial failure, has been proposed by Urquhart and Davis (Fig. 20–4). They propose that the primary mechanism for the control of aldosterone secretion is mediated by extracranial structures and that the aldosterone-stimulating factor is renin, an enzyme secreted by the juxtaglomerular cells of the kidney. This agent transforms the angiotensinogen substrate to a decapeptide, angiotensin I. A plasma-converting enzyme subsequently degrades this material to an octapeptide, angiotensin II, the immediate aldosterone-stimulating factor and an active pressor agent. Since the juxtaglomerular cells are located in the renal afferent arterioles, there is good presumptive evidence that the system functions as a volume receptor. Under these circumstances a decrease in stretch will stimulate juxtaglomerular cell secretion. Situations characterized by hypersecretion of aldosterone are usually accompanied by hemodynamic abnormalities leading to decreased pressure and volume in the afferent arterioles. According to Davis:

"The principal components of the renal aldosterone-regulatory system are: (1) the renal afferent arterioles with juxtaglomerular cells; (2) the renin-angiotensin system; (3) the zona glomerulosa of the adrenal cortex; (4) aldosterone; and (5) the renal tubule cells. The afferent signal to the system is provided by a decrease in renal arterial pressure and in renal blood flow which is associated with a decrease in the degree of stretch of the walls of renal afferent arterioles. The efferent signal is conveyed by the renin-angiotensin system. Renin is secreted by the juxtaglomerular cells and results in the production of angiotensin II, which acts directly on the zona glomerulosa of the adrenal cortex to increase the production of aldosterone. Aldosterone promotes Na transport by the renal tubule cells and Na retention occurs. Sodium retention is accompanied by retention of water and expansion of the circulating blood volume takes place; blood pressure and blood flow through vital organs, including the kidney, is thus increased. These changes increase the stretch of the renal afferent arterioles and tend to restore the secretion of renin to normal. In congestive heart failure, most of the retained fluid is filtered as edema into tissue spaces or as effusion into serous cavities, preventing the retained fluid from restoring renal arterial hemodynamics to normal. Thus, hypersecretion of renin and aldosterone continues and brings about chronic fluid retention." Although this hypothesis seems to be a reasonable one, it has not been proved, and some other as yet unknown factor may be responsible for renin release.

Much recent evidence has accumulated, however, which suggests that although aldosterone production is increased in congestive heart failure, it cannot in itself account for the early appearance and persistence of sodium retention. Other puzzling findings include the absence of striking hyperaldosteronism in some cases of true congestive heart failure, a finding that is particularly common in the early, untreated state. In addition, there is no accumulation of edema in the patient with primary hyperaldosteronism and little evidence of sodium retention after infusion of aldosterone into the renal artery of the normal dog, although sodium retention could be demonstrated when this experiment was repeated in the dog with congestive heart failure (? altered sensitivity in the presence of cardiac decompensation). Some investigators have even questioned whether an increase in release of aldosterone does not occur in response to the intensive therapy of congestive heart failure, involving as it does both sodium restriction and drugs that increase sodium excretion and reduce extracellular fluid volume. Persistent use of a regimen of this type would certainly provide a continuous stimulus for adrenal release of this hormone.

Free Water Clearance in Congestive Heart Failure

In the patient with congestive heart failure, an increase in antidiuretic substances in blood and urine simultaneously with the retention of free water has led to what may be an unwarranted conclusion regarding an exclusive relationship between the two. The decrease in free water clearance is particularly troublesome since patients with an average intake of water may develop dilutional hyponatremia and anasarca with a concentrated urine even though body sodium is abnormally increased. Recent reports of studies with the osmotic diuretic mannitol have shown that the limitation in free water excretion may be at least in part attributable to a decrease in volume flow to the diluting segment of the tubule. This state may be brought about by enhanced iso-osmotic proximal renal tubular reabsorption of glomerular filtrate. Mannitol increases free water clearance by osmotically carrying filtrate down to the diluting segment and permitting the production of a dilute urine.

An increase in renal venous pressure will also increase tubular reabsorption of sodium and water. This effect may be transient, however, and its true significance has yet to be determined.

Disagreement among the proponents of these several theories continues. Although a unitary explanation is always preferable, most objective observers agree that retention of sodium and water is the final expression of most, if not all, of these complex and subtle mechanisms acting in concert.

Myocardial Metabolism

It is generally conceded that the primary event in congestive heart failure, the factor that initiates the secondary hemodynamic and renal responses already discussed, as well as the symptoms and signs to be discussed shortly, is a fall in effective cardiac output. Very early in the disease cardiac output at rest may be normal. There may be no evidence of circulatory congestion, filling pressures may be within normal limits and indeed the diagnosis itself may have been made on evidence of an inadequate response to exercise, that is, a demonstrable reduction in cardiac reserve.

With myocardial failure there is a progressive decline in contractility; cardiac reserve, which is normally capable of an output of two to four times the resting level (as seen

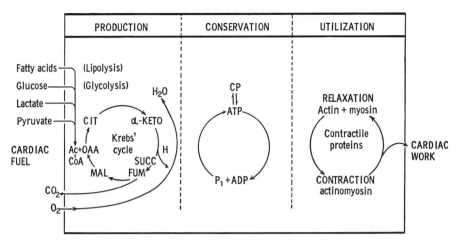

Figure 20–5. Steps involved in the transfer of substrate energy to cardiac work. (After Olson.)

in patent ductus arteriosus and valvular insufficiency) and blood pressure of close to twice the normal, may now gradually or suddenly (and frequently without an apparent precipitating event) be unable to sustain a normal or augmented load. Although transient increases in work may precipitate decompensation, the failing heart is not only unable to meet an increased hemodynamic demand, but eventually loses its ability to sustain a work effort it had previously supported quite adequately.

Since the ultimate source of the energy necessary to maintain adequate contractility is derived from the biologic oxidation of substrate carried to the heart by the coronary circulation, congestive heart failure may ultimately be defined in terms of a biochemical defect severe enough to interfere with the transduction of the potential chemical energy of the substrate into useful mechanical work.

Development of the coronary catheter permits sampling of myocardial venous drainage. This and other techniques, including those for measurement of myocardial blood flow, have enabled the investigator to determine the myocardial extraction (A-V) and consumption (arterial-venous concentration times coronary flow) of oxygen and substrate. For comparison of hearts of different weights such data are usually expressed per 100 gm. of myocardium. The technique is subject to the obvious limitations inherent in studies of this type and in some cases may fail to detect subtle abnormalities in myocardial metabolism. It must also be noted that substrate storage may occur and therefore consumption of substrate cannot always be equated with its immediate utilization (oxidation). The

accuracy of such studies also depends on homogeneous myocardial perfusion and the establishment of a true steady state of performance, often difficult to achieve in biologic systems and particularly important when monitoring coronary blood flow.

Wollenberger and, more recently, Olson have utilized the schema illustrated in Figure 20–5 as a guide to understanding the energetics of the metabolism of cardiac muscle. If indeed the etiology of this syndrome proves to be a biochemical one, the actual defect in myocardial energetics could be due to insufficient production of energy (liberation), defective storage of energy (conservation) or an inability to utilize this energy efficiently (utilization).

Energy Liberation and Conservation

The myocardial cell shows a greater dependence upon aerobic metabolism than any other tissue in the body. It has a low content of anaerobic enzymes and many giant mitochondria filled with the cristae necessary for the production of stores of cellular energy. The cardiac mitochondria perform few accessory enzymatic activities and are more resistant to inhibitors of oxidative phosphorylation than those from other tissues. The heart demonstrates wide substrate adaptability and is capable of utilizing most nutritional substances made available to it by the coronary circulation. It will normally extract glucose, pyruvate, lactate, free and esterified fatty acids, acetate, ketone bodies and amino acids. Extraction patterns for individual substrates are influenced by many factors, the most important being their absolute and relative arterial concentration and the permeability of the cell membrane which sets specific concentration thresholds. Olson has shown that the threshold for pyruvate and lactate extraction is very close to zero and that extraction is linear and proportional to arterial concentration.

The rate of glucose uptake is determined by a mobile, carrier-mediated sugar transport system which shows substrate stereospecificity and is responsive to a variety of influences. It is accelerated principally by insulin and by anoxia. The threshold for transport appears to approach 60 mg./100 ml. The extraction slope is curvilinear and approaches a maximum at about 200 mg./100 ml.

Myocardial extraction of free fatty acids (FFA) seems to bear a direct but variable relationship to arterial concentration. When individual fatty acids are compared, extraction is inversely related to chain length (C12-C18). Saturation also influences extraction. The monoenoic fatty acids, palmitoleic and oleic, the most abundant fatty acids of animal lipids, are extracted in preference to saturated fatty acids of equal chain length. Extraction of FFA in excess of the needs of aerobic metabolism leads to their conversion and storage as tissue triglyceride. There is as yet incomplete agreement as to the factors controlling extraction of esterified fatty acids. Bing and associates reported that in fasting human subjects esterified acids account for 58 per cent of total lipid extraction, FFA making up the other 42 per cent. The norepinephrine-mediated increase in FFA extraction reported by several workers is probably related to increased arterial concentrations resulting from catechol-induced lipolysis.

The state of nutrition of the organism plays a related role in the choice of substrate by myocardium. Goodale and Olson have reported that in the postprandial state the heart utilizes mainly glucose, lactate and pyruvate; the respiratory quotient approaches 1.0; and carbohydrates may account for 92 per cent of oxygen utilization. Under fasting conditions or in the diabetic, the arterial concentration of FFA and ketones is high and the myocardium extracts increasing quantities of these compounds. The heart is equally affected by the general metabolic defect of diabetes and demonstrates the same inability to adequately utilize carbohydrates as do other tissues. The respiratory quotient drops to 0.80 and oxygen utilized in the catabolism of fatty acids may rise from 5 to 58 per cent. After prolonged fasting, up to 70 per cent of total energy production is derived from the oxidation of fatty acids.

In sufficient concentrations, ketones compete successfully with fatty acids and glucose, even in the presence of insulin, and may account for over 90 per cent of myocardial respiration. Ordinarily amino acids do not contribute significantly to energy production. When infused in high concentrations, however, extraction is increased, and as much as 40 per cent of oxygen consumption may be accounted for by their aerobic metabolism.

This flexibility in substrate utilization has no effect either on work performance or capacity. Fuel mixtures available to the heart may vary, but energy production continues at a persistent fixed level despite these variations, as long as sufficient oxygen is provided. Increases in myocardial needs for energy are normally mediated by increases in coronary blood flow. Substrate extraction (A-V concentration) remains unchanged, its pattern being set by the conditions outlined above.

The immediate source of energy to the cell, permitting synthetic, transport and contractile activity, is stored in the high energy phosphate bonds of adenosine triphosphate (ATP) and creatine phosphate (CP). Controlled hydrolysis of the terminal phosphate bond of ATP releases energy from this chemical storage battery in a graded manner conserving it and making it available as needed. The supply of ATP is constantly replenished by rephosphorylation of adenosine diphosphate (ADP). Resynthesis of these phosphate bonds requires an input of energy approximately equal to that released by their hydrolysis.

$$F + Pi + ADP \rightleftarrows ATP$$

Free energy (F) derives from the intracellular oxidation of organic substrates, in reality a series of enzymatically regulated dehydrogenations, with the ultimate oxidation of hydrogen to the level of water. Pi represents inorganic phosphate.

Dehydrogenases catalyze the transfer of the hydrogen (electrons pairs) released from substrate to coenzyme hydrogen carriers. The principal carriers, the closely related nucleotides, diphosphopyridine nucleotide (DPN) and flavin-adenine dinucleotide (FAD) are thereby reduced and subsequently oxidized and reconstituted in the mitochondria of the cell by delivery of hydrogen atoms to the electron transport chain. In this system electrons are passed, in a stepwise manner, to progressively lower energy levels by a series of interrelated oxidation-reductions of the flavoproteins, coenzyme Q, and the cytochrome system. The process, known as oxidative phosphorylation, liberates free energy and chemically binds it as the energy-rich pyrophosphate bonds of CP and ATP. Three molecules of inorganic phosphate are consumed, and three molecules of ADP are rephosphorylated to ATP for each atom of oxygen utilized in the formation of a molecule of water. The chemical reaction is shown in 1 below. The thermodynamic efficiency of oxidative phosphorylation associated with a P:O ratio of 3.0 for the oxidation of fatty acids and glucose indicates that from 50 to 65 per cent of their chemical bond energy is converted into high energy phosphate bonds.

The cellular utilization of substrate extracted by the heart actually proceeds in two stages. The first stage is concerned with the production of a metabolic target compound common to both carbohydrates and lipids. It is a small key molecule and is composed of a two-carbon acetyl fragment activated by coenzyme A (acetyl Co-A). The initial pathways of lipid catabolism produce these molecules, *in the presence of oxygen,* by hydrolysis, acylation and beta-oxidation and thereby release the first 25 per cent of the potential chemical energy of fatty acids.

Glycolysis, the initial stage of carbohydrate catabolism, follows a different chemical pathway, an important one to those interested in cardiac function. Glucose enters the cell and in the process is phosphorylated to glucose-6-PO_4 by ATP in the presence of the enzyme hexokinase. Glycogen stored in the cell may also be made available for energy release after debranching (debranching enzyme), phosphorylation to glucose-1-PO_4 (Pi + phosphorylase-*a*, and isomerization. A small quantity of the glucose-6-PO_4 so formed may be directly oxidized via the TPN-dependent hexose monophosphate shunt (pentose phosphate shunt). The remainder enters the glycolytic pathway described by Embden and Meyerhof, illustrated in 2 below:

Glycolytic ATP is produced via two mechanisms. An oxidative reaction frees hydrogen for reduction of DPN^+ and electron transport, as described above for aerobic or respiratory

chain phosphorylation. In addition, certain intermediate compounds of glucose-6-PO_4 metabolism may directly transfer their high energy phosphate to ADP. Such coupling, known as substrate-linked phosphorylation, is not quantitatively significant, but is qualitatively important since this ATP is produced in the absence of oxygen. The reactions are governed by enzyme systems found in the cytoplasmic cell sap. In this manner four molecules of ATP are produced per molecule of glucose consumed in the production of pyruvate, the functional end product. Net production is only two molecules of ATP, however, since the reactions themselves consume two molecules of ATP. The total energy yield is thus rather meager and represents 56,000 cal., or about 8 per cent of the potential energy of glucose. Under aerobic conditions the pyruvate so formed is decarboxylated to an acetyl fragment and condenses with coenzyme-A to form a molecule of acetyl Co-A.

The Krebs (Citric Acid) Cycle

The second stage of metabolism has an extremely high energy yield, is common to the products of carbohydrate, lipid and protein degradation, and is confined to the enzyme systems of the mitochondria. The cycle will function only in an aerobic environment and utilizes almost all of the acetyl coenzyme A produced in the reactions described above. The acetyl group is freed and, in the presence of a condensing enzyme richly concentrated in heart muscle, is coupled to oxaloacetate to form citrate. Operation of the cycle and its production of ATP is tightly coupled to the electron transport chain and consequently requires regeneration of sufficient DPN^+ and FAD to meet the demands of its several enzymatic dehydrogenations. DPN is present in only catalytically small amounts, and its oxidation is essential for the maintenance of aerobic energy production. In the absence of an adequate supply of oxygen, DPN^+ availability becomes rate-limiting, and the cycle is disrupted.

As illustrated in Figure 20–6, the stoichiometric coupling is such that 36 of the 38 moles of ATP produced per mole of glucose oxidized are formed as a result of aerobic

(1) $DPN + H^+ + \frac{1}{2} O_2 + 3 ADP + 3 Pi \rightleftharpoons DPN^+ + H_2O + 3 ATP$

(2) Glucose $+ ADP + 2 Pi + 2 DPN^+ \rightleftharpoons 2$ Pyruvic Acid $+ 2 ATP + DPNH + 2 H^+$

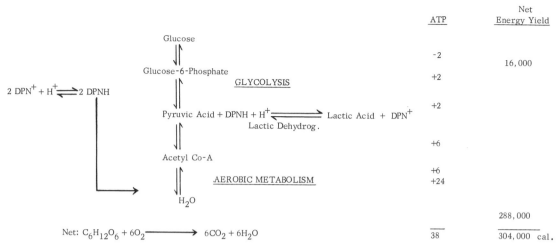

Figure 20–6. Carbohydrate metabolism = Energy yield.

mitochondrial activity. Thus, aerobic oxidation of glucose yields approximately 12 times more energy per mole than does anaerobic glycolysis.

Anaerobic Myocardial Metabolism

During glycolysis only one oxidative reaction occurs (see **1** below).

Extramitochondrial DPN is the obligatory electron acceptor in this *cytoplasmic* reaction catalyzed by the enzyme triose phosphate dehydrogenase. An efficient mechanism for continuous oxidation of DPNH is therefore essential for the maintenance of glycolysis. Recent investigations indicate that the mitochondrial membrane is relatively impermeable to cytoplasmic DPNH, and thus it prevents its direct mitochondrial oxidation. This impermeability may be a major regulatory factor in cell metabolism. An indirect route, by which electrons may be carried from extramitochondrial DPNH to the intramitochondrial electron transport chain, is probable. In principle any metabolite that can oxidize cytoplasmic DPNH, pass the mitochondrial membrane, and release its electrons, by serving as substrate for mitochondrial oxidation, can perform this shuttle function. One such system utilizes dihydroxyacetone phosphate, which is reduced by extramitochondrial

DPNH to alphaglycerol phosphate. The latter enters the mitochondria, is oxidized, and then passes back into the cytoplasm as dihydroxyacetone phosphate (see **2** below).

In the aerobic state these pathways maintain an adequate supply of DPN in its oxidized state (DPN^+). During partial or complete anoxia, however, the mitochondria are no longer capable of performing this function, and glycolytic energy production will halt unless alternate means for reoxidizing DPNH become operative. Some of the reduced coenzyme is utilized in the synthesis of fatty acids, cholesterol, and amino acids, reductive synthetic reactions which require reduced coenzyme. Most of it is utilized by a regulatory system that directs glycolysis to its classic terminal reaction, the reduction of pyruvate to lactate in the presence of lactic acid dehydrogenase (Fig. 20–6). In the anoxic state lactate, instead of being utilized by the myocardium as substrate for aerobic energy liberation, is produced by an actively glycolyzing metabolic system. Its tissue concentration and that of alphaglycerol phosphate and other products of DPNH-linked redox systems are increased as these systems shift toward a more reduced state. Lactic acid appears to be a fortuitous end product of metabolism and its production, happily, is an efficient emergency measure. Accumulation of lactate, besides

(**1**) Glyceraldehyde-3-PO_4 + Pi + DPN^+ $\rightleftharpoons$ 1,3 diphosphoglycerate + DPNH

(**2**) H^+ + DPNH + dihydroxyacetone-P $\longrightarrow$ DPN^+ + alphaglycerol-P (Cytoplasm)

Alphaglycerol-P + FAD $\longrightarrow$ dihydroxyacetone-P + $FADH_2$ (Mitochondria)

causing a slight drop in intracellular pH, does not interfere with other metabolic reactions. Actually, since it diffuses freely through the cell membrane, high intracellular concentrations are rapidly dissipated as lactate passes into the general venous circulation. Its concentration in myocardial venous blood provides a valuable clue to the extent of intra-myocardial anaerobic metabolism.

Huckabee has demonstrated that infusions of pyruvate, hyperventilation, and other factors may also cause an elevation in the concentration of myocardial venous lactate and has devised a formula which, by relating lactate to pyruvate concentration in both arterial and venous blood, permits a more controlled expression of glycolysis. Expressed as *"excess lactate,"* this approach and the use of the ratio of lactate to pyruvate have proved of value both in diagnosing and investigating ischemic heart disease. When aerobic production of energy is depressed by experimental cyanide intoxication, about 12 per cent of the total energy needs of the heart are met by anaerobic glycolysis. Utilization of anaerobic energy in myocardial contraction is supported by experiments demonstrating that external mechanical work exceeded the energy available from aerobic metabolism alone. For at least brief periods a portion of total energy can be released without simultaneous consumption of oxygen.

Although contractility is depressed, energy derived solely from anaerobic metabolism is sufficient to enable the cells of the sinus node to generate impulses and the conducting tissue to function adequately. Normally, stores of myocardial glycogen can sustain energy requirements by glycolysis alone for only about 4 minutes. Anoxic dependence on glycolytic energy production therefore implies an increase in glucose consumption for even marginal cellular function. Pasteur first recognized that glucose consumption was greater under anaerobic than under aerobic conditions. Anoxia has been shown to increase membrane transport of glucose as much as six times. There is a simultaneous reduction in the Km for glucose phosphorylation and an increase in the velocity maximum (V max) for the hexokinase reaction. This increased transport is matched by increased phosphorylation. Glycogenolysis is stimulated by an increase in phosphorylase-*a* activity, and glycogen stores are rapidly depleted. The enzyme systems of the Embden-Meyerhof system are also stimulated by the increase in the concentration of ADP and inorganic phosphate (Pi) accumulating as a result of breakdown of ATP without its active aerobic reconstitution. Further evidence for the increased activity of glycolytic pathways was obtained by Brachfeld and Scheuer who demonstrated that, under conditions of partial anoxia, the coefficient of glucose extraction increases 400 per cent and absolute glucose consumption increases 100 per cent.

Clinically, myocardial ischemia is more often acute and temporary, and less frequently complete. In these borderline states production of glycolytic ATP may make an important contribution to the maintenance of cell life, the functioning of nodal and conducting tissue, and myocardial contractility. When coronary blood flow is reestablished after induced occlusion, a reactive hyperemia results and both flow and oxygen debts are overpaid. Mechanisms for hydrogen storage are reversed and reduced substrate is oxidized by newly available DPN^+. Lactate may be oxidized to pyruvate and may enter the Krebs cycle or aid in the reaccumulation of cellular glycogen stores.

Energy Utilization; Excitation Contraction Coupling; Cardiac Relaxing Factor

The third phase of myocardial energetics is that of energy utilization. It is concerned with the coupling of the potential chemical energy of substrate, stored as ATP and CP to the contractile mechanism itself.

For many years investigators have been puzzled by the fact that muscle may remain in a state of relaxation, despite the presence in its cytoplasm of all the factors necessary for shortening, until an excitation stimulus triggers a contraction. Indeed, the true meaning of excitation and its mechanism of action are largely unknown. Recent studies have begun to provide some of the answers to these questions. According to current concepts of excitation-contraction coupling, as described by Lee for skeletal muscle, the function of the excitation wave, as it travels along the cell membrane, is to initiate the release of ionic calcium (Ca^{++}) from storage depots. These consist of membrane-enclosed intracellular structures known as *sarcoplasmic reticulum* and sometimes referred to as *relaxing factor vesicles*. The released Ca^{++} initiates the interaction of the myofibril with ATP, and muscle contraction results. Following contraction the Ca^{++} is taken up by a process of active transport and passes from its cytoplasmic locale back through the sarcoplasmic membrane, where it is once again stored so that relaxation is permitted to occur. Lee demonstrated under experimental conditions that the sarcoplasmic reticulum of heart muscle was as potent as that of skeletal muscle with regard to Ca^{++} uptake. Leonard pointed out that skeletal muscle is a self contained unit in which this process may cycle independent of the ionic concentration of the external medium. Sufficient Ca^{++} is present in the vesicles to permit contraction when it is released from vesicle to cytoplasm. During relaxation "salvage" and reaccumulation of Ca^{++} is great enough to permit subsequent cycling. Although the sarcoplasmic reticulum of heart muscle may sequester Ca^{++}, it does not appear to be able to do so in quantities sufficient to trigger contraction and must therefore depend upon an accessory extracellular source of these ions. Since the magnitude of the influx of extracellular Ca^{++} seems to influence the strength of contraction, the concentration of extracellular Ca^{++} has a direct bearing on the strength of myocardial contractility. This observation, should it be supported by further investigation, provides a mechanistic explanation for what have been until now well known empirical observations of the effects of extracellular Ca^{++} concentration on myocardial contractility. Furthermore, the myocardial cell membrane must provide a calcium pump mechanism since extracellular calcium transport is an active, energy requiring process and must occur with each excitation-contraction cycle. One may

only speculate at this time as to the role a defect in Ca^{++} transport may play in the depressed myocardial contractility of congestive heart failure.

COMPARISON OF HEMODYNAMICS AND METABOLISM OF MYOCARDIAL AND SKELETAL MUSCLE

Table 20–1 compares myocardial and skeletal muscle and emphasizes the significant differences between these two types of contractile tissue, each best adapted for its major function. Myocardial contraction is a continuous process; the myocardium has an extensive vascular network, particularly at the capillary level, providing at least one capillary per muscle fiber. Its blood flow is 10 to 20 times that of skeletal muscle. Its myolemma, the cellular membrane, is especially thin and permits rapid diffusion of substrate and oxygen from the capillary to the interior of the cell. Myoglobin also facilitates oxygen transport. Myocardial glycogen content is maintained; indeed, it is higher in the fasting state than in the immediate postprandial period. In diabetes it may reach extremely high levels. These apparently parodoxical findings, quite the opposite of those in liver and skeletal muscle, are probably due to a glucose-sparing effect brought about by the large amounts of FFA and ketones which are oxidized (mediated by high arterial concentrations and membrane transport) under these circumstances. There is a decrease in utilization of

TABLE 20–1. COMPARISON OF THE HEMODYNAMICS AND METABOLISM OF MYOCARDIAL AND SKELETAL MUSCLE.

	Myocardial	Skeletal
Number of capillaries	4 ×	1 ×
Mean blood flow	10 to 20 ×	1 ×
Myolemma (sarcolemma)	Thin, low resistance	Thicker, higher resistance
Myoglobin	Present	Present in red skeletal muscle
Sarcomere length	1 ×	1.7 ×
Glycogen concentration	Maintained	Depleted by fasting, diabetes
Glycolytic enzyme systems	1 ×	2 ×, strongly developed
Creatine phosphate concentration	1 ×	6 ×
Anaerobic energy production	Beating—2 min. Arrested—30–90 min.	Up to 40% total energy
Production of lactic acid	Terminal mechanism	Frequent, when incurring O_2 debt
Mitochondria	Abundant, giant	Fewer, smaller
Krebs cycle enzymes	2 to 3 ×	1 ×
Cytochrome C	6 ×	1 ×
Ability to incur O_2 debt	1 ×	4 ×
An increase in O_2 requirement met primarily by:	Increased flow	Increased extraction
Oxygen consumption	3 ×	1 ×
Oxygen extraction at rest	Near maximal	Significant reserve
Increase in oxygen consumption with an increase in work	2 ×	30 ×

the glucose entering the cell, much of it being transformed into glycogen storage granules. Storage in this form provides a readily available supply of substrate for emergency anaerobic energy production. A relatively low concentration of glycolytic enzymes and creatine phosphate, relatively poor anaerobic energy production and an insignificant ability to incur an oxygen debt accentuate the primarily aerobic metabolic status of the myocardium and its limited reserve of high energy phosphate linkages. So, too, do the abundant giant mitochondria and the high concentration of Krebs cycle enzymes and of cytochrome C. Anaerobiosis and production of lactic acid, constantly present in exercising skeletal muscle when incurring an oxygen debt, are emergency measures utilized by cardiac muscle only under extreme conditions of ischemia or anoxia.

Myocardial oxygen extraction is near maximal at rest and is greater than that of any other tissue of the body. There is little change from resting myocardial oxygen extraction when a subject exercises and, indeed, in some cases the percentage of extraction may actually fall with exercise. The heart does not have the large reserve available to skeletal muscle for increasing extraction when a greater amount of oxygen is needed. An increase in demand for oxygen in response to an increase in work load is met primarily by utilization of its large reserve capacity to increase coronary blood flow. This response may be great enough to provide flow in excess of myocardial oxygen needs and normally will easily satisfy an increase in oxygen consumption of from 40 to 60 per cent. In addition, left ventricular mechanical efficiency may increase as much as 30 per cent during exercise and allow greater work per unit of oxygen consumed.

Myocardial Metabolism in Congestive Heart Failure

Congestive heart failure could result from a defect occurring at any stage of the schema outlined in Figure 20–5, whether it be partial failure in energy liberation or conservation or an inability to utilize energy efficiently in the development of tension.

High Output Congestive Heart Failure. This category includes a heterogeneous group of diseases which meet the criteria for failure outlined previously; that is, these hearts are unable to maintain a cardiac output sufficient to supply the metabolic and hemodynamic demands of the body. There is retention of salt and water, an increase in blood volume and extracellular fluid volume, elevation of venous pressure, cardiac dilatation and all the classic signs of vascular congestion. This group differs from the more common type of congestive heart failure in that cardiac output may be normal or in some cases as high as two or three times normal. It is most commonly seen when heart failure is precipitated by arteriovenous fistula, Paget's disease, patent ductus arteriosus and chronic cor pulmonale—essentially hemodynamic defects. It occurs less frequently with severe chronic anemia, beriberi and thyrotoxicosis, all of which demonstrate a potential defect in myocardial energy liberation including the generation and storage of high energy phosphate bonds. In both types the hypervolemia, the marked decrease in total peripheral resistance and the sustained demand for an increase in cardiac output may exhaust cardiac reserve. The clinical and physiologic manifestations of failure are otherwise indistinguishable from low output failure. Correct diagnosis is vital since many patients are completely and in some cases dramatically and rapidly cured by definitive therapy of the inciting cause.

The defect may result from an anatomic abnormality or may be secondary to a systemic process. Renal retention of salt and water is apparently due to a decrease in the ratio of renal blood flow to total cardiac output caused by a disproportionate decrease in the extrarenal fraction of total peripheral resistance. The decrease in renal blood flow and glomerular filtration rate sets the stage for the mechanisms of abnormal retention of salt and water outlined earlier. In many cases of high output failure, the primary lesion is remote from the heart, and it may be affected only secondarily by the persistent excessive demands of a reduced peripheral resistance and the compensatory hypervolemia it calls forth. Eventually the ventricles must dilate, the law of Laplace becomes operative and the cost of maintaining tension is prohibitive. In many cases a fall in cardiac output supervenes, further accentuating the signs and symptoms of heart failure.

The marked generalized vasodilatation accompanying chronic anemia affects the coronary vascular bed. When faced with a decrease in the oxygen-carrying capacity of the blood and its limited ability to increase extraction of oxygen, the heart must depend upon the adequacy of its coronary bed to dilate and increase flow. In moderate anemia, or hypoxia from poisoning, or breathing at low oxygen tensions, this compensation may be complete. In more severe cases or in patients with superimposed coronary vascular disease, the ability to maintain the increased work load is lost when coronary reserve becomes exhausted. Oxidative phosphorylation is compromised by a lack of oxygen. An increase in the anaerobic metabolic rate is evinced by a decrease in myocardial glycogen stores, an increase in glucose consumption and an increase in lactate production. The heart, instead of utilizing lactate by its conversion to pyruvate and entrance into the respiratory cycle, is now producing it as an end product of glycolysis. Inadequate resynthesis of ATP and CP eventually leads to inadequate energy stores for maintaining optimal myocardial function.

Beriberi is a classic example of metabolic heart disease. Thiamine pyrophosphate or co-carboxylase is a critical coenzyme needed for decarboxylation of pyruvate to acetyl coenzyme A, for α-ketoglutarate dehydrogenation and for the transketolase reaction. When the supply is limited, heart muscle, like other tissues, is unable to utilize lactate and pyruvate normally, and blood levels of these substrates rise. The carbohydrate contribution to total myocardial energy production is curtailed, and decreased levels of ATP may be observed experimentally. In our contemporary western society chronic alcoholism is the most common cause of this type of dietary deficiency. The full-blown syndrome is fortunately somewhat rare and occurs as "wet" beriberi in which there is both reduction in myocardial co-carboxylase and significant peripheral vasodilatation. Although administration of thiamine usually restores the patient to normal, such treatment, if vigorous, may lead to further cardiac dilatation since venous tonus is restored. In the presence of hypervolemia this may trigger an increase in venous pressure and return.

Congestive heart failure is often associated with the generalized hypermetabolism of thyrotoxicosis; the *cause* of the failure, however, is not clear. Although a potent uncoupler of oxidative phosphorylation in other tissues, there is disagreement as to whether thyroid hormone decreases concentrations of ATP or CP in myocardial tissue. The lack of an apparent relationship between the severity of hyperthyroidism and the onset of congestive heart failure has puzzled many workers in this field. Thyroid "storm" may occur without evidence of heart disease, and conversely thyroid heart disease may be the first manifestation of hyperthyroidism. This disease, accompanied by auricular fibrillation, occurs most frequently after forty, and although thyroid heart disease has occasionally been reported in patients without other heart ailments, it is uncommon. Several studies give evidence of associated heart disease in 67 to 90 per cent of cases. There is little doubt that thyrotoxicosis may overwhelm a heart functioning in a state of borderline compensation produced by other factors.

Rowe reports that the circulation of such patients *at rest* resembles that of the normal person after exercise. There is an increase in heart rate, oxygen consumption, cardiac output, pulmonary arterial pressure, right and left ventricular work and coronary blood flow, and a decrease in coronary vascular and peripheral resistance. It is significant that myocardial efficiency *decreases*.

The atria appear to be exquisitely sensitive to the effects of this hormone and may increase their oxygen consumption as much as 77 per cent. Such sensitivity may help to explain not only the tachycardia but the frequency of atrial fibrillation in thyrotoxicosis. Depressed protein anabolism and contractility of ventricular muscle strips after treatment with thyroxin are other etiologic clues. Since there is little agreement as to whether myocardial stores of ATP are decreased in this disease, it is not yet possible to locate the defect at the level of energy liberation or conservation.

Low Output Congestive Heart Failure. The most common type of congestive heart failure is characterized by a low cardiac output and is seen in congenital or acquired disease of the valves or great vessels, hypertension, coronary artery disease, and fibrosis or other types of muscle fiber degeneration. In biochemical investigations heart failure has been induced in a variety of species, and the results of such studies at times appear to be contradictory and difficult to organize into a coherent metabolic picture. For example, we are as yet unable to define accurately a biochemical defect that will account for the inability of the heart in failure to respond to an increase in diastolic tension by an increased force of contraction. There is evidence that the processes of energy liberation and conservation are normal. Coronary blood flow and oxygen extraction and consumption per 100 gm. of heart muscle are unchanged in the failing heart. Myocardial substrate consumption, metabolic enzyme systems, and oxidative phosphorylation are usually reported as being comparable to controls. Chidsey et al. studied mitochondria isolated from failing human myocardium removed at operation and found that they possessed a high degree of structural and functional integrity. These and other workers have reported that the myocardial concentration of high energy phosphate compounds was adequate and did not differ significantly from resting controls. Such evidence indicates that the biochemical defect in low output failure, expressed mechanically as a decrease in efficiency, is an inadequate conversion of available chemical energy into mechanical work. In terms of the Olson schema the defect lies at the stage of energy utilization. The target molecules for energy utilization are, of course, the contractile proteins themselves. Abnormalities in their molecular structure, perhaps caused by the chronic stretch of contracting at a mechanical disadvantage, were long thought to be the responsible biochemical lesion. More recent studies, however, have failed to confirm earlier reports of differences in the molecular weight and physical-chemical properties of myosin extracted from normal and failing hearts.

Two other observations may help to explain an apparent defect in energy utilization despite normal protein structure. The first, based on disorganization of the contractile elements at a supramolecular (ultrastructural) level, was discussed earlier (see Pathologic Changes in Congestive Heart Failure). The second attempts to explain the diminution of contractility of actomyosin bands prepared from failing human hearts obtained at autopsy and of glycerol-extracted muscle strips taken from animals with experimentally induced heart failure. Such studies indicate that the contractile proteins, although structurally normal, may be unable to utilize phosphate bond energy efficiently. There is a constant association between the rate of ATP hydrolysis and the extent of shortening or tension development in muscle models. Adenosine triphosphatase (ATPase), the enzyme responsible for this hydrolysis, has been assayed by Alpert in normal and failing hearts and found to be considerably depressed in failure. Although these findings are as yet unsupported and difficult to interpret, they do suggest that a biochemical defect, unrelated to the liberation or conservation of energy, interferes with the coupling of energy to an otherwise normal contractile protein. The measurable decrease in contractility has not yet been

satisfactorily explained, nor has it been possible to reconcile the conflicting reports that the oxidative phosphorylating capacity of mitochondria is depressed in the failing heart of the guinea pig and dog, nor that ATP, CP, and total creatine is decreased significantly in these species when failure is induced by a chronic increase in outflow resistance. Clearly more work is needed before these differences can be resolved.

PRIMARY MYOCARDIAL DISEASE AND CONGESTIVE HEART FAILURE

A miscellaneous group of comparatively rare systemic diseases, congenital, hereditary or acquired in nature, may affect the heart severely enough to cause congestive heart failure. Patients afflicted with ailments classified as "primary myocardial disease" show progressive cardiomegaly accompanied by arrhythmias, conduction defects and congestive heart failure and not infrequently die suddenly. Disease is confined to the myocardium itself and occurs in the absence of valvular deformity, hypertension or occlusion of coronary arteries. Each disease entity will be briefly discussed in categories determined by their pathogenetic characteristics.

Failure may result from the infiltration of abnormal material into or between muscle fibers. Amyloidosis, glycogen storage disease, lipochondrodystrophy (gargoylism) hemochromatosis, fatty infiltration, tumor invasion, metastases and primary myocardial neoplasms may all induce myocardial failure by purely mechanical means.

Myocarditis may be specific and secondary to infection by bacterial, viral, mycotic, protozoal or rickettsial agents, to bacterial toxins or toxic chemicals, or to physical trauma such as electrical current or radiation. Nonspecific myocarditis may be an immunologic response to unknown agents or an autoimmune hypersensitivity reaction. Both commonly produce severe, resistant and often fatal congestive heart failure. Primary myocardial disease may be associated with three heredofamilial neuromuscular disorders (*myotonic dystrophy, progressive muscular dystrophy,* and *Friedreich's ataxia*) in which the myocardium, as well as striated muscle, is involved in a chronic degenerative process.

Metabolic disease, resulting from abnormal production of hormone as in pheochromocytoma, adrenal insufficiency, hyperaldosteronism, Cushing's syndrome, acromegaly, hyperinsulinism and hyperthyroidism, may be associated with cardiac enlargement and heart failure. Segmental myocardial necrosis has been identified in the clinical syndrome of hypokalemic cardiomyopathy, a not infrequent complication of adrenal disease.

In pregnancy the heart rate, plasma and total blood volume and cardiac output are increased. About 8 weeks before term these changes become maximal. The incidence of failure is therefore at its peak during this period. Although failure most commonly occurs in patients with rheumatic, congenital or hypertensive heart disease, over 100 cases of a late *puerperal cardiomyopathy* have been reported. Decompensation is seen both during the last trimester and in the postpartum period. Recurrences are not infrequent in subsequent pregnancies. The heart is dilated and flabby, and there is evidence of myocardial degeneration, emboli from ventricular mural thrombi, myocardial hypertrophy, and focal and diffuse areas of myocardial necrosis. Similar pathologic changes have been described in patients with *chronic alcoholism, cardiovascular collagenosis, nephritis* and *toxemia.* The etiology of these changes remains obscure and may represent the end stage of many different metabolic or endocrine derangements.

Severe progressive congestive heart failure is also seen as a result of asymmetric or generalized myocardial hypertrophy, which is idiopathic and produces anatomic or functional obstruction of the outflow tract of one or both ventricles.

Finally, cardiac hypertrophy and dilatation of obscure nature may appear with or without myocardial or endomyocardial fibrosis. This is a large, somewhat miscellaneous group of idiopathic myocardiopathies and includes congenital, adult and familial forms. It has been variously described under a somewhat confusing and as yet unclassified number of subtypes. One of the more frequently encountered, endocardial fibroelastosis, becomes apparent during infancy and is characterized by the appearance of thick, pearly endocardial bands of fibrous and elastic tissue, which impair myocardial contractility and cause severe, unremitting congestive heart failure. The more exotic members of this category, grouped under the heading of *"cryptogenic heart disease,"* include *endomyocardial fibrosis,* the so-called Uganda heart, seen in many countries in tropical Africa. The patient suffers a progressive sclerosing process infiltrating the endocardium and myocardium of both sides of the heart. When valves and papillary muscles become involved, mitral or tricuspid

insufficiency or both result. The clinical picture is almost always that of right heart failure with severe dyspnea. Response to therapy is poor, as is the prognosis. Death from severe congestive heart failure usually occurs within 20 months.

An entirely distinct type of cryptogenic heart disease is seen in Rhodesia and the Republic of South Africa. It is generally known as *"idiopathic cardiac hypertrophy"* and is the most frequent type of heart disease among the Bantu. It is also seen, although to a far lesser extent, in the white population. The heart is markedly dilated and hypertrophied and shows but slight endocardial fibrosis with rare involvement of the valves. The patient presents with the insidious onset of dyspnea, peripheral edema, and other signs of congestive heart failure. Although there is an initial response to treatment, relapses are common and death may ensue in a few weeks. Five and six year survivals, however, are not rare.

TOTAL BODY METABOLISM IN CONGESTIVE HEART FAILURE—CARDIAC CACHEXIA

Cardiac cachexia, characterized by a striking degree of malnutrition, often follows the onset of chronic congestive heart failure. In a recent review of the pathogenesis of this state, Pittman and Cohen point out that although other factors may be evident, the wasting process seems to be related directly to the cellular hypoxia accompanying a persistent reduction in cardiac output. The wide arteriovenous oxygen differences noted earlier, and excessive production of lactate in the postexercise state indicate an increase in anaerobic glycolysis, an inefficient method of energy production, wasteful of substrate and fostered by chronic stagnant tissue anoxia. Anorexia frequently accompanies heart failure and may be the expression of several abnormalities including poor splanchnic perfusion, interstitial edema, reduced gastric capacity, retarded gastric emptying, and generalized fatigue and weakness. Cachexia is often accentuated by iatrogenic factors such as a therapeutic regimen which may include opiates, diuretics, potassium chloride, exchange resins, digitalis (to the point of toxicity), aminophylline, and other agents. Restrictive and, in some cases, unpalatable diets decrease food intake still further. This negative nutritional state is abetted by the malabsorption and steatorrhea found in the majority of patients with congestive heart failure.

High renal venous pressures frequently lead to proteinuria, at times so severe as to mimic the nephrotic syndrome. Protein is also lost as a result of therapeutic removal of pleural and peritoneal effusions and by the protein-losing gastroenteropathy most often associated with constrictive pericarditis. Hypoalbuminemia is accentuated by a shift of protein from the intra- to the extravascular space. Pittman and Cohen point out that compensatory adaptation to the semistarvation of congestive heart failure is interfered with by (1) a generalized *hypermetabolism* brought on by increased activity of the respiratory muscles, (2) enhanced oxygen consumption of a large dilated heart, (3) a marked increase in the rate of erythropoiesis, (4) overactivity of the sympathetic nervous system, and (5) elevation in body temperature, brought on by impairment of the mechanisms of cutaneous heat dissipation. These factors further accentuate nutritional deficits. The treatment of cardiac cachexia is the same as that for congestive failure. In many cases increased appetite often attends improved cardiac function.

Signs and Symptoms of Congestive Heart Failure

We noted earlier that the heart muscle is a spiral syncytium and that disease of one chamber is often associated with disease of the other. In many patients, however, particularly if hypertrophy develops, the syncytial concept is not evident in functional terms, and one ventricle may dilate and "fail" while the other remains compensated (see Univentricular Heart Failure). Clinically the classic examples are failure of the left ventricle after an acute hypertensive crisis or failure of the right ventricle before severe cor pulmonale. The predominant symptoms, signs and laboratory findings are governed by whether the right, the left or both chambers are involved. At the onset of congestive heart failure, in contrast to many other diseases, initial attention is rarely directed to the heart itself. Symptoms and signs are reflections of changes produced in other organs by congestion and by a decrease in effective cardiac output. They may result from the accumulation of an excessive volume of venous blood at high pressures or from interstitial edema, or they may reflect the response of the individual organ to a decrease in perfusion. The brain, skin, muscle, lung, liver, kidney and vascular system are the most frequent target

organs responsible for clinical evidence of myocardial failure.

When left-sided failure predominates, diagnosis frequently is made earlier than is usual during isolated right heart failure. The patient becomes aware of troublesome, sometimes frightening pulmonary symptoms and consults his physician. In isolated right ventricular failure, *symptoms* are sometimes obscure and may be misleading to the patient, although the *signs* of failure are clearly evident to the physician. A critical delay may intervene before a physician is consulted. Some of the signs to be discussed are not unique for congestive heart failure. Dyspnea, orthopnea, paroxysmal nocturnal dyspnea, pulmonary rales, peripheral edema, hydrothorax, ascites, and a tender enlarged liver may also be manifestations of extracardiac disease. Note also that mitral stenosis, tricuspid stenosis, and pericardial tamponade may produce many of the symptoms of congestive heart failure brought on by mechanical obstruction despite normal myocardial contractility and normal end diastolic pressures.

MANIFESTATIONS OF LEFT-SIDED HEART FAILURE

The most marked symptoms and signs of left heart failure are noted in the pulmonary system and are caused by elevated pressures in the pulmonary vascular bed because of elevated diastolic pressures in the left ventricle and atrium. The patient may complain of dyspnea, orthopnea, paroxysmal dyspnea, cough, hemoptysis, and occasional chest pain. On physical examination one notes tachypnea, pulmonary rales, particularly at the lung bases, and, on occasion, hydrothorax. There is a measurable decrease in pulmonary compliance, a rise in the left atrial, pulmonary arterial and pulmonary venous pressure, and a prolongation of the pulmonary circulation time.

Chronic, severe fatigue is a less dramatic but an almost universal symptom of congestive heart failure. It is often overlooked since it is not easily measured. It is most often expressed as excessive exertional fatigue and is due in large part to inadequate flow of blood to skeletal muscle.

A fall in effective cardiac output stimulates a redistribution of blood to essential areas. The skin responds by vasoconstriction which may cause a secondary elevation of body temperature. The kidney retains salt and water. The liver may not properly inactivate circulating hormones, particularly those leading to retention of fluid. Function of the central nervous system is compromised by inadequate cardiac output, by increased venous pressures and by a fall in arterial pO_2. There may be an elevation of spinal fluid pressure, a decrease in cerebral blood flow, and cerebral edema. Patients frequently demonstrate an inability to concentrate and undergo personality changes; in severe cases coma or psychosis may ensue. Periodic breathing, so-called "Cheyne-Stokes respiration" is at least in part also due to impaired cerebral function.

Dyspnea

Dyspnea, a feeling of need for increased breathing, is the most marked symptom of left ventricular failure. It is characterized by rapid, shallow respiration often punctuated by cough. In most cases the symptom is brought on by exertion, but in severe decompensation, dyspnea and tachypnea may occur at rest. Dyspnea is not restricted to congestive heart failure. It is seen with anemia, obesity, pregnancy, neuromuscular disease, pleural effusion or pneumothorax and as a neurotic symptom. It is almost always present with intrinsic pulmonary disease. Whether seen at rest or after exertion, it is a nonspecific response to an intense respiratory stimulus. Testing the various parameters of pulmonary function may help in differentiating cardiac dyspnea from that due to other causes.

The pathogenesis of cardiac dyspnea is uncertain and probably represents the final expression of many separate afferent stimuli to the respiratory center.

A generalized sympathetic discharge and vasoconstriction accompany onset of failure and cause an increase in venous return to the right side of the heart. In isolated left heart failure a temporary imbalance in output between the two ventricles is thought to occur. The disproportionate output of the uninvolved right ventricle contributes to the increase in left ventricular end diastolic pressure and residual volume associated with failure of that chamber. There is displacement of a significant volume of blood from the systemic to the highly distensible pulmonary reservoir. Eventually the increase in volume causes the pressure in the pulmonary vascular bed to rise. In this manner a pressure gradient of about 8 mm., necessary to insure forward flow between the pulmonary veins and the left ventricle in end diastole, is maintained. These volume readjustments are necessarily transitory. The decrease in cardiac output rapidly reduces venous return and reestablishes the balance in stroke volume between the two ventricles. Pulmonary engorgement persists, however, until left ventricular performance improves.

Pulmonary venous distention reduces the elasticity of the lungs by interposing large inelastic columns of blood between the air-containing portions. The lungs become stiffer, more rigid, and less distensible. Pulmonary compliance—that is, the ratio of change in lung volume to a given change in intra-thoracic or transpulmonary pressure—is consistently decreased. There is a greater resistance to breathing, and it soon becomes impossible to expand the lungs to maximal normal capacity. Inflation and deflation require progressively greater effort. Longstanding pulmonary congestion eventually leads to fibrosis caused partially by continuous phagocytosis of exuded red blood cells; thus the lungs are further indurated by proliferation of connective tissue.

Arterial content of carbon dioxide is reduced in the dyspneic patient, and there is an increase in the alveolar-arterial oxygen gradient. Respiratory rate and minute ventilation are increased; maximum breathing capacity, air velocity index, total lung volume, functional residual capacity and vital capacity are decreased, although timed vital capacity may be normal. The increase in pulmonary blood volume is not solely responsible for the measurable decrease in pulmonary compliance. Cardiomegaly, pleural effusions, and elevation of the diaphragm because of hepatomegaly, ascites or meteorism contribute to a decrease in total lung capacity and help to increase the viscous resistance to breathing.

Dyspnea is proportional to the decrease in vital capacity and to the amount of vital capacity utilized as tidal volume. It is well to remember, however, that dyspnea is a sensation and as such is almost impossible to quantitate. Its expression varies from patient to patient and depends on many factors, not the least of which is the cortical threshold of appreciation. Changes in oxygen saturation, arteriovenous oxygen difference, carbon dioxide content, or hydrogen ion concentration are not in themselves sufficient either in degree or direction to account wholly for this symptom.

Pulmonary congestion induces an intense bombardment of the respiratory center by afferent stimuli arising in the stretch receptors of the pulmonary vascular tree (Churchill-

Cope reflex) and left atrium, in the inflation and deflation receptors of the lungs (Hering-Breuer reflex), and as a chemoreceptor response to tissue anoxia. In the normal subject at exercise or after pulmonary vascular engorgement has been experimentally induced, the center responds by causing an increase in the rate and depth of respiration. When the resting state is resumed or the pulmonary congestion relieved, inhibitory impulses from the stretch receptors of the lungs suppress inspiratory cell activity. In heart failure this response is inadequate and inappropriate, pulmonary congestion is not relieved, and the respiratory center continues to discharge excessively. The decreased compliance of the congested lung prevents an increase in tidal air volume so that respiratory center hyperactivity is expressed largely as an increase in respiratory rate. The pathway by which this activity is appreciated in areas of consciousness as the sensation of dyspnea is not known. The patient may perceive this intense respiratory discharge as an unrelated stimulus which "spills over" into the sensorium.

Orthopnea

Orthopnea is a symptom characterized by the initiation or intensification of respiratory distress when lying down. Defined by Altschule as "dyspnea of recumbency," it is predominantly a symptom of left-sided heart failure usually occurring in the absence of right-sided heart failure. The severity of orthopnea is often decreased by onset of right ventricular decompensation probably because systemic engorgement causes partial relief of pulmonary congestion.

Assumption of the supine or prone position redistributes blood from the lower extremities and dependent parts of the body to the central pulmonary reservoir, venous return is increased, and the diaphragm shifts to a more cephalad position because of the pressure of abdominal viscera. In congestive heart failure these changes are accentuated, tidal volume and vital capacity are decreased, and respiratory rate is increased in contrast to the normal subject who demonstrates a slowing of respiration and an increase in tidal volume when changing from the sitting to the lying position. Recumbency therefore reduces pulmonary compliance to still lower levels. The work of breathing may increase as much as 25 per cent by this additional increase in viscous resistance to lung expansion. Aeration is diminished and the oxygen saturation of arterial blood may fall.

Changes in cerebral blood flow may also play a role in orthopnea. Assumption of the recumbent position intensifies cerebral venous engorgement. Ernstene and Blumgart pointed out that flexing the neck and thus raising the height of medullary centers relative to the atria facilitates venous drainage and relieves orthopnea. These observations have been corroborated by others. An elevation in cerebral venous pressure may be a significant cause of orthopnea—however, only when it occurs in conjunction with some degree of pulmonary engorgement. By raising his head on several pillows the orthopneic patient invariably relieves his symptoms and is able to sleep despite the absence of an improvement either in vital capacity or tidal volume.

Orthopnea does not imply an intermittent or temporary intensification of the degree of myocardial decompensation induced by changes in body position. In left ventricular failure it is a reflection of the patient's inability to sustain the number of physiologic adjustments consequent upon changing from the upright to the lying position.

Cough, Cardiac Asthma and Paroxysmal Nocturnal Dyspnea

Cough, often productive of a frothy pink sputum, is a prominent symptom of left ventricular failure. It may be severe, frequently intensifies the degree of dyspnea and can precipitate attacks of cardiac asthma. Its etiology is in part traceable to the anatomic relationship of the bronchial and pulmonary vasculature. The bronchial circulation drains into the pulmonary system, and a flow gradient cannot be maintained unless bronchial venous pressure exceeds that of the pulmonary veins. Pulmonary hypertension is quickly reflected back into the bronchial vasculature distending these vessels and raising their capillary hydrostatic pressure. Bronchial mucous membranes rapidly become congested and edematous and produce an increased amount of viscid mucus which exudes into the tracheobronchial tree. Coughing is stimulated by excessive secretions but is unable to clear large accumulations of mucus. Its effects are blunted by a decrease in pulmonary compliance and by elevation of the diaphragms. Airway resistance is markedly increased as the luminal cross section is encroached upon by the swollen mucosa and because of reflex bronchospasm. On physical examination ronchi, wheezing respiration and rales at the lung bases are heard. The examiner may find that the differential diagnosis between cardiac asthma and allergic bronchial asthma is difficult but very important in determining his therapeutic approach. Morphine has proved extremely effective in the treatment of severe cardiac asthma and epinephrine in treating allergic bronchial asthma. They are obviously not interchangeable agents and depend upon entirely different mechanisms to provide relief. When administered for the wrong type of paroxysmal asthma their secondary effects may prove fatal.

A vicious circle of events tends to prolong attacks of cardiac asthma. Paroxysmal coughing requires an excessive muscular effort, one that increases the load on the left ventricle, increases the degree of failure and thus intensifies pulmonary congestion.

An enlarged left atrium due to mitral valvular disease or the grossly dilated heart and pulmonary artery of severe congestive heart failure may compress the left recurrent laryngeal nerve, causing paralysis of the left vocal cord, chronic hoarseness and cough.

Paroxysmal Nocturnal Dyspnea

A specific type of cardiac asthma often occurs one or two hours after the patient has fallen asleep. This is a particularly frightening symptom. The patient awakens with a sensation of suffocation, his dyspnea markedly intensified and cough and wheezing prominent. He rarely obtains relief by merely sitting up in bed but sits at the edge of the bed or moves to a chair before an open window. In both cases his feet are usually dangling or planted on the floor. These attacks may occur as the patient slips from his pillows, which are almost universally propped up upon retiring so as to maintain him in an orthopneic position. Perhaps attacks are precipitated by a cardiovascular response to the frightening dreams to which such patients seem especially prone.

Although these factors undoubtedly play some role, most investigators agree that the most prominent cause of this delayed type of paroxysmal dyspnea and cardiac asthma relates to changes in blood volume and distribution. When the body is positioned in a horizontal plane, there is a gradual increase in total blood volume. In congestive heart failure, this increase is magnified. The distended veins of the lower extremities tend to collapse and blood is redistributed to the trunk. The fall in hydrostatic fluid pressure, no longer supported by gravity, permits the slow resorption of edema fluid into the vascular space from previously dependent tissues. The increase in intravascular volume is appreciable and may reach the quantitative equivalent of 10 to 15 per cent of the total plasma volume. It causes an increase in venous return to the right ventricle and in this way intensifies the degree of pulmonary congestion.

When the patient assumes a static sitting position with his feet dangling, he seems to be making good physiologic sense. Such body orientation tends to reverse these volume changes and blood is once again sequestered in the extensive venous network of the lower extremities. Lagerlof studied subjects on a tilt table and found that a change from the vertical to the horizontal position will decrease venous return and lower pulmonary blood volume and pressure.

During sleep, the respiratory center is less sensitive and respiratory rate falls. Since tidal volume is already reduced by pulmonary congestion, hypercapnia and/or anoxia may be gradually established. Another theory suggests that when this new, elevated respiratory threshold is reached by the gradual change in pO_2 and pCO_2 there is an intense stimulus and the patient awakens to a sensation of marked dyspnea. The decrease in arterial oxygen saturation permitted by changes in center sensitivity during sleep may be a prime factor in the etiology of the terrifying dreams mentioned earlier.

Acute Pulmonary Edema

Acute pulmonary edema is a symptom complex characterized by the paroxysmal occurrence of severe dyspnea, cardiac asthma and cough. The cough is characteristically productive of a pink, frothy, protein-rich sputum, similar in composition to inflammatory effusions. The patient is extremely anxious, he may be cyanotic and his skin may be cold and sweaty. In severe cases he may literally drown in the enormous amounts of foam which pour out of his respiratory tract. Although attacks are more frequent at night, they may occur at any time. On physical examination, ronchi and wheezing respiration are intense. Both fine and coarse inspiratory rales are heard throughout both lung fields. When precipitated by occlusion of a large coronary vessel, the pulse is often rapid and thready and the blood pressure quickly drops to shock-like levels. When due to other causes, the pulse is frequently full and the blood pressure normal or elevated.

If such attacks are superimposed on the clinical states described earlier (cardiac asthma), they usually signify an increase in the severity of chronic congestive heart failure and are produced by similar mechanisms. They differ from other pulmonary indications of left ventricular failure not only by their intensity and associated physical findings but also by the fact that attacks may occur de novo as the first indication of severe left ventricular decompensation. The precipitating event may be a sudden marked elevation of systemic blood pressure, as seen with malignant hypertension, pheochromocytoma, or glomerulonephritis. In other cases attacks follow acute myocardial infarction, acute rheumatic carditis, severe coarctation of the aorta, acute and subacute bacterial endocarditis, aortic stenosis or severe aortic insufficiency, particularly that caused by leutic heart disease or after excessive transfusions of blood or intravenous fluids into patients whose hearts are in borderline compensation.

It must be borne in mind, however, that acute pulmonary edema is not synonymous with severe left ventricular failure and indeed may occur in the total absence of intrinsic heart disease. As example of the latter, one may cite the occurrence of pulmonary edema with mitral stenosis, in some cases of chronic cor pulmonale and in the uninvolved portions of a lung otherwise stressed by pulmonary embolism. Noncardiac cases of pulmonary edema are seen with disease of the brain (trauma to the skull, tumor, subarachnoid hemorrhage, cerebrovascular accidents, inflammatory disease), with severe pulmonary disease (pneumonia, respiratory obstruction, inhalation of toxic gases, respiratory burns, trauma to the chest), with serum sickness and after ingestion or injection of many chemical poisons.

Accumulation of extravascular interstitial tissue fluid is quantitatively determined by a balance between several forces, not the least of which is the mechanical resistance to stretch of the tissues themselves (see Edema). The unique construction of the lung offers little mechanical resistance to leakage of fluid from capillary to alveolus. The maintenance of a dry lung must depend upon the integrity of the pulmonary capillary membrane and a very low hydrostatic pressure so that non-protein-containing fluid may be resorbed from alveolus to capillary. There is also an especially competent lymphatic network which is able to rapidly clear non-protein- and protein-containing transudates from interstitial tissue and alveoli. The capacity of the lymphatic system to perform this function normally far exceeds the demands made

upon it and can maintain the lung in a dry state despite great increases in the rate of capillary filtration. Pulmonary edema is caused by an imbalance between these forces so that the volume of transudate exceeds pulmonary vascular absorptive capacity.

Cases of noncardiac pulmonary edema are usually due to severe damage to the capillary endothelium. Anoxia and superimposed neurogenic reflex mechanisms also increase capillary permeability and contribute to flooding of the lungs. It is thought that pulmonary edema associated with disease of the central nervous system is caused by reflex stimulation of the sympathetic nervous system leading to a sudden, marked increase in peripheral resistance. As a result, increased resistance to left ventricular outflow accompanies a shift of blood volume from the periphery to the lungs. Reflex mechanisms may also favor pulmonary vasodilatation and increased capillary permeability. The resultant tendency toward pulmonary flooding is accentuated by the presence of preexisting left ventricular strain or incipient heart failure from other causes.

In severe left ventricular failure, whether it be an acute episode caused by a sudden coronary occlusion or hypertensive insult, or accentuation of failure due to the superimposition of an additional load on a ventricle already showing signs of decompensation, *all* the factors necessary to upset pulmonary fluid balance occur simultaneously. If the left ventricular failure is of a chronic nature, the already elevated pulmonary capillary pressure is raised to still higher levels by the increased load which initiates the attack of pulmonary edema. Because of the number of mechanisms involved there is only a general correlation between the absolute capillary pressure attained and the onset of pulmonary edema. Levels always exceed the oncotic pressure of blood and may vary from 25 to 40 mm. Hg. Unfortunately, the factors which favor increased transudation are not balanced by an adequate increase in reabsorption. To the contrary, although lymphatic flow is increased, its maximal capacity is quite seriously impaired by the same factors that favor transudation. The elevation of systemic venous pressure mechanically decreases emptying of the main lymphatic channels by increasing the resistance at the thoracic duct and at other venolymphatic junctions. With progression of the attack, arterial pO_2 falls and the slight initial increase in permeability due to dilatation alone is markedly aggravated. Edema fluid, containing 2 to 4 per cent protein, passes from the capillaries into the alveolar septa and into the alveoli themselves. Gas exchange is impeded by increased airway resistance, by thickening of alveolar walls due to interstitial edema and by actual flooding of alveoli and bronchioles by fluid and foam. Foaming is a particulary pernicious consequence of pulmonary edema and is a major cause of the collapse and obstruction of gas exchange units. The foam is rich in surface-active material derived from and leading to a decrease in pulmonary surfactant. Pulmonary edema foam bubbles are extremely stable and not only lead to premature alveolar closure but may occlude large airways and cause extensive atelectasis. The perfused, nonventilated areas of lung serve as venoarterial shunts and intensify the degree of arterial oxygen desaturation caused by impaired gas exchange. Tidal volume is further reduced by these atelectatic areas, and in more severe cases deep cyanosis, respiratory acidosis, coma and death may ensue unless vigorous treatment is immediately begun.

Cheyne-Stokes Breathing

The true pathogenesis of Cheyne-Stokes respiration, sometimes called periodic breathing, is not entirely clear. Clinically this symptom is characterized by a gradual increase in respiratory rate and depth which extends over 30 to 40 respiratory cycles and progresses from shallow, barely perceptible respiratory movements to deep, full, hyperpneic breathing, At the peak of this respiratory crescendo the cycle is reversed, and there is a graded decrease in depth often followed by a brief period of apnea. On occasion, apnea may be prolonged for as long as 20 to 30 seconds. Cheyne-Stokes respiration undoubtedly bears some etiologic relationship to the depression of respiratory center sensitivity discussed previously and may be precipitated in patients with left ventricular failure, by the injudicious administration of sedatives and by other central nervous system depressants. As might be expected, these episodes are most frequently nocturnal and seem to be triggered by the decreased sensitivity of the respiratory center during sleep. If they occur during waking hours, the patient is rarely aware of their cyclic nature and does not differentiate this state from his awareness of coincident dyspnea. The hyperpnea which occurs during the crescendo phase blows off large amounts of carbon dioxide and produces a drop in arterial pCO_2. At this moment arterial oxygen saturation may be normal. The apneic period

which follows is probably related to the absence of sufficient stimulus to drive the already depressed respiratory center. If it is prolonged sufficiently, it leads to hypoxemia and hypercapnia. Low oxygen tensions stimulate carotid body chemoreceptors and respiration is again initiated and intensified by hypercapnia. This sequence of events soon leads to a recurrence of hyperpnia and the cycle is repeated. The time lag noted between changes in blood gases and the onset of apnea or hyperpnea may be in part due to a delay in the circulation of blood from lungs to brain.

Signs of Left Ventricular Failure

A familiarity with the pathologic physiology of congestive failure should enable the clinician to predict most of the signs found on physical examination. Many of the respiratory signs have already been discussed. Pulmonary rales, often characterized as fine or crepitant, are usually heard in showers just prior to the peak of inspiration and are not cleared by coughing. They are the result of air flow through the secretions or exudate in the terminal bronchioles or alveoli. In the early stages of failure they may be heard only at the lung bases, posteriorly. In advanced failure, or during pulmonary edema, these sounds are scattered throughout both lung fields. Coarse rales, wheezing respiration and ronchi reflect edematous changes, and excess mucus accumulation in the trachea and bronchi. In rare cases, usually those in which fluid films and foam have obstructed bronchioles and caused atelectasis of pulmonary lobules and a marked reduction in vital capacity, there may be few audible rales despite other evidence of left ventricular failure.

Hydrothorax or pleural effusion is rarely seen in isolated right heart failure, occurs frequently in left ventricular failure and is most commonly seen with biventricular failure. It is due to the accumulation of a high protein-containing fluid in the pleural cavity. The mechanism of this accumulation is obscure and probably depends upon several factors, including the increase in extracellular fluid volume brought about by renal retention of salt and water, interference with adequate venous drainage of the pleura into the superior vena cava and pulmonary veins by elevation of the venous pressures in these systems, and by a similar depression of lymphatic drainage (by mechanisms already discussed). The high protein content of this fluid may be caused by inadequate lymphatic drainage or by an increase in capillary permeability associated with pleural irritation. The high cytologic counts of the fluid would tend to support the latter possibility. The greater incidence of right-sided (as opposed to left-sided) hydrothorax is unexplained. Such accumulations decrease pulmonary expansion by mechanically occupying space within the thorax and by causing atelectasis. The weight of the fluid also causes diaphragmatic compression and flattening, limiting its excursion and contributing to inefficient respiration.

The heart is enlarged to percussion, and when aortic or mitral valvular insufficiency is present there is a prominent ventricular heave. The component of the second heart sound produced by pulmonary valve closure is intensified by pulmonary hypertension and may be louder than that due to aortic valve closure. In early or mild failure there is a modest sinus tachycardia. In more advanced decompensation, heart rate may be very rapid and one may note premature contractions, arrhythmias, gallop rhythm or pulsus alternans. The latter two findings provide especially valid evidence of a severe impairment in contractility. A gallop rhythm is common in untreated or inadequately treated failure and is a grave prognostic sign if it persists despite optimal therapy. This sign consists of a pathologic triple rhythm, heard in diastole. It is most clearly audible when the bell of the stethoscope is placed over the apex of the heart with the patient lying on his left side. It is rarely evident in the absence of tachycardia.

The so-called *protodiastolic* or *ventricular gallop* is identical in timing with the physiologic third heart sound, and is heard about 0.14 second after the second heart sound. It is low pitched and corresponds temporally to the descent of the "v" wave of the jugular venous pulse and to the summit of the rapid filling wave of the apex cardiogram. The mechanism of its production is still incompletely understood. It is most probably caused by the vibrations set up in the stiffened left ventricular wall (its compliance reduced by dilatation) by rapid filling under an increased head of pulmonary pressure. The sound persists despite atrial fibrillation.

A *presystolic* or *atrial gallop* may also be heard in congestive heart failure, although less frequently than the ventricular gallop. It is the pathologic equivalent of the fourth heart sound and corresponds in timing to the inscription of the peak of the "a" wave of the apex cardiogram. This presystolic sound is most probably an intensification of the usually inaudible sound of atrial systole. It is brought about by an increased resistance to ventricular filling, by an increase in atrial pressure or by atrial dilatation or hypertrophy. It is heard at the apex but is often loudest in the third or fourth intercostal space to the right or left of the sternum. Atrial gallop is most common when failure is associated with hypertension, myocardial infarction, anemia, large shunts or myocarditis. Its atrial origin is supported by the fact that it disappears with the onset of atrial fibrillation and is best heard when the P-R interval of the electrocardiogram is prolonged.

Most clinicians agree that the so-called "summation" gallop is the most common triple rhythm of congestive heart failure. The third sound of summation gallop is a composite which results from the almost simultaneous production of the protodiastolic and presystolic gallop. It occurs when the diastolic period is markedly shortened by a rapid rate and when the P-R interval is relatively prolonged. Under these conditions ventricular filling and atrial systole may be almost simultaneous. When the heart rate is slowed by carotid sinus stimulation, the two components of this sound can be separated and identified. Whatever the type, the pathologic sound is a product of both dilatation and increased filling pressure and can sometimes be eliminated by phlebotomy, effective treatment of congestive failure or maneuvers which tend to decrease circulating blood volume.

MANIFESTATIONS OF RIGHT-SIDED HEART FAILURE

Failure of the right ventricle may occur as an isolated phenomenon. This is a relatively infrequent finding and is usually due to an excessive pressure load induced by an increase in pulmonary vascular resistance. More commonly, right ventricular failure occurs in association with or is secondary to left ventricular failure. The most prominent manifestations of right ventricular failure are expressed by the signs of intense, generalized, systemic, venous engorgement rather than by subjective symptoms so prominent in left ventricular failure. Central venous pressure is elevated, venous reservoirs are congested (liver, spleen, splanchnic bed, peripheral veins) and there is an accumulation of low protein fluid in the interstitial spaces of all body tissue, but most evident in dependent subcutaneous areas (edema). Serous effusions into pleural and peritoneal spaces may also occur.

Blood Volume

Early reports of a universal elevation in total blood volume with congestive heart failure have been modified due to recent studies with P^{32}, Cr^{51} labeled red blood cells and I^{131} labeled albumin. Technical difficulties, including problems presented by the need for adequate mixing, leakage of dye or radioactive tracer outside the vascular tree and methods of hematocrit calculation, may interfere with accurate measurements. Current data show that blood volume may be normal or decreased in early left-sided failure but is almost always elevated in chronic failure of either or both ventricles. The increase in plasma volume is due in great measure to renal retention of salt and water. Red cell volume increases as a result of enhancement of erythropoietic activity, demonstrated by erythroid hyperplasia in bone marrow studies and by a low grade reticulocytosis and normoblastemia in the peripheral blood. With cardiac compensation the elevated plasma volume may decrease 10 to 20 per cent and the red cell volume 5 to 15 per cent. Although an elevated blood volume is uniformly associated with an increase in venous pressure above 15 cm. of water, there is only a rough correlation between the degree of expansion of blood volume and the elevation of venous pressure.

The mechanism by which the elevated blood volume is maintained is not completely understood. It might be expected that the continual loss of intravascular fluid into tissue edema and into serous cavities would cause a decrease rather than an increase in blood volume. Landis suggested that these patients undergo repeated transient elevations in venous pressure due to injudicious activity which increases venous return to a ventricle unable to respond by an increase in filling volume or stroke output. This causes a transfer or trapping of blood in a distended venous system, an increase in hydrostatic pressure and increased filtration of fluid into tissue spaces, particularly those with weak supporting tissues, i.e., the liver, intestines, lungs, and subcutaneous tissue. The result is an intermittent reduction in effective circulating blood volume which in turn stimulates a compensatory vasoconstriction by mechanisms already discussed (the same response may occur after sudden blood loss or with prolonged standing). This undifferentiated signal stimulates the kidney to decrease excretion of salt and water and also leads to overproduction of erythrocytes and plasma proteins.

Edema

Starling originally outlined the general mechanisms which govern the exchange of fluid between the vascular and interstitial spaces. Since his time it has been found that the factors of greatest importance in governing the accumulation of tissue edema include the heart, vascular system and the composition of the fluid it contains, the adrenal cortex, kidney and hypothalamic-posterior hypophyseal axis. These systems serve to regulate the environment whereby the normal balance between capillary (hydrostatic) blood pressure which tends to drive fluid out of the vascular compartment and the colloid osmotic (oncotic) pressure which tends to draw fluid into this compartment is maintained. They are so well integrated that it has proved extremely difficult to produce tissue edema experimentally in the normal subject. During congestive heart failure elevation of pressure at the venous end of the capillary may be inordinate and fluid may enter the interstitial space faster than it can be removed. This elevation in capillary pressure is not necessarily uniform and indeed may be quite localized. It is a significant factor in determining the distribution of capillary fluid loss and is positional to some degree since its magnitude is subject to the effects of· gravity. Interstitial osmotic and hydrostatic pressure also play an important role in the regulation of fluid movement, particularly in terms of its tissue distribution. Thus, edema fluid will accumulate at any site at which capillary hydrostatic pressure has risen high enough to exceed the reabsorptive capacity of the plasma osmotic pressure and of the lymphatic system.

The limit of edema formation is determined by a balance between the height of the capillary pressure and the resistance of the interstitial tissue to stretch, that is, the elasticity of the supporting connective tissues and skin. On rare occasions edema accumulation may be so severe as to cause poorly nourished skin to rupture and permit direct fluid leakage. Consideration of these factors helps to explain why edema associated with the fluid retention caused by primary renal disease, or that precipitated when normal subjects are given excessive amounts of salt and water, shows a diffuse distribution governed by local capillary and tissue pressures. During left ventricular failure, the primary area of high capillary and low tissue pressure is the lung. Pressures rise to even higher levels when these patients are recumbent and the lungs may be flooded by fluid transudation. With right-sided or biventricular failure the distribution of cutaneous edema tends to be determined by gravity. In the upright position fluid accumulates in dependent areas, usually in the lower extremities. With recumbency much of this fluid is slowly resorbed and redistributed to new dependent areas, usually the sacral region and the genitalia, the peritoneum, and, on occasion, the lungs.

Starling also commented on the important role played by lymph transport in the prevention of edema formation. Indeed, these channels have recently been shown to be extremely efficient in draining fluid, and can compensate completely for a *moderate* increase in the rate of capillary transudation. They also provide a means of reducing the colloid osmotic pressure of interstitial fluid since they permit transport of protein molecules which may escape through dilated, more permeable capillary walls. During frank right or biventricular failure, lymphatic compensation is no longer adequate, venous pressure rises and the markedly distensible thin walled lymph channels are overloaded as resistance at the venolymphatic junction rises. There may be a two- to fourfold increase in the diameter of the thoracic duct and a potential rate of lymph flow that is three to twelve times greater than normal. When the thoracic duct is experimentally cannulated and vented to the exterior, a rapid flow of lymph is re-established and there follows a decrease in venous pressure and in signs of circulatory congestion.

The osmotic pressure of the plasma is usually normal or slightly lowered in congestive failure, and at best plays a minor role in the production of edema. When plasma protein is more markedly decreased, the resultant fall in osmotic pressure would, of course, contribute to the decrease in reabsorption of fluid into the venous capillaries and increase any tendency to edema formation. In contrast to the protein content of serous effusions, edema fluid contains less than 0.5 per cent protein and is an insignificant factor in the perpetuation of tissue fluid accumulations.

Enlargement of the Liver

Hepatomegaly is a constant finding in chronic congestive heart failure and it may be massive, depending upon the degree and duration of elevation of the venous pressure. Pathologically, this is known as chronic passive congestion of the liver and is usually described grossly as "nutmeg liver." Distention of the central vein and its neighboring capillaries may be so pronounced as to produce flattening of the liver cells, atrophy or fatty degeneration, and, if longstanding, may be followed by necrosis, focal regeneration and fibrotic repair (cardiac cirrhosis). Similar changes have been produced by experimental obstruction of the vena cava, the sequence and degree of change depending upon the degree and duration of the obstruction. Venous pressures in the hepatic vein have been measured in man by passage of a catheter into this system via the saphenous vein and right atrium. Such studies have shown that the venous pressure in right-sided heart failure is elevated in the hepatic vein and is roughly of the same magnitude as that observed in the antecubital vein.

Rapid engorgement of the liver may lead to upper abdominal pain, which is believed to result from sudden stretching of the liver capsule and may rarely be the presenting complaint given by a patient with congestive heart failure. Manual pressure in the right upper quadrant over an engorged liver will result in a further rise in peripheral venous pressure, often detectable clinically by increased filling of the cervical veins (hepatojugular reflex).

Ascites

Effusion of fluid into the peritoneal cavity is not an uncommon occurrence in right-sided heart failure and is probably caused by an elevation of portal venous pressure, although true measurements of portal venous pressure during congestive heart failure have not been reported.

Presumably, elevation of the hepatic venous pressure is transmitted to the portal vein, since all the structures of the liver are contained in the same relatively inelastic capsule, and variations in pressure (in the absence of fibrotic changes) should be relatively uniform. It has long been known that the portal pressure is elevated in cirrhosis and that ascites is consequent to this elevation. The accumulation of ascites thus appears to require an increase in hepatic and portal venous pressure and an increase in extracellular fluid. This combination of factors causes leakage of high protein fluid in quantities great enough to exceed the capacity of centripetal lymph drainage. Ascitic fluid forms in droplets on the surface of the liver and drains down into the peritoneal cavity where it may assume some of the characteristics of an obligatory extracellular fluid dead space.

Hydrothorax and hydropericardium frequently accompany ascites and peripheral edema in severe congestive heart failure.

Cyanosis

Cyanosis is relatively uncommon in uncomplicated chronic congestive heart failure but when present is manifested by a faint reddish-blue tint usually confined to the ear lobes, lips and fingernails. According to Harrison, this type of cyanosis is not uniformly associated with a decrease in the oxygenation of either the arterial or the venous blood and is presumably caused by an increase in both the number and volume of the venous capillaries, a result of increased systemic venous pressure. The same type of cyanosis may be produced without any decrease in oxygen saturation when a blood pressure cuff is inflated to 60 mm. of mercury. Furthermore, under this stimulus the increase in the number and the degree of dilatation of the capillaries is comparable to that seen in chronic right-sided heart failure. In other words, the normal color of the venous blood imparts a "cyanotic" hue to the skin.

The deep purplish cyanosis commonly seen in congenital heart disease or chronic pulmonary disease, however, is almost entirely due to diminished oxygen saturation of the arterial and venous blood caused by physiologic or anatomic venoarterial shunts. Cyanosis appears when the concentration of reduced hemoglobin is 5 gm. per cent or greater. The greatest degree of desaturation is usually present in the lungs (pulmonary artery). The administration of oxygen often dramatically relieves such cyanosis when it is caused by pulmonary diseases alone.

If the cardiac output is suddenly reduced, as in shock or in acute cardiac failure consequent to myocardial infarction, there is a prompt decrease in the oxygen saturation of the venous blood due to increased tissue extraction and a widening of the arteriovenous oxygen difference. This results in an ashen-gray type of cyanosis.

Thus, cyanosis in heart disease may be due to an increase in the venous pressure with capillary distention, to deficient oxygenation in the lungs or to increased concentrations of reduced oxyhemoglobin in the capillaries. One or a combination of these factors may be the cause of cyanosis in any patient.

Venous congestion may cause splenomegaly, as well as the renal, gastrointestinal and central nervous system symptoms already discussed.

Treatment of Congestive Heart Failure

In valvular heart disease, recent advances in surgical procedures have made it possible, in many cases, to repair or eliminate inciting factors and definitively treat increasing numbers of patients. In other types, treatment of the provocative states noted previously may result in cure without use of specific cardiotonic agents. For the vast majority, however, and regardless of etiology, the rationale for the treatment of congestive heart failure should be found in the pathophysiology described earlier.

The aim of therapy is to reduce the work of the heart and whenever possible to eliminate those factors that increase the demand load. The reduction in load factors is combined with the use of drugs that increase mechanical efficiency, decrease the energy costs of contraction and improve contractility. The increase in stroke volume and cardiac output facilitates delivery of oxygen to the tissues and, when combined with a decrease in load factors, reduces venous pressure and the symptoms and signs of congestion. Rest, both physical and emotional, is the most effective way of reducing cardiac load. Measures should be instituted to lessen both pulmonary and systemic hypertension when they exist. A decrease in heart rate will prolong diastole and decrease cardiac tension per unit time, a factor of major significance in defining the work of the heart and one that may also be decreased by a reduction in the mean radius of the dilated heart. The slower, smaller, more efficient heart can produce a relative increase in stroke volume and cardiac output at a much lower oxygen cost. Reduction in heart size and in pulmonary congestion also helps to alleviate hypermetabolism in congestive failure. Elevation of pulmonary and systemic venous pressure causes most of the symptoms of congestive failure and is responsible for volume loading. Improvement in cardiac function by use of

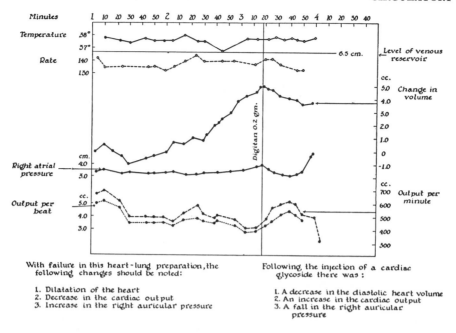

With failure in this heart-lung preparation, the following changes should be noted:

1. Dilatation of the heart
2. Decrease in the cardiac output
3. Increase in the right auricular pressure

Following the injection of a cardiac glycoside there was :

1. A decrease in the diastolic heart volume
2. An increase in the cardiac output
3. A fall in the right auricular pressure

After Cohn and Steele

Figure 20–7.

cardiotonic drugs will often in itself initiate diuresis, which may be enhanced by maintaining the patient on a low sodium diet and by use of diuretics to lower circulating blood volume and venous return. Paracentesis, thoracentesis and the application of Southey tubes will rapidly reduce massive accumulations of fluid in body cavities and extremities.

In the management of congestive heart failure digitalis is unquestionably the drug of choice. The genus Digitalis is not unique in containing cardiotonic glycosides, and such agents have been purified from *Strophanthus gratus* (the major ingredient of an African arrow poison), which yields ouabain, and from other plants. The precise mechanism of digitalis action is unknown but its target organs include the kidneys, central nervous system and skeletal muscle as well as its primary site of action, the cardiovascular system. It decreases systemic vascular resistance, venous tone and venous pressure. The diuresis that follows results not only from an improvement in cardiac function but also from a direct action on renal ion transport causing a profound natriuresis and chloruresis. It is the only inotropic agent in common use which will improve the efficiency of the failing heart, i.e., increase contractility without increasing oxygen consumption and enhance the ability of the contractile proteins to convert chemical energy to mechanical work. Al-

though the position of the heart on the Starling curve is not altered, the entire ventricular function curve is shifted to the left, cardiac output is improved and there is a decrease in the size of the dilated failing heart. Its chronotropic action in slowing heart rate is both a reflex response to its positive inotropic activity and due to a direct depression of AV conduction.

Figure 20–7 illustrates the response to digitalis in the heart-lung preparation of Starling after failure has occurred. Heart rate, right atrial pressure and cardiac output were monitored. Note the decrease in diastolic volume, the increase in cardiac output and the fall in right atrial pressure after injection of the digitalis glycoside. Figure 20–8 shows the effects of digitalis on cardiac output, cardiac size and ventricular rate during artificial atrial fibrillation.

Table 20–2 shows the trend of reaction in 10 patients with severe cardiac failure and normal sinus rhythm, after 2 to 8 days bedrest. Eight cc. (1.6 mg.) of lanatoside C was given intravenously and the measurements were taken at intervals of 5 to 10 minutes. A second kymogram was taken 30 minutes to 2 hours later, depending upon the patient's response. The diastolic heart volume usually decreased and cardiac output rose slightly; venous pressure decreased, and pulse pressure increased. The work performance of the heart

EFFECT of GIVING DIGITALIS on CARDIAC OUTPUT, CARDIAC SIZE VENTRICULAR RATE, DURING ARTIFICIAL ATRIAL FIBRILLATION

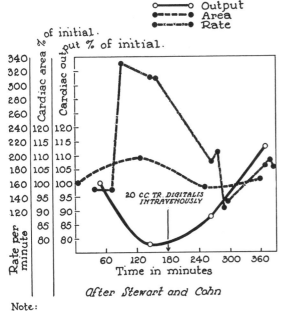

After Stewart and Cohn

Note:
1. The slowing of the heart rate
2. The decrease in the heart size
3. The increase in the output of the heart

Figure 20–8.

increased, whereas the diastolic heart volume diminished slightly indicating a corresponding improvement in mechanical efficiency.

The response of the failing human heart to the administration of a cardiac glycoside is comparable to that seen in a heart-lung preparation. The data of the teleroentgeno-kymogram are analogous to those of cardi-ometer tracings of the heart-lung prepara-tion, for both measure changes in systolic and diastolic heart volume. Measurements of venous and arterial pressure in man are com-parable to those of right atrial and aortic pressures in the heart-lung preparation.

Figure 20–9 shows the changes in the roent-genokymogram and Figure 20–10 the im-provement of a patient as manifested by changes in the blood pressure, heart rate, circulation time, vital capacity, venous pres-sure, diastolic heart volume, stroke output, cardiac output per minute, heart work in kilo-gram-meters per minute and percentage in-crease in mechanical efficiency.

In three of the patients studied minute out-put was greater at the height of congestive failure than it was 3 to 6 weeks later when these patients were completely compensated, although an immediate increase in cardiac output had been noted 2 hours after the in-travenous injection of the cardiac glycoside. Two of these patients were restudied re-spectively 3 and 13 months later while fully compensated. In one, cardiac output was slightly elevated, but in the other it had de-creased to approximately the level observed before the administration of the cardiac gly-coside. However, in both patients the diastolic heart volume was 300 cc. less than at the time of the first, or control, kymogram.

These observations suggest that the signifi-cant circulatory changes initiating the onset or remission of congestive heart failure can be observed only during transition from a state of compensation to a state of failure of the circulation. That such a transition may oc-cur with relative rapidity is suggested by the observations just discussed. In other words, small changes in cardiac output occurring over a relatively short period may result in rapid disappearance of congestive phenomena or, conversely, in their rapid appearance.

Earlier we discussed the mechanisms by

TABLE 20–2. AVERAGES OF THE CIRCULATORY MEASUREMENTS MADE ON 10 PATIENTS BEFORE THE INTRAVENOUS INJECTION OF LANATOSIDE C, 2 HOURS AFTER INJECTION AND, IN 7 CASES, AT THE TIME OF DISCHARGE. TWO PATIENTS WERE RESTUDIED 3 AND 13 MONTHS, RESPECTIVELY, AFTER THE INTRAVENOUS INJECTION OF LANATOSIDE C.

Time	Pulse Pressure	Circulation Time	Venous Pressure	Diastolic Heart Vol. (cc.)	Stroke Output	Minute Vol.	Work in Gm. Meters per Minute	% Increase in Mechanical Efficiency	Number of Cases
Before lanatoside C	45.2	34.0	20.3	1021	44.4	4.2	6453		10
½–2 hours after lanatoside C	73.3*	26.6*	15.0*	986	54.6	5.0	8518*	22	10
At discharge	76.2*	30.0*	6.2*	755.5*	55.8	4.3	6990	25	7
3–13 months later	73.0	21.05	6.5	691	58.2	4.8	8255	30	2

* Statistically significant changes.

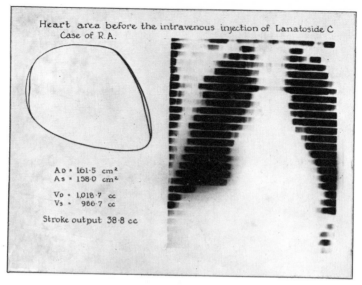

A

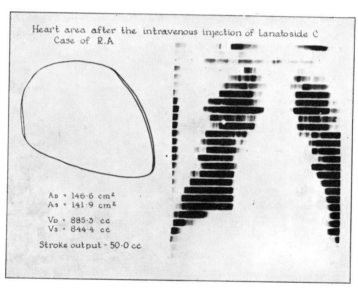

B

Figure 20–9. Teleroentgenokymogram and derived systolic and diastolic tracings obtained from a patient. *A*, Before the intravenous injection of lanatoside C. *B*, Thirty minutes after the intravenous injection of lanatoside C. *C* (see facing page), Nineteen days after the intravenous injection of lanatoside C.

The cardiac output and diastolic heart volume were determined by the method of Keys and Friedell, where the volume = 0.64 × A1.45, stroke output = 1.45ΔV, when Δ = change, V = volume, A = heart area.

Key
A_D = diastolic heart area
A_S = systolic heart area
V_D = diastolic heart volume
V_S = systolic heart volume

which a decrease in cardiac output and *effective* circulating blood volume, as well as a shift of blood to the venous reservoirs, initiates an inappropriate afferent baroreceptor response from receptors located in the ar-terial wall. The response, similar to that occurring after hemorrhage or any other cause of a *true* decrease in total blood volume, is governed by renal retention of salt and water. Normal feedback controls do not effectively

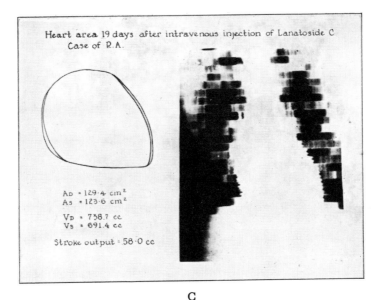

C

Figure 20–9 (*Continued*).

terminate such retention since salt and water leak from the intravascular to the extravascular compartment, cardiac output is not restored, and effective circulating blood volume remains depressed. Diuretic agents may be used to reduce these accumulations of edema fluid in the interstitial spaces, and their use will help to reduce left ventricular volume and improve cardiac efficiency. There is little true increase in cardiac output unless digitalis is administered or the load factor on the heart is reduced. Satisfactory diuresis relieves congestion and eliminates many of the most bothersome symptoms of congestive heart failure. As the rigidity of the lungs decreases there is a corresponding lessening of dyspnea, reflex tachypnea, and orthopnea; gas exchange and tissue oxygenation are improved. The fall in venous and capillary pressure permits more efficient lymphatic drainage of edema fluid; gastrointestinal and hepatic function is improved, and the appetite is increased.

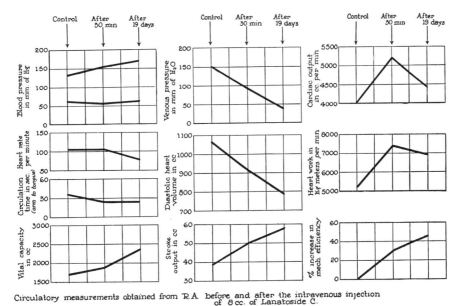

Figure 20–10. Circulatory measurements obtained from the patient noted in Figure 20–9, before and after the intravenous injection of 8 cc. of lanatoside C.

The term *diuretic* may be a misnomer in the context in which we use it. We must aim not only to increase urinary flow, which may be accomplished without loss of edema fluid, but to increase the net loss of sodium (natriuresis) by inhibiting the reabsorption of sodium from the tubular lumen. With effective osmoreceptors, such solute loss will induce water loss to restore osmotic pressure to normal and cause a decrease in extracellular fluid volume. Some patients in advanced stages of failure may prove highly resistant to the usual diuretic techniques. Osmoreceptor function is disturbed, there is increased excretion of antidiuretic hormone, and a state of hyponatremia may develop.

Most sodium is reabsorbed isosmotically in the proximal tubule; the remainder may be reabsorbed against an ionic gradient in the loop of Henle and in the distal segment. At present there is disagreement on the site of action of the more commonly used agents and on their biochemical activities. Fortunately such knowledge is not essential to the effective use of these drugs.

With the exception of drugs whose action is related to inhibition of aldosterone, all the agents in common use may induce varying degrees of hypokalemia by mechanisms intrinsic to their mode of action. Sodium is normally reabsorbed as sodium chloride or exchanged for hydrogen (made available by the hydration of CO_2 under the enzymatic control of carbonic anhydrase) by substitution of the buffer pairs in the urine or by exchange for ammonium ion. Almost all potassium is secreted in the distal tubule. Sodium ions reaching this site may be exchanged for potassium, and indeed this is the principal mechanisms for potassium excretion. Normally little sodium reaches the distal portions of the tubular system. When diuretics are administered, however, more proximal reabsorption is inhibited, an increased amount of sodium is delivered for exchange, and potassium excretion is enhanced. Much of the potassium is excreted with chloride ion (ammonium also accounts for chloride loss) and, as a result, the excretion of chloride commonly exceeds that of sodium.

The organic mercurials (meralluride, mercaptomerin, mersalyl) are powerful inhibitors of sulfhydryl-containing enzymes and liberate ionic mercury in the renal cortex. Both functions may play a part in their mode of action. Sodium reabsorption may be inhibited in both the proximal and distal tubular segments. Despite a direct inhibitory ef-

fect on potassium secretion by mercurials, excretion of this ion may be increased by the mechanisms described before. Loss of chloride in excess of sodium may complicate therapy by causing hypochloremic alkalosis, a state particularly common in patients on low-salt diets and one that can lead to a poor response or refractoriness to mercurials. Treatment with ammonium chloride, potassium chloride, L-lysine monohydrochloride or one of the carbonic anhydrase inhibitors not only reverses hypochloremia but, when given for 2 or 3 days before diuresis, causes hyperchloremic acidosis and thus provides an optimal background for mercurial responsiveness.

The carbonic anhydrase inhibitor acetazolamide (Diamox) causes diminution in the supply of hydrogen ion available to the acidification mechanism of the distal tubule. Exchange of sodium for hydrogen is inhibited, and there is diuresis of sodium bicarbonate in an alkaline urine. Unfortunately, levels of potassium are lowered when hydrogen ion is less available, and significant hypokalemia may occur. The onset of systemic hyperchloremic acidosis soon blocks the diuretic action of acetazolamide.

The benzothiadiazine diuretics have a more far reaching effect and cause a direct inhibition of tubular reabsorption of sodium *and* chloride. Thus acid-base disorders are rarely induced. Hydrochlorothiazide, a typical example of this group, has about 50 per cent of the potency of the mercurials. It is presumed to act at some point distal to the ascending limb of the loop of Henle, at a site differing from that of the mercurials. These drugs have an additive effect when administered simultaneously. Thiazides should be used cautiously in patients with renal insufficiency since their use has been associated with elevated levels of blood urea nitrogen.

The use of the aldosterone antagonists as diuretic agents is based on the observation that, although the normal renal tubule may "escape" from the effects of this hormone, susceptibility continues in congestive heart failure, perhaps caused by an expansion of extracellular fluid volume or later, as a direct result of diuretic therapy. The spironolactones (Aldactone) are structurally similar to aldosterone and probably act by competing with it at its locus of action in the distal tubule. As a result of their use the sodium-potassium exchange mechanism is inhibited, sodium is excreted, and renal loss of potassium and hydrogen is lowered. They remain effective in patients on low-sodium diets, but have no diuretic activity in the presence of a high-sodium intake, which inhibits aldosterone secretion. In themselves rather weak diuretics, they potentiate the activity of the thiazides or other agents which increase the amount of sodium reaching the distal tubule.

Triamterine, a pteridine derivative, increases urinary excretion of sodium, chloride and bicarbonate while the excretion of potassium is either decreased or unchanged.

Ethacrynic acid and furosemide are at least as potent as the mercurials and do not require establishment of acidosis to potentiate their effect. Diuresis is not impaired by alkalosis, hypochloremia or hyponatremia, and resistance to their action is rare. These drugs are relatively nontoxic, but the massive fluid loss that they induce can produce serious changes in electrolyte balance, particularly in concentrations of potassium and sodium chloride. Extracellular fluid space may contract acutely without significant loss of bicarbonate and produce a rise in arterial pH and metabolic alkalosis. Side effects are analogous to those seen with the thiazides.

Although numerous and effective diuretic agents are available, moderate restriction of sodium intake is necessary in all patients with congestive heart failure.

Promise is also seen in current attempts to develop an intra- or extracorporeal mechanical pumping device to serve as a temporary or perhaps permanent substitute for the heart in terminal decompensation.

Angina Pectoris, Coronary Insufficiency and Myocardial Infarction

These three entities are so similar in etiology, pathogenesis, symptomatology and their effects upon the cardiovascular system that they may be regarded as stages of the same pathologic process. Over a period of time one or all three may be observed in the same patient. There is little question that they are caused by a complete or incomplete, localized or generalized reduction in coronary blood flow and that they represent differences in the degree of myocardial damage as determined by the intensity and duration of ischemia. The location of the obstruction to flow contributes to the clinical significance of the myocardial ischemia so produced. The most common cause of such reduction in flow is a narrowing or obstruction of one or more coronary arteries by the intimal and medial lesions of atherosclerosis. Less frequently, it may be caused by congenital abnormalities in coronary anatomy, by obstruction of coronary ostia brought about by the pathologic changes of luetic aortitis, or by coronary embolization. Conversely, the pain of myocardial ischemia may occur in the absence of coronary artery disease when myocardial hypertrophy or other causes of an increased demand for flow are so marked that they outstrip the vascular supply of the heart.

Most patients fall into one of two easily distinguishable groups: (1) The patient with classic *angina pectoris* is subjected to intermittent, reversible ischemia and most probably does not suffer permanent myocardial damage. His pain is brief and confined to the attacks. Between attacks he shows little evidence of heart disease. (2) *Myocardial infarction* is usually accompanied by total occlusion of one or more coronary arteries which causes ischemia so severe as to lead to cellular necrosis. These tissue changes are not reversible and are potentially lethal. The pain with which they are associated may be so severe as to defy description and can last for hours or days unless relieved by opiates. Serious arrhythmias and congestive heart failure are common sequelae of myocardial infarction, and permanent changes in the electrocardiogram (EKG) are the rule.

In a small but diagnostically worrisome group of patients, ischemia of intermediate severity, falling just short of causing immediate cell necrosis, may occur. This syndrome, most commonly termed *coronary insufficiency,* has also been identified as preinfarction angina, status anginosis, coronary failure and impending coronary occlusion—all expressions of a relatively unstable and therefore frequently confusing diagnostic category. Characteristically the signs and symptoms in this group seem to lie midway between angina pectoris and myocardial infarction. Pain is often severe and is prolonged, usually lasting for more than 30 minutes. In some cases there may be minimal although permanent cell damage, but evidence of recent coronary thrombosis or chronic coronary occlusion is usually absent on pathologic examination. Changes in the electrocardiogram are usually not diagnostic, and nonspecific signs of tissue necrosis may be absent. In some cases and on the same day, a patient may have attacks of angina and episodes of coronary insufficiency.

Experience in evaluating chest pain, the use of the EKG, and the diagnostic tests to be described have helped to simplify the differential diagnosis of these syndromes.

Angina Pectoris

It should be emphasized that angina pectoris is characterized by the *sudden* onset of substernal pain usually associated with apprehension or fear of death and relieved *completely* and without sequelae of any kind by a few minutes of rest (1 to 5) or sublingual administration of nitroglycerin. Attacks may be precipitated by exertion, emotional tension, ingestion of a large meal, tachycardia or arryhthmias associated with paroxysmal rapid heart action, smoking cigarettes, exposure to cold (particularly to a cold wind), as an idiosyncrasy to coffee or other drugs, as part of an allergic reaction or by terrifying dreams. Nocturnal angina accompanied by diagnostic EKG changes correlates well with the rapid eye movement (REM) periods that occur during sleep. This activity coincides with stage B of sleep, a period of physiologic arousal during which systolic blood pressure and heart and respiratory rates may show striking minute-to-minute variation and compromise an already borderline coronary blood supply. All these factors have the common denominator of an increase in the work of the heart. Although spontaneous angina has been described at rest, such attacks rarely occur in the presence of a physician; when carefully observed these patients are usually tense and anxious. Most demonstrate an increase in blood pressure or pulse rate during an attack. In a small group originally described by Prinzmetal, a variant form of angina is seen which occurs when the subject is truly at rest, or while performing ordinary activity during the day or night. These attacks do not seem to be precipitated by effort. This group and the group in whom pain is triggered by large meals or during sleep when examined pathologically usually show disease of all three major coronary arterial trunks. Angina seems to be more frequent in patients with aortic regurgitation, hypertrophy and dilatation, hypertension, pheochromocytoma or other sources of circulating catecholamines, anemia, polycythemia, thyrotoxicosis and atrial fibrillation. Many of these associated conditions respond to therapy, and unless corrected may produce intractable symptoms.

Afferent pathways for transmission of cardiac pain have been anatomically established; nevertheless, agreement is lacking as to the actual mechanisms involved in the production or appreciation of the pain of angina pectoris. Kisch has recently described an extensive capillary innervation of the atria and ventricles. He believes that these nerves are pain-sensitive and respond to the effects of acute ischemia. There is certainly good evidence that pain fibers are stimulated by focal hypoxia and that they become more sensitive in the presence of an adjacent, well oxygenated, normally functioning myocardium than when subjected to the effects of ischemic metabolites alone. When myocardial involvement becomes more generalized, with congestive failure and decreased cardiac output, the pain often abates. Angina may also disappear when myocardial infarction destroys the gradient between well oxygenated and relatively ischemic myocardium. These observations are supported by the work of Fauteux, who reported that when both coronary arteries of the dog were simultaneously ligated, neither ventricular fibrillation nor signs of pain were as likely to develop as when only one was obstructed.

On questioning, some patients will admit to what might be called an anginal equivalent; it is manifested as sudden dyspnea, fatigue, lightheadedness, palpitations, cold sweats or sudden weakness following a provocation that would otherwise lead to typical pain symptoms in the majority of patients with significant coronary vascular disease. These symptoms are relieved in much the same manner as typical angina, by rest or administration of nitroglycerin. Absence of pain is especially common in elderly diabetic patients, a high-risk coronary group, and is thought to be evidence of diabetic neuropathy or of ischemia of afferent pain fibers. When present, the pain is most frequently confined to the upper substernal region, but may be felt from the sternal notch to the xiphoid process. The radiation of pain, in order of frequency, is to the left shoulder and arm, neck and face, epigastrium, right shoulder and arm, right upper abdomen and upper spine. Not uncommonly it is described as "going clear through to the back" and in some cases is appreciated as an aching, soreness, numbness, sticking or tingling sensation, or a vague sense of discomfort in the regions involved.

Etiology of Angina Pectoris, Coronary Insufficiency, and Myocardial Infarction

Before discussing the physiologic approaches to recognition of myocardial ischemia, a review of the mechanisms con-

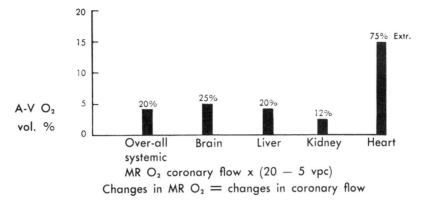

MR O_2 coronary flow x (20 — 5 vpc)

Changes in MR O_2 = changes in coronary flow

Figure 20–11. This chart illustrates the striking difference in oxygen extraction by the heart and by other organs. Myocardial oxygen consumption (MR O_2) is determined by coronary blood flow and oxygen extraction. Normally, 12 to 15 vol. per cent O_2 is extracted by the heart. Because extraction is near maximal at rest, changes in oxygen need are met by changes in coronary flow when reserve capacity is adequate.

trolling myocardial blood flow may be of value. As noted in the previous chapter, the heart is particularly dependent on aerobic metabolism. This concept is substantiated by its low content of anaerobic enzymes, its high concentration of cytochromes and by the fact that it cannot perform a normal work load without oxygen. The heart may "live," i.e., sustain cellular integrity, for as long as an hour (in the noncontractile state) without oxygen, but such an environment will not permit contractile activity sufficient to maintain normal cardiac output or blood pressure. This continuing need for oxygen is met by coronary blood flow and by the ability of the myocardium to extract a very large proportion of the oxygen contained in each milliliter of blood with which it is perfused. The coronary circulation is totally different from any other in the body, since 75 per cent of the oxygen brought to the myocardium is extracted from the blood. Thus, oxygen extraction is ordinarily near maximum and varies but slightly from resting levels (Fig. 20–11). This high extraction ratio exists even at rest and permits little flexibility. Changes in need for oxygen are largely mediated therefore by changes in coronary blood flow. Thus, an increase in extraction, a common means of providing more oxygen to other tissues, will occur in the heart only as a final defense, when flow alone can no longer meet oxygen demand. This is at best a limited but, on occasion, most important reserve. Evidence of increased oxygen extraction (not seen in the normal state) may provide valuable evidence of myocardial ischemia.

Figure 20–12 illustrates the interrelationship of factors governing coronary blood flow.

The upper half of the figure presents stimuli which must be met by a change in flow. Factors which increase the oxygen demand on the heart are shown on the left. An increase in the work of the heart is the most common cause of an increased need for oxygen. Acceleration of heart rate increases oxygen demand in direct proportion to systolic contraction time. Likewise, epinephrine and thyroid hormone, as well as the changes in the diastolic fiber length seen in congestive heart failure, increase overall myocardial oxygen cost.

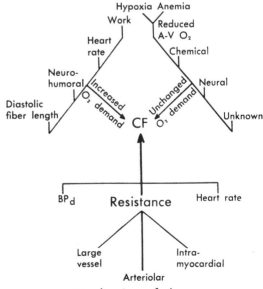

Figure 20–12. Regulation of coronary blood flow. See text.

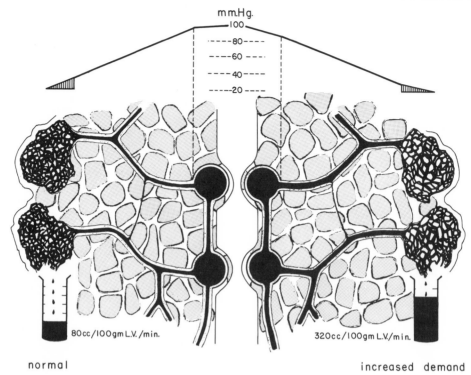

Figure 20–13. Response of the normal coronary vascular system to an increase in demand for flow. Increased need for oxygen is met by arteriolar vasodilatation and a decrease in vascular resistance. Since mean aortic pressure remains constant or increases, an increase in flow occurs.

Factors affecting the normally low flow-extraction ratio are shown on the right of Figure 20–12. This ratio is most commonly influenced by a reduction in the oxygen content of coronary arterial blood as in anemia or anoxemia. Under these circumstances even the normal need for oxygen can be met only by increased coronary blood flow. Certain chemical and neural and other, unknown mechanisms may also alter the flow-extraction ratio.

The lower half of Figure 20–12 illustrates the hemodynamic mechanisms responsible for meeting these demands. The major hydraulic factor is the aortic perfusion pressure. Because the coronary arteries are perfused primarily in diastole, the mean blood pressure is of particular importance. Increased cardiac rate exerts a deleterious action on coronary hemodynamics not only by increasing consumption of oxygen as a function of the maintenance of tension, but also by decreasing diastolic inflow time and mean blood pressure.

The second most important factor in regulating coronary flow is vascular resistance. Resistance to flow may result from myocardial compression of intramyocardial vessels, direct obstruction of the large coronary ar-

teries, or constriction of the arterioles. Increased demand for coronary blood flow, unaccompanied by an increase in aortic perfusion pressure, is usually met by arteriolar dilation and decreased coronary vascular resistance. When the diastolic pressure head in the aorta is compromised or rendered less effectual, as with the low diastolic pressure of aortic insufficiency or with tachycardia, or when the intramyocardial resistance in systole is infinite, as in aortic stenosis, there is a compensatory coronary vasodilation (Fig. 20–13). The increased need for oxygen and the resultant increased coronary flow required by these pathologic states can only be met by still further arteriolar dilatation. Similarly, when coronary artery disease is diffuse, with narrowing or obstruction of several large vessels, the coronary circulation cannot be maintained at an adequate functional level without significant arteriolar vasodilation (Fig. 20–14). Thus, as coronary sclerosis progresses, collateral anastomoses open up and arterioles distal to the obstructed vessel dilate. The corollary of this response is that if vascular disease progresses, the available coronary arteriolar reserve for dilation under stress may already be exhausted, and flow will be inadequate to meet demand. The severity of this deficit would seem to be the factor of greatest importance in determining whether angina pectoris, coronary insufficiency or myocardial infarction will follow.

As noted earlier, a precise description of the pathogenesis of angina pectoris has eluded investigators for almost 200 years. The evanescent nature of the pain and other factors have made it difficult to study this syndrome adequately, and it has therefore been most frequently attributed to locally produced anoxia secondary to spasm of a coronary artery. Evidence in support of this formulation is the acute onset, the fact that it rises to the same peak of severity regardless of the cause, and the "all or nothing" response to nitrites, which are known vasodilators. A specific attack is usually completely terminated, and pain recurs only in response to a new inciting cause. In addition, Gorlin and others have demonstrated coronary vasospasm by angiographic techniques. There is little objective evidence to support this concept, however. Many interested in the problem cannot accept the premise that acute hypoxia, perhaps the most potent stimulus for vasodilata-tion in nonrigid arteries of other vascular systems, would be associated with vasospasm in the coronary tree. After embolization of the coronary arteries in animals there is a decrease in coronary vascular resistance and a prolonged *increase* in coronary flow. In man, examination at autopsy of the coronary arteries supplying areas of presumed ischemia demonstrates rigid, frequently calcified segments characteristically associated with the arteriosclerotic process and hardly amenable to spasm *or* vasodilation. Gorlin has been unable to demonstrate the relationship of pain or any other symptom to coronary spasm and, in many cases, attributes spasm of nonarteriosclerotic vessels to direct stimulation by the tip of the angiographic catheter.

Although a more definitive discussion must await further study, there is sufficient evidence for thinking that angina is due to a sudden unmet myocardial demand for oxygen. It occurs most frequently when an area of normal, well perfused myocardium lies adjacent to what may be a small, localized area of hypoxic tissue. It appears to be a transitory state and one that passes when the cause is removed.

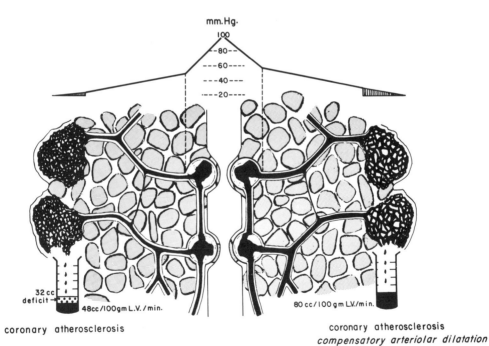

Figure 20–14. Illustration of the decrease in arteriolar perfusion pressure produced by significant coronary atherosclerosis. The left half of the diagram illustrates a presumptive flow deficit of 32 cc. from a normal mean flow of 80 cc. per 100 gm. left ventricle (L.V.) per minute. A deficit may be avoided if arteriolar reserve is sufficient to meet this challenge, enabling these vessels to dilate and maintain capillary pressure and perfusion. This type of compensation is illustrated by the right half of the figure.

Attacks of coronary insufficiency indicate an intensification of the degree of myocardial ischemia and are usually superimposed on a history of more classic angina pectoris. Some authors challenge the wisdom of characterizing these patients as members of a specific group and feel that they actually represent a variant form of myocardial infarction. It is undoubtedly and unfortunately true that lending a name to any syndrome implies a degree of knowledge that, at least for coronary insufficiency, does not exist. Such patients nevertheless demonstrate an intensification of the severity, frequency or duration of pain, or pain may differ from classic angina by occurring spontaneously, at rest. This condition has a much graver prognosis than that of angina pectoris and often indicates impending myocardial infarction. In many cases it is precipitated by extracoronary factors, which increase the demand on, or reduce the flow to, an already ischemic myocardium. Prolonged paroxysmal tachycardias or hypertensive episodes, massive pulmonary embolism, or shock from whatever cause often provokes coronary insufficiency. Successful treatment of these insults may terminate an attack and prevent permanent myocardial damage.

When the disparity between need and supply of oxygen is such that viability can no longer be maintained, cellular necrosis, i.e., myocardial infarction, is precipitated. The patient may recover, or shock, acute ventricular failure with pulmonary edema or serious arrhythmias may lead to death.

The most common methods for assessing the coronary circulation are indirect ones. The electrocardiogram (EKG) was the first and is still the most valuable tool for differential diagnosis of chest pain. Unfortunately, only positive findings are helpful; a negative EKG does not exclude functionally significant coronary arteriosclerosis.

BIOCHEMICAL AND PHYSIOLOGIC CORRELATES OF MYOCARDIAL ISCHEMIA

During the past two decades a variety of physiologic correlates to myocardial ischemia have evolved and may be of help when a diagnosis cannot be made by history and physical examination alone.

In 1928, Wasserman first described relief from the pain of angina pectoris after *carotid sinus pressure*. In this country Dr. Samuel Levine popularized this test in the differential diagnosis of angina-like chest pain. If the patient's pain occurs or can be induced in the physician's presence and if it can be relieved by carotid sinus pressure, an almost certain diagnosis of angina pectoris can be made. Among its many advantages are ease of performance and a definite end point. The maneuver is useful only when pain is relieved.

Unfortunately, no reports have been published of physiologic or biochemical studies simultaneously performed. Although not proved, relief is most likely obtained by slowing the heart to permit a relative lengthening of the diastolic filling period and thus of coronary perfusion time. A decrease in heart rate also decreases time spent in systole (high ventricular wall tension) and thus lessens myocardial oxygen requirements. Finally, a reflex inhibition of cardiac sympathetic discharge may decrease myocardial catecholamine release, a factor of potential significance in myocardial oxygen consumption.

The *electrocardiogram* taken at rest helps immeasurably to confirm a clinical impression of myocardial infarction, but is of little or no help in the diagnosis of angina pectoris. When recorded during a spontaneous attack of angina or after an induced stress of coronary reserve (usually exercise), the EKG will record specific changes in the majority of patients. All authors emphasize that a negative test result does not exclude the presence of significant coronary sclerosis. Conversely, grade 4 sclerosis may be present in one major artery even though the postexercise electrocardiogram fails to reveal an abnormality. In about 50 per cent of patients with valvular heart disease or cardiopulmonary or hypertensive cardiovascular disease, the EKG will demonstrate ST segment abnormalities after exercise in the absence of myocardial ischemia and therefore yield false positive test results. Except for such cases, a positive test signifies diffuse, advanced coronary arterial insufficiency and is of prognostic as well as diagnostic significance.

Refinements in telemetering techniques now permit the recording of an electrocardiogram *during* exercise. The electric impulse is broadcast by a lightweight radio transmitter and utilizes a specially designed bipolar electrode, which is taped to the patient. This technique obviates the need for fixed cable connections and provides a steady and stable base line. It permits a more accurate quantitation of the amount of exercise needed to produce significant changes and may prove valuable in following the course of progressive disease and in evaluating the response to specific therapeutic measures.

The measurement of absolute *resting coronary flow* is of little or no diagnostic value since such studies reveal little difference between the normal subject with an unused reserve and the anginal patient whose coronary reserve is exhausted. A quantitative estimate of coronary reserve must be sought.

Nitroglycerin, a potent vasodilator of the normal coronary vascular bed, increases flow in the normal person by as much as 150 per cent, but has little or no effect on flow or coronary vascular resistance in the patient with advanced coronary insufficiency. This diminished or absent reserve serves as the basis for the nitroglycerin vasodilator test. The coronary sinus is catheterized and coronary blood flow measured by the nitrous oxide desaturation method of Kety and Schmidt or by more recent techniques with iodine 131-labeled antipyrine or krypton 85.

Figure 20–15 illustrates the effect of nitroglycerin on coronary flow and diastolic vascular resistance. In the normal patient there is an average increase in coronary flow of 100 per cent, and a decrease in coronary vascular resistance of 50 per cent, thus demonstrating a reserve capacity for vasodilatation. In coronary artery disease with angina pectoris, blood flow changes little after nitroglycerin is given, and coronary vascular resistance is virtually fixed. The majority of patients with angina demonstrate a fixed flow. Nevertheless, there is a group of patients who retain borderline responsiveness and in whom minimum dilative capacity may remain, but when compared to that of the normal subject is markedly diminished. A striking lack of response indicates a critical reduction in coronary reserve.

An excellent index of an exhausted coronary reserve can be obtained by a determination of *myocardial oxygen extraction after exercise.* Since myocardial oxygen extraction is nearly maximum at rest, the normal subject shows a remarkably constant coronary sinus oxygen saturation despite the stress of exercise. In the diffusely diseased coronary vasculature, flow cannot increase sufficiently to meet the increased demands of exercise, and the myocardium is forced to increase its extraction of oxygen to absolute physiologic limits. Under these circumstances, it may extract an additional 1.5 to 2.0 cc. of oxygen per 100 ml. of whole blood. The test, like that previously described, requires coronary sinus

catheterization and blood sampling for oxygen determination after an exercise period. In a study by Messer et al. myocardial oxygen extraction increased in 82 per cent of patients with clinical coronary insufficiency.

The *transcoronary circulation time* is a somewhat different and simpler approach to the measurement of reactivity. It eliminates the necessity for the multiple-sample analysis needed to determine coronary flow. The coronary sinus is catheterized and a second catheter placed in the pulmonary artery or at the root of the aorta. Tracer substances injected via the second catheter are sampled from the coronary sinus and will thus provide a measure of the transcoronary circulation time. When radioactive iodinated serum albumin (RISA) is used, the injection may be made into the pulmonary artery or the aortic root. Continuous sampling from the coronary sinus catheter through a gamma detector permits an accurate determination of the myocardial transit time.

Another technique utilizes hydrogen gas as the tracer substance and platinum-tipped hydrogen-sensitive catheter electrodes as detectors.

Raab and co-workers introduced a most provocative theory for the cause of angina based on neurohumoral *studies of catecholamine release.* Under the influence of these hormones, oxygen consumed by the myocar-

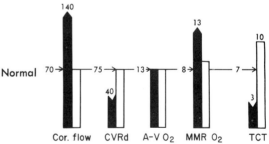

Figure 20–15. Response of the normal and the diseased coronary circulation to a vasodilator stimulus. The direction of the arrow indicates direction of change with nitroglycerin. Figures to the left of the black columns indicate resting normal values; figures at the tops of the columns show the response after nitroglycerin administration. Coronary flow = ml./100 gm./min.; CVRd = diastolic coronary vascular resistance, dynes second cm.$^{-5}$ × 10^3; A-V O$_2$ = coronary arteriovenous oxygen difference, cc./100 ml. blood; MMR O$_2$ = myocardial metabolic rate for oxygen, cc./100 gm./min.; TCT = transcoronary circulation time, sec.

dium may be inefficiently utilized. This theory has been most helpful in explaining the occurrence of angina in those cases which lack objective evidence of an acute increase in cardiac load. The effects of exposure of a myocardium, whose vessels are already nearly maximally dilated, to a catecholamine stimulus are self-evident.

Several investigators have demonstrated a significantly increased level of plasma catecholamines (epinephrine, norepinephrine) coincident with the onset of angina. Elevations were also noted after myocardial infarction. Noncardiac causes of chest pain failed to produce a similar elevation. Although the possibility of adrenal medullary release of hormone has not been entirely excluded, other studies indicate that postganglionic adrenergic nerve endings are the most probable source of these increased levels. Unlike levels of serum enzymes (serum glutamic oxaloacetic transaminase, serum glutamic pyruvic transaminase, lactic acid dehydrogenase, isoenzymes), serum catecholamine concentration is elevated during *angina pectoris* as well as subsequent to myocardial infarction.

When coronary reserve has been exhausted and neither coronary flow nor oxygen extraction can be increased to meet a stress state, the myocardium may *increase its rate of anaerobic metabolism* and utilize glycolysis as a small supplemental source of energy. This switching of metabolic gears will be reflected by the myocardial production of lactate and its subsequent appearance in coronary sinus samples.

When dogs are made hypoxic by breathing 10 per cent oxygen or by cyanide intoxication, there is a significant increase in coronary sinus lactate concentration (expressed as excess lactate). Such evidence of increased anaerobic metabolism indicates that oxygen delivery is not adequate to meet cardiac tissue requirements. In other studies, coronary patients were exercised to the point of pain or tested by infusion of isoproterenol. Patients with presumptive evidence of myocardial ischemia demonstrated significant levels of excess lactate in coronary sinus blood samples. Excess lactate was not present when normal subjects were so exercised.

As direct surgical techniques for the treatment of localized occlusive coronary artery disease continue to improve, the need to pinpoint the site of these lesions has increased. A variety of methods are now available for recording distribution of radiopaque substances injected directly into the coronary ostia. In a recent report on *coronary arteriography*, Kattus et al. outlined four different types of coronary arterial abnormalities which may lead to angina pectoris and which can be demonstrated by angiography: (1) the classic multiple occlusive lesion, (2) elongated narrow segments without occlusion, (3) multiple narrow segments and (4) the strategic local narrow segment which may lead to nocturnal angina. Sones et al., using cinecoronary arteriographic techniques, obtained important information by demonstrating collateral arterial channels from one major artery to the area of distribution of another totally occluded segment. Angiography is of the greatest value when it anatomically localizes coronary inadequacy previously diagnosed by history, the electrocardiogram, or one of the techniques described above.

THE DIAGNOSIS OF MYOCARDIAL INFARCTION AND CORONARY INSUFFICIENCY

The size and location of the infarction is determined by the site of the coronary occlusion, the presence and functional capacity of adjacent collateral vessels and the adequacy and location of other coronary vessels. In general, *anterior* infarcts are caused by occlusion of the left anterior descending coronary artery. When the left circumflex coronary artery is occluded, the infarct is usually located in the free left ventricular wall near the atrioventricular sulcus and is designated as a *lateral* or *high lateral* infarct. In 10 per cent of patients this type of occlusion may lead to ischemia of the A-V node and a predisposition to atrial arrhythmias. *Posterior* or *diaphragmatic* infarction may involve the diaphragmatic surface of the heart, the crux and the posterior left ventricular free wall. These infarcts are precipitated by occlusion of the right coronary artery. James has emphasized that this type of infarct is treacherous and most often leads to sudden death produced by associated disturbances in rhythm and conduction. By a series of meticulous dissections he has demonstrated that both the A-V node artery and the sinus node artery arise from the right coronary artery in 44 per cent of human hearts. Thus a single occlusion of the proximal right coronary artery may cause serious and frequently fatal conduction disturbances.

Most cases of myocardial infarction develop abruptly without an obvious provoking incident and frequently in the absence of a history of angina pectoris. In patients who have antecedent angina there may be an abrupt increase in the severity and frequency of attacks of pain. Such patients also have a poorer immediate and long-term prognosis than those without antecedent agnina. The location, radiation, and quality of the pain of myocardial inforction resemble that of angina, but may be less sharp, though of increased severity, and may be described as having an oppressive, pressing, crushing, or squeezing quality. Most patients demonstrate acute anxiety, and many describe a sensation of intense apprehension. Less commonly, myocardial infarction occurs without pain, the so-called "silent" myocardial infarction. It may be suggested by the appearance of sudden severe weakness, syncope, convulsion, arrhythmia, a sense of precordial or substernal uneasiness, severe diaphoresis, pain in the upper back, vague gastrointestinal discomfort or nausea and vomiting, manifestations of cardiogenic shock, or the pulmonary symptoms of acute severe left ventricular failure.

The *EKG* is undoubtedly the most useful aid in the diagnosis of acute myocardial infarction. The recent introduction of vectorcardiographic analysis has increased its value so that 85 per cent of cases can be accurately diagnosed. Unfortunately accuracy falls to 50 per cent if prior infarctions have occurred. Serial studies are often particularly helpful in patients with a history of prior infarction. In contrast, the most common EKG alterations of coronary insufficiency are ST depressions or T wave inversions. The Q wave of frank myocardial infarction is not seen.

In the absence of EKG abnormalities, studies of serum enzymes may be the most sensitive index of myocardial infarction. A clear correlation has been established between myocardial necrosis and elevation of the serum concentration of glutamic oxaloacetic transaminase (GOT), lactic dehydrogenase (LDH) and its isoenzymes, aldolase (ALD), glutamic dehydrogenase (GDH), α-hydroxybutyric dehydrogenase (HBD), acid phosphatase (ACP), malic dehydrogenase (MDH), hexose isomerase (HSO), succinic dehydrogenase (SUC) and creatine phosphokinase (CPK). These changes are noted for several days after a transmural infarct and appear to be quantitatively proportional to the size of the infarcted muscle. The concentrations of these enzymes in tissue are normally three to 5000 times those in serum. Pathologic studies have demonstrated that tissue activity diminishes in proportion to the age of the infarct, suggesting that the eleva-

tions are due in part to enzyme leakage from ischemic or necrotic cells. Other mechanisms undoubtedly play an important role in causing or sustaining such findings. The serum concentrations of many cardiac tissue enzymes are not elevated after infarction. In addition, there is poor correlation between serum enzyme concentration and the extent of necrosis produced experimentally or resulting from disease of skeletal muscle or acute hepatic necrosis. Finally, intravenous injection of GOT and LDH has shown that these enzymes are rapidly cleared from the blood of the normal subject. Enzyme concentration in the infarcted myocardium would not in itself appear to be great enough to maintain high serum levels for days.

There has been widespread clinical experience with GOT and LDH and elevated levels in serum correlate with clinical and autopsy findings of myocardial infarction in over 97 per cent of patients. An increase in GOT is measurable within 6 to 12 hours after a transmural infarction, reaches a peak within 24 to 48 hours and returns to a normal level in from 4 to 7 days. The diagnostic value and specificity of GOT are diminished somewhat since abnormal elevations may derive from extracardiac tissue sources. Congestive hepatomegaly, central necrosis of the liver, shock, dissecting aneurysm of the aorta, hemorrhagic pericarditis, acute pancreatitis, disease of skeletal muscle and of the extrahepatic biliary tract, and infarction of the kidney, spleen and lung (late rise) resulting from embolization will elevate levels of serum GOT. Administration of Dicumarol, Tromexan, opiates, and salicylates may also cause abnormal elevations.

Serum LDH activity rises and peaks somewhat later than GOT and remains elevated for several days longer. Unfortunately it is no more specific than GOT. An elevation of LDH may confirm a diagnosis of myocardial infarction and helps in the differential diagnosis of pulmonary infarction. In the latter, early elevations of LDH may occur without elevation of GOT, a circumstance rarely seen with myocardial infarction.

Many attempts have been made to increase the specificity and thus the diagnostic accuracy of these tests. Wroblewski has studied the isoenzyme pattern of LDH and determined that its five electrophoretic components have characteristic tissue distributions. He reports that isoenzyme 5 (LDH_5) is specific for the myocardium, appears earlier, and remains elevated for 5 to 10 days longer than total enzyme activity. Serum CPK activity may also prove to be a more specific diagnostic tool. Abnormal levels are measurable within 6 hours, peak between 18 and 24 hours, and remain elevated for about 3 days. Elevations from extracardiac causes are seen only after damage to skeletal muscle and in some patients with acute cerebrovascular disease, conditions rarely confused with acute myocardial infarction.

Elevations of serum enzymes are not seen in angina pectoris, but a moderate rise, not nearly as great as that seen with infarction, has been described in about 50 per cent of patients with coronary insufficiency.

Treatment of Angina Pectoris

Ischemia, whether expressed as angina, coronary insufficiency or myocardial infarction, is due to a deficit between oxygen demand and supply. Efforts to improve coronary vascular reserve (with certain exceptions to be discussed) have been disappointing, and have necessarily been directed toward prophylaxis rather than therapy, i.e., they are aimed at decreasing the number, frequency and severity of attacks by reducing inordinate demands on an already embarrassed coronary vascular system. The patient is advised to avoid heavy meals, maintain normal or lean weight and avoid *extremes* of temperature. Exertion connected with work, sports or sexual activity and emotional or mental stress frequently triggers attacks. Cumulative evidence supports the theory that reasonable activity below the threshold usually associated with pain is a valuable adjunct to therapy. Not only does it maintain body tone and function, but it encourages growth of collateral coronary vessels.

There seems to be little need for a *chronic* chemical vasodilator since hypoxia has already been shown to be the most potent stimulus for increasing coronary flow when reserve has not been exhausted. The patient with angina pectoris certainly has no need for an increase in *resting* coronary blood flow. Oxygen extraction is near maximal at rest, and flow must be normal as there would otherwise be a measurable decrease in myocardial oxygen consumption, a hemodynamic state not seen at rest in patients with angina.

Since in these patients cardiac work is usually normal or above normal, it is unlikely that the diseased myocardium should require less oxygen for the same basal work load. At rest there is little difference in measured flow between the normal patient with a large, still unused reserve capacity and the patient with angina in whom measured flow actually represents the result of near maximal vascular dilatation.

Generalized coronary vasodilation chemically induced unfortunately may result in more harm than benefit. These secondary vasodilators include epinephrine, norepinephrine, theophylline ethylenediamine (aminophylline), quinidine, salicylates, nikethamide, angiotensin and other long-acting nitrates. Such agents increase myocardial blood flow by increasing myocardial oxygen demand. The "primary vasodilators," the "benign dilators" of Gregg's classification, enhance flow without significantly increasing oxygen consumption. They are characterized by an elevation of oxygen saturation in the coronary sinus and by a decrease in the oxygen extraction coefficient. Among the few agents in this category are isoproterenol, papaverine, serotonin, adenosine compounds, including several purine and pyrimidine derivatives, and an active agent found in urine. The nitrites, and nitroglycerin in particular, are undoubtedly the most effective agents available for the treatment of angina. Administered sublingually at the onset of pain, they may abort an incipient attack or terminate an attack in 1 to 3 minutes. Pain diminishes, the electrocardiogram pattern reflects improvement, and there is increased exercise tolerance. Their true mechanism of action remains unknown. The nitrites are potent secondary vasodilators in *responsive* blood vessels, but do not cause vasodilation in the arteriosclerotic arteries of patients with angina.

Pathologic studies reveal that occlusive thrombi or severe stenosis usually involves only one or two of the three functional coronary vessels. Restriction of flow in the involved vessels results in a state of borderline vascular compensation for the myocardium it supplies. There is maximal dilatation of the distal vascular tree in response to this hypoxic stimulus and eventual exhaustion of coronary reserve. The actual areas affected may be quite small and localized. Uninvolved adjacent vessels maintain their normal reserve capacity for dilatation and their responsiveness to vasodilator agents. By acting on responsive uninvolved vessels, nitroglycerin may lead to an increase in the pressure gradient across collateral channels thus causing them to open and permitting a shunt of blood to the widely dilated low pressure vessels of the ischemic myocardium. Gorlin and Brachfeld exercised coronary patients until the onset of pain. Symptoms terminated promptly when nitroglycerin was administered, but simultaneously recorded measurements failed to demonstrate a significant change in coronary blood flow (Fig. 20–15). In a control group, flow increased as much as 100 per cent. These observations were confirmed by others as well as by Fam and McGregor, who concluded that nitroglycerin may act only in the presence of a well-developed collateral circulation, redistributing flow to these channels without significantly altering total coronary artery flow.

Nitroglycerin may act through mechanisms totally unrelated to its vasoactive properties. A recent review by Brachfeld describes the extensive pharmacologic activity of this drug and emphasizes its far-reaching effects. Nonvascular hemodynamic and biochemical responses to administration of nitrites are diverse and may contribute to, or be primarily responsible for, their effectiveness. They include a decrease in myocardial work, contractility and efficiency, a shortening of cardiac size and diastolic filling period in both ventricles, possible uncoupling of oxidative phosphorylation, inhibition of adenosine triphosphatase activity, reversal of acute left ventricular failure (often associated with anginal attacks) and potent antiadrenergic activity.

There is little theoretic rationale for use of the so-called "long-acting nitrites," no experimental evidence that they have prolonged hemodynamic or biochemical activity, and no clinical proof that patients given these drugs require decreased amounts of nitroglycerin.

Initial reports of the use of Propanolol, a beta adrenergic blocking agent, have been most encouraging. This drug reduces the mechanical work of the heart and permits a decrease in myocardial oxygen requirement of as much as 25 per cent with an associated decrease in the severity and frequency of anginal attacks.

The sedative effects of alcohol, when used in moderation, and the administration of barbiturates and psychotropic agents have proved to be valuable adjunctive measures in many patients. Analogues of radioiodine or thiouracil relieve a limited number of patients by reducing basal metabolic activity thus decreasing demand upon the heart. In many patients, however, the stigmata of myxedema become intolerable, and the use of exogenous thyroid extracts is accompanied by a resumption of angina.

Over the years many surgical procedures have been tried and abandoned. These include ligation of the internal mammary artery, epicardial operations that have attempted to develop collateral flow by producing pericardial adhesions, ligation of the great cardiac vein, and a variety of anastomoses including communication of the coronary sinus with the aorta, the ventricular wall with the ventricular cavity, and the left atrium with the pulmonary artery. These procedures have in common their lack of physiologic rationale and clinical success. Coronary endarterectomy has been made possible by contemporary improvements in surgical technique and equipment. Unfortunately mortality is high and further refinement is needed before this operation will become general. Several techniques, which attempt to revascularize the heart by implanting the internal mammary artery in the myocardium (an operation originally reported by Vineberg in 1954), have been described. Some workers have been able to demonstrate patency and significant flow through the anastomoses which seem to develop. Mortality is not as high as in endarterectomy and this technique may prove of value if its effectiveness is confirmed by future studies.

TREATMENT OF CORONARY INSUFFICIENCY AND MYOCARDIAL INFARCTION

Death or survival after an acute myocardial infarction is usually determined in the immediate postinfarction period. The principal hazard is sudden death resulting from conduction disturbances which trigger ventricular fibrillation, asystole or profound cardiovascular collapse.

The pain which inevitably accompanies myocardial infarction must be immediately controlled by use of opiates. Narcotics should be supplemented with atropine when evidence of thrombosis of the right coronary artery indicates potential conduction disturbances or excessive vagal stimulation. Sedation with long-acting hypnotics is begun after acute pain has been relieved and is continued as long as necessary to allay anxiety, decrease physical activity and permit the patient to rest in a state of tranquil drowsiness. Oxygen, administered by mask or nasal catheter, can raise the oxygen content of the blood by 10 to 15 per cent (in physical solution) and improve oxygen supply to the areas of borderline ischemia usually surrounding the site of infarction. Tight face masks or positive pressure devices are uncomfortable for the patient, increase his anxiety and should be reserved for those in shock, with considerable cyanosis or in congestive heart failure with pulmonary edema. Chambers in which hyperbaric oxygen pressures may be maintained are now available in several institutions and are being evaluated for the treatment of myocardial infarction, but data are insufficient at present to support their routine use.

In 1937, Levine advocated chair rest in the treatment of myocardial infarction except for patients in shock or whose blood pressure appeared to be too low to maintain adequate cerebral circulation. The upright position decreases venous return to the right side of the heart and thus lowers pulmonary and central venous pressure. The load on the heart is decreased, and there is less tendency to develop dyspnea. Breathing is eased as pulmonary blood volume falls, and diaphragmatic and respiratory muscle function improves because of unencumbered movement of the thorax. Postural reflexes are maintained when the patient is upright, and functioning of bowel and bladder improves. Despite pooling of blood in the lower extremities, Levine found a striking decrease in the incidence of thrombophlebitis when compared to traditional bed-care management; this may be due to the maintenance of reflex activity and movement of the extremities fostered by chair rest. Patients on this regimen seem to be less fearful, to be in better spirits and to require less medication for relief of pain than those kept in bed.

Anticoagulants, chiefly Dicumarol or heparin, in the treatment of myocardial infarction have been the subject of international debate since first introduced by Wright in 1953. These agents have no effect on the coronary thrombosis that is responsible for the myocardial infarction, but there is good evidence that they decrease the incidence of subsequent mural and vascular thrombosis, pulmonary embolism, and infarction. In general it would appear that the chief value of the anticoagulants is in the improved chances of survival when administered immediately after infarction and continued for 1 year thereafter. There seems to be a statistically significant decrease in mortality when they are used in patients under 50 years of age and in those with prior vascular disease, shock, or circulatory or congestive heart failure—the so-called "poor risk" group described by Russek and Zohman.

Epidemiology of Coronary Artery Disease

The investigations of many epidemiologists and biochemists indicate that atherosclerosis and its clinical manifestations are not an inevitable feature of the aging process. Preventive measures cannot be instituted until all the characteristics of the "coronary-prone" individual are known. Current studies on making a "profile" of the victim of atherosclerosis and determining the risk factors he should avoid are encouraging, but conclusions have only just begun to be formulated. Investigations conducted in such places as Framingham, Massachusetts, and Albany, New York, have shown that genetic factors, hypertension, obesity, diabetes, elevated levels of serum triglycerides, cigarette smoking and physical inactivity significantly increase the risk of myocardial infarction in middle-aged men. Many of these factors may be modified or eliminated, and long-term studies are underway to determine if such measures can effectively reduce the incidence of this disease.

REFERENCES

Alpert, N. R., and Gordon, M. S.: Myofibrillar adenosine triphosphatase activity in congestive heart failure. Am. J. Physiol., 202:940, 1962.

Barger, A. C.: The kidney in congestive heart failure. Circulation, 21:124, 1960.

Bing, R. J., Siegel, A., Ungar, I., and Gilbert, M.: Metabolism of the human heart. Am. J. Med., 16:504, 1954.

Brachfeld, N.: Coronary vasomotor response to pharmacologic agents. Am. J. Cardiol., 13:1, 1964.

Brachfeld, N., Bozer, J., and Gorlin, R.: Action of nitroglycerin on coronary circulation in normal and mild cardiac subjects. Circulation, 19:697, 1959.

Brachfeld, N., and Gorlin, R.: Physiologic evaluation of angina pectoris. Dis. Chest, 38:658, 1960.

Bradlow, B. A., Zion, M., and Fleishman, S. J.: Heart disease in Africa with particular reference to Southern Africa. Am. J. Cardiol., 13:650, 1964.

Braunwald, E. W.: The control of ventricular function in man. Brit. Heart J., 27:1, 1965.

Burch, G. E., Ray, C. T., and Cronvich, J. A.: Certain mechanical peculiarities of the human cardiac pump in normal and diseased states. Circulation, 5:504, 1952.

Case, R. B., and Brachfeld, N.: Surgical therapy of coronary artery diseases with special reference to myocardial revascularization. Am. J. Cardiol., 9:425, 1963.

Chidsey, C. A., Braunwald, E., Morrow, A. G., and Mason, D. T.: Myocardial norepinephrine concentration in man: Effects of reserpine and of congestive heart failure. New England J. Med., 269:653, 1963.

Chidsey, C. A., Weinbach, E. C., Pool, P. E., and Morrow, A. G.: Biochemical studies of energy production in the failing human heart. J. Clin. Invest., 45:40, 1966.

Danforth, W. H., Bailard, F. B., Kako, K., Choudhury, J. D., and Bing, R. J.: Metabolism of the heart in failure. Circulation, 21:112, 1960.

Dumont, A. E., Clauss, R. H., Reed, G. E., and Tice, D. A.: Lymph drainage in patients with congestive heart failure. New England J. Med., 269: 949, 1963.

Eichna, L. W.: Circulatory congestion and heart failure. Circulation, 22:864, 1960.

Feinstein, M. B.: Effects of experimental congestive heart failure, ouabain, and asphyxia on the high-energy phosphate and creatine content of the guinea pig heart. Circ. Res., 10:333, 1962.

Fox, A. C., Wikler, N. S., and Reed, G. E.: High energy phosphate compounds in the myocardium during experimental congestive heart failure. Purine and pyrimidine nucleotides, creatine and creatine phosphate in normal and in failing hearts. J. Clin. Invest., 44:202, 1965.

Freiman, A. H., Tolles, W., Carbery, W. J., Ruegsegger, P., Abarquez, R. F., and La Due, J. S.: The electrocardiogram during exercise. Am. J. Cardiol., 5:506, 1960.

Gorlin, R.: Recent conceptual advances in congestive heart failure. J.A.M.A., 179:441, 1962.

Gorlin, R., Brachfeld, N., MacLeod, C., and Bopp, P.: The effect of nitroglycerin on the coronary circulation in patients with coronary artery disease or increased left ventricular work. Circulation, 19:705, 1959.

Gorlin, R., Brachfeld, N., Messer, J. V., and Turner, J. D.: Physiologic and biochemical aspects of the disordered coronary circulation. Ann. Int. Med., 51:698, 1959.

Green, D. E., and Goldberger, R.: Pathways of metabolism in heart muscle. Am. J. Med., 30:666, 1961.

Guyton, A. C., and Miss, J.: The systemic venous system in cardiac failure. J. Chron. Dis., 9:465, 1959.

James, T. N.: Arrhythmias and conduction disturbances in acute myocardial infarction. Am. Heart J., 64:416, 1962.

Kako, K., and Bing, R. J.: Contractility of actomyosin bands prepared from normal and failing human heart. J. Clin. Invest., 37:465, 1958.

Katz, A. M.: The descending limb of the Starling curve and the failing heart. Circulation, 32:871, 1965.

Katz, L. N., Feinberg, H., and Shaffer, A. B.: Hemodynamic aspects of congestive heart failure. Circulation, 21:95, 1960.

Lee, K. S.: Present status of cardiac relaxing factor. Fed. Proc., 24:1432, 1965.

Levine, J., and Wagman, R. J.: Energetics of the human heart. Am. J. Cardiol., 9:372, 1962.

Lewis, B. M., Houssay, H. E. J., Haynes, F. W., and Dexter, L.: The dynamics of both right and left ventricles at rest and during exercise in patients with heart failure. Circ. Res., 1:312, 1953.

Linzbach, A. J.: Heart failure from the point of view of quantitative anatomy. Am. J. Cardiol., 5:370, 1960.

Lown, B., and Levine, S. A.: The carotid sinus: Clinical value of its stimulation. Circulation, 23:766, 1961.

Luisada, A. A., and Cardi, L.: Acute pulmonary edema; pathology, physiology and clinical management. Circulation, 13:113, 1956.

Master, A. M., Friedman, R., and Dack, S.: The electrocardiogram after standard exercise as a functional test of the heart. Am. Heart J., 24:777, 1942.

Master, A. M., and Rosenfeld, I.: Master two-step exercise test. J.A.M.A., 172:265, 1960.

Mattingly, T. W.: The postexercise electrocardiogram. Am. J. Cardiol., 9:395, 1962.

Mattingly, T. W.: Changing concepts of myocardial diseases. J.A.M.A., 191:127, 1965.

Olson, R. E.: Myocardial metabolism in congestive heart failure. J. Chron. Dis., 9:442, 1959.

Pittman, J. G., and Cohen, P.: The pathogenesis of cardiac cachexia. New England J. Med., 271:403, 1964.

Pittman, J. G., and Cohen, P.: The pathogenesis of cardiac cachexia (concluded). New England J. Med., 271:453, 1964.

Procita, L., Schwartz, A., and Lee, K. S.: Oxidative phosphorylation in the failing dog heart-lung preparation. Circ. Res., 16:391, 1965.

Raab, W., Van Lith, P., Lepeschkin, E., and Herrlich, H. C.: Catecholamine-induced myocardial hypoxia in the presence of impaired coronary dilatability independent of external cardiac work. Am. J. Cardiol., 9:455, 1962.

Ross J., Jr., and Braunwald, E. A.: Studies on Starling's law of the heart. IX. The effects of impeding venous return on performance of the normal and failing human left ventricle. Circulation, 30:719, 1964.

Said, S. I., Avery, M. E., Davis, R. K., Banerjee, C. M., and El-Gohary, M.: Pulmonary surface activity in induced pulmonary edema. J. Clin. Invest., 44:458, 1965.

Sarnoff, S. J.: Myocardial contractility as described by ventricular function curves: Observations on Starling's law of the heart. Physiol. Rev., 35:107, 1955.

Sarnoff, S. J., and Mitchell, J. H.: The regulation of the performance of the heart. Am. J. Med., 30:747, 1961.

Scheuer, J., and Brachfeld, N.: Myocardial ischemia: EKG, hemodynamic and metabolic correlates. Clin. Res., 12:192, 1964.

Schwartz, A., and Lee, K. S.: Study of heart mitochondria and glycolytic metabolism in experimentally induced cardiac failure. Circ. Res., 10:321, 1962.

Sonnenblick, E. H., Spiro, D., and Spotnitz, H. M.: The ultrastructural basis of Starling's law of the heart. The role of the sarcomere in determining ventricular size and stroke volume. Am. Heart J., 68:336, 1964.

Sonnenblick, E. H., Spotnitz, H. M., and Spiro, D.: Role of sarcomere in ventricular function and the mechanism of heart failure. Circ. Res., 15 (Suppl. II):70, 1964.

Starling, E. H.: The Linacre Lecture on the Law of the Heart. London, Longmans, Green and Co., 1918, p. 27.

Uhley, H. N., Leeds, S. E., Sampson, J. J., and Friedman, M.: Role of pulmonary lymphatics in chronic pulmonary edema. Circ. Res., *11:* 966, 1962.

Vander, A. J., Malvin, R. L., Wilde, W. S., and Sullivan, L. P.: Re-examination of salt and water retention in congestive heart failure. Significance of renal filtration fraction. Am. J. Med., *25:*497, 1958.

Wasserman, A. J., Mauck, H. P., and Patterson, J. L.: The nature and pathogenesis of dyspnea. Heart Bull., *11:*1, 1962.

Wroblewski, F.: Serum enzyme and isoenzyme alterations in myocardial infarction. Prog. Cardiov. Dis., *6:*63, 1963.

Part VII

Respiratory System

Chapter Twenty-One

Pulmonary Ventilation and Respiration; Tests of Respiratory Function

JOHN H. SEABURY

Introduction

The structural and functional specialization of the lungs is aimed at maintaining tensions of oxygen and carbon dioxide in the arterial blood which will permit life without conscious effort during ordinary conditions of living, and provide a sufficient reserve to maintain these tensions within safe limits under a variety of stressful situations.

Air must be brought in through the upper airway, moved along the trachea and major bronchi, and distributed to myriad alveoli. The movement of air to and from the alveoli and the mixing of gases are collectively termed *ventilation.*

Ventilation in man is complex. Movement of air through tubes of varying sizes with repeated branching involves problems of airway resistance during both laminar and turbulent flows. In normal people resistance to flow in the upper airway is a significant part of total airway resistance, but in the evaluation of abnormal ventilatory mechanics the intrathoracic airways are of primary concern. Inertial pressure drop in the airways is of minor importance in disease states as compared with the frictional pressure drop. Whereas the frictional resistance of the upper airway in normal individuals accounts for approximately 49 per cent of total frictional resistance, this segment of the airway is responsible for about 19 per cent of frictional resistance in the emphysematous patient. Inspiratory frictional resistance in the lower airway is approximately 85 per cent of the expiratory resistance in normal individuals, whereas in the emphysematous person inspiratory frictional resistance in the lower airway is only about 65 per cent as large as expiratory resistance. Regional differences in resistance to air flow are extremely important in pulmonary disease, particularly when the altered distribution of ventilation is not matched by a similar alteration and distribution of blood flow.

Ventilation is accomplished by the muscles of respiration: the diaphragm, intercostals, and accessory muscles. Alteration in the physical characteristics of the pulmonary parenchyma, the airways, and both the bony and soft tissue components of the thorax may require greater mechanical work and oxygen expenditure on the part of these muscles to maintain adequate ventilation. This constitutes the total work of breathing, and is one of the most important considerations in disease states involving ventilation primarily.

The *circulation* of blood through the lung is in many ways analogous to ventilation. The pulmonary capillary bed is extremely distensible and operates normally with low resistance and, therefore, low intravascular pressures.

The distribution of the circulating blood is not completely uniform in health, and is easily altered in disease. Distribution may be altered reflexly, or by regional differences in resistance to flow through the vascular tree. Reflex changes may be beneficial in that they tend to divert the greatest flow of blood to areas of lung which are best ventilated. The factors which alter resistance to flow of blood through tubes are discussed elsewhere (see p. 277).

Between the circulating, or perfusing, blood in the pulmonary capillary and the ventilating air in the alveolus is an area of variable width. Normally, this barrier consists of an extremely thin alveolar epithelium on one side, a capillary endothelium on the other, with both basement membranes and a few collagen fibrils and extracellular fluid between. This blood-air barrier is often called the alveolar-capillary membrane. The membranes are normally highly permeable to oxygen and carbon dioxide. Small differences in partial pressure are sufficient to produce *diffusion* of gas across the membranes. Normal or abnormal diffusion is an important segment of *respiration*.

The term *respiration* includes much more than pulmonary function. Respiration is concerned with the absorption of oxygen and the elimination of carbon dioxide. The pulmonary fraction of respiration is concerned with the passage of these gases through the alveolar-capillary membrane to the fluid tissue, blood. From the functional point of view, the pulmonary vascular bed is better regarded as a part of the lung, and the relation of this bed to the movement of gases as a part of the pulmonary fraction of respiration. Once the gases are brought to the cellular or noncellular fraction of the blood, the circulatory phase of respiration is entered. The exchange of gases is ultimately a cellular process.

Anatomico-Physiologic Relations

When the infant takes its first breath, changes in the thoraco-pulmonary relations are great, and normally take place rapidly. The anterior thorax is elevated, moving upward and forward. This increases the anteroposterior diameter of the chest and, therefore, the circumference. The lungs are inflated by the pull of the thoracic cage and diaphragm as they enlarge the volume of the thoracic cavity. Despite the fact that the size of the hemithorax is made considerably greater than the resting volume of the lung, expansion might not take place were it not for the presence of a substance or substances on the alveolar membranes that greatly reduce surface tension during deflation or during reduction in pulmonary volume (expiration). The importance of this surface acting substance requires separate consideration. When initial expansion of the lung occurs, the pleural investment of the thorax and its reflection over the lung, being a closed potential space, together with the molecular cohesion between the pleural surfaces, keep the external surface of the lung in close contact with the thoracic pleura and thereby keep the lung parenchyma and bronchial tree slightly on the stretch.

The rapid increase in volume of the thoracic cage during infancy is greater than the growth of the lung. This disproportion results in a further stretching (i.e., distention) of the lung. The distention is opposed by the inherent elasticity of the lung, thereby creating a force which is negative with reference to atmospheric pressure. Since the disproportion between the growth of the lungs and that of the thorax is greater in early childhood than at birth, the normal intrapleural pressures will be more highly negative in the child than in the newborn.

There is a lipoprotein, and probably an acid mucopolysaccharide, distributed over the surface of the alveolar membrane of normal lungs. This substance, or group of substances, is active in changing surface tension at the tissue-gas interface. Appropriately termed "surfactant," the material can be shown to lower surface tension as the area of the film decreases (expiration) and to increase surface tension when the area increases (inspiration). Consequently, distention requires less work when the lung is deflated and more work as the lung is inflated. This would appear to favor alveolar stability and also uniform ventilation, provided the distribution of surfactant is not altered regionally. There is evidence that deficiency or inactivation of surfactant, except in premature infants, is related to impaired alveolar circulation. Consequently, alveolar surfactant may be very important in determining ventilation-perfusion relationships.

Because isolated lungs have greater elastic recoil when distended with gas than they do when distended with physiologic saline, it has been concluded that the surface tension of the tissue-gas interface (which is abolished by a fluid-fluid interface) is a very important part of total pulmonary elasticity. It is easy to deduce that many pathologic states of the lung are intimately related to alterations in pulmonary surfactant, either primarily or secondarily, but caution is necessary in evaluating the importance of this factor in normal lung function since studies of its effects and quantitation are almost entirely indirect and open to criticism. The Mendenhalls believe that their studies of hysteresis loops of alveolar surfactant fail to indicate any important contribution of surfactant to either lung elasticity or alveolar stability.

Intrathoracic Pressure

For functional purposes, the term "intrathoracic pressure" may be considered equivalent to the term "intrapleural pressure" under normal conditions. This is true only because the intrapleural "space" is potential and normally nonexistent. Because of its elasticity and surfactant activity, the lung opposes the strain exerted on it by the intrapleural force, and these forces of stress tend to return it to its original size. If the pleural space were open to the air, the elastic stress of the lung would be unopposed by the chest wall, diaphragm and muscles of respiration, and the lung would immediately return to its resting size —the size at which stress is zero.

With the basic condition of an elastic, distensible body in contact with an envelope which may vary in size, but is always larger than the contained body, it is easy to understand that the lung, even at rest, is under strain and the intrapleural pressure is negative relative to atmospheric pressure. Increase in chest volume (inspiration) will normally increase the negativity of the intrapleural pressure, and decreasing chest size (expiration) will decrease the negative pressure. The vascular channels and spaces within the substance of the lung and contiguous to it are subject to the various forces transmitted to the lung, to the elastic recoil of the pulmonary parenchyma, and to changes in surface tension. It is evident that profound disturbances must be created by any process which greatly modifies the elasticity or distensibility of the lung. The great reserve of pulmonary function prevents, as a rule, serious consequences from regional changes in elasticity.

The forces of the muscles of respiration and the change in volume of the bony thoracic cage will be transmitted by the lung in a more or less radial manner toward the hilus, and will be dissipated in part on the columns of air in the respiratory passages. The resistance of these passages to the flow of air will modify the pressures produced by the lung in the alveoli themselves. Intra-alveolar pressure will be negative during inspiration (but less so than the intrapleural pressure), but will be slightly positive during expiration. Pathologic intra-alveolar pressures will modify the intrapleural pressure and the movements of the thoracic cage. For convenience of reference, the important approximate pressures within the chest are given in Table 21–1.

The amplitude of intrapleural pressure change can be used as a measure of the discrepancy in volume between the lung and the hemithorax. These pressures also measure the change in stress of the pulmonary parenchyma and indicate the changing forces to which the vascular bed is subjected. During aging, and during the course of *chronic obstructive emphysema*, the antero-posterior diameter of the chest is increased. However, the elasticity of lung is decreased. Therefore, the intrapleural pressure does not become more negative. As a matter of fact, it usually becomes less negative.

The larynx with its vocal cords serves several important functions in thoracopulmonary dynamics. In the first place, the larynx is the narrowest portion of the upper airway, and this obstruction is made abrupt and ledge-like at the rima glottidis. Consequently there is resistance to both inspiration and expiration. The vocal cords normally widen the airway slightly with inspiration and narrow it with expiration. The net effect of this abrupt obstruction is to facilitate the development of intrapulmonary negativity during the beginning of inspiration and favor intrapulmonary mixing by interposing slight expiratory resistance.

Much more important is the sphincteral

TABLE 21–1. IMPORTANT APPROXIMATE PRESSURES WITHIN THE CHEST.

	Inspiration	*Expiration*
Intrapleural (quiet breathing, recumbent)	− 7 cm. H_2O	− 2 cm. H_2O
Intra-alveolar (quiet breathing, recumbent)	− 0.5 cm. H_2O	+ 0.5 cm. H_2O
Forced inspiration, glottis closed	− 55 cm. H_2O	
Forced expiration, glottis closed		+ 65 cm. H_2O

action of the larynx. The closure of the larynx during rapid increase in intrathoracic pressure, and rapid opening of this organ, are essential to effective *cough*. The sphincteral action of the larynx is also protective against foreign bodies, especially fluids.

The smooth muscle that is distributed along the tracheobronchial tree is arranged so that these ducts may be altered in both length and diameter. The lung is likewise rich in elastic tissue, not only along the tracheobronchial tree, but also as a loose and rather poorly organized network of fibers which extend out into the alveolar septa. The trachea, bronchi, and bronchioles normally elongate and dilate during inspiration, and constrict and shorten during expiration. Since this actually alters the volume of the air conduit between the nose and the respiratory bronchiole, the dead space will increase during inspiration and decrease during expiration.

Work of Breathing

It is obvious that more work is required to meet the respiratory demands of great exertion than to meet the demands at rest. However, it was only after careful measurement of the mechanical work of breathing and the oxygen cost of breathing at different ventilatory volumes, and in different pathologic states, that it was realized that a large part of pulmonary disability may be due to the work performed in attempting to maintain adequate gas exchange.

In the normal individual, only about a third of the total work of breathing is due to airway and tissue resistance. Streamline or laminar flow occurs at ordinary flow rates along the relatively straight and smooth portions of the airway which are of relatively uniform bore. Streamline flow will be transformed to turbulence or eddying turbulence by marked change in direction of flow or sudden change in cross-sectional diameter of the airway. Turbulence is also produced at high velocity flows. Turbulence, and particularly eddying turbulence, is produced by anything which introduces an irregularity or partial obstruction within the airway. Turbulent flow requires a greater expenditure of work to move gas along the ventilatory ducts than is necessary during streamline flow.

Airway resistance is greater in bronchi of small internal diameter than in those of large diameter. Resistance to air flow is altered by changes in the diameter of the airway during normal inspiration and expiration. Disease may greatly increase resistance to air flow by a variety of mechanisms. Edema or congestion decreases the internal diameter of the tubes, thereby increasing resistance. Loss of ciliary action allows secretions to pool and accumulate, introducing airway obstruction and promoting edema and infection. The production of thick secretions may both decrease the diameter of the airway and also produce projections into the air stream which bring about turbulent flow and partial obstruction. Anything which tends to obstruct or narrow the airways will greatly increase the work of breathing.

Some of the mechanical work of breathing is determined by the elastic properties of the lungs and thorax. The term *compliance* is used to designate the resistance of the lung to increase in volume. It is a measure of distensibility. Compliance is expressed as change in volume (in liters) produced by a change in pressure (centimeters of water). The elastic properties which greatly assist in expiration must be overcome during inspiration. In the normal individual, the greatest part of the work of breathing at rest is expended in overcoming this elastic resistance of the lung.

Anything which stiffens the lung will decrease its compliance. Compliance may be decreased by fibrosis, whether perivascular, peribronchiolar or septal. It will be decreased by multiple granulomata, by diffuse infiltration of inflammatory or neoplastic origin, and by vascular congestion due to any cause. Stiffening processes may not only make it more difficult to distend the lung, but also impair its elastic recoil. Such pathologic changes, together with obstruction to air flow, greatly increase the work required to accomplish expiration. Instead of being an essentially passive act, as in the normal individual at rest, a great portion of the total work of breathing may be required to force air from the lung. The mechanical properties of the thoracic wall may be altered by some diseases, especially obesity, so that the work required for both inspiration and expiration is increased.

Disease can increase the ventilatory volume necessary to maintain adequate gas exchange. Disease may also increase greatly the amount of mechanical work required to accomplish this hyperventilation. The oxygen required by the muscles of respiration under such conditions may exceed the oxygen gained by hyperventilation, and hypoxia may increase unless a high oxygen mixture is substituted for room air.

Pulmonary Volumina

The methods of studying pulmonary function in man have changed greatly due to the requirement of thoracic surgery and the age of space, depth, and speed. Formerly, the experienced thoracic surgeon felt that by seeing the patient, taking his pulse, asking pertinent questions about exercise tolerance, and knowing the clinical background, he could predict whether or not the patient could withstand the operation planned so far as pulmonary function was concerned. Needless to say, this judgment was based on learning from error, and was subject to the limitations of all impressions. Equally inexact was judgment aided by determination of the "vital capacity" since limitations of this measurement were rarely appreciated. At present, estimation of pulmonary function is fairly adequate for clinical purposes. The biophysics of pulmonary function in relation to altitude, depth, acceleration, and rate of compression and decompression are being extensively studied by both military and civilian groups.

It is desirable to consider pulmonary function under two main subdivisions: ventilatory and respiratory. This is not an arbitrary division, but has its basis not only in the separate predominate functions of anatomic entities (e.g., the respiratory tract down through the respiratory bronchiole is almost entirely ventilatory), but also in the surprising degree to which they are independently variable. Ventilatory function is better understood, and will be discussed first.

Because of the rhythmicity of breathing and the ease with which displaced air may be graphically registered, the study of pulmonary ventilation was early concerned with the analysis of spirograms. Such tracings allow the measurement of various phases into which the act of breathing seems to divide naturally. These divisions are referred to as the *pulmonary volumina* (Fig. 21–1).

These volumes have been variously defined in the past both within the United States and abroad. In an attempt to reduce the confusion, a group of North American physiologists suggested the terminology illustrated in Figure 21–2. Note that the primary subdivisions of lung volume occupy the right half of the diagram and contain no overlapping volumes. These are true for any level of breathing effort. The left half of the diagram illustrates the more common volumes which are determined from spirograms in the clinical estimate of pulmonary function. Note that

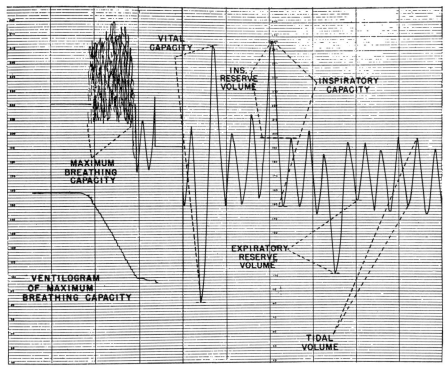

Figure 21–1. Pulmonary volumina. Spirogram of a normal subject illustrating the principal lung volumes. Kymograph set at fast speed. Horizontal lines are 2 mm. apart and are equivalent to 41.46 ml. Reduction factor for ventilometer is 25. The carbon dioxide absorber has been removed from the system.

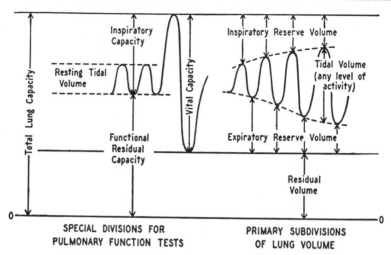

Figure 21–2. Subdivisions of the lung volume. (Federation Proc., Vol. 9.)

the term "capacity" is used for the clinical volumes, whereas the term "volume" is reserved for the primary subdivisions of lung volume.

Useful as this terminology is, the needs of clinical spirometry were not met, and there is again a confusion of terms in the literature. Gandevia and Hugh-Jones made recommendations that were approved by the Thoracic Society in Great Britain. The recommended nomenclature has been accepted by many workers, modified by others and ignored by some. The terminology which follows is in keeping with most of the recommendations of Gandevia and Hugh-Jones.

The most obvious lung volume is the amount of air breathed in or out during a single breathing cycle. This is termed the *tidal volume*. In the average adult it amounts to about 500 ml. This value may be multiplied by the minute respiratory rate to give the *minute ventilation*. The minute ventilation is subject to considerable variation unless the conditions under which it is determined are rigidly defined. For clinical purposes, the *resting* minute ventilation seems most important and should always be determined under the same conditions required for estimation of the basal metabolic rate. The minute ventilation at rest may represent a more or less minimal ventilatory requirement and can be compared with the respiratory requirement during exercise and the maximum voluntary ventilation.

The inspiratory and expiratory reserve volume may be measured at any level of activity, but in pulmonary function studies the resting state is usually used. *The inspiratory reserve volume* is the maximum amount of

gas that can be inspired from the spontaneous end-inspiratory (tidal) position. *The expiratory reserve volume* is the maximum amount of gas that can be expired from the spontaneous end-expiratory (tidal) position.

The *vital capacity* is the maximum amount of air that can be expired after a maximum inspiration. At times, one will encounter the term *inspiratory vital capacity*, which is the maximum amount of gas that can be inspired after a maximum expiration. The *inspiratory capacity* is the maximum volume of gas that can be inspired from the resting end-expiratory position.

The *forced vital capacity* (FVC) is the maximum volume of air which can be exhaled during rapid, forced expiration after a maximal inspiration. Although this is almost identical with the vital capacity in normal individuals, it will be less than the latter in the presence of obstructive airway disease. The same tracing, or maneuver, may be used to determine the *forced expiratory volume* for a given unit of time (FEV_t). The time unit may vary from ½ second to 3 seconds, but the volume at 1 second seems to have the greatest clinical usefulness. The forced expiratory volume often is expressed not only in relation to time but also as a percentage of the *observed* and *predicted* forced vital capacity ($FEV_t\%$). At 1 second, the forced expiratory volume should exceed 75 per cent ($FEV_1 = 75\%$) of the FVC, and this percentage should be at least 93 per cent at 3 seconds ($FEV_3 = 93\%$). The FEV_1 is probably the most useful single test of ventilatory function in common use, particularly when it is viewed as a percentage of the observed and predicted FVC.

Obstructive lung disease always reduces the volume of a gas which can be exchanged per unit of time, and it has been customary to determine the maximum volume of air that a patient will exchange during a period of forced rapid ventilation. The rate and depth of breathing may be varied to achieve a maximum result, but volume per breath is usually subordinate to rate because the extremes of inspiration and expiration are wasteful of time and energy. This measurement, usually termed the *maximum breathing capacity* (MBC), requires instruction and example on the part of the examiner, and motivation and cooperation by the patient. For these reasons, Gandevia and Hugh-Jones suggested that the term be replaced by *maximal voluntary ventilation* (MVV). The test is dependent upon the neuromuscular status and other extrapulmonary factors to a greater degree than is the volume exhaled during the first second of a forced expiration. In addition, volitional factors are less likely to alter the first second of a forced expiration. Therefore, the relationship between ventilatory capacity and pulmonary factors may be more clearly expressed in the FEV_1 than in the MVV. The MVV is usually determined in the standing or sitting position, using a breathing valve and tubing of low resistance. With those spirometers which have attached recording ventilometers, the maximum voluntary ventilation is best determined on the same graphic recording paper as is used for the registration of the pulmonary volumina, provided the resistance of the spirometer is not excessive. The rate and depth of breathing can be easily determined, and the form of the rapid excursions and changes in the end-expiratory position are helpful in the recognition of ventilatory disturbances and the adequacy of the patient's effort. A Tissot gasometer or Douglas bag can be used for collecting the expired air if a recording ventilometer is not available. The mechanics of breathing are demonstrated to the patient, and he is asked to breathe as rapidly and forcefully as possible during a specified period of time. Because of the symptoms of hypocapnia and the amount of muscular work required, the test is usually limited to either 12 or 15 seconds. If the patient is allowed to select his own frequency of breathing, the abbreviation MVV_F is used to indicate freedom of choice. For comparative purposes, it may be desirable to indicate the actual frequency selected by the patient as an additional subscript.

The FEV_1 can be a useful means of estimating the validity of the MVV. The FEV_1 multiplied by 40 should give a close approximation of the MVV (and has been called "the indirect MVV").

Although the FEV_1 is more truly a measure of airway resistance than is the MVV, the latter has had great clinical usefulness in evaluating the suitability of a patient for major chest surgery. The use of assisted ventilation during and after chest surgery has decreased the value of the MVV as a measure of anesthetic risk, but it retains its value for predicting ventilatory incapacity after convalescence.

A rapidly moving spirometer drum or similar device for inscribing a tracing during forced expiration permits the measurement of other volume-time relationships. One of these has been called the *maximal expiratory flow rate* (MEFR), and is defined as the volume exhaled per unit of time between the 200 and 1200 ml. volumes of FVC. Since this is not an instantaneous measurement of maximal flow, the designation *forced expiratory flow* ($FEF_{200-1200}$) recommended by Gandevia and Hugh-Jones is preferable.

Another volume-time measurement which is used frequently was designated the *maximal mid-expiratory flow* (MMF) and defined as the volume exhaled per unit of time during the middle 50 per cent of the FVC. This, likewise, is not a maximal measurement and is better termed *forced mid-expiratory flow* ($FEF_{25-75\%}$).

Peak flow during expiration can be measured by a flow meter which records the maximal instantaneous flow achieved at any point during the forced vital capacity. Since peak flow should relate to the emptying of the upper airway, there is objection to this measurement as an index of total airway resistance.

The *anatomical dead space* is the volume of the ventilatory passages from nose through bronchioles within which there is no rapid exchange of respiratory gases. This volume is about 100 ml. in adult women and 150 ml. in adult men.

The *physiological dead space* includes the anatomical dead space plus the volume of gas ventilating unperfused alveoli and the volume ventilating alveoli in excess of the requirement for full oxygenation. It is of primary importance in estimating ventilatory adequacy. The total minute ventilation at the nose or mouth is determined by the respiratory rate and tidal volume, but the actual volume that participates in gas exchange is

TABLE 21–2. USEFUL PREDICTION FORMULAS FOR NORMAL SUBJECTS.

Vital capacity (liters, BTPS), adults	Men*	0.052 Hcm. − .022A − 3.60
	Women†	0.041 Hcm. − .018A − 2.69
Vital capacity (milliliters, BTPS), children	Boys‡	$2.157 \times 10^{-3} \times$ Hcm.$^{2.81}$
	Girls‡	$1.858 \times 10^{-3} \times$ Hcm.$^{2.82}$
Maximum voluntary ventilation (MVV_f in liters/min., BTPS), adults	Men*	1.34 Hcm. − 1.26A − 21.4
	Women§	$(92 - \dfrac{A}{2})M^2$ BSA
One second forced expiratory volume (FEV_1 in liters, BTPS), adults	Men*	0.037 Hcm. − .028A − 1.59
	Women†	0.028 Hcm. − .021A − .867
Functional residual capacity (milliliters, BTPS), children	Boys‡	$7.312 \times 10^{-4} \times$ Hcm.$^{2.93}$
	Girls‡	$4.781 \times 10^{-3} \times$ Hcm.$^{2.54}$
Ratio of residual volume to total lung capacity (RV/TLC × 100%), adults	Men¶	0.43A + 16.3
	Women¶	0.33A + 22.7

Hcm = Height in centimeters. A = age in years. Standard deviations are not indicated, but normal range for volumina will be between ± 15–20 per cent of predicted.

* Kory, Callahan, Boren and Syner: Am. J. Med., *30:*243, 1961.
† Kory, Smith and Callahan, unpublished.
‡ DeMuth, Howatt, and Hill: Pediatrics, *35:*162, 1965.
§ Miller, Johnson and Wu: J. Appl. Physiol., *14:*510, 1959.
¶ Needham, Rogan and McDonald: Thorax, *9:*313, 1954.

the *alveolar volume,* which is determined by the magnitude of the physiological dead space in addition to the respiratory rate and tidal volume.

Total lung capacity, functional residual capacity, and residual volume cannot be determined spirometrically. The *functional residual capacity* (the volume of gas remaining in the lung at the end of a resting expiration) is usually measured by either a closed circuit rebreathing method depending upon helium dilution or an open circuit nitrogen washout with oxygen. If the functional residual capacity (FRC) is known, the *residual volume* (volume of gas in the lungs at end of a maximal expiration) can be determined by subtracting the spirometrically measured expiratory reserve volume from the FRC.

The *total lung capacity* (amount of gas in the lung at the end of maximal inspiration) can be found by adding the spirometrically measured inspiratory capacity to the FRC. The total lung capacity can be determined by whole-body plethysmography. When carefully performed, this method is more accurate than gas methods. The latter fail to measure the volume of lung which is not actively participating in ventilation at the time of study.

Figure 21–1 shows a typical clinical spirogram. A faster drum speed is necessary for accurate measurement of the FEV_1 and forced expiratory flow rates. Useful prediction formulas are in Table 21–2.

Regulation of Pulmonary Ventilation

The act of breathing is exceedingly complex in its controls and integration. The primary mechanisms of control are neural and chemical. Regulation and integration involve not only mechanisms initiated by the act of breathing, but also the chemical changes of respiration, chemical changes unrelated to the pulmonary segment of respiration, peripheral and central neuromuscular relations and purely voluntary cerebral modifications.

Changes in the act of breathing after experimental modification of alveolar and blood carbon dioxide and oxygen tensions, change in blood and respiratory center *p*H, stimulation of stretch reflexes and similar manipulation of factors known to modify breathing and respiration are too frequently accepted as separate factors, all having a basic position in the control of breathing. These are all important singly, but knowledge of these factors and of the manner in which they may modify breathing and respiration fails to give any clear idea of the integration of breathing.

The rhythmic change in thoracic capacity occurring in the normal adult about 16 cycles per minute constitutes the act of breathing. The known mechanisms which modify and control the act of breathing can be rather briefly presented.

Central Regulation of Breathing

Within the medulla are bilateral groups of neurons which are intrinsically active in effecting inspiration and expiration in a more or less rhythmic manner. In man, this center is essential for coordinated breathing and may be considered as the primary respiratory center. This center receives modifying afferents from both higher and lower centers.

There is good evidence for a separate bilateral center on the surface of the medulla which responds either to P_{CO_2} or $[H^+]$, but probably to the latter. This medullary chemoreceptive area is not stimulated by hypoxia, and may be primarily concerned with the regulation of hydrogen ion concentration in the cerebrospinal fluid. The normal cerebrospinal fluid pH (7.31) is lower and the CO_2 tension (47.9 mm. Hg) higher than arterial blood.

In the pons is a center which sends efferent impulses to the inspiratory neurons in the medulla, stimulating them to sustained discharge and consequent prolonged inspiration. This has been called the *apneustic center*. Although this center is subservient to vagal afferents and its function modified from descending impulses, it may be of some importance in intact man. At a higher level in the pons there is an area, called the *pneumotaxic center*, which facilitates expiration. Its importance in the regulation of breathing in man is not known.

Breathing may be modified by the cerebral cortex either in the direction of facilitation or inhibition. It is possible, in part, to delineate certain anatomic areas and pathways. Whether in response to emotion, special sensory afferents or simple volition, the cerebral cortex is of secondary importance, and is not involved in the maintenance of basically rhythmic breathing.

Reflex Control

Among the many reflexes mediated by the vagi, the stretch reflexes are probably best known. The Hering-Breuer inflation reflex is initiated by stimulation of receptors in the bronchioles or alveolar ducts. Action potentials increase in frequency as inspiration progresses in depth or rate and are carried to the medullary respiratory center to inhibit inspiration specifically and perhaps to serve as one factor in adjusting the rate and depth

of breathing for minimal muscular work. The deflation reflex increases the rate of breathing by means of vagal afferents, but its central connections and importance in man are not known.

Stretch receptors in the wall of the ascending aorta and the carotid sinuses send impulses to medullary centers which inhibit inspiration. When these receptors are stimulated by a decrease in vascular wall tension, they act to increase minute ventilation. Although the afferents from the ascending aorta are carried by the vagus and those from the carotid sinuses by the glossopharyngeal nerve, they both terminate in the nucleus of the fasciculus solitarius. It is doubtful that these reflexes are important in the regulation of breathing in man.

The pulmonary stretch receptors are probably of real importance in certain types of dyspnea. An unpleasant acceleration of breathing can be produced by pulmonary vascular congestion or edema, diffuse interstitial processes or atelectasis. All these abnormalities reduce the compliance of the lung and sensitize the stretch receptors.

There are other receptors within the vascular bed and small airways of the lung. The small airways are essentially unresponsive to mechanical stimulation but are extremely active through vagal afferents in the production of cough and bronchoconstriction as a response to chemical irritation. Receptors within the vascular bed are stimulated by embolism, and there is reflexly produced an initial apnea which is followed by rapid shallow breathing, bradycardia, hypotension and bronchoconstriction. This reflex is probably mediated through both the vagi and the sympathetic afferents.

Proprioceptive stimuli from the muscles of respiration modify and help to integrate breathing, both in rate and amplitude. Proprioceptives from the extremities seem to aid in the regulation of breathing, but their importance is doubtful. Tugging and pressure stimulation of abdominal viscera will modify the act of breathing. Cough and sneeze may be provoked by either mechanical or chemical stimulation of subepithelial receptors which give rise to vagal and glossopharyngeal afferents.

Breathing is modified by peripheral reflexes. The nociceptive cutaneous reflexes are striking. Immediate gasping breathing followed by hyperventilation can be produced by the sudden flow of cold water over the skin. Pain also modifies the act of breathing.

Some primarily protective reflexes from the larynx may give rise to considerable medical concern. Mechanical stimulation or increase in intraluminal pressure, both of which occur during intubation, may give rise to laryngospasm with apnea, bradycardia and cardiac arrhythmias, and bronchoconstriction.

Peripheral chemoreceptors are present in the carotid and aortic bodies, and give rise to dominant inspiratory afferents. They are experimentally sensitive to changes in P_{O_2}, P_{CO_2}, [H^+], and various drugs and chemicals which may be circulated through them. The carotid bodies particularly are important in severe hypoxic states.

Anoxemia produces an increase in the minute ventilation due to increased tidal exchange when moderate, but with an additive factor of increased rate when chronic anoxemia is severe. Hypoxic hyperventilation depends on actual oxygen tension and not on the oxygen content of the blood. These chemoreceptors do not alter ventilatory response significantly during mild hypoxemia. Although there is individual variation in sensitivity to decreased arterial oxygen tension, increased ventilation of significant degree does not usually occur until the breathing mixture contains approximately 12 per cent oxygen. However, if the carbon dioxide tension is increased slightly or moderately, the response to hypoxemia is greater and begins at a higher arterial P_{O_2}.

Under experimental conditions, an increase in P_{CO_2} or of hydrogen ion concentration of the arterial blood will produce an increase in action potentials in the carotid nerve. There is little evidence that these chemoreceptors are important in producing hyperventilatory response to change in P_{CO_2} under usual circumstances.

There is a good reason to believe that during the hyperventilation that occurs in acute hypoxia, carbon dioxide contributes little to the maintenance of ventilation. In such situations hyperventilation occurs reflexly due to hypoxia of the peripheral chemoreceptors; the reduction in carbon dioxide tension from hyperventilation makes no difference. Ordinarily CO_2 responsiveness is determined by the central medullary chemoreceptors, and when they are depressed or adapted to high P_{CO_2}, the carotid and aortic bodies respond as usual to hypoxia but not to hypercapnia.

In chronic hypoxia, such as may occur during acclimatization to altitude, the respiratory center becomes more sensitive to carbon dioxide. The threshold is lowered to the point

at which the alveolar P_{CO_2} exceeds the threshold and is responsible for at least part of the hyperventilation which occurs. However, it is the low atmospheric oxygen tension stimulating the peripheral chemoreceptors which maintains hyperventilation. The carotid chemoreceptors do not adapt to low oxygen tension.

An important clinical application of this primacy of hypoxic control of ventilation is seen in those patients with chronic alveolar hypoventilation. Carbon dioxide accumulation may be quite high in the chronic state without producing coma. Since these patients are frequently cyanotic and dyspneic, high oxygen mixtures may be given for breathing. The arterial oxygen tension can thus be raised to abolish cyanosis. Unfortunately this removes the hypoxic respiratory drive, and ventilation may become greatly reduced, thereby allowing further accumulation of carbon dioxide. Unless some means of mechanical hyperventilation is provided to remove CO_2, the abolition of hypoxia in such circumstances may lead to carbon dioxide narcosis and even death.

Voluntary Control

It has been indicated that the cerebral cortex may modify breathing without having any basic position in inherent rhythmicity. Breathing is fundamentally an involuntary act, yet there is abundant evidence of cortical modifications in both the waking and sleeping states. Breathing is modified during speaking and swallowing, but this is partially voluntary and partially reflex. Many individuals exhibit slight coughs or sniffs at frequent intervals on a habitual basis. These may be similar to the type of periodic sighing seen in psychoneurotics and others during states of anxiety. However, it must be remembered that periodic hyperinflation is essential to normal lung function. Fear and other emotions may greatly modify breathing, and variations are seen during different stages of sleeping and dreaming.

Pulmonary Respiration and Its Regulation

It has been stated that the pulmonary segment of respiration is concerned with the movement of oxygen and carbon dioxide between the gaseous compartment in the alveoli and the fluid compartment in the pulmonary capillaries. This process of diffusion must take place through both the alveolar membrane and the capillary barrier.

Electron microscopy has revealed the presence of an epithelium lining the alveolar wall. Except for the perinuclear region, the cytoplasm of these cells appears to be very thin, but capable of some modification in thickness. In addition, these cells rest upon a basement membrane. Also in the alveolar walls are loosely arranged fibrils of collagen which are more numerous by far than the elastic fibers present. The alveolar epithelial cells are believed to secrete surfactant by means of organelles called "lamellar inclusion bodies."

The capillary barrier is formed by the capillary endothelium and its basement membrane. Where the capillary approaches the alveolar epithelial surface most intimately, the endothelial and epithelial basement membranes are close together, but are not adherent. Diffusion of gases across this barrier may well be influenced by histochemical changes which have not yet been explored.

Pulmonary Diffusion

Although the movement of gases from one region to another because of purely physical considerations involves concentration gradients as well as pressure gradients, the "diffusion capacity of the lung" is defined in pressure terms: namely, the milliliters of a gas at standard conditions diffusing across the alveolocapillary membrane per minute per mm. Hg of partial pressure difference between alveolar air and pulmonary capillary blood. Actual diffusion for oxygen (or CO) from alveolar air to intraerythrocytic hemoglobin must also involve consideration of solubilities and tension differences in surfactant, interstitial fluid, plasma and intracellular fluid. Therefore, the "diffusion capacity of the lung" (D_L) consists of at least two phases which can be separated at present: D_M, the membrane diffusing capacity; and θV_c, the diffusing capacity of the erythrocytes within the pulmonary capillary bed.

Despite the much greater affinity of hemoglobin for CO than for O_2, the use of CO for measurement of the pulmonary diffusing capacity involves competition between O_2 and CO for hemoglobin and thereby nullifies the assumption that capillary CO tension is negligible. The diffusing capacity for CO ($D_{L_{CO}}$) decreases when the alveolar O_2 tension increases and vice versa. This difference is independent of the alveolocapillary membrane. Consequently, by measuring diffusing capacity for CO with both a high and low oxygen mixture, one can estimate the $D_{M_{CO}}$ and the volume of blood in the pulmonary capillary bed (V_C).

$D_{M_{CO}}$ is the membrane diffusing capacity for CO defined as the rate in ml. per minute under standard conditions divided by the difference in tension (in mm. Hg) between alveolar air and the plasma. The value obtained in normal individuals varies with the method used for measurement as well as with other factors (e.g., body size, age, exercise) known to influence the diffusing capacity. The single breath (breath-holding) method is probably used most widely, and gives a $D_{L_{CO}}$ of approximately 30 ml./(min. $\times$ mm. Hg) and $D_{M_{CO}}$ of 57 ml./(min. $\times$ mm. Hg).

The diffusing capacity between the plasma and the intracellular hemoglobin can be expressed as $\theta_{CO}V_C$, which can be defined as the diffusing capacity in ml./(min. $\times$ mm. Hg) of the average number of erythrocytes in the pulmonary capillaries at any instant. θ_{CO} is the *rate* of combination of 1 ml. of blood with CO in ml. CO/(min. $\times$ mm. Hg), and is dependent upon the P_{O_2} present, being lower at high P_{O_2} and higher at low P_{O_2}. θ_{CO} can be determined in vitro on erythrocyte suspensions and, at constant P_{O_2}, is dependent upon the erythrocyte concentration in the pulmonary capillaries. Since this latter is unknown, the hematocrit of venous blood can be substituted. If θ_{CO} is known for high and low levels of P_{O_2} together with the CO capacity of the peripheral blood, the value of V_C can be estimated. Capillary volume at any instant is normally somewhere between 60 and 100 ml. in the resting state.

In health, with variation in physiologic conditions (e.g., exercise), D_L seems to be determined primarily by V_C. This is to be expected since capillary volume is rapidly responsive to change in physiologic factors affecting the pulmonary vascular bed and cardiac output, whereas no such responsiveness is known for the physical characteristics of the alveolar membrane.

As one might expect, $D_{M_{CO}}$ and $D_{L_{CO}}$ are approximately halved by pneumonectomy; but although both surface area of the diffusing membrane and the dimensions of the capillary bed are, in fact, approximately halved, the ventilation-perfusion ratios in the remaining lung are usually improved so that $D_{L_{CO}}$ is reduced (in the resting state) to less than 50 per cent.

Diffuse alveolar surface alterations (e.g., bronchiolar cell carcinoma) and some diffuse "interstitial" processes (e.g., pulmonary scleroderma) will reduce $D_{M_{CO}}$ more than V_C. On the other hand, significant anemia will reduce θV_C without necessarily altering D_M.

$D_{L_{CO}}$ increases with body size and exercise, but decreases with age. Changes in $D_{L_{CO}}$ with changes in alveolar volume, blood flow, hyperventilation, and vascular pressure vary somewhat with the method of measurement.

The Circulation in the Lung

In normal man, the pulmonary circulation carries the entire output of the right ventricle. Between the outgoing pulmonary arteries and the incoming pulmonary veins lies a vast vascular bed consisting of pulmonary arterioles, capillaries, and venules. The normal pulmonary arterioles are not rich in smooth muscle. The capillaries are extremely thin with little supporting tissue. The distensibility of the normal vascular bed is great and its resistance low. Although not entirely a passive system, the immensity of the capillary bed and the normal lack of resistance-producing muscular arterioles permit the existence of a rather gradual fall in intravascular pressures between the right ventricle and the left heart. Pulmonary resistance to flow is about one-eighth that of the systemic circulation. The main pulmonary artery pressure at rest is approximately 14 mm. Hg, and the left atrial pressure is approximately 5 mm. Hg, giving a pressure drop of only 9 mm. Hg.

In normal man the greater circulation, through the bronchial arteries, contributes a small amount of blood to the venous return from the lungs. This contribution is of no known consequence in health, but may be significant in many diseases affecting the pulmonary parenchyma and vasculature.

So far as is known, the right heart is subject to the same general regulatory mechanisms as the left, and these are not discussed here. The pulmonary circulation distal to the heart is influenced or regulated by a variety of mechanisms which, on the whole, are less well known than those controlling ventilation.

The capillary bed normally contains only a small volume of blood per moment (75 to 100 ml.), but is capable of expansion to a relatively enormous volume without increasing the intracapillary pressure to a level which could have significantly detrimental effects. As a consequence of low intravascular pressure and delicate walls, the capillary bed is influenced significantly by changes in the in-trapulmonary and intrapleural pressures and changes in the gradient between them. Capillary blood flow is normally pulsatile due to the very low pulmonary arteriolar resistance. Pulsatile flow probably is maintained during obstruction of lobar pulmonary arteries, whereas it disappears during embolization from multiple small emboli due to bacterial endotoxin.

Resistance to flow develops within the pulmonary bed in many diseases of the pulmonary vasculature and parenchyma. It is difficult to measure the changes in resistance which may occur regionally or locally and which participate in the regulation of pulmonary blood flow. It has been suggested that in small vessels, such as those constituting a large portion of the pulmonary vascular bed, the patency of the vessel is dependent upon the equilibrium existing between the intravascular pressure, which tends to keep the vessel open, and the tension in the vascular wall, which tends to close it. If the tension in the wall, from whatever source, exceeds the intravascular pressure, the blood vessel will tend to close actively and completely. The pressure necessary has been called the *critical closing pressure*. Since the pulmonary circulation is a low pressure system, it would be advantageous for the arterioles to have a small critical closing pressure. Present evidence suggests that either the critical closing pressure is, indeed, small or for practical purposes nonexistent. This does not mean that pressure-flow relationships of the whole lung are not complicated or regional, but rather that flow through individual vessels depends simply upon the balance between intra- and extravascular pressures.

If one assumes that the colloid osmotic pressure is the same in both the pulmonary and systemic circulations, then the much lower hydrostatic pressure in the pulmonary system will tend to protect the lung from the movement of intravascular fluid into the alveoli. If the pulmonary capillary pressure becomes greatly elevated, edema is likely to occur. Pulmonary hypertensive mechanisms are discussed later.

Control of the Pulmonary Circulation

The anatomic structure and relations of the pulmonary vasculature are such that changes in the pressures and flow are measured more easily in pathologic states than in normal man. Even such an obvious factor as gravity is difficult to demonstrate by ordinary methods until failure of the circulation brings about orthopnea.

It was stated previously that flow in individual vessels depends upon the balance between intra- and extravascular pressure and that the latter varies with changes in intrapulmonary and intrapleural pressure as well as the gradient between them. Inspiration and expiration must, therefore, exert a modifying effect on pulmonary blood flow. This effect is small during ordinary breathing, but both forced inflation and deflation produce a rise in pulmonary vascular resistance.

The remarkable distensibility and reserve vascular volume of the lungs make possible a great increase in volume flow with little increase in perfusing pressure. It is probable that flow can be increased by "conditioning" without comparable change in perfusing pressue (in athletes), although high altitude studies indicate that a consequence of such residence is some increase in this pressure.

Pneumonectomy increases the pulmonary vascular pressures very little if the contralateral lung is normal. This fact is useful in the preoperative evaluation of patients proposed for pneumonectomy. Balloon occlusion of the artery to the involved lung should produce only a small sustained rise in main pulmonary artery pressure if the contralateral pulmonary vascular bed is essentially normal.

One of the most important controls is the response to oxygen tension. Hypoxemia or local hypoxia results in increased vascular resistance. Hypoxemia produces a rise in pulmonary artery pressure which is not an acute adaptive mechanism since residence at high altitude is accompanied by a variable degree of pulmonary hypertension. Local hypoxia brings about shunting of blood away from poorly ventilated or unventilated areas to improve ventilation-perfusion ratios. If anoxemia is severe, pulmonary arterial pressure falls and cardiac output rises in an attempt to produce maximal pulmonary flow.

The neurohumoral control of the pulmonary circulation is incompletely known. Pressoreceptors are present in both the pulmonary arterial and venous systems. Vasoconstriction and vasodilatation can also occur on the effector side. The known innervation is the expected vagal and sympathetic divisions of the autonomic system.

Epinephrine and norepinephrine undoubtedly affect the pulmonary circulation, but the mechanism of the effects is not known for man. It is probable that hexamethonium can block the vasoconstrictor fibers. Other blocking agents, such as tetraethylammonium, also affect the pulmonary circulation. The measurable effects of such humoral agents are much more obvious in the presence of disease with pulmonary hypertension.

O_2-CO_2 Exchange and Respiratory Hydrogen Ion Regulation

Dissociation of a substance in a solvent to form a positively charged ion (cation) and a negatively charged ion (anion) is not equivalent to dissociation into an "acid radical" and a "basic radical." To be an acid, the substance must be in a solution which can accept protons. The metal cations (Na^+, K^+, Ca^{++}) are neither acids nor bases since they cannot donate or accept hydrogen ions (protons). Electrical charge and balance of charges (electronegativity) are important in the regulation of biologic electrolytes, but are not equivalent to acid-base balance.

Solutions containing both weak acids or bases and their salts reduce the magnitude of change in pH resulting from the addition of an acid or base to the solution. This phenomenon is called buffering. It is simply a matter of reducing the dissociation of the proton donor or acceptor. The respiratory system is concerned with the carbonic acid-bicarbonate buffer pair. Carbonic acid is weak (not highly dissociated), and the bicarbonate salt is fully dissociated. If a nonvolatile acid is added to this buffering solution, the resulting hydrogen ion activity will be considerably less than it would be if the added acid were in water alone. This is simply a matter of reduced dissociation of the carbonic acid (thereby reducing hydrogen ion concentration) due to the relatively large amount of conjugate base supplied by the fully dissociated salt and the excess conjugate base available to accept hydrogen ions from the added acid. Although the buffer systems are present to regulate hydrogen ion, clinical chemistry has emphasized the changes in anions and cations because of available measurements.

In biological systems, the glass electrode is standard for pH measurement as is saturated KCl for the salt bridge. Despite cogent pleas to discard pH in favor of some direct notation of hydrogen ion concentration, the negative logarithm of the hydrogen ion concentration is likely to remain in use because the voltage developed by our usual hydrogen ion measuring instruments is proportional to the logarithm of the hydrogen ion concentration (activity). Furthermore, the mathematical manipulations and connotations of pH are not as difficult to understand as many clinicians seem to think.

With this brief background, it is convenient to consider the transport of carbon dioxide and oxygen, the means of doing so with little change in hydrogen ion concentration, and the function of the carbonic acid-bicarbonate buffer system in the regulation of hydrogen ion derived from nonvolatile acids.

O_2-CO_2 *transfer*, whether from the metabolizing cells to the blood or back and forth between the blood and the pulmonary alveoli, depends directly upon the partial pressures of each gas and its solubility coefficient when dissolved. The difference in partial pressures and membrane permeability factors determines the rate and direction of diffusion of gases at all body interfaces.

The solubility coefficient for O_2 in blood is low (0.023 ml. O_2/ml. of blood at 38° C.). Therefore, the amount of oxygen in physical solution in arterial blood is small (0.003 ml./ml. of blood) at the normal P_{O_2} of 100 mm. Hg.

The solubility coefficient for CO_2 is much higher (0.488 ml. CO_2/ml. arterial blood at 38° C.), but the partial pressure of carbon dioxide is lower (40 mm. Hg in arterial blood) so that the amount of dissolved CO_2 (0.026 ml./ml. of blood) is also small.

It is evident from this that *transport* of both O_2 and CO_2 must be accomplished for the most part by means other than physical solution. Transport of both gases, and a considerable portion of hydrogen ion regulation, depends primarily upon hemoglobin.

Oxygen has a partial pressure of approximately 155 mm. Hg in air at sea level, and this is reduced to 100 mm. by dilution in the alveoli. Mixed venous blood has an oxygen tension of about 40 mm. when entering the pulmonary capillary so that the oxygen gradient is large. In the normal individual, equilibration takes place within the capillary passage time, but arterial blood has a slightly lower oxygen tension (5 to 10 mm. Hg) than alveolar air due to some admixture of venous blood (bronchial and thebesian veins).

As already stated, oxygen *transport* is primarily by binding with hemoglobin. The amount of oxygen which can be carried by hemoglobin (at full saturation) is 1.34 ml./gm. or 20.1 ml. in 100 ml. of blood containing 15 gm. of hemoglobin.

The actual percentage saturation of hemoglobin is dependent upon the partial pressure of oxygen, but in a nonlinear fashion. The oxygen dissociation curve for hemoglobin is such that during reasonably normal states *arterial* oxygen tensions can change widely with only small change in saturation, whereas at the tensions prevailing at the tissue level, large changes in saturation occur with small changes in partial pressure, thus making abundant oxygen available.

The oxygen dissociation curve of hemoglobin is altered by pH. At higher than normal hydrogen ion concentrations, dissociation of oxygen from hemoglobin is increased. This tends to make more oxygen available at the tissue level and during acidosis.

Cellular metabolism yields large amounts of CO_2 which must be transferred from the cell to the liquid and cellular constituents of the blood. Since the membrane permeability for CO_2 is high and carbonic anhydrase is not present in the bulk of tissues, transfer is dependent upon the development of an intracellular CO_2 tension which exceeds that of the interstitial fluid and blood. The CO_2 tension of venous blood (46 mm. Hg) is only 6 mm. higher than the arterial gas tension.

A small amount of carbon dioxide is hydrated ($CO_2 + H_2O \rightleftarrows H_2CO_3$) in the plasma, but in the absence of carbonic anhydrase this is a minor mode of transport. The hydrated CO_2 combines with sodium in the plasma to form a small portion of the plasma bicarbonate.

Major transport is by means of bicarbonate ion ($H_2CO_3 \rightleftarrows H^+ + HCO_3^-$) in the plasma, and is dependent upon the acceptance of the released hydrogen ion by intracellular hemoglobin and ion exchange by the chloride shift.

Most of the CO_2 enters the red blood cells where, under usual circumstances, the greater part is hydrated very rapidly due to the high content of carbonic anhydrase. Thus there is created a large pool of hydrogen ion which must be "inactivated" to avoid a wide shift in pH. To explain how this is accomplished without change in pH requires some digression.

Hemoglobin is an amphoteric protein (ampholyte) whose pK is 7.9, whereas the pK for oxyhemoglobin is 6.7. This means that hemoglobin ("reduced hemoglobin") is a weaker acid than oxyhemoglobin. This change in behavior (i.e., as acid or base) is believed due to the —NH group of the imidazole ring of hemoglobin which changes molecular position during oxygenation. These groups have been called "oxylabile" because their dissociation (ionic) changes with oxygenation. By this mechanism, hemoglobin can bind approximately 0.7 hydrogen ion for each molecule of O_2 given up (within the usual pH range). Consequently, if the respiratory quotient were 0.7, a person could bind all the hydrogen ions liberated during ordinary metabolism without change in pH or utilization of any true buffer system. The change from oxyhemoglobin to hemoglobin occurs at the tissue level where CO_2 is produced. Since there is no change in pH, this has been called "the isohydric shift."

Whereas the greater part of the $[H^+]$ is bound by hemoglobin, the bicarbonate combines with the intracellular potassium made available by isohydric conversion. Potassium bicarbonate is highly dissociated. The red blood cell membrane is permeable to negatively charged ions, but not to cations. Therefore, bicarbonate ions traverse the red cell membrane. To preserve electronegativity, anions must enter the red cell to replace the migrated $[HCO_3^-]$. Chloride ion is the most abundant anion in the plasma and is the major replacement. This exchange of chloride for bicarbonate ions in accordance with the Donnan equilibrium principle is called the chloride shift. It is now evident that the major portion of bicarbonate (CO_2) transport is ultimately in the plasma, although it must first enter the red cell, and most of the hydrogen ion released is bound within the red blood cell. Plasma bicarbonate becomes a major alkali donor (Na^+) in electrolyte regulation as well as the largest transport mechanism for CO_2 under normal circumstances.

Some of the CO_2 which enters the red cell combines directly with hemoglobin and oxyhemoglobin as carbamino compounds. This reaction is also dependent upon oxylabile groups and is greater with hemoglobin than oxyhemoglobin. It probably accounts for more than half of the CO_2 transported within the red cell. The oxylabile group involved in the carbamino reaction is $-NH_2$, not the $-NH$ of the isohydric shift.

Oxygen-CO_2 transfer is in opposite directions at the tissue level and within the pulmonary alveoli. The general mechanisms of tissue transfer and transport in the blood have been briefly described. Exchange at the pulmonary level is no different in principle since the equations involved are reversible.

The difference in partial pressures between oxygen in the alveoli and oxygen in the mixed venous blood is the most important single factor in the transfer of O_2 in the normal person. Most of the hemoglobin is converted to oxyhemoglobin (changing pK from 7.9 to 6.7) thus freeing hydrogen ions. The excess hydrogen ions are taken up by bicarbonate.

The difference in partial pressures of CO_2 between mixed venous blood and alveolar gas is small, but sufficient to initiate diffusion of CO_2 into the alveoli because of the high membrane permeability for CO_2. The low partial pressure of CO_2 in air makes it possible to increase the unloading of CO_2 by hyperventilation (increasing the difference in partial pressures). This simple mechanism can maintain a nearly normal CO_2 output in people whose carbonic anhydrase has been inhibited by the administration of acetazolamide, although both tissue and mixed venous blood CO_2 tensions will be elevated. Because hemoglobin cannot be supersaturated, hyperventilation can alter O_2 content in the blood very little in the normal individual despite elevation of the alveolar PO_2. Hyperventilation can serve as a compensatory mechanism, if the oxygen cost of hyperventilatory effort is not too great, when hypoxemia is present to a degree sufficient to place the arterial oxygen saturation on the steep portion of the O_2 dissociation curve of hemoglobin.

Under normal circumstances, most of the CO_2 blown off in the lungs will be derived from the bicarbonate load due to the liberation of H^+ ions in the hemoglobin-oxyhemoglobin conversion and the activity of carbonic anhydrase. This requires that bicarbonate move back into the red cell where the enzyme can catalyze the breakdown of carbonic acid, although some carbonic anhydrase is present in lung tissue and alveolar CO_2 equilibrates with lung tissue in about 1 second. The sequence can be summarized by the equation at the bottom of this page. The CO_2 diffuses readily across the red cell membrane into the plasma and across the alveolar membranes.

The carbamino mechanism of CO_2 transport is also reversible, and therefore CO_2 is given up when hemoglobin is oxygenated. It is the reversibility of all these transport mechanisms and the interrelationships of CO_2 and O_2 with hemoglobin that make O_2-CO_2

$$H^+ \text{ (oxygenation of hemoglobin)} + HCO_3^- \longrightarrow H_2CO_3 \text{ (red cell)} \underset{CA}{\longrightarrow} H_2O + CO_2\uparrow.$$

exchange a system with tremendous reserves without serious swings in hydrogen ion concentration.

Acid-Base Balance

Despite the fact that the pK for the bicarbonate-carbonic acid buffer system is 6.1, it holds a predominant place in the regulation of hydrogen ion derived from acids stronger than carbonic. This is due to the fact that the stronger acid reacts with bicarbonate, substituting the weaker and volatile carbonic acid for the stronger acid. Carbonic acid dissociates into H_2O and CO_2 and the latter is blown off in the lungs.

When the law of mass action is applied to the dissociation of the weak acid H_2CO_3, $\frac{[H^+] \times [HCO_3^-]}{[H_2CO_3]} = K$, K being the dissociation constant. If rearranged to solve for $[H^+]$ and converted to the negative logarithm (to the base 10), the expression becomes the Henderson-Hasselbalch equation: $pH = pK + \log \frac{[HCO_3^-]}{[H_2CO_3]}$

For clarity, two modifications are necessary: (1) The pH of the buffer system depends not only on the ratio of $[HCO_3^-]$ to $[H_2CO_3]$ but also on the specific ionic concentration present. The pK can be corrected for this ionic strength and is then designated pK^1. (2) The carbonic acid is present as such in very small concentration, most being present as CO_2 (dissolved) $+ H_2O$. Hence, we can substitute the solubility coefficient of CO_2 in plasma (a) expressed in millimols/liter/mm. Hg multiplied by the P_{CO_2} for the denominator. The final equation becomes: $pH = pK^1 + \log \frac{[HCO_3^-]}{a (P_{CO_2})}$. At 38° C., the equation is: $pH = 6.1 + \log \frac{[HCO_3^-]}{0.03 P_{CO_2}}$ where $[HCO_3^-]$ is expressed in millimols per liter and the P_{CO_2} in mm. Hg.

For normal blood pH of 7.4, the ratio of $[HCO_3^-]$ to $[H_2CO_3]$ is 20 to 1, and it is the maintenance of this ratio that preserves a fixed pH. For example, in normal status one could have:

$$pH = 6.1 + \log \frac{[24 \text{ mM./L } HCO_3^-]}{0.03 \times 40 \text{ mm. Hg } P_{CO_2}}$$

$$= 6.1 + \log \frac{24}{1.2} = 6.1 + \log 20 = 7.4.$$

With an increase in blood P_{CO_2} to 60 mm. Hg ($0.03 \times 60 = 1.8$), the pH of 7.4 can be preserved by raising the $[HCO_3^-]$ to 36 mM./L.

The physiologic significance of this buffer system is obvious for protection against added acids (other than carbonic) because CO_2 is volatile and can be blown off rapidly in the lung. The buffer ratio of 20 bicarbonate to 1 CO_2 is such that the handling of added acid is facilitated. This ratio is far from the maximum buffering capacity for this system and would appear to be a poor one for the control of added nonrespiratory base. However, CO_2 (H_2CO_3) is being added constantly from cellular metabolism.

We are not concerned here with the mechanisms of production of so-called metabolic acidosis and alkalosis. Their origins may be far removed from metabolic sources, but the bicarbonate-carbonic acid buffer system is the first line of defense against both.

Granted that the buffering systems may be seriously depleted in their efforts to maintain a physiologic pH and that this knowledge is important to the understanding of the patient's physiologic stability, it is still a matter of hydrogen ion concentration that determines "acidosis" or "alkalosis." If the pH is below the physiologic range, acidosis is present, and if the pH exceeds this range, the patient is alkalotic. Compensatory mechanisms may be indicated by the values of serum electrolytes and CO_2 content, tension, and combining power, but the blood pH (preferably arterial) must be known for accurate classification. There is no longer any valid reason why capillary or arterial pH cannot be obtained on any hospitalized patient. The clinical picture of moderate respiratory alkalosis may be like that of metabolic acidosis, and the total plasma CO_2 content, or CO_2 combining power, or arterial P_{CO_2} will be low in both. True differentiation rests upon the elevated arterial blood pH in respiratory alkalosis and the lowered value in metabolic acidosis.

When the hydrogen ion concentration in arterial blood is increased from sources other than carbonic acid, the sequence already described takes place. The stronger acid combines with bicarbonate (decreasing bicarbonate) to substitute the weaker acid, H_2CO_3, which after dissociation into H_2O and CO_2 can be controlled (partially) in the lungs by blowing off CO_2. This still leaves a decrease in $[HCO_3^-]$ which can be reestablished (compensated) only by the kidney which reabsorbs $[HCO_3^-]$, converts H_2CO_3 to CO_2 and H_2O (because of the presence of carbonic anhydrase), and exchanges a hydrogen ion for a sodium ion. Immediate adjustment is via the large reserve of bicarbonate. Intermediate response is hyperventilation (stimulated by increased $[H^+]$ and P_{CO_2}) which lowers the blood P_{CO_2} but rarely completely restores normality; ultimate compensation depends upon renal mechanisms.

If the hydrogen ion concentration in arterial blood is reduced from sources other than bicarbonate, pH increases and alkalosis is present. Carbonic acid will be rapidly depleted by the added base, and although continued CO_2 production will tend to restore carbonic acid, the respiratory centers will respond to both $[H^+]$ and P_{CO_2} by hypoventilation to restore the H_2CO_3. Hypoventilation will continue to increase P_{CO_2} in the blood and tissues until pH returns nearly to normal. Again, ultimate regulation of $[H^+]$ will depend upon the kidney to excrete the excess bicarbonate. Since renal mechanisms for compensation are considerably slower than respiratory ones and since renal function may be impaired in many pathologic states involving serious alterations of $[H^+]$, careful monitoring of both pH and P_{CO_2} is frequently necessary to prevent therapy from worsening the acid-base status. This will be discussed later.

Respiratory acidosis and alkalosis are primary disturbances of CO_2 regulation by the lungs and although immediately altered by the non-(bicarbonate/carbonic acid) buffer systems, depend upon renal mechanisms for correction.

Respiratory acidosis begins when either alveolar ventilation is primarily reduced or is unable, for any reason, to increase commensurately with elevated CO_2 production. The initial change is an increase in arterial P_{CO_2}. This must be followed, as already explained, by a rise in total plasma CO_2 due to an increase in dissolved CO_2 (H_2CO_3) and bicarbonate. The equation: $CO_2 + H_2O \rightleftarrows H_2CO_3 \rightleftarrows H^+ + HCO_3^-$ is being driven to the right. The non-(bicarbonate/carbonic acid) buffers can handle the initial increase in hydrogen ion concentration, but experiments in normal individuals breathing high CO_2 mixtures (7 per cent and 10 per cent) show that the "whole body titration curve" for CO_2 has little depth during acute change and a drop in pH is quick to appear. A steady-state elevation of P_{CO_2}, $[H^+]$, and $[HCO_3^-]$ is achieved within 10 minutes under these conditions. Bicarbonate increase is not great, and is quite insufficient to significantly modify the hydrogen ion increase which appears to be nearly linear with the rise in P_{CO_2}. Thus, respiratory acidosis is characterized by an increased arterial CO_2 tension and total CO_2 together with an increased hydrogen ion concentration (lowered pH). The hemoglobin and other protein buffers are perhaps less protective than has been thought.

Chronic respiratory acidosis is not so clear cut. Quite aside from the mechanisms responsible for its existence, duration alone alters the picture due to the renal compensations which excrete hydrogen ion and increase bicarbonate. Sufficient renal compensation may take place to raise serum bicarbonate to twice its normal value with consequent decrease in chloride ion and a pH which does not directly reflect the P_{CO_2}.

The patient with a stable chronic respiratory acidosis may appear to be much better than his precarious biochemical state. Like the patient with chronic uremia, the seriousness of his disturbance may not even be investigated until acute insult destroys his compensation and he is near death.

The causes of alveolar hypoventilation are many, but those most often encountered are basically due to obstructive ventilatory dysfunction, such as chronic bronchitis, emphysema, asthma and those diseases obstructing alveoli or bronchioles such as diffuse bronchopneumonia and alveolar proteinosis. Obstruction of the upper airway is an unusual cause, but chronic respiratory acidosis and hypoxemia can be produced in children by marked enlargement of the tonsils and adenoids. Oversedation and anesthesia are not infrequently associated with hypercapnia, and are somewhat analogous (at least temporarily) to what occurs in hypoventilation due to muscular or neuromuscular insufficiency (myasthenia gravis, poliomyelitis).

It is only a step from respiratory center depression due to drugs to alveolar hypoventilation due to infarction or other destructive disease of the respiratory centers, and from muscular inadequacy due to intrinsic or neuromuscular disease to the inadequate ventilation of extreme thoracoabdominal obesity. The lungs may be normal in all these conditions, yet hypoxemia and hypercapnia can be serious.

The relationship of hypercapnia to hypoxemia in CO_2 retention is now well known and needs no belaboring. Patients with CO_2 retention show a decreased responsiveness of the respiratory center to CO_2 elevation, and the principal stimulus to ventilation is the hypoxia of the peripheral chemoreceptors. Therefore if oxygen is administered to such a one, the hypoxic drive is removed, and alveolar hypoventilation increases abruptly with a consequent sharp rise in P_{CO_2} and $[H^+]$.

Excess blood CO_2, whether acute or chronic, produces symptoms and signs which are explicable on the basis of the physiologic effects already enumerated. These occur rapidly because of the great membrane permeability to CO_2. Cerebral blood flow and spinal fluid pressure increase. Headache is the most common symptom. Increase in systemic blood pressure often appears relatively early during acute or subacute CO_2 retention. Hyperventilation, when permitted by the neuromusculoskeletal system, occurs in response to acute increase in P_{CO_2} if the respiratory centers are intact and not already too depressed. However, responsive hyperventilation is much more obvious in otherwise normal individuals suffering from acute hypercapnia than in chronic respiratory acidosis during exacerbation. Most patients with chronic respiratory acidosis are unable to raise alveolar ventilation to normal without mechanically controlled ventilation. In the previously normal patient developing hypercapnia, confusion or retarded cerebration with restlessness is common, whereas in the chronic hypercapnic undergoing acute intensification, coma with tremor and papilledema are frequent.

Respiratory alkalosis is being recognized far more frequently than in the past. There are two primary reasons for this: blood pH is being determined more frequently, and inhalational therapy, particularly controlled and assisted breathing, is becoming a part of the facilities of the general hospital. Respiratory alkalosis is characterized by a low P_{CO_2} and total CO_2 and some elevation of the blood pH.

Anything that increases alveolar ventilation to supernormal levels (hyperventilation), whether encephalitis or mechanical ventilation, decreases the alveolar P_{CO_2} and thus the arterial blood P_{CO_2}. Without actual monitoring of both tidal volume and breathing frequency it may be difficult to know the adequacy of ventilation. Slow, deep breathing may result in alveolar hyperventilation, whereas rapid, shallow breathing may result in the same minute volume but actual alveolar hypoventilation due to the increase in dead space ventilation.

Primary hyperventilation is best known in

the form of the *"hyperventilation syndrome"* of psychoneurotics. No pathologic damage to lung is involved, and the changes are acute in response to not only the excessive blowoff of CO_2 but also some apparent increased sensitivity of the central reflex mechanisms to the acute changes in cerebrospinal fluid engendered by hyperventilation.

Hyperventilation may be produced by such involuntary means as encephalitis, other poorly understood neurologic lesions, mechanically controlled breathing, and primary elevation of hydrogen ion concentration (metabolic acidosis).

In primary respiratory alkalosis, the initial event is a decrease in P_{CO_2}. There is, directly, a decrease in H_2CO_3 and consequently a rise in pH according to the Henderson-Hasselbalch equation. However, a decrease in P_{CO_2} also produces a decrease in $[HCO_3^-]$ due to the blood protein buffers, and pH change may be less than expected.

Compensation for respiratory alkalosis is not as clear as is the case for acidosis. Excretion of $[HCO_3^-]$ with both Na^+ and K^+ is increased, and excretion of $[H^+]$ together with phosphate and ammonia is decreased. The renal loss of $[HCO_3^-]$ is insufficient to account for the degree of compensation which can occur. It is probable that an increase in lactic and pyruvic acids accomplishes a large part of the compensation. If hypocapnia is continued, $[HCO_3^-]$ will also continue to be lost until metabolic acidosis develops. It is probable that the transition from respiratory alkalosis to metabolic acidosis is simply one of degree of loss of $[HCO_3^-]$.

The patient with "hyperventilation syndrome" usually complains of facial paresthesias and numbness and tingling of the extremities which may progress to tetany. The feeling of impending syncope is probably due to the decreased systemic blood pressure and reduced cerebral blood flow (cerebral vasoconstriction), but the pathogenesis of the paresthesias and tetany is not known. Alteration in serum calcium is not responsible. It is probable that the rapid movement of CO_2 from the central nervous system cells into the extracellular fluid produces a temporary intracellular alkalosis (HCO_3^- excess) that is responsible for the paresthesias at least.

Less obvious is the patient with periodic or sustained mild hyperventilation, usually complaining of chest pain or discomfort, whose electrocardiogram shows inverted T waves with or without S-T segment depression. These patients are usually young to middle-aged females. Although the pathogenesis has not been precisely delineated, it is related to intracellular-extracellular K^+ concentration since it can be abolished by a modest potassium load.

The ease and rapidity with which CO_2 can be excreted by the lungs makes possible the conversion of a CO_2 excess to a CO_2 deficiency by means of mechanical hyperventilation. This will be discussed in the section "Pulmonary Function in Disease."

Anoxia

Anoxia refers to a lack of oxygen at the tissue level. Since blood is a tissue, the term "anoxemia," which refers to a deficiency of oxygen in the blood, somewhat overlaps the term "anoxia." In general usage the term "hypoxia" is largely neglected, although it is etymologically to be preferred to anoxia. Wiggers suggested that hypoxia be used when the arterial oxygen saturation is not less than 80 per cent, and that anoxia be used for levels lower than 80 per cent. The distinction is based on the observation that this is about the level at which serious manifestations of oxygen lack appear. It does, however, further confuse the use of the terms "anoxia" and "anoxemia."

Anoxia may be divided into four fundamental types: anoxemic anoxia, anemic anoxia, stagnant anoxia, and histotoxic anoxia. In clinical medicine, superimposition of one type on another is not infrequent.

In *anoxemic anoxia* the volume of oxygen in the arterial blood is reduced, as is the oxygen tension. It may be produced by reducing the alveolar oxygen tension either by reduced barometric pressure or by a decreased percentage volume of oxygen in the inspired air at 760 mm. of mercury pressure, or by inadequate pulmonary ventilation or respiration such as occurs in extensive pneumonia or pulmonary edema. It is one of the principal concerns of life at high altitudes and is the main type of anoxia due to truly pulmonary disease, whether ventilatory or respiratory. It may be combated by breathing a gaseous mixture of higher oxygen content or by increasing the compression of the gaseous mixture, or both. Ventilation should be improved if possible. In aviation and mountain climbing the inhalation of pure oxygen at altitudes between 12,000 and 40,000 feet will maintain the arterial oxygen saturation at 80 per cent or above. At greater altitudes pressurized oxygen is necessary. Increasing the available oxygen will not completely solve the problem when anoxemic

anoxia is due to alveolar hypoventilation, and can correct only partially large right to left shunts.

Life at high altitude is especially interesting to the physiologist since it permits study of the effects of hypoxemia and hypoxia without concomitant CO_2 retention, which usually accompanies hypoxia due to disease. With the decrease in barometric pressure at high altitudes, there is a decrease in alveolar oxygen tension which ultimately shifts arterial oxygen tension to the point where only the shape of the oxyhemoglobin dissociation curve maintains a near normal mixed venous oxygen tension despite arterial hypoxemia. Consequently, exercise (increased O_2 demand) will produce a fall in arterial oxygen saturation which is parallel to the drop in oxygen tension.

There are several interesting consequences of life at altitudes above 10,000 feet. Minute ventilation is increased by hypoxia and this lowers the alveolar (and arterial) P_{CO_2} and raises oxygen tension slightly. Nevertheless, arterial hypoxemia is present. By increasing the hemoglobin concentration (polycythemia), tissue hypoxia can be prevented so long as the altitude does not reduce alveolar oxygen tension much below 50 mm. Hg.

The hyperventilation induced by altitude must inevitably lead to some degree of alkalosis because of the lowered arterial P_{CO_2}. Since this is a chronic state, renal compensation can be essentially complete and the blood pH can be normal or nearly so. This compensation brings about an increased central sensitivity to P_{CO_2}. Therefore, if O_2 is given, or if the person suddenly returns to sea level, ventilation will decrease less than one would predict, but will decrease enough to give rise to CO_2 retention and acidosis. The initial hypoxic drive is replaced by responsiveness to both hypoxia and P_{CO_2}.

An interesting disturbance is *high altitude pulmonary edema*. This affects a small percentage of those exposed to high altitude who are not acclimatized or who have broken their acclimatization by a variable period of residence at low altitude. Acute pulmonary edema is usually preceded by some degree of tachycardia, palpitation, and dizziness. The symptoms of acute pulmonary edema usually appear within 1 to 3 days after reaching high altitude. The exact etiology of this affliction is not known, but it does involve the individual's susceptibility to hypoxia. It has been suggested that at least part of the pathogenesis is myocardial, but the evidence is best for a primary pulmonary vascular response. Pulmonary hypertension and pulmonary edema develop, and it is believed that constriction of the pulmonary veins in response to hypoxemia is the initial event. When detected early, the syndrome is reversed promptly by high oxygen breathing.

Anemic anoxia, as the name implies, is due to decreased functioning hemoglobin. This state may be due to anemia from any cause or to decreased oxygen-carrying capacity of hemoglobin because of its change to methemoglobin, or carbon monoxide hemoglobin (carboxyhemoglobin). Since the oxygen tension is normal, the dissociation of oxyhemoglobin will be in the physiologic portion of the curve and the volume per cent of oxygen in blood which will support life without serious symptoms can be much lower in anemic anoxia than in anoxemic anoxia. Oxygen therapy can aid to the extent of the 2 ml. of oxygen per 100 ml. of blood which can be held in physical solution regardless of the cause of the anemic anoxia. Transfusion of whole blood or washed erythrocytes is indicated in those states due to true anemia, and may be helpful in the treatment of methemoglobinemia or carboxyhemoglobinemia. In the latter condition, oxygen therapy is definitely indicated to increase the P_{O_2} of the alveolar air and thus aid in the dissociation of carbon monoxide hemoglobin. Hyperbaric oxygenation (100 per cent O_2 at 2 or 3 atmospheres pressure) is being used for carbon monoxide poisoning. If given with careful observation, its value probably exceeds its hazards.

Stagnant anoxia is due to disturbances of circulation such that the capillary flow, at least to some tissues, is inadequate to supply the tissue needs for oxygen even if the arterial oxygen be normal as it leaves the heart. This type of anoxia is frequently superimposed on one of the other types, as would be expected, since cardiocirculatory failure occurs terminally in many states, including anoxia. Therapy must be directed at the underlying causes.

Histotoxic anoxia is due to interference with cellular respiration. The respiratory enzyme system of the cells is inactivated or impaired. The best known example of this type of anoxia is cyanide poisoning. Although cyanide will combine with hemoglobin to form cyanhemoglobin, this is not the cause of the disturbances seen in poisoning. Indeed, the best method of combating cyanide poisoning depends on the conversion of part of the circulating hemoglobin to methemoglobin, with

which cyanide will combine rapidly to form a relatively stable and inactive compound, cyanmethemoglobin.

Symptoms. The symptoms of oxygen lack differ in the acute and chronic states. In the acute state of anoxia there is no physiologic adaptation. In pure, uncomplicated form, acute anoxia is rarely seen except as the acute anoxemic anoxia of high altitude. Acute anemic and stagnant anoxia are almost always complicated by other factors, such as low circulating blood volume and myocardial failure, to which the anoxic state is usually secondary. Acute histotoxic anoxia may occur, but the chemical agents which produce it are protoplasmic poisons, and other cellular functions are likely to be damaged, in most instances concomitantly rather than as a result of inadequate cellular respiration. The acute anoxemic anoxia of acute pulmonary edema, whether due to cardiac failure, shock or noxious gases, is accompanied by other preexisting pathologic changes.

The nervous system is more vulnerable to anoxia than any other. A decrease in peripheral vision and in dark adaptation is probably the first symptom. Subsequently the respiration and pulse rate increase. Between 10,000 and 15,000 feet of altitude, respiration and heart rate are further stimulated, and emotional instability and defects in judgment become evident. Some of these effects are due to the hypocapnia produced by the increased ventilation. Indeed, the emotional reactions at such altitudes are not unlike those seen in hysterical hyperventilation. When the arterial oxygen saturation falls to about 85 per cent (12,000 feet), some cyanosis becomes evident if no significant anemia is present. Headache, nausea, difficult concentration and often lassitude are experienced by many persons at levels between 10,000 and 15,000 feet. With greater degrees of anoxia, vomiting, dulling of the intellect, neuromuscular incoordination, weakness, faintness, rapid thready pulse and finally unconsciousness appear more or less in the order given. Exercise will, of course, accentuate the symptoms of anoxia.

Chronic anoxia may occur as a result either of continuous residence at high altitudes or of disease. If the body is constantly presented with a mixture of gases which cannot afford to the circulating blood enough oxygen to meet tissue demands, compensatory mechanisms must be evoked or death will result. Two obvious mechanisms may serve to correct or alleviate the deficiency: increased pulmonary ventilation with, therefore, increased

P_{O_2} of alveolar air, and increased oxygen-carrying capacity. This latter may be achieved by increasing the circulating hemoglobin, either by increasing the erythrocyte concentration, hemoglobin concentration, or both, or by increasing the minute circulating blood volume. These mechanisms of homeostasis have physiologic limitations. There is no proof that hyperventilation can lead to emphysema, but emphysema of the hypertrophic type is a frequent manifestation of high altitude disease (Monge's disease), and when it occurs, decompensation is inevitable.

Cyanosis

Inasmuch as anoxemia is the most common cause of cyanosis, this physical finding is usually considered with the abnormalities of respiration. Actually "cyanosis" is used as a descriptive term in physical diagnosis to cover any blue, gray or purple appearance of the skin due to changes in the circulating blood rather than to pigmentary changes in the skin. The appearance of the skin is determined by many factors other than the color of the blood itself, but especially is it modified by the state of the vascular bed, the thickness and pigmentation of the overlying skin and the light in which the skin is seen.

In cyanosis produced by anoxemia it is the amount of the reduced hemoglobin present which determines the presence and depth of the blue color. Five grams of reduced hemoglobin per 100 ml. of blood must be present before cyanosis appears. The relative amount of reduced hemoglobin is not a determining factor. Anoxia may be severe without cyanosis being present, as in anemic anoxia and histotoxic anoxia. On the other hand, cyanosis may be recognized in people with polycythemia when only slight anoxemia is present. In these patients slight degrees of stasis will result in a sufficient increase in the capillary unsaturation to give cyanosis. Polycythemia vera is characterized by a normal, or nearly normal, arterial oxygen saturation. This fact has been used to differentiate polycythemia vera from secondary polycythemia, in which arterial oxygen saturation is always low. One should remember that in the presence of significant pulmonary dysfunction in a patient with polycythemia vera the arterial oxygen saturation may be low.

Many factors, singly or in combination, may operate to produce anoxemic cyanosis. These factors may be strictly pulmonary, such as inequalities of ventilation and perfusion or impairment of the process of diffusion. On the other hand, purely extrapulmonary factors such as low oxygen content of inspired air, both right-to-left and left-to-right intracardiac shunts, and vascular stasis may be responsible.

Cyanosis may be produced by methemoglobin when this compound is present in the blood stream in amounts of about 3 gm. per 100 ml. The same is true of sulfhemoglobinemia. The color produced is not the same as that due to reduced hemoglobin, being more violaceous or gray, depending upon the degree of capillary dilatation.

Oxygen Poisoning

Although oxygen is "the breath of life" for man, it can be quite poisonous when present at high partial pressures. There is variation in susceptibility from individual to individual and in the same individual at different times. An oxygen tension of only 250 mm. Hg has been tolerated for 17 days without serious consequences, but irritating effects on the lungs and tracheobronchial tree were noted. A partial pressure of 350 mm. Hg of oxygen is usually tolerated for at least 48 hours. In general, toxic manifestations are directly proportional to the oxygen tension and the duration of exposure. In addition to its irritant properties, high oxygen concentration inhibits certain enzyme systems within the cells and the growth and reproduction of cells.

Aside from retrolental fibroplasia in premature infants, the tissue effects of high oxygen breathing at normal atmospheric pressure have been recognized primarily in the lung. Capillary congestion, dilatation, and finally proliferation are accompanied by pulmonary edema and increased thickness of the alveolar septa. Hyaline membranes may be formed with many small areas of atelectasis. Pulmonary surfactant is reduced in amount, probably due to inhibited production.

Clinical manifestations are variable. A sensation of retrosternal "tightness" is fairly frequent together with increased minute ventilatory volume. Headache, anorexia, nausea, and digital paresthesias are not infrequent. Reduction in the vital capacity does not usually appear until after 48 hours of exposure to a minimum of 350 mm. Hg partial pressure. The formation of hyaline membranes interferes with the diffusion of oxygen, and the multiple areas of "microatelectasis" result in right to left shunting.

The breathing of oxygen at pressures greater than 1 atmosphere is much more dangerous than the administration of a 100 per cent oxygen at atmospheric pressure. There is a wide variation in individual responsiveness to hyperbaric oxygen, and the central nervous system manifestations of oxygen poisoning may appear in susceptible individuals after relatively brief exposure at less than 3 atmospheres of pressure. The cerebral vasoconstriction which is produced by oxygen under high pressure is insufficient to prevent pronounced elevation of the cerebral tissue oxygen tension. Coma, convulsions, and paralytic phenomena may occur more or less in sequence.

The dangers of high oxygen administration to patients with chronic hypoventilation are well known and are not a manifestation of oxygen toxicity in itself. The paradoxical tissue hypoxia which can be produced by high oxygen inhalation after a preceding period of hypoxia or in association with hyperventilation is also well known. These are matters which can be controlled by the intelligent administration of oxygen and maintenance of a reasonable minute ventilation and are not primarily related to the concentration of oxygen.

The administration of oxygen mixtures during ordinary inhalational therapy in hospitals probably does not present much of any hazard from oxygen poisoning so long as the ordinary precautions concerning humidification and maintenance of adequate ventilation are observed. However, since oxygen concentrations of 90 per cent or more can be maintained by intermittent inspiratory positive pressure breathing with one-way valves and particularly by endotracheal intubation, there is reason to exercise extreme caution in the administration of oxygen by this method for prolonged periods.

Abnormalities of Breathing

The simplest types of respiratory arrhythmia are quantitative disturbances of rate, depth and minute volume. Medical terminology is not consistent, and, except for the forms of periodic breathing, the nomenclature is none too precise or uniform. It is unfortunate that a standard terminology is not available. Indeed, the New International Dictionary defines polypnea, tachypnea and hyperpnea as rapid respiration, quickness of breathing and abnormally rapid breathing. The term "hyperpnea" may be restricted to abnormally rapid respiration due to deficient arterialization of the blood. Such etymologic

looseness is unsatisfactory, and I do not hesitate to define some of these terms more precisely in discussing the abnormal types of breathing.

Quantitative Arrhythmias

Eupnea means easy breathing or normal respiration. Minor variations in minute rate and rhythm together with occasional changes in the tidal volume are acceptable within this definition. Ranges are difficult to assign, but at sea level the rate of breathing for the average resting adult should fall somewhere between 24 and 10 cycles per minute.

Tachypnea is simply rapid breathing. It is properly applied when the depth of breathing is not modified significantly, but the rate is in excess of 24 cycles per minute. The increased rate with nearly normal tidal volume produces an increase in the minute ventilation. This type of breathing may be seen in states of fear or passion.

Bradypnea may be used to characterize breathing of a rate less than 10 cycles per minute so long as the tidal volume is not greatly modified. As a general rule this type of breathing will lead to some reduction in the minute ventilation. It is often seen following administration of depressing amounts of sedatives and narcotics and when increased intracranial pressure is present.

When increased depth of breathing is the main abnormality, the term *hyperpnea* should be applied. The breathing of a well-conditioned athlete after strenuous exercise exemplifies this type of ventilation: the tidal volume is considerably increased, the rate to a lesser degree. Above all, the term should not be applied if breathing is difficult.

Hypopnea should be used to denote breathing that is greatly reduced in depth; but the change in rate is less striking. Sleep itself may produce hypopnea. Poor posture, spondylitis rhizomelica and paretic muscles of respiration are examples of mechanical factors which may produce hypopnea. Sedatives and narcotics may depress the depth of breathing more than the rate in some persons.

Polypnea and *oligopnea* may be used to characterize breathing in which the minute ventilation is increased or decreased, regardless of whether this change is due to abnormal rate or tidal volume. However, I prefer to use hyperventilation and hypoventilation in such a generic sense and to restrict the meaning of polypnea to that of striking increase in both rate and depth of breathing. Kussmaul breathing is sometimes an example of polypnea, but as a rule Kussmaul breathing is truly dyspneic. I likewise restrict the use of the term "oligopnea" to those states in which both rate and depth of breathing are significantly reduced.

Both hyperventilation and hypoventilation can be normal compensatory states. On the other hand, attacks of hyperventilation are a common manifestation of anxiety states, and the excessive blowoff of carbon dioxide may produce numbness and tingling, especially about the face, and even tetany. Hypoventilation may lead to carbon dioxide accumulation before there is any clinical evidence of hypoxemia, and often may be suspected when the hypoventilating patient complains of headache, shows a rising arterial blood pressure, or appears alert but somewhat disoriented.

Periodic Breathing

A second group of respiratory arrhythmias involving primarily quantitative changes is known as periodic breathing. In this group the rate, depth and tidal volume change strikingly from one interval to the next, the pattern of change being reproduced in a periodic manner.

The best known type of periodic breathing is an involuntary arrhythmia in which a period of apnea (or striking oligopnea) is followed by a series of ventilations in which each successive tidal volume is increased and the rate simultaneously quickens until actual dyspnea may be present, at which time the breathing decreases in depth and rate, often more rapidly than it increased, and lapses into another period of apnea. The periodicity is more or less regular. This type of periodic breathing was described by John Cheyne (1818) and William Stokes (1846) and is known as *Cheyne-Stokes* breathing. The probable mechanism of its production in most instances has been described in Chapter 20. It is encountered frequently in clinical medicine, especially in severe heart failure and uremia. It may be seen in a less well-developed form in normal persons at high altitudes before adaptation has occurred.

A second type of periodic breathing was described by Camille Biot and is known as *Biot's breathing*. It is not seen frequently. Periods of tachypnea and usually hypopnea abruptly alternate with apnea. The duration of the periods is more variable than in Cheyne-Stokes breathing, so that Biot's breathing may be considered an irregular irregularity. It is seen occasionally in the presence of meningitis, encephalitis, heat stroke, brain abscess and head trauma. It may be recognized in a poorly developed form during sleep.

Qualitative Arrhythmias

The second main group of the respiratory arrhythmias involves changes which are primarily qualitative. In this category belong dyspnea and orthopnea, in both of which respiratory rate, depth and minute volume may be abnormal, but are not defining characteristics.

Dyspnea, or difficult breathing, is a term which is frequently misused. The breathlessness of moderate exertion is neither painful nor difficult for the *normal* person, and may or may not be for the person with reduced cardiac reserve. Shortness of breath refers to quick respiration and is not necessarily difficult or painful in any way. Its affectual content may indeed be pleasurable, as is exemplified by the shortness of breath which occurs during erotic acts. Suffocation is commonly used to describe the strangling or choking asphyxia associated with obstruction of the upper airway. It is also applied to acute pulmonary edema. In both instances it implies an unpleasant or painful state. However, suffocation is also used at times to describe states of asphyxia in which consciousness is lost without known appreciation of pain or distress (e.g., high concentration of carbon monoxide). The truth is that physicians themselves are not careful in the use of such terminology and are vague about the distinguishing features of the breathing in different pathologic states.

Dyspnea means difficult or painful breathing and is thus a subjective state. The fact that it is most frequently seen in those persons whose breathing reserve (B.R.) is low does not alter the fact that the recognition of dyspnea, like that of angina pectoris, depends upon what the patient says. The breathlessness experienced by the runner may not be greatly different objectively from that observed in the patient with reduced cardiac reserve after mild exertion. In the patient with heart disease, oxygen demand and lactic acid production (and accumulation) are present to the same degree after much less exercise, and not only are the stretch receptors stimulated by the increased inspiration, but also the pulmonary vascular congestion which may occur gives rise to inspiratory excitation.

Both will have rapid, deep breathing with little pause between expiration and inspiration. However, the patient with heart disease may have sufficient pulmonary edema and bronchospasm to make breathing difficult. Furthermore, he may experience a feeling unknown to the runner—apprehension. It appears that the neurohumoral elements of exertional breathlessness and exertional cardiac dyspnea are similar, but the two states are quite different.

It is difficult to evaluate the role of the emotions in disturbances of breathing. Indeed, the origin of the emotional tone evoked is often obscure. In some persons voluntary forced hyperventilation will result in hypocapnia and mild to moderate symptoms in a short time. At times the hyperventilation escapes from voluntary control and is identical with the hyperventilation syndrome of anxiety psychoneurosis. Such people may experience the same apprehension and dyspnea, but no tetany, with forced hyperventilation, even when the breathing mixture is adjusted to prevent the development of hypocapnia. Other people will tolerate voluntary forced overbreathing for more than five minutes without significant emotional disturbance. Just as there are many causes of breathlessness, so likewise for dyspnea, which may be purely painful in pleurisy and purely difficult in emphysema.

It has been stated that a large part of pulmonary disability may be due to the work performed in attempting to maintain adequate gas exchange. Sustained muscular work, particularly in breathing against obstruction, may account for much of the sensation of dyspnea.

An explanation for dyspnea is not at hand, and it may be that we are seeking too much simplicity. One facet seems clear: whatever the afferent mechanisms, the emotional state is not dependent solely upon either pulmonary or cardiovascular adequacy. "Conditioning" in the normal person involves central adaptation at least as much as peripheral.

Orthopnea implies that breathing must be performed in an erect posture. In such a position the patient may be quite comfortable, but more often some degree of dyspnea is present even then. Orthopnea is usually present in congestive heart failure. As one would expect, the erect posture serves to reduce the venous pressure and pulmonary congestion and thus diminish the resistance to breathing. In this manner the result is similar to that of phlebotomy or digitalization.

The Clinical Evaluation of Pulmonary Function

One of the most informative approaches to the determination of functional capacity is the measurement of the *maximum capacity of the function,* and the expression of the measurement in relation to the average normal maximum capacity. It is even more useful to know by how much the maximum capacity exceeds the actual requirement at rest and under stress. This gives a measurement of the available reserve. However, if the actual requirement at rest or under stress is abnormal, it is essential to know that the abnormality is due to malfunction of the modality under consideration, and not to an interrelated function.

Suppose, for example, that a patient with chronic pulmonary tuberculosis has had unilateral partial thoracoplasty. Study reveals a low maximum breathing capacity and a high resting minute ventilation with little breathing reserve. Dyspnea is observed after slight exertion. It would seem unwise, therefore, to perform lobectomy or pneumonectomy beneath the thoracoplasty in order to remove active cavitary disease.

This information has a different meaning when it is also known that the lung beneath the thoracoplasty absorbs little oxygen despite a significant share of the total ventilation. The high resting minute ventilation may be due to ventilation of a poorly respiring lung (increased dead space), with consequent inability of the contralateral lung to meet the respiratory requirement without increased ventilation. Increased ventilation requires more work. This may lead to dyspnea.

Knowing that the lung beneath the thoracoplasty partakes significantly of ventilation, but does not absorb significant oxygen, one can state that resection of the underlying lung should not result in increased ventilatory insufficiency, since it will reduce the amount of air diverted to nonrespiring lung. If one can further demonstrate that the lung beneath the thoracoplasty is being perfused without adequate oxygenation of the blood, one can be even more helpful to the surgeon. This additional information permits one to state that this patient's pulmonary function should be improved by resection of the underlying lung. The blood which has been circulating through the lung without oxygenation (venous admixture effect) will now be diverted to the contralateral lung. This lung has been maintaining fairly adequate function at rest despite the handicap of a diseased lung which robs it of a portion of each tidal volume and accepts mixed venous blood from the right ventricle only to return it essentially unchanged to the left side of the heart.

In the final analysis, ventilatory sufficiency or insufficiency is determined by the respiratory requirement. What is needed is to present to the alveolo-capillary network a sufficient movement of suitable air to supply enough oxygen and to remove enough carbon dioxide to meet the demands of the particular metabolic state. Absolute ventilatory insufficiency will be present when the maximum ventilatory capacity of the person is insufficient to meet the respiratory requirement—if one assumes that the functional elements of true respiration are within normal limits.

Pulmonary function testing is aimed at trying to determine not only quantitative but also qualitative impairment. It is much easier to measure than it is to know what one is measuring. Tests of ventilation, gaseous diffusion and pulmonary circulation are all utilized to evaluate pulmonary function. It is realized that disease processes usually alter several functions, that these alterations may be unequally distributed to various parts of the lung, and that it may not be possible to distinguish deviations of one factor from the deviation of another in the presence of diffuse disease.

Measurement

Assessment of pulmonary function has an obvious place in preoperative evaluation, disability studies, and the management of patients in respiratory failure. Increasing importance is being attached to the long-term study of ventilatory and respiratory function of patients with degenerative lung disease with and without treatment. There is a growing interest in similar studies of population groups exposed to various types and concentrations of air pollutants.

What should be measured and how should it be done? Much depends upon the purpose of the study. The tuberculous patient with thoracoplasty, previously cited, presents a problem quite different from the "average" patient with a bronchogenic cancer whose ventilatory studies alone are quite sufficient, unless marginal, to indicate suitability for the type of surgery planned. If one is trying to evaluate the effects of a bronchodilator, measurement of change in the total vital capacity, forced expiratory volume at 1 sec-

ond, or the MVV may be sufficient. However, if one finds that intrapulmonary mixing (as measured by N_2 washout) does not necessarily parallel change in airway resistance, it may become necessary to expand testing. Measurement of arterial and alveolar tensions of O_2 and CO_2 during rest and exercise together with response to 32 per cent oxygen breathing may be quite adequate to detect clinically significant impairment of total lung diffusion if the ventilatory volumina and mechanics of breathing are typical of restrictive ventilatory dysfunction and the clinical picture is known. On the other hand, if one is studying the course of a diffuse interstitial disease, or attempting to detect impaired diffusion as a part of degenerative lung disease, this approach is not sufficiently sensitive or precise, and serial measurements of $D_{L_{CO}}$ are necessary.

What should be measured is also determined by the abilities of the examiner. One possessing a solid background in physiology who has subsequently become a good clinician in thoracic medicine can arrive at valid conclusions with much less testing data than can either the pure physiologist or the pure clinician. Simple fluoroscopy during quiet and deep, forced breathing can yield not only a knowledge of the mechanics of breathing, not otherwise obtainable, but also estimation of the relations of the ventilatory volumina, one to the other, and their distribution between the two lungs. This ability is acquired only by prolonged correlation of actual measurements with fluoroscopic observations of the same patient at approximately the same time.

There is a tendency at present to worship gadgetry: the more tests, the more valuable the study. Yet multiple tests of the same function yield only an index of variability of test results. The value of a test or tests should be measured by the validity of information when equated against other tests. For example, Ariza-Mendoza and Woolf found that measurement of the total forced vital capacity could predict the development of respiratory insufficiency during surgery with cardiac bypass almost as well as a whole battery of tests, including pulmonary diffusion and intracardiac pressures. Simple spirometry will suffice for most *clinical* purposes unless one suspects an impairment of diffusion or circulation unassociated with ventilatory dysfunction of classic type. Tests of pulmonary function should be selected in accordance with the clinical problem except in population surveys where highest yield of abnormality together with simplicity are paramount.

If the resting minute ventilation is carefully determined, it has usefulness in relation both to its magnitude and to the maximum voluntary ventilation (MVV). By considering the resting minute ventilation as a minimum ventilatory requirement, one may subtract this value from the MVV to find the *breathing reserve*.

The ratio $\frac{\text{Breathing reserve}}{\text{MVV}} \times 100$ may be used to express the breathing reserve as a percentage of the maximum voluntary ventilation, and affords a numerical estimate which can be related to the level at which dyspnea usually appears. The maximum voluntary ventilation in liters per minute is sometimes divided by the minute ventilation (in liters) to indicate the number of times per minute the person could ventilate above that of the minute requirement. This has been called the *ventilatory reserve*. Unless the maximum voluntary ventilation is more than twice the minute ventilatory requirement, dyspnea will be present.

An expression which correlates oxygen absorption with ventilation is the *ventilatory equivalent*. This is used to express the number of liters of air which must be ventilated in order to absorb 100 ml. of oxygen. The ventilatory equivalent finds its greatest usefulness in bronchospirometry, in which it may serve as an index of the efficiency with which each lung absorbs oxygen. If abnormally high, it gives no idea of the reason for such inefficiency.

As indicated in the discussion of the pulmonary volumina, analysis of the form of the tracings (spirograms) will give considerable information about the mechanical factors of breathing. This type of information is easily obtained and should be supplemented by careful fluoroscopic observations of the diaphragm and its motions, the mediastinum during forced inspiration and expiration, the movements of the costal cage, the relative changes in lucency of the lung fields during deep breathing, and the relative position and movement of the hili. The spirogram in patients with air trapping and loss of pulmonary elasticity will show a prolongation and retardation of expiration which will be most obvious in the registration of successive vital capacity breaths and the maximum voluntary ventilation. It should be remembered that the vital capacity may be only slightly or moderately disturbed even in the presence of serious pulmonary disease.

Normally, the residual volume does not exceed 35 per cent of the total capacity. Many things may alter the total lung capacity, both musculoskeletal and pulmonary. The residual volume may be increased with hyperinflation, temporary or chronic. A ratio over 35 per cent is not diagnostic of emphysema, and ratios below 35 per cent do not rule out mild or regional emphysema. If the total lung capacity (TLC) is low, a normal residual volume will give a high ratio of RV/TLC in the absence of obstructive airway disease. The TLC may be enlarged considerably in emphysema. The residual volume or functional residual capacity must be known in order to determine or calculate some measurements of pulmonary function (e.g., single breath $D_{L_{CO}}$), and is essential to investigational studies, particularly where serial quantitation is desirable or necessary. The information afforded does not justify the time required for duplicate determinations in the routine study of ventilation in the general hospital laboratory. Substantial increase in the residual volume can usually be inferred from examination of the patient and the spirogram.

The maximum voluntary ventilation represents a satisfactory measurement of ventilatory capacity when properly performed. Like any pulmonary function test involving considerable exercise and cooperation, it is determined by too many factors. If the flow of gases into and out of the chest bellows is relatively unobstructed, the vital capacity can be greatly decreased without much decrease in the maximum voluntary ventilation. When the vital capacity is reduced much more than the maximum voluntary ventilation, the term "restrictive ventilatory dysfunction" is often used.

On the other hand, anything that decelerates breathing will significantly reduce the MVV. Obstruction to expiration, or reduced pulmonary compliance—such as may be present in emphysema, bronchospasm or edema, or intrabronchial exudate and tumor—will greatly reduce the MVV. Under these circumstances, the vital capacity may be within normal range, slightly or moderately reduced if no time limit is placed on expiration and the expulsive powers are relatively normal. When the MVV is reduced much more than the vital capacity, the term "obstructive ventilatory dysfunction" has been used if there is good correlation between the MVV and the $FEV_1 \times 40$ (the indirect MVV).

Determination of the VC, FEV_1, and MVV before and after the administration of effective bronchodilators is a valuable means of distinguishing relievable from unrelievable airway obstruction. This type of study can also be used for the evaluation of bronchodilating substances.

Studies of gas flows at the mouth or in subdivisions of the tracheobronchial tree are a relatively recent advance. Various types of flow meters have been designed for recording respiratory flows. In order to analyze better the work of breathing, studies of the relation of ventilatory gas flows to intrathoracic pressures can be performed. Intrathoracic pressures may be closely approximated by recording intra-esophageal pressures by means of an esophageal balloon. Pressure-flow curves can be constructed to study the intrathoracic pressures required to overcome the resistance to gas flow in health and various disease states. In this manner some differentiation can be made between pressures required to overcome resistances inherent in the pulmonary parenchyma and pressures required to overcome the resistances offered to air flow through the airway from alveolus to mouth. Pulmonary compliance can be measured from pressure-volume loops and gives important information about the elastic and nonelastic components of the total work of breathing. It has real meaning only when related to lung volume (specific compliance), and is not the type of measurement that would be done routinely in a hospital pulmonary laboratory.

Poor distribution of inspired air is the commonest of the significant ventilatory disturbances. When distribution is unequal because of regional changes in elasticity or regional obstruction of the airway, it can be detected by intelligent use of fluoroscopy. It cannot, however, be quantitated by this means. When poor distribution is due to regional changes in distensibility of the lung, such as may be seen in congestive processes and various fibroses, it must be demonstrated by such methods as the single breath nitrogen washout. Measurable degrees of distribution defect may not be present in some patients with radiographically evident fibrosis, whereas in others with similar radiographic appearance the defect may be considerable.

Both helium and nitrogen are gases which are relatively inert and insoluble in the blood. Such gases can be used to study the distribution of inspired mixtures without relation to the factors of diffusion or circulation. During ordinary air breathing a patient will be both inhaling and exhaling a gaseous mixture containing approximately 80 per cent of nitrogen. If he is made to take a single deep inspiration of 100 per cent oxygen, the succeeding expiration will consist of several gaseous stages. The first portion exhaled will be pure oxygen from the dead space, and this will be followed by an increasing nitrogen concentration which reflects a varying mixture of dead space and alveolar gases. The last fraction, the alveolar gas, will have much less dilution of the nitrogen. If the single breath of oxygen has been uniformly distributed throughout the lung, then the alveolar gas will have a uniform concentration of nitrogen throughout the forced alveolar sample. If the distribution has been uneven, then the best ventilated alveoli will contain more oxygen and less nitrogen and will be emptied first during the expulsion of the alveolar sample. Consequently, unevenness of distribution can be estimated from the slope of the nitrogen excretion curve during the expiration of the alveolar fraction. The Lilly-Hervey nitrogen meter makes possible the continuous analysis of single or multiple breathing cycles. If the patient expires directly into a flow meter, the sampling needle for the nitrogen meter may be inserted at the mouthpiece. By this means a continuous and simultaneous record can be made of the rate and volume of flow of expiration and the nitrogen content of the expired gas.

When pulmonary diffusion is to be measured specifically, whether as D_L or D_M, it is almost always measured for carbon monoxide. A number of methods are available, but the single breath (breath-holding) technique is simplest. Just as there are regional differences in ventilation and perfusion, so there are also for diffusion. The $D_{L_{CO}}$ gradient parallels the perfusion gradient (from apex to base) in normals and people with obstructive ventilatory dysfunction when erect or sitting. This gradient is abolished by the supine position, and it would seem that testing in this position might yield less variation in resting values.

Estimation of the diffusing capacity of the lungs is subject to many variables, and these differ with the method used. The steady-state CO methods are best adapted to measurements during exercise (where breath-holding may be impossible), and since exercise $D_{L_{CO}}$ appears to be more reproducible and a measure of maximal diffusional capacity, one of these methods may be used. In patients with uneven ventilation/perfusion ratios, small errors in the values for CO_2 or CO can result in large errors in D_{LCO}. The steady-state methods give much lower values in maldistribution of ventilation than does the single breath method, and are more subject to error at rest than during exercise.

Rapid rebreathing of a mixture of gases containing 0.5 per cent CO and 10 per cent helium in a bag of slightly greater than vital capacity volume can be used to calculate D_{LCO} after about 1 minute of rebreathing. Rebreathing reduces the effect of uneven ventilation/perfusion ratios, but not all patients can breathe effectively as rapidly as desired (rate of 25/min.).

It is also possible to measure D_{LCO} by the regular breathing of a mixture of 0.1 per cent to 0.2 per cent CO in air to steady-state and then plotting the end-tidal concentrations of N_2 and CO during 100 per cent O_2 washout. This equilibration method has many advantages but requires regular breathing.

In an excellent analysis of the single breath method of measuring D_{LCO}, Morton and Ostensoe determined the chief sources of significant error in the ordinary laboratory application of the method, and suggested ways in which the validity of the method could be improved. Although the actual period of breath-holding was sufficiently variable to introduce significant error in some patients, this can usually be minimized by measuring the actual breath-holding time and making an appropriate correction in the calculations.

A more serious source of error is due to inadequate dead space washout. Patients with a vital capacity of 2000 ml. or less were liable to the greatest error. Unless 750 ml. was expired before beginning collection of the alveolar sample, the latter would be contaminated with dead space gas, giving an erroneous diffusing capacity. This type of error is particularly likely in the patients with reduced vital capacity and obstructive airway disease because of the reduction in expired volume which occurs during forced expiration (trapping). For some patients in this group, adequate dead space washout leaves an alveolar sample which is too small for accurate analysis of CO, helium, and carbon dioxide.

Morton suggests with considerable logic that the residual volume used for the calculation of the single breath diffusing capacity should be that calculated from the single breath helium dilution (effective residual volume) rather than the true residual volume determined separately by the closed circuit helium dilution method.

Ventilation and perfusion are not the same in various parts of the lung. In general, there is reason to believe that in the healthy human being those areas having hypoventilation have roughly equivalent hypoperfusion. The presence of a decreased oxygen tension is capable of producing pulmonary vasoconstriction tending to shunt the blood away from such poorly ventilated alveoli. There is not, however, a perfect ventilation-perfusion ratio throughout the lungs in health. In disease there is frequently a greater divergence of ventilation and perfusion within the same area. The same statements apply to the process of diffusion. The two most obvious factors which can alter pulmonary diffusion are the area of blood surface exposed to the alveolar gases and the thickness of the alveolo-capillary membrane. Little is known concerning the normal alterations of the alveolar membrane, but it is probable that alterations in thickness do occur. In pathologic states both the capillary walls and the alveolar membranes may be altered in thickness and composition. Alveolar exudates and transudates as well as interstitial fluid changes may likewise impair diffusion.

Information concerning the probable existence of diffusion defects can be obtained by simple analysis for alveolar and arterial P_{CO_2} and P_{O_2}. Where impaired diffusion is present, the alveolar P_{O_2} will be normal or high and the arterial P_{O_2} will be reduced; whereas, except in the presence of hypoventilation or severe diffuse parenchymal disease, the alveolar P_{CO_2} will be approximately the same as the arterial P_{CO_2}.

If the capillary bed is expandable, exercise will result in an increased diffusing surface and a consequent rise in arterial P_{O_2}. If the capillary bed cannot be expanded during exercise, then the velocity flow in the capillaries must increase unless cardiac output falls. The increased velocity flow may so shorten the exposure of blood to the alveolo-capillary surface that the maximum diffusion of which the membrane is capable will not take place, and the P_{O_2} falls during exercise.

Exercise will, therefore, make a diffusion defect more obvious when the capillary bed is not expandable.

If the arterial P_{O_2} falls during exercise while the patient is breathing room air, the difficulty must lie either in the intrapulmonary or extrapulmonary circulation (shunting) or in impaired diffusion. If the exercising patient is now given 100 per cent oxygen to breathe, the greatly increased alveolar P_{O_2}

will overcome the diffusion impairment (alveolo-capillary block) and the arterial oxygen saturation should be 100 per cent and the P_{O_2} above 500 mm. Hg.

The effects of large intracardiac or intrapulmonary shunts will not be abolished by 100 per cent oxygen breathing, and thus impairment of circulation can be differentiated from impairment of diffusion. However, 100 per cent oxygen breathing will not distinguish between anatomic shunt and so-called "virtual" shunts which may be produced by unequal ventilation-perfusion.

Since hypoventilation (failure to maintain alveolar P_{O_2} and P_{CO_2} at normal or near-normal levels) may be produced by a wide variety of extra- and intrapulmonary factors, it may present a greater clinical than physiologic challenge. It always results in an increase in CO_2. The diffusibility of CO_2 is such that an increase in CO_2 never occurs from impaired membrane diffusing capacity except in those with such a loss of diffusing capacity that life must be sustained by 100 per cent oxygen inhalation or hyperbaric conditions.

Impaired circulation per se can be ignored for practical purposes as a cause of increased arterial P_{CO_2}. Elevation of arterial P_{CO_2} can be accepted as evidence of ventilatory inadequacy or severely altered ventilation-perfusion ratios.

The study of the pulmonary circulation requires cardiac catheterization. The pulmonary blood flow, pulmonary arterial pressure and the so-called pulmonary end-capillary pressure may be determined during catheterization. Changes which occur during exercise may give important information.

This discussion of the evaluation of pulmonary function is intended as a general introduction to the methods currently in use. In most general hospitals the evaluation will fall short of what can be accomplished by the methods which have been discussed. On the other hand, in certain research centers more refined and exhaustive studies of pulmonary function can be made.

It is more or less agreed that the needs of purely clinical evaluation can be met by (1) the patient's history, with signs and symptoms at rest and during exercise, (2) dynamic fluoroscopy correlated with the measurements of the pulmonary volumina, (3) determination of the arterial pH, and the arterial oxygen saturation and arterial carbon dioxide content, both at rest and during exercise while breathing room air and during exercise when breathing 100 per cent oxygen. The arterial P_{CO_2} can be derived from these measurements. Simultaneous sampling and later analysis of the alveolar gas tensions may give additional information and can usually be done in any laboratory equipped to determine the arterial carbon dioxide content.

In the author's laboratory the direct determination of arterial P_{O_2} and P_{CO_2} by the bubble equilibration method of Lilienthal, Riley, Proemmel and Franke has proved both reliable and not too difficult technically. By this method one can detect subnormal blood oxygenation in patients whose arterial blood saturation will fall within normal limits for the laboratory. Because of the shape of the oxyhemoglobin dissociation curve, the difference between 96 and 98 per cent arterial oxygen saturation is equal to a difference of 25 mm. of mercury in arterial oxygen tension (88 mm. and 113 mm.).

The development of the Clark oxygen electrode has made the polarographic measurement of oxygen tension practical over a range of tensions which could not be covered by the bubble-equilibration method. The polarographic method for determining P_{O_2} and P_{CO_2} is both rapid and accurate when done properly. Rapid determination of pulmonary gas mixtures is also readily available. Many more determinations can be made per day without increase in personnel. Expense and maintenance remain serious considerations.

When pulmonary or thoracic surgery is contemplated, the changes in ventilation and respiration which must result from surgery are usually predominantly unilateral. If the question is whether or not a patient can stand left lobectomy or pneumonectomy, knowledge of total function may not be sufficient, particularly if it is seriously reduced. Under such conditions it is necessary to know the *distribution* of function between the two lungs. This type of information is obtainable with much less difficulty, danger and inconvenience to the patient than is generally supposed.

By means of a flexible, double-barreled rubber catheter, *bronchospirometry* may be done. The bronchial catheter is inserted into the left main stem bronchus (under fluoroscopic control) and its balloon snugly inflated. The other catheter opens into the trachea, and inflation of its balloon will seal the trachea so that air from the right lung must pass through it. The two catheter openings are connected to separate spirometers which record on the same kymograph.

Because of the factor of stenosis, absolute ventilation and oxygen absorption values are not valid. However, the relative values may be used if no block of the catheters is encountered and they are properly placed. *If the catheter is so constructed that the lumina to the right and left bronchi have unequal flow characteristics, this is the same as a partial block of one of the catheters.* The tracings may be analyzed exactly as are those spirograms obtained in recording the pulmonary volumina. The minute ventilation can be calculated and the oxygen absorption estimated from the slope of the tracing (or from gas analysis if Douglas bags are used) and expressed separately. By this means one can determine the percentage of the total ventilation and oxygen absorption carried out by each lung. Bronchospirometry should be done during both quiet breathing and hyperventilation in order that trapping of air due to partial bronchial obstruction will become apparent. In a relative sense, this indicates the distribution of the maximum voluntary ventilation. By correlating the results of bronchospirometry with the observations of careful fluoroscopy, it can be shown that one can predict with surprising accuracy (within 10 per cent) the distribution of ventilatory function in *most* patients by means of fluoroscopy alone.

Oxygen absorption cannot be so closely estimated by fluoroscopy, particularly in patients with borderline total function in whom the greatest possible accuracy is desirable, and it is in this group that bronchospirometry is essential. Normally, the left lung contributes between 40 and 50 per cent of the total ventilatory and respiratory function.

Catheterization techniques make possible the study of the ventilation of individual segments of lung. When combined with gas analysis, segmental bronchospirometry gives us additional information concerning oxygen absorption and carbon dioxide excretion in the segment under study.

Pulmonary Function in Disease

Pulmonary function testing can determine, within the limitations of present methods, the presence of disturbed pulmonary function, and to a considerable extent identify the fraction or fractions impaired. In many instances such testing will allow a comparison of the patient's function with predicted normal function based on the study of apparently normal persons of the same age and sex. Serial studies will allow one to evaluate progression or regression of disease processes and perhaps to evaluate treatment. Cardiopulmonary studies are helpful in the study of those patients who suffer from dyspnea or cyanosis without obvious relation to either cardiac or pulmonary disease. Pulmonary function testing has many applications in industry, both in relation to the pre-employment screening for hazardous occupations and also in relation to problems of compensation. However, these studies cannot produce etiologic diagnoses, nor in themselves establish disability.

Above all, one should avoid the notion that clinical diseases of the lung can be specifically excluded on the basis of pulmonary function testing. A patient may have functional studies which fall within normal or near normal limits and still have actual disability.

The evaluation of disability, particularly in compensation cases, can sometimes be difficult or impossible. In those claiming respiratory disability, thorough pulmonary function testing will usually reveal impairment of one or more functions. However, when this impairment is borderline and not beyond possible variation due to aging, the separation of disability due to psychologic factors or malingering from disability due to changes which have actually occurred within the lung may rest upon opinion rather than knowledge. It is difficult to tell a court of law that after extensive pulmonary function testing one is unable to state that the amount of disability claimed is excessive when other physicians, qualified as expert witnesses, have no difficulty in making such a decision on the basis of physical and x-ray examinations and a vital capacity.

It is to be remembered that pulmonary function studies are intended to detect alterations of function that may occur in disease and possible mechanisms of disease. Clinical diseases rarely have any constant abnormalities of pulmonary function.

It was stated in the introduction that pulmonary function consists primarily of two phases—ventilation and respiration. They may fail singly, disproportionately one to the other, or more or less equally.

Ventilatory deterioration is manifested first by a measurable increase in minute ventilation during exercise, which may be expressed by the patient as "short of breath" or "out of breath" and which later becomes dyspnea.

However, by increasing ventilation and work of breathing, the blood gases are maintained within normal range.

The patient with a beginning pure impairment of diffusion may have the same complaints, and the nervous person who hyperventilates and the patient with beginning diffusion impairment may show the same findings. Woolf has shown that the psychoneurotic increases his respiratory work during hyperventilation, but the uptake of CO is almost linear, so that the respiratory work equivalent for CO does not parallel respiratory work alone. We can detect the patient with early diffusional impairment by specific measurement of diffusing capacity.

What is commonly called chronic obstructive emphysema is still a disease of unknown etiology. There is evidence to suggest that it may be a disease which is anatomically first manifest in the bronchial circulation. It has been postulated that the changes in elasticity and alveolar size are related to nutritional changes stemming from disease of the bronchial arteries. On the other hand, there is much other evidence to support the view that chronic bronchiolitis or bronchitis, with alteration of bronchomotor tone, produces alveolar hypertension and thereby brings about secondary vascular changes due to alteration of the critical closing pressure of the pulmonary capillaries.

At the time of clinical recognition the most obvious disturbance in emphysema is that of pulmonary ventilation. The total lung capacity is either increased or remains within normal range. The residual volume and functional residual capacity are *usually* increased. There is, however, no correlation between the amount of increase in the residual volume and the amount of disability. There is increased resistance to expiratory flow. This may be seen in the reduction of the MVV and FEV, which will be out of proportion to the reduction in the total vital capacity. Distribution of inspired air is likewise faulty. In moderate or severe emphysema the percentage of nitrogen in the expired air after seven minutes of 100 per cent oxygen breathing will exceed 2.5 per cent. However, in mild emphysema this effect may be abolished by hyperventilation and the percentage of nitrogen will then be less than 2.5 per cent. The single breath nitrogen washout curve is more likely to be abnormal even in mild emphysema.

Disturbances in the circulation are not so readily demonstrated in early or mild emphysema. There can be considerable obliteration of the capillary bed before the pulmonary arterial pressure will rise even with exercise. Furthermore, at this stage the arterial blood oxygen saturation may be normal both at rest and after exercise. Even with considerable inequality of ventilation-perfusion the arterial oxygen saturation, P_{CO_2} and pH may be within normal limits. In mild emphysema the capillary bed seems to respond to hypoxia in the poorly ventilated or unventilated alveoli by shunting its blood away from such alveoli, thereby maintaining normal alveolar ventilation-perfusion ratios.

However, as the disease increases in severity, circulation is less well able to maintain its functional integrity, and the alveolar-arterial P_{O_2} difference will increase and the arterial P_{O_2} will fall during exercise to be revealed as some decrease in arterial oxygen saturation. Similarly, one may expect some rise in the pulmonary arterial pressure, certainly with exercise and perhaps at rest. There may or may not be any abnormality of the alveolar or arterial P_{CO_2}. Pulmonary compliance decreases, and the total work and oxygen cost of breathing increase.

In still more severe emphysema the capillary bed will be further decreased and definite pulmonary arterial hypertension will result. There will be marked disproportion between alveolar ventilation and perfusion, and the capillary bed will be too small to adjust perfusion to ventilation. The arterial oxygen saturation may be low at rest and will fall even further with exercise. Carbon dioxide retention will occur with elevation of both the arterial P_{CO_2} and the alveolar P_{CO_2}. The blood pH will be decreased and respiratory acidosis appears.

Diffusing capacity changes may not show up so long as the pulmonary capillary bed can adjust its perfusion to avoid hypoventilated or unventilated alveoli. As the capillary bed becomes restricted and the inequality of perfusion and ventilation becomes greater, reduction in diffusing capacity will become evident. The severity of emphysema probably correlates more closely with the alteration in maximal diffusing capacity than with rising pulmonary arterial pressure.

In this one disease there are alterations of ventilation due to obstruction and loss of elasticity, with uneven distribution. There are also alterations of circulation and diffusion. If one wishes to measure the ventilation defect in terms of increased physiologic dead space and the altered ventilation-perfusion ratios in terms of venous admixture or shunt, the variability of this disease remains just as obvious. Ventilation of unperfused or hypoperfused alveoli (dead space effect) may be as great as 60 per cent of the tidal air, and perfusion of underventilated or unventilated alveoli (venous admixture effect) may represent up to 40 per cent of the cardiac output. However, these two changes do not occur equally in either degree or time. Emphysema may be associated with markedly reduced alveolar ventilation, without much evidence of physiologic shunt, or it may be associated with marked evidence of impaired alveolar circulation and much less ventilatory disturbance.

Uneven ventilation and perfusion is the most common cause of arterial hypoxemia. In chronic obstructive emphysema the combined volume of poorly ventilated lung is large and perfusion of these areas is usually relatively greater than ventilation, resulting in significant unsaturation of the perfusing blood. Hyperventilated areas can contribute very little toward increasing arterial saturation. Consequently, the oxygen saturation of the systemic arterial blood is determined primarily by the volume and ventilation/perfusion ratio of the poorly ventilated lung. The hypoxic drive tends to maintain ventilation and reduce *chronic* alveolar hypoventilation. However, the patient is now subject to acute episodes of hypoventilation which may be precipitated by depressant drugs, high oxygen breathing or infection.

Zonal distribution of ventilation can be measured by a closed-circuit rebreathing technique utilizing Xenon-133 in air. The same isotope can be injected intravascularly and its washout used to measure regional perfusion. These studies indicate that in many patients with emphysema there are considerable zonal differences in distribution of function. Tidal volume and blood flow may be relatively even and directed to an area where parenchymal structure is relatively good. However, there appears to be one group of patients whose disease is diffuse from the beginning and a second group with primarily localized or zonal involvement. The prognosis, and quite possibly the etiology, may be different.

Most patients with chronic obstructive and degenerative lung disease die from added insults. Infection is the greatest killer with its abrupt production of acute ventilatory failure. Clinically unrecognized pulmonary embolism or thrombosis is found in 44 per cent of autopsied patients with severe emphysema.

The effects of sedation and diuretics or corticosteroids are more subtle.

The assessment of O_2-CO_2 exchange and the control of hydrogen ion concentration has become essential to the management of patients with pulmonary insufficiency, especially those with obstructive airway disease in failure. The danger of producing a worsening respiratory acidosis and CO_2 narcosis by administering high oxygen mixtures to patients with alveolar hypoventilation is common knowledge. The effects of controlled or assisted mechanical ventilation with a variety of gaseous mixtures are not as well appreciated as the rather general use of inhalational therapy dictates. One cannot predict the development of increasing respiratory acidosis or the production of alkalosis from the initial levels of Pa_{CO_2}, Pa_{O_2}, and pH. Frequent monitoring and regulation of ventilation and gas mixture is necessary. One should try to maintain the arterial pH above 7.25 and oxygen tension above 50.

The dangers of alkalosis are not the only reasons for advocating a slow correction or incomplete correction of respiratory acidosis. One must remember that mild acidosis increases alveolar ventilation and improves ventilation/perfusion relationships. It also increases oxyhemoglobin dissociation and thereby increases the volume of oxygen available at the tissue level (without change in arterial oxygen tension). Furthermore, rapid reduction of arterial P_{CO_2} can lead to cardiac arrhythmias.

Rapid lowering of the CO_2 tension may produce coma, convulsions, fever, and focal evidence of neurologic excitation, which are associated with alkalosis. CO_2 is rapidly blown off by hyperventilation, but bicarbonate ion crosses cell membranes slowly and must be excreted by the kidneys. In most patients of this type, chloride ion is already low as compensation for the chronic respiratory acidosis (or as a consequence of diuretic therapy), and this further delays bicarbonate excretion. Shift of arterial pH to the alkalotic side can be rapid once hyperventilation is started. Because of the composition of the cerebrospinal fluid, it is believed that central nervous system cells are even more alkalotic (and slower to compensate) than arterial blood.

Since the greatest danger of both acidosis and alkalosis is to the central nervous system, it is desirable to serially measure spinal fluid pH during treatment.

The patient with chronic obstructive bronchitis, even though more responsive to medical treatment, is in a more precarious position without treatment than one with obstructive emphysema alone. Alveolar destruction may be absent or minor in chronic obstructive bronchitis, but obstructive underventilation of well perfused areas is great, and chronic alveolar hypoventilation results in a degree of hypoxemia and hypercapnia which cannot be corrected by voluntary attempts at increased ventilation. Controlled ventilation is indicated as part of the therapeutic management for many patients who are in acute respiratory failure superimposed on chronic obstructive bronchitis. Even with frequent monitoring of the arterial blood gases, pH and electrolytes, it is very difficult to maintain adequate oxygenation without dangerous or lethal effects of altered hydrogen ion concentration during the days required for renal compensation.

The alteration of pulmonary function during the course of granulomatous or fibrosing diseases of the lung is also variable. Small granulomas or areas of fibrosis may be unaccompanied by any detectable alterations of pulmonary function. Solid lesions or fibrosis may be much more extensive without significantly altering ordinary pulmonary function studies when these abnormal processes are confined to one lung. Bronchospirometry and pneumoangiography may detect definite abnormalities in this situation.

In more diffuse fibrosing and nodular disease there may be almost entirely restrictive ventilatory dysfunction. The total lung capacity, vital capacity and residual volume may be reduced, with lesser decrease of the maximum voluntary ventilation. This may represent a "tight" lung, and the loss of distensibility may stimulate stretch reflexes which provoke significant hyperventilation on even mild exertion.

In many more instances of such nodular and fibrosing diseases there will be a definite impairment of oxygen diffusing capacity with hyperventilation at rest as well as during exercise. In such persons the alveolar P_{O_2} will be normal or frequently increased if hyperventilation is marked. The arterial oxygen saturation at rest may be nearly normal (but the P_{O_2} will be decreased), but will fall significantly during exercise. The arterial P_{CO_2} however, will be normal or reduced if hyperventilation is significant. When this type of process involves the capillary bed extensively, there will be pulmonary arterial hypertension during exercise.

Pulmonary embolism is one of the more frequent accidents to previously normal as well as diseased lungs. Multiple small emboli escape recognition more often than large thromboembolism, especially when they occur intermittently over a period of weeks.

Cyanosis may not be produced by multiple small emboli, but when present, the mechanism for hypoxemia is uncertain. It has been attributed to the opening of arterial-venous anastomoses, to retrograde flow through the azygous-mediastinal-bronchial-pulmonary venous system, to decreased diffusing capacity, and to altered ventilation-perfusion relationships. It seems reasonably certain that altered diffusing capacity does not contribute significantly to hypoxemia. Altered ventilation-perfusion ratios are the most likely explanation at least in those situations where embolization has not been sufficient to permanently reduce the pulmonary capillary volume below a critical level. Perfusion of poorly ventilated areas may occur as a consequence of regional pulmonary edema, change in surfactant, followed by atelectasis of small air units. Reflex shifting of ventilation away from nonperfused areas occurs but is incomplete, and an increase in alveolar dead space results which may be reflected in a significant arterial-alveolar (low) P_{CO_2} difference.

Pulmonary hypertension is produced by multiple small pulmonary emboli, both acutely and permanently if embolization is episodic. The hypertension which accompanies the initial episode is due not only to reduction of the vascular bed but also to a reflex pulmonary vasoconstriction.

Massive pulmonary embolism, when not rapidly fatal, does produce hypoxemia by great expansion of the alveolar dead space. A significant lowering of the alveolar P_{CO_2} with normal or near-normal arterial P_{CO_2} can be used as a means of diagnosis, although angiography and isotopic scanning offer more useful information. The lowered alveolar P_{CO_2} will, if the patient lives long enough, bring about reflex bronchoconstriction in the area of thromoboembolism and reduce the amount of ventilation going to the nonperfused lung.

Pulmonary hypertension may occur in a variety of destructive or fibrosing pulmonary diseases, whether they involve blood vessels primarily (e.g., Wegener's granulomatosis, multiple emboli) or incidentally (e.g., tuberculosis, obstructive emphysema, silicosis). It may also be a late result of primarily cardiac disease (mitral stenosis). Pulmonary hypertension can be produced together with the pathologic picture of pulmonary hypertensive

polyarteritis by experimentally diverting sys
temic arterial blood to a lobar pulmonary
artery.

Primary pulmonary hypertension involves
the muscular arteries, and its pathogenesis is
not understood. Since it may occur in very
early life, it has been suggested that it may
represent a persistence of the thickened and
narrowed pulmonary arteries which are found
in fetal life.

The pulmonary hypertension that occurs
at high altitudes involves muscular arteries.
It has been shown to improve the perfusion
of the apices and thus has real biologic value
in increasing O_2 transfer in erect man. This
type of hypertension does not appear to be
symptomatic or to have serious consequences.
It has been suggested that hypertension of
altitude may be produced by the relative
hypoventilation which occurs during exercise
(arterial P_{CO_2} rises and P_{O_2} falls). The hypertensive response may be due either to a local
tissue reflex which produces medial hypertrophy over a period of time or to a central
reflex mechanism which produces the same
result.

The purpose of these examples is to emphasize the limitations of pulmonary function
testing in the study of lung diseases. The air
spaces, alveolar structures, parts of both the
pulmonary and bronchial vascular tree, and
the entire system of airways are intimately
associated. Disease is unlikely to affect one
structural unit only, and the degree of involvement of one or another structure is
variable during the course of a single disease.
Many different diseases may produce structural alterations which will result in similar
or indistinguishable functional disturbances.
The ranges of normal for the results of the
various lung function tests are wide, and
most testing procedures are incapable of detecting small, or at times moderate, alterations.
Localized structural changes of severe degree
may not be reflected by abnormal measurements of pulmonary function. There is real
reason, therefore, to try to analyze functional
impairment of the lung without expecting

the results to give an anatomic or etiologic
diagnosis.

REFERENCES

Ariza-Mendoza, F., and Woolf, C. R.: The value of
pulmonary function studies in the assessment of
patients for cardiac surgery. Canad. Med. Assn.
J., 91:1250, 1964.
Baldwin, E. deF., Cournand, A., and Richards, D. W.,
Jr.: Pulmonary insufficiency. I. Physiological
classification, clinical methods of analysis, stand-
ard values in normal subjects. Medicine, 27:243,
1948.
Brackett, N. C., Jr., Cohen, J. J., and Schwartz, W. B.:
Carbon dioxide titration curve of normal man.
New England J. Med., 272:6, 1965.
Christie, R. V.: The lung volume and its subdivisions.
I. Methods of measurement. J. Clin. Invest., 11:
1099, 1932.
Christie, R. V., and McIntosh, C. A.: The measurement
of the intrapleural pressure in man and its sig-
nificance. J. Clin. Invest., 13:279, 1934.
Comroe, J. H., Jr., Forster, R. E., II, Dubois, A. B., Bris-
coe, W. A., and Carlsen, E.: The Lung, Clinical
Physiology and Pulmonary Function Tests, 2nd
ed. Chicago, Year Book Publishers, 1962.
Cournand, A., Richards, D. W., Jr., and Darling, R. C.:
Graphic tracings of respiration in study of pulmonary disease. Am. Rev. Tuberc., 40:487,
1939.
Handbook of Physiology. Section 3: Respiration, Vol. I.
Am. Physiol. Soc., Washington, D. C., 1964.
Liebow, A. A., Hales, M. R., Harrison, W., Bloomer,
W., and Lindskog, G. E.: The genesis and functional implications of collateral circulation of
the lungs. Yale J. Biol. & Med., 22:637, 1950.
Mendenhall, R. M., and Mendenhall, A. L., Jr.: Lung
alveolar surfactant, lung elasticity, and lung stability. Nature, 204:747, 1964.
Morton, J. W., and Ostensoe, L. G.: A clinical review
of the single breath method of measuring the
diffusing capacity of the lungs. Dis. Chest, 48:
44, 1965.
Pinner, M., Leiner, G. C., and Zavod, W. A.: Bronchospirometry, Ann. Int. Med., 22:704, 1945.
Respiratory Failure. Ann. New York Acad. Sc., 121:
651 (article 3), 1965.
Riley, R. L.: Pulmonary gas exchange. Am. J. Med.,
10:210, 1951.
Woolf, C. R.: The relationships between minute ventilation, pulmonary gas diffusion and respiratory
work measured simultaneously during a standard exercise test. Dis. Chest, 47:616, 1965.

Chapter Twenty-Two

Protective Mechanisms of the Lungs; Pulmonary Disease; Pleural Disease

JOHN H. KILLOUGH

Introduction

In order for the lungs to perform their basic function as a membrane for two-way gaseous exchange between the external and internal environments, it is necessary that they be in constant contact with air. Thus the lungs are exposed to air which may contain dust, bacteria, fungi, viruses, and various other noxious agents. For defense against these potentially harmful materials the lungs possess a complex of protective mechanisms. Disruption of these mechanisms by internal changes or overwhelming onslaught from without accounts for many pulmonary diseases. To understand these disease processes some knowledge of the structure and function of the various elements of the respiratory system is necessary.

Although the respiratory tract is divided arbitrarily into upper and lower portions, it functions as a physiologic unit directed toward the cleansing, warming, and humidification of ventilated air and gaseous exchange. From the nasopharynx to the alveoli there are many gross and microscopic changes in structure which reflect these different physiologic functions.

Nasopharynx

Air entering the upper passage is grossly filtered by hairs in the nose and further fil-tered, warmed, and humidified as it comes in contact with the moist mucous membranes of the turbinates. At sites where air currents strike the membrane, cilia are present which beat in a coordinated fashion so that particles are swept toward areas where they can be expectorated, swallowed, or expelled by nose blowing. Absorption from the olfactory area occurs rather freely; thus, various allergens and infectious agents as well as medications may enter at this level.

Trachea and Bronchi

The trachea branches into the right and left bronchi, and this pattern of dichotomous as well as monopodial division is repeated with decreasing cross-sectional diameters to the level of the respiratory bronchioles. Here the branching becomes much more extensive and gives rise to alveolar ducts, alveolar sacs, and alveoli.

Structurally the trachea and bronchi contain more or less the same elements, although there are important quantitative variations. They have been divided into layers on cross-section: the epithelial, the subepithelial, the muscular, and the adventitial layers. The first three layers are most important in terms of protective mechanisms and diseases and will be briefly described.

The *epithelial layer* consists of ciliated co-

539

lumnar cells among which are interspersed goblet cells. This pattern persists throughout the trachea and bronchi until bronchioles are reached which are 0.4 mm. in diameter. Here the goblet cells disappear and the cilia-bearing cells become cuboidal and interspersed with nonciliated cuboidal cells. Finally in bronchioles of 0.3 mm. in diameter the ciliated cells disappear altogether.

Sensory fibers of the trigeminal, glossopharyngeal, and vagal nerves are present at various levels in the mucous membranes of the pharynx, larynx, trachea, and bronchi. Stimulation of these fibers by irritating substances results in cough. Whether ciliary action is under nervous control is not known at present. However, it is quite evident that the activity of the cilia is coordinated by some means.

The *subepithelial layer* lies between the basement membrane upon which the epithelial cells rest and the muscular layer. It is composed largely of connective tissue elements, arterioles, venules, and capillaries of the bronchial vasculature. There are also fibers of the vagi and sympathetics distributed to the blood vessels. The lymphatic vascular system is found in this layer and it should be appreciated that it represents one of the most extensive in the body. The lymphatic capillaries do not extend to the alveoli, but appear at the level of the alveolar ducts. From Miller's diagrams it is evident that the lymphatics form a plexus about the arteries and the airways and anastomose at the level of the alveolar ducts with a somewhat separate system about the pulmonary veins. Lymph flow in the periarterial and peribronchial vessels is believed to be centrifugal, whereas the flow in the perivenous vessels is centripetal and into the hilar lymph glands. Peripheral connections are made with the lymphatic plexus in the pleura. The pleural lymphatics form a separate set which unite into a variable number of trunks and drain into lymph nodes at the hilum. One of the peculiarities of the pulmonary lymphatic system is that nearly all the lymph from both lungs drains into the right lymphatic duct. Only lymph from the left upper lobe drains into the thoracic duct. There are, however, frequent connections between the two sides, so that this separation is not entirely complete. These patterns are of importance in the understanding of metastatic spread of infection and malignancies.

The *muscular layer,* composed entirely of smooth muscle, is so extensive that it is said to be impossible to cut through a cubic mil-

limeter of lung without encountering muscle. It extends from the trachea to bronchioles approximately 0.1 mm. in diameter. The more or less circular arrangements of the muscle fibers are such as to provide for efficiency in constriction as well as to provide strength against high intraluminal pressures. Innervation of the musculature is via the vagi and sympathetics, which, by their activity, may produce constriction and relaxation respectively. However, it is most likely that the changes in bronchial diameter during normal respiration are a passive phenomenon without an element of alternating vagal and sympathetic activity. Beneath the smooth muscle are the longitudinal elastic fibers which passively resist the expansion of inspiration and by elasticity alone bring the airways back to their resting length on expiration.

The submucosal glands which extend throughout the three outer layers produce a mucoprotein secretion of varying viscosity. Secretion occurs on vagal stimulation but the effect is largely a quantitative rather than a qualitative one. When various factors such as dehydration, drugs, and shallow respiration are combined to affect volume and viscosity of the secretion, ciliary activity may become ineffective and permit airways to become obstructed.

Cartilage, which at first is regularly disposed and almost surrounds the trachea and large bronchi, eventually becomes fragmented into irregular plaques, and in bronchioles of 0.6 mm. diameter disappears altogether. Where cartilaginous support is absent, the encircling muscle fibers can produce maximal constriction.

Alveoli

The respiratory bronchiole divides twice giving rise to three orders of respiratory bronchioles. The third order then divides into two alveolar ducts which in turn divide five to eight times and terminate as alveolar sacs or infundibula. There are occasional small projecting spaces called alveoli on the walls of the first order respiratory bronchioles. With continued branching, the frequency of these increases markedly until at the level of the alveolar sacs the walls are beset solidly with alveoli. The walls of the alveoli consist of a moist surface (see surfactant, p. 542), a thin alveolar membrane which is one cell thick, a narrow "basement membrane," and the underlying capillary membrane. Through these tissues, gaseous diffusion occurs between the air and the blood. Various mononuclear cells are found on and within these thin structures as histiocytes, fibroblasts, and undifferentiated mesenchymal cells. Some of these cells may become active phagocytes to remove offensive matter which, by damaging the alveolar membrane, would interfere with the essential process of gaseous diffusion.

Minute openings called alveolar pores have been described between adjacent alveoli by Kohn and others. Whether these pores are present in normal lungs as well as in the presence of pathologic processes is not entirely certain. However, when they are present, they are of importance for they permit the direct passage of air from alveolus to alveolus. This situation is referred to as collateral ventilation since it allows the ventilation of alveoli even in the presence of obstruction of their normal ventilatory pathways.

Protective Mechanisms

The protective mechanisms of the lung are directed toward maintaining the integrity of the alveoli, their blood supply, and ventilation. This requires the cleansing, humidification, and temperature regulation of relatively large volumes of air. The size of the task is impressive when one realizes that air contains bacteria, fungi, viruses, and many other forms of particulate matter which are potentially damaging to the 70 to 80 m.^{2} of alveolar surface area. Air that seems clean may contain as many as 3 million particles per cubic foot, whereas visibly dusty air may contain over 100 million particles per cubic foot. The efficiency of these protective mechanisms is evident from the fact that the alveoli are maintained essentially sterile and free of foreign matter in the presence of these agents and a necessary basal alveolar ventilation of approximately 4 liters each minute.

A large portion of the cleansing of air, humidification, and temperature adjustment occurs in the nose. From the moment air enters the nose, the processes for removing particulate matter are at work. Larger material is immediately trapped by hairs in the nose and those particles getting past this gross filter still may be removed in the nose by coming in contact with the moist turbinates. If this happens, the particles are swept away by cilia for elimination by swallowing or nose blowing.

In the trachea and bronchi the process becomes somewhat more elaborate. Mucus, produced by the goblet cells and mucous glands, enters the lumen of the bronchi and forms a continuous, moist, sticky surface. Beneath the surface lies the ciliated epithelium. The wave-like movements of the cilia are coordinated in such a way as to move the mucus sheet upward at a rate of a centimeter or so each minute. Thus a tubular "conveyer belt" is provided which continuously moves upward in the normal individual and is being replenished continuously throughout the airways from the level of the alveolar ducts on up. The ciliated epithelium is interrupted only by stratified squamous epithelium over the vocal cords, but recurs again above them. It is believed that the mucus sheet is drawn uninterrupted over the vocal cords through its cohesive and elastic properties. Airways are somewhat tortuous, and, where particles impinge upon the walls, they adhere and are swept out of the respiratory tract. As will be noted in the subsequent discussion of lung disorders, there are many factors which alter the efficiency of this self-cleansing mechanism. For example, cold, sedatives, and anesthetics may directly depress ciliary action; and ciliary efficiency may be disrupted seriously by dry air and various drugs which render the mucus sheet too viscous and sticky for efficient ciliary action. Even here there is considerable latitude, for as much as 50 per cent of the water may be removed from mucus before there is a great increase in its consistency.

The movement of the mucus sheet and the expelling of foreign matter are assisted to some extent by changes in the diameter of airways on inspiration and expiration. Bronchi have been observed to widen and elongate on inspiration and narrow and shorten on expiration. The narrowing on expiration increases the rate of air flow considerably and therefore has a tendency to blow out mucus and other intraluminal matter.

Normally the cleansing secretions of the lung are handled entirely by ciliary action with some assistance from the expulsive forces of quiet respiration. However, when bronchial or tracheal secretions become slightly excessive, acceleration of the expiratory air flow by clearing of the throat may be necessary to clear the nonciliated vocal cords. If this is ineffective, a more forceful mechanism, the cough, may be called forth to blast the secretions upward. The cough reflex is initiated by stimulation of afferent nerve endings in the laryngeal, tracheal or bronchial mucosa. The act itself can be divided into three parts. First, there is a deep inspiration followed immediately by closure of the glottis. Second, with the glottis still closed, positive pressure is developed in the thorax by contraction of muscles of the chest and the abdominal wall. Lastly, the glottis is suddenly opened and the air under pressure is rapidly expelled. If the offending substance is eliminated, or if it is moved upward to an insensitive area, coughing ceases. There may, however, be continuous paroxysms of coughing which move the offensive matter little by little until it is eliminated or until the cough reflex is suppressed by medication.

In addition to the cleansing action of the mucus sheet, and the expulsive forces of normal respiration and coughing, peristaltic movements in the finer bronchi probably assist in eliminating secretions. Jarre and Di Rienzo, using radiopaque material, separately have demonstrated peristalsis in the bronchi of man. It is believed that the peristaltic waves assist in moving foreign material to larger airways where coughing may be more effective.

Up to this point the mechanisms of defense that have been described are the ones which are at work in the airways lined with a ciliated epithelium and coated with a moving mucus sheet. However, some respired matter may penetrate beyond these barriers. Very small particles, 10 microns or less in diameter, are respirable, and after inhalation can be found rather uniformly deposited over the alveolar walls. Heppleston has observed this in coal miners who have died very shortly after exposure in dusty mines. Disposal of foreign material at this level of the respiratory tree is quite different from what has been described thus far. It depends upon phagocytosis and, from the observations of Heppleston, must occur rapidly. If the ingested material is bacterial, it may be destroyed within the phagocyte. If, as in the case of various dusts, it is resistant to digestion, the phagocyte moves upward to an alveolar duct. This is the level of termination of both the ciliated epithelium and the lymphatic system. Disposition may then be accomplished by ciliary action sweeping the phagocyte upward, or the cell may enter the lymphatic vessels and arrive in nearby lymphoid collections or hilar lymph nodes. Some of the variations in this process of removing dust particles are discussed in the section on pneumoconiosis.

The mechanisms which trap inspired dry material are not so successful against liquids or even insoluble material suspended in a liquid. For example, Barclay found in his experimental studies that finely powdered lead-glass when insufflated into lungs did not reach the alveoli and frequently was eliminated from the larger airways within a matter of hours. Yet, the same material suspended in a liquid reached the alveoli and might still be visible on roentgenography for weeks. The significance of this observation to patients with sinusitis, bronchitis, and other morbid conditions characterized by excessive pulmonary secretions is quite obvious.

The inhalation of irritating fumes may elicit reflex constriction of the bronchioles. This is similar to the response in asthma and although it may be looked upon as a mechanism for protecting the alveoli, it is a two-edged sword. If the irritation is long maintained, as in the case of industrial fumes, it can produce bronchitis and asthmatic symptoms. Voluntary breath holding or limitation of ventilation is an obvious defense against inhalation of noxious material which can be effective for only short periods of time.

Defensive mechanisms can be active to extremes which are disadvantageous. The dry cough which does not become productive even when expectorants are employed may be exhausting to the patient and accomplish nothing toward removing the irritative focus. Occasionally the cough reflex has been incriminated in the spread of infection from one area of the lung to another. The risk of spreading infection which is inherent in excessive liquid secretions has been alluded to above. In general, however, the effectiveness of the self-cleansing mechanisms of the lungs is quite impressive when one considers how much extraneous material must be removed even from air that seems to be clean.

Maintenance of the integrity of alveoli depends not only on defense mechanisms against foreign matter, but also against the tendency of surface tension of the moist lining to collapse the alveoli. Patency of alveoli is accomplished in part by negative intrathoracic pressure and supporting tissues; however, these alone do not prevent collapse under certain pathologic conditions. The relationship between pressure (P) within a sphere, tension (T) in the wall and the radius (r) of the sphere is expressed in the Laplace equation, $P = \dfrac{2T}{r}$. A moist sphere such as an alveolus with airway connections to the atmosphere would tend increasingly to collapse as the radius diminished were it not for the presence of a substance which adjusts surface tension in relation to radius. Normally there is a film of lipoprotein substance lining the alveolar membrane. This surface active agent, or surfactant, lowers surface tension as the surface area of alveoli decreases. By thus varying the surface tension of the alveolar wall (in relation to radius) the right side of the equation $\left(\frac{2T}{r}\right)$ is maintained relatively constant so that an antiatelectic effect is produced.

Pulmonary Disease

A virulent infectious organism introduced into the respiratory tract in one individual may result in progressive disease. In another, the organism may obtain a temporary foothold only to be eliminated later or held in a quiescent state, though still alive. In still another, the infectious agent may be eliminated promptly without any measurable effect on the host. Thus, there are varying degrees of effectiveness of the protective mechanisms. Pulmonary disease, whether infectious or not, may be looked upon as the result of the disruption or undesirable response of one or more of these mechanisms. The pulmonary protective mechanisms probably are modified by many factors, including heredity, age, sex, nutritional status, and ill-defined fluctuations in individual resistance to disease. It must be remembered that very little information is available concerning the physiologic effects of these factors. The bodily defenses are many and varied so that the failure of one mechanism is generally compensated for by other processes. As a consequence, many pulmonary disorders are reversible and on recovery the functional status of the lungs is little or none the worse for the experience.

In the consideration of pulmonary disorders, it is desirable to interpret the pathologic alterations in terms of effects on physiologic processes. Thus, pulmonary diseases should be considered in the light of the various components of pulmonary function that are discussed in the preceding chapter. When doing this, however, it must be remembered that a patient may have pulmonary disease without significant deviation from normal in functional studies. This may be due to the statistical range of normal values, limited extent of the pathologic process, or the inherent inaccuracies of current testing techniques.

Bronchial Asthma

Bronchial asthma is characterized by diffuse bronchial obstruction which is generally reversible. It is usually regarded as allergic in origin, but even the most experienced are unable to discover evidence for an antigen-

antibody reaction in all instances. Except in those cases in which there is a clear allergic origin and the manifestations occur in acute seizures, it is not always possible to establish a clear separation of bronchial asthma from exacerbations of obstructive emphysema with bronchitis. This is as true of the pulmonary and hemodynamic changes as it is of the clinical features.

The obstructive characteristics of asthma arise mainly from two physical changes in the airways which increase the resistance of gas flow: irregularities of the walls and narrowing of the lumina. Slight irregularities in larger airways such as the bronchi increase the resistance to flow by producing turbulence. The physical accompaniment of this is audible wheezing. In smaller airways, turbulence, if it occurs at all, is less important, and viscosity of the air becomes dominant because of the extreme degrees of bronchiolar narrowing.

The narrowing is brought on by at least three factors. One is the inflammatory reaction with its accompanying vascular engorgement, edema, leukocytic infiltration and eventual fibroblastic proliferation. Another is the excessive, tenacious sputum produced by the hyperactive mucous glands. This sticky material adheres, narrows, blocks, and produces irregularities and increased thickness in the walls of the bronchi and bronchioles. Lastly, there is constriction of smooth muscle in the bronchial walls.

The mechanism which initiates these narrowing processes is not known. Acetylcholine, which may be produced by the antigen-antibody reaction, is known to simulate asthmatic attacks by causing the production of excessive mucus and bronchial constriction. Histamine or a histamine-like compound also can cause edema of mucous membranes and smooth muscle spasm. Serotonin has a similar action. Each of these substances may produce an asthmatic attack in an asthmatic subject; but no one substance has been clearly incriminated as a factor in the pathogenesis of bronchial asthma.

The ventilatory alterations of bronchial asthma are those of bronchiolar obstruction and as such are not diagnostic for asthma alone, but occur with any process obstructing these small airways. Diffusing capacity, however, remains relatively normal in uncomplicated asthma. The primary value in function tests is that they are objective and allow better evaluation of the disability as well as the results of therapy. In the early stages there is a high degree of reversibility of the changes in bronchial asthma, and the lungs may be normal between paroxysms. This is the chief point of functional differentiation from emphysema which is characterized by relative irreversibility. As paroxysms of asthma are repeated over and over again, the narrowing of airways may become permanent. There is disruption of alveolar walls, and the pulmonary-cardiac abnormalities become indistinguishable from those of obstructive emphysema. Thus the pathophysiologic changes described in the section on emphysema are applicable in various degree to bronchial asthma.

Emphysema

Chronic obstructive pulmonary emphysema is a pathologic entity characterized by obstructive phenomena at the level of the smaller bronchioles. As such, it is clearly distinguished from compensatory emphysema and senile emphysema which lack the obstructive element. Etiological factors generally cited are bronchial asthma, chronic bronchitis, the pneumoconioses, sarcoidosis, bronchiectasis, tuberculosis, and other serious pulmonary infections.

As a consequence of edema and exudate in infectious processes or of hyperactivity of the muscular layers as in asthma, there is narrowing of the pulmonary airways particularly at the bronchiolar level. When this occurs, air becomes trapped in the alveoli distal to the narrowing. There are several factors which facilitate the passage of air beyond the partial obstruction in inspiration yet do not assist in its egress on expiration. One of these is the fact that airways are wider on inspiration than on expiration. Thus an obstruction which is of minor significance on inspiration may increase to a serious degree on expiration. If the narrowing is further increased, the discrepancy between the forces of inspiration and those of expiration comes into play. Air is taken into the lungs by the powerful contraction of the diaphragm supplemented by the levator muscles of the ribs which enlarge the diameter of the thorax. Forces of expiration consist of fiber-elastic recoil of the lungs, the use of depressor muscles of the ribs, relaxation of the diaphragm, and contraction of the abdominal muscles so as to force the diaphragm up. From the studies of von Neergard, it is clear that the surface tension of the air-liquid interface of the approximate 300 million alveoli is also a significant contributory factor in expiration. These com-

bined forces do not approximate those of inspiration; thus, with airway narrowing, air can be forcibly pulled into the alveoli, but expiration is less effective in discharging it. Even with complete obstruction, the alveoli distal to the obstruction may receive air via alveolar pores from alveoli which are normally aerated. The alveolar pores also narrow on expiration, and, in addition, this pathway of collateral ventilation is tortuous so that air-trapping is continued. On expiration, and particularly when expiration is forced, there is a sharp, abnormal rise in pressure in the areas of trapped air leading to compression and further narrowing of adjacent bronchi and bronchioles. All these processes lead to an increasing accumulation of air and a rising pressure beyond the obstruction. Eventually distention becomes so great that there is disruption of alveolar walls and the encircling mesh of musculo-elastic tissues about the smaller airways. Paroxysms of coughing increase the intrapulmonary pressures still further and contribute to the overdistention.

With repetition of acute exacerbations of the underlying disease there may be excessive amounts of tenacious mucus or mucopurulent secretion, hypertrophy, and spasm of bronchial muscle and permanent thickening of the mucosa. Each of these, by interfering with mechanisms such as ciliary action, cough, and collateral ventilation, serves to increase the obstructive process and trapping of air in the lungs. The lungs enlarge, their bases push the diaphragm downward toward its position of maximal inspiration so that its excursion becomes less and less. As distention continues, the intrapleural pressure becomes less negative and, during expiration, actually may be 1 or 2 cm. of water pressure above atmospheric, so that, when the sternum is removed at autopsy, the lungs balloon out of the thoracic cavity. With increasing intrapleural pressure the ribs elevate, the chest barrels, and the diaphragm flattens. This is the position of full inspiration; hence, the ability to inspire additional air and maintain effective ventilation is markedly impaired. An improvement in ventilation might be anticipated if the diaphragm could be returned to a more normal position on expiration—the rationale behind the use of emphysema belts, breathing exercises, and pneumoperitoneum.

In emphysema, as during acute attacks of asthma, the vital capacity is reduced and the total lung volume is increased. This is the result of expiratory air-trapping beyond narrow airways producing an increase in the residual volume. As noted previously, rapid expiration increases the obstructive element and augments air-trapping still further. Under these circumstances, therefore, the total vital capacity varies with the speed of expiration; hence the importance of the timed vital capacity as a measure of obstruction.

The physiologic and pathologic changes are not uniform throughout the lungs; some areas are better ventilated than others. The effect of this variation is that inspiratory and expiratory gaseous mixing is poor or absent in some regions and relatively better in others. Venous blood passing through poorly ventilated regions with impaired mixing of gases is exposed to a low pressure of oxygen and high pressure of carbon dioxide. If this defect is pronounced, there will be a fall in the oxygen saturation of arterial blood and a rise in the partial pressure of carbon dioxide. Contributing to the fall in oxygen saturation is a reduction of diffusing capacity. This reduction is not due to alveolar-capillary block but rather to a disruption of normal alveolar architecture and a decrease in the functioning capillary bed—all of which decrease the effective surface area for diffusion.

In advanced obstructive emphysema, cyanosis and respiratory acidosis develop and the same may occur in acute asthmatic attacks if the attack continues long enough. With severe respiratory acidosis the medullary respiratory centers lose their sensitivity to the normal carbon dioxide stimulus for respiration. In this circumstance, hypoxia provides the respiratory drive. If this is not recognized and high concentrations of oxygen are given to relieve cyanosis without mechanical aids to respiration, the termination may be fatal.

Several factors operate to reduce pulmonary blood flow, viz., destruction of interalveolar septa, which diminishes the area of the capillary bed, vasoconstriction due to hypoxia, increased viscosity of blood due to secondary polycythemia, high intra-alveolar pressure coincident to air-trapping, and secondary arteriosclerotic changes in the pulmonary arteries. Although with severe hypoxemia without pulmonary heart disease there may be a high cardiac output, cardiac output falls with the development of cor pulmonale. Pulmonary vascular resistance rises sufficiently to produce a net effect of pulmonary hypertension, right heart strain, and, if the process continues, cardiac failure. Elevated intrapleural pressures and prolonged expiration add to the elevation of venous pressure by impeding venous return to the heart.

Senile emphysema is a nonobstructive form of pulmonary overdistention in which the chest is barrelled but in which the functional impairment of the lungs is slight. The disease is primarily of the spine, and pulmonary involvement is secondary. With aging, degenerative changes occur in the vertebral discs and there may be sufficient loss of mineral content to lead to partial collapse of the vertebral bodies. It is believed that in the erect position the greatest stress on the intervertebral discs and body of the vertebrae is anterior; hence the tendency for these degenerative changes to lead to increase of the normal thoracic kyphosis. As kyphosis increases, the ribs rotate so that the sternum is pushed forward and the chest becomes barrel-shaped. The lungs accommodate themselves to the expanding chest and, in doing so, may overdistend to the point of thinning and rupture of alveolar walls. Diaphragmatic movements remain good.

Functional changes are slight and, in the absence of complicating pulmonary disease, of little note. Vital capacity is slightly reduced and the maximal breathing capacity may be reduced by half. At the same time there is an increase in the residual volume. These changes apparently are related to a slight reduction of pulmonary compliance and are not inconsistent with decreased elasticity in other tissues. Arterial oxygen and carbon dioxide values remain within the limits of normal.

Compensatory emphysema is a physiologic, nonobstructive process called forth by a decrease in volume of lung parenchyma, most commonly from atelectasis, surgical resection, or fibrosis. The remaining pulmonary tissues overdistend to fill the available space and, to this extent, compensate for the loss. If the diseased pulmonary segment becomes functional again, the emphysema disappears. But, if the emphysema persists, as after pneumonectomy, there is a gradual loss of pulmonary elasticity with some associated functional impairment.

Interstitial emphysema occurs when air from ruptured alveoli or bronchi enters the interstitial tissues of the lung and dissects along the peribronchial and perivascular sheaths into the mediastinum. From here it may enter the pleural space or travel to the subcutaneous tissues of the suprasternal notch and extend over the neck, face, arms, and trunk. Pain, which may simulate angina pectoris, often heralds the onset of interstitial emphysema. Hamman in 1937 called attention to the presence of a peculiar crunching, crackling sound heard over the heart and synchronous with each beat. Most commonly interstitial emphysema occurs in association with trauma, surgery, asthma, obstructive pulmonary processes, and pulmonary infections.

Eosinophilic Pulmonary Infiltration (Loeffler's Syndrome)

Eosinophilia associated with transient, migratory, and symptomless roentgenographic shadows was described first by Loeffler in 1932. Subsequently he suggested that an allergic mechanism might be responsible, and this seems compatible with later opinions. The meager amount of autopsy material indicates that the lesion is a pneumonitis composed largely of aggregates of eosinophils together with histiocytes and giant cells in a background of edema fluid. Eosinophils are predominant in both the interstitial and alveolar exudates and in the sputum. The size of the lesions is such that significant alterations in pulmonary function have not been described. Similar areas of eosinophilic pulmonary infiltrates with systemic eosinophilia have been reported in bronchial asthma, helminthiasis, chronic brucellosis, tropical eosinophilia, coccidioidomycosis, drug sensitivities, chemical sensitivities, and polyarteritis nodosa.

Pulmonary Alveolar Proteinosis

This chronic disease of the lungs, characterized by the deposition of proteinaceous material in alveoli, was described first by Rosen, Castleman, and Liebow in 1958. To date the etiology remains unknown. Certain histologic similarities to pneumocystis infection have led to intensive but unsuccessful searches for this parasite. Efforts to isolate other infectious agents or to identify an inhalant or aspirant common to all cases have also been unsuccessful.

In the early stages of pulmonary alveolar proteinosis, septal cells in the walls of alveoli increase in both size and number. Increasing further, they may line the alveoli, project into the lumina, slough, disintegrate, and give rise to PAS-positive granular and floccular material with numerous small acicular spaces. Continuation of this sequence leads to the filling of the alveoli and distal air spaces, including respiratory bronchioles. In these areas of consolidation there is a striking absence of cellular infiltration into the interalveolar septa and there is no evidence of vascular conges-

tion. The ultimate histologic fate is not clearly defined, although it is known from clinical studies that regression may occur. Biopsy studies of areas believed to have been involved previously have shown slight interstitial fibrosis of questionable significance and some residual granularity of the alveolar lining cells.

In this disease, although the distal parenchyma is not normal and air containing, there is no primary involvement of the airways. Hence, spirographic studies show no evidence of obstruction to air-flow. There is, however, filling of alveoli by proteinaceous material and replacement of functioning lung volume by consolidation. As a consequence of this, there is a restrictive pattern of ventilation with a decrease in vital capacity. The patient may complain of dyspnea and there may even be objective hyperventilation at rest. Inspiration of high concentrations of oxygen does not relieve the hyperventilation, although it does decrease any arterial unsaturation which may be present. As in many other forms of diffuse lung disease, this hyperventilation is believed to be due to an alteration in the proprioceptive reflex mechanism within the diseased lung.

The increase in size and number of alveolar septal cells and the early partial coating of alveoli with proteinaceous material interferes with the diffusion of oxygen across the alveolar-capillary membrane. This does not permit full saturation of hemoglobin passing such alveoli, and results in various degrees of arterial unsaturation and its clinical manifestation, cyanosis. Further arterial oxygen unsaturation is caused by venous blood passing through the intact vasculature of consolidated alveoli which contain no air at all. Thus the pathophysiology of pulmonary alveolar proteinosis is a consequence of both alveolar-capillary block and increased venous admixture. There is no evidence of impaired carbon dioxide excretion. If clinical improvement occurs, the alveolar-capillary block diminishes and the venous admixture may return to normal.

From clinical studies thus far published, patients with pulmonary alveolar proteinosis seem unusually susceptible to superimposed infections. In the presence of pulmonary insufficiency such infections, even though minor in extent, may lead to death. Those who have died without recognized infection showed progressive respiratory failure in the form of dyspnea and cyanosis.

Congenital Cystic Disease

Although it is difficult in a given case to be certain that a cystic pulmonary lesion did not develop after birth, there is little doubt as to the existence of true congenital cysts. It is believed that if intrauterine lung development is arrested at an early stage, a large solitary cyst may be formed; whereas, if the arrest occurs later, multiple cysts may result. The cysts, as observed in the patient, may be walled off and filled with serous fluid or they may be partly or entirely air containing if there are small communications to functioning bronchi. The lining epithelium of the cyst may be invested partially with cartilage and smooth muscle. Other cysts may be thin walled and lined by a flattened epithelium.

There is a great tendency for these lesions to become infected because bacteria gaining access to cysts cannot be removed by normal mechanisms. The absence of any connections to an airway or the inadequate size where a connection does exist prevents drainage of infected material and elimination of ciliary action and coughing. In those cysts connected to airways, infection, mucus accumulation and the valvelike mechanism from changes in duct sizes on inspiration and expiration cause air-trapping.

Pulmonary Arteriosclerosis

The pathogenesis of pulmonary arteriosclerosis is not clearly understood, although its relationship to certain lung diseases and congenital cardiac lesions has been noted. With the exception of pulmonary valvular stenosis, most of these conditions lead to significant pulmonary arterial hypertension. The possible role of pulmonary hypertension in pulmonary arteriosclerosis has been investigated extensively. Dammann and his associates, by anastomosing systemic arteries to pulmonary arteries in animals, have produced various degrees of pulmonary vascular damage. Following anastomosis, there is fragmentation of the elastic layer of the pulmonary arteries, hemorrhage, interstitial edema, capillary dilatation, medial hypertrophy, and the deposition of fibrous material in the adventitia and intima. As the vascular narrowing progresses, capillary dilatation disappears, macrophages appear, and there is resorption of alveolar and interstitial hemorrhage and edema. The end result is restoration of normal appearing alveolar walls and the persistence of arteriosclerosis. However, pulmonary arteriosclerotic changes also occur in the absence of hyper-

tension in pulmonary valvular stenosis, suggesting that another etiologic factor may be operative. Duguid and others, on the basis of experimental studies, have developed the concept that pulmonary arteriosclerotic changes are secondary to thromboembolism. Small clots of fibrin particles are converted into intimal thickenings showing hyaline or fibrinoid changes and incorporated lipid droplets. The end result has the morbid appearance of pulmonary arteriosclerosis and cannot be distinguished from that produced by hypertension. Whether pulmonary arteriosclerosis in pulmonary diseases such as emphysema develops as a consequence of hypertension or whether thromboembolism or some unrecognized factor is involved is not known at this time. At any rate, the reaction of the arteries to insults from hypertension and from thromboembolism is the development of arteriosclerotic changes, a defensive mechanism which may initially protect alveoli but in itself may be harmful. Still, in severe hypertension the changes have some protective value since they apparently prevent the acute arteritis with hemorrhage and edema in alveolar walls observed in the studies of Dammann.

Pulmonary Embolism

The pulmonary vascular tree is an efficient filter which can remove emboli of neoplastic cells, bacteria, blood clots, fat globules, air, and the debris of amniotic fluid. A few particles of less than 75 microns diameter may escape through normally occurring precapillary arteriovenous anastomoses, but this is not of clinical significance. Frequently overlooked is the fact that pulmonary infarction is not an invariable accompaniment of embolism. Pulmonary embolism alone is much more common than pulmonary infarction. The collateral bronchial circulation is, in many cases, adequate to maintain viability of the area involved. In the presence of conditions such as diminished ventilation, pulmonary infection, or congestion which tend to produce vascular stasis, an embolus is much more likely to produce frank infarction.

Embolic obstruction leads to hyperemia and edema, which, if some of the above conditions are present, will progress in about 24 hours to infarction with alveolar wall necrosis and hemorrhage into the alveoli and associated bronchi. This gives rise to the so-called meaty sputum which contains dark red clots. Within two weeks, fibroblastic proliferation is in progress and the end result is a contracted scar which may not be visible on roentgenographic examination.

The severity of response to embolization is a function of whether the embolus obstructs a large or small pulmonary artery. Obstruction of a small pulmonary artery may be silent, whereas occlusion of the main trunk of the pulmonary artery is followed by a cessation of cardiac output, gasping respirations, and death. If an artery of intermediate size is plugged, the systemic blood pressure falls suddenly and there is a concomitant rise in the pulmonary artery pressure, and dilatation of the right cardiac chambers and the peripheral veins. There is a sudden onset of dyspnea, which has been variously explained as a consequence of anoxia and reflexes from stimulation of receptors in the pulmonary artery. The Hering-Breuer type of reflex from distention and collapse of air spaces, and the fever associated with pneumonic consolidation may also be factors in dyspnea. Tachycardia occurs as a response to the fall in systemic blood pressures, anoxia, fever, and apprehension. Cyanosis is a consequence of arterial unsaturation rather than the stasis cyanosis seen after myocardial infarction. The unsaturation may be a consequence of shunting through the normal arteriovenous anastomoses, and a decreased area of functional pulmonary capillaries producing in turn a decreased diffusing capacity of the lung. Fever and leukocytosis are essentially a response to tissue necrosis although infection in the embolus may contribute. When cough occurs, it is probably in response to the inflammation of bronchial mucosa within the area of infarction. With involvement of the visceral pleura by infarction there is frequently pleuritic pain, but there may also be substernal discomfort reminiscent of myocardial ischemia. This discomfort may be attributable to the mechanical block of pulmonary arteries reducing, in turn, the cardiac output and coronary blood flow. Distention of the right cardiac chambers may also impede coronary flow by interfering with coronary venous return. Since pulmonary hypertension of other types has been noted to produce an anginal pain, it is also possible that some of the pain may result directly from distention of the pulmonary arteries. To explain the death of patients from emboli blocking only a small portion of the pulmonary arterial tree, it has been postulated that pulmonary arterial constriction occurs. Serotonin released from platelet agglutination has been suggested as the mediator of the constriction.

In fact, the question of constriction in response to emboli has not been settled and it is believed by many that all the manifestations are explainable on a mechanical basis.

One consequence of pulmonary embolism is that alveoli may continue to be ventilated although there is no capillary circulation. In the absence of effective circulation, the CO_2 tension in these alveoli will fall to very low levels instead of remaining approximately equal to the CO_2 tension of arterial blood, as in the normal. On the basis of this, it was thought that a pulmonary embolus could be detected and quantitated on the basis of a comparison of arterial CO_2 and the mixed expired alveolar CO_2. In practice this has not been too successful for three reasons: first, any pulmonary disease such as obstructive emphysema with altered ventilation-perfusion relationships may give similar results; second, when an area of lung loses its circulation there is, in fact, reduction of ventilation of the area; and third, the effects of smaller emboli are not detected. In the presence of obstruction of large areas of the pulmonary bed or with the use of differential bronchospirometry, the theory has some practical application.

Pneumoconiosis

If large air-borne particles are inhaled, they impinge upon the walls of the tortuous airways and are either swept out in the mucus sheet by ciliary action or expelled by the cough mechanism. However, if the particles are small, less than 10 microns in diameter, they are respirable and as such a portion of them will reach the alveoli and become scattered evenly over the walls. With surprising rapidity these particles are engulfed by phagocytes and transported toward the respiratory bronchioles. Even in normal lungs this is a relatively inefficient process, and silting up of these dust cells occurs in the respiratory bronchioles. Thus, not all the material reaches the continuous layer of ciliated epithelium which could expel the dust from the lung. Those cells which do not progress up the bronchial tree enter the interstitial tissues. Furthermore, some of the dust cells take a short cut via interstitial routes, arriving in the walls of other alveoli; or they aggregate about venules. The possibility that some dust particles enter the interstitial tissues without previous phagocytosis is not ruled out.

Once within the interstitial tissues, the dust particles may remain in situ or enter the lymphatics lying in relation to the airways, arteries, and veins. Much of this dust is arrested in foci of lymphoid collections at the divisions of the airways or vessels, while the remainder is carried to the tracheobronchial and hilar lymph nodes. In many instances, more distant lymph nodes such as those in the supraclavicular area also contain the inspired particles. There is no clear-cut evidence that phagocytes have any destructive action on the contained inorganic particles. Apparently, they act merely as vehicles to free the alveoli from foreign matter.

As dust particles arrive within the pulmonary tissues, a foreign-body type of response is elicited. Reticulum cells are transformed into fibroblasts and there is a deposition of fibrous tissue. When this reaction occurs about small bronchioles, there is impairment of airflow at the site, distortion and disruption of alveoli, the development of focal emphysema, and a sequence of events similar to that in obstructive emphysema. In advanced pneumoconiosis where conglomerate lesions appear, there will be a decrease in lung volume in such areas from scarring and a compensatory emphysema in other areas. If the process is extensive, not only is the ventilatory function affected, but there is disruption of the pulmonary capillary bed. Fibrosis occuring within the lymphatics impedes lymph flow so that the irritating dust and phagocytes escape into the areolar tissue about the blood vessels. In this position further fibrosis, with the added element of decreased capillary bed, contributes to the development of pulmonary arterial hypertension. In time this may eventuate in cor pulmonale and right heart failure. The obstruction of the lymphatics is possibly related to the known susceptibility of these patients to superimposed pulmonary infections. The severe ventilatory disturbances are those which are found in emphysema and fibrosis. In a given patient the changes may be predominantly those of emphysema, or fibrosis, or a combination of the two. The decreases in arterial blood oxygen saturation are due primarily to poorly ventilated or non-ventilated alveoli which are perfused with blood. This, in effect, is a right-to-left shunt of blood and, if severe, will be attended by cyanosis, secondary polycythemia, and clubbing of the fingers.

Each type of dust invokes a particular response, and there is considerable variation in the pathologic characteristics and the attendant physiologic alterations. In general, carbon particles cause only mild changes in the lymphatic vessels and nodes with which they come in contact; iron dust promotes tubercle formation; silica, intense fibrosis; asbestosis, nodular necrosis. The sputum produced in pneumoconiosis can be revealing. With anthracosis it may be black with carbon. When iron oxide is inhaled in large amounts, the sputum is reddish. In asbestosis, asbestos bodies may be found. Chronic infection is a common complication of the pneumoconioses, and the mucopurulent sputum produced is suggestive of tuberculosis. The possibility of superimposed tuberculosis always must be considered for it is a frequent secondary invader, particularly in silicosis and anthracosilicosis.

Pulmonary Fibrosis

Etiologically, pulmonary fibrosis is not an entity. It may occur in the course of pulmonary tuberculosis, scleroderma, sarcoidosis, roentgen irradiation of the lungs, the inhalation of various noxious dusts and industrial fumes, eosinophilic granuloma of the lung, the diffuse interstitial pulmonary fibrosis of Hamman and Rich, and as a consequence of the organization of inflammatory exudates of lobar pneumonia or bronchopneumonia. Systemic symptoms in this group of diseases vary widely and are generally characteristic of the particular clinical entity, but the pulmonary manifestations may be strikingly similar. The spectrum of pulmonary signs and symptoms varies from none at all in the earlier stages to cough, mucopurulent sputum, chest pain, cyanosis, clubbing of the digits, and severe dyspnea. As fibrosis progresses, cor pulmonale and cardiac failure ensue. The common denominator pathologically is interstitial fibrosis, which may be localized, as in the case of irradiation pneumonitis following therapy for cancer of the breast, or diffuse, as in many of the other diseases. When the lesions are small, there may be no detectable alteration of pulmonary function. However, if the lesions become diffuse and the fibrosis extensive, the lung will lose its elastic distensibility and there will be a decrease in total lung capacity, vital capacity, and residual volume. If the fibrosis is not evenly distributed throughout the lungs, compensatory emphysema develops in the uninvolved tissue. An element of airway obstruction may also be present from fibrosis about bronchioles. Frequently the fibrosis disturbs the relationship between the air-containing alveoli and the alveolar capillaries so as to impair gaseous diffusion. This defect has been discussed in the preceding chapter and is referred to as an "alveolar-capillary block." It may be the predominant aberration of pulmonary physiology in the Hamman-Rich syndrome, miliary tuberculosis, sarcoidosis, scleroderma, beryllium granulomatosis, and certain neoplasms with lymphangitic spread in the lungs.

Atelectasis

A bronchus may become obstructed either by an intraluminal mass or by external pressure so that the passage of air beyond is prevented. When obstruction occurs and is complete, gas in the segment supplied by the bronchus is absorbed into the blood stream, leaving the lung airless and collapsed. Concomitant with the mechanical obstruction, absorption of gas, loss of volume, and diminution of alveolar surface area, there is a decrease of surfactant in the affected area of the lung. Thus, as the alveolar surface area decreases, there is an increase in surface tension which probably contributes to the mechanism of collapse. Adjacent, normal lung retains normal activity of the antiatelectic surfactant.

Depending upon the size of the atelectatic area, various aberrations in pulmonary function may be observed. The vital capacity is reduced through the absolute reduction in functioning lung tissue. Arterial oxygen saturation is reduced due to the passage of desaturated venous blood through alveolar capillaries which are no longer in contact with air. Pulmonary elasticity is reduced. If the collapsed volume of lung is large, these physiologic changes are manifested as dyspnea and cyanosis. Fever is usual and is due either to the process initiating the atelectasis or to bacteria already present in the bronchi or introduced from aspiration, blood stream, or lymphatics. In most cases, antibody and leukocytic activity controls the infective agents but at times pulmonary abscess or chronic bronchiectasis may develop in the affected area. If infection does not intervene, restoration of normal function may occur after removal of the obstruction, even though atelectasis has been long persistent.

A type of atelectasis which is not obstructive may occur in the presence of processes which decrease the effective intrathoracic space. This is commonly observed in patients with sizeable pleural effusions or pneumothorax and may also be noted with the high diaphragm and retracted intercostal spaces of patients with respiratory paralysis. The atelectasis is a consequence of compression from outside the lung and represents an adjustment of a new intrathoracic volume. Among the terms used for this entity are adjustment atelectasis, compression atelectasis and disc, or platelike, atelectasis.

Atelectasis in association with pneumonia may occur as a consequence of obstruction of airways by viscid bronchial secretions, inflammatory exudate, or edema. It also may occur in the absence of obstruction and in any stage of the disease, including even convalescence. The mechanism is not entirely clarified. There is evidence in diseased lungs and somewhat debatable evidence in normals that the smooth muscle elements may extend as far distal as alveolar walls. It is postulated that these muscular elements are under autonomic control and might under certain circumstances give rise to "contraction atelectasis." There is also a decrease in surfactant activity in infected portions of lungs and contiguous areas which might result in pulmonary collapse. There is the possibility that when contraction or other mechanisms have reduced lung volume to a critical level, the increased surface tension in infected areas completes the collapse.

At birth, various degrees of atelectasis might well be anticipated since intrauterine life is essentially aquatic. A certain amount of physiologic atelectasis exists in the normal full-term infant, but generally disappears during his first week of life. Avery has suggested that in premature infants with atelectasis and infants with hyaline membrane disease, the pulmonary collapse may be due to an absence of the normal surfactant lining of airways and alveoli. The success of therapeutic maneuvers designed to lower the surface tension would seem to support this theory.

In children atelectasis has no predilection for a particular area, presumably because all of the bronchi are narrow. Adults, however, are particularly vulnerable to obstruction of the right middle lobe. This fact led E. A. Graham to coin the term "middle lobe syndrome." Since the etiologic factors are many, this unusual susceptibility would seem to be on an anatomic basis. The middle lobe bronchus is not only relatively narrow, but it is also more compressible by virtue of the acute angle that it forms with the main bronchus. Brock has emphasized that this situation is made more precarious by the fact that the bronchus is surrounded closely by lymph nodes draining not only the middle lobe but also the lower lobe. Thus infection in any part of these two lobes may produce sufficient lymphadenopathy to be obstructive.

Atelectasis as a postoperative complication is attributed to bronchial obstruction from retained secretions. Many of the processes which normally protect the bronchi from occlusion by secretions are rendered ineffective by surgery. Anesthesia, narcotics, pain, and fear of damage to the wound interfere with the expulsion of secretions by eliminating or making ineffective the cough reflex and by diminishing the tidal volume and associated bronchial movements. Also, as shown by Brock, lying on one side for long periods of time allows secretions to gravitate to the dependent lung segments. Aggravating each of these deficiencies is the increased viscosity of the sputum as a consequence of drugs administered for premedication, anesthesia, and postoperative pain. Not only is the sputum so sticky that it is difficult to move by coughing, but this same viscid characteristic impairs the movement of the cilia which are otherwise unchanged. Consideration of these various surgical effects on the pulmonary protective mechanisms provides the rationale for effective therapy of atelectasis—thinning of the sputum, restoration of the cough, changing body positions, alleviation of pain on respiration, and increasing the depth of respiration.

Tumor of the Lung

The respiratory symptoms of tumor of the lung are largely manifestations of partial or complete mechanical obstruction of an airway. Intraluminal tumors obstruct by direct growth into a bronchus, whereas parenchymal tumors produce similar effects through external pressure on the airways. As the tumor enlarges, asthmatic type breathing or stridor may be observed over the area of one lung or lobe in approximately 10 per cent of the cases. Since bronchi enlarge on inspiration and narrow on expiration, there may be localized emphysema beyond the tumor. This can be demonstrated often if roentgenograms are taken in both full inspiration and full expiration. Cough is an early symptom which is difficult to evaluate since most of these patients are heavy smokers and chronic cough is such a prevalent symptom in this group. However, as ulceration occurs the sputum changes and there may be blood streaking or frank hemoptysis. Drainage from the bronchus is impaired and secondary infection appears. The sputum becomes more abundant and is mucoid or mucopurulent. Pneumonia may develop and respond to antibiotics only to recur again. Lung abscess, either distal to the obstructing lesion or within the necrotic tumor, is relatively common. With complete obstruction there is atelectasis. All these symptoms are predominantly attributable to mechanical effects of the tumor and are not indicative of its origin or cell type, benign or malignant.

As the malignant tumor spreads to the pleura, or as a consequence of pneumonia, there is pleuritis with pain and effusion. Extension to the mediastinum may produce back pain and obstruction to the superior vena cava. Rarely a primary or metastatic carcinoma in the lungs may have a lymphangitic spread throughout the lungs. Pulmonary hypertrophic osteoarthropathy, which may resemble rheumatoid arthritis, is said to occur in approximately 10 per cent of malignant lung tumors.

Pulmonary Infections

The remarkable effectiveness of protective mechanisms of the lung maintains the alveoli essentially free of particulate matter such as dust and bacteria. This is in striking contrast to the upper respiratory tract, where there is a wide variety of bacteria which, if permitted to travel downward into the alveoli, would produce serious disease. However, like all defensive mechanisms, those of the lung are not perfect, and infectious diseases of the lung still rank first among infections as a cause of death.

Consideration of the fact that mechanisms are in action to remove particles from the air from the moment it enters the nares until the time it reaches the alveoli would suggest that the major onslaught would be in the trachea and bronchi. Experimentally, this theory is supported by the radiologic studies of Jarre, in which opaque dusts insufflated into lungs did not appear to enter the alveoli although bronchi were rendered opaque. Clinically, it is supported by the fact that the majority of respiratory tract infections actually are limited to the trachea and bronchi. Ordinarily the mucus lining of the bronchi and trachea is being constantly swept upward for elimination of foreign material deposited on it from ventilation. When the foreign material is irritating and produces inflammation of the larger airways, the cough mechanism and orally directed peristaltic waves help to move the mucus sheet more rapidly. Yet this constant cleansing action is not impregnable. During sleep, for example, defenses are lowered and septic material from the nose and pharynx, particularly if it is abundant, gravitates readily into the lungs. Other factors which must be taken into consideration when there is a breakdown of protective mechanisms are the virulence of organisms inhaled, the dosage of the infectious material and variation in the patient's native resistance to pathogenic organisms. Once an organism invades and produces an inflammatory reaction, secondary defenses involving phagocytes and antibodies, still assisted by the expulsive mechanisms, are manifested.

Acute Tracheitis and Bronchitis

The inflammatory reaction may be a consequence of infectious diseases such as influenza or pertussis, drainage from suppurative sinusitis, allergies, dust, or chemical irritants. Among the latter, excessive smoking of tobacco and atmospheric pollution are relatively common. Treatment is directed toward assisting the normal protective mechanisms. Termination of exposure to dust or chemical irritants, thinning of secretions with expectorants, steam, or aerosols, antihistaminics for allergy, and correctly directed antibiotic or chemotherapeutic agents for infections are used as indicated in a given situation. Occasionally bronchodilators are useful when there is a bronchospastic element. If the cough is excessive or nonproductive, it may be desirable to suppress this reflex to avoid undue exhaustion of the patient.

Chronic Bronchitis

When the etiologic factors considered in the section on acute tracheitis and bronchitis are constant or frequently repeated so that the bronchial inflammation cannot be completely eliminated, chronic bronchitis is said to exist. In the British Isles, chronic bronchitis as a reported cause of death is exceeded only by heart disease, cerebrovascular accidents, and carcinoma. By contrast, chronic bronchitis is not a frequently appearing diagnosis on death certificates in the United States. The difference in incidence may be in part real, but it is certainly in part a matter of definition. Gaensler and Lindgren in the United States reinvestigated the medical histories of their patients who had been given a diagnosis of chronic obstructive emphysema on the basis of pulmonary function tests. They found that 68 per cent of their patients with the physiologic alterations of obstructive emphysema met the British criteria for chronic bronchitis. Patients with chronic bronchitis had a progressive increase of a productive cough, worse in the mornings and in cold or inclement weather and, ultimately, dyspnea. In patients who had a productive cough with chronic obstructive emphysema, the dyspnea antedated the cough. This study suggests that chronic bronchitis is an important etiologic factor in most of the patients presenting with obstructive emphysema.

This etiologic relationship of chronic bronchitis to obstructive emphysema emphasizes the need for more serious regard of "bronchial troubles." Chronic bronchitis may lead to rigidity and thickening of the bronchial mucosa from vasodilation, congestion, and edema. There is infiltration of the mucosa by lymphocytes and polymorphonuclear cells and there may be an increase in the tonicity of the bronchial musculature. Mucous glands are enlarged and the excessive secretion interferes with ciliary activity so that the cough mechanism must assist in the expulsion of mucus. The pathologic changes also involve the smaller bronchi and bronchioles.

Thickening of the bronchial mucosa, excessive mucus secretion and increased tone of the bronchial musculature first slow the rate of maximal expiratory air-flow and subsequently that of maximal inspiratory flow. As the disorder continues, the functional pulmonary tests become those of obstructive emphysema.

Treatment is directed along physiologic lines of assisting the normal pulmonary defenses: antibiotics for infectious elements; removal from airborne irritants; thinning of secretions with expectorants and aerosols; and treatment for allergy, if such is present. Histologic examination of the secretion is of considerable value in establishing the type of bronchitis.

Lung Abscess

Aspiration of infectious material from the upper air passages is probably the most common cause of lung abscess. When dental or surgical procedures on the mouth or surgical procedures on the paranasal sinuses are performed under general anesthesia, the incidence of acute pulmonary abscess is relatively high. Blood clots and other material, along with organisms from the mouth, are inhaled into the lungs at a time when the cough reflex is depressed by general anesthetics and sedatives. Simultaneously viscosity of the bronchial secretions is increased, as a consequence of premedication, anesthesia, and dehydration, rendering ciliary action ineffective. With the inactivation of these mechanisms for clearing foreign material and the presence of a culture medium in the form of blood, the groundwork is laid for bacterial multiplication and abscess formation. Abscess as a consequence of aspirated vomitus has much the same pathogenesis. The anatomic distribution of these bronchogenic abscesses has been presented admirably by Brock.

All pulmonary abscesses, however, are not sequels to *aspiration* of infectious material. Bronchogenic mechanisms such as strictures and tumors may disrupt the processes which normally remove foreign material from the lower respiratory tract. Abscesses may arise from hematogenous spread of organisms in septicemias and in septic pulmonary infarcts. Even aseptic infarcts, by devitalizing pulmonary parenchyma, may precipitate abscess formation. Necrotizing pneumonitis caused by Friedlander's bacillus, staphylococci, streptococci, mixed flora, and poorly drained bronchogenic cysts may also overwhelm local defenses. It is rare for a simple pneumococcal pneumonia to progress to abscess formation. Infrequently, pulmonary abscess may result from transdiaphragmatic spread of infectious material. Amebic hepatic abscess is generally considered in this situation if the abscess is in the base of the right lung, but this same route may be taken by any subdiaphragmatic abscess. Progress of the infection is usually slow enough to allow symphysis of the pleura so that the lung is invaded without empyema occuring first.

In most cases of simple abscess the defense mechanisms discussed in the section on pneumonia, when aided by antibacterial agents, bronchoscopy, and postural drainage, will be adequate. The abscess wall collapses, fibrosis occurs, and the end result may be a scar which is invisible on roentgenography. The chronic abscess with a thick fibrous wall which will not collapse even on adequate bronchial drainage is seen less frequently than in the past—even in tuberculosis—because of earlier diagnosis and effective antibiotic agents.

Bronchiectasis

There is continuing controversy as to the pathogenesis of acquired bronchiectasis. Mallory has emphasized that it is a disease of the pulmonary parenchyma as well as of the bronchi and implies that the parenchymal disease occurs first. Among the most frequently cited parenchymal diseases are pulmonary atelectasis, chronic bronchial infection with parenchymal scarring, pneumonitis, and pulmonary fibrosis. Although the pathogenesis varies somewhat, each of these is characterized by some reduction in air-containing lung

and a concomitant reduction of lung volume. With the reduction of lung volume there is an increase in the negativity of intrathoracic pressure. This increases the traction on bronchial walls and produces dilatation. Weakening of the bronchial walls by infection may contribute. Fleischner has demonstrated with mechanical models how the traction may be exaggerated about certain bronchi. When the parenchymal process is reversible and of short duration, so is the bronchiectasis. Pneumonia and atelectasis are notable examples of this type of clinically reversible bronchiectasis. In mucoviscidosis there is production of an excessive tenacious mucus with bronchial obstruction and infection as in chronic bronchitis. Bronchostenosis does not regularly induce ectasia, and, when it does, it may be through atelectasis or infection and the mechanism proposed above. There is adequate evidence for a congenital form of bronchiectasis in which embryologic development is arrested after the outgrowth of bronchial buds, but before there is differentiation into alveolar tissue. This is more frequently referred to as congenital cystic disease.

In the diseases mentioned there is a relative lack of aerated alveoli distal to the bronchiectasis. As a consequence, the current of air generated in coughing is inadequate to expel secretions from the bronchi. Thus, secretions tend to stagnate and become secondarily infected because the weakened cough mechanism cannot eliminate completely the dependent secretions. The accumulated secretions destroy much of the bronchial wall, including muscle and cilia, if the disease is long continued. Large anastomotic communications develop between the bronchial and pulmonary vasculature and may give rise to hemoptysis. Since the bronchiectatic lung is often functionless in terms of gaseous exchange, these segments may constitute a considerable area of arteriovenous shunting. It is, therefore, not surprising that pulmonary osteoarthropathy is a frequent finding. So-called dry bronchiectasis does exist as a clinical entity, but it is confined most commonly to the upper lobes where gravitational drainage exists.

Pneumonia

When an acute infectious process involves the alveoli, pneumonia results. The route of transport of the infectious agent to the alveoli varies somewhat with the organism, being either via the airways, blood vessels, or lymphatics.

The pattern of response to a particular organism has a tendency to be characteristic. For example, the pneumococcus and Friedlander's bacillus tend to elicit a lobar type of consolidation, whereas the streptococcus is more apt to lead to bronchopneumonia and the staphylococcus to abscess formation. With earlier etiologic diagnosis and specific treatment this anatomic differentiation has lost much of its diagnostic significance and infections are frequently arrested at the stage of scattered consolidation, resulting in bronchopneumonia.

Among the bacterial pneumonias, the pathogenesis of pneumococcal pneumonia has been the most extensively studied. The current concept is that the bacteria reach the alveoli via the airway in droplets of mucus or saliva. Because of the absence of acute angles of the bronchi leading to the right lower and left lower lobes, these areas are the most frequently involved. Once established in the alveolus, the pneumococcus elicits an acute outpouring of edema fluid with neutrophilic leukocytes and small numbers of erythrocytes. This fluid constitutes not only a favorable culture medium for the organisms but also the vehicle for spread. With respiration and coughing this watery exudate laden with bacteria is carried via the smaller air passages and pores of Kohn to adjacent areas. As the lesion enlarges it may be divided into three zones. The peripheral zone consists largely of bacteria floating in edema fluid and represents the advancing wave of infection. Beneath this there is an area of leukocytes, fibrin, and bacteria where phagocytosis is occurring. In the central zone the infection is under control and advanced consolidation is present. The alveoli contain many leukocytes, but there is a relative absence of bacteria. It is in this inner zone that resolution first appears.

With increasing numbers of leukocytes and the appearance of macrophages, the outer zone is invaded by the phagocytes and the lesion ceases to progress in size. When, or whether, this occurs is a function of many factors, including the dose, virulence, and rate of multiplication of the infecting bacteria, antibody formation, and the general health of the patient.

In the early stages, when the infection is spreading rapidly, bacteremia is commonly observed. However, it may occur at any stage should the defense mechanisms of the host be overwhelmed. When bacteremia occurs it is believed that the organisms gain access to the blood stream via the lymphatics. The consequence of bacteremia may be metastatic lesions such as meningitis, bacterial endocarditis, peritonitis, and arthritis.

The development of antibodies such as precipitins, lysins, and opsonins constitutes an important aspect of host defense. Before the development of chemotherapeutic and antibiotic agents, type-specific antipneumococcus serum was an important agent in therapy. This serum is thought to be effective largely by its enhancement of phagocytosis. Pneumococci in the presence of opsonins tend to agglutinate, presumably through altered surface tension, and agglutinated organisms are more readily ingested by phagocytes.

By the time of crisis, living bacteria have been disposed of and the temperature falls to normal. Consolidation is still present but liquefaction sets in rapidly and the debris is removed largely by the lymphatics but in part by coughing and ciliary activity. Complete resolution may be delayed for several weeks, particularly in older individuals, but in the absence of complications proceeds in most patients with striking rapidity. Rarely the process is not completely resolved and the involved area is replaced by fibrous tissue. Lung abscess is an extremely rare complication of pneumococcal pneumonia, apparently because there is little or no necrosis of lung tissue. The pleura is involved in most instances and small pleural effusions occur. If there is delay in the initiation of specific therapy, an empyema may develop.

Systemic manifestations depend upon the characteristics of the organism, host, and the degree of impairment of lung function. Fever and cyanosis, if the process is extensive, are constant. At the outset of lobar pneumonia and throughout bronchopneumonia, cyanosis is due to imperfect oxygenation of the blood which passes through the affected lobes. As a consequence of consolidation of alveoli and obstruction of airways, the venous blood is not exposed to high levels of oxygen and, in effect, venous blood is shunted through these areas into the pulmonary veins and systemic circulation. When consolidation of one lobe is complete, cyanosis improves somewhat since all the alveoli have lost their function and there is a decrease in pulmonary blood flow to the lobe.

When pain occurs in pneumonia, it is indicative of involvement of the parietal pleura. The localization of pain by the patient is generally accurate because the impulse travels over fibers of the corresponding spinal nerves. The pulmonary parenchyma and the visceral pleura are themselves devoid of pain fibers. When the diaphragmatic pleura is involved, pain may be referred less accurately to the abdomen and simulate acute disorders for which surgery is indicated. Similarly, as a consequence of the cervical origin of the phrenic nerves, pain of diaphragmatic pleuritis may be experienced in the shoulder region.

Pneumonia also is associated with many viral and rickettsial infections such as influenza, parainfluenza, measles, mumps, chickenpox, respiratory syncytial virus, adenovirus and several related viruses, psittacosis and *Coxiella burnetii* (Q fever). *Mycoplasma pneumoniae* (Eaton agent), which is a pleuropneumonia-like organism (PPLO), has been identified as the cause of primary atypical pneumonia (PAP) in from 10 to 85 per cent of cases. Adenovirus also has been frequently identified in civilian and military populations as an agent in PAP. "Primary atypical pneumonia" was coined to describe a clinical syndrome. Now that approximately 50 per cent of acute viral lower respiratory tract infections can be identified etiologically, several authorities have suggested that the term be dropped. Pathologically the lesion of PAP is an acute bronchiolitis with interstitial pneumonitis characterized by mononuclear infiltration into alveolar walls, septa, and peribronchial tissues. The alveoli are relatively free of polymorphonuclear leukocytes and are either air containing or are collapsed.

Lipoid Pneumonia

Certain oils, particularly mineral oil and vitamin oils, when introduced into the lungs produce an acute pneumonitis which may progress to fibrosis. Access to the airways is through the use of oily nasal drops or sprays, forceful administration of oily preparations to crying infants, defective swallowing mechanisms or the aspiration of oily laxatives taken at bedtime.

The lesion produced is an organizing bronchopneumonia with an abundance of macrophages and desquamated alveolar lining cells. In time it may progress to fibrosis with obliteration of the pulmonary vasculature and contraction of the area, producing bronchial distortion and even bronchiectasis. Oil is partly ingested by macrophages and carried off into the lymphatics and partly eliminated in sputum. When the latter occurs, the etiology of the pneumonitis may be established by cytologic and histochemical studies of 24-hour sputum specimens. The clinical spectrum varies from the asymptomatic to simulation of most of the usual pulmonary diseases, including carcinoma.

Tuberculosis

In pulmonary tuberculosis, the bacilli are usually inhaled and arrive at the alveoli in the same manner as other particulate matter. There, depending upon the number of organisms, their virulence, and the native resistance of the host, there may be either little prompt reaction or the formation of an acute inflammatory exudate. In either case, with multiplication of the bacilli there develops bronchopneumonia with many leukocytes, mostly neutrophils initially but subsequently monocytes, acid-fast bacilli, and thickened, congested, and infiltrated alveolar walls. As hypersensitivity develops, caseation of the exudate and alveolar walls occurs, and a surrounding zone of tuberculous granulation tissue, consisting of blood vessels, lymphocytes, epithelioid and Langhans cells, and collagen fibrils, develops. If adequate acquired resistance develops, proliferation of the bacilli ceases and a hyalinized connective tissue capsule is formed from the zone of granulation, with a consequent reduction in the size of the lesion. The caseous material may be resorbed or inspissated and calcified. Bacilli in such a primary lesion may be completely eliminated or they may remain quiescent, but virulent, for years.

Simultaneous with the development of the pulmonary lesion, bacilli appear in the hilar lymph nodes. Although these areas of involvement are always larger than those in the pulmonary parenchyma, the progressive anatomic changes are similar. If the hilar lesion and the pulmonary parenchymal lesion both become calcified, a Ghon complex is formed.

It is believed that, in the evolution of the primary lesion, bacilli reach the blood stream either directly from the parenchyma or lymph node or via the thoracic duct into the subclavian vein. Generally, the seeding is slight, the lesion minute, and the end result is encapsulation, calcification, or complete absorption. Infrequently, persistent, viable bacilli in these extrapulmonary sites may later give rise to progressive disease in the organ in which they are situated.

In the so-called reinfection or adult tuberculosis, tuberculous lobular pneumonia is followed by caseation and cavitation. As the disease progresses, extension of the process in one area and healing by fibrosis in another may continue simultaneously. Hilar lymph node involvement is less than in the childhood form and calcification, if it occurs at all, is minimal.

The gross mechanism of defense against tuberculous pulmonary infection is evident from the preceding account. As in other infectious processes, it is an inflammatory reaction with exudation, phagocytosis, fibrosis, and walling off of the involved area. There are, however, unique characteristics of tuberculosis and the host response which make it inadvisable, if not impossible, to make dogmatic statements regarding other protective mechanisms. The mechanism of variation of racial resistance, for example, is not understood although it is an evident fact. White adults respond to the presence of tubercle bacilli by inhibiting their multiplication and spread by marked reparative fibrosis. Negroes of all age groups and white children are deficient in these responses and hence less well protected. Hereditary constitutional characteristics, age, and sex are factors influencing the course of tuberculosis in the individual; yet the role of these parameters in causing fluctuations in the level of resistance to infection is not understood. Although antibodies develop in response to the tuberculous focus, their role in acquired resistance is not yet clear. Still, acquired resistance can be demonstrated in experimental animals and there is indirect evidence for its occurrence in man. Marfan in 1886 observed that individuals who had healed cervical adenitis before puberty subsequently did not develop pulmonary tuberculosis as frequently as others. This "Law of Marfan" has been held to be true even in African natives who are highly susceptible to tuberculosis. Rich has indicated the important role of mononuclear phagocytes in ingesting free bacilli as well as dead polymorphonuclear cells with their contained bacilli. In the susceptible host bacilli may not only survive, but also multiply within the monocytes. Yet, once resistance is acquired through infection, these mononuclear phagocytes not only continue to ingest bacilli, but in addition they then inhibit multiplication and increase the rate of destruction of bacilli.

When tuberculin is injected into a person who has never had a tuberculous infection, the material is harmless and no significant reaction occurs. When injected into the skin of a person who has or has had a tuberculous infection, a sterile inflammatory reaction occurs. Using a pure culture of tubercle bacilli rather than tuberculin, Koch observed this altered reactivity in infected guinea pigs, and subsequently the altered reaction to reinfection has been referred to as the "Koch phenomenon." This hypersensitiveness has been a source of considerable controversy. Some investigators have considered it an important protective mechanism since acceleration and augmentation of the inflammatory response occurs in response to tubercle bacilli in the hypersensitive organism. This and the concomitantly accelerated tubercle formation are believed to represent an acceleration of the normal body defense. Others have regarded hypersensitivity as undesirable because of the associated necrosis of connective tissue, epithelium, blood vessels, and even the inflammatory cells themselves. In considering this problem, Rich comes to the conclusion that acquired resistance and hypersensitivity are separate phenomena and that hypersensitivity is at times decidedly deleterious and at other times is neither deleterious nor beneficial. The role of hypersensitivity as an advantageous defense mechanism remains an unsettled question, and it is even doubted by many that it in any way participates in the development of acquired immunity.

From the standpoint of systemic symptoms the presence or absence of hypersensitivity is important. The very hypersensitive patient with a focus producing tuberculoprotein may have malaise, fever, headache, anorexia, and the other constitutional symptoms of tuberculosis. But another individual who is anergic may have a more extensive process with active bacilli and yet fail to develop any appreciable systemic response. The experimental counterpart of this is the desensitized tuberculous animal that will tolerate enormous doses of tuberculin which would be fatal to a hypersensitive but similarly infected animal.

The tendency of tuberculosis to localize in the posterior portions of the upper lobes is well recognized, but the mechanism of the localization has not been defined clearly. Various theories have been proposed based upon diminished respiratory movement in the apices, direct retrograde spread from cervical lymphatics, streaming of blood flow to the lungs so that blood from the superior vena cava flows preferentially to the apices, and relative anemia of the apices due to man's erect posture. There is now increasing evidence that the hydrostatic effect of gravity diminishes circulation to the apical areas of the lung. It is postulated that there is also a decreased transport of humoral factors and possibly a decrease in lymph flow. All these factors might contribute to increased susceptibility to infection in the apices. Nevertheless, there must still be a factor of acquired resistance, for it is in reinfection that this odd distribution is seen. The lesion of primary infection is ordinarily situated anywhere in the lung.

The functional alterations in advanced pulmonary tuberculosis are secondary to parenchymal infiltration, loss of lung substance, fibrosis, and pleural disease. Infiltrations result in destruction of alveoli and localized stiffening of the lung. The loss of lung substance in itself is infrequently serious due to the large pulmonary reserve. The normal minute ventilation is of the order of 5 liters and this can be increased, on demand, to as much as 150 liters. However, the loss may be critical when combined with extensive fibrosis of the lung substance and pleura, resulting in increased lung stiffness (loss of compliance) and slowing of both inspiration and expiration, defects in gas mixing, and compensatory emphysema. Pulmonary function tests reveal these pathologic changes as decreases in vital capacity, an increase in dead space, an increase in the ratio of the residual air to total lung capacity and a decrease in arterial oxygen saturation on exercise. Although cor pulmonale is less common in tuberculosis than in chronic bronchitis and emphysema, it does occur in long standing cases as a consequence of extensive vascular destruction from inflammation and fibrosis and increased shunting of blood from the bronchial arteries into the pulmonary veins.

In recent years it has become evident that mycobacteria other than *M. tuberculosis* and *M. bovis* may produce human pulmonary disease. These strains have been called unclassified mycobacteria, anonymous mycobacteria, and atypical acid-fast organisms. Early skepticism as to their pathogenicity was based on the lack of virulence for guinea pigs. Repeated recovery in culture from sputa and tissue specimens in the absence of other organisms has been convincing of their primary role in certain patients. Although pulmonary disease caused by these unclassified mycobacteria is uncommon, it is now evident that the disease produced is indistinguishable from tuberculosis both clinically and pathologically. Although not yet demonstrated, it is supposed that the pathologic physiology will closely resemble that of tuberculosis.

Fungus Infections

There are many systemic mycoses which at times involve pulmonary tissues. Among the more important are histoplasmosis and coccidioidomycosis. Others, less frequently encountered, are actinomycosis, nocardiosis, cryptococcosis, candidiasis, blastomycosis, aspergillosis, geotrichosis, and mucormycosis. These various mycoses may occur as independent infections, but it is not unusual for them to appear as complications in the terminal stages of diseases such as the lymphomas, leukemia, and cancer. Candidiasis is often reported as a complication of broad spectrum antibiotic therapy and mucormycosis as a complication of uncontrolled diabetes mellitus.

As a group, the fungi are poor antigens, and they do little to stimulate resistance mechanisms. In some the response is more reminiscent of that to a foreign body than to a living infectious agent. Like the tubercle bacillus they have a tendency to elicit hypersensitivity in the patient, and it is believed that the necrosis of tissue and abscess formation is a consequence of this.

Clubbing of Fingers and Toes

The bizarre phenomenon of clubbing is associated with pulmonary neoplasms and various chronic disorders of the lung as well as chronic disorders of the heart, gastrointestinal tract, liver, thyroid and parathyroids and subacute bacterial endocarditis. In its more advanced stages, clubbing may be associated with periostitis and synovitis in the triad referred to as pulmonary hypertrophic osteoarthropathy. The sequence, however, may be reversed so that the osteoarthropathy precedes the clubbing, and at times the manifestations may be unilateral or unidigital. There are also two hereditary-familial conditions, congenital clubbing and idiopathic hypertrophic osteoarthropathy, which are of little clinical significance except that their presence may be interpreted incorrectly.

Clubbing is a process of soft tissue proliferation at the base of the nail which elevates the nail root. The bony aspect is a proliferative periostitis which most commonly involves the distal portion of long bones of the forearms and legs and metacarpals and metatarsals. When joints are involved, there is osteoporosis, chronic synovitis and nonspecific changes in the cartilage.

The pathogenesis is not clearly understood. Increased peripheral blood flow is a constant feature, but the flow is believed to be largely through dilated arteriovenous anastomoses. Limitation to fingers, toes, and occasionally the nose is attributed to the fact that these areas are endowed richly with arteriovenous anastomoses. Various hypotheses as to how clubbing is brought about have included endocrine imbalance, reduced oxygen tension of the blood, and reflex circulatory changes mediated through efferent nerves of the lung. Hall has postulated that digital clubbing may be the result of long-term action of a vasoactive substance on the arteriovenous anastomoses. On the basis of experimental studies he suggests the substance to be reduced ferritin which has not been oxidized by circulation through normal lung tissue. At present, however, one need not assume that there is a single cause of clubbing.

Pleural Disorders

The pleura is a thin, serous membrane. It is composed of an outer mesothelial layer, which rests on an avascular elastic layer, and an areolar layer, consisting of elastic and collagenous fibers, blood vessels, lymph vessels, and nerves. The blood vessels are derived from the bronchial artery and, after breaking up into capillaries, reunite into branches of the pulmonary vein. The lymphatics drain into the hilar lymph nodes.

Since the relationship of the pleura to the subpleural alveoli is an intimate one, disorders involving these alveoli are readily reflected in pleural disease. This is well illustrated by the pleurisy and serous exudate which occur as a result of a small tuberculous focus in the lung. Cardiac decompensation, trauma to the thoracic duct, or any generalized disease affecting blood vessels or lymphatics also may lead to the appearance of fluid in the pleural space. Pleural effusion associated with the ascites of hepatic cirrhosis or solid ovarian tumors is occasionally observed. Examination of such fluid for its physical, clinical, and cellular characteristics is a useful clinical procedure.

Although there are various means of driving fluid into the pleural space, there are probably only two defense mechanisms for its subsequent removal. In those circumstances in which the protein concentration of the fluid is low, the resorption is probably at the venous end of the pleural blood capillaries. This a consequence of the colloidal osmotic pressure of the blood plasma. However, in the presence of fluid of high protein content, the hydrostatic effect is nullified and the absorption of fluid, as well as any particulate matter, is through pleural lymphatics.

Tumors of the Pleura

The true, primary pleural origin of tumors which are found in the pleura is under considerable doubt. In a given case it is extremely difficult to rule out the possibility of a primary pulmonary origin with growth of secondary lesions in the pleura. The localized tumors have the characteristics of lipomas, fibromas, fibrosarcomas, and differentiated neural tissue. As a group, they are slow growing and may reach huge size without evidence of metastases. The only diffuse tumor is the mesothelioma, and it may involve the entire pleural surface. Whether metastases of this neoplasm ever extend beyond mediastinal lymph nodes is open to question. The clinical course may be rapidly downhill. The symptoms of pain, dyspnea, and cyanosis associated with pleural tumors are due to the interference with ventilation from the space occupied by the tumor, stiffening of the lung, and the accompanying effusion. Clubbing of the fingers may occur. Cytologic examination of the massive serous or serosanguineous fluid may be diagnostic.

Pleuritis

Inflammatory reaction of the pleura is almost always a consequence of spread of infection from contiguous structures. Thus the primary site may be within the lungs, mediastinum, chest wall, diaphragm, or subdiaphragmatic area. Pulmonary infarctions, neoplasms, and systemic diseases such as the so-called collagen diseases are at times the causes of pleurisy. The early reaction to insult is erythema and edema of the pleura, followed promptly by the exudation of cellular elements and fibrin deposition. As the inflammatory reaction involves the parietal pleura and as the rough fibrinous surface stimulates parietal pain receptors during respiration, the symptoms and signs of pleurisy are evident. The pain of diaphragmatic pleuritis may be referred to the abdomen or the shoulder area, whereas involvement of the parietal pleura of the chest wall is rather accurately localized by the patient. Partial relief is obtained by voluntary and involuntary splinting which, by decreasing the amplitude of pleural excursions, reduces the stimulation of parietal pleural nerves. This limitation of tidal ventilation is partially compensated for by an increase in the rate of respiration. The clinical manifestation is tachypnea and the patient may complain of dyspnea if he resorts to any exertion. Pleural pain is absent in interlobar pleurisy, and any symptoms produced are those of the primary lesion or those of decreased lung volume should the effusion be very large.

If the disease progresses from the stage of dry pleurisy, an exudate which is usually serofibrinous is produced and this may become frankly purulent. As fluid separates the inflamed pleural surfaces, there will be alleviation of the acute pleuritic pain and the appearance of a more generalized chest pain. With large effusions dyspnea is largely a consequence of volume displacement and reduced vital capacity.

Protective mechanisms brought into play are those that deal with the pulmonary problem precipitating the pleuritis, as well as absorption of fluid through the pleural capillaries and lymphatics and formation of adhesions that tend to seal the pleural surfaces together and wall off the process. The latter is readily induced, particularly when pulmonary movement is retarded, as it normally is at the apices.

At times the needle aspiration of pleural fluids is attended by symptoms of dizziness and faintness, even in the absence of pain. This is attributable to a fall in blood pressure, and its degree is a rough function of the volume aspirated and the rate of removal. Infrequently, the reaction to thoracentesis may be more serious and has even been reported to be a cause of death. Capps and Lewis studied this phenomenon in dogs and demonstrated that the aspiration of fluid with stimulation of the visceral pleura in the presence of inflammation is attended by a much greater risk than in the absence of inflammation. Their studies indicated that two different reflex mechanisms are involved. One is cardio-inhibitory, with slowing of the cardiac rate and usually slowing of respiration. This type of reflex is infrequently fatal. The other reflex is of the vasomotor type and is characterized by a rapid fall in blood pressure and more frequent termination in death unless therapy is directed toward the restoration of arteriolar tone.

Empyema

In thoracic empyema the pleural surfaces are abscess walls which are thickened, inflamed, and granular. Initially there is an acute pleuritis which may be a consequence of pulmonary infection, surgery, trauma, or extension of an infection from the subdiaphragmatic area, mediastinum, or esophagus.

When the origin is neither traumatic nor iatrogenic, the infectious agent most generally reaches the pleural space by direct extension from the lung, by rupture of a subpleural abscess, by lymphatic drainage into an effusion, or by septic embolization. Once the organism is established, an inflammatory exudate appears and the previously glistening pleural surface becomes a dull, thickened, granulating surface and pyogenic membrane. Further progress results in fibrous bands crisscrossing the empyema space and loculation of the exudate so that complete removal by thoracentesis is not possible. The wall of the empyema becomes organized into elastic fibrous tissue which may, as in tuberculosis empyema, effectively limit the infection and lead to quiescence for years.

If the empyema is small, the only alteration in pulmonary function may be a decrease in the excursions of the diaphragm and ribs. This is secondary to pain and reduces the vital capacity and maximal breathing capacity. If the empyema is large, the lung is compressed and the mediastinum is shifted toward the opposite lung, decreasing its volume also. The total pulmonary volume is reduced, vital capacity decreases, and pulmonary blood flow diminishes. Reduced oxygenation of the blood is generally evident. Although the loss of volume may not be great, the development of a nonelastic fibrous peel over the pleurae will reduce ventilatory function by mechanically limiting changes in volume. With maturation of the fibrous tissue, contraction occurs, which may reduce the lung volume severely by pulling the mediastinum toward the affected side and elevating and fixing the diaphragm. Particularly when this develops in early life, there may be a deforming scoliosis. With the decrease in volume on the side of disease, there is an absolute increase in volume in the normal hemithorax which results in a compensatory emphysema.

The principles of management are directed toward the elimination of the infection by use of appropriate antibiotics, aspiration of the exudate and enzymatic debridement if the purulent exudate is thick. If this is delayed or unsuccessful, surgical drainage of the abscess or decortication of the fibrous peel will be required to restore more normal pulmonary function. It has been observed repeatedly that bacteria may occur in pleural effusions and be eliminated by host defenses so that empyema does not develop. This situation, however, is a risky one, for, if empyema does develop, the defense mechanisms walling off the empyema may in themselves result in crippling pulmonary disease.

Epidemic Pleurodynia

Epidemic pleurodynia, or Bornholm disease, is an acute febrile illness due to Coxsackie virus, Group B. In experimental animals the typical lesion in striated muscle resembles Zenker's hyaline degeneration. In man, the histologic changes are unknown because the illness is self-limited and followed by complete recovery. There may be severe pain and tenderness of muscles in the trunk and extremities, suggesting that the basic lesion is perhaps a myositis which also involves the diaphragm. Pleuritis, pleural effusion, and pulmonary infiltrations have been noted mostly when there was an associated pericarditis. There are no described significant alterations in pulmonary function. Recovery is characterized by a rise in complement-fixing antibody.

Pneumothorax

Pneumothorax occurs when air enters the pleural space. If entry of the air is via the bronchial tree, the condition is termed closed pneumothorax; if via the thoracic wall, open pneumothorax. The latter is a consequence of trauma, whereas the causes of closed pneumothorax are many. Formerly, tuberculosis was believed to be the etiologic factor in 80 per cent of the cases of closed pneumothorax, but now blebs or bullae associated with localized obstructive bronchitis are considered to be the most common causes. Other disease entities occasionally incriminated are abscess, carcinoma, staphylococcal infections, and congenital cysts. As a rule, patients with generalized pulmonary emphysema do not have spontaneous pneumothorax.

The physiologic complications are related to the loss or, at least, decrease in normal intrapleural negative pressure, which in turn interferes with the return of venous blood to the heart. If there is a valvelike mechanism at the site of the tear in the visceral pleura, a tension pneumothorax with pressures many times atmospheric may be obtained. Valsalva-type maneuvers associated with sneezing or coughing continue to force air into the pleural space. The lung first collapses with the loss of negative pressure and eventually is compressed toward the mediastinum. This structure may be forced toward the opposite side, resulting in partial compression of the intact lung, and the diaphragm may be forced

downward. Dyspnea and cyanosis may occur as a consequence of pain, impairment of the volume of ventilation and the passage of blood through non-aerated lung.

The vast majority of pneumothoraces are simple in that the pressures developed are not strikingly elevated and the process does not proceed beyond partial collapse. The pleural opening closes spontaneously and the healthy pleura absorbs the air within a matter of a few weeks. Complications such as tension pneumothorax, hemopneumothorax, bilateral spontaneous pneumothorax, and infectious processes require intervention to remove air, halt bleeding and eradicate infection.

REFERENCES

Altschule, M. D.: Physiology in Diseases of the Heart and Lungs. Cambridge, Harvard University Press, 1949.

Avery, M. E., and Mead, J.: Surface properties in relation to atelectasis and hyaline membrane disease. A.M.A. Dis. Child., 97:517, 1959.

Barclay, A. E., Franklin, K. J., and Macbeth, R. G.: Roentgenographic studies of the excretion of dusts from the lungs. Am. J. Roentgenol., 39:673, 1938.

Basch, F. P., Holinger, P., and Poncher, H. G.: Physical and chemical properties of sputum. I. Factors determining variations in portions from different parts of the tracheobronchial tree. Am. J. Dis. Child., 62:981, 1941.

Basch, F. P., Holinger, P., and Poncher, H. G.: Physical and chemical properties of sputum. II. Influence of drugs, steam, carbon dioxide and oxygen. Am. J. Dis. Child., 62:1149, 1941.

Blanshard, G.: Sputum viscosity and postoperative pulmonary atelectasis. Dis. Chest, 37:75, 1960.

Brock, R. C.: The Anatomy of the Bronchial Tree with Special Reference to the Surgery of Lung Abscess. London. Oxford University Press, 1954.

Capps, J. A., and Lewis, D. D.: Observations upon certain blood-pressure-lowering reflexes that arise from irritation of the inflamed pleura. Am. J. Med. Sc., 134:868, 1907.

Cobb, B., and Nanson, E. M.: Further studies with serotonin and experimental pulmonary embolism. Ann. Surg., 151:501, 1960.

Comroe, J. H., Jr.: Physiological and biochemical effects of pulmonary artery occlusion. In de Reuck, A. V. S., and O'Connor, M. (eds.): Ciba Foundation Symposium on Structure and Function. Boston, Little, Brown & Co., 1962, pp. 176–193.

Comroe, J. H., Jr., Forster, R. E., II, Dubois, A. B., Briscoe, W. A., and Carlsen, E.: The Lung. Clinical Physiology and Pulmonary Function Tests. Chicago, Year Book Publishers, 1962.

Corpe, R. F., Runyon, E. H., and Lester, W.: Status of disease due to unclassified mycobacteria. Am. Rev. Resp. Dis., 87:459, 1963.

Corpe, R. F., and Stergus, I.: Is the histopathology of nonphotochromogenic mycobacterial infections distinguishable from that caused by mycobacterium tuberculosis? Am. Rev. Resp. Dis., 87:289, 1963.

Corssen, G.: Changing concepts of the mechanism of pulmonary atelectasis. J.A.M.A., 183:314, 1963.

Cudkowicz, L., and Armstrong, J. B.: The bronchial arteries in pulmonary emphysema. Thorax, 8: 46, 1953.

Dammann, J. F., Jr., Baker, J. P., and Muller, W. H., Jr.: Pulmonary vascular changes induced by experimentally produced pulmonary arterial hypertension. Surg. Gynec. & Obst., 105:16, 1957.

Dickson, J. A., Clagett, O. T., and McDonald, J. R.: Cystic disease of the lungs and its relationship to bronchiectatic cavities. J. Thoracic Surg., 15: 196, 1946.

Di Rienzo, S.: Radiologic Exploration of the Bronchus. Springfield, Charles C Thomas, 1949.

Divertie, M. B., and Olsen, A. M.: Pulmonary infiltration associated with blood eosinophilia (P.I.E.): A clinical study of Loeffler's syndrome and of periarteritis nodosa with P.I.E. syndrome. Dis. Chest, 37:340, 1960.

Drinker, C. K.: The Clinical Physiology of the Lungs. Springfield, Charles C Thomas, 1954.

Duguid, J. B.: The arterial lining. Lancet, 2:207, 1952.

Ellis, F. H., Jr., and Carr, D. T.: The problem of spontaneous pneumothorax. M. Clin. North America, 38:1065, 1954.

Finley, T. N., Tooley, W. H., Swenson, E. W., Gardner, R. E., and Clements, J. A.: Pulmonary surface tension in experimental atelectasis. Am. Rev. Resp. Dis., 89:372, 1964.

Fleischner, F. G.: The pathogenesis of bronchiectasis. Radiology, 53:818, 1949.

Fletcher, C. M.: Chronic bronchitis. Its prevalence, nature and pathogenesis. Am. Rev. Resp. Dis., 80:483, 1959.

Fraimow, W., Cathcart, R. T., and Taylor, R. C.: Physiologic and clinical aspects of pulmonary alveolar proteinosis. Ann. Int. Med., 52:1177, 1960.

Gaensler, E. A., and Lindgren, I.: Chronic bronchitis as an etiologic factor in obstructive emphysema. Symposium on Emphysema and the "Chronic Bronchitis" Syndrome. Am. Rev. Resp. Dis., 80:185 (No. 1, Part 2), July, 1959.

Golden, A.: Pathologic anatomy of "atypical pneumonia, etiology undetermined." Acute interstitial pneumonitis. A.M.A. Arch. Path., 38:187, 1944.

Gordon, R. B., Lennette, E. H., and Sandrock, R. S.: The varied clinical manifestations of Coxsackie virus infections. A.M.A. Arch. Int. Med., 103: 63, 1959.

Hall, G. H.: The cause of digital clubbing. Testing a new hypothesis. Lancet, 1:750, 1959.

Hamman, L.: Spontaneous interstitial emphysema of the lung. Tr. A. Am. Physicians, 5:311, 1937.

Hamman, L., and Rich, A. R.: Acute diffuse interstitial fibrosis of the lungs. Bull. Johns Hopkins Hosp., 74:177, 1944.

Hauser, T. E., and Steer, A.: Lymphangitic carcinomatosis of the lungs: Six case reports and a review of the literature. Ann. Int. Med., 34:881, 1951.

Head, J. R.: Cystic disease of the lung with emphasis on emphysematous blebs and bullae. Am. J. Surg., 89:1019, 1955.

Heppleston, A. G.: The pathogenesis of simple pneu-

mokoniosis in coal workers. J. Path. & Bact., 67: 51, 1954.

Huber, H. L., and Koessler, K. K.: The pathology of bronchial asthma. A.M.A. Arch. Int. Med., 30: 689, 1922.

Jarre, H. A.: Roentgenologic studies on physiologic motor phenomena. Radiology, 15:377, 1930.

Jillson, O. F.: Mycology. New England J. Med., 249: 523, 1953.

Johnston, R. F., and Loo, R. V.: Hepatic hydrothorax. Ann. Int. Med., 61:385, 1964.

Klosk, E., Bernstein, A., and Parsonnet, A. E.: Cystic disease of the lung. Ann. Int. Med., 24:217, 1946.

Lewis, P. A., and Sanderson, E. S.: The histological expression of the natural resistance of rabbits to infection with human type tubercle bacilli. J. Exper. Med., 45:291, 1947.

Liebow, A. A.: Atlas of Tumor Pathology. Tumors of the Lower Respiratory Tract. Washington, D.C., Armed Forces Institute of Pathology, 1952.

Loeffler, W.: Zur Differential-Diagnosis der Lungeninfiltrierungen. II. Über flüchtige Succendan-Infiltrate (mit Eosinophilie). Beitr. Klin. Tuberk., 79:368, 1932.

Lowell, F. C.: Bronchial asthma. Am. J. Med., 20:778, 1956.

Macklin, C. C.: The dynamic bronchial tree. Am. Rev. Tuberc., 25:393, 1932.

Mallory, T. B.: The pathogenesis of bronchiectasis. New England J. Med., 237:795, 1947.

Mayer, E., and Rappaport, I.: Developmental origin of cystic, bronchiectatic and emphysematous changes in the lungs. A new concept. Dis. Chest, 21:146, 1952.

McLean, K. H.: The pathogenesis of pulmonary emphysema. Am. J. Med., 25:62, 1958.

Mead, J., Whittenberger, J. L., and Radford, E. P., Jr.: Surface tension as a factor in pulmonary volume-pressure hysteresis. J. Appl. Physiol., 10: 191, 1957.

von Meyenburg, H.: Eosinophilic pulmonary infiltration: Pathologic anatomy and pathogenesis. Schweiz. med. Wehnschr., 72:809, 1942.

Michelson, A. L., and Lowell, F. C.: Blood acetylcholine in bronchial asthma. J. Lab. & Clin. Med., 47:119, 1956.

Miller, W. S.: The Lung. Springfield, Charles C Thomas, 1947.

Motley, H. L.: Pulmonary function impairment in pneumoconioses. J.A.M.A., 172:1591, 1960.

Negus, V. E.: The action of cilia and the effect of drugs on their activity. J. Laryng. & Otol., 49:571, 1934.

Norris, R. F., and Tyson, R. M.: The pathogenesis of congenital polycystic lung and its correlation with polycystic disease of other epithelial organs. Am. J. Path., 23:1075, 1947.

O'Neal, R. M., and Thomas, W. A.: The role of pulmonary hypertension and thromboembolism in the production of pulmonary arteriosclerosis. Circulation, 12:370, 1955.

Parker, B. M., and Smith, J. R.: Pulmonary embolism and infarction. Am. J. Med., 24:402, 1958.

Proetz, A. W.: Essays on the Applied Physiology of the Nose. St. Louis, Annals Publishing Co., 1941.

Pump, K. K.: The morphology of the finer branches of

the bronchial tree of the human lung. Dis. Chest, *46:*379, 1964.

Rich, A. R.: The Pathogenesis of Tuberculosis. Springfield, Charles C Thomas, 1951.

Robertson, O. H.: Phagocytosis of foreign material in the lung. Physiol. Rev., *21:*112, 1942.

Robin, E. D.: Some aspects of the physiologic disturbances associated with pulmonary embolism. M. Clin. North America, *44:*1269, 1960.

Rosen, S. H., Castleman, B., and Liebow, A. A.: Pulmonary alveolar proteinosis. New England J. Med., *258:*1123, 1958.

Rytel, M. W.: Primary atypical pneumonia: current concepts. Am. J. Med. Sc., *247:*84, 1964.

Smyth, C. J., et al.: Rheumatism and arthritis: Review of American and English literature of recent years. Part II. Ann. Int. Med., *50:*664, 1959.

Snider, G. L.: Pulmonary tuberculosis and centrilobular emphysema. A.M.A. Arch. Int. Med., *111:*762, 1963.

Sodeman, W. A., and Stuart, B. M.: Lipoid pneumonia in adults. Ann. Int. Med., *24:*241, 1946.

Steinberg, I.: Lipoid pneumonia associated with paraesophageal hernia. Angiocardiographic study of a case. Dis. Chest, *37:*157, 1960.

Stewart, P. B.: The rate of formation and lymphatic removal of fluid in pleural effusions. J. Clin. Invest., *42:*258, 1963.

Sturm, A.: Der Lungenkrampf (Kontraktionsatelektase durch Pulmonalen Spasmus). Deutsch. Med. Wschr., *71:*201, 1946.

Sundberg, R. H., Kirschner, K. E., and Brown, M. J.: Evaluation of lipoid pneumonia. Dis. Chest, *36:*594, 1959.

Sutnick, A. I., and Soloff, L. A.: Atelectasis with pneumonia. A pathophysiologic study. Ann. Int. Med., *60:*39, 1964.

Vogl, A., Blumenfeld, S., and Gutner, L. B.: Diagnostic significance of pulmonary hypertrophic osteoarthropathy. Am. J. Med., *18:*51, 1955.

Von Neergard, K.: Neue Auffassungen ueber einen Grundbegriff der Atemmechanik, abhaengig von der Ober-flaechenspannung in den Alveolen. Z. Ges. Exp. Med., *66:*373, 1929.

West, J. B., Holland, R. A. B., Dollery, C. T., and Mathews, C. M. E.: Interpretation of radioactive gas clearance rates in the lung. J. Appl. Physiol., *17:*14, 1962.

Wood, W. B., Jr.: Studies on the mechanism of recovery in pneumococcal pneumonia. I. The action of type specific antibody upon the pulmonary lesion of experimental pneumonia. J. Exper. Med., *73:*201, 1941.

Wood, W. B., Jr., Smith, M. R., and Watson, B.: Studies on the mechanism of recovery from pneumonia. The mechanism of phagocytosis in the absence of antibody. J. Exper. Med., *84:*355, 1946.

Yoo, O. H., and Ting, E. Y.: The effects of pleural effusion on pulmonary function. Am. Rev. Resp. Dis., *89:*55, 1964.

Zimmerman, L. E.: Fatal fungus infections complicating other diseases. Am. J. Clin. Path., *25:*46, 1955.

Zohman, L. R., and Williams, M. H., Jr.: Cardiopulmonary function in pulmonary fibrosis. Am. Rev. Resp. Dis., *80:*700, 1959.

Part VIII

Digestive System

Chapter Twenty-Three

The Esophagus

JOSEPH B. KIRSNER

Mechanism of Esophageal Pain

The mucosa of the normal esophagus is sensitive to heat and cold, but insensitive to tactile stimuli. Irritants, such as dilute hydrochloric acid, evoke painful sensations from the pharyngeal end of the viscus only where there is overlapping of the spinal and autonomic innervations. In the esophagus proper, pain often is related to tension of the muscle fibers; either distention or spasm may be an adequate stimulus. Pain is more frequent with sudden distention of the esophagus, as by a foreign body, than in a slow-growing neoplasm, permitting gradual adjustment of the esophagus to the lesion. The pain tends to be burning in quality when the stimulus acts continuously, and griping when it is intermittent and intense. The pain of esophageal distention is not attributable to interference with propulsive movement along the esophagus. Esophageal pain also may be induced by the reflux of acid gastric content (pH 1.0 to 2.0) into the lower portion of the esophagus, the acid inducing a chemical inflammation of the mucosa. Vascular engorgement and inflammation of the esophageal mucosa diminish the local pain threshold. As with pain elsewhere in the body, esophageal pain is influenced by individual variations in sensitivity and by fluctuations in the pain threshold of the same person.

Heartburn is an intermittent, wavelike, burning, or searing painful sensation, experienced retrosternally in the midline, between the xiphoid and the manubrium, and often relieved by antacids. The distress may radiate to the upper abdomen, the anterior chest wall, and the jaws. Heartburn ordinarily is caused by irritation of the esophagus, secondary to the reflux of acid gastric content; but it also may be induced by the reflux of alkaline intestinal content, as in patients with total gastrectomy. Impairment of the normal barrier to esophageal reflux, therefore, is an important predisposing condition. Rapid distention or overdistention of the stomach, such as during eating, or the excessive drinking of water or carbonated beverages, also predisposes to gastroesophageal reflux and heartburn. Increased tension of the muscle fibers in the wall of the esophagus, proximal to the cardia, contributes to the discomfort. The mechanism of the heartburn induced by the ingestion of orange juice, sweet rolls, or cake icing in patients with hiatus hernia or gastroesophageal reflux is not known, though it may involve changes in pH of the esophageal content. The mechanism of pain in peptic ulcer of the esophagus is the same as in gastric and duodenal ulcer.

Pain is referred usually to the midline beneath the sternum, and occasionally to the back, neck, face, or arms. Lesions in the upper esophagus project painful sensations to an area near the manubrium or suprasternal notch; those in the middle esophagus cause discomfort behind the midsternum; and lesions in the lower esophagus, proximal to the

565

cardia, produce pain at or immediately proximal to the xiphoid. Clinically, the topographic location of esophageal pain usually corresponds with the level of the lesion in the esophagus. The distress produced by esophageal spasm or hiatus hernia may radiate from the substernal area into the left shoulder and arm, and thus simulate the pain of angina pectoris. The similarity of esophageal pain induced by balloon distention to the pain of angina pectoris in some patients has been ascribed to the faulty localization of visceral pain, and to the correspondence of the sensory innervation of the esophagus, at least in part, with that of the heart.

The surface area to which all pain from the esophagus is referred is innervated from the third cervical to the seventh and eighth dorsal spinal segments. The sympathetic nerves provide the chief pathways. The uppermost part of the esophagus is supplied by branches from the pharyngeal plexus, lower down from the cardiac branches of the superior cervical ganglia, and, occasionally, from the middle cervical or vertebral ganglia of the sympathetic trunks. Other fibers reach the esophagus in the delicate nerve plexuses accompanying the fine arteries of its blood supply. The abdominal portion of the esophagus is supplied from the terminal part of the left greater splanchnic nerve and from the right inferior phrenic plexus. Observations with balloon distention of the esophagus in patients with angina pectoris have suggested that at least the upper five thoracic nerves are involved in the esophageal sensory innervation. Since pain from the esophagus, as studied experimentally, can be experienced as low as the umbilicus, the possibility exists that the lower thoracic nerves also contain esophageal pain fibers. The vagi may contain sensory fibers, but conclusive proof of this has not been adduced. The parasympathetic fibers supplying the upper esophagus arise in the nucleus ambiguus; those supplying the lower esophagus arise from the recurrent laryngeal nerves and anterior and posterior vagal trunks.

The pain of esophageal disease thus may resemble or mimic that of cardiac disease and disorders of the stomach, duodenum, gallbladder, and biliary tract. In a patient with both gastrointestinal and cardiac disease, the diagnostic problem may be difficult. More precise characterization of esophageal pain is aided by cineradiography of the esophagus, the acid perfusion and esophageal motility tests, and by measurement of intraluminal pH. The response to the intraesophageal perfusion of 0.1N hydrochloric acid, as employed in the reproduction of ulcer pain in the stomach and duodenum, is helpful in confirming the diagnosis of esophagitis. The esophageal motility test, measuring resting pressures and deglutition sequences with appropriate apparatus including multiple-pressure sensors, may facilitate the diagnosis of a hyperreacting gastroesophageal sphincter and of diffuse esophageal spasm. Simultaneous measurements of intraesophageal pH and intraluminal pressures are useful in demonstrating the presence of gastroesophageal reflux.

Functional Disorders of the Esophagus

Spasm of Functional Origin

Roentgenologically demonstrable spasm of the esophagus usually is associated with an intrinsic lesion, but primary spasm occurs. Globus hystericus ordinarily is attributed to spasm of the esophagus, but proof is difficult to obtain because the phenomenon is transitory. True hysterical dysphagia is not rare and may be the outstanding manifestation of the psychiatric disorder. Primary spasm of the nonsphincteral parts of the esophagus may consist in (1) diffuse irregular spasm of the lower third or half of the esophagus, (2) diffuse narrowing of the lower third or half, or (3) multiple spastic segments of concentric narrowing, with the formation of so-called functional esophageal "diverticula."

Esophageal motor activity often is disorganized in aged individuals, with tertiary contractions as the predominant esophageal response to swallowing, and a motility pattern resembling that of diffuse esophageal spasm. The esophagus may undergo nonpropulsive contraction, narrowing a considerable segment and simulating the appearance of a corkscrew, a state described as "curling." The cause is not known. The chief symptoms are intermittent difficulty in swallowing and substernal pain of varying severity. Regurgitation is the predominant manifestation of esophageal spasm in children. In some patients, spasm of the esophagus is a coincidental roentgenologic finding, not accompanied by symptoms.

ACHALASIA (CARDIOSPASM; MEGAESOPHAGUS; APERISTALSIS)

Anatomic Features

Achalasia is characterized anatomically by a variable dilatation of the entire thoracic esophagus and by an undilated lower segment, the gastroesophageal vestibule of Lerche varying in length from 1.5 to 4.5 cm. There is no evidence of stricture or of hypertrophy of the muscle in the undilated segment. In early cardiospasm, the esophagus dilates only slightly. The muscular layers, especially the circular, are thickened, as are the circular elastic fibers. In advanced achalasia, the esophagus is dilated to a degree seldom observed in obstruction from stricture or carcinoma. The muscle layers and the elastic tissue are thinned, and the esophagus is stretched lengthwise, so that bends and kinks occur. Inflammation, erosion, and ulceration may develop, especially in the lower half of the esophagus. The principal histologic features of achalasia are diminution or the complete absence of ganglion cells from the myenteric plexus, as conspicuous in the undilated as in the dilated parts of the esophagus; mucosal and submucosal infiltration with mononuclear cells, often associated with focal areas of sclerosis; proliferation of fibrous tissue; newly formed blood vessels; and lymphocytic infiltration. When studied with the electron microscope, the esophageal smooth muscle manifests three principal types of cellular change consistent with denervation atrophy: myofilament detachment from surface membranes, an increased number of ribosomes, and cellular atrophy. Electron microscopic examination of the extraesophageal vagus nerves in achalasia has demonstrated wallerian degeneration of both myelinated and nonmyelinated axons.

The motor activity of the esophagus in achalasia, as observed roentgenologically, differs from the normal and from that of the obstruction produced by fibrosis or neoplasm. In moderate or advanced cardiospasm, the deep, primary peristaltic wave begins normally in the pharynx, but instead of progressing to the region of the diaphragm, it ceases at or slightly below the level of the suprasternal notch or the superior margin of the aortic arch. Shallow, nonpropulsive contractions are noted, especially in the lower half of the esophagus. These undulating movements may be accompanied by generalized tonic contractions, diffusely narrowing the esophageal lumen.

The resting pressure within the esophagogastric sphincter is normal; but swallowing fails to elicit the usual fall in pressure, indicating nonrelaxation of the sphincter; and there is early nonperistaltic contraction of the sphincter after deglutition. After effective treatment with mechanical dilatation or cardiomyotomy, the resting pressures in the sphincter area decrease significantly, with restoration of a positive gastroesophageal pressure gradient for the entire respiratory cycle. However, the deglutition response of the sphincter and of the esophagus proper remains abnormal.

Pathogenesis

Achalasia is not attributable to a failure of the diaphragmatic pinchcock to open during the process of deglutition. No obstruction is found at operation or autopsy examination, and a bougie passes readily through the cardia. The junction of the dilated and undilated segments occurs at varying levels, not always at the hiatus. Physiologically, achalasia is attributable to failure of the gastroesophageal vestibule to relax with the advancing peristaltic wave, as a consequence of a neuromuscular deficit. Experimentally, complete bilateral cervical section of the vagus in the cat and dog results in dilatation of the esophagus and obstruction at its lower end; sympathectomy relieves the obstruction; and simultaneous vagotomy and sympathectomy do not result in obstruction. Clinically, mild cardiospasm occasionally occurs in man after vagotomy for duodenal ulcer and after potent anticholinergic medication. In both instances, the abnormality seems related to the predominant action of the sympathetic nerves. Achalasia of the esophagus also can be produced in dogs and rabbits by freezing the cardia thereby destroying the sensitive nerve elements but not the other esophageal components. Similarly, in Chagas' disease (South American trypanosomiasis), the intramural nerve plexus of the esophagus apparently is destroyed by the neurotoxin released from the dead parasites, producing dilatation of the esophagus and a histologic appearance resembling achalasia.

Ingelfinger, Code, and their associates, among others, have demonstrated by simultaneous pressure recordings and cinefluorographic studies that the distal esophageal segment (vestibule) functions physiologically as an intrinsic sphincter. This mechanism apparently maintains esophagogastric competence, preventing regurgitant esophagitis. In cardiospasm, the parasympathetic stimuli to the esophagus are weak and incoordinated. The cholinergic drug methacholine, given intramuscularly, induces a tetanic and painful contraction of a variable extent of the distal esophagus—a response not observed otherwise, except in diffuse spasm of the esophagus.

There is, thus, convincing evidence that achalasia or "cardiospasm" is the result of a neuromuscular dysfunction of the esophagus proper, a disorder of the cholinergic innervation and motor integration of the entire esophagus; in effect, a postganglionic denervation of the esophagus. The myenteric ganglia, particularly in the region of the cardia, seem to be primarily involved, but the cause is not known. The degenerative changes in the ganglia presumably impede the vagal inhibitory impulses, and sympathetic motor impulses are dominant. The lower end of the esophagus fails to relax with each peristaltic wave and esophageal peristalsis is not sufficiently powerful to overcome the resistance of the tonically contracting, unrelaxed muscle of the terminal esophageal segment.

Symptoms

The onset of symptoms in achalasia is variable, often gradual and occasionally abrupt, as after an emotional disturbance. The course tends to be intermittent, at least initially. The chief manifestations are substernal distress or pain, dysphagia, and regurgitation. There is an intermittent substernal discomfort, a choking feeling on attempting to swallow, and a sense of pressure caused by delay in the passage of food. The patient often develops the habit of forcing food into the stomach during or after eating by a type of Valsalva maneuver; that is, assuming the erect position, drinking one or two glasses of water, then taking a deep breath; the thorax is compressed by flexing the head so that the chin rests on the chest and a forced expiratory effort is made. This procedure may be utilized several times during the course of a meal to obtain relief. Waves of peristalsis descend intermittently along the esophagus in an effort to propel the contents into the stomach. Pain in achalasia is attributable to spasm and distention of the esophagus. It occurs intermittently, during or after eating. The pain is experienced usually in the lower retrosternal area, with radiation to the interscapular region or to the base of the neck. With sufficient distention of the esophagus, pain also may occur independent of deglutition and during sleep. In some instances the distress simulates the pain produced by insufficiency of the coronary arteries. In advanced cardiospasm, pain may be mild or absent, since esophageal tonus is diminished and peristaltic activity is confined to irregular, weak contractions.

The dysphagia is not a difficulty in the act of swallowing, but rather delay in the passage of food from the esophagus into the stomach. The dysphagia is not consistently related to the type of food. Solids may be swallowed more readily than liquids, and hot foods more readily than cold, but this is variable. Regurgitation of the esophageal contents initially may occur with each meal, especially when the patient is in the recumbent position. As the esophagus dilates the regurgitation occurs less often. The regurgitated food is unchanged from that eaten. The regurgitated material contains a large amount of thick mucus, resulting from irritation of the mucous glands. The nutritional state of the patient is maintained early in the course of achalasia; but in persistent achalasia considerable loss of weight occurs as a result of the interference with the passage of food into the digestive tract. Pressure of the distended esophagus upon the trachea, bronchi, and mediastinal structures causes dyspnea and cough. The aspiration of esophageal material into the bronchi may produce basal pneumonitis, pulmonary abscess, bronchiectasis, pleural effusion, and pulmonary fibrosis. In children nocturnal regurgitation and recurrent pulmonary infections resulting from the aspiration of food may be the presenting manifestations of achalasia. Pressure upon the diaphragm by the distended esophagus may cause hiccup. Palpitation and cardiac arrhythmias, including heart block and atrial fibrillation, may occur, presumably from pressure of the dilated esophagus upon the heart.

Organic Diseases of the Esophagus

PLUMMER-VINSON (PATERSON-KELLY) SYNDROME

The Plummer-Vinson (Paterson-Kelly) syndrome is a symptom complex of dysphagia, glossitis, and hypochromic microcytic anemia attributable to deficiency of iron and vitamin B. The upper esophagus is characterized by atrophy and hyperkeratinization of the epithelium, areas of desquamation with degeneration of the underlying tissue, and by thin fibrous strictures or webs. The muscle coats are thin; Auerbach's plexus is normal. The disorder is observed almost exclusively in women. Symptoms occur intermittently over a period of months or years. Patients tend to be apprehensive lest attempts to swallow precipitate choking spells; prolonged or careful mastication ("mincing of food") is characteristic. The dysphagia results from inflammation and spasm in the initial phase, and from the thin cicatricial webs in the later stage of the illness. The buccal mucosa is atrophic and dry; the tongue is smooth, glossy, and devoid of papillae, and there are fissures at the corners of the mouth, and fissuring of the finger tips, changes possibly attributable to deficiency of the vitamin B group. The anemia results from deficiency of iron; some observers have ascribed the entire syndrome to iron deficiency. Enlargement of the spleen is common. Achlorhydria has been common, but this feature requires re-examination with maximal tests of gastric secretion. Carcinoma of the mouth, hypopharynx, and upper esophagus may develop.

LOWER ESOPHAGEAL RING

Intermittent difficulty in swallowing also may be associated with a sharply defined contractile ring of the lower esophagus, an annular constriction, located at a level 0.5 to 2.5 cm. above the diaphragm. Muscular hypertrophy of the inferior esophageal sphincter has been implicated as the underlying defect, but the nature of the disorder remains unclear. The frequent association of an esophageal ring with a hiatus hernia has suggested the possibility that the ring represents the esophagogastric junction. In one case studied histologically, the esophageal ring was covered above by esophageal mucosa and below by gastric glands. The core consisted of connective tissue, an overgrowth of muscularis mucosae, and groups of smooth muscle fibers, forming an annular band. Mucous glands, excretory ducts, blood vessels, nerves, and lymphatics also were present. The radiologic appearance of an esophageal ring characteristically is that of a constant, symmetrical, sharply defined narrowing of the distal portion of the esophagus. Symptoms frequently are absent. When symptoms are present, the usual clinical picture is that of intermittent esophageal obstruction, often becoming apparent during the rapid eating of meat or bread, commonly at a steak dinner; hence the designation "steak-house syndrome." The occurrence and severity of the dysphagia depend upon the diameter of the esophageal lumen at the level of the ring.

SCLERODERMA OF THE ESOPHAGUS

The esophagus is involved often and early in the systemic disease scleroderma. The process is characterized by thickening of the submucosa, sclerosis of the connective tissue, and atrophy and fibrosis of the muscularis. The infiltration of the esophageal wall produces characteristic alterations in esophageal motor activity, including decreased to absent contractile activity of most of the esophagus, nonrelaxation in the area of the esophagogastric sphincter, and absence of the normal elevation in intraesophageal resting pressure upon swallowing. Esophageal symptoms occur in at least 50 per cent of patients; roentgen examination discloses abnormal esophageal findings in approximately 70 per cent of patients. These findings include atony and varying degrees of dilatation of the lower four-fifths (smooth muscle portion) of the esophagus, decreased to complete absence of normal peristaltic activity and ineffectual transport of food and esophageal content when the patient is recumbent. Gastroesophageal reflux is common, producing esophagitis and esophageal stricture. Dysphagia is the principal symptom of esophageal scleroderma, on the basis of the anatomic and physiologic changes described.

INFLAMMATION OF THE ESOPHAGUS

Nonspecific Esophagitis

Acute nonspecific esophagitis is the most common disease of the esophagus. It may accompany acute infectious diseases, the trauma produced by a foreign body, the ingestion of irritating or caustic substances, and in debilitated patients the use of antibiotics, increasing the susceptibility to infection with Monilia. The esophagus is vulnerable to infection with organisms from the oral cavity since its mucous glands open freely on the epithelial surface. Infection also may come from the blood and from the abdominal cavity via the lymphatic drainage. Chronic nonspecific esophagitis is a frequent concomitant of esophageal obstruction, particularly in achalasia and carcinoma, because of the prolonged contact of the mucosa with stagnant esophageal content containing many bacteria.

Pain is the most frequent symptom of esophagitis. It usually is mild or burning, but in the presence of esophageal spasm it may be so severe as to require opiates. It is aggravated by the swallowing of food and is experienced usually beneath the lower end of the sternum and in the back. Dysphagia in acute esophagitis is due to spasm. Painful deglutition is encountered more often than is obstruction to the passage of food, and it is observed with liquid as well as solid food.

Peptic Esophagitis

Peptic esophagitis is a chronic disease of the lower end of the esophagus, produced by the corrosive effect of acid gastric juice secreted by ectopic gastric glands or, more commonly, regurgitated from the stomach, in situations associated with prolonged vomiting, during gastric intubation, or incompetence of the sphincteric mechanism of the lower esophagus, as in hiatus hernia and after gastroesophageal anastomosis. Diminution or loss of the protective layer of mucus, the presence of an atypical, embryonic type of epithelium susceptible to the irritant action of hydrochloric acid, and mucosal erosions produced by excessive muscular activity, as in vomiting, predispose to peptic esophagitis. The mucosa is red, granular, and eroded. The histologic appearance is characterized by acute and chronic inflammation, superficial erosions, hemorrhage, and areas of thickened epithelium. The symptoms of peptic esophagitis include heartburn and retrosternal discomfort or pain, occasionally radiating to the neck, to the back, or down both arms. The complaints are experienced shortly after eating, on bending over, or while lying down, since these positions facilitate the reflux of gastric contents into the esophagus. Swallowing may be painful, especially after drinking fruit juices or alcoholic beverages and ingesting either hot or ice cold foods. Spasm, edema of the esophagus, and cicatricial stenosis produce dysphagia. Bleeding from the congested esophageal mucosa is common, and massive hemorrhage may occur. Diffuse esophagitis and localized ulcers often coexist. Not infrequently patients with peptic esophagitis also have stenosing duodenal ulcers and gastric hypersecretion.

Peptic Ulcer of the Esophagus

Acid-peptic lesions of the gastroesophageal junction tend to be of two types: (1) superficial erosions of the squamous mucosa of the lower esophagus, with friability of the esophageal surface and, in chronic cases, development of fibrosis and stricture formation; and (2) deep ulcers penetrating areas lined by columnar epithelium. Localized ulcerations resemble chronic peptic ulcers of the stomach and duodenum and are located usually on the posterior wall of the esophagus. Hiatus hernia, cardioesophageal incompetency after surgical procedures, and prolonged esophageal intubation predispose to its formation by facilitating acid reflux. The ulcer varies in size from a diameter of a few millimeters to a lesion completely encircling the esophageal lumen. The principal symptoms are pain, hematemesis, and dysphagia. The pain often is described as a burning sensation of varying intensity, located beneath the lower part of the sternum or in the epigastrium, or as a boring pain extending to the back below the shoulder blades. It may be induced by eating or may not occur until several hours after eating, as in the typical ulcer distress, and may be relieved by antacids and food. The pain mechanism is the same as that of gastroduodenal ulcer, intensified by spasm or by the passage of food over the ulcer. Bleeding, if present, usually consists in the intermittent or persistent oozing of blood from congested submucosal veins. Rarely the ulcer erodes into an artery with consequent massive hematemesis. Dysphagia may be mild or severe, intermittent or persistent. Initially, the difficulty in swallowing is slight and momentary and is due to spasm. Later, when cicatricial stenosis has developed, dysphagia is pronounced, more persistent, and accompanied by regurgitation of food. The ulcer may penetrate the entire thickness of the esophageal wall and perforate into the pleura, pericardium, mediastinum or a bronchus.

Mechanical Obstruction

The most important mechanical causes of obstruction to the passage of food and liquid through the esophagus are benign cicatricial stenosis and neoplasm. Mechanical obstruction also may be produced by extrinsic compression of the esophagus by masses, such as pulmonary and mediastinal tumors, substernal goiter, aneurysm of the aorta, and breast carcinoma extending to the mediastinum.

Benign Stricture

Stricture of the esophagus frequently is caused by the swallowing of lye and other caustic agents, alkaline or acid. The degree of injury depends upon the concentration and quantity of the corrosive, the duration of contact with mucosa, and the protection afforded by the contents of the esophagus and by the mucus layer. Stenosis may follow the ingestion of inorganic acids, bichloride of mercury, and ammonia; it may occur as a sequel to infectious diseases, trauma of the esophagus by ingested foreign bodies, prolonged vomiting, esophagitis, and peptic ulcer. In some cases the etiology is unknown. Temporary slowing of the esophageal contents probably explains the frequency of the lesion at the normal sites of narrowing of the esophagus. The stricture not infrequently develops 2 or 3 inches above the diaphragm, a level at which the irritant is temporarily arrested. The size and type of the deformity vary from a purse-string narrowing to a long, tubular stenosis. Cicatricial narrowing develops usually within 4 to 6 weeks after the ingestion of a caustic substance. The degree of dilatation proximal to the stenosis depends upon the location, duration, and severity of the stricture.

Difficulty in swallowing develops gradually and increases progressively, depending upon the extent of the stricture and the diameter of the lumen. Solid food is the first to cause trouble; it may temporarily obstruct the lumen completely and thus produce intermittent symptoms suggesting spasm. The patient often attempts to facilitate the passage of food by sipping liquids or by repeated swallowing movements. If the material cannot pass the obstruction, it is sooner or later regurgitated. Pain is seldom present after the initial trauma subsides.

Carcinoma of Esophagus

Carcinoma of the esophagus is predominantly a disease of men above the age of 50. Its cause is as obscure as that of neoplasm elsewhere in the body. Mechanical and chemical irritation, dental sepsis, and various esophageal diseases, including achalasia and hiatus hernia, are regarded as predisposing factors, perhaps because of the associated leukoplakia of the esophagus. Esophageal obstruction by webs, lye stricture, and congenital and inflammatory stenosis also may predispose to the development of esophageal carcinoma. Epidemiologic observations have implicated excessive smoking and intake of alcohol as possible contributory factors, but the evidence is inconclusive.

Carcinoma may involve any region of the esophagus, but occurs often at one of the areas of physiologic narrowing. The lower and middle thirds of the esophagus are affected more often than the upper segment. The growth usually is annular and may become very extensive before producing stenosis of the lumen. Three gross types of tumor are distinguished: (a) the polypoid variety, causing early obstruction; (b) the soft ulcerative type, associated with bleeding, anemia, and early metastases; and (c) the scirrhous or infiltrating tumor, tending to encircle the esophagus and to obstruct the lumen gradually. Carcinoma of the upper part of the esophagus usually is squamous cell in type; carcinoma of the lower portion of the esophagus often is adenocarcinoma in type. Carcinoma of the lower third frequently originates in the cardiac glands present in the esophagus and is of either type. Secondary infection is common, particularly with the spirochetal and fusiform organisms of the mouth, and may lead to perforation of the lesion and mediastinitis.

The symptoms vary with the type, extent, and location of the lesion. Before actual difficulty in swallowing arises, the patient may experience a sense of weight, oppression, or fullness beneath the sternum, or a persistent burning discomfort retrosternally. These sensations usually are noticed during swallowing, but they also occur independently. Substernal discomfort may be intermittent for long periods, depending upon the presence or absence of inflammation and spasm of the esophagus in the area of the tumor.

The most common and usually the initial symptom of carcinoma is dysphagia, first in the swallowing of coarse foods, typically meat, followed by increasing difficulty in the swallowing of soft foods as the esophageal lumen is further reduced. Well-chewed food may pass without apparent difficulty through a channel as small as 5 mm. in diameter. Gradually, as the lumen becomes further occluded, complete inability to swallow either food or liquid ensues, and regurgitation is frequent. Pain seldom is present during the early stages of the disease, and is more common in ulcerating or infiltrating tumors than in the polypoid growths. Pain is experienced most frequently in the substernal region, the location tending to correspond with the actual position of the tumor. The presence of pain often signifies extension of the tumor beyond the confines of the esophagus, and invasion of adjacent structures, especially when it occurs independently of swallowing. The pain varies from a mild burning sensation to severe distress requiring opiates for relief. Occasionally, the pain is referred to the back, abdomen, neck, or face. The anorexia and difficulty in eating lead to a rapid loss of weight and strength. The lesion may erode into a blood vessel and precipitate a massive hemorrhage.

Carcinoma associated with achalasia usually involves the middle third of the esophagus. It tends to occur at a younger age than the average for the usual esophageal cancer (approximately 50 years of age vs. 60 years).

When the tumor involves the distal esophagus, obstructive symptoms may be delayed, since the esophagus already is dilated. The upper two-thirds of the esophagus anatomically is in close relation to many important structures, such as the trachea, left bronchus, recurrent laryngeal nerves, aortic arch, and carotid and subclavian arteries. Consequently, extension of a tumor in this region may produce symptoms and signs earlier than lesions located below the bifurcation of the trachea. Hoarseness, aphonia, and a persistent irritating cough indicate involvement of the recurrent laryngeal nerves and paralysis of the vocal cords. Involvement of the sympathetic nerve trunk on either or both sides produces initially a dilatation of the pupil on the corresponding side and a slight degree of exophthalmos; later, paralysis is associated with enophthalmos and the pupil becomes contracted and fixed. Cough, dyspnea, and hemoptysis indicate extension of the tumor into the trachea, bronchus, or lung. Hiccup may signify neoplastic involvement of the diaphragm and the phrenic nerve.

Esophageal Varices

Esophageal varices are dilated branches of the azygos veins, caused by increased pressure within the veins of the portal system anastomosing with the esophageal veins, i.e., the splenic and short gastric veins. This increased pressure is produced usually and classically by portal cirrhosis of the liver, the scarring and disorganization of the hepatic architecture interfering with normal flow of blood through and from the liver. The high pressure gradient in the portal system is transmitted to the esophageal veins via the coronary or left gastric vein. Another cause is thrombosis of the portal or splenic veins or of both, with resultant increase in portal pressure.

The rupture of esophageal varices is attributable to an increased hydrostatic pressure. The immediate exciting factors include a sudden increase in venous pressure, as in physical exertion, coughing, vomiting, and an expanded blood volume. Rupture may take place through an apparently normal esophageal mucosa or through an area of mucosa involved in inflammation or ulceration. Reflux of acid gastric juice into the esophagus is a contributory factor.

The symptoms produced by esophageal varices are hematemesis and melena, usually developing suddenly, and the manifestations of acute loss of blood. The vomited blood may be bright or dark red. However, in many patients there are no symptoms.

Esophageal Diverticula

Diverticula are pouches opening from hollow viscera and composed of one or more layers of the organ of origin. Esophageal diverticula are of two types, pulsion and traction, although combined forms occur.

Pulsion Diverticula

True pulsion, or Zenker's diverticula, arise from the posterior wall of the pharynx, between the inferior constrictor of the pharynx and the lower fibers of this muscle composing the cricopharyngeus or superior constrictor muscle of the esophagus. The protrusion occurs in the presence of a congenital anatomic weakness and in response to long-continued intrapharyngeal pressure. The wall of the sac consists of mucosa, submucosa, and fibrocellular connective tissue.

Zenker's diverticula occur predominantly in males. They are comparatively infrequent, but are most likely to produce symptoms with significant frequency. The most common initial symptom is a sense of irritation of the throat with excessive secretion of mucus or the sensation of a foreign body in the throat. Occasionally the patient may hear a gurgling sound in the neck when liquids are swallowed. Usually the regurgitated material is identical in odor and taste with that swallowed earlier. The growth of the sac ordinarily is slow. Eventually it becomes so large that it descends into the superior mediastinum, deviating somewhat to the left, producing pressure upon the esophagus and trachea and altering the alignment of the pharynx and the esophagus. The pharynx is permanently in line with the large pouch; the entrance to the esophagus becomes oblique and consists of a narrow slit on the anterior border of the neck of the sac. Distention of the sac with food increases the obliquity of the entrance of the esophagus, causing the dysphagia. In some cases, the difficulty in swallowing is less noticeable with solid foods than with liquids, and is less pronounced with the first few mouthfuls than later when the sac is full. Dysphagia is accompanied by the regurgitation of food that has passed into the diverticulum. Compression of the trachea by the diverticulum produces an irritating cough and dyspnea. Overflow from the pouch during sleep and intrabronchial aspiration of the pouch contents cause a reflex paroxysmal cough and pulmonary infection. Pain is uncommon unless inflammation or ulceration develops. Loss of weight may be pronounced as a result of the failure of food to enter the digestive tract.

Traction Diverticula

Traction diverticula are caused most frequently by adhesions from an adjacent tracheobronchial lymph node, the adhesions holding the wall when the esophagus contracts, or pulling out the wall of the esophagus as the scar tissue contracts. Traction diverticula usually occur on the anterior or anterolateral wall of the thoracic esophagus, opposite the bifurcation of the trachea, or near the left main bronchus. All the muscular coats of the esophagus are involved. The opening of the diverticulum is located at the lower end of the sac, and inasmuch as it empties readily and usually is small it rarely causes symptoms. Infection of the pouch may lead to the development of a mediastinal abscess. Rupture of the diverticulum into the left bronchus produces an esophagobronchial fistula.

Traction-pulsion diverticula occasionally develop in the lower esophagus near the diaphragmatic hiatus. They produce symptoms infrequently. However, they may enlarge to considerable size, causing a sense of pressure discomfort in the lower substernal area and upper abdomen associated with nausea.

Diaphragmatic (Hiatus) Hernia

A diaphragmatic hernia is a protrusion of abdominal viscera into the thoracic cage through a normal or abnormal opening in the diaphragm. It is the result of imperfect development, anatomic weakness, or trauma. Most hernias are false hernias in that they do not contain a sac of peritoneum. Herniation occurs predominantly on the left. The infrequency of right-sided diaphragmatic hernias is ascribed to the protection afforded by the liver. Large diaphragmatic hernias, which may follow abdominal trauma, usually include the stomach, transverse colon, and greater omentum.

Diaphragmatic hernia may be classified as congenital, traumatic, or acquired. A *congenital* hernia is present at birth. The absence of a sac indicates that the hernial opening is due to failure of development or to lack of fusion of one or more of the anlagen of the diaphragm. The presence of a sac composed of pleura and peritoneum is evidence of hernial formation after complete separation of the pleural and peritoneal cavities. The most common form of congenital diaphragmatic hernia in children is through the *trigonum lumbocostale,* a posterior area of fibrous tissue normally closing a space between the attachment of the lumbar muscle to the vertebra and to the twelfth rib, called the *foramen of Bochdalek.* The congenital diaphragmatic hernia most often seen in adults is through the esophageal opening in the diaphragm, the so-called hiatus hernia.

The congenitally short esophagus or partially thoracic stomach is not a true hernia. The stomach originates as an enlargement of the foregut in the thorax in the 11- to 12-mm. embryo. It migrates downward with the elongation of the esophagus and coincident descent of the septum transversum and, by the time the diaphragm is complete, normally lies below it. If any part of the stomach fails to reach its normal position at the time of diaphragmatic closure, it will remain intrathoracic, constituting a congenitally short esophagus and thoracic stomach. The degree of esophageal shortening and the amount of stomach remaining above the diaphragm vary; the entire stomach may be intrathoracic.

A *traumatic hernia* results from a penetrating injury to the diaphragm, by a bullet or stab wound, or from sudden, violent abdominal or thoracic compression, produced by a fall, blow, or crushing impact, with tearing or rupture of the diaphragm. Traumatic diaphragmatic hernias range from rupture of the muscle to tears in the peripheral attachments. The attachment of the diaphragm by fibrous loops or arches loosely bound down to the underlying abdominal muscles increases its susceptibility to peripheral tears. Ninety per cent of traumatic hernias occur in males. Traumatic herniations usually take place through the dome of the diaphragm. They are more likely to contain viscera other than the stomach and to cause symptoms and serious complications, such as volvulus.

An *acquired hernia* develops gradually after birth in an area such as the esophageal hiatus, or at the parasternal or lumbocostal trigone, presumably weakened in muscular support of the diaphragm. The most common type is the hiatus hernia, acquired in the same sense as an inguinal hernia. The most apparent cause is increased intra-abdominal pressure, produced by coughing, vomiting, straining at defecation, or sudden physical exertion; acute trauma does not appear to be a significant factor. Small hiatus hernias may represent physiologic deviations from the normal during later life as a result of weakening of the muscular tissue surrounding the hiatus. Obesity, pregnancy, and ascites may play a role by increasing intra-abdominal pressure.

A useful clinical classification defines three types of hiatus hernia. The sliding or short esophagus type results from the stomach sliding directly through both the membranous and muscular openings of the diaphragm, so that the gastroesophageal junction is above the diaphragm. The rolling or paraesophageal hernia results from herniation of the gastric cardia through the hiatus so that the stomach is adjacent to the normally situated gastroesophageal junction. The third category involves a combination of the sliding and rolling types. In the sliding hernia, the cardia is patulous, the cardioesophageal junction is incompetent, and reflux esophagitis and esophageal stricture are more common.

Symptoms

The clinical manifestations of hiatus hernia are extremely variable. Frequently there are no symptoms. The distress, when present, may be mild or severe, intermittent or constant. Small protrusions, although usually asymptomatic, may be associated with severe discomfort. Large hernias often do not produce distress until after unusual physical exertion. The occurrence of symptoms is determined not only by the size of the hernia and degree of narrowing or compression of the esophagogastric junction, but also by the presence of venous congestion, erosion, or ulceration of the gastric mucosa, and, most often, by the degree of gastroesophageal reflux. The absence of gastroesophageal reflux normally, despite a negative pleuroperitoneal pressure gradient, may be attributed to several mechanisms, chiefly the physiologic sphincteric action. The high resting pressures in the lower few centimeters of the esophagus appear to be the result of tonic contractions of the circularly arranged muscle fibers. This sphincteric segment acts as a barrier against esophageal reflux because the pressures are higher than those in the gastric fundus. Presumably, watertight closure of the lower end of the esophagus is maintained by the apposition of mucosal folds. The action of the diaphragm may be important when the normal mechanism has been disturbed, as in hiatus hernia (maintenance of the esophagogastric angle and attachment of the esophagus to the diaphragm by the esophagophrenic ligament).

Normally pressure within the lower esophageal sphincter is higher than intragastric pressure, preventing reflux from the stomach. In the presence of a hiatus hernia, this zone of high pressure is altered; intragastric pressure exceeds intraesophageal pressure and reflux ensues.

The immediate symptoms of a traumatic hernia may be those of shock, hemorrhage, or pneumothorax. The later manifestations are determined by the size and position of the hernial opening, by its content, and by the mobility of the hernia.

Pain probably is the most common symptom of diaphragmatic hernia. It varies from a sensation of a lump, pressure, or burning at the level of the xiphoid process or beneath the lower end of the sternum to a viselike and severe pain. It may be referred to the epigastrium, along both costal margins, especially the left, to the back, upper thorax, and arms. It may be precipitated or aggravated by bending, reclining, coughing, overeating, or physical exertion, all of which increase intra-abdominal pressure; it may be relieved by assumption of the erect position, especially if the hernia is of the sliding type. The burning distress also may be precipitated by the ingestion of orange juice or sugarcoated rolls and cakes. Less often distress occurs after only a few mouthfuls of food, the pain becoming so severe as to interrupt the meal. After the patient walks about for several minutes, the discomfort disappears abruptly. The sequence of events apparently consists in filling of the herniated part of the stomach, with compression of the esophagus. The herniated stomach empties itself with the movement of the patient, and the distress disappears.

Pain in diaphragmatic hernia thus is attributable to a combination of factors, including distention of the herniated part of the stomach, inflammation or ulceration of the gastric mucosa, and spasm and inflammation of the lower portion of the esophagus. Pressure upon the central part of the diaphragm induces pain in the shoulder and occasionally in the neck or face; the pain may radiate along the radial side of the arm to the base of the thumb. Irritation of the peripheral portion of the diaphragm evokes painful sensations in the segmental distributions of the seventh to twelfth intercostal nerves, along the costal margins, and in the epigastrium.

In addition to producing symptoms resembling those of coronary insufficiency, a hiatus hernia may act as the "trigger" mechanism precipitating angina pectoris. Dysphagia usually indicates esophageal spasm associated with inflammation and/or stricture formation. Narrowing or compression of the esophagogastric junction interferes with the passage of food into the stomach and causes dysphagia and regurgitation, intensified by exertion or by change of position. Compression of the herniated part of the stomach by the diaphragmatic hiatus may prevent normal venous drainage and produce hyperemia of the gastric mucosa. The congested mucosa is easily traumatized, and superficial erosions or ulcerations develop. The slow but persistent loss of blood leads to a hypochromic microcytic anemia; occasionally the bleeding is abrupt and severe. Bleeding in some cases arises in a concomitant esophageal, gastric, or duodenal ulcer. Compression of the lung by a large hernia into the pleural cavity may produce a sense of fullness or suffocation, dyspnea, cyanosis, and a persistent cough. Pressure upon the heart and great vessels may result in tachycardia, palpitation, vertigo, and attacks of syncope, but these problems are rare.

REFERENCES

Barrett, N. R.: Achalasia of the cardia: Reflections upon a clinical study of over 100 cases. Brit. Med. J., *1*:1135, 1964.

Bockus, H. L.: Gastroenterology. Volume I: Examination of the Patient—the Esophagus and the Stomach, 2nd ed. Philadelphia, W. B. Saunders Co., 1963.

Bremer, J. L.: The diaphragm and diaphragmatic hernia. Arch. Path., *36*:539, 1943.

Brown, H. G.: The applied anatomy of vomiting. Brit. J. Anaesth., *35*:136, 1963.

Cassella, R. R., Brown, A. L., Jr., Sayre, G. P., and Ellis, F. H., Jr.: Achalasia of the esophagus: I. Pathologic and etiologic considerations. Ann. Surg., *160*:474, 1964.

Cassella, R. R., Ellis, F. H., Jr., and Brown, A. L., Jr.: Fine-structure changes in achalasia of the esophagus. II. Esophageal smooth muscle. Am. J. Path., *46*:467, 1965.

Code, C. F., and others: Atlas of Esophageal Motility in Health and Disease. Springfield, Charles C Thomas, 1958.

Franklin, R. H., Bain, J. I., and Lynch, G.: Carcinoma of the esophagus. Brit. J. Surg., *51*:178, 1964.

Ingelfinger, F. J.: Disorders of esophageal motor functions. Adv. Int. Med., *8*:11, 1956.

Ingelfinger, F. J.: Esophageal motility. Physiol. Rev., *38*:533, 1958.

Jones, C. M.: Digestive Tract Pain. New York, Macmillan, 1938.

Kramer, P., and Hollander, W.: Comparison of experimental esophageal pain with clinical pain of angina pectoris and esophageal disease. Gastroenterology, *29*:719, 1955.

Lerche, W.: The Esophagus and Pharynx in Action. A Study of Structure in Relation to Function. Springfield, Charles C Thomas, 1950.

Lindsay, J. R., Templeton, F. E., and Rothman, S.: Lesions of the esophagus in generalized progressive scleroderma. J.A.M.A., *123*:745, 1943.

Lipkin, M., and Sleisenger, M. H.: Studies of visceral pain: Measurements of stimulus, intensity and duration, associated with the onset of pain in esophagus, ileum and colon. J. Clin. Invest., *37*:28, 1958.

MacMahon, H. E., Schatzki, R., and Gary, J. E.: Pathology of a lower esophageal ring. New England J. Med., *259*:1, 1958.

Moersch, H. L., and Miller, J. R.: Esophageal pain. Gastroenterology, *1*:821, 1943.

Morgan, E. H., and Hill, L. D.: Objective identification of chest pain of esophageal origin. J.A.M.A., *187*:921, 1964.

Templeton, F. E.: X-ray Examination of the Stomach: A Description of the Roentgenologic Anatomy, Physiology, and Pathology of the Esophagus, Stomach, and Duodenum, 2nd ed. Chicago, University of Chicago Press, 1964.

Van Trappen, G., Texter, E. C., Jr., Barborka, C. J., and Vandenbroucke, J.: The closing mechanism at the gastroesophageal junction. Am. J. Med., *28*:564, 1960.

Vinson, P. P.: Diagnosis and Treatment of Diseases of Esophagus. Springfield, Charles C Thomas, 1940.

Winkelstein, A.: Peptic esophagitis. J.A.M.A., *104*:906, 1935.

Chapter Twenty-Four

The Stomach

JOSEPH B. KIRSNER

Anatomic Variations

The form and position of the stomach vary in different persons and in the same person at various times, depending upon the degree of filling, the size and position of the adjacent organs, the condition of the anterior abdominal musculature, and the physical habitus. In the relatively short, thick person with a tense abdominal wall the stomach lies high in the left upper abdomen and is steer-horn in shape, whereas in the tall, lean person the greater curvature may extend to the brim of the true pelvis in the shape of the letter J. This condition often is called gastroptosis, and a symptomatology erroneously is attributed to it. Such variations in the position of the stomach are of no clinical significance; they do not produce symptoms. The important consideration is not the location, but rather the structure and physiologic activity of the stomach.

Congenital Anomalies

Hypertrophic Stenosis of the Pylorus

Obstructive narrowing of the pylorus by hypertrophy of the pyloric muscle is most common in infants 2 or 3 weeks old, although it may be observed at any time between the ages of 10 days and 3 or 4 months. Occasionally, more than one member of a family is affected. The condition generally is attrib-

uted to congenital hypertrophy, with or without spasm. The pylorus is represented by an oval tumor of muscular tissue, with hypertrophy, especially of the circular layer of the muscularis propria, and fibrotic thickening of the submucosa. Symptoms begin usually during the second to fourth weeks after birth, and consist of projectile vomiting after a feeding, constipation or obstipation, and rapid loss of weight. The nutritional depletion may be pronounced. Dehydration and alkalosis develop as a consequence of the loss of fluid and electrolytes.

Hypertrophy of the pylorus occurs in adults with and without stenosis, and with and without symptoms. The congenital origin of the hypertrophy is less certain, although some instances may represent persistence of pyloric hypertrophy from infancy into adulthood. The condition may be associated with acquired gastric disease, such as peptic ulcer or gastritis, and may be the result of work-hypertrophy of the muscle or of chronic inflammation. The chief symptoms are nausea, vomiting, and epigastric discomfort aggravated by the ingestion of food. Pain may or may not be present; if present, it usually is caused by the associated lesion. Hematemesis may occur from hemorrhagic gastritis or mucosal erosions.

Diverticula

Diverticula of the stomach are rare. True diverticula contain all the coats of the normal

576

stomach and are either congenital or secondary to pulsion and traction. False diverticula lack the muscular coats and are attributed to weakening of the gastric wall. Any region of the stomach may be involved, but diverticula occur most frequently near the cardia and in the antrum. Duodenal diverticula, on the other hand, are much more common. Almost all diverticula of the duodenal bulb are "pseudodiverticula," produced by the scarring associated with duodenal ulcer. Gastric and duodenal diverticula do not cause distress, except unusually, in the presence of inflammation or ulceration, or unless they are huge in size and are so situated as to fill readily with food and gastrointestinal contents but empty poorly, resulting in stagnation and increased tendency to bacterial infection and inflammation. The belching and abdominal discomfort or pain described by some patients usually are attributable to accompanying disease or to a functional disturbance independent of the diverticulum.

Sensory Disturbances

Appetite and Hunger

The sensations of appetite and hunger are closely related. Appetite is a pleasant sensation, conditioned by previous agreeable experiences with the smell, taste, and appearance of food. Hunger is an unpleasant sensation of abdominal emptiness, epigastric discomfort, or pangs of dull pain, produced by the intermittent contractions of the empty stomach and/or intestine. The distinction between hunger and appetite is not always sharp, and accentuation of the appetite often is interpreted as a part of the total complex of hunger. The following sensory components may be enumerated:

1. Pleasant olfactory and gustatory sensations with their associated pleasant memories of the taste and smell of food constitute the classic features of appetite.

2. Painful hunger pangs result from contractions of the empty stomach and intestines.

3. An indefinite, unpleasant, generalized, steady, and continuous sensation is interpreted as hunger and is vaguely referred to the abdomen.

4. Accessory phenomena such as lassitude, weakness, drowsiness, faintness, irritability, restlessness, and headache may occur concomitantly.

As summarized by Janowitz: "At the physiologic level of regulation of intake, deficits of the body's stores of calorically significant nutrients activate feeding reflexes which are facilitated by areas in the lateral hypothalamus and are inhibited by the ventromedial hypothalamus. These deficits concomitantly give rise to hunger sensations which may be cues for food intake. These hypothalamic centers are sensitive to local temperature and appear to be influenced by body stores of water. Day-to-day regulation of the amount of food consumed is regulated in part by oropharyngeal receptors; and the size of an individual meal is controlled by gastric and upper intestinal receptors responding to distention, probably mediated by the vagus nerve. The hypothalamic areas also are believed to be influenced by the metabolic consequences of food absorbed and assimilated. The specific dynamic action of food, the utilizable blood glucose, the concentration of other metabolites in the blood, the level of protein in the diet and depot fat, all have been proposed as cues to the central nervous system, but none has been firmly established as governing short or long-term control."

Excessive appetite and hunger occur in various conditions, as in convalescence from an acute infectious disease, but the mechanism is unexplained. A similar situation obtains in thyrotoxicosis, in which the requirement of food is maintained at a high level because of the excessive metabolism. In diabetes mellitus the glucose in the blood is not available to the tissues; hunger and polyphagia result. Excessive appetite also may be a feature of the emotionally disturbed individual. In peptic ulcer the distress may be interpreted as hunger, because the patient fails to differentiate it from a hunger pang or because it occurs when the stomach is thought to be empty and is relieved by eating.

Loss of appetite is a variable but common symptom in various diseases. It is an early and prominent feature of hepatitis and of gastric or pancreatic neoplasm. Loss of appetite often is functional in origin, a manifestation of an emotional disturbance, usually depression. As such it is the outstanding symptom of anorexia nervosa, a psychoneurotic state observed chiefly in young women.

Vomiting

Vomiting is defined as the forceful expulsion of gastric and intestinal contents through the mouth. Immediately preceding vomiting are tachypnea, copious salivation, dilatation of the pupils, sweating, pallor, and rapid heartbeat, signs of widespread autonomic discharge. Vomiting begins with deep inspiration. The glottis is closed and the nasopharynx is shut off partly or completely. Inspiration is converted to an expiratory effort, with simultaneous contraction of the abdominal muscles. Because the glottis is closed, the increase in intrathoracic and intra-abdominal pressure is transmitted to the stomach and esophagus. The body of the stomach and the muscle of the esophagus relax. At the same time a strong annular contraction, at approximately the angulus of the stomach, nearly divides the body from the antrum. While the body of the stomach remains flaccid, peristaltic waves sweep aborally over the antrum. Owing to the positive intrathoracic and intra-abdominal pressures, the gastric contents are expelled from the mouth. The esophagus then is emptied partly by the elevated intrathoracic pressure and partly by peristaltic waves stimulated by vomitus in the esophagus and mouth. Finally the voluntary muscles relax and respiration resumes.

The vomiting center is situated in the dorsolateral border of the lateral reticular formation, lying just ventral to the tractus solitarius and its nucleus, near the sensory nucleus of the vagus. It may be excited directly by mechanical stimuli, such as increased intracranial pressure, by chemical stimuli in the form of such drugs as digitalis or emetine, by afferent impulses produced by distention of the stomach and duodenum, or by impulses from any region of the body. The afferent impulses reach the center along many routes, the chief ones being the vagal and sympathetic nerves from the stomach and other abdominal viscera. The efferent fibers are contained chiefly in the phrenic, vagus, and sympathetic nerves. Vomiting may be produced in susceptible persons by impulses from the higher cerebral centers, as when unpleasant subjects are discussed or when offensive odors are encountered. Nervous vomiting is a manifestation of a psychiatric difficulty; the characteristic feature is the continued, effortless vomiting of food, usually immediately after eating, without loss of weight. The symptom presumably reflects a neuromuscular disorder, with reverse peristalsis in the intestine and the stomach initiated by stimuli from the central nervous system.

Nausea

Nausea denotes an unpleasant sensation, ordinarily referred to the back of the throat, the epigastrium, or both, and often culminating in vomiting. It may be accompanied by vasomotor manifestations of autonomic stimulation, such as weakness, faintness, salivation, sweating, vertigo, headache, and tachycardia. The clinical significance of nausea is related closely to that of vomiting. It may be produced by gastric or pancreatic disease, by pyloric or intestinal obstruction, by reverse peristalsis of functional or physiologic origin, or by intense pain from any source.

Belching

Belching is the eructation of swallowed air. Normally a small amount of air is swallowed in the process of eating; with the rapid swallowing of food, the chewing of gum, or excessive smoking the quantity may be large. Most of the air does not reach the stomach, but is regurgitated immediately from the lower esophagus as a part of the act of belching. Some of the gas passes into the stomach and accumulates in the gastric air bubble, until it is eliminated in a more or less spontaneous belch. The chronic belcher then renews the cycle of swallowing more air, most of which he regurgitates with each belch, but some of which passes on into the stomach, until once more a spontaneous belch occurs. In time, the act becomes almost involuntary and automatic. Belching does not result from the alleged fermentation of food, nor is it related specifically to disease of the gallbladder, stomach, or any other organ. It is primarily a functional disturbance, often induced by a sensation of abdominal fullness or discomfort which the patient attempts to relieve by the expulsion of air.

Motor Disturbances

Gastric tone and peristalsis are subject to wide physiologic variations. Added bulk in the diet, pleasant sensory stimuli, and emotional reactions such as anxiety, resentment, or hostility increase the motor activity of the stomach, whereas the presence of fat in the food, unpleasant sensory stimuli, fear, and sadness depress it. Tone and peristalsis are not dependent upon secretion; there is, however, some relation between the motor and secretory functions. Vagal stimulation increases and vagal section decreases both. After vagotomy gastric tonus is reduced, the peristaltic waves are shallow, and gastric emptying is delayed. With the passage of time, there is more or less recovery, attributable perhaps to control regained by the intrinsic neurogenic mechanism. Gastric peristalsis may be decreased in patients with diabetes mellitus, resembling the situation after vagotomy; indeed, a neuropathy involving the vagus nerve has been implicated. Symptoms may be absent or include gradual loss of weight, vague upper abdominal discomfort, nausea or vomiting, and unexplained difficulty in controlling the diabetes. According to some observers, gastric motility is reduced in gastric ulcer and the decreased motor activity contributes to the stimulation of the antrum, implicated in the pathogenesis of the lesion. Hyperperistalsis and hypertonicity of the stomach, observed in nervous persons, are not the basis for symptoms.

Spasm of the entire stomach or of a segment of the stomach has been described in tabes dorsalis, in other lesions of the central nervous system, and also in the presence of cholelithiasis or pancreatic disease. The relationship of such spasm to abdominal pain is questionable, for the pain of tabetic crisis seems not to arise in the stomach itself, and segmental gastrospasm is observed without pain. On the other hand, painful gastric spasms are noted occasionally in the apparently normal stomach. Localized muscular spasm occurs not infrequently with gastric lesions, as in hourglass contracture with a benign ulcer, the contracture disappearing when the ulcer heals. Painless spasm of the pylorus, as evidenced by rather persistent closure, occurs frequently with intrapyloric peptic ulcer, with gastric and duodenal lesions adjacent to the pylorus, and occasionally with gastric ulcers located several centimeters proximal to the pylorus, on the lesser curvature.

Secretory Disturbances

PHYSIOLOGIC CONSIDERATIONS

The secretion of hydrochloric acid physiologically is a composite of three interrelated phases: neurogenic (vagal), gastric (gastrin), and to a very small extent intestinal. The neurogenic phase is initiated by stimuli such as the sight, smell, or taste of food acting upon receptors in the cerebral cortex, and subsequent stimulation of the vagal nucleus. The process presumably is mediated chemically by acetylcholine acting upon the parietal cells, in conjunction with gastrin from the antrum and probably with histamine. Stimulation of the vagus nerve elicits a copious secretion of gastric juice, rich in acid and pepsin. Complete division of the vagi is followed by a pronounced reduction in the volume and acidity of the excessive gastric secretion in patients with duodenal ulcer, but the production of hydrochloric acid is not eliminated completely. Stimulation of the splanchnic nerves evokes an alkaline secretion, chiefly from the pyloric glands, rich in mucus and poor in peptic activity. The effects of neurogenic stimuli are determined to some extent by the state of gastric function at the time of stimulation. Emotional disturbances exert an important influence upon the secretory and motor functions of the stomach. Prolonged anxiety, guilt, conflict, hostility, and resentment cause engorgement of the gastric mucosa and increased secretion, whereas depression and fear induce pallor of the mucosa and a reduction in acid output. The significant decrease in gastric acid secretion after complete vagotomy in patients with duodenal ulcer suggests that the hypersecretion is caused by excessive stimuli over the vagus nerves, although other mechanisms probably are involved.

The prolonged administration of large quantities of corticotropin and adrenal steroids may increase gastric secretion, but this effect is neither frequent nor consistent. This observation and the occasional development or recurrence of peptic ulcer during the administration of adrenal corticosteroids has suggested a relationship of "stress" and increased gastric secretion to sequential effects upon the hypothalamus, pituitary gland, and adrenal glands. Excitation of the anterior hypothalamus presumably activates the vagal stimulatory component, whereas excitation of the posterior hypothalamus apparently exerts an effect through the pituitary-adrenal system. This concept is yet to be established conclusively, for gastric secretion does not increase and peptic ulcer does not occur in many patients during the prolonged administration of adrenal steroids.

The gastric phase of secretion is mediated by the hormone gastrin, produced by the antrum in response to distention by food and fluid, vagal stimulation, and probably by exposure of the mucosa of the antrum to the products of protein digestion. Gastrin now has been identified as two nearly identical peptides (gastrins I and II), each much more potent than histamine in stimulating acid secretion when given in low concentrations, but inhibiting acid secretion when administered in high concentrations. Both gastrins also stimulate pepsin production, the secretion of gastric intrinsic factor, the volume and enzyme content of pancreatic secretion, and gastrointestinal motility. The mechanism of release of gastrin from the antrum and the gastrin-secreting cells has not been defined as yet. The intestinal phase of gastric secretion is initiated by the entrance of partly acidified or neutralized food into the small intestine, initiating a humoral mechanism, with the release of gastrin, a hormone resembling gastrin, or a secretory stimulant produced by the digestion of food.

The best known chemical stimulant of gastric secretion is histamine, which elicits from the parietal cells a large amount of hydrochloric acid and relatively small quantities of pepsin and mucus. An analogue of histamine, 3-beta aminoethyl pyrazole (Histalog), stimulates gastric secretion similarly, but with much fewer side effects; it also is an effective stimulant when administered by mouth. Reserpine given intravenously may evoke a still larger output of hydrochloric acid, perhaps via the liberation of histamine from tissue mast cells. The pronounced gastric hypersecretion after experimental diversion of the portal vein and after portacaval transposition presumably involves the effect of a secretory stimulant, possibly histamine, produced in the alimentary canal and not inactivated within the liver, as a consequence of the shunt. Loss of this histamine-destroying mechanism in the liver and the consequent gastric hypersecretion may explain at least partially the apparently increased incidence of peptic ulcer in patients with cirrhosis of the liver treated by portacaval shunt.

The target of these secretory stimuli is the parietal cell, with varying numbers of cells responding at a given time, depending upon the physiologic state of the stomach and upon the strength of the stimulus. The total number of responding parietal cells represents the parietal cell mass, and a correlation exists between the number of parietal cells and the hydrochloric acid produced in response to the maximal histamine (0.04 mg./kg. body weight) or Histalog (1.5 mg./kg. body weight) test.

Gastric secretion may be inhibited under various circumstances, such as emotional disturbances, presumably via inhibitory fibers in the vagus and splanchnic nerves. Gastric secretion also is influenced by at least two autoregulatory mechanisms: inhibition of gastrin release by exposure of the antral mucosa to a pH of 1.5 or lower; and release of the inhibitory hormone enterogastrone, probably interfering with the formation or release of gastrin, produced in the upper small intestine in the presence of bile salts and pancreatic lipase. An additional inhibitory influence may be the action of pancreatic secretin, produced by the action of acid content in the upper small intestine.

The principal components of gastric secretion are hydrochloric acid; mucus; proteolytic enzymes including at least three pepsins; nonproteolytic enzymes; gastric intrinsic factor; the anions chloride, phosphate, and sulfate; and the cations sodium, potassium, calcium, and magnesium. The alkaline component of gastric secretion is a mixture of various constituents, including mucus from the surface mucous cells, cytoplasm of desquamated cells, and a transudate of interstitial fluid. Pepsinogen is secreted by the chief cells and is converted to pepsin in the gastric lumen. Three fractions of pepsinogen and pepsin have been identified chromatographically in the gastric content, including the proteolytic enzyme formerly identified as gastricsin. The relative proportions of the different pepsinogens in human gastric mucosa and of the pepsins in human gastric juice apparently vary from person to person. Vagally mediated influences are the major stimuli to the sustained secretion of pepsin. The output of pepsin also may be increased by gastrin and by large quantities of histamine. A very small proportion of pepsinogen is secreted into the plasma and thence into the urine. Electrophoretic studies of the gastric mucous substances, as well as of other high molecular components of gastric content, provide additional quantitative parameters of gastric secretion. Paper electrophoresis and other techniques have demonstrated the passage of serum albumin from the blood into the gastric lumen in patients with giant rugae or gastric cancer, probably accounting for the hypoproteinemia in these patients.

The volume of gastric juice secreted daily under fasting conditions in the average normal adult ranges from 1000 to 1500 cc., with an acid concentration of approximately 40 mEq./L. Although the normal stomach may secrete gastric juice as acid as that in disease, significant quantitative differences may be observed. In duodenal ulcer, the 24 hour volume often exceeds 2000 cc., with an average acid concentration of approximately 100 mEq./L; the output of hydrochloric acid may exceed normal by three to 20 times. The volume of secretion in patients with gastric ulcer is similar to that of normal persons, but the concentration of acid usually is lower. The output of acid is smallest in patients with gastric carcinoma; the decreased secretory activity may antedate the development of cancer by many years.

Under theoretically optimal conditions, hydrochloric acid is secreted by the parietal cells as a relatively pure solution, with an initial acid concentration of 160 to 170 mEq./L. and a pH of slightly less than 1.0. The lower acid values observed clinically are the result of (1) neutralization by buffer substances such as protein, phosphate, and bicarbonate present in food, saliva, gastric, and regurgitated intestinal secretions; (2) dilution by these fluids; and (3) rediffusion of hydrogen ions into the blood or tissues. Hollander has postulated that hydrochloric acid is formed by the hydrolysis of the neutral chlorides (chiefly sodium chloride) of the cytoplasm, the residual alkali being neutralized immediately by the intracellular buffers. The wall of the intracellular canaliculus is conceived as a membrane permeable to water and to hydrogen and chloride ions. The application of any secretory stimulus to the parietal cell initiates a process driving water from the cell in two directions. The fluid passing forward into the intracellular canaliculus carries hydrogen and chloride ions with it, thus effecting a membrane hydrolysis of the neutral chloride, with simultaneous separation of the hydrochloric acid so formed. At the same time, the "alkalinized" buffers of the cytoplasm are transported across the cell wall proper back into the tissue fluids and into the general circulation, obviating pronounced or prolonged elevation of the intracellular pH. Davies regards the fundamental reaction as that expressed in the formula $H_2O \rightarrow H^+ OH^-$. The hydrogen ions are thought to be elaborated by means of energy available from the metabolism of glucose. The hydrogen ions are secreted, and the OH^- ions are finally neutralized by the carbon dioxide and passed into the blood. This process is regarded as comparable with the theory of membrane hydrolysis. The secretion of hydrochloric acid requires large amounts of energy, and during active secretion blood flow through the stomach is greatly increased.

Pathologic Disturbances in Gastric Secretion

Pathologic alterations in gastric secretion apparently occur more often in the direction of depression in total volume, acid concentration, or both. These variations do not correspond consistently with gross changes in the mucosa, although true anacidity occurs most frequently in association with atrophy of the stomach. Normal persons with apparently normal mucosae, gastroscopically, exhibit a wide variety of secretory responses, ranging from achlorhydria, with a pH value of approximately 8.0, to a highly acid juice with a pH of 1.0. These differing secretory rates are not correlated with specific symptoms or disease, except that chronic peptic ulcer does not occur in the continued absence of acid gastric juice. The complete absence of all gastric juice (achylia gastrica) is rare, for some secretion containing enzymes in small amounts is almost always present. The term "achlorhydria" or "anacidity," therefore, may be preferable.

Anacidity may be defined as a decrease in the pH of the gastric content less than one unit or a pH above 6.0 following maximal stimulation of the gastric secretory mechanism with histamine or Histalog. The hydrogen ion concentration of anacid specimens obtained after histamine stimulation varies in different diseases, although not consistently. The pH of the gastric secretion in pernicious anemia ranges usually between 7.0 and 8.0; the pH in atrophy of the gastric mucosa unaccompanied by other disease is similar, although more variable; values between 3.5 and 7.0 may be observed in gastric carcinoma.

Anacidity is not a "normal" variant, since it is associated with an almost total loss of functioning parietal cells, as in severe gastric atrophy. Studies with the maximal histamine test indicate that anacidity is rare in patients with gastric carcinoma and gastric polyps. Patients with true anacidity who do not have overt pernicious anemia require careful observation for the later development of pernicious anemia or gastric carcinoma. Histologic studies indicate that the number of parietal cells in the fundus of the stomach is relatively high in patients with duodenal ulcer and decreases progressively in benign gastric ulcer and in gastric cancer, especially in patients without acid; parietal cells are virtually absent in pernicious anemia. Human gastric content also contains a substance which inhibits the production of hydrochloric acid. Gastric contents from patients with pernicious anemia and gastric atrophy contain relatively more of this inhibitory substance.

Hypersecretion of hydrochloric acid refers to an excessive quantity of acid rather than to an increased concentration. The clinical conditions associated with gastric hypersecretion are duodenal ulcer, stomal ulceration, the

Zollinger-Ellison syndrome, and retained, excluded antrum after gastric surgery.

An excessive output of hydrochloric acid is observed in approximately 50 per cent of patients with duodenal ulcer. The hypersecretion is demonstrable continuously, between meals, during the night, and after the ulcer has healed. The Zollinger-Ellison syndrome is characterized by extremely high basal outputs of hydrochloric acid, usually with less than a 50 per cent rise following stimulation with maximal doses of histamine or Histalog.

The cause of the gastric hypersecretion in duodenal ulcer is not established completely. Anatomically it appears to be correlated with an increased number of parietal cells, possibly a genetically determined trait or perhaps the result of chronic stimulation by neurogenic and humoral influences. Physiologically the continuous hypersecretion of gastric juice in duodenal ulcer is chiefly of neurogenic origin and decreases significantly after vagotomy.

The development of gastric ulcer experimentally in association with gastric stasis or with antral hyperfunction as induced by explantation of the antrum to the colon, and the gastric ulcers developing in patients with pyloric stenosis secondary to duodenal ulcer have suggested the concept of hypersecretion of gastrin as the cause of the gastric ulcer. However, thus far direct evidence of gastric hypersecretion in the usual sense and of gastrin overproduction is lacking.

Mechanism of Pain

The normal gastric mucosa is insensitive to touch, cutting, pinching, tearing, and exposure to solutions of varying hydrogen ion concentration. Heat and cold are experienced as such. Vigorous pressure applied to the gastric wall elicits a steady, dull, gnawing pain, experienced approximately in the region of the stimulus. This pain, like that produced by distention or by powerful contractions, arises from stretching of the muscular and peritoneal layers of the stomach. Its mechanism is assumed to comprise a local rise in smooth muscle tension produced by spasm, obstruction or rapid distention, and subsequent contraction or stretching of the nerve terminals lying between the circular muscle fibers. The intensity of the distress is proportional to the state of contraction of the stomach at the time and to the rapidity of the stimulus. The entire reflex involved in the transmission of such impulses may be via the afferent visceral fibers accompanying the sympathetic pathways; the cerebrospinal nerves need not participate. The threshold for pain in the stomach and, therefore, for the development of symptoms is influenced by the condition of the gastric mucosa. Vascular engorgement and acute inflammation diminish the threshold for pain, and in their presence stimuli such as hydrochloric acid or gastric contractions not causing discomfort when the mucosa is normal elicit painful sensations. This mechanism may explain the distress described by some patients with severe erosive or hemorrhagic gastritis.

Clinically, the relation of spasm and gastric distention to abdominal pain is variable. Segmental gastrospasm may be observed in the absence of distress; painful gastric spasm occasionally is noted in the apparently normal stomach. Contractions of the pylorus and stomach ordinarily are independent of the sensation of pain, as indicated, for example, by its infrequency during the powerful peristalsis accompanying pyloric obstruction. However, such contractions may be painful in the empty stomach, the "hunger pang," or when they pass over a sensitive peptic ulcer.

The pain of peptic ulcer is caused primarily by the hydrochloric acid in the gastric content. The acid evokes a chemical inflammation and thereby lowers the pain threshold of the nerve endings present in large numbers in the base and in the edges of the ulcer. The pain is a true visceral sensation, arising directly at the site of the lesion. Physiologic and roentgenologic studies demonstrate that it is not dependent upon hyperperistalsis, gross spasm of the musculature, pylorospasm, or distention of the antrum. However, the acid may activate not only the pain mechanism but also motor activity; under these circumstances, ulcer pain originating in a sensitive ulcer may be increased by motility or muscle spasm. The temporary decrease or disappearance of pain in patients with duodenal ulcer after gastric "freezing," without apparent change in the gastric secretory pattern, is an intriguing phenomenon. Reduction in gastroduodenal motility has been implicated, but the evidence is insufficient.

The importance of acid in the development of ulcer pain is further indicated by the occurrence of the distress only when the gastric content is acid. The concentration of hydrochloric acid at the time of distress is not necessarily excessive, nor does it exceed that present in the same stomach without pain when the ulcer is healed or in the healing phase. The threshold of acidity necessary to evoke pain varies from one patient to another and in the same patient from time to time. The presence of pain at any given moment is dependent, therefore, upon the presence of both an inflamed lesion lowering the pain threshold and of an adequate stimulus, acid gastric juice. The pain is relieved by emesis or aspiration of the stomach, which removes the acid, or by the ingestion of food or alkali, which neutralizes hydrochloric acid.

When the pain mechanism is sensitive, pain may be induced by the introduction of hydrochloric acid in physiologic concentrations (0.1N) or by acid gastric juice; it is alleviated by withdrawal or neutralization of the acid. The pain induced by the hydrochloric acid is not prevented by prior parenteral or oral administration of anticholinergic compounds. Pain sensitivity disappears quickly, presumably as the acute inflammatory process in the ulcer subsides. The absence of pain in some instances and the occurrence of hemorrhage or perforation without antecedent pain are difficult to explain, except on the rather vague basis of an individually high pain threshold, protection of the ulcer crater from the hydrochloric acid by blood during the course of hemorrhage, and the formation of an acute perforating ulcer, so rapid as to encompass development and perforation of the lesion within hours.

Location of Pain

Ulcer pain is located almost always in the epigastrium and usually is limited to an area several centimeters in diameter. The pain of gastric ulcer is likely to be experienced in the left epigastrium or just below the xiphoid process, and, with ulcers in the upper portion of the stomach, occasionally in the anterior or left lateral portion of the chest. In duodenal ulcer, the pain is located in the right epigastrium and slightly above the umbilicus. In jejunal ulcer, it is located usually in the left midabdomen and also in the left lower abdominal quadrant. The pain may be referred laterally to the left chest in the area supplied by the sixth and seventh thoracic nerves or may extend through to the back at the level of the eighth to tenth dorsal vertebrae. This latter radiation is more common in duodenal ulcer located on the posterior wall. Sudden, severe abdominal pain frequently indicates an acute perforation. Its subsequent distribution depends partly on the course taken by the escaping gastric contents. Gravitation of the gastroduodenal contents to the right paracolic gutter produces pain in the right lower abdominal quadrant. Pain in front, behind, or on top of the shoulder and at the base of the neck denotes involvement of the diaphragm and the phrenic innervation.

Pain in Gastric Carcinoma

The pain originating in gastric carcinoma may be of several types. In the presence of hydrochloric acid, the pain often is indistinguishable from that produced by benign peptic ulcer, because the mechanism is the same: acid irritation. In the absence of acid and peptic activity, gastric cancer is painless until the tumor progresses beyond the confines of the stomach and involves somatic tissue. The pain then becomes constant, is unrelated to the nature of the gastric content, and is relieved only by opiates. This pain is attributable to malignant infiltration of both the somatic and splanchnic nerves.

Transmission of Pain

At least three distinct mechanisms may be involved in pain originating within the abdomen: true visceral pain with impulses transmitted over afferent visceral fibers accompanying the sympathetic trunks; referred pain, with impulses carried over both afferent visceral and cerebrospinal nerve fibers; and the peritoneocutaneous reflex of Morley, with impulses transmitted only via cerebrospinal nerves. True visceral pain alone may be present accompanied by a referred pain, or all three mechanisms may participate, as in the perforation of peptic ulcer with peritonitis.

Pain impulses arising in the stomach and duodenum are conducted along sensory fibers in the splanchnic branches of the sympathetic nerves. The splanchnic nerves enter first the celiac ganglion, travel via the greater splanchnic nerves to the spinal cord, probably to the corresponding posterior roots of the eighth through thirteenth thoracic spinal nerves, and thence to the higher centers by way of the spinal thalamic tract. The parasympathetic supply of the stomach and duodenum arises in the dorsal vagal nucleus in the floor of the fourth ventricle, and the afferent fibers end in the same nucleus, which is a mixture of visceral efferent and afferent cells. The fibers are conveyed to and from the abdomen through the vagus nerves, esophageal plexus, and vagal trunks. The reproduction of ulcer pain after complete section of the vagi, by introducing hydrochloric acid into the stomach of a patient with a sensitive ulcer, demonstrates that pain impulses travel via the splanchnics. The skin area to which visceral pain is referred is determined by the segment of the cord receiving the visceral afferent (sympathetic) fibers. Referral of the pain sometimes is attributed to stimulation of the somatic nerve fibers of the peritoneum or mesentery. However, ulcer distress arising from lesions not penetrating to the serosa does have a cutaneous reference, indicating that visceral nerves are capable of mediating pain referred to somatic segments.

Chronic Nonspecific Gastritis

A gastric mucosa is normal histologically when the parietal and chief cells of the gastric glands display a regular arrangement and normal nuclei; there are no abnormalities in the surface epithelium or in the foveolae; the glands are normal in outline and are disposed regularly throughout the mucosal surface; the lamina propria is complete at both its surface and deep layers, with capillaries, collagenous fibers, and cellular elements; the lumina of the foveolae are empty; and the muscularis mucosae forms a lamina at the bottom of the glands, with fibers extending all along the lamina propria. An absolutely normal mucosa is found only during infancy or the first decade of life. Subsequently there is a progressive interstitial infiltration with lymphocytes, plasma cells and eosinophils, and metaplasia of the glandular epithelium in virtually every adult stomach. When these changes are accompanied by hemorrhages in the superficial layers of the mucosa, erosion of the papillae, and cellular infiltration of the submucosa, muscularis, and serosa, the diagnosis of gastritis may be regarded as established.

Clinically chronic gastritis is classified on the basis of gastroscopic observation into three types. (1) In superficial gastritis the mucosa is reddened, edematous, and covered with adherent mucus; mucosal hemorrhages and small erosions are frequent. The histologic findings include flattening and irregularity of the epithelium, distortion and dilatation of the glands, penetration of the glandular epithelium by polymorphonuclear cells, and lymphocytic infiltration of the deep layers of the lamina propria. (2) Atrophy is characterized by a thinned, gray, or greenish-gray hemorrhagic mucosa; the submucosal vessels are visible as red or blue ramifications; the folds are diminished in number and size so that the mucosa presents an unusually smooth surface; the atrophy usually is distributed irregularly, but the entire stomach may be af-

fected. The histologic features are atrophy of all layers of the stomach, distortion and disappearance of the glandular structure, decreased numbers of parietal and chief cells, so-called intestinal metaplasia of the glandular epithelium, the presence of Paneth cells and Russell bodies, and proliferation of fibrous tissue. (3) In hypertrophic gastritis the mucosa is dull, spongy, or nodular in appearance; the rugae are irregular, thickened, or nodular; hemorrhages and superficial erosions are frequent. This category is reserved for the unequivocal evidence of enlarged, inflamed gastric rugae; too often, variations in the normal appearance of the gastric mucosa are misinterpreted as "hypertrophic gastritis." Gastritis occurring after gastroenterostomy or partial gastric resection combines the manifestations of all three types. Giant gastric rugae (Menetrier's disease) are noted most commonly in the midportion of the stomach along the greater curvature, although there may be diffuse involvement of the stomach. The appearance is not unlike that of the cerebral convolutions and may suggest a tumor or polyposis. Histologically, the mucosal folds are thickened enormously, with infiltration of round cells, and edema.

The etiology and pathogenesis of chronic gastritis are not known. Dietary indiscretions, alcohol, tobacco, coffee, infections, and nutritional deficiencies have been implicated, but the evidence is inconclusive. The stomach is subjected constantly to a variety of influences, physiologic, psychogenic, physical, chemical, and bacterial, whose individual significance is difficult to evaluate. The appearance of the healthy gastric mucosa varies within a wide physiologic range. Small hemorrhages and pigment spots are not indicative of chronic gastritis. Large gastric rugae per se likewise do not signify chronic inflammation, and have been attributed to increased contractility of the muscularis mucosae. Erosive and ulcerative gastritis probably are induced by the same mechanism that produces peptic ulcer. The erosions may heal or, rarely, increase in size until a definite ulcer develops. All types of chronic gastritis are observed in association with peptic ulcer, but atrophy is more frequent in gastric than in duodenal ulcer, whereas a hyperplastic mucosa is more common in duodenal ulcer than in gastric ulcer. Atrophy of the gastric mucosa is invariably present in pernicious anemia and gastric polyposis, and not infrequently in patients with sprue, pellagra, and iron-deficiency anemia. Although atrophy may be observed in young people, it is more common in the older age groups. Chronic gastritis also may be associated with various diseases of the stomach, including sarcoidosis, tuberculosis, syphilis, hemochromatosis, and amyloidosis. An isolated granulomatous gastritis also has been observed, distinct from regional enteritis or sarcoidosis. The condition often presents clinically as pyloric obstruction with radiologic features of antral narrowing, simulating neoplasm.

A possible immune mechanism in the development of gastric atrophy has been suggested on the basis of interesting observations in patients with pernicious anemia: resemblance of the gastric mucosal lesion in pernicious anemia to that of the thyroid in autoimmune thyroiditis; the frequent clinical interrelations of pernicious anemia with autoimmune disease of the thyroid (thyroiditis, myxedema, Hashimoto's disease); the high incidence of circulating thyroid antibodies in patients with pernicious anemia, and, conversely, the high incidence of gastric antibodies in serum from patients with these thyroid diseases; the familial tendencies in both disorders; the frequent presence of circulating antibodies reacting specifically with parietal cell cytoplasmic antigen and/or gastric intrinsic factor in patients with pernicious anemia; and the presence of the same parietal cell antibody in serum from patients with atrophic gastritis without pernicious anemia, presumably candidates for the later development of pernicious anemia. Treatment with corticosteroids may permit regeneration of gastric mucosal glands with recovery of acid and intrinsic factor secretion and normal absorption of vitamin B_{12}. This beneficial steroid effect may reflect suppression of immunologic phenomena in the gastric mucosa. The clinical evidence thus is intriguing but not decisive. There is no evidence as yet that parietal cell antibodies exact a cytopathic effect upon parietal cells; nor has it been possible consistently to produce atrophic gastritis in experimental animals by immunologic techniques.

The consequences of chronic nonspecific gastritis are not known. The course seems to be persistent or recurrent, with unpredictable variations in type, severity, and distribution in the same person. Minor surface alterations, such as erosions, hemorrhages, and hyperemia, usually heal completely. Severe and complete atrophy of the stomach generally tends to continue unchanged. In elderly patients, especially among women, minimal deficiency

of vitamin B_{12} may develop; but it does not progress to pernicious anemia. The associated clinical manifestations include weakness, loss of memory, mental depression, paresthesias, and abdominal discomfort with flatulence, responding to treatment with B_{12}. Deficiencies of iron and other vitamins also may be associated with atrophy of the gastric mucosa.

The evaluation of symptoms in patients with chronic gastritis often is difficult. Experimentally, acute inflammation and sustained hyperemia of the gastric mucosa lower the threshold for pain. Chronic inflammation, therefore, may be expected a priori to facilitate the development of gastric symptoms. Clinically, however, chronic gastritis may be observed in the absence of abdominal distress. In patients with chronic gastritis the symptoms are varied and vague; their incidence, type, or severity cannot be correlated with the character and degree of the gastritis. The most frequent complaints enumerated by patients found to have gastritis are loss of appetite, fullness, belching, vague epigastric pain, nausea, and vomiting. These also are the symptoms of functional distress; they may be relieved by the use of a bland diet and antispasmodic drugs, even though the gastroscopic evidence of gastritis persists. On the other hand, erosive and ulcerative gastritis may cause symptoms, not only epigastric distress identical with that of peptic ulcer, but also massive gastric hemorrhage; the mechanism presumably is the same as in peptic ulcer.

Benign Gastric Tumors

Gastric neoplasms may be classified pathologically as of mesenchymal or epithelial origin. Their clinical differentiation, however, is difficult. The mesenchymal tumors include myoma, fibromyoma, leiomyoma, hemangioma, angioma, lipoma, and the malignant sarcomas. Gastric teratomas arise from the visceral wall, the embryonic splanchnopleure, and are composed of tissues representing all three embryonic germ layers. They apparently occur exclusively among males. Benign epithelial or mucosal neoplasms include adenoma, papilloma, and adenomatous polyps of various kinds. Tumors originating in the nerve tissue, such as neurofibroma, neuroepithelioma, and neurilemoma, also may occur. The pathogenesis of most benign gastric tumors is as obscure as that of carcinoma of the stomach. The formation of polyps in an atrophic gastric mucosa with regenerative hyperplasia has been demonstrated, but the underlying mechanism is not known.

There is no clinical syndrome characteristic of benign tumor of the stomach. Symptoms are determined by the size and position of the lesion and by its tendency to ulcerate, bleed, or become malignant. Small tumors located away from the orifices of the stomach are symptomless until complicated by ulceration or hemorrhage. Large tumors indicate their presence by the mechanical effects of pressure, causing sensations of fullness and distention and such variable symptoms as distress after meals, heartburn, and nausea. Tumors, sessile or pedunculated, situated near the pylorus may produce an intermittent pyloric obstruction, with episodes of pain, nausea, and vomiting; complete pyloric obstruction may develop. Pain, as a rule, is mild or absent; it occurs usually when a tumor prolapses into or intussuscepts through the pylorus or is sufficiently large to be caught and pulled by gastric peristalsis. Benign gastric tumors usually are discovered accidentally or during a search for the cause of gastrointestinal bleeding. Hemorrhage and anemia are the important clinical manifestations. Bleeding occurs more readily in adenomas, leiomyomas, and hemangiomas, and more often in larger tumors than in small growths. The hemorrhage is attributed usually to torsion of the pedicle with vascular congestion, ulceration of the overlying mucosa, and sloughing of the polypoid tumor.

Carcinoma of the Stomach

The cause of gastric carcinoma remains obscure, but current evidence indicates that it is not congenital, that it does not develop from embryonal rests, that it is not directly inherited (although a predisposition to it may be inherited), and that it is neither infectious nor contagious, although a viral etiology remains a possibility. The use of alcohol, tobacco, coffee, and condiments apparently is of no etiologic significance. The possible relationship between gastric carcinoma and various chemical carcinogenic substances, especially their ingestion in foods, continues to be intriguing. The pronounced variations in incidence of gastric cancer in different countries (decreasing in the United States, Canada, and England, and remaining high in Finland, Iceland, Chile, and Japan), the higher incidence in higher latitudes, and the inverse correlation with economic status suggest environmental, principally dietary, influences (hot liquids and foods, seasonings, smoked fish). The importance of mucus and the mucous cells as a barrier to the diffusion of carcinogens and of bile and gastric juice as vehicles for carcinogenic agents remains unclear. Trauma appears to be significant only in relation to the sequelae of corrosion of the mucosa, as in acid or alkali poisoning. While a sequence of ulceration and inflammation, regenerative hyperplasia, and unregulated cell growth is appealing theoretically, there is no conclusive evidence that benign gastric ulcer undergoes neoplasia. There may be a relationship between polyps of the stomach and gastric carcinoma, though direct evidence also is lacking.

The relationship of atrophic gastritis to carcinoma is obscure. Some degree of atrophy is observed in almost all cancer-bearing stomachs. Extensive atrophy of the gastric mucosa is invariably present in pernicious anemia and gastric polyposis, diseases in which the incidence of gastric carcinoma is distinctly higher than among similar age groups of the general population. The transitional changes from chronic atrophic gastritis with small areas of hyperplasia to papilloma and to carcinoma have been demonstrated. On the other hand, atrophic gastritis occurs in association with gastric disease other than carcinoma, and in the absence of any other apparent disorder. The high incidence of cancer of the stomach among both Japanese men and women is noteworthy and unexplained; the average age of appearance of gastric cancer in Japan is at least a decade earlier than in the white population of the United States. An increased incidence of blood group A among patients with gastric cancer has been alleged; even if this finding should be confirmed, the biologic significance of the observation is unclear.

The possible role of achlorhydria in the development of gastric carcinoma is closely related to that of atrophic gastritis. Complete anacidity, as determined by the maximal histamine or Histalog test, is present in only a very small proportion of patients with carcinoma; in many the output of hydrochloric acid is reduced; but in some instances the acidity is high. The cause of the decreased gastric secretion has not been established. Neither the atrophy nor the anacidity appears to be of direct etiologic significance; rather, they represent detectable abnormalities produced by some as yet undefined defect in the cells of the gastric mucosa.

Gastric carcinoma thus may be regarded as

an acquired disease, developing in an abnormal gastric mucosa, and probably arising on the basis of cellular reaction to continued injury, presumably from unknown chemical carcinogens. The frequency of gastric carcinoma in the United States seems to have decreased during the past 25 years, for some obscure reason, whereas the incidence of carcinoma of the pancreas appears to have risen.

Carcinoma may involve any part of the stomach, but is found most frequently in the pyloric antrum, an area probably more exposed to carcinogenic influences. The majority of gastric cancers are adenocarcinomas, originating in the mucus-secreting cells of the mucosa. The tumor does not necessarily begin with a single cell, but many cells throughout an area of variable size may undergo neoplasia, as in multiple polyposis and frank multicentric carcinoma. Gastric carcinoma, like other neoplasms, varies enormously in its rate of growth, from the "acute," rapidly metastasizing tumors to "subacute" and "chronic" neoplasms. Nothing is known of the factors accelerating its progress in some instances and retarding it in others, nor of the conditions inhibiting growth in some directions and favoring it in others. Some cancers project into the lumen with little penetration into the wall, others extend directly through the gastric wall, and still others spread chiefly along the wall, primarily along the mucosa, the so-called superficial spreading carcinoma.

The resistance of the body to cancer is not well understood, but it exists, as indicated in part by the sharp circumscription of some tumors, with atrophy and pyknosis of cancer cells at the margins of the lesion and the proliferation of fibrous tissue. Some lesions are associated with early ulceration; in others it is a late manifestation, and in some ulceration never occurs. Acid gastric juice can digest neoplastic as well as non-neoplastic mucosa, submucosa, and muscularis, and produce a lesion closely resembling a benign ulcer. The clinical course of such ulcerating carcinomas may be similar to that of benign ulcer, at least initially.

Symptoms

There are no symptoms pathognomonic of early gastric carcinoma. The onset of the disease usually is so insidious and its course so latent that it is seldom suspected by the patient or the physician until it is advanced. An interval of 6 to 12 months usually elapses between the initial manifestations and establishment of the diagnosis. The development and nature of the symptoms depend chiefly upon the location of the growth, the presence of hydrochloric acid, the size and extent of the carcinoma, and its tendency to ulcerate, bleed, or metastasize. A tumor at the cardiac end of the stomach, sufficiently large to narrow the lumen of the esophagus, causes the progressive difficulty in swallowing characteristic of esophageal neoplasm. Intractable vomiting often is the first indication of neoplasm obstructing the pylorus. On the other hand, a carcinoma on the lesser or greater curvature of the stomach, or one confined to the body, may not cause symptoms until ulceration, bleeding, secondary infection, or metastases develop.

Symptoms include some type of indigestion, such as vague upper abdominal discomfort, a sense of fullness, ulcer-like distress but without the usual relief after the taking of food or antacid, or continuous epigastric pain. Anorexia is common, although in many instances the appetite initially may be unimpaired. The patient experiences a sense of fullness after eating less than the customary amount of food. The cause of the anorexia is not known. Loss of appetite in later stages is attributed generally to a diminution of gastric tone and peristalsis secondary to neoplastic infiltration, but this explanation is not entirely satisfactory. The decreased desire for food reduces the total caloric intake and results in progressive loss of weight. The inadequate diet and the loss of nutrient substances by vomiting or diarrhea may lead to protein and vitamin deficiencies; in patients with pyloric obstruction, the malnutrition may become extreme.

Pain may occur early or late in the disease, or occasionally not at all. It is seldom severe until the carcinoma has ulcerated or invaded the wall of the stomach. The distress may consist only in a vague sensation of fullness or burning in the epigastrium. When hydrochloric acid is present, the pain often is indistinguishable from that of benign peptic ulcer and follows a similar pattern. In general the pain tends to appear earlier and to be more severe in patients with acid gastric secretion than in those with anacidity, presumably because of peptic ulceration, inflammation, and acid stimulation of exposed nerve fibers. In many cases, however, the distress of carcinoma differs from that of peptic ulcer in that it is aggravated by the ingestion of food and relieved only partially or not at all by alkali or emesis. With progression and extension of the carcinoma to involve the celiac plexus and the spinal nerves, the pain may become severe, constant, and relieved only by opiates.

Nausea and vomiting may occur relatively early in the disease, regardless of the location of the lesion, but are much more frequent when the tumor obstructs the pylorus. The vomitus may or may not contain food, bile, or blood, but the so-called coffee-ground emesis is common. Dysphagia and substernal distress are characteristic of a tumor involving the cardiac orifice of the stomach and the lower end of the esophagus, interfering with the passage of food. Ulceration of a comparatively small tumor located in a "silent" area, with penetration into the wall of a blood vessel, may cause hematemesis or melena before other symptoms appear. Anemia is frequent, usually hypochromic and microcytic in type, and is caused by the loss of blood. However, the hematologic picture may be that of a true pernicious anemia, owing probably to coexistence of the two diseases. Weakness, increasing fatigue, and lack of energy are related usually to the loss of weight and anemia, but they may precede these latter manifestations. Diarrhea is not uncommon, and in patients with diffusely infiltrating linitis plastica of the stomach may be ascribed to rapid gastric emptying. An elevation of body temperature may originate in an associated pyogenic gastritis. Infrequently, the "initial" manifestations are those of metastatic lesions such as carcinomatosis of the peritoneum, massive enlargement of the liver, or severe backache caused by extension of the neoplasm into the celiac plexus or the spine.

Peptic Ulcer

Pathogenesis

Pure acid gastric juice is capable of destroying and digesting all living tissues, including the stomach. Under normal circumstances, the gastric mucosa is protected, partially at least, by a thick layer of tenacious adherent mucus. Protection also is afforded by the regenerative capacity of the mucosal cells, the alkaline, bile, pancreatic and intestinal secretions, and by an adequate blood supply; there are other protective factors, but their nature is not known. Under certain conditions the resistance of the stomach to digestion fails. The mechanism of this failure is not clear. In duodenal ulcer there is an excessive secretion of acid, neurogenic and possibly humoral in origin, and abnormal in that it continues when the stomach is empty

and in the absence of the usual stimuli for gastric secretion. Presumably, the hydrogen ion concentration and the proteolytic activity of the gastric juice exceed in destructive effect the defensive capacity of the mucosa.

Experimentally, peptic ulcer may be produced by various operations interfering with the normal neutralization of the acid by the intestinal content, by the administration of acid, or by the continuous stimulation of highly acid gastric secretion. The contributory role of vascular spasm with local ischemia of the mucosa, perhaps caused by contractions of the muscle layers of the stomach, is an attractive but unproved concept.

The healing of peptic ulcer in the presence of hydrochloric acid, the low output of acid in benign gastric ulcer, and the localized nature of the lesion emphasize the role of tissue vulnerability in its pathogenesis. The nature of this susceptibility remains unexplained. It may involve excessive exposure of the mucosal vessels to hydrochloric acid; impairment in the defense against mechanical, chemical, and other irritants provided by the mucous layer and the mucus-secreting cells; and/or the pronounced gastritis noted in some patients with gastric ulcer. On the other hand, the gastric mucosa has a remarkable capacity for regeneration of cells; the absence of chronic peptic ulcer in pernicious anemia, associated with pronounced gastric atrophy, suggests that atrophy alone, in the absence of hydrochloric acid, is insufficient to produce chronic peptic ulceration.

The factor of decreased tissue resistance is implicated in both duodenal and gastric ulcer, but appears to be especially important in patients with gastric ulcer, in whom the output of hydrochloric acid may be normal or less than normal. Nevertheless, complete neutralization of the acid or its prolonged inhibition invariably results in healing of the ulcer. The lower incidence and lesser severity of duodenal ulcer and its complications in women, and the apparently beneficial influence of pregnancy in women with peptic ulcer suggest a sex-linked influence, but the nature of this factor, if indeed present, is not known.

Regardless of the initial causes, the subsequent development and extension of the lesion, its chronicity, and its failure to heal are all attributable to the destructive action of acid gastric juice upon a susceptible mucosa. Tissue necrosis and digestion result eventually in the typical peptic ulcer. The ulcerogenic effects of certain drugs, such as phenylbutazone (Butazolidin), the adrenal steroids, and the salicylates, seem attributable both to the local stimulation of acid secretion and to direct irritation and inflammation of the mucosa, and perhaps also to a depletion of gastric mucus whereas the ulcerogenic effect of reserpine seems to be related more completely to its potent stimulation of gastric secretion.

The general incidence of peptic ulcer approximates 15 per cent. It is more common in patients with rheumatoid arthritis, obstructive bronchopulmonary disease, and possibly in patients with cirrhosis of the liver treated by portacaval shunt. The mechanisms involved are not known entirely. Duodenal ulcer appears to be more frequent in individuals with blood group O, especially those not secreting A, B, and H blood group factors in saliva and gastric juice. The significance of this relationship is not apparent, but suggests perhaps that duodenal ulcer represents the outcome of an interplay between environmental and hereditary factors. Constitutional factors are suggested by the occurrence of ulcers occasionally in families and in twins living separately.

Gastric ulcer resembles duodenal ulcer in its chronicity, recurrences, complications, and in its tendency to healing, especially when the acid gastric content is neutralized or abolished. Gastric ulcer differs from duodenal ulcer in its lower output of hydrochloric acid and the intermittency of the secretion, and in its increased frequency among women, older age groups, and among the poorly nourished and impoverished social classes.

Endocrine abnormalities are not involved in most patients with peptic ulcer, although duodenal ulcer may be more common in patients with parathyroid adenomas and hyperparathyroidism, especially among men. The Zollinger-Ellison syndrome is characterized by refractory, occasionally multiple peptic ulcerations, located in the esophagus, stomach, duodenum, and jejunum, with enormous gastric hypersecretion, in association with single or multiple nonbeta islet cell adenomas of the pancreas. The 12-hour volumes of gastric secretion range from 2 to 4 and up to 6 liters; the acid outputs greatly exceed the normal value of 18 mEq./L. (Table 24-1). The hypersecretion is humoral in origin, and gastrin or a gastrin-like material has been isolated from the pancreatic tumor and its metastases. Low gastric secretion is observed in approximately 5 per cent of patients. Diarrhea is a prominent symptom in about 25 per cent of cases, and is attributable probably to inactivation of the normally secreted pancreatic enzymes interfering with the digestion of fat, as well as to the possibly direct instant effect

of the excessive acid secretion. Total gastrectomy is the recommended treatment at present. The Zollinger-Ellison syndrome resembles multiple endocrine adenomatosis (Wermer's syndrome), a familial disorder characterized by the presence of multiple tumors or hyperplasia of the parathyroid glands, pancreatic islets, and pituitary gland, and, less often, of the thyroid and adrenal glands. Peptic ulcer is demonstrated in more than 50 per cent of cases. Multiple endocrine adenomatosis appears to have a genetic basis attributable to the action of a mutated gene which is dominant, carried in an autosome, and is of high penetrance.

Peptic ulcer is a penetrating process, beginning in the mucosa, gradually extending through the muscularis mucosae into the muscularis propria, in some cases perforating through the wall, and in others eroding into blood vessels. Regenerative activity is present almost always and may at any time lead to healing of the ulcer, especially if it is protected from gastric juice.

Clinically, chronic peptic ulcer occurs only in those parts of the digestive tract exposed to the action of acid gastric juice: the lower part of the esophagus, the stomach, the upper part of the duodenum, or in the small bowel adjacent to a patent gastroenterostomy or a Meckel's diverticulum containing ectopic gastric glands. It occurs only in patients whose gastric glands are able to secrete acid. It does not develop in patients with complete and persistent achlorhydria. Prolonged emotional turmoil tends to produce vascular engorgement, increased secretory and motor activity of the stomach, and heightened susceptibility of the mucosa to injury. The mechanism may include neurogenic and hormonal stimulation of the gastric secretory mechanism. Frequently, a chronologic parallelism exists between the onset, recurrence, and course of peptic ulcer and emotional disturbances. The

TABLE 24-1. COMPARATIVE OUTPUTS OF HYDROCHLORIC ACID

	Basal (mEq./hr.)	Maximal Histamine (mEq./hr.)	Nocturnal (mEq./12 hr.)
Normal	2	20	18
Gastric ulcer	4	20	8
Duodenal ulcer	8	35	60
Zollinger-Ellison syndrome	30	45	120

development of gastric ulcer in patients with stenosing duodenal ulcers and delayed gastric emptying has been attributed to stimulation of the gastric antrum and the consequent overproduction of gastrin. However, evidence of gastric hypersecretion associated with an excessive production of gastrin is yet to be demonstrated.

Thus, peptic ulcer may be described as the product of a pathologic physiology in which the mucosa fails to withstand the destructive action of acid-pepsin gastric juice. The local factors responsible probably include a diminution of cellular resistance, possibly a loss of protective intracellular substances, decreased cellular protection from an insufficient secretion of mucus, excessive secretion of hydrochloric acid, or a combination of these. The central nervous system probably plays a significant role, perhaps by producing hyperemia of the stomach and duodenum, possibly localized areas of ischemia, hypermotility, and hypersecretion, thereby increasing the vulnerability of the gastric mucosa to injury.

Symptoms

The outstanding symptom of peptic ulcer is pain, characterized by its chronicity, periodicity, and relation to the ingestion of food. The average duration at the time the patient is first seen by the physician is 6 or 7 years; in occasional cases the symptoms have been present for only a few days or weeks; in others they have continued for 40 or 50 years. The periodicity of the distress is striking, the symptoms lasting a few days, weeks, or months, with periods of remission of similar duration. The explanation for this intermittent pattern remains unknown. Periodicity of ulcer distress is observed under all circumstances: environmental, social, and climatic. Exacerbations of peptic ulcer occur at all times of the year, but in some patients they may be confined to the spring and fall seasons of the year. In some patients the tendency is for the periods of distress to become more frequent and of longer duration, whereas the remissions are less frequent and shorter. On the other hand, progression is not inevitable; in many individuals recurrences become less frequent and eventually the ulcer may heal completely.

The pain is usually a gnawing or aching sensation, sometimes described as burning, boring, heartburn or pressure in the upper abdomen, cramplike, or, indeed, as hunger. It differs from the intermittent pangs of true hunger in that ulcer distress is almost always steady and continuous for 15 minutes to an hour or more unless relieved, whereas the hunger pang lasts for only a minute or so. The rhythm of pain in peptic ulcer is related to the digestive cycle; it is the same for both gastric and duodenal ulcer. Pain attributable to peptic ulcer usually is absent before breakfast, appears 1 to 4 hours after breakfast, and lasts 30 minutes or more, perhaps until relief is obtained at the noon meal. The distress recurs 1 to 4 hours later and usually is more severe than in the forenoon. The afternoon pain likewise may disappear spontaneously, but more often food or alkali is required to obtain relief. In the evening, the pain may recur 1 to 4 hours after eating; it may be less severe than in the afternoon. The patient may be awakened with pain, usually between midnight and 3:00 in the morning. Rarely does nocturnal pain appear unless pain has been present in the evening, and rarely indeed does pain attributable to ulcer develop later in the night, unless it has been present earlier. The presence of nocturnal pain often is interpreted as evidence of pyloric obstruction or high-grade stenosis, but it occurs also in non-obstructive, acutely inflamed lesions. There is no characteristic syndrome for ulcers located in the pyloric canal, although delayed gastric emptying and retention are frequent and are associated with nausea and vomiting.

Ulcer pain usually is localized in the epigastrium, to the left of the midline and in the left upper quadrant in gastric ulcer, and halfway between the xiphoid and umbilicus to the right of the midline or immediately above the umbilicus in duodenal ulcer. The pain of jejunal ulcer often is in the left midabdomen and in the left lower quadrant. Pain in the back at the level of the eighth to tenth thoracic vertebrae may occur in the presence or absence of a penetrating ulcer. With penetration of an ulcer into the pancreas or other adjacent structures, ulcer pain becomes more persistent and more severe. In young children with peptic ulcer the distress may lack the usual rhythmicity and periodicity, the pain is vague and diffuse, and vomiting is common. In older children the symptoms resemble those of adults. Nausea, vomiting, anorexia, and weight loss, as in older patients with gastric ulcer, initially may suggest the presence of malignancy. A curious and as yet unexplained observation is the subsidence of ulcer pain after gastric "freezing" in patients with duodenal ulcer in the absence of any demonstrated alteration in gastric secretion. Hypothermic damage to the terminal vagal (parasympathetic) and sympathetic nerve endings in the gastroduodenal wall has been postulated.

Nausea is not a common symptom. Vomiting may result from severe pain, but usually indicates pyloric obstruction. Painless vomiting may occur with nonobstructive ulcer, presumably owing to a reflex disturbance of the intrinsic neuromuscular coordination. The appetite and weight usually are well preserved, but severe loss of weight may result from continued vomiting or the patient's fear of eating. The frequent ingestion of food to relieve pain, on the other hand, may produce a gain of weight. Constipation and flatulence reflect an associated irritable colon. Diarrhea may result from various causes: the excessive use of laxative antacids; gastric hypersecretion, the acid inactivating intestinal and pancreatic enzymes and thus interfering with normal digestive processes; and a gastrojejunocolic fistula, short-circuiting the gastrointestinal content.

Bleeding occurs in the life history of at least 25 per cent of patients with peptic ulcer. It is caused by penetration of the ulcer into an artery, vein, or capillary at the base of the lesion. In gastric ulcer the vessels involved usually are branches of the gastric coronary, splenic, right gastroepiploic, hepatic, or pyloric arteries. In duodenal ulcer the vessels usually affected are branches of the superior pancreaticoduodenal or gastroduodenal arteries. The ulcers usually are on the posterior wall. The anterior surfaces of the stomach and duodenum do not contain major vessels, and the vascular channels are smaller than on the posterior wall. The associated symptoms are determined by the rapidity and severity of the blood loss. The manifestations of severe hemorrhage include sudden weakness, faintness, perspiration, dizziness, headache, thirst, dyspnea, syncope, and collapse as a consequence of the pronounced decrease in blood volume. These symptoms respond promptly to the transfusion of whole blood and other supportive measures.

Pyloric or duodenal obstruction results from spasm, edema, and inflammation in an active pyloric or duodenal ulcer, from cicatricial stenosis, or from a combination of these factors. The obstruction in the majority of patients is temporary and disappears during medical treatment, as the inflammation and edema subside. Permanent narrowing may result from frequent recurrences of ulcer. Each episode results in the proliferation of connective tissue, followed eventually by cicatricial contraction. The end result is a firmly contracted scar narrowing the lumen. The most significant symptoms of obstruction are the vomiting of retained food and gastric content, loss of weight, and weakness.

The loss of large quantities of chloride ion and a smaller but significant amount of sodium, as well as of potassium and fluid, in the vomitus produces an alkalosis, characterized by an increase in the carbon dioxide content and pH and a decrease in the concentration of chloride and sodium ions in the plasma. The consequent diminution in blood volume, reduction in the flow of blood through the kidneys, and tissue dehydration lead to a temporary impairment of renal function. The symptoms of the electrolyte imbalance (alkalosis) include loss of appetite, distaste for food, increased nausea, weakness, lassitude, headache, nervous irritability, and occasionally coma. Tetany is rare, since the carbon dioxide tension of the blood usually is maintained above the critical level, but muscular twitchings and hyperirritability of the reflexes may be present. These manifestations disappear rapidly with correction of the biochemical disturbance by the intravenous administration of appropriate amounts of chloride, sodium, and water.

Perforation

Approximately 1 to 2 per cent of all ulcers perforate, and perforations recur in 1 to 2 per cent of these cases. Pyloroduodenal perforations exceed gastric perforations in a proportion of 20:1 for men and 5:1 for women. Males exceed females in a ratio of 50:1. The ulcers usually are on the anterior wall of the stomach or duodenum, unsupported by contiguous structures. Ulcers on the posterior wall tend to penetrate rather than perforate, and their further extension is limited by adjacent solid organs. Perforations occur more often after eating and during the latter part of the afternoon or evening. Ulcers perforate at all times of the year, but probably less often during the summer and more frequently during the winter. The symptoms begin with sudden, extremely severe pain in the upper abdomen, extending rapidly throughout the abdomen as a consequence of the escape of the irritating gastric and intestinal contents and the development of a chemical peritonitis. The pain may be referred to one or both shoulders because of irritation of the diaphragm, innervated by the phrenic nerves. Gravitation of the escaping gastroduodenal contents to the right paracolic gutter produces pain in the right lower abdominal quadrant. The sudden severe pain is replaced within 6 to 12 hours by a dull discomfort, and may disappear within 24 hours. The subsequent development of a bacterial peritonitis produces fever, tachycardia, increasing abdominal distention, and toxemia. Death occurs within 5 to 7 days if surgical and medical management proves inadequate.

Other Complications

A gastrojejunocolic fistula may develop from penetration of an ulcer at the anastomosis between the stomach and jejunum into the adjacent transverse colon. The principal symptoms are the pain of peptic ulceration and diarrhea of varying intensity. The diarrhea and the bypass of small intestine result in rapid and severe loss of weight, electrolytes, and water. Regurgitation of colonic contents into the stomach produces fecal vomiting. The associated malnutrition often is pronounced. Rarely duodenal ulcer may cause an obstructive jaundice as a consequence of ulceration into the common bile duct, inflammatory obstruction of the duct, penetration into the head of the pancreas causing pancreatitis, or penetration into the gastrohepatic ligament, obstructing the common bile duct proximally.

REFERENCES

Ballard, H. S., Frame, B., and Hartsock, R. J.: Familial multiple endocrine adenoma-peptic ulcer complex. Medicine, 43:481, 1964.

Bonney, G. L. W., and Pickering, G. W.: Observation on the mechanism of pain in ulcer of the stomach and duodenum. I. The nature of the stimulus. II. The location of the pain nerve endings. Clin. Sc., 6:65, 91, 1946.

Brunschwig, A., Prohaska, J. V., Clarke, T. H., and Kandel, E. V.: A secretory depressant in gastric juice of patients with pernicious anemia. J. Clin. Invest., 18:415, 1939.

Clarke, J. S., Ozeran, R. S., Hart, J. C., Cruze, K., and Creuling, V.: Peptic ulcer following portacaval shunt. Ann. Surg., 148:551, 1958.

Davies, R. E., Longmuir, N. W., and Crane, E. E.: Elaboration of hydrochloric acid by gastric mucosa. Nature, 159:468, 1947.

Dragstedt, L. R.: The cause of peptic ulcer. J.A.M.A., 169:203, 1959.

Dragstedt, L. R., Woodward, E. R., Linares, C. A., and De La Rosa, C.: The pathogenesis of gastric ulcer. Ann. Surg., 160:497, 1964.

Ellison, E. H., and Wilson, S. D.: The Zollinger-Ellison syndrome: Reappraisal and evaluation of 260 registered cases. Ann. Surg., 160:512, 1964.

Fisher, J. M., and Taylor, K. B.: A comparison of autoimmune phenomena in pernicious anemia and chronic atrophic gastritis. New England J. Med., 272:499, 1965.

Gregory, R. A., and Tracy, H. J.: The constitution and properties of the two gastrins from hog antral mucosa. I. The isolation of two gastrins from hog antral mucosa. II. The properties of two gastrins isolated from hog antral mucosa. Gut, 5:103, 107, 1964.

Grossman, M. I., Kirsner, J. B., Gillespie, I. E., and Ford, H.: Basal and histalog-stimulated gastric secretion in control subjects and in patients with peptic ulcer or gastric cancer. Gastroenterology, 45:14, 1963.

Hollander, F.: The chemistry and mechanics of hydrochloric acid formation in the stomach. Gastroenterology, 1:403, 1943.

Irvine, W. T., Duthie, H. L., Ritchie, H. E., and Watson, N. G.: The liver's role in histamine absorption from the alimentary tract. Lancet, 1:1064, 1959.

Janowitz, H. D.: Hunger and appetite—physiologic regulation of food intake. Am. J. Med., 25:327, 1958.

Kirsner, J. B.: A Study of Alkalosis with Special Reference to the Electrolyte Composition of the Blood Serum and the Role of the Kidney. Chicago, University of Chicago Press, 1942.

Kirsner, J. B.: The problem of peptic ulcer. Am. J. Med., 13:615, 1952.

Kirsner, J. B.: Drug-induced peptic ulcer. Ann. Int. Med., 47:666, 1957.

Kirsner, J. B.: Peptic ulcer. In Beeson, P. B., and McDermott, W. (eds.): Cecil-Loeb Textbook of Medicine. Philadelphia, W. B. Saunders Co., 1963, p. 891.

Kirsner, J. B., Clayman, C. B., and Palmer, W. L.: The problem of gastric ulcer. A.M.A. Arch. Int. Med., 104:995, 1959.

Kirsner, J. B., and Palmer, W. L.: Gastritis. Cyclopedia of Medicine, 13:157. Philadelphia, F. A. Davis Co., 1951.

Kirsner, J. B., and Palmer, W. L.: Symposium on Peptic Ulcer. Multiple authors. Am. J. Med., 29:5, 1960.

Kirsner, J. B., Levin, E., and Palmer, W. L.: Observations on the excessive nocturnal gastric secretion in patients with duodenal ulcer. Gastroenterology, 11:598, 1948.

Kirsner, J. B., Nutter, P. B., and Palmer, W. L.: Studies on anacidity: The hydrogen-ion concentration of the gastric secretion, the gastroscopic appearance of the gastric mucosa and the presence of a gastric secretory depressant in patients with anacidity. J. Clin. Invest., 14:619, 1940.

Palmer, W. L.: The mechanism of pain in gastric and duodenal ulcers. II. The production of pain by means of chemical irritants. Arch. Int. Med., 38:694, 1926.

Palmer, W. L.: The "acid test" in gastric and duodenal ulcer. J.A.M.A., 89:1778, 1927.

Palmer, W. L.: Causality in peptic ulcer. Arch. Int. Med., 106:786, 1960.

Schindler, R.: Gastroscopy. The Endoscopic Study of Gastric Pathology, 2nd ed. Chicago, University of Chicago Press, 1950.

Sparberg, M., and Kirsner, J. B.: Gastric secretory activity with reference to HCl. Arch. Int. Med., *114*:508, 1964.

Templeton, F. E.: X-ray Examination of the Stomach. A Description of the Roentgenologic Anatomy, Physiology and Pathology of the Esophagus, Stomach and Duodenum, 2nd ed. Chicago, University of Chicago Press, 1964.

Thompson, J. E., and Vane, J. R.: Gastric secretion induced by histamine and its relationship to the rate of blood flow. J. Physiol., *121*:433, 1953.

Walters, W., Gray, H. L., and Priestley, J. T.: Carci-noma and Other Malignant Lesions of the Stomach. Philadelphia, W. B. Saunders Co., 1942.

Wermer, P.: Endocrine adenomatosis and peptic ulcer in a large kindred. Am. J. Med., *35*:205, 1963.

Wolf, S., and Wolff, H. G.: Human Gastric Function. New York, Oxford University Press, 1943.

Zollinger, R. M., and Ellison, E. H.: Primary peptic ulceration of the jejunum associated with islet cell tumors of the pancreas. Ann. Surg., *142*: 709, 1955.

Chapter Twenty-Five

The Small Intestine

LEON SCHIFF

Anatomico-Physiologic Considerations

The small intestine is divided into three parts: the duodenum, 20 to 30 cm. long; the jejunum, about 2.5 meters; and the ileum, about 3.5 meters long. As a functioning structure, however, its effective length is probably somewhat less than the autopsy measurements just given, for intestinal tubes only 3 meters long may pass to the cecum. Functionally and radiographically, the duodenum is a distinct structure. The duodenal antrum, the so-called cap or bulb, seen with opaque media radiographically is frequently the site of peptic ulcer and is discussed with that subject in Chapter 24. Radiologically, it differs from the rest of the duodenum and from the jejunum and ileum, for it lacks valvulae conniventes. The jejunoileum is the mobile mesenteric part of the small intestine, extending from the duodenojejunal flexure to the ileocecal junction. The transition from jejunum to ileum is a gradual one, and, in general, the caliber of the small intestine gradually diminishes toward the ileum. This accounts for the fact that foreign bodies—for example, gallstones—obstruct the lower small intestine rather than the duodenum or upper jejunum.

From the standpoint of diagnosis, one of the most important anatomic characteristics of the mucosa of the small intestine is the presence of transverse circular ridges, the plicae circulares or kerkringi, formed by mucosal duplications. These are most prominent in the fourth portion of the duodenum and diminish in size toward the terminal jejunum. Functionally, they increase the digestive and absorptive surfaces. These folds produce the "herringbone" pattern seen in opaque meal studies of the small intestine by radiography. In the lower jejunum they take on a feathery, flaky appearance. Disturbance in this pattern is one of the important roentgenologic signs of impaired function of the small intestine.

In their review on electron microscopy of the small intestine, Trier and Rubin state that "the glandular mucosa of the small intestine in man consists of finger-like villi covered with columnar epithelium which merge with the crypts at their bases. Absorptive and goblet cells cover the villi and undifferentiated, goblet, Paneth and enterochromaffin cells line the crypts. The connective tissue core of the villus contains capillaries, lacteals, smooth muscle, plasma cells, nervous elements, lymphocytes, eosinophils, fibroblasts, macrophages, reticulum cells and mast cells. Interposed between these cellular elements is a homogeneous matrix containing collagen and reticular fibrils."

There is general agreement that the width of the microvillus is approximately 0.1μ. It has been estimated from various calculations that the microvilli increase the surface of the absorptive cells 14- to 39-fold.

The cells covering the villous tip are known to have maximal absorptive capacity, and this may be related to the structure and enzyme content of their microvilli. The endoplasmic reticulum is known to play important roles in the synthetic functions of cells, the granular reticulum being important in protein synthesis, while the agranular reticulum is concerned with the synthesis of nonprotein substances such as steroids and with the secretion of electrolytes.

Cell renewal in the gastrointestinal tract of man has been studied by identifying proliferating cells with H^3 thymidine (H^3TdR) and microautoradiography. In normal gastrointestinal tissue there is rapid renewal of epithelial cells in contrast to other cells which renew very slowly, e.g., connective tissue and muscle cells, and parietal and zymogen cells of the stomach.

Proliferating epithelial cells of the stomach, ileum, colon, and rectum are produced at a mean rate of about one to two cells per 100 cells per hour, and most of the epithelial lining of the gastrointestinal tract is replaced in 3 to 6 days. The S (DNA synthesis) phase of proliferating epithelial cells is about 10 to 15 hours, the minimum G_2 (premitotic) phase about 1 to 2 hours, and M (mitosis) in the order of an hour or less.

Motility

Posey and Bargen, using the tandem balloon kymographic technique, recorded the same three types of motility waves in the human ileum as originally described by Templeton and Lawson in the canine colon and by Adler, Atkinson, and Ivy in the human colon (see Chap. 26). Type I contractions are the most frequent. They average about eight per minute, are small, rhythmical, and nonpropulsive. They include what were formerly designated as segmentation and pendular movements. They are myogenic in origin and serve to knead and mix the intestinal contents and facilitate absorption. Type II contractions are larger and slower, each contraction lasting about $\frac{1}{2}$ to $1\frac{1}{2}$ minutes. They may or may not be rhythmic, and are potentially propulsive. Type III contractions are tonus waves, surmounted by type I and II patterns, last from 1 to 15 minutes, and are least commonly seen. Posey and Bargen described the intestinal motor function as "a complex form of activity made up of three basic compounds: tone, motility of various types, and the intersegmental relationships including coordination and incoordination. Tone provides the general background upon which motility is superimposed. It is possible for excessive tone markedly to inhibit mo-

tility. . . . The intestinal tract is composed of functional segments smaller in the ileum than the colon, which usually behave independently of one another. This normal intersegmental incoordination is of prime importance in acting as a physiological 'brake' to prevent the too rapid aboral progression of intestinal contents. The intestine cannot transport its contents unless adjacent functional segments become coordinated to act together, in phase, as single motor units." Excessive intersegmental coordination has been recorded from both the ileum and colon in patients with chronic ulcerative colitis and produces cramping and discomfort. Under certain circumstances peristaltic waves may travel for several meters and propel material for long distances down the intestine. Such peristaltic activity is termed peristaltic rush and probably occurs three or four times daily in normal persons, particularly after a meal, is seen in certain types of diarrhea, and may follow the use of irritant cathartics.

There is great variability in the rate of movement of food through the small intestine. Disturbances in motility may be responsible for symptoms in many types of disease, so that an understanding of the time sequence of passage of food is important. On the average, food reaches the terminal ileum in $1\frac{1}{2}$ to 3 hours after ingestion, but may arrive there in 15 to 30 minutes. It may remain there until the sixth or seventh hour, being discharged by the gastroileal reflex when food again enters the stomach. Food passes through the ileocecal valve into the cecum at intervals. The action of this valve is said to result from contraction of circular fibers or through a true valvelike action. The mechanism is disputed. However, distention of the cecum closes the valve, and low pressures in the ileum may open it. In this way the contents of the large intestine, now bacteria-laden, are prevented from entering the ileum.

Innervation

The small intestine is innervated by parasympathetic and sympathetic fibers. In general, parasympathetic impulses augment intestinal motility and tone, while the sympathetics are usually inhibitory. According to traditional concepts, sympathetic denervation should augment the motor activity of the gastrointestinal tract. Bingham, Ingelfinger, and Smithwick, reporting on this phenomenon, state that, on the basis of balloon-kymograph recordings, gastrointestinal and biliary motility in man are not significantly changed by a preganglionic sympathectomy. They suggest that the role of the sympathetic nerves in the control of gastrointestinal motility under ordinary conditions is unimportant and that they are not constantly holding the gut in check by a flood of inhibitory impulses. Under conditions of stress, however, the effects of sympathetic denervation might become apparent. Thus an intestine which is unprotected by sympathetic "brakes" might be provoked to severe hypermotility if exposed to irritative stimuli, and such a mechanism may account for the rather distressing diarrhea experienced by a few patients after sympathectomy. Most studies of small intestinal motility have shown no change following vagotomy. The delay in the passage of barium which has often been noted is usually attributed to the slow emptying of the stomach. On the other hand, diarrhea is a common postoperative symptom, and hyperirritability of the bowel has often been described in animals after vagotomy. Sectioning of both sympathetic and parasympathetic fibers may produce temporary disturbances, but essentially normal activity returns—thus tone and segmenting movements, although influenced by the nervous system, are dependent solely upon the inherent rhythmical property of the muscle itself. Furthermore, the somewhat contradictory and unpredictable effects of sectioning intestinal nerves cast serious doubts on the traditional conception of constant antagonism between the two divisions of the autonomic nervous system and, according to Thomas, favor a more rational concept involving coordination and frequent synergistic action.

That gastrointestinal disturbances often accompany emotional stress has been recognized for many years. Thus, with abnormal stimulation from central areas or other organs, functional derangements occur. These are organ expressions of fear, anxiety, rage, and other emotions, manifested in irregularities of function, with spasm, hypermotility, and hypersecretion, in an otherwise normal gastrointestinal tract. The theory that such disturbances lay the groundwork for organic change in the gastrointestinal tract—for example, peptic ulcer and ulcerative colitis—represents the psychosomatic approach to such diseases, which is further discussed in Chapters 24 and 26.

Secretions

Digestion in the intestine results chiefly from the enzymes of pancreatic and intestinal juice, aided by the bile salts. Pancreatic secretion, a clear alkaline fluid, accounts for several ferments. *Trypsinogen* interacts with *enterokinase* from the succus entericus to form *trypsin* which carries protein digestion beyond the stage of peptones and proteoses into smaller amino acid groups, peptides. *Erepsin* acts on the peptides and converts them into amino acids. An *amylase* which converts starch into sugars, and a *lipase* which hydrolyzes triglycerides into fatty acids, monoglyceride, and glycerol, are also present. The lipase is relatively inactive when secreted, but is activated by the bile salts. According to Borgström, a lipase concentration in intestinal content of less than 10 per cent of normal leads to steatorrhea. Chymotrypsinogen, maltase, and protaminase are also secreted.

Pancreatic secretion is stimulated by the liberation of gastric contents into the duodenum.

The duodenal juice from Brunner's glands, as well as the *succus entericus* from the small intestine in general, contains mucus and many enzymes, including lactase, maltase, invertase, lipase, erepsin, phosphatase, nucleinases, nucleotidases, and nucleosidases. It is now known that the chief action of the disaccharidases takes place within the intestinal cells and not in the intestinal lumen (succus entericus) as formerly believed. Enterokinase, also present, is in reality a coenzyme. The intestinal juices, under nervous and hormonal influences, complete digestion of all types of foodstuffs. The goblet cells of the small and large intestines are stimulated by mechanical and chemical irritation to secrete mucus.

Symptomatology of Small Intestinal Disease

The functions of the various segments of the bowel are becoming more clearly defined. Disturbances of folic acid, xylose, and iron absorption when the jejunum is involved in disease processes, and impairment of vitamin B_{12} absorption (in the presence of adequate intrinsic factor), with involvement of the distal ileum, can be expected. The main site of fat absorption in man is in the last portion of the duodenum and proximal jejunum, whereas the main part of the bile acids is absorbed in the distal small intestine. This dissociation of absorption sites explains why fat absorption may be more severely disturbed by distal than proximal small bowel resection. Lesions of differing etiology affecting the small intestine may be associated with essentially similar clinical pictures, and, conversely, conditions of similar etiology can give rise to differing clinical pictures according to the length and area of the intestinal tract involved.

Symptoms may result from disturbances in the principal activities of the small intestine, which are *motility, secretion, digestion,* and *absorption.* These activities are intimately coordinated by nervous and humoral mechanisms, a disturbance of one generally affecting the others. When disease produces disturbed function of the small intestine, symptoms arising from any or all of these activities may appear. If any one activity becomes sufficiently abnormal, a disturbance in nutrition results.

Disorders of the small bowel may be characterized by hemorrhage, pain, distention, borborygmi, tenderness, nausea, vomiting, diarrhea, and constipation.

Hemorrhage from the small bowel may produce bright red, dark red, dark brown, or tarry stools, depending, according to Hilsman, more on the length of time the blood remains in the intestine than on the level at which the bleeding occurs. A similar experience was reported by Luke and associates following introduction of blood into the cecum. In the presence of intestinal hypermotility, bleeding from the duodenum may result in a bright red stool. Bleeding from lesions below the ligament of Treitz seldom produces hematemesis. Though tarry stools are most commonly the result of a bleeding peptic ulcer, they may be due to hemorrhage from any part of the small bowel or from the cecum. They have not been observed, as far as I am aware, in bleeding distal to the cecum. Azotemia may follow extensive hemorrhage from the small bowel, but does not occur in bleeding from the colon.

Intramural hemorrhage may occur in the wall of the small intestine, particularly the duodenum, in patients on anticoagulant therapy, in those suffering from a blood dyscrasia, or most frequently following abdominal trauma. Epigastric or periumbilical pain is usually the initial symptom and may be followed by nausea and vomiting. On roentgen examination the involved segment of bowel is apt to appear rigid, with spikelike projections giving a picket fence or coiled-spring appearance. A mass is sometimes demonstrable and intestinal obstruction may supervene. Gross blood may rarely appear in the stool. Felson and his associates have reproduced

the roentgen appearance in vivo by injecting water into the bowel wall.

Abdominal pain is often the earliest, and not infrequently the sole or outstanding, expression of intestinal disease. The alimentary tract is insensible to ordinary forms of stimulation from about the middle of the esophagus to the anal canal. Yet pain is one of the frequent manifestations of visceral disease. To the clinician a careful interpretation of abdominal pain is requisite, and not infrequently affords the sole means of arriving at a diagnosis. Visceral pain is experienced when the nerve endings in the musculature or submucosa of a hollow viscus are adequately stimulated, the stimulus usually being an increase in the intramural tension. Sudden distention in the presence of muscular tone or marked contraction involving a broad band of musculature constitutes an adequate stimulus. Before visceral pain due to distention can occur, the distention must be overcome or at least resisted by active muscular contraction. The intensity of the pain is proportionate to the speed with which the intravisceral tension develops and the height which it attains; it is usually inversely proportional to the total duration of the disorder. Figure 25–1 depicts a record of intraluminal pressure in the jejunum during the absence and presence of periumbilical pain (obtained by means of an ingestible pressure-sensitive radiotelemetering capsule).

Pain arising in viscera is usually not well localized and is referred by most patients to some somatic or skeletal part which is innervated by the cerebrospinal nerves originating in those segments of the cord which innervate the viscus. Ivy has classified the pain of visceral disease into five types:

1. *True visceral pain,* which is accurately localized by the patient in the viscera.

2. *Referred pain,* in which the pain is not localized by the patient in the diseased viscus, but in somatic parts, deeper than the superficial surface of the skin, and related phylogenetically to the innervation of the viscus.

3. *Habit reference of pain,* in which the pain from a newly diseased viscus is referred to an area sensitized by the former or long-standing disease of another viscus.

4. *Secondary visceral or referred pain,* in which disease of one viscus reflexly causes a functional disturbance in another viscus which in turn gives rise to pain in an area not primarily diseased.

5. *Associated somatic pain,* in which the

INTRALUMINAL PRESSURE OF SMALL INTESTINE

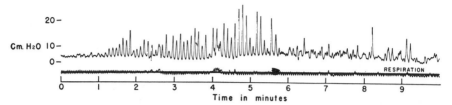

PROXIMAL JEJUNUM OF NORMAL PATIENT

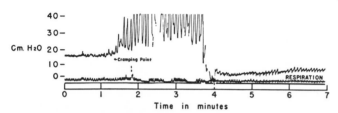

JEJUNUM IN PATIENT WITH PERIUMBILICAL PAIN

Figure 25–1. Intraluminal pressure of small intestine in two patients. The upper record is from a normal patient. The lower record was obtained while patient was complaining of periumbilical pain. (From Farrar: in Rider, J. A., and Moller, H. C. (eds.): Disturbances in Gastrointestinal Motility. Springfield, Charles C Thomas, 1960.)

disease of the viscus spreads to involve adjacent somatic nerves or parietal serous surfaces, which are innervated by somatic pain nerves.

Jones and others have studied experimentally the pain resulting in human beings from balloon distention of various segments of the digestive tract from the esophagus to the rectum. As a rule, the pain induced by small intestinal distention was normally felt in a relatively discrete area somewhere in the midline between the xyphoid and the umbilicus. Distention of the duodenal cap produced for the most part sharply localized midline or right epigastric pain, while distention of the duodenojejunal angle produced pain in the umbilical zone. Distention of the jejunum and the ileum caused umbilical pain that was fairly well localized in the midline, pain arising from the jejunum being felt a little higher than that arising from the ileum. Distention of the terminal ileum sometimes also caused pain below the umbilicus and occasionally about McBurney's point. At the ileocecal valve, distention produced pain at McBurney's point with radiation toward the epigastrium, simulating the distribution of appendiceal pain. After unilateral sympathectomy, according to Bingham, Ingelfinger, and Smithwick, small intestinal pain caused by distention is referred to the contralateral, untreated side and the threshold of pain is elevated. Ray

and Neill were unable to ascertain such lateralization of pain. After bilateral sympathectomy, pain could not be elicited by small bowel distention.

Jones found that distention of the ascending, transverse, or descending colon produced pain which was usually referred to the hypogastrium toward the midline, while distention of the hepatic flexure, splenic flexure, and sigmoid colon produced pain over that part of the bowel which was being stimulated. Distention of the rectosigmoid area produced suprapubic or sacral pain. As a rule, the pain produced by distention of the large bowel was much less acute and less well localized than that noted at upper levels of the digestive tract. Pain in the back was a not uncommon finding when local disturbances were brought about at any level of the gastrointestinal tract, particularly in hypersensitive patients. At times midline back pain was the only symptom caused by distention of a segment of the gut.

Previous abdominal disease, as evidenced by operational scars, seemed to modify the production of pain in such a way that it was no longer referred to the usual sites. Bingham and associates along with Ray and Neill have shown that bilateral lumbodorsal sympathectomy abolishes pain from the ascending, transverse, and descending colon, but not from the lower sigmoid colon and rectum.

Vascular disease of the mesentery can cause abdominal pain in the absence of gangrene or peritoneal irritation. It has been suggested that the pain so caused is the result of anoxia of the intestinal musculature and is a true visceral pain conducted by sensory neurons on the sympathetic nerves independent of the musculocutaneous pathways.

Awareness of the earlier manifestations of occlusive arterial disease in various parts of the body, including the abdomen, is steadily growing due to the advances in angiography and surgical techniques. *Intestinal* (or abdominal) *angina* is being increasingly recognized as an important forerunner of complete mesenteric vascular occlusion, as in a case reported by Dunphy in 1936. (An outstanding propensity to infarction has recently been questioned by Reiner.) Intestinal angina may exist for weeks, months, or years before complete massive and usually irremediable mesenteric vascular occlusion occurs, according to Mikkelsen and Berne. It is characterized by abdominal discomfort or pain, usually centered in the upper midabdomen, occurring 15 to 30 minutes after a meal, gradually increasing in severity, reaching a plateau, and slowly abating in 1 to 3 hours. The pain appears to be produced only by the ingestion of food; the larger the meal, the greater its intensity and duration. The relationship to meals leads to a reluctance on the part of the patient to eat and results in impairment of nutrition and loss of weight in which secondary malabsorption may also play a role. The pain is caused by relative ischemia of the small bowel and would appear analogous in its mechanisms to that of angina pectoris or intermittent claudication. Characteristically the pathologic process causing intestinal angina is localized arteriosclerotic narrowing of the orifice or the first 2 cm. of the celiac and superior mesenteric arteries. According to Mikkelsen and Zaro, involvement of both vessels is usually necessary to produce the syndrome because of rich collateral communications between them. A chronic midgut ischemia with steatorrhea has been reported in a case of polycythemia vera. Chronic vascular insufficiency of the bowel may also occasionally produce segmental lesions of either the small or large intestine simulating an inflammatory lesion or stricture or a combination of the two (see Fig. 26–9).

Distention may be *mechanical,* due to increased intraluminal pressure developing behind an obstruction and gradually stretching the intestine, or *functional,* due to a failure of the bowel to maintain its normal motor functions, particularly its tone. Gas-distended small and large intestines are sometimes observed in psychoneurotic patients and are thought to be produced by aerophagia.

Borborygmi are audible peristaltic noises which occur when a gross mixture of gas and fluid is agitated in the bowel. Ingelfinger has said that they may normally arise from the colon, but are produced in the small intestine under conditions characterized by active motility and excessive accumulation of gas—mechanical obstruction, for instance.

Intestinal motor activity normally produces intermittent but continual bursts of fine, crackling noises which can be heard by application of the stethoscope to the abdomen. In the presence of a diarrheal state these sounds are loud and frequent; in functional distention the "quiet belly" is characteristic; in mechanical obstruction peristaltic noises are pronounced, but their usual low-pitched crackle becomes a high-pitched tinkle as the taut bowel wall is increasingly stretched. Hyperactive peristalsis on the part of the small bowel also may make itself visible as a directionless, writhing movement near the umbilicus, but visible peristalsis usually means that the abdominal wall is thin or that the intestine has become hypertrophied.

Tenderness and involuntary spasms of muscle usually result from impulses arising in the mesenteric and parietal peritoneum and suggest involvement of these surfaces. Some tenderness may occur from pressure on intravisceral lesions or from the palpation of contracted abdominal muscles. It is of interest that Bingham and associates did not observe tenderness or reflex muscle spasm following artificial distention of the gut. This is in keeping with the findings in simple bowel obstructions.

Nausea and vomiting may be classified as central or reflex in nature. As far as the small intestine is concerned, nausea has been observed to be accompanied by duodenal spasm which forces the duodenal contents back into the stomach by a simple reversal of the intestinal gradient, while the aboral flow of contents may be hastened beyond the duodenum. The study of Abbot and associates indicates that duodenal spasm is not essential to the sensory experience of nausea, but may well be a part of the motor mechanism of vomiting. Nausea and vomiting may be caused by excessive distention or irritation of the duodenum. According to Ivy, the duodenum is the most sensitive portion of the tract in this regard and has been called the "organ of nausea."

Diarrhea and constipation may be caused by a markedly accelerated or retarded flow of contents through the small bowel even though compensatory activity of the colon may mask the abnormal transport. In patients with malabsorption, diarrhea may be caused by the irritative action of organic acids formed as a result of intestinal bacterial activity. Bacterial fermentation of carbohydrates to form lactic, acetic, formic, and other acids has been well documented in patients with disaccharidase malabsorption. As James et al. have indicated, the active principle of castor oil, ricinoleic acid, is a hydroxylated fatty acid similar to the bacterially synthesized hydroxy acids isolated from the feces of some patients with steatorrhea. It is possible that the conversion of conjugated bile salts to toxic unconjugated compounds by abnormal bacterial activity in the small intestine might contribute to the production of diarrhea by interfering with absorption or by a direct "irritating" effect. A complete organic obstruction of the small gut obviously is characterized by pronounced constipation. The same symptoms may be present with partial obstruction, but frequently material on the distal side of the obstruction flows rapidly through the intestine and causes diarrhea. According to Ingelfinger, with functional disorders the rate of transport depends not on any single factor, but on the total motility pattern. A high tone retards transport almost as effectively as complete atony, for no matter how frequently peristaltic waves may occur, their effectiveness is reduced by the lack of "diastole" between waves. Conversely, a few peristaltic waves traveling down a relatively atonic gut may initiate rapid transport.

The symptoms arising from a lesion of the small bowel are often not sufficiently characteristic to implicate this structure. The historical data may suggest a gastric or colonic disturbance, either functional or organic. Physical examination, because of the relative inaccessibility of the small intestine, may show little or no abnormality, and radiologic studies may likewise prove negative. Fecal analysis may indicate faulty digestion or absorption or the presence of blood. Mucus in small particles well mixed with feces may have its origin in the small intestine or in the proximal colon in contrast to the large pieces or bands of mucus which originate in the distal part of the large bowel. Green discoloration of the mucus of the stool by biliverdin again incriminates the small bowel and indicates a rapid transit through the small bowel ("jejunal diarrhea"). Intestinal intubation with the Miller-Abbot tube may, with roentgenologic aid, localize lesions and yield intestinal juices for examination. Peroral small bowel biopsies are now widely used and, particularly with the advent of electron microscopy, are proving an invaluable tool in furthering our knowledge of intestinal physiology and disease. A new capsule for culture of the gastrointestinal juice has been devised by Shiner.

Effects of Diseases of the Small Intestine on Disturbances in Small Bowel Function: Mechanisms of Symptom Production

Intestinal Obstruction

Intestinal obstruction may be classified as follows:

I. Organic or mechanical obstruction
   A. Simple obstruction, in which the continuity of the bowel alone is blocked
   B. Strangulating obstruction, in which there is interference with the blood supply as well as interruption of continuity of the bowel lumen
II. Functional obstruction
   A. Inactive (adynamic or paralytic ileus)
   B. Active (dynamic ileus)

Most of the damaging effects from obstruction are due primarily to dehydration and distention. When the obstruction is in the duodenum or high in the jejunum, the distention is slight and there is early vomiting of large amounts of bile-stained material. There may be enormous water loss with anhydremia. When the lesion is lower in the small intestine, distention may be considerable before vomiting of dark brown intestinal contents occurs.

Organic Obstruction. According to Speed, when a normally functioning bowel becomes obstructed, that portion above the point of obstruction undergoes relatively violent peristalsis. After a short time, usually several hours, paresis ensues and distention begins, mainly due to swallowed air and also to fermentation. Distention is really a temporizing and protective measure, since it tends to lower the intraluminal pressure or at least to delay temporarily an increase. With increasing distention there is a decrease in absorption, an accumulation of intestinal fluids and an impediment of venous return with a resultant increase in the venous pressure and capillary permeability. Plasma extravasates into the gut lumen and through the bowel wall into the peritoneal cavity. As the circulatory changes progress and weaken the bowel wall, it becomes permeable to bacteria. Thus infection can actually reach the peritoneal cavity before perforation occurs. The late results of obstruction are increasing ischemia, gangrene, and a virulent peritonitis.

Strangulation causes the loss of considerable blood into the wall and lumen of the strangulated segment. When the veins alone are tied experimentally to a segment 3 or 4 feet in length, enough blood is lost in 4 or 5 hours to produce shock and frequently death. When the arteries and veins together or the arteries alone are tied, the survival period is considerably longer (16 to 20 hours), and, though fluid of a high protein content accumulates in the peritoneal cavity, the blood loss is not great.

As previously stated, if the obstruction is high in the small bowel, the immediate result is a marked loss of electrolytes and fluid through vomiting. This results in a trend toward alkalosis or acidosis, depending on the proportionate loss of gastric juice, bile, and pancreatic and intestinal juices. Alkalosis is more likely to be present in pyloric obstruction than in duodenal or jejunal obstruction, for the loss of hydrochloric acid readily leads to an increase of the bicarbonate ion in the plasma. Gamble and his associates showed that the cause of elevation of the nonprotein blood nitrogen, decrease in blood chlorides, and alkalemia with an increased carbon dioxide-combining power was the loss of fluid and electrolytes from the stomach and upper reaches of the bowel. With the loss of intestinal and pancreatic fluid there is depletion of sodium and bicarbonate resulting in metabolic acidosis. The resultant dehydration, due to sodium loss, causes a reduction in blood volume and finally a decrease in the intracellular fluid and electrolytes. The eventual outcome is renal suppression with nitrogen retention. In addition to the loss of electrolytes, the transudation of fluid and blood into the gut lumen and peritoneal cavity represents large losses of protein and red blood cells. This adds materially to the shock and prostration. The protein loss initiates osmotic pressure disturbances, and edema, both generalized and local, may occur.

In low obstructions the amount of essential electrolyte and fluid lost by vomiting is not so immediate or marked, and the deleterious effects of distention predominate.

The most prominent findings to be considered in small bowel obstruction are abdominal pain, nausea, vomiting, distention, change in bowel habits, hyperperistalsis, and tenderness. *Pain* is usually crampy, colicky, and periumbilical in location. A distinguishing characteristic is that a given wave of pain may start mildly and then proceed in rapid crescendo to a maximum intensity which is maintained for 2 to 3 minutes. There is then a steady diminuendo until the next spasm commences. The *vomiting* of obstruction is early, copious, frequent, and accompanied by *nausea*. Vomiting coincides with the spasm of pain, but does not relieve it, and, in spite of the eructation of much air with each act of vomiting, there is increasing *distention*. The patient usually complains of distention or a "swollen abdomen," whether or not any enlargement is discernible. Almost half of the patients complain of inability to move the bowels, but the absence of *obstipation* should not rule out the possibility of obstruction. In some instances of obstruction the patient may have one or more loose movements after the onset of pain and vomiting—the reflex emptying of the gut below the occlusion. *Borborygmi* are heard in increasing volume as the pain spasm rises to its peak of intensity and then become less audible as the pain diminishes. A patient with simple obstruction usually shows no *tenderness* or rigidity of the abdominal wall. If, however, strangulation occurs with a resultant escape of serosanguineous fluid into the peritoneum, abdominal wall tenderness ensues. If the fluid has gravitated to the pelvis, tenderness may be detected on rectal examination. A type of strangulation obstruction in which tenderness may not be observed is intussusception. This is explained by the fact that the infarcted part of the gut is invaginated into a sound portion of the intestine, the bloody exudate is at a minimum, and there is no infarcted or gangrenous part to come in contact with the parietal peritoneum.

Chronic obstructions of the small bowel are usually produced by granulomatous and neoplastic processes which slowly encroach on the intestinal lumen. The symptoms and signs are similar to those of acute obstruction, but milder and of longer duration. Diarrhea or constipation may predominate, depending on the nature of the lesion, its site, and the degree of encroachment on the intestinal lumen. Thus a granulomatous lesion, such as regional ileitis, typically produces loose, frequent stools; whereas a narrow, annular, constricting lesion, such as occurs in neoplasm, produces constipation. Visible peristalsis is frequently evident. Anemia, usually hypochromic, but occasionally hyperchromic, may result from deficient iron intake, poor absorption, or actual bleeding from the obstructing lesion. Evidences of vitamin deficiencies and hypoproteinemia may appear.

Functional Obstruction. Functional obstructions, both active and inactive, result from imbalance between those intestinal motor forces which promote and those which resist evacuation. The *inactive* variety (adynamic ileus) is by far the more common and occurs when the propulsive forces are strongly inhibited by intestinal anoxia or by adrenergic impulses which are reflexly activated and reach the bowel by way of its extrinsic nervous system. Many stimuli may activate this inhibitory reflex, including peritonitis, operative trauma to the intestines, overwhelming infections, severe visceral pain, drugs, and spinal injuries. The term "paralytic ileus," which has been used to describe this type of intestinal obstruction, has largely been discarded because, as reported by Wangensteen, the contractile power of the gut is not lost in this condition. There is a rapid and generalized dilatation of the intestine; the abdomen becomes distended and the patient may complain of a steady aching pain, but there is no colic such as occurs in mechanical obstruction. Physical examination reveals a tender, tympanitic, and usually completely silent abdomen. When the condition has lasted for some days, extreme dehydration is seen. The tongue is dry, the eyes are sunken, and the skin shows a loss of tissue turgor. There is extreme thirst, yet any ingested fluid is at once regurgitated; the vomitus may at first be merely bile stained, but later, owing to putrefactive changes, it becomes yellowish brown and foul in odor.

Active functional obstruction (dynamic ileus) is rare and is characterized by actual spastic contraction of a segment of the bowel, usually the colon. This, according to Ingelfinger, results in a block of the intestinal lumen in spite of strong, but often abnormal, peristaltic activity. Various causative factors have been observed, including lead poisoning, injuries, intestinal worms, ulcers, renal colic, neurasthenia, and hysteria.

Mesenteric Vascular Occlusion

Mesenteric arterial occlusion may occur suddenly as a result of an embolism or thrombosis or insidiously from a stenotic process. Emboli produce mesenteric arterial occlusion in 42 per cent of cases, are twice as common in men than women, and usually occur between the third and sixth decades. According to Jackson, obliterative arteriosclerosis causes obstruction in 38 per cent of cases, while no obstructing lesion may be demonstrable in the mesenteric vessels in the remaining 20 per cent. Almost all emboli originate in the left heart from thrombi in the atria, ventricles, or on the heart valves. Infrequently emboli arise from atheromatous patches in the aorta or thrombi which have developed in the pulmonary veins. Auricular fibrillation initiates migration of the thrombus in 80 per cent of the cases, according to Jackson. A translumbar aortogram demonstrating complete occlusion of the superior mesenteric artery by an embolus at the level of the middle colic artery is shown in Figure 25–2.

Venous thrombosis of the mesenteric vessels is usually associated with infection in organs or viscera that contribute tributaries to the portal vein. The conditions usually antedating the thrombosis are appendicitis, pelvic inflammatory disease, diverticulitis, ulcerative colitis, or colonic neoplasm. Abdominal operations, however, account for venous thrombosis in about one-third of cases. In venous occlusions the amount of hemorrhage is usually greater because of venous congestion following the infarction.

The pathologic condition resulting from vascular occlusion is infarction, usually involving the lower part of the jejunum and the ileum. Pain is frequently agonizing, sudden in onset, and continuous, but may show temporary diminution of intensity or may be colicky. According to Whittaker and Pemberton, the pain is more frequently sudden and prostrating in arterial occlusion and more frequently progressively severe in venous occlusion. They also feel that vomiting is more common in arterial occlusion and that, when arterial and venous occlusion occur together, vomiting will be seen in 75 per cent of the cases. The stools and vomitus occasionally contain blood. Constipation is common, although diarrhea associated with tenesmus or alternating constipation and diarrhea may be present. The abdomen displays moderate abdominal tenderness and rigidity, but rarely a palpable mass. Shock is frequently marked and is due to the violent visceral pain and the loss of blood into the infarcted bowel. Distention of both small and large intestines is usually seen in a roentgenogram. The leukocyte count is usually high, varying between 15,000 and 25,000.

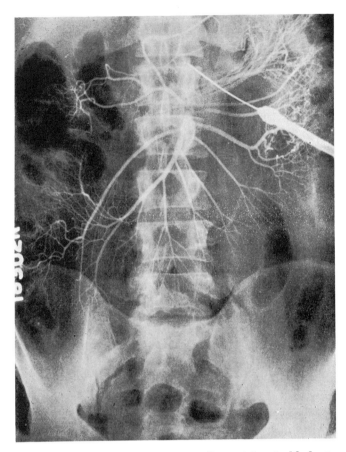

Figure 25–2. Translumbar aortogram demonstrating complete occlusion of the superior mesenteric artery by an embolus at the level of the middle colic artery. Note rippling of arterial wall in major branches from spasm suggesting the toxic effects of the contrast media. (From Jackson, B. B.: Occlusion of the Superior Mesenteric Artery. Springfield, Charles C Thomas, 1963.)

Neoplasms

Neoplasms demonstrate the differences in symptoms based on the nature and type of lesion. They may be stenosing, infiltrating, ulcerative, or polypoid. The location of the tumor as well as the gross morphology may influence the character of the symptoms. Periampullary neoplasms produce obstructive *jaundice* through occlusion of the terminal portion of the common bile duct. Sloughing or ulceration of growth may result in temporary regression of jaundice. Tumor ulceration may produce gross or occult *hemorrhage,* which may result in either acute or chronic anemia. Bleeding is more often occult in ulcerating mucosal tumors, and massive and later in its appearance, and at times fatal, in excavating connective tissue tumors of muscular origin (leiomyomas). Symptoms and signs of *obstruction* may be caused by a stenosing lesion or a polypoid tumor obstructing the bowel lumen. Vague epigastric distress, bloating, and anorexia may result from incomplete obstruction. As the obstruction becomes more complete, pain and discomfort

are apt to increase and vomiting is likely to occur. Intussusception is a fairly frequent complication of small bowel tumors and is much more common in benign than in malignant tumors. The development of intussusception depends on the location of the tumor and whether or not it is polypoid or pedunculated. Submucous lipomas, pedunculated leiomyomas, and polyps are most prone to intussusception (Ackerman and Regato). *Diarrhea* may result from a small bowel neoplasm which causes a marked irritability of the involved segments and hurries the intestinal contents, which are still of liquid consistency, distalward. Ulceration may cause attacks of circumscribed abdominal pain, due to spasm or irritability of the intestine, before either bleeding or obstruction appears. The patient's initial complaint may depend upon the development of localized *peritonitis* due to necrosis of the growth, a walled-off abscess, or a fistulous communication between the lumen of the intestine and the necrotic center of an extraluminal growth. A localized peritonitis occurs in some cases of leiomyoma, carcinoma, and sarcoma. Free perforation due to ulceration or necrosis of the growth may exceptionally be the first indication of abdominal disease.

Symptoms caused by similar tumors may differ, depending upon whether they are subserosal or submucosal. Submucosal leiomyomas tend to remain small, rarely exceed 4 cm. in diameter, and do not metastasize. Subserosal leiomyomas grow much larger, frequently attracting the patient's attention by their size. In about 16 per cent of the cases these tumors behave as leiomyosarcomas with metastasis to the mesenteric lymph nodes. Progressive central liquefaction in the tumor, evacuating into the intestinal tract, produces a pseudodiverticulum which may be noted roentgenologically at the site of the tumor after hemorrhage.

An unusual condition which warrants special consideration and is familial in occurrence is that of generalized intestinal polyposis (usually small intestine) with melanin spots of the oral mucosa, lips, and digits (Peutz-Jeghers syndrome). The diagnosis can be made clinically in a young patient who presents the history of intestinal bleeding or recurrent episodes of intestinal obstruction due to transient enteric intussusceptions and who on physical examination is found to have brown or black spots about the lips, oral mucosa, and digits.

Carcinoid Tumors

Much interest has been aroused in these tumors since they have been shown to produce excessive amounts of biologically active 5-hydroxytryptamine (5-HT) or serotonin. (Blood serotonin levels of carcinoid patients have been shown to range from 0.5 to 2.7 μg. per ml. as compared to normal values of 0.1 to 0.3 μg. per ml.) The physiologic effects comprise vasomotor changes in the skin with characteristic flushing and cyanosis, particularly of the face; stimulation of intestinal peristalsis with diarrhea, borborygmi, and colic often associated with the flush; bronchial spasm resulting in dyspnea and asthmatic attacks; and increased pressure in the pulmonary artery with thickening of the valves (and endocardium) of the right side of the heart with the development of pulmonic stenosis and/or tricuspid insufficiency. An important aspect of the metabolic abnormality in the carcinoid syndrome is the conversion of the serotonin pathway from a minor to a major route for the metabolism of tryptophan, resulting in secondary tryptophan deficiency with decreased formation of other products such

as protein and niacin. Cutaneous lesions of pellagra have been noted, and hypoalbuminemia and edema are frequent manifestations. Normally only 1 per cent of dietary tryptophan is said to be converted into 5-hydroxyindoles, whereas in the carcinoid syndrome as much as 60 per cent may be metabolized in this manner.

Carcinoids are epithelial tumors which arise from the Kultschitzky cells in the mucous membrane of the gastrointestinal tract and have the pathologic features of very slowly growing malignant tumors. They are most commonly found in the appendix and the small intestine, usually the terminal ileum. They are usually small and circumscribed, submucosal in location, and cause little ulceration. They may also arise in the pancreas or lung. Metastases occur primarily to the liver, generally in those arising in organs other than the appendix. The main source for the circulating 5-HT is believed to be the distant deposits, which are apt to be much larger than the primary tumor (or tumors).

The circulating 5-hydroxytryptamine is believed to be derived mostly or entirely from ingested tryptophan, and, when released into the blood stream, it is actively absorbed by platelets and finally stored in and transported by the platelets. The following steps in the metabolism of 5-hydroxytryptamine have been proposed: Tryptophan is hydroxylated to 5-hydroxytryptophan, which is decarboxylated to 5-hydroxytryptamine (serotonin) and then converted by oxidative deamination by the enzyme monoamine oxidase to the pharmacologically inactive 5-hydroxyindole acetic acid (5-HIAA) (Fig. 25–3). It seems quite probable that 5-HT is broken down to a large extent in the liver and lungs, which contain the largest amounts of monoamine oxidase. The 5-HIAA is to a large extent excreted as such in the urine where its detection in excess has become accepted as a simple diagnostic test. Urinary excretion of 5-HIAA may range from 76 to 580 mg. per day, as compared to 2 to 9 mg. in normal human subjects. Benson and associates report urinary excretion of 9.3 to 21.0 mg. of 5-HIAA per 24 hours with a mean of 13.3 $\pm$ 2.8 mg. in 21 patients with untreated adult celiac disease, with a frequent decrease to normal during therapy with a gluten-free diet. Similar moderately increased levels of 5-HIAA excretion have been reported in tropical sprue and Whipple's disease.

The role of serotonin as the sole mediator of carcinoid flushes has been questioned in view of the observations that the intravenous injection of serotonin does not produce a typical flush in patients with carcinoid tumors, and that the levels of free plasma-serotonin do not correlate well with attacks of flushing. Oates and associates have adduced evidence that during flushes a kinin peptide is released into the circulation of patients with the carcinoid syndrome, and that an enzyme which catalyzes the formation of a kinin is present in metastatic carcinoid tumors. Injection of one of the kinin peptides—bradykinin—produced flushing episodes which resembled those which may occur spontaneously or be otherwise induced in carcinoid patients. The role of kinins in the pathophysiology of the carcinoid syndrome awaits further developments.

It is well to keep in mind that the concentration of 5-HT or 5-HIAA in the tumor tissue, blood, or urine of a patient with carcinoid disease does not depend solely on the amount of 5-HT produced, but also on the rate of release from the tumor, the mode of transport and binding in the blood, and the rate of 5-HT destruction in the body. This may well explain the discrepancies between biochemical and clinical findings which have been reported. Thorson has stressed the point that the clinical syndrome produced by these tumors occurs only when a considerable amount of tumor tissue is drained by the caval system without passage through the liver parenchyma, as in the case of hepatic metastases.

According to Davis, a marked variation of serotonin content in carcinoid tumor nodules can occur in an individual case suggesting significant differences in the capacity of the nodules to form or metabolize serotonin. The differing serotonin concentrations are not due to variable amounts of fibrous tissue stroma in the nodules.

5-hydroxytryptamine is said to be a mild histamine liberator and cases of carcinoid tumor have been described with histamine or histamine-like substances in the urine and with 5-hydroxytryptophan in addition to 5-HT, 5-HIAA, and histamine in the urine. It has been suggested that there exists a distinct clinical group of tumors producing 5-hydroxytryptophan.

The "malignant carcinoid syndrome" may be associated with noncarcinoid tumors. Moertel and associates have recently reported the eighth such case involving a metastatic solid carcinoma that was assumed to have its origin in the thyroid gland. These authors point out that "all the cases reported with known primary sources have originated in tissues derived from the entoderm of pouches of the primitive foregut—that is, pancreas, lung and thyroid gland. The possibility of a stem cell common to all these tumors, therefore, can be considered."

Anderson and associates have shown that monkeys excrete much more 5-HIAA when bananas are added to their diet; Waalkes and associates attributed this to the large amount of serotonin contained in bananas. Connel and associates have found that the ingestion of as few as three bananas is sufficient to raise the excretion of 5-HIAA above the normal limits in man. The rate of elimination from the body is rapid, the greater proportion being excreted in the first 8 hours, when the level of urinary 5-HIAA may be well within the range found in patients with carcinoid tumors.

A group of patients has been described by Majcher and associates with clinical findings of flushing, abdominal cramps, telangiectasias, diarrhea, and peptic ulcer, without carcinoidosis or systemic mastocytosis but associated with abnormal histamine metabolism. The blood histamine level was elevated in all the

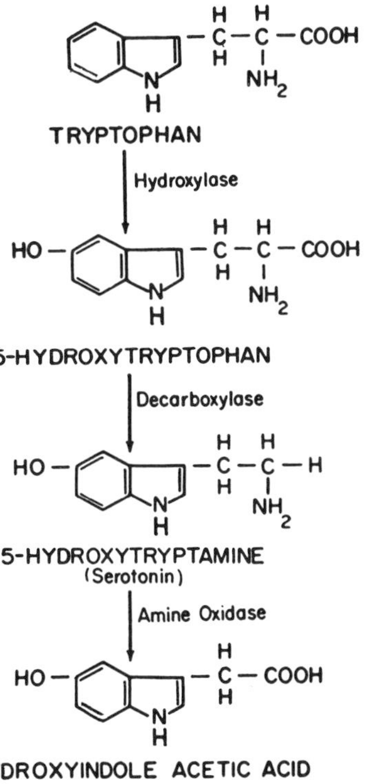

Figure 25–3. The 5-hydroxyindole pathway of tryptophan metabolism. (From Sjoerdsma, A.: Am. J. Med., *20*:520, 1956.)

patients except one, and in two of four patients studied the mean 24-hour urinary histamine levels were markedly elevated, one of these having shown normal blood histamine values.

Diverticula

Outpouching of the intestine, if it produces symptoms, does so on altogether different grounds from the tumors encroaching upon the lumen. True diverticula, thought by many to occur at points of weakness in the intestinal wall where blood vessels pass through the muscularis, rarely occur in the first part of the duodenum. Most of the pouches described as diverticula of the first part of the duodenum are actually pseudo-diverticula, resulting from either duodenal ulcer or traction on the duodenum by adhesions.

Most diverticula are asymptomatic unless they are large, show abnormal retention of barium, exhibit irregularity, or are tender on pressure. Symptoms which have been described include vague abdominal pain and soreness, flatulence corresponding in time incidence with the pain, nausea, vomiting, and diarrhea. The symptoms, usually intermittent over periods of months or years, have, as a rule, no demonstrable relation to meals or bowel movements. Edwards attributed the symptoms to retention in the diverticula, particularly when relief follows operation. Acute diverticulitis of the small bowel occasionally develops and may be due to irritation or occlusion by fecal concretions and foreign bodies. Edema and local swelling produce stasis in the diverticulum. The inflammation tends to involve adjacent segments by direct extension and is accompanied by pain, tenderness, and spasm. Peritonitis, localized or generalized, may result from perforation. If the local inflammation subsides prior to perforation, areas of fibrosis with partial stenosis or complete obstruction may subsequently develop.

Multiple jejunal diverticulosis may express itself as a malabsorption syndrome. Cooke and associates found a disturbance of vitamin B_{12} metabolism and absorption in 16 of 33 patients with jejunal diverticula, and neuropathy in 12 of these patients. They ascribed an important role to the abnormal bacterial activity in the small intestine in these cases.

Meckel's diverticulum is a special variety of a small evagination of the intestine resulting from a persistence of the proximal end of the omphalomesenteric duct, located most frequently on the antimesenteric border of the ileum. From 15 to 20 per cent contain islands of jejunal or duodenal mucosa, and an additional 15 to 20 per cent, islands of gastric mucosa. These areas give rise at times to peptic ulcer which, in Meckel's diverticulum, is said to be seven times as common in males as in females. It usually has a wide mouth and is thus able to empty itself. When the mouth of the diverticulum is small and emptying is difficult, inflammation is more likely to occur. Congenital bands, adhesions, and inflammatory masses resulting from chronic diverticulitis, acute diverticulitis, volvulus, or intussusception (frequently associated with a tumor in the diverticulum) may cause obstruction. Ulceration is due to involvement of the heterotopic gastric mucosa, which may produce pain, hemorrhage, or perforation resembling that due to duodenal ulcer. Peptic ulceration of Meckel's diverticulum must be seriously suspected in boys who complain of pain in the lower part of the abdomen and who pass dark, clotted blood by rectum. Of considerable interest is the occurrence of symptoms simulating appendicitis in the presence of heterotopic gastric mucosa without inflammatory change in the diverticulum at operation. Such symptoms have been attributed to spasm of the bowel as a result of irritation by acid and pepsin.

Enteritis

Van Patter and associates, in a study of 600 patients with *regional enteritis,* have listed the following symptoms and signs in order of frequency: diarrhea, pain, weight loss, fever, abdominal mass, and blood in the stool. *Diarrhea,* usually consisting of four to five loose stools a day, is a result of the partial obstruction caused by the lesion. Any increased activity of the small bowel required to overcome an obstruction is paralleled by increased activity of the large intestine and causes a rapid transit of intestinal contents and frequent, loose bowel movements. It is theoretically possible that the diarrhea may have some relation to the numerical increase in the bacterial flora of the upper small bowel. *Pain* is usually dull and aching, and is located in the right lower quadrant. Early in the course of the disease, edema limited to the mucosa or submucosa may produce tension on the nerve plexuses and result in pain. When severe involvement of the intestinal wall or cicatrization occurs, the resultant stenosis causes obstruction with an increase in the severity of the pain. *Weight loss* may be explained on the basis of anorexia, the fear of the pain which eating may initiate, and the rapid passage of food through the intestinal canal. Thus inadequate intake or absorption may result in emaciation and avitaminosis. *Fever* occurs after the appearance of ulceration and secondary inflammation. A marked elevation of temperature may signify that inflammation involves a long segment of bowel or that fistula and abscess are developing. Once the acute inflammation is replaced by a chronic granulomatous process, the temperature often returns to normal. An *abdominal mass* is frequently palpable, usually in the right lower quadrant, and usually consists of the lesion itself together with the edematous, thickened mesentery. *Bleeding* occurs from areas of hyperemic, eroded mucosa and granulation tissue and usually manifests as red streaking of the stools, but it may appear as profuse red blood or as tarry stools.

The anemia of regional enteritis is most frequently of the hypochromic, microcytic variety. In some cases the anemia is hyperchromic, macrocytic, and associated with a megaloblastic bone marrow, due presumably to defective absorption and utilization of the hemopoietic substances. A spruelike syndrome may be present in those cases with extensive involvement of the jejunum and ileum. However, the macrocytic anemia seen in these patients does not respond to liver extract, but does improve after surgical procedures. Cameron and his associates reported the development of macrocytic anemia after a short-circuit operation for regional enteritis in a patient in whom, at a second operation, multiple constrictions and areas of distention were present in the by-passed loop. The anemia disappeared after excision of the loop, although liver therapy before the second operation was ineffective. On the basis of clinical observation and the study of macrocytic anemia in rats induced by surgically produced blind loops or intestinal stenosis, the authors believe that the anemia is probably due to stagnation of intestinal contents and a change in the bacterial flora of the small intestine (see Blind Loop Syndrome, p. 620).

Since the broad-spectrum antibiotics gained wide acceptance, there has been much concern about the gastrointestinal complications that accompany their administration. *Staphylococcal enteritis* is a condition which appears usually between the third and sixth days after the institution of broad-spectrum antibiotic therapy and is characterized by a diarrhea which may be mild, moderate, or extremely severe, with copious greenish-colored stools. Fever is usually present, the temperature varying from 100 to 106° F., and is often mistaken for a recurrence of the original disease or for a reaction of tolerance, while actually superinfection with a highly pathogenic and resistant microorganism is occurring. Anorexia, nausea, vomiting, and distention may also occur. Dehydration and loss of electrolytes rapidly develop when the diarrhea is intense. Shock may supervene if the systemic reactions are severe, may prove irreversible and terminate in death.

According to Dearing and Heilman, the normal bacterial flora of the intestinal tract is inhibited or removed by the administration of Terramycin, Aureomycin, or other broad-spectrum antibiotics, and resistant strains of *Micrococcus pyogenes* (staphylococci) overgrow. The resultant gastrointestinal and systemic symptoms are due to effects produced by the intestinal staphylococci. The organisms are found in large numbers or in pure culture in the watery feces. Occasionally no micrococci can be cultured from the stool. Fairley and Kilner feel that the phenomenon is not merely the result of a simple suppression of the intestinal flora permitting overgrowth of staphylococci, but that other factors are involved which might include the introduction of a particular strain of staphylococci or a direct stimulation of toxin production by staphylococci under the influence of antibiotics.

An uncommon but catastrophic hazard attending surgical operations is sloughing of large tracts of the intestinal mucous membrane, known as *postoperative pseudomembranous enterocolitis*. Although first described by Finney in 1893, the entity received little attention until Penner and Bernheim reported a series of 40 cases in 1939. Recent renewed interest may be partly ascribable to the possible relation of this entity to the type of enteritis just described. Pseudomembranous enteritis, proved at necropsy, may occur both with and without culturable *Staph. aureus* in the intestine, and severe postantibiotic staphylococcic enteritis may exist without demonstrable intestinal lesions. Fatal pseudomembranous enteritis (without *Staph. aureus* in the intestine) may occur in patients who have not had an operation, although in the majority of cases the patients have undergone some type of surgical procedure. The destruction of the mucous coat of the intestine in the past has been attributed by Penner and Bernheim to acute ischemia secondary to operative or postoperative shock, an opinion shared by others. Pettet and associates in a report dealing with 94 cases believe, on the contrary, that the shock is secondary to the extreme fluid and electrolyte imbalance that occurs as the result of the intestinal lesions. Bruce has observed one case quite in accord with Penner and Bernheim's view, but three others in which the factors of shock and hypotension were "less clearly operative."

The cause of this disturbance and the factors determining the localization of these changes to the intestinal mucosa are not known. It is of interest, accordingly, that the operative diagnosis in 44 of the 94 cases of Pettet and associates was carcinoma of the colon, that 64 per cent of these had some degree of obstruction before operation and that the pseudomembranous lesions were always proximal to the site of obstruction in these cases. In a group of 14 cases previously reported from the same clinic by Kleckner and associates, in which the pseudomembranous enterocolitis was not preceded by an abdominal operation, obstruction of the large intestine was present in five cases and the cause of the obstruction was carcinoma in four of the five. The authors postulate the possible role of prolonged intestinal obstruction with increase in intra-enteric pressure in producing ischemia of the mucosa with necrosis or infarction.

In the cases reported by Pettet and associates an abrupt change in the patient's condition took place a few days after operation and was heralded by the onset of abdominal pain and distention, frequently leading to a clinical diagnosis of peritonitis. These symptoms were often accompanied or followed by fever, nausea, and vomiting. Diarrhea occurred in 48 per cent of the cases and when it did occur was of great help in making the clinical diagnosis. Almost all the patients went into profound and unremitting shock terminally, but this usually followed the onset of abdominal distention, vomiting, or diarrhea. Bruce stresses as an important diagnostic sign the persistence of bowel sounds in the presence of marked distention and diarrhea or, in cases undergoing suction, the aspiration of much foul intestinal contents.

Another condition of unknown cause, which at present appears to be separate from the forms of enterocolitis previously described, is *acute hemorrhagic enterocolitis*. It is usually seen in middle-aged or elderly persons suffering from chronic cardiovascular disease or other debilitating illness. The clinical picture is one of abrupt onset with watery or bloody diarrhea, abdominal pain, and moderate abdominal distention, accompanied by shock which is usually irreversible. The outstanding pathologic features are edema and hemorrhage in the wall of the small and large intestines (Wilson and Qualheim).

Sprue and Spruelike Syndromes (Malabsorption Syndromes)

Tropical sprue, adult celiac disease (idiopathic steatorrhea, nontropical sprue) and celiac disease are disorders of the small intestine characterized by functional motor disturbances and impaired absorption of foods, particularly fats and fat-soluble materials. Although there has been a tendency to consider these three disturbances as varied manifestations of the same disorder, there are important differences. Tropical sprue is strikingly localized and occurs in India and the Far East, in the Caribbean area but not in Africa. In tropical sprue, the bone marrow is almost always megaloblastic, tetany and hypoprothrombinemia are rare, and response to folic acid therapy, contrary to that seen in nontropical sprue, is striking. On the other hand, the gluten-free diet, so beneficial in celiac disease and chronic idiopathic steatorrhea, has been reported ineffective in tropical sprue. According to French et al., approximately 50 per cent of patients with adult idiopathic steatorrhea have a history of presumptive celiac disease in childhood, which, together with reports of familial occurrences (including occurrences in identical twins), suggests a genetic factor in celiac disease and idiopathic steatorrhea. Specific disorders which interfere with intestinal absorption may produce a sprue-syndrome clinically. These include tuberculosis of the mesenteric lymph nodes, abdominal Hodgkin's disease, mesenteric lymphadenopathy of various types, lymphosarcoma, Whipple's disease or amyloidosis, certain forms of ileo-jejunitis, multiple intestinal diverticula, irradiation injury, and mesenteric arterial insufficiency. Jacobson et al. have reported a malabsorptive syndrome resembling those observed in idiopathic steatorrhea following administration of neomycin, 8 to 12 gm. daily for 7 to 10 days. Jejunal biopsy specimens obtained at operation and by means of the Crosby peroral jejunal biopsy capsule revealed histologic changes similar to those observed in idiopathic steatorrhea, viz., clubbing of the villi, edema of the lamina propria, and increase in the number of lymphocytes and plasma cells within the lamina propria. "Secondary" sprue may also occur in cases in which there is a short-circuiting of intestinal contents from the upper to the lower part of the gastrointestinal tract as the result of improper intestinal anastomoses or fistulous communications resulting from gastrojejunal ulcers or carcinoma of the stomach or colon. Experimental observations indicate that the passage of food is actually not short-circuited in these cases, but that there is a disturbance in intestinal absorption and motility secondary to an enteritis resulting from the passage of feces through the small bowel. Figure 25–4 lists the causes of the malabsorption syndrome.

It is generally accepted that the biliary and pancreatic secretions are normal in sprue and hence cannot be implicated in the defective absorption of fat. It is now recognized that the absorptive defect is associated with characteristic pathologic changes in the proximal small intestine characterized by atrophy of villi, with thinning, clubbing, and flattening of villar tufts and resulting in a marked decrease in absorptive surface (Fig. 25–5). There may be varying degrees of cellular infiltration in the lamina propria, particularly with lymphocytes and plasma cells.

Holmes and associates have stressed the importance of examining intestinal biopsy specimens under a dissecting microscope before they are fixed and prepared for histologic examination. They believe that this greatly facilitates orientation of the biopsy in readiness for section and also enables the observer to make an accurate diagnosis within minutes of taking a biopsy specimen. The three-dimensional view obtained under a dissecting microscope is said to reveal abnormalities of the intestinal mucosa which cannot be recognized using conventional histologic techniques. Thus viewed, "the villi project like delicate long fingers from the mucosa and the blood vessels are easily seen through the transparent layer of columnar cells which covers them" (Figs. 25–6 to 25–8). Rubin has emphasized the importance of correct orientation of the fresh biopsy specimen by an experienced physician before fixation and serial sectioning in a plane exactly perpendicular to the mucosal surface by an adept histology technician in order to avoid erroneous diagnosis.

In their review dealing with electron microscopy of the small intestine, Trier and Rubin summarize the changes described in adult celiac disease as follows:

"There is general agreement that the mi-crovilli of surface absorptive cells of the small intestine of patients with clinically active celiac-sprue are shorter, wider, less numerous and more irregular than the microvilli of normal absorptive cells. . . . Some investigators have indicated that the cytological lesion in sprue is confined to the brush border. . . . Others have noted additional cytoplasmic changes including a poorly developed, irreg-

Diseases that may be associated with malabsorption

Etiology	Disease state
Inadequate digestion	Gastric resection
	Pancreatic insufficiency
	Liver and biliary tract disease
Biochemical abnormality	Disaccharidase deficiency
	Abetalipoproteinemia
	Cystinuria
	Celiac disease (gluten enteropathy)
	Diabetes mellitus
	Hypo- and agammaglobulinemia
Altered gastrointestinal mucosa	Pernicious anemia
	Regional enteritis, ileojejunitis
	Lymphoma
	Amyloid
	Radiation injury, radiomimetic drugs
	Neomycin
	Acute enteritis
	Parasitic infestation
Altered bacterial flora	Jejunal diverticula
	Blind loop, afferent loop obstruction
	Stricture, fistula
	Tropical sprue
	Scleroderma
Lymphatic obstruction	Intestinal lymphangiectasia
	Whipple's disease
Inadequate absorptive surface	Intestinal resection
	Intestinal bypass
Alterations in motility	Vagotomy
Endocrine	Carcinoid syndrome
	Systemic mast cell disease
	Adrenal insufficiency
	Hypoparathyroidism
	Hypothyroidism
	Pancreatic adenoma
Vascular	Congestive heart failure
	Constrictive pericarditis
	Mesenteric artery insufficiency

Figure 25–4. (From Jeffries, G. H., Weser, E., and Sleisenger, M. H.: Gastroenterology, *46*:434, 1964.)

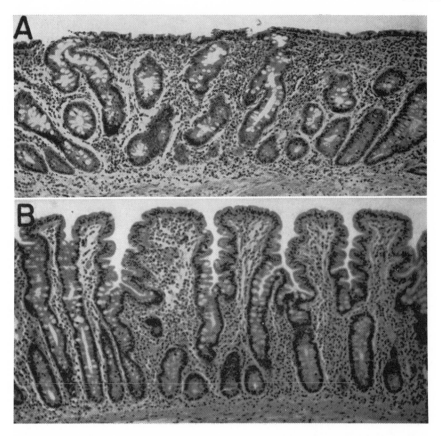

Figure 25–5. Celiac-sprue lesion (×100): *A*, severe; *B*, ? mild or moderate. (From Rubin, C. E., Brandborg, L. L., Phelps, P. C., and Taylor, H. C., Jr.: Gastroenterology, *38*:28, 1960.)

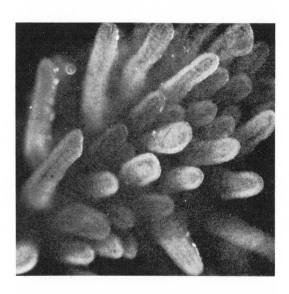

Figure 25–6. Normal finger-shaped jejunal villi under dissecting microscope (×42). (From Booth et al., in Ciba Foundation Study Group No. 14 on Intestinal Biopsy. Boston, Little, Brown & Co., 1962.)

Figure 25–7. Leaf-shaped villi from the jejunum of a control subject (×33). Such villi are often seen in the duodenum. (From Booth et al., in Ciba Foundation Study Group No. 14 on Intestinal Biopsy. Boston, Little, Brown & Co., 1962.)

Figure 25–8. Entirely convoluted jejunal mucosa from an adult patient with idiopathic steatorrhea (×26). (From Booth et al., in Ciba Foundation Study Group No. 14 on Intestinal Biopsy. Boston, Little, Brown & Co., 1962.)

ular terminal web . . . , an abundance of ribosomes with an associated decrease in membranous elements of the endoplasmic reticulum . . . , a decrease in the number of small membrane-bounded vesicles in the apical cytoplasm . . . , increased numbers of lysosome-like structures in the apical cytoplasm . . . , and discontinuities of the epithelial cell basement membrane. . . ."

Zetterqvist and Hendrix point out that the sparseness and rudimentary appearance of the microvilli act to reduce absorption, not only by decreasing the absorbing area, but also by altering concentration and spatial arrangement of enzymes at the absorbing surface. In one of their patients with adult celiac disease, electron micrographs showed an absence of the brush border when intestinal absorption was impaired, with regeneration to normal after disappearance of the malabsorption on a gluten-free diet. Electron microscopic changes before and after treatment with a gluten-free diet are shown in Figure 25–9.

The abnormal motor function, which consists in atony and hypomotility, most pronounced in the upper small intestine, accounts for only a part of the absorption defect, according to Ingelfinger and associates. Frazer and associates have demonstrated excessive mucus secretion by radiologic studies in both tropical sprue and idiopathic steatorrhea which they believe may cause mechanical interference with absorption.

Senior has comprehensively reviewed the intestinal absorption of fats and stressed the great progress made in our understanding of the mechanisms of fat absorption during the past 15 years and the importance of the contributions of the Swedish investigators Bergström and Borgström and their coworkers, the

work of Deuel, and the recent surveys of Wilson and Johnston and others.

Most dietary fat is ingested in the form of mixed triglycerides from meats, dairy products, or vegetable oils and emulsified in the

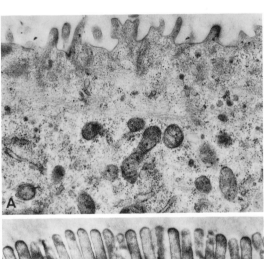

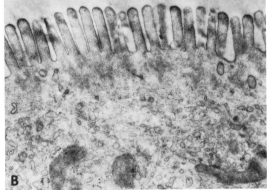

Figure 25–9. *A,* Untreated celiac sprue. *B,* After 5 months of a gluten-free diet (approx. ×20,000). (From Rubin et al., in Ciba Foundation Study Group No. 14 on Intestinal Biopsy. Boston, Little, Brown & Co., 1962.)

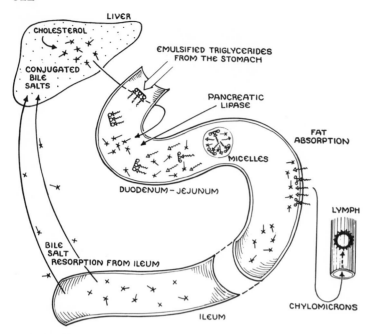

Figure 25–10. A scheme of intraluminal formation and fat and bile salt absorption. x—, conjugated bile salt; x, unconjugated bile salt, free fatty acid; ooo, free glycerol. (From Senior, J. R.: J. Lipid Res., 5:495, 1964.)

stomach by its mechanical squirting and churning movements. In the small intestine it is hydrolyzed by pancreatic lipase to form free fatty acids, monoglyceride, and a small amount of free glycerol. Hofmann and Borgström have very recently shown that in the duodenum and jejunum conjugated bile salts form complexes or micelles with fatty acids and monoglycerides which are absorbed readily and may represent the major pathway of fat absorption (Fig. 25–10). The glycerol formed is water soluble and quickly absorbed by passive transport, most of it entering the mesenteric venous blood, although a small fraction may be phosphorylated by enzymes in the cytoplasm of the intestinal cells. Short-chain fatty acids tend to be transported into the mesenteric portal blood without being activated and incorporated into triglycerides. Most lipid is transported across the cell membrane in the micellar form; the quantitative importance of transport by pinocytosis is yet to be evaluated. Within the cell the fatty acids are activated to fatty acyl-CoA in the presence of ATP and Mg^{++}. The activated fatty acids are used in the intracellular resynthesis of triglycerides. The newly synthesized triglyceride is wrapped in a thin envelope of protein also synthesized by the epithelial cell and discharged into the lacteals as chylomicrons. From these lacteals the chylomicrons are collected into the lymphatic channels and distributed throughout the body via the venous and arterial channels. Triglycerides of short- and medium-chain fatty

acids are probably absorbed directly into the epithelial cells where they are hydrolyzed and transported via the portal vein as free fatty acids bound to serum albumin.

According to Frazer, impairment of absorption of long-chain fatty acids is the primary defect in sprue. He believes that more extensive hydrolysis of long-chain fats occurs in sprue because of delayed glyceride absorption. He found that feeding fat as glyceride in animals and man usually has little effect on the emptying of the stomach or gastric acidity, but feeding the fats as fatty acid invariably caused delay in gastric emptying and inhibition of gastric secretion—changes which are common to sprue. Furthermore, the glyceride usually had no apparent effect upon intestinal mucus secretion in animals, while the fatty acids contained in the glyceride caused a marked increase of mucus secretion, which also occurs in sprue. He believes, therefore, that the more extensive hydrolysis of long-chain fats with its resultant increase in fatty acids might thus explain some of the changes observed in the sprue syndrome.

The abnormal motility and slow transit that occur in the small intestines of patients with sprue would favor bacterial overgrowth, as would the presence of increased quantities of unabsorbed nutrients.

Studies of the bacterial population of the jejunum of patients with tropical sprue and of volunteer control patients as determined by intestinal intubation revealed no alteration of the bacterial flora in sprue patients when compared to volunteer subjects without malnutrition. Frazer believes it probable that overgrowth of intestinal flora, due to improved supply of food materials consequent upon faulty absorption, may be largely responsible for many characteristics of the classic steatorrheic stool and may also contribute to the absorptive defect itself in some patients. He also believes that floral changes may affect the long-chain fecal fat content of the stools as indicated by the fact that in certain cases with sprue the fecal fat was reduced from a grossly abnormal level (20 to 30 gm. a day) to normal (less than 5 gm. a day) by antibacterial therapy. If the various foodstuffs are not rapidly absorbed they may undergo more extensive decomposition by the action of enzymes and bacteria. "Thus, the carbohydrates may be fermented with the formation of short-chain fatty acids and gas. The fats may be more completely hydrolyzed with the liberation of poorly absorbed long-chain saturated fatty acids. Amino acids may be decarboxylated to form amines that have many pharmacologic actions, including inhibition of intestinal motility. Fermenting intestinal organisms are known to be a potent source of decarboxylases" (Gale, 1946). Increased activity of intestinal bacteria in patients with various types of malabsorption is suggested by the increased urinary excretion of bacterial metabolites of tryptophan observed in such patients. Patients with gluten-induced enter-

opathy, tropical sprue, and pancreatic insufficiency excrete increased quantities of indolacetic acid in the urine, an abnormality that is corrected by broad-spectrum antibiotics. Although the relation between bacteria and the appearance of the intestinal mucosa remains unsettled, the absence of microorganisms results in marked cecal enlargement in certain species. Striking increase in cecal size, associated largely with an increase in the contents of the cecum, has been observed in germ-free guinea pigs, rats, and mice.

Volwiler has listed at least twelve different clinical effects of intestinal malabsorption: hemorrhagic phenomena, diarrhea, tetany, osteomalacia and/or osteoporosis, general malnutrition, edema, amenorrhea, megaloblastic or iron-deficiency anemia, glossitis, and cheilosis and peripheral neuritis (see Fig. 25–11).

Some observers have shown that the steatorrhea in nontropical sprue can be favorably influenced by administration of cortisone or related substances. It seems likely that cortisone reduces the tissue reaction in the intestine to the injurious agent, but, according to Frazer, no direct study of this point has yet been published. Adrenal steroids have been shown to enhance phosphatase activity, including that within the gut wall. The possibility is thus raised that the beneficial effect of steroids on malabsorptive disease is related to an effect on phosphorylating systems. This is of potential importance since phosphoryla-

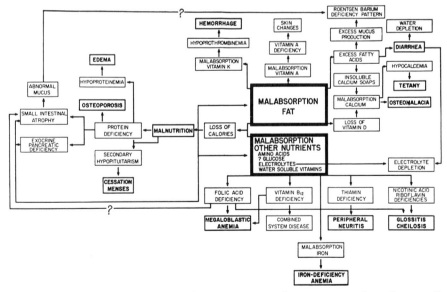

Figure 25–11. Pathophysiology of the major signs and symptoms resulting from small intestinal malabsorption. The various typical presenting symptoms and findings are recorded in heavy lettering. (From Volwiler, W.: Am. J. Med., 23:259, 1957.)

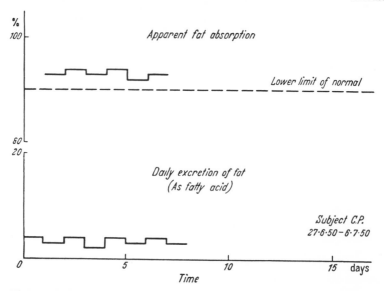

Figure 25–12. Day to day fatty acid excretion and fat balance in a normal subject on a daily fat intake of 50 gm. Normal absorption exceeds 90 per cent; daily variations are small and regular. (From Frazer, A. C., in Jones, F. A. (ed.): Modern Trends in Gastro-enterology. London, Butterworth & Co., Ltd., 1952.)

tion has been implicated in the absorption of many compounds from the intestinal lumen.

Ingelfinger and Moss state that in the markedly atonic small intestine of sprue large peristaltic waves and stationary spasms occur irregularly at scattered points and believe that this disorganization of motility accounts for the diarrhea, cramps, and meteorism. Bowel obstruction is said to occur in a small percentage of cases, and Badenoch would attribute this to the glutinous nature of the intestinal contents. Typically, the diarrheal stools are bulky, tan-colored, and foul smelling and contain large amounts of undigested fats. In 32 cases of idiopathic steatorrhea Badenoch found that only 19 had the typical bulky, foamy diarrhea, while four patients suffered from chronic constipation. Cooke and his associates found that, though feces containing abnormal amounts of fat are often pale and more bulky than usual, they may be perfectly normal in color and consistency.

Normal stools contain, on the average, less than 5 gm. of fat a day when the daily fat intake is from 50 to 150 gm.

According to Frazer, the levels of increased fat commonly encountered in the malabsorption syndrome range from 10 to 30 gm. a day, but sometimes greater amounts are found. On a fat-free diet, normal subjects may excrete up to 3 gm. of fat per day, which indicates the importance of endogenous sources of fat, such as desquamated mucosal cells and in-

testinal lymph. The normal fecal fat content increases with increasing dietary intake, but the coefficient of excretion (fecal fat expressed as a percentage of intake) remains below 7 per cent with fat intakes varying between 50 and 300 gm. In normal persons receiving 61 gm. of fat per day, the fecal fatty acid composition was independent of the composition of the dietary fat; in patients with malabsorption, however, the fatty acid composition of the feces varied with that of the diet and the feces contained abnormal fatty acids (isomers and hydroxy derivatives of C-18 fatty acids) that were not present in the diet but were produced by bacterial modification of unabsorbed fatty acids. Gas liquid chromographic analyses have shown that in patients with steatorrhea shorter chain saturated fatty acids (C-10-14) and longer chain unsaturated fatty acids (C-18) are better absorbed than long-chain saturated acids. However, determination of the excreted fat without knowledge of the quantity ingested may not clarify the diagnosis, because patients with steatorrhea may absorb between 75 and 85 per cent of the ingested fat. Cooke has therefore emphasized the importance of utilizing a fat-balance technique, in which 90 per cent absorption has been set as the lower limit of normal, while results below 85 per cent absorption are abnormal. When values between 85 and 90 per cent are obtained, further tests should be made to decide whether or not the fat absorption is consistently at this level. Frazer prefers the method based on the technique of van Kamer, Huinik, and Weijers, in which the total fatty acid excreted each day in the feces is determined with the patient on a known fat intake. The absorption is calculated as the difference between intake and output—the 3-day sliding mean being used to obviate sampling errors. Typical normal and abnormal absorption nomographs are shown in Figures 25–12 and 25–13.

Although flat curves were found following ingestion of I[131] triolein among the 11 subjects with untreated sprue as compared with 18 normal subjects, Butterworth et al. found that the wide range in values makes the procedure of very limited value in the diagnosis of sprue. It was noted that 15 normal subjects excreted a mean of 2.6 per cent of the dose (standard deviation, ± 2.1 per cent) in the total 3-day stool collection. Patients with sprue excreted 30.2 per cent (mean) ± 19.9 per cent (standard deviation). In eight subjects the triolein radioactivity of feces showed no correlation with the chemical measurement of fecal fat. The limitations of the radiotriolein absorption test have since been stressed by other observers.

It is believed that the vitamin deficiencies are secondary factors in sprue, and Frazer believes that this also holds true for folic acid. The fasting blood levels of vitamin A and carotene are low, and little or no rise in the plasma vitamin A concentration follows the standard (oily) test dose of vitamin A. The low carotene level is a significant diagnostic point in that it is rarely encountered in any other disease. Vitamin A deficiency may result in night blindness. The occurrence of hypocalcemic tetany and osteoporosis may be attributable to inadequate absorption of vitamin D or to the formation of insoluble calcium soaps in the stools. The binding of calcium by the excess unabsorbed fatty acids sets free phosphoric acid, which is absorbed by the intestine and excreted in the urine. This effect is said to lead to low serum phosphorus values. Because of defective vitamin K absorption, patients may exhibit extensive subcutaneous hemorrhages, massive hematoma, melena, or hematuria. Deficient absorption of vitamin E has been considered the basis of the deposits of "ceroid" sometimes found in the organs of patients dying of sprue (Pappenheimer and Victor). Vitamin B complex deficiency may initiate glossitis, stomatitis, or sometimes a fullblown picture of pellagra. In most cases of nontropical sprue there is a moderate or severe defect of vitamin B_{12} absorption which does not improve when cobalt-60-labeled vitamin B_{12} is given with added intrinsic factor, nor following a course of broad-spectrum antibiotics, but which may revert to normal after institution of the gluten-gliadin-free diet. Serum cholesterol is also reduced in most patients with gluten-induced enteropathy and sprue. The reason for this is not known. There is, however, no consistent evidence of adrenal inadequacy in patients with gluten-induced enteropathy or sprue.

Elevated values of 5-hydroxyindolacetic acid are found in the urine of symptomatic cases of nontropical sprue which revert to nor-

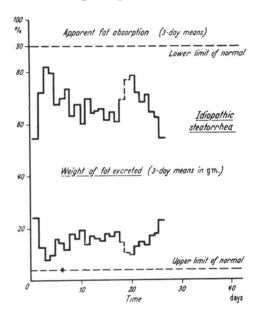

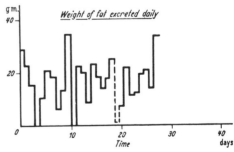

Figure 25–13. Fat balance on a 50-gm. fat diet in idiopathic steatorrhea (fat estimated by total saponification method of van de Kamer). Defective fat absorption is less than 90 per cent; daily variations are marked and irregular. (From Frazer, A. C., in Jones, F. A. (ed.): Modern Trends in Gastro-enterology. London, Butterworth & Co., Ltd., 1952.)

mal during treatment with the gluten-free diet. This increased excretion seems to be related to increased endogenous serotonin production as it is independent of diet or bacterial metabolism in the gut. Urinary excretion of skatole derivatives, derived from tryptophan, is elevated in malabsorption. These substances, possibly formed by bacterial action, are cellular toxins. There may also be considerable excretion of indole-3-acetic acid in various malabsorptive states, including multiple diverticulosis of the small intestine. Sterilization of the intestinal tract of a patient with nontropical sprue resulted in a marked reduction of urinary indole-3-acetic acid. The finding of increased excretion of p-hydroxyphenylacetic acid (a metabolite of phenylalanine) by patients acutely ill with tropical sprue may possibly be related to the attendant inanition and depression of enzyme systems.

Black observed salt deficiency in tropical sprue. Abnormal loss of sodium and, to a lesser extent, of chloride occurs in the feces. Some degree of acidosis may result from the preponderant loss of sodium over chloride in the stools. Loss of electrolyte in copious watery stools is thought to be the main cause of the salt deficiency, but diminished intake of salt in anorexic patients is also a factor. The normal person passes 100 to 200 ml. of water per day in the stools, together with 2 to 5 mEq. of sodium and 10 to 15 mEq. of potassium. Increase in the amount of water in the stools, as for example in patients with diarrhea, is associated with an increase in the excretion of sodium in quantities which indicate a direct relationship between the two. The amounts of sodium that may be found in severe diarrhea can be as much as 200 to 250 mEq. per day. In patients with nontropical sprue there is an increased fecal loss of potassium; the daily excretion of potassium may be about 25 mEq., with as much as 60 mEq. being found on occasion. Flear and associates showed that the total exchangeable potassium averaged 58 per cent of the mean normal value in 23 patients with steatorrhea, some of whom had no diarrhea. Potassium deficiency may play a part in the production of intestinal distention and ileus, as well as the peripheral neuropathy and mental disturbances, weight loss, and renal tubular nephropathy occurring in patients with steatorrhea. Poor diuresis follows oral ingestion of water in patients with severe steatorrhea and suggests that the nocturnal diuresis which occurs is related to the retention of large volumes of water in the intestines during the prolonged period necessary for the digestion and absorption of food.

Gastric analysis reveals that free hydrochloric acid is more often present than absent, the usual picture being one of hypoacidity. Marked anemia is characteristic. It is usually of the macrocytic variety and is usually accompanied by a megaloblastic bone marrow. The anemia may be due to folic acid, B_{12} or iron deficiency. It is of interest that a macrocytic anemia which fails to disappear with large and regular dosage of B_{12} and folic acid should spontaneously disappear with improvement on a gluten-free diet.

Faulty absorption of glucose is a prominent feature of sprue and in the past formed the basis of a diagnostic test. The diagnostic value of the test has been questioned because of the influence on the results of variations in gastric emptying and glucose utilization and the occurrence of "flat" curves in 40 per cent of normal subjects. The absorption of fructose and xylose has also been shown to be defective as may be that of disaccharides, particularly lactose. In a series of 114 normal subjects, Butterworth et al. found the 5-hour excretion of xylose after a 25-gm. oral dose to be 5.7 gm. (mean) $\pm$ 1.4 gm. (standard deviation). A result of less than 3.0 gm. is presumptive evidence of malabsorption. In 49 patients with sprue in relapse the mean excretion was 1.5 gm. in 5 hours. Reduced absorption of xylose is not necessarily specific for sprue as it has been noted in regional ileitis, gastric resection, and intestinal diverticula. The results of the xylose absorption test are reliable except in renal insufficiency and at times in elderly individuals. Increased absorption and excretion of xylose may accompany clinical improvement on a gluten-free diet, but this may not necessarily be accompanied by normal fat absorption.

Hypoproteinemia is chiefly caused by inadequate protein intake, anorexia, profound diarrhea, increased loss of serum proteins into the intestinal lumen, and probable defective hepatic synthesis. It may result in edema, ascites, or hydrothorax. The absorption of urea is also impaired in sprue.

The role of wheat and rye flour in celiac disease, the beneficial effects of their withdrawal from the diets of children and adults with celiac disease, and the subsequent demonstration that the offending portion of wheat and rye flour lay in the gluten or gliadin (protein) rather than in the starch fraction have become increasingly recognized. Dramatic clinical response has been reported by numerous observers following withdrawal of wheat and rye from the diet with disappearance of steatorrhea, diarrhea, weight loss, and replenishment of electrolyte losses and body nitrogen stores. Dietary resumption of gluten and gliadin has usually resulted in return of steatorrhea (Fig. 25–14).

A rise in the blood glutamine level in celiac disease has been shown after oral loading with 350 mg. of gliadin per kg. of body weight. The elevation of blood glutamine— shown to be peptide-bound rather than free —occurs in practically all celiac disease patients, whether the diet contains wheat or not. A rise greater than 40 mg. per cent is thought to be indicative of wheat sensitivity. A working hypothesis states that the peptides which contain glutamine cause the harmful action of wheat in patients with celiac disease. It has been suggested that the presence of peptides in the blood may reflect an incomplete development of the proteolytic enzyme systems in the intestinal cells so that food proteins are not completely broken down to amino acids but are taken up in the form of peptides. The proteolysis can also be inhibited by accumulation of breakdown products because of the hypotonicity of the small intestine and the associated defective circulation.

Gliadin, especially with its high glutamine content, might be able to exert an extra harmful influence in this respect when the ammonia formed from the glutamine is not sufficiently eliminated.

Rubin and associates have demonstrated direct damage to the intestinal mucosa by instilling wheat flour (three times daily for 9 days) into the proximal ileum of two patients with sprue in remission. This resulted in anorexia, flatulence, distention, cramping, and diarrhea, with considerable marked decrease in fat absorption. The characteristic sprue lesion developed in the vicinity of wheat instillation where the mucosa had been normal previously.

It has been found that the celiac sprue lesion is apparently irreversible in some patients. Similar observations on the improvement in intestinal absorptive function despite the persistence of the histologic changes have been noted. Persistence of malabsorption after long periods of successful gluten-free dietotherapy has been demonstrated.

The roentgenologic picture of the small bowel in sprue is said to be sufficiently characteristic to be of diagnostic value in 70 per cent of the patients. The principal findings are dilatation, segmentation, thickening of folds, scattering hypersecretion, and fluid

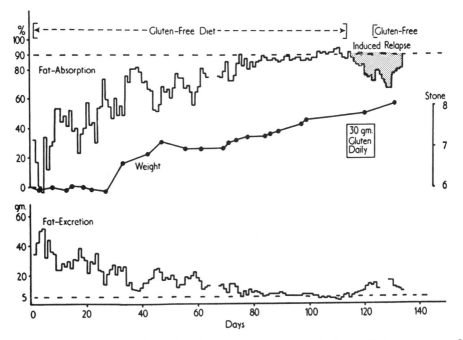

Figure 25–14. Effect of gluten-free diet on fat absorption and body weight in a woman aged 50, with a 25-year history of idiopathic steatorrhea. Relapse was induced with wheat gluten. Note length of time on a wheat-free diet before complete remission was obtained. (From French, J. M., Hawkins, C. F., and Cooke, W. T.: Gastroenterology, 38:592, 1960.)

levels. The dilatation is usually best visualized in the midjejunum and distal jejunum. Both correlation and lack of correlation have been reported between the radiologic abnormalities and the histologic and biochemical changes in patients with tropical sprue and adult celiac disease. Jejunal dilatation was seen in the patients with hypokalemia or hypomagnesemia.

Disaccharide Intolerance

The carbohydrates in our diet are chiefly present as oligosaccharides and polysaccharides and require hydrolysis to monosaccharides in the intestine before they can be utilized in the body. It has recently been demonstrated that the intestinal disaccha-

ridases exert their physiologic action in the mucosal cells and not in the intestinal lumen (in the succus entericus), as formerly thought. It is believed that the microvilli or brush borders are the site of most of the disaccharidases. They are in the outer protein coat of the cellular membrane and are formed in the maturation and differentiation of the brush borders as they migrate up the side of the villus.

A number of specific congenital and acquired diseases exist in which disaccharide intolerance occurs as a result of a deficiency of one or more of a group of intestinal disaccharidases (Figs. 25–15 to 25–18). The deficit may be demonstrated by a specific enzyme assay of an intestinal biopsy specimen or may

SPECIFICITY OF HUMAN INTESTINAL DISACCHARIDASES
IN RELATION TO SPECIFIC SUGAR INTOLERANCE

PERCENT OF TOTAL HYDROLYTIC CAPACITY AGAINST

	LACTOSE	SUCROSE	ISOMALTOSE	MALTOSE
LACTASE	100	–	–	–
INVERTASE	–	100	–	25
ISOMALTASE	–	–	100	50
MALTASE	–	–	–	25

(DATA OF DAHLQVIST)

Figure 25–15. (From Crane, R. K.: The Annual Clinical Conference of The Chicago Medical Society, March 2, 1965.)

ENZYME ACTIVITIES PRESENT IN
MUCOSAL BIOPSIES

(UNITS/GRAM PROTEIN)

	ALKALINE PHOSPHATASE	MALTASE	INVERTASE	ISOMALTASE	LACTASE
NORMAL	802	266	87	97	44
LACTOSE INTOLERANT	778	234	77	83	2

(DATA OF DUNPHY, DAHLQVIST, HAMMOND, FORSTNER, LITTMAN and CRANE)

Figure 25–16. (From Crane, R. K.: The Annual Clinical Conference of The Chicago Medical Society, March 2, 1965.)

ENZYME ACTIVITIES PRESENT IN
MUCOSAL BIOPSIES

(UNITS/GRAM PROTEIN)

	ALKALINE PHOSPHATASE	MALTASE	INVERTASE	ISOMALTASE	LACTASE
NORMAL	430	180	82	80	50
NONTROPICAL SPRUE	69	50	19	14	1.4

(DATA OF PLOTKIN AND ISSELBACHER)

Figure 25–17. (From Crane, R. K.: The Annual Clinical Conference of The Chicago Medical Society, March 2, 1965.)

be suspected if the patient fails to show a normal rise in the blood of the monosaccharide present when the disaccharide is given as an oral load.

The most frequently observed and most studied of this group of "brush border disorders" is lactose intolerance. When patients with intolerance of this disaccharide are given a test dose of 100 gm. of lactose dissolved in 200 to 250 cc. of water, blood glucose curves obtained at half hour intervals for a period of 2 hours will show a maximum elevation of less than 20 mg. per cent, in contrast with normals in whom the peak elevation is at least 20 mg. per cent. When a mixture of 50 gm. of glucose and 50 gm. of galactose is given, the blood sugar elevation reaches the same levels as in normals and no diarrhea results.

Peternel found that a blood glucose elevation of at least 20 mg. per 100 cc. above the fasting value in nondiabetic subjects following ingestion of 100 gm. of lactose correlated well with normal intestinal lactase activity as demonstrated by assay of jejunal mucosal biopsy specimens. Conversely, an elevation of blood glucose of less than 20 mg. per 100 cc. above the fasting values in diabetic as well as nondiabetic individuals correlated with low intestinal lactase activity.

In cases of lactose intolerance, abdominal cramps, bloating, borborygmi, and diarrhea develop within a couple of hours following ingestion of milk or lactose. The stools are apt to be watery and acid, and may contain lactose, which through its osmotic effect contributes to the diarrhea. The fecal pH falls to as low as 4.5, and according to Weijers and associates, total bacterial counts are increased during diarrheal periods with preponderance of fecal streptococci. Furthermore, bacterial fermentation of lactose within the colon produces organic acids, mainly lactic and acetic, which may stimulate peristalsis and interfere with the digestion and absorption of fat. Withdrawal of milk results in disappearance of the abdominal symptoms.

A history of "milk intolerance" may not necessarily indicate an intestinal deficiency of lactase. As a matter of fact, such a deficiency is demonstrable in only about half the cases giving such a history, according to Littman and to Haemmerli. Allergy may play a role as well as factors which are as yet unknown.

The lactase deficiency may be congenital, appearing in the newborn infant in whom it may prove disastrous, or may manifest itself

or be acquired in adult life. Lactase deficiency has been demonstrated in jejunal biopsy specimens without any clinically recognizable lactose intolerance. According to Littman, deficiency of this enzyme may occur in about 30 per cent of a general hospital population, and many "flat" lactose tolerance curves which have been reported in normals have probably been obtained in patients with asymptomatic lactase deficiency. Blood glucose curves obtained during an oral tolerance test may, of course, be influenced by such factors as gastric emptying, intestinal motility, and glucose utilization.

Littman and associates have observed lac-

TENTATIVE CLASSIFICATION OF DISACCHARIDE INTOLERANCES DUE TO INTESTINAL MUCOSAL ENZYME AND/OR TRANSPORT DEFECTS

Congenital (primary) syndromes
  Congenital lactose intolerance with lactosuria (Durand's syndrome) probably due to increased absorption of molecular lactose
  Congenital lactose malabsorption (Holzel's syndrome)
  Congenital sucrose-isomaltose malabsorption
  Congenital sucrose malabsorption
  Disaccharide intolerance due to congenital glucose-galactose malabsorption
  Physiological lactose-induced diarrhea of breast-fed newborns

Acquired (probably primary) syndromes
  Acquired lactose malabsorption (milk intolerance in the adult)
  Acquired sucrose malabsorption ? ?

Symptomatic (secondary) syndromes
  Disaccharide malabsorption in nonspecific diarrhea of childhood
  Lactose malabsorption in severe *Giardia lamblia* infestation
  Disaccharide malabsorption in severe malnutrition of infancy
  Lactose malabsorption in kwashiorkor
  Disaccharide malabsorption in celiac disease and idiopathic sprue
  Lactose malabsorption after extensive small bowel resections
  Lactose malabsorption after gastrectomy
  Lactose malabsorption in the irritable colon syndrome
  Lactose malabsorption in cystic fibrosis of the pancreas
  Lactose malabsorption in ulcerative colitis

(From Haemmerli et al.: Amer. J. Med., 38:7, 1965.)

Figure 25–18.

tase deficiency without clinical symptoms in patients drinking as much as 2 liters of milk a day who were unable to tolerate 100 gm. of lactose given at one time, which corresponds to the amount of the sugar contained in this quantity of milk. This suggests that the size of the load at a given time may determine the actual production of symptoms.

Lactose malabsorption may occur even with normal lactase activity when the small intestinal absorbing surface is greatly reduced as in elective intestinal resection. Disaccharidase deficiency especially of lactase has been demonstrated in the intestinal mucosa of a variety of malabsorption states, especially adult celiac disease. The decreased mucosal disaccharidase levels are probably a reflection of both a reduction in the number of the epithelial cells and alterations in the function of individual cells. During remission intestinal disaccharidase levels tend to return to normal, according to Plotkin and Isselbacher.

Human subjects affected by sucrose malabsorption cannot hydrolyze sucrose, isomaltose, and palatinose (isomaltulose) in their intestines, while maltose and lactose are digested normally. Determinations of disaccharidase activities in the intestinal mucosa obtained from patients with sucrose malabsorption have shown normal lactase activity, while sucrase activity is absent, isomaltase activity is reduced to traces, and maltase activity is reduced to 10 to 20 per cent of the normal. The observations of Auricchio and associates make it very likely that in sucrose malabsorption only maltases 4 and 5 (and probably 3) are absent or inactive, whereas maltases 1 and 2 are essentially normal. The lack of maltases 4 and 5 (and probably 3) in a disease which is transmitted by a single genetic factor indicates that these enzymes are under a common genetic control mechanism. Semenza and associates point out the interesting feature that maltases 4 and 5 (and probably 3) occur in the brush border close to each other and are activated by Na^+, whereas maltases 1 and 2 are not. In another disease also transmitted by a single genetic factor, Parr et al. have reported the absence of two enzymes, both phosphorylase and glycogen-synthetase activity.

Isomaltose intolerance can be expected to occur as an isolated defect if isomaltase (maltase I a) is absent. The disease can be expected to give symptoms on the ingestion of starch-rich meals, because isomaltase is formed from the branching points of starch during its digestion by amylase. Isolated isomaltose intolerance has thus far not been found, according to Dahlqvist.

(It is interesting to note that a syndrome of congenital glucose-galactose malabsorption has been described recently in which fructose may be substituted without ill effect.)

Blind Loop Syndrome

Any intestinal lesion which produces stasis within the lumen of the gut and bacterial proliferation, either as a result of a stricture, intestinal anastomotic surgery (usually to relieve obstruction), or multiple jejunal diverticulosis, may produce the various manifestations of a malabsorption syndrome. Restoration of the normal anatomy or sterilization of the gut by antibiotics may be curative. The macrocytic anemia which is frequently encountered may be due to utilization of folic acid and vitamin B_{12} by bacteria which reside in the loop and require these vitamins for their own metabolism or to diminished synthesis of folic acid by the suppression of essential bacteria. Absorbable broad-spectrum antibiotics, such as chlortetracycline, have been shown to improve the anemia and the absorption of labeled vitamin B_{12}. It is of interest that the anemia in the blind loop syndrome may be unaffected by neomycin, which is not readily absorbed (and may therefore fail to appear in sufficient concentration in the "blind loop"). Absorption of vitamin B_{12} has been shown to be inhibited by a metal chelating agent, and this can be reversed by calcium ions. The suggestion has been made that decreased B_{12} uptake during malabsorption is due to a relative deficiency of calcium, inasmuch as calcium is bound to fatty acids and lost in the stool.

Surgical blind loops, strictures, enteroenterostomies, fistulas, and diverticula involving the small intestine may all be associated with macrocytic anemia. If surgical correction of the small bowel abnormality involves resection or bypass of distal ileum, then vitamin B_{12} malabsorption will persist since intact ileal mucosa is necessary for normal absorption of the vitamin.

Massive Intestinal Resection

Resection of up to two-thirds of the small bowel can be compatible with good health. With more extensive ileal resection, there may be complete malabsorption of vitamin B_{12}. If less than 18 inches is left, death from inanition is likely. Surgical resection of the proximal intestine may be tolerated better than resection of the distal small bowel in experimental animals and man. Resection of the upper small bowel seldom causes malabsorption unless the resection is massive. The distal small bowel is presumably capable of performing the functions of the resected proximal portion. According to Booth and associates, the total amount of fat absorbed increases with increasing fat intake, but so does the degree of steatorrhea.

In a patient whose entire colon, except for a small segment of rectum, had been excised for multiple polyposis and who subsequently had resection of most of the small intestine with anastomosis of the proximal jejunum to the rectal segment, no significantly measurable amounts of blood serotonin or urinary 5-hydroxyindole acetic acid have been found. This observation supports the thesis that 5-hydroxyindoles in blood and urine represent mainly the contribution of the gastrointestinal tract. Some intestinal function studies following resection of varying amounts of the distal small intestine are shown in Figure 25–19.

Porus has reported mucosal cell hyperplasia—an increase in the number of epithelial cells per unit length of villus—with no villus hypertrophy in two patients with 75 per cent and 80 per cent distal small bowel resections, but not in two patients with 50 per cent resection. He believes that this is the first evidence in man of mucosal cell hyperplasia following small bowel resection.

Irradiation Effects

Damage to the intestinal mucosa of animals subjected to irradiation was reported as early as 1906. Crypt epithelium, which possesses a high rate of regeneration, is the area of the alimentary tract most sensitive to the detrimental action of radiation. Intestinal motility is altered and each of the absorptive mechanisms may be affected to a different extent. According to Scudamore and Green, a malabsorption syndrome, intermittent small intestinal obstruction, and hypochromic anemia due to chronic blood loss are the main conditions that may develop 2 to 20 years after radiation of the abdomen for malignant disease, the response depending on the amount of radiation administered and host tissue sensitivity.

Sodium loss is said to be relatively greater than potassium loss in postirradiation diarrhea. Damage to the small bowel, which may follow x-ray therapy for carcinoma of the cervix, has been reported to produce a malabsorption syndrome.

"Protein-Losing Gastroenteropathy"

Under normal conditions albumin is eliminated and catabolized mainly in the upper part of the gastrointestinal tract. It is now well known that the loss of abnormal amounts of protein into the gastrointestinal tract may prove a major factor in the hypoproteinemia associated with a variety of diseases. These include cases of giant gastric rugae, gastric

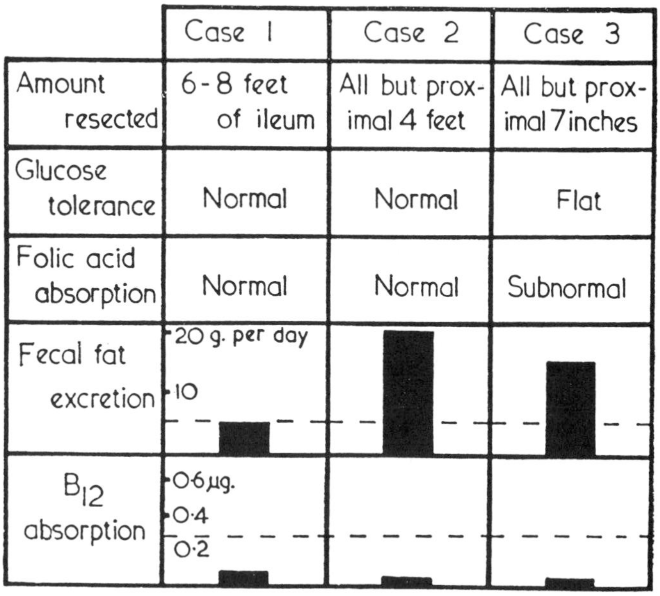

Figure 25–19. Intestinal function studies after resection of varying amounts of the distal small intestine (Cases 1 to 3). In this and subsequent figures, the interrupted lines indicate the upper limit of normal fecal fat excretion (6 gm. per day) and the lower limit of normal B_{12} absorption (0.3 μg.), using an oral test dose of 1.0 μg. (From Booth, C. C.: Brit. J. Radiol., 33:201, 1960.)

	Case 1	Case 2	Case 3
Amount resected	6-8 feet of ileum	All but proximal 4 feet	All but proximal 7 inches
Glucose tolerance	Normal	Normal	Flat
Folic acid absorption	Normal	Normal	Subnormal
Fecal fat excretion	20 g. per day / 10		
B_{12} absorption	0.6 μg. / 0.4 / 0.2		

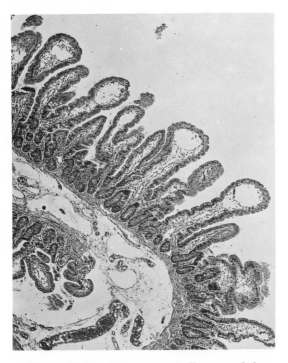

Figure 25–20. Jejunum surgically resected from 11 year old girl with clinically classic "exudative enteropathy," severe hypoproteinemia, responding temporarily to resection. Note striking dilatation of lymphatics at the tip of the villus and in the submucosa (×110). (Courtesy of Dr. Eugene V. Perrin, Children's Hospital, Cincinnati, Ohio.)

carcinoma, regional enteritis and ulcerative colitis, sprue, Whipple's disease, cardiac lesions, especially constrictive pericarditis, and cases of hypogammaglobulinemia.

"Intestinal lymphangiectasia" has become increasingly recognized as an important cause of enteric protein loss, particularly in young individuals. In this disorder there is dilatation of the lacteals and villi of the small intestine (which may contain foamy lipophages) and thickening of the wall of the mesenteric vessels with narrowing of the lumen (Figs. 25–20 to 25–23). Dilated lymphatic vessels containing chyle may be seen on the serosal surface, and chylous effusions may be present. Recent reports would indicate that the intestinal disorder represents only one manifestation of a more generalized disease of the lymphatic system which may be demonstrated by lymphangiography (Figs. 25–24 and 25–25).

Waldmann and associates have postulated that the gastrointestinal protein loss in these patients may result from rupture of the dilated mucosal lymphatics with discharge of their contents into the bowel lumen, or by protein transudation through the intact epithelium as a result of obstruction of the mesenteric lymphatics. While the presence of lymph has been demonstrated in the intestinal lumen of such patients, directly by intubation studies

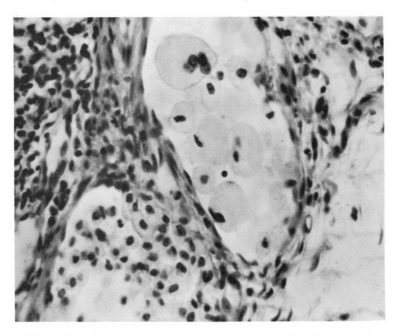

Figure 25–21. Submucosal lymph vessels of jejunum dilated and filled with great lipophages. Patient, age 7, had lymphangiectatic gigantism of a leg and the corresponding flank, and severe exudative enteropathy (×480). (Courtesy of Dr. Eugene V. Perrin, Children's Hospital, Cincinnati, Ohio.)

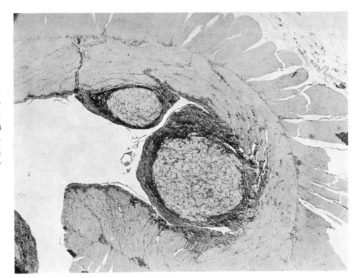

Figure 25–22. Laparotomy specimen: mesenteric vessel with lumen partially occluded by fibrosis (elastic Van Gieson stain ×55). (From Waldmann et al., in Schwartz, M., and Vesin, P.: Plasma Proteins and Gastrointestinal Tract in Health and Disease. Baltimore, Williams & Wilkins Co., 1963.)

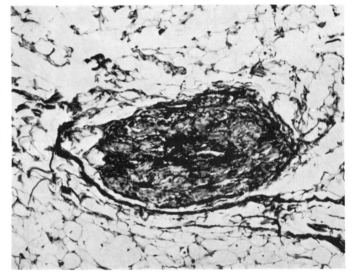

Figure 25–23. Laparotomy specimen: serosal lymph vessels occluded by foamy lipophages (H & E ×27). (From Waldmann et al., in Schwartz, M., and Vesin, P.: Plasma Proteins and Gastrointestinal Tract in Health and Disease. Baltimore, Williams & Wilkins Co., 1963.)

and indirectly by lymphangiography (Figs. 25–26 and 25–27), the actual proof of rupture of the dilated lymphatics with discharge of their contents into the intestinal lumen remains to be obtained.

The occlusion of the lymphatic channels would also explain the steatorrhea which occurs in these patients. Waldmann believes that these lymphatic disorders are most likely due to congenital malformation, particularly in those with onset at birth and a family history of hypoproteinemia and chylous effusions, while in other instances the defect may possibly be acquired.

In adult patients who are usually not severely incapacitated by the disease, the symptoms include dependent edema secondary to hypoproteinemia, abdominal distention, and diarrhea, and occasionally intermittent vomiting. In childhood severe secondary hypoglobulinemia may result in repeated bacterial infections, and growth may be retarded by disturbances of calcium and protein metabolism.

Methods to determine the excessive enteric protein loss have included the use of I^{131}-tagged albumin, I^{131}-tagged PVP and Cr^{51}-labeled albumin. At present Waldmann and Gordon prefer the use of Cr^{51}-labeled albumin, since the advantages over I^{131} PVP "include easy labeling of a variety of normal plasma and cellular proteins, negligible absorption from or excretion into the intestinal tract, and marked difference in stool excretion of radioactivity between controls and patients with gastrointestinal protein loss." Following

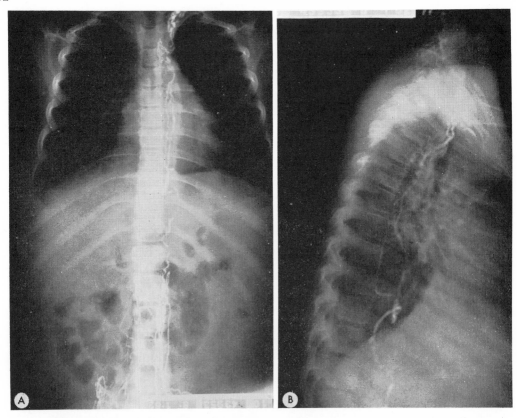

Figure 25–24. Double tortuous thoracic duct. *A,* Posterior-anterior view. *B,* Lateral view. (From Pomerantz, M., and Waldmann, T. A.: Gastroenterology, *45:*703, 1963.)

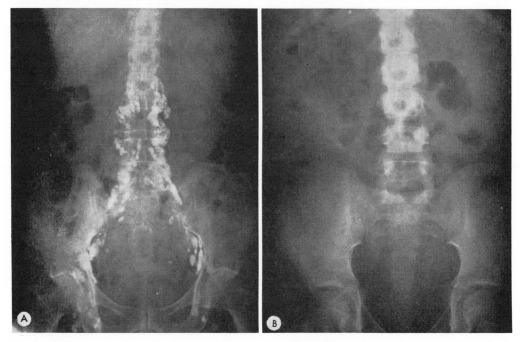

Figure 25–25. *A,* Delayed (24 hours) lymphangiogram x-ray of the abdomen of a normal control opacifying in a homogeneous fashion the pelvic and retroperitoneal lymph nodes. *B,* Delayed (24 hours) lymphangiogram x-ray revealing lack of opacification of the pelvic and retroperitoneal lymph nodes. (From Pomerantz, M., and Waldmann, T. A.: Gastroenterology, *45:*703, 1963.)

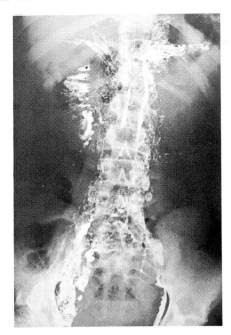

Figure 25-26. Lymphogram showing dilated and tortuous retroperitoneal and pelvic lymphatics, partial block at the level of the diaphragm, dilated and numerous intestinal lymphatics, and retrograde passage of dye with contrast medium in the duodenum and jejunum. (From Mistilis, S. P., Skyring, A. P., and Stephen, D. D.: Lancet, 1:77, 1965.)

Figure 25-27. Lymphogram demonstrating passage of the contrast medium along the small bowel. (From Mistilis, S. P., Skyring, A. P., and Stephen, D. D.: Lancet, 1:77, 1965.)

intravenous administration of Cr^{51} albumin the greatest fecal excretion by a control was 0.7 per cent with a mean of 0.25 per cent, in comparison with an upper limit for controls of 1.6 per cent with PVP and a mean of 0.7 per cent. In patients with hypoproteinemia and a shortened albumin survival in the absence of proteinuria, Waldmann and Gordon found that from 5 to 27 per cent of the intravenous dose of Cr^{51} albumin was excreted in a 4-day stool specimen with a mean of 12 per cent compared to a mean of 5 per cent

in the patients given I^{131} PVP. In contrast to iodine, the chromium ion is not secreted into the gastrointestinal tract. Supplementing an orally administered anion exchange resin Amberlite (RIA-400) to the intravenous injection of I^{131}-labeled albumin has been advocated to chelate iodide in the intestinal lumen and to prevent its reabsorption.

Reduction of the dietary fat intake may not only lessen the steatorrhea but also the enteric protein loss. Mistilis reported fecal excretion of 8.5 gm. of fat per day on a fat-free diet and felt that this was evidence of excessive enteric loss of fat as opposed to

Figure 25-28. Twenty-four-hour fecal-fat output. Dietary fat intake in the first 3 days was 70 gm. per day and during the last 5 days 130 gm. per day. (From Mistilis, S. P., Skyring, A. P., and Stephen, D. D.: Lancet, 1:77, 1965.)

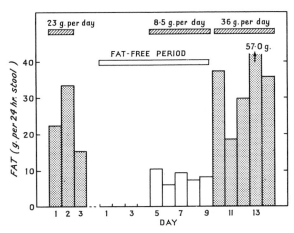

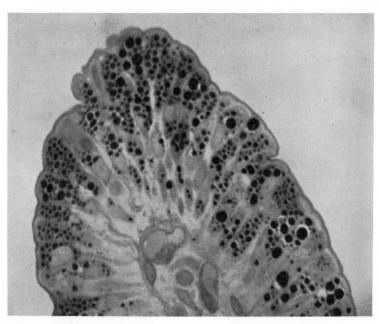

Figure 25–29.   Jejunal biopsy after 18 hours of fasting. Epithelial cells at tip of villus are filled with many dark staining lipid droplets; none are visible in submucosa. (Osmium counterstained with Giemsa; ×800.) (From Isselbacher, K. J., Scheig, R., Plotkin, G. R., and Caulfield, J. B.: Medicine, *43:*347, 1964.)

malabsorption. Increasing the fat intake to 130 gm. per day resulted in a marked increase in the steatorrhea, which was interpreted as indicative of overloading an already obstructed lymphatic system (Fig. 25–28). He believes that the partial block of the intestinal lymphatic system producing retrograde lymph flow is likely to become more complete on a high fat diet, which would result not only in an increase in the degree of steatorrhea but also in the degree of enteric protein loss.

In Whipple's disease, treatment with antibiotics and steroids may effect a reversal of the enteric protein loss.

In the cases of constrictive pericarditis, the excessive enteric protein loss may be stopped by surgical correction of the cardiac lesion. In this connection the observations of Blalock following occlusion of the superior vena cava in dogs with its obstruction to the outflow of lymph from the thoracic ducts and its resultant chylous effusion, as well as stasis and dilatation of the lymphatics of the gastrointestinal system, are of interest.

Waldmann and associates have observed patients with severe hypoproteinemia and edema in association with marked eosinophilia. Some of these patients had asthmatic-like symptoms and marked amelioration of the gastrointestinal protein loss following corticosteroid administration. They would speak of an "allergic enteropathy" in which an important allergen appears to be milk.

Circumferential Small Bowel Ulcer

An increasing frequency of small bowel ulcer has been noted in patients taking oral diuretics and enteric-coated potassium chloride tablets for hypertensive cardiovascular disease. Recurrent attacks of crampy abdominal pain associated with nausea and occasionally with vomiting are prominent. Intermittent abdominal distention and postprandial pain have also been noted. Intestinal obstruction is common, and hemorrhage and perforation have also been reported. The ulcers are circumferential, overlying a zone of cicatricial narrowing with the mucosa and musculature of the proximal bowel showing varying degrees of edema and hemorrhagic infiltration. There is no accompanying evidence of vascular occlusion. Boley et al., on the basis of experimental observations in dogs, believe that a high concentration of potassium chloride in the veins of the absorbing segment results in venous spasm and stasis, submucosal edema, and subsequent ulceration. Morgenstern and Panish found that in the dog local application of potassium chloride in high concentration not only produces a tonic contraction of the intestine, but also a superficial mucosal lesion which promptly heals in the absence of further injury. They were unable to produce any lesion with chlorothiazide alone.

Congenital Beta-Lipoprotein Deficiency (A-Beta-Lipoproteinemia, Acanthocytosis)

A hereditary disorder has been recently described characterized by steatorrhea, neurologic disorder (progressive ataxic neuropathy), atypical retinitis pigmentosa, and abnormal red cells with spinelike or thornlike projections (acanthocytes) resembling crenated erythrocytes. The blood levels of cholesterol, triglyceride, and phospholipid are greatly reduced, and beta-lipoproteins are either absent or markedly deficient. The villi and epithelial cells of the intestinal mucosa have been reported normal in structure but filled with numerous fat droplets (Fig. 25–29). The major clinical and laboratory features are given in Figure 25–30.

Isselbacher and associates have adduced evidence that the steatorrhea and mucosal accumulation of lipid are not due to impaired synthesis of triglycerides but to an interference in the formation of chylomicrons and thus the transport of lipid from the intestinal cells into the lymph. The mechanisms explaining the neurologic changes and acanthocytosis are unknown.

Salt and his associates first reported the absence of beta-lipoproteins and chylomicrons and considerable depletion of alpha lipoprotein in this disorder. Ways and his associates found that the linoleic acid content of the acanthocytes was depressed to levels of only 20 per cent of normal. In addition, linoleic acid was decreased in all the lipid fractions of the plasma where it normally occurs. Isselbacher believes that the primary defect is not in the absorption or metabolism of linoleic acid, as has been suggested by others, but in the congenital inability to form the beta-lipoprotein molecule. In support of this are the facts that essential fatty acid deficiency does not produce the changes characterizing this disease and that the administration of linoleic acid in liberal doses is without recognizable benefit. The tissue depletion of linoleic acid is probably secondary to the impaired intestinal absorption of long-chain fatty acids. Furthermore, Sebesin and Isselbacher have observed similar biochemical and morphologic changes when intestinal protein and lipoprotein synthesis are experimentally inhibited by puromycin.

Major Clinical and Laboratory Features in Patients with Congenital β-Lipoprotein Deficiency

A. *Red Blood Cells*
 1. Appearance and shape—
  a. Spiny or thorny—hence *acanthocytes.*
  b. Shape prevents rouleaux formation; extremely low sedimentation rate.
  c. Acanthocytes converted to normal cells in vitro by Tween (33).
 2. Composition of membrane phospholipids—
  a. Fatty acids—decreased linoleic acid content (38).
  b. Phospholipid distribution—decreased lecithin; increased sphingomyelin (23, 38).
B. *Serum Lipids*
 1. β-lipoproteins—low to absent.
 2. Cholesterol and phospholipids—low.
 3. Triglycerides—very low.
 4. Free fatty acids—slightly depressed.
C. *Intestinal Tract*
 1. Steatorrhea; impaired fat absorption; onset in infancy.
 2. Mucosa—normal shaped villi; fat in epithelial cells.
 3. Often normal absorption of glucose, xylose, Vitamin B_{12}.
D. *Neurologic Features*
 1. Cerebellar, posterior column, peripheral nerve involvement.
 2. Great resemblance to Friedreich's ataxia.
 3. Onset usually after age 5.
E. *Retina—Retinitis Pigmentosa*
 1. Not present in all patients.
 2. May be late in onset.

Figure 25–30. (From Isselbacher, K. J., Scheig, R., Plotkin, G. R., and Caulfield, J. B.: Medicine, *43:* 347, 1964.)

In the patient studied by Salt and his associates, a gluten-free diet for 10 weeks failed to improve fat absorption, while a low-fat diet (20 gm. daily) resulted in weight gain, improvement in the general condition, and cessation of diarrhea.

REFERENCES

Abbot, F. K., Mack, M., and Wolf, S.: The relation of sustained contraction of the duodenum to nausea and vomiting. Gastroenterology, 20:238, 1952.

Ackerman, L. V., and del Regato, J. A.: Cancer: Diagnosis, Treatment and Prognosis. St. Louis, C. V. Mosby Co., 1947.

Adlersberg, D., et al.: The roentgenologic appearance of the small intestine in sprue. Gastroenterology, 26:548, 1954.

Almy, T. P.: A refractory case of idiopathic steatorrhea (nontropical sprue), with observations on the therapeutic effects of salt-poor human albumin and of the adrenocorticotropic hormone. Ann. Int. Med., 34:1041, 1951.

Anderson, C. M., et al.: The influence of gluten and antibacterial agents on fat absorption in the sprue syndrome. Gastroenterologia, 81:98, 1954.

Anderson, C. M., and Townley, R. R. W.: The effects of a gluten-free diet on intestinal histology in coeliac disease. In Ciba Foundation Study Group No. 14 on Intestinal Biopsy. Boston, Little, Brown & Co., 1962.

Anderson, J. A., Ziegler, M. R., and Doeden, D.: Banana feeding and urinary excretion of 5-hydroxyindolacetic acid. Science, 127:236, 1958.

Armstrong, F. B., Margen, S., and Tarver, H.: Plasma protein. VII. Site of degradation of serum albumin. Proc. Soc. Exper. Biol. Med., 103:592, 1960.

Ashworth, C. T., and Chears, W. C., Jr.: Follow-up of intestinal biopsy in nontropical sprue after gluten-free diet and remission. Fed. Proc., 21: 880, 1962.

Ashworth, C. T., Chears, W. C., Jr., Sanders, E., and Pearce, M. B.: Nontropical sprue. Fine structure of the intestinal epithelial lesion. Arch. Path., 71:13, 1961.

Auricchio, S., et al.: Intestinal glycosidase activities in congenital malabsorption of disaccharides. J. Ped., 66:555, 1965.

Badenoch, J.: The blind loop syndrome. In Jones, F. A. (ed.): Modern Trends in Gastroenterology, Second Series. New York, Paul B. Hoeber, Inc., 1958.

Baker, D. R., Schrader, W. H., and Hitchcock, C. R.: Small-bowel ulceration apparently associated with thiazide and potassium therapy. J.A.M.A., 190:586, 1964.

Barker, W. H., and Hummel, L. E.: Macrocytic anemia in association with intestinal strictures and anastomoses. Bull. Johns Hopkins Hospital, 64: 215, 1939.

Bassen, F. A., and Kornzweig, A. L.: Malformation of the erythrocytes in a case of atypical retinitis pigmentosa. Blood, 5:381, 1950.

Bennett, L. R., Bennett, V. C., Shaver, A., and Grachus, T.: Absorption and distribution of vitamin A in x-irradiated rats. Proc. Soc. Exper. Biol. Med., 74:439, 1950.

Benson, G. D., Kowlessar, O. D., and Sleisenger, M. H.: Adult celiac disease with emphasis upon response to the gluten-free diet. Medicine, 43:1, 1964.

Bergström, S., and Borgström, B.: Intestinal absorption of fats. In Holman, R. T., Lundberg, W. O., and Malkin, T. (eds.): Progress in the Chemistry of Fats and Other Lipids, Vol. 3, p. 351. London, Pergamon Press, 1955.

Berson, S. A., Yalow, R. S., Schreiber, S. S., and Post, J.: Tracer experiments with I131 labeled human serum albumin: Distribution and degradation studies. J. Clin. Invest., 32:746, 1953.

Bickel, G., and Rentchnick, P.: The acute staphylococci enterocolitis of antibiotic therapy. Internat. Med. Digest, 64:325, 1954.

Bingham, J. R.: The effects of sympathectomy on abdominal pain in man. Gastroenterology, 15:18, 1950.

Bingham, J. R.: Effect of combined sympathectomy and vagectomy on the gastrointestinal tract. J.A.M.A., 146:1406, 1951.

Bingham, J. R., Ingelfinger, F. J., and Smithwick, R. H.: The effects of sympathectomy on the motility of the human gastrointestinal and biliary tracts. Gastroenterology, 15:6, 1950.

Birke, G., et al.: The role of the gastrointestinal tract in the protein metabolism under normal conditions. In Schwartz, M., and Vesin, P. (eds.): Plasma Proteins and Gastrointestinal Tract in Health and Disease. Baltimore, Williams & Wilkins Co., 1963.

Black, D. A. K.: Salt deficiency in sprue. Lancet, 2:671, 1946.

Blainey, J. D., Cooke, W. T., Quinton, A., and Scott, K. W.: The measurement of total exchangeable potassium in man, with particular reference to patients with steatorrhea. Clin. Sci., 13:165, 1954.

Blalock, A. R., Cunningham, R. S., and Robinson, C. S.: Experimental production of chylothorax by occlusion of the superior vena cava. Ann. Surg., 104:359, 1936.

Blomstrand, R.: Studies on fat absorption in the malabsorption syndrome with the aid of labeled fatty acids. In Proceedings of the World Congress of Gastroenterology, vol. 1. Baltimore, Williams & Wilkins Co., 1959.

Boley, S. J., et al.: Experimental evaluation of thiazides and potassium as a cause of small-bowel ulcer. J.A.M.A., 192:763, 1965.

Bookstein, J. J., French, A. B., and Pollard, H. M.: Protein-losing gastroenteropathy; concepts derived from lymphangiography. Am. J. Dig. Dis., 10:573, 1965.

Booth, C. C.: I. Classification of malabsorption syndrome. Brit. J. Radiol., 33:201, 1960.

Booth, C. C.: The metabolic effects of intestinal resection in man. Postgrad. Med. J., 37:725, 1961.

Booth, C. C., Alldis, D., and Read, A. E.: Studies on the site of fat absorption. 2. Fat balances after resection of varying amounts of the small intestine in man. Gut, 2:168, 1961.

Booth, C. C., and Mollin, D. L.: The site of absorption of vitamin B_{12} in man. Lancet, 1:18, 1959.

Booth, C. C., Stewart, J. S., Holmes, R., and Brackenbury, W.: Dissecting microscope appearances of intestinal mucosa. In Ciba Foundation Study Group No. 14 on Intestinal Biopsy. Boston, Little, Brown & Co., 1962.

Borgström, B.: Metabolism of Glycerides. In Bloch, K. (ed.): Lipide Metabolism. New York, John Wiley & Sons, 1960.

Borgström, B.: Digestion and absorption of fat. Gastroenterology, 43:216, 1962.

Borgström, B., Lundh, G., and Hofmann, A.: The site of absorption of conjugated bile salts in man. Gastroenterology, 45:229, 1963.

Brown, A. L., Jr.: Microvilli of the human jejunal epithelial cell. J. Cell. Biol., 12:623, 1962.

Bruce, J.: Post-operative necrosis of the intestinal mucous membrane. Gastroenterology, 81:74, 1954.

Butterworth, C. E., Jr., et al.: Folic acid absorption, excretion, and leukocyte concentration in tropical sprue. J. Lab. & Clin. Med., 50:673, 1957.

Butterworth, C. E., Jr., and Perez-Santiago, E.: Jejunal biopsies in sprue. Ann. Int. Med., 48:8, 1958.

Caird, D. M., and Ellis, H.: Intramural haematoma of the duodenum: A report of a case and a review of the literature. Brit. J. Surg., 45:389, 1957–58.

Cameron, D. G., Watson, G. M., and Witts, L. J.: The clinical association of macrocytic anemia with intestinal stricture and anastomosis. Blood, 4: 793, 1949.

Cameron, D. G., Watson, G. M., and Witts, L. J.: Experimental production of macrocytic anemia by operations on intestinal tract. Blood, 4:803, 1949.

Card, W. I.: "Blind loop" syndrome. In Symposium on disorders of the small intestine (excluding the duodenum). Proc. Roy. Soc. Med., 52:28, 1959.

Christensen, A. K., and Fawcett, D. W.: The fine stricture of testicular interstitial cells in the opossum. Anat. Rec., 136:333, 1960.

Citrin, Y., Sterling, K., and Halsted, J. A.: The mechanism of hypoproteinemia associated with giant hypertrophy of the gastric mucosa. New England J. Med., 257:906, 1957.

Clayton, B. E., and Cotton, D. A.: A study of malabsorption after resection of the entire jejunum and the proximal half of the ileum. Gut, 2:18, 1961.

Coniglio, J. G., et al.: The effect of x-irradiation on fat metabolism. Peaceful Uses of Atomic Energy, New York, United Nations, 11:306, 1956.

Connell, A. M., Rowlands, E. N., and Wilcox, P. B.: Serotonin, bananas and diarrhea. Gut, 1:44, 1960.

Cooke, W. T.: Steatorrhea and regional ileitis. In Jones, F. A. (ed.): Modern Trends in Gastro-enterology. London, Butterworth & Co., Ltd., 1952.

Cooke, W. T.: Water and electrolyte upsets in the steatorrhea syndrome. J. Mt. Sinai Hosp., 24: 221, 1957.

Cooke, W. T., Fowler, D. I., Cox, E. V., Gaddie, R., and Meynell, M. J.: The clinical significance of seromucoids in regional ileitis and ulcerative colitis. Gastroenterology, 34:910, 1958.

Cooke, W. T., Thomas, G., Mangall, D., and Cross, H.: Observations on the faecal excretion of total solids, nitrogen, sodium, potassium, water and fat in the steatorrhea syndrome. Clin. Sc., 12: 223, 1953.

Cooke, W. T., et al.: The clinical and metabolic significance of jejunal diverticula. Gut, 4:115, 1963.

Cox, E. V., Meynell, M. J., Cooke, W. T., and Gaddie, R.: The folic acid excretion test in the steatorrhea syndrome. Gastroenterology, 35:390, 1958.

Crane, R. K.: Hypothesis for mechanism of intestinal active transport of sugars. Fed. Proc., 21:891, 1962.

Crane, R. K.: Enzymes and malabsorption: A concept of brush border membrane disease. Gastroenterology, 50:254, 1966.

Crane, R. K.: Personal communication.

Crohn, B. B., and Yarnis, H.: Regional Ileitis, 2nd ed. New York, Grune & Stratton, 1958.

Crosby, W. H., and Kugler, H. W.: Intraluminal biopsy of the small intestine. Am. J. Dig. Dis., 2:236, 1957.

Curran, R. C., and Creamer, B.: Ultrastructural changes in some disorders of the small intestine associated with malabsorption. J. Path. Bact., 86:1, 1963.

Dagliesh, C. E., Kelly, W., and Horning, E. C.: Excretion of a sulphatoxy derivative of skatole in pathological states in man. Biochem. J., 70:13P, 1958.

Dahlqvist, A.: Specificity of the human intestinal disaccharidases and implications for hereditary disaccharide intolerance. J. Clin. Invest., 41: 463, 1962.

Dahlqvist, A.: The intestinal disaccharidases and disaccharide intolerance. Gastroenterology, 43: 694, 1962.

Dahlqvist, A.: Intestinal disaccharides. In Durand, P. (ed.): Disorders Due to Intestinal Defective Carbohydrate Digestion and Absorption. Rome, Il Pensiero Scientifico, 1964.

Dahlqvist, A., Hammond, J. B., Crane, R. K., Dunphy, J. V., and Littman, A.: Intestinal lactase deficiency and lactose intolerance in adults. Preliminary report. Gastroenterology, 45:488, 1963.

Dahlqvist, A., Hammond, J. B., Crane, R. K., Dunphy, J. V., and Littman, A.: Assay of disaccharidase activities in peroral biopsies of the small-intestinal mucosa. Acta Gastroent. Belg., 27:543, 1964.

Davis, R. B.: Observations on the occurrence and significance of serotonin in carcinoid tumors. Am. J. Path., 41:693, 1962.

Dawson, A. M., and Isselbacher, K. J.: Studies on lipid metabolism in the small intestine with observations on the role of bile salts. J. Clin. Invest., 39:730, 1960.

Dearing, W. H., and Heilman, F. R.: Micrococcic (staphylococcic) enteritis as a complication of antibiotic therapy. Its response to erythromycin. Proc. Staff Meet., Mayo Clin., 28:121, 1953.

Deuel, H. J., Jr.: The Lipids, vol. 2. New York, Interscience Publishers, Inc., 1955.

Dicke, W. K.: Coeliakie. M.D. Thesis, Utrecht, 1950.

Dickinson, C. J., Hartog, M., and Shiner, M.: A report of two cases of Whipple's disease diagnosed by peroral small intestinal biopsy. Gut, 1:163, 1960.

Dixon, C. F., and Weismann, R. E.: Acute pseudomembranous enteritis or enterocolitis: A complication following intestinal surgery. S. Clin. North America, 28:999, 1948.

Dixon, J. M. S., and Paulley, J. W.: Bacteriological and histological studies of the small intestine of rats treated with mecamylamine. Gut, 4:169, 1963.

Donaldson, J. K., and Stout, B. F.: Mesenteric thrombosis (arterial and venous types as separate clinical entities): A clinical and experimental study. Am. J. Surg., 29:208, 1935.

Donaldson, R. M., Jr.: Normal bacterial populations of the intestine and their relation to intestinal function. New England J. Med., 270:938, 994, 1050, 1964.

Dormandy, T. L.: Peutz-Jeghers syndrome. In Jones, F. A. (ed.): Modern Trends in Gastroenterology, Second Series. New York, Paul B. Hoeber, Inc., 1958.

Duncan, R. D., Ferrell, T. E., and Hansbro, G. L.: Acute mesenteric venous thrombosis. Am. J. Surg., 83:205, 1952.

Dunphy, J. V.: Abdominal pain of vascular origin. Am. J. Med. Sc., *192:*109, 1936.

Dunphy, J. V., et al.: Intestinal lactase deficit in adults. Gastroenterology, *49:*12, 1965.

Edwards, H. C.: Diverticulosis of the small intestine. Ann. Surg., *103:*320, 1936.

Estren, S.: The blood and bone marrow in idiopathic sprue. J. Mt. Sinai Hosp., *24:*304, 1957.

Fairley, N. H., and Kilner, T. P.: Gastrojejunocolic fistula with megalocytic anemia simulating sprue. Lancet, *2:*1335, 1931.

Farrar, J. T.: Study of gastrointestinal motility by a radiotelemetering capsule. In Rider, J. A., and Moller, H. C.: Disturbances in Gastrointestinal Motility. Springfield, Charles C Thomas, 1959.

Fawcett, D. W.: Morphological considerations of lipid transport in the liver. In Proceedings of an International Symposium on Lipid Transport. Springfield, Charles C Thomas, 1964.

Feldberg, W., and Smith, A. N.: Release of histamine by tryptamine and 5-hydroxytryptamine. Brit. J. Pharm., *8:*406, 1953.

Felson, B., and Levin, E. J.: Intramural hematoma of the duodenum: Diagnostic roentgen sign. Radiology, *63:*823, 1954.

Fernandes, J., van de Kamer, J. H., and Weijers, H. A.: Differences in absorption of the various fatty acids studied in children with steatorrhea. J. Clin. Invest., *41:*488, 1962.

Finney, J. M. T.: Gastro-enterostomy for cicatrizing ulcer of the pylorus. Bull. Johns Hopkins Hosp., *4:*53, 1893.

Flear, C. T. G., Cawley, R., Quinton, A., and Cooke, W. T.: The simultaneous determination of total exchangeable sodium and potassium and its significance with particular reference to congestive cardiac failure and the steatorrhea syndrome. Clin. Sc., *17:*81, 1958.

Floch, M. H., Caldwell, W. L., and Sheehy, T. W.: A histopathologic basis for the interpretation of small bowel roentgenography in tropical sprue. Am. J. Roentgenol., *87:*709, 1962.

Fone, D. J., et al.: Jejunal biopsy in adult celiac disease and allied disorders. Lancet, *1:*933, 1960.

Fowler, D., and Cooke, W. T.: Diagnostic significance of d-xylose excretion test. Gut, *1:*67, 1960.

Frazer, A. C.: A new mechanism of vitamin deprivation, with special reference to the sprue syndrome. Brit. Med. J., *2:*731, 1949.

Frazer, A. C.: The physiology of fat absorption. In Jones, F. A. (ed.): Modern Trends in Gastroenterology. London, Butterworth & Co., Ltd., 1952.

Frazer, A. C., French, J. M., and Thompson, M. D.: Radiographic studies showing the induction of a segmentation pattern in the small intestine in normal human subjects. Brit. J. Radiol., *22:*123, 1949.

French, J. M., Hawkins, C. F., and Cooke, W. T.: Clinical experience with the gluten-free diet in idiopathic steatorrhea. In Proc. World Congress of Gastroenterology. Baltimore, Williams & Wilkins Co., 1959, vol. 1, p. 615.

Gamble, J. L., and McIver, M. A.: A study of the effects of pyloric obstruction in rabbits. J. Clin. Invest., *1:*531, 1925.

Gamble, J. L., and Ross, S. G.: The factors in the de-

hydration following pyloric obstruction. J. Clin. Invest., *1:*403, 1925.

Gardner, F. H., and Perez-Santiago, E.: Oral absorption tolerance tests in tropical sprue. Arch. Int. Med., *98:*467, 1956.

Gellman, D. D.: Diverticulosis of the small intestine with steatorrhea and megaloblastic anemia. Lancet, *2:*873, 1956.

Girdwood, R. H., and Doig, A., cited by Card, W. I.: "Blind loop" syndrome. In Symposium on disorders of the small intestine (excluding the duodenum). Proc. Roy. Soc. Med., *52:*28, 1959.

Gitlin, D.: Genetic defects in protein metabolism. Pediat. Clin. North America, *10:*319, 1963.

Glenert, J., Jarnum, S., and Riemer, S.: Animal investigations on the normal albumin breakdown in the digestive tract. In Schwartz, M., and Vesin, P. (eds.): Plasma Proteins and Gastrointestinal Tract in Health and Disease. Baltimore, Williams & Wilkins Co., 1963.

Gold, M. A., and Sawyer, J. G.: Diverticula of the gastrointestinal tract. Ann. Int. Med., *36:*956, 1952.

Goodman, R. D., Lewis, A. E., and Schuck, E. A.: Effects of x-irradiation on gastrointestinal transit and absorption availability. Am. J. Physiol., *169:*242, 1952.

Gordon, R. S.: Exudative enteropathy. Lancet, *1:*325, 1959.

Gordon, R. S., Bartter, F. C., and Waldmann, T.: Idiopathic hypoalbuminemias. Clinical staff conference at the National Institutes of Health. Ann. Int. Med., *51:*553, 1959.

Goulston, S. J. M., and McGovern, V. J.: Pseudo-membranous colitis. Gut, *6:*207, 1965.

Grasbeck, R., and Nyberg, W.: Inhibition of radio-vitamin B_{12} absorption by ethylenediamine tetraacetate (EDTA) and its reversal by calcium ions. Scand. J. Clin. & Lab. Invest., *10:*448, 1958.

Green, P. A., Wollaeger, E. E., and Scudmore, H. H.: Nontropical sprue, functional efficiency of small intestine after prolonged use of gluten-free diet. J.A.M.A., *171:*2157, 1959.

Haemmerli, U. P., et al.: Acquired milk intolerance in the adult caused by lactose malabsorption due to a selective deficiency of intestinal lactase activity. Am. J. Med., *38:*7, 1965.

Halsted, J. A., Lewis, P. M., and Gasster, M.: Absorption of radioactive vitamin B_{12} in syndrome of megaloblastic anemia associated with intestinal stricture or anastomosis. Am. J. Med., *20:*42, 1956.

Harrison, R. J., and Booth, C. C.: Massive resection of the small intestine after occlusion of the superior mesenteric artery. Gut, *1:*237, 1960.

Hartman, R. S., and others: An electron microscopic investigation of the jejunal epithelium in sprue. Gastroenterology, *38:*506, 1960.

Haverback, B. J.: Serotonin and gastrointestinal tract. Clin. Res., *6:*57, 1958.

Haverback, B. J., and Davidson, J. D.: Serotonin and the gastrointestinal tract. Gastroenterology, *35:*570, 1958.

Haverback, B. J., Dyce, B., and Thomas, H. V.: Indole metabolism in the malabsorption syndrome. New England J. Med., *262:*754, 1960.

Haverback, B. J., Sjoerdsma, A., and Terry, L. L.: Urinary excretion of the metabolite 5-hydroxyindolacetic acid in various clinical conditions. New England J. Med., 255:270, 1956.

Hilsman, J. H.: The color of feces following the instillation of citrated blood at various levels of the small intestine. J.M.A. Georgia, 39:402, 1950.

Hofmann, A. F.: Clinical implications of physicochemical studies on bile salts. Gastroenterology, 48:484, 1965.

Hofmann, A. F., and Borgström, B.: Physicochemical state of lipids in intestinal content during their digestion and absorption. Fed. Proc., 21:43, 1962.

Holman, H., Nickel, W. F., Jr., and Sleisenger, M. H.: Hypoproteinemia antedating intestinal lesions, and possibly due to excessive serum protein loss into the intestine. Am. J. Med., 27:963, 1959.

Holmes, R., Hourihane, D. O'B., and Booth, C. C.: The mucosa of the small intestine. Postgrad. Med. J., 37:717, 1961.

Holmes, R., Hourihane, D. O'B., and Booth, C. C.: Dissecting-microscope appearances of jejunal biopsy specimens from patients with "idiopathic steatorrhea." Lancet, 1:81, 1961.

Horning, E. C., and Dalgliesh, C. E.: The association of skatole-forming bacteria in the small intestine with the malabsorption syndrome and certain anemias. Biochem. J., 70:13P, 1958.

Ingelfinger, F. J.: Diseases of the small intestine. In Portis, S. A. (ed.): Diseases of the Digestive System, 3rd ed. Philadelphia, Lea & Febiger, 1953.

Ingelfinger, F. J.: Panel symposium. Chronic vascular insufficiency of the gastrointestinal tract: Abdominal angina. Gastroenterology, 45:789, 1963.

Ingelfinger, F. J., and Moss, R. E.: The motility of the small intestine in sprue. J. Clin. Invest., 22:345, 1943.

Isselbacher, K. J.: Personal communication.

Isselbacher, K. J., Scheig, R., Plotkin, G. R., and Caulfield, J. B.: Congenital β-lipoprotein deficiency: An hereditary disorder involving a defect in the absorption and transport of lipids. Medicine, 43:347, 1964.

Isselbacher, K. J., and Senior, J. R.: The intestinal absorption of carbohydrate and fat. Gastroenterology, 46:287, 1964.

Ito, S., and Winchester, R. J.: The fine structure of the gastric mucosa in the bat. J. Cell. Biol., 16:541, 1963.

Ivy, A. C.: Lecture notes: Physiology of Symptoms. Dept. Physiology, Northwestern University Medical School, 1945–1947.

Jackson, B. B.: Occlusion of the Superior Mesenteric Artery. Springfield, Charles C Thomas, 1963.

Jackson, W. P. U.: Massive resection of the small intestine. In Jones, F. A. (ed.): Modern Trends in Gastroenterology, Second Series. New York, Paul B. Hoeber, Inc., 1958.

Jacobson, E. D., Chodos, R. B., and Faloon, W. W.: An experimental malabsorption syndrome induced by neomycin. Am. J. Med., 28:524, 1960.

James, A. T., Webb, J. P. W., and Kellock, T. D.: The occurrence of unusual fatty acids in faecal lipids from human beings with normal and abnormal fat absorption. Biochem. J., 78:333, 1961.

Jarnum, S., and Petersen, V. P.: Protein-losing enteropathy. Lancet, 1:417, 1961.

Jarnum, S., and Schwartz, M.: Hypoalbuminemia in gastric carcinoma. Gastroenterology, 38:769, 1960.

Jarnum, S., and Schwartz, M.: Diagnosis of gastrointestinal protein loss by means of ^{131}I-labeled albumin. In Schwartz, M., and Vesin, P. (eds.): Plasma Proteins and Gastrointestinal Tract in Health and Disease. Baltimore, Williams & Wilkins Co., 1963.

Jeejeebhoy, K. N.: Cause of hypoalbuminaeminia in patients with gastrointestinal and cardiac disease. Lancet, 1:343, 1962.

Jeejeebhoy, K. N.: The use of an ion-exchange resin to measure gastrointestinal albumin catabolism (a new method). In Schwartz, M. and Vesin, P. (eds.): Plasma Proteins and Gastrointestinal Tract in Health and Disease. Baltimore, Williams & Wilkins Co., 1963.

Jeejeebhoy, K. N., and Coghill, N. F.: Measurement of gastrointestinal protein loss by a new method. Gut, 2:123, 1961.

Jeffries, G. H., Chapman, A., and Sleisenger, M. H.: Low-fat diet in intestinal lymphangiectasia. New England J. Med., 270:761, 1964.

Jeffries, G. H., Holman, H. R., and Sleisenger, M. H.: Plasma proteins and the gastrointestinal tract. New England J. Med., 266:652, 1962.

Jeffries, G. H., and Sleisenger, M. H.: Abnormal enteric loss of protein in gastrointestinal diseases. In Schwartz, M., and Vesin, P. (eds.): Plasma Proteins and Gastrointestinal Tract in Health and Disease. Baltimore, Williams & Wilkins Co., 1963.

Jeffries, G. H., Weser, E., and Sleisenger, M. H.: Malabsorption. Gastroenterology, 46:434, 1964.

Jeghers, H., McKusick, V. A., and Katz, K. H.: Generalized intestinal polyposis and melanin spots of the oral mucosa, lips and digits. New England J. Med., 241:993, 1949.

Johnston, J. M.: Recent developments in the mechanism of fat absorption. In Paoletti, R., and Kritchevsky, D. (eds.): Advances in Lipid Research, Vol. 1. New York, Academic Press, 1963.

Jones, C. M.: Digestive Tract Pain, Diagnosis and Treatment: Experimental Observations. New York, Macmillan, 1938.

Joske, R. A., Shamma, M. H., and Drummey, G. D.: Intestinal malabsorption following temporary occlusion of the superior mesenteric artery. Am. J. Med., 25:449, 1958.

van de Kamer, J. H., Huinik, H. T. B., and Weijers, H. A.: Rapid method for the determination of fat in feces. J. Biol. Chem., 177:347, 1949.

van de Kamer, J. H., and Weijers, H. A.: Coeliac disease. Some experiments on the cause of the harmful effect of wheat gliadin. Acta Pediat., 44:465, 1955.

Kern, F., Jr.: Fat absorption. American College of Physicians Postgraduate Course No. 15 on Current Concepts in Gastroenterology. Montreal, Canada, May 24–26, 1965.

Kinder, C. H.: Paralytic ileus. Guys Hosp. Rep., 100:362, 1951.

Kinney, J. M., Goldwyn, R. M., Barr, J. S., Jr., and Moore, F. D.: Loss of the entire jejunum and ileum, and the ascending colon. Management of a patient. J.A.M.A., 179:529, 1962.

Kleckner, M. S., Bargen, J. A., and Baggenstoss, A. H.: Acute pseudomembranous enterocolitis. Proc. Staff Meet., Mayo Clin., 28:313, 1953.

Kowlessar, O. D., Williams, R. C., Law, D. H., and Sleisenger, M. H.: Urinary excretion of 5-hydroxyindolacetic acid in diarrheal states, with special reference to nontropical sprue. New England J. Med., 259:340, 1958.

Kremen, A. J., Linner, J. H., and Nelson, C. H.: Experimental evaluation of nutritional importance of proximal and distal small intestine. Ann. Surg., 140:439, 1954.

Laplane, R. et al.: L'intolérance aux sucres à transfert intestinal actif. Ses rapports avec l'intolérance au lactose et le syndrome coeliaque. Arch. Franc. Pédiat., 19:895, 1962.

Laster, L., Waldmann, T. A., Fenster, L. F., and Singleton, J. W.: Reversible enteric protein loss in Whipple's disease. American Gastroenterological Association, April 27, 1962, New York.

Lawrason, F. D., Alpert, E., Mohr, F. L., and McMahon, F. G.: Ulcerative-obstructive lesions of the small intestine. J.A.M.A., 191:641, 1965.

Laws, J. W., Shawdon, H., Booth, C. C., and Stewart, J. S.: Correlation of radiological and histological findings in idiopathic steatorrhoea. Brit. Med. J., 1:1311, 1963.

Leading Articles: Carcinoid flush. Lancet, 1:676, 1962.

Leading Articles: New light on carcinoid flush. Lancet, 1:539, 1964.

Leading Articles: Lymphatics and the gut. Brit. Med. J., 1:1062, 1964.

Lesher, S.: Cytologic changes in the mouse intestine under daily exposure to gamma rays. J. Nat. Cancer Inst., 19:419, 1957.

Levine, R. J., and Sjoersma, A.: Pressor amines and the carcinoid flush. Ann. Int. Med., 58:818, 1963.

Lewis, G. T., and Partin, H. C.: Fecal fat on an essentially fat-free diet. J. Lab. & Clin. Med., 44:91, 1954.

Lewis, T., Pickering, S. W., and Rothchild, P.: Observations upon muscular pain in intermittent claudication. Heart, 15:359, 1931.

Lewis, W. H.: Pinocytosis. Bull. Johns Hopkins Hosp., 49:17, 1931.

Lindholmer, B., Nyman, E., and Räf, L.: Nonspecific stenosing ulceration of the small bowel: A preliminary report. Acta Chir. Scand., 128:310, 1964.

Lindquist, B., and Meeuwisse, G. W.: Chronic diarrhoea caused by monosaccharide malabsorption. Acta Paediat., 51:674, 1962.

Lindquist, B., Meeuwisse, G., and Melin, K.: Glucose-galactose malabsorption. Lancet, 2:666, 1962.

Lipkin, M.: Cell proliferation in the gastrointestinal tract of man. Fed. Proc., 24:10, 1965.

Littman, A.: Personal communication.

Littman, A., and Hammond, J. B.: Progress in gastroenterology: Diarrhea in adults caused by deficiency in intestinal disaccharidases. Gastroenterology, 48:237, 1965.

Luke, R. G., Lees, W., and Rudick, J.: Appearances of

the stools after the introduction of blood into the caecum. Gut, 5:77, 1964.

Majcher, S. J., Stubrin, M. I., Dyce, B. J., and Haverback, B. J.: Flushing, diarrhea, and peptic ulcer associated with abnormal histamine metabolism. Gastroenterology, 48:832, 1965.

Masson, N. L., and Stayman, J. W., Jr.: Intestinal angina. Am. J. Surg., 104:500, 1962.

Meyer, L. M., et al.: Oral administration of Co⁶⁰ B₁₂ in tropical sprue and hepatic cirrhosis and diarrhea. Proc. Soc. Exper. Biol. Med., 83:681, 1953.

Mickelsen, O.: Intestinal synthesis of vitamins in the nonruminant. Vitamins & Hormones, 14:1, 1956.

Mier, M., Schwartz, S. O., and Boshes, B.: Acanthrocytosis, pigmentary degeneration of the retina and ataxic neuropathy: A genetically determined syndrome with associated metabolic disorder. Blood, 16:1586, 1960.

Mikkelsen, W. P., and Berne, C. J.: Intestinal angina. S. Clin. North America, 42:1321, 1962.

Mikkelsen, W. P., and Zaro, J. A., Jr.: Intestinal angina: Report of a case with preoperative diagnosis and surgical relief. New England J. Med., 260:912, 1959.

Miller, D., and Crane, R. K.: The digestive function of the epithelium of the small intestine. II. Localization of disaccharide hydrolysis in the isolated brush border portion of intestinal epithelial cells. Biochem. Biophys. Acta, 52:293, 1961.

Mistilis, S. P., Skyring, A. P., and Stephen, D. D.: Intestinal lymphangiectasia. Lancet, 1:77, 1965.

Moertel, C. G., Beahrs, O. H., Woolner, L. B., and Tyce, G. M.: "Malignant carcinoid syndrome" associated with noncarcinoid tumors. New England J. Med., 273:244, 1965.

Mollin, D. L., Booth, C. C., and Chanarin, I.: The pathogenesis of deficiency of vitamin B₁₂ and folic acid in idiopathic steatorrhea. In Proceedings of the World Congress of Gastroenterology, vol. 1. Baltimore, Williams & Wilkins Co., 1959.

Moore, R. M.: Some experimental observations relating to visceral pain. Surgery, 3:534, 1938.

Morgenstern, L., Freilich, M., and Panish, J. F.: The circumferential small bowel ulcer. J.A.M.A., 191:637, 1965.

Morgenstern, L., and Panish, J.: The pathogenesis and clinical diagnosis of the circumferential small bowel ulcer. Gastroenterology, 48:835, 1965.

Morris, G. C., Jr., and DeBakey, M. E.: Abdominal angina—diagnosis and surgical treatment. J.A.M.A., 176:89, 1961.

Morson, B. C.: Pathology of carcinoid tumors. In Jones, F. A. (ed.): Modern Trends in Gastroenterology, Second Series. New York, Paul B. Hoeber, Inc., 1958.

Moss, W. T.: The effect of irradiating the exteriorized small bowel on sugar absorption. Am. J. Roentgenol., 78:850, 1957.

Nadel, H., and Gardner, F. H.: Bacteriologic assay of small bowel secretion in tropical sprue. Am. J. Trop. Med., 5:686, 1956.

Norman, A., and Sjovall, J.: On the transformation and enterohepatic circulation of cholic acid in the rat. J. Biol. Chem., 233:872, 1958.

Nunez-Montiel, O., Bauza, C. A., Brunser, O., and Sepulveda, H.: Ultrastructural variations of the jejunum in the malabsorption syndrome. Lab. Invest., *12:*16, 1963.

Nusslé, D., et al.: Pertes digestives de protéines et syndrome néphrotique. In Schwartz, M., and Vesin, P. (eds.): Plasma Proteins and Gastrointestinal Tract in Health and Disease. Baltimore, Williams & Wilkins Co., 1963.

Nusslé, D., et al.: Diagnostic et localisation des pertes de protéines dans le tube digestif par l'analyse immunochimique du contenu gastro-intestinal. In Schwartz, M., and Vesin, P. (eds.): Plasma Proteins and Gastrointestinal Tract in Health and Disease. Baltimore, Williams & Wilkins Co., 1963.

Oates, J. A., et al.: Release of a kinin peptide in the carcinoid syndrome. Lancet, *1:*514, 1964.

Padykula, H. A.: Recent functional interpretations of intestinal morphology. Fed. Proc., *21:*873, 1962.

Padykula, H. A., Strauss, E. W., Ladman, A. J., and Gardner, F. H.: A morphologic and histochemical analysis of the human jejunal epithelium in nontropical sprue. Gastroenterology, *40:*735, 1961.

Palade, G., Siekevitz, P., and Caro, L. G.: Structure, chemistry and function of the pancreatic exocrine cell. In The Exocrine Pancreas: Normal and Abnormal Functions. Boston, Little, Brown & Co., 1961.

Palay, S. L., and Karlin, L. S.: An electron microscopic study of the intestinal villus. II. The pathway of fat absorption. J. Biophys., Biochem., & Cytol., *5:*363, 1959.

Palay, S., and Revel, J. P.: The morphology of fat absorption. In Proceedings of an International Symposium on Lipid Transport. Springfield, Charles C Thomas, 1964.

Pappenheimer, A. W., and Victor, J.: "Ceroid" pigment in human tissues. Am. J. Path., *22:*395, 1946.

Parkins, R. A.: Protein-losing enteropathy in the sprue syndrome. Lancet, *2:*1366, 1960.

Parr, J., Teree, T. M., and Larner, J.: Symptomatic hypoglycemia, visceral fatty metamorphosis, and aglycogenosis in an infant lacking glycogen synthetase and phosphorylase. Pediatrics, *35:*770, 1965.

Patzelt, V.: Der Darm. In von Mollendorff, W. (ed.): Handbuch der Mikroskopischen Anatomie des Menschen. Berlin, Springer, 1936.

Penner, A., and Bernheim, A. I.: Acute postoperative enterocolitis, a study on the pathologic nature of shock. Arch. Path., *27:*966, 1939.

Peternel, W. W.: Lactose tolerance in relation to intestinal lactase activity. Gastroenterology, *48:*299, 1965.

Petersen, V. P., and Hastrup, J.: Protein-losing enteropathy in constrictive pericarditis. Acta Med. Scand., *173:*401, 1963.

Pettet, J. D., Baggenstoss, A. H., Judd, E. S., Jr., and Dearing, L. H.: Generalized postoperative pseudomembranous enterocolitis. Proc. Staff Meet., Mayo Clin., *29:*333, 1954.

Phelps, P. C., and Rubin, C. E.: The fine structure of intestinal mucosa in celiac-sprue. Unpublished data.

Phelps, P. C., Rubin, C. E., and Luft, J. H.: Electron microscope techniques for studying absorption

of fat in man with some observations on pinocytosis. Gastroenterology, *46:*134, 1964.

Phillips, B. P., and Wolfe, P. A.: The use of germfree guinea pigs in studies on the microbial interrelationships in amoebiasis. Ann. New York Acad. Sc., *78:*308, 1959.

Pietz, D. G.: Nutritional and electrolyte evaluation in massive bowel resection; study of one case and review of the literature. Gastroenterology, *31:*56, 1956.

Plotkin, G. R., and Isselbacher, K. J.: Secondary disaccharidase deficiency in adult celiac disease (nontropical sprue) and other malabsorption states. New England J. Med., *271:*1033, 1964.

Pomerantz, M., and Waldmann, T. A.: Systemic lymphatic abnormalities associated with gastrointestinal protein loss secondary to intestinal lymphangiectasia. Gastroenterology, *45:*703, 1963.

Portman, O. W.: Importance of diet, species, and intestinal flora in bile acid metabolism. Fed. Proc., *21:*896, 1962.

Porus, R. L.: Epithelial hyperplasia following massive small bowel resection in man. Gastroenterology, *48:*753, 1965.

Posey, E. L., Jr., and Bargen, J. A.: Observations of normal and abnormal human intestinal motor function. Am. J. Med. Sc., *221:*10, 1951.

Ray, B. S., and Neill, C. L.: Abdominal visceral sensation in man. Ann. Surg., *126:*709, 1947.

Reiner, L.: Mesenteric arterial insufficiency and abdominal angina. Arch. Int. Med., *114:*765, 1964.

Rider, J. A., and Moeller, H. C. (eds.): Disturbances in Gastrointestinal Motility. Springfield, Charles C Thomas, 1959.

Robertson, J. I. S., Peart, W. S., and Andrews, T. M.: The mechanism of facial flushes in the carcinoid syndrome. Quart. J. Med., *31:*103, 1962.

Rosebury, T.: Microorganisms Indigenous to Man. New York, McGraw-Hill, 1962.

Roth, T. F., and Porter, K. R.: Yolk protein uptake in the oocyte of the mosquito, Aedes aegypti L. J. Cell. Biol., *20:*313, 1964.

Rubin, C. E.: Malabsorption: Celiac sprue. Ann. Rev. Med., *12:*39, 1961.

Rubin, C. E., Brandborg, L. L., Phelps, P. C., and Taylor, H. C., Jr.: Studies of celiac disease. I. The apparent identical and specific nature of the duodenal and proximal jejunal lesion in celiac disease and idiopathic sprue. Gastroenterology, *38:*28, 1960.

Rubin, C. E., et al.: The effect of wheat instillation into the proximal ileum of patients with idiopathic sprue. J. Clin. Invest., *39:*1023, 1960.

Rubin, C. E., et al.: Biopsy studies on the pathogenesis of coeliac sprue. In Ciba Foundation Study No. 14 on Intestinal Biopsy. Boston, Little, Brown & Co., 1962.

Ruffin, J. M., et al.: Gluten-free diet for nontropical sprue. Immediate and prolonged effects. J.A.M.A., *188:*42, 1964.

Sakula, J., and Shiner, M.: Coeliac disease with atrophy of the small intestine mucosa. Lancet, *2:*876, 1957.

Salt, H. B., Wolff, O. H., Lloyd, J. D., Fosbrooke, A. S., Cameron, A. H., and Hubble, D. V.: On having no beta-lipoprotein. A syndrome comprising a-beta-lipoproteinaemia, acanthocytosis, and steatorrhoea. Lancet, 2:325, 1960.

Sandler, M., and Snow, P. J. D.: Atypical carcinoid tumor secreting 5-hydroxytryptophan. Lancet, 1:137, 1958.

Sauer, W. G.: Factitial enteritis; An unusual cause of intestinal obstruction, chronic blood loss or malabsorption syndrome. J. Iowa Med. Soc., 50:1, 1960.

Schiffer, L. M., Faloon, W. W., Chodos, R. B., and Lozner, E. L.: Malabsorption syndrome associated with intestinal diverticulosis: Report of a case with jejunal biopsy. Gastroenterology, 42:63, 1962.

Schwartz, C. J., Acheson, E. D., and Webster, C. U.: Chronic mid-gut ischaemia with steatorrhoea in polycythaemia rubra vera. Am. J. Med., 32:950, 1962.

Schwartz, J. F., Rowland, L. P., Eder, H., Marks, P. A., Osserman, E. F., Hirschberg, E., and Anderson, H.: Bassen-Kornzweig syndrome: Deficiency of serum β-lipoprotein. Arch. Neurol., 8:438, 1963.

Schwartz, M., and Jarnum, S.: Gastrointestinal protein loss in idiopathic (hypercatabolic) hypoproteinaemia. Lancet, 1:327, 1959.

Schwartz, M., and Thomsen, B.: Idiopathic or hypercatabolic hypoproteinaemia. Brit. Med. J., 1:14, 1957.

Schwartz, M., and Vesin, P. (eds.): Plasma Proteins and Gastrointestinal Tract in Health and Disease. Baltimore, Williams & Wilkins Co., 1963.

Schwartz, M., et al.: The effect of a gluten-free diet on fat, nitrogen and mineral metabolism in patients with sprue. Gastroenterology, 32:232, 1957.

Scudamore, H. H., and Green, P. A.: Secondary malabsorption syndromes of intestinal origin. Postgrad. Med., 26:340, 1959.

Sebecin, S. M., and Isselbacher, K. J.: Protein synthesis inhibition: Mechanism for the production of impaired fat absorption. Science, 147:1149, 1965.

Semenza, G.: Enzymes and carbohydrate absorption. Personal communication.

Semenza, G., et al.: Lack of some intestinal maltases in a human disease transmitted by a single genetic factor. Biochim. Biophys. Acta, 105:386, 1965.

Senior, J. R.: Intestinal absorption of fats. J. Lipid Res., 5:495, 1964.

Senior, J. R., and Isselbacher, K. J.: Activation of long-chain fatty acids by rat-gut mucosa. Biochim. Biophys. Acta, 44:399, 1960.

Senior, J. R., and Isselbacher, K. J.: A novel metabolic pathway of fat absorption in the intestinal mucosa. J. Clin. Invest., 41:1399, 1962.

Senturia, H. R., Susman, N., and Shyken, H.: Roentgen appearance of spontaneous intramural hemorrhage of the small intestine associated with anticoagulant therapy. Am. J. Roentgenol., 86:62, 1961.

Seymour, W. B., and Liebow, A. A.: "Abdominal intermittent claudication" and narrowing of the celiac and mesenteric arteries. Ann. Int. Med., 10:1033, 1937.

Shearman, D. J. C., Girdwood, R. H., Williams, A. W., and Delamore, I. W.: A study with the electron microscope of the jejunal epithelium in primary malabsorptive disease. Gut, 3:16, 1962.

Sheehy, T. W., and Floch, M. H.: The Small Intestine, Its Function and Diseases. New York, Harper & Row, 1964.

Sheenan, D.: Clinical significance of nerve endings in the mesentery. Lancet, 1:409, 1933.

Shiner, M.: Small intestinal biopsies by the oral route, histopathologic changes in the malabsorption syndrome. J. Mt. Sinai Hosp., 24:273, 1957.

Shiner, M.: Coeliac disease: Histopathological findings in the small intestinal mucosa studied by a peroral biopsy technique. Gut, 1:48, 1960.

Shiner, M., and Birbeck, M. S. C.: The microvilli of the small intestinal surface epithelium in coeliac disease and in idiopathic steatorrhoea. Gut, 2:277, 1961.

Shiner, M., and Doniach, I.: Histopathologic studies in steatorrhea. In Proceedings of the World Congress of Gastroenterology, vol. 1. Baltimore, Williams & Wilkins Co., 1959.

Shiner, M., Lacy, D., and Hudson, R. H.: Electron microscope study of fat absorption in normal subjects and in patients with idiopathic steatorrhoea. In Ciba Foundation Study Group No 14 on Intestinal Biopsy. Boston, Little, Brown & Co., 1962.

Shiner, M., Waters, T. E., and Allan Gray, J. D.: Culture studies of the gastrointestinal tract with a newly devised capsule. Gastroenterology, 45:625, 1963.

Singer, K., Fisher, B., and Perlstein, M. A.: Acanthocytosis. A genetic erythrocytic malformation. Blood, 7:577, 1952.

Sjoerdsma, A.: Serotonin. Medical progress. New England J. Med., 261:181, 231, 1959.

Sjoerdsma, A., Weissbach, H., Terry, L. L., and Udenfriend, S.: Further observations on patients with malignant carcinoid. Am. J. Med., 23:5, 1957.

Smith, A. N., et al.: Further observations on endocrine aspects of argentaffinoma. Scottish Med. J., 2:24, 1957.

Speed, T.: Mechanical obstruction of the small bowel. Surg. Clin. N. Am., 32:1445, 1952.

Spencer, R., Bateman, J. D., and Horn, D. L.: Intramural hematoma of the intestine, a rare cause of intestinal obstruction. Surgery, 41:794, 1957.

Spencer, R. P.: The Intestinal Tract, Structure, Function and Pathology in Terms of the Basic Sciences. Springfield, Charles C Thomas, 1960.

Spiro, H. M., et al.: Functional histochemistry of the small bowel mucosa in malabsorptive syndromes. Gut, 5:145, 1964.

Steinfeld, J. L., Davidson, J. D., and Gordon, R. S.: A mechanism for hypoalbuminemia in patients with ulcerative colitis and regional enteritis. J. Clin. Invest., 36:931, 1957.

Steinfeld, J. L., Davidson, J. D., Gordon, R. S., Jr., and Greene, F. E.: The mechanism of hypoproteinemia in patients with regional enteritis and ulcerative colitis. Am. J. Med., 29:405, 1960.

Stoelinga, G. B. A., van Munster, P. J. J., and Sloof, J. P.: Chylous effusions into the intestine in a patient with protein-losing gastroenteropathy. Pediatrics, 31:1011, 1963.

Taylor, A. B., Wollaeger, E. E., Comfort, M. W., and Power, M. H.: The effect of cortisone on nontropical sprue (idiopathic steatorrhea). Gastroenterology, 20:203, 1952.

Templeton, R. D., and Lawson, H.: Studies in the motor activity of the large intestine. I. Normal motility in the dog, recorded by the tandem balloon method. Am. J. Physiol., 96:667, 1931.

Ten Thije, O. J.: Electronenmicroscopisch Onderzoek. In Darmslijmvlies en Sprue. Groningen, Van Denderen, 1963.

Thorson, A. H.: Studies on carcinoid disease. Acta Med. Scand., 161 (suppl. 334):1, 1958.

Toh, C. C.: Release of 5-hydroxytryptamine (serotonin) from dog's gastrointestinal tract. J. Phys., 126:248, 1954.

Toh, C. C.: Release of 5-hydroxytryptamine (serotonin) and histamine from platelets by tissue extract. J. Phys., 133:402, 1956.

Tolentino, P., Spirito, L., and Jannuzzi, C.: Celiac syndrome, retinal dystrophy, acanthocytosis, without defect of beta lipoprotein. Ann. Paediat., 203:178, 1964.

Trier, J. S., Phelps, P. C., and Rubin, C. E.: Electron microscopy of mucosa of small intestine. J.A.M.A., 183:768, 1963.

Trier, J. S., and Rubin, C. E.: Electron microscopy of the small intestine: A review. Gastroenterology, 49:574, 1965.

Turner, P., Sowry, G. S. C., and O'Donnell, P. M.: Hypoalbuminaemia due to protein loss from gastric carcinoma. Gut, 4:155, 1963.

Van Patter, W. N., et al.: Regional enteritis. Gastroenterology, 26:347, 1954.

Verzar, F., and McDougall, E. J.: Absorption from the Intestine. London, Longmans, Green & Co., 1936.

Vesin, P., et al.: Entéropathie avec perte de protéines et stéatorrhée. Étude par le PVP-I^{131} et la trioléin-I^{131}. Action du régime sans gluten. Bull. Mem. Soc. Med. Hop. Paris, 76:261, 1960.

Vesin, P., Troupel, S., Renault, H., and Cattan, R.: Entérocolite de Crohn. Étude de la déperdition intestinale de protéines par le PVP-I^{131}. In Schwartz, M., and Vesin, P. (eds.): Plasma Proteins and Gastrointestinal Tract in Health and Disease. Baltimore, Williams & Wilkins Co., 1963.

Waalkes, T. P., Sjoerdsma, A., Creveling, C. R., Weissbach, H., and Udenfriend, S.: Serotonin, norepinephrine and related compounds in bananas. Science, 127:648, 1958.

Waldenstrom, J., and Ljungberg, E.: Studies on the functional circulatory influence from metastasizing carcinoid (argentaffinoma, enterochromaffine) tumors and their possible relation to enteramine production. I. Symptoms of carcinoidosis. II. The chemistry of carcinoid tumors. Acta Med. Scand., 152:293, 311, 1955.

Waldmann, T. A.: Gastrointestinal protein loss demonstrated by ^{51}Cr-labelled albumin. Lancet, 2:121, 1961.

Waldmann, T. A.: Personal communication.

Waldmann, T. A., and Gordon, R. S., Jr.: The use of I^{131}-albumin, I^{131}-PVP and Cr^{51}-labeled albumin to detect gastrointestinal protein loss. In Schwartz, M., and Vesin, P. (eds.): Plasma Proteins and Gastrointestinal Tract in Health and Disease. Baltimore, Williams & Wilkins Co., 1963.

Waldmann, T. A., Gordon, R. S., Jr., Davidson, J. D., and Goodman, D. S.: Gastrointestinal protein loss secondary to cardiac lesions. In Schwartz, M., and Vesin, P. (eds.): Plasma Proteins and Gastrointestinal Tract in Health and Disease. Baltimore, Williams & Wilkins Co., 1963.

Waldmann, T. A., Gordon, R. S., Jr., Dutcher, T. F., and Wertlake, P. T.: Syndromes of gastrointestinal protein loss. In Schwartz, M., and Vesin, P. (eds.): Plasma Proteins and Gastrointestinal Tract in Health and Disease. Baltimore, Williams & Wilkins Co., 1963.

Waldmann, T. A., and Laster, L.: Abnormalities of albumin metabolism in patients with hypogammaglobulinemia. J. Clin. Invest., 43:1025, 1964.

Waldmann, T. A., Steinfeld, J. L., Dutcher, T. F., Davidson, J. D., and Gordon, R. S., Jr.: The role of the gastrointestinal system in "idiopathic hypoproteinemia." Gastroenterology, 41:197, 1961.

Wangensteen, O. H.: Intestinal Obstructions. A Physiological and Clinical Consideration with Emphasis on Therapy, Including Description of Operative Procedures, 2nd ed. Springfield, Charles C Thomas, 1942.

Watson, G. M., Cameron, D. G., and Witts, L. J.: Experimental macrocytic anemia in the rat. Lancet, 2:404, 1948.

Watson, M. R.: Primary nonspecific ulceration of the small bowel. Arch. Surg., 87:600, 1963.

Ways, P., Reed, C. F., and Hanahan, D. J.: Abnormalities of erythrocyte and plasma lipids in acanthocytosis. J. Clin. Invest., 40:1088, 1961.

Ways, P., Reed, C. F., and Hanahan, D. J.: Red-cell and plasma lipids in acanthocytosis. J. Clin. Invest., 42:1248, 1963.

Webb, J. P. W., James, A. T., and Kellock, T. D.: The influence of diet on the quality of faecal fat in patients with and without steatorrhoea. Gut, 4:37, 1963.

Weibel, L. A., Jorgenson, E. J., and Keasbey, L. E.: A clinical study of small bowel tumors. Am. J. Gastroenterol., 21:466, 1954.

Weijers, H. A., and van de Kamer, J. H.: Coelic disease: Rapid method to test wheat sensitivity. Acta Paediat., 44:536, 1955.

Weijers, H. A., and van de Kamer, J. H.: Some biochemical investigations into the cause of wheat sensitivity in celiac disease. Proceedings of the World Congress of Gastroenterology, vol. 1. Baltimore, Williams & Wilkins Co., 1959.

Weijers, H. A., van de Kamer, J. H., Dicke, W. K., and Ijsseling, J.: Diarrhoea caused by deficiency of sugar-splitting enzymes. Acta Paediat., 50:55, 1961.

Weiner, P.: Über Fettablagerung und Fettresorption in Darm. Ztschr. f. mikr.-anat. Forsch., 30:197, 1928.

Weissbach, H., King, W., Sjoerdsma, A., and Udenfriend, S.: Formation of indole-3-acetic acid and tryptamine in animals: Method for estimation of indole-3-acetic acid in tissue. J. Biol. Chem., 234:81, 1959.

Welch, C. E.: Diverticulosis and Diverticulitis. DM, Chicago, Year Book Publishers, June, 1958.

Wenger, J., Kirsner, J. B., and Palmer, W. L.: Blood carotene in steatorrhea and the malabsorptive syndromes. Am. J. Med., 32:373, 1957.

Wetterfors, J., et al.: Hypoalbuminemia in cancer of the stomach. In Schwartz, M., and Vesin, P. (eds.): Plasma Proteins and Gastrointestinal Tract in Health and Disease. Baltimore, Williams & Wilkins Co., 1963.

Whittaker, L. D., and Pemberton, J. de J.: Mesenteric vascular occlusion. J.A.M.A., 111:21, 1938.

Wilson, R., and Qualheim, R. E.: A form of acute hemorrhagic enterocolitis afflicting chronically ill individuals: A description of 20 cases. Gastroenterology, 27:431, 1954.

Wilson, T. H.: Intestinal Absorption. Philadelphia, W. B. Saunders Co., 1962.

Wiot, J. F., Weinstein, A. S., and Felson, B.: Duodenal hematoma induced by coumarin. Am. J. Roentgenol., 86:70, 1961.

Wiseman, G.: Absorption from the Intestine. New York, Academic Press, 1964.

Wollaeger, E. E., Comfort, M. W., and Osterberg, A. E.: Total solids, fat and nitrogen in feces: Study of normal persons taking test diet containing moderate amounts of fat; comparison with results obtained with normal persons taking test diet containing large amount of fat. Gastroenterology, 9:272, 1947.

Yardley, J. H., Bayless, T. M., Norton, J. H., and Hendrix, T. R.: Celiac disease. A study of the jejunal epithelium before and after a gluten-free diet. New England J. Med., 267:1173, 1962.

Zetterqvist, H.: The Ultrastructural Organization of the Columnar Absorbing Cells of the Mouse Jejunum. Monograph. Stockholm, Aktiebolaget Godvil, 1956.

Zetterqvist, H., and Hendrix, T. R.: A preliminary note on an ultrastructural abnormality of the intestinal epithelium in adult celiac disease (nontropical sprue) which is reversed by a gluten-free diet. Bull. Johns Hopkins Hospital, 106:240, 1960.

Chapter Twenty-Six

The Large Intestine

LEON SCHIFF

The large intestine, or colon, is about 150 cm. long. The cecum is the widest part, about 7.5 cm. in diameter; like the small intestine, the colon gradually diminishes in diameter to the rectosigmoid junction, where it is about 2.5 cm. wide. At the rectosigmoid junction the bowel lumen is smallest and a sharp angle occurs, factors which are thought to control, in part, the passage of feces into the rectum. Here, too, is a favorite site of polyps and carcinoma. The reflection of the peritoneum from the anterior surface of the upper rectum at a point about 7.5 cm. from the anus is a site of metastatic lesions from gastric carcinoma and is within reach of the index finger.

The three longitudinal muscular bands, or taeniae coli, running from the cecum to the rectosigmoid are shorter than the colon itself, causing the colon to be drawn up into haustral sacculations, rows of pouches separated internally by folds. According to Weintraub, these sacculations are largest in the cecum and ascending colon, most regularly formed in the transverse colon and gradually disappear as the sigmoid is reached. In Weintraub's experience the haustrations are usually absent in the descending and sigmoid portions of the normal colon. It is important to bear this in mind, for clinicians and roentgenologists have been wont to ascribe the absence of such haustrations to irritability or inflammation of the colon.

The large intestine has considerable mobility. This is especially noticeable in the transverse and pelvic colon where the long mesentery permits a wide range of movement. The cecum, ascending colon, and hepatic flexure also possess considerable motility, while the splenic flexure, descending colon, and rectum are relatively fixed. The floating character of the colon permits great variation of position in response to posture, respiration, gas distention, and especially variation in smooth muscle tone (Barclay, Quigley).

The colon is relatively large and distensible. Thus it is especially designed to provide large capacity. According to Quigley, this factor and its specialized musculature permit long retention of its contents.

The ascending and right half of the transverse colon are supplied with blood from the superior mesenteric artery, which also supplies the small intestine. Like the small intestine, this part of the colon has an important absorptive function. The left half of the colon receives its blood from the inferior mesenteric artery. The venous return is similarly divided. The lack of valves in the mesenteric veins permits hypertension to develop in the presence of portal stasis, and varicosities to develop where collateral circulation occurs, as in the hemorrhoidal plexuses.

Like the small intestine, the colon is supplied with sympathetic and parasympathetic fibers. The sympathetic impulses come from the eleventh and twelfth thoracic and first and second lumbar levels. The parasympa-

637

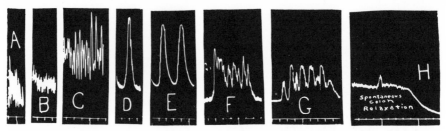

Figure 26–1. Excerpts of tracing from the colon of man. *A, B, C,* Type I contractions at various tonus levels. *D, E,* Type II contractions. *F, G,* Type III contractions. *H,* Demonstrating spontaneous relaxation. (From Adler, H. F., Atkinson, A. J., and Ivy, A. C.: Am. J. Dig. Dis., 8:197, 1941.)

thetic impulses probably come from the vagus and the second, third, and fourth sacral nerves. In discussing the innervation of the colon Quigley has stated the following: "The colon is similar to other portions of the gut, since it possesses considerable autonomy, especially in the proximal portion, and the haustral contractions may be intrinsic phenomena. Local reflexes may be produced through the myenteric plexuses; but these reflexes, colonic tone, and the mass movements are greatly influenced by the autonomic nervous system through the thoracicolumbar and sacral fibers. Although the influence from the sympathetics usually reduces colonic tone and motility, other effects have been reported. Strong emotions, which are usually associated with a generalized sympathetic discharge, may result in diarrhea and other manifestations of colonic stimulation." Parasympathetic denervation of the colon occurs as the result of spinal injury and may handicap the defecation reflex, although less specialized motor functions of the colon may be unimpaired. The gastrointestinal tract, when deprived of its central connections through the autonomic nervous system, carries on its rhythmic movements capably.

Functions

The functions of the colon are absorption, storage, and excretion. The main function is to render waste products of digestion fit for elimination in a form and at a time giving little inconvenience. This is brought about by absorption of water to reduce the liquid character of the intestinal contents, by storage of the mass until a time convenient for excretion, and, finally, by expulsion of the excreta. As already stated, the right half of the colon is concerned with absorption and dehydration, and the left half with storage and expulsion.

A significant amount of water and salts is absorbed from the proximal colon, relatively little absorption taking place in the distal colon. According to Quigley, the feces contain about one-fifth as much water as the ileal discharge, and in the human being this involves the absorption of approximately 500 cc. of water per day from the 620 cc. passed through the ileocolic sphincter, leaving 120 cc. in the form of feces. (If the discharges from a normal ileum following ileostomy are taken as a guide to the normal daily discharge of ileal contents into the colon, then volumes of water up to 2 liters or more per day containing sodium in at least isotonic concentration are presented to the colon for reabsorption each day.) Although the absorptive function of the large intestine is performed primarily by the right half of the colon, some salt and sugars (dextrose and sucrose) are absorbed throughout the colon, and certain drugs may be absorbed from the rectum.

There is no proof that absorption of "toxic" products occurs in intestinal stasis. In the past, "intestinal toxemia" was thought to result from the absorption of the products of putrefactive bacteria, such as indole, skatole, phenol, cresol, and hydrogen sulfide compounds. These substances, when absorbed, are detoxified to indoxyl, indican, and other products. Histamine is produced from histidine and is detoxified in passing through the intestinal wall. No one has proved that these detoxified products are the cause of symptoms or that they are harmful. In fact, the bacteria of the lower intestine have a function in the destruction of food residues and in vitamin production.

Functionally, the movements of the alimentary tract may be classified primarily as either propulsive or nonpropulsive. The three types of contraction waves originally described by Templeton and Lawson in canine colons were likewise found to occur in the human colon by Adler and associates (Fig. 26–1). They have since been studied by other investigators, including Almy and associates, Code and associates, and Posey and Bargen. Type I contractions are small simple waves with their amplitude seldom representing a pressure of more than 10 cm. of water or their duration more than 10 seconds. They occur at a rate of from three to eight per minute, and their amplitude varies. When displaying their basic rhythm, their rate in the pelvic colon is 13 per minute, while in the descending colon it may be about one-half of this (Code and associates). They are not propulsive.

Type II waves are also simple waves, but they are uniformly of greater duration and almost always of greater amplitude than type I waves. When in rhythmic sequence, their frequency is almost exactly two per minute. In normal persons they account for more than 90 per cent of the recorded activity and represent slow contractions which migrate slowly over short distances. Their function is one of mixing rather than propelling, and available evidence indicates that they account for the haustral contractions observed roentgenologically.

Type III waves are complex and are composed of a change in the baseline pressure or a change in tonus upon which are superimposed type I or II waves, or both. They often last for about a minute, sometimes for many minutes, and are not common. "The function of these waves may be one of aiding absorption by increasing intraluminal pressure."

Almy and associates have corroborated the three types of motility waves and also the variation in the pattern and in the amount of contractile activity that may occur (Fig. 26–2). Their observation that the balloon has never been passed from the rectum by a person with a normal colon is indicative of the nonpropulsive character of all these wave types.

The validity of this classification of colonic waves has recently been questioned, since the tracings were obtained with tandem balloons connected with water manometers, in contrast with the present-day methods of using open-ended polyethylene tubes connected with optical manometers recording on photographic paper or electromanometers with direct writing systems. Chaudhary and Truelove feel that the water manometer is obsolete and has many drawbacks, that the presence of a balloon is unphysiologic, and that distention by the balloon often induces activity so that the recorded motility is in-

duced rather than spontaneous. They propose a new nomenclature: "phasic waves" and "tonus waves" of short and long duration, respectively.

Kern and associates describe the type IV wave as a simple wave lasting from 2 to 5 minutes with an amplitude approximately twice that of the usual type II contractions (Fig. 26–3). It has a relatively sharp ascending limb and a gentler descending limb. The surface area beneath such a wave was eight times that beneath an average type II contraction. This wave occurred only in those

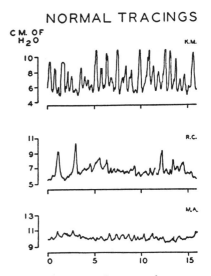

Figure 26–2. Sigmoid tracings from persons with anatomically normal colons, illustrating the usual variations in amount and type of wavelike activity. This activity is usually continuous. (From Kern, F., Jr., Almy, T. P., Abbot, F. K., and Bogdonoff, M. D.: Gastroenterology, 19:492, 1951.)

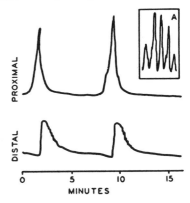

Figure 26–3. The amplitude, duration and progressive character of type IV waves, recorded on tandem sigmoid balloons. On the insert (A) are typical type II waves, drawn to the same scale. (From Kern, F., Jr., Almy, T. P., Abbot, F. K., and Bogdonoff, M. D.: Gastroenterology, 19:492, 1951.)

patients who otherwise had a marked diminution of the usual rhythmic activity. Passage of the balloon per rectum indicates that these waves are definitely propulsive. Code and associates are also convinced of the propulsive nature of these waves and found that when they were present in the colon adjacent to a colonic stoma, the fecal material gushed out onto the surface, and when obtained in records of activity of the pelvic colon, passage of gas or feces was almost always associated. Code and his associates observed a type IV wave only once in tracings from normal persons, and that occurred when the subject defecated just after eating a meal. They believe that type IV waves represent mass peristalsis or mass movement.

Although most phasic activity in the colon is nonpropulsive, the feces move onward by brief peristaltic rushes which occur infrequently. The usual stimulus to such propulsive activity is the ingestion of food or fluids, and the pathway is the gastrocolic reflex. Studies made in dogs by Welch and Plant and later by Slive and Fogelson indicate that the reflex is not due to gastric filling as Hurst believed, but is rather an appetite or a feeding reflex. According to Alvarez, the gastrocolic reflex in dogs is not affected by bilateral vagotomy, and the observation of Grace and associates in one of their subjects would indicate that the same holds true in man. Connell and associates state that there is no reason why the gastrocolic reflex should not initiate a mass movement at one time or in one part of the colon and segmenting or delaying contractions in the other. In their patients with abdominal pain associated with colonic hypermotility after meals the effect of the gastrocolic reflex was clearly to hold up the passage of feces through the sigmoid.

Adler and associates pointed out that two adjacent segments of the colon do not necessarily manifest the same type of motility at the same time; that is, they may manifest phases of activity which obviously are not conducive to propulsion of contents from one segment to another. It would appear that the motor activity of the colon as a whole is not "organized" or coordinated at all times, so that propulsive activity in one segment may affect transport of contents to an adjacent segment. It is not surprising, therefore, that under certain conditions the disorganization may be increased and the syndrome of so-called spastic or unstable colon may occur in the absence of easily recognized roentgenologic evidence.

Motor activity in the colon, except during defecation, is sluggish. In performing motility studies, some have noted that complete quiescence of the normal colon may persist for as long as 6 hours. In the cecum and ascending colon, filling results chiefly from ileal activity, and peristalsis is weak. At times, especially on the right side, mild antiperistaltic waves appear in order, some investigators believe, to retain the fecal mass until it is of proper consistency to enter the left side.

Movement of feces in the left colon is achieved by the same discontinuous process as in the right, but is even slower. Dehydration continues, and the feces accumulate in the sigmoid and lower descending colon.

Defecation normally occurs after the fecal mass has passed beyond the sigmoid colon, which is the usual reservoir of feces. Mass peristaltic waves, often initiated when food is ingested in the morning, carry the feces into the rectum. Distention of the rectum produces the desire to defecate, but, if the act is not completed, the rectum relaxes and the desire disappears. Further distention is then necessary to reactivate the desire, or voluntary activation may be effected by increasing the intra-abdominal pressure, which causes the entrance of more feces into the rectum and increases the rectal pressure. This distention reflexly stimulates peristalsis in the colon and contraction of the voluntary muscles of the abdomen, including the levator ani muscles, and causes a relaxation of the anal sphincters. The reflex center for the external sphincter ani is in the conus terminalis of the spinal cord. Destruction of the lower cord relaxes the external sphincter, whereas destruction of the afferent nerves permits fecal accumulation without any sensation.

In normal persons, feces are passed 8 to 72 hours after the corresponding food has been eaten. The stool is 70 to 85 per cent water and weighs on an average of 100 to 250 gm. Delay in defecation with greater absorption of water can result in exceedingly small, dry stools. With more rapid propulsion and reduced absorption of water the stool may be more voluminous and mushy or liquid in character. A large intake of water does not increase the fecal water content (Ingelfinger). The feces consist in large part, not of ingested food, but of secretions and products of the intestinal tract. When vegetables and cereals are excluded from the diet, feces rather constantly contain about 65 per cent water and 35 per cent solids, which may be divided into ash (15 of the 35 per cent), chiefly calcium, phosphate, iron, and magnesia; ether-soluble material (15 of the 35 per cent), chiefly fatty acids; and nitrogen (5 of the 35 per cent). A large part of the fecal mass is epithelial cells and bacteria. Ingested cellulose in cereals and vegetables passes out in the feces unchanged and increases the bulk of the stool. Such materials also accelerate the passage of food through the gastrointestinal tract and increase the amount of undigested food in the feces.

The secretion of the colon differs entirely from that of the succus entericus. It is chiefly a protective mucus which also acts as a lubricant. The goblet cells, which are in general increased in number from the upper to the lower regions of the gastrointestinal tract, are stimulated directly to produce mucus. Mucus is increased in amount by irritative agents, be they chemical, bacterial, or mechanical, or by psychologic factors. Enemas increase the amount, as do strong cathartics or colonic irrigations and inflammatory processes. In fistulous subjects the mucus secretion is thin, watery, and relatively scant during periods of cheerfulness and relative tranquility, but becomes thick, tenacious, and opalescent, and often profuse—resembling that seen in the stools of patients with chronic ulcerative colitis—during periods of anger, resentment, and anxiety.

Symptoms and Signs of Colonic Disease

Much of what has been said of the symptomatology of disease of the small intestine (Chap. 25) applies to the colon as well, and the remarks on pain, tenderness and related symptoms, and hemorrhage should be reviewed under that heading.

Again, symptoms depend on the nature of the lesion as well as on its location. The history, unlike that obtained in cases of disease of the small intestine, often discloses symptoms which directly suggest colonic involvement. This holds particularly true for abdominal distress (mostly lower abdominal), which is relieved by the passage of gas or evacuation of feces or which may be increased by the ingestion of food (as a result of stimulation of the gastrocolic reflex with increased sigmoid motor activity) or by cathartics (as a result of secondary spasm). The passage of small stools points to colonic disturbance.

Physical examination of the colon is more satisfactory than that of the small intestine because the colon is more accessible to palpation. The colon may be palpable and tender and is most commonly felt in the left lower quadrant. The terminal 8 cm. of the colon can be palpated internally and the final 25 to 30 cm. inspected with the sigmoidoscope. Radiologic examination of the colon is also simpler than that of the small intestine because of the greater ease of manipulation under fluoroscopic control. Contrast studies with barium and air may reveal abnormalities of the mucosal pattern or lesions not seen otherwise. Below the rectosigmoid junction, radiologic studies are not satisfactory. The palpating finger may be the only means of detecting lesions in the "hollow" of the sacrum. A spastic anal sphincter may be encountered in ulcerative colitis.

Examination of excreta will often disclose findings compatible with disease anywhere along the intestinal tube. Examination of material aspirated at sigmoidoscopy may reveal motile parasites, pus, macrophages, and blood or mucus indicative of local (colonic) disease. In bacillary dysentery, for example, the exudate is rich in pus cells and macrophages, while in amebic infection mucus, red blood cells, and motile amebae predominate and there is little cellular debris. Chemical and bacteriologic examinations may furnish additional valuable information. Finally, tissue for biopsy examination may be taken through the sigmoidoscope.

As in the small intestine, *focal symptoms* arise as a result of disturbances in the principal activities of the large intestine, particularly that of motility. In addition to abdominal pain, which was discussed on page 597, the most important effects of disturbance of motility are constipation and/or diarrhea.

Constipation

Constipation in the objective sense means delayed passage of feces. To the patient it may mean the infrequent passage of stools, the passage of dry, hard, and small stools, or the sensation of incomplete emptying of the rectum after a bowel movement. At present two principal forms of constipation are recognized: (1) that due to impairment of colonic motility with the delay occurring at the sigmoid level or higher (so-called spastic constipation) and (2) that due to rectal insensibility or a defect in the integrated mechanism of defecation—so-called rectal constipation, or dyschezia. Not infrequently the two forms may be combined in the same person. The so-called atonic constipation seems to be falling into disrepute as the result of further clinical studies and observations

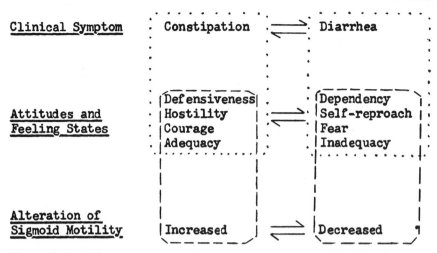

Figure 26–4. Schema of relations between symptoms, feeling states, and physiologic changes. Heavy rings indicate associations observed in laboratory. Dotted rings indicate clinically observed associations. (From Almy, T. P., Kern, F., Jr., and Abbot, F. K.: A. Res. Nerv. & Ment. Dis. Proc., 29:724, 1950.)

of colonic motility both by roentgen examination and balloon-kymographic techniques.

According to Almy, constipation may develop because the gastrocolic reflex, with resulting mass peristalsis, does not get started or is blocked. He points out that fasting man is constipated and that marked reduction in the bulk of fluid or food, or in its residue, diminishes the vigor of peristaltic rushes in the lower bowel. Diminished gastric motility due to various causes may impair the gastrocolic reflex and produce constipation. Inhibition of the gastrocolic reflex has been observed during feelings of sadness and dejection and suggests that this mechanism may account for the constipation which occurs during phases of depression in patients with ulcerative colitis.

Almy and his co-workers have thrown considerable light on the effects of psychologic factors on colonic motility in general, and constipation (and diarrhea) in particular (Fig. 26–4). They observed the sigmoid colon proctoscopically for long periods of time in human subjects. "When the thoughts of the subject were occupied with neutral topics, the bowel was widely patent. When the experimenters made the subject angry, hostile and defensive the lumen was occluded by a vigorous and sustained contraction." They further demonstrated the physiologic effects on the colon of psychologic factors by kymographic studies in which single or tandem balloons were passed by rectum. They found the sigmoid motility of resting subjects to be constant for the individual over a period of two to three hours. "When involved in an emotionally disturbing interview heightened contractions frequently developed. The pattern of these non-propulsive contractions seems appropriate for retaining feces and suggests that the sigmoid is truly a sphincteric zone, overactivity of which is associated with constipation." These motility changes seemed to be consistently accompanied by feelings of tension, hostility, defensiveness, and tenacity, attitudes which they have commonly observed in their patients with constipation. They expressed the view that "colonic motility is usually disturbed as part of a defensive reaction against life stress which has characteristic emotional colorings and involves diminished gastrocolic reflexes and increased segmental contractions of the distal colon."

In cases of constipation due to impaired colonic motility the rectum is usually empty of all but exceedingly small and hard pellets of feces, in contrast with cases in which the defect lies in the process of defecation in which the rectum contains large masses of stool of normal or softer consistency. In the former the point of retardation of motility is usually at the sigmoid, which manifests an excessive degree of nonpropulsive activity, commonly referred to as spasm. This spasm of the sigmoid retards the normal progress of the feces, which in turn results in dehydration of the stools. As a result the stool enters the rectum in small driblets (rather than a sizable bolus) which do not initiate the usual evacuating mechanisms of the rectum.

The rectal form of constipation is frequently seen in debilitated persons. Almy believes that the fact that the rectum is found to contain large masses of stool of normal or softer consistency in this form of constipation suggests that the rate of passage of contents is normal until the rectum is reached and that the defect lies in the process of defecation. In addition to the impairment of rectal sensibility as a result of the habitual neglect of the call to stool, the "negative conditioning" of the defecation reflex which occurs with growth as the result of increasing awareness of social pressures, and the repeated disruption of the defecation reflex by alterations in the habits of daily life and by abuse of cathartics, several other factors may play a role in this type of constipation. These include (1) local inhibition because of pain such as occurs in anal fissures or fistulas or thrombosed or inflamed hemorrhoids, which prevent relaxation of the sphincter, (2) cord compression involving the reflex center in the sacral cord or damage to the efferent or afferent nerves as in lesions of the cauda equina, and (3) weakening of the effector muscles or damage as the result of multiple pregnancies, birth injuries, anterior horn cell disease, or muscular dystrophy.

Of much interest is the observation that voluntary contraction of the perineal and rectal muscles, as is done to avoid having a bowel movement, produces inhibition of colonic motor activity and attenuation of the gastrocolic reflex. This further adds to the complexity of the various factors that may operate to produce constipation.

Among the less common forms of constipation are megacolon, and that due to opiates, lead poisoning, hyperparathyroidism, and myxedema. Opiates have been shown to increase the segmental, nonpropulsive activity of the intestines of both man and dog. Almy suggests that the hypercalcemia of hyperparathyroidism may possibly play a role by impairing the contractility of muscle. He points out that adequate studies on the constipation of myxedema are lacking and suggests the possible role of the lack of a vigorous appetite which strengthens the gastrocolic reflex and the lack of attention to toilet habits which healthy persons require for optimum bowel function.

Most unusual of all the diseases causing constipation is *megacolon*. This is a congenital dilatation of extreme grade, usually found in children. Circumferences up to 100 cm. and fecal masses weighing 50 pounds have been reported. There is hypertrophy of the muscularis, chiefly of the circular layer, and the mucosa is "thick, vascular, edematous, and sometimes ulcerated." The muscularis mucosae is also hypertrophic, and the mesenteric nodes are enlarged and hyperplastic. The accumulation of intestinal contents leads to severe constipation and infrequency of bowel movements, which may occur at intervals of weeks or months. The dilatation of the colon produces prominent abdominal distention.

Recently adduced evidence strongly suggests that the absence of normal propulsive waves in the rectum and rectosigmoid in cases of megacolon constitutes a physiologic defect that results in chronic obstruction. There is evidence that the disease consists of a congenital defect in the pelvic parasympathetic system resulting in an aganglionic segment of colon which is normally supplied by this portion of the autonomic system. The resulting absence of peristalsis in the involved colon accounts for the accumulation of fecal material in the colon proximal to the lesion. This malfunctioning segment is identical with the narrow, irregular bowel visualized roentgenologically. Removal of this segment results in cure with return of the colon to normal size and peristalsis as evidenced by barium enema.

Diarrhea

Patients complaining of diarrhea may pass frequent semiliquid to mushy stools or may pass only one or two soft stools a day with considerable urgency and tenesmus. The increased number of bowel movements is associated with vigorous rhythmic contractile activity of the right side of the colon, while the region of the sigmoid undergoes longitudinal contraction with shortening and no rhythmic contractions of the circular muscle. The importance of sigmoid hypomotility as part of the mechanism of diarrhea has been shown. In keeping with the view that hypomotility of the sigmoid is part of the mechanism of diarrhea are the observations that wavelike colonic contractions were abolished during defecation in the dog and that expulsion of a barium enema by patients was accomplished without visible wavelike contractions of the distal colon. Injection of Mecholyl, which produces diarrhea, reduces motility of the sigmoid and simultaneously increases that of the ascending colon. This combination of physiologic changes is the probable mechanism of diarrhea. Furthermore, reduction in sigmoid motility has been observed in patients with ulcerative colitis during periods of diarrhea with a return of the motility pattern to normal during remission of the disease.

Almy distinguishes between large-stool diarrheas and small-stool diarrheas, and points out that, when the stools are consistently large, the underlying disorder is likely to be in the small intestine or the proximal colon. The diarrhea is thought to result from the stimulation of a functionally normal colon by exceptionally large or unusually irritating intestinal contents. "The stimulus thus presented is similar to that of an enema, leading to expulsion of loose stools of large size despite the normal irritability of the lower bowel."

Diseases of the Colon and the Mechanism of Symptom Production

Irritable Colon

Lumsden, Chaudhary, and Truelove divide patients with the "irritable colon syndrome"

into those with spastic colon, which comprise the majority, and those with diarrhea as the predominant symptom. In the former, colonic pain is the outstanding symptom, being most commonly experienced over the descending and sigmoid colon. Attacks of pain may be related to periods of emotional stress. The pain itself may arise or become increased at a definite time interval after meals or may be relieved by defecation. The patients with spastic colons often have normal bowel habits, but some show a tendency to constipation when their colonic pain is severe and then may pass clear mucus from the rectum.

Diarrhea may be continuous over long periods of time or intermittent and be unaccompanied by any blood in the stools.

In patients with symptomatic spastic colon, the resting pattern of colonic motility is much more active than in normals or asymptomatic patients. In those with active diarrhea, the resting pattern shows normal or reduced activity, in contrast with normal activity dur-

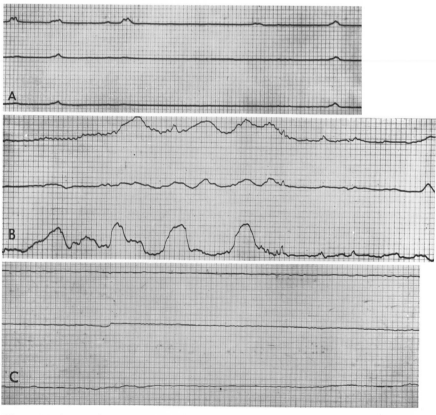

Figure 26–5. Intraluminal colonic pressure recordings of three human subjects at rest, each recording representing 6 minutes. *A,* A normal patient showing a few small pressure waves. *B,* A patient with spastic colon in a stage of symptoms, showing increase in number and size of pressure waves. *C,* A patient with chronic diarrhea in a stage of symptoms, showing a "flat" pressure tracing such as is often found in these patients. (From Lumsden, K., Chaudhary, N. A., and Truelove, S. C.: J. Fac. Radiologists, *14:*54, 1963.)

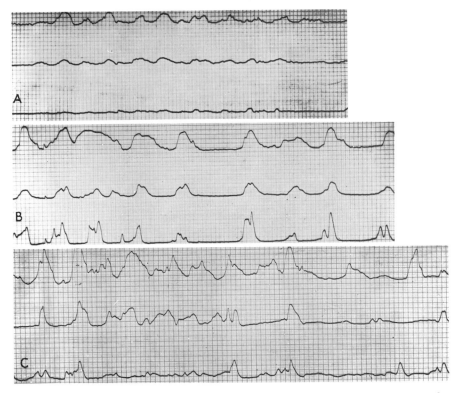

Figure 26–6. Intraluminal colonic pressure recordings of the same three human subjects whose resting patterns are shown in Figure 26–5, after intramuscular injection of 1 mg. Prostigmin methylsulfate. *A,* The normal subject shows a considerable increase in number and size of pressure waves. *B,* Marked motor activity displayed by the patient with spastic colon. *C,* Equally marked motor activity displayed by the patient with chronic diarrhea, although the resting pattern was a flat one. (From Lumsden, K., Chaudhary, N. A., and Truelove, S. C.: J. Fac. Radiologists, *14*:54, 1963.)

ing a symptomless stage (Fig. 26–5). Following intramuscular injection of 1 mg. of Prostigmin, normal subjects show considerable enhancement of activity as compared with their resting patterns, while the irritable colon group show much more colonic activity after Prostigmin than do the normals, regardless of whether or not symptoms are present when they are studied (Fig. 26–6).

Pain is probably due to distention of the bowel with gas or to vigorous sustained or rhythmic contraction of the muscular coats, with the quality of fullness, dull deep ache, rhythmic cramping, steady deep griping, or sudden knifelike jabs. The *constipation* is the most frequent form of that due to impairment of colonic function and is due to exaggerated nonpropulsive contractions ("spasm") of the distal colon, particularly the sigmoid. It is believed that these "holding back" contractions of the left portion of the colon, together with diminished propulsive movements throughout the colon, are primarily responsible for the constipation. In most patients the

mechanism is complicated by distortion of bowel habits and abuse of laxatives. *Diarrhea* is frequently severest after meals, especially breakfast, which suggests that the diarrhea is due to exaggeration of the normal colonic mechanism of the propulsion of feces. Though of chronic duration, it is not accompanied by loss of weight, a point of value in diagnosis. *Small stools* occur in the presence of both constipation and diarrhea and are regarded as a manifestation of "irritability" in which a smaller than normal accumulation of feces evokes a defecation reflex. Excessive dehydration of the stool in constipation may come into play with the passage of mucus as a coating for the stool as an aid to the passage of hard stools, the mucus probably representing hypersecretion of the goblet cells under cholinergic stimulation. *Dyspepsia* may be associated with reduced motility of the stomach, which in turn may be coincident with sigmoid spasm. *General vascular instability*—weakness, faintness, flushing, sweating, palpitation—simulates the symptoms of neu-

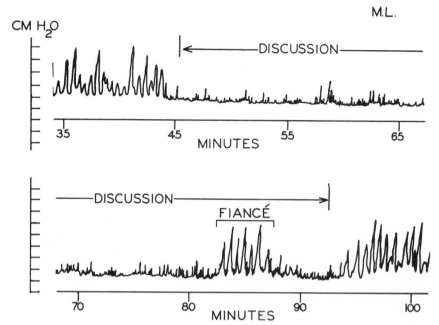

Figure 26–7.   Kymographic record in a woman, aged 29, with complaint of constipation, showing sigmoid motility during recital of personal problems. (From Almy, T. P., Abbot, F. K., and Hinkle, L. E., Jr.: Gastroenterology, *15*:95, 1950.)

rocirculatory asthenia, and their occurrence has been considered evidence of disordered activity throughout the autonomic nervous system.

In a group of patients with irritable colon, Almy observed "two distinct and opposite patterns of altered motility of the sigmoid colon" associated with periods of induced emotional tension. These patterns consisted in (1) increased tone, increased frequency and amplitude of the sigmoid contractions which were usually associated with expressed hostility and aggression, and (2) disappearance of the wavelike contractions, often with a decrease in tone in "striking association with a change in the attitude of the subject from one of self-confidence, aggression, or even hostility, to one of hopelessness, personal inadequacy or self-reproach." The hypomotility of the sigmoid frequently corresponded exactly to periods of weeping, lasting as long as 12 minutes (Figs. 26–7 and 26–8). The alternation of constipation and diarrhea so characteristically seen in patients with irritable colon has been attributed to fluctuations in mood between the aggressive, hostile, defensive attitudes associated with constipation and the fearful, self-reproachful attitudes accompanying diarrhea.

According to Lumsden and associates, patients with both spastic colon and diarrhea yield closely similar appearances on barium

enema examination, with evidence of "irritability" in the great majority of cases. This similarity of the barium enema appearances corresponds with the motility patterns observed after injection of Prostigmin.

Ulcerative Colitis

The relation between periods of emotional stress and the onset and exacerbation of symptoms in patients with chronic ulcerative colitis has been well established. In periods of tranquility the bowel has been found to be pale in color, relatively immobile, with a scant, thin watery mucous secretion low in lysozyme content. During phases of anger and resentment, the bowel may be engorged, hyperactive, and covered with a thick, opalescent, tenacious mucus, high in lysozyme concentration. These observations would indicate that hyperfunction of the colon results in increased fragility of the mucous membrane and that sustained hyperfunction of the colon associated with sustained feelings of anger and resentment results in submucosal bleeding and ulceration. Petechial lesions have been observed at sigmoidoscopy in patients with ulcerative colitis during anger.

The diarrhea of ulcerative colitis is apparently due to the reduction of sigmoid motility plus the increase in motility of the proximal colon, plus the abnormal appearance of mass peristalsis (type IV waves). *Consti-*

pation is sometimes present in patients with ulcerative colitis, and the barium meal has been observed to remain in the right half of the colon in spite of frequent evacuations, the "paradox of constipation in the presence of diarrhea." It is of interest that Engel found that the earliest abnormality in 22 of 32 patients with ulcerative colitis was the passage of blood with accompanying constipation in ten; he observed normally formed stools in six, and diarrhea in the remaining six. He points out that the prominence of bleeding rather than diarrhea as the presenting symptom is not generally recognized. He found diarrhea to be associated with more widespread involvement of the bowel. "When the disease is confined to rectum or rectosigmoid there may be frequent passage of blood, pus and mucus, but stools may remain normal in consistency or even continue to be constipated. When the disease involves segments proximal to the sigmoid or when more than the distal half of the descending colon is affected, diarrhea is a much more consistent symptom."

The *abdominal pain* is due to disturbance in colonic function which in turn is affected by environmental stresses as well as by the inflammatory process in the bowel, and such complications as perforation or abscess formation. As is true of colonic pain in general, temporary relief may be afforded by bowel movements. The *blood* in the stools is bright because the bleeding arises from the areas of ulceration in the colon and is usually rapidly evacuated. The presence of *pus* in the stools is the result of the inflammatory process, as is the presence of fever and leukocytosis during acute exacerbations. The *anemia* which may be prominent in more severe and chronic cases has been ascribed to a number of factors. These include (1) the degree of iron deficiency produced by chronic hemorrhage and inadequate intake or absorption; (2) nutritional status of the patient, as indicated by the degree of weight loss, evidences of avitaminosis, and the level of the serum protein; (3) toxemia and infection with their presumable impairment of the ability of the body to utilize iron and protein in the formation of hemoglobin, as postulated by Cartwright and his associates; (4) the anatomic extent of the disease (rather than its duration); (5) the occurrence of exacerbations of the disease as contrasted with remissions; and (6) the sex of the patient, the anemia being more common and more severe in females, presumably because of their normally increased require-

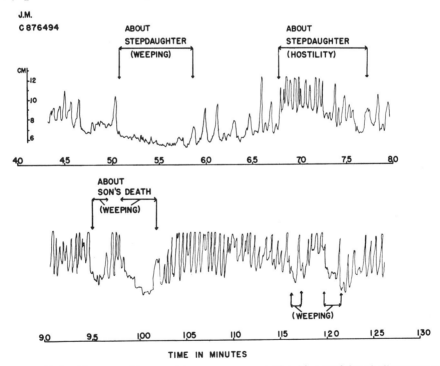

Figure 26–8. Kymographic record in a woman, aged 47, with complaint of alternating constipation and diarrhea, showing sigmoid motility during discussion of disturbing features of personal history. Note changes associated with weeping. (From Almy, T. P., Abbot, F. K., and Hinkle, L. E., Jr.: Gastroenterology, *15*:95, 1950.)

ments for iron associated with menstruation and pregnancy.

It is generally agreed that deficiency states are commonly encountered in ulcerative colitis, particularly in the more severe cases, and that they contribute to the clinical features and pathologic physiology of the disease. The deficiency states are not primary in the sense of antedating the onset of the colitis. The possible mechanisms involved in their production are anorexia, faulty therapeutic diets, increased gastrointestinal motility, hemorrhage and exudation, and impaired absorption independent of intestinal hypermotility. The buccal and lingual mucous membranes may present abnormalities analogous to those encountered in sprue, pellagra, and pernicious anemia. The skin may show changes similar to those reported in vitamin A deficiency and in pellagra. Nutritional edema occurs in advanced cases. Nutritional deficiency may play a role in the production of fatty liver and, less frequently, hepatic cirrhosis. Ascorbic acid and vitamin K deficiencies may contribute importantly to the degree of blood loss.

Some patients present a reduction in blood calcium and disturbance of the acid-base mechanism. According to Posey and Bargen, osseous demineralization occurs frequently. They list a multiplicity of factors contributing to the development of osteoporosis, including steatorrhea, reduced concentrations of vitamin C, hypoproteinemia, malnutrition, and "diminished protein anabolism of corticoadrenal steroids." They reported diminished urinary excretion of 17-ketosteroids, abnormal urinary excretions of corticosteroids, and impairment of adrenal reserve function.

According to Jones, renal calculi may occur in some cases, owing presumably to (1) dehydration as a result of chronic fluid loss and (2) increased loss of calcium in the urine due to confinement to bed for long periods. He points out that the abdominal or flank pain produced by these calculi may be overlooked because of the coexisting colitis. Maratka and Nedbal report increased incidence of calculi in the urinary tract of patients who have had ileostomies, and suggest that the loss of water and sodium through the ileostomy results in a fall in urinary output and urinary sodium loss and a tendency to form stones.

Clinical and roentgenologic studies indicate that frequently there is a significant disorder of the small bowel in ulcerative colitis. There may be an inability to absorb an amino acid mixture from the upper jejunum to a degree comparable with that of normal persons. The degree of impairment of absorption may correlate with the severity of clinical evidence of malnutrition. Abnormal oral sugar tolerance curves occurred in two-thirds of a series of patients with ulcerative colitis, the majority of the abnormal curves being of the low or flat types. There may be low fasting plasma vitamin A levels.

An abnormally large fecal excretion of nitrogen (five to six times the normal) may result in negative nitrogen balance. The fecal nitrogen loss is largely due to colonic exudate, since it is not rapidly diminished during total abstinence from food (Almy). Increased excretion of sodium, chloride, and potassium in the feces is probably the result of large losses of intestinal fluids and may lead to shock in some instances. The loss of sodium through the intestinal tract is greater than the loss of chloride, which may be explained by the fact that the intestinal fluid contains relatively less fixed acid than it does fixed base. Posey and Bargen noted instances of potassium deficiency accompanied by characteristic electrocardiographic alterations.

Patients with ulcerative colitis may possess a total exchangeable I^{131} albumin pool that is much smaller than the normal value of approximately 360 gm. Following administration of radioactive albumin to such patients, there occurs a 10 to 50 per cent fecal loss of the radioactive tag. The small albumin pool may thus be due to prolonged fecal loss and inadequate replacement. Immunologic techniques demonstrate the presence of typical blood albumin and globulin in the intestinal lumen of patients suffering from active ulcerative colitis, showing that there is a true protein "leak" across the mucosa.

In 1961 Truelove described a small group of patients with ulcerative colitis in whom a remission followed removal of milk and milk products from the diet, while resumption of milk was followed by relapse in the course of a few days or weeks. It is quite likely that some of these patients were suffering from lactose intolerance. Taylor and Truelove found that patients with ulcerative colitis were much more liable to have high titer serological reactions to purified cow's milk proteins than healthy subjects, but were unable to determine whether the findings had any direct clinical significance. Acheson and Truelove found patients with ulcerative colitis twice as liable as a control group to have been weaned from the breast within the first months of life.

Truelove has reported rapid clinical remission in nearly three-fourths of a series of cases of ulcerative colitis of mild or moderate severity following local treatment with a water-soluble corticosteroid (hydrocortisone hemisuccinate sodium or prednisolone 21-phosphate), applied by means of a nightly rectal drip. Only about one-third of the patients treated with oral prednisolone went into rapid clinical remission. With combined systemic and local treatment, the results depended on the particular combination used. When oral prednisolone was combined with local prednisolone 21-phosphate, the results were similar to those of local treatment used alone. When oral prednisolone was combined with local hydrocortisone hemisuccinate sodium, all the patients so treated showed rapid remission. Since the hydrocortisone hemisuccinate sodium is apparently poorly absorbed, the beneficial action of topical hydrocortisone hemisuccinate in ulcerative colitis is presumably a local one upon the mucosa. As Truelove has pointed out, the observation of Nugent and associates that different metabolic pathways may be involved in the breakdown of hydrocortisone and prednisolone in the body is of considerable interest in this connection.

The assumption that autoimmune processes may be involved in ulcerative colitis has received increasing support from the studies of Broberger and Perlman, and Kirsner and associates. The former have demonstrated that most of the sera obtained from 30 children suffering with ulcerative colitis contained a precipitating and hemagglutinating factor, reacting with a constituent of human colonic tissue and behaving electrophoretically as a gamma globulin. The autoantibodies were present in considerable amounts in saline extracts of regional colonic glands, possibly indicating production of antibodies near the ulcerative lesions. Kirsner and Bregman report circulating antibodies to colon tissue in the sera of patients with ulcerative colitis, although not uniformly. On the other hand, Soergel was unable to detect any electrophoretic differences between rectal mucus from normal persons and that from patients with ulcerative colitis, and various precipitation tests failed to reveal antibodies to rectal mucus in the sera of patients with ulcerative colitis. Calabresi and associates have demonstrated the presence of antinuclear globulins by the fluoroescent antiglobulin technique in a large proportion of patients with longstanding ulcerative colitis; the antinuclear factor was not found in patients who had previously undergone colectomy. Although the role of autoimmune mechanisms remains uncertain, Taylor and Truelove believe that there is a strong possibility that they are an important factor in the perpetuation of the disease even if they are not responsible for its initiation.

The beneficial effect of steroid therapy noted in ulcerative colitis would be in keeping with the assumption that an autoimmune disorder could be involved. Thus it is possible that the adrenal steroids, in addition to their anti-inflammatory effects, also inhibit the production of autoantibodies. It should also be noted that high levels of gamma globulin are often observed in sera from patients with ulcerative colitis.

Hepatic disease is a common complication of chronic ulcerative colitis. It may take the form of fatty vacuolization, chronic hepatitis, cirrhosis, or pericholangitis with recent studies indicating that pericholangitis is probably the most common. The pathogenesis of pericholangitis in patients with colitis is still not proved, but strong suspicion has been cast on the bacteria or bacterial products absorbed from the diseased colon. The pericholangitis may be reflected biochemically primarily by elevation of the serum 5-nucleotidase, the major source of which is the bile canaliculi. Mistilis and associates found no correlation between the presence and severity of liver disease and the presence of severe colitis.

Arthritis is also common and often occurs in association with skin lesions, especially erythema nodosum. The arthritis most commonly affects one or more of the big joints, especially the knees or ankles. The clinical picture may at times resemble rheumatoid arthritis. Ankylosing spondylitis may also be associated with ulcerative colitis and not infrequently precedes the bowel symptoms.

Cooke and associates found a raised value for seromucoids in ulcerative colitis (and regional enteritis) to be associated with other evidence of clinical activity of the lesion. The most seriously ill patients had the highest seromucoid values. (They found the mean value for seromucoids in normals to be 77.3 [S.D. 14.6] mg. per 100 cc., with a range of 46 to 110 mg. per 100 cc.) They found a close inverse relation between seromucoid and serum albumin in patients with regional ileitis, but a less close one in ulcerative colitis. The test proved a more sensitive index of activity of the lesion than the erythrocyte sedimentation rate.

Ulcerative colitis may become fulminant

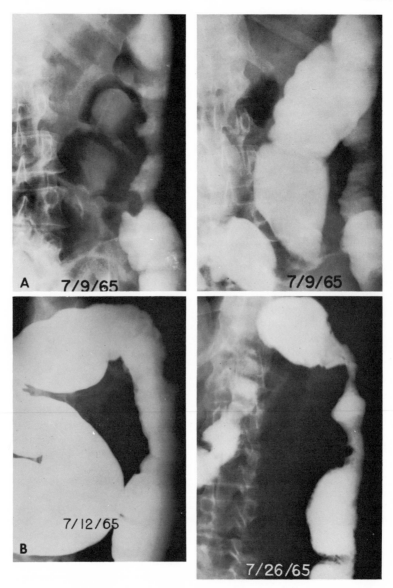

Figure 26–9. *A,* Edema, spasm, and "thumbprinting" of segment of descending colon in middle-aged female with sudden onset of pain and tenderness in area. Note change in appearance during same examination. *B,* Three days later the segment is more rigid and shows less edema. Over next 14 days progressive stricture formation has occurred. (Courtesy of Dr. Jerome Wiot.)

with sudden development of severe symptoms, both colonic and systemic. Diffuse or segmental acute dilatation of the colon—"toxic megacolon"—may ensue and presage perforation. Fulminant colitis may seemingly be precipitated by anticholinergics and opiates used to control diarrhea or by the performance of a barium enema.

It has recently been recognized that segmental involvement of the bowel as a result of intestinal ischemia may assume the characteristics of inflammation or stricture or both (Fig. 26–9).

Much interest has recently been aroused in granulomatous colitis or Crohn's disease of the large intestine, which is thought to be increasing in frequency. About one-third of these patients have associated involvement of the terminal ileum, while the rectum is normal in half the cases in sharp contrast with ulcerative colitis. The mucosal surface has a characteristic cobblestone appearance with intercommunicating fissures or linear ulcers between the "cobblestones." Spontaneous abdominal fistulas are occasionally present. Sarcoid tubercles occur in three-fourths of the cases. Anal lesions were found by Lockhart-Mummery and Morson in 61 of 75 patients. Diarrhea is the most frequent symptom, while grossly bloody stools are present in less than half the cases.

Lymphopathia Venereum

Bleeding is a direct consequence of the replacement of a part of the mucosa by granulation tissue resulting from the local action of the virus. Bacterial infection of the raw surface and the pyogenic property of the virus soon cause the anal discharge to be purulent. Contraction of the fibrous elements of the granulation tissue produces a narrowing of the lumen of the bowel which may be partial (stricture) or complete (stenosis). There is little or no pain until the development of stricture, when abdominal cramps and tenesmus are likely to appear. Constipation may be progressive, and the passage of blood and pus may be increased after catharsis. The smallest diameter of the lumen of the bowel compatible with evacuation, aided by cathartics, has been demonstrated to be approximately 8 mm.

Amebiasis

The location of the tissue reaction may in part be responsible for the wide variation in clinical pictures in the same infection from time to time. While this variation may be partly due to differences in virulence of organisms and in the host factor, location of the tissue reaction is important. In amebiasis, for example, although all areas of the colon may be involved, two are more frequently involved than any others, namely, the cecal region and the rectosigmoid region. In the former group, diarrhea is uncommon, and vague intestinal symptoms, symptoms of appendicitis (with actual involvement of the appendix), and reflex symptoms simulating gallbladder disease and peptic ulcer occur. When the infection has attacked the sigmoid and rectal regions, diarrhea or dysentery occurs, the latter especially when the colon is diffusely involved. Thus the location of the lesion determines whether diarrhea with liquid stools is present or whether formed stools, even to constipation, are passed. Exacerbations of the disease may occur in situations of stress which it is thought may make the resulting more fragile colonic mucosa more susceptible to invasion by amebae.

Shigella Infections

The diffuse and active process produces diarrhea almost routinely. The toxin of B. *dysenteriae* causes acute inflammation of the colon, leading to coagulation necrosis of the mucosa and ulceration. In general, the sigmoid and rectum are most frequently and severely affected.

The mucosa, in the early stages of most cases of acute bacillary dysentery, when coagulation necrosis has developed, has a grayish-green necrotic appearance and shows hemorrhagic areas. A few days later ulceration may be observed with sloughing of the necrotic mucosa. In milder cases the mucosa is of a strawberry-red tint with diffuse inflammation and hyperemia, bleeding when traumatized.

Diverticula

Variations in symptoms as a result of local reactions occur in some diseases having similar anatomic backgrounds. Diverticula of the colon produce a different symptom complex from those in the small intestine. This difference may be caused by the level of the lesion, as discussed previously, but may also rest on a difference in the causative factors, even though the defect has the same name. In the colon, diverticula are commonest in the sigmoid portion and generally occur after the age of fifty. They are probably more common than is generally realized. It is well to keep in mind, as Welch has noted, that routine barium examinations are more accurate in revealing them than are routine autopsies, since diverticula are found readily by the radiologist but require particular search by the pathologist. The usual site is between the mesocolic and antimesenteric taeniae. Roentgen evidence strongly supports the viewpoint that colonic diverticula increase in number and size as the age of the patient increases. Diverticula form at the points of penetration of the muscularis by blood vessels. They are formed by herniation of the mucosa through a gap in the intestinal muscle layer.

It has recently been shown that hypertrophy of the sigmoid musculature with significant increase in the thickness of both circular and longitudinal muscle bundles may be encountered in the incipient stages of diverticulosis and in the total absence of inflammation. This anatomic finding, revealed roentgenologically by narrowing, corrugation, and a saw-tooth appearance of the barium-filled sigmoid, had in the recent past been wrongly considered secondary to advanced diverticulitis (Fig. 26–10). The basis of the hypertrophy is presumably the increased motor activity of the sigmoid colon as expressed in

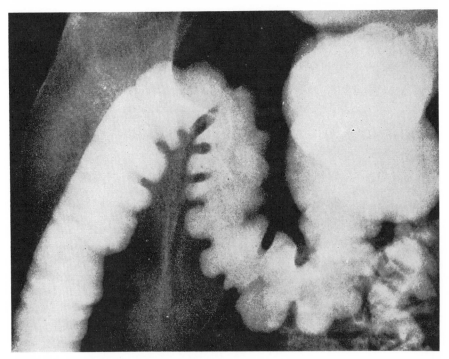

A

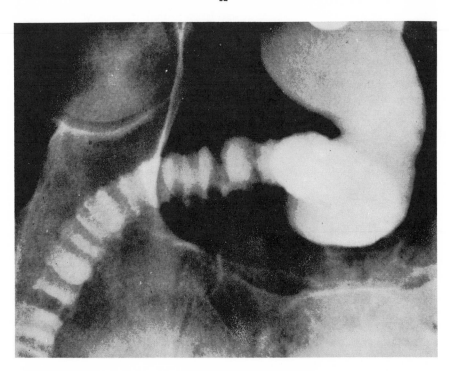

B

Figure 26–10. Radiograms of the sigmoid colon in a patient in whom the recorded intra-sigmoid pressure and number of strong waves were unusually high, but diverticula were not demonstrable. The sigmoid seemed to be drawn together lengthwise and had a corrugated appearance. The haustra were small and separated by often quite broad and circular indentations. *A*, Early stage and *B*, late stage of barium enema. (From Arfwidsson, S.: Acta Chir. Scand., Suppl. 342, 1964.)

intrasigmoid pressure and the number of strong waves (greater than 30 cm. of water) recorded during a 30-minute period of study (Fig. 26–11). The motor activity is increased even at rest and is further augmented by meals and by parasympathetic stimulation with injection of Prostigmin (Figs. 26–12 and 26–13).

Hypodermic injection of morphine produces further increase in motor activity in diverticular disease in contrast with injection of meperidine. Arfwidsson has adduced evidence to indicate that the high intrasigmoid pressure caused by increased sigmoid motor activity contributes to the pathogenesis of the diverticula and to much of the symptomatology of diverticular disease of the colon. High intrasigmoid pressures evoked by morphine have been shown by Painter and associates to be accompanied by distention of neighboring diverticula, sometimes to an extreme degree.

Although the necks of the diverticula may shut under the influence of morphine, they do not remain closed but open intermittently and allow colonic contents to be squirted into the diverticula. It thus appears possible that the use of morphine in acute diverticulitis may predispose to rupture of inflamed diverticula. Painter and associates have shown that these effects of morphine can be abolished by an intravenous injection of Probanthine.

The early symptoms of diverticular disease are remarkably similar to those of the irritable colon; as Almy has stated, "the knowledge that increased wavelike contractions of the sigmoid are a normal body accompaniment of emotional tension suggests that this ubiquitous phenomenon may play a major role in the formation of diverticula." Symptoms may be due to the increased motor activity of the sigmoid colon and the factors which further

Age group in years	Normal subjects			Diverticular patients		
	Case no.	Total pressure in cm²	Number of waves ≥ 30 cm H_2O	Case no.	Total pressure in cm²	Number of waves ≥ 30 cm H_2O
20—29	1	2.4	0	21	60.9	1
30—39	2	0	0	22	8.0	0
	3	1.8	0	23	43.9	7
	4	6.4	0	24	45.6	3
	5	26.7	0	25	109.6	20
40—49	6	0	0	26	95.8	13
	7	0	0	27	25.3	1
	8	3.4	0	28	64.5	13
	9	57.9	7	29	80.7	13
50—59	10	0	0	30	12.6	4
	11	0	0	31	56.7	0
	12	8.1	0	32	45.6	10
	13	18.4	0	33	79.5	6
	14	33.5	7	34	211.2	33
60—69	15	3.4	0	35	10.5	2
	16	3.7	1	36	11.5	3
	17	6.3	0	37	34.7	3
	18	7.3	0	38	20.6	0
	19	16.3	0	39	88.1	17
70—79	20	19.8	1	40	26.8	3
		215.4	16		1132.1	152
Mean		10.77 ± 3.3	0.80 ± 0.5		56.61 ± 10.6	7.60 ± 1.9

Figure 26–11. The total intrasigmoid pressure and number of strong waves in the sigmoid colon at rest in normal subjects and in patients with diverticular disease. (From Arfwidsson, S.: Acta Chir. Scand., Suppl. 342, 1964.)

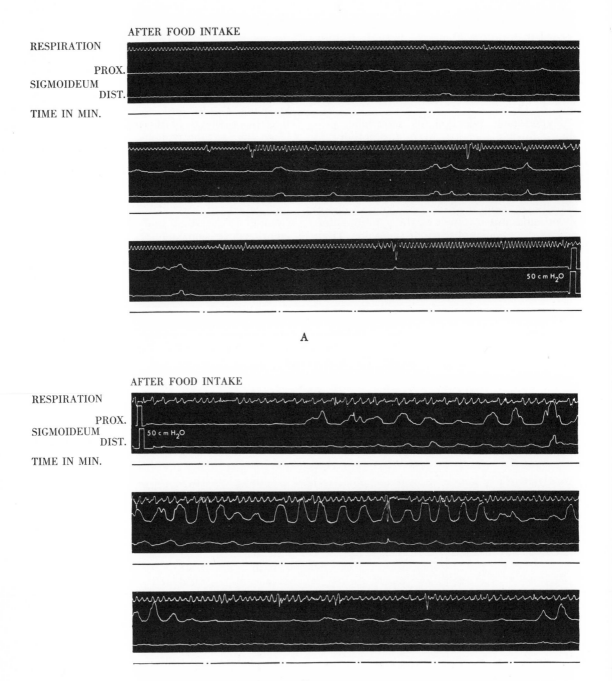

Figure 26–12. *A*, Postprandial record from a normal subject showing three consecutive periods of 6 minutes each. There were 20 pressure waves in the whole 30-minute period with a maximal amplitude of 25 cm. water, and the total pressure was 26.7 cm.² *B*, Postprandial record from a diverticular patient showing three consecutive periods of 6 minutes each. There were 65 pressure waves in the whole 30-minute period, 32 of them with an amplitude greater than 30 cm. water, and the total pressure was 235.4 cm.² (From Arfwidsson, S.: Acta Chir. Scand., Suppl. 342, 1964.)

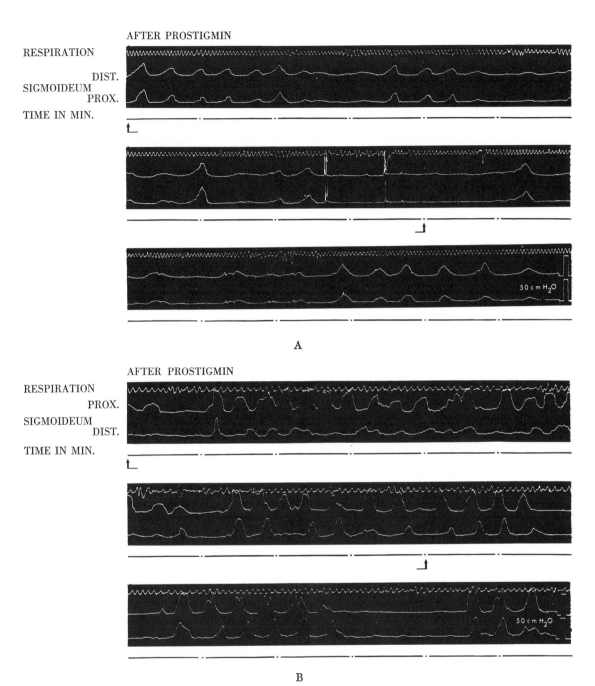

Figure 26–13. *A*, Record of sigmoid motor activity in a normal subject starting 10 minutes after i.v. injection of 0.5 mg. Prostigmin, three consecutive periods of 6 minutes each; the 10-minute period used for calculation is indicated. There were four pressure waves with an amplitude greater than 30 cm. water, and the total pressure was 52.0 cm.² *B*, Record of sigmoid motor activity in a diverticular patient starting 10 minutes after i.v. injecion of 0.5 mg. Prostigmin, three consecutive periods of 6 minutes each; the 10-minute period used for calculation is indicated. There were 25 pressure waves with an amplitude greater than 30 cm. water, and the total pressure was 204.1 cm.² (From Arfwidsson, S.: Acta Chir. Scand., Suppl. 342, 1964.)

enhance it, and take the form of pain in the left lower abdomen, occurring or increasing in severity at a definite time interval after meals or following emotional disturbance, and being relieved or temporarily abolished by a bowel movement. Symptoms may also be produced by recurring attacks of acute inflammation, to low grade chronic inflammation, or to a gradually developing chronic obstruction associated with narrowing of the sigmoid colon and distention of the right colon. In the last-named type of case, right-sided pain may predominate (Allen), as would be expected, from distention of the right colon. Because of the lack of a muscular layer, the diverticulum is thought to be incapable of emptying itself and thus to be predisposed to the development of an inflammatory process. The contents of the diverticulum become solidified and cause ulceration in the mucosa with ensuing infection. The neck of the sac, which is the narrowest part, becomes constricted because of edema and hyperemia, and its failure to empty results in a pathologic process similar to that observed in obstructive inflammation of the vermiform appendix. The process rarely goes on to acute perforation, but much more commonly to a chronic perforation with formation of peridiverticulitis or peridiverticular abscess. The abscess may perforate (1) into the bowel, resulting in discharge of pus; (2) into the bladder, producing a vesicocolic fistula with bladder irritability and passage of pus, feces, and air through the urethra; (3) into the surrounding tissues and become walled off; or (4) into the pelvic floor and simulate an ischiorectal abscess or fistula in ano.

In chronic diverticulitis there has usually developed a marked inflammatory hyperplasia with partial intermittent bowel obstruction in association with adhesions. A mass may be present at the site of the inflammatory reaction, usually in the left lower abdominal quadrant. It is well to remember that a mass may represent only the hypertrophied sigmoid, particularly in the absence of fever and leukocytosis. The signs and symptoms of low grade intermittent bowel obstruction may intervene. Later, in rare instances, complete bowel obstruction may develop. Diarrhea frequently occurs just before or after an exacerbation of diverticulitis and may be extremely troublesome in chronic stages of the disease.

Hemorrhage is probably a more common complication of diverticulitis of the colon than is generally realized and may be explained by the fact that the diverticula form at the points of penetration of the muscularis by blood vessels. An incidence of 15 per cent has been found in 200 unselected cases, and at the Massachusetts General Hospital it was observed in 27 per cent of patients who required a resection.

Tumors and Polyps

According to Welch, there are four important varieties of polypoid lesions of the bowel: simple adenoma, papillary adenoma, polypoid carcinoma, and cancer developing from papillary adenoma—which in toto comprise 95 per cent of all the polypoid lesions of the colon and rectum. Adenomas, particularly when situated in the sigmoid or descending colon, tend to develop long pedicles, presumably because of greater peristaltic "pull," while pedicles are rare with invasive cancer (Fig. 26–14).

The symptoms which polypoid lesions of the bowel produce will, as in the small intestine, depend upon their location and number, the distribution, rate of growth, size, shape, and tendency to ulceration, infection, and malignant change. Small adenomas, not enlarging, but retaining normal epithelial characteristics and located high in the colon where the contents are liquid, may persist for long periods of time without symptoms. Factors which produce symptoms are numerous. Although they rarely obstruct the colon because of the size of the lumen, colocolic intussusception with obstruction or prolapse of the rectum and obstruction may result from peristaltic propulsion of a pedunculated adenoma. Ulceration with or without malignant change will result in bleeding, and inflammation or erosion may produce irritative bowel symptoms.

One of the characteristic features of the papillary or villous adenoma, particularly that with a very large surface area, is the secretion of considerable mucus that contains large amounts of electrolytes, particularly potassium. As much as 1000 cc. of mucus may be secreted from one of these tumors in 24 hours and severe hypokalemia may ensue. The villous adenoma frequently involves more than half the circumference of the bowel wall, with numerous characteristic fronds protruding from its surface.

The occurrence of polyps singly or in small numbers in the cecum, ascending and transverse parts of the colon is less frequent than in the left half of the colon. In the right half of the colon they are subject to little trauma, owing to the liquid character of the stool; as a consequence, ulceration and bleeding occur less often. Blood is likely to be occult and well mixed with the stools. For this reason, and because of the absence of other symptoms, most polyps in the right colon probably go unrecognized until long after malignant change has occurred. In rare instances colocolic intussusception occurs and irritative diarrhea may result from inflammation in ulcerated areas.

In the left colon and rectum, polyps are more subject to trauma because of the solidity of the stool, and accordingly are more liable to bleed or become inflamed. Blood coming from the left colon is often visible and may be mixed with the stool when it comes from the sigmoid colon, or may coat the stool when it comes from the rectum. Periods of diarrhea may result from peristaltic attempts to propel an adenoma or from the irritative effect of inflammation. In the latter instance excessive amounts of mucus may be found in the stools. Prolapse of the sigmoid to a degree resulting in intussusception is rare, but varying degrees of prolapse of the left colon and rectal mucosa are common. Partial or complete prolapse of rectal mucosa through the anal orifice may be initiated by polyps.

Familial polyposis is a rare disorder and is characterized by its familial occurrence, diffuse involvement of the colon, and a tendency for the patient to develop carcinoma at an early age. The polyposis is transmitted as a heterozygous dominant trait. Diarrhea is usually the initial symptom; it is followed by abdominal cramps, blood loss, weakness, and finally by the development of carcinoma. A number of observers have noted the regression and even disappearance of some of the adenomas of the rectum after colectomy and ileoproctostomy. It has been suggested by Cole and associates that ileal contents might inhibit the development and growth of rectal adenomas after subtotal colectomy, since the adenomas close to the ileorectal anastomosis are the first to disappear and adenomas are much less common in the right side of the colon where there is greater exposure to ileal contents.

Gardner's syndrome is an inheritable disease characterized by polyposis of the colon, multiple osteomatosis, and multiple cutaneous or subcutaneous tumors.

Pseudopolyps grossly resemble pedunculated or sessile adenomas, but are composed entirely of inflammatory granulomas with an adenomatous element and are most commonly associated with ulcerative colitis.

Carcinoma is the most common malignant tumor. About one-half of all colonic carcinomas occur in the rectum, one-quarter in the sigmoid, and one-quarter in the remainder of the colon. Ninety-nine per cent of the carci-

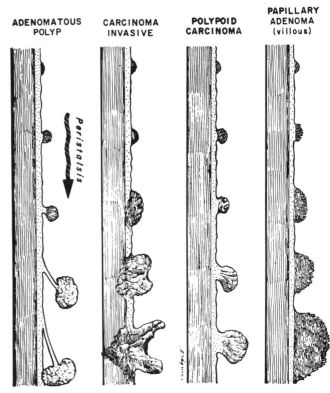

ADENOMATOUS POLYP **CARCINOMA INVASIVE** **POLYPOID CARCINOMA** **PAPILLARY ADENOMA (villous)**

Peristalsis

Figure 26–14. Castleman's conception of pedicle formation. With papillary adenomas, the broad base prevents prolapse so that pedicles are rare. Polypoid cancer may develop with a short pedicle. Invasive cancer rapidly fixes mucosa to muscularis so that pedicle formation becomes impossible. Simple adenomas, by proliferation at the tip, develop large heads, so that the underlying mucosa is soon pulled into a pedicle by peristalsis. (From Welch, C. E.: Polypoid Lesions of the Gastrointestinal Tract. Philadelphia, W. B. Saunders Co., 1964.)

nomas of the large intestinal tract are adeno-carcinomas and about 1 per cent are squamous carcinomas arising from the anal canal. Sarcomas of the colon are relatively rare, occurring mostly in children, in whom they are more common than carcinoma. Carcinoma of the colon originates either in a pre-existing polyp or in a sessile, indurated nodule in the mucosa; this has been recently debated. Some have classified the growths into four types; nodular, scirrhous, mucinous, and papillary (villous).

The arbitrary division of the colon into two halves helps to clarify the evolution of symptoms produced by tumors of the large intestine. Differences in the manifestations of tumors of the right and left halves of the colon are due to structural and functional differences between these parts and to the differences in the character of the tumors invading them. Notwithstanding the tendency of tumors in the right half of the colon to become large, fungating growths, the liquid nature of the fecal content and the greater diameter of the lumen tend to prevent the development of obstruction. Furthermore, the location of the tumor on the lateral wall and the tendency toward penetration of the bowel rather than encirclement also militate against the development of obstruction. On the other hand, in tumors of the left half of the colon the smaller bowel lumen, the thicker contents, and the tendency of the tumors to be scirrhous and to encircle the lumen of the bowel (producing the so-called napkin-ring type of growth) explain the much greater frequency of obstruction in this half. According to Wangensteen, about one-third of the cases of carcinoma of the colon give rise to acute or chronic intestinal obstruction, and nine of every ten cases of colonic obstruction are due to carcinoma.

The mechanism of the anemia which is frequent and striking in carcinomas of the right half of the colon and which is usually not ascribable to blood loss is not clear. The anemia seems definitely related to some perverted function of the mucous membrane of the large intestine which permits the absorption of toxins from the extensively infected surface of the growth and neighboring segment of the bowel.

Blood in the stools is much more frequently observed by patients with lesions in the left half of the colon than by those with lesions in the right half, and is most frequently noted by those with carcinoma of the rectum. Abdominal cramps and pain are much more fre-quent when the tumor is located in either the right or left colon than in the rectum.

Tumefaction is more common in the left half of the colon because of the greater accessibility of this part and the predominance of obstructive features which dam back the bowel content, producing impaction and dilatation.

Colonic obstructions due to tumor are essentially simple. Wangensteen has emphasized the role of the ileocecal valve and sphincter in converting an occlusion of the colon into a strangulating obstruction with necrosis, gangrene, and perforation of the cecum. According to him, perforation is more likely to develop in acute obstruction than when the occlusion develops slowly and permits thickening and hypertrophy of the bowel wall. Volvulus may occur, especially when the obstruction is in the sigmoid flexure. Intussusception also occurs, but is unusual; it occurs with predilection in the presence of polypoid tumor in the sigmoid flexure and cecum, with the intussusception usually of the chronic type. According to Welch, approximately 80 per cent of acute obstructions of the colon seen at the Massachusetts General Hospital are due to cancer, 15 per cent to diverticulitis and 5 per cent to other causes, of which volvulus is the most common.

REFERENCES

Acheson, E. D., and Truelove, S. C.: Early weaning in the aetiology of ulcerative colitis. Brit. Med. J. 2:929, 1961.

Adler, H. F., Atkinson, A. J., and Ivy, A. C.: A study of the motility of the human colon: An explanation of dysynergia of the colon, or of the "unstable colon." Am. J. Dig. Dis., 8:197, 1941.

Allen, A. W.: Surgery of diverticulitis of the colon. Am. J. Surg., 86:545, 1953.

Almy, T. P.: Experimental studies on the irritable colon. Am. J. Med., 10:60, 1951.

Almy, T. P.: Diverticular disease of the colon—the new look. Gastroenterology, 49:109, 1965.

Almy, T. P., and Lewis, C. M.: Ulcerative colitis: A report of progress, based upon the recent literature. Gastroenterology, 45:515, 1963.

Alvarez, W. C.: An Introduction to Gastro-Enterology. New York, Paul B. Hoeber, 1940.

Arfwidsson, S.: Pathogenesis of multiple diverticula of the sigmoid colon in diverticular disease. Acta Chir. Scand., Suppl. 342, 1964.

Barclay, A. E.: Note on the movements of the large intestine. Arch. Roentgen Ray, 16:422, 1912.

Broberger, O., and Perlmann, P.: Autoantibodies in human ulcerative colitis. J. Exper. Med., 110:657, 1959.

Calabresi, P., Thayer, W. R., Jr., and Spiro, H. M.: Demonstration of circulating antinuclear globulins in ulcerative colitis. J. Clin. Invest., 40:2126, 1961.

Chaudhary, N. A., and Truelove, S. C.: Colonic motility. A critical review of methods and results. Am. J. Med., *31*:86, 1961.

Chaudhary, N. A., and Truelove, S. C.: Human colonic motility: A comparative study of normal subjects, patients with ulcerative colitis, and patients with the irritable colon syndrome. I. Resting patterns of motility. Gastroenterology, *40*:1, 1961.

Chaudhary, N. A., and Truelove, S. C.: Human colonic motility: A comparative study of normal subjects, patients with ulcerative colitis, and patients with the irritable colon syndrome. II. The effect of Prostigmin. Gastroenterology, *40*:18, 1961.

Chaudhary, N. A., and Truelove, S. C.: Human colonic motility: A comparative study of normal subjects, patients with ulcerative colitis, and patients with the irritable colon syndrome. III. Effects of emotions. Gastroenterology, *40*:27, 1961.

Chaudhary, N. A., and Truelove, S. C.: The irritable colon syndrome. A study of the clinical features, predisposing causes, and prognosis in 130 cases. Quart. J. Med., *31*:307, 1962.

Code, C. F., Wilkinson, G. R., Jr., and Sauer, W. G.: Normal and some abnormal colonic motor patterns in man. In The colon: Its normal and abnormal physiology and therapeutics. Ann. New York Acad. Sc., *58*:317, 1954.

Cole, J. W., McKalen, A., and Powell, J.: The role of ileal contents in the spontaneous regression of rectal adenomas. Dis. Colon Rectum, *4*:413, 1961.

Connell, A. M., Jones, F. A., and Rowlands, E. N.: Motility of the pelvic colon. IV. Abdominal pain associated with colonic hypermotility after meals. Gut, *6*:105, 1965.

Cooke, W. T., et al.: The clinical significance of seromucoids in regional enteritis and ulcerative colitis. Gastroenterology, *34*:910, 1958.

Davis, J. E., Seavey, P. W., and Sessions, J. T., Jr.: Villous adenomas of the rectum and sigmoid colon with severe fluid and electrolyte depletion. Ann. Surg., *155*:806, 1962.

Dunning, M. W. F.: The clinical features of haemorrhage from diverticula of the colon. Gut, *4*:273, 1963.

Engel, G. L.: Studies of ulcerative colitis. II. The nature of the somatic processes and the adequacy of psychosomatic hypotheses. Am. J. Med., *16*:416, 1954.

Findlay, C. W., Jr., and O'Connor, T. F.: Villous adenomas of the large intestine with fluid and electrolyte depletion. J.A.M.A., *176*:404, 1961.

Fleischner, F. G., Ming, S. C., and Henken, E. M.: Revised concepts on diverticular disease of the colon. I. Diverticulosis: Emphasis on tissue derangement and its relation to the irritable colon syndrome. Radiology, *83*:859, 1964.

Goldgraber, M. B., and Kirsner, J. B.: The arthus phenomenon in the colon of rabbits: A serial histological study. A.M.A. Arch. Path., *67*:556, 1959.

Goldgraber, M. B., Kirsner, J. B., and Palmer, W. L.: On the histopathology of ulcerative colitis and its pathogenic implications. In Proceedings of the World Congress of Gastroenterology, vol. 1. Baltimore, Williams & Wilkins Co., 1959.

Grace, W. J., Wolf, S., and Wolff, H. G.: The Human Colon. An Experimental Study Based on Direct Observation of Four Fistulous Subjects. New York, Paul B. Hoeber, Inc., 1951.

Gray, S., and Reifenstein, R. W.: Antilysozyme and steroid therapy in ulcerative colitis. In The colon: Its normal and abnormal physiology and therapeutics. Ann. New York Acad. Sc., *58*:474, 1954.

Hurst, A. F.: Constipation and Allied Intestinal Disorders. London, Henry Frawde, 1921.

Ingelfinger, F. J.: The treatment of chronic constipation. In The colon: Its normal and abnormal physiology and therapeutics. Ann. New York Acad. Sc., *58*:503, 1954.

Jacobson, M. A., and Kirsner, J. B.: The basement membranes of the epithelium of the colon and rectum in ulcerative colitis and other diseases. Gastroenterology, *30*:279, 1956.

Jones, C. M.: Medical aspects of chronic ulcerative colitis. Am. J. Surg., *86*:608, 1953.

Kern, F., Jr., Almy, T. P., Abbot, F. K., and Bogdonoff, M. D.: The motility of the distal colon in nonspecific ulcerative colitis. Gastroenterology, *19*:492, 1951.

Kirsner, J. B., and Bregman, E.: Immunologic studies in ulcerative colitis, abstr. Gastroenterology, *38*:970, 1960.

Kirsner, J. B., and Elchlepp, J. G.: The production of an experimental ulcerative colitis in rabbits. Tr. Assoc. Am. Phys., *70*:102, 1957.

Kirsner, J. B., and Goldgraber, M. B.: Hypersensitivity, autoimmunity, and the digestive tract. Gastroenterology, *38*:536, 1960.

Koelle, G. B.: Autonomic and pharmacologic control of colonic activity. In The colon: Its normal and abnormal physiology and therapeutics. Ann. New York Acad. Sc., *58*:307, 1954.

Korelitz, B. I., and Janowitz, H. D.: Dilatation of the colon, a serious complication of ulcerative colitis. Ann. Int. Med., *53*:153, 1960.

Kratzer, G. L., and Hamandi, W. J.: Acute fulminating ulcerative colitis. Dis. Colon Rectum, *4*:424, 1961.

Lagercrantz, R., Winberg, J., and Zetterstrom, R.: Extra-colonic manifestations in chronic ulcerative colitis. Acta Paediat., *47*:675, 1958.

Lockhart-Mummery, H. E., and Morson, B. C.: Crohn's disease of the large intestine. Gut, *5*:493, 1964.

Lumsden, K., Chaudhary, N. A., and Truelove, S. C.: The irritable colon syndrome. J. Fac. Radiologists, *14*:54, 1963.

Maratka, Z., and Nedbal, J.: Urolithiasis as a complication of the surgical treatment of ulcerative colitis. Gut, *5*:214, 1964.

Marshak, R. H., Wolf, B. S., and Eliasoph, J.: Segmental colitis. Radiology, *73*:707, 1959.

Mendeloff, A.: Chronic diarrhea, a diagnostic approach to the patient. Am. J. Dig. Dis., *3*:801, 1958.

Mistilis, S. P.: Pericholangitis and ulcerative colitis: I. Pathology, etiology, and pathogenesis. Ann. Int. Med., *63*:1, 1965.

Mistilis, S. P., Skyring, A. P., and Goulston, S. J. M.: Pericholangitis and ulcerative colitis. II. Clinical aspects. Ann. Int. Med., *63*:17, 1965.

Morson, B. C.: The muscle abnormality in diverticular disease of the sigmoid colon. Brit. J. Radiol., *36*:385, 1963.

Nabarro, J. D. N., Moxham, A., Walker, G., and Slater, J. D. H.: Rectal hydrocortisone. Brit. Med. J., 2:272, 1957.

Noer, R. J.: Hemorrhage as a complication of diverticulitis. Ann. Surg., 141:674, 1955.

Nugent, C. A., Eik-Nes, K., and Tyler, F. H.: A comparative study of the metabolism of hydrocortisone and prednisolone. J. Clin. Endocr., 19:526, 1959.

Painter, N. S., and Truelove, S. C.: The intraluminal pressure patterns in diverticulosis of the colon. I. Resting patterns of pressure. Gut, 5:201, 1964.

Painter, N. S., and Truelove, S. C.: The intraluminal pressure patterns in diverticulosis of the colon. II. The effect of morphine. Gut, 5:207, 1964.

Painter, N. S., and Truelove, S. C.: The intraluminal pressure patterns in diverticulosis of the colon. III. The effect of prostigmine. Gut, 5:365, 1964.

Painter, N. S., and Truelove, S. C.: The intraluminal pressure patterns in diverticulosis of the colon. IV. The effect of pethidine and probanthine. Gut, 5:369, 1964.

Painter, N. S., Truelove, S. C., Ardran, G. M., and Tuckey, M.: Effect of morphine, prostigmine, pethidine, and probanthine on the human colon in diverticulosis studied by intraluminal pressure recording and cineradiography. Gut, 6:57, 1965.

Palmer, W. L., Kirsner, J. B., and Rodaniche, E. C.: Studies on lymphogranuloma venereum infection of the rectum. J.A.M.A., 118:517, 1942.

Pollard, H. M., Block, M., and Bachrach, W. H.: Causes and management of anemia associated with chronic ulcerative colitis. J.A.M.A., 134:341, 1947.

Posey, E. L., and Bargen, J. A.: Metabolic derangements in chronic ulcerative colitis. Gastroenterology, 16:39, 1950.

Quigley, J. P.: Normal physiology of the colon of animals. In The colon: Its normal and abnormal physiology and therapeutics. Ann. New York Acad. Sc., 58:297, 1954.

Rankin, J. G., Goulston, S. J. M., Boden, R. W., and Morrow, A. W.: Fulminant ulcerative colitis. Quart. J. Med., 29:375, 1960.

Roth, J. L. A., Valdez-Dapena, A., Stein, G. N., and Bockus, H. L.: Toxic megacolon in ulcerative colitis. Gastroenterology, 37:239, 1959.

Rowe, P. B.: A mucus-secreting villous adenoma of the rectum. Gut. 5:250, 1964.

Schwartz, S., Boley, S. J., Lash, J., and Sternhill, V.: Roentgenologic aspects of reversible vascular occlusion of the colon and its relationship to ulcerative colitis. Radiology, 80:625, 1963.

Schwartz, S., Boley, S. J., Robinson, K., Krieger, H., Schultz, L., and Allen, A. C.: Roentgenologic features of vascular disorders of the intestines. Radiol. Clin. N. A., 2:71, 1964.

Slack, W. W.: Diverticula of the colon and their relation to the muscle layers and blood vessels. Gastroenterology, 39:708, 1960.

Sline, A., and Fogelson, S. J.: Colon motility: An experimental study of the colon in the dog. Am. J. Dig. Dis., 4:17, 1937.

Smith, F. W., Law, D. H., Nickel, W. F., Jr., and Sleisenger, M. H.: Fulminant ulcerative colitis with toxic dilation of the colon: Medical and surgical management of eleven cases with observations regarding etiology. Gastroenterology, 42:233, 1962.

Soergel, K.: Electrophoretic and immunologic properties of rectal mucus in normals and patients with ulcerative colitis. Clin. Res., 8:206, 1960.

Spencer, R. P.: The Intestinal Tract. Structure, Function and Pathology in Terms of the Basic Sciences. Springfield, Charles C Thomas, 1960.

Steinfeld, J. L., Davidson, J. D., and Gordon, R. S., Jr.: A mechanism for hypoalbuminemia in patients with ulcerative colitis and regional enteritis. J. Clin. Invest., 36:931, 1957.

Sunderland, D. A., and Binkley, G. E.: Papillary adenomas of the large intestine: A clinical and morphological study of forty-eight cases. Cancer, 1:184, 1948.

Swenson, O.: Classification and treatment of children with severe chronic constipation. Am. J. Surg., 86:497, 1953.

Swenson, O., Rheinlander, H. F., and Diamond, I.: Hirschsprung's disease: A new concept of the etiology. Operative results in 34 patients. New England J. Med., 241:551, 1949.

Taylor, K. B., and Truelove, S. C.: Circulating antibodies to milk proteins in ulcerative colitis. Brit. Med. J., 2:924, 1961.

Templeton, R. D., and Lawson, H.: Studies in the motor activity of the large intestine. I. Normal motility in the dog, recorded by the tandem balloon method. Am. J. Physiol., 96:667, 1931.

Truelove, S. C.: Systemic and local corticosteroid therapy in ulcerative colitis. Brit. Med. J., 1:464, 1960.

Truelove, S. C.: Ulcerative colitis provoked by milk. Brit. Med. J., 1:154, 1961.

Truelove, S. C., and Reynell, P. C.: Diseases of the Digestive System. Philadelphia, F. A. Davis Co., 1963, pp. 395–419.

Vinnik, I. E., and Kern, F., Jr.: Biliary cirrhosis in a patient with chronic ulcerative colitis. Gastroenterology, 45:529, 1963.

Vinnik, I. E., and Kern, F., Jr.: Liver diseases in ulcerative colitis: A review. A.M.A. Arch. Int. Med., 112:41, 1963.

Vinnik, I. E., Kern, F., Jr., and Corley, W. D.: Serum 5-nucleotidase and pericholangitis in patients with chronic ulcerative colitis. Gastroenterology, 45:492, 1963.

Wade, A. P., Slater, J. D. H., Kellie, A. E., and Holliday, M. E.: Urinary excretion of 17-ketosteroids following rectal infusion of cortisol. J. Clin. Endocrin., 19:444, 1959.

Wangensteen, O. H.: Intestinal Obstructions. Springfield, Charles C Thomas, 1942.

Weintraub, S.: The roentgenological aspects of the normal and abnormal colon. In The colon: Its normal and abnormal physiology and therapeutics. Ann. New York Acad. Sc., 58:345, 1954.

Welch, C. E.: Polypoid Lesions of the Gastrointestinal Tract. Philadelphia, W. B. Saunders Co., 1964.

Welch, P. B., and Plant, O. H.: A graphic study of the muscular activity of the colon with special reference to its response to feeding. Am. J. Med. Sc., 172:261, 1926.

Williams, I.: Changing emphasis in diverticular disease of the colon. Brit. J. Radiol., 36:393, 1963.

Chapter Twenty-Seven

The Liver

FRANZ J. INGELFINGER

Changes in Hepatic Structure

The liver may be regarded as comprising four main systems: the blood vessels, the reticuloendothelial Kupffer cells, the parenchyma, consisting of hepatocytes or polygonal cells, and the biliary channels, all four being supported by a connective tissue framework, the stroma. On microscopic examination, these various hepatic components appear arrayed in a lobular pattern, but no real lines of demarcation between lobules exist in the normal adult human liver. Hence, the definition of the hepatic lobule is a matter of conceptual choice. The preponderant view regards the central vein as at the center of the lobule and the portal tracts at the periphery, but others prefer to think of the "acinus of Rappaport," defined as a mass of hepatic tissue with a portal tract as its axis.

When any of the major hepatic systems is affected by an acute disorder, specific morphologic changes of the involved system appear initially. The anatomic relation of blood vessel, Kupffer cell, bile duct, and hepatocyte is so intimate, however, that the consequences of a continuing disorder spread beyond the system primarily affected. Sooner or later the others also undergo changes in structure. At the same time the defenses of the liver are mobilized. Mesenchymal reaction (multiplication of Kupffer cells, infiltration by inflammatory cells, and deposition of collagen), parenchymatous regeneration, and prolifera-

tion of biliary passages appear to varying degrees, depending upon the type and chronicity of tissue damage. Consequently the structural changes which eventuate during the course of any hepatic disorder are determined, not only by its nature and duration, but also by the balance achieved between tissue destruction and hepatic response. These variables, of course, are also instrumental in shaping the gross characteristics of the liver: whether large, small, hard, or soft.

PARENCHYMATOUS DISORDERS

Parenchymatous affections of the liver are caused by infectious agents, toxins, states of hypersensitivity, anoxia, metabolic disorders, and nutritional deficiencies. A sharp distinction between the morphologic effects of these etiologic factors is frequently impossible for a number of reasons: (1) except for some specific toxins and anoxia, the etiologic agents are themselves poorly defined and sometimes may act in combination rather than individually to produce liver damage; (2) the variety of hepatic reactions to injury is limited; and (3) the defenses marshalled by the liver tend to obscure any specific structural changes that may characterize the initial injury. Occasionally toxic injury to the liver exhibits a characteristic zonal distribution; i.e., the damaged area in each hepatic lobule forms a bandlike circular zone about the central vein. Damage is zonal, it is usually assumed, because the relative concentration of toxins and protective agents reaches a value optimum for tissue damage in a rather sharply defined zone as blood flows from the periphery to the center of the lobule. This explanation, however, ignores the characteristics of sinusoidal blood flow, and it is possible that the distribution of certain enzyme systems in lobular zones may determine the localization of specific toxic effects.

Outstanding examples of the determining role exercised by the quantitative aspects of hepatic damage are provided by the variable effects of viral hepatitis. In the average case, edema, mesenchymal reaction, and cholestasis are prominent, but cellular damage is spotty, often confined to an area surrounding the central vein, and characterized more by degenerative changes than by outright destruction. Since the inflammatory reaction outweighs the necrotic process, the liver is large and moderately tense and presents a rounded edge. The stroma is little damaged and serves, when healing occurs, as a framework for normal alignment of regenerating liver cells, even if parenchymatous changes have been severe. The inflammatory response likewise tends to resolve completely, and eventually the normal structure of the liver is reconstituted in all but a few cases. In the mildest forms of hepatitis, which often run an anicteric course, structural changes seen under the light microscope appear limited to focal areas of infiltration.

When viral hepatitis is fulminant, cellular necrosis is extensive and the stroma is swept clear of the destroyed parenchyma, which is replaced by hemorrhages in the center of each lobule and by densely packed inflammatory cells at the periphery. Grossly, such a liver is of relatively normal size, but its consistency is flabby. If the process is somewhat less acute, parenchymatous destruction is partial instead of complete, and the patient does not die immediately. During the period of survival, necrosis of parenchyma is followed by collapse, but not destruction, of the supporting framework. Some atypical regeneration of liver cells occurs, but the destroyed parenchyma and collapsed stroma more than offset the combined effect of regenerative activity and cellular infiltration. The liver, consequently, becomes small and atrophic—"yellow atrophy." If necrosis is sufficiently restricted to permit clinical recovery, remaining lobular fragments coalesce to form irregular nodules of parenchymal cells that are imbedded in a dense matrix of collagen and are

totally devoid of their normal supportive pattern of portal triads and central veins. Further growth and irregularity of the nodules is brought about by regeneration of hepatocytes, but the extensive fibrotic scars prevent general enlargement, and a hard, knobby, and irregular liver of small or normal size results. This picture, once called "healed yellow atrophy," today is known as *postnecrotic, coarsely nodular, multilobular,* or *postcollapse cirrhosis.*

The foregoing example illustrates that one possible (although unusual) outcome of viral hepatitis may be chronic liver disease with the structural features of postnecrotic cirrhosis. Similarly, viral hepatitis is only one (and probably unusual) cause of postnecrotic cirrhosis. Other causes include nutritional, toxic, and immunologic damage to the liver, and in many instances the cause is unknown. The point should be clear: hepatic pathology often does not mirror etiology.

In *portal cirrhosis* (also known as *Laennec's, nutritional, fatty, alcoholic, diffuse septal, monolobular,* or *microlobular cirrhosis*), one of the early pathologic manifestations is fatty infiltration, which produces a large liver of relatively normal shape and consistency. Coincident with fatty infiltration, degeneration of hepatocytes with the appearance of amorphous, eosinophilic material known as Mallory's alcoholic hyaline, inflammatory infiltrate often containing polymorphonuclear as well as mononuclear elements, fibrosis, ductular proliferation, and cholestasis are present to a variable degree. The fibrotic process is characterized by the formation of multiple thin septa that radiate between portal tract and central vein to dissect the normal liver lobule and thus produce a pattern of small, fairly regular nodules that may appear to be centered around portal tracts and thus emphasize the acinus of Rappaport. In this process, the central veins undergo sclerosis and tend to disappear altogether. According to Popper, the continuing exogenous insult to which the liver affected with portal cirrhosis is exposed (e.g., alcohol) accounts for the diffuse and progressive nature of the pathologic features. In gross terms, the liver tends to be large, greasy, firm, and characterized by a fine nodularity not detectable on physical examination.

The existence of a third type of parenchymatous cirrhosis has been convincingly argued by Gall. In terms of nodularity and fibrous septa, it appears to occupy a position midway between postnecrotic and portal cirrhosis, the nodules being of multilobular origin and of irregular size, but not nearly to the degree seen in postnecrotic cirrhosis. Fibrous septa are thinner than in the postnecrotic variety, and some vestiges of the normal position and relation of central veins and portal triads are preserved. Fatty infiltration and hyaline degeneration are not seen, but signs of a chronic inflammatory process are striking. Gall has termed this type of chronic liver disease *posthepatitic cirrhosis,* whereas Popper uses the term *incomplete septal cirrhosis.* To the extent that "posthepatitic" implies an etiology, it is unfortunate, for the varieties of cirrhosis do not permit confident identification of their several etiologies.

BILIARY DISORDERS

Biliary disorders are characterized by *cholestasis,* a term used to signify a retarded or interrupted flow of bile. Its causes may be extra- or intrahepatic. Extrahepatic causes are usually explainable on simple mechanical grounds: the lumen of the hepatic or common duct is compromised by some lesions such as neoplasm, stone, or inflammation. Similar lesions may occlude the major intrahepatic ducts to produce cholestasis in the hepatic lobes they drain. As one proceeds upstream, however, to the small peri- and intralobular bile ducts, to the ductules, to the bile capillaries, and even to the very interior of the hepatocytes themselves, the causes of cholestasis become more subtle and correspondingly more difficult to analyze.

To be sure, morphologic evidence of cholestasis may be found in some or all of these structures. The perilobular bile ducts may be involved in an inflammatory reaction, ductules may be proliferating within a matrix of mesenchymal reaction, bile capillaries may be dilated and may contain what appear to be masses of inspissated bile pigment known as bile thrombi, the microvilli lining the bile capillaries may appear plump, distorted, and numerically deficient under the electron microscope, and the same instrument may show that intracellular organelles believed to be concerned with the secretion of bile (e.g., lysosomes and Golgi apparatus) are abnormal in structure and number.

Among such pathologic manifestations, however, it may be difficult to distinguish cause and effect. A bile thrombus in a bile capillary, for example, may be the result (1) of distal obstruction in the ductules, (2) of a disorder permitting excessive leakage of water and/or solvating agents out of the bile capillary, (3) of parenchymal cell disease leading to formation of an abnormal bile pigment by the hepatocyte, and even (4) of hepatic excretion of some exogenous substance or abnormal metabolite. An unnatural bile acid, for example, may be selectively secreted by the liver but may precipitate rapidly, because of its low aqueous solubility, in the small channels of the intrahepatic biliary system.

Cholestasis is believed to cause *regurgitation* of biliary constituents into the blood. The routes by which conjugated bilirubin, bile salts, cholesterol, phospholipids, test dyes, electrolytes, and water may regurgitate are several. If the common duct of a laboratory animal is suddenly ligated, conjugated bilirubin, alkaline phosphatase, and BSP appear first in higher concentration in thoracic duct lymph than in the plasma. As seen under the electron microscope, the dilated bile capillary of an obstructed biliary system and extensions of the space of Disse are separated by such a fine partition of tissue that regurgitation of bile by leakage or perhaps by rupture seems quite possible. Thus the lymphatics may be accepted as a major pathway of biliary regurgitation. It is also possible that regurgitated substances in the space of Disse may pass readily into the sinusoidal blood through the porous sinusoidal lining. In the presence of frank parenchymal necrosis, normal barriers are disrupted and presumably permit ducts perhaps may also exercise an absorptive function with subsequent direct or indirect seepage of bile into the hepatic substance. Finally, the endothelium of obstructed bile (i.e., via lymphatics) passage of biliary constituents into the blood.

Two aspects of cholestasis deserve emphasis. In the first place, an impaired flow of bile brings about the same functional derangements whether the cause diffusely affects the bile capillaries in the liver or blocks the common duct in the form of an isolated tumor. In either case the flow of bile is impaired, and the patient manifests the clinical and biochemical phenomena that characterize the accumulation of biliary constituents in the blood and tissues. For the same reason, various liver function tests may be expected to indicate whether or not cholestasis is present, but they will not localize the cause of the cholestasis.

The second point is that cholestasis refers to the stasis of whole bile and all its components, including bile pigment, bile salts, alkaline phosphatase, and cholesterol. It should be distinguished from conditions which specifically impair the hepatic secretion of conjugated bilirubin, of test dyes, or of any isolated components of bile.

Intrahepatic Causes of Cholestasis

Examples of intrahepatic biliary disease are provided by many varieties of drug hepatitis and by cases of viral etiology in which the virus, for unknown reasons, attacks primarily the ductules, or that portion of the polygonal cell wall that lines the bile capillaries, or the secretory organelles of these cells. In some instances, such as the jaundice that may attend methyl testosterone therapy, little morphologic change except bile stasis is found in the liver. The 17-α substituted steroids, of which methyl testosterone is one, apparently interfere with the biliary secretory process by some mechanism that is not otherwise harmful. In other cases, such as the hepatitis caused by chlorpromazine, parenchyma as well as bile capillaries and ductules appear involved; and in still other instances, perhaps caused by a virus or a drug such as arsphenamine, the picture is one of bile stasis, proliferation of ductules, cellular infiltration, and early perilobular fibrosis. Cases of this last variety have been called *cholangiolitic hepatitis* to emphasize the fact that the intrahepatic biliary system is principally affected. Since cholestasis and portal inflammation are added to a normal amount of parenchyma, the liver is large, moderately firm, and not very irregular.

Some cases of cholangiolitic hepatitis resolve. Others, possibly because of an auto-immune mechanism, appear to enter a chronic phase in which extensive fibrosis superimposed on bile stasis, bile duct proliferation, and cellular infiltration is responsible for a large, hard, and irregular liver. The pathologic picture, in short, is that of *biliary cirrhosis;* but, since no evidence whatsoever exists of obstruction or bacterial infection of the larger biliary channels, the condition is designated as *"primary biliary cirrhosis."* The terms *Hanot's cirrhosis* and *xanthomatous biliary cirrhosis* have also been used to indicate chronic and intrinsic liver disease with primary biliary and secondary parenchymal effects.

Extrahepatic Causes of Cholestasis

Hepatic changes following mechanical obstruction of the hepatic and common ducts are modified by the degree and acuteness of the obstruction, by infection and by gallbladder function. Because these determinants differ in the two main clinical types of choledochal obstruction, i.e., neoplastic or benign, the hepatic effects are correspondingly different. *Neoplastic obstructions,* steadily progressive and usually uninfected, bring about an extensive dilatation of the entire biliary tract. Morphologic damage to the polygonal cells is, however, limited, and uncomplicated cholestasis appears to stimulate relatively little reaction by way of parenchymal regeneration, inflammatory infiltration, and fibrosis. Except for distention of the biliary tree, there are consequently no intrahepatic processes leading to hepatomegaly.

Even more important in preventing hepatic enlargement is the gallbladder, which, by means of its storing and concentrating functions, cushions the effects of increasing backpressure, at least until cholestasis is so advanced as to arrest the secretory activity of the liver itself. Neoplastic occlusions of the *common* duct are therefore characterized by a distended gallbladder (Courvoisier's Law) and only slight hepatic enlargement; growths that exclude cholecystic function by their situation at or above the junction of hepatic and cystic ducts may cause considerable hepatomegaly. In either case, the liver is firm but not hard, regular in shape, and very bile-stained.

Benign extrahepatic obstructions of the biliary tract are caused by gallstones or strictures. Such obstructions are rarely complete. There course, if unrelieved by surgery, is intermittent and chronic, secondary infection is almost invariable, and the gallbladder is either absent or nonfunctioning. Under such conditions the biliary passages are not only distended, but also are elongated to form a tortuous network which responds with new and irregular bile duct proliferation. As biliary stasis and infection persist, edema, cellular infiltration, parenchymatous degeneration, and fibrosis appear, particularly in the portal areas about the interlobular bile ducts. The degree of cellular infiltration is obviously related to the element of infection. If this is unchecked, the biliary channels become the site of a purulent inflammation which may develop into multiple abscesses.

The usual end result of chronic and partial obstruction of the common duct is biliary cirrhosis. The liver is large and hard, for parenchymal destruction is limited, and new bile ducts, cellular infiltration, and fibrosis contribute to the hepatic mass. The architecture of the liver, though distorted, is not completely destroyed, and the intrahepatic circulation preserves some of its original configuration. Eventually, however, the sinusoidal circulation may be sufficiently impaired to expose the parenchymal cells to undernutrition and anoxia, and the structural abnormalities of postnecrotic cirrhosis are gradually superimposed on those of biliary cirrhosis.

FATTY LIVER AND THE RELATION OF NUTRITION TO STRUCTURAL CHANGES

About 3 to 6 per cent of the wet weight of the normal human liver is contributed by fatty substances: phospholipids, triglycerides, fatty acids, cholesterol, cholesterol esters, and fat-soluble vitamins. This material, being finely dispersed or solubilized, is not seen in routine histologic sections examined by light microscopy, but small lipid droplets can be detected by special stains and also with the electron microscope in normal parenchymal and Kupffer cells. Under various abnormal conditions, however, fat accumulates to produce droplets visible by light microscopy. Such droplets, when present in profusion, enlarge the liver, sometimes massively, and the organ becomes greasy even to gross inspection. A fatty liver, in terms of wet weight, may contain 10 to 40 per cent lipid consisting predominantly of triglycerides.

The accumulation of fat in the liver has been called fatty infiltration, fatty metamorphosis, fatty degeneration, steatosis, or hepatosis, some of these terms having been introduced to indicate the origin and nature of the excess lipid. The responsible mechanisms, however, have not been clearly identified, and at least two major etiologic views must be considered. One holds that the fatty liver is the consequence of nutritional deficiency; the other contends that the direct action of a toxic substance is responsible.

One classical scheme of how and why a liver becomes fatty is exemplified by the rat consuming a choline-deficient diet. Choline, a nitrogenous substance with three methyl groups, is combined in the liver with phosphorus, glycerol, and two fatty acids to form phospholipids. If choline or another methyl donor is unavailable, phospholipid production is impaired, and fat accumulates in the liver, possibly because phospholipids, as lipoprotein components, are required to facilitate normal transport of fat from the liver, or because a block in the pathway of phospholipid synthesis may displace diglyceride fragments into the pathway that produces triglycerides. Some evidence indicates that choline promotes normal oxidation of fatty acids. Whatever the biochemical mechanism, choline deficiency in the rat leads to an accumulation of fat droplets in the liver. At first these droplets accumulate within the hepatocytes, but, as they grow larger, they break the cell membrane, escape, and coalesce with other collections of extracellular fat to form small fatty cysts. If choline is given to the animal, these fatty changes can be prevented or reversed. For this reason, choline and other dietary agents with similar properties (e.g., methionine, inositol, vitamin B_{12}) are called *lipotropic* substances.

The second view is based on the fact that some toxins, whether carbon tetrachloride or excessive amounts of alcohol, appear capable of causing excessive fat accumulation in the liver in both man and experimental animals without the prerequisite of nutritional deficiency. That alcohol may by itself produce a fatty liver is subject to a number of reasonable biochemical explanations. Alcohol, in the first place, stimulates lipolysis of depot fat, with increased release of free fatty acids into the circulation. These fatty acids may then be deposited in re-esterified form in the liver, a possibility supported by the fact that the accumulating hepatic triglycerides predominantly contain the type of fatty acids found in peripheral depot fat. Second, alcohol is oxidized in the liver to acetaldehyde and then to acetate, steps that require the presence of a hydrogen acceptor, DPN (NAD), which is reduced to DPNH ($NADH_2$). An excess of DPNH relative to DPN affects fatty acid synthesis in that the liver may produce more or different kinds of fatty acids, which then accumulate as triglycerides. Third, alcohol may alter hepatic metabolism of fatty acids by inhibiting their oxidation and/or by causing preferential synthesis of triglycerides over other pathways of fatty acid metabolism. Finally, the liver that is exposed to large amounts of alcohol may not release lipids normally into the circulation. A damaged liver, for example, may not be able to synthesize the protein necessary to form lipoproteins, the form in which lipid of hepatic origin is usually transported in blood.

Which of these four mechanisms is predominantly responsible for the fatty liver induced by alcohol is quite controversial. Both free fatty acids and triglyceride blood levels have been observed to be increased following administration of alcohol, but these changes are inconstant and appear to depend on a number of factors such as the previous condition of the animal, the amount of alcohol given, and the time interval between administration of alcohol and the measurement of serum lipids. Actually, it is difficult to imagine that one mechanism alone is responsible, for an excessive supply of fatty acids to the liver could not cause triglyceride deposition in this organ unless metabolic and disposal mechanisms were overtaxed.

It also appears reasonable to conceive of a fatty liver in man not as a pure deficiency of a lipotropic factor, nor as pure alcohol toxicity, but as a combination of these factors, with enzymatic function impaired by nutritional deficiency and hence unable to cope with toxins, or with caloric loads imposed by alcohol or by other forms of carbohydrate. Thus, whether a human fatty liver is blamed on overeating, on diabetes, on genetic enzyme deficiency (i.e., galactosemia), on dietary restrictions imposed by geography and poverty (e.g., kwashiorkor), on infection, on excessive use of alcohol, or on exposure to toxins, it appears reasonable that the enzymatic functions responsible for fat metabolism are both impaired and exposed to bizarre proportions of nutrients.

Fatty infiltration is often associated with portal cirrhosis in man, and sometimes it appears to precede cirrhotic changes. In choline-deficient rats, a morphologic progression from fatty liver to a cirrhosis can clearly be shown. One theory, consequently, holds that fatty infiltration is a direct cause of cirrhosis. It is argued that liver cells are destroyed by the pressure of intracellular fat droplets, that the fat-laden cells compromise the sinusoidal circulation sufficiently to cause anoxic damage to centrilobular tissues, and that fibrous deposits forming about extracellular fatty cysts condense, as the fat is resorbed, into fibrotic trabeculae. Some of these contentions, however, are quite mechanistic and do not account for the facts that fatty livers in man may persist for years without progressing to cirrhosis and, vice versa, that portal cirrhosis can develop without associated fatty infiltration. In addition, the frequently invoked explanation of sinusoidal "compression" by fat-laden cells has never been established by direct measurement; indeed, development or disappearance of fatty liver in man does not appear to change hepatic blood flow appreciably. An alternative and possibly better theory, therefore, is that fatty and cirrhotic changes are frequently associated, not because one leads to the other, but because the same conditions that cause fatty infiltration also damage liver cells directly.

As opposed to fatty liver and cirrhosis, *acute hepatic necrosis* can also be produced in laboratory animals by dietary means. If the animal survives, a *postnecrotic cirrhosis* develops. Diets producing hepatic necrosis are characterized by a deficiency of tocopherol (vitamin E), of an unidentified factor containing selenium, or of the sulfur-containing amino acids methionine and cystine; the necrogenic properties of such deficiencies appear potentiated if much fat, certain yeasts, or cod liver oil is incorporated in the diet. The mechanisms underlying dietary hepatic necrosis are not clear; it is possible that hepatic cells are being deprived of agents that can perform essential catalytic functions in oxidative phosphorylation, or that the diets, which are deficient in antioxidants, may lead to abnormal oxidation of lipid substances. In man, hepatic necrosis and postnecrotic cirrhosis are usually ascribed to viral or toxic liver disease. A nutritional etiology is possible but has not been documented. In many patients, however, the etiology of postnecrotic cirrhosis is completely mysterious.

CIRRHOSIS: COMMON DENOMINATORS

The common denominator of all types of cirrhosis appears to be distortion of the normal connective tissue framework of the liver with loss of the normal lobular pattern and deposit of varying amounts of collagenous tissue. This architectural distortion particularly affects the liver's vasculature so that the sinusoidal circulation is no longer neatly arrayed between afferent and efferent vessels. The absence or abnormal position of efferent central veins, so evident in postnecrotic and portal cirrhosis, offers, in effect, a postsinusoidal block to the drainage of blood from the liver. This, in turn, leads to intrahepatic congestion and portal hypertension.

An additional vascular abnormality is the formation of multiple shunts connecting arterial, portal venous, and hepatic venous radicles. Abnormal communications between the arterial and portal venous systems may permit the transmission of arterial pressures into the portal system, thus contributing to portal hypertension. Indeed, if postsinusoidal venous outflow block is severe, some arterial blood may drain from the liver by means of retrograde flow through the portal system and thence, via collateral channels, to the systemic venous system (see Portal Hypertension). In addition to its effects on portal pressure, it is obvious that the distorted vasculature of cirrhosis permits arterial and portal venous blood to bypass the sinusoidal circulation, and thus denies both oxygen and nutrients to a struggling parenchyma. In many chronic cases of cirrhosis, the sinusoidal lining is thickened by a process called "capillarization" by Popper; to the extent that this is present, parenchymal nutrition may be further impaired.

Postsinusoidal vascular obstruction is also held responsible for increasing hepatic lymph flow and, in turn, thoracic duct lymph flow. Thus, in cirrhotic patients with ascites, thoracic duct lymph flow ranges between 2 and 12 ml./min., as opposed to a normal value of less than 1 ml./min., and thoracic duct pressure, believed to reflect sinusoidal pressure, ranges between 15 and 17 cm. of water as opposed to normal values of 6 to 15 cm. Moreover, thoracic duct lymph in cirrhotic patients with severe postsinusoidal block may contain abundant red cells that apparently leak from blood to lymph as a result of intrahepatic congestion.

Common but not invariable features of cirrhosis are parenchymal cell degeneration, mesenchymal reaction, and ductular proliferation. When one or more of these is evident, the process is considered active; when they are all in abeyance, the cirrhosis is inactive. Inactive cirrhosis may cause portal hypertension and its sequelae. Metabolic function is abnormal only to the extent that it is limited by an abnormal parenchymal blood supply. Hence, under ordinary conditions and in the absence of stress, no clinical or biochemical evidences of deranged protein, lipid, carbohydrate, or bile pigment metabolism may be evident. Similarly, there are no clinical or laboratory evidences of an inflammatory or hyperimmune state.

When cirrhosis is active, the clinical and biochemical phenomena reflect the pathologic changes in the liver to a reasonable degree. Degeneration of hepatocytes usually leads to marked deterioration of hepatic metabolic functions and impaired secretion of bile (cholestasis). Certain active types of degeneration, as may be seen when acute alcoholic hepatitis is superimposed upon portal cirrhosis, lead to an inflammatory reaction in the liver with the predominant accumulation of polymorphonuclear white cells and the systemic manifestation of fever. When the process is more chronic, the infiltrate is composed principally of mononuclear cells, and the pattern is that of a mesenchymal reaction.

The mesenchymal reaction, consisting of an accumulation of Kupffer cells, macrophages, lymphoid cells, and plasma cells, is believed to exercise phagocytic functions and to play a role in the deposition of collagen. In addition, the presence of lymphoid and plasma cells, as well as the demonstrable presence of gamma globulin in Kupffer cells, provide strong indications that the mesenchymal reaction expresses immunologic phenomena. Some of these phenomena may properly be regarded as the consequences of cellular injury. On the other hand, in certain forms of cirrhosis, particularly in such disorders as active postnecrotic cirrhosis, plasma cell or "lupoid" hepatitis, and primary biliary cirrhosis, immunologic phenomena may represent not only defense mechanisms but may act aggressively to attack cellular components, thus accounting for the apparent self-perpetuation of many chronic but active cirrhoses.

The hepatic cellular component that appears most involved in chronic antibody-antigen reactions appears to be the epithelial cell lining the small bile channels that connect the bile capillaries to the interlobular bile ducts. These channels, known as ductules or cholangioles, undergo active proliferation not only in the biliary varieties of cirrhosis but also in any chronic liver disease that is active. Ductular proliferation and mesenchymal reaction appear in close proximity to each other, and the gamma globulins of patients with chronic liver disease exhibit a high affinity, as shown by immunofluorescent techniques, for antigens within proliferating ductular cells. Finally, in conditions in which intrahepatic bile channels appear particularly involved, as in certain stages of primary biliary cirrhosis, mesenchymal cells in the liver may contain a 19S macroglobulin, and the blood serum is apt to contain a high titer of antibody to nuclear substances in a variety of tissues.

Although postnecrotic cirrhosis occasionally represents the inactive residual of a once serious process, most cirrhoses of all types, including the postnecrotic variety, tend to be active, with cellular destruction and repair, fibrotic deposition and resorption, and mesenchymal defense and attack going on in a manner that may fluctuate but is nevertheless continuous. Under such dynamic conditions, it is hard to imagine that the overall pathologic pattern remains static and that a single pathologic type of cirrhosis becomes immutably established in a given patient. Hence, although all would not agree, the view is entertained here that the structural abnormalities of chronic but active liver disease are subject to constant change and with the passage of time tend to assume the pathologic pattern of postnecrotic cirrhosis, irrespective of the histologic abnormalities present during the earlier stages of the disease. Only such a dynamic formulation permits comprehension of reports showing that primary biliary cirrhosis, in its early stages, may be indistinguishable on pathologic grounds from posthepatitic cirrhosis, and that its end-stages exhibit the scarred lobulations of postnecrotic cirrhosis.

Disorders of Hepatic Blood Flow

Under basal conditions the blood flow through the normal human liver averages 1500 ml. per minute, with a range of 1000 to 2000 ml. per minute.

In the intact human subject, "estimated hepatic blood flow" (EHBF) is measured by injecting a test substance intravenously and by determining (1) the overall amount of the substance that is removed from the blood per minute and (2) the amount extracted from each milliliter of blood or plasma as it passes through the liver. If the test substance is removed from the blood exclusively by the liver, then division of value 1 by value 2 yields a figure for the volume of blood or plasma that must have passed through the liver per minute.

Commonly used test substances are either water-soluble dyes removed by hepatic parenchymal cells (e.g., Bromsulphalein, rose bengal, indocyanine green) or isotopically labeled colloidal particles removed by Kupffer cells (e.g., radioactive chromic oxide, gold, or denatured albumin). If, for example, 5 mg. of Brom-sulphalein is given per minute by constant intravenous infusion, and a constant peripheral arterial or venous plasma level is achieved, the removal rate is assumed to be 5 mg. per minute also. Assuming that the peripheral venous plasma level is 1.2 mg. per 100 ml. and, at the same time, hepatic venous plasma obtained by hepatic venous catheterization contains 0.7 mg. per 100 ml., the liver is removing 0.5 mg. from each 100 ml. of plasma, or 0.005 mg. from each ml. Therefore, estimated hepatic plasma flow is:

$$\frac{5.0 \text{ mg./min.}}{0.005 \text{ mg./ml.}} = 1000 \text{ ml. per min.}$$

To obtain EHBF, this figure is divided by the plasmacrit:

$$\text{EHBF} = \frac{1000 \text{ ml./min.}}{0.6} = 1,666 \text{ ml./min.}$$

Modifications of this technique have been proposed to permit administration of the test substance by a single intravenous injection, and to eliminate the need for hepatic venous catheterization by injecting colloids that are nearly completely extracted on their initial circulation through the liver; but with each additional simplification the chance of error grows, partly because of inaccuracies introduced by external monitoring, and partly because the assumption that hepatic extraction of the colloid is 100 per cent may be quite unjustified.

All the methods used are inaccurate to the extent that the overall removal rate is determined by other than hepatic activity. The dye methods, which depend on both parenchymal and biliary tract integrity, become less accurate when the parenchyma is deranged or the biliary channels blocked. Colloidal test substances may yield more reliable values in hepatitis, cirrhosis, and biliary obstruction since Kupffer cell activity is not necessarily grossly altered in these conditions.

About three-fourths of the blood reaches the liver through the portal vein; the other fourth is supplied by the hepatic artery. Some experimental evidence indicates that portal blood is not homogeneously mixed, but is channeled, with blood from the splenic, gastric, and inferior mesenteric veins being carried principally to the left hepatic lobe, and blood reaching the liver from the small bowel and the right colon via the superior mesenteric vein being delivered to the right lobe. This channeling of blood is said to determine to some extent the distribution of hepatic metastases from splanchnic organs and may explain why amebic abscess appears to be more frequent in the right than in the left lobe of the liver, the cecum being the favorite habitat of these parasites. It should be noted, however, that channeling of the portal blood is best demonstrated by injecting particulate matter into the portal system. When water-soluble radiopaque substances are injected, either directly or via the spleen, the dye appears to be equally distributed to both hepatic lobes.

Within the liver, arterial and portal venous pathways remain distinct until they join at the periphery of, or within the lobule. Thus sinusoidal blood may be purely arterial, purely venous, or mixed. Vascular shunts bypassing hepatic parenchyma have been demonstrated in animals, but the existence of shunts in the normal human liver is disputed. A throttling mechanism found in dogs near the orifice of the hepatic veins is not demonstrable in man, and there is little evidence that the human liver acts as a reservoir for the storage of large amounts of blood.

The dual nature of its blood supply affords the liver some protection if portal venous or hepatic arterial flow is impaired. Dogs survive and live fairly normally if the portal vein is severed and the entire portal circulation shunted into the inferior vena cava (Eck fistula). This procedure, however, reduces total hepatic blood flow, leads to moderate hepatic atrophy, diminishes the capacity of the liver to withstand stress, and may induce cerebral disorders ("meat intoxication"). In man portosystemic shunts are usually used in patients with portal hypertension. Such patients already have decreased portal flow through the liver, and a shunt causes no *additional* damage to hepatic structure and function. Like dogs with Eck fistulas, however, patients with portacaval shunts may suffer disorders of the central nervous system (see Hepatic Coma).

The mechanisms by which the liver compensates for exclusion of portal blood are increased arterial flow and greater extraction of oxygen and metabolites. A portacaval shunt, for example, may reduce total blood flow through a cirrhotic liver from 1200 to 600 ml. per minute, but, since oxygen extraction may increase from 3.25 to 6.5 volumes per cent, the liver uses 40 ml. of oxygen per minute after as well as before operation. For identical reasons the overall disappearance rate of a hepatic test substance like Bromsulphalein may be unaffected by a portacaval shunt even though total hepatic blood flow is diminished. Increased extraction of oxygen and other substances may take place in cirrhosis after portacaval anastomosis, possibly because hepatic circulation is slower, is less congested, and makes less use of abnormal intrahepatic shunts.

Since portal venous blood is relatively well oxygenated (fasting arterial-portal venous oxygen difference = 2± volumes per cent), portal flow can to some extent compensate for hepatic arterial occlusion. It cannot, however, compensate for total arterial exclusion; sudden and complete deprivation of arterial blood is fatal to the human liver. For this reason, when any attempt is made to reduce arterial pressure in the liver, the hepatic artery is ligated near its origin from the celiac axis, a procedure which assures the liver a remaining supply of collateral arterial blood.*

A normal liver appears to tolerate hypoxia of systemic origin (i.e., hypotension, shock) quite satisfactorily, partly because extraction of oxygen increases as hepatic blood flow decreases. Severely anoxic liver cells, on the other hand, may affect the general circulation. Dogs in experimental shock survive longer if hepatic circulation is selectively maintained, and it has been claimed that the anoxic liver elaborates vasodepressor substances. In contrast to the normal organ, however, the damaged liver appears most susceptible to oxygen lack. As a result of even brief periods of hypotension, the function of a cirrhotic liver may deteriorate irrevocably, and a patient with hepatitis may suffer progressive liver failure if exposed to surgery and the hypoxia that may attend many anesthetic procedures. The impaired hepatic circulation which often accompanies severe liver disease provides, moreover, a proper background for focal ischemic injury. Under such conditions a suddenly superimposed hepatic arterial occlusion or portal venous thrombosis sometimes causes either true infarcts or hemorrhagic infarcts without necrosis (Zahn's infarcts).

Vascular Congestion: Extrahepatic Causes. The principal extrahepatic cause of vascular congestion of the liver is an increased systemic venous pressure attributable to right-sided heart failure, but occasionally hepatic venous outflow is retarded by stasis of the pulmonary circulation (e.g., pulmonary infarct), by pericardial disease that restricts right atrial inflow, or by obstruction of the inferior vena cava at the orifice of the hepatic veins.

As an initial result of elevated hepatic venous pressure, the volume of blood normally present in the liver at any one time (200 to 400 ml.) increases and may nearly double. Fluid, which resembles plasma because of the porous nature of the hepatic vascular endothelium, leaks into the space of Disse lying between sinusoids and hepatic cells. This edema formation, if acute, may expand the liver mass by about 25 per cent; if chronic, the connective tissue framework of the liver probably stretches to permit a much greater augmentation of hepatic volume, creating a large, tense liver with a rounded edge palpable at the umbilical level or even lower. In spite of the increased venous pressure, the enlarged liver of right-sided heart failure rarely pulsates, presumably because the venous pulses produced by the atrial and ventricular contractions are dampened by the spongy and congested hepatic mass. Pulsations of the liver, however, are detectable under certain conditions: (1) Right intra-atrial pressure must rise sharply with cardiac systole, as may happen with tricuspid stenosis or regurgitation; (2) the orifice of the inferior vena cava must not be obstructed by the eustachian valve or pericardial disease; and (3) the liver must be relatively afibrotic.

If the plethora, edema, and increased venous pressure characteristic of the acutely

---

* Almost all dog's livers, some diseased human livers, but few normal human livers harbor anaerobes which lie dormant as long as exposed to normal concentrations of oxygen. After hepatic artery ligation and its attendant hypoxia, however, these anaerobes may flourish and damage the liver fatally unless their growth is inhibited by antibiotics.

congested liver continue, further changes supervene. The parenchymal cells most exposed to anoxia, i.e., the cells adjoining the central veins of the lobules, are destroyed, and their place is taken by red cells and a few infiltrating leukocytes. Iron-containing pigment derived from the extravasated red cells is found in the Kupffer cells, and fatty infiltration suggests that the metabolism of the surviving parenchyma is impaired. Eventually, the walls of the hepatic venous system undergo sclerotic thickening, and an exuberant fibrosis, predominantly centrilobular, develops. These changes take place in about half the cases that have increased hepatic venous pressures for as long as a year. In patients that survive for longer periods, patients with constrictive pericarditis or tricuspid lesions, for example, the fibrosis becomes truly massive and extends to the hepatic capsule, which, according to Moschcowitz, thickens to "Zuckerguss" proportions in response to the chronically increased vascular tension within the liver.

Grossly, the fibrotic changes characteristic of chronic hepatic congestion produce a liver that is large and hard, with a sharp and often irregular edge. Whether such a liver manifests "cardiac cirrhosis" is a disputed semantic point. Certainly if it is merely meant that fibrosis and some structural distortion occur in the chronically congested liver, the term seems apropos.

Portal Hypertension. The pressure in the human portal vein normally varies between 6 and 10 cm. of water. This pressure is increased (1) when elevated pressures in the systemic venous system are transmitted backward through an engorged liver, as often happens in cardiac failure, or (2) when the portal venous system is selectively affected by processes that impede either the afferent or efferent venous blood flow of the liver. Examples of afferent block are (1) thrombosis or cavernomatous transformation of the portal vein, and (2) the "pipe-stem cirrhosis" of chronic hepatic schistosomiasis in which ova and sometimes worms lodge in and alter the radicles of the portal venous system. Efferent block may be caused by (1) thrombosis or neoplastic occlusion of the hepatic veins (Budd-Chiari syndrome), and by (2) venoocclusive disease, a process that causes sclerotic narrowing of the tributaries of the hepatic venous system; but the most common cause is (3) the postsinusoidal block of postnecrotic and portal cirrhosis (see Cirrhosis:

Common Denominators).* Obviously a mixed type will be seen in some cases of cirrhosis in that the delicate ramifications of both the hepatic and portal venous systems are replaced by a gnarled and stunted vasculature. Contracting fibrous tissue and regenerating parenchyma further impede the intrahepatic circulation. The end result is a portal pressure amounting to 25 to 50 cm. of water.

Presumably because of the higher pressures in the arterial system, arterial flow through the liver is not greatly impaired in cirrhosis; in fact, it may actually be increased with the result that total hepatic blood flow is reduced by no more than 20 to 50 per cent. Since the postsinusoidal block also impedes drainage of hepatic arterial blood and since abnormal communications may open up between arterial and portal venous branches, arterial pressures may be transmitted directly to the portal venous system. The concept that arterial pressure in this manner contributes to the degree of portal hypertension provides a rationale for two surgical procedures advocated for treating this condition. One of these, no longer practiced today, consisted of ligating the hepatic artery. The other is use of a side-to-side anastomosis in creating a portacaval shunt for the relief of portal hypertension. Once this shunt is created, hepatic arterial blood, finding its normal outflow passages blocked, may drain off by flowing through the portal vein between the liver and the anastomosis, the direction of blood flow in this section of the portal vein therefore being the opposite of usual.

When portal hypertension is merely a reflection of increased pressures in the systemic veins, the portal circulation, though engorged and sluggish, continues to flow through its usual channels. Selective vascular obstruction

---

* Pressures in the portal venous system may be measured directly at laparotomy, by needling the spleen transcutaneously and measuring splenic pulp pressure, or by catheterization of the hepatic vein to obtain a "wedge" pressure reading. In this maneuver, the venous catheter is advanced so as to wedge the catheter tip into an hepatic venous tributary and thus to occlude it. This theoretically creates a head of pressure that builds up until it approximates the pressure in the blood distal to the obstructed hepatic venule, i.e., portal pressure. In practice, the results are affected by the degree to which the vascular outflow of a hepatic segment can be wedged effectively without dissipation of pressure via natural channels or shunts to adjoining segments. Increased portal pressures caused by obstruction of the afferent, portal venous system can obviously not be detected by the wedge method.

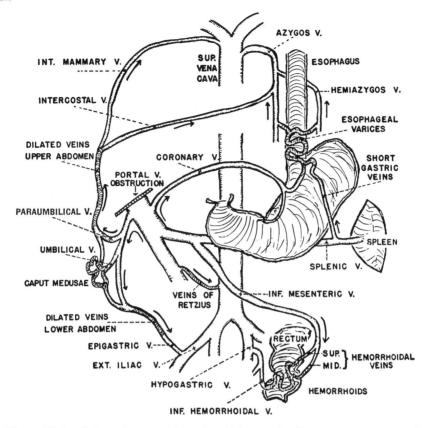

Figure 27–1. Collateral venous channels which may develop as a consequence of portal obstruction.

of the portal system, however, forces blood draining from this area to seek the normal pressures of the systemic veins through collateral pathways. The routes taken in this attempt to circumvent portal obstruction are illustrated in Figure 27–1. The degree of development of the various collateral channels varies from patient to patient, but from the clinical viewpoint esophageal varices and the dilated veins of the anterior body wall are most important. Hemorrhoids have no clinical significance, since they occur in many otherwise normal persons and are often absent in cirrhotic patients.

Esophageal varices occur in 60 to 70 per cent of patients with portal cirrhosis, are demonstrable by careful x-ray examination in 40 per cent, lead to hematemesis in 25 to 30 per cent, and are the principal cause of death through hemorrhage in 20 to 25 per cent. Dilated abdominal and thoracic veins are diagnostic of portal hypertension, provided the blood flows toward the thorax in the upper abdomen and toward the femoral vein in the groin. In obstruction of the inferior vena cava a similar dilation of the veins in the groin and

lower abdomen may take place, but in this instance blood flows up the abdomen, away from the femoral veins.

Dilated veins clustering around the umbilicus, a *caput Medusae*, are frequently cited as a sign of portal hypertension, but the picturesque name has lent this collateral venous pattern an unwarranted importance. Actually, a caput Medusae occurs rarely, for, as shown in Figure 27–1, it can develop only if the fetal umbilical vein fails to become obliterated. Even more uncommon is the *Cruveilhier-Baumgarten syndrome,* the eponym applied when vascular eddies in dilated periumbilical veins produce a loud bruit.

PAIN SENSATION

Painful sensations arising in the liver are carried to the central nervous system by pathways which pass with the sympathetic nerves but without synapses through the celiac plexus and thence to the seventh through twelfth paravertebral ganglia. The end organs of these nerves lie in the capsule of Glisson, which not only invests the surface of the liver, but also enters the liver with the portal vessels and is distributed with them throughout the substance of the organ. Like the sensory nerves of the gut and biliary tract, hepatic nerves are susceptible only to certain stimuli. Burning the liver is not usually painful, nor is puncturing the organ, except at the moment of penetration. Any process which alters the tension within Glisson's capsule or its ramifications may, however, be distressingly painful.

The disorders most likely to produce hepatic pain are acute congestion or inflammation in the liver. Acute congestion, such as occurs typically in a patient with a tight mitral stenosis, obviously stretches the fibrous elements of Glisson's capsule both within and on the surface of the liver. It is often assumed that the external capsule is particularly sensitive to distention, but rapid infusion of physiologic saline solution via catheter into one of the major radicles of the hepatic vein also may evoke a severe, boring midepigastric pain. Pain in this instance would seem to arise from increased tension on the intrahepatic capsular elements.

Acute inflammatory processes, whether hepatitis or scattered pyogenic abscesses, presumably give rise to pain if Glisson's capsule is either stretched by hepatic edema or is directly involved by an inflammatory reaction. Since these are variable factors, the incidence and degree of pain are inconstant in hepatic inflammations.

Chronic benign disorders of the liver, whether congestive, inflammatory, or any other type, rarely produce significant hepatic pain unless an acute process is superimposed. Chronic disorders apparently progress so slowly that Glisson's capsule can adjust itself by gradual stretching and fibroblastic proliferation without subjecting the nerve endings to abnormal tension.

Since the hepatic nerves are limited in their detection of painful stimuli, carcinomas and indolent abscesses of the liver are often not painful. When an abscess or a neoplasm is situated near the surface of the liver, however, the closely contiguous parietal peritoneum, well supplied by deep somatic nerves, may be irritated.

Changes in Hepatic Function

Correlation of Structure and Function

In the study of liver disease, correlation between specific changes in structure and function is constantly being sought. To a great extent this is helpful. On the other hand, too great emphasis on isolated aspects of structure as related to function leads to an artificial dissection of hepatic physiology, which, for its proper understanding, actually requires an appreciation of the remarkable functional integration of the various structural units that comprise the liver. The processing of a metabolite, for example, not only may require a series of enzymatic reactions within a certain cell, but also may depend on an orderly sequence, including removal of the metabolite from the blood, its transformation in the hepatocyte, and its excretion by the specialized structures that characterize that portion of the polygonal cell wall which abuts on the bile capillary. It should be understood, consequently, that many an explanation of a functional abnormality in terms of morphologic change is admittedly mechanistic and is here presented, like a diagram, merely to promote understanding.

The hepatocytes appear principally responsible for the metabolic functions of the liver. These functions, consequently, are affected by diffuse parenchymal diseases such as hepatitis and portal cirrhosis, conditions which may or may not destroy many polygonal cells, but which involve nearly all of them. On the other hand, the reserve capacity of the liver is so great that conditions which permit survival of some normal cells do not impair hepatic function appreciably, even if patchy destruction of parenchyma is marked. A liver enormously enlarged by metastatic cancer, for example, or peppered with localized abscesses often exhibits normal function.

Kupffer cells are the reticuloendothelial elements within the liver; their response to liver injury may or may not parallel that of the hepatocytes. In hepatitis or cirrhosis with marked mesenchymal reaction, indeed, Kupffer cells multiply and may actually move into the liver from the spleen. Consequently, reticuloendothelial functions such as phagocytosis and immunologic reactions are often enhanced when hepatocyte function is seriously depressed.

Disorders of the biliary tract exert their initial effect on the formation and excretion of bile. Metabolic functions, not significantly affected at first, are subsequently depressed as secretory obstruction or infection gradually embarrasses the parenchyma. Complete and unrelieved biliary obstruction eventually leads to total parenchymal failure, but partial obstruction, even if chronic, often permits enough parenchyma to survive so that metabolic functions are only moderately depressed.

Since disorders of the extrahepatic biliary tract are often amenable to surgical treatment, whereas those of the intrahepatic biliary system deserve medical ministration, a sharp distinction between these two types of biliary tract disease is necessary clinically. From the functional viewpoint, however, the effect on bile flow and, secondarily, on the liver is the same whether an obstructive process affects the bile capillaries or the common duct; neither clinical phenomena nor liver function tests may suffice to distinguish the "medical" jaundice caused by intrahepatic biliary tract disease from its "surgical" counterpart caused by obstruction of the extrahepatic bile channels (see Cholestasis).

The effects of a deranged hepatic blood flow are usually discussed in terms of cellular hypoxia and malnutrition. The blood flow, however, can affect hepatic function much more directly, for the total work done by a hepatic cell depends not only on its functional capacity, but also upon the load with which it is presented. In a chronic case of portal cirrhosis, for example, the rate of removal of some metabolite, such as ammonia, from the blood may be limited more by the decreased hepatic blood flow than by any cellular disease.

ENZYME SYSTEMS

The basic determinants of how well the liver exercises its functions are the integrity and vitality of its enzyme systems. Many of these systems are known and have been identified in specific cytoplasmic structures, or organelles, such as mitochondria, endoplasmic reticulum, and lysosomes. The mitochondria are the sites of oxidative phosphorylation, the reaction whereby oxidation of nutrients is coupled with the production of energy-rich adenosine triphosphate. The endoplasmic reticulum, which on cellular homogenization and differential centrifugation yields the microsomal fraction, appears to be made up of convoluted membranes that line a complex system of tiny intracellular channels and puddles. In the granular endoplasmic reticulum, rich in ribonucleic acid, enzyme systems for the synthesis of proteins from amino acids are located; and the enzymes of the agranular reticulum may play a role in glycogen metabolism and in detoxification.

Certain enzymes are suspected by virtue of their position to play a role in the uptake and excretion of various substances by the hepatocytes. Thus 5-nucleotidase, a phosphatase, is concentrated at the cellular surface facing the sinusoids, and at the other pole of the cell, bordering the bile capillaries, adenosine triphosphatase and alkaline phosphatase are found. Between the ends are vacuoles and lysosomes, rich in acid hydrolases such as acid phosphatase, and believed to act as "dispose-alls" at the sink-end of cellular metabolism; in addition, they may exercise some transport function. Certain pigments, such as lipofuscin and that which accumulates intracellularly in the Dubin-Johnson syndrome, are found in the general area where lysosomes predominate.

In some but not all types of experimental liver damage, depression of hepatocellular enzymatic activity, disorganization of mitrochondrial structure, and various changes in the distribution and appearance of cytoplasmic organelles precede other evidences of liver damage. Altered hepatic enzyme activity may also be detected by histochemical reactions which reveal not only quantitative changes, but also loss of the striking zonal distribution of various enzymes within the lobule (e.g., according to some methods of analysis, enzymes participating in anaerobic glycolysis are more active at the periphery, and those participating in aerobic metabolism of carbohydrates are more active near the center). In hereditary metabolic disorders affecting the liver, specific enzyme defects have been implicated (see Jaundice, Carbohydrate Metabolism). The finding of low concentrations of zinc in the cirrhotic livers of alcoholics may have some pathogenetic significance in view of the fact that zinc is indispensable to the activity of alcohol dehydrogenase, an enzyme instrumental in the oxidation of ethanol. In general, however, the present state of knowledge of hepatic enzymes, their normal function, and their specific response to injury is still quite circumscribed and precludes the delineation of hepatic disorders as snowballing sequences of primary enzymatic defects, secondary metabolic derangements, and ultimate structural dissolution.

Most of the enzyme systems found in liver cells are also present in the cells of other tissues, particularly in other cells engaged in transport, such as intestinal epithelial cells. The peculiarities of hepatic metabolism must therefore be attributed to the quantity and organization of the enzyme systems within the liver cells. Presumably because of this wide systemic distribution of basic enzyme systems, many functions that might be considered inherently hepatic can be performed by other tissues, but at such slow rates, as compared to normal hepatic metabolism, that the contribution by extrahepatic tissues is of moment only if liver function is impaired. Hepatectomized animals, for example, can remove Bromsulphalein from the blood, but extrahepatic Bromsulphalein removal is negligible when a healthy liver is functioning. The glucuronyl transferase activity of the kidney and gastrointestinal tract presumably has little to do with bilirubin metabolism under normal conditions, but when the liver is seriously damaged, these extrahepatic transferases may participate in some bilirubin conjugation. Both intra- and extrahepatic enzyme systems can, moreover, adapt themselves under certain circumstances to meet changing demands.

Derangements of various hepatic functions neither begin simultaneously nor progress in a parallel fashion. Some functions, such as the formation of albumin, appear to be affected by even minor injury, whereas others, such as the utilization of amino acids, are impaired only when liver damage is severe. The usual explanation offered for this variable sensitivity to injury is that some liver functions possess great reserve capacity. In more specific terms, "great reserve capacity" may mean that some hepatic enzyme systems are less susceptible than others to noxious factors such as hypoxia, lack of essential metabolites, or accumulation of inhibitory factors.

The concentration in peripheral blood of hepatic enzymes has been used increasingly by clinicians to assess the status of the liver. Several types of such enzyme tests must, however, be clearly differentiated on the basis of their rationale and significance. One type measures the blood concentration of enzymes synthesized by the liver and appearing in the blood under normal conditions, such as acetylcholine esterase. Since this enzyme is made exclusively by hepatic cells, its concentration in serum is depressed in proportion to hepatic cellular damage, and, in terms of liver damage, its plasma levels and those of albumin have a similar significance.

A second type of enzyme test measures the blood concentration of hepatic enzymes that normally appear in the plasma to a slight extent or not at all, but which exhibit increased blood levels when the liver is acutely damaged, presumably because necrosis destroys cellular integrity and allows the escape of intracellular enzymes into the blood. A large number of such tests have been proposed utilizing enzymes active in many metabolic pathways (e.g., aldolase involved in the breakdown of glucose, isocitric dehydrogenase active in the tricarboxylic acid cycle, and ornithine carbamyl transferase active in the urea cycle), but the most popular tests have depended upon measuring transaminase activity. Glutamic oxalacetic transaminase (GOT) catalyzes the transfer of amino groups from aspartic acid to alpha-ketoglutaric acid, with the formation of glutamic and oxalacetic acid (Fig. 27–2). Glutamic pyruvic transaminase (GPT) is measured by the same reaction, except that alanine and pyruvic acid replace aspartic and oxalacetic acid, respectively. The concentration of GOT in hepatic tissue normally exceeds that of GPT, but, since high concentrations of GOT are also found in other organs, elevations of GPT in the blood are more specific for hepatic injury than elevations of GOT.

A third type of enzyme test involves the measurement of enzymes that manifest increased blood concentrations when the intra- or extrahepatic biliary passages are damaged or obstructed, e.g., alkaline phosphatase and leucine aminopeptidase. The normal role of these enzyme systems in biliary tract function (if any) is not known.

Jaundice

Jaundice is caused by the accumulation of bile pigments in the blood and tissues. These pigments principally consist of bilirubin and bilirubin diglucuronide.* Most bilirubin is formed in the reticuloendothelial system as a degradation product of hemoglobin liberated by the breakdown of mature erythrocytes (1 gm. of hemoglobin yields approximately 35 mg. of bilirubin); the bilirubin so formed in the spleen and bone marrow is carried to the liver via the blood, where it is held in solution by forming a reversible complex with albumin. Some bilirubin, however, may be synthesized directly in the liver from precursors such as glycine, and another fraction appears to be derived from hemoglobin or hemoglobin precursors in the bone marrow.

---

* In this discussion, "bilirubin," unmodified by an adjective, always refers to the unconjugated pigment. Conjugates other than the diglucuronide may exist but have not been firmly identified. A pigment identified as bilirubin monoglucuronide for example may merely represent a mixture of bilirubin and bilirubin diglucuronide; the status of a bilirubin sulfate conjugate is uncertain.

These two "early appearing" fractions (so called because they appear in the blood too soon following injection of labeled precursors to be derived from broken down red cells) account for some 10 to 15 per cent of bilirubin formed normally; but under abnormal conditions, this proportion may more than double. Bilirubinemia caused by excessive production of "early appearing" bilirubin is known as "shunt" bilirubinemia, because the responsible mechanisms bypass the usual sequence of heme metabolism.

In the liver, bilirubin is taken up by the hepatocyte, transported across the cell, and excreted into the bile capillaries. An obligatory feature of pigment movement across the hepatic cell is its conjugation with glucuronic acid to form bilirubin diglucuronide. Bilirubin, before its conjugation, is lipid soluble and relatively water insoluble, may act, in high concentrations, as a protoplasmic poison (e.g., in neonatal hyperbilirubinemia with kernicterus), and cannot be excreted by either the liver cell or kidney. Conjugated bilirubin is water soluble and can be excreted in bile and urine. The normal conjugated product, bilirubin diglucuronide, is formed only by the liver; perhaps other conjugates may be formed extrahepatically.

The synthesis of bilirubin diglucuronide in the hepatocyte depends on a microsomal enzyme, glucuronyl transferase. In this synthesis, the transfer of two molecules of glucuronic acid to one molecule of bilirubin is possible only if the glucuronic acid is first incorporated in a donor compound, uridine diphosphate glucuronic acid. In schematic form, the sequence of reactions is as follows:

ing agent, methyl alcohol in case of the van den Bergh reaction, to form its colored diazo compound. When the van den Bergh reaction is carried out in the presence of methyl alcohol, consequently, both bile pigments are responsible for the color produced, and *total* serum bilirubin is measured. Total serum bilirubin minus the "one minute direct" value provides a value for serum "indirect" bilirubin. "Indirect" bilirubin, so measured, thus consists principally of bilirubin.

As measured by the van den Bergh reaction, normal serum contains from 0.4 to 0.8 mg./100 ml. indirect bilirubin, and from 0 to 0.2 mg./100 ml./one minute direct bilirubin, the concentration of total bile pigments thus ranging from 0.4 to 1.0 mg./100 ml. The presence of bilirubin, which is being carried to the liver from extrahepatic reticuloendothelial cells, is readily explained. The reason for the apparent presence of conjugates is more puzzling: perhaps some bilirubin diglucuronide leaks back into the blood via the hepatic lymph even under normal conditions, or perhaps native solubilizing agents in the blood allow some bilirubin to participate in the first minute of the reaction.

Bilirubin diglucuronide, upon reaching the intestine, is not reabsorbed as such but is converted by bacterial action to several related compounds usually grouped together under the name urobilinogen. Much of this is excreted in the feces (50 to 250 mg./24 hrs.). The remainder is reabsorbed* into the portal circulation, carried to the liver, and there to a large extent extracted and re-excreted into the bile. Urobilinogen thus has an enterohepatic circulation. A small amount, however,

1. Glucose ⟶ glucose-6-phosphate
   hexokinase
2. Glucose-6-phosphate ⟶ glucose-1-phosphate
   phosphoglucomutase
3. Glucose-1-phosphate + uridine triphosphate ⟶ uridine diphosphate glucose
   uridyl transferase
4. Uridine diphosphate glucose ⟶ uridine diphosphate glucuronic acid
   dehydrogenase
5. Uridine diphosphate glucuronic acid + bilirubin ⟶ bilirubin diglucuronide
   glucuronyl transferase

The van den Bergh reaction affords an approximate separation of unconjugated and conjugated bilirubin pigments. Conjugated bilirubin yields a magenta color almost immediately upon the addition of Ehrlich's diazo reagent to serum containing this pigment. If "almost immediately" is defined as "within one minute," conjugated bilirubin is what is measured as "one minute direct" bilirubin. Bilirubin requires the addition of a solubiliz-

escapes hepatic removal mechanisms and reaches the systemic circulation, whence it is excreted in the urine. The actual amount so

---

* Absorption of urobilinogen is much more rapid in the small than in the large bowel, but the total amount absorbed in the colon may be greater, for the indigenous flora of this organ probably forms much more urobilinogen than the limited bacterial population of the small intestine.

excreted depends upon several factors which may vary independently:

1. The amount of bilirubin diglucuronide excreted into the gut by the liver.

2. The rate and degree of intestinal conversion of bilirubin diglucuronide to urobilinogen. (This rate is decreased when intestinal bacteria are depressed by antibiotics.)

3. The proportion of intestinal urobilinogen absorbed into the portal circulation.

4. The proportion of absorbed urobilinogen removed by the liver from the portal circulation.

Normally, urine contains less than 1 mg./100 ml. of colorless urobilinogen. When urine is exposed to light and air, its urobilinogen content is oxidized to yellow urobilin.

In jaundice, the amount and partition of bile pigments in the blood and urine and of the urobilinogen group of compounds in the feces and urine depend upon the nature of the icterogenic mechanism. Mechanisms possibly responsible for the types of jaundice seen in various clinical conditions are listed in Table 27–1. It should be recognized, however, that many of the mechanisms are hypothetical or based on indirect evidence. In the entire sequence between the uptake of bilirubin from the blood and the excretion of its diglucuronide conjugate in the bile, for example, only the conjugation reaction and its pertinent enzymatic activities have been identified with reasonable certainty. In spite of this identification, it is unknown to what extent impaired conjugation accounts for the degree of bilirubinemia in most varieties of jaundice. Thus a specific and genetic absence of glucuronyl transferase has been pinpointed as responsible only in the rare Crigler-Najjar syndrome and in its animal counterpart, the Gunn rat. In "physiologic" jaundice of the newborn (some consider "physiologic" a misnomer since the condition is potentially dangerous), some immaturity of glucuronyl transferase is probable, but excess destruction of the red cells contributes to the degree of jaundice. In practically any case of active hepatitis or cirrhosis glucuronyl transferase activity is presumably impaired, but the relative importance of this impairment with respect to other defects of bilirubin metabolism and excretion is unknown.

Perhaps most controversial is the role of glucuronyl transferase deficiency in the pathogenesis of Gilbert's syndrome. Homogenates of hepatic tissue obtained from some cases diagnosed as having this syndrome may exhibit deficient bilirubin conjugation with glucuronide when this reaction is tested in vitro. In other cases, glucuronide conjugation has been tested by means of nonbilirubin substances that the liver conjugates with glucuronic acid. Thus phenols or salicylamides have been given to patients and the amounts of the conjugated compound appearing in plasma or excreted in the urine determined. Discrepancies in the results obtained by such tests in patients with Gilbert's syndrome are partly explained by the possibility that hepatic conjugation of the various test substances used does not require the same transferase system specifically instrumental in bilirubin conjugation. An even more likely explanation is that Gilbert's syndrome, which in essence consists of an unexplained, usually mild, unconjugated hyperbilirubinemia without overt hemolysis or any evidence of hepatic dysfunction, is a clinical category that encompasses several conditions from the viewpoint of pathogenesis.

Examination of the possible mechanisms listed in Table 27–1 indicates that it is difficult to construct a uniformly applicable classification of the various types of jaundice on the basis of abnormalities in the handling of bilirubin and related compounds. If a classification has to be used, a division of jaundice into (1) hemolytic, (2) parenchymatous, (3) intrahepatic obstructive, and (4) extrahepatic obstructive types, though far from ideal, has at least the advantage of being straightforward and sanctioned by popular usage. Furthermore, it emphasizes the need of separating the surgically treatable extrahepatic obstructive types from the first three "medical" types of jaundice which cannot be helped by surgical means and are apt to be aggravated by inappropriate operative intervention.

As emphasized previously, the functional changes resulting from cholestasis should be and are the same, whether the cholestasis is caused by intra- or extrahepatic disease. Thus bilirubin diglucuronide regurgitates and is the predominant bile pigment in the blood whether the patient has methyltestosterone hepatitis or cancer of the pancreatic head. In jaundiced cases of hepatitis and cirrhosis, regurgitation also takes place because the widespread damage disrupts both liver cells and the finer radicles of the biliary system. The increased levels of unconjugated bilirubin in jaundiced patients with choledochal obstruction are usually attributed to hepatic parenchymal damage caused by "back pressure," but it is more likely that the uptake, transfer, and excretory mechanisms of the

TABLE 27-1. BILIRUBINEMIA: MECHANISMS, CLINICAL SYNDROMES, AND DISTRIBUTION OF BILE PIGMENTS IN BLOOD AND URINE.

Major Mechanisms, Identified or Postulated	Clinical Syndromes	Approximate Partition of Bile Pigments in Blood According to van den Bergh Reaction*	Bile Pigment in Urine	Urobilinogen or Derivatives	
				In Feces	In Urine
1. Excessive bilirubin production a. Excessive red cell breakdown b. Excessive production by liver or bone marrow of "early appearing bilirubin" that never enters mature red cells	a. Hemolytic disorders b. "Shunt bilirubinemia"—idiopathic, or as part of hematologic (e.g., pernicious anemia) or other disorder	90% or more indirect 90% or more indirect	0 0	increased increased	increased increased
2. Impaired uptake of bilirubin into hepatocyte a. Inhibition by toxic effects or by competition b. "Primary" disorder	a. Perhaps agents contained in male fern; perhaps a variety of other drugs or hormones b. Perhaps some cases of Gilbert's syndrome	90% or more indirect 90% or more indirect	0 0	? normal	? normal
3. Glucuronide conjugation—specific defects a. Glucuronyl transferase absence b. Transferase immaturity or deficiency c. Transferase inhibition	a. Crigler-Najjar syndrome b. "Physiologic jaundice" of newborn (mechanism 1.a. also active) Perhaps some cases of Gilbert's syndrome c. By pregnane-3α, 20β-diol in mother's breast milk By inhibitors in serum of pregnant women Hypothetically, by substances competing for conjugating mechanism	90% or more indirect 90% or more indirect 90% or more indirect	0 0 0	decreased variable ?	decreased variable ?
4. Intracellular storage or transport disorder	4. Hypothetical at present, but presumably a secondary effect of all types of cholestasis	(hypothetical mechanism at present)			
5. Impaired transport from hepatocyte into bile capillary a. Competitive b. Inhibitory or toxic c. "Primary" disorder	a. Substances secreted in bile: bile salts, test dyes, cholecystographic media b. Estrogens. Perhaps other steroids and their derivatives c. Dubin-Johnson syndrome Rotor's syndrome	60–80% direct 20–40% indirect 60–80% direct 20–40% indirect 60–80% direct 20–40% indirect	+ + +	decreased or normal decreased or normal normal	decreased or normal decreased or normal normal
6. Cholestasis a. Bile capillary disorder b. Bile ductular disorder c. Obstruction of hepatic or common duct	a. "Drug hepatitis" caused by methyltestosterone and other 17α substituted steroids Perhaps effect of other hormones (estrogens) or of infections b. Cholangiolitic hepatitis caused by virus, bacteria, drugs (e.g., chlorpromazine), or autoimmunity Primary biliary cirrhosis c. Stone, stricture, inflammation Neoplasm	60–80% direct 20–40% indirect 60–80% direct 20–40% indirect 60–80% direct 20–40% indirect 60–80% direct 20–40% indirect	+ + + +	decreased decreased decreased very low	decreased or normal decreased or normal decreased or normal; occasionally increased very low or absent
7. Mixed: Impaired uptake, conjugation, transport, and excretion with variable cholestasis	7. Most varieties of hepatitis and cirrhosis	30–70% direct 30–70% indirect	+	decreased or normal	decreased, normal, or increased

* As noted in the text, the van den Bergh reaction does not identify the bile pigments with exactness; hence some "direct" bilirubin may be falsely measured as present even if serum contains no bilirubin conjugates.

polygonal cell are saturated by bile pigments that cannot be moved along, and hence the removal of bilirubin from the blood is impaired.

Since the kidney can excrete only the water-soluble conjugates of bilirubin, the urine is bile-stained only in those jaundiced states characterized by an accumulation of conjugated bilirubin; thus bilirubinuria does not occur in the first three categories listed in Table 27–1. As measured by the van den Bergh reaction, the concentration of direct bilirubin necessary to produce bilirubinuria is variable. Early in infectious hepatitis, bile pigment may be detected in the urine when there is but a slight increase in direct bilirubin and practically no increase in the plasma concentration of total bile pigments. Late in the disease, several milligrams per 100 ml. of direct bilirubin may appear to be in the plasma without any bilirubinuria occurring. Perhaps the type of conjugate accounting for the direct bilirubin is responsible for this inconstant renal threshold; perhaps conjugated bile pigments in the blood may, over a period of time, be held more firmly in protein aggregates, or perhaps an increase of plasma solubilizing agents may cause a falsely high determination of direct bilirubin, or perhaps glomerular permeability is altered during the course of viral hepatitis. This last possibility is consistent with recent evidence suggesting (but not proving) that conjugated bilirubin enters the urine principally as a result of glomerular filtration. Until pure preparations of bilirubin diglucuronide become available, further elucidation of the mechanism of renal bile pigment excretion will probably be thwarted.

The output of fecal and urinary urobilinogen substances follows readily comprehensible patterns in conditions such as hemolytic states or complete choledochal obstruction by neoplasm. In some cases of hepatic disease and of choledocholithiasis, however, urobilinogen output may be quite variable because the various determinants of this output are working in opposite directions. In an early case of hepatitis, for example, intrahepatic cholestasis is so pronounced that the quantity of bilirubin diglucuronide reaching the bowel is greatly reduced. Hence the total amount of urobilinogen formed is reduced, and so is the amount of urobilinogen absorbed into the portal circulation. The liver, however, since it is damaged by hepatitis, cannot handle adequately even this reduced amount of absorbed urobilinogen. Thus one abnormal mechanism cancels the effects of the other, with the result that the urinary output of urobilinogen falls within the normal range. In the case of patients jaundiced because of choledocholithiasis, a decreased fecal and urinary urobilinogen output is reasonably expected, since conjugated bilirubin excretion into the gut is reduced and liver function should not be much impaired. Yet patients

with this disorder may intermittently excrete much urinary urobilinogen. Shifting of the stone to permit occasional discharges of dammed-up bile into the gut may in part explain this phenomenon, but other mechanisms, as yet obscure, probably play a role as well. Intermittent discharges of bile into the gut with consequent intermittent urobilinogenuria may also take place in the case of cancers of the ampulla of Vater, which are sufficiently necrotic and erosive to open up temporary communications between bile ducts and duodenum. With respect to the differential diagnosis of hepatobiliary disorders, either a very high or very low output of urinary urobilinogen is most significant—a persistent extremely high output is uncommon except in parenchymatous disorders of the liver, and the persistent finding of no or minimal urobilinogen in the urine strongly suggests neoplastic obstruction of the common duct.

The liver's excretory function can be tested by a bilirubin tolerance test, but bilirubin for this purpose is neither readily available nor easily given. Alternatively, hepatic excretory function is assessed by measuring the disappearance rate of injected dyes, such as Bromsulphalein, indocyanine green, or rose bengal, which are excreted by the same anatomic pathways but not the same biochemical mechanisms as bilirubin. Bromsulphalein, for example, does not require glucuronide conjugation for its excretion; instead the dye is mainly conjugated with glutathione. In the presence of any jaundice with increased direct bilirubin (i.e., with conjugated bilirubin in the plasma), these tests are of limited value, for they add little to the information provided by the very presence of conjugated bilirubin in the blood, namely, that excretory function is impaired; and the excretion of dyes can in no way differentiate whether the cause of the impairment is to be found in the parenchymal cell, the biliary channel, or the common duct. When jaundice is slight or absent, however, the removal of injected dyes from the blood provides an excellent index of hepatic function. In clinical practice, this removal is usually measured in terms of "retention," i.e., the percentage of the dye remaining in the blood after a given interval following its injection. By taking more frequent samples and subjecting the data to mathematical manipulation, various disappearance or removal constants can be calculated. Normally, for example, 90 per cent of an injected dose of

Bromsulphalein is removed from the plasma at a rate of 11 to 15 per cent/min. of the amount present in the blood at a given time.

The overall excretion of Bromsulphalein may be separated into two components: (1) uptake and storage in the parenchyma, and (2) metabolism and excretion into the biliary system. Storage appears to be unlimited and is a function of the plasma dye level. In man, normal Bromsulphalein storage is 63 ± 25 mg./mg./100 ml. Excretion, however, is rate-limited; in normal man maximal excretion (called Tm or transport maximum) is 8.6 ± 1.9 mg./min.

There is no substantial evidence that any aspect of the hepatobiliary excretion of bilirubin or of dyes is affected by adrenocortical steroids under normal conditions. In patients with jaundice, particularly those with hemolytic disorders or parenchymatous inflammation, but also to some extent in those with choledochal obstruction, adrenocorticotropic hormone or adrenocortical steroids may lessen the concentration of bile pigments in the blood, but this result is attributable to the effect of the steroid therapy on the pathologic mechanism, and not to enhancement of a normal mechanism. As shown in Table 27–1, however, a variety of estrogenic and 17α-substituted androgenic agents may affect the secretion of bile and of test dyes in a significant manner.

BILE CONSTITUENTS OTHER THAN BILIRUBIN

Besides bilirubin, such biliary constituents as *bile salts, alkaline phosphatase,* and *lipids* assume significance when the formation and flow of bile are affected by disease.

The bile acids, cholic (a trihydroxy compound) and deoxycholic (a dihydroxy compound) acid, are formed in the liver from cholesterol, are there conjugated with taurine or glycine by a reaction which requires microsomal enzymes, coenzyme A, and ATP, and are excreted in the bile as sodium salts.* In the intestine, bile salts facilitate the digestion and absorption of lipids and then are in large part themselves reabsorbed to be resecreted by the liver, thus participating in an enterohepatic circulation. Man produces about 1 gm. of bile acids per day, their half-life is approximately 3 days, and the total bile acid pool, which is believed to circulate twice following each meal, amounts to 4 gm. Certain resins such as cholestyramine bind bile acids in the intestinal lumen, thus preventing their reabsorption and promoting their fecal excretion. Hence, in conditions with elevated blood levels of bile acids but with some continuing excretion of bile acids into the gut (e.g., primary biliary cirrhosis, partial stricture of common duct), oral cholestyramine may be used to reduce the body's bile acid content and thereby to alleviate the itching.

Another portion of bile salts in the intestines is degraded or altered by bacteria. A product of bacterial action on cholic acid is the dihydroxy bile acid chenodeoxycholic acid, which also enters the enterohepatic circulation and quantitatively is one of the three major bile acids of man. A monohydroxy product, lithocholic acid, is less soluble in water than the more common bile acids and is reabsorbed only to a slight extent under normal conditions. If bile contains excessive amounts of an abnormal bile acid such as lithocholic acid, or a bile acid stereoisomer (known as an allo-bile acid), the stability of bile is grossly impaired.

Bile salts tend to accumulate in the blood when the intra- or extrahepatic biliary channels are obstructed. Under such conditions, bile acids continue to be made but regurgitate into the blood because of the obstructive process. The resultant excess of bile salts in blood and tissues is generally held responsible for the itching which accompanies most forms of obstructive jaundice. On the other hand, jaundice produced by extensive parenchymal damage is rarely accompanied by itching, presumably because the damaged liver cells cease to produce bile acids. The distribution of bile acids in the blood is also altered by the nature of the icterogenic disease. In parenchymatous liver diseases, the dihydroxy bile acids predominate; in essentially cholestatic states, the trihydroxy compounds are more prevalent.

Because bile salts are surface-active agents, their accumulation in the blood in obstructive jaundice has other biochemical and physiologic consequences. The permeability of cellular membranes may be altered, and the extent to which lipids, such as cholesterol, are

---

* Sodium taurocholate, a typical human bile salt, is formed from sodium, cholic acid and taurine. Naturally occurring bile salts of this type should be distinguished from many commercial preparations which are oxidized and unconjugated derivatives of cholic acid. The administration of such preparations stimulates the flow of a watery, diluted bile without increasing the output of biliary constituents; whereas natural bile salts promote the output of a normally concentrated bile.

held in the blood is partly determined by the activity of regurgitated bile salts.

The alkaline phosphatase activity of the serum also is increased by cholestasis associated with relatively little parenchymal liver damage: in obstructions of the common duct, cholangiolitic hepatitis or biliary cirrhosis, serum alkaline phosphatase usually exceeds 10 Bodansky units (normal is less than 5 units). The responsible mechanisms are, however, obscure, as indeed is the physiologic significance of alkaline phosphatase itself (the optimum activity of this enzyme, or enzymes, is at the decidedly unphysiologic pH of 9!). Under normal conditions alkaline phosphatase is presumed to be made in bone, carried in the blood, and excreted in the bile. One explanation for increased serum alkaline phosphatase in obstructive jaundice consequently rests on the simple assumption that the normal excretory pathway of the enzyme is blocked. This explanation is controverted, however, by experimental evidence: the alkaline phosphatase that is derived from bone, and that which accumulates in the blood when bile flow is obstructed, can be distinguished on the basis of electrophoresis, differential inhibition, and immunologic techniques. In addition, it is clinically evident that cholestasis with marked jaundice, when associated with considerable parenchymal damage (as in the usual case of hepatitis), is not necessarily accompanied by an increase in serum alkaline phosphatase; and that primary and secondary cancers involving the liver may cause high serum levels of alkaline phosphatase even in the total absence of jaundice. It is probable that the increased alkaline phosphatase of cholestatic jaundice is of hepatogenous origin, possibly elaborated by hepatocytes where their borders face bile capillaries and sinusoids. According to this view, serum alkaline phosphatase might not rise in jaundiced cases of hepatitis and cirrhosis because production as well as excretion of alkaline phosphatase could be affected. Proliferating tissue, particularly connective tissue, is also rich in alkaline phosphatase; perhaps this is the source of the increased alkaline phosphatase often found in the blood of patients with hepatic malignancy.

"White bile," i.e., a nearly colorless, mucoid material, is occasionally found in the biliary tract after prolonged and complete obstruction, especially if gallbladder function is negligible. Under such conditions biliary pigment appears to be resorbed and a clear or whitish mucus is secreted by the mucosal cells lining the biliary passages. "White bile" is not a product of the liver.

CARBOHYDRATE METABOLISM

Carbohydrate in the liver is chiefly in the form of glycogen, a complex aggregate of glucose molecules. When sugars are plentifully available and the energy requirements of the body are satisfied, absorbed molecules of glucose, fructose, and galactose are assimilated by the liver to build up its glycogen stores (glycogenesis). The liver also changes an excess of ingested carbohydrates to lipids suitable for storage in the fat depots of the body. Conversely, during fasting states the liver breaks down glycogen (glycogenolysis) to maintain the blood glucose level and to supply calories for the energy needs of the body. The capacity of the hepatic glycogen depot, however, is limited; in man it can supply only about 500 calories. The fasting person would consequently soon suffer from hypoglycemia were it not for hepatic gluconeogenesis and glyconeogenesis, processes by which glucose and glycogen are formed, by way of pyruvic acid, from the deaminated residue of certain amino acids and from glycerol. If these mechanisms are not adequate to satisfy caloric requirements, depot lipid is mobilized and hepatic fat metabolism is accelerated to provide fuel in the form of ketone bodies to extrahepatic tissues.

Though the liver plays an integral part in all the phases of carbohydrate metabolism, few of these phases depend only on hepatic function. The endocrines, in particular the pancreas, the pituitary, and the adrenal cortex, also play major roles. Furthermore, extrahepatic utilization of glucose is extensive. The blood sugar and the intermediary products of carbohydrate metabolism, consequently, depend upon many interplaying factors and do not mirror hepatic function specifically.

Total removal of the liver in experimental animals causes a precipitous fall in blood sugar. In man, however, pronounced hypoglycemia is rarely seen as an expression of liver damage, even if extreme. In addition, unusual alimentary hyperglycemia with glycosuria, or moderate hypoglycemia on fasting is evident in only the occasional patient with hepatitis or cirrhosis, although such fluctuations in blood sugar might be expected on the basis of decreased hepatic glycogen storage and impaired gluconeogenesis. Considerable hepatic reserve function and participation by extrahepatic tissues apparently enable the patient with liver disease to maintain fairly normal glucose levels in response to moderate metabolic demands. When, however, the mechanisms regulating the blood sugar are severely taxed, impairment of hepatic glycogenolysis and gluconeogenesis may become apparent. Thus an unusually labile response to insulin with prolonged hypoglycemia presents a serious clinical problem in some patients with both diabetes and cirrhosis. Deficient hepatic glycogen storage in hepatitis and cirrhosis is also revealed by the feeble elevations in blood glucose that take place in response to epinephrine or glucagon. When patients with these diseases are given ACTH or cortisone, on the other hand, fasting blood sugar levels may increase, possibly because adrenal hormones stimulate gluconeogenesis more rapidly than the liver can convert glucose to glycogen.

Another abnormality pertaining to carbohydrate metabolism in patients with advanced liver disease is the finding of elevated blood pyruvic acid levels (1.5 to 3.0 mg. per 100 ml. as opposed to the normal range of about 1.0 mg.). This key substance in the intermediary metabolism of all foodstuffs may accumulate because the damaged liver cannot adequately provide with sufficient rapidity the enzymes necessary for the further metabolism of pyruvate. Thus the crucial step which links pyruvate and the Krebs citric acid cycle via acetyl coenzyme A requires thiamine pyrophosphate as a coenzyme; and the liver is a main site for converting ingested thiamine hydrochloride (vitamin B_1) to the phosphorylated coenzyme. Hepatic enzyme systems also play a role in the synthesis of coenzyme A from pantothenic acid, cysteine, and other precursors. On the other hand, blood lactate may also be increased by advanced hepatic failure, and accumulation of various metabolites of glycolysis may reflect such a total metabolic disorder that the pin-pointing of specific enzymatic deficiencies is quite speculative. Indeed, the central position of glucose in total metabolism is such that severe hepatic parenchymal damage is reflected not so much by abnormal blood glucose levels as by decreased synthesis of proteins, fatty acids, nucleoproteins, cholesterol, and urea, all of which may suffer indirectly when the metabolism of glucose is impaired. It is not known whether liver damage primarily affects aerobic and anaerobic glycolysis or the oxidative phosphogluconate pathway, both of which sequences the normal liver can accomplish in the metabolism of glucose.

Two hepatic diseases associated with genetically determined disorders of carbohydrate metabolism are galactosemia and glycogen storage disease. In galatosemia, the normal sequence converting galactose-1-phosphate to glucose-1-phosphate is interrupted because the enzyme galactose-1-phosphate uridyl transferase is congenitally deficient. Because UDP-galactose cannot be formed, ingested galactose accumulates as galactose-1-phosphate and by unknown mechanisms causes cerebral damage, cataracts, aminoaciduria, and liver damage characterized by fatty infiltration, necrosis, fibrosis, hepatomegaly, and jaundice. The enzymatic deficiency can also be demonstrated in circulating red cells. As surviving children with galactosemia grow older, however, they manifest an increased tolerance of galactose, possibly because tissues become more resistant to whatever noxious factors accumulate when galactose metabolism is deranged. The next step in the conversion of galactose-1-phosphate to glucose-1-phosphate, namely the conversion of UDP-galactose to UDP-glucose, is dependent upon the action of UDP-galactose-4-epimerase. Excessive alcohol ingestion depresses the activity of this enzyme because of the large amounts of DPNH ($NADH_2$) produced when alcohol is oxidized.

Glycogenosis refers to a group of inherited disorders affecting infants and children. Four of these disorders (Cori types I, III, IV and VI) may be considered examples of hepatic glycogen storage, or *von Gierke's disease*, in that glycogen accumulates predominantly but not always exclusively in the liver. The responsible enzymatic deficits have been identified as type I: glucose-6-phosphatase; type III: amylo-1,6-glucosidase, a debranching enzyme also found in erythrocytes; the very rare type IV: amylo-(1,4 → 1,6)-transglucosidase and type VI: phosphorylase, also found in leukocytes. The increase in liver glycogen content from a normal of 3-6 to 12-16 per cent of wet weight (except in type IV) causes hepatomegaly with variable but usually moderate hepatic functional impairment. Because glycogen is not normally available, fasting hypoglycemia, acidosis, and lipemia are common. Nitrogen retention is impaired because proteins are converted to carbohydrates in an effort to sustain the blood sugar; as a result, growth is often retarded.

Glucose tolerance curves in liver disease yield results that are variable and not easily interpreted because the blood sugar reflects the activity of so many organs. Galactose and fructose tolerance tests, on the other hand, have been proposed as satisfactory in the belief that the rate of removal of these sugars from the blood depends primarily on the liver. Of the two, the galactose test, especially if given intravenously to eliminate the variable of intestinal absorption, appears the more reliable. Although the normal liver removes fructose from the blood approximately twice as rapidly as it removes glucose, other tissues also take up fructose, and results of fructose tolerance tests in liver disease have been inconsistent. To test the liver's ability to convert lactic acid to glycogen, sodium d-lactate has been injected and its removal rate determined, but this procedure has not been widely used.

NITROGEN METABOLISM

In the digestion of protein to its constituent amino acids and in their absorption, the liver plays no direct role; in hepatic disease, therefore, the digestion and absorption of proteins is not impaired except insofar as secondary disorders of the gastrointestinal tract are present.

Once absorbed, amino acids immediately enter the "dynamic equilibrium" of nitrogen metabolism. On one side the equilibrium is maintained by all the extrahepatic organs, each of which is constantly synthesizing and degrading its specific proteins. In these processes plasma amino acids, peptides, and proteins are consumed, but only amino acids and perhaps peptides are returned to the blood. The other side of the equilibrium is supported by the liver. Here nitrogen metabolism is both much more versatile and rapid than in other organs, the half-life of liver protein being 10 days, as opposed to the 180-day half-life of muscle protein. The means of exchange between the liver and other tissues is provided by the blood, whose nitrogenous constituents thus reflect the general state of protein metabolism. If the liver is damaged, this state necessarily is changed, but the change is modified both qualitatively and quantitatively by the adjustments made by extrahepatic tissue.

The pathways of hepatic amino acid metabolism are: (1) formation of new amino acids, (2) synthesis into proteins and nucleoproteins, and (3) removal of amino groups with conversion of amino groups to urea, and of non-nitrogenous residues to glucose or ketone bodies. In these reactions, a central role is played by transamination, a process which exchanges the NH$_2$ group of an amino acid with the double-bonded oxygen of a keto acid to form a different amino and a different keto acid. Transaminations are reversible. The important transamination shown in Figure 27–2 proceeds from right to left in the sequence there outlined, but the laboratory procedure used to measure glutamic oxalacetic transaminase (GOT) employs aspartic

and α-ketoglutaric acids as starting reagents. If the amino acid alanine is used in place of aspartic acid, the products of transamination are pyruvic and glutamic acids, and the hepatic enzyme catalyzing the reaction is glutamic pyruvic transaminase (GPT).

When the liver deaminates an amino acid, glutamic acid for example, the NH$_2$ group is used for urea synthesis without formation of NH$_3$ as an intermediate (see Fig. 27–2). The liver, however, is also responsible for converting ammonia from other sources to urea, and two possible pathways for this conversion are outlined in Figure 27–2. It is to be noted that the Krebs-Hanseleit cycle essentially picks up two NH$_2$ groups and combines them with one molecule of CO$_2$ to form urea.

In liver disease, decreased conversion of ammonia to urea is a sign of advanced hepatic damage, and its clinically important result is to increase blood ammonia to several times its normal value of about 1 mcg. ammonia nitrogen/1 ml. blood. Theoretically this excess blood ammonia could result if the injured liver deaminated more rapidly than it converted the resultant amino groups to urea, and this happens when large amino acid loads are imposed on dogs deficient in arginine. In human liver disease, however, removal from amino acids of amino groups and their conversion to urea are probably impaired in parallel fashion, and hepatic release of NH$_3$ into the circulation is not recognized as significant. The major cause of high blood ammonia levels in advanced liver disease is inadequate removal of ammonia reaching the liver from other sources (see Fig. 27–2), especially from the intestines. In part, the deficient removal rate can be ascribed to impairment of the hepatic mechanisms outlined in Figure 27–2, in part through portosystemic vascular shunts, spontaneous or surgically created, permitting ammonia of intestinal origin to bypass the liver. The kidney's role in elevating blood ammonia is probably not large, but its ammoniagenic activity is enhanced by hypokalemia, a complication that may take place when edematous patients with liver disease are given diuretics such as chlorothiazide.

Other possible results of an amino acid metabolism impaired by liver disease are changes in the amino acid pattern in the plasma, an increase in total plasma amino acids, aminoaciduria, and a decreased blood urea; but these phenomena are found only in very advanced or terminal liver disease,

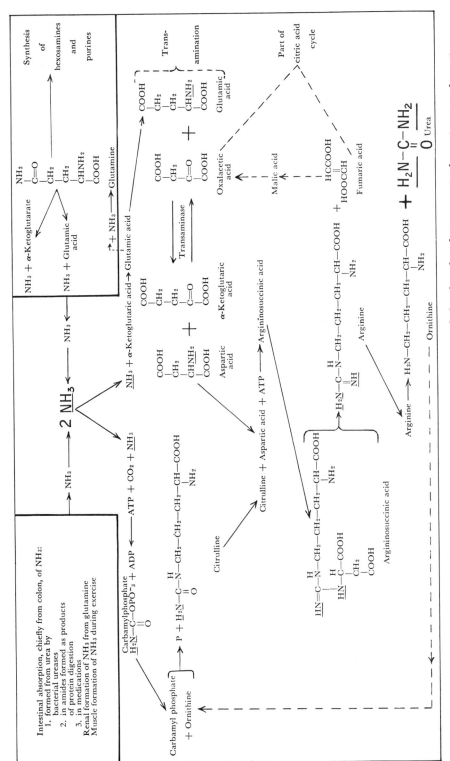

Figure 27–2. Hepatic urea formation from ammonia. The ammonia groups are underlined so that their course in the various transformations may be more easily followed. It is to be noted that ammonia enters the Krebs-Hanseleit cycle via two substances, citrulline and aspartic acid.

and inconstantly at that. Because of the renal functional depression that often attends liver failure, blood urea may actually be increased, a complication which causes more urea to enter the gut and hence more ammonia to be generated there. The occurrence of leucine and tyrosine crystals in the urine, described in the case of patients dying of hepatic necrosis, is believed to reflect rapid lysis of hepatic tissue itself.

The degree of decreased gluconeogenesis and ketogenesis from deaminated amino acid residues in liver disease is not clearly defined. Presumably these deficiencies make the patient less able to fulfill energy requirements and to withstand hypoglycemia.

The liver is the sole source of plasma albumin, several clotting factors, fibrinogen, and cholinesterase, and it is a major source of all other plasma proteins except gamma globulin. With progressive liver disease, the levels of most plasma proteins tend to fall, but the clinically most important decreases are those affecting albumin and the clotting factors (see Effects of Hepatic Disease on Blood). Fibrinogen formation, however, is apparently quite resistant to injury, and fibrinogenopenia of a degree affecting blood clotting is practically never seen in liver disease. The physiologic function of the so-called "pseudo" cholinesterase of the plasma is unknown. The plasma concentration of alpha globulin, containing glycoproteins and mucoproteins, may not change because decreased formation by hepatic parenchyma may be offset by increased synthesis of mucoproteins, a response characteristic of many chronic inflammatory states. Beta globulins, which include a major lipoprotein fraction, do exhibit low plasma levels in advanced hepatic disease, and this effect may be responsible for inefficient lipid transport. As far as gamma globulins are concerned, their plasma concentration is usually elevated in chronic liver disorders because of their increased production by mesenchymal elements throughout the body.

Decreased plasma albumin levels have two far-reaching implications: (1) the resultant decreased plasma osmotic pressure is a major factor in the pathogenesis of ascites and edema, and (2) in view of the dynamic equilibrium that characterizes protein metabolism, hypoalbuminemia also means decreased tissue proteins. The hypoalbuminemic patient is thus a depleted patient, and his resistance to stress and infections of all types is impaired. Parenteral administration of albumin or plasma to such a patient raises plasma albumin levels evanescently, for the whole body as well as the plasma has to be repleted.

Abnormalities of protein metabolism as revealed by electrophoresis, by flocculation or precipitation tests, by the serum albumin-globulin (A:G) ratio, and by serum cholinesterase levels are often used to diagnose or evaluate liver disease clinically. Though flocculation tests are superficially similar, their mechanisms are not necesarily identical. Flocculation of a cephalin-cholesterol emulsion, for example, takes place if the stabilizing components of serum proteins, albumin and alpha-1-globulin, are decreased; thymol turbidity and flocculation tests depend upon (1) increased and abnormal gamma globulins, (2) decreased albumin, and (3) the presence of plasma lipids; whereas the zinc sulfate test principally responds to an increase in precipitable gamma globulin. As opposed to the flocculation tests, which reflect early and acute hepatic disease, reversal of the A:G ratio, as determined by routine chemical methods, usually does not appear until hepatic damage is chronic or extensive.

Although the dietotherapy of liver disease fluctuates continuously, the present tendency is to give normal or increased amounts of protein to patients with hepatic disorders except those verging on hepatic coma. If hepatic protein metabolism is impaired, how can the practice be justified? The rationale is as follows: (1) The major factor limiting protein metabolism in many patients with liver disease is not hepatic function, but anorexia with decreased food intake. (2) To repair damaged hepatic enzyme systems, dietary amino acids, especially essential amino acids, must be liberally available. (3) Even in the face of advanced hepatic disease, positive nitrogen balances can be maintained if enough protein is given, probably because of direct extrahepatic utilization. (4) In spite of the theoretical danger of "overloading" a damaged organ, no good evidence exists that an excess of amino acids causes further liver injury.

LIPID METABOLISM

In the small bowel, ingested lipids (neutral fats, phospholipids, sterols, steroids, carotenes) are first finely emulsified by virtue of the surface-active properties of bile salts. Hydrolysis under the influence of pancreatic enzymes then takes place with the formation of fatty acids, monoglycerides, and some diglycerides. These substances, as well as other lipid moieties, are then solubilized in the aqueous medium of intestinal chyme by the micelle-forming properties of the bile salts. Bile salts thus play a crucial role in preparing lipids for absorption.

If bile of normal quantity and quality is prevented from reaching the intestine, the fat lost in the feces, normally less than 10 per cent of the intake, may increase up to 50 per cent of the amount ingested. The magnitude of the steatorrhea obviously depends upon the nature and severity of the hepatobiliary disorder. If the common duct is blocked, fecal fat loss is roughly proportional to the degree of obstruction. In parenchymatous disorders with jaundice the picture is more complex, for not only is the formation of new bile salts impaired, but their excretion is retarded by intrahepatic biliary obstruction. On the other hand, parenchymal diseases associated with relatively patent biliary channels—portal cirrhosis, for example—may not affect fat absorption strikingly. Parenchymal damage, to be sure, decreases the formation of bile acids, but the enterohepatic circulation of these acids partly compensates for their decreased synthesis and thus prevents gross steatorrhea.

After absorption, unesterified short-chain (12-carbon or less) fatty acids are transported to the liver by the portal vein, but the great bulk of absorbed lipid is carried in the form of chylomicra (protein-stabilized particles of tri-, di-, and monoglycerides, cholesterol esters, cholesterol, and phospholipids) via the intestinal lymph channels, and thus bypasses the liver in reaching the systemic circulation. This anatomical arrangement would seem to permit extrahepatic tissue to utilize absorbed fatty substances directly, but some experiments with labeled compounds indicate that lipids contained in dietary chylomicra are first taken up by the liver and there converted to phospholipids before being transported to peripheral fat depots. In the fasting state, unesterified fatty acids, freed from depot fat by lipoprotein lipase, are brought to the liver for utilization.

Whatever the nature or source of fatty substances reaching the liver, these substances are here broken down, reshaped or combined in a variety of reactions. Fatty acids, which are degraded to acetyl coenzyme A, may by this route enter the citric acid cycle, may be diverted to the formation of ketone bodies, or may be used in the synthesis of new fatty acids and steroids. Much of the normal liver lipid is in the form of phospholipids, which the liver is constantly synthesizing and which, as major constituents of plasma lipoproteins, may be instrumental in transporting fat from the liver to other tissues.

When obstruction of the biliary passages occurs, the lipids of the plasma tend to rise, particularly phospholipids and cholesterol.

The increase in cholesterol is chiefly confined to the free fraction, but some elevation of cholesterol esters also takes place. Since free cholesterol and a small quantity of phospholipids are normally excreted in the bile, an increase in the plasma content of these lipids is a reasonable consequence of biliary obstruction. This mechanism, however, is not adequate to explain all the observed changes. A more important cause appears to be the increased plasma content of regurgitated bile salts, which, by virtue of their surface activity, hold cholesterol and other lipids in solution and prevent their uptake by the tissues. In spite of its high lipid content, the serum of obstructive jaundice is clear, probably because the formation of chylomicron aggregates is prevented by the relatively high concentrations of bile salts and phospholipids. In addition, because of poor fat absorption, the number of chylomicra delivered to the blood from the thoracic duct is limited.

Severe parenchymatous disease of the liver with minimal obstructive phenomena is usually attended by a drop in plasma phospholipids, a normal or low total cholesterol, and a marked depression of cholesterol esters, which, in severe cases, may practically disappear from the blood. Depressed phospholipids in the plasma may be attributed to decreased hepatic synthesis of these substances. Esterification of cholesterol, however, may be achieved quite efficiently by the intestine, and a relative increase of cholesterol esters actually takes place within the liver substance during many hepatic disorders. Perhaps mobilization rather than hepatic synthesis of cholesterol esters is impaired.

Values for plasma free, esterified, and total cholesterol have been used to differentiate jaundice caused by hepatic and biliary tract disease; a normal or low total cholesterol with a depressed ester fraction is considered characteristic of liver disease, and a high total cholesterol with a normal proportion of cholesterol esters (66 per cent of total) is regarded as typical of cholestatic disorders. These changes in plasma cholesterol content and partition are, however, only moderately reliable in the differential diagnosis of jaundice and, as expected, are inadequate for separating cholestasis of intrahepatic and extrahepatic origin. In primary biliary cirrhosis, for example, jaundice is marked and fat absorption impaired; yet such huge amounts of phospholipids and cholesterol accumulate in the blood that abnormal fat deposits appear in the skin.

All the plasma lipids, whether neutral fats, unesterified fatty acids, phospholipids, or cholesterol, exist in the form of protein-containing aggregates known as lipoproteins. In the presence of hepatobiliary disorders, various lipoprotein fractions may be altered qualitatively and quantitatively, but a specific trend has not been delineated for any one type of liver or biliary tract disease. Perhaps this is not surprising, for the plasma lipoprotein pattern is theoretically subject to many influences when liver function is damaged or bile secretion is blocked; e.g., abnormal lipid synthesis or breakdown, deranged protein metabolism, impaired excretion of lecithin and free cholesterol in the bile, or the accumulation of surface-active bile acids in the blood.

Since the liver is responsible for the production of ketone bodies, ketosis is rarely observed when hepatic damage is advanced. The significance of this disability is probably limited to the fact that the body under such conditions cannot depend upon fats to satisfy its fuel requirements.

A number of abnormalities of lipid metabolism are of obscure origin. These include (1) *primary xanthomatoses* characterized by an intensively lipemic plasma, and (2) disorders such as *Gaucher's disease, Niemann-Pick disease,* and eosinophilic granulomas in which abnormal deposits of lipid accumulate in many tissues, presumably because of some derangement of intracellular metabolism. The cells of the liver are involved as are the cells of other organs, but evidence is lacking that either hepatic dysfunction or damage is primarily responsible for disorders of this type.

Vitamin Metabolism

Fat-Soluble Vitamins

Absorption of the fat-soluble vitamins A, D, K, and E tends to be impaired in hepatobiliary disorders, particularly if accompanied by steatorrhea. In part, these vitamins are held in solution by unabsorbed fats and hence are washed out of the bowel. The main reason, however, for the poor absorption of fat-soluble vitamins in diseases of the liver or biliary tract is an inadequate supply of bile acids. This is particularly true of vitamin K and carotene, the precursor of vitamin A.

Ingested vitamin A is available to the body immediately upon absorption, but carotene must first be converted to vitamin A, a process which takes place to a large extent in the intestinal wall. Excess vitamin A is stored in the liver, where it is ready for mobilization in response to tissue demands. In the normal liver, vitamin A is found in the esterfied form and is distributed, according to fluorescence microscopy, in both polygonal and Kupffer cells. After liver injury the vitamin-containing droplets are coarse, irregular, and principally in the Kupffer cells. Apparently the phagocytic system can still take up the vitamin, but normal intercellular exchange, storage, and metabolism are disrupted.

In hepatic disease or obstruction of the biliary tract, plasma vitamin A levels fall precipitously, and large oral doses of vitamin A are not followed by the usual increase in plasma vitamin A levels. These changes can be blamed on decreased absorption, on impaired hepatic mobilization, and on impaired transport mechanisms in the blood. In spite of their apparent sensitivity to hepatobiliary disorders, neither plasma vitamin A levels nor vitamin A tolerance tests are very satisfactory tests of hepatic function; they are affected by too many other diseases. Plasma carotene levels bear no clear-cut relation to the liver's activity.

Although plasma vitamin A levels are depressed, clinical evidences of vitamin A deficiencies are not common in liver disease. Occasionally a history of night blindness is elicited, or poor dark adaptation can be demonstrated. Conjunctival keratinization and follicular keratosis of the skin are not found to an unusual degree in liver disease.

Many functions have been attributed to vitamin E, not the least interesting of which are its protective action against nutritional hepatic necrosis in animals (see Fatty Liver) and its antioxidant action in preventing the deposition of ceroid in hepatic and other tissues, but its role in man is uncertain. By analogy with other fat-soluble vitamins, the absorption and metabolism of vitamin E may be abnormal in hepatic disorders; plasma tocopheral levels are depressed.

Vitamin K is needed by the liver in the formation of prothrombin and Factors VII, IX and X (see Effect of Hepatic Disease on Other Organs—Blood). In the course of hepatobiliary disorders the concentration of prothrombin in the plasma may fall for one of two basic reasons:

1. Insufficient bile salts are entering the intestine for the normal absorption of vitamin K.

2. The liver is so damaged that it cannot utilize vitamin K, even if the supply of this material is adequate.

Obstruction of the extrahepatic biliary passages typically leads to hypoprothrombinemia based on deficient absorption of vitamin K. Ordinarily the plasma prothrombin does not fall until biliary obstruction has persisted for a few weeks, but the limited stores of vitamin K normally available may be reduced by previous hepatic disease or may be rapidly consumed during the course of an acute infection or after surgical trauma. Parenteral administration of vitamin K in cases of this type makes this substance readily available to the liver, which usually can restore normal levels of plasma prothrombin within 1 or 2 days. For this purpose the huge doses of vitamin K used to combat excessive effects of coumarin derivatives are not necessary.

In the ordinary mild or moderate case of hepatitis, absorption and utilization of vitamin K are not sufficiently diminished to lower the plasma prothrombin. With more severe hepatitis, however, these processes are affected and hypoprothrombinemia develops. Patients with advanced cirrhosis may absorb sufficient amounts of vitamin K, but cannot maintain normal plasma prothrombin levels because parenchymal damage interferes with the use of this vitamin. By contrast with the cases of biliary tract obstruction, the hypoprothrombinemia of hepatic parenchymal disease cannot be corrected by parenteral injections of vitamin K.

The response of the prothrombin time to parenterally administered vitamin K may be used as a measure of liver function. A prolonged prothrombin time persisting after vitamin K is given parenterally indicates pronounced hepatic damage. When the prothrombin concentration in the plasma is sufficiently reduced, a diffuse bleeding tendency may appear, leading to such clinical phenomena as purpura of the skin and hemorrhages from the gastrointestinal or genitourinary tract. Such hemorrhagic manifestations are said to occur when the prothrombin level is 20 per cent of normal, but this figure is only approximate and cannot be considered a constant "critical level."

Water-Soluble Vitamins

The absorption of water-soluble vitamins is not directly affected by liver disease, but their metabolism may be deranged to an uncertain extent. Although liver cells use water-soluble vitamins for the synthesis of essential coenzymes, other tissues can also perform this function, and no vitamin is known to be entirely dependent upon hepatic function for conversion to its metabolically active form. Liver disease consequently would not be expected to abolish utilization of water-soluble vitamins, but their incorporation into enzyme systems might be retarded. Thus the rate of phosphorylation of thiamine (see Carbohydrate Metabolism) is reported as decreased

in cirrhosis. Nicotinic acid is used by the liver for the synthesis of nicotinamide adenine dinucleotide (DPN), and a major urinary excretory product, N^1-methyl nicotinamide, is formed by methylation of nicotinamide in the liver. Like other hepatic methylations (exchange of methyl groups to form choline or methionine, synthesis of creatine by methylation of guanidoacetic acid), this process may proceed less efficiently when the liver is damaged. Folic acid is converted to its active coenzyme form, tetrahydrofolic acid. In a patient with liver disease, consequently, any associated evidence of vitamin deficiency may be ascribable not only to improper diet, but also to damaged hepatic metabolism.

INACTIVATION AND DETOXIFICATION

The liver inactivates a large number of endogenous and exogenous substances, including hormones produced by other glands, bacterial toxins, and noxious agents absorbed from the gastrointestinal tract. Hepatic function with respect to hormones is of particular interest because many of the clinical and biochemical phenomena of liver disease are explained in terms of impaired inactivation of this or that glandular product. Such explanations, however, usually are gross oversimplifications. The liver doubtlessly decreases the activity of hormones by three major means, often exercised in sequential fashion: (1) reduction, hydroxylation, or oxidation; (2) conjugation with UDP-glucuronic acid* or sulfate; and (3) excretion in bile with subsequent intestinal absorption and biliary reexcretion (enterohepatic circulation). On the other hand, hepatic function with respect to hormone metabolism cannot be considered purely destructive. Normal synthetic activity on the part of the liver may be necessary to create hormone precursors, to activate humoral agents, and to change one active agent into another. In addition, the feedback control mechanism exercised through the hypothalamus and hypophysis tends to maintain the plasma level of various hormones in the normal range. Consequently, although failure of inactivation of various humoral agents is a

---

* Steroid conjugation with glucuronic acid is usually by means of a glycosidic linkage and thus differs from the ester bond characterizing the linkage of the propionic side chain of bilirubin with glucuronic acid. This may explain in part why there is no obvious clinical association between defects in bilirubin and steroid conjugation.

definite feature of liver damage, the plasma levels and the biological activity of these agents is not increased a priori in hepatic disease.

Studies on the role of the normal and abnormal liver in *estrogen* metabolism have yielded conflicting results. Hepatic inactivation of estrogens, for example, is easily demonstrable in rats, but not in monkeys. In man an increased urinary output of estrogens occurs in male patients with cirrhosis, and patients with advanced hepatic disease do not appear to handle parenterally administered estrogen normally. On the other hand, normal endogenous estrogen levels have been found in pregnant women with hepatitis, even in those suffering from severe liver damage and hepatic coma. Since the estrogenic metabolites participate to a greater extent in the enterohepatic circulation than those of other steroid hormones, some of the variable results may be related to the opposing influences exerted by parenchymatous disease on one hand, and by cholestasis on the other. A high urinary output of estrogenic substances, for example, may merely reflect obstruction of the biliary route of excretion.

From the clinical viewpoint inadequate inactivation of estrogens by the liver has been held responsible for some of the most interesting physical signs often, but not invariably, found in patients with chronic hepatic disease: (1) loss of hair, (2) fine, soft skin, (3) testicular atrophy, (4) gynecomastia, (5) palmar erythema, (6) arterial spiders (spider angiomas, telangiectases), (7) vascular dilatation or engorgement on face, on buccal mucosa, in nares, and in conjunctivae.

Loss of hair, skin changes, testicular atrophy, and gynecomastia—physical signs which are often accompanied or preceded by loss of libido and by impotence—are reasonable consequences of an excessive amount of circulating estrogens. The relation of estrogens and the vascular phenomena, including the arterial spider typical of chronic cirrhosis, is, however, less obvious. Also unexplained is the fact that 99 per cent of the spiders seen in cirrhosis appear above the belt line.

The liver inactivates *cortisol* (*hydrocortisone*) by first reducing it to tetrahydrocortisol, and then by conjugating it with uridine diphosphate-activated glucuronic acid or sulfate. The water-soluble conjugated compound is excreted in the urine and to a lesser extent in bile. Similar hepatic mechanisms play a role in the conversion of other *adrenocortical hormones*. If liver function is impaired, the rate of inactivation of adrenocortical steroids is depressed, formation of the tetrahydrocompounds rather than conjugation being primarily affected by hepatic malfunction. The circulating plasma level of free 17-hydroxycorticoids is, however, not grossly abnormal, and patients with liver disease do not have clinical evidence of excessive glucocorticoid activity, probably because the rate of adrenal glucocorticoid production is also decreased. Liver damage per se does not impair the adrenal response to adrenocorticotropic stimulation.

The marked inability of the cirrhotic patient to excrete sodium in the urine (see Edema and Ascites) is blamed, in part at least, on excessive aldosterone activity, and the high urinary output of aldosterone in cirrhotic patients accumulating ascites is consistent with this view. In addition, urinary sodium and water output often increase in edematous patients with liver disease if the adrenal is surgically ablated or if aldosterone antagonists are given. The reasons for enhanced aldosterone activity in cirrhotic patients are not entirely clear, but in many animals an intricate hepatic-renal-adrenal mechanism may exist. It is thus postulated that the kidney, when its perfusion is threatened in the course of severe hepatic disease, releases renin. Renin in turn liberates angiotensin from a circulating globulin; angiotensin, in its turn, stimulates the secretion of aldosterone by the adrenal cortex.

The liver also plays a major role in the metabolism of *progesterone, androgens, thyroxine,* and *pituitary hormones;* the blood level or urinary excretion of some of these agents or their products is altered in hepatic disease. Abnormal production of hormones as well as abnormal utilization doubtless accounts for the changes observed. In spite of the fact that liver tissue inactivates posterior pituitary hormone, it cannot be established unequivocally that this hormone accumulates to excess in the blood of patients with cirrhosis, that physiologic amounts of antidiuretic hormone cannot be inactivated by the damaged liver, or that this hormone plays a primary role in causing water retention in liver disease.

A number of *drugs* are inactivated by the liver. In some cases this hepatic activity is supplementary rather than essential, but in other instances, notably that of morphine, the effect of the drug is unusually potent and prolonged if the liver is damaged. Patients with cirrhosis or hepatitis also tolerate sedatives and hypnotics poorly. This intolerance, particularly with respect to short-acting barbiturates, has been ascribed to impaired hepatic inactivation, but a more important cause is the increased cerebral sensitivity of the patient with cirrhosis to central nervous system depressants of all types. No sound basis exists, therefore, for assuming that chloral hydrate or paraldehyde is better tolerated by the liver patient than barbiturates.

The ability of the liver to conjugate various substances with glucuronic acid has been tested with phenolic and other compounds (see Jaundice), but the most popular test of hepatic detoxification has been the hippuric acid test. This consists of administering sodium benzoate and determining, by measuring urinary hippuric acid excretion, the degree to which the liver conjugates benzoic acid with the amino acid glycine to form hippuric acid.

Effects of Hepatic Disease on Other Organs

SPLEEN

Splenic enlargement is common in liver disease. In acute processes, such as hepatitis or cirrhosis in exacerbation, hepatic and splenic damage probably proceed concomitantly in response to common noxious agents. In chronic hepatic disorders with portal hypertension, splenomegaly is ascribed to vascular congestion. Thus one of the causes of Banti's syndrome (portal or splenic venous obstruction, splenomegaly, ascites, leukopenia, and anemia) is chronic cirrhosis.

BLOOD

Anemias are frequently associated with hepatic disease, particularly with cirrhosis, but the type of anemia is not constant. In those patients who have suffered from hypoprothrombinemic hemorrhages or ruptured esophageal varices, the microcytic, hypochromic erythrocytes of iron deficiency are found. Normocytic and macrocytic anemias seen in many cases of cirrhosis are ascribable to increased erythrocyte destruction or to nutritional deficiency, such as folic acid deficiency (see Disorders of Blood, Chap. 30). Occasionally, hemolysis and/or thrombocytopenia complicate liver disease; under such circumstances a diffusely acting autoimmune mechanism is suspected.

During infectious hepatitis the neutrophils are often decreased, whereas the monocytic elements may be both increased and atypical. These changes are probably a part of the general mesenchymal reaction to the infectious agent and are not specifically related to hepatic function. In more chronic hepatic diseases neutropenia is frequent, and a decrease in lymphocytes, monocytes, and platelets occasional. Though this leukocytic distribution pattern may be influenced by the changes in the liver, the effect of concomitant or secondary alterations in the spleen (i.e., "hypersplenism") is probably predominant.

Bleeding tendencies, when they occur in the course of hepatobiliary tract disease, are usually caused by hypoprothrombinemia or by deficiency of the accessory factors proaccelerin (Factor V) and proconvertin (Factor VII), both of which are also made in the liver. Not infrequently, however, a patient with hepatic disease manifests hemorrhagic phenomena in spite of prothrombin times that are not grossly abnormal. In such instances thrombocytopenia, increased capillary fragility, or deficiencies in Christmas (IX) Factor or in Stuart (X) Factor must be considered. Hepatic synthesis of fibrinogen appears to be maintained in the face of severe parenchymal damage, but excessive fibrinolysis is a characteristic finding in patients with advanced cirrhosis. The reasons for this enhanced fibrinolytic activity are not clear, but one possibility is that the damaged liver does not synthesize sufficient amounts of a normally occurring inhibitor of fibrinolysin.

Serum iron and vitamin B_{12} levels are often elevated in the active stages of hepatitis; the mechanism is not definitely known, but iron and vitamin B_{12} are probably liberated from destroyed hepatic parenchyma. Depression of serum copper levels in hepatitis is a nonspecific effect found in many inflammatory conditions.

Patients with hepatic damage, biliary obstruction, or both excrete abnormal amounts of coproporphyrins in the urine, probably because the normal hepatobiliary excretory route for these substances is damaged or blocked. Type III coproporphyrin appears to be excreted in large amounts, particularly by patients with alcoholic cirrhosis. Increased urinary coproporphyrin excretion, known as porphyrinuria, is thus a secondary phenomenon and of relatively little clinical significance. It must be distinguished from porphyria, which refers to the several primary abnormalities that may affect porphyrin metabolism and that are characterized by the urinary excretion of porphobilinogen and uroporphyrins. The hepatic type of porphyria is believed to be caused by abnormal or excessive formation of porphyrin compounds in the liver, but the incidence of associated hepatic abnormalities is inconstant. In some cases, cirrhotic changes are found; in others, no defects in liver structure or function are detectable beyond those pertaining to porphyrin metabolism.

KIDNEY

The functions of the kidney may be affected so profoundly in the course of severe hepatic disease that the concept of a "hepatorenal" syndrome has gained wide recognition. The clinical manifestations of this syndrome, embodying as it does the combined effects of acute hepatic and renal failure, are striking, but the responsible mechanisms are disputed. In certain conditions, such as intoxications by carbon tetrachloride or heavy metals, the noxious agent probably damages both the kidney and the liver. A similar situation obtains in the hepatorenal syndromes seen in Weil's disease and yellow fever. On the other hand, oliguria and anuria have been observed to follow damage restricted to the liver or biliary tract.

When renal failure supervenes on severe cirrhosis, it does so rather rapidly and progressively, but renal function tests, in spite of marked oliguria, may show no more than decreased renal plasma flow and glomerular filtration rate. At death, renal structural changes are unimpressive. Thus it appears that the association of renal with hepatic failure may be ascribed to vascular insufficiency and to a general deterioration of living processes rather than to any specific nephrotoxic substance elaborated by the liver. Since the hepatorenal syndrome also occurs in such a variety of conditions as poisoning, sepsis, specific infectious diseases, liver trauma, acute adrenal insufficiency, fever therapy, prolonged choledochal obstruction, hepatic necrosis, and postoperative "liver death," it is suggested that the term, while perfectly proper as a clinical description, should not be used to express a direct causal relation between hepatic and renal failure.

Prolonged cholestatic states, whether of extrahepatic or intrahepatic origin, are often associated with pathologic changes in the kidney known as cholemic or bile nephrosis.

In this condition the kidney may be swollen, and the tubules exhibit a variable degeneration with bile casts in their lumina. Bile nephrosis may account for the albumin, casts, and cellular elements often found in the urine of icteric patients, but a good correlation between renal pathology and function is not obtained, nor is bile nephrosis held to account for the renal failure of the hepatorenal syndrome. Since bile nephosis usually occurs with regurgitation jaundice, the tubular changes have been attributed to a toxic effect of some biliary constituent, particularly the bile salts.

BONES

The bones of patients or laboratory animals with obstructive jaundice or external biliary fistula may show demineralization. Presumably the following chain of events takes place: Absence of bile salts from the intestine impairs the absorption of vitamin D and of calcium that is bound to unabsorbed fats. Consequently the absorption and metabolism of calcium are deranged, and the blood level of calcium has to be maintained and the bodily needs satisfied at the expense of the bones.

GASTROINTESTINAL TRACT

Gastrointestinal manifestations such as anorexia, nausea, vomiting, meteorism, flatulence, cramps, diarrhea, and constipation occur frequently with hepatic disease. Many of these symptoms are caused by disorders of gastrointestinal motility which occur as nonspecific responses to many illnesses. In some cases, a deficient supply of bile salts, or an increased bacterial flora of the small bowel, may interfere with normal digestion and absorption. Finally, gastrointestinal disorders may bespeak organic changes in the digestive tract. Thus an acute viral or toxic process of the liver may be associated with structural changes in the stomach or bowel, or the gut may be congested or edematous because of portal hypertension or hypoalbuminemia.

CENTRAL NERVOUS SYSTEM

Morphologic changes of the central nervous system may occur in liver disease. In some instances cerebral and hepatic damage are independent effects of the same agent. Dietary deficiencies (e.g., beriberi) or metabolic disorders (e.g., Wilson's disease) may injure both brain and liver, and viruses may be both neurotropic and hepatotropic. In other cases cerebral changes may be regarded as definite sequelae of hepatic damage. The edema and bleeding tendencies of severe liver disease may compromise the cerebral circulation, and toxins or abnormal concentrations of metabolites may injure cerebral tissue directly (see Hepatic Coma). Perhaps as a result of such irritants, a hyperplasia of protoplasmic astrocytes develops in the cortex, lenticular nuclei, thalamus, substantia nigra, and pontine nuclei of patients with chronic portal cirrhosis. From the functional viewpoint, animals with chronic liver damage have impaired cerebral metabolism as judged by in vitro tests. These abnormalities may explain in part why patients with severe liver disease are exquisitely sensitive not only to opiates and sedatives, but also to electrolyte imbalance, moderate oxygen lack, and ammonia.

CARDIOVASCULAR SYSTEM

Bradycardia has a variable incidence in jaundice. When it does occur, it may be the result of vagal stimulation, perhaps by some regurgitated biliary constituent such as the bile salts. It is also possible that the damaged liver fails to inactivate vasoactive peptides, such as bradykinin, in a normal fashion. Hemodynamic phenomena seen in many patients with chronic cirrhosis are increased cardiac output at rest, decreased peripheral vascular resistance, decreased arterial oxygen saturation, and small arteriovenous oxygen differences. Because of these findings it is possible that "high output" cardiac failure may occasionally be the result of chronic liver disease, but the cardiac reserve of cirrhotic patients in response to moderate exercise does not appear abnormally low. Perhaps the wide-open peripheral vascular bed is related to the clinical phenomena of "liver palms" and spider telangiectases. In cirrhotic patients with marked arterial oxygen unsaturation, evidence for the existence of right-to-left shunts has been found. These shunts have been identified as minute arteriovenous anastomoses in the lungs ("pulmonary spider nevi") but more frequently as communications leading from portal to bronchial and pulmonary veins via periesophageal and mediastinal connections. Such venoarterial shunts have been held responsible for the clubbed fingers and cyanosis sometimes evident in patients with chronic hepatic cirrhosis.

Manifestations Produced by Multiple Factors

For purposes of analysis, the functions of the liver have been regarded as individual units which are altered under the influence of hepatic disease to produce a chain of biochemical and structural aberrations. In a patient with liver disease, symptoms and signs are produced by an intricate combination of many disordered functions which may contribute in varying proportion to the observed abnormalities. The intense fatigue characteristic of infectious hepatitis, or the lassitude and weakness of cirrhosis, for example, represent the end result of many metabolic disorders. Similarly, the wasted, spindly arms and legs of the patient with chronic hepatic disease cannot be ascribed to one functional defect; rather the liver's inability to handle all types of food normally must be held responsible. Multiple factors must also be sought to explain ascites, edema, coma, and the clinical phenomena of liver failure.

EDEMA AND ASCITES

The patient with liver disease retains sodium and water. Patients with active hepatitis cannot excrete a water load promptly; with improvement a copious diuresis may presage a turn for the better. In more serious cases of liver disease, sodium and water retention are manifested characteristically by ascites, and sometimes by pleural effusion and/or peripheral edema. In addition to systemic fluid retention, major causes of ascites are portal hypertension and hypoalbuminemia.

The pressure gradient causing fluid to filter from splanchnic and intrahepatic capillary beds is increased in liver disease by two factors: (1) hydrostatic pressure, tending to force fluid out, is increased because of portal hypertension; and (2) colloid osmotic pressure, tending to pull fluid into the capillaries, is decreased. Colloid osmotic pressure depends principally upon the albumin content of the plasma. Consequently, when plasma albumin decreases because of impaired hepatic synthesis, colloid osmotic pressure drops in a roughly parallel fashion. An average normal plasma colloid osmotic pressure of 37 cm. of water, for example, may drop to 20 cm. if plasma albumin concentration falls from 4.5 to 2.0 gm./100 ml. A contributing factor occasionally present is an abnormal capillary permeability that allows increased leakage of protein into the tissues, thus flattening the gradient between intra- and extravascular concentrations of the colloids chiefly responsible for osmotic pressure.

Portal hypertension alone does not cause peritoneal effusion. Patients with extrahepatic portal venous block, or dogs with ligated portal veins, do not usually accumulate ascites. Even if the radicles of the *portal* venous system within the liver are compromised but hepatic circulation is otherwise little affected (as in the pipe-stem cirrhosis of schistosomiasis), ascitic fluid is rare. Once the vascular block is postsinusoidal, however, as in the common varieties of cirrhosis, in veno-occlusive disease affecting the *hepatic* venous radicles, in the Budd-Chiari syndrome with occlusion of the major hepatic veins, or in the dog with the inferior vena cava ligated just above the orifices of the hepatic veins, then ascitic fluid tends to accumulate rapidly. Under such conditions, albumin synthesis by liver parenchyma is presumably altered either because of deranged blood supply or because of concurrent disease.

Although portal hypertension and hypoalbuminemia are two key factors in the pathogenesis of ascites, there is a third: the patient who is accumulating ascites puts out negligible amounts of sodium in his urine—sometimes no more than 1 to 3 mEq./24 hrs. This antinatriuretic phenomenon is regarded by some as secondary; i.e., fluid pouring into the peritoneal cavity decreases blood volume with the following possible consequences:

1. Decreased renal blood flow → decreased glomerular filtration rate → decreased urine flow through renal tubules → nearly complete reabsorption of water and solute → oliguria.

2. Decreased renal blood flow → increased renin release by juxtaglomerular apparatus → increased formation of angiotensin in blood → adrenal stimulation by angiotensin to release aldosterone → increased tubular sodium (and hence water) reabsorption.

3. Decreased renal blood flow → increased release of sodium-retaining factors other than aldosterone.

4. Stimulation of vascular "volume receptors" → release of antidiuretic hormone (ADH) by the posterior pituitary → increased renal water retention.

5. Decreased hepatic inactivation of aldosterone and/or other humoral factors leading to salt and water retention by kidney.

Several observations support the reality of these postulated secondary mechanisms. In particular, plasma aldosterone levels and urinary output of aldosterone are elevated in the fluid-retaining cirrhotic. Plasma angiotensinase levels are also high. On the other hand, the renin-angiotensin-aldosterone hypothesis is in some respects controversial, and no direct evidence has been found in cirrhotic patients of an excessive circulating level or increased activity of ADH. Perhaps most disconcerting is the fact that measurement of blood volume in the fluid-accumulating cirrhotic yields normal or even increased rather than decreased values. This has forced the adoption of the rather ill-defined concept of a reduced "effective" blood volume in cirrhosis —i.e., an inadequate regional volume and flow of blood in spite of an apparently normal total amount in the body.

The alternate view is that the release of salt and water retaining agents by the damaged liver is primary; i.e., that liver cells under the influence of vascular congestion, of anoxia, or of some other harmful situation, release substances which directly or indirectly cause excessive renal retention of sodium and water. Thus, some experimental evidence exists that the anoxic liver puts out a ferritin-like material said to have an antidiuretic effect; cross-circulation experiments in dogs suggest that the congested liver elaborates an agent that causes the adrenal to release aldosterone. At present, the primary event which initiates the accumulation of ascitic fluid remains unidentified; once the process has been set in motion, loss of transudate into the peritoneal cavity and systemic fluid retention obviously may aggravate each other cyclically.

Since ascites is the result of several interacting forces, there is no absolute level of portal hypertension, of plasma colloid osmotic pressure, of hypoalbuminemia, or of aldosteronemia that causes ascitic fluid to appear. An effort has been made to take into consideration the combined influence of portal pressure and serum albumin levels by means of the following formula:

$$\frac{10 \times \text{serum albumin (gm./100 ml.)} + 4}{\text{Intrasplenic pressure (cm. H}_2\text{O)}} = \text{"Ascites quotient"}$$

When the "ascites quotient" is less than one, ascites tends to form, but even this approach is an oversimplification. It should also be noted that many patients severely ill with cirrhosis are hyponatremic and retain more water than can be accounted for merely on the basis of sodium retention. Apparently the kidney under such conditions retains free water (i.e., water without sodium) because of the reduced glomerular filtration rate and because of the marked reabsorption of an isotonic solution of sodium in the proximal tubule, thus delivering such a small volume of urine to the distal tubule that adequate amounts of free water cannot be produced there.

Part of the transudate that characterizes the ascites of liver disease leaks into the peritoneal cavity from the splanchnic capillary bed. In addition the postsinusoidal block so often present and the consequent intrahepatic congestion cause variable amounts of fluid to weep from the liver itself. Absorption of fluid from the peritoneal cavity is primarily via lymphatics in the area of the diaphragm. In some patients, lymphatic vessels on the peritoneal side of the diaphragm communicate freely with those on the pleural side (a situation particularly true of the right hemidiaphragm), with the result that peritoneal fluid passes readily via lymphatic passages into the pleural spaces, particularly on the right side, in about 20 per cent of patients with ascites. In addition, lymph flow from the congested liver is markedly enhanced and increases the pressure in the thoracic duct. If the thoracic duct is opened and drained, lymph pours out of this channel, which apparently acts as a vent for decompressing the ascitic accumulation as long as drainage remains copious.

Depending on the amount of fluid in the peritoneal cavity, and on the resistance of the abdominal musculature, intraperitoneal pressure is increased and is transmitted to the inferior vena cava. By this mechanism, hydrostatic pressure in the veins of the lower extremities is increased and promotes edema formation in these areas, particularly in those patients with hypoalbuminemia.

HEPATIC COMA

Irrational behavior, drowsiness, flapping "tremors," delirium, convulsions, stupor, deep coma, and electroencephalographic abnormalities may appear during the course of severe liver disease. The responsible mechanisms are two: (1) an abnormal concentration of metabolites or other substances in the central nervous system, and (2), just as important but usually ignored, increased sensitivity of cerebral tissue to abnormalities of its milieu (see Effect of Hepatic Disease on Other Organs: Central Nervous System).

Hepatic coma (also called hepatic, portosystemic, or shunt encephalopathy) may be attended by many biochemical derangements, such as elevated pyruvate and lactate and depressed sodium and potassium levels in the blood, but the most significant abnormalities appear to be an increased concentration of blood ammonia, an elevated arterial pH with reduced carbon dioxide tension, and a diminished cerebral oxygen uptake. Blood ammonia levels, which normally are less than 1 mcg. ammonia N/ml. whole blood, are elevated to levels of 2 to 4 mcg./ml., the degree of cerebral deterioration and the ammonia level evidencing a general but not perfect correlation. The alkalosis is of the respiratory type secondary to hyperventilation, but the mechanism providing the respiratory stimulus is unknown. The resultant increased arterial pH, however, may increase intracellular ammonia levels because un-ionized blood ammonia (NH_3), which diffuses more readily across the cellular membrane than ionized NH_4^+, tends to move on the side of the membrane where the pH is lower.

Although the complexities of Figure 27–2 are admittedly frightening, a tracing of the sequence of biochemical events indicates (1) the extrahepatic sources of blood ammonia that are important in the production of hepatic coma; (2) the role the liver would play in inactivating this ammonia were it not damaged or bypassed; and (3) the rationale of such therapies for hepatic coma as low protein diet, antibiotics to depress intestinal bacterial activity, glutamic acid, and arginine. All these methods aim either to reduce the amount of ammonia that can enter the portal circulation or to fortify the metabolic mechanisms that can dispose of it. It may be noted, however, that glutamic acid therapy is in this respect a "dead-end" treatment: ammonia is bound as glutamine, but eventually most of the ammonia so stored must be given up and eliminated by other mechanisms (Fig. 27–2, upper right-hand box).

How does increased ammonia, alone or in combination with other metabolic aberrations, injure cerebral metabolism? The answer is speculative. Perhaps excess ammonia combines with so much α-ketoglutaric acid (Fig.

27–2) that the dynamics of the citric acid cycle are altered. Perhaps the combination of α-ketoglutaric acid with ammonia consumes so much ATP that little is left over for synthesizing the crucial neurotransmitter substance acetylcholine.

None of the nitrogenous substances so far implicated in the pathogenesis of hepatic coma can be held responsible for the pungent, sweet-sour odor of fetor hepaticus. The odor, also detectable in the urine, has been tentatively identified as that of methyl mercaptan (CH_3SH), the possibility being that methionine, instead of serving as a methyl donor, is abnormally handled by the damaged liver to yield CH_3S-groups. The nose refuses to accept the identity, however, of fetor hepaticus and the mercaptan odor of the urine of the asparagus eater.

LIVER FAILURE

Liver failure may be described as a progressive deterioration of all the functions of the liver, with the consequent effects on metabolism and other organs that have been described in this section. The outstanding biochemical and clinical phenomena of liver failure are not always the same. In the fulminating necrosis of epidemic hepatitis, for example, edema, hemorrhagic phenomena, and cerebral symptoms dominate the clinical picture. In Weil's disease or carbon tetrachloride intoxication, jaundice and renal failure are striking. The "liver death" which may follow thyroid or biliary surgery is characterized by hyperpyrexia; and the usual picture in terminal cirrhosis is starvation, salt and water retention, oliguria, and coma. In most cases, however, extreme hepatic injury appears to initiate a vicious cycle in which anoxia, hemorrhage, circulatory insufficiency, metabolic aberrations, and specific organ damage interact to create the complex pattern of liver failure.

REFERENCES

Adams, R. D., and Foley, J. M.: The neurological disorder associated with liver disease. A. Res. Nerv. & Ment. Dis. Proc., 32:198, 1953.

Ahrens, E. H., Jr., Payne, M. A., Kunkel, H. G., Eisenmenger, W. J., and Blondheim, S. H.: Primary biliary cirrhosis. Medicine, 29:299, 1950.

Ames, R. P., Borkowski, A. J., Sicinski, A. M., and Laragh, J. H.: Prolonged infusions of angiotensin II and norepinephrine and blood pressure, electrolyte balance, and aldosterone and cortisol secretion in normal man and in cirrhosis with ascites. J. Clin. Invest., 44:1171, 1965.

Arias, I. M., Gartner, L. M., Seifter, S., and Furman, M.: Prolonged neonatal unconjugated hyperbilirubinemia associated with breast feeding and a steroid, pregnane-3 (Alpha), 20 (Beta)-diol, in maternal milk that inhibits glucuronide formation in vitro. J. Clin. Invest., 43:2037, 1964.

Atkinson, M., and Losowsky, M. S.: Mechanism of ascites formation in chronic liver disease. Quart. J. Med., 30:153, 1961.

Bean, W. B.: The cutaneous arterial spider: A survey. Medicine, 24:243, 1945.

Billing, B. H., and Lathe, G. H.: Bilirubin metabolism in jaundice. Am. J. Med., 24:111, 1958.

Bradley, S. E., Ingelfinger, F. J., and Bradley, G. P.: Hepatic circulation in cirrhosis of the liver. Circulation, 5:419, 1952.

Brauer, R. W.: Mechanisms of bile secretion. J.A.M.A., 169:1462, 1959.

Brauer, R. W.: Liver circulation and function. Physiol. Rev., 43:115, 1963.

Brauer, R. W.: Hepatic blood flow and its relation to hepatic function. Am. J. Dig. Dis., 8:564, 1963.

Chalmers, T. C.: Pathogenesis and treatment of hepatic failure. New England J. Med., 263:23, 77, 1960.

Counseller, V. S., and McIndoe, A. H.: Dilatation of the bile ducts (hydrohepatosis). Surg. Gynec. & Obst., 43:729, 1926.

Crigler, J. F., Jr., and Najjar, V. A.: Congenital familial nonhemolytic jaundice with kernicterus. Pediatrics, 10:160, 1952.

Dubin, I. N.: Chronic idiopathic jaundice, a review of fifty cases. Am. J. Med., 24:268, 1958.

Dumont, A. E., and Mulholland, J. H.: Alterations in thoracic duct lymph flow in hepatic cirrhosis. Ann. Surg., 156:668, 1962.

Elias, H.: A re-examination of the structure of the mammalian liver. I. Parenchymal architecture. Am. J. Anat., 84:311, 1949.

Elias, H.: A re-examination of the structure of the mammalian liver. II. The hepatic lobule and its relation to the vascular and biliary systems. Am. J. Anat., 85:379, 1949.

Fletcher, A. P., Biederman, O., Moore, D., Alkjaersig, N., and Sherry, S.: Abnormal plasminogen-plasmin system activity (fibrinolysis) in patients with hepatic cirrhosis: Its causes and consequences. J. Clin. Invest., 43:681, 1964.

Foulk, W. T., Butt, H. R., Owen, C. A., Jr., Whitcomb, F. F., Jr., and Mason, H. L.: Constitutional hepatic dysfunction (Gilbert's disease): Its natural history and related syndromes. Medicine, 38:25, 1959.

Fritts, H. W., Jr.: Systemic circulatory adjustments in hepatic disease. M. Clin. North America, 47:563, 1963.

Gall, E. A.: Posthepatitic cirrhosis, fact and fancy. In Ingelfinger, F. J., Relman, A. S., and Finland, M. (eds.): Controversy in Internal Medicine. Philadelphia, W. B. Saunders Co., 1966.

Gilbert, A., and Lereboullet, P.: La cholémie simple familiale. Semaine méd., 21:241, 1901.

Hanger, F. M.: The meaning of liver function tests. Am. J. Med., 16:565, 1954.

Hanger, F. M., Jr., and Gutman, A. B.: Postarsphenamine jaundice apparently due to obstruction of intrahepatic biliary tract. J.A.M.A., 115:263, 1940.

Hartroft, W. S.: Diagnostic significance of fatty cysts in cirrhosis. Arch. Path., 55:63, 1953.

Himsworth, H. P.: Lectures on the Liver and Its Diseases. Cambridge, Harvard University Press, 1947.

Isselbacher, K. J., and Greenberger, N. J.: Metabolic effects of alcohol on the liver. New England J. Med., 270:351, 402, 1964.

Josephson, B.: The circulation of the bile acids in connection with their production, conjugation, and excretion. Physiol. Rev., 21:463, 1941.

Klatskin, G.: Effect of alcohol on the liver. J.A.M.A., 170:1671, 1959.

Lathe, G. H.: Disorders of bilirubin metabolism. Clin. Chem., 11:309, 1965.

Lester, R., and Schmid, R.: Intestinal absorption of bile pigments. III. The enterohepatic circulation of urobilinogen in the rat. J. Clin. Invest., 44:722, 1965.

Levine, R. A., and Klatskin, G.: Unconjugated hyperbilirubinemia in the absence of overt hemolysis. Am. J. Med., 36:541, 1964.

Lieber, C. S., Jones, D. P., and DeCarli, L. M.: Effects of prolonged ethanol intake: Production of fatty liver despite adequate diets. J. Clin. Invest., 44:1009, 1965.

Lucké, B.: I. The pathology of fatal epidemic hepatitis. II. The structure of the liver after recovery from epidemic hepatitis. Am. J. Path., 20:471, 1944.

Lucké, B., and Mallory, T.: The fulminant form of epidemic hepatitis. Am. J. Path., 22:867, 1946.

Metge, W. R., Owen, C. A., Jr., Foulk, W. T. and Hoffman, H. N.: Bilirubin glucuronyl transferase activity in liver disease. J. Lab. Clin. Med., 64:89, 1964.

Miller, L. L., and Bale, W. F.: Synthesis of all plasma protein fractions except gamma globulins by the liver. J. Exper. Med., 99:125, 1954.

Moschcowitz, E.: The morphology and pathogenesis of cardiac fibrosis of the liver. Ann. Int. Med., 36:933, 1952.

Novikoff, A. B., and Essner, E.: The liver cell. Some new approaches to its study. Am. J. Med., 29:102, 1960.

Papper, S.: The role of the kidney in Laennec's cirrhosis of the liver. Medicine, 37:299, 1958.

Paronetto, F., Schaffner, F., and Popper, H.: Immunocytochemical and serologic observations in primary biliary cirrhosis. New England J. Med., 271:1123, 1964.

Popper, H.: What are the major types of hepatic cirrhosis? In Ingelfinger, F. J., Relman, A. S., and Finland, M. (eds.): Controversy in Internal Medicine. Philadelphia, W. B. Saunders Co., 1966.

Popper, H., and Schaffner, F.: Liver: Structure and Function. New York, McGraw-Hill Book Co., Inc., 1957.

Popper, H., and Schaffner, F.: Pathology of jaundice resulting from intrahepatic cholestasis. J.A.M.A., 169:1447, 1959.

Popper, H., and Schaffner, F.: Progress in Liver Disease. New York, Grune and Stratton, 1961.

Popper, H., and Schaffner, F.: Fine structural changes of the liver. Ann. Int. Med., 59:674, 1963.

Ratnoff, O. D.: Hemostatic mechanisms in liver disease. M. Clin. North America, 47:721, 1963.

Ratnoff, O. D., and Patek, A. J., Jr.: The natural history of Laennec's cirrhosis of the liver. An analysis of 386 cases. Medicine, 21:207, 1942.

Rich, A. R.: Pathogenesis of forms of jaundice. Bull. Johns Hopkins Hosp., 47:338, 1930.

Rotor, A. B., Manahan, L., and Florentin, A.: Familial non-hemolytic jaundice with direct van den Bergh reaction. Acta med. philippina, 5:37, 1948.

Rouiller, C. (ed.): The Liver. Morphology, Biochemistry, Physiology. Two volumes. New York, Academic Press, 1963.

Schiff, L.: Diseases of the Liver, 2nd ed. Philadelphia, J. B. Lippincott Company, 1963.

Schiff, L., and Billing, B. H.: Congenital defects in bilirubin metabolism as seen in the adult. Gastroenterology, 37:595, 1959.

Schmid, R.: Jaundice and bilirubin metabolism. Bull. New York Acad. Med., 35:755, 1959.

Sebesta, D. G., Bradshaw, F. J., and Prockop, D.: Source of the elevated serum alkaline phosphatase activity in biliary obstruction: Studies utilizing isolated liver perfusion. Gastroenterology, 47:166, 1964.

Segal, S., Blair, A., and Roth, H.: The metabolism of galactose by patients with congenital galactosemia. Am. J. Med., 38:62, 1965.

Sherlock, S.: Pathogenesis and management of hepatic coma. Am. J. Med., 24:805, 1958.

Sherlock, S.: Diseases of the Liver and Biliary System, 3rd ed. Springfield, Charles C Thomas, 1963.

Sherlock, S.: Jaundice due to drugs. Proc. Roy. Soc. Med., 57:881, 1964.

van Creveld, S., and Huijing, F.: Glycogen storage disease. Am. J. Med., 38:554, 1965.

van den Bergh, A. A. H., and Grotepass, W.: An improved method for the determination of bilirubin in blood. Brit. M. J., 1:1157, 1934.

van den Bergh, A. A. H., and Muller, P.: Ueber eine direkte und eine indirekte Diazo Reaktion auf Bilirubin. Biochem. Zeitschr., 77:90, 1916.

Victor, M., Adams, R., and Cole, M.: The acquired (non-Wilsonian) type of chronic hepatocerebral degeneration. Medicine, 44:345, 1965.

Vorhaus, L. J., and Kark, R. M.: Serum cholinesterase in health and disease. Am. J. Med., 14:707, 1953.

Wachstein, M.: Enzymatic histochemistry of the liver. Gastroenterology, 37:525, 1959.

Walker, J. G., Doniach, D., Roitt, I. M., and Sherlock, S.: Serological tests in diagnosis of primary biliary cirrhosis. Lancet, 1:827, 1965.

Watson, C. J., and Hoffbauer, W. F.: The problem of prolonged hepatitis, with particular reference to the cholangiolitic type and to the development of cholangiolitic cirrhosis of the liver. Ann. Int. Med., 25:195, 1946.

Wheeler, H. O., Meltzer, J. I., and Bradley, S. E.: Biliary transport and hepatic storage of sulfobromophthalein sodium in the unanesthetized dog, in normal man, and in patients with hepatic disease. J. Clin. Invest., 39:1131, 1960.

Yamamoto, T., Skanderbeg, J., Zipursky, A., and Israels, L. G.: The early appearing bilirubin: Evidence for two components. J. Clin. Invest., 44:31, 1965.

Chapter Twenty-Eight

The Gallbladder and Pancreas

FRANZ GOLDSTEIN

The gallbladder and pancreas will be considered in the same chapter because of their anatomic proximity, their related functions in fat digestion, and their not infrequent interrelations in disease. For the sake of clarity each organ will be discussed separately.

The Gallbladder

The gallbladder is a pear-shaped distensible hollow organ with an average capacity of about 50 cc. The thin wall of the normal gallbladder consists of mucosa and muscularis but has no submucosa, and the mucosa contains no glands. The delicately woven mucosal folds and villi normally project into the muscular layer as crypts and sinuses. In diseased gallbladders these mucosal invaginations may become larger and more deeply penetrating, imitating on histologic cross sections actual gland formation. These pseudoglandular sacculations are known as Rokitansky-Aschoff sinuses and signify either chronic inflammation or degenerative gallbladder disease.

The cystic duct connects the gallbladder with the juncture of the common hepatic and common bile ducts. It is tortuous and its mucous membrane is thrown into folds forming the spiral valves of Heister. A true sphincter is probably not present, and the direction of bile flow to and from the gallbladder is determined primarily by pressure differences between the gallbladder and bile ducts. The

tortuosity of the cystic duct presents an obstacle to the passage of solid objects such as stones.

The gallbladder is not essential to life, and some mammalian species (e.g., mouse, horse) have no gallbladder. Extirpation of the gallbladder in man does not interfere with good health and usually causes mild and temporary, if any, physiologic disturbances.

The older literature emphasized the intimate lymphatic connections between the gallbladder and the liver which were believed to be the cause of frequent hepatitis in the presence of chronic cholecystitis. More recent investigations provide little support for such a pathologic relationship.

The *functions* of the gallbladder are (1) storage, concentration, and complexing of bile, (2) discharge of stored bile into the duodenum during periods of digestion, and (3) stabilization of bile pressure within the biliary system. Normally the liver secretes about 800 to 1000 ml. of bile per day. Instead of entering the duodenum directly, part of the bile is diverted through the cystic duct into the gallbladder whenever the lower end of the common bile duct is closed by contraction of the sphincter of Oddi and whenever the pressure in the common duct exceeds the pressure in the gallbladder. The sphincter is closed most of the time and thus prevents entry of intestinal contents into the biliary tract. Relaxation of the sphincter occurs nor-

696

mally in response to the ingestion of fat-containing food and is synchronized with gallbladder contractions. The secretory pressure of bile normally varies between 15 and 25 cm. of water. The sphincter of Oddi offers resistance to bile flow at pressures of the same order of magnitude. When the gallbladder is filled and a pressure of 25 cm. is reached in the common duct, the sphincter resistance is overcome and bile trickles into the duodenum. Bile secretion ceases if, due to obstruction, the pressure within the biliary duct system rises above 35 cm. of water. After prolonged bile duct obstruction all bile pigment proximal to the obstruction is absorbed, and the bile ducts become filled with white fluid and mucus ("white bile") produced by the lining cells of the ducts.

The gallbladder concentrates bile four to ten times through the absorption of water. The main solids of bile—bile acids, bile pigments, cholesterol, and lecithin—are concentrated to a comparable extent, whereas the ordinary electrolytes are partially absorbed with water to maintain osmotic equilibrium with plasma. Even though bile is isotonic with plasma, the total cation concentration of bile may greatly exceed that of plasma and may reach 300 mM./L. This phenomenon is explained by the presence of large molecular aggregates, known as *micelles*. Bile micelles, consisting chiefly of bile salts, cholesterol, and lecithin, contain on their surface many negative charges which bind cations, especially sodium and calcium. The bound cations exert no osmotic pressure. It has been debated whether the gallbladder is able to secrete cholesterol. Evidence in favor of cholesterol secretion derives mostly from the presence of cholesterol underneath the mucosa of the gallbladder, at times in large quantities (cholesterolosis of the gallbladder or "strawberry gallbladder"). However, this does not constitute proof of secretion and may reflect absorption and deposition of cholesterol in the submucosa. There is evidence of absorption, through the normal gallbladder mucosa, of the organic constituents of bile.

The volume and concentration of liver bile is affected by certain agents. Substances which increase the volume flow of bile are called *hydrocholeretics,* whereas those which increase the concentration of bile solids are called *choleretics.* Naturally occurring bile salts are the most potent agents with both hydrocholeretic and choleretic activities. Unconjugated, oxidized bile acid derivatives are potent hydrocholeretics; they produce copious flow of dilute bile.

Substances which stimulate the evacuation of the gallbladder are called *cholagogues.* They include fats, magnesium sulfate, and the hormone *cholecystokinin.* The latter is released from the duodenal and upper jejunal mucosa in response to fat ingestion and appears to be the most important physiologic agent producing gallbladder contraction. In response to cholecystokinin, the sphincter of Oddi relaxes simultaneously with the evacuation of the gallbladder. Caroli and his associates have recently claimed the existence of an anticholecystokinin and have expressed the hypothesis that the relative amounts of the two hormones control the tone and contraction of the gallbladder, bile ducts, and sphincter of Oddi. Autonomic nervous stimuli and autonomic drugs also affect gallbladder motor activity. While some investigators believe that gallbladder evacuation is a purely passive process brought about by reduction in both sphincter tone and intraductal pressure, there is good evidence for the presence of active gallbladder contractions. This is illustrated clinically by the occasional dissociation between the action of the gallbladder and that of the sphincter of Oddi in which forceful gallbladder contraction occurs in the absence of sphincter relaxation (biliary dyskinesia).

Bile acids have strong surface tension-lowering effects and upon entry into the duodenum exert important actions on fat digestion. Bile acids aid the solubilization of fats, and appear to activate pancreatic lipase. Both actions are necessary for adequate digestion and subsequent absorption of fats.

Among the numerous substances excreted in bile and concentrated in the gallbladder are certain organic iodinated radiopaque compounds called dyes. The recognition of this fact led Graham and Cole to the development of oral cholecystography. At a suitable interval after the ingestion of a dye such as iodopanoic acid, roentgen films of the gallbladder area are taken which permit visualization of the gallbladder shadow, demonstrate radiolucent stones as filling defects, and document evacuation of the gallbladder after the administration of a cholagogue (a fat meal or intravenous cholecystokinin). Nonvisualization of the gallbladder indicates a nonfunctioning and, usually, diseased gallbladder provided the following conditions can be excluded: (1) failure of the patient to have ingested the dye, (2) vomiting of dye,

(3) pyloroduodenal obstruction, (4) poor excretory liver function as evidenced by jaundice or marked Bromsulphalein retention, (5) unsuspected cholecystectomy, (6) intrahepatic gallbladder obscured by the liver shadow, and (7) congenital absence of gallbladder. Diarrhea may follow the intake of gallbladder dyes but does not usually interfere with their absorption. In rare instances the gallbladder does not concentrate dye because it is filled with thick mucus after prolonged periods of inactivity resulting from a fat-free diet. Following the ingestion of fatty foods for several days, a normal cholecystogram may be obtained. Apparent lack of filling may also be produced by irritability of the gallbladder in some cases of cholecystosis.

Stones in the common duct and gallbladder of mildly jaundiced patients can occasionally be demonstrated by the 4-day oral administration of dye (calculography). When the oral administration of dyes is not feasible, or when higher concentrations of dye are required for optimal outlining of the biliary tree, especially after cholecystectomy, intravenous cholangiography is often used. However, none of the above procedures are applicable in the presence of more than minimal jaundice. Cholangiography is carried out in selected cases during or after the performance of biliary tract surgery, the dye being injected through a catheter or a T-tube inserted into the common bile duct (operative and T-tube cholangiography). Transhepatic percutaneous cholangiography has more recently become accepted as a method of visualizing the biliary tree in frankly jaundiced patients.

An older test which retains limited usefulness is biliary drainage (Lyon test). The recovery of calcium bilirubinate and cholesterol crystals from bile obtained by duodenal intubation may clinch the diagnosis of cholelithiasis in an occasional nonjaundiced or mildly jaundiced patient with a poorly or nonfunctioning gallbladder. Duodenal drainage also permits the recovery of parasites (e.g., *Giardia lamblia*) and pathogenic bacteria (e.g., *E. typhosa*) residing in the duodenum or gallbladder.

These tests have done much to place the diagnosis of gallbladder disease on a sound objective basis but have not totally eliminated the misconceptions about gallbladder disease created around the turn of the century.

Cholelithiasis (the presence of gallstones) constitutes the pivotal problem in gallbladder disease. Gallstones not only may give rise to symptoms, but may lead to cholecystitis and its various complications and, rarely, to the development of carcinoma of the gallbladder. Despite much interest and work concerning the pathogenesis of gallstones, the exact mechanism of their formation remains in doubt. Several types of gallstones may be distinguished. Gallstones may consist of cholesterol, bile pigment, or both, with some admixture of calcium salts and organic matter; rarely do stones consist only of calcium carbonate; most commonly stones are mixed and made up of cholesterol, pigment, and calcium salts. Pure cholesterol and pure pigment stones are not radiopaque; mixed stones and pigment stones become increasingly radiopaque as their calcium content rises. Stones may be single or multiple; in some instances thousands of small stones have been recovered from a diseased gallbladder.

The formation of *cholesterol stones* is influenced by a variety of local and metabolic factors. Pregnancy predisposes to stone formation, possibly due to metabolic alterations favoring the development of hypercholesterolemia, and local factors, especially bile stasis and alkalinization in the sluggishly emptying gallbladder. Pigment stones most commonly occur in patients with increased pigment formation secondary to increased hemoglobin breakdown (hemolytic anemias).

Infection rarely appears to be the initiating factor in gallstone formation. However, infection and inflammation of the gallbladder are frequently superimposed on cholelithiasis. By favoring bile salt absorption, raising the pH, and providing desquamated epithelial nuclei, infection and inflammation lead to further gallstone formation, stone growth, and the development of mixed stones.

The vast majority of gallstones contain cholesterol and probably start out as cholesterol stones with later additions of other components. The solubility of cholesterol in water is low, the maximal quantity of cholesterol soluble in water at 20° C. being 260 mg. per 100 ml. Yet cholesterol concentrations in bile, an aqueous medium, range up to 1.5 gm. per 100 ml. The problem of cholesterol solubility in bile has undergone intensive investigations in recent years because an understanding of the factors controlling cholesterol solubility should lead to a better understanding of gallstone formation.

The role of bile salts in the stabilization of cholesterol in aqueous bile has long been known, but until relatively recently it was believed that bile salts and cholesterol formed coordination compounds, known as choleic acids. Isaakson in 1951 discovered that human bile contains large amounts of lecithin which was subsequently shown to enhance the dissolving power of bile salts for cholesterol. It is now established, by the work of Verschure, Hofmann, Juniper, and others, that bile salts, lecithin, and cholesterol are present in bile in the form of micellar, macromolecular complexes, and it is this physicochemical phenomenon which explains the presence of high concentrations of cholesterol in clear solution in bile.

Micelles are aggregates of molecules in solution. They are formed by substances which have surface-active properties and have both polar and nonpolar regions in their molecules (detergents). In aqueous solution, under favorable conditions, these molecules may arrange themselves in a sphere or other geometric form with their polar or water-soluble portions facing the outside and the nonpolar fat-soluble portions oriented toward the center. This orientation gives the micelle the ability to dissolve lipid in its center. The micelles present in bile are mixed micelles because they contain lecithin, in addition to the detergent bile salt and cholesterol. Lecithin itself has surface-active properties but is too insoluble to form micelles alone. In the mixed bile micelles, lecithin appears to be interposed between the bile salt and cholesterol molecules. As a result, the bile micelles are larger in size and have a greater solubilizing capacity for cholesterol. The mixed bile micelles are relatively stable within fairly wide ranges of temperature and individual component concentrations. However, when the ratio of bile salt to cholesterol drops below approximately 12:1, cholesterol precipitation will occur. Theoretically, either increases in cholesterol concentration or decreases in bile salt or lecithin concentration could lead to a breakdown of micellar aggregates and to precipitation of cholesterol. The available evidence points to reductions in bile salt concentration as the critical factor in this system.

Impaired bile salt secretion can occur in liver disease, or there may be selective absorption of bile salts from bile by a damaged gallbladder mucosa. The exact nature of the events which directly lead to cholesterol precipitation and gallstone formation has yet to be clarified, but it is known that in bile obtained from patients with cholelithiasis the macromolecular complex is reduced or absent. The importance of bile salts in preventing cholesterol from precipitation is also emphasized by experiments in which rabbits fed a fully saturated cholesterol analogue produce allo-bile acids which are deposited as calcium salts in the gallbladder. These abnormal bile acids do not form micelles and the animals invariably develop cholesterol gallstones.

The incidence of gallstones varies depending upon age, sex, race, economic status, living habits, state of nutrition, and other factors. A high incidence has been noted among certain ethnic groups such as Italians, Jews, and Chinese. The incidence is considerably lower in Negroes, although it appears to be rising, perhaps due to a higher standard of living and better nutrition. The highest incidence is found in parous, obese women past age 40, but gallstones are certainly not limited to obese people. About 20 per cent of all patients coming to autopsy have gallstones, considerably more in the oldest age groups. In a recent clinical survey of healthy, mostly asymptomatic, male executives of a mean age of under 50, 7.5 per cent had cholecystographic evidence of gallstones and an additional 7.0 per cent had other evidence of gallbladder disease (Wilbur and Bolt).

Small stones may migrate from the gallbladder through the ductal system into the duodenum. Examples of complete disappearance of stones, due to passage or dissolution, have been documented but are rare. The lodgment of stones in, or passage through, the cystic and common duct usually is accompanied by a pain syndrome known as "biliary colic." This pain is not actually colicky, if colic is to denote a crampy intermittent pain. The pain produced by stone passage, resulting in spasm of the ducts and forceful contraction of the gallbladder with or without dilatation, is an example of visceral pain. Like most abdominal visceral pain, it is referred to the midline, usually the midepigastrium, and depending upon its intensity may radiate diffusely along both costal margins and through to the back. The pain usually builds up in crescendo fashion, then remains constant for hours and may subside either spontaneously when the stone drops back into the gallbladder or passes into the duodenum, or following the injection of antispasmodics or opiates. The pain is frequently accompanied by nausea and vomiting.

If the stone remains impacted in the cystic duct, obstruction and distention of the gallbladder (hydrops) may lead to impairment of its blood supply and to the development of acute cholecystitis. Attacks of biliary colic tend to occur at unpredictable intervals (episodic pain), in contrast to the rhythmic and periodic recurrence of peptic ulcer pain. Most attacks follow heavy meals, usually by several hours, probably related to events in the digestion of fats and forceful gallbladder contractions. Single large stones are less commonly set in motion by gallbladder contractions, and hence less commonly give rise to colic. Larger stones, by exerting constant pressure, may erode the wall of the gallbladder and produce fistulous communications with surrounding structures such as the common bile duct, duodenum, or colon. Despite the presence of stones in it, the gallbladder may continue to function, as evidenced by the results of cholecystographic examination and biliary drainage. There are no demonstrable effects upon fat digestion and absorption unless the common duct becomes blocked by stones. When this happens, other clinical manifestations usually appear, especially jaundice and intermittent fever and chills (Charcot's fever).

It is difficult to understand the alleged causation of chronic "dyspeptic symptoms," "flatulent indigestion," gaseousness, and fatty food intolerance by the mere presence of stones in the gallbladder. Recent objective analyses of symptoms by Price in England and by Koch and Donaldson in this country have shown that indigestion and dyspeptic symptoms occur with equal frequency in patients with and without gallstones. Interestingly, around the turn of the century leading medical authorities considered most gallstones to be asymptomatic and held biliary colic to be the only symptom reliably attributable to gallstones. Moynihan, a highly influential British surgeon, was the chief champion of a causative relationship between gallstones and indigestion. His belief was based on the finding of gallstones and the absence of gastric lesions on autopsies of patients with histories of indigestion, and the untenable conclusion that the stones had to cause the indigestion since the stomachs were normal.

When digestive symptoms are encountered in patients with gallstones, they are likely caused either by organic disease of other gastrointestinal structures or are functional in origin, associated with the irritable bowel syndrome, aerophagia, or the prolonged abstinence from fatty foods. The latter may in itself lead to intolerance of fats, manifested by delayed gastric emptying and nausea following the unaccustomed ingestion of fat. Even a *nonfunctioning diseased gallbladder*, with or without stones, offers no adequate ex-

plantation for indigestion and flatulence. Digestive symptoms are not usually encountered following the removal of the gallbladder for painful calculous cholecystitis in patients without digestive symptoms preoperatively. The removal of a *nonfunctioning* gallbladder does not produce any change in the transport and character of bile and could hardly be expected to affect digestive functions. Cholecystectomy cannot, therefore, be expected to ameliorate dyspeptic symptoms and should not be recommended for that purpose.

The most common cause of *cholecystitis* has already been mentioned. In about 90 per cent of cases a calculus blocking the cystic duct or the gallbladder neck can be demonstrated. Other causes of cystic duct obstruction account for a small percentage of cases of cholecystitis. Obstruction to the outflow of bile from the gallbladder is believed to be the key factor leading to inflammation of the gallbladder. The initial inflammation is chemical in nature, and bacterial cultures during the early stage of inflammation have usually been sterile. After prolonged distention of the organ resulting in stasis of gallbladder contents and impairment of the blood supply, bacterial invasion is likely to occur. While *E. coli* is the most common bacterial organism involved, almost all known pathogens may be encountered with the exception of pneumococci, which are bile soluble and hence unable to survive in the gallbladder.

In about half of all patients with acute cholecystitis the initial symptom is midepigastric pain of visceral origin, the above-described biliary colic. Unless specific inquiry is made, the early pain may not be mentioned by the patient who may be too preoccupied with the later right upper quadrant pain caused by local inflammation of the gallbladder and parietal peritoneal irritation. The pain of cholecystitis is frequently referred to the right scapula or the interscapular area. Examination of the patient will usually reveal local and systemic signs of inflammation such as localized tenderness, muscle guarding over the gallbladder area, and mild fever and leukocytosis. When the gallbladder is distended it can often be palpated. Slight hyperbilirubinemia (rarely exceeding 2.0 mg. per 100 ml.) may be encountered in the absence of choledocholithiasis and is explained by edema of the cystic duct and its encroachment on the lumen of the common duct. The acute inflammation may either subside or progress to empyema, gangrene, and rupture of the gallbladder with resulting peritonitis or abscess formation. In other instances a low-grade chronic cholecystitis may ensue. The diagnosis of the latter should not be accepted without cholecystographic proof of impaired gallbladder function; in many instances stones can be demonstrated, as well, in a shrunken contracted gallbladder.

Patients with chronic cholecystitis may be totally asymptomatic; others experience repeated attacks of symptoms as described for acute cholecystitis; others may complain of mild right upper quadrant pain and tenderness especially after fatty meals, and they may tend to avoid the ingestion of fatty foods.

Jaundice due to common duct stones is associated in about 80 per cent of cases with chronic cholecystitis and hence with a contracted and rigid gallbladder. In contrast, jaundice due to carcinomatous obstruction of the common bile duct is usually accompanied by a dilated gallbladder (Courvoisier's law), unless previous unrelated cholecystitis prevents distention of the diseased organ.

Occasionally obstruction of the cystic duct and low grade chronic cholecystitis lead to the absorption of all bile pigment. The material filling the gallbladder in such patients, mostly mucus and calcium salts secreted by the mucosa of the gallbladder, is white and pasty and contains much calcium carbonate; hence the term "milk of calcium" bile. The high calcium content is responsible for the radiopacity of the affected gallbladder on scout films of the abdomen.

Jutras and his associates have in recent years described under "hyperplastic cholecystoses" a condition or group of conditions of alleged degenerative gallbladder disease. Included are previously recognized forms of gallbladder disease such as cholesterolosis, adenomyomatosis, and Rokitansky-Aschoff sinuses. Jutras postulates that in the degenerative cholecystoses hyperplasia of mucosal, muscular, and neural elements takes place and leads to a "hyperfunctional state" which in turn may produce severe and lasting pain, intermittent colics, and indigestion. The diagnosis is based mostly on radiologic criteria. Further work will be required to show whether the described condition constitutes a pathologic entity or a conglomeration of unrelated conditions, some possibly of inflammatory or congenital origin. The clinical significance of the hyperplastic cholecystoses is also not clearly defined at this time, but it is likely that a "hyperfunctional state" of the gallbladder exists and is characterized clinically by postprandial gallbladder pain and

radiologically by poor gallbladder visualization.

Carcinoma of the gallbladder is a relatively rare malignancy, found in about 0.35 per cent of autopsies in this country, and not necessarily related to the cause of death. Most but not all cases follow calculous cholecystitis with chronic inflammation and irritation believed to be predisposing factors. Since this cancer is rare and encountered mostly in older age groups (peak incidence in the seventh decade) and since cholelithiasis is rather common, cholecystectomy in all calculous individuals for the prevention of carcinoma is not generally recommended. The number of lives lost from the resulting operative mortality would exceed the number of lives saved by the prevention of carcinoma occurrence, and the disparity would even be greater if the loss of years of life rather than crude mortality figures are compared.

Functional disorders of the biliary tract include *biliary dyskinesia* and the *postcholecystectomy syndrome*. The basic disturbance in biliary dyskinesia is a loss of synchronization of gallbladder contraction and sphincter relaxation. The net result is the inability of the gallbladder effectively to empty itself because of sphincter spasm with or without sphincter stenosis. The term dyskinesia is often used loosely and incorrectly in connection with flatulence and indigestion before or following cholecystectomy. The rarity of the condition has made some clinicians dubious of its actual existence. The diagnosis should be made only if rigid criteria can be met, especially the demonstration of impaired gallbladder evacuation despite common duct filling after adequate stimulation (Fig. 28–1), accompanied by pain which is relieved by nitroglycerin.

More frequent than functional dyskinesia is "mechanical dyskinesia," a condition of mechanical noncalculous partial obstruction of the cystic duct which leads to normal or exaggerated gallbladder filling but impaired emptying associated with typical biliary pain. Cystic duct strictures and external fibrous bands and adhesions are among the more common causes. This condition has been known for over 40 years under various designations but was most recently termed the *cystic duct syndrome*. Its diagnosis is also best confirmed radiologically by the demonstration of impaired gallbladder evacuation with minimal or no common duct filling after the injection of cholecystokinin (Fig. 28–2). The reproduction of a patient's spontaneously

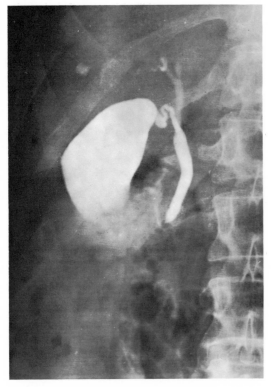

Figure 28–1. Biliary dyskinesia—dilatation of common duct and minimal egress of dye into the duodenum, after injection of dye into the gallbladder during laparotomy. Cystic duct is patent. Dilated common duct and failure of the gallbladder to contract after cholecystokinin injection were demonstrated preoperatively.

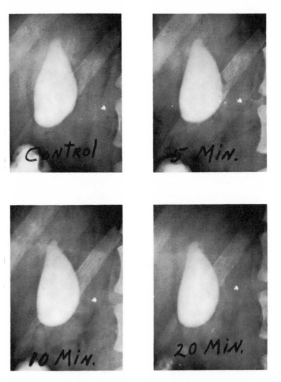

Figure 28–2. Cystic duct syndrome—lack of gallbladder contraction and failure of visualization of common duct after stimulation with cholecystokinin. Normally gallbladder volume decreases by 50 per cent or more within 20 minutes of cholecystokinin injection.

experienced gallbladder pain by the injection of cholecystokinin is a requirement for diagnosis. The pain in biliary dyskinesia and in the cystic duct syndrome is produced by forceful contractions of the gallbladder against resistance, occurs characteristically within 30 minutes after a fat-containing meal, and is experienced either directly over the gallbladder area or in the epigastrium.

The use of the term *"postcholecystectomy syndrome"* has been deplored because it erroneously implies a uniform cause or pathogenesis. The term has come to denote any gastrointestinal symptoms present after cholecystectomy and, by implication, related to it or the pre-existing gallbladder disease. When such a broad definition is used, organic causes such as a remaining common duct stone, stricture, or pancreatitis are found in a small minority of patients. The most common cause of this "syndrome" is erroneous preoperative diagnosis, i.e., the patient's preoperative symptoms were unrelated to the gallbladder and remained unaffected by its removal.

The Pancreas

The pancreas is a digestive gland which embryologically originates as a pair of outpouchings from the primitive gut. It is located retroperitoneally and stretches transversely from the bend of the duodenum to the region of the hilum of the spleen. The pancreas consists of two functionally separate units, an exocrine portion consisting of the pancreatic acini and ducts, and an endocrine portion consisting of the islets of Langerhans. The hormones elaborated by the latter, *insulin* and *glucagon,* and their functional significance are discussed elsewhere. The exocrine portion of the pancreas secretes a watery fluid rich in bicarbonate and containing a number of digestive enzymes including *amylase, lipase, trypsinogen, chymotrypsinogen A and B, procarboxypeptidases A and B, ribonucleases,* and *elastase.* The polypeptide nature and amino acid sequence of several of the proteolytic enzymes have recently been elucidated. The existence of another enzyme, *collagenase,* has been both claimed and doubted. *Amylase* probably exists in several forms referred to as isoamylases. According to Dreiling and associates, the amylase predominantly found in serum of normal individuals moves electrophoretically with albumin, whereas in patients with acute pancreatitis amylase activity was greatest in the gamma globulin fraction. There is suggestive evidence that the isoamylase attached to albumin is of hepatic origin, whereas the globulin-bound isoamylase more likely originates from the pancreas.

The prime *function* of the external pancreatic secretion is to help split or digest complex foods—proteins, fats, and carbohydrates—into their components, an action necessary before adequate absorption of food can occur. The high bicarbonate content, and hence highly alkaline pH of the secretion, helps to neutralize the acid gastric juice upon its entry into the duodenum. Extirpation of the pancreas leads to the expected disturbances in food digestion due to absence of digestive enzymes, and to disturbances in carbohydrate metabolism due to loss of insulin and glucagon. In addition, still unexplained disturbances in lipid metabolism occur which include fatty infiltration of the liver and decreased concentrations of blood lipids, possibly caused by deficiency of lipocaic or lipase. Recent investigations have suggested that pancreatic secretions influence the absorption of both iron and vitamin B_{12}, but the exact nature of the effects is not known.

There is evidence for a functional subdivision within the exocrine portion of the pancreas. Bicarbonate solution appears to be elaborated by the cells lining the pancreatic ducts, whereas the enzymes are produced by the acinar cells. The latter cells are stimulated by vagal and local reflex mechanisms, and by a hormone, *pancreozymin,* manufactured chiefly by the duodenal and upper jejunal mucosa and released in response to chyme reaching these areas. The ductal secretion appears to be produced chiefly in response to *secretin,* another hormone of upper small intestinal origin and released in response to both hydrochloric acid and chyme entering the duodenum. Secretin was discovered in 1902 by Bayliss and Starling and was the first substance called a hormone. It is presently available commercially in highly purified form, free of pancreozymin effects and containing 15,000 to 25,000 cat units per milligram. Further purification has been obtained by Jorpes and Mutt. Pancreozymin, also purified to a high degree, has so far remained inseparable from cholecystokinin. The importance of secretin and pancreozymin in the physiologic regulation of pancreatic secretion has been re-emphasized by Wang and Grossman and by Harper, but a full understanding of the interrelations between nervous and humoral control of pancreatic secretion is still lacking.

Both secretin and pancreozymin have been used to *test pancreatic function* since the first attempts performed by Chiray in 1926 with a crude secretin preparation. Such tests are important because they are able to detect mild degrees of functional impairment in the absence of pancreatic insufficiency. Like most organs, the pancreas has an ample functional reserve, and signs of overt pancreatic insufficiency do not appear until the major portion of the pancreas is destroyed or prevented, by ductal obstruction, from discharging its secretions into the intestine. In the performance of the so-called secretin test a double-lumened tube is placed so that the distal lumen opens in the duodenum and the proximal lumen in the stomach to permit continuous removal of gastric juice. Following the intravenous injection of secretin, with or without added pancreozymin, the volume and bicarbonate concentration of the aspirated duodenal juice are measured over at least a 1-hour or an 80-minute period. Normally, the 1-hour volume after secretin measures 1.3 cc. per kilogram of body weight or more.

Depressions in volume output suggest obstruction of the pancreatic ducts. Patients with ductal obstruction may also show rises in serum enzyme activities after secretin-pancreozymin injections. Signs of obstruction are encountered far more frequently in patients with pancreatic carcinoma than with pancreatitis. Marked elevations in volume of pancreatic secretion occur in liver disease, presumably due to failure of secretin inactivation by diseased liver cells. The bicarbonate concentration normally is at least 80 mEq./L. in any one 10-minute specimen. Low bicarbonate concentration is indicative of impaired secretory activity of the gland. The enzyme concentrations in duodenal juice have been more frequently measured since pancreozymin became available for investigative purposes. The sensitivity of any of the pancreatic enzyme determinations in detecting mild pancreatic functional impairment is probably no greater than the sensitivity of bicarbonate determinations. However, the finding of slightly depressed values for both bicarbonate and one or more enzymes reduces the likelihood of random scatter to account for low values and more strongly supports a diagnosis of pancreatic functional impairment. In recent years cytologic examination of duodenal juice for malignant cells has been developed into a practical test with an accuracy of better than 50 per cent.

In the total diagnostic evaluation of the pancreas it is helpful to obtain a roentgen examination of the stomach and duodenum with particular reference to pressure effects of an enlarged pancreas on these organs. Calcifications of the pancreas are indicative of advanced chronic pancreatitis, usually of the alcoholic variety. The pancreatic ductal system can be outlined by the injection of radiopaque dye through a catheter inserted into the main pancreatic duct during laparotomy (pancreatography). Progress has also been made with attempts to visualize the pancreas and detect diseased nonfunctioning areas by means of radioactive photoscanning, using radioactive selenomethionine. Examination of the stools for fat globules and meat fibers is easy to perform and permits detection of gross malabsorption. Intestinal absorption can be studied quantitatively by means of fat and nitrogen balance techniques, I^{131} labeled triolein excretion measurements, and other methods. In conjunction with other evidence of pancreatic disease, the documentation of malabsorption helps to establish the diagnosis of pancreatic insufficiency. Despite the various and many diagnostic advances made in recent years, structural and functional abnormalities of the pancreas remain difficult to detect in early stages.

Disease processes affecting the exocrine portion of the pancreas may do so by means of two mechanisms working separately or together—obstruction to the outflow of pancreatic juice into the duodenum and to smaller pancreatic ductal radicles, or replacement of glandular by inflammatory or neoplastic tissue.

Inflammation of the pancreas, *pancreatitis,* is the most common disorder affecting the exocrine portion of the pancreas. Since the original description by Opie in 1901 of an autopsied case of pancreatitis in which a gallstone was found impacted in the common channel formed by the distal common bile and pancreatic ducts, the *common channel theory* of acute pancreatitis has been widely debated. As pointed out by Rich and Duff, impacted gallstones in the ampulla of Vater are clearly responsible for only about 6 per cent of cases of pancreatitis and certainly cannot account for pancreatitis in patients

without biliary tract disease, without a common channel (absent in about 35 per cent of the population), or in cases of pancreatitis limited to the area drained by the duct of Santorini or to the distal pancreas.

Although it is widely accepted that obstruction to the outflow of pancreatic juice is an important factor in the pathogenesis of pancreatitis, obstructive causes other than gallstones have been invoked. Among them have been spasm and edema of the ampulla of Vater secondary to duodenitis, metaplasia of pancreatic ductal epithelium, and edema of the gland secondary to infectious (mumps), toxic and nutritional (methanol poisoning, alcoholism) causes. Obstruction of pancreatic ducts by parasites, especially Ascaris, has been observed. An actively secreting gland is the other prerequisite for the development of acute pancreatitis. The increased intraductal pressure caused by a gland actively secreting against increased resistance probably leads to disruption of pancreatic ducts and to the escape of activated enzymes into the gland parenchyma where the characteristic inflammatory changes are then produced.

In the original common channel theory it was believed that regurgitation of bile was necessary to activate the enzyme precursors. However, experimental observations have shown that bile can be perfused through the pancreas at normal pressures without harm. It has also been pointed out from measurements at the operating table and from short-term animal experiments that normally the intraductal pressure is higher in the pancreas than in the common bile duct and that in the presence of a blocked common channel the direction of flow would be from pancreas to bile duct. More recent work by Elliott, Williams, and Zollinger has shown that in experiments extended past 24 hours, bile duct pressure often equaled or exceeded pancreatic ductal pressures and that bile indeed could enter the pancreatic ducts. Furthermore, incubation of stagnant bile with pancreatic juice was shown to produce chemical changes, including the activation of trypsin. Severe pancreatitis resulted from perfusion of the pancreas with the incubated mixture at low pressures. Although these experiments demonstrate that bile, after incubation with pancreatic juice, may cause activation of pancreatic enzymes, they do not prove the necessity for bile reflux in pancreatitis. It should be pointed out again that pancreatitis may be limited to the area drained by the duct of Santorini where bile reflux plays no part.

Others have postulated that toxic factors such as an abnormal hemin pigment, produced by the incubation of blood with pancreatic juice, may be significant in the pathogenesis of pancreatitis. Still others state that the mere mechanical rupture of pancreatic ductules is sufficient to initiate pancreatitis in the absence of extraneous factors and activators, assuming that small amounts of trypsin are activated on contact with tissue juices and that these traces of trypsin then serve to activate further enzyme from its precursor. It is likely that the pancreatitis produced by traumatic injuries or by direct surgical trauma to the pancreas is produced by leaking of pancreatic enzymes from ruptured ducts.

Pancreatitis can also be produced by a variety of causes in which ductal obstruction is unlikely involved. Pancreatitis has been produced in animals by the administration of ACTH and adrenocortical steroids and may have clinical counterparts in spontaneous "stress" situations, including surgical operations not involving the pancreas or surrounding structures, and following the administration of steroids. Pancreatitis has been attributed to toxic effects of chlorthiazide. Pancreatitis is seen in association with certain metabolic disorders such as hyperlipemia, hemochromatosis, malnutrition, pregnancy, hyperparathyroidism, and liver disease. Thal has produced pancreatitis experimentally by means of sensitization of pancreatic blood vessels to bacterial products, inducing a local Shwartzman reaction. Other vascular injuries both to the venous and arterial sides of the circulation may induce or aggravate pancreatitis. It has been shown by Popper and Necheles that the state of the circulation is important in determining the extent and severity of acute pancreatitis, a compromised vascular supply and ischemia adding to the primary insult and facilitating the occurrence of pancreatic necrosis.

Clinically, the vast majority of patients with acute pancreatitis have either associated biliary calculous disease or are alcoholics, but low-grade chronic pancreatitis or pancreatic fibrosis not uncommonly occurs in association with the various metabolic disturbances listed. Despite the great frequency of so-called alcoholic pancreatitis, the precise mechanism by which alcohol induces pancreatitis remains uncertain. While the production of nutritional deficiencies and a direct toxic effect of alcohol on the pancreas cannot be excluded, the presently most plausible mechanism is a combination of pancreatic stimulation, mediated through acid and secretin, and partial obstruction of the ampulla of Vater by edema and inflammation caused directly by alcohol.

When activated pancreatic juice enters the gland parenchyma, a process of autodigestion ensues, mediated primarily by trypsin. The recently described enzymes elastase and collagenase are said to dissolve the elastic tissue and collagen of blood vessels not affected by trypsin and thus lead to hemorrhage into the damaged gland ("hemorrhagic pancreatitis"). Escaped lipase on contact with tissue fat causes its hydrolysis into glycerol and fatty acids. The latter combine with calcium to precipitate as soaps and form areas of so-called fat necrosis seen grossly as white plaques on the surface of the pancreas, the omentum, and a times at distant sites. In severe cases substantial quantities of blood plasma and fluid may leak into the abdominal cavity from the surface of the necrotic pancreas.

The clinical manifestations of acute pancreatitis depend on the above pathologic changes. Severe abdominal pain probably is due to edema and swelling of the inflamed gland, ductal spasm and obstruction, and peritoneal irritation. Peritoneal irritation appears responsible in part also for the symptoms of nausea, vomiting, abdominal distention (sentinel loops of small bowel seen on scout films of the abdomen), and for the local abdominal tenderness. Shock is most likely produced by the decreased blood and plasma volumes, resulting from leakage of plasma into the abdominal cavity; intravenous plasma infusions have been effective in combating the shock of pancreatitis. Toxins released by bacteria which secondarily invade the necrotic pancreas probably contribute to the production of shock.

In the past, shock was thought to be caused by trypsin absorbed into the blood stream, but shock does not follow the therapeutic administration of trypsin solutions in thromboembolic disease. The determination of serum trypsin levels, which might help clarify the clinical significance of trypsin, remains to be satisfactorily worked out.

The most consistent and diagnostically helpful laboratory alterations in acute pancreatitis are increases in serum amylase and lipase activities and reductions in blood calcium levels in severe cases. The hypocalcemia is caused chiefly by the binding of calcium in the process of fat necrosis. The serum enzyme elevations are due to absorption of these enzymes from the venules of the injured pancreas and from lymphatic channels draining the peritoneal cavity. Fairly good correlation between the degree of ductular disruption or pancreatic injury and the height of serum amylase elevations has been reported. Elevations of serum enzyme activities beyond 10 to 14 days are suggestive of complicating abscess or cyst formation. Serum amylase elevations are not pathognomonic of pancreatitis and occur also in mumps, with or without pancreatic involvement, in renal insufficiency (because of impaired renal excretion of amylase), in intestinal obstruction, perforated peptic ulcer, ruptured ectopic pregnancy, abdominal and extra-abdominal trauma, and following the administration of opiates which induce sphincter spasm. However, in most instances of hyperamylasemia from causes other than acute pancreatitis, the degree of elevation is moderate and rarely exceeds five times the normal value of serum amylase. Serum lipase is less commonly elevated in conditions not associated with pancreatic necrosis. Disturbances in digestive functions and in glucose metabolism are usually insignificant and transient in acute pancreatitis.

The treatment of acute pancreatitis is based on physiological principles. All oral food intake is withheld and gastric contents are continuously aspirated through a tube to prevent gastric juice from entering the duodenum and stimulating the secretin mechanism. Anticholinergic drugs in large doses have been used in attempts to reduce both gastric and pancreatic secretion and to relieve spasm of the sphincter of Oddi, although it is realized that these drugs are only partially effective. Analgesic opiate drugs are given in smallest possible dosage because they have a tendency to increase sphincter spasm in larger doses. Papaverine and nitrites have been used for their sphincter-relaxing effects. Broad spectrum antibiotic coverage is recommended to counteract secondary bacterial infection not infrequently superimposed upon pancreatic necrosis. Surgical intervention is reserved for cases complicated by abscess or pseudocyst formation when drainage becomes necessary. The administration of adrenocortical steroids and ACTH has been proposed as a possibly lifesaving measure in severely ill patients with shock. The use of these agents should be approached with caution because of their demonstrated capacity to produce pancreatitis in animals and because of the reported high incidence of acute pancreatic lesions at autopsy

in patients who received these agents for other illnesses. Recent clinical trials with an enzyme inhibitor, Trasylol, have given promising, though somewhat conflicting and inconclusive results in the treatment of acute pancreatitis.

Chronic pancreatitis and pancreatic fibrosis may follow bouts of acute pancreatitis. Extensive destruction of pancreatic parenchyma and variable degrees of ductal obstruction may cause a reduction in the amount of enzyme secretion to the point of producing pancreatic insufficiency. The absence from the small intestine of sufficient quantities of amylase, lipase, and trypsin leads to incomplete hydrolysis of starches, fats, and proteins. Without this preliminary digestion these materials are incompletely absorbed. Hence, varying amounts of undigested food material appear in the stools which may become bulky, oily, and malodorous and contain an excess of microscopically visible fat globules and meat fibers. Starch digestion is least impaired due to the extremely high potency of pancreatic amylase active in dilutions up to 1:100,000,000 and because amylase is produced also by the salivary glands. As the result of the incomplete assimilation of food, patients may eat excessive amounts of food yet lose weight and become malnourished. There is also impaired absorption of fat-soluble vitamins which may lead to clinical vitamin deficiencies. The prolonged excretion of fats combined with calcium in the form of soaps may lead to hypocalcemia and clinical tetany. Some patients with chronic relapsing pancreatitis continue to have bouts of pain, at times of great severity, throughout their illness. Pancreatitis without pain has occasionally been observed. Jaundice may result from compression of the common bile duct by fibrous contracture of the pancreas. In late stages of pancreatitis the destructive process frequently involves the islets of Langerhans and may cause the appearance of clinical diabetes mellitus. Therapeutic measures are directed mainly at replacement of deficient pancreatic enzymes and bicarbonate and at attempts to relieve pain, when present.

A hereditary form of pancreatitis transmitted through nonsex-linked mendelian dominance, has been described in several families. This form of pancreatitis clinically resembles nonhereditary chronic relapsing pancreatitis but occurs at an earlier age with onset often in adolescence, and is associated neither with cholelithiasis nor alcoholism. An important distinguishing feature encountered in about half the affected subjects is the presence of aminoaciduria, predominantly of lysine and cystine.

Cystic fibrosis of the pancreas is another hereditary disease characterized by dysfunction of exocrine glands including the pancreas, liver, bronchi, and mucous glands throughout the body, as well as salivary and sweat glands. The underlying defect appears to be a physicochemical abnormality of mucus and other exocrine secretions. The abnormally viscid mucus obstructs ducts and passages and thereby leads to the typical pathologic features in the individual organs affected. The pancreas is commonly, but not always, diseased in cystic fibrosis. The pathologic findings in the pancreas have been compared to those seen following experimental ligation of the pancreatic duct in animals and consist chiefly of atrophy, fibrosis, replacement by fat, cystlike dilatations, and at times prominent inflammatory changes. The clinical manifestations are those of pancreatic insufficiency, as described for chronic pancreatitis. However, diabetes mellitus occurs infrequently and pain is also quite rare.

Since pancreatic insufficiency and malnutrition in cystic fibrosis usually have their onset in childhood, physical growth may be stunted. Symptoms of pulmonary insufficiency and liver disease may overshadow the pancreatic aspects, and 90 per cent of all deaths from cystic fibrosis are due to pulmonary insufficiency and infection. The diagnosis of cystic fibrosis can be made even in mild subclinical cases from characteristic elevations in the concentration of sodium and chloride in sweat which are independent of adrenal function or the state of hydration.

Carcinoma of the pancreas has shown an increasing incidence in this country during the past several decades. Early diagnosis has been difficult and the results of treatment have been disappointing. The chief manifestations are abdominal pain, jaundice, weight loss, and disturbances in carbohydrate metabolism.

The pain in carcinoma of the pancreas is often severe, persistent, and very disturbing to the patient. The location of the pain may be right or left-sided, usually but not invariably with involvement of the back. The pain is often worst at night and typically is ameliorated by the sitting position, especially leaning forward. Invasion of perineural lymphatics has been invoked to explain the pain of pancreatic neoplasm and perhaps also the relief of pain by postural measures through release of pressure on the involved nerves, but the exact significance of nerve invasion remains to be established. The wide variation in pain distribution is best explained by the location and extent of the neoplasm, whether it involves the head, body, or tail of the pancreas, and what contiguous structures are invaded.

Jaundice may be an early sign of pancreatic malignancy if the primary lesion is in the head of the pancreas and encroaches upon the distal common duct. The jaundice caused by pancreatic carcinoma is often associated with a palpably distended gallbladder (see Courvoisier's law in the section on the gallbladder) and more often than not is accompanied by pain.

Weight loss may be due to lack of desire of the patient to eat, to sitophobia resulting from pain after eating, to diabetes, to malabsorption of food when pancreatic insufficiency is produced by tumor, or possibly to utilization of nutrients by rapidly growing tumor tissue.

Disturbances in carbohydrate metabolism are surprisingly common, occurring in about half of all cases, and may consist of a decreased glucose tolerance, the appearance of clinical diabetes mellitus, or the sudden increase in severity of existing diabetes mellitus. The exact mechanism by which carcinoma of the pancreas affects carbohydrate metabolism is not fully understood, since microscopically detectable destruction of islet tissue is usually not sufficient to explain the metabolic disturbances. Immunologic phenomena may be involved. Peculiar neurotic disturbances have been described, at times appearing as the earliest manifestations of carcinoma of the pancreas or following the onset of initially unexplained pains and perhaps related to the unbearable discomfort.

Thromboembolic phenomena have been reported to accompany carcinoma of the pancreas, at times before the onset of other symptoms. Most reports have represented isolated cases, or were derived from autopsy material which permits no conclusion as to causative factors other than mechanical ones. Various coagulation disturbances, related either to the release of clot-producing enzymes or destruction of clot-preventing substances, have been claimed, but none have been fully substantiated. A satisfactory explanation has not been offered to explain the mechanism by which an early pancreatic neoplasm can cause thromboembolism before invasion or compression of larger blood vessels has occurred.

Of great interest has been the association of noninsulin-producing islet cell tumors of the pancreas with intractable peptic ulceration, first described in 1955 and since known as the *Zollinger-Ellison syndrome* after the names of the discoverers. These tumors have subsequently been shown to produce enormous quantities of gastrin, or a gastrin-like substance, which is responsible for the excessive stimulation of gastric acid and the resulting ulcerations. Approximately 20 per cent of affected patients also manifest severe watery diarrhea which may lead to dangerous losses of potassium and other electrolytes. Another group of patients with the Zollinger-Ellison syndrome manifests steatorrhea, caused apparently by inhibition of enzymatic food digestion in the small bowel lumen rendered acid by the overwhelming outpouring of acid gastric juice. Several patients with islet tumors have been described as having watery diarrhea but no hyperacidity or ulcers, giving rise to the hypothesis that another hormone, separate from gastrin, may be produced by these tumors and specifically causes diarrhea. The finding of gastrin in pancreatic tumor tissue naturally led to a search for gastrin in normal pancreatic tissue and to the question of any role this might play in the pathogenesis of peptic ulcers generally. To date gastrin has not been recovered from normal pancreatic tissue, but gastrin-like activity has been demonstrated in extracts of atrophic or severely fibrotic glands.

Over half the tumors reported in association with the Zollinger-Ellison syndrome have shown metastases or local invasiveness. About 20 per cent of the primary tumors have occurred in aberrant locations, especially the wall of the duodenum, and in about 10 per cent of cases diffuse adenomatosis of the pancreas has been encountered. Because of these anatomic peculiarities it has rarely been possible to resect all involved tissue and check the ulcer diathesis. In most instances the only available and lifesaving treatment has been total gastrectomy, even small gastric remnants left behind having led to renewed ulcerations and ulcer complications.

Approximately 20 per cent of reported Zollinger-Ellison tumors have occurred in association with other endocrine adenomas, possibly as part of a familial and hereditary syndrome. However, only the pancreatic tumors have been found to contain gastrin and to cause peptic ulceration.

REFERENCES

Gallbladder

Berk, J. E.: Postcholecystectomy syndrome: A critical evaluation. Gastroenterology, *34:*1060, 1958.

Bockus, H. L.: Gastroenterology. Volume III. Philadelphia, W. B. Saunders Co., 1965.

Caroli, J., Plessier, J., and Plessier, B.: Endogenous cholecystokinin and its inhibitor: Method of assessment in humans; its role in normal and pathologic physiology. Am. J. Dig. Dis., n.s., *6:*646, 1961.

Cozzolino, H. J., Goldstein, F., Greening, R. R., and Wirts, C. W.: The cystic duct syndrome. J.A.M.A., *185:*920, 1963.

Goldstein, F., Ginsberg, D. K., and Johnson, R. G.: Biliary dyskinesia—report of two cases with physiologic studies. Am. J. Gastroenterol., *36:*268, 1961.

Hofmann, A. F.: Clinical implications of physicochemical studies on bile salts. Gastroenterology, *48:*484, 1965.

Isaakson, B.: On the lipid constituents of bile from human gallbladder containing cholesterol gallstones. Acta Soc. Med. Upsal., *59:*277, 1954.

Isaakson, B.: On the dissolving power of lecithin and bile salts for cholesterol in human bile. Acta Soc. Med. Upsal., *59:*296, 1954.

Ivy, A. C., and Sandblom, P.: Biliary dyskinesia. Ann. Int. Med., 8:115, 1934.

Jorpes, J. E., and Mutt, V.: Secretin, pancreozymin and cholecystokinin. Gastroenterology, *36:*377, 1959.

Juniper, K., Jr.: Chemical and ultracentrifugal studies on the macromolecular complex in normal bile of the human gallbladder. Am. J. Surg., *107:*371, 1964.

Juniper, K., Jr.: Physico-chemical characteristics of bile and their relation to gallstone formation. Am. J. Med., *39:*98, 1965.

Jutras, J. A.: Hyperplastic cholecystoses. Am. J. Roentgenol., *83:*795, 1960.

Koch, J. P., and Donaldson, R. M., Jr.: A survey of food intolerances in hospitalized patients. New England J. Med., *271:*657, 1964.

Kornblum, K., and Hall, W. C.: The roentgenologic significance of "milk of calcium" bile. Am. J. Roentgenol., *33:*611, 1935.

Lichtman, S. S.: Diseases of the Liver, Gallbladder and Bile Ducts. Philadelphia, Lea & Febiger, 1953.

Machella, T. E.: Diagnosis of diseases of the gallbladder. Gastroenterology, *34:*1050, 1958.

Mann, F. C., and Giordano, A. S.: The bile factor in pancreatitis. Arch. Surg., *6:*1, 1923.

McMaster, P. D., and Elman, R.: On the expulsion of bile by the gallbladder and a reciprocal relationship with the sphincter of Oddi. J. Exper. Med., *44:*173, 1926.

Moeller, H. C., and Texter, E. C., Jr.: Problems in the management of biliary tract disease. Am. J. Dig. Dis., n.s., *2:*521, 1957.

Moynihan, B.: Gall stones. Brit. Med. J., *1:*8, 1913.

Price, W. H.: Gallbladder dyspepsia. Brit. Med. J., *2:*138, 1963.

Rains, A. J. H.: Gallstones. Springfield, Charles C Thomas, 1964.

Roberts, B.: Primary carcinoma of the gallbladder. Surg. Gynec. & Obst., *98:*530, 1954.

Salzman, E., Spurck, R. P., and Watkins, D. H.: X-ray diagnosis of bile duct calculi. Gastroenterology, 37:587, 1959.

Sherlock, S.: Diseases of the Liver and Biliary System, 3rd ed. Philadelphia, F. A. Davis Co., 1963.

Tumen, H. J.: What is the "postcholecystectomy syndrome"? Am. J. Dig. Dis., n.s., 2:289, 1957.

Verschure, J. C. M., and Mijnlieff, P. F.: The dominating macromolecular complex of human gallbladder bile. Clin. Chim. Acta, 1:154, 1956.

Wheeler, H. O.: Flow and ionic composition of bile. Arch. Int. Med., 108:156, 1961.

Wilbur, R. S., and Bolt, R. J.: Incidence of gallbladder disease in "normal" men. Gastroenterology, 36:251, 1959.

Pancreas

Archibald, E.: The experimental production of pancreatitis in animals as the result of the resistance of the common duct sphincter. Surg. Gynec. & Obst., 28:529, 1919.

Banga, I., and Balo, J.: Elastomucoproteinase and collagenomucoproteinase, the mucolytic enzymes of the pancreas. Nature, 178:310, 1956.

Biggs, J. C., and Davis, A. E.: Relationship of diminished pancreatic function to haemachromatosis. Lancet, 2:814, 1963.

Blau, M., and Bender, M. A.: Se^{75}-selenomethionine for visualization of pancreas by isotope scanning. Radiology, 78:974, 1962.

Blumenthal, H. T., and Probstein, J. G.: Pancreatitis. Springfield, Charles C Thomas, 1959.

Bockus, H. L., Kalser, M. H., Roth, J. L. A., Bogoch, A. L., and Stein, G.: Clinical features of acute inflammation of the pancreas. A.M.A. Arch. Int. Med., 96:308, 1955.

Burton, P., Hammond, E. M., Harper, A. A., Howat, H. T., Scott, J. E., and Varley, H.: Serum amylase and serum lipase levels in man after administration of secretin and pancreozymin. Gut, 1:125, 1960.

Carone, F. A., and Liebow, A. A.: Acute pancreatic lesions in patients treated with ACTH and adrenal corticoids. New England J. Med., 257:690, 1957.

Deller, D. J.: Iron^{59} absorption measurements by whole-body counting: Studies in alcoholic cirrhosis, hemochromatosis, and pancreatitis. Am. J. Dig. Dis., n.s., 10:249, 1965.

di Sant'Agnese, P. A.: Cystic fibrosis of the pancreas. Am. J. Med., 21:406, 1956.

Dreiling, D. A.: Technique of secretin test: Normal ranges. J. Mt. Sinai Hosp., 21:363, 1954.

Dreiling, D. A., Janowitz, H. D., and Josephberg, L. J.: Serum isoamylases: Electrophoretic study of blood amylase and patterns observed in pancreatic disease. Ann. Int. Med., 58:235, 1963.

Dreiling, D. A., Janowitz, H. D., and Perrier, C. V.: Pancreatic Inflammatory Disease. New York, Hoeber Medical Division, Harper & Row, 1964.

Elliott, D. W.: Treatment of acute pancreatitis with albumin and whole blood. A.M.A. Arch. Surg., 75:573, 1957.

Elliott, D. W., Williams, R. D., and Zollinger, R. M.: Alterations in the pancreatic resistance to bile in the pathogenesis of acute pancreatitis. Ann. Surg., 146:669, 1957.

Exocrine Pancreas: Ciba Foundation Symposium, A.V.S. de Reuck and M. P. Cameron (eds.). Boston, Little, Brown & Co., 1961.

Goldstein, F., Wirts, C. W., Cozzolino, H. J., and Menduke, H.: Secretin tests of pancreatic and biliary tract disease. Arch. Int. Med., 114:124, 1964.

Gross, J. B., Gambill, E. E., and Ulrich, J. A.: Hereditary pancreatitis. Am. J. Med., 33:358, 1962.

Gullick, H. D.: Carcinoma of the pancreas: A review and critical study of 100 cases. Medicine, 38:47, 1959.

Harper, A. A.: Physiologic factors regulating pancreatic secretion. Gastroenterology, 36:386, 1959.

Janowitz, H. D., and Dreiling, D. A.: The plasma amylase. Am. J. Med., 27:924, 1959.

Jorpes, E., and Mutt, V.: Secretin, pancreozymin and cholecystokinin: Their preparation and properties. Gastroenterology, 36:377, 1960.

Miller, E. M., Dockerty, M. B., Wollaeger, E. E., and Waugh, J. M.: Carcinoma in the region of the papilla of Vater. Surg. Gynec. & Obst., 92:172, 1951.

Moshal, M. G., Marks, I. N., Bank, S., and Ford, D. A.: Trial of trasylol in treatment of acute pancreatitis. South African Med. J., 37:1072, 1963.

Nelp, W. B.: Acute pancreatitis associated with steroid therapy. Arch. Int. Med., 108:702, 1961.

Nemir, P., Jr., and Drabkin, D. L.: The pathogenesis of acute necrotizing hemorrhagic pancreatitis: An experimental study. Surgery, 40:171, 1956.

Opie, E. L.: The relationship of cholelithiasis to disease of the pancreas and to fat necrosis. Am. J. Med. Sc., 121:27, 1901.

Popper, H. L., Necheles, H., and Russell, K. C.: Transition of pancreatic edema into pancreatic necrosis. Surg. Gynec. & Obst., 87:79, 1948.

Raskin, H. F., Wenger, J., Sklar, M., Pleticka, S., and Yarema, W.: The diagnosis of cancer of the pancreas, biliary tract, and duodenum by combined cytologic and secretory methods. Gastroenterology, 34:996, 1958.

Rich, A. R., and Duff, G. L.: Experimental and pathological studies on the pathogenesis of acute hemorrhagic pancreatitis. Bull. Johns Hopkins Hosp., 58:212, 1936.

Thal, A., and Brackney, E.: Acute hemorrhagic pancreatic necrosis produced by local Shwartzman reaction. J.A.M.A., 155:569, 1954.

Thomas, J. E.: The external secretion of the pancreas. Springfield, Charles C Thomas, 1950.

Veeger, W., Abels, J., Hellemans, N., and Nieweg, H. O.: Effect of sodium bicarbonate on absorption of vitamin B$_{12}$ and fat in pancreatic insufficiency. New England J. Med., 267:1341, 1962.

Wang, C. C., and Grossman, M. I.: Physiological determinations of release of secretin and pancreozymin from intestine of dogs with transplanted pancreas. Am. J. Physiol., 164:527, 1951.

Yaskin, J. C.: Nervous symptoms as earliest manifestations of carcinoma of the pancreas. J.A.M.A., 96:1664, 1931.

Zollinger, R. M.: Observations on the relationship of the pancreas to peptic ulcer. Bull. New York Acad. Med., 39:617, 1963.

Zollinger, R. M., and Craig, T. V.: Endocrine tumors and peptic ulcer. Am. J. Med., 29:761, 1960.

Part IX

Urinary Tract

Chapter Twenty-Nine

The Kidney

A. C. CORCORAN
and
J. M. WELLER

The primary function of the kidney is homeostatically to "defend the internal environment," i.e., it maintains the constancy of volume and composition of extracellular fluid by formation of urine of appropriately varied composition. This is a complex process that depends on vascular and tubular receptor and effector sites that recognize and respond to neural and humoral "signals." The best characterized renal endocrine function is the renal-adrenal, renin-aldosterone interplay concerned with regulation of sodium output, defense of arterial pressure, and, abnormally, "renal" hypertension. A second is renal formation of erythropoietin, which stimulates red blood cell formation. An antihypertensive endocrine function may enter into the mechanism of "renoprival" or even "renal" hypertension. These endocrine functions are incompletely characterized as compared with excretory urinary function. But they assume importance in disease, which may impair one or several aspects of renal function.

Excretory Function

Renal Blood Flow

The blood volume of the kidneys is about 20 per cent of their weight, which is only 0.5 per cent of body weight. Perfusion with blood is large and very rapid since it amounts to about 1 liter per minute or 20 per cent of the cardiac output. Comparison indicates rates of flow in the kidney of about 3.5, in the left ventricle of 0.9 and in the brain of about 1 ml. per gm. tissue per minute. Clearly renal flow exceeds metabolic need because it is directed primarily toward excretion, so that renal arteriovenous O_2 difference is small, i.e., 1.7 ml. per 100 ml. as compared with mixed venous blood at 4 to 6. The kidney, or at least the renal cortex, is in this respect an arteriovenous fistula. This comparison arises in part from the fact that renal arteriovenous O_2 difference is constant over a wide range of flow, whereas in other active tissues this function varies inversely with flow. One reason for this is that close apposition of renal arterial and venous capillaries makes for an "oxygen shunt" (Levy). Another, probably more significant, is that most of the kidneys' 20 ml. per minute of resting O_2 consumption is spent in providing energy for reabsorption of Na; ischemia involves impairment or suppression of filtration, so that, with little or no Na to be reabsorbed, resting O_2 consumption falls to about 4 ml. per minute.

Blood enters through major arteries that form the interlobar and then arcuate or arciform arteries. The subterminal interlobar arteries run off from these at right angles toward the cortex and through short branches give rise to the afferent arterioles, each of which supplies a glomerulus. These branch to form the glomerular capillary loops which segregate into five to eight lobules and then fuse to form the efferent arteriole. Cortical efferents rapidly divide into anastomosing peritubular capillary plexuses; juxtamedullary nephrons differ in that efferents form small peritubular plexuses, but also give rise to long looped vessels (arteriolae et venulae rectae spuriae, grouped as vasa recta) that dip down into the medulla. Many of the nephrons in the cortex are short; some have longer loops of Henle that reach down with these vessels into the outer medulla, and some (about one in eight in the human) have very long loops that enter the inner medulla and return in association with the vasa recta.

This unique arrangement of vessels has several important concomitants. One is that rate of renal blood flow is relatively constant over a wide range of arterial pressure (e.g., 80 to 200 mm. Hg mean). The autonomy or autoregulation of the renal circulation is at least partly myogenic, i.e., afferent vessels constrict during a rise and dilate during a fall in arterial pressure. Other vascular beds, such as those of the brain, do this to a degree.

The unusual capacity of the kidney to maintain flow despite varying pressure requires explanation. Pappenheimer and Kinter explained this from the curious rapid branching of the arteries and, assuming axial flow of red cells in interlobular arteries, postulated that pressure would skim plasma off into the proximal glomeruli and deliver an increasingly viscous blood to the outer cortex; an increase in pressure would enhance and a fall would diminish skimming of cells and thus vary resistance so as to maintain constant flow. This does not seem to be an adequate concept, although it is very stimulating, since autoregulation persists in kidneys perfused with cell-poor media. Other mechanisms, including the renin-angiotensin system, probably participate. Autoregulation is, in any event, primarily a cortical function, whereas medullary flow is relatively small (cortex ca. 4.7, outer medulla 1.3, inner medulla 0.17 ml. per gm. per minute) and passive. Some degree of skimming does occur, since medullary blood is cell poor. The vasa recta also seem relatively protein permeable, since medullary interstitial fluid is albumin rich.

The juxtaglomerular apparatus (JGA) is a differentiation of the media of afferent arterioles, just before they enter the glomerulus, into a mass of swollen, afibrillar and granular "myoepitheloid" cells that form pillows (polkissen) at the glomerular pole. They were also known as "Goormaghtigh bodies" since he was the first to postulate their endocrine function. These are apparently pressure-sensing sites of renin secretion. They also respond to changes in Na balance, by changes in granule content (renin?). Serum Na concentration physiologically varies over a narrow range and it is unlikely the polkissen can sense these small changes. Closely applied to the vascular pole is a differentiated set of distal convoluted tubule cells, the macula densa, which is in a position to sense changes in Na balance as they are reflected in composition of distal tubular fluid and, by contiguity, to transfer this "signal" to the JGA. The two areas are related and form the juxtaglomerular complex, which may be a mechanism of self-regulation of arterial pressure, extracellular fluid volume and Na output that operates through secretion of renin and changes in secretion rate of aldosterone (see below).

Glomerular Filtration

The liter of blood that perfuses the kidneys each minute carries with it about 600 ml. of plasma. More than 90 per cent of this flow perfuses glomeruli and peritubular structures and contributes to excretory functions. As indicated above, some deep glomeruli may be relatively plasma rich and some peripheral glomeruli plasma poor, with proportionate differences in rates of ultrafiltration into tubules. Inequalities among nephrons occur in other respects, and function tests show diversities in the normal nephron population. It is therefore an oversimplification to consider renal function as merely an average of the sum of identical activities of the 1.5 million glomeruli of each kidney. With this reservation, it is a useful visualization didactically. Thus, since the overall percentage of plasma water filtered off is 20 per cent, or about 120 ml. per minute, it is useful to consider this fraction as representing an average glomerular filtration rate.

The relationship between glomerular function and structure was first described by Bowman more than a century ago: "It would indeed be difficult to conceive a disposition of parts more calculated to favor the escape of water from the body, than that of the malpighian body. A large artery (the inter-lobular) breaks up in a very direct manner into a number of small branches (afferent arterioles) each of which suddenly opens into an assemblage of vessels (the glomerular capillaries) of far greater aggregate capacity than itself, and from which there is but one narrow exit (the efferent arterioles)."

It would be interesting to know what Bowman's reaction would be to the complexity of glomerular structure as shown by electron microscopy (Fig. 29–1). This technique has shown that the glomerulus normally contains only two types of cells, endothelial and epithelial, which establish three ultramicroscopic layers of capillary wall. The inner layer is formed by nuclei and spreading cytoplasm of endothelial cells. This forms a membrane which seems to be coarsely fenestrated with pores that would retain cells but not plasma. This, the *lamina fenestrata,* is closely applied to a continuous, structureless layer of muco-protein which is the ultimate filtering membrane and represents a specialized and unusually retentive capillary basement membrane. Applied to the outer face of this are epithelial cells. These are large cells arranged like interdigitating octopuses; their cytoplasmic arms carry ribbed or foot-like processes called *pedicles,* which give the cells their name of *podocytes* (foot-bearing cells). The slits between the points of contact of these feet or ribs are about 80 Å wide, so that they would retain most hemoglobin molecules. These slits supply the effective filtering surface; they communicate with each other under the podocytes' arms, or trabeculae, forming spaces that are ultimately continuous with the glomerular space. There is therefore no true intercapillary space, and what the light microscope indicates as basement membrane is a complex composed principally of lamina densa and pedicles. A cluster of mesangial cells at the root of the lobule seems not to enter into filtration.

The rate of glomerular filtration tends, as a rule, to be more constant than renal blood flow. Falls or rises in renal blood (or plasma) flow are apparently associated with reciprocal changes in transglomerular resistance. This depends on relationships between afferent and efferent arteriolar constriction. Thus, renal hyperemia consequent on a pyrogenic reaction may double renal blood flow; however, filtration rate may be unchanged or even decreased, apparently because efferent arteriolar vasodilation has reduced the plasma

fraction filtered from about 20 to about 10 per cent. Contrariwise, a decrease in renal blood flow, such as occurs in congestive heart failure, is associated with an increased filtered or "filtration" fraction consequent on increased intraglomerular pressure. This pressure is normally very high—some 65 mm. Hg—as compared to that in capillaries elsewhere in the body. Apparently glomerular capillaries are able to sustain this and also to maintain a very high relative degree of protein impermeability by reason of their supporting lamina densa and its enveloping podocytes. Net or effective filtration pressure is normally about 40 mm. Hg (hydrostatic minus plasma colloid osmotic pressure of some 25 mm. Hg). Vari-

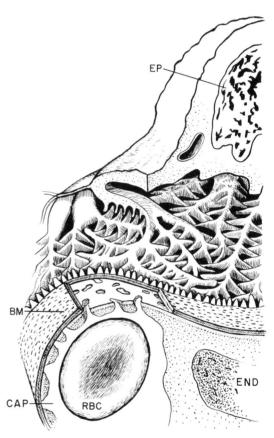

Figure 29–1.   A schematic view, based on electron microscopy, of a portion of a glomerulus. In the upper right is the nucleus of an epithelial cell (EP), or podocyte. The foot processes of this cell and its neighbor extend out, like the tentacles of an octopus, with their feet, the pedicles, resting tightly upon the basement membrane (BM). The basement membrane is shown cut away, revealing the fenestrated cytoplasmic investment of the endothelial cell (END), which is closely applied to the basement membrane and lines the lumen of the glomerular capillary (CAP) which contains a red blood cell (RBC).

GLYCOSURIA MECHANISMS

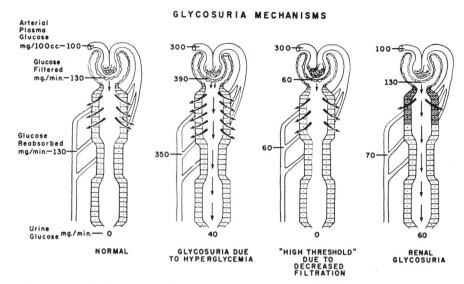

Arterial
Plasma
Glucose
mg./100cc.—100

Glucose
Filtered
mg./min.—130

Glucose
Reabsorbed
mg./min.—130

Urine
Glucose mg./min.— 0

NORMAL   **GLYCOSURIA DUE TO HYPERGLYCEMIA**   **"HIGH THRESHOLD" DUE TO DECREASED FILTRATION**   **RENAL GLYCOSURIA**

Figure 29–2. Glycosuria. Mechanisms of normal glucose retention (normoglycemia, total reabsorption indicated by arrows, and no glycosuria); of glycosuria due to hyperglycemia (increased arterial glucose, fully loaded reabsorptive mechanism, excess excreted, i.e., indicated as 350 mg. per minute: 390 mg. filtered, —40 mg. excreted); of a "high renal threshold" due to decreased functioning glomerular surface, as in glomerulosclerosis, with filtration rate reduced to 20 mg. per minute, so that glucose load filtered from plasma of 300 mg. per 100 ml. is 300/100 times 20 = 60 mg. per minute; lastly, typical familial renal glycosuria with deficient proximal tubular system for glucose reabsorption, so that $Tm_G = 70$ mg. per minute.

ables other than hydrostatic and colloid osmotic pressure that may affect filtration are renal intratubular and intrapelvic pressures, interstitial pressure, and, to a small degree, venous pressure. The last, at least in arcuate veins of the dog, is as high as 20 mm. Hg. Diseases such as glomerulonephritis that affect the filtering membrane impair both filtration and protein impermeability.

Proximal Tubule

Even the most primitive kidneys have proximal tubules. Their structure under the electron microscope is nearly as surprising as that of the glomerulus. The light microscopist's brush border is seen as bundles of microvilli that lead into little intracellular pools formed by invaginations of cell membrane and that are enzyme rich, notably in alkaline phosphatase. Cellular structures, especially the nucleus, Golgi apparatus, "fluorescent bodies," vacuoles, and mitochondria, stand out in detail. Most of the energy enzyme-rich mitochondria are packed into the bases of the cells, where they are infolded by invaginations of basal cellular membranes that create canaliculi extending deep into the cell. These form a relatively vast "intracellular" interstitial space almost continuous with surrounding capillary basement membranes.

Functional connotations of these structures

have yet to be unraveled in detail. It is evident that the microvilli enormously increase the absorbing surface; the size and chemistry of the mitochondria accord with the relatively high metabolic activity of the cells, while their basal infoldings must facilitate transfer of substances into or out of the capillary blood. Many of these transfers involve "active transport," a term that implies movement of a substance against a concentration or electrochemical gradient. This transport may be either reabsorptive, from lumen to capillary, or excretory, from capillary to lumen. In both cases, energy sources of active transport systems involve resynthesis of ATP, and materials that stimulate this (e.g., thyroxine) enhance and those that interfere (e.g., dinitrophenol) suppress these transport systems. Compounds subject to active transport apparently pass through cells in some conjugated form, so that agents that interfere with specific conjugases (e.g., Benemid, in the case of uric acid reabsorption and of secretion of substances such as p-aminohippuric acid, or PAH) also suppress transport. The processes are visualized in terms of (1) entry of the compound X into the tubule cell from lumen (reabsorption) or interstitial fluid (secretion), (2) coupling or conjugation with transfer substance Y, of which there may be more than one compound or one step, (3) movement through the cytoplasm and (4) decomposition of compound XY, with regeneration of Y, which then moves to cycle in transport, with (5) discharge of free X into tubular or capillary fluid. Saturation of the medium with compound X and determination of maximum rate of transport thereof is a measure of the amount of available Y (or of coenzymes) and is therefore an index of mass of tubular cells (Tm).

A substance may be completely or incompletely reabsorbed or secreted. Glucose is normally completely absorbed; phosphate, some amino acids, sulfate, uric and ascorbic acids are not. Some of the seeming vagaries of K, phosphate and urate excretion are attributable to three-phase (filtration, reabsorption and secretion) excretion systems. These reabsorptions are sometimes associated so that, for example, saturation of glucose transport impairs phosphate reabsorption; others, such as those of different groups of amino acids, are quite distinct in their energy sources and limits. Application of the concept of Tm to problems of glycosuria is shown in Figure 29–2; however, it should be noted that, while some renal glycosurics show low overall glucose Tm's, others do not, and are apparently glycosuric because of inequalities in glucose reabsorptive capacities of individual nephrons. The Fanconi syndrome and its variants, as well as the renal injury that occurs in Wilson's disease (heavy metal poisoning of proximal tubules, in this case by copper), are indicative of defects of proximal tubular function manifested as phosphaturia, aminoaciduria and glycosuria; the full-blown syndrome in infants is associated with a corresponding cellular hypoplasia in the proximal portion of the tubule, the "swan neck" deformity.

Secretory systems of the proximal tubule account for excretions of a variety of organic acids, many of them derivatives of hippuric acid; the same transport system carries penicillin, Diodrast, acetylated sulfonamides and phenolsulfonphthalein (PSP). A distinct system transports certain organic bases, notably N-1-methylnicotinamide. As with tubular reabsorption, maximum rates of tubular secretion (Tm's) can be measured by saturating the transport system with a substance X, typically PAH (see Fig. 29–4) and measuring this function as total amount in urine less amount filtered per unit time.

Some of the droplets and granules that appear in proximal tubules under the electron microscope represent macromolecular substances in course of transport and/or cellular digestion. This process is quite distinct from micromolecular reabsorption. Mass capacity of these systems is very small and a sufficient overload results in retention of aggregates of the compound (e.g., protein) or its product (e.g., in the cases of a lipoprotein, lipid). The phenomenon is of most significance in relation to proteinuria (Fig. 29–3). Retentive as it is, some serum protein, principally albumin, escapes through the glomerular filter and is

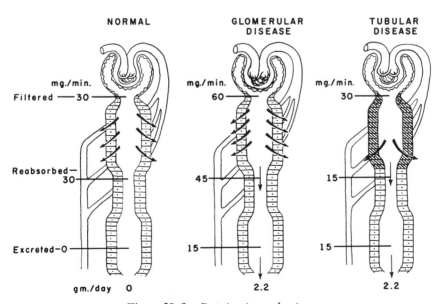

Figure 29–3. Proteinuria mechanisms.

CLEARANCE TESTS

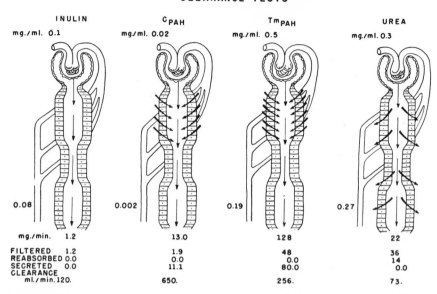

	INULIN	C_{PAH}	Tm_{PAH}	UREA
mg./ml.	0.1	0.02	0.5	0.3
	0.08	0.002	0.19	0.27
mg./min.	1.2	13.0	128	22
FILTERED	1.2	1.9	48	36
REABSORBED	0.0	0.0	0.0	14
SECRETED	0.0	11.1	80.0	0.0
CLEARANCE ml./min.	120.	650.	256.	73.

Figure 29–4. Schematic representation of examples of clearance mechanisms and measurement for inulin (arrows indicate filtration alone), PAH (arrows indicate filtration and secretion) at low and high (Tm measurement) plasma concentrations, and of urea (arrows indicate filtration and reabsorption primarily by diffusion). In each case the value recorded in milligrams per minute is UV (urinary concentration times rate of urine flow) and that indicated opposite afferent arteriole is plasma concentration P, so that clearance is UV/P. The numerals at end of schematic peritubular capillary plexus indicate estimated renal venous plasma concentrations.

taken up in this manner from tubule fluid, so that urine is normally protein free, or nearly so. Sufficient tubular injury may paralyze this system and establish proteinuria of tubular origin. However, most proteinurias probably originate in transglomerular leak of protein into tubular fluid as a result of functional or structural damage that disorganizes podocyte function and/or structure of the lamina densa. One sequel to such proteinuria is, as might be anticipated, appearance of lipid droplets in tubule cells. This may eventually give the kidney the appearance of being fatty and was formerly interpreted as a "degenerative" change; actually, fatty tubules occur normally in some species, such as cats and, in the case of most proteinurias, they are more indicative of cellular surfeit than damage.

Clearance

The concept of renal clearance is introduced at this point in the discussion of nephron function because it underlies some of the views stated above and many that will follow. The usage began with D. D. Van Slyke as a convenient way of expressing the amount of a substance that *seemed* to be wholly extracted or "cleared" from blood in one minute's time; clearance is, in effect, the *least* volume of blood or plasma that contains enough of a substance to account for the amount of that substance present in one minute's urine. It is a calculated, not a real volume.

The concept is schematized in Figure 29–4 in terms of inulin, a levulose polymer that is small enough to be freely filterable, but too large and inert to be actively or passively reabsorbed. Inulin clearance is therefore equal to the rate of glomerular filtration, and the discovery of this fact was one of the first great contributions Homer Smith made to renal physiology; it provided a base point around which to describe excretory (secretory) and reabsorptive functions. Thus, the clearance of PAH at low plasma levels is much greater than that of inulin because nearly all (90+ per cent rather than 20 per cent) is extracted from plasma in one renal passage. It is so high that it is nearly equal to renal plasma flow and is accepted as indicative of plasma flow to excretory tissues or "effective renal plasma flow." At high plasma concentrations PAH clearance is "self-suppressed" by saturation of the transfer system —a phenomenon that cannot occur with inulin, which is excreted purely by filtration; such saturation enables measurement of Tm_{PAH}. Clearance of urea is less than that of inulin because, while it is filtered, it is also reabsorbed, apparently by diffusion, and, in some species, may also be subject to tubular excretion. A clearance less than that of inulin does not establish the absence of secretion; this is notably the case with potassium; most filtered potassium is reabsorbed since nearly all that appears in urine is secreted. As indicated above, the same is true of urate and probably phosphate.

The Loop of Henle

Animals that have to retain water according to need have a hairpin loop of tubule leading back to the distal convolution. This loop structure was once assumed to have some association with water conservation. However, the appearance of the thin segment, especially under the electron microscope, is much more consistent with the view that this region functions only in osmotic equilibration, much in the manner of capillary endothelium, and with a minimum of active transport. Since it could not be assumed that antidiuretic hormone (ADH) could act here, the significance of its morphology was not appreciated; indeed, most thinking on the point may have been channeled by an "Idol," viz., the simplicity of a schematized rectilinear nephron.

It can still be assumed that most (80 to 85 per cent) salt and water is reabsorbed in the proximal tubule iso-osmotically and by "obligatory" (independent of extrarenal controls) reabsorption of sodium, with chloride and water following. Hence the descending limbs of the loops receive a fluid with an osmolality of about 300 mOsm. in a total volume of about 20 ml. per min.

The countercurrent concept, developed by chemists Hargitay and Kuhn, physiologist Wirz and variously elaborated by others and by new evidence from tubule punctures, is based primarily on the facts that renal interstitial and intraluminal fluids (during antidiuresis) increase in osmolality and in Na, Cl and urea concentrations as the loops dip into medulla, while intraluminal and interstitial osmolalities diminish as the ascending limb returns to the cortex, where it delivers hypotonic fluid into the distal tubule. The engineering principle is similar to that of various cooling and heating devices; in the case of the loop, the function is described as a countercurrent osmotic multiplier. This requires a hairpin structure in osmotic equilibrium with interstitial fluid and with each side of the loop, in which one side (ascending limb) extracts Na from tubule fluid, driving

it into interstitial fluid and descending limb. The vasa recta, similarly looped, but lacking active transport, remove fluid and salt from the concentrated interstitial fluid by functioning as slowly flowing countercurrent exchange systems.

The former postulate that concentration is achieved by active transport of water against a concentration gradient, has been abandoned; all that need be supposed is that distal and collecting tubules are poorly permeable to water in the absence of ADH, although facultatively responsive to hormonal and metabolic regulation of Na reabsorption. When ADH is present, permeability of these structures increases, and they come into osmotic equilibrium with their hypertonic surroundings; the result is formation of a small volume of hypertonic urine, the vasa recta returning conserved water to the body. The concept clarifies the manner in which urea, a highly diffusible solute, participates in enhancing water conservation. Urea, present in high concentration in medullary interstitial fluid and, by equilibration, in collecting tubules, increases the osmotic "ceiling" without imposing a transcellular osmotic gradient. Lack of urea, and not renal damage, explains the low concentrating powers found in patients on protein-deficient diets.

This synopsis, even with the aid of Figure 29–5, should be supplemented by reference to specific discussions of the concept which develop principles in more detail. The phenomenon these discussions describe is one of the greatest recent advances in our understanding of renal functions.

This concept bears on the mechanism by which partial ligation of a renal artery, a procedure that tends to decrease filtration and blood flow relative to tubular mass, results in formation of a small volume of hypertonic, sodium-poor urine, even in the absence of ADH. Decreased filtration load promotes greater fractional sodium reabsorption by the intact proximal tubule system; decreased blood flow in vasa recta permits a very high buildup of osmotic concentration in the medullary interstitial fluid. Then, if one assumes some water permeability of distal and collecting tubules, equilibration between tubular and interstitial fluids reduces volume and increases osmolality. Again, predominance of renal injury in medulla and collecting ducts rather than cortex may bear on the observation that many patients with pyelonephritis show impairment of concentrating power out of proportion to other tests of excretory func-

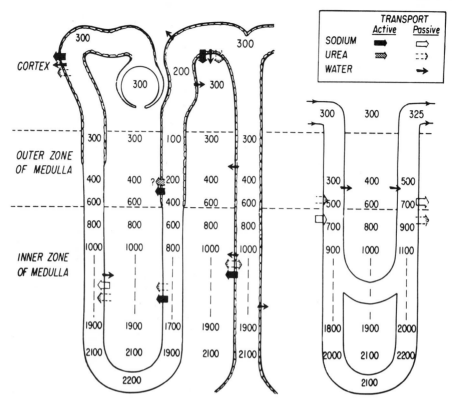

Figure 29–5. Diagram illustrating the countercurrent mechanism as it is believed to operate in a nephron with a long loop and in the vasa recta. Numbers represent hypothetic osmolality values. No quantitative significance is attached to the numbers of arrows and only net movements are indicated. As is the case with the vascular loops, all loops of Henle do not reach the tip of the papilla and hence the fluid in them does not become as concentrated as the final urine, but only as concentrated as the medullary interstitial fluid at the same level. (Courtesy of Dr. C. W. Gottschalk and the publishers of Circulation and the American Journal of Physiology. A recent personal communication from Dr. Gottschalk states that he sees no reason to alter this view, although others have reported variant data on site of sodium transport from thin limbs.)

tion. Similarly, the inability to form concentrated urine found in patients with nephrocalcinosis and hypercalcemia may be explained from the locale of their lesions; however, associations between parathyroid activity, polyuria, thirst and phosphate and calcium excretion are still uncertain. Unless it can be assumed that there may occur a state in which distal and collecting tubular segments cannot increase basic water permeability, even in the absence of lesions by electron microscopy, the mechanism of the rare, familial, "Pitressin-resistant" form of diabetes insipidus is unexplained, as is also the nature of the defect that impairs concentration function but not water reabsorption ($Tm^C_{H_2O}$) during osmotic diuresis in sickle-cell anemia.

Ion Exchange: Acidification

These processes are primarily functions of the distal tubule, a zone of columnar epithelium which shows even more extensive infoldings of basement membrane than the proximal tubule and many evidences of high metabolic activity. Actually, ion transport, which in the proximal tubule is substantially sodium transport, probably is always and everywhere in the kidney a matter of ion exchange, notably of exchange of sodium for hydrogen ion. However, it is in the distal tubule that the fluid actually may become acid and that the concentration of sodium may be so reduced as to bring a third ion, potassium, into the pattern of exchange, as well as a fourth, ammonium ion, formed there. Such ion exchange accounts also for tubular reabsorption of bicarbonate, a function normally set as if Tm were reached at a serum HCO_3 level of about 28 mEq. per liter, i.e., about 3 mEq. of filtered HCO_3 per minute.

The basic chemical exchanges are schematized in Table 29–1. Two of the major reactions are dependent on integrity of the carbonic anhydrase system; these provide hydrogen ion for bicarbonate reabsorption and also for formation of titratable acid (NaH_2PO_4). These reactions are deficient in renal tubular acidoses, are suppressed by carbonic anhydrase inhibitors (e.g., sulfanilamide, acetazoleamide) and are impaired in potassium deficiency. The reactions making for ammonia secretion are not affected by these enzyme inhibitors or by potassium deficiency (which seems to stimulate this process), but are usually impaired in renal acidoses. The hydrogen ion secretion is the immediate line of renal defense of blood pH; it can lower urinary pH to about 4.5, a level at which hydrogen ion may substitute for sodium ion of some weak acids, so that organic acids begin to appear in the urine. The basic stimulus to hydrogen ion secretion is determined by carbon dioxide tension or pH within the tubule cell. Hence, metabolic acidosis is an instant stimulus to secretion of hydrogen ion, while alkalosis normally instantly suppresses this function and, with it, reabsorption of bicarbonate. Actually, since our net residue from food is acid, urine is normally acid and serum HCO_3 nearer 25 than 28 mEq. per liter. The ammonia mechanism is a less immediate line of defense; it is capable of stimulation by acidosis of some days' duration. Hence, agents intended to act by acidifying the urine, such as NH_4Cl, or by carbonic anhydrase inhibition are most effective when administered only for 2 to 3 days at a time.

Potassium. Potassium ion forms a significant fraction of the solute mixture only in the distal tubule, where it enters into ion exchange with sodium and hydrogen. Hence, impairment or deficiency of the carbonic anhydrase system results in urine rich in sodium and potassium, but low in hydrogen. Similarly, organic acid excess, as in diabetic acidosis, depletes "fixed base" (Na and K) once it exceeds the capacity of the exchange systems for acidification of the urine.

The association is the more complex because intracellular potassium is intimately related to carbon dioxide tension and pH in the cell. Provision of excess potassium leads to formation of a potassium-rich, hydrogen-poor urine, even though extracellular HCO_3 decreases to the point of acidosis. Again, deficit of potassium tends (initially at least) toward formation of acid urine, even though the systemic state is one of alkalosis and chloride deficiency. A further complication arises from the role of adrenal hormones, notably aldosterone. This acts to promote distal sodium reabsorption at the expense of potassium loss. Further, whereas the several mechanisms that contribute to avid sodium retention in the face of a deficit act rapidly and effectively, those that would make for potassium retention (presumably by the single channel of suppressing its cellular secretion) are less prompt and intense; indeed, they may be less than ineffective, since the conditions that make for potassium deficit often stimulate adrenal secretions that make for potassium loss.

Hence syndromes of potassium deficit are

TABLE 29–1. BASE CONSERVATION BY ACIDIFICATION AND AMMONIA SECRETION.

a Cell	b Transfer Product	c Lumen	d Transfer Product	e Cell	f Blood
A. Carbonic anhydrase dependent					
1. $CO_2 + H_2O$ $H·HCO_3$	H^+	$Na·HCO_3$ $H·HCO_3$ $CO_2 + H_2O$ H_2O	Na CO_2	$H_2O + CO_2$ $H·HCO_3$ $NaHCO_3$	$NaHCO_3$
2. $CO_2 + H_2O$ $H·HCO_3$	H^+	Na_2HPO_4 NaH_2PO_4	Na	$H·HCO_3$ $NaHCO_3$	$NaHCO_3$
B. Ammonia formation					
Glutamine (glutaminase)	NH_3	H^+, NaCl NH_4^+		$H·CO_3$	
Amino acids (amine oxidase)	NH_3	NH_4Cl	Na	$NaHCO_3$	$NaHCO_3$ NaCl

Reactions are listed from above down in each category and from left to right in sequence of (*a*) intracellular reaction, (*b*) transcellular transfer, (*c*) luminal reaction, (*d*) transfer, and (*e*) cellular reaction with (*f*) final exchange into blood.

relatively common, whereas noteworthy potassium retention occurs only in severe renal failure. The potassium deficiency syndromes occur (1) in diarrheal states, (2) with massive diuresis or glycosuria, (3) in the renal tubular acidoses, including those resulting from carbonic anhydrase-suppressing agents, and (4) in adrenal hypercorticoidism, viz., in Cushing's syndrome often and in primary aldosteronism regularly. If the deficiency is sufficiently severe, functional and structural renal effects ensue. The structural lesion is substantially one of vacuolation; functional effects are impairment of PAH transport and extraction and polyuria with Pitressin-resistant isosthenuria, relieved by providing enough potassium and, in some cases, by restricting sodium; in primary aldosteronism the urine is also slightly alkaline and ammonium rich. Indeed, the finding of these urinary signs in a patient with hypertension suggests the likelihood of primary aldosteronism. What seem to be less severe degrees of deficit may be encountered in patients with severe, especially malignant, hypertension; these may develop states of alkalosis and/or hypokalemia and show definite aldosterone oversecretion in the absence of sodium lack, volume deficit or congestive heart failure (Laragh et al., 1960).

Stop-Flow Technique

Most of the localizations of renal functions have been based on data from nephron punctures or duct cannulation, highly specialized techniques that have limited application. The "stop-flow" procedure of Malvin et al. (1958) has been humorously described by Pitts as the "poor man's micro-puncture." It consists in clamping the ureter during osmotic diuresis thereby stopping urine flow and rapidly building up intratubular pressure which *nearly* stops filtration. Just before the occlusion is released, inulin is injected into the renal artery as a marker of resumption of filtration. The urine that gushes out is collected second by second, and the sequence of changes in its composition establishes the order in which specific tubular activities modified their fluid content during the period of stopped flow.

Diuresis and Diuretics

The following discussion is proposed only as an outline of a complex field considered in a monograph by Pitts (1959).

Normally, diuresis and antidiuresis depend on excretion of more or less water, according to needs imposed by solute load and water availability. The ultimate determinant of decreased water output is secretion of ADH in response to increases of body fluid osmolality of as little as 2 per cent. Intracerebral osmoreceptors respond to such changes by stimulating the hypophyseal-hypothalamic area to discharge impulses that initiate this secretion. A secretion of only 0.2 *milli*unit per kg. body weight per hour establishes an adequate physiologic antidiuretic state. Secretion normally is inhibited by decreased osmolality of body fluid or by ethyl alcohol. The "set" of the receptor system seems to be lowered in compulsive water drinkers who establish a functional diabetes insipidus. Normally, and in these neurotic states, the receptors can be stimulated by a sharp upward shift in osmolality (Hickey-Hare test). They can also be stimulated by emotion, nicotine, and acetylcholine in the absence of osmotic changes. Further, volume receptors may modify ADH output; the antidiuretic effect of veratrum alkaloids may depend on stimulation of these and other cardiovascular receptors. As stated above, the ultimate effect of secreted ADH is exerted by increasing permeability of collecting tubules.

Both ADH and aldosterone secretion seem to be stimulated in edematous states, including congestive heart failure and the nephrotic syndrome. Cerebral injuries or disease may also affect both. Diabetes insipidus may reflect injury to the ADH secretory system, or to the hypophyseal-hypothalamic nuclei. Deficiency of ADH secretion may also be associated with impairment of osmoreceptor function, with resultant insensitivity of the thirst mechanism and establishment of a hyperosmolar state. An analogous defect of aldosterone-controlling receptors can be postulated in those cases of meningitis and poliomyelitis that develop salt-losing syndromes.

Today the common meaning of the word diuresis is *increased* urine flow, but literally it implies merely that there is *some* urine flow. In its present sense, there are two major physiologic mechanisms of diuresis, *water diuresis* and *osmotic diuresis*. A third mechanism may operate when discharge of both salt and water is accelerated by a decrease in extracellular fluid volume. The urine formed in water diuresis is hypotonic with reference to plasma, that formed in osmotic diuresis is hypertonic over a wide range and, other things being equal, that formed during discharge of extracellular fluid tends to be isotonic and, of course, sodium rich.

Water diuresis is due to ADH inhibition,

physiologically by water loading or pharmacologically by alcohol. In this sense, water is the ideal diuretic and alcohol a useful one. However, in edematous states such as congestive heart failure excess water may not be excreted and, when retained, leads to water intoxication. Hence, what is usually a reasonable provision of water to such patients may not be desirable and marked restriction of water administration may be necessary.

Osmotic diuresis is characterized by formation of urine whose osmolality decreases asymptotically toward the isohydric line or even below it as the volume flow increases. Anything that contributes to osmotic load (urinary osmolal concentration times volume) is an osmotic diuretic, since its excretion carries with it some water. Typical osmotic diuretics are small molecular substances (urea, mannitol, glucose in large amounts) that are incompletely reabsorbed by tubules. Because they persist in tubular fluid they osmotically hold water, increasing flow rate from proximal tubules into loops, through which flow is thereby increased. Increased loop flow decreases the efficiency of the loop as an osmotic multiplier and dilutes medullary interstitial fluid, so that even in the presence of an excess of ADH, urine concentration falls. During water deprivation and in subjects on diets adequate in protein (to provide urea) and NaCl, maximum medullary and urinary osmolality is about 1200 mOsm. per kg. water, i.e., $U_{Osm}/P_{Osm} \doteq 3$. As concentration falls during an osmotic diuresis and solute load excretion increases, net reabsorption of solute-free water ("free water") is increased, and reaches a maximum of about 5 ml. per minute. This limit is expressed as $Tm^C_{H_2O}$; it is calculated as the osmolal clearance (C_{Osm}) less urine flow (V). At high rates of flow and osmotic load it describes an upper limit of water reabsorption, much as $Tm_{Glucose}$ describes glucose reabsorption, although it is not as fixed or reproducible a datum.

A side-effect of osmotic diuresis is the washout of increased amounts of NaCl, and the urine formed at high rates of osmotic diuresis can be regarded as very similar to proximal tubular effluent. At such forced rates of flow, tubules dilate and tubular electrolytes are diluted, fluid movement is accelerated and medullary blood flow increases. Possibly all these factors, as well as dilution effects on electrolyte concentration gradients, tend to interfere with electrolyte reabsorption.

In some cases (urea, mannitol, water) classification of the mechanisms of the actions of diuretic drugs is very easy (although side-effects on electrolyte excretion may occur). But the mechanisms of actions of most diuretics in clinical use may involve osmotic and water mechanisms and also hemodynamic changes that complicate their consideration. Table 29-2 presents a classification that may be useful.

Some clinical connotations of these agents and notes on mechanisms that indicate the defects in classification are mentioned below. For more detailed considerations, the reader is referred to Pitts' monograph and the Hahnemann Symposium on Edema (1960).

Among the physiologic group, colloids are indeed active under normal conditions; however, they are most diuretic when they correct hypovolemia, restoring plasma volume, cardiac output, filtration and thereby urine flow while also suppressing stimuli from "volume-receptors" that make for salt and water retention. They pay a modest dividend in promoting loss of NaCl; passage of some smaller molecules of the colloid into tubular fluid may add a slight osmotic effect. Digitalis glycosides certainly alter cellular ion fluxes and

TABLE 29-2. FUNCTIONAL CLASSIFICATION OF DIURETIC AGENTS (MODIFIED FROM PITTS, 1959).

A. Physiologic
  1. Those that increase filtered Na and/or Cl loads
    a. Colloids: albumin, dextran, etc.
    b. Cardiac glycosides: (only in congestive heart failure)
    c. Afferent vasodilators: aminophylline
    d. Acidifying agents: NH_4Cl
  2. Those that impair Na and/or Cl reabsorptions
    a. Aldosterone anti-secretory agents: amphenone—experimentally only
    b. Aldosterone antagonists: spirolactones, prednisone (?)
    c. Agents that increase flow rate or impair ion gradients in distal tubules: water, osmotic diuretics—urea, mannitol
B. Pharmacologic
  1. Those that specifically impair Na and/or Cl transport
    a. Xanthines: caffeine, theophylline
    b. Aminouracils: aminoisometridine
    c. Mercurial diuretics
    d. Thiazide diuretics
    e. Triamterene
    f. Ethacrynic acid
    g. Furosemide
  2. Those that interfere with Na:K ion exchange, impairing HCO_3 transport
    a. Potassium salts
    b. Carbonic anhydrase inhibitors: sulfanilamide, acetazoleamide

thereby may have some direct renal action. Verification of this has been sought since Withering's time; it is not a primary therapeutic mechanism. They are effective diuretics only in those conditions in which they restore renal circulation by enhancing efficiency of cardiac action, i.e., in heart failure. Acidifying agents provide excess chloride ions that trap sodium as the limit of urinary acidification is reached. They are useful as adjuncts to mercurials; diuretic activity of organic mercurials is suppressed in an alkaline medium and enhanced in an acid, possibly by increased splitting off of inorganic mercury. They have the disadvantage that they cause acidosis, so that the renal mechanisms of acidification become "resistant." Amphenone is of experimental interest only, being very toxic. The aldosterone antagonists of the spirolactone group act apparently by competing with aldosterone for receptor sites; they are most useful as adjuncts to other diuretics, since they inhibit the action of excess aldosterone secretion and thereby suppress the tendency to potassium loss. However, they may cause severe hyperkalemia. Triamterene has a similar net, albeit nonendocrine effect. Diuretic activities of the corticosteroids and their derivatives, such as prednisone, are very complex; in part there may be suppression of aldosterone and of other adrenal hormones; in adrenal insufficiency at least the effect is largely hemodynamic and possibly also one of altered membrane permeability that increases water output.

Activities and limitations of the pharmacologic agents are well recognized. The largest innovation in this field has been the advent of chlorothiazide and its congeners and their use in hypertension. The parent drug shares properties of a carbonic anhydrase inhibitor and a salt-with-water eliminating (saluretic) diuretic, such as a mercurial. Mercurials seem to act by complexing with sulfhydryl-rich enzymes, possibly Na-K-activated, Mg-dependent, ouabain-inhibited, "membrane ATP-ase," that provide some of the energy for sodium (or chloride) reabsorptive transport, primarily in the proximal tubule; impairment of sodium reabsorption at this level has the net effect of an osmotic diuretic. The type substance among the carbonic anhydrase inhibitors, acetazoleamide, impairs reabsorption of sodium, potassium and bicarbonate, tending thereby to provoke a metabolic hyperchloremic acidosis, and has not been a satisfactory agent in heart failure. Chlorothiazide is useful in failure because it also suppresses proximal and distal Na and/or Cl reabsorptions, apparently by a mechanism distinct from that of mercurials, to which its effect may therefore be additive. It has the disadvantage that it tends to promote hypokalemia and metabolic alkalosis, while its proximal tubular action also impairs excretion (promotes reabsorption?) of urate, leading to hyperuricemia, sometimes gout. Its newer derivatives, beginning with hydrochlorothiazide, are in general more active, weight for weight.

Two newer diuretic agents are ethacrynic acid, a phenoxyacetic acid derivative, and furosemide, a benzothiadiazine analogue having a furfuryl group substituted on the amino nitrogen of the anthranilic acid. Both appear to act by blocking renal tubular sodium reabsorption in a manner similar, but not identical, to that of the organic mercurials. These new compounds appear to be of considerable efficacy in promoting intense, brief diuresis.

Diuretic therapy of hypertension on a large scale is relatively new, although it was shown several years ago that sufficient dosage with mercurials might have the same net effect as prolonged, severe restriction of dietary sodium. However, blood pressures of only a minority of patients with hypertension are responsive to low-sodium dietotherapy or to diuretics. Nevertheless these drugs have come to be used widely, sometimes alone, but more commonly in association with other antihypertensive drugs, notably those that tend to impair sympathetic vasomotor reflexes and tone (e.g., reserpine, the ganglion blockers) and the new peripherally acting agents (e.g., guanethedine, alpha-methyldopa). Saluresis, however accomplished, assuming a reasonably constant and limited sodium intake, has the same net effect as sodium restriction and greatly enhances the antihypertensive effect of these neurotropic drugs. The first effect is that sufficient saluresis depletes plasma volume and that the hypertensive's response to this is increased vasomotor tone; if, concurrently, he is receiving a drug that impairs ability to increase vasomotor tone, blood pressure decreases, particularly when standing; later in the course of therapy other mechanisms may participate in maintaining low pressure levels.

TESTS OF EXCRETORY FUNCTION

The tests of excretory function are either (1) qualitative or semiquantitative or (2) directly quantitative.

Qualitative and semiquantitative tests include (1) detection and estimation of proteinuria, (2) estimates and descriptions of urinary sediment, either crystalline or organized (red blood cells, white cells and casts), and (3) estimation of excretory function from determinations of blood urea or nonprotein nitrogen.

The tests which quantitatively measure excretory function are: (1) tests of excretion rates (e.g., phenolsulfonphthalein test), (2) clearance tests, and (3) tests of the function of water reabsorption. (4) Quantitative measurements of urinary protein and sediment may be included in this category.

The quantitative tests of renal function are only a little more complicated to perform and usually much easier to interpret than qualitative or semiquantitative procedures. Mean normal values for these measurements of renal function are given in Table 29–3.

Tests of Rate of Excretion

The most commonly used test of excretory rate depends on measurement of percentile excretion of 6 mg. of intravenously injected phenolsulfonphthalein. This dye is excreted almost entirely by the same tubular mechanism as is concerned with Diodrast, hippuran or PAH, all of which, as also probenecid (Benemid), block its excretion. The rate at which it appears in urine depends on (1) the rate of renal blood flow, (2) the percentage of dye removed from blood during one renal circulation (normally about 50 per cent), and (3) the rate at which fluid moves down the renal tubules, through the pelvis and ureter to the bladder. Severe renal diseases impair both renal blood flow and tubular secretion and thus reduce excretion of dye by impairing their mechanisms. Obstructive uropathies reduce blood flow and also slow the rate of movement of tubular fluid and urine and, in obstructions below the renal pelvis, dilute the excreted dye in the hydronephrotic accumulation of urine. Oliguria also tends to slow the rate of dye excretion.

Normally, 30 per cent of the injected dye is excreted in 15 minutes after intravenous injection. Slower excretion reflects delay in the urinary tract or renal damage. In the proved absence of obstructive uropathy or extreme oliguria, a decreased excretion of dye in urine collected at 15 minutes indicates a reduction of renal blood flow. Because it is more easily seen through the cystoscope than phenolsulfonphthalein, indigo carmine is used as a semiquantitative test of excretion time (blood to bladder) in urologic practice.

The rate of appearance and depth of shadow seen by the radiologist during intravenous urography are other indices of excretory rate. Two of the radiopaque substances used in this procedure (hippuran and Diodrast) are excreted almost entirely by tubular secretion; another (Neo-iopax) is excreted largely by glomerular filtration. While the degree of radiopacity of the pyelographic shadow and the time of its appearance vary with renal excretory function, the shadow will also depend on the degree to which the dye is diluted. The estimate of function provided by this method is useful secondary information. It should not be referred to as dye "clearance," since it does not correspond to quantitative clearance tests properly so-called.

TABLE 29–3. APPROXIMATE AVERAGE VALUES FOR VARIOUS MEASURES OF RENAL FUNCTION IN NORMAL ADULTS.

Test		Mean
Effective renal blood flow	Men	1150 ml./1.73 sq. m./min.
	Women	950 ml./1.73 sq. m./min.
Effective renal plasma flow (Diodrast, PAH clearance)	Men	700 ml./1.73 sq. m./min.
	Women	600 ml./1.73 sq. m./min.
Glomerular filtration rate (inulin, mannitol clearance)	Men	130 ml./1.73 sq. m./min.
	Women	115 ml./1.73 sq. m./min.
PAH(Tm_{PAH})	Men	80 mg./1.73 sq. m./min.
	Women	70 mg./1.73 sq. m./min.
Tubular reabsorptive capacity, glucose	Men	375 mg./1.73 sq. m./min.
	Women	300 mg./1.73 sq. m./min.
Urea clearance, percentage of normal		$100 \pm 30\%$
Creatinine clearance (12 or 24 hr. collection)		about 140 ml. per min.
Phenolsulfonphthalein excretion (6 mg. injection, i.v.)	15 min.	30% excreted
Radio-iodo-hippurate	20 min.	$64 \pm 8.6\%$ excreted
Urinary concentration (Fishberg)		1.023 sp. gr. or greater. U_{Osm}/P_{Osm} about 2.8
Urinary concentration (Addis)		1.026 sp. gr. or greater. U_{Osm}/P_{Osm} about 3.0

Preop

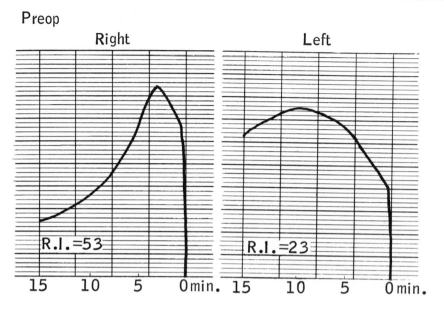

Postop

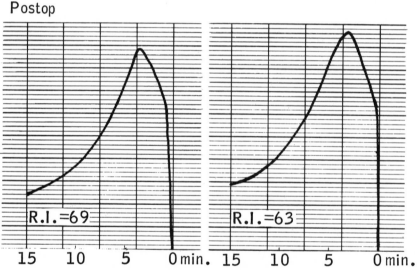

Figure 29–6. I[131]-hippurate renograms, right and left; *above*, before and *below*, after repair of renal arterial occlusion. (Courtesy of John R. Caldwell, M.D., Division of Hypertension, and William R. Eyler, M.D., Department of Radiology, Henry Ford Hospital, Detroit, Mich.)

Related to the above is the "radioisotope renogram." This procedure consists in plotting graphically radioactivity over the two kidneys for 10, 15 or 20 minutes after injection of a radioactively iodinated, renally excreted agent, preferably iodo-hippurate (Hipputope) since hepatic excretion does not interfere. The graphs show an initial "vascular spike" representing inflow of the tag in a bolus of blood into the kidney and great vessels followed by a slow rise, representing tubular uptake and secretion of activity, followed by a fall as urine flows out of the kidney more

rapidly than dye is being stored (Fig. 29–6). Abnormalities may be detected in the "vascular" phase, representing decreased inflow of blood, the tubular phase of accumulation (suppressed in severe renal disease) or the outflow phase, absent or impaired in hydronephrosis. Quantitation has been approximated by the use of the renogram index (Fig. 29–7). Other parameters, e.g., "peak" time, half-time of down-slope, should be noted. In our experience to date, it seems to be useful in screening for renal abnormalities, including renal arterial occlusive disease. It is relatively insensitive to small variations in total renal function.

Although not truly a test of renal excretory function, renal scintiscans utilizing a mercurial diuretic tagged with Hg^{197} are easy to perform and may be useful for delineating the size and approximate position of the kidneys and detecting renal vascular abnormalities or space-occupying lesions.

Clearance Tests

The principle of clearance measurement and its applications to PAH, inulin and urea were discussed above. Utilization of this concept in a test merely implies that the result is interpreted with reference to some standard of normality, best of all the patient's but, if need be, to means and ranges of data from normal subjects, appropriately corrected for body surface when the patient's body size varies substantially from adult normal. Measurement of inulin (or mannitol) and PAH clearance remains substantially an investigative procedure. Conventional methods require steady intravenous infusion, repeated plasma sampling and collections of urine by catheterization and bladder washing. This last imposes some risk of activation of urinary tract infections; the risk is diminished by instillation of 0.1 gm. of neomycin into the bladder at the time the catheter is withdrawn. However, this is still a cumbersome and uncomfortable, if very informative, procedure.

For these reasons two clearance tests are in clinical use. The one used most often is the measurement of urea clearance. Changes in urea reabsorption, complicated perhaps by "wash-out" of medullary urea tend to make the results of this test uncertain at low or rising rates of urine flow. However, at a stable or slowly falling urine flow somewhat in excess of 2 ml. per minute, urea reabsorption

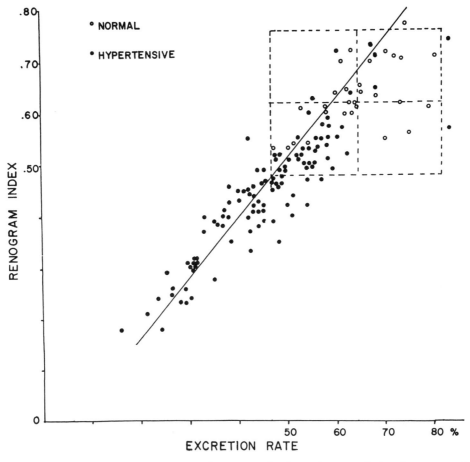

Figure 29–7. The mean renogram index of normal subjects (open circles) and patients with hypertensive or other bilateral renal disease (closed circles) is plotted against the 20-minute radiohippurate excretion rate. Dotted lines outline means ± 2 S.D.'s of these two functions in normal subjects. (From Hirakawa, A., and Corcoran, A. C.: J. Lab. & Clin. Med., *61*:795, 1963.)

is nearly constant at about 40 per cent of that filtered, and urea clearance is normally about 75 ml. per minute and bears a fairly reproducible relation to glomerular filtration rate. In fact, since the test is usually reported as per cent normal (ml. cleared $\times$ 1.33 at volume greater than 2 ml. per minute), and filtration rate is normally about 120 ml. per minute, reported values of urea clearance multiplied by 1.2 nearly equal concurrent filtration rate. The test requires no injection of test materials and the laboratory techniques are in common use. It is therefore adapted to routine clinical studies, provided sufficient care is taken to maintain urine flow by adequate prehydration, by recumbency during the test period and no smoking.

The second test used for clinical purposes is measurement of endogenous creatinine clearance, usually over fairly long periods of urine collection, of 12 or 24 hours. Again, no injection is required, and the chemical procedures are familiar. However, great care has to be used in measuring creatinine at low (normal) plasma concentrations and there is some advantage in the adsorption techniques that eliminate some noncreatinine chromogen. Excretion rate is independent of urine flow, which is an advantage. In dogs and rats creatinine clearance is as good a measure of glomerular filtration rate as inulin or mannitol. Extensive comparison of simultaneous mannitol and endogenous creatinine clearances (adsorption technique) in patients with hypertension indicates a mean somewhat greater than filtration rate, with ranges of creatinine/mannitol clearance from about 0.6 to 2.0. Possibly the pattern of creatinine excretion is fairly constant in any one person, so that the test can be considered quantitative in serial measurements on that individual. From technical and nursing aspects, it is easier to do than urea clearance.

Water Tests

Tests directed at measuring water excretion are variously intended as tests of renal or extrarenal water function. Those in common use, the concentration-dilution tests, are aimed at detecting abnormalities in the renal tubular mechanisms responsible for altering the osmolality of tubular fluid by reabsorption or excretion of osmotically unobligated "free water." Others, which measure diuretic responses to standard water or salt loads, are directed usually at possible abnormalities of extrarenal (pituitary, adrenal or circulatory) regulatory mechanism.

The concentration-dilution tests measure the degree to which tubular cells bring about differences in osmotic concentrations between glomerular filtrate and urine. Dilution tests are little used. They consist in measuring the ability to achieve a low specific gravity after a standard water load. The range of measurement is small (10 points on the hydrometer), the influence of extrarenal factors (adrenal, pituitary, hepatic, intestinal, cardiac, hemic) large, and the function aimed at is that measured in concentration tests.

Concentration tests measure the ability to form urine of high osmolar concentration in response to ADH stimulation of the mechanisms of water reabsorption. In these, ADH stimulation is elicited by endogenous release under the stimulus of water deprivation, or by giving ADH by injection of Pituitrin or vasopressin. The simplest of these tests in form is that of Fishberg. Hourly urine specimens are collected during continuance of nocturnal water deprivation begun 12 hours before; one of the specimens should yield a specific gravity greater than 1.023. The Addis test is more rigid in that water deprivation is practiced for 24 hours and the urine collected during the last 12 (nocturnal) hours of this time. It should yield a specific gravity of 1.026 or more, and the specimen serves also for measurement of proteinuria and for the sediment count. The osmolality of urine which is achieved on a concentration test should be at least 850 mOsm. per Kg. water, i.e., U/P osmolal ratio should be 2.9 or more.

Substitution of Pituitrin or vasopressin for water deprivation is used to speed the test, and to provide a standard stimulus which is independent of the patient's interpretation of water deprivation. The test is done by measuring specific gravities of specimens collected at intervals after subcutaneous injection of 10 pressor units of pituitary extract. However, the test has the disadvantage that it requires injection of a substance which is sometimes uncomfortable and occasionally lethal. Further, the amount injected is very large as compared with calculated maximum physiologic rates of ADH release. Lastly, dehydration as such independently of ADH, promotes urine concentration, so that the "ceilings" indicated by these tests are not as high as in the Addis procedure.

Comparison of the Pituitrin, Fishberg and Addis tests indicates fair correspondence between the first two, both of which yield lower and more variable mean specific gravities than the Addis test. The variability of the Pituitrin test results from the fact that maximum anti-diuresis is obtainable only at low initial rate of urine flow and solute output; that of the Fishberg test presumably reflects the varying degree of ADH stimulation elicited by a short period of water deprivation. In both the Fishberg and Addis tests the collection of specimens during or after a night's fast tends naturally to decrease solute load, much of which is excreted during the day, and thus facilitates formation of uniformly concentrated urine.

The nature of either concentration or dilution tests is that they vary from a baseline specific gravity of 1.010, which represents excretion of a urine which is only slightly hypertonic to a protein-free plasma filtrate (specific gravity 1.008). In the common forms of renal disease the ability to concentrate or dilute the urine becomes considerably diminished when urea clearance is about 30 per cent of normal and the number of nephrons remaining in function about 40 per cent of normal. Beyond this degree of renal damage the progress of renal failure must be measured by other means.

It is important to recognize that even at a stage of "fixed" specific gravity there may be no real concentrating defect in the remaining nephrons. They may be responding perfectly to the osmotic diuresis elicited by azotemia, which increases solute (nonprotein nitrogen) concentration in the glomerular filtrate. This follows from the nature of osmotic diuresis, in which the urine tends to an osmolar concentration of 300 mOsm. per Kg. water as solute load increases, even in the presence of maximally effective water-reabsorbing mechanisms. This fact has other implications. Thus it has been assumed that excretion of urine of specific gravity of 1.010 (about 300 mOsm. per Kg. water) implies that the tubules are doing a minimum of osmotic work and that they are called upon to do more osmotic work when the urine is either very dilute or very concentrated. From this it has been argued that protein should be restricted in the presence of renal disease, because excretion of urea requires the kidney to do osmotic work. Without prejudice to other unrelated, perhaps sufficient reasons which might justify protein restriction, this rationalization at least is unjustified. Urea excretion is passive once arterial pressure has forced urea through the glomerulus. Further, from what is known of the many mechanisms of active transport which operate in urine formation, it follows that the only condition in

which the kidney would do a clear minimum of osmotic work would be one in which it excreted unmodified glomerular filtrate.

The concentration tests remain as useful indices of renal function which reflect in varying degree defects in water reabsorption in the nephrons or the response of remaining nephrons to an osmotic load. They have value primarily in the detection of early renal disease. In the presence of any considerable azotemia they are essentially noninforming and the imposition of hydropenia may be harmful. It is essential to a proper concentration test that the conditions be such as to provide reasonable standardization of solute load and water deficit, so that the volume of fluid which the tubule is called upon to concentrate is small and relatively constant, and the ADH stimulus maximal. The tests are therefore subject to artefacts, such as prior restriction of protein and salt (e.g., rice diet) which diminish the osmoreceptor stimulation caused by water deprivation; another such is receding edema, which unpredictably adds isotonic fluid to the urine.

Early experience with what was termed "electrometric urinometry" indicated that such measurements of freezing point are at least as convenient as and much more accurate than the rough equivalent provided by measurements of specific gravity. Furthermore, measurement of urine osmolality is of much greater physiologic significance than is specific gravity as it directly evaluates the amount of osmotic work done by the renal

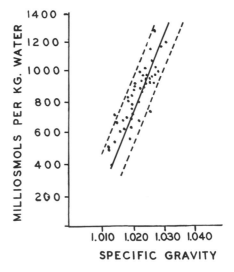

Figure 29–8. Graph of the relationship between urine osmolality and specific gravity. (Adapted from Dustan, H. P., and Corcoran, A. C.: M. Clin. North America, 39:947, 1955.)

tubular cells when compared with simultaneous plasma (or serum) osmolality. Cost of the apparatus may be a limiting factor. In hospitals this should not be a determinant in view of the significant results obtained. The relationship between urine osmolality and specific gravity of patients with hypertension on a normal mixed diet is shown in Figure 29–8. The slope changes during sodium restriction.

Pressor-Antipressor (Endocrine) Functions

Bright suggested in 1827 and more or less desultory studies during the following century confirmed an association between albuminuric renal disease and increased arterial pressure. One of the major efforts of one of Bright's London successors, Frederick Mohamed, was the definition of what was termed "pre-albuminuric Bright's disease," now recognized as essential hypertension. Establishment of this concept directed attention away from the kidney until Goldblatt's experiments of 1933–1934 showed that hypertension of varying severity could be produced in dogs and other animals by partial, permanent compression of the renal artery. Among methods described to evoke such hypertension, none seems more satisfactory than that of Page, in which hypertension follows perinephritis elicited by silk or cellophane.

The stimulus to hypertension in both these cases is apparently a change in the character, possibly in the distribution, but not necessarily in the total volume of renal blood flow. Hence, excretory function may be normal or nearly so during persistence of severe hypertension. Alternatively, as in Selye's "endocrine kidney," excretory function can be unilaterally abolished and the kidney still serve as a cause of rapidly fatal renal hypertension. Thus, excretory and pressor functions of the kidney can be completely disassociated.

Nearly 20 years ago it seemed that the mechanisms of renal hypertension would be rather readily worked out. The initial charge was visualized as liberation of a proteolytic enzyme, renin, which now seems to be present in or near the cells of the juxtaglomerular body. Renin then acts on a globulin (renin substrate, angiotensinogen) of hepatic origin, present in plasma in very low concentrations. This highly specific reaction releases a polypeptide, known at that time as angiotonin or hypertensin. More recently, and by mutual agreement, it is known as angiotensin. This material, as it is split off from renin substrate, is a 10-amino-acid polypeptide which is vasoinactive (angiotensin-1). Splitting off of two amino acids converts this (a converting enzyme is present in plasma) to angiotensin-2, which is weight for weight more vasoconstrictor than anything known. This product is dissipated by more or less nonspecific peptic enzymes grouped as angiotensinases. Angiotensin has been detected in blood in experimental renal and severe clinical hypertension. Angiotensin is carried in the blood to the adrenal cortex where it stimulates the output of aldosterone. Aldosterone in turn circulates back to the kidney where it promotes renal tubular reabsorption of Na. Renin is also released on quiet standing, during plasma volume depletion and in congestive heart failure. Its biological status and that of aldosterone have been surveyed in part by Denton.

Hypertension also appears in animals that have been bilaterally nephrectomized and kept alive by dialysis. This is "renoprival" hypertension and, at first glance, would seem wholly distinct from renal hypertension. However, it points to an antipressor function of the kidneys. Such an antipressor effect of a normal kidney can be demonstrated by placing the kidney into the circulation of an animal with either renal or renoprival hypertension. It may be therefore that the two hypertensions are not so different as they seem. Possibly the renin system acts much more by suppressing the antipressor function of the kidney than it does by directly elevating pressure. Still, the volume and sodium dependence of "renoprival hypertension" are consistent with some less complicated mechanism.

It is well to remember that chronic renal hypertension in dogs is partly sustained by upward "resetting" of moderator nerves, so that they tend to buffer blood pressure at high rather than normal levels. Thus, what started out as a renal hypertension continues as a predominantly neurogenic hypertension. Certainly the returns are not all in; altered neural regulation and impaired renal antipressor activity may account for persistence of hypertension in the seeming absence of significant pressor amounts of circulating angiotensin.

Angiotensin shows an interesting direct effect on excretory function in many hypertensives, in whom it induces an osmotic diuresis of salt and water; in normal subjects it reduces excretion of both. Its diuretic effect in hypertensives is somewhat irregular and more constant in Peartt's observations than in ours.

To us the phenomenon is reminiscent of our finding with del Greco and McCubbin that renin is regularly a cause of intense osmotic saluresis in dogs with sectioned moderator (buffer) nerves. It also brings to mind the observation by Miles and de Wardener that many hypertensives, but few normotensives, often show an "emotional" diuresis of salt and water when frightened or excited. Perhaps the explanation, when found, may bear on basic mechanisms of hypertension. It may simply result from the fact that a hypertensive's capacitance system is already reduced in capacity and that angiotensin vasoconstriction wrings the fluid out, much as hypertonic saline loads are rapidly excreted by hypertensive subjects.

Erythropoietin

Another endocrine function of kidney is the formation of a substance, still poorly characterized, that has to do with red cell formation. Clinically, the lack of formation of this substance may account for the anemias of patients with severe renal damage and, when produced in excess, for the polycythemias that have been described in patients with hypernephroma and with renal cysts.

Clinical Manifestations of Renal Disease

Any means of examination that will point to the presence or absence of renal disease is, broadly speaking, a test of renal function. In the strict sense this term applies only to the quantitative tests, principles of which have been reviewed; clinically, it includes qualitative and semiquantitative procedures which are usually positive in the presence of renal disease. Consideration of the latter has been deferred to this heading, which concerns primarily the phenomena of renal disease rather than "tests" as such.

These phenomena can be conveniently grouped as (1) proteinuria, hematuria, pyuria and cylindruria; (2) hyposthenuria, oliguria and anuria; (3) renal edema and the nephrotic syndrome; (4) renal hypertension and hypertensive disease; (5) excretory failure and uremia.

Proteinuria and the Organized Sediment

Proteinuria. Urine protein estimations are usually semiquantitative only (e.g., heat and acetic acid); quantitative measurement (e.g., Shevky-Stafford) of proteinuria per unit time (usually 24 hours) is almost as convenient and much more interpretable. New urine protein test strips facilitate estimates which are fairly quantitative.

The protein content of normal urine is small and, by specific measurements, appears to be about 50 mg. daily. The usual test commonly indicates normal excretions of 50 to 100 mg. daily; the smaller part of this is albumin derived from normal seepage and the rest from membrane desquamation, diapedesis and secretion of accessory glands; in the absence of lower urinary tract disease which would account for increased contributions of this sort, proteinuria in excess of 100 mg. daily is presumed to be abnormal and of renal origin. The significance of quantitative estimates is such that those who say they are forced (?) to rely on semiquantitative tests should find for themselves quantitative means of reference by performing the tests on normal urine with added albumin or plasma. As a guide, in the heat and acetic acid test, "trace" should correspond to about 0.3 to 0.5 gm. per liter, + to 0.5 to 1, ++ 1 to 3, +++ to 3 to 8, and ++++ (boils *solid*) to 10 gm. per liter or more.

The mechanism of proteinuria was illustrated in Figure 29–3. It is due either to a capillary leak greater than the (presumed) maximum of 30 mg. per 100 ml. of glomerular filtrate which the tubules can normally absorb or to diminished proximal tubular capacity for colloid ingestion.

Thus visualized, proteinurias are preglomerular, glomerular or tubular in origin.

PREGLOMERULAR. A normally retentive glomerulus permits the escape of circulating colloids of low molecular size. Thus earlier dextran solutions were composed of a "cut" of molecules of varying span, and the total amount excreted depended on the average molecular weight of the sample; because the smaller particles will pass through parts of the glomerular surface which will retain larger particles, dextran clearance was high at first and decreased progressively as the smaller molecules were excreted. The comparatively large hemoglobin molecule (molecular weight 68,800) can pass through about 12 per cent of the glomerular surface (inulin through 100 per cent); the relatively great glomerular permeability to hemoglobin as compared to albumin (molecular weight 72,000) presumably reflects differences in the shape and charge of the hemoglobin molecule. With hemoglobin the amount which will appear in urine depends in part on the amount which the tubules can reabsorb. Hemoglobin, which is normally of constant molecular size, shows a "threshold" at about 100 mg. per 100 ml. of plasma, which at normal rates of filtration reflects tubular absorption of about 20 mg. per 100 ml. of filtrate. Demonstration of haptoglobulin binding of hemoglobin may require revision of this estimate.

The excretion of abnormal amounts of a circulating protein of somewhat smaller size occurs in the case of Bence Jones proteinuria. Bence Jones protein, an immunoglobulin, is formed in excess by the proliferating plasma cells in certain patients having multiple myeloma. It is unique in that it precipitates between 45° and 60°C. as urine is heated, then becomes soluble as the urine is heated further to boiling, but reprecipitates with cooling between 60° and 45°C. It has been shown that Bence Jones protein consists of light polypeptide chains having molecular weights of about 22,000 for the monomer and 44,000 for the dimer, in which pairs of light chains are linked by intermolecular disulfide bonds. Light chains isolated from myeloma protein and light chains from normal human immunoglobulin of the Ig G class (7S, γ_2-globulin) appear to be identical with those of Bence Jones protein and show similar reversible thermosolubility properties. Indeed, from both urine and plasma of normal individuals low molecular weight globulins have been isolated which resemble the light chains of normal Ig G human globulin, i.e., they appear to be the normal counterparts of Bence Jones protein.

Thus the variables which determine "renal threshold" in preglomerular proteinuria are (1) the size, shape and charge of the abnormal plasma protein, (2) the rate of glomerular filtration, and (3) tubular capacity for protein pinocytosis, while (4) glomerular permeability is assumed to be normal and constant.

GLOMERULAR. This assumption is not true in the relatively common, glomerular proteinurias; in these the essential defect is focal increase in glomerular permeability. The "pore" concept of the glomerulus supposes that the surface is not uniform, but is interrupted by "pores" of varying size, few of which are large enough to permit the passage of albumin molecules, while perhaps 20 per cent of the surface is permeable to a small molecule like myoglobin (molecular weight 16,400). Glomerular proteinuria would then arise from the creation of pores of abnormal size. Such can readily be visualized as occurring in damaged glomeruli in hypertensive or primary glomerular disease; that this focal change, rather than an overall increase in glomerular permeability, is the case is suggested by the association between proteinuria in these conditions and impaired excretion of a marginally filterable grass polysaccharide (Beattie and Corcoran). Glomerular origin of proteinuria in malignant hypertension is suggested by the fact that arterial pressure—which is a large factor in determining increased intraglomerular pressure—is a partial determinant of the rate of this form of proteinuria (Piette and Corcoran). Further, in the nephrotic syndrome comparisons of albumin clearance (measured directly or from excretion of Evans blue and concurrent filtration rate) usually show that the filtrate contains more than 30 mg. of protein per 100 ml., presumably because of increased capillary leak. Electron microscopy has been particularly informative in glomerular disease. Acute glomerulonephritis is shown to be associated with intense endothelial cell proliferation and, apparently as a consequence, with formation of irregular, thickened bands of *lamina densa* in bars and strands, with monocytic aggregation. In contrast, in the nephrotic syndrome the endothelial cells and lamina seem relatively intact, but there is swelling and disorganization of the pedicles of podocytes. Presumably the variations in interpedicle slits determine proteinuria in the latter, and the changes in lamina densa account for hematuria and proteinuria in the former.

The common association of increased capillary leak with a diminished or damaged surface is, at first glance, paradoxical. However, the physical factors of pressure and permeability which determine true filtration through a normally retentive glomerular surface of water and dissolved substances up to the size of inulin or grass polysaccharide are basically different from those which would permit a leak of occasional protein molecules through a focus of diminished retentiveness. They are qualitatively distinct and quantitatively of widely different orders; thus, at a plasma albumin concentration of 4 gm. per 100 ml., proteinuria of 20 gm. daily represents a plasma albumin clearance of 0.5 liter daily, while filtration rate is 360 times greater. One way of visualizing the phenomenon is in terms of the separation of a precipitate (e.g., $BaSO_4$) from water. When the suspension is poured into a filter formed by one layer of normally retentive paper, the precipitate is wholly retained and filtrate formed at a normal, rapid rate; when the filter is formed with two layers of the same paper, but pierced at one or two points with a pin, the total *rate* of true filtration is diminished, but some particles of precipitate appear in the filtrate. This reflects the common situation in which glomerular disease diminishes filtration rate by decreasing average *permeability,* while it results in proteinuria as a result of focal capillary lesions which here and there increase *porosity.*

Because glomerular proteinuria is due to abnormal spans of porosity, the glomerulus still shows differential retentiveness of larger molecules, and the bulk of the proteinuria consists of serum albumin molecules, while the larger globulins are retained. The amounts of globulin which enter the urine vary from case to case, and, because the composition of urinary protein is thus variable, the term "proteinuria" is preferred to the common term "albuminuria." Presumably entry of molecules larger than albumin (such as globulin) into glomerular filtrate reflects a more severe change in porosity than a true albuminuria, and therefore a more serious and less reversible disease.

TUBULAR PROTEINURIA. Proteinuria of tubular origin results from diminished capacity of renal tubular cells to take up and digest protein. This impairment may be due to structural or functional damage of essential cellular mechanisms or to surfeit. The latter situation was noted as a presumptive explanation of the accumulations of granules, vacuoles and lipid in tubule cells in many proteinuric states. Clearly, when cellular mechanisms of protein ingestion are fully occupied in digestion, capacity for further uptake of protein must suffer. Consequently, glomerular or preglomerular proteinurias have an associated tubular component. This is most apparent in the case of hemoglobin; in rats, injected bovine albumin passes through the glomerulus and is subject to cellular ingestion; during this time the "renal threshold" for injected hemoglobin is decreased because of decreased tubular absorption. Prolonged hemoglobinuria is associated with a decrease in the "renal threshold" for hemoglobin and with albuminuria because of decreased tubular reabsorption of both hemoglobin and the albumin of normal glomerular filtrate. The initial proteinuria of mercury bichloride or bichromate poisoning reflects tubular injury. Possibly some of the proteinuria which occurs during renal ischemia is due to functional impairment of these mechanisms, although such situations are associated with hemodynamic changes which could of themselves alter glomerular porosity. Thus proteinuria primarily of tubular origin is probably uncommon and usually inconsequential; there seem to occur cases of "familial proteinuria" that may be tubular, but these must be rare and this comforting diagnosis cautiously reserved.

CLINICAL CONSIDERATIONS. From what has been said, most proteinurias are evidences of glomerular damage, primary or secondary, structural or functional; some reflect the presence of abnormal circulating proteins, and a few are primarily tubular. Altered tubular mechanisms contribute to the extent of preglomerular or glomerular proteinurias, which they may augment by rejection of albumin which would be normally absorbed. Consequently, the mechanisms are hard to sort out in detail in a given case and, for clinical purposes, the proteinurias are grouped descriptively.

Thus considered, *proteinurias* are either *inconstant* or *constant.* The inconstant proteinurias are *occasional, postural* or *orthostatic,* and *exertional.* The association of proteinuria with severe exercise in normal people is usually obvious. Proteinuria which is demonstrably occasional and transient may be due to some hemodynamic change, such as the proteinuria which may be associated with a cold pressor test, with emotional disturbance or central nervous injury, or to transient change in glomerular porosity occasioned by allergy, fever or infection.

Orthostatic proteinuria is a poor term; many proteinurias are either increased or even made overt by standing and exercise. *Lordotic* proteinuria would be a better term, since the condition is associated with exaggerated lumbar lordosis which, in some, causes the liver to compress the inferior vena cava. The condition is usually seen in normal, spare, adolescent males, in whom it tends to remit as their muscles and postural habitus catch up with their growth. It is benign and recoverable and important only as a source of disqualifications for military service or life insurance.

The condition is detected by having the patient void a timed urine specimen one hour after going to bed; he should void again on waking, while still in bed; he is then placed in exaggerated lordosis by putting small pillows under the small of his back for 30 minutes, when he collects another specimen. The proteinuria will thus be established as constant (present in the three specimens), re-

TABLE 29–4. COUNTS OF URINARY SEDIMENT IN NORMAL SUBJECTS FREE FROM RENAL DISEASE (THE RANGE GIVEN BY ADDIS USUALLY ACCEPTED AS NORMAL).

Group	RBC Millions per 12 Hours	WBC Millions per 12 Hours	Casts Thousands per 12 Hours	Author
Adult	0–0.5	0.03–1.8	0–4	Addis
Adult	0–1.5	0.02–0.3	0–9	Goldring
Adult	0–1.1	0.05–4	0–9	Naeraa
Children	0–0.13	0.009–2.8	0–12	Lyttle
Aged males	0–2.3	0.2–2	0–15	Naeraa

lated to the erect posture primarily (specimen one) or to lordosis (specimen three) by quantitative measurement in grams per hour. Proteinuria, regardless of its cause, will usually be accentuated by the erect posture.

More significant among the inconstant proteinurias are the bursts of protein excretion which occur in some patients with essential hypertension, since these often mark eruptions of nephrosclerotic activity, and the exercise proteinuria that occurs in congestive heart failure. Both presumably reflect renal ischemia, which, in heart failure, is primarily functional.

The constant proteinurias are of more general concern, since they are the rule in patients with renal disease. As noted, these are usually intensified by the factors which, of themselves, result in inconstant proteinuria. Thus, during recovery from acute glomerulonephritis, *orthostatic* proteinuria, not increased during lordosis, is not uncommon, and, as suggested, proteinuria of severe hypertension is partly a function of blood pressure. Such variations are presumably related to temporary, recoverable increases in glomerular porosity due to stretching of glomerular capillaries; the interpretation is by analogy with the albuminuria which can be induced by large infusions of albumin in normal people or the administration of renin or angiotensin to normal animals, notably rats. Dogs seem to have more "retentive" glomerular membranes than either rats or people. In general, the presence of constant proteinuria is presumptive evidence of a glomerular lesion which has created foci of increased porosity. Its ultimate significance depends on its cause and, to some extent, on its degree. Large, constant proteinurias are usually associated with the nephrotic syndrome, to which their discussion will be deferred.

The Organized Sediment. The principal elements are casts and red and white blood cells. Occasionally, adventitious components, such as sperm, olive pits and pomegranate seeds, may be found. The customary method of examination and characterization in "units per high power field" (observed with various objectives and oculars, from drops of great or little thickness, obtained with more or less dilution by random observation of a casual sample of urine of uncontrolled concentration and uncertain vintage) leaves almost everything to be desired. In spite of this, people still are encouraged to futile argument as to the occurrence of these elements in normal urine, basing their contentions on these inexcusable methods, which are practically throwbacks to urinoscopy. The fact is (Table 29–4) that urine of healthy people may contain these elements in considerable numbers so that there is no substitute for their enumeration by sediment count.

This technique was established by Addis and recently reviewed by Lippman. Our custom is to do the counts on aliquots from a 10 cc. portion of a freshly voided 3-hour morning urine collected during the last 3 hours of a 15-hour period of fluid deprivation. This is centrifuged at 1600 revolutions a minute for 10 minutes in an Addis sediment tube. The sediment is suspended evenly in a varying volume of supernatant (more when there is much sediment, but usually 0.2 ml.), and a drop of the mixed suspension placed under the cover slip on each side of a standard hemocytometer slide. Casts are searched for under low power with reduced illumination in the 0.9 square millimeter of each side and cells counted under high power in the central 0.1 square millimeter of each side. The multiplying factors are then calculated from the volume of urine counted, its dilution and the duration of the collection, so that results can be expressed in units per 12 or 24 hours.

Casts are literally coagulated protein casts of the tubule lumen in which they were formed. Hence proteinuria, diffuse as in glomerulonephritis, or lobular as in nephrosclerosis, is a usual primary condition of cast formation. The fact that some appear in the urine leaves open the question of how many are left behind to obstruct the tubule.

Casts are formed in distal tubules and collecting ducts; this localization is determined by the concentration and acidification of urine in these sites, but these are not the sole determinants of cast formation. The variables considered by Oliver are (1) osmotic concentration of the urine, (2) concentration and nature of its protein, (3) hydrogen ion concentration, (4) concentration of an unidentified substance (X-body), which is possibly a polysaccharide. Other factors being equal, increases in (1) and, paradoxically, (2) favor stability of the urinary colloid, while increases in (3) and (4) create instability which favors precipitation. Globulins by definition require some minimum salt concentration to be maintained in solution; consequently globulins tend more than albumin to precipitate out in casts, and those globulins of very low isoelectric point and high precipitability, such as form in myeloma, precipitate out even in the proximal tubules, where hydrogen ion concentration is low and the tubule fluid still isotonic.

Most casts are washed away as they form by intratubular pressure, which pushes them on and dilates tubules around them. However, collecting tubules may form as traps to retain them, and renal disease with interstitial fibrosis may distort tubules and prevent their discharge. As a result, Oliver considers casts to have "a most important part in the production of alterations of organ architecture." Hence the more serious prognosis of proteinuria in which there is considerable globulinuria may result not only from the greater severity of the glomerular lesion—as suggested above—but also from the greater tendency of globulins to precipitate out in the tubules. Hemoglobin and myoglobin are similarly precipitable; pigment casts due to one or the other occur in a wide variety of conditions that cause acute renal failure, such as "acute tubular necrosis" (Oliver). This latter condition was formerly termed "lower nephron nephrosis." In its initial phases one usually finds large or small amounts of circulating hemoglobin or myoglobin, decreased renal blood flow, filtration rate and urine flow. The extent to which the heme pigment casts obstruct or specifically injure and thus contribute to renal failure and tubular necrosis is unknown and probably widely variable. In some situations, as after large mismatched transfusion or in black-water fever or severe myoglobinuria, obstruction and tubular damage (liberated ferriheme or ferric ion?) by the pigment may be a large factor. However, in most of these conditions the main event is renal ischemia and tubular necrosis is primarily ischemic; pigment casts merely mark the kidney as one which has been subject to these abnormalities during hemoglobinemia

or myoglobin release. "Crush syndrome" can be simulated in rats by limb crush and myo-hemoglobin injection; an osmotic diuretic (Na_2SO_4 or mannitol) was found partly protective by Corcoran and Page (1947).

The noncellular casts are classified as hyaline, finely and coarsely granular, waxy, fatty and pigmented. The distinction between hyaline and finely granular casts depends largely on the conditions of their precipitation, granularity being more evident when the urine is more acid. The "granules" of some granular casts frequently represent the remnants of degenerate cells. Some coarsely granular materials are actually accumulations of lipid in which the presence of cholesterol may be identified with the polarizing microscope. Such casts are common in the nephrotic syndrome. The nature of "waxy" casts is obscure. Possibly they represent lipoproteins which have not yet separated. Pigmented casts are either common types of casts colored with bilirubin or are composed of heme pigment. Casts of heme pigment are usually dense and short. Their granularity sometimes gives the impression that they are composed of degenerate red blood cell aggregates.

Cellular casts are casts in which blood, pus or renal epithelial cells have adhered in the renal tubule, so that they testify to the presence of cellular exudation in nephrons. Lastly, *renal failure* casts are distinguished by great breadth and comparatively short length. They are formed in the terminal collecting ducts —the ducts of Bellini. Cast formation can hardly occur in this position, where the flow of urine is normally rapid, unless flow has been slowed. Such slowing is most commonly the result of death or disability of the majority of nephrons that lead from the lobule into the duct in which the cast is formed. Consequently their presence in urine is evidence of severe structural loss.

Hematuria. Red blood cells may be liberated in either the upper or lower urinary tract. The simple two-glass voiding test is commonly used to establish the cause as a lesion of the lower tract (verumontanitis, seminal vesiculitis, prostatitis). Cystography and cystoscopy may establish the source as vesical, and ureteral catheterization may determine whether prevesical bleeding is due to unilateral or bilateral lesions of the upper tract. Supportive diagnostic evidence is of course obtained from the history and clinical features, from tests of renal function and from intravenous and retrograde urography.

Typically, hematuria due to lesions of the

upper tract is characterized by an even suspension of the red blood cells in the urine, so that the urine may become smoky and brownish because of the suspended cells in which some red hemoglobin has been changed to bronze methemoglobin. Such gross hematuria is easily differentiated from hemoglobinuria and myoglobinuria, in which heme pigments are in solution, by centrifuging the urine and examining the sediment. Hematuria which is less severe may be diagnosed either chemically or microscopically. Chemical procedures are superficially attractive because they seem convenient and quantitative. Actually, results cannot be easily evaluated because of interference with the benzidine reaction by vitamin C and other constituents of urinary sediment. Microscopy is therefore more accurate. The result it yields may be "semiquantitative" (cells per high power field) or quantitative. The method of choice is the Addis count of the sediment, especially when hematuria is scant and its detection significant. A simple, semiquantitative alternative for ward or office is a count of cells present in the ruled area (0.1 cu. mm.) of a hemacytometer, using fresh morning urine without centrifugation. Such counts are most useful in following the day to day course of acute glomerulonephritis.

Hematuria of prevesical origin is evidence of a lesion in the renal pelvis, tubule system or glomerular apparatus. The presence with it of red cell casts is presumptive evidence that the lesion involves the renal parenchyma. The causative lesions may be functional, as in the faint hematurias which may result from renal vasoconstriction, whether from effort, extrarenal trauma, injection of epinephrine, or congestion—as in congestive heart failure—or may be due to temporarily increased vascular permeability, as from injection of histamine, or to vigorous treatment with heparin. So-called essential hematuria is believed to be due to anomalies of the submucosal venules of the renal papillae. Transient bleeding may be caused by trauma to renal parenchyma or tubular mucosa (renal rupture, crystalluria, lithuria). The remaining causes of hematuria are various forms of vascular damage, either primary, as in hypertensive arteriolar disease, glomerulonephritis, polyarteritis, and so forth, or parenchymal disease, as in pyelonephritis, renal tuberculosis, sickle cell disease, renal infarction and neoplasia.

The degree of hematuria is an index of the activity of the underlying lesion in "medical" types of renal disease. Thus the severe inflammatory glomerular change in acute hemorrhagic glomerulonephritis is characterized by gross hematuria. The attenuated exudative lesions of chronic glomerulonephritis cause persistent microscopic hematuria and pyuria; exacerbations and remissions can be estimated from the counts of the urinary sediment. Similarly the slow course of occlusive vascular renal disease in essential hypertension causes at most only a slight and persistent increase in the sediment count, while the acute necrotizing arteriolar lesions of malignant hypertension may lead to gross urinary bleeding. The lesions in these conditions are glomerular or preglomerular, and hematuria is nearly always bilateral, since they occur equally in both kidneys. In contrast, unilateral hematuria is prima facie evidence for the presence of a unilateral postglomerular lesion which may be as benign as "essential" hematuria or as ominous as chronic pyelonephritis, renal tuberculosis or carcinoma. In "malignant hypertension" it suggests unilateral main renal artery occlusion disease with contralateral necrotizing or malignant nephrosclerosis.

Pyuria. The conditions which lead to the appearance of abnormal numbers of white blood cells in bladder urine differ from those which cause hematuria in that they are all exudative and none of them is due to vessel rupture. Localization of the lesion is carried out in the same manner as with hematuria, and, as with the latter, the presence of casts to which the cells are adherent is presumptive evidence of a parenchymatous focus.

The most common cause is infection, although the sterile exudates and degenerative changes of chronic glomerulonephritis or other destructive renal lesions may lead to increased numbers of white blood cells in the urine. The comparatively large number of white cells which may be present in normal urine are presumably derived from ameboid wandering of leukocytes through the mucosa of urinary epithelium, and are principally polymorphonuclear leukocytes. Unfortunately, the recent trend towards critical diagnostic examination of the cellular content of exudates has not been as successfully applied to urinary sediment, largely because of difficulties in staining. Thus, while it seems likely that the differential study of urinary white cells may lead to new diagnostic criteria, the lack of good data requires that the significance of pyuria be evaluated almost entirely from the accompanying clinical and urinary abnormalities.

Enzymes. Acute renal injuries may be associated with increased outputs of enzymes of renal origin, many of them in cellular debris. Thus, in rats, x-irradiation of the kidney provokes a large increase in alkaline phosphatase in urine, with concurrent depletion from tubular cells. Estimates of lactic dehydrogenase in the urine of patients with chronic renal disease suggest an association with the disease process. However, such tests are still much in the exploratory phase.

Hyposthenuria, Oliguria, Anuria. Hyposthenuria signifies inability to form hypertonic urine. Its mechanism has been discussed and shown to be either neurogenic (hypothalamico-hypophyseal) or renal.

Renal hyposthenuria results from suppression or permanent loss of distal and collecting tubular ability to concentrate (or sometimes to dilute) isotonic tubular fluid. A major defect occurs in sicklemia and is attributable to occlusion of medullary vessels and/or ischemia due to sickling therein with resultant increased medullary blood viscosity. In hypertensive renal disease some of the defect seems to result from ischemia created by reversible vasoconstriction, and is to this degree recoverable. However, major defects in concentrating power are usually associated with irrevocable loss of nephrons. In hypertension increased intraglomerular pressure tends commonly to maintain filtration rate at levels high in relation to renal blood flow or residual functioning tissue and may increase relative medullary blood flow and thus impair concentration more than filtration. Hence, in this condition, a concentration test of renal function is commonly a more sensitive clinical index of the presence and extent of incipient renal damage than is the urea clearance, which depends on filtration rate. Reduction of concentrating power in hypertensive disease is sometimes much greater than would be estimated from other indices of functional capacity, such as excretory Tm_{PAH}.

Azotemia also results in excretion of urine which tends to be isotonic, but, in this case, the mechanism is one of osmotic diuresis, and concentrating power may be quite normal in residual nephrons.

Symptomatically, hyposthenuria results in nocturnal formation of a large volume of urine of low specific gravity, i.e., nocturia. It is important to remember that nocturia has other causes. It may be habitual and reflect an insomniac's loss of the normal rhythm of concentration and osmolal excretion. More significantly, it may be an early sign of congestive heart failure. In this latter situation, as in famine edema, latent edema accumulates hypostatically during the day and is discharged during the night. Exercise and insomnia lead the patient in a truly vicious cycle.

Another consequence of hyposthenuria is that the minimal urinary volume required for excretion of the urinary osmotic load is increased. A normal person can excrete some 35 gm. of urinary solid in a 24-hour volume of about 500 cc. at a specific gravity of about 1.028, while a patient with hyposthenuria may require three times as much water to excrete the same metabolic load. Failure to provide for this minimal volume results in azotemia and uncomfortable deyhdration and, in the presence of advanced renal disease, may precipitate uremia. The summation of true hyposthenuria with azotemic diuresis is dramatically demonstrated in the severe diuresis which may occur during recovery from acute tubular necrosis, especially when the injury is largely medullary, as in Far Eastern epidemic hemorrhagic fever (Russ. nephrosonephritis); azotemia accumulated during the anuric phase contributes the factor of osmotic diuresis, and tubular injury causes impairment of concentrating power; the result is a situation in which urine flow may reach levels of several liters daily but in which tolerance to excess fluid loads may be very poor and pulmonary edema easily precipitated.

Anuria is failure to form urine, while *oliguria* is failure to form urine in amounts sufficient to meet metabolic demand. The daily urine volume at which oliguria begins is therefore a function of concentrating power and solute load and varies from 400 to about 1500 cc. per day. Anuria due to renal lesions begins or terminates in oliguria, so that the two may be regarded as one.

Oliguria may be (1) extrarenal, as in dehydration, cardiac failure, arterial hypotension or painful stimulation, (2) renal, and the result of damage or loss of renal tissue, or (3) obstructive. The obstructive anurias may be intrarenal, from obstruction of renal tubules and collecting ducts, or extrarenal and due to extrinsic or intrinsic obstruction of the lower urinary tract.

A clue to the mechanism primarily at fault is given by the specific gravity. From this aspect, oliguria may be considered either hypersthenuric or hyposthenuric. In hypersthenuric oliguria the volume of urine formed is inadequate, and the specific gravity is high, i.e., more than 1.023, whereas it is only 1.010 in hyposthenuric oliguria.

Hypersthenuric oliguria can result from inadequate intake of water or from a decrease of glomerular filtration which does not otherwise severely affect tubular function. Such a decrease in glomerular filtration may result from decreased arterial pressure, renal blood flow and filtration, i.e., from circulatory failure or diffuse glomerular lesions.

In contrast, hyposthenuric oliguria is an indication that the primary lesion is one which injures or destroys the concentrating power of the renal tubules. Such injury may result from an extrarenal cause, as when in prolonged shock there results renal anoxia, or it may be due to tubular damage by toxins or tubular loss from disease, or to blockage of either intrarenal or extrarenal origin. Thus parenchymal damage is the rule in hyposthenuric oliguria.

More than one mechanism can participate in causing urinary suppression, and, once the injury has been done, the clinical courses of conditions of the most varied origin may be indistinguishable. This is the case in the conditions which have been grouped as "lower nephron nephrosis" or "hemoglobinuric nephrosis" and, more recently, as "acute tubular necrosis." The causes of the condition range from trauma (burns, battle wounds, hypotension, crush injury, obstetrical accident) through mismatched transfusions, other acute hemolytic states, some infections, notably Far Eastern hemorrhagic fever, and a variety of intoxications (mercury bichloride, ethylene glycol, carbon tetrachloride and sulfonamides). Oliver's studies indicate that there are two basic types of renal injury; the one, often associated with circulating nephrotoxins, is ischemic necrosis which occurs diffusely in the epithelium of the *proximal* convoluted tubules, but which leaves the basement membrane intact as an orienting scaffold for regeneration of the tubule; the other is focal disruption of nephrons, proximal and distal, as the result of locally intense cortical ischemia. In the primary atraumatic injuries the primary lesion is nephrotoxic, but secondary events (vomiting, dehydration, prostration) superimpose the lesions of renal ischemia. Both types of injury are followed by regeneration of the necrotic epithelium; however, loss of the continuity of the basement membrane at the sites of tubulorrhexis may interfere with orderly reformation of a functioning nephron. When regeneration is sufficiently advanced, the tubular fluid, some of which had been passively diffusing back into the blood through the sites of tubular necrosis (functional glomerulotubulovenous fistulas), again

begins to appear as urine. However, the damage to the kidney is such that there ensues a hyposthenuric state with osmotic diuresis which is also complicated by inability of the kidney to regulate the output of electrolytes. This diuretic phase subsides over several days or even weeks (hemorrhagic fever) until, at the end of 6 or 12 months, functional recovery is nearly complete.

Acute renal failure uncomplicated by major trauma or infection is usually recoverable; renal failures complicated by major wounds and infection impose a heavy mortality (about 50 per cent) under best available conditions, including dialysis, partly because of the nature of the injury which may be inconsistent with prolonged survival.

Edema of Renal Origin

Strictly, this term includes all edema due to excretory inadequacy. Thus it would comprise edema due to overtreatment with parenteral saline solution and the edema of congestive cardiac failure, for both result from relative inadequacies of urinary excretion. But, in the more restricted sense of this discussion, edema of renal origin is taken to mean edema which is part of the natural evolution of renal disease; it includes the edema of acute glomerulonephritis, that of eclamptogenic toxemia of pregnancy, and the nephrotic syndrome.

Edema in Acute Nephritis and Eclamptogenic Toxemia. The clinical features of *acute glomerulonephritis* and *severe toxemia of pregnancy* are strikingly similar, and it seems likely that some of the underlying mechanisms are identical. Edema in these conditions begins in a sudden increase in interstitial fluid and plasma volumes with rapid gain in body weight. Clinically, the edema is "rubbery" and is characteristically evident in the loose subcutaneous tissues around the eyes. The hypervolemia often mimics congestive heart failure.

Two mechanisms seem principally at fault. One is a decrease in glomerular filtration, the result of glomerular exudation and, to some degree, of afferent renal vasoconstriction or swelling. This change is not associated with equivalent tubular damage, and, at least in the early stages of these diseases, renal blood flow is well maintained or even increased. The result of this disparate renal change is glomerulotubular imbalance. The amount of sodium filtered is decreased; the still intact renal tubular structure reabsorbs sodium and water at approximately a normal absolute rate. This results in hypersthenuric oliguria, with retention of sodium and water.

The distribution and character of the edema in toxemia of pregnancy indicate that another mechanism plays some part in localizing the fluid accumulations. The occurrence of signs of generalized damage to small vessels, as in the retina, brain and heart, suggests that the second factor in the edema is exudative, probably as a result of severe subcutaneous arteriolar constriction with capillary prestasis and peristasis and/or, as recently demonstrated, widespread microvascular thrombosis.

Hypoproteinemia is usually a minor factor in this form of edema. It is not present at the onset of acute glomerulonephritis, and is only somewhat more common in women with eclamptogenic toxemias, probably because so many of them are poorly nourished, than in those who go through pregnancy without edema. However, hypoproteinemia with nephrotic edema may rapidly supervene as acute glomerular damage persists, and one of us (A.C.C.) has some evidence this may be partly a homeostasis of colloid osmotic pressure.

The Nephrotic Syndrome. The term "nephrotic syndrome" denominates a state characterized by edema, which is accompanied by profuse proteinuria and hypoproteinemia with lipemia, usually measured as hypercholesterolemia. The edema is most obvious in dependent subcutaneous tissue, although measurements of extracellular fluid volume show that it extends throughout the body. It often gives rise to ascites and pleural effusions; there may be renal edema; and it may extend to the submucosa of the intestines, where it can be demonstrated radiologically. Plasma volume is frequently decreased. The edema does not involve significantly the liver, brain or heart.

The nephrotic syndrome appears most commonly in the adult during the intermediate course of chronic glomerulonephritis, and is often the first sign of glomerulonephritis of insidious onset (type II nephritis in Ellis' grouping: pathologically chronic membranous glomerulonephritis). It probably develops in every patient suffering from glomerulonephritis and is certainly a characteristic of the preuremic course in at least three-fourths of the cases. In contrast, the nephrotic syndrome is uncommon in renal disease due to hypertensive arteriolosclerosis and in chronic pyelonephritis. It is characteristic of diabetic intercapillary glomerulosclerosis, in which it

persists during uremia. It is not uncommon in the "lupus kidney" of systemic lupus erythematosus. Most of the aspects of the nephrotic syndrome appear in the late stage of renal amyloidosis. Prolonged states of toxic nephrosis due to various causes elicit some of its components. Finally, it may be the solitary manifestation of an entity called idiopathic nephrosis, which seems to be frequently a recoverable disorder of podocytes which is more common in childhood.

The principal cause of edema in the nephrotic syndrome is sodium retention which is associated with secondary hyperaldosteronism. In addition the decrease in plasma protein content results in increased filtration into and decreased reabsorption of fluid from tissue spaces so far as it decreases plasma colloid osmotic pressure. The osmotic activity of the albumin fraction is roughly four times that of the globulin, so that hypoalbuminemia is a major cause of hypoproteinemic edema, and the primary mechanism is a net continuing increase in formation of interstitial fluid at the relative and dynamic expense of plasma volume. The onset of edema therefore shows no correlation with total plasma globulin content, which, in this condition, tends to remain constant or is often slightly increased. Actually, gamma globulin is typically low and the lipoprotein beta globulin is increased. Edema appears in most adults at plasma albumin concentrations of about 2.5 gm. per 100 ml., which correspond to a total protein content of 5.5 gm. per 100 ml. These critical levels are 0.5 to 1 gm. lower in children, who have better tissue elasticity and perhaps lymph flow, than adults.

It is tempting to attribute the hypoproteinemia to a negative protein balance due to urinary loss of protein (loss and lack theory). Undoubtedly, this is an important mechanism, for the loss of 10 gm. of protein in the urine daily is roughly equivalent to the drainage of the albumin from more than 200 ml. of plasma. It is likely that a loss of this kind may surpass the possibilities of protein regeneration in some circumstances. The apparent limiting factors in regeneration are (1) protein intake and (2) protein synthesis, especially the synthesis of albumin. The intake of protein in such cases is unfortunately too often limited by the thoughtless, "rule of thumb" prescription of a low protein diet, which adds to lack without controlling loss. It is furthered by anorexia. This is probably the result of edema of the stomach and small bowel, which tends toward a vicious cycle of edema and protein lack. Unfortunately, also, these deficiencies may not be wholly correctable, for prolonged protein loss and lack inhibit the regenerative and synthetic ability of the liver. The dietary factor is therefore obvious, important and deserving of early correction so far as possible by the provision of a diet rich in good biologic protein calculated to give the nonazotemic patient a maintenance intake of at least 1 gm. per kilogram daily of protein plus whatever is needed to supplement urinary loss.

But it is common experience that the diet of these patients may be adequate in all respects and the mechanism of protein synthesis apparently unimpaired, so that nutritional defects are rapidly corrected and protein actually stored, while the hypoproteinemia and edema persist unchanged. Indeed, it is characteristic that the level of plasma protein tends to be unchanged for long periods until some factor, such as mild infection, alters the homeostasis and is sometimes followed by inexplicable loss of edema and increase in plasma protein content. Such is the case in the idiopathic nephrotic syndrome of the child who responds favorably to steroid administration. Again, proteinuria in some patients, especially in those with chronic glomerulonephritis, need not be severe (less than 5 gm. daily), and the diet may be ample for regenerative need, while edema and hypoproteinemia may be as extensive as in patients whose proteinuria is severe. We (A.C.C.) have elsewhere suggested the possibility that hypoproteinemia in the nephrotic syndrome may be due to a lowered "set" of plasma colloid osmotic pressure which would act homeostatically to restore filtration through a poorly functioning glomerular filtering surface. Certainly, in chronic glomerulonephritis, intercapillary glomerulosclerosis or other states in which filtration tends to be disproportionately depressed, a lowered plasma colloid osmotic concentration has the possible advantage that it tends to maintain glomerular filtration in patients in whom calculations show it would be suppressed were the plasma colloid osmotic pressure normal.

However the hypoalbuminemia may originate, the question arises as to the usefulness of intravenous replacement by transfusion of blood or albumin. Plasma volume is usually decreased. Anemia is not the important factor, so that transfusion of blood is not required. Transfusion of plasma or, more specifically, of albumin would seem to be the principal need. Unfortunately, such transfusion can hardly repair the enormous deficit of circulating albumin and, in practice, the excess albumin is rapidly excreted so that there is no lasting change in plasma protein concentration. Colloid infusions, however, tend temporarily to mobilize water from the tissues and dilute plasma electrolytes and thus stimulate water loss in the urine. Such loss is beneficial and clinically indicated insofar as it relieves edema which has become a hazard or a nuisance. Perhaps a major, although usually temporary, benefit of such treatment is the relief of anorexia.

The edema of the nephrotic syndrome has the primary element of sodium retention by the renal tubular cells because of the secondary hyperaldosteronism and is therefore advantageously treated by sodium restriction with careful use of agents such as spironolactone and/or triamterene. Figure 29–9 schematizes the sequence of altered mechanisms which enter into the nephrotic state.

The mechanism of lipemia in the nephrotic syndrome is still obscure. It is not due to deficient thyroid function and it is not an ineffective homeostatic compensation for lowered colloid osmotic pressure. Rather, it may represent the response to renal reabsorption into the blood of nearly all the lipid from the protein which appears in the tubular fluid. Proteinuric urine contains very little lipid. Possibly cells that are protein-stuffed can still hydrolyze lipoproteins and take up the lipid moiety. Hence, in part, their fatty appearance and Bright's "large white" and greasy kidney. Another cause of the visible lipemia is deficiency in the free fatty acid carrier albumin.

The tendency of patients with massive proteinuria to excrete significant amounts of complement has been noted. This, the general low level of nutrition, and resistance probably explain the tendency to infection in nephrosis. Another, possible explanation of low serum complement concentration in patients with chronic glomerulonephritis is that the continuing antigen-antibody reaction which characterizes the disease binds the available complement as it is formed. Especially common, although easily controlled by antibacterials and antibiotics, are erysipeloid infections of the edematous skin of the abdomen, scrotum and face.

Treatment of the nephrotic syndrome with ACTH and/or corticosteroids has now roughly a 15 year background of experience. As with steroid therapy generally (Addison's disease is an exception), the treatment is

EDEMA IN THE NEPHROTIC SYNDROME

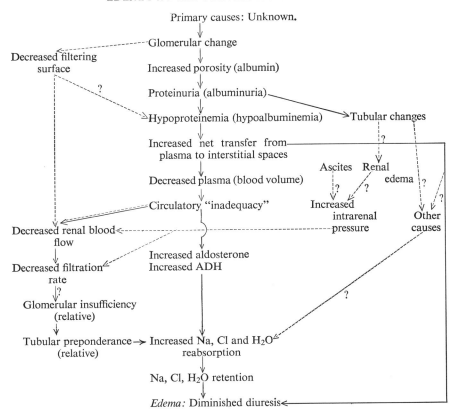

Figure 29–9. Summary of sequential changes in the nephrotic syndrome. (Modified from Eder, Lauson, Chinard, Greif, Cotzias and Van Slyke: J. Clin. Invest., Vol. 33.) Solid lines connect processes occurring in established sequence indicated by arrows; dashed lines connect processes which are still either speculative or of irregular occurrence (e.g., some patients show minimal glomerular lesions and maintain high rates of glomerular filtration.)

wholly empirical. The aim is to reproduce the set of circumstances which, during the course of measles or of a round of typhoid vaccine, precipitates diuresis and remission in a substantial proportion of "nephrotics"; the same rationale supports the use of nitrogen mustard or newer immunosuppressive agents. The net experience is that corticosteroids will induce diuresis, especially in many children and some adults with the idiopathic nephrotic syndrome, and that diuresis is often associated with diminished proteinuria and relief of hypoproteinemia (remission) which, in some cases, is apparently complete and prolonged. Recent experience demonstrates the advantage of prolonged steroid therapy in preventing relapse. However, even when prolonged treatment is duly carried out, a disappointingly large proportion of patients follow the slow, relentless progression into chronic renal failure of chronic glomerulonephritis and lose their edema and hypoproteinemia terminally.

Functional Patterns in Renal Disease

Terminal renal failure of whatever origin involves such losses of functional and structural characteristics that, in chronic conditions, diagnosis and correlation of structural and functional changes are often inconclusive and retrospective. At this stage, using Oliver's phrase, "the kidney is not a kidney," but a barely recognizable something else, although Bricker postulates that some few nephrons are intact. This is likely in pyelonephritis.

Earlier in their courses renal diseases have more or less characteristic effects on functions, some of which were noted above.

Essential Hypertension

The earliest change in function in essential hypertension is really no change at all. Plasma flow, filtration rate, tubular excretory and reabsorptive capacities, as well as protein and sediment tests, are all normal, because there has occurred an increase in afferent, presumably arteriolar, resistance that maintains a normal intraglomerular pressure and rate of blood flow in the face of increased arterial pressure. As noted before, some of this increased resistance may depend on increased peripheral cortical viscous resistance, with increased plasma skimming into deep glomeruli.

Persistence or increased severity of the hypertensive state intensifies this change, increasing afferent resistance in part by causing arteriolosclerosis; whether by release of renin from stretched "J-G" bodies and formation of angiotensin or otherwise, there also occurs an increase in efferent resistance and intraglomerular pressure; increased vascular resistance depresses blood flow and increased intraglomerular pressure increases the filtered fraction ("filtration fraction" = filtration rate/plasma flow) and results in glomerular injury that causes minor proteinuria and cylindruria, although filtration rate is well maintained. Levels of Tm_{PAH} tend to fluctuate downward at this stage, but to a lesser degree than plasma flow; glucose reabsorption is well maintained; concentration tests often show some impairment. Administration of a load of hypertonic NaCl solution intravenously results in more rapid saluresis than occurs in normal persons. Increasing severity of the hypertension tends to speed the rate of these changes, although progress of renal damage in sequential observations (A.C.C.) seems often to be more episodic than linearly progressive.

The syndrome of malignant hypertension, which may develop at fairly adequate but usually at low levels of excretory function, intensifies all these changes and, untreated, results in more or less rapidly progressive functional deterioration; proteinuria is the rule and bursts of gross with continuing microscopic hematuria common.

Adequate control of moderately severe and severe hypertension tends to stabilize function and prevent further deterioration. A few patients show very distinct improvement. Another few, after a period of stabilization, slowly progress into renal failure, apparently as the result of fibrous hyperplasia of larger renal arteries. The nephrosclerosis that has occurred causes profound changes in architecture of many nephrons, with formation of irregularities and dilatations that provide foci of potential stasis. It is therefore not surprising that patients who have these renal lesions show an increased rate of pyelonephritis in the absence of detectable ob-struction in the lower urinary tract. In brief, pyelonephritis may be primary in hypertension, but it seems to us, as to Oliver, more often secondary, with the nephrosclerotic horse pulling the pyelonephritic cart. Hence, urine cultures and sediment counts should be done in follow-up as well as at first examination of all hypertensive patients who show signs of renal disease.

Lastly, it should be noted that, in an extensive experience, functional changes in patients with essential hypertension are equal and symmetrical in the two kidneys.

Renal Hypertensions

Renal Arterial Occlusion. Advent of aortography and renal angiography led to recognition of occlusive lesions of renal arteries as causes of onset or exacerbation of hypertension. The proportions of patients having such lesions is not known, and may be between 1 and 5 per cent. The condition is therefore 10 to 50 times more common than pheochromocytoma and is often as remediable.

Lesions may affect main or branch (segmental) arteries and may be unilateral or bilateral; they range from atheromatous plaques or emboli to fibrous hyperplasia in secondary and smaller branches and "fibromuscular" of main and major arteries. One more or less characteristic syndrome has been defined; this is hypertension in early youth with bilateral orificial stenosis of both main renal arteries by fibrous cushions and, usually, some degree of coarctation of the abdominal aorta. Much more common are patients, often with pre-existing hypertension, who suddenly develop hypertension or an exacerbation thereof, as the result of atheromatous occlusion, sometimes with a history of recent flank pain, and occasionally presenting murmurs or thrills over the loins or upper abdomen. Changes in intravenous urograms may not be recognizable; the radioisotope renogram has, perhaps, its best use in screening such patients for subsequent anatomical diagnosis by aortography.

Description of the "Howard test" suggested the possibility of a simple diagnostic and prognostic procedure. In principle, this consists in demonstrating that ureteral urine from one side has a considerably lower volume and sodium content (and higher osmolality) than urine from the other. For reasons outlined above, such a change occurs when there is partial occlusion of one main renal artery; hypertension due to this cause can be cured by appropriate surgical means viz., shunt bypass or endarterectomy. However, in our experience, lesions of main arteries are often bilateral, in which case the *more* affected side gives the "positive test" but relief by by-pass may be only partial. Again, the lesion may be in a branch artery; depending on the mass of kidney affected, there results some depression of functions such as plasma flow and filtration rate, but without noteworthy differences in sodium concentrations or osmolality, so that the functional pattern resembles that found in many patients with bilateral chronic pyelonephritis and is not diagnostic.

Pyelonephritis. Chronic pyelonephritis is common. In Brod's study (1956), it was recognized in 6 per cent of routine autopsies but was not diagnosed and was not associated with lower urinary tract obstruction in two-thirds of cases. It was associated with hypertension in one-third of those with and two-thirds of those without recognized obstructive lesions and the hypertension was not infrequently malignant.

The functional pattern is one of overall depression of plasma flow, filtration rate, tubular excretory and reabsorptive capacities with, commonly, disproportionate decreases in concentration ceilings. Proteinuria is usually less than 2 gm. per 24 hours. One kidney is commonly affected more than the other. A noteworthy recent addition to diagnosis is the quantitative culture, obtained on clean-voided urine without catheterization. Other elements in diagnosis are repeated sediment counts, with demonstration of abnormal viable (vital-staining) leukocytes by the Sternheimer-Malbin or like techniques.

Glomerulonephritis. The basic change is cellular proliferation, basement membrane disorganization and, ultimately, fibrous replacement of glomeruli with atrophy of the rest of the nephron. Acute glomerulonephritis is often associated with an increase in renal plasma flow. However, both acute and chronic lesions result in disproportionate depression of filtration rate and decrease in filtration fraction. Concentrating power is impaired in proportion to overall functional loss and, ultimately, by establishment of azotemic osmotic diuresis.

The glomerular lesion results in proteinuria which may be very great and commonly exceeds levels found in both severe hypertension and chronic pyelonephritis. With this is associated hematuria and increased sediment counts of white and renal epithelial cells that tend to be persistent, rather than episodic

as in pyelonephritis. The lesion in many cases of the nephrotic syndrome is basically a disorganization of podocyte structure and function, which makes for massive proteinuria, without major changes in urine sediment or severe depression of filtering ability, which is sometimes increased. This lesion is reversible, but the condition often continues into proliferative nephritis and renal failure. Other primary glomerular diseases (systemic lupus erythematosus, intercapillary glomerulosclerosis, etc.) yield functional patterns substantially indistinguishable from that of chronic glomerulonephritis and also tend to be associated with a nephrotic state and hypoproteinemia. Ultimately, the relationship between C_{PAH} and true renal plasma flow is severely distorted by nephron hypertrophy and atrophy, so that functional connotations of clearance tests cannot be interpreted in strict physiologic terms.

Tubular Dysfunctions

The human, more than other species, is prone to hereditary tubular dysfunctions, most of them familial, which may affect single or multiple reabsorptive or excretory functions. Renal glycosuria was noted above. Cases have been reported in which, as in the Dalmatian dog, there is hypouricemia due to impaired urate reabsorption. Nephrogenic diabetes insipidus was also noted; it is a disorder of "porosity" of distal and collecting tubules that makes them unresponsive to ADH. Study of these more-or-less "isolated" functional defects has clarified knowledge of some tubular functions; in the case of cystinuria—which had been presumed to be a defect of systemic cystine metabolism—renal studies have shown that there is absence of tubular reabsorption of one set of amino acids, viz., cystine, lysine, arginine and ornithine.

Many of the defects are multiple and sometimes partial, as in the Fanconi syndrome, and several are associated with skeletal lesions, usually with increased phosphate clearance. The number and variety prevents any adequate review. This, and more, is provided in Stanbury, Wyngaarten and Fredrickson (see References). However, the Lignac-Debré-de Toni-Fanconi series, with phosphaturia, glycosuria and aminoaciduria, require special mention because they are sometimes acquired lesions resulting from heavy metal (lead, copper in Wilson's disease) or myeloma. A similar acquired tubular disorder with associated severe renal tubular acidosis occurs following ingestion of degraded tetracycline. The hereditary type is either infantile, appearing about the fifth month and associated with cystinosis or—apparently as an unrelated condition—adult, without cystinosis. Sometimes the full series of defects is absent. Thus, there may be phosphaturia with "vitamin D resistant rickets" and moderate aminoaciduria, but no glycosuria; in what seems to be a milder expression of the same defect, the skeletal lesions may not appear until adult life, as after pregnancy, when they may respond to dihydrotachysterol or other vitamin D-like agents and there is no aminoaciduria or glycosuria.

Renal tubular acidosis of hereditary origin is more common than any of these. It is often associated with renal lithiasis, nephrocalcinosis and/or remediable metabolic and skeletal defects. The basic abnormality is inability to acidify urine and retain bicarbonate; ammonia formation is also impaired. The nature of the defect is not entirely clear, although it is apparently not a selective or total deficiency of the carbonic anhydrase system; children seem often to "grow out of it." Inability to retain one anion, bicarbonate, is countered by increased reabsorption of the other major anion, chloride, with resultant hyperchloremic metabolic acidosis. Sodium is lost in excess, and the condition may be complicated by a secondary hyperaldosteronism, which, if it occurs, adds to the already high rate of potassium loss and results in potassium deficit. At the renal level, this deficit is a factor contributing to decreased urinary citrate concentration. Lack of this chelating and solubilizing anion, in the presence of hypercalciuria (calcium loss is increased with that of other cations), makes for deposition of calcium phosphate in the alkaline medium of tubules and collecting ducts, and for renal lithiasis. Meanwhile, the calcium deficit leads to skeletal lesions. Treatment is by replacement with sodium bicarbonate or citrate, potassium and, in patients with skeletal lesions, calcium and/or vitamin D.

Treatment usually stabilizes renal function levels, which sometimes improve considerably. Occasionally, renal failure supervenes as a result of idiopathic diffuse large vessel sclerosis.

Renal Failure; Uremia

Deterioration of renal function advances through a stage in which changes in body chemistry are not demonstrable except after stress or during a test of renal function (subclinical renal failure). As this state persists, evidence of generalized metabolic disturbance may appear in the form of resistant anemia, anorexia and fatigability. Early in renal failure the patient's economy is in a precarious balance which an unusual stress, easily tolerable when renal function is normal, may seriously disturb. Ultimately, the loss of function is lethal even when the patient is protected from situations of special strain.

Uremia is the clinical *syndrome* which indicates that renal failure has changed the chemistry of the body so seriously as to disable normal functions. Its presence is demonstrated by a combination of clinical and chemical evidence. Since it is the result of a summation of excretory defects, the manifestations of uremia vary as one or another change in body chemistry tends for a time to outweigh the others. Consequently its course differs according to whether it is due to sudden loss of excretory power or to a remediable upset in the unsteady equilibrium of partial renal failure or whether it supervenes terminally in chronic renal disease.

The symptoms of uremia are weakness, headache, somnolence, apathy and confusions, twitchings, convulsions, pruritus, nausea, vomiting, dyspnea, stomatitis and diarrhea. The resistant anemia invariably present in terminal chronic renal disease is usually associated with a hemorrhagic diathesis which leads to epistaxis, bruising and melena. Unexplained fibrinous pericarditis occurs in most cases of terminal chronic renal failure. The uremic state may be associated with severe extrarenal vascular injury, so that to the symptoms of renal failure are added those of cardiac and cerebral damage. This summation is almost characteristic of the uremia of malignant hypertension. In uremia due to primary renal disease congestive heart failure is a common complication and is due both to overhydration and an obscure myocardial weakness.

Results of Renal Failure. Since renal failure merges insensibly into the physical deterioration of uremia, and since uremia may be precipitated by undue stress in the presence of early renal failure, the underlying mechanisms of the two phases may be considered together. They are (1) decrease in glomerular filtration, (2) decrease in tubular reabsorption, (3) decrease in tubular secretion, and (4) hypothetically at least, loss of a detoxifying renal function.

The consequence of decreased glomerular filtration is that at some point, usually when about 60 per cent of normal function is lost, there develops retention in the blood of substances normally excreted by filtration. This change is manifested in elevated blood non-protein nitrogen and among its constituents, especially urea. Decreased tubular reabsorption results in loss of major electrolytes and of water. Such a salt-losing tendency is most commonly seen in chronic pyelonephritis. Failure of tubular secretion is principally reflected in loss of ability to excrete hydrogen ions and to form ammonia. The relative well-being of patients with severe excretory loss due to congenital cystic kidney has been attributed to the detoxifying function of the clusters of normal nephrons that remain. Adaptation to slowly developing changes in body fluids seems a more likely explanation in some patients with chronic renal disease. In brief, a "detoxifying" function is as hard to show as it is to define.

ACUTE FAILURE. The nature of the predominant changes in body fluids which result from renal failure depends largely on the rate at which function is lost and on the volume of urine which is formed. Most renal failures of sudden onset (acute renal failure) are complete and result in oliguria or anuria. The predominant change is therefore retention, while loss of electrolytes and fluids is minimal. Such renal failure results in azotemia, which may be severe, but, for reasons which are not thoroughly understood, the mental and nervous manifestations of uremia are scant and limited perhaps to a natural anxiety and brief periods of confusion. The cause of death is very often cardiac arrest by potassium poisoning. Such death is sudden and occurs about the end of the first week of anuria. This is rarely the case in chronic renal disease.

The importance of potassium intoxication and nitrogenous accumulation is shown by the fact that survival time in anuric rats is inversely proportional to their intakes of potassium and protein. In some conditions, notably in burns and after crushing injuries to muscles, potassium intoxication is unusually severe because mobilization of tissue fluid releases large amounts of potassium into the circulation; in some of these sodium loss (burns, vomiting) further aggravates the ionic imbalance.

Accumulation of potassium in plasma results in characteristic electrocardiographic changes. First the T waves increase in vertical amplitude, their base is narrowed and the pattern peaked. This is followed by an increase in R and S waves, and then by patterns of atrioventricular and interventricular block.

The next striking change consists in a loss of P waves. This is followed by depression of the S-T segment (obliteration of the segment with the T wave originating from the S wave) and then, finally, by a spread of QRS and T waves into a smooth biphasic curve. T wave elevation occurs in man when plasma potassium reaches about 7 mEq. per liter. P waves disappear at about 9 mEq. per liter, and spread of the QRS complex and death follow at levels of about 10 mEq. per liter. However, the toxic myocardial effects of potassium vary with the balance of other ions, notably Na^+, H^+ and Ca^{++}, so that there can be no exact correlation between serum potassium and the electrocardiogram.

Hyperkalemia is countered in several ways. Those which are suppressive only consist in giving sodium chloride, bicarbonate or lactate; glucose (40 per cent with insulin) by venous drip with the aim of depositing potassium with glycogen; or taking advantage of the K/Ca antagonism, to administer large amounts of calcium gluconate (Meroney and Herndon). More lasting relief is obtained by removal of excess potassium, either by dialysis (peritoneal or blood) or by oral or rectal administration of a cationic resin in the Na^+ cycle usually with a demulcent such as mannitol or sorbitol.

Practical hemodialysis (Kolff) had to await the availability of cellophane tubing and peritoneal dialysis the antibiotics. Both are now well established procedures in the management of acute renal failure (or in some intoxications). In essence the procedures consist in dialysis against an isotonic electrolyte solution, to which glucose is added; the aim is to restore electrolyte and fluid balance and to remove the constituents of the nonprotein nitrogen. Dialysis is occasionally useful in chronic renal disease. It may tide over patients with acute exacerbations of chronic pyelonephritis until their pre-existing level of depressed function is restored. Sometimes it will enable patients with chronic renal failure to endure a severe catabolic stress, such as operation, injury, infection, or heart failure. Usually, it only postpones the fatal issue by a few weeks. An exception occurs in cystic disease; these patients often build up very high levels of urea before becoming clinically uremic and, when they do, dialysis may be lifesaving; possibly removal of a large part of the accumulated urea decreases osmotic diuresis in residual nephrons, diminishes intrarenal pressure and enables the useful nephrons to resume sufficient function to maintain the patient, often for several months. A similar situation is seen in chronic pyelonephritis, especially when uremia has been precipitated by acute fluid and electrolyte loss.

The greatest accomplishment in the management of acute renal failure is the now widespread recognition of the fact that these patients cannot excrete water and that they must inevitably drown in any large excess. This is especially the case in post-traumatic or postinfectional failure, in which provision of endogenous water of oxidation by accelerated catabolism may decrease water needs well below amounts estimated from external balance.

CHRONIC FAILURE. The most common type of renal failure and uremia results from chronic renal disease. In such patients the urine volume is usually large until shortly before death. Hyperkalemia is not as significant as in acute renal failure. Indeed, the mechanism of potassium excretion, inadequately balanced by concurrent hydrogen ion formation, may be so active as to cause potassium clearance to rise to levels well above filtration rate, so that there ensues an actual depletion of plasma potassium with resultant weakness and paresis of skeletal muscles and cardiac failure. Such cases, however, are less common than those in which, as in acute renal failure, terminal potassium intoxication results from failure of urine flow. Possibly some that have been described as "potassium-losing" nephritis are cases of primary hyperaldosteronism with secondary renal damage due to potassium deficiency.

Muscular twitching and, far less usually, convulsions are thought by some clinicians to be caused by a decrease in the ionized calcium of blood due to renal retention of phosphate. But the relation of symptoms to plasma calcium is tenuous, and it has been suggested that the defect in calcium is in the nervous system itself. Observations in nephrectomized dogs indicate that the onset of twitching is more closely related to increased inorganic phosphate in cerebrospinal fluid than to the increase in plasma. The ionized calcium of the cerebrospinal fluid is often significantly lowered (3 mg. per 100 ml. as compared to a normal 4.3 in dogs, and 3.8 as compared to 4.3 in patients, with a rise in inorganic phosphate from 1.3 to 2.7 mg. per 100 ml.). Intravenous administration of calcium tends to relieve twitching, and oral dosage with aluminum hydroxide tends at once to relieve the deficiency in ionizable calcium and some

of the acidosis by causing fecal excretion of insoluble aluminum phosphate.

The defect in calcium metabolism extends much further and reaches earlier into the course of renal failure. The tendency to depression of ionized calcium acts as a stimulus to parathyroid hyperplasia, which is manifested functionally and structurally. Functionally, it results in decalcification. This, in the ages of bony growth, accounts in part for some of the syndromes of renal rickets. In adults the bony changes may not be obvious, although areas of decalcification are commonly found in the vertebrae. The result of this hyperfunction is that the clinical and chemical patterns of renal failure with secondary hyperparathyroidism are confusingly similar to that of primary hyperparathyroidism which has resulted in renal failure.

Vomiting, anorexia and apathy tend to occur early in uremia, often preceding other serious disturbances. It is therefore difficult to ascribe them to retention of identified substances. They result in undernutrition with loss of weight. But in some patients, again for undetermined reasons, the loss of weight and strength seems to precede other manifestations of renal failure. Apathy and depression in patients and increased blood phenols are certainly associated phenomena, but a definite correlation cannot be established.

Stomatitis and diarrhea and pruritus are common in uremia when blood urea is greatly elevated. It has been suggested that these are due to liberation of ammonia from the action of oral, intestinal or cutaneous bacterial ureases on the urea of saliva, intestinal fluid and sweat. Such liberation accounts for the ammoniacal odor of the breath of such patients, which, since it is distasteful, may be relieved by a mouthwash containing sodium acid phosphate.

The plasma electrolyte pattern in chronic renal failure is characteristically subject to wide variations. Typically, there are increases in plasma potassium, SO_4 and PO_4. The loss of sodium and HCO_3 in urine due to failure of reabsorption and of H^+ and NH_4^+ secretion tends to deplete plasma sodium, decrease extracellular fluid and lead to acidosis with decrease in plasma HCO_3.

In patients whose renal function is normal or nearly so, deficits in NaCl and HCO_3 can be rapidly repaired by administration of solutions of sodium chloride, depending on the kidney to partition out the excess chloride from the salt, so that sodium bicarbonate is restored to plasma and chloride excreted. Such dependence is unwise in renal failure. The situation is met by intravenous administration of these salts, apportioning them roughly as two volumes of 0.9 per cent NaCl to one volume of 1.3 per cent $NaHCO_3$.

When acidosis is the predominant feature, with resultant dyspnea and discomfort, the administration of alkali is the most urgent need. It is met by infusion of $NaHCO_3$. The amount given in grams is calculated as 0.3 times body weight in kilograms times deficit in plasma HCO_3 in milliequivalents per liter, times 0.084 (times 0.112 when sodium lactate is used instead of bicarbonate). After correction of acidosis, treatment is completed by administration of sodium chloride solution in an amount sufficient to correct the weight deficit. Patients in chronic renal failure can be kept in relative comfort for long periods by oral maintenance doses of sodium chloride and sodium bicarbonate adjusted by periodic checks of plasma chloride and HCO_3 content. Failure to give such attention in chronic renal failure hastens uremia as a result of oligemia.

The treatment of uremia therefore consists in remedying as best one can the deficits which nature has imposed on the patient. The inevitable polyuria of chronic renal disease is treated by administration of adequate volumes of water, and of this thirst is the physiologic and desirable criterion. Salt restriction, practiced during the nephrotic phase, is substituted by judicious replacement of the salt lost as the result of tubular insufficiency. The deficit of sodium and tendency to acidosis consequent on deficient H^+ and NH_4^+ formation are treated by administration of the required amounts of bicarbonate, either as such or as sodium lactate. Calcium may be administered to increase the available supply and to prevent osseous changes, while extrarenal excretion of phosphate is accelerated by oral administration of aluminum hydroxide. Uremic osteodystrophy due to secondary hyperparathyroidism in the young may respond to massive doses of vitamin D, *cautiously* given. The meat of the diet may be restricted, and other proteins, notably lactalbumin and casein, substituted with the aim of decreasing potassium intake in cases in which potassium is being retained, and with the secondary aim of decreasing the exogenous sources of phenols. The aim is the maintenance as long as possible, by somewhat artificial means, of the delicate equilibrium of body fluids which the kidney should normally balance.

In chronic renal failure, as in acute, reversible failures, provision of diet rich in nonprotein calories tends at once to spare protein catabolism and to prevent azotemia. Special efforts should be made to devise palatable mixtures of fat and carbohydrate. Transfusions are of supportive value in the anemia of renal failure if they actually relieve symptoms that are due to the anemia. They should be given with care as they may precipitate heart failure. It is preferable to give only the red cells. There is some evidence that this anemia will respond to oral cobalt. Lastly, anabolic androgen-like substances may be helpful. Among these the safest seems (A.C.C.) to be a long-lasting testosterone (the caprinoyl acetate ester). It is available in Canada.

Platt took as the theme of his Lumleian lectures "Structural and Functional Adaptations in Renal Failure"; he noted that in experimental subtotal renal ablations, as also in chronic renal disease, there occurs hypertrophy of remaining nephrons, especially of their proximal tubules, and osmotic diuresis which maintains the total rates of urea or creatinine excretion in spite of low clearance rates. Further adaptations are decreased relative reabsorptions of sodium and potassium, parathyroid hyperplasia and slowed water diuresis; conceivably hypertension and anemia fit in this category, since hypertension would tend to maintain filtration rate by pressure, and anemia to do the same by increasing the volume of plasma per unit blood flow. He considers that "our concept of renal failure should not be one of disordered function, but rather one of extremely efficient function by a renal remnant too small for its task." And this is a good philosophy on which to base our approach to a disease process in which our present knowledge only permits us to assist rather than contend with nature.

REFERENCES

Addis, T.: Glomerular Nephritis, Diagnosis and Treatment. New York, Macmillan, 1952.

Berliner, R. W. (guest editor): Symposium on the kidney. Am. J. Med., 36:641, 1964.

Black, D. A. K. (ed.): Renal Disease. Philadelphia, F. A. Davis Co., 1962.

Brod, J., Prat, V., and Dejdar, R.: Early functional diagnosis of chronic pyelonephritis with remarks on the pathogenesis of the pyelonephritic contracted kidney. In Quinn, E. L., and Kass, E. H. (eds.): Biology of Pyelonephritis (Henry Ford Hospital Symposium). Boston, Little, Brown & Co., 1959.

Chinard, F. P.: Kidney, water and electrolytes. Ann. Rev. Physiol., *26:*187, 1964.

Corcoran, A. C.: Edema. Cleveland Clin. Quart., *12:* 117, 1945.

Corcoran, A. C.: Renal circulation in hypertension. M. Clin. North America, *45:*301, 1961.

Denton, D. A.: Evolutionary aspects of the emergence of aldosterone secretion and salt appetite. Physiol. Rev., *45:*245, 1965.

Dustan, H. P., Corcoran, A. C., and Page, I. H.: Separate renal functions in patients with renal arterial disease, pyelonephritis and essential hypertension. Circulation, *23:*34, 1961.

Gottschalk, C. W.: Osmotic concentration and dilution of urine. Am. J. Med., *36:*670, 1964.

Gottschalk, C. W.: Personal communication, May, 1965.

Hamburger, J., Richet, G., Crosnier, J., and Funck-Brentano, J. L.: L'Insuffisance renale. In Alken, C. E., et al. (eds.): Handbuch der Urol., etc., Volume 4. Berlin, Springer, 1962.

Laragh, J. H., Ulick, S., Januszewicz, V., De Ming, Q. B., Kelly, W. G., and Lieberman, S.: Aldosterone secretion and primary and malignant hypertension. J. Clin. Invest., *39:*1091, 1960.

Malvin, R. L., Wilde, W. S., and Sullivan, L. P.: Localization of nephron transport by stop flow analysis. Am. J. Physiol., *194:*135, 1958.

Moyer, J. H., and Fuchs, M. (eds.): Hahnemann Symposium on Salt and Water Retention. Philadelphia, W. B. Saunders Co., 1960.

Oliver, J.: Architecture of the Kidney in Chronic Bright's Disease. New York, Paul B. Hoeber, Inc., 1939.

Perillie, P. E., and Epstein, F. H.: Sickling phenomenon produced by hypertonic solutions: A possible explanation for the hyposthenuria of sicklemia. J. Clin. Invest., *42:*570, 1963.

Pitts, R. F.: The Physiological Basis of Diuretic Therapy. Springfield, Ill., Charles C Thomas, 1959.

Pitts, R. F.: Physiology of the Kidney and Body Fluids. Chicago, Year Book Publishers, 1963.

Smith, H. W.: Principles of Renal Physiology. New York, Oxford University Press, 1956.

Stanbury, J. B., Wyngaarten, J. B., and Fredrickson, D. S. (eds.): The Metabolic Basis of Inherited Disease. New York, McGraw-Hill, 1960.

Strauss, M. B., and Welt, L. G.: Diseases of the Kidney. Boston, Little, Brown & Co., 1963.

Van Slyke, D. D., Stillman, E., Moller, E., Enhrich, W., McIntosh, J. F., Leiter, L., MacKay, E. M., Hannon, R. R., Moore, N. S., and Johnston, C.: Observations on the courses of the different types of Bright's disease and on the resultant changes in renal anatomy. Medicine, *9:*257, 1930.

Part X

Blood and Spleen

Chapter Thirty

Disorders of the Blood and Blood-Forming Tissues

WILLIAM B. CASTLE

General Functions of the Blood

The blood functions conservatively as a medium for maintaining a suitable and nearly constant environment for the growth and function of the innumerable cells of the body. It also serves the liberal function of a modifiable medium of exchange between the external environment and the various tissues of the body. Essential for a successful administration based on a compromise of these opposing policies is the delicate adjustment of the circulation to the local needs of various organs. The blood is also concerned in specialized mechanisms for controlling the functions of such organs as the lungs, kidneys, liver, bone marrow, spleen and endocrine glands which in various ways maintain the relative constancy of the volume and composition of the blood with respect to both its formed and its liquid components.

The formed elements of the blood and the blood-forming organs include both those corpuscles maintained in suspension in the plasma by virtue of its turbulence while in motion in the blood vessels and those fixed cells in process of growth and development in the bone marrow, spleen, lymph nodes and elsewhere prior to entering the circulation. Because of the numerous excellent descriptions of the origin, development and mor-

phologic characteristics of the cells of the blood and blood-forming tissues elsewhere available, these somewhat controversial topics will be referred to only so far as descriptive morphology appears to be useful for a better comprehension of the pathologic physiology of the disorders of the blood under consideration.

The primary function of the circulating red cells is to maintain in the circulation the high concentration of hemoglobin essential for the transport of the large amount of oxygen necessary for the respiration of the tissues of the warm-blooded animal. The circulation forms a pathway for the white cells on the way to those areas where, by virtue of their phagocytic or other properties, they may assist in arresting invasion of microorganisms or in the repair of tissues. The third formed element of the peripheral blood, the platelet, is concerned in maintaining the integrity of the vascular endothelium, and so in preventing the escape of blood from the blood vessels. In this effort the coagulating properties of the plasma are also of fundamental importance when trauma ruptures a blood vessel wall. The fixed cells of the reticuloendothelial system are characterized by their powers of phagocytosis of particulate matter, whether foreign material including microorganisms, or fragments of dead tissue cells. The reticuloendothelial system is concerned in the conversion of hemoglobin to bilirubin and in the storage of iron. The aggregations of plasma cells or lymphocytes in the spleen and lymph nodes are involved in the production and delivery of antibodies to the circulating blood. The pathologic physiology of the spleen and reticuloendothelial system is discussed in Chapter 31.

Disorders Affecting Erythrocytes

It is appropriate to begin a discussion of the pathologic physiology of disorders of the blood with a description of normal red cell production and destruction, because this background information is essential for an understanding of the pathologic processes involved. Moreover, in many instances disturbances of white cell or platelet production affect the circulating levels of red cells and hemoglobin. Thus, in leukemias, polycythemia is sometimes found early and anemia eventually is almost always present. Again, if the platelets in circulation are sparse, or coagulation of the blood is defective, anemia may develop, owing in varying proportions to blood loss or to disturbance of red cell formation.

Morphology of Erythrocyte Production

The absolute as well as the relative size of the tissues which are actively engaged in the formation of red cells varies with age. In the adult the weight of the bone marrow has been estimated at 1600 to 3700 gm., of which about half is active in blood formation and so is approximately equal to the weight of the liver. Donohue has calculated that for every 100 circulating adult erythrocytes there are 1 circulating and 1.5 marrow reticulocytes and 1.5 nucleated marrow erythrocytes. The total blood volume of the newborn child is about 275 ml., and in the female increases in a roughly linear fashion to reach about 3800 ml. at the age of sixteen. In the male at puberty the total blood volume begins to increase more rapidly than in the female and reaches nearly 5000 ml. at the age of sixteen. Plasma volume is estimated, with some uncertainty due to losses of label to extravascular space, as dilution of a known amount of injected albumin labeled with a dye or with I^{131}; whereas red cell volume measurements employ more reliably a red cell label such as Cr^{51}. When plasma and red cell volumes are independently determined, the latter is found to represent only about 91 per cent of the value calculated from the large vessel hematocrit. This is because of the relatively low hematocrit of blood in the minute vessels where the plasma film adjacent to the endothelial surface is, for geometrical reasons, large relative to cell content. The reverse effect, due to hemoconcentration of red cells in the spleen, is discussed in Chapter 31.

At birth the entire bone marrow is active in blood formation. However, a few months later some fat cells begin to appear in the centers of the peripheral long bones. This process begins in the most distal bones of the extremities and gradually advances centrally with respect to each bone, until by the age of puberty most of the marrow of the long bones has been converted into a largely fatty tissue in which active hematopoiesis is no longer apparent. Thus, in the normal adult, the areas of the bone marrow active in the formation of the red cells, white cells and platelets include only the ribs, vertebrae, sternum, skull, os innominatum and the proximal ends of the humerus and femur. Consequently, for trephine or needle biopsies in the adult, the sternum, rib or crest of the ilium offer acceptable areas containing representative cellular marrow, whereas in the child up to the age of 14 the tibia is a satisfactory site.

In areas of cellular marrow, erythropoiesis is active in relation to collapsed capillaries, whereas white cell formation is more likely to be manifest where vascularity is more prominent. The total nucleated cell count of active marrow ranges from 20,000 to 100,000 per cubic millimeter. Leukopoiesis involves roughly two to four times the number of erythropoietic cells. It is now established that both red cells and granulocytes are produced outside the vascular sinusoidal bed, as has long been known for megakaryocytes. The sinusoidal walls are composed of a single layer of reticular cells without a basement membrane except adjacent to fat cells, so that the germinal blood cells have access to protein-bound as well as to diffusible substances. Moreover, the sinusoidal reticular cells may become phagocytic or differentiate leaving gaps in the wall. The red cell precursors on losing their nuclei become reticulocytes and simply penetrate the walls of the sinusoids as do the leukocytes.

The nucleated precursors of the erythrocytes normally develop as clusters of maturing normoblasts derived from pronormoblasts that originally differentiated by division from inconspicuous and infrequent reticulum or stem cells, which are close relatives of the phagocytic or endothelial cells of the marrow sinusoids. According to Erslev, erythropoiesis in the bone marrow can be divided roughly into three stages (Fig. 30–1). In Stage I the stem cells, which are capable of initiating the formation of any type of marrow cell, divide. Thereupon, one differentiates into the earliest red cell progenitor, the pronormoblast, while the other remains a stem cell, presumably in order to maintain the basis of future marrow cell differentiation. Stage II represents the period in which, during perhaps three or four successive mitotic divisions of normoblasts at intervals of about 20 hours, increasing maturity of both nucleus and cytoplasm is observed. With the beginning of Stage III, reached after perhaps two days of erythroid cell division and maturation, mitoses are no longer seen and the nucleus is pyknotic. About 10 per cent of the red cell precursors die in the bone marrow, a process that is greatly increased in certain anemias displaying ineffective erythropoiesis. This explains part of the so-called "early labeling" peak of stercobilin, which appears within a few days and so prior to significant labeling of its normal precursor the circulating hemoglobin. An even earlier portion of the labeled stercobilin is apparently derived within hours from porphyrin synthesis in liver cells. A few cells skip mitotic divisions and appear in the circulation as large reticulocytes, a prominent feature of the early marrow response to acute blood loss or hemolysis. If hemoglobin synthesis is delayed, as with iron deficiency, more than the usual number of cell divisions may take place, resulting in small adult red cells.

The early normoblasts display basophilia, indicating nuclear deoxyribonucleotides and cytoplasmic ribonucleotides that are involved, respectively, in nuclear division and cytoplasmic protein synthesis. Porphyrin appears later in polychromatophilic normoblasts and, when combined with iron to form heme, couples with globin in increasing amounts as the acid-staining properties of hemoglobin become fully manifest in the orthochromatophilic normoblast. Conversion to the reticulocyte involves discarding of the pyknotic nucleus—a phenomenon said to account for much of the rise in hemoglobin concentration from 20 to 25 to the normal 34 per cent. This loss of volume perhaps also changes the shape of the cell from the spherical to the biconcave adult form. After the nucleus has been lost, deoxyribonucleic acid (DNA) is no longer available to code the formation of protein through messenger ribonucleic acid (RNA). However, the residual instructed polyribosomes of the cytoplasm continue briefly to make hemoglobin and account for the diffuse cytoplasmic basophilia of the young cell visible with Romanowsky dyes. This material is more readily detected by the use of supravital dyes such as brilliant cresyl blue in the form of the granular network characteristic of the reticulocyte. The fact that, like their precursors, reticulocytes appear to adhere more readily to glass slides than do adult erythrocytes has been suggested as a factor in the retention of red cells by the marrow until fully mature. Reticulocytes have a lower specific gravity than do adult cells, and so can be concentrated by centrifugation. They are normally 20 per cent larger, and their osmotic fragility may or may not differ from that of the adult red cell. The entire erythropoietic process within the marrow probably occupies from three to six days. In the blood stream the life of the reticulocyte is two days or

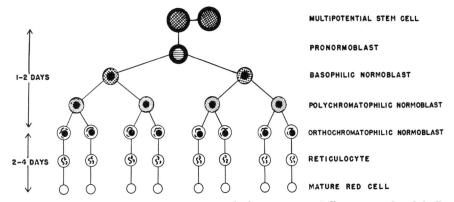

Figure 30–1. Diagram of erythropoiesis in the bone marrow. Cells are stained with brilliant cresyl blue and Wright's stain. Note division and differentiation of stem cells, mitotic division and maturation of normoblasts and eventual formation of reticulocytes from normoblasts with pyknotic nuclei without further division. (Slightly modified from Erslev: Blood, *14*:386, 1959.)

less, that of the adult cell from 100 to 120 days.

In the peripheral fatty marrow of the adult the sinusoidal vascular bed is compressed by the fat cells, and its endothelial lining bears few germinal cells. However, this provides for the central cellular marrow an effective peripheral reserve space which may be called upon whenever a demand is made for increased production of circulating hemoglobin. In order for the increase to take place, either the maturation and/or division rate of the entire series of erythroid cells must be accelerated or the number of erythropoietic cells at some level must increase by division so that the number of their mature descendants ready to enter the circulation at any moment will be increased. The latter process is the principal effect, based upon an increase in the number of pronormoblasts differentiated from stem cells with a corresponding increase in the number of the collateral lines of descent (Fig. 30–1). Experimentally, acute blood loss anemia of only a few hours' duration stimulates stem cell division, after which the erythropoietic response of the marrow proceeds automatically even if the anemia is abolished by retransfusion of the blood. A wave of cell division and accelerated maturation sweeps over the marrow, and only two or three days later breaks into the blood stream as reticulocytes. Prior to this some large reticulocytes, whose nucleated precursors have presumably skipped one or more mitotic divisions with consequently undivided cytoplasm, appear in the circulation. Although following blood loss or hemolysis the younger erythroid cells initially increase, the original ratios of such cells to their descendants are soon restored because the older cells increase in proportion. Thus, apparently the rate of red cell production is largely governed by the rate of stem cell differentiation into pronormoblasts, while the rate of subsequent erythroid cell maturation is somewhat increased by the anemia stimulus. Persistent anemia of course increases the number of nucleated erythroid cells absolutely and in relation to myeloid cells per unit of active marrow.

Chronically increased blood loss or destruction reverses the normal prepubertal fatty involution of the bone marrow and causes the disapparance of fat cells at the margin of the marrow cavity and adjacent to the cellular portion of the marrow, as the latter extends peripherally in the long bones. Indeed, in chronic hemolytic anemias a considerable resumption of erythropoietic activity may take place in the long bones, especially in young children, in whom the reserves of fatty marrow are characteristically small. Further enlargement of the marrow cavities may occur by actual resorption of cortical bone. This invasion of the cortex may cause the appearance of "hairs-on-end" in x-ray films of the skull in children with Cooley's anemia or sickle cell anemia and sometimes in those with congenital hemolytic jaundice or hypoxic polycythemia. When even more erythropoietic tissue is needed, extramedullary foci of hematopoiesis may appear, especially in the spleen and lymph nodes and to a less extent in the liver. Gross tumors of such tissue may develop along the vertebral column and in the hilum of the kidney in chronic hemolytic anemia.

PHYSIOLOGY OF ERYTHROCYTE PRODUCTION

Clinical and experimental evidence indicates that, for normal erythropoiesis to occur, the anatomic structure, local temperature, nutritional requirements and endocrine influences of the marrow must be satisfactory. There must also be no toxic inhibitory influences of internal or external origin. That under these circumstances the level of circulating hemoglobin is normally so perfectly controlled and yet the erythropoietic response to a sudden fall of hemoglobin level is so effectively augmented clearly indicates the existence of homeostatic control. It is well known that when the oxygen tension or content of the arterial blood is diminished, the tissue oxygen tension falls and there eventually results an increase in the concentration of red cells and hemoglobin in the peripheral blood stream. In men exposed to low barometric pressure for even a few hours the rates both of the disappearance of injected plasma-bound radioiron and of its subsequent incorporation into new circulating hemoglobin are increased. In occasional patients who have experienced partial asphyxia—for example, as a result of an attack of status asthmaticus—a reticulocyte response takes place within the next few days that chronologically resembles that seen after the development of anemia as a result of acute red cell loss or destruction. Conversely, an increase in the oxygen tension or content of the arterial blood in experimental animals or in man causes an increase in the tissue oxygen tension, and a suppression of the delivery of young red cells into the circulation. In man the regulatory influence of the arterial oxygen tension is best demonstrated in hemolytic anemias with rapid red cell formation (Fig. 30–2). The effect of polycythemia induced by transfusions in suppressing reticulocytosis in such conditions is also well known. In normal subjects so rendered polycythemic the erythroid cellularity of the marrow is diminished after a few days and reticulocytes virtually disappear from the circulation. The progressive "anemia" of the premature newborn is associated with a decreasing number of reticulocytes during the first few days of life and probably represents a similar phenomenon resulting from the increase to a normal level of the oxygen tension of the infant's arterial blood consequent upon the establishment of pulmonary respiration.

These observations suggest that the rate of hemoglobin production is normally critically controlled by the amount of oxygen carried by the arterial blood during a given period of time to some regulatory tissue. If so, an increased rate of blood flow should increase its oxygen tension and so depress erythropoietic effort. Possibly this is the cause of the so-called physiologic anemia of pregnancy, which is most marked at the beginning of the last trimester when the cardiac output is greatest and the plasma volume is increased by about 25 per cent. Certainly the commonly offered explanation of hemodilution as its

cause is unsatisfactory because during the preceding months there would be plenty of time for the plasma-diluted hemoglobin concentration to stimulate erythropoiesis unless in some way this was inhibited. That increased peripheral blood flow does annul the erythropoietic stimulus of hemodilution has been shown by Erslev in animals in which the hemoglobin concentration was lowered by maintaining an increased circulating plasma volume with daily injections of dextran. However, when a comparable fall of hemoglobin concentration was created by bleeding and prompt restoration of blood volume to normal with dextran, typical reticulocyte responses followed. These animals were equally "anemic" but were without the compensatory increase in cardiac output of those with increased plasma volume.

It is of interest that, as measured both in capillary tubes in vitro and in the circulation of hypotensive dogs in vivo, blood with a hematocrit of about 45 per cent appears to transport the most oxygen at a given perfusion pressure. This transport capacity is a function of blood flow (reciprocal of viscosity) $\times$ oxygen capacity $\times$ percentage oxygen saturation of the hemoglobin. Oxygen capacity is a linear function of the hematocrit, while the blood flow is inversely related to the

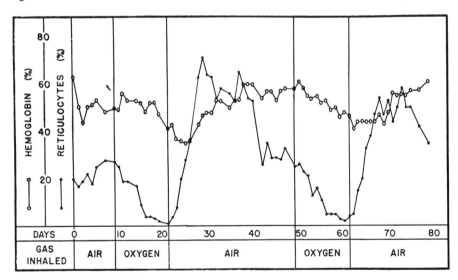

Figure 30–2. Depressant effect of oxygen inhalation on erythropoiesis in a patient with sickle cell anemia. Note that during each 12-day period of oxygen inhalation there is a progressive fall of reticulocytes and of hemoglobin, and that immediately after these periods there is a sharp rise of reticulocytes and later of hemoglobin. This presumably indicates that when the patient breathed oxygen, the anoxic stimulus to erythropoiesis due to the anemia was abolished and recurred only when the patient again began to breathe room air. This effect dominated any lessened red cell destruction that may have occurred from diminished sickling in the tissue capillaries. (Redrawn from Reinhard and others: J. Clin. Investigation, 23:682, 1944.)

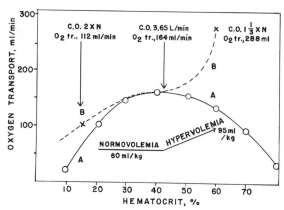

Figure 30–3. Homeostasis of oxygen transport and erythropoiesis. In vitro the rate of flow of samples of the same oxygenated blood adjusted to various hematocrit levels (by adding or subtracting plasma) varies inversely with the hematocrit in an Ostwald viscosimeter. The rate at which the blood transports oxygen through the viscosimeter can be calculated by multiplying the rate of flow by the hematocrit of the sample. Experimentally it is found that with a low hematocrit, despite a fast rate of blood flow, the oxygen transported is small; despite a high hematocrit, because of the slow rate of blood flow, the oxygen transported is also small. There is thus an optimal value for oxygen transport at about the normal hematocrit, as shown by the upward convexity of curve A.

If these conditions held in vivo, any degree of polycythemia would diminish oxygen transport and stimulate erythropoiesis increasingly as the hematocrit rose. This would prevent the homeostatic regulation of erythropoiesis required to maintain a normal hematocrit. However, in vivo as the hematocrit increases, so does the blood volume (see Fig. 30–39), and consequently the cardiac output. As a result the oxygen transport is enhanced and erythropoiesis is suppressed by the polycythemia. Curve B is based on clinical measurements showing that as the hematocrit declines the blood volume remains constant (Fig. 30–39), but the cardiac output is increased. For example, when the hematocrit is one-third of normal the cardiac output is roughly doubled. Data concerning the cardiac output in polycythemia vera obtained by Cobb, Kramer, and Finch (J. Clin. Invest., 39:1722, 1960) indicate that with a hematocrit of 60 per cent the cardiac output is about 1⅓ times normal. These data from patients with polycythemia vera have been applied to the construction of curve B showing the transport of oxygen in vivo at different hematocrits. Note that the oxygen transport is diminished by anemia and enhanced by polycythemia.

hematocrit. Consequently, an intermediate hematocrit value of 40 to 45 per cent results in a maximal value for oxygen transport capacity. A decline in hematocrit, as with anemia, produces a fall in oxygen transport despite the partial compensation of an increased cardiac

output (Fig. 30–3). That an increase in hematocrit (and blood viscosity) does not also cause a fall in oxygen transport depends upon the accompanying increase in blood volume, which results in a more than compensatory increase in cardiac output and oxygen transport. On these interrelated phenomena of the circulation and blood depends the homeostasis of the normal hemoglobin level.

The peculiar location of the bone marrow within a rigid bony shell completely filled at all times by incompressible germinal cells, fat cells or blood suggests an anatomic arrangement whereby changes in the hemoglobin concentration, rather than in blood flow, would be the dominant factor influencing the rate of oxygen delivery. Nevertheless, direct measurement of the oxygen saturation of the blood perfusing the active marrow of anemic animals and men has failed to show consistent decreases. Exposure of marrow suspensions in vitro to hypoxia does not increase the rate of heme synthesis or of mitosis of nucleated red cells. Moreover, much evidence has now been presented for an indirect or humoral control of erythropoiesis.

Thus, in 1950, Reissmann found that parabiotic rats develop a similar degree of normoblastic hyperplasia in the bone marrow when only one breathes air with lowered oxygen tension. Stohlman and others have shown that, in patients with right-to-left flow through a patent ductus arteriosus and, consequently, with cyanosis and hypoxia of the lower part of the body, the resulting degree of erythropoietic hyperplasia in specimens of bone marrow from the upper part of the body was equally great. Erslev and others have demonstrated the presence of a nondialyzable substance in the serum of rabbits rendered anemic by bleeding or made hypoxic by low oxygen tension of the inspired air that will cause reticulocyte responses and increases in nucleated red cells in the marrow and in circulating hemoglobin when injected intravenously into normal homologous recipients (Fig. 30–4). Others have reported such activity to be present in filtrates of boiled plasma or urine from anemic or hypoxic animals. It has been detected by animal assay in the plasma and urine of many anemic patients, especially those with aplastic anemia and thalassemia as well as in hypoxic polycythemia. It has been reported by Halvorsen to be present in the amniotic fluid surrounding anemic infants in utero.

Erythropoietin is a glycoprotein of molecular weight from 10,000 to 40,000 or, assuming aggregation, perhaps even smaller. It travels electrophoretically with the alpha-1- and alpha-2-globulins of serum. It can be detected in the plasma of experimental animals after only six hours of anemia or of arterial hypoxia. Its concentration varies with the degree of chronic anemia and small amounts are found in normal urine. The principal effect of erythropoietin is to enhance red cell formation from the stem cell level. However, some workers have reported effects upon more mature erythroblasts, and even a prompt release of reticulocytes from rat bone marrow in vivo and in vitro.

A homeostatic control of erythropoiesis such as clearly exists requires that, unless the blood itself is a self-contained regulatory system, somewhere in the body its oxygen content must be sampled with precision by a tissue that it perfuses. At the present time, as a result of the work initiated by Jacobson in 1957, the kidney is considered to be an important source. Bilateral nephrectomy in rats, as opposed to ureteral ligation, decreases greatly the erythropoietic response to blood loss or hypoxia. All such animals presumably suffer equally from the suppressive effects of uremia upon erythropoiesis. Recent experiments suggest that a renal factor becomes active as erythropoietin by reacting with a serum component. Evidence that the kidney is a source of erythropoietic factor has been further substantiated by animal experiments demonstrating that perfusion of isolated rabbit kidneys with hypoxic, but not with oxygenated blood, causes the production of erythropoietin. There is, moreover, a growing

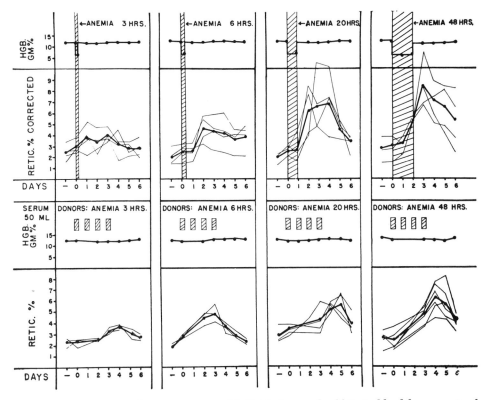

Figure 30–4. Reticulocyte responses of individual normal rabbits to blood loss anemia of various durations. The charts in the *upper row* depict the drop in the average hemoglobin level and its duration induced by bleeding 20 ml. per kilogram followed by immediate restoration of blood volume with infusions of 6 per cent dextran in saline. In the various groups of rabbits the anemia was terminated after 3, 6, 20 and 48 hours by reinfusion of the blood previously removed. Note the reticulocyte responses of individual bled rabbits. The charts in the *lower row* depict the effect upon the reticulocyte percentages of other normal rabbits who received infusions of 50 ml. of serum on 4 successive days from groups of rabbits (comparable to those in the upper series of charts) after 3, 6, 20 and 48 hours of anemia respectively. Note the comparable reticulocyte responses in the nonanemic plasma-recipient rabbits. (From Erslev: J. Lab. & Clin. Med., 50:543, 1957.)

number of reports of patients with renal cysts or neoplasms and polycythemia. In some of these it is claimed that increased amounts of erythropoietic factor are present in the circulation. However, it is clear that in man, with surgical absence of kidney tissue, erythropoiesis is reasonably well sustained if uremia is prevented by repeated dialysis.

BIOCHEMISTRY OF ERYTHROCYTE AND HEMOGLOBIN PRODUCTION

The nucleated red cells of the bone marrow contain the necessary subcellular particles and enzymes for replication, differentiation and maturation. These processes involve the production of lipids, carbohydrates and proteins. The most important of these proteins are nucleoproteins, stromatin, hemoglobin and various enzymes. Stromatin, the protein of the erythrocyte envelope, begins to form during the early stages of normoblast maturation, together with basophilic nucleoproteins containing deoxyribonucleic acid (DNA) and ribonucleic acid (RNA) in the nucleus and cytoplasm, respectively. As already described this is followed by the rapid production of acidophilic hemoglobin. Cytoplasmic polyribosomes direct globin synthesis, while in the mitochondria iron is incorporated into protoporphyrin to become heme. Subsequently, heme is released to unite with globin. The energy for this and for other functions is furnished by the well-known pathways of carbohydrate metabolism, the Krebs tricarboxylic acid cycle, the Embden-Myerhof pathway for anaerobic glycolysis and the closely linked pentose phosphate oxidative pathway together with the cytochrome oxidase system of the mitochondria. The loss of the nucleus deprives the reticulocytes of the master-molecules of DNA and so of ability to divide or synthesize RNA. However, the already instructed RNA persisting in the cytoplasm directs the completion of hemoglobin synthesis (Fig. 30–5).

The all-important red protein hemoglobin, a grooved, slightly ellipsoidal molecule with a weight of 66,000, consists of globin, to which are linked by their propionic groups four bivalent iron-porphyrin complexes called heme units. Each heme unit contains an atom of ferrous iron in the center of the four pyrrole groups composing the protoporphyrin ring whose vinyl groups are essential for the insertion of the iron. The ability of its iron atoms to accept (and to release) oxygen without oxidation renders hemoglobin useful for the transport of oxygen. This ability is due to the attachment of the iron through one of its six coordinate bonds to an imidazole group in one of the histidine residues in which globin is especially rich. This leaves the sixth bond free for reversible attachment to oxygen. The globin molecule of adult hemoglobin is composed of two identical half molecules, each of which carries two different folded peptide chains, alpha and beta, of 141 and 146 amino acids, respectively, in a genetically determined sequence. Fetal hemoglobin, normally present for the first three or four months of life, has similar alpha chains but different beta chains called gamma. Thus, the adult hemoglobin molecule is described as $\alpha^2\beta^2$, that of fetal hemoglobin as $\alpha^2\gamma^2$. Fetal hemoglobin, normally present for the first three or four months of life, and the various abnormal types of hemoglobin found in disease, including sickle hemoglobin, differ with respect to the composition of one or both of their peptide chains, which results in diagnostically useful differences in their electrophoretic mobility and solubility.

Heme synthesis begins with condensation of glycine and succinyl coenzyme A to form delta-aminolevulinic acid for which pyridoxal phosphate is required as activator of glycine (Table 30–1). Next, two molecules of delta-aminolevulinic acid condense to form the monopyrrolic substance porphobilinogen. Then four molecules of porphobilinogen combine to form a series of tetrapyrroles: uroporphyrinogen III, coproporphyrinogen III, protoporphyrinogen III and finally, by oxidation, protoporphyrin IX. On the reticulocyte, but not on the adult red cell, are located the receptor sites for plasma iron on its way to the interior (Fig. 30–6). Jandl has shown that, when bound to plasma transferrin, iron has selective affinity for reticulocytes and, presumably, for their precursors in the bone marrow. The adult red cell no longer possesses transferrin-specific receptors and has ceased to make hemoglobin.

Adult red cells are composed of about 70 per cent water. Ninety per cent of the dried substance is hemoglobin, the rest being stroma, carbohydrate and inorganic salts, chiefly potassium. The red cell envelope contains stromatin, a protein with qualities very much like those of keratin, the protein of hair and nails. It also contains lipids, chiefly phospholipids, cholesterol (mostly in the free form) and some neutral fat. The biconcave,

TABLE 30–1. SYNTHESIS OF PORPHYRINS AND HEME.

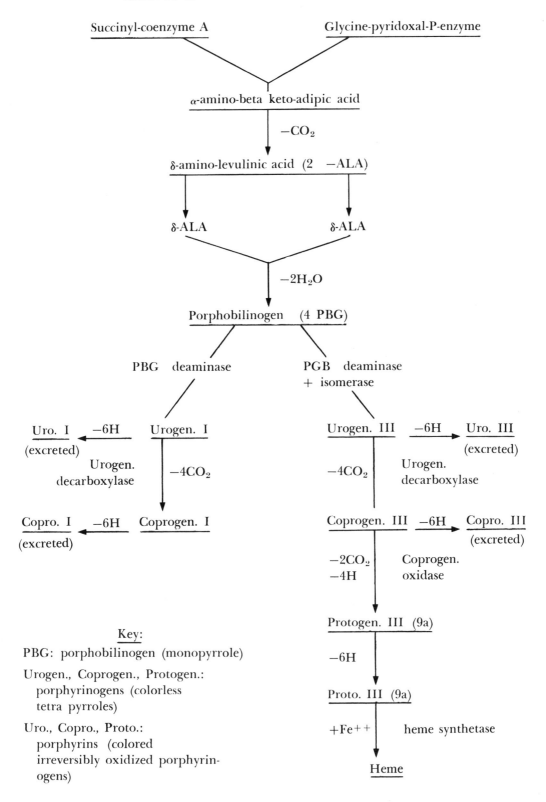

Succinyl-coenzyme A   Glycine-pyridoxal-P-enzyme

α-amino-beta keto-adipic acid

$-CO_2$

δ-amino-levulinic acid (2 —ALA)

δ-ALA δ-ALA

$-2H_2O$

Porphobilinogen (4 PBG)

PBG deaminase   PGB deaminase + isomerase

Uro. I   —6H   Urogen. I   Urogen. III   —6H   Uro. III
(excreted)   (excreted)

Urogen.   Urogen.
decarboxylase $-4CO_2$ $-4CO_2$ decarboxylase

Copro. I   —6H   Coprogen. I   Coprogen. III   —6H   Copro. III
(excreted)   (excreted)

$-2CO_2$ Coprogen.
$-4H$ oxidase

Protogen. III (9a)

$-6H$

Key:

PBG: porphobilinogen (monopyrrole)

Urogen., Coprogen., Protogen.:
    porphyrinogens (colorless
    tetra pyrroles)

Uro., Copro., Proto.:
    porphyrins (colored
    irreversibly oxidized porphyrin-
    ogens)

Proto. III (9a)

$+Fe^{++}$ heme synthetase

Heme

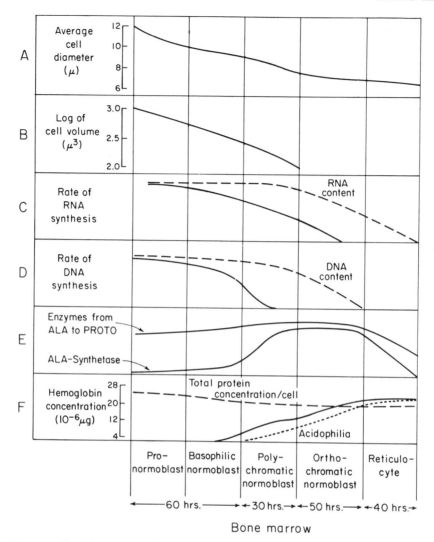

Figure 30–5. Changes in cell size and of various substances in the bone marrow during normal erythroid differentiation and maturation. Unless otherwise specified, the graphs represent the relative values of the substances listed in the left hand column. (From Granick and Levere, in Moore and Brown (eds.): Progress in Hematology, Volume IV. New York, Grune and Stratton, 1964.)

discoidal shape of the red cell persists after the contents have been released by osmotic lysis, possibly, as Murphy has recently suggested, because of the concentration of cholesterol near the edges of the disc with resultant higher interfacial tension.

The red cell envelope is thought to be from 100 to 500 angstroms thick with birefringent properties indicating a radial orientation of lipids and a tangential orientation of proteins. The red cell surface has a negative charge and is freely permeable to water and small anions such as Cl^- and HCO_3^- but to a far less extent to cations such as Na^+ and K^+. The principal function of the adult red cell is to maintain the integrity of the cell envelope and the volume of its contents and to preserve from oxidative denaturation its packaged hemoglobin burden during a normal life span of 120 days. Meanwhile the hemoglobin has loaded oxygen in the lung and partially unloaded it in the tissues thousands of times, and the red cell has traveled hundreds of miles in the vascular bed.

The energy for maintaining cellular integrity and the high internal concentration of potassium, as well as for preventing the oxidation of heme, is derived from the only two carbohydrate pathways remaining to the adult red cell (Fig. 30–7). The Embden-

Myerhof pathway carries out through a series of phosphorylated intermediates the anaerobic conversion of glucose to lactate with the net production of potential energy in the form of two moles of adenosine triphosphate (ATP) for each mole of glucose. ATP is essential for maintaining the normal cation concentration and balance of the red cells. Reduced diphosphopyridine nucleotide (DPNH) is also produced by this pathway. DPNH is important for the function of enzymes such as methemoglobin reductase. When the phosphogluconate pathway oxidizes one mole of glucose to carbon dioxide and water, it produces two moles of a compound with high reductive capacity, reduced triphosphopyridine nucleotide (TPNH). Critical to cell survival in the circulation is the action of glutathione reductase upon thiols of the red cell envelope. This enzyme is linked to TPNH. Normally, the glycolytic pathway utilizes about ten times as much glucose as does the phosphogluconate shunt. With aging of the adult red cell in the circulation the ability of some of the enzymes of both pathways declines, as do the lipids of the red cell envelope.

Except for iron, the chemical composition of the adult red cells provides little suggestion as to the dietary factors which may under clinical circumstances limit the production of red cells and of hemoglobin. This is presumably because the necessary amino acids for the production of globin, keratin and heme are present in the normal diet. Dietary protein deficiency per se has not been established as a cause of anemia in man, but in rats it decreases the hemoglobin production within a few days, apparently by an indirect effect through the decreased formation of erythropoietin. Clinically, in iron deficiency anemia with hypoproteinemia, administration of iron while patients are maintained on low protein diets causes the formation of red cells and hemoglobin at the expense of plasma protein. Moreover, animal dietary protein unless carefully purified contain vitamins in-

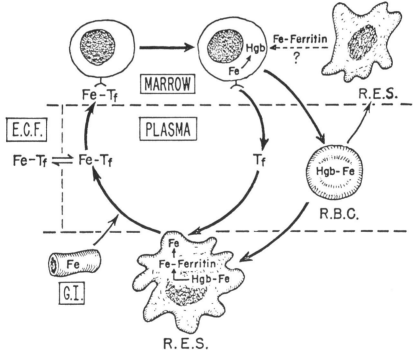

Figure 30–6. A diagrammatic representation of the cyclic mechanisms involved in the delivery of iron to the immature red cell. No attempt has been made to illustrate a feedback of iron from an "erythropoietic labile pool," nor the relatively small exchange in transferrin-bound iron with sites other than the bone marrow. Attachment of transferrin to the cell receptors is necessary before the iron can enter the cell. Thereafter the transferrin molecule leaves the cell and is ready to accept two more trivalent iron molecules. Attachment of iron to transferrin renders it highly effective in competing for red cell receptor sites with iron-free transferrin. In the diagram Tf is transferrin; Fe-Tf, trivalent iron bound to transferrin; E.C.F., extracellular fluid; R.E.S., reticuloendothelial system or cell; G.I., gastrointestinal tract. (From Katz: Scand. J. Haematol., Suppl. 6:15, 1965.)

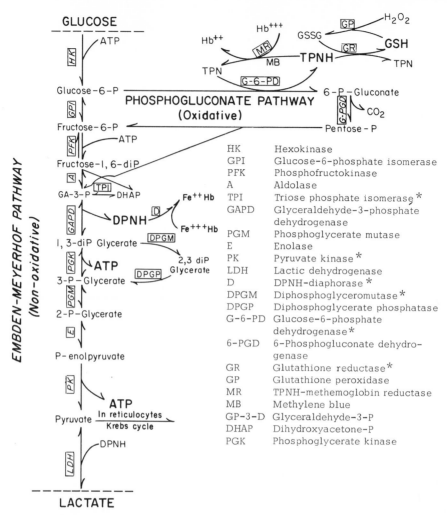

Figure 30–7. Erythrocyte metabolic pathways in adult erythrocytes. Asterisks indicate recognized hereditary enzyme deficiencies. In the glycolytic pathway, deficiencies of pyruvate kinase, triose phosphate isomerase and diphosphoglyceromutase are responsible for shortening cell survival. In the oxidative pathway, deficiencies of glucose-6-phosphate dehydrogenase, glutathione reductase or GSH itself provide a liability to exogenous or endogenous oxidative stress and thus to acute hemolysis with oxidant drug exposure, or, if severe enough, to chronic hemolysis without oxidant drug administration. (From Simon, Giblett, and Finch: Red Cell Manual. Seattle, University of Washington Press, 1966.)

volved in erythropoiesis. In experimental animals, however, under controlled conditions of nutritional deficiency or chronic blood loss, the rate of hemoglobin production can be shown to be increased by the addition of various individual amino acids, of constituents of the vitamin B complex such as riboflavin, pyridoxine, vitamin B_{12}, pteroylglutamic (folic) acid and its conjugates. Such nutritional deficiencies in man may lead to anemia as a result of inadequate erythropoiesis. On the other hand, hereditary or acquired defects of the energetic processes of the circulating red cells or of their surfaces can shorten their

life span and so produce hemolytic anemias. The pathologic physiology of these contrasting, though sometimes combined, situations will be discussed below.

PRODUCTION RATES OF ERYTHROCYTES AND HEMOGLOBIN

To comprehend the nature of clinical anemias, it is valuable to know whether the rates of red cell and hemoglobin production are significantly decreased or increased and, especially, whether a change can be induced in those processes. Red cell production rates may often be estimated roughly from the ratio of erythroid to myeloid cells in the marrow, usually about 1:3 when erythroid and myeloid production are both normal. The most useful morphologic index of the rate of red cell production is the number of reticulocytes in the peripheral blood (normally about 0.8 per cent or 60,000 per cubic millimeter), especially at times when significant changes in the rate of erythropoiesis occur (Figs. 30–2 and 30–4). When in severe anemia the peripheral blood contains numerous polychromatophilic and somewhat macrocytic erythrocytes accompanied by nucleated red cells, there is probably a premature release of reticulocytes into the blood with consequently a longer than normal persistence of their reticulum. Finch has suggested that an arbitrary allowance be made for these circumstances by dividing the number of reticulocytes by two. By the use of tracer amounts of radioactive iron bound to transferrin by incubation with plasma and given intravenously, the half-time of its disappearance from the plasma may be determined in a few hours and its percentage reappearance in circulating hemoglobin after a few days. Normally, the half-time for plasma iron is about 90 minutes; and this together with the plasma iron level shows that the plasma iron turnover is at the average rate of 0.6 mg. per 100 ml. of blood per day. However, from data on red cell utilization of radioiron it is apparent that about 0.15 mg. does not represent iron entering into erythropoiesis. In the normal subject, over 75 per cent of the injected radioiron reappears in labeled hemoglobin in fourteen days, indicating a daily utilization of about 0.45 mg. of iron per 100 ml. blood, and equivalent to about 0.83 per cent of the circulating hemoglobin mass. In addition, by scanning over such organs as the sternal and sacral marrows, the liver and spleen, the normal rapid transit of radioiron from the plasma into the bone marrow and thence progressively into the circulating red cells can be followed (Fig. 30–8). In aplastic anemia with defective erythropoiesis the radioiron may fail to go to the marrow and instead be deposited chiefly in the liver cells. In hemolytic anemia, the radioiron rapidly enters and leaves the bone marrow and accumulates progressively in the liver and/or spleen depending on the site of sequestration of the short-lived, labeled red cells.

The results reported in most anemias have correlated well with reasonable expectations, including those of therapeutic procedures with known effects upon the rate of erythropoiesis. However, in pernicious anemia and thalassemia major, determinations of the plasma iron turnover have given 80 to 90 per cent higher values than those for red cell utilization. Consequently, Finch has developed the concept of "ineffective" erythropoiesis which was originally proposed by Whipple because of the large bile pigment output relative to the hemoglobin production in pernicious anemia. This idea was later confirmed by London using N^{15} glycine as a heme and bile pigment precursor and appears to account for the discrepancy existing between increased erythroid : myeloid ratios and fecal stercobilin on the one hand and decreased reticulocytes on the other. It is consistent with the ferrokinetic data indicating a far greater iron utilization by the marrow than can be accounted for by the delivery of viable red cells containing labeled hemoglobin to the circulation (Fig. 30–8).

Another measure of erythropoiesis requires the determination of the daily excretion of coproporphyrin type I in urine and feces. These difficult collections and chemical determinations are principally of interest for the insight given into the synthesis of hemoglobin. An outline of this process is shown in Table 30–1. The numerical type of the isomeric porphyrins, which contain four pyrrole nuclei united by four methene bridges in a ring, is defined by the arrangement of four methyl and four ethyl radicles on the pyrrole nuclei. When hemoglobin is synthesized in the erythroid cells of the bone marrow, with the formation of type III protoporphyrin, a certain proportion of type I porphyrin is also formed. The latter does not chelate iron to form heme and is subsequently excreted in the bile and urine as coproporphyrin type I. This is in contrast to the fate of the porphyrin type III of hemoglobin, which becomes bilirubin when the porphyrin ring is opened. On the other hand, porphyrin rings not containing iron cannot be opened and are excreted as such. Consequently when hemoglobin synthesis is increased in response to anemia, the excretion of coproporphyrin type I in the feces is also increased as, for example, in congenital spherocytic anemia and in pernicious anemia. Splenectomy in the former and vitamin B_{12} therapy in the latter result in a decreased excretion of coproporphyrin type I, because in both, but for different reasons, such therapy decreases the production of hemoglobin. Thus, in spherocytic anemia, this is patently the result of the rapid lessening of the

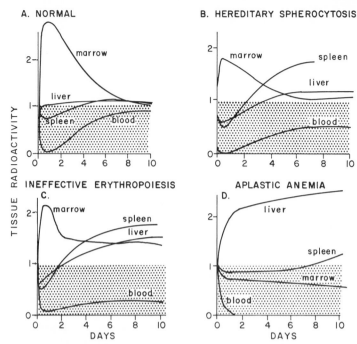

Figure 30–8. Profiles of radioiron distribution. The unit 1 represents radioactivity in the indicated tissue immediately after the injection of radioiron. In the normal individual (*A*) as the radioiron leaves the plasma, there is a corresponding rise in marrow radioactivity. Marrow activity then falls as the radioiron is incorporated into the hemoglobin of newly formed erythrocytes. Since all developing red cell precursors, including the reticulocytes, take up the injected radioiron, the circulating red cells contain some radioactivity within 24 hours of injection. Radioactivity in the liver and spleen shows little change. In pathologic states other patterns of iron distribution are observed. For example, in *hereditary spherocytosis* (*B*) the marrow produces cells which are trapped and subsequently destroyed in the spleen, here indicated by the accumulation of radioactivity in the spleen and the reduced proportion of activity appearing in the circulating erythrocytes. In *ineffective erythropoiesis* (*C*) the marrow is active as shown by its initial uptake of radioiron. However, radioactivity subsequently accumulates in the liver, spleen and marrow, indicating that a large portion of the erythroid activity is concerned with the production of nonviable erythrocytes, which are removed by the reticuloendothelial cells of these organs. The ferrokinetics of a patient with *aplastic anemia* lacking erythroid marrow function is shown in *D*. There is no marrow uptake of radioiron and none appears in the circulating red cell mass. Instead, there is pathologic deposition of iron in the parenchymal cells of the liver. (From Simon, Giblett, and Finch: Red Cell Manual. Seattle, University of Washington Press, 1966.)

anemia. In pernicious anemia with more "effective" erythropoiesis, the intramedullary loss of hemoglobin-containing precursors is abolished by vitamin B_{12} therapy. Coproporphyrin type III appears in significant amounts in the urine and feces only when there are perversions in the synthesis of hemoglobin.

Normally, the rates of red cell and hemoglobin production and destruction are balanced so that the same numbers of red cells and amounts of hemoglobin enter and leave the circulating red cell mass daily. In response to anemia, the plasma iron turnover increases within hours as pronormoblast differentiation begins and proceeds to the delivery of reticulocytes to the circulation within three or four days. Anemia, due to sus-

tained increased red cell destruction (or loss), becomes progressively more severe unless and until the rate of red cell production increases to equal the rate of destruction. When that occurs, the levels of circulating red cells and hemoglobin again become constant, but now at an anemic level. The principles of a homeostatic mechanism, such as is clearly involved here, require that for a continued response to take place there must be a continued stimulus. Therefore, for even slight compensatory red cell production to persist, some degree of anemia must continue. Instances of "compensated" chronic hemolysis without anemia appear to provide unexplained exceptions. With severe chronic hemolytic anemias, the rate of effective red cell production may be increased

ERYTHROCYTE DESTRUCTION

The average normal life-span of the red cell in the circulation is from 100 to 120 days. Transfused red cells which persist normally in circulation are removed in linear fashion, presumably indicating that in any sample of normal blood, there are equal quotas of red cells of from 1 to 120 days of age. Each quota apparently survives for its expected life-span. This conclusion is based upon determinations of the survival of transfused compatible normal red cells identified by appropriate antiserums, either as unagglutinable (group O) or as M or N specificities different from those of the red cells of the recipient, as well as by calculations from red cell radioiron utilization. The red cells of either donor or recipient may also be labeled in vitro with radioactive chromium in the form of sodium chromate, which has an initial loss by in vivo elution of 5 per cent the first day and 1 per cent a day thereafter. The normal biological half-life of the Cr^{51} label is about 26 days, and it has the additional advantage of emitting gamma irradiation by which the sites of red cell sequestration (liver or spleen) can be detected by body surface scanning. In the normal person approximately 0.83 per cent of the total number of red corpuscles, or those contained in about 45 ml. of blood, are presumed to be destroyed each day. When transfused red cells are destroyed by an active hemolytic process, their removal is to a greater or less extent independent of their age and may be so increased that the average cell may survive only a few days. Under these circumstances the survival curve of the labeled cells is nonlinear and approaches an exponential form, indicating the destruction of a constant percentage of the transfused red cells daily. In the absence of bleeding, a rate of decline of red cells, hemoglobin or of hematocrit values of more than 1 per cent a day is prima facie evidence of a hemolytic process. Complete failure of erythropoiesis alone could account for only a 1 per cent decline. An elevated serum level of indirect (unconjugated) bilirubin and a substantial increase in the daily excretion of fecal urobilinogen are indicative of increased hemoglobin catabolism, although, for reasons already given, not necessarily derived from red cells in circulation. Finally, of course, evidences of increased red cell production not resulting in a gain in circulating blood values imply a corresponding rate of hemolysis.

There are at least four ways in which the red cell may be destroyed normally or in hemolytic anemias. Although the first of these, *phagocytosis* of entire red cells by cells of the reticuloendothelial system, is often mentioned, and indeed is observed in certain pathologic conditions, the quantitative aspects of the process are difficult to evaluate and seem inadequate, at least as a primary mechanism for increased red cell destruction, however important it may be as a "mopping up" process. Unless phagocytosed red cells are released into the plasma again, erythrophagocytosis itself cannot be responsible for the changes in osmotic and mechanical fragilities of the red cells observed in certain hemolytic anemias. Phagocytosis of red cells by granulocytes may develop within minutes in incubated blood samples from patients with acquired hemolytic anemias, and it may be induced in mixtures of normal red cells and white cells with serum containing incompatible antibodies or active hemolysins. Heating of the serum to destroy complement inhibits, but does not abolish, phagocytosis. Phagocytosis in the spleen and bone marrow is observed in many conditions, including pernicious anemia, and at postmortem examinations, but biopsies during life do not show this to be an important finding.

The second method, that of *hemolysis* of red cells by specific agents in the plasma, is rare, but is indubitably exemplified in certain hemolytic anemias in which a lytic system requiring complement may be demonstrated in vitro. Lysis of human red cells in vitro by complement-requiring antibodies, despite obvious release of hemoglobin, is *not* accompanied by swelling or change in osmotic fragility of the surviving red cells. Recent observations with the electron microscope suggest that immune lysis is caused by the rapid formation of numerous holes in the red cell envelope (Fig. 30-9) of a size sufficient to permit leakage of hemoglobin and, of course, cations and water, so that colloid osmotic pressure differentials with plasma proteins do not develop. Nonspecific lytic agents have also been reported to develop in "unmoved" incubated plasma (lysolecithin) and to be present in saline extracts of certain normal tissues, such as the lung, liver, kidney and spleen. Whether these are physiologically active is difficult to ascertain, because both serum and tissues contain powerful inhibitors. However, because in vitro such tissue lysins,

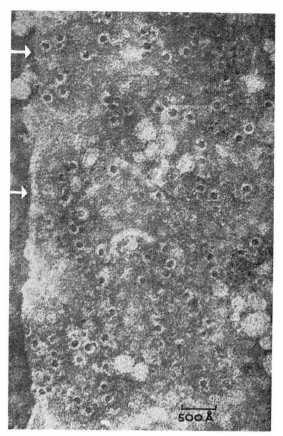

Figure 30–9. Electron microphotograph of part of the membrane of a sheep erythrocyte lysed with Forssman antibody and guinea pig complement. Numerous "holes" are seen, each surrounded by a clear zone. (From Borsos, Dourmashkin, and Humphrey: Nature, 202:251, 1964.)

in contrast to immune lysins, are able to increase the osmotic fragility of normal red cells, their influence will be considered in connection with the secondary effects of agglutination of red cells in vivo. In acquired hemolytic anemia autoagglutination in vitro of the red cells, which in such clumps are sometimes observed to be spheroidal, is much more commonly demonstrable than autohemolysis. Red cells coated with "incomplete" antibodies are not lysed in vitro, but are readily sequestered by spleen or liver in vivo and there destroyed.

The third method, that of *osmotic lysis,* is suggested by the well-known phenomenon of increased osmotic fragility of the red corpuscles in congenital spherocytic anemia. Radioiron labeling of a cohort of normal red cells has shown this osmotic fragility to increase toward the end of their life-span. Several observers have also noted slightly increased osmotic fragility of the red cells in

the splenic vein or pulp in normal animals and in man. It is doubtful, however, whether this characteristic of the red cell is normally of direct importance in red cell destruction, because osmotic lysis of the cell is manifest in vitro only in considerably hypotonic solutions. Anything like a comparable degree of hypotonicity clearly does not exist in the body. The normal summation curve of percentage hemolysis in a range of hypotonic salt solutions is symmetrically S-shaped (see Fig. 30–12). In certain types of congenital and acquired hemolytic anemia this curve, as pointed out by Dacie, is asymmetrical with a "tail" because of the presence of an increased proportion of red cells with greater than normal osmotic fragility. However, the most osmotically fragile red cells rarely approach the point of osmotic lysis in isotonic serum, and in that medium such red cells are invariably increased in their mechanical fragility. This is probably an expression of weakness of the cell envelope and is accompanied by the loss of normal cation impermeability together with cell swelling associated with holes in the cell envelope insufficient in size to permit leakage of hemoglobin until further damage has been done. Recent observations by Jacob have shown that reduced sulfhydryl inhibitors acting upon the red cell membrane, but not affecting the cell's metabolic activities can initiate osmotic swelling. This can be prevented initially by the addition of a nonpenetrating molecule such as sucrose to the suspension medium. Moreover, as will be discussed below, a primary metabolic failure of the red cell may allow secondary damage to membrane sulfhydryl groups and cause red cell sequestration and destruction before "colloid osmotic" swelling of the red cells has become significant. A different situation occurs, as has already been mentioned, when complement-mediated lysis rapidly produces large holes or clusters of holes in the red cell membrane. Here hemoglobin escapes without the intervention of cell swelling due to a colloid osmotic differential with that of the plasma.

The fourth method, that of *mechanical destruction* due to the traumatic effect of the motion of the circulation on the red cells, has much to recommend it as that most likely in normal and in many pathologic conditions. Such observations as those of Krogh upon the distortions of red cells in traversing small capillaries are graphic testimony to the mechanical stresses so imposed upon the red cell. Reliable values may be obtained for the percentage of red cells in a given sample that are destroyed in vitro by mechanical trauma of specified amount and duration. This does not destroy the red cells by progressive fragmentation, as first suggested by Rous and Robertson, but apparently by an all or none rupture of the cell membrane with more or less complete escape of the cell contents. Shen has demonstrated the influence of such factors as increased hematocrit and strong agglutination of red cells as well as the effect spheroidicity and of inherent membrane weakness in causing increased mechanical fragility in vitro. Recently the mystery of "march hemoglobinuria" was shown by Davidson to depend upon trauma to the red cells in the vessels of the feet during running on a hard surface. In the susceptible athletes it was readily prevented by the use of rubber foot pads in their shoes.

A mechanism involving the exhaustion of the energy-supplying chemical processes would seem best to explain the facts concerning the predictable longevity of the normal red cell in circulation. Allison and Burn have demonstrated a decline in some of the enzymatic activities of the red cell with age, and others have shown the increased susceptibility of old red cells to osmotic, immune and oxidant drug-induced hemolysis. Young and his associates have shown that the mechanical fragility of dog red cells undergoes gradual increase, after more than half the lifetime of the red cell in the circulation. Finally, the fact that the mechanical fragility of a sample of blood increases in exponential fashion with its hematocrit may offer a homeostatic device for increasing the rate of erythrocyte destruction as the red cell concentration rises, and vice versa. In experimental hemolytic anemias following the injection of anti-red cell immune serum and the administration of oxidant drugs, the mechanical as well as the osmotic fragility of the red cells is increased. This is also the case in several types of clinical hemolytic anemias, including for example, congenital spherocytic jaundice. Whenever the osmotic fragility of red cells is increased, their mechanical fragility is also increased. Indeed, increased mechanical fragility of the red cells in certain hemolytic anemias may not be accompanied by increased osmotic fragility an illustration of the facts that the red cell membrane may be slightly damaged without necessarily a change in permeability to cations.

SPLENIC FUNCTIONS

Because the functions of the spleen and reticuloendothelial system will be considered in detail in Chapter 31, only the high points of the relation of the spleen to the sequestration and destruction of red cells will be touched upon here. Some authors have considered the spleen to have a suppressive effect upon hematopoiesis. Incontrovertible evidence for such an action is actually meager when the secondary effects of the cell-sequestering functions of the spleen upon red cells, granulocytes and platelets are excluded from consideration. On the other hand, because splenectomy for a time tends to lower the normal plasma iron level, it is probable that the reticuloendothelial cells of the spleen, like those of the bone marrow, normally facilitate the return of iron from destroyed red cells to the plasma, and so promote erythropoiesis indirectly.

It is well established that the spleen is a filter with a high degree of discrimination. "Flat" (target) cells or cells containing nuclear remains (Howell-Jolly bodies) or iron-containing granules (siderocytes) are found in the peripheral blood for many months or even years after splenectomy. In congenital absence of the spleen and in patients given oxidant drugs following splenectomy, granules of denatured hemoglobin (Heinz bodies) in the red cells are frequently seen. These effects may well be the result of the loss of a filter. Crosby has shown that the spleen can remove the iron granules from siderocytes, but that it sequesters and destroys red cells containing Heinz bodies produced experimentally in animals. These observations are respectively consistent with Dacie's suggestion of a local splenic influence accelerating the final stages of the incorporation of iron into heme and with the anticipated destructive effect of splenic sequestration upon red cells containing Heinz bodies, which are evidence of denatured hemoglobin and of presumptive cell injury.

The reticulocytopenia of some patients with splenomegaly has been put forward as evidence of the spleen's inhibitory influence upon erythropoiesis. However, recently Berendes found that in congenital spherocytic anemia the percentage of reticulocytes in the splenic pulp blood considerably exceeded that in the circulating blood, suggesting a quite different explanation for the apparent inhibitory influence of the spleen upon erythropoiesis. Such reticulocyte sequestration may well be the result of their greater size or "stickiness." Indeed, Jandl observed that reticulocytes suspended in serum can be separated from adult red cells by filtration at low pressure through

Millipore filters. Young has shown that perfusion of a human spleen with a compatible mixture of normal and congenital spherocytic anemia red cells resulted in the selective retention of the latter type of cell. Emerson and Ham achieved similar results in vivo with transfusions of compatible normal red cells to patients with congenital spherocytic anemia a few days prior to splenectomy. With such a fine degree of discrimination between individual red cell size or shape established as a function of the spleen, it becomes easy to understand that this organ may easily retain other morphologically altered or agglutinated red cells; for example, as in sickle cell disease or in certain types of acquired hemolytic anemia. This has now been fully confirmed in such conditions by surface scintillation counting over the spleen after the reinjection of patients' cells labeled with radioactive chromium.

It is still not clear how the spleen (or other tissues) discriminates between normal and abnormal red cells of apparently entirely similar morphology and behavior in vitro in the patient's serum. However, Jandl has shown that autologous or homologous Rh-positive red cells weakly or even undetectably sensitized with the "incomplete" antibody of anti-Rh serum and labeled with radioactive chromium are selectively retained by the spleen of both Rh-positive and Rh-negative subjects (Fig. 31–1). Jacob has recently shown that red cells, some of whose surface sulfhydryl groups have been inhibited by a nonpenetrating organic mercurial, are retained by the spleen, although their morphology, metabolism and osmotic fragility were not affected. Archer has also found that red cells sensitized with incomplete Rh antibody adhere to monocytes (possibly with physical characteristics similar to those of reticuloendothelial cells) after being brought into contact by brief centrifugation. This may be the essence of the physical process of selective retention of Rh-sensitized red cells which neither are agglutinated nor appear to be morphologically abnormal when suspended in the patients' serum. However, many large red cell agglutinates are found in blood from the splenic pulp of such patients at operation while none may be present in samples of the peripheral blood.

The phenomenon of intravascular retention of red cells in the splenic pulp or elsewhere has been termed *erythrostasis* and appears to have important physiologic implications. Of necessity it leads to concentration of red cells relative to plasma and so to diminished opportunities for metabolic exchanges between cells and plasma. When erythroconcentration occurs in a living tissue, its circulation is diminished or impeded and ischemia or even infarction may ensue. Another result of erythrostasis is the enhanced opportunity for erythrophagocytosis by tissue and blood leukocytes, for their competitive utilization of glucose and other protective substances or for their release of lytic principles. Changes in the osmotic and mechanical fragility of red cells occur in the spleen under these circumstances and may be reflected in the circulating red cell population if these cells escape from the area of erythrostasis before they are destroyed.

In vitro the cells of patients with congenital spherocytosis are unusually susceptible to autohemolysis upon incubation of several hours' duration, for reasons to be discussed below. Incubation of normal red cells with liver pulp in vitro causes marked changes in their osmotic and mechanical fragilities within two to four hours. However, even supposing that autohemolysis is accelerated in some way by contact with living tissue, it is difficult to extrapolate to the rapid lytic process following the injection of otherwise compatible weakly Rh-sensitized Cr51-labeled red cells into a normal subject. Under these circumstances, after 30 minutes half the injected red cells were sequestered in the spleen and the plasma hemoglobin began to rise within a few minutes to reach a small peak after an hour. Thus, it must be supposed that some active type of lytic process was involved other than that represented by erythrostasis of red cells even with a severe primary metabolic defect. Knowledge of the pathologic physiology of red cell sequestration in the spleen appears now to explain the beneficial results of splenectomy in congenital spherocytic anemia and in some instances of acquired hemolytic anemia. Splenectomy should prove to be beneficial whenever, for one reason or another, the spleen serves as an organ of erythrostasis. Evaluation of this function appears to be possible most directly by surface counting over the organ after the removal of a sample of the patient's red cells, their labeling with radioactive chromium, and intravenous reinjection.

HEMOGLOBIN CATABOLISM

In some way effete red cells are recognized on contact by the cells of the reticuloendothelial system of the spleen, liver, lymph nodes and bone marrow, which proceed after their ingestion to break down their hemoglobin to bilirubin, globin and iron. Consequently, the amount of bilirubin in the blood coming from the spleen and bone marrow is greater than that in the blood and entering those organs. It is uncertain whether the conversion of hemoglobin to bilirubin begins with the oxidative splitting off of the globulin within the reticuloendothelial cell or with the formation of the intermediate choleglobin. With either pathway iron is lost in the form of a hydroxide (Fig. 30–10). Thereafter, the globin enters the body protein pool, whereas the ferric iron may remain stored in the retic-

uloendothelial cells or be released to combine with transferrin, the iron-binding protein of the plasma, for transport to the bone marrow for reconversion into hemoglobin. Iron is stored in the reticuloendothelial cells of the liver, spleen or other organs as ferritin and hemosiderin. Recently deposited hemosiderin appears as small granules which apparently enlarge with time and further accretion of iron.

Biliverdin, the first bile pigment, forms with the opening of the porphyrin ring and loss of a molecule of carbon monoxide. It is then quickly reduced to bilirubin and released

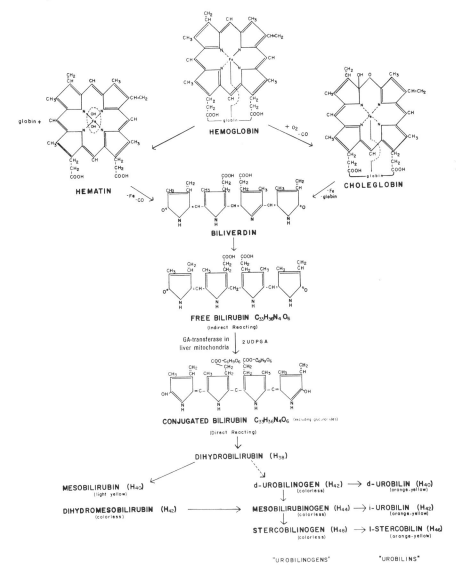

Figure 30–10. Hemoglobin breakdown through bilirubin-urobilinogen pathways. It is not known whether the in vivo pathway proceeds through hematin, choleglobin, or both, in the initial steps. (From Harris: The Red Cell. Cambridge, Mass., Harvard University Press, 1963.)

into the plasma where it is normally carried on an alpha-1-globulin fraction, and when in excess also on albumin. This bilirubin, which gives the so-called indirect-acting van den Bergh reaction, in passing through the liver cells becomes converted to water-soluble, direct-acting bilirubin by conjugation with 2 moles of glucuronic acid and to a small extent with sulfate. Studies with isotopic nitrogen incorporated in dietary glycine indicate that bilirubin is not reused in the formation of hemoglobin. Iron, on the other hand, is so carefully conserved by the body that the adult male probably loses less than 1 mg. a day.

Normally, the plasma contains only traces of hemoglobin, perhaps 2 to 5 mg. per 100 ml. An elevated plasma hemoglobin level indicates active intravascular hemolysis. Crosby has found normal hemoglobin levels in congenital spherocytosis in which splenic red cell sequestration is prominent, but levels between 20 and 25 mg. per 100 ml. in severe sicklemia in which the spleen is usually absent. In one patient with moderately severe thalassemia and a normal plasma hemoglobin level splenectomy caused much clinical improvement, but the plasma hemoglobin rose to 25 mg. per 100 ml. This may have been the result either of relatively more intravascular hemolysis or of less removal of plasma hemoglobin by the reticuloendothelial tissue remaining after splenectomy. Thus, the site and rate of cell lysis may have much to do with whether hemolysis is regarded as "intravascular" or otherwise. In rapid blood destruction with severe and progressive anemia, free hemoglobin in the plasma may reach values of 200 to 500 mg. per 100 ml. Under those circumstances, according to Fairley, another pigment, methemalbumin, also forms as the result of oxidative degradation of hemoglobin into ferric hematin and globin. The hematin promptly unites with plasma albumin to form methemalbumin.

With severe hemolysis the hemoglobin in the plasma may be sufficiently elevated to give rise to hemoglobinuria, which, though often more obvious, is always secondary to a rise in plasma hemoglobin. Following extensive thermal burns or hemolytic transfusion reactions, massive hemoglobinuria may result in anuria. The idea of a "renal threshold" thought to prevent hemoglobinuria until the plasma hemoglobin level reaches 135 mg. per 100 ml. or over has been modified through the work of Laurell and others producing evidence for a plasma "haptoglobin." This glycoprotein, unique in its ability to combine stoichiometrically and irreversibly with two molecules of hemoglobin in vitro, to form a complex of molecular weight about 300,000 is normally present in the alpha-2-globulin fraction at about 90 mg. per 100 ml. of plasma. The large haptoglobin-hemoglobin complex is not excreted by the kidney but is rapidly removed by the reticuloendothelial cells. The rate of formation of haptoglobin is such that, in hemolytic anemias when the rate of red cell destruction merely exceeds twice the normal, haptoglobin is absent from the plasma. Thereafter, additional hemoglobin is filtered through the glomeruli but does not appear in the urine until the capacity of the tubules for reabsorption has been exceeded. Hemoglobin is degraded in the tubule cells to form ferritin and hemosiderin. The latter appears a few days after an episode of hemoglobinemia in desquamated tubule cells in the urine which contain iron-staining granules.

EXCRETION OF BILIRUBIN

Ducci and Watson found that in the normal person the value for direct-acting bilirubin (bilirubin diglucuronide), read one minute after mixture of serum and diazo reagent, was not over 0.2 mg. per 100 ml.; while the total bilirubin, read fifteen minutes after the addition of alcohol to the serum and including both direct- and indirect-acting bilirubin (free bilirubin), usually did not exceed 1 mg. In hemolytic anemias the total serum bilirubin usually becomes significantly increased and may reach values of 3 or more mg. per 100 ml., only because the amount of bilirubin formed exceeds the excretory capacity of even the healthy liver. The much higher values for unconjugated bilirubin observed in erythroblastosis fetalis are the result of a hemolytic process superimposed upon the reduced glucuronide-forming enzyme systems of the neonatal liver. However, in severe hemolytic anemias without evidence of liver disease or obstruction of the biliary passages the increased total bilirubin content of the blood is often due in part to an increased amount of conjugated bilirubin which has reached the bile canaliculi after traversing the hepatic cells and has been regurgitated into the blood stream. This indicates some degree of liver damage, either secondary to the anoxia created by the anemia or the result of injury to the liver cells caused by the accumulation of red cell debris in the liver capillaries, or possibly the result of hypothetical pigment stasis in the biliary canaliculi. The excessive excretion of bile pigment is probably the basis for the frequent occurrence of pigment stones in the gallbladders of patients with chronic hemolytic anemias.

After the bilirubin has reached the intestine it is reduced by the activity of bacteria, chiefly in the colon, to one or more colorless compounds giving the Ehrlich diazo reaction, mesobilirubinogen, stercobilinogen and other chromogens, usually referred to collectively as urobilinogen. From total collections of the feces and urine over several days the average daily output of urobilinogen can be determined and used as a measure of the rate of hemoglobin destruction. In hemolytic anemia the urobilinogen of the feces is significantly increased, and the urobilinogen in the urine also is augmented absolutely as well as relatively with respect to the amount excreted in the feces. This is due to the fact that, when large amounts of urobilinogen are formed from the large amounts of bile pigments excreted in hemolytic anemias or when the function of the liver is defective, that organ is unable to free the blood of the urobilinogen reabsorbed from the gut, and the excess is excreted in the urine. The details of this relationship were described in Chapter 27.

According to Watson, the normal daily excretion of urobilinogen in the feces is usually from 100 to 200 mg.; that in the urine, such as 0.5 to 4 mg. In hemolytic anemias, such as congenital hemolytic jaundice, the urobilinogen in the feces commonly ranges from 600 to 2000 mg. daily; that in the urine, from 5 to 30 mg. Theoretically, these absolute values should be corrected for the reduction in circulating hemoglobin mass due to the anemia, but other sources of error are probably of greater importance. From such data it is theoretically possible to calculate the rate of hemoglobin destruction on the basis of the assumption that 1 mg. of urobilinogen is derived from 23.9 mg. of destroyed hemoglobin. Thus a daily total excretion of 150 mg. of urobilinogen would represent the catabolism of 150 times 23.9, or 3.585 gm. of hemoglobin. There is an obvious difference between this value and the figure for the average daily amount of blood destroyed, 45 ml. containing about 7 gm. of hemoglobin. The latter value is based on the reasonable assumption that about 0.83 per cent (1/120) of the circulating red cell mass is destroyed daily. This discrepancy is possibly to be explained on the basis that, although bilirubin is quantitatively derived from hemoglobin and excreted in the bile, in the intestine a more or less constant amount is converted to mesobilifuscin, a brownish pigment substance containing only two pyrrole nuclei and not measurable as urobilinogen.

A further objection to the estimation of the rate of red cell destruction on the basis of the Ehrlich reaction and suggesting an error in the opposite direction is the evidence that some of the bile pigment output is derived from the breakdown of heme, possibly before its incorporation in formed red cells. This effect was observed by London, who showed that in normal subjects as much as 15 per cent of isotopic nitrogen ingested in the form of glycine appears to be incorporated into fecal stercobilin within a few days and so before any of the red cells in the circulation containing isotopic nitrogen in their hemoglobin have been destroyed. In pernicious anemia this pigment "short circuit" or indicator of "ineffective erythropoiesis" may account for 60 per cent of the isotopic nitrogen assimilated; in congenital porphyria, for as much as 85 per cent. More recent studies by Israels have shown that this so-called "early labeling" peak of stercobilin includes a portion appearing within a few hours and apparently derived from porphyrin synthesis in liver cells. These matters have been further clarified by the use of radioiron in so-called ferrokinetic studies discussed above.

CONSERVATION OF IRON

Of the three breakdown products of hemoglobin, iron is apparently the most highly prized. Its conservation is an axiom of the wisdom of the body. Indeed, in man, except when in certain hemolytic anemias the rate of blood destruction is so rapid that hemoglobin appears in the urine, the loss of iron from the body in the form of desquamated skin and intestinal cells and in bile and urine combined is insignificant, probably normally amounting to about 1 mg. a day. When blood destruction is increased without hemoglobinuria, the small amount of iron normally present in the bile may be increased tenfold, but even so, reabsorption from the bowel apparently limits its excretion from the body to 3 per cent of that in the bile or a total of 1.5 mg. a day. Of the 12 to 15 mg. of food iron

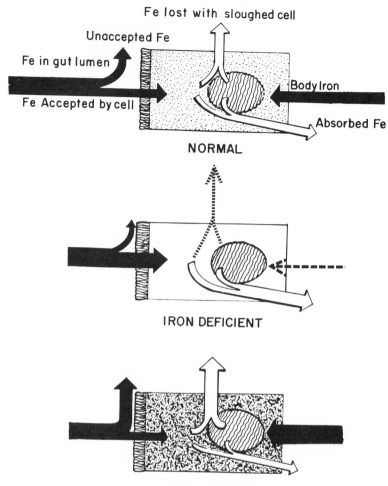

Figure 30–11. A concept of control of iron absorption by the intestinal mucosa. It is predicated that iron absorption is regulated primarily through the columnar epithelium of the small intestine. In normal, iron-replete subjects the mucosal cells may contain a variable amount of iron supplied from the body store. This deposit regulates—within limits—the quantity of iron which can enter the cell from the gut lumen. After the iron has entered the cell it may proceed into the body to fulfill a requirement. Alternatively, a portion of the iron may become fixed in the epithelial cytoplasm, to be lost when the cell is sloughed at the end of its life-span. In iron-deficient subjects there appears to be little or no mechanism to inhibit entrance of iron into the villous epithelial cells or to retain it. Thus dietary iron readily proceeds into the body. In iron-loaded subjects the body iron which is incorporated in the epithelial cells is eventually lost, but during the life-span of the cells its presence inhibits the entrance of iron into the cells. (From Conrad and Crosby: Blood, 22:406, 1963.)

in the normal daily diet, only about 10 per cent is absorbed. Thus the balance between intake and excretion is only slightly favorable.

Storage iron in three states of accessibility for the formation of hemoglobin has been described by Granick. The least available are the yellow, coarse granules of hemosiderin in the reticuloendothelial cells of liver, spleen and marrow. The most available is in the form of monomolecular ferrous and ferric hydroxides. Intermediate is colloidal iron in the

form of ferritin which is ordinarily derived from the breakdown of effete red cells. According to Rath and Finch, microscopic inspection of bone marrow smears for hemosiderin affords a practical measure of the available iron stores. Ferritin is a combination of a protein, apoferritin, with ferric iron. This particular kind of ferric hydroxide-phosphate is distributed in micellar units on the surface of the protein molecule, which sometimes contains as much as 23 per cent of the ferric compound. The presence of iron stabilizes the apoferritin with which it combines.

After the oral administration of iron it is absorbed in ferrous form by the mucosal cells of the duodenum and becomes ferritin in the ferric form. In 1946 Granick proposed that this ferritin produced a "mucosal block" that regulated the iron uptake. Recently this concept has been extended by Crosby, who suggests that as the columnar cells of the mucosa are formed in the crypts, they incorporate iron in proportion to the body's stores. Normally these cells are only partially saturated with intrinsic iron and consequently will accept dietary iron in inverse proportion (Fig. 30–11). Depending on erythropoietic needs, perhaps signaled by the level of serum iron, the assimilated iron leaves the columnar cells and passes into the blood stream. If there is no need for such assimilation, the columnar cells, with their iron burden intact, can be cast off two or three days later when they reach the tips of the villi.

Iron is carried in the plasma in the ferric state by the so-called iron-binding beta-1-globulin, transferrin or siderophyllin, specifically to enter the erythropoietic cells of the bone marrow. This process is facilitated by the fact, demonstrated by Jandl in vitro, that transferrin molecules loaded with iron will displace transferrin molecules that have unloaded their iron burden on the surface of the reticulocyte (Fig. 30–6) and presumably its nucleated precursors. Normally with a serum iron level of from 50 to 150 micrograms per cent the transferrin is about a third saturated with iron. Only with abnormally high saturations of the transferrin is such iron deposited for storage in the reticuloendothelial cells of the liver and spleen. The usual source of the storage iron in those cells is phagocytosis of worn-out red cells or haptoglobin-bound hemoglobin in the plasma.

GENERAL EFFECTS OF ANEMIA

As mentioned above the physical characteristics of the blood are such that, for a given amount of cardiac work, its capacity to transport oxygen is optimal when the hematocrit and the hemoglobin concentration are both normal. Consequently the outstanding defect common to all types of anemia is the decreased capacity of the blood to transport oxygen. In addition, severe leukopenia may allow infection to occur, usually in the oral cavity or about the rectum or vagina; and thrombocytopenia may result in purpura and

bleeding into the skin, mucous membranes or internal organs. The pathologic physiology of special varieties of anemia relates also to specific underlying causes, such as nutritional deficiency, intoxication, infection, physical injury and the effect of local or generalized malignant disease.

The immediate effect of sudden loss of blood is a proportionate reduction in circulating blood volume which is subsequently restored, at first by the entry of fluids from the extracellular space and later by regeneration of plasma protein and red cells. In chronic anemias of moderate degree, according to Gibson, the *total blood volume*, owing to a nearly compensatory increase in plasma volume, is only slightly reduced. With extreme degrees of anemia Sharpey-Schafer finds some decrease in total blood volume, which he regards as a means of maintaining a somewhat higher hemoglobin concentration. In contrast to certain animals, in normal man there are apparently no important reserves of red cells which are not in circulation. With splenomegaly, however, especially in congenital spherocytic jaundice, the splenic pulp, as in the dog, may serve as a considerable reservoir of concentrated red cells.

The *oxygen consumption* of the body is not reduced in anemia. Actually, it is increased by 10 or 20 per cent because of the increased work of the heart, but two important mechanisms provide partial compensation for the decreased ability of the blood to transport oxygen. The first of these results in an *increased cardiac output* and blood flow velocity (Fig. 30–3). The heart beats faster, its systolic size is smaller, and it ejects more blood with each beat. A forceful apex beat, a murmur most commonly systolic, and changes in the S-T segment and T waves of the electrocardiogram are common findings with severe anemia. The peripheral vascular resistance is diminished with increased pulse pressure; and the many open capillaries are manifest in the capillary pulsation visible in the finger tips. In the moderately anemic patient there may be little evidence of such circulatory changes while at rest, though on exertion weakness, palpitation and dyspnea may be prominent symptoms. When the hemoglobin is decreased to about a third of its normal value, the cardiac output at rest is stated to be about double the normal, and at even lower hemoglobin values the venous pressure is increased as cardiac failure threatens.

The second method of partial compensation,

that of a proportionately *increased extraction of oxygen* from the blood during its passage through the capillary bed, is maximally evoked in severe anemia. However, it is apparent only on blood gas analysis that 90 per cent of the available oxygen may have been removed, because the bluish color of reduced hemoglobin is not evident to the eye when circulating hemoglobin values are less than 5 gm. per 100 ml. Another method of compensation which has received inadequate study in anemia may be the increase in the concentration of tissue enzymes concerned with oxygen transport, such as the cytochromes or myohemoglobin. In this connection the observations of Hurtado showing increased amounts of myoglobin in the muscles of dogs which have resided at high altitudes are suggestive, but have not been confirmed for man.

In the absence of intrinsic cardiac disease the patient often displays no discomfort while at rest in bed unless the hemoglobin level falls below a fifth of the normal. Dyspnea, orthopnea or cough are noted only on exertion or excitement or when, with even more severe anemia, failure of circulatory compensation is imminent. Occasionally in elderly patients who presumably have intrinsic disease of the coronary vessels, angina pectoris or signs of *decompensation* of either the left or the right side of the heart may appear with only moderate anemia. In children, especially, the compensatory adjustment seems most effective, but even adults may be forced to enter the hospital only after the hemoglobin has fallen to 10 per cent of the normal concentration.

Many of the symptoms and signs referable to other systems of the body are also attributable to *tissue anoxia*. Presumably anoxia of the nervous system causes headache, easy fatigue, dimness of vision and tendency to fainting. On the other hand, in pernicious anemia the symptoms and signs of degeneration of the dorsal and lateral columns of the spinal cord and even of the brain are sometimes observed with little or no anemia and are due to the underlying nutritional deficiency indicated by the low serum level of vitamin B_{12}. Except for appetite, the function of the gastrointestinal tract does not seem to be much affected by tissue anoxia. Again this is in contrast to the striking glossitis, "indigestion" and diarrhea of pernicious anemia and especially of sprue and sometimes of iron deficiency anemias, on occasion even when hemoglobin values are little reduced. Thus disturbances in the motor function and absorptive capacity of the bowel appear to be

related to the underlying deficiency state rather than to the severity of the anemia.

Renal function is sometimes disturbed in anemias. Polyuria, hyposthenuria (especially in sicklemia) and, occasionally in severe anemias, moderate azotemia and proteinuria are observed. Bradley has shown that in chronic anemia the effective renal whole blood flow is greatly reduced: 31.8 per cent in females and 46 per cent in males. The smaller reduction in percentage of plasma filtered by the glomerulus implies constriction of afferent and efferent glomerular arterioles, especially the former. This vasoconstriction of the kidney vessels may be of value to the anemic organism by diverting blood to other tissues more sensitive to oxygen lack and could best account for the azotemia of some severely anemic patients. Tubular excretion values for Diodrast are also significantly reduced. These findings help to explain the edema that occurs in certain patients with anemia in whom plasma oncotic pressure is normal and heart failure is absent. Strauss found, independently of these factors, a direct relation between water retention following salt administration and hemoglobin levels except in pernicious anemia, in which condition significant water retention did not occur in response to salt loading until shortly after the institution of remission with liver extract therapy when the plasma volume is now known to increase.

Erythrocyte Characteristics

The red cell represents a device by which a high concentration of hemoglobin is maintained in the capillary blood of the lungs and the tissues without the undue increase in colloid osmotic pressure that would ensue if the hemoglobin were in solution in the plasma. The discoidal shape of the red cell permits it safely to traverse capillaries of caliber less than its own diameter because, not being spherical, the necessary deformation of the red cell can be accomplished without destructive stretching of its envelope. Moreover, such molding of the red cell to fit the bore of the capillary shortens the average distance through which oxygen must diffuse in passing from the red cell to the tissue. Owing to the "drag" of the plasma adjacent to the capillary wall, the faster central flow produces an "Indian file" of cuplike red cells.

The *size, color and shape* of the red cell and certain other characteristics are of interest in anemia. Table 30–2 shows values for the average characteristics of the red cells of normal persons at various ages. The mean corpuscular volume (MCV) is calculated by dividing the percentage volume of the sample of blood occupied by the red cells (hematocrit) by their number. The mean corpuscular hemoglobin concentration (MCHC) is obtained by dividing the hemoglobin content in grams per cent of a sample of blood by its hematocrit, or by the number of red cells if the mean corpuscular hemoglobin (MCH) of the individual red cell is the value desired. The average cell diameter (MCD) is determined in blood films by the method of Price-Jones. The average thickness (MCT) of the cell can be calculated on the basis of von Boros' assumption that the red cell is a right cylinder of known diameter (MCD) and volume (MCV).

In anemias the average *volume* of the red cells (MCV) may be as large as 160 or as small as 50 cubic microns. In macrocytic anemias the average red cell diameter may be as great as 9.0, and in microcytic anemias the small red cells, usually also hypochromic, may have an average diameter of only 6.0 microns. As pointed out by Price-Jones, in anemias there is a greater spread of red cell diameters than in normal blood, and their distribution frequency curve may be asymmetric. Diminished stem cell differentiation into pronormoblasts in the early (Stage I) phase of the process of erythropoiesis (Fig. 30–1 and Table 30–3), as in aplastic anemias with hypocellular marrows, results in normocytic, normochromic red cells. Large red cells are the descendants of large parents in the bone marrow, a result characteristic of defects of nucleoprotein synthesis during the middle (Stage II) phase of erythropoiesis. A copious supply of pigment precursors is usually present with macrocytosis, which, though characteristic of nutritional macrocytic anemias, may occur in anemias usually normocytic, especially when there is reticulocytosis or other evidence of increased erythropoiesis. Macrocytosis associated with a diminished MCHC is often noted during the reticulocyte response to severe acute blood loss and in hemolytic crises. It is the result of skipped cell divisions in the marrow or of premature release into the circulation. Moderate macrocytosis, often less impressive than the increase in cell diameter in blood films, is characteristic of the anemia of chronic liver disease. Obstructive jaundice and acute hepatitis with jaundice quickly result in increased cell diameter without, however, increase in cell volume. Small and hypochromic red cells indicate difficulty in the synthesis of hemoglobin, a late (Stage III) process in erythropoiesis, and are characteristic of the anemias of iron deficiency, lead poisoning and in thalassemia major and minor. Various degrees of macrocytosis and hypochromia appear when chronic deficiency of vitamin B_{12} or of folic acid and of iron are combined, as in nutritional deficiency associated with gastrointestinal bleeding, and result in the blood picture of so-called "dimorphic" anemia.

The color, that is, the average *hemoglobin concentration* of the red cells (MCHC), rises above the normal value of 34 ± 2 per cent only in congenital spherocytosis, but may, in hypochromic anemias, go as low as 21 per cent. Hypochromia is the hallmark of insufficient hemoglobin production due to deficiency of iron. It is characteristic also of

TABLE 30–2. NORMAL VALUES FOR ERYTHROCYTES AT VARIOUS AGES.

Age	R.B.C. (Mils.)	HB. (Gm. %)	Hematocrit	Corpuscular Values				
				M.C.V. (cu. μ)	M.C.H. (γγ)	M.C.H.C. (%)	M.C.D. (μ)	M.C.T. (μ)
Day 1	5.1 ± 1.0	19.5 ± 5.0	54.0 ± 10.0	106	38	36	8.6	1.82
Week 3–9	4.7 ± 0.9	14.0 ± 3.3	42.0 ± 7.0	90	30	33	8.1	1.75
Month 3–5	4.5 ± 0.7	12.2 ± 2.3	36.0	80	27	34	7.7	1.72
Month 6–11	4.6	11.8	35.5 ± 5.0	77	26	33	7.4	1.79
Year 1	4.5	11.2	35.5	77	25	32	7.3	1.84
Year 3	4.5	12.5	36.0	80	27	35	7.4	1.86
Year 6–10	4.7	12.9	37.5	80	27	34	7.4	1.86
Adult female	4.8 ± 0.6	14.0 ± 2.0	42.0 ± 5.0	87 ± 5	29 ± 2	34 ± 2	7.5 ± 0.3	1.97
Adult male	5.4 ± 0.8	16.0 ± 2.0	47.0 ± 7.0	87 ± 5	29 ± 2	34 ± 2	7.5 ± 0.3	1.97

M.C.V. = mean corpuscular volume; M.C.H. = mean corpuscular hemoglobin; M.C.H.C. = mean corpuscular hemoglobin concentration; M.C.D. = mean corpuscular diameter; M.C.T. = mean corpuscular thickness.

Slightly modified from Wintrobe, M. M.: Clinical Hematology.

TABLE 30–3. PATHOPHYSIOLOGIC CLASSIFICATION OF THE ERYTHROPOIETIC DISORDERS.*

Category	Stage of Erythropoiesis Principally Affected	Apparent Functional Defect	Marrow Morphology	Red Cell Morphology	Causes
Aplastic anemias	Early	Defect of differentiation	Hypoplastic normal cytology	Normocytic, normochromic	Chemical poisoning, radiation damage, inflammation, renal insufficiency, carcinomatosis, idiopathic
Megaloblastic anemias	Middle	Defect of DNA synthesis	Hyperplastic, maturation arrest (megaloblastic)	Macrocytic, normochromic	Vitamin B$_{12}$ or folic acid deficiency, miscellaneous defects in DNA synthesis
Hypochromic anemias	Late	Defect of hemoglobin synthesis	Hyperplastic, deficient hemoglobinization	Microcytic, hypochromic	Iron deficiency, thalassemia, pyridoxine deficiency, chronic lead poisoning, sideroblastic (sideroachrestic) anemias

* Table kindly supplied by Dr. J. H. Jandl.

pyridoxine responsive anemia and of intoxications such as lead poisoning, in which the metabolism of iron and of porphyrins is patently disturbed resulting in decreased rates of formation of hemoglobin. In thalassemia decreased rate of formation of beta (or alpha) peptide chains in hemoglobin production predicates an extremely variable supply of hemoglobin to individual red cells, on the average a subnormal concentration.

The *shape* of the normal red cell observed in vivo and in plasma is that of a biconcave disk with a slightly depressed central part. The stroma, or envelope, retains the biconcave shape of the original cell even after rupture of the cell in hypotonic solutions. The red cell suspended in plasma is isotonic with it, and its membrane is readily permeable with respect to anions, but far less so to cations and not at all to proteins. A solution of about 0.85 per cent sodium chloride is isotonic with the interior of the red cell and hence causes it neither to swell nor to shrink. At body temperature such substances as water, urea and glucose penetrate the membrane freely, as do oxygen, nitrogen and carbon monoxide. For this reason a solution of glucose in water equal in calculated osmotic pressure to an isotonic solution of sodium chloride hemolyzes the red cells because, unlike sodium chloride, which remains outside, glucose soon distributes itself equally between the inside and the outside of the red cell. Increase in plasma carbon dioxide

results in an increase in plasma bicarbonate anion and, because of the effects described by the Donnan equilibrium, in a shift of chloride anion into the red cell and a shift of bicarbonate anion out of the red cell. This causes, as does acidification of the blood by other substances, slight augmentation of the volume and spheroidicity of the red cell. For this reason the red cells of venous blood are slightly larger and more osmotically fragile than those of arterial blood.

Hypochromic red cells, such as those of iron deficiency or of thalassemia and other hemoglobinopathies, sometimes appear in stained blood films as "target" cells. Such cells tend to be "thin," especially in the central part, even relative to their small diameter, and also are seen in patients with jaundice, due to either extra- or intrahepatic obstruction and following splenectomy. The red cells of congenital spherocytic anemia though slightly small in volume are relatively "thick" or spheroidal even after splenectomy, probably because of their greater content of hemoglobin relative to surface. Provided the red cell envelope has not lost its normal relative impermeability to cations the so-called *osmotic fragility*, that is, the concentration of hypotonic salt solution initiating leakage of hemoglobin is determined roughly by the average diameter-thickness ratio; in functional terms, by the difference between the original discoidal volume of the red cell in isotonic plasma and that of a sphere of equal surface. This is because, short of lysis, red cells of different so-called osmotic fragilities actually behave alike osmotically. That is, the percentage increases above their original volumes, in isotonic plasma, of red cells of *different* osmotic fragilities, when placed in a given hypotonic plasma, are *identical*. When, however, a red cell swells to such an extent that its shape has become completely spherical, further increase in volume is impossible without increase in surface. Under these circumstances the fact that the surface of a red cell is "plastic but not elastic," as Haden has expressed it, causes stretching of the cell envelope and the development of numerous holes eventually large enough to permit hemoglobin to leak out.

Normally the range of red cell shapes results in a symmetrical, S-shaped, summation curve of percentage hemolysis in a range of hypotonic saline solutions (Fig. 30–12). In a given sample of normal blood relatively spheroidal ("thick") red cells are hemolyzed by relatively small increases in hypotonicity,

while the more discoidal ("thin") red cells are hemolyzed only by larger increases in hypotonicity. If the majority of the red cells are abnormally "thick," as in hereditary spherocytic anemia, as in iron-deficiency anemia, the main body of the S-shaped curve will be symmetrically shifted to the left or to the right, respectively. If, however, only a portion of the red cells is so altered, only the extremities of the curve will be extended to the left or to the right due to hemolysis in the relatively less and more hypotonic solutions, respectively.

In any severe anemia the range and variation in cell shape is increased and "club," "tailed," "teardrop" and other bizarre forms are frequent. However, when the marrow is the site of invasion by foreign cells, for instance, granulomas or cancer cells or organized tissue (fibrosis or osteosclerosis) even with little anemia, the variations in red cell size and shape may be impressive. Because such anomalies of shape are seen in nucleated red cells in the bone marrow or cells that may

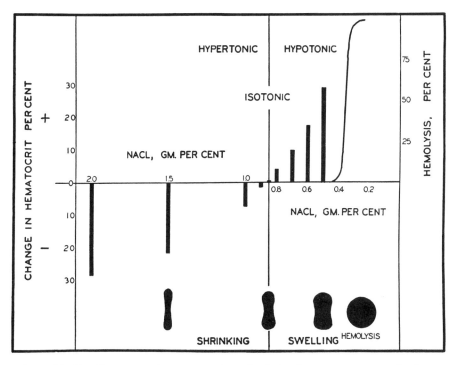

Figure 30–12. Diagrammatic representation of relation between tonicity and volume and shape of red cells. Note that in hypertonic solutions the cell volume becomes smaller and the cells become "flatter." In hypotonic solutions the cell volume increases and the shape of the cell approaches that of a sphere which is critical for the destruction of the cell. The S-shaped summation curve of percentage hemolysis in hypotonic salt solution begins at about 0.44, attains a value of 50 per cent at about 0.35 and reaches a value of 100 per cent at about 0.26 per cent sodium chloride. With normal blood the curve is symmetrical, suggesting that it represents variation in relative spheroidicity about a mean. (Reproduced from a figure kindly supplied by Dr. T. Hale Ham.)

escape in small numbers into the blood, the aberrations are thought to be of production. Under other circumstances "microangiopathic hemolytic anemia" is featured by blood films with "triangular" or "helmet" forms of red cells. This has been ascribed to mechanical injury in the circulation, because similar appearances have been noted in patients with regurgitant jets of blood impinging on teflon grafts or other prostheses inserted during cardiac surgery.

So-called "burr" cells may be seen in the anemia of uremia and in the hemolytic anemia of the rare patients with absence of serum beta lipoprotein in whom the red cells are seen to be "spiny," the so-called acanthocytes. This is one type of the familiar crenation of red cells which probably arises from a variety of causes affecting the lipid composition and negative charge of the red cell envelope. Red cells suspended in saline between slide and and cover glass promptly become covered with small projections which are instantly dispelled by a drop of serum. As Murphy has recently shown, the loss of cholesterol to plasma through esterification also causes crenation. The most dramatic change in red cell shape is that of "sickling" due to the unique physical behavior of an abnormal hemoglobin which causes the characteristic deformity of the red cell envelope when the blood is de-oxygenated in vivo or in vitro. Re-exposure to oxygen at once restores the discoidal form of the red cells. Therefore the inevitable exposure to oxygen involved in preparation prevents sickled cells from being seen in the blood films of patients with sicklemia unless the red cells have acquired a fixed deformity in vivo as is characteristically the case for a small percentage. Twenty-four hour incubation of deoxygenated sickle red cells in vitro produces similar "irreversible" sickled forms, probably because of fixed changes in the cell envelope.

Several types of basophilic inclusion bodies are seen in red cells stained with Romanowsky dyes. Nuclear remains (DNA) in the form of a blackish dot (Howell-Jolly body) are common in pernicious anemia. RNA in the form of disseminated ribosomes gives the bluish color to the young red cells in blood films described as showing polychromatophilia. When aggregated, as in slowly dried blood films or in lead poisoning, clumps of ribosomes appear as numerous uniform small bluish dots with the even distribution characteristic of the so-called *stippled cells*. When supravitally stained with brilliant cresyl blue,

the ribosomes coalesce to form the bluish network that gives its name to the *reticulocyte*. One to a few-medium sized nonuniform granules representing iron-protein complexes may stain blue with Romanowsky dyes (Pappenheimer bodies) or with the Prussian blue reaction (siderotic granules) and are normally present in a variable percentage of marrow normoblasts, but rarely in normal red cells and never in those of iron deficiency anemias. These bodies represent iron in mitochondria, not yet incorporated into hemoglobin. *Siderocytes* are especially prevalent when there is difficulty in heme synthesis as in thalassemia in which the mitochondria are loaded with excess iron. In the bone marrow of these patients numerous iron granules may surround the nucleus giving the appearance known as "ringed sideroblasts." They are especially prevalent (40 to 80 per cent) in conditions known variously as sideroachrestic anemia (Heilmeyer) or refractory normoblastic anemia (Dacie). *Heinz bodies,* which are aggregates of oxidatively denatured hemoglobin, the result of either drug administration or of unstable hemoglobins, can be shown by the electron microscope to form initially near mitochondria and to grow by coalescence and eventually to come to lie just beneath the red cell envelope, and sometimes to distort and project through it. These bodies require supravital staining with cresyl violet or inspection of fresh preparations with the phase microscope for their demonstration. They are not visible with Romanowsky stains, although the resulting deformities of the red cell envelope may be. Because, as Crosby has shown, the granules of siderocytes are removed by the spleen and the entire cell containing Heinz bodies is destroyed by that organ, both types of abnormality are more prevalent in patients with splenic agenesis or after splenectomy. Other important abnormal characteristics of the red cell will be discussed in the section on Hemolytic Anemias.

PERIPHERAL BLOOD IN ANEMIA

Because red cells, granulocytes and platelets develop in the bone marrow, observations of their number and type in the peripheral blood frequently yield important information about the nature of the underlying disturbance and the functional state of the bone marrow. In general, when the bone marrow is physiologically hyperactive—as, for example, in congenital spherocytic anemia—the peripheral blood exhibits an increased percentage of reticulocytes, and at least normal numbers of granulocytes and platelets. Sometimes moderate leukocytosis with a relative increase of young granulocytes and increased numbers of platelets testify to the ability of the marrow precursors of these elements to respond to some stimulus, not necessarily simply the anemia. When, on the other hand, the bone marrow is physiologically hypoactive, as indicated by cellular aplasia or hypoplasia—as, for example, in acute benzol poisoning—the peripheral blood usually exhibits few reticulocytes and decreased numbers of white cells and platelets. The granulocytes are reduced in number and are mostly fully mature.

A peripheral blood picture suggesting physiologic hypofunction does not, however, necessarily mean a scarcity of germinal cells in the bone marrow. Thus the immature and increased erythroid cellularity of the bone marrow in anemias responding to vitamin B_{12}, folic acid or iron administration has led to the concept of so-called nutritional maturation arrest, a topic which has already been discussed in connection with ineffective erythropoiesis. Again, in studies by Bomford and Rhoads of so-called refractory anemias, some of which resulted from chronic exposure to benzol, the bone marrow findings varied from hypoplasia or fibrosis of the marrow to hyperplasia with cellular immaturity. In these patients also hypercellularity may have been associated with some type of ineffective erythropoiesis as in anemias due to vitamin B_{12} or folic acid deficiency.

In certain anemias in which disturbances in the production of red cells are seemingly at fault, the peripheral blood has mixed characteristics. Thus, despite increased reticulocytes or even occasional nucleated red cells in the periphery, there may be leukopenia or thrombocytopenia. Classically, these circumstances obtain early in the course of anemias in which the bone marrow is invaded by leukemic or by foreign, neoplastic cells or becomes infiltrated by fibrous or bony tissue. Here it is presumed that one type of element in the bone marrow is impinged upon more than another by the foreign cellular invasion. On the other hand, it is possible that an excessive destruction of red cells or other formed elements is taking place in situ. Because hypoxia, the chief stimulus to erythrocyte production, does not appear to be critically concerned in promoting leukocytosis or thrombocytosis, it is perhaps not surprising that consistency in the responses of the three formed elements of the peripheral blood is often lacking. Moreover, the filtering effect of a large or hyperfunctional spleen may decrease somewhat the number of circulating reticulocytes and more commonly the granulocytes or platelets.

DEFINITION AND CLASSIFICATION OF ANEMIA

The importance to the organism of the capacity of the blood to transport oxygen suggests the appropriateness of defining anemia as a decrease in the concentration of the hemoglobin in the peripheral blood irrespective of the concomitant number of red cells. However, except in rare instances of moderate anemia in which, because of hypochromia of the red cells, their number is above normal while the hemoglobin concentration is below normal. The number of red cells and the percentage volume occupied by them are also reduced. Anemia develops when the rate of hemoglobin loss or destruction exceeds that of hemoglobin production. Whether this results, on the one hand, from an abnormally great increase in blood loss or blood destruction, or, on the other hand, from an abnormally decreased rate of blood production is a question of fundamental importance to an understanding of the pathologic physiology of the anemia. In most anemias one or the other process predominates and the extent of the participation of each can be determined, for example, by the use of radioactive iron as a measure of erythropoiesis and of chromium-51 as a measure of the life-span of a sample of the circulating red cells and the site of their demise.

The distinction between anemias due mainly to *increased red cell loss or destruction* (Table 30–4) and those due mainly to *decreased red cell production* (Table 30–8) is here based on evaluation of the quantitative rather than the qualitative aspects of erythropoiesis. Thus, for example, because the rate of hemoglobin formation in congenital spherocytosis is greatly increased, this condition is regarded as a hemolytic anemia despite the fact that the red cells produced are inherently defective. On the other hand, in pernicious anemia the deficiency of vitamin B_{12} clearly results in a quantitatively diminished rate of effective erythropoiesis that produces a limited number of qualitatively defective red cells. By the present definition, the rate of effective erythropoiesis being decreased, it is irrelevant to our classification that the cells have a shortened survival time. Therefore pernicious anemia is classified here as an anemia mainly due to decreased red cell production. Finally, in the anemia of chronic blood loss, the classification depends on the stage of the disease. Initially, the anemia results from the increased rate of red cell loss, but eventually the loss of available iron results in a decreased rate of erythropoiesis, so that recovery does not occur, even after the cessation of bleeding, unless iron is administered. In any combination of decreased red cell production and increased red cell destruction the intensity of these phenomena must obviously be reciprocally related within certain limits if the patient is to survive.

Anemia of Acute Erythrocyte Loss

A classification of the anemias of acute erythrocyte loss and of increased erythrocyte destruction based as far as possible on recognized pathologic physiology is shown in Table 30–4.

The initial effect of sudden loss of blood is to produce a proportional reduction in the circulating blood volume, which, if reduced by a third, may result in a state of circulatory shock. Until diluted by the entrance of fluids

TABLE 30–4. Classification of Anemias Due Mainly to Increased Erythocyte Loss or Destruction (Bone Marrow Physiologically Hyperactive).

I. Acute erythrocyte loss
  A. Hemorrhage, external
  B. Hemorrhage into tissue
II. Increased erythrocyte destruction
  A. Extrinsic causes:
    1. Septicemias: streptococcus, Welch bacillus, malaria, bartonella
    2. Chemicals: lead, arsine, oxidants, sulfonamides, venoms
    3. Heat: extensive burns
    4. Trauma: artificial heart valves, march hemoglobinuria
    5. Immunity, natural: transfusion of ABO incompatible plasma
    6. Immunity, acquired: Rh factor, fava beans, Fuadin, penicillin
  B. Intrinsic causes:
    1. Abnormal erythrocytes: hereditary hemolytic (spherocytic and nonspherocytic) anemias, thalassemia, sickle cell anemia, glucose-6-phosphate dehydrogenase, paroxysmal nocturnal hemoglobinuria, and pyruvate kinase and triose phosphate isomerase deficiencies
    2. Abnormal plasma: paroxysmal hemoglobinuria due to cold (syphilis); acquired hemolytic anemia due to cold, warm or acid-activated agglutinins or hemolysins
    3. Hypersplenism: portal hypertension, cellular infiltration, infectious hyperplasia, lupus erythematosus

from the extracellular space, a lowering of the concentration of circulating red cells and hemoglobin does not occur. Thereafter the development of anemia indicates actual progress toward restoration of the circulating blood volume, a most useful physiologic effect without which adequate cardiac output and circulation of the remaining red cells cannot be achieved. Depending upon the rate of entry of tissue fluid, the red blood cell and hemoglobin values do not reach their lowest point until forty-eight to seventy-two hours after a single blood loss.

The first effect of a large external hemorrhage upon the blood picture is often, but by no means regularly, manifested within an hour or two by a moderate leukocytosis. In experimental animals such a leukocyte response to hemorrhage or anoxia, but not to the injection of foreign protein, depends on the presence of the adrenal medulla. When the hemorrhage is into tissue or body cavities, leukocytosis is more certain and more marked, probably as a result of the local delivery into the circulation of the leukocytosis-promoting substance described by Menkin and more recently studied by Gordon and others. The leukocyte count may reach 20,000 per cubic millimeter or more with relative increase in granulocytes, including band forms. A few nucleated red cells and myelocytes also may appear in the peripheral blood, probably as a result of physical displacement from the marrow. Rarely, a marked leukemoid response develops after a few hours. Epinephrine injections or asphyxia may cause thrombocytosis, sometimes to as high as a million platelets per cubic millimeter, according to Aster by release from a splenic pool. The factors resulting in an increase in platelets after hemorrhage are unknown, but it is clear that their production is not closely geared to a circulating concentration as in the case of red cells. Despite variable reports, uncomplicated and severe external blood loss has little effect upon platelet levels except perhaps to cause a slight fall during the first few days and a small sustained rise after the first week.

In patients and in experimental animals after hemorrhage the reticulocytes in the peripheral blood do not increase significantly until the second or third day. Thereafter the percentage of reticulocytes increases in a regular manner to a peak value on the fifth to seventh day and then declines somewhat more slowly to the base line. There is temporarily some macrocytosis at the time of the reticulocyte response (Fig. 30–13), and the erythroid cellularity of the marrow will be found to have begun to increase. If the hemorrhage is considerable, and especially if the patients' iron stores are minimal, the serum iron falls and the serum iron-binding protein (transferrin) rises somewhat over a period of a few days. As the reticulocyte peak is reached, the red cells and hemoglobin begin to increase together, and usually within four to six weeks the red cell count has become normal. In the later stages of this recovery period the hemoglobin may lag behind the red cell count despite iron administration, so that the mean corpuscular hemoglobin concentration falls somewhat. At this time the mean corpuscular volume of the red cells and their hemoglobin concentration are both somewhat reduced. This tendency of red cell regeneration to exceed the rate of hemoglobin regeneration is apparently a characteristic bone marrow reaction to anemia or anoxia and is exaggerated by relative iron deficiency and not always prevented by iron therapy. A deficiency of readily available iron, confirmed by low serum iron levels, produces the hypochromic red cells in blood films during the middle stages of the response. Hypochromia may develop despite the presence of

considerable amounts of stainable ferritin-hemosiderin in the reticuloendothelial cells of the bone marrow.

When the hemorrhage is internal, especially when diffusely into tissues rather than into a body cavity, the effect on hemoglobin regeneration is not simply that of external blood loss, but may resemble that of increased blood destruction. This is because, depending on the rate of red cell disintegration, the hemoglobin iron released becomes available for reutilization in the formation of new hemoglobin. Thus, in the severe normocytic or slightly macrocytic anemia sometimes observed in florid clinical scurvy, in which massive hemorrhages may occur into the skin, subcutaneous tissue, muscles and elsewhere, studies by Vilter have demonstrated anemia with reticulocytosis and signs of increased blood destruction such as elevated bilirubin in the serum. Vitamin C administration obviously prevents further hemorrhages, and to this hemostatic effect is probably due the resulting elevation of blood values accompanied by a decline of reticulocytes and bilirubin. Daily intramuscular injections of washed red cells derived from 30 ml. of normal blood have been shown to initiate reticulocyte responses and increases

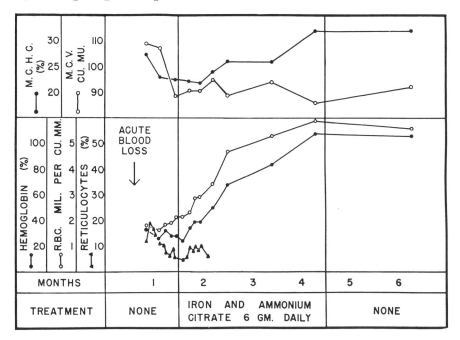

Figure 30–13. Effect of acute blood loss and subsequent iron administration. The patient had previously suffered repated small blood losses. Note the initial reticulocyte response to the final large hemorrhage (at arrow) associated with an elevation of the mean corpuscular volume and for some time a reduced mean corpuscular hemoglobin concentration. As the reticulocytes declined, the red cells began to increase. Hemoglobin production was presumably accelerated by the administration of iron, which gave a small second reticulocyte response. Eventually the red cell count temporarily exceeded its normal value, but only while the hemoglobin was below its normal level. (Slightly modified from Heath: New England J. Med., *209*:173, 1933.)

of hemoglobin in patients with chronic hypochromic anemia. Hemorrhage into a tissue is thus to be considered, from the point of view of iron and of pigment metabolism, as at least qualitatively similar to delayed intravascular blood destruction.

ANEMIAS OF INCREASED ERYTHROCYTE DESTRUCTION

The outstanding characteristics of the peripheral blood in anemias due to increased red cell destruction are the signs of increased hemoglobin catabolism and of compensatory red cell production. The red cells are usually normal or slightly above normal in size and are hypochromic only in hemoglobinopathies with decreased or defective hemoglobin formation such as thalassemia. The leukocytes and platelets are frequently increased if the anemia is the result of severe acute blood destruction. Indeed, even more often than with sudden severe blood loss, a myeloid type of blood picture in the periphery is seen with some nucleated red cells and even late myelocytes in considerable numbers. On the other hand, in chronic hemolytic anemias, especially with prominent splenomegaly, moderate granulocytopenia and thrombocytopenia may be present. If the hemolytic process is very mild, the red cell and hemoglobin values may be only slightly reduced, and the blood picture may appear superficially to be normal. However, careful measurements will usually show slight increases of reticulocytes and possibly of bilirubin, as well as a perceptible shortening of the half-life of labeled red cells. In moderately severe anemia the increased bilirubin and reticulocytosis are obvious, and with rapid intravascular hemolysis, depending on the degree of severity, free hemoglobin and methemalbumin may be present in the plasma in amounts ranging from 25 to 500 mg. per 100 ml. If intravascular red cell destruction exceeds twice the normal rate, serum haptoglobin will be used up by combining with the released hemoglobin. The serum bilirubin rarely exceeds 4 mg. per 100 ml. unless there is evidence of liver or biliary tract dysfunction, when the presence of regurgitated conjugated bilirubin in the plasma leads to bilirubinuria.

The cellular bone marrow is frequently considerably increased in its gross size; the nucleated erythroid cells are increased including in proportion their early stages. The frequent enlargement of the liver, especially in chronic hemolytic anemias, is partly due to the increased number of reticuloendothelial cells necessary for dealing with the increased

pigment metabolism and to the development of the process of blood formation designated as extramedullary hematopoiesis. Splenic enlargement as in many congenital and acquired hemolytic anemias is due to reticuloendothelial hyperplasia as well as to a vast quantity of red cells sequestered in the pulp, which may be released into the circulation as an "autotransfusion" as the spleen contracts under the hand of the surgeon.

The particular causes of hemolytic anemia may be divided rather arbitrarily into those extrinsic or intrinsic to the body, as shown in Table 30–4.

Extrinsic Causes of Increased Erythrocyte Destruction

A variable amount of information is available about the mechanism of blood destruction in different anemias due to extrinsic causes. *Hemolytic snake venoms* contain an enzyme, lecithinase, which converts the lecithin of the red cells to the hemolytic agent, lysolecithin, which in turn injures the red cell membrane and causes hemolysis and the increased osmotic and mechanical fragilities observed with this agent in vitro. In *septicemias* due to hemolytic streptococci and the Welch bacillus it is probable that increased red cell destruction is the result of a bacterial lecithinase demonstrably hemolytic in vitro. At least in the experimental *malarial infections* of monkeys and in the hemolytic anemia of *Bartonella infection* in man increased osmotic and mechanical fragilities of the parasitized red cells are demonstrable. Other mechanisms, however, are probably involved in the fulminating acute hemolytic anemia of blackwater fever in man, which is observed in recurrent *falciparum* malaria. Otherwise, as discussed below, certain antimalarial drugs may produce in usual therapeutic doses hemolytic anemia and sometimes hemoglobinuria in individuals with red cells susceptible to oxidants. *Lead* salts in vitro are stated to increase the mechanical fragility of red cells. The mechanical origin of the hemolysis in *march hemoglobinuria* has already been referred to and is also involved when regurgitant blood gets impinged on *prosthetic heart valves*. The irregularly angular red cells ("triangular" or "helmet" forms) are presumably the result of such trauma. Similar red cells are also seen in the blood of patients with "microangiopathic hemolytic anemia" associated with *thrombotic thrombocytopenic purpura, bilateral cortical necrosis* of the kidneys or *disseminated cancer*.

Exposure to certain *chemicals*, such as amino and nitro compounds of phenol, benzol and toluol, as well as to arsine or naphthalene may produce hemolytic anemia. The therapeutic administration of quinine, primaquine, acetanilid, phenacetin, sulfonamides or sulfones sometimes produces hemolytic anemia as a result of changes in the physical properties of the red cell envelope that render it susceptible to osmotic lysis or to splenic sequestration. Patients exposed to such compounds may exhibit transient cyanosis due at least in part to methemoglobin formation. Their red cells also form small spheroidal, refractile inclusions visible in fresh preparations supravitally stained with brilliant cresyl blue (Heinz bodies). Similar appearing clumps of spheroidal bodies can be produced in vitro in the presence of oxygen in either red cells or pure hemoglobin solutions in contact with phenylhydrazine, a drug formerly used in polycythemia vera for the express purpose of destroying red cells. In vitro, loss of reduced glutathione is followed by methemoglobin (oxidized hemoglobin) formation and then by partly soluble brown to green derivatives of hemoglobin before still more insoluble aggregates of oxidized hemoglobin (Heinz bodies) appear in the red cells.

Emerson and Ham demonstrated an increase in the osmotic fragility of the red cells in the early stages of these hemolytic anemias. They also showed that small concentrations of these drugs in vitro rapidly produce methemoglobin and increases in the osmotic and mechanical fragilities of human red cells, but only in the presence of oxygen. Unlike the active oxidants studied, sulfanilamide did not produce anemia in experimental animals and in vitro did not cause changes in the red cells. However, persons who acquire hemolytic anemia with sulfanilamide administration have been shown to form metabolically oxidant derivatives such as para-amino-phenol and hydroxylaminobenzine sulfonamide that have been detected in the urine. These and other compounds have the capacity to transmit the high oxidation potential of oxygen through redox intermediates to cellular components such as glutathione and thereafter to hemoglobin.

Alving, Beutler, Carney and their associates have shown that increased *susceptibility to primaquine* and other potential oxidants resides in the red cells of 15 to 20 per cent of American Negroes or members of relatively dark-skinned Caucasian population groups. In vitro their washed red cells, when exposed to phenylhydrazine or other oxidants, form Heinz bodies with unusual speed, apparently because of a deficiency of reduced glutathione (GSH). This, in turn, depends upon an inadequate reduction mechanism resulting from a sex-linked incompletely dominant hereditary trait causing diminished activity of a red cell enzyme, glucose-6-phosphate dehydrogenase, of which also unstable species have been found. With sufficient lack in some Caucasian males congenital hemolytic anemia results. Normally this enzyme is involved in the initial step of the so-called phosphogluconate pathway, the principal source of reduced triphosphopyridine nucleotide (TPNH), the coenzyme for the reduction of oxidized glutathione (GSSG) to GSH by the enzyme glutathione reductase (Fig. 30–7). Without sufficient GSH, hemoglobin and certain enzymes, as well as the proteins of the red cell envelope, presumably become denatured by oxidation of their sulfhydryl groups. Indeed, treatment of normal red cells with a nonpenetrating inhibitor of GSH groups in the cell envelope renders the red cells osmotically fragile in vitro or susceptible to sequestration and subsequent lysis in the spleen. Mature normal red cells, in contrast to reticulocytes, whose GSH and enzyme contents in general are higher, are more susceptible to oxidants in vitro than are reticulocytes. This is also true in vivo, where, after the initial hemolysis of the older red cells, the relative resistance of the younger cells renders them insusceptible to damage despite renewed administration of the oxidant at the original dosage. The development of hemolytic anemia following primaquine administration is shown in Figure 30–14.

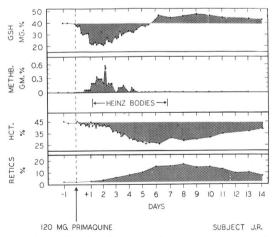

Figure 30–14. Sequence of events associated with acute hemolysis following administration of a single large dose of primaquine to a drug-sensitive individual. Note the initial fall of reduced glutathione followed by the formation of methemoglobin and the further oxidation of hemoglobin to form Heinz bodies. Owing to hemolysis, the hematocrit declines and evokes a prolonged reticulocyte response. (From Brewer and others: J. Lab. Clin. Med., 59:905, 1962.)

Shortly after extensive *thermal burns* the presence of hemoglobinuria may draw attention to free hemoglobin in the serum. In such patients the red cells exhibit increased osmotic and mechanical fragilities for several hours, and anemia may develop rapidly. Experimentally, heating of red cells in vitro causes entirely similar effects, accompanied by the development of spheroidal forms with later subdivisions of individual red cells by a process of "budding," not necessarily with loss of hemoglobin. Because Brown and his associates, however, found that red cells transfused into subjects who had received burns were rapidly destroyed, some other type of mechanism producing hemolytic anemia may also be present; and diminished red cell production, as in chronic infection, is clearly an anemia-producing factor during the late stages of recovery from burns.

Natural or *acquired antibodies* against red cells are a cause of red cell destruction. Thus, the severe constitutional reaction associated with lysis of donor's red cells after transfusion of incompatible blood is well known. On the other hand, relatively insignificant symptoms accompany the more gradual destruction of the red cells of the *recipient* which sometimes occurs as a result of the transfusion of incompatible plasma of high natural potency against the red cells of recipients of groups A, B or AB. Acquired antibodies may develop against fetal red cells if they leak into the maternal circulation and if the mother has a different major blood group. The maternal antibodies are at first like natural iso-antibodies, complement-fixing and "complete," with macroglobin (19S) characteristics, but later "incomplete" antibodies develop, and, after entering the fetal circulation, produce hemolytic anemia, spheroidicity and increased osmotic fragility of the infant's red cells. Ultra-centrifugation of fetal plasma shows that these placenta-penetrating antibodies are of low density (7S) and are not inhibited by A and B substances, such as occur in fetal tissue. Presumably, therefore, their attack is concentrated on the fetal red cell. Statistically Type O mothers have more affected ABO incompatible infants than do type A or B mothers, apparently because they tend to form 7S rather than the larger 19S antibodies as do Type A and B mothers. Major blood group incompatibility tends to prevent maternal sensitization to Rh antigen (to be discussed below) probably because of the rapid initial destruction by natural isoantibodies of fetal red cells penetrating the placenta.

In the classic type of erythroblastosis fetalis, hemolysis of the infant's red cells occurs as a result of "incomplete" anti-Rh antibodies in the mother's serum. Irrespective of her major blood group, such antibodies may develop in the Rh-negative mother (15 ± per cent of the population) because of the presence in utero of an Rh-positive fetus. This occurs when the father, even though of the same major blood group as the mother, is the transmitter of the dominant Rh-positive gene (85 ± per cent of the population) to his child.* After one or more pregnancies, under these genetic circumstances, anti-Rh antibodies develop in the plasma of a small proportion of mothers because of leakage of fetal red cells into the maternal circulation, and may then enter the fetal circulation by traversing the placenta. There they cause destruction of the Rh-positive red cells of the fetus. The resulting clinical manifestations are those of a hemolytic anemia with elevated bilirubin and signs of rapid red cell regeneration, including many reticulocytes and nucleated red cells in the peripheral blood. There is also hyperplasia of the blood-forming organs, including pronounced extramedullary blood formation in the liver and spleen. The anemia increases after delivery, partly because the infant's bone marrow is no longer subjected to the stimulus of the hypoxia of intrauterine life. Also, after the transplacental route of excretion of bilirubin is eliminated, the inability of the neonatal liver to conjugate and so to excrete bilirubin results in rapidly increasing bilirubinema of the indirect reacting type. In contrast to conjugated bilirubin this bilirubin is fat-soluble and hence may stain and damage the central nervous system of the infant to produce the histological picture of kernicterus. Treatment includes the removal of circulating anti-Rh antibodies and bilirubin by venesection of large amounts of blood and its immediate replacement by the blood of Rh-negative donors.

Rh-negative persons may also acquire anti-Rh antibodies in the serum as a result of transfusion or even from the intramuscular injection of small amounts of Rh-positive blood. Homologous skin or other living tissue grafts (probably not including corneal transplants) might also be antigenic. Subsequent transfusions of Rh-positive blood of a compatible major group may result in a severe or even

---

* Limitations of space compel this greatly oversimplified view of the complex and important genetic and serologic aspects of the Rh factor problem. Appropriate references are given at the end of the chapter.

fatal hemolytic transfusion reaction accompanied by rapid destruction of the transfused red cells. Erythroblastosis fetalis may develop in a first pregnancy of such an already sensitized woman.

The mechanism of the destruction of incompatible donor's red cells by a recipient whose serum contains a complement-fixing *hemolysin* rapidly active in vitro against the donor's cells seems obvious. In its activated form one of the components of complement C_1 displays esterase activity and is capable of producing large holes (Fig. 30–9) in the red cell envelope through which hemoglobin readily escapes. Hemolysins, however, have not been convincingly demonstrated in anti-Rh serum which contains "incomplete" antibodies capable of agglutinating Rh-positive red cells in serum but not in saline. Moreover, according to Wiener, in 70 per cent of fresh human serums, isoagglutinins active in saline and in serum are not accompanied by demonstrable hemolysins against red cells of incompatible major blood groups. How, then, is it possible to explain increased red cell destruction in vivo in the absence of demonstrable hemolysins in vitro? Many years ago Banti noted that the hemolysis induced by a given amount of anti-red cell immune serum in experimental animals was delayed but was eventually much greater than that promptly and maximally produced by the same amount of immune serum in the test tube. He observed, as did Wasastjerna more recently, that, although increases of the osmotic fragility of the red cells accompanied the development of the hemolytic anemia, such changes did not take place when the red cells were exposed to the antiserum in vitro. Ebert and Emerson have shown that the destruction of the red cells of patients of blood groups A, B or AB as a result of transfusion of large amounts of group O plasma was associated with increased osmotic fragility of the recipients' red cells. However, as already discussed above, group O plasma, like anti-red-cell immune serum, does not affect the osmotic fragility of group A or B human red cells in vitro even when considerable hemolysis takes place.

Consequently, it is not possible to ascribe *directly* to the hemolysins present the increases in osmotic fragility of the red cells observed, for example, by Dameshek and Schwartz with anti-guinea-pig-red-cell immune serum. In the first place, such serums contain agglutinins as well as hemolysins. Second, Shen has produced marked and progressive red cell destruction by using anti-dog-red-cell serum intravenously in such final dilutions in the blood of the animal as to agglutinate the red cells, but to be entirely without hemolytic effect on comparable blood samples in vitro. Third, as already noted, in hemolytic transfusion reactions due to Rh sensitization, incomplete agglutinins, but not hemolysins, active against Rh-positive red cells are demonstrable in the recipient's serum. These facts suggest that agglutination of the red cells, which is the phenomenon present both in vitro and in vivo, is an essential primary stage of the hemolytic mechanism when complement-fixing hemolysin is not demonstrable in vitro.

Although strongly *agglutinated red cells* exhibit increased mechanical fragility in vitro, this effect is negligible with the relatively weak agglutination of red cells required experimentally to initiate progressive hemolysis in vivo. In the vascular bed such "agglutination" may well take place between red cells and reticuloendothelial elements of the spleen or liver, and would be expected to be especially significant in capillaries or sinusoids where the flow of blood is characteristically slow, because the perfusion pressure is low. Archer has recently shown that human red cells coated with Rh antibodies adhere to monocytes on contact (but not to granulocytes) when the blood sample is centrifuged. Red cell agglutination in the dog injected with anti-dog-red-cell serum is maximal at once; it is only after an hour or two that the osmotic and mechanical fragilities of the red cells become distinctly increased. Although immediately after the injection of the immune serum in the experimental animal agglutinated red cells appear in the peripheral blood and the hematocrit falls sharply, free hemoglobin appears in significant amounts in the plasma only after an hour or more. The hemoglobinemia thereafter gradually increases as the increases in osmotic and mechanical fragilities of the red cells become manifest. Such effects can be obtained even with sufficient dilution of the immune serum with dog serum prior to injection to abolish its hemolytic (but not agglutinating) effects upon dog red cells in vitro (Fig. 30–15). From these facts it is inferred that the initial effect of the agglutination of erythrocytes produces erythrostasis and sequestration of red cells in the capillaries of various organs. Because sterile incubation in vitro of red cells with liver or muscle pulp accelerates increases in their osmotic and mechanical fragilities, it

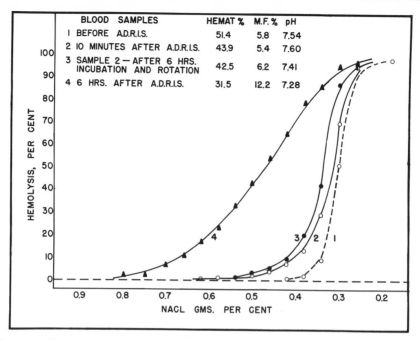

Figure 30–15. The effect of anti-dog-red-cell immune serum (A.D.R.I.S.) showing, after dilution with dog serum in vitro, a high agglutination titer but no hemolysis of dog red cells. Following an intravenous injection of diluted A.D.R.I.S. into a dog, there were progressive increases in the osmotic (curves 1 and 4) and mechanical fragilities of the red cells during the next 6 hours. Note, however, that the essentially normal osmotic fragility (curve 2) of a sample of the dog blood taken 10 minutes after the injection of A.D.R.I.S. showed an insignificant increase in osmotic fragility (curve 3) during 6 hours of incubation and rotation of the oxygenated sample in vitro. (Kindly supplied by Dr. S. C. Shen.)

is inferred that the local ischemia produced by *erythrostasis* causes the liberation of substances from the tissues, which in turn bring about the changes in the red cells noted in vivo. It is thus of interest that Cohn has described the probable release of hydrolytic enzymes from granules adjacent to vacuoles in monocytes in which individual red cells are being lysed.

Jandl has determined the site of *sequestration* of red cells, labeled with radioactive chromium, by means of body surface counting subsequent to their intravenous injection. In observations on patients, red cells incompatible with the major blood group of the recipient and agglutinated but not hemolyzed by his serum in vitro were removed within minutes after transfusion, while low levels of hemoglobin promptly appeared in the plasma and a heavy accumulation of radioactivity developed over the liver. Similar surface-counting methods showed that otherwise compatible or even autologous Rh-positive red cells, after being sensitized with anti-Rh serum, although morphologically normal and not demonstrably agglutinated by the plasma of either Rh-positive or nonimmunized Rh-negative recipients, were promptly removed by the spleen (Fig. 31–1). The probable

mechanism of this sequestering effect is discussed above under Functions of the Spleen and also in Chapter 31. However, the rapidity of the release of hemoglobin from such sensitized red cells has so far not been equaled by incubation of normal blood with liver or spleen pulp in vitro. It seems necessary to suppose that either leukocytes or R-E cells "activate" an incomplete agglutinating antibody to become a hemolytic one or release an independent hemolytic principle unusually active against sensitized red cells. The sequence of postulated events leading to and resulting from the sequestration of red cells in various types of hemolytic anemias is outlined in Table 30–7.

Many varieties of *peas* and *beans* contain globulins which agglutinate particulate matter, including red cells. Especially in Sardinia, hemolytic anemia of great severity is said to result in a few persons from the ingestion of fava beans, which many persons eat with impunity. Most of the susceptible individuals have now been shown to have red cells hereditarily deficient in glucose-6-phosphate dehydrogenase. It is not clear why the resulting susceptibility to oxidants should be a hazard in favism. Inhalation of the pollen of the fava bean and of certain flowers growing near Baghdad is also said to produce hemolytic anemia. Because the amounts of material that could be absorbed by inhalation must of necessity be minute, individual sensitization to an antigen is almost certainly involved. This is supported by the evidence that, during an attack of hemolytic anemia, positive skin tests with fava bean extract may become temporarily negative. It has also been established that a plasma factor develops in response to fava bean ingestion that agglutinates red cells that have been coated with fava bean extract. The immediate mechanism of red cell destruction remains obscure, but may be analogous to the findings of Harris with the drug Fuadin, a disulfonated heptahydrate of trivalent antimony. On retreatment his patient had a severe hemolytic anemia with increased osmotic and mechanical fragilities of the red cell and a positive antiglobulin (Coombs') test. A thermostable factor in the plasma strongly agglutinated the patient's or normal red cells in vitro only when Fuadin was present. Transfusion of the patient's plasma to a normal recipient caused agglutination of the recipient's red cells only when he was subsequently given Fuadin. It is of interest that closely analogous observations in vitro have been made in both drug-induced agranulocytosis and thrombocytopenic purpura, as will be discussed later.

Intrinsic Causes of Increased Erythrocyte Destruction

The mechanisms of the so-called intrinsic causes of increased red cell destruction are in many instances still obscure. However, the biochemical basis of several of the hereditary defects has now been clarified and some of the so-called "idiopathic autoimmune" hemolytic anemias may turn out to be the late result of exposure to external agents as yet unrecognized. A recent retrospective study in England has shown that about a quarter of a group of such patients were receiving an antihypertensive drug that frequently causes a positive direct anti-gamma globulin test.

Abnormal Erythrocytes. In hereditary spherocytic and nonspherocytic anemias, in sicklemia and in paroxysmal nocturnal hemoglobinuria there are demonstrable abnormalities of the red cells of patent significance for increased blood destruction. In thalassemia major and minor there are, especially in the former, striking variations in the size, color and shape of the red cells. The available observations indicate that the red cells of patients with these conditions do *not* survive normally when transfused into normal recipients, whereas normal red cells usually will survive in these patients.

HEREDITARY SPHEROCYTIC ANEMIA. This is a chronic, congenital condition, transmitted as a mendelian dominant by either parent. It is closely resembled by a form of hereditary spherocytosis in the deer mouse, inherited as an autosomal recessive. The characteristic spheroidal red cell is of normal volume but has a decreased diameter to thickness ratio and a uniquely increased hemoglobin concentration, which is sometimes from 2 to 4 per cent above normal. The anemia and jaundice may be severe, or so mild as to escape detection unless a critical examination of the blood is made. Splenomegaly is probably invariable if there is anemia.

In this disease the mechanism of increased blood destruction now seems clearly to reside in certain properties of the congenitally abnormal erythrocytes. The transfusion experiments of Dacie and Mollison demonstrated that red cells from patients with congenital spherocytic anemia were quickly destroyed in the circulation of normal persons, even when the blood samples transfused were taken some time after clinically successful splenectomy. On the other hand, red cells from normal donors survived normally in patients with clinically active congenital spherocytic anemia and intact spleens. According to Emerson, Shen and Ham, the peculiarity of the red cells in congenital spherocytic anemia which renders them liable to abnormal destruction is their unusual susceptibility to increase in osmotic and mechanical fragilities upon sterile incubation in vitro and presumably when sequestered in the characteristically congested spleen. Comparisons of the fragilities of serologically distinct but compatible normal red cells transfused into patients with congenital spherocytic anemia several days before splenectomy with those of the patient were made at operation. It was found that, whereas there was little change in the normal red cells, either in the peripheral blood or in the splenic pulp, the osmotic and mechanical fragilities of a portion of the patient's red cells in the splenic pulp greatly exceeded those of the normal red cells as well as those of the patient's red cells in the peripheral circulation. Moreover, the proportion of patient's to normal red cells in the splenic pulp was found considerably to exceed that in the general circulation. The ability of the normal, as well as of the patient's own spleen, to sequester Cr^{51}-labeled spherocytes has been directly confirmed by Jandl. In these observations the radioactivity over the liver remained low, while the rate of increase over the normal spleen exceeded that over the patient's spleen probably because the competition for splenic sequestration of spherocytes was less in the normal individual.

In hereditary spherocytic anemia the spleen contains a quantity of red cells, sometimes sufficient, when expelled in operative manipulation, to increase at once the circulating red cell and hemoglobin values by 15 per cent or more. This is presumably the result of the selective retention of spheroidal cells observed by Young when a mixture also containing normal discoidal red cells was perfused through a surgically removed human spleen; and by Jandl using a Millipore filter with apertures 5 microns in diameter. After splenectomy, in patients not receiving transfusions, the spheroidicity and the osmotic and mechanical fragilities of the circulating red cells decline rapidly toward, but do not usually reach, entirely normal values. However, the characteristic tendency to abnormal increase of their osmotic and mechanical fragilities upon sterile incubation persists, a phenomenon utilized by Young in order to detect evidence of subclinical disease in relatives of affected individuals.

Hemolysins have not been demonstrated in the plasma of patients with hereditary spherocytic anemia, nor have serum globulins, possibly representing antibodies of an immune type, but very rarely been found adsorbed on the red cells. Consequently, the weight of evidence suggests that the mechanism of increased red cell destruction in this disease depends upon the peculiar characteristics of the red cell. These become of clinical significance only when splenic sequestration can occur. On leaving the marrow the red cell is already slightly spheroidal and remains abnormally liable to further increase in spheroidicity when even temporarily sequestered in the splenic pulp. Moreover, as suggested by Prankerd, once a sufficient degree of spheroidicity has developed, apparently among older members of the red cell population, these cells become subject to preferential sequestration and further metabolic injury whenever they enter the splenic pulp. As pointed out by Dacie, in some patients the peripheral blood contains a proportion of red cells of considerably increased osmotic fragility. These resemble the much larger proportion of such cells demonstrated by Emerson and Ham in the splenic pulp at operation and presumably destined mostly to

be destroyed there by osmotic lysis (Fig. 30–16). After splenectomy the unusually osmotically and mechanically fragile cells disappear from the peripheral blood within a few days, and so are known already to be sufficiently damaged as to be destroyed in the general circulation.

These alterations of the red cells in hereditary spherocytic anemia probably result from their lack of free access to plasma when the cells are sequestered in the spleen. An important metabolic deficit so induced is the diminished availability of glucose which, as in the normal red cell, is required for glycolysis. In 1954, in comparative studies with normal red cells in vitro, Selwyn and Dacie found that in congenital spherocytic anemia, during sterile incubation in vitro the rates of autohemolysis, of sodium intake and of potassium loss were excessive. Both for normal and for spheroidal red cells, these degenerative processes were distinctly retarded by the presence of glucose. No specific enzymatic defect has been discovered, but recently Jacob has shown that there is an abnormal increase in the active transport of sodium accompanied by an appropriate increase, rather than by a decrease, in glycolysis. Apparently the primary abnormality is a "leaky" cell envelope which allows sodium to enter at twice the normal rate with the result that adenosine triphosphate (ATP) is broken down to adenosine diphosphate (ADP) and pyrophosphate. This stimulates anaerobic glycolysis and an increased rate of sodium extrusion from the cell associated with an accelerated turnover of cell membrane phospholipids, especially phosphatidylserine. As long as the hereditary spherocyte has free access to glucose, the extra energy for sodium "pumping" is produced and the cell survives well in the blood stream.

In some families with the usually benign anomaly of *elliptocytosis*, moderate or severe hemolytic anemia, splenomegaly and relief by splenectomy have been recorded. In some of these patients, the abnormally increased autohemolysis of the red cells upon incubation was diminished by glucose; and the associated anomaly may resemble that of hereditary spherocytosis or result from a coincidental metabolic defect like one of those now to be discussed.

HEREDITARY NONSPHEROCYTIC ANEMIAS. As a result of studies of autohemolysis during incubation in vitro, a variety of metabolic defects of the red cells have now been recognized. Selwyn and Dacie found that in some patients autohemolysis and other changes during incubation did not exceed those of normal red cells, but were only partially inhibited by glucose.

These patients were classified by them as Type I. In some instances the red cells are now known to be deficient in glucose-6-phosphate dehydrogenase (G-6-PD) activity. In affected Negro males the enzyme defect, discussed above, is moderate and requires the administration of oxidant drugs for hemolytic effects to appear. The defect has been demonstrated in Negroes only in non-nucleated cells such as erythrocytes and the lens of the eye. In dark-skinned Caucasian ethnic groups the defect in reducing mechanisms is usually more severe and is sometimes associated with target cells, Heinz bodies or basophilic stippling, which do not require the administration of oxidant drugs for their development. In these susceptible Caucasians the enzyme defect is found in leukocytes, skin, liver cells and saliva. In other Caucasian subjects unstable variants of G-6-PD have been found as well as various other defects in the provision of adequate amounts of reduced glutathione. In the newborn physiologic hypoglycemia renders the red cells of otherwise normal infants sensitive, as may be the case in diabetic acidosis. In renal and liver disease the plasma concentration of an oxidant drug administered in usual dosage may be abnormally increased.

The red cells of still other patients deteriorated during incubation even more rapidly than did those of patients with spherocytic anemia, but this process was totally unresponsive to glucose. These patients were assigned by Selwyn and Dacie to Type II; and many of them were later shown by DeGruchy to have a limited ability to produce ATP. Their red cells have now been found by Tanaka to be deficient in pyruvate kinase (PK), an enzyme normally active in the late stage in the Embden-Myerhof pathway for anaerobic glycolysis, the principal source of ATP (Fig. 30–7). The hemolytic anemia is characterized by macrocytosis and minor degrees of red cell deformity associated after splenectomy with a striking reticulocytosis and some clinical benefit. According to Keith this is due to the fact that the nonreticulated cells are selectively destroyed in the liver. On the other hand, the reticulated cells are able to produce ATP by oxidative phosphorylation in their mitochondria. After removal of the spleen, a site of temporary detention for reticulocytes, these cells spend more of their life-span in the circulation.

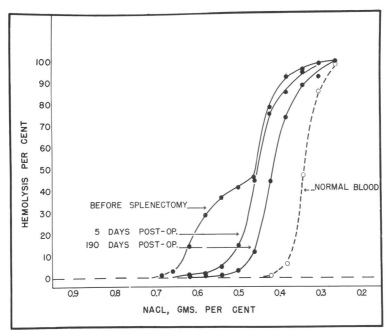

Figure 30–16. The effect of splenectomy upon the osmotic fragility of the red cells of the peripheral blood in hereditary spherocytic anemia. Note the "hump" on the curve of blood taken before splenectomy, reflecting the influence of erythrostasis in the spleen in producing a population of more osmotically fragile cells. By 5 days after splenectomy these have disappeared, indicating a short survival of these damaged red cells. The osmotic fragility of the red cells produced by the bone marrow in this disease remains somewhat increased even 190 days after splenectomy, as does their increased susceptibility to glucose deprivation during incubation.

In other patients, Prankerd has produced indirect evidence of a deficiency of 2,3-diphosphoglyceromutase and Schneider has clearly defined a marked hereditary deficiency of a glycolytic enzyme, triosephosphate isomerase (TPI), apparently also on a recessive hereditary basis. However, the hurdle imposed by TPI deficiency can be circumvented partially through the hexosemonophosphate shunt. Thus both added glucose and adenosine (which provides pentose) partially inhibit autohemolysis in vitro. In hereditary spherocytosis, abnormal sodium influx seems to be the primary event, but in these non-spherocytic hemolytic anemias, the primary defect in energy production leads to a defect in potassium retention.

SICKLE CELL ANEMIA AND OTHER HEMOGLOBINOPATHIES. Sickle cell anemia occurs in the United States in only about one out of forty Negroes whose red cells exhibit the characteristic trait, which is transmitted by either parent in about 7 per cent of the Negro population. Persons with the heterozygous state are usually completely asymptomatic and have no anemia. However, Allison has proposed that, in areas of endemic malaria in Africa, the higher incidence of the sickle cell gene results from the relative resistance to the parasite conferred by the presence of sickle cell hemoglobin, especially in children. The active disease is characterized by symptoms of the constant anemia, attacks of pain in the limbs, resembling acute rheumatism, and in the abdomen, mimicking an abdominal catastrophe, as well as by frequent leg ulcers. Many patients fail to reach adult life. The hemolytic anemia is usually severe with elevated reticulocytes, plasma hemoglobin and bilirubin. In children the spleen and liver are often palpable; the former rarely in adults.

In the homozygous condition, these clinical manifestations, associated with multiple thromboses and infarcts of many organs and usually with atrophy of the spleen in the adult, are the result of the abnormal physical behavior of the red cells. Displacement of their oxygen by exposure to gases such as nitrogen or carbon dioxide, or by the addition of reducing agents, results in changes in shape typified by the development of sickle- or oat-shaped forms. These begin to appear at oxygen tensions of about 35 to 45 mm. of mercury and rapidly increase as the oxygen tension is further reduced. The sickled cell immediately reverts to the discoidal form when reexposed to normal oxygen tension. In persons with the heterozygous sickle cell trait the red cells are less susceptible to hypoxia, but are still capable of sickling if the oxygen tension is sufficiently lowered or if the fresh blood is mixed with a reducing agent such as sodium bisulfite. Transfused trait cells survive normally except in subjects with arterial oxygen unsaturation or, as shown by Watson and her associates, in certain young patients with large spleens. The cells of patients with sickle cell anemia are rapidly destroyed in normal persons or in persons with the heterozygous condition.

Brewster and Ham found that, beginning at about 30 to 40 mm. of mercury, the oxygen tension of the capillary blood, the viscosity of homozygous sickle cell blood rapidly increases until it reaches nearly maximal values at about 10 mm. of oxygen tension. When fully deoxygenated, such samples also exhibit large increases in the mechanical fragility of the red cells, which, according to Diggs, is the cause of the hemolytic anemia. Specimens of normal blood show no such changes on being deprived of oxygen, and sickle trait blood begins to sickle and to become viscous only at oxygen tensions well below physiologic. Millipore filters with apertures 5 microns in diameter readily separate sickled from normal red cells but only when the mixture is deoxygenated. In the peripheral blood of patients with active sickle cell disease a small percentage of the red cells remain sickled even after thorough exposure to oxygen as in the preparation of a stained blood film. Similar "permanently" sickled forms are numerous in blood from splenic puncture in children and are produced by incubation in vitro in the absence of oxygen for several hours, a process accompanied by loss of cell potassium and "fixation" of the cell membrane. Such observations, as well as the widespread thrombosis and infarction observed post mortem, testify to the prevalence of erythrostasis during life. The increased destruction of red cells in sickle cell disease may thus be attributed either to mechanical destruction of the sickled forms as the viscous and mechanically fragile blood traverses the capillaries and venules or to lysis by tissue factors if the circulation is sufficiently impeded.

The high proportion of fetal hemoglobin in the blood despite the relatively hypoxic conditions of intrauterine life protects the homozygous fetus. However, four months after birth when the fetal hemoglobin has been largely replaced by sickle hemoglobin, nearly all the red cells will sickle and painful crisis may develop, classically in the form of a tender, hot, swollen hand or foot, due to infarction of the active marrow of one of the bones. Rarely, an extreme degree of red cell sequestration in the spleen in children may lead to fatal hypovolemic shock with extreme anemia, and at autopsy a greatly swollen spleen distended with sickled red cells. More commonly venous congestion or impaction of masses of sickled cells in the capillaries of various organs is responsible for the rheumatic pains, abdominal distress sometimes with jaundice, local aseptic necrosis of bones, especially of the head of the femur, pulmonary infarction, and the splenic atrophy invariably found in the adult. The process of sickling is not instantaneous, but requires some seconds for its development. This may explain the exemption of the myocardium from infarction. Thus, despite the distinctly low oxygen tension of the coronary sinus blood, its rapid flow may allow insufficient time for sickling to occur. On the other hand, hyperosmolarity favors the sickling process, is characterisic of the renal medulla, and may explain the occurrence of hematuria and the development of hyposthenuria, at first reversible by transfusions.

A relationship between infections and painful crises has sometimes been noted. The rise in oxygen utilization by the tissues and the increase in the plasma viscosity and sedimentation rate caused by an increase in plasma fibrinogen as a result of infection may well play a part in initiating a vicious cycle of tissue anoxia and red cell sickling. As shown by Hahn and Gillespie in 1927, sickling is enhanced by the lowered percentage saturation of hemoglobin at a given oxygen tension when the acidity of the blood is increased by carbonic, lactic or other metabolically produced acids. Consequently, it is of interest that painful crises have been precipitated by administration of ammonium chloride and perhaps relieved by the vigorous use of intravenous sodium bicarbonate. In Negro aviators with sickle cell trait ascent to high altitudes with consequent anoxia of the arterial blood has led to splenic infarctions. Since a rise in the oxygen tension of the arterial blood suppresses red cell formation and consequently increases the anemia (Fig. 30–2), oxygen inhalation is not a useful therapeutic method. Transfusion of normal red cells in severely anemic patients may be beneficial because such cells do not become sickled in the patient, and because the resultant increase in hemoglobin suppresses the production of sickle cells by the bone marrow.

In 1949 Pauling and his associates demonstrated that the hemoglobin in the red cells of sickle cell disease has a different isoelectric point and a different electrophoretic mobility from those of normal hemoglobin. They suggested that these peculiarities may allow alignment of the molecules within the cell when its hemoglobin is reduced. This would explain the birefringence under polarized light previously observed by Sherman. Harris then showed that when 15 to 25 per cent solutions of sickle cell hemoglobin were rendered anoxic, their viscosity became greatly increased. Moreover, they displayed birefringence and, under the phase microscope, "tactoid" or "liquid crystal" formation. These bodies closely resembled sickled red cells (Fig. 30–17) and promptly disappeared with reoxygenation of the hemoglobin. Thus, the characteristic deformity of the sickled red cell was explained as accommodation of its membrane to the aggregate of oriented hemoglobin molecules within it, being in fact a "thinly veiled hemoglobin tactoid."

In sickle cell anemia the abnormal S hemoglobin may account for nearly all the hemoglobin in the cell. Normal A hemoglobin is not present but fetal F hemoglobin, which is present in certain other types of anemia in adults, accounts for the rest. The protective influence of F hemoglobin in the infant against painful crises is due to its inability to complex with S hemoglobin molecules. This benignant effect is also seen in those adults with sickle cell disease whose red cells contain various amounts of F hemoglobin averaging up to 25 per cent. The clinical findings are uniformly mild in double heterozygotes for S hemoglobin and the hereditary anomaly known as "high F" whose red cells may contain uniformly as much as 30 per cent of F hemoglobin. In the red cells of the heterozygous sickle trait less than half of the total hemoglobin is S hemoglobin, the rest being normal hemoglobin. The widespread use of paper electrophoresis and hemoglobin solubility studies have disclosed the existence of many other varieties of abnormal hemoglobin, running almost through the alphabet and into place-names. Of those found in combination with S hemoglobin are especially notable C, D and G, mostly in Negroes. During electrophoresis on moist filter paper at pH 8.6, a streak of C hemoglobin moves slowly; D and S move together but more rapidly, while G and finally normal A hemoglobin move still more rapidly toward the positive electrode. When homozygous, C and D hemoglobins cause no disability and many target cells. When heterozygous with normal A

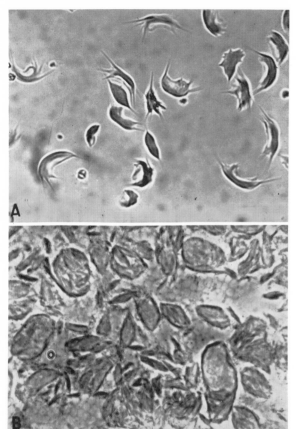

Figure 30–17. The sickling phenomenon as observed with the phase microscope: *A*, Sickling produced in a drop of fresh SS hemoglobin-containing blood by chemical reduction of the hemoglobin with sodium metabisulfite. *B*, Sickling produced in a solution of S hemoglobin reduced by exposure to nitrogen. Note the resemblance of the hemoglobin "tactoids," which form in the hemoglobin solution as a result of aggregation and alignment of the relatively insoluble reduced S hemoglobin molecules, to the shape of the intact sickled cell. Reduction of both blood and hemoglobin solutions greatly increases their viscosity of flow. (From Harris: Proc. Soc. Exper. Biol. & Med., 75:197, 1950.)

hemoglobin, target cells are less numerous. However, in genetic combination with S hemoglobin, C and D hemoglobins cause significant hemolytic anemia, splenomegaly (because the spleen does not become totally infarcted in childhood) and crises that are painful but not so severe as those of sickle cell disease. This is presumably because C hemoglobin, to a greater degree than A hemoglobin, and unlike F hemoglobin, can complex to form polymers with S hemoglobin, demonstrable in vitro. G and S hemoglobin genes in combination do not cause disease. The combination of the sickling and thalassemia traits results in red cells containing a predominance of S over A hemoglobin, but often also considerable F hemoglobin and/or A_2 hemoglobin, normally present in only trace amounts. As will be discussed in the next section, under the influence of the thalassemia gene, S and A_2 or F hemoglobins are more readily formed than is A hemoglobin. Greenberg has shown that, when the mean corpuscular sickle hemoglobin concentration (MCSHC) is below 15 gm. per cent, as in sickle cell trait, sickling does not develop at physiologic capillary oxygen tensions. In sickle cell disease, the MCSHC is

above 25 gm. per cent. In the combination of S and C hemoglobins, the MCSHC usually falls between 15 and 25 gm. per cent and the clinical disease is correspondingly milder than the homozygous sickle cell disorder.

The globin portion of the normal A hemoglobin molecule contains two pairs of polypeptide chains, designated as alpha and beta, respectively. Fetal, or F, hemoglobin normally present at birth displays resistance to denaturation by alkali and also differs from A hemoglobin in possessing a distinctly different sequence of amino acids in the partner of its normal alpha chains. Consequently, F hemoglobin is said to contain alpha and gamma polypeptide chains. Remarkable progress has recently been made in the understanding of even more subtle biochemical differences between other kinds of hemoglobin molecules. Thus, Ingram has shown that the basis of the different electrophoretic properties of S and A hemoglobins consists in a change of but a single amino acid in one of the 28 peptide fragments derived by tryptic hydrolysis from the beta chains of their respective molecules. There, in the peptide derived from S hemoglobin, a single valine replaces the glutamic acid of the A hemoglobin peptide. In C hemoglobin, lysine is substituted for glutamic acid. The different electric charge conferred on the entire molecule by these single substitutions apparently determines their electrophoretic behavior, as well as the sickling phenomenon. Here one gene controls the nature of a single amino acid and so of a disease, designated as "molecular" by Pauling.

Besides sickle hemoglobin certain abnormal hemoglobins condition hemolytic anemias with short red cell survival, but by a quite different mechanism. The rare disorder H hemoglobin disease is probably the genetic result of double heterozygosity with the gene for alpha thalassemia. Up to 40 per cent of the red cell hemoglobin migrates rapidly during electrophoresis and contains 4 beta polypeptide chains. The physiologically significant feature is that this hemoglobin undergoes irreversible oxidative denaturation either spontaneously, after the native GSH content of the red cells declines with age, or as a result of oxidant drug administration. Upon incubation in vitro the red cells develop Heinz bodies which appear in the blood especially after splenectomy, a procedure which is beneficial, but not curative. Two other abnormal hemoglobins, so-called Zurich and Ube I, are also susceptible to drug-induced or spontaneous oxidation respectively, with the formation of methemoglobin and Heinz bodies, despite the absence of defects in the red cell's reducing mechanisms. In Zurich hemoglobin there is a single substitution of arginine for histidine normally in A hemoglobin at the 63 position of the beta chain. In Ube I hemoglobin there is a blockade of unknown nature of the cysteine residue at the 93 position of the beta chain which is next to the 92 positioned histidine residue attached to and essential for the preservation of the heme's ferrous iron in A hemoglobin. With oxidation of the ferrous iron a reaction takes place with the internal ligand and the molecule is no longer a suitable substrate for methemoglobin reductase.

THALASSEMIA. Thalassemia, or Mediterranean anemia, occurs in two forms, major and minor, sometimes designated as Cooley's anemia and familial microcytic anemia, respectively. Thalassemia major is a severe microcytic anemia with moderate hypochromia appearing in infants of geographical origin from the Mediterranean eastward through Indonesia to the Philippines. It is usually fatal before the patient becomes adult. Siblings are often affected, and both parents exhibit the mild form of microcytic anemia char-

acteristic of thalassemia minor. The severe disease is the homozygous state transmitted by an autosomal gene from each parent when heterozygous in each. The mild, heterozygous disorder may be transmitted directly when only one parent is affected. Overlapping in the clinical severity of the two genetic types is well documented.

The peripheral blood in thalassemia major is characterized by signs which may be interpreted as increased (though qualitatively abnormal) production of red cells, including erythroblasts and inconstantly increased numbers of reticulocytes. There is often a granulocytic leukocytosis, sometimes even of a myeloid character. The adult red cells exhibit marked variations in size and in hemoglobin content, up to half of which may be of fetal type. The average red cell is small and "flat" and has markedly decreased osmotic and possibly increased mechanical fragility and a short survival time in the patient as well as in normal subjects. The serum hemoglobin and bilirubin are usually increased. However, despite increased plasma radioiron turnover and urobilinogen in the feces, the decreased radioiron labeling of the red cells indicates ineffective erythropoiesis with relative lack of response to the increased red cell destruction. The iron-binding capacity of the serum may be fully saturated, and the tissue hemosiderin is increased. With iron stains the bone marrow exhibits ringed sideroblasts and in the peripheral blood the reticulocytes contain many siderotic granules, which with the electron microscope appear to be iron-laden mitochondria. An enlarged head and mongoloid facies are due in part to the enlargement of the marrow cavities of the cranial bones. The spleen is often very large and the liver moderately so. Splenectomy may have a favorable effect upon the hemoglobin level and especially the transfusion requirements of certain patients with large spleens in whom, unlike others, normal red cells do not survive normally. In thalassemia minor there is little clinical disability and the blood picture is that of a mild microcytic, and rarely slightly hypochromic, anemia with decreased osmotic fragility of the red cells. Because the red cell count is often distinctly above normal, cases have been reported as "familial polycythemia." Defective hemoglobin and red cell production are more important than increased red cell destruction. Splenectomy is not effective in raising the hemoglobin level in thalassemia minor. Iron therapy is without benefit in either form of the disease.

A diagnostic feature of the red cells of patients with thalassemia major is their content of from 40 to almost 100 per cent of F hemoglobin. Most of the rest of the hemoglobin, at least by present criteria, appears to be normal A hemoglobin. In thalassemia minor about half of the patients have up to 10 per cent of F hemoglobin; the rest have none. Another frequent anomaly of the red cells in both types of thalassemia is the presence of A_2 hemoglobin in increased amounts. This hemoglobin, electrophoretically slow-moving compared to A hemoglobin, is present in trace amounts in normal red cells and requires starch block electrophoresis for its demonstration. The defect in hemoglobin synthesis is not of quality but of quantity. Linkage of the thalassemia gene to the gene controlling the beta polypeptide chain of normal A hemoglobin interferes with its formation. Consequently, compensatory gamma chain polypeptide production takes place with the result that F (alpha and gamma chain) hemoglobin instead of A (alpha and beta chain) hemoglobin is preferentially formed. Increased A_2 hemoglobin indicates increased production of an alpha and delta chain variety. What has been said so far applies chiefly to the genetic type called "beta thalassemia". In another variety, the so-called "alpha thalassemia", the production of alpha instead of beta chains is inhibited in some instances to such a degree that an abnormal globin containing four beta chains (H hemoglobin) is produced. In alpha thalassemia A, A_2 and F hemoglobins, all of which contain an alpha chain, are usually evolved with difficulty. Consequently, these infants in utero cannot compensate, as does the infant with the beta variety of thalassemia, by producing F hemoglobin, and are severely anemic at birth. Recent isotopic studies of the comparative rates of globin and of heme synthesis in vitro in beta thalassemia show that the lag in beta chain synthesis slows the production of globin and that this in turn interferes with the synthesis of heme. The electron microscope demonstrates heavily iron-laden mitochondria in the thalassemic reticulocytes. Excess iron apparently inhibits the synthesis of the porphyrin precursor of heme, delta aminolevulinic acid, in these subcellular structures.

As already mentioned, double heterozygotes of beta thalassemia and S hemoglobin occur with uninhibited production of F and S hemoglobins and consequent clinical features of sickle cell disease and its painful crises. In combination with other types of hemoglobin, such as C and E, the clinical state and degree of microcytic anemia of the relatively few patients studied are perhaps those of a more severe thalassemia minor. On the other hand, G hemoglobin in combination with the thalassemia gene appears not to be clinically important. In some families with heterozygous thalassemia-sickle cell disease the genetic factors do not behave like alleles. Thus both traits or neither trait may go to one offspring.

PAROXYSMAL (NOCTURNAL) HEMOGLOBINURIA. Chronic hemolytic anemia with paroxysmal nocturnal hemoglobinuria is a rare disorder usually appearing in adults sometimes as a sequel to aplastic anemia. It is characterized by somewhat macrocytic, normochromic anemia, moderate jaundice and splenomegaly and sometimes hepatomegaly. The patient may notice that urine passed after sleep is red, more commonly dark brown, in appearance. The urine gives a positive test for hemoglobin, but does not contain red cells. In contrast to the peripheral blood picture of other hemolytic anemias, the leukocytes and platelets are often decreased and hemoglobinemia or methemalbuminemia giving a brownish color to the plasma is invariably present, though accompanied by only a moderate increase in bilirubin.

According to Dacie and Mollison, normal red cells transfused into patients with paroxysmal nocturnal hemoglobinuria survive normally, while in normal subjects a portion of the patient's transfused cells are destroyed rapidly, the rest more slowly. Autologous red cells labeled with Cr^{51} are not sequestered by the patient in either liver or spleen. Ham's observations showed that the mechanism causing the increased blood destruction is the result of a peculiarity of the red cells, many of which, although normal with respect to osmotic and mechanical fragilities, are readily lysed in vitro when incubated in unheated, slightly acidified serum. After treatment with tannic acid normal red cells become susceptible. Reticulocytes are no less sensitive than mature cells. Heinz has shown that magnesium ion, properdin and complement-like components of patients' or normal serum are essential for hemolysis. No antibody has been found on the red cells or in the plasma, but the patients' red cells are abnormally sensitive to lysis by various antibodies with agglutinating and hemolytic properties, for the detection of which they are usefully employed. The hypersensitivity depends upon a structural anomaly of the red cell that allows C' complement to create more large holes in its abnormal membrane than in normal cells. Less than half the usual concentration of acetyl cholinesterase is consistently found in these red cells, but this apparently bears no relation to their susceptibility. Thus, complete inhibition of this enzyme in the red cells of normal subjects does not shorten their lifespan.

That increased local acidity of the blood is responsible for accelerating blood destruction in the patient was demonstrated by Ham in several ways (Fig. 30–18). Normally during sleep the pH of the blood falls slightly, probably as a result of insensitivity of the respiratory center. The usual effect of sleep in producing an increased hemoglobin excretion in the urine was abolished by hyperventilation of a sleeping patient in a respirator, with resultant slight alkalosis. The rate of red cell destruction, as determined chiefly by measurement of the hemoglobin excreted in the urine during sleep, was increased by the administration of ammonium chloride and temporarily decreased by sodium bicarbonate. Repeated transfusions of washed red cells may raise the patient's hemoglobin and suppress autogenous red cell production and hence the hemolytic process. Removal of an enlarged spleen may decrease hemolysis little or temporarily or may only abolish the increases in hemoglobinuria previously observed during sleep. That the red cells are destroyed in other internal organs in which the pH of the blood may be slightly low as a result of erythrostasis is suggested by the venous thromboses occurring in the portal system and by central and midzonal necrosis of the liver. The free hemoglobin in the serum does not, curiously enough, result in striking elevations of the serum bilirubin, nor, unless the patient has received many transfusions, in the diffuse distribution of hemosiderin characteristic of most hemolytic anemias. Instead, probably because of the constant hemoglobinuria the free iron pigment is found largely in the convoluted tubules and ascending loops of Henle of the kidney. The appearance in the urinary sediment of iron-containing tubule cells or casts accounts for a considerable loss of iron.

Abnormal Plasma. In this group of hemolytic anemias the immediate mechanism of blood destruction appears to reside in abnormalities of the plasma. In some instances the operation of the plasma factor responsible for the hemolytic mechanism is demonstrable in vitro; in others it is inferred only because transfused normal red cells are rapidly removed from the patient's circulation.

PAROXYSMAL (COLD) HEMOGLOBINURIA. Paroxysmal hemoglobinuria due to *cold* is a rare phenomenon manifested clinically by the passage of dark urine containing hemoglobin within minutes or a few hours after local or general exposure of the body to cold. Pain in the back, chills, fever and prostration are characteristic of a severe attack. Hemoglobinuria is invariably the result of hemoglobinemia, with moderate increase in serum bilirubin. In response to the hemolytic anemia signs of increased erythrocyte production appear in the peripheral blood.

Two entirely different mechanisms for the sudden increased red cell destruction may be involved in different patients and can be demonstrated in vitro. The first mechanism involves an immune hemolysin essentially without agglutinating properties and is usually displayed by patients with a positive Wassermann reaction. The antibody can be separated from the Wassermann factors and was formerly most common as a late manifestation of syphilis, congenital or acquired. It may also develop following infectious diseases or be a concomitant phenomenon of idiopathic acquired hemolytic anemia. The serum (but uniquely only in the presence of complement) will sensitize the patient's or normal red cells at 16° C. or below, and will subsequently hemolyze them at body temperature. This is the so-called Donath-Landsteiner reaction. The patient's serum upon chilling and rewarming also causes clumping of leukocytes and phagocytosis by them of the red cells of the patient or of normal subjects of the same blood group. After immersion of an arm or leg in cold water with or without tourniquet applied, hemoglobinemia with or without hemoglobinuria is observed. Leukopenia with relative lymphocytosis is accompanied by erythro-

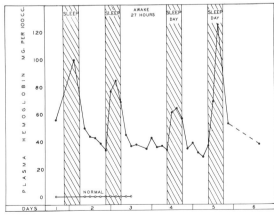

Figure 30–18. The effect of sleep in increasing hemoglobinemia in a patient with paroxysmal nocturnal hemoglobinuria. Note that the hemoglobin level of the patient's plasma did not increase during 27 hours without sleep, but was increased by sleep during the daytime. (From Ham: Arch. Int. Med., *64:*1271, 1939.)

phagocytosis in incubated blood samples. If due to syphilis, penicillin therapy will usually abolish the clinical, but not entirely the laboratory, manifestations of exposure of the blood to cold.

The second mechanism involves the presence of a *cold agglutinin,* sometimes in high titer. Usually, according to Dacie, the patient's red cells taken directly into warm saline are agglutinated by antihuman rabbit (Coombs) serum, and a weak hemolysin for normal red cells can frequently be demonstrated in the patient's serum, especially if it is slightly acidified. With high titers of agglutinin the red cells may begin to clump at room temperature, and when strongly agglutinated in chilled blood are abnormally susceptible in vitro to mechanical trauma. In the patient, clumps of red cells may be seen in cooled conjunctival and nail bed capillaries, which by obstructing the flow of blood give rise to the Raynaud-like manifestations and purpura or even to local gangrene of the extremities. Chronic hemolytic anemia, more severe in winter, may be present. Hemoglobinemia, but not necessarily hemoglobinuria, can be induced in such patients by immersion of the arm in cool water. The cause of the development of the cold agglutinins is often obscure. They may accompany a hemolysin in idiopathic acquired hemolytic anemia of chronic type, or unaccompanied by a hemolysin may appear in patients with leukemia or lymphosarcoma or in the recovery period after "atypical" pneumonia due to *Mycoplasma pneumoniae.* Occasionally in this last the titer may exceed 1:30,000 and a cold sponge bath has been known to precipitate a hemolytic crisis. However, agglutination by even a high titer of cold agglutinin declines sharply between 20 and 25° C., and rarely extends above 32° C.

Transfusion of red cells of *incompatible blood groups* induces a classic form of increased red cell destruction affecting, however, only the donor's erythrocytes. The mechanisms of red cell destruction in these circumstances have already been discussed (see pp. 784 and 785). The most practical screening test for compatibility remains the mixing of a drop or two of the donor's blood (not red cells in saline solution) with a drop of the recipient's serum on an uncovered microscopic slide. Agglutination under these circumstances as the slide is gently rocked on an illuminated surface at body temperature will usually appear within five minutes if a dangerous incompatibility is at hand. This procedure, as devised by Diamond for the detection of incomplete antibodies, provides automatically inhibition of cold agglutination, slight concentration of plasma through drying, approximation of red cells and visualization of particulate flow due to incomplete Rh antibodies. Another test of red cell sensitization with incomplete antibody is the addition of large anisometric molecules such as fibrinogen, gelatin or polyvinylpyrrolidine (PVP) to a suspension of the (unwashed) red cells on a slide or in a test tube. Rouleaux formation with nonsensitized cells can be dispelled at once by dilution with saline solution while agglutination of sensitized red cells persists. Nevertheless, some incomplete Rh antibodies such as D_u variants do not cause agglutination under either of these circumstances. Such incompatibility may be detected by testing with antihuman-globulin rabbit serum for the presence of adsorbed globulin on the saline-washed red cells of the prospective donor after they have been incubated with the recipient's serum (indirect Coombs' test). There still remains, as Swisher and Young have shown in dogs, and as Jandl and Greenberg have observed in patients, no available method for detecting in advance those properties of red cells that may on rare occasions prejudice their survival in certain patients who have previously been transfused and who tolerate perfectly red cells from some but not from other persons. Fortunately the clinical reaction is mild, and is usually delayed for a few days until presumably fixation of the otherwise undetectable antibody on the surface of the red cells has taken place.

The misfortune of a hemolytic transfusion reaction may become manifest with restlessness, back pain, chill, fever, nausea and vomiting. The circulatory collapse attending these signs, which include agglutination and hemolysis of the transfused cells with release of histamine and serotonin following antigen-antibody union, may itself prove fatal or contribute to oliguria and subsequent renal failure with death in uremia. A febrile response following multiple transfusions does not necessarily imply immune hemolysis. If not due to bacterial pyrogen it may be obviated by prior removal of leukocytes from whose subsequent immune destruction endogenous pyrogen may be derived. When a transfusion reaction occurs in a patient under general anesthesia, the premonitory signs do not appear.

ACQUIRED HEMOLYTIC ANEMIA. Acquired hemolytic anemia is a term used here to designate a heterogeneous group of acute, more usually chronic or remitting hemolytic anemias, exclusive of hereditary hemolytic anemias and of hemolytic anemias ascribable to the extrinsic and intrinsic causes of hemolysis already discussed. Acquired hemolytic anemia is sometimes associated with liver cirrhosis, Hodgkin's disease, leukemia, nonleukemic myelosis, carcinomatosis, infectious mononucleosis, miliary tuberculosis, lupus erythematosus, sarcoid and cysts and tumors of the ovary (Table 30–5). In about two-thirds of the patients the hemolytic anemia occurs without association with recognizable disease. The spleen is often enlarged, sometimes greatly.

In many patients, beyond the fact that the survival of the patient's and often of transfused normal red cells is reduced, the immediate basis of the hemolytic process is obscure. Frequently, the patient's labeled red cells are sequestered by the spleen, especially when it is enlarged. In the few instances tested, short survival of a portion of patients' red cells in normal recipients has been observed with normal survival of the remainder. Survival may be normal in the normal recipient when, during remission of the anemia, survival in the patient is still somewhat short. Characteristic of acquired "autoimmune" hemolytic anemias are alterations of red cell surface and presence of substances in the serum with a general affinity for human red cells of all types. For the most part these serum substances are 7S gamma globulins that behave like incomplete antibodies and in a few instances display specificity for Rh antigens, most frequently anti-e. When transfused into the patient, normal red cells acquire within 24 to 72 hours a positive test for adsorbed serum globulin (Coombs test), if the patient's red cells are Coombs-positive. Autoagglutination of the red cells of fresh blood when the plasma is slightly concentrated by evaporation is a common finding. An increase of agglutination on cooling indicates that a cold agglutinin is present. The microscopic appearances may include clumps of spheroidal cells with increased osmotic and mechanical fragility. Labeled normal red cells injected into such a patient show an increase in osmotic fragility within two or three days, and those remaining unhemolyzed through the next few days approach in their osmotic fragility that of the patient's red cells. Only in rare instances is a hemolysin for normal red cells demonstrable unless the patient's serum is acidified to between pH 6.5 and 7. Otherwise, its affinity for the red cell would result in its adsorption by agglutinated or hemolyzed red cells in vivo.

Boorman, Dodd and Loutit were the first to show that the saline-washed red cells of patients with "acquired acholuric jaundice," in contrast to those with "congenital acholuric jaundice," were agglutinated by rabbit serum containing antibodies developed against human serum (direct Coombs test). The interpretation offered was that an immune globulin from the patient's serum had become adsorbed on the surface of the circulating red cells which were consequently agglutinated by the antiglobulin antibodies in the immune rabbit serum. Thus the Coombs test has often been interpreted as evidence of adsorbed "autoantibodies" on the red cells in idiopathic acquired hemolytic anemia. This inference is, of course, entirely correct in the case of Rh sensitization and in instances of hemolytic anemia due to antigenic alteration of the red cells by such drugs as Fuadin and penicillin. Equally plausible is the assumption that in idiopathic acquired hemolytic anemia the avidity of the adsorbed globulin for the red cell is merely fortuitous, and is an incidental property of anomalous globulin formation in response to an infection or by neoplastic cells. Possible analogies to such processes are agglutinins for sheep red cells in infectious mononucleosis and the M protein of the serum of myeloma, respectively. The fact that, according to Dacie, agglutinins in the patient's serum may be specific for certain Rh antigens of the patient's red cells or, according to Davidsohn, may be more active against the patient's than against other red cells of similar antigenic type adds no weight to the evidence in favor of "autoantibodies." Indeed, for example, plants of the legume

TABLE 30–5. FREQUENCY OF "AUTOANTIBODIES" IN ACQUIRED HEMOLYTIC ANEMIA.*

		Percentages
I. Warm type	(75%)	
A. Idiopathic		58
B. Secondary		
1. Chronic lymphatic leukemia		6
2. Lymphomas		4
3. Disseminated lupus erythematosus		4
4. Other		3
II. Cold type	(25%)	
A. Idiopathic		12
B. Secondary		
1. Atypical (mycoplasma) pneumonia		7
2. Lymphoma		4
3. Other		2

* Data from Dacie, J. V.: The Haemolytic Anaemias: Congenital and Acquired. Part II: The Autoimmune Haemolytic Anaemias. New York, Grune & Stratton, 1962.

TABLE 30–6. USUAL CHARACTERISTICS OF "AUTOANTIBODIES" IN ACQUIRED HEMOLYTIC ANEMIA.*

I. Warm type
  A. Electrophoretic mobility: "slow" gamma (γG)
  B. Sedimentation: 7S, mol. wt. 160,000
  C. In vitro characteristics:
    1. Usually "incomplete" agglutinins
    2. Peak activity at 37° C.
    3. Demonstrated by Coombs test (usually "gamma" type), 25% albumin, PVP, etc.
    4. Nonhemolytic (do not bind complement)
  D. May pass placenta
II. Cold type
  A. Electrophoretic mobility: "fast" gamma (γM)
  B. Sedimentation: 19S, mol. wt. 1,000,000 ±
  C. In vitro characteristics:
    1. Often "complete" agglutinins, sometimes lytic
    2. Peak activity at 0 to 4° C., and high thermal range with increasing titer
    3. Demonstrated by cold agglutination and by Coombs test (usually "nongamma" type)
    4. Potentially hemolytic (bind complement)
    5. Do not pass placenta

* Kindly supplied by Drs. M. Kaplan and J. H. Jandl.

species may contain highly specific agglutinins for certain major red cell groups. Moreover, Jandl has shown that the natural presence of transferrin, a normal serum protein, on the surface of reticulocytes renders them agglutinable by antiglobulin serum; and that chromium or iron salts apparently cause attachment of serum proteins to the red cell surface, which then results in red cell agglutination in the presence of the Coombs serum. Such observations indicate the lack of a necessarily "immunologic" basis for the adsorption of the globulin detected by the serum.

Under various and often unphysiologic conditions, *anomalous behavior of the patient's serum* toward red cells can be demonstrated. Thus, incubation of the serum of many patients with acquired hemolytic anemia together with normal compatible red cells may cause the cells to become agglutinable with antiglobulin serum (indirect Coombs test). This may occur because of the presence of either warm or cold, complete or incomplete "antibodies" (Table 30–6). Slight acidification of the serum often enhances the effect. The action of antiglobulin serum is competitively inhibited by gamma globulin when warm antibodies are involved. The patient's serum may irreversibly agglutinate normal red cells previously treated with trypsin or papain or the peculiarly sensitive red cells of paroxysmal nocturnal hemoglobinuria (PNH). In both types of system, hemolysis may accompany the agglutination to a similar degree of dilution. The detection of adsorbed cold agglutinins by Coombs serum is only slightly inhibited by gamma globulin, and is thought to be due to the attachment of complement, a nongamma globulin, by the weak hemolysin present. Cold agglutinins may accompany warm agglutinins or be present independently. When a hemolysin is present, if serum containing cold antibodies is acidified to between pH 6.5 and 7, normal red cells may be rapidly hemolyzed in the presence of complement. Trypsinized and PNH red cells are even more sensitive. However, in vitro, strong cold agglutination may give rise to difficulties in blood grouping and to falsely positive tests for the presence of hemolysins when the cooled and agglutinated red cells are pipetted or otherwise subjected to mechanical trauma. Stats showed that the mechanical fragility of the agglutinated red cells at icebox temperature and, to some extent, at room temperature may be greatly increased.

The pioneer clinical observations of Widal and his pupils to the effect that *autoagglutination* of red cells is a distinguishing feature of acquired hemolytic anemia have now developed manifest functional significance. Wasastjerna, using slit-lamp microscopy of the superficial vessels of the scleral conjunctiva, saw a "granular" flow of blood indicating intravascular erythroagglutination. This varied with the intensity and severity of the disease in patients with positive Coombs tests. Jandl's as well as Mollison's observations with Cr[51]-labeled red cells detect from scanning of body surface gamma emission the sequestration of red cells in the spleen and liver. When hemolysis is very active and spherocytosis and autoagglutination of red cells are seen in the peripheral blood, the liver uptake predominates, but when a positive Coombs test is the only abnormality, the spleen is the principal site of red cell removal. Splenomegaly, classically associated with multiple areas of thrombosis and infarction and with extensive congestion of the splenic pulp, is presumably the result of agglutination of the red cells. Autoagglutination of the red cells, greater in the spleen than in the peripheral blood, has been observed at the time of splenectomy. Wagley has shown that exposure of normal red cells to the washed splenic pulp of such patients for an hour in the incubator caused globulin to be adsorbed by the normal red cells. The development of a positive Coombs test did not occur in similar experiments with the pulp from spleens of hemolytic anemias and other conditions with Coombs-negative red cells.

In summary, when a complement-requiring hemolytic system active against normal red cells in vitro is present, there is no difficulty in understanding the hemolytic mechanism in the patient. However, the presence of such a system is a rarity. Much more frequent is the finding only of autoagglutination or of potential agglutinability of the patient's red cells, that is, agglutination in slightly concentrated patient's or normal plasma. The influence of actual or potential agglutination in the patient's plasma on sequestration of labeled red cells in the liver and/or spleen of the patient has been amply documented. As already mentioned, mononuclear cells, perhaps resembling the reticuloendothelial cells of the splenic and hepatic sinusoids, ingest red cells coated with Rh antibodies after contact is brought about mechanically by centrifugation. The nature of the subsequent lytic process, especially the means of its rapid initiation, which clearly involves participation by vascular or tissue cells, is, however, still obscure. Whether the observed hemolysis is due to the release of tissue lysins or of substances capable of "activating" potentially hemolytic globulins on the surfaces of the red cells is unknown. Table 30–7 is a schema of the postulated sequence of events leading under various circumstances to eventual red cell lysis.

Dameshek has clearly demonstrated the value of splenectomy in acquired hemolytic anemia. This procedure is distinctly beneficial, at least for a time, in about half the patients, presumably both because it removes an important source of "antibodies" and/or because it removes a filter for weakly agglutinated red cells. For both reasons irradiation of an enlarged lymphomatous spleen in acquired hemolytic anemia associated with leukemia may be useful. Again, in one patient with acquired hemolytic anemia, removal of an ovarian tumor (source?) was effective; in another, splenectomy (filter?) in addition to removal of the tumor was required for relief. If splenectomy is effective, a fall in the titer of the Coombs test may or may not occur, together with clinical recovery progressive over a period of weeks.

ACTH or more conveniently cortisone is often useful both before and after splenectomy in suppressing the hemolytic process (Fig. 30–19). By analogy with their prompt effects in decreasing the adhesion of cells to blood vessel walls as observed by Ebert, and in suppressing lymphoid tissue, their action is possibly due in part to a diminution of the filtering effect of the spleen, liver sinusoids and other vascular structures upon sensitized red cells. Indeed, Coleman and Finch demonstrated an inhibitory effect of steroids upon hemolysis in hereditary spherocytic anemia, a condition in which antibodies are not present. Adrenocortical steroids also may eventually inhibit antibody production, with a resulting decline of both direct and indirect Coombs test titers in some patients, who thereafter presumably have less tendency to autoagglutination of the red cells. Agglutination of the "coated" red cells by PVP seems to correlate better than the Coombs test with the rate of hemolysis.

Hypersplenism. The hypersequestering action of the spleen upon red cells is usually secondary to primary abnormalities of red cells or plasma as just discussed. However, in occasional instances, an independent increase in the filtering efficiency of the spleen or of other tissues can result in the sequestration of initially normal red cells as well as of leukocytes and platelets. This is most surely illustrated by certain patients with considerable splenomegaly as the result of infiltration by Gaucher's or lymphosarcoma cells. Again, "acute splenic tumor" associated with infections such as typhoid fever or infectious mononucleosis or chronic splenomegaly as a result of increase in splenic vein pressure as in cirrhosis have likewise been shown to cause enhanced splenic sequestration of the patient's Cr^{51}-labeled red cells. Finally, in thalassemia major and in combined S and C hemoglobinopathy, splenomegaly induced by congestion with the patient's red cells may secondarily lead to sequestration of transfused normal red cells. For a full discussion the reader should consult Chapter 31.

ANEMIAS OF DECREASED ERYTHROCYTE PRODUCTION

In these anemias there is presumptive evidence of failure on the part of the bone marrow to supply sufficient red cells to keep pace with a more or less normal rate of red cell destruction. In some instances, however, the increased cellularity of the bone marrow reflects the fact that to some extent an increased local rate of erythroid precursor destruction may be involved. This supposition is fortified in pernicious anemia and in certain instances of refractory macrocytic anemia by

TABLE 30–7.   POSTULATED SEQUENCE OF EVENTS RESULTING IN INCREASED
ERYTHROCYTE DESTRUCTION IN HEMOLYTIC ANEMIAS.

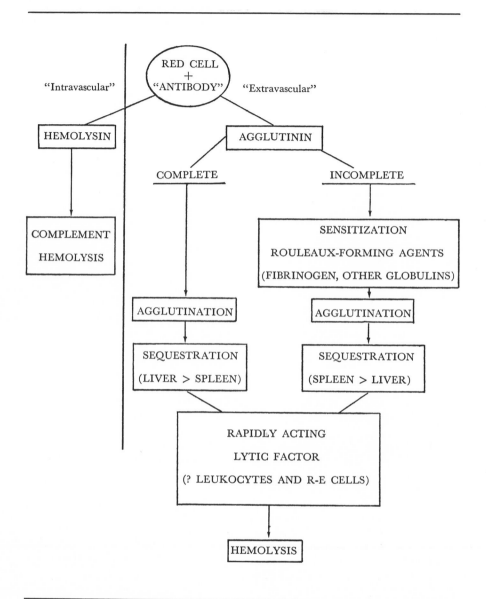

the presence of increased amounts of bile pigment in the feces and by ferrokinetic studies indicating "ineffective erythropoiesis." Characteristic of the group as a whole is the fact that, even in the presence of severe anemia, the precentage of reticulocytes is not significantly increased. Moreover, those therapeutic measures which are beneficial and cause elevation of the blood values promptly initiate an increase in the percentage of the reticulocytes in circulation. With the excep-

tion of the hypochromic iron deficiency and sideroachrestic anemias, the erythrocytes tend to be normal or increased in size and to contain a normal or only slightly diminished concentration of hemoglobin. In general the granular leukocytes, except in the anemia of leukemia and in anemias due to chronic local infection, are normal or reduced in number. The platelets are also likely to be reduced. Table 30–8 presents a classification of these anemias which may serve to define the order of discussion, even if not acceptable to all on the basis of pathogenesis.

Nutritional Deficiency of Erythropoiesis

Nutritional deficiency is an important cause of deficient erythropoiesis by the bone marrow. The defect in marrow function may be mainly a decreased rate of effective red cell production as a result of deficiency of vitamin B_{12}, folic acid, or of both folic and ascorbic acids; or it may be mainly a diminished rate of hemoglobin production as a result of a deficiency of iron or possibly of copper. In each instance abolition of the specific deficiency results in increased red cell and hemoglobin production as a consequence of a return towards normal of bone marrow morphology and function. This is heralded in the peripheral blood by an orderly rise and subsequent decline in the number of reticulocytes, and is followed by a subsequent restoration to normal of blood values and

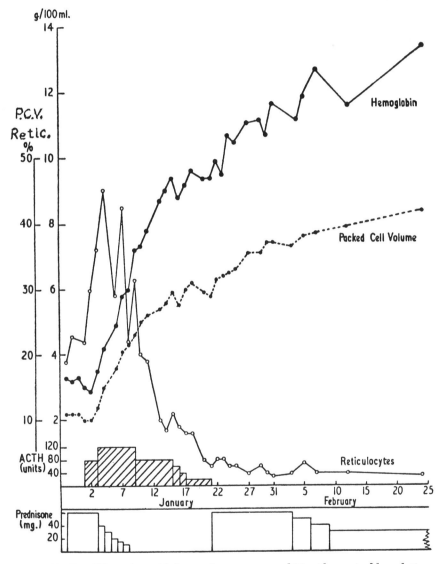

Figure 30–19. Effect of steroid therapy in a woman aged 26 with acquired hemolytic anemia associated with disseminated lupus erythematosus. Prednisone by mouth was supplemented with injection of ACTH. Note the prompt increase in reticulocytes despite the rise in hemoglobin. This suggests that the steroid therapy either caused increased erythropoiesis or more probably decreased (splenic?) sequestration of reticulocytes. (Modified from Dacie: Brit. Med. Bull., 15:67, 1959.)

TABLE 30–8. CLASSIFICATION OF ANEMIAS
DUE MAINLY TO DECREASED ERYTHROCYTE
PRODUCTION (BONE MARROW PHYSIOLOGICALLY
HYPOACTIVE).

I. Nutritional deficiency
  A. Vitamin B_{12} (macrocytic anemia)
    1. Defective diet: nutritional macrocytic anemia (vegans)
    2. Defective absorption:
      a. Intrinsic factor deficiency: gastrectomy, achylia gastrica, pregnancy, sprue
      b. Intestinal disease: ileal resections, short circuits, sprue, "receptor" lack
      c. Competitive parasites: broad tapeworm, bacteria in diverticuli, stenoses, "blind loop"
  B. Folic acid (macrocytic anemia)
    1. Defective diet: megaloblastic anemia of infants, tropics, pregnancy
    2. Defective absorption: intestinal short circuits, stenoses, steatorrhea, sprue
    3. Metabolic derangement: folic acid antagonists, liver disease, pregnancy
  C. Folic and ascorbic acids (macrocytic anemia)
    1. Defective diet: megaloblastic anemia of infantile and adult scurvy
    2. Defective metabolism: liver disease (?)
  D. Iron (hypochromic anemia)
    1. Increased requirement: growth
    2. Increased loss: menstruation or pregnancy, chronic hemorrhage
    3. Decreased intake: defective diet, gastric anacidity, diarrhea, steatorrhea
  E. Pyridoxine (hypochromic anemia)
    1. Defective diet (?)
    2. Defective metabolism
II. Endocrine deficiency (normochromic anemia)
  A. Thyroid, adrenal, testicular or anterior pituitary hormones
III. Toxic inhibition (normochromic anemia)
  A. External poisons: benzol, insecticides, antibacterial and antileukemic drugs
  B. Internal toxins: chronic infections, renal failure, cancer (local or metastatic)
IV. Physical injury (normochromic anemia)
  A. X-rays, radium, radioactive phosphorus
V. Mechanical interference (normochromic anemia)
  A. Inadequate marrow capacity: anemia of newborn and of prematurity
  B. Myelophthisis: leukemia, myelo- and lymphoproliferative disorders, metastatic carcinomatosis, reticuloendothelioses, primary xanthomatoses, myelofibrosis and osteosclerosis
VI. Idiopathic (normochromic anemia)
  A. Refractory (aplastic) anemias

---

bone marrow morphology. This is taken to mean that with the abolition of the specific nutritional deficiency the bone marrow is enabled to respond to the pre-existing anemia. In addition, possibly as a result of a metabolic block, there are patients with microcytic hypochromic red cells and high serum iron levels who respond to pyridoxine administration.

The Antianemia Principles of Liver. Shortly after the discovery of the efficacy of liver feeding in pernicious anemia in 1926, Cohn, Minot and their associates began the chemical fractionation of beef liver. This soon led to the preparation of extracts of high potency at first for oral, and by 1930 in Germany, for parenteral injection. However, during the next twenty years progress in efforts on both sides of the Atlantic to identify the active principle was slow, owing to the lack of physical methods of separation, such as chromatography, and the necessity for clinical testing of each fraction. In 1945 "folic acid" in the form of a synthetic preparation of pteroylglutamic acid was unexpectedly found by Spies to be hematopoietically and clinically effective in pernicious and related macrocytic anemias, including those of sprue, pregnancy and infancy. Folic acid was therefore at first thought to be the antipernicious anemia principle of liver. However, because purified liver extract, highly active in pernicious anemia, contained insignificant amounts of folic acid, this misconception was soon appreciated. Moreover, although synthetic pteroylglutamic (folic) acid was active initially in 1 to 5 or more milligram daily dosage in causing remissions in pernicious anemia, as time passed the blood values were not maintained. In some patients glossitis reappeared, and the appearance or progress of lesions of the spinal cord was noted. Within a short time it was found that megaloblastic anemias responsive to crude but not to refined liver extracts responded to much smaller doses of folic acid.

With the isolation in 1948 of vitamin B_{12} from highly purified liver fractions as cyanocobalamin by members of the pharmaceutical industry both in America and in England, the goal of the identification of the unique antipernicious anemia principle of liver was at last reached. When injected daily in pernicious anemia 1 microgram of cyanocobalamin produces maximal hematopoietic effects. Consequently, it must be regarded as one of the most potent therapeutic agents known.

It is certain from studies of the growth requirements of bacteria and of the histochemical changes in patients and animals resulting from deficiencies of vitamin B_{12} or of folic acid that derangements of nucleic acid metabolism are involved. As with the toxic effects of folic acid antagonists or of x-rays, the rapidly dividing cells of the body, such as those of the bone marrow or intestinal tract, are among the first affected. Thus large cells with relative nuclear immaturity are found not only among the red and white cell and platelet precursors in the bone marrow in pernicious anemia, but also in gastric washings and in buccal and vaginal scrapings as well as in the epithelial cells of the small intestine in sprue. The characteristic biochemical abnormality of megaloblastic erythropoiesis, whether due to lack of vitamin B_{12} or folic acid, is a relative increase of cytoplasmic ribonucleic acid (RNA) compared to nuclear deoxyribonucleic acid (DNA). These master molecules are composed of specific purines and pyrimidines combined with the two varieties of ribose sugars respectively and phosphoric acid. According to Beck, vitamin B_{12} deficiency interferes with the reduction of all four ribosyl nucleotides to deoxyribosyl nucleotides at the diphosphate level, whereas folic acid deficiency interferes with the methylation of a single DNA precursor, deoxyuridylate to deoxythymidylate at the monophosphate level. The effect of either deficiency is to delay nuclear maturation and division.

Deficiency of these vitamins also interferes with biochemical reactions less directly concerned with hematopoiesis and probably of less physiologic importance. A biochemical interrelation, perhaps having a bearing on the ability of large amounts of folic acid to produce hematopoietic effects in vitamin B_{12} deficiency (Fig. 30–20), as well as the less impressive clinical effect of large amounts of vitamin B_{12} in folic acid deficiency, is the requirement of vitamin B_{12} as coenzyme for the conversion of homocysteine to methionine (Fig. 30–21). Here donation of methyl from N-5-methyltetrahydrofolate is involved. Again, the excretion of abnormal amounts of formiminoglutamic acid, an intermediary metabolite of histidine, serves as a clinical indication of folic acid deficiency but is also increased in vitamin B_{12} deficiency. Normally, tetrahydrofolate, having lost a methyl group to methionine, is ready to accept the formimino group and so to convert formiminoglutamic to the normal urinary metabolite, glutamic acid. Of possibly greater physio-

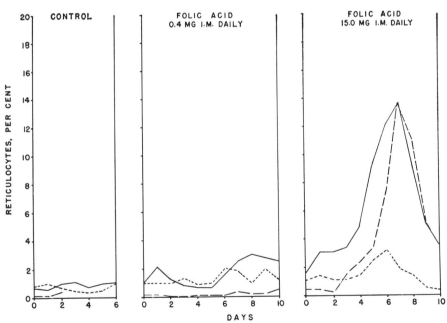

Figure 30–20. Reticulocyte responses of three patients with vitamin B_{12} deficiency to "physiologic" followed by "pharmacologic" dosage of pteroylglutamic (folic) acid. These patients were *not* deficient in folic acid. Note the absence of response until the larger dosage was given. Patients with folic acid deficiency (not shown) respond readily to the "physiologic" dosage of folic acid employed here. (From Marshall and Jandl: Arch. Int. Med., *105:*352, 1960.)

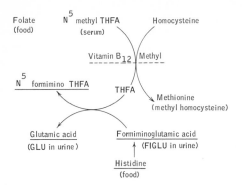

Figure 30–21. Diagrammatic representation of an important metabolic relationship between vitamin B$_{12}$ and folic acid. Note that the conversion of homocysteine to methionine requires the donation of a methyl group from N^5 methyl tetrahydrofolate (N^5 methyl THFA) to homocysteine with the help of vitamin B$_{12}$. The observed increase of N^5 methyl THFA activity in the serum of patients deficient in vitamin B$_{12}$ may be due to block of methyl transfer. Deficiency of either vitamin can fail to provide tetrahydrofolate (THFA) for later acceptance of the formimino group of the abnormal metabolite formiminoglutamic acid (FIGLU). (Modified slightly from Herbert and Zalusky: J. Clin. Invest., 41:1263, 1962.)

logic interest is the role of vitamin B$_{12}$ in the methylmalonyl CoA isomerase reaction to succinate, a key step in propionate metabolism. In vitamin B$_{12}$ deficiency, but not in folic acid deficiency in man, the abnormal intermediate methylmalonic acid appears in the urine, perhaps in especially large amounts in those patients exhibiting neural disturbances. There is current interest in the possible relationship of the methylmalonate abnormality to combined system disease in man. Possibly an abnormality of propionate metabolism could affect the lipid integrity of the myelin sheaths of spinal cord neurons.

In vitamin B$_{12}$ deficiency, partial responses to precursors of more complex nucleosides have been obtained with uracil, orotic acid and thymine. Moreover, methyl group donors such as choline and methionine plus uracil have some effect, and gram-sized doses of thymine (5 methyl uracil) imitate the erythropoietic effects of milligram doses of folic acid in the pernicious anemia of pregnancy. Sustained erythropoietic responses follow the administration of "physiologic" daily parenteral doses of either vitamin B$_{12}$ (1 microgram) or folic acid (150 to 400 micrograms) only in megaloblastic anemias due, respectively, to each deficiency.

Deficiency of Vitamin B$_{12}$. Deficiency of vitamin B$_{12}$ or of folic acid causes morphologically similar varieties of macrocytic normochromic anemia which, when established, are usually associated with granulocytopenia and thrombocytopenia. The large red cells appear oval in blood films. The bone marrow is featured by an erythroid hyperplasia preponderantly of large erythroid precursors (megaloblasts) and especially of the younger cells corresponding to the proliferative stage II of normal erythropoiesis (Fig. 30–1). The specifically impaired production of DNA increases the time required for its doubling, a necessary prelude to cell division, whereas there is no impediment to RNA production in the cytoplasm. Consequently the maturity of the nuclear structure lags behind that of the hemoglobiniferous cytoplasm. This is reflected in the decreased DNA/RNA ratio of the marrow. Large metamyelocytes and polymorphonuclear leukocytes with increased numbers of nuclear lobes, as well as large megakaryocytes with nuclear immaturity are also seen. Yet, whereas the causes of the two kinds of vitamin deficiency are strikingly different, as will be detailed below, their hematologic abnormalities are identical. Only some of their associated clinical manifestations are similar. Thus, glossitis is common to both, and mild intestinal unrest or constipation sometimes accompanies vitamin B$_{12}$ deficiency in pernicious anemia, while diarrhea with steatorrhea is prominent in patients with sprue and folic acid deficiency. On the other hand, combined system disease of the spinal cord is strictly confined to vitamin B$_{12}$ deficiency, usually in association with gastric achylia in pernicious anemia.

Vitamin B$_{12}$, a cobalamin, is found in many foods of animal origin. In milk, muscle, serum and liver it is closely associated with proteins. It is conveniently prepared as cyanocobalamin from hydrolyzed liver and crystallizes in red needles with a molecular weight of 1356. The molecule contains 4 per cent cobalt, which, as a trivalent cobalt coordination complex, is responsible for the red color. One of the six coordinate bonds of the cobalt atom is attached to a cyan group; four are attached to the nitrogens of the four substituted pyrrole rings surrounding it and making a planar macroring, resembling in form and in biological synthesis the iron-centered macroring of the porphyrins. The remaining bond is attached to a 5,6-dimethylbenzimidazole riboside, which is joined to the macroring again through phosphate esterified

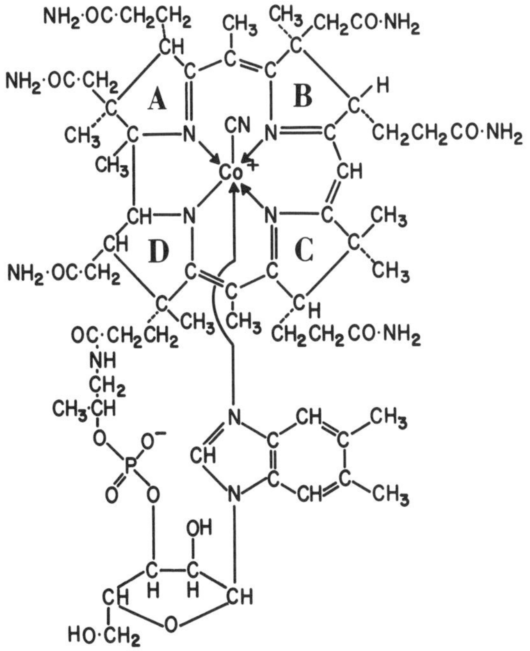

Figure 30–22. The cyanocobalamin molecule. Note in the upper part of the figure the central cobalt atom linked to four reduced pyrrole rings forming a macroring, the "planar" portion of the molecule. Below is the "nucleotide" portion which in nature lies in a plane nearly at right angles. The base joined to the cobalt atom is 5,6-dimethyl benzimidazole, and the sugar is a ribose attached to the D portion of the macroring through phosphate esterified with 1-amino-2-propanol. In cyanocobalamin the sixth coordinate bond of the cobalt atom is attached to a cyan group. In the native coenzyme form of the vitamin active in mammals, the cyan group is replaced with a 5'-desoxyadenosyl group above the plane of the macroring. (Modified from Beck: New England J. Med., 266:708, 1962.)

with 1-amino-2-propanol (Fig. 30–22). According to the recent work of Barker, vitamin B_{12} occurs in animal tissues as a very labile coenzyme in which an adenosine-like ligand above the planar ring replaces the cyan group of the therapeutic preparation. Thus the coenzyme is the native form of vitamin B_{12} whose adenosine-like group is readily displaced by a hydroxy group to form hydroxycobalamin (vitamin B_{12}a). Because cyanide was used to stabilize the commercial extraction process from liver the vitamin was isolated in the cyanocobalamin form. These three cobalamins have similar biologic activity clinically and in promoting the growth of certain lactobacilli and flagellates requiring them for growth on synthetic media.

Vitamin B_{12} is unique among water-soluble vitamins in not being formed by higher plants or animals. Only certain bacteria and molds seem capable of its synthesis. Bacterial growth in the rumen is probably responsible for the high concentration of vitamin B_{12} in the livers of cows and sheep. In nonruminants vitamin B_{12} is probably largely derived from animal protein in the food. Although in man, including patients with pernicious anemia, bacterial synthesis in the colon produces daily 5 micrograms or more of vitamin B_{12}, this is not absorbed. Cobalt deficiency in sheep produces a "conditioned" vitamin B_{12} secondary to a cobalt-depleted bacterial flora in the rumen. Commercial advantage was fortunately taken of the fact that vitamin B_{12} is a by-product of streptomycin production.

Because the various macrocytic anemias listed in Table 30–8 under deficiency of vitamin B_{12} respond characteristically to the parenteral administration of a few micrograms of vitamin B_{12}, a common basic deficiency may be inferred. In untreated pernicious anemia and its allied conditions, the serum vitamin B_{12} level, as determined by the growth of the green flagellate *Euglena gracilis*, is almost invariably less than 100 micromicrograms per milliliter, or less than a fifth of the normal value. Girdwood has shown that the livers of patients dying of pernicious anemia do not contain vitamin B_{12}, and from his data on normal subjects it has been estimated that the normal adult body contains from 1 to 2 mg. of vitamin B_{12}, of which perhaps half is in the liver.

Following the parenteral administration of vitamin B_{12} to anemic patients there is initially a prompt fall of the elevated plasma bilirubin and iron values. Declines in the excessively rapid plasma iron turnover and shortly thereafter of the increased fecal urobilinogen indicate the cessation of the intramedullary conversion of heme to bilirubin involved in ineffective erythropoiesis. Within a day or two the megaloblastic proliferation of the bone marrow is converted to normoblastic. A reticulocyte response appears on the third to the fifth day (Fig. 30–23), which thus resembles the time relations of the reticulocyte response to acute hemorrhage or hypoxia (Fig. 30–13). In the later stages of the restoration of a normal hemoglobin evidence of iron deficiency may become apparent in the development of hypochromic red cells. Under these circumstances the serum vitamin B_{12} level may have become normal, but the serum iron level is low and a reticulocyte response to iron administration may

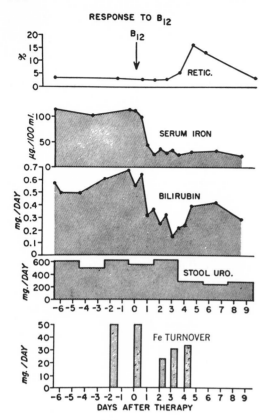

Figure 30–23. Effect of a therapeutically active injection of vitamin B_{12} in pernicious anemia. Note the prompt initial fall in the elevated serum iron, iron turnover and serum bilirubin values. These were followed within a few days by a reticulocyte peak and a decline in the excessive excretion of fecal urobilinogen. (Reproduced from Finch and others: Blood, *11:*807, 1956.)

be shown. Thus the abolition of one nutritional deficiency may bring to light or create another which in turn may be abolished by appropriate specific therapy.

Immediate Mechanisms of Vitamin B_{12} Deficiency. Vitamin B_{12} deficiency is rarely a consequence solely of a dietary lack of the vitamin, although it may appear on this basis in so-called "vegans," persons subsisting on diets completely lacking in animal protein. Most commonly, as indicated in Table 30–8, it is a "conditioned" failure of assimilation of the vitamin resulting specifically from lack of secretion of the so-called intrinsic factor of the normal stomach, from nonspecific or possibly specific defects of intestinal absorption or from competition by intestinal parasites for the available vitamin B_{12}. In individual patients these limitations occur singly or in combination and may participate to different degrees at different stages of the disease. For example, with vitamin B_{12} as-

similation already embarrassed by achylia gastrica, pernicious anemia may be precipitated by change to a diet of lower vitamin B_{12} content.

Observations leading to modern knowledge of the conditioning mechanisms of vitamin B_{12} deficiency began in 1929 when it was shown that normal human gastric juice and beef muscle given daily together produced a reticulocyte response that was followed by increases of red cells and hemoglobin quite as if moderate doses of liver extract had been administered. However, when given individually, separated by only a 12 hour interval, they were hematopoietically ineffective. It was therefore assumed that the increased blood production depended upon "interaction" of two factors—one in the beef muscle (extrinsic) and one in the normal human gastric juice (intrinsic). The negative effect of administering beef muscle alone made it clear that in the patient with pernicious anemia and achylia gastrica the gastric factor is virtually lacking.

Shortly after the isolation of the antipernicious anemia principle of liver in the form of vitamin B_{12}, Berk and his associates discovered that 5 micrograms of vitamin B_{12} could be substituted for 200 gm. of beef muscle with essentially similar results in such clinical observations. Erythropoietic effects were detectable with the simultaneous oral administration of as little as 1 microgram of vitamin B_{12} and 10 cc. of gastric juice daily (Fig. 30–24). However, the effect of 1 microgram of vitamin B_{12} given parenterally was always greater than that of up to 10 micrograms of vitamin B_{12} and 150 cc. of gastric juice given orally. Bethell showed that the activity of desiccated hog stomach or duodenum when orally administered is due to the presence of both vitamin B_{12} and intrinsic factor.

It thus became clear that vitamin B_{12} was both the antipernicious anemia principle of purified liver extracts and also the so-called extrinsic factor of beef muscle. It was soon shown that the function of the intrinsic factor was merely to augment the assimilation of vitamin B_{12} as such from the gastrointestinal tract. Thus, Heinle, in 1952, showed that when 0.5 microgram of Co^{60}-labeled vitamin B_{12} was given to patients with pernicious anemia, most of the radioactivity was excreted in the feces. However, simultaneous administration of an active source of intrinsic factor resulted in distinctly less fecal excretion. Similar results were obtained by Halsted in postgastrectomy patients shortly after the operative procedure. That intrinsic factor enhanced the uptake of the labeled vitamin B_{12} as such was demonstrated by Schilling, who, by using a large parenteral injection of nonradioactive vitamin B_{12}, "flushed" the absorbed source of radioactivity into the urine and showed that its solubility in butanol and its chromatographic distribution indicated the presence of Co^{60}-B_{12}.

In man the intrinsic factor is apparently secreted by the entire gastric mucosa with the possible exception of the pyloric gland area, but not by the duodenum. This corresponds to histologic studies of the stomach in pernicious anemia indicating marked degeneration of the glands of the fundus without significant changes in the pyloric gland area or duodenum. Only total gastrectomy may thus be expected to abolish completely the known sites of secretion of intrinsic factor in the human stomach. Radioautographs of sections of human stomach after immersion in solutions of Co^{60}-B_{12} indicate binding of the vitamin by the parietal (acid-secreting) cells, a phenomenon specifically inhibited by anti-intrinsic factor serum. Gastric intrinsic factor is thermolabile and nondialyzable, but will pass a Berkefeld V filter. It is not inactivated by alkali at pH 10. Pepsin, rennin, gastric lipase, alpha-aminopolypeptidase, prolinase or hyaluronidase do not act as intrinsic factor.

Ternberg and Eakin found that normal human gastric juice prevented utilization of vitamin B_{12} by cultures of lactobacilli and suggested, though without clinical evidence, that such "binding" is the basis of its physiological action with respect to vitamin B_{12} in man. Although it was soon shown that *binding* is a property of many proteins, the purest preparations of intrinsic factor possess strong vitamin B_{12} binding capacity. Moreover, intrinsic factor is protected against gastrointestinal enzymes when bound to vitamin B_{12}. Glass found a close correlation between soluble, glandular mucoprotein and intrinsic factor activity. Current work indicates that intrinsic factor will prove to be a mucopolysaccharide or mucopolypeptide, containing, besides amino acids, hexose, hexosamine and sialic acid. The molecular weight, approximately 50,000, of some preparations may represent a polymer of subunits of smaller size which have been reported to be active. All preparations active in pernicious anemia bind vitamin B_{12}, for example, 6.6 micrograms of vitamin B_{12} per milligram of intrinsic factor protein, of which 100 micrograms has been shown to be active in the Schilling test in pernicious anemia when administered with

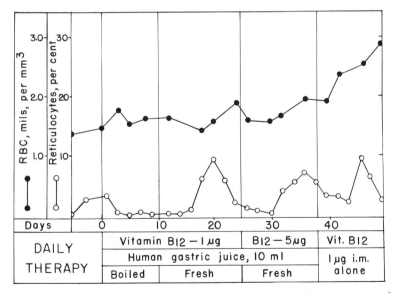

Figure 30–24. Successive reticulocyte responses demonstrating the potentiation of vitamin B_{12} by simultaneous daily oral administration of normal human gastric juice. Note the negative effect of 10 ml. of boiled gastric juice and 1 microgram of vitamin B_{12} daily. This was followed by a first reticulocyte response when 10 ml. of fresh gastric juice was substituted. When the vitamin B_{12} was increased to 5 micrograms daily a second reticulocyte response developed. However, the parenteral administration of 1 microgram of vitamin B_{12} then produced a third reticulocyte response indicating its greater erythropoietic activity. (From Castle: Med. Clin. North America, 50:1245, 1966.)

0.5 microgram of Co^{60}-labeled vitamin B_{12}. Possibly one mole of intrinsic factor binds one mole of vitamin B_{12}.

Dialysis experiments in vitro indicate that the first action of intrinsic factor is competitively to bind the low concentrations of vitamin B_{12} present in ingested animal protein. This process is favored by the gastric acidity. Observations in pernicious anemia suggest that Co^{60}-B_{12} bound to intrinsic factor is preferentially absorbed over "cold" vitamin B_{12} given simultaneously by mouth to the patient. Observations with perfused loops of rat small intestine with intact blood supply and with everted intestinal segments in vitro indicate that this second action of intrinsic factor involves adsorption of the vitamin B_{12}-intrinsic factor complex to the intestinal mucosa as a physical process requiring, according to Herbert, the presence of calcium ions and a pH near neutrality. Because of the polarity, fat insolubility and large molecular radius (8 angstroms) of the vitamin B_{12} molecule (Fig. 30–22) and especially of the intrinsic factor molecule (44 angstroms) specifically required for its assimilation, Wilson has proposed that the next step in the absorption of the complex into the intestinal cell might be by the process of "pinocytosis," a kind of phagocytosis at a molecular level requiring the expenditure of cell energy and consistent with the morphologic appearance under the electron microscope of the epithelial cells of the ileum (microvilli, etc.).

After adsorption to the intestinal mucosa, there is, according to Doscherholmen, a delay of some four hours before the radioactive vitamin begins to appear in the blood stream. This is not due to a temporary accumulation in the liver as the delay is not reduced in patients with portacaval anastomosis. Consequently, some metabolic process located in the bowel wall must be involved, perhaps concerned with release of vitamin B_{12} from intrinsic factor or its intracellular transport. When oral doses of 100 micrograms or more of vitamin B_{12} are given, intrinsic factor is not required for their partial assimilation, which occurs without the delay characteristic of the physiologic transport process. This pharmacologic effect presumably explains the classic oral activity in pernicious anemia of liver and liver extract which are relatively concentrated sources of vitamin B_{12}.

The ability of intrinsic factor to prevent the microbial utilization of vitamin B_{12} has suggested that intrinsic factor protects vitamin B_{12} in the small intestine from bacterial utilization and so makes it available for assimilation. However, in pernicious anemia antibiotics rarely enhance the uptake of labeled vitamin B_{12} while intrinsic factor regularly does. On the other hand, in patients with multiple diverticula of the upper small intestine, intestinal anastomosis or "blind loop" as a result of surgery, or with tropical sprue and macrocytic anemia, labeled vitamin B_{12} may not be absorbed, even when given with intrinsic factor, until after a few days of tetracycline therapy. In such patients hydrochloric acid and intrinsic factor are secreted by the stomach but luxuriant bacterial growth occurs in the blind pouches and overflows into the adjacent intestine. Presumably, the avid assimilation of dietary vitamin B_{12} by the bacteria allows it to be carried out of the body in nutritionally inaccessible form. This situation resembles at a microscopic level the deleterious influence of the broad tapeworm, which takes up vitamin B_{12} and eliminates it from the body in the worm segments, thus producing pernicious anemia, especially in patients with a dwindling secretion of intrinsic factor. Expulsion of the worm again permits vitamin B_{12} to be absorbed.

The mechanism of the defective absorption of vitamin B_{12} and of other nutrients in patients with small intestinal resections seems self-evident. When blind loops, short circuits or stenoses are present, bacterial contamination of the bowel is also of importance. Mollin's scanning observations of the small bowel of nonpernicious anemia patients at laparotomy a few hours after the oral administration of a dose of radioactive vitamin B_{12} and intrinsic factor, as well as studies of patients with local disease or resection of various portions of the small intestine, indicate surprisingly that vitamin B_{12} is normally assimilated only in the distal ileum (Fig. 30–25). When the upper regions of the small bowel are also involved, where other nutrients are normally absorbed, deficiencies of iron and folic acid and of fat and fat-soluble substances, such as vitamins A, D and K and calcium soaps, can be added. Deficiencies of vitamin B_{12} and folic acid so induced may then lead to further dysfunction of the alimentary tract. Probably for this reason, therapy with each of these two vitamins may produce dramatic amelioration of the intestinal symptoms in tropical sprue and occasionally in other chronic diarrheas, accompanied by rapid improvement of the abnormal roentgenologic appearance of the small intestine sometimes referred to as the "deficiency pattern." An isolated intestinal defect of vitamin B_{12} absorption, perhaps due to a lack of the intestinal receptors for vitamin B_{12} bound to intrinsic factor, has been found in a few infants and adults without clinical or histologic evidence of intestinal disease. A few suggestive observations indicate that normal small intestinal secretions may enhance the assimilation of vitamin B_{12} in some of these patients.

Pinpointing the basis of vitamin B_{12} deficiency in a given patient requires analysis of the defects of its intake, assimilation and utilization. The same participation of such factors may not exist in a given patient at all times. That before the introduction of liver therapy it was often possible in the early stages of pernicious anemia to produce temporary remissions by the use of high caloric diets rich in meat, suggests that some intrinsic factor was still present. This was apparently much more frequently the case in patients with early sprue. In at least some patients with the relatively rare type of

pernicious anemia of pregnancy due to vitamin B_{12} deficiency, the administration of beef muscle, a source of vitamin B_{12}, before delivery produced no effect on blood formation. After delivery, however, this material induced clinical improvement and a reticulocyte response, which was further augmented when normal gastric juice was added. The implied diminution of the intrinsic factor of the gastric juice during pregnancy is occasionally paralleled by the disappearance of the hydrochloric acid, which likewise may spontaneously return after delivery.

The participation of dietary deficiency (B_{12}), intrinsic factor deficiency (IF) and intestinal malabsorption (IM) in limiting the amount of vitamin B_{12} assimilated may be empirically expressed as: $\dfrac{B_{12} \times IF}{IM} = B_{12}$ absorbed. From this it can be seen that decrease of either or both factors in the numerator or increase of the denominator will diminish the value of each side of the equation. Moreover, because so long as some potential for secretion of IF remains, a dietary increase in B_{12} may increase IF and to some extent

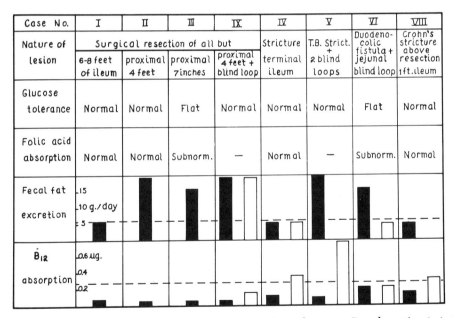

Case No.	I	II	III	IX	IV	V	VI	VIII
Nature of lesion	Surgical resection of all but				Stricture terminal ileum	T.B. Strict. + 2 blind loops	Duodeno-colic fistula + jejunal blind loop	Crohn's stricture above resection
	6-8 feet of ileum	proximal 4 feet	proximal 7 inches	proximal 4 feet + blind loop				1ft. ileum
Glucose tolerance	Normal	Normal	Flat	Normal	Normal	Normal	Flat	Normal
Folic acid absorption	Normal	Normal	Subnorm.	—	Normal	—	Subnorm.	Normal
Fecal fat excretion								
B_{12} absorption								

Figure 30–25. Results of oral glucose, folic acid, fat and vitamin B_{12} absorption tests in patients with previous surgical resection and/or disease of the small intestine. The interrupted horizontal lines indicate the upper limit of normal fat excretion on diets containing 50 or 100 gm. of fat and the lower limit of normal vitamin B_{12} absorption following oral administration of 1 microgram of radioactive cyanocobalamin. Solid bars indicate values before and open bars indicate values after oral administration of Aureomycin. The results suggest that glucose and folic acid are readily absorbed from even short lengths of the upper small intestine, fat with more difficulty, while vitamin B_{12} is absorbed chiefly from the distal ileum. The suppressive effect of Aureomycin upon intestinal bacteria growing above strictures or in blind loops of bowel was presumably responsible for the improved absorption of vitamin B_{12} in 3 of the 4 patients so treated. (Redrawn from illustrations in the article by Booth and Mollin, Proc. Roy. Soc. Med., 53:658, 1960.)

TABLE 30–9. "Autoantibodies" in Pernicious Anemia and Thyroiditis: Patients and Relatives.*

| Immunofluorescence | Percentage of Positive Reactors | | | | Hospital Controls |
| | Pernicious Anemia | | Hashimoto's, Myxedema | | |
	Pts.	Rels.	Pts.	Rels.	
Gastric parietal cytoplasm	89	36	32	20	2–16†
Thyroid acinar cytoplasm	55	49	87	52	0–15†

* Modified from table and figure by Doniach and Roitt: Seminars Hemat., 1:313, 1964.

† The figures for pernicious anemia and thyroiditis are for approximately age 60; those of the hospital controls are greater in females and increase with age.

decrease IM, the factors in the equation can influence one another and an unstable equilibrium is implicit. Moreover, DeGowin's studies of red cell survival suggest that vitamin B_{12} deficiency produces not only defective red cells, but also a hostile environment for their survival in the circulation. Consequently, at least two mechanisms are disclosed for producing the classic remissions and relapses of the disease, at least in its early stages; one enteral and one parenteral. Consistent with either explanation is the great rarity of so-called spontaneous remissions in pernicious anemia in our experience when such patients are maintained in a metabolic ward on diets low in vitamin B_{12}.

REMOTE CAUSES OF ALIMENTARY TRACT DYSFUNCTION. Miller and Rhoads produced a rather chronic dietary deficiency ("black tongue") in swine. The intrinsic factor normally present in the gastric juice was lacking in these animals. It is therefore of interest that statistical studies indicate a greater incidence of achlorhydria and of digestive disturbances in persons living on diets deficient in meat, green vegetables and fruit, than in persons eating these foods liberally. More frequently, however, the tendency to achlorhydria appears to be a hereditary trait expressing itself progressively during adult life and with greater frequency in the families of patients with pernicious anemia. Homozygosity of a recessive gene may be important in juvenile pernicious anemia. Of eight children with this disease, six had siblings with the same disease and three had parental consanguinity. In such patients hydrochloric acid but not intrinsic factor may be secreted by a histologically normal stomach. Histamine-fast achlorhydria does not develop later. In other children defective intestinal absorption of vitamin B_{12} occurs despite presence of intrinsic factor. This, according to Imerslund, is due to a hereditary lack of intestinal receptors for the vitamin B_{12}-

intrinsic factor complex, presumably formed by their acid- and intrinsic factor-containing gastric juice. Albuminuria is an unexplained associated finding.

The development by Wood in 1949 of a gastric mucosal biopsy tube with a grasping mechanism activated by suction has permitted extensive study of the histology of the living stomach as well as of the small intestine. In pernicious anemia microscopic appearances range from "gastritis" with varying degrees of infiltration with lymphocytes to severe "gastric atrophy." Recently it has been shown that "autoantibodies" specifically directed against the parietal cells of the stomach are found in the serum of about 90 per cent of patients with pernicious anemia (Table 30–9). Moreover, such antibodies, demonstrable by the use of fluorescein-labeled anti-gamma globulin serum on fresh frozen sections of normal human stomach (Fig. 30–26) are found in the serums of patients with histologic evidence of gastritis and in a considerable percentage of the asymptomatic relatives of patients with pernicious anemia. In the clinically manifest disorder with low serum vitamin B_{12} levels, half of the patients have, in addition, an "antibody" directed against intrinsic factor, at any rate a gamma globulin capable of preventing the specific binding of radioactive vitamin B_{12} by intrinsic factor, both in vitro and in the Schilling test. Ordinarily, unless the patient's serum "leaked" into the intestinal tract, the anti-intrinsic factor antibody would seem to play no part in limiting the absorption of vitamin B_{12}. Thus, in a patient immunized against hog intrinsic factor with specific antibodies in the serum, hog intrinsic factor given by mouth was fully active in promoting the absorption of radioactive vitamin B_{12}. Nevertheless, in a few patients with pernicious anemia the scanty gastric secretions have been shown to contain either an anti-intrinsic factor antibody or an anti-B_{12} intrinsic factor complex antibody that might interfere with the intestinal absorption of the complex, especially with a limited secretion of intrinsic factor.

The idea that the basis of the longstanding "gastritis" of the adult patient with pernicious anemia is associated with some type of underlying "autoimmune" process on a hereditary basis rests on the work of Doniach, Taylor and others showing that in about half the patients with pernicious anemia and their close relatives are found antibodies against thyroid acinar cytoplasm (Fig. 30–26), while about a third of patients with Hashimoto's syndrome or myxedema have antibodies against gastric parietal cell cytoplasm (Table 30–9). Antibodies against either or both types of cells have been found in some of the few patients studied with nontuberculous Addison's disease. In the entire group of such patients the incidence of the so-called lupus erythematosus (LE) factor is less frequent than in the controls.

GASTROINTESTINAL AND NEURAL MANIFESTATIONS. In vitamin B_{12} deficiency, in addition to the anemia, there are often manifestations of greater or less severity in the alimentary tract and in the nervous system. Therapy with vitamin B_{12} has a prompt effect in healing the lesions of the oral mucosa and in causing the papillae of the tongue to grow again. After vitamin B_{12} therapy, the "macrocytic" epithelial cells characteristic of oral, gastric and vaginal washings disappear. The apathy, anorexia and weakness, characteristic of other nutritional deficiency diseases, begin to disappear after a few days and distinctly before any significant rise in hemoglobin values has occurred.

Neural disturbances develop most commonly in pernicious anemia, but also in rare instances in patients with absorptive defects of the intestine and diminished serum vitamin B_{12}. The classic lesion is a myelin degeneration and loss of nerve fibers in the dorsal and lateral columns of the spinal cord and in some cases in the white matter of the brain. Somewhat similar sensory neuron degeneration has been produced in animals given diets deficient in pyridoxine and pantothenic acid and has been prevented by liver extracts effective in pernicious anemia. In man subacute combined degeneration of the spinal cord is arrested effectively by vitamin B_{12} given parenterally in sufficient doses. Pteroylglutamic acid, however, does not prevent this disability; and advance or development of neural lesions, occasionally with great rapidity, has been reported as beginning several days or weeks after the initiation of a satisfactory hematologic remission, especially when 2 milligram or larger daily amounts of folic acid are given.

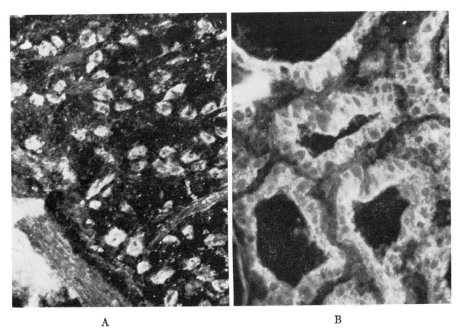

A   B

Figure 30–26. A, The result of immunofluorescent staining of normal gastric parietal cell cytoplasm by serum from a patient with pernicious anemia. B, A similar effect on normal thyroid acinar cell cytoplasm by serum from a patient with Hashimoto's thyroiditis. Note the unstained (dark) nuclei of the cells in both tissues. The two microsomal autoantigens show close biochemical similarities. (From Doniach and Roitt: Seminars Hemat., 1:313, 1964.)

Under these conditions the already low serum levels of vitamin B_{12} descend further. This, together with the observations of Ross and Chodos, indicating that even miminal amounts of parenterally administered vitamin B_{12} afford protection of the spinal cord against large daily doses of folic acid, suggests a "mass action" depletion of residual vitamin B_{12} by folic acid administration. The speculative relation of disturbed propionate metabolism to demyelination has already been mentioned.

POSSIBLE DEFECTS OF INTERNAL METABOLISM. Thomas has shown that vitamin B_{12} added to bone marrow cultures from pernicious anemia patients in vitro will enhance DNA production. According to Reisner, despite contradictory reports by others, vitamin B_{12} may bring about maturation of megaloblasts in bone marrow cultures in vitro. Normal serum, but not pernicious anemia serum (deficient in vitamin B_{12}), is also effective. Consequently, once in the blood stream there would appear to be no impediment to the erythropoietic activity of vitamin B_{12}. According to Beck cyanocobalamin is converted in the erythroid cell to hydroxycobalamin, which is then collected on a special class of ribosomes. There it is converted to the coenzyme form, metabolically active in the reduction of ribose to deoxyribose nucleotides.

Beard considers that alpha globulin is the most important transport protein for vitamin B_{12} in the serum. Theoretically, an abnormality of this or other serum proteins might result in a failure of vitamin B_{12} to be transported from the intestine to the marrow or might allow the unbound vitamin to be rapidly excreted by the kidney en route. A possible example of such a situation is the unique patient reported by Horrigan and Heinle who responded only to an unusually large parenteral dose of vitamin B_{12} or to 250 ml. of normal plasma. In this connection also comes to mind the enormous requirement for vitamin B_{12} of the patient with splenomegaly and chronic myelogenous leukemia reported by Conley. It is possible that a local deficiency of vitamin B_{12} (or of folic acid) can be brought about by the competitive requirements of neoplastic cells infiltrating the marrow or that the enhanced binding capacity of the serum in myelogenous leukemia for vitamin B_{12} may prevent its utilization by the erythroid precursor cells. The interest that attaches to such observations far outweighs their frequency. Defects of internal metabolism of vitamin B_{12} are undoubtedly rare, except possibly as a result of toxic inhibition by fever or drugs of metabolic processes dependent upon vitamin B_{12}, as discussed below.

Deficiency of Folic Acid. In 1937 Wills and her associates studied a nutritional macrocytic anemia which developed in monkeys maintained on defective diets resembling those of patients in India with macrocytic anemia. They showed that, in contrast to autolyzed yeast or a relatively crude liver extract, purified liver extract, now known to contain only vitamin B_{12}, was hematopoietically ineffective. Similar therapeutic differences were then found in the patients in India and in certain instances of the macrocytic anemia of pregnancy, of infancy and of celiac disease in Europe and elsewhere. When pteroylglutamic (folic) acid became available, it was found to be active in these patients, in the tropical macrocytic anemia of India and in sprue with macrocytic anemia in Puerto Rico.

Pteroylglutamic acid, a yellow compound with a molecular weight of 335, was synthesized as a result of extensive studies of the nutritional requirements of microorganisms and of laboratory animals, for example, the prevention of nutritional cytopenia and a spruelike syndrome in monkeys. The term "folic acid" was originally used for a substance in spinach required for the growth of *Streptococcus lactis R*. Pteroylglutamic acid is found in yeast, liver, green leaves, cereals and other foods chiefly in the form of "conjugates" containing three or seven molecules, rather than only one, of glutamic acid. Conjugates of a reduced form of the vitamin folinic acid, to be discussed, are also present and account for much of the folic acid activity of liver. Pteroylglutamic acid has a molecule composed of a pteridine (related to the yellow color in butterfly wings), linked by para-aminobenzoic acid, a well known antagonist of sulfonamides, to glutamic acid, an amino acid. Conjugates of this substance are erythropoietically effective in animals or in patients with folic acid deficiency when given by mouth; and the monoglutamate is readily released from the conjugate by enzymes present in various tissues, including intestine, pancreas and kidney.

In 1949, Sauberlich noted that a growth factor for *Leuconostoc citrovorum* was present in various amounts in certain liver extracts and was excreted in the urine of rats and of men after the ingestion of folic acid. This "citrovorum factor," also known as folinic acid because of its close chemical similarity to folic acid, is found in yeast, liver and kidney. Nichol and Welch showed that ascorbic acid or reducing conditions in vitro augmented the conversion in liver slices of folic acid to citrovorum factor, subsequently shown to be a reduced form of folic acid to which four hydrogens and a formyl group have been added. In monkeys and in man, ascorbic acid deficiency inhibits the conversion of folic to folinic acid, one of several reduced (tetrahydro) forms in which the biologically active one-carbon group is attached either to N^5 or N^{10} or balanced between them (Fig. 30–27). Another such is N^5 methyl tetrahydrofolate, which is detected in the serum of normal individuals by its growth promoting effect upon *Lactobacillus casei* under defined conditions, and is decreased in clinical folic acid deficiency.

As already stated, the morphologic features of the peripheral blood and megaloblastic bone marrow of folic acid deficiency are indistinguishable from those of vitamin B_{12} deficiency. However, free hydrochloric acid is almost always present in the gastric contents and neural manifestations are absent.

Overt or latent steatorrhea is presumably an index of defective intestinal assimilation. Because of an associated iron deficiency, the red cells sometimes exhibit less macrocytosis and more hypochromia than is usual in pernicious anemia and the serum bilirubin level may be normal. Such patients have been shown to respond to physiologic doses, 150 to 400 micrograms daily, of pteroylglutamic acid after therapeutic failure with parenteral vitamin B_{12}. The assimilation of the synthetic monoglutamate pteroylglutamic (folic) acid given by mouth is excellent even in patients with malabsorption syndromes. The serum vitamin B_{12} level is not abnormally low, but the serum activity for *L. casei* (Herbert) is decreased, being equivalent to 3 or less, as compared to a lower limit of normal of 5 millimicrograms of pteroylglutamic acid per milliliter. In addition, the accelerated disappearance rate of injected folic acid (Chanarin) indicates that the internal deficiency in these patients is not that present in addisonian pernicious anemia. An increased urinary ex-

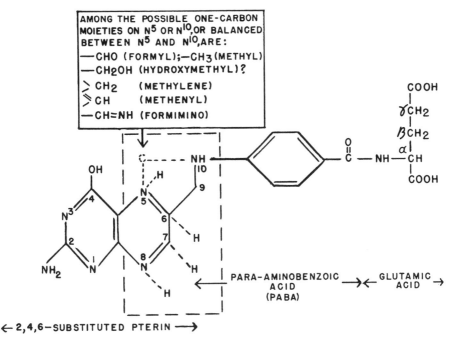

FOLIC ACID (PTEROYLGLUTAMIC ACID)
AREA IN BROKEN RECTANGLE IS THE "ACTIVE CENTER" IN 1-CARBON TRANSFERS.

BROKEN LINES OUTLINE THE BASIC 1-CARBON ACCEPTOR (5,6,7,8—TETRAHYDROFOLIC ACID) (THFA) (FH₄), AND THE VARIOUS 1-CARBON-DONATING COENZYMES DERIVED FROM IT.

Figure 30–27. Diagram of the molecule of pteroylmonoglutamic acid showing the component parts and the metabolic "active" center provided by reduction to the tetrahydro form. Native food forms contain additional glutamic acid residues attached by gamma linkages. (From Herbert and Zalusky: J. Clin. Invest., *41*:1263, 1962.)

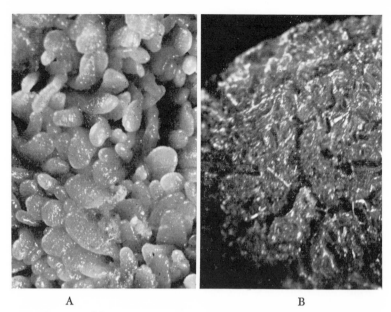

A   B

Figure 30–28. Jejunal biopsies as seen magnified × 25 with the dissecting microscope. *A,* The normal appearance of the villi. *B,* The fused and distorted appearance of the villi in primary malabsorption disease. (From Girdwood: Symposium: The Study of Normal and Disordered Function of the Small Intestine. Edinburgh, The Royal College of Physicians, 1962.)

cretion of formimino glutamic acid may result from deficiencies of either folic acid or vitamin B_{12}. For metabolic reasons this may also occur in liver disease and in iron deficiency.

Immediate Mechanisms of Folic Acid Deficiency. In contrast to vitamin B_{12} deficiency for which years of inadequate assimilation are required, dietary folate deficiency has been induced in an adult man within weeks. The conjugated forms of folic acid found in leafy vegetables, beans, fruit, liver and kidney are diminished by cooking. Infants on an exclusive milk diet receive insufficient folic acid and iron, and sometimes ascorbic acid. Infants reared on goat's milk, a poor source of folic acid, are especially liable to develop megaloblastic anemia. Folic acid deficiency is both a result and a cause of intestinal malabsorption.

The primary cause of *tropical sprue* remains obscure, but probably involves a factor of individual susceptibility unfavorably modified by dietary deficiency and/or intestinal infection. Low serum levels of both folic acid and vitamin B_{12} have been found. Achlorhydria is frequent, and malabsorption of both water-soluble and fat-soluble vitamins occurs in established tropical sprue or celiac disease. Intestinal biopsy discloses severe atrophy and blunting of the intestinal villi, with macrocytosis of the intestinal epithelial cells (Fig. 30–28), reversible by therapy with

folic acid. Dramatic cessation of the fatty diarrhea and disappearance of the typical roentgen picture of "puddling" in the small bowel often follow the administration of effective doses of folic acid and sometimes of vitamin B_{12}. This is presumably because of the inevitably multiple nature of the nutritional defects conditioned in malabsorption syndromes. In *celiac disease,* which may appear clinically in infancy or not until adult life, there is apparently a primary disorder of the small intestine. The sensitivity of the intestine to contact with wheat gluten probably indicates an enzymic defect which prevents conversion of gluten to a nontoxic digestive product. The use of gluten-free diets may strikingly relieve intestinal symptoms, but the atrophied intestinal villi do not become normal. Folic acid, unlike vitamin B_{12}, is readily absorbed from the upper small bowel. The adverse influence of resections, strictures and blind loops consists of a combination of loss of absorptive surface and of the detrimental effects of bacterial growth either by competing for folic acid or by causing injury to the absorptive surface of the intestine. Booth and Mollin's studies in individual patients of the role of such factors in causing defective assimilation of fat, folic acid and vitamin B_{12} are illustrated in Figure 30–25.

The increased demand of the *growing infant* for folic acid both in utero and thereafter is probably a factor in the development of the corresponding maternal and infantile deficiencies of folic acid. Maternal folic acid deficiency is more marked in the last trimester of pregnancy and with the greater gestational demands of twins (Fig. 30–29). In liver cirrhosis the metabolic conversion of folic to folinic acid may be disturbed. In addition to dietary deficiency as a cause of megaloblastic anemia in such patients, Sullivan has demonstrated the inhibitory effects of alcohol upon the erythropoietic action of small doses of folic acid (75 mg.). *Local cellular competition* for this essential precursor of nucleic acid synthesis may also explain the development of megaloblastic erythropoiesis in certain other patients. Examples occur with leukemic hyperplasia of the bone marrow in acute leukemia, occasional instances of the so-called myeloproliferative disorders of adults, including myelogenous leukemia and the di Guglielmo syndrome, as well as in thalassemia. In such patients transient erythropoietic responses to large doses of folic acid have been observed. The precipitation of "aplastic crises" with megaloblastic bone marrows responsive to folic acid administration as a consequence of the increasing metabolic demands of hemorrhage or hemolysis has been well documented. Infection may have a similar effect when the availability of folic acid is marginal. Administration of the 4-amino analogs of folic acid quickly produces megaloblastosis in animals and in man. Likewise, *anticonvulsants,* such as phenytoin and primidone, and especially the antimalarial agent, pyrimethamine, which have chemical structures analogous to the pteridine ring of folic acid or to nucleic acid precursors, are thought to be causative of megaloblastic anemias responsive to folic acid administration. Critical observations with physiologic doses of folic or of folinic acid in such types of anemia demonstrating competitive inhibition by the drug are yet to be done. Consequently, the merely circumstantial role of dietary inadequacy or of subclinical malabsorption still requires exclusion.

Nearly all patients with macrocytic anemia and megaloblastic bone marrow due to vitamin B_{12} deficiency respond at least initially to large, daily doses (5 mg. or more) of folic acid. Thus, in order to distinguish patients in whom the controlling deficiency is of vitamin B_{12} from those in whom folic acid deficiency is responsible, it is necessary either to determine the serum vitamin B_{12} and folic acid activity levels or to conduct a therapeutic trial employing the daily physiologic dosages

referred to above: cyanocobalamin, 1 to 5 micrograms parenterally; pteroylglutamic acid, 100 to 400 micrograms orally or parenterally. Unfortunately, in many instances of tropical macrocytic anemia and of sprue this has not been done, and the basis of the internal deficiency remains obscure. Moreover, especially in sprue or other intestinal disease, a deficiency of both vitamin B_{12} and of folic acid may coexist.

Deficiency of Folic and Ascorbic Acids. From what has already been said concerning the importance of ascorbic acid for the conversion of folic acid to, or its preservation as, the metabolically active tetrahydro forms (e.g., folinic acid), it is clear that dietary deficiency of ascorbic acid may cause an otherwise barely adequate intake of folic acid to become insufficient. May has shown that in experimental megaloblastic anemias of monkeys induced by a deficiency of both folic and ascorbic acids, folinic acid was much more erythropoietically active than was folic acid. Presumably such a double deficiency is the basis for certain megaloblastic anemias that have appeared in infants fed exclusively on unsupplemented formulas based on dried milk preparations which were deprived of ascorbic acid in the manufacturing process. About a quarter of these patients showed clinical signs of scurvy.

The anemia of adult scurvy is commonly normocytic and due to extensive bleeding into tissues (in effect, red cell destruction)

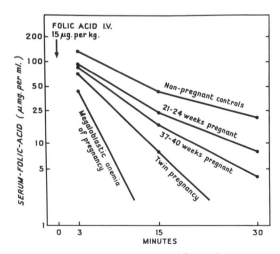

Figure 30–29. Mean serum folic acid concentration, after the intravenous injection of 15 micrograms per kilogram in 30 healthy nonpregnant women, 31 women 21 to 24 weeks pregnant, 31 women 37 to 40 weeks pregnant, 11 women with twin pregnancy, and 11 patients with megaloblastic anemia of pregnancy. (From Chanarin: Lancet, 2:634, 1959.)

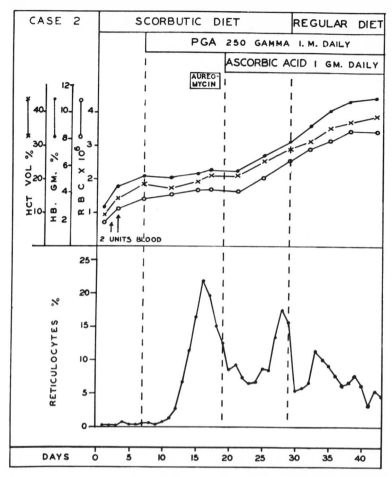

Figure 30–30. Potentiation of the erythropoietic effect of pteroylglutamic (folic) acid by ascorbic acid in a 49-year-old male chronic alcoholic with signs of liver dysfunction and scurvy. Initial hematologic studies showed a severe macrocytic anemia with leukopenia and thrombocytopenia. The bone marrow aspirate showed a predominance of abnormal macrocytic red and white cell precursors, including numerous megaloblasts. Free HCl was present in the gastric juice. Total serum vitamin B_{12} level was 193 micromicrograms per ml. (low normal), and ascorbic acid was not found in the leukocytes or serum. The successive reticulocyte peaks indicate, first, a partial response to pteroylglutamic (folic) acid; second, potentiation by the addition of orally administered ascorbic acid, presumably because of increased formation of citrovorum factor (folinic acid); and third, an undefined additional effect of normal diet. (From Jandl and Gabuzda: Proc. Soc. Exper. Biol. & Med., *84:452,* 1953.)

to account for the reticulocytosis. Ascorbic acid quickly abolishes the hemorrhagic tendency and the reticulocytes fall as the hemoglobin rises. In occasional patients, especially those with alcoholic liver disease, macrocytic anemia and clinical scurvy coexist, and ascorbic acid may be lacking in the leukocytes, while the serum vitamin B_{12} level is normal. The bone marrow may or may not be suggestively megaloblastic but the serum folate level is low. In such patients Jandl and Gabuzda have shown that the erythropoietic effect of as little as 125 micrograms of folic

acid given parenterally and daily was significantly augmented by the daily oral administration of 1 gm. of ascorbic acid (Fig. 30–30). Although contrary to our experience, isolated reports indicate that in scorbutic patients with macrocytic anemia, in whom presumably the deficiency of ascorbic acid was the controlling influence, response may occur to ascorbic acid alone. Usually, however, folic acid deficiency is the controlling influence, and no erythropoietic response occurs with ascorbic acid administration until folic acid is given. This distinction is difficult to make clinically because considerable amounts of folic acid are present in most hospital diets even when the diets are low in ascorbic acid.

Deficiency of Iron. Anemias due to deficiency of iron are frequently encountered, affect persons of all ages, and are widely distributed geographically. The blood picture is characterized by hypochromic microcytic red cells. Usually the leukocyte and platelet values are little altered. The bilirubin is normal or reduced, and the fecal urobilinogen excretion is reduced. In the marrow the meager bluish cytoplasm of the dominant pyknotic normoblasts, the absence of the siderotic granules normally present in these cells, and the consistent lack of hemosiderin testify to the dearth of available iron. In 1936, Heath showed that in hypochromic anemia intramuscularly injected iron appears during the initial gain in circulating hemoglobin more or less quantitatively. Consequently, as has been amply confirmed by modern ferrokinetic studies, iron deficiency may be presumed to be the dominant factor in the production of such anemia. Indeed, when iron is administered to patients with hypochromic anemia while they are maintained on diets low in protein, hemoglobin is actually formed at the expense of plasma protein. Finally, the plasma iron, which is usually much reduced, sometimes to values of less than 35 micrograms per 100 ml., rises rapidly as the result of iron therapy, while the moderately increased iron-binding capacity of the plasma returns toward normal.

The problem of the causation of hypochromic anemia therefore resolves itself mainly into how the supply of iron available for hemoglobin production in the body becomes depleted. The iron in the body of an adult man, normally 3 to 5 grams in all, has the following approximate distribution: hemoglobin 55 per cent, myoglobin 15 per cent and storage 25 per cent, with the small but important remainder in tissue respiratory enzymes (e.g., cytochromes). Of this only the hemoglobin iron and the storage iron, together about three quarters of the total body iron, are available for hemoglobin production. It has been estimated that the normal person may lose about half the iron in circulation or about 1.32 gm., and still regain normal blood values. This figure is not greatly different from that given for the amount of storage iron available to meet such demands, or 1.20 gm.

The liberation of iron during the catab-olism of hemoglobin and its assiduous retention by the body have already been described. Unlike anemias due to deficiency of vitamin B_{12} or of folic acid, in which the principle is metabolized or excreted, the development of hypochromic anemia in man implies an adventitious and positive mechanism causing a reduction of the iron available for hemoglobin production. Aside from loss of blood to the exterior, the theoretical causes of such an effect are the demands of growth, menstruation and pregnancy (Table 30–10). The frequent hypochromia of the red cells of patients with polycythemia and high red cell levels presumably results from the depletion of the body iron stores in the effort to sustain the greatly increased circulating red cell mass. The barely favorable iron balance of the normal adult male has been mentioned on page 771.

Whether, then, hypochromic anemia will develop depends on the magnitude of the demand for iron created by these conditions relative to the available stores of iron, the iron content of the food and the effectiveness of its absorption from the alimentary tract. After the stores of iron have become depleted, aside from its actual iron content, the availability of iron in the food is probably of greatest importance. When erythropoiesis is stimulated by hypoxia or by certain anemias, especially iron deficiency anemia, the uptake of radioactive iron given by mouth is increased. Hypertransfusion and hyperoxia have the opposite effect, as do pernicious and hemolytic anemias in which the serum iron level is high. Callender has shown that inorganic iron is more readily absorbed by both normal and iron-deficient subjects than is

TABLE 30–10. ESTIMATED TOTAL IRON REQUIREMENT IN GRAMS DURING INCLUSIVE AGE PERIODS INDICATED.*

Age, Years	Males	Females
1–6	0.656	0.659
7–12	0.641	0.700
13–18	1.550	2.162
19–21	0.301	1.175
22–24	0.000	0.894
	Total 3.148	Total 5.590

Annual loss by menstruation	0.298 gm.
Average loss per pregnancy	0.374 gm.

* Data from Heath and Patek: Medicine, *16*:267, 1937.

organic iron in hemoglobin with or without cooking. The percentage absorption of inorganic iron varies inversely with the size of the dose. Smith and Pannaciulli found that when 1 mg. of labeled ferrous sulfate was given the average absorption by normal persons was 0.3 mg.; in hypochromic anemia it was 0.53 mg. With a dose of 100 mg. the corresponding figures were 12.6 and 37.5 mg., respectively. Iron assimilation is apparently favored by a high calcium, and inhibited by a high phosphorus, content of the food. Efficient parenteral iron therapy requires that sufficient inorganic iron be chelated with some substance (e.g., dextran) in order to avoid the toxicity of the ionized element if the serum transferrin binding capacity is exceeded.

In man, iron is probably not absorbed unless it becomes ionized and reduced to the ferrous state. Present in the food in relatively insoluble ferric forms, it is presumably dissolved in the acid gastric secretions and then reduced by the ascorbic and other weak acids of the food. Added ascorbic acid increases the uptake of radioiron from labeled foods. The concept of the regulation of iron absorption by the ferritin content of the duodenal mucosa has recently been modified by Crosby to involve the desquamating epithelial cells of the villi as already described (Fig. 30–11). In the congenital absence of serum transferrin and in normal subjects whose transferrin was kept saturated by intravenous infusion of iron, the assimilation of orally administered iron was not suppressed. Instead, in the experimental situation orally administered radioactive iron was deposited on first reaching the liver capillaries and did not enter the systemic circulation unless a portacaval shunt had been performed. Ferritin serves there as elsewhere as a conveniently labile repository of ferric iron in un-ionized form.

Achlorhydria is common in adult women with hypochromic anemia and may be supposed to affect the absorption of iron adversely, especially as this takes place principally in the upper part of the small intestine, where the influence of gastric acidity would be greatest. Mettier and Minot showed that small doses of iron administered by stomach tube to patients with iron deficiency anemia were more effective in promoting blood formation when given in a strongly buffered meat-acid mixture than when given at neutrality. Although subsequent studies

with radioactive iron have appeared to deny the relevance of gastric anacidity to the development of iron deficiency, Goldberg recently showed that when radioactive iron was given together with a standard test meal containing 12 mg. of iron to iron-deficient anemic subjects, the assimilation averaged 57.5 per cent in those with free hydrochloric acid in the stomach, but only 18.5 per cent in those patients without ability to secrete acid. There is ample evidence that hypochromic anemia may follow gastrectomy and operations upon the stomach in animals, as well as in man. The dysphagia and intestinal disturbances in patients with achlorhydria and hypochromic anemia suggest, moreover, a general alimentary tract dysfunction and hence other difficulties in the absorption of iron from the intestinal tract. The prompt relief of such symptoms, as well as the occasional reappearance of hydrochloric acid in the stomach secretion following therapy with iron, indicates a secondary influence of iron deficiency possibly due to a lack of heme-containing tissue enzymes. Hypochromic anemia is frequently found in chronic intestinal diseases such as sprue or idiopathic steatorrhea. A superimposed chronic infection may inhibit the regeneration of hemoglobin that would otherwise occur after blood loss or during growth.

IMMEDIATE MECHANISMS OF IRON DEFICIENCY ANEMIAS. The *hypochromic anemia of infants* is fundamentally due to an increase, with natural growth, in the amount of hemoglobin needed to maintain a normal concentration of hemoglobin in the ever-increasing circulating blood volume. For this the iron endowment at birth is insufficient, especially in premature babies and twins. The effects of such deficiency of the stores of iron are, however, not likely to become apparent before the fourth month of life, and are not often observed thereafter unless, during the first year of life, the infant is kept on a diet low in iron, such as is provided by food restricted largely to cow's milk. Hypochromic anemia may persist or appear later in childhood because of the continued demands of the increasing volume of circulating red cells for hemoglobin, especially when diets low in iron or gastrointestinal abnormalities are present. *Chlorosis* was confined largely to adolescent girls and was thus presumably an expression of the demand for iron in the period of increased growth occurring with sexual development and especially with the onset of blood loss from menstruation. In the adult male, iron deficiency anemia never develops without preceding chronic overt or occult blood loss. If it is occult, the blood loss is usually from the alimentary tract. In adult females the iron balance is normally precarious because of a slightly lower dietary intake and especially because of the increased physiological losses in menstruation, which is sometimes profuse, and in pregnancy (Table 30–10).

During pregnancy, the restrictions on diet imposed by nausea or ill-advisedly by physicians, and, as shown by Strauss, the tendency to the development of hypochlorhydria or even temporary achlorhydria, presumably diminish the amount of iron available for supplying the fetal demands. The effectiveness of iron therapy in preventing the development of such hypochromic anemia seems to eliminate inhibitory influences specific to the gravid state. In women past the child-bearing age, "idiopathic" chronic hypochromic anemia appears in most instances in association with either an absence or a reduction of free hydrochloric acid in the stomach contents. For economic or other reasons diets poor in iron are common in these patients. The clinical features, such as atrophy of the papillae of the tongue, dysphagia and concave and brittle fingernails, are believed by Waldenström to be due to disturbances of tissue metabolism possibly conditioned by defective function of iron-containing intracellular enzymes. Therapy with iron gives a sense of increased well-being within a few days and so before any rise in circulating hemoglobin has taken place. In time it relieves the dysphagia, may abate menorrhagia, and causes the fingernails to resume normal growth. Beutler believes that chronic fatigue relievable by iron therapy occurs in some women with little or no hypochromic anemia because of a depletion of their iron-containing tissue enzymes.

Various pathologic causes of *chronic blood loss* result in hypochromic anemia. When the hemorrhage is external and obvious, the cause of the anemia is equally so. Otherwise, gastrointestinal abnormalities such as varices, hiatus hernia, ulcer or cancer are common findings. Such lesions are, moreover, likely to result in dietary restriction by the patient or as a result of professional advice. The anemia of *hookworm disease* represents a complex of factors in which blood loss due to the worm burden and to a lesser extent dietary deficiency are outstanding, but in which the presence of the parasites does not inhibit the effectiveness of orally administered iron. In *congestive splenomegaly,* or Banti's syndrome, in which portal hypertension is demonstrable at operation, massive or subtle bleeding from esophageal varices is responsible for the hypochromia of the red cells, and in addition there is probably a component of inhibition of red cell production and of increased red cell destruction based on the liver dysfunction. The usual leukopenia and thrombocytopenia are presumably the result of sequestration of these elements by the enlarged spleen (see Chap. 31), as can readily be shown with red cells labeled with radioactive chromium.

Pyridoxine Responsive Anemia. In 1953 Snyderman observed a severe microcytic hypochromic anemia in an infant subsisting on a pyridoxine-deficient diet which responded to the administration of pyridoxine with a prompt reticulocyte rise and further hematologic improvement. In another infant, convulsions occurred and disappeared after pyridoxine therapy. Only after 1956, when Harris described two adult patients with a similar blood picture who also responded to the parenteral administration of pyridoxine, were other such patients reported. Well over 50 patients have now been observed, predominately males, in a quarter of whom there is a family history of some abnormality of iron metabolism. One patient was shown repeatedly to respond to the intravenous administration of normal human plasma with or without red cells. None of these adult patients subsisted upon a deficient diet, and none has shown other clinical signs of pyridoxine deficiency. In other patients given such metabolic antagonists of pyridoxine as desoxypyridoxine or isoniazid, no anemia has developed despite the appearance of signs in the skin, mucous membranes or nervous system characteristic of pyridoxine deficiency in animals. Moreover, in most of the adult anemic patients, despite initial improvement accompanied by a rapid fall of serum iron and reticulocytosis, and despite continued therapy with pyridoxine and return to a normal hemoglobin level, microcytic hypochromic red cells have persisted. This suggests that some type of disturbance in hemoglobin synthesis underlies and conditions the need for more than the normal level of dietary pyridoxine.

Whatever the underlying cause, the superimposed microcytic hypochromic anemia with low reticulocyte levels closely resembles that produced by dietary deficiency of pyridoxine in such animals as dogs and swine. The serum iron is elevated nearly to the saturation point of the slightly low plasma transferrin, while bilirubin and stercobilin output have been normal. Hemosiderosis of bone marrow, liver and spleen is pronounced. The erythropoietic cells of the marrow are moderately increased, chiefly normoblastic, with many containing perinuclear iron granules (ringed sidero-blasts). In a few instances marrows have been megaloblastic. When the patient is given a loading dose of tryptophan, abnormal metabolites such as xanthurenic and kynurenic acid are excreted in the urine until pyridoxine is administered. Ferrokinetics indicate ineffective heme production in iron-loaded mitochondria, due apparently to a specific defect at the key position of the metabolically active form of pyridoxine, pyridoxal-5-phosphate, in activating glycine to condense with succinic acid and form delta-aminolevulinic acid, a precursor of the monopyrrole, porphobilinogen and subsequently of the tetrapyrrole nucleus of hemoglobin.

It is of interest that in thalassemia major a similar metabolic block has been reported in the synthesis of hemoglobin just at the normal point of action of pyridoxine. The findings are similar in congenital sideroachrestic anemia: microcytic hypochromic red cells, saturated serum-iron binding capacity, hemosiderosis and many ringed sideroblasts in the bone marrow as well as ferrokinetic studies showing ineffective erythropoiesis. A few of these patients show partial responses to pyridoxine administration.

Endocrine Deficiency of Erythropoiesis

Anemia is observed in patients with anterior pituitary or with thyroid, adrenal and possibly male gonadal insufficiency.

In hypophysectomized rats the bone marrow gradually becomes hypoplastic and anemia develops, probably as a result of lack of one or more of the tropic principles of the anterior pituitary. In such animals growth hormone, thyrotropic hormone and gonadotropic hormone, or the products of their target organs, are all stated to cause hematopoietic effects. According to Crafts, the anemia produced by hypophysectomy in female rats is duplicated by removal of the thyroid and adrenals instead. Testosterone raises and estrogen lowers the hemoglobin in rats of both sexes. Castration of male rats results in the characteristically lower female hemoglobin level. Male hemoglobin levels are regained by testosterone administration. The anemia developing in thyroidectomized rats can be alleviated by the oral administration of small amounts of thyroid hormone. The response is accompanied by reticulocytosis and bone marrow hyperplasia.

Patients with *anterior pituitary insufficiency* may have a deceptive degree of pallor, and many have a moderate degree of anemia. The leukocyte levels tend to be reduced with absolute granulocytopenia and relative lymphocytosis as in deficiency of the adrenal cortex. The marrow is somewhat hypocellular. Gastric anacidity is not infrequent. Therapy with thyroid extract and testosterone or with cortisone and testosterone brings about a gradual restoration of blood values.

The mild normocytic normochromic anemia of uncomplicated *primary myxedema* is associated with a hypocellular and sometimes gelatinous marrow. It is abolished by therapy with thyroxine alone. In other patients with hypothyroidism, especially those with gastric anacidity, who comprise about half the total, more pronounced anemias of both macrocytic and hypochromic types occur. Of these the latter is the more common, especially in women. These anemias are the results of complicating deficiencies of vitamin B_{12} or of iron, respectively. The peripheral blood and marrow findings are characteristic of these deficiencies in every way, as are their immediate causes and responses to specific nutritional therapy prior to administration of thyroid extract (Fig. 30–31). About half the patients have gastric anacidity; and intrinsic factor has been found to be lacking in those with pernicious anemia and myxedema in combination. Their possible common basic cause in terms of an "autoimmune" process involving both the stomach and the thyroid gland has been discussed above. It is well known that lack of thyroid hormone causes a diminished oxygen consumption by the cells of the body. According to Bomford, with a constant rate of blood flow this might actually result in a higher than normal oxygen tension in the cells of the bone marrow (or in some other tissue responsible for the control of erythropoiesis). By analogy with the erythropoietic depression resulting from a rise in the oxygen tension of the arterial blood, the rate of red cell production should be depressed as it is in hypothyroidism, which is said to be the only condition in which the red cell life-span is supernormal. Thyroid deficiency, unlike, for example, iron deficiency, appears to depress only the final hemoglobin level attained rather than notably to impede hemoglobin production below that level.

In *Addison's disease*, mild normocytic normochromic anemia with leukopenia, relative lymphocytosis and increased eosinophils are often seen. After restoration of the patient's contracted plasma volume, the anemia may be more impressive. It gradually disappears with replacement therapy. In *eunuchoid males* and *hypogonadal females* mild anemia with leukopenia and sometimes thrombocytopenia is observed. The responses to endocrine replacement therapy are in general like those of the experimental animals described above. However, according to Kennedy, the administration of androgens to anemic patients with metastatic breast carcinoma will even raise the hemoglobin to levels above normal. Shahidi and Diamond have reported remissions in children with aplastic anemia. This "pharmacologic" effect, which Gardner has usefully employed in adult patients with cellular marrows and refractory anemia or myeloid metaplasia, renders difficult the estimate of the "physiologic" replacement dose and its interpretation. The recent work of Gurney indicates that the hematopoietic effect of testosterone is mediated by stimulation of the production of erythropoietin of renal origin. The occasionally elevated hemoglobin level in Cushing's disease and also that following prolonged therapy with corticosteroids suggest that these streoids also have "pharmacologic" effects upon erythropoiesis.

Toxic Inhibition of Erythropoiesis

The anemias of this group are considered to be due to interference with normal bone marrow function by toxic substances, whether absorbed from outside the body or elaborated by perversions of its internal metabolism.

Among the various poisons of external origin, the classic effects of *benzol* have received the most careful clinical study. In acute poisoning the outstanding manifestations are bleeding from the mucous membranes, due to thrombocytopenia, liability to the development of necrotic lesions in the oral cavity because of granulocytopenia, and normocytic or macrocytic normochromic anemia, due either entirely to toxic depression of the bone marrow or partly to blood loss. In these patients the bone marrow may be aplastic and fatty, with failure of proliferation beyond the stem cell level, as in experimental animals acutely poisoned with benzol.

It has also been recognized that in chronic poisoning with benzol or other *cyclic compounds* the bone marrow may be hyperplastic rather than hypocellular, even when the peripheral blood picture is fairly characteristic

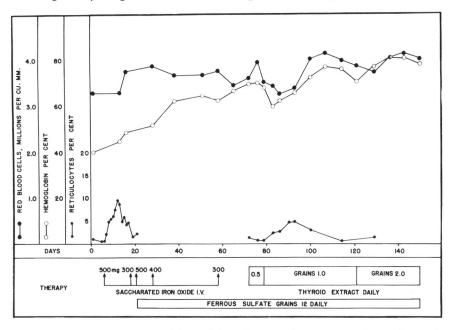

Figure 30–31. Effect of iron and later of thyroid extract therapy in a patient with myxedema and hypochromic anemia due to menorrhagia. Note the effect of intravenous iron administration in causing an initial reticulocyte response and increase in red cell level together with progressive elevation of the hemoglobin. Thereafter, oral iron therapy was continued throughout. Thyroid extract therapy begun after 72 days caused initially a characteristic sharp fall in red cells and hemoglobin because of hemodilution, then, following a second reticulocyte response, over a period of 80 days, the hemoglobin and red cell levels gradually increased with disappearance of hypochromia of the red cells. (From Werner: The Thyroid, New York, Paul B. Hoeber, 1955.)

of acute benzol poisoning. Dacie has confirmed the presence of numerous megaloblasts or other early forms in the marrow of such patients. Hypoplasia may later develop, followed by, in rare instances, a characteristic picture of myelogenous leukemia. Bomford and Rhoads, in a study of 66 patients with refractory macrocytic anemia, many of whom had hypercellular marrows, discovered suggestive histories in 34 of exposure to potentially toxic substances, including benzol, arsphenamine, insecticides, hair dyes, photographic developers and analgesic drugs. The feces contained an increased amount of coproporphyrin types I and III. An increased output of coproporphyrin type III has been demonstrated in poisoning with lead, salvarsan and sulfanilamides and in diseases of the liver, including hemochromatosis. Judged by the output of urobilinogen in the feces and from the increased reticulocytes, more than half the patients had some increase in the rate of blood destruction, which may partly explain the hypercellularity of bone marrow. Some eventually went into remission while taking crude liver extract by mouth and may thus have suffered from folic acid deficiency originally, or later as a complication of the action of the toxic agent. The basis of the failure of the marrow to regenerate after removal of the toxic agent is suggested by the successful use of isogenic bone marrow infusions (derived from identical twins) in five of ten such patients. This indicates that systemic intoxication is not the cause, but rather a persistent abnormality of the patient's marrow stem cells.

An explanation of why certain drugs are injurious to erythropoiesis, usually with damage to the formation of white cells and platelets as well, in a small proportion of the large number of patients receiving them remains a challenging problem. The clinical evidence to date does not serve to distinguish a "toxic" from an "allergic" basis. Volini has shown that hematologic recovery may occur after short exposure to *chloramphenicol,* and Erslev found that, even after longer exposure, stopping the drug may result in a prompt reticulocyte response and disappearance of the anemia. No antibodies capable of adversely affecting red cell, granulocyte and/or platelet precursors in the bone marrow, as well as their descendants in the peripheral blood, have been found for this offender. The relatively rare clinical incidence of aplastic anemia with pancytopenia, as well as of agranulocytosis or thrombocytopenia, some-

times following repeated chloramphenicol administration, suggests an idiosyncrasy, but might equally well be determined by genetic or acquired lack of a detoxifying enzyme system. However, Rubin's ferrokinetic studies detected early suppression of erythropoiesis with cessation of plasma iron turnover and consequently a striking rise in the percentage saturation of the iron-binding protein in 5 of 15 patients given this drug for only a few days. Withdrawal of the antibiotic led to restoration of erythropoiesis with reticulocytosis and fall of serum iron.

Follette found that chloramphenicol suppressed the oxygen consumption of leukocytes in vitro, and Ward showed that it blocks RNA activity, especially in very young erythroblasts. Saidi has described the appearance of large vacuoles in the marrow erythroid precursors of patients receiving chloramphenicol, as well as its suppressive effect upon the reticulocyte responses to specific therapy in patients with vitamin B_{12} or iron deficiencies (Fig. 30–32). Similar cytoplasmic vacuoles are seen in acute alcoholics and in infants with phenolketonuria while receiving a diet deficient in phenylalanine. Simultaneous administration of phenylalanine will abolish the cytoplasmic vacuoles in the bone marrow of children receiving the antibiotic. Sullivan has shown that alcohol ingestion can inhibit the response to minimal doses of folic acid in patients with megaloblastic anemias due to such deficiency.

Examples of common causes of the usually moderate anemia of chronic local infection are seen in *rheumatic fever, chronic tuberculosis* and *osteomyelitis.* The red cells are usually normocytic or slightly microcytic and are rarely hypochromic unless blood loss has occurred. Leukopenia is infrequent because the infection itself usually causes leukocytosis. In exceptional instances thrombocytopenia with purpura is observed. It is inferred that the moderate immaturity of the erythroid cells of the bone marrow is the result of inhibition by toxic products elaborated by the organisms or by the tissues destroyed by them. In addition, occasionally enlargement of the spleen is associated with its increased red cell sequestration.

The inhibitory action of infection on the bone marrow was at one time best illustrated by the occasional instances in which, in the course of a response to liver therapy in pernicious anemia, an intercurrent infection resulted in prompt suppression of reticulocytes and of red cell production (Fig. 30–33). In patients with chronic hemolytic anemias who acquire the "grippe," as originally shown by Owren, this effect is even more dramatic because the short survival time of the red cells causes the rapid increase of anemia associated with lessening of jaundice, temporary hypoplasia of the marrow and disappearance of reticulocytes from the peripheral blood. Occasionally the marrow becomes megaloblastic, suggesting that an abnormally great requirement for folic acid induced by the chronic hemolytic process has created, under the influence of the infection, an acute nutritional embarrassment to erythropoiesis. Similar suppression of erythropoiesis by infection in normal persons produces too little anemia to be observed without special attention to slight changes in reticulocyte levels. On the other hand, certain exotic viral (?) infections (e.g., hemorrhagic fever, onyalai) may produce prolonged suppression of all marrow elements with eventual, gradual recovery.

The fact that the excretion of fecal urobilinogen is rarely increased is consistent with the concept that the anemia of infection is due chiefly to decreased blood production; the increased erythrocyte protoporphyrin and excretion of coproporphyrin type III suggest a disturbance of hemoglobin synthesis. Wintrobe and his associates have shown that the plasma iron level drops within a day or two after the development of an infection, often to values of 40 micrograms per 100 ml. or less. Later, decrease in the iron-binding protein of the serum and increases in serum copper and erythrocyte protoporphyrin appear. Iron-labeled senescent red cells and even iron compounds, when injected intravenously, fail to elevate the serum iron or relieve the anemia, and the iron is stored in the liver and spleen. On the other hand, Freireich and associates have shown in dogs with turpentine abscesses that iron previously bound to plasma transferrin is promptly incorporated into new circulating hemoglobin. This suggests that chronic infection causes anemia in part by inhibiting the release of iron from storage forms into the plasma. The influence of chronic infection in causing anemia in growing children is clinically prominent. It is of interest that some observers have noted a moderate increase in number and immaturity of the erythroid cells of the bone marrow in such patients. Indeed, this may be a striking feature of intercurrent infection in untreated pernicious anemia. May has reported experimental development of megaloblastosis of the bone marrow and of lower values of folic acid in the livers of monkeys on diets poor in folic acid after infection was simulated by the creation of turpentine abscesses. Such changes in the marrow could be prevented by folic acid but not by vitamin B_{12}.

Inhibition of erythropoiesis is also the basis of the common normochromic, normocytic anemia of *cancer* whether or not metastatic to bone marrow. The low grade fever and cachexia of such patients resemble those of infection. Several instances of aplastic anemia developing in association with *thymoma* in

Figure 30–32. Effect of chloramphenicol in suppressing response to vitamin B_{12} administration in pernicious anemia. Note the striking delayed peak of reticulocytes after the discontinuance of chloramphenicol therapy, accompanied by an exaggerated rise of white cells and platelets. (From Saidi, Wallerstein, and Aggeler: J. Lab. & Clin. Med., 57:247, 1961.)

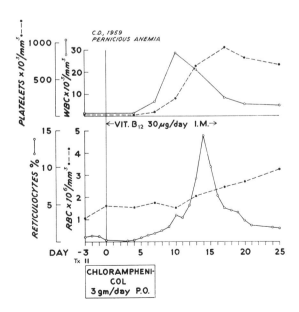

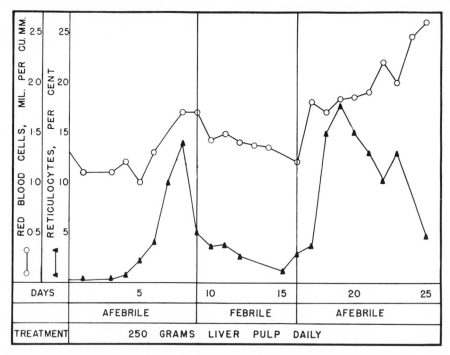

Figure 30–33. Depressant effect of infection upon erythropoiesis in a patient with pernicious anemia. Note that, despite the daily administration of liver pulp throughout the entire period of observation, the reticulocyte response and associated rise of red cells were interrupted during the febrile period (highest temperature, 102° F.). When the patient again became afebrile, the reticulocytes rose rapidly to a second peak and the upward progress of the red cell values was re-established. (Slightly modified from Minot and Castle: Lancet, 2:319, 1935; from data kindly supplied by Dr. O. H. Robertson.)

adults have been reported, with remission of the anemia in a few following removal of the tumor. In most of these patients the production of granulocytes and platelets was not affected.

Like chronic infections, *chronic disturbances of renal function* often result in anemia. Significant lowering of the blood values is not common unless the nonprotein nitrogen of the blood remains for some time above 100 mg. per 100 ml. Usually the more severe the anemia, the higher the maintained level of nonprotein nitrogen. The retention of nitrogen may be due to chronic nephritis, congenital cystic kidneys, surgical removal of one kidney or prostatic obstruction. The red cells are usually normochromic, reticulocytes are few, and the leukocytes and platelets little altered. When azotemia is severe, so-called "burr" cells may appear in blood films. The bone marrow shows some decrease in cells of the erythroid series, but does not become aplastic or hyperplastic in response to severe anemia. It is of interest that the blood phenols are said to be elevated in this type of anemia, because benzol is well recognized as a cause of injury to the bone marrow. The exact basis for decreased red cell formation remains obscure, but failure of erythropoietic factor production by the kidney has recently been invoked. Thus, Naets found increased serum erythropoietic levels in only one of 39 uremic patients with anemia. Nevertheless, as recently shown by Nathan, patients surgically deprived of kidneys and maintained by dialysis were no more anemic (7 to 9 gm. of hemoglobin) than patients with damaged kidneys and a similar degree of chronic uremia. Indeed, these patients showed erythropoietic responses to intercurrent hypoxia or blood loss. Despite lack of other evidence of increased red cell destruction, transfused normal red cells may be destroyed more rapidly than normally.

Physical Injury of Erythropoiesis

Undue exposure to *roentgen rays* or *radioactive material* is causative of this as yet relatively rare type of anemia. The usual therapeutic dose of regional roentgen ray has little inhibitory effect on erythrocyte production, except on the bone marrow directly exposed; and modern methods of protection render occupational exposure slight. When severe anemia develops in the course of roentgen ray therapy—for example, of leukemia or Hodgkin's disease—it is usually the result of invasion of the bone marrow by the disease process and not of the radiation. However, in the treatment of polycythemia vera, spray x-ray or radioactive phosphorus may produce definite leukopenia and prolonged inhibition of excessive erythropoiesis and sometimes of platelet production. When roentgen therapy is properly applied in the treatment of chronic leukemia, the more radiosensitive abnormal leukocyte production in the bone marrow may be inhibited and more space may so become available for red cell and platelet production.

Besides the effect of the concussion and of radiant heat, the biologic action of atomic bombs is chiefly the result of penetrating gamma rays and neutrons, to which the most sensitive tissues are the bone marrow, lymphoid apparatus, ovary, testis and intestinal epithelium. In Nagasaki, with intense exposure in the acute radiation syndrome, early symptoms were weakness, vomiting and diarrhea, sure signs of a fatal outcome. The effect of the penetrating gamma rays and neutrons on the bone marrow occurred within days with granulocytopenia and thrombocytopenia often to the extent of agranulocytosis and complete absence of platelets. As in acute benzol poisoning, the immediate complications were infection and hemorrhages. Later, after partial recovery, a picture of aplastic anemia developed in some patients. The mutagenic effects of this large single exposure of the population to irradiation were clearly manifest five years later among the survivors in a peak incidence of leukemia, chiefly myelogenous in type, but not associated with the Ph^1 chromosome anomaly characteristic of the "spontaneous" disease.

In experimental studies in animals of the effect of irradiation it has been observed that hypoplastic or aplastic changes appear in the irradiated, and compensatory hyperplasia in the unirradiated, portions of the bone marrow. Thus it is doubtful whether irradiation produces important effects except where the energy is directly absorbed. Clinical effects apparently contradictory to this supposition may be explained on the basis that the cells of the lymph nodes, spleen and bone marrow are not fixed tissue cells, but migrate from organ to organ. Irradiation of leukopoietic or erythropoietic tissue thus directly affects not only these tissues, but also the rate at which their cellular products reach and accumulate in other organs. Thus it has clearly been shown by Jacobson that in otherwise totally and lethally irradiated mice, shielding of the spleen to some extent favors regeneration of irradiated marrow, even if the spleen is removed only an hour later. Shielded cellular, but not fatty, marrow has a similar influence, as do other tissues containing reticuloendothelial cells. Intravenous injections of isologous spleen or marrow are protective, but cell-free extracts of these organs are inert. Depending on the species, the degree of genetic homogeneity and the thoroughness of the elimination of the hematopoiesis cells by the x-rays, homologous or even heterologous marrow may be so used.

The nature of the action of irradiation on blood-forming tissues is not well understood. At the time of the exposure reducing agents such as cysteine and glutathione and oxygen deprivation or cyanide intoxication inhibit the injurious effects. This may possibly be through their influence upon the formation or toxic effects of the hydrogen peroxide produced by irradiation, or by their direct protective effects on sulfhydryl-containing enzymes.

The well-known effect of roentgen rays in producing genetic mutations in fruit flies suggests a profound effect on nuclear functions. Osgood stated that irradiation prevents both mitotic and amitotic cell division. Further evidence of a disturbance of vital substances within the nucleus is apparent from the work of Mitchell, who showed that the synthesis of deoxynucleic acid in the nucleus is inhibited and that ribonucleotides accumulate in the cytoplasm.

The mature cells of the blood except the lymphocytes are not affected by irradiation, but their precursors in the lymphoid tissues and in the bone marrow show various degrees of sensitivity. The parent cells of the lymphocytes and of the red cells are the most sensitive, while those of the granulocytes, monocytes and platelets are decreasingly so in that order. After a single exposure to irradiation this is by no means accurately reflected in the peripheral blood because of the different lengths of life of the mature elements (Fig. 30–34). The sensitivity of the lymphocytes and lymphoid tissues results in a detectable, prompt decline in their number in the peripheral blood with the smallest amount of irradiation that produces any effect upon hematopoiesis. With a larger exposure the lymphocytes may reach a low level in a few hours. Granulocytes are less sensitive and, because of the large marrow reserves, granulocytosis of short duration may precede

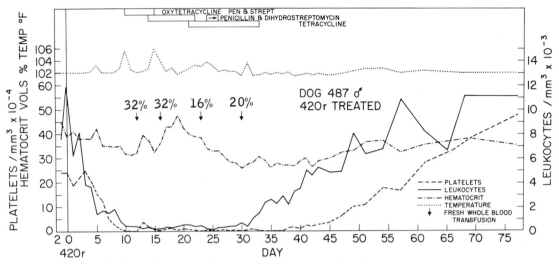

Figure 30–34. Effect of irradiation (460 r) on peripheral blood values of a dog. Note the decline of leukocytes and platelets to base line at 5 and 10 days respectively, and the much slower decline of the hematocrit. Platelet-rich plasma transfusions and antibiotics were given in order to minimize hemorrhage and infection respectively. Rapid recovery of granulocyte levels began on about the twenty-fifth day and of platelets on about the thirtieth day. (From Perman and others: Blood, *19*:724, 1962.)

granulocytopenia, which becomes maximal in about six days. The platelets may require a little longer to reach their lowest value. Although reticulocytes disappear in a day or two, unless bleeding occurs, anemia may not be significant until four to eight weeks later at a time corresponding to about one-half the average life of the red cell. With lesser exposures, the full development of the hematologic abnormalities requires 2 to 3 weeks, at a time when regeneration is beginning in the marrow, accompanied by persistent morphologic abnormalities of erythropoiesis and myelopoiesis. As stated by Minot and Spurling, "the greater the dose, the more profound is the blood damage, the more rapidly it develops, and the more slowly it is repaired." The effects of chronic moderate occupational exposure upon the blood picture are variable and include slight polycythemia or anemia, moderate granulocytopenia and relative or absolute leukocytosis. Lymphocytes with double nuclei have been observed, and the circulating lymphocytes may show in supravitally stained preparations an increase in the number of refractive neutral red absorbing bodies.

Present evidence indicates that there is not a significant difference in the effect of irradiation on the blood-forming organs, whether of external or internal origin. Roentgen and gamma rays or neutrons generated by ex-

ternal sources readily penetrate the body. On the other hand, sources of alpha and beta particles, in order to produce biological effects, must be absorbed in order to be sufficiently close to the cells that are affected. The energy of disintegration of radium is manifest in alpha particles, beta particles and gamma rays; that of radioactive phosphorus in beta particles, with a maximum range of penetration of slightly under a millimeter.

The localization of radioactive phosphorus is selectively determined by the amount and rate of turnover of phosphorus in the tissues. Thus in experimental animals and in leukemia patients radiophosphorus first is present in the greatest concentration in the bone marrow, lymph nodes, spleen and liver. Later the greatest concentration appears in bone. The half-life of radioactive phosphorus is only 14.3 days. This means that within two weeks after administration of any given dose of radioactive phosphorus half its activity will have been lost by transformation of the artificial element into stable sulfur. Consequently the irradiation desired will largely be delivered with some degree of selectivity for rapidly growing cells within a few days and can be calculated in advance and repeated as indicated.

On the other hand, as a result of the long half-life of radium, the final disastrous results of the absorption of radium as seen in industry, chiefly in connection with the painting of luminous instrument dials, may not appear until years after the termination of the exposure. Radium, like calcium, is absorbed by the skeleton and in that strategic position has an enduring opportunity to exert its destructive action on the bone marrow. Because of the devitalization of the tissues of the jaw bones, the extraction of teeth may result in a progressive osteomyelitis. Later, progressive anemia and, finally, the development of osteogenic sarcomas appear to be the outstanding clinical manifestations. According to Martland, the anemia of these patients was often severe. It was always normochromic, frequently macrocytic and invariably associated with leukopenia of greater or less degree, but not usually with much thrombocytopenia. The bone marrow at first shows hypercellularity distinctly resembling that of pernicious anemia, with young red and white cell precursors and megakaryocytes. Eventually a replacement fibrosis of the marrow occurs, and in the end stage the blood picture is consistent with that of aplastic anemia, said to be the cause of death of Madame Curie, who certainly had an ample exposure to radium emanations.

Mechanical Interference with Erythropoiesis

Certain types of anemias may be explained on the supposition that the volume of the marrow cavity available for red cell production is inadequate because of either congenital or acquired circumstances. The first situation is illustrated by the anemia which progressively develops during the first few weeks of extrauterine life in *premature infants* and which is at least qualitatively similar to the milder process observed in the full term baby. According to Gairdner and his associates, at birth the normal erythroid cell count of the bone marrow is about 40,000, but after ten days it declines to about 2800 per cubic millimeter. At the same time the reticulocytes of the peripheral blood, elevated at birth to 3 or 4 per cent in the production of the neonatal polycythemia, decline sharply. These events would be expected from the fact that only after birth does the oxygen tension of the infant's arterial blood rise to a normal value consequent upon its coming into equilibrium with air in the lung rather than, as previously, with the mother's capillary blood in the placenta. The development of the anemia may thus be due to an abnormally early loss of the stimulating effect of the

partial anoxia that would have been maintained in utero. Lacking this stimulus, even the erythropoietic tissue filling the entire bone marrow cavities of the normal infant is apparently no longer able to maintain normal red cell and hemoglobin values. This phenomenon is probably also in part responsible for the rapid fall of the circulating red cell level of the erythroblastotic baby after birth, despite separation from the maternal source of antibody, and is analogous to the effect of pure oxygen breathing in hemolytic anemia (Fig. 30–2). The proof of this hypothesis appears from Gairdner's observation that in the newborn infant who is cyanotic because of congenital heart disease, reticulocytes continue to be increased, and the elevated hemoglobin level at birth may be maintained or even increased, while the erythroid activity of the bone marrow does not diminish. During the first three or four months of life of the premature but otherwise normal infant the relatively more rapid increase in blood volume probably creates a greater demand for red cells than in the normal child. Consequently, during these early weeks of life, the fall in hemoglobin level of the premature infant is greater than that of the full term baby (Table 30–2). The phenomena of the initial phases of the development of this anemia appear to have been duplicated reasonably well in animal experiments (Fig. 30–35).

That the inadequate space available for hematopoiesis in the infant persists for a time in maintaining the anemia is suggested by the observation that the first signs of development of fat cells in the marrow, that is, of reserve spatial capacity, are said to appear during the fourth to fifth month as the anemia ceases to increase and then begins to lessen. That initial development of the anemia of prematurity is not due to nutritional deficiency is consistent with the fact that the red cell and hemoglobin values fall at the same rate and that the administration of vitamin B_{12}, folic acid, iron and copper has usually been unsuccessful in its prevention. However, when increase of red cells begins, their number may increase more rapidly than does the hemoglobin, suggesting that iron deficiency then becomes a factor. This is exaggerated in the infant born of an iron-deficient mother.

Other types of anemia may be explained on the theory that the marrow cavity becomes extensively occupied by cells other than those concerned with red cell produc-

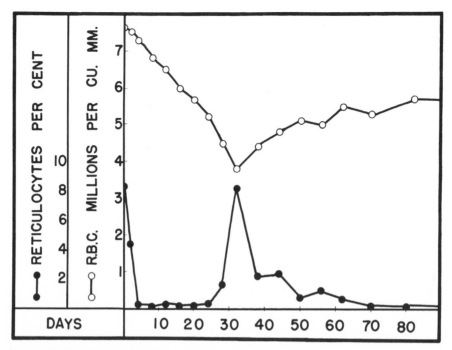

Figure 30–35. Depressant effect of induced polycythemia upon erythropoiesis in experimental animals. Polycythemia was caused to develop in guinea pigs by exposure to air at low barometric pressure. The figure is based on average data from four representative animals and begins with the return of the animals to normal atmospheric pressure. Note the rapid fall in the reticulocytes and the slower fall in red cells to a minimum after about 30 days. Shortly before the minimum red cell value was obtained the reticulocytes began to increase and the red cells then returned to their normal value of about 5.5 million per cubic millimeter after 80 days. (From data by Gordon and Kleinberg: Proc. Soc. Exper. Biol. & Med., 37:507, 1937–38.)

tion (Fig. 30–36). The histology of the bone marrow then leaves little doubt of the importance of mechanical interference with red cell production in acute and chronic *leukemias, Hodgkin's disease, miliary tuberculosis* and in patients with extensive *carcinomatosis* of the bone marrow, *marble bone disease* and *osteosclerosis.* According to Block, there must be more than 85 per cent infiltration of the marrow by leukemic cells before moderate anemia will develop when red cell survival in the circulation is normal. The infarction and fibrosis of the bone marrow sometimes seen in carcinomatosis may also result from a progressive occlusion of the vascular bed of the marrow by the tumor or its stroma. In the myelophthisic anemias certain areas of the bone marrow unaffected by the invading cells may still have normal function. However, the total ability of the organ to produce red cells is reduced. Nevertheless, this purely mechanical theory does not explain the anemia of the majority of patients with metastatic cancer, because little or no cellular invasion of the marrow may be present. Indeed, Shen has shown that the severity

of the anemia is independent of the degree of involvement of the marrow and is not associated with a hemolytic process. More likely, judging from such clinical evidences of intoxication as fever and an elevated sedimentation rate, is the general depression of erythropoiesis analogous to that in chronic inflammation. However, in occasional cases of widespread carcinomatosis of the bone marrow and of myeloid metaplasia or lymphatic leukemia, hemolytic processes seemingly dominate the picture, especially in its terminal stages.

An appearance of active red cell production in the presence of progressive anemia without blood loss or satisfactory evidence of increased blood destruction is frequently seen in the peripheral blood of patients with widespread involvement of the bone marrow by the various conditions that have been referred to. Blood films frequently show, with relatively little anemia, an elevated percentage of reticulocytes, but with a disproportionately large number of nucleated erythrocytes and marked variation in size and shape of the adult red cells. In such marrows, as in those of patients with various types of leukemic invasion, although erythropoiesis is predominantly normoblastic, a few cells may be found which resemble megaloblasts such as are seen in considerable numbers in pernicious anemia. In certain instances of leukemia a macrocytic anemia may even precede the appearance of frank leukemia; and the cases of erythremic myelosis of di Guglielmo may represent an association in which the leukemic process is further obscured by the manifest abnormalities of erythropoiesis. Vaughan was the first to propose a nutritional basis for the resemblances of the erythropoietic processes in such patients to those of pernicious anemia. That this is possibly the result of the competitive nutritional demand of the adjacent cancer or leukemia cells is further supported by the occasional small but definite reticulocyte responses to folic acid or vitamin B_{12} that have been observed in patients with agnogenic myeloid metaplasia or chronic myelogenous leukemia. The vitamin B_{12} content and binding capacity of the serum of patients with myelogenous leukemia are often greatly increased. Possibly the vitamin is not therefore so readily available as normally for erythropoiesis, which must also compete for it and for folic acid locally with the enormous myeloid proliferation.

Erf and Herbut have described the many disorders that may end in *myelofibrosis.* Several begin with moderate to intense hypercellularity. Among these last are the anemias of absorbed radioactive substances, miliary tuberculosis, Hodgkin's disease, Gaucher's disease and especially the pleomorphic conditions, sometimes collectively called myeloproliferative syndromes (Fig. 30–38), and individually known as atypical myelogenous leukemia, nonleukemic myelosis, leukoerythroblastosis and agnogenic myeloid metaplasia. Myelosclerosis of the bone marrow has been experimentally produced by the repeated injection of myeloid-stimulating substances extracted from the urine of patients with myelogenous leukemia and may represent a form of "scar-tissue" response to many types of injury. The characteristic "myeloid metaplasia" and enormous enlargement of the spleen in agnogenic myeloid metaplasia are not secondary or "compensatory" to failure of bone marrow function. Indeed, the marrow was highly cellular when the spleen was already large in 13 of 30 patients studied by

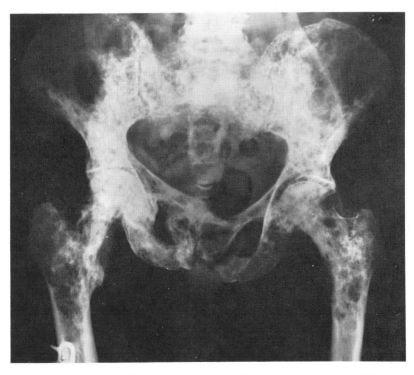

Figure 30–36. X-ray film of pelvis of a patient with metastatic carcinoma of the breast. Note extensive bone destruction in areas normally occupied by red marrow, as, for example, the pelvis and upper ends of the femora.

Wyatt and Sommers. Later when the marrow has been largely replaced by fibrous or even sometimes by bony tissue, the dependence of the anemia upon mechanical interference with erythropoiesis is clear. This is readily confirmed following the intravenous injection of Fe^{59} by ferrokinetic studies that show the absence of the characteristic early accumulation of gamma radiation over the sacrum or other sites of normally active erythropoiesis. If, under these circumstances, erythropoiesis is active in the enlarged spleen, the early build-up of gamma radiation over that organ will be impressive.

Like other anemias of this group, *nonleukemic myelosis*, or *osteosclerotic anemia*, is characterized by a normocytic or slightly macrocytic anemia with a certain number of somewhat immature granulocytes and occasional nucleated red cells in circulation. The degree of immaturity of the leukocytes is suggestive of, but usually not definitely consistent with, leukemia, and their alkaline phosphatase content is not reduced as in myelogenous leukemia. In some patients thrombocytopenia may be present and may result in purpura at various stages of the disease, which may progress slowly for many years. Gardner has demonstrated improvement in the hemoglobin level with testosterone administration, usually with an increase in the size of the spleen and rise in blood uric acid. On occasion there may develop a peripheral blood picture consistent with a diagnosis of acquired hemolytic anemia and characterized by reticulocytosis, jaundice and sometimes increased mechanical and osmotic fragilities of the red cells. Red cells labeled with radioactive chromium are rapidly sequestered in the enormous spleen, which under these circumstances may be removed with benefit.

Polycythemias

An increase above the normal range at sea level of the concentration of circulating hemoglobin, the physiologically significant component of the red cells, should logically distinguish "polycythemia" from anemia. Without this, an increase in the number of red cells per cubic millimeter, sometimes seen in mild hypochromic anemias, does not represent an increase in the oxygen-carrying capacity of a unit of circulating blood. An etiologic classification of the various kinds of polycythemia is shown in Table 30–11.

TABLE 30–11. ETIOLOGIC CLASSIFICATION OF POLYCYTHEMIAS.

I. Relative polycythemia: hemoconcentration with decreased plasma volume
   A. Loss of water: deprivation
   B. Loss of water and electrolytes: gastrointestinal, renal and adrenocortical "stress"
   C. Loss of whole plasma: extensive burns
II. Absolute polycythemia: increased erythrocyte and hemoglobin concentrations and circulating blood volume
   A. Secondary: erythrocytosis (cf. leukocytosis)—physiologic hyperactivity
      1. Tissue hypoxia: from decreased arterial oxygen transport
         High altitude: low alveolar pO_2
         Newborn: low pO_2 in umbilical veins
         Alveolar hypoventilation: obesity, ascites, depressed respiratory center, emphysema
         Alveolar diffusion defects: berylliosis, sarcoid
         Venoarterial shunts: septal defects, ductus arteriosus, pulmonic A-V aneurysms
         Abnormal hemoglobins: met-, carboxy-, and Chesapeake
      2. Pharmacologic agents: nonspecific erythropoietic stimulants
         Cobalt: histoxic hypoxia (?) and secondary erythropoietin production
         Testosterone: increased renal erythropoietin production
      3. Neoplasms: erythropoietic stimulation
         Subtentorial brain tumors: respiratory center depression (?)
         Renal, hepatic and uterine tumors: excess erythropoietic factor(s)
      4. Miscellaneous:
         Cushing's and adrenogenital syndromes: excess androgens
         Hydronephrosis and cystic renal disease: excess erythropoietic factor
         Monovular (polycythemic-anemic) twins: placental vascular anomalies
   B. Primary: erythremia (cf. leukemia)—a form or phase of a neoplastic (?) "myeloproliferative disorder" (see Fig. 30-38)

RELATIVE POLYCYTHEMIA

This condition may result transiently from an abnormal loss of whole plasma as in extensive burns or a sudden ascent to high altitude or from excessive loss of water and electrolytes as a result of persistent vomiting, severe diarrhea, copious sweating, acidosis or adrenal insufficiency. J. H. Lawrence has noted mild relative polycythemia as a result of persistent, unexplained reduction in plasma volume in a group of nervously tense persons characteristically displaying obesity, plethoric appearance and moderate hypertension. Such patients may be similar to those described by Gaisböck. The total blood volume is actually reduced because of the decrease in plasma volume. In normal men, in contrast to the large effect in dogs, transient polycythemia due to slight increases in red cells and hemoglobin has been reported by some observers after emotional stress or the injection of epinephrine. According to Taylor and Page, this does not occur in splenectomized men or dogs.

ABSOLUTE POLYCYTHEMIA

In this condition, which includes a variety of *secondary types* as well as the *primary variety,* both the circulating hemoglobin concentration and mass are increased above normal, usually without decrease in plasma volume.

Secondary Polycythemias

The evidence that reduction in the amount of oxygen carried in the arterial blood increases the rate of red cell production by the bone marrow has been discussed in a previous section. Recent observations suggest that the resulting polycythemia is not the direct result of anoxia of the bone marrow. Thus, Stohlman and Schmid independently noted that the polycythemia of patients with right-to-left flow through a patent ductus arteriosus and, consequently, cyanosis of the lower but not the upper extremities was due to erythroid hyperplasia of the bone marrow in *both* areas. The work of others discussed above under Physiology of Erythrocyte Production indicates the presence of erythropoietic factors in the serum and urine of anemic patients and in the serum and urine of anemic and hypoxic animals. Some observers have reported similar findings in human hypoxic polycythemia and in animals treated with cobaltous chloride, a stimulant of erythropoiesis in several species, including man. This chemical probably works indirectly, probably by interfering with tissue transport of oxygen, thus causing an increased renal output of erythropoietin.

Polycythemia as a result of hypoxia of the arterial blood, usually with cyanosis even in a warm environment, is brought about by several clinical circumstances. The polycythemia of the *infant in utero* and of the newborn (Table 30–2) is probably due to the fact that the infant's blood has derived its oxygen from the capillaries of the placenta rather than, as it does after birth, from the capillaries of the aerated lung. In *congenital heart disease,* polycythemia may result from a short circuit within the heart such that the venous blood passes from the right to the left side without traversing the lung, as in septal defects or in the tetralogy of Fallot. In pulmonary cavernous hemangioma and arteriovenous fistula the vascular short circuit for venous blood is within the lung. In those forms of *acquired heart disease* in which the diffusion of oxygen into the blood in the lung is interfered with by edema or thickening of the alveolar septa, the arterial blood is also unsaturated with oxygen. This may happen also in the *alveolar-capillary block syndrome* as a consequence of such primary diffuse pulmonary disorders as miliary tuberculosis, sarcoidosis, berylliosis and the Hamman-Rich syndrome. Deficient oxygenation of the arterial blood, eventually with increased carbon dioxide retention, may result either from restricted or obstructed pulmonary or alveolar ventilation in various forms of *chronic pulmonary disease:* emphysema, chronic bronchitis, pulmonary tuberculosis or silicosis. *Hypoventilatory disturbances* and polycythemia may also develop from idiopathic hypofunction of the respiratory center, marked obesity with carbon dioxide retention and narcosis (Pickwickian syndrome) and perhaps from subtentorial intracranial tumors. This may also be the mechanism involved in some of the reports of polycythemia with huge hydronephroses or uterine myomata and of its relief by surgical removal of the mass. *Ayerza's syndrome,* as indicated by the usual history of slowly developing asthma, bronchitis, dyspnea, cyanosis and finally polycythemia, is a result of chronic pulmonary disease with secondary changes in the pulmonary arteries. Enlargement of the liver and spleen is a common finding in chronic pulmonary disease, probably as a result of infections and secondary right-sided heart failure. Clubbing of the fingers and, less often, of the toes is associated with arterial anoxia, possibly enhanced by local agglutination of the red cells in the digital capillaries as a result of cold agglutinins in the plasma or of vasospastic changes interfering with local tissue oxygenation. Clubbing may be confined to one upper extremity with impaired blood flow. In a patient with reverse flow through a patent ductus arteriosus, the cyanotic toes were clubbed but the normally oxygenated fingers were not.

According to Hurtado, in the polycythemia of permanent residents at various *high altitudes* there is an inverse correlation between the hemoglobin concentration in the circulating blood and the percentage of arterial oxygen saturation (Table 30–12). This last is directly related to the progressive lowering of the oxygen tension of the atmosphere with

TABLE 30–12. EFFECT OF ALTITUDE UPON OXYGEN CONTENT, CAPACITY AND PERCENTAGE SATURATION OF THE ARTERIAL BLOOD OF RESIDENTS AT VARIOUS ALTITUDES IN THE ANDES.*

Height, Thousands of Feet	Arterial Blood Values		
	O_2 Content, Vol. %	O_2 Capacity, Vol. %	O_2 Saturation, %
0	20.6	21.4	96.0
4.8	20.9	22.2	93.8
12.0	22.1	25.2	87.6
14.7	22.3	27.5	81.0
17.4	23.0	30.2	76.2

* Data from Hurtado, Merino, and Delgado: Arch. Int. Med., 75:284, 1945.

altitude. It should be obvious that owing to the polycythemic response to arterial unsaturation the oxygen capacity (oxyhemoglobin content) of the blood increases more rapidly with adjustment to altitude than does the oxygen content. The resulting increase in circulating hemoglobin and oxygen content will not enhance the decreased oxygen tension of the arterial blood, but, by conveying more oxygen even at a lower tension, may sustain a somewhat higher tissue oxygen tension than would a normal concentration of equally unsaturated hemoglobin.

In pulmonary disease with arterial oxygen unsaturation, the increase in the circulating hemoglobin level is usually less than would be expected from the values displayed in Table 30–12, because of the inhibitory effect of the frequently associated chronic pulmonary infection upon erythropoiesis. The total blood volume is increased as the result of the increased volume of circulating red cells. The survival time of labeled red cells is normal, and the rate of red cell production is increased, and the reticulocytes and the serum bilirubin of the peripheral blood, but not the leukocytes, are elevated. A tendency to hemorrhage resembling that of polycythemia vera has been reported. In patients with *Monge's disease* the polycythemia is more marked than in other residents at the same altitude. The long history of frequent bronchitis and laryngitis, diminished vital capacity, marked cyanosis and the improvement resulting from a return to sea level suggest that the condition is the result of an unusual decrease in the arterial oxygen saturation as a consequence of the combined effects of the lowered oxygen tension in the inspired air and of pulmonary disease. With the extreme polycythemia of Monge's disease, leukocytosis

may be present at times, and epistaxis, hemoptysis, bleeding gums and purpura may also occur.

Since *abnormal forms of hemoglobin* are inefficient in the transport of oxygen, chronic exposure to *carbon monoxide* and the excessive use of *coal tar products* yielding oxidant derivatives may result in "polycythemia" in experimental animals and occasionally in man. However, despite the increases in red cells and total heme pigments resulting from chronic low-grade exposure, the physiologic ability of the blood to transport oxygen is less than normal. This is also illustrated in the rare condition of *congenital methemoglobinemia,* in which the normal enzyme systems for reducing the spontaneously formed methemoglobin are lacking. Abnormal hemoglobin pigments may be suspected upon obvious change in the color of blood samples to cherry red (carboxyhemoglobin) or to brown (methemoglobin). Usually spectroscopy is required for identification of the relatively small amounts of abnormal pigments present. With brown methemoglobinemia the patient often is cyanotic (bluish) because of the loss by diffusion in the skin of the red reflected light rays (e.g., carbon black tattoo looks blue). Recently mild familial polycythemia has been reported in association with hemoglobin Chesapeake, which has an abnormally great affinity for oxygen that probably interferes with its delivery to the tissues.

The *treatment* of secondary polycythemia obviously depends upon the nature of its underlying cause. Oxygen inhalation will raise the percentage saturation of the arterial blood only in patients with ventilatory or pulmonary diffusion defects and in the former may induce carbon dioxide narcosis. Venesection as a symptomatic measure may help by reducing the viscosity of the blood or by relieving pulmonary congestion, but it always carries the risk of still further reducing the oxygen content of the arterial blood and of decreasing the blood volume and so of reducing the elevated cardiac output (Fig. 30–3).

Recently interest has been aroused in the occasional association of *renal tumors* or *hydronephrosis* with polycythemia without hypoxia or morphologic alteration of the arterial blood. It is possible that patients with renal ischemia, caused either by tumor or hydronephrosis, would secrete increased amounts of the so-called erythropoietic factor evoked in normal animals by anemia or hypoxia, provided that the kidney is (one of) its source(s). However, renal carcinoma tissue devoid of normal renal tissue has been shown to contain erythropoietic factor activity. Excision of the tumor has relieved the polycythemia, and this has later reappeared when distal metastases developed. In addition, subtentorial cerebellar hemangiomas, hepatocellular carcinomas, uterine myomata and a pheochromocytoma have been reported in association with polycythemia. In a few instances, erythropoietic activity has been demonstrated in extracts of the tumor; and where removal of the tumor has been possible relief of the polycythemia has followed. The association with polycythemia in *Cushing's syndrome*, and so with hyperplasia of the adrenal cortex, is better known. A possible common endocrine influence is suggested by the now well-documented pharmacologic effects of *androgenic* therapy in causing polycythemia. It is of interest that in experimental animals the erythropoietic effect of testosterone requires the presence of the kidney and seems to depend upon increased formation of erythropoietin by that organ.

Substances such as cyanide, acetone and urethan, to mention a few, interfere with the ability of tissue cytochromes to take up or release oxygen. A similar function has been suggested for cobalt, an agent which regularly produces polycythemia in animals and in man when given in pharmacologic amounts. In cobalt-treated animals, the oxygen tension in subcutaneous "gas pockets" is elevated, indicating a defect in oxygen utilization by the adjacent tissue cells.

Polycythemia Vera

This disease, of gradual onset and occurring usually in middle life, runs a chronic course characterized by a striking absolute increase in the concentration and total volume of circulating red cells and of hemoglobin. The hematocrit may reach 80 per cent, the hemoglobin 25 gm. per 100 ml. These are frequently but not necessarily accompanied by signs of increased bone marrow activity, including slight increase of the reticulocytes, leukocytosis or even a leukemoid response and sometimes marked thrombocytosis. A moderate degree of iron deficiency, sometimes due to previous unrecognized blood loss but also due to the demands of the increased red cell mass, probably explains the not infrequent

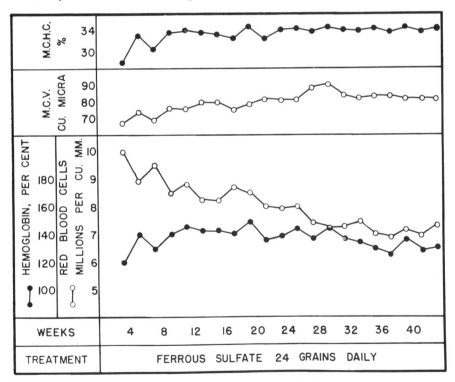

Figure 30–37. Effect of iron administration in reducing red cell count in a patient with polycythemia vera. Note that after an initial rise during the first 10 weeks from 120 to 140 per cent, approximately, the hemoglobin level was maintained or declined slightly. The initial red cell count of almost 10 million per cubic millimeter, however, progressively declined during a period of about 36 weeks to a level of about 7 million red cells per cubic millimeter. During this period the mean corpuscular volume and mean corpuscular hemoglobin concentration which were initially somewhat low, became normal.

TABLE 30–13. DISTINGUISHING FEATURES OF PRIMARY VS. SECONDARY (HYPOXIC) POLYCYTHEMIA.

	Primary	Secondary
Clinical		
Cyanosis (warm)	0	+
Heart or lung disease	0	+
Splenomegaly	+ (¾)*	0
Blood		
Arterial O₂ sat.	Normal	Decreased
Volume	Increased	Increased
Reticulocytes	Increased	Increased
Nucleated RBC	Often present	Absent
Granulocytes	Increased (⅘)	Normal
Platelets	Increased (⅔)	Normal
Marrow		
Erythroid	Increased	Increased
Myeloid	Increased	Normal
Megakaryocytes	Increased	Normal
Erythropoietin	Normal	Increased

* Numbers in parentheses indicate proportion of patients with the finding indicated at the initial examination, according to Gardner: Disease-a-Month, June 1962, Chicago, Year Book Medical Publishers.

moderate microcytosis and hypochromia of the red cells. Iron therapy will abolish the hypochromia (Fig. 30–37). Familial polycythemia, not to be confused with thalassemia minor or microcytic anemia in which the red cells, but not the hemoglobin, may be increased above normal, has been reported in a few instances, and may appear in youth. The majority of patients with polycythemia vera show enlargement of the spleen and later also of the liver.

In contrast to the findings in secondary (hypoxic) polycythemia is the normal oxygen saturation of the arterial blood (Table 30–13). Abnormal hemoglobins are absent, and the oxygen dissociation curve is normal. Consequently the flushed or cyanotic appearance (depending on the degree of local vasoconstriction) of the facies and mucous membranes, the dyspnea, lassitude, weakness, headache and irritability are probably the result of the increased volume and viscosity of the blood. Evidences of disease of the peripheral arteries, including coronary thrombosis, claudication without occlusion or actual gangrene and thromboangiitis obliterans, have been noted. Venous or arterial thromboses also occur in many patients. Thrombosis of the hepatic or portal vein radicles is probably the cause of the liver cirrhosis observed in some patients, and, when acute and extensive, is a serious event. Peripheral vascular thromboses are the result partly of the increased blood viscosity and partly, when arterial, of

primary arteriosclerotic changes in the blood vessels. Although the coagulation time of the blood is normal, there is an increased tendency to hemorrhage, due in part to the increased red cell volume and consequent vascular congestion. Also, despite elevated platelet counts, the increased proportion of red cells results in large, friable clots which retract poorly, at least in vitro. Hemorrhage from engorged veins in the esophagus, stomach or bowel is common and may even be fatal.

Labeled isotopes have shown that polycythemia vera is not due to increased longevity of the red cells. There appears, however, to be a double type of red cell population, some with short and some with normal survival times. This net average slightly increased rate of destruction is compensated for by an increased rate of red cell and hemoglobin production (measured by an increased rate of removal of injected Fe^{59} from the plasma), which maintains the elevated total red cell volume. A mere doubling of the normal rate of erythropoiesis is required to sustain double the number of circulating red cells, if their life-span is normal. The facts that the attainment of a normal concentration of circulating hemoglobin fails to prevent a further rise by inhibition of erythropoietic activity as in the normal person and that erythropoietin is not found in the plasma or urine unless the patient has been rendered anemic by therapy, demonstrate the primary nature of the increased erythropoiesis.

Neoplastic versus Physiologic Control of Erythropoiesis

Current thinking regards polycythemia vera as an idiopathic hyperplastic or neoplastic process involving to a variable degree at different times the precursors of the three marrow-derived elements of the peripheral blood: red cells, granulocytes and platelets. A peripheral and often marked increase of one (or sometimes two) of these elements in the peripheral blood may for some time precede evidence of the disturbance of the others. Eventually, however, the blood picture of some patients comes to resemble that of chronic myelogenous leukemia; and there is sometimes an acute final myeloblastic process. Some observers have sought an explanation of the disease in locally induced hypoxia of the bone marrow. However, analyses of blood removed from the bone marrows of anemic animals and from those of patients with anemia and polycythemia vera lend no support to such a concept. Moreover, no increase of erythropoietic factor in the plasma has been consistently reported. However, erythropoiesis in polycythemia vera, as pointed out below, is clearly to a certain extent under physiologic control. The situation may be analogous to that of certain cancers or leukemias which, though neoplastic, are for a time controllable by appropriate endocrine or antimetabolic therapy.

Lawrence, in acute observations with oxygen inhalation, was unable to depress the rate of hemoglobin production as measured by the rate of disappearance of Fe^{59} from the plasma, although this occurred in similar observations in patients with secondary (hypoxic) polycythemia. This difference is not unexpected because the arterial oxygen unsaturation (not present in polycythemia vera) was of course greatly decreased by oxygen inhalation in the patients with hypoxic polycythemia. Therefore a more appropriate comparison would have been between polycythemia vera and normal subjects. However, Castle and Strauss found that the changes occurring in the peripheral blood of patients with polycythemia vera which resulted from repeated blood loss, increased red cell destruction, iron administration and irradiation were *qualitatively* similar to those seen in patients without polycythemia when submitted to similar procedures. Particularly striking was the effect of the administration of iron (Fig. 30–37). Instead of the further elevation of both red cell and hemoglobin values, which might have been anticipated with an uncontrollable neoplastic disease of the red cells, there resulted an initial rise of hemoglobin concentration of about 20 per cent, which was thereafter maintained. This was accompanied by a steady decline of the red cell count to a level corresponding to that of the hemoglobin. This effect is similar to that occasionally seen in the late stages of the therapeutic responses of patients with pernicious or hypochromic anemia when the red cells temporarily exceed their normal value at a time when the hemoglobin has not yet reached its normal value (Fig. 30–13).

Certain clinical instances of polycythemia suggest that an increase of other types of cells in the bone marrow may in some way promote increased local erythropoiesis. Such an interpretation might be placed upon Turnbull's observation that zones of increased hematopoietic activity may surround discrete secondary metastases of carcinoma in fatty marrow. Occasionally, in the early stages of chronic poisoning by benzol and by radium, in which there is a marked increase in cellularity of the bone marrow, polycythemia of

mild degree is observed. Jaffe has pointed out that in leukemias, especially the acute variety, the bone marrow may display evidence of intense red cell production. Association between polycythemia and lymphatic leukemia is rare, as it is with multiple myeloma. In one instance transient polycythemia preceded terminal histiocytic leukemia by ten years. On the other hand, polycythemia is well known to occur in the early stages of myelogenous leukemia, in which eventually anemia develops as the bone marrow becomes more extensively invaded by leukemic cells. The condition of "erythroleukemia," in which the peripheral blood is characterized by numerous nucleated red cells and immature white cells, is possibly a dramatic example of the stimulating effect of a leukemic invasion of the bone marrow on red cell production. Thus Rundles and Jonnson have shown that in occasional patients with myelogenous leukemia treatment with urethan may not only abolish the anemia, but may even raise the hemoglobin to polycythemic levels. Similar effects have been observed by Moloney in multiple myeloma treated with urethan. Examination of the bone marrow in polycythemia vera indicates manifest hyperactivity and immaturity of the leukopoietic cells as well as of the erythropoietic cells.

It is becoming increasingly well recognized that certain cases of polycythemia vera, after a period of months or usually of years, develop the characteristics of the condition known as nonleukemic myelosis or agnogenic myeloid metaplasia or less commonly of myelogenous leukemia. Early in the development of polycythemia vera, and often at a time when the bone marrow is still hypercellular, the spleen becomes enlarged and the peripheral blood exhibits leukocytosis with differential counts suggesting a leukemoid type of response. The terminal stage of the disease process may be acute myelogenous leukemia or more commonly may be characterized as osteosclerotic anemia. Turnbull has drawn attention to the invariable presence of hematogenous marrow in areas where osteosclerosis is prominent. Upton and Furth have described a spontaneous disease of mice transmissible by particle-free extracts of spleen cells and characterized by splenomegaly and early myeloid and erythroid hyperplasia of the marrow later followed by myelosclerosis. Valentine and his associates have found that the alkaline phosphatase activity of the leukocyte population in polycythemia vera, although the leukocytes may be morphologically indistinguishable from those of myelogenous

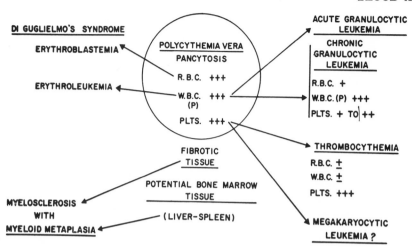

Figure 30–38. Clinical and possibly etiologic relations between polycythemia vera and related blood disorders, the so-called myeloproliferative syndromes. Clinical evidence indicates that cellular proliferation begins in the marrow, spleen and probably liver simultaneously and that the myeloid metaplasia of liver and spleen is not the secondary result of marrow fibrosis. Other conditions associated with primary hypercellularity of the bone marrow sometimes terminate with hypoplasia or fibrosis; e.g., benzol poisoning and Hodgkin's disease. (From Dameshek: Bull. New England Med. Center, *16*:53, 1954.)

leukemia, is twenty times as great as in the latter. In this respect the leukocytes of polycythemia resemble those of infection. However, because there is presently no convincing evidence for a physiologic cause of polycythemia vera, the conventional view is that the enhanced erythropoiesis, leukopoiesis and thrombocytopoiesis of the various "myeloproliferative syndromes" associated with polycythemia vera, early and late (Fig. 30–38) are part of a fundamental and single neoplastic process of varying expression, originating in the multipotential stem cells of the marrow.

General Aspects of Polycythemia Vera

The flow of polycythemic blood through a capillary tube under a given head of pressure is slow compared to that of normal blood, which in turn is slow compared to that of anemic blood. These differences are inversely related to blood viscosity which in polycythemia may be from five to six times that of normal blood. This increase in viscosity is due to the increased hemoglobin content (equivalent to hematocrit), and is independent of the number and size of the individual red cells. Thus, the ability of the polycythemic blood to transport oxygen through a capillary tube in vitro is limited by its high viscosity, and that of anemic blood by its low hemoglobin content. Direct measurements made on blood in vitro show that the optimum for oxygen

transport lies between these extremes: blood with a normal hematocrit of about 45 per cent (Fig. 30–3).

Quite a different situation obtains in the body, however, because in polycythemia the disability imposed by the high viscosity of the blood upon oxygen transport to the tissues is more than compensated for by the increased cardiac output which results from the increased blood volume. The effect of this is to distend the peripheral venous bed, and so to diminish its resistance and permit a larger venous return to the heart with a corresponding increase in cardiac output. However, such a compensatory effect cannot apply to fixed local arterial narrowings where, unless the perfusion pressure is increased, the flow of polycythemic blood is inevitably restricted by its high viscosity. For reasons not at all clear, the risk of hemorrhage and thrombosis during or following operative procedures remains high until some time after blood viscosity and volume have been brought to normal by treatment. The frequently elevated basal metabolic rate can be ascribed to the leukemic or leukemoid process underlying many cases of polycythemia vera. Another resemblance to leukemia is the increased output of uric acid in the urine, despite which few patients have attacks of gout, even after roentgen-ray therapy by which large numbers of leukocytes are destroyed.

The *treatment* of polycythemia vera is of interest in connection with its pathologic physiology. There have been three common methods.

In the first, increased destruction of the blood is caused by the administration of *acetylphenylhydrazine,* the hemolytic action of which has already been described under the section on Hemolytic Anemias. Because this increased red cell destruction leads to further increased red cell production by a bone marrow well supplied with the iron derived from the red cells destroyed by the drug, this is an illogical method of treatment that is no longer used. Moreover, increased production of platelets may favor venous thrombosis.

A second and time-honored method is the use of *venesection,* which has the useful primary effect of reducing the circulating blood volume and viscosity and eventually the secondary effect of creating a progressive iron deficiency through loss of hemoglobin in the venesections. As a result the bone marrow becomes less and less able to produce hemoglobin and red cells. Consequently, after several bleedings venesection is required at progressively longer intervals in order to maintain the same reduced hemoglobin level. The therapeutic objective is thus to produce what amounts to "hypochromic anemia" in a patient with polycythemia vera. Sufficient venesection to reduce the hematocrit toward the normal value decreases the need for increased cardiac output and thus brings beneficial results. However, it should be kept in mind that the first effect of blood loss is to diminish the blood volume and, hence, the cardiac output, which in polycythemia compensates for the excessive blood viscosity (Fig. 30–3). Only after tissue fluids have entered the blood stream will the hematocrit be decreased. For this reason blood letting should be performed slowly in well hydrated patients, and saline or plasma expanders in equal volume should be infused at the same time into another vein.

The third method of treatment also involves inhibition of red cell production by various agencies. Among these is the use of *irradiation,* whether by roentgen rays or radioactive phosphorus. Irradiation is always associated with depression of leukopoietic activity and sometimes with a fall of platelets. Because it affects the precursors, but not the circulating blood cells themselves, even total cessation of erythropoiesis will not cause much fall in red cell values before 4 to 6 weeks. *Potassium arsenite,* in the form of Fowler's solution, as well as *benzol,* has also been used. Both are leukopenia-producing agents. Both have now been abandoned, largely because of toxic effects. The modern antitumor agents such as *nitrogen mustard,* triethylenemelamine and recently *busulfan* are also effective. That these agents, like irradiation, directly or indirectly inhibit red cell formation rather than hemoglobin production is clearly brought out when they are used in a patient who, as a result of previous phlebotomies, has a depressed hemoglobin level relative to that of the red cells and whose blood thus has a low corpuscular hemoglobin concentration. After irradiation or the effective use of antitumor

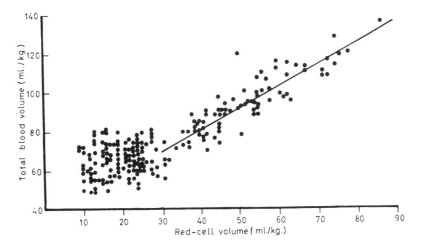

Figure 30–39. Relationship of red cell volume and total blood volume. The effect of the increased circulating red cell volume is shown to increase the total blood volume more or less correspondingly in polycythemia. Note the insignificant changes in blood volume when red cell volume is normal or below normal as in anemia, in which the contraction of the circulating red cell volume is replaced by a corresponding increase of plasma volume. (From Huber, Lewis, and Szur: Brit. J. Haemat., *10*:567, 1964.)

agents the diminished numbers of newly formed red cells are no longer hypochromic; the red cell count progressively declines and eventually corresponds with the hemoglobin level so that the red cells at length display a normal hemoglobin concentration. This, with a normal hematocrit, will provide maximal oxygen transport capacity without increased cardiac output. Recent statistical studies by Modan have shown that when treated by irradiation, whether by x-rays and/or by P^{32}, about 10 per cent of patients will eventually develop acute myelogenous leukemia, whereas this will occur in less than 1 per cent of those not receiving some form of irradiation. The life expectancies of other series of patients treated with or without P^{32} were similar, 13.3 and 13.6 years, respectively.

Disorders of the Leukocytes

Various types of pathologic responses of the white cells, including leukocytosis, leukopenia and leukemia, are recognized by clinicians by means of examination of the peripheral blood or of the bone marrow, reticuloendothelial or lymphoid structures. In contrast to the situation in disturbances of the red cells in which the oxygen-carrying capacity of the peripheral blood is directly a measure of the essential pathologic physiology, the abnormalities of the leukocyte formula of the peripheral blood are merely somewhat blurred reflections of responses to antigens or of effects of inflammation or necrosis of the fixed tissues or of neoplasia of the various germinal lines of white cells. Except for agranulocytosis, a lack of leukocytes in the blood stream creates no obvious defect of body function. Indeed, lack of granulocytes in the blood is merely an indication of the functional lack at a tissue level.

LEUKOCYTE CHARACTERISTICS

In the peripheral blood the relatively mature forms of three series of white cells can normally be recognized: the myeloid or granular leukocyte, the lymphocyte, and the monocyte. Unlike the red cell's, the white cell's nucleus is retained throughout life, although not necessarily with capacity for division. Neither space nor the limitations of the methods of study permit a discussion of the morphology of their proliferation, which, together with the various theories concerning their origins, are well described in many textbooks of hematology. Bloom has stated in

effect that when leukocytes are sufficiently primitive they cannot be distinguished as to type by any of the methods proposed in the last half century unless identified by association with their presumptive progeny. The granulocytes are formed extravascularly in the bone marrow, probably from a stem cell common also to erythrocytes and megakaryocytes, as has recently been confirmed by the finding of an anomalous chromosome in the nuclei of each of the three types of descendants; the lymphocytes, largely in the spleen and lymph nodes; the monocytes, largely in the bone marrow, but also, like histiocytes, from reticuloendothelial cells. However, many observers since the days of Metchnikoff have noted that lymphocytes may become mononuclears or histiocytes in appearance and function in injured tissue or in tissue culture and may finally become converted to fibroblasts. The lymphocyte enters the blood stream through the thoracic duct and, as shown by Blalock, largely disappears if the venous portals of entry of the duct and all its collaterals are obliterated. Large, but not small, lymphocytes may divide in the blood stream.

The life-span of the granulocyte comprises formative, intravascular and extravascular or tissue phases. Observations with labeling of nuclear DNA by such precursors as C^{14}-adenine or H^3-thymidine indicate that in man production and storage in the marrow granulocyte reserve occupy from 5 to 10 days. The marrow reserve of maturing granulocytes is from 20 to 25 times the number in the circulation. Cartwright et al. have shown, by labeling a sample of blood granulocytes in vitro with di-isopropylfluorophosphate (DFP^{32}) and reinjecting it, that from the dilution of the isotope, the total pool is about 700 million granulocytes per kilogram of body weight. About 45 per cent of these cells are in active circulation, the rest in a marginal pool, presumably close to the walls of small blood vessels and so can be readily mobilized by epinephrine injection or exercise. The mature granulocyte circulates for about 10 hours and the blood pool turns over 2.3 times a day. Once the granulocyte leaves the blood pool to enter the tissues, it does not return, and its survival time is unknown, except in areas of inflammation where granulocyte disintegration begins within a few hours. No firm conclusions can presently be drawn about the life-span of the lymphocyte. Data with H^3-thymidine show prompt labeling of precursors in thymus, lymph nodes, and thoracic duct lymph with peak labeling of large lymphocytes or mononuclear cells in the blood after 2 or 3 days. The work of Gowans indicates extensive recirculation of blood lymphocytes via the thoracic duct. They reenter the lymph nodes through the cortex by way of postcapillary veins, and via the splenic sinuses, but do not return to the thymus. Small lymphocytes label during incubation in vitro to a minor extent only; large lymphocytes up to 40 per cent, indicating a clear potential for mitotic division. Continuous infusion of the label into rats shows that lymphocytes initially unlabeled may survive for over 100 days, confirming other studies suggesting a life-span of 100 to 300 days. The lymphocyte may well require a long life-span in order to preserve a long memory for immunologic events.

According to Bierman, enormous numbers of granulocytes are normally trapped in the lungs—sometimes more than 16,000 per cubic millimeter of blood per minute. Forced expiration causes a drop within seconds of the arterial leukocyte count, and the opposite respiratory manuever increases it somewhat above the passive level. The liver and spleen apparently also sequester granulocytes, at least under pathologic conditions; and the intestinal mucosa is infiltrated with lymphocytes, which may be excreted in this way, as are the leukocytes in the saliva and bronchial secretions. Granulocytes continue to leave the pulmonary capillaries and to enter the bronchial secretions unless their concentration in the blood is less than 1000 per cubic millimeter. Myriads of eosinophils characterize the mucous discharges in allergic vasomotor rhinitis.

Craddock's leukopheresis experiments with dogs have indicated homeostatic control of the circulating granulocyte pool. More recently Gordon and associates have demonstrated in the plasma of rats subjected to loss of leukocytes by peritoneal lavage a plasma globulin factor effecting a leukocytosis in a parabiont partner and specifically active in causing release of granulocytes and lymphocytes from perfused hind leg preparations. The prompt action of this humoral substance is distinct from that of erythropoietin, which primarily affects stem cell proliferation. Here the effect seems to be to release mature granulocytes and so to make way for their replacement by cell proliferation. The action of the leukocyte releasing factor is probably mediated by an increase in marrow blood flow and is inhibited by an increase in the number of leukocytes in the perfusing blood. Vasodilator drugs and endotoxin do not simulate the blood flow pattern, although after an initial leukopenia the latter causes a leukocytosis.

Relatively rapid, random ameboid mobility at a rate up to 60 microns per minute is characteristic of granular leukocytes. In vitro, when less than 1 mm. distant from a target, these leukocytes respond to chemical stimuli arising from bacteria or injured or necrotic tissue. In vitro, granulocytes are, for example, attracted by pneumococci, are rather indifferent to tubercle bacilli, and are repelled by typhoid bacilli. Antigen-antibody complexes, when formed in the presence of complement, exert a chemotactic effect in vitro. Phagocytosis in the neutrophils is characteristically directed against bacteria and small particles, and is most active in the one-, two- and three-lobed cells. Once a leukocyte has reached the target, phagocytosis of the organism may occur without antibodies if the cell can trap it against a suitable surface. Phagocytosis is facilitated in vitro by the coating of the bacteria with antibody and by the presence of complement. It is opposed by the mucoid capsule of some organisms. Chemotropism in the monocytes or histiocytes is sluggish, but these cells can ingest not only bacteria, but also protozoa and larger particulate matter, including red cells. The lymphocytes exhibit moderate motility but no phagocytic activity or chemotropism.

Warburg, in 1930, initiated the active study of cell metabolism, noting the high rate of anaerobic glycolysis in neoplastic cells. The granular leukocytes exhibit active, aerobic as well as anaerobic glycolysis with lactic acid production from glucose. Oxygen consumption is rapid, and the Embden-Myerhof cycle, the hexosemonophosphate shunt and the Krebs cycle are functional. About 90 per cent of the glucose utilized can be recovered as lactate. Glucose utilization by leukocytes in vitro is greatly augmented by the act of phagocytosis, whether of bacteria or of inert particles. This probably explains the fall of spinal fluid glucose in bacterial meningitis as opposed to aseptic (viral) meningitis with leukocytic reaction. The entry of the particle is accompanied by a burst of oxygen consumption due to massive stimulation of the hexosemonophosphate shunt. This activation is thought to be due to oxidases present on or released from cell granules termed lysosomes by DeDuve. These granules that give the leukocyte its name subsequently burst, releasing acid and alkaline phosphatases and a dozen other hydrolytic enzymes from the "bag" into the adjacent vacuole surrounding the phagocytized particle. This process may be fatal to the cell and contributory to the pathology of inflammation. (See also Chapter 31.) DNA and RNA are of course present in large amounts in young and dividing leukocytes. The maturing cell contains increasing amounts of glycogen dispersed throughout its cytoplasm, and of various enzymes. Its granules stain with oil-soluble dyes. Lipase, amylase, trypsin and acid and alkaline phosphatase are present, as are also nucleases which split nucleoproteins and, probably, enzymes that split nucleic acid and its digestion products, including carbohydrate moieties. Increases of both eosinophils and basophils appear to correlate with local increases of histamine and heparin. Among trace elements zinc is present in considerable amounts and is required for the activation of alkaline phophatase. About half the normal blood histamine is present in the few basophils, a third in the eosinophils and the rest in the neutrophils. Histamine is produced by the basophil through decarboxylation of histidine. The large metachromatic granules of the basophils and tissue mast cells exhibit staining reactions characteristic of heparin, which has been isolated from the mast cell tumors of dogs. Heparin, which in vivo evokes a lipid "clearing action" on plasma, is thought to be released by degranulation of basophils after a meal containing enough fat to give visible lipemia.

The *neutrophils* represent a second line of defense against pathogenic organisms which have successfully traversed the skin or mucous membranes, especially in persons in whom humoral immune bodies have not yet developed. Menkin has shown that the local collection of leukocytes at the site of injury or infection is caused by a polypeptide, "leukotaxine." This material can be separated from a euglobulin, "necrosin," which causes leukopenia and accelerates the clotting of blood in vitro. Leukotaxine itself, however, in contrast to crude exudative material, when injected into dogs does not produce the marked leukocytosis and hyperplasia of the myeloid elements of the bone marrow caused by the crude material. Instead, another substance, the "leukocytosis-promoting factor" (? endotoxin), which is associated with the alpha globulins of the exudates, enters the circulation from the site of inflammation and stimulate production of immature leukocytes by

the bone marrow. The blood stream then serves as a means of transportation of the granulocytes from the bone marrow to the tissue in which the infection is located.

Certain constitutional anomalies of the granulocytes produce morphologic changes apparent in blood smears. The sex chromatin characteristic of the female may be seen in the "drumstick" projecting from the nuclear membrane of about 1 per cent of the granulocytes. "Dumbbell" or "spectacle" shaped bilobate nuclei with coarse chromatin, not to be confused with the band forms of normal young granulocytes, reflect the hereditary Pelger-Huët anomaly transmitted as an autosomal dominant. Another anomaly is the presence of large neutrophils with multilobate nuclei, which may closely resemble those of pernicious anemia. The Chediak-Higashi anomaly is a serious clinical condition in which albinism, mental retardation, hepatosplenomegaly and anemia with leukopenia and thrombocytopenia are inherited as an autosomal recessive trait. There are abnormalities in the granulation and nuclear structure of all types of leukocytes. In the granulocytes, the lysosomes are enlarged, malformed and few in number. In addition, cytoplasmic inclusions and Döhle bodies may be seen. The association between albinism and abnormalities of the granulocytes led Windhorst to examine the hair bulb of such patients with the electron microscope. The melanosomes, like the lysosomes, were seen to be large and poorly pigmented, suggesting that the syndrome may be an expression of a genetic disease of the limiting membranes of such granules.

Despite earlier evidence apparently relating this function to the phagocytic cells of the reticuloendothelial system, it now appears that immature plasma cells and certain lymphocytes are directly concerned in *antibody production*. Lymphocytes are not phagocytic, but the handle of the typical "hand mirror" form of the living cell in vitro ends in a number of thread-like projections. In leukocyte cultures McFarlane has observed contact between these filaments and adjacent macrophages that may in this fashion be passing instructive material concerning antigens or antibodies to the lymphocytes. Transmission of labeled RNA to lymphocytes has been demonstrated in vitro. Harris and Ehrich showed that typhoid antigen or sheep red cells injected into the footpad of rabbits cause a general increase in lymphatic tissue. Free antigen appears locally and in the regional lymph nodes within two days and disappears after four days. Antibodies specific for these antigens appear in the regional lymph nodes in maximum titer on the fifth or sixth day. In lymphoid cells present in the lymph draining the lymph nodes the concentration of antibodies was five to seven times that in the lymph plasma.

The observations of many European workers, including Bing, Bjorneboe, and Fagraeus, have now made it clear that the less conspicuous plasma cells of the red pulp of the spleen, of the medullary areas of the lymph nodes, of the portal connective tissue and of the villi of the ileum are sources of antibodies. The first response to antigenic stimulation is the production of gamma macroglobulins or γM (19S) globulins which remain in the plasma, but are rapidly degraded. After a few days γG globulin (7S) appears and replaces the other. In animals injected with a bacterial antigen for the second time after an interval, young plasma cells were shown by Ehrich and his associates specifically to adsorb the antigenic bacteria, and this has been repeatedly confirmed by Coons' fluorescent method. The deep blue coloration of the cytoplasm of the plasma cell with the Romanowsky stain is characteristic of the presence of ribonucleic acids, and this indicates the rapid production of protein. The association between plasma cells and elevated serum globulin in multiple myeloma is well known and is strikingly exemplified in such diverse types of chronic infection as lymphogranuloma venereum, kala-azar and subacute bacterial endocarditis. Conversely, it has now been shown that patients with agammaglobulinemia fail to respond to antigenic stimulation, permanently accept homologous skin grafts and exhibit no plasma cells in their tissues. The lymphoid thymus of immunized animals contains no antibodies, but is apparently necessary in the newborn animal for the subsequent development of the lymphoid apparatus and its ability to produce antibodies. Such failure in the infant may lead to absence of both lymphocytes and plasma cells and so to lack of all immune globulins. In the absence of plasma cells, very low levels of gamma globulins are found or absence of certain kinds only may be disclosed by electrophoretic analysis.

Passive transfer of delayed skin sensitivity to drugs and to tuberculin in guinea pigs cannot be achieved unless the material injected contains living white cells, presumably lymphocytes or plasma cells derived from the sensitized animals. However, recently Lawrence has readily transferred such sensitivity in man with soluble extracts of lymphocytes containing protein-free material of relatively low molecular weight. Presumably the altered characteristics of the reticuloendothelian system in Hodgkin's disease in some way condition an early failure to respond to primary immunization and to exhibit a delayed skin reaction to tuberculin (anergy). It is of interest that lymphocytes from Hodgkin's disease may fail to transfer delayed skin sensitivity and that profound lymphopenia is characteristic of the late stages of the disease. For a fuller discussion of the cellular and humoral aspects of immunity and the role of the thymus, the reader should consult Chapters 3 and 31.

The *monocytes* can digest microorganisms containing protein and carbohydrate, but in addition have the special property of containing lipase, an enzyme that enables them to attack bacteria with a fat-containing capsule, such as the tubercle and leprosy bacilli. The monocytes apparently play a specific role in immunity to tuberculosis. Monocytes from tuberculous guinea pigs are susceptible to injury by tuberculin in vitro and retain this property through successive generations in tissue culture in which it has recently been shown that ascorbic acid is necessary for their conversion to fibroblasts.

LEUKOCYTOSIS

Though hemoconcentration of the red cells amounting to 10 or 20 per cent is impressive, such a change in the number of leukocytes would pass almost unnoticed because of the normal range of fluctuation. Consequently the twofold or greater increase in the leukocyte levels of the peripheral blood that is often seen in dehydration is not ascribable directly and simply to hemoconcentration. Instead, this indicates a true leukocytic response to dehydration or other noxious stimuli. On the other hand, the so-called physiologic leukocytosis present during pregnancy, in the newborn infant, after strenuous exercise, and in patients experiencing severe pain, nausea or some emotional disturbance is probably similar to that following adrenalin injection and merely represents displacement of the marginal pool of granulocytes into active circulation.

Clare and his associates have shown that, after removal of the adrenal medulla of rats, procedures leading to stimulation of the sympathetico-adrenal system—

that is, convulsions induced by Metrazol, electric shock and anoxia—fail to cause the leukocytosis seen in normal animals after these stimuli. The injection of bacterial vaccines, however, produces leukocytosis in both the operated and the normal animals, indicating a direct action on the bone marrow. Experimental leukopheresis in dogs causes within an hour or two a marked but brief leukopenia. Thereafter there is an accelerated movement of relatively mature granulocytes from the marrow reserve, which contains about twenty times the number normally in circulation, into the blood stream. Clinical estimates of this marrow reserve can be made by the intravenous injection of 0.1 to 0.2 gamma of purified bacterial endotoxin which normally causes a prompt fall followed by a doubling of the base line granulocyte level often from 6 to 10 hours. Labeling with P^{32} shows that, despite repeated leukopheresis, newly formed granulocytes do not begin to leave the bone marrow until after the third day.

Granulocytosis

This is the usual response to a pyogenic infection which causes an absolute increase in the number of neutrophils as well as in their proportion. With maintained rise in the number of white cells in the circulating blood, the proportion of immature neutrophils increases, but, although formation of new granulocytes is involved, does not usually include cells less mature than the metamyelocyte. According to Craddock, in severe infections and in other toxemias the appearance of newly formed granulocytes in the blood stream is accelerated by a day or two over the normal delivery, but their survival in the circulation does not seem to be much shortened. Deeply staining basophilic granules appear in the neutrophils and are usually referred to as "toxic granules." These and the amorphous bluish cytoplasmic inclusions known as Döhle bodies are also induced by cytotoxic agents such as cyclophosphamide. In experimental animals toxic granules are sometimes associated with the necrosis of tumor masses, such as in Brown-Pearce carcinomatosis of the rabbit, and also appear experimentally after the intravenous injection of nucleic acid and its derivatives.

Monkeys receiving for the first time an inoculation with streptococci react with an immediate and marked leukocytosis, without, however, any increase in the phagocytic capacity of the granulocytes against the organism. Reinoculation with the same microorganism three to six months later causes no appreciable leukocytosis, but a prompt and definite increase in the phagocytic capacity of the granulocytes and a rise in serum antibody.

Acute infections, especially when due to cocci and localized, or when present as complications of conditions not usually associated with neutrophilia, e.g., typhoid fever, classically cause a neutrophilic response. The essential local process for which the granulocytes are being transported in the blood stream concerns the localization of the foreign antigen and its destruction by the phagocytic and digestive activities of the granulocytes. Rebuck has shown that at the site of scarification and application of a foreign protein to the human forearm granulocytes rapidly appear, but degenerate and fragment within a few hours. The particles of cell debris are then ingested by hypertrophied small lymphocytes and by monocytes and macrophages which dominate the picture by 12 to 14 hours after the injury. According to Good, unless intact granulocytes are available during the initial response, lymphocytes do not leave the local blood vessels and enter the area of inflammation. Such observations, as well as study of antigen-stimulated cell cultures, indicate the local conversion of small lymphocytes and monocytes to larger cells with increased phagocytic and antibody-forming abilities and other characteristics of macrophages or plasma cells.

Metabolic disturbances such as uremia, diabetic acidosis, eclampsia, gout and burns or poisoning with various chemicals and drugs, sterile necrosis of tissues such as occurs in operative procedures, coronary thrombosis or malignant neoplasm call forth neutrophilic responses. The hypoxia produced by acute hemorrhage or severe hemolytic anemia is a less certain stimulus. In general, the more severe the stimulus, the greater the neutrophilic response and the more marked the proportion of young neutrophils. However, in elderly individuals leukocytic responses are less certain, and in other patients overwhelming infection with pyogenic organisms or massive exudates may even cause leukopenia with extreme increase in the proportion of immature granulocytes. As might be anticipated from the work of Menkin, a localized infectious process is more likely to be a cause of leukocytosis than is a generalized septicemia without metastatic infection in the tissue.

In any of the conditions causing a severe neutrophilic leukocytosis the total height of the white cell count and the relative immaturity of the white cells may be suggestive of leukemia, especially when accompanied, as sometimes, by the presence of nucleated red cells in the peripheral blood. In contrast to myelogenous leukemia the alkaline phosphatase of the granulocytes is usually normal or elevated; but there is no wholly definitive way of drawing a distinction except on the basis of the chromosome anomaly (Ph¹) present in many cases of myelogenous leukemia. The so-called *myeloid* or *leukemoid reactions* have been observed in infections, such as pneumonia, empyema and septicemia. Sudden and severe hemolysis of blood is regularly followed by marked leukocytosis of the myeloid type, and this is sometimes the case after severe hemorrhage. Myeloid blood pictures have also been noted in tuberculosis, particularly of the miliary variety and when involving the lymph nodes, spleen and presumably the bone marrow. In rare instances extreme leukocytosis has been observed in eclampsia, liver necrosis and after severe burns. An occasional association is with malignancy without bone metastases, sometimes with large tumors of the lung or liver, perhaps especially when necrosis of the tumor is present. More commonly a myeloid blood picture is associated with widespread infiltration of the bone marrow, such as in multiple myeloma, myelosclerosis and Hodgkin's disease.

Eosinophilia occurs especially in allergic disorders, skin diseases, parasitic infections accompanied by tissue invasion and occasionally in certain infections such as scarlet fever and in a miscellaneous group of disease such as Hodgkin's disease, periarteritis nodosa, Loeffler's syndrome and tropical eosinophilia. It may also be a familial condition, and has recently been reported in magnesium-deficient rats.

Experimentally, eosinophils respond promptly to the first injection of protein only in large amounts and when it has the properties of relative insolubility, antigenicity and the presence of sulfhydryl groups. According to Homma, there is first a local accumulation of eosinophils which may result in temporary blood eosinophilopenia, which in turn after twelve hours stimulates marrow eosinophil production. Curiously, Speirs found that insoluble asbestos fibers cause eosinophils to accumulate rapidly at the site of their injection. In the sensitized animal blood stream eosinophilia at once results from the injection of the protein antigen. Litt suggests that eosinophils are attracted by the antigen-antibody reaction itself. They may counteract the local effects of histamine, as can be demonstrated experimentally with extracts of eosinophils. Adrenalectomy enhances the eosinophil response in animals; and repeated failure of adrenocorticotropin to at least halve the eosinophil level in patients suggests adrenal failure. The eosinophilopenic effect of adrenocorticotropin is probably upon formation rather than upon destruction of the eosinophils. Cortisone lowers the eosinophil level in peritoneal fluid in experimental animals only after blood levels have declined. Blockade of the reticuloendothelial system with colloidal dyes inhibits the removal of eosinophils from the circulation.

An increased number of eosinophils often follows the termination of infectious disease and presumably indicates either a cessation of stress or the presence of antigen-antibody in combination. Charcot-Leyden protein crystals are formed in some way by degenerating eosinophils in local accumulations such as the bronchial secretions in asthma.

Basophilic leukocytosis is sometimes observed in myelogenous leukemia, polycythemia vera, chronic sinusitis and following splenectomy and exposure to x-rays. In chronically inflamed or in irradiated tissues mast cells or tissue basophils, which are perhaps more mature forms of the circulating basophil, also are numerous. Recently histamine, long associated with eosinophils, has been shown to be released from the mast cells of the rat mesentery accompanied by loss of their granulation. Similar observations have been made upon tissue mast cells of patients with local urticaria on exposure to cold, whose blood basophils are similarly affected in vitro. The maculo-papular lesions of urticaria pigmentosa, which contain many mast cells, also release histamine upon trauma or exposure to cold, sometimes in amounts sufficient to produce systemic effects: headache, flushing and diarrhea.

Lymphocytosis

An absolute lymphocytosis, in contrast to the relative lymphocytosis often accompanying leukopenia, is found in the blood of infants. Lymphocytosis is also characteristic of certain infections which are usually nonpyogenic, as in the early stages of pertussis, infectious mononucleosis and acute infectious lymphocytosis. Marked lymphocytosis often accompanied by plasma cells has been described in whooping cough and chickenpox. Lymphocytosis and sometimes an increase of plasma cells occur during the secondary stages of such infections as mumps, German measles, undulant fever, tuberculosis and syphilis, probably as a reflection of continued antibody production. During the stage of convalescence from acute pyogenic infections lymphocytosis sometimes with eosinophilia is common. Finally, relative as well as absolute lymphocytosis accompanies hyperthyroidism, especially when lymph node enlargement is also present. The lymphocytes in the blood stream may be large and distinctly abnormal in appearance in any of these conditions.

The atypical lymphocytosis of infectious mononucleosis and the normal-appearing lymphocytes of acute infectious lymphocytosis, as well as the lymphocytosis sometimes occurring in association with purpura haemorrhagica, are of particular interest to hematologists. In all probability these are manifestations of infections with specific viruses, although this is not proved. Infectious mononucleosis, especially because of the associated sore throat, enlargement of the lymph nodes and splenomegaly, together with the presence of immature lymphocytes in the blood film and occasionally associated thrombocytopenia with purpura, has been mistakenly diagnosed as acute leukemia. Recently similar particles visible with the electron microscope and interpreted as "myxovirus-like" have been reported in both conditions. Others suspect them to be particles from disintegrated platelets. The Paul-Bunnell test for heterophile antibodies capable of causing agglutination of sheep cells is positive in about 90 per cent of cases, presumably as a response to the infection. Falsely positive serologic reactions for syphilis are occasionally observed, but persist after removal by absorption of the heterophile antibodies. Naturally present heterophile antibodies are found in low titer in the serum of normal persons and, like young lymphocytes and plasma cells, may be greatly increased in "serum sickness" after the injection of horse serum. They can be distinguished from those present in infectious mononucleosis because the latter are absorbed by ox cells, but not by guinea pig kidney.

Monocytosis

This refers to an absolute increase in the number of monocytes in the peripheral blood, which occurs in certain bacterial infections such as tuberculosis, subacute bacterial endocarditis, brucellosis and typhus fever. Occasionally the cells resemble histiocytes with more voluminous cytoplasm displaying vacuoles and erythrophagocytosis. Because of their large size, such cells may accumulate in capillaries of the dependent ear lobe and be demonstrable in blood films obtained with needle puncture. Monocytosis also occurs in certain protozoal infections such as malaria, spotted fever, kala-azar and trypanosomiasis. Monocytosis sometimes appears in Hodgkin's disease and in the primary form of xanthomatosis. *Plasma cells* are rarely found in the circulating blood in acute infections, except occasionally in German measles, scarlet fever, measles and chickenpox. Plasma cells are sometimes also seen in drug and serum reactions and in patients with chronic localized infections, presumably as an indication of antibody production. In very rare instances plasma cells in the peripheral blood reflect the presence of multiple myeloma (plasmacytoma).

LEUKOPENIA

The mechanisms producing leukopenia, usually due to granulocytopenia, are not well understood, but in theory consist in decreased production by the bone marrow, redistribution after delivery to the circulation, and increased loss or destruction. Clinical and experimental evidence at least suggests examples of each.

Depression of *granulocyte formation* in the bone marrow often results in mild chronic leukopenia on the basis of *nutritional deficiency*. Thus in pernicious and related macrocytic anemias the characteristic leukopenia responds to the administration of folic acid or vitamin B_{12} if such deficiencies exist. It is featured by large adult granulocytes with increased numbers of nuclear lobes and must not be confused with the occasional familial incidence of a minor population of "giant neutrophils" in normal subjects. The granulocytopenia is not secondary to the anemia or to the megaloblastic hyperplasia of the bone marrow, since erythropoiesis can be suppressed by multiple transfusions without causing an increase of leukocytes or platelet formation. Granulocytopenia has been observed in experimental animals receiving various forms of purified diets, when it has been ascribed to deficiency of folic acid, tryptophan, pantothenic acid or riboflavin. Such specific nutritional deficiencies may be involved in the causation of the leukopenia which is often seen in debilitated or aged persons. Zuelzer has described an idiopathic form of granulocytopenia, "myelokathexis," due to premature senescence of such cells within the marrow. Neutropenia with a cycle of about 3 weeks, accompanied by markedly diminished marrow precursors, has been reported in about 40 patients, in several of whom there was a familial incidence.

Leukopenia is also the result of toxic action or of sensitivity to certain *drugs and chemicals*. Therapeutic administration of sulfur and nitrogen mustards may cause an extreme degree of leukopenia apparently because they directly affect nuclear structure and function of leukocytes and their precursors. Irradiation also, whether by roentgen rays or radioactive phosphorus, produces somewhat similar results. An initial lymphopenia is followed by granulocytopenia which may persist for a month or more (Fig. 30–34). Also, with considerable regularity benzol, and, in rare instances, amidopyrine, dinitrophenol, the sulfonamides, thiouracil, phenylbutazone, chloramphenicol and chlorpromazine have caused leukopenia often associated with depression of red cell and platelet production. Granulocytopenia also may result from limited marrow reserves in alcoholics due either to the toxic effects of alcohol or to deficiency of folic acid. Vacuoles in the cytoplasm of marrow precursors appear in alcoholics and with chloramphenicol administration in children in whom they can be abolished by phenylalanine. Various analogs of pteroylglutamic acid such as aminopterin and amethopterin are used with temporary benefits in the chemotherapy of acute leukemia because they inhibit the production of leukemic (as well as normal) leukocytes. It is possible that the sulfonamides produce leukopenia by a similar direct action on leukopoiesis, although the usual explanation for this effect in animals is interference with the synthesis of folic acid by the bacteria of the alimentary tract. Antagonisms to purines and pyrimidines involved in nucleoprotein synthesis may account for the leukopenic action of 6-mercaptopurine and 5-fluorouracil. The limiting factor in the use of all such antitumor chemotherapeutic agents is the tendency to pancytopenia (Fig. 30–40).

Decreased production of leukocytes is probably illustrated clinically by *certain infections* with bacteria, such as those of the typhoid group and of undulant fever, viruses such as influenza and measles, and protozoal infections such as malaria and kala-azar. However, in the last two the influence of splenomegaly in sequestering granulocytes is probably also involved. Depression of white cell formation is readily understood when the marrow is largely acellular, and is also occasionally the result of invasion of the marrow by foreign cells such as those of metastatic carcinoma or xanthomatosis or by infiltration with fibrous or bony tissue in various types of *myelophthisic anemia.* It is also possible that the distinction between aleukemic and leukemic leukemia is based on different rates of delivery of abnormal cells from the marrow, conceivably, as is suggested by the occasional difficulty in removing such cells by needle

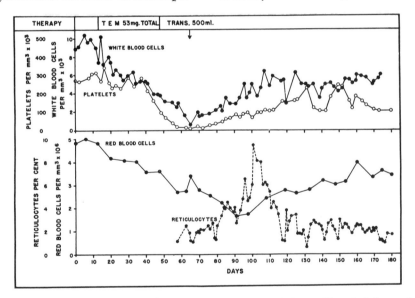

Figure 30–40. Development of pancytopenia in association with triethylenemelamine (TEM) therapy in a 74-year-old woman with papillary adenocarcinoma of the ovary and peritoneal metastases. Because of the repeated accumulation of ascites, the patient was treated with TEM, initially 1 mg., increasing to 2.5 mg. daily from the tenth to the fortieth day. At this time because of nausea, mild anemia, and thrombocytopenia, the medication was discontinued, but during the next 10 days the red cells, white cells and platelets continued to decline and leukopenia and thrombocytopenia became extreme. Thereafter there was a progressive rise in all hematologic values accompanied by a prolonged reticulocyte response reaching a peak only about 50 days after the cessation of TEM therapy, and so indicating its lessening suppressive influence upon erythropoiesis during this time. No agglutinins for white cells or platelets were demonstrated in vitro, but moderate anemia, leukopenia and thrombocytopenia continued and perhaps indicate some degree of irreversible injury to hematopoiesis. No significant changes in the microscopic appearance of the bone marrow were, however, noted before, during or in the recovery period from TEM therapy. (Figure kindly supplied by Dr. Shu Chu Shen.)

puncture, as a result of their unusual adhesiveness in the aleukemic variety. The severe leukopenia of *overwhelming bacterial invasion* may also be the result of intoxication of leukopoiesis. Leukopenia sometimes accompanies the so-called aplastic crises observed in hemolytic anemias, presumably as a result of viral infections sometimes complicated by an induced folic acid deficiency. Recovery is associated with granulocytosis, including immature cells.

Redistribution of leukocytes in the vascular channels results in leukopenia from their mechanical entrainment following the intravenous injection of hydrophilic colloids such as gelatin, or of macroglobulin or fibrinogen. Likewise, leukopenia develops shortly after the intravenous injection of the antigen into a sensitized subject or in any subject in response to the intravenous injection of purified endotoxin (exogenous pyrogen) from typhoid or other gram-negative organisms. In view of the rapidity of white cell release from marrow reserves, this can be at best only a transient phenomenon and is followed within an hour or so by fever due to production of endogenous thermolabile pyrogen, and a leukocytosis reaching its peak some hours later. In experimental animals it can be directly observed that the white cells, particularly the neutrophils, assume a marginal position in the venules in certain internal organs, such as the liver, lung, spleen and omentum. Similar effects are considered to be involved in anaphylactoid shock and in the early stages of the reaction to foreign protein. Injury to granulocytes is thought to be the source of the endogenous pyrogen. White cell counts of blood from the human ear lobe are normally statistically slightly higher than those from venous or fingertip blood and often contain slightly greater percentages of the larger and perhaps "stickier" monocytes or histiocytes. In disease this selective filtering may be marked. For example, five- to tenfold elevations of the leukocyte count in blood from the ear lobe compared to that of the venous blood may be found in patients with subacute bacterial endocarditis. Prominent among the increased numbers of leukocytes are large histiocytes sometimes actively phagocytosing red cells. According to Chatterjea and his associates, the injection of epinephrine caused in normal subjects a transient pancytosis usually maximal by thirty minutes. As the increase in leukocytes involved only mature forms, was no different in splenectomized patients and showed no correlation with the degree of splenomegaly, it did not represent a test of splenic "reservoir" function, but more probably of that of the various vascular beds of the body, including the bone marrow. More recent observations, however, suggest that in congestive splenomegaly the enlarged organ does contain a larger number of mobilizable granulocytes.

Increased loss or destruction of leukocytes is becoming more clearly recognized in the development of the leukopenic state. With repeated saline irrigations of the peritoneal cavity of rabbits or as a result of rapidly repeated phlebotomies, removal of leukocytes and reinfusion of the rest of the blood in dogs, enormous numbers of leukocytes can be removed and within hours leukopenia of the circulating blood will appear. However, owing to the large marrow reserves, backed up by increased granulocyte production from myeloblasts, increased destruction or loss, according to Craddock, in order to be effective in maintaining leukopenia must be a continuous process. In experimental animals the injection of antineutrophilic serum causes a maximal fall of leukocytes within six hours to a level which is maintained for 24 to 28 hours. In such experiments, however, there is no certainty that the leukopoietic cells of the bone marrow are not also affected by the antiserum. Analogous considerations probably apply to patients with chronic or recurrent granulocytopenia whose plasma may induce leukopenia in hematologically compatible recipients and may agglutinate suspensions of their leukocytes in vitro (Fig. 30–41). According to Dausset, the leukopenic effect is due to a thermolabile plasma component, probably a gamma globulin, which he found in the serums of only nineteen of 102 patients with leukopenia. All but one patient had received transfusions, and none had evidence of "collagen disease." On the other hand, Killman found clinical diagnoses of lupus erythematosus, Felty's syndrome, panarteritis nodosa and rheumatoid arthritis in 30 of 71 patients with leukopenia and leukocyte agglutinins of a somewhat different specificity. Fifteen of these 30 patients had never been transfused and eight had neither been transfused nor had been pregnant.

The association of *hepatomegaly* and especially of *splenomegaly* with some instances of chronic leukopenia, sometimes with accompanying thrombocytopenia and anemia, was proposed by Wiseman and Doan as evidence of hypersplenism or increased ability of the spleen to destroy white cells, allegedly by increased phagocytic activity. Certainly the removal of the spleen in these cases often causes a rise in the peripheral white cell count, and the concept, at least of functional hypersplenism secondary to a variety of conditions, is favored by recent observations indicating the selective removal of labeled red cells and platelets by the spleen. Others, however, believe that the spleen effects a suppressive action on the bone marrow, instead of being the graveyard for the leukocytes. Thus, in the rat, Palmer has shown that insertion of a fragment of the spleen into the abdominal wall will prevent the 90 day leukocytosis characteristic of splenectomy alone. However, it can be shown that the splenic fragment undergoes hypertrophy in the new location and resumes the sequestering effect of the normal spleen at least for labeled red cells. For the present a humoral influence of the spleen upon marrow function remains improved; and the possible sequestering effect of accessory splenic tissue cannot be denied. This subject is discussed more fully in Chapter 31.

Systemic lupus erythematosus is often associated with chronic leukopenia, hemolytic anemia and various serologic abnormalities: elevated serum gamma globulin, rheumatoid factor, anti-tissue antibodies and false positive *Wassermann* reactions. Incubated blood samples exhibit a special type of dissolution and depolymerization of nuclear deoxyribonucleic acid of the granulocytes. Subsequently there is attraction to and phagocytosis of the round,

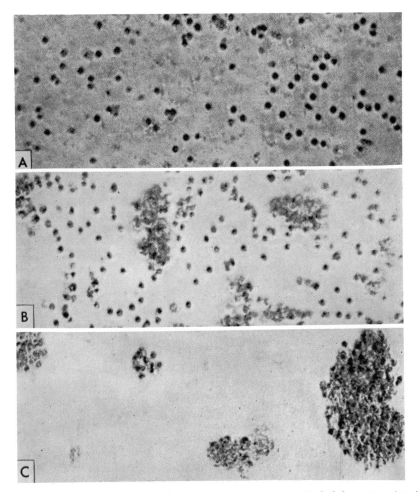

Figure 30–41. Results of leukoagglutination tests: *A,* negative; *B,* slightly positive (1+); and *C,* highly positive (3+). Photomicrographs of mixtures of 0.1 ml. of test serum following heating at 56° C. for 10 to 30 minutes and addition to 0.05 ml. of normal leukocyte suspension derived by sedimentation with PVP from defibrinated bloods of donors with compatible blood groups. Leukoagglutination was consistently present in at least 50 tests with the serums of 19 of 102 patients with leukopenia unassociated with collagen disease. Except for one instance of temporary leukopenia following pyramidon administration, previous transfusions had been given to all 19 patients, who had various hematologic disorders. (From Dausset and others: Blood, 9:696, 1954.)

homogeneous-appearing nuclear masses by other granulocytes. This "LE cell" phenomenon was first observed by Hargraves in 1946 in biopsy specimens of heparinized sternal bone marrow. The primary event in vitro is depolymerization of the polymorphonuclear material with secondary attraction of and phagocytosis by another granulocyte. It is now known that falsely positive serologic reactions may precede the development of systemic lupus by months or years and that the basis of the LE cell phenomenon is an abnormal serum gamma globulin. Indeed, normal human, leukemic human or animal leukocytes react with the lupus serum. Hydralazine therapy may induce such events in patients, and crossing of an inbred strain (NZB) of mice with another (NZW) produces hybrids whose serum will induce LE cell formation. Kurnick has suggested that the abnormal serum factor causes release of normal intracellular deoxyribonuclease from an intracellular inhibitor. Using fluorescein-labeled anti-human-globulin rabbit serum which has been absorbed with rabbit bone marrow, Calabresi has shown nuclear labeling of granulocytes in lupus erythematosus (sometimes before the LE cell test became positive), in rheumatoid arthritis and strongly in Felty's syndrome. Such lupus serum antibodies appear to be directed against either nuclear DNA or a DNA-histone complex.

AGRANULOCYTOSIS

This is perhaps the most striking clinical manifestation of leukopenia. The disorder is characterized by an acute course, fever, necrotic lesions usually in the pharynx, together with leukopenia and pronounced granulocytopenia. The failure of defense against bacteria normally present in such areas as the mouth or rectum may lead to local infection and development of necrosis, generalized infection with chills and fever, and finally overwhelming sepsis with death. There is no significant degree of anemia or thrombocytopenia. In 1934 the etiologic importance of the drug amidopyrine was recognized by Madison and Squier. This relationship has been extended to numerous compounds, including the sulfonamides, antihistamines, antithyroid, anticonvulsant drugs and phenothiazine tranquilizers. Severe leukopenia, due to an adverse drug effect, may develop without the dramatic clinical sequelae of sudden, complete lack of granulocytes and secondary infection. Agranulocytosis as discussed here is restricted to the

rare phenomenon of allergic or metabolic sensitivity to a drug and does not include the leukopenia that can regularly be induced with sufficient amounts of such myelotoxic agents as antifolic or antipurine compounds (Fig. 30–40).

Sensitization occurs in few persons exposed to suitable drugs, apparently as a result of a drug-serum combination acting as an antigen for the development of an antibody. It is not known whether the antibody coats the leukocytes nonspecifically and later reacts with the drug or whether the antibody remains in the serum until the drug causes an antigen-antibody complex to precipitate nonspecifically on the leukocytes. Most of the sensitized subjects tested have shown striking clinical effects, such as headache, malaise, fever and muscular aches, within a few hours. The granulocytes sometimes promptly disappeared from the blood stream, but usually decreased more gradually after an initial rise accompanied by the appearance of immature granulocyte forms, including myelocytes, which lasted several hours or even a few days. The lymphocytes and monocytes were often initially reduced, but then after some days returned to normal or even temporarily to higher values. In the bone marrow the early forms of granulocyte precursors disappeared. In severe and fatal cases the marrow became hypocellular. This has been interpreted as a hypersensitive reaction on the part of the bone marrow affecting the granulocyte precursors with secondary disappearance of the more mature granulocytes in circulation. On the other hand, Moeschlin has shown that the plasma of persons known to be sensitized to amidopyrine and who had received three hours previously 0.3 gm. of the drug possesses leukopenia-producing properties. This was demonstrated by a prompt fall of the white cell count of normal recipients that persisted for three to five hours after the transfusion of 300 ml. of blood from the sensitized donor. In vitro such donor plasma caused agglutination of patients' and of normal granulocytes. This effect disappeared after a few days, when presumably the drug had been excreted. Scratch, patch and intradermal tests with the drug in patients who have recovered from agranulocytosis have been negative in the hands of most workers. However, Dameshek and Colmes found that amidopyrine, after exposure to human serum for several days, produces strongly positive reactions on intradermal injection in susceptible patients and suggested that this is on the basis of a drug-protein linkage. In a few patients, despite most critical questioning, a history of exposure to an offending drug has not been discovered. This is especially true of certain patients with chronic recurrent episodes of granulocytopenia rather than of agranulocytosis.

Other drugs that have caused agranulocytosis, usually but not necessarily through a sensitivity mechanism, are dinitrophenol, the sulfonamide compounds, barbiturates and, more recently, methimazole, chlorpromazine and chloramphenicol. With the sulfonamides, leukopenia, not necessarily associated with complete disappearance of the granulocytes, has been observed to appear gradually after several days of the administration of the drug, possibly as a result of competitive interference with the metabolism of pteroylglutamic acid. However, in the majority of instances severe leukopenia or agranulocytosis following the use of sulfonamides or thiouracil is accompanied by evidences of sensitization such as fever and skin rashes. Persons who once have exhibited sensitization to a given sulfonamide are stated to be more likely to exhibit toxic reactions to that drug when it is readministered at a later time. Finland has observed, however, that only 15 per cent of such patients will not tolerate any other sulfonamide. Sensitization to any one of the three sulfadiazine derivatives almost always extends to the others. That sensitivity to amidopyrine sufficient to cause immediate collapse of the patient may not necessarily be associated with detectable changes in the leukocytic formula was demonstrated in one instance by Strauss.

The seriousness of the condition makes therapeutic observations of a controlled sort difficult. However, there is no doubt that lives have been saved by the use of sulfonamide compounds other than those specifically involved in causing the condition. More recently penicillin or the broadspectrum antibiotics have successfully resisted spread of infection until the patient has had time to recover spontaneously an adequate leukocyte formula. Claims for the beneficial effects of ACTH or cortisone appear to be based more

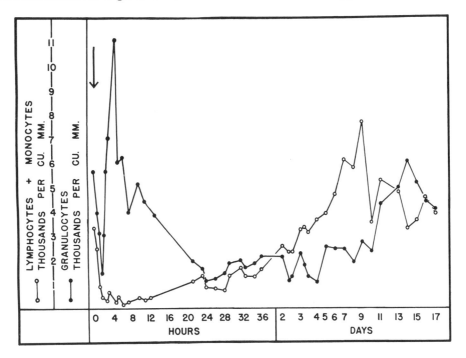

Figure 30–42. Effect of administration of amidopyrine upon leukocyte values of a recovered case of severe agranulocytosis. At the point marked by arrow, the patient was given 0.2 gm. of amidopyrine by mouth. One hour later the patient had a chill and rising temperature which reached 104° F. a few hours later. Note the prompt fall of granulocytes, lymphocytes and monocytes. This was followed by a transitory rise of granulocytes, perhaps due to a response of the marrow reserves to the initial drop in the periphery. However, the level fell to just above 1000 per cubic millimeter at the end of 24 hours. The lymphocyte and monocyte values remained depressed, although slowly rising, until the end of the third day, and thereafter were normal or above. The granulocyte values remained in the vicinity of 2000 until the end of the tenth day, when they returned to normal. (Slightly modified from Plum: Lancet, 1:14, 1935.)

on immediate subjective improvement, sometimes with defervescence, than on prompt reappearance of granulocytes; and the possible therapeutic benefits must be weighed against the known effects of steroid therapy in promoting the dissemination of infection.

LEUKEMIAS AND MALIGNANT LYMPHOMAS

Leukemia and the localized forms of tumors arising from certain cells of the blood-forming organs are potentially fatal conditions characterized by local or widespread overproduction and invasion of the body by neoplastic leukocytes. The close relation between tumor formation and blood stream invasion by young leukocytes in both animals and man renders it improbable that leukemia is fundamentally a condition due to failure of normal removal mechanisms for leukocytes. Such a process, however, may exert a modifying influence upon the height of the circulating leukocyte level. Astaldi has questioned the classic concept that leukemia represents an increased rate of cell proliferation and peripheral delivery. Bierman, by means of leukopheretic observations in man, has concluded that the major defect in acute and chronic granulocytic leukemia is inability of the cells to enter the circulation, thus creating a picture of "maturation arrest" in the hematopoietic tissues. The apparent increase in the rate of cell proliferation in acute leukemia has been shown by Craddock, using H_3 thymidine and P^{32} labeling in vitro and the latter in vivo, to be instead attributable to a lengthening of the individual cell generation time. Thus, there is an enormous, slowly dividing, immature cell population with consequent prolonged survival in the circulation. Craddock, however, points to a difference in chronic leukemias in which a relatively small proportion of immature cells exhibits a growth, mobilization and death cycle of approximately normal duration.

Clinically, leukemias, especially the acute varieties, resemble infections in that fever and intoxication are prominent features. Leukemia-like blood pictures have been observed occasionally in association with various infections, as already described. The literature contains references to many types of bacteria, viruses and parasites cultured from patients with leukemia or malignant lymphoma. The lack of consistency in such reports and the possibility that the various organisms in the blood and other tissues cultured do not necessarily have an etiologic relation to the underlying disease process render this evidence of doubtful significance. The same problem presently complicates the interpretation of reports of viruses visualized in human leukemic tissues by the electron microscope and of pleuropneumonia-like organisms cultured from them. The transition in Hodgkin's disease from granuloma to sarcoma suggests a change from an infection to a neoplastic condition. The clinical course and the histologic studies, especially in those types of leukemia associated with localized processes in lymph nodes and other organs, seem entirely consistent with a neoplastic process. Human leukemia has never been transmitted by transfusion of blood from one patient to another, although obviously such occurrences are few and accidental. Leukemia in the mother is not transmitted to the newborn child, nor does it subsequently develop, although this is a regular occurrence with viral mouse leukemias. Local clusters of children with acute leukemia have been reported in two communities in association with an increased incidence of congenital heart disease, well-known as a sequel of maternal rubella. However, this may be no more than a chance distribution rather than evidence for a common and communicable basis for the two conditions.

Leukemias in animals are probably analogous to the process in man, and a study of these conditions has consequently yielded information of value. According to Furth, the most important characteristic of the leukemic cell is its ability to overcome the forces which restrain the growth of normal immature cells of its kind, so that it invades tissues and organs and ultimately kills its host. The basic change is intrinsic in the cell, since it is maintained in tissue culture and probably involves fundamental enzymatic and metabolic capacities. The best available test for this autonomy of the leukemic cell is its ability to survive and propagate its kind in the body of a susceptible host, as in the transmissible leukemias of mice. Such bioassays made during the preleukemic phase of spontaneous leukemia have disclosed the presence of malignant blood cells unsuspected on histologic examination. The leukemic cell is not simply an excessively immature cell. Thus, although malignant lymphocytes of mice and men grow rapidly in tissue culture, variable survival only is achieved for normal myeloblasts or lymphoid cells in this medium. Greene has been able to grow various human embryonic tissues and neoplasms in the anterior chamber of the rabbit's eye. However, of the various forms of lymphoma tested, only Hodgkin's sarcoma has been successfully propagated in this manner.

The basic change in the leukemic cell may be the result of (1) an alteration of the reproductive material of the cell by somatic mutation, or (2) the presence of a self-perpetuating exogenous factor such as a virus or (3) the presence of an endogenous growth factor multiplying autocatalytically and resulting in abnormal cell differentiation. The difficulty in clearly separating these possibilities is indicated by studies demonstrating that the type conversion factor of the pneumococcus, certain viruses, and the substances in the chromosomes of neurospora that result in mutation after experimental irradiation with ultraviolet light contain specific forms of nucleic acid (DNA). Indeed, perhaps we shall discover that they are merely one and the same. The proof that the neoplastic change is analogous to somatic mutation requires evidence that neoplasia results in modification of the chromosomes (DNA) or of reproductive cytoplasmic particles (RNA). Exclusively present in the myeloid cells of many patients with chronic myelogenous leukemia is a miniscule acrocentric chromosome No. 21, the so-called Ph[1]; and transplantation experiments in mice have provided indirect evidence of a genetic basis for the leukemic alteration in highly inbred stocks. The heterozygosity of the human population and the strong influence of nonleukemic stock apparently serve to mask such genetic tendencies. However, several instances of familial leukemia have been noted, sometimes involving two or three generations. The lymphatic has been more common than the myelogenous, and in identical twins has been noted to develop in about a fifth of the partners of the affected siblings.

Human leukemia patients have been reported to show in the serum or cells particles visible with the electron microscope of the order and magnitude of viruses. Other workers suspect that these are merely granules from disintegrated platelets; and so far no related virus has been cultured, although a pleuropneumonia-like organism has been consistently found in human beings with leukemia—perhaps only as a fellow traveler. In birds, leukemia and sarcoma occur which are readily transmissible by cell-free agents or, on the other hand, only by living cells. In the latter instance the virus can be considered to be a part of the reproductive matter of the normal cell. It is thus only incidental that the virus can be separated from the cell in some neoplastic processes, as, for example, with the milk factor in the transmission of hereditary breast cancer in mice. Indeed, Gross has reported the transmission of mouse leukemia of the lymphocytic type to newborn mice of an insusceptible (C3H) strain which were injected with cell-free filtrates of (AK) strain leukemic organs. After ultracentrifugation such filtrates induced carcinoma of the parotid gland with subsequent metastasis instead of leukemia. Friend was able to initiate a form of myelogenous leukemia in young adult Swiss mice with cell-free filtrates from Ehrlich mouse ascites tumor. Moreover, Gross and also Kaplan induced lymphatic leukemia by means of x-rays in normally low-leukemia strains of mice and were then able to transmit it to unirradiated newborn mice of the same strain by cell-free filtrates. Perhaps for immunologic reasons removal of the thymus delays or inhibits the development of leukemia, whether spontaneous or virus- or radiation-induced. In man the immunologic deficiency associated with thymic dysfunction and agammaglobulinemia relates to an increased susceptibility to malignant lymphoma. In filtrates and in the induced leukemia tumors of mice spherical particles 60 to 100 millimicrons in diameter were observed with the electron microscope. These virus particles replicate not only in leukemic cells but also in apparently normal hematopoietic cells, particularly megakaryocytes. The virus is apparently transmitted vertically through the fetus, but also by the leukemic nursing female mouse through the milk, in which viral particles are numerous. Mouse leukemia has also been induced in hybrid newborn mice by the injection of purified nucleic acid from the lymphoid tissues of a high-leukemia donor strain. In view of such experiments, the etiologic differentiation between a virus and an autocatalytic specific protein of endogenous origin (DNA or RNA), becomes difficult indeed. Consequently, the effects of x-rays and of carcinogens may be regarded as either inducing a chromosomal change or of activating a virus itself capable of taking over the cellular genetic machinery.

Leukemia has been observed to develop in persons exposed to the action of certain *chemicals*, particularly benzol, pyridine and aniline dyes, sometimes after a period of aplastic anemia. Likewise, in mice, leukemia has been produced in about 15 per cent of animals by the injection of benzol and other agents, such as methylcholanthrene, indole and dibenzanthracene. These leukemias are usually of the lymphatic type. Leukemia has been described a number of times in persons exposed chronically to *irradiation*, and the incidence of leukemia in radiologists is eight to ten times as great as in other physicians. A similarly disproportionate increase in terminal, acute myelogenous leukemia has been observed in patients with polycythemia who have received irradiation or P^{32} as compared to those who have not. Likewise, both myelogenous and lymphatic leukemias have been produced in mice by roentgen rays, which are, of course, capable of causing genetic modifications in cells. In general, however, irradiation is a weak agent and acts only after a long latent period. Thus Moloney found that among atomic bomb survivors of a single exposure an increased incidence of leukemia became detectable two years later and was maximal five years after irradiation. The leukemia was chiefly myelogenous, as is the spontaneous leukemia characteristic of the Japanese population. In man leukemia is more common in males than in females, although this may be the result of greater exposure to carcinogenic agents in the occupational than in the domestic environment. Evidence that physical trauma may produce leukemia is unconvincing. In general, coal tar derivatives, sex hormones and radiation produce atrophy of the blood-forming organs, in which leukemia subsequently arises.

The factors which cause focal areas of regeneration to become neoplastic are not understood. Reduction in food intake has an inhibitory effect on the occurrence of spontaneous leukemia, and lack of cystine in the diet is stated to have reduced the incidence of leukemia in mice treated with methylcholanthrene. On the other hand, it is possible that nutritional deficiency may predispose to the development of neoplastic disease or to the modification of the tissue essential to its development. In experimental animals and in man, cirrhosis of the liver and subsequent primary liver cancer are definitely related to diets chronically defective in protein and probably in other nutritional elements. There is, however, no clinical evidence that in man nutritional deficiency predisposes to the development of leukemia.

The resemblance of *leukemoid reactions* to leukemia and the appearance of leukocytosis or lymphocytosis for some time preceding the development of leukemia in man suggest that hyperplastic responses may precede the development of neoplasia of the white cells. More probable, however, is the supposition that the increased white cells in circulation are simply not recognizable as neoplastic or are the result of the nonspecific metabolic effects of an already established leukemic process. Indeed, in chronic monocytic or histiocytic leukemia the peripheral blood sometimes exhibits cells suggestive of an associated nonspecific myeloid response. In man, extreme leukemoid reactions have been produced by certain infections and by necrotic carcinomas. In rabbits with Brown-Pearce carcinomatosis, for example, bone marrow hyperplasia is observed even when the tumors are entirely outside the marrow cavity. These tumors invariably show extensive central necrosis, which is believed to result in the release of nucleic acid and related products into the circulation.

For the most part, *biochemical and histochemical comparisons* of normal and neoplastic leukocytes have not been especially revealing, and may well be more related to different degrees of maturity or of rate of cell growth than specifically to neoplasia. The anaerobic glycolysis of lymph nodes and spleen shows no definite difference between control and leukemic mice. Significant or consistent differences between normal and leukemic cells have not been observed with respect to DNA and RNA, sulfhydryl content, glycogen, oxidative enzymes, dehydrogenases, esterases or beta-glycuronidase. However, according to Wachstein, there are striking differences in nonspecific alkaline phosphatase as determined histochemically. Thus, in patients with infectious diseases, 90 per cent of the neutro-

phils show a positive reaction, as do the cells in leukemoid responses and in myeloid metaplasia and polycythemia vera. On the other hand, few or no mature phosphatase-positive polymorphonuclears are found in myelogenous and other forms of leukemia. Exceptions are not infrequent, but in general there is such clinical correlation and it is in good agreement with the biochemical results of Valentine and his associates. According to Hayhoe continued study of the DNA structure of the leukemic cell is most likely to disclose the essential biochemical difference from the normal, because this complex molecule is presumably responsible for the transfer of the specific abnormality from one generation of leukemic cells to the next. The consistent occurrence of the abnormal autosomal No. 21 chromosome (Ph^1) in chronic myelogenous leukemia has already been mentioned. A variety of anomalies appear in the chromosomes of patients with acute leukemia, each, however, unique and persistent in the individual patient. Recently a specific chromosome anomaly (Ch^1) has been found in the No. 21 chromosome of members of a family exhibiting lymphatic leukemia in siblings. Trisomy of this chromosome is found in mongolism, a condition in which the incidence of leukemia is 20 times that expected. It has been suggested that the No. 21 chromosome may genetically control the alkaline phosphatase level because in trisomy it is high, whereas in chromic myelogenous leukemia, with its dwarf chromosome No. 21 anomaly, it is low.

Clinical Features

The *clinical classification of leukemias and related processes* depends upon (1) the cell type affected, as myelocytes, lymphocytes, monocytes, and so on; (2) the tendency of the process to remain localized to certain organs, to metastasize widely or to invade the blood stream profusely, as sarcoma, aleukemic leukemia or leukemia; (3) the aggressiveness of the process, which is usually correlated with the degree of differentiation of the typical cells and described as acute, subacute or chronic. The origin and relation of the various cell types, though useful in prognosis and treatment, are not considered to be germane to a discussion of the pathologic physiology of leukemias. Table 30–14 presents a possible view of the etiologic relations between apparently dissimilar clinical manifestations of neoplastic processes of various cell types.

Illustrated by extremes, giant follicle lymphoma is in itself essentially a benign process and assumes malignant characteristics only when it becomes converted into Hodgkin's disease, reticulum cell sarcoma or lymphosarcoma. In children acute leukemias may be fatal within a few days of the first symptom. In middle-aged adults chronic myelogenous leukemia may be a slowly progressive disorder, and in even older persons chronic lymphatic leukemia sometimes seems scarcely to alter life expectancy. Lymphoblastic or lymphocytic lymphoma is often manifested clinically as chronic aleukemic lymphatic leukemia or lymphatic leukemia. Gall and Mallory concluded that it is impossible to distinguish the leukemic from nonleukemic conditions by means of lymph node histology. This is well illustrated by the lymphadenopathy that sometimes occurs with prolonged anticonvulsant (Mesantoin) therapy, which under the microscope may show numerous atypical reticulum cells of the type seen in Hodgkin's disease. In mouse leukemias the same strain of leukemic cells may form either localized tumors or widespread systemic disease without localization, depending on whether the cells are inoculated subcutaneously or intravenously. Neoplastic processes of myeloid cells, as perhaps might be expected from their widespread distribution in the bone marrow, are usually manifested as myelogenous leukemia. They sometimes occur, however, as aleukemic myelogenous leukemia and rarely

as myelochloroma in a localized form. Whether a localized tissue form of monocytic leukemia exists is doubtful.

The *effects of leukemias* are both general and local. Early or late, the effects of invasion of the bone marrow make themselves apparent in the peripheral blood. Thus, in the early stages of myelogenous leukemia, polycythemia may appear, to be replaced later by anemia, as has already been discussed under Polycythemia Vera. As the bone marrow becomes progressively replaced by the leukemic infiltration, it seems clear why red cell formation should be disturbed and in some instances crowded out into areas of extramedullary blood formation such as the spleen, liver and lymph nodes. In addition, and especially in certain patients with lymphatic leukemia, lymphosarcoma or Hodgkin's disease, a hemolytic process associated with Coombs-positive red cells and usually with splenomegaly may become the main cause of anemia, as discussed earlier. The secondary effects of anemia on circulatory and renal function have already been covered.

Invasion of the bone marrow by leukemic cells presumably is responsible for the decreased number of platelets in the peripheral blood. Thrombocytopenia appears with onset in acute leukemia and often early in chronic lymphatic leukemia and almost invariably in all types of leukemia when anemia is well established. The secondary effects of the low platelet counts are discussed later under Hem-

TABLE 30–14. CLINICAL MANIFESTATIONS OF LEUKEMIAS AND RELATED CONDITIONS WITH EMPHASIS ON THE ESSENTIAL ETIOLOGIC SIMILARITIES BETWEEN SEEMINGLY DIFFERENT CLINICAL ENTITIES.*

Cell Series	Local Tissue Form	Bone Marrow Involvement Without Prominent Blood Stream Invasion—Subleukemic or Aleukemic Leukemia	Bone Marrow Involvement With Blood Stream Invasion by Typical Leukocytes—Leukemia
Myeloid	Myelochloroma (rare)	+	+
Monocytic	?	+	+
Lymphoid	→Lymphoblastic sarcoma	+	+
	→Lymphocytic sarcoma	+	+
Plasma cell	Plasmacytoma (myeloma)	+	Rare
Stem cell	Stem cell lymphosarcoma	?	0
Histiocytic (clasmatocytic)	Histiocytic sarcoma (reticulum cell sarcoma)	+	Rare
Giant follicle lymphoma	←Giant follicle lymphoma	Very rare	?
Hodgkin's	↳H. lymphoma (granuloma)	+	0
	↓		
	H. sarcoma	+	0

* The presentation is schematic rather than inclusive or accurate in detail. The arrows suggest some recognized histologic transitions.

orrhagic Diseases. The hemorrhagic tendency may be present in many organs and, when it occurs in the central nervous system, is a frequent cause of death. In patients with sudden increases in blast cells and leukocyte counts of over 300,000, such hemorrhages occur around leukemic nodules in the white matter, probably as a result of intravascular stasis of leukemic cells followed by vascular injury, escape of leukemic cells, and subsequent hemorrhage. In contrast to idiopathic thrombocytopenic purpura, spontaneous bleeding often does not appear until the platelets number less than 25,000 per cubic millimeter.

With leukemia the white cell count in the peripheral blood is usually high, with varying proportions of immature and relatively normal-looking cells depending upon the cell type and "acuteness" of the process. In the aleukemic variety the total white cell count may be reduced and the remaining leukocytes may or may not be obviously representative of the cell type of the leukemic process. In acute lymphocytic leukemias the granulocytes may be largely replaced by lymphoblasts, and in myelogenous leukemia most of the cells may be myelocytes or myeloblasts. Despite these disturbances, *secondary infection* due to a decreased number of granulocytes is a relatively rare manifestation of aleukemic leukemia. Using a skin window technique, Stuart Finch has found the exudative response on granulocytes to be delayed and quantitatively deficient, although differential counts were similar to those of normal subjects. No blast forms appeared. The oral sepsis common in acute leukemias, especially the monocytic variety, is encouraged by the mononuclear infiltration and local thrombosis of small vessels in the gingival tissues.

Fever is rare in chronic leukemia unless the anemia is severe or unless an obvious secondary infection is present. In acute leukemia, fever is usually present when the process is active, and at such times secondary infection, such as of the oral cavity, is often found. The intermittent Pel-Ebstein fever of Hodgkin's granuloma is classic. Because it is sometimes associated with enlargement and tenderness of the involved lymph nodes, it is perhaps the result of the necrosis characteristic of these structures. Fundamentally, elevation of temperature is related to reduction in the ability of the patient to dissipate heat. In addition the *basal metabolic rate* and consequently the body's heat production is increased in most cases of chronic myelogenous leukemia and in acute leukemia. In lymphatic leukemia the metabolic rate is not increased until the

disease has become well established, and in aleukemic leukemia the phenomenon is variable. In general, the increased metabolic rate is roughly proportional to the intensity of the leukemic process as measured by the height of the white cell count, the degree of immaturity of the leukocytes and the pulse rate. Because irradiation, which arrests white cell formation in the bone marrow, is usually followed after a transient rise in the metabolic rate by a more or less sustained fall, it is commonly inferred that the increased metabolic rate in leukemia is due to the increased oxygen consumption of the many immature leukocytes. Unlike the situation in hyperthyroidism, normal or low values for protein-bound iodine in the blood (thyroid hormone) are usually found, the radioiodine uptake is not increased and total thyroidectomy does not reduce the basal metabolic rate to as low a level as in myxedema.

The *increased metabolic activities of the white cells* in leukemia are presumably reflected in certain chemical findings. Thus the nonprotein nitrogen and uric acid of the blood are increased, and the endogenous uric acid elimination is greater than normal, and can be dangerously increased by leukocyte-destroying therapy. Perhaps as a result of disturbances in food intake, the nitrogen balance is variable in chronic leukemia and usually negative in acute leukemia. The total plasma proteins are decreased, especially in myelogenous leukemia, and the albumin-globulin ratio may be reversed. However, because of an increased binding capacity of the transport protein, the serum vitamin B_{12} level may be greatly elevated. In lymphatic leukemia abnormal globulins may be produced and coat the red cells resulting in Coombs-positive hemolytic anemia; late in the disease antibody production may be seriously impaired, whereas in Hodgkin's disease cutaneous anergy to tuberculin and other antigens is an early development.

The classic example of *dysproteinemia* due to aberrant protein synthesis by clones of neoplastic cells widely scattered in bone marrow and parenchymatous tissues is found in multiple myeloma (plasmacytoma). Hyperproteinemia, sometimes of extreme degree, is due to increase of various abnormal plasma globulins of which the first indication may be an elevated sedimentation rate. The globulin abnormality is highly consistent for a given patient. The increased amount and striking homogeneity of the anomalous protein causes a sharp peak to appear upon electrophoretic analysis, that may range in mobility from slower than gamma to (less commonly) as fast as beta globulin. Except for homogeneity these so-called myeloma "M" proteins resemble the *normal serum globulins* which include the bulk of the antibodies (immunoglobulins) and are designated: γG, γA and γM. The normal serum levels of these globulins are 1.24, 0.39, and 0.12 grams per cent, respectively. A typical γG globulin sediments in the ultracentrifuge as 7S and has a molecular weight of about 150,000, being composed of two light polypeptide chains (mw 22,000) and two heavy polypeptide, carbohydrate-containing chains (mw 55,000) held together by disulfide bonds (Fig. 30–43). The character of the heavy chains determines whether the antibody is γG, γA or γM. Its antigenic specificity depends primarily upon the heavy chains, each of which, with the help of the adjacent light chain, forms an antigen-binding site at an opposite end of the 240 × 57 angstrom-sized molecule. The γA (β₂A) globulins sediment at from 6.5 to 13S. The γM globulins (19S) have a molecular weight of about a million and can be dissociated by reduction of S-S bonds into 7S components. The light chains are common to all three classes of antibodies, but are of two species (Type I and Type II) in different molecules, normally produced separately by different plasma cells. Thus, depending on the composition of three heavy and two light chains, normal gamma globulin can be of six different varieties according to genetic directions given to plasma cells.

The myeloma globulins represent a highly homogeneous overproduction of one (rarely two) molecules closely resembling γG or γA globulins. However, only one type of light chain (I or II) is present, presumably because a neoplastic clone of myeloma cells has largely taken over production. In many patients with myeloma Bence Jones proteins are also synthesized and appear in the serum, but being of small molecular size, rapidly pass unaltered into the urine. These small proteins consist of light chains only which correspond in type (I or II) to those of the myeloma globulin of the same patient. Bence Jones protein was originally detected in the urine of patients with myeloma because of its anomalous precipitation on heating to about 55° C. Instead of remaining insoluble at 100° C., it begins to dissolve as that temperature is approached.

Lawson has shown that even large increases in myeloma gamma globulin may have little or no functional capacity as antibodies. Indeed, the serum of patients with multiple myeloma may progressively decline in its titers of the antibodies normally present, and even of complement, to the vanishing point. According to Zinneman, such patients may demonstrate poor capacity to form antibodies in response to pneumococcus and brucella polysaccharide test antigens; and this, together with loss of opsonic activity for phagocytosis, probably explains the frequency of bacterial infections commonly due to the pneumococcus.

Additional secondary effects of dysproteinemia are the frequent damage to renal tubules and later glomeruli as well as the occasional primary type of amyloidosis, both perhaps due to the capillary-penetrating ability of Bence Jones protein. Moreover, when the plasma protein is high, the serum calcium is usually increased, partly as a result of the increased amount of calcium bound to the protein. Hypercalcemia is also partly responsible for eventual renal failure. The neoplastic properties of multiple myeloma cells either produce diffuse decalcification of the skeleton or the characteristic osteolytic lesions of skull, spine and other bones which cause pain and may lead to pathologic fracture. In Table 30–15 are shown the various abnormal serum globulins found by Osserman in a series of 400 patients, mostly associated with plasmacytoma or lymphocytoma. There is a striking correlation between the incidence of

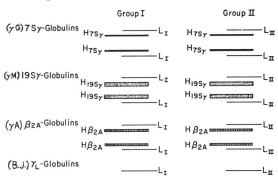

Figure 30–43. Schematic representation of four classes of immunoglobulins. Each of the three pairs of H (heavy) chains is different. They are held together as well as tied to two of one or the other of the two types of L (light) chains by S-S bonds. Bence Jones (B. J.) globulins are individual L chains of one type or the other. In the gammopathies classified in Table 30–15, one or another of the abnormal proteins becomes increased. The abnormal molecular species is highly homogeneous, and the same type of L chain is found in Bence Jones protein, if present. (Slightly modified from Mannik and Kunkel in Samter and Alexander: Immunological Diseases. Boston, Little, Brown & Co., 1965.)

TABLE 30–15. DIAGNOSTIC CLASSIFICATION
AND GAMMOPATHIES IN 400 PATIENTS
(1953–1963).*

	Number of Cases
Multiple myeloma	
Gamma G	97
Gamma G + Bence Jones	45 (6)
Gamma A	41
Gamma A + Bence Jones	17 (23)
Bence Jones protein only	59 (1)
No abnormality	3
Heavy chain (Franklin's) disease	
Heavy chain of gamma G	3
Waldenström's macroglobulinemia	
Gamma M	41 [1]
Lymphoma with "monoclonal gammopathy"	
Gamma G	23
"Monoclonal gammopathy" without neoplasm	
Gamma G	32
Gamma A	7
Gamma M	1
"Monoclonal gammopathy" with neoplasm	
Gamma G (rectosigmoid, prostate, breast, oropharynx, etc.	28
Gamma A	1
Gamma M	2

Numbers in parentheses indicate number of cases
with "primary" paramyloid; number in brackets indicates case with "secondary" paramyloid.

* Modified from table by Osserman and Takatsuki: Medicine, *42:*357, 1963.

Bence Jones protein and primary amyloidosis.
Other workers have noted some degree of
correlation between γA globulin and nonosseous plasmacytomas. Abnormal globulins are
in some instances associated with adenocarcinoma of breast or bowel, found to be heavily
infiltrated and surrounded by plasma cells.
Five reported patients, mainly with spleen
and lymph node enlargement, have been
found to have an abnormal serum globulin
composed of heavy polypeptide chains only.
Finally, in elderly patients abnormal serum
globulins may be present for years before (or
without) the appearance of myeloma.

Waldenström's *macroglobulinemia* is characterized by marked increase in viscosity
of the plasma due to increased amounts of
γM-like globulin of a molecular weight of
about one million. Like multiple myeloma,
macroglobulinemia is an instance of anomalous plasma protein formation by diffusely
scattered potentially neoplastic cells resembling lymphocytes or lymphoid plasma cells
and often exhibiting pyronine (mucopolysaccharide) staining. Macroglobulins normally
represent about 7 per cent of the serum

immunoglobulins and include the well-known
polysaccharide-containing isohemagglutinins.
Pathologic macroglobulins, with a sedimentation constant of 12 to 19S (Svedberg) units
in the ultracentrifuge, are polymers and can
be dissociated in vivo and in vitro into 6.5S
unit monomers of much less viscosity by
antisulfhydril agents such as penicillamine.
Normal serum, containing about 0.12 gram
per cent of γM globulin, has a viscosity relative to water of from 1.4 to 1.8. Because of
the high axial length-to-width ratio of this
globulin, an increase markedly affects the
serum viscosity, especially when the concentration reaches more than 3 grams per
cent. According to Fahey, at 5 grams per
cent the serum viscosity may be from 10 to
12 times that of water, and plasmapheresis
with consequent reduction of viscosity abolishes such symptoms as headache, vertigo,
postural hypotension or even cardiac failure
(Fig. 30–44). Spontaneous crystallization of
protein in the blood plasma may be noted
on cooling (cryoglobulins), and precipitates
may occur when the serum is heated to 60°
C. (pyroglobulins). Cryoglobulins are sometimes associated with Raynaud's phenomenon,
purpura and skin necroses of the extremities.
The hemorrhagic tendency associated with
macroglobulins is in part due to interference
by the abnormal proteins with platelet function or with various stages of the coagulation
process. Unlike multiple myeloma, bone and
renal lesions are very rare and hepatosplenomegaly and lymphadenopathy are frequent.
Anemia with marked rouleaux formation of
the red cells, leukopenia and thrombocytopenia are common findings.

Local enlargement of the lymphatic structures in lymphatic leukemia, and especially
in the malignant lymphomas, may lead to
various untoward results. Enlargement of the
tonsils, of peripheral lymph nodes and of the
spleen, unless of massive proportions, is usually
unimportant. A large spleen may cause weight
loss by reducing the reservoir capacity of the
stomach for food, and may sequester red
cells and platelets. The filtering action of the
spleen and lymph nodes on leukocytes is
suggested by the occasional rapid enlargement of the liver and peripheral nodes in
chronic lymphatic leukemia after splenectomy for secondary acquired hemolytic anemia. If the marrow is experimentally depleted
of granulocytes by leukopheresis, lymphocytes move in. If the venous circulation is
disturbed by lymph node enlargement, edema
may develop, especially in the lower extrem-

ities. In such patients enlarged retroperitoneal lymph nodes and distended lymphatics are clearly visible by the recently developed radiologic technique of lymphangiography with radiopaque material. Lymph node enlargement in the thorax, however, may be the cause of tracheal obstruction and hence of asphyxia, especially because the incautious administration of roentgen ray causes further temporary increase in lymph node volume. Pressure of enlarged lymph nodes upon the renal veins leads to albuminuria and disturbances of renal function. Pressure on the mesenteric veins or lymphatics may interfere with absorption from the intestinal tract, and rarely pressure on the common bile duct or its main divisions may cause obstructive jaundice.

Leukemic infiltration rather than gross tumors may result in dysfunction of various organs. Thus in all types of acute leukemia, and especially in monocytic leukemia, hypertrophy and necrosis of the gums and oral mucosa with secondary infection may accompany the invasion of the tissues and thrombosis of the local blood vessels supplying them. Rapid loosening of the teeth results from the early necrosis of dental periosteum. Lesions of the skin are found in all types of leukemia, but are most common in the chronic lymphatic, monocytic and his-tiocytic varieties, perhaps because of the large size or greater "stickiness" of their characteristic cells, referred to earlier. Various skin lesions are found in lymphosarcoma and in Hodgkin's disease in which infiltration occurs. True leukemic invasion results in local reddening or thickening of the skin, rarely in ulceration. In other instances a generalized erythematous or exfoliative process may appear. The local release of histamine by dermal mast cell tumors in urticaria pigmentosa has already been mentioned. Bleeding into the skin is the result of thrombocytopenia. Herpes zoster has been reported in several instances, mostly in lymphatic leukemia. In some patients the lesions have been attributed to involvement of the posterior nerve roots and have been followed by nerve palsies. In others a generalized vesicular eruption has raised the question of chickenpox or disseminated herpes zoster. Leukemic infiltration of various parts of the gastrointestinal tract or enlargement of abdominal lymph nodes may lead to gastrointestinal symptoms, such as pain, colic, intestinal obstruction or malabsorption. The liver is often enlarged as a result of leukemic infiltration, but jaundice or other evidences of liver dysfunction are rare, as is ascites. Chylous ascites or chylothorax is said to occur with lymphomas because of obstruction or rupture of the

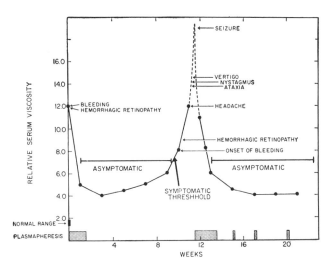

Figure 30–44. Correlation of clinical findings and serum viscosity in a patient with macroglobulinemia. With low serum macroglobulin levels a small increase in macroglobulin (from 1 to 2 gm./100 ml.) causes only a small increase in serum viscosity, whereas a similar increase (from 4 to 5 gm./100 ml.) results in a marked increase in viscosity of the serum. These effects would be correspondingly greater in whole blood where red cells and fibrinogen add substantially to the absolute viscosities observed. Note the effect of repeated plasmapheresis in lowering the serum viscosity and causing an abatement of symptoms. (From Fahey, Barth, and Solomon: J.A.M.A., 192:464, 1965.)

thoracic duct below or above the diaphragm, respectively.

Lesions of the bones demonstrable by roentgen ray are much more frequent in children than in adults, owing to the presence of active marrow in the peripheral bones and the nonunion of their epiphyses. Various forms of infiltration lead to the widening of epiphyses, periosteal elevation, fractures and areas of destruction or absorption of bone. Such abnormalities are visible in x-rays and may give rise to pain seemingly referable to joints. In the adult, bone lesions are restricted to the areas occupied by the active cellular marrow and are most common in multiple myeloma. Invasion of the bones, in acute leukemia, and sometimes in chronic myelogenous leukemia because of extensive marrow hyperplasia, may lead to spontaneous bone tenderness or pain when pressure is applied over such a bone as the sternum. The pain in normal subjects produced by suction with a syringe during needle biopsies of the sternum suggests that in leukemia the cell growth within the marrow cavity may cause pain because of an increase of pressure, which has now been measured in leukemias by Petrakis and found to be highest in the acute types. Bone infarction occurs in acute lymphatic leukemia only when the marrow is packed with cells. Difficulty in aspiration of cells from such marrows is associated with reticulin fibrosis.

Besides infiltration of the nervous system, there the manifestations of leukemia may take the form of tumor-like growths, of hemorrhage or thrombosis. Clinical evidence of neurologic complications may be found in as many as 20 per cent of patients. Intracranial lesions such as hemorrhage or meningeal or brain tissue invasion are common. Less frequent are infiltrations of the spinal cord or meninges, and involvement of the spinal extradural or peripheral nerves. Spinal fluid pressure may be increased, or there may be increased cells and protein in accordance with the nature of the lesions. Myeloma and Hodgkin's disease do not directly invade the central nervous system, but produce neurologic lesions by extension from adjacent structures or by destruction of vertebrae with subsequent collapse.

Treatment

The objectives of the treatment of leukemia and lymphomas can best be understood in terms of the pathologic physiology of the disease. Therapeutic agents, whether acting locally or generally, depend for their effectiveness upon the selective suppression or destruction of neoplastic leukocytes, whether invading the bone marrow, the spleen, the lymph nodes or other tissues or organs. Table 30–16 presents a summary of the kind and nature of the principal agents available. In Figure 30–45 are illustrated differential susceptibilities between various normal and abnormal cell types to several kinds of antileukemic agents. It should be noted that the therapeutic differential is only partial.

What little is known of the intimate nature of the action of *irradiation* has been described earlier under anemias due to physical injury. It damages cells to which the energy is delivered, including those of the neoplastic process. There is thus no inherent advantage in supervoltage over other methods such as rotational filtered x-ray therapy with less penetration as long as the energy is absorbed by the neoplastic cells and not too extensively by the normal proximal structures such as the skin. It is not certain that young cells are more susceptible to injury than are old cells. They are perhaps only apparently so because of their more rapid rate of development and of multiplication. As leukemias are diffuse processes, usually involving the entire active bone marrow, all of this organ should receive irradiation, but not necessarily at one time. A theoretical advantage of local exposure over "spray" irradiation is the beneficial effect upon marrow recovery of the "shielding" inherent in the former method. Pertinent experiments with irradiated animals are referred to under the Anemias of Physical Injury. Destruction of leukemic cells in the bone marrow will usually diminish the abnormality of the peripheral white cell count and may also provide more space for the production of red cells and platelets. Because, however, the biologic effect of irradiation cannot always be accurately anticipated in advance, the interval between irradiation exposures should be sufficiently long, a matter of several days, in order to allow the effect of one exposure to become manifest before another is given. In practice, with acute processes this is not always possible or even desirable. When the disabling effect of the disease process is limited to bone, lymph nodes or spleen, and when, in the absence of anemia, it may be assumed that the bone marrow is not extensively invaded, the local use of roentgen ray can be extremely useful. Because of continuous "colonization" by cells conveyed to distant sites by the blood, local irradiation, for example, of the spleen, may affect distal marrow; and even extracorporeal irradiation of blood may be therapeutically effective.

Immediately after irradiation in leukemias the usually elevated basal metabolic rate is promptly raised to a higher level and then declines toward normal over a period of several days. This initial effect is accompanied by the development of a negative nitrogen balance, which in turn gradually becomes normal and is followed by a period of positive nitrogen balance. The pathologic physiology of irradiation sickness depends upon the amount of irradiation given, the amount of tissue affected, the part of the body irradiated, as well as to some extent upon the general and psychologic condition of the patient. Experimental and clinical data suggest that direct injury to the intestinal mucosa is importantly concerned and that cell injury, after a latent period of a few hours, releases proteins and their breakdown products into the circulation. Together, these may explain the usual nausea, vomiting, leukocytosis, malaise and fever. However, observations by Thomas and others have shown that, provided the dosage rate is sufficiently slow, ordinarily lethal doses of total body irradiation of from 800 to 1200 r can be given over a period of 24 hours without undue discomfort. As previously in experimental animals, these dosages were applied in efforts to destroy all the leukemic cells as well as those "immunologically competent" to inhibit

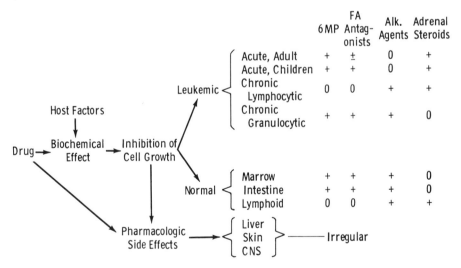

Figure 30–45. Differences in susceptibility of various cell types to a given agent are represented. To 6-mercaptopurine (6-MP) cells of normal marrow and intestine in chronic granulocytic leukemia are regularly susceptible, stem cells in children with acute leukemia are frequently susceptible, morphologically similar stem cells in adults with acute leukemia are infrequently susceptible and chronic lymphatic leukemia is not susceptible. It is apparent that in relation to 6-MP, the folic acid antagonists and alkylating agents, there is a uniformity of response of normal marrow and intestinal epithelium which is closely paralleled by the response of chronic granulocyte leukemia but not by other leukemic cells. The susceptibility to adrenal steroids follows a different pattern, chronic granulocytic leukemia again responding in a manner similar to that of normal tissues. (From Krakoff: Am. J. Med., 28:735, 1960.)

subsequently transfused bone marrow elements from normal subjects. Except possibly in the instance of identical twins, one of whom had acute leukemia, this method has so far been, despite its great theoretical interest, of no long term value. At best the marrow of the twin only temporarily repopulates the marrow of the recipient, and later the leukemic process reappears. In blood dyscrasias such as Hodgkin's disease with perhaps areas of uninvolved marrow, low temperature storage of samples of the patient's marrow prior to heavy irradiation has been of help in tiding the patient over a temporary period of marrow depression. The use of fetal marrow should theoretically obviate the graft-versus-host reaction of marrow transplants from unrelated subjects, but has failed to do so in practice.

Radioactive phosphorus, P³², differs from ordinary phosphorus only in that it is an unstable isotope with a half-life of 14.3 days as a source of beta particles with a penetrating distance for tissue averaging 2 mm. It has a theoretical advantage over external irradiation in that, when administered, it is selectively withdrawn from the blood by those cells which are multiplying fastest. Consequently, relatively high concentrations of radioactivity are reached in those organs principally involved in the leukemias and lymphomas—bone marrow, lymph nodes, spleen and liver. Nevertheless, in these organs other cells, including normal cells, are also irradiated. In the bone marrow in leukemia, for example, sufficient radioactive phosphorus to destroy leukemic cells has an injurious effect on erythroid and megakaryocytic cells as well. Radioactive phosphorus treatment has not been shown to be definitely superior to irradiation by roentgen ray except in the matter of convenience, in any of the leukemias. Both are useful palliative agents in chronic leukemias, especially the myelogenous, and both are usually said to fail to be beneficial in the acute leukemias.

The so-called *nitrogen mustards,* especially bis-beta-chloroethylmethylamine hydrochloride (HN₂), dichloroethyl aminophenyl butyric acid (chlorambucil) and the polyethyleneamine, triethylenemelamine (TEM), have received extensive study. More recently other nitrogen mustards such as cyclophosphamide and a phenylalanine derivative (melphalen) have been employed. Experimentally, these highly active alkylating agents for biological substances, like roentgen rays, can produce

inheritable chromosomal abnormalities in fruit flies without effect on other cellular entities. Cell mitosis is inhibited in the resting phase of the mitotic cycle, possibly as the result of inactivation of essential cellular enzymes, the phosphokinases. Clinically, depending on dosage and patient susceptibility, lymphopenia and, later, leukopenia may be moderate or severe within ten days and may last as long as a month. Normocytic anemia and, occasionally, bleeding tendencies due to thrombocytopenia may occur. In instances of nonlymphoid tumors, this injury to the hematopoietic organs exceeds the effect on the tumor (Fig. 30–40). In suppressing abnormal cell proliferation in Hodgkin's disease, in multiple myeloma, in macroglobulinemia and in lymphatic leukemia and lymphosarcoma, the nitrogen mustards appear to be distinctly useful, sometimes after roentgen ray therapy has ceased to be beneficial. In diffuse visceral disease or in patients with fever and "intoxication," great improvement may promptly appear and persist for a time.

Arsenic in the form of Fowler's solution was formerly used in the treatment of chronic myelogenous leukemia with somewhat useful results. Its action may be ascribed to the arrest of mitosis, which in turn may depend on the affinity of arsenic for sulfhydryl groupings. Recently another alkylating agent, 1:4 dimethane sulfonyloxybutane (*busulfan* or *Myleran*), has been used in chronic myelogenous leukemia with therapeutic results resembling those of roentgen rays. In contrast to the effects of the nitrogen mustards, cells of the lymphoid germinal tissue and of the intestinal tract are, fortunately, not much affected by busulfan. *Ethyl carbamate* (urethan), a mitotic poison, is effective in chronic myelogenous leukemia and, to some extent, in lymphatic leukemia. However, its special asset is its ability to produce rather striking improvement in symptoms, x-ray appearances of bone lesions and levels of the anomalous serum proteins in certain cases of multiple myeloma. At present phenylalanine mustard is regarded as superior. In acute leukemias, especially of children, *chemical analogs of pteroylglutamic acid,* such as 4-amino-pteroylglutamic acid (Aminopterin), and 4-amino-N¹⁰-methylpteroylglutamic acid (Amethopterin), appear to be able to reduce greatly the abnormal cells in the bone marrow. Although clinical remissions have followed, toxic effects resembling those of pteroylglutamic acid deficiency in animals are frequently observed because these agents interfere with the normal reduction of folic acid to its metabolically active tetrahydro forms (see page 812). Eventually the synthesis of nucleoproteins is inhibited, and so cell division is delayed. Another substance useful in acute leukemias is 6-mercaptopurine (Fig. 30–46), which is an antagonist, at least in bacteria, of purine metabolism. Other purine antagonists such as 6-thioguanine and azathiopurine have no practical advantage in leukemia, but the latter has found a clinical use in suppressing rejection responses in kidney transplantation. Pyrimidine analogs such as fluorouracil and fluorodeoxyuridine are sometimes useful in the palliation of breast cancer, but despite a strongly leukopenic and myelosuppressive effect are not beneficial in leukemia.

Demecolcin, an alkaloid from the common plant "meadow rue," is a mitotic poison long used experimentally but of limited value clinically. Recently two alkaloids from the plant "periwinkle," vinblastine and vincristine, have been idiopathically efficacious in acute leukemias. ACTH and cortisone are useful for their lympholytic effects and because they increase capillary resistance and may elevate platelet levels, as well as for their anti-inflammatory and euphoria-producing qualities. Androgen therapy, when given for periods of over two months in large dosage, can nonspecifically stimulate erythropoiesis in myeloid

metaplasia and in some cases of chronic myelogenous and lymphatic leukemias as well as in multiple myeloma.

On the whole, it does not seem likely that the presently available chemotherapeutic agents, the effectiveness of which depends on their action on fundamental metabolic processes common to many types of cells, are sufficiently selective to be especially promising. However, the optimists point to the remarkable remissions produced by amethopterin in women with choriocarcinoma (but not in the teratoma in men). Nevertheless, because this tumor arises in women from trophoblast tissue, it resembles a nonindigenous transplantable tumor. In experimental animals, a much greater rate of incorporation of the purine analog, 8-azaguanine, into tumor than into normal tissues has been observed; and in experimental leukemias in mice 8-azaguanine is found in the ribonucleic acid of leukemic cells sensitive to this agent in 100 times greater concentration than in strains of cells dependent on the presence of the agent for growth. Just as with antibacterial chemotherapy, in animal as well as in human leukemias the failure of control by chemotherapeutic agents is in part due to the development of "resistance" by genetic mutations, enzyme adaptation or otherwise. Other strains of cells develop dependence for growth upon these substances. The probability of the occurrence of a single

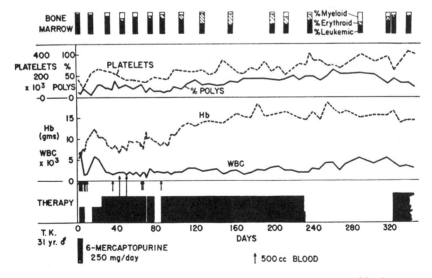

Figure 30–46. Effect of therapy with 6-mercaptopurine in a 31-year-old white man with acute lymphatic leukemia. Although the leukemic cells and lymphocytes in the patient's bone marrow never reached a level of less than 40 per cent, the hemoglobin, platelets and percentage of polymorphonuclear leukocytes in the peripheral blood returned to normal levels, and the patient appeared to be in perfect health for 9 months. Thereafter his disease became resistant to therapy. (From Burchenal and others: Am. J. Med. Sc., 228:371, 1954.)

mutation that will result in simultaneous resistance to two drugs is far less than the probability of such an event's occurring with respect to either drug alone. It is thus possible that the combined use of antitumor chemotherapeutic agents in man will more successfully prevent development of resistance than has so far been possible with one agent alone. In transplantable acute lymphocytic leukemia of the mouse both resistant and dependent mutant strains that have developed through exposure to antipurines show a striking increase in sensitivity to antifolic agents. On the other hand, cells that have become resistant to or dependent on antifolics are not more sensitive to purine analogs. Recent observations of the effects of virus infections in prolonging the life of leukemic mice perhaps also imply antagonistic effects against the specific reproductive material of the leukemic cell.

The inherent character of the disease process in the particular patient is still the most important single factor in determining the success of therapy. In general, too much attention is paid in the evaluation of therapeutic agents for leukemia to their effect in lowering the white cell count in the peripheral blood. Admittedly, especially in chronic myelogenous leukemia, this is a useful therapeutic index. Drug-induced granulocytopenia invites bacterial infection, which can be combated with antibiotics. Unfortunately the absence of bacteria then leaves the field ready for seeding by yeasts and fungi. Besides infection, the development of severe anemia or thrombocytopenia with consequent hemorrhage is the feature of the disease most likely to cause morbidity and death. Consequently, in estimating the responsiveness of the disease, the more important physiologic concern is whether, in addition to suppression of abnormal leukocytic formation, a rise in circulating hemoglobin and in platelet values will occur. Otherwise resort must be had to transfusion in order to elevate artificially the hemoglobin values and to concentrated infusions of platelets in order to prevent hemorrhage by temporary provision of platelets. Transfusions of leukocytes from normal bone marrow or even blood of patients with chronic myelogenous leukemia have been reported to provide all too brief a respite from granulocytopenia.

Hemorrhagic Disorders

Hemorrhagic disorders constitute a variety of hereditary and acquired defects of hemo-

stasis, ranging in severity from dangerous and disabling to mere cosmetic annoyance. Their clinical manifestations appear when the blood escapes from the vessels. This may occur "spontaneously" or as a result of trauma ordinarily inadequate to produce such a result in a normal person. The complex of integrated mechanisms that would normally have prevented or limited such bleeding by promoting hemostasis can be outlined by an experimental illustration. If a small arteriole is ruptured with a fine needle, blood escapes into the surrounding tissue for only a few seconds. In that short interval, however, several chemical and physical agencies have cooperated to cause cessation of the bleeding. First the flow of blood in the vessel itself is diminished, probably by local contraction of its smooth muscle. This is first effected by axonic reflexes, later by the blood platelets that become adherent to the edges of the vascular wound and at once partially close the orifice. This retardation of the flow of escaping blood permits material exuded by the damaged tissues and to some extent by the platelets to initiate the formation of a clot which, if the platelets have not already done so, completely seals the wound. Then the autocatalytic nature of the intermediate stages of the coagulation process rapidly reinforces the barrier with fibrin clot. Finally, activated by the adherent platelets, a contraction of the fibrin strands of this clot helps to approximate the edges of the wound. The extravasated blood outside the vessel wall also clots, either under the stimulus of substances formed by the initial clotting process or because of thromboplastic substances present in the injured tissues.

In the skin the small hemorrhage just described appears to the unaided eye as a small red spot, or petechia. The reddish color may deepen within a few minutes to purple or blue as the reduction of the oxyhemoglobin of the extravasated erythrocytes takes place. Within 24 to 48 hours a yellowish or greenish hue at the periphery of larger extravasations of blood indicates the conversion of hemoglobin to bilirubin by tissue phagocytes. In a few days only careful inspection will show a brownish discoloration due to the iron-staining pigment left behind in the tissues. Depending on its size and location, the hemorrhage may obviously produce either trivial or important systemic and local effects on the circulation or on the function of adjacent structures such as airways or nerves.

In all hemorrhagic diseases a lesion of the vascular wall due to inherent defect or pro-

TABLE 30–17. CLASSIFICATION OF HEMOR-
RHAGIC DISEASES

I. Vascular purpura
  A. Congenital
    1. Hereditary telangiectasia
    2. Hereditary vascular defect?: von Wille-
       brand's disease
  B. Inelastic tissues
    1. Senile purpura
    2. Cushing's syndrome, Ehlers-Danlos syn-
       drome
  C. Infections
    1. Toxic: hemorrhagic scarlet fever, measles
    2. Embolic: septicemias, e.g., meningococcus,
       typhoid, endocarditis
  D. Nutritional
    1. Vitamin C deficiency
  E. Metabolic
    1. Diabetes mellitus
    2. Arteriosclerosis
  F. Allergic
    1. Schoenlein-Henoch purpura
    2. Drugs, focal infections
    3. Serum sickness
II. Platelet defects
  A. Primary
    1. Thrombocytopenia: "idiopathic" numerical
       defect
    2. Thrombocytoasthenia: "Spreading defect"
       (Glanzmann's disease)
    3. Thrombocytopathy: phospholipid defect
    4. Thrombocythemia: myeloproliferative dis-
       orders, carcinoma
  B. Secondary to:
    1. Myelophthisis: aplastic anemia, leukemia,
       myelofibrosis
    2. Immunization: transfusion, pregnancy, lupus
       erythematosus, drugs
    3. Vasculitis: thrombohemolytic thrombocyto-
       penic purpura, purpura fulminans
    4. Splenomegaly: congestive splenomegaly,
       lymphoma, Gaucher's disease
III. Coagulation defects
  A. Prothrombinase formation
    1. Hereditary: individual factors V, VII, VIII,
       IX, X or XI
    2. Acquired: vitamin K deficiency, Factors VII,
       IX, and X (and prothrombin), hemophilia
       neonatorum, steatorrhea
      a. Dicumarol therapy, Factors VII, IX and
         X (and prothrombin)
      b. Liver disease, Factors V, VII, IX, and
         X (and prothrombin)
  B. Thrombin formation
    1. Hereditary: prothrombin
    2. Acquired: prothrombin (and Factors VII,
       IX and X) (see A.2 above)
  C. Fibrinogen formation
    1. Hereditary: fibrinogenopenia, fibrin stabiliz-
       ing factor, fibrinogen (Baltimore)
    2. Acquired: severe liver failure, congestive
       heart failure
  D. Fibrinolysis
    1. Primary: lung surgery, shock, prostatic cancer
    2. Secondary to intravascular coagulation,
       snake venom

E. Consumption coagulopathies
  1. Amniotic fluid embolism, renal cortical
     necrosis, purpura fulminans
F. Circulating anticoagulants
  1. Anti-Factors: V, VIII, IX or XI
  2. Antithrombins: fibrinogen degradation prod-
     ucts, macroglobulins,
     heparin therapy

duced by external violence is involved. Thus in the so-called *purpuras* defective function of the system of defense against bleeding, involving vessel wall or blood platelets or both, is chiefly concerned. The hemorrhagic lesions are widely scattered and on the whole do not involve much extravasation at any one point unless significant trauma has occurred, but with platelet defects oozing of blood from around teeth or the gastrointestinal tract may be prolonged or occur in a vital area, such as the central nervous system. To ordinary clinical tests the clotting of the blood appears to be normal, although with sufficiently decreased platelet levels this is not the case when prothrombin consumption is critically evaluated. In *coagulation defects*, exemplified by such conditions as hemophilia and hypoprothrombinemia, profuse bleeding or large extravasations of blood occur locally, usually as a result of obvious trauma or injury to relatively large vessels. Here delay in the formation of the clot fails to back up the normal action of the platelets in checking the flow of blood from the wound. Tocantins has defined three groups of factors that are normally involved in *hemostasis*, defects of which are consequently concerned in the manifestations of hemorrhagic disease: (1) extravascular factors, (2) vascular factors and (3) intravascular factors, including platelets and the coagulation mechanism of the blood itself. Table 30–17 presents a classification of the various forms of hemorrhagic disease.

EXTRAVASCULAR FACTORS

The elasticity of the tissues surrounding the blood vessels protects them from damage and resists the escape of blood from the site of injury. When, however, a vessel runs close to the surface, it lacks support from the tissues on its external aspect. This is especially true when the vessel runs parallel to the surface for some distance, as, for example, in the mucous membrane of the nasal septum, where the vasculature is exposed under a thin mucous membrane on one side and on the other is adjacent to a rigid surface. There, as a result of slight injury or vascular weakness, the escaping blood pours out into the nasal cavity with little help from the extravascular tissue in closing the opening. It is probably for this reason that the nasal septum is a frequent site of bleeding in hypertension, purpuras and in rheumatic fever. The exposed position of the capillary loops in the gums and possibly the ease of bacterial invasion may be responsible for the frequency of bleeding around the teeth in thrombocytopenias. The surface vessels of the mucous or serous membranes of the gastrointestinal, respiratory or urogenital tracts are likewise only half supported by the tissues and are, moreover, located in organs of considerable mobility. In *hereditary hemorrhagic telangiectasia* the vessels in the small congenital nevi, which are usually distributed about the oral or nasal cavity and the finger tips, are enlarged, have unusually thin walls and are covered with only a thin layer of epithelium. The bright red hue of these lesions, which are in effect small arteriovenous fistulas, implies increased blood pressure in their capillaries. Their superficial location renders them readily susceptible to trauma. Internal nevi, sometimes corresponding to the segmental distribution of peripheral nevi, may cause intracranial or enteric hemorrhage.

The closure of small cuts in the skin may prevent anything more than an insignificant loss of blood in healthy young persons. On the other hand, in the aged and in the debilitated the loss of elasticity of the skin is probably responsible for the so-called *senile purpura* or the facility with which hematomas develop even after carefully performed venipunctures. In senile purpura the lesions are rather characteristic in their sharply circumscribed, reddish rather than purple color and sometimes slightly raised appearance, which leads to the impression that they occupy a superficial position in the epidermis. Resistance offered by the body tissues to forcible distention of their spaces also influences the amount of blood which may escape from injured vessels. This tissue resistance varies in different areas of the body and is naturally most effective in preventing hemorrhages from vessels with relatively low blood pressure, such as capillaries and veins. The distended overlying skin of an extremity or a fascial plane may, however, limit the progress of even a large hemophiliac hemorrhage. On the other hand, the substance of certain organs such as the brain offers little resistance

to the extravasation of blood. Similarly, the loose areolar tissue of the orbit and that surrounding the vessels of the antecubital and inguinal regions provide favorable sites for diffuse subcutaneous hematomas.

The widespread extent of subcutaneous hemorrhage that may occur as a result of vascular weakness unassociated with a coagulation defect—as, for example, in scurvy—suggests that the intercellular spaces are penetrated by the blood without sufficient injury to the tissue cells themselves to result in the release of thromboplastic agents. The tissues vary in their content of thromboplastic materials; and anticoagulant substances, such as heparin, may be extracted from them. The brain, lung and testes are especially rich in thromboplastic substances, which the studies of Chargaff indicate to be a complex containing a high molecular lipoprotein, which Spaet has recently separated into a protein (enzyme?) and a phosphatide. Possibly, as with hemorrhage into body cavities or in menstrual flow, the blood is incoagulable because it has already clotted and the red cells are diffused in serum or defibrinated transudates. Finally, it has been suggested that tissue autolysis may destroy the clot-accelerating substances.

Vascular Factors

The relative thickness and strength of the walls of the arteries, veins and capillaries are obviously consistent with the pressure and volume of the blood to be conveyed by each. All except the capillaries, which are without smooth muscle, share the property of contractility upon injury. This in a small vessel, with the assistance of normal platelets even in the presence of defective coagulation, may successfully limit the amount of hemorrhage, as in a needle puncture in hemophilia or even in afibrinogenemia. On the other hand, when a larger vessel is wounded, as in hemophilia, such mechanical responses by platelets and vessel wall may be unable to arrest the bleeding when unassisted by the coagulation of the blood.

In the conditions listed as *vascular purpura* in Table 30–17, local or general weakness of the capillary walls seems to be the factor chiefly involved. The platelets are normal in number and, so far as known, in function; probably for this reason the bleeding time is also normal. The coagulation of the blood is without defect. The limitation of purpura, like edema, in some instances to the dependent parts of the body emphasizes the relation of increased hydrostatic pressure to both. The Rumpel-Leede, or tourniquet, test provides a rough measure of the resistance of the capillaries to a rise in their blood pressure—for example, 80 mm. of mercury maintained for eight minutes by a blood pressure cuff applied just above the bend of the elbow. At the conclusion of the test the pressure in the cuff is released and the petechial hemorrhages which have appeared in a circular area 5 cm. in diameter are counted. Humble studied the effect of the tourniquet test upon the formation of petechial hemorrhages in the nail bed capillaries. He found that with or without thrombocytopenia the petechiae occurred exclusively in the arterial end of the capillary loop. At this site Landis has shown that the precapillary vessel suddenly dilates into the capillary loop, and it is here that intracapillary pressure is highest. Retinal hemorrhages in anemias without platelet decreases are probably the result of the increased blood flow and capillary pressure.

Purpura is observed with the onset of certain acute *infectious diseases* and, when not associated with striking thrombocytopenia, is assumed to be due to the action of toxins on the vascular endothelium. The erythrotoxin of the scarlet fever streptococcus is obviously able to cause widespread capillary injury, and substances have been obtained by autolysis of pneumococci which are capable of producing purpura in experimental animals. An unusual degree of vascular injury presumably accounts for the occasional diffuse hemorrhagic manifestations of ordinarily erythematous or vesicular exanthemata. In various types of septicemia scattered purpura is presumably also due to local bacterial emboli. The rose spots of typhoid fever, the splinter hemorrhages of subacute bacterial endocarditis and the variable purpura of meningococcal septicemia are illustrative of this mechanism. It is sometimes possible to demonstrate organisms in these skin lesions. The reduction of the platelets that is frequently observed at the onset of many infections may contribute to the extensive purpura occasionally associated with vascular collapse and adrenal hemorrhage. Usually due to meningococcus septicemia, it is known as the Waterhouse-Friderichsen syndrome and may well be analogous to the Sanarelli-Shwartzman phenomenon in animals given two successive injections of endotoxin.

The *familial incidence of a hemorrhagic condition* affecting both sexes, but especially females, without abnormality of platelet count or of blood coagulation but with prolongation of the bleeding time and a positive tourniquet test, was first described by von Willebrand. The findings suggested that in such families there was some type of constitutional weakness of the blood vessels. Macfarlane observed abnormal contractility of the capillaries of the nail bed under the microscope after injury, but this is not always confirmed. These patients are reported to bleed easily, sometimes fatally, from various mucous membranes, from minor abrasions of the skin, and to suffer from an unusual frequency of fatal hemorrhages into the central nervous system. Bleeding in some is complicated by alleged defects of platelet aggregation or adhesiveness, a plasma "vascular factor" or clearly by a non-sex-linked deficiency of plasma antihemophilic globulin (AHG). To be discussed subsequently under Coagulation Defects is the fact that transfusion of plasma from classical hemophilia A patients produces a gradual rise in the AHG titer of the plasma of the von Willebrand type patient. Hereditary hemorrhagic *telangiectasia* presents purely local causes of abnormal bleeding except for rare instances of associated thrombocytopenia, which may be extreme in infants with large vascular nevi capable of sequestering, or destroying platelets. In females, bleeding from telangiectases may occur principally during the first day or two of menstruation, at which time certain normal women show the phenomenon of "easy bruising" and distinct reduction of the platelets. In many women easy bruising is present at all times without thrombocytopenia. In extremely rare instances, according to Gardner and Diamond, autosensitization to red cells may cause larger painful ecchymoses to develop over the course of a few days at the sites of initial minor bruises. However, according to Ratnoff these patients are highly neurotic females and can be caused to develop such lesions in specified areas by suggestion. Patients with somewhat similar painful ecchymoses have been shown to react to phosphatidylserine, autologous leukocytes or calf thymus DNA when injected subcutaneously.

The experimental demonstration of the function of vitamin C in the laying down of intercellular collagen provides a suggestive explanation of the hemorrhagic tendency in scurvy. In experimental wounds, while there is no lack of growth capacity in the capillary endothelial cells, fully formed capillaries do not develop with deprivation of vitamin C. In scurvy the tourniquet test is positive, but the petechial hemorrhages so induced are largely into the hyperkeratotic hair follicles on the extensor surfaces of the forearm utilized in the test. The bleeding and clotting times are normal as is the number of platelets, unless there is thrombocytopenia because of an associated folic acid deficiency. The hemorrhages may vary from small purpuric spots, especially on the dependent parts of the body and characteristically in the hair follicles, to enormous extravasations of blood. Subperiosteal hemorrhage is confined to children in whom the ununited epiphysial junctions provide a point of origin for bleeding. In adults the posterior aspect of the thigh is an especially common site of extensive hemorrhage. The administration of crystalline ascorbic acid promptly corrects the hemorrhagic tendency and the capillary fragility. In vitamin K deficiency, of which purpura is a common manifestation, it is also probable that there is lack of a poorly specified vascular protective substance in addition to a depression of the levels of prothrombin and other liver-produced clotting factors.

Another type of purpura in which a vascular lesion is clearly present is the so-called *anaphylactoid* or *allergic purpura*. Clinically, this condition often develops a few days after an acute infection or a flare-up of a chronic one. It may follow the ingestion of certain foods or drugs. Osler pointed out the clinical resemblances between allergic purpura and serum sickness, and the rheumatic symptoms described by Schoenlein and the abdominal pains with purpuric manifestations noted by Henoch are found also in serum sickness. Frequently the constitutional signs due to the initial infection may have subsided entirely before the purpura appears. This characteristic latent interval between an acute infection and the onset of acute hemorrhagic nephritis is paralleled by cases of purpura with bleeding from the kidney. Indeed, according to Christian, the urinary findings are sometimes indistinguishable from those of acute glomerular nephritis.

The typical manifestations suggest dilatation or change in permeability of the capillaries in various locations in the body, probably as a result of the liberation of histamine in the walls of the blood vessels. Presumably the extent of the injury to the vascular wall and the relative proportions of serum, leukocytes and erythrocytes leaking through it determine the appearance of the lesions in the skin and the descriptive nomenclature applied by the dermatologist. Thus, associated with purpura of the skin or internal organs, are also erythema, urticaria, or edema, serous effusions or even local necroses. The amount of blood lost, even with widespread lesions, is usually far less than in thrombocytopenic purpura. The platelets are usually normal in number, and the bleeding and clotting times are normal. The tourniquet test, however, may or may not be positive. It occasionally causes the development of local urticaria rather than purpura.

INTRAVASCULAR FACTORS

The cooperative activity in preventing blood loss of such intravascular factors as the platelets and the coagulation of the blood has already been briefly described. An outline of the main phases of their joint effort is given in Table 30–19. Of these, in view of the frequently prolonged periods of relative freedom from hemorrhage in hemophilia and in fibrinogenopenia, we must conclude that the coagulation factors are of secondary importance in the absence of overt trauma. As originally stated by Hayem, the *mechanical* effect of the platelet adherence in wholly or partially sealing the vascular wound would appear to be the primary and more important event in normal hemostasis. This requires a delay at the vascular wound of at least ten or eleven seconds in order for the coagulation of blood to take place. Cessation of bleeding from true capillaries appears to be an exception in that platelet thrombi do not form, and indeed are perhaps unnecessary because the small intravascular pressure permits only a slow escape of blood. The demonstration by Quick and by Brinkhous of the interaction of platelet cofactors and plasma factors to form prothrombinase has established the importance of the *chemical* effect of the platelets in initiating blood coagulation. In so doing, the disintegration of the platelets releases phospholipids, chiefly phosphatidyl serine and phosphatidyl ethanolamine, which participate in prothrombinase generation and thus accelerate the conversion from prothrombin to thrombin and the formation of fibrin. Finally, clot retraction is a critical measure of normal platelet function and, in contrast to other platelet properties, is readily destroyed by superficial injury of the platelets or by supersonic disintegration.

Platelet Defects

Deficiency of platelet number or function is often associated with, if not entirely the cause of, certain types of pathologic bleeding. The megakaryocytes of the bone marrow are the most important source of blood platelets, although megakaryocytes are found in caval blood and are retained in the lung. The granular cytoplasm of the megakaryocytes projects into the vascular sinusoids of the marrow, and the small segments broken off by the force of the blood stream or by some other mechanism become the platelets of the circulating blood. There they are observed as thin, round or oval bodies, 2 to 4 microns in diameter containing many granules near the center (granulomere) and a clear peripheral zone (hyalomere). With the electron microscope mitochondria have been observed and various tubules and microvesicles. About 25 per cent of the platelet's dry weight is lipid, 60 per cent protein and 10 per cent carbohydrate. RNA and various enzymes have been identified as part of the glycolytic pathway, pentose phosphate shunt and tricarboxylic acid cycle. In fact, although the platelet does not contain a nucleus or DNA, it is very active metabolically with an ATP content 150 times that of the red cell. ATP has been shown to activate a contractile protein present in platelets and clot retraction will not occur in the absence of glucose.

The first step in hemostasis, prompt adherence of platelets to the injured vessel wall is perhaps the result of an electrostatic effect; and platelet agglutination in vitro is brought about by ADP in the presence of calcium and magnesium. The next event, change in the appearance of platelets called "viscous metamorphosis," which is associated with extrusion of microscopic pseudopodia, signals the beginning of their hemostatic action. It is probably induced by traces of thrombin acting on fibrinogen normally adsorbed on the platelet surface. The final contribution of the platelets to coagulation is the shortening of the fibrin strands that results in clot retraction.

It has been estimated that the normal rate of platelet production is about 40,000 to 100,000 platelets per cubic millimeter per day. Schulman has recently demonstrated the effect of normal human plasma in raising the platelet count of a unique patient with congenital thrombocytopenic purpura. Plasma filtrates were active in normal rats as well as in certain children with acute idiopathic thrombocytopenic purpura, suggesting a factor normally involved in platelet level regulation. Marked increases in the platelet count may occur in response to trauma and partial asphyxia. Fractures of bone, surgical operations and especially splenectomy result in rises of platelets. In these circumstances so-called giant platelets are sometimes seen in the peripheral blood stream. Aas and Gardner found that Cr^{51}-labeled platelets transfused into normal recipients survived in linear fashion for 9 to 11 days irrespective of the compatibility of the major blood groups. With subsequent transfusions platelet survival became progressively shorter, presumably because of the development of antiplatelet antibodies. It has been claimed and Shulman has demonstrated by complement-fixation methods that platelets from different persons may contain different isoantigens, which do not, unfortunately, correspond to those of their red cell blood groups. Thus, a patient who had received transfusions suddenly developed thrombocytopenia after an interval of a few days. Later it was shown that the recipient's serum contained an antibody against the donor's, but not the recipient's, platelets; and it was necessary to assume that in some way the foreign platelets had provided an antigen and, in addition, had transferred it to the recipient's platelets, so that both were attacked by the patients' developing antibody.

Moderate degrees of thrombocytopenia are often associated with increased capillary fragility, though not necessarily sufficient to produce spontaneous purpura; and in swine sulfur-35 peak labeling of platelets is followed after 12 to 24 hours by peak labeling of the endothelium. These facts suggest that blood, in passing through the capillaries, gives up some of its platelets for the purpose of sealing off minute lesions in the blood vessels which are the natural consequence of mechanical or metabolic stresses. A pathologic exaggeration of this process may be responsible for the diffuse platelet thromboses in small arterioles described by Baehr, Singer and others. This condition, *thrombotic or thrombohemolytic thrombocytopenic purpura,* is clinically manifest as thrombocytopenia, hemolytic anemia with spherocytes and other marked anomalies of red cell shape, negative Coombs' test, variable neurologic signs and fever. The absence of red cell and platelet agglutinins favors a primary vascular lesion to account for the local adherence of platelets and mechanical injury to circulating red cells. Occasionally the resulting intravascular events invoke sufficient coagulation to reduce secondarily, in addition to platelets, such plasma coagulation factors as fibrinogen and prothrombin and to evolve cryofibrin. *Purpura fulminans,* a drastic condition occurring in children 2 or 3 weeks after an infection, has these hematologic features and is manifest by extensive tissue hemorrhage and necrosis due to local thrombosis of small blood vessels. It is thought to have analogies to the Arthus phenomenon and has been successfully treated with heparin.

Thrombocytopenia is clinically suggested by the appearance of numerous petechiae often, of course, accompanied by larger purpuric areas. It is detected by a decreased platelet count, positive tourniquet test, prolonged bleeding time and absent or diminished clot retraction. The *positive tourniquet* test implies either that there is defective strength of the small blood vessels apart from a deficiency of platelets, or that the platelets are insufficient in number or function to plug effectively the lesions in the capillaries produced by the increased intravascular pressure. *Prolongation of the bleeding time* for minutes or even hours is presumably the result of failure of the platelets to agglutinate and so to occlude the small lesions in the blood vessels produced by the needle puncture. Failure or delay of *clot retraction* usually occurs when the platelets number 70,000 per cubic millimeter or less. This is the result of deficiency of a second important function of the platelets, which, according to Tocantins, normally form complex knots at the points of contact of interlacing strands of fibrin and so cause the clot to contract. According to Quick, the normal coagulation time usually observed in thrombocytopenic purpura is merely due to the crudity of the method used. With reduction of the number of platelets below a critical level, which varies in different patients, the consumption of prothrombin virtually ceases. This is the result of deficiency of a third function of the platelets: their essential participation in the formation of plasma prothrombinase.

Such disturbances are usually the result of insufficient numbers of platelets, but may also indicate defective function of normal numbers of platelets. The latter clinical syndromes are not clearly defined. However, Glanzmann was the first to describe a familial hemorrhagic condition in which the only measurable defect was poor clot retraction (thrombocytoasthenia). In such patients the platelets are normal in number, but in blood smears do not appear in clumps and look large and ill formed. Under the electron microscope, unlike normal platelets, they fail to develop the dendritic appearance subsequently enveloped in a cytoplasmic veil, known as

"spreading" (Fig. 30–47). In vitro the addition of ADP fails to cause platelet clumping, but the addition of ATP and magnesium ions corrects the defective clot retraction, thought to be due to lack of high energy phosphate as a consequence of defective glycolysis.

In a variety of other mild hemorrhagic syndromes with normal numbers of platelets, platelet morphology is only occasionally abnormal, but platelet function is defective with respect to chemical participation in prothrombinase generation (*thrombocytopathy*). These conditions may be either congenital or acquired (liver disease, uremia, macroglobulins) and may be either due to lack of or inability to release the essential platelet phospholipids. According to Bowie this type of platelet abnormality can be diagnosed when decreased prothrombin consumption in the Quick test is returned to normal by addition of soy bean phospholipid (Inosthin). Deficit can then be distinguished from dysfunction by showing that prothrombinase generation improves after sonic disintegration of the platelets. Finally, in rare instances thrombocytoasthenia may be combined with thrombocytopathy and the latter with one of the coagulation factor defects found in hemophilia A or B.

According to Bigelow, in patients with a paradoxical tendency to bleed despite platelet levels of a million or more per cubic millimeter (thrombocythemia), which is a condition sometimes preliminary to the development of polycythemia vera or myelogenous leukemia, the elevated platelet count may be associated with a diminished amount of serotonin activity. Excess of platelets inhibits the thromboplastin generation test or may produce in vivo thrombi with infarction and secondary depletion of plasma coagulation factors. Levin has recently shown that platelet counts above 400,000 are frequent in patients with various malignancies and may be responsible for the occasional association of migratory thrombophlebitis with cancer of lung, breast, ovary, stomach and pancreas. The thrombocytosis is not due to marrow involvement and, in contrast to myeloproliferative thrombocythemia, is not a cause of bleeding.

Thrombocytopenic purpura is observed clinically in rare congenital instances and either secondary to some recognizable cause of platelet reduction or in the little understood primary condition, idiopathic thrombocytopenic purpura. Of especial interest are infants with huge vascular tumors and thrombocytopenia relieved by destruction of the platelet-sequestering vascular mass by irradiation. The initial effect of *infection* in producing purpura has already been ascribed either to a generalized vascular injury or less certainly to a fall in platelets which is usually only of moderate degree. Likewise, the manifestations of easy bruising coincidental to a fall of platelets in the first day or two of the menstrual cycle has already been referred to.

In certain instances *allergy to food* has been claimed as responsible for thrombocytopenic purpura, but not always in a convincing manner. The evidence connecting certain *drugs* with thrombocytopenic purpura on an allergic basis is, however, unquestionable. Thus the organic arsenicals, sulfonamides, quinine, quinidine and especially the drug Sedormid (allyl-iso-propyl-acetylcarbamide) have clearly

A

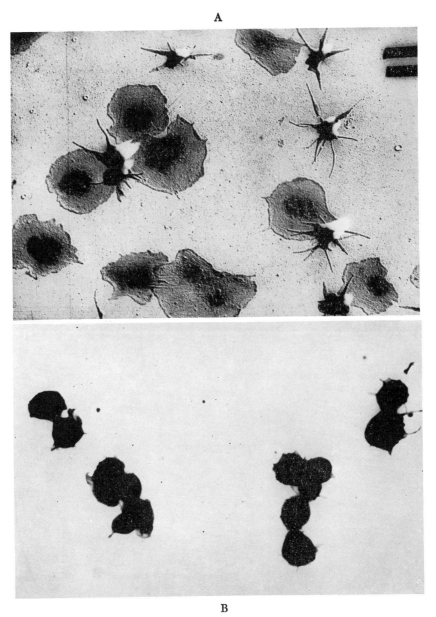

B

Figure 30–47. *A,* Electron microphotographs of normal platelets exhibiting numerous pseudopods and spreading of the hyaloplasm. *B,* Platelets from a patient with thrombocytoasthenia. There is defective pseudopod formation and complete lack of spreading. (From Braunsteiner: Chapter 43 in Henry Ford Hospital Symposium: Blood Platelets. Boston, Little, Brown & Co., 1961.)

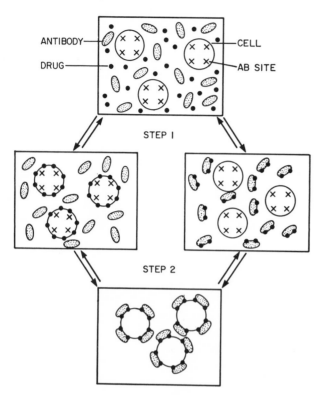

STEP I

STEP 2

Figure 30–48. Two possible mechanisms are depicted for the first step of the reaction leading to attachment of drug antibodies to cells in instances of drug-induced thrombocytopenia. It is known that antibodies will not attach to platelets unless the drug is present. Shulman's observations using equilibrium dialysis as a measure of drug binding show that the right-hand diagram in Step 2 is the probable mechanism. Thus, the association between cells and drug is too weak to account for the large amount of antibodies that the platelets can absorb, whereas in the absence of platelets the serum antibodies avidly bind drug and in some instances may act as precipitins. (From Shulman: Tr. A. Am. Phys., 76:72, 1963.)

produced sensitivity in certain persons, in whom the experimental readministration of small doses of these substances has been followed within a few minutes by a pronounced fall in platelets in the peripheral blood and the subsequent development of extensive purpura. Ackroyd has shown that Sedormid, when mixed with the plasma of such sensitized persons, produces agglutination of either their own or of normal platelets. The platelets are lysed in the presence of complement, which is fixed by platelets when the drug and the patient's plasma are present, but not in the absence of either. The essential abnormality thus lies in the patient's plasma which supplies the antibody. This was originally thought to be formed by the sensitized patient in response to an antigen composed of a drug-platelet combination. However, Shulman's recent observations suggest instead that the antigen is a drug-plasma protein complex that, when the drug is readministered, specifically combines with the antibody (Fig. 30–48). This antigen-antibody complex then nonspecifically coats the platelets and leads to their rapid sequestration in spleen or liver. In patients with sensitivity to quinidine its optical isomer, quinine, is not capable of inducing a fall in platelets in vivo or platelet agglutination in vitro, but will do so in other patients

with thrombocytopenia clinically induced by quinine. Drugs that cause thrombocytopenic purpura in some persons may cause vascular purpura in others. The development of platelet isoagglutinins and purpura of the newborn when there is an antigenic difference between the infant's and the mother's platelets will be discussed below.

Nutritional deficiency, with the exception of Vitamin C deficiency, in which the hemorrhagic tendency is due to vascular weakness and not to thrombocytopenia, unless complicated by folic acid deficiency, is rarely associated with purpura as a prominent manifestation. In pernicious anemia the platelet count is usually somewhat reduced and hemorrhages are often observed in the eyegrounds. Because severe anemia following blood loss without thrombocytopenia may produce similar hemorrhages, the anemia itself is probably an important factor in their production. Administration of vitamin B_{12} or pteroylglutamic acid in corresponding nutritional deficiency anemias causes prompt elevation of the platelet count, which precedes the rise of hemoglobin concentration in the blood and hence is clearly not merely secondary to an overcrowded erythropoietic marrow. Moreover, Epstein has described the presence of megakaryocytes with multiple or large nuclei and abnormal chromatin distribution in the bone marrow before treatment.

Marked diminution of the platelets in the peripheral circulation is found in anemias considered to be due to *inhibition of bone marrow function* by benzol, arsphenamine, stilbestrol, most antileukemic chemotherapeutic agents and gold compounds, or as the result of absorption of radium and exposure to roentgen ray. Experimentally, the last also leads to defective coagulation of the blood, due to the presence of circulating heparin. Low platelet counts are also found in *myelophthisic anemias* resulting from invasion of the marrow by foreign neoplastic cells, such as those of cancer or leukemia. Similar disturbances may arise from infiltration with lipid-containing cells in such conditions as Niemann-Pick or Gaucher's disease, or when the bone marrow becomes the seat of extensive fibrosis or osteosclerosis, as in the conditions known as nonleukemic myelosis or osteosclerotic anemia.

Idiopathic thrombocytopenic purpura in children occurs in an acute form with extreme thrombocytopenia, which sometimes follows by a week or two an infection such as rubella. In this latent period, the not infrequent lymphocytosis and eosinophilia as well as the complete recovery within a few weeks suggest an immune response. In adults the condition is usually more chronic with only partial remissions and without consistent relation to an infection at onset. In both types the clinical hallmark is petechiae, and these may be accompanied by ecchymoses in the skin and by persistent oozing of blood from the mucous membranes and by hemorrhages into various tissues. Except for the primary reduction of the number of platelets in circulation and the changes secondary to hemorrhage, the morphology of the blood is normal, and the number of megakaryocytes in the bone marrow is normal or increased. Bleeding may occur when the platelets number as many as 100,000 and is usually profuse if the platelets are less than 20,000 per cubic millimeter. With such low platelet counts the clotting time of the blood, as usually determined, may be slightly increased, and the prothrombin consumption is moderately diminished. In addition to its serious clinical consequences for the mother as a complication of pregnancy, thrombocytopenic purpura of more or less severity may appear in her infant, usually as a phenomenon lasting only a few days or weeks after birth.

The frequent discrepancies between the number of platelets in circulation and the intensity of the hemorrhagic manifestations in idiopathic thrombocytopenic purpura necessarily raise the question whether, in addition to a deficiency of platelets, there is not also a defect of the capillary wall or of precapillary contraction. Roskam has shown that subcutaneous injections of antiplatelet serum cause local purpura without producing a fall of platelets in the blood. Moreover, in cross circulation experiments purpura does not appear in normal vascular areas perfused with blood from another animal previously rendered deficient in platelets by antiplatelet serum. On the other hand, by means of biopsies of experimental wounds, Zucker has demonstrated failure of the platelets in thrombocytopenic purpura to become adherent to the edges of the vascular lesion. The fact that symptomatic purpura commonly occurs with various disturbances of the bone marrow, as a result of which the blood contains a diminished number of platelets, strongly suggests that a deficiency of platelets alone may sometimes be sufficient to cause the hemorrhage in thrombocytopenic purpura.

The immediate *causation* of many instances of idiopathic thrombocytopenic purpura seems now to have been established as a result of the presence of a plasma factor. This conclusion is compatible with the cardinal features of the disorder: thrombocytopenia, normal or increased numbers of megakaryocytes in the bone marrow, and a variable degree of effectiveness of splenectomy. Harrington reported in 1951 that the transfusion of 500 ml. of blood from patients with idiopathic thrombocytopenic purpura to normal compatible recipients caused within a few hours a 50 per cent or greater decrease in the level of the recipient's platelet level that persisted for four to seven days. The fall in platelets in the recipient was too rapid to be explained as an inhibition of platelet production. It occurred with blood or plasma from patients who had never been transfused or pregnant. Different plasmas varied in platelet-reducing potency. High titer plasma induced a fall of platelets in both normal and splenectomized subjects, low titer plasma only in recipients with intact spleens (Fig. 30–49). It was not abolished by splenectomy of the donor, but did diminish or disappear with spontaneous remission or sometimes after cortisone therapy. Stefanini's observations with high potency platelet agglutinating serum from a patient with idiopathic thrombocytopenic purpura showed that intravenous injection of the serum not only caused a prompt fall of cir-

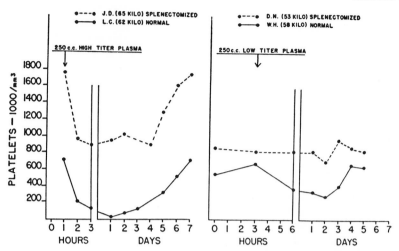

Figure 30–49. Results of studies on the response of normal and splenectomized subjects to transfusions of plasma from donors with idiopathic thrombocytopenic purpura. Plasmas with platelet-agglutinating properties of both high and relatively low potency, respectively, were used. Thrombocytopenia was induced in normal recipients on all occasions; but in splenectomized subjects by only the high potency plasma, presumably because of the absence of the critical splenic filter for platelets. (From Harrington and others: Ann. Int. Med., 38:433, 1953.)

culating platelets in normal recipients, but also produced degenerative changes in their bone marrow megakaryocytes with apparent temporary cessation of platelet formation. In the reverse type of observation, Hirsch and Gardner observed a fall of transfused normal platelets to previous thrombocytopenic levels in aplastic anemia in five or six days while in acute idiopathic thrombocytopenic purpura the previous platelet level was sometimes reached in less than a day. In chronic idiopathic thrombocytopenic purpura the interval was one to five days. Aster has recently shown that infused normal, chromium-51 labeled platelets are quickly destroyed in the liver of patients with acute idiopathic thrombocytopenic purpura and slowly sequestered by the spleen in the chronic variety. In general the lower the platelet count the greater the liver uptake relative to that of the spleen. In such observations or with the infusion of patient's plasma into normal recipients the possibility exists of platelet-plasma isoimmune incompatibility, even though undetectable by in vitro methods. However, this possibility has now been eliminated by Shulman's recent work showing that plasma harvested from a patient with idiopathic thrombocytopenic purpura prior to splenectomy was later promptly effective in lowering the same patient's restored platelet count when infused in small amounts.

The demonstration of *platelet agglutinating activity* in vitro peculiar to patients with idio-

pathic thrombocytopenic purpura has nevertheless been more often announced than confirmed. Such agglutination has been attributed to persisting traces of prothrombin in the plasma of the thrombocytopenic patient, which was converted to thrombin upon contact with the test platelets. Agglutination did not occur when the adsorbed fibrinogen on the test platelets were removed by previous exposure to trypsin. It is also curious that although Wilson confirmed Harrington's original observations in which platelet counts were made by the indirect method, he was unable to do so on the basis of direct platelet counts. Nor has complement fixation, the most sensitive in vitro method of detecting platelet incompatibility, been able to find evidence of isoantibody in the plasma of patients with acute or chronic idiopathic thrombocytopenic purpura. This, of course, does not deny the clinical evidence of a platelet-destroying effect of the patient's plasma in vivo.

Thrombocytopenic purpura may appear in the newborn and persist for a few weeks, presumably because of the passive transfer of a maternal platelet-sequestering factor across the placenta of a mother with idiopathic thrombocytopenic purpura. Consequently, the mother may have chronic thrombocytopenia, the infant low platelets only temporarily. Previous splenectomy of the mother does not necessarily prevent a recrudescence of her thrombocytopenic purpura during pregnancy or the subsequent appearance of thrombocytopenia in the infant at birth unless the maternal antiplatelet factor has disappeared. According to Harrington, thrombocytopenia of the newborn may also develop on a basis analogous to Rh disease as a result of active immunization of the mother by the fetal platelets during pregnancy. The recent demonstration of dominant autosomally controlled differences in platelet iso-antigens has confirmed the analogy. When the father's platelet iso-antigen differs from that of the mother, the maternal plasma may develop an agglutinin-blocking or complement-fixing isoantibody which may cross the placenta and affect the infant's platelet level. Despite severe thrombocytopenic purpura of the mother at the time of delivery, the infant will not be affected if the mother's thrombocytopenia is not due to antiplatelet factors (aplastic anemia), or if isoantibodies are present in her plasma, but are incapable of crossing the placental barrier.

Entirely without evidence of any antiplatelet plasma factor, *splenomegaly* may be associated with decreased levels of circulating platelets with a normal life-span of eight to ten days. It is thus possible that the thrombocytopenia is due to diminished platelet production. However, Aster using chromium-51 labeled autologous platelets found reciprocal fluctuations in the amount of radioactivity over the spleen and in the circulation. Consequently, studies were made before, during and after the slow (20 minute) intravenous infusion of epinephrine at a constant rate into normal, splenectomized and splenomegalic patients: those with congestive splenomegaly (Fig. 30–50), chronic lymphatic leukemia and polycythemia vera. The results were similar whether the platelets were autologous or homologous. Without a spleen there was no rise in platelets. Aster concluded that normally pulmonary or marginal vascular pools of platelets are insignificant, but that about a third of the total platelet mass is in the spleen, where it is readily able to exchange with the platelets in the circulation. In patients with large spleens as much as 50 to 90 per cent of the platelets were in the splenic pool (Fig. 31–13). These observations yield no support for a regulating effect of the spleen upon platelet production and demonstrate a novel basis for thrombocytopenia without either decreased production or increased destruction of platelets in splenomegaly.

Splenectomy in normal persons and in various forms of splenomegaly causes increases

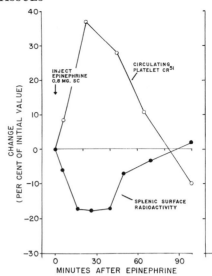

Figure 30–50. Effect of epinephrine infusion in congestive splenomegaly. Note the prompt increase in the Cr^{51}-platelet label in the circulation and the simultaneous decline in splenic surface Cr^{51} radioactivity. After the cessation of the infusion these values returned to their preinjection levels, indicating the exchangeability of the splenic platelets with those in the circulation. (Kindly supplied by Dr. R. H. Aster.)

in circulating platelet values, either because of displacement of the splenic platelet pool or removal of a platelet-destroying organ or from a combination of these factors. In thrombocytopenic purpura it causes a prompt shortening of the bleeding time and an increase in capillary resistance. These presumably nonspecific humoral effects, probably due to increased endogenous ACTH secretion, are followed only after many hours by the elevation of platelets that follows splenectomy in this condition as well as in normal subjects (Table 30–18). Because splenectomy does not necessarily result in permanent im-

TABLE 30–18. TIME REQUIRED TO ACHIEVE NORMAL HEMOSTATIC VALUES AFTER SPLENECTOMY IN IDIOPATHIC THROMBOCYTOPENIC PURPURA.*

Observation	Twelve Patients
Bleeding time	12–100
	Av. 48 minutes
Capillary resistance	12–360
	Av. 125 minutes
Platelet count	8–480
	Av. 79 hours

* Based on data from Robson: Quart. J. Med., 18:279, 1949.

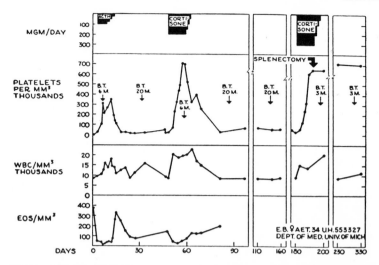

Figure 30–51. Effects of ACTH, cortisone and splenectomy upon a 34-year-old woman with idiopathic thrombocytopenic purpura. An episode of purpura at the age of 25 was followed by a spontaneous remission during which there was an uneventful full term delivery. Six months before admission purpura recurred and continued with minimal clinical manifestations, but with a platelet count of 9000 per cubic millimeter and a bleeding time (B.T.) of 16 minutes just prior to therapy. As indicated in the figure, temporary clinical improvement with increases of platelets and decreases of bleeding time accompanied brief periods of administration of ACTH and cortisone. Following splenectomy the second cortisone-induced remission was maintained for at least 9 months. (From Meyers and others: Ann. Int. Med., 37:352, 1952.)

provement in platelet levels, it has always been difficult to accept the idea that splenic dysfunction is the primary cause of idiopathic thrombocytopenic purpura. Aster has recently demonstrated the rapid sequestration of chromium-51 labeled platelets by the liver in thrombocytopenic patients with a short platelet life-span, and the slower splenic sequestration of labeled platelets in other patients with a longer platelet survival time. These results resemble similar observations made in acquired hemolytic anemia by Jandl. By analogy with that condition, the variable results of splenectomy can best be understood on the basis that the spleen is not the only tissue in the body with capacity to sequester and destroy platelets.

Nevertheless, splenectomy for chronic thrombocytopenic purpura remains the form of treatment most likely to be permanently effective. Alternatively, or as a preparation for splenectomy, the use of ACTH or cortisone (Fig. 30–51) will usually lessen bleeding within two or three days, presumably by decreasing the permeability of the capillaries, as shown by the observations of Ebert on the blood vessels of the rabbit's ear. In patients a beneficial effect on bleeding time and tourniquet test can sometimes be demonstrated at this time, and may or may not be followed by a rise in platelets. Discontinuance of ste-

roid therapy is often followed within a few days by relapse. Whole blood and platelet-rich plasma transfusions are beneficial only during the short survival time of the platelets, and may develop antiplatelet antibodies that shorten the survival of subsequently transfused platelets.

Coagulation Factor Defects

Coagulation deficiencies contribute to blood loss following injuries to blood vessels which are sufficiently large to prevent obliteration of the lesion by vascular contraction and by the adhesiveness of the platelets. Extravasations of blood much larger than petechiae occurring in skin and muscles as a result of definite trauma are characteristic, as is prolonged bleeding from wounds. Normally the amount of the hemorrhage depends to a considerable extent on the rapidity with which the fibrin clot forms, adheres to the vessel wall, and draws the edges of the wound together by secondary contraction. Fibrin formation is the physical end point of the chemical reactions involved in the process of blood clotting.

In 1905 Morawitz published a description of blood coagulation consisting of the two consecutive phases depicted in Table 30–19. Today, this still forms the framework of the concept of blood coagulation. Morawitz was aware that the work of predecessors had recognized the participation and characteristics of fibrin, fibrinogen and calcium, and had inferred the existence of thrombokinase and thrombin. He stated that all the reagents essential for the physicochemical process involved in blood coagulation were present in the blood. In the plasma were prothrombin, calcium and fibrinogen and in the platelets and leukocytes was an activating enzyme, thrombokinase, for the conversion of prothrombin to thrombin. He conceived that normally the blood remained fluid because the clot-promoting effect of the constant disintegration of the formed elements was opposed by hypothetical plasma antithrombins. However, with minor damage to the vascular wall platelets agglutinated and leukocytes gathered locally to stop the leak and to release the small amounts of thrombokinase necessary for completing the minuscule clot. With major hemorrhage the injured tissues became an important additional source of thrombokinase for blood extravasated outside the vessel wall.

The assumption that the process of blood coagulation involves enzyme reactions was strongly suggested by subsequent evidence that each phase of the process could be independently activated by an enzyme foreign to blood. Thus purified trypsin is able to convert prothrombin to thrombin, but not fibrinogen to fibrin. Papain, however, rapidly converts fibrinogen to fibrin, but will not change prothrombin to thrombin. An example of the

TABLE 30–19. EVOLUTION OF KNOWLEDGE CONCERNING BLOOD COAGULATION.

| | *Two-Stage Hypothesis* | |
Substrate	*Activating Enzyme*	*Product*
1. Prothrombin	Platelets and calcium (Trypsin)	Thrombin
2. Fibrinogen	Thrombin (Papain)	Fibrin

activation of one enzyme by another is provided in the conversion of chymotrypsinogen to chymotrypsin by small quantities of trypsin.

Subsequent observations have shown that the formation of Morawitz' thrombokinase (more accurately prothrombokinase) requires the participation of other factors. Consequently, an initial third stage, that of prothrombinase formation, has been added to Morawitz' hypothesis concerning the clotting process. Thus, the clotting process is much more complex than as just described. Moreover, it involves autocatalytic reactions, that is, processes that are, according to Milstone, *progressively accelerated* by their own end products. These appear to be initiated by the formation of a minute amount of thrombin. Thereafter, thrombin begets more and more thrombin by lysing platelets and activating plasma factors to produce plasma prothrombinase which in turn converts prothrombin to thrombin (Table 30–20). Thereafter, one part of thrombin may convert 10,000 times

TABLE 30–20. EVOLUTION OF KNOWLEDGE CONCERNING BLOOD COAGULATION (CONTINUED).

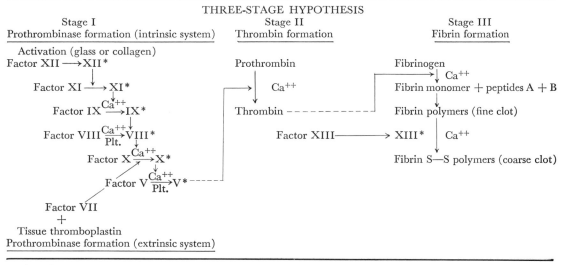

* Indicates activated form of factor.

TABLE 30–21. SYNONYMS, PROPERTIES AND DEFICIENCY STATES OF BLOOD CLOTTING FACTORS.*

Factor No.	Synonyms	Present in Serum	Adsorbed by $BaSO_4$	Stable in Bank Blood	Clinical State
I	Fibrinogen	No	No	Yes	Afibrinogenemia
II	Prothrombin	No	Yes	Yes	Aprothrombinemia
III	Thromboplastin	—	—	—	None
IV	Calcium	Yes	No	Yes	None
V	Labile factor, proaccelerin (Ac-globulin)	No	No	Poor	Parahemophilia
VII	Serum prothrombin conversion acceler- ator (SPCA)	Yes	Yes	Yes	SPCA deficiency
VIII	Antihemophilic globulin (AHG)	No	No	50% in 3 weeks	Classic hemophilia A
IX	Plasma thromboplastin component (PTC)	Yes	Yes	Yes	Christmas disease Hemophilia B
X	Stuart-Prower factor	Yes	Yes	Yes	S-P deficiency
XI	Plasma thromboplastin antecedent (PTA)	Yes	Partly	Yes	Hemophilia C
XII	Hageman factor	Yes	Partly	Yes	None
XIII	Fibrin stabilizing factor (FSF)	Yes	?	Yes	FSF deficiency
Platelets	Phospholipid, platelet Factor 3	No	No	Yes	Thrombocytopathies

* Modification of table from Hougie: Fundamentals of Blood Coagulation in Clinical Medicine. New York, McGraw-Hill, 1963.

its weight of fibrinogen to fibrin. Such a self-augmented mechanism doubtless presents inherent advantages in the vital biologic problem of quickly and progressively converting a liquid to a solid at the point of rupture of a vascular system containing blood that flows initially through and later past the break in continuity. The integrity of the mechanism is further insured by the presence in great excess of the key factors. Moreover, the injured tissues provide an extrinsic source of thromboplastic material that can cause blood to clot with greater rapidity without the help of platelets. With termination of the hemorrhagic emergency, plasma antithrombins destroy excess thrombin and plasma fibrinolysin assists in the removal of the no longer essential intravascular clot.

The ancient recognition of hemophilia as a hereditary defect of blood coagulation was followed only in the present century by comprehension in detail and accurate delineation of other hereditary anomalies. To a large extent the study of rare patients with novel defects of the clotting mechanism, subsequently recognized as genetically controlled, has brought the concept of blood coagulation after many revisions to its present form. However, at any time the discovery of a new hereditary defect may require a further modification.

During the 1930's, studies were made of the rate and amount of prothrombin formation by the so-called one-stage (Quick) test and the two-stage (Warner) test respectively. In the one-stage method tissue thromboplastin and calcium are added simultane-

ously to oxalated plasma, which then normally clots in 12 seconds. Delay may be due to decrease of prothrombin or of various accessory factors to be discussed below. In the two-stage test this same mixture is allowed to reach an end point during a preliminary incubation period. In the second stage an aliquot from the first-stage test tube is added to a fibrinogen solution, the coagulation time of which is measured in seconds. Delay is strictly due to a deficiency of the prothrombin quantitatively converted to thrombin in the first test tube and measured as such in the second.

During the 1940's, study of patients with prolonged coagulation or Quick prothrombin times led to the recognition of a labile factor V, a stable factor VII, and an antihemophilic globulin factor VIII. Although it had been known for some time that the mixing of the bloods of certain "classic" hemophilic patients with those of others sometimes resulted in mutual correction of the clotting time, it remained for Aggeler and for the Oxford group independently in 1952 to recognize a second variety of hemophilia due to lack of plasma thromboplastin component (PTC), now called Factor IX. Soon study of other patients with anomalous coagulation defects disclosed three other new clotting factors: the Stuart-Prower Factor X, the plasma thromboplastin antecedent (PTA) or Factor XI by Rosenthal and the Hageman Factor XII by Ratnoff. Recently, a hemorrhagic disease due to a deficiency of a fibrin stabilizing Factor XIII has been described by Duckert. In Table 30–21 are listed some of the synonyms and properties of these factors. The latest defect to be discovered involves an abnormal species of fibrinogen (Baltimore). The clinical conditions due to such abnormalities will be discussed below.

Morawitz' conception that thrombokinase was released from leukocytes and platelets when blood was brought into contact with a wettable surface such as glass, as well as by injured tissues, was reemphasized in 1953 by the Oxford group more specifically in terms of *an intrinsic and an extrinsic system of blood clotting*. These systems can now be described in considerable detail. By itself the first or intrinsic system provides only a slow formation of prothrombinase, as is shown by the clotting time of whole blood in glass at body temperature (8 to 12 minutes). On the other hand, the production of prothrombinase initiated by tissue thromboplastin in the extrinsic system of clotting is rapid, as shown by the clot accelerating effect of adding tissue thromboplastin to whole blood or more clearly in the one-stage prothrombin test at body temperature where clotting occurs in 12 seconds. In this test it is now thought that the formation of the essential prothrombinase requires, in addition to tissue thromboplastin, the plasma Factors VII, V, X and calcium (Table 30–22). Obviously a deficiency of prothrombin itself or of any of these coagulation factors will be reflected in a prolonged one-stage prothrombin time. Experience indicates that unless, as is rarely the case, the fibrinogen level of the plasma tested is less than 100 mg. per cent, the prothrombin time will not be affected.

A defect of any of the plasma factors involved in the *intrinsic system* can be detected by the so-called partial thromboplastin time, which differs from the one-stage prothrombin time only in that platelets or a platelet substitute rather than tissue thromboplastin are added (Table 30–22).

The factors involved in the intrinsic system have now been analyzed as a result of the introduction of the thromboplastin generation test developed by Macfarlane and associates at Oxford in 1952. In a test tube equal parts of normal serum and normal BaSO$_4$-adsorbed plasma are mixed with a saline suspension of normal platelets. Calcium chloride is then added and at two-minute intervals aliquots are removed and added to a series of test tubes containing normal oxalated plasma as a source of prothrombin and fibrinogen. As prothrombinase is generated in the incubation mixture the clotting time of the oxalated plasma in successive test tubes decreases. The shortest time, a matter of seconds, is recorded. It is now known that in the first test tube the normal serum supplies Factors IX, X, XI and XII, whereas BaSO$_4$-adsorbed plasma contains Factors V and VIII (Table 30–21). Factor VII is also present in the serum but does not enter into the reaction. When the test is performed using a patient's serum, BaSO$_4$-adsorbed plasma and a saline suspension of platelets, deficiency of any of the specified coagulation factors will obviously prolong the clotting time. By substituting, one at a time, each of the three patient-derived "reagents" for the corresponding normal item, the identification can be narrowed to a reagent, but not to a single plasma factor, an achievement beyond the scope of this discussion.

The essentials of the modern scheme of blood coagulation are diagrammatically represented in Table 30–20. Ratnoff believes that Factor XII is activated by contact with glass or collagen and that this substance then activates Factor XI. Indeed, it has recently been suggested by Macfarlane that each successive factor, after being activated, activates the next below in the order shown in Table 30–20 in what has been called a "cascade" ending in "prothrombinase." Unless the rapid ex-

TABLE 30–22. FACTORS PARTICIPATING IN TESTS FOR COAGULATION DEFECTS (AT 37° C.).[*]

One-Stage Prothrombin Time	Partial Thromboplastin Time	Thromboplastin Generation Test
Plasma factors: V, VII, X	Plasma factors: V, VIII, IX, X, XI, XII	BaSO$_4$-plasma factors: V, VIII, XI, XII
Prothrombin	Prothrombin	Serum factors: IX, X, XI, XII
Fibrinogen	Fibrinogen	
Tissue thromboplastin	Platelet substitute	Platelets
CaCl$_2$	CaCl$_2$	CaCl$_2$
12–14 seconds (normal)	12–14 seconds (normal)	Serial aliquots[†]

[*] Modified from Hougie: Fundamentals of Blood Coagulation in Clinical Medicine. New York, McGraw-Hill, 1963.

[†] Removed at 2-minute intervals and added to tubes containing plasma (prothrombin and fibrinogen) which then *normally* clot, e.g., 60, 20, 10, 10 seconds.

trinsic system has been activated by contamination with tissue juice during the venipuncture, the clotting time of whole blood is slow because of the time consumed in the successive activation of Factors XII, XI, and IX, after which the action is rapid. For this reason, prolongation of the clotting of whole blood due to partial deficiencies of subsequent factors in the chain is not impressive. Calcium is required in the activation of each step of the process following the activation of Factor XI. The end point for both the extrinsic and intrinsic systems of prothrombinase formation appears to be the activation of Factor X. Thus, activated Factor X is the junction point of the two systems and thereafter proceeds to activate Factor V in the presence of calcium and platelet phospholipid. Activated Factor V then acts directly on prothrombin to convert it quantitatively to thrombin.

The work of van Creveld and others indicates that substances (probably phospholipids) derived from platelets take part in every stage of the coagulation process. In addition to the inherent difficulties of comprehending a biologic process described either in terms of the activities of unidentified substances in a natural mixture or of substances of uncertain purity in a synthetic system, there has been no great tendency among investigators to admit possible discovery of the same substance under different names. In the interests of scientific communication, in 1954 an international committee was set up and has approved the numerical designations shown in Table 30–21 with their principal synonyms.

There is no general agreement on the mechanisms which maintain the circulating blood in liquid form. Some theories are concerned with the presence of physiologic anticoagulants that are inactivated when a break in the vascular endothelium occurs. More generally accepted is the concept that the stability of the blood platelets in circulation prevents the activation of prothrombin until injury to the vascular wall results in their attraction and provides tissue thromboplastin. Defective coagulation of the blood is the result of deficiencies of one or more of the components of the three reactions outlined in Table 30–20: (I) formation of prothrombinase (extrinsic or intrinsic), (II) formation of thrombin, or (III) formation of fibrin. Only when the calcium is reduced to 2.5 mg. per 100 ml. or less is coagulation delayed in vitro. Such a calcium level is incompatible with life, and for this reason calcium deficiency is probably never a cause of prolonged blood coagulation in vivo. In addition, in rare clinical instances of hemorrhagic disease, anticoagulants are present in the circulating blood stream. These and the problems of fibrinolysis and excessive platelet and plasma factor utilization in intravascular clotting (consumption coagulopathies) will be discussed below.

Congenital Defects of Prothrombinase Formation (Coagulation Stage I). Deficiency of prothrombinase due to aberrations of the *intrinsic system* (Table 30–20) may occur with sufficient reduction of platelets or lack of availability of their phospholipids and has been discussed on page 868. The clinical manifestations are mild unless reduction in number of platelets is marked or there is abnormality of their physical properties (Glanzmann's disease). On the other hand, the effect of lack of an essential plasma factor is exemplified by *hemophilia A,* which is the classic illustration of a serious hemorrhagic disease due to failure of the shed blood to clot properly, affecting one in 25,000 persons. This occurs because the level of the plasma antihemophilic globulin (AHG) Factor VIII is 20 per cent or less of normal. Hemophilia A is inherited as a sex-linked mendelian recessive character transmitted from affected males to unaffected female "carriers." In such heterozygous females genotypically XhX, the somatic influence of the defective Xh chromosome is counteracted by the other normal X chromosome. In the hemizygous male, XhY, however, the normal Y chromosome does not prevent the full clinical expression of the coagulation defect. Estrogen therapy in male hemophilia is without effect. The consistent mildness of the disease in some families with Factor VIII levels of 2 to 20 per cent of normal has led to the conclusion that it is transmitted by a gene allelomorphic to that of the more severe condition in which the level is less than 2 per cent. Hemophilia in females, the consequence of the double genetic defect resulting from the union of a hemophilic male with a female "carrier" and long regarded as lethal to the embryo, has now been reported in several instances. Moreover, Pitney and Arnold, using a sensitive modification of the thromboplastin generation test, have found some reduction of the AHG level in a majority of female carriers. Female patients with prolonged clotting time and seeming male hemophiliacs without evidence of hereditary taint, reported before the modern era of critical analysis of the coagulation factors in the blood, were probably examples of congenital or acquired hypoprothrombinemia or of anticoagulants in the blood of spontaneous origin.

Hemorrhage from various parts of the body, either spontaneously or from slight trauma, is a main cause of disability in hemophilia. Subcutaneous and intramuscular hemorrhages are frequent and may lead to serious consequences if they involve areas where the pressure of the blood mass interferes with the circulation or respiration, as in an extremity or in the neck. Bleeding from the mucous membranes of the mouth is common and often difficult to control. Tooth extraction constitutes, when not handled appropriately, a hazard to life. A characteristic site of hemorrhage is into the joints with the development of hemarthrosis and consequent deformity and limitation of motion. Fortunately, hemorrhage into the central nervous system is relatively rare.

In hemophilia A the bleeding time is not prolonged because of the adequacy of platelet clumping to occlude a needle prick and because of the normal activation of the extrinsic clotting mechanism by tissue thromboplastin. However, if a few hours later the clot is gently dislodged, bleeding may persist because tissue thromboplastin is no longer released and clotting must now rely on the defective intrinsic mechanism. This phenomenon is a cause of delayed hemorrhage after trauma or surgical procedure and can affect any of the clinical conditions with defects of the intrinsic system of prothrombinase formation. In hemophilia A the clotting time of the blood may range from 30 minutes to several hours in different patients, but shows relatively little spontaneous variation in the same patient observed at different times.

When hemophilic blood at long last clots spontaneously, the amount of prothrombin converted to thrombin is small. However, the addition either of tissue thromboplastin (rabbit brain extract) which activates the extrinsic prothrombinase system, or of fresh normal platelet-free plasma, which supplies AHG, quickly clots the blood and causes a normal utilization of prothrombin. Consequently, Quick reported in 1949 that the fundamental defect in hemophilia was a lack of "plasma thromboplastinogen," and that this was responsible for the delayed conversion of prothrombin to thrombin. The missing factor (AHG) had already been characterized by Taylor and his associates as a euglobulin present in fresh, normal plasma but not in serum, and distinct from prothrombin and fibrinogen. Later it was found to be present in Cohn

Fraction I and to persist in banked blood for at least three weeks, provided thrombin formation is prevented. Subsequently it became recognized that in different "hemophiliacs" different types of defective prothrombinase formation are involved. Thus, as already mentioned, in addition to platelet phospholipid and AHG Factor VIII, several other plasma factors are required by the intrinsic prothrombinase system: the so-called plasma thromboplastin component (PTC) Factor IX, the plasma thromboplastin antecedent (PTA) Factor XI, labile Factor V, Stuart-Prower Factor X, and finally the so-called Hageman Factor XII. This last is not required for hemostasis in vivo but is activated by contact with glass. Consequently, in its absence the blood fails to clot in the test tube but there is no associated bleeding disorder.

PTC Factor IX deficiency (Christmas disease, Hemophilia B) exhibits a clinical and genetic picture indistinguishable from that of AHG deficiency (hemophilia A) and apparently constitutes about one-fifth of the patients formerly considered to have classical hemophilia. PTA Factor XI deficiency is a mild disease and is clinically unimportant except for epistaxis. Bleeding has sometimes followed tooth extractions or surgery. It is rare except in New York and Los Angeles, where it appears to be transmitted as an autosomal dominant trait and may affect females. Factor V deficiency occurs as a rare bleeding disorder, transmitted as a highly penetrant, incompletely recessive, autosomal trait affecting both sexes. The clinical hemostatic level in plasma is between 5 and 10 per cent of the normal. Activation of Factor V by activated Stuart-Prower Factor X is the common end point of both prothrombinase formation systems. Factor X deficiency, as described by Graham, is inherited as a rare autosomal recessive with mild symptomatology in heterozygotes. Homozygotes of both sexes with less than one per cent of the normal plasma level of Factor X exhibit a condition resembling classic hemophilia with epistaxis, hematomas and hemarthroses. Lack of identity with congenital Factor VII deficiency was finally recognized because Factor X, but not Factor VII, is required for the formation of intrinsic prothrombinase. These four types of defective intrinsic prothrombinase formation can be distinguished by laboratory tests because oxalated plasma, after absorption with barium sulfate, corrects the defect in AHG and PTA deficiency, but not in PTC or Stuart-Prower Factor deficiency; while normal serum corrects the defect in PTA, PTC and Stuart-

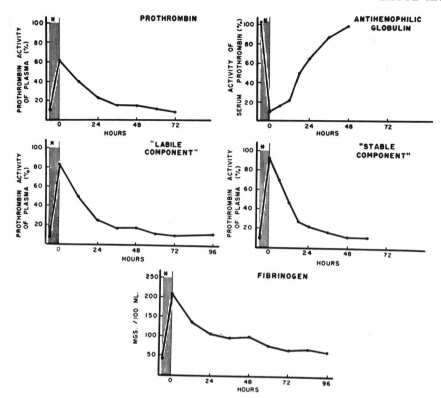

Figure 30–52. Persistence of activity of coagulation factors following their intravenous injection in patients with severe congenital deficiencies of the various factors investigated. Presumably correction of the physiologic defect was temporarily complete in each. *Prothrombin* activity following administration of purified prothrombin from 1.5 liters of oxalated human plasma. Data partly influenced by contemporary administration of "stable component." *Antihemophilic globulin* following administration of 1 liter of fresh plasma. *Labile component* following administration of 1 liter of lyophilized, deprothrombinized and reconstituted plasma. *Stable component* following administration of 1 liter of fresh serum. *Fibrinogen* following administration of 1.5 liters of lyophilized and reconstituted plasma. These relatively short survivals compared to that of plasma albumin suggest that physiologic utilization of blood coagulation factors constantly occurs. However, the turnover rates are probably not so rapid in the undepleted normal subject. (Slightly modified from Stefanini: Am. J. Med., *14*:64, 1953.)

Prower, but not in AHG deficiency. Di-sodium EDTA, according to Didisheim, selectively removes AHG from whole blood, thus converting it into a diagnostic reagent. The duration of the corrective effect upon the residual serum prothrombin of a single injection of AHG in the form of 1 liter of fresh plasma is shown in Figure 30–52.

Preparations of the euglobulin derived from hemophilia A plasma have little or no AHG activity. The clotting time of the blood of hemophilic patients can be maintained in many instances close to the normal range by the repeated intravenous injection at four or six hour intervals of sometimes as little as 50 ml. of citrated normal blood or dried preparations of a few hundred milligrams of the active fraction of human plasma. Even animal

preparations of Factor VIII (AHG) have been used in great emergencies, and recently simple methods of concentrating Factor VIII from human plasma by exposure to cold have been described. Elevation of the Factor VIII in the patient's plasma by such means and local application to bleeding wounds of preparations of rabbit or beef thrombin, together with appropriate local mechanical support, constitute the most important measures for the control of bleeding. With the exception of labile Factor V and to some extent Factor VIII, the stability of the plasma factors concerned in prothrombinase formation is good in banked citrated blood less than 21 days old. The treatment of Factor V deficiency requires fresh plasma and this is desirable for supplying Factor VIII from this source. The efficacy of stored citrated blood in the treatment of deficiencies of Factors VIII, IX, X and XI depends upon the hemostatic level of each factor and the persistence of the activity of the factors introduced by transfusion (Fig. 30–52). Serum is a rich source of Factors VII, IX, and X, but its use may cause thrombocytopenia.

Patients with hereditary *von Willebrand's disease*, in addition to possible vascular defects and lack of platelet adhesiveness, have a deficiency of Factor VIII which is, however, not sex-linked. They also show an interesting difference in their response to transfusion of normal blood. Thus, instead of an immediate and predictable increase in the concentration of Factor VIII in the recipient's plasma, there is a slow progressive increase that may reach a peak in 48 hours and persist for longer than 72 (Fig. 30–53). Moreover, a similar result follows when plasma from hemophilia A, lacking in Factor VIII, is transfused. This stimulating effect in von Willebrand's disease has not been ascribed to any known clotting factor, and may not be accompanied by shortening of the prolonged bleeding time. Plasma from von Willebrand's disease has no effect on the Factor VIII level in hemophilia A.

It is doubtful that a lack of tissue thromboplastin exists as a cause of *defective extrinsic prothrombinase formation* in a fresh wound. Inspection of Table 30–20 shows that Factors VII, X and V are required for the formation of extrinsic prothrombinase, but of these only Factor VII is not involved in the intrinsic system as well. Hereditary deficiency of Factor VII is transmitted as a highly penetrant, incompletely recessive, autosomal trait affecting one in 500,000 persons of either sex. The hemorrhagic manifestations are usually but not always mild, consisting of petechiae, purpura and hemorrhages, rarely into the joints. The bleeding time is usually prolonged, perhaps due to the fact that in the absence of Factor VII tissue thromboplastin does not successfully activate the rapid extrinsic prothrombinase system normally invoked by needle puncture, and so leaves coagulation to the slow intrinsic system. Deficiencies of Factors V and X would have the same adverse effect upon the extrinsic system and, in addition, would compromise the intrinsic prothrombinase system.

Acquired Defects of Prothrombinase Formation (Coagulation Stage I). Whereas hereditary or congenital defects of this or of any stage of blood coagulation are with rare exceptions the result of genetically determined deficiencies of single blood coagulation factors, those that are acquired are often multiple. Moreover, they may include factors involved in more than one coagulation stage (Table 30–20). For that reason, although hemorrhagic conditions due to vitamin K deficiency, coumarin therapy and liver disease affect both prothrombinase formation and the level of prothrombin itself, they will be discussed at this point. Multiple factor disturbances due to circulating anticoagulants arising in disease, fibrinolysis and the so-called consumption coagulopathies will be considered later.

Vitamin K deficiency results in failure of formation by the liver of Factors VII, IX, and X as well as of prothrombin itself. Consequently, both the extrinsic and the intrinsic

Figure 30–53. Reciprocal compatible plasma transfusions between patients with hemophilia A and von Willebrand's disease. Plasma was obtained from each patient and thereafter each was transfused with the other's plasma. Note the slow, progressive increase in antihemophilic (AHF) Factor VIII activity shown in curve A (that of the patient with von Willebrand's disease), and the lack of any effect shown in curve B (that of the patient with hemophilia A). (Modified from Barrow and Graham: Progress in Hematology, Volume IV, p. 203. New York, Grune & Stratton, 1964.)

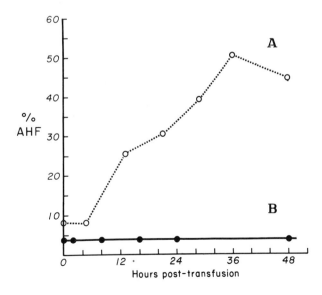

prothrombinase systems as well as Stage II of coagulation are involved (Table 30–20). There is also suggestive evidence that vascular integrity may be compromised, perhaps on the basis of the associated Factor VII deficiency, which in its hereditary form may result in purpura and a prolonged bleeding time. The body's supply of vitamin K is normally derived in large part from synthesis by the intestinal bacteria. Recent work indicates that after being absorbed from the intestine and reaching the liver, the vitamin serves as a physiologic electron carrier in oxidative phosphorylation in the liver cell mitochondria. Vitamin K is thought to be essential to the prosthetic group of an enzyme system necessary for the formation of the clotting factors mentioned above.

Despite the importance of such bacterial synthesis, at least in the coprophagic rat, it is uncertain whether inadequacy of food intake alone can induce vitamin K deficiency in man. Postoperative bleeding in obstructive jaundice was a serious and little understood complication of surgery of the biliary passages until the recognition of the relation between vitamin K and prothrombin deficiency. Before the development of the one-stage prothrombin test this type of coagulation defect usually went undetected in advance, owing to the fact that the clotting time of blood in glass may be normal with less than 10 per cent of the normal concentration of prothrombin and associated liver-produced factors. It is now clearly understood that vitamin K deficiency may occur with *extrahepatic biliary obstruction* or *biliary fistula* when for some days bile acids do not enter the intestinal tract. Likewise in patients in whom *steatorrhea* is present, as in sprue, celiac disease or idiopathic ulcerative colitis, there may be defective absorption of the fat-soluble vitamin. Lack of bacterial synthesis may be brought about by bowel sterilization with *broad spectrum antibiotics,* but deleterious effects on hepatic synthesis cannot be excluded.

Hemorrhagic disease of the newborn, though strictly congenital, is a nonhereditary, self-limited condition which occurs in the first few days of life. It is manifested by spontaneous external or internal hemorrhages and a low prothrombin concentration in the blood. Deficiencies of other liver-produced Factors VII, IX, and X are also involved and are even more pronounced. The condition appears in less than one per cent of newborn infants and seems to be an exaggeration of the normally decreased levels of prothrombinase-forming factors and prothrombin detected by the one-stage prothrombin test during the first five days of life. Low values have been observed especially in full-term infants born during the winter months or of mothers whose diets were deficient during pregnancy. At birth the maternal source of vitamin K is cut off. There appears to be no reserve of vitamin K in the newborn, which either fails to synthesize prothrombin and its congeners because of immaturity of liver function or does not produce vitamin K until after 4 or 5 days when the intestinal bacterial flora has been established. Therapy with vitamin K applied to both mother and child is clearly a wise precaution. However, the levels of prothrombin and of Factor VII do not achieve adult values even in the normal infant for some months after birth.

Link's study of the hemorrhagic disease of cattle fed spoiled, sweet clover hay led to the isolation of a toxic principle, *bishydroxycoumarin,* now available to medicine as Dicumarol. Resemblances between the naphthoquinone-like structural formulas of Dicumarol and of vitamin K suggest the possibility that the former induces hypoprothrombinemia by competing with the latter in the synthesis of prothrombin in the liver cells. Thus, mitochondria from rat liver cells are unable to produce prothrombin in vitro if the rat has been receiving Dicumarol. According to Jacques, salicylates are effective in lowering prothrombin levels only when given orally; this action is prevented by sulfonamides. For these reasons it is thought that Dicumarol may be formed in the gut from salicylates as a result of bacterial action. Dicumarol administration induces deficiency of prothrombin as well as of Factors VII, IX and X because all require vitamin K for their formation. Factor VII is more responsive than is prothrombin production both to vitamin K therapy and the administration of Dicumarol. Tromexan, phenylindandione and related drugs act in similar fashion by inhibiting formation of these coagulation factors.

For reasons that are now obvious the most common cause of hypoprothrombinemia in the adult is defective formation of prothrombin as a result of *liver disease,* for example, acute yellow atrophy or cirrhosis. In contrast to biliary obstruction or fistula, which when relieved allows the absorption of vitamin K as a result of the entry of bile salts into the alimentary tract, is the inability of even parenterally administered vitamin K to promote the synthesis of prothrombin in some instances of hepatic dysfunction. In severe liver disease the production not only of prothrombin but also of Factors VII, IX, and X and to a lesser degree of Factor V may be defective.

Defects of Thrombin Formation (Coagulation Stage II). The stoichiometric conversion of prothrombin to thrombin is brought about by activated Factor V, the final product of both the extrinsic and intrinsic prothrombinase systems (Table 30–20). Also required are probably calcium and the presence of phospholipids from platelets. However, the latter can be supplied by tissue extracts in the extrinsic system. Prothrombin is a sulfur-containing glycoprotein, which, as already stated, is formed by the liver. In general, chemicals affecting disulfide but not those affecting sulfhydryl groups inhibit the activity of prothrombin. Normally there is a five fold excess of prothrombin over the amount required to produce effective hemostasis. Less than ten instances of pure *congenital deficiency of prothrombin* have been reported and are of uncertain heredity. Surprisingly the bleeding tendency is usually mild. On the other hand *acquired deficiency of prothrombin* is common in association with deficiencies of the vitamin K dependent coagulation factors discussed above (VII, IX, X) as a result of vitamin K deficiency (biliary obstruction or steatorrhea), severe liver disease or Dicumarol therapy.

Defects of Fibrin Formation (Coagulation Stage III). Defective function of this third and last stage of the process of blood coagulation (Table 30–20) is rare. A few patients have been studied and found to have bleeding tendencies due to *hereditary fibrinogen deficiency,* or, very recently, to *hereditary abnormal fibrinogen* (Baltimore) or to *hereditary deficiency of fibrin-stabilizing Factor XIII.* So far as is known, these are transmitted independently as autosomal recessive traits of variable expressivity. The blood clots formed in any of these deficiency states may be thin, friable and apparently mechanically ineffective. However, with deficiency of fibrinogen and with the abnormal fibrinogen anomaly the bleeding tendency is mild in contrast to the serious bleeding tendency with hereditary lack of Factor XIII which clinically resembles fairly severe hemophilia. Normally, thrombin, a proteolytic enzyme removes two pairs of peptides A and B from the fibrinogen molecule by attacking its arginyl-glycine bonds. Fibrinogen is a large tripeptide with a molecular weight of about 300,000. The fibrin monomers polymerize to form an intermediate fibrin polymer with hydrogen bonding and with further tridimensional polymerization form a coarse fibrin clot which perhaps reflects disulfide bond formation. On the other hand, if purified fibrinogen is treated with purified thrombin, only a fine fibrin clot forms due to the absence of Factor XIII. Addition of normal serum then results in the normal coarse fibrin clot, which is no longer soluble in 5-M urea. Defective fibrin formation is readily detected by the prolonged clotting time of patients' plasma after the addition of thrombin.

Fibrinogen solutions exhibit double refraction of flow, a characteristic of linear macromolecules in solution. The fibrinogen molecule is stated to be thirty times as long as it is wide, as compared to a ratio of 4:1 for human serum albumin. This asymmetry is responsible for the increased viscosity of plasma containing increased amounts of fibrinogen and for causing increased rouleaux formation and consequently increased sedimentation velocity of red cells. Like prothrombin, fibrinogen is formed principally in the liver. Increased production follows within hours the stimulus of many toxic, traumatic or inflammatory conditions. Curiously, in congestive heart disease, increased fibrinogen production fails to take place, perhaps because of inhibition of production by congestion of the liver. The plasma normally contains from 180 to 400 mg. per 100 ml. Hemorrhage as a result of fibrinogen deficiency occurs only with extremely low values, such as 60 mg. or less. The conversion of fibrinogen to fibrin does not share in the autocatalytic aspects of blood coagulation but is of tremendous efficiency itself.

A few cases of *hereditary fibrinogen deficiency* have been reported in which the plasma fibrinogen is either completely lacking or greatly reduced. In the former circumstance the blood is completely incoagulable, and yet surprisingly the hemorrhagic defect may be less than in mild hemophilia. In fibrinogen deficiency some diminution of the platelets has been observed, which may account for diminished capillary resistance and purpura. Of the patients with no fibrinogen in the blood, several have died of blood loss as children, sometimes, however, after long periods of freedom from hemorrhage. Lawson has reported the case of a young woman who even menstruated regularly without excessive blood loss. In explanation it has been suggested that some intermediate product of blood coagulation may cause agglutination of platelets as a partial hemostatic substitute for

TABLE 30–23. MECHANISMS OF ACTIVATION AND EFFECTS OF FIBRINOLYSIS.*

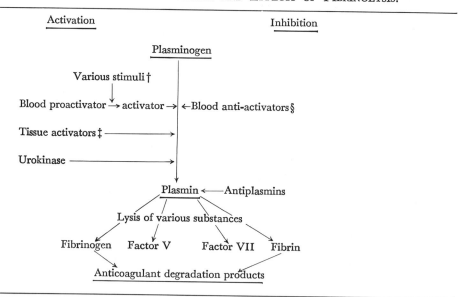

* Modified from figure by Pechet: New England J. Med., *273*:966, 1965.
† Stress, major surgery and shock.
‡ Also blood activators such as thrombin and activated Factor XII.
§ Point of action of synthetic ε-aminocaproic acid (EACA) and of Trasylol (bovine parotid extract) which also blocks plasmin and prothrombinase formation.

fibrin. Reduced amounts of fibrinogen in the plasma occasionally occur in pernicious anemia, scurvy, pellagra, leukemia and metastatic cancer of the bone marrow and especially in severe liver damage. In the last, however, hemorrhage is usually due to prothrombin and prothrombinase precursor factor deficiencies rather than to lack of fibrinogen, which is rarely, if ever, sufficiently reduced. The fibrinogen level of patients with lack of fibrinogen can usually be elevated only by transfusions of plasma, of whole blood or of fraction I of Cohn and then only for a few days (see Fig. 30–52).

Fibrinolysis. An exaggeration of this normal "cleaning up" operation may wantonly dissolve blood clots formed in the course of hemostasis of operative wounds or on eroded surfaces. The continuing need for fibrin formation so created may significantly reduce not only the fibrinogen but also the coagulation Factor V and VIII content of the blood. In vitro the blood clot formed is more or less promptly dissolved, and the blood remains incoagulable because it then contains neither fibrinogen nor fibrin. Recent studies attribute this fibrolytic activity to *plasmin,* a trypsin-like enzyme with a strong affinity for fibrinogen and fibrin. Like thrombin, it attacks the arginyl-lysine peptide bonds of fibrinogen;

but unlike thrombin it does not cleave the bonds and renders fibrinogen incoagulable by thrombin. In fact, the subsequent action of thrombin results in the release of fibrinogen fragments with anticoagulant activity, directed against thrombin-fibrinogen interaction, platelet adhesion and the polymerization of fibrin monomers. Plasmin is formed from *plasminogen,* a plasma euglobulin, by various activators evoked in blood or present in tissue and normally kept in check by excess of plasma *inhibitors* directed against plasmin as well as against its *activators* (Table 30–23). Tissues with a high content of activator are lung, kidney, and uterus where it appears to be concentrated around veins and capillaries rather than arteries. Plasmin was discovered because of the effect of streptococcal products (streptokinase) in causing the lysis of fibrin in blood clots, a process now understood as an activation of their contained plasminogen. Another activator of plasminogen, *urokinase,* a potent esterase, is excreted in the urine, although it is probably not formed in the urinary tract. Fibrinolytic activity can be detected by early clot lysis (normally 48 hours or more), by digestion of heated fibrin coatings or by release of peptides from casein or of amino acids from synthetic peptides. The incoagulable state of the blood of patients dying suddenly without previous disease is probably due to fibrinolysis. It can be induced transiently by emotion, vigorous voluntary exertion or an epileptic convulsion. Fibrinolysis has been reported in the blood of patients during the first days of menstruation, in toxemia of pregnancy, after intravenous injection of typhoid vaccine and mercurial diuretics, and in shock due to transfusion reactions, extensive hemorrhage or flame burns.

Disastrous consequences may follow activation of plasminogen in *thoracic* or *pancreatic surgery*. In *premature separation of the placenta* or with the onset of labor after fetal death in utero two mechanisms for reducing the plasma fibrinogen level have been implicated. In the first, it is assumed that the inactive precursor, plasminogen, is activated by substances in amniotic fluid, decidua or placenta. Alternatively, it is presumed that *tissue thromboplastin* derived from these tissues may enter the maternal circulation and result in progressive "defibrination" of her blood. A tissue source of fibrinolysin appears normally to be present in the prostate and to enter the circulation briefly and harmlessly after prostatic massage, but sometimes continuously and with serious consequences in instances of *prostatic cancer* or surgery. In this last the presence of *urokinase* may be a factor.

The successful treatment of fibrinolysis depends upon its early recognition and its distinction from that secondary to excessive thromboplastic activity to be discussed below. Obviously, fresh blood and plasma containing adequate amounts of fibrinogen and of Factors V and VII as well as inhibitors of further plasmin activity should be used. Nevertheless death may ensue from uncontrollable bleeding with continuing shock and fibrinolysis, unless concentrated preparations of fibrinogen such as Cohn fraction I are injected. A very effective new therapeutic agent has been contributed by Sherry in the form of ε-aminocaproic acid (EACA) and shown to inhibit the activators of plasminogen present in tissue and plasma. The drug is rapidly absorbed from the alimentary tract and has few direct toxic effects.

Consumption Coagulopathies. Defective blood coagulation may be the paradoxical result of disseminated or locally excessive intravascular blood coagulation. This, as already stated, may secondarily activate the fibrinolytic (plasmin) system with consequent destruction of fibrinogen and production of anticoagulant cleavage products. Moreover, in the primary process of *intravascular coagulation*, in addition to fibrinogen, there may be excessive consumption of Factor V and Factor VIII and of platelets. According to Rodriguez-Erdmann, the partially altered fibrinogen may be precipitated at 4° C. in vitro as cryoprofibrin (Table 30–24). This finding, together with low prothrombin and platelet levels, is the hallmark of consumption coagulopathy in contrast to primary fibrinolysis.

In 1760, Hewson observed that in the venisection of men and animals, "the blood that issued first, coagulated last." This was the first evidence that hemorrhage and shock could hasten blood coagulation as a result of the common denominator of *all types of shock*, including that due to extensive surgery and burns: inadequate perfusion of the visceral vascular bed. According to McKay, shock induced by bleeding in dogs causes progressive hypercoagulability of the blood in silicone-coated tubes, accompanied by a progressive fall in fibrinogen and associated at autopsy with microscopic capillary thrombi and tissue necrosis. Heparin prevents these events. Other initiating factors for consumption coagulopathy may be released by the hemolysis of red cells in *transfusion reactions,* and in *hemolytic anemias* such as those of paroxysmal nocturnal hemoglobinuria, sickle cell disease and malaria. In *late pregnancy* a variety of intravascular clotting syndromes associated with the characteristically elevated fibrinogen levels may occur: eclampsia, abruptio placentae, amniotic fluid embolism and bilateral cortical necrosis of the kidneys. The histologic findings at autopsy of such patients show intracapillary fibrin deposition in the glomeruli and other lesions of the small vessels very much resembling those of the so-called *Sanarelli-Shwartzman phenomenon*.

TABLE 30–24. COMPARISON OF CONSUMPTION COAGULOPATHY AND FIBRINOLYTIC STATE WITH RESPECT TO CHANGES IN COAGULATION FACTORS. *

Activity	Consumption Coagulopathy	Fibrinolytic State
Platelets	Decreased	Normal
Fibrinogen	Decreased	Decreased
Prothrombin	Decreased	Normal
Factor V	Decreased	Decreased
Factor VIII	Decreased	Decreased
Cryoprofibrin	Present	Absent
Fibrinolysis	Variable	Increased
Antithrombin	Decreased initially	? Normal

* Modified from Rodriguez-Erdmann: New England J. Med., *273:*1370, 1965.

This remarkable reaction occurs in experimental animals following the second of two injections of endotoxin (derived from gram-negative bacteria) separated by an interval of 24 hours. Serum prothrombin, platelets and Factor V drop to low levels in a few hours. The pregnant animal requires only one injection.

In patients similar vascular effects are thought to occur in *purpura fulminans, the Waterhouse-Friderichsen syndrome, gram-negative septicemias* and perhaps in *thrombohemolytic thrombocytopenic purpura.* The occurrence in cancer of superficial migratory thrombophlebitis is well known and recently the additional association of high platelet levels with a variety of cancers has been pointed out. The intravascular coagulation underlying the manifest fibrinolysis in a patient with *carcinoma of the prostate* was unmasked by the use of the plasmin inhibitor ε-aminocaproic acid with fatal results, due to widespread vascular thrombosis. On the other hand, bleeding with fibrinolysis and low platelet levels in a patient with diffuse vasculitis, diagnosed as *thrombohemolytic thrombocytopenic purpura,* responded brilliantly to the administration of heparin, suggesting the secondary nature of the fibrinolysis. These patients exemplify the clinical importance of distinguishing the basic pathophysiology of primary fibrinolysis from that of primary intravascular blood coagulation with secondary fibrinolysis.

Circulating Anticoagulants. Without the presence of natural *physiologic anticoagulants,* once the evolution of thrombin was activated in a local cause it might generalize to become massive intravascular clotting. Moreover, it is probably desirable that in the "enzyme cascade" involved in the formation of prothrombinase by the intrinsic system, once some of each activated participant has activated the next in the series, the excess of the precursor remaining should be removed. Thrombin or its activator is opposed by several mechanisms referred to as *antithrombins.* These include adsorption by fibrin, the refractory modification of fibrinogen produced by plasmin, and the inhibitory effect of subsequent thrombin-produced degradation products upon fibrin monomer polymerization. The property of normal serum that slowly inactivates added thrombin is readily measured in vitro and is usually referred to as "antithrombin." There is also a well-defined, relatively heat-stable, property of plasma that is not adsorbed by barium sulfate which promotes

the deterioration of fully formed prothrombinase (activated Factor V) in vitro. Recently Deykin has shown the importance of an in vivo "clearing mechanism" in the perfused liver for removing activated Factor IX, which triggers the formation of blood clots in isolated segments of uninjured veins.

Most of these physiologic anticoagulants act upon the clotting mechanism subsequent to the formation of prothrombinase (Table 30–20). On the other hand, the *anticoagulant activity that may develop in disease states* is directed toward precursors of prothrombinase in the intrinsic system such as Factors VIII and IX, deficiencies of which are found in hemophilias A and B, respectively. In rare instances in women, usually some months after parturition, and more commonly in elderly individuals of either sex, circulating anticoagulants directed against Factor VIII have been found. Although usually clinically mild in the elderly, the unrecognized condition may be a serious hazard to surgical hemostasis. In the presence of these pathologic anticoagulants the thromboplastin generation test is abnormal, but the one-stage prothrombin test is normal (Table 30–22). The anticoagulants are present in the gamma globulin fraction of serum or plasma and are relatively heat- and storage-stable. As might be expected from the early participation of Factors VIII and IX in the intrinsic clotting mechanism, addition of a small amount of the anticoagulant-containing plasma to freshly drawn blood prolongs the clotting time, but has little effect if added shortly before the appearance of the fibrin clot.

These anticoagulants, as well as those recently detected against Factors V and XI, are thought to be the result of immunization, sometimes but not always clearly following prior therapeutic administration of blood or blood products. Those directed against Factors VIII and IX may develop in about 10 per cent of patients with hemophilia due to lack of these factors, respectively. They are a serious obstacle to treatment because of the greatly increased requirement for the anticoagulant-opposed factors required. Moreover, the intravenous injection of fresh plasma in treatment brings about a subsequent anamnestic rise in the levels of the anticoagulants. In *lupus erythematosus* less than 10 per cent of patients develop an anticoagulant and this is rarely responsible for clinical bleeding unless thrombocytopenia is present. The anticoagulant has usually been directed against Factor VIII; but in one patient of Hougie's, a male with a positive L.E. test, the anticoagulant opposed the conversion of prothrombin to thrombin even when the patient's plasma was diluted 80 times.

Failure of the blood to clot in cases of *anaphylactic shock* in animals appears to be due to the presence of heparin. *Heparin* is present in animal liver and lung, but is not found in the blood of normal dogs, and does not appear in the blood of sensitized *hepatectomized* dogs after anaphylactic shock. Irradiation with roentgen rays also causes a rise in the heparin content of the plasma of dogs. Heparin, a mixture of compounds having a mucoitin polysulfuric acid structure, has not been shown to have a physiologic role in man. However, it prevents coagulation of whole blood both by retarding the formation of prothrombinase and by acting as antithrombin. It has almost no inhibitory action on a mixture of purified fibrinogen and thrombin. Consequently its action may be directly upon some other protein in the plasma (albumin X) with which its strongly acid groups permit it to form stable salts. The anticoagulant action of heparin is neutralized both in vitro and in vivo by the strongly basic protamine, salmine.

As a drug, *heparin* has been used to render the blood of transfusion donors temporarily incoagulable and to prevent intravascular thrombosis. *Hirudin,* a substance extracted from leeches, renders blood incoagulable by preventing the action of thrombin upon fibrinogen. *Cysteine, glutathione,* taurine and taurocolic acid probably prevent coagulation by inhibition of disulfide groups which are known to be present in prothrombin. *Dicumarol,* in contrast to these substances, is effective only in vivo. Its pharmacologic action and that of salicylic acid in preventing the formation of prothrombin and of other liver-produced Factors VII, IX and X as a result of antagonism to the function of vitamin K have already been discussed.

In Waldenström's *macroglobulinemia* and sometimes in multiple myeloma, skin purpura or even greater hemorrhage from the mucosa of the nasopharynx or gastrointestinal tract has been observed. The platelet count and bleeding time, the coagulation time and the concentration of prothrombin and fibrinogen are normal; however, clots formed may be friable and retract poorly. The tourniquet test is frequently positive. Again, the elevated plasma globulins appear to be responsible by opposing the action of thrombin in converting fibrinogen to fibrin, and possibly by altering the electrostatic charge or the ability of platelets to release phospholipids. This is of interest in view of the reports of hemorrhagic episodes in a few patients with other types of hyperglobulinemia. These include patients with globulins precipitating at ice box or even at room temperature (cryoglobulinemia). In the case reported by Lerner and Watson, purpura first appeared on the extremities after exposure to cold and was accompanied by transient urticaria. Stefanini finds the hemorrhagic tendency in liver disease particularly impressive when the globulin levels are elevated, even if specific coagulation studies fail to indicate any significant laboratory abnormality.

REFERENCES

General

Cartwright, G. E.: Diagnostic Laboratory Hematology, 3rd ed. New York, Grune & Stratton, 1963.

Daland, G. A.: Color Atlas of Morphologic Hematology: With a Guide to Clinical Interpretation. (Revised) Cambridge, Mass., Harvard University Press, 1959.

de Gruchy, G. C.: Clinical Haematology in Medical Practice, 2nd ed. Philadelphia, F. A. Davis Co., 1963.

McDonald, G. A., Dodds, T. C., and Cruickshank, B.: Atlas of Hematology. Baltimore, Williams & Wilkins Co., 1965.

Smith, C. H.: Blood Diseases of Infancy and Childhood. St. Louis, C. V. Mosby Co., 1960.

Stanbury, J. B., Wyngaarden, J. B., and Frederickson, D. (eds.): The Metabolic Basis of Inherited Disease, 2nd ed. New York, McGraw-Hill Book Co., 1966.

Wintrobe, M. M.: Clinical Hematology, 5th ed. Philadelphia, Lea & Febiger, 1961.

Erythrocyte and Hemoglobin Production

Allen, D. W.: Hemoglobin metabolism within the red cell. Chapter 8 in The Red Blood Cell. New York, Academic Press, 1964.

Allen, D. W., and Jandl, J. H.: Factors influencing relative rates of synthesis of adult and fetal hemoglobin in vitro. J. Clin. Invest., *39:*1107, 1960.

Berk, L., Burchenal, J. H., and Castle, W. B.: Erythropoietic effect of cobalt in patients with and without anemia. New England J. Med., *240:*754, 1949.

Birkhill, F. R., Maloney, M. A., and Levenson, S. M.: Effect of transfusion polycythemia upon bone marrow activity and erythrocyte survival in man. Blood, *6:*1021, 1951.

Borsook, H.: A picture of erythropoiesis at the combined morphologic and molecular levels. Blood, *24:*356, 1964.

Bruce, W. R., and McCulloch, E. A.: The effect of

erythropoietic stimulation on the hemopoietic colony-forming cells of mice. Blood, 23:216, 1964.

Caffey, J.: Skeletal changes in chronic hemolytic anemias (erythroblastic anemia, sickle cell anemia and chronic hemolytic icterus). Am. J. Roentgenol., 37:293, 1937.

Crosby, W. H.: The control of iron balance by the intestinal mucosa. Blood, 22:441, 1963.

Dacie, J. V., and White, J. C.: Erythropoiesis, with particular reference to its study by biopsy of human bone marrow: A review. J. Clin. Path., 2:1, 1949.

Erslev, A. J.: The effect of anemic anoxia on the cellular development of nucleated red cells. Blood, 14:386, 1959.

Giblett, E. R., and others: Erythrokinetics: Quantitative measurements of red cell production and destruction in normal subjects and patients with anemia. Blood, 11:291, 1956.

Granick, S., and Levere, R. D.: Heme synthesis in erythroid cells. In Progress in Hematology, Vol. IV, p. 1. New York, Grune & Stratton, 1964.

Harris, J. W.: The Red Cell: Production, Metabolism, Destruction: Normal and Abnormal. Cambridge, Mass., Harvard University Press, 1963.

Hosain, F., and others: Nature of internal iron exchange in man. Tr. A. Am. Physicians, 75:59, 1962.

Huff, R. L., and others: Ferrokinetics in normal persons and in patients having various erythropoietic disorders. J. Clin. Invest., 30:1512, 1951.

Ingram, V.: Control mechanisms in hemoglobin synthesis. Medicine, 43:759, 1964.

Lange, R. D., and Pavlovic-Kentera, V.: Erythropoietin. In Progress in Hematology, Vol. IV, p. 72. New York, Grune & Stratton, 1964.

London, I. M., Bruns, G. P., and Karibian, D.: The regulation of hemoglobin synthesis and the pathogenesis of some hypochromic anemias. Medicine, 43:789, 1964.

Lowman, R. M., Bloor, C. M., and Newcomb, A. W.: Roentgen manifestations of thoracic extramedullary hematopoiesis. Dis. Chest., 44:154, 1963.

Rath, C. E., and Finch, C. A.: Sternal marrow hemosiderin. J. Lab. & Clin. Med., 33:81, 1948.

Simon, E. R., Giblett, E. R., and Finch, C. A.: Red Cell Manual. Seattle, University of Washington Press, 1966.

Stohlman, F., Jr., and others: Regulation of erythropoiesis. XVI. Cytokinetic patterns in disorders of erythropoiesis. Medicine, 43:651, 1964.

Erythrocyte and Hemoglobin Destruction

Amorosi, E. L.: Hypersplenism. Seminars Hemat., 2:249, 1965.

Berlin, N. I., Waldmann, T. A., and Weissman, S. M.: Life span of red blood cell. Physiol. Rev., 39:577, 1959.

Brus, I., and Lewis, S. M.: The haptoglobin content of serum in haemolytic anaemia. Brit. J. Haemat., 5:348, 1959.

Crosby, W. H.: Normal functions of the spleen relative to red blood cells: A review. Blood, 14:399, 1959.

Keene, W. R., and Jandl, J. H.: The sites of hemoglobin catabolism. Blood, 26:705, 1965.

Noyes, W. D., Bothwell, T. H., and Finch, C. A.: The role of the reticuloendothelial cell in iron metabolism. Brit. J. Haemat., 6:43, 1960.

Schmid, R.: Hyperbilirubinemia. Chapter 37 in Metabolic Basis of Inherited Disease, 2nd ed. New York, McGraw-Hill Book Co., 1966.

Yamamato, T., and others: The early appearing bilirubin: Evidence for two components. J. Clin. Invest., 44:31, 1965.

General Effects of Anemia

Bartlett, D., Jr., and Tenny, S. M.: Tissue gas tensions in experimental anemia. J. Appl. Physiol., 18:734, 1963.

Bradley, S. E., and Bradley, G. P.: Renal function during chronic anemia in man. Blood, 2:192, 1947.

Campbell, J. A.: Tissue oxygen tension and haemoglobin. J. Physiol., 65:255, 1928.

Crowell, J. W., Ford, R. G., and Lewis, V. M.: Oxygen transport in hemorrhagic shock as a function of the hematocrit ratio. Am. J. Physiol., 196:1033, 1959.

Fudenberg, H., Baldini, M., and Dameshek, W.: The body hematocrit/venous hematocrit ratio and the "splenic reservoir." Blood, 17:71, 1961.

Gibson, J. G., II, Harris, A. W., and Swigert, V. W.: Clinical studies of the blood volume. VIII. Macrocytic and hypochromic anemias due to chronic blood loss, hemolysis and miscellaneous causes, and polycythemia vera. J. Clin. Invest., 18:621, 1939.

Hatcher, J. D.: The physiological responses of the circulation to anaemia. Mod. Concepts Cardiovas. Dis., 23:235, 1954.

Huber, H., Lewis, S. M., and Szur, L.: Influence of anemia, polycythemia and splenomegaly on relationship between venous hematocrit and red cell volume. Brit. Haematol., 10:567, 1964.

Murray, J. F., Gold, P., and Johnson, B. L., Jr.: The circulatory effects of hematocrit variations in normovolemic and hypervolemic dogs. J. Clin. Invest., 42:1150, 1963.

Roughton, F. J. W.: Transport of oxygen and carbon dioxide. Chapter 3 in Handbook of Physiology, Vol. I. Am. Physiol. Soc., 1964.

Strauss, M. B., and Fox, H. J.: Anemia and water retention. Am. J. Med. Sc., 200:454, 1940.

Wells, R. E., and Merrill, E. W.: The variability of blood viscosity. Am. J. Med., 31:505, 1961.

Erythrocyte Characteristics

Bowman, W. D., Jr.: Abnormal (ringed) sideroblasts in various hematologic and nonhematologic disorders. Blood, 18:662, 1961.

Castle, W. B., and Daland, G. A.: Susceptibility of mammalian erythrocytes to hemolysis with hypotonic solutions. Arch. Int. Med., 60:949, 1937.

Fessas, P.: Inclusions of hemoglobin in erythroblasts and erythrocytes of thalassemia. Blood, 21:21, 1963.

Jacob, H. S., and Jandl, J. H.: Effects of sulfhydryl inhibition on red blood cells II. Studies in vivo. J. Clin. Invest., 41:1514, 1962.

Jandl, J. H.: Agglutination and sequestration of immature red cells. J. Lab. & Clin. Med., 55:663, 1960.

Jandl, J. H.: Leaky red cells: An analytical review. Blood, 26:367, 1965.

Jandl, J. H., and Allen, D. W.: Oxidative hemolysis and precipitation of hemoglobin: Heinz body anemias as an accelerated form of red cell aging. J. Clin. Invest., 39:1000, 1960.

Jensen, W. N., Moreno, G. D., and Bessis, M. C.: An electron microscopic description of basophilic stippling in red cells. Blood, 25:933, 1965.

Price-Jones, C.: Red Blood Cell Diameters. London, Oxford Medical Publications, 1933.

Rifkind, R. A., and Danon, D.: Heinz body anemia: An ultra-structural study. I. Heinz body formation. Blood, 25:885, 1965.

Wintrobe, M. M.: Macroscopic examination of the blood. Am. J. Med. Sc., 185:58, 1933.

Increased Erythrocyte Loss

Conrad, M. E., and Crosby, W. H.: The natural history of iron deficiency induced by phlebotomy. Blood, 20:173, 1962.

Ebert, R. V., Stead, E. A., Jr., and Gibson, J. G., II: Response of normal subjects to acute blood loss. Arch. Int. Med., 68:578, 1941.

Vilter, R. W., Woolford, R. M., and Spies, T. D.: Severe scurvy; A clinical and hematological study. J. Lab. & Clin. Med., 31:609, 1946.

Increased Erythrocyte Destruction

(a) CONGENITAL ERYTHROCYTE DEFECTS

Beutler, E.: Glucose-6-phosphate dehydrogenase deficiency and non-spherocytic congenital hemolytic anemia. Seminars Hemat., 2:91, 1965.

Chanarin, I., Burman, D., and Bennett, M. C.: The familial aplastic crisis in hereditary spherocytosis: Urocanic acid and formiminoglutamic acid excretion in a case of megaloblastic arrest. Blood, 20:33, 1962.

Chanarin, I., Dacie, J. V., and Mollin, D. L.: Folic acid deficiency in haemolytic anaemia. Brit. J. Haematol., 5:245, 1959.

Conley, C. L., and others: Hereditary persistence of fetal hemoglobin: A study of 79 affected persons in 15 Negro families in Baltimore. Blood, 21:261, 1963.

Cutting, H. O., and others: Autosomal dominant hemolytic anemia characterized by ovalocytosis. Am. J. Med., 39:21, 1965.

Dacie, J. V.: The Hemolytic Anaemias: Congenital and Acquired. Part I. The Congenital Anaemias. New York, Grune & Stratton, 1960.

Dacie, J. V., and others: Hereditary Heinz-body anemia. Brit. J. Haemat., 10:388, 1964.

Desforges, J. F.: Erythrocyte metabolism in hemolysis. New England J. Med., 273:1310, 1965.

Emerson, C. P., Jr., and others: Quantitative methods for determining the osmotic and mechanical fragility of red cells in the peripheral blood and splenic pulp; the mechanism of increased hemolysis in hereditary spherocytosis (congenital hemolytic jaundice) as related to the functions of the spleen. Arch. Int. Med., 97:1, 1956.

Harris, J. W., and others: Biophysics and biology of sickle cell disease. Arch. Int. Med., 97:145, 1956.

Heller, P.: Analytical review: The molecular basis of the pathogeneity of abnormal hemoglobins: Some recent developments. Blood, 25:110, 1965.

Ingram, V.: Control mechanisms in hemoglobin synthesis. Medicine, 43:759, 1964.

Jacob, H. S.: Hereditary spherocytosis: A disease of the red cell membrane. Seminars Hemat., 2:139, 1965.

Jaffe, E. R., and Heller, P.: Methemoglobinemia in man. In Progress in Hematology, Vol. IV, p. 48. New York, Grune & Stratton, 1964.

Jandl, J. H., Simmons, R. L., and Castle, W. B.: Red cell filtration and the pathogenesis of certain hemolytic anemias. Blood, 18:133, 1961.

Jensen, W. N., Rucknagel, D. L., and Taylor, W. J.: In vivo study of the sickle cell phenomenon. J. Lab. & Clin. Med., 56:854, 1960.

Marks, P. A., and Gerald, P. S.: The thalassemia syndromes: Biochemical, genetic and clinical considerations. Am. J. Med., 36:919, 1964.

McCurdy, P. R.: Erythrokinetics in abnormal hemoglobin syndromes. Blood, 20:686, 1962.

Perillie, P. E., and Epstein, F. H.: Sickling phenomenon produced by hypertonic solutions: Possible explanation for hyposthenuria of sicklemia. J. Clin. Invest., 42:570, 1963.

Rieder, R. F., Zinkham, W. H., and Holtzman, N. A.: Hemoglobin Zurich: Clinical, chemical and kinetic studies. Am. J. Med., 39:4, 1965.

Schneider, A. S., and others: Hereditary hemolytic anemia with triosephosphate isomerase deficiency. New England J. Med., 272:229, 1965.

Selwyn, J. G., and Dacie, J. V.: Autohemolysis and other changes resulting from the incubation in vitro of red cells from patients with congenital hemolytic anemia. Blood, 9:414, 1954.

Sturgeon, P., and Finch, C. A.: Erythrokinetics in Cooley's anemia. Blood, 12:64, 1957.

Tanaka, K. R., Valentine, W. N., and Miwa, S.: Pyruvate kinase (PK) deficiency hereditary non-spherocytic hemolytic anemia. Blood, 19:267, 1962.

Zuelzer, W. W., Robinson, A., and Booker, C. R.: Reciprocal relationship of hemoglobins A₂ and F in beta chain thalassemias. A key to the genetic control of hemoglobin F. Blood, 17:393, 1961.

(b) ACQUIRED ERYTHROCYTE DEFECTS

Allen, F. H., Jr., and Diamond, L. K.: Erythroblastosis fetalis. New England J. Med., 257:659, 705, 761, 1957.

Beal, R. W., Kronenberg, H., and Firkin, B. G.: The syndrome of paroxysmal nocturnal hemoglobinuria. Am. J. Med., 37:899, 1964.

Bennett, J. M., and Healey, P. J. M.: Spherocytic hemolytic anemia and acute cholecystitis caused by Clostridium welchii. New England J. Med., 268:1071, 1963.

Brain, M. C., Dacie, J. V., and Hourihane, D. O'B.: Microangiopathic haemolytic anaemia: Possible role of vascular lesions in pathogenesis. Brit. J. Haemat., 8:358, 1962.

Castle, W. B., Ham, T. H., and Shen, S. C.: Observations on the mechanism of hemolytic transfusion reactions occurring without demonstrable hemolysin. Tr. A. Am. Physicians, 63:161, 1950.

Chertkow, G., and Dacie, J. V.: Results of splenectomy in autoimmune haemolytic anaemia. Brit. J. Haemat., 2:237, 1956.

Dacie, J. V.: The Haemolytic Anaemias: Congenital and Acquired. Part II. The Autoimmune Haemolytic Anaemias. New York, Grune & Stratton, 1962.

Davidson, R. J. L.: Exertional hemoglobinuria: Report of three cases with studies on hemolytic mechanism. J. Clin. Path., 17:536, 1964.

Freedman, A. L., Barr, P. S., and Brody, E. A.: Hemolytic anemia due to quinidine. Am. J. Med., 20:806, 1956.

Ham, T. H.: Chronic hemolytic anemia with paroxysmal nocturnal hemoglobinuria. Arch. Int. Med., 64:1271, 1939.

Harris, J. W.: Studies on the mechanism of a drug-induced hemolytic anemia. J. Lab & Clin. Med., 47:760, 1956.

Jandl, J. H.: The anemia of liver disease: Observations on its mechanism. J. Clin. Invest., 34:390, 1955.

Jandl, J. H., Engle, L. K., and Allen, D. W.: Oxidative hemolysis and precipitation of hemoglobin. I. Heinz body anemias as an acceleration of red cell aging. J. Clin. Invest., 39:1818, 1960.

Jandl, J. H., and Kaplan, M. E.: The destruction of red cells by antibodies in man. III. Quantitative factors influencing the patterns of hemolysis in vivo. J. Clin. Invest., 39:1145, 1960.

Leddy, J. P., and others: The unitary nature of "complete" and "incomplete" pathologic cold hemagglutinins. Blood, 19:379, 1962.

Lewis, S. M., Dacie, J. V., and Szur, L.: Mechanism of hemolysis in cold-hemagglutinin syndrome. Brit J. Haemat., 6:154, 1960.

Mackell, J. V., and others: Acute hemolytic anemia due to ingestion of naphthalene moth balls. Pediatrics, 7:722, 1951.

Pisciotta, A. V.: Cold hemagglutination in acute and chronic hemolytic syndromes. Blood, 10:295, 1955.

Reynafarje, C., and Ramos, J.: Hemolytic anemia of human bartonellosis. Blood, 17:562, 1961.

Rosenthal, M. C., and others: The autoimmune hemolytic anemia of malignant lymphocytic disease. Blood, 10:197, 1955.

Sears, D. A., and Crosby, W. H.: Intravascular hemolysis due to intracardiac prosthetic devices: Diurnal variations related to activity. Am. J. Med., 39:341, 1965.

Wasastjerna, C., Dameshek, W., and Komninos, Z. D.: Direct observations of intravascular agglutination of red cells in acquired autoimmune hemolytic anemia. J. Lab. & Clin. Med., 43:98, 1954.

Decreased Erythrocyte Production

(a) Nutritional deficiency

Beck, W. S.: The metabolic basis of megaloblastic erythropoiesis. Medicine, 43:715, 1964.

Bok, J., and others: Effect of pteroylglutamic acid administration on serum vitamin B_{12} concentration in pernicious anemia in relapse. J. Lab. & Clin. Med., 51:667, 1958.

Bothwell, T. H., and Finch, C. A.: Iron Metabolism. Boston, Little, Brown & Co., 1962.

Callender, S. T., and Denborough, M. A.: A family study of pernicious anaemia. Brit. J. Haemat., 3:88, 1957.

Castle, W. B.: Factors involved in the absorption of vitamin B_{12}. Gastroenterology, 37:377, 1959.

Chanarin, I.: Urocanic acid and formimino-glutamic acid excretion in megaloblastic anaemia and other conditions: The effect of specific therapy. Brit. J. Haemat., 9:141, 1963.

Chanarin, I., and others: Folic acid deficiency in pregnancy. Lancet, 2:634, 1959.

Cox, E. V., and others: Scurvy and anemia. Am. J. Med., 32:240, 1962.

Cox, E. V., and White, A. M.: Methylmalonic acid excretion: An index of vitamin B_{12} deficiency. Lancet, 2:853, 1962.

Doig, A., and Girdwood, R. H.: The absorption of folic acid and labelled cyanocobalamin in intestinal malabsorption. Quart. J. Med., 29:333, 1960.

Doniach, D., and Roitt, I. M.: An evaluation of gastric and thyroid autoimmunity in relation to hematologic disorders. Seminars Hemat., 1:313, 1964.

Finch, C. A., and others: Erythrokinetics in pernicious anemia. Blood, 11:807, 1956.

Gardner, F. H.: Tropical sprue. New England J. Med., 258:791, 835, 1958.

Glass, G. B. J.: Gastric intrinsic factor and its function in the metabolism of vitamin B_{12}. Physiol. Rev., 43:529, 1963.

Goldberg, A., Lockhead, A. C., and Dagg, J. H.: Histamine-fast achlorhydria and iron absorption. Lancet, 1:848, 1963.

Goldfarb, T. G., and Popp, B. J.: Excessively high levels of lactic acid dehydrogenase activity in pernicious anemia. Am. J. Med., 34:578, 1963.

Gräsbeck, R.: Physiology and pathology of vitamin B_{12} absorption, distribution and excretion. Adv. Clin. Chem., 3:299, 1960.

Gräsbeck, R., and others: Selective vitamin B_{12} malabsorption and proteinuria in young people: A syndrome. Acta Med. Scand., 167:289, 1960.

Harris, J. W.: Notes and comments on pyridoxine-responsive anemia and the role of erythrocyte mitochondria in iron metabolism. Medicine, 43:803, 1964.

Hawkins, C. F., and Meynell, M. J.: Macrocytosis and macrocytic anaemia caused by anticonvulsant drugs. Quart. J. Med., 27:45, 1958.

Heath, C. W., and Patek, A. J., Jr.: The anemia of iron deficiency. Medicine, 16:267, 1937.

Heilmeyer, L., and others: Congenital atransferremia in child aged seven. Deutsche Med. Wchnschr., 86:1745, 1961.

Herbert, V.: The Megaloblastic Anemias. Modern Medical Monographs 18. New York, Grune & Stratton, 1959.

Hoedemaeker, P. J., and others: Site of production of intrinsic factor in man. Lab. Invest., 13:1394, 1964.

Jacobs, A.: Iron-containing enzymes in the buccal epithelium. Lancet, 2:1331, 1961.

Jandl, J. H., and Gabuzda, G. J., Jr.: Potentiation of pteroylglutamic acid by ascorbic acid in anemia of scurvy. Proc. Soc. Exper. Biol. Med., 84:452, 1953.

Jandl, J. H., and Greenberg, M. S.: Bone marrow failure due to relative nutritional deficiency in Cooley's hemolytic anemia. New England J. Med., 260:461, 1959.

Johns, D. G., and Bertino, J. R.: Folates and megaloblastic anemia: A review. Clin. Pharm. Therap., 6:372, 1965.

Marshall, R. A., and Jandl, J. H.: Responses to "physiologic" doses of folic acid in megaloblastic anemias. Arch. Int. Med., 105:352, 1960.

McIntyre, O., and others: Pernicious anemia in childhood. New England J. Med., 272:981, 1965.

Mollin, D. L., Booth, C. C., and Baker, S. J.: The absorption of vitamin B_{12} in control subjects, in Addisonian pernicious anemia and in the malabsorption syndrome. Brit. J. Haemat., 3:412, 1957.

Nyberg, W.: Absorption and excretion of vitamin B_{12} in subjects infected with *Diphyllobothrium latum* and in noninfected subjects following oral administration of radioactive B_{12}. Acta Haemat., 19:90, 1958.

Resnick, R. H., and others: Abnormal Schilling test corrected by intestinal juice. New England J. Med., 268:926, 1963.

Sheehy, T. W., and others: The effect of "minute" and "titrated" amounts of folic acid on the megaloblastic anemia of tropical sprue. Blood, 18:623, 1961.

Smith, M. D., and Pannacciulli, I. M.: Absorption of inorganic iron from graded doses. Brit. J. Haemat., 4:428, 1958.

Toohey, J. I., and Barker, H. A.: Isolation of coenzyme B_{12} from liver. J. Biol. Chem., 236:560, 1961.

Wheby, M. S., and Crosby, W. H.: The gastrointestinal tract and iron absorption. Blood, 22:416, 1963.

Williams, A. M., Chosy, J. J., and Schilling, R. F.: Effect of vitamin B_{12} in vitro on incorporation of nucleic acid precursors by pernicious anemia bone marrow. J. Clin. Invest., 42:670, 1963.

Wilson, T. H.: Intestinal absorption of vitamin B_{12}. The Physiologist, 6:11, 1963.

Zalusky, R., and Herbert, V.: Megaloblastic anemia in scurvy with response to 50 μg. folic acid daily. New England J. Med., 265:1033, 1961.

(b) ENDOCRINE DEFICIENCY

Daughaday, W. H., Williams, R. H., and Daland, G. A.: The effect of endocrinopathies on the blood. Blood, 3:1342, 1948.

Fisher, J. W., and Crook, J. J.: Influence of several hormones on erythropoiesis and oxygen consumption in the hypophysectomized rat. Blood, 19:557, 1962.

Gardner, F. H., and Pringle, J. C., Jr.: Androgens and erythropoiesis. Arch. Int. Med., 107:846, 1961.

Greig, H. B. W., and others: Anaemia in hypopituitarism: Treatment with testosterone and cortisone. South African J. Lab. & Clin. Med., 2:52, 1956.

Muldowney, F. P., Crooks, J., and Wayne, E. J.: The total red cell mass in thyrotoxicosis and myxoedema. Clin. Sc., 16:309, 1957.

Tudhope, G. R., and Wilson, G. M.: Anaemia in hypothyroidism: Incidence, pathogenesis and treatment. Quart. J. Med., 29:513, 1960.

Van Dyke, D. C., and others: Hormonal factors influencing erythropoiesis. Acta Haemat., 11:203, 1954.

(c) TOXIC INHIBITION

Bierman, H. R., and Nelson, H. R.: Hematodepressive virus disease of Thailand. Ann. Int. Med., 62:867, 1965.

Callen, I. R., and Limarzi, L. R.: Blood and bone marrow studies in renal disease. Am. J. Clin. Path., 20:3, 1950.

Cartwright, G. E., and others: The anemia of infection. J. Clin. Invest., 25:65, 81, 1946.

Dacie, J. V., and others: Refractory normoblastic anaemia: Clinical and haematological study of seven cases. Brit. J. Haemat., 5:56, 1959.

Freireich, E. J., and others: The effect of inflammation on the utilization of erythrocyte and transferrin-bound radio iron for red cell production. Blood, 12:972, 1957.

Gervirtz, N. R., and Berlin, N. I.: Erythrokinetic studies in severe bone marrow failure of diverse etiology. Blood, 18:637, 1961.

Loge, J. P., Lange, R. D., and Moore, C. V.: Characterization of the anemia associated with chronic renal insufficiency. Am. J. Med., 24:4, 1958.

May, C. D., and others: Infection as a cause of folic acid deficiency and megaloblastic anemia: Experimental induction of megaloblastic anemia by turpentine abscess. Am. J. Dis. Child., 84:718, 1952.

Miller, A., and others: Studies of anemia and iron metabolism in cancer. J. Clin. Invest., 35:1248, 1956.

Moore, C. V.: The concept of relative bone marrow failure. Am. J. Med., 23:1, 1957.

Movitt, E. R., Mangum, J. F., and Porter, W. R.: Idiopathic true bone marrow failure. Am. J. Med., 34:500, 1963.

Roberts, F. D., and others: Evaluation of the anemia of rheumatoid arthritis. Blood, 21:470, 1963.

Rubin, D., and others: Changes in iron metabolism in early chloramphenicol toxicity. J. Clin. Invest., 37:1286, 1958.

Saidi, P., Wallerstein, R. O., and Aggeler, P. M.: Effect of chloramphenicol on erythropoiesis. J. Lab. & Clin. Med., 57:247, 1961.

Schmid, J. R., and others: Thymoma associated with pure red cell agenesis: Review of literature and report of four cases. Cancer, 18:216, 1965.

Scott, J. L., Cartwright, G. E., and Wintrobe, M. M.: Acquired aplastic anemia. Medicine, 38:119, 1959.

Shahidi, N. T., and Diamond, L. K.: Testosterone-induced remissions in aplastic anemia of both acquired and congenital types: Further observations in 24 cases. New England J. Med., 264:953, 1961.

Willison, G. W.: The effects of bacterial toxins on erythrogenesis. J. Lab. & Clin. Med., 24:383, 1939.

Yunis, A. A., and Bloomberg, G. R.: Chloramphenicol toxicity: Clinical features and pathogenesis. In Progress in Hematology, Vol. IV, p. 138. New York, Grune & Stratton, 1964.

(d) PHYSICAL INJURY

Cronkite, E. P., and Bond, V. P.: Radiation Injury in Man. Springfield, Charles C Thomas, 1960.

Goswitz, F. A., Andrews, G. A., and Kniseley, R. M.: Effects of local irradiation (Co⁶⁰ teletherapy) on the peripheral blood and bone marrow. Blood, 21:605, 1963.

Lorenz, E., and Congdon, C. C.: Radioactivity: Biologic effects of ionizing radiations. Ann. Rev. Med., 5:323, 1954.

Martland, H. S.: The occurrence of malignancy in radio-active persons. Am. J. Cancer, 15:2435, 1931.

Perman, V., and others: The regenerative ability of hemopoietic tissue following lethal X-irradiation in dogs. Blood, 19:724, 1962.

(e) MECHANICAL INTERFERENCE

Carpenter, G., and Flory, C. M.: Chronic non-leukemic myelosis. Arch. Int. Med., 67:489, 1941.

Gairdner, D., Marks, J., and Roscoe, J. D.: Blood formation in infancy. II. Normal erythropoiesis. Arch. Dis. Childhood, 27:214, 1952.

Korst, D. R., Clatanoff, D. V., and Schilling, R. F.: On myelofibrosis. Arch. Int. Med., 97:169, 1956.

Shen, S. C., and Homburger, F.: The anemia of cancer patients and its relation to metastases to the bone marrow. J. Lab. & Clin. Med., 37:182, 1951.

Upton, A. C., and Furth, J.: A transmissible disease of mice characterized by anemia, leukopenia, splenomegaly and myelosclerosis. Acta Haemat., 13:65, 1955.

Wasi, P., and Block, M.: The mechanism of the development of anemia in untreated chronic lymphatic leukemia. Blood, 17:597, 1961.

Polycythemias

Aggeler, P. M., and others: Polycythemia in childhood: Studies of iron-kinetics with Fe⁵⁹ and blood clotting factors. Blood, 17:345, 1961.

Cobb, L. A., Kramer, R. J., and Finch, C. A.: Circulatory effects of chronic hypervolemia in polycythemia vera. J. Clin. Invest., 39:1722, 1960.

Damon, A., and others: Polycythemia and renal carcinoma. Am. J. Med., 25:182, 1958.

Escobar, M. A., and Trobaugh, F. E., Jr.: Erythrocythemia. M. Clin. North America, 46:253, 1962.

Gardner, F. H.: Polycythemia. Disease-a-Month. Chicago, Year Book Publishers, June, 1962.

Goldwasser, E., and others: The effect of cobalt on the production of erythropoietin. Blood, 13:55, 1958.

Jaworski, Z. F., and Wolan, C. T.: Hydronephrosis and polycythemia: A case of erythrocytosis relieved by decompression of unilateral hydronephrosis and cured by nephrectomy. Am. J. Med., 34:523, 1963.

Kennedy, B. J., and Gilbertson, A. S.: Increased erythropoiesis induced by androgenic hormone therapy. New England J. Med., 256:719, 1957.

Lawrence, J. H., Berlin, N. I., and Huff, R. L.: The nature and treatment of polycythemia: Studies on 263 patients. Medicine, 32:323, 1953.

Mendlowitz, M.: The effect of anemia and polycythemia on digital intravascular blood viscosity. J. Clin. Invest., 27:565, 1948.

Modan, B., and Lilienfeld, A. M.: Polycythemia vera and leukemia. The role of radiation treatment: A study of 1222 patients. Medicine, 44:305, 1965.

Rodman, T., and others: Alveolar hypoventilation due to involvement of the respiratory center by obscure disease of the central nervous system. Am. J. Med., 32:208, 1962.

Van Liew, H. D.: Oxygen tension of subcutaneous gas pockets in cobalt-treated mice and adrenalectomized mice. Proc. Soc. Exper. Biol. Med., 94:112, 1957.

Wasserman, L. R., and Bassen, F.: Polycythemia. J. Mt. Sinai Hosp., 26:1, 1959.

Wasserman, L. R., and Gilbert, H. S.: Surgery in polycythemia vera. New England J. Med., 269:1226, 1963.

Leukocytosis

Archer, R. K.: The Eosinophil Leukocytes. Oxford, Blackwell Scientific Publications, 1963.

Askoe-Hansen, G., and Clausen, J.: Mastocytosis (urticaria pigmentosa) with urinary excretion of hyaluronic acid and chondroitin sulfuric acid. Am. J. Med., 36:144, 1964.

Boyden, S.: Chemotactic effect of mixtures of antibody and antigen on polymorphonuclear leukocytes. J. Exper. Med., 115:453, 1962.

Braunsteiner, H., and Zucker-Franklin, D.: The Physiology and Pathology of Leukocytes. New York, Grune & Stratton, 1962.

Brittingham, T. E., and Chaplin, H., Jr.: Febrile transfusion reactions caused by sensitivity to donor leukocytes and platelets. J.A.M.A., 165:819, 1957.

Cline, M. J.: Metabolism of the circulating leukocyte. Physiol. Rev., 45:674, 1965.

Craddock, C. G., Jr., Perry, S., and Lawrence, J. S.: The dynamics of leukopenia and leukocytosis. Ann. Int. Med., 52:281, 1960.

Davidson, W. M., Milner, R. D. G., and Lawler, S. D.: Giant neutrophil leukocytes: Inherited anomaly. Brit. J. Haemat., 6:339, 1960.

Fahey, J. L.: Antibodies and immunoglobulins. I. Structure and function. J.A.M.A., 194:71, 1965.

Gordon, A. S., and others: Leukocytic functions. Ann. New York Acad. Sc., 59:665, 1955. (Extensive monograph composed of 25 articles.)

Gordon, A. S., and others: Evidence for circulating leukocytosis-inducing factor. Acta Haemat., 23:323, 1960.

Itoga, T., and Lazlo, J.: Döhle bodies and other granulocytic alterations during chemotherapy with cyclophosphamid. Blood, 20:668, 1962.

Karnovsky, M. L.: Metabolic basis of phagocytic activity. Physiol. Rev., 42:143, 1962.

McFarland, W., and Heilman, D.: Lymphocyte foot appendage: Its role in lymphocyte function and in immunologic reactions. Nature, 205:887, 1965.

Norman, A., and others: Lymphocyte lifetime in women. Science, 147:745, 1965.

Oski, F. A., and others: Leukocyte inclusions—Döhle bodies—associated with platelet abnormality (May-Hegglin anomaly). Report of family and review of literature. Blood, 20:657, 1962.

Petersdorf, R. G.: Relationship of phagocytosis to the fall in spinal fluid glucose in experimental meningitis. J. Clin. Invest., 39:1016, 1960.

Petrakis, N. L.: In vivo cultivation of leukocytes in diffusion chambers: Requirement of ascorbic acid for differentiation of mononuclear leukocytes to fibroblasts. Blood, 18:310, 1961.

Shelby, W. B., and Juhlin, L.: Degranulation of the basophil in man induced by alimentary lipemia. Am. J. Med. Sc., 242:211, 1961.

Skendzel, L. P., and Hoffman, G. C.: Pelger anomaly of leukocytes: 41 cases in seven families. Am. J. Clin. Path., 37:294, 1962.

Smith, M. R., and Wood, W. B.: Surface phagocytosis. J. Exper. Med., 107:1, 1958.

Weiseman, G.: Lysosomes. Blood, 24:594, 1964.

Windhorst, D. B., Zelickson, A. S., and Good, R. A.: Chediak-Higashi syndrome: Hereditary gigantism of cytoplasmic organelles. Science, 151:81, 1966.

Wintrobe, M. M.: Diagnostic significance of changes in leukocytes. Bull. New York Acad. Med., 15:223, 1939.

Leukopenia and Agranulocytosis

Aisenberg, A. C.: Studies on the mechanism of the lupus erythematosus (L.E.) phenomenon. J. Clin. Invest., 38:325, 1959.

Craddock, C. C., Jr., and others: Evaluation of marrow granulocyte reserves in normal and disease states. Blood, 15:840, 1960.

Daland, G. A., and others: Hematologic observations in bacterial endocarditis: Especially the prevalence of histiocytes and the elevation and variation of the white cell count in blood from the ear lobe. J. Lab. & Clin. Med., 48:827, 1956.

Follette, J. H., and others: Effect of chloramphenicol and other antibiotics on leukocyte respiration. Blood, 11:234, 1956.

Good, R. A.: Failure of plasma cell formation in bone marrow and lymph nodes of patients with agammaglobulinemia. J. Lab. & Clin. Med., 46:167, 1955.

Hartl, W.: Drug allergic agranulocytosis. Seminars Hemat., 2:313, 1965.

Killman, S.: Occurrence of leukocyte agglutinins. Acta Med. Scand., 163:149, 1959.

Lalezari, P., and others: Neonatal neutropenia due to maternal isoimmunization. Blood, 15:236, 1960.

Moeschlin, S., and Wagner, K.: Agranulocytosis due to the occurrence of leukocyte-agglutinins (pyramidon and cold agglutinins). Acta Haemat., 8:29, 1952.

Palmer, J. G., and others: The experimental production of splenomegaly, anemia and leukopenia in albino rats. Blood, 8:72, 1953.

Payne, R.: The development and persistence of leuko-

agglutinins in parous women. Blood, 19:411, 1962.

Pisciotta, A. V., and Kaldahl, J.: Studies on agranulocytosis. IV. Effects of chlorpromazine on nucleic acid synthesis of bone marrow cells in vitro. Blood, 20:364, 1962.

Pisciotta, A. V., and others: Agranulocytosis following administration of phenothiazine derivatives. Am. J. Med., 25:210, 1958.

Wiseman, B. K., and Doan, C. A.: A newly recognized granulopenic syndrome caused by excessive splenic leukolysis and successfully treated by splenectomy. Ann. Int. Med., 16:1097, 1942.

Leukemias and Related Disorders

Aisenberg, A. C.: Hodgkin's disease: Prognosis, treatment and etiologic and immunologic considerations. New England J. Med., 270:508, 575, 617, 1964.

Arnason, B. G., Jankovic, B. D., and Waksman, B. K.: A survey of the thymus and its relation to lymphocytes and immune reactions. Blood, 20:617, 1962.

Bertino, J. R., and others: Increased level of dehydrofolate reductase in leukocytes of patients treated with amethopterin. Nature, 193:140, 1962.

Bierman, H. R., and others: Leukopheresis in man. III. Hematologic observations in patients with leukemia and myeloid metaplasia. Blood, 21:164, 1963.

Boggs, D. R., Wintrobe, M. M., and Cartwright, G. E.: The acute leukemias: Analysis of 322 cases and review of the literature. Medicine, 41:163, 1962.

Bouroncle, B., and Doan, C. A.: Myelofibrosis: Clinical hematologic and pathologic study of 110 patients. Am. J. Med. Sc., 243:697, 1962.

Brittingham, T. E., and Chaplin, H., Jr.: The antigenicity of normal and leukemic human leukocytes. Blood, 17:139, 1961.

Cline, M. J., and others: Anemia in macroglobulinemia. Am. J. Med., 34:213, 1963.

Craddock, C. G., and Nakai, G. S.: Leukemic cell proliferation as determined by in vitro desoxyribonucleic acid synthesis. J. Clin. Invest., 41:360, 1962.

Cronkite, E. P., Moloney, W., and Bond, V. P.: Radiation leukemogenesis. Am. J. Med., 28:673, 1960.

Dameshek, W., and Gunz, F.: Leukemia, 2nd ed. New York, Grune & Stratton, 1964.

Fahey, J. L.: Antibodies and immunoglobulins. II. Normal development and changes in disease. J.A.M.A., 194:141, 1965.

Firat, D., and others: Giant follicular lymph node disease: Clinical and pathological review of sixty-four cases. Am. J. Med., 39:252, 1965.

Gall, E. A., and Mallory, T. B.: Malignant lymphoma. Am. J. Path., 18:381, 1942.

Gavosto, F., Maraini, G., and Pileri, A.: Proliferative capacity of acute leukemia cells. Nature, 187:611, 1960.

Grace, J. T., Jr.: Viruses as etiologic agents in acute leukemia. CA, 14:135, 1964.

Gross, L.: Viral etiology of leukemia and lymphomas. Blood, 25:377, 1965.

Gruenwald, H., and others: Philadelphia chromosome

in eosinophilic leukemia. Am. J. Med., *39:*1003, 1965.

Gunz, F. W., and Fitzgerald, P. H.: Chromosomes and leukemia. Blood, *23:*394, 1964.

Hayhoe, F. G. J.: Leukaemia: Research and Clinical Practice. Boston, Little, Brown & Co., 1960.

Heller, E. L., Lewisohn, M. G., and Palin, W. E.: Aleukemic myelosis: Chronic nonleukemic myelosis, agnogenic myeloid metaplasia, osteosclerosis, leukoerythroblastic anemia, and synonymous designations. Am. J. Path., *23:*327, 1947.

Hunt, W. E., Bouroncle, B. A., and Meagher, J. N.: Neurologic complications of leukemias and lymphomas. J. Neurosurg., *16:*135, 1959.

Krakoff, I. H.: Mechanisms of drug action in leukemia. Am. J. Med., *28:*735, 1960.

Kundel, D. W., and others: Reticulin fibrosis and bone infarction in acute leukemia: Implications for prognosis. Blood, *23:*526, 1964.

Lawson, H. A., and others: Observations on the antibody content of the blood in patients with multiple myeloma. New England J. Med., *252:* 13, 1955.

Mackay, I. R.: Macroglobulins and macroglobulinemia. Austral. Ann. Med., *8:*158, 1959.

Miller, A., and Sullivan, J. F.: Some physicochemical properties of vitamin B_{12} binding substances of normal and chronic myelogenous leukemic sera. J. Lab. & Clin. Med., *53:*607, 1959.

Mitus, W. J., and others: Alkaline phosphatase of mature neutrophils in chronic forms of the myeloproliferative syndrome. Am. J. Clin. Path., *30:*285, 1958.

Nathan, D. G., and Berlin, N. I.: Studies of the rate of production and life span of erythrocytes in acute leukemia. Blood, *14:*935, 1959.

Osserman, E. F., and Takatsuki, K.: Plasma cell myeloma: Gamma globulin synthesis and structure. Medicine, *42:*357, 1963.

Osserman, E., and Takatsuki, K.: Clinical and immunochemical studies of four cases of heavy ($H_{\gamma 2}$) chain disease. Am. J. Med., *37:*351, 1964.

Perillie, P. E., and Finch, S. C.: Quantitative studies of local exudative cellular reaction in acute leukemia. J. Clin. Invest., *43:*425, 1964.

Primikirios, N., Stutzman, L., and Sandberg, A. A.: Uric acid excretion in patients with malignant lymphomas. Blood, *17:*701, 1961.

Ritzmann, S. E., and others: The syndrome of macroglobulinemia. Arch. Int. Med., *105:*939, 1960.

Ritzmann, S. E., Coleman, S. L., and Levin, W. C.: Effect of some mercaptans on macrocryogelglobulin: Modifications induced by cysteamine, penicillamine and penicillin. J. Clin. Invest., *39:*1320, 1960.

Ritzmann, S. E., and Levin, W. C.: Cryopathies: Reviews, classification, diagnostic and therapeutic considerations. Arch. Int. Med., *107:*754, 1961.

Rosenberg, S. A., and others: Lymphosarcoma: A review of 1269 cases. Medicine, *40:*31, 1961.

Schwab, P. J., and Fahey, J. L.: Treatment of Waldenström's macroglobulinemia by plasmapheresis. New England J. Med., *263:*574, 1960.

Scott, R. B., Ellison, R. R., and Ley, A. B.: A clinical study of twenty cases of erythroleukemia (di

Guglielmo's syndrome). Am. J. Med., *37:*162, 1964.

Szweda, J. A., and others: Systemic mast cell disease: A review and report of three cases. Am. J. Med., *32:*227, 1962.

Utz, J. P., Frei, E., III, and McCullough, N. B.: Fever, infection and host resistance in acute leukemia. Am. J. Med., *24:*25, 1958.

Zinneman, H. H., and Hall, W. H.: Recurrent pneumonia in multiple myeloma and some observations on immunologic response. Ann. Int. Med., *41:*1152, 1954.

Zucker-Franklin, D.: Structural features of cells associated with the paraproteinemias. Seminars Hemat., *1:*165, 1964.

Hemorrhagic Disorders

(a) GENERAL

Biggs, R., and Macfarlane, R. G.: Human Blood Coagulation and its Disorders. Philadelphia, F. A. Davis Co., 1962.

Hougie, C.: Fundamentals of Blood Coagulation in Clinical Medicine. New York, McGraw-Hill, 1963.

Ratnoff, O.: Blood clotting mechanism and its disorders. Disease-a-Month. Chicago, Year Book Publishers, Nov., 1965.

(b) VASCULAR AND PLATELET DEFECTS

Ackroyd, J. F.: Allergic purpura, including purpura due to foods, drugs and infections. Am. J. Med., *14:*605, 1953.

Adelson, E., Rheingold, J. J., and Crosby, W. H.: The platelet as a sponge: A review. Blood, *17:*767, 1961.

Aster, R. H.: Splenic platelet pooling as a cause of "hypersplenic" thrombocytopenia. Tr. A. Am. Physicians, *78:*362, 1965.

Aster, R. H., and Jadl, J. H.: Platelet sequestration in man. II. Immunological and clinical studies. J. Clin. Invest., *43:*856, 1964.

Borchgrevink, C. F.: Platelet adhesion in vivo during secondary bleeding in normal individuals and in patients with clotting defects. Acta Med. Scand., *170:*245, 1961.

Bowie, E. J. W., Thompson, J. H., Jr., and Owen, C. A., Jr.: The blood platelet. Mayo Clin. Proc., *40:* 625, 1965.

Bradlow, B. A.: Liberation of material with plateletlike coagulant properties from intact red cells and particularly from reticulocytes. Brit. J. Haemat., *7:*476, 1961.

Braunsteiner, H., and Pakesch, F.: Thrombocytoasthenia and thrombocytopathia: old names and new diseases. Blood, *11:*965, 1956.

Corn, M., and others: Components of blood necessary for clot retraction. Bull. Johns Hopkins Hosp., *107:*90, 1960.

Corn, M., and Upshaw, J. D., Jr.: Evaluation of platelet antibodies in idiopathic thrombocytopenia purpura. Arch. Int. Med., *109:*157, 1962.

Ebert, R. H., and Wissler, R. W.: In vivo observations of the effects of cortisone on the vascular reaction to large doses of horse serum using the rabbit ear chamber technique. J. Lab. & Clin. Med., *38:*497, 1951.

Fulton, G. P., and Berman, H. J.: The defective vascular wall as a factor in bleeding. Ann. New York Acad. Sc., 115:56, 1964.

Gardner, F. H., and Diamond, L. K.: Autoerythrocyte sensitization: A form of purpura producing painful bruising following autosensitization to red blood cells in certain women. Blood, 10:675, 1955.

Gilon, E., Ramot, B., and Sheba, C.: Multiple hemangiomata associated with thrombocytopenia. Blood, 14:74, 1959.

Gunz, F. W.: Hemorrhagic thrombocythemia: A critical review. Blood, 15:706, 1960.

Humble, J. G.: The mechanism of petechial hemorrhage formation. Blood, 4:69, 1949.

Inglefield, J. T., Jr., Tisdale, P. D., and Fairchild, J. P.: A case of hemangioma with thrombocytopenia in newborn infant treated by total excision: Review of the literature. J. Pediat., 59:238, 1961.

Jackson, D. P., and others: Nature of a platelet-agglutinating factor in serum of patients with idiopathic thrombocytopenic purpura. J. Clin. Invest., 42:383, 1963.

James, T. N., and others: Histology of platelet-plasma clots from normal subjects and patients with abnormal coagulation. Blood, 19:751, 1962.

Johnson, S. A., and others: The mechanism of the endothelial supporting function of intact platelets. Exper. Molec. Path., 3:115, 1964.

Levin, J., and Conley, C. L.: Thrombocytosis associated with malignant disease. Arch. Int. Med., 114:497, 1964.

Marcus, A. J., and Zucker, M. B.: The Physiology of Blood Platelets. New York, Grune & Stratton, 1965.

Marcus, A. J., and others: Studies on human platelet granules and membranes. J. Clin. Invest., 45:14, 1966.

McKenna, J. L., and Pisciotta, A. V.: Fluorescence of megakaryocytes in idiopathic thrombocytopenic purpura (ITP) stained with fluorescent antiglobulin serum. Blood, 19:664, 1962.

Meyers, M. C.: Results of treatment in 71 patients with idiopathic thrombocytopenic purpura. Am. J. Med., Sc., 242:295, 1961.

Pearson, H. A., and others: Isoimmune neonatal thrombocytopenic purpura: Clinical and therapeutic considerations. Blood, 23:154, 1964.

Robson, H. N.: Idiopathic thrombocytopenic purpura. Quart. J. Med., 18:279, 1949.

Salzman, E. W.: Measurement of platelet adhesiveness: Simple in vitro technic demonstrating abnormality in von Willebrand's disease. J. Lab. & Clin. Med., 62:724, 1963.

Schulman, I., and others: A factor in normal human plasma required for platelet production: Chronic thrombocytopenia due to its deficiency. Blood, 16:943, 1960.

Schwartz, R. S., Lewis, F. B., and Dameshek, W.: Hemorrhagic cutaneous anaphylaxis due to autosensitization to desoxyribonucleic acid. New England J. Med., 267:1105, 1962.

Shulman, N. R., and Rall, J. E.: Mechanism of blood cell destruction in individuals sensitized to foreign antigens. Tr. A. Am. Physicians, 76:72, 1963.

Singer, K., Motulsky, A. G., and Shanberge, J. N.: Thrombotic thrombocytopenic purpura. II. Studies on the hemolytic syndrome in this disease. Blood, 5:434, 1950.

Spaet, T. H., and Zucker, M. B.: Mechanism of platelet plug formation and role of ADP. J. Physiol., 206:1267, 1964.

Weiss, H. J., and Eichelberger, J. W.: The detection of platelet defects in patients with mild bleeding disorders: Use of a quantitative assay for platelet factor 3. Am. J. Med., 32:872, 1962.

Zucker, H. D.: Platelet thrombosis in human hemostasis: A histologic study of skin wounds in normal and purpuric individuals. Blood, 4:631, 1949.

(c) Coagulation defects

Anderson, L.: Fibrinolytic states in prostatic disease and their treatment with ε-aminocaproic acid. Acta Chir. Scand., 126:251, 1963.

Barnhart, M. I., and Riddle, J. M.: Cellular localization of profibrinolysis (plasminogen). Blood, 21:306, 1963.

Barrow, E. M., and Graham, J. B.: von Willebrand's disease. In Progress in Hematology, Vol. IV, p. 203. New York, Grune & Stratton, 1964.

Biggs, R., and Denson, K. W. E.: Fate of prothrombin and factors VIII, IX and X transfused to patients deficient in these factors. Brit. J. Haemat., 9:532, 1963.

Conrad, F. G., Breneman, W. L., and Grisham, D. B.: A clinical evaluation of plasma thromboplastin antecedent (PTA) deficiency. Ann. Int. Med., 62:885, 1965.

Deykin, D.: The role of the liver in serum-induced thrombosis. J. Clin. Invest., 45:256, 1966.

Gaston, L. W.: The blood clotting factors. New England J. Med., 270:236, 290, 1964.

Henstell, H. H., and Feinstein, M.: Interference of abnormal plasma proteins with the clotting mechanism. Am. J. Med., 22:381, 1957.

Macfarlane, R. G.: An enzyme cascade in the blood clotting mechanism, and its function as a biochemical amplifier. Nature, 202:495, 1964.

Margolius, A., Jackson, D. P., and Ratnoff, O. D.: Circulating anticoagulants: A study of 40 cases and a review of the literature. Medicine, 40:145, 1960.

McKay, D. G.: Disseminated Intravascular Coagulation. New York, Harper & Row, 1965.

Merskey, C., and others: Pathogenesis of fibrinolysis in defibrination syndrome: Effect of heparin administration. Blood, 24:701, 1964.

Nemerson, Y., and Spaet, T. H.: The activation of factor X by extracts of rabbit brain. Blood, 23:657, 1964.

Nussbaum, M., and Morse, B. S.: Plasma fibrin stabilizing factor activity in various diseases. Blood, 23:669, 1964.

Owen, C. A., and others: Congenital deficiency of Factor VII (hypoconvertinemia). Am. J. Med., 37:71, 1964.

Pechet, L.: Fibrinolysis. New England J. Med., 273:966, 1024, 1964.

Rapoport, S. I., Ames, S. B., and Duvall, B. J.: A plasma coagulation defect in systemic lupus erythematosus arising from hypoprothrombinemia combined with antiprothrombinase activity. Blood, *15*:212, 1960.

Ratnoff, O. D., Pritchard, J. A., and Colopy, J. E.: Hemorrhagic states during pregnancy. New England J. Med., 253:63, 97, 1955.

Rausen, A. R., and others: A study of fibrinogen turnover in classical hemophilia and congenital afibrinogenemia. Blood, *18*:710, 1961.

Rechnic, J., and others: Afibrinogenemia and thrombocytopenia in guinea pigs following injection of *Echis colorata* venom. Blood, *20*:735, 1962.

Rodriguez-Erdmann, F.: Bleeding due to increased intravascular blood coagulation: Hemorrhagic syndromes caused by consumption of blood-clotting factors (consumption-coagulopathies). New England J. Med., *273*:1370, 1965.

Sawyer, W. D., and others: Studies on the thrombolytic activity of human plasma. J. Clin. Invest., *39:* 426, 1960.

Soulier, J. P., Wartelle, O., and Menache, D.: Hageman trait and PTA deficiency: The role of contact of blood with glass. Brit. J. Haemat., *5:*121, 1959.

Spaet, T. H.: Clinical implications of acquired blood coagulation abnormalities. Blood, *23*:839, 1964.

Spaet, T. H., and others: Reticuloendothelial clearance of blood thromboplastin by rats. Blood, *17*:196, 1961.

Verstraete, M., and others: Excessive consumption of blood coagulation components as a cause of hemorrhagic diathesis. Am. J. Med., *38*:899, 1965.

Chapter Thirty-One

The Spleen and Reticuloendothelial System

JAMES H. JANDL

The Structure and Composition of the Reticuloendothelial System

The cellular components of the reticuloendothelial system (RES) are so widely scattered, so diverse in their structural associations and so pleomorphic that there exists a confusion of terms and concepts concerning their morphology and function. The structural association of a family of round or stellate cells with a system of connecting fibrils (reticulin or reticulum) was given functional significance by the studies of Metchnikoff and others demonstrating that many of these cells were engaged in the vital function of phagocytosis. Later Aschoff provided a unifying definition of the RES as a system of cells capable of taking up dyes or particles. Hortega and others, on the basis of metallophilic staining, also recognized the close association and overlapping between reticulum formation and a potentiality for phagocytosis in cells found in a great variety of tissues, particularly in the spleen, liver, marrow and lymph nodes.

Although phagocytic and tinctorial properties serve to identify the cells that form the structural skeleton of the RES, the histologic picture is complicated by the presence of similar but less differentiated cells that ordinarily are not phagocytic: the "primitive reticular" cells of Maximow. In addition, the population of phagocytes or macrophages contains several morphologically distinct variants,

some of which are found primarily in the circulation. Furthermore, the fixed reticuloendothelial cells described above are closely associated with, and in some instances are progenitors of, a number of cell types that are distinctly different in appearance and function and that lack the telltale metallophilia: these are the lymphocytes and plasma cells produced in the lymphatics and spleen and the red cells, granulocytes and platelets produced in the bone marrow. Thus, in its broadest sense the RES has come to be defined not only as the system of mesenchymal cells that form and are supported by reticulum and are capable of phagocytosis, but also all cells that normally derive from such cells.

In order to avoid ambiguity and to minimize uprofitable semantics, the known or commonly proposed functions and origins of the various major cell types encountered in the RES are presented in Table 31--1. With the exception of the monocyte, which is a freely circulating macrophage or phagocyte that appears to be derived largely, if not entirely, from the marrow, these cells of the RES can be grouped generally into (1) the fixed RE cells that form the filtering and phagocytic structure of the RES, and (2) the immunologically active cells, the lymphocytes and plasma cells. These two major cell populations exist in close combination in the spleen and lymph nodes. In the human liver and bone marrow, however, the RE cells are

897

not usually structurally associated with appreciable numbers of immunologically competent cells. It is true that discrete plasma cells are scattered through the marrow and that nests of lymphocytes also may be encountered, particularly in childhood; however, most of these cells appear to be in transit, there being little generation of such cells in the marrow.

Thus, the spleen and lymph nodes are able both to filter particulate matter from the intravascular and extravascular fluids, respectively, and to form antibodies; the liver and bone marrow, on the other hand, act as filters for the blood but normally form little or no antibody.

Functions of the RES

FILTRATION AND PHAGOCYTOSIS

Whereas the general system of lymphatics and lymph nodes is concerned with "policing" the extravascular fluids, the principal highly vascular organs of the RES—the liver, spleen and bone marrow—provide the essential function of clearing particulate matter from the blood (Table 31–2). This vital role serves to preserve the normal fluidity of the blood and to rid it of toxic or infectious particles and of effete blood cells. Among the particulate materials with which this system may deal in everyday life are effete or injured red cells,

leukocytes and platelets; bacteria, microemboli, fibrin and other coagulation products; antigen-antibody complexes; and probably certain lipids. In addition a host of particulate, colloidal or poorly soluble materials have been shown under experimental conditions to be removed from blood by the RES, among them being carbon particles, metallic colloids, denatured or aggregated proteins, bacterial endotoxin and a variety of macromolecules such as dextran, methylcellulose, zymosan and polyvinylpyrrolidone.

The overall process by which the RES clears particles from the blood is often referred to as phagocytosis because of the fact that inspection of the tissues shortly after injection of material such as suspended carbon (India ink) or thorium dioxide reveals these particles to be localized in the cytoplasm of phagocytic cells. In most if not all instances, however, it appears that the particles first are physically trapped in the RES by adherence between the surfaces of RE cells or by aggregation in the sinusoids. In some instances, especially with foreign particles or markedly altered endogenous materials, phagocytosis occurs within a few minutes; thereafter the engulfed material may be carried by the phagocytes some distance from the initial site of particle sequestration. In other instances, as is evident with altered red cells during hemolytic processes, physical trapping or sequestration may be striking, particularly in the spleen, but phagocytosis

TABLE 31–1. DISTRIBUTION AND FUNCTION OF CELLS OF THE RES.*

Cell Type	Subtypes	Principal Distribution	Mobility	Principal Functions
Reticuloendothelial cells (RE cells)	Reticulum cells Endothelial cells Tissue phagocytes (histiocytes and Kupffer cells)	Spleen Lymphatics Liver Bone marrow	Remain in tissue of origin, except for histiocytes, small numbers of which circulate	RES structure Filtration of particles Phagocytosis ? Stem cell compartment
Lymphocytes	Small lymphocytes Large lymphocytes Thymocytes	Spleen Lymphatics Thymus Blood	Circulate readily through blood and lymphatics	Immunologic responsiveness ? Stem cell compartment
Plasma cells	—	Spleen Lymphatics Bone marrow	Circulate to a minor extent in blood	Antibody formation
Monocytes	—	Blood (probably formed in bone marrow)	Circulate readily in blood	Phagocytosis

* The principal cells derived from bone marrow (red cells, granulocytes and platelets) are discussed in Chapter 30. The macrophage systems of the lungs and of the central nervous system are separate specialized regional systems that are considered elsewhere in this text.

TABLE 31–2. PRINCIPAL FUNCTIONS OF THE RES ORGANS IN MAN.

Organ	Cellular Composition	Estimated Blood Flow	Principal RES Functions
Lymph nodes	RE cells Lymphocytes Plasma cells	Small (probably <1% of cardiac output)	Filtration of extravascular fluids, antibody formation
Spleen	RE cells Lymphocytes Plasma cells	Approximately 3–5% of cardiac output	Filtration of blood, antibody formation
Liver	RE cells Hepatocytes	20–25% of cardiac output	Filtration of blood
Bone marrow	RE cells Blood cell precursors Fat cells	Approximately 5% of cardiac output	Filtration of blood, blood cell formation

may be delayed and limited in extent; in this case, destruction of the particle largely takes place within the sinusoid (see below).

As a generalization, blood-borne particles that are highly abnormal are removed principally by the liver, and phagocytosis of the particles (by the resident Kupffer cells) is rapid and extensive. Particles that are less aberrant may be sequestered and destroyed, mainly by the spleen or bone marrow, and phagocytosis may be restrained. The special properties of the spleen as a filter will be discussed in more detail later in this chapter.

In studies of the clearance from the blood of carbon particles of about 250 Å diameter, Benacerraf, Biozzi, Halpern and their coworkers have found that the bulk (about 80 per cent) is removed by the liver, mainly in the most actively phagocytic of the hepatic littoral cells, the Kupffer cells. In these studies small amounts of carbon were cleared very rapidly at a rate limited only by the voluminous blood flow of the liver, representing about 25 per cent of the cardiac output. Large amounts of carbon were cleared more slowly, reflecting not only the factor of blood flow but also the phagocytic efficiency of the littoral phagocytes. These relationships are defined by the constancy of the product of the particle dose and the "phagocytic index" (K), which expresses the clearance rate as an exponential function of time. In analogous studies of the clearance of red cells injured by prolonged storage, Noyes and his associates similarly noted the inverse relation between cell dose and clearance rate and found that, in contrast to carbon particles, an absolute saturation limit was reached; the RES of normal man was capable of removing about 50 or 60 ml. of effete red cells per hour—a rate about 40 times that involved in the normal

steady state removal of senescent red cells. Each kind of particle, cell or colloid is removed from the blood at its individual rate. When two or more kinds of particles are being removed simultaneously there may be competition between them, with preferential removal of one or another species of particle.

SPECIAL ATTRIBUTES OF IMMUNOLOGIC MECHANISMS AND OF OPSONINS

Some particles are cleared largely by virtue of the action of serum factors, usually antibodies, acting as opsonins, in which case the extent of clearance may be influenced by the concentration of antibody and, in many instances, of complement. The amount of antibody minimally required for opsonizing red cells is small and may not even be measurable by ordinary techniques in vitro. Indeed the RES is able to "recognize" and filter out cells so slightly injured that no present techniques in vitro are adequate for demonstrating the abnormality. If, on the other hand, the RES is temporarily saturated by being presented with a very large mass of altered cells, as during a hemolytic anemia or severe transfusion reaction, altered red cells may pile up in the circulation.

The role of antibodies in immunologic destruction is complex, but in general the principal mechanism is that of altering the surface of the cells or particles, thereby causing them to be sequestered by the RES. When cells such as red cells or platelets are coated with a large amount of antibody, or when the antibody is an agglutinin or fixes complement to the affected cell, the liver is the main site of sequestration; when lesser amounts of antibody are involved or when the antibody is an incomplete agglutinin and does not fix complement, the spleen is the primary erythro-clastic organ (Fig. 31–1).

Because of its high blood flow the liver can potentially remove altered red cells at rates as fast as 20 or 30 per cent per minute. With its much lesser blood flow, the spleen is normally capable of removing cells at rates of no more than 3 or 4 per cent per minute. The bone marrow appears to play a relatively small role in destroying red cells during acute hemolytic processes, although it may be important in some chronic processes or in the destruction of normal red cells by senescence. When the amount of antibody available is limiting, as in patients undergoing primary immunization by transfused blood or as in agammaglobulinemic patients given incompatible blood, it may take several days for sufficient antibody to coat the transfused cells to cause their removal. When a critical degree of opsonization is achieved, the cells may be removed over the course of a few days, the cell survival curve having a sigmoidal or "collapse" shape (Fig. 31–2). When antibody concentrations are low it is relatively easy to absorb out the opsonizing activity of the serum, allowing cells subsequently injected to survive normally for a time.

Although it is clear that serum antibody plays an important part in determining the rate of removal of bacteria and viruses by the RES, less is known about the importance of the kind of antibody involved or the distribution patterns within the RES. Nevertheless, mechanisms appear to operate that are quite similar to those described for red cells. There is some evidence that serum factors which might be considered to be opsonins play a role in the clearance of particles that are believed to be immunologically inert, but that the clearance of all particles depends upon preliminary interactions with serum proteins is not established. The efficiency with which the spleen clears abnormal red cells, metallic colloids and certain bacteria during perfusion with buffered saline ex vivo argues against a necessity for serum factors apart from those involved in true immunologic processes.

RES BLOCKADE AND STIMULATION

The use of quantitative measures of overall phagocytosis in vivo permits observations as to relative rates of particle clearance. These have revealed a general pattern in the response of the RES to the "work" of particle clearance. Initially there is a phase of saturation for the particle which may create a state of "blockade" with respect to other particles of comparable or of lesser affinity for the RES. This RES blockade, which is usually only a

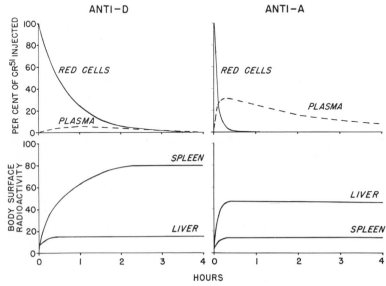

Figure 31–1. Patterns of red cell destruction by the RES. As depicted on the left, Cr[51]-labeled red cells coated with "incomplete" Rh (anti-D) antibodies are cleared from the blood largely by the spleen, with very little escape of radioactivity (or of hemoglobin) into the plasma. When red cells are acted on by agglutinins or complement-fixing antibodies such as anti-A, however, clearance of the altered cells is very rapid, the uptake of cells is primarily in the liver and relatively large amounts of labeled hemoglobin escape into the plasma. (Figure derived from data in Jandl, J. H., Jones, A. R., and Castle, W. B.: J. Clin. Invest., 36:1428, 1957.)

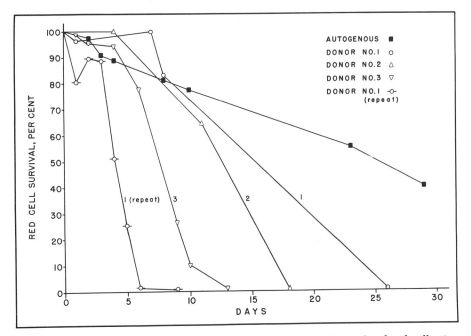

Figure 31–2. Progressive shortening in the survival of normal transfused red cells. At no time did the recipient show antibodies that could be demonstrated in vitro against the various donors' red cells. This "collapse" type of red cell survival curve is characteristic of early or minimal antibody formation and can be demonstrated in over one-quarter of normal individuals given transfusions of normal, apparently compatible cells despite the absence in most of the demonstrable antibodies. Such data illustrate the facility with which the RES can detect slight antigenic differences in cells and cause their destruction. (Redrawn from Jandl, J. H., and Greenberg, M. S.: J. Lab. & Clin. Med., 49:233, 1957.)

relative impairment of RES activity, generally persists for no more than a day or two, and is usually (but not invariably) followed by a transient period of heightened avidity for the same or for other particles (Fig. 31–3).

In some instances blockade by such agents as Thorotrast has involved toxic injury to the phagocytic cells, reduction in liver blood flow and even vascular occlusions and shock. In many experiments the findings reported are confused by the presence of contaminating endotoxin or even intact bacteria in the "blocking" suspensions. In addition many instances of blockade actually represent depletion of opsonizing antibody or of complement. Nevertheless, it is clear that the RES can be temporarily saturated, that the act of phagocytosis often tends to reduce the lifespan of the phagocytic cell and that recovery of function may be associated with a period of overshoot. Kelly and her co-workers have provided evidence that this phase of stimulated activity in the liver after an injection of foreign colloids reflects a proliferative response on the part of the hepatic RE cells, which results in a transient increase in the mass of RE tissue. Studies of DNA synthesis

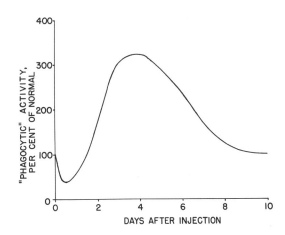

Figure 31–3. Sequential "blockade" and stimulation of the RES after an injection of particulate matter. Most particulate matter temporarily suppresses the "phagocytic" activity of the RES with respect to clearing other particulate matter injected subsequently. Usually, although not always, this period of blockade, lasting anywhere from a few hours to a few days, is followed by a period of stimulation of variable degree and duration. Studies by L. S. Kelly and her co-workers indicate that the stimulated phase reflects a proliferative reaction.

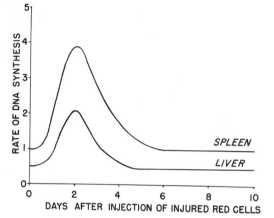

Figure 31–4. Proliferative response of the spleen and liver to an episode of hemolysis. Within 24 hours of the injection of injured red cells into rats there is a sharp increase in the overall rates of DNA synthesis in the spleen and liver, as determined by the incorporation of tritiated thymidine into DNA. (Drawn from data presented by Jandl, J. H., Files, N. M., Barnett, S. B., and MacDonald, R. A.: J. Exper. Med., *122:299*, 1965.)

in animals during and after acute episodes of hemolysis (Fig. 31–4) indicate that such a proliferative reaction occurs in the spleen and liver in response to the destruction of autologous blood cells.

Although there are certain disorders, such as hemolytic anemia or thrombocytopenic purpura, in which it may be desirable as a therapeutic measure to block the function of the RES for a protracted period, efforts to do so have been thwarted by this proliferative rebound. To some extent the rebound from blockade can be delayed or inhibited by cortisone or x-radiation, but the net effect of repeated injections of blockading materials or of chronic hemolysis or infection is to create an inexorable increase in the size and activity of the RES, even despite simultaneous administration of cortisone.

As implied above, cortisone has a modest ability to inhibit RES activity, an action most evident in the liver and one which explains in part the beneficial effect of corticosteroids in certain hemolytic anemias (see Chap. 30). Although the lymphocytes and the parenchymal cells of the marrow are highly susceptible to cytotoxic agents such as mechlorethamine (HN2) or radiation, the population of RE cells that are engaged in filtration and phagocytosis is unusually resistant to these agents, and particle clearance may continue undiminished and may even increase, despite exposure to amounts of these agents that eventually prove lethal.

Striking clinical evidence of the radioresistance of RE tissue was illustrated by the author's observations in two patients with immunohemolytic anemia and splenic sequestration. Whereas x-radiation in the amount of only 50 or 100 r to the spleen is usually more than enough to destroy a large proportion of its small lymphocytes and to reduce appreciably the total circulating mass of lymphocytes, the administration of 3000 r through multiple ports to the spleens of these patients with marked splenic sequestration of red cells had no beneficial effect on the rate of hemolysis or of splenic uptake of red cells; splenectomy, on the other hand, later proved dramatically effective.

INTRACELLULAR EVENTS DURING PHAGOCYTOSIS

Generally phagocytosis eventuates in the degradation of the engulfed particle. Actually such may not be the case with particles such as carbon or heavy metal colloids, as no chemical mechanism exists for their destruction. Such phagocytized particles may be carried to central structures of the RES and are presumed to undergo repeated rephagocytosis on the death of each successive phagocyte, possibly creating thereby a chronic "irritation" to the RES. In some instances, for reasons not well understood, destructible particles such as bacteria may be phagocytized, and then at some later time be ejected with little or no apparent harm. In some instances, in fact, bacteria, plasmodia and possibly viruses may reside and even multiply within phagocytes, thereby creating a "tissue phase" of a disease process. In most situations, however, the entrance of an opsonized bacterium or blood cell stimulates a sharp hostile reaction within the phagocyte. Much of this reaction is due to special cytoplasmic granular structures described by de Duve. These granules, called lysosomes, are essentially packages of destructive enzymes, including proteases, lipases, phosphatases, nucleases and lysozymes (enzymes that lyse cell walls) that are set free on appropriate stimulation.

With high-speed cinematography, Hirsch and Cohn and others have shown that the presence of particles in the cytoplasm of phagocytes (granulocytes) induces an explosive swelling of contiguous lysosomes with the release of lytic and noxious agents into the phagocytic vacuole encasing the intruder, resulting usually in its fragmentation and dissolution. The phagocyte may use up its supply of lysosomes and ultimately become ineffectual and die, but the phagocytic capacity of a single macrophage is remarkable and may allow the ingestion within a short time of numerous red cells and scores of bacteria. The time required for degradation of the ingested particle may vary considerably. As determined by the release of I^{131} from iodinated, heat-aggregated albumin, proteolysis is quite rapid. When hemoglobin is taken up by the RE cells in vivo, either as free hemoglobin or as hemoglobin within altered red cells, it is degraded to bile pigments as early as 30 minutes after its sequestration (Fig. 31–5). With respect to hemoglobin, and possibly with respect to most serum proteins, proteolysis within RE cells is a physiologic form of catabolism, probably an essential one.

Although effective against proteins, lipids and cell walls, lysosomes appear to lack the necessary enzymes for splitting many polysaccharides and these may persist for many years. It is not certain whether cells containing lysosomes are able to excrete their lytic enzymes into the milieu and thereby to destroy cells or particles that are contiguous to, but not within, the phagocyte, although there is suggestive evidence for such a mechanism. It is known, however, that such cells as tissue mast cells and the blood granulocytes do release or excrete toxic substances, including histamine, serotonin and probably endogenous pyrogen, when exposed to antigen-antibody complexes in vitro. This release of these packaged chemicals appears to account for many of the symptoms of allergic reactions, including anaphylaxis, edema and fever.

The processes of phagocytosis and pinocytosis stimulate a sharp increase in the metabolic activity of the phagocyte, characterized by increased respiration, activation of the hexose monophosphate shunt, heightened glycolysis, and increased production of lactic acid. Karnovsky and his associates have reported that a basic step is the activation of a DPNH oxidase; they view the metabolic response as a mechanism for repairing the defect in the membrane resulting from phagocytosis. In addition, it is probable that some of the energy is set free by the lysosomes and possibly some is utilized in initiating DNA synthesis preparatory to the later proliferative reaction described above. In some instances, particularly evident with granulocytes that are engaged in phagocytosis in tissues outside the RES, the metabolic reaction of the phagocytic cell may actually cause the

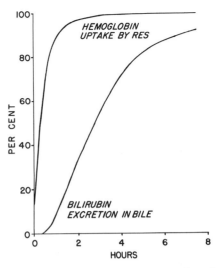

Figure 31–5. Formation of bilirubin from hemoglobin by the RES. Beginning within 30 minutes after the injection of C^{14}-labeled hemoglobin into rats, C^{14}-labeled bilirubin begins to appear in the bile. The interval between hemoglobin uptake and bilirubin excretion appears to vary from less than 30 minutes to several hours, depending on variations within the RES. (Drawn from data presented by Ostrow, J. D., Jandl, J. H., and Schmid, R.: J. Clin. Invest., *41:*1628, 1962.)

major inflammatory manifestations of a disease or a reaction. Thus, the necrotizing inflammation seen in the Arthus reaction and in analogous inflammatory processes observed clinically results from the granulocytic reaction to the antigen-antibody precipitates, rather than being caused by the precipitates themselves. Similarly the manifestations of gout appear to be due to the lactic acid and other metabolites released by granulocytes as they phagocytize the spiculated urate crystals.

IMMUNITY

The second major function of the RES is that of immunity. This is a highly complex subject, certain essential aspects of which are presently obscure. Fundamentally, however, the initial immune mechanism may be divided into three general phases. First, antigen must be trapped, ingested and, when appropriate, solubilized. This phase is accomplished by the mechanisms described previously and appears to be the province of the phagocytic RE cells. Second the trapped antigen is in some way identified and "coded," presumably by eliciting a ribonucleic acid message, one that may be based upon an inherited "alphabet." The identity of the cells involved in coding antigens is uncertain, but much of the evidence points to the radiosensitive lymphocyte. The third phase is that of producing antibody, a function largely carried out by plasma cells and by lymphoid cells having some of the cytoplasmic features of plasma cells. The plasma cell is well qualified for the task of secreting protein by possessing a heavy endoplasmic reticulum richly studded with ribosomes.

The "primary response" to a soluble, non-toxic antigen involves little cytologic reaction in the RES. Usually the level of circulating antibody first becomes measurable between 1 and 2 weeks after entry of the antigen, and the bulk of antibody formed is the Ig M variety, a 19S macroglobulin of about 1 million molecular weight. As noted in early studies of Rh sensitization this antibody may not persist very long after primary stimulation and in many instances may be succeeded by the appearance of the smaller 7S antibody denoted as Ig G; in hematologic terms an early "saline" agglutinin is largely replaced by an "incomplete" agglutinin, or, to use earlier expressions, by "blocking" or "hyperimmune" antibodies. There is some disputed evidence to suggest that the Ig M antibodies may be formed by the lymphoid plasma cells, while there is general agreement that the Ig G antibodies which form the bulk of serum gamma globulin, are produced chiefly by characteristic plasma cells and that these cells also produce some of the Ig M antibodies.

The secondary response to a strong antigen generally involves a violent cytologic reaction in the spleen and lymph nodes, characterized by a sharp proliferation of primitive cells, especially around the lymphatic sheaths. These primitive cells undergo several maturation divisions over the course of 3 to 4 days to create a large new population of plasma cells and lymphocytes, thus enlarging the spleen (acute splenic tumor) and lymph nodes. Attending this there may appear unusual numbers of atypical lymphocytes (i.e., young lymphocytes relatively rich in RNA), and of plasma cells in the peripheral blood. This marked cytoproliferative reaction is associated with a sharp acceleration in antibody synthesis and serum antibody levels within a few days. It should be noted that when antigen is present in large amounts or persists by resisting catabolism, the quiescent primary response may progress into the more vigorous secondary type response. The stimulus for the cellular proliferation seen in secondary responses is not fully understood, but it is probable that noxious interaction with preformed antibody is accountable in part. It is clear at any event that certain noxious materials, such as bacterial endotoxin, that are taken up by the RES markedly potentiate the cytoproliferative, and thereby the serologic, response to antigens.

Although the intention of immunity is to suppress or prevent disease, the reactions of the RES to antigens may create symptoms which, when troublesome, are called allergies. As the result of the normal reactivity of the RES many clinical or subclinical illnesses, particularly childhood infections, are accompanied by lymphadenopathy, sometimes splenomegaly and often the appearance in the blood of normal and atypical lymphocytes, plasma cells and a few histiocytes. Similar changes occur in adults in response to a number of viral and some bacterial infections or during drug reactions or serum sickness. When the offending antigen or haptene is unknown, such immunologic or allergic reactions may be misinterpreted as autoimmune phenomena. Since cell proliferation and hyperplasia are a characteristic part of the RES response to antigens, particularly to infectious agents, it is not surprising that in clinical situations uncertainty may arise as to whether enlargement of the spleen or lymph nodes is a physiologic reaction or a pathologic and possibly malignant one. When the lymphoid hyperplasia is unusually marked or the underlying disorder obscure, a tissue biopsy may be necessary for distinguishing normal reactions from malignant processes. Even on biopsy the distinction between reactive hyperplasia of RE tissue and malignant reticuloendotheliosis or lymphoma is at times difficult. Indeed, in the RES, as in many tissues, sustained hyperplasia may ultimately predispose to a malignant transformation.

OTHER FUNCTIONS OF THE RES: HEMATOPOIESIS

During embryonic and fetal life, hematopoiesis or blood formation (i.e., generation of red cells, granulocytes and platelets) takes place throughout much of the RES, including the liver and spleen. During the last trimester of intrauterine life the marrow gradually predominates, and normally in man there is no appreciable blood formation outside the marrow thereafter. This specialized component of the RES is described in detail in Chapter 30.

In many animals the spleen is normally a blood-forming organ or rapidly becomes so in response to anemia. In man, however, splenic hematopoiesis usually occurs to only a comparatively moderate extent when at all. Even in patients with chronic anemia, and splenic enlargment resulting from this, extramedullary hematopoiesis is seldom marked. A specific exception to this generalization is the myeloproliferative disease, myelofibrosis, wherein hematopoiesis in the spleen and liver is pronounced and wherein extraordinary enlargement of these organs occurs.

Pathologic Disorders of the RES

The human disorders in which changes in the RES, whether primary or secondary, may dominate the clinical picture can be divided broadly into hypoplastic and hyperplastic processes. Aplasia or hypoplasia of one or more of the cellular elements of the RES entails a loss of specific function, and in fact some of the most convincing evidence as to the different roles played by lymphocytes and plasma cells was derived from observations of diseases involving specific deficiencies or excesses of these cells. The various principal disorders of the cellular components of the RES are categorized in Table 31–3. Organized disorders principally affecting the spleen will be discussed later in this chapter.

THE LYMPHOPENIAS

There is no known example of absence or severe depletion of the reticulum cells or of the endothelial cells, although a significant regional loss is seen in splenic agenesis or after splenectomy. It is doubtful that life is possible in the absence of these basic RE cells.

It is doubtful as well whether life is possible in the complete absence of lymphocytes, but natural and experimental situations do exist in which lymphocyte depletion is of pathogenic importance. Because of their marked susceptibility to radiation or to radiomimetic drugs, abnormalities in lymphocyte nuclear morphology and a reduction in their numbers is a very early and sensitive sign of exposure both in vivo and in vitro. In some way not understood, cortisone and its congeners have a rather specific lytic effect upon lymphocytes.

An important advance in our understanding of the RE system was the demonstration in recent years that the thymus is concerned with the regulation of the lymphocyte population and with immunologic behavior. Although the thymus had fallen into disrepute when it was realized that so-called "status thymolymphaticus" was a spurious concept, interest in its possible functions was reawakened by a number of clinical observations by Good and others which associated thymic abnormalities (involution, absence or, more often, dysplastic thymomas) with immunologic deficiency states. Miller and others demonstrated that, when performed very early in life, thymectomy in animals led to impaired immunologic function and a reduction in lymphocyte numbers.

In part, at least, the influence of the thymus early in life is humoral. In a similar way, the intestinal and appendiceal lymphatic tissue, analogous to the bursa of Fabricius found in birds, appears to represent a precursor population for much of the lymphatic tissue of adult life. These observations and the known tendency of some lymphomatous tumors, par-

TABLE 31–3. PRINCIPAL DISORDERS OF THE RES.

| | | Hyperplasias | |
Cell Type	Hypoplasias	Secondary (reactive)	Primary (usually malignant)
"RE" cells	None described	Infection Antigenic stimulation Blood cell destruction Congestive splenomegaly Hypersplenism Some lipidoses	Certain lymphomas Histiocytic leukemia Reticuloendothelioses Some lipidoses
Lymphocytes	Postirradiation or -radiomimetic drugs Hyperadrenocorticism Hodgkin's disease Thymic insufficiency	Many viral infections Infectious mononucleosis Antigenic stimulation Hyperthyroidism Rarely bacterial infections	Most lymphomas Lymphatic leukemia Macroglobulinemia
Plasma cells	Most agamma globulinemias	Infection Antigenic stimulation	Multiple myeloma
Monocytes	None described	Chronic infection	Monocytic leukemia

ticularly in the pharynx, to involve cells of a mixed lymphoepithelial character have led to recent studies suggesting that the lymphocyte is formed as the result of an inductive effect of mesenchymal tissues upon primitive epithelial cells. These studies imply that the lymphocyte—which might be considered the "sensory cell" of the immunologic apparatus—is essentially epithelial in origin, and that it arises from juxtaepithelial masses and colonizes the fibrillar meshwork provided by the mesenchymal RE cells. On the other hand, in its phylogeny, the lymphocyte seems to evolve from a primitive ancestor having the potential to form both lymphoid and myeloid cells, implying a common mesenchymal derivation.

At any event it appears that much of the cell population involved in immunity is derived from or governed by lymphoid tissues first appearing in the pharyngeal and gut wall and that the full development and organization of this lymphatic tissue takes place rather late in ontogeny. As a consequence the newborn is morphologically partially deficient in lymphocytes and phagocytic RE cells and is almost totally deficient in plasma cells. Concomitantly the newborn is immunologically poorly responsive and depends for the first several weeks on the maternal antibody with which it was born.

In phylogeny adaptive immunity first appears in the lowest vertebrates, and again, as shown by Good and his associates, immunologic competence (primarily as "cellular immunity") is associated with the development of a lymphocyte-like cell and the appearance of a definitive thymus. As in the ontogeny of man, there is an association of the plasma cell with the appearance of circulating antibody during phylogeny. At a somewhat higher stage (Amphibia), plasma cells are seen in the lamina propia of the gut, ultimately organized into the bursa of Fabricius in birds and later into tonsillar and intestinal lym-

phatics and the general system of lymphatics, as seen in higher mammals. Generally speaking the thymus of mammals appears most critical to the lymphocytic function of delayed or cellular type immunity, whereas the bursa of fowl is associated with the evolution of an efficient antibody-forming system. To what extent these two systems develop separately during fetal and neonatal life in man is presently unclear.

It is evident from this that disorders of the thymus, particularly if congenital, may affect the lymphocytic apparatus, either by impairing or by exaggerating its functions. Table 31–4 presents a list of a number of disorders associated with early thymic abnormalities. These abnormalities are diverse and include simple hypoplasia or hyperplasia, cystic degeneration, replacement by stromal or spindle cells and the abnormal presence of germinal centers. Most of these disorders appear to have some immunologic aspect, but the specific pathogenetic mechanisms relating the thymus to disease manifestations are not clear. The frequent association of thymic disease with acquired aplastic anemia and with certain types of acquired agammaglobulinemia suggests that the thymus may influence specific steps in cell differentiation during maturity as well as regulating and instructing the mass of competent lymphocytes during early life. The striking incidence of thymomas in acquired aplastic anemia supports the view that the blood-forming and lymphatic tissues derive from a common ancestor.

Hodgkin's disease is a noteworthy lymphopenic affliction in that there is an associated malignant change in the other elements of the RES causing it to be classified anomalously as a lymphoma. Moderate lymphopenia usually becomes evident in the blood and lymph nodes, and despite an adequate capacity to form serum antibodies there is a characteristic impairment in the mechanism for delayed hypersensitivity and for homograft rejection.

PLASMA CELL HYPOPLASIA

Unlike lymphocytes, plasma cells are normally lacking in the newborn and only appear in appreciable numbers after several weeks, at which time the first traces of nonmaternal antibody are first detectable. Early thymectomy has a less definite effect on plasma cell numbers than on the lymphocyte population, but the fact that many thymectomized animals do show a plasma cell deficit and that thymomas are found in over 10 per cent of

TABLE 31-5. ANTIBODY DEFICIENCY DISEASES
(AGAMMAGLOBULINEMIAS).*

Congenital forms
    Sex-linked recessive
    Sporadic
    Lymphopenic (Swiss type)
    Ataxia telangiectasia
Adult-onset forms
    Primary "acquired"
    Secondary (usually to multiple myeloma or
        chronic lymphatic leukemia)

---

* The term agammaglobulinemia is employed recognizing the facts that some gamma globulin is always present in these patients and that in certain instances (e.g., multiple myeloma) the presence of the myeloma proteins may actually increase considerably the total amount of gamma globulin even though functional antibody is virtually absent.

patients with primary "acquired" agammaglobulinemia suggests a fundamental relationship. Most forms of agammaglobulinemia (Table 31-5) involve a severe deficit or absence of plasma cells and a lack of the normal plasma cell response to antigenic stimulation. In some patients (e.g., with the sex-linked recessive type) there may be a partial depletion of lymphocytes as well; in the more severe autosomal recessive disorder known as the Swiss type of agammaglobulinemia the deficiency in lymphocytes and in lymphoid tissue including the thymus and tonsils is extreme.

Most patients, whether with hereditary or acquired agammaglobulinemia, suffer repeated episodes of bacterial infection and may develop general RE hyperplasia as the result. Usually viral and fungal infections are handled reasonably well despite the lack of serum antibodies, and delayed hypersensitivity reactions may be normal. However, certain viruses, particularly that of serum hepatitis, may prove highly virulent in agammaglobulinemia. When lymphopenia is involved, however, the general resistance to fungal and viral diseases is also impaired and the ability to manifest delayed hypersensitivity reactions may be lost. Among patients with established agammaglobulinemia there is a rather high incidence of lymphoma and lymphatic leukemia. Conversely, some degree of hypogammaglobulinemia commonly complicates widespread chronic lymphatic leukemia, lymphoma and multiple myeloma.

SECONDARY (REACTIVE) HYPERPLASIAS

Persistent antigenic stimulation, subacute or chronic infection of any kind, or repeated injections of particulate or colloidal matter may cause such a degree of hyperplasia as to create disabling overfunction of the RES. Commonly these situations are attended by a syndrome of lymphadenopathy, splenomegaly and hyperglobulinemia, with increased numbers of plasma cells visible in the bone marrow and, less often, in the blood. Such a process may also lead to a special syndrome known as hypersplenism (to be discussed presently). Examples of infectious diseases that often cause such reactions are subacute bacterial endocarditis, tuberculosis and brucellosis.

Some infections elicit an extraordinarily strong immunologic response by the RES. Most common of these are the communicable "childhood" illnesses—measles, pertussis, rubella, mumps and chickenpox—in which disorders the brisk "physiologic" response of the RES may at times border on the "pathologic." In some patients with measles, rubella or chickenpox plasmacytosis may be striking. In some patients with pertussis, chickenpox or mumps a leukemoid lymphocytosis may appear and persist for several weeks. A special example of this sort of pathologic hyperreaction to an infectious agent is the disorder infectious mononucleosis, in which all the cell elements and functions of the RES are stimulated, in rare instances with dire results. An intriguing example of extreme hyperreactivity to a viral agent is seen in the veterinary disorder, Aleutian mink disease, in which there is an intensive plasma cell response, hyperglobulinemia and often progression to a disorder resembling multiple myeloma.

The tendency for certain viruses to cause lymphocytic and plasmacytic reactions is notable and presumably relates to their great antigenicity. Perhaps it is more mechanistic to state that man has evolved an unusually brisk responsiveness to these prevalent, highly communicable agents whose potential destructiveness is very evident in patients with lymphopenic disorders or in isolated peoples who have not previously been exposed.

PRIMARY HYPERPLASIA OF THE RES

As indicated in Table 31-3 each of the main cellular constituents of the RES is capable of undergoing malignant change, to form a lymphoma or a leukemia, depending on the cell type and its distribution between blood and tissues. In addition to the lymphomas and leukemias which have been discussed in Chapter 30, there is a closely-related group of hyperplastic diseases having a wider spectrum of involvement and of severity. When disease of the RE cells leads to a typically lymphomatous, malignant process, it is termed reticulum cell (or histiocytic) sarcoma; in some patients, however, the hyperplasia may be difficult to classify and the terms reticuloendothelioses or histiocytoses may be employed.

However different in their specific manifestations, the reticuloendothelioses share certain features. These are (1) RE cell (histiocytic or reticulum cell) hyperplasia, (2) granuloma formation, (3) a tendency to involve bone, lymphatics, liver, spleen, lung and skin and (4) a tendency for lipids to accumulate in the affected RE cells. A benign form highly localized to bone is eosinophilic granuloma. When bone involvement is more destructive and some involvement of the skin or general RES occurs, the clinical term may be Schüller-Christian syndrome. When RES involvement and enlargement is pronounced, skin and lung infiltrates are widespread and a febrile downhill course ensues, the diagnosis may be made of Letterer-Siwe syndrome.

By and large the earlier in onset the more disseminated and severe is the disease. The most benign form, eosinophilic granuloma, may be cured by excision or local irradiation. The intermediate forms may be materially benefited by radiation, chemotherapy or corticosteroids. The most malignant forms may pursue a course rather like that of leukemia, and in some instances numerous histiocytes may be seen in the peripheral blood, in which case the disease might well be called histiocytic leukemia. Although the granulomatous pattern found in the involved viscera strongly suggests an infectious or foreign agent, no such agents have been uncovered.

The Lipidoses

Another group of diseases, mostly uncommon, are the lipidoses: constitutional metabolic disorders in which the underlying lipid abnormality may involve the RES. The most important are Gaucher's disease and Niemann-Pick disease.

Gaucher's disease is usually recessive in inheritance and involves an accumulation of cerebrosides in RE cells which may result in splenomegaly, bone lesions and skin pigmentation. Because of the elongate, tubular form of these intracellular cerebroside microdeposits as seen on electron microscopy, the cytoplasm of the "Gaucher cell" has a characteristic wrinkled or scroll-like appearance on routine microscopy and Wright's stain. In its milder, more slowly evolving form, Gaucher's disease may still be serious, principally by enlarging the spleen and causing hypersplenism with thrombocytopenic purpura.

Niemann-Pick disease is a recessively inherited disorder, usually fatal before 2 years of age, characterized by accumulations of sphingomyelin and to some extent other lipids in RE cells. The resulting foam-cells cause enlargement of liver and spleen and in addition—as with many of the lipidoses—there may be extensive neurologic involvement. Unlike Gaucher's disease, a relatively isolated hypersplenism is not encountered and splenectomy has little or no place in therapy.

The Spleen

Historical

Although recognition of the existence and workings of the RES was understandably slow in coming, the spleen has been the object of curiosity since early antiquity. Puzzled by its variable size and obscure function Galen regarded the spleen as an organ "full of mystery" and believed it to be the source of "black bile" or melancholy. The mystical association of the spleen and the psyche has persisted idiomatically in such contemporary expressions as Milzsucht, hypochondriasis and "venting" one's spleen. In ancient Greece it was recognized that the spleen may become an impediment, and it was alleged by Pliny that some Greek athletes suffered their spleens to be destroyed by hot irons in a determined effort to improve their running. Although careful observations of the spleen in man and animal had to await the seventeenth century, two fundamental facts about the spleen emerged over the centuries: first, the spleen is not essential to life; second, marked enlargement of the spleen is usually accompanied by poor health.

With the advent of histology and pathology it was realized that the spleen is essentially a mixed lymphatic and vascular organ. The lymphoid tissue, which ensheaths the arterial vessels and which sprouts budlike structures, the lymph follicles of Malpighi, was termed the *white pulp*. The red spongy matrix in which the white pulp is embedded was called the *red pulp*. Although the histology of the white and red pulp has been reasonably well characterized for many years, a true understanding of the functions and mechanisms of the spleen has been painfully slow in coming. Apart from the difficulties alluded to earlier in differentiating and identifying the various cells of the RES on morphologic grounds, a major obstruction to progress has been the lack of knowledge concerning the "intermediate" circulation of the spleen: does the perfusing blood remain within a "closed" system of endothelial-lined vascular channels, or does it escape into an "open" unlined meshwork and then seep back into venous channels? Only very recently, by means of tracer studies and electron microscopy, is this controversy being resolved, albeit important areas of uncertainty still remain. Because of the complexity of splenic histology and the recent developments in knowledge of its cytologic reactions, the anatomy will be discussed in further detail.

ANATOMY OF THE SPLEEN

Among the higher vertebrates the relative proportions of white pulp and red pulp are fairly comparable. There are considerable differences in size, however, the rabbit spleen being disproportionately small, the human and rat spleens relatively large. There are also numbers of structural variations among the different species that account for numerous conflicting statements in the literature concerning spleen histology and function. The dog spleen, for example, possesses a muscular capsule capable of contracting that organ; conversely, the dog spleen has a notorious capacity for swelling up with blood during sleep or anesthesia to assume a weight several times greater than its "true" weight. In some species (rabbit) the arterioles possess a remarkably thick cuboidal epithelium; in others (especially dogs) there are specialized and prominent periarteriolar or capillary sheaths, sometimes called ellipsoid bodies. In the rat, and to a lesser extent in man, there is a highly developed marginal zone of nonreticular cells. The following descriptions will apply to splenic structures that are known or believed to exist in man.

In man as in other animals the spleen is deficient in lymphatic (white pulp) components at birth and does not reach its full size until early adult life, when its weight is about 150 gm. Thereafter spleen weight declines gradually to approximately 100 gm. in older adults. The organ is encased in a thin fibrous capsule from which trabeculae enter its substance, dividing it into compartments. The notably large artery and vein penetrate the capsule in a hilar notch on the medial aspect of the organ, and the artery arborizes within the trabeculae in company with veins and with an efferent system of lymphatics.

On departing from the trabeculae to enter the parenchyma the arterial vessels are enveloped along their course by a lymphatic mantle, the *periarterial lymphatic sheath*. Because of the symmetry of this sheath of lymphocytes, each such artery is termed a *central artery*. The sheath has for a skeleton a concentrically aligned, lacy network of reticulum cells linked together by reticulum fibers, in the interstices of which are enmeshed the abundant lymphocytes, smaller numbers of macrophages and a few plasma cells. Spaced along these cylindrical sheaths are organized spherical colonies of cells that comprise the so-called *lymphatic follicles*. These interesting structures, which appear to arise during the secondary response to antigenic stimulation and are sometimes called "secondary follicles," are grossly visible as malpighian corpuscles in human spleens. Histologically they are usually seen in cross section, forming in their union with the lymphatic sheath an oval structure in which the central artery has become eccentric (Fig. 31–6).

Seen at the center of most lymphatic follicles are loose, irregular aggregations of cells that are larger and paler than the surrounding lymphocytes. These *germinal center* cells appear to be a mixture of primitive cells, many of which are undergoing mitosis or DNA synthesis and many of which are phagocytic. A remarkable feature of the abundant, phag-

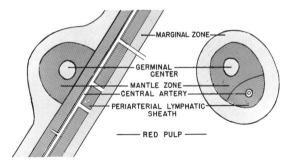

Figure 31–6. Diagrammatic scheme of spleen histologic structure. It appears from studies by Weiss and Snook and others that most of the central arterial blood passes through arterioles that penetrate the white pulp and empty into the loose "marginal zone." These blood cells then pass either into the sinuses or the cords of the red pulp; most of the cells entering the relatively constricted and discontinuous cords must slip through a fenestrated basement membrane in order to escape out the venous end.

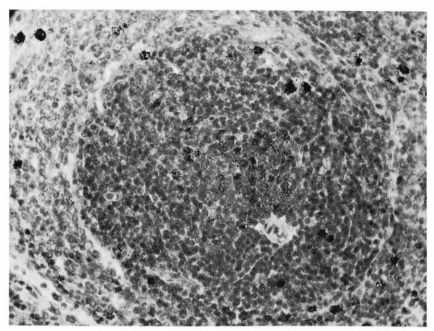

Figure 31–7. Autoradiograph of a spleen lymphatic follicle shortly after injection of tritiated thymidine into a normal adult rat. As indicated by the black grains over the cells at the center of the follicle above the central artery, the germinal center cells are very actively engaged in DNA synthesis, albeit grain counts are characteristically low. Scattered in small numbers throughout the surrounding dark lymphatic mantle, and to a greater extent in the lighter-stained, larger cells of the marginal zone and red pulp, are occasional individual cells that are heavily labeled. Very few lymphocytes show evidence of DNA synthesis. The marginal sinus, which visibly separates the lymphatic follicle from the marginal zone, is prominent in the rat.

ocytosed debris (the *tingible bodies*) in the cytoplasm of these cells, is that it consists largely of nuclear remnants, derived particularly from lymphocytes and plasma cells. The evidence both for cell generation and for cell death has led to disagreement as to whether this structure is primarily a center of cell formation or of cell destruction. Labeling studies with tritiated thymidine (H³TDR) revealed that an extraordinary proportion (almost half) of the germinal center cells are in the synthetic (S) phase of the cell cycle (Fig. 31–7). Studies by Fliedner, Cronkite and their associates indicate that germinal centers do not generate most of the lymphocytes that surround them, but rather that they behave as "micro-organs" which go through a continuous internal cycle of cell birth and death. The functional significance of this curious arrangement is uncertain, but the salient fact that these cells appear both to conserve and to utilize DNA has raised the conjecture that this may provide a mechanism for "immunologic memory."

Although some disagreement continues as to the origins of the lymphocytes surrounding germinal centers, it has been established by Gowans and others that the lymphocytes of the periarterial lymphatic sheath are accumulated there from the circulation and that this portion of the white pulp represents a tissue or resting stage of their circulatory cycle. When Gowans labeled rat thoracic duct lymphocytes with tritiated adenosine and injected them back into rats, he found that most small lymphocytes left the blood and "homed" into the lymphoid tissue surrounding the central arterioles of spleen and lymph nodes (Fig. 31–8). Very few of these labeled lymphocytes showed up in the marginal zones and essentially none entered the adult thymus. This physiologic migration appeared to involve the passage of blood lymphocytes through, as well as between, the endothelial cells lining the postcapillary venules of the lymphatic follicle. It is this population of recirculating lymphocytes which contributes most of the cells recovered during thoracic duct drainage.

Enveloping the compact lymphatic sheath and follicle is an ill-defined, variable mass of cells which constitute the *marginal zone* (Figs. 31–6 and 31–7). This junctional tissue separates the lymphatic tissue (white pulp) from the true red pulp, and consists of a mixture of RE cells, predominantly pale, somewhat flattened, endothelial-like cells that lack reticulum, and large lymphocytes. These cells are distributed in ill-defined vascular spaces that are roughly concentric in orientation to the follicle. Although virtually devoid of phagocytes, the marginal zone appears to be a structure crucial to the special filtering function of the spleen, for it is here that particulate matter first accumulates after intravenous injection (Fig. 31–9).

Beyond the marginal zone is the highly vascular red pulp which constitutes the bulk of the spleen mass. Two principal vascular structures have been recognized, and it seems likely that these correspond to the two hemodynamic compartments of the spleen (see below). The main conduits of the red pulp are the splenic sinuses, the lumina of which are large (30 to 40 μ in diameter) relative to those of the perfusing arterioles. The sinus-lining cells are elongate, tapered reticulum cells which become variably phagocytic when aroused. These cells are perched on a fenestrated, screenlike type of basement membrane (Fig. 31–10). Because of discontinuity

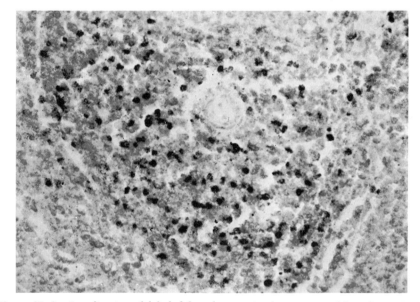

Figure 31–8. Localization of labeled lymphocytes in the periarterial lymphatic sheath of the rat spleen. On their reinjection these previously labeled (black-grained) lymphocytes accumulated in the lymphocytic sheath by a sort of "homing instinct." Contrast this "lymphatic" pattern of sequestration with the usual perifollicular pattern found after the injection of non-lymphocytic cells or particles, as depicted in Figure 31–9. (Reproduced with the kind permission of the author and publisher, from Gowans, J. L., in Good, R. A., and Gabrielsen, A. E. (eds.): The Thymus in Immunobiology. New York, Hoeber Medical Division, Harper & Row, 1964.)

Figure 31–9. Localization of particulate matter in the rat spleen. Ten minutes after the injection of chlorazol black E, the particulate dye is concentrated intercellularly between the marginal zone (MZ) cells surrounding the lymphatic nodule (LN), as shown in A. Eight hours after a similar injection, most of this particulate matter had been moved off into the red pulp (RP) by macrophages, as shown in B. Injured red cells show the same initial pattern of sequestration in the spleen. Contrast this perifollicular distribution with that for lymphocytes shown in Figure 31–8. (Reproduced and modified with the kind permission of the author and publisher, from Snook, T.: Anat. Rec., *148:* 149, 1964.)

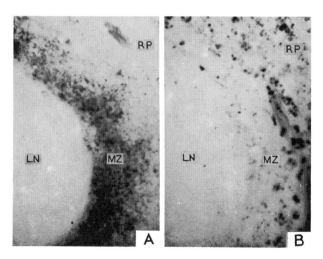

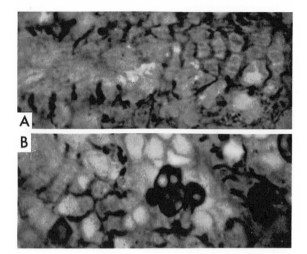

Figure 31–10. Characteristic fenestrated basement membrane separating the sinus and cord structures of the red pulp of human spleen. In *A* the overlying endothelium was uncovered on the right, revealing the lattice-like pattern. *B* reveals the branching of a sinus, with a cluster of dark-stained granulocytes at the bifurcation. PAS stain. (Reproduced with the kind permission of the author and the publisher, from Weiss, L.: J. Biophys. & Biochem. Cytol., 3:599, 1957.)

of the lining cells, intercellular gaps are numerous and red cells are frequently found in the process of slipping through. The sinuses terminate by emptying into the splenic veins.

Alternating with the blood-filled sinuses are irregular, comparatively narrow vascular structures called *splenic cords*. The cords differ from the sinuses in that the reticulum cells are less flattened, often dangle into the narrow lumen and frequently have processes that cross the lumen and interrupt its continuity. These lining cells appear to be more actively phagocytic than those of the sinuses, and it appears that many of them let go of their moorings during sequestration of particles and move into and along the lumen of the cords. The content of the potential cord lumen varies considerably in number of blood cells and contains relatively high concentrations of lymphocytes and monocytes.

In recent years the disputed vascular course within the spleen has been studied intensively by Weiss and Snook and others by means of electron microscopy. There is not as yet certainty or full agreement, but the following summarizes the present understanding. The central artery of the white pulp sends off at right angles a number of thin capillaries that enter into and terminate within the lymphatic mantle (Fig. 31–6). These narrow channels contain relatively few blood cells, and it is probable that they provide the plasma-skimming mechanism that functions in essence as an afferent lymphatic system. It is also through this network of capillaries that blood lymphocytes re-enter the lymphatic sheath, and one may consider this as a lymphocyte-trapping structure (Fig. 31–8). Most of the larger branches of the central artery terminate

in the marginal zone. In the rat, at least, much of this blood enters a marginal sinus and then percolates outward through the enveloping network of the marginal zone (Figs. 31–6 and 31–7); blood emerging from the outer fringe of the marginal zone may enter into cords or into sinuses and continue out through veins. A minority of the branches of the central artery, including the main stem, pass through the marginal zone and enter directly into the red pulp, entering either into cords or into sinuses.

Thus, apart from a system of fine capillaries that perfuse the white pulp, the bulk of the blood cells appear to enter into the marginal zone; thereafter, these cells either pass through the sinuses and out, or must first wend their way through the cords and then slip out through the basement membrane into the sinuses or veins.

Hemodynamic Features of Normal and of Enlarged Spleens

THE SPLENIC RED CELL POOL

In normal man under physiologic conditions, the total blood content of the spleen, despite its rich vascularity, is only about 50 ml., representing approximately one-third of the spleen weight and about 1 per cent of the total blood volume. Most of this blood appears to exchange rapidly with peripheral blood. Judged by indirect methods the blood flow to the normal human spleen is believed to be about 3 or 4 per cent of the cardiac output or roughly 150 ml. per minute. If all the intrasplenic blood is in transit, through serial conduits, as is true of most organs, one would expect that the mean transit time would be about 20 seconds.

Direct studies of normal spleen blood mixing in man have been made by injecting Cr51-labeled autologous red cells into a peripheral vein and monitoring radioactivity over the spleen. Such studies have shown that the time for complete mixing of peripheral blood with spleen blood is as short as 20 seconds and no more than about 2 minutes (Fig. 31–11). Although it is quite conceivable that in such studies there is concealed a minor slowly exchanging compartment, it is clear that the transit time for most of the blood flowing through the spleen is only slightly slower than in the other organs.

In patients having splenomegaly for any of a variety of reasons the hemodynamics are altered. In most splenomegalic patients the total number of labeled red cells entering the spleen pool is increased, often severalfold. Moreover, the period required for the systemic pool of labeled cells to equilibrate with the splenic pool may be markedly prolonged, frequently requiring 30 or 40 minutes (Fig. 31–11), sometimes taking over an hour. Studies by Harris, McAlister and Prankerd revealed that whereas normal mixing of blood in the spleen followed a single exponential function of time, many patients with splenomegaly and delayed mixing showed two-component curves.

Such studies in man and in experimental animals provide strong kinetic evidence for two vascular compartments. One conducts blood rapidly with a transit time of less than 2 minutes, and is the predominant normal pathway; the second vascular compartment exchanges much more slowly and in splenomegaly may be much the larger. The general result is that splenomegaly tends to detain red cells, and splenomegalic states are usually associated with an appreciable "extravascular" red cell pool. The anatomic counterparts of these two kinetic vascular compartments are not yet established. It is reasonable to suppose, however, that the alternative chance as to whether the blood cell enters a cord or a sinus may be the basis for these compartments. If so, one must assume that the more capacious and patent sinuses provide the rapid-flowing normally predominant compartment, and that under certain conditions the second (cordal) compartment is entered or opened up.

In addition to the pooling of blood, the investigations of Barcroft and others demonstrated that the spleen has a rather unique ability to induce hemoconcentration. If blood is obtained from the spleen pulp by puncture or by incising the organ and collecting the oozings, it is found that the hematocrit may be considerably higher than that of spleen artery or spleen vein blood. This phenomenon is particularly evident in animals such as dogs, in which the red cell reservoir function of the spleen is highly developed, especially in dogs that are asleep or under the influence of barbiturate anesthesia or tranquilizing drugs. In anesthetized dogs the red pulp hematocrit may even exceed 95 per cent! Dog spleen blood was also found to be somewhat dehydrated as revealed by increased plasma protein concentrations; thus, the plasma skimmed was relatively watery as is true of most lymph.

Normal human spleens do not show striking evidence for hemoconcentration, but studies by Rothschild and others revealed that in splenomegalic individuals there is a decisive increase in the total body hematocrit as compared to the peripheral hematocrit, indicating the existence of a hemoconcentrated splenic pool. Subsequent calculations by others have revealed that the red cell pool in splenomegaly is highly variable, depending presumably on whether enlargement represents vascular or nonvascular tissue; in many patients with splenomegaly, however, studies with Cr51-

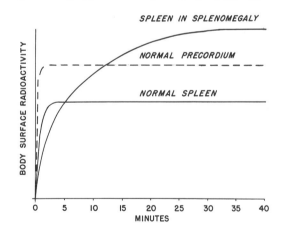

Figure 31–11. Rates of mixing of red cells in normal and enlarged spleens. Following the intravenous injection of normal Cr51-labeled red cells, mixing of labeled and unlabeled cells can be monitored with a directional scintillation counter. As indicated by the interrupted line, radioactivity over the normal precordium reaches a plateau indicating complete mixing within less than a minute, and that over the normal spleen is very slightly slower. However, mixing of circulating and intrasplenic blood often is not completed for 30 or 40 minutes in patients with splenomegaly and may require longer than an hour.

labeled red cells indicate that as much as 20 or 25 per cent of the total circulating red cell mass may be in the splenic pool.

THE SPLENIC PLATELET POOL

The observations, largely in dogs, cats and sheep, that the spleen may normally function as an important reservoir which stores blood during calm or sleepy states and discharges it on exertion or nervous excitement created much interest as to the relevance of this to man and his diseases. Doan and others showed that epinephrine caused a shrinkage of the spleen that could be observed at the bedside in splenomegalic individuals, and that epinephrine injected into the splenic artery at operation caused a reduction in spleen size and a rise in certain blood elements in the spleen vein blood. By and large, as would be expected from the foregoing discussion, epinephrine had very little effect upon the peripheral blood hematocrit, although appreciable rises sometimes occurred in patients with hereditary spherocytosis. Frequently, however, there was a sharp rise in leukocyte and platelet levels after epinephrine and in some instances spleen vein platelet levels were found to rise sharply on stimulation. This led to use of epinephrine in the diagnosis of splenic disorders, the intention being to "flush out" incriminating cell types. However, the general experience that patients lacking spleens showed similar leukocyte changes after epinephrine or exercise led to the view that the response was largely due to mobilization of the "marginal pool" of leukocytes from vessels throughout the body, rather than reflecting the specified contents of the spleen. Accordingly the diagnostic injection of epinephrine in splenic disorders was largely discontinued, and the concept that the spleen was an important reservoir for blood cells went out of vogue.

Very recently investigations in man by Aster and by Penny, Rozenberg and Firkin have established that with respect to the third formed element of blood, the platelet, the spleen reservoir concept is indeed a physiologic fact.

A remarkable fact that has been known for years concerning the spleen is that after splenectomy there is usually a rapid and often a profound rise in blood platelet levels. This is most dramatic in some patients with thrombocytopenia (Fig. 31–12), or myeloproliferative disorders (see Chap. 30), but the effect is evident in relatively normal individuals.

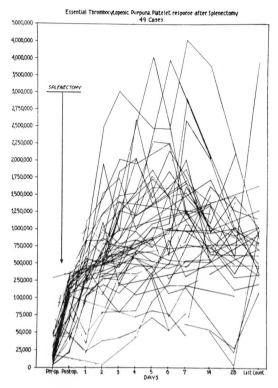

Figure 31–12. The effect of splenectomy on peripheral blood platelet levels in 49 consecutive cases of thrombocytopenic purpura. An immediate rise in platelet levels occurred in all but five patients at the operating table on the day of surgery. In most patients platelets rose steadily thereafter to reach a peak level within a week. (Reproduced with the kind permission of the author and publisher, from Doan, C. A.: Bull. New York Acad. Med., 25:625, 1949.)

Usually some increase in platelet numbers occurs within the first day or two after splenectomy and reaches a peak on the average at 6 or 7 days (Fig. 31–12). Sometimes, however, the rise in platelets does not begin until a few days or occasionally weeks after splenectomy. Thereafter, levels gradually decline at rather variable rates over a period of weeks or months, but some degree of thrombocytosis often persists for years. Persistent thrombocytosis after splenectomy is particularly striking in patients with continuing hemolytic anemia.

Although compatible with the view that the spleen normally destroys platelets, this finding did not satisfactorily explain why the marrow is usually so slow to adjust the rate of production after splenectomy, so as to restore presplenectomy platelet levels. Furthermore, later studies with Cr[51]-labeled platelets showed the liver to be the principal normal site of platelet removal. Finally, the observation by Cohen, Barnett and Gardner that, in congestive splenomegaly with thrombocytopenia, platelet survival was only slightly diminished, made it seem doubtful that an increased splenic destruction of platelets was operative. Nevertheless, the studies of Doan and his associates and of Reimann and coworkers showed without question that platelet levels in the spleen were often high. Penny et al. perfused human spleens removed at operation and found that from 40 to 1100 billion platelets could be flushed out, representing in some instances more platelets than were found in the general circulation. Using Cr^{51} platelets Aster demonstrated that the spleen contains an exchangeable pool for platelets that varies roughly in magnitude with spleen size and that can be discharged into the circulation by epinephrine infusion. Aster's studies indicate that normally about one-third of the total platelet mass is concentrated in the spleen.

In splenomegaly the spleen platelet pool may be greatly enlarged and may contain up to 90 per cent of the total platelet mass (Fig. 31–13). Since the total platelet mass of a normal man would amount to only 10 or 15 gm., it is evident that variation in this pool of cells has little effect on spleen size; the entry of 90 per cent of the red cell mass into the spleen, on the contrary, would add over 2 kg. to its weight. Analysis of the kinetic data indicates that normal platelets enter into a slow-mixing compartment that may resemble that described previously for red cells in enlarged spleens or for abnormal red cells in normal spleens. Since Björkman had shown that starch granules similar in size to platelets are found in the cords rather than in the sinuses, Aster postulates that platelets normally enter the slow-moving (probably cordal) compartment; assuming a blood flow of 4 per cent of cardiac output, the normal spleen would contain about 30 per cent of the total platelets if the average platelet transit time were 7 or 8 minutes. The effect of epinephrine appears to be that of excluding platelets from the slow compartment and allowing those already present to escape, probably at a normal rate.

Although further work is needed, it appears likely that the phenomenon of spleen pooling accounts for the effects on platelet levels of splenectomy, stress, exercise and splenomegaly. That the marrow seems to adjust its rate of platelet production more to some function of total platelet mass or turnover than to circulating levels suggests a homeostatic feed-

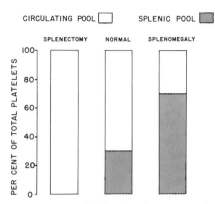

Figure 31–13. Platelet distribution in splenectomized, normal and splenomegalic individuals. As depicted here, the majority of the platelet mass may be in transit through an exchangeable splenic pool in patients with splenomegaly. (Figure kindly provided by Dr. Richard H. Aster.)

back mechanism quite different from that regulating red cell levels.

THE SPLEEN LEUKOCYTE POOL

The extent and significance of granulocyte pooling in the spleen is less well understood, but it is certain that the normal spleen plays only a minor role. It may be considered a major pool for recirculating lymphocytes, however, for as discussed earlier, a large fraction of the lymphocyte mass undergoes continuous turnover between the lymphatic tissue, a large portion of which is in the spleen, and the circulation by way of the thoracic duct.

Specialized Functions of the Spleen

The two major functions of the RES in general are also the principal activities of the spleen. By virtue of its unique organization and vascular structure, however, the spleen may perform these functions in unique ways or with special proficiency. The most singular clinical consequences of its specialized functions are seen in hematologic disorders involving increased blood cell destruction; it plays an important but not as unique a role in infection and immunity.

THE ROLE OF THE NORMAL SPLEEN IN CELL SEQUESTRATION

Red Cell Destruction

That the human spleen with its rich sinus structure is sometimes a major site of red cell destruction has been evident for years,

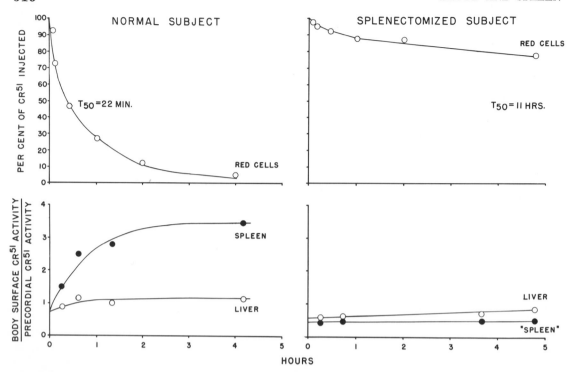

Figure 31–14. Selective splenic sequestration of mildly injured red cells. The special facility of the spleen for trapping and destroying red cells is revealed here by injecting autogenous red cells that had been exposed to low concentrations of the sulfhydryl-blocking agent, NEM. As shown on the left, such cells are cleared readily by the spleen at a rate probably limited by its blood flow. In a splenectomized individual, however, clearance is markedly impaired. (Reproduced with the permission of the publisher, from Jacob, H. S., and Jandl, J. H.: J. Clin. Invest., *41*:1514, 1962.)

from the fact that in certain anemias the organ is darkly engorged with red cells, many of which may ooze forth from its cut surfaces. Furthermore, examination of spleen vein blood reveals higher levels of bilirubin than are found in the arterial blood, indicating actual red cell destruction and hemoglobin breakdown within the spleen. A series of observations by Emerson, Shen, Ham and Castle provided evidence that the spleen detained red cells in hereditary spherocytosis and subjected them to "erythrostasis," (Chap. 30), and direct perfusion studies by Dacie and by Young demonstrated ex vivo that the spleen can indeed selectively retain red cells. It was apparent, then, that a spleen that permits normal red cells to pass through unmolested can trap and destroy certain abnormal cells.

The use of red cells labeled with the gamma-emitting isotope, Cr^{51}, allowed further study of such processes in vivo. It was found that certain kinds of abnormalities of the red cells caused the cells to be sequestered very selectively in the spleen, with little or no sequestration elsewhere in the RES. Examples of alterations predisposing to

splenic sequestration are cell-coating with "incomplete" antibodies (e.g., 7S anti-Rh) or metalloprotein complexes; spherocytosis induced by exposure of cells to mild heat or to lecithin; and certain chemical alterations, such as inhibition of membrane sulfhydryl groups with N-ethylmaleimide (NEM) (Fig. 31–14).

In normal individuals red cells mildly injured in these ways are cleared from the circulation at slow or moderate rates, the half-survival time not being less than about 20 minutes. In splenomegalic individuals sequestration by the spleen may be faster, giving half-survival times as short as 8 or 10 minutes. In splenectomized individuals red cells similarly altered are cleared much less rapidly, half-survival times being from 5 to 10 or more hours (Fig. 31–14). Such data indicate that with certain red cell abnormalities the spleen may be 20 or 30 times as proficient a filter as the entire remainder of the RES, despite the fact that its blood flow is very much smaller.

When red cells are altered in certain other ways or when the alterations described above are inflicted more severely, other portions of the RES, particularly the liver, participate in red cell sequestration and destruction. Examples of injuries predisposing to hepatic sequestration are "complete" (19S) agglutinins and complement-fixing antibodies (e.g., anti-A or anti-B), injury by prolonged storage or incubation and injury by large concentrations of NEM or by more intensive heating. In such processes, the rate of clearance is potentially very fast by virtue of the high blood flow of the liver, and the half-time of clearance may be as short as 2 minutes. As a generalization, alterations which invoke this nonspecific or "hepatic" pattern of cell destruction involve gross changes in cell morphology or injuries that in vitro are signified by increased spontaneous autohemolysis. A "splenic" pattern of sequestration usually signifies mild morphologic change, if any, and may operate against cells having little or no tendency for autohemolysis in vivo.

As with other particles or cells, red cells are initially trapped between the cells of the marginal zone and in the neighboring red pulp. Later, masses of red cells accumulate throughout the red pulp, where erythrophagocytosis may or may not become striking. Mildly altered cells trapped in this way undergo an accelerated change in osmotic fragility (Fig. 31–15), indicative of imminent lysis. It is not certain whether the relatively rapid deterioration and lysis of mildly injured cells that are sequestered in the spleen is the result of specific lytic chemicals or of an impairment or an acceleration of metabolism, or both.

Sequestration Without Cell Destruction

In some instances altered red cells may be sequestered by a normal spleen for many minutes or even several hours and then be released back into the circulation to survive fairly normally thereafter (Fig. 31–16). This indicates that the act of trapping of cells is a probationary phase and that the secondary phase of cell lysis does not necessarily follow.

The likelihood that splenic sequestration may in some instances be constructive rather than destructive was suggested by Crosby's observation indicating that transfused red cells containing iron granules (siderocytes) lost these granules in normal spleens, without the cells themselves being destroyed (Fig. 31–17). Further evidence by others indicated that the spleen normally sequesters immature red cells, including many reticulocytes, and it appears that most of these are allowed to ripen there and then to proceed. The finding that immature red cells possess a protein-coating (largely as attached transferrin) and behave like antibody-coated cells in vitro suggests a common mechanism for their splenic sequestration. Recent observations by Keene

Figure 31–15. Changes in the osmotic fragility of antibody-coated red cells trapped in the spleen. In this study in rats, red cells labeled with Cr^{51} and coated with antibody underwent no significant change in osmotic fragility in vitro or, as shown in the upper portion of this figure, in the peripheral blood. Those labeled red cells that were trapped in the spleen meanwhile, however, underwent rapid increase in osmotic fragility and lysis. (Reproduced with the kind permission of the publisher, from Jandl, J. H.: Mechanisms of immune hemolysis in vivo, in Thomas, L., Uhr, J. W., and Grant, L. (eds.): Injury, Inflammation, and Immunity. Baltimore, Williams & Wilkins Co., 1964.)

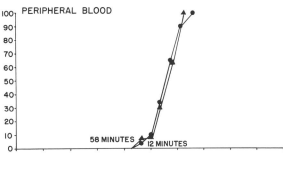

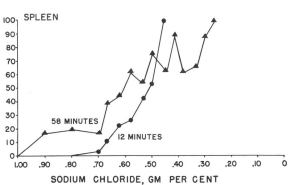

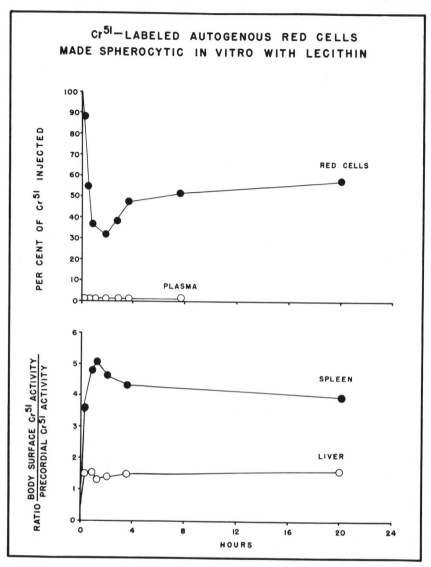

Figure 31–16. Temporary sequestration of injured red cells. Cells that had been injured by lecithin, which makes red cells spheroidal in shape, were at first taken up by the spleen of this normal individual. After about an hour many of the trapped cells were released from the spleen (lower portion) into the circulation (upper portion), which releasing continued for several hours thereafter. Presumably in this instance splenic sequestration exerted a beneficial or at least a temporizing influence, for the survival of the labeled cells thereafter was normal. (Reproduced with the kind permission of the publishers, from Jandl, J. H., and Tomlinson, A. S.: J. Clin. Invest., 37:1202, 1958.)

reveal that the bone marrow and spleen are the two RES organs most avid in trapping nucleated red cells. Till and McCulloch and their associates have utilized the ability of mouse spleens to trap primitive nucleated blood cells that were injected in the form of marrow cell suspensions, for evaluating the behavior of stem cells. Since the recipients are previously irradiated "lethally" in order to destroy autogenous stem cells, the number of spleen colonies or clones arising after

injection of marrow is used to assay the number of stem cells as well as to observe their individual behavior.

These various findings show that the spleen may indeed be a receptive site for colonization by certain dividing cells and may provide a temporary sanctuary for viable cells having reversible defects or requiring additional maturation. It is evident in this light that the spleen provides a form of "quality control" for cells formed in and released by the marrow. In most instances the marrow only releases cells that have been adequately formed and matured. Occasionally red cells escape the marrow sinuses that are still nucleated or that possess such manifestations of immaturity as siderotic granules or nuclear remnants. Such cells are caught up in the sinuses of the spleen where they are altered, ripened or destroyed. The magnitude of this task when the marrow is normal is probably not great; in diseases with disturbed marrow function or architecture, however, this role of the spleen may be considerable.

The result is that splenectomy in the normal results in a relatively minor accumulation of peculiar cells, principally evident by occasional cells having siderotic granules and Howell-Jolly bodies. On the other hand, splenectomy in myelopathic anemias such as thalassemia or congenital inclusion body anemias results in dramatic changes in blood morphology in which various inclusions and nucleated forms may be numerous. In marrow-replacement disorders such as myelofibrosis or carcinomatosis, in which the marrow cell-releasing mechanism is affected, splenectomy may uncover the presence of numerous immature blood cells of all types, including erythroblasts and myeloblasts. In

certain nonspherocytic hemolytic anemias splenectomy may result in a substantial rise in reticulocyte levels without a fall in hemoglobin levels, presumably indicating removal of a reticulocyte-detaining compartment.

An analogous situation in which the splenic sequestration of red cells serves a useful function is in latent, endemic bartonellosis. In this disorder, as seen in rats or dogs, apparently healthy animals develop a severe, often fatal, hemolytic disease after splenectomy. This bacilliform organism clings to red cell surfaces, causing their destruction. Evidently the intact spleen efficiently removes minimally "infected" red cells from the blood, destroys the organism and thereby suppresses the disease. Removal of the spleen allows the Bartonella organisms to remain and survive in the circulation, to proliferate and within a few days to hemolyze the red cells. It is probable that the spleen may play a similar, if less effectual role in such protozoan disorders as malaria.

A more subtle and less understood influence of splenic conditioning is that on the shape of the red cell. After splenectomy in hematologically normal patients there is a gradual flattening of the circulating red cell population, with the appearance of target cells. This

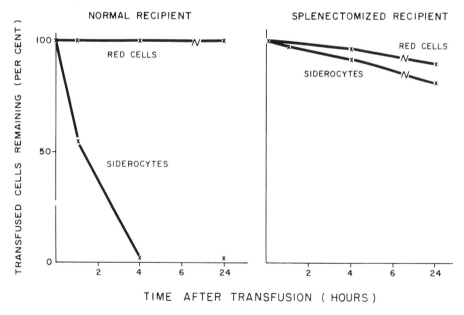

Figure 31–17. Removal of red cell inclusion granules by the normal spleen. When blood containing numerous siderocytes (red cells possessing inclusion granules of iron) was transfused to a normal recipient, as depicted on the left, these red cells survived normally but the inclusions were removed. When the same blood was transfused to a splenectomized recipient (right), these iron granules persisted. This attribute of the spleen was termed by Crosby the "pitting function." (Reproduced with the kind permission of the author and publisher, from Crosby, W. H.: Blood, 14:399, 1959.)

A. Red cells
   1. No change in numbers or life span
   2. Flattening of cell, increase in surface, target cells
   3. Usually slight increase in reticulocytes
   4. Inclusion bodies: siderocytes, Howell-Jolly bodies,
       basophilic stippling, Heinz bodies
   5. Occasional nucleated red cells
B. Leukocytes
   1. Leukocytosis, moderate at first; later usually slight
       or moderate
   2. Occasional immature forms
   3. Frequently a delayed increase in lymphocytes,
       monocytes and eosinophils
C. Platelets
   1. Thrombocytosis; may be striking at first, later
       usually slight
   2. No change in life span
   3. Occasionally atypical and giant forms

shape change after splenectomy is essentially the opposite of that seen during "conditioning" by the spleen of hereditary spherocytes, and it is assumed that repetitious passage through the normal spleen tends to diminish the surface area of red cells and to increase slightly their thickness-to-diameter ratio. Since the lifespan of normal red cells is influenced little, if at all, by splenectomy, the importance of this aspect of normal splenic conditioning is in doubt. Furthermore, a possible disturbance in iron metabolism after splenectomy has not been excluded. The hematologic "syndrome" of the postsplenectomy or asplenic state is listed in Table 31–6.

Sequestration of Leukocytes and Platelets

Apart from its ability to retain reversibly lymphocytes and platelets as a physiologic "pooling" function (discussed earlier), the normal spleen also has the capacity to trap irreversibly and to destroy altered leukocytes and platelets. Relatively little is known of this mechanism with respect to leukocytes, except that acute granulocytic destruction, as during a pyrogenic reaction to immune hemolysis, to drugs or to endotoxin, is accompanied at the histologic level by large numbers of granulocytes seemingly trapped in the sinuses of the spleen and liver. The effect in vivo of injury to platelets has been studied by methods very similar to those used on red cells with analogous results. Thus, when platelets are exposed in vivo to relatively small amounts of isoantibody there is a highly selective sequestration in the spleen (Fig.

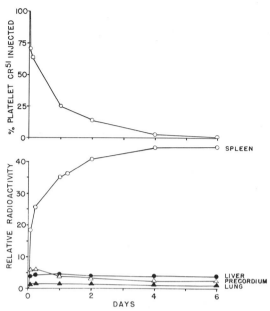

Figure 31–18. Splenic sequestration of Cr[15]-labeled platelets in an isoimmunized recipient. As with red cells, transfused platelets exposed to low levels of antibody are cleared from the blood (upper portion) rather selectively by the spleen (lower portion). High concentrations of platelet antibody, detectable by complement fixation in vitro, cause more rapid, hepatic sequestration. (Reproduced with the kind permission of the publisher, from Aster, R. H., and Jandl, J. H.: J. Clin. Invest., *43*:856, 1964.)

31–18). Large amounts of antibody cause more rapid destruction with predominantly hepatic destruction. In patients with idiopathic thrombocytopenic purpura, mild or moderate curtailment of platelet survival has been found to be associated with a "splenic" uptake pattern; very rapid rates of platelet destruction have been associated with a "hepatic" pattern of platelet sequestration.

Sequestration of Tumor Cells

Tumor cells or leukemia cells released into the blood are taken up by the RES components of the liver, bone marrow and spleen. These cells appear to proliferate readily in the liver and marrow to form gross colonies, and these two organs are the commonest sites of hematogenous metastases. The spleen, despite its extraordinary competence for filtering unusual cells, is rather infrequently a site of gross metastases. Microscopic clusters of tumor cells are not infrequent in the spleen, and are encountered in at least 10 per cent of patients with metastatic carcinoma. However, these implants seem to flourish poorly in the spleen as compared to the other organs of the RES, apparently as the result of a more aggressive population of phagocytic cells. Occasionally, however, the spleen tissue may be replaced by tumor cells, although marked enlargement thereby is rare.

Some patients with tumor develop a "reactive" splenic hyperplasia resembling that invoked by antigens or infections, and it has been suggested that this is a manifestation of an immunologic defense mechanism. Some patients with carcinoma, particularly of the gastrointestinal tract, develop a homogeneous or "monoclonal" hyperglobulinemia, possibly for the same reason. The hyperplasia of the RES in some patients with carcinoma may be so impressive as to create a clinical and pathologic picture resembling or identical with reticulum cell sarcoma; it is difficult to be certain whether this malignant-appearing hyperplasia of RE cells is a reaction to the tumor or is a second, coincidental neoplasm.

THE ROLE OF THE SPLEEN IN INFECTION AND IMMUNITY

There is little direct information as to any special ability of the spleen for filtering out bacteria and other infectious particles, although it may be assumed that splenic sequestration of blood-borne bacteria accounts for the relatively high frequency of septic foci in spleens of patients with bacterial endocarditis, tuberculosis and diverse septicemias. As judged by studies of red cells, it may be surmised that splenic trapping of bacteria is particularly important when antibody levels are low and when complement-fixing antibodies are absent. Occasionally the initial site of infection may recover to the extent that the spleen is the only apparent infected organ. In such instances one may speak of "primary tuberculosis of the spleen," or of a splenic abscess. The presence of such an isolated infection of the spleen should be considered particularly in patients with persistent signs of infection, splenomegaly and pain in the left upper quadrant.

The spleen is a major source of antibody and accounts for about one-quarter of the total lymphatic mass. Removal of the spleen has little effect on the net potential for antibody production, however, and there is no serious alteration in most of the immunologic reactions. In one important respect, however, splenectomy creates an immunologic impairment; this is in the initial response to particulate, blood-borne antigens. Splenectomized individuals form antibody to subcutaneous antigens quite normally and respond well to soluble intravenous antigens. However, when a particulate antigen is injected intravenously for the first time, as by injecting Rh-positive red cells into an unsensitized Rh-negative recipient, the splenectomized individual forms little or no antibody. Even highly antigenic, heterologous red cells elicit little or no response when given in small amounts. With repeated stimulation, however, splenectomized individuals eventually do produce normal or, in some instances, even increased amounts of antibody against cellular antigens, albeit the peak titers may be achieved more slowly than in normals.

This special role of the spleen in forming antibodies against cellular antigens is logically attributable to the fact that in the spleen special mechanisms exist for trapping intravascular particles, whether or not antibodies are present, and that particles or cells so trapped are brought into close proximity to immunologically competent tissue. In addition, when the quantity of antigen is small, the spleen concentrates intravascular antigens so as to create a high-density antigenic stimulation. Presumably patients with large hyperplastic spleens may have an enhanced ability to form antibody against particulate antigens, although this is yet to be proved.

An immunologic deficit similar to that observed in splenectomy is observed in situations in which preformed antibody to one cellular antigen interferes with a primary response to a second antigen. It has been known for some time that erythroblastosis fetalis due to Rh antibodies usually occurs in infants who are ABO-incompatible with the mother's serum. Similarly Rh-positive type A or B cells seldom induce anti-Rh when injected into Rh-negative recipients having anti-A or anti-B. Since, as noted earlier, ABO antibodies normally cause a swift lysis or sequestration of red cells in the liver, such antibodies would greatly reduce the exposure of other cellular antigens to the lymphoid tissue of the spleen.

Although most infections are handled normally in splenectomized individuals, there is evidence that such individuals and congenitally asplenic patients are prone to fall victim to overwhelming, often fatal septicemias. The number of such catastrophic infections is very small in normal or relatively normal individuals who have been splenectomized, but it is rather high in patients splenectomized for serious disorders such as thalassemia or thrombocytopenic purpura. Although there has been debate as to the frequency of serious infections in splenectomized individuals, there is little doubt that these infections tend to be unusually fulminant, with fatalities often occurring between 10 and 18 hours of the onset of symptoms. The most common offending organism is the pneumococcus, the usual course involving septicemia and pneumonia or meningitis. About three-fourths of the fatal infections take place within 2 years of splenectomy, the incidence being higher in younger than in older patients. Accordingly, when patients are to be splenectomized electively it is considered advisable to delay surgery beyond early childhood if possible, and to regard all postsplenectomy infections as potentially hazardous and deserving of prompt, appropriate therapy.

Splenomegaly: Regulation of Spleen Size and Function

The phenomenon most responsible for the reputation of the spleen as a sinister organ is its remarkable capacity for enlargement. Whereas enlargement of most organs to twice their normal size is most unusual, the spleen very commonly increases to two or three times its normal size, and often enlarges to five to ten times of normal; it is not unusual in certain disorders for the spleen to achieve a size of 20 to 30 times normal. When greatly enlarged, this organ may displace the stomach, bowels and left kidney, may fill the entire left side of the abdominal cavity as well as part of the right side and may mechanically interfere with body movements.

Lists of potential causes of splenomegaly are so lengthy as to be virtually useless clinically. It is helpful, however, to distinguish certain magnitudes of splenomegaly, for the list of conditions leading to massive splenomegaly is relatively short. In Table 31–7 the common causes of splenomegaly (as seen in

the temperate regions) are categorized in terms of the characteristic magnitude of the enlargement. Obviously, all these disorders may at one stage or another manifest "slight" splenomegaly; furthermore, disorders such as the infections listed may at times induce "moderate" splenomegaly. In certain regions the list of common causes of marked splenomegaly would include kala-azar and chronic malaria.

It should be pointed out that in a large proportion of patients having slight splenomegaly, the underlying cause of the enlargement is never ascertained. Furthermore, the splenic enlargement resulting from a transient illness regresses quite variably thereafter, persisting often for weeks, frequently for months and occasionally for years after the apparent removal of the underlying cause. It is evident, therefore, that for some time after an illness splenomegaly, usually of slight degree, may be discovered during a routine examination of a symptomless patient; it is generally advisable in otherwise healthy subjects to view slight splenomegaly as more likely benign than serious and to be inquisitive but restrained.

In some instances much of the added bulk of enlarged spleens is provided by deposits of extraneous materials as in the lipidoses, by engorgement with blood as during an acute hemolytic anemia or transfusion reaction, or by implantation of ectopic tissue such as tumor or as in extramedullary hematopoiesis. In the majority of instances, however, splenomegaly reflects splenic hyperplasia.

On reaching their mature size, most organs of the body are quite stable and exhibit little evidence of cell turnover or DNA synthesis. In brain and muscle, for example, the cell population is fixed. Among the liver parenchymal cells only about one cell in 1000 nor-

TABLE 31–7. Common Causes of Splenomegaly.

Category	Magnitude of Splenomegaly		Causative Diseases
	Cm. Below Left Costal Margin	Spleen: Weight, gm.	
Normal	0	100–200	None
Slight	0–4	200–500	Infections (tuberculosis, SBE, hepatitis), hypersensitivity reactions, connective tissue disorders
Moderate	4–8	500–2000	Cirrhosis, hemolytic anemia, infectious mononucleosis, leukemia and lymphoma, polycythemia vera
Marked	>8	>2000	Chronic granulocytic leukemia, myelofibrosis

TABLE 31–8. COMPARISONS OF CELL NUMBERS AND PROLIFERATIVE ACTIVITIES IN
THE SPLEENS AND LIVERS OF NORMAL RATS.*

Measurement	Spleen	Liver	Approximate Ratio Spleen/Liver
Weight, gm.	0.8	14.4	1/18
DNA, mg. total	11.2	32.2	1/3
Total number of cells*	1.9×10^9	3.2×10^9	3/5
Total number of RE cells*	1.0×10^9	1.2×10^9	1/1
H³TDR uptake			
C.p.m./mg. DNA	63,000	10,800	6/1
C.p.m., total	641,500	336,300	2/1
% of cells labeled	4.1	0.57	7/1

* From Jandl, et al.: J. Exp. Med., *122:*299,1965. The number of cells was calculated from DNA analysis by utilizing the constancy of nuclear DNA in somatic cells. The term RE cells here excludes hepatocytes and lymphocytes.

mally is engaged in DNA synthesis, as can be seen by injecting the labeled DNA precursor, tritiated thymidine (H³TDR), and performing autoradiographs. In certain tissues, on the other hand, the cells are exfoliated and need to be replaced at a constant relatively high rate. Tissues having a rapid DNA turnover are the bone marrow and the gastrointestinal tract; in both tissues the cells formed are exfoliated from that tissue in a period of several days after their initial differentiation from the resident or sessile stem cells. Skin has a similar exfoliative pattern of cytokinetics, albeit the rate is much slower. In some situations the rate of proliferation may be markedly accelerated. When red cells are removed from the circulation rapidly, the erythroid marrow increases its rate of proliferation. Rates of red cell formation may be increased abruptly by three- or four-fold, and with time rates of over ten times normal are achieved. The skin responds similarly in such disorders as psoriasis, and even quiescent organs such as the liver become actively proliferative when liver tissue is partly removed or destroyed.

The proliferative behavior of the spleen and RES has been studied recently by use of H³TDR, and it is clear that the normal "resting" spleen is a relatively proliferative organ and that its rate of DNA synthesis and turnover is rather high.

Although much smaller than the liver, the spleen contains many more cells per given volume of tissue because of their small cytoplasmic volume. Thus, the rat spleen, which is only 5 or 6 per cent the weight of the liver, contains about 60 per cent as many cells as the liver as determined by DNA analysis (Table 31–8). About 38 per cent of the liver cells are RE cells, and roughly 50 per cent

of the spleen cells are nonlymphocytic RE cells. Thus, these two disparate organs appear to possess comparable numbers of cells capable of participation in filtration or phagocytosis. The turnover of cells in the spleen is higher, however, and thus the normal rat spleen is actually synthesizing about twice as much DNA as the normal liver.

There are two principal patterns of cell labeling in the spleen after injections of H³TDR. As shown in Fig. 31–7, a very high proportion of the cells of the germinal center take up thymidine and are engaged in DNA synthesis, although the radioautographic grain counts are characteristically low. Elsewhere in the spleen, particularly in the marginal zone and red pulp, there are scattered cells in the DNA synthetic (S) phase of the cell cycle, and in these the grain counts are very high. Overall, about 4 per cent of the spleen cells of the adult rat are engaged in DNA synthesis, indicating an appreciable daily turnover of the spleen cell population.

When the spleen is engaged in particle removal, as during hemolytic anemia, or when it is stimulated by antigens, there is a marked proliferative reaction whereby the rate of DNA synthesis and cell formation may be increased severalfold. Thus, an acute hemolytic process, as may be induced by injecting altered red cells, provokes a sharp rise in H³TDR uptake and a slower accumulation of new DNA and of cells (Fig. 31–4), i.e., there is a mild hyperplasia. The principal site of new cell labeling is in the marginal zone and in the red pulp (Fig. 31–19). This hyperplastic reaction subsides over a period of several days. If the stimulus is sustained, the hyperplasia is cumulative and gross splenomegaly ensues. Presumably this chain of events accounts for the hyperplastic spleno-

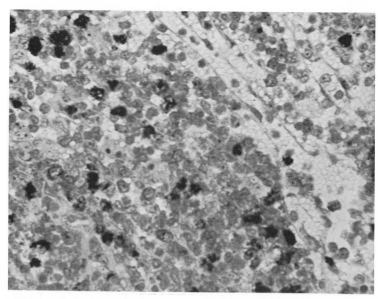

Figure 31–19. Autoradiograph of rat spleen 24 hours after the injection of heat-injured red cells and 2 hours after tritiated thymidine. The view centers on the marginal zone, with the adjacent red cell-filled sinuses of the red pulp showing in the upper right and the outer edge of the lymphatic follicle visible in the lower left corner. A marked increase in DNA synthesis is indicated by the heavy labeling of cell nuclei with tritium. (Reproduced with the kind permission of the publisher, from Jandl, J. H., Files, N. M., Barnett, S. B., and MacDonald, R. A.: J. Exper. Med., *122*:299, 1965.)

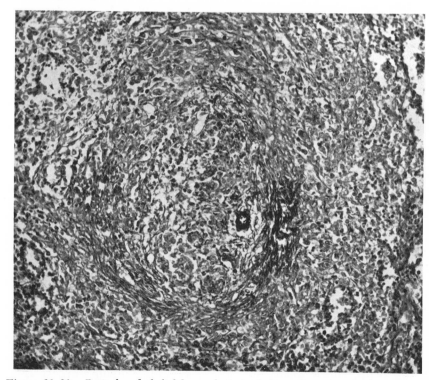

Figure 31–20. Reticuloendothelial hyperplasia in thalassemia major. As the result of continuous destruction of defective red cells in the spleen, and usually of transfused cells as well, the spleen undergoes gradual hyperplasia and may add an additional burden of "hypersplenism" to this grave disorder. (Reproduced with the kind permission of the authors and publisher, from Blaustein, A. U., and Diggs, L. W.: Pathology of the spleen. In Blaustein, A. (ed.): The Spleen. New York, McGraw-Hill Book Co., 1963.)

megaly observed in patients with intrinsic disorders of red cells, as in thalassemia (Fig. 31–20) or hereditary spherocytosis.

Analyses of human spleens reveal a DNA content of about 850 mg., indicating a spleen cell population of about 140 billion. In adults with hereditary spherocytosis who have never been transfused the spleen cell population may be 10 to 20 times this and may exceed the cellular population of the liver by five- or ten-fold. It may be inferred that the maintenance of so large a population of actively proliferating cells is comparable from a metabolic standpoint to having a large neoplasm. As is true in the bone marrow of patients with chronic hemolytic anemias, wherein "relative deficiencies" may develop, particularly of folic acid, the patient with marked splenomegaly may have an appreciable nutritional and metabolic burden. In addition, the maintenance of this large proliferating mass may contribute to the inanition and the gouty diathesis of certain splenomegalic disorders.

It is thus evident that increasing the functional demands of the spleen stimulates its growth; presumably the lymph nodes have similar responses.

What determines the size of the normal spleen? Some early insight was provided by the studies of Marine and Manley, who studied the growth of pieces of spleen tissue implanted elsewhere in the same animal. These implants, when not infected, were found to undergo successive necrosis and then regeneration, and it was noted that regeneration was usually more extensive in animals that had had all other spleen tissue removed than in those in which part of the spleen was left in its original site. In subsequent years, it was observed that spleen autotransplants protected animals against the bartonellosis that otherwise followed splenectomy in animals harboring that organism. Palmer and his associates noted that small autotransplants also inhibited the leukocytosis of splenectomy. These observations encouraged the view that humoral factors affected spleen growth and that spleen tissue secreted substances having an effect upon the levels of blood cells.

Later studies of spleen autotransplants revealed that regeneration was associated with the acquisition of sequestering function as determined by injecting labeled red cells (Fig. 31–21). These studies revealed that an absence of spleen tissue markedly stimulated regeneration in the transplant during the period of maximal proliferation, between 2 and 4 weeks after implantation, and concomitantly

sequestering function in the transplant increased more rapidly and extensively in splenectomized than in hemisplenectomized animals. When a particulate "work load" was imposed by creating a hemolytic process, spleen transplant growth and sequestering function were markedly stimulated. As shown in the lower part of Figure 31–21, the relatively sustained platelet rise and, to a lesser extent, the leukocytosis after splenectomy were inhibited as the transplant acquired the ability to trap cells. Spleen transplants inserted within membrane filter chambers had none of these functional influences.

These observations indicate that most, if not all, of the effects of spleen autotransplants can be attributed to the resurrection of the splenic filter, even though it be relatively

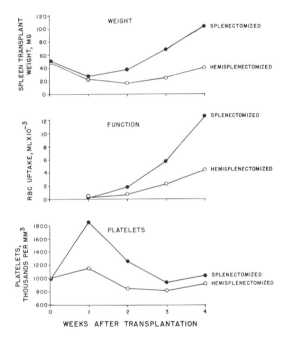

Figure 31–21. Effect of splenectomy on the growth and function of autotransplanted spleen tissue. When a small piece of spleen tissue is transplanted subcutaneously, its subsequent growth (top portion) is stimulated by removal of all other spleen tissue ("splenectomized"); leaving half of the original spleen in its natural location ("hemisplenectomized") suppresses growth. Similarly the functional activity of the autotransplant, expressed as the rate of uptake of abnormal red cells (middle portion) increased in splenectomized animals. In the bottom portion the effect of transplant regeneration on blood platelet levels is portrayed. In splenectomized rats lacking transplants (not shown), platelet levels remained high during the period of observation. (Reproduced with the kind permission of the publisher, from Jacob, H. S., MacDonald, R. A., and Jandl, J. H.: J. Clin. Invest., 42:1476, 1963.)

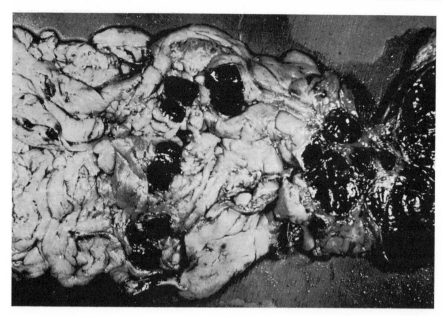

Figure 31–22. Splenosis in a patient who had ruptured his spleen 20 years earlier. The gross appearance of this benign dissemination may resemble that of endometriosis or carcinomatosis. (Reproduced with the kind permission of the authors and publisher, from Blaustein, A. U., and Diggs, L. W.: Pathology of the spleen. In Blaustein, A. (ed.): The Spleen. New York, McGraw-Hill Book Co., 1963.)

small. Furthermore, they emphasize that its usual anatomic relations are not crucial to the spleen's functions. Taken together these observations suggest that spleen size and function are principally governed by the total particulate "work load." There is also evidence that the total mass of the RES is similarly determined and that after splenectomy there is a gradual compensatory hyperplasia of other RES organs which partially offsets the lost splenic functions.

SPLENOSIS AND ACCESSORY SPLEENS

A clinical counterpart of experimental autotransplantation is seen in some patients who have had splenic trauma or surgery. When spleen cells are liberated by traumatic rupture or during surgery, some of these may seed on the peritoneum to form regenerated splenuli or splenunculi, sometimes in very large numbers (Fig. 31–22). This form of accidental autotransplantation is especially prone to occur when the spleen is excised at the same time. When seedings are numerous the condition is termed splenosis, and occasionally these disseminated implants may cause intestinal obstruction or other symptoms necessitating later surgery. In one or two instances the return of spleen function through splenosis has caused a relapse of the underlying hemolytic disorder (hereditary spherocytosis) for which splenectomy was performed.

Occasionally patients who have responded well to splenectomy for disorders such as idiopathic thrombocytopenic purpura have had relapses attributable to the presence of "accessory" spleens, for some people do have aberrant spleen tissue which may be overlooked during the initial surgery. Some so-called accessory spleens are probably autotransplants; others presumably reflect very small bits of aberrant tissue which was stimulated to grow when the true spleen was excised. Although single small accessory spleens or regenerated splenuli may well cause a relapse of thrombocytopenic purpura, wherein the process requires very little spleen mass, it is unlikely that a hemolytic anemia would relapse unless the splenulus was at least of a size approaching that of a normal spleen. Such a hemolytic relapse has been documented by Mackenzie et al., in a splenectomized patient with hereditary spherocytosis; at surgery the splenunculus was found to weigh 217 gm. The total mass of spleen tissue in Stobie's patient with splenosis and relapsing hereditary sperocytosis appeared to be of similar or greater magnitude.

TRAUMATIC RUPTURE OF THE SPLEEN

The rich vascularity of the human spleen makes it liable to hemorrhagic rupture as the result of violent impact, and an unsuspected "ruptured spleen" is a major cause of delayed death resulting from accidental or athletic trauma. When the spleen capsule is actually torn, internal bleeding may be massive. More often the tear is subcapsular or deep within the spleen substance, and a large growing hematoma may develop; although at first compartmented, the extravasation may gradually expand throughout the spleen and distend the capsule, causing tender splenomegaly. Gradual "blood loss" and eventual rupture of the capsule, with shock, may ensue.

In a fairly large proportion of ruptured spleens, especially those arising from mild trauma or occurring apparently spontaneously, there is underlying pathology of the spleen. Among the conditions predisposing to rupture of the spleen are malaria, infectious mononucleosis, hemolytic anemia, polycythemia vera, myelofibrosis, leukemias and lymphomas and certain acute or subacute infections. In animals the writer has noted that the spleen is much more readily broken up in a tissue homogenizer when it is engorged with sequestered red cells; presumably the trapped red cells separate and stretch out the comparatively firm interlocking planes of tissue in the red pulp, reducing elasticity.

A notable example of a relatively benign disorder which predisposes to splenic rupture, particularly in young adults, is infectious mononucleosis. In this disorder, there is a characteristic cellular infiltration around the intratrabecular vessels, which separates them from their connective tissue sheaths (Fig. 31–23). This loosening of the supporting structure, partially evident during the second and third week of illness, markedly increases the fragility of the vessels and sets the stage for traumatic hematomata and rupture.

In many parts of the world malaria is the chief underlying cause of "spontaneous" splenic rupture.

SPLENIC INFARCTION

In trapping and holding masses of blood cells in the red pulp, often for many hours, the spleen does not usually undergo apparent ischemic damage. Presumably the alternating sinus-and-cord arrangement creates a dual circulation in the red pulp, whereby the cordal RE cells continue to be nourished by sinus blood even when the cord is impacted. Furthermore, the RE cells are hardy cells,

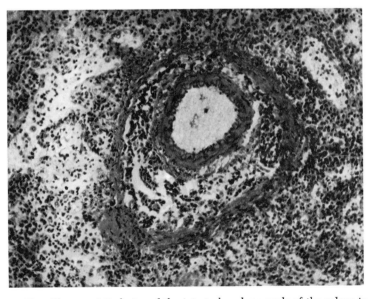

Figure 31–23. Characteristic lesion of the intratrabecular vessels of the spleen in infectious mononucleosis. The separation of the vessels from their supporting connective tissue sheaths by the lymphocytic infiltrate and edema creates vascular friability and predisposes to splenic hematoma or rupture. Similar changes may occur in leukemia. Other disorders such as malaria or congestive splenomegaly appear to predispose to rupture by causing simple vascular engorgement. (Reproduced with the kind permission of the authors and publisher, from Jambon, M., and Bertrand, L.: Sang, *31*:235, 1960.)

able to withstand metabolic deprivations that would destroy others. If, on the other hand, both the cords and sinuses are impacted or if the hemostasis "backs up" the arterial side into the white pulp, infarction may in fact occur. Such appears to happen in a variety of splenomegalic states, including lymphomas, leukemias and myelofibrosis, wherein episodes of left upper quadrant pain, splenic tenderness and friction rubs may occur episodically. The most readily understood pathogenic mechanism for splenic infarction is in sickle cell anemia, for in that hemolytic disorder, spleen trapping of red cells inherently predisposes through stasis to increased sickling in all adjacent red cells (see Chap. 30). Accordingly, splenic infarction is so continuous and gradually becomes so extensive in sickle cell anemia that by adulthood the spleen is invariably reduced to a few grams of scar tissue and the patient may be regarded as "autosplenectomized."

CLINICAL EVALUATION OF SPLENIC ABNORMALITIES

Usually spleens in excess of 300 or 400 gm. in weight are palpable in adults, and most palpable spleens are enlarged to a size of 300 gm. or more. In some instances, as with ascites, pregnancy or abnominal spasm, palpation may be hindered. In others there may be uncertainty as to whether the left upper quadrant mass is truly spleen, confusion sometimes arising with masses of the left kidney, stomach, colon or rarely ovary. Often a clear oblique or left lateral x-ray film of the abdomen may help to identify the mass and to quantitate its size. In special instances, apart from its use in studying hemolytic anemias, the injection of Cr^{51}-labeled red cells may provide helpful data by indicating the mass to be a site of red cell sequestration, as determined with a directional scintillation counter. In this usage, it is preferable to employ the patient's own cells after these have been suitably altered by chemical or physical agents (e.g., Fig. 31–14).

A refinement of this technique is the utilization of automatic scintillation scanning devices to obtain a scintiscan picture of the splenic site of sequestration of the Cr^{51}-labeled cells (Fig. 31–24). Although somewhat higher amounts of radioactivity are required in this method, the exposure is justified when the issue is important. Older methods of injecting heavy metal contrast material such as Thorotrast are probably much

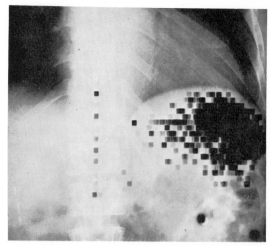

Figure 31–24. Scintiscan of the normal spleen after injection of Cr^{51}-labeled altered red cells. When information is desired concerning the specific size, shape or location of the spleen, the technique of scintiscanning may be utilized. In this technique red cells, preferably derived from the patient, are labeled with Cr^{51} and then are injured in vitro by sulfhydryl inhibitors, heat or incomplete antibodies. On reinjection, scintiscanning of the abdomen gives a clear image of the spleen which can be superimposed on abdominal x-ray film, as shown here. (Reproduced with the kind permission of the authors and publisher, from Winkelman, J. W., Wagner, H. N., Jr., McAfee, J. G., and Mozley, J. M.: Radiology, 75:465, 1960.)

more hazardous in terms of potential long-range effects. The use of scintiscanning should prove particularly helpful in determining the emergence of regenerated or accessory spleen tissue after splenectomy, particularly in patients with recurrent idiopathic thrombocytopenic purpura.

HYPERSPLENISM

Perhaps there is no medical term, with the exception of the expression "autoimmunity," which has elicited as many definitions, debates and diatribes, as has the term "hypersplenism." Originally used by Chauffard and others to describe the role of the spleen in hereditary spherocytosis, the term hypersplenism was revived years later by Dameshek and by Doan to encompass a spectrum of disorders in which splenomegaly was associated with diminution in the levels of one or more of the formed elements of the blood. It has become the common, although not universal, usage to regard as hypersplenism only those disorders wherein the blood cytopenia appears to be secondary to splenic hyperfunction. Accordingly, the hemolytic anemias in which the red cell defect is primary and the splenomegaly is secondary—as in the original sense of Chauffard's term—are no longer regarded by most as true examples of hypersplenism.

Regardless of postulated mechanisms, the following are the principal features of hypersplenism in its usual sense:

1. Splenomegaly.
2. Blood cytopenia or cytopenias.
3. Hyperplasia of the bone marrow.
4. Correction of the cytopenia(s) by splenectomy.

Dameshek and his associates have attributed this syndrome to an influence of the spleen on bone marrow function, notably to the exaggerated release of a humoral substance which affects the maturation and delivery of immature blood cells. Doan and his co-workers have interpreted the same syndrome to reflect an increased phagocytic activity on the part of enlarged spleens, with compensatory marrow hyperplasia following.

There have been innumerable experimental attempts to demonstrate a splenic humor affecting bone marrow activity. Although some are suggestive of a humoral mechanism, most of the experiments have been unsuccessful or difficult to interpret. It may well be that such a regulatory influence exists, but it still awaits firm proof. The evidence that larger spleens sequester and destroy red cells at an increased rate is unequivocal, and in a variety of splenomegalic states red cell survival has been found to be diminished and splenic uptake of labeled cells to be increased (Fig. 31–25).

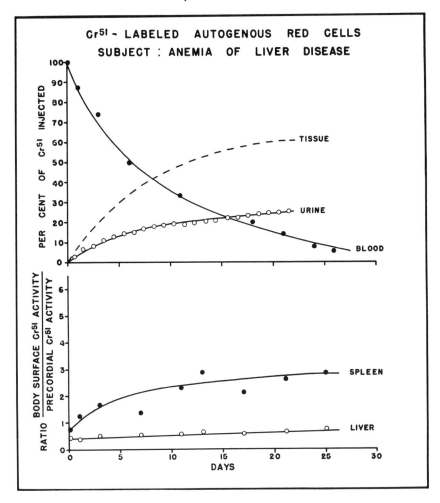

Figure 31–25. Hemolytic anemia and splenic sequestration of red cells in congestive splenomegaly. A common cause of hypersplenism with increased red cell destruction in the spleen is congestive splenomegaly secondary to cirrhosis of the liver. (Reproduced with the kind permission of the publisher, from Jandl, J. H., Greenberg, M. S., Yonemoto, R. H., and Castle, W. B.: J. Clin. Invest., 35:842, 1956.)

The Mechanism of Hemolysis in Hypersplenism

By virtue of the hemodynamic changes occurring in splenomegaly, as discussed earlier, the normal red cell is exposed to a degree of erythrostasis comparable to that which the normal spleen inflicts on the mildly abnormal red cell. The manner in which slow transit through a large spleen stresses red cells can be understood by imagining a single cell that has entered the spleen. According to the mixing studies referred to earlier, this cell may spend as much as an hour in the slow-mixing (probably cordal) chambers of the enlarged spleen before being returned to the venous system and heart. If the spleen flow should represent 5 per cent of cardiac output, this cell has a 5 per cent chance of immediately returning for another hour's sojourn to the spleen and then faces a similar risk of still a third period of erythrostasis shortly thereafter.

It is presently conjectural as to what metabolic stresses are actually applied to a red cell wedged within a cord or sinus and how long the stress can be withstood. Almost certainly glucose deprivation, lactate accumulation and a fall in pH take place and, judging from studies in vitro, viability is lost within a few hours of erythrostasis when cells are packed together. Undoubtedly this injury is much more rapid when red cells are packed in close proximity to cells having high metabolic requirements, as would be the case in the splenic red pulp. The ability of red cells to withstand this repetitious splenic "conditioning" will be a function of the length of time spent in the spleen, as opposed to their metabolic capacity to recuperate while circulating elsewhere. When the red cell is essentially normal the process of conditioning will cause the destruction of only relatively limited numbers of cells, as is usually the case in hypersplenism. When the cell is defective to begin with, splenic conditioning may produce a much more severe hemolytic process. In either situation splenic conditioning usually generates a minor population of injured red cells, evident morphologically as spherocytes.

Generally speaking hemolytic anemia in hypersplenism is mild or moderate, not necessitating splenectomy. On the other hand, when hypersplenism develops in patients with impaired marrow function or with pre-existing intrinsic defects of the red cell, as may be the case in thalassemia or myelofibrosis, splenectomy may alleviate the anemia and may greatly diminish transfusion requirements.

Leukopenia in Hypersplenism

Although less frequent than anemia, leukopenia of mild or moderate degree is often encountered in splenomegalic individuals. Usually the granulocytes are principally affected. Occasionally granulocyte depression is sufficiently marked to be regarded as "agranulocytosis," and life-threatening infections may supervene.

This severe situation is particularly likely to occur in Felty's syndrome (rheumatoid arthritis, splenomegaly and leukopenia), wherein direct studies of spleen vein blood have demonstrated splenic removal of leukocytes, and it is presumed that hypersplenic leukopenia is the result of splenic sequestration of granulocytes. It is uncertain as to why leukopenia is especially prominent in that disorder, which has some of the characteristics of disseminated lupus erythematosis. It may be noted, however, that the spleen in severe Felty's syndrome usually is of a size seldom seen except when secondary to actual overproduction of granulocytes (i.e., myeloproliferative disorders). The occasional patients with congestive splenomegaly who develop leukopenia are usually those with unusually large spleens.

In patients with "splenic neutropenia," as in Felty's syndrome, splenectomy may be dramatically effective in raising the white count and quelling infections, although in some this benefit is transient or incomplete.

Thrombocytopenia in Hypersplenism

Thrombocytopenia is relatively frequent in patients with big spleens, and thrombocytopenic purpura is the most common indication for splenectomy in hypersplenism. Although platelet levels seldom fall to the extremely low levels encountered in so-called idiopathic thrombocytopenic purpura (ITP), the hypersplenic patients often have complicating factors that make the moderate reduction in platelet level hazardous. In patients with cirrhosis, low prothrombin levels and esophageal varices, for example, a "hypersplenic" platelet level of 40,000 or 50,000 may dispose to protracted or fatal bleeding. Hypersplenic thrombocytopenia and ITP usually can be differentiated promptly on the basis of spleen size alone, the spleen being large in the former and not enlarged in the latter.

As noted earlier, observations on platelets have provided some of the strongest arguments for the view that the spleen affects blood levels by inhibiting marrow function. Particular emphasis has been placed on the appearance of the marrow megakaryocytes, which appear to be increased in number and which are described as having smooth margins that appear not to be releasing new platelets. Although such morphologic findings are most striking in ITP, in which platelet destruction is greatly increased and thrombocytopenia often is extreme, similar changes may be observed in hypersplenism. The conclusion that these smooth, "nonproductive" megakaryocytes have been functionally inhibited by a splenic hormone is brought into considerable doubt by the finding by Craddock and his associates that simple platelet removal in dogs induces similar megakaryocyte changes. Others have reported these changes in rat megakaryocytes after platelet depletion by exchange transfusion. Thus it appears that the smooth megakaryocytes of thrombocytopenic states reflect cellular immaturity and rapid platelet utilization and do not necessarily imply suppressed production.

Whereas the anemia and perhaps the leukopenia of hypersplenism appear to result from excessive splenic destruction of those cells, the studies of Aster and of Penny et al., alluded to earlier, indicate that the thrombocytopenia is caused primarily by displacing platelets into an enlarged splenic platelet pool, rather than by actually destroying them. In patients with large spleens the majority of platelets may be found within the red pulp of the spleen. Although these pooled platelets are still functional and can be shown to exchange with those in the circulation, the result is that the systemic platelet concentration may be greatly diminished despite relatively normal rates of platelet production and destruction. Whereas even a very large spleen seldom contains more than about 20 per cent of the total circulating red cell mass, it may contain as much as 80 or 90 per cent of the total platelet mass.

There remain a number of unsettled aspects of spleen structure and function and of the effects of disease thereon. However, many of the principal mysteries have been clarified in recent years. It appears that this elusive and mysterious organ, deprived of her ancient secrets, may soon fully submit to the dependable, if unromantic, terms of Science.

REFERENCES

Spleen and RES Structure and Development

Abramson, D. I. (ed.): Blood Vessels and Lymphatics. New York, Academic Press, 1962.

Drinker, C. K.: The lymphatic system: Its part in regulating composition and volume of tissue fluid. Lane Medical Lectures. Stanford, Stanford University Press, 1942.

Good, R. A., and Gabrielsen, A. E. (eds.): The Thymus in Immunobiology. Structure, Function, and Role in Disease. New York, Hoeber Medical Division, Harper & Row, 1964.

Good, R. A., and Papermaster, B. W.: Ontogeny and phylogeny of adaptive immunity. In Dixon, F. J., and Humphrey, J. H. (eds.): Advances in Immunology, Vol. 4. New York, Academic Press, 1964.

Knisely, M. H.: Spleen studies. I. Microscopic observations of the circulatory system of living unstimulated mammalian spleens. Anat. Rec., 65:23, 1936.

Marshall, A. E. H.: An Outline of the Cytology and Pathology of the Reticular Tissue. London, Oliver and Boyd, 1956.

Rebuck, J. W., and Lo Grippo, G. A.: Characteristics and interrelationships of the various cells in the RE cell, macrophage, lymphocyte and plasma cell series in man. Lab. Invest., 10:1068, 1961.

Snook, T.: Studies on the perifollicular region of the rat's spleen. Anat. Rec., 148:149, 1964.

Volkman, A., and Gowans, J. L.: The origin of macrophages from bone marrow in the rat. Brit. J. Exp. Path., 46:62, 1965.

Weiss, L.: The structure of fine splenic arterial vessels in relation to hemoconcentration and red cell destruction. Am. J. Anat., 111:131, 1962.

Weiss, L.: The structure of intermediate vascular pathways in the spleen of rabbits. Am. J. Anat., 113:51, 1963.

Yoffey, J. M., and Courtice, F. C.: Lymphatics, Lymph and Lymphoid Tissue. Cambridge, Harvard University Press, 1956.

Spleen and RES Functions and Reactions

Barcroft, J., and Florey, H. W.: Some factors involved in the concentration of blood by the spleen. J. Physiol., 66:231, 1928.

Benacerraf, B.: Functions of the Kupffer cells. In Rouiller, C. H. (ed.): The Liver, Vol. 2. New York, Academic Press, 1964, p. 37.

Benacerraf, B., and Selbestye, M. M.: Effect of bacterial endotoxins on the reticuloendothelial system. Federation Proc., 16:860, 1957.

Björkman, S. E.: The splenic circulation. With special reference to the function of the spleen sinus wall. Acta med. Scand., 128, Suppl. 191:1, 1947.

Crosby, W. H.: Normal functions of the spleen relative to red blood cells: A review. Blood, 14:399, 1959.

de Duve, C.: The lysosome. Sci. Amer., 208:64, 1963.

Dixon, F. J.: Morphology of immune reactions. In Conceptual Advances in Immunology and Oncology. New York, Hoeber Medical Division, Harper & Row, 1963, pp. 77–84.

Gowans, J. L., and Knight, E. J.: The route of recirculation of lymphocytes in the rat. Proc. Roy. Soc. B., *159*:257, 1964.

Halpern, B. N. (ed.): Physiopathology of the Reticuloendothelial System. Springfield, Charles C Thomas, 1957.

Jacob, H. S., and Jandl, J. H.: Effects of sulfhydryl inhibition on red blood cells. II. Studies in vivo. J. Clin. Invest., *41*:1514, 1962.

Jacob, H. S., MacDonald, R. A., and Jandl, J. H.: The regulation of spleen growth and sequestering function. J. Clin. Invest., *42*:1476, 1963.

Jandl, J. H.: Mechanisms of immune hemolysis in vivo. In Thomas, L., Uhr, J. W., and Grant, L.: Injury, Inflammation and Immunity. Baltimore, Williams & Wilkins, 1964.

Jandl, J. H., Files, N. M., Barnett, S. B., and MacDonald, R. A.: Proliferative response of the spleen and liver to hemolysis. J. Exper. Med., *122*:299, 1965.

Jandl, J. H., Jones, A. R., and Castle, W. B.: The destruction of red cells by antibodies in man. I. Observations on the sequestration and lysis of red cells altered by immune mechanisms. J. Clin. Invest., *36*:1428, 1957.

Karnovsky, M. L.: Metabolic basis of phagocytic activity. Physiol. Rev., *42*:143, 1962.

Kelly, L. S., Dobson, E. L., Finsey, C. R., and Hirsch, J. D.: Proliferation of the reticuloendothelial system in the liver. Am. J. Physiol., *198*:1134, 1960.

Langevoort, H. L.: The histopathology of the antibody response. I. Histogenesis of the plasma cell reaction in rabbit spleen. Lab. Invest., *12*:106, 1963.

Marshall, A. H. E., and White, R. G.: Reactions of the reticular tissues to antigens. Brit. J. Exper. Path., *31*:157, 1950.

Thorbecke, G. J., and Benacerraf, B.: The reticuloendothelial system and immunological phenomena. Prog. Allergy, *6*:559, 1962.

White, R. G.: Immunological functions of lymphoreticular tissues. In Gell, P. G. H., and Coombs, R. R. A. (eds.): Clinical Aspects of Immunology. Philadelphia, F. A. Davis Co., 1962, p. 213.

Wissler, R. W., and Fitch, F. W.: The reticuloendothelial system in antibody formation. Ann. New York Acad. Sc., *88*:134, 1960.

Disorders of Spleen and RES

Blaustein, A. U., and Diggs, L. W.: Pathology of the spleen. Chapter 3 in Blaustein, A. (ed.): The Spleen. New York, McGraw-Hill Book Co., 1963.

Good, R. A., Kelly, W. D., Rötstein, J., and Varco, R. L.: Immunological deficiency diseases. Prog. Allergy, *6*:187, 1962.

Moeschlin, S.: Spleen Puncture. London, William Heinemann Medical Books, Ltd., 1951.

Szabo, K. de L.: Splenosis. Am. J. Surg., *101*:208, 1961.

Thannhauser, S. J.: Lipidoses: Diseases of the Intracellular Lipid Metabolism. New York, Grune & Stratton, 1958.

Wright, C. S., Doan, C. A., and Gardner, E. J.: The spleen. In Sloan, L. (ed.): Practice of Medicine, Hagerstown, Md., W. F. Prior Co., 1962.

Hypersplenism and Splenic Pooling

Aster, R. H.: Pooling of platelets in the spleen: Role in the pathogenesis of "hypersplenic" thrombocytopenia. J. Clin. Invest., *45*:645, 1966.

Bowdler, A. J.: Theoretical considerations concerning measurement of the splenic red cell pool. Clin. Sc., *23*:181, 1962.

Crosby, W. H.: Hypersplenism. Ann. Rev. Med., *13*: 127, 1962.

Giblett, E. R., Motulsky, A. G., Casserd, F., Houghton, B., and Finch, C. A.: Studies on the pathogenesis of splenic anemia. Blood, *11*:1118, 1956.

Harris, I. M., McAlister, J., and Prankerd, T. A. J.: Splenomegaly and the circulating red cell. Brit. J. Haemat., *4*:97, 1958.

Leffler, R. J.: The spleen in hypersplenism. Am. J. Path., *28*:303, 1952.

Motulsky, A. G., Casserd, F., Giblett, E. K., Broun, G. O., and Finch, C. A.: Anemia and the spleen. New England J. Med., *259*:1164, 1215, 1958.

Penny, R., Rozenberg, M. C., and Firkin, B. G.: The splenic platelet pool. Blood, *27*:1, 1966.

Toghill, P. J.: Red-cell pooling in enlarged spleens. Brit. J. Haemat., *10*:347, 1964.

Von Haam, E., and Awny, A. J.: The pathology of hypersplenism. Am. J. Clin. Path., *18*:313, 1948.

Selected Historical Treatises and Classic Descriptions

Aschoff, L.: Das reticulo-endothelial System. Ergeb. inn. Med. u. Kinderheilk, *26*:1, 1924.

Aschoff, L., and Kiyono, K.: Zur Frage der grossen Mononukleären. Folia Haemat., *15*:383, 1913.

Banti, G.: La Splénomégalie hemolytique. Semaine med., *32*:265, 1912; *33*:313, 1913.

Chauffard, A., and Troisier, J.: Des Rapports de certaines anémies splénomégaliques avec l'ictère hémolytique congénital. Bull. et Mem. Soc. Med. des Hop. de Paris, *27*:293, 1909.

Eppinger, H.: Zur pathologie der Milzfunktion. Berl. klin. Wchnschr., *50*:1572, 1913.

Larrabee, R. C.: Chronic congestive splenomegaly and its relationship to Banti's disease. Am. J. Med. Sc., *188*:745, 1934.

McNee, J. W.: The spleen: Its structure, functions, and diseases. The Lancet, pp. 951, 1009 and 1063, 1931.

Metchnikoff, E.: Immunity in Infective Disease, translated by F. G. Binnie. Cambridge, England, University Press, 1905.

Pearce, R. M., Krumbhaar, E. B., and Frazier, C. H.: The Spleen and Anaemia. Experimental and Clinical Studies. Philadelphia, J. B. Lippincott Co., 1918.

von Pirquet, C., and Schick, B.: Serum Sickness (reissue in English). Baltimore, Williams & Wilkins Co., 1951.

Part XI

Musculoskeletal System

Chapter Thirty-Two

The Joints

RICHARD H. FREYBERG

Satisfactory function of the locomotor apparatus depends upon the properly coordinated operation of the nervous system, the muscles and their attachments, and the skeletal system and its articulations. In health these systems function in a highly coordinated fashion so that movement of the body is accomplished in a purposeful manner with ease and efficiency. The coordinated functions of these highly integrated systems are complicated. For clearest analysis the student and investigator should consider simply (1) the skeletal supports of the body, the bones, (2) the joints between these osseous structures and (3) the neuromuscular mechanism for moving the supporting parts. As in visceral organs, normal function of somatic tissues depends upon proper circulation of blood through, and normal utilization of nutrients in, the component parts. Should there be important interference with coordinated function of any one of these systems, locomotion is made difficult or becomes impossible, the patient may be disabled for activities which require movement of the body, and he may suffer great discomfort.

In this chapter only the articulations and the disturbances of their function which result from diseases of the joints and their supporting and motivating structures will be considered.

Anatomy and Physiology of Joints

Disease states of the musculoskeletal system can be understood only if the normal structure and physiology are known. The embryologic anlage of the joint, which is complete at the third month, consists of two chondrogenous zones with an interposed remnant of mesenchyma. Later, liquid hyaloplasm, probably elaborated by mesenchymal cells, appears, and the mesenchyma retracts peripherally to enclose densely packed fibrils. This is the future joint cavity, and its lining is the embryologic equivalent of the synovial membrane. Simple gliding joints (diarthroses) are composed of two bone ends held in apposition by a strong fibrous tissue capsule, reinforced by ligaments, and lined with a thin layer of specialized connective tissue cells—synovium, or synovialis. The articular surfaces of bone are covered with hyaline cartilage (Fig. 32–1). Within the joint space is a small amount of synovial fluid.

The joint capsule is composed of specialized connective tissue with a collagenous matrix richly supplied with blood vessels, lymphatics and nerves, few elastic fibers and characteristic connective tissue cells (fibroblasts, histiocytes and others). Near the surface of the joint, aggregates of modified fixed connective tissue cells occur. Villi extend into the joint space. There is no direct communication or barrier separating the articular cavity from the intercellular spaces of the synovialis. Thus the joint cavity is not a body cavity such as the pleura, pericardium or peritonium, but is a tissue space.

Maintenance of normal relationship of all joint structures is required for stability and for normal movement of joints. Proper alignment

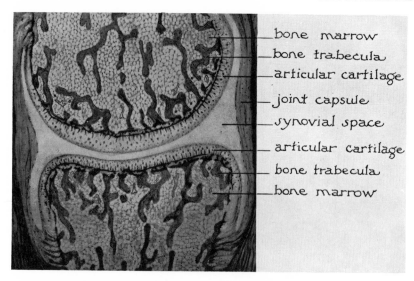

bone marrow
bone trabecula
articular cartilage
joint capsule
synovial space
articular cartilage
bone trabecula
bone marrow

Figure 32–1. Sketch of a normal diarthrodial joint.

articulating surface
chondrocyte
bone

horizontal fibrils
tangential fibrils
perpendicular fibrils
anchoring substance

Figure 32–2. Sketch showing the structure of articular cartilage as revealed by polarized light. Note the three zones of fibrils arranged in horizontal, tangential and radial positions.

and stability of joints are maintained partly by barometric pressure (in joints such as the hip joint), by the molecular cohesive force of synovial fluid, but mostly by the strong, fibrous, outer part of the joint capsule and its reinforcing ligaments. These specialized connective tissue structures are largely responsible for the stability of most joints; when they are significantly weakened, joint stability and function are threatened or destroyed.

Articular Cartilage

Joint cartilage is the recipient of most blows and jolts on the skeleton. The extremely efficient buffer action of articular cartilage is accounted for by the great resilience of this tissue, readily explained by the anatomic structure of articular cartilage (Fig. 32–2). This tissue consists of fibrils which extend in a looping curve resembling a croquet wicket, the ends of which are fixed in a calcium-rich anchoring substance. The fibrillar arrangement is divided into three zones. The surface layer is made up of the middle sections of the fibrils lying closely packed, horizontal

to the surface; the middle zone contains fibrils in tangential arrangement; in the lower zone the fibrils are in a position perpendicular to the joint surface. Chondrocytes exist in the lowermost interfibrillar substance; there is no serous covering at the surface.

Expansion of the cartilage under pressure provides a cushioning effect to protect the subchondral bone. Because of its fibrillar arrangement, when pressure is exerted on the cartilage surface it expands laterally and diminishes in thickness; when pressure is relieved, it rebounds because of the elasticity of the fibrils (Fig. 32–3). Thus, under pressure, the cartilage mass changes in shape, but not in volume.

The irregularity of the subchondral surface of epiphysial bone protects the cartilage surface from blows to the shaft of the bone, and also serves to prevent separation of cartilage from bone during ordinary function (Fig. 32–4). Decalcification of severe degree allows such separation.

Under frequent intermittent pressures, cartilage continues to be very elastic; however, under continuous compression its expansile power is decreased and the recovery period is lengthened. Elasticity is also lost with desiccation. These facts form the basis for the changes noted with aging.

Another function of joint cartilage is to provide a smooth, gliding surface for the opposing bone ends. This is accomplished by the surface arrangement of the cartilage fibrils, providing a slightly irregular surface which prevents adhesion of the surfaces, and the lubrication by synovial fluid.

Cartilage has no blood supply. It derives nourishment from three sources: (1) from subchondral bone, which is richly provided with blood, but from which cartilage nutrient is poorly supplied, owing to the interface barrier, (2) from subsynovial vessels located at the junction of the capsule and the cartilage, and (3) through the synovial fluid, which is its chief source of nutrition. That this alone can sustain cartilage viability is well demonstrated by the long life of loose cartilage bodies free in the joint space.

It is presumed that metabolites pass along the intercellular system of fibrils; it is possible that there is a physical factor of alternating positive and negative pressure—a "pumping" action—which aids the flow of nutriment and which may augment the permeability of cartilage cells themselves. The changes in cartilage occurring with aging and disease are primarily due to changes in nutrition and dehydration.

Cartilage contains glycogen, lactic acid, collagen, chondroitin sulfuric acid and calcium salts. The presence of dehydrogenase (a hexophosphate enzyme) has been demonstrated in cartilage. Studies of the metabolism of articular cartilage show that its respiration is almost negligible. Like muscle, cartilage has the faculty of anaerobic oxidation. The metabolic rate of cartilage tissue is about one-tenth that of soft connective tissue, owing to the low cellularity of cartilage. The rate of metabolism per cartilage cell appears to be of the same order as that of other connective tissue cells.

Growth in adult cartilage is entirely amitotic. Apposition of articular surfaces is required for maintenance of integrity in the articular cartilage. It has been demonstrated that after experimental immobilization for 62 days only the separated parts of the joint cartilage showed degeneration. Reaction of cartilage to injury differs, depending upon the depth of the injury. Superficial cuts remain essentially unchanged for many months; if lesions do not extend into the subchondral bone or do not involve the perichondrium, there is only slight proliferation. Wounds which extend into the bone or which damage the cartilage or synovial surfaces are filled in rapidly with fibrous tissue. Regeneration of cartilage is virtually negligible.

Joint Capsule and Synovium

The mechanical properties of the joint capsule are determined by its fibrous layers. The synovial tissue has little elasticity. Its elastic resistance is 30 times that of a sheet of pure rubber of equal thickness. Hence there is only a small increase in the surface of the synovium from elastic expansion; some stretching of the membrane may take place, but, like tendinous connective tissue, it has high resistance to tear. The marked pliability of the synovium is an important characteristic which helps it to withstand the stresses of

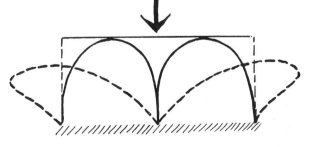

Figure 32–3. The dotted lines show the response to pressure (arrow) applied to surface of the articular cartilage—the fibrils flatten and widen. When the force is relieved, the fibrils quickly resume the original high-arched resting shape (solid lines).

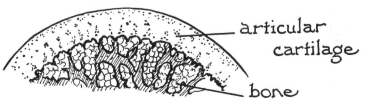

Figure 32–4. Sketch showing the rough subchondral bone surface which helps to secure the cartilage to the bone.

Table 32–1. The Cytology of Normal Synovial Fluid.

	Ropes and Bauer	Kling	McEwen
Total white blood cells per cu. mm.	13–180	0–50	125–200
Polymorphonuclear cells	6.5%	0–15%	7–27%
Lymphocytes	24.6%	5–35%	8–16%
Monocytes	47.9%	0–20%	5–10%
Macrophages	....	Counted with monocytes	5–8%
Indeterminate macrophages	4.9%	......	0–13%
Synovial cells	4.3%	35–60%	3–7%
Clasmatocytes	10.1%	......	......
Undifferentiated connective tissue cells	......	......	12–16%
Degenerated cells (not identified)	......	......	21–44%
Unclassified	2%	......	......

joint motion. The metabolism of synovial cells is comparable to that of other soft connective tissue cells. Because of its rich vascularity, synovial tissue has pronounced regenerative ability; within 60 days after experimental hemisynovectomy, new synovium may be regenerated.

Synovial Fluid

Investigations of normal synovial fluid from human beings and animals indicate that the cell content may vary considerably. The reported cytology is shown in Table 32–1. The experimental injection of saline solution into the joints of rabbits promptly causes a rise in polymorphonuclear cells in synovial fluid, probably from mild irritation of subsynovial capillaries leading to intra-articular migration. There is slower migration of mononuclear cells into synovial fluid after various types of irritation.

Normal joint fluid is approximately 95 per cent water; the specific gravity ranges from 1.009 to 1.012, with an average of 1.010; it has a pH of 7.3 to 7.4. It is under slightly negative pressure, −2 to −12 cm. of water. The total protein concentration is between 1 and 2 per cent; the albumin-globulin ratio is high—it may be as high as 20:1. The high proportion of albumin is thought to be due to the ease of diffusion of this smaller molecule in contrast to globulin. There is no fibrinogen in synovial fluid. Relative viscosity varies from 51 to 209, with an average of 124. This high value is due to an abundant mucoprotein content, and varies with the amount and degree of polymerization of this material. Mucoprotein (a glycoprotein) exists in an average concentration of 0.85 gm. per cent. The hyaluronic acid (polysaccharide) in this conjugated protein is identical with that present in vitreous and aqueous humor, in Wharton's jelly of the umbilical cord, in skin, in some mesodermal tumors and in group A hemolytic streptococci; according to Bauer, it is the same as the polysaccharide found in the mucinous substance of subcutaneous tissue.

The amount of nonprotein nitrogenous substances and uric acid in synovial fluid is slightly below that of normal blood plasma. The average urea content is 8.2 mg. per 100 ml. Sugar diffuses freely into the joint fluid and is found in varying concentrations. Cholesterol and fatty acids are normally absent.

Little is known about the enzyme content and activity of synovial fluid. No measurable amount of hyaluronidase has been demonstrated in articular cartilage; only small amounts exist in synovial fluid. (See the discussion of connective tissue chemistry and function which follows.)

Results of studies of the origin of joint fluid have not been conclusive. The electrolyte pattern agrees with that of a dialysate of plasma, as would be expected according to the Gibbs-Donnan theory of membrane equilibrium. Other theories hold that the fluid is (1) a product of glandular activity of synovial tissue cells, (2) a mixture of the products of disintegration of synovial tissue in a transudate from blood capillaries and lymphatics, (3) a formation from the products of attrition of articular cartilage, (4) a mixture of substances elaborated from synovial cells in a transudate, or (5) a liquid matrix of connective tissue lining the joint cavity considered to be simply an enlarged tissue space. Bauer and his collaborators support the theory that the joint fluid is entirely a transudate and that it is a dialysate to which mucin is added from connective tissue cells through which the fluid passes. Other investigators have contended that mucin is secreted by specialized cells lining the synovial surface of the capsule-cells which have true secretory function. Reports that goblet cells containing mucin have been grown on tissue culture are cited to support this view. Although there is no final proof for the origin of some substances in synovial fluid, it is indeed highly reasonable to consider joint fluid a dialysate of plasma, enriched by the addition of mucin from another source, either ordinary connective tissue cells surrounding the large tissue space (joint cavity) or from secretory cells in its surface layer.

Synovial fluid serves two purposes: (1) to lubricate the joint surfaces and (2) to nourish the articular cartilage.

Exchange of Substances through the Articular Membrane

The relation between the articular cavity and the circulatory system is of great importance, for the maintenance of normal joint function depends in a large measure upon the entrance of nutrient materials and the removal of toxic or potentially injurious substances. In various musculoskeletal disorders this physiology is disrupted in the disease, sometimes to a striking degree.

The passage of substances in solution across the border of the joint cavity is unique. Extensive investigations have shown that there is unobstructed and easy passage of electrolytes in homogeneous solution between the joint space and the blood. The manner in which colloidal substances enter and leave joints depends chiefly on the size of the particles. Colloidal particles of small molecular weight are readily diffusable and, when experimentally placed in the joint cavity, are removed by the subsynovial blood capillaries. Motion of the joint markedly increases the rate of removal, presumably by raising the intra-articular pressure and by increasing the capsular blood flow.

The passage into and out of the joint cavity of large colloidal particles is more complex. The mechanism of passage of large particles *into* the joint space is not well understood. That the vascular membrane is somewhat permeable to larger molecules is shown by the finding of some plasma albumin and globulin in synovial fluid. It is also known that microorganisms get into joint fluid more readily than into cerebrospinal fluid, aqueous humor and urine, thus explaining the greater likelihood of joint metastasis of systemic infection. However, proteins injected into the intra-articular space are removed by the lymphatics. Carbon particles injected into the cavity of a normal joint are found in three different places: some pass directly into the intercellular spaces of the synovialis; some are phagocytized by polymorphonuclear leukocytes and by fixed connective tissue phagocytes; some particles remain in the cavity to be organized there. From all these places, by repeated phagocytosis, the carbon particles are moved into regional lymph channels and finally into distal lymphatics. Removal of particles from the joint space by the lymph system also is augmented by exercise of the joint.

Alterations in Joint Fluid Produced by Disease

Changes in the physiology of joints depend primarily upon two factors: (1) altered permeability of synovial and capsular tissue and (2) disturbances of intra-articular metabolism.

Permeability changes permit passage into the joint space of an increased amount of water, electrolytes, readily diffusible colloids, proteins, fibrinogen, antibodies, leukocytes and probably enzymes. An increase in protein concentration in synovial fluid commonly characterizes inflammatory joint disease. The amount of protein entering the joint space varies directly with the intensity of the inflammation; it is only slightly increased in traumatized joints, whereas in septic joints and in those affected by severe rheumatoid disease it is usually markedly increased. The proportion of globulin increases with increase in membrane permeability; a larger amount of globulin enters, and less is absorbed or leaves the joint space, accounting for the increased protein content and the decrease in the albumin-globulin ratio in the persistent joint effusion commonly seen in late stages of rheumatoid arthritis. Abnormally high concentration of colloid material in joint fluid increases the osmotic pressure and may be a factor in the persistence of the effusion.

Disturbances in metabolism affect chiefly the sugar and mucoprotein of joint fluid. The sugar in the fluid of septic joints is reduced, sometimes completely disappears, as a result of a number of factors, including the use of this substance as a nutrient by the great number of leukocytes and bacteria present, the increased activity of fixed tissue cells and the enhanced nutrition of cartilage. In non-

TABLE 32–2. CHARACTERISTICS OF SYNOVIAL FLUID IN COMMON
FORMS OF ARTHRITIS.

	Appearance	Viscosity	Mucin Clot	Cell Count	Urate Crystals	Cartilage Fibers	Bacteria
Normal	Straw color, clear	High	Good	200–600 WBC 25% neutro.	0	0	0
Traumatic arthritis	Yellow to bloody, cloudy	High	Good	2000 ± WBC 30% neutro. Many RBC	0	0 or +	0
Septic arthritis	Gray or bloody, turbid	Low	Poor	80,000 ± WBC 90% neutro.	0	0	+
Tuberculous arthritis	Yellow, cloudy	Low	Poor	25,000 ± WBC 50–60% neutro.	0	0	+
Osteoarthritis	Yellow, clear	High	Good	1000 ± WBC 20% neutro.	0	+	0
Rheumatic fever	Yellow, sl. cloudy	Low	Good	10,000 ± WBC 50% neutro.	0	0	0
Rheumatoid arthritis	Yellow to green, cloudy	Low	Poor	15,000 ± WBC 65% neutro.	0	0	0
Systemic lupus erythematosus	Straw, sl. cloudy	High	Good	5000 ± WBC 10% neutro.	0	0	0
Gouty arthritis	Yellow to milky, cloudy	Low	Poor	12,000 ± WBC 60% neutro.	±	0	0

purulent synovitis the sugar content of the joint fluid is reduced at least in part because of decreased permeability of the thickened synovium to sugar solution. Changes in the mucin content of the fluid of diseased joints are due either to an alteration in its formation or destruction. In some situations there is an increased production of synovial fluid mucin; in other circumstances, such as infection in joint tissue with infected synovial fluid there is destruction of mucin, probably due to an increase in concentration of bacterial mucinase.

Synovial fluid shows characteristic changes in many types of joint disease. Study of the joint fluid is oftentimes very helpful in diagnosis and differentiation of types of arthritis, and periodic re-examination of synovial fluid may help to assess the course of the arthritis in that joint and to evaluate treatment. Characteristics of synovial fluid in the more common forms of arthritis that can be simply demonstrated by fluid examination are shown in Table 32–2.

Joints as Units

Joints serve the primitive purposes of bearing weight and providing motion. Joints are constructed so as to afford greatest stability and motion; their capsules, ligaments, tendons and muscular tone impart stability to joints; the articular cartilage buffers impacts because of its remarkable elasticity. Viscous synovial fluid aids in maintaining proximity of articular components and forms a strong fluid interface at the cartilage surfaces so that motion may occur with negligible friction. Articular cartilage is subjected to rigorous wear and tear unequaled by any other tissue except the integument. It has no direct blood supply, it subsists largely upon the synovial fluid—hence the maintenance of adequate synovial fluid is of prime physiologic importance. The volume of joint fluid depends upon the balance between two opposing forces, that of capillary pressure, and the osmotic pressure gradient between synovial fluid and plasma. The synovialis has greater permeability than true membranes.

Deviations in articular physiology result chiefly from alterations in synovial tissue and intra-articular metabolism. The former accounts for qualitative and quantitative disturbances of exchange equilibriums, and the latter results in deficient nutrient for cartilage and reduction in mucoprotein. Injury to articular cartilage is of profound importance because it has virtually no regenerative power; repair is accomplished to a limited degree by fibrous tissue invasion from the joint margins and subchondral bone marrow.

Periarticular Connective Tissue

Knowledge of the chemistry of connective tissue serves to increase understanding of the many problems of rheumatic diseases.

Connective tissue is composed of two main structures of quite different composition—fibrous elements and cement substances. *Fibers* are composed of insoluble denatured proteins of high molecular weight and are of three types: collagen, reticulin, and elastic fibers. Collagen and reticulin fibers have essentially the same chemical structure; both derive from a common origin. The collagen and elastic fibers are alike in that each type is rich in glycine and proline, but they differ in content of other amino acids. Studies by means of roentgenography and electron microscopy show that fibers of collagen are composed of fine crystalline fibrils having alternating bands of higher and lower density regularly spaced along their length. Collagen fibers are slowly digested by proteolytic enzymes. Crystalline collagen in aqueous solution is changed by heat into soluble gelatin.

Cement substances appear to be of considerable importance in certain rheumatic diseases. The chemical nature of the proteins in cement substances is not known, but it has been demonstrated that they are bound to highly polymerized mucopolysaccharides of four different types: hyaluronic acid, hyalurono-sulfuric acid (found only in cornea), chondroitin sulfuric acid, and sulfuric acid ester (in amyloid disease). These polysaccharides account for the mucinous nature of connective tissue. Hyaluronic acid contains n-acetyl glucosamine and glucuronic acid. It is hydrolized by specific enzymes—hyaluronidases. Different types of connective tissue are characterized in part by their mucopolysaccharide content. Synovial fluid contains only hyaluronate, while cartilage contains only chondroitin sulfate, a compound of n-acetylgalactosamine, glucuronic acid and sulfuric acid.

From what is known of the chemistry of connective tissue correlated with histologic studies and tissue culture, the following mechanism of development of connective tissue is suggested. Young growing fibroblasts secrete hyaluronic acid and later chondroitin sulfate and a collagen precursor which is denatured by the polysaccharides. Hyaluronate is then largely removed by enzymes, leaving the more firmly bound chondroitin sulfates on the surface of the fibers. By cross-linking, these fibers grow into mature insoluble fibers.

Although alterations in connective tissue chemistry during disease are being vigorously studied, little is known of the changes. The finding of an increased concentration of hyaluronate in joint effusions in patients with rheumatoid arthritis suggests that inflamed synovial cells elaborate excessive hyaluronic acid. Similar changes may occur in other mesenchymal tissue spaces and account for an increase in interfibrillar cement substances which, because they are highly viscous, could slow down metabolic processes in this connective tissue. The exact roles of different enzyme systems, catalysts, ascorbic acid, vitamin E and other vitamins are unknown and may be of importance.

Muscle Function in Relation to Movements of Joints

Good posture depends upon the maintenance of proper tone in muscles located about the supporting skeletal structures. Bones are moved at their articulations by a system of muscle levers, energy for which is inherent in the contractility of the muscle tissue. Movement at a joint requires the forceful contraction of muscles about a fixed point at the articulation. Figure 32–5 shows that when a contracting muscle (M) pulls upon a bone at the site of its tendinous insertion, the force is in two primary components which are at right angles; one component (A) moves the bone at the joint; the other component (B) produces a thrust along the bone toward the joint. The ratio A/B is the expression of the part played by the muscle in any given position of the joint, whether it is acting primarily

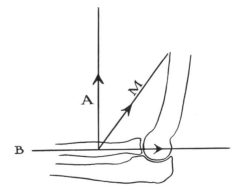

Figure 32–5. Sketch showing the relation of muscle function to movement at the joint.

as a *mover* or as a *stabilizer*. Depending upon the relative strength of these components of muscle force, various skeletal muscles are classified as those which are primarily sources of energy of movement and those which approximate the bones at the joints. The kinetics of a single hinge (diarthrodial) joint, such as the knee, depends upon balanced function of two sets of muscles, the joint movers and the stabilizers. If the *functional* insertion of muscles be reversed, owing to different position of the joint at the time force is applied, or to reversal of the fixed side of the hinge, a muscle which is ordinarily a prime mover may become a joint stabilizer.

Tendon sheaths serve to keep long tendons near the joints they span so that the tendon in its sheath behaves as if passing around a pulley. Many long tendons which pass to the hands and feet are enclosed in separate sheaths and are firmly secured about the wrists and ankles, respectively, in such a way as to make the tendons act as stabilizers of these joints. In this way the enclosures of tendons about the wrists allow a person to hold weights in the hands, and the tendons enclosed about the ankles allow one to stand in many comfortable positions for long periods of time.

These few examples illustrate the importance of proper muscle function to the operation of joints. Further details of kinesiology would be inappropriate in this section.

Pathologic Physiology of the Musculoskeletal System

The rheumatic diseases affect the connective tissue of the musculoskeletal system predominantly. To this group of diseases attention is now directed, with the primary purpose of bringing into focus the manner in which the pathologic changes alter function and cause disability and abnormalities which characterize these diseases. Different pathologic processes alter the structure and function of connective tissue in different ways.

Effects of Trauma

The simplest type of joint disease is that which results from injury. This may be slight, causing only a strain of the ligaments or the fibrous capsule of the joint, in response to which edema and congestion produce swelling about the joint, which in turn causes stiffness at the joint and pain from stimulation of the sensory nerve endings abundant in the periarticular tissue. Because the tissues affected are richly supplied with blood, healing is usually rapid and complete.

If the injury is greater, the synovium may be traumatized and sterile inflammation may ensue, effecting additional alteration in the dynamics and metabolism of the articular structures because of the traumatic synovitis; usually such synovitis persists for a relatively short time and recovery is complete. Severe blows may traumatize the cartilage and/or underlying bone, and may provoke changes in the dynamics of the joint which, after a period of time, result in degenerative changes in the joint—"post-traumatic degenerative joint disease." If the cartilage injury is in the central position, regeneration cannot take place and an irregular joint surface results which, in a weight-bearing joint, causes strain at the joint margins, stimulating osteogenic proliferation resulting in marginal spurs and lipping. If the original cartilage injury occurs at the articular margin, abnormal bone formation may result sooner. Thus dysfunction follows severe joint injury, and its speed of development depends on the nature and location of the trauma. Injury to a weight-bearing joint during childhood is frequently a cause of degenerative changes in that joint years later, usually relatively early in adult life. The late changes resulting from severe joint trauma are those of osteoarthritis.

Osteoarthritis—Degenerative Disease of Joints. Articulations are subject to a great amount of attrition during normal function, so that after years of use degenerative changes make their appearance. Postmortem studies reveal that all persons beyond the age of 45 years have degenerative joint disease, although in many persons the changes are mild and cause no clinical problem.

Degenerative changes appear first in that part of the articular cartilage which receives the greatest wear and has the poorest nutrition. The weight-bearing joints of the lower extremities and spine are subjected to greater wear and tear, and most commonly show earlier and more severe degenerative changes. The first pathologic changes are dehydration and softening of the cartilage; these are followed by separation of the fibers, resulting in fissuring and, later, disintegration of the cartilage. Degenerated cartilage soon thins, and postural strain occurs at the edges of the joint; this irritates the perichondrium and periosteum, which in turn stimulates proliferation of cartilage and bone at the joint margins. As the cartilage wears thin, the subchondral bone becomes eburnated. The evolution of these changes is sketched in Figure 32–6.

Because of the occurrence of marginal osteophytes and the subchondral sclerosis of bone this disease is called "*osteo*arthritis." It is evident also why this type of joint disease is sometimes referred to as "hypertrophic" and "senile" arthritis and, when it occurs in the hip joint, "*malum coxae senilis.*" Degenerative changes frequently occur at the terminal interphalangeal finger joints, where the characteristic hypertrophic spurs give rise to swellings called "Heberden's nodes."

Abnormalities in synovium and joint capsule are infrequent; if synovitis occurs, it is late in the disease and results from irritation caused by rough surfaces of articular cartilage and bone. Liberal use of the affected joint during the existence of synovitis may lead to villous proliferation of the synovium at the articular margins and thickening of the capsule may result. Function of the joint is disturbed by the thin cartilages with rough surfaces and by mechanical interference with motion caused by the bony proliferations.

This disease is a local joint disturbance, not a systemic disease. The patient is usually in good general health, often obese—another important factor contributing to the degeneration of cartilage.

Aging of cartilage is attended by decrease in water content and in the proportion of cells to the matrix—changes which predispose to degeneration. Some investigators emphasize the gradually decreasing oxidative power of aging cartilage which augments the susceptibility of cartilage to degeneration. Bollet has shown that the chondromalacic lesions in osteoarthritic articular cartilage are due to loss of chondroitin sulfate. In abnormal cartilage chondroitin sulfate concentration averaged 33 per cent that of normal areas, and there was correlation between the decrease in concentration and in polymerization. Studies suggested but did not prove that the loss of chondroitin sulfate was due to digestion by hyaluronidase. Stecher showed that there is a hereditary factor in the development of Heberden's nodes. Other poorly understood factors may also be important in pathogenesis. Certainly there must be important variations in the composition of connective tissue in different persons to explain why some persons have significant osteoarthritis, while others who experience the same degree of trauma have degenerative joint changes so slight that they produce no symptoms or disability. Reasons for this difference and whether they are structural, chemical, physiochemical or a combination of these and other factors are not known.

In women osteoarthritis may first become symptomatic at the time of menopause; if it has been present previously, symptoms may be sharply accentuated with the development of menopause. This fact suggests that there

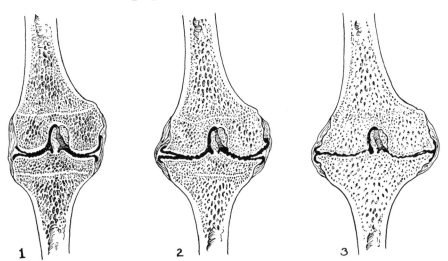

Figure 32–6. Sketches showing progression of the joint abnormalities in osteoarthritis: *1,* early degenerative changes in cartilages; *2,* more extensive cartilage degenerative and early hypertrophic changes of bone at joint edges; *3,* late stage with almost complete destruction of articular cartilages, irregular subchondral bone surfaces, underlying eburnated bone and extensive hypertrophic spur formation at margins of the joint.

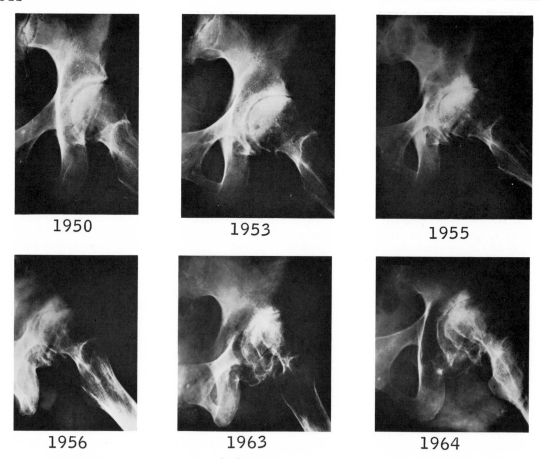

1950   1953   1955

1956   1963   1964

Figure 32–7. Roentgenograms of a hip joint in various stages of evolution of degenerative joint disease—osteoarthritis (*malum coxae senilis*).

may be an endocrine factor in the pathogenesis of osteoarthritis. The Silberbergs, Kling and others have reported that ovarian hormones retard maturation of cartilage and suggest that this partially explains the degenerative joint changes of osteoarthritis. Similarly, in patients with eosinophilic anterior pituitary adenoma (causing acromegaly), frequently there are extensive osteoarthritic changes at many joints. These observations suggest that there may be endocrine factors in the pathogenesis of degenerative joint disease.

Examples of the pathologic joint changes of osteoarthritis and the way in which they are responsible for the disturbances of joint function are well shown in the evolution of osteoarthritis of the hip. When osteoarthritis develops in only one hip, trauma often has occurred many years previously, and such injury sets up the changes that result in chondromalacia (discussed earlier). Slowly the cartilage loss progresses as shown in the roentgenograms (Fig. 32–7). Restricted motion in the early stage of disease is due chiefly

to pain. As the cartilage damage increases, osteophytes develop which act to block movement mechanically. Later, after the subchondral bone crumbles and the femoral head flattens, there is further restriction of movement, or none—a very disabling situation.

The degenerative changes in the spine very often begin and progress in the intervertebral cartilaginous discs rather than in the true joints (facets) of the spine. The affected discs become thin, and the borders of the adjacent vertebrae become rough from osteophyte formation (Fig. 32–8). The vertebrae become closer together as the disc thins, and movement is restricted and painful. Secondary muscle spasm may be induced adding to the stiffness. Frequently osteophytes project into the foramina and produce nerve root pressure, or the degenerated disc itself or a fragment of it may produce nerve root pressure. When this occurs, in addition to the restriction of movement, there are the disabilities of the neuropathy—motor weakness, neurologic pain, paresthesia, dysesthesia, etc.—in the part of the extremity enervated by the segment involved.

Neuropathic Joint Disease

The changes of neuropathic disease of joints (Charcot's joint) are in some ways similar to those of osteoarthritis, but in some ways distinctly different. With spinal tract disease of tabes dorsalis there is diminution in pain sensibility, together with "trophic" changes which allow degenerative changes to develop especially in the larger joints of the lower extremities and spine. These degenerative changes, similar to those of osteoarthritis, usually progress rapidly and result in much cartilage damage. With such neurologic disorder there is less pain than normally results from strain on the joint capsule, and continued use of the articulation results in extensive damage to cartilages and subchondral bone. These structures fragment, leaving loose bodies of cartilage and bone free in the joint cavity. Extensive erosion of bone irritates the synovium; proliferative synovitis results, and there is usually an accumulation of fluid in the joint. Lack of reactive muscle spasm about a Charcot's joint, the relaxation and stretching of the joint capsule, and the fragmentation of bone act to produce an unstable joint, albeit with little or no pain because of the underlying nervous disorder. The patient frequently falls because of the instability of the joint, causing further damage to the joint.

Syringomyelia and the neurologic lesions which occur in pernicious anemia and uncontrolled diabetes may also be the basis for neuropathic joint disease. Because syringomyelia usually occurs in the upper part of the spinal cord, Charcot's joints more frequently occur in the upper extremities with this neuropathy; joints of the lower extremities are more commonly involved in all other neuropathies.

Specific Infectious Arthritis

Microorganisms of all types may infect joint structures and cause arthritis. Entry may be through a laceration; in such cases usually only one joint is affected. Most frequently bacterial invasion occurs through the blood, when usually several joints are involved; the chief exception is tuberculous joint disease, which is commonly monarticular. All types of infectious arthritis are uncommon since the advent of effective antimicrobial treatment.

Tuberculous infection of a joint provokes a slowly progressive, low grade synovitis; the synovium proliferates and frequently causes destruction of some of the joint cartilage at the periphery of the joint. Classical signs of inflammation are found at the tuberculous joint; however, increased local heat may be slight or imperceptible. In the tuberculous joint, usually there is an increase in joint fluid which shows the changes indicated in Table 32–2. Tuberculous exudate may extend into adjacent tissues causing an abscess about the affected joint, or it may travel between muscle or fascia planes and drain exteriorly through sinus tracts. In these ways tuberculosis of the joint is a destructive lesion. As damage to articular cartilage and bone progresses, joint dysfunction increases.

Bacteria most frequently responsible for purulent inflammation of joints are the staphylococcus, streptococcus, gonococcus, meningococcus and pneumococcus. Pus in the cavity of a joint infected with any type of organism rapidly destroys the articular cartilage as a

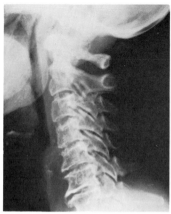 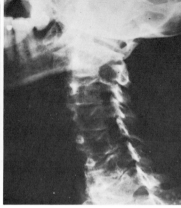 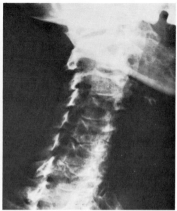

R OBLIQUE   L OBLIQUE

Figure 32–8. Roentgenograms of the cervical spine of a patient showing characteristic degenerative changes which are the cause of the pathologic physiology of this disorder.

result of the lytic effect of digestive ferments in leukocytes. It has been shown that cartilage is digested in vitro by proteolytic enzymes in leukocytic autolysates. Purulent synovial fluids containing upward of 110,000 leukocytes per cubic millimeter are capable of digesting small pieces of cartilage, whereas synovial fluids containing 6000 to 20,000 polymorphonuclear leukocytes are not. This lytic property varies considerably and depends upon the amount of free proteolytic enzyme present in the fluid. Natural repair of articular tissue which has harbored prolonged purulent inflammation may result in fibrous tissue ankylosis.

Diffuse Connective Tissue Diseases

A group of nonpurulent inflammatory diseases affect primarily the soft connective tissue of joints and the surrounding connective tissue. In this category belong rheumatoid arthritis, rheumatic fever, systemic lupus erythematosus, progressive systemic sclerosis (scleroderma), polymyositis (dermatomyositis) and polyarteritis. The more important diseases of this large group will be considered separately.

Rheumatoid Arthritis

The most common chronic diffuse connective tissue disease and the one which produces the most joint dysfunction and disability is rheumatoid arthritis. Its etiology is unknown, but its cellular pathology is well understood. The most important disability arises from the articular pathology and the damages which result therefrom.

Sometimes without a prodromal illness, but usually after several weeks of symptoms of systemic disease which may have no distinguishing characteristics, one or many joints of the extremities show signs of inflammation. In its early stage this inflammation is localized in the joint capsule and primarily in the synovium. The tissue becomes thickened from congestion and edema, but at no time is the inflammation purulent. Soon a characteristic inflammatory response develops in the form of a synovial proliferation, rich in fibroblasts, which invades the interior of the joint. This inflammatory tissue (pannus) extends into the interior of the joint along the surface of the articular cartilage to which it may be tightly adherent, so that it interferes with nutrition of the cartilage. By lysis, starvation and invasion this inflammatory tissue slowly destroys the articular cartilage. Similar pro-

liferative inflammatory tissue frequently develops in the subchondral bone and invades the cartilage from its osseous border, adding to the destruction. The capsular inflammation and the proliferative tissue tend to persist and to progress usually slowly and with partial or complete remissions and relapses causing increasing damage to the joint cartilage and subchondral bone. Frequently there is an increase in synovial fluid in the inflamed joints. The metaphysial bone becomes osteoporotic. These damages, all of which are consequent to the original inflammation, account for the deformities and crippling that characterize the late stages of rheumatoid arthritis. As a result of all these pathologic changes, *function of the affected joints is interfered with* in a proportional degree. After extensive cartilage damage has occurred, the synovitis lessens and may subside completely; then the inflammatory tissue becomes invaded with tough fibrous tissue which inhibits or prevents motion at the joint (fibrous ankylosis). If it has not already subsided, synovial inflammation at this stage rapidly abates. The fibrous tissue may then become calcified and may undergo metamorphosis to osseous tissue, resulting in firm bony union (bony ankylosis) —the final stage of the joint pathology.

Characteristically, then, if it is not arrested, joint pathology evolves through four stages: (1) synovitis, (2) pannus formation which causes cartilage and bone destruction, (3) fibrous ankylosis, and (4) bony ankylosis (Fig. 32–9). The time required for this evolution varies greatly, from months to years, and, by natural means or as a result of treatment, evolution may stop at any stage. The amount of pathologic change and the speed of its progress usually vary greatly at different joints in the same patient, so that there is wide variation in the clinical manifestations of each patient who has rheumatoid arthritis.

Although the principal disorder of rheumatoid arthritis involves the joints, there is much disease of the nonarticular connective tissue. In about 15 per cent of patients subcutaneous fibrous nodules occur, arising from tendon sheaths, bursal walls, periosteum or fascia. Frequently they are found a few centimeters distal to the olecranon process on the dorsal surface of the forearm. Wherever they occur they have the same characteristic structure which varies only in size or age. The nodule is composed of a central portion of fibrinoid degeneration (of disintegrated collagen), quite avascular; about this there is a zone of inflammatory reaction consisting of large mononuclear cells (endothelioid in nature), usually arranged in a radial fashion; at the periphery is a fibrous tissue capsule (Fig. 32–10). Nodules may occur singly or in a conglomerate mass. The fibrous tissue nodule is one of the most characteristic lesions of rheumatoid arthritis. When such nodules occur close to joints they may interfere with free movement of the joint, and when they occur at bony prominences pressure on them causes pain.

Elsewhere in fibrous tissue small (usually microscopic) foci of inflammatory cells are characteristically found. These occur along perineurium, intramuscular fibrous tissue septa, fascia, and similar tissue. These cellular collections are found early in the course of the disease. They emphasize the widespread systemic nature of this disease, and probably account for some of the "muscle pain," stiffness, tenderness and paresthesia.

Adding greatly to disability are the poorly understood changes in muscle and fibrous tissue which account for the troublesome stiffness of periarticular structures. This feature of rheumatoid arthritis is called "secondary fibrositis" and is thought to be the same sort of change that characterizes "primary fibrositis" (not associated with arthritis). The fibrous tissue becomes stiff and achy, and the muscles behave as though they were partly gelled and had lost their fluidity; the muscles feel tight and usually are tender. These symptoms are always worse after rest ("morning stiffness") and in cold and are relieved with motion and warmth.

Wright and Johns have extensively studied the joint stiffness associated with rheumatoid

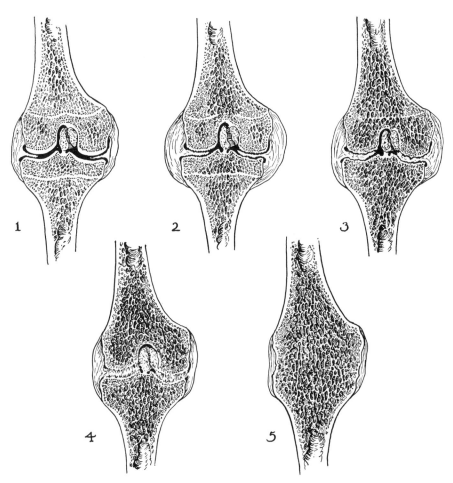

Figure 32–9. Sketches showing the joint pathology in rheumatoid arthritis. *1,* Inflammation of the joint capsule with synovitis; beginning proliferative changes. *2,* Progression of inflammation with pannus formation; beginning destruction of cartilage and mild osteoporosis. *3,* Advanced synovitis with extensive pannus, cartilage destruction and osteoporosis. *4,* Inflammation subsided; fibrous ankylosis. *5,* Bony ankylosis.

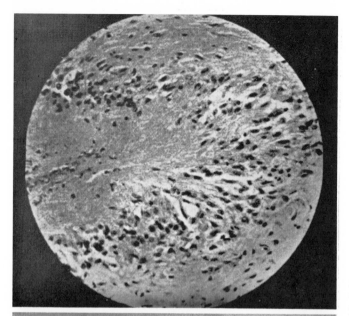

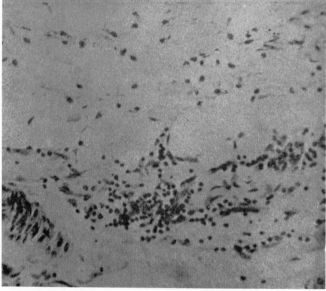

Figure 32–10. *Upper,* Subcutaneous rheumatoid nodule. Note the central zone of degenerated tissue, the middle palisading zone of epithelioid cells, and the outer fibrous capsule. *Lower,* Microscopic aggregate of inflammatory cells in perineurium. (Ragan and Tyson: Am. J. Med., Vol. 1.)

arthritis and other connective tissue diseases. They found that frictional stiffness accounted for only 1 per cent, and viscous stiffness of connective tissues accounted for less than 10 per cent of overall stiffness. The major component was increased elastic stiffness. Frictional stiffness was small even in the most badly damaged rheumatoid joint in which crepitus could be felt and in which roentgenograms showed major cartilage and bone erosions, destruction of joint surfaces and loss of joint space. This directs attention away from damaged joint surfaces to *changes in the capsule* of the joint when seeking explanation of stiffness in arthritic disorders. Stiffness

measured at the joints was found to be elastic stiffness of tendons and the joint capsule, and a small amount in the skin over the joint. Attempts to move the rheumatoid joint cause pain and a subjective sensation of stiffness.

Besides these various connective tissue lesions, there are other significant changes. Recent studies emphasize the extensive changes in blood vessels (especially arterioles and venules) and circulating blood sludge commonly found in this disease. The sticky red blood cells form clumps and aggregates which impede the flow in small vessels; they adhere to the intima and cause leakage with resultant edema. Such changes in blood and vessels contribute to anemia, malnutrition of regional tissue and edema.

Anemia, common in rheumatoid arthritis, is characteristically hypochromic, microcytic or normocytic and, although significant, usually it is not severe. There are no consistent bone marrow changes. The white blood cells are not characteristically altered; they may be normal in number and in distribution of the various components. Slight or moderate leukocytosis is frequently found in early cases, especially when there is fever. Leukopenia is not uncommon in chronically ill, undernourished patients. It is characteristically present with anemia, splenomegaly, lymphadenopathy and undernutrition seen in the variant of rheumatoid arthritis frequently referred to as "Felty's syndrome." Eosinophilia is sometimes encountered; it is usually transient, and factors responsible for it are unknown.

The fasting blood glucose value is usually normal, but in approximately 50 per cent of patients with rheumatoid arthritis, glucose tolerance is decreased as measured by the oral test, so that the glucose tolerance curve simulates that of a mild diabetic. If a high carbohydrate diet is administered a few days before the test is performed, a normal tolerance curve is obtained in about half of the patients who formerly showed decreased tolerance. This is frequently observed in chronically ill, undernourished rheumatoid arthritics, suggesting that in some patients the carbohydrate utilization is delayed because of malnutrition.

Various visceral lesions are found in rheumatoid arthritis. The spleen is sometimes enlarged, and usually there is a considerable degree of generalized lymphadenopathy, often without splenomegaly. Hepatomegaly may occur and various degrees of hepatic dysfunction are encountered in some cases. Studies in our laboratory indicate that liver function is normal in most patients with rheumatoid arthritis; when dysfunction exists, it is usually mild. Plasma proteins are frequently altered; usually the globulin fraction is increased, sometimes to a high level. When hyperglobulinemia occurs, the plasma albumin may be comparably reduced, so that the total plasma protein may not be elevated. Such changes in circulating protein occur more often in severe cases with extensive systemic illness.

At postmortem examination the heart has been found to contain fibrous granulomatous lesions indistinguishable from those of rheumatic fever in about 50 per cent of cases. These findings have not been adequately explained; most investigators of rheumatic diseases judge that these cardiac lesions are not due to rheumatic fever but are in most instances focal myocardial and fibrous tissue lesions of rheumatoid disease.

Extensive studies during the past decade have elucidated the protein dyssynthesis which commonly can be demonstrated in rheumatoid disease and which results in formation of a macroglobulin characteristic for this disease—"rheumatoid factor." This macroglobulin usually has a Svedberg coefficient of 19S, but recent studies indicate that there are different macroglobulins—some with a coefficient of 22S. These different rheumatoid factors may exist in the same patient. By fluorescent dye technique it has been shown that rheumatoid factor is formed by plasma cells in germinal centers of lymph nodes and in the cellular infiltrates in inflamed synovial tissue. Sometimes it is possible to demonstrate the macroglobulin (rheumatoid factor) in the inflammatory tissue before it can be found in the blood. By tests usually used, rheumatoid factor can be found in the blood of about 80 per cent of patients with classical rheumatoid arthritis; by more sophisticated methods is has been shown to be present in about 95 per cent of rheumatoid patients. It is usually not found until months after the onset of the disease. Sometimes it cannot be demonstrated by usual methods even in severe late stage classical disease.

The rheumatoid factor reacts with human gamma globulin coated on blood cells, latex or bentonite particles so as to agglutinate the sensitized cells, to fix latex particles or flocculate bentonite particles coated with gamma globulin—so that this reaction is used in standardized methods to identify the presence of rheumatoid factor. Such tests are commonly used now for confirmation of diagnosis; when the macroglobulin is demonstrated in persons with arthritis it is strong support for the diagnosis of rheumatoid disease, but it cannot be depended upon for critical differential diagnosis, especially early in the illness.

The rheumatoid factor is distinguished from other 19S macroglobulins by this specific serologic reactivity with gamma globulin. It has also been shown that rheumatoid sera can react directly to produce a precipitin reaction with aggregated—essentially partially denatured—human gamma globulin added to them. This reaction has been a great aid in more sophisticated studies of the serologic reactions of rheumatoid sera and in isolation of "pure" rheumatoid factor for chemical studies. The rheumatoid factor is closely akin to classical antibodies which are Ig M gamma globulins and has other features to put them in a protein group of "immuno-globulins." Its estimated molecular weight is nearly one million. It has a low tyrosine content. It can be depolymerized by disulfide-bond-reducing agents, and this abolishes all serologic activity. The monomers do not reaggregate when reducing agent is withdrawn.

Demonstration of the rheumatoid factor has clearly indicated a disturbance in the immune mechanism associated with rheumatoid disease, but just what role is played by the rheumatoid macroglobulin is not known. Some similarities to known antibodies have led to the suggestion that rheumatoid factor is an antibody and that it is important in etiology of the disease. This has led to the currently popular consideration that rheumatoid arthritis is an autoimmune disease and that rheumatoid factor is an autoantibody against altered gamma globulin. Proof of this has not been produced. Further studies are needed to clarify the importance and physiologic or pathophysiologic role of this gamma globulin.

In 1949 Hench and his co-workers first reported the remarkable effects of cortisone on rheumatoid arthritis. The quick and dramatic relief of stiffness, reduction of pain, increased muscle and joint function and general improvement in practically all instances when glucocorticosteroid is administered or when its production is stimulated by appropriate amounts of corticotropin have aroused interest as to whether rheumatoid arthritis is caused by adrenal disease or improper utilization of adrenal cortical hormone in the tissues. There is no support for the suspicion that adrenal deficiency exists in patients with rheumatoid arthritis. It appears likely that the fault lies outside the adrenals, probably in the connective tissue. The remarkable relief of stiffness observed within 24 hours after the first administration of cortisone, long before the synovitis is significantly reduced, strongly suggests than in intracellular connective tissue function is disturbed, and it seems likely that the cortisone effect is exerted through an enzyme system. The slower resolution of the joint inflammation, the prompt appearance of improved muscle function and general euphoria emphasize the nonarticular aspects of rheumatoid arthritis and also affirm the systemic nature of the disease. Relapse quickly follows the cessation of administration of cortisone, which indicates that etiologic abnormalities are not corrected, but rather that they are only temporarily suppressed.

The hormonal effects, which certainly are of great importance in rheumatoid arthritis, particularly from the standpoint of pathologic physiology, point the way for further research. As further investigations based on these observations proceed, many problems of rheumatoid arthritis undoubtedly will be solved.

Synovial fluid is frequently increased in the inflamed joints. This pathologic fluid has many consistent characteristics (see Table 32–2). The quantity may be small or large. The protein content is always increased, and globulin makes up approximately half of the total. Niedermeier, Cross and Beetham have recently shown that synovial fluid from patients with rheumatoid arthritis contained haptoglobin in mean concentration 5.4 times greater than in normal subjects. It accounted for 0.68 per cent and 1.65 per cent of total protein concentration of synovial fluid from normal subjects and patients with rheumatoid arthritis respectively. These findings suggest that synovial membranes normally possess a means of excluding haptoglobin from synovial fluid and that in patients with rheumatoid arthritis this mechanism is blocked. Synovial fluid mucin is slightly reduced, the fluid is less viscous, and the sugar content slightly increased compared to normal joint fluid. Changes in the fluid depend upon the severity of the synovitis, the chronicity of the effusion, the thickness of the joint capsule, its vascularity and probably other factors as yet unknown.

Early in 1965 Hollander and McCarty et al. reported the finding of cytoplasmic inclusions in polymorphonuclear leukocytes in the synovial fluid from inflamed joints of patients with rheumatoid arthritis. The proportion of cells with such inclusions correlated roughly with the intensity and duration of the joint inflammation. The cells were called by these investigators "R.A. cells." By proper treatment these cells could be fractured so as to liberate rheumatoid factor. Cells without inclusions did not liberate rheumatoid factor. The authors postulated the pathogenesis of inflammation of the rheumatoid joint as follows: The synovial tissue could be the source of materials forming the complex of rheumatoid factor and altered gamma globulin. If the particles of complex are deposited onto or near the synovial surface, they may fix, complement or act as foreign bodies attracting by chemotaxis polymorphonuclear leukocytes into the joint. Phagocytosis of the particles by the neutrophils may lead to degeneration of the phagocytizing cells and the release of lysosomal enzymes, causing damage (inflammation) to joint tissues. The cells, with their phagocytosed particle complex, may be the "R.A. cells" described. To test this hypothesis, Hollander and associates injected into the joints of rheumatoid patients autologous rheumatoid 7S gamma globulin and observed an acute inflammatory response in five of six trials. This tends to support the hypothesis and suggests that autologous rheumatoid 7S gamma globulin may be specifically antigenic. It further suggests that one of the steps in pathogenesis of rheumatoid inflammation might be the alteration of 7S gamma globulin to provide antigenic stimulation.

In the foregoing section have been recounted the more important disturbances of physiology which characterize the clinical picture of rheumatoid arthritis. Knowledge of these is important to the understanding of this disease. Of importance to the patient and his management is the appreciation of the disturbances of function which the disease causes—disturbances which account for the incapacitation imposed by this crippling disease.

In early stages when the disease is confined to inflammation of the joint capsule, articular function is interfered with chiefly by pain and the swelling of articular tissues, tension within the capsule if there is effusion, and the disturbance of the connective tissues about the joint. If joint inflammation is severe and these pathologic changes are extensive, there is usually much limitation of joint motion. If joints in the hands are affected, tight fists cannot be made, the grasp becomes weak, and dextrous motions are impaired or lost. If wrists are involved, positioning of the hands is interfered with, and, even though finger joints may not be affected, the strength of grasp is diminished because of the interference with movement of the flexor and extensor tendons to the fingers as they lie adjacent to the inflamed wrist joints. Invasion of the tendons at the wrists by rheumatoid inflammation and attrition of the tendons as they move over rough bone edges often cause fraying or rupture of extensor tendons to the fingers and cause finger drop. Inflammation at the elbows makes it difficult to lift things and to get the hands to the head for feeding and attending to personal toilet—combing the hair and the like. Arthritis in the shoulder joints interferes with most of the motions of the entire upper extremity; besides interfering with motion commonly used in many sorts of labor, it may make dressing difficult or impossible.

If joints of the lower extremities are inflamed, locomotion is difficult or impossible, and arising from a seated position, sitting, climbing and descending stairs may be impossible because the legs cannot serve as levers to lift the body. These functions are interfered with when hips or knees are affected; if both the hip and knee of one or both lower extremities are involved, the disability is greater. Inflammation of ankles or joints of the feet also interferes with standing or walking, the more so because the entire column of weight is borne by these articulations.

When only joint synovitis exists, these functional abnormalities may be great, but when there is coexisting affection of regional fibrous connective tissue and muscles, the joint dysfunction is even greater, for upon these nonarticular structures much of the function of the joint depends. Irritation and pain in muscles limit the extent and strength of muscle contraction, and may initiate muscle spasm which prevents effective muscle function. Periarticular fibrous tissue disease also may stiffen the joint and limit its motion.

If rheumatoid arthritis becomes arrested in the early stage, completely normal function may be regained. If the disease continues until destructive changes of cartilage and bone result, joint dysfunction will persist even after the inflammation is arrested. Extensive joint destruction may result in ankylosis which will leave the joint stiff and motionless, or coexisting relaxation of the joint capsule and ligaments and imbalance of muscles which operate it may account for dislocations or deformities as well as decreased movement of the joint. When such extensive articular pathology occurs, almost without exception there is much nonarticular connective tissue disease and muscle atrophy—changes which further decrease the function of the irreparably damaged and deformed joints. Muscle weakness and atrophy make movement of the joint more difficult and more limited. Articular cartilage and subchondral bone damage, by reason of the roughened joint surface, impede movement by mechanical interference. Joint deformity may contribute greatly to functional impairment. When such changes occur in weight-bearing joints, locomotion becomes difficult or impossible. If there are flexion deformities at the hips or knees, the postural defects add great strain to the joint capsules and other supporting structures. Ankylosis of the knees or hips may make it impossible for the patient to get out of bed or a chair without assistance, and of course walking is difficult or impossible.

Rheumatic Fever

The locomotor system may be significantly involved in rheumatic fever, a disease characterized by acute inflammation of articular synovia, tendons, tendon sheaths and other connective tissue, particularly about joints. The chemical, metabolic and pathogenic physiology differs from rheumatoid arthritis chiefly because of the differences in evolution of the pathology. This illness characteristically begins abruptly, and the articular changes evolve rapidly. Joint inflammation is intense and tends to subside after a short period of disease activity. Pannus does not form, so that cartilage and bone damages do not occur. The synovitis subsides rather quickly, and deformities, crippling and incapacity, which are caused by the damage of *chronic* articular capsule inflammation, do not result. Functional disturbances of this disease are only those which result from the active inflammation and are similar to those existing in the early stage of rheumatoid arthritis. When the disease becomes inactive, the patient has no residual functional disturbance of the locomotor system.

Other Diffuse Connective Tissue Diseases (Collagen Diseases)

Other diseases in the group commonly referred to as diffuse connective tissue diseases are systemic lupus erythematosus, dermatomyositis, polyarteritis, and progressive systemic sclerosis (scleroderma). All these connective tissue diseases have similar basic pathologic changes in the connective tissue. The differences in the clinical syndromes depend upon the location of the connective tissue pathology. In systemic lupus erythematosus, articular, fascial, tendinous, and bursal changes with pathology exactly like that of rheumatoid arthritis may exist, but usually these rheumatic manifestations exist to a lesser degree than in classical rheumatoid arthritis, and usually the most important abnormalities exist in viscera. The prognosis of this illness is worse because of the greater visceral pathology, and failure of one of the vital organs is the usual cause for death.

In patients who have systemic lupus erythematosus the connective tissue inflammation is similar to that of rheumatoid arthritis, but usually there is a different amount in organ systems and more in viscera than in joint and periarticular connective tissue structures. Likewise there is characteristically a different immunologic disturbance usually demonstrable by serologic studies. LE cells are found in the blood of most patients with clinically characteristic systemic lupus erythematosus. These cells are polymorphonuclear leukocytes which have phagocytosized nucleoprotein—"hematoxylin bodies" that have been extruded by damaged leukocytes. LE gamma globulin is necessary for association with whole nuclei or nucleoprotein to form the hematoxylin body. It has been considered that the combination of LE factor and nucleoprotein is an antigen-antibody reaction and that systemic lupus erythematosus is truly an autoimmune disease.

It has also been shown that some patients with systemic lupus erythematosus have an antibody to whole cell nuclei, others have antibody to desoxyribonucleic acid, and others have an antibody to histone or to ribosomes. Any or all of these antibodies may be found in a patient with systemic lupus erythematosus, but in about 20 per cent of patients with typical disease no antibody or LE factor can be identified.

The autoimmune aspects of this disease are discussed in Chapter 3. All joint functional disturbances which occur in this illness are similar to those of rheumatoid arthritis, discussed in earlier sections of this chapter.

If diffuse connective tissue inflammation and degenerative changes occur chiefly in skin and subcutaneous tissues, the illness has clinical features of progressive systemic sclerosis (scleroderma). Joint changes with dysfunction identical with those of classical rheumatoid arthritis may occur with this type of diffuse connective tissue disorder, but in a small minority of patients. Frequently, rheumatoid factor tests are positive in patients with scleroderma without arthritis, another indication of the similarity of these disorders, suggesting a common pathogenesis. Sclerosis frequently occurs as a result of connective tissue pathology in the gut, bronchi, lungs, heart or kidneys—and accounts for visceral organ disease even to failure resulting in death.

Polyarteritis may be the chief involvement of diffuse connective tissue disease and may cause visceral dysfunction, depending on which arteries are principally affected. Joints are rarely affected with this disorder, but peripheral nerves are frequently affected because of disturbance of their blood supply when nutrient arterioles of the nerve are involved. Thus various types of neuropathy result, especially affecting lower extremities, and result in different sensory or motor deficits.

Muscles are predominantly inflamed in the diffuse connective tissue disease labeled polymyositis. When skin changes accompany the myopathy it is referred to as dermatomyositis. In this disorder muscle pain, tenderness, weakness and atrophy are the predominant troubles and if progressive may lead to death from respiratory paralysis if muscles of respiration are predominantly affected, or from starvation if muscles of deglutition are involved.

The pathologic changes are similar in all these diffuse connective tissue diseases, but the pathologic physiology differs depending upon the organ systems principally affected. Many times clinical features of two or more of these disorders exist simultaneously in the same patient giving rise to diagnoses of undifferentiated diffuse connective tissue disease, overlap syndrome and multiple system disease. This mixture of clinical features of differently labeled diffuse connective tissue disorders strongly suggests the likelihood that there is a common basic pathogenesis for all, the nature of which is as yet unclear.

Ankylosing Spondylitis

Chronic inflammation indistinguishable from the joint pathology characteristic of classical rheumatoid arthritis frequently occurs in the articulations of the spine and pelvis. But added to this pathology is the unusual subligamentous calcification along the spine which tends to accompany the progress of the inflammation. This perispinous calcification and other features which differ distinctly from those of rheumatoid disease (predominance in young males, absence of rheumatoid factor, lack of occurrence of rheumatoid fibrous tissue nodules and different response to same forms of therapy) have led to the current belief that this is not a variant of rheumatoid arthritis but more likely a different disease of connective tissue, and consequently this form of spinal rheumatic disease is usually labeled ankylosing spondylitis rather than rheumatoid spondylitis as it was

usually diagnosed between 1940 and 1960. The pathologic physiology of this disorder is unique chiefly because of the location of the pathology and the ankylosing process.

The disease usually begins in the sacroiliac joints, where the sacroiliitis goes through an evolution similar to the joint inflammation of peripheral rheumatoid arthritis, frequently to complete fusion. But, because there is little motion in these articulations, there is little or no functional disturbance. Along with the early inflammation in the sacroiliac joints there is usually much fibrous tissue and muscle irritation which contribute to back pain, stiffness and limitation of motion. Spasm of paraspinous muscles may be extensive and add significantly to discomfort and to limitation of motion.

As the disease progresses, joint inflammation and accompanying periarticular changes involve the lumbar back, later the dorsal and even the cervical segments, causing inflammatory changes in the facets of the spine and involvement of paraspinous tissue in characteristic fashion. In early stages, movements of the low back are limited and painful, and motion at the hips may be impaired because of irritation of muscles and ligaments which originate adjacent to the diseased joints and which operate these articulations. During this stage of the arthritis, picking things up from the floor, pulling on shoes and all movements requiring lumbar back flexion and extension are usually difficult to perform; turning in bed is difficult and painful. Spasm of the lumbodorsal muscles adds to stiffness and pain in the back. When the disease affects the dorsal spine there is involvement of the costovertebral articulations so that expansion of the chest becomes diminished and breathing usually is painful. If the disease extends to the cervical spine, movements of the head and neck are restricted and painful.

The progress of this disease may become arrested at any stage in its evolution. If arrested early in its course function of the spine may return to normal. If the disease becomes chronic, as it does usually, the joints become damaged, just as do the joints of the extremities in rheumatoid arthritis; ankylosis results, and in addition there is usually extensive calcification underneath the longitudinal spinous ligaments causing fixation of the spine. These changes are irreversible; hence limitation of function persists even after the disease becomes arrested. The subligamentous calcification may become continuous, giving the

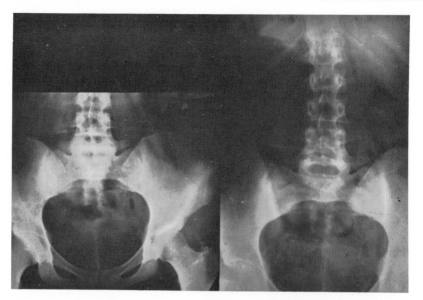

A

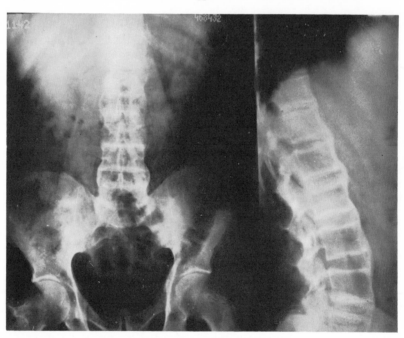

B

Figure 32–11. Roentgenograms of pelvis and lumbar spine in ankylosing spondylitis. *A, Early stages:* left, sacroiliac arthritis, cartilages well preserved; right, later stage of sacroiliac arthritis with extensive articular cartilage destruction and slight subligamentous calcification in upper lumbar segments. *B, Late stage:* left, fusion of sacroiliac joints and extensive subligamentous calcification; *right,* "bamboo spine" produced by solid calcification beneath the longitudinal spinous ligaments.

spine a bamboo appearance in the roentgenogram (Fig. 32–11), and the spine is completely stiff. If the patient's posture has been essentially normal, there will be a straight, stiff ("poker") spine; a round back deformity results from dorsal kyphosis, causing a

"rocker" spine. When ankylosis of costovertebral joints accompanies ankylosed kyphotic spine, breathing is entirely diaphragmatic and greatly restricted. In late stages of spondylitis the cervical spine sometimes is fixed at an angle projecting forward from the kyphotic dorsal spine, and, if the atlanto-occipital and atlanto-axial joints are ankylosed, the head cannot be moved on the spine and the patient's horizon is low. This presents a potentially dangerous as well as an embarrassing handicap to the ambulatory patient.

Shoulder and hip joints frequently are inflamed with this type of spondylitis. Stiffness of the shoulders combined with an immobile spine causes much interference with function, but when there is ankylosis of both hips in a patient with a stiff back, incapacity is extreme. There is no combination of arthritic damages so devastating. Without assistance the patient cannot rise from bed or lie down once he is up. If both hips are ankylosed in a position of extension, he cannot sit, and walking is accomplished with very short steps, for progression requires swinging the pelvis. If the hips are ankylosed in considerable flexion, the patient becomes a chair or bed invalid.

Ankylosing spondylitis may occur with classical rheumatoid arthritis of the extremity joints; then the functional disturbance is great due to the combined stiffness of the back and the extremity joint disability.

Gouty Arthritis

Gout is a metabolic disorder of purine metabolism which is usually hereditary, but which may be acquired, whose main clinical problem is arthritis. The metabolic disorder is characterized by an increase in tissue urates, caused in some instances by increased production as a result of abnormal metabolic degradation of purines, in other instances by a decreased excretion of urates, or by a combination of both factors. The unusual metabolic features of this disease are elevation of uric acid in the blood, decreased urinary excretion of urates and deposition of sodium monourate crystal masses (tophi) usually in or adjacent to cartilages at joints or in the ears.

The physiologic disturbance accounting for the acute synovitis which characterizes gouty arthritis had been considered a mystery until the recent work of McCarty and his associates. These investigators have clearly shown that sodium urate crystals can cause synovitis under certain conditions, and their explanation for the acute inflammation seems logical. Conditions being suitable, sodium monourate crystals are formed at or near the surface of the synovial lining of a joint; by chemotaxis polymorphonuclear leukocytes are attracted to the foreign substances and phagocytize the crystals; the phagocytes disintegrate and free lysosomes liberate enzymes which cause inflammation of the synovium. The acute synovitis of gout is therefore a crystal deposition disease.

The functional disturbances which characterize an acute gouty attack are due to the synovitis which constitutes the connective tissue pathology. The extremely severe joint synovitis, which develops rapidly, may completely incapacitate the victim of this disease, but the attack ends quickly and the inflammation subsides completely, so that the affected joints return to normal anatomic and functional state. After repeated attacks of gouty arthritis, urate deposits in and about joint structures may become large and, together with the inflammatory changes, may produce severe damage to articular cartilage and subchondral bone, causing persistent dysfunction similar to that which occurs in chronic joint changes from any cause. In the chronic tophacious stage of gouty arthritis the pathologic physiology of the locomotor system is due to a combination of acute and chronic articular disease.

Nonarticular Rheumatism

Besides the rheumatic diseases which affect the joints, there are several disorders of the locomotor system which are confined to nonarticular structures. These conditions include affections of the tendon sheath, tendons, bursae, fascia and periarticular connective tissue.

Primary Fibrositis

This common disease, often called "muscular rheumatism," actually is a disease of the fibrous connective tissue more than in the muscles. It may occur in acute attacks, causing painful stiff neck or lumbago, or it may begin insidiously and become a nagging, chronic ailment affecting many parts, including the back, shoulders, hands, thighs and legs. Its etiology is unknown, but chemical changes are thought to be responsible.

Although the patient is well systemically, the connective tissue becomes irritated and painful, interfering with movements of the joints. The tissue changes have been discussed in the section on rheumatoid arthritis. In primary fibrositis the connective tissue changes exist without joint synovitis, but the pathologic physiology is chiefly the stiff, difficult, painful and often limited movement of the joints.

If the cervical structures are affected, the

patient has pain when attempting to move the head and neck, and little or no motion is accomplished. Cervical muscle spasm may be severe. Acute low back fibrositis accounts for the syndrome of lumbago. Chronic fibrositis may involve many structures at once or may migrate from one to another part. The involved parts are usually tender and stiff, worse with rest and cold, better with exercise, heat and massage. Since movement of the joints depends upon function of the periarticular connective tissue and muscles, when these structures are irritated limitation of movement occurs; but, since the joints are not affected there is no permanent dysfunction.

Bursitis may occur at any of the many periarticular bursae. If the subacromial bursa, which lies in intimate proximity to the shoulder joint, is inflamed, movement at this joint is limited and painful. The supraspinatus tendon forms the floor of this bursa so that abduction of the shoulder is difficult and limited. Deposits of calcium may occur in the tendon, close to its attachment, and cause further interference with shoulder motion. If abduction can be initiated, it may be limited by impingement of the calcific deposit or the inflamed bursa against the acromion. Usually there is a varying degree of periarticular fibrositis at the involved shoulder which adds to the stiffness, pain and functional disturbance. If it is not possible to relieve the condition in a short while, muscle atrophy develops rapidly and periarticular stiffness may prevent motion, causing a "frozen shoulder," even though the joint itself is not diseased.

Activities which require shoulder movements, such as putting on and taking off shirts, coats and dresses, may be difficult or impossible. Shoulder function returns quickly following acute "bursitis," but if it becomes chronic irreparable stiffness and impairment of function may result. Many times paresthesias are noted in the fingers because of irritation of the axillary nerves located close to the disease process.

Inflammation of bursae located about the elbows, knees, ischial tuberosities and the attachment of the tendo Achillis causes impairment of function of the adjacent joint similar to, but seldom as troublesome as when the bursae about the shoulder are involved.

Tenosynovitis and Other Forms of Fibrositis

Tenosynovitis may interfere with free passage of the enclosed tendon. Function of the joints moved by these tendons will be im-

paired. A common place for such inflammation is the sheaths of the flexor tendons to the fingers, where frequently fibrous tissue reaction results in adhesive tenosynovitis, so that, if the finger is flexed, it cannot be extended by the extensor apparatus without assistance ("trigger finger"). In some cases inflammation of the flexor tendon sheaths and the palmar fascia may cause adhesions so strong as completely to prevent movement of the fingers, which then become deformed in a partially flexed position. Inflammation of the palmar fascia may cause adhesions with contractions so that flexion deformities of the affected fingers (Dupuytren's contracture) result (usually affecting digits number 5, 4 and 3 in decreasing order).

Diseases of Muscles

Function of the locomotor system may be interfered with by primary myositis or muscular dystrophy. The inflammatory reaction set up by the parasitic infection, such as trichinosis, causes pain and tenderness in the regions infected; contraction of the muscle aggravates the discomfort, so that the patient avoids use of the muscle whenever possible. Weakness and atrophy result if the infection becomes chronic. Since the joints are not diseased, no deformities result, and, when the infection is arrested, function returns to normal, unless there is weakness due to severe atrophy.

Muscular dystrophies, such as pseudohypertrophic myodystrophy, disturb function of joints only by reason of weakness of the affected muscles.

Nervous System Disease

Many neurologic disorders cause dysfunction of the locomotor system, chiefly or entirely as a result of muscle weakness or total paralysis. Motor nerve paralysis, from whatever cause, results in complete absence of function of the muscle supplied by the affected nerve. Such paralysis results from central nervous system tumors, infections, vascular disease or degeneration of the nerve tracts. Various sensory disturbances may accompany the motor disorder.

In poliomyelitis two types of muscle change occur as a result of the infection in the anterior horn cells. The muscles innervated by the nerves whose nuclei have been destroyed become paralyzed and atrophic, and the flaccid paralysis characteristic of this disease results. The spotty affection of the cord explains the disorganized paralysis of this disease. Nonparalyzed muscles often become spastic and account for pain and dysfunction. Muscle spasm contributes greatly to the deformities formerly thought to be caused by the paralysis. The lumbodorsal muscles are commonly spastic, even when paralysis has not affected any muscles of the back. Stiffness and limitation of motion of the lumbar and low dorsal back are, therefore, common in patients with poliomyelitis.

When a focal point of pain persists, a sympathetico-somatic reflex may be set up, which, through the internuncial pool in the spinal cord, may be continued for weeks or months, resulting in sympathetic neuromuscular dystrophies. For example, "shoulder-hand syndrome" may follow myocardial infarction, chronic thoracic diseases, paraplegia and other affections of the upper part of the body. Early in this disease there is intense pain in the shoulder and hand. Movement of the shoulder is restricted by pain; stiffness tends to develop rapidly and may be difficult to overcome after the pain has subsided. In the early stage the hand usually is swollen and painful, and the grasp is remarkably weak, and in severe cases the fingers cannot be flexed because of the resultant pain. The fingers usually are held partially flexed, in which position they may become stiffened irreparably if the condition is not promptly relieved. Swelling subsides sooner or later, and atrophy about the hand and shoulder becomes evident. Movement can usually be recovered unless pain has persisted for a long time. Functional return depends upon the amount of effort put forth by the patient to exercise the affected parts throughout the active illness.

If this disease is bilateral, the resulting disability is great. If the condition remains active for long, permanent stiffness may remain in the hand or the shoulder, or both. This condition is different from other rheumatic diseases, from which it should be differentiated as early as possible.

Diseases of Bone

Various pathologic conditions of bone, including fracture, infection, neoplasm, osteoporosis and necrosis, may cause pain or irritation of surrounding tissue, so as to interfere with function of involved parts, through muscle spasm or mechanical interference with movement. Disability, even complete incapacitation, may result. The mechanism of the pathologic physiology is no different from that resulting from disease of other tissue of the locomotor system, except that it has its origin in bone. If the disease can be eradicated, dysfunction ceases for the joints and the motivating nerve-muscle apparatus are not damaged.

Diseases of the muscles, the nervous system and bones are major specialties; they are referred to in this chapter only in regard to their importance in causing pathologic physiology of the joints.

REFERENCES

Aho, K., and Simons, K.: Studies of the antibody nature of the rheumatoid factor. Arth. & Rheumat., 6:676, 1963.
Astorga, C., and Bollet, A. J.: Diagnostic specificity and possible pathogenetic significance of inclusion body cells in synovial fluid. Arth. & Rheumat., 7:288, 1964.
Barnett, E. F., Bienstock, J., and Block, K. J.: Antinuclear factors in synovial fluid: Possible participants in the rheumatoid inclusion body. Arth. & Rheumat., 7:726, 1964.
Bauer, W., Ropes, M. W., and Waine, H.: Physiology of articular structures. Physiol. Rev., 20:272, 1940.
Bayles, T. B.: Rheumatoid arthritis and rheumatic heart disease in autopsied cases. Am. J. Med. Sc., 205:42, 1943.
Bayles, T. B.: Bursitis and fibrositis, clinical and therapeutic aspects. M. Clin. North America, 39:1483, 1955.
Bennett, G. A., Waine, H., and Bauer, W.: Changes in the Knee Joint at Various Ages. New York, Commonwealth Fund, 1942.
Bollet, A. J.: Is hyaluronidase responsible for the loss of chondroitin sulfate from osteoarthritic cartilage? Abstract. Arth. & Rheumat., 8:433, 1965.
Bunim, J. J., Sokoloff, L., Williams, R. R., and Block, R. L.: Rheumatoid arthritis: A review of recent advances in our knowledge concerning pathology, diagnosis and treatment. J. Chron. Dis., 1:168, 1955.
Calkins, E., and Bauer, W.: The protean manifestations of the connective tissue disease. M. Clin. North America, 39:325, 1955.
Collins, D. H.: Recent advances in pathology of chronic arthritis and rheumatic disorders. Postgrad. Med. J., 31:602, 1955.
Cruikshank, B.: The arteritis of rheumatoid arthritis. Ann. Rheumat. Dis., 13:136, 1954.
de Duve, C.: Lysosomes, a new group of cytoplasmic particles. In Hayashi, T. (ed.): Subcellular Particles. New York, The Ronald Press Co., 1959.
Dresner, E.: Aetiology and pathogenesis of rheumatoid arthritis. Am. J. Med., 18:74, 1955.
Fessel, J. M., and Chrisman, O. D.: Enzymatic degradation of chondromucoprotein by cell-free extracts of human cartilage. Arth. & Rheumat., 7:398, 1964.

Franklin, E. C., Holman, H. R., Muller-Eberhard, H. J., and Kunkel, H. G.: An unusual protein component of high molecular weight in the serum of certain patients with rheumatoid arthritis. J. Exper. Med., *105*:425, 1957.

Freyberg, R. H.: Non-articular rheumatism. Bull. New York Acad. Med., *27*:245, 1951.

Fudenberg, H., and Martensson, L.: The GM and INV, and the rheumatoid factors: Interrelations, interpretations and implications. Bull. Rheumat. Dis., *13*:313, 1963.

Gardner, E. D.: Physiology of blood and nerve supply of joints. Bull. Hosp. Joint Dis., *15*:35, 1954.

Gear, J.: Autoantibodies and the hyperreactive state in the pathogenesis of disease. Acta Med. Scand., Supp., *306*:39, 1955.

Graham, W.: Fibrositis and non-articular rheumatism. Physiotherapy Rev., *35*:128, 1955.

Gross, J.: Some structural and chemical properties of connective tissue. Scientific Conferences (Hosp. for Special Surgery), New York, 149, 1955.

Grubb, R.: The Gm groups and their relation to rheumatoid arthritis serology. Arch. & Rheumat., *4*:195, 1961.

Hargraves, M. M., Richmond, H., and Morton, R.: Presentation of two bone marrow elements; "tart" cell and "L.E." cell. Proc. Staff Meet., Mayo Clin., *23*:25, 1948.

Heimer, R.: The macroglobulins and connective tissue disease. Arth. & Rheumat., *2*:266, 1959.

Heimer, R., Federico, O. M., Schwartz, E. R., and Freyberg, R. H.: Studies on macroglobulins of rheumatoid arthritis. Abstract. Fifth Interim Scientific Session. Am. Rheum. Assn., December 1958.

Heimer, R., and Schwartz, E. R.: Isolation of rheumatoid factors. Arth. & Rheumat., *4*:153, 1961.

Hench, P. S., Kendall, E. C., Slocumb, C. H., and Polley, H.: Effect of a hormone of the adrenal cortex (17-hydroxy-11-dehydrocorticosterone (Compound E)) and of pituitary adrenocorticotropic hormone on rheumatoid arthritis: Preliminary report. Proc. Staff Meet., Mayo Clin., *24*:181, 1949.

Hollander, J. L.: The most neglected differential diagnostic test in arthritis. Arth. & Rheumat., *3*:364, 1960.

Hollander, J. L., and collaborators: Comroe's Arthritis and Allied Conditions, 6th ed. Philadelphia, Lea & Febiger, 1960.

Hollander, J. L., Jessar, R. A., and McCarty, D. J.: Synovianalysis: An aid in arthritis diagnosis. Bull. Rheumat. Dis., *12*:263, 1961.

Hollander, J. L., McCarty, D. J., Jr., Astorga, G., and Castro-Murillo, E.: Studies on the pathogenesis of rheumatoid joint inflammation. I. The "R.A. cell." Ann. Int. Med., *62*:271, 1965.

Jacox, R. F., and Feldmahn, A.: Variation of beta glucuronidase concentration in abnormal human synovial fluid. J. Clin. Invest., *34*:263, 1955.

Jeffrey, M. R.: Some observations on anemia in rheumatoid arthritis. Blood, *8*:502, 1953.

Johnston, J. P.: The viscosity of normal and pathological human synovial fluids. Biochem. J., *59*: 633, 1955.

Kellgren, J. H.: Rheumatic Diseases. Philadelphia, W. B. Saunders Co., 1952.

Kellgren, J. H.: Non-articular rheumatism. Scientific

Conferences (Hosp. for Special Surgery), New York, 149, 1955.

Klemperer, P.: The significance of the intermediate substances of the connective tissue in human disease. Harvey Lect., *49*:100, 1953–1954.

Mannick, M., and Kunkel, H. G.: The immuno-globulins. Bull. Rheumat. Dis., *13*:309, 1963.

Mason, G. D., Selle, W. A., and McKee, J. W.: Some physiological aspects of joints in health and disease. Part II. Physiology of abnormal joints. Am. J. Phys. Med., *33*:239, 1954.

McCarty, D. J., Jr., Gatter, R. A., Brill, J. M., and Hogan, J. M.: Crystal deposition diseases. J.A.M.A., *193*:129, 1965.

Mellors, R. C., Heimer, R., Corcos, J., and Korngold, L.: Cellular origin of rheumatoid factor. J. Exper. Med., *110*:875, 1959.

Niedermeier, W., Cross, R., and Beetham, W. P., Jr.: The concentration of haptoglobin in synovial fluid of patients with rheumatoid arthritis. Arth. & Rheumat., *8*:355, 1965.

Patterson, M., and Freyberg, R. H.: Blood sludge in patients with arthritis. In Slocumb, C. H. (ed.): Rheumatic Diseases. Based on Proceedings of Seventh International Congress on Rheumatic Diseases. Philadelphia, W. B. Saunders Co., 1952.

Ragan, C.: The history of the rheumatoid factor. Arth. & Rheumat., *4*:571, 1961.

Randall, J. T.: Observations on the collagen system. Nature, *174*:853, 1954.

Rawson, A. J., Abelson, N. M., and Hollander, J. L.: Studies on the pathogenesis of rheumatoid joint inflammation. II. Intracytoplasmic particulate complexes in rheumatoid synovial fluids. Ann. Int. Med., *62*:281, 1965.

Restifo, R. A., Lussier, A. J., Rawson, A. J., Rockey, J. H., and Hollander, J. L.: Studies on the pathogenesis of rheumatoid joint inflammation. III. The experimental production of arthritis by the intra-articular injection of purified 7S gamma globulin. Ann. Int. Med., *62*:285, 1965.

Robbins, W. C., Holman, H. R., Deicher, H., and Kunkel, H. G.: Complement fixation with cell nuclei and DNA in lupus erythematosus. Proc. Soc. Exper. Biol. Med., *96*:575, 1957.

Robinson, W. D., Duff, I. F., and Smith, E. M.: Joint fluid changes in rheumatoid arthritis. J. Michigan M. Soc., *54*:270, 1955.

Ropes, M. W., and Bauer, W.: Synovial Fluid Changes in Joint Disease. New York, Commonwealth Fund, and Cambridge, Harvard University Press, 1953.

Rosenberg, E. F., Baggenstoss, A. H., and Hench, P. S.: Causes of death in 30 cases of rheumatoid arthritis. Ann. Int. Med., *20*:903, 1944.

Rothfield, N. F., Phythyon, J. M., McEwen, C., and Miescher, P.: The role of antinuclear reactions in the diagnosis of systemic lupus erythematosus: A study of 53 Cases. Arth. & Rheumat., *4*: 223, 1961.

Silberberg, M., and Silberberg, R.: Age changes in bones and joints in various strains of mice. Am. J. Anat., *68*:69, 1941.

Smyth, C. J., and Gum, O. B.: Mast cells in connective tissue diseases. Arth. & Rheumat., *1*:178, 1958.

Smyth, C. J., et al.: Rheumatism and arthritis: Review of American and English literature of recent years. (Fifteenth Rheumatism Review.) Ann. Int. Med., 59:supp. 4, pp. 1–146, 1963.

Stecher, R. M.: Hereditary factors in arthritis. M. Clin. North America, 39:499, 1955.

Sturgill, B. C., and Carpenter, R. R.: Antibody to ribosomes in systemic lupus erythematosus. Arth. & Rheumat., 8:213, 1965.

Weissman, G., Barland, P., and Weidermann, G.: Role of lysosomes in streptolysin S induced arthritis. Clin. Res., 12:240, 1964.

Wright, V., and Jones, R. J.: Physical factors concerned with the stiffness of normal and diseased joints. Bull. Johns Hopkins Hosp., 106:215, 1960.

Wright, V., and Jones, R. J.: Observations on the measurement of joint stiffness. Arth. & Rheumat., 3:328, 1960.

Ziff, M.: Some immunologic aspects of the connective tissue diseases. Ann. Rheumat. Dis., 24:103, 1965.

Zucker-Franklin, D.: Electron microscope study of cytoplasmic inclusions in leukocytes of patients with rheumatoid arthritis. Arth. & Rheumat., 7:760, 1964.

Zvaifler, N. J.: A speculation on the pathogenesis of joint inflammation in rheumatoid arthritis. Arth. & Rheumat., 8:289, 1965.

Part XII

Nervous System

Chapter Thirty-Three

The Nervous System

BERNARD J. ALPERS
and
ELLIOTT L. MANCALL

Introduction

Organic disease of the nervous system is associated with permanent or transitory damage of the nervous system tissues or with abnormal mechanisms producing disturbance of function with or without recognizable damage to the nervous tissues. Recognition of the nature of the damage is usually possible because of what is known as a result of pathological studies, but it is not always possible to be certain even with these studies, and the mechanism of production of symptoms is often obscure, both with and without a knowledge of the underlying pathology. On the other hand, much may be known regarding the mechanism, as in seizures and migraine, without a clear conception of the underlying organic process.

The pathogenesis of symptoms of nervous system origin is too varied to be considered in detail. Help concerning the production of symptoms may be derived from their *level of origin* (although the division into levels has its artificial aspects). Symptoms may be due to involvement at the peripheral nerve, spinal cord, brain stem and cortical levels, or at all or most of them simultaneously or intermittently. A recognition of the level at which symptoms appear to be produced tends to confine the possible causes and mechanisms,

making due allowance for the fact that many diseases, such as poliomyelitis, may be focal or diffuse in their involvement of the nervous system.

For a clear image of the pathogenesis, however, it is necessary not only to determine the level at which symptoms are produced, and whether they are focal or diffuse, but also to have an idea of the underlying cause or mechanism responsible for them.

Little is known regarding the *selectivity* of diseases which affect nervous tissue. The mechanism of such selectivity differs in various diseases, but it may be different even in the same disease, and may be dependent on divergent factors. It is not known why acute infectious polyneuritis, though not a single entity, involves almost exclusively the peripheral nerves in a parenchymatous form of neuritis. Nor is it clear, even when due allowances are made for the associated vascular changes, why diabetes is responsible at times for neuritis, and at other times for central nervous system symptoms. This is even more true in the case of alcohol intoxication, which may be responsible for a severe multiple neuritis in one instance, an encephalopathy in another, and a combination of the two in still other instances.

The mystery of selectivity is illustrated further in the case of poliomyelitis, which is

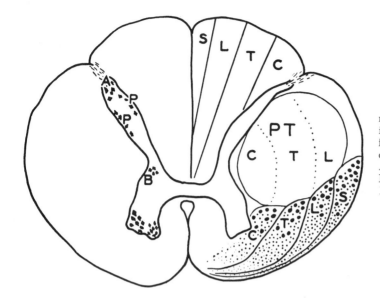

Figure 33–1. Segmental arrangement of fibers in ascending and descending columns of spinal cord. *S,* sacral fibers; *L,* lumbar; *T,* thoracic; *C,* cervical; *PT,* pyramidal tract. (From Walker, A. E.: Central representation of pain. Proc. A. Res. Nerv. & Ment. Dis., 23:63, 1943.)

exclusively an anterior horn cell disease at various levels of the nervous system, even to the Betz cells of the motor cortex. Similar anterior horn cell selectivity is seen in progressive spinal muscular atrophy. A striking example is to be found in the subacute combined degeneration of pernicious anemia which is confined to the spinal cord level (with very rare exceptions), with remarkable selectivity of the long tracts of the posterior, lateral or anterolateral areas of the spinal cord and with sparing of the anterior and posterior roots. So too is the case in syringomyelia, which is usually seen at the spinal cord level, but may involve the brain stem. Not only is the selectivity of amyotrophic lateral sclerosis for the anterior horn cells and pyramidal tracts of the spinal cord and brain stem, with extension of the pyramidal involvement to the cerebral cortex, in itself a puzzle, but the predominance in some instances of one level involvement over another (brain stem or spinal cord), and of anterior horn or pyramidal tract symptoms is equally perplexing. Examples could be multiplied indefinitely to illustrate the obscurity of the problem of selectivity, but little is known regarding the reason, except that some viruses are neurotropic and that, empirically, some diseases are associated with involvement of the nervous system at specific levels, with the implication of specific systems.

It has long been known that the symptoms associated with destruction of tissue in the nervous system are the result of *unopposed activity* of other parts of the nervous system.

This is true of the spasticity of hemiplegia, the intention tremor and incoordination of cerebellar disease, and of other symptoms. Hughlings Jackson pointed out that the paralysis in hemiplegia could be attributed to the loss of tissue, but that positive symptoms such as spasticity were due to the action of other parts. Involuntary movements of various sorts can be viewed in the same light. The specific areas or mechanisms involved are not clearly known for many of the released symptoms, but the available evidence will be given consideration in relation to specific symptoms.

The explanation of *symptoms at a distance* from the lesion often offers great difficulties. They are sometimes explainable by anatomical facts, but at other times the mechanism is unknown. The paresthesias of the feet and legs occurring early in a compressing lesion of the cervical portion of the spinal cord are due to stimulation of the foot and leg fibers on the periphery of the spinal cord because of the special anatomical arrangement of these fibers in the spinothalamic tract (Fig. 33–1). Symptoms at a distance from a focal cerebral lesion have occupied the attention of neurologists for many years, since errors in diagnosis and in cerebral localization have resulted from failure to recognize the principle involved in such symptoms. For their explanation, Monakow suggested the hypothesis of *diaschisis,* or *cerebral shock,* which has been defined as follows: "Diaschisis is a transient state of diminished or abolished function to which regions distant from the region primarily involved may be submitted. Thus, diaschisis is a remote effect, due to the interruption of pathways relating the distant parts to the part involved in a lesion" (Riese). There are two important implications in the theory of diaschisis which are not generally accepted. These are (1) the concept of a working unit with its complex connections, which is interrupted in the development of a focal lesion of any nature, and (2) the concept of each cerebral unit as a source of excitation for each other, and the denial of the effects of inhibition. The recovery from aphasia in a 79-year-old subject would not be attributed by Monakow to the assumption of speech functions by the opposite hemisphere or adjacent parts of the affected hemisphere. Rather, "it seems more intelligible to assume that a lesion throws out of function, though only temporarily, proximate as well as remote cerebral structures, which regain their previous and habitual functions after a certain interval subject to individual variations" (Riese).

Probably related to this is the complete interruption of function, simulating in all respects that of severance of the nerve in the case of concussion of a nerve trunk. Complete interruption of function, with complete return, may follow a direct blow to the spinal cord in dislocation of a vertebra or as a result of an indirect blow to the spinal cord through injury of the vertebra by, for example, a bullet or a fall.

The Motor System

THE NEUROMUSCULAR JUNCTION AND MUSCLE

The normal sequence of events of muscular contraction in response to stimulation of a motor nerve may be considered as being comprised of three relatively distinct stages: transmission of the nerve impulse across the myoneural junction with activation of the motor end-plate, propagation of the impulse along the muscle itself, and, finally, the actual physical phenomenon of muscular contraction with its attendant biochemical changes. In the normal individual, these are blended together in a smooth continuum, but specific abnormalities confined to one or another of these phases can be recognized under a variety of pathological conditions. It is therefore appropriate to consider both normal and abnormal functioning of muscle under these three general categories.

The Neuromuscular Junction

Morphologically, the neuromuscular junction is a rather complex structure, consisting of a highly specialized infolded portion of muscle membrane (sarcolemma) called the motor end-plate, into which the terminal filaments or motor nerves penetrate. This structure is essentially discontinuous, in that the nerve fibers are not in direct contact with the sarcolemmal membrane, but are separated from it by a distinct, albeit very narrow, gap. The exact nature of the transmission of an impulse from nerve to muscle across this junctional complex has been the subject of considerable controversy; the bulk of the evidence presently available indicates that the release and activity of a neurohumoral agent, presumably acetylcholine, is basic to the transmission of the impulse.

The most widely accepted theory of the nature of the impulse transmission may be briefly stated in this way: Acetylcholine is stored in tiny, discrete packets, or "quanta," inside the nerve terminals. The size of these packets is relatively fixed and not particularly subject to external influences. These minute accumulations of acetylcholine constantly leak from the nerve endings, spontaneously and at random time intervals, and cross the narrow gap between nerve and sarcolemma to encounter and combine with the motor end-plate receptor. This receptor is in all likelihood a special protein component of the sarcolemmal membrane with reactor sites exposed on its external surface. When the acetylcholine combines with the reactor sites, the physical properties of the muscle membrane become altered in such a way as to produce an increase in permeability to ions, a drop in membrane potential and a resultant electrical excitation or impulse formation. In response to the random bombardment of the receptor by the spontaneous leakage of humoral quanta, small local depolarizations of the membrane occur. These low amplitude responses, the so-called miniature end-plate potentials, are in themselves insufficient to initiate an impulse capable of being propagated along the muscle membrane, and no muscular contraction results. However, when a nerve impulse arrives at the terminal twigs of a motor nerve, a simultaneous discharge of large numbers of such acetylcholine packets occurs. When these arrive at the receptor site, depolarization is sufficiently widespread and intense to establish the true end-plate potential; this is an electrical impulse of sufficient amplitude to be propagated along the sarcolemmal membrane as the muscle action spike potential, which in turn initiates muscular contraction. The effective end-plate potential appears to represent the summation of several hundred miniature units. The acetylcholine itself survives only for a matter of a few milliseconds, being rapidly deactivated and destroyed by the enzyme cholinesterase normally present at the end-plate.

As Marshall has stressed, disturbances in transmission at the myoneural junction theoretically may arise in four fundamentally different ways. First, acetylcholine production at the terminations of the motor nerve may be deficient. Second, acetylcholine may be produced normally but destroyed before it can reach the reactor sites of the motor end-plate. Third, a substance may compete with acetylcholine for the receptor sites. Fourth, acetylcholine may be produced and transferred adequately, and react in the usual fashion with the receptor sites, but may then persist for an abnormal period of time on the end-plate, i.e., there is an inadequate or delayed enzymatic destruction of acetylcholine.

A *disturbance of acetylcholine production* in the nerve terminals is rare, but may be observed in botulism, the *botulinus* toxin appearing to prevent the release of the neurohumor. Disturbed production also follows the administration of the agent hemicholinium HC_3 which appears to inhibit acetylcholine synthesis. There are no established examples of blockage of transmission by destruction of acetylcholine before it reaches the end-plate.

Curare, as well as its alkaloid d-turbocurarine, paralyzes by competing with acetylcholine for the receptor sites, a type of interference called *competitive antagonism* or *inhibition*. This competition is probably founded on the similarity in chemical structure of the substances concerned, acetylcholine and curare both being organic quaternary compounds. A similar antagonism is seen with bis-quaternary compounds such as hexamethonium or tetraethylammonium (TEA), although it should be stressed that the action of these drugs predominates at the autonomic cholinergic ganglionic synapses, the effect at the myoneural junction being minimal. Although these various quaternary compounds interfere with the combination of acetylcholine with the receptor sites, in themselves they have no action upon the end-plate, and

no depolarization or potential change is observed following their administration.

An *abnormal persistence of acetylcholine activity* at the end-plate also blocks transmission, but the mechanism here is quite different from that of the competitive blocking agents. When acetylcholine remains active at the receptor sites, depolarization of the membrane persists; since repolarization is necessary to make the end-plate "receptive" to new stimuli, an effective block is maintained. This type of interference with transmission is termed a *depolarization block*, and may be produced in a variety of ways. An intra-arterial injection of acetylcholine will flood the junctional region with a superabundance of acetylcholine in amounts exceeding that which the cholinesterase normally present can deactivate; similarly, rapid repetitive stimulation of the motor nerve will cause an accumulation of acetylcholine beyond the inactivating capacity of the enzyme. Under both of these circumstances, persistent depolarization occurs, with resultant paralysis, although cholinesterase activity per se has not been disturbed. A depolarization block may also be produced by an impairment of cholinesterase activity; this is the mode of action of the so-called *anticholinesterases*, such as neostigmine, Tensilon, eserine, and diisopropyl fluorophosphate (DFP), all of which combine directly with cholinesterase and prevent it from destroying acetylcholine. It is of some interest that these compounds also exhibit a quaternary structure; in addition to their anticholinesterase activity, they may also have some direct cholinergic effect on the receptor sites, mimicking the action of acetylcholine itself. A third type of depolarization block is exemplified by the action of the drug decamethonium, a bis-quaternary substance. Decamethonium does not increase the amount of acetylcholine present, and has no effect on cholinesterase, but it does have a direct cholinergic effect on the end-plate itself, with resultant depolarization, at least in normal muscle. Succinylcholine, widely used as an anesthetic adjunct to obtain muscular relaxation, is thought to act in the same way.

On clinical grounds alone, one cannot ordinarily distinguish between a depolarization block and a competitive block of neuromuscular transmission; the use of an anticholinesterase agent such as neostigmine or Tensilon permits a differentiation to be made fairly readily. As would be expected, a competitive block is promptly relieved by an anticholinesterase, since such a drug allows acetylcholine to build up sufficiently to overcome the competitive inhibition. On the other hand, a depolarization block is not overcome by such an agent, and may actually be worsened.

It is logical at this juncture to consider the enigma of *myasthenia gravis*. This disease, characterized clinically by muscular hyperfatigability, has long been recognized as a disorder of neuromuscular transmission, and the therapeutic restoration of strength with anticholinesterase agents is a well-established clinical practice. The exact nature of the disturbance of transmission, however, still awaits elucidation. Comparative physiologic studies of myasthenic patients and of animals injected with hemicholinium HC₃ suggest that defective synthesis of acetylcholine in the presynaptic portions of the neuromuscular apparatus may play a significant role in myasthenia. The in vitro observation of faulty release of acetylcholine packets from nerve terminals would also support the contention that at least one of the abnormal sites in myasthenia may be the terminal arborization of the motor nerve. In addition, however, a number of observations would seem to indicate that myasthenia is due to a circulating toxic substance which has its main action at the end-plate itself, acting either as a competitive inhibitor or as a depolarizing blocking agent. For example, a transient myasthenic syndrome may occur in infants born of mothers with myasthenia gravis, suggesting that a toxin of some sort has crossed the placental barrier and entered the fetal circulation. Again, a myasthenic syndrome has been observed on a number of occasions in individuals with bronchogenic carcinoma and other neoplasms; the possibility of a toxic agent somehow elaborated as a by-product of the metabolism of the tumor immediately suggests itself. The improvement in at least some individuals following thymectomy again might suggest the presence of a toxin, perhaps removed from the circulation by removal of its source. Interestingly, it has been shown that serum from myasthenic patients may impede neuromuscular transmission in the experimental animal, although Marshall has emphasized that the neuromuscular block produced in these experiments does not fulfill all the expected criteria of myasthenia gravis, viz., reversal by neostigmine, ability to transmit low rates of stimulation better than high, and preservation of the reactivity of the muscle to direct stimulation.

Even allowing the possibility of toxic causation of myasthenia, however, these data alone do not permit one to distinguish between competitive inhibition and depolarization blockade. The beneficial therapeutic action of anticholinesterase agents would indicate that myasthenia is essentially a problem of competitive inhibition (*vide supra*) by a curare-like substance. In recent years, a number of additional features have come to light which, though quite complex, may aid in clarifying the problem. These have recently been reviewed extensively by McArdle, and need only be mentioned briefly here. Decamethonium, which produces a depolarizing block in the normal subject, appears to produce a competitive block in muscles involved in myasthenia; curiously, in muscles which appear unaffected in the myasthenic patient there is heightened resistance to the depolarizing action of this drug. These findings indicate some change in the response to pharmacologic agents at the end-plate in myasthenic individuals. Similarly, acetylcholine, which in a normal muscle produces depolarization, causes a competitive type of inhibition in the myasthenic following a brief latent period, as pointed out by Grob, Johns and Harvey. The same authors found that choline, a hydrolysis product of acetylcholine, gives rise to a competitive block when injected into myasthenic patients, a block which can be alleviated by a further injection of choline. These observations suggest that choline itself, or, more likely, an abnormal conversion product of choline at the end-plate, may well be responsible for the interruption of transmission in myasthenia gravis.

In addition to probable affection of both the nerve twig and end-plate, however, there is an increasing body of evidence indicating a different type of abnormality probably affecting the myofibrils themselves. Circulating antibodies have been repeatedly demonstrated in the sera of myasthenic patients, and with appropriate immunologic techniques binding of these antibodies to skeletal muscles is apparent. Observations such as these have opened an entirely new area of speculation and investigation in the study of myasthenia gravis, introducing the concept that myasthenia may be in fact autoimmune in nature. The relationship between myasthenia and the thymus thus becomes still more intriguing in view of the recognized role of this gland in immune mechanisms. In this connection, of course, clinical benefit from thymectomy need not indicate removal of an unknown toxic substance, as mentioned above, but might equally well imply interference with antibody formation. Similarly, passage of circulating maternal antibodies across the placenta might well explain the occurrence of neonatal myasthenia.

One is thus left with at least three potential mechanisms in myasthenia gravis: (1) faulty formation or release of acetylcholine from the terminus of the motor nerve, (2) local "toxic" competitive inhibition at the end-plate itself, and (3) an immunologically determined abnormality of the myofibrillary apparatus. Finally, mention should be made of the morphologic alterations of the end-plate apparatus noted by Coers and Desmedt, Zacks and others. These structural changes may represent a secondary phenomenon in longstanding myasthenia; it is interesting to speculate as to whether these changes in turn could be responsible for the muscular atrophy noted clinically in some patients late in the course of the disease.

One cannot dismiss the problem of myasthenia gravis without at least a passing reference to the not infrequent occurrence of profound muscular weakness developing during the course of therapy with anticholinesterase agents. In view of the fluctuating requirement for such agents which is characteristic of many of these patients, a distinction must often be made between weakness due to inadequate therapy and weakness due to overmedication, i.e., the weakness of a persistent depolarization block as part of a so-called cholinergic crisis.

A cholinergic crisis is essentially a massive parasympathetic mobilization coupled with the weakness of a depolarization block and muscle fasciculations; increased activity of the gastrointestinal tract, with hyperperistalsis and diarrhea, increased bladder tone, excessive salivation, bradycardia, pupillary constriction, and paradoxical sweating are all characteristic features. In some instances, the muscle weakness overshadows the other associated phenomena, and it may be impossible, on clinical grounds alone, to distinguish between under- and overmedication. On such an occasion, the use of the short-acting anticholinesterase agent Tensilon is of crucial importance. If the weakness is due to inadequate medication, improvement follows an injection of this drug; if due to excessive medication, obviously no improvement is possible, and, in fact, some transitory worsening may be seen. On the basis of this test, the medication may be adjusted in the appropriate

direction. When a depolarization block has been demonstrated, atropine is often administered; unfortunately, the cholinergic blocking activity of atropine predominates at the receptors on glands and smooth muscle, with no direct effect on striated muscle. The recent development of the so-called *cholinesterase activators*, the aldoxines, e.g., pyridine aldoxine methiodide (PAM) and duodecyl aldoxine methiodide (DAM), promises a more direct effect on striated muscle under these circumstances; these substances appear capable of rapidly splitting the anticholinesterase-cholinesterase linkage, the cholinesterase so released being free to deactivate the excessive amount of acetylcholine which has accumulated.

The Sarcolemmal Membrane

As has been pointed out, an end-plate potential of sufficient amplitude to be propagated along the sarcolemmal membrane is set up in response to a motor nerve impulse. The nature of transmission of this impulse, the muscle action potential, is, as far as is known, identical with transmission of an impulse along a nerve membrane, and is based largely on the ionic permeability of the membrane concerned. Both the nerve and muscle membranes appear to be freely permeable to potassium and chloride ions, but relatively impermeable to sodium ions. Sodium is maintained at a high concentration outside the membrane by the "sodium pump," a mechanism of active transport of these ions from inside the membrane to without. Because of the very high concentration of sodium ions external to the membrane, the potassium and chloride ions also become distributed irregularly, in accordance with Donan equilibrium. Potassium becomes concentrated inside the membrane, chloride outside, along with the sodium. As a result of the differential ionic concentration, a potential difference exists across the membrane, the interior zone being negative to the exterior. The arrival of an electrical impulse lowers the resting potential across the membrane, and a rapid influx of sodium ions occurs; this further lowers the resting potential, permitting still more sodium ions to enter. The result of this inflow is a reversal of the resting potential, the interior now becoming positive to the exterior; this change of polarity constitutes the action potential. The resting potential is restored by the compensatory flow of potassium ions from within outward; subsequently the activity of the sodium pump and a reversed flow of potassium ions brings the distribution of the various electrolytes back to the initial state. During the course of the ionic flow as described, an electrotonic field is created in portions of the membrane adjacent to the site originally affected; this reduces the resting potential in these regions, and the same ionic flow repeats itself. By this means, the impulse is transmitted the length of the membrane. In mammalian skeletal muscle, transmission is very rapid, the impulses traveling along the sarcolemmal membrane at about 3 meters per second.

In view of the critical role of electrolytes in transmission along the sarcolemmal membrane, one would anticipate that derangements of electrolyte metabolism might interfere significantly with this mechanism. That this is indeed the case, at least insofar as potassium is concerned, is attested to by the frank muscular paralysis which may occur in association with either abnormally high or abnormally low blood potassium levels. A variety of conditions which lead to *potassium depletion,* such as excessive vomiting or diarrhea, potassium-losing nephritis, and primary aldosteronism, may all be associated with attacks of muscular weakness. This is presumably due to a fall in intracellular potassium and disruption of the normal ionic pattern on either side of the cell membrane.

A somewhat more complex alteration occurs in the syndrome of *familial periodic paralysis.* Here, a fall in serum potassium appears associated with a shift of the potassium ion into cells which have not previously been depleted of the ion. Theoretically this paralysis could result from hyperpolarization of the cell membrane with an elevation in threshold of the membrane and a resulting conduction block; however, the recent studies of Shy et al. utilizing intracellular recordings have failed to demonstrate such an hyperpolarization. There is some evidence pointing to an abnormality of carbohydrate metabolism as the basis for this syndrome: attacks of weakness often follow a carbohydrate debauch, and attacks may be precipitated by giving repeated doses of glucose, by a combined dose of glucose and insulin, and occasionally by the administration of epinephrine. Further, lactate and pyruvate tend to be elevated during attacks, and inorganic phosphorus is low. McArdle has suggested a partial block of carbohydrate metabolism at the hexose phosphate stage, pointing out that intracellular hexose phosphates act as indiffusible anions; an increase of these substances would tend to draw extracellular potassium ions and water into the cells. Some support for this suggestion is found in the observations of Shy et al. that vacuoles containing granules which appear to be carbohydrate in origin (possibly glycogen) appear within muscles during an attack. Utilizing electron microscopy, these vacuoles are seen to represent dilated portions of the endoplasmic reticulum. A curious feature of familial periodic paralysis is the remarkably long duration of the hypopotassemia, which may be present for days. This would suggest that for some reason the biochemical abnormality is self-perpetuating. There is also some evidence that the cell membrane itself is abnormal in this disease, with a resultant disturbance in transport of potassium ions. Occasionally, a syndrome remarkably similar to familial periodic paralysis may be encountered in association with thyrotoxicosis; the underlying mechanism is unknown.

Weakness also is known to occur in *hyperkalemic states,* particularly in renal disease with anuria and potassium retention. A rare familial type of periodic paralysis associated with high serum potassium levels, called *adynamia episodica hereditaria* (Gamstorp's syndrome), has also been recognized; that this condition is not caused by retention of potassium at the renal level is indicated by the high urinary potassium excretion in the course of an attack. It appears that the elevated serum and urinary potassium levels in this condition reflect a loss of potassium from the muscle cells, with a shift in the ion from the intracellular to the extracellular compartment and alteration of the ionic pattern across the excitable membrane. Attacks may be precipitated by the administration of potassium chloride. Increased sensitivity to intra-arterial acetylcholine, both during and between attacks, suggests that the site of abnormality may actually be at the neuromuscular junction rather than at the more distal sarcolemma. A third variety of periodic paralysis with normal potassium levels has also been recognized in recent years.

Alterations in the concentrations of sodium and chloride are not known to affect propagation of the impulse along the sarcolemmal membrane. Changes in muscle function with alterations in the concentrations of other serum electrolytes are occasionally seen. The most readily recognized of these is the state of *tetany* associated with *hypocalcemia;* this appears to be due to the effect of low calcium levels on transmission along the motor nerve fiber, with no specific effect on sarcolemmal transmission as such.

Muscular Contraction

The basic physiologic unit of muscle contraction is the so-called motor unit, a group of muscle fibers all innervated by the terminal branches of a single motor axon. In general, a motor unit is made up of from 100 to 200 muscle fibers, but in certain small muscles, such as the extraocular muscles, such a unit consists of only 10 to 15 fibers. Following denervation, the atrophy observed in the muscle follows the anatomic pattern of these motor units.

The muscle action, or sarcolemmal, potential initiates the essential function of the individual muscle fiber, i.e., contraction. In contrast to the brief duration of the action potential (a few milliseconds), the contraction response of the muscle lasts considerably longer, up to 0.1 second or more. The duration of this response varies considerably, being relatively brief in muscles which ordinarily partake in rapid small-amplitude movements, such as the extraocular muscles, and most prolonged in muscles called upon for more protracted action, such as those utilized in postural mechanisms. The muscle response itself far outlasts the very transient refractory period of the sarcolemmal membrane, and it therefore follows that a muscle fiber may be restimulated while still responding to an initial stimulus, with a resultant summation of the mechanical effect. When a repetitive series of stimuli is delivered and conducted along the sarcolemmal membrane, a smooth and sustained summated contraction is obtained; this fused contraction is called *tetanus*. The frequency rate at which tetanus can be produced varies with the type of muscle; more rapidly acting muscles such as the extraocular group require a very high frequency of stimulation, the more slowly contracting postural muscles a relatively low frequency. One should emphasize that the term tetanus, as used in this way by muscle physiologists, is clearly not synonymous with the clinical disease bearing the same name, which is characterized by recurrent spasms and, later, contractures of muscles in response to abnormal firing of anterior horn cells under the influence of the exotoxin elaborated by the bacillus *Clostridium tetani*.

Random, spontaneous, coarse, rather slow twitchings of entire motor units are a prominent feature of a number of disease processes affecting motor neurons (particularly anterior horn cells) or their processes. These contractions, or *fasciculations*, are most characteristically seen in amyotrophic lateral sclerosis, and apparently indicate an abnormal state of excitability of the neural apparatus, the motor unit itself being normal. It should be emphasized, however, that fasciculations per se cannot be taken as absolute indicators of disease of the motor neuron, because the same phenomenon may be seen with cholinergic crisis (*vide supra*) and salt deprivation. Fasciculations are also characteristic of the poorly understood clinical entity of *myokymia* (benign fasciculations). In this disorder, the fasciculations occur in the same muscle group, or groups, for long periods of time, and are usually brought on or intensified by fatigue; no evidence of any other disease of the neuromuscular apparatus can be found. The phenomenon of fasciculations should be clearly distinguished from that of *fibrillations*. These are rapid twitches of individual muscle fibers which appear soon after denervation of a muscle and which persist as long as any fibers remain. Fibrillations are of small amplitude as compared with fasciculations, and thus are not visible through the intact skin. They appear based on the activity of individual fibers rather than of the larger motor units. It has been suggested that fibrillation is an inherent property of the muscle cell in vivo, suppressed by an intact motor supply and released when the motor nerve is interrupted. An excessive sensitivity to certain pharmacologic agents, particularly acetylcholine, is also seen after denervation of a muscle, and the administration of small amounts of this drug markedly increases the fibrillary activity.

Three other states of disordered muscle contractility warrant at least brief mention, viz., spasms, cramps and myo-edema. Muscle *spasms* may be defined as repetitive activation of entire motor units associated with repetitive firing of the motor nerve. They are seen in a variety of conditions, such as tetanus and hypocalcemic tetany, and during the regeneration of damaged peripheral nerves (particularly the facial nerve). Muscle *cramps,* on the other hand, consist of a rapid disordered firing of portions of motor units, with a tendency for the activity to spread from part of one motor unit to parts of adjacent ones. Spontaneous twitching of isolated fibers may also be seen. Adams et al. contend that the underlying defect is an irritable focus in the terminal branching of a motor nerve, involving only a portion of its network. Since muscle cramps are most commonly encountered in electrolyte disturbances, one is drawn to the supposition that an abnormality in conduction on the basis of ionic disequilibrium exists in the presynaptic nerve twigs and perhaps in the postsynaptic sarcolemma as well. *Myo-edema*, or "idiomuscular contractions," refers to the abnormal persistence of a local contraction in a muscle induced by direct percussion, which may be propagated along the muscle as a small, slowly moving wave without any recognizable change in the electromyogram. This phenomenon is usually encountered in states of cachexia; its relationship to the muscle atrophy commonly found under such circumstances is not clear.

In addition to abnormal states of contractility, one occasionally encounters a delay in muscular relaxation. Certain drugs, such as veratrine and 2,4-Dichlorphenoxyacetate (2,4-D), prolong the period of relaxation following a muscular contraction induced by a single stimulus to a motor nerve. The effect seems to be due to excitation of the neuromuscular apparatus distal to the myoneural junction, with independent contractions of isolated muscle fibers. 2,4-D also acts to heighten the response of a muscle to mechanical stimulation. From the standpoint of naturally occurring disease, a delay in relaxation, termed *myotonia,* is characteristic of two probably unrelated states, viz., myotonia congenita (Thomsen's disease) and myotonic dystrophy. It may also be encountered in cases of hyperkalemic periodic paralysis (adynamia episodica hereditaria of Gamstorp).

The basic abnormality in the myotonic phenomenon appears remarkably similar to that observed with veratrine and 2,4-D, and consists of incoordinated excitation of isolated muscle fibers following contraction, i.e., of fibrillation-like activity. It is noteworthy that a single excitation cannot initiate the myotonic discharge, repeated excitations being necessary to elicit this phenomenon; thus, myotonia is not strictly comparable with the drug-induced activity already described. The nature of its occurrence suggests that myotonia may be due to the cumulative effect of some by-product of the contraction itself. The appearance of myotonia in affected patients, not only after voluntary effort but also following direct percussion of a muscle, is explained by the fact that percussion produces

a brief but intense repetitive excitation of the muscle. In addition to the rather specific myotonic phenomenon seen in these patients, widespread muscle afterspasms also occur, interpreted by Denny-Brown and Nevin as reflex spasms produced by abnormal proprioceptive discharges induced by the myotonic phenomenon itself. The beneficial effects of both quinine and calcium in the patient with myotonia have been attributed by Adams et al. to their property of lengthening the refractory period of excitable tissue in general. A similar mechanism, i.e., stabilization of the polarized muscle membrane, has been suggested as the explanation for the improvement following the use of procaine amide.

The relative importance of abnormal excitability of the end-plate itself as contrasted with abnormal excitability of the sarcolemmal membrane distal to the myoneural junction in the production of myotonic after-contractions is difficult to judge. Competitive inhibition by d-tubocurarine and depolarization blocking by decamethonium appear to have no effect on the myotonic phenomenon per se, implying that the basic defect is distal on the neuromuscular junction; on the other hand, the therapeutic agent quinine has a curarelike action capable of raising the threshold of the end-plate, so that a state of abnormal excitability at this site cannot be entirely ruled out in the consideration of the pathogenesis of the myotonic phenomenon.

An additional feature of myotonia, as yet unexplained, is the commonly noted worsening of the abnormality on exposure to cold. Some writers isolate a group of patients in whom the myotonic after-contractions appear only following such an exposure, applying the term *paramyotonia* to this state; the validity of such a distinction is uncertain. Slowness of muscular relaxation, along with weakness and muscle cramps, may also be found in association with hypothyroidism; although clinically this may suggest true myotonia, electromyographic studies do not substantiate such an impression.

Finally, mention should be made of the so-called "stiff-man" syndrome of Moersch and Woltman. This is a chronic and gradually progressive illness characterized by muscular tightness and spasms involving particularly the muscles of the back and abdominal wall. The spasms are often triggered by a variety of external stimuli. Electromyographic studies have demonstrated constant activity of motor units in this disorder. A resemblance between this illness and tetanus has been stressed, and it has been postulated that the abnormalities in these patients are due to interference with the function of the inhibitory internuncial neurons of the spinal cord.

Chemical Aspects of Muscular Contraction. The contractile elements of muscle, the myofibrils, exhibit a complex and intriguing chemical composition, the principal components of which are the structural proteins actin and myosin. These proteins are organized into an overlapping system of longitudinally oriented filaments a few hundred Å apart. The filaments are of two types, those approximately 110 Å in thickness (myosin), and those approximately 40 Å in thickness (actin). The space between these structural proteins is presumably filled with a dilute solution of proteins, electrolytes and triphosphates. During muscular contraction, the overlapping sets of protein filaments slide past each other, the filaments themselves varying little in length. This movement seems produced by obliquely oriented cross linkages between the actin and myosin; the metabolism of adenosine triphosphate (ATP) is somehow concerned in this interaction. In fact, the key to the entire process of muscular contraction appears to be ATP, although its exact role, and that of the other triphosphates also found in muscle (inosine triphosphate, uridine triphosphate, guanosine triphosphate), is not yet clear.

ATP seems to be the predominant source of energy for muscle contraction by virtue of its high energy phosphate bond; its breakdown by the enzyme adenosine triphosphatase, present in the myosin fibrils, is the energy-releasing event closest to the contraction itself. Certain electrolytes, particularly calcium, potassium and magnesium, are clearly related to the activity of this ATP-ase system, suggesting that perhaps the muscle weakness seen in such states as hyper- and hypopotassemia (*vide supra*) may be due at least in part to disturbances of cofactor-enzyme activity at the ATP-ase level. It is generally assumed that the dephosphorylation of ATP is necessary for contraction to occur, although there is some evidence to indicate that a binding of ATP to the contractile apparatus may be the event immediately producing contraction, dephosphorylation actually occurring following the contraction itself. ATP is rapidly resynthesized from its dephosphorylated form, adenosine diphosphate (ADP), the energy for resynthesis being derived from both carbohydrate and creatine phosphate breakdown. In vitro, ATP produces a remarkable change in the vis-

cosity of the actomyosin system. Both actin and myosin exist in solution as long filaments, the viscosity of such a solution being very high. When ATP is added to a solution of this sort, the viscosity falls, a change attributed to breakage of linkages between the two proteins permitting them to exist independently. This phenomenon is probably related to contraction in vivo, the breakage of certain linkages conceivably allowing the filaments to slide by each other. The difference between living, resting muscle and dead muscle in a state of rigor mortis can be satisfactorily explained on the basis of the viscosity change induced by ATP: resting muscle contains an adequate amount of ATP, so that the protein filaments are free to move on each other and the muscle is extensible; in rigor mortis, on the other hand, ATP is either absent or present in very low concentrations, the filaments are linked together, and no movement is possible.

A variety of biochemical abnormalities occurs in patients with *myopathy* (e.g., polymyositis, muscular dystrophy), but the relationship of these changes to the actual biochemistry and physical chemistry of contraction is obscure. Thus, certain findings, such as the high excretion of creatine in the urine, diminished excretion of creatinine, and the abnormal creatine tolerance test, simply reflect the reduction in muscle mass in such disorders. Creatine is synthesized in the liver and stored in the muscle under normal circumstances both in an uncombined form and as creatine phosphate; with loss of muscle tissue this normal site of storage is lost in the face of continuing hepatic synthesis, and creatinuria results. Excretion of pentoses in the urine in cases of dystrophy may also reflect a simple loss of muscle mass, although the absence of ribosuria in neuronal atrophy or cachexia, emphasized by Drew, suggests that the loss of the carbohydrates may be more specific and perhaps related to ATP itself (the adenosine base is constituted of ribose plus the purine adenine). The aminoaciduria found in patients with muscular dystrophy may likewise be due to a loss of muscle bulk, but here too the matter may be more complex; the finding of a similar biochemical abnormality in clinically normal siblings and parents raises the possibility of a more specific, perhaps inborn, alteration.

Another group of abnormalities appears related, not to a loss of muscle bulk, but to a leakage of substances through an abnormally permeable muscle membrane. The loss of myoglobin observed in cases of acute paroxysmal myoglobinuria, in some acute cases of polymyositis and following crushing injuries of muscle, is in all likelihood due to such leakage, and the raised serum levels of aldolase, transaminase, and hexose-6-phosphate isomerase found in dystrophic individuals are probably based on the same mechanism.

The characteristic elevation of creatine phosphokinase in certain dystrophies may also be due to leakage through an altered membrane. However, a significant elevation of this serum enzyme may be found before appreciable muscular weakness is present, and in fact this enzyme is also increased in nonaffected carriers. Since histologic abnormalities may be found in muscle before weakness becomes apparent clinically, the pathogenetic significance of this enzyme elevation remains uncertain.

A variety of muscle disorders of presumed metabolic origin is occasionally encountered, but for the most part very little is known of their pathogenesis. Thus, endocrinopathies, and in particular thyrotoxicosis, may be accompanied by a chronic myopathy, and myopathy has been reported following the prolonged use of steroids. The exact biochemical and physiologic derangements underlying such muscle disorders have not been clarified.

In diffuse familial glycogenosis (glycogen storage disease of muscle, Pompe's disease), glycogen accumulates in abnormal amounts within skeletal muscle fibers, as well as within the liver, kidneys, myocardium, nerve cells and other structures. The muscular weakness is probably due at least in large part to mechanical disruption of the normal constituents of the muscle fibers by the masses of glycogen. A deficiency of α-glucosidase has recently been described in this disorder, though it has not yet been proved that glycogen can accumulate in significant quantities as a result of a lack of this enzyme alone.

Another variety of glycogen "storage" disease affecting only muscles is that known as McArdle's syndrome. This disorder is characterized clinically by the development of weakness, muscle stiffness, cramping pain and occasional myoglobulinuria with moderate exercise. A number of detailed biochemical investigations have demonstrated a specific hereditary absence of myophosphorylase in affected individuals. As a result of this deficiency, there is inadequate glycogenolysis under anaerobic conditions; failure to obtain a rise in blood lactic acid during exercise is considered characteristic of this disease.

Several other rare diseases of muscle have recently been described, such as central core disease and nemaline myopathy; though possibly metabolic in origin, the proper categorization of disorders such as these remains unsettled. A syndrome of myopathy with abnormal mitochondria and hypermetabolism has been reported by Luft et al. In this condition a defect in mitochondrial metabolism has been defined which consists primarily of a separation of the functions of respiration and oxidative phosphorylation, in contrast to the obligatory coupling of these two phenomena in normal mitochondria. The abnormal mitochondria are unable to adjust the respiratory rate according to their access to phosphate acceptor, and thus exhibit a nearly maximal rate of respiration even in the absence of a continuous supply of adenosine diphosphate. Clinical features associated with this metabolic derangement include excessive sweating, polydipsia, weight loss, muscular wasting and weakness, and an elevated basal metabolic rate in the presence of normal thyroid function.

In the experimental animal, abnormalities of muscle function may be produced by the inhibitor monoiodoacetic acid (the Lundsgaard effect), and frank necrosis of muscle follows the administration of the myotoxic agent plasmocid; destruction of muscle fibers may also be found in experimental deficiency of either vitamin E or vitamin C. The mechanisms underlying these experimental myopathies are not understood, and their relationship to naturally occurring disease in the human is obscure.

Electrodiagnosis in Muscle Disease

Electromyography is often a useful tool in distinguishing between disease of the motor neuron and intrinsic disease of the muscle itself. In a normal muscle, insertion of a needle electrode results in a transient burst of action potentials (the insertion action potentials) from the motor units. When complete relaxation is attained, no further electrical activity is seen. With voluntary contraction, action potentials recur, building up in both number and frequency as the strength of the contraction increases, eventually resulting in a confused "interference pattern" in which, with ordinary techniques, individual potentials can no longer be isolated. Normal action potentials, at least in the extremities, are of an amplitude of 0.2 to 2.0 millivolts, with a duration of 5 to 10 milliseconds.

Following denervation, and usually after

a time lag of approximately 3 weeks, a number of abnormalities appear in the electromyogram. Fibrillation potentials are seen; these are small rapid spikes lasting only 1 to 2 milliseconds, with an amplitude of less than 0.2 millivolt and a frequency of 2 to 10 per second. These fibrillation potentials are thought to represent the activity of individual fibers which are hypersensitive to acetylcholine consequent to interruption of the motor nerve. The normal insertion activity may be replaced by this fibrillation activity. Fasciculations, or spontaneous, often rhythmical, discharges of entire motor units, also occur with denervation, as do the so-called "positive sharp waves," defined as large amplitude (up to 4 or more millivolts), slow (up to 200 milliseconds), nonpropagated positive potentials. The interference pattern accompanying voluntary contraction becomes altered with denervation, due to a diminution in number of available motor units. Polyphasic potentials and giant potentials also may be seen under such circumstances. It is noteworthy that the site of disease of the motor neuron may significantly affect the "usual" denervation pattern. Fasciculations tend to be associated with disease of the anterior horns, such as amyotrophic lateral sclerosis, rather than with a more peripheral affection of the motor nerve, although this is not invariably true; similarly, reduction of the interference pattern and the presence of polyphasic and giant waves are more in keeping with anterior horn cell disease than with peripheral neuropathy. On the other hand, fibrillation activity tends to be more common with peripheral lesions than central ones.

Myopathy, or intrinsic disease of the muscles themselves, gives quite a different electromyographic picture from denervation. Fibrillations and fasciculations do not occur, there is no increase in insertion activity, and the interference pattern may be nearly normal. The primary change appears to be one of the action potentials themselves, the presence of rapid low amplitude potentials with an increase in polyphasic potentials being characteristic. The alterations in myotonia have previously been noted, and consist basically of postcontraction fibrillation activity.

Electromyographic techniques have largely supplanted other forms of electrodiagnosis, in particular the differential response to faradic and galvanic stimulation of the motor point (defined as the site of entry of a motor nerve into the muscle itself). Under normal circumstances, the application of a faradic current (short-duration) at this point initiates contraction, the nerve rather than the muscle being stimulated by this type of current. Following denervation, no reaction to faradic currents occurs. On the other hand, a rise in excitability to galvanic stimulation (long-duration current) occurs under the same circumstances (a phenomenon called the reaction of degeneration). This may be quantitated by plotting the so-called intensity-duration curve, which is derived from observations of the intensity of threshold stimuli at varying durations of current. An index of excitability may be calculated (the chronaxie) from a determination of the minimal voltage required to excite the muscle when applied for an indefinite period of time; the term rheobase is applied to this minimal voltage.

THE PERIPHERAL NEURON

Both clinically and physiologically, the peripheral neuron is best conceived as being composed of elements in the entire reflex arc —afferent and efferent roots, anterior horn cells and roots and the peripheral nerve itself. Clinically, there is good reason for this concept, since there are many conditions which primarily involve one part of the reflex arc to the exclusion of others, but which simultaneously affect other parts of it as well. There are forms of peripheral neuritis which affect the entire reflex arc, as in diabetes, arsenic poisoning, acute infectious polyneuritis, and triorthonesylphosphate intoxication. In herpes zoster, there is involvement not only of the posterior root ganglions and roots, but also of the posterior horns; and even in acute anterior poliomyelitis, posterior horn infiltration is found. Hence, diseases which affect the peripheral neuron must be regarded as not being confined to a single element of the reflex arc in the visualization of the correlation of clinical and pathological features.

Peripheral Nerve

The reaction of the peripheral nerve to disease varies under a variety of circumstances. This is best illustrated by its reaction in neuritis. There are forms of neuritis in which motor fibers are damaged almost exclusively and others in which damage of sensory fibers predominates. The reason for this selectivity is not clearly known, but there are helpful observations. In tourniquet experiments it was found that the sensation of touch was lost before that of pain, and pain before motion. Compression experiments indicate that the interruption of conduction is due to ischemia and not to compression. At the pressures employed by these investigators the failure of conduction was selective in that conduction of motor impulses failed before transmission of sensation. It was found further that after pressure of 2 hours or less, sensation recovered in a few hours, but that the loss of motor conduction lasted from 2 to 18 days. The disturbances in conduction are associated with changes in the myelin sheaths and axis cylinders which outlast the return of conductivity.

Following injection of cocaine around a nerve, as well as after compression and in asphyxia, there is a preferential block of sensation and movement. After blocking by cold and asphyxia, movement is affected early, but after injection of cocaine it is one of the last modalities to disappear. After blocking by cocaine the order of disappearance is cold, warmth, pain and touch. The smallest fibers are apparently blocked first. "In contrast to block produced by a local anesthetic, application of pressure over a limb of man leads to disappearance of sensations usually in the following order: touch, cold, warmth, pain" (Rose and Mountcastle). In animal experiments it seems clear that the failure of conduction does not follow an orderly sequence according to fiber size. It is also clear that the observation that one type of peripheral fiber is devoted to a single type of sensory modality has not been definitely proven.

It is difficult to correlate the evidence from compression experiments with the circumstances found in neuritis in the human. There is no good explanation for the predominant involvement of motor and/or sensory fibers in neuritis by toxic-infectious processes. The remarkable feature of neuritis is that so many diverse causes are capable of producing such similar pathological and clinical changes. Some conditions are associated with parenchymatous forms of neuritis, which may be found in vitamin deficiency, disturbance of pyruvate oxidation and of enzyme metabolism. In other conditions, such as diphtheria and lead poisoning, there develops a segmental type of neuritis; and in still others an interstitial form. The mechanism of their production remains to be determined in most instances.

The selection of specific types of fibers is illustrated by *tabes*, in which the long ascending fibers of the posterior columns are destroyed, probably in the Obersteiner-Redlich space, where the roots penetrate the meninges before entering the spinal cord.

There are forms of neuritis in which the posterior root area is most severely affected. This is reported to be the case in *acute infectious polyneuritis* (Guillain-Barré) in sensory radicular neuropathy.

Anterior Horn

The results of denervation are seen in interruption of the neuron at many parts of the reflex arc, but they are best illustrated by disease of the anterior horn cells. The main features, paralysis, atrophy and loss of reflexes, are found also in peripheral nerve disease, but in anterior horn cell disease there are also fasciculations, and in peripheral nerve disease pain and sensory disturbances are present.

Muscle *fasciculations* are characteristic of anterior horn cell disease. They have been reported in peripheral nerve disease, but in such instances there is associated disease of anterior horn cells, either by involvement of the entire reflex arc or by retrograde degeneration. The fasciculations seen in denervated muscle result from isolated contraction of one or more motor units. They can be seen by the naked eye and recorded in the electromyogram. *Fibrillation* occurs as a result of contraction of individual muscle fibers. *Fasciculation* develops from contraction of several motor units, causing twitching of the muscle which can be seen through the skin. Fibrillations develop after the fifth day of denervation, and are characterized by twitches in individual muscle fibers, accompanied by a small, rapid action potential, at intervals of 2 to 10 seconds. They can be detected as fibrillation potentials in the electromyogram.

The site of origin of the *fasciculations* seen in striated muscle in disease of the anterior horn cells in amyotrophic lateral sclerosis and in other diseases associated with anterior horn cell damage is uncertain. The best evidence appears to indicate that their origin is at the myoneural junction. They are unaffected by procaine injection into the muscle and by spinal anesthesia. They are increased by injection of neostigmine. They are eliminated by curare and denervation of the muscle. Fasciculations were found to decrease 4 days after denervation from section of the axillary nerve in humans with amyotrophic lateral sclerosis. They disappeared with disappearance of the peripheral nerve. Extreme dilutions of acetylcholine produce prolonged enhancement of fibrillation. From this it has been concluded that fibrillation is due to the effect of traces of acetylcholine normally present in tissue fluids, and that it is but an index of the increase in the excitability of the muscle fiber following denervation. Fibrillation action potentials have been reported in the electromyogram from the resting muscle of patients with progressive muscular dystrophy following prolonged strong contraction.

Sustained fibrillation potentials in the electromyogram appear relatively late after denervation, and do not appear to be present until about the third week.

Atrophy develops after muscle denervation, but little is known regarding its mechanism. "There is no evidence of any special trophic innervation of muscle, except that which is derived through continuity of the motor nerve fiber" (Adams, Denny-Brown and Pearson). Intact innervation appears to be the essential factor, and "anatomic continuity is more important in preventing atrophy than the receipt of nerve impulses" (Adams et al.). Section of the dorsal roots or the autonomic nerve supply induces no atrophy, but section of the ventral roots produces the same changes as seen in interruption of the peripheral nerve.

Muscle atrophy may develop at times in disease of the parietal lobe. It may develop slowly in progressive lesions such as tumor, or appear rapidly with vascular lesions in the course of a few days to a few weeks. The arm is usually affected, but the leg may be involved in some cases. The hand and shoulder girdle are affected early, and the atrophy of the small hand muscles may simulate closely that due to peripheral denervation. The affected muscles are flabby and soft, and the hand is of a feminine type. The muscles become hypotonic and flaccid. No fasciculations are seen. The skin becomes thin and soft and changes occur in the nails. Hemiplegia or hemiparesis is usually present but not always found. Hemianesthesia of varying degree is present in many, but not in all instances. There may be only loss of position sense in the digits or in some instances astereognosis. The type of atrophy described is associated with disease of the parietal lobe. No more specific localization can be made, though efforts have been made to correlate it with disease of the postcentral gyrus. The reason for the atrophy is not known. Of the many hypotheses which have been put forward, the trophic has most merit. This presupposes a cortical center which controls the nutrition of the peripheral musculature.

Atrophy in denervation has been ascribed to continued fibrillary activity, with resulting loss or depletion of glycogen and other substances normally stored in muscle. This view has been challenged, since similar degrees of atrophy were found in the first 10 days in denervated muscle and in inactivated muscle with intact nerve supply, though only the former had fibrillations. Repeated doses of quinidine and atropine abolish or inhibit fibrillary activity, but have no effect on retardation of loss of weight in denervated muscles. Drugs which increase fibrillary activity (neostigmine, acetylcholine, Mecholyl) do not affect the rate of atrophy. Electrical stimulation is effective in delaying atrophy if it is done under conditions which result in effective tension development in the muscle. Observations are available in disuse atrophy produced by application of a cast, by tenotomy or by isolation of muscles through intact spinal cord segments leaving the motor nerve intact. Atrophy after tenotomy and skeletal fixation is slower than that following denervation. Studies in disuse atrophy emphasize the fact that maintenance of muscle tension and activity are of the greatest importance in preventing muscle atrophy. "Much evidence has been found to indicate that atrophy results from the absence of tension development by denervated muscle" (Hines).

There is wide variation in the degree and the rate of development of atrophy in disease of the anterior horn cells and peripheral nerves in humans. The severity of the atrophy is probably related to the quantitative destruction of motor units at any point along the lower motor nerve pathway. It is safe to assume that the greater the atrophy, the larger is the number of motor units destroyed. Whether the same principle can be maintained for the rate of development of atrophy is impossible to say. Clinical observation records great variation in the rate of development of atrophy. It is strikingly rapid in some instances and slow in others.

Conflicting observations regarding the appearance of atrophy in lower animals are available. In monkeys denervation of the gastrocnemius-soleus muscles is followed by evident atrophy in 1 week, progressing over a period of 12 weeks to 88 per cent of the muscle bulk. After anterior hemisection of the gastrocnemius-soleus and anterior tibial groups, atrophy was evident in 10 to 20 days. Histological studies throw some light on the development of atrophy. After section of the muscular nerves or the motor nerve roots, the earliest changes are in the sarcolemmal nuclei and can be seen in the first week. In the first 2 weeks it is difficult to demonstrate reduction in size of individual muscle fibers, though there is beginning loss of weight and bulk of the whole muscle. There is perceptible decrease in the diameter of muscle fibers at the end of a month, at the end of 2 months the decrease in diameter of all the muscle fibers is far advanced, and after 4 months "it is progressing less rapidly" (Adams, Denny-Brown and Pearson). Chronic experiments in the Australian opossum show a 30 per cent weight loss in the first 29 days and a 50 to 60 per cent loss in 60 days. It progressed more slowly after this period, reaching a value of 60 to 80 per cent at 120 days and longer. Reduction in the size of the fibers was rapid in the first 30 days, and by 60 days it was about 70 per cent of normal.

Important changes take place in the chemistry during muscle atrophy. Calcium and chlorides increase and potassium decreases. Phosphorus decreases rapidly, especially phosphocreatine and adenosine triphosphate. Phosphocreatine and glycogen decline rapidly with the onset of fibrillation and creatine is progressively lost after the fifteenth day. The decrease in phosphate compounds, creatine and potassium is in proportion to muscle loss.

Pyramidal System

There are many features of the *anatomy* of the pyramidal system which have bearing on clinical problems. One of the most important is that not all the pyramidal fibers arise from the Betz cell area in the motor cortex (area 4). There are only 25,000 to 30,000 Betz cells, and about one million axons in the pyramidal tract in the medulla. The Betz cells comprise, therefore, only about 2 to 3 per cent of the fibers in the pyramidal tract. The other fibers are thought to arise from the smaller cells in area 4 as well as from the premotor area (area 6), and the postcentral cortex (areas 1, 3, 5). It is presumed that the pyramid in the medulla receives fibers from subcortical levels, since about half the fibers in this structure remain intact after hemispherectomy. A substantial portion of the pyramidal tract remains uncrossed (10 to 20 per cent). Direct synaptic connection with the anterior horn cells is achieved only by 10 to 15 per cent of fibers in the pyramidal tract; the majority end in relation to cells in the intermediate zone.

Spasticity. The spasticity which follows lesions of the pyramidal tract may be defined as an increased resistance to passive movement with clasp-knife character and with over-active reflexes. Section of the pyramids in the monkey results in flaccid paresis which persists throughout the period of postoperative recovery. Spasticity is regarded as an exaggeration of the spinal stretch reflexes. Impairment of central inhibitory influences which normally reduce spinal stretch reflexes is requisite for the appearance of spasticity. Release from such descending inhibitory activity (presumably channeled through, if not actually originating in, the descending reticular formation) permits hyperactivity of the *gamma* motor system of innervation of the muscle spindles. Heightened activity of this neural apparatus, particularly in antigravity muscles, results in those clinical phenomena such as increased reflex activity which we recognize as spasticity. Persistent spasticity follows ablation of area 6 in the monkey after area 4 has been ablated. Removal of the strip area (area 4S) in the transitional cortex between areas 4 and 6 in the monkey results in spasticity, which becomes more pronounced with the removal of areas 4 and 6. In monkeys and chimpanzees "the phenomenon of spasticity is an extrapyramidal release of cortical origin" (Fulton). Inhibitory extrapyramidal mechanisms are mediated through a corticobulbar-reticular projection. There appears to be a powerful inhibitory mechanism in the bulbar reticular formation, and inhibitory influences are mediated also from the striatum (caudate and putamen). Influences from the vestibular nuclei appear to contribute to spasticity. Not all the influences involved in spasticity are inhibitory. There appear to be excitatory mechanisms as well. These are propriospinal and brain stem, and even area 4 has been shown to have a tonic excitatory action on lower motor neurons. "Spasticity, then, is caused by a combination of inhibitory influences mostly from above and by the remaining activity of various excitatory mechanisms" (Chatfield).

Flaccidity. Hemiplegia in the human may result in flaccidity of the limbs, often transitory and followed by spasticity, but sometimes permanent. In monkeys and chimpanzees ablation of area 4 results in flaccidity which persists indefinitely in the proximal joints, but is succeeded sometime between the third and fifth week by spasticity in the wrist and digits. In the human, removal of areas 4 and 6 results in flaccid paralysis immediately after ablation, but is succeeded by spasticity in 4 to 16 days.

Atrophy. Atrophy develops in the chimpanzee after ablation of area 4, affecting particularly the distal muscles. Similar atrophy

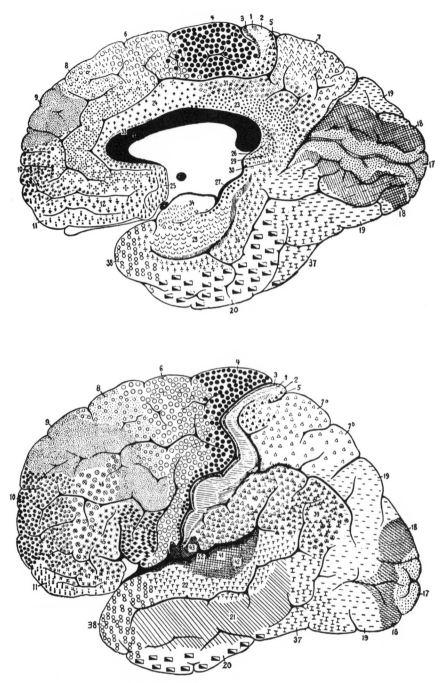

Figure 33–2. Map of the cytoarchitectonic areas of the human cerebral cortex. (After Brodmann, from Bailey, P., and von Bonin, G.: The Isocortex of Man. Urbana, University of Illinois Press, 1951.)

has been observed in the human, especially when there is simultaneous involvement of the postcentral gyrus. The mechanism is not definitely known and has been attributed to disuse or to a trophic influence.

The increased *reflexes* which develop after

lesions of the pyramidal tract may occur in the human without evidence of spasticity. Flaccid hemiplegia immediately following interruption of the pyramidal tract may be associated with unobtainable tendon reflexes. These are often followed by overactive reflexes despite flaccidity. In the monkey, after ablation of area 4, the reflexes are depressed. "Despite the flaccidity, however, the deep reflexes generally become moderately increased in all parts of the extremity" (Fulton). The Babinski sign is seen following a lesion restricted to area 4 and is characterized by simple extension of the toes. Fanning of the toes is also present when there is an associated lesion of area 6. The Babinski sign has been found after section of the pyramid in the medulla in monkeys and of the cerebral peduncle in man. Some investigators believe that the pyramidal tract may be involved without the presence of a Babinski sign, and that, conversely, a Babinski sign may be present without involvement of the pyramidal tract. The sign of Chaddock is also found after a lesion restricted to area 4.

Posture in Pyramidal Tract Lesions. It is a well-known clinical fact that not all the muscles are paralyzed on the opposite side of the body after a pyramidal tract lesion, and that not all those paralyzed are similarly affected. The arm is flexed and adducted and the hand and fingers flexed; the leg is extended. In spinal shock the limbs are flaccid and reflexes abolished, a state which is usually followed by spasticity and overactive reflexes. Extensor spasm predominates in transverse lesions of the spinal cord. The occurrence of extensor spasticity has been regarded as evidence of an incompletely divided spinal cord, but the mechanism has not been satisfactorily clarified. It is presumed that the integrity of the pyramidal tract or of the vestibulospinal tract is essential for the maintenance of extensor posture. Recent studies indicate that complete transection of the spinal cord may be associated with the development of extensor reflexes. In some instances, transection of the spinal cord is followed by *paraplegia-in-flexion.* In such states the legs are held in firm flexion, which is usually intermittent and, on external stimulation, such as throwing back the bed covers or pinprick of the lower limbs, is associated with strong flexor spasm. Paraplegia-in-flexion is also regarded as indicative of incomplete spinal cord section. Incomplete transection of the brain stem in humans, usually by tumor or demyelinating processes such as multiple sclerosis, may be associated with *decorticate rigidity.* The posture in such instances parallels that found in chronic decorticate animals, and is characterized by head extension, flexion of the arms and extension of the legs.

Extrapyramidal System

There is no general agreement on what constitutes the extrapyramidal system. In general it may be said to consist of the *basal ganglia* and the extrapyramidal portions of the cerebral cortex. Strictly speaking, it is composed of all the motor structures and neurons subserving motor functions, apart from those of the pyramidal tract. The basal ganglion portion is formed by the striatum (caudate and putamen), the pallidum and the substantia nigra. To these are often added the red nucleus, the corpus subthalamicum and the cerebellum. The cortical areas pertinent to the extrapyramidal system are not well defined. Many areas have been recorded from work on lower animals (areas 4, 4S, 6, 8, 9, 24, 2, 19, 3, 1, 5 and 7). The main cortical projections arise from the posterior part of the frontal lobe, especially from the motor area and the portion anterior to it. There appears to be an important connection between the striatum and the premotor cortex.

Disease of the extrapyramidal system is characterized by disturbance of movement, by decreased movement as seen in paralysis agitans, and by involuntary movements such as tremor, chorea, athetosis and dystonia found in a variety of clinical conditions associated with disease of this system.

Rigidity. Paralysis agitans is associated with disturbance of muscle tone referred to as rigidity, which differs from the spasticity of pyramidal tract disease in the absence of the clasp-knife reaction and the presence of plastic resistance to passive movement and the cogwheel phenomenon. It involves both flexors and extensors. The rigidity of paralysis agitans appears to be of myotatic origin, and is dependent on the integrity of posterior roots and proprioceptive nerve endings in muscle. The electromyogram in rigidity, unlike that in spasticity, reveals action potentials and basic activity in resting muscle. Voluntary movement in rigidity is characterized by synchronization of impulses, and increased myotatic reflexes, and increased activity in protagonists and antagonists. Rigidity is found also in other forms of extrapyramidal disease—hepatolenticular degeneration, dystonia musculorum deformans.

Chorea and Athetosis. The pathological studies of chorea indicate that this symptom may be associated with lesions in more than a single area. The evidence is conflicting. Supporters of the striatal origin of chorea find their strongest support in cases of Huntington's chorea, in which disease of the striatum is constant and pronounced. Further support is found in the isolated cases of Sydenham's chorea and of chorea gravidarum which have revealed evidence of infectious process in the striatum. Opposed to these are the many instances of vascular softenings involving the striatum, without clinical evidence of chorea.

Severe hemichorea or hemiballismus is found in vascular lesions, as well as in reported instances of tuberculoma and metastatic carcinoma, involving the contralateral corpus subthalamicum or its immediate vicinity. Hemiballismus has been described in rare cases without apparent involvement of the corpus subthalamicum. Choreiform movements have also been reported with lesions of the thalamus.

Experimental studies of the basal ganglia have been, on the whole, unrewarding. Striate lesions have produced no disturbance of function. Lesions in the subthalamus of primates have produced involuntary movements of the opposite side of the body and these have been likened to hemiballismus. Stimulation experiments of the striatum have produced fleeting involuntary movements. Lesions of the basal ganglia in chimpanzees produce irregular, jerking, involuntary movements which disappear after a few days. Hyperkinesia can be produced in the monkey consistently by localized lesions in the corpus subthalamicum, provided 20 per cent of the volume of the nucleus is destroyed, and the integrity of the pallidum and the pallidofugal fibers is preserved. Preservation of the latter is important. Conversely, subthalamic hyperkinesia can be improved or abolished contralaterally in the monkey by lesions destroying the pallidum. Electromyographic studies of chorea and athetosis reveal no action potentials in the resting phase, but show asynchronization of motor impulses during activity.

The physiological basis of *athetosis* and *dystonia* is not known. Even the pathological background is not clear, particularly in the case of the dystonias. In athetosis lesions have been described in the striatum, the thalamus and the pallidum. In congenital double athetosis there is usually found a marbled appearance of the striatum (status marmoratus) due to an increased number of medullated fibers. In some instances there is found status dysmyelinisatus of the striatum, associated with a decrease in the number of medullated fibers.

Chorea and athetosis disappear from the affected limbs after the development of hemiplegia. There has been no adequate explana-tion for the disappearance of involuntary movements in sleep.

It has been suggested that the involuntary movements of athetosis are due to nerve impulses from the pyramidal tract and that these impulses come by way of the parapyramidal fibers in areas 4 and 6, passing to subcortical centers and thence to the anterior columns of the spinal cord by way of secondary neurons.

Tremor. Tremor is a disabling symptom, not only in paralysis agitans, but in hepato-lenticular degeneration and in other extra-pyramidal diseases. Its anatomical basis in paralysis agitans is not firmly established, but it is said to be due to lesions in the pallidum and/or substantia nigra. Hemiplegia has been reported to abolish the tremor of paralysis agitans. Electromyograms of muscles with tremor reveal rhythmic bursts of motor-unit discharges.

Experimental efforts to produce tremor by lesions of the basal ganglia, the subthalamic nucleus or substantia nigra have been unsuccessful. Intention tremor can be produced consistently by lesions in the cerebellum or its efferent pathways. In monkeys, small electrolytic lesions placed in the lateral portion of the reticular formation of the mesencephalic tegmentum between the red nucleus and the substantia nigra result in the development of a spontaneous tremor at rest. Lesions restricted to the mesencephalic reticular formation without injury to the superior cerebellar peduncle are reported to yield a simple tremor. The mechanism of these various tremors remains to be clarified.

Stimulation of the pallidum in the human "is able to induce a typical tremor or to increase the amplitude of an existing tremor which effect continues for several seconds after cessation of the stimulation" (Spiegel and Wycis). The same authors report that "tremor could be produced by stimulation of the midbrain tegmentum not only in animals but also in a Parkinson patient."

Operations for the relief of the symptoms of paralysis agitans provide some information regarding the source of origin of the tremor. Tremor has been abolished by removal of the precentral cortex. It has been reported to be abolished, not always permanently, by destruction of the opposite pallidum in humans by the injection of alcohol and procaine. It has also been abolished by destruction of the opposite ansa lenticularis and by destruction of the opposite thalamus, in particular the ventrolateral nucleus. The beneficial effects on tremor and rigidity in thalamic operations are attributed to interruption of cerebellothalamic and other afferent systems to the thalamus, including pallidothalamic and rubrothalamic fibers. Relief of tremor by ansotomy has been explained by interruption of pallidofugal facilitating impulses to lower centers.

The Sensory System

For clinical purposes disturbances of sensation may affect the superficial sensations (touch, pain, heat, cold) or the deep, or proprioceptive, sensations (position, muscle sense), either separately or together. These may be affected at any level of the nervous system, from the periphery to the cerebral cortex, in varying degree.

Specificity of Sensory Receptors

The skin and subcutaneous structures contain receptors of many types (Meissner's corpuscles, Merkel's disks, Krause's end-bulbs, Ruffini's corpuscles). It has been generally accepted that the sensory receptors give rise to a specific sensation and to no other, regardless of the nature of the stimulus. Thus, pain, heat and cold spots have been identified; stimulation of a cold spot by warmth produces a sensation of cold. The concept of specificity has been challenged by the recent observations that only naked nerve terminals and basket endings around the base of the hairs have been found in certain hair-bearing areas of the skin, although they are sensitive to all forms of sensation. Similar observations were made in the cornea and pinna. On the basis of these observations it has been suggested that touch and pain are felt when a small number of fibers discharge simultaneously, the lowest frequency giving rise to touch, the highest to sharp pain. Cold is felt when endings in the superficial skin layer discharge; warmth is felt when the deep endings discharge. These observations favor a lack of specificity of receptors, the type of sensation experienced representing difference in the pattern of stimulation. Despite these observations there appears to be good evidence for specific tactile and thermal receptors, as well as evidence that fiber size may be related to specific receptors.

Of clinical importance is the relationship between the types of fiber in the *compound action potential* and disorders of the peripheral nerve. The fastest fibers are in the A group, the intermediate in the B group, and the smallest, most poorly myelinated and slowest in conduction in the C group. Intimate correlation between fiber size and action potential and clinical deficits is hard to determine. It has been shown that A fibers, which have to do with motion and proprioception, are affected early in anoxia, while the C fibers carrying pain are affected later. In procaine blocking, on the other hand, the C fibers are affected early.

Posterior Column System

The disturbance of movement of limbs and trunk in disease of the posterior column system, referred to as *ataxia*, is dependent upon impairment or loss of proprioception (position and muscle sense) in the joints. Generally speaking, the severity of the ataxia parallels the loss of proprioception from joints. The difficulty in gauging direction in ataxia is well explained by the loss of joint sense. The same holds true of the tremor which is seen in the course of disease of the posterior columns. This is in reality a tremor associated with the irregular movement of ataxia and is similarly dependent on impairment or loss of proprioception. As in the case of cerebellar disease, there may be truncal but no limb involvement, but this may be in part an expression of the cause of the posterior column disease. In tabes dorsalis both limbs and trunk are usually affected, whereas in the subacute combined degeneration of pernicious anemia, limb and trunk ataxia may be dissociated.

Two types of receptors have been found in the knee joint. The most common are the spray-type endings, similar to the Ruffini receptors in the skin. They are found in the connective tissue capsule of the joint, but not in the synovial membrane, and they are supplied by myelinated fibers (7 to 10 microns). They respond at low threshold by a slowly adapting process, signaling the steady position of the joint and the direction, rate and extent of joint movement. A second type of receptor resembles the Golgi tendon organ and is found in the ligaments of the joint. It has properties similar to the spray-type receptor. Proprioception in the knee joint appears to be carried out by one type of ending which discharges continuously at a fixed position and another which discharges temporarily during any change in position.

There is good evidence that the receptors in and around the joints project into the posterior column (lemniscal) system. Mechanical stimulation of the joint tissues and stimulation of articular nerves evoke responses in the ventral thalamus and the somatic sensory cortex. On the other hand, the stretch receptors of muscle do not inform of joint position, and the stretch afferents from muscle do not project in the posterior column system, but by the column of Clarke into the cerebellum.

Despite the relationship between ataxia and impairment of joint and muscle sense, position sense disturbance may be found without evidences of ataxia by clinical examination. It is not an uncommon experience to find impairment of position sense of the toes in subacute combined degeneration or multiple sclerosis without evidence of ataxia.

The impairment or loss of position sense may be associated with loss of *vibration sense,* but there is often a dissociation of the two modalities of sensation in posterior column disease. Vibration sense may be lost without involvement of position sense, but it is unusual to find severe position sense loss without simultaneous loss of vibration. There is much dispute concerning the loss of vibration sense in lesions involving the sensory cortex. It is said that pure cortical lesions are characterized by loss only of position sense.

Vibration sensation appears to result from repetitive stimulation of touch receptors in the skin and deep receptors in the tissue. Tactile sensation is conveyed not only in the trigeminal pathways but in the anterolateral columns as well. There appears to be no adequate explanation for the loss of vibration sense in lesions of the posterior columns of the spinal cord (multiple sclerosis, subacute combined degeneration, syringomyelia) with intact touch and pressure sensations in the periphery.

The *hypotonia* which is found in some diseases of the posterior columns (tabes dorsalis) is probably the result of associated disease of the posterior roots rather than of the posterior columns.

Localization of fibers is to be found at all levels of the posterior column-lemniscal system. In the spinal cord the leg, trunk and arm fibers are separate, and there is evidence that this lamination is maintained within the median lemniscus and the ventrolateral thalamus. Pressure upon the spinal cord in the cervical region is therefore associated not infrequently with loss of position sense in the toes without involvement of the hand or arm. In the brain stem and thalamus this is not likely to occur, but loss of position sense in the digits of the hand or foot is quite consistent with cortical lesions. In the crural monoplegia associated with a tumor of the parasagittal region, usually a meningioma, there is not only impairment of leg and foot movement and other evidences of pyramidal tract disease, but also impairment or loss of position of the great toe.

Spinothalamic System

Through the spinothalamic system are conveyed pain and temperature fibers and probably also fibers subserving touch sensation. The evidence for tactile fibers within this system is not conclusive, but some observations indicate that after anterolateral cordotomy in the human there is an increase in threshold for tactile stimuli and a decrease in the number of sensory spots.

At the *peripheral nerve* level, pain and temperature, as well as touch, are markedly affected. Touch is more likely to be lost than either pain or temperature because of overlap from adjacent nerves. As has been pointed out, there is often considerable dissociation in peripheral nerve disease between motor and sensory involvement, and in the degree of implication of separate sensory modalities. The reasons for this have been discussed under Peripheral Neuron.

Although there is nothing specific about the spontaneous pain associated with peripheral nerve disease, one type of pain is of particular significance. This is the type referred to as *causalgia,* a pain which is the aftermath of peripheral nerve injury. Though it is often a burning pain, it is not always so, and this feature may be overemphasized at the expense of its post-traumatic nature. The mechanism of the pain is not clear. Several possibilities have been suggested: (1) Since sympathectomy relieves the pain, it has been suggested that the sympathetic fibers contain afferents. It is impossible, however, to demonstrate sensory changes following sympathectomy. (2) There is an artificial synapse between sympathetic and sensory fibers at the site of the nerve lesions, causing short-circuiting. Resection of the damaged nerve segment fails to relieve the causalgia. It is believed, however, that, because of the short-circuiting, impulses pass centrally and distally and that antidromic impulses cause the release of a histamine-like substance at the periphery which either lowers the threshold of sensory stimulation or causes pain impulses in the sensory fibers which summate with impulses arising directly at the artificial synapse.

The pain is refractory to all treatment except blocking or interrupting the sympathetic nerve supply to the injured limb.

Sensory disturbances involving the *posterior roots* are characterized by decrease or loss of touch and pain sensations. These are difficult to detect by ordinary clinical methods unless more than one root is affected because of the extensive overlap of adjacent posterior root zones. In compressing lesions, hyperesthesia is often present, and is always a feature of herpes zoster. The increase of pain on cough and strain which is characteristic of posterior root disease is unfortunately not always present.

Within the spinal cord, pain and temperature sensations may be lost in disease involving the *posterior horn* before its decussation. In such instances, usually associated with a linear cyst due to syringomyelia, the sensory loss is ipsilateral.

Segmental disorders of the pain and temperature fibers seen in the commissural syndrome associated with syringomyelia or other diseases of the central grey matter offer no difficulties. There are difficult problems, however, associated with involvement of the spinothalamic pathways within the spinal cord after their decussation and the formation of the spinothalamic tracts.

The pain and temperature fibers in the spinal cord are projected into the spinal cord so that the caudal portions of the body lie lateral to the oral portions at any level of the cord. Extramedullary compression tends to involve the sacral segments first and other segments later. The opposite is true of intramedullary processes (sacral sparing). The same arrangement holds true in the medulla, pons, midbrain and in the thalamus. Despite the topical arrangement, there seems to be considerable intermingling of fibers from different dermatome segments. The evidence for this lies primarily in the observation that superficial or shallow sections of the spinothalamic tract produce only transitory loss of pain and temperature of higher segmental levels and that deep section is necessary to produce lasting loss of sensation. Pain and temperature sensations are carried in separate pathways in the spinal cord, but it is difficult to produce a differential disturbance of sensation either by selective section or spontaneously by disease.

Pain and temperature sensations are usually equally affected in tract lesions involving the spinal cord and brain stem. Because of the intermingling of fibers in the tract, the level of analgesia is usually below the level of compression in spinal cord tumor or other compressive lesions, the area of absolute sensory loss covering one or two segments. The type of spinothalamic tract disturbance in the brain stem differs in no way from that in the spinal cord. It is localized by the presence of other appropriate segmental signs.

The segmental arrangement of pain and temperature fibers is illustrated in sensory disturbances involving the face when the descending root of the trigeminal nerve is affected. The sensory disturbance is usually described as of a concentric or onion-peel type, the outermost segments representing pontine levels and the innermost, cervical levels. This description has been challenged by some investigators.

In lesions of the *thalamus* the loss of pain and temperature sensation is usually absolute and involves the entire half of the body, including the head and face. There may also be typical thalamic pain characterized by a raised pain threshold and a spreading quality, as well as by its extremely unpleasant character. Pain of this nature has been described elsewhere along the spinothalamic tract.

Pain and temperature sensations are not affected in lesions of the somatic *sensory cortex*. Stimulation of the sensory cortex rarely causes frank pain, but severe pain from tumors or cysts involving the sensory cortex has been observed on rare occasions. Destructive lesions involving the sensory cortex may result in hypalgesia, but this is never pronounced. *Asymbolia for pain (pain asymbolia)* is quite the opposite of the organic pain deficits, since it is characterized by absence of the psychic reaction to pain without organic loss of pain sensation. The localization of this phenomenon has been variously ascribed to the supramarginal gyrus, the inferior parietal region and also to no specific localization but to a defect in the premorbid personality, characterized by a tendency to withdraw and the avoidance of stress.

Vestibular System

The *vestibular system* is only one of a number of structures concerned with the maintenance of equilibrium. It is probably the most important of the structures responsible for maintenance of posture, the others including (1) the retina and the proprioceptors in ocular muscles, (2) proprioceptors from the muscles and joints and (3) exteroceptors of the skin. The vestibular system consists of the labyrinths, the vestibular nerve, the vestibular nuclei in the brain stem, and their central projections in the brain stem and in the cerebral cortex.

The central connections of the vestibular apparatus are intricate and imperfectly

known. In brief, impulses pass from the labyrinth via the vestibular nerve to the vestibular
nuclei. These consist of a lateral (Deiter)
nucleus, a medial (Schwalbe) nucleus, a
superior (Bechterew) nucleus and a descending, or spinal (Roller), nucleus, which form
a single functioning unit. The vestibular nuclei of each side are connected with one another. Some of the vestibular impulses pass
directly to the cerebellum. Fibers from the
medial and superior vestibular nuclei form
the medial longitudinal fasciculus (posterior
longitudinal bundle), which terminates in the
nuclei of the oculomotor nerves of the same
and opposite sides. Fibers from the vestibular
apparatus reach the cerebral cortex. Descending fibers are conveyed to the anterior horn
cells by the vestibulospinal tract from the
lateral vestibular nucleus. There are also descending fibers from the reticulospinal tract
by way of rich connections between the vestibular nuclei and the reticular formation.
The medial longitudinal fasciculus also contributes descending fibers.

Vertigo

Vertigo is the outstanding feature of disease of the vestibular system, which may be
affected anywhere from the periphery to
the cerebral cortex. The term should be restricted to those instances in which there is
a sense of movement either of the patient or
his environment. This movement sense is often
one of rotation, but it may be described as
an up-and-down movement or as one in which
the floor comes up to meet the subject, or in
other dramatic terms.

The *mechanism* of production of vertigo
varies and may involve either peripheral or
central pathways. In disease involving the
labyrinth, many mechanisms are responsible
for vertigo. In Meniere's disease the vertigo
is due to hydrops of the labyrinth, but neither
the cause of the hydrops nor the mechanism
of production of the vertigo is clear. The
best evidence indicates that the vertigo in
hydrops of the labyrinth results from increased endolymphatic pressure which stimulates the sensory epithelium. Some doubt is
cast upon this concept by the fact that vertigo
is not an invariable concomitant of brain
tumors and of other conditions in which the
cerebrospinal fluid pressure is increased and
fluctuating, with parallel increases and fluctuations in the endolymph. In other forms of
labyrinthine disease vertigo may result from
stimulation of the sensory endings due to inflammation, hemorrhage (trauma), toxic fac-

tors (drugs) and tumors. Circulatory mechanisms are probably a factor in some instances
of labyrinthine vertigo. Because of the distribution of the internal auditory artery, there
appears to be evidence for terminal artery
supply of both branches of the internal auditory artery, which permits interference with
circulation by embolus, spasm or vascular
insufficiency. Vertigo due to involvement of
the *vestibular nerve* is not so frequent as that
due to involvement of the labyrinth. It may
occur in cerebellopontine angle tumor, usually as a late symptom, and in fractures involving the base of the skull. Inflammation
of this nerve is not common, but it has been
reported in central nervous system syphilis
and in vestibular neuronitis which involves
the vestibular neurons either in Scarpa's ganglion or more centrally. Severe vertigo may
result from disease involving the *vestibular
nuclei* in the medulla. This occurs most often
from vascular occlusion (posterior inferior
cerebellar artery) and multiple sclerosis. It
may result however from any type of disorder
in this area. A wide variety of causes and
mechanisms involving the ascending pathways in the brain stem (medial longitudinal
fasciculus, reticular formation) may be associated with vertigo. In disease of the *cerebellum* vertigo develops with involvement of
the connections with the flocculo-nodular
lobe, either by direct implication or by pressure in association with cerebellar tumors.
It is seen frequently in disease involving the
cerebrum, more often with vascular disease
than with tumor.

The vertigo of *labyrinthine disease* is usually rapid in onset, sometimes as in Meniere's
disease, and associated with prodromes which
provide warning of the attack. It occurs in
paroxysms or episodes, varying in duration
from minutes to 2 or 3 days. Cochlear symptoms are usually present. These consist of
tinnitus and/or varying degrees of hearing
impairment. In contrast to this, the vertigo
of central nervous system disease is not paroxysmal, is more prolonged, and, because of
the bilateral distribution of the ascending
acoustic pathways, is not associated with hearing loss. There are notable exceptions to this
generalization, but they are found in areas
which may be regarded physiologically as
parts of the peripheral mechanism—the vestibular nerve and the vestibular nuclei in
the medulla. Auditory symptoms are usually
present in disease involving the vestibular
nerve, especially tumor and trauma, since the
vestibular and cochlear fibers are carried in

the auditory nerve and lie in close conjunction with one another. Severe, acute vertigo may occur with disease of the vestibular nuclei, simulating that of labyrinthine vertigo, especially in vascular disease, but it is not episodic, except in cases of multiple sclerosis or encephalitis. *Recurrent vertigo* may develop in association with brain stem disease above the level of the vestibular nuclei, especially in association with vascular disease, but it is not so severe as in labyrinthine vertigo, it does not have its paroxysmal features, and hearing impairment is not found.

Postural Vertigo. Vertigo occurs frequently with change of posture. The history of precipitation of dizziness is encountered frequently in vertigo of labyrinthine and central origin. On rare occasions, a specific type of postural vertigo is encountered in the Bruns syndrome, and has special significance. It is characterized by (1) severe vertigo and vomiting, sometimes with loss of consciousness, on change of posture of the head. It may be induced by any movement—lateral, rotation, flexion or extension, (2) freedom from symptoms between attacks, induced by change of posture, and (3) fixation of the anterior or lateral flexion in order to avoid precipitation of attacks. The syndrome is almost always associated with a cyst or tumor of the fourth or third ventricle. It has been reported in multiple sclerosis.

The *loss of consciousness* encountered in severe vertigo is usually seen in instances of Meniere's disease. It is syncopal in character.

The *autonomic symptoms*—nausea, vomiting, sweating, pallor, tachycardia, fear and anxiety—occur with surprising irregularity in patients with vertigo. Their absence, even in some instances of severe vertigo, is striking. Their presence or absence provides no reliable information regarding the localization of the mechanism responsible for the vertigo. It is possible that their presence may be roughly correlated with the location and severity of the underlying cause. Nausea, vomiting and accompanying autonomic symptoms are usually found in Meniere's disease and in occlusion of the posterior inferior cerebellar artery, but are often absent in brain stem vertigo.

Vertiginous Epilepsy. Vertigo is a common aura in epilepsy. It may occur as an epileptic seizure, sometimes as paroxysmal vertigo. It is usually but not always associated with loss of consciousness, but when this is lacking there is often amnesia for the attack. In the vertigo associated with epilepsy, there is no consecutive giddiness or dizziness. The vertigo is over as soon as the attack is completed, without after-discharge, and in this respect it differs from vertigo due to vestibular disorders. Discharges may be seen in one or both temporal lobes in the electroencephalogram. The epileptogenic zone in patients with vertigo is found in the posterior-superior portions of the temporal lobe and in the temporo-parietal border regions, but vertigo may be produced also by stimulation of the superior parietal cortex. Electrical stimulation of the vestibular nerve in animals reveals that the receiving area in the cerebral cortex lies in the anterior ectosylvian gyrus and the posterior bank of the anterior suprasylvian gyrus. The projection is chiefly contralateral, but stimulation of the ipsilateral nerve activates a part of the same region.

Nystagmus

Except for the loss of balance and the inconstant autonomic symptoms in the course of an acute attack, nystagmus is the only objective sign of disease involving the vestibular system.

The localizing value of nystagmus is difficult to assess. The chief differentiation lies almost exclusively, except in the case of ataxic nystagmus, between a peripheral (labyrinthine) and central mechanism and cause. Spontaneous nystagmus is found in labyrinthine and brain stem disease. It is rare in cerebral disease. In labyrinthine disease the nystagmus subsides after a few weeks because of central compensation. If it is persistent, the probabilities favor a central nervous system localization at some point in the brain stem. The precise localization must be made on the basis of associated symptoms and signs.

The *nature* of the nystagmus sometimes provides valuable information. The nystagmus of labyrinthine disease is said to be horizontal-rotatory in character, but the rotatory component is often lacking in spontaneous nystagmus; and, when present, it is not possible to determine that the underlying process is in the labyrinth on the basis of the nystagmus alone. Horizontal nystagmus has no precise localizing value in itself. When it is bilateral it is more likely the result of central brain stem mechanisms, but unilateral horizontal nystagmus may be found in both labyrinthine and central disorders. *Monocular nystagmus* is seen in the syndrome of internuclear ophthalmoplegia, in which there is paralysis of the internal rectus muscle on attempted conjugate lateral gaze, with preservation of convergence. Horizontal nystagmus is often, but not always, present, usually exclusively in the abducting eye; if it is present in both eyes it is much more marked in the abducting eye. Vertical divergence of the eyes (skew deviation) is often present. The syndrome results from a lesion of the medial longitudinal fasciculus, involving the anterior part of this bundle. It has been reproduced experimentally in the monkey by a lesion of the medial longitudinal fasciculus at the level of the facial colliculi. The syndrome of internuclear ophthalmoplegia with monocular nystagmus is found usually, but not exclusively, in multiple sclerosis. Unilateral cases are regarded as being of vascular origin. *Ataxic nystagmus* is probably the same as monocular nystagmus. In this type of nystagmus there is weakness of the internal rectus on lateral conjugate gaze, with coarse nystagmus of the abducting eye. The symptom is found in multiple sclerosis.

Vertical nystagmus, often referred to as neurological nystagmus, is seen usually on upward gaze, but may be present also on downward gaze. It is fine and usually sustained. It is seen usually in diseases involving the vestibular pathways in the brain stem, but it may be found in labyrinthine disease. *Positional nystagmus* associated with vertigo may occur with the head in some positions. It is induced as follows: The patient sits on a table with the head turned to one side and the gaze fixed on the examiner's forehead. The examiner grasps the patient's head between his hands and pushes him back briskly into the supine position with the head 30 degrees below the level of the couch, and rotated 30 to 45 degrees to one side. If nystagmus occurs, the head is held in this position for 30 seconds, after which the patient is brought upright, and the test is repeated with the head turned to the opposite side. In the *fatigable type,* the nystagmus appears after a latency of 2 to 10 seconds and subsides in 5 to 30 seconds. In the *nonfatigable type* the nystagmus appears without latency, as soon as the head is put in the critical position, and persists as long as this position is maintained. The fatigable type is associated with lesions of the utricle or saccule, and the nonfatigable type with central lesions. The precise localization of the central lesion is not known.

Cerebellum

Though the cerebellum has been investigated extensively in the experimental animal, the application to human disorders involving this structure is limited. The syndrome of the *flocculo-nodular lobe* in the monkey is quite clearly defined. Anatomically, this complex is closely associated with vestibular function, and it receives and sends out fibers to the vestibular nuclei. Removal of the nodulus, flocculus and uvula produces disturbance in posture and equilibrium without loss of motor power, with resulting difficulty in walking and standing and inability to run. In the human, truncal incoordination without involvement of the limbs is not infrequently seen. Such patients perform well while lying down and have no disturbance of limb movement or coordination. When they attempt to walk and stand, the truncal incoordination becomes clearly apparent. The syndrome is seen in the midline tumors of childhood, particularly the medulloblastomas, which are said to arise in the nodulus in the inferior vermis. Since these tumors often spread into an adjacent cerebellar hemisphere or peduncle or crowd the fourth ventricle, the syndrome may not be seen in its pure form, except in the early stages of development.

The syndrome of the *neocerebellum* or of the cerebellar hemispheres is well defined in the human, but there are important differences from the syndrome which is elicited in lower animals. The symptoms are more pronounced in the human and, in lower animals, tend to vary from one species to another. They are more enduring in chimpanzees than in monkeys. The outstanding features of cerebellar disease in man are dyssynergia and tremor and hypotonia; hypotonia is, as a rule, less striking than the other symptoms.

The mechanism of the decomposition of movement, or *dyssynergia,* seen in cerebellar disease is not definitely known. The associated hypotonia may contribute to the difficulty. Dyssynergia has been regarded as probably the result of loss of postural tone in the muscles, the irregular movements representing an effort on the part of the cerebellar patient to overcome the lack of tone by voluntary efforts. Or there may be "failure of the cerebellum to adjust the background of inhibition and facilitation necessary at various levels of the nervous system for smooth coordinated movement" (Marshall).

Tremor is a striking feature of disease of the neocerebellum. It is an intention or volitional tremor, which is not present at rest and occurs only on voluntary movement. It is usually detected at the end of a purposive movement, but it varies in degree from a few coarse movements to severe and intense tremor. Intention tremor may occur in any form of disease involving the cerebellum, in tumor, multiple sclerosis, parenchymatous cerebellar degeneration and in other forms. It is found in other disorders, however, in which there is no definite evidence of cerebellar disease clinically, but in which there may be disturbance of cerebellar function. It is seen at times in paralysis agitans, usually in conjunction with the typical static tremor. It is also seen in senile tremor, in hereditary tremor and in idiopathic tremor. In none of these can it be said that cerebellar disease is present on clinical examination, but typical intention tremor of the cerebellar type is characteristic of them.

Intention tremor of the cerebellar type is seen in disease involving the cerebellar hemispheres (neocerebellum). It is more pronounced in disease which implicates the cerebellar nuclei, especially the dentate nucleus. It is quite severe in *Benedikt's syndrome*, which involves the superior cerebellar peduncle (brachium conjunctivum), and in occlusion of the superior cerebellar artery with involvement of the superior cerebellar peduncle. In primates, involvement of the dentate and emboliform nuclei causes ipsilateral tremor during voluntary and involuntary activity. Recovery is never complete when the nuclei are affected. On the other hand, it is not striking in lesions of the spinocerebellar pathways which implicate the arm fibers, and it is not found in disease of the inferior cerebellar peduncle (corpus restiforme). Occlusion of the posterior inferior cerebellar artery, with softening in the inferior cerebellar peduncle, causes dyssynergia, but tremor is not usually present. Tremor of the upper or lower limbs is not seen after section of the spinocerebellar pathways in anterolateral chordotomy.

The genesis of cerebellar tremor is not known. It is said to result from a loss of postural control by the cerebellum, but its actual basis has not been clarified. It has been attributed also to the loss of the steadying effect which antagonists give to voluntary movements. It is also attributed to irregularities in the rate of muscle contraction. There is good evidence to indicate that the motor cortex (areas 4 and 6a) is intimately involved in the mechanism of tremor. Removal of these areas after contralateral section of the cerebellar peduncles abolishes the tremor. On the other hand, removal of area 6a in a hemide-

cerebellate preparation is followed by marked accentuation of cerebellar signs. The intention tremor of cerebellar disease appears, then, to represent imperfect compensation of the cerebral cortex. Little is known regarding the basis of senile tremor. Changes have been observed in the striatum in tremor of this type, but nothing of significance was found in the cerebellum.

Under rare circumstances, patients with subtentorial tumors may develop *cerebellar fits* or seizures. These are tonic postural seizures with sudden onset of body rigidity and with extension of the arms and legs. The posture resembles that of decerebrate rigidity. The seizures are usually associated with loss of consciousness, which last usually for a few minutes, but may last for a few hours. The seizures have nothing to do with the cerebellum itself, since stimulation of the cerebellum has never produced a typical seizure. The cerebellar seizures result from activity within the brainstem, "a sudden neuronal discharge within the upper pons or lower midbrain" (Penfield and Jasper), or they are said to "represent functional decerebration near the junction between the pons and medulla" (Fulton).

Special Senses

Olfaction

Relatively little is known concerning disordered function in the olfactory system. The specialized sensory ganglia, the olfactory bulbs, project via the olfactory tracts and the medial and lateral olfactory striae upon the anterior perforated space, amygdala, and prepyriform and periamygdalar areas. No secondary olfactory projections are recognized in man; the hippocampal complex and other portions of the primitive limbic system which are anatomically related to the olfactory system appear to have lost any recognizable olfactory function in the course of evolution, and to have acquired a significant role in behavioral regulation.

Anosmia, or loss of smell, results from interruption of the distal portions of the olfactory apparatus, as by compression of the olfactory tract by a subfrontal meningioma. A loss of smell rarely if ever occurs on the basis of a central lesion. However, olfactory hallucinations have long been recognized as a component of so-called uncinate fits, i.e., focal seizures initiated in the anterior and medial portions of the temporal lobe or insula, and characterized by hallucinations of smell and taste associated with a "dreamy state."

Vision

The visual apparatus may be grossly subdivided into three distinct anatomic regions: the retina, the conducting pathways, and the primary receptive and associative portions of the cerebral cortex. Since the specific nature of visual dysfunction under any given set of circumstances depends to a large extent upon the site of involvement, these dysfunctions may be suitably considered according to these morphologic headings.

The Retina. The receptor cells of the retina, the rods and cones, are photosensitive elements of differential sensitivity and distribution. Cones are the exclusive receptors at the macula, subserve central and color vision, and function particularly under conditions of good illumination; they diminish in number as the periphery of the retina is approached. On the other hand, rods are distributed everywhere but at the macula, subserve peripheral and achromatic vision, and function especially when illumination is poor. Relatively little is known of the photochemical reactions by which light initiates activity of the receptor cells; pigments have been described in both types of elements (visual purple in the rods, visual violet in the cones) which are undoubtedly concerned in this conversion of energy. At least one abnormality of vision, *night blindness,* appears directly related to such pigments. The visual purple, or rhodopsin, of the rods is broken down by exposure to light into visual yellow (retinene) and a protein, a process which is reversed in darkness; this breakdown of rhodopsin may be the event setting off the nerve impulse. Retinene is an aldehyde of vitamin A and, with continued exposure to light, becomes broken down to vitamin A itself. A shortage of vitamin A is known to cause night blindness, presumably since a lack of this vitamin produces a lack of retinene, and thus of rhodopsin.

Another deficiency of vision which may be directly attributable to an intrinsic abnormality of the photosensitive cells is that of *color blindness.* Following the trichromatic Young-Helmholtz theory of color vision, the cones are considered to be of three distinct sorts, sensitive to different portions of the spectrum. A lack of one or more of these elements results in varying types of color blindness, from isolated color deficiencies to total color blindness; interestingly, total color blindness is generally associated with central scotoma, implying a total, or nearly total, absence, presumably congenital, of all the cones. It must be emphasized, however, that color blindness does not in itself necessarily mean intrinsic abnormality of the cones; in certain types of complete color blindness, there is no central scotoma and pupillary responses are preserved, suggesting that the lesion is behind the retina, perhaps in the lateral geniculate bodies or cortex. Further, acquired defects of color vision may be seen with lesions of the cerebral cortex itself (*vide infra*).

The Conducting Pathways. The visual conducting pathway may be considered to begin in the bipolar and ganglion cells of the retina itself, extend through the optic nerves, chiasm and tracts to the lateral geniculate bodies, and then proceed via the geniculocalcarine or visual radiation to the occipital cortex surrounding the calcarine fissure, the so-called striate or visual cortex. It is far beyond the scope of this section to review the alterations in visual fields which may be seen in a variety of disease states; details of such changes may be found by consulting the works of Traquair, Walsh and others. Suffice to say that the exact disturbance of the visual field depends almost exclusively on the site of interruption of the conducting pathway and on the extent of that interruption.

Characteristic types of defects are associated with lesions of specific portions of these pathways: Thus, arc-shaped *sector defects* are commonly seen with lesions of the conducting apparatus of the retina itself, and *altitudinal defects* with compression of the optic nerve, generally from above. *Central scotomata* are found with lesions of the optic nerves involving the papillomacular bundle, as may be seen in cases of multiple sclerosis and deficiency amblyopia. *Bitemporal hemianopsia* occurs with suprasellar lesions involving the optic chiasm from below, impinging on the decussating nasal fibers; the much less common *binasal hemianopsia* results from compression of the chiasm laterally with involvement of the nondecussating temporal fibers, as with bilateral fusiform aneurysms of the internal carotid arteries. A variety of *homonymous field defects* (quadrantic and hemianopic, congruous and incongruous, and with or without sparing of the macular region) are noted with lesions behind the chiasm, i.e., of the optic tracts or radiations. Regardless of the type of field deficit, visual acuity is preserved if the fibers from the macula (the papillomacular bundles and their projections) have not been implicated in the lesion.

It should be emphasized that the apparent size of the field defect, and particularly of a scotoma, depends to a large extent upon the size and color of the object used in testing. Defects appear larger with small white test objects as compared with large white objects, since small objects afford a less intense visual stimulus. Similarly, scotomata appear larger when mapped with a colored test object, especially one that is red or green, than when a white object of equal size is used, reflecting the less intense degree of stimulation obtained with colored objects. Finally, it should be remembered that the pupillary light reflexes are often lost with lesions involving the visual pathways up to the lateral geniculate bodies, whereas these reflexes are usually preserved with lesions beyond the geniculates.

The Cerebral Cortex. The simplest and most common visual abnormality encountered with lesions of the cerebral cortex is the *homonymous hemianopsia* which follows unilateral destruction of the visual cortex itself, as by neoplasm or infarction. When such destruction is bilateral, the patient is totally blind, a state referred to as *cortical blindness.* On occasion, and particularly with softening due to occlusive disease of the posterior cerebral arteries, the macular cortical projection area is spared, and the patient may be left with macular or tunnel vision.

A number of other unusual, often puzzling, defects in visual function may occur with lesions of the cerebral cortex; these have been critically and extensively reviewed by Critchley. Patients with cortical blindness may be unaware of, and actually deny, the existence of their own visual defect; such a state of nonrecognition is a specific variety of anosognosia, often called *Anton's syndrome.* An individual may also be unaware of a hemianopic defect, particularly when the hemianopsia is on the basis of a lesion in the occipital cortex or visual radiation in association with a lesion in the nondominant parietal lobe. Disturbances of color sense, so-called *color agnosia,* may be seen with a variety of bilateral cerebral lesions, particularly when such lesions involve the occipital cortex.

Visual agnosia (psychic blindness) may occur with bilateral lesions of the cerebral hemispheres, generally of the occipital lobes. Characterized by the loss of the ability to recognize objects or persons by visual cues alone, visual agnosia may be looked upon as a breakdown in stages of Gestalt formation. A similar defect has been described in monkeys after removal of both temporal lobes, in association with a phenomenon called *hypermetamorphosis,* defined as a compulsive tendency to attend to, and react to, visual stimuli. It is not certain whether visual agnosia can occur as an isolated neurological deficit in man. A special variety of visual agnosia consists of the inability to recognize human faces; this is termed *prosopagnosia,* and is said to occur with bilateral lesions in the posterior parietal, posterior temporal, and occipital regions. A specific disturbance of the ability to comprehend the meaning of written or printed symbols is called *dyslexia;* this usually is found with lesions of the dominant hemisphere, often though not invariably in the vicinity of the angular gyrus. It is apparent that dyslexia may occur as part of the syndrome of visual agnosia, but it also commonly occurs as part of a more generalized disorder of language, i.e., as part of an aphasic syndrome.

Metamorphopsia, or apparent alterations in size, shape, orientation, or movement of objects, may be noted with lesions in the posterior half of the brain, but may occur under a variety of other circumstances. For example, a sudden apparent increase in size of objects (macropsia) or decrease (micropsia) may be encountered as part of the aura of temporal lobe seizures; tilting and other distortions may be seen under the same circumstances. Similarly, metamorphopsia may occur in febrile delirium, in drug intoxication (as with mescaline) in vertiginous states (such as Meniere's disease) and with abnormalities of the ocular apparatus itself. Finally, such symptoms may occur as manifestations of psychiatric disease, e.g., schizophrenia.

A very rare phenomenon is that referred to as *visual perseveration,* in which visual stimuli or events repeat themselves, apparently in a hallucinatory fashion, or extend beyond their normal bounds, in an illusory manner; this occurs with posteriorly placed hemispheral lesions, and also in drug intoxications and as part of an epileptic aura. Bilateral lesions of the parietal lobes may result in a state of *visual disorientation,* in which the patient is unable to localize objects either in an absolute fashion or relative to one another, to compare the dimensions of two visualized objects, or to recognize movement in a sagittal plane; disturbance in counting and in visual attention may be found, and the patient so afflicted may find it difficult to get about because he cannot avoid obstacles in his path. The inability to "conjure up" visual images or memories, so-called defective re-visualization or "irreminiscence," is often referred to as the *Charcot-Wilbrand syndrome;* this has been attributed to lesions in the junctional zone between parietal and occipital lobes. *Visual inattention,* or extinction, may develop with a lesion of one parietal lobe, more often in the nondominant hemisphere. A patient with such a defect can see and recognize objects in any part of the visual field when called upon to do so, but will neglect that part of the field opposite the site of the lesion when stimuli are presented simultaneously in both halves of the visual field, a situation analogous to the tactile inattention or extinction frequently encountered with parietal lobe disease.

Visual hallucinations may be considered as being of two general types, viz., crude and relatively unformed images, such as amorphous blobs, colored globules, streaks of light, etc., and complex formed images of recognizable individuals or objects. Both types occur under a wide variety of circumstances in which no focal lesions are evident, such as drug intoxication with hallucinogenic agents (mescaline, LSD), febrile delirious states, drug withdrawal syndromes (e.g., classical delirium tremens occurring with abstinence from alcohol), and psychosis, particularly schizophrenia. Hallucinations also occur with focal epilepsy, particularly in those cases exhibiting foci in the posterior temporal and occipital areas; crude hallucinatory activity tends to be associated with posteriorly placed foci (approaching the primary cortical receptive area), whereas formed hallucinations tend to occur with more anterior foci (presumably involving the visual association cortical areas). In this connection, the findings of Penfield and Jasper as to the results of cortical stimulation in the conscious human are of some interest. On stimulation of areas 17, 18, and 19, i.e., the striate cortex itself and the immediately surrounding cortical areas, only crude visual hallucinations were elicited, usually but not always contralateral to the site of stimulation. Complex formed hallucinations were not recorded until the stimuli were applied in the posterior parietal and posterior temporal regions. Stimulation still more anteriorly in the temporal lobe elicited panoramic memories, of which formed visual hallucinations were often a significant part. Visual hallucinations also occur very commonly with migraine headaches; they are crude in quality and generally contralateral to the side of the hemicrania. Finally, visual hallucinations may occur in conjunction with lesions of, or adjacent to, the upper brain stem, a phenomenon usually referred to as the *peduncular hallucinosis* of Lhermitte; it is tempting to ascribe hallucinations under these circumstances to an effect upon the upper portion of the brain stem reticular formation, but there is no clear-cut evidence to substantiate this.

FLICKER AND FLICKER FUSION. If an individual is exposed to a flickering light, the frequency of flicker being gradually increased, a point is reached at which a discontinuous flicker can no longer be recognized, only a steady light being seen. The level at which the transition from a discontinuous to an apparently continuous stimulus occurs is termed the critical flicker fusion frequency. The explanation for the failure of discrimination of independent stimuli once this threshold level is attained is not known; it is assumed that overlapping firing in the visual conducting pathways eventually exceeds the ability of the receptor cortex to distinguish between isolated stimuli in time. A decrease in the frequency requirement for flicker fusion may be found with a variety of cerebral lesions.

Electroencephalographically, changes may appear over the occipital cortex in response to a flickering light, so-called "photic driving" of the EEG; this was once thought to be due to a "driving" of the alpha rhythm, but differential frequency analysis indicates that the alpha rhythm and the flicker-induced potential changes are independent processes. The mechanism of neuronal activation by photic stimulation remains unknown; that this is not simply a localized electrical change with no practical significance is emphasized by the appearance of facial myoclonus with the same frequency as the flicker itself in patients subject to spontaneous myoclonus. Furthermore, flicker may induce spreading epileptiform discharges in the EEG; for this reason, photic stimulation has found widespread application as a rather simple device for activating the EEG in an attempt to bring out abnormalities not discernible in an ordinary recording. Frank clinical seizures may result from such stimulation, and, in fact, some epileptics are so susceptible to this form of activation that flickering produced by driving along a tree-lined road with rays of sunlight streaming between the trees may be sufficient to precipitate a seizure. A flickering television image may have the same effect. Some of these individuals, and particularly children so affected, may willfully precipitate a seizure by staring at a light source and passing their fingers rapidly and repetitively before their eyes.

AMBLYOPIA EX ANOPSIA. Amblyopia ex anopsia, or strabismic amblyopia, may be defined as a loss of vision in one eye occurring as a result of an uncorrected monocular strabismus in the infant or child. This loss is often attributed to disuse of the affected eye, the nonsquinting eye being used for fixation and, thus, for useful vision. Occlusion of the nonsquinting eye may cause an improvement in vision in the offending eye, and a loss of the nonsquinting eye, as by trauma, often results in a startling improvement in the previously poor eye. A central scotoma may be found in the field of the amblyopic eye. No morphologic changes have been found to explain the amblyopia under these conditions; it has been suggested that the loss of vision results from cortical inhibition in the macular projection site. The suppression of the false image following the development of an acquired squint with diplopia is probably related to amblyopia ex anopsia, and is presumably due to a process of readjustment in the visual cortex with suppression of the macular image from the offending eye; there is consequently a loss of the initial complaint of double vision.

Hearing

The primary receptive mechanisms and conducting neuronal pathways subserving auditory sensation are exceedingly complex, but on the basis of our present knowledge abnormalities of hearing need be considered only under two broad categories, i.e., dysfunction of the peripheral apparatus (the cochlea and the cochlear division of the eighth cranial nerve) and dysfunction of the central connections thereof (the cochlear nuclei and their ascending projections).

Lesions in the middle or inner ear, or of the auditory nerve itself, result in a loss of hearing on the affected side. *Tinnitus* frequently accompanies this loss. The cause of the tinnitus is not known; besides its occurrence with destructive lesions in these regions, transitory tinnitus may also be encountered in the course of acute drug intoxication (as in cinchonism or salicylism). It is often mandatory to differentiate a loss of hearing due to local disease of the ear, such as otosclerosis or otitis media, from that due to a lesion of the auditory nerve itself, e.g., auditory neurinoma, or following a fracture of the petrous portion of the temporal bone; the former type is referred to as conduction deafness, the latter as nerve deafness. In general, this distinction can be made on the basis of the difference between air and bone conduction of sound. In the normal individual, air conduction is louder than bone conduction, as determined by the response to a vibrating tuning fork held variously just outside the external auditory meatus (thus testing air conduction) or directly upon the mastoid (testing bone conduction); this is the technique of the *Rinne test.* The patient with a conduction type of deafness exhibits a reversal of the normal formula, bone conduction being louder than air conduction, whereas the normal formula is maintained in cases of nerve deafness. The *Weber test* may be of additional help in distinguishing between these two types of deafness. This is carried out by placing a vibrating tuning fork on the midline of the forehead; if the deafness is of the conduction variety, the vibration is referred to the affected ear, but with a nerve deafness it is referred to the sound ear.

A most interesting phenomenon, *loudness recruitment,* is frequently found in conjunction with disease in the inner ear, and particularly with Meniere's disease, but is encountered only rarely with lesions of the auditory nerve itself. It is characterized by an insensitivity to sounds of low intensity in the affected ear, with normal or heightened sensitivity in that ear as the intensity of the sound is increased. Although the exact mechanism responsible for this reaction is not known, it is thought to be due to a lesion of the hair cells of Corti in the cochlea itself. An occurrence of a somewhat different order is *hyperacusis,* or painful sensitiveness to loud sounds, which may be found with lesions in the facial canal involving the nerve to the stapedius muscle; hyperacusis has also been noted in cases of diffuse cerebral lipidosis, e.g., Tay-Sachs disease.

In contrast to the frequent loss of hearing associated with lesions in the peripheral structures, hearing is only rarely lost with centrally placed lesions. If the cochlear nuclear complex is destroyed on one side, deafness ensues in the ipsilateral ear. However, because of the partial decussation of the secondary auditory pathways in the brain stem, unilateral supranuclear lesions cause no discernible loss, deafness being found only with bilateral lesions involving the ascending auditory connections. Although such bilateral lesions unquestionably do occur, as in some cases of multiple sclerosis, intrinsic tumor of the brain stem, etc., this combination of events is distinctly unusual, so that a loss of hearing due to brain stem lesions is quite uncommon. Similarly, because of the bilateral cortical representation of hearing in the temporal lobes, cerebral lesions are only rarely followed by deafness, although a few cases of bilateral temporal lesions, both cortical and subcortical, in which such a deficit was found have been recorded.

Disorders of auditory perception characterized by distortions of sounds, such as alterations in pitch and loudness, are not infrequently observed. They are analogous to the visual phenomena known as metamorphopsia (*vide supra*), and tend to occur under much the same circumstances, particularly with drug intoxication and temporal lobe seizures. Auditory hallucinations are also commonly observed. They may be either crude in quality, characterized by indistinguishable muttering, rumbling, whistling, etc., or quite complex, with distinctly meaningful sounds and voices; the latter variety may be so vivid that the afflicted patient may hold prolonged conversations with, and carry out actions directed by, the voices. As with visual hallucinations, the comparable auditory phenomena occur under a variety of circumstances in which there is no focal cerebral lesion, including drug intoxications, drug withdrawal states (as in so-called alcoholic auditory hallucinosis) and psychoses. In certain clinical states, such as delirium tremens due to abstinence from alcohol, it may be difficult to differentiate between frank auditory hallucinations bearing no relationship to objective stimuli and the more subtle subjective misinterpretations of real auditory stimuli. Auditory hallucinations may also be encountered with focal epileptic seizures, particularly those with epileptogenic foci in the temporal lobe. One should also note in this connection the actual precipitation of seizures by auditory stimuli in certain epileptic patients, and in particular that variety of seizures referred to as "musicogenic epilepsy," in which the hearing of a given strain of music is sufficient to precipitate an attack. Stimulation studies of the human cerebral cortex have shed further light on the localization of auditory hallucinatory phenomena. Stimulation of the first temporal convolution gives rise to elementary auditory sensations, such as noises of various sorts, usually though not always referred to the contralateral ear; occasionally, the negative phenomenon of deafness may be produced by such a stimulation. On the other hand, complex auditory hallucinations, e.g., music and/or voices, are elicited by stimulating areas over much of the remainder of the temporal lobe, particularly anteriorly.

A loss of the ability to recognize the significance of auditory stimuli in the presence of intact hearing is referred to as *acoustic* or *auditory agnosia*. Such a defect may be quite general, applying to auditory stimuli of all sorts, or may be quite specific, involving only the understanding of the spoken word. The latter variety is called *acoustic verbal agnosia*, and is usually accompanied by other language dysfunctions, i.e., other stigmata of aphasia; the lesion responsible for such an abnormality is usually found in the middle third of the first temporal convolution of the dominant hemisphere. Some writers also distinguish a syndrome of pure word deafness, characterized by an isolated acoustic verbal agnosia without other aphasic defects; this is also called *subcortical acoustic verbal agnosia*, and is said to be due to bilateral lesions of the temporal lobes or to an extensive subcortical lesion in the dominant temporal lobe alone. Occasionally, a child may exhibit the syndrome of acoustic agnosia, called *congenital word deafness* under these circumstances, with a resulting retardation in the acquisition of speech. This tends to appear as a familial trait; the underlying pathologic changes, if any, are unknown. Still another special and quite uncommon variety of auditory agnosia is *amusia,* or acoustic musical agnosia, the deficit here being one of a failure of recognition of musical notes or compositions; this is thought to follow lesions in the dominant temporal lobe.

Taste

As with the sense of smell, and in a general way of hearing as well, a loss of taste sensation regularly follows interruption of the peripheral conducting pathways, but occurs quite uncommonly with central lesions. It will be recalled that there is a differential sensory innervation of different portions of the tongue, the anterior two-thirds of the tongue being supplied by the chorda tympani, joining the facial nerve in the facial canal, the posterior third by the glossopharyngeal nerve. Thus, lesions of the facial canal involving the chorda tympani cause a loss of taste over the anterior two-thirds of the tongue, taste over the posterior third being preserved; the reverse obtains with lesions of the glossopharyngeal nerve. A loss of taste may occur with lesions in the lower brain stem which destroy the nucleus and tractus solitarius, as in the vascular syndrome of the lateral medullary plate (the so-called syndrome of the posterior inferior cerebellar artery), but supranuclear lesions rarely if ever cause any observable alterations. Hallucinations of taste (gustatory hallucinations) are not infrequently encountered with uncinate fits (usually considered to be due to epileptogenic foci in the anterior and medial temporal-insular structures); such hallucinations may occur independently, but more commonly are combined with an olfactory element. Stimulation deep beneath the fronto-parietal operculum, adjacent to the cortical representation of salivation and alimentary activity, produces gustatory experiences in the conscious human. Whether occurring spontaneously in epileptic patients, or as a result of cortical stimulation, the tastes elicited are almost always described as "bad" or unpleasant in quality.

The Autonomic Nervous System

CENTRAL ORGANIZATION OF VEGETATIVE ACTIVITY

The Hypothalamus

Although other portions of the neuraxis are intimately concerned with the regulation of activity of the autonomic nervous system (*vide infra*), the region of the hypothalamus seems to occupy a central position insofar as vegetative functions are concerned. A vast amount of experimental data has been accumulated indicating the variety of functions under the influence of this region of the brain; these may be briefly summarized as follows: The hypothalamus has a significant control over *temperature regulation;* a loss of heat with a fall in body temperature, achieved by accelerated respiration, panting, and sweating, follows stimulation in the anterior parts of the hypothalamus, whereas conservation of heat with shivering, piloerection and a rise in body temperature follows stimulation in the posterior hypothalamus. *Water metabolism* is under the direct influence of osmoreceptors in the supraoptic and paraventricular nuclei; these nuclei are connected with the posterior lobe of the pituitary (neurohypophysis) and control the secretion of antidiuretic hormone. Active secretion of the hormone may also occur in the pituitary stalk, and perhaps in the hypothalamus itself. The hypothalamus also appears to play a role in the *regulation of anterior pituitary activity*, particularly as concerns the secretion of gonadotrophic, thyrotrophic and adrenocorticotrophic hormones and perhaps the growth hormone as well. A relationship of the hypothalamus to *appetite,*

or at least to the amount of food ingested, is indicated by the fact that lesions, generally bilateral, in the vicinity of the tuber cinereum in animals produce hyperphagia (bulimia) and resultant obesity, whereas more laterally placed lesions lead to refusal to eat and starvation. *Gastrointestinal motility* and *secretion* are clearly influenced by the hypothalamus, increased peristalsis and an increase in the flow of gastric juice following stimulation in the region of the tuber cinereum and diminished peristalsis and decreased flow of gastric juice following stimulation in the posterior hypothalamus. *Vasomotor activity* is also under the influence of the hypothalamus, as has been shown both in the experimental animal and in man; stimulation anteriorly in this region results in bradycardia and hypotension, whereas tachycardia and an elevation of blood pressure follow stimulation more posteriorly.

There is no convincing evidence that carbohydrate metabolism is directly affected by the hypothalamus itself, but it is of interest that Bond et al. have described persistent hyperglycemia following lesions in the septum, fornix and anterior thalamus, areas closely related to the hypothalamus. Similarly, the hypothalamus seems to play no direct role in sexual behavior, but stimulations in the related septal region clearly produce sexual manifestations. The hypothalamus has also been implicated in certain alterations of emotion and behavior, e.g., the state known as sham rage, elicited by stimulation of the anterior hypothalamus; since these are not strictly autonomic functions, they will be considered elsewhere.

A variety of clinical manifestations occur with affection of the hypothalamus in man which bear out much of the experimental data noted above, although admittedly in a rather crude way. Destructive lesions in the hypothalamus frequently are associated with a profound disorder of temperature regulation, generally expressed as persistent hyperthermia. Lesions in or near the hypothalamic-posterior pituitary system are prone to produce diabetes insipidus, characterized by polyuria with an insatiable, presumably secondary, craving for water. It is assumed that lesions in this area interfere with the production of the antidiuretic hormone; the large urinary output reflects a faulty reabsorption of water in the distal renal tubules, this reabsorption ordinarily being promoted by the antidiuretic hormone. Both precocious puberty and genital atrophy have been noted with lesions of the hypothalamus itself or with mass lesions compressing the hypothalamic region from below (as with craniopharyngioma); extreme obesity may be seen under the same circumstances. Thus, the combination of precocious puberty and obesity known as Fröhlich's syndrome may be due to lesions in or around the hypothalamus, but it should be noted that the same combination occurs with disease, usually neoplastic, elsewhere in the body. Transient epileptiform discharges may occur in the hypothalamus, the so-called "diencephalic epilepsy" of Penfield, with episodes of fever, slowing of respiration, flushing, sweating, lacrimation, salivation and pupillary dilatation. A less well delineated episodic disorder possibly related to abnormal activity in the hypothalamus is the Kleine-Levin syndrome, characterized by periodic attacks of hyperphagia and somnolence.

In recent years, Hess has advanced a plan of functional organization of the diencephalon on the basis of extensive experimental studies, largely in the cat. Although admittedly these concepts have not gained universal acceptance, nonetheless they are of sufficient theoretical interest to be reviewed briefly at this point. Hess subdivides the *diencephalon* into two fundamentally distinct zones: (1) the *ergotrophic,* or *dynamogenic,* zone, extending from the anterior midbrain into the posterior hypothalamus, and (2) the endophylactic-trophotrophic zone, encompassing the anterior and lateral hypothalamus, septum, supra- and preoptic areas and the ventral nuclei. Stimulation in the ergotrophic field produces pupillary dilatation, rise in blood pressure, tachycardia, and an increased respiratory rate and depth, along with a state of heightened motor excitability; in the trophotrophic field, the opposite effects are observed, viz., pupillary constriction, hypotension, diminished respiratory activity and a state of relative adynamia and lethargy, as well as a variety of other phenomena including salivation, retching, vomiting, urination and defecation. The activity of the ergotrophic field is considered to be sympathetic in nature, that of the trophotrophic field, parasympathetic. Exteroceptive mechanisms (visual, auditory or painful stimuli) are considered to play a significant role in the activation of the ergotrophic system, enteroceptive stimuli from a variety of viscera activating the trophotrophic system. Thus, Hess postulates two mutually antagonistic systems, one oriented toward catabolic events and energy utilization, the ergotrophic, the other toward anabolic mechanisms and the preservation of energy, the trophotrophic.

Brodie and Baker have advanced this scheme still further by relating the action of various psychotherapeutic agents to neurohumeral transmission within these two systems. The neurohumeral transmitting agent within the ergotrophic system is considered to be norepinephrine, in the trophotrophic system, serotonin. The tranquilizing and parasympathetic, or cholinergic, effects of the Rauwolfia alkaloids are thought to be due to a direct stimulation of the trophotrophic system by releasing the stored mediator substance serotonin, whereas the similar clinical effects of the phenothiazine derivatives are due to a direct blockage of the norepinephrine-ergotrophic system (a so-called adrenergic blockade). Stimulants such as amphetamine and mescaline are adrenergic agents and activate the ergotrophic system, probably by virtue of the phenylethylamine grouping common to these drugs as well as to norepinephrine itself. LSD-25 also activates the ergotrophic system, presumably because it too contains a phenylethylamine grouping. Since an indole group is also part of its chemical structure, LSD-25 may in addition compete with the indole-containing serotonin for reactor sites. The monoamine-oxidase inhibitors, the "psychic-energizers," similarly have an adrenergic, ergotrophic action, but the mechanism here is still different in that these compounds appear to act by interfering with the destruction of norepinephrine by enzymatic activity.

The Cerebral Cortex

There is ample experimental evidence to indicate that the cerebral cortex plays a significant role in the regulation of autonomic activity. The frontal, orbital, cingulate and insular regions seem particularly important in this regard, though autonomic representation has been found elsewhere as well. Thus, stimulation of the orbital cortex produces a rise in blood pressure and respiratory arrest, as well as increased gastric secretion. Stimulation and ablation studies of different portions of the frontal cortex demonstrate alterations in blood pressure, pulse rate, pupillary size, gastric motility and flow of gastric juice; both bulimia and piloerection have also been noted after bilateral ablations. Bladder control may be lost after bilateral lesions of the paracentral lobule. When the cingulate gyrus is stimulated, piloerection, bradycardia, slowing of respiration, and pupillary dilatation occur, and hypotension and inhibition of respiration and gastric motility follow stimulation of the insular cortex. Pupillary constriction may also be seen after stimulation of the occipital regions, at least in the cat. As with the frontal regions, bilateral ablations of the temporal regions also produce bulimia.

In the course of their studies of cortical stimulation in the awake human, Penfield and Jasper have described a number of autonomic phenomena following stimulation in the insula and peri-insular grey matter; these changes were mostly gastrointestinal in nature, but alterations in pupillary size and heart rate were also encountered. Respiratory arrest was noted following stimulation of the anterior cingulate gyrus in their patients. (Pool has stressed vasomotor and gastrointestinal changes under the same circumstances.) Interestingly, these authors never observed urination, lacrimation, pilomotor change, shivering or sweating, regardless of the site of stimulation. The common clinical observation of vasodilatation, and later pallor and sweating, in paralyzed limbs following the onset of a hemiplegia implies that some form of control over both vasomotor and sweating functions is probably present in the human cortex or adjacent subcortical regions.

The Amygdala

There seems little doubt that the amygdaloid complex is also intimately related to autonomic functions, particularly the corticomedial division thereof. A variety of autonomic changes follow stimulation of this structure, including salivation, piloerection, respiratory inhibition, hypotension and pupillary dilatation. An increase in gastric secretions and gastric acidity has also been noted, as well as uterine activity, premature labor, and ovulation. An increase in pituitary-adrenocortical activity has also been found following stimulation of the amygdala. Some similar phenomena, e.g., ovulation, can also be elicited by stimulation of the septal region. In addition, behavioral responses, both affective and sexual, have been seen when the amygdaloid complex is stimulated; these will be referred to presently. Alterations of autonomic function in the human with pathological conditions affecting the amygdaloid complex per se have not been established.

Brain Stem Structures

Besides the diencephalic and supradiencephalic structures already discussed, portions of the brain stem must also be considered insofar as regulation of certain vegetative functions is concerned. Two mechanisms in particular, control of respiration and of cardiovascular activity, appear segmentally represented at the brain stem level, though both are obviously under the influence of more rostral structures as well. An inspiratory center is present in the ventral reticular formation low in the medulla, an expiratory center in the dorsal reticular formation either just adjacent to the inspiratory center or more posteriorly. The expiratory center appears subject to inhibitory influences from the inspiratory center; both are under the control of an apneustic center found in the lateral reticular formation of the pons, and this in turn is influenced by the pneumotaxic center located still higher in the pons, in the dorsolateral reticular formation. In addition to presumed diencephalic and cortical control, this complex also appears regulated by vagal afferents mediating the Hering-Breuer reflexes, by chemoreceptors in the brain stem (not yet discretely localized) responding to circulating carbon dioxide, and by chemoreceptors in the aortic and carotid bodies which respond to oxygen lack. As far as the regulation of cardiovascular activity is concerned, a pressor center is present in the lateral reticular formation of the rostral medulla, and a depressor center in the medial reticular formation in the caudal medulla, influencing the spinal (sympathetic) vasomotor neurons and the vagal (parasympathetic) outflow; these centers are under the influence of baroreceptors and chemoreceptors in the aortic arch and carotid body, and are regulated by higher centers as well.

A number of other mechanisms related to autonomic functioning are also segmentally represented in the brain stem, particularly in the medulla; these include coughing, sneezing, swallowing, salivation and sucking reflex mechanisms. The vomiting reflex is still another example: an *emetic center* is found in the lateral reticular formation, under the direct influence of the vagus, glossopharyngeal, vestibular, and perhaps the splanchnic nerves; this center is also under the control of a chemoreceptor, the so-called chemoreceptor trigger zone (probably situated in the area postrema), which is itself responsive to a variety of blood-borne metabolites (as in cases of uremia) or toxic substances (such as apomorphine). The threshold of this chemoreceptor trigger zone is raised by the phenothiazine derivates, explaining the antiemetic action of these agents.

It is thus apparent that one cannot speak of a single center for autonomic activity within the brain. A variety of structures partake in the regulation of the vegetative nervous system, including the cerebral cortex, subcortical gray masses (such as the amygdala), septum, diencephalon and portions of the reticular formation of the brain stem. A point worthy of special emphasis is that much of this regulating activity takes place in the rhinencephalon (the so-called limbic system) or in its immediate connections, viz., frontal and orbital cortices, cingulate gyrus, insula, amygdala, septum and hypothalamus. Certain aspects of behavior also appear related to this same primitive neuronal complex; although arbitrarily, and perhaps artificially, excluded here, they will be considered subsequently.

PERIPHERAL ORGANIZATION OF VEGETATIVE ACTIVITY

The peripheral portion of the vegetative nervous system consists of two divisions, the *craniosacral parasympathetic* and the *thoracolumbar sympathetic*. Preganglionic parasympathetic fibers tend to be long, postganglionic short, the synapse occurring at ganglia in or near the specific structure innervated. On the other hand, sympathetic preganglionic fibers are very short, the ganglia lying adjacent to the vertebral canal, whereas the postganglionic fibers are quite long and distributed to a variety of structures. As a result, widespread effects follow stimulation of a preganglionic sympathetic fiber, but only restricted effects follow stimulation of a preganglionic parasympathetic fiber. Stimulation of sympathetic fibers produces sweating, constriction of blood vessels in the skin and viscera, piloerection, relaxation of the muscular walls of hollow viscera, tachycardia, pupillary dilatation, and deepening of respiration; stimulation of parasympathetic fibers causes contraction of the walls of hollow viscera, bradycardia, pupillary constriction and glandular secretion. Synaptic transmission within the ganglia of both sympathetic and parasympathetic divisions is in all likelihood mediated by the neurohumor acetylcholine. Postganglionic transmission in the sympathetic nervous system is mediated by sympathin (epinephrine) and is thus adrenergic; in the parasympathetic nervous system it is mediated by acetylcholine and is thus cholinergic. The sole exception concerns the innervation of the sweat glands, which is cholinergic, although anatomically they are a part of the sympathetic nervous system.

Although the spinal and peripheral autonomic mechanisms are normally under the influence of higher centers (*vide supra*), removal of higher level controls does not necessarily imply total failure of vegetative activity at the periphery. The peripheral autonomic system is capable, at least in part, of acting at segmental spinal levels free of influence from above. This is best illustrated by the changes occurring after complete transection of the spinal cord. Transection of the cord above the lumbar segments results in a loss of sweating under conditions in which sweating usually occurs on a central basis, e.g., with hyperthermia; however, following recovery from the initial state of spinal shock, sweating may occur on a segmental reflex basis in response to distention of rectum or bladder, or as part of the "mass reflex" (a marked withdrawal of the lower limbs following the application of a noxious cutaneous stimulus, associated with involuntary urination and defecation as well as sweating). Similarly, with lesions above the midthoracic level, a loss of vasomotor tone ensues, especially in the legs and splanchnic areas, and the patient becomes a victim of postural hypotension; nonetheless, an intense reflex vasoconstriction may occur in the toes as well as in the fingers when the bladder is distended.

Changes in micturition may occur with a variety of lesions, the specific type of alteration depending in large part on the site of the lesion and its extent. The bladder is innervated both by the sympathetic division, via the hypogastric nerves, and by the parasympathetic, via the pelvic nerves. The act of voiding itself is essentially parasympathetic, with contraction of the muscle wall and relaxation of the internal sphincter; the stimulus initiating such activity is a stretch stimulus evoked by increased intravesical pressure. Much uncertainty has existed concerning the types of disturbance of bladder function seen under different circumstances, and the terminology which has been used is conflicting and confusing. The following classification is essentially derived from Ruch, who recognizes four basically different disturbances.

The first, the so-called *uninhibited neurogenic bladder,* occurs with damage to the cerebrum or with subtotal interruption of the corticospinal pathways, and is characterized by urgency, frequent micturition with emptying of the bladder, small-volume threshold of activity, and normal or increased bladder tone. These changes have been attributed to either of two mechanisms, viz., release of a spinal bladder reflex from cortical inhibition, or facilitation of the spinal reflex from the brain stem reticular formation; obviously, both may play a significant role. The second, the *automatic bladder* (the so-called "cord bladder," or spastic reflex neurogenic bladder) is seen following complete transection of the spinal cord above the sacral segments. Immediately following such a transection, there is complete areflexia, the state of spinal shock, with loss of bladder sensation; it is probable that at this stage there is interruption of the brain stem facilitating pathways, the local or segmental afferent influx from the bladder being insufficient to excite the sacral motor neurons. Subsequently, as somatic reflex activity returns, reflex bladder activity appears. Under these circumstances, one characteristically encounters frequent voiding with complete emptying of the bladder, absence of warning of the immediacy of micturition, and absence of significant inhibitory or voluntary control; the bladder capacity is quite small and the tone usually increased, a rapid rise in intravesical pressure occurring with filling. Stimulation by a noxious cutaneous stimulus at the periphery causes immediate voiding associated with other phenomena, already described as the mass reflex, explicable perhaps as a strong segmental facilitation or reinforcement of subliminal bladder afferent activity with resultant reflex contraction. Manual compression of the abdominal wall may also initiate a voiding reflex under these circumstances.

The third type is the *autonomous bladder*, or denervated bladder, which occurs after interruption of the afferent and efferent portions of the parasympathetic reflex arc by lesions of the conus medullaris, cauda equina, sacral roots or pelvic nerve. This is characterized by a loss of bladder sensation, loss of both voluntary and spinal reflex bladder activity, heightened bladder capacity (at least in the earlier stages), and small frequent voiding with ineffectual emptying. The bladder contractions under these circumstances are considered to represent autonomous activity on the part of the intrinsic intramural nerve fiber network of the bladder. The fourth type, the *tabetic* or *atonic bladder*, follows interruption of the sacral posterior roots, the anterior roots remaining intact. Overdistention of the bladder results in thinning of the bladder wall and overflow incontinence with a large residual urinary volume. No reflex contraction of the detrusor muscle is possible, and there is a loss of the desire to void, although some poorly defined bladder sensation may persist. The lack of activity of the intramural plexus in this set of circumstances has not been explained.

Changes in defecation also appear following transection of the cord above the sacral level, a loss of tone of the anal sphincter and rectum with failure of defecation being observed in the state of spinal shock, with at least partial return of reflex activity as the spinal shock disappears; this reflex activity can be augmented by appropriate cutaneous stimulation, as with the mass reflex. The fact that defecation may occur even when the sacral cord is destroyed implies that a peripheral reflex pattern can be set up, perhaps analogous to that seen with the autonomous bladder.

Sexual activity in the male, particularly erection and emission of semen, is basically a function of the vegetative nervous system, erection appearing to be a parasympathetic phenomenon, emission sympathetic. Although these functions are undoubtedly influenced by higher centers, reflex activity may occur at the segmental spinal level; following the state of spinal shock with cord transection, both erection and emission may occur in response to peripheral cutaneous stimuli. The impotence seen in cases of tabes is probably due to interference with the afferent portion of the reflex arc in its course through the posterior roots. Priapism, a state of prolonged erection, may be seen with intrinsic disorders of the spinal cord; the mechanism is not known.

A large number of clinical syndromes have been attributed to dysfunction of the peripheral autonomic system. Although a simple listing of these disorders would be far beyond the scope of this section (the interested reader is referred to the work of Kuntz), a few of the more commonly accepted disorders of this type may be mentioned briefly. Among the multitude of vasomotor phenomena which have been attributed to an abnormality of the peripheral sympathetic system, *Raynaud's disease* is perhaps the best known. This is a form of peripheral vascular disease due to tonic contraction of the small arterioles on the basis of sympathetic overactivity. The vascular spasms are intermittent, and are precipitated by emotional stimuli or exposure to cold; sweating with either cyanosis or pallor may accompany the vascular change. Interruption of the peripheral sympathetic pathways by either sympathetic block or sympathectomy may be remarkably beneficial in relieving these symptoms. *Erythromelalgia*, a condition characterized by burning pain in the extremities with erythema of the involved areas and dilatation of peripheral vessels, is also considered to be due to some variety of peripheral autonomic dysfunction. Attacks may be precipitated by exertion, heat or by placing the limbs in a dependent position; sympathetic ganglionectomy is useful in the treatment.

Vasomotor changes may also be observed in cases of *causalgia,* a syndrome of persistent, often burning, pain in an extremity following injury, usually partial, of a peripheral nerve. Cutaneous hypalgesia and dysesthesias and trophic changes in the skin are often present. The mechanism underlying the disturbances is not clear. Retrograde activity (so-called antidromic firing) in the sympathetic fibers is thought to stimulate sympathetic vasoconstrictor fibers at the segmental spinal cord level; irritation of somatic afferent fibers at the site of injury is considered responsible for the pain and dysesthesias. Sympathetic block or sympathectomy may alleviate the symptoms to a considerable extent. Causalgia-like pain may also be encountered in the so-called "thalamic syndrome" of Déjérine and Roussy, following a lesion in the ventrolateral nucleus of the thalamus; the relationship of this pain to that of true causalgia is uncertain. *Trophic changes,* such as edema, glossiness of the skin, excessive sweating, and bone atrophy, are often observed in an extremity following injuries, even of a minor degree, of roots and peripheral nerve trunks. The underlying factors are not understood, but the changes are usually considered to be due to abnormal sympathetic activity, presumably initiated, as in the causalgic syndrome, by partial nerve damage.

Abnormal lacrimation is found in the *syndrome of crocodile tears,* and facial sweating occurs in the *auriculotemporal syndrome,* both of which follow the faulty regeneration of nerve fibers in the facial nerve which may occur during recovery from a bout of Bell's palsy. Fibers normally destined for the salivary glands may reach instead the lacrimal glands, so that eating, with its normal reflex salivation, is accompanied by lacrimation, the "crocodile tears." Similarly, salivary gland fibers may innervate the preauricular and temporal sweat glands; in this instance eating is accompanied by sweating in these regions. *Pathological sweating* (hyperhydrosis) may also be seen as an isolated phenomenon limited to the hands and feet; occasionally, cyanosis and coldness may be found in the same areas. Sympathectomy may be of aid in the treatment of severe cases of this sort. A rare disturbance of glandular activity is the state of pathological dryness of the mucous membranes called *Sjögren's syndrome,* characterized by faulty secretion on the part of lacrimal,

salivary, gastric and sweat glands. The etiology of this syndrome is unknown, but in many cases it appears associated with one of the collagen diseases. Since the clinical picture is one of adrenergic overactivity, parasympathomimetic (cholinergic) drugs are used therapeutically.

Pupillary abnormalities are well known to be associated with peripheral disorders of the autonomic system. Of these, perhaps the best known is the pupillary constriction which occurs with *Horner's syndrome,* along with anhydrosis over the same side of the face and a variable degree of enophthalmos and ptosis. This syndrome frequently follows damage to the cervical sympathetic chain, as with lesions of the stellate ganglion, and may be considered the result of a loss of sympathetic innervation in the structures involved. Lesions in the lateral portion of the medulla, such as those consequent to occlusion of the posterior inferior cerebellar artery, may also produce this syndrome, presumably by interrupting descending sympathetic pathways. Destructive processes in the vicinity of the intermediolateral column of the cervical cord may have the same effect, either by interrupting descending pathways or by destroying the sympathetic "motor" neurons in that part of the spinal cord directly.

Miotic pupils which fail to react to light but which still exhibit the accommodation reflex are often found in cases of neurosyphilis, particularly with tabes; these are the so-called *Argyll Robertson pupils.* This abnormality is often attributed to lesions within the Edinger-Westphal nucleus of the midbrain, but this has not been well substantiated, and lesions of the ciliary ganglia have also been proposed as a suitable explanation. Pupillary changes also occur in the course of herniation of supratentorial structures due to increased intracranial pressure, pupillary constriction being the initial event, with subsequent dilatation. Although the cause of these alterations in pupillary size is not entirely clear, it is thought that compression of the oculomotor nerve by the protruding uncus may initially stimulate the parasympathetic pupilloconstrictor fibers within the nerve, resulting in the early constriction of the pupil. The later dilatation would then be due to physiologic interruption of these same fibers as a result of continued and increasing pressure. Other affections of the oculomotor nerve, as by a compressing tumor or aneurysm, may also be accompanied by changes in the size of the pupil.

The basis for the curious phenomenon referred to as the tonic or Adie's pupil remains unknown. This term describes a pupillary abnormality, often unilateral, characterized by delayed and slow but ultimately excessive reaction of the pupil to both light and accommodation, most strikingly the latter. The pupillary constriction under these circumstances often continues after removal of the stimulus itself. The tonic pupil may initially appear nonreactive to light; the patient may have to be confined in the dark for a period of time to allow full dilatation to occur before the tonic light reaction becomes evident. The term "Adie's syndrome" refers to those cases, most commonly females, in which the tonic pupil is associated with a loss of tendon reflexes.

A variety of disorders of the gastrointestinal tract have also been attributed to abnormal autonomic activity or autonomic imbalance. The most clearly defined of these is *congenital megacolon* (Hirschsprung's disease). In this condition, there is an absence of the intramural (parasympathetic) ganglia in a segment of the large bowel. The aganglionic segment is constricted and unable to partake in peristaltic activity; dilatation of the more proximal portion of bowel results. Sympathectomy is valueless in the therapy of this disease, resection of the constricted aganglionic segment being the only rational mode of treatment.

Alterations in heart rate and blood pressure occur with *vasovagal attacks* and with the syndrome of the *hyperirritable carotid sinus* or so-called vasovagal syncope. In the former, a variety of emotional stimuli result in bradycardia, hypotension, pallor, sweating and syncope, presumably on the basis of vagal activation due to stimulation of the medullary depressor centers from higher in the neuraxis; similar effects may occur in response to deep pain, e.g., that from joints or viscera. In the latter, the carotid sinus seems unusually sensitive to direct stimulation such as the application of external pressure, and a vagal reflex is set up with the same clinical effects as already described.

A rather uncommon form of dysfunction of the autonomic nervous system is *familial dysautonomia* (the Riley-Day syndrome), a hereditary disease transmitted as a mendelian recessive, usually encountered in Jewish children. This is characterized by defective lacrimation, with secondary corneal ulcerations, transient erythematous blotching of the skin, excessive sweating, drooling, labile blood pressure and frequent bouts of unexplained fever. Seizures and mental retardation may be found, as well as disturbances of swallowing and sucking of sufficient magnitude to produce distinct feeding problems in infancy. Motor incoordination, hyporeflexia and indifference to pain are occasionally encountered. This complex is looked upon as a mixture of excessive activity on the part of both the sympathetic and parasympathetic divisions; there is no agreement as to the cause, although in isolated cases a degeneration of the brain stem reticular formation has been described.

Consciousness and Higher Integrative Functions

Consciousness

The evaluation of problems of awareness and consciousness is immediately made difficult by the lack of a suitable definition of that state which comprises normal consciousness. One may initially define such a state as that condition of awareness or alertness in which the individual's actions and responses appear regulated by events in the environment to the same degree as those of the examiner. Unfortunately, even such a simple definition has obvious deficiencies. Thus, the introverted autistic individual, the severely depressed patient, or the catatonic schizophrenic all appear unmindful of, and fail to react to, stimuli to which the examiner may react, and yet such individuals are generally considered conscious and aware; in fact, following recovery the catatonic patient may recall perfectly all that went on about him. At the other end of the scale may be found the patient with delirium tremens, who is excessively attentive and reactive to minor stimuli in the environment which are ordinarily neglected, while disregarding other, often more significant events or stimuli; although such a patient may be spoken of as normally conscious, the state is actually one of heightened, albeit selective, alertness, a state of "hyperconsciousness."

In view of this basic semantic difficulty, definitions or descriptions of states of altered consciousness are often confusing and generally lack precision, a fact which makes quantitative clinical evaluation of these states most difficult. Nonetheless, a few descriptive terms may be suitably employed, if this basic difficulty is kept in mind. (These will be defined rather briefly here; a detailed description of most of these states of altered awareness and consciousness may be found by referring to Adams, and Victor and Adams.)

Lethargy is a state of sleepiness or drowsiness, a tendency to fall asleep under inappropriate conditions, as during the course of an examination or conversation. A lethargic patient may be readily roused by verbal auditory stimuli, and responds appropriately and usually briskly to painful stimuli. *Stupor* may be defined as a state in which physical and mental activity is minimal, the patient being inaccessible to many stimuli. Poor or inadequate responses to verbal stimuli or commands are characteristic, and stereotyped or restless motor activity may be noted. Reflexes are generally intact. A stuporous patient may open his eyes and follow events about him, though often with little recognizable reaction to such events. An individual who does not respond to verbal stimuli, but who can be roused, at least to some degree, by painful stimuli, is considered to be in a state of *semicoma*. Reflex activity may be preserved at this level of depressed consciousness, but the plantar responses are often extensor in type. *Coma* is a state characterized by a lack of reaction to either verbal or painful stimuli, with the exception of occasional fragmentary and abnormal motor responses such as decerebrate posturing. The tendon and plantar reflexes are absent, as are the corneal, pupillary and pharyngeal reflexes; periodic or depressed respiration is common.

Confusional states are phenomena of a somewhat different order from simple states of depressed consciousness, but may suitably be considered here as well. A state of confusion is defined as that state in which an individual is unable to think with accustomed clarity and coherence. Disorientation in time and place is one of the earliest signs, along with some irrelevancy of thought processes; a severe retardation of speech and frank unawareness of the surroundings may be encountered in more serious forms. A confusional state associated with reduced alertness, attentiveness and responsiveness is referred to as *primary mental confusion;* lethargy may be prominent, and perceptual misinterpretations are common. Confusion coupled with an increase in psychomotor and autonomic activity is spoken of as *delirium;* overalertness, insomnia, speech overactivity, perceptual disorders with hallucinations and a low seizure threshold are characteristic features of such a state. The term *beclouded delirium* refers to

the addition of a confusional syndrome to a pre-existing dementing illness.

A wide variety of toxic and metabolic disorders alter the state of consciousness to varying degrees, presumably by adversely affecting neuronal metabolism *en masse;* these include acute alcoholic and other drug intoxications, hypoglycemia, hypoxia, diabetic acidosis, hepatic coma, uremia, porphyria, deficiencies of thiamin, nicotinic acid, pyridoxine, and vitamin B_{12}, and hypo- and hyperthermia. Severe systemic infections such as meningococcemia, pneumonia and typhoid fever may also act in the same way. Cerebral ischemia due to circulatory collapse, as in cases of heart block, also produces disordered consciousness by a global depressing effect on neuronal activity. Narcotic and anesthetic agents may similarly have a generalized action within the nervous system, although there is some evidence to indicate that their major site of action may be within the ascending reticular formation (*vide infra*). A depression of consciousness also is a characteristic feature of any pathological process in the brain which destroys nerve cells in large numbers in a diffuse fashion, such as viral encephalitis, cerebral lipidosis, or cortico-striato-cerebellar degeneration (Jakob-Creutzfeldt disease).

In addition to these generalized disorders, focal lesions within the central nervous system may also lead to a profound alteration in the state of awareness. An impressive amount of experimental data coupled with a number of clinical-pathologic observations have emphasized the importance of the ascending reticular formation insofar as wakefulness and consciousness are concerned. Of particular importance are the mesencephalic and posterior hypothalamic portions of the reticular formation itself, and the related midline and intralaminar thalamic nuclei, as well as the diffuse "nonspecific" cortical afferent system. Stimulation of the reticular activating system directly, or indirectly via a variety of ascending sensory pathways, produces an arousal and alertness response in the sleeping experimental animal, accompanied by the fast desynchronized electroencephalographic pattern of arousal. Destructive lesions in these same areas, both in animal and man, lead to a prolonged state of coma. On the basis of such evidence, there has been an increasing tendency to regard the reticular system as a true center of consciousness; this is probably an oversimplification because the cerebral cortex itself probably participates actively in its own arousal and in the maintenance of the waking state by virtue of corticofugal impulses to the reticular formation. The opposite of the arousal response, i.e., drowsiness and sleep, has been described by Hess following stimulation in the more anterior portion of the diencephalon. In view of these and other findings (see p. 994), Hess proposes the existence of two mutually antagonistic diencephalic regions: the ergotrophic (posterior diencephalic) zone, stimulation of which leads to arousal, alertness, and certain autonomic changes, all bringing the organism into an optimal state for reaction with the environment, and the trophotrophic (anterior diencephalic) zone, stimulation of which predisposes to withdrawal from active participation with the environment, sleep and restoration of the "milieu interne."

As has already been indicated, intrinsic destructive lesions, such as softening or hemorrhage involving the mesencephalic-diencephalic system, lead to coma. The comatose state found with expanding supratentorial lesions is presumably explicable on the basis of herniation of the medial surface of the temporal lobe through the tentorium with resultant compression of the midbrain. The altered state of awareness accompanying and following epileptic seizures is probably due to firing into the central gray masses from cortical epileptogenic foci, with suppression or inactivation of the reticular activating system; in cases of petit mal (or centrencephalic epilepsy in Penfield's terminology) the focus of abnormal activity may reside directly within this system. The prolonged somnolence which was such a characteristic feature of encephalitis lethargica (epidemic encephalitis, von Economo's encephalitis) was almost certainly a reflection of the predominance of the lesions in the midbrain, hypothalamus and subthalamus. The curious state of episodic irresistible pathologic sleepiness referred to as *narcolepsy* may also be due to intrinsic activity, seemingly inhibitory, within the reticular formation. The occurrence of a depressed state of consciousness following head trauma is perhaps due to convergence of lines of force upon the diencephalic centers, with temporary disorganization and failure of function of these activating mechanisms.

There are no known naturally occurring examples of the reverse of depression of consciousness, i.e., sleeplessness, consequent to destruction of the "sleep center" described by Hess.

The Limbic System and Behavior

The limbic system (the *rhinencephalon* or "visceral brain") is composed anatomically of a complex related and interconnected series of phylogenetically primitive portions of the cerebral cortex and subcortical nuclear masses, and includes the hippocampus, fasciola cinereum, induseum griseum, pyriform cortex, orbital frontal cortex, hippocampal gyrus, cingulate gyrus, insula, amygdaloid complex, septal nuclei, anterior and perhaps dorsomedial thalamic nuclei, habenula, and portions of the diencephalon and brain stem reticular formation. The medial forebrain bundle, diagonal band of Broca, stria terminalis, fornix, mammillothalamic tract (of Vicq d'Azyr), mammillotegmental tract, cingulum, anterior commissure, supraoptic decussations (of Meynert, Ganser and Gudden), stria medullaris and habenulopeduncular tract serve as the principal connecting pathways within this system. The cortical portions of the limbic system may be further subdivided into *archipallium* and *mesopallium;* the more anterior portions are often referred to as olfactory cortex in view of their afferent projections from the olfactory tracts via the medial and lateral olfactory striae. Olfactory function is in fact localized to this part of the brain in lower mammals, but in higher mammals, particularly primates and man, little if any specific and recognizable olfactory function can be assigned to these regions. These areas seem to have acquired a different function in the course of evolution, viz., regulation of certain forms of behavior and perhaps of emotion as well. This was originally inferred by Herrick, who suggested that the olfactory cortex might serve as a nonspecific activator for all cortical activities, but was later propounded in an elaborate fashion by Papez. Subsequent investigators have made a number of experimental and theoretical contributions to this concept.

A variety of behavioral changes appear consequent to ablations of, or stimulation within, parts of this system in the experimental animal. A loss of fear, diminished aggressive behavior, hypersexuality, bulimia, and pronounced oral tendencies follow bilateral temporal lobectomy in the monkey (Klüver and Bucy). Identical alterations may be noted after relatively isolated ablations of the amygdaloid complex and surrounding structures; lesions in the ventromedial hypothalamic nuclei or mammillary bodies can prevent the occurrence of such a syndrome, or can abolish it if previously established. Loss of fear and of "social consciousness" may also follow bilateral ablations of the cingulate gyrus, though this is not a consistent finding. In contrast to the relative docility and placidity evoked by lesions in the vicinity of the amygdala, as noted by most workers, a paradoxical increase in activity and frank rage reactions have been noted following lesions in the same general area by Spiegel et al. and Bard and Mountcastle; the reason for this discrepancy is not clear. Wood and also Green have pointed out that fractionation of the Klüver-Bucy syndrome may be obtained by producing restricted lesions involving isolated parts of the amygdala.

Anger or rage reactions (so-called "sham rage") frequently follow extensive decortication (although this can be avoided if the pyriform cortex, hippocampus, amygdala and anterior cingulate gyrus are preserved intact), and may also be observed after an isolated ablation of area 14 in the orbital frontal cortex; a lesion in the ventromedial nucleus of the hypothalamus may have the same effect. Stimulation of the amygdala or of the anterior hypothalamus also elicits a rage reaction; stimulation in the lateral hypothalamic area produces a state of placidity. Aimless hyperactivity, restlessness, loss of fear, and distractibility may result from bilateral lesions in the dorsomedial nuclei of the thalamus. Finally, pleasure reactions and sexual manifestations have been found with stimulation in the hippocampus and septal region.

Gloor has concluded from data of this sort that the limbic system is concerned primarily with affective and sexual behavior; he doubts that this system is critically involved in the integration of somatomotor or autonomic mechanisms, although it undoubtedly does exert some influence over functions in these spheres, particularly the latter. MacLean has stressed the role of this system insofar as preservation of both self and species is concerned, and has discussed at length the possible psychiatric implications of limbic activity. Gloor has also pointed out the possible role of this system in the production and regulation of emotions by virtue of its modulating activities as a mediating link between neocortex and diencephalon.

One cannot immediately transpose the data derived from animal studies to the human. Thus, Scoville has indicated that in man bilateral resections of the uncus, amygdala and anterior hippocampus produce no demonstrable behavioral abnormality. Nonetheless, some clinical data do appear to substantiate to some degree the theoretical and experimental considerations noted above. For example, patients with temporal lobe epilepsy, with epileptogenic foci in the hippocampus, periamygdalar region, or insula, often report a variety of affective reactions in the course of their seizures, such as fear, or, less commonly, a sensation of pleasure or exhilaration. The affective aspect of the *déjà vu* phenomenon, i.e., a sense of familiarity, is also frequently remarked upon. In certain patients with this variety of epilepsy, seizures may actually consist of attacks of rage and assaultive behavior. Irritability and aggressive behavior may also be encountered in individuals with tumors compressing the floor of the diencephalon and frontal lobes. The opposite state, i.e., a state of apathy and dullness, may be observed in patients with hippocampal lesions, and is characteristic of patients suffering from Korsakoff's psychosis (in which instance lesions are present in the mammillary bodies). A similar state of indifference is associated with tumors of the corpus callosum much more commonly than is found with growths elsewhere; it is tempting to ascribe these changes to involvement of the overlying cingulate gyrus.

A number of other pertinent behavioral changes have been sporadically reported in man. Nymphomania has been observed in conjunction with a vascular tumor of the paracentral lobule, adjacent to the cingulate gyrus. Vivid daydreams and difficulty in distinguishing between fantasy and reality have been found following anterior cingulectomy, but no other psychological changes were evident in these individuals. Finally, all the elements of the Klüver-Bucy syndrome have been reproduced at least once in man by extensive bilateral temporal lobectomy. One may therefore conclude that there is at least some evidence in man indicating that the limbic system is of importance as regards affect and behavior, and that disturbances within this portion of the brain may lead to aberrations in these spheres.

Memory

A disturbance of memory is commonly found in association with many generalized or poorly localized diseases of the nervous system, such as chronic hydrocephalus, cerebral arteriosclerosis with multiple infarcts, viral encephalitis and a variety of metabolic and degenerative conditions. Expanding intrahemispheral mass lesions very often give rise to memory difficulty, regardless of the site of the lesion, and large subdural hematomata, whether unilateral or bilateral, have the same effect. The loss of memory in these instances occurs as part of a widespread neurological and psychological defect; it would be unjustifiable under such circumstances to consider memory as a separate and isolatable psychological function localized to a specific region within the brain. Nonetheless, an increasing amount of data, both clinical and pathological, suggests that an isolated disorder of memory may be observed as the expression of focal disease involving a specific portion of the brain, the limbic system; the hippocampal complex, hippocampal commissure (psalterium), fornix and mammillary bodies seem particularly significant in this regard. A profound loss of memory has been noted following radical resections of the mesial portions of both temporal lobes, or following a unilateral resection in individuals with evidence of disease in the opposite temporal lobe. The deficit so produced is often described as a loss of recent memory, but probably should be designated more accurately as an inability to form new memories, i.e., a defect in learning and retention. Pathologic studies of the brains of individuals who suffered from a similar memory deficit during life, presumably on the basis of vascular disease, have demonstrated relatively isolated focal lesions involving the hippocampal complex and/or psalterium bilaterally. It is noteworthy that patients exhibiting this type of defect in learning and retention in association with hippocampal lesions may have relatively little difficulty with memory for events of the remote past, and "gnostic memory" (recognition of people and objects by involuntary recall) appears unimpaired. It is as yet uncertain as to whether bilateral lesions of the hippocampal complex are necessary for the development of this type of amnestic syndrome, or whether a sufficiently extensive unilateral lesion can have the same effect.

There is much more evidence supporting the contention that the integrity of the hippocampal complex and/or its connections is essential for normal memory function. In some cases of senile dementia, a serious loss of memory may be the principal clinical feature; in these individuals, the pathological alterations appear predominantly in the hippocampus and hippocampal gyrus. Similarly, a remarkable loss of memory may be encountered in cases of inclusion body encephalitis, in which the inferomesial portions of the temporal lobes may be particularly involved. Sweet and his co-workers have reported an identical memory defect following section of the columns of the fornix (the principal efferent hippocampal fiber system), and a loss of memory has often been reported in conjunction with tumors of the third ventricle, in the vicinity of the pillars of the fornix and the mammillary bodies. Finally, in cases of Korsakoff's psychosis, in which an amnestic syndrome characterized by a defect in learning and retention is the cardinal feature, symmetrically placed lesions are consistently found in the mammillary bodies (the sites of termination of the fibers of the fornix) or in the anterior thalamic nuclei (the points of termination of the mammillothalamic tract). The conclusion seems inescapable that normal, uninterrupted activity of the hippocampal-fornical-mammillary-thalamic system is necessary for a normal memory status, at least insofar as the formation of "new memories" is concerned.

It is probable that the overall function of memory is actually divisible into three major and theoretically distinct processes, viz., *acquisition, retention* and *recall*. The importance of the rhinencephalic structures appears centered primarily around the first two of these. The elicitation of "panoramic memories" by stimulation over a broad expanse of temporal isocortex suggests that the process of recall of stored memories may be, at least in large part, a function of this phylogenetically more recent portion of the brain. The precise manner, biophysical or chemical, by which memory traces are formed and stored is as yet unknown.

One should also note in passing the affective aspect of memory function, e.g., the sensation of familiarity, which is an integral part of recognition. In many patients with temporal lobe epilepsy, an unexpected sense of familiarity may occur as part of the aura of an attack, a phenomenon referred to as *déjà vu;* an identical experience may occasionally be noted by normal individuals, particularly during adolescence. The reverse phenomenon, i.e., a sense of unfamiliarity in admittedly familiar surroundings (*jamais vu*), is also encountered in patients with temporal lobe seizures, though much more rarely.

The Body Image

On the basis of a variety of sensory experiences, particularly visual, postural and tactile, the normal individual acquires an imaginal conception of his own body, a psychological representation and awareness of self as a unified whole whose significance exceeds the sensory building blocks of which it is composed; it is this psychological conception of self which is called the *body image,* or body schema. A number of disorders of the body image may be encountered in organic cerebral disease, often, although not invariably, associated with a lesion in the right (nondominant) parietal lobe. *Unilateral neglect* of one side of the body, usually the left, may occur in respect to either motor or sensory functions. Thus, early in the course of an expanding right parietal lesion, a patient may disregard the left arm and leg in spontaneous movements, with a resulting poverty of movement on that side; nonetheless, he is quite capable of using those limbs adequately when attention is drawn specifically to their use. In a more advanced form, and generally in association with some degree of mental confusion, the affected individual may actively neglect the left side of the body in such acts as bathing or shaving, and may dress only the right side of the body; the latter disorder is spoken of as *dressing apraxia,* and is thought to indicate some degree of extension of the defect from neglect of self to neglect of extracorporeal space. Sensory neglect (or sensory inattention or extinction) usually affects the left side as well. A patient may be perfectly capable of perceiving tactile or painful stimuli independently on either side of the body, but, when identical stimuli are applied simultaneously to both sides, he is only aware of the stimulus on the right, neglecting that on the left. A similar defect, an inattention hemianopsia, may be found in the visual sphere, again generally on the left side, and indicates neglect of that portion of the patient's surroundings.

Disturbances of the body schema may be found in association with frank motor deficits, as in the syndrome of *anosognosia,* a term introduced by Babinski to describe an unawareness of a left-sided hemiplegia. Different degrees of such unawareness may be found, from a mild unconcern or tendency to minimize the paralytic defect to a frank denial of the existence of such a defect; the latter is often accompanied by confabulation. Some degree of mental confusion is usually found in conjunction with the anosognosia, and a loss of sensibility, especially of position sense, is almost invariably found in the affected extremities. There has been a widespread tendency to attribute this syndrome to specific

dysfunction of the minor parietal lobe, but Weinstein and Kahn, and others, have emphasized that the responsible lesion need not be located here. It should be noted that the term anosognosia is often used in a much wider sense than originally defined, being applied to unawareness or denial of illness of any sort rather than to a specific unawareness of a left-sided hemiplegia only.

A still more striking disruption of the body image, found most often with lesions of the nondominant parietal lobe, is that disorder known as *hemisomatotopagnosia* (asomatognosia, imperception of one-half of the body, hemidepersonalization). This is characterized by a feeling of loss or nonexistence of the entire left side of the body, resulting in a failure on the part of the patient to recognize his limbs as his own, and, in fact, actual denial of the possession of such limbs. Hemiparesis may be present on the affected side, but not invariably so; sensory loss, particularly of position sense, is almost always found. This syndrome is quite unusual; when present it not uncommonly is found in conjunction with anosognosia. It is worthy of emphasis that both anosognosia and hemisomatotopagnosia tend to follow rapidly developing lesions, such as infarction. Feelings of depersonalization not strictly limited to one side of the body, i.e., feelings of being drawn out of or becoming separated from one's own body, are not uncommonly encountered in a variety of psychiatric disorders, and may also occur as part of the aura in certain cases of temporal lobe epilepsy. Total asomatognosia, a feeling of complete disappearance of the entire body, is a rare syndrome, and is usually found in individuals with a major psychosis.

Portions of the *Gerstmann syndrome* may also be looked upon as disturbances of the body image. This syndrome, characterized by agraphia, acalculia, right-left disorientation and finger agnosia (the inability to recognize and properly identify digits) is due in the majority of cases to a lesion in the vicinity of the angular and supramarginal gyri of the dominant cerebral hemisphere. Both of the latter two features, i.e., right-left disorientation and finger agnosia, appear related to a breakdown of the body scheme; the particular significance of the hand and the digits in this regard has been discussed at length by Critchley.

Still another disorder related to the body image, although not strictly a disorganization of this image, is the syndrome of the *phantom limb.* A phantom limb may be defined as a "model" of a lost extremity, which arises to conscious awareness and which is perceived as feeling and acting in much the same manner as a real limb. A phantom usually develops in adult life following the sudden loss of a limb, less often of a breast, nose, or penis. It may be felt as a normal extremity, or as a distorted, fragmentary, or foreshortened one, and its configuration and apparent position may change involuntarily. A phantom may be painless, or may be the source of considerable discomfort; the pain in the latter case may be due to changes in the severed peripheral nerves at the amputation site. Relief of pain by excision of an amputation neuroma or by chordotomy may leave the phantom itself intact. Excision of the contralateral parietal region may eradicate the phantom limb; however, painless phantoms may fade away of their own accord. Psychologically, the phenomenon of a phantom limb may be looked upon as an attempt to preserve the integrity of the body image.

Highest Integrative Functions

In addition to the varieties of behavioral patterns previously discussed, a number of other phenomena may suitably be considered as being "higher" or "highest" cerebral functions. Among these are such variegated aspects of mental activity as *attention, orientation, judgment* and *discrimination, intellectual capacity, abstract and symbolic thinking processes, creativity, moral and ethical sensibilities, the ability to plan, initiate, and carry out meaningful acts with definite goals, etc.* Despite common usage, it is difficult to define exactly many of the terms used in this connection, such as "mentation" or "intelligence." It is equally difficult to set forth precisely the attributes, both qualitative and quantitative, of normal "mental" activities, or to categorize these attributes in a meaningful way.

Chapman and Wolff have proposed four basic categories of functions they consider the "highest integrative functions of man," and have described in detail the alterations that occur with disease of the brain. Briefly, these categories are: *First,* those functions concerned with the expression of needs, appetites and desires; these are reflected in the responses to such basic requirements as food and shelter, in sexual activity, and in imagination, striving toward definite goals and the establishment of interpersonal relationships. *Second,* functions concerned with goal achievement and the capacity to respond to symbols as substitutes for biologically significant events, as expressed in anticipation, planning, arranging, inventing, exploring, perceiving, learning, remembering, postponing and discriminating. *Third,* functions operating under conditions of stress to integrate defensive or protective behavior into sustained, adequate and socially acceptable patterns of activity and adaptation. *Fourth,* functions which maintain the stability of the organism during stress and which ensure rapidity of response to a variety of stimuli.

Attempts have often been made to correlate disturbances of these "highest functions" with lesions restricted to certain parts of the brain and particularly to the frontal lobes. Thus, the term *"frontal lobe syndrome"* is often encountered. This is usually defined as a combination of personality change and intellectual impairment often with some associated motor deficit. The personality changes usually noted are instability, superficiality, facetiousness, shallow emotional responses, errors in judgment, indifference and lack of concern, and sexual excesses; the intellectual impairment is described as a lack of concentration, shortened attention span, faulty memory, lack of initiative, inability to direct and sustain meaningful activity, loss of the capacity to think in abstract terms, difficulties with calculations, etc. It has become increasingly evident, however, that at least the majority of such functions cannot be localized to a specific portion of the brain, and that a frontal lobe syndrome in the sense defined above does not exist. Chapman and Wolff emphasize that impairment of these highest integrative functions appears directly related to the mass of cerebral tissue lost, independent of site or side of involvement. The degree of impairment under any given set of circumstances seems to reflect the total number of inadequately functioning neurons, regardless of site or regardless of whether the abnormality is focal or diffuse.

As may be discerned from the preceding sections concerning the body image, limbic system and behavior and memory, there are obvious objections to the complete acceptance of such a formulation. Certain of the psychological functions considered by Chapman and Wolff to be general functions of the brain as a whole do in fact appear, on the basis of sound evidence, to be primarily localized to restricted portions of the brain. A dilemma is thus posed by these conflicting concepts, which cannot be resolved completely on the basis of present knowledge. The relative importance of involvement of neocortex as opposed to involvement of archi- and mesocortex in this connection has not been elucidated.

In clinical parlance, the terms *dementia,* or *organic mental syndrome,* are often used. These have a limited application, and refer to an acquired enfeeblement of intellectual capacities and forgetfulness. Impaired orientation, lack of interest, faulty judgment, perseveration, lability of mood, a shortened attention span and lack of insight often accompany the intellectual deficit. Dementia may occur with large focal lesions, such as vascular softening or tumor, regardless of site, and with a number of diffuse neuronal affections. Among the latter are general systemic metabolic disorders such as bromide intoxication, pellagra, pernicious anemia, hypothyroidism and hepatolenticular degeneration, as well as more specific degenerative disorders of the nervous system, including Huntington's chorea, cerebral lipidosis, Jakob-Creutzfeldt disease, Alzheimer's disease and senile dementia. That dementia is not necessarily due to involvement of the cerebral cortex itself is indicated by its occurrence in diffuse cerebral sclerosis and also in Marchiafava-Bignami disease, in which the predominant and consistent changes appear in the corpus callosum.

Seizures

The problem of seizures is a complicated one, and much remains to be clarified, but there are many available experimental studies which provide background for clinical application.

Grand Mal Seizures. These can be produced "by any measure acting as a diffuse assault on the brain and causing a sufficiently widespread disorder of cerebral metabolism," such as a strong electric current to the whole of the brain, injection of analeptic drugs, or sudden withdrawal of barbiturates.

Generalized convulsions have a subcortical origin. They can be seen in the diencephalic, mesencephalic and rhombencephalic animal possessing only medulla and pons, but they are not found in the spinal animal. The discharge presumably takes place through the brain stem reticular formation. While seizures are readily produced by stimulation of the motor cortex, these are focal in nature. They may become secondarily generalized by spread of the impulse, but it has been demonstrated that seizures occur in animals after bilateral destruction of the pyramidal tracts. Generalized seizures presumably originate in

diencephalic structures, radiating out to the whole of the brain. Stimulation of the median diencephalon, the thalamic reticular formation, results in bilaterally synchronous discharges, chiefly frontal. The relationship of the EEG manifestations to grand mal seizures is not clear. "One may try to explain grand mal epilepsy in terms of a hypersynchronous discharge, but one cannot postulate the existence of hypersynchronous discharge in an affection which (until we know more about it) is characterized only by convulsions and loss of consciousness" (Gastaut and Fischer-Williams). The clinical and EEG manifestations are not necessarily linked.

On the basis of a study of experimentally produced convulsions by anoxia, strychnine and other poisons, analeptics and pentylenetetrazol it has been possible to make observations which correlate to some extent with human convulsions. The hypothesis has been put forth, based on considerable evidence, that grand mal epilepsy "is related to a subcortical mechanism corresponding first to a paroxysmal discharge of the thalamic reticular system transmittted to the cortex by the diffuse thalamocortical projection pathways, which explains the loss of consciousness. This discharge results in functional exclusion of the thalamocortical formations, thus liberating 'normal' or reinforced activity of the caudal reticular system; this release, by putting into play the tonicogenic reticulospinal system, explains the peripheral convulsions" (Gastaut and Fischer-Williams). There are no demonstrable reticular lesions in the majority of patients with generalized grand mal seizures. In a small number a focal or diffuse irritative lesion in the reticular formation has been found.

Petit Mal Seizures. Unlike grand mal seizures, the absences or blank periods of petit mal have not been reproduced in the experimental animal. The brief loss of consciousness induced by focal cerebral disturbances and electrical stimulation of indwelling electrodes resembles psychomotor rather than petit mal absences. On the other hand, it is possible to reproduce the typical slow spike-and-wave EEG pattern in animals. Studies in man indicate that the spike-and-wave discharge takes place simultaneously in the cortex and thalamus, though it is believed by some that it has a localized cortical origin and that it is transmitted rapidly to the whole of the cortex of both hemispheres chiefly by the corpus callosum. The opposite view states that the petit mal attack begins in the thalamus and is propagated to the cortex. The slow wave appears to have its origin in the thalamus, and the spike in the cerebral cortex.

Focal (Partial) Epilepsy. Focal seizures can be produced experimentally by a variety of methods. Of these, the most widely employed is the application of aluminum hydroxide to the brain. Generally speaking, the experimentally produced focal seizures are due to direct action on the nerve cells (electric current, heat or cold, or a chemical irritant), or to indirect action, resulting from a lesion produced by an irritating substance (aluminum hydroxide).

The discharge in focal epilepsy usually begins in the immediate neighborhood of the epileptogenic lesion due to overexcitability of the neurons. In some cases the discharge begins at a distance from the epileptogenic lesion, presumably due to heightened neuronal excitability at a distance from the lesion. "One concludes therefore that, although the existence of a sporadic spike or a rhythmic discharge in an EEG or a corticogram constitutes the most reliable proof of a local epileptic process, it in no way guarantees that the epileptogenic lesion is seated in the same place" (Gastaut and Fischer-Williams). This observation is carried farther in a group of pertinent observations: (1) The epileptogenic lesion may not coincide with an EEG focus, and may even be at some distance from it. (2) The existence of an EEG spike focus is valuable physiologically, but it never permits one to incriminate a lesion of the underlying cortex with certainty. (3) The presence of several concomitant or independent foci does not necessarily signify a corresponding number of lesions. Also, a focus of bilateral and symmetrical spikes does not necessarily signify a bilateral lesion. The precipitating factor in focal epilepsy is a volley of afferent stimuli which usually is not clinically apparent and may assume many forms.

An epileptogenic focus appears from the outset to be able to stimulate other areas which are anatomically connected with it or even with the whole brain and in these circumstances to produce a generalized grand mal seizure. The discharge in such cases appears to be from the epileptogenic focus along normally functioning nerve fibers to anatomically healthy areas. The discharge originates as a lesional phenomenon and is propagated as a functional phenomenon. For this propagation it is necessary to have: (1) Hyperexcitability of the neuronal population allied to the epileptic focus. "Not only the primary focus is hypersensitive, but this hypersensitivity is found in the other cortical and subcortical structures with which it is intimately connected" (Johnson and Walker). (2) Effective bombardment from the epileptogenic focus, if the discharge is to be propagated. This is dependent on many factors, all of which are not necessarily present at one time. These factors are high frequency of the bombardment discharges, activation of a sufficient number of terminals on the cells to produce spatial summation, and continuation of the bombardment long enough to produce a progressive effect.

The partial or focal epilepsies are divided into two major groups: (1) the localized focal epilepsies and (2) the diffuse focal epilepsies. In the *localized* variety the discharge originates in a structure connected to one single other structure constituting a functional system, the discharge always being limited within this system. The EEG manifestations in such instances are localized to a single sector and reveal an epileptogenic focus. The localized focal epilepsies are caused by a superficial lesion, atrophic or neoplastic. Among the causes are head injuries, localized infections, vascular malformations or thromboses, and small tumors. The lesions are discrete and usually cortical. In the *diffuse* focal epilepsies the causal discharge originates in a venous structure more or less diffusely connected with several other cerebral regions. The EEG manifestations consist of focal seizure discharges in the temporal or occipital lesions, or diffuse discharges more or less generalized over one or both hemispheres but often predominantly in the frontotemporal region. The interseizure discharges may be diffuse but are most often localized in the anterior temporal region of one or both hemispheres. This form of focal epilepsy is due to diffuse sclerosis involving the inferomedial portion of the cerebral hemisphere. There are three main groups of causes: severe and prolonged compression of the head during delivery, cerebral edema in infancy and childhood, and closed head injuries in the adult. "The principal pathogenic mechanisms in these three conditions are wedging of the hippocampal gyrus and the blood vessels supplying it into the tentorial incisure during compression of the brain at birth, or during intracranial hypertension secondary to cerebral edema in childhood, and injury of the orbito-insulotemporal region by the sharp edge of the lesser wing of the sphenoid from the contrecoup accompanying closed head injuries" (Gastaut and Fischer-Williams).

Little is known regarding the events which occur within the brain tissue during the course of an epileptic seizure, except in terms of neuronal discharge. The duration and termination of a grand mal seizure depend on a negative process of neural exhaustion and a positive process of inhibition. EEG studies indicate that neuronal fatigue and exhaustion are responsible for the progressive slowing of the cortical and muscular discharge in the tonic phase, while the thalamocaudate inhibitory system is responsible for the relaxation in the clonic phase.

Clinical Correlations. Generalized grand mal seizures represent diffuse neuronal discharge physiologically, but in clinical experience they are often associated with focal lesions, particularly tumors. They may develop with or without evidence of focal onset, more frequently without such evidence. In instances in which the grand mal seizure is ushered in by focal motor twitching of an arm or leg, or by turning of the head and eyes, or by other focal symptoms which spread to develop a generalized seizure, clinical evidence is provided of the location of the lesion or of its focal point of discharge. More frequently, however, a grand mal seizure associated with a brain tumor in an adult subject develops with no focal symptoms. This appears to bear no relationship to the location or nature of the tumor. It is as likely to develop in one part of the cerebral hemisphere as in another, and the occurrence of a grand mal seizure as the first symptom of a brain tumor in an adult provides no clue to the location of the tumor. The mechanism of a generalized grand mal seizure in a diffuse process such as general paresis or cerebral arteriosclerosis is somewhat easier to visualize. Here it can be assumed that there is general neuronal discharge from irritative or anoxic-ischemic processes.

The occurrence of a focal seizure clinically —a motor seizure involving face and hand of one side, or a sensory seizure with the same or other distribution, or an uncinate seizure— indicates the point of discharge of the seizure, and almost always indicates also the location of the lesion producing the seizure. In some instances, however, the lesion may be at a distance from the point of discharge, and the focal discharge may reflect mechanisms different from that of the primary lesion. Focal motor seizures have been described in occipital lobe meningiomas, and focal seizures at a distance are well known in temporal lobe tumors.

The EEG is a valuable adjunct in the diagnosis of convulsive seizures, but it must be correlated with the clinical findings, and care is required in its evaluation. It has been pointed out that a focal discharge in the EEG is indicative of a physiological disturbance, but does not indicate the location of the anatomical lesion. Furthermore, a focal lesion may be associated with diffuse discharges. Interseizure discharges are not always present in the EEG examination, particularly in grand mal and psychomotor seizures.

Vascular System

The normal human adult brain, comprising about 2 per cent of the total body weight, accounts for approximately 15 per cent of the total resting cardiac output. The high rate of cerebral blood flow is necessary to maintain a comparably greater metabolic rate of oxygen consumption for the brain. By means of the nitrous oxide technique of Kety and Schmidt, the normal cerebral blood flow in man is 54 cc./100 gm. brain/min. Modifications of this method, such as the krypton desaturation technique, have corroborated these findings with the value of 57.5 cc./100 gm. brain/min. Measurements of blood flow of the total brain by various methods have given findings of between 700 and 1200 cc. per minute, averaging around 950 cc. per minute. The normal cerebral oxygen consumption is 3.5 cc. of oxygen per 100 gm. brain/min. or approximately 57 cc. of oxygen per minute for the total brain. About 75 mg. of glucose is consumed by the brain per minute. The cerebral circulation is largely regulated by the cerebrovascular resistance, which in normal individuals is 1.7 mm. of mercury per cc. per 100 gm. brain per min. These hemodynamics and metabolic factors have been studied experimentally using the nitrous oxide technique and its krypton modifications over the past 20 years.

One of the effects of interruption of the brain circulation, partial or complete in an affected vessel, is cerebral anoxia or stagnant anoxia. In adults the effects of anoxia are reversible for up to 5 or 6 minutes, but anoxia of more than 10 minutes' duration causes irreversible changes. In the newborn the ability to survive anoxia is greater than in the adult. This greater resistance to anoxia on the part of the newborn is due in part to the lower oxygen requirement of the brain. Among other factors the newborn infant is poikilothermic at birth, and the energy requirements of the brain are decreased. Differences in the enzyme system may also play a role since the young fetus is able to obtain energy through glycolysis, the oxidase use of glucose developing during growth. With growth the brain becomes increasingly dependent on oxidation as a means of energy. Finally, in the newborn the blood-brain barrier is not yet developed, and its protective function with the accumulation of toxic metabolites is not yet at work.

The resistance to anoxia varies inversely with the basal metabolic rate and is increased by thyroidectomy and diminished by thyroxin administration. Resistance to anoxia is also increased by reducing the body temperature. Blood glucose and oxygen tension act synergistically, and the effect of anoxia on the EEG is greatly increased by insulin hypoglycemia.

The oxygen consumption of the brain is decreased in severe anoxia, and impairment of function occurs. The cerebral circulation adjusts to anoxia by dilatation of the blood vessels in response to increased carbon dioxide or decreased oxygen tension, and by an increase in volume of the brain (5 to 6 per cent). "The uptake of oxygen by the cerebral cortex continues at a normal rate even when the oxygen tension in the brain has fallen to a very low value; and conversely, it is not affected if the oxygen tension is increased to more than three times the normal" (Richter).

Oxygen consumption is much higher in the gray matter than in the white. It is particularly high in the cerebellum and the cerebral cortex, and the highest oxygen uptake has been found to be in the dendritic layers of the cerebral cortex, where the highest concentration of synapses is found.

Cerebral anoxia is associated with changes in brain metabolites—a decrease in glucose, glycogen and high-energy phosphate bonds, a several hundred per cent increase in lactic acid, a fall in phosphocreatine, a fall in acetylcholine, a liberation of free ammonia, and a shift in the electrolytes, with potassium ions passing out from the nerve cells into the extracellular space, while sodium ions enter the cell. The accumulation of metabolites is greatly reduced under conditions of lowered body temperature.

In man the brain is supplied with blood entirely by means of the paired internal carotid arteries. Although there are several anasto-moses with extracerebral arteries, these play a relatively minor role in the maintenance of cerebral blood flow. In general the internal carotid arteries supply the anterior and middle portions of the brain on each side, while the basilar arteries, formed by the union of the two vertebral arteries, supply the occipital lobes, portions of the temporal lobe, the cerebellum, and the major part of the brain stem and upper spinal cord.

The carotid and vertebral arteries connect by the posterior connecting arteries from a hexagonal anastomotic circle of arteries at the base of the brain called the circle of Willis. The circle of Willis fails frequently to conform to textbook ideals, and a high percentage of deficiency is found in its anatomical pattern. A study of 350 carefully dissected circles reveals a normal configuration in 52.3 per cent and deficient circles in 47.7 per cent. Absent vessels are uncommon, and duplication and triplication of vessels, particularly the anterior communicating and anterior cerebral arteries, are frequently seen. The deficiencies in the circle of Willis consist chiefly of variations in the size of the lumen, resulting in stringlike vessels with narrowed patent lumina (more or less). Multiple deficiencies of many combinations are frequent (43 per cent). The anomalies are most common in the posterior communicating arteries, where one or both vessels are stringlike (22 per cent), but stringlike anterior communicating and anterior cerebral arteries are also seen. A common anomaly involves the posterior cerebral artery, which is not infrequently derived directly from the internal carotid, perpetuating its embryonic origin (14.6 per cent). There is no evidence that the anomalies of the circle of Willis cause any embarrassment to the cerebral circulation under normal circumstances.

The Regulation of Cerebral Blood Flow

Both mechanical and chemical phenomena are concerned with the intrinsic control of the cerebral circulation and regulation of cerebral blood flow. The mechanical phenomena are related to the regulation of intravascular pressure and cerebrovascular resistance in the brain, and the general homeostatic regulation of blood pressure by the cardiovascular system through its reflex mechanisms. The chemical control of cerebral circulation and cerebrovascular resistance is related to variations in cerebral metabolism, oxygen consumption, and carbon dioxide production.

The driving force of the cerebral circulation is the pressure difference between the cerebral arteries and veins. Since the pressure in the cerebral veins is only a few millimeters above atmospheric pressure, the blood pressure at the level of the head represents the *cerebral perfusion pressure*. Until quite recently, it was generally believed that the arterial blood pressure was the only factor that determined cerebral blood pressure and consequently blood flow of the brain. The circulation of blood in the brain was considered passively to follow changes in the systemic blood pressure. Maintenance of a relatively constant cerebral blood flow was thought merely to be the result of the homeostatic regulation of the cardiovascular system through reflex mechanism, such as the carotid sinus reflexes.

Recent quantitative studies of cerebral blood flow in man have demonstrated that within a wide pressure range, the cerebral blood flow is not dependent on changes of the arterial blood pressure. Only with extreme variations in blood pressure will the cerebral circulation be affected. Lassen plotted 376 individual cerebral blood flow values (from 11 different studies of blood pressure alterations) against the mean arterial blood pressure. He demonstrated that the cerebral blood flow remains at a relatively normal level with variations in the mean blood pressure from 150 mm. Hg to less than 50 mm. Hg. In marked hypotension, when the mean arterial pressure falls below 50 mm. Hg, the cerebral blood flow decreases significantly. This has been demonstrated by cerebral blood flow studies in the presence of syncope and of drug-induced hypotension. In hypertension the mean arterial pressure may increase over 150 mm. Hg without changes in the cerebral blood flow.

These studies in man are in general agreement with the early experimental observations in animals by Fog and Forbes. They observed that when the systemic blood pressure increased, the pial arteries on the surface of the brain contracted and vice versa. Numerous investigators have subsequently shown that the arterial wall behaves in the manner common to smooth muscle, that is, it responds to a reduction in tension by relaxation, and to an increase in tension by contraction. The arteries thus contract (vasoconstriction) with an increase in intraluminal pressure, and relax (vasodilatation) with a fall in intravascular pressure. It was further demonstrated that the vascular reactivity to pressure changes was not affected by blocking the vagus, cervical sympathetic, sinus, and aortic nerves. Fog concluded that the active regulation of cerebrovascular tone in the face of fluctuations in blood pressure was a kind of autoregulation, due to a direct effect of the pressure changes on the inherent smooth muscle tone. This principle of the mechanical control of the myogenic tone of arteries is referred to as the *Bayliss effect*.

In addition to the role of the blood pressure systemically in the regulation of the cerebral circulation, *cerebrovascular resistance* plays a significant role in the phenomena of autoregulation. Over a wide range of arterial pressure, the cerebral circulation is regulated by the factors that govern the resistance of blood flow through the cerebral vessels. The cerebrovascular resistance, which is the ratio of the cerebral perfusion pressure to the cerebral blood flow, is the net effect of a number of factors. When the mean arterial blood pressure falls, in order to maintain cerebral blood flow there is a fall in the cerebral vascular resistance from vasodilatation. Conversely, when the pressure rises, vasoconstriction occurs with an increase in cerebrovascular resistance. These phenomena are mediated by the Bayliss effect. The cerebrovascular resistance depends on the viscosity of the blood, the intracranial pressure, and on the state of the intracranial vascular bed.

Changes in the physical viscosity of the blood play an important role in cerebral blood flow. Blood viscosity varies with red cell concentration and also with the temperature of the blood. With anemia cerebrovascular resistance is decreased and cerebral blood flow is increased. In polycythemia the cerebrovascular resistance is increased and very low values for cerebral blood flow may be experimentally obtained.

The pressure of cerebrospinal fluid within the rigid cranial cavity is exerted on the thin-walled cerebral vessels. This pressure is particularly significant on cerebral veins. Normally the intracranial pressure is nearly the same as the pressure in the thin-walled pial veins. Even marked variations in absolute pressure in the veins, for example those produced by changes in posture, result in little change in the actual distending pressure of these vessels. At the same time that the cranial pressure increases, the venous pressure increases. By this mechanism the cerebral veins are protected against collapse as well as against any extreme extension.

The intracranial pressure is also of importance for circulation in the cerebral arteries.

The intracranial pressure reflects the external pressure upon the walls of the cerebral arteries and is, thus, one of the pressures which determine the degree of distention of the cerebral arteries. It has been demonstrated by Kety and his colleagues that the intracranial pressure must increase to over 450 mm. of water before there is an effect on cerebral blood flow. If the cerebrospinal fluid pressure is greater than the systolic arterial pressure, blood flow to the brain will markedly diminish because of the extreme increase in cerebrovascular resistance. This phenomenon has been graphically demonstrated by arteriography in the presence of markedly increased cerebrospinal fluid pressure from intracranial tumors or infarction.

Under normal conditions regulation of cerebrovascular resistance appears to be accomplished primarily by carbon dioxide and secondarily by oxygen tension of the blood. It has been repeatedly demonstrated in animals and experiments in man that the respiratory gases appear to have a greater influence on vascular tone than other physiological or pharmacological factors. Increased arterial carbon dioxide tension produced by the inhalation of 5 to 7 per cent carbon dioxide increases the cerebral blood flow up to 75 per cent by cerebral vasodilatation. The increased arterial carbon dioxide concentration results in relaxation of the intrinsic myogenic tone of the smooth muscles of the walls of the cerebral vessels. Hyperventilation on the other hand with a reduction in carbon dioxide tension results in an increase in cerebrovascular resistance because of vasoconstriction. Alterations in oxygen tension are less effective than alterations in carbon dioxide tension. A fall in blood oxygen dilates cerebral vessels and an increase in oxygen tension has the opposite effect. They are the factors responsible for chemical phenomena in the regulation of the cerebral circulation and control of cerebral blood flow.

The role of vasospasm must be considered when one is discussing the state of the blood vessels in relation to the cerebrovascular resistance. Pool has demonstrated experimentally in animals and at operation in man that trauma, such as by traction on a large branch of the circle of Willis, will cause intense spasm of the vessel. The vessel will narrow to as much as one-third of its former diameter. This phenomenon has been demonstrated clinically by arteriography in patients who have had a subarachnoid hemorrhage from a ruptured aneurysm. The local vascular trauma from the rupture of the aneurysm will cause spasm distally in the vessel.

Severe vasospasm with increased cerebrovascular resistance and impairment of blood flow can be experimentally induced by suddenly increasing the intravascular pressure. If saline is rapidly injected into a cerebral venule against the direction of blood flow, complete blanching of the area of brain develops due to intense spasm of the cerebral arteries in the area drained by the vein. A comparable condition in man has been described by Denny-Brown. Through too energetic injection of contrast media into the carotid artery, a large infarction was produced in the carotid distribution without any evidence of occlusion of vessels.

Vascular disease itself produces alterations in the size and state of the cerebral vessels that produce increase in cerebral vascular resistance. Atherosclerosis of the carotid or vertebral arteries from their origins to their termination at the circle of Willis offers significant resistance to flow. The overall effects of abnormalities of the vascular wall are of primary importance, rather than a single lesion in a specific vessel. Asymptomatic occlusion of one carotid vessel is not rare. Similarly disease of arterioles, such as occurs with hypertension, will cause a marked elevation in vascular resistance. Byron has shown transient spasm of cerebral cortical vessels in the hypertensive rat. Denny-Brown and Rodda have found similar spasm in the monkey. They point out that hypertensive changes affect the anastomotic arterioles. This prevents the formation of effective collateral circulation in the presence of vascular occlusion and hypertension.

The dynamic effects of cerebral arteriosclerosis and arteriolar sclerosis in the alteration of the local and overall cerebral vascular resistance and flow are complex. The mechanism by which cerebral vessels alter their tone in response to vascular occlusion at distant sites is based on a type of autoregulation, locally in the affected area, and the response elsewhere in the cerebral vascular system.

Adjustment of regional blood flow following local vascular occlusion appears to be a situation similar to that of maintaining total cerebral blood flow in the presence of systemic hypotension. This has been demonstrated in a series of animal experiments by Denny-Brown, Meyer, and others. These authors devised a method of registering the oxygen saturation in the cerebral cortex by using a platinum polargraph electrode. Thermocouples and thermistors were used to measure changes in the blood flow in cortical vessels. Arterioles and capillaries in the cortex were also observed directly by a stereoscopic microscope.

When a middle cerebral artery is occluded in the normal monkey, there is an immediate and widespread reduction in the intravascular pressure in the middle cerebral artery over the lateral aspect of the cerebral hemisphere to a level of between 10 and 30 mm. Hg. This results in prompt dilatation of small arterioles (up to 200 microns), and a drop in blood flow of the middle cerebral territory, associated with a fall in oxygen saturation. The oxygen tension in the center of the affected area reaches a low level, and then slowly climbs again to high or normal levels.

In the normal animal with maintenance of adequate systemic arterial pressure, middle cerebral artery occlusion does not produce symptoms. With maintenance of adequate perfusion pressure the compromised area is supplied with blood and oxygen from collateral channels through subarachnoid arterial anastomoses and through the communicating arteries of the circle of Willis. The degree of the initial fall and subsequent recovery of oxygen tension in the middle cerebral territory is related to the size and state (tone) of the communicating and collateral vessels. Clipping one or more of these vessels will correspondingly decrease the extent of recovery of the tissue oxygen tension.

The ultimate effects of middle cerebral or carotid artery occlusion have been shown experimentally to be dependent upon the level of the systolic blood pressure. Cerebral ischemic anoxia with the production of infarction occurs only when the blood pressure falls below critical levels with the result that the collateral channels are unable to maintain an adequate oxygen supply to the compromised area. The collateral circulation requires a minimum systemic systolic blood pressure of 50 mm. Hg. If the blood pressure falls below this the collateral circulation fails. Prolonged occlusion of the middle cerebral artery in the presence of low blood pressure thus results in tissue infarction. In animals with chronic occlusion of one middle cerebral artery, Meyer was able to produce transient hemiplegia at will by the use of hypotensive drugs, bleeding, nitrogen breathing, or the induction of hypoglycemia.

The role of the oxygen supply in occurrence of ischemia or infarction was demonstrated by having an animal breathe 7 per cent oxygen in nitrogen. In spite of the diminished supply of oxygen and relative hypoxia, there is no embarrassment of cortical function as long as the systemic blood pressure is maintained. When the circulation in a cerebral vessel is impaired by vascular occlusion, the consumption of oxygen rapidly exceeds the supply and anoxia develops. If the animal is then allowed to breathe pure oxygen, the available oxygen in the tissue of the affected area rises though the main artery to it remains occluded. This is due to the fact that the blood brought to the area by collateral circulation has the elevated oxygen tension of the systemic blood. Oxygenation from the collateral supply becomes inadequate if the systemic blood pressure is reduced.

The stimulus to function of the collateral circulation has been experimentally demonstrated by Meyer. The regional cerebral arterial pressure and blood flow were measured in contiguous fields of collateral blood supply in order to elucidate the relationship between pressure and flow changes within these fields after vascular occlusion. Following occlusion of a middle cerebral artery, the widespread reduction of pressure within the pial vessels in the middle cerebral artery field is not communicated to adjacent vascular fields. A pressure differential develops in the collateral zone between contiguous arterial fields. Under these circumstances the extension of the blood supply from adjacent vascular fields into the area of their occluded neighbor is assured because of the development of the pressure differential between the two fields. The redistribution of blood is further enhanced by vasodilatation (described above) in the field of supply of the occluded vessel.

Occlusive Vascular Disease

It is a well-known fact that following occlusion of one of the major cerebral arteries there may result no softening, minimal softening, or complete softening. In the last instance, the extent of the softening or infarct formation is never so great as the anatomical distribution of the artery would lead one to expect. This more or less complete confinement of the softening is presumptive evidence that collateral channels exist in the cerebral circulation.

A study of a large group of subjects with brain softenings (194 cases) by Berry and Alpers indicates that there is a higher incidence of anomalies of the circle of Willis in instances with extensive softening. The anomalies are found chiefly in a higher incidence of stringlike posterior communicating arteries (50 per cent as compared with a normal of 22 per cent), and in a higher incidence of embryonically derived posterior cerebral arteries (27 per cent as compared with 15 per cent). No such difference was found in a comparable group of subjects with massive cerebral hemorrhage.

Collateral or compensatory circulation following occlusive cerebral vascular disease may be established through various channels. Probably the most important is through the *circle of Willis* itself. Under normal conditions there is no mingling of blood between the internal carotid and vertebral-basilar segments of the circle, an interface existing between the two segments in the posterior communicating artery. A similar interface is presumed to exist in the anterior communicating artery, with no intermingling of the circulation of the two carotid systems. An interface has also been postulated along the basilar artery with separation of the circulation from the two vertebral arteries. With occlusion of one of the major arteries, or with decrease of circulation through its lumen by arteriosclerosis (stenosis), pressure relationships change sufficiently so that blood may enter the internal carotid circulation from the vertebral-basilar system, or conversely; or there may be collateral circulation across the midline from one internal carotid artery to the opposite internal carotid circulation. The most important factor controlling adjustments of circulation in the collateral vessels appears to be the intraluminal pressure. A localized reduction in intraluminal pressure results in dilatation of the vessel and an increased flow from neighboring collaterals having a higher head of pressure. The dependence of the two segments of the circulation through the circle of Willis is dramatically demonstrated by two recently reported cases of softening of the cerebellum after occlusion of an internal carotid artery. In these instances, the embarrassed circulation in the vertebral artery due to an arteriosclerotically narrowed artery was helped by circulation from the internal carotid, but when occlusion of the latter developed, the vertebral artery was unable to maintain circulation on its own.

Occlusion of the common and external carotid artery in humans produces a reduction of maximum and minimum systolic pressures to 50 per cent of the original values prior to occlusion, and in cervical carotid occlusion the percentage drop in pressure in all portions of the internal carotid artery and its branches is the same as far down as vessels 0.4 mm. in diameter. It is not known definitely how long this fall in pressure persists. Confirmatory evidence of fall in systolic pressure following occlusion of the internal carotid artery is supplied by ophthalmodynamometry, the recorded fall varying from 30 to 49 per cent.

By means of arteriography it is clear that collateral channels may be established through the *extracranial circulation*. It is probable that not all the channels are seen in the arteriogram in such instances, but the possibility has been confirmed by studies in cadavers. Not all extracranial channels have been determined, but the more important ones thus far appear to be (1) from the external carotid artery of the same side into the ophthalmic artery by various channels of the external carotid (facial, internal maxillary, middle meningeal) and (2) from the external carotid into the vertebral system. By these channels blood is routed circuitously into the internal carotid circulation. The possible extracranial channels in the vertebral circulation have not been determined. It has been suggested that collaterals may develop between the external carotid and vertebral arteries through the occipital branches of the two vessels.

Anastomoses have been demonstrated to exist between the major cerebral arteries. The precise role of the *meningeal anastomoses* is not clear. Injection experiments of the human brain reveal end-to-end anastomoses between anterior and middle cerebral, and middle cerebral and posterior cerebral arteries. Other anastomoses are found between the anterior and posterior cerebrals, as well as between the cerebellar arteries. The anastomoses lie in the pia, in the depths of the sulci, and are of relatively large size, varying from 200 to 600 microns in diameter. Other injection studies indicate that major anastomoses occur between the three major cerebral arteries and between the branches of the basilar artery, and that the presence and competency of these superficial anastomoses vary greatly from one individual to another. While the actual presence of meningeal anastomoses is well established, their role in collateral circulation has not been demonstrated. They may serve to confine the area of softening and to contain it well within the limits of the anatomical supply of the vessel. Or they may make possible flow from one area of distribution to another.

The *time factor* becomes significant in determining the role of collateral circulation. The rapidity with which it is established is not definitely known. There is evidence to indicate that it takes place very quickly. The adjustments in collateral blood flow are rapid and occur within 30 seconds after occlusion.

The adequacy of the collateral circulation is dependent not only on the anatomical channels, but on the adequacy of the systemic circulation and the condition of the blood vessels.

An interesting instance of the dynamic interplay between the cerebral and extracerebral circulation is found in the so-called "subclavian steal syndrome." This generally arises in patients with occlusion of the subclavian artery proximal to the origin of the vertebral artery. In response to increased metabolic demand distal to the site of occlusion, as with exercise of the pulseless arm, siphoning of blood from the contralateral to the ipsilateral vertebral artery occurs. Thus, a vertebro-vertebral shunt is instituted, which expresses itself clinically with symptoms of basilar artery insufficiency.

Softening or Infarction Without Occlusion.
Softening of the brain has been reported without evidence of vascular occlusion, and from this has developed the concept that frank softening, with complete breakdown of the deprived tissue, may result from vascular insufficiency. It is also maintained, as an outgrowth of these observations, that vascular thrombosis is uncommon as a cause of brain softening.

There is no doubt that in any series of brain softenings or infarcts there is always a group in which no occluded vessel can be found. The incidence of such cases varies widely from one reported series to another. Most of the observations have been made on gross studies and thus leave unsettled the crucial issue. In many of the reported cases small branches are involved, as in instances of softening in the internal capsule, and the offending vessel in such instances is easily overlooked in gross section. Serial section studies of the vessels are essential before it can be safely asserted that softening may develop without evidence of occlusion of a vessel.

Dissection of the blood vessels of the brain in cases in which a vascular occlusion is clinically presumed to be present reveals evidence of occlusion by thromboembolism in a high percentage of cases. In a study by Berry of 172 specimens, thrombosis was found to be responsible in 75 per cent, and in only 25 per cent was no occlusion demonstrable. It was clear from this study that in the 25 per cent without demonstrable gross occlusion, microscopic study of the vessels was necessary before it could be said that no occlusion was present.

Factors Involved in Recovery from Occlusive Vascular Disease.
The factors involved in recovery from a hemiplegia, aphasia, hemianopsia or other forms of focal symptoms due to vascular occlusion are numerous and not altogether clear. The circumstances differ in cases with rapid recovery and in those with prolonged recovery. In the latter group, several factors contribute to either partial or complete restitution of function. Recession of *edema* of the brain is important, but probably of less significance than other factors. This factor is best seen in occlusion of the internal carotid artery. Postmortem studies of such cases reveal brain edema in the distribution of the middle cerebral artery which is present up to 12 or 14 days. Histological study of the nerve cells in such areas reveals cloudy swelling and other evidences of edema in the tissue. The changes are reversible. How much they interfere with function is a matter of speculation. More important than edema is the establishment of *collateral circulation*. This is probably the most important factor in the re-establishment of function of the deprived areas. In the case of hemiplegias it is possible that some return of function takes place by way of *ipsilateral pathways,* the uncrossed pyramidal fibers. The importance of this factor is difficult to evaluate. It is possible that subcortical or extrapyramidal mechanisms may play a role in recovery. It is possible that the post-central gyrus may contribute to recovery. "It has been demonstrated that the post-central gyrus is essential to the partial restitution and improvement of motor performance in the monkey, following removal of the precentral gyrus" (Peele).

Cerebral Vascular Insufficiency.
The mechanism of transient cerebral symptoms such as aphasia, hemiparesis or hemiplegia, monoplegias, hemianopsias, and similar focal symptoms is under dispute. These are presumably the result of temporary ischemia, but whether they result from cerebral vascular spasm or from cerebral vascular insufficiency has not been determined.

Vascular spasm has been observed in the larger cerebral arteries in the human, and has been reported in the internal carotid artery during and after angiography. There is doubt whether the arteries beyond the circle of Willis are capable of developing spasm, or, if they do, whether this is significant for clinical purposes. Vasospasm has been observed after stimulation of the cerebral cortex in the human. The concept of cerebral vascular spasm has been challenged on two counts: (1) An adequate local stimulus is absent. Arteries do not contract without a stimulus, and there is no evidence regarding the nature of such a stimulus. (2) The cerebral blood vessels are among the least reactive in the body. They are thin-walled, and the media contains little muscle. That a vasoconstrictor mechanism exists by way of the cervical sympathetic nerves has been demonstrated in the cat, but whether this is a physiologically useful and important mechanism is not clear.

The concept of cerebral vascular insufficiency has been proposed in order to explain transient cerebral ischemic episodes. This is dependent on deficiency of the cerebral arterial blood flow due to inadequate systemic arterial blood pressure or to impairment of the cardiac output, usually in the presence of narrowed cerebral arteries. The transient cerebral disorders which are cited as examples of "vasospasm" have in common a defective collateral circulation. The primary event is occlusion of a cerebral vessel, not by spasm but by endarteritis. The repeated transient disorders reflect the sensitivity of the tissue, thus indirectly supplied by collateral vessels, to fluctuations in systemic blood pressure. Transient ischemic episodes in the internal carotid and basilar artery circulation have been explained on the basis of vascular insufficiency. One of the most significant bits of evidence in support of the theory of vascular insufficiency is supplied by the cases which have been treated with anticoagulants. Recurrent episodes of vascular insufficiency in the internal carotid or basilar circulation, due presumably to partial occlusion, can be controlled by the use of anticoagulants. The mode of action of the anticoagulants is not understood. It has been suggested that they alter the flow in the collateral channels.

It has been suggested that transient cerebral symptoms are the result of embolism, and that the recovery in such cases is the result of rapid establishment of collateral circulation, recession of edema and migration of the embolus. Though this mechanism of embolism may be significant in some cases, there are many instances of transient ischemic episodes in which no source of embolism can be demonstrated.

Cerebral Embolism

Cerebral embolism is regarded by some as a frequent cause of occlusive vascular disease. The clinical diagnosis of embolism is not possible without a known source, but in a study of brains with occlusive vascular disease, embolism appears to be more frequent than has hitherto been recognized. The pathological diagnosis of cerebral embolism must, however, be accepted with caution in those instances in which there is no recognized source. The diagnosis of cerebral embolism in such cases is made by inference and is based on the absence of evidence of vascular occlusive disease, the absence of a cause for a thrombus, such as arteriosclerosis, infarcts in other organs, hemorrhagic infarction, and the clinical history of acute, abrupt onset of symptoms. The occurrence of a hemorrhagic softening or infarct is good evidence in favor of embolism, but similar infarcts are found in thrombosis of the dural sinuses and of cerebral veins.

The manner in which embolism reaches the brain from the venous side of the circulation offers difficult problems. It is now generally assumed that emboli and metastases to the brain by-pass the pulmonary circulation by way of the paravertebral veins or the "vertebral vein system." This system of valveless veins parallels the vertebral column, by-passes the cavity veins, and unites the superior vena cava to the inferior vena cava. Coughing or straining is capable of pushing embolic material into the vertebral vein system, by-passing the portal, caval and pulmonary systems.

In the *paradoxical brain abscess* associated with congenital heart disease, embolus is assumed to reach the brain by right-to-left shunts, by which means venous blood enters the left heart or the systemic arteries without passing through the pulmonary capillary bed.

Cerebral Hemorrhage

The mechanism of production of cerebral hemorrhage has long occupied neuropathologists, but little light has been shed on the problem by recent investigations. Charcot suggested that massive brain hemorrhage resulted from the rupture of minute, miliary aneurysms. Later studies revealed that the aneurysms were, in fact, intra-adventitial hemorrhages, and probably not the source of the bleeding. More recent investigations indicate that cerebral hemorrhage may result from a diffuse aneurysm consisting of intramural hemorrhage with bulging of the adventitia. This is to all intents a dissecting aneurysm which may rupture through the adventitia and cause hemorrhage into the brain. Hemorrhage has been explained by primary softening of the brain tissue, with later rupture of a cerebral artery due to lack of support or resistance of the softened tissue. On the other hand, there are many instances of softening without evidence of hemorrhage in hypertensive brains. In essential hypertension it has been suggested that the primary source of the hemorrhage is to be found in angiospasm, followed by stasis and dilatation of the capillaries, with eventual rupture.

The source of the bleeding in meningeal hemorrhage varies with the location. In *extradural hemorrhage* the bleeding is almost always due to rupture of a branch of the middle meningeal artery associated with head injury and fracture of the skull which transects the groove of the artery in the skull. The fracture is not always seen radiologically if it involves the base of the skull, but it can be found on postmortem study. In rare instances extradural hemorrhage is venous in origin, due to bleeding from a dural sinus. In *subdural hemorrhage* the bleeding develops from bridging cerebral veins. The source of bleeding in *subarachnoid hemorrhage* of nontraumatic origin is usually to be found in a cerebral aneurysm. This may develop as a first symptom, without previous clinical evidence of presence of the aneurysm, or in the presence of known aneurysm. In some instances the bleeding may result from telangiectasis on the surface of the brain or from arteriovenous malformations. Rarely, subarachnoid hemorrhage is due to a cerebral angioma and is associated with cerebral hemorrhage from the same cause. In the group of primary or spontaneous subarachnoid hemorrhage the bleeding has been attributed to a miliary aneurysm, but it is usually impossible to find the source of the bleeding after rupture of the offending vessel.

REFERENCES

Adams, R. D.: Coma and related disturbances of consciousness. In Harrison, T. R. (ed.): Principles of Internal Medicine, 3rd ed. New York, McGraw-Hill Book Co., Inc., 1958.

Adams, R. D., Denny-Brown, D., and Pearson, C. M.: Diseases of Muscle: a Study in Pathology. New York, Paul B. Hoeber, Inc., 1953.

Adie, W. J.: Tonic pupils and absent tendon reflexes: A benign disorder *sui generis;* its complete and incomplete forms. Brain, 55:98, 1932.

Alexander, R. S.: Tonic and reflex functions of medul-

lary sympathetic cardiovascular centers. J. Neurophysiol., 9:205, 1946.

Alpers, B. J.: Vertigo and Dizziness. New York, Grune and Stratton, Inc., 1958.

Alpers, B. J., Berry, R. G., and Paddison, R. M.: Anatomical studies of the circle of Willis in normal brains. A.M.A. Arch. Neurol. & Psychiat., 81:409, 1959.

Anand, B. K., Dua, S., and Shoenberg, K.: Hypothalamic control of food intake in cats and monkeys. J. Physiol., 127:143, 1955.

Aring, C. D., and Fulton, J. F.: Relation of the cerebrum to the cerebellum. Arch. Neurol. & Psychiat., 35:439, 1936.

Baker, W. W.: Pharmacology of the central nervous system. Prog. Neurol. & Psychiat., 14:103, 1959.

Beutner, E. H., Witebsky, E., Ricken, D., and Adler, R. H.: Studies on autoantibodies in myasthenia gravis. J.A.M.A., 182:46, 1962.

Blahd, W. H., Bloom, A., and Drell, W.: Qualitative study of aminoaciduria in muscular dystrophy and myotonia dystrophica. Proc. Soc. Exper. Biol. & Med., 90:704, 1955.

Bremer, F.: The neurophysiological problem of sleep. In Delafresnaye, J. F. (ed.): Brain Mechanisms and Consciousness. Oxford, Blackwell Scientific Publications, 1954.

Brierley, J. B., and Beck, E.: The effects upon behavior of lesions in the dorsomedial and anterior thalamic nuclei of cat and monkey. In Neurological Basis of Behavior (Ciba Foundation Symposium). Boston, Little, Brown and Co., 1958.

Brodie, B. B., Prockop, D. J., and Shore, P. A.: An interpretation of the action of psychotropic drugs. Postgrad. Med., 24:305, 1958.

Bucy, P. C.: The Precentral Motor Cortex. Urbana, University of Illinois Press, 1944.

Bunn, J. P., and Everett, J. W.: Ovulation in persistent estrous rats after electrical stimulation of the brain. Proc. Soc. Exper. Biol. & Med., 96:369, 1957.

Chapman, L. F., and Wolff, H. G.: The cerebral hemispheres and the highest integrative functions of man. A.M.A. Arch. Neurol., 1:357, 1959.

Chatfield, Paul O.: Fundamentals of Clinical Neurophysiology. Springfield, Charles C Thomas, 1957.

Churchill-Davidson, H. C., and Richardson, A. T.: Neuro-muscular transmission in myasthenia gravis. J. Physiol., 122:252, 1953.

Cogan, D. G., Kubik, C. S., and Smith, W. C.: Unilateral internuclear ophthalmoplegia. A.M.A. Arch. Ophthal., 44:783, 1950.

Critchley, M.: The Parietal Lobes. London, Edward Arnold, Ltd., 1953.

Dahlbäck, O., Elmquist, D., Johns, T. R., Radner, S., and Thesleff, S.: An electrophysiologic study of the neuromuscular junction in myasthenia gravis. J. Physiol., 156:336, 1961.

Denny-Brown, D., Recurrent cerebrovascular episodes. Arch. Neurol., 2:194, 1960.

Denny-Brown, D., and Brenner, C.: Paralysis of nerve induced by direct pressure and tourniquet. A.M.A. Arch. Neurol. & Psychiat., 51:1, 1944.

Denny-Brown, D., and Foley, J. M.: Evidence of a chemical mediator in myotonia. Tr. A. Am. Physicians, 62:187, 1949.

Denny-Brown, D., and Pennybacker, J. B.: Fibrillation and fasciculation in voluntary muscle. Brain, 61:311, 1938.

Engel, W. K., Foster, J. B., Hughes, B. P., Huxley, H. E., and Mahler, R.: Central core disease—an investigation of a rare muscle cell abnormality. Brain, 84:167, 1961.

Erickson, T. C.: Erotomania (nymphomania) as an expression of cortical epileptiform discharge. Arch. Neurol. & Psychiat., 53:226, 1945.

Fatt, P.: Skeletal neuromuscular transmission. In Field, J., Magoun, A. W., and Hall, V. E. (eds.): Handbook of Physiology, Section I: Neurophysiology, Vol. I. Washington, D. C., American Physiological Society, 1959.

Fernandez de Molina, A., and Hunsberger, R. W.: Affective reactions obtained by electrical stimulation of the amygdala. J. Physiol., 134:29P, 1957.

Forster, F. M., Borkowski, W. J., and Alpers, B. J.: Effects of denervation on fasciculations in human muscle. Arch. Neurol. & Psychiat., 56:276, 1946.

French, J. D.: The reticular formation. J. Neurosurg., 15:97, 1958.

Gamstorp, I.: Adynamia episodica hereditaria. Acta Paediat., Suppl. 108, 1956.

Gastaut, H., and Fischer-Williams, M.: The physiopathology of epileptic seizures. In Field, J., Magoun, H. W., and Hall, V. E. (eds.): The Handbook of Physiology, Section I: Neurophysiology, Vol. I. Washington, D. C., American Physiological Society, 1959.

Gastaut, H., and Roger, A.: Les Grandes Activités du Lobe Temporal. Paris, Masson, 1955.

Geschwind, N., and Simpson, J. A.: Procaine amide in the treatment of myotonia. Brain, 78:81, 1955.

Glees, P., and Griffith, H. B.: Bilateral destruction of the hippocampus (cornu ammonis) in a case of dementia. Monatsschrift für Psychiatrie und Neurologie, 123:193, 1952.

Gloor, P.: Telencephalic influences upon the hypothalamus. In Fields, W. S., Guillemin, R., and Carton, C. A. (eds.): Hypothalamic Hypophysial Interrelationships. Springfield, Charles C Thomas, 1956.

Grob, D., Johns, R. J., and Liljestrand, A.: Potassium movement in patients with familial periodic paralysis. Am. J. Med., 23:356, 1957.

Guillemin, R., and Schally, A. V.: Recent advances in the chemistry of neuroendocrine mediators originating in the central nervous system. Chapter 10 in Nalbandov, A. V. (ed.): Advances in Neuroendocrinology. Urbana, University of Illinois Press, 1963.

Haber, W. B.: Observations on phantom-limb phenomena. Arch. Neurol. Psychiat. Chic., 75:624, 1956.

Harris, G. W.: Central control of pituitary secretion. In Field, J., Magoun, H. W., and Hall, V. E. (eds.): Handbook of Physiology, Section I: Neurophysiology, Vol. II. Washington, D. C., American Physiological Society, 1960.

Harvey, A. M., and Johns, R. J.: Myasthenia gravis and the thymus. Am. J. Med., 32:1, 1962.

Herman, R. H., and McDowell, M. K.: Hyperkalemic paralysis (Adynamia episodica hereditaria). Am. J. Med., 35:749, 1963.

Hess, W. R.: The diencephalic sleep centre. In Delafresnaye, J. F. (ed.): Brain Mechanisms and Consciousness. Oxford, Blackwell Scientific Publications, 1954.

Hess, W. R.: The Functional Organization of the Diencephalon. New York, Grune and Stratton, Inc., 1957.

Hines, H. M.: Neuromuscular denervation, atrophy and regeneration. Fed. Proc., 3:231, 1944.

Huxley, H. E.: The ultra-structure of striated muscle. Brit. Med. Bull., 12:171, 1956.

Ironsides, R., and Guttmacher, M.: The corpus callosum and its tumors. Brain, 52:452, 1929.

Katz, B.: The role of the cell membrane in muscular activity. Brit. Med. Bull., 12:210, 1956.

Keller, A. D.: Separation in the brain stem of the mechanisms of heat loss from those of heat production. J. Neurophysiol., 1:543, 1938.

Kling, A., and Hutt, P. J.: Effect of hypothalamic lesions on the amygdala syndrome in the cat. A.M.A. Arch. Neurol. & Psychiat., 70:511, 1958.

Klüver, H., and Bucy, P. C.: "Psychic blindness" and other symptoms following temporal lobectomy in Rhesus monkeys. Am. J. Physiol., 119:352, 1937.

Kuhn, R. A.: Physiologic observations on spinal cord function in paraplegics. J. Nerv. & Ment. Dis., 113:301, 1951.

Kuntz, A.: The Autonomic Nervous System. Philadelphia, Lea & Febiger, 1953.

Lambert, E. H., Rooke, E. D., Eaton, L. M., and Hodgson, C. H.: Myasthenic syndrome occasionally associated with bronchial neoplasm: Neurophysiologic studies. Chapter 4 in Viets, H. R. (ed.): Myasthenia Gravis. Springfield, Charles C Thomas, 1961.

Lassen, N. A.: Cerebral blood flow and oxygen consumption in man. Physiol. Rev., 39:183, 1959.

Lewis, T., Pickering, G. W., and Rothschild, P.: Centrepetal paralysis arising out of arrested blood flow to the limb, including notes on a form of tingling. Heart, 16:1, 1931.

Lloyd, C. W.: Central nervous system regulation of endocrine function in the human. Chapter 14 in Nalbandov, A. V. (ed.): Advances in Neuroendocrinology. Urbana, University of Illinois Press, 1963.

Luft, R., Ikkos, D., Palmieri, G., Ernster, L., and Afzelius, B.: A case of severe hypermetabolism of nonthyroid origin with a defect in the maintenance of mitochondrial respiratory control. J. Clin. Invest., 41:1776, 1962.

MacLean, P. D.: The limbic system with respect to self-preservation and the preservation of the species. J. Nerv. & Ment. Dis., 127:1, 1958.

Magoun, H. W.: The ascending reticular system and wakefulness. In Delafresnaye, J. F. (ed.): Brain Mechanisms and Consciousness. Oxford, Blackwell Scientific Publications, 1954.

Magoun, H. W., and Rhines, R.: Spasticity. Springfield, Charles C Thomas, 1947.

Magoun, H. W., Harrison, F., Brobeck, J. R., and Ranson, S. W.: Activation of heat loss mechanisms by local heating of the brain. J. Neurophysiol., 1:101, 1938.

Mancall, E. L., Aponte, G. E., and Berry, R. G.: Pompe's disease (diffuse glycogenosis) with neuronal storage. J. Neuropath. Exper. Neurol., *24:*85, 1965.

Marshall, J.: Clinical Neurophysiology. Springfield, Charles C Thomas, 1959.

McArdle, B.: Biochemical aspects of disorders of muscle. In Cumings, J. N., and Kremer, M. (eds.): Biochemical Aspects of Neurological Disorders. Springfield, Charles C Thomas, 1959.

McArdle, B.: Metabolic and endocrine myopathies. Chapter 15 in Walton, J. N. (ed.): Disorders of Voluntary Muscle. Boston, Little, Brown & Co., 1964.

McHenry, L. C., Jr.: Quantitative cerebral blood flow determination, application of krypton-85 desaturation technique in man. Neurology, *14:* 785, 1964.

van der Meulen, J. P., Gilbert, G. J., and Kane, C. A.: Familial hyperkalemic paralysis with myotonia. New England J. Med., *264:*1, 1961.

Meyer, J. S., and Denny-Brown, D.: The cerebral collateral circulation. Neurology, *7:*447, 1957.

Moersch, F. P., and Woltman, H. W.: Progressive fluctuating muscular rigidity and spasm ("stiffman" syndrome): Report of a case and some observations in 13 other cases. Proc. Staff Meet., Mayo Clin., *31:*421, 1956.

Nachmansohn, D.: Chemical and Molecular Basis of Nerve Activity. New York, Academic Press, 1959.

Nathan, P. W., and Smith, M. C.: The Babinski response. J. Neurol. Neurosurg. Psychiat., *18:*250, 1955.

Nauta, W. J. H.: Central nervous organization and the endocrine motor system. Chapter 2 in Nalbandov, A. V. (ed.): Advances in Neuroendocrinology. Urbana, University of Illinois Press, 1963.

Ngai, S. H., and Wang, S. C.: Organization of central respiratory mechanisms in the brain stem of the cat: Localization by stimulation and destruction. Am. J. Physiol., *190:*343, 1957.

Olafson, R. A., Mulder, D. W., and Howard, F. M.: "Stiff-man" syndrome: A review of the literature, report of three additional cases and discussion of pathophysiology and therapy. Proc. Staff Meet., Mayo Clin., *39:*131, 1964.

Oosterhuis, H. J. G. H., van der Geld, H., Feltkamp, T. E. W., and Peetoom, F.: Myasthenia gravis with hypergammaglobulinaemia and antibodies. J. Neurol. Neurosurg. Psychiat., *27:*345, 1964.

Pearson, C. M., Rimer, D. G., and Mommaerts, W. F. H. M.: A metabolic myopathy due to absence of muscle phosphorylase. Am. J. Med., *30:*502, 1961.

Penfield, W., and Jasper, H.: Epilepsy and the Functional Anatomy of the Human Brain. Boston, Little, Brown & Co., 1954.

Penfield, W., and Milner, B.: Memory deficit produced by bilateral lesions in the hippocampal zone. A.M.A. Arch. Neurol. & Psychiat., *79:*475, 1958.

Pennington, R. J.: Biochemical Aspects of Muscle Disease. Chapter 10 in Walton, J. N. (ed.): Disorders of Voluntary Muscle. Boston, Little, Brown & Co., 1964.

Perry, S. V.: Interactions of actomyosin and adenosine-triphosphate. Brit. Med. Bull., *12:*188, 1956.

Pitts, R. F.: Organization of the respiratory center. Physiol. Rev., *26:*609, 1946.

Pool, J. L.: The visceral brain of man. J. Neurosurg., *11:*45, 1954.

Pribram, K. H., and Fulton, J. F.: An experimental critique of the effects of anterior cingulate ablations in monkey. Brain, *77:*34, 1954.

Ranson, S. W., Kabat, H., and Magoun, H. W.: Autonomic responses to electrical stimulation of the hypothalamus, preoptic region and septum. Arch. Neurol. Psychiat., *33:*467, 1935.

Reichlin, S.: Neuroendocrinology. New England J. Med., *269:*1182, 1246, 1963.

Riese, W.: The principle of diaschisis. Internat. Rec. Med., *171:*73, 1958.

Rose, J. E., and Mountcastle, V. B.: Touch and kinesthesis. In Field, J., Magoun, H. W., and Hall, V. E. (eds.): Handbook of Physiology, Section 1, Neurophysiology, Vol. 1. Washington, D. C., American Physiological Society, 1959.

Rowland, L. P., Hoefer, P. F. A., and Aranow, H., Jr.: Myasthenic syndromes. Res. Publ. ARNMD, *38:*548, 1961.

Rushworth, G.: Muscle tone and the muscle spindle in clinical neurology. Chapter 3 in Williams, D. (ed.): Modern Trends in Neurology, 3rd ed. Washington, D. C., Butterworth, 1962.

Samaha, F. J.: Hyperkalemic periodic paralysis. Arch. Neurol., *12:*145, 1965.

Schilder, P.: The Image and Appearance of the Human Body. New York, International Universities Press, 1950.

Schmid, R., and Hammaker, L.: Hereditary absence of muscle phosphorylase (McArdle's syndrome). New England J. Med., *264:*223, 1961.

Schmidt, C. F.: The Cerebral Circulation in Health and Disease. Springfield, Charles C Thomas, 1950.

Scoville, W. B., and Milner, B.: Loss of recent memory after bilateral hippocampal lesions. J. Neurol. Neurosurg. Psychiat., *20:*11, 1957.

Sen, R. N., and Anand, B. K.: Effect of electrical stimulation of the limbic system of brain ("visceral brain") in gastric secretory activity and ulceration. Indian J. M. Res., *45:*515, 1957.

Shealy, C. N., and Peele, T. L.: Studies on amygdaloid nucleus of cat. J. Neurophysiol., *20:*125, 1957.

Sheehan, D.: The hypothalamus and gastro-intestinal regulation. Res. Publ. ARNMD., *20:*589, 1940.

Shy, G. M., and Magee, K. R.: A new congenital nonprogressive myopathy. Brain, *79:*610, 1956.

Shy, G. M., Wanko, T., Rowley, P. T., and Engel, A. G.: Studies in familial periodic paralysis. Exper. Neurol., *3:*53, 1961.

Spatz, H.: Brain injuries in aviation. In German Aviation Medicine in World War II. U. S. Air Force, 1950.

Spiegel, E. A., and Wycis, H. T.: Pallido-anatomy. In Felds, W. S. (ed.): Pathogenesis and Treatment of Parkinsonism. Springfield, Charles C Thomas, 1958.

Terzian, H., and Ore, G. D.: Syndrome of Klüver and Bucy reproduced in man by bilateral removal of the temporal lobes. Neurology, *5:*373, 1955.

Victor, M., Angevine, J. B., Jr., Mancall, E. L., and Fisher, C. M.: Memory loss with lesions of hippocampal formation. Arch. Neurol., *5:*244, 1961.

Voris, H. C., and Adson, A. W.: Tumors of the corpus callosum, a pathologic and clinical study. A.M.A. Arch. Neurol. & Psychiat., *34*:965, 1935.

Walker, A. E.: Recent memory impairment in unilateral temporal lesions. A.M.A. Arch. Neurol. & Psychiat., *78*:543, 1957.

Ward, A. A., Jr.: The cingular gyrus: Area 24. J. Neurophysiol., *11*:13, 1948.

Wechsler, D. The Measurement and Appraisal of Adult Intelligence. Baltimore, Williams & Wilkins Co., 1958.

Weddell, G.: The pattern of cutaneous innervation in relation to cutaneous sensibility. J. Anat., *75*:346, 1941.

Wheatley, M. D.: The hypothalamus and affective behavior in cats. Arch. Neurol. Psychiat., *52*:296, 1944.

White, J. C.: Autonomic discharge from stimulation of the hypothalamus in man. Res. Publ. ARNMD, *20*:854, 1940.

White, J. C., and Cobb, S.: Psychological changes associated with giant pituitary neoplasms. A.M.A. Arch. Neurol. & Psychiat., *74*:383, 1955.

Whitty, C. W. M., and Lewin, W.: Vivid day-dreaming. An unusual form of confusion following anterior cingulectomy. Brain, *80*:72, 1957.

Whitty, C. W. M.: The neurological basis of memory. Chapter 16 in Williams, D. (ed.): Modern Trends in Neurology, 3rd ed. Washington, D.C., Butterworth, 1962.

Wood, C. D., Schottelius, B., Frost, L. L., and Baldwin, M.: Localization within the amygdaloid complex of anaesthetized animals. Neurology, *8*:477, 1958.

Zacks, S. I.: The Motor Endplate. Philadelphia, W. B. Saunders, 1964.

Index

NOTE: Page numbers in *italics* refer to material in illustrations and tables.

1021

Ulcer (*Continued*)
  peptic, of Meckel's diverticulum, 606
    pain of, 582
    perforation of, 591
    symptoms of, 590
Ulcerative colitis, 646–651
Ultrasonic energy, 235–236
Urea, clearance of, 718, *718*
  tests for, 727
Uremia, 744–747
  acidosis in, 747
  treatment of, 746
Urethan, in treatment of leukemia, 860
Urinary tract, 713–747. See also *Kidney(s)*.
Urination, control of, 996
  anuria and, 737
  bile pigments in, in jaundice, 676, *677*
  blood in, 735
  casts in, 734, *734*
  diuresis and, 722, *723*
  enzymes in, 737
  hyposthenuria and, 737
  in paroxysmal nocturnal hemoglobinuria, 794
  oliguria and, 737
  protein in. See *Proteinuria*.
  pus in, 736
  renal excretion tests and, 724–730, *725*
  sediment counts in, 734, *734*
Urinometry, electrometric, 729
Urobilinogen, 675
  in hemolytic anemias, 771
  output of, in hepatic disease, 678
Urography, intravenous, renal excretory rates and, 725
Urokinase, 884
Uterus, dysfunctional bleeding from, 172

Vaccines, in defense against infection, 214
Vagina, in defense against infection, 213
Vagus nerve, gastric secretion and, 579
Valves, cardiac, 315
    diseases of, 391–412. See also names of specific cardiac valves.
    in cardiac cycle, 341–344
van den Bergh reaction, 675, 770
Varices, esophageal, 572
Varicose veins, 307
Vascular disease, occlusive, 1012
  peripheral, 284–290
Vasoconstriction, 294
Vasodilatation, 294
Vasopressin, 140
Vasospasm, 1011
Vasovagal syncope, 999
Vater, ampulla of, pancreatitis and, 704
Vector, in infectious disease, 200
Vectorcardiography, 373–377, *374, 375, 376*
Veins
  anomalous pulmonary, atrial septal defect and, 416
  blood pressure in, 305–309. See also *Blood pressure, venous*.
  of neck, distention of, 433
  pulse and, 284, *284*
  varicose, 307
Vena caval syndromes, 309
Venesection, in treatment of polycythemia vera, 837

Venography, 289
Venopressor mechanism, venous pressure and, 306
Ventilation, pulmonary, 505
  in disease states, 534–538
  regulation of, 512–514
Ventricles
  arrhythmias of, 348
  dilatation and hypertrophy of, 386–391
  excitation and recovery in, electrocardiogram and, 360–366, *361*
  fibrillation of, 349
  function of, adrenergic nervous system and, 452
  in cardiac cycle, 341–344
  in cardiac decompensation, 448–457
  paroxysmal tachycardia in, 349
  premature systole in, 350
Ventricular failure, left, 479
  right, 480
Ventricular septal defect, 418–421, *419, 420*
  cardiac catheterization in, 427
  surgery for, 430, *430*
  tetralogy of Fallot and, *413, 414*, 420
Vertigo, 984–985
Vestibular system, 983–986
Vibration sense, 982
Vibrio cholerae, 199
Virulence, of microorganisms, in infectious disease, 197
Vision, 988–991
Vitamin(s), 78–90
  deficiencies of, hemorrhage and, 865, 866
    in ulcerative colitis, 647
  metabolism of, hepatic, 686–687
Vitamin A, deficiency of, 79
  in sprue, 615
  metabolism of, liver disorders and, 686
Vitamin B complex, 80–85
  deficiency of, in sprue, 615
Vitamin B_1, deficiency of, 80–82
Vitamin B_6, deficiency of, 80, 819
Vitamin B_{12}, 85
  chemical structure of, 804, *805*
  deficiency of, erythropoiesis and, 804–812
    in sprue, 615
    mechanisms of, 806
  malabsorption of, in blind loop syndrome, 620
Vitamin C, 85–86
  deficiency of, erythropoiesis and, 815
  hemorrhage and, 865
Vitamin D, 86–88
  deficiency of, in sprue, 615
  in treatment of uremic osteodystrophy, 747
Vitamin E, 88
  deficiency of, in hepatic necrosis, 666
    in sprue, 615
  metabolism of, liver disorders and, 686
Vitamin K, 88–89
  deficiency of, coagulation defects from, 881
    hemorrhage and, 866
    in newborn, 88
    in sprue, 615
  metabolism of, liver disorders and, 686
Volt, 250
Volumina, pulmonary, classification, 509–512, *509, 510, 512*
Volvulus, in colonic tumors, 658
Vomiting, 577
  autonomic control of, 995